D1327786

INFECTIOUS DISEASE EPIDEMIOLOGY
Theory and Practice

THIRD EDITION

Edited by

Kenrad E. Nelson, MD
Professor, Departments of Epidemiology, International Health, and Medicine
The Johns Hopkins Medical Institutions
The Johns Hopkins University
Baltimore, Maryland

Carolyn Masters Williams, PhD, MPH
Chief, Epidemiology Branch, Basic Science Program
Division of AIDS
National Institute of Allergy and Infectious Diseases
National Institutes of Health
Bethesda, Maryland

*Dr. Williams contributed to the book in her personal capacity. The views expressed are her own and do not necessarily represent the views of the National Institutes of Health or the United States Government.

JONES & BARTLETT
LEARNING

World Headquarters
Jones & Bartlett Learning
5 Wall Street
Burlington, MA 01803
978-443-5000
info@jblearning.com
www.jblearning.com

Jones & Bartlett Learning books and products are available through most bookstores and online booksellers. To contact Jones & Bartlett Learning directly, call 800-832-0034, fax 978-443-8000, or visit our website, www.jblearning.com.

Substantial discounts on bulk quantities of Jones & Bartlett Learning publications are available to corporations, professional associations, and other qualified organizations. For details and specific discount information, contact the special sales department at Jones & Bartlett Learning via the above contact information or send an email to specialsales@jblearning.com.

Infectious Disease Epidemiology: Theory and Practice, Third Edition is an independent publication and has not been authorized, sponsored, or otherwise approved by the owners of the trademarks or service marks referenced in this product.

Some images in this book feature models. These models do not necessarily endorse, represent, or participate in the activities represented in the images.

The screenshots in this product are for educational and instructive purposes only. All trademarks displayed are the trademarks of the parties noted therein. Such use of trademarks is not an endorsement by said parties of Jones & Bartlett Learning, its products, or its services, nor should such use be deemed an endorsement by Jones & Bartlett Learning of said third party's products or services.

This publication is designed to provide accurate and authoritative information in regard to the Subject Matter covered. It is sold with the understanding that the publisher is not engaged in rendering legal, accounting, or other professional service. If legal advice or other expert assistance is required, the service of a competent professional person should be sought.

Production Credits
Publisher: Michael Brown
Managing Editor: Maro Gartside
Editorial Assistant: Chloe Falivene
Associate Production Editor: Rebekah Linga
Senior Marketing Manager: Sophie Fleck Teague
Manufacturing and Inventory Control Supervisor: Amy Bacus
Composition: CAE Solutions Corp.
Cover Design: Michael O'Donnell
Cover Image: © Fenton/ShutterStock, Inc.
Printing and Binding: McNaughton & Gunn
Cover Printing: McNaughton & Gunn

To order this product, use ISBN: 978-1-4496-8379-5

Library of Congress Cataloging-in-Publication Data
Infectious disease epidemiology : theory and practice / [edited by] Kenrad E. Nelson and Carolyn Masters Williams. — 3rd ed.
    p. ; cm.
  Includes bibliographical references and index.
  ISBN 978-0-7637-9533-7 (hard cover) — ISBN 0-7637-9533-X (hard cover)
  I. Nelson, Kenrad E. II. Williams, Carolyn Masters.
  [DNLM: 1. Communicable Diseases—epidemiology. 2. Disease Outbreaks. 3. Epidemiologic Methods. WC 100]

614.5—dc23

2012039132

6048

Printed in the United States of America
25 24 23 22 21 20   10 9 8 7 6 5 4 3

Contents

Chapter 28   Epidemiology of Helminth Infections   917

Clive J. Shiff

Contributors

William R. Bishai, MD, PhD
Professor
Departments of Medicine and Molecular
    Microbiology and Immunology
The Johns Hopkins Medical Institutions
The Johns Hopkins University
Baltimore, MD

Robert E. Black, MD
Professor and Chairman
Department of International Health
Bloomberg School of Public Health
The Johns Hopkins University
Baltimore, MD

David Blythe, MD, MPH
Associate Director
Maryland State Department of Health
    and Mental Hygiene
Baltimore, MD

Karen C. Carroll, MD
Professor of Pathology and Medicine
School of Medicine
The Johns Hopkins University
Baltimore, MD

David D. Celentano, ScD, MHS
Charles Armstrong Professor and Chair
Department of Epidemiology
Bloomberg School of Public Health
The Johns Hopkins University
Baltimore, MD

Richard E. Chaisson, MD
Professor
Departments of Medicine, Epidemiology,
    and International Health
Schools of Medicine and Public Health
The Johns Hopkins University
Baltimore, MD

Jacqueline S. Coberly, PhD
Senior Epidemiologist
The Johns Hopkins Applied Physics Laboratory
National Security Technology Department
The Johns Hopkins University
Laurel, MD

Derek A. T. Cummings, PhD
Associate Professor
Department of Epidemiology
Bloomberg School of Public Health
The Johns Hopkins University
Baltimore, MD

Wendy W. Davis, EdM
Senior Research Associate
Department of Epidemiology
Bloomberg School of Public Health
The Johns Hopkins University
Baltimore, MD

Diane M. Dwyer, MD, MS
Medical Director
Center for Cancer Surveillance and Control
Deputy Director
Maryland State Department of Health
    and Mental Hygiene
Baltimore, MD

Christa L. Fischer Walker, PhD, MHS
Associate Scientist
Bloomberg School of Public Health
The Johns Hopkins University
Baltimore, MD

John S. Francis, MD, PhD
Yale-New Haven Hospital
Nathan Smith Clinic
Internal Medicine
Division of Infectious Diseases
New Haven, CT

Stephen J. Gange, PhD
Professor
Department of Epidemiology
Bloomberg School of Public Health
The Johns Hopkins University
Baltimore, MD

Charlotte A. Gaydos, MS, MPH, DrPH
Professor
Department of Medicine
Division of Infectious Disease
School of Medicine
The Johns Hopkins University
Baltimore, MD

Elizabeth T. Golub, PhD, MPH
Associate Scientist
Department of Epidemiology
Bloomberg School of Public Health
The Johns Hopkins University
Baltimore, MD

Jonathan E. Golub, PhD
Associate Professor
Departments of Medicine
    and Epidemiology
The Johns Hopkins Medical Institutions
Baltimore, MD

Gregory E. Glass, PhD
Professor
W. Harry Feinstone Department of Molecular
    Microbiology and Immunology
Bloomberg School of Public Health
The Johns Hopkins University
Baltimore, MD

Diane E. Griffin, MD, PhD
Professor and Chairman
W. Harry Feinstone Department of Molecular
    Microbiology and Immunology
Bloomberg School of Public Health
The Johns Hopkins University
Baltimore, MD

Carmela Groves, RN, MS
Chief
Division of Outbreak Investigation
Epidemiology and Disease Control
    Program
Maryland Department of Health
    and Mental Hygiene
Baltimore, MD

Susan M. Harrington, MT, MPH, PhD
Associate Medical Director
The Cleveland Clinic Foundation
Cleveland, OH

Claudio F. Lanata, MD, MPH
Senior Researcher
Instituto de Investigacion Nutricional
Lima, Peru

Justin Lessler, PhD
Assistant Professor
Department of Epidemiology
Bloomberg School of Public Health
The Johns Hopkins University
Baltimore, MD

Anita M. Loughlin, MS, PhD
Assistant Professor
Department of Epidemiology
School of Public Health
Boston University
Boston, MA

Joseph B. Margolick, MD, PhD
Professor
Departments of Molecular Microbiology &
    Immunology, Environmental Health Sciences,
    and Epidemiology
Bloomberg School of Public Health
The Johns Hopkins University
Baltimore, MD

Richard B. Markham, MD
Professor
W. Harry Feinstone Department of Molecular
    Microbiology and Immunology
The Johns Hopkins University
Baltimore, MD

Richard H. Morrow, MD, MPH
Professor
Department of International Health
Bloomberg School of Public Health
The Johns Hopkins University
Baltimore, MD

William J. Moss, MD, MPH
Professor
Department of Epidemiology
Bloomberg School of Public Health
The Johns Hopkins University
Baltimore, MD

Kenrad E. Nelson, MD
Professor
Departments of Epidemiology, International
    Health and Medicine
Bloomberg School of Public Health and School
    of Medicine
The Johns Hopkins University
Baltimore, MD

Martin O. Ota, MD, FWACP, PhD
Medical Research Council Unit
Fajara, Gambia

Leilani Paitoonpong, MD, MSc
International Research Fellow
Hospital Infection Control and Epidemiology
Department of Medicine
The Johns Hopkins University Hospital
Baltimore, MD

Nicole M. Parrish, PhD, MS
Assistant Professor
Department of Pathology
School of Medicine
The Johns Hopkins University
Baltimore, MD

Trish M. Perl, MD, MSc
Professor and Director
Infection Control and Epidemiology
Departments of Medicine and Epidemiology
The Johns Hopkins University Hospital
Baltimore, MD

Stefan Riedel, MD, PhD, D(ABMM)
Department of Pathology
School of Medicine
The Johns Hopkins Bayview
    Medical Center
Baltimore, MD

Richard D. Semba, MD, MPH
Professor
Department of Ophthalmology
School of Medicine
The Johns Hopkins Medical Institutions
The Johns Hopkins University
Baltimore, MD

Alan L. Scott, PhD
Professor
W. Harry Feinstone Department of Molecular
    Microbiology and Immunology
Bloomberg School of Public Health
The Johns Hopkins University
Baltimore, MD

Clive J. Shiff, PhD, MSc
Associate Professor
W. Harry Feinstone Department of Molecular
    Microbiology and Immunology
Bloomberg School of Public Health
The Johns Hopkins University
Baltimore, MD

Ellen Smit, PhD
Associate Professor of Epidemiology
School of Biological & Population
    Health Sciences
College of Public Health & Human Sciences
Oregon State University
Corvallis, OR

Mark C. Steinhoff, MD
Director
Children's Global Health Center
Professor
Pediatric Infectious Disease
Cincinnati Children's Hospital
    and Medical Center
Cincinnati Children's Research Foundation
Cincinnati, OH

Steffanie A. Strathdee, PhD
Professor and Harold Simon Chair
Division of International Health and Cross
    Cultural Medicine
Department of Family Medicine
University of California at San Diego
San Diego, CA

Catherine G. Sutcliffe, PhD, ScM
Assistant Scientist
Department of Epidemiology
Bloomberg School of Public Health
The Johns Hopkins University
Baltimore, MD

Alice M. Tang, PhD, MS
Associate Professor
Department of Public Health and Community
    Medicine
Tufts School of Medicine
Boston, MA

David L. Thomas, MD, MPH
Professor of Medicine and Epidemiology
Schools of Medicine and Public Health
Chief
Division of Infectious Diseases
Department of Medicine
The Johns Hopkins University School of Medicine
Baltimore, MD

Carolyn Masters Williams, PhD, MPH
Chief, Epidemiology Branch
Basic Science Program
National Institute of Allergy
    and Infectious Diseases
National Institutes of Health
Bethesda, MD

Chun Kwan Bonnie Wong, MD
International Research Fellow
Hospital Infection Control
    and Epidemiology
Department of Medicine
The Johns Hopkins University Hospital
Baltimore, MD

Preface to the Third Edition

Although the second edition of this book was published only 5 years ago, it is apparent that another edition is needed to keep pace with important recent advances in epidemiology and the prevention of infectious diseases. The chapters in the third edition have been revised to reflect current knowledge, concepts, and approaches to understand and investigate the epidemiology of infectious diseases so as to develop effective prevention strategies.

- Among the recent beneficial changes to preventing many important infectious diseases is the recent focus of attention on global health by academic institutions, international funding agencies, governmental organizations, and nongovernmental organizations (NGOs). The global pandemics of severe acute respiratory syndrome (SARS), influenza, human immunodeficiency virus (HIV)/acquired immunodeficiency syndrome (AIDS), tuberculosis, and other infectious diseases have taught us once again that infectious diseases do not respect borders, socioeconomic classes, or geopolitical divisions. Nevertheless, as a result of the refocusing of these scientific efforts and financial commitments, millions of lives have been saved. There is now talk of eventually ending the HIV/AIDS pandemic in the next 40–50 years and shrinking the region where malaria is endemic. One very important victory over a recurring infectious disease was the control of meningitis epidemics in the African meningitis belt with the development and massive deployment of an effective meningococcal type A vaccine to millions of persons in the target population in central Africa, thereby averting the tragedy so often associated with this disease in the past.
- Despite these important successes, new infectious disease challenges have continued to emerge and some chronic infectious disease problems have become more serious. During the last 5 years, ongoing problems with antibiotic-resistant pathogens have become more serious. We are now confronted with the specter of multidrug-resistant (MDR) tuberculosis and extremely resistant (X-DR) strains of *Mycobacterium tuberculosis*. Methicillin-resistant *Staphylococcus aureus* (MRSA) infections have become a major health issue, and the distinction between hospital/healthcare-associated and community-associated strains has become blurred. Emerging resistance to multiple available antibiotics has complicated the effective treatment of *Neisseria gonorrhea* infections. Moreover, although the arsenal of effective antiretroviral drugs and drug combinations to treat HIV has grown impressively, inadequate adherence to therapy after patients' symptoms are controlled has led to treatment failure and the emergence of resistant viruses among many patients. The concepts of "treatment as prevention" and prophylactic treatment (PREP) to prevent infection are important new strategies that have emerged in the past few years as a means to control the spread of HIV infections. Unfortunately, the effectiveness of PREP, as well as vaginal microbicides to prevent HIV transmission, has often been seriously compromised by poor adherence to the drug regimens. Although an HIV/AIDS vaccine remains a hope, an effective vaccine that will provide meaningful long-term protection is not likely to be launched in the foreseeable future. Therefore, many challenges remain for the control of existing and emerging infectious diseases.
- The chapters in this text have all been updated since the second edition, and many have been completely rewritten. We have also added a new chapter, which reviews the methods and principles of the prevention of infections acquired by various means, including contact, foodborne, vector-borne, and airborne routes of transmission. We believe this critical review of prevention strategies is a valuable addition to the book.
- The HIV/AIDS chapter reviews and evaluates the global epidemiology of HIV. In addition, it assesses the many prevention trials that have been published in the last few years.

- The chapter on hepatitis has been updated to include recently published information on the genetic polymorphisms affecting host susceptibility to hepatitis C virus infection and the virus's natural history. In addition, new information on the natural history, reservoirs, and risks factors for infection with the other four human hepatitis viruses (A, B, D, E) has been included in this chapter.

- The chapter on emerging infectious disease has been updated to include several newly recognized infections. The chapter on infectious disease dynamics has been rewritten and expanded to include methods of modeling the dynamics of infectious disease transmission in populations where various scenarios for transmission, natural history, and immunity prevail. The use and importance of mathematical models has increased in recent years as epide-miologists have sought to better understand infectious disease dynamics. Models are now commonly employed to estimate the potential efficacy and possible consequences of a prevention strategy or the consequences of delaying the age of infection with a specific pathogen. We believe it is important for infectious disease specialists and students to understand the interpretation and use of various models to describe the dynamics of an infection in a population.

We hope that those individuals who read and use our text will find it useful and informative. We enjoyed and learned from the process of reviewing and analyzing the mass of relevant information to assemble this book. We continue to find the pursuits of research and application of infectious disease epidemiology to be very exciting, rewarding, and important.

Methods in Infectious Disease Epidemiology

1

Early History of Infectious Disease: Epidemiology and Control of Infectious Diseases

Kenrad E. Nelson and Carolyn Masters Williams

INTRODUCTION

Epidemics of infectious diseases have been documented throughout history. In ancient Greece and Egypt, accounts describe epidemics of smallpox, leprosy, tuberculosis, meningococcal infections, and diphtheria.[1] The morbidity and mortality of infectious diseases profoundly shaped politics, commerce, and culture. In epidemics, no one was spared. Smallpox likely disfigured and killed Ramses V in 1157 BCE, although his mummy has a significant head wound as well.[2] At times, political upheavals exacerbated the spread of disease. The Spartan wars caused massive dislocation of Greeks into Athens, triggering the epidemic of 430–427 BCE that killed up to half of the population of ancient Athens.[3] Thucydides' vivid descriptions of this epidemic make clear its political and cultural impact, and provide valuable clinical details of the epidemic.[4] Several modern epidemiologists have speculated about the causative agent. Langmuir et al.[5] favor an influenza and toxin-producing *Staphylococcus* epidemic, while Morrens and Chu suggest Rift Valley fever.[6] A third researcher, Holladay believes the causative agent no longer exists.[7]

From the earliest times, humans have sought to understand the natural forces and risk factors affecting the patterns of illness and death in society. These theories have evolved as our understanding of the natural world has advanced—sometimes slowly; sometimes, when there are profound breakthroughs, with incredible speed. Remarkably, advances in knowledge and changes in theory have not always proceeded in synchrony. Although wrong theories or knowledge has hindered advances in understanding, one can also cite examples of great creativity when scientists have successfully pursued their theories beyond the knowledge of the time.

THE ERA OF PLAGUES

The sheer magnitude and mortality of early epidemics are difficult to imagine. Medicine and religion both strove to console the sick and dying. However, before advances in the underlying science of health, medicine lacked effective tools, and religious explanations for disease dominated. As early communities consolidated people more closely, severe epidemics of plague, smallpox, and syphilis occurred.

The bubonic plague and its coinfections, measles and smallpox, were the most devastating of the epidemic diseases. In 160 CE plague contributed to the collapse of the Han Empire,[8] and six years later the Roman Empire was ravaged by the Antonine Plague (165–180 CE), which likely killed both coemperors Lucius Verus (130–169 CE) and Marcus Aurelius (121–180 CE) along with 5 million others.[9,10] Plague and other communicable diseases flourished in the cities of the Roman Empire and surely contributed to its final demise.[11] The devastating Justinian plague (541 CE) was caused by a distinct strain of *Yersinia pestis*. This epidemic killed approximately 40% of Constantinople and heralded the end of the second plague era. From 700 CE until the massive epidemics of the 14th century, bubonic plague was much less common. However, the plague—or

Black Death, as it was then called—struck again in 1345 and swept across Europe. Starting in the lower Volga, it spread to Italy and Egypt in 1347 on merchant ships carrying rats and fleas infected with the plague bacillus, *Yersinia pestis*.[1] During the next five years (1347–1351), the Black Death killed 3 Europeans out of 10, leaving 24 million Europeans dead and causing a total of 40 million deaths worldwide.[1,12–14] These waves of bubonic plague fundamentally affected the development of civilizations as well as imposed a genetic bottleneck on those populations exposed to the pathogen. In fact, Europeans may be able to attribute their lower susceptibility to leprosy and human immunodeficiency virus (HIV) to the selective pressure of bubonic plague.[15] To survive in an ancient city was no small immunologic feat— and populations that had the immunologic fortitude had an advantage over others when exploration and colonization brought them and their pathogens together.[11]

The first recorded epidemic of smallpox was in 1350 BCE, during the Egyptian–Hittite war.[1] In addition to Ramses V, typical smallpox scars have been seen on the faces of mummies from the time of the 18th and 20th Egyptian dynasties (1570–1085 BCE). Smallpox was disseminated during the Arabian expansion, the Crusades, the discovery of the West Indies, and the colonization of the Americas. Mortality ranged from 10% to 50% in many epidemics. The disease apparently was unknown in the New World prior to the appearance of the Spanish and Portuguese conquistadors. Cortez was routed in battle in 1520 but ultimately proved victorious as smallpox killed more than 25% of the Aztecs over the next year.[8] Mortality rates of 60–90% were described by the Spanish priest Fray Toribio Motolinia. He reported that 1000 persons per day died in Tlaxcala, with ultimately 150,000 total dead.[16] Smallpox then traveled north across the Americas, devastating the previously unexposed Native American populations.[11]

At that time, there was a reasonable understanding of the epidemiology of smallpox transmission. At the least, it was appreciated that the skin lesions and scabs could transmit the disease. Survivors of the infection were recognized as being immune to reinfection after further exposure. The practice of inoculation, or variolation, whereby people were intentionally exposed to smallpox was practiced in China, Africa, and India centuries before the practice would be adopted in Europe and the Americas.[17]

Syphilis is another epidemic infectious disease of great historical importance. Syphilis became epidemic in the 1490s as a highly contagious venereal disease in Spain, Italy, and France. By the 1530s, the venereal spread of this infection was widely recognized in Europe.[18] The name *syphilis* originated from the popular, and extremely long, poem by Girolamo Fracastoro "Syphilis sive morbus Gallicus." Written in 1546, the poem recounts the causes of disease and the origin and treatment of syphilis.[12,18] Fracastoro describes the legend of a handsome young shepherd named Syphilis, who, because of an insult to the god Apollo, was punished with a terrible disease, "the French Disease"—or syphilis. The origins of venereal syphilis are debated. One theory proposes that it began as a tropical disease transmitted by direct (nonsexual) contact.[18] In support of this theory, the causative organism, *Treponema pallidum*, was isolated from patients with endemic (nonvenereal) syphilis (bejel) and yaws. After the first accounts of syphilis appeared, it was reported to spread rapidly through Europe and then North America. In keeping with the hypothesis that syphilis was a recently emerged disease, mortality from syphilis was high in these early epidemics.[11]

EARLY EPIDEMIOLOGY

In Western medicine, Hippocrates (460–377 BCE) was among the first to record his theories on the occurrence of disease. In his treatise *Airs, Water and Places*, Hippocrates dismissed supernatural explanations of disease and instead attributed illness to characteristics of the climate, soil, water, mode of life, and nutrition surrounding the patient.[2,19–21] It is Hippocrates who coined the terms *endemic* and *epidemic disease* to differentiate those diseases that are always present in a population (endemic) from those that are not always present but sometimes occur in large numbers (epidemic). It was Claudius Galen (131–201 CE), however, who codified the Hippocratic theories in his writings. Galen combined his practical experience caring for gladiators with experiments, including vivisections of animals, to study the anatomy and physiology of humans.[22] His voluminous writings carried both his correct and incorrect views into the Middle Ages. It was more than 1000 years before Andreas Vesalius (1514–1564), who based his work on dissections of humans, was able to correct Galen's errors in anatomy.[22]

That infectious diseases were contagious was recognized in early epidemics, but because knowledge of the true epidemiology of diseases was lacking, efforts to control the spread of such diseases were flawed. Plague was recognized to be contagious; however, the control measures focused primarily on quarantine and disposal of the bodies and the possessions (presumably contaminated) of the victims. Although it was observed that large numbers of rats appeared during an epidemic of plague, the role of rats and their fleas was not appreciated.

As far back as biblical times, leprosy was believed to be highly contagious. Afflicted patients were treated with fear and stigmatization. Given that leprosy progresses slowly, quarantine of cases late in disease likely had little effect on the epidemic spread. In the Middle Ages, lepers were literally stricken from society as leprosy became increasingly equated with sin. Some even required lepers to stand in a dug grave and receive the "Mass of Separation" from a priest after which they were considered "dead." One example of a Mass of Separation reads as follows:

> I forbid you to ever enter a church, a monastery, a fair, a mill, a market or an assembly of people. I forbid you to leave your house unless dressed in your recognizable garb and also shod. I forbid you to wash your hands or to launder anything or to drink at any stream or fountain, unless using your own barrel or dipper. I forbid you to touch anything you buy or barter for, until it becomes your own. I forbid you to enter any tavern; and if you wish for wine, whether you buy it or it is given to you, have it funneled into your keg. I forbid you to share house with any woman but your wife. I command you, if accosted by anyone while traveling on a road, to set yourself downwind of them before you answer. I forbid you to enter any narrow passage, lest a passerby bump into you. I forbid you, wherever you go, to touch the rim or the rope of a well without donning your gloves. I forbid you to touch any child or give them anything. I forbid you to drink or eat from any vessel but your own.[23]

Persons with leprosy, or suspected leprosy, were forced to carry a bell to warn others that they were coming (see **Figure 1-1**).

Fracastoro (1478–1553) was much more than just an author of the popular poem on syphilis. A true Renaissance man, he was also an astronomer and doctor. In his book published in 1546, *De contajione, ontagiosis morbis et curatine* (*On Contagion, Contagious Diseases, and Their Treatment*), he proposed the revolutionary theory that infectious diseases were transmitted from person to person by minute invisible particles.[12,24] Fracastoro conceived of the idea that infections were spread from person to person by minute invisible seeds, or *seminaria*, that were specific for individual diseases, were self-replicating, and acted on the humors of the body to create disease. Although his theory was revolutionary, Fracastoro did not realize that the seeds of a disease were microbes, and he held to ancient beliefs that they were influenced by planetary conjunction particularly "nostra trium superiorum, Saturni, Iovis et Martis" ("our three most distant bodies: Saturn, Jupiter, and Mars"). He postulated that the environment became polluted with seminaria and that epidemics occurred in association with certain atmospheric and astrologic conditions.[12,24] Fracastoro proposed three modes of transmission of contagious disease: by direct contact from one person to another, through contact with *fomites* (a term for contaminated articles still used today), and through the air. His theories were respected and certainly far ahead of their time. Fracastoro was able to persuade Pope Paul III to transfer the Council of Trent to Bologna because of the prevalence of contagious disease in Trent and the risk of contact with contaminated fomites.[1] Nevertheless, it would take the discovery of the microscope 200 years later to prove his theories.

Figure 1-1 The leper was required to dress in recognizable clothing and to carry a bell. © Science Source/Photo Researchers, Inc.

THE OBSERVATION AND CARE OF PATIENTS

Medical practice was gradually transformed by the introduction of disease-specific treatments during the Renaissance era. Peruvian bark, or cinchona, was imported into Europe for the treatment of malaria around 1630.[25] Its active ingredient, quinine, was the first specific treatment for the disease. Based on the observation that smallpox disease conferred immunity in those who survived its ravages, intentional inoculation of healthy people to induce immunity was attempted. This process, which was known as variolation, was advocated by Thomas Jefferson (1743–1826), Benjamin Franklin (1706–1790), and Cotton Mather (1663–1728). Mather learned of it from a man he enslaved, Onesimus, who was inoculated with smallpox in a cut as a child in Africa.[17]

In 1796, Edward Jenner (1749–1823), based on the observation that milkmaids were immune to smallpox, greatly improved the process by substituting cowpox in place of the human pathogen. He performed the first vaccine clinical trial by inoculating 8-year-old James Phipps (1788–1853) with lesions containing cowpox (vaccinia virus) and later showed that the boy was immune to variolation, or challenge with variola virus.[26] Thus was born the science of vaccination, which led eventually (180 years later) to the eradication of smallpox.[26] Napoleon (1769–1821) showed his support by vaccinating his army, declaring that "anything Jenner wants shall be granted. He has been my most faithful servant in the European campaigns."[27]

It is worthy of mention that other empiric attempts were proposed during the 1700s to induce protection by intentional inoculation, such as for measles (called morbillication) and syphilis. Neither of these efforts was successful, however.

Changes in the practice of clinical medicine in the 1600s began to differentiate diseases from one another. One of the earliest advocates of careful observation of patients' symptoms and their disease course was the London doctor Thomas Sydenham (1624–1689). He classified various febrile illnesses plaguing London in the 1660s and 1670s in a book entitled *Observations Medicae*. Sydenham's approach departed from that employed by Galen and Hippocrates, who focused on the individual and their illness rather than on trying to differentiate specific diseases. After Sydenham, the Italian physician Giovanni Morgagni (1682–1771) inaugurated the method of clinicopathologic correlation. His book *De sedibus et causis morborum per anatomen indagatis* (*On the Seats and Causes of Diseases, Investigated by Anatomy*), based on more than 700 autopsies, attributed particular signs and symptoms to pathologic changes in the tissues and organs. The influence of Sydenham and Morgagni on medicine can be seen in Benjamin Rush's (1745–1813) description of dengue among patients afflicted in the 1780 Philadelphia epidemic:

> The pains which accompanied this fever were exquisitely severe in the head, back, and limbs. The pains in the head were sometimes in the back parts of it, and at other times they occupied only the eyeballs. In some people, the pains were so acute in their backs and hips that they could not lie in bed. . . . A few complained of their flesh being sore to the touch, in every part of the body. From these circumstances, the disease was sometimes believed to be a rheumatism. But its more general name among all classes of people was the Breakbone fever.[28]

This new way of thinking about diseases, requiring careful clinical observation, differentiation, and specific diagnosis, led naturally to the search for specific, as opposed to general, causes of illness.

Expanding on the concept of careful clinical observation of individuals, epidemiologists in the 1800s observed unusual epidemics and performed controlled studies of exposed persons. Epidemiologic theories about the means of transmission of various infectious diseases often preceded the laboratory and clinical studies of the causative organisms. Peter Panum (1820–1885) recorded his observation of an epidemic of measles on the Faroe Islands in 1846.[29] Measles had not occurred on these remote Scandinavian islands for 65 years. Remarkably, the attack rate among those younger than 65 years old was near 97%, but older persons were completely spared. This selectivity demonstrated that immunity after an attack of natural measles persists for a lifetime. Further, Panum described the mean 14-day incubation period between cases.[29] Observations of outbreaks of mumps and other contagious diseases in isolated populations also contributed to the early understanding of the epidemiology of these diseases.[30,31]

The epidemiology of bacterial diseases also progressed at this time. John Snow (1813–1858) performed classic epidemiology of the transmission of cholera in the mid-1850s, nearly 30 years prior to the identification of the causative organism.[32] William Budd (1868–1953) demonstrated the means of transmission of typhoid fever and the importance of the human carrier in transmission

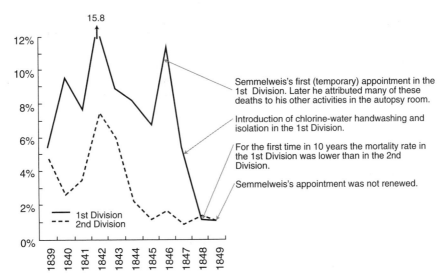

Figure 1-2 Semmelweis's Mortality rates in the first and second divisions of the Department of Obstetrics in the Vienna Lying-in Hospital between 1839–1984. Reproduced from Iffy L & Kaminetzky H, eds., Principles of Obstetrics and Perimatology, Volume 2, © 1981.

35 years prior to the isolation of *Salmonella typhi*.[33] Ignatz Semmelweiss (1818–1865) demonstrated with a retrospective record review that an epidemic of puerperal fever, or childbed fever, in 1847 at the Vienna Lying-In hospital was due to transmission of infection on the hands of medical students and physicians who went from the autopsy room to the delivery room without washing their hands. In contrast, the women who were delivered by midwives, who used aseptic techniques (by immersing their hands in antiseptic solution prior to contact with the patient), had much lower rates of puerperal sepsis (**Figure 1-2**).[34] Unfortunately, while Semmelweiss was correct, bacteria had not yet been identified and his theories were not welcomed by the medical profession. This factor, combined with his more liberal political views, resulted in his leaving the hospital in 1849.[27] These early epidemiologic theories would have to wait for scientific knowledge to catch up.

THE DEVELOPMENT OF STATISTICS AND SURVEILLANCE

Meanwhile, the fields of probability and *political arithmetic*—a term coined by William Petty (1623–1687) to describe vital statistics on morbidity and mortality[27]—were advancing. Gerolamo Cardana (1501–1576) introduced the concept of probability and described that the probability of any roll of the dice was equal so long as the die was fair.[35] Jacques Bernoulli (1654–1705) carried this concept further

with the central limit theorem, which states that the observed probability approaches the theoretical probability as the number of observations increases.[35]

One of the early leaders in the use of statistics to help understand the natural occurrence and epidemiology of infectious diseases was John Graunt (1620–1674), a wealthy haberdasher; he became interested in bills of mortality and published the *Natural and Political Observations—The Bills of Mortality* in 1662.[27,36] In this document, he detailed the number and causes of deaths in London during the preceding third of a century. Graunt used inductive reasoning to interpret the mortality trends and noted the ratio of male to female births and deaths, mortality by season, and mortality in persons living in rural versus urban locations. He examined several causes of deaths over time and constructed the first life tables.[36] Subsequently, other observers used public health data for the study of epidemics of infectious diseases. For example, Daniel Bernoulli (1700–1782), the son of Jacques Bernoulli, analyzed smallpox mortality to estimate the risk-benefit ratio of variolation.[12] His calculations determined that the fatality rate of variolation exceeded the benefit in population survival.[37]

In England, numerous improvements in public health sanitation and vital registries were made in the 1800s. Edwin Chadwick (1800–1890), an arrogant zealot, managed to institute numerous sanitary reforms when he was not annoying his peers.[27] Chadwick used health statistics to effectively change public policy. His 1842 report "to the Poor Law

Commission" outlined the cost-effectiveness of public health. His report emphasized the understanding that hygiene was closely related to health, but Chadwick also linked morality to hygiene and health. He made the following pronouncements:

- That the formation of all habits of cleanliness is obstructed by defective supplies of water.
- That the younger population, bred up under noxious physical agencies, is inferior in physical organization and general health to a population preserved from the presence of such agencies.
- That the population so exposed is less susceptible of moral influences, and the effects of education are more transient than with a healthy population.
- That these adverse circumstances tend to produce an adult population short-lived, improvident, reckless, and intemperate, and with habitual avidity for sensual gratifications.
- That defective town cleansing fosters habits of the most abject degradation and tends to the demoralization of large numbers of human beings, who subsist by means of what they find amidst the noxious filth accumulated in neglected streets and bye-places.
- That the expense of public drainage, of supplies of water laid on in houses, and of means of improved cleansing would be a pecuniary gain, by diminishing the existing charges attendant on sickness and premature mortality.[38]

Chadwick's countryman William Farr (1807–1883) made important contributions to the improvement and analytical use of public health statistical data. His careful documentation of deaths was used by John Snow to investigate the 1849–1953 London cholera epidemics. Farr initially disagreed with Snow's hypothesis that cholera was transmitted by water, instead preferring the miasma theory. However, he was eventually convinced, and his book based on the 1866 epidemic demonstrated that contaminated water was a risk for cholera.[39]

THE DISCOVERY OF MICROORGANISMS

A significant leap forward in scientific understanding came with the visualization of microorganisms. Anton van Leeuwenhoek (1632–1723) invented the microscope, and in 1683 he described how materials such as rainwater and human excretions contained cocci, bacilli, and spirochetes.[8] He did not evaluate these organisms as agents of disease, however, and considerable controversy arose over the origin of these minute forms. Because they were often present in decaying or fermenting materials, some people maintained that they were spontaneously generated from inanimate material. However, Leeuwenhoek believed that they were derived from animate life.[27]

Louis Pasteur (1822–1895) demonstrated the dependence of fermentation on microorganisms in 1857 and showed that these organisms came from similar organisms present in the air.[40] Subsequently, Robert Koch (1843–1910) demonstrated in 1876 that he could reproducibly transmit anthrax to mice by inoculating them with blood from sick cattle and that he could then recover the same rodlike bacteria from the sick mice as came from the cattle. Further, he could pass the disease from one mouse to another by inoculating the animals with these microorganisms.[12] Based on these experiments he proposed the "Henle-Koch postulates" as proof that a microorganism was the cause of an infectious disease.

In the next 50 years, numerous microorganisms were identified as the causative agents of important human diseases (**Table 1-1**) and their epidemiology was elucidated. Among these pathogens was the causative agent of plague, identified in 1894 by Alexander Yersin (1863–1943) and Shibasaburo Kitasato (1852–1931). They discovered the organism in both rats and humans who had died of plague during an epidemic in Hong Kong.[12,13] Two years later in Bombay, Paul-Louis Simond (1858–1947) of France established that the link between rats and humans was the rat flea, *Xenopsylla cheopis*. Once a rat flea becomes infected with *Yersinia pestis*, the plague bacillus, it cannot digest its food—that is, rat blood. Starving, it looks aggressively for another animal to feed on and, in so doing, passes the organism on to humans. After it is infected, the rat flea can hibernate for as long as 50 days in grain, cloth, or other items and spread the disease to humans who come into contact with these items of commerce.[12]

To study disease in a controlled setting, some researchers resorted to self-experimentation—sometimes with great success, other times not. The first specific published account of human hookworm disease was provided in 1843 by Angelo Dubini (1813–1902) from Milan.[41] He had found hookworms in the intestines of nearly 20% of autopsies. However, the means of spread was commonly believed to be by the fecal–oral route until the observation of Arthur Looss in Cairo, Egypt, in

Table 1-1	Scientists Credited with the Discovery of Important Human Pathogens and the Years of Their Discoveries	
Year	Disease or Organism	Scientist
1874	Leprosy	Hansen
1880	Malaria typhoid (organism seen in tissues)	Laveran and Eberth
1882	Tuberculosis glanders	Koch, Loeffler, and Schutz
1883	Cholera *Streptococcus* (erysipelas)	Koch and Fehleisen
1884	Diphtheria	Klebs and Loeffler
	Typhoid (bacillia isolate)	Gaffky
	Staphylococcus	Rosenbach
	Streptococcus	Rosenbach
	Tetanus	Nicolaier
1885	*Escherichia coli*	Escherich
1886	*Pneumococcus*	Fraenkel
1887	Malta fever	Bruce
	Soft chancre	Ducrey
1892	Gas gangrene	Welch and Nuttall
1894	Plague	Yersin and Kitasato
	Botulism	Van Ermengen
1896	*Haemophilus influenzae*	Pfeiffer
1898	Dysentery bacillus	Shiga

1898.[42] Looss was studying *Strongyloides stercoralis* and swallowed several larvae of this organism to infect himself. When he examined his stools, however, he found only hookworm eggs. Then he recalled that he had accidentally spilled a fecal inoculum on his hands that caused a transitory itchy red rash. He then intentionally exposed his skin to another hookworm inoculum and, after a few minutes, was unable to find the organisms on his exposed skin. After several additional careful experiments, he reported the entrance of hookworms into humans by skin penetration of the parasites, rather than by ingestion.

One self-experimenter who succumbed to the pathogen he was studying was Daniel Carrion (1858–1885), a medical student in Lima, Peru. Carrion injected himself with the material from a chronic skin lesion called Verraga peruana. This self-experiment was designed to determine whether the same organism (later identified to be *Bartonella bacilliformis*) could also cause another disease, known as Oroya fever. Oroya fever was a more serious disease, involving the red blood cells. When Carrion developed Oroya fever, he proved that the two diseases were caused by the same infectious organism—but the experiment cost him his life.[43]

In subsequent decades, numerous scientists began to focus their investigations on vector-borne disease. The explosive epidemic nature of yellow fever and malaria when they occurred in Europe and the United States, not to mention the military and commercial interests in their control, spurred researchers and their governments to support studies.

The first proof that an animal disease was spread by an arthropod was the report in 1893 by Smith and Kilbourne on the transmission of Texas cattle fever by a tick.[44] Another group of landmark studies was organized in Cuba, which led to an understanding of the biology and epidemiology of yellow fever.[45] Although epidemics of yellow fever had been reported as far north as Philadelphia in the 1700s and 1800s, the means of transmission of the disease were unclear. Some believed that the disease was spread directly from person to person. However, Stubbins Firth (1784–1820) in 1804 observed that secondary cases among nurses or doctors caring for patients with the disease were unheard of. To prove that person-to-person transmission was not a risk, he undertook a remarkable series of self-experiments, in which he exposed himself orally and parenterally to the hemorrhagic vomitus, other excretions, and blood of patients dying of yellow fever. He was unable to transmit the infection in these experiments, and he concluded that yellow fever was not directly transmitted from person to person.[12]

Early in the 1800s, several physicians suggested that yellow fever might be spread by mosquitoes.[12] This theory was restated by the Cuban physician Carlos Finley (1833–1915) in 1881, but experimental proof was lacking.[12,43] When the United States occupied Cuba during the Spanish–American War, a yellow fever study commission was established and Walter Reed (1851–1902) was dispatched to Cuba in 1899 to study the question further. The commission studied the transmission of yellow fever by *Stegomyia fasciata* mosquitoes, now named *Aedes aegypti*, using human volunteers (because there were no animal models). In the course of the investigation, one of the volunteers, a member of the committee named Jesse H. Lazear (1866–1900), contracted yellow fever following a mosquito bite and succumbed to the disease. After several definitive experiments, the commission was able to report that yellow fever was transmitted to humans by the bite of an infected mosquito.[45]

In 1898, Loeffler and Frosh had shown that hoof-and-mouth disease of cattle was caused by an agent small enough to pass through a filter capable of retaining the smallest bacteria.[46] Reed and colleagues demonstrated that the agent of yellow fever was present in filtered blood, leading them to conclude that the causative agent of yellow fever was a virus.[45] This conclusion made yellow fever the first identified viral cause of human disease. Furthermore, Reed et al.'s studies showed that yellow fever had an obligate insect cycle and was not transmitted directly from person to person.

Mosquitoes were also suspected of transmitting malaria, although early researchers were unsure as to whether they were a marker of poor sanitation or a necessary part of the malaria life cycle. In *De Noxiis Palodum Effloriis* (*On the Noxious Emanations of Swamps*), published in 1717, Giovanni Maria Lancisi (1654–1720) speculated on the manner in which swamps produced malaria epidemics.[12] Lancisi theorized that swamps produced two kinds of emanations capable of producing disease—animate and inanimate. The animate emanations were mosquitoes, and these, he thought, could carry animalcules. More than 150 years later, the microscope was the tool used to wage an intense scientific competition to identify the malaria life cycle. The malaria parasite, *Plasmodium falciparum*, was originally discovered by Alphonse Laveran (1845–1922), a French army surgeon working in Algeria. On November 5, 1880, he "was astonished to observe, [in a soldier's blood specimen] . . . a series of fine, transparent filaments that moved very actively and beyond question were alive."[47]

After this discovery, researchers from England and Italy began working on the malaria problem around the globe. The Italian research team took a wrong turn and concluded that the parasite might be an amoeba or other spore outside of the human; thus they concentrated on collecting materials from malarious locations, including but not limited to mosquitoes. It was the tireless work of Ronald Ross (1857–1932) in India that finally uncovered the life cycle of avian malaria. Painstakingly dissecting

mosquitoes, he searched for malaria parasites and finally found the salivary glands packed with the germinal rods of malaria. He described the excitement of his discovery in a letter to Sir Patrick Manson (1844–1922) on July 6, 1898:

> I think that this, after further elaboration, will close at least one cycle of proteosoma, and I feel that I am almost entitled to lay down the law by direct observation and tracking the parasite step by step—Malaria is conveyed from a diseased person or bird to a healthy one by the proper species of mosquito and is inoculated by its bite. Remember, however, that there is virtue in the "almost." I don't announce the law yet. Even when the microscope has done its utmost, healthy birds must be infected with all due precaution. . . . In all probability it is these glands which secrete the stinging fluid which the mosquito injects into the bite. The germinal rods . . . pass into the ducts . . . and are thus poured out in vast numbers under the skin of the man or bird. Arrived there, numbers of them are probably instantly swept away by the circulation of the blood, in which they immediately begin to develop into malaria parasites, thus completing the cycle. No time to write more.[47]

Ross was able to demonstrate that birds fed upon by these mosquitoes were infected, and Patrick Manson presented these results to the British Medical Association in Edinburgh at the end of July 1898.[48] Unfortunately for Ross, the British Army required him to work on kala-azar until February 1899, giving the Italians Amico Bignami, Giovanni Battista Grassi, and Giuseppe Bastianelli the opportunity to finish verifying that anopheline mosquitoes were the vector for malaria and to confirm that the avian life cycle was the same in humans.[49] The heated rush to decipher the remaining questions in the malaria life cycle pitted the Italians against the near-celebrity Koch (**Figure 1-3**), who arrived on invitation from the Italian government to "solve the malaria problem."[47] The Italians, bitterly jealous of the German scientific superstar, rushed to publication and failed to give due credit to Ross. The ensuing battle between Ross, Grassi, and Koch is legendary in the scientific annals. In fact, when the Nobel committee considered splitting the 1902 Nobel Prize in medicine between Ross and Grassi,[49] Koch's vehement opposition prevented it, allowing Ross the honor alone.[47]

Following the elegant demonstration of yellow fever and malaria transmission, the epidemiology of several other arthropod diseases was described

Figure 1-3 Dr. Robert Koch, center seated figure, is glorified in this photograph of him conducting yellow fever research. The photograph's composition is a hyperbole today in how it strives to show his command of the situation and the exotic nature of the tropical patients. Courtesy of the National Library of Medicine.

Table 1-2	Scientists Credited with the Discovery of Important Vector-Borne Pathogens and the Years of Their Discoveries		
Disease	**Disease Vector**	**Investigator**	**Year**
Babesiosis (Texas cattle fever)	Deer tick	Smith and Kilbourne	1893
Yellow fever	Mosquito	Reed, Carroll, and Lazaer	1900
Dengue	Mosquito	Bancroft, Craig, and Asburn	1906
Rocky Mountain spotted fever	Wood tick	Ricketts, King	1906
Typhus, epidemic	Body louse	Nicolle	1909
Sandfly fever	Sand fly	Doerr, Franz, and Taussig	1909
Murine typhus	Rat louse	Mooser	1931
	Rat flea	Dyer	1931
Colorado tick fever	Wood tick	Topping, Cullyford, and Davis	1940
Rickettsial pox	Mite	Huebner, Jellison, and Pomerantz	1946
Lyme disease	Deer tick	Burgdorfer	1982
Cat scratch fever and bacillary angiomatosis	Cat flea	Koehler	1994
Human monocytic ehrlichiosis	Dog tick and lone star tick	Maedo et al.	1986
Human granocytic ehrlichiosis	Deer tick	Chen et al.	1994

(**Table 1-2**). Also, many other human diseases caused by viruses were defined in the ensuing decades. The second mosquito-borne human viral infection to be identified was dengue, a reemerging viral infection of increased importance today. Dengue is spread by the same mosquitoes that transmit yellow fever, *A. aegypti*. The means of transmission and the fact that dengue was a filterable virus were discovered by the Australian Thomas Bancroft et al.[12] in the Philippines in 1906.

THE TWENTIETH CENTURY

The identification of the causative microorganisms of specific infections allowed for a much better understanding of their epidemiology, which in turn informed prevention strategies. The disciplines of microbiology, virology, and immunology paralleled and complemented the disciplines of epidemiology, statistics, and public health in the prevention of infectious diseases. Despite these advances, however, epidemic diseases continued to occur in the United States, particularly in the nation's port cities. Cholera (which was first seen in the Western Hemisphere in 1832),[27] yellow fever, malaria, and plague were constant concerns. Although public health authorities had a better understanding of the diseases, treatments for them lagged behind, and quarantine remained the staple tool of prevention.

Several U.S. congressional acts in 1887, 1901, and 1902 were responsible for creating what would ultimately become the National Institute of Health (NIH). Congress charged the future NIH with the study of "infectious and contagious diseases and matters pertaining to the public health." The agency's first employee was Joseph J. Kinyoun, who promoted the science of health and introduced laboratory diagnostics for the confirmation of cholera cases. The Public Health Service was instrumental in addressing sanitation issues during World War I as well as during the influenza epidemic of 1918. In 1930, a financially strapped U.S. government still found funds under the Ransdell Act to further expand the NIH and charged it with investigating basic medical and clinical science. During World War II, the NIH concentrated on diseases of particular importance to the military, including yellow fever and typhus vaccines. After the war, the 1946 Public Health Service Act established the NIH's grant mechanism to fund nonfederal scientists. Finally, in 1948, the National Institute of Health was given its last name change and became the National Institutes of Health, reflecting the diversity of diseases under study at the NIH.[50]

Greater understanding of the biology of disease pathology also led to better treatments. Treatments for diphtheria with antitoxin and the development of vaccines for rabies, anthrax, diphtheria, and tetanus were developed. However, many of the antisera that were developed and antiseptics that were tried for the therapy of infectious diseases were of only limited effectiveness. Complicating their use was the risk of contamination in the production of these medications. Kinyoun worked hard to establish standards in the production of drugs and vaccines. After the death of 13 children in Saint Louis from contaminated diphtheria antitoxin, the U.S. Congress passed the Biologics Control Act.[51] Under this act, standards in biologics were developed and licenses granted to pharmaceutical companies for specific medications or vaccines. In 1924, investigators at the Bayer pharmaceutical company in Germany synthesized a new antimalarial drug, pamaquine (Plasmoquine). Shortly thereafter, company researchers synthesized other antimalarial compounds, including quinacrine (Atabrine).[52] The development of these new drugs gave some hope that specific, effective antimicrobial treatments could be developed for infectious diseases.

One of the earliest scientists to contribute to the development of compounds to treat specific diseases was Paul Ehrlich, who found that organic chemicals could have different and specific staining interactions with cells and tissues. His research defined the cells in the blood as neutrophils, eosinophils, basophils, lymphocytes, and reticulocytes. While working in Robert Koch's laboratory, Ehrlich developed the acid-fast stain for the tubercle bacillus. He also collaborated with Emil von Behring and Shibasaburo Kitasato in the development of an antiserum against diphtheria. Subsequently he developed a compound—called at the time a "magic bullet"—named Salvarsan arsphenamine and neoarsphenamine, or compound 606 (the 606th compound tested), that was able to kill *Treponema pallidum* and cure syphilis. It was the first chemical to effectively and specifically kill an important known pathogen. Ehrlich was awarded the Nobel Prize in 1909.[53–55]

In 1932, Gerhardt Domagk, experimenting with synthetic dyes, discovered that Prontosil could cure mice challenged with lethal doses of hemolytic streptococci.[52] This work led to the development of several sulfa drugs. The sulfonamides were shown during World War II to be quite effective against a number of highly fatal infections, such as meningococcal meningitis. In the 1930s and 1940s, Alexander Fleming, Howard Florey, and Ernst Chain at Oxford University conducted experiments that led to the demonstration that penicillin, a mold product, was effective against many pathogenic organisms.[52] Penicillin was shown to be effective against syphilis, gonorrhea, and pneumococcal infections. For the first time, it became possible to effectively treat a wide range of infections, and this advance gave birth to the search for new antibiotics produced by organisms in nature or synthesized in the laboratory.

After the conclusion of World War II in 1946, the Center for Disease Control (CDC) was established in Atlanta, Georgia.[56] The CDC grew out of an organization known as "Malaria Control in War Areas," which had the mandate to control malaria and other tropical infections, especially scrub typhus and hookworm, in the southern United States. Its founder, Dr. Joseph Mountain, was a visionary public health leader who had high hopes that the CDC would eventually play an important role in public health in the United States. Subsequently, the role of CDC, under the leadership of Dr. Alexander Langmuir, grew dramatically to include surveillance of infectious and noninfectious diseases, provision of expert scientific advice on health issues to policymakers in the United States, service as a reference laboratory to the states, and education of the public about health issues through the *Morbidity and Mortality Weekly Report*. Today, epidemiologists from the CDC routinely assist state health departments in investigating and controlling outbreaks of infectious and noninfectious diseases. In its role in the field investigation of outbreaks, the CDC is unique among national public health organizations. Since its establishment the CDC has grown to provide leadership, often in partnership with the World Health Organization (WHO), in controlling emerging infectious diseases worldwide.

Although some vaccines were developed earlier, the number and impact of vaccines developed in the 20th century were monumental. In 1999, the renamed Centers for Disease Control and Prevention published a review of the 10 greatest public health achievements in the United States during the 1900s.[57] At the top of its list was vaccination. The vaccines developed and licensed to prevent various diseases are shown in **Table 1-3**, and an estimate of their effect on reported infectious disease morbidity is shown in **Table 1-4**.

During the 20th century, the average life span of persons in the United States was lengthened by approximately 30 years, and 25 years of this gain has been attributed to advances in public health. The public health actions to control infectious diseases in the 1900s, which included marked improvements in sanitation, chlorination of nearly all public water supplies, and development and use of vaccines to prevent infectious diseases and antibiotics for their treatment, along with improved methods for diagnosis, were reviewed recently by the CDC (**Figure 1-4**). During the 1900s, infectious disease mortality declined from approximately 800 per 100,000 population to less than 50 per 100,000 and accounted for most of the improvement in U.S. life expectancy. In 1900, 30.4% of all deaths occurred in children younger than 5 years of age; in 1997, the proportion of total mortality in this age group was only 1.4%.[58,59]

WHAT LIES AHEAD

The science of health moved forward at breakneck speed in the 20th century. The effectiveness of treatments and vaccines coupled with increased financial support fueled spectacular advances as the underlying science of diseases was unraveled. Although many advances are noteworthy, perhaps the discovery of the structure of DNA and ultimately the determination of the entire human genome will have the greatest impact on the future of health research.

It was February 28, 1953, when James Watson and Francis Crick first determined the double-helix structure of DNA and the mechanism by which it could copy itself and, therefore, serve as the basis for hereditary information. Rosalind Franklin and

Table 1-3	Years in Which Effective Vaccines Were Developed Against Different Human Diseases		
Smallpox*	1798[†]	Mumps*	1967[‡]
Rabies	1885[†]	Rubella*	1969[‡]
Typhoid	1896[†]	Anthrax	1970[‡]
Cholera	1896[†]	Meningitis	1975[‡]
Plague	1897[†]	Pneumonia	1977[‡]
Diphtheria*	1923[†]	Adenovirus	1980[‡]
Pertussis*	1926[†]	Hepatitis B*	1981[‡]
Tetanus*	1927[†]	*Haemophilus influenzae* type b*	1985[‡]
Tuberculosis	1927[†]	Japanese encephalitis	1992[‡]
Influenza	1945[‡]	Hepatitis A	1995[‡]
Yellow fever	1953[‡]	Varicella*	1995[‡]
Poliomyelitis*	1955[‡]	Lyme disease	1998[‡]
Measles*	1963[‡]	Rotavirus*	1998[‡]

* Vaccine recommended for universal use in U.S. children. For smallpox, routine vaccination was ended in 1971.
† Vaccine developed (i.e., first published results of vaccine usage).
‡ Vaccine licensed for use in the United States.

Table 1-4	A Comparison of Morbidity from Infectious Diseases Before and After the Availability of Vaccines		
Disease	Baseline 20th-Century Annual Morbidity	1998 Provisional Disease Morbidity	% Decrease
Smallpox	48,164*	0	100%
Diphtheria	175,885[†]	1	100%[§]
Pertussis	147,271[¶]	6,279	95.7%
Tetanus	1,314**	34	97.4%
Poliomyelitis (paralytic)	16,316[††]	0[§§]	100%
Measles	503,282[¶¶]	89	100%[§]
Mumps	152,209***	606	99.6%
Rubella	47,745[†††]	345	99.3%
Congenital rubella syndrome	823[§§§]	5	99.4%
Haemophilus influenzae type b	20,000[¶¶¶]	54****	99.7%

* Average annual number of cases during 1900–1904.
[†] Average annual number of reported cases during 1920–1922, 3 years before vaccine development.
[§] Rounded to nearest tenth.
[¶] Average annual number of reported cases during 1922–1925, 4 years before vaccine development.
** Estimated number of cases based on reported number of deaths during 1922–1926 assuming a case-fatality rate of 90%.
[††] Average annual number of reported cases during 1951–1954, 4 years before vaccine licensure.
[§§] Excludes one case of vaccine-associated polio reported in 1998.
[¶¶] Average annual number of reported cases during 1958–1962, 5 years before vaccine licensure.
*** Number of reported cases in 1968, the first year reporting began and the first year after vaccine licensure.
[†††] Average annual number of reported cases during 1966–1968, 3 years before vaccine licensure.
[§§§] Estimated number of cases based on seroprevalence data in the population and on the risk that women infected during a childbearing year would have a fetus with congenital rubella syndrome.[12]
[¶¶¶] Estimated number of cases from population-based surveillance studies before vaccine licensure in 1985.[39]
**** Excludes 71 cases of *Haemophilus influenzae* disease of unknown serotype.

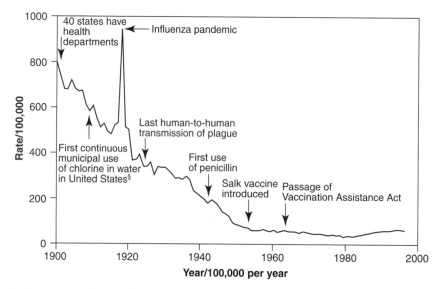

Figure 1-4 Crude death rates for infectious diseases, United States 1990–1996. Reproduced from the Centers for Disease Control and Prevention (1999). *MMWR*, Vol. 48 No. 29 p. 621–648.

Maurice Wilkins from King's College in London created images of DNA with X-ray diffraction, and these images, combined with cardboard models, allowed Watson to finally determine the binding of adenine, thymine, guanine, and cytosine to form the ladder rungs of the double helix.[60] Franklin (**Figure 1-5**) died of cancer in 1958, and was unable to share in the Nobel Prize with Watson, Crick, and Wilkins in 1962.

Since that time, gradual progress in deciphering and manipulating the genetic code of animals and plants has occurred. Dolly the sheep, born July 5, 1996, was the first higher animal to be cloned, and several other animals have followed in her hoofprints.[60] In 1990, the U.S. Human Genome Project was undertaken to identify all of the approximately 25,000 genes in human DNA. This project was completed ahead of schedule, and in

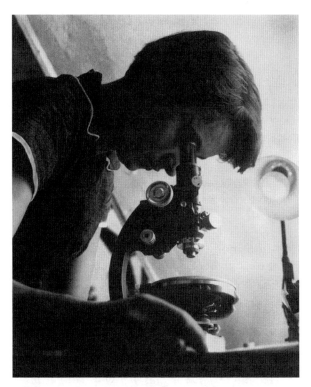

Figure 1-5 Rosalind Franklin was an outspoken feminist in a field of science dominated by men. She tragically died of breast cancer, possibly caused by radiation exposure in the course of her work. © Lebrecht 3/Corbis

April 2003 the human genome was published in several articles in *Nature* and *Science*.[61,62] The sequencing project has identified more than 10 million locations where single-base DNA polymorphisms (SNPs) occur.[63] Today it is recognized that differences in SNPs between individuals directly affect a person's susceptibility to infection and disease. The fields of genomics and proteomics (the study of protein expression) are rapidly evolving areas that hold great promise for understanding the interaction of humans with infectious pathogens.

Genetics also promises to play a role in unlikely places. On August 11, 2005, the genome of rice was reported; it was the first of the cereal grains to be deciphered. This genome will be informative for all grains, because rice, corn, and wheat diverged from a common grass ancestor only 50,000 years ago.[64] Cereals make up the majority of calories in most of the world. Earlier researchers manipulated the rice genome to insert a daffodil gene, which added vitamin A to rice.[65,66] Vitamin A is crucial to immunologic health,[67] and the use of enhanced food products holds promise for improving global health. However, genetically modified foods are also highly controversial. Hardier plants, enhanced with insect repellant genes or drought resistance, threaten

to drive out native plants, which could ultimately reduce global genetic diversity. Highly successful seeds are patented, in a practice that elevates the cost of seed beyond the reach of subsistence farmers. The concentration of ownership of seeds is high, with only a handful of companies owning the rights to most of the food seed sold in the world.[68] These controversies, and those surrounding manipulation of the human and other genomes, will determine the ethical boundaries and ultimate potential of genomic and proteomic science.

THE INFECTIOUS DISEASES CHALLENGE

In the previous century, such spectacular progress was made in infectious disease control that many health professionals believed that antibiotics and vaccines would soon eliminate infectious disease threats from most developed nations. The confidence of the 1970s was shattered during the 1980s, when the AIDS pandemic exploded. The first scientific report of AIDS (acquired immunodeficiency syndrome) came on June 5, 1981, in *Morbidity and Mortality Weekly Report*.[69] In this report, cases of *Pneumocystis* pneumonia in previously healthy gay men were described by Dr. Michael Gottlieb. Since that time the magnitude and severity of the HIV/AIDS epidemic have not abated; more than 5 million people continue to become infected with HIV every year. Because most people infected with HIV acquired the disease through sexual contact, it is predominately a disease of young adults. The introduction of highly active antiretroviral therapies (HAART) has modified the disease course for those able to afford these medications, but to date neither an effective cure nor a vaccine has been developed. HIV and the immune suppression it causes have also allowed for a resurgence of tuberculosis in much of the world. Unfortunately, drug-resistant strains of tuberculosis have emerged, making control of this infection even more difficult. In addition, several other diseases emerged, or reemerged, in the last of the previous century. The unfounded optimism of the mid-1900s has been replaced by greater resolve to solve some of the most intractable problems in infectious diseases.

The remainder of this book lays out the techniques and tools of infectious disease epidemiology and describes some of the important infectious diseases. The book is not intended to be a comprehensive study of all infectious diseases, but rather an introduction to the fundamental tools and knowledge necessary to advance the reader's understanding of infectious disease epidemiology.

● ● ● **REFERENCES**

1. Watts S. *Epidemics and History: Disease, Power and Imperialism.* New Haven, CT: Yale University Press; 1997.

2. Ruffer MA, Ferguson AR. Note on an eruption resembling that of variola in the skin xof a mummy of the Twentieth Dynasty (1200–1100 BC). *J Pathol Bacteriol.* 1911; 15:1–4.

3. Garrett L. *The Coming Plague.* New York, NY: Penguin Books; 1994:236.

4. Poole JCF, Holladay AJ. Thucydides and the plague of Athens. *Classic Q.* 1979;29:282–300.

5. Langmuir AD, Northern TD, Solomon J, Ray CG, Petersen E. The Thucydides syndrome. *N Engl J Med.* 1985;313:1027–1030.

6. Morens DM, Chu MC. The plague of Athens. *N Engl J Med.* 1986;314:855.

7. Holladay AJ. The Thucydides syndrome: another view. *N Engl J Med.* 1986;315: 1170–1173.

8. Lee HSJ, ed. *Dates in Infectious Diseases.* Boca Raton, FL: Parthenon Publishing Group; 2000.

9. Fears JR. The plague under Marcus Aurelius and the decline and fall of the Roman Empire. *Infect Dis Clin North Am.* 2004;18:65–77.

10. Antonine plague. Wikipedia. Available at: http://en.wikipedia.org/wiki/Antonine_Plague. Accessed February 22, 2006.

11. Porter R, ed. *Cambridge Illustrated History of Medicine.* New York, NY: Cambridge University Press; 1996.

12. Rosen G. *A History of Public Health.* Baltimore, MD: Johns Hopkins University Press; 1993.

13. McNeill WH. *Plagues and Peoples.* New York, NY: Doubleday; 1977.

14. Hirst LF. *The Conquest of Plague.* London, UK: Oxford University Press; 1953.

15. Duncan SR, Scott S, Duncan CJ. Reappraisal of the historical selective pressures for the CCR5-Delta32 mutation. *J Med Genet.* 2005;42:205–208.

16. Cook ND. *Born to Die, Disease and the New World Conquest, 1492–1650.* Cambridge, UK: Press Syndicate of the Cambridge University Press; 1998.

17. National Library of Medicine. Smallpox and variolation. Available at: http://www.nlm.nih.gov/exhibition/smallpox/sp_variolation.html. Accessed February 22, 2006.

18. Pusey EW. *The History and Epidemiology of Syphilis.* Springfield, IL: Charles C. Thomas; 1933.

19. Temkin O. *Hippocrates in a World of Pagans and Christians.* Baltimore, MD: Johns Hopkins University Press; 1991.

20. Adams F, trans. *The Genuine Works of Hippocrates, Francis Adams Translation.* Baltimore, MD: Williams & Wilkins; 1939.

21. Sigerist HE. *The Great Doctors.* New York, NY: WW Norton & Company; 1933.

22. University of Virginia Health Sciences Library. Antiqua medicina. Available at: http://www.med.virginia.edu/hs-library/historical/antiqua/galen.htm. Accessed February 22, 2006.

23. Mass of Separation. Cistercian Scholars Quarterly. Available at: http://www2.kenyon.edu/Projects/margin/lepers.htm. Accessed February 22, 2006.

24. Hall MB. *The Scientific Renaissance, 1450–1630.* Minneola, NY: Dover Publications; 1994.

25. Bruce-Chwatt LJ, de Zulueta J. *The Rise and Fall of Malaria in Europe: A Historico-Epidemiological Study.* London, UK: Oxford University Press; 1981.

26. Fenner F, Henderson DA, Anita I, Jezek Z, Ladnyl IR. *Smallpox and Its Eradication.* Geneva, Switzerland: World Health Organization; 1988.

27. Porter R. *The Greatest Benefit to Mankind: A Medical History of Humanity.* New York, NY: W. W. Norton and Company; 1997.

28. Rush B. An account of the bilious remitting fever as it appeared in Philadelphia in the summer of 1780. In: *Medical Inquiries and Observations.* Philadelphia, PA: Richard & Hall; 1789.

29. Panum PL. *Observations Made During the Epidemic of Measles in the Faroe Island in the Year 1846.* [Reprinted by the Delta Omega Society.] New York, NY: FH Newton; 1940.

30. Nelson KE. Invited commentary on observations on a mumps epidemic in a "virgin" population. *Am J Epidemiol.* 1995;142:221–222.

31. Philips RN, Reinhardt R, Lackman DB. Observations on a mumps epidemic in a "virgin" population. *Am J Hyg.* 1959;69:91–111.

32. Snow J. *On Cholera.* New York, NY: Commonwealth Fund; 1936.

33. William B. *Typhoid Fever: Its Nature, Mode of Spreading and Prevention, London 1873.* New York, NY: Delta Omega; 1931.

34. Semmelweiss IP. The etiology, the concept and the prophylaxis of childbed fever. Murphy FP, trans-ed. *Med Classics.* Jan–Apr 1941:5.

35. Timeweb. Statisticians through history. Available at: http://www.bized.ac.uk/timeweb/reference/statisticians.htm#2 Accessed February 22, 2006.

36. Graunt J. *Natural and Political Observation Made upon the Bills of Mortality.* Wilcox WF, ed. [Reprint of first ed., 1662.] Baltimore, MD: Johns Hopkins University Press; 1937.

37. Shodor Education Foundation. Case studies and project ideas: smallpox. Available at: http://www.shodor.org/succeed/biomed/labs/pox.html.

38. Victorian Web. Edwin Chadwick. Available at: http://www.victorianweb.org/history/chadwick2.html Accessed February 22, 2006.

39. LaborLawTalk.com. William Farr. Available at: http://encyclopedia.laborlawtalk.com/William_Farr. Accessed February 22, 2006.

40. Pasteur L. *The Physiological Theory of Fermentation in Scientific Papers.* Eliot CW, ed. New York, NY: PF Collier and Sons; 1910.

41. Dubini A. Nvove verme intestinalumano (Ancylostoma duodenale) constitutente un sestro gemere dei nematoide: proprii del-luomo. *Aanali Universali de Medicina.* 1843:106;5–13. In: Kean B, Mott KE, Russell AJ, trans. *Tropical Medicine and Parasitology.* Vol. 2. Ithaca, NY: Cornell University Press; 1978:287–291.

42. Looss A. Uber das eindringen der ankylosto-malarrea in die meatschliche haut. *Zeatral Blatt for Bakteriologic and Parisitenkunde.* 1898;24:441–448,483–488.

43. Altman LK. *Who Goes First? The Story of Self-Experimentation in Medicine.* New York, NY: Random House; 1986:134.

44. Assadian O, Stanek G. Theobald Smith: the discoverer of ticks as vectors of disease. *Wien Klin Wochenschr.* July 31, 2002;114 (13–14):479–481.

45. Reed W, Carroll J. The prevention of yellow fever. *Med Rec NY.* 1901;60:641–649.

46. Mahy BW. Introduction and history of foot-and-mouth disease virus. *Curr Top Microbiol Immunol.* 2005;288:1–8.

47. Harrison G. *Mosquitoes, Malaria and Man: A History of the Hostilities Since 1880.* New York, NY: E. P. Dutton; 1978.

48. Ronald R. *The Prevention of Malaria.* New York, NY: E. P. Dutton; 1910.

49. http://www.britannica.com/nobel/micro/369_83.html

50. National Institutes of Health. Office of History. Available at: http://history.nih.gov. Accessed February 22, 2006.

51. Food and Drug Administration. Biologics centennial. Available at: http://www.fda.gov/oc/history/2006centennial/biologics100.html. Accessed February 22, 2006.

52. Sepkowitz KA, One hundred years of Salvarsan. *N Engl J Med.* 2011;365:291–292.

53. Schwartz RS. Paul Ehrlich's magic bullets. *N Engl J Med.* 2004;350:1079–1080.

54. Gensini GF, Conti AA, Lippi D. The contributions of Paul Ehrlich to infectious disease. *J Infection.* 2007;54:221–224.

55. Dowling HF. *Fighting Infection.* Cambridge, MA: Harvard University Press; 1977.

56. Etheridge EW. *Sentinel for Health: A History of the Centers for Disease Control.* Berkeley: University of California Press; 1992.

57. Centers for Disease Control and Prevention. Ten great public health achievements—United States, 1900–1999. *MMWR.* 1999;48:241–248.

58. Batelle Medical Technology Assessment and Policy Research Program, Center for Public Health Research and Evaluation. *A Cost Benefit Analysis of the Measles-Mumps-Rubella (MMR) Vaccine.* Arlington, VA: Batelle; 1994.

59. Centers for Disease Control and Prevention. Ten great public health achievements—United States, 1900–1999, control of infectious diseases. *MMWR.* 1999;48:621–629.

60. Davies K. *Cracking the Genome: Inside the Race to Unlock Human DNA.* New York, NY: Free Press; 2001.

61. Venter JC, Adams MD, Myers EW, et al. The sequence of the human genome. *Science.* 2001;291:1304–1351.

62. Genome International Sequencing Consortium. Initial sequencing and analysis of the human genome. *Nature.* 2001;409:860–921.

63. National Institutes of Health. National Human Genome Research Institute. Available at: http://www.genome.gov. Accessed February 22, 2006.

64. International Rice Genome Sequencing Project. The map-based sequence of the rice genome. *Nature.* 2005;436:793–800.

65. Burkhardt PK, Beyer P, Wunn J, et al. Transgenic rice (*Oryza sativa*) endosperm expressing daffodil (*Narcissus pseudonarcissus*) phytoene synthase accumulates phytoene, a key intermediate of provitamin A biosynthesis. *Plant J.* 1997;11:1071–1078.

66. Paine JA, Shipton CA, Chaggar S, et al. Improving the nutritional value of golden rice through increased pro-vitamin A content. *Nat Biotechnol.* 2005;23:482–487.

67. Villamor E, Fawzi WW. Effects of vitamin A supplementation on immune responses and correlation with clinical outcomes. *Clin Microbiol Rev.* 2005;18:446–464.

68. Institute for Science in Society. Monsanto vs. farmers. Available at: http://www.i-sis.org.uk/MonsantovsFarmers.php. Accessed February 22, 2006.

69. Centers for Disease Control and Prevention. Kaposi's sarcoma and *Pneumocystis* pneumonia among homosexual men—New York City and California. *MMWR.* 1981;30:305–308.

2

Epidemiology of Infectious Disease: General Principles

Kenrad E. Nelson

INTRODUCTION

Studies of the epidemiology of infectious diseases include evaluation of the factors leading to infection by an organism, factors affecting the transmission of an organism, and factors associated with clinically recognizable disease among those who are infected. Epidemiologic concepts such as the incubation period and resistance were originally developed in studies of infectious diseases and later applied to noninfectious diseases.

Epidemiologic characterization is the first step in defining a new disease, although diseases can also be classified according to their clinical or microbiologic features. For the public health professional, it is the epidemiologic features—for instance, the prevalence, incidence, transmission route, and susceptible populations—that are of paramount importance in developing a control program. In contrast, a clinician whose primary role is to treat a disease may be more concerned with the clinical symptoms or pathophysiology. For example, an infectious agent that causes secretory diarrhea will be treated empirically with fluid replacement and symptomatic management of the pathophysiology, irrespective of how the infection was acquired or what the infectious organism is. A microbiologist will be concerned primarily with the characteristics of the organism and will focus on the tasks of isolation, identification, and development of targeted treatments.

The control, treatment, and prevention of an epidemic usually requires the cooperative efforts of all three groups of specialists—clinicians, microbiologists, and epidemiologists. However, each has a unique orientation and contribution to make to this field. The perspectives from each of these three areas

of study can best be appreciated by considering how infectious diseases are classified by each specialist.

THE CLASSIFICATION OF INFECTIOUS DISEASES

Clinicians tend to classify infectious diseases according to their most common or most important clinical manifestation or by the organ systems that are primarily affected. An example of a clinical classification is given in **Table 2-1**.

Microbiologists use classification schemes focused on the characteristics of the causative organism. An example of a typical microbiologic classification of infectious diseases is shown in **Table 2-2**.

Epidemiologists focus on the epidemiologic characteristics of a disease and classify diseases according to either the means of transmission or the reservoir of the organism. Infectious diseases can be classified according to their means of transmission into five distinct categories, as shown in **Table 2-3**. With the epidemiologic classification of infectious diseases according to where the pathogen is found, the most generalized form of categorization is based on whether a pathogen is either native to humans, animals, soil, or water. Some common examples of infectious diseases classified according to their reservoir are shown in **Table 2-4**.

When a new disease appears on the scene, the detailed microbiologic characteristics of the organism are typically unknown. Likewise, the full clinical manifestation may be undefined. For example, the fact that infection with *Borrelia burgdorferii*, the cause of Lyme disease, was responsible not only for the classical skin

Table 2-1	Clinical Classification of Infections
Classification	**Infection**
Diarrheal diseases	Secretory
	Invasive
Respiratory diseases	Upper respiratory
	Lower respiratory
Central nervous system infection	Meningitis (bacterial vs. aseptic)
	Encephalitis
	Abscess
Cardiovascular infection	Endocarditis
	Myocarditis
	Vasculitis
Sepsis	Disseminated

Table 2-2	Microbiologic Classification of Infectious Diseases
Classification	**Organism**
Bacterial	Gram-negative
	Gram-positive
Viral	DNA virus
	RNA virus
	Enveloped vs. nonenveloped viruses
Fungal	Disseminated (biphasic)
	Localized
Parasitic	Protozoa
	Helminths
	Trematodes
	Cestodes
Prion	Protein

Table 2-3	Classification of Infectious Organisms by Their Means of Transmission
Transmission	**Characteristics**
Contact	Requires direct or indirect contact (indirect = infected fomite, blood, or body fluid; direct = skin or sexual contact)
Food- or water-borne	Ingestion of contaminated food (outbreaks may be large and dispersed, depending on distribution of food)
Airborne	Inhalation of contaminated air
Vector-borne	Dependent on biology of the vector (mosquito, tick, snail, etc.), as well as the infectivity of the organism
Perinatal	Similar to contact infection; however, the contact may occur in utero during pregnancy or at the time of delivery

Table 2-4	Classification of Infectious Organisms by Their Reservoir in Nature
Reservoir	**Some Typical Organisms**
Human	*Treponema pallidum, Neisseria gonorrhoeae,* HIV, hepatitis B and C virus, *Shigella, S. typhi*
Animals (zoonoses)	Rabies, *Yersinia pestis, Leptospira,* nontyphoid *Salmonella, Brucella*
Soil	*Histoplasma capsulatum* (and other systemic fungi), *Clostridium tetani, Clostridium botulinum*
Water	*Legionella, Pseudomonas aeruginosa, Mycobacterium marinum*

lesion, erythema chronica migrans (ECM), but also for acute and chronic arthritis, vascular and cardiac disease, and neurologic symptoms, including Bell's palsy and encephalitis, was not appreciated initially. In fact, the full range of clinical manifestations of infection with *B. burgdorferii* is still being defined.

If one is aware of the reservoir of the agent in addition to the means of transmission, it is generally possible to develop a strategy to prevent transmission, even when the microbiologic characteristics of the organism are not known. The demonstration of the water reservoir of cholera by John Snow in London in 1853 preceded the identification of the *Vibrio* cholera by Robert Koch in 1884.[1] In this case, the epidemiologic information alone was sufficient to develop public health strategies to limit exposure to contaminated water and prevent human infections. Similarly, the demonstration of the importance of human carriers of *Salmonella typhi* as the important reservoir in outbreaks of typhoid fever by Budd in 1858 antedated by 22 years the isolation of the infectious organism in the laboratory by Eberth in 1880. Walter

Reed succeeded in transmitting yellow fever by the bite of infected *Aedes aegypti* mosquitoes in 1901, but it was not until 1928 that Stokes and colleagues isolated the causative virus in the laboratory. In more recent times, investigation of pneumonia at the American Legion convention in Philadelphia in 1976 demonstrated that disease was due to airborne spread of microorganisms from the air-conditioning system and suggested that infection could be prevented by avoiding the air in the hotel.[2] The implicated organism, *Legionella pneumophila*, was not isolated and characterized in the laboratory until 1978, when it was identified by McDade and Sheppard at the Centers for Disease Control and Prevention (CDC).

Knowledge of the reservoir often is essential before one can devise rational and effective means of preventing transmission of infectious diseases. Prior to John Snow's demonstration that contaminated water was the reservoir of *Vibrio cholerae* in the outbreak in London in the 1850s, the predominant theories were that miasma—that is, exposure to foul or malodorous air—was the critical exposure leading to infection. However, there were no successful efforts to control the outbreak that were based on the miasma theory. When Snow demonstrated that attack rates of cholera were highest in those persons who received their water from one particular water company and subsequently terminated an epidemic by closing down the pump at one water source, the evidence was persuasive.[1]

Infectious Diseases Transmitted by More Than One Means

Some organisms may be spread by several different means, depending on the epidemiologic circumstances. Therefore, it is important for an epidemiologist to keep an open mind to detect unusual epidemiologic features of an infection. A few examples of infectious diseases that have been spread by multiple means are described here.

Tularemia

Perhaps a typical example of a disease that can be spread by more than one means is tularemia, which can be acquired by the bite of infected ticks or deer flies,[8] by contact with infected rabbits or other animals during the hunting season,[9,10] or by inhalation of an aerosol.[11,12] In addition, nosocomial infection among microbiology laboratory workers has been reported from inhalation of infected aerosols of the causative organism, *Francisella tularensis*.[13] Curiously, none of the investigators who have studied epidemics of tularemia have found evidence of human-to-human transmission.[14]

Plague

Plague—the disease that has been associated with perhaps the most serious and extensive epidemic in human history—is caused by the plague bacillus, *Yersinia pestis*. This zoonotic disease of rodents is transmitted to humans and other mammalian hosts from infected rodents by rat fleas. Percutaneous inoculation of the plague bacillus in humans initiates inflammation of lymph nodes draining the inoculation site, resulting in bubonic plague. Bloodstream invasion may lead to septicemic plague or to infection of other organ systems, such as the lung or meninges. Involvement of the lungs may result in pneumonic plague, which can then be transmitted from person to person via the respiratory route.

Historically, many epidemics of plague have spread rapidly through populations, causing very high mortality. The earliest description of plague dates from the sixth century AD in Egypt, when the epidemic spread throughout North Africa and into Europe. Epidemic plague reappeared in the Far East in the 1300s and subsequently spread to Europe. During the "Great Plague" epidemic in London, which peaked in August and September 1665, 7,000 deaths per week were reported in a population of an estimated 500,000 persons. For unknown reasons, plague gradually disappeared from Europe in the 1700s, and the entire continent was free of plague by 1840.[15] Zinsser considers the disappearance of epidemics of plague from Europe to be one of the great mysteries of the epidemiology of infectious diseases.[16]

However, epidemics of plague did occur in Asia in the late 1800s and more recently in Vietnam, during the war between 1962 and 1975.[17] An epidemic of plague was reported in India in 1994.[18] Sporadic cases of plague have occurred throughout the American Southwest for the past several decades, related to epizootics in infected prairie dogs.[19,20] The infectious organism was first isolated by Yersin in Hong Kong in 1894.[21] Although a vaccine is available, its efficacy in preventing pneumonic plague is unknown.

Anthrax

Anthrax is an infection with *Bacillus anthracis*, a gram-positive spore-forming organism that causes a zoonotic disease in herbivorous animals. The pathogen can be transmitted to humans from contact with infected animals, and the resulting disease has three clinical forms in humans: cutaneous, gastrointestinal, and inhalation anthrax.

The organisms from infected animals most often infect humans by contact with contaminated animal hides or pelts; this disease has been called *woolsorter's disease.*[22] Infection can also occur by inoculation of organisms into the skin during butchering of an infected animal; this type of exposure usually leads to cutaneous anthrax, consisting of a black eschar on the skin with swelling and inflammation of the draining lymphatics. Consumption of meat from an infected animal leads to gastrointestinal anthrax, which has a much higher mortality than does cutaneous anthrax. Inhalation anthrax occurs when an infectious aerosol of *B. anthracis* spores is inhaled and germinates in the pulmonary lymphatic tissues. This form of anthrax is rare, which is fortunate because it usually proves rapidly fatal.

An epidemic of inhalation anthrax occurred among persons living in Sverdlovsk, Union of Soviet Socialist Republics, in April and May 1979. At least 96 cases and 66 deaths occurred. The outbreak also affected cattle within 50 kilometers of the city. Interestingly, Sverdlovsk was known to have a military facility that was suspected of manufacturing biologic weapons, including anthrax spores, for potential use in warfare. Initially, the Soviet authorities maintained that this outbreak was from gastrointestinal exposure due to the consumption of contaminated meat from cattle that had died of anthrax. However, in 1992, Meselson and colleagues visited the site of the epidemic and were able to conduct an epidemiologic investigation, together with Russian scientists. Their study found that all of the human cases were living or working in a narrow belt south of the city on the day the outbreak occurred.[23] Furthermore, the animal deaths also occurred in this belt, up to 50 kilometers distant (**Figure 2-1**). The wind pattern on the day of the outbreak could explain the geographic distribution of cases. Subsequently, evidence was discovered that many of the human cases had pneumonic anthrax. The researchers concluded that this outbreak—the largest outbreak of human inhalation anthrax ever recorded—was due to an infectious aerosol emanating from the military facility.

One very interesting finding in this study was that human cases continued to occur for as long as 6 weeks after the initial point-source exposure. Apparently, spores were inhaled and continued to germinate and cause disease for several weeks after they were inhaled. This outbreak has raised considerable concern among scientists and policymakers about the potential for the use of aerosolized *B. anthracis* spores as an agent of biologic terrorism. Indeed, these fears were confirmed in 2001 when an outbreak of 22 cases of anthrax occurred in the United States from intentional contamination of the U.S. mail delivered to a number of persons by the U.S.

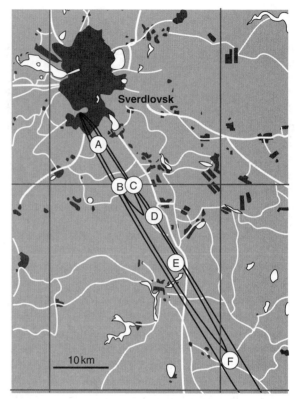

Figure 2-1 Russian villages with animal anthrax. Six villages where livestock died of anthrax in April 1979 are shown. Settled areas are shown in gray, roads in white, and calculated contours of constant dosage in black. From M. Meselson et al, The Sverdlovsk Anthrax Outbreak of 1979. *Science*, Vol. 266, Figure 3, p. 1205. © 1994. Reprinted with permission from AAAS.

Postal Service. This outbreak is described in detail in the chapter on emerging infections.

Rabies

Rabies is a nearly uniformly fatal infection of the central nervous system that is almost always transmitted by a bite from an animal infected with the rabies virus. Historically, rabies has nearly always been acquired by a bite from an infected dog, skunk, fox, bat, or other animal. It has been regarded as a typical contact-transmitted infection, in that percutaneous inoculation of rabies virus by a bite is usually required. Nevertheless, a few persons have developed rabies from exposure to infected aerosols in caves that harbored by many infected bats.[24] In addition, rabies has occurred in a laboratory worker who was exposed to an infectious aerosol[25] and in persons who have received corneal transplants from a donor who died of undiagnosed rabies.[26] In recent years, in the United States, only 2–3 cases have occurred annually; however, reported bite exposures in these cases has been unusual. Of the 32 cases of rabies that were diagnosed in the United States between 1980 and 1996, 25 (78%) had no history of a bite exposure.[27] Some of these non-bite-transmitted cases in the United States have occurred in persons exposed in the same room (or closed space) to an infected bat; presumably, the transmission in these cases was by aerosol. Genetic analysis of the viruses has shown that 17 (53%) of these cases in the United States were related to rabies viruses found in insectivorous bats.

Brucellosis

Brucellosis is an infectious disease of humans acquired through contact with an infected animal (i.e., a zoonosis). Four species of *Brucellae* have infected humans: *B. abortus* (from cattle), *B. melitensis* (from goats or sheep), *B. suis* (from pigs), and *B. canis* (from dogs). Human infections with the two other known species, *B. ovis* (from sheep) and *B. neotomae* (from desert wood rats), have not been reported. Clinically, the most serious human infections are seen with *B. melitensis*. However, in the early decades of the 1900s, infections with *B. abortus* were common, and these infections often were acquired by the consumption of contaminated milk from infected cows.

After World War II, the U.S. Department of Agriculture (USDA) undertook a campaign to eliminate milk-borne brucellosis as a human health problem in the United States. The program included testing of cattle for *B. abortus* and slaughtering of infected animals or animals from infected herds, and pasteurization of all milk and dairy products.[28] This program was quite successful. More than 6000 cases of human brucellosis were reported each year at the start of this program; the rate had declined to 4.5 cases per 100,000 population in 1948. In the 1990s, only about 100 cases per year were reported; 0.05 case per 100,000 population was reported in 1993.

In recent years, persons affected brucellosis have usually had an occupation that directly exposed them to infected animals, such as slaughterhouse workers, farmers, or veterinarians. Brucellosis in these workers was acquired by direct contact with infected animals, not through consumption of infected milk. Also, *B. suis* infections from infected pigs have become proportionally more common, because the brucellosis control program was directed at eliminating the disease in cattle.

Transmission of Microbial Agents by Transfusions

Evidence shows that several microbial agents can be transmitted by blood transfusion or contaminated injection if exposure occurs during a time when the organisms are present in the bloodstream. For example, hepatitis B virus, hepatitis C virus, and HIV are commonly transmitted by the transfusion of blood or blood products. *Trypanosoma cruzii*, a protozoan parasite that causes Chagas's disease, is usually transmitted to humans by the bite of a reduviid bug but can be transmitted by blood transfusion from a carrier.[29] Malaria usually is caused by the transmission of one of four species of *Plasmodium* parasites by the bite of an infected female *Anopheline* mosquito, but it can also be transmitted by blood transfusion or to an infant by perinatal transmission. Hepatitis A virus is generally transmitted by ingestion of contaminated food or water but can be transmitted by blood transfusion during the brief viremic stage early in the infection.

Perinatal Infections

Infections of an infant may be acquired from the mother in utero via placental transfer, during passage through the birth canal, or in the postpartum period.

Rubella

The dramatic effect of rubella infections during the first trimester of pregnancy in producing congenital anomalies in the infant was first reported by Sir Norman Gregg following an outbreak of rubella in Australia in 1940.[30] Gregg noted ocular defects and cardiac lesions in the affected infants. Subsequently, these findings were confirmed by studies conducted during rubella outbreaks in Australia, the United States, and the United Kingdom. These studies further defined the congenital rubella syndrome (CRS) from intrauterine exposure to rubella during the first trimester of pregnancy to include cataracts and other ocular abnormalities, cardiac defects, deafness, microcephaly, and mental retardation. Infants exposed during the first trimester of pregnancy have a 90% risk of developing congenital rubella syndrome; during the early second trimester, the risk of congenital abnormalities from exposure to rubella declines to 20–40% and often involves only deafness.

In 1962, the rubella virus was isolated by investigators at Harvard University[31] and independently by scientists at the Walter Reed Army Institute of Research.[32] Shortly thereafter, in 1964, a major epidemic of rubella and CRS occurred in the United States.[33] An attenuated live rubella virus vaccine was developed and licensed in the United States in 1969.[34] Subsequently, congenital rubella infections have become rare in the United States, due to routine immunization of infants and screening and selective immunization of susceptible women of childbearing age.

Cytomegalovirus

Cytomegalovirus (CMV) infections during the first trimester of pregnancy are known to lead to congenital malformation, especially of the central nervous system. Cytomegalovirus was first isolated in human fibroblast cultures in 1956.[35–37] It is possible to screen pregnant women for susceptibility to infection during pregnancy. Epidemiologic studies suggest that CMV infection may occur in about 1% of all U.S. births, or approximately 40,000 infants annually.[38] In most instances, these infections are asymptomatic.

In 1990, the CDC established a national surveillance registry in the United States to monitor congenital CMV infections.[39] The most common clinical manifestation reported was petechiae, observed in 50% of cases, which was often accompanied by hepatosplenomegaly, intracranial calcification, and thrombocytopenia.

Herpes Simplex Virus

In contrast to CMV and rubella, in utero infection with herpes simplex virus (HSV) is rare, and when it does occur, it is most likely to lead to a miscarriage, rather than a congenital malformation. However, infants can be infected when passing through the birth canal if the mother has an active infection, especially with HSV type 2 (HSV-2), which causes recurrent genital tract infection. When the mother has an active HSV infection at the time of delivery, the infant can develop a generalized infection, which is quite serious. The risk to the newborn is higher when the mother has a primary HSV infection than when the HSV is a recurrence; the risk to the newborn is approximately 40% when exposed to a mother with primary infection, compared with 2–5% when the mother has a recurrent infection. In the latter situation, the infant's risk is modified by maternal passive transfer of antibodies to HSV-2 and by lower maternal viral load.

Cesarean section is recommended to prevent neonatal herpes in children born to women with active HSV at the time of delivery. Nevertheless, most cases of neonatal HSV occur where the mother was not identified as having active HSV infection. For example, during an 18-month hospital-based surveillance study, CDC identified 184 cases of neonatal herpes, but only 22% of the mothers had a history of genital HSV infection, and only 9% had lesions at the time of delivery.[40]

Toxoplasmosis

Congenital infection with *Toxoplasma gondii* occurs when a pregnant woman develops a infection with this pathogen, especially early in pregnancy. Clinical manifestations in the infant at birth may include a maculopapular rash, generalized lymphadenopathy, hepatomegaly, splenomegaly, jaundice, or thrombocytopenia. In addition, the infant can develop meningoencephalitis with cerebrospinal fluid abnormalities, hydrocephalus, microcephaly, chorioretinitis, and convulsions. More typically, congenital infection is asymptomatic at birth, although sequelae can become apparent several years later. Sequelae of congenital *Toxoplasma* infection include mental retardation and learning disability.

Ocular toxoplasmosis most often results from reactivation of a congenital infection, but it can occur from an acquired infection as well. Ocular toxoplasmosis usually occurs among adults.

Syphilis

Syphilis is caused by infection with a spirochete, *Treponema pallidum*. It is usually transmitted sexually but can be transmitted by the perinatal (congenital) route by infection through the placenta, especially in the second and third trimester of pregnancy. More rarely, transmission may occur during delivery by contact of an infant with the mucosa of a woman with primary or secondary syphilis during the birth process.

Congenital syphilis can be asymptomatic or it may manifest as multisystem involvement, including osteitis, hepatitis, lymphadenopathy, pneumonitis, mucocutaneous lesions, anemia, and hemorrhage. Late manifestation may involve the central nervous system, bones, teeth, and eyes. Rates of congenital syphilis parallel the rates of primary and secondary syphilis in women and can be prevented by treatment of infected pregnant women with penicillin, to which the organism is uniformly sensitive. Rates of congenital syphilis increased in the late 1980s and early 1990s, in part related to the epidemic of crack cocaine use in the United States.[41]

Because newborns infected with each of the agents so far have similar clinical symptoms, pediatricians often consider all of them in the differential diagnosis of perinatal infections. The syndrome of congenital infection is often referred to by the abbreviation *TORCHS* to signify the most common etiologies: toxoplasmosis, rubella, CMV, HSV, and syphilis.

Hepatitis B Virus

Women who are carriers of hepatitis B virus (HBV) may transmit the virus to their infants in utero or at the time of birth (peripartum). Infection of a newborn with HBV carries a very high risk of chronic infection, with the possibility of subsequent chronic active hepatitis, cirrhosis, or liver cancer when

Table 2-5	Effects of Transplacental Fetal Infection				
	Effect of Infection on the Fetus and Newborn Infant				
Organism or Disease	**Prematurity**	**Intrauterine Growth Retardation and Low Birth Weight**	**Developmental Anomalies**	**Congenital Disease**	**Persistent Postnatal Infection**
Viruses					
Rubella	–	+	–	+	+
Cytomegalovirus	+	+	+	+	–
Herpes simplex	+	–	–	+	+
Varicella-zoster	–	(+)	–	+	–
Mumps	–	–	–	(+)	–
Rubeola	+	–	–	+	–
Vaccinia	–	–	–	+	–
Smallpox	+	–	–	+	–
Coxsackieviruses B	–	–	(–)	+	–
Echoviruses	–	–	–	–	–
Polioviruses	–	–	–	–	–
Influenza	–	–	–	–	–
Hepatitis B	+	–	–	+	+
Human immunodeficiency virus	(+)	(+)	(–)	+	+
Lymphocytic chorio-meningitis virus	–	–	–	+	–
Parvovirus	–	–	–	(+)	–

Notes: +, evidence for effect; –, no evidence for effect; (–), association of effect with infection has been suggested and is under consideration.
Reprinted from Epidemiologic Concepts and Methods, in Viral Infections of Humans, 4th Edition. A.S. Evans and R.A. Kaslow, eds., p. 30. ©1997, Plenum Publishing Corporation. With kind permission from Springer Science+Business Media B.V.

carriage persists for decades. Most perinatal transmission of HBV can be prevented by screening pregnant women for hepatitis B surface antigen (HBsAg) and administering hepatitis B immunoglobulin and a course of HBV vaccine to the infants of HBsAg carriers, beginning immediately after birth.

Human Immunodeficiency Virus

Human immunodeficiency virus (HIV) is an important viral infection that can be transmitted perinatally from an infected woman to her newborn infant. Worldwide, the number of infected infants born each year in the 1990s was estimated to be approximately 500,000.

Although the risk of the prenatal transmission of HIV can be reduced to 5–10% or less by screening pregnant women and treating them with antiviral drugs, perinatal transmission still commonly occurs in sub-Saharan Africa. The various reported studies and research strategies to reduce perinatal HIV transmission are discussed in detail in the chapter on HIV.

Other Infectious Agents

The most important infectious diseases that are transmitted by the perinatal route were discussed in the preceding subsections; however, some evidence indicates that transmission of several other agents—such as parvovirus B-19, varicella-zoster virus, and others—via this route is possible. The most common agents incriminated in perinatal infection and the effects of perinatal infection with these agents on the fetus and newborn infant are listed in **Table 2-5**.

EPIDEMIOLOGIC CHARACTERISTICS OF INFECTIOUS DISEASES

Incubation Period

The incubation period of an infectious disease is the time between exposure to an infectious agent and the onset of symptoms or signs of infection. Each infectious disease has a typical incubation period that requires multiplication of the infectious agent to a threshold necessary to produce symptoms or laboratory evidence of infection, such as antibodies, viral isolation, and nucleic acids in the host. The incubation period for infectious diseases shows some variation, which occurs for a variety of reasons, including the dose or inoculum of the infectious agent, the route of inoculation, and the rate of replication of the organism. Even when numerous persons are exposed at the same time to a similar inoculum of the same strain of an infectious agent, such as consumption of food contaminated with *Salmonella* at a picnic, the length of the incubation period varies between individuals. A plot of the incubation period for persons exposed at the same time usually follows a log normal distribution. The antilogarithm of 1 standard deviation from the mean log incubation period has been referred to

by Sartwell as the *dispersion factor*.[45] The dispersion factor multiplied by the mean log of the incubation period will define an interval above which 16% of the periods will fall, and the mean divided by the dispersion factor will define the period below which 16% will occur. Even diseases with very long incubation periods have been shown to follow similar patterns of distribution of their incubation periods. A recent study of the incubation periods of AIDS found that a log normal distribution reasonably described the incubation period of this disease as well.[46]

The usual ranges of the incubation periods for a number of infectious diseases are shown in **Figure 2-2**. These incubation periods range from 6 to 12 hours for *B. cereus* and staphylococcal food poisoning to 5–10 years for AIDS and leprosy. The extrinsic

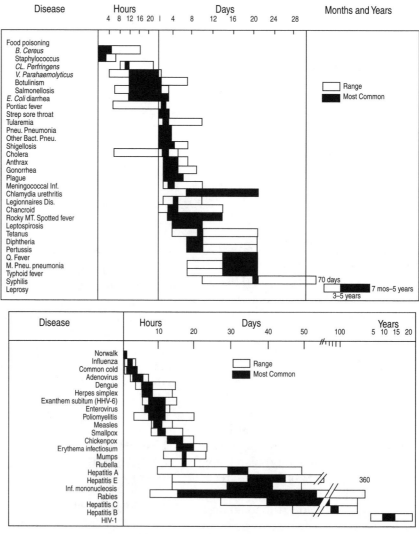

Figure 2-2 Incubation periods of common bacterial disease (top panel) and viral disease (bottom panel). Reprinted from *Epidemiologic Concepts and Methods*, in *Viral Infections of Humans*, 4th Edition. A.S. Evans and R. A. Kaslow, eds., p. 30. © 1997, Plenum Publishing Corporation. With kind permission from Springer Science+Business Media B.V.

incubation period applies to vector-borne infections; it is the time that a vector-borne agent requires for maturation to infectivity in the vector before the organism becomes infectious to humans. The extrinsic incubation period also has a median and range that are unique to each organism. The extrinsic incubation period can be affected by environmental conditions as well. For example, when *A. aegypti* mosquitoes were infected with dengue type 2 virus and held at 30°C, the mean extrinsic incubation period before they become infectious was 12 days, whereas between 32°C and 35°C, they became infectious after only 7 days.[47] The extrinsic incubation periods for various species of *Plasmodium* are discussed in more detail in the chapter on malaria.

Biologic Characteristics of the Organism

Infectivity

Infectivity is defined as the ability of an agent to cause infection in a susceptible host. The basic measure of infectivity is the minimum number of infectious particles required to establish infection. In diseases spread from person to person, the proportion of susceptible individuals who develop infection after exposure—the secondary attack rate—is a measure of the infectivity of an organism.

Pathogenicity

Pathogenicity refers to the ability of a microbial agent to induce disease. Diseases such as rabies, smallpox, measles, chickenpox, and rhinovirus colds have high pathogenicity. Others, such as polio and arbovirus (mosquito-borne) infections, have low pathogenicity.

Virulence

Some dictionaries use the terms *virulence* and *pathogenicity* interchangeably. However, it is useful to consider them to be separate properties of an infectious agent. *Virulence* can be defined as the severity of the disease after infection occurs. For example, although smallpox and rhinoviruses both usually cause symptoms (both are pathogenic), smallpox infections are much more virulent. Virulence can best be measured by the case fatality rate or as the proportion of clinical cases that develop severe disease. It is possible to classify organisms based on their infectivity, pathogenicity, and virulence. Only a few diseases, such as smallpox, airborne anthrax, and Ebola virus, rank high in all three characteristics.

It is important to recognize that these properties of an infection may change over time under different circumstances. At one time, syphilis and streptococcal infections were highly virulent infections with high mortality rates, but these diseases are now much less virulent. Changes in the epidemiologic characteristics of infectious diseases will be discussed in greater detail later in this chapter and elsewhere in this book.

Immunogenicity

Immunogenicity is the ability of an organism to produce an immune response after an infection that is capable of providing protection against reinfection with the same or a similar organism. Contact with some organisms, such as measles, polio, HBV, and rubella, leads to solid, lifelong immunity after an infection. Other organisms, such as *Neisseria gonorrhoeae* and *Plasmodium falciparum*, are weakly immunogenic, so that reinfection commonly occurs. Studies of the antigens that produce protective immunity after natural infections often have led to the development of effective vaccines.

Some microorganisms may provoke an immune response that is not protective from future infections. In a sense, they are immunogenic. Even so, these immune responses may sometimes be deleterious to the host. Several types of group A streptococci can provoke an immune response that leads to glomerulonephritis or acute rheumatic fever because of cross-reactive antibodies elicited in response to the streptococcal infection that react with endocardial or glomerular basement membrane antigens. Pathogenesis research in HIV infection is examining the role of immune activation in disease outcome. Inflammation of the immune system is a contributor to cardiovascular, renal, hepatic, and neural disease, and is also being studied as a component of aging and the development of frailty.

In other instances, antibodies may be generated that are markers of a previous or current infection but do not provide immunity to the organism or terminate an ongoing infection. These so-called *binding antibodies* react to non-neutralizing antigens (or epitopes) of the organism. Examples of such antibodies are found in patients with hepatitis C virus infection, HIV infection, and HSV-2 infection. Persons with these antibodies have been or are infected with the virus and have antibodies but are not immune.

Inapparent Infections

An inapparent infection is an infection that can be documented by isolation of an organism by culture, demonstration of the presence of a nucleic acid by polymerase chain reaction (PCR) amplification, or demonstration of a specific immune response in a

Table 2-6	Classification of Several Infections Diseases by their Epidemiologic Characteristics		
Severity	Infectivity	Pathogenicity	Virulence
High:	(Secondary AR) Measles Pertussis Ebola HPV SARS/ COV Influenza	(Illness=Infection) Measles Rabies Pertussis Ebola Smallpox Rhinovirus-URI SARS/COV Influenza	(Severe/Fatal) Rabies Ebola SARS/COV Smallpox
Intermediate	Smallpox Rubella Mumps Polio Rhinovirus URI	Rubella Mumps	Polio Pertussis Measles Tuberculosis Leprosy Influenza
Low	Tuberculosis Leprosy	Polio Tuberculosis Leprosy	Rhinovirus-URI Rubella Mumps

person who remains asymptomatic. The proportion of individuals with asymptomatic or clinically inapparent infections is a measure of the pathogenicity of the organism, as defined previously. Inapparent infections are quite common in many infections and may play an important role in the propagation of an epidemic in some circumstances.

The proportion of infected individuals who do not develop symptoms varies with different organisms. For example, most polio infections are inapparent. Likewise, inapparent nasopharyngeal carriage of meningococci is quite common, especially during an epidemic. Identification and treatment of carriers of meningococci or *Staphylococcus aureus* have been shown to help control epidemic transmission, because healthy carriers may play an important role in transmission. In the United States, persons who convert their tuberculin skin test and are infected but asymptomatic carriers of *Mycobacterium tuberculosis* are often treated to prevent clinically active tuberculosis from developing later in their life and to curtail the subsequent spread of infection to their contacts. Inapparent infections with other organisms are quite rare—for example, most persons with measles, varicella, smallpox, or hanta virus infection are symptomatic.

The proportion of infections that are symptomatic is of considerable importance in understanding the transmission of a disease during an epidemic and in designing methods to control epidemic or endemic transmission. The proportion of infections that are

clinically inapparent among individuals infected with some important organisms is shown in **Table 2-6**.

The Carrier State

The epidemiologic importance of the asymptomatic carrier in the transmission of infectious diseases has been recognized for some time. An early classic example was an Irish cook in New York City in the early 1900s, Mary Mallon, who became known as "Typhoid Mary." She was quite healthy but had worked as a cook in many homes where the residents developed typhoid fever after she was hired. Eventually, 53 cases of typhoid fever were traced to her. After Mallon was located and cultures of her stool consistently grew *S. typhi*, she was confined and not allowed to work in food service between 1907 and 1910. After her release, she disappeared and changed her name. Two years later, outbreaks of typhoid fever involving more than 200 persons were detected in hospitals in New York and New Jersey that were traced to her.[48] This remarkable story illustrates the potential importance of the carrier state in the transmission of typhoid fever. Patients infected with *S. typhi* may carry the organism in their gallbladders and excrete the organism in their stool for many years. Generally, antibiotic therapy is ineffective in curing their infections, but many chronic carriers can be cured by cholecystectomy.[49]

Another, more modern example is that of "patient zero," who was at the center of a large cluster of men who developed Kaposi's sarcoma (KS), with or without *Pneumocystis carinii* pneumonia (PCP), in 1980–1981. This patient was a male homosexual flight attendant who had visited several large U.S. cities. He had sexual contact with all of the men who later became ill. This cluster of cases of KS and PCP was one of the early outbreaks of AIDS in the United States.[50] The carrier state may be of epidemiologic importance in any infectious disease that is transmitted from person to person. However, the average length of the carrier state, the site of replication and infectivity of the organism, and the usual means of spread determine the epidemiologic importance of asymptomatic carriers.

Outbreaks have been documented from persons who chronically carried organisms in their respiratory tract, stool, genital tract, or blood. Nosocomial transmission from hospital workers to patients, from one patient to another, or from patients to health care workers is common. Currently, transmission of antibiotic-resistant staphylococci by healthy carriers of these organisms is of major concern in hospitals in the United States. Patients who are chronic carriers of hepatitis B virus pose a significant risk to healthcare workers. As a result, use of HBV vaccine is routinely recommended for healthcare professionals who are likely to be exposed to this virus. These issues are covered in more detail in the chapter on nosocomial infection.

Transfusion-Transmitted Infection

The transmission of infections by transfusion has received increasing attention in the last 20 years. Although transfusion-transmitted HBV was recognized for several decades, the introduction of screening of donors for HBsAg in 1973 reduced this risk. Subsequently, it became apparent that after screening of blood donors for hepatitis virus was introduced, post-transfusion hepatitis declined to roughly half of the previous rate but was not eliminated. The hepatitis C virus was identified and screening for it implemented in 1990. Also, the occurrence of HIV infection and AIDS among transfusion recipients and hemophiliacs has highlighted the risks of the transmission of infection by transfusion of blood or blood products from healthy carriers.

Currently, blood donors undergo extensive questioning about their risks related to a variety of infectious agents, and they are screened for the presence of several pathogens. Pooled plasma products also undergo several viral inactivation steps and are heat-treated prior to their use. Nevertheless, the list of agents that may possibly be transmitted by the transfusion of blood or blood products continues to expand (**Exhibit 2-1**).

Exhibit 2-1	**Infections Transmitted by Transfusion**

- Viruses
  - HIV, HTLVI/II
  - HBV, HCV, HAV (rare)
  - Parvovirus B-19
  - CMV
  - KSHV (HHV-8)
  - West Nile Virus
  - Chikungunya Virus
  - Dengue
  - Others
- Bacteria
  - T. pallidum (rare)
  - Y. enterocolitica
  - Various gram-positive organisms by platelet transfusion (especially)
  - Ehrlichea (rare)
- Parasites
  - Trypanosoma cruzii
  - Plasmodium species
  - Babesia necrotica
- Other agents
  - New variant Creutzfeldt-Jakob disease prion

The Host–Parasite Relationship
Patterns of Natural History

After infection occurs, the subsequent course or natural history of an infection can be quite variable. Many infections are characterized by acute symptoms, some of which may be severe and even terminate fatally. In some infections, the proportion of patients with asymptomatic or clinically inapparent infections varies, but once the acute phase is over, the patient is immune to reinfection with the same agent. The common childhood contagious diseases, such as measles, mumps, and rubella, are characterized by this type of natural history.

In other infections, some patients may develop chronic or recurring infection, and others may recover and develop lasting immunity. Hepatitis B virus and herpes virus types 1 and 2 typify this type of natural history. Infection with some agents may lead to chronic sequelae, due to an autoimmune reaction or chronic tissue damage that occurs after the acute infection has subsided and without persistence of the organism or chronic infection. Poststreptococcal glomerulonephritis and rheumatic fever are typical of this type of natural history.

Some infectious agents may recur or relapse, even after the acute infection has resolved without sequelae. Typical of this pattern are HSV-1 and HSV-2, varicella-zoster virus, and cytomegalovirus infections. Some infections may become chronic, with a variable proportion leading to progressive

Table 2-7	Natural History Patterns of Some Important Infectious Diseases
Natural History	**Disease**
Acute with recovery and long-term immunity	Measles, mumps, rubella, polio, diphtheria
Acute with some chronic carriers	HBV, HSV-1 and HSV-2, VZV, *Chlamydia trachomatis* infections
Acute disease, chronic sequelae without carrier state	Group A streptococcal (ARF, AGN), syphilis, Lyme disease
Chronic carriers common (or usual)	HIV, HBV, HSV-2, HPV, HCV, *H. pylori* infections, *Opisthorchis viverrini*, *Schistosoma* infections
Chronic carriers may develop cancer	HBV—Hepatocellular CA HCV—Hepatocellular CA HPV—Cervical or laryngeal CA *H. pylori*—Gastric CA HTLV-1—T-cell leukemia EBV—Nasopharyngeal carcinoma HHV-8—Kaposi's sarcoma Opisthorchis—Cholangiocarcinoma

Table 2-8	Infection and the Burden of Cancer Worldwide, 2008		
Cancer	**Incidence, *N* (age standardized rate per 100,000)**	**Mortality, *N* (age standardized rate per 100,000)**	**Infectious Agent**
Stomach	988,602 (14.0)	737,419 (10.3)	*H. pylori*
Liver	749,744 (10.8)	695,726 (9.9)	HBV, HEV
Cervix uteri	530,232 (15.2)	275,008 (7.8)	HPV
Bladder	382,660 (5.3)	150,282 (2.0)	*S. hematobium*
Larynx	150,677 (2.2)	81,892 (1.2)	HPV
Hodgkin's lymphoma	67,919 (1.0)	29,902 (0.4)	EBV
Non-Hodgkin's lymphoma	356,431 (5.1)	191,599 (2.7)	HBV, HCV, EBV
Leukemia	350,434 (5.0)	257,161 (3.6)	HTLV-1

Data from GLOBOCAN 2008 (IARC), Section of Cancer Information. Fact Sheets, Country Fast Stat IARC. World Health Organization. Available at: http://globocan.iarc.fr/factsheet.asp. Updated May 17, 2012. Accessed May 17, 2012.

tissue damage at the primary site of the infection. Typical of this pattern are hepatitis C virus, HBV, and HIV.

Finally, some infections may become chronic and eventually lead to cancer in the target organ of the infection. Typical of this type of infection are human papillomavirus, HBV, and *Helicobacter pylori* infections. Infections that often exhibit each of these various natural history patterns are listed in **Table 2-7**.

The World Health Organization (WHO) estimates that more than 15% of human cancers worldwide are caused by chronic infections. The proportion and types of human cancers associated with infectious agents are shown in **Table 2-8**.

The Immune Response to Infection

A detailed discussion of the immune responses to infection is well beyond the scope of this chapter. Instead, this topic is covered fully in the chapter on immunology. For now, however, it is useful to provide a very brief overview to introduce some concepts and nomenclature relative to the immune responses to infection.

Protection against infection consists of both specific immune responses against particular pathogens and nonspecific defenses directed against organisms or foreign antigens. Several compounds present in the normal intact skin, including lipids, lipoproteins, and peptides, are toxic to many organisms. Lysozyme in the tears and several proteins in the oral cavity have

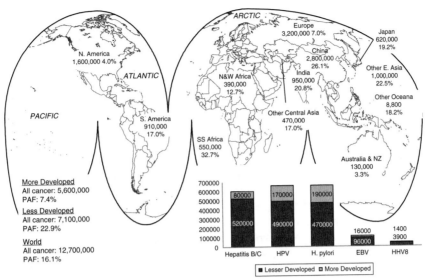

Figure 2-3. Socio-Economic, Geographic and Agent Variability in the Distribution of Cancers due to Infectious Agents*
All cancer cases and the Population Infectious Agent Attributable Fraction (PAF%). Data from de Matel, et al (2012). Global burden of cancers attributable to infections in 2008: a review and synthetic analysis. *Lancet Oncol.* 2012; 13: 607–15.

bactericidal activity. The acidic pH of the stomach is lethal to moderate doses of many enteric pathogens. The normal ciliary activity of the respiratory tract and the mucous layer coating the bronchus and bronchioles represent an important first line of defense against respiratory organisms. The low pH of the vagina serves as a first line of defense against many sexually transmitted pathogens. Furthermore, natural killer (NK) cells and cells of the monocyte–macrophage lineage can provide some nonspecific defense against a pathogen, although the immune responses generated by cells and antibodies that have been stimulated to respond to a specific pathogen usually are more effective.

The immune system consists of a few main classes of cells and a large variety of cell subsets. Lymphocytes provide direction for the main activities of the immune system and govern the nature of the immune response. Those that originate in the bone marrow are called *B lymphocytes*; those that originate in or traffic through the thymus are called *T lymphocytes*. Other cells of the immune system include circulating monocytes and macrophages, tissue macrophages, dendritic cells, Langerhans cells, NK cells, mast cells, eosinophils, and basophils. Granulocytes are involved in phagocytosis of bacterial pathogens, and eosinophils are involved in the reaction to parasitic pathogens and in allergic and autoimmune reactions.

B Lymphocytes and Humoral Immunity The B lymphocytes are responsible for humoral immunity. These cells produce antibodies in the form of immunoglobulins (Ig) that are reactive with foreign anti-

gens. Five different isotypes of antibody are produced by B cells—namely, IgM, IgD, IgG, IgE, and IgA. Generally, the acute response to infection is characterized by a predominance of IgM antibodies, but later an IgG predominance emerges. This pattern is useful in differentiating a recent infection (i.e., within the past 3–6 months) from a more remote infection. For example, persons with IgM antibodies to hepatitis A virus (HAV) or the core antigen of HBV have had their primary HAV or HBV infections in the past 6 months. Persons with only IgG antibodies to HAV or HBV but no IgM antibodies were infected longer than 6 months ago.

Antibodies of the IgA class may provide neutralization of pathogens on mucosal surfaces. IgE antibodies are often involved in the immune responses to parasites and in allergic reactions to foreign protein antigens.

Local Immunity: The Mucosal Secretory IgA System
B lymphocytes secrete IgA antibodies, both in the blood and at the mucosal surfaces. These antibodies may play critical roles in resistance to infection in the respiratory, intestinal, and urogenital tracts. They are secreted after natural infection or following the administration of some whole-virus vaccines. Vaccines given parenterally are less effective in inducing mucosal IgA. Therefore, some live virus vaccines, such as oral polio virus vaccines, may be more effective in preventing infection than killed vaccines because the former provide resistance to mucosal infection as well as resistance to invasive infection.

T Lymphocytes and Cell-Mediated Immunity T lymphocytes are important regulatory cells of the immune system. They interact with antigen-presenting cells and secrete numerous cytokines that activate effector cells and interact with cells through the major histocompatibility complex (MHC) proteins at the cell surface. T lymphocytes can be classified as helper cells if they have CD4+ markers on their surface. The CD4+ helper cells activate B cells, monocytes–macrophages, and other helper T cells by binding directly to these cells or by secreting specific cytokines that stimulate cell proliferation. The cells that have CD8+ markers on their surface are cytotoxic T cells; they lyse other cells that contain foreign proteins or viruses. Also, CD8+ T cells can help modulate the immune response by suppressing the activation of effector cells, such as macrophages.

Granuloma reactions to an infection with mycobacteria consists of an organized cellular immune response with phagocytic effector cells, surrounded by CD4+ cells and CD8+ T-suppressor cells on the periphery to provide a localized and controlled immune response to the organism. Natural killer cells resemble lymphocytes but have some distinctive properties, such as expression of a specific receptor for the Fc portion of IgG. In some circumstances, these NK cells can kill virus-infected or neoplastic cells by secretion of interferon-gamma (IFN-γ), especially when induced to do so by tumor necrosis factor (TNF) and other cytokines produced by macrophages. Macrophages and monocytes function to process and deliver antigens for recognition by lymphocytes. Macrophages also can destroy intracellular virus-infected cells. These cells can respond to IFN-γ secreted by the T cell, which activates the toxic oxygen and enzymatic pathways of the macrophage.

Granulocytes and Complement Granulocytes are phagocytic cells that become involved in protection of the body against bacterial infections by ingesting and killing extracellular bacteria. The complement system comprises a set of enzymes and other proteins that attach to bacteria or foreign proteins and promote their destruction by phagocytosis. Persons who are deficient in some components of the complement system (especially C6, C7, or C8) have markedly increased susceptibility to recurrent infection with meningococci.[51]

Innate Immunity In addition to benefiting from acquired immunity, animals are protected from invasion by pathogenic organisms by a system of innate or native immunity. The innate immune system is prepared to control a range of pathogens immediately after they enter a host and does not have to develop and activate as the adaptive immune system does. A transmembrane receptor, named Toll, was first identified in Drosophila embryogenesis and subsequently found to be responsible for protecting insects against fungal infections. Toll-like receptors (TLRs) have since been identified in invertebrates, vertebrates, bacteria, and even plants. Given this diversity, they are probably among the most ancient of immune responses. These proteins recognize patterns of non-self molecules, such as bacterial lipopolysaccharides or viral DNA or RNA; such recognition triggers the intracellular defenses, including cytokines and enzymes, to destroy the foreign material.

Quantification of Infectious Diseases

Epidemiologists use a variety of measurements to quantify the occurrence of disease. Fundamentally, these measurements are intended to estimate the burden of disease in a population or the incidence of disease—that is, the rate at which the disease is spread among persons in the population. The prevalence of disease in a population is the number of people who are infected divided by the number of people in the population. The numerator is the number of persons who are ill, who have specific symptoms of the illness, or who have microbiologic evidence of infection but do not exhibit symptoms. Each of these definitions yields different information, and each is a valid measure of prevalence. No matter which definition is used, it is critical that what constitutes infection be defined. The denominator in the prevalence equation is also defined by the epidemiologist. It may be the number of persons in the population, regardless of known exposure status, or it may be only those persons who were exposed to the disease. In the former case, the measurement of prevalence defines the burden of disease in the population overall; in the latter case, the definition gives the prevalence of disease among those exposed. Where exposure is common, age-specific population prevalence is typically measured. Where exposure is rare, prevalence rates by exposure group are more frequently used.

The other commonly used measure in epidemiology is the incidence of disease. The incidence is either the rate at which persons acquire the disease or the rate at which the infectious agent is being transmitted throughout the population. The incidence of disease always includes a unit of time—the number of cases of influenza in a given year, month, or week, for example.

The incidence and prevalence of disease are related to each other by the duration of disease. In cases where the duration of disease is short, the prevalence of disease will be approximately equal to the incidence of disease because most infections will be relatively recent. In contrast, if the duration of the disease is long, the prevalence of disease will include both new and former cases of disease and will be larger than the incidence of disease. This relationship can be described by the following equation:

$$Prevalence = Incidence \times Duration$$

At times, the incidence of a disease may be decreasing at the same time that the prevalence is rising. Such may be the case with HIV infections in the United States and Western Europe at present, because combined antiretroviral therapy has prolonged survival and thereby increased the prevalence; concurrently, because of the effect of the drugs in reducing viral load, the transmission—that is, the incidence of new cases—may be decreasing.

In other infectious diseases that have short duration but for which infected persons remain susceptible to reinfection, the incidence may exceed the point prevalence. Affected persons may have several episodes of diarrheal disease or rhinovirus respiratory infections per year that last only a few days. In these diseases, the point prevalence may be low but the annual incidence may be quite high. In this scenario, it may be preferable to measure the impact of a disease by determining its annual incidence rate. In contrast, in malaria hyperendemic areas, young children may receive hundreds of bites from infected mosquitoes every year. In this situation, the annual incidence of malaria is so high that it is difficult to measure. However, a blood film will allow determination of the point prevalence of infection, because the parasites persist in the blood for some time. Malaria prevalence data are more useful to differentiate populations at very high risk or of hyperendemic foci in an endemic area.

SURVEILLANCE OF INFECTIOUS DISEASES

Surveillance of infectious diseases is essential to understand their epidemiology. *Surveillance* can be defined as the ongoing and systematic collection, collation, and analysis of data, and the dissemination of the results to those who need to know to avoid or prevent infections or epidemics.

In the United States, surveillance of infectious diseases is done by physicians and other healthcare workers, laboratories, clinics, and public health departments. Cases or outbreaks of selected infectious diseases are reported to the local health department by healthcare providers, laboratories, or hospitals. These reports are analyzed and forwarded to each state's health department, which reports the data to the CDC in Atlanta.

TEMPORAL TRENDS OF INFECTIOUS DISEASES

Many infectious diseases undergo temporal variation in incidence. This temporal variability is sometimes easy to explain by changes in the exposure to the agent over time, such as in different seasons of the year or in different years.

Seasonal Variation

Vector-transmitted diseases, such as malaria, dengue, and St. Louis encephalitis (SLE), depend on exposure to infected mosquito vectors for their transmission. Therefore, these diseases are present only during the warm months of the year in temperate climates when the appropriate mosquito vectors are present. The seasonal distribution of SLE virus infections of the central nervous system in the United States that were reported to the CDC between 1988 and 1997 is shown in **Figure 2-4**. The marked and consistent seasonality of SLE is readily apparent and easily understood, because the transmission depends on bites of susceptible humans by infected *Culex pipiens* or other related mosquitoes. These mosquitoes breed only in the summer in temperate climates and must reach a certain density and level of infection with SLE virus before human infections occur. **Figure 2-5** depicts the epidemiologic cycle of SLE in nature.

The important reservoir hosts for SLE are infected birds, both wild and domestic, that carry the virus without illness and develop high-level, persistent viremia with SLE virus after infection. These birds serve as the reservoir to infect mosquitoes. Because humans and other animals that may be bitten by SLE-infected mosquitoes have low levels of virus in the blood and the virus is very transient, they are not effective as reservoir hosts to infect additional mosquitoes and maintain the epidemic. For this reason, they are termed *dead-end hosts*. In other mosquito-borne arboviral infections, such

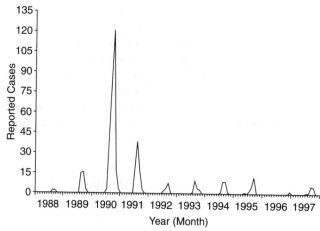

Figure 2-4 Arboviral infections of the central nervous system-reported laboratory confirmed cases caused by St. Louis encephalitis virus, by month of onset, United States 1988–1997. Reproduced from *MMWR*. November 20, 1998/46(54); 1–87. Figure 6.

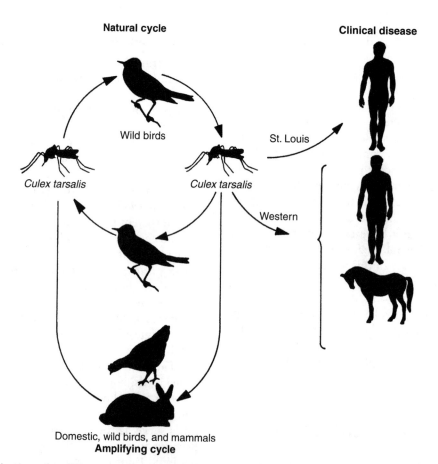

Figure 2-5 The sylvatic cycles of Western and St. Louis encephalitis viruses. The natural inapparent cycles is between *Culex tarsalis* and nesting and juvenile birds, but this cycle may be amplified by infection of domestic birds and wild and domestic mammals. Western encephalitis virus can replicate in mosquitoes at cooler temperatures, so epidemic disease in horses and humans may occur earlier in the summer and farther north into Canada. St. Louis encephalitis virus in the eastern United States involves *Culex pipiens* and other urban mosquitoes and causes urban epidemics. Reprinted from Richard T. Johnson, *Viral Infections of the Nervous System*, © 1982. Raven Press, Lippincott Williams & Williams; p. 113.

as Eastern equine encephalitis, Western encephalitis, or Venezuelan encephalitis, horses may commonly be infected when bitten by infected mosquitoes and develop symptomatic, even fatal, illness after infection. The rate of inapparent infections in humans may be 1000 to 1 or higher, whereas a much higher proportion of infected horses are symptomatic. Therefore, severe or fatal encephalitis in horses may serve as a harbinger that a subsequent human epidemic may follow.

Substantial variations in the number of reported SLE infections by year are seen in the CDC data. Beyond the seasonal pattern, however, the year-to-year variation in the number of cases is not readily predictable. These mosquito-borne viral infections vary in relation to the number of mosquitoes, which may vary in density due to rainfall and temperature patterns, the number of reservoir hosts (especially wild birds) that are infected, and contact patterns between mosquitoes and birds and between infected mosquitoes and susceptible humans. Because of the interaction of these variables, it is difficult to predict from one year to the next whether an epidemic will occur. The important arthropod-borne virus infections of humans are discussed further in the chapter on emerging vector-borne infections.

Annual Variation

Prior to the development of effective vaccines for the prevention of many of the common childhood infections (measles, mumps, rubella, and varicella), these infections exhibited marked and repetitive

cyclical trends, which depended largely on an epidemic exhausting the susceptible population and another birth cohort replenishing it. For measles, the cycle for a major epidemic in an urban population in the United States was repeated every other year, at which time the number of cases roughly doubled, compared with the preceding and following years. With the widespread routine use of effective measles vaccine, however, the rates of measles have decreased dramatically, and the cyclical occurrence of cases has changed. In contrast, cycles at 3- to 4-year intervals persisted quite stubbornly for reported cases of pertussis between 1967 and 1997 (**Figure 2-6**). This cyclical pattern indicates that persistent transmission of pertussis related to contact between an infected case and a susceptible host still occurs, despite the availability of a vaccine that has been used quite widely. In part, this persistence may relate to waning of the immunity induced by the whole-cell pertussis vaccine over time, the role of older children and adults in maintaining the transmission cycle of pertussis, and the periodic replenishment of the susceptible population. Most of the childhood infections are more common in the winter and early spring seasons. This seasonality has been postulated to be related to greater transmissability when populations spend more time indoors during the winter. Also, the low humidity of indoor air and the presence of other respiratory infections, which cause coughing and sneezing, may be critical factors in promoting the transmission during the winter.

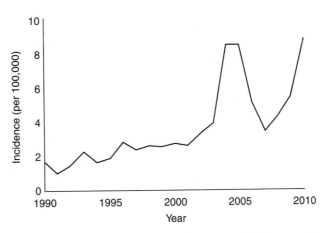

Figure 2-6 Pertussis (whooping cough) by year, United States, incidence per 100,000 persons from 1990–2010. Reproduced from the Centers for Disease Control and Prevention, National Center for Immunization and Respiratory Diseases, Division of Bacterial Diseases (2011). Surveillance and Reporting: Trends. http://www.cdc.gov/pertussis/surv-reporting.html. Accessed June 22, 2012.

Herd Immunity

Prior to the epidemiologic theories proposed by Kermack and McKendrick and by Reed and Frost from Johns Hopkins, the predominant theory was that epidemics occurred due to variation in the infectivity of the organism. The investigations carried out by these researchers showed that, in fact, patterns of epidemics could be explained by the proportion and distribution of susceptible persons. In certain diseases that are spread from person to person, the level of immunity of the population may be critical in determining whether an epidemic will occur and, therefore, the risk of infection for a susceptible individual in the population. Because transmission is based on contact between an infected person and a susceptible person, if the number of immune persons is large enough that it is unlikely that a susceptible individual will have contact with an infected person, the population is said to have *herd immunity*. Even though some susceptible persons remain in the population, epidemics are not sustained because the day-to-day contacts between persons do not result in contact between infected persons during the period that they are contagious and others who are still susceptible.

The level of immunity required to attain herd immunity depends on the characteristics of the infectious disease. Those diseases that are spread more readily will require a higher level of immunity in the population than will those that are less infectious.

The levels of herd immunity and individual susceptibility to infections are major epidemiologic factors that have influenced the periodicity and secular trends observed in many diseases, such as measles, rubella, varicella, and polio. A new epidemic of measles, prior to the era of widespread immunization, was dependent on the existence of a large cohort of susceptible individuals. A large enough pool of susceptible individuals to sustain an epidemic occurred every other year as new children were born. After an effective measles vaccine became available, however, epidemics were less common, were less predictable, and often involved older individuals. Epidemics occurred even in immunized populations when clusters of susceptible persons were exposed to an infectious case, such as on college campuses. The theoretical modeling of epidemics is covered more thoroughly in the chapter on modeling.

Variations of Infectious Diseases Over Decades
Tuberculosis

Many classic infectious diseases, such as tuberculosis, have decreased in incidence and mortality in the United States and Europe during the past century.

Tuberculosis remains one of the most important infectious diseases globally. However, in the United States, the mortality rates from tuberculosis began to decline in the late 1800s. Between 1950 and 1985, tuberculosis morbidity declined at a rate of approximately 5% per year.

Tuberculosis mortality by age in the United States is highest in older age groups.[52] However, the age-specific tuberculosis mortality data were studied in another way by Wade Hampton Frost. He examined the risk of tuberculosis death by birth cohort, rather than as cross-sectional age-specific mortality.[53] When the data are studied in this way (as the risk of mortality from tuberculosis in a cohort of persons born in the same year), different conclusions are reached about the age-specific risk of mortality. In **Figure 2-7**, the mortality rates are depicted as age-specific mortality by birth cohort. This cohort analysis shows tuberculosis mortality. The reason for the higher mortality among older persons is that they were born at a time when the risk of tuberculosis was higher than it is at present. Their higher mortality reflects their elevated risk of infection due to subsequent activation of an infection that originally occurred when the incidence of tuberculosis was higher than in more recent cohorts.[53,54]

Changes in Infectious Disease Morbidity and Mortality During the 1800s and 1900s

During the 1700s, 1800s, and early 1900s, infectious diseases were the major cause of morbidity and mortality. Reliable mortality data are available from the United Kingdom from the 1800s because early leaders, such as John Graunt and William Farr, recognized the importance of surveillance data to evaluate improvements in public health and promoted routine reporting of infectious disease mortality. The mortality rates from whooping cough, enteric fevers, and tuberculosis decreased more than 100-fold between 1900 and 1960 in persons living in the United Kingdom. The mortality rates from these diseases decreased in the United States and other developed countries in Europe in a parallel fashion to those reported from the United Kingdom. In 1900, the death ratio from 10 of the most common infectious diseases varied from 202.2 deaths per 100,000 population for influenza and pneumonia to 6.8 deaths per 100,000 population for meningococcal infections. By 1970, only influenza and pneumonia infections were associated with mortality rates greater than 3 per 100,000 (**Table 2-9**).

A recent analysis of the trends in infectious disease mortality in the United States during the 1900s documented the effect of the control of infectious diseases. The overall mortality from infectious diseases,

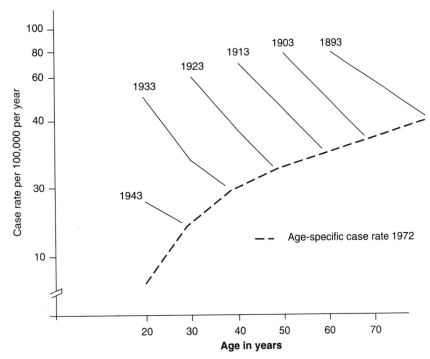

Figure 2-7 Cohort analysis of effect of age on tuberculosis incidence. Reproduced from G.W. Comstock, Frost Revisited: The Modern Epidemiology of Tuberculosis, *American Journal of Epidemiology*, Vol. 101, p. 424. © 1975. By permission of Oxford University Press.

Table 2-9	Death Rates for Common Infectious Diseases in the United States in 1900, 1935, and 1970		
	Mortality Rate per 100,000 Population		
Infectious Disease	**1900**	**1935**	**1970**
Influenza and pneumonia	202.2	103.9	30.9
Tuberculosis	194.4	55.1	2.6
Gastroenteritis	142.7	14.1	1.3
Diphtheria	40.3	3.1	0.0
Typhoid fever	31.3	2.7	0.0
Measles	13.3	3.1	0.0
Dysentery	12.0	1.9	0.0
Whooping cough	12.0	3.7	0.0
Scarlet fever (including streptococcal sore throat)	9.6	2.1	0.0
Meningococcal infections	6.8	2.1	0.3

Data from the National Office of Vital Statistics, U.S. Public Health Service, and from the Centers for Disease Control and Prevention.

which was 797 deaths per 100,000 in 1900, declined to 36 deaths per 100,000 in 1980.[55] However, this decline in mortality was reversed between 1980 and 1995, when the death rate increased to 63 deaths per 100,000 persons.[56] In the early 20th century, the trend of a steady decline in infectious disease mortality was interrupted by a sharp spike of increased mortality during the 1918 influenza epidemic. Between 1938 and

1952, the decline was particularly rapid, with mortality decreasing by 8.2% per year. Pneumonia and influenza were responsible for the largest number of infectious disease deaths throughout the century. Tuberculosis caused a large number of deaths early in the century, but mortality from this cause declined sharply after 1945. Although the crude mortality rate for infectious diseases was dramatically reduced during the first eight

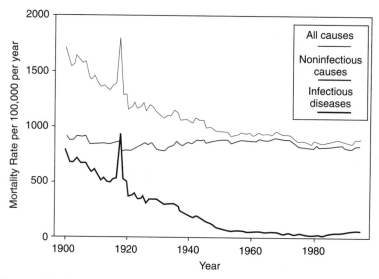

Figure 2-8 Crude mortality rates for all causes, noninfectious causes, and infectious diseases. Reproduced from GL Armstrong, L.A. Conn, and R.W. Pinner. Trends in Infectious Disease Mortality in the United States during the 20th century. *JAMA* Vol. 281, pp. 61–66, 1999.

decades of the 1900s, the mortality from all noninfectious diseases has not shown a similar trend (**Figure 2-8**). In fact, most of the decline in mortality during the 1900s can be attributed to the dramatic reduction in infectious disease mortality. In the last two decades of the 1900s, the mortality from coronary heart disease declined substantially, but this trend was offset by increasing mortality for lung cancer and other diseases. Clearly, the decline in mortality from infectious diseases during the 1900s stands as a tribute to the advances in public health and safer lifestyles, compared with that in previous centuries.

What caused these remarkable reductions in the mortality from common infectious diseases? One might surmise that the development of modern microbiology with the understanding the discipline provided about

the pathogenesis of specific infections led to the creation of vaccines and effective antibiotics to prevent or treat infections. In reality, for most of these infections, the evidence suggests a more complex scenario. The decline in the annual death rates for tuberculosis in England and Wales antedated the identification of the tuberculosis bacillus; however, the slope of the declining mortality increased after 1948, with the availability of streptomycin, isoniazide, and other chemotherapeutic agents (**Figure 2-9**). Similarly, death rates from scarlet fever, diphtheria, and whooping cough (pertussis) in children younger than age 15 in England and Wales began to decline well before these organisms were identified in the laboratory, and the availability of effective antibiotics had a small effect on the overall mortality decline (**Figure 2-10**).[57] In addition, dramatic

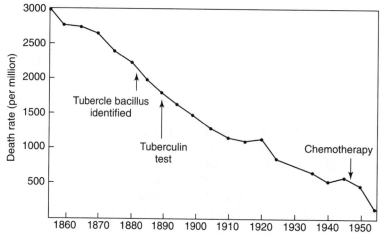

Figure 2-9 Mean annual death rate from respiratory tuberculosis, England and Wales. Reproduced from E. Kass. Infectious Diseases and Social Change. *Journal of Infectious Diseases*, Vol. 23(1):110–114. © 1971. By permission of Oxford University Press.

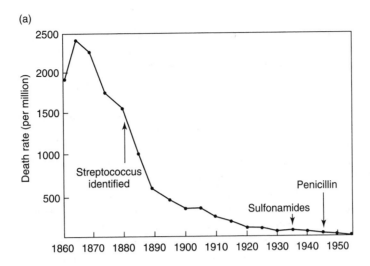

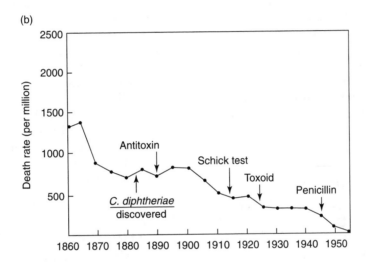

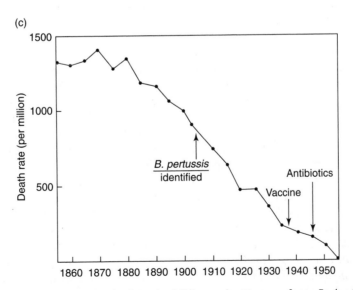

Figure 2-10 (a) Mean annual death rate from scarlet fever in children under 15 years of age, England and Wales; **(b)** Mean annual death rate from diptheria in children under 15 years of age, England and Wales; and **(c)** Mean annual death rate from whooping cough in children under 15 years of age, England and Wales. Reproduced from E. Kass. Infectious Diseases and Social Change. *Journal of Infectious Diseases*, Vol. 23(1):110–114. © 1971. By permission of Oxford University Press.

declines in the death rates from measles and pertussis were seen among children in England and Wales decades prior to the identification of these organisms and the availability of vaccines or antibiotics to treat infected persons.

What might account for these declines in mortality? Recent experience with some of these diseases in poor and often malnourished children from developing countries in Africa has shown that some of these diseases still have high mortality in certain populations. For example, measles, which is rarely fatal when it occurs in children in the United States, is still associated with a 15–20% mortality rate in infants and children in sub-Saharan Africa. Hypotheses to explain this difference have included poorer nutritional status, earlier ages at exposure, other concomitant infections, higher infectious dose, and greater crowding during epidemic spread among infants in Africa.[58,59] All of these factors may play a role, but it is difficult to evaluate their independent contribution. Clearly, the complex changes that have occurred in society, hygiene, and lifestyle in the United States and in Europe during the late 1800s and early 1900s have had a profound effect on these diseases.

RECENT TRENDS IN INFECTIOUS DISEASE MORBIDITY AND MORTALITY IN THE UNITED STATES

Although the mortality from the classical infectious diseases declined dramatically in the late 1800s and the first 80 years of the 1900s, several cultural and environmental changes occurred that fostered the emergence of a number of new infections and the re-emergence of older, well-recognized infections. Indeed, it has been estimated that a larger number of new infections have emerged in the last decade or so than in the hundred years previously.

The most heralded, of course, is the HIV/AIDS epidemic, which probably originated as a mutant or recombinant primate retrovirus that was spread to humans from monkeys in West Africa possibly as early as the turn of the 20th century. The ensuing pandemic of AIDS has led to the emergence of many new and previously recognized but rare human pathogens, such as *P. carinii*, *Mycobacteria avium*, *Cryptosporidia parvum*, *Microsporidia*, *Bartonella rochelimea*, and *Penicillium marneffei*. In addition to HIV and AIDS, modern chemotherapy of neoplasms, aging of the population, increased invasive therapeutic procedures in hospitalized patients, crowding of elderly patients in nursing homes and infants and children in daycare centers, widespread use of broad-spectrum antibiotics, environmental pollution, and other factors have fostered the emergence of infectious diseases.

An analysis was done by investigators for the CDC of all deaths in the United States between 1980 and 1992.[56] In this interval, the death rate due to infectious diseases as the underlying cause increased 58%, from 41 to 65 deaths per 100,000 population in the United States. Age-adjusted mortality from infectious diseases increased 39% during the same period. Infectious disease mortality increased 25% among those aged 65 years or older, from 271 to 338 per 100,000 population, and 5.5 times among 25- to 44-year-olds, from 6.9 to 38 deaths per 100,000 population. Mortality due to respiratory tract infections increased 20%, the death rate from septicemia increased 83%, and AIDS emerged as a major cause of death. These national data are quite sobering because they clearly demonstrate that an increased infectious disease mortality has occurred recently in the U.S. population, and that this trend is not limited to newly emerging diseases, such as AIDS. The 10 leading underlying causes of mortality caused by infectious diseases in the United States in 1980 and 1992 are listed in **Table 2-10**.

RECENT WORLDWIDE TRENDS IN INFECTIOUS DISEASE MORBIDITY AND MORTALITY

Infectious diseases play a leading role in mortality and morbidity globally, due in large part to the continued importance of infectious diseases in sub-Saharan Africa, Asia, and Latin America. Data were published recently from the Global Burden of Disease Study, which was initiated in 1992 through a collaboration of the World Bank and the WHO. The goals of this study were to make reasonable estimates from the available data of the impact of various diseases as causes of disability, to develop unbiased assessments for major disorders, and to quantify the burden of disease with a measure that could be used for cost-effectiveness analysis. This study found that 98% of all deaths in children younger than 15 years of age occur in the developing world, and 50% of deaths in persons between ages 15 and 59 years of age happen in the developing world.[60] The probability of death between birth and 15 years of age ranges from 22% in sub-Saharan Africa to 1.1% in the established

Table 2-10	Leading Underlying Causes of Mortality Caused by Infectious Diseases in the United States, 1980, 1992					
	1980			**1992**		
Rank	Infectious Disease Group	No. of Deaths	Mortality per 100,000	Infectious Disease Group	No. of Deaths	Mortality per 100,000
1	Respiratory tract infections	56,966	25.1	Respiratory tract infections	77,336	30.3
2	Septicemia	9,438	4.2	HIV/AIDS	33,581	13.2
3	Infections of kidney/ urinary tract	8,006	3.5	Septicemia	19,667	7.7
4	Infections of the heart	2,486	1.1	Infections of kidney/ urinary tract	12,399	4.9
5	Tuberculosis	2,333	1.0	Infections of the heart	3,950	1.5
6	Bacterial meningitis	1,402	0.6	Hepatobiliary disease	2,494	1.0
7	Gastrointestinal tract infections	1,377	0.6	Mycoses	2,298	0.9
8	Hepatobiliary disease	1,227	0.5	Tuberculosis	1,851	0.7
9	Perinatal infections	1,035	0.5	Gastrointestinal tract infections	985	0.4
10	Mycoses	680	0.3	Perinatal infections	965	0.4
	Total infectious diseases	93,407	41.1		166,047	65.1
	All deaths	1,989,841	878.0		2,175,613	852.7

Reproduced from Pinner RW et al. Trends in infectious disease mortality in the United States. *JAMA* 1996;275(3):189–193.

market economics. Probabilities of death between 15 and 50 years of age range from 7.2% for women in established market economics to 39.1% in sub-Saharan Africa. Worldwide in 1990, communicable, maternal, perinatal, and nutritional disorders accounted for 17.2 million deaths, noncommunicable diseases for 28.1 million deaths, and injuries for 5.1 million deaths. The leading causes of death in 1990 were ischemic heart disease (6.3 million deaths), cerebrovascular accidents (4.4 million deaths), lower respiratory infections (4.3 million deaths), diarrheal diseases (2.9 million), perinatal disorders (2.4 million), chronic obstructive pulmonary disease (2.2 million), tuberculosis (2.0 million), measles (1.1 million), road traffic accidents (1.0 million), and lung cancer (0.9 million).

This WHO–World Bank study also concluded that effective treatment of tuberculosis is the most cost-effective health measure that could be implemented in developing countries in terms of preventing mortality and increasing disability-adjusted life years (DALY).[61] The analysis of tuberculosis programs in Malawi, Mozambique, and Tanzania has shown that treating smear-positive tuberculosis costs $20–52 per death averted. The cost per discounted year of life saved, therefore, is $1–3. Few other interventions are as cost-effective as tuberculosis case treatment. The WHO analysis estimated that $150 million would be needed to treat 65% of smear-positive cases in low-income countries and 85% of smear-positive individuals in middle-income countries with short-course chemotherapy.

Clearly, the interaction between HIV and tuberculosis has made the tuberculosis problem more acute and intractable. The rapid and extensive spread of AIDS in countries in the developing world, where a high proportion of the population has latent tuberculosis, indicates that a public health strategy that is limited to treating active cases is unlikely to control the emerging tuberculosis epidemic effectively. The roll-out of antiretroviral therapy for HIV infection coupled with a new resolve to tackle the TB epidemic holds promise that this combined effect may be successful. To be sure, the emergence of multidrug-resistant TB (MDR-TB) and extremely resistant TB (XDR-TB) has added new challenges to the control of TB. Nevertheless, it should be emphasized that active tuberculosis is usually sensitive to current chemotherapeutic regimes and can be controlled in both HIV-negative and -positive patients.

Other health interventions that are cost-effective for the prevention of infectious disease morbidity and mortality include effective sexually transmitted disease (STD) treatment; oral rehydration therapy for diarrhea; immunization for childhood diseases, including HBV; ivermectin for the treatment and prevention of onchocerchiasis and schistosomiasis; and zidovudine for the prevention of the perinatal transmission of HIV. The chemotherapy and chemoprophylaxis of malaria and antibiotic prophylaxis for the prevention of postsurgical infections are also cost-effective measures in this sense.

Currently, the world's population is in a very delicate balance with respect to infectious diseases. The continual emergence of new infectious diseases and the reemergence of old infections, together with the potential for their global spread, underline the need for accurate surveillance and the development of newer strategies for their control and prevention. At the same time, the successes of the last century provide reason for hope that infectious diseases can be controlled with the proper understanding and effort.

• • • REFERENCES

1. Snow J. On Cholera. New York, NY: Commonwealth Fund; 1996.

2. Fraser DW, Tsai TR, Orenstein W, et al. Legionnaire's disease: Description of an epidemic of pneumonia. N Engl J Med. 1977;297:1189–1197.

3. Dondero TJ, Rentdorff RL, Mallison GF, et al. An outbreak of Legionnaire's disease associated with a contaminated air-conditioning cooling tower. N Engl J Med. 1980;302:365–370.

4. Cords LG, Fraser DW, Skailly P, et al. Legionnaire's disease outbreak at an Atlanta, Georgia, country club: evidence for spread from an evaporative condenser. Am J Epidemiol. 1980;111:425–431.

5. Garbe PL, Davis BJ, Weisfeld JS, et al. Nosocomial Legionnaire's disease: epidemiologic demonstration of cooling towers as a source. JAMA. 1985;254:521–524.

6. Morris GK, Patton CM, Feeley JC, et al. Isolation of the Legionnaire's disease bacterium from environmental samples. Ann Intern Med. 1979;90:664–666.

7. Moraca E, Yu VC, Goetz A. Disinfection of water distribution system for Legionella: a review of applicator procedures and methodologies. Infect Control Hosp Epidemiol. 1990;11:79–88.

8. Francis E. Deer-fly fever: a disease of man of hitherto unknown etiology. Public Health Rep. 1991;34:2061–2062.

9. Waring WB, Ruffin JJ. A tick-borne epidemic of tularemia. N Engl J Med. 1946;234:137.

10. Young LS, Bickewell DS, Archer BG, et al. Tularemia epidemic: Vermont 1968: forty-seven cases linked to contact with muskrats. N Engl J Med. 1969;280:1253–1260.

11. Teutsch SM, Martone WJ, Brink EW, et al. Pneumonic tularemia on Martha's Vineyard. N Engl J Med. 1979;301:826–828.

12. Dahlstrand S, Ringertz O, Zetterberg B. Airborne tularemia in Sweden. J Infect Dis. 1971;3:7–16.

13. Barbeito MS, Alg RL, Wedum AG. Infectious bacterial aerosol from dropped Petri disk cultures. Am J Med Technol. 1961;27:318–322.

14. Hornick RB. Tularemia. In: Evans A, Brachman PS, eds. Bacterial Infections of Humans: Epidemiology and Control. 3rd ed. New York, NY: Plenum Publishing; 1998:823–837.

15. Hirst CF. The Conquest of Plague. London, UK: Oxford University Press; 1953.

16. Zinsser H. Rats, Lice and History. Boston, MA: Little, Brown; 1934.

17. Marshall JD Jr, Joy RJT, Ai NY, et al. Plague in Vietnam 1965–1966. Am J Epidemiol. 1967;86:603–616.

18. Campbell GL, Hughes JM. Plague in India: a new warning from an old nemesis. Am Int Med. 1995;122:151–153.

19. Eskey CR, Haas V. Plague in the western part of the United States. *Public Health Bull.* 1940;254:1–82.

20. Mann JM, Martone WJ, Myoce JM, et al. Endemic human plague in New Mexico: risk factors associated with infections. *J Infect Dis.* 1979;140:397–401.

21. Butler T. *Plague and Other Yersinia Infections.* New York, NY: Plenum Publishing; 1983.

22. Laforce FM. Woolsorter's disease. *Acad Med.* 1978;54:956–963.

23. Meselson M, Guillemin J, Hugh-Jones M, et al. The Sverdlovsk anthrax outbreak of 1979. *Science.* 1994;266:1202–1208.

24. Constantine DG. Rabies transmission by non-bite route. *Public Health Rep.* 1963;77:287–289.

25. Winkler WG, Fashinell TR, Leffingwell C, Howard P, Conomy JP. Airborne rabies transmission in a laboratory worker. *JAMA.* 1973;226:1219–1221.

26. Hooff SA, Burton RC, Wilson RW, et al. Human-to-human transmission of rabies by a corneal transplant. *N Engl J Med.* 1979;300:603–604.

27. Noah DC, Drenzik CL, Smith JS, et al. Epidemiology of human rabies in the United States, 1980 to 1996. *Ann Intern Med.* 1998;128:922–930.

28. Brown GM. The history of the brucellosis eradication program in the United States. *Ann Selavo.* 1977;19:20–34.

29. Grant IH, Gold JW, Witner M, et al. Transfusion-associated Chagas' disease acquired in the United States. *Ann Intern Med.* 1989;111:849–851.

30. Gregg NM. Congenital cataract following German measles in the mother. *Trans Ophthalmol Soc.* 1941;3:35–46.

31. Weller TH, Neva FA. Propagation in tissue culture of cytopathic agents from patients with rubella-like illness. *Proc Soc Exp Biol Med.* 1962;11:215–225.

32. Parkman PD, Bueschler EL, Artenstein MS. Recovery of rubella virus from army recruits. *Proc Soc Exp Biol Med.* 1962;111:225–230.

33. Krugman S, ed. Rubella symposium. *Am J Dis Child.* 1965;110:345–476.

34. Krugman S, ed. International conference on rubella immunization. *Am J Dis Child.* 1969;118:2–410.

35. Smith MG. Propagation in tissue culture of a cytopathic virus from human salivary gland virus (SGV) disease. *Proc Soc Exp Biol Med.* 1956;92:424–430.

36. Rowe WP, Hartley JW, Waterman S, Turnan HC, Huebner RJ. Cytopathic agent resembling human salivary gland virus recovered from tissue culture of human adenoids. *Proc Soc Exp Biol Med.* 1956;92:418–424.

37. Weller TH, MaCaulay JC, Craig JM, Wirth P. Isolation of intranuclear inclusion producing agents from infants with illness resembling cytomegalic inclusion disease. *Pro Soc Exp Biol Med.* 1957;94:4–12.

38. Gershon AH, Gold E, Nankervis GA. Cytomegalovirus. In: Evans AS, Kaslow RA, eds. *Viral Infections of Humans, Epidemiology and Control.* New York, NY: Plenum Publishing; 1997:229–251.

39. Dobbins JG, Stewart JAS. Surveillance of congenital cytomegalovirus disease 1990–1991. *MMWR.* 1992;41:SS–2.

40. Stone KM, Brooks CA, Guinan ME, Alexander ER. National surveillance for neonatal herpes virus infections. *Sex Transm Dis.* 1989;16:152–156.

41. Mcllinger AK, Goldberg M, Wade A, et al. Alternative case-finding in a crack-related syphilis epidemic—Philadelphia. *MMWR.* 1991;40:77–80.

42. Conner EM, Sperling RS, Gelber R, et al. Reduction of maternal–infant transmission of human immunodeficiency virus type 1 without zidovudine treatment. *N Engl J Med.* 1997;31:1173–1180.

43. Shaffer N, Chunchoonong R, Mock PA, et al. Short-course zidovudine for perinatal HIV-1 transmission in Bangkok, Thailand. *Lancet.* 1999;353:773–780.

44. Guay CA, Musoke P, Fleming T, et al. Intrapartum and neonatal single-dose nevirapine compared with zidovudine for prevention of mother-to-child transmission of HIV-1 in Kampala, Uganda: HIVNET 012 randomized trial. *Lancet.* 1999;254:795–802.

45. Sartwell PE. The distribution of incubation of disease. *Am J Epidemiol.* 1950;51:310-318.

46. Muñoz A, Kirby AJ, He DY, et al. Long-term survivors with HIV-1 longitudinal patterns of CD4$^+$ lymphocytes. *J Acquir Immunodeficiency Syndr.* 1995;8:496–505.

47. Watts DM, Burke DS, Harrison BA, et al. Effect of temperature on the vector efficiency of *Aedes aegypti* for dengue 2 virus. *Am J Trop Med Hyg.* 1987;36:143–152.

48. Soper GA. The curious case of Typhoid Mary. *Acad Med.* 1939;15:698–712.

49. Anders W, Conde F, Stephen W. Surgical treatment of the chronic typhoid carrier: report of 102 operated cases. *Dtsch Med Wochenschr.* 1955;89:1637–1648.

50. Shilts R. *And the Band Played On.* New York, NY: St. Mortons Press; 1987.

51. Peterson BH, Lee TJ, Snyderman, Brooks GF. *Neisseria meningitidis* and *Neisseria gonorrhoeae* bacteremia associated with C6, C7, C8 deficiency. *Ann Intern Med.* 1979;90:917–920.

52. Rieder HL, Cauthen GM, Kelly GD, et al. Tuberculosis in the United States. *JAMA.* 1989;262:385–389.

53. Frost WH. The age selection of mortality from tuberculosis in successive decades. *Am J Hyg.* 1939 (Section A);30:91–96.

54. Doege TG. Tuberculosis mortality in the United States, 1900 to 1960. *JAMA.* 1965;192:1045–1048.

55. Armstrong GL, Conn LA, Pinner RW. Trends in infectious disease mortality in the United States during the 20th century. *JAMA.* 1999;281:61–66.

56. Pinner RW, Teutsch SM, Simonsen L, et al. Trends in infectious diseases mortality in the United States. *JAMA.* 1996;225:189–193.

57. Kass EM. Infectious disease and social change. *J Infect Dis.* 1971;123:110–114.

58. Aaby P, Bakh J, Lisse IM, Snits AJ. Measles mortality, state of nutrition, and family structure: a community study on Guinea-Bissau. *J Infect Dis.* 1983;147:693–701.

59. Aaby P. Malnutrition and overcrowding-exposure in severe measles infection: a review of community studies. *Rev Infect Dis.* 1988;10:478–491.

60. Murray CJ, Lopez AD. Alternative projections of mortality and disability by course, 1990–2020: global burden of disease study. *Lancet.* 1997;349:1498–1504.

61. Murray CJ, Lopez AD. Mortality by cause for eight regions of the world: global burden of disease study. *Lancet.* 1997;349:1269–1276.

3

Study Design

Stephen J. Gange and Elizabeth T. Golub

INTRODUCTION

Epidemiologic methods constitute the scientific frameworks, concepts, and tools that are used for epidemiological evaluations. This chapter presents an overview of these methods in the context of evaluating the epidemiology of infectious diseases. As an organizational framework, it is useful to conceptualize epidemiologic methods as addressing key questions (**Figure 3-1**):

- *Who is to be studied?* Epidemiologists study diseases in *populations* of individuals. While studies of entire populations may be of interest, typically only a sample of individuals contributes to an epidemiologic evaluation, selected according to specific *study designs*.
- *Which data will be collected?* Observing the occurrence of diseases and their determinants requires *measurement* for purposes of constructing *measures of disease occurrence*.
- *Which inferences will be made from the analysis?* Epidemiology, as the study of the distribution, determinants, and control of

disease, is predicated on the fact that disease occurrence in humans does not occur at random. Epidemiologic evaluations play an important *descriptive* role in characterizing diseases among populations. When evaluating the determinants of diseases, epidemiologic evaluations typically require *comparisons of populations* for making *causal inferences*.

In infectious disease epidemiology, an intricate network of causal determinants influences the susceptibility to and development of disease. A useful framework for organizing these important determinants is the *epidemiologic triangle* (**Figure 3-2**), a diagram that emphasizes the interrelationship between three components:

- **Host.** Human hosts differ in susceptibility to infections because of genetic, environmental, behavioral, and other characteristics. Major epidemic diseases, such as malaria, tuberculosis, smallpox, and plague, have led to selective genetic changes in human populations. For example, the evolution of several genetic mutations among Africans and Asians has resulted primarily from the selective pressure of hyperendemic malaria. Sickle hemoglobin, glucose-6-phosphate dehydrogenase deficiency, thalassemia, hemoglobin C, and hemoglobin E may be disadvantageous in homozygous individuals, but these traits have evolved in certain populations because they confer significant protection from malaria in heterozygous individuals.[1]
- **Agent.** The agent constitutes the infecting pathogen (e.g., virus, bacterium, parasite, or fungus). Agents have certain characteristics that influence their infectivity. For example, one important characteristic of a pathogen is its escape mechanism, such as the evolution of resistance to antibiotics and antiviral

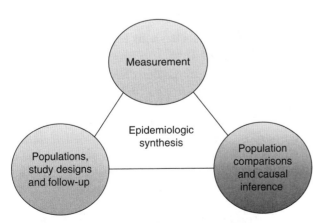

Figure 3-1 A Framework for Epidemiologic Methods

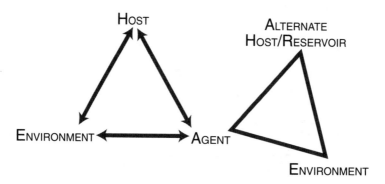

Figure 3-2 Epidemiologic Triangle (agent/host/environment)

therapies. This capability is recognized as a growing threat to public health and was presciently predicted in 1945 by the discoverer of penicillin, Sir Alexander Fleming, who said, "The greatest possibility of evil in self-medication is the use of too-small doses, so that, instead of clearing up the infection, the microbes are educated to resist penicillin and a host of penicillin-fast organisms is bred out which can be passed on to other individuals."[2]

- **Environment.** The environment constitutes the setting in which transmission occurs. It is important to understand and characterize the environment in which transmission occurs and to be aware of environmental factors that may facilitate the agent's survival or infectivity. It is not difficult to envision the role of environment for some agents, such as hookworm, where soil humidity, temperature, and other soil characteristics can influence the development of infectious *Ancylostoma duodenalae* larvae. However, the environment is also important in the transmission of airborne viruses, such as influenza and varicella, because it affects the length of time that the viral particles remain infective as an aerosol. The winter environment in temperate climates also facilitates transmission of influenza by bringing people indoors. Conversely, influenza epidemics have been interrupted by extreme cold weather that has forced schools to close, thereby interrupting transmission among children and introduction of the virus into the home.[3]

By understanding these determinants and their interrelationship, we can identify and implement interventions for disease prevention and treatment. While the prescription and use of individual medications (e.g., antibiotics, antivirals, antifungals) may be

the natural "intervention" that comes to mind when thinking about infectious diseases, it is important to recognize that "interventions" actually include the vast breadth of public health measures, policies, and guidance that affect large populations (e.g., vaccination programs, chlorination of the water supply, social marketing).

POPULATIONS

Epidemiologists take a multifaceted approach to defining populations. First, populations are generally identified in terms of three basic characteristics: person, place, and time. Second, it is rarely possible to study the entire population about which we want to make inferences for a particular disease (the "target population"). Instead, we must identify a source from which study participants can be identified and then define a study population of those persons who will ultimately be included in the study. Finally, we must consider multiple factors that influence study populations, such as eligibility criteria, feasibility of enrollment, and the refusal rate among those invited to participate.

How Epidemiologists Describe Populations: Person, Place, and Time

The central focus of studying diseases in populations reflects an assumption that individual persons can be aggregated by some common characteristics. The population chosen for study ultimately depends on the purpose of the investigation. We usually describe populations in terms of factors that are well known to influence disease risk. Epidemiologists generally classify such factors as those that are related to *person, place,* and *time.*

Attributes of *person* include individual-level characteristics believed to influence disease. These might include demographic characteristics (e.g., age, sex, race/ethnicity), socioeconomic characteristics (e.g., education, income), or biologic factors (genetics).

The description of *place* spans different geographical characteristics, which can be as broad as a continent, more mid-level such as a country or city, or as specific as a neighborhood. It might also include even more specific attributes, such as place of employment, patients in a certain clinic or hospital ward, or distance from a certain environmental site. The characteristics of *place* add to those of *person* in providing a specific description of our population; for example, we might describe our population as women ages 18–59 living in Baltimore, Maryland.

It is clear that defining a population using these two criteria alone may be insufficient. Continuing the preceding example, are we studying women in that age group who *ever* lived in Baltimore? To provide more specificity, we can include in our definition an aspect of *time*. *Time*, like the attributes of *person* and *place*, can be thought to influence disease. For example, it is reasonable to assume that a 25-year-old woman in Baltimore in 1882 had a much different disease risk profile than a woman of the same age living in Baltimore today. Likewise, *time* might refer to a scale other than calendar time—we might characterize individuals in terms of their life-course—although most commonly we choose calendar time as our parameter of *time* when describing a population.

Types of Populations: Target, Source, and Study Populations

Epidemiologists conceptualize several different types of populations (**Figure 3-3**). A *target population* comprises those individuals about whom we will want to make inferences based on the results of our study. Identifying a target population is often subjective because the group to which we want to make inference may be a conceptual construct and not a group of individuals who can be specifically enumerated. Ideally, this population is most relevant to the research question being investigated, in terms of its person, place, and time characteristics.

The target population serves as the background for the *source population*. A source population is a subset of the target population that *can be enumerated* and further studied. For example, in a study of the prevalence of sexually transmitted infections (STIs), we may wish to make inferences from the findings to a broad community and, therefore,

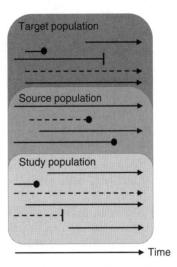

Figure 3-3 Populations Moving Through Time

identify as our target population sexually active men and women ages 18–49 living in the United States during 2005–2010. Of course, it would not be feasible to enumerate, or enroll into a study, all individuals meeting those criteria. Instead, we might identify a source population from which we can enroll study participants. One example of a source population for this study might be individuals attending specific STI clinics in Chicago or Baltimore during a certain period of time. There are, of course, alternative source populations that could be chosen to conduct a study whose results would be relevant to the same target population.

A *study population* comprises those individuals in the source population who contribute data to an epidemiologic investigation. In some settings, the study population might be equal to an entire source population (or even to an entire target population). Whether a member of the source population ultimately becomes a study participant is influenced by a number of factors. Eligibility criteria are those characteristics that are necessary for an individual to be considered for enrollment, and may include attributes of person, place, and/or time. It may also not be feasible to study the entire source population (due to cost or logistics). Finally, some individuals in the source population may decline the invitation to participate.

In summary, identifying the characteristics of these different populations is an essential component of epidemiology. In the next section, we outline various descriptive and analytical designs that are used in epidemiology as applied to infectious diseases.

EPIDEMIOLOGIC STUDY DESIGNS

Epidemiologic studies of infectious diseases aim to evaluate the contributions of various factors in the transmission and acquisition of infectious pathogens, as well as those factors favoring endemic transmission and epidemics. The design of such studies must optimize the researcher's ability to measure and evaluate the relationships between exposures and the occurrence of disease in the study population.

Studies of infectious disease can be designed to explore landmarks along the entire temporal process during which an individual is at risk, acquires infection, develops an infectious disease, or succumbs to it. The duration of this process can be short, such as with highly virulent infections (e.g., Ebola virus), or it can be very long, as with chronic infectious diseases such as HIV/AIDS. Epidemiologists strive to understand the population-level burden of disease, including the reasons for increased susceptibility of one population relative to another, the factors that affect the susceptibility of particular individuals in a population, and the factors leading to epidemics.

Several study designs are used to address research questions regarding the risk factors for, and burden of, disease in human populations. For example, descriptive designs are typically not initiated to make comparisons across populations but rather provide an opportunity to describe important characteristics of individuals with disease. Such descriptive designs include case reports, case series, and ecological and surveillance studies. In contrast, analytical designs are initiated to draw particular conclusions regarding the association between exposures and outcomes; they include cohort studies, case-control and other nested studies, and randomized clinical trials. Meta-analysis and systematic reviews, wherein either primary or published data from individual studies are systematically combined to investigate a research question, are also being conducted with increasing frequency. The optimal study design is a function of the hypothesis under investigation. In this section, we review several important and frequently used epidemiologic study designs and illustrate their use in evaluating infectious diseases.

Descriptive Study Designs

When a new disease is recognized, it may be of interest to describe the nature of the disease and to evaluate the probable means of transmission, reservoir, and natural history. Sometimes a new disease can be quickly linked to a specific organism, such as staphylococcal toxic shock syndrome. More often, however, epidemiologic studies contribute to the discovery and characterization of new pathogens, as with hantavirus pulmonary syndrome, Legionnaires' disease, and AIDS.

Early studies may consist of descriptions of cases that may be linked by a route of transmission or common exposure. Descriptive studies do not typically make inferential comparisons of cases to individuals without disease (controls); rather, they only describe aspects of the disease and circumstances surrounding the acquisition and occurrence of disease. Surveillance methods capture cases of disease and are an excellent source for identifying individuals for further follow-up. At times, case reports or case series provide considerable insight into the epidemiology of an infectious disease.

Case Reports

Case reports involve a careful evaluation of a single case of disease, and may describe the transmission, natural clinical history, and/or response to treatment. Although case reports are based on an infection in a single patient, they may yield important new epidemiologic information regarding the disease. Examples of illustrative case reports follow.

Rabies Rabies is a zoonotic viral infection that is spread to humans by contact with body fluids (most commonly saliva) from an infected animal. Prior to rabies vaccination of domestic animals, most transmissions of this disease in the United States were associated with domestic animal bites.[4] Rabies transmission was initially believed to require direct inoculation via a bite or other invasive contact with the infected animal. Infection is initially confined to the site of exposure without systemic viremia; hence the rabies vaccine can be given after exposure to prevent infection of the central nervous system (CNS). Such postexposure prophylaxis is usually successful. Moreover, it was universally believed that, in the absence of such treatment, rabies was fatal once the virus infected the CNS and signs and symptoms of CNS infection occurred. Early case reports of rabies overturned these long-held beliefs about the means of transmission of the virus and its natural history.

Aerosol transmission of rabies was described in a cave explorer, a spelunker, who developed rabies after exploring a cave inhabited by large numbers of bats in Frio, Texas.[5] In this case, there was no history of a bite. This case was followed by a series of experiments in which animals were placed in the cave and protected from bites and even insect transmission but were exposed to the air in the infected cave. After several animals developed rabies during this exposure, the classic concepts of rabies transmission were challenged.[5] This hypothesis was confirmed in additional laboratory studies that showed rodents could be infected by aerosol inoculation.[6,7] This route of infection was further explored by a review of case reports of rabies in the United States between 1980 and 1996, which found that, in the majority of human cases, there was no clear documented evidence of a bite; however, the reports also suggested that an unreported or undetected bite remained the most plausible hypothesis regarding route of transmission.[8] The control of rabies in domestic animals in the United States has resulted in fewer human cases, with a higher proportion of cases being attributed to wild animal exposures. These exposures are not as readily recognized as rabies risks, so preventive vaccination and postexposure prophylaxis may not be initiated. Reports of individual cases continue to provide information that contributes to our general understanding of the transmission of rabies.

The uniform fatality of rabies has also been challenged. In October 1970, a 6-year-old boy was bitten by a rabid bat. He was given 14 doses of duck embryo rabies vaccine but developed rabies 21 days later. He eventually recovered completely after treatment in an intensive care unit for nearly 2 months.[9]

A second report of survival from clinical rabies was reported in October 2004 in a previously healthy 15-year-old Wisconsin girl who was bitten on the left finger after handling a bat.[10,11] Three weeks later she complained of fatigue, double vision, vomiting, and tingling in her left arm. Within 3 days she developed diploplia, and subsequently slurred speech and an unsteady gait. On the sixth day of her illness, the diagnosis of rabies was considered when the history of a bat bite was obtained. The patient was transferred to a tertiary care hospital and treated aggressively with a series of medications that included ketamine, midazolam, ribavirin, and amantadine. Ketamine had been shown in laboratory studies to inhibit rabies viral transcription.[12] The use of gamma-aminobutyric acid (GABA) receptor agonists with benzodiazepines and barbiturates was intended to reduce excitotoxicity, brain metabolism, and autonomic reactivity. Clinical reports of rabies cases had suggested that death resulted from the secondary complications of infections, primarily "neurotransmitter imbalance" and autonomic failure, rather than from direct cytolysis of the rabies virus. The patient survived and regained most of her cognitive function and has, so far, been able to live without major impairments.[13] This was the first case of human rabies reported to have survived without the use of rabies vaccine or rabies immunoglobulin; since then, the same aggressive treatment protocol has been used on additional cases and is credited with saving the life of an 8-year-old

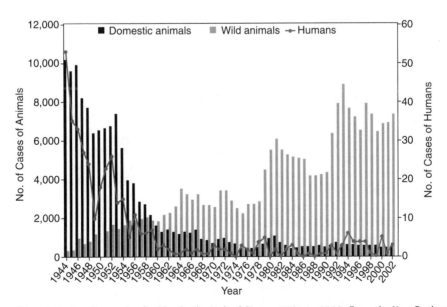

Figure 3-4 Temporal trends in the diagnosis of rabies in the United States, 1994 to 2002. From the New England Journal of Medicine, Rupprecht, C.E., Gibbons, RV Prophylaxis against Rabies, Vol. 351; 25 pp. 2627, Figure 1. Copyright © 2004 Massachusetts Medical Society. Reprinted with permission from Massachusetts Medical Society.

Table 3-1	Sources of Human Exposure to Rabies in the United States				
Year	Domestic Animal*	Wildlife	Other Sources†	Unknown‡	Total No. of Cases
		number of cases (percent)			
1946–1955	86 (72)	8 (7)	0	26 (22)	120
1956–1965	21 (55)	7 (18)	0	10 (26)	38
1966–1975	6 (38)	7 (44)	1 (6)	2 (12)	16
1976–1985	6 (30)	1 (5)	2 (10)	11 (55)	20
1986–1995	2 (12)	1 (6)	0	14 (82)	17
1996–2003	4 (19)	2 (10)	0	15 (71)	21

* After 1979, there were no cases involving documented exposure to a domestic animal known to be rabid or probably rabid. Thereafter, all cases originated in countries where canine rabies was endemic.
† Other sources of exposure include laboratory aerosol (in 1972 and 1977) and corneal transplantation (in 1978).
‡ If a definitive source of exposure was not identified in the patient's history, the source of exposure was considered to be unknown, regardless of the source suspected on the basis of antigenic or genetic characterization.

From the New England Journal of Medicine, Rupprecht, C.E., Gibbons, RV Prophylaxis against Rabies, Vol. 351; 25 pp. 2627, Figure 1. Copyright © 2004 Massachusetts Medical Society. Reprinted with permission from Massachusetts Medical Society.

girl in Cali, Colombia. A third patient, a 15-year-old boy in Brazil, was also successfully administered this treatment protocol, after receiving postexposure prophylaxis.[14]

Although rabies still has among the highest case fatality rates, the successful treatment of these patients provides important insight into the pathophysiology of human rabies and offers promise for advances in treatment.

HIV/AIDS: Cure of HIV HIV is unique among infectious diseases in that clearance of disease was not believed to ever occur. Bryson and her colleagues from the University of California at Los Angeles reported the case of an infant who was born after 36 weeks' gestation to an asymptomatic HIV-infected woman.[15] The pregnancy was uncomplicated, and the mother had a CD4+ T-cell count of more than 1000 cells/mm³ at the time of delivery. At birth, the infant required hospitalization for 8 days because of mild respiratory distress syndrome. Laboratory studies on the newborn found a negative culture of cord blood for HIV. However, the infant's blood culture was positive at 19 and 51 days of age, and the PCR was positive at 33 days of life. Subsequently, HIV antibodies disappeared by 12 months of age. Multiple cultures of peripheral blood lymphocytes and plasma for HIV were negative between 3 months and 5 years of age. The child was asymptomatic and had no laboratory evidence of HIV infection at 5 years of age. The authors believed that the infant was infected but cleared the HIV infection by immunologic or other mechanisms. This case report was followed up by a search for similar cases of spontaneous resolution of perinatal HIV infection in infants by other investigators; to date, no such cases have been reported.

More recently, physicians reported a case of an HIV-infected man who may have been cured with allogeneic stem-cell transplantation. The biological mechanism by which HIV binds to cells during infection has been well established: attachment occurs with a primary receptor (CD4) and with a co-receptor (either CCR5 or CXCR4). Epidemiologic studies played a critical role in identifying the importance of these co-receptors, whereby individuals with certain mutations (Δ32/Δ32 homozygosity) were at greatly reduced risk for HIV infection.[16] In this case, an HIV-infected man who was undergoing allogeneic stem-cell transplantation to treat acute myeloid leukemia was specifically given cells from a matched donor who was also homogeneous for the Δ32/Δ32 mutation. The initial report in 2009 documented a lack of detectable virus through 20 weeks.[17] A 2011 follow-up study documented continued absence of evidence of viral infection and recovery of the patient's immune system through 3.5 years.[18] The impact of these case reports has helped propel the search for a cure for HIV as a top research priority.

Case Series

A second type of descriptive epidemiologic study is the case series. In this kind of study, data from a cluster or series of cases are reported. No comparison is made with controls; instead, the case series may be reported in sufficient epidemiologic detail that it is possible to infer the means of transmission and the risk factors for infection. A case series of AIDS patients, which was reported early in the epidemic and prior to the identification of HIV, is described next.

AIDS Cluster A cluster of homosexual men with Kaposi's sarcoma (KS) and/or *Pneumocystis carinii* pneumonia (PCP) was reported in 1984, prior to the identification of HIV.[19] The investigators enumerated the sexual contacts of the first 19 homosexual male AIDS patients reported from Southern California. One man reported sexual contact with 12 of the AIDS patients within 5 years of the onset of their symptoms. Four of the patients from Southern California had contact with a non-California AIDS patient, who was also the sex partner of four AIDS patients from New York City. Ultimately, 40 AIDS patients in 10 cities were linked by sexual contact in this extensive sexual network (**Figure 3-5**). At the epicenter of this cluster was "patient zero," who estimated that he had had approximately 250 different male sexual partners each year from 1979 through 1981 and was able to name 72 of his 750 partners during this 3-year period; 8 of these

partners had developed AIDS. The sexual network linking these patients with the new disease (AIDS) was remarkably similar to the networks of patients with syphilis that were described four decades earlier. This remarkable study led the investigators to conclude that AIDS was caused by a sexually transmitted agent.

Ecologic Studies

Ecologic studies utilize populations with different levels of exposure and examine the correlation of exposure levels with population-level disease frequency. In a typical ecologic study, data are not available at the individual level to determine whether those individuals who are truly exposed have a higher (or lower) occurrence of disease; the researcher simply knows that in the population with greater exposure, there is more (or less) disease.

Ecologic studies may be useful in exploring hypothesized associations by comparing disease frequencies among populations from different geographic regions or from different time periods. Population-level data may be available from national

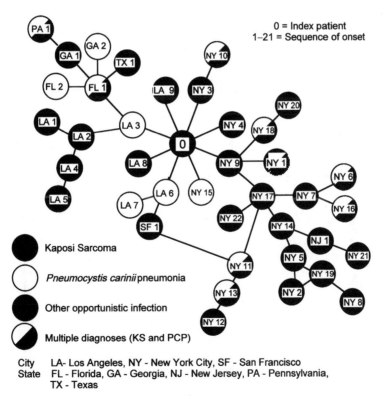

Figure 3-5 Sexual contacts among homosexual men with AIDS. Each circle represents an AIDS patient. Lines connecting the circles represent sexual exposures. Indicated city or state is place of residence of a patient at the time of diagnosis. "0" Indicates Patient 0. Reprinted from the American Journal of Medicine, Vol. 76, D. Auerbach et al, *Cluster of Cases of the Acquired Immune Deficiency Syndrome Patients linked by Sexual Contact*, pp. 487–492, © 1984, with permission from Excerpta Medica Inc.

or community-wide surveys of exposure frequencies and disease rates, which can often be obtained inexpensively. Ecologic studies also allow for comparisons where the range of exposure in one particular population may be too narrow to correlate with a disease outcome at the individual level. For example, the association of vitamin A deficiency with an infectious outcome would be difficult to evaluate in a population consisting of only vitamin A-deficient individuals. Alternatively, an ecologic study comparing infection outcomes across populations with varying prevalence of vitamin A deficiency would permit a better assessment of the correlation. Similarly, studies of the relationship between infectious agents and unusual outcomes—such as the liver fluke *Opisthorchis viverrini* and bile duct cancer, and *Helicobacter pylori* and stomach cancer—can be strengthened by ecologic data from populations with widely varying levels of infections and cancer.

Two ecologic studies, one of rheumatic fever and one of HIV infection, are described here.

Crowding and Rheumatic Fever Early studies led to the hypothesis that household crowding was an important environmental factor in the transmission of group A streptococci and high rates of acute rheumatic fever. Moreover, it has been hypothesized that the reduction in household crowding may have been one factor leading to the decreased rates of acute rheumatic fever in the last half of the 1900s in comparison with earlier periods.[20] The data in **Figure 3-6** show the association between the incidence of rheumatic heart disease and crowding (as measured by household size) in various districts in the city of Bristol, England, 1927–1930. Compared to districts with high household crowding, those with low crowding show lower rates of disease.

Circumcision and HIV Transmission Male circumcision (removal of the foreskin) is a common surgical procedure undertaken for a variety of cultural and medical reasons. Biologically, the foreskin is rich in immune cells and may develop micro-tears that may

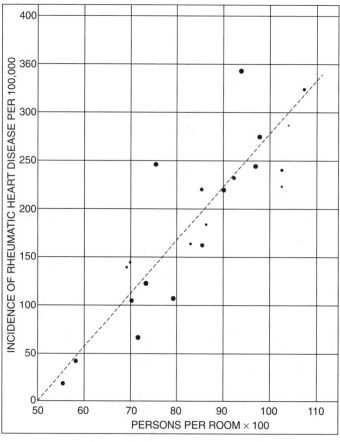

Figure 3-6 The correlation between the incidence of rheumatic heart disease per 100,000 and the number of persons per room (x100), as found by Perry and Robers in various districts of the city of Bristol, England, in 1927–1930. (The size of the dots indicates roughly the comparative population size of the districts.) Reproduced from E. Kass. Infectious Diseases and Social Change. *Journal of Infectious Diseases*, Vol. 23(1):110–114. © 1971. By permission of Oxford University Press.

serve as an entry point for HIV. The foreskin may also trap HIV in a warm moist environment, allowing more time for infection to occur. Given these factors, it is not surprising that circumcised men have been found to have lower rates of sexually transmitted diseases.[21]

In the late 1990s, data began to emerge suggesting that circumcised men were at lower risk for HIV infection. An ecologic study contributed to this evidence by examining the association of the prevalence of circumcision and HIV in several African countries.[22] Data on circumcision practices were extracted from an ethnographic database and were combined with published HIV seroprevalence data. By mapping these data, the authors identified a strong correlation between the practice of male circumcision and the prevalence of HIV infection among males (**Figure 3-7**).

The challenge in conducting this analysis was that a variety of behavioral, cultural, and religious differences between ethnic groups may alter the risk of HIV acquisition. Most notably, circumcised men in the study were more likely to be Muslim, and it was possible that behavioral factors may have contributed to their lower risk of infection. As noted by Gray:

[M]arried Muslim men are predominantly polygamous, and polygamous unions may provide a closed sexual network reducing the risk of HIV introduction. Also, Muslim men abstain from alcohol consumption, and alcohol is associated with high-risk behaviors. Key informant interviews suggest that penile hygiene may be important. Under Islam, individuals are considered unclean after intercourse, and Muslim men and women are required to perform post-coital ablutions. In addition, observant Muslims will often wash before daily prayer. Hygienic practices

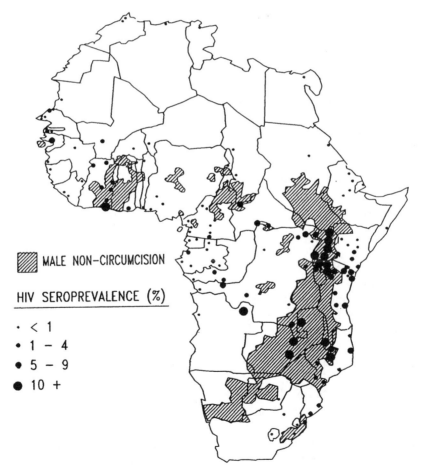

Figure 3-7 Map of Africa showing political boundaries and usual male circumcision practice, with point estimates of general adult population HIV seroprevalence superimposed. Reproduced from Moses et al., Geographical Patterns of Male Circumcision Practices in Africa: Association with HIV Seroprevalence. International Journal of Epidemiology, Vol. 19, pp. 693–697. © 1990. By permission of Oxford University Press.

associated with religion may thus partly explain the protective effects of circumcision among Muslims.[23]

Because an ecologic study design does not collect individual-level data, it cannot account for differences in cultural or hygienic practices that may differ between those men who are and are not circumcised.

Based on the strength of the ecologic studies and other emerging data, three randomized clinical trials of male circumcision were initiated in 2001 in Kenya, South Africa, and Uganda. The results of these studies demonstrated convincingly that male circumcision reduced the incidence of HIV acquisition by more than 50%.[24–26] Although no benefits were seen for circumcision of HIV-infected men in protecting against transmission to their female partners,[27] additional studies have demonstrated benefits of circumcision for genital ulcer disease[28] and high-risk human papillomavirus.[29] The next generation of studies will need to evaluate the expansion of circumcision as part of national HIV prevention strategies and the impact on regional HIV incidence—again requiring further ecologic designs.

Analytical Study Designs

Analytical study designs are fundamental tools for epidemiological inference. In contrast to descriptive study designs, analytical studies collect individual-level data and compare the occurrence of disease with exposure. These designs are best described in the context of a study population moving through time, as illustrated in Figure 3-3, which emphasizes several interrelated methodological considerations:

1. **Selection of the study population from the target and source populations.** As noted previously, there are usually individuals who are part of the target population but who are outside the study population. Thus the manner in which individuals are selected (or self-select) for participation into the study population is an important consideration in evaluating the inferences of a study.
2. **Determination of time metric and follow-up.** The choice of an appropriate metric for conceptualizing the study population moving through time is an important design consideration. Typically, studies are described in terms of the calendar time during which individuals are enrolled and followed. Keep in mind, however, that time can be defined by any number of measures, such as chronological age, biological

life stages (e.g., before or after menopause), or other events (e.g., jobs, marriage, retirement).[30]

Each line in Figure 3-3 represents the time when an individual begins and ends his or her time at risk for experiencing the disease outcome. Determining whether an individual is at risk incorporates both biological and methodological considerations. For example, individuals vaccinated against *Morbillivirus* will not be susceptible to measles and, therefore, cannot be considered at risk for this outcome. Furthermore, if an individual moves out of a study catchment area, he or she would also no longer be considered at risk (if the event occurred, it would not be recorded by the study). Depending on the time metric of interest, not all study participants might enter into a study at the same time. For example, if "time" is measured by age, then participants might enter at different ages, even if they are all enrolled during the same calendar period.

The importance of a well-defined and relevant time metric becomes more evident when we are thinking about the group of individuals who are at risk for an event at a particular time point—the *risk set*. As we will discuss in more detail later, risk sets are important in both the design and the analysis of epidemiologic studies.

1. **Exposure assessment.** In the simplest studies evaluating the link between a particular exposure (e.g., "exposed" and "unexposed," illustrated as solid and dashed lines, respectively, in Figure 3-3) and outcome, it is important to determine whether and how exposure may change over time. Some exposures may be unchanging ("fixed") within an individual (e.g., genetics). Others may be time varying but may change in different ways. For example, some infectious exposures may be transitory and recurrent (e.g., influenza), whereas others are persistent and lifelong once acquired (e.g., HIV). When exposures can change, an important aspect of the study design is the time when they are assessed. It is vital that they are measured at a relevant time point so that they can be temporally linked to a disease outcome.
2. **Outcome assessment.** At the end of the period at risk, some individuals in the study population may develop the disease of interest (Figure 3-3, circles). Like exposures, some disease outcomes may be transient and recur; others are lifelong or defined that way in the analysis (e.g., defining a disease outcome as the first occurrence).

Furthermore, a study will usually end before all individuals develop disease; the term we use for those individuals whose period of follow-up ends while they are still disease-free and at risk is "censored." Thus we need to think about the different types of censoring that may occur within our study design. Individuals may be censored due to logistics of cutting off their follow-up time for an analysis (e.g., administrative censoring). Alternatively, censored individuals may include those who drop out or otherwise become lost to follow-up during the course of the study.

In this section, we provide a brief survey of the various study designs used in epidemiologic analysis, highlight key issues for each design in light of these four methodologic characteristics, and provide examples in the context of infectious disease studies.

Randomized Clinical Trials

Clinical trials evaluate the effect of planned interventions in an experimental manner. The investigator assigns certain participants to receive one treatment—the experimental group—and others to receive another treatment—the control or comparison group. In this subsection, we highlight several key methodological issues in clinical trial designs.

Selection of the Study Population from the Target & Source Populations Clinical trials are initiated to make inferences about an intervention among a specific target population. Thus the eligibility criteria that apply to the study population are a key element of the design. Some trials aim to produce widely generalizable results, exemplified by the advocacy for "large simple trials."[31] With this design, study investigators impose few specific eligibility criteria, with the goal of making inferences about a large and diverse population. More typically, however, clinical trials incorporate strict eligibility criteria, with the goal of eliminating potential factors that might obscure the evaluation of the safety and efficacy of an intervention. This effort would include identifying participants who will be compliant with the study protocol and are either healthy enough to gain some benefit from the intervention or more ill with fewer clinical options.

The decision to impose strict eligibility criteria may particularly affect the enrollment of minorities, women, and persons who have other comorbidities. While not limited to studies of infectious diseases, several studies have documented these effects in HIV disease.[32,33] These disparities remain despite evidence that minorities are willing to participate in research studies.[34,35]

Determination of Time Metric and Follow-up The natural time origin in a clinical trial is the date of randomization, and the time elapsed since randomization is the natural metric for measuring follow-up. The study protocol will usually specify the target minimal time for follow-up of the primary endpoint after which data are analyzed—for example, the trial may continue until all patients have a minimum follow-up of 5 years. Completeness of follow-up is a vital part of clinical trials to ensure the results are not subject to selection bias. The Consolidated Standards of Reporting Trials (CONSORT) Group has developed a variety of initiatives and recommendations that address problems arising from inadequate reporting of randomized controlled trials (RCTs).[36]

Many studies conduct planned interim analyses, with the possibility of stopping a trial early for futility or if strong safety and/or efficacy signals are observed. A substantial number of statistical issues arise with interim analyses, and careful planning and adaptation of specialized methods are necessary to ensure the study maintains its statistical integrity.[37] Further, the decision to stop a study early requires the study team, usually in collaboration with an independent data safety and monitoring board, to balance a variety of complex considerations.[38,39]

Exposure Assessment In an RCT, the exposure of interest (i.e., the intervention) is randomized and administered to participants according to a prespecified study protocol. In the classic double-masked (or double-blinded) trial, subjects are assigned by a random procedure to receive either an experimental treatment or placebo, and neither the subject nor the investigator knows which treatment the subject is receiving. Under some circumstances, this type of trial is not possible, for a variety of reasons. It may not always be possible to conceal the treatment group from the trial participants or the investigators. For instance, trials of medical procedures may be obvious, or medications may have certain side effects. Also, there may be times where a suitable placebo is not available.

In an ideal setting, all individuals would receive and adhere to the intervention to which they were randomized. However, issues of crossovers between treatment groups and adherence are important and raise a key consideration of whether individuals should be analyzed as they are randomized ("intention to treat" analysis) or as they actually use the treatment ("as-treated" analysis). Describing the crossover and adherence in a standardized manner is aided by guidelines such as the CONSORT statement.

An increasing number of design choices are becoming available beyond the traditional two-group, one-to-one randomization schemes for clinical trials. Adaptive randomization schemes attempt to alter the balance of allocation toward the more favorable treatment group based on accumulated outcomes. While potentially reducing the time for a trial, this process may also introduce bias.[40,41] Alternatively, in some situations, clinical trials may be conducted in which it is more appropriate to randomize communities, rather than individuals. This is the case when the intervention is ecologic and is applied at the community level, rather than at the individual level. For example, health education using mass media is this type of intervention. Also, in infectious diseases with a human reservoir where transmission occurs on a person-to-person basis, an intervention targeted at decreasing the prevalence of infected persons or the duration of their infectivity would be expected to decrease the risk of new infection among individuals in the community.

As an example, a community-based randomized trial of insecticide-treated bednets (ITN) was initiated in 1997.[42] The study was conducted in Asembo and Gem, two rural areas of western Kenya, adjacent to Lake Victoria. In this trial, villages were randomized by public lottery to receive ITN or not, and then mortality and morbidity due to malaria were assessed in children up to 5 years of age. Every 6–11 months, study personnel returned to the houses to retreat the bednets. Adherence with use of the ITN was assessed through unannounced visits to the homes in the early morning, 4:30–6:30 A.M. To be considered as adherent, children younger than the age of 5 years had to have their body completely covered by the hanging net. Prior to the start of the study, a cross-sectional survey of the communities was conducted to assess malaria-specific morbidity and mortality. Because of the substantial burden malaria has on the health of young children, the study team included broad measures of health such as weight and diarrheal disease as well as specific markers of malaria morbidity such as anemia and parasitemia. At 14 and 22 months after deployment of the ITN intervention, study personnel returned to the villages to conduct additional cross-sectional surveys of morbidity and mortality.

In the baseline survey, 70% of children had parasitemia; however, only 4% were symptomatic with a fever. *Plamodium falciparum* accounted for the majority of cases (86%). A majority of the children had hemoglobin levels less than 11.0 g/dL (90%),

and nearly one-third (30%) had severe anemia with hemoglobin levels less than 7.0 mg/dL. The follow-up surveys found a reduction in all-cause morbidity by 15%, an increase in anemia by 0.5 mg/dL overall, and a corresponding decrease in severe anemia (39%) reduction in ITN-recipient villages as compared to control villages. The prevalence of malaria parasitemia was reduced by 19% and clinical cases of malaria were decreased by 44% in ITN-recipient villages as compared to control villages. Subsequent research on this population has found that ITN benefits are sustained for as long as 6 years of follow-up.[43]

A variant of the community randomized design that has been of increasing interest is the *stepped-wedge* design. With this approach, an intervention is phased into a group of communities; thus the communities that received the intervention late can serve as controls for the communities that received the intervention at an earlier time.[44] This design is particularly useful for evaluating routine implementation of public health measures.[45] Some examples where this design has been used in infectious disease studies include evaluating the impact of water distribution systems on diarrheal disease outcomes in South Africa,[46] integrated antiretroviral therapy care in antenatal care clinics in Zambia,[47] and training of health personnel for reducing TB disease in Brazil.[48]

Outcome Assessment Assessment of outcomes in a clinical trial is usually rigorous, with the study protocol providing definitions of primary outcomes (those that determine the trial sample size) versus secondary outcomes. Trials typically employ a variety of quality assurance techniques—such as external study adjudication committees—to ensure standardized quality of outcomes.

An issue that often arises in infectious disease trials is the choice of an appropriate outcome. For example, because sexually transmitted HIV infection occurs due to high-risk sexual behavior, interventions to reduce this risk are very important. However, designing, implementing, and evaluating behavioral intervention trials are quite difficult. Problems arise in designing an intervention to be applied to a group of high-risk people. Moreover, valid measurement of the reduction in risk behavior is difficult because the behavior is private and cannot be observed. Some social scientists have relied on risk behavior change reported by study subjects as an endpoint. Even so, after subjects have received extensive counseling, it may be difficult to differentiate socially desirable reporting from true reductions in high-risk behavior.

Clinical trials of behavioral change for preventing HIV infection as an outcome have not been done frequently because of these difficulties and the large number of subjects required for such a trial. One alternative to a trial requiring HIV incidence as an endpoint is to measure the incidence of other STDs as a surrogate marker for HIV risk behavior; the rationale is that those persons who develop other STDs are engaged in behaviors that can result in HIV transmission if the partners are discordant for HIV infection. For example, two randomized controlled clinical trials have been conducted in the United States to study the efficacy of a standardized behavioral intervention to prevent sexually transmitted HIV; incident STDs and reported high-risk behaviors were the endpoints.[49,50]

In one trial, 3706 sexually active adults were recruited from 37 clinics in the United States.[51] Participants were HIV-negative persons who had recently engaged in high-risk sexual behavior, as evidenced by unprotected high-risk vaginal or anal sex in the past 90 days with a new partner, more than one partner, an injection-drug user, or a person infected with HIV. Participants were then assigned randomly to either the control counseling group ($N = 1855$) or the intensive behavioral counseling group ($N = 1851$). Controls received a single 1-hour AIDS education session, whereas those in the intervention group received seven 90- to 120-minute HIV risk-reduction counseling sessions. Reported condom use increased above baseline in both the intervention and control groups at 3 months, but there was a 47% greater increase in reported condom use in the intervention group, which persisted for 12 months. Overall, the rates of reported STDs were not different in the two groups. However, in the participants recruited from an STD clinic, the rate of newly diagnosed gonorrhea in the intervention group was half the rate in the control group. Incident HIV was not studied in this population.

Novel Trial Design: Vaccines Used as Probes to Assess Infectious Diseases

A standard vaccine efficacy trial measures disease to learn about the vaccine efficacy. A "vaccine probe study" uses a vaccine of known efficacy to estimate disease incidence. Thus the intent of the two types of studies is reversed, but the methods are similar. Such a study must be done with a proven, well-characterized vaccine with known efficacy in the prevention of standard clinical outcomes. Like a vaccine efficacy trial, the probe trial needs careful randomization between vaccines and controls, blinding or masking of participants to the intervention, high-quality nondifferential surveillance in both study groups, standard disease definitions with well-characterized specificity, and, of course, an adequate sample size.

Vaccine efficacy is usually expressed as a *relative difference* or percentage reduction in realized disease between the placebo group and the vaccine group. In a probe study to determine disease burden, one can calculate both the relative and *absolute difference* in incidence between the two groups. The incidence difference is the measurement of the incidence of vaccine-prevented cases or *vaccine-prevented incidence (VPI)*; it is a pragmatic direct measure of the effect of the vaccine, in the local setting, without concern for variable and often insensitive microbiological estimates. VPI also incorporates all local effects of immune response, vaccine storage and handling, the actual age of immunization, and other local variations. It has an understandable direct application for local policy. In the example in **Table 3-2**, the VPI would be 110/100,000, or approximately 1 case prevented for every 1000 immunized children.

One of the oldest examples of this kind of assessment was a reanalysis of a cholera vaccine trial in Bangladesh. The original trial evaluated a cholera vaccine with a tetanus toxoid vaccine as a control. The reanalysis evaluated mortality in children of women who received tetanus toxoid vaccine compared with the children of women who received the cholera vaccine. Deaths in the 0- to 28-day neonatal period were reduced by 50% in vaccine recipients' children. Earlier surveillance had not revealed that tetanus was responsible for so high a proportion of infant deaths.[52]

In another example, several studies of *Haemophilus influenzae* type b (Hib) vaccine have shown its effectiveness in reduction of laboratory-confirmed Hib meningitis and blood culture-positive Hib pneumonia. The new data related to analyses of the reduction of clinical syndromes suggest that use of Hib vaccine reduces severe pneumonia requiring hospitalization by approximately 20% in the Gambia and by approximately 4% in Indonesia.[53,54] In contrast, when analyzed for the absolute reduction of illness, the incidence per 100,000 population of vaccine-preventable clinically severe pneumonia was estimated as 83 in children younger than 5 years in the Gambia and as 264 in children younger than 2 years in Indonesia. These rates of Hib vaccine-preventable severe pneumonia are far higher than rates previously estimated by standard blood culture studies and are likely a better measure of disease burden. Similarly, in a prospective trial, the incidence of laboratory-proven Hib meningitis in control group children younger than 2 years of age in Indonesia was 19/100,000. However, the use of Hib vaccine prevented 67/100,000 meningitis cases in children

Table 3-2	Summary of Basic Analytic Study Designs		
Study Design	**Temporal Nature**	**Characterization of Subjects at Enrollment**	**Measures of Association**
Cross-sectional	Point in time May collect retrospective data	Exposure and disease status measured simultaneously	Prevalence = $\dfrac{\text{N with disease}}{\text{N in total population}}$ Odds ratio = $\dfrac{\frac{\text{N exposed with disease}}{\text{N exposed without disease}}}{\frac{\text{N unexposed with disease}}{\text{N unexposed without disease}}}$
Case-control	Point in time May collect retrospective data	Diseased and nondiseased	Odds ratio = $\dfrac{\frac{\text{N exposed with disease}}{\text{N exposed without disease}}}{\frac{\text{N unexposed with disease}}{\text{N unexposed without disease}}}$
Cohort	Follow participants over time	Exposed and nonexposed	Incidence of disease = $\dfrac{\text{N with new disease}}{\text{N in total cohort}}$ Relative risk = $\dfrac{\frac{\text{N exposed with new disease}}{\text{Total N exposed}}}{\frac{\text{N unexposed with new disease}}{\text{Total N unexposed}}}$ Odds ratio = $\dfrac{\frac{\text{N exposed with disease}}{\text{N exposed without disease}}}{\frac{\text{N unexposed with disease}}{\text{N unexposed without disease}}}$
Clinical trial	Follow participants over time	Similar with respect to disease status, randomly assigned an exposure status (treatment)	Incidence of disease = $\dfrac{\text{N with new disease}}{\text{N in total cohort}}$ Relative risk = $\dfrac{\frac{\text{N exposed with new disease}}{\text{Total N exposed}}}{\frac{\text{N unexposed with new disease}}{\text{Total N unexposed}}}$ Odds ratio = $\dfrac{\frac{\text{N exposed with disease}}{\text{N exposed without disease}}}{\frac{\text{N unexposed with disease}}{\text{N unexposed without disease}}}$

admitted to hospital with lumbar puncture. These data on Hib vaccine-prevented meningitis cases suggest that only 28% of all Hib meningitis cases were detected through routine hospital surveillance and standard culture techniques, again showing the true burden of vaccine-preventable illness.

The use of vaccines and such a design that provides for careful analysis of their effect can provide substantial new information regarding the full spectrum of morbidity associated with specific vaccine-preventable agents.[55,56]

Cohort Studies

The word *cohort* was originally used to describe a unit of 300–600 men in the ancient Roman army. In epidemiology, a cohort is a group of individuals with similar characteristics who are followed over time. The characteristic(s) used to define the cohort (i.e., study population) may be—as discussed earlier in this chapter—an exposure, an occupation, a genetic trait, a geographic location, or other population characteristics describing person, place, and time. The cohort study design most closely mimics the fundamental framework of a population moving through time as mentioned previously (Figure 3-3). In its simplest form, participants who are disease free at baseline and at risk for the disease of interest are enrolled in the study and followed over time to measure the occurrence of disease. In this manner, exposures measured at baseline and updated throughout the course of the study can be linked to the occurrence of disease.

A cohort study is best suited for diseases with high incidence among exposed persons and high prevalence of exposure in the source population. This design requires adequate numbers of individuals who are exposed, and who develop disease after enrollment, to have sufficient statistical power to detect a true association between exposure and disease. If the disease of interest were rare, an unrealistically large cohort would have to be assembled to have enough incident outcomes for analysis. If exposures were uncommon, that fact could also affect the size of the cohort needed.

As with other analytic designs, when describing characteristics of a cohort study, epidemiologists are generally interested in four considerations, as profiled next.

Selection of the Study Population from the Target and Source Populations Cohort study populations can be assembled from any number of source populations, be they community based or utilizing specialized resources available for follow-up. For example, members of health maintenance organizations (HMOs) or occupational groups with employment records can be selected as the source population. In one study, a cohort of healthcare providers at San Francisco General Hospital was invited to participate in an investigation of the risk of HBV, HCV, CMV and HIV transmission.[57]

Determination of Time Metric and Follow-up Not all cohort studies need to solicit participation and enroll new members who volunteer and engage in prospective follow-up. The timing of follow-up in a cohort study can be either prospective or retrospective; such studies are distinguished by when the cohort is assembled and follow-up data are collected.

A *prospective* design is one in which the cohort is assembled by the investigator in present time and followed into the future. Advantages of this design include quality control of the exposure and outcome measurement, as assessments are conducted prospectively and can be as detailed and standardized as desired. This design also protects against temporal ambiguity between exposure and outcomes because exposures are captured prior to the development of disease outcomes. Disadvantages of prospective studies are related to resources and time: the enrollment and prospective follow-up of a cohort requires infrastructure (e.g., clinical facilities, staff, laboratory and repository space) and months to years of data collection.

A *retrospective* cohort, or historical cohort design, takes advantage of records and specimens collected in the past, and assesses outcomes that have occurred until the present. This design often utilizes an existing database from which the cohort is assembled, taking advantage of the infrastructure, data, and even specimens already collected. Some examples of such databases might include the General Practice Research Database or Kaiser Permanente;[58] the retrospective design is fairly common in pharmacoepidemiology and occupational settings. The retrospective cohort study can generate results more rapidly, and is typically less expensive, than a prospective design, which must wait for the development of disease. On the downside, this design depends largely on data that have already been collected, thereby removing any control or input by the investigators regarding exposure measurement.

Finally, *ambispective* (also termed "ambidirectional") cohort studies incorporate design aspects of both the retrospective and prospective designs. These studies involve assembling a cohort from the past and assessing outcomes not only until the present, but on an ongoing basis into the future.

Exposure Assessment The timing of the measurement of exposures in a cohort study must take several factors into account. In particular, it depends upon both operational concerns (i.e., logistics, cost) and biological aspects of the disease under study.[59] We can conceptualize the time period during which the effect of a given exposure can have an effect on the risk of disease (i.e., the etiologically relevant time window). For example, in a study of the effect of CD4+ lymphocyte count on HIV disease progression, one might choose to measure CD4+ count at baseline, just prior to the initiation of treatment, or repeatedly over time (more on this later in the chapter). Similarly, we might consider the biologically effective dose (i.e., the dose most pertinent to the etiology of disease). For example, in a study of the effects of alcohol consumption, we might measure exposure as the number of drinks per week over a 6-month period, the number of days on which participants consumed more than 1 drink per day, or some other metric.

Outcome Assessment Generally, two approaches to the ascertainment of outcomes in a cohort study are possible: active and passive. With the active approach, the investigator initiates (or attempts to initiate) direct contact with participants and tries to determine whether the outcome has occurred. Examples might include in-person contact during a study visit (whether clinic based or at home), telephone contact, or mailed surveys. Direct contact with a proxy, such as a close family member who can provide outcome information about the participant, qualifies as active ascertainment. In contrast, passive ascertainment involves indirect tracking of participants' outcome status. This method of assessing outcomes does not require direct contact with the participant, but it requires an established infrastructure that routinely and completely captures events. Examples include Social Security Administration records, the National Death Index (a record of all U.S. deaths since 1978), state vital statistics and registries, or other established data sources.

Cohort studies—and particularly those with a prospective design—can be very expensive and often require a large staff and great motivation on the part of the study participants to remain in follow-up. Studies with significant losses to follow-up may not yield data that are interpretable, because the risks for disease outcomes may be different in those subjects lost to follow-up than in those subjects who were successfully followed (see the later section on selection bias). Next, we outline two examples of cohort studies, one that enrolled new participants and the other that obtained data from an existing database.

HIV Infection and Risk Behaviors in the ALIVE Study Between February 1988 and March 1989, the AIDS Link to the Intravenous Experience (ALIVE) study in Baltimore, Maryland, recruited a cohort of 2960 participants. Criteria for enrollment were as follows: age 18 years or older, a history of injection-drug use (IDU) in the past 10 years, and AIDS-free status at baseline. The target population included current and former injection-drug users in Baltimore; hence the study population was recruited from a source population that included local agencies having contact with injection-drug users: emergency departments, homeless shelters, drug treatment programs, parole and probation, STD clinics, and AIDS prevention programs.[60] Those persons who were HIV-seropositive at baseline were enrolled in a study of the natural history of HIV infection among IDUs; a sample of HIV-negative IDUs was followed prospectively to determine the incidence of HIV infection. Study participants made semiannual visits to the researchers; the visits included interviewer-administered questionnaires, physical exam, and venipuncture. Risk factors of interest in this study were active drug use within the past 6 months, age (younger than 35 years versus 35 years or older), and gender.[61] These factors, as well as other relevant exposures, were captured and updated (where applicable) every 6 months. HIV seroconversion outcomes among those uninfected at baseline were assessed via active ascertainment; blood samples were obtained at every visit and tested for the presence of HIV. Among the 1532 HIV-negative baseline participants, plus an additional 338 who were subsequently enrolled in 1994, a total of 277 (15%) had seroconverted by December 1998.[62]

Oral Contraceptives and Venous Thromboembolism in the GPRD This next example describes a cohort study that was assembled from an existing database, rather than enrolling new participants. This study was initiated to examine the potentially causal association between the use of specific oral contraceptives (OCs) and the incidence of venous thromboembolism (VTE). The target population for this study included women of reproductive age in the United Kingdom between 1993 and 1999. The source population was the General Practice Research Database (GPRD), a clinical database containing data on prescription drugs and clinical diagnoses for more than 3 million people in the United Kingdom. From this source, the study population was identified; the cohort included 1,340,776 women in the GPRD who were between the ages of 15 and 39 years. Because previous studies had suggested a causal relationship between third-generation OC use and the risk of VTE, a warning advising against their use was issued to U.K. doctors and pharmacists in October 1995. To compare the association of third-generation OC use with incident VTE before and after the issuance of this warning by the Committee on Safety of Medicines, the study follow-up considered two time periods: January 1993–October 1995 and January 1996–December 1999. Follow-up began at the date of the first prescription until OC use ceased or the type of OC changed; a woman died, transferred away from her clinical practice, or developed VTE; or the end of the study period. The exposure of interest was the use of OCs containing gestodene or desogestrel (so-called third-generation OCs) versus the use of second-generation OCs, which contained levonorgestrel. The outcome, VTE, was assessed via passive ascertainment methods. This entailed careful individual review of the computerized medical information for each patient with a first diagnosis of VTE. The incidence of VTE was compared in the two time periods for women with and without the exposure; in each time period, those taking third-generation OCs (the exposed group) had approximately twice the incidence of VTE than those taking second-generation OCs (the unexposed group).[63]

Case-Control Studies

Case-control studies can be envisioned as a natural extension of a descriptive case series study. Within the context of a population moving through time (Figure 3-3), the goal of a case-control design is to compare the exposure characteristics of cases with a representative sample of the target population within which the cases occurred. This fundamental characteristic of this study design overcomes some of the disadvantages of cohort studies. It is possible to study rare diseases because resources can be efficiently used to evaluate known or readily available cases of a disease. More than one exposure can be evaluated because the original study population was not restricted with respect to exposure. Typically, case-control studies involve smaller sample sizes than do cohort studies, allowing for greater resources to be expended per participant and for lower costs to the study overall. In this subsection, we highlight several key methodological issues for case-control studies using the framework outlined previously and refer the reader to several other resources for more details.[64–67]

Selection of the Study Population from the Target and Source Populations The target and source populations for a case-control study are an important aspect of the design: understanding how cases are identified aids in the choice of the most appropriate controls. While controls will ideally be drawn from the same source population of the cases, a variety of methodological options exist for identifying and selecting individuals to study. In the most general design, termed "population based," a source population for cases is identified and methods are used to select controls from the same source. The population might be defined geographically (e.g., from a particular country or neighborhood) or from some other defined population (e.g., patients from a particular hospital).

An excellent example of a population-based case-control study was published by Munoz et al.[68] In this study, the investigators conducted an analysis evaluating the link between HPV infection and cervical cancer among women in nine provinces of Spain and one city in Colombia. To do so, the investigators initiated an active case-finding approach to identify all the new cases of invasive squamous-cell cervical carcinoma in these regions. Women free of cancer were selected from the general population in each of these areas to serve as controls. In Spain, provincial census lists were used to randomly identify households; in Colombia, aerial photographs of the region were used to identify homes from which a random sample was drawn. This large study was very important for demonstrating HPV as a causal agent associated with cervical neoplasia.

In contrast to drawing subjects from a general population, a different source population for cases and controls may be identified in an established

cohort study or clinical trial. This type of study design is termed a *nested case-control study*. While a cohort study or trial may capture a wide variety of exposure information, specific and/or new information or tests may emerge that were not anticipated when the longitudinal study was initiated. Instead of making new measurements on the entire cohort, a more efficient design is to initiate a nested case-control study to make measurements only among selected cases and a set of controls.

Nested studies capitalize on some of the advantages of longitudinal studies that follow large study populations over time for the development of outcomes. For studies that prospectively establish biological repositories of specimens for later study, particularly specimens collected at repeated intervals, nested case-control studies offer immense potential for integrating evolving technology and research questions that significantly extend the value of a cohort study or clinical trial. With repeated specimens, these studies provide the opportunity to confirm whether the exposure occurred prior to the onset of disease. For example, epidemiologists for many years questioned whether Hodgkin's disease (HD) was caused by an infectious agent, with some investigations finding evidence of an increased prevalence of Epstein-Barr virus (EBV) antibodies in patients with HD. Although EBV infection is not uncommon, it is known to cause other tumors, especially nasopharyngeal carcinoma, and to persist after the initial infection. To show a causal association, it was necessary to demonstrate that EBV infection preceded the development of HD.

A community-based public health epidemiologic study in Washington County, Maryland, afforded the opportunity to test the hypothesis that EBV might be etiologically related to HD.[69] In this study, a sera repository was established for a population-based cohort study in 1963. More than two decades later, specimens from persons who had developed HD in the interim were selected, matched with controls, and tested for serologic evidence of EBV. The data showed a significant association between EBV antibodies prior to the onset of HD in cases, compared with matched controls (relative risk [RR] = 2.6–4.0 for various serologic markers of infection). This evidence strengthened the argument that EBV infection might be part of the causal pathway for HD, given that EBV infections were more common in the HD cases and preceded the onset of HD. Similar nested study designs have been used to establish other associations, including establishing a causal link of herpes virus variants and Kaposi's sarcoma.[70–73]

A disadvantage of nested case-control groups is the need to select different control groups for each outcome of interest. For example, if a study is interested in examining different cancer outcomes after HPV infection (e.g., cervical cancer, head and neck cancer, oral cancer), a nested case-control study would need to select separate control groups for each group with cancer. Alternatively, another method for selecting controls is to select a random subset of the entire cohort at baseline and use this group as a control group for each of the case groups. Then, if a new type of outcome needs to be studied, only the new cases need to be tested and the original baseline subset can be used as a comparison group. This design, termed a *case-cohort* study, provides an efficient way to study the association of the exposure and outcome.

One example of a nested case-cohort study is an evaluation of the risk of HIV seroconversion among healthcare workers (HCWs) in France, the United Kingdom, and the United States.[74] This study was done to determine whether treatment with zidovudine (or other antiretroviral drugs) after parenteral exposure in HCWs reduced the rate of HIV transmission. Several animal studies suggested that post-exposure prophylaxis conferred protection after challenge with simian immunodeficiency virus (SIV). Furthermore, at the time of the study, zidovudine had been shown to be effective in preventing vertical transmission of HIV. Prospective studies had suggested that the risk of HIV transmission after parenteral exposure was only 0.35%.[57] Therefore a prospective study, or clinical trial, would need to be extraordinarily large to have sufficient statistical power to evaluate the benefit of therapy. Also, recruitment of participants for a randomized clinical trial would be difficult given that zidovudine was generally believed to be effective in preventing HIV transmission, and participants who were randomized to the control arm might insist on receiving the unproven antiretroviral therapy. In this study, available data from the United States and France were analyzed in which the exposure and treatment history of all known cases of HIV

transmission to HCWs ($N = 31$ cases) was compared with that of all reported uninfected exposed HCWs ($N = 679$, cohort). Exposure was defined as a documented penetrating injury with an instrument contaminated by blood from an HIV-positive patient. Cases and cohort members had received either zidovudine or no antiretroviral prophylaxis and had been followed at least 6 months, as of August 1994. The risk factors for HIV infection and protective effect of zidovudine are shown in **Table 3-3**.

Based on the findings from this study, the CDC recommended that all HCWs receive zidovudine after percutaneous exposure to HIV-infected blood. However, it is clear that some potential biases were present in this study. For example, if there was significant underreporting of HCWs in whom transmission failed to occur and who had not received prophylaxis, the transmission rate in the control group could be inflated. This referral (or enrollment) bias would decrease the measured odds ratio (OR) and increase the apparent protective efficacy of zidovudine postexposure prophylaxis above the actual efficacy. Certainly, a randomized controlled clinical trial could provide more valid data. Clinical trials are not always feasible or ethical to conduct, however, and other study designs must often be used to answer important policy questions.

Lastly, sometimes an opportunity arises to use individuals as their own control. A *case-crossover* design[75] is an approach that can be best used to study transient exposures that have a short-term impact on an outcome. With this design, the investigator selects cases and evaluates their exposure immediately preceding the occurrence of the outcome. Instead of making comparisons to a different individual without disease, this design determines a period of time for the case when the outcome could have occurred but did not (typically at an earlier time point). After defining this "control period," the exposure during this time can be evaluated. The advantage of this design is readily apparent: all person-level factors are similar

Table 3-3	Risk Factors for HIV Infection Among Health Care Workers After Percutaneous Exposure to HIV-Infected Blood		
Risk Factors		**Adjusted OR**	**(95% CI)**
Deep injury		16.1	(6.1–44.6)
Visible blood on device		5.2	(1.8–17.7)
Procedure involving needle placed directly in vein or artery		5.1	(1.9–14.8)
Terminal illness in source patient		6.4	(2.2–18.9)
Postexposure use of zidovudine		0.2	(0.1–0.6)

Notes: OR, odds ratio; CI, confidence interval.
Reproduced from the Centers for Disease Control and Prevention (1995). *MMWR*, Vol. 44, pp. 929–931.

and, therefore, cannot serve to confound the analysis. However, a key assumption of this study design is that there are no temporal trends that might influence the occurrence of the exposure or disease. If such temporal trends do play a role, the design can be extended (i.e., *case-time-control design*[76]) to add information from controls to correct the estimates from the impact of temporal trends.

As an example, these designs were used[77] to investigate behavioral factors associated with T-cell homeostasis failure (TCHF), which is a rapid decline in total T-cell counts among individuals with HIV infection that typically occurs 1.5 years prior to the onset of clinical AIDS in the absence of therapy. The case-crossover design was thought to be ideal because the research question of interest dealt with short-term triggers that might perturb a precarious immune system and push it toward greater disease progression. Using extensive data available in the Multicenter AIDS Cohort Study, an initial analysis demonstrated unexpected results that showed strong *protective* effects of sexual and drug use behaviors. Further investigation of the trend in the full cohort showed that there were strong downward trends over time—an intuitive result given that individuals were more ill and aged, and thus tended to report fewer partners and less recreational drug use. To compensate for these trends, the change in exposures occurring over time among a set of control individuals without TCHF was used to adjust the case-crossover results. After this adjustment, the association disappeared, illustrating the importance of the assumptions underlying the design and analysis.

Determination of Time Metric and Follow-up

The concept of a time metric for case-control studies may not seem as directly important as in cohort studies or clinical trials. However, it represents a salient issue when considering the manner by which controls are selected: If there is a time metric that is strongly related to the occurrence of the disease, it is best that cases and controls have a similar distribution of this variable that so a systematic difference does not arise that would potentially affect the association (i.e., confounded, discussed more later in this chapter). Thus, for example, if age were known to alter the occurrence of an outcome (as it typically does), then the investigator would want to make sure cases and controls are chosen to be of similar ages.

Matching is the primary method used to ensure similarity of controls to cases. With case-control studies, when the investigators match by a time metric and select controls from among all non-cases at times similar to the time that the cases occur, the type of sampling is called "incidence density sampling." This type of sampling is particularly easy to accomplish with studies that are nested within cohort studies, but other choices are possible.[66]

Exposure Assessment The issue of exposure assessment in case-control studies is similar to that in other study designs. One issue that arises more often with this study design, when exposure assessment is made retrospectively for cases and controls, is the potential for *information bias*—that is, distortion of the association between exposure and outcome because of how data are measured. Of particular concern is *recall bias*, in which the recall of exposure in cases may be more or less accurate than the recall of exposure in controls.

Distinguishing between different exposures that might be correlated with an outcome also poses a challenge. For example, the first case-control study of Reye's syndrome was conducted in Phoenix, Arizona, in 1976. This study showed a significant association between the use of aspirin during influenza illness and the occurrence of Reye's syndrome.[78] However, the study also showed controls with influenza were more likely to use other antipyretics, such as acetaminophen. With the rising incidence of Reye's syndrome in the United States between 1972 and 1983, a number of case-control studies were done, and all of them showed a significant association with a similar OR.[78–80] Because of some lingering concerns about the representativeness of controls in these studies, the CDC conducted a case-control study in which controls were selected from four different populations for each case.[81] The findings in this case-control study agreed with the results of the other studies—namely, they showed a significant association between aspirin use for influenza and Reye's syndrome. Because of these findings, the CDC[82] and the American Academy of Pediatrics recommended that physicians warn parents of the risk of Reye's syndrome. The Food and Drug Administration mandated warning labels about this hazard on aspirin bottles. Subsequently, Reye's syndrome has virtually disappeared as aspirin use during influenza season declined (**Figure 3-8**).[83]

Outcome Assessment Similar to other epidemiologic study designs, the choice of outcome is dependent on the study question of interest but several issues arise with how cases are identified in case-control studies. The source of cases is important for establishing the relevant target population. Once a source is identified, investigators need to decide the diagnostic criteria that define a case. For new diseases, this may be difficult, as illustrated by the different case-reports in the early HIV/AIDS epidemic. Consider

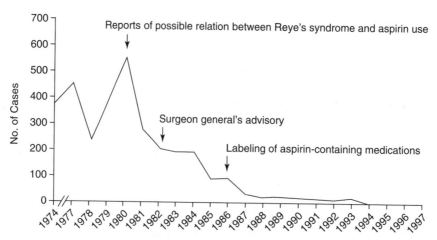

Figure 3-8 Number of reported cases of Reye's syndrome in relation to the timing of public accouncements of the epidemiologic association of Reye's syndrome with aspirin ingestion and the labeling of aspirin-containing medications. From Belay et al., Reye's Syndrome in the United States from 1981 through 1997, New England Journal of Medicine, Vol. 340, pp. 1379, Figure 1. Copyright © 1999 Massachusetts Medical Society. Reprinted with permisison from Massachusetts Medical Society.

the following CDC report from 1982, which offered a specific definition of AIDS:

> CDC defines a case of AIDS as a disease, at least moderately predictive of a defect in cell-mediated immunity, occurring in a person with no known cause for diminished resistance to that disease. Such diseases include KS, PCP, and serious other opportunistic infections . . . Diagnoses are considered to fit the case definition only if based on sufficiently reliable methods (generally histology or culture). However, this case definition may not include the full spectrum of AIDS manifestations, which may range from absence of symptoms (despite laboratory evidence of immune deficiency) to non-specific symptoms (e.g., fever, weight loss, generalized, persistent lymphadenopathy) (4) to specific diseases that are insufficiently predictive of cellular immunodeficiency to be included in incidence monitoring (e.g., tuberculosis, oral candidiasis, herpes zoster) to malignant neoplasms that cause, as well as result from, immunodeficiency (5). Conversely, some patients who are considered AIDS cases on the basis of diseases only moderately predictive of cellular immunodeficiency may not actually be immunodeficient and may not be part of the current epidemic. Absence of a reliable, inexpensive, widely available test for AIDS, however, may make the working case definition the best currently available for incidence monitoring.[84]

Another decision that needs to be made in case-control studies is whether all cases will be included or whether the study will restrict participation to only newly identified cases. The latter criterion is often implemented to eliminate "prevalence–incidence bias," which may occur when the duration of disease is affected by exposure. Prevalence–incidence bias can either increase or decrease the observed association between an exposure and a disease. If persons who are exposed to a factor experience a more rapid course of disease, they may die before they can be identified by researchers—a factor that will spuriously reduce the association. Conversely, if exposure increases survival, the association measured by the study will be greater than the true association. For studies of infectious disease with long incubation periods (e.g., HIV, HCV), this issue is particularly important.

Systematic Reviews and Meta-analyses

Systematic reviews are investigations that attempt to answer specific research questions through existing study reports instead of through direct data collection. The design of systematic reviews focuses on defining criteria by which a search is conducted and how reports are chosen for inclusion. A meta-analysis is a statistical analysis of a collection of data identified in selected reports, typically using summary data as reported in study tables or figures. Meta-analysis is commonly employed by epidemiologists to synthesize data for which various studies have created controversy, or sometimes to arrive at an overall summary estimate of a relationship when individual studies are underpowered. One of the problems associated with meta-analysis relates to the effects of publication

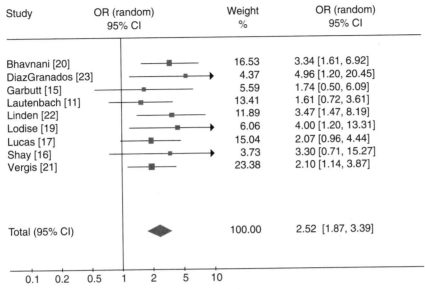

Study	OR (random) 95% CI	Weight %	OR (random) 95% CI
Bhavnani [20]		16.53	3.34 [1.61, 6.92]
DiazGranados [23]		4.37	4.96 [1.20, 20.45]
Garbutt [15]		5.59	1.74 [0.50, 6.09]
Lautenbach [11]		13.41	1.61 [0.72, 3.61]
Linden [22]		11.89	3.47 [1.47, 8.19]
Lodise [19]		6.06	4.00 [1.20, 13.31]
Lucas [17]		15.04	2.07 [0.96, 4.44]
Shay [16]		3.73	3.30 [0.71, 15.27]
Vergis [21]		23.38	2.10 [1.14, 3.87]
Total (95% CI)		100.00	2.52 [1.87, 3.39]

0.1 0.2 0.5 1 2 5 10

Figure 3-9 Meta-analysis plot using a random effects model. The dots represent the point estimates for the measure of effect of each study. The horizontal lines represent the 95% CIs for each study. The rhomboidal figure represents the summary measure and 95% CI. The right column shows the numeric values for each study and summary measure. Reproduced from Diaz Grandos CA, Zimmer SM, Klein M and Jernigan JA. Comparison of mortality associated with Vancomycin-resistant and Vancomycin-susceptible enterococcal bloodstream infections: A meta-analysis. Clin Infect Dis 2005; 41:330, Figure 2. © 2005. By permission of Oxford University Press.

bias, which can occur when negative studies are not published. Also, the combined analysis of data from studies in which the exposure measurements or outcomes are significantly different may not clarify an association but rather lead to erroneous conclusions.

Example: A Meta-analysis of Mortality Associated with Vancomycin-Resistant and Vancomycin-Sensitive Enterococcal Bloodstream Infections

Enterococcal infections have emerged as the third or fourth most frequent cause of nosocomial bloodstream infections in hospitalized patients in the United States.[85] Moreover, the prevalence of vancomycin resistance has increased such that it now accounts for 14–25% of all nosocomial enterococcal bacteremic strains. In 1995, the CDC published guidelines to prevent transmission of vancomycin-resistant enterococci (VRE), and several pharmaceutical firms are developing antibiotics to use against VRE. However, some clinicians have argued that VRE strains are not commonly virulent and have questioned whether they should be given special attention. To address this question, a meta-analysis of the mortality rates associated with vancomycin-resistant (VR) compared to vancomycin-sensitive (VS) nosocomial bacteremia was performed. All articles listed in the MEDLINE database from January 1988 through March 2003 were identified, as well as those compiled in the Cochrane Library through

March 2003. Studies were included if they assessed mortality after enterococcal bloodstream infection (BSI), compared mortality after VRE BSI with VSE BSI, and adjusted for underlying severity of illness. Individual study validity was assessed, with attention being paid to selection bias and misclassification bias.

Of 114 studies, nine met the inclusion criteria. All of the nine studies found a significant increased OR for mortality associated with VRE BSI compared to VSE BSI;, however, the 95% confidence interval of three studies overlapped (**Figure 3-9**).[85]

MEASUREMENT AND MEASURES OF DISEASE OCCURRENCE

A famous quotation by British physicist Lord Kelvin emphasizes the importance of measurement to scientific investigations:

> I often say that when you can measure what you are speaking about and express it in numbers you know something about it: but when you cannot measure it, when you cannot express it in numbers, your knowledge is of a meagre and unsatisfactory kind: it may be the beginning of knowledge, but you have scarcely, in your thoughts, advanced to the stage of science, whatever the matter may be.[86]

This is no less true in epidemiology. In this section, we describe several key areas where measurement issues intersect with epidemiological studies.

Obtaining Data: Measurement on the Individual

A variety of theoretical frameworks have been developed for describing the processes of taking measurement, including breaking down the process into those related to "mensuration" and "quantification" by Feinstein[87] and the ideas of "practical" and "representational" measurement by Hand.[88] Regardless of the framework, data collection must ensure meaningful and accurate translation of observations into numerical summaries.

Infectious disease epidemiology shares many such considerations common to epidemiologic studies of other diseases. Data collection itself may involve review of employment or medical records, personal interviews, clinical exams, environmental measurements, collection of biologic specimens, or other relevant measures. Interviews may be conducted in person (either self- or interviewer-administered), by phone, by mail, or by computer. Each of these methods has its advantages and disadvantages in terms of reliability, minimization of bias, and resource burden.

To conduct an epidemiologic study of an infectious disease, one must measure the occurrence of infection. When doing so, the infection might be treated as an exposure for evaluating sequelae and subsequent disease, or the infection in itself might be an endpoint (e.g., to study the factors leading to infection). The choice of measures, the selection of instruments, and interpretation of the results represent an area where epidemiology intersects with other sciences and subject-matter experts—for example, microbiology, immunology, and clinical practice. Depending on the study question, infections may be ascertained via self-reports, abstracted from medical charts or laboratory reports, or identified through direct study-related testing. While this may seem straightforward, the occurrence of infectious exposures and outcomes may be difficult to define and/or costly to ascertain (**Figure 3-10**).

In addition to measuring the occurrence of a particular infectious agent, measures of "intensity" or "degree" of infection are often of interest. With chemical exposures, this kind of information is captured by the concept of "dose," which has long been part of an assessment of the degree to which individuals have been exposed. With some infectious agents, viral titers often serve a similar role and help to distinguish those individuals who may have more virulent infections. Testing for viral loads is now routine in studies of HIV infection, for example, based on the evidence that it predicts disease progression;[89] for those exposed to antiretroviral therapy, the association of viral load with nonadherence and resistance is a key consideration.[90]

Measurement and Time

Measurements of exposures, outcomes, and other variables in epidemiology are taken in the context of populations evolving through time (Figure 3-3).

Many infectious diseases result in the formation of antibodies. Antibodies are generally long lasting and indicate that a person has been exposed to a disease. However, using antibodies as a marker of disease is more complicated than it first appears:

1. **When was the person exposed?** Antibodies to mumps are long lasting and could indicate infection in the distant past or a recent infection. Immunoglobulin type M (IgM) antibodies are the first to form, and high levels of these antibodies indicate that the infection is recent. IgG antibodies form later in the course of infection. Variation in the timing (but not the sequence) of the different antibody classes is seen among individuals and for different infections.
2. **Has immunity waned or never formed?** Antibodies are not long lasting for some infectious agents. Antibodies form several months after exposure to *B. burgdorferi* (the agent of Lyme disease) and may either wane or not form at all in persons who are treated early.
3. **Was the person exposed or vaccinated?** It may not be possible to differentiate those who are vaccinated from those who had disease. Vaccination against polio with the inactivated injection and oral inoculation will generate immunity that cannot be differentiated from immunity from polo infection. In contrast, the hepatitis B vaccine results in antibodies against only one viral protein (HBsAg). An infected individual will have antibodies to other viral proteins not included in the vaccine.
4. **Did the person have the disease or just infection?** Antibody formation can occur in those who suffered severe disease and in those with subclinical symptoms. The presence of antibodies only demonstrates infection, not disease status. Cholera has low rates of clinical disease, and the prevalence of antibodies to cholera are not a measure of the mortality and morbidity of a cholera epidemic.

Figure 3-10 Issues in determining the occurrence of an infectious disease

It is important to consider whether, and by how much, exposures may change over time. Fixed exposures are those that change neither over the follow-up period nor with additional measurement. These parameters may be things that are truly immutable (e.g., date of birth, host genetics), or they may be factors measured at a particular time point in the study that remain constant over additional follow-up (e.g., CD4$^+$ cell count at initiation of antiretroviral therapy). In contrast, time-varying exposures can change over time—for example, behaviors (e.g., smoking, alcohol use, diet, medications), environmental/occupational factors (e.g., employment), and most biological disease parameters (e.g., CD4$^+$ cell counts over the course of HIV disease progression).

Epidemiologists consider how other factors, both intrinsic and external to the individual, may change over time and can influence the occurrence of disease. In addition to the effect of aging on the risk of disease, other susceptibility factors, biological precursors, and additional exposures might also alter the occurrence of disease. The decision to measure these factors, and the relevant time window in which to measure them, are additional considerations that influence study design. When exposures are time-varying, it is important to consider the time at which these variables are measured when attempting to link them to a disease outcome. We use the idea of *etiologically relevant time windows* to describe the appropriate timing of exposure measurement.[91]

With time-varying exposures, it is important to think about how the frequency, duration, and accumulation of exposure may impact the disease of interest. Measures can be constructed that summarize an individual's cumulative exposure into a single value. For example, epidemiologists have long used the measure of "pack-years" for summarizing the duration and intensity of smoking history; a similar measure for viral burden has also been proposed.[92]

Measurement in Populations: Incidence and Prevalence

Epidemiologists quantify the occurrence of disease in populations with a variety of measures; the two fundamental measures are *prevalence* and *incidence*. While both are estimates of the burden of disease in a given population, they have very different interpretations. Prevalence measures the proportion of the population who has the disease at a given time (*point prevalence*) or during a given interval (*period prevalence*). Alternatively, we can assess the occurrence over time of incident (new) cases of disease among those who are disease free at the start of follow-up. The choice of measure is largely determined by the study design.

Prevalence

Prevalence estimates are often generated by survey or cross-sectional studies. A one-time measure of the number of individuals in the population who have the disease, expressed as a proportion of the size of the population at risk (i.e., those persons deemed susceptible to the disease), measures the prevalence of that disease. However, prevalence can also be estimated in the context of a longitudinal study (Figure 3-3). At any point in the study (e.g., often at baseline but also possible at any point during follow-up), we could assess the number of individuals in the population who have the disease; this measure of disease burden at a particular point in time is called *point prevalence*. Alternatively, we could estimate the prevalence during an interval of time; for example, we could assess the number of individuals who had the disease of interest during the year 2010, as a proportion of the population at risk during 2010. This type of measure is called *period prevalence*.

One strength of prevalence measures is that they provide a snapshot of the burden of disease at a particular time. Thus they are useful as descriptive characterizations of a population and vital for informing public health practice, such as where to target interventions. However, prevalence measures are not useful for estimating an individual's risk for developing disease over time, nor are they helpful for identifying determinants of disease. These issues are better addressed with incidence measures.

Incidence

Incidence refers to new cases that develop among individuals known to have previously been disease free. Incidence can be expressed either as a proportion of at-risk individuals who develop the disease by a certain time (*cumulative incidence*) or as a function of follow-up time contributed at risk (*incidence rate*).

Cumulative Incidence **Figure 3-11** shows a hypothetical cohort, consisting of 10 individuals followed over a 5-year study period. Each horizontal line represents the follow-up experience of an individual participant. The circles (participants 2, 8, and 10) indicate outcomes (i.e., incident disease), the vertical bars (participants 3 and 6) represent losses to follow-up, and the arrows (all remaining participants) show that those individuals remained in the study for the entire follow-up period, with no disease outcome (termed "administrative censoring"). To assess the burden of disease in this study population, we could calculate the *cumulative incidence* of disease that, in its simplest form, is the number of events as a proportion of the

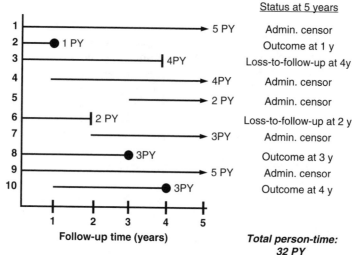

Figure 3-11 A Cohort of 10 Individuals

size of the population at risk. Cumulative incidence is expressed as a proportion; in this case, 3 events ÷ 10 individuals at risk = 0.3 or 30%. This measure represents the probability of disease developing in an individual over a 5-year interval.

Despite their misnomer as "rates" (a rate is a ratio in which time is in the denominator), attack rates are among the most common measures of cumulative incidence in infectious disease epidemiology. These are a staple measure for outbreak investigations. In these settings, choices must be made as to the criteria that define both the numerator and the denominator. The numerator depends on establishing a specific case definition, which will reflect the symptoms being reported. This typically results in cases being classified as suspect, probable, or confirmed, based on the spectrum of reported symptoms, laboratory confirmation, or other criteria. The choice of an appropriate denominator is less clear, as it is often derived once common links can be made between cases, and may be too broad to define.

For example, in August–September 2011, the Colorado Department of Public Health and Environment reported an outbreak of listeriosis to the CDC.[93] Laboratory analysis led to a case definition, which included illness with one of four outbreak strains isolated in cases occurring on or after August 1. Cantaloupe consumption was implicated in all of the first 19 cases reported. By September 29, 84 cases had been identified in 19 states; among those cases for which data was available on food consumption, 92% reported eating cantaloupe within the month before the onset of illness. Food tracing methods led investigators to one particular

farm in Colorado, which had issued a voluntary recall of its cantaloupe on September 14.

In this example, identification of the case definition (i.e., the numerator of the attack rate) was determined by symptoms and laboratory analysis. However, the attack rate denominator was less clear. Because this was a large outbreak (involving two serotypes, multiple states, and the highest number of deaths of any U.S. foodborne outbreak since a previous listeriosis outbreak in 1998,[94] the identification of an appropriate denominator was debatable and was too broadly defined to be enumerable. In such cases, the case definition is often sufficient to characterize the breadth of the outbreak and provide direction for identifying the source of the illness.

Incidence Rates A limitation of cumulative incidence calculated in the manner described previously is that the contributions of all study participants are weighted equally. As Figure 3-11 shows, this tactic is often not appropriate. Participants who are not at risk during the entire period of follow-up because they enter the cohort late (participants 4, 5, 7, and 10) and/or leave the risk set early (due to developing the outcome or being lost to follow-up) contribute less time under observation than do those subjects who remain in the study for the entire follow-up period. The Kaplan-Meier method estimates the cumulative incidence by incorporating the different person-time contributions across the cohort.

An alternative measure of incidence is the *incidence rate*. This measure expresses the occurrence of disease by incorporating the amount of follow-up time rather than simply the population size. The numerator in the incidence rate is the same as that in the cumulative incidence: the number of new cases of disease over the follow-up period. The denominator, however, is not the number of individuals in the study; rather, it is the accumulated amount of time over all individuals (termed *person-time* and often expressed as person-years [PY]) contributed by those at risk for the outcome. In Figure 3-11, the accumulated person-time for each individual is shown at the end of his or her follow-up and totals 32 PY. The incidence rate would then be 3 events ÷ 32 person-years = 9.4 per 100 person-years.

POPULATION COMPARISONS AND EPIDEMIOLOGIC INFERENCE

Incidence and prevalence measures are important components of an epidemiologic study that enable us to assess the burden and risk of disease. While often calculated to characterize the entire population, these measures are more frequently calculated among subgroups of individuals with particular characteristics. In etiologic studies evaluating an exposure–disease relationship, these measures would be calculated and compared between different exposure groups. Such comparisons form the basis for inference from epidemiologic studies.

Measures of Association

Epidemiologists use a variety of measures to describe the association between exposures and disease in etiologic studies. The choice of which measure to use is determined by the study design and the nature of the data. In its simplest form, we can consider a scenario in which there are two exposure categories (typically "exposed" and "unexposed") and two outcome categories ("disease" and "no disease").

The cross-classification of individuals into the four possible exposure–disease combinations is called a "2 × 2 table," as illustrated in **Figure 3-12**. The 2 × 2 table is useful for visualizing the distribution of exposure and disease across the study population. Using this tool, and based on the study design, we can construct the appropriate measure for the association between exposure and disease. Epidemiologists make comparisons using both relative and absolute scales; here we will focus on the more common relative measures.

For cohort studies and clinical trials that are measuring incidence, the most natural measure of association is the ratio of cumulative incidence in the exposed versus unexposed groups. This ratio is usually termed the relative risk (RR) or risk ratio. Using the 2 × 2 table format as shown in Figure 3-12, the relative risk is expressed as follows:

$$RR = \frac{A/(A+B)}{C/(C+D)}$$

This equation shows that if the cumulative incidence of disease among those exposed is greater than that among the unexposed, the RR will be greater than 1, meaning the exposed are more likely to have the disease (i.e., the exposure increases risk of the disease). Conversely, if the incidence in the exposed is less than that among the unexposed, the RR will be less than 1, indicating that the exposed are less likely to have disease (i.e., the exposure is protective).

Similar ratio estimates can be calculated if we are estimating the incidence rate. That is, we can calculate the ratio of incidence rate in the exposed group as compared to the unexposed group. This ratio, which is called the incidence rate ratio (IRR), is a measure of association similar in its interpretation to the RR.

Epidemiologic data can be presented according to the disease and exposure status of the study participants. In the simplest case, the data may be presented as a 2 × 2 table. In instances where there are multiple exposures, the 2 × 2 table may be generalized to include as many exposure categories as necessary.

2 × 2 Table		Disease Status +	Disease Status -
Exposure Status	Yes	A	B
	No	C	D

2 × N Table		Disease Status +	Disease Status -
Exposure Status	High	A	B
	Medium	C	D
	Low	E	F
	None	G	H

Figure 3-12 Epidemiologic data presentation

In case-control studies, we cannot use the RR and IRR measures because of how individuals are selected for study and because we are not estimating incidence. Instead, the study design evaluates the distribution of exposures for the case and control groups. The numbers of individuals with and without the disease are fixed by the investigator at enrollment. Cornfield's famous result[95] shows the relative risk can be approximated in a case-control study when the disease is rare using the ratio of the odds of exposure among the cases as compared to the controls, as can be seen in this formula:

$$OR = \frac{\text{Odds of exposure among cases}}{\text{Odds of exposure among controls}} = \frac{A/C}{B/D} = \frac{AD}{BC}$$

The further away the measure of association (e.g., RR, IRR, OR, or other measure) from the null value (1.0), the stronger the association between the exposure and the disease.

Statistical tests are used to determine whether the measured RR is likely to be a true effect or due to chance; it is important to note that the magnitude of the effect and the level of statistical significance are not equivalent. For instance, a very small effect size can be statistically significant, and vice versa; statistical significance depends on sample size. As a consequence, a result may be highly statistically significant, yet medically unimportant. Alternatively a result that is not statistically significant could indicate a potentially important finding that needs further study to confirm it.

Causation and Epidemiologic Inference

After identifying individuals for a study population, and making measurements of exposure and disease and their measures of association, epidemiologists conduct analyses and report on what was found in their study population. While descriptive data are important, epidemiologists typically conduct analytical studies with the goal of making inferences from the associations observed in their study population back to the target population.

Ideally, any associations that are investigated in epidemiological studies will be *causal*. The definition and concepts surrounding causality are vast, cross multiple scientific and philosophical domains, and have deep historical roots. In epidemiology and public health, identifying causal associations is important not only for uncovering underlying mechanisms of disease, but also for serving as a basis for intervention and prevention.

One of the key threats to establishing a causal association is confounding. As defined by Porta,[96] confounding is "the distortion of a measure of the effect of an exposure on an outcome due to the association of the exposure with other factors that influence the occurrence of the outcome." In other words, when confounding is present the comparison between an exposed and unexposed group is "unfair" because the two groups differ relative to a third variable. For example, studies of the association of male circumcision with acquisition of HIV were described earlier in this chapter. One area of concern in the observational studies of this association was the potential for confounding due to cultural and behavioral factors among Muslims. In Gray et al.'s study,[23] for example, 80% of the circumcised men were Muslim while only 0.2% of the men who were not circumcised were Muslim. If being Muslim were also related to acquiring HIV, then this variable would confound the ability to distinguish the true impact of male circumcision on HIV acquisition.

How do epidemiologists discern causal associations that are not affected by confounding? Fortunately, a variety of approaches are available that address confounding and make the exposed and unexposed groups more similar (and thus the comparison "more fair"). In interventional clinical trials of a treatment exposure, randomization aims to ensure balance on all variables (observed and unobserved) in those treated and not treated. In observational studies, methods include aspects that can be implemented at the time the study is designed, such as restriction to individuals in a certain group (e.g., only the Muslim men in the circumcision–HIV study) or matching to ensure an equal proportion of individuals with the third factor in both the exposed and unexposed groups (e.g., equal proportion of circumcised and uncircumcised men who are Muslim).

Alternatively, methods can be implemented to mitigate confounding factors at the time of analysis, such as stratification, weighting, and regression adjustment. Good statistical practice aids in the assessment of causal associations. The armament of statistical concepts and tools provides a powerful set of approaches for the analysis of data. Nevertheless, it is important to distinguish statistical associations that reflect correlation between variables from true causal associations. The ultimate evaluation of whether an association is causal is a central challenge for epidemiologists and is not something that can be determined from statistical analysis alone.

Epidemiologic Inference

Epidemiologists use the term *internal validity* to reflect the goal of obtaining inferences from a study population that are applicable to the target population. The *external validity* of a study—also termed *generalizability*—refers to the relevance of these inferences to other target populations. The degree to which results are generalizable to other populations cannot be assessed statistically but instead relies upon evaluating the myriad biological and clinical factors that might influence the occurrence of disease.

How do epidemiologists ultimately make internally valid inferences? The answer to this question relies upon understanding all the components described in the framework depicted in Figure 3-1. *Bias* is the term used to describe the general deviation of an estimated measurement from its underlying true value. To make unbiased inferences, we need to know how the study population was selected relative to the target population and how the study design and follow-up were selected in the context of individuals moving through time (Figure 3-3). We need to know if individuals were chosen for our study population (or self-selected, such as what might occur with follow-up in a longitudinal study) from the target population in a way that might influence our association. This type of bias is termed *selection bias*. Comparisons should be made between the actual study sample and the population targeted for study, the response rate of subgroups, and the composition of the population from which the sample was drawn.

For example, in case-control studies, the researcher attempts to determine the exposures among the cases and controls. Because the analysis is based on comparisons within the study sample, generalizability of the results to the overall population is less important than the appropriate selection of the control population. The overriding consideration in the selection of controls is to choose them in such a way that they are truly representative of the same population from which the cases arose. For example, studies have sought controls from other patients in hospitals or clinics, friends of the cases, family members of cases, neighborhood or geographic controls, or other accessible populations. Whereas the risk of disease may differ between cases and controls, controls should be similar enough to cases that they, too, have a risk of developing the disease under study. If the controls were completely immune to developing a disease, the risk factor of importance in the case group may not be different between the groups. For instance, in a study of genetic traits and ovarian cancer, men should not be used as the control group. A less extreme example is that HIV-seronegative persons are not suitable controls for a study of AIDS patients with Kaposi's sarcoma; the researcher should instead choose individuals who have a similar level of immune suppression but are KS free. Researchers

must also decide whether controls should be chosen from populations with other diseases or from nondiseased persons. Frequently, data are often available on persons diagnosed with another disease as a result of diagnosis or treatment that can be used to compare risk factors between cases and controls. When controls with other diseases are selected, it is important to ensure that the exposure being evaluated is not also related to the control's disease. Sometimes, it may be difficult to rule out the presence of disease in persons who have not received certain diagnostic procedures. However, if a study requires that the controls have undergone extensive diagnostic tests, that criterion may compromise generalizability or external validity because only a select group of people will have met the testing requirements.

To make unbiased inferences, we also need to know something about the means by which the measurements in our study were done and the quality of the data. Was the study performed in the manner in which it was designed? Did any deviations from the design alter the quality of the results? Variability in our study inferences as reflected in the size of confidence intervals can be introduced because of the use of poor-quality measurements. *Information bias* can arise from obtaining measurements in a way that affects the association. For example, while case-control studies are useful for evaluating potential risk factors in an outbreak of an infectious disease, the determination of exposure data may be difficult. Sometimes, the exposure may have occurred many years prior to the onset of the disease, and the individuals who had the disease are more likely to remember the circumstances in the past than those who did not get the disease. In this scenario, a difference will arise in the quality of how the data are measured, which in turn may lead to a distortion (termed *recall bias* in this situation) in the measures of association. This outcome is not inevitable, however. For example, in acute outbreaks of infectious diseases, such as with the toxic shock syndrome or foodborne outbreaks, the exposures are recent, so recall bias may be less important than in circumstances when the time from exposure to disease is long.

Lastly, to make unbiased inferences, we need to make appropriate comparisons and aim for associations that are causal. Confounding was described earlier as a distortion of an effect that can occur in the comparison of populations, particularly in observational studies where randomization is absent to ensure exposed and unexposed populations are comparable. The best epidemiological studies take advantage of the tools described previously to attempt to elucidate the factors that may be obscuring causal associations.

Conclusion

Epidemiological inference is challenging and requires an appreciation for the framework in Figure 3-1. In this chapter, we provided an overview of how epidemiologists use the components of this framework to describe the burden and determinants of disease in populations.

• • • REFERENCES

1. Miller L. Impact of malaria on genetic polymorphism and genetic disease in Africans and African Americans. In: Bernard Roisman B, ed. *Infectious Disease in an Age of Change: The Impact of Human Ecology and Behavior on Disease Transmission.* Washington, DC: National Academies Press; 1995:99–111.

2. Penicillin's finder assays its future. *The New York Times,* June 26, 1945, p.21.

3. Glezen WP, Couch RB, Taber LH. Epidemiologic observations on influenza B virus infections in Houston, Texas, 1976–1977. *Am J Epidemiol.* 1980;111(1):13–22.

4. Rupprecht CE, et al. Prophylaxis against rabies. *N Engl J Med.* 2004;351:262–2635.

5. Constantine D. Rabies transmission by non-bite route. *Public Health Rep.* 1962;77:287–291.

6. Hronovsky V, Benda R. Development of inhalation rabies infection in suckling guinea pigs. *Acta Virol.* 1969;13:198–202.

7. Hronovsky V, Benda R. Experimental inhalation of infection of laboratory rodents with rabies virus. *Acta Virol.* 1969;13:193–197.

8. Noah D, Drenzek C, Smith J, et al. Epidemiology of human rabies in the United States. *Ann Intern Med.* 1998;128:922–930.

9. Hattwick M, Weis T, Stechschulte J, Baer GM, Gregg M. Recovery from rabies: a case report. *Ann Intern Med.* 1972;76:931–942.

10. Centers for Disease Control and Prevention. Recovery of a patient from clinical rabies—Wisconsin, 2004. *MMWR.* 2004;53:1171–1173.

11. Willoughly RE, Jr, Tieves KS, Hoffman GM, et al. Survival after treatment of rabies with induction of coma. *N Engl J Med.* 2005;352:2508–2514.

12. Luckhart BP, Tordo N, Tsiáng H. Inhibition of rabies virus transcription in rat cortical neurons with the dissociative anesthetic ketamine. *Antimicrob Agents Chemother.* 1992;36:1750–1755.

13. Lite J. Medical mystery: only one person has survived rabies without vaccine—but how? *Sci Am.* October 8, 2008. Available at: http://www.scientificamerican.com/article.cfm?id=jeanna-giese-rabies-survivor.

14. Juncosa B. Hope for rabies victims: unorthodox coma therapy shows promise. *Sci Am.* November 21, 2008. Available at: http://www.scientificamerican.com/article.cfm?id=hope-for-rabies-victims-unorthodox-coma-therapy-shows-promise.

15. Bryceson Y, Pang S, Wei L, et al. Clearance of HIV infection in a perinatally infected infant. *N Engl J Med.* 1995;332:833–838.

16. Lederman MM, Penn-Nicholson A, Cho M, Mosier D. Biology of CCR5 and its role in HIV infection and treatment. *JAMA.* 2006;296(7):815–826.

17. Hütter G, Nowak D, Mossner M, et al. Long-term control of HIV by CCR5 Delta32/Delta32 stem-cell transplantation. *N Engl J Med,* 2009;360(7):692–698.

18. Allers K, Hütter G, Hofmann J, et al. Evidence for the cure of HIV infection by CCR5Δ32/Δ32 stem cell transplantation. *Blood.* 2011;117(10):2791–2799.

19. Auerbach D, Darrow W, Jaffe H, et al. Cluster of cases of the acquired immune deficiency syndrome: patients linked by sexual contact. *Am J Med.* 1984;76:487–492.

20. Kass E. Infectious disease and social change. *J Infect Dis.* 1971;123:110–114.

21. Cook L, Koutsky L, Holmes K. Circumcision and sexually transmitted diseases. *Am J Public Health.* 1994;84:197–201.

22. Moses S, Bradley J, Hagelkerke N, Ronald A, et al. Geographical patterns of male

circumcision practices in Africa: association with HIV seroprevalence. *Int J Epidemiol.* 1990;19: 693–697.

23. Gray RH, Kiwanuka N, Quinn TC, et al. Male circumcision and HIV acquisition and transmission: cohort studies in Rakai, Uganda. Rakai Project Team. *AIDS.* 2000;14(15):2371–2381.

24. Auvert B, Taljaard D, Lagarde E, et al. Randomized, controlled intervention trial of male circumcision for reduction of HIV infection risk: the ANRS 1265 Trial. *PLoS Med.* 2005;2(11):e298.

25. Gray RH, Kigozi G, Serwadda D, et al. Male circumcision for HIV prevention in men in Rakai, Uganda: a randomised trial. *Lancet.* 2007;369(9562):657–666.

26. Bailey RC, Moses S, Parker CB, et al. Male circumcision for HIV prevention in young men in Kisumu, Kenya: a randomised controlled trial. *Lancet.* 2007;369(9562): 643–656.

27. Wawer MJ, Makumbi F, Kigozi G, et al. Circumcision in HIV-infected men and its effect on HIV transmission to female partners in Rakai, Uganda: a randomised controlled trial. *Lancet.* 2009;374(9685):229–237.

28. Gray RH, Serwadda D, Tobian AA, et al. Effects of genital ulcer disease and herpes simplex virus type 2 on the efficacy of male circumcision for HIV prevention: analyses from the Rakai trials. *PLoS Med.* 2009;6(11):e1000187.

29. Gray RH, Serwadda D, Kong X, et al. Male circumcision decreases acquisition and increases clearance of high-risk human papillomavirus in HIV-negative men: a randomized trial in Rakai, Uganda. *J Infect Dis.* 2010;201(10):1455–1462.

30. Samet JM. Concepts of time in clinical research. *Ann Intern Med.* 2000;132:37–44.

31. Yusuf S, Collins R, Peto R. Why do we need some large, simple randomized trials? *Stat Med.* 1984;3:409–420.

32. Gifford AL, Cunningham WE, Heslin KC, et al. Participation in research and access to experimental treatments by HIV-infected patients. *New Eng J Med.* 2002;346(18): 1373–1382.

33. Gandhi M, Ameli N, Bacchetti P, et al. Eligibility criteria for HIV clinical trials and generalizability of results: the gap between published reports and study protocols. *AIDS.* 2005;19(16):1885–1896.

34. Adeyemi OF, Evans AT, Bahk M. HIV-infected adults from minority ethnic groups are willing to participate in research if asked. *AIDS Patient Care STDs.* 2009;23(10):859–865.

35. DeFreitas D. Race and HIV clinical trial participation. *J Natl Med Assoc.* 2010;102(6):493–499.

36. Schulz KF, Altman DG, Moher D, for the CONSORT Group. CONSORT 2010 statement: updated guidelines for reporting parallel group randomised trials. *Ann Intern Med.* 2010;152.

37. Cook TD, DeMets DL. *Introduction to Statistical Methods for Clinical Trials.* Boca Raton, FL: CRC Press; 2008.

38. Friedman LM, Furberg CD, DeMets DL. *Fundamentals of Clinical Trials.* New York, NY: Springer; 2010.

39. Ellenberg SS, Fleming TR, DeMets DL. *Data Monitoring Committees in Clinical Trials: A Practical Perspective.* West Sussex, UK: John Wiley & Sons; 2003.

40. Bretz F, Koenig F, Brannath W, et al. Adaptive designs for confirmatory clinical trials. *Stat Med.* 2009;28(8):1181–1217.

41. Guidance for industry: adaptive design clinical trials for drugs and biologics. February 2010. Available at: http:// www.fda.gov/downloads/Drugs/ GuidanceComplianceRegulatoryInformation/ Guidances/ucm201790.pdf.

42. Phillips-Howard PA, Nahlen BL, Alaii JA, et al. The efficacy of permethrin-treated bednets on child mortality and morbidity in western Kenya, I: development of infrastructure and

description of study site. *Am J Trop Med Hyg.* 2003;68(suppl 4):3–9.

43. Linblade K, Eisele TP, Gimnig JE, et al. Sustainability of reductions in malaria transmission and infant mortality in western Kenya with use of insecticide-treated bednets: 4 to 6 years of follow-up. *JAMA.* 2004;291(21):2571–2580.

44. Hussey M, Hughes JP. Design and analysis of stepped wedge cluster randomized designs. *Contemp Clin Trials.* 2007;182–191.

45. Mdege ND, Man MS, Taylor Nee Brown CA, Torgerson DJ. Systematic review of stepped wedge cluster randomized trials shows that design is particularly used to evaluate interventions during routine implementation. *J Clin Epidemiol.* 2011;64(9):936–948.

46. Bailey IW, Archer L. The impact of the introduction of treated water on aspects of community health in a rural community in Kwazulu-Natal, South Africa. *Water Sci Technol.* 2004;50(1):105–110.

47. Killam WP, Tambatamba BC, Chintu N, et al. Antiretroviral therapy in antenatal care to increase treatment initiation in HIV-infected pregnant women: a stepped-wedge evaluation. *AIDS.* 2010;24(1):85–91.

48. Moulton LH, Golub JE, Durovni B, et al. Statistical design of THRio: a phased implementation clinic-randomized study of a tuberculosis preventive therapy intervention. *Clin Trials.* 2007;4(2):190–199.

49. Methodological overview of a multisite HIV prevention trial for populations at risk for HIV. NIMH Multisite HIV Prevention Trial. *AIDS.* 1997;11(suppl 2):S1–S11.

50. Kamb M, Fishbein M, Douglas J Jr, et al. Efficacy of risk-reduction counseling to prevent human immunodeficiency virus and sexually transmitted diseases: a randomized controlled trial. Project RESPECT Study Group. *JAMA.* 1998;280:1161–1167.

51. The NIMH Multisite HIV Prevention Trial: reducing HIV sexual risk behavior. *Science.* 1998;280:1889–1894.

52. Black RE, Huber DH, Curlin GT. Reduction of neonatal tetanus by mass immunization of non-pregnant women: duration of protection provided by 1 or 2 doses of aluminum-absorbed tetanus toxoid. *Bull WHO.* 1980;58:927–930.

53. Mulholland K, Hilton S, Adegbola R, et al. Randomised trial of *Haemophilus influenzae* type-b tetanus protein conjugate vaccine for prevention of pneumonia and meningitis in Gambian infants. *Lancet.* 1997;349:1191–1197.

54. Gessner BD, Sutanto A, Linehan M, et al. Incidence of vaccine-preventable *Haemophilus influenzae* type b pneumonia and meningitis in Indonesian children: hamlet-randomized vaccine-probe trial. *Lancet.* 2005;365:43–52.

55. Orenstein WA, Bernier RH, Hinman AR. Assessing vaccine efficacy in the field: further observations. *Epidemiol Rev.* 1988;10: 212–241.

56. Clemens J, Brenner R, Rao M, et al. Evaluating new vaccines for developing countries. Efficacy or effectiveness? *JAMA.* 1996;275:390–397.

57. Gerberding J. Incidence and prevalence of human immunodeficiency virus, hepatitis B virus, hepatitis C virus, and cytomegalovirus among healthcare personnel at risk for blood exposure and final report studies. *J Infect Dis.* 1994;170:1410–1417.

58. Strom BL. *Pharmacoepidemiology.* West Sussex, UK: John Wiley & Sons; 2000.

59. White E, Armstrong BK, Saracci R. *Principles of Exposure Measurement in Epidemiology,* 2nd ed. New York: Oxford University Press; 2008.

60. Vlahov D, Anthony JC, Munoz A, et al. The ALIVE study, a longitudinal study of HIV-1 infection in intravenous drug users: description of methods and characteristics of participants. *NIDA Res Monogr.* 1991;109:75–100.

61. Nelson K, Vlahov D, Solomon L, et al. Temporal trends of incident human immunodeficiency virus infection of injecting drug users in Baltimore, MD. *Arch Intern Med.* 1995;155:1305–1311.

62. Nelson KE, Galai N, Safaeian M, et al. Temporal trends in the incidence of human immunodeficiency virus infection and risk behavior among injection drug users in Baltimore, Maryland, 1988–1998. *Am J Epidemiol.* 2002;156(7):641–653.

63. Jick H, Kaye JA, Vasilakis-Scaramozza C, Jick SS. Risk of venous thromboembolism among users of third generation oral contraceptives compared with users of oral contraceptives with levonorgestrel before and after 1995: cohort and case-control analysis. *BMJ.* 2000;321(7270):1190–1195.

64. Wacholder S, McLaughlin JK, Silverman DT, Mandel JS. Selection of controls in case-control studies. I. Principles. *Am J Epidemiol.* 1992;135(9):1019–1028.

65. Wacholder S, Silverman DT, McLaughlin JK, Mandel JS. Selection of controls in case-control studies. II. Types of controls. *Am J Epidemiol.* 1992; 135(9):1029–1041.

66. Wacholder S, Silverman DT, McLaughlin JK, Mandel JS. Selection of controls in case-control studies. III. Design options. *Am J Epidemiol.* 1992;135(9):1042–1050.

67. Armenian HK. *The Case-Control Method: Design and Applications.* New York: Oxford University Press; 2009.

68. Muñoz N, Bosch FX, de Sanjosé S, et al. The causal link between human papillomavirus and invasive cervical cancer: a population-based case-control study in Colombia and Spain. *Int J Cancer.* 1992;52:743–749.

69. Mueller N, Evans A, Harris NL, et al. Hodgkin's disease and Epstein-Barr virus: altered antibody pattern before diagnosis. *N Engl J Med.* 1989;320(11):689–695.

70. Chang Y, Cesarman E, Pessin M, et al. Identification of herpesvirus-like DNA sequences in AIDS-associated Kaposi's sarcoma. *Science.* 1994;266:1865–1969.

71. O'Brien T, Kedes D, Ganem D, et al. Evidence for concurrent epidemics of human herpesvirus 8 and human immunodeficiency virus type 1 in US homosexual men: rates, risk factors, and relationship to Kaposi's sarcoma. *J Infect Dis.* 1999;180:1010–1017.

72. Jacobson L, Yamashita T, Detels R, et al. Impact of potent antiretroviral therapy on the incidence of Kaposi's sarcoma and non-Hodgkin's lymphomas among HIV-1–infected individuals. Multicenter AIDS Cohort Study. *J AIDS.* 1999;suppl 1:S34–S41.

73. Dore G, Li Y, Grulich A, et al. Declining incidence and later occurrence of Kaposi's sarcoma among persons with AIDS in Australia: the Australian AIDS cohort. *AIDS.* 1996;10: 1401–1406.

74. Centers for Disease Control and Prevention. Case-control study of HIV seroconversion in health-care workers after percutaneous exposure to HIV-infected blood—France, United Kingdom, and United States, January 1988–August 1994. *MMWR.* 1995;44: 929–933.

75. Maclure M. The case-crossover design: a method for studying transient effects on the risk of acute events. *Am J Epidemiol.* 1991;133(2):144–153.

76. Suissa S. The case-time-control design: further assumptions and conditions. *Epidemiology.* 1998;9:441–445.

77. Schneider MF Gange SJ, Margolick JB, et al. Application of case-crossover and case-time-control study designs in analyses of time-varying predictors of T-cell homeostasis failure. *Ann Epidemiol.* 2005;15:137–144.

78. Starko K, Ray C, Domingues L, et al. Reye's syndrome and salicylate use. *Pediatrics.* 1980;66:859–864.

79. Waldman R, Hall W, McGeeh H, et al. Aspirin as a risk factor in Reye's syndrome. *JAMA.* 1982;247:3089–3094.

80. Halpin T, Holtzhauer F, Campbell R, et al. Reye's syndrome and medication use. *JAMA.* 1982;248:687–691.

81. Pinsky P, Hurwitz E, Schonberger L, et al. Reye's syndrome and aspirin: evidence for a dose-response effect. *JAMA.* 1988;260:657–661.

82. Centers for Disease Control and Prevention. Surgeon General's advisory on the use of salicylates and Reye's syndrome. *MMWR*. 1982;31(22):289–290.

83. Belay E, Bresee J, Holman R, et al. Reye's syndrome in the United States from 1981–1987. *N Engl J Med*. 1999;340: 1377–1382.

84. Centers for Disease Control and Prevention. Update on acquired immune deficiency syndrome (AIDS)—United States. *MMWR*. 1982;31:507–508, 513–514.

85. Diaz Grandos CA, Zimmer SM, Klein M, and Jernigan JA. Comparison of mortality associated with vancomycin-resistant and vancomycin-susceptible enterococcal bloodstream infections: a meta-analysis. *Clin Infect Dis*. 2005;41:327–333.

86. Merton RK, Sills DL, Stigler SM. The Kelvin dictum and social science: an excursion into the history of an idea. *J Hist Behav Sci*. 1984;20:319–331.

87. Feinstein AR. *Clinical Epidemiology: The Architecture of Clinical Research*. Boston: Little, Brown; 1985.

88. Hand DJ. *Measurement Theory and Practice*. New York: Wiley; 2009.

89. Mellors JW, Rinaldo CR Jr, Gupta P, et al. Prognosis in HIV-1 infection predicted by the quantity of virus in plasma. *Science*. 1996;272(5265):1167–1170.

90. Sethi AK, Celentano DD, Gange SJ, et al. Association between adherence to antiretroviral therapy and human immunodeficiency virus drug resistance. *Clin Infect Dis*. 2003;37:1112–1118.

91. Rothman KJ. Induction and latent periods. *Am J Epidemiol*. 1981;114:253–259.

92. Cole SR, Napravnik S, Mugavero MJ, et al. Copy-years viremia as a measure of cumulative human immunodeficiency virus viral burden. *Am J Epidemiol*. 2010;171:198–205.

93. Centers for Disease Control and Prevention. Multistate outbreak of listeriosis associated with Jensen Farms cantaloupe—United States, August–September 2011. *MMWR*. 2011;60(39):1357–1358.

94. Mead PS, Dunne EF, Graves L, et al. Nationwide outbreak of listeriosis due to contaminated meat. *Epidemiol Infect*. 2006;134:744–751.

95. Cornfield J. A method of estimating comparative rates from clinical data: applications to cancer of the lung, breast, and cervix. *J Natl Cancer Inst*. 1951;11:1269–1175.

96. Porta M Ed. *A Dictionary of Epidemiology*, 5th ed. New York: Oxford University Press; 2008.

4

Prevention of Infectious Diseases

Catherine G. Sutcliffe, Wendy W. Davis, and David D. Celentano

INTRODUCTION

Contracting many of the infectious diseases that cause illness worldwide is avoidable. Preventing exposure and infection remains the most effective way of obviating the significant morbidity and mortality associated with these diseases. Many prevention measures exist that cover a wide array of viruses, bacteria, and parasites. These measures usually apply to multiple pathogens with similar modes of transmission and can be categorized as individual or community measures. Individual measures are those that an individual can implement to prevent exposure or infection, whereas community measures are those that a community can implement to reduce transmission so that individuals within the community are at lower risk of exposure and infection. Many of these measures are relatively simple and easy to implement, and have been known to humans for a long time. For example, the importance of hand washing was first raised in the 1840s when Ignaz Semmelweiss identified the mode of transmission of puerperal sepsis and introduced hand washing for male physicians in hospitals as part of an effort to reduce maternal mortality.[1]

Despite the simplicity and effectiveness of many prevention measures, implementation is often not widespread among individuals, households, or communities. Changing behaviors around prevention can be difficult, as many factors related to knowledge, motivation, and available resources determine whether a measure will be implemented.

This chapter covers some of the most common individual and community prevention measures. Some of these steps are applicable to everyone regardless of setting, whereas others may be more specialized to personal circumstance or local environment. Prevention measures that are extensively covered in other chapters, such as vaccination and measures specific to

healthcare infections, are not included here. Individual prevention measures that are discussed include hand washing, food sanitation, male condoms, and measures against vector-borne diseases. Community measures that are discussed include sanitation and water safety; isolation, quarantine, and contact tracing; screening of the blood supply; and measures directed against vector-borne diseases. These measures can be implemented to prevent most sexually transmitted infections and infections transmitted by vectors, blood, food, air, and water.

INDIVIDUAL PREVENTION MEASURES

Hand Washing

The simple act of hand washing with soap has been associated with significant decreases in the prevalence of many common infections, in both low- and high-income countries. The most common infections averted globally by the introduction of hand hygiene practices are diarrheal diseases, primarily among young children, and acute respiratory infections (**Table 4-1**). An estimated 1.5 million children die due to diarrhea annually,[2] and pneumonia-associated diseases lead to the premature deaths of approximately 1.4 million children each year.[3] Other important sources of morbidity prevented by hand washing include helminth infections in sub-Saharan Africa and other tropical locales, and conjunctivitis, which is highly transmissible.

A person's hands can become contaminated with pathogens after coming into contact with human or animal feces, bodily fluids (e.g., nasal excretions), or foods and liquids. These pathogens can then be transmitted from person to person, through either direct contact (e.g., touching other people) or indirect contact (e.g., touching surfaces or fomites).[4] Hand washing works by removing pathogens

Table 4-1	Clinical Classification of Infections	
Diarrheal Diseases	**Acute Respiratory Infections**	**Helminth Infections**
Campylobacter sp.	Influenza virus	*Trichuris trichiura*
Cryptosporidium parvum	Human metapneumovirus	*Ascaris lubricoides*
Entameba histolytica	Respiratory syncytial virus	
Enteropathogenic *E. coli*	Parainfluenza virus	
Enterotoxigenic *E. coli*	Adenovirus	
Giardia lamblia		
Rotavirus		
Salmonella sp.		
Shigella sp.		

from the hands and preventing disease transmission, but how it works depends on the techniques and products used. Hand washing with water dislodges visible dirt from the hands through rubbing and friction but does not break down the grease and oils on the hands that carry many pathogens; thus this technique is not recommended.[4,5] Using soap to wash hands is more effective, as it increases the time spent washing hands; in addition, most soaps are detergents and will actively break down grease, oils, and other organic matter. When hands are washed properly (**Figure 4-1**), all soaps are equally effective at removing pathogens.[4] Antimicrobial soaps, alcohol-based rubs, and other specialized products, including chlorhexadine, chloroxylenol, and triclosan, have direct antimicrobial activity and have been developed to increase the effectiveness of hand washing, particularly in healthcare settings, but are not widely available to the general population in many settings.[5] Critical times for hand washing to prevent the spread of infections include after using the toilet, after changing dirty diapers or cleaning a child, and before handling any food.[4]

Additional components of hand washing include the quality of the water used and the methods for drying hands after hand washing. The efficacy of hand washing with soap in decontaminating hands can be reduced if clean water is not used. Waterborne pathogens may readily be found in available water supplies, including bacteria (*Campylobacter jejuni* and *coli, Escherichia coli, Legionella* species, *Shigella typhi,* and *Vibrio cholerae,* among others), viruses (e.g., adenoviruses, enteroviruses, hepatitis A, rotaviruses), protozoa (*Giardia lamblia, Toxoplasma gondii, Cryptosporidium parvum*), and helminths (*Dracunculus medinensis, Schistosoma* species).[6] Thus, even if soap is used, contamination of hands

may result from contaminated water supplies. A particular problem is the use of communal bowls of water for hand washing prior to eating, which may promote contamination and infection rather than prevent it. In these cases, washing hands under running water would be preferable. A second source of contamination is hand drying. Hand drying may be a problem in settings where clean towels or other wiping materials are not available, and touch-contact may undo the effects of hand washing. In these cases, air drying would be preferable to using dirty or communal towels.

A number of studies have demonstrated that hand washing with soap reduces the quantity of microbes on the hands far more than rinsing with water alone.[7,8] In one study, the prevalence of bacteria of fecal origin (primarily *Enterococcus* and *Enterobacter* spp.) was significantly reduced from 44% to 23% after washing with water alone, and to 8% after washing with plain soap and water.[9] The length of time spent hand washing is also important. In one study, bacterial counts on the skin were reduced by $0.6–1.1 \log_{10}$ after hand washing with soap and water for 15 seconds and by $1.8–2.8 \log_{10}$ after hand washing for 30 seconds.[10]

The importance and effectiveness of hand washing in reducing infection and disease were first recognized by Ignaz Semmelweiss and Oliver Wendell Holmes in the mid-19th century, when they hypothesized that puerperal fever acquired in maternity wards was transmitted directly by the hands of healthcare workers.[1] The solution was hand washing with a chlorinated lime solution before each patient encounter; upon initiation of this practice among healthcare providers, mortality rates dropped precipitously. Since then, many studies have evaluated the effectiveness of hand washing in preventing

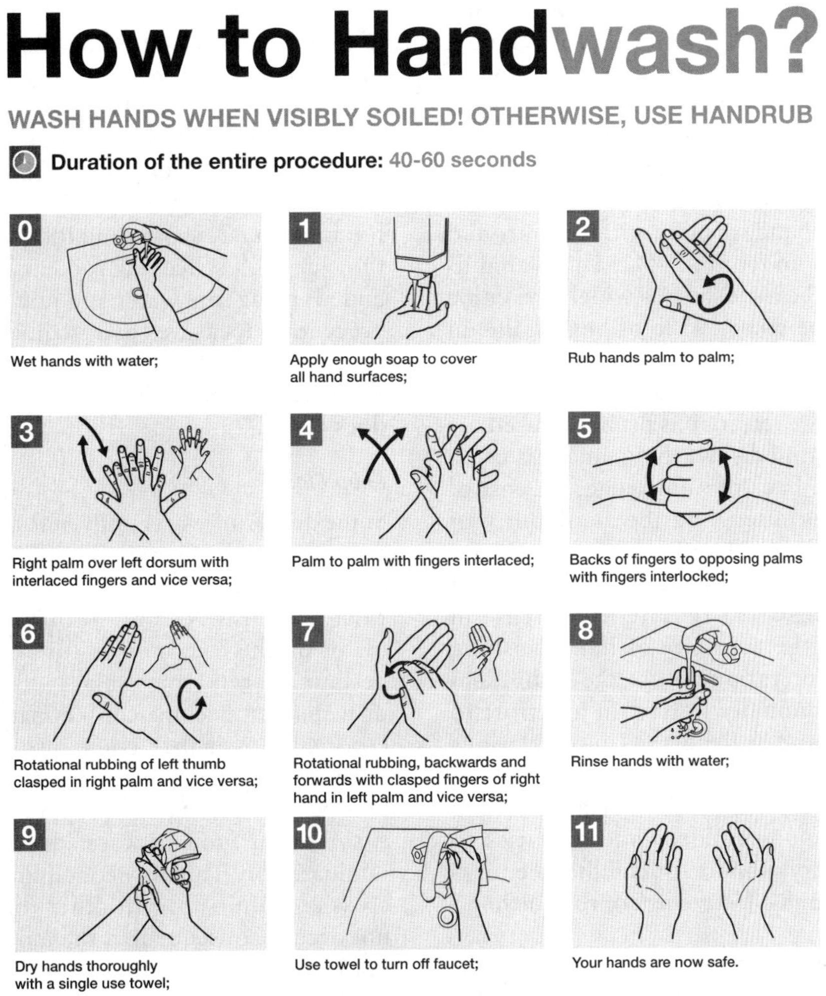

How to Handwash?

WASH HANDS WHEN VISIBLY SOILED! OTHERWISE, USE HANDRUB

🕐 **Duration of the entire procedure:** 40-60 seconds

0 Wet hands with water;

1 Apply enough soap to cover all hand surfaces;

2 Rub hands palm to palm;

3 Right palm over left dorsum with interlaced fingers and vice versa;

4 Palm to palm with fingers interlaced;

5 Backs of fingers to opposing palms with fingers interlocked;

6 Rotational rubbing of left thumb clasped in right palm and vice versa;

7 Rotational rubbing, backwards and forwards with clasped fingers of right hand in left palm and vice versa;

8 Rinse hands with water;

9 Dry hands thoroughly with a single use towel;

10 Use towel to turn off faucet;

11 Your hands are now safe.

Figure 4-1 WHO recommended guidelines on how to wash your hands. Reproduced from the World Health Organization (2009). How to Handwash? http://www.who.int/gpsc/5may/How_To_HandWash_Poster.pdf. Last updated May 2009. Accessed February 25, 2012.

disease. The most extensive and strongest evidence comes from studies of diarrhea prevention.[11–19] These community-based studies suggest that hand washing reduces the incidence of diarrhea by 32–47%.[11,13,18] In addition, significant evidence shows that hand washing is effective in reducing acute respiratory infections by an estimated 24%.[20] The evidence for other infections is not as extensive or robust, but does suggest that hand washing is effective in reducing the incidence of helminth infections,[21–24] particularly ascariasis and trichuriasis, and eye infections.[25]

The importance of hand washing has also been recognized and extensively studied in healthcare settings, where acquisition and transmission of nosocomial infections represent a significant source of patient morbidity and mortality.[26] Poor

hand hygiene among healthcare workers has been associated with many outbreaks in healthcare settings, and most studies have shown a transient improvement in infection rates associated with better adherence to hand washing recommendations.[5] Consequently, hand washing is the cornerstone of infection control in healthcare settings. Hand hygiene guidelines for healthcare settings were first promulgated in the United States by the Centers for Disease Control and Prevention in the 1980s,[27] and updated in 1996[28] and 2002.[29]

In addition to being an effective method for reducing the incidence of disease, hand washing has been found to be the most cost-effective intervention for diarrheal diseases. To avert a single disability-adjusted life year (DALY) with hand washing costs $3.35, compared with $11.15 for latrine promotion, $527–2001 for breastfeeding promotion programs, and $1658–8274 for cholera immunizations.[4]

Despite the demonstrated efficacy of proper hand hygiene measures in decreasing infection in both community and healthcare settings, hand washing with soap has not been widely adopted. Observed rates of hand washing with soap around the world range from zero to 34%.[4] The availability of soap is not the issue, as it is widely available worldwide—in one study, 95% of households in Uganda, 97% of households in Kenya, and 100% of households in Peru were found to have soap.[4] In many areas, however, soap is primarily used for laundry, bathing, and dishwashing, and less often for hand washing. Lack of knowledge, the cost of soap for additional uses, and the availability of water may all influence hand washing practices. Increasing initiation and sustained adoption of proper hand hygiene will require an increase in the awareness of the necessity of hand washing with soap and motivation to change individual behaviors and community norms. In an effort to promote proper hand hygiene, the United Nations declared October 15 to be Global Handwashing Day.[4] In 2008, the inaugural Global Handwashing Day focused on young children and activities to mobilize community support for childhood education on the utility and effectiveness of routine hand washing.[4,30]

The success of hand hygiene requires constant and continuous dedication on the part of individuals to implement proper techniques at all critical times. Health education campaigns promoting hand hygiene will require the same level of vigilance and commitment to maintain awareness of the risks in a community and improve health outcomes. Hand hygiene has been shown to be one of the simplest, yet most difficult human behaviors to affect.

Food Safety

Measures to ensure food safety are implemented to protect against foodborne or waterborne infections. Foodborne or waterborne infections are some of the most common infections, causing an estimated 2.2 million deaths annually, with the majority of the mortality occurring among children.[31] Infections occur through ingestion of food or water that is contaminated with pathogenic microorganisms. Contamination may occur either naturally or from fecal–oral transmission from an infected individual who is handling the water source or preparing the food. Infections can be caused by bacteria,

parasites, or viruses (**Table 4-2**) and generally result in diarrhea, fever, and vomiting. Food safety has increasingly been recognized as an essential measure in public health. To protect the world's population from foodborne or waterborne infections, the World Health Organization has developed the Five Keys to Safer Food, which include: (1) keeping foods clean, (2) separating foods, (3) cooking food thoroughly, (4) keeping food at safe temperatures, and (5) using safe water and raw materials.[32] These prevention measures are intended to prevent contamination of food and water and to kill microorganisms or inhibit their growth if contamination does occur.

Keep Clean

Some food or water may naturally contain microorganisms; other food and water may become contaminated during the process of preparation. Microorganisms can reside in human or animal feces or on the feet, mouths, or skin of animals and pests (e.g., rats, mice, birds, cockroaches). Food or water can become contaminated with these microorganisms if they come into contact with surfaces containing infected fecal matter or animals and pests. Keeping the preparation process clean ensures that food or water does not become contaminated or, if already contaminated, ensures that cross-contamination to other food or water does not occur. Consequently, the individual and others in the household consuming the food or water will not become infected.

Keeping clean encompasses two components: the individual preparing the food and the surfaces and equipment being used. Keeping the individual clean involves washing hands before handling food, during food preparation, and anytime after going to the toilet, handling garbage, changing diapers, or playing with pets. Hands should especially be washed after slaughtering animals and after handling raw meat or poultry. Hands should be washed with soap and water (refer to the earlier section on hand washing for proper techniques) or, if soap is not available, with coal ash. Studies of hand washing interventions have estimated that increasing the frequency of hand washing can reduce the incidence of diarrheal episodes by approximately 32–47%.[11,13,18]

Keeping surfaces and equipment clean involves washing and sanitizing them before preparing food and after they have any contact with raw meat or seafood. Sanitizing is distinct from cleaning, in that the former implies the process of disinfecting or killing microorganisms rather than simply clearing debris.

Table 4-2	Common Causes and Sources of Foodborne and Waterborne Illnesses	
Type	**Agent**	**Common Sources**
Bacteria	*Campylobacter* species (commonly *C. jejuni* and *C. coli*)	Poultry Raw milk Water
	Escherichia coli	Meat products Raw milk and milk products Raw fruits and vegetables Water
	Salmonella species (commonly *S. enteritidis* and *S. typhimurium*)	Meat Poultry Eggs Raw milk and milk products Raw fruits and vegetables
	Shigella dysenteriae, flexneri, boydii, or sonnei	Food Water Humans
	Listeria species (commonly *L. monocytogenes*)	Raw milk and milk products Deli meats Hot dogs
	Vibrio cholerae	Raw shellfish Water
Parasites	*Giardia lamblia*	Raw meat Water Contaminated food
	Trichinella spiralis	Raw/undercooked meat
Viruses	Hepatitis A	Shellfish Raw produce Water Uncooked or cooked contaminated foods
	Norovirus	Shellfish Contaminated foods from feces or infected by food handlers

To sanitize a surface or piece of equipment, it can be washed in boiling water or with a sanitizing solution (mix 5 mL of household bleach with 750 mL of water). Keeping surfaces and equipment clean also involves protecting them from insects, pests, and other pets or domestic animals.

Separate Raw and Cooked Foods

Raw food—especially meat, poultry, and seafood—can contain microorganisms that can be transferred onto other foods during food preparation and storage. Cross-contamination of other types of food can be prevented by keeping them separate while shopping for, refrigerating, preparing, and storing food. While preparing food, cross-contamination can be prevented by using separate equipment and utensils for meat, poultry, seafood, and other types of food, and for raw and cooked food.

Cook Thoroughly

Most microorganisms do not survive at high temperatures; therefore cooking to temperatures greater than 70°C (160°F) can render contaminated food safe for consumption. At these temperatures, almost all dangerous microorganisms are killed within 30 seconds. Microorganisms generally reside on the outer surfaces of food, particularly intact pieces of meat, so cooking foods thoroughly to these temperatures is not necessary and eating meat with a red center can be safe. Minced meat, rolled roasts, and poultry are exceptions: they need to be cooked thoroughly, as microorganisms can be found on the surfaces as well as in the center. To ensure proper

Table 4-3	Proper Cooking Procedures		
Cooking Temperatures (°F)		**How to Use a Thermometer Properly**	
Ground meat/meat mixtures:		• Place the thermometer in the center of the thickest part of the meat.	
• Beef, pork, veal, lamb	160	• Make sure the thermometer is not touching a bone or the side of the container.	
• Turkey, chicken	165	• Make sure the thermometer is cleaned and sanitized between each use to avoid cross-contamination between raw and cooked food.	
Fresh beef, veal, lamb	145		
Poultry	165	**If a Thermometer Is Not Available**	
Pork and ham	145	• Cook poultry until the juices are clear and the inside is no longer pink.	
Egg dishes	160	• Cook eggs and seafood until piping hot throughout.	
Leftovers and casseroles	165	• Bring liquid-based foods such as soups and stews to a boil and continue to boil for at least 1 minute.	

Reproduced from Food Safety.Gov. Keeping Food Safe: Safe Minimum Cooking Temperatures. http://www.foodsafety.gov/keep/charts/mintemp.html. Accessed February 25, 2012.

cooking temperatures, liquids should be brought to a boil and a thermometer should be used for meats (see **Table 4-3** for instructions on how to use a thermometer and proper cooking temperatures).

Keep Food at Safe Temperatures

Microorganisms require the right environment to thrive, and this generally occurs at temperatures between 5°C and 60°C. Keeping temperatures below 5°C or above 60°C can slow and even stop microorganisms from multiplying; therefore keeping food at room temperature for longer than 2 hours should be avoided. Food should be thawed in the refrigerator, kept hot before serving, and refrigerated as soon as possible after eating to keep it at a safe temperature. If no refrigerator is available, a hole can be dug in the ground for storage or cold water can be used. To decrease the cooling time of cooked food, it should be stored in smaller quantities. As microorganisms can still grow at low temperatures, food should not be stored in the refrigerator for longer than 3 days and should not be reheated more than once.

Use Safe Water and Raw Materials

Raw materials may be contaminated with microorganisms and, therefore, may contaminate any food that they are prepared with. Purchasing fresh foods and clean water or sanitizing food and water in the home can minimize this risk of contamination. For example, purchasing foods that have been processed, such as pasteurized milk and cheeses, can reduce the risk of purchasing contaminated products. In addition, washing fruits and vegetables with clean water, especially if they will be consumed raw, can reduce the risk of consuming contaminated products.

Water is used in many steps of food preparation and consumption: it is used for washing foods, as an additive to many liquid-based foods, for cleaning hands and cooking equipment, and to make up drinks or ice. Consequently, it is important to use safe water in all steps of food preparation and consumption. If safe water is not available in the household and cannot be purchased, individuals can inactivate microorganisms by boiling the water or using chlorine (3–5 drops of chlorine to 1 liter of water), or can physically remove these organisms by filtering the water.[33] Studies have found that use of improved water sanitation procedures by individuals can significantly reduce contamination of water sources[34–36] and decrease the risk of diarrheal disease in the household by as much as 35%.[13]

By following these procedures, individuals can effectively remove significant sources of microorganisms and protect themselves against foodborne and waterborne infections. However, these procedures must be followed every day to be effective, as any lapse can result in infection.

Male Condoms

Male condoms have been used for more than 400 years[37] and remain a highly effective means of protection against sexually transmitted infections (STIs).[38] STIs can be transmitted through either vaginal or anal sex and may be caused by viruses, bacteria, and parasites (**Table 4-4**). STIs mainly fall into two categories: discharge diseases and genital ulcer diseases. The infectious agents of discharge diseases, including human immunodeficiency virus (HIV), gonorrhea, chlamydia, and trichomoniasis, are present in genital secretions (semen or vaginal fluids) and are transmitted through contact of infected secretions with a partner's mucosal surfaces (i.e., urethra, rectum, vagina, or cervix). The infectious agents of genital ulcer diseases, including genital

Table 4-4	Common Sexually Transmitted Infections	
	Type	**Agent**
Discharge Diseases		
HIV	Virus	Human immunodeficiency virus
Gonorrhea	Bacteria	*Neisseria gonorrhoeae*
Chlamydia	Bacteria	*Chlamydia trachomatis*
Trichomoniasis	Parasite	*Trichomonas vaginalis*
Genital Ulcer Diseases		
Genital herpes	Virus	Herpes simplex virus types 1 and 2
Chancroid	Bacteria	*Haemophilus ducreyi*
Syphilis	Bacteria	*Treponema pallidum*
Other		
HPV	Virus	Human papillomavirus

herpes (HSV), syphilis, and chancroid, are present in sores and ulcers or may be shed into secretions and are transmitted through contact with infected lesions. Another STI, human papillomavirus (HPV), which is the cause of cervical cancer and genital warts, is transmitted through contact with infected cell surfaces, even in the absence of fluid or tissue exchange.

Male condoms provide protection against STIs by putting a physical barrier between surfaces (i.e., between penis and vagina or between penis and rectum). They are typically made of latex and are impermeable to the smallest STI pathogen.[38] Condoms can provide different levels of protection depending on the mode of transmission. These products protect against discharge diseases by preventing infected bodily fluids from coming into contact with mucosal surfaces. When used properly (**Box 4-1**) and in the absence of breakage or leakage, condoms completely contain male pre-ejaculate and ejaculate and completely cover the male urethra. As a consequence, they provide a high level of protection against discharge diseases for uninfected male and female partners.[38] Condoms protect against genital ulcer diseases and HPV by preventing contact between infected and uninfected skin and mucosal surfaces.[38] As sores or infected cells may be present outside of the area protected by the condom, however, condoms may provide less protection against genital ulcer diseases or HPV for uninfected partners.[38]

Efficacy—that is, the protection afforded by condoms under ideal conditions—cannot be measured and evaluated using randomized controlled trials, as it would be unethical to discourage their use in one group. Instead, effectiveness—that is, the protection afforded under actual conditions of use—must be

Box 4-1	How to Use a Condom Consistently and Correctly

- Use a new condom for every act of vaginal, anal, and oral sex throughout the entire sex act (from start to finish).
- Before any genital contact, put the condom on the tip of the erect penis with the rolled side out.
- If the condom does not have a reservoir tip, pinch the tip enough to leave a half-inch space for semen to collect. Holding the tip, unroll the condom all the way to the base of the erect penis.
- After ejaculation and before the penis gets soft, grip the rim of the condom and carefully withdraw. Then gently pull the condom off the penis, making sure that semen does not spill out.
- Wrap the condom in a tissue and throw it in the trash where others will not handle it.
- It you feel the condom break at any point during sexual activity, stop immediately, withdraw, remove the broken condom, and put on a new condom.
- Ensure that adequate lubrication is used during vaginal and anal sex, which might require water-based lubricants. Oil-based lubricants (e.g., petroleum jelly, shortening, mineral oil, massage oils, body lotions, and cooking oil) should not be used because they can weaken latex, causing breakage.

Modified from the Centers for Disease Control and Prevention (2011). Condom Fact Sheet in Brief: How to Use a Condom Consistently and Correctly. http://www.cdc.gov/condomeffectiveness/brief.html#Condom. Last updated April 11, 2011. Accessed February 24, 2012.

assessed through self-report in observational studies. Under these circumstances, the degree to which condoms protect against STIs depends not only on the properties of the condom but also on how properly and consistently condoms are used by the individuals in the study.[38] In such studies, because of the difficulty in quantifying partial condom use, effectiveness is typically measured by comparing the incidence of STIs among individuals who report never using a condom with the incidence among individuals who report always using a condom. Many studies are conducted among discordant couples, where one partner is infected and one partner is not, or among individuals with high exposure to STIs.

The effectiveness of condoms has been best evaluated for heterosexual transmission of HIV, for which estimates indicate that consistent and correct use of condoms can reduce the risk by approximately 80%.[39] Estimates of effectiveness for anal sex among heterosexual and homosexual partners are limited, but may be lower given the potentially greater risk of breakage and slippage during anal sex as compared to vaginal sex.[40] Studies have also demonstrated that condoms are effective in reducing the risk of gonorrhea (49–90%)[38,41,42] and HSV-2 (30%).[43] Studies of HPV have generally found that condoms do not result in a reduced risk of HPV infection; however, condom use has been found to reduce the risk of genital warts in men and cervical neoplasia in women.[38,44] Studies for chlamydia, trichomoniasis, chancroid, and syphilis have produced inconclusive results or have been insufficiently rigorous to draw conclusions.[38]

Condoms are most effective when used correctly and consistently with all types of sexual partners, including both casual and long-term partners. For infections that are easily transmitted, such as gonorrhea, failure to use a condom during even one sexual act may result in exposure and infection.[38] Incorrect use and behaviors that compromise the integrity of the condom may increase the risk of breakage, thereby decreasing its effectiveness. In the United States, studies of condom slippage and breakage during use have estimated the frequency of breakage to range from 0.4% to 2.3% and the frequency of slippage to range from 0.6% to 1.3%. Combined estimates of failure (breakage and slippage) range from 1.6% to 3.6%.[38] Instruction on how to correctly put on a condom and other practical issues related to their correct use—including the need to protect condoms from sharp objects such as jewelry, fingernails, or teeth; the need to avoid oil-based lubricants; and the ability to choose a condom that is the right size—can improve an individual's ability to use condoms effectively.[45,46]

Consistent condom use with both heterosexual and same-sex partners can be a challenge in many settings. A national survey in the United States in 2002 reported that among heterosexual men and women aged 15–44 years, only 28.6% of men and 27.2% of women used condoms some or all of the time in the past 4 weeks,[47] although use has been increasing over the past two decades.[38] A review of surveys of

men who have sex with men (MSM) in 44 low- and middle-income countries revealed that slightly more than half of MSM reported using a condom in their last sexual encounter with a man.[48] Rates of condom use vary with cultural setting, with the lowest rates reported in South and Southeast Asia (38%), intermediate rates reported in sub-Saharan Africa (57%) and Eastern Europe and Central Asia (58%), and the highest rates reported in Latin America (73%).[48]

Practical, individual, social, cultural, and religious factors may all influence consistent condom use. Practical considerations include cost and availability. While condoms are relatively inexpensive, even a minimal cost can be prohibitive for individuals in low- and middle-income settings.[49] For individuals who can afford condoms, it can be embarrassing to actually purchase them. This embarrassment can significantly negatively impact consistency of condom use.[50] Indeed, neighborhoods that have a greater number of stores requiring assistance from store personnel to purchase condoms are more likely to have higher rates of HIV, STIs, and teen pregnancy.[51]

Consistent condom use also requires individuals to initiate and negotiate their use with partners. This process can be hindered by substance use[49,52] (use of alcohol or drugs often precedes sexual activity), by partner type, and, within heterosexual partnerships, by gendered power imbalances.[53] For example, in relation to partner type, condom use may be seen as appropriate when visiting a sex worker[54] but not within a more established partnership for both heterosexual individuals and MSM.[52,55] Among heterosexual adolescents, a similar dynamic occurs where condoms are used with partners who are "dirty," and young women who have condoms or suggest using them are stigmatized for being sexually experienced.[56] Younger age (e.g., younger than age 24) is itself associated with condom use that is more likely to be inconsistent.[57,58]

Cultural norms or religious beliefs or traditions, such as those that suggest that condom use can make men "ill" or waste "bodily powers,"[54] or that flatly forbid condom use given its association with preventing procreation, can also discourage consistent condom use. At the same time, structural interventions that turn condom use into a norm, including several measures that have been implemented among sex workers,[59] have been associated with decreased HIV incidence.

Despite the practical, behavioral, and societal challenges discussed previously, condoms remain perhaps the most valuable preventive measure against most STIs. When used consistently and correctly, they are highly effective. They are relatively inexpensive, and countries and communities can have a demonstrated positive impact in ensuring their broad accessibility and acceptability.[60] In the absence of vaccines for most STIs, they remain an essential and important prevention tool.

Personal Prevention Measures Against Vector-borne Diseases

Many infectious diseases, such as malaria and dengue, are transmitted to humans by a vector (**Table 4-5**). For these vector-borne diseases, part of the life cycle of the pathogen depends on a nonhuman host—most commonly an arthropod—carrying the organism from one host to another. This can be done either biologically, by multiplying within the vector and then being transmitted by a bite, or mechanically, by physically being carried from one place to another on the vector. Consequently, the main protection measures that an individual can implement to prevent infection focus on limiting contact between the person and the vector. This can be accomplished by avoiding or eliminating areas where vectors reside and by using a physical or chemical barrier.[61] In addition, chemoprevention can be used to prevent infection if contact does occur.

Avoidance and Elimination

In many cases, contact with vectors can be limited by avoiding areas that are infested with the vector or avoiding the time of day or year when vectors are actively circulating. For example, to prevent Lyme disease, which is transmitted by ticks, the Centers for Disease Control and Prevention recommends avoiding wooded and bushy areas with high grass and a lot of leaf litter, particularly in May, June, and July, when ticks are most active.[62]

Contact with vectors can also be limited by managing the environment around the home so that conditions are not conducive to vector survival, thereby eliminating or reducing the density of vectors in the immediate surroundings. This can be done through landscaping, such as clearing yard debris and standing water, which might serve as potential breeding sites for mosquitoes; creating a sunny and dry landscape that does not provide an optimal habitat for ticks; and actively eliminating the vector population by applying insecticides. For example, acaricides are used against ticks and, if properly applied at the end of May, can reduce tick populations by 68–100%.[62]

Physical Barriers

Contact with vectors can also be limited by putting a physical barrier between human and vector. Physical barriers include screens on windows and doors to prevent vectors from entering the house, protective clothing, and untreated bednets. Protective clothing can be as simple as wearing ankle-high footwear with trousers tucked into socks and shirts tucked into trousers when walking in tick-infested areas or wearing loose-fitting long sleeves and trousers made from tightly woven fabric to prevent bites from mosquitoes or flies; alternatively, it can be as complicated as taping the junction of footwear, trousers, and shirts and protecting the hands and face with gloves and nets.[61] Untreated bednets hung over sleeping places provide a physical barrier between humans and vectors at night, and have

Table 4-5	Selected Diseases of Common Vectors		
Vector	Disease	Type	Agent
Ticks	Lyme disease	Bacteria	*Borrelia burgdorferi*
	Rocky Mountain spotted fever	Bacteria	*Rickettsia rickettsii*
	Tularemia	Bacteria	*Francisella tularensis*
Mosquitoes	Dengue	Virus	Dengue virus
	Malaria	Parasite	*Plasmodium falciparum, vivax, ovale,* or *malariae*
	Yellow fever	Virus	Yellow fever virus
	West Nile encephalitis	Virus	West Nile virus
	Lymphatic filariasis	Parasite	*Wuchereria bancrofti, Brugia malayi, Brugia timori*
Flies	Leishmaniasis	Parasite	*Leishmania* species
	Onchocerciasis	Parasite	*Onchocerca volculus*
	Trypanosomiasis	Parasite	*Trypanosoma brucei gambiense* or *rhodesiense*
Lice	Epidemic typhus	Bacteria	*Rickettsia prowazekii*
Fleas	Plague	Bacteria	*Yersinia pestis*

been used to protect against infections such as malaria, dengue, leishmaniasis, filariasis, and Chagas disease. Untreated bednets are estimated to provide half the protective effect of insecticide-treated nets, which provide additional chemical barriers as discussed next, when properly used and maintained.[63,64]

Chemical Barriers

In addition to physical barriers, several chemical barriers, in the form of repellents or toxicants, are available to limit contact with vectors. Natural or synthetic repellents can be used directly on the skin or on fabrics to repel vectors for several hours. Naturally occurring repellents are generally derived from the leaves (e.g., pyrethrum) and oils (e.g., thyme, clove, citronella, quwenling, neem) of plants. They have been found to reduce mosquito biting rates by as much as 80% for a period of time.[61] The most commonly employed synthetic repellent is DEET, which has been in use since the 1950s. It is effective against mosquitoes, biting flies, chiggers, fleas, and ticks, and is available in many different forms (e.g., sprays, foams, lotions, sticks, towelettes).[61] The protective effect of DEET has recently been demonstrated in several studies,[65,66] with one trial finding 56% efficacy against *Plasmodium falciparum*.[65]

Repellents and toxicants can also be applied to fabric. Toxicants are preferable to repellents for this usage, as they have the added benefit of killing or incapacitating insects that come in contact with the fabric. Toxicants—most commonly pyrethroids—are generally applied to bednets or curtains and used in the home to provide protection for several months or years. Traditionally, insecticide-treated nets (ITNs) were created by dipping existing bednets in a WHO-recommended insecticide, with retreatment being necessary after three washes or at least once a year. More recently, long-lasting ITNs have been developed that are applied in the factory and utilize netting material that has insecticide incorporated within or around the fibers (**Table 4-6**). These long-lasting ITNs retain their insecticidal activity for at least 20 washes over 3 years.[63]

Many trials have been conducted to evaluate the efficacy of ITNs in reducing the morbidity and mortality associated with malaria. A review and meta-analysis of these studies found that ITNs were effective in reducing all-cause child mortality by 18% and uncomplicated clinical episodes of malaria by approximately 50%.[67] The protective efficacy of ITNs has also been demonstrated for anemia, maternal and placental malaria, birth-weight outcomes, and fetal loss among pregnant women.[68,69] The effectiveness of ITNs outside of the trial setting has been documented in both small- and large-scale program settings. Studies have found reductions of 25–40% in all-cause mortality, 59–76% in mild disease, 62% in parasitemia, and 63% in anemia with the use of

Table 4-6	WHO-Recommended Long-lasting Insecticidal Mosquito Nets
Product Name	**Product Type**
DawaPlus 2.0	Deltamethrin coated on polyester*
Duranet	Alpha-cypermethrin incorporated into polyethylene*
Interceptor	Alpha-cypermethrin coated on polyester*
LifeNet	Deltamethrin incorporated into polypropylene*
MAGNet	Alpha-cypermethrin incorporated into polyethylene*
Netprotect	Deltamethrin incorporated into polyethylene*
Olyset	Permethrin incorporated into polyethylene†
PermaNet 2.0	Deltamethrin coated on polyester†
PermaNet 2.5	Deltamethrin coated on polyester with strengthened border*
PermaNet 3.0	Combination of deltamethrin coated on polyester with strengthened border (side panels) and deltamethrin and PBO incorporated into polyethylene (roof)*
Royal Sentry	Alpha-cypermethrin incorporated into polyethylene*
Yorkool LN	Deltamethrin coated on polyester†

*Status of WHO recommendation: interim.
† Status of WHO recommendation: full.

Reproduced from the World Health Organization (2011). WHO recommended long-lasting insecticidal mosquito nets. http://www.who.int/whopes/Long_lasting_insecticidal_nets_Jul_2011.pdf. Last updated July 2011. Accessed February 29, 2012.

these products.[68] ITNs have also been found to protect against other vector-borne diseases, including leishmaniasis, Japanese encephalitis, lymphatic filariasis, and Chagas disease.[63]

Other Barriers

Electronic devices are also available to either repel or kill vectors, including electric light traps with electrocution grids, ultrasound devices, and audible sound devices. These devices have generally been found to be ineffective in reducing mosquito bite rates and repelling the target vector.[61]

In general, avoidance, elimination, and barrier strategies can be very effective in preventing infections, as they are simple and easy for individuals to implement, they are easily accessible, and most measures can be used to protect against multiple vector-borne diseases. No single strategy is 100% effective, however, so the various techniques are best used in combination. The downside to these strategies is that they require consistent use throughout the high-transmission season, as any lapse in use could result in contact with the vector and infection. In addition, to be most effective, avoidance and elimination strategies require a thorough understanding of vector ecology and population dynamics, and recognition that prevention strategies that work for one pathogen and vector may be ineffective against another. For example, remaining indoors from dusk until dawn to reduce transmission of malaria by *Anopheles* mosquitoes may be completely ineffective in preventing dengue fever, yellow fever, or chikungunya—the latter diseases are transmitted by *Culex* mosquitoes, which that can bite any time during the day. ITNs also require proper use and maintenance to be most effective, with continuous retreatment every 1–3 years depending on the type of net. ITN programs have not found high retreatment rates, even with large education campaigns,[64] indicating that many individuals receive only the limited protection of an untreated net after the initial insecticide application wears off. In addition, with the use of insecticides on nets or for environmental management, there is always the risk of increasing insecticide resistance among vectors, thereby reducing the effectiveness of these measures in areas where resistance is high.

Chemoprophylaxis

Chemoprophylaxis is widely used to prevent vector-borne diseases among travelers in high-transmission areas. Intermittent preventive treatment with antimalarial drugs can also be used to prevent malaria in high-risk groups, including pregnant women and children, in high-transmission areas. With intermittent preventive treatment for infants (IPTi), antimalarial drugs are provided to children at the time of routine vaccination in the first year of life regardless of symptoms so as to provide prophylactic protection and reduce infections in this high-risk group. In several trials, this strategy was found to reduce rates of clinical malaria by 30%, anemia by 21%, and all-cause hospitalization by 23% in infants up to 12 months of age.[70] Studies of the effectiveness of IPTi are ongoing,[71] although one study in Tanzania reported reductions in malaria parasitemia and mild anemia following the introduction of IPTi into communities.[72]

With intermittent preventive treatment for pregnant women (IPTp), full curative treatment is provided at specific intervals to reduce the adverse effects of malaria during pregnancy. This strategy is currently recommended by the WHO in areas of stable malaria transmission.[73] In a trial setting, IPTp was found to be effective,[74-78] reducing peripheral parasitemia by 85%[74] and anemia by 39–51%.[74,77,78] IPTp was also found to reduce placental infection and maternal anemia in Ghana,[79] Gabon,[80] and Burkina Faso[81] in communities that introduced IPTp.

Providing preventive treatment to pregnant women and children has many advantages. These groups are at high risk of experiencing adverse effects of malaria infection; thus targeting them for treatment can be a highly cost-effective way of diminishing disease burden.[71,73] In addition, both of these populations are often already being seen by healthcare providers at antenatal clinics and through the WHO Expanded Programme for Immunisation, so treatment can be delivered through the existing infrastructure and health services. They also do not require additional laboratory capacity, as all women and children are treated regardless of symptoms. Of course, use of the existing infrastructure and services requires that a high proportion of women have access to antenatal care and that areas have good vaccination coverage—conditions that are not always met in high-transmission areas. Moreover, resistance to sulfadoxine-pyrimethamine, the main drug used with this strategy, is spreading through Africa; the safety and effectiveness of other drugs will need to be evaluated in areas where drug resistance is high. In addition, with IPTi, concerns have been raised that providing preventive treatment may impair the development of naturally acquired immunity to malaria and put the child at risk of malaria later in childhood, although no evidence of this phenomenon has yet been found.[71]

COMMUNITY PREVENTION MEASURES

Sanitation and Water Safety

Sanitation and water safety are measures that are implemented to prevent the transmission of diseases through water contaminated with human or animal waste. These diseases are caused by bacteria, viruses, protozoa, and helminths, with pathogens including, among others, *Vibrio cholerae*, *E. coli*, *Salmonella* species, hepatitis A, and worms.[82] Infection primarily occurs after ingesting contaminated water and results in symptoms ranging from mild gastroenteritis to severe, and often fatal, diarrhea, dysentery, and hepatitis. An estimated 2.6 billion people globally do not have access to adequate sanitation, and 900 million do not have access to safe water.[82] The people most affected by these deficiencies are those living in poverty in rural regions of sub-Saharan Africa, southern Asia, and Oceania. While individuals can certainly take some measures to protect themselves and their households (see the earlier section on food safety), system-wide measures can also be implemented to protect an entire village or community from these waterborne infections.

Sanitation

Sanitation involves the safe disposal and hygienic separation of human or animal excreta (feces or urine) from water sources and further human contact. It deals with the collection, storage, treatment, disposal, reuse, or recycling of excreta as well as the drainage, disposal, recycling, and reuse of wastewater, storm water, and solid waste.[83] What constitutes "basic sanitation" has been defined in various ways. In the Millennium Development Goals, basic sanitation is described as "the lowest-cost option for securing sustainable access to safe, hygienic, and convenient facilities and services for excreta and sullage disposal that provide privacy and dignity, while at the same time ensuring a clean and healthful living environment both at home and in the neighborhood of users"[84]; therefore, what constitutes basic sanitation will be specific to each context. The Joint Monitoring Program for Water Supply and Sanitation provides another definition based on the facilities available,[85] identifying "improved" and "unimproved" sanitation facilities (**Table 4-7**) based on the risk of contamination and, therefore, based on the health risks associated with use of the facilities. Improved facilities are associated with the lowest risk of harm.

Regardless of the definition, the health benefits of improved sanitation are well documented. Several reviews of sanitation interventions have found that improving sanitation results in a reduction of approximately 30–40% in the incidence of diarrhea.[12,13,83,86] It also has indirect benefits on health, particularly for children who are most at risk for diarrheal diseases, given that children with diarrhea are at increased risk for respiratory infections and under-nutrition.[87,88] Improved sanitation can also help to improve childhood development and education, not only by reducing the number of absences from school due to illness, but also by reducing the stunting and cognitive impairment

Table 4-7	Improved and Unimproved Sanitation and Water Facilities	
	Sanitation	**Water Supply**
Improved	Flush or pour-flush to piped sewer system, septic tank, pit latrine Ventilated improved pit latrine Pit latrine with slab Composting toilet	Piped water into dwelling, plot, or yard Public tap or standpipe Tubewell or borehole Protected dug well Protected spring Rainwater collection
Unimproved	Flush or pour-flush to street, yard, plot, open sewer, ditch, drainage way Pit latrine without slab or open pit Bucket latrine Hanging toilet or hanging latrine No facilities or bush or field (open defecation)	Unprotected dug well Unprotected spring Cart with small tank/drum Bottled water Tanker-truck Surface water (river, dam, lake, pond, stream, canal, irrigation channels)

Data from WHO/UNICEF Joint Monitoring Programme (JMP) for Water Supply and Sanitation (2010). Types of drinking-water sources and sanitation. http://www.wssinfo.org/definitions-methods/watsan-categories/. Accessed March 26, 2012.

associated with chronic malnutrition and helminth infection.[87,88] In addition, when safe toilet facilities are made available, girls are at lower risk of experiencing violence at public latrines or in the bush and are less likely to be absent or drop out of school at menarche.[88]

While improving sanitation facilities at the community level requires large investments on the part of communities (**Box 4-2**) and governments, the evidence indicates that such interventions are cost-effective, as these diseases are associated with an estimated $7 billion in healthcare-related costs every year.[88] For every dollar invested in sanitation, there is an estimated beneficial yield of $3–46,[87] and for every $1000 spent, an estimated 90 disability-adjusted life years (DALYs) are averted, making sanitation one of the most cost-effective health interventions available.[87]

Water Safety

Water safety at the community level involves interventions at the source of the water supply or in the distribution system, including physically removing pathogens (i.e., through filtration, adsorption, sedimentation, or other methods); chemically treating the water, commonly with chlorine, to kill or deactivate pathogens; and disinfecting water using heat (i.e., boiling or pasteurization) or ultraviolet radiation (i.e., sun or artificial lamp).[89] Alternatively, protected sources of water can be created, such as springs, wells, and boreholes, which are generally free from contaminants. As for sanitation, improved and unimproved water facilities have been defined based on their risk of contamination (Table 4-7).[85]

To achieve the greatest benefits, water safety must consider not only the quality of the water being supplied, but several other factors as well:

- The quantity that is either available or can be transported, as safe water is necessary for drinking as well as for food preparation and personal and household hygiene
- Access to the water supply in terms of distance from a household (less than 1000 meters is generally considered appropriate) as well as social and economic barriers
- Reliability of the water supply throughout the day, month, or year
- The cost of safe water if a fee is paid by the user
- How easy or necessary it is for users to operate, maintain, and manage the water supply[90]

In addition, water safety at the community level must be accompanied by education and water safety at the individual level, as contamination of the water supply can still occur during transport, storage, and use in the household.

The direct and indirect health benefits of safe water are similar to those realized with adequate sanitation in terms of reducing the morbidity and mortality associated with diarrheal diseases, respiratory infections, and under-nutrition, as well the impact on child growth and development. In addition, improving the water supply may lead to improvements in hygiene and sanitation, as safe and clean water are necessary prerequisites for both activities. Studies of the impact

---

Box 4-2	The Success of Community-Led Total Sanitation

The Community-Led Total Sanitation (CLTS) approach was developed in Bangladesh in 1999–2000 in response to the recognition that top-down approaches focused on subsidies and hardware were not effective. Instead, the CLTS approach mobilizes community members to take action against open defecation and change their own behavior. It does so by helping the community to assess and analyze its own level of sanitation and then come up with an action plan to combat open defecation. In this way, communities become aware of their own level of sanitation and decide together how they will create a clean and hygienic environment for everyone to enjoy. CLTS works because communities take ownership of the program, take responsibility for changing their collective behavior, and come up with innovative local solutions that are sustainable.

The CLTS approach involves four steps:

1 Pre-triggering: selecting a community, introducing the program, and building rapport
2 Triggering: having the community participate in a sanitation profile analysis
3 Post-triggering: action planning by the community
4 Scaling up and going beyond CLTS: in its fullest sense CLTS encompasses hand washing, proper handling of food and water, proper disposal of animal and domestic waste; it can also serve as an entry point for changing other behaviors

The CLTS approach has been successfully implemented in communities across South America, the Middle East, Asia, and Africa. For example, it was piloted in 2007 in several rural communities in Southern Province, Zambia, where sanitation coverage was estimated to be only 23%. With the support of traditional leaders, facilitators brought the CLTS approach to 12 communities. Within 2 months, sanitation coverage increased to 88% and 75% of the villages were certified as open defecation free.

Data from Community-Led Total Sanitation (2011). Handbook on Community Led Total Sanitation. http://www.communityledtotalsanitation.org/sites/communityledtotalsanitation.org/files/cltshandbook.pdf; and Zambia. http://www.communityledtotalsanitation.org/country/zambia. Both accessed March 26, 2012.

of community-level interventions to improve the water supply generally indicate that they lower the risk of diarrhea by an estimated 30–50%.[89,91]

Water safety requires large investments on the part of communities and governments, but studies have provided ample evidence that these interventions are cost-effective. Every dollar spent on water and sanitation facilities has the potential to yield a return of $5–46 by reducing healthcare costs and improving productivity, with the highest returns possible in the least developed settings.[90]

Water safety, sanitation, and hygiene go hand in hand, as good sanitation reduces contamination of the water supply, and a safe water supply is necessary to improve sanitation and promote good hygiene. Improving sanitation and ensuring a safe water supply not only impact the health of a population by reducing the direct and indirect morbidity and mortality associated with waterborne infections, but arguably are necessary for economic development and growth.[90]

Isolation, Quarantine, Case Finding, and Contact Tracing

Isolation and Quarantine

Isolation and quarantine are measures that can be used by health officials to protect the public and limit the spread of disease by preventing contact between healthy individuals and those who are infected or have been exposed to an infectious disease.[70] These measures have been used for centuries. For example, in the 14th century, ships in Italy were required to remain anchored at sea for 40 days before they were allowed to land to protect coastal cities from plague epidemics (the term "quarantine" is derived from *quaranta giorni*, the Italian term for "40 days").[70] Isolation and quarantine are typically used for diseases that are transmitted by person-to-person contact and have relatively short incubation or infectious periods, such as influenza and severe acute respiratory syndrome (SARS). However, they can also be used for diseases transmitted through other routes, such as fecal–oral routes in the case of typhoid.

Isolation involves the separation of infected and sick individuals from healthy individuals. The duration of isolation depends on the availability of treatment, and can last a few hours or days if curative therapy is available or a few days to weeks if isolation for the duration of the infectious period is necessary.[72] Isolation is commonly used in hospitals to prevent the spread of disease between patients, as in the case of infectious tuberculosis.[70]

Quarantine involves the separation or restriction of movement of well individuals who may have been exposed to an infectious disease to see if they become sick.[70] Individuals under quarantine who become sick may then be put under isolation. The duration of quarantine depends on available information and preventive measures; it may last a few hours or days if tests are available to assess whether a person is infected and preventive therapy or vaccination can be administered, or a few days to weeks if quarantine for the duration of the incubation period is necessary.[72] While quarantine traditionally involves the sequestration of individuals in their homes or a quarantine facility, modern quarantine can also take the form of home curfew, restrictions on the assembly of groups such as at school or religious events, cancellation of public events, suspension of public gatherings, and closure of public places such as theaters or schools. In addition, restrictions on air, rail, water, motor vehicle, or pedestrian travel and closure of mass-transit systems can be implemented to restrict passage into and out of an area.[72]

Although these measures are commonly implemented on a voluntary basis, they can also be implemented under "police power" to forcefully detain individuals for the benefit of society. In an emergency setting, health authorities can implement these measures to contain epidemics by preventing the spread of diseases within and between communities. In the United States, the Division of Global Migration and Quarantine in the CDC is empowered with the authority to detain and isolate or quarantine individuals suspected of being infected with an infectious disease. Each state also has the authority to declare and enforce quarantines within its borders. In the United States, the list of quarantinable diseases includes cholera, diphtheria, infectious tuberculosis, plague, smallpox, yellow fever, viral hemorrhagic fevers, SARS (**Box 4-3**), and influenza that is causing, or has the potential to cause, a pandemic.[70]

The efficacy and effectiveness of these measures are difficult to define. It is not possible to conduct trials of their use, and during public health emergency situations isolation and quarantine are generally not implemented alone, so the impact of any one intervention is problematic to determine. Nevertheless, a review of studies evaluating control measures to prevent the spread of respiratory infections found evidence for the effectiveness of isolation and quarantine for respiratory syncytial virus, SARS, and other respiratory tract infections.[92] When trials are not possible, mathematical modeling can provide a method for evaluating the effectiveness of control measures. Such modeling studies indicate that for isolation to be effective, the majority of the infectious period must occur after the onset of symptoms. If this condition

| Box 4-3 | Use of Quarantine to Control the Outbreak of Severe Acute Respiratory Syndrome |

In the spring of 2003, an outbreak of atypical pneumonia, later termed severe acute respiratory syndrome (SARS), began in China and quickly spread around the world. The outbreak was caused by a previously unknown coronavirus and was spread primarily by person-to-person contact through respiratory secretions. Globally, there were 8422 cases and 916 deaths, with the majority of cases occurring in China, Hong Kong, Taiwan, Singapore, and Canada.

Quarantine and isolation were instrumental in the global effort to control the spread of SARS. Quarantine was used at a global level to restrict travel, with the World Health Organization issuing travel advisories recommending postponement of all but essential travel to Hong Kong, Toronto, Taipei, and parts of mainland China. Quarantine and isolation were also used at a local level. Examples from the response to the SARS outbreak in Toronto, where the majority of the cases from Canada occurred and which began on February 23, 2003, include the following measures:

- In hospitals, isolation units were created for all suspected SARS patients, all nonessential services were suspended, visitation was limited, and protective equipment was issued to all staff.
- At airports, incoming and outgoing passengers were screened for symptoms of SARS. Approximately 6.5 million people were screened, and more than 9000 were referred to screening nurses or quarantine officers. None met the criteria for a suspect or probable case.
- Contacts of all SARS patients, either in the home, in the workplace, or at the hospital, were asked to comply with a 10-day home quarantine and were monitored, usually by telephone, by a local public health worker. At least one school was closed and all students and teachers asked to stay at home for the 10-day period after one student displayed symptoms of SARS.
- Approximately 30,000 people in Toronto were quarantined during the outbreak.

In the SARS outbreak in Canada, both federal and provincial laws were passed to authorize the use and enforcement of quarantine and isolation. In most cases, people submitted to home quarantine voluntarily. In only a few instances were written orders required. To increase acceptance of these control measures, the government increased public awareness of SARS by providing timely information through websites, a SARS hotline, community meetings, and other community outreach at schools, workplaces, and community groups. On July 2, 2003, Toronto was removed from the list of areas with recent local transmission, and on July 5, 2003, the World Health Organization declared the end of the SARS outbreak.

Adapted from the World Health Organization (2012). Health topics: Severe acute respiratory syndrome. http://www.who.int/topics/sars/en/. Accessed February 29, 2012; and Rothstein MA, et al. Quarantine and isolation: lessons learned from SARS. A report to the Centers for Disease Control and Prevention. Institute of Bioethics, Health Policy and Law, University of Louisville School of Medicine, November 2003.

is met and isolation is done efficiently, transmission can be greatly reduced.[93] For quarantine to be effective, asymptomatic individuals must be effectively identified and put into quarantine and a large proportion of transmission must occur during the asymptomatic period. Even if transmission occurs only after symptom onset, quarantine can contribute to controlling transmission of the disease if individuals under quarantine who develop symptoms are effectively isolated.[94]

While quarantine and isolation can be effective in limiting the spread of diseases, they are difficult to implement. If done on a voluntary basis, they require the trust and participation of the public. For this to happen, the public must be well informed about the risks and consequences of infection and about the control measures to follow during the epidemic. If these measures are not implemented on a voluntary basis, their use can be controversial, as they can infringe upon individual rights and freedoms. In addition, considerable economic and social costs are associated with housing and caring for individuals under isolation and quarantine, as well as with restricting movement within and between communities.

Contact Tracing and Case Finding

Contact tracing and case finding can be used to enhance implementation of isolation and quarantine. *Contact tracing*, in which contacts of infected individuals are identified and investigated, can be used to identify potentially exposed individuals so that they can be put under quarantine. *Case finding*, in which infected individuals are identified, can be used to identify individuals with the disease so that they can be isolated or treated. Case finding is used as part of the "Stop TB Strategy" to control tuberculosis[95] and as part of the trypanosomiasis control program in West Africa,[96] so that individuals infected with these diseases can be effectively treated. Case finding and contact tracing were also used extensively in the eradication program for smallpox so that infected individuals could be isolated and their contacts vaccinated.[97]

Case finding, through screening, and contact tracing (also called partner notification in this context) are also used extensively for the control of STIs, including syphilis, gonorrhea, chlamydia, and HIV. The goal of partner notification is to test and treat potentially exposed sexual partners of infected individuals. Partner notification can be done by the health provider, the infected individual, or a combination of both, where the infected individual notifies his or her sexual partners and the health provider follows up if they do not come in for an appointment. In the case of hard-to-reach populations who are unlikely to come to health facilities for testing, presumptive treatment can be given to the infected individual to distribute to his or her sexual partners. An estimate of the case yield of partner notification for bacterial infections is that 1 new case is found for every 4–5 infected index individuals interviewed for partner notification.[98] The yield is estimated to be half as high for HIV. Several studies have found that intensive partner notification programs have been associated with lower incidence rates.[98]

New cases are consistently found through case finding and contact tracing. In the context of STIs, however, these strategies are difficult to implement. Given the large amount of stigma surrounding STIs, infected individuals may not want to disclose their sexual partners and identified contacts may refuse to come in for testing and treatment. In addition, long asymptomatic periods for these infections can make it difficult to identify all exposed contacts or to find them in enough time to prevent further transmission.

Screening of the Blood Supply

Procedures for screening and handling donated blood components are designed to preserve their utility for blood transfusions and to protect individuals against transfusion-transmissible infections (TTIs), such as HIV, hepatitis B and C, and syphilis. From the selection of potential donors, to the screening of donated blood, to the transfusion of donated blood to individuals in need, these procedures are applied with varying degrees of effectiveness in clinical settings throughout the world. In 2007, 85.4 million blood donations were collected by 162 countries that had some sort of national procedure for blood screening in place.[99]

Donor selection is an essential first step in reducing the risk of disease transmission. The WHO recommends that all blood transfusion services rely on nonremunerated, volunteer blood donors. TTIs are more prevalent in family, replacement, or paid donors, whose motivations to donate may lead them to respond inaccurately to donor screening questionnaires.[100] Fifty-four of 193 countries have achieved 100% voluntary blood donation. Of these, 68% are among high-income countries, 23% are among middle-income countries, and 9% are among low-income countries.[99] Countries that have 100% voluntary blood donation are more likely to have a higher number of individuals in the population donating

blood (31 per 1000 individuals versus 9 per 1000 for populations with less than 50% voluntary donations) and a higher percentage of regular donors.[99] Regular donors are between 10 and 50 times less likely to have markers for TTIs than first-time donors when their blood is tested.[101]

Comprehensive donor questionnaires, such as the Uniform Donor History Questionnaire (UDHQ),[102] which has been approved for use in the United States, assess the presence of medical, behavioral, or geographical risk factors that have been epidemiologically associated with TTIs among potential donors (**Table 4-8**).[101] In some instances, assays for these TTIs may exist, such as HIV and hepatitis C; for others, such as Creutzfeldt-Jacob disease, donor screening questionnaires are the only protection from TTIs for recipients of blood components. Donor screening may also prevent the collection of blood from individuals with recent infections who may not be identified by blood screening assays. Although donor questionnaires have low specificity and sensitivity and include questions that have never been validated, they are effective in yielding a population of donors who have between 75% and 97% fewer risk factors for TTIs than the general population.[101]

The development of blood screening assays over the last several decades has transformed healthcare systems' capacity to protect against TTIs, which are characterized by a long incubation period and infectious organisms that are stable in blood stored at 4°C or lower. Assays that can be employed to test blood for evidence of TTIs include immunoassays, which detect antibodies or antigens of an infectious agent; nucleic acid amplification technology (NAT) assays, which reveal the presence of viral nucleic acid (DNA or RNA); and, more recently, nanoparticle-based assays, which can detect antibodies, antigens, and gene sequences.[101,103] When someone is infected with a TTI, nucleic acids from the infection are the first markers to be detected by assays, followed by antigens and then ultimately antibodies as the body begins to build an immune response. The window periods for detection of each of these markers vary within each TTI as well as across TTIs.[103]

The decision of which assay to use depends on a variety of factors within a setting, including the number of overall assays to be conducted; the capacity for automation; lab and staff capabilities including equipment maintenance, controlled storage conditions, and availability of a constant power supply; the system of procurement; and test kit supply availability and reliability. Ultimately, assays should be selected based on their ability to reach sensitivity and specificity levels of at least 99.5% within the

Table 4-8	Selected (30 of 48) Questions from the Uniform Donor History Questionnaire	Yes	No
In the past 12 months have you			
Had a blood transfusion?		☐	☐
Had a transplant such as organ, tissue, or bone marrow?		☐	☐
Had a graft such as bone or skin?		☐	☐
Come into contact with someone else's blood?		☐	☐
Had an accidental needle-stick?		☐	☐
Had sexual contact with anyone who has HIV/AIDS or has had a positive test for the HIV/AIDS virus?		☐	☐
Had sexual contact with a prostitute or anyone else who takes money or drugs or other payment for sex?		☐	☐
Had sexual contact with anyone who has ever used needles to take drugs or steroids, or anything *not* prescribed by their doctor?		☐	☐
Had sexual contact with anyone who has hemophilia or has used clotting factor concentrates?		☐	☐
Female donors: Had sexual contact with a male who has ever had sexual contact with another male?		☐	☐
Had sexual contact with a person who has hepatitis?		☐	☐
Lived with a person who has hepatitis?		☐	☐
Had a tattoo?		☐	☐
Had ear or body piercing?		☐	☐
Had or been treated for syphilis or gonorrhea?		☐	☐
Been in juvenile detention, lockup, jail, or prison for more than 72 hours?		☐	☐
From 1980 to the present, did you			
Spend time that adds up to five (5) years or more in Europe?		☐	☐
Receive a blood transfusion in the United Kingdom or France?		☐	☐
From 1977 to the present, have you			
Received money, drugs, or other payment for sex?		☐	☐
Male donors: Had sexual contact with another male, even once?		☐	☐
Have you EVER			
Had a positive test for the HIV/AIDS virus?		☐	☐
Used needles to take drugs, steroids, or anything *not* prescribed by your doctor?		☐	☐
Used clotting factor concentrates?		☐	☐
Had hepatitis?		☐	☐
Had malaria?		☐	☐
Had Chagas disease?		☐	☐
Had babesiosis?		☐	☐
Had sexual contact with anyone who was born in or lived in Africa?		☐	☐
Been in Africa?		☐	☐
Have any of your relatives had Creutzfeldt-Jakob disease?		☐	☐

Adapted from the U.S. Food and Drug Administration. Full-Length Donor History Questionnaire, prepared by the AABB Donor History Task Force. http://www.fda.gov/downloads/BiologicsBloodVaccines/BloodBloodProducts/ApprovedProducts/LicensedProductsBLAs/BloodDonorScreening/UCM213552.pdf. Accessed February 29, 2012.

proposed setting.[103] In many settings, immunoassays are best able to meet these criteria.[103]

Different settings will also need to evaluate the TTIs for which they need to screen. The WHO recommends that every system screen for HIV (including HIV-1 and HIV-2 and epidemiologically relevant subtypes), hepatitis B, hepatitis C, and syphilis; decisions about additional screening assays should be based on local epidemiological evidence. For example, in regions where malaria, Chagas disease, and HTLV I/II are endemic, screening assays for these conditions should also be employed. The efficacy of assays varies within settings and between TTIs. In more sophisticated settings, where NAT can be employed, screening against a TTI can be highly effective. The estimated risk of transmission via transfusion, for example, can be as low as 0.14–1.1 per million units transfused for HIV and 0.10–2.33 per million units transfused for hepatitis C.[104]

The efficacy of blood screening is greatest when such testing occurs within a regulated national system of strategically located regional facilities where uniform standards (e.g., for labeling of blood donations, samples, and components and linking test results to the correct donations and donors) can be applied and economies of scale realized.[103] National systems need to have cold-chain systems in place for the reliable transport of test kits and reagents, and must also have a reference laboratory sophisticated enough to conduct confirmatory testing on reactive donations, provide quality-control samples, and evaluate and validate assay equipment and systems.[103] Mechanisms for notifying donors of positive screening test results and for avoiding the unnecessary transfusion of blood also contribute to the prevention of TTIs.

Established regional blood collection and screening services that have an adequate blood supply, rely on nonremunerated volunteer blood donors, apply comprehensive sensitive and specific assays, and ensure appropriate use of transfusions remain difficult to achieve. In a recent survey of 46 countries in the African region, 38 had a national blood transfusion service and 32 had a national blood transfusion policy. Only 11 countries had a blood transfusion policy that was supported by legislation.[105] The extent to which blood is adequately screened for HIV, hepatitis B, hepatitis C, and syphilis can be difficult to assess in countries that lack regional blood collection programs or reliable testing systems. In sub-Saharan Africa, where these conditions exist, however, modeling has been able to offer some analysis of risk of TTIs; the results suggest that the infection risk is 1 per 1000 units transfused for HIV, 2.5 per 1000 units transfused for hepatitis C, and 4.3 per 1000 units transfused for hepatitis B.[106]

In 2007, the WHO surveyed 162 countries, representing 92% of the global population, about their blood donation practices. The survey revealed that of a total of 85.4 million donations, the majority (65%) were collected in high-income countries, which represented only one-fourth of the surveyed population.[107] High-income countries collected, on average, 13,600 donations per center, nearly five times the 2800 donations per center that low-income countries were able to collect. It is estimated that a rate of 10 donations per 1000 population is necessary to meet a nation's most basic requirements for blood. Average donation rates in low-income countries were 2.3 per 1000 population as compared to 38.1 in high-income countries. In 73 countries, donation rates of less than 10 per 1000 population were reported.[107]

While terrific advances have been made in the collection and screening of blood components in the last several decades, structural challenges continue to hamper the safe collection and efficient delivery of blood to individuals in need in many settings throughout the world. Resolution of many of these structural challenges will require the coordinated effort of local and national governments and healthcare practitioners. Individuals and communities can have an impact, however, by encouraging and participating in voluntary, nonremunerated blood donation.

Community Prevention Measures Against Vector-borne Diseases

In addition to measures that individuals can implement to protect themselves against vector-borne diseases, two kinds of community measures can reduce the density of vectors or reservoirs in the community. First, measures that target the vector population, including environmental management and larval control, may be undertaken. Second, measures may be implemented by individuals but provide indirect protection to others in the community, including insecticide-treated nets, indoor residual spraying, and mass treatment.

Environmental Management

The environment within and around a community can be modified to deprive the target vector population of its optimal habitat, thereby reducing the possibilities for contact between the vector and humans and rendering conditions less conducive to disease transmission.[108] Examples of environmental management programs include periodic flushing of streams by small dams with siphons and sluice gates to control mosquito populations in Malaysia, changing the salinity of breeding habitats for mosquitoes in Indonesia, and managing deer populations to control ticks in the United States.[108] These approaches can be very effective in controlling vector populations if a high proportion of breeding sites are included in the areas targeted for management.

Larval Control

Vector populations can also be controlled by applying insecticides or other biological methods, such as bacterial toxins, larvivorous fish, or polystyrene beads, to the environment.[108] These methods can be very effective: in the 1930s, the insecticide Paris green was used to successfully eradicate *Anopheles gambiae* from Brazil, although it is too toxic for modern use; larvivorous fish housed in confined water containers have been found to effectively control malaria in Bombay, India, and Somalia.[108]

Both of these methods—environmental management and larval control—can impact the vector population in both the short and long term and can be used to supplement other control measures implemented in a community. However, they require a thorough understanding of vector ecology as well as complete identification of vector breeding sites. Specifically, the breeding sites must be of manageable size and a large proportion of breeding sites within range of the community to be protected must be covered by the intervention if it is to be effective. In addition, these strategies require both financial and human resources, community involvement, and coordination of multiple sectors of the population, which is not always possible to achieve in areas where vector-borne diseases are prevalent.

Chemotherapy

Mass or targeted drug administration is used as a control strategy for several vector-borne diseases, including onchocerciasis,[109] trypanosomiasis,[96] and lymphatic filariasis.[110] This technique protects not only those who are given treatment, but also individuals who are not treated directly by reducing the density of reservoirs in the community and eventually interrupting disease transmission. For example, ivermectin is used as a primary component of onchocerciasis control programs in Africa and South America (**Box 4-4**). Twice-yearly mass administration of the drug over a period of up to 7 years resulted in the elimination of onchocerciasis from communities in Guatemala, Mexico, Ecuador, and Colombia. Similar successes have not yet been achieved in West Africa, although evidence suggests that mass treatment has interrupted transmission and that elimination of the disease may be possible.[109]

Box 4-4	Successful Use of Ivermectin in Onchocerciasis Control Programs in Latin America

The Onchocerciasis Elimination Program for the Americas (OEPA) was launched in 1991–1992 with the goal of eliminating the morbidity associated with river blindness and, where possible, interrupting transmission in Latin America. The OEPA operates in six endemic countries, including Brazil, Colombia, Ecuador, Guatemala, and Mexico, and is a partnership between the Pan American Health Organization (PAHO), Merck & Company, the Centers for Disease Control and Prevention, and local nongovernmental organizations (e.g., The Carter Center, Lions Clubs International Foundation, and CBM). The program is based on a strategy of mass treatment with ivermectin every 6 months and aims to achieve coverage of at least 85% in communities at risk.

The OEPA has been quite successful, and evidence suggests that transmission has been interrupted in local areas. For example, in the Santiago River focus in Ecuador, the onchocerciasis control program began mass treatment with ivermectin for a period of 7 years from 1990 to 1997. The control program was integrated into the existing primary healthcare structure and used specially trained healthcare workers from each community to deliver the drugs biannually to hyperendemic communities and annually to mesoendemic and hypoendemic communities. The total population of the region was estimated to be 4900 individuals. An average coverage of 92% of all eligible individuals in the communities was achieved throughout the program. To monitor the success of the program a cohort of infected individuals at baseline was followed over the 7 years, a survey of children younger than 5 years of age (who would not have received ivermectin) was carried out at the end of the program, and entomological studies were done. By the end of the program, the prevalence of infection in the cohort had decreased from 100% to 0%. In the survey of children younger than 5 years of age, no infections were detected, compared to a prevalence of infection of 64.3% in this age group in 1985. Lastly, entomological studies found that the prevalence of infection in the black fly populations had decreased from 1.1% prior to the program to 0.08% in 1996, a level thought to be low enough to interrupt transmission.

By the end of 2007, no new cases of blindness attributable to onchocerciasis had been reported and eye lesions had been eliminated in the majority of endemic areas in Latin America.

Data from World Health Organization (2012). Onchocerciasis Elimination Program for the Americas (OEPA). http://www.who.int/blindness/partnerships/onchocerciasis_oepa/en/. Accessed March 26, 2012; and Guderian RH. Successful control of onchocerciasis with community-based ivermectin distribution in the Rio Santiago focus in Ecuador. *Top Med & Int Health*. 1997;2(10):982–988.

Insecticide-Treated Bednets

As previously described, ITNs are an effective tool that individuals can implement to protect themselves against vector-borne diseases, primarily those transmitted by mosquitoes. Because the toxicant is lethal to mosquitoes, however, its use can also provide indirect protection to households without ITNs by reducing the overall size of the vector population in the community. Studies have demonstrated that community-wide use of ITNs in areas where mosquitoes are highly anthropophilic* shortens their mean life span and results in large-scale mosquito death.[64] Evaluations of malaria morbidity and all-cause mortality in children without ITNs and in communities adjacent to those with widespread ITN use have found improved survival and health, thereby demonstrating the indirect community-level protection provided by ITNs. This community-level effect has been observed in Ghana,[111] Kenya,[112,113] Papua New Guinea,[64] and the United Republic of Tanzania.[114] The community-level effect of ITNs appears to be as large as the individual-level effect, such that achieving a high level of coverage of ITN use in a community can greatly enhance the effectiveness of this control measure.[64]

Indoor Residual Spraying

With indoor residual spraying (IRS), a long-acting chemical insecticide is applied to the walls and roofs of all houses and domestic animal shelters in a given area. The goal of IRS is to kill adult vectors that land on indoor surfaces, thereby reducing the vector population within the community. IRS is not a personal protection measure—it does not prevent individuals from being bitten—but rather kills vectors that rest on indoor surfaces after biting, thereby providing protection for other individuals from future infection.[115] IRS is used as a primary control measure for malaria, but has also been used to control leishmaniasis,[116] Chagas disease,[117] and lymphatic filariasis.[110] Only a few trials have been conducted evaluating the efficacy of IRS in controlling malaria—specifically, in Tanzania, Nigeria, Mozambique, India, and Pakistan.[118] These studies found IRS to be effective in reducing the incidence of infection (protective efficacy: 31–88%) and reinfection (54%), parasite incidence (14%), and parasite prevalence (6–74%).[118]

These methods of controlling the vector population and reservoirs of infection—including chemotherapy, ITNs, and IRS—can have a rapid and effective short-term impact on the burden of disease.

They can also be targeted to high-risk communities and can prove responsive to changing transmission patterns and geographic locations. On the downside, these tools require a high level of human and financial resources as well as infrastructure to efficiently distribute the drugs or nets or apply the insecticide. These methods also require a high level of community participation and coverage in space and time to be effective. For mass drug treatment, a high proportion of the community is required to participate in the program at each distribution and agree to take the drugs. For ITNs, a high proportion of the community has to not only acquire an ITN but sleep under it every night. For IRS, a large proportion of the community has to live in permanent dwellings and agree to have them sprayed 1–2 times per season and to preserve the integrity of the surfaces that have been sprayed. While enthusiasm may be high at the beginning of a program, it may wane over time, thereby compromising the program's effectiveness. With all methods, resistance of the agent to the drugs or the vector to the insecticides remains a concern.

CONCLUSIONS

Preventing infectious diseases can be as simple as using soap and water or as complicated as implementing an integrated service delivery system. In either instance, widespread adoption of a prevention measure can be daunting to effect and maintain. Communities may struggle with practical deterrents such as expense, expertise, and environment as well as systemic or social constraints. Individuals can face these same challenges. Coordinated efforts and broad educational campaigns can overcome these obstacles, however, and many heartening examples of successful implementation of infection prevention measures can be cited. For example, in 2004, Togo was able to increase the percentage of households that owned at least one ITN from 8% to 62.5% by distributing ITNs to every child between the ages of 9 and 59 months during a 6-day National Integrated Health Campaign.[119] Togo capitalized on its high rates of vaccination (more than 90%) as a means of combating devastatingly high malaria-associated death rates among its children. In December 2004, every child who received a vaccination also received a bednet. One month after the campaign, 93.1% of children in Togo had their own bednet.

Brazil tackled another worrisome public health problem by harnessing the power of popular culture. Recognizing a disproportionate increase in cases of HIV/AIDS among young women, the Brazilian

---

* Feeding preferentially on humans and not at all or to a less degree on other animals.

Ministry of Health devoted one of its annual public communication carnival campaigns to promoting condom use among adolescents, especially girls and young women, aged 13–19 years.[120] Campaign messages were disseminated for 3 weeks via television, radio, posters, and billboards, and showed a popular young female Brazilian singer purchasing condoms. Television and billboard exposure had a positive and significant effect on a norm of women purchasing condoms among sampled 13- to 19-year-old females. Examples such as these make clear that real change can happen when communities work collaboratively, creatively, and with determination to overcome obstacles to the adoption of prevention measures.

One-time campaigns, even when they are well-conceived and coordinated efforts, are typically not enough to obviate a public health concern. A recent study evaluating the eradication of Chagas disease in La Joya, Peru, uncovered evidence of a nearly forgotten, yet very successful previous campaign that had occurred in the region in 1995. Evidence of this campaign was almost nonexistent 13 years later, when researchers returned to the region to redeploy eradication efforts.[121] This study and decades of experience in public health send a clear message: communities, individuals, and researchers must remain vigilant in the application of prevention measures. A beautifully executed campaign with demonstrated efficacy must almost always be accompanied by a realistic acceptance of the place of any individual campaign in the longer battle of adoption of prevention measures. The ultimate measure of the methods described in this chapter, then, is not simply their efficacy, strengths, and weaknesses, but also their capacity to be successfully applied, not just in one instance or in one campaign, but again and again and again until their use is routine and the dangers they prevent no longer pose a threat.

• • • REFERENCES

1. Semmelweis IP. *Die Aetiologie, der Begriff und die Prophylaxis des Kindbettfiebers*: Pest, Vienna, & Leipzig: C. A. Hartleben; 1861.

2. World Health Organization. Diarrhoeal disease. 2012. Available at: http://www.who.int/mediacentre/factsheets/fs330/en/index.html. Accessed January 19, 2012.

3. World Health Organization. Pneumonia. 2012. Available at: http://www.who.int/mediacentre/factsheets/fs331/en/index.html. Accessed January 19, 2012.

4. World Health Organization. *Global Handwashing Day Planner's Guide*. Geneva, Switzerland: WHO; October 15, 2008.

5. World Health Organization. *WHO Guidelines on Hand Hygiene on Health Care*. Geneva, Switzerland: WHO; 2009.

6. World Health Organization. *WHO Guidelines on Drinking-Water Quality*. Geneva, Switzerland: WHO; 2006.

7. Hoque B, Briend A. A comparison of local handwashing agents in Bangladesh. *J Trop Med Hyg*. 1991;94:61–64.

8. Kaltenthaler E, Waterman R, Cross P. Faecal indicator bacteria on the hands and effectiveness of hand-washing in Zimbabwe. *J Trop Med Hyg*. 1991;94:358–363.

9. Burton M, Cobb E, Donachie P, Judah G, Curtis V, Schmidt WP. The effect of handwashing with water or soap on bacterial contamination of hands. *Int J Environ Res Public Health*. 2011;8(1):97–104.

10. Rotter M. Hand washing and hand disinfection. In: Mayhall C, ed. *Hospital Epidemiology and Infection Control*. Philadelphia: Lippincott Williams; 1999.

11. Curtis V, Cairncross S. Effect of washing hands with soap on diarrhoea risk in the community: a systematic review. *Lancet Infect Dis*. 2003;3(5):275–281.

12. Esrey SA, Feachem RG, Hughes JM. Interventions for the control of diarrhoeal diseases among young children: improving water supplies and excreta disposal facilities. *Bull WHO*. 1985;63(4):757–772.

13. Fewtrell L, Kaufmann RB, Kay D, Enanoria W, Haller L, Colford JM Jr. Water, sanitation, and hygiene interventions to reduce diarrhoea in less developed countries: a systematic review and meta-analysis. *Lancet Infect Dis*. 2005;5(1):42–52.

14. Luby SP, Agboatwalla M, Feikin DR, et al. Effect of handwashing on child health: a randomised controlled trial. *Lancet*. 2005;366(9481):225–233.

15. Luby SP, Agboatwalla M, Painter J, et al. Combining drinking water treatment and hand washing for diarrhoea prevention, a cluster randomised controlled trial. *Trop Med Int Health*. 2006;11(4):479–489.

16. Luby SP, Agboatwalla M, Painter J, Altaf A, Billhimer WL, Hoekstra RM. Effect of intensive handwashing promotion on childhood diarrhea in high-risk communities in Pakistan: a randomized controlled trial. *JAMA*. 2004;291(21):2547–2554.

17. Luby SP, Halder AK, Huda T, Unicomb L, Johnston RB. The effect of handwashing at recommended times with water alone and with soap on child diarrhea in rural Bangladesh: an observational study. *PLoS Med*. 2011;8(6):e1001052.

18. Ejemot RI, Ehiri JE, Meremikwu MM, Critchley JA. Hand washing for preventing diarrhoea. *Cochrane Database Syst Rev*. 2008;1:CD004265.

19. Huttly SR, Morris SS, Pisani V. Prevention of diarrhoea in young children in developing countries. *Bull WHO*. 1997;75(2):163–174.

20. Rabie T, Curtis V. Handwashing and risk of respiratory infections: a quantitative systematic review. *Trop Med Int Health*. 2006;11(3): 258–267.

21. Olsen A, Samuelsen H, Onyango-Ouma W. A study of risk factors for intestinal helminth infections using epidemiological and anthropological approaches. *J Biosoc Sci*. 2001;33(4):569–584.

22. Han A, Hiaing T, ML K, Saw T. Hand washing intervention to reduce ascariasis in children. *Trans R Soc Trop Med Hyg*. 1988;82:153.

23. Kightlinger L, Seed J, Kightlinger M. Ascaris lumbricoides intensity in relation to environmental, socioeconomic, and behavioral determinants of exposure to infection in children from southeast Madagascar. *J Parasitol*. 1998;84:480–484.

24. Nishiura H, Imai H, Nakao H, et al. *Ascaris lumbricoides* among children in rural communities in the Northern Area, Pakistan:

prevalence, intensity, and associated sociocultural and behavioral risk factors. *Acta Trop*. 2002;83(3):223–231.

25. Wilson JM, Chandler GN, Muslihatun, Jamiluddin. Hand-washing reduces diarrhoea episodes: a study in Lombok, Indonesia. *Trans R Soc Trop Med Hyg*. 1991;85(6):819–821.

26. Emori TG, Gaynes RP. An overview of nosocomial infections, including the role of the microbiology laboratory. *Clin Microbiol Rev*. 1993;6(4):428–442.

27. Garner JS, Favero MS. CDC guideline for handwashing and hospital environmental control, 1985. *Infect Control*. 1986;7(4):231–243.

28. Recommendations for preventing the spread of vancomycin resistance. *Infect Control Hosp Epidemiol*. 1995;16(2):105–113.

29. Boyce JM, Pittet D. Guideline for hand hygiene in health-care settings. Recommendations of the Healthcare Infection Control Practices Advisory Committee and the HICPAC/SHEA/ APIC/IDSA Hand Hygiene Task Force. Society for Healthcare Epidemiology of America/ Association for Professionals in Infection Control/Infectious Diseases Society of America. *MMWR Recomm Rep*. 2002;51(RR-16):1–45, quiz CE41–44.

30. United Nations. UN stresses effectiveness of handwashing with soap to prevent diseases. 2011. Available at: http://www.un.org/apps/ news/story.asp?NewsID=40047&Cr=hygiene &Cr1.

31. World Health Organization. Food safety. 2011. Available at: http://www.who.int/foodsafety/ en/.Accessed March 30, 2011.

32. World Health Organization. *Five keys to safer food manual*. Geneva, Switzerland: WHO; 2006.

33. Sobsey MD. *Managing Water in the Home: Accelerated Health Gains from Improved Water Supply*. Geneva, Switzerland: World Health Organization; 2002.

34. Roberts L, Chartier Y, Chartier O, Malenga G, Toole M, Rodka H. Keeping clean water clean

in a Malawi refugee camp: a randomized intervention trial. *Bull WHO.* 2001;79(4):280–287.

35. Quick RE, Venczel LV, Mintz ED, et al. Diarrhoea prevention in Bolivia through point-of-use water treatment and safe storage: a promising new strategy. *Epidemiol Infect.* 1999;122(1):83–90.

36. Sobel J, Mahon B, Mendoza CE, et al. Reduction of fecal contamination of street-vended beverages in Guatemala by a simple system for water purification and storage, handwashing, and beverage storage. *Am J Trop Med Hyg.* 1998;59(3):380–387.

37. Youssef H. The history of the condom. *J R Soc Med.* 1993;86(4):226–228.

38. National Institute of Allergy and Infectious Diseases. *Workshop Summary: Scientific Evidence on Condom Effectiveness for Sexually Transmitted Disease (STD) Prevention.* Herndon, VA: NIAID; 2001.

39. Weller S, Davis K. Condom effectiveness in reducing heterosexual HIV transmission. *Cochrane Database Syst Rev.* 2001;3:CD003255.

40. Silverman BG, Gross TP. Use and effectiveness of condoms during anal intercourse: a review. *Sex Transm Dis.* 1997;24(1):11–17.

41. Warner L, Newman DR, Austin HD, et al. Condom effectiveness for reducing transmission of gonorrhea and chlamydia: the importance of assessing partner infection status. *Am J Epidemiol.* 2004;159(3):242–251.

42. Niccolai LM, Rowhani-Rahbar A, Jenkins H, Green S, Dunne DW. Condom effectiveness for prevention of *Chlamydia trachomatis* infection. *Sex Transm Infect.* 2005;81(4):323–325.

43. Martin ET, Krantz E, Gottlieb SL, et al. A pooled analysis of the effect of condoms in preventing HSV-2 acquisition. *Arch Intern Med.* 2009;169(13):1233–1240.

44. Manhart LE, Koutsky LA. Do condoms prevent genital HPV infection, external genital warts, or cervical neoplasia? A meta-analysis. *Sex Transm Dis.* 2002;29(11):725–735.

45. Crosby R, Yarber WL, Sanders SA, Graham CA, Arno JN. Slips, breaks and "falls": condom errors and problems reported by men attending an STD clinic. *Int J STD AIDS.* 2008;19(2):90–93.

46. Crosby RA, Sanders SA, Yarber WL, Graham CA, Dodge B. Condom use errors and problems among college men. *Sex Transm Dis.* 2002;29(9):552–557.

47. Centers for Disease Control and Prevention. National Survey of Family Growth. Accessed December 6, 2011.

48. Adam PC, de Wit JB, Toskin I, et al. Estimating levels of HIV testing, HIV prevention coverage, HIV knowledge, and condom use among men who have sex with men (MSM) in low-income and middle-income countries. *J Acquir Immune Defic Syndr.* 2009;52(suppl 2):S143–S151.

49. Sarkar NN. Barriers to condom use. *Eur J Contracept Reprod Health Care.* 2008;13(2):114–122.

50. Moore SG, Dahl DW, Gorn GJ, Weinberg CB, Park J, Jiang Y. Condom embarrassment: coping and consequences for condom use in three countries. *AIDS Care.* 2008;20(5):553–559.

51. Rizkalla C, Bauman LJ, Avner JR. Structural impediments to condom access in a high HIV/STI-risk area. *J Environ Public Health.* 2010;2010:630762.

52. Lo SC, Reisen CA, Poppen PJ, Bianchi FT, Zea MC. Cultural beliefs, partner characteristics, communication, and sexual risk among Latino MSM. *AIDS Behav.* 2011;15(3):613–620.

53. Dworkin SL, Ehrhardt AA. Going beyond "ABC" to include "GEM": critical reflections on progress in the HIV/AIDS epidemic. *Am J Public Health.* 2007;97(1):13–18.

54. Bhattacharya G. Sociocultural and behavioral contexts of condom use in heterosexual married couples in India: challenges to the HIV prevention program. *Health Educ Behav.* 2004;31(1):101–117.

55. Foss AM, Hossain M, Vickerman PT, Watts CH. A systematic review of published evidence

on intervention impact on condom use in sub-Saharan Africa and Asia. *Sex Transm Infect.* 2007;83(7):510–516.

56. Marston C, King E. Factors that shape young people's sexual behaviour: a systematic review. *Lancet.* 2006;368(9547):1581–1586.

57. East L, Jackson D, O'Brien L, Peters K. Use of the male condom by heterosexual adolescents and young people: literature review. *J Adv Nurs.* 2007;59(2):103–110.

58. Larmarange J, Wade AS, Diop AK, et al. Men who have sex with men (MSM) and factors associated with not using a condom at last sexual intercourse with a man and with a woman in Senegal. *PLoS One.* 2010;5(10).

59. Shahmanesh M, Patel V, Mabey D, Cowan F. Effectiveness of interventions for the prevention of HIV and other sexually transmitted infections in female sex workers in resource poor setting: a systematic review. *Trop Med Int Health.* 2008;13(5):659–679.

60. Charania MR, Crepaz N, Guenther-Gray C, et al. Efficacy of structural-level condom distribution interventions: a meta-analysis of U. S. and international studies, 1998–2007. *AIDS Behav.* 2011;15(7):1283–1297.

61. Barnard DR. *Global Collaboration for Development of Pesticides for Public Health.* Geneva, Switzerland: World Health Organization, Communicable Disease Control, Prevention and Eradication WHO Pesticide Evaluation Scheme; 2000.

62. Centers for Disease Control and Prevention. Lyme disease prevention and control. Available at: http://www.cdc.gov/ncidod/dvbid/lyme/ld_prevent.htm. Accessed December 7, 2010.

63. World Health Organization. *Insecticide-Treated Mosquito Nets: A WHO Position Statement.* Geneva, Switzerland: WHO Global Malaria Programme; 2011.

64. World Health Organization. *Malaria vector Control and Personal Protection: Report of a WHO Study Group.* Geneva, Switzerland: WHO; 2006.

65. Rowland M, Downey G, Rab A, et al. DEET mosquito repellent provides personal protection against malaria: a household randomized trial in an Afghan refugee camp in Pakistan. *Trop Med Int Health.* 2004;9(3):335–342.

66. Rowland M, Freeman T, Downey G, Hadi A, Saeed M. DEET mosquito repellent sold through social marketing provides personal protection against malaria in an area of all-night mosquito biting and partial coverage of insecticide-treated nets: a case-control study of effectiveness. *Trop Med Int Health.* 2004;9(3):343–350.

67. Lengeler C. Insecticide-treated bed nets and curtains for preventing malaria. *Cochrane Database Syst Rev.* 2004;2:CD000363.

68. Hill J, Lines J, Rowland M. Insecticide-treated nets. *Adv Parasitol.* 2006;61:77–128.

69. Gamble C, Ekwaru JP, ter Kuile FO. Insecticide-treated nets for preventing malaria in pregnancy. *Cochrane Database Syst Rev.* 2006;2:CD003755.

70. Aponte JJ, Schellenberg D, Egan A, et al. Efficacy and safety of intermittent preventive treatment with sulfadoxine-pyrimethamine for malaria in African infants: a pooled analysis of six randomised, placebo-controlled trials. *Lancet.* 2009;374(9700):1533–1542.

71. IPTI Consortium. Intermittent preventive treatment of malaria in infants (IPTi) with antimalarial medicines delivered through the Expanded Programme on Immunisation (EPI). Available at: http://www.ipti-malaria.org. Accessed December 7, 2010.

72. Armstrong Schellenberg JR, Shirima K, Maokola W, et al. Community effectiveness of intermittent preventive treatment for infants (IPTi) in rural southern Tanzania. *Am J Trop Med Hyg.* 2010;82(5):772–781.

73. World Health Organization. *A Strategic Framework for Malaria Prevention and Control During Pregnancy in the African Region.* Brazzaville, Republic of the Congo: WHO Regional Office for Africa; 2004.

74. Shulman CE, Dorman EK, Cutts F, et al. Intermittent sulphadoxine-pyrimethamine to prevent severe anaemia secondary to malaria in pregnancy: a randomised placebo-controlled trial. *Lancet.* 1999;353(9153):632–636.

75. Schultz LJ, Steketee RW, Macheso A, Kazembe P, Chitsulo L, Wirima JJ. The efficacy of antimalarial regimens containing sulfadoxine-pyrimethamine and/or chloroquine in preventing peripheral and placental *Plasmodium falciparum* infection among pregnant women in Malawi. *Am J Trop Med Hyg.* 1994;51(5):515–522.

76. Parise ME, Ayisi JG, Nahlen BL, et al. Efficacy of sulfadoxine-pyrimethamine for prevention of placental malaria in an area of Kenya with a high prevalence of malaria and human immunodeficiency virus infection. *Am J Trop Med Hyg.* 1998;59(5):813–822.

77. Njagi JK, Magnussen P, Estambale B, Ouma J, Mugo B. Prevention of anaemia in pregnancy using insecticide-treated bednets and sulfadoxine-pyrimethamine in a highly malarious area of Kenya: a randomized controlled trial. *Trans R Soc Trop Med Hyg.* 2003;97(3):277–282.

78. Asa OO, Onayade AA, Fatusi AO, Ijadunola KT, Abiona TC. Efficacy of intermittent preventive treatment of malaria with sulphadoxine-pyrimethamine in preventing anaemia in pregnancy among Nigerian women. *Matern Child Health J.* 2008;12(6):692–698.

79. Hommerich L, von Oertzen C, Bedu-Addo G, et al. Decline of placental malaria in southern Ghana after the implementation of intermittent preventive treatment in pregnancy. *Malar J.* 2007;6:144.

80. Ramharter M, Schuster K, Bouyou-Akotet MK, et al. Malaria in pregnancy before and after the implementation of a national IPTp program in Gabon. *Am J Trop Med Hyg.* 2007;77(3):418–422.

81. Sirima SB, Cotte AH, Konate A, et al. Malaria prevention during pregnancy: assessing the disease burden one year after implementing a program of intermittent preventive treatment in Koupela District, Burkina Faso. *Am J Trop Med Hyg.* 2006;75(2):205–211.

82. World Health Organization. Water sanitation and health. Available at: http://www.who.int/water_sanitation_health/en/. Accessed April 28, 2011.

83. Clasen TF, Bostoen K, Schmidt WP, et al. Interventions to improve disposal of human excreta for preventing diarrhoea. *Cochrane Database Syst Rev.* 2010;6:CD007180.

84. United Nations Millennium Project. *UN Millennium Project Task Force on Water and Sanitation:- Health, Dignity and Development: What Will It Take?* London: Earthscan; 2005.

85. World Health Organization/United Nations Children's Fund. WHO/UNICEF Joint Monitoring Programme (JMP) for water supply and sanitation. Available at: http://www.wssinfo.org. Accessed May 7, 2011.

86. Schmidt WP, Genser B, Barreto ML, et al. Sampling strategies to measure the prevalence of common recurrent infections in longitudinal studies. *Emerg Themes Epidemiol.* 7(1):5.

87. Bartram J, Cairncross S. Hygiene, sanitation, and water: forgotten foundations of health. *PLoS Med.* 7(11):e1000367.

88. Mara D, Lane J, Scott B, Trouba D. Sanitation and health. *PLoS Med.* 7(11):e1000363.

89. Clasen T, Roberts I, Rabie T, Schmidt W, Cairncross S. Interventions to improve water quality for preventing diarrhoea. *Cochrane Database Syst Rev.* 2006;3:CD004794.

90. Hunter PR, MacDonald AM, Carter RC. Water supply and health. *PLoS Med.* 7(11):e1000361.

91. Clasen T, Schmidt WP, Rabie T, Roberts I, Cairncross S. Interventions to improve water quality for preventing diarrhoea: systematic review and meta-analysis. *BMJ (Clinical Research Ed).* 2007;334(7597):782.

92. Jefferson T, Del Mar C, Dooley L, et al. Physical interventions to interrupt or reduce the spread of respiratory viruses: a Cochrane review. *Health Technol Assess.* 2010;14(34):347–476.

93. Fraser C, Riley S, Anderson RM, Ferguson NM. Factors that make an infectious disease outbreak controllable. *Proc Natl Acad Sci USA.* 2004;101(16):6146–6151.

94. Day T, Park A, Madras N, Gumel A, Wu J. When is quarantine a useful control strategy for emerging infectious diseases? *Am J Epidemiol.* 2006;163(5):479–485.

95. World Health Organization. *The Stop TB Strategy. Building on and Enhancing DOTS to Meet the TB-Related Millennium Development Goals.* Geneva, Switzerland: WHO; 2006.

96. Fevre EM, Picozzi K, Jannin J, Welburn SC, Maudlin I. Human African trypanosomiasis: epidemiology and control. *Adv Parasitol.* 2006;61:167–221.

97. The intensified smallpox eradication programme, 1967–1980. In: Fenner F, Henderson DA, Arita I, Jezek Z, Ladnyi ID, eds. *Smallpox and Its Eradication.* Geneva, Switzerland: World Health Organization; 1988.

98. Brewer DD. Case-finding effectiveness of partner notification and cluster investigation for sexually transmitted diseases/HIV. *Sex Transm Dis.* 2005;32(2):78–83.

99. World Health Organization. *Towards 100% Voluntary Blood Donation: A Global Framework for Action.* Geneva, Switzerland: WHO; 2010.

100. World Health Organization. Blood transfusion safety: voluntary non-remunerated blood donation. 2012. Available at: http://www.who.int/bloodsafety/voluntary_donation/en/.

101. Epstein JS. Alternative strategies in assuring blood safety: an overview. *Biologicals.* 2010;38(1):31–35.

102. American Association of Blood Banks. Blood donor history questionnaire. 2008. Available at: http://www.aabb.org/resources/donation/questionnaires/Pages/dhqaabb.aspx. Accessed January 19, 2012.

103. World Health Organization. *Screening Donated Blood for Transfusion-Transmissible Infections.* Geneva, Switzerland: WHO; 2010.

104. Bihl F, Castelli D, Marincola F, Dodd RY, Brander C. Transfusion-transmitted infections. *J Transl Med.* 2007;5:25.

105. Bloch EM, Vermeulen M, Murphy E. Blood transfusion safety in Africa: a literature review of infectious disease and organizational challenges. *Transfus Med Rev.* Aug 25, 2011.

106. Jayaraman S, Chalabi Z, Perel P, Guerriero C, Roberts I. The risk of transfusion-transmitted infections in sub-Saharan Africa. *Transfusion.* 2010;50:433–442.

107. World Health Organization. Blood safety and availability: facts and figures from the 2007 Blood Safety Survey. 2009. Available at: http://www.who.int/mediacentre/factsheets/fs279/en/index.html. Accessed January 19, 2012.

108. World Health Organization. *Vector Control for Malaria and Other Mosquito-borne Diseases: Report of a WHO Study Group.* Geneva, Switzerland: WHO; 1995.

109. Boatin BA, Richards FO, Jr. Control of onchocerciasis. *Adv Parasitol.* 2006;61:349–394.

110. Ottesen EA. Lymphatic filariasis: Treatment, control and elimination. *Adv Parasitol.* 2006;61:395–441.

111. Binka FN, Indome F, Smith T. Impact of spatial distribution of permethrin-impregnated bed nets on child mortality in rural northern Ghana. *Am J Trop Med Hyg.* 1998;59(1):80–85.

112. Hawley WA, Phillips-Howard PA, ter Kuile FO, et al. Community-wide effects of permethrin-treated bed nets on child mortality and malaria morbidity in western Kenya. *Am J Trop Med Hyg.* 2003;68(4 suppl):121–127.

113. Howard SC, Omumbo J, Nevill C, Some ES, Donnelly CA, Snow RW. Evidence for a mass community effect of insecticide-treated bednets on the incidence of malaria on the

Kenyan coast. *Trans R Soc Trop Med Hyg.* 2000;94(4):357–360.

114. Maxwell CA, Msuya E, Sudi M, Njunwa KJ, Carneiro IA, Curtis CF. Effect of community-wide use of insecticide-treated nets for 3–4 years on malarial morbidity in Tanzania. *Trop Med Int Health.* 2002;7(12):1003–1008.

115. World Health Organization. *Indoor Residual Spraying: Use of Indoor Residual Spraying for Scaling up Global Malaria Control and Elimination: WHO Position Statement.* Geneva, Switzerland: WHO; 2006.

116. World Health Organization. Surveillance and control of leishmaniasis. 2011. Available at: http://www.who.int/leishmaniasis/surveillance/en/. Accessed December 14, 2010.

117. Yamagata Y, Nakagawa J. Control of Chagas disease. *Adv Parasitol.* 2006;61:129–165.

118. Pluess B, Tanser FC, Lengeler C, Sharp BL. Indoor residual spraying for preventing malaria. *Cochrane Database Syst Rev.* 2010;4:CD006657.

119. Wolkon A, Vanden Eng JL, Morgah K, et al. Rapid scale-up of long-lasting insecticide-treated bed nets through integration into the national immunization program during child health week in Togo, 2004. *Am J Trop Med Hyg.* 2010;83(5):1014–1019.

120. Porto MP. Fighting AIDS among adolescent women: effects of a public communication campaign in Brazil. *J Health Commun.* 2007;12(2):121–132.

121. Delgado S, Castillo Neyra R, Quispe Machaca VR, et al. A history of Chagas disease transmission, control, and re-emergence in peri-rural La Joya, Peru. *PLoS Negl Trop Dis.* 2011;5(2):e970.

5

Outbreak Epidemiology

Diane M. Dwyer, Carmela Groves, and David Blythe

INTRODUCTION

Outbreak epidemiology is the investigation of a disease cluster or epidemic with the goal of controlling or preventing further disease in a population. The word *epidemic*—defined as an increase in the number of cases of a disease above what is expected—is derived from the Greek *epi* and *demos*, meaning "that which is upon the people." This meaning enriches our understanding of epidemics by emphasizing the burdensome toll they have on a population or "a people." This definition also allows us to realize that epidemics are not always caused by infectious agents. Many other hazards, such as chemicals or physical conditions, can cause unusually high numbers of cases of disease in a given population. Regardless of the etiology of the disease, the techniques used to investigate and control outbreaks are generally similar.

Accounts of outbreaks have been recorded throughout the centuries. Cholera, influenza, malaria, smallpox, and the plague are extensively documented as causes of epidemics and pandemics that have altered the outcome of wars, disrupted political structures, killed millions of people, and affected the lives of countless others.[1] The prevention of disease through measures such as improved sanitation, as well as isolation and quarantine, was recognized even before the causes of these diseases had been identified.

New challenges continue to arise in the control of infectious diseases. Public health officials and healthcare providers face the emergence of new diseases and the reemergence of diseases that were no longer thought to be a threat to the public's health.[2] The threat of the use of biologic agents or their toxins (e.g., anthrax, plague, botulism, and smallpox) as weapons of bioterrorism has resulted in increased attention being paid to the possibility of outbreaks caused by intentionally released agents.[3] Changes in the environment; industrial practices; agriculture and food processing; international transportation of people, foods, and goods; and changes in human behaviors have increased the risk of disease and the speed at which communicable disease can spread.

Concurrently, the number of people at increased risk of infection and the density of human populations have increased. People with immune dysfunction (e.g., because of human immunodeficiency virus infection, rheumatologic conditions, hematologic conditions, organ transplantation, cancer chemotherapy, or chronic use of corticosteroids), infants, and the elderly are more susceptible to infectious diseases, including those caused by infectious agents that may not have been medical concerns in the past. These compromised individuals may present with lower temperature or with unusual symptoms that complicate the diagnosis, and their infections may be more difficult to treat. Immunosuppression may also increase the infectiousness of the individual, either by increasing the number of infectious organisms that the individual sheds or by increasing the length of time during which the individual is infectious.[4] Meanwhile, the increasing density of the human population, especially in some developing nations, creates situations that foster the spread of new and old infectious diseases.

Nevertheless, the advantage is not all to the microbes. Advances in laboratory techniques, medical interventions (such as antibiotics), sanitation, technology, and epidemiology have increased our ability to identify and control infectious diseases.[5]

The news media and other media such as the Internet and social media have enhanced outbreak awareness. Names of organisms and events such as *Escherichia coli* O157:H7, Ebola virus, *Cryptosporidium*, group A *Streptococcus* ("the flesh-eating bacteria"), antibiotic-resistant organisms (methicillin-resistant *Staphylococcus aureus* [MRSA]), severe acute respiratory syndrome, and pandemic influenza conjure up reports of outbreaks that have been brought to the attention of the public through the media. That *E. coli* O157:H7 can cause fatal hemolytic uremic syndrome, especially in children, was demonstrated in U.S. outbreaks caused by contaminated ground beef and fresh spinach and in the Japanese outbreak caused by contaminated radish sprouts.[6-8] The speed at which international diseases could become threats to U.S. citizens was underscored by the reports of Ebola virus isolated in monkeys in Reston, Virginia.[9] Reports of outbreaks involving strains of *Mycobacterium tuberculosis,* MRSA, and *Streptococcus pneumoniae* that are resistant to antibiotics have raised public awareness of the danger of inappropriate or excessive antibiotic use. Investigation of such events allows epidemiologists to identify risk factors and to determine preventive measures that will limit and control the spread of disease.

An outbreak may occur for a variety of reasons, including poor food handling practices and personal behaviors, environmental contaminants, and intentional acts of terrorism. An epidemiologist must investigate cases of disease with an awareness of all these possibilities. However, the basic techniques in investigation remain the same. This chapter reviews the methods used to investigate and control outbreaks of infectious disease.

SURVEILLANCE AND OUTBREAK DETECTION

Outbreaks may come to the attention of health professionals through a report from a doctor's office, a hospital, a nursing home, a laboratory, or even a patient's call to the health department. Alternatively, outbreaks may be recognized through analysis of routine public health surveillance reports of individual cases of disease or through active surveillance for specific syndromes. Refer to the chapter on surveillance for additional information and methods relating to surveillance of diseases.[10]

Each state has its own individual laws, regulations, or both that govern which diseases and conditions are reportable and specify the method and timing of reporting; thus there are some variations across states. Nevertheless, reporting of outbreaks is generally included in most states' disease reporting systems. The list of diseases for inclusion in national surveillance is established by the Council of State and Territorial Epidemiologists (CSTE) and the federal Centers for Disease Control and Prevention (CDC) and is updated yearly.[11] States then voluntarily report to the CDC cases of diseases that are on the "nationally notifiable" list.

In traditional passive public health surveillance, reports can originate from a variety of sources, including physicians, laboratories, hospitals, schools, childcare centers, vital records departments, and other facilities (**Figure 5-1**).[12] Cases are generally reported to state or local health departments with information such as diagnosis, name, age, gender, address, and date of onset. Reports may also include other information, such as laboratory results, treatment, occupation, setting of occurrence, and risk factors (**Figure 5-2** and **Figure 5-3**).[13,14] Case reports, without personal identifiers, are then transmitted weekly from states to the CDC for inclusion in national summary data published in *Morbidity and Mortality Weekly Report.*[15]

Information collected as part of the disease reporting system is compiled and evaluated at local, state, and federal levels. Outbreaks are often first identified at the local or state health department level. Multistate outbreaks can sometimes be detected at the federal level by identification of increases in routine surveillance reports to CDC, the Foodborne Disease Active Surveillance Network (FoodNet), or early detection systems such as PulseNet. FoodNet, a collaborative project among CDC, 10 state health departments, the U.S. Department of Agriculture (USDA), and the U.S. Food and Drug Administration (FDA), consists of active surveillance for foodborne diseases; surveys of laboratories, physicians, and the general population; and population-based epidemiologic studies. Personnel in state health departments contact local laboratories to obtain reports of selected foodborne infections diagnosed in residents of these areas.[16] PulseNet, whose activities are also coordinated by CDC, is a network of public health and food regulatory agency laboratories that perform molecular subtyping of foodborne bacteria; this information is submitted electronically to CDC and maintained in a standardized database. This national database allows for rapid comparison of molecular patterns.[17] Detection of outbreaks can also occur through specialized analytic routines for aberration detection or other systems that use early indicators such as "syndromic surveillance"[10,18] or surveillance for syndromes of diarrhea, rash, or respiratory symptoms.

The information collected as part of the surveillance network is made available for additional epidemiologic evaluation. These data represent years of continuous data collection and, therefore, can be used to examine disease trends in a community.

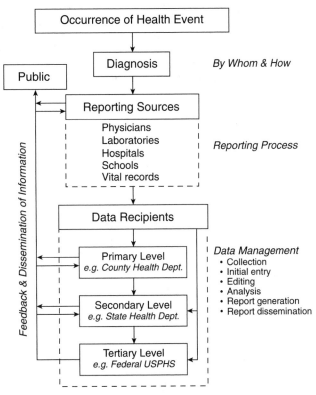

Figure 5-1 The major steps in a public health surveillance system. Reproduced from *Public Health Surveillance.* Halperin W and Baker E, eds., p. 30, © 1992, John Wiley & Sons.

However, these data are not collected primarily for the conduct of research or study. Rather, surveillance data are collected to detect disease, to describe cases found in a specific community, and to guide public health actions. Ideally, epidemiologic research data would be collected to address specific hypotheses and to produce generalizable knowledge. Surveillance data are collected according to those procedures that maximize consistency and minimize the barriers to reporting. For example, surveillance databases often include data collected by passive reporting and have only minimal information on cases. In contrast, more detailed data collection may be required for research purposes to examine specific hypotheses, such that employees may be dedicated to managing complex data collection systems. Because of these differences, surveillance data may be inadequate to answer some epidemiologic questions. Even so, surveillance data are an excellent source of information to establish baseline rates and detect outbreaks, to identify new problems or trends in a community, to guide public health actions, to evaluate programs, to assist health professionals in estimating the magnitude of a health problem, and to identify possible hypotheses that

can be explored by enhancing surveillance or by a research study.

Because outbreak epidemiology is concerned primarily with the control of disease, the sensitivity of the surveillance or reporting network is of paramount importance. If cases of disease are not reported, an outbreak may not be detected or may continue unabated.

OUTBREAK INVESTIGATION

Based on experience with outbreak investigations, a series of steps has been identified that can be used to guide any epidemiologic field investigation.[19–24] The outbreak epidemiologist is the "disease detective" of public health. Outbreak investigation is a systematic process of evaluating data to form hypotheses, and then collecting additional data to test the hypotheses. An understanding of the basic steps of outbreak epidemiology can guide the investigator in determining which types of data to collect and how to collect them; each outbreak is unique, however, so it is also important to be aware of how an outbreak

MARYLAND CONFIDENTIAL MORBIDITY REPORT (DHMH 1140)

(For use by physicians and other health care providers, but not laboratories. Laboratories should use forms DHMH 1281 & DHMH 4492.)

SEND TO YOUR LOCAL HEALTH DEPARTMENT

STATE DATA BASE NUMBER (Completed by Health Department)

NAME OF PATIENT – LAST   FIRST   M

DATE OF BIRTH MONTH DAY YEAR   **AGE**   **SEX** M ☐ F ☐

ETHNICITY (Select independently of RACE)
HISPANIC or LATINO: YES ☐   NO ☐   UNKNOWN ☐

TELEPHONE NUMBERS   Home: Workplace:

RACE (Select one or more. If multiracial, select all that apply)
American Indian/Alaskan Native ☐   Asian ☐   Black/African American ☐
Hawaiian/Pacific Islander ☐   White ☐   Unknown ☐
Other (Specify):

ADDRESS   UNIT#   CITY OR TOWN   STATE   ZIP CODE   COUNTY

OCCUPATION OR CONTACT WITH VULNERABLE PERSONS
(Check all that apply - include volunteers)
☐ HEALTH CARE WORKER (Include any PATIENT CARE, ELDER CARE, "AIDES," etc.)
☐ DAYCARE (Attendee or Worker)
☐ PARENT of a child in DAYCARE
☐ FOOD SERVICE WORKER
☐ NOT EMPLOYED
☐ OTHER (SPECIFY):

WORKPLACE, SCHOOL, CHILD CARE FACILITY, ETC. (Include Name, Address, ZIP Code)

DISEASE OR CONDITION
PATIENT HAS BEEN NOTIFIED OF THIS CONDITION YES ☐   NO ☐

DATE OF ONSET MONTH DAY YEAR   **ADMITTED** YES ☐ NO ☐   **DATE ADMITTED** MONTH DAY YEAR   **HOSPITAL**

CONDITION ACQUIRED IN MARYLAND YES ☐ NO ☐ UNKNOWN ☐
(IF NO, INTERSTATE ☐, or INTERNATIONAL ☐)   **SUSPECTED SOURCE OF INFECTION**

DIED YES ☐ NO ☐   **DATE DIED** MONTH DAY YEAR   **PREGNANT** YES ☐ NO ☐ UNKNOWN ☐ NOT APPLICABLE ☐
WEEKS PREGNANT _____ DUE DATE _____

LABORATORY TESTS - VIRAL HEPATITIS
POS NEG DATE
HAV Antibody Total ☐ ☐ ____
HAV Antibody IgM ☐ ☐ ____
HBV surface Antigen ☐ ☐ ____
HBV e Antigen ☐ ☐ ____
HBV core Antibody Total ☐ ☐ ____
HBV core Antibody IgM ☐ ☐ ____

LABORATORY TESTS - VIRAL HEPATITIS
POS NEG DATE
HBV surface Antibody ☐ ☐ ____
HBV Viral DNA ☐ ☐ ____
HCV Antibody ELISA ☐ ☐ ____
HCV ELISA Signal/Cut Off Ratio
HCV Antibody RIBA ☐ ☐ ____
HCV RNA (eg., by PCR) ☐ ☐ ____

LABORATORY TESTS - VIRAL HEPATITIS
HCV Viral Genotyping ____ DATE ____
ALT (SGPT) Level ____ DATE ____
ALT - Lab Normal Range: ____ to ____
AST (SGOT) Level ____ DATE ____
AST - Lab Normal Range: ____ to ____
NAME of LAB: ____

ADDITIONAL LAB RESULTS
(SPECIMEN - TEST - RESULT - DATE - NAME of LAB)
(Please attach copies of lab reports whenever possible.)

PERTINENT CLINICAL INFORMATION + OTHER COMMENTS

HUMAN IMMUNODEFICIENCY VIRUS (HIV) and ACQUIRED IMMUNODEFICIENCY SYNDROME (AIDS) – ADDITIONAL CASE INFORMATION

CONDITIONS	HIV LAB TESTS	DATE	RESULT
WEIGHT LOSS OR DIARRHEA ☐	CD4+ T-cells < 200 per microliter or < 14%		
SECONDARY INFECTIONS (PCP, TB, etc.) ☐	ELISA		
PERINATAL EXPOSURE OF NEWBORN ☐	WESTERN BLOT		
OTHER CONDITIONS ATTRIBUTED TO HIV INFECTION ☐ (SPECIFY):	OTHER (SPECIFY):		

PHYSICIAN REQUESTS LOCAL HEALTH DEPARTMENT TO ASSIST WITH: NOTIFICATION TO PATIENT YES ☐   NO ☐   PARTNER SERVICES YES ☐   NO ☐

SEXUALLY TRANSMITTED INFECTION (STI) – ADDITIONAL CASE INFORMATION

SYPHILIS: PRIMARY ☐   SECONDARY ☐   EARLY LATENT (LESS THAN 1 YR) ☐   CONGENITAL ☐   OTHER STAGE ☐ (SPECIFY):
GONORRHEA: CERVICAL ☐   URETHRAL ☐   RECTAL ☐   PHARYNGEAL ☐   OPHTHALMIA NEONATORUM ☐   PID ☐   OTHER ☐ (SPECIFY):
CHLAMYDIA: CERVICAL ☐   URETHRAL ☐   RECTAL ☐   PHARYNGEAL ☐   PID ☐   OTHER ☐ (SPECIFY):
OTHER STI (Specify):

STI LABORATORY CONFIRMATION AND TREATMENT

| Specify STI Lab Test (e.g., RPR Titer, FTA – TPPA, Darkfield, Smear, Culture, NAAT, EIA, VDRL - CSF) | | | STI Treatment Given ☐ (Specify date – drug – dosage below) | | No Treatment Given ☐ |
DATE	TEST	RESULT	DATE	DRUG	DOSAGE

TUBERCULOSIS (Suspect or Confirmed) – ADDITIONAL CASE INFORMATION

MAJOR SITE: PULMONARY ☐   EXTRAPULMONARY ☐   ATYPICAL ☐ (SPECIFY)   **ABNORMAL CHEST X-RAY:** ☐
COMMENTS:

REPORTED BY   ADDRESS   TELEPHONE NUMBER   DATE OF REPORT MONTH DAY YEAR
☐ Check here if completed by the Health Department

NOTES: Your local health department may contact you following this initial report to request additional disease-specific information.
To print blank report forms or get more information about reporting, go to http://ideha.dhmh.maryland.gov/SitePages/what-to-report.aspx.

DHMH 1140   REVISED JANUARY 26, 2012

Figure 5-2 Confidential Morbidity Report form for transmission to a state or local health department. Reproduced from the Maryland Department of Health & Mental Hygiene (2012). Maryland Confidential Morbidity Report (DHMH 1140). http://ideha.dhmh.maryland.gov/IDEHASharedDocuments/what-to-report/DHMH1140.pdf. Revised January 26, 2012. Accessed January 4, 2013.

under current investigation differs from previous outbreaks.

Most commonly, outbreak investigations, including laboratory support, occur at the local or state public health level. Generally, the CDC is consulted in multistate outbreaks or in outbreaks of diseases that require resources or skills that state and local agencies are unable to provide. The laboratory and epidemiologic capabilities of the CDC are enlisted to assist with domestic and international disease outbreaks of unusual etiology or of major public health significance.

Local and state health departments decide to conduct an outbreak investigation based on health regulations and/or policies and on the professional judgment of staff regarding the outbreak and its

Gastroenteritis Case Report Form
Maryland Department of Health & Mental Hygiene
Epidemiology & Disease Control Program

Source of Case Report ______
Date of Case Report ______

Disease ☐ Campylobacteriosis ☐ Shigellosis ☐ Unknown ☐ Salmonellosis ☐ Other ______

Status ☐ Sporadic Case ☐ Outbreak

Patient Data

Name Last First

Telephone Home Work

Address Street County City State Zip

Age | Date of Birth / /

Race ☐ White ☐ Hispanic ☐ Other ☐ Black ☐ Asian ☐ Unknown

Occupation, Student, or Situation

Name of Employer, School or Day Care

Clinical and Lab Data

Data of Onset ___/___/___ Time ______ am or pm

☐ Diarrhea ☐ Bloody Stool ☐ Cramps
☐ Fever ☐ Vomiting ☐ Other ______

Duration of Symptoms ____ days
Outcome ☐ Survived ☐ Died
Hospitalized ☐ Yes ☐ No
Name of Hospital
Date Admitted / / Date Discharged / /
Date of Death / /
Name of Lab confirming diagnosis

Was the culture of specimen sent to the State Lab for serotyping or confirmation? ☐ Yes ☐ No ☐ Unknown

Agent (Check one)
☐ Campylobacter Serotype ______
☐ Giardia
☐ Salmonella Group ___ Serotype ______
☐ Shigella Serotype ______
☐ Other ______

Type of Specimen ☐ Bacterial ☐ Viral ☐ Ova and Parasite ☐ Serological

Source of Specimen ☐ Stool ☐ Urine ☐ Blood ☐ Other ______

Travel

Did patient travel to another state or country in the 2 weeks prior to symptom's onset? ☐ Yes ☐ No

Where ______ When ______

Animal Contact

Did patient have contact with the following animals [ ] hours/days* prior to symptom's onset?

☐ Dogs ☐ Parakeets ☐ Cows
☐ Cats ☐ Chickens ☐ Turtles
☐ Ducks ☐ Other ______

Food History

Did patient eat any of the following within [ ] hours/days* prior to onset of illness?

	Yes	No	Unknown
1. Eggs			
a. Cooked eggs: scrambled, hard fried, other ____	☐	☐	☐
b. Undercooked eggs: poached, soft, scrambled, sunny side up, other ____	☐	☐	☐
c. Raw eggs: egg nog, Caesar salad, hollandaise sauce, meringue, bearnaise, other ____	☐	☐	☐
2. Raw or undercooked poultry (chicken, turkey)	☐	☐	☐
3. Raw or undercooked red meat	☐	☐	☐
4. Raw (unpasteurized) milk	☐	☐	☐
5. Homemade/unpasteurized cheese	☐	☐	☐
6. Raw or undercooked fish/shellfish	☐	☐	☐

Other Exposure

Within [ ] hours/days* prior to onset of symptom(s) did patient:

	Yes	No	Unknown
1. Handle raw poultry?	☐	☐	☐
2. Have exposure to a day care or nursery?	☐	☐	☐
3. Have household member or sexual partner with similar symptoms?	☐	☐	☐
4. Hike, camp, fish, swim?	☐	☐	☐
5. Drink from a spring, stream or lake?	☐	☐	☐
6. Take antibiotics in month prior to onset of illness?	☐	☐	☐

Disposition

Work or school restrictions? ☐ Yes ☐ No
Is yes, specify ______
Was patient advised of appropriate precautions? ☐ Yes ☐ No
Is yes, how?
☐ Telephone ☐ Fact Sheet ☐ In Person ☐ In Writing

DHMH 4458 (June 1992)

Figure 5-3 Maryland Gastroenteritis Case Report Form. Reproduced from the Maryland Department of Health & Mental Hygiene, Epidemiology & Disease Control Program (2003). Gastroenteritis Case Report Form. http://ideha.dhmh.maryland.gov/IDEHASharedDocuments/case_reports/gastroenteritis.pdf. Revised January 2003. Accessed January 4, 2013.

(*Continued*)

Food History for Food-borne Diseases. List the foods eaten within [   ] hours/days* prior to onset:

[12 hours]   [24 hours]   [48 hours]   [72 hours]

Breakfast _____

_____

_____

Lunch _____

_____

_____

Dinner _____

_____

_____

_____

Household Members. List household contacts, even if asymptomatic; give onset if symptomatic:

Name	Age	Relationship to Case	Symptoms Y/N?	Onset of Symptoms	lab Testing (Date Collected, Result)	Occupation/Employer School/Grade, Day Care

Summary of Investigation - action taken on patients and contacts - outcome:

_____

_____

_____

_____

_____

_____

_____

_____

Name of person completing form   Date of Interview

* Use the incubation period which applies to the agent/disease under investigation: e.g., bacillus cereus (1–24 hours), Campylobacter (1–10 days), Clostridium (6–24 hours), E. coli (9–60 hours), Giardia (5–25 days), Listeria (3–70 days), Salmonella (6–72 hours), Shigella (12–96 hours), Staphylococcus (30 min.–7 hours), Typhoid fever (1–3 weeks), Vibrio (4–96 hours), Viral agent (24–72 hours).

Figure 5-3 (*Continued*)

public health impact or implications. Regardless of the etiologic agent, the setting in which the disease may have been transmitted, or the population at risk, it is possible to summarize the basic steps and goals of the investigation. The primary motivation of any outbreak investigation is to control the spread of disease within the initial population at risk or to prevent the spread to additional populations. Many outbreaks occur in defined populations, groups, or settings, such as a foodborne outbreak at a wedding banquet or a potluck dinner. Fortunately, these outbreaks generally have a single exposure, where the contaminated vehicle may have been consumed or discarded before the first cases are apparent and no more people are at risk. In other outbreaks, where transmission may be ongoing, such as legionellosis among hospitalized patients or disease caused by commercial products or fruits and vegetables, the epidemiologic investigation must be initiated quickly and control measures implemented to halt further transmission. Prevention of disease requires that the investigation identify the etiologic agent, its source,

Prepare and plan for the investigation
Confirm the existence of an outbreak—verify
    the diagnosis
Identify and count cases and exposed persons
    Select a case definition
    Identify cases, population at risk, and
        controls
Choose a study design
Collect risk information
Tabulate the data in terms of time, place, and
    person
Collect specimens for laboratory analysis
Conduct an environmental investigation
Institute control measures
Formulate and test hypotheses
Conduct additional systematic studies
Communicate the findings

Figure 5-4 Steps in an outbreak investigation. Modified from the Centers for Disease Control and Prevention (2006). Principles of Epidemiology in Public Health Practice: An Introduction to Applied Epidemiology and Biostatistics, 3rd edition. http://www.cdc.gov/osels/scientific_edu/SS1978/SS1978.pdf. Updated May 2012. Accessed January 10, 2013.

the mode of transmission, and the vehicle. The information learned during the course of investigation is important in preventing and controlling outbreaks of the same disease in the future and may be useful in linking sporadic cases to the same source.

The steps for conducting an outbreak investigation are outlined in **Figure 5-4**.[24] A hallmark of outbreak epidemiology is that these steps do not necessarily proceed in a specified sequence. In actuality, several steps in the investigation usually occur simultaneously. These steps are tailored to the situation and depend on factors such as the urgency of implementing control measures; the availability of staff, resources, and time; and the difficulty of obtaining the data. Multiple persons may perform activities concurrently. Action and reaction proceed based on new and cumulative information. Because implementation of control measures is central to the goal of any outbreak investigation, measures to control the spread of disease must be implemented early in the investigation and may be altered as data are collected and analyzed.

Prepare and Plan for the Investigation

Preparing for the outbreak investigation and planning the investigation are critical to a successful outcome. It is imperative to identify the investigation team members, to assign responsibilities, to begin the investigation as soon as possible, and to conduct progress meetings at regular intervals. The multidisciplinary investigative team may include epidemiologists, healthcare professionals, laboratorians, and sanitarians, among others. Often, the personnel who initiate an outbreak investigation are predetermined: health departments, hospitals, schools, or nursing homes commonly have personnel responsible for disease control who are dedicated to outbreak activities when the need arises. For many small-scale epidemiologic investigations, the initial outbreak "team" will be a single epidemiologist or other professional who will assess the situation and determine what needs to be done. As the investigation proceeds, personnel may need to be added or reassigned to carry out the investigation.

Successful investigations require effective communication at all levels of authority. Summaries or specific findings need to be shared on an ongoing basis (as appropriate and as allowed by confidentiality laws) with critical individuals and parties, such as facilities or businesses where the outbreak occurred, colleagues, healthcare providers, other regulatory agencies, the media, and the public. In the United States, communication among the local health department, state health department, and federal agencies such as the CDC, the FDA, and the USDA is routine in multijurisdictional outbreaks or outbreaks of national importance, and helps ensure that roles and responsibilities are clear from the outset of the investigation onward.

Confirm the Existence of an Outbreak: Verify the Diagnosis

An early step of any outbreak investigation is to confirm the existence of an outbreak. Important questions to ask include the following: Are there cases in excess of the expected baseline rate for that disease and setting? Is the reported case actually a case of the disease or a misdiagnosis? Do all (or most) of the "suspect cases" have the same infection or similar manifestations?

For some diseases, a single case is sufficient to warrant an outbreak investigation. For example, anthrax, human rabies, foodborne botulism, polio, and bubonic plague are very rare in the United States and are serious diseases; thus an investigation would be initiated with a single suspected case. This is illustrated by the single case of anthrax reported in October 2001[25]; the report initiated the full-scale investigation of the intentional release of anthrax in multiple locations across the eastern United States. Investigators must also be aware of the background level of disease in a population under surveillance.

For example, malaria infection acquired in the United States would be treated quite differently than a case of malaria acquired in sub-Saharan Africa. A review of existing state, local, or facility baseline rates of disease can be compared with the current case number. It is important to take into account the population in which the cases are occurring. Several cases of diarrhea in a nursing home may be a common occurrence, whereas the same number would represent an outbreak if they occurred clustered in time among healthy adults after a picnic. When trying to determine whether more cases of an illness are occurring than would be expected, it is also important to consider seasonal variations in disease rates. Influenza outbreaks can be expected to occur in the winter, whereas bacterial enteric diseases are more common in the summer.

As an outbreak investigation is initiated, it is important that the diagnosis be confirmed—and that the specificity of the case definition is good. This involves a review of available clinical and laboratory findings that support the diagnosis and often entails obtaining more clinical or laboratory information than is initially reported. For example, before deciding that *Neisseria meningitidis* is the organism causing meningitis, the investigator must confirm that the specimen was taken from a sterile body site (e.g., blood or cerebrospinal fluid), rather than from a body site where the organism might be a part of the normal flora (e.g., throat). Several cases of rash illness in a school may signal a chickenpox (varicella) outbreak if the diagnosis is confirmed, or they may simply represent a cluster in time of rashes of different etiologies and, therefore, not an outbreak.

Identify and Count Cases and Exposed Persons; Select a Case Definition

A case definition is needed to identify and count cases in a consistent way so as to determine who may be affected by the outbreak. Components of the case definition may include information about time and place of exposure, laboratory findings, and clinical symptoms. Case definitions should be applied consistently and investigators should be clear and specific about any component of a case definition. However, it is also important to appreciate that case definitions might be refined or different case definitions used at different points in an investigation.

In general during an outbreak investigation, the initial case definitions used are broader rather than narrow. For example, an early definition in a foodborne outbreak might take the following form: "A case of illness is defined as any diarrhea, vomiting, abdominal cramps, headache, or fever that developed after attending the implicated event." This broad definition neither assumes that all cases will have the same symptoms, nor does it make any assumptions about the risk factors for illness (e.g., those who ate a particular food or had contact with specific people). This initial case definition has greater emphasis on sensitivity than on specificity. As additional information is gathered about the cases, the nature of exposure, and the symptoms, the case definition can be refined as appropriate to improve the specificity. A subsequent case definition may state: "A case of illness is defined as diarrhea or vomiting with onset within 96 hours of consuming food served at the implicated meal." This refined definition is more specific and will serve to exclude unrelated cases of gastroenteritis or other illnesses, so that the etiologic exposure is more reliably identified.

In outbreak investigations, as in routine surveillance, cases of disease are commonly separated into those that are *confirmed* and those that are *probable*. Confirmed cases are generally those with laboratory findings for the organism (such as a positive culture or antigen test, antibody titer rise, or a positive polymerase chain reaction [PCR]), and probable cases are those who have certain symptoms meeting a clinical case definition but without laboratory confirmation.[26] For some diseases (e.g., pertussis), a case is considered confirmed if a compatible clinical illness is present and the case is epidemiologically linked to a laboratory-confirmed case.

Frequently, laboratory confirmation is complicated by a number of factors: People may test positive for the organism for only a short time around the acute phase of illness; some pathogens produce toxins for which there is no laboratory test; the organism may be shed only transiently or intermittently; antibody tests may be difficult to interpret if individuals have been exposed to the pathogen in the past; persons with mild disease may not seek medical attention and, therefore, will not have laboratory tests completed; and persons may be treated at different medical facilities with different laboratory procedures. If laboratory confirmation is important and the outbreak is identified rapidly enough, the outbreak investigation team may want to collect samples promptly or obtain multiple specimens to confirm the initial cases so as to establish the agent responsible for the outbreak. However, this commitment of resources may not be necessary to confirm every case during the investigation. If the case definition can be made sufficiently specific without the use of laboratory tests, collecting and testing specimens may simply represent an additional burden and expense to the exposed population and the investigation team.

Identify Cases, Population at Risk, and Controls

During the outbreak investigation, the investigator should seek to identify additional cases not known or reported at the time of the initial report. Case-finding techniques used to enhance surveillance for additional cases include reviewing existing surveillance data (e.g., morbidity reports received by a health department or monthly summaries of illness) for other cases of the same illness; reviewing outbreak–complaint logs kept by a local health department; reviewing past laboratory data; surveying hospitals, emergency rooms, or physicians; and obtaining credit card receipts or shopper card information. In certain outbreaks, such as those occurring in a restaurant where there is no list of attendees, a useful technique for finding additional cases and controls is questioning known cases to identify others who were in attendance. (See the section on case-control studies.) In some situations, other techniques might be appropriate, such as the use of the Internet, social media, or other media notices.

The investigator should identify the population at risk or the exposed group in which to conduct expanded surveillance for cases. The exposed group or cohort will vary depending on the setting, and it may not always be possible to identify or enumerate the entire population at risk. Examples of exposed groups include a group of persons who attended a wedding banquet; all people who dined in a food establishment on one particular day; children who attend a daycare center, their household members, and the employees of the center; and all persons who were exposed to an implicated manufactured lot or shipment of a commercial product. The exposed population, therefore, can range from as few as one person to as many as thousands of individuals in multiple locations. Records maintained by the establishments involved can facilitate identification of persons at risk. Party invitation lists, guest books, credit card receipts, and customer lists are often available and are very helpful to investigators. Of course, individuals located by release of their names from credit card receipts may be concerned about how the investigators got their names and may fear credit card theft! Explaining the purpose of the investigation and how information will be handled may be vital to securing their cooperation in the investigation. State and federal public information laws vary in terms of which information is to be held confidential in outbreak situations.

Choose a Study Design

During an outbreak investigation, the study design is chosen based on factors such as the size and availability of the exposed population, the speed with which results are needed, and the available resources. The characteristics of the exposed population are generally determined after interviewing a few of the initial cases. Exposed populations fall into four broad categories: small enumerable exposed groups, large enumerable exposed groups, large or small groups where the exposure situation can be pinpointed but where the exposed population cannot be enumerated, and cases of disease where the exposed population is not known or identifiable. The study design that is chosen will then dictate the appropriate analysis and hypothesis testing, as discussed next.

Cohort Studies

Cohort studies, which include persons based on their exposure status, are appropriate when it is possible to enumerate or assemble a list of persons potentially exposed and to contact the people in a timely manner. Outbreaks that are suspected to have occurred at a specific event, such as a party, or in a specific place, such as a worksite or cruise ship, are often suited to cohort investigations. If the group is small enough, a study can be designed to include all of the people in the exposed cohort. Alternatively, a selection (using a random number table or selecting a random starting point and then choosing, for example, every fourth name) can be made from a large enumerated exposed population. The demographic statistics, attack rates, and relative risks are calculated when data are collected on the cohort or on a randomly selected fraction of the cohort. (See the section on formulating and testing hypotheses.)

Case-Control Studies

For outbreaks associated with large events (such as a convention or a state fair), or for community-wide outbreaks or uncommon diseases reported from a population, especially where the potential exposure is unknown, it may not be possible or economically feasible to obtain or assemble a list of all those exposed or to interview all people in the cohort or exposed population. Such outbreak investigations lend themselves to studies that include all or a selected group of cases, and a selected group of not-ill individuals for comparison. A full description of the types of case-control studies, their nomenclature, and their analyses can be found in several references.[27–29]

When a list of a large cohort of potentially exposed people is available (i.e., the cohort can be enumerated) but a cohort study is not desirable or feasible, information on identified cases can be included and compared with information from a random sample of not-ill persons chosen from the baseline cohort, such as the list of those exposed (called a case-control study within a specific cohort, a case cohort study,[29] or a cumulative ["epidemic"] case-control study[28]). The number of not-ill people for comparison and the manner in which the not-ill participants are chosen differentiate these studies from traditional case-control studies. Such investigations maximize the number of cases included, and include a manageable number of not-ill people for comparison. The analysis of data is based on odds ratios, but attack rates and relative risks can also be calculated if the study group is a known fraction of the total cases and not-ill people.

Another common outbreak situation arises when cases are occurring within a known exposed population (e.g., attendees at a state fair or a specific restaurant) but the exposed population cannot be enumerated and there is no list of attendees from which to identify cases and controls. In this situation, it is important to secure data on a representative sample of people who were potentially exposed. Cases can be identified from reports of illness. Both cases and controls can be identified from the exposed group through friends of cases or through media reports, credit card receipts, lists of hospital patients, and so on. Publicizing details of the outbreak through a press release in local print or on television and radio may be necessary to secure a sufficient number of not-ill participants. People who know someone who became ill are more likely to know about the outbreak investigation and volunteer to participate. The volunteers, however, may share characteristics with those who are cases and may not represent all of those who attended the event. Small groups may be identified who attended a larger event, such as a church group who attended a national convention or a state fair, and the group members may serve as a source of investigation participants. The use of such identified groups can aid recruitment because they may have a list of participants for inclusion. For these types of outbreaks, analysis of the data would necessarily proceed using odds ratios as in a case-control study because data are not available for either the entire cohort or a known fraction of the group of exposed persons.

For situations in which an exposed cohort or population is not known or identifiable, a case-control study design is appropriate to determine risk factors for disease. Examples of this situation include increases in the number of community-wide cases of an unusual *Salmonella* serotype, and the need to identify risk factors for sporadic cases of *Campylobacter* infection. In these situations, cases are selected based on their disease status rather than their exposure status. All known cases are included in the study along with a group of controls; the controls are selected, for example, by random digit dialing or from friends or neighbors of cases. For increased statistical power, as many as four controls per case may be selected.

A further refinement of the case-control study is the matched case-control design. In these studies, controls are matched to cases with respect to potentially confounding variables. In matched case-control studies, the effect of these matched variables is removed from the analysis so that the effect of other factors can be more readily observed. For example, to determine the risk factors for a cluster of cases of a rare *Salmonella* serotype, all known cases would be interviewed. Controls may be identified by randomly calling homes with incrementally higher or lower telephone numbers from the case's telephone number. If a household is found in which a member matches the case within a certain age grouping, that person is included as a control in the study and is interviewed.

Because outbreak investigations are primarily concerned with the prevention of the spread of disease, the speed at which case-control studies can be assembled makes them an attractive alternative to cohort studies. The case-control design is also efficient with respect to collection of data and the expense of conducting the study. The toxic shock syndrome epidemic of 1980 was alarming for the speed at which cases occurred and the severity of the illness.[30–32] Investigation was needed as rapidly as possible. Using a case-control study design, investigators assembled study populations using cases and selecting as controls their friends of the same sex. Controls were matched to cases within 3 years of age. Lives were saved because of the speed at which these investigations were completed and the subsequent speed at which health interventions were initiated (**Figure 5-5**).[33]

Collect Risk Information

As the case investigation continues, the investigator accumulates information about the affected population to answer questions regarding the outbreak's person, place, and time characteristics (also referred to as who, what, when, and where). As part of the investigation, the investigator may use a questionnaire or survey instrument to collect pertinent data (**Figure 5-6**). Questionnaires should be administered as soon as possible. The ability to recall one-time exposures after an event is poor, even in the best of circumstances, and will diminish rapidly with time.

Identified as a severe systemic illness in children, toxic-shock syndrome (TSS) burst on the national scene when cases suddenly appeared, first in Wisconsin and Minnesota and then nationwide, among young adult women during their menstrual periods. The disease was serious and caused substantial mortality. Recovery was complete among survivors; however, recurrences were common during a subsequent menses unless the *S. aureusvaginal* infection was effectively treated with antibiotics. Eventually, 941 cases were reported from every state in the United States. However, 247 (26%) of the cases occurred in Minnesota and Wisconsin.

In the interest of speed and because the number of cases was small, a case-control study design was chosen. To control for unknown confounders and to assemble a study population rapidly, the investigators chose to use friends of cases for the initial investigation. Controls were the same gender as the cases (female) and matched to cases within 3 years of age. In the initial investigations, conducted June 13–19, 1980, one control was matched to each case. These studies implicated tampons and hormonal contraception as risk factors for TSS during menstruation. However, women had been using tampons and hormonal contraception for years. Why an outbreak now? And why were the cases concentrated in Wisconsin and Minnesota? The epidemiologic team was aware that a new brand of tampons had been marketed in these states, and they suspected that these super-absorbent tampons might be associated with the outbreak. Although a few brands of tampons were common among women with TSS, these tampon brands were found to be popular with women in general (as measured by market share). A third case control outbreak investigation was conducted September 5–8, 1980. In this study, cases were matched to three age- and gender-matched controls. To reduce misclassification bias, participants were asked to get any boxes of tampons they had in the house and to read the brand information to the telephone interviewer. In this investigation, one brand of super-absorbent tampons was identified and subsequently recalled on September 22, 1980. The incidence of TSS declined dramatically and fell even further when polyacrylate tampons (super-absorbent tampons) were withdrawn altogether, although some cases are still reported.

Figure 5-5 Investigation of toxic shock syndrome. Reproduced from the Centers for Disease Control (1982). Epidemiologic notes and reports of Toxic-shock syndrome, United States, 1970–1982. *MMWR*. 31:201–204.

Initially, questionnaires may need to be broad and to capture as much information as possible on suspected exposures, such as in widely distributed or geographically clustered outbreaks like the large cryptosporidiosis outbreak in Milwaukee.[34]

The questionnaire instrument collects pertinent information about the exposed population or the cases and controls, and about the situation under investigation. Questionnaires usually include variables sufficient to define cases and to identify exposures. Each survey must be tailored to the outbreak and the possible routes of exposure for the agent involved. Demographic information allows the investigator to answer the *who* question and usually includes personal identifiers, such as the person's name, home address, telephone number, age, gender, race/ethnicity, occupation/school, and work address.

These variables are used to characterize both the ill and well populations. Clinical information helps the investigator with the *what* and *when* questions and includes symptoms of illness, date and time of onset and length of symptoms, specimen collection dates and results, severity of illness, medical care sought, and outcome information, such as hospitalization or death. These variables allow the characterization of identified cases and assist with hypothesis generation. Exposure information helps the investigator to answer the *where* and *when* questions and details the suspected event or situation that put the individuals at risk. The questionnaire should consider exposures other than the most obvious exposure. For example, if ill individuals all attended a wedding, they should be asked not only about the wedding but also about events related to the wedding, such as a common hotel swimming pool exposure, or attendance at other events, such as the rehearsal dinner.

Errors in recall can result in "baseline noise" or misclassification bias. Misclassification bias occurs when persons are randomly incorrectly classified with respect to exposure or illness. Misclassification bias results in the measured risk of disease for

The Health Department is investigating some reports of illness that occurred after the _____ (event) _____ on __ day, _____.
It is important that anyone who attended fill out a questionnaire, even if you did not get sick.

Last name _____ First name _____ Age _____
Home phone number: (__ __ __) __ __ __ -__ __ __ __   Sex: M F (circle one)
Did you eat at this event?   Yes   No

Please circle YES for any food item you ate at the event and circle NO for each item that you did not eat. **All items should be marked.**

Ate item?   Ate item?

Food 1 .... Yes   No   Food 7 .... Yes   No
Food 2 .... Yes   No   Food 8 .... Yes   No
Food 3 .... Yes   No   Food 9 .... Yes   No
Food 4 .... Yes   No   Food 10 .... Yes   No
Food 5 .... Yes   No   Food 11 .... Yes   No
Food 6 .... Yes   No   Food 12 .... Yes   No

Did you have any drinks on ice?   Yes   No
Did you have any soft drinks on ice?   Yes   No
Did you have any alcoholic drinks on ice?   Yes   No   (Number_____)
Did you have any non-iced alcoholic drinks?   Yes   No   (Number_____)

Was anyone in your household ill with diarrhea or vomiting in the week preceding the event?
Yes   No   (If yes, Who? & When?_____)

Have you become ill **since** attending the event?   Yes   No

If yes, please circle   YES   or   NO   for **each** of the following symptoms:

Diarrhea   Yes   No   If yes, total number of stools on worst day ____
                                     Was there any blood in your stool? Yes   No
Stomach cramps   Yes   No
Nausea   Yes   No
Vomiting   Yes   No
Fever   Yes   No   If yes, what was your highest temperature?_____
Headache   Yes   No
Body aches   Yes   No
Chills   Yes   No

Date illness began: _____   Time illness began: ___:___ AM? or PM? (circle answer)

Still having symptoms?   Yes   No
   (If no, symptoms ended: Date: ___ Time: ___:___ AM? or PM?)
Did you take any medicines for this illness?   Yes   No   If yes, what medicines? _____
Did you go to your doctor or an emergency room for this illness?   Yes   No
   If yes, did they collect specimens?   Yes   No   If yes, name of doctor: _____
Were you admitted to the hospital for this illness?   Yes   No   If yes, name of hospital:_____

Figure 5-6 Sample questionnaire for a foodborne illness outbreak

persons exposed being lower than the actual risk. As a consequence, a study could underestimate or miss a significant exposure. **Figure 5-7** shows an example of how a 20% misclassification of exposure among all attendees at a dinner underestimates the true relative risk by half. One technique used to aid respondents is to ask directed questions of what they "usually" would eat. Using these questions in combination with more traditional food survey questions may help to reduce misclassification bias. For example: "If given a choice between chicken salad and roast beef, which would you usually take?" In addition to improving the quality of data collected, timely collection of data allows for a faster public health response, such as closure of a facility or a product recall or embargo.

Ate Birthday Cake	Ill	Not Ill	Attack Rate	Relative Risk
Yes	30	30	30/60 = 50%	50%/10% = 5.0
No	15	135	15/150 = 10%	

Now, assume that, on the questionnaire, 20% of all attendees made an error in whether or not they ate birthday cake. The table below shows the resulting calculation with the relative risk underestimated at 2.5.

Ate Birthday Cake	Ill	Not Ill	Attack Rate	Relative Risk
Yes	30 − 6 + 3* = 27	30 − 6 + 27 = 51	27/78 = 34.6%	34.6%/13.6% = 2.5
No	15 − 3 + 6 = 18	135 − 27 + 6 = 114	18/132 = 13.6%	

*Note: 30 people ate birthday cake, minus 20% (or 6) who make an error and say they did not eat cake, plus 20% of the 15 (or 3) people who did not eat cake but in error say that they did.

Figure 5-7 Effect of misclassification on a relative risk calculation

The Tennessee Department of Health and Environment conducted a planned study to determine the degree of misclassification of food consumption after a luncheon.[35] By comparing videotapes of the luncheon to participants' answers on a subsequent food survey, investigators found that 32 attendees failed to report 58 food items actually selected and reported selecting 24 items not actually chosen, or a total of 82 errors. Only 12.5% of participants made no errors.

Figure 5-7 shows the true exposures to birthday cake and true illness in a cohort of 210 people who attended a banquet: 50% of those who ate cake became ill, compared with only 10% of those who did not eat the cake. The true relative risk of illness is 5.0, or "Those who ate birthday cake were five times as likely to become ill, compared with those who did not eat cake."

The design of the survey instrument is determined by how much the investigative team already knows. In cases where some of the epidemiologic questions have been answered, the questionnaire can be more specific. Questions can be in a closed format with "yes" or "no" answers or they can be quantitative (e.g., maximum number of stools per day or amount of food consumed). This assures consistency in response and facilitates analysis of the data. In cases where less is known, investigators must apply an open survey instrument to collect any information that may be of use. In such instances, the initial interview or survey instrument should include open-ended questions to encourage people to recall how, where, and over which period they may have been exposed. The questionnaire must be flexible enough to take into account the variable incubation periods for different diseases. For example, two diseases that might initially be reported

as diarrheal diseases, salmonellosis and giardiasis, have incubation periods of 1–3 days and 7–10 days, respectively. Until the agent is known through laboratory results, the questionnaire would need to be broad enough to cover exposures during both periods of risk. The epidemiologist must evaluate all the completed questionnaires to see whether any common links can be found. This sort of evaluation requires knowledge about the clinical syndrome, incubation period, duration, possible etiologies, and possible routes of transmission. This detailed initial process may be conducted even verbally, with only a few participants, so as to define the outbreak better. Once the questionnaire can be made more specific, a new questionnaire without open-ended questions may be administered to a larger group of participants to complete the investigation.

As noted, more than one questionnaire may be used during an investigation to capture the necessary information. The initial questionnaire may not be specific enough to answer all of the epidemiologic questions of interest, such as the qualitative and quantitative details of exposure. Furthermore, different populations affected by the epidemic may have different roles in its transmission. For example, a survey of patrons of a food establishment might be administered to the exposed group to find cases and to record clinical and risk information. A different questionnaire would be administered to food service workers that would collect information on illnesses prior to the event, food preparation and handling, hygiene practices, food intake at the event, and any illnesses after the event. Similarly, in a hospital nursery outbreak, the questionnaires completed on newborn cases and controls would be very different from the questionnaires for hospital personnel.

Tabulate and Orient the Data in Terms of Time, Place, and Person

The organization of data is critical to the timely and successful analysis of the outbreak data. A useful tool to organize data is the line listing. An example of a line listing is provided in **Figure 5-8**. Using a spreadsheet-style format, key variables on each ill person are listed, either on paper or in a computerized form. Information on well persons can also be included. A line listing allows the investigator to visualize and summarize pertinent variables quickly, including the total number of cases, the number of individuals with specific symptoms, their ages, gender, hospitalization, date and time of onset, exposures, and rates of

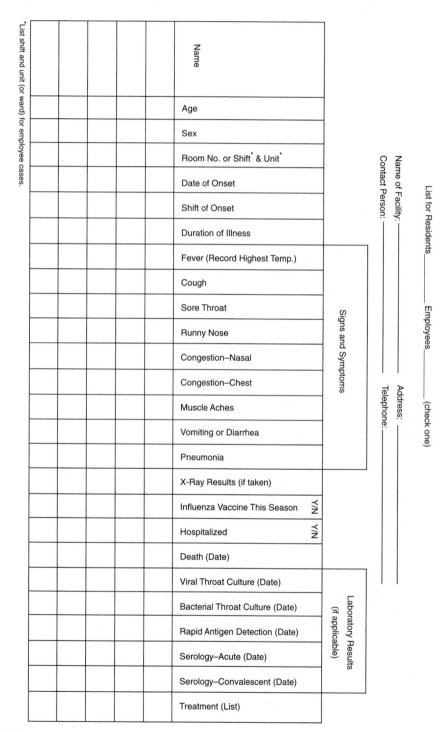

Figure 5-8 Line listing for respiratory illness outbreaks

illness. Another traditional method for organizing outbreak data is to use cards, where each person's characteristics are recorded on a single index card. Sorting the cards in different ways allows investigators to determine risk factors for cases.

Obviously, card and paper methods were devised prior to the advent of computers, and any of the spreadsheet or database programs available today can be employed for data management and analysis. The CDC has developed the EpiInfo computer software program, in which questionnaires can be created, data entered and analyzed, and line listings produced. This program is currently in worldwide use because it is free, is easy to use, has modest computer requirements, is designed specifically for surveillance systems and outbreak epidemiology, and is sufficiently powerful for most investigations. Information on EpiInfo can be obtained from the CDC.[36]

Visual representations of data can be helpful in understanding an epidemic. Spot maps of cases by residence, site of care, or location in a facility can help explain the occurrence of cases, for example. More complex methods of combining outbreak data with other sources of data are explained in the chapter on geographical information systems (GIS).

Graphs, such as an epidemic curve, or epi-curve, provide a visual summary of data (**Figure 5-9**). The epidemic curve depicts the frequency of cases over time by plotting the number of cases by date or time of onset. This provides information regarding the nature and time course of the outbreak. The epi-curve can allow an estimate of the incubation time of the infection, which may help in the identification of the organism. The time from the presumed exposure to the peak of the epidemic curve is the hypothesized median incubation time. The epi-curve can also give an indication of whether transmission is continuing or has ended. This information is vital to knowing whether control measures may be needed because the current outbreak is continuing and whether control measures are containing the outbreak.

Epidemics in which the number of cases rises abruptly and falls again in a log linear fashion are possible *point source epidemics*: the population at risk was exposed at one point in time. In this scenario, cases occur suddenly after the minimum incubation time and continue for a brief period of time related to the variability in the incubation time in infected individuals. Unless there is secondary spread of the pathogen to others not exposed originally, the epidemic

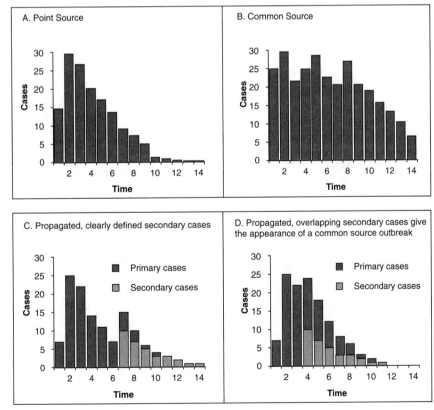

Figure 5-9 Examples of epidemic curves illustrating that the shape of the curve give clues to the mode of transmission and incubation period

ends. In contrast, a *common source epidemic* occurs in situations where there is continued exposure of individuals. On the epi-curve for this scenario, cases rise suddenly after the minimum incubation time but do not disappear completely because more individuals continue to be exposed to the source. The epi-curve for a *propagated outbreak* will show an increase in cases after exposure, then a fall in the number of cases after the epidemic has exhausted those susceptible from the initial exposure. Later, a second increase in cases occurs one incubation period after the peak of the first cases, due to secondary cases infected by person-to-person spread. Because an incubation period may be shorter than the rate at which case rates decline after the initial exposure, propagated outbreaks and common source outbreaks can be difficult to distinguish on the basis of their epi-curves alone.

Perform Laboratory Analysis

The laboratory investigation consists of collecting and testing appropriate specimens. To identify the etiologic agent, the collection of laboratory specimens needs to be appropriately timed. Examples of specimens include food and water samples, other environmental samples (e.g., air settling plates), and clinical specimens (e.g., stool, blood, sputum, or wound specimens) from cases and controls. Hypotheses about the suspected agent and source should guide the laboratory tests that are performed. Further description of organisms through speciation and other specialized laboratory testing, such as pulsed field gel electrophoresis (PFGE),[37] plasmid analysis,[38] polymerase chain reaction (PCR),[39–41] restriction fragment length polymorphism (RFLP) analysis, or multiple loci variable number of tandem repeats analysis (MLVA),[42] is useful to link cases with each other and with the hypothesized source(s). For example, to confirm the source in a legionellosis investigation, it is important to obtain an isolate of *Legionella* from the patient and from the epidemiologically implicated water source to determine whether the isolates are identical.

Conduct an Environmental Investigation

An assessment of the environment where the exposure occurred should be performed when appropriate. The environmental investigation assists in answering the *how* and *why* questions. This includes an inspection of the facility, a review of practices and procedures for the operation, and an assessment of employee illness. Staff members (including paid employees and volunteers) at facilities such as daycare centers, restaurants, and healthcare facilities may play a key role in outbreaks and may be either the

source of the problem or cases in the outbreak. Their evaluation as potential sources and cases, as well as the information they provide in the environmental investigation, may be critical.

The facility assessment may include an inspection by an environmental specialist or other investigator to review procedures and compliance with existing regulations and to identify breakdown of preventive measures. Timely inspection of facilities is of utmost importance to the control of an outbreak. When violations are noted, corrective actions are recommended and compliance monitored. In a foodborne outbreak, an inspection should focus on the kitchen and food preparation areas, whereas in a legionellosis outbreak, inspection should focus on water sources, such as the cooling tower, heating and ventilation systems, potable hot water and plumbing systems, and other areas of water aerosolization, such as showers, decorative fountains, and respiratory equipment. In a nursing home outbreak with person-to-person spread, inspection and interviews should focus on adherence to appropriate infection control procedures, including hand washing and exclusion of ill employees from working while ill.

While conducting the physical inspection of the facility, the investigator must pay careful attention to the details of the suspected procedure, such as food preparation, administration of medications, hand washing, or endoscope cleaning. Investigating each step in a procedure with observations of their use and open-ended questions enables the epidemiologist to identify potential problem areas or violations. A review of existing standard operating procedure manuals or materials is helpful in the process. In the United States, food providers are recommended (or, in some states, required) to have a hazard analysis, critical control point (HACCP) procedure outlined for each food product they serve.[43] The HACCP plan outlines the ingredients, food preparation techniques, storage until serving, serving conditions, and handling of leftover food (for an example, see **Figure 5-10**). However, the investigator must assess how the procedure was done *at the time of the outbreak*, instead of how the procedure should be done or how it is usually done. For example, in an outbreak of egg-associated *Salmonella* serotype *enteritidis* in Maryland, pasteurized eggs were always used in the preparation of crab cakes, and the crab cakes were reportedly cooked to an adequate internal temperature according to their procedure. On one occasion when no pasteurized eggs were available and the facility was exceptionally busy, the facility used fresh shell eggs in the mixture and the crab cakes were not cooked to an internal temperature necessary to kill

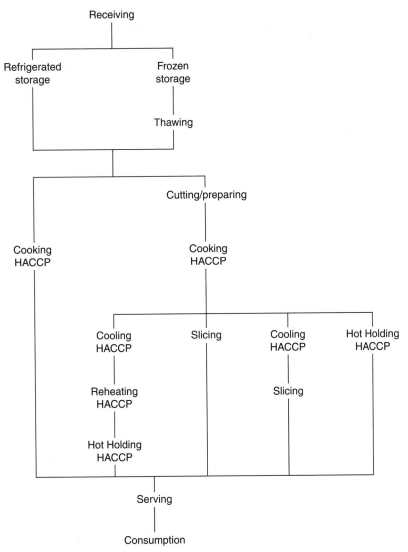

Figure 5-10 Sample hazard analysis, critical control point (HACCP) chart that follows an item (e.g., raw meat) from the point of receiving the raw product through storage and cooking to the point of consumption

Salmonella. Thus *Salmonella* in the raw shell eggs and breaks in the usual operating procedures were responsible for the outbreak.[44]

Sometimes the investigator may need to replicate the process described to determine where the break in food handling procedures occurred. A Maryland outbreak of cholera was found to be associated with a coconut dessert prepared in an individual's home.[45] The cook explained that the commercial, fresh-frozen coconut milk had been brought to a boil. After replicating the recipe and cooking procedures, investigators found that coconut milk brought to a low boil reached only 160° F. After "boiling," the coconut milk had been allowed to sit on the counter for several hours at room temperature in the summer before

being eaten, offering an excellent opportunity for the *Vibrio cholerae* organisms to multiply.

Implement Control Measures

As soon as preliminary data indicate the magnitude and severity of the outbreak, a hypothesis should be developed regarding the time, place, and person; the suspected etiologic agent(s); and the mode of transmission. Steps should be taken to contain the outbreak. Additional recommendations for control may be developed as the investigation progresses and new information is gathered. Appropriate control measures depend on knowledge of the etiologic agent, the mode of transmission, and other contributing factors. Public health law gives health officials substantial authority to take action to prevent the spread of disease to others. Some examples of control measures include the following:

- Recalling or destroying remaining contaminated food products[45, 46]
- Restricting infected workers from high-risk occupations[47]
- Closing affected facilities to prevent continued exposure
- Correcting procedural practices identified as inadequate or improper (such as food handling in a salmonellosis outbreak[48] or patient care practices in a MRSA outbreak[49])
- Recommending a prophylactic therapeutic agent and/or vaccine (e.g., use of antibiotics in an outbreak of meningococcal disease)[50]
- Enforcing hand washing (e.g., in an outbreak of nosocomial gastroenteritis)
- Educating the public about risk and prevention (e.g., recall of beef contaminated with *E. coli* O157:H7, coupled with the message to cook hamburger to a temperature greater than or equal to 160° F)[46]

Surveillance for additional cases will allow the investigator to evaluate how the control measures are working. Depending on the disease and the incubation period, additional reports of cases may be expected, even after control measures have been implemented and control achieved. For example, successful control of an outbreak of hepatitis A (with an incubation period of 2–6 weeks) does not prevent additional cases from occurring that were exposed in the past and incubating at the time that control measures were implemented.

Recommendations or control measures from an outbreak investigation may lead to the development of procedural changes, guidelines, regulations, or laws that will be applied more broadly as public health policy and are intended to prevent additional cases or outbreaks in similar settings in the future.

Formulate and Test Hypotheses

As the outbreak is investigated, data are assessed informally so that control measures can be implemented and hypotheses can be developed that may lead to further data collection or data analysis. Data are also assessed formally, using standard descriptive and analytic epidemiologic techniques to determine the specific cause(s) of the epidemic.

A primary goal of data analysis is to determine the means of transmission and the source and the vehicle of the agent, so that the most effective preventive measures can be implemented. Laboratory data can be conclusive but may not be available, especially at the beginning of an outbreak. An evaluation of symptoms, including their description, frequency, and severity, is a first step in determining the probability of the causal agent. Also, the mean, median, mode, and range of the incubation period can be determined from the epi-curve or by direct calculation. As mentioned earlier, it is important to separate primary and secondary cases of disease, when possible, to avoid errors in estimating the incubation period. The epi-curve and interviews can be used to determine whether the epidemic is most likely a point source, a common source, or a propagated epidemic.

Another goal of data analysis is to determine the risk factors for disease. As has been done throughout the investigation, analysis starts by answering global questions and works toward answering more specific questions—nesting more specific questions within the context of having answered the broader ones. Initially, analysis will be directed toward determining which population is at risk for disease. Initial hypotheses will include questions such as "Are people who attended the wedding at greater risk of disease than the general public (i.e., was there an outbreak)?" Subsequently, the question will be modified to "Among those who participated in the wedding party events, are people who ate at the wedding buffet, or swam in the pool, or attended the rehearsal dinner at greater risk of disease than people without these exposures?" More specifically, the hypotheses will later be in the form, "Among those who ate at the buffet, are people who ate the Caesar salad (or other specific food item) at greater risk than those who did not?" To answer these questions, measures of risk will be calculated.

The measure of risk used in outbreaks investigated using cohort design is the risk-specific attack rate (e.g., the food-specific attack rate for foodborne outbreaks), which is the number of persons who became ill who reported the risk behavior divided by the total number of people who reported that risk behavior. Commonly, the risk-specific attack rate is expressed as a percentage. **Figure 5-11**, **Figure 5-12**, and **Figure 5-13** illustrate the nested hypothesis testing in a typical outbreak of diarrheal disease associated with a picnic. In Figure 5-11, 42.9% (30 of 70) of attendees who ate hors d'oeuvres became ill (that is, the risk-specific attack rate for hors d'oeuvres was 42.9%, higher than the attack rates for other risk factors examined).

Risk Factor Present	Cases N = 35	Not Cases N = 100	Risk-Specific Attack Rate (AR)
Swimming	15	39	$\frac{15}{54} = 27.7\%$
Volleyball	5	20	$\frac{5}{25} = 20.0\%$
Ate box lunch	20	95	$\frac{20}{115} = 17.3\%$
Ate evening hors d'oeuvres	30	40	$\frac{30}{70} = 42.9\%$

Figure 5-11 Example of attack rates in a typical outbreak

		Case	Not Case	AR	
Swimming	Yes	15	39	$\frac{15}{54} = 27.7\%$	Relative Risk $= \frac{27.7\%}{24.7\%} = 1.1$
	No	20	61	$\frac{20}{81} = 24.7\%$	

		Case	Not Case	AR	
Ate hors d'oeuvres	Yes	30	40	$\frac{30}{70} = 42.9\%$	Relative Risk $= \frac{42.9\%}{7.7\%} = 5.6$
	No	5	60	$\frac{5}{65} = 7.7\%$	

Figure 5-12 Follow-up analysis to determine the risk of disease according to specific exposures

The second step of analysis is to compare the attack rates for different groups. In this way, it can be determined whether persons reporting a particular behavior are at higher risk of illness than those who do not report the risk behavior. The relative risk (RR) is the attack rate among those exposed to the risk factor divided by the attack rate in those who were not exposed. Continuing the example, if those who ate hors d'oeuvres were no more likely to become ill than those who did not, the attack rates would be equal, and the RR would be 1. If those who ate hors d'oeuvres were more likely to become ill than those who did not, this ratio would be greater than 1, and hors d'oeuvres would be a risk factor for illness. Conversely, if the ratio is less than 1, having that factor would be protective against illness. In Figure 5-12, the attack rate in those who ate hors d'oeuvres is divided by the attack rate in those who did not, or 42.9% divided by 7.7%, for an RR of 5.6. In this example, the statement could be made

that those who ate hors d'oeuvres were more than five times as likely to become ill as those who did not eat hors d'oeuvres. Usually, additional statistical calculations are made, including the confidence interval around this point estimate of risk and the probability that this result occurred by chance.

In a case-control study, the total population exposed to the risk factor is not available; the ratio of cases to controls is determined by the investigator. Therefore, in the case-control study design (or, frequently, in the case cohort design, unless the cases and not-ill individuals are a known fraction of the cohort of ill and not-ill individuals), it is not possible to measure the risk-specific attack rates. However, it is possible to measure the number of cases who reported the risk behavior and compare this to the number of controls who report the same risk behavior. In the example in Figure 5-12, a small case-control study was done within the picnic cohort to determine which hors d'oeuvre was the culprit. Fifteen cases and 30 controls

The investigators were concerned that one of the ingredients used in the preparation of the stuffed mushrooms was also used in a dipping sauce for chips. In particular, they were concerned about a prepared meat product used to stuff the mushrooms and to flavor the dipping sauce. To determine whether the two hors d'oeuvres were independent risk factors for illness, the investigators first reviewed the risk of disease for participants who ate the mushrooms and for those who ate the dipping sauce. They then conducted a cohort study because they were using data from the entire cohort who ate the evening hors d'oeuvres ($N = 70$), and they were able to calculate relative risks.

		Case	Not Case	AR	
Ate Stuffed	Yes	15	9	$\frac{15}{24} = 62.5\%$	Relative Risk = 1.9
Mushrooms	No	15	31	$\frac{15}{46} = 32.6\%$	

		Case	Not Case	AR	
Ate Dipping	Yes	16	14	$\frac{16}{30} = 53.3\%$	Relative Risk = 1.5
Sauce	No	14	26	$\frac{14}{40} = 35.0\%$	

Next, they conducted a stratified analysis to determine the risk-specific attack rates of people who ate both of the hors d'oeuvres, dipping sauce only, stuffed mushrooms only, and neither item.

Ate Dipping Sauce

Yes / No

Ate Stuffed Mushrooms		Case	Not Case	AR		Case	Not Case	AR
	Yes	4	1	$\frac{4}{5} = 80.0\%$	Yes	11	8	$\frac{11}{19} = 57.9\%$
	No	12	13	$\frac{12}{25} = 48.0\%$	No	3	18	$\frac{3}{21} = 14.3\%$

Based on these results, investigators concluded that both stuffed mushrooms and dipping sauce were risk factors for illness, without evidence of additive interaction between them. An investigation was initiated into the common ingredient—prepared meat. Further laboratory tests confirmed that packages of prepared meat were contaminated, and appropriate control measures instituted.

Figure 5-13 Additional analysis to determine whether there was interaction between foodstuffs consumed at the picnic

were asked additional questions. In this case-control study, the question was "How many *cases* ate stuffed mushrooms?" rather than "How many of those who ate stuffed mushrooms became cases?" as would be asked in a cohort study. The odds ratio (OR) is used to compare the odds of risk behaviors between cases and controls. The odds of eating stuffed mushrooms in cases (9/6, or 3:2) is divided by the odds in controls (6/24, or 1:4). Thus the OR or relative odds is 6.0. The OR is interpreted in the same manner as the relative risk: values significantly greater than 1

indicate that the risk behavior is associated with being a case (a risk factor), whereas values less than 1 indicate that the risk behavior is associated with being a control (a protective factor). An OR greater than 1 would be stated as "The relative odds of eating stuffed mushrooms among cases compared to controls was 6.0." Confidence intervals and probabilities can be calculated for the OR as well.

In an outbreak investigation, it is important to consider the possibility that relationships between the variables may influence their association with the risk of disease. Three commonly seen relationships are interaction, effect modification, and confounding of the data. Variables are said to interact if the presence of one variable changes the risk of disease associated with another variable. In an additive model, the effect of one variable increases the risk of the other as though the risks were being added. If the risk of disease in those people exposed to both risk factors exceeds the sum of the two individual risks, the two factors are said to show positive additive interaction or synergism. Similarly, the presence of a multiplicative interaction is evaluated against a multiplicative model for disease risk where the baseline risk is multiplied in the presence of one or more factors.[27]

In the example provided in Figure 5-13, a third analysis of the picnic data was conducted to examine additive interactions. All of the guests who had eaten the evening hors d'oeuvres were further queried about whether they had eaten specific items, including stuffed mushrooms and dipping sauce. First, a two-by-two table was constructed for each item, and it was found that the relative risk of disease was 1.9 for those who had eaten the stuffed mushrooms and 1.5 for those who had eaten the dipping sauce. Second, a stratified analysis was performed, where the risk of disease after eating stuffed mushrooms was stratified according to whether the guest also ate the dipping sauce. In this analysis, it was found that those persons who ate both the mushrooms and the dipping sauce were more than five times more likely to be cases than those who ate neither item (80% versus 14.3%; the risk attributable to consuming both items above the baseline rate of disease is 80% minus 14.3%, or 65.7%). The risk of disease after consuming both was slightly lower than the sum of the risks of eating only stuffed mushrooms and the risk of eating only the dipping sauce (i.e., 65.7% is slightly lower than 77.3%)—that is, the sum of the individual risks (57.9% − 14.3%) + (48.0% − 14.3%). An additive risk model makes biological sense in this example: if both items were equally contaminated and people ate equal amounts of both items, then those who ate both items would get twice the dose of the pathogenic agent. Although the number of people in the example is small, the combined risk is approximately the sum of the risk of the two items alone—there is no evidence of additive interaction.

Another type of relationship is effect modification. Effect modification arises when the value of one variable affects the relative risk or odds ratio of another variable. For example, age is often an effect modifier: the risk of disease is higher among infants and the elderly who consume a particular food.

Confounding occurs when the causal effect of one variable is modified by the value of another variable. For example, it may initially appear that gender is a risk factor for a particular disease until it is determined that a second factor is differentially distributed by gender. A preliminary review of the data might show that male participants at an event were more likely to be cases than were female participants. After additional investigation, it may be found that the water fountain near the men's restrooms was contaminated; thus more men were exposed than were women. In this scenario, the variable gender is confounded by whether the participant drank from a contaminated water fountain. When investigating an outbreak, it is important to consider the possibility of interaction or confounding and to continue to explore the relationships between variables to ensure that any of these effects in the data have been evaluated.

The OR and RR are similar measures of risk that can be used and interpreted interchangeably when the attack rate in the population being studied is less than 5%. This is done because many people find it simpler to describe or to conceptualize the risk and relative rate of disease than the odds and relative odds of disease. The assumption that the OR approximates the RR is known as the "rare disease assumption"; mathematically, the OR estimates the RR at low attack rates. Although the rare disease assumption is usually valid in epidemiologic research on diseases with low prevalence, it is generally not valid in outbreak investigations. Attack rates of 30% or more are common in outbreak studies—clearly much higher than the 5% cutoff used by convention. It is important to realize that the OR and the RR are both valid measures of the association between disease and the risk factor at any level of attack rate. However, when the disease is common, the investigator may not be able to use the OR to estimate the RR. For example, the OR in Figure 5-12 for stuffed mushrooms is 6.0, whereas the RR in Figure 5-13 is 1.9. Both measures point to an association between the mushrooms and illness.

Some associations that are found may be due to chance, rather than reflecting any true association between the risk factor and disease. Statistical tests (e.g., p-values and confidence intervals) are used to evaluate the possibility that the findings are due to chance alone. These statistical tests assess the possibility that the distribution of cases by risk group could have happened by chance alone. In other words, how likely is it that, by chance alone, 30 of the 70 people who ate hors d'oeuvres became ill, versus 5 of the 65 people who did not eat these items? If the possibility that this distribution of data would occur by chance is less than 5% ($p < .05$), the distribution of the data is attributed to an association between the factors, meaning the exposure is associated with disease. In outbreak studies, it is common for multiple comparisons to be made; for example, the risk of disease may be compared for exposure to 20 different foods. If the cutoff value for statistical significance is set at 5% ($p < .05$), it would be expected that one of 20 comparisons would appear to be a significant association by chance alone. To correct for multiple comparisons, the most conservative approach is to lower the p-value, according to the number of comparisons being made.

To assess the possibility that the distribution arose by chance alone, the statistical test will make some assumptions about the distribution of data. For instance, the test will commonly assume that the data are "normally distributed." This means that the test is comparing the distribution of data found in the study to a hypothetical data set, where the distribution of data would fit a normal curve. If the study includes very few people (fewer than 40), the assumption of normally distributed data may not be warranted, however. Some corrections have been devised to overcome this assumption of normality, such as Cornfield or Fisher's exact test. These alterations to the basic statistical equations are available in most software packages, including EpiInfo. In any event, it is important to note that statistical significance is influenced by sample size, and for some outbreak investigations, sample size is fixed and relatively low. Investigators should not ignore potential factors with elevated ORs or RRs simply because the association is not statistically significant. Such risk factors might be truly associated with illness, and should still be considered when implementing control measures or taking other public health actions.

In some outbreak investigations, the data are sufficiently complex that analysis using 2×2 tables is difficult or insufficient. In such scenarios, stratifying the data may be necessary to remove confounding factors. Logistic regression may also be used to control for certain variables. However, the basic goal remains the same: to determine the important risk factors for disease and to prevent its spread or recurrence.

Outbreak investigations should look beyond the current circumstances to determine how to prevent future outbreaks. In foodborne outbreaks, determination that a particular food was responsible for the disease is just the first step. It may be possible to follow the flow diagram of the food production to determine how the food became contaminated with the pathogen or how the food was improperly handled so that a pathogen could persist or multiply. Corrections to the handling of the food should then be made to prevent similar problems in the future. This step may take the investigation across state or national boundaries. In Figure 5-13, once the prepared meat in the stuffed mushrooms is determined as the most likely cause of illness, the investigators can further query the food handlers who prepared the item by developing an HACCP chart, detailing the procedures for food preparation, storage, and serving. Laboratory data, if available, will be used to support the epidemiology.

In the case of the cholera outbreak in Maryland, epidemiology and laboratory results pointed to the coconut milk as the vehicle for *V. cholerae*.[45] It was determined that raw coconut was washed in stream water in the country of origin. Subsequently, the coconut milk was not pasteurized, but instead was frozen and shipped to the United States. The contamination from the stream water exposed United States residents to pathogens from thousands of miles away. Changes in United States import laws may be required to reduce the risk of future outbreaks.

Plan Additional Studies

The data derived from the outbreak investigation may lead to questions that can be answered only with further planned studies, including epidemiologic research or laboratory investigation at academic, private, or governmental agencies. Outbreaks of *E. coli* O157:H7 have identified undercooked hamburger and apple cider as vehicles for contamination. As part of the follow-up, institutional review board–approved case-control studies of sporadic cases of diarrhea in numerous states caused by this pathogen were conducted to determine additional specific risk factors. Similarly, nationwide outbreaks of *Salmonella* serotype *enteritidis* linked to grade A shell eggs led to studies of chickens, the henhouse environment, the heat lability of the pathogen, the transport and storage requirements of eggs, and other factors, with the goal of preventing future cases.

Communicate Findings

Investigators communicate their interim findings and recommendations verbally and in writing during the investigation to those needing to know, such as the facility where the outbreak occurred or public health agencies. At the conclusion of the investigation, the investigators should write a summary report to document the investigation, the actions taken, and the outcome. If the investigation was conducted by a local, state, or federal health agency, the report becomes a document that will provide feedback to the personnel at the facility or site where the outbreak occurred.

Background: In November 1993, we investigated an outbreak of gastroenteritis associated with eating raw oysters.

Methods: We interviewed 14 groups of two or more ill persons who had eaten raw oysters together. Source beds for oysters were identified using oyster sack tags and dealer records. Oyster harvesters were interviewed. Stool samples from ill persons were tested by electron microscopy (EM) and reverse transcription-polymerase chain reaction (RT-PCR) for Norwalk-like virus (NLV); viral genome was also sequenced.

Results: Of 78 raw oyster eaters, 65 (83%) became ill, compared with 2 (5%) of 41 associated persons who did not eat raw oysters (Risk Ratio [RR] = 17.1, 95% Confidence Interval [CI] 4.4–66.3). The 67 persons had vomiting (71%) or diarrhea (92%) 5–60 hours after eating (median 31 hours). Nine stool samples from persons in three of the groups were tested for NLV; six were positive by EM, and nine were positive by RT-PCR. Viruses sequenced to date are identical. In the 13 outbreaks where tracing information was available, implicated oysters were harvested November 9–13 from a single area of beds remote from sewage contamination and ship traffic. Four harvesters who did not eat oysters were ill with vomiting and diarrhea while working in the implicated beds on November 7–9 and disposed of their feces and vomitus overboard.

Conclusions: Because the infectious dose for NLV is small (1–10 virus particles) and because oysters concentrate enteric pathogens, virus-containing stool from four ill harvesters may have contaminated a sufficient number of oysters to cause this outbreak. Enforcement of regulations governing waste disposal by fishing boats might prevent similar outbreaks from occurring.

Figure 5-14 An outbreak of oyster-related Norwalk-like virus gastroenteritis traced to fecal contamination from fishing boats. Data from M.A. Kohn et al., An Outbreak of Oyster-Related Norwalk-Like Virus Gastroenteritis Traced to Fecal Contamination from Fishing Boats, presented at the Epidemic Intelligence Service 43rd Annual Conference, 1994, Centers for Disease Control and Prevention.

A summary might also be completed and submitted to the CDC-maintained National Outbreak Reporting System.[51] Final reports may, in some instances, lead to recommendations, publications, or regulatory changes that will prevent disease and improve outbreak response in the future (see **Figure 5-14**).[52]

CONCLUSION

Outbreaks afford opportunities to gain information about diseases, pathogens, and changing risk factors for disease. Epidemiologic field investigations or outbreak investigations involve a series of steps geared toward the collection and analysis of data. Armed with the knowledge of how to investigate an outbreak, the epidemiologist is able to execute a timely and thorough investigation of the cause and contributing factors of an outbreak while quickly taking measures to control the outbreak. Cooperation and communication are key elements in the smooth operation of this process. Issues of confidentiality and the release of information should be taken into account, with the operating procedure of the jurisdiction guiding the action to release information. Public health officials in local, state, and federal agencies can provide expert advice and assistance in the investigation of outbreaks.

••• REFERENCES

1. Zinsser H. *Lice and History—The Biography of a Bacillus: A Bacteriologist's Classic Study of a World Scourge.* Boston, MA: Atlantic, Little, Brown; 1963.

2. Institute of Medicine. Lederberg J, Shope RE, Oaks SC Jr, eds. *Emerging Infections: Microbial Threats to Health in the United States.* Washington, DC: National Academies Press; 1992.

3. Ashford A, Kaiser RM, Bales ME, Shutt K, Patrawalla A, McShan A, Tappero JW, Perkins BA, Dannenberg AL. Planning against biological terrorism: lessons from outbreak investigations. *Emerg Infect Dis.* 2003;9(5):515–519.

4. Khanna N, Steffen I, Studt JD, et al. Outcome of influenza infections in outpatients after allogeneic hematopoietic stem cell transplantation. *Transpl Infect Dis.* 2009;11(2):100–105.

5. Centers for Disease Control and Prevention. Public health then and now: celebrating 50 years at *MMWR*. *MMWR*. 2011;60 (suppl):1–124.

6. Bell BP, Goldoft M, Griffin PM, et al. A multistate outbreak of *Escherichia coli* O157:H7-associated bloody diarrhea and hemolytic uremic syndrome from hamburgers: the Washington experience. *JAMA*. 1994;272:1349–1353.

7. Centers for Disease Control and Prevention. Multi-state outbreak of *E. coli* 0157:H7 infections from fresh spinach. October 6, 2006. Available at: http://www.cdc.gov/foodborne/ecolispinach/100606.htm.

8. Yukioka HK. *Escherichia coli* O157 infection disaster in Japan 1996. *S Eur J Emerg Med*. 1997;4:165.

9. Centers for Disease Control. Ebola virus infection in imported primates—Virginia, 1989. *MMWR*. 1989;48:831–838.

10. Nelson K, Williams CM. *Infectious Disease Epidemiology: Theory and Practice*. Burlington, MA: Jones & Bartlett Learning; 2012: Chapter 4.

11. http://www.cdc.gov/nndss.

12. Douglas N. Klaucke. Chapter 3. Evaluating Public Health Surveillance Systems. In Halpern W, Baker E, eds. *Public Health Surveillance*. New York, NY: John Wiley and Sons;1992: 30.

13. http://ideha.dhmh.maryland.gov/IDEHAShared Documents/what-to-report/DHMH1140.pdf.

14. http://ideha.dhmh.maryland.gov/IDEHAShared Documents/case_reports/gastroenteritis.pdf.

15. http://www.cdc.gov/mmwr.

16. http://www.cdc.gov/foodnet.

17. http://www.cdc.gov/pulsenet.

18. CDC framework for evaluating public health surveillance systems for early detection of outbreaks. *MMWR*. 2004;53(RR-05).

19. Goodman RA, Buehler JW, Koplan JP. The epidemiologic field investigation: science and judgment in public health practice. *Am J Epidemiol*. 1990;132:9–16.

20. Dwyer DM, Strickler H, Goodman RA, Armenian HK. Use of case-control studies in outbreak investigations. *Epidemiol Rev*. 1994;16:109–123.

21. Reingold AL. Outbreak investigations: a perspective. *Emerg Infect Dis*. 1998;4:21–27.

22. El-Gazzar RE, Marth EH. Foodborne disease: investigative procedures and economic assessment. *Environ Health*. 1992;55:24–26.

23. http://www.cdc.gov/outbreaknet/investigations/investigating.html.

24. *Principles of Epidemiology: A Introduction to Applied Epidemiology and Biostatistics*, 3rd ed. Available at: http://www.cdc.gov/osels/scientific_edu/SS1978/SS1978.pdf.

25. Centers for Disease Control and Prevention. Notice to readers: ongoing investigation of anthrax—Florida, October 2001. *MMWR*. 2001;50(40);877.

26. http://wwwn.cdc.gov/NNDSS/script/SearchResults.aspx?Searchfor=

27. Schlesselman JJ. *Case-Control Studies: Design, Conduct, Analysis*. New York, NY: Oxford University Press; 1982.

28. Rothman KS, Greenland S. *Modern Epidemiology*, 2nd ed. Philadelphia, PA: Lippincott-Williams & Wilkins; 1998:108–111.

29. Szklo M, Nieto FJ. *Epidemiology: Beyond the Basics*. Gaithersburg, MD: Aspen Publishers; 1999:1–51.

30. Langmuir AD. Toxic-shock syndrome: an epidemiologist's view. *J Infect Dis*. 1982;145:588–591.

31. Centers for Disease Control. Epidemiologic notes and reports of toxic-shock syndrome, United States, 1970–1982. *MMWR*. 1982;31:201–204.

32. Donawa ME, Schmid, GR, Osterholm MT. Toxic shock syndrome: chronology of state and federal epidemiologic studies and regulatory decision-making. *Public Health Rep*. 1984;99(4):342–350.

33. Davis JP, Chesney PJ, Wand PJ, LaVenture M. Toxic-shock syndrome: epidemiologic features, recurrence, risk factors, and prevention. *N Engl J Med.* 1980;303:1429–1435.

34. MacKenzie WR, Hoxie NJ, Proctor ME, et al. A massive outbreak in Milwaukee of *Cryptosporidium* infection transmitted through the public water supply. *N Engl J Med.* 1994;331:161–167.

35. Decker MD, Booth AS, Dewey MJ, et al. Validity of food consumption histories in a foodborne outbreak investigation. *Am J Epidemiol.* 1986;124:859–863.

36. http://www.cdc.gov/epiinfo.

37. Centers for Disease Control and Prevention. Multistate outbreak of *Salmonella* serotype *agona* infections linked to toasted oats cereal—United States, April–May 1998. *MMWR.* 1998;47:462–464.

38. Morris JG Jr, Dwyer DM, Hoge CW, et al. Changing clonal patterns of *Salmonella enteritidis* in Maryland: evaluation of strains isolated between 1985 and 1990. *J Clin Microbiol.* 1992;30:1301–1303.

39. Kohn MA, Farley TA, Ando T, et al. An outbreak of Norwalk virus gastroenteritis associated with eating raw oysters: implications for maintaining safe oyster beds. *JAMA.* 1995;273:466–471.

40. Dowell SF, Groves C, Kirkland KB, et al. A multistate outbreak of oyster-associated gastroenteritis: implications for interstate tracing of contaminated shellfish. *J Infect Dis.* 1995;171:497–503.

41. Moe CL, Gentsch J, Ando T, et al. Application of PCR to detect Norwalk virus in fecal specimens from outbreaks of gastroenteritis. *Clin Microbiol.* 1994;32:642–648.

42. Braden CR, Templeton GL, Cave MD, et al. Interpretation of restriction fragment length polymorphism analysis of *Mycobacterium tuberculosis* isolates from a state with a large rural population. *J Infect Dis.* 1997;175:1446–1452.

43. Food and Drug Administration. *Food Code: Annex 4-5.* Washington, DC: FDA; 2009. Available at: http://www.fda.gov/Food/FoodSafety/RetailFoodProtection/FoodCode/default.htm.

44. Maryland Department of Health and Mental Hygiene, Epidemiology and Disease Control Program, Division of Outbreak Investigation. Unpublished data.

45. Taylor JL, Tuttle J, Pramukul T, et al. An outbreak of cholera in Maryland associated with imported commercial frozen fresh coconut milk. *J Infect Dis.* 1993;167:1330–1335.

46. Centers for Disease Control and Prevention. *Escherichia coli* O157:H7 infections associated with eating a nationally distributed commercial brand of frozen ground beef patties and burgers—Colorado. *MMWR.* 1997;46:777–778.

47. Rodriguez E, Parrott C, Rolka H, et al. An outbreak of viral gastroenteritis in a nursing home: importance of excluding ill employees. *Infect Control Hosp Epidemiol.* 1996;17:587–592.

48. Meehan PJ, Atkeson T, Kepner DE, Melton M. A food-borne outbreak of gastroenteritis involving two different pathogens. *Am J Epidemiol.* 1992;136:611–616.

49. Boyce JM, Jackson MM, Pugliese G, et al.; the AHA Technical Panel on Infections within Hospitals. Methicillin-resistant *Staphylococcus aureus* (MRSA): a briefing for acute care hospitals and nursing facilities. *Infect Control Hosp Epidemiol.* 1994;15:105–115.

50. Jackson LA, Schuchat A, Reeves MW, Wenger JD. Serogroup C meningococcal outbreaks in the United States: an emerging threat. *JAMA.* 1995;273:383–389.

51. http://www.cdc.gov/outbreaknet/nors/

52. Berg DE, Kohn MA, Farley T, McFarland LM. Multi-state outbreaks of acute gastroenteritis traced to fecal-contaminated oysters harvested in Louisiana. *J Infect Dis.* 2000:181:S381–S386.

6

Infectious Disease Dynamics

Derek A. T. Cummings and Justin Lessler

INTRODUCTION

Infectious disease dynamics is the study of how the distribution and transmission of infectious disease vary across space and time. While this term is often used synonymously with infectious disease modeling, the study of infectious disease dynamics is more general and employs a variety of statistical and mathematical techniques to understand the dynamics of disease transmission. Questions that fall under the purview of infectious disease dynamics include the following:

1. Given the introduction of a pathogen to a population, will cases increase?
2. If so, how quickly and how far will they spread?
3. Will the pathogen persist in the population?
4. What are the drivers of spatial and temporal variation in disease incidence?
5. What is the best way to intervene to minimize the spread and burden of disease?
6. Can transmission be eliminated?

Central to answering these questions and others surrounding the dynamics of transmission is the contagion process, which distinguishes infectious diseases from other areas of epidemiology.

In this chapter, we present a brief survey of concepts, methods, and applications in infectious disease dynamics. We begin with a brief history of the field and then introduce the basic building blocks of the theory, including metrics of transmission and the structure of simple models of transmission. Extensions of this basic model account for heterogeneities in host population structure, different modes of transmission, pathogen population structure, and the dynamic interactions between multiple components of these systems. We next present examples where infectious disease dynamics research has played an important role in informing public health responses or understanding observed patterns of disease. We close with a discussion of future directions in the field.

A BRIEF HISTORY

The 18th-century mathematician, physicist, and statistician Daniel Bernoulli (developer of Bernoulli's principle in aerodynamics and nephew of probability pioneer Jakob Bernoulli) is often credited for creating the first epidemic model in his 1766 examination of smallpox.[1] In truth, Bernoulli's model cannot be considered a model of epidemic dynamics per se, as it treated smallpox as other researchers had treated other noninfectious health hazards, assuming a constant hazard of infection and including no hypothesis as to the mechanisms driving transmission. While such a model may be useful for understanding long-term risks from an endemic disease (Bernoulli used his model to understand the effect of variolation on long-term survival), it does not explain the ebbs and flows of epidemics.

William Farr, the contemporary and sometimes rival of John Snow, worked at the general register's office as compiler of statistical abstracts and later Superintendent of the Statistical Department from 1838 until his retirement in 1880.[2] Farr was one of the first epidemiologists to attempt to explain the dynamic shape of an epidemic. Farr's method of doing so was to use the "assumption of the second ratio"—essentially fitting a normal distribution to an epidemic curve. His approach involved no

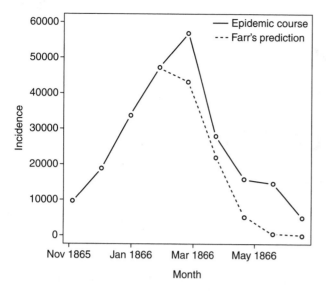

Figure 6-1 Epidemic course of an 1865–1866 epidemic of cattle plague in England compared with predictions using William Farr's "assumption of the second ratio" (first predicted date is February 24, 1866). Data from Brownlee J. Historical Note on Farr's Theory of the Epidemic. *British Medical Journal* 1915;2(2850):250–2.

assumptions about the underlying process that led to a given shape. Farr used his method to predict the course of an epidemic of the cattle plague that occurred in England from 1865 to 1866 (**Figure 6-1**).[3] While Farr's selection of an arbitrary curve happened to fit this epidemic with reasonable success, his work does not clarify the mechanisms leading to this shape. However, his observation that propagated epidemics tend to follow a roughly normal distribution is still used to help distinguish between propagated and point source outbreaks (which tend to follow the log-normal distribution of the incubation period) today (see the discussion of incubation periods later in this chapter).

Arthur Ransome was perhaps the first to articulate what is one of the most important principles of infectious disease dynamics: that the depletion of susceptible individuals in the population can cause an epidemic to recede, even if not everyone in the population has been infected.[4] In doing so, he anticipated modern efforts to use the principles of infectious disease dynamics to understand and predict epidemics much as we do the weather: "Like the cyclones of the atmosphere, these storms of disease can only be tracked, and the laws of their course discovered, by the combined efforts of many observers."[4] Ransome developed his ideas on the importance of susceptible dynamics and postulated

that multiyear cycles in epidemics are likely the result of an accumulated density of susceptible individuals through births over time.[5]

While Ransome recognized the important role played by susceptible hosts in epidemic dynamics, he never developed a precise mathematical formulation of his hypothesis. Perhaps the first to do so was a Russian physician, Pyotr Dimitrievich En'ko,[6] who presented his model in an 1889 paper, "On the course of epidemics of some infectious diseases."[7] En'ko's model is similar to one later developed by Lowell Reed and Wade Hampton Frost (discussed later in this section), calculating the number of infectious cases expected to occur in a generation of an epidemic based on the probability of members of the current susceptible population making contact with a member of the current infectious population.[7] En'ko used his model to model the course of epidemics and was one of the first to observe that there exists a density of susceptible individuals below which an epidemic will not occur. Despite the importance of En'ko's model, it did not gain wide adoption until Reed and Frost's formulation was popularized in the 20th century.

Separately, Ronald Ross, a British medical doctor with a strong interest and aptitude in mathematics, was working in India to understand the transmission of malaria.[8] Ross received the Nobel Prize for his discovery that mosquitoes transmit malaria. Subsequent to this discovery, Ross developed a model of malaria transmission that would lay the foundation for decades of malaria research and for mechanistic descriptions of contagion. Using this model, he identified thresholds of mosquito populations below which transmission of malaria would not be sustained. Ross argued that mosquito control could eliminate malaria transmission—a position that many of his contemporaries rejected, as they believed that mosquito populations of even very small numbers could continue to sustain transmission. Decades after Ross's work, MacDonald used his framework to advocate for mosquito control when effective insecticides were available and public health authorities were considering large-scale malaria control efforts.[9]

Wade Hampton Frost was a professor of epidemiology and Lowell Reed was a professor of biostatistics at the Johns Hopkins School of Public Health, and both eventually went on to serve as deans of the School of Public Health. Frost and Reed developed and refined a statistical model of epidemics similar to that developed by Pyotr En'ko that considered a series of distinct generations of infection. Under the Reed–Frost model, the number of cases seen in a generation is calculated as follows:[10]

$$C_{t+1} = S_t(1 - q^{ct}) \qquad \text{(Equation 1)}$$

where C_t is the number of new cases occurring in generation t, S_t is the number of individuals that remains susceptible to infection in generation t, $q = 1 - p$ is the probability that a susceptible individual avoids contact with any given case (p is the probability of such a contact), and q^{ct} is the probability that a susceptible individual avoids infectious contact with all C_t infectious cases. Reed and Frost predominantly used their model as a teaching tool, but it was resurrected and popularized by other authors. Reed and Frost were also responsible for what may be the first epidemic simulator. Created before the computer era, this mechanical device used small beads to represent individuals and could be used to simulate stochastic epidemics.[11] The chain binomial models of En'ko and Reed and Frost are the foundation of analysis of transmission and intervention effects in households, schools, and other tightly interacting social units.[12]

Another thread of scientific development that helped lay the foundation for much of modern infectious disease dynamics focused on the use of mass-action kinetics to describe the interactions of infectious and susceptible individuals. Here Ronald Ross again played a central role. Ross supervised Anderson Gray McKendrick, a Scottish physician, during an antimalarial campaign in Sierra Leone. At this time, Ross introduced McKendrick to his model of malaria and encouraged McKendrick to extend his work. McKendrick used ideas from chemical reaction kinetics to formulate a model of transmission that treats the interaction of susceptible and infectious individuals as similar to the collision of molecules.[13] He published a model that represented transmission dynamics as a compartmental model expressed as continuous time ordinary differential equations.[14] Later, McKendrick worked with William Ogilvy Kermack, a chemist by training, to develop this model and identify key conclusions, including the critical density of susceptible persons needed for an epidemic to propagate.[15]

Since the early 20th century, there has been an ever-growing interest in infectious disease dynamics. The history and main ideas developed during this period have been reviewed in many excellent texts, including, in no particular order, those by Anderson and May (1991);[16] Dietz (1975);[17] Bailey (1957, 1975);[18,19] Keeling and Rohani (2007);[20] Halloran (2010);[12] and Heesterbeek (2005).[13] We refer the reader to these texts for a more detailed review of the history of ideas in this field.

DETERMINANTS OF EPIDEMIC GROWTH

The rate at which an epidemic grows (or recedes) is determined by the number of infections that occur in each successive generation of pathogen transmission and the time between these generations. These two quantities, which are referred to as the reproductive number and the generation time, respectively, form the basis for much of our thinking about the dynamics of the epidemic process.

The Reproductive Number

The reproductive number, R, is the number of secondary cases expected to be caused by a single, typical infected individual in a population with some level of susceptibility. If the population is fully susceptible, this is termed the basic reproductive number and denoted as R_0 (estimates of R_0 for some common disease are shown in **Table 6-1**). The reproductive number is the primary metric used to quantify the transmission of a disease in infectious disease dynamics; it provides a measure of how fast an outbreak will grow across subsequent generations of transmission. For instance, for influenza $R_0 \approx 2$; hence we would expect a single infected case to cause 2 cases after one generation, 4 cases after two generations, 8 cases after three generations, and so on. For measles, where $R_0 \approx 11$, we would expect to see 11 cases in one generation, 121 cases in two generations, and 1331 cases in three generations. However, the observed speed of growth does not depend only on R_0, as the average time between generations of transmission varies by disease (see the discussion of generation time in the next subsection) and the number of people available to be infected decreases over time as the pool of susceptible individuals is depleted by infection.

While R_0 refers to the number of cases caused by a typical individual in a completely susceptible population, R refers to the number of cases caused by a typical infectious individual given the proportion of individuals still available to be infected at the current time. R changes over time and is sometimes denoted R_t, whereas R_0 refers to a theoretical time 0 when the entire population is susceptible. R accounts for the reduction in transmission due to some individuals being immune (**Figure 6-2**). For instance, if R_0 is 4, but half of a primary case's contacts are immune due to previous infection or vaccination, then we would expect

Table 6-1	R_0 for Multiple Pathogens	
Pathogen	R_0	**Generation Time**
Cholera	5.0*,[121] 2.6,[122] 4–15[123]	7.1–9.3 days,[124] 7–10 days[123]
Dengue	1.3–6.3[125]	19–22 days,[126] 24 days[127]
Influenza	1.5–2[57]	3.6 days (s.d. 1.6 days); [128] 2.3 days (H1N1, range 1.5–2.7 days),[30] 3.1 days (H3N2, range 2.2–4.0 days),[30] 2.7 days (H1N1 pdm)[73]
Malaria	1–10 low transmission areas/100–1000 high transmission areas, [123] 1–3000[129]	~60–120 days,[123] > 200 days[129]
Measles	7.7,[130] 7.1–29.3,[131] 11–18[16]	9–17 days,[132] 12 days[19]
Rubella	2.9–7.8,[131] 3.4–5.6[133]	22 days,[133] 15–23 days[134]
SARS	2.7,[135] 1.2,[136] 2.2–3.6[137]	8.4 days[137]
Smallpox	3.2,[138] 3.5–6,[139] 6.87 (95% CI 4.52–10.1)[140]	14–16 days,[138] 16 days (s.d. 4 days),[141] 14–20 days[132]

*reproductive number estimate, not R_0 estimate.

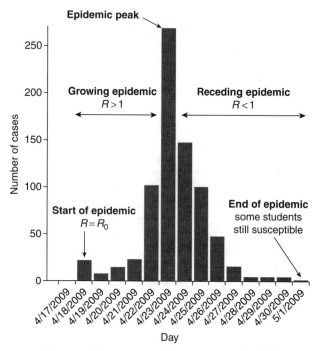

Figure 6-2 Dynamics of an emergent influenza epidemic. Adapted from Lessler J, Reich NG, Cummings D a T, et al. Outbreak of 2009 pandemic influenza A (H1N1) at a New York City school. *New England Journal of Medicine*. 2009;361(27):2621.

that case to infect only 2 individuals; in this scenario, R would be equal to 2. In general, if s_t is the proportion of the population still susceptible to infection at time t, then R_t is $R_0 s_t$.

When R is less than 1, then the infectious individuals will no longer replace themselves; that is,

there will be fewer infectious individuals in the current generation than in the previous generation. At this point the epidemic will begin to wane and eventually die out. Likewise, when R is less than 1 in a population, introduction of a disease will not cause a widespread epidemic—a state usually referred to as herd immunity. When a population has herd immunity against a disease ($R < 1$), it is protected from sustained transmission of the disease (note that herd immunity is also used to refer to the protection that susceptible individuals in the population get from the immunity of others, even when R is greater than 1). Because of the relationship between susceptibility and $R(R = R_0 s)$, we can derive an expression for the proportion of the population that must be immune for herd immunity to occur. In other words, we can determine the proportion of the population that must be successfully vaccinated to induce herd immunity: the critical vaccination threshold V. Based on the previously discussed relation, it follows that:

$$V = 1 - \frac{1}{R_0} \qquad \text{(Equation 2)}$$

The role of vaccination in inducing herd immunity will be discussed in more detail with specific reference to rubella later in this chapter.

R_0 and R depend on both the pathogen and the setting. Table 6-1 shows some typical estimates of the basic reproductive number for multiple pathogens. Estimates vary considerably by pathogen, but we emphasize that they also vary from setting to setting. Setting-to-setting variability results from aspects of the transmission process that vary between locations, including environmental characteristics,

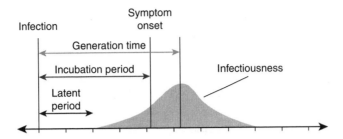

Figure 6-3 Schematic of an infected individual's progression in relation to time of infection. Gray indicates infectiousness over time. Incubation period is defined by the time from infection to symptom onset. The latent period is defined by the time from infection to non-zero infectiousness. The generation time is the mean time from infection to time of infection in those individuals that this person infects. We expect this to be equal to the latent period plus the time from the start of non-zero infectiousness to the probability weighted center of the infectiousness distribution.

crowding, underlying health status of the population, and cultural factors that affect the rate at which individuals make potentially infectious contacts.

The inclusion of the word "typical" in the definition of the basic reproductive number admits the possibility that infectiousness across individuals may be heterogeneous. The basic reproductive number is the *average* number of secondary infections created by a single infectious individual in an entirely susceptible population, *averaging* over all types of individuals who may be first infections in a population.

Generation Time

The generation time (or generation interval) of an infectious disease is the time separating the onset of infection in an individual (the infector) and the time that person transmits to another individual (the infectee). While the reproductive number dictates the number of infections produced by each generation of transmission, the generation time specifies a time scale at which these transmissions accumulate. The generation time is also referred to as the serial interval, a term coined by Hope-Simpson that is often used to refer to the time between symptom onset in successive generations of infection.[21]* The generation time is not fully observable, as the precise moment of infection is difficult, if not impossible, to detect.

A proxy that is often used to estimate the generation time is the time separating the onset of symptoms in infector and infectee (i.e., the serial interval). Two other time periods—the latent period and the infectious period—also affect the generation time. The latent period is the time between infection and the onset of

infectiousness. The infectious period is the duration of time for which individuals are infectious. The infectiousness of individuals may vary over the infectious period. The mean generation time can be approximated by the mean latent period plus the time until the center of the infectious period weighted by transmissibility (**Figure 6-3**).

ELEMENTS OF THE COURSE OF INFECTION

The course of infection within individuals has its own dynamics, which need to be well characterized for a full description of the dynamic disease process. While the within-host disease process has been modeled at varying degrees of complexity, the distribution of three time periods characterize the essentials of the infectious process: the incubation, latent, and infectious periods.

Incubation Period

The incubation period is the time between infection with a disease and the development of symptoms (see Figure 6-3). It plays an important role in the dynamics of disease transmission because it dictates when cases will be detected relative to individuals' time of infection. This delay must be accounted for when determining the true infectious burden and evaluating the effect of control measures based on symptomatic surveillance.[22]

While statements of a mean incubation period or range for the incubation period are common in the infectious disease literature, they are often too vague for use in dynamic models of disease transmission.[23] Typically, in dynamic models, incubation periods are assumed to follow some statistical distribution. Common choices for this distribution are exponential, log-normal, Weibull, and gamma distributions.[24,25]

---

* Phillip Sartwell coined the term *generation time* to describe the slightly different length of time between infection and the time when an infector is most likely to infect others (rather than the average time).

Latent Period

The latent period is the time between when an individual is infected and when he or she becomes infectious (see Figure 6-3). While in some cases the latent period and the incubation period have the same length, for many diseases this is not the case. Perhaps the most dramatic example of such a discrepancy involves HIV/AIDS, for which the incubation period can last years longer than the latent period. Care should be taken when reading the literature, as not all authors are precise in distinguishing the incubation period from the latent period, often referring to the latter as the former.

When exploring the dynamics of epidemics, it is usually the latent period, rather than the incubation period, in which we are interested because the latent period has the more profound effect on the generation time, and hence epidemic growth. However, the incubation period may also be important, especially when attempting to interpret observed case counts, which may not include all infections that have already occurred.

The distinction between the incubation period and the latent period is especially important when evaluating the effect of control methods based on symptomatic surveillance. If infectiousness proceeds symptom onset (i.e., the latent period is shorter than the incubation period), as in HIV, then interventions based on targeted controls toward symptomatic individuals are unlikely to be effective.[26] Diseases where symptom onset is coincident with, or even proceeds, infectiousness (e.g., smallpox) are more likely to be controlled using methods based on symptomatic surveillance. Hence, the proportion of transmission that takes place before the onset of symptoms may be an important metric of controllability.[26]

As with the incubation period, the latent period is usually modeled as following an exponential, lognormal, Weibull, or gamma distribution.

Infectious Period

The infectious period is clearly one of the most important determinants of infectious disease dynamics. The infectious period for an infection can range from days (e.g., influenza) to years (e.g., HIV) and plays an important role in determining the reproductive number for that disease. Even a difficult-to-transmit infection may cause a large number of secondary cases if individuals remain infectious for a long period of time. For instance, HIV has a fairly low per-act probability of transmission (0.001 per heterosexual act, 0.008 per male-homosexual act),[27,28] but individuals remain infectious for years, leading to a relatively high basic reproductive number (2–5).[26] In

contrast, measles has a comparatively short infectious period (approximately 1 week)[29] but is highly infectious during that period and has a very high basic reproductive number (7 to over 20, see Table 6-1).

The dynamic effects of infectious disease control measures are often best understood by considering their effects on the infectious period. The primary effect of treatment, in terms of epidemic dynamics, is to decrease the infectious period. Similarly, case isolation can be seen as decreasing the effective infectious period of those isolated. In some circumstances a treatment may increase the infectious period—for instance, supportive care that prevents death but does nothing to prevent transmission.

The infectious and latent periods play a primary role in determining the generation time of an infection. If infectiousness in evenly distributed across the infectious period, then the mean generation time will be equal to the mean latent period plus one-half the mean infectious period. In general, infectiousness may not be uniform during the infectious period, though the mean timing of infection may still be determined through more sophisticated techniques (see Carrat et al.'s work for an example).[30]

DYNAMIC MODELS OF THE EPIDEMIC PROCESS

As stated previously, the reproductive number is the product of the basic reproductive number and the susceptible fraction. A central challenge of infectious disease dynamics is to describe the dynamics of transmission given changes in the susceptible and infectious populations. Compartmental models provide a method to integrate our understanding of the constituent parts of disease transmission and the course of infection into dynamic models of the epidemic process.

Compartmental Models

In compartmental models, each individual in the population exists within a compartment (or state) based on that person's current role in the transmission process. For immunizing infections (i.e., those that induce a protective immune response), compartmental models usually consist of (at least) compartments for individuals who are susceptible to infection (the S compartment), infectious (the I compartment), or recovered and immune from further infection (the R compartment). This last compartment can also be thought of as consisting of all those individuals who have been removed from the infectious dynamics in the population, which explains why it is sometimes referred to as the removed compartment. The state of the model at any given point in time is the number of individuals who reside in each of the model compartments. For mathematical clarity, the population is usually considered to be continuous; hence partial individuals may reside in any particular compartment.

In simple compartmental models, the compartments in the model are usually listed in the order in which individuals travel through them. For example, a model in which susceptible individuals become infectious and then recover is an SIR model, one in which recovered individuals can eventually lose immunity and become susceptible again is an SIRS model, and one in which individuals reside in an exposed but not yet infectious compartment during their latent period (the E compartment) is referred to as an SEIR model. **Figure 6-4** provides examples of some compartmental model structures.

The dynamics of an infection in a population is defined by the rate at which members of the population move between compartments. In some cases, this rate will be dictated by the biology of the disease process—for instance, the rate at which individuals

recover, moving from the I compartment to the R compartment. In other cases, the rate will depend on the state of the population—for instance, the rate at which susceptible individuals become infectious (i.e., move from the S compartment to the I compartment) is driven by the number of infectious individuals in the population. The rates at which individuals transition between compartments define a set of differential equations that capture the epidemic dynamics of the disease (under a set of assumptions to be discussed later). For instance, a basic SIR model can be defined by the following set of equations:

$$\frac{ds}{dt} = -\beta SI \qquad \text{(Equation 3.1)}$$

$$\frac{dI}{dt} = \beta SI - \gamma^I \qquad \text{(Equation 3.2)}$$

$$\frac{dR}{dt} = \gamma^I \qquad \text{(Equation 3.3)}$$

The Basic Model

A) In the basic model, Susceptible, Infectious, and Recovered individuals start out susceptible (in S). They are infected by infectious individuals (I) at the rate β, at which point they become infectious (enter I). They eventually recover (move to R at rate γ), at which point they are immune from further infection. This basic model is appropriate for explosive epidemics of diseases with a short latent period relative to the infectious period and immunity lasting the course of an epidemic. For example, an emerging influenza virus in a single town.

Extensions of the Basic Model

B) To capture the long term dynamics of a childhood infection such as measles, the basic model needs to be extended to take into account population dynamics and important epidemiologic aspects of the infection. Since measles confers life-long immunity, we must account for the accumulation of susceptibles through births and deaths, here considered to occur at a constant rate μ. Upon entering the population, children are protected by maternal antibodies (they are in M), which they lose at the rate δ, at which point they become susceptible. Since the latent period of measles is long compared to the infectious period, we introduce an exposed compartment (E), which cases enter upon becoming infected and leave at the rate ε, at which point they become infectious.

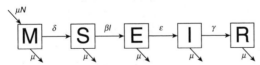

C) If we want to model a disease process where there is no lasting immunity, such as nasal staphylococcus colonization, we may actually want to use a reduced model on the infectious process. In this case, the model has two states, susceptible and infectious. When an individual does clear the bacteria, they are instantly susceptible to reinfection.

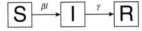

D) For vector borne diseases such as dengue, the rate of infection in humans is driven by the number of infected mosquitos (i.e., humans are infected at the rate αI_m). and the rate of mosquito infection is in turn driven by the rate of infection in humans (at rate βI_h). Hence we model two populations with their own population dynamics and interrelated rates of infection. Similar model structures can be used to model zoonotic infections, paired human populations and age groups.

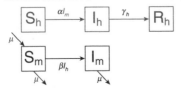

Figure 6-4 Examples of important types of compartmental models.

That is, susceptible individuals become infected at rate βI, at which point they instantly become infectious. Infectious individuals remain infectious for an average of $1/\gamma$ days (i.e., they recover at the rate of γ), at which point they recover and are permanently immune. In this formulation, the transmission coefficient, β, combines the contact process by which the disease spreads with the per-contact infectiousness of the disease considered. The product of the number of susceptible and infectious individuals in the population ($S \cdot I$) represents all of the potential infectious contacts between infectious and susceptible individuals in this population. Hence, the parameter β is the probability that a potential infectious contact actually occurs *and* that the contact results in an infection. What constitutes an "infectious contact" varies by disease and setting, in some cases requiring direct person-to-person contact (e.g., for Ebola virus), and in others representing contamination and subsequent contact with some environmental reservoir (e.g., hepatitis A contamination of a salad bar). When the contact process is well understood, it is often useful to break β into its constituent parts: the rate at which potentially infectious contacts are made and the proportion of those contacts that result in infection. This formulation is particularly useful when describing sexually transmitted infections.

Force of Infection

An important metric of the infection pressure that susceptible individuals experience is the force (or hazard) of infection. The force of infection is the rate at which susceptible individuals acquire infection at a particular time, regardless of the source. In other words, it is the total hazard a susceptible individual encounters given all exposures to infectious individuals. In the basic SIR model, the force of infection is βI. The force of infection is often easier to estimate from empirical data than the basic reproductive number, as it can be directly estimated from longitudinal data on infection status for a cohort of susceptible individuals without any information on the size of the infectious population. Estimation of the force of infection can be an intermediate step in estimating the basic reproductive number and other parameters describing epidemic dynamics.

Transmission Rates: Density and Frequency Dependent Transmission

In the basic SIR model presented earlier (Equations 3.1–3.3), we assume that susceptible individuals become infected at a rate that is directly proportional to the number of infectious individuals, βI. Under

this formulation, the basic reproductive number is the product of the transmission coefficient (β), the length of infectiousness (γ), and the total population size (N):

$$R_0 = \beta N/\gamma \qquad \text{(Equation 4)}$$

Under this formulation, R_0 is not consistent in populations of differing sizes if β is assumed to be constant. For example, a disease for which R_0 is 2 in a population of 10,000 individuals would fail to spread in a population of 4000 ($R_0 = 0.8$), but would demonstrate far more explosive spread in a population of 100,000 individuals ($R_0 = 20$). Models like those defined by equations 3.1–3.3 are called "density-dependent" models because they suggest that members of a population existing in a fixed area all come in contact with one another no matter how many individuals are present in the population. Thus it is assumed that the rate at which contacts are made scales with density, such that all members of a population of 100,000 have contact with one another just as a population of 10 would. Hence, the disease will spread more effectively in larger populations. In many cases, this outcome makes intuitive sense, especially for pathogens in animal and plant populations where the frequency of contact with individuals of the same species may be driven predominantly by population density.

However, empirical evidence for infectious diseases in humans suggests that R_0 is surprisingly consistent across a variety of contexts. Estimates of the basic reproductive number for the 2009 pandemic involving H1N1 influenza ranged from 1.2 to approximately 3.[31-33] Despite a 20-fold difference in population density, similar reproductive number estimates were obtained for New Zealand (1.9) and Japan (2.3).[32,33] This consistency is not completely surprising given the contexts in which most close human interactions take place. Whether in Manhattan or rural Wyoming, most households in the United States contain between 1 and 5 individuals, and even across the entire world, variation in household size will be less than variation in total population density. Workplaces, restaurants, and entertainment venues will fall within a similarly narrow range of sizes. Because the density dependence assumption often appears not to hold, an alternative "frequency dependent" formulation of the SIR model is often used:

$$\frac{ds}{dt} = -\beta \frac{SI}{N} \qquad \text{(Equation 5.1)}$$

$$\frac{dI}{dt} = \beta \frac{SI}{N} - \gamma I \qquad \text{(Equation 5.2)}$$

$$\frac{dR}{dt} = \gamma I \qquad \text{(Equation 5.3)}$$

In the frequency-dependent formulation, the interpretation of the transmission coefficient changes. The term S/N is the probability that any random contact that someone in I makes will be with someone susceptible to infection. The transmission coefficient β now combines the number of contacts that I is expected to make during a single time step and the probability a contact results in a new infection (note that β in the two models has different units). Under this formulation, the expression for the basic reproductive number becomes:

$$R_0 = \beta/\gamma \qquad \text{(Equation 6)}$$

which is invariant to the size of the population. Similarly, the epidemic dynamic from a frequency dependent model is the same when expressed as a percentage of the population regardless of the size of the population.

HOST POPULATION STRUCTURE

Homogeneous Mixing

One critical assumption of compartmental models is that of homogenous mixing. In these models, we assume that populations behave similarly to how a gas behaves in a container: people move about randomly and have an equal probability of contacting any member of the population of a particular type. For instance, in a simple SIR model every infectious individual has an equal probability of coming into contact with every susceptible individual (i.e., there is no clustering, hyperinfectivity, or other type of aggregation influence). Human populations are highly structured, and homogenous mixing is clearly an over-simplification; nevertheless, over some scales, models built on this assumption can accurately model epidemic data.[34,35]

Introducing Structure

Thus far we have assumed that all individuals in the same disease state are identical. In reality, important heterogeneities exist between individuals that can affect the dynamics of transmission. It is possible to relax the assumption of identical, homogenously mixing individuals by introducing additional model compartments and specifying transmission coefficients based on the interactions between these compartments.

Age

Age can alter a person's risk of acquiring and transmitting an infectious disease through multiple pathways. For example, young individuals may be protected by maternal antibodies or have increased susceptibility

because of immaturity of their immune response. Infectious contacts that might transmit respiratory and gastrointestinal infections may occur at increased rates among young individuals because of reduced hygienic practices. Age has been shown to be a predictor of whom individuals have social contact with, with the age distribution of contacts showing a strong tendency for contacts to occur between individuals of a similar age, but also reflecting family structure.[36] Models that incorporate this heterogeneity may exhibit fundamentally different behavior than models that do not. In addition, age dictates the timing of immunization targeting many pathogens. Models that incorporate age structure can compare multiple alternative age-specific immunization programs.

Age is often modeled by adding age-specific compartments for each disease state and specifying transmission coefficients capturing the rates at which members of these age compartments interact.[37-39] For example, consider the model shown in **Figure 6-5**, which divides the population into three groups: preschoolers, school-aged children, and adults. Each of these groups has a different level of interaction both within their group and with people in other groups. School-aged children might have the most interaction among themselves ($\beta_{22} > \beta_{11}, \beta_{33}$, but the least interaction with preschoolers or adults. Preschool-aged children, in contrast, may interact less among themselves than school-aged children do ($\beta_{11} < \beta_{22}$), but likely have a closer relationship to adults ($\beta_{13} > \beta_{23}$). For many questions and diseases, the use of models with population structure is critical, as important heterogeneities might change our conclusions about the effectiveness of interventions and other factors (see the example of rubella later in this chapter).

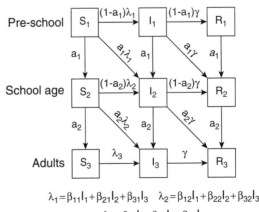

$$\lambda_1 = \beta_{11}I_1 + \beta_{21}I_2 + \beta_{31}I_3 \quad \lambda_2 = \beta_{12}I_1 + \beta_{22}I_2 + \beta_{32}I_3$$
$$\lambda_3 = \beta_{13}I_1 + \beta_{23}I_2 + \beta_{33}I_3$$

Figure 6-5 A simple age structured SIR model where individuals move through (1) pre-school, (2) school aged and (3) adult categories.

The average age of infection can be derived from compartmental models and expressed as a function of model parameters. Empirical data on the average age of incident cases can be used to parameterize these models and obtain estimates of the basic reproductive number.[16] With certain assumptions about the demographic structure of the population, the basic reproductive number is related to the average age of infection by the following expression:

$$R_0 = \frac{L}{A} + 1 \qquad \text{(Equation 7)}$$

where L is the average life expectancy of individuals in the population.

Gender

Sexually transmitted infections may be transmitted asymmetrically with respect to gender, with different rates of transmission being noted from women to men, men to women, men to men, and women to women. Rates of sexual partnership may vary across these different types of couplings in any population. Models of sexually transmitted infections (STIs) introduce host heterogeneity to account for these differences in contact rates and transmission rates. Models of STIs among exclusively heterosexual couples are similar in structure to models of vector-borne diseases where each host transmits the disease exclusively to the other host type. A key challenge in crafting models of STIs with multiple genders and types of partnerships is to balance partnerships across genders. Reconciling empirical data on partnership formation in a way that balances sexual contacts made by each group is often difficult and may require reinterpretation of empirical data.

When host heterogeneities are present, the individual basic reproductive numbers within each age group bounds the overall basic reproductive number, but this quantity must be estimated while accounting for the typical infective individual in the population. Later in this chapter, we present methods to estimate the basic reproductive number from models with structured host populations.

Agent/Networks

One of the key assumptions of compartmental models of infectious disease is that all individuals within the population, or within subpopulations, have the same chance of having an infectious contact with other individuals within that population. This is never truly the case, but for many diseases transmitted by person-to-person contact (e.g., measles, rubella), this assumption is close enough to reality to give accurate predictions. However, for some diseases, particularly STIs, individual variations in contact may have a profound effect on disease dynamics. Furthermore, even in the cases of constant contact probability, the specifics of how contact occurs may be important to disease dynamics. For instance, "concurrent" contacts in STIs can greatly increase the speed of disease spread and population risk.[40]

One approach to dealing with heterogeneities in contact, as well as other types of heterogeneity (e.g., differences in host susceptibility), is to explicitly model each individual in the population and his or her infection status. In network models, individuals are depicted as nodes in a network of potentially infectious connections. In agent-based models, individuals are depicted as "agents" that exist in some virtual environment where they contact (or do not contact) other agents based on some set of behaviors. These definitions are somewhat malleable, and the distinction between the two approaches is not always clear. Agent-based models typically incorporate some process by which agents can gather and interpret information on the state of other agents in the model.[41] For example, in dynamic network models, contacts between nodes (i.e., agents) may change based on some set of rules analogous to agent behaviors.[41] In both approaches, individuals are considered to have a disease state (analogous to the compartmental model states), such as "susceptible," "infectious," or "immune." Individual-based approaches, however, allow for an expansion of the state space to include subtle differences between infected hosts; for example, each host may have a different transmission probability to those around the host.

Agent-based models have been built at a variety of spatial scales, from single hospital unit up to entire countries,[42–44] and have played a particularly important role in pandemic preparedness planning. Network-based models have proved particularly useful in modeling the transmission of STIs, where contact networks tend to be heterogeneous, and their structure can play an important role in epidemic dynamics.[45]

Network- and agent-based models are intuitively appealing because they can, in theory, represent almost any level of realism and complexity in the disease transmission process. However, this power and flexibility come at a cost. Greater realism generally requires more background information or assumptions about host behavior and the disease process. The number of assumptions needed often makes it difficult to directly estimate model parameters from a disease process or to perform adequate sensitivity analyses of the results. Furthermore, it is easy to embed arbitrary structural assumptions in agent-based models that are difficult to communicate to other researchers or to replicate, which in turn may make replication, comparison, and generalizable inferences challenging. Despite these caveats, agent-based and

---

Box 6-1	Modeling Methodologies

Branching Processes

Basic branching processes assume that infection occurs in discrete non-overlapping, overlapping generations. The number of infections in each generation is a function of the number of infections in the previous generation times the reproduction number, R.

Model Inputs

Branching models assume a known distribution of "child" infections for each "parent" infection occurring in the previous generation. In their simplest form, this is simply R.

Compartmental Models

Compartmental models divide the population into "compartments" based on infectious state and demographics—for example, the S compartment for susceptible individuals and the I compartment for infectious individuals. At any given time, the state of the population is defined by the number of people in each compartment. It is assumed that the population is homogeneous within each compartment (i.e., an individual in the population is fully defined by his or her compartment) and that homogeneous mixing occurs between compartments.

Model Inputs

In general, a transmission coefficient and the average time that individuals remain infectious must be specified. More complex models may require the length of the latent period (SEIR models), birth and death rates (open population models), and seasonal variations in the transmission coefficient to be known. The number of parameters that must be specified generally scales with the number of compartments modeled.

Network- and Agent-Based Models

Network- and agent-based models explicitly represent each individual in the population and his or her potentially infectious contacts. These contacts may be represented by a static or a dynamic network structure (network-based models) or may be the result of an individual's changing status and behavior over time (agent-based models). These models make few assumptions other than that the specification of the model capture the important aspects of the infectious process.

Model Inputs

Network- and agent-based models often require a large amount of information about the population, although simplified models can be sometimes revealing. In addition to disease natural history (e.g., latent and infectious periods) and per-contact infection probabilities, it is often necessary to know the population distribution of contact patterns, the daily movements and other behaviors of the members in the population, and the way in which population members of different types are distributed across geographic space.

---

network-based approaches remain powerful methods to model dynamic disease processes, and are often the only tool flexible enough to handle certain problems.

TYPES OF PATHOGENS

There is huge diversity in the types of pathogens that cause infectious disease. In terms of epidemic dynamics, two differences are of primary importance: (1) how the pathogen induces (or does not induce) host immunity and whether this affects future transmission, and (2) how the pathogen is transmitted between hosts.

Immune Status and Pathogen Population Structure

In the simplest formulation, hosts are born susceptible, then are infected, and then recover and are forever immune to future infection. Although there are few diseases for which this simple formulation is completely true, depending on the question of interest such a simplified structure may be adequate to capture the essential disease dynamics. For instance, while the period of maternal protection to measles may be very important for setting vaccine policy, it is unimportant in predicting the course of a measles outbreak in a measles-naive population. While in many cases it may be necessary to develop a disease-specific immune model, most diseases fall into one of the following major classes.

Pathogens Conferring Lifelong Immunity (SIR, SEIR)

Pathogens such as measles, smallpox, and rubella confer lifelong immunity to future infection. For these diseases, a simple susceptible–infected–recovered (SIR) model is usually adequate to capture the epidemic dynamics (Figure 6-4A). Even when full immunity is temporary (e.g., cholera), models that assume full immunity after infection are adequate for capturing the dynamics at shorter time scales (e.g., over the course of a single epidemic).

Pathogens with Protective Maternal Antibodies (MSIR, MSEIR)

Many diseases are characterized by a period following birth where infants are immune to infection due to the presence of maternal antibodies transplacentally transferred from mother to infant.[46] This phenomenon can have important implications for disease dynamics, especially for diseases such as measles, where the presence of maternal antibodies interferes with the action of vaccines.[47] When maternal antibodies are important, a maternally immune (M) compartment is usually added to models to account for the period of maternal protection (and possible reduced vaccine efficacy) (Figure 6-4B).

Pathogens Conferring No Immunity (SIS)

Some pathogens, particularly some bacterial infections, confer no significant immunity even within the course of a single epidemic. In these cases, a susceptible–infectious–susceptible (SIS) model, in which individuals immediately return to the susceptible compartment after treatment or recovery, is appropriate (Figure 6-4C). The reasons for continued immunity vary. In some cases (e.g., cutaneous *Staphylococcus* infection), the host mounts no permanent immune response; in others, the diversity of pathogen strains is such that individuals are effectively susceptible to another infection with a different strain immediately after recovery.

Pathogens Conferring Temporary or Waning Immunity (SIRS)

In some cases, a pathogen may induce temporary immunity but this immunity may wane eventually, making a susceptible–infectious–recovered–susceptible (SIRS) model appropriate. The reasons for returning susceptibility vary between pathogens. In the case of influenza, an SIRS model allows epidemiologists to approximate the effect of the influenza virus changing over time through the process of antigenic drift, eventually becoming different enough that individuals are no longer are immune to the circulating virus.[46] In contrast, cholera immunity is temporary not because of a changing bacterium but due to a waning in host immunity itself,[48] yet an SIRS model is still appropriate. In many cases, a pathogen that is truly SIRS can be modeled as SIR (if we are interested in only a single epidemic) or as SIS (if the period of immunity is insignificant on the timescale being studied).

Pathogens Conferring Partial Immunity or Cross-Immunity Between Strains

In some cases, an individual's immune status and infection history must be modeled in more detail than is captured by a single compartment. This is often true when infection confers partial immunity to future infections with the same pathogen (for instance, protecting against systemic disease) or when multiple pathogen strains exist that provide partial protection between one another. There are also cases, such as dengue, where previous infection increases the probability of severe disease in a subsequent infection. Modeling these systems can be quite complex, requiring a large number of susceptible, infectious, and recovered compartments.

Figure 6-6 shows a simplified model of a dengue-like system with two strains. Infection with one strain gives immunity to that strain, but individuals remain susceptible to the other strain. After infection with both strains, individuals are immune to all future infection.

Mode of Transmission

Direct Contact

The default assumption of most of the models presented so far is that infection is primarily transmitted by direct contact. Even within the range of what are considered directly transmitted infections, however, there can be a range of contact types. For instance, influenza may be transmitted by touch, by small droplet particles that travel some distance in the air, and by pathogens being deposited on surfaces (i.e., fomites).[49] In most models, the combined effect of all of these modes of transmission are collapsed into a single β term, which encompasses both the probability of each type of contact occurring and the probability of successful transmission if it does occur. In other models, particular modes of contact are considered independently, as in explicit modeling of fomite-mediated transmission.[50]

Sexually Transmitted Infections

While these diseases are technically transmitted by "direct contact," the dynamics of STIs are often highly dependent on the special nature of sexual

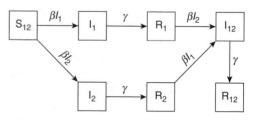

Figure 6-6 A model of a two strain (dengue-like) disease where individuals can be infected once with each strain but are permanently immune after infection with both.

contact. In part, we can exploit the fact that sexual contacts may be clear, easy-to-recall events that can be measured, at least when compared to the person-to-person transmission of a respiratory virus. For this reason, it is often useful to decompose the transmission coefficient into the average number of contacts that occur per unit time, c, and a per-contact transmission probability, β'. Hence $\beta = c\beta'$, which leads to the oft-cited formula for R_0, $R_0 = c\beta'D$, where D is the average duration of infection.

The population and contact structure also plays a particularly important role for STIs. Most notable is the existence of two distinct populations, males and females, whose members for the most part have contact with those in the opposite group and have less contact with others in their group. This distinction can be especially important in a number of contexts, such as when a pathogen causes disease in one group but not the other (e.g., HPV), if the probability of sexual transmission differs between homosexual and heterosexual contacts (e.g., HIV),[27,28] or in cultures when the ages of males and female partners vary significantly.

Nevertheless, male–female differences are not the only variations in sexual partnering that have an important impact on the transmission of STIs. There is a large distribution in the number of sexual partnerships that individuals have, with most having a small number of partners and a few having a large number.[51] The pattern of partnerships in a population forms its sexual network; not surprisingly, as their name implies, network models have proved especially useful for modeling such networks. **Figure 6-7** shows two sexual networks. In both networks, the average number of partnerships is 1.33 (i.e., $c = 1.33$). However, in network A an STI introduced in a random part of the network could cause at most 3 infections. By comparison, in network B an STI introduced into a random part of the network could cause as many as 11 infections. In fact, if every sexual partnership successfully transmitted the infection, we would expect 3 infections to result from a random introduction in network A and 8.33 infections to occur in network B [$(11 \times 11 + 4)/15$].

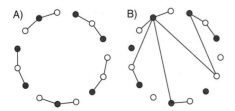

Figure 6-7 Two hypothetical sexual networks where individuals have on average 1.33 sexual partnerships.

Vector-borne Diseases

Vector-borne diseases are often be treated in the same way as directly transmitted infections given that vectors may be dispersed fairly evenly through the population, resulting random vector-mediated infectious "contacts" between members of the population.[52,53] However, if we need a more sophisticated understanding of the disease dynamics, it is often necessary to explicitly model the vector population. This is particularly true if we are interested in the effect that vector control measures (e.g., insecticide spraying) or interventions to reduce vector–human interactions (e.g., bednets) have on the spread of disease.

One of the first useful dynamic models of infectious disease, Ronald Ross's malaria model (see **Box 6-2**), explicitly modeled the mosquito population and its interaction with the human population. Ross's model encompasses many important aspects of the mosquito–human interaction: the density of mosquitoes, the percentage living long enough to transmit disease, the frequency with which they bite humans, and the percentage of humans who are infectious (i.e., have gametocytes in their blood). This model makes it possible to estimate how interventions affecting each of these compartments will affect the dynamics of malaria

---

Box 6-2	The Malaria Model of Ronald Ross

Ronald Ross's 1911 model of malaria transmission is perhaps the first mathematical model of an infectious disease used in public health practice. Ross's model was later refined by George MacDonald and served as the basis for the malaria eradication efforts starting in the 1950s and continuing through the 1970s.

In Ross's model of malaria transmission, the number of individuals infected with malaria in a given month t follows the equation:

$$m_{t+1}p = m_t p + b^2 sai(1 - m_t)m_t p - rm_t p$$

where:

- m_t is the proportion of the population infected with malaria at time
- p is the population of the area
- b is the proportion of Anopheles mosquitoes that succeed in biting a human
- s is the proportion of Anopheles mosquitoes surviving long enough to transmit malaria
- i is the proportion of humans with gametocytes in their blood
- r is the proportion of humans recovering from malaria in a month
- a is the number of Anopheles mosquitoes biting each person per month

transmission: insecticides would decrease the number of mosquitoes living long enough to transmit the infection, bednets can decrease biting frequency, and treatment reduces the number of people with gametocytes in their blood.

A simple, compartmental version of a vector-based model is shown in Figure 6-4D. Not dissimilar from Ross's model, this model contains compartments for susceptible, infectious, and recovered humans as well as susceptible and infectious mosquitoes. The rate at which susceptible humans become infected is determined by the number of infectious mosquitoes (I_m). Likewise, the rate at which mosquitoes become infected is determined by the number of infected humans (I_n).

Zoonoses

Zoonotic diseases can be modeled in a similar manner to vector-borne diseases, by creating linked models including the reservoir species and the humans at risk for infection. The chief difference between models of zoonotic infections and those of vector-borne disease is that the infection dynamics assumes that the reservoir species is generally completely independent of the state of the human population, whereas vectors generally acquire infection from infected humans. Zoonotic diseases can be considered to have two separate, independent reproductive numbers: R_0^Z for the reservoir species and R_0^H for the human host. In many cases, R_0^H will be at or near 0, and the dynamics in humans can be effectively ignored (e.g., rabies).[54] In other situations, R_0^H may excess 0 to such an extent that some modeling of the dynamics of infection in humans may be important (e.g., monkeypox, zoonotic influenza).[55-57] Consideration of chains of transmission in humans becomes especially important when we consider that zoonotic infections may become adapted to their human hosts and R_0 may move above 1, allowing for a wider epidemic and the emergence of a new infectious disease.[55]

Environmental Reservoirs

Some infectious agents, particularly bacteria, are able to replicate outside of their hosts in environmental reservoirs. In many ways these pathogens behave much like zoonosis, with humans acquiring infection from the environmental reservoir based on the amount of pathogen in that reservoir. Nevertheless, direct transmission may occur in addition to infection from the environmental reservoir—cholera is an example. The pathogen in an environmental reservoir will have its own population dynamics, which can often be quite complex. For instance, cholera is host to its own infectious disease: the bacteriophage,

which can have a profound effect on the amount of cholera in the environment.[48] Pathogens with no true environmental reservoir can also be spread through the environment. In these cases, the environment can serve as a component of the "direct" contact process (see the earlier discussion of fomites) or behave like any other noninfectious environmental contaminant.

For pathogens where an environmental reservoir plays an important part in transmission, person-to-person transmission, as characterized by R_0, may tell only part of the story. If a pathogen is ever-present in the environment, then modeling a constant (or seasonally varying) risk of infection from the environment may be appropriate, as in the following expression:

$$\frac{dI}{dt} = \beta IS + \psi S - \gamma I \qquad \text{(Equation 8)}$$

where ψ is the risk of infection from the environment.

Sometimes environmental transmission may be periodic, resulting from human contamination. For example, person-to-person transmission may be somewhat efficient, with an R_0 value slightly greater than 1, but if someone contaminates the environment, the result might be hundreds, or even thousands, of secondary infections. In this case it might be useful to model the contamination process itself:

$$\frac{dI}{dt} = \beta IS + \psi XS - \gamma I \qquad \text{(Equation 9.1)}$$

$$\frac{dX}{dt} = \phi I + rX - \delta X \qquad \text{(Equation 9.2)}$$

where X is the pathogen population in the environmental reservoir, ϕ is the rate at which infectious humans contaminate the reservoir, r is the reproductive rate of the pathogen in the environment, and δ is the pathogen's natural death rate in the environment.

Spatial Spread

The model formulations described so far implicitly assume a population that exists in a single homogenous spatial unit, though this may be at the scale of a city, state, country, or even the entire world. Many scientific questions may require a more explicit spatial representation of the disease process. For example, the spread of a pathogen from city to city across an entire country or between countries may be of central interest when modeling the spread of an emerging pathogen. Compartmental models can be extended in two basic ways to incorporate spatially distinct populations (sometimes called patches): by incorporating mass-action mixing terms between patches and by introducing migration between patches. These two formulations correspond to different conceptions about how interaction between spatial patches occurs, and some models may incorporate both types of interaction. Both types of model are often referred to as patch models or meta-population models.

Mass-action coupling assumes that individuals have some probability of interacting with individuals in other spatial patches, but remain tied to their home patch. For instance, individuals may work in a different patch from the one in which they live or temporarily visit different patches on vacations or business trips. The following system of equations describes a model where transmission proceeds as a result of mass-action coupling of two distinct spatial patches:

$$\frac{dS_1}{dt} = -\beta_{11}S_1I_1 - \beta_{12}S_1I_2 \qquad \text{(Equation 10.1)}$$

$$\frac{dI_1}{dt} = \beta_{11}S_1I_1 + \beta_{12}S_1I_2 - \gamma I_1 \qquad \text{(Equation 10.2)}$$

$$\frac{dR_1}{dt} = \gamma I_1 \qquad \text{(Equation 10.3)}$$

$$\frac{dS_2}{dt} = -\beta_{22}S_2I_s - \beta_{21}S_2I_1 - \ S_2 \qquad \text{(Equation 10.4)}$$

$$\frac{dI_2}{dt} = \beta_{22}S_2I_2 + \beta_{21}S_2I_1 - \gamma I_2 \qquad \text{(Equation 10.5)}$$

$$\frac{dR_2}{dt} = \gamma I_2 \qquad \text{(Equation 10.6)}$$

Generally, we expect the rates β_{11} and β_{22} representing contact within a patch to be higher than β_{12} and β_{21}, which represent the rate at which infectious contacts are made between patches. This model makes some curious assumptions about contact. Individuals can contribute to the force of infection in two patches at once. This makes sense if spatial interactions occur on a small time scale relative to the disease process (e.g., commuting to work), but is inappropriate for spatial shifts occurring over a longer time scale.

Spatial interactions occurring over a longer time scale can be modeled by introducing migration terms into the model. In this approach, individuals actually move between patches, becoming members of the new patch to which they travel. Once in this new patch, they have an equal probability of migrating out as every other member of the patch. Migration models are appropriate for modeling actual migration and any spatial interaction that occurs on a time scale that is long compared to the disease process

(e.g., a week-long vacation might be best modeled as migration if we are interested in the dynamics of influenza). The following system of equations defines a two-patch migration model:

$$\frac{dS_1}{dt} = -\beta S_1I_1 - \varepsilon S_1 + \iota S_2 \qquad \text{(Equation 11.1)}$$

$$\frac{dI_1}{dt} = \beta S_1I_1 - \gamma I_1 - \varepsilon I_1 + \iota I_2 \qquad \text{(Equation 11.2)}$$

$$\frac{dR_1}{dt} = \gamma I_1 - \varepsilon R_1 + \iota R_2 \qquad \text{(Equation 11.3)}$$

$$\frac{dS_2}{dt} = -\beta S_2I_2 - \varepsilon S_2 + \iota S_1 \qquad \text{(Equation 11.4)}$$

$$\frac{dI_2}{dt} = \beta S_2I_s - \gamma I_2 - \varepsilon I_2 + \iota I_1 \qquad \text{(Equation 11.5)}$$

$$\frac{dR_2}{dt} = \gamma I_2 - \varepsilon R_2 + \iota R_1 \qquad \text{(Equation 11.6)}$$

In this model, individuals migrate between patches via the migration terms ε and ι, and once they have migrated are indistinguishable from any other members of their new patch.

A key consideration in choosing between these models is the time scale of disease progression, transmission, and human movement between patches. If movement between patches is relatively fast compared to the rate of progression through infectious state, mass-action coupling might be assumed to roughly hold. In contrast, if movement is slow, this may be more consistent with the migration model.

DYNAMIC POPULATIONS AND PATHOGENS

Open Populations

In the basic SIR model, there is no process by which individuals enter the population (by birth or immigration) or leave (by death or emigration). This may be a convenient and appropriate simplification for epidemics that occur on fast time scales, but to understand longer-term dynamics these processes must be included. A simple adaptation of the basic model is to add some constant rate of birth into the susceptible class and some constant rate of death from each compartment (as in Figure 6-4B). The rate at which deaths occur can be specific to each disease class, allowing for increased mortality among those that are infected compared to those that are not.

Box 6-3	The Importance of Births

The rate at which susceptible individuals enter the population is dictated by the birth rate in a population. Populations with high birth rates can experience frequent epidemics due to the rapidity with which births replenish the pool of susceptible individuals. Births have been found to be an important predictor of periodicity in many predator–prey systems, including lynx and hares (Moran, see file), and red grouse (Moss, see file). Measles dynamics show a distinct response to birth rates (Earn, 10650003). The graph shown here plots the incidence of measles in New York City from 1928 to 1960. Peaks in incidence occur each year, but clear biennial patterns can also be seen, with much larger peaks in even years from 1946 to 1960. This biennial pattern persists during a period when birth rates are high (gray curve). However, earlier in the series, following a period of low birth rates in the 1930s, large peaks in incidence are separated by up to 3 years.

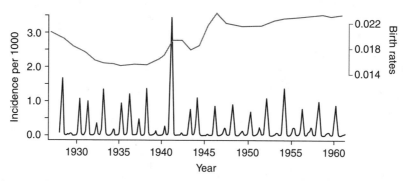

Reproduced from Yorke JA and London WP. Recurrent outbreaks of measles, chickenpox and mumps II. Systematic differences in contact rates and stochastic effects. *American Journal of Epidemiology*. 1973;98(6):469–482. By permission of Oxford University Press.

Including vital dynamics—that is, births and deaths—allows for the inclusion of population turnover and is critical to modeling endemic diseases over long time scales. Without the introduction of new individuals into the population, infections in closed populations will die out if individuals recover and become immune or die after infection. With the inclusion of vital dynamics, pathogens can persist in models over many years, as they are observed to do in human populations. Incidence may reach a relatively stable level over time, or it may go through cycles due to the influence of cyclic extrinsic drivers of transmissibility or oscillations in immunity in the population as the number of susceptible individuals waxes and wanes. The flow of susceptible individuals into a population through is a critical determinant of incidence patterns for many infectious diseases (**Box 6-3**). Next, we present a discussion of sources of seasonal oscillations in extrinsic drivers of transmission and their impact on transmission dynamics (seasonality) and the interaction of seasonality with intrinsic cycles of immunity in populations.

Seasonality

Many diseases demonstrate clear seasonal patterns of infection. In temperate regions, influenza and measles epidemics tend to occur during the winter,[58,59] and in tropical regions, these diseases have seasonal patterns that seem to bear a stronger relationship to local factors. Vector-borne diseases are often highly seasonal (e.g., peaks in dengue incidence in Thailand typically occur between July and December),[60] as are waterborne diseases that require particular environmental conditions for efficient transmission.

The drivers of seasonality vary between diseases and are not always clear. For diseases transmitted by direct contact, it is generally assumed that either weather conditions or seasonal variations in social mixing lead to seasonal variation in incidence. For example, differences in the efficiency of influenza transmission at different absolute humidity levels has been postulated as a possible reason for the seasonal variation in flu transmission.[61] The timing of school terms has been considered as a possible prime driver of both flu and measles transmission.[59] Possible drivers of seasonality are often location specific. For instance, Niger experiences a yearly regional migration to the capital during the dry season, driven by agricultural cycles. This large migration, in turn, results in strong seasonal forcing of the measles epidemic in that country.[62]

In compartmental modals, seasonality is usually modeled by a time-varying transmission coefficient, β_t. One of the simplest functional forms used

A) If seasonality is due to smoothly varying climactic factors such as temperature a sine wave captures the rise and fall in transmission around an overall mean.

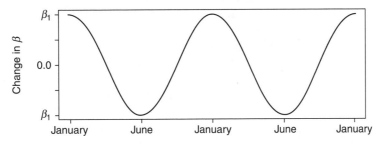

B) The timing of school terms may divide the year into discrete period where school is in session and β is high, or school is out of session and β is low.

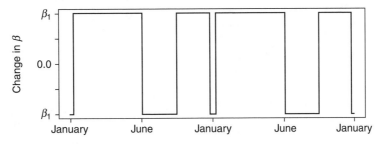

C) Seasonality might also be driven by hightened levels of social mixing and travel during specific, short, times of the year (e.g., the lunar new year in China).

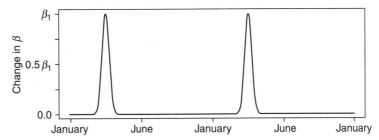

Figure 6-8 Different formulations of seasonal forcing functions.

to represent time-varying transmission is that of a sine wave with a yearlong periodicity:

$$\beta_t = \beta_0(1 + \beta_1 \sin(2\pi t + c)) \quad \text{(Equation 12)}$$

where t is the time in years and c is an offset that governs the timing of peak seasonality. A sine is a good representation of seasonal forcing if we believe smoothly varying climactic factors (e.g., temperature) to be driving the seasonality of epidemics. Alternatively, we may choose other functional forms for β_t if we believe seasonality to result from a different process (**Figure 6-8**).

The peak of an epidemic curve does not often coincide exactly with the time at which β_t is the highest. If sustained transmission can occur (i.e., R_0 is greater than 1) only during the periods of most efficient transmission (i.e., when β_t is highest), then the epidemic will peak after the peak in β_t. In contrast, if sustained transmission has been occurring for some time before β_0 peaks, then the epidemic may already be receding due to the depletion of susceptible individuals.

An example of these phenomena could be seen in the 2009 H1N1 influenza pandemic. In the United States, in most years the epidemic peak in influenza cases occurs late in the winter (i.e., late January through mid-March); during the 2009–2010 influenza season, however, the epidemic peak occurred in late October and early November.[63] While we do not know the timing of peak β_t for influenza, it is unlikely to vary between seasonal and pandemic strains. The reason for the early peak in 2009 is that more people were susceptible to the novel pandemic strain, which meant that sustained transmission could start earlier in the season. In normal years, fewer people are susceptible to influenza, so β_t must rise higher before sustained transmission can occur, leading to a later epidemic.

Multiannual Cycles

The combination of seasonality and transmission and population demography often combine to create multiannual patterns in disease dynamics. During the mid-1900s, the size of measles epidemics in New York City, London, and other locations varied dramatically between years, often showing a biennial pattern with alternating big- and small-incidence years (see Box 6-3). These biennial patterns show the impact of cycling of the susceptible fraction in time. Such oscillations are predicted by simple models such as the SIR model. SIR models that include vital dynamics exhibit oscillatory dynamics as they approach an equilibrium level of incidence. As incidence slows and R approaches 1, the system has momentum in the form of infectious individuals who give rise to less than one infection, but more than zero on average. These cause the model to overshoot its equilibrium point. From any starting point, the basic SIR model will experience damped oscillations until it reaches a fixed equilibrium in each state variable. If transmission is driven seasonally, the seasonality will cause these natural oscillations to persist, much like a child being pushed on a swing. The period at which large increases in incidence occur is called the natural period of oscillations of a system; it is dictated by birth rates as well as the natural history of the pathogen. The measles system often exhibits a natural two-year oscillation. Surprisingly, this dynamic can be reproduced using a simple SEIR model with only annual forcing.[34,59,64]

Changing and Diverse Pathogens

Many pathogens exist as multiple, genetically distinct, but related strains. The genetic diversity of a pathogen can have a dramatic impact on the dynamics of human disease for a family of pathogens. Strain structure may sometimes be irrelevant to human immune response, with exposure to one eliciting a protective response to all variants (e.g., measles). In that scenario, individuals are infected at most once in their life. For other pathogens, infection with one strain may yield a partially protective immune response to other strains of the pathogen (e.g., RSV). Strains that invoke a protective immune response to one another

upon infection are antigenically similar to one another; that is, they present a similar antigen profile to the human immune system. Conversely, pathogens that exhibit multiple antigenically distinct strains, either at any time or over time, can infect humans multiple times over their lifetime.

The genetic diversity of pathogen populations may also have implications for the effectiveness of interventions such as vaccines and antimicrobial agents. For example, multiple strains of pneumococcal bacteria cause invasive disease, but vaccines can target only a subset of strains that circulate, leaving the possibility of infection with uncovered strains as well as the possibility of selection for strains not covered by the vaccine (i.e., serotype replacement). Genetic diversity also makes it possible that the selective pressure of antimicrobial agents will result in the evolution of resistant pathogens.[65,66]

Multiple-strain pathogens have been modeled in several ways. If the strains have little cross-reactive immune response, they can be treated as independent pathogens. If interaction occurs, it may result in several different epidemiologically relevant phenomena. The risk of infection in persons with preexisting immunity to an antigenically distinct strain may be reduced compared to immunologically naive individuals. Upon infection, individuals with preexisting immunity may experience a lower pathogen load and lower transmissibility to others. Both of these changes can be represented in extensions of the basic SIR framework by expanding the state space to include separate compartments for those experiencing their first, second, third, and later infections (see Figure 6-6). This representation is called a history-based model,[67,68] as it classifies each susceptible host in terms of past history of infection.

A difficulty in formulating these models for pathogens with a large number of strains is that the number of compartments that must be included becomes very large, as each distinct history must have its own compartment. An alternative formulation is a status-based model,[69] which represents each individual's current status of immunity to all circulating strains. Infection with particular strains updates this status, given the former status of the host. Thus the state space is defined by the unique sets of strains to which hosts are immune, and the scheme allows for representation of a fuller range of cross-immunity (including expanding the types of partial immunity that can be represented).

A key phenomenon that has been investigated with these models is the generation, persistence, and loss of diversity of pathogen populations. Ecological theory would predict that in the presence of a cross-protective immune response, heterogeneity between pathogens in transmissibility would result in competitive exclusion of pathogen strains that are less transmissible.[70] In fact, many pathogens exhibit heterogeneity in transmissibility but still show sustained diversity; the mechanisms that maintain this diversity are not well understood.[68,71]

STOCHASTICITY AND RANDOMNESS

When we predict the dynamics of an infection by solving the system of differential equations that define a compartmental model, we get only the expected behavior of a pathogen in that population. In reality, random events govern the epidemic process, and a large amount of variation may occur in the course of an epidemic that we might actually see if identical pathogens are introduced into identical populations multiple times. One of the most important of these possibilities is whether an index case entering a population causes an epidemic in the first place. In a deterministic SIR model, when an infectious individual enters the population, an epidemic will always result. For instance, if a pathogen has an R_0 of 1.1, the index case will result in exactly 1.1 additional cases, triggering epidemic growth. However, 1.1 is actually the *average* number of cases caused in a fully susceptible population—over 10 introductions, we might see the index case cause 3 cases once, 2 cases once, 1 case six times and no cases two times. When no secondary cases are caused, obviously no epidemic occurs.

The basic compartmental model framework can be extended to account for the randomness in the epidemic process by using the rates in the differential equations defining the model to define random variables that govern how many people move between states as we step through time. A simple stochastic SIR model would consist of a series of binomial draws from the S and I compartments of the number of individuals who should move to the I and R compartments, respectively:

$$SI \sim BINOMIAL\ S, \frac{\beta I}{N} \quad \text{(Equation 13.1)}$$

$$\Delta IR \sim BINOMIAL\ (I, \gamma) \quad \text{(Equation 13.2)}$$

$$S_{t+1} = S_t - \Delta SI \quad \text{(Equation 13.3)}$$

$$I_{t+1} = I_t + \Delta SI - \Delta IR \quad \text{(Equation 13.4)}$$

$$R_{t+1} = R_t - \Delta IR \quad \text{(Equation 13.5)}$$

In practice, refinements of this crude model are often used. Because the epidemic dynamics

produced by stochastic models can be influenced by the time-step size if it is too large, the time-steps used in simulations are often smaller than the scale at which the rates are specified. An alternative to taking time-steps is to use an event-driven approach, whereby a stochastic draw determines when the next state transition occurs in the system based on its current state.

Often individual state transitions are estimated to follow a more intricate distribution than a simple constant rate. For instance, the SEIR assumption of an exponentially distributed incubation period (i.e., that people leave the E compartment at a constant rate) is clearly at odds with evidence that incubation periods tend to follow a log-normal distribution. In a stochastic model we may solve this problem by drawing a time in the E compartment for each individual when he or she becomes infected. In this case, we need to begin to track the infection histories of individuals in our population, as opposed to simply performing aggregate counts of the number in each compartment, making implementation more difficult (in these cases, the lines between compartmental and agent-based models begin to blur).

Inference using a stochastic model is performed by simulating thousands of random epidemics using the model. The average behavior in these epidemics (i.e., the average number of people in each compartment on each epidemic day) gives the expected course of infections. In addition to the mean behavior, confidence intervals, percentage of index cases resulting in an epidemic, and other descriptive statistics can be estimated from these simulations.

One key result of stochastic epidemic simulations is the distribution of epidemic sizes obtained over multiple simulations. For any given R_0, we expect a particular distribution of final epidemic sizes (although this distribution is somewhat sensitive to other model assumptions). In general, these distributions tend to follow a particular form. In situations where R is greater than 1, some percentage of epidemics will die out after only a few cases. Conversely, in those that reach a certain threshold, the number of cases all go on to cause large epidemics of a size similar to that predicted by the deterministic models (**Figure 6-9**). When R is less than 1, most introductions will result in only a few cases, but occasionally larger epidemics will occur. Because the distribution of sizes reflects a particular R value, it can be used to estimate R if we see multiple introductions where we expect similar levels of susceptibility (e.g., human epidemics of a rare zoonosis).

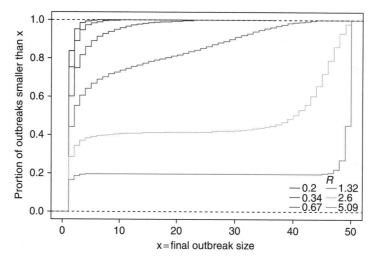

Figure 6-9 Cumulative distribution functions of final epidemic sizes in a population of 50 individuals after one introduction.

Other Methods of Including Stochasticity

In cases where host populations of interest are assumed to be large, alternative methods can be used to introduce stochasticity. Demographic stochasticity in large populations can be represented by including additive or multiplicative noise in each of the state variables in a system of differential equations. For example, a normal random deviate could be added to each of the state variables with a distinct variance in each state variable:

$$\frac{dS}{dt} = \mu - \beta SI - \mu S + N(0, \sigma_S) \qquad \text{(Equation 14.1)}$$

$$\frac{dI}{dt} = \beta SI - \gamma I - \mu I + N(0, \sigma_I) \qquad \text{(Equation 14.2)}$$

$$\frac{dR}{dt} = \gamma I - \mu R + N(0, \sigma_R) \qquad \text{(Equation 14.3)}$$

The result is called a system of stochastic differential equations. This approach is often taken to test the robustness of deterministic results to the inclusion of some stochasticity without specific interest in the structure and mechanism of introduced noise.

METHODS OF ESTIMATION

"The aim of mathematical epidemiology is to integrate biological and circumstantial data into one coherent whole." —George MacDonald

Dynamic models of the infectious disease process are useful conceptually and can be used to derive some important results from core principles. However, the ultimate utility of this approach depends on our ability to match our models with processes that truly occur in nature. Without this link to real data, infectious disease models are merely representations of an idealized system, being studied for their own sake. While this approach has yielded some important results, for application to real infectious diseases it is necessary to estimate the parameters that govern disease dynamics. There are two main approaches for doing so: (1) estimating individual model parameters and (2) fitting the full system to a set of infectious disease outcomes (usually a time series of incidence). The former approach has the advantage of combining the best science from many subfields and very tractable estimation tasks; the latter is assured to produce a model with dynamics consistent with reality in at least one case. In practice, many studies end up using a combination of the two approaches, deriving some estimates from existing literature and obtaining other problems based on the optimal model fit to data. Regardless of the approach used, a strong link to data is essential to developing scientifically grounded dynamic models of infectious disease.

Time Periods

Two main approaches are used in the estimation of time periods such as the generation time, incubation period, and infectious period. The first strategy is to directly estimate the distribution of times seen using statistical techniques from survival analysis. The second involves simultaneous fitting of the constituent time periods and other aspects of the dynamic process.

Direct Estimation

Direct estimation has the advantage of being grounded in a lengthy and well-established body of literature on statistical survival analysis and requiring few assumptions about other aspects of the epidemic process. In general, censored observations of the time period of interest are used to fit an assumed underlying distribution of times. One such approach is to place upper and lower limits on the time period of interest based on the time period of interest based on data (i.e., make singly interval censored observations); see the work of Lessler et al. for an example of this technique applied to the incubation period.[23] More accuracy can be achieved if the start and the end of the potential period can both be constrained (e.g., if we can bound both the time of infection and the time of symptom onset in an incubation period observation).[72]

The problem with direct estimation is that these periods are difficult to observe; hence limited data are available to use. For some diseases, experimental studies have been performed, but these investigations are not common and would often be unethical to perform. Observations of naturally occurring cases can provide additional data, but appropriate observations are limited (for instance, in one highly observed epidemic more than 800 cases yielded only 16 cases with information that could be used to estimate the generation time).[73]

Simultaneous Estimation of Time Periods and Parameters

An alternative approach that uses all of the available data in an epidemic is to simultaneously estimate time periods and other aspects of the epidemic. If a highly structured model is assumed (e.g., one of the compartmental models described previously), an epidemic curve can be fit using any number of techniques (e.g., minimization of mean square error, maximum likelihood).

An alternative approach has been to consider only the generation time and R_0 as parts of the epidemic process.[74] This strategy has the advantage of minimizing model assumptions while using the full epidemic data, but can still result in substantial uncertainty because of the close relationship between R_0 and the generation time.[75]

Basic Reproductive Number

Many techniques can be used to estimate the basic reproductive number. Estimates of R_0 can be calculated using at least four different methods: (1) calculation using rates of the multiple constituent processes of transmission, (2) estimation using the initial growth rate of cases in epidemics, (3) estimation using the final size of outbreaks, and (4) estimation from equilibrium age-specific prevalence.

Calculation from Constituent Processes

Numerous biological processes are involved in a single generation of transmission. These processes might include the biting rate of a vector, the per-bite probability of acquisition of a pathogen by a vector from an infectious human, the rate at which the pathogen disseminates from the midgut of the vector to the salivary glands, the daily survival probability of the vector, and the per-bite probability of infection of a human by an infectious vector. Each of these quantities could be measured empirically. For example, in Ross's malaria model, new infections are a product of the rate at which mosquitoes bite humans, survival of the mosquito, the gametocyte rate in humans, and the recovery rate of humans (see Box 6-2). A challenge in estimating reproductive numbers from constituent processes is the need to obtain data on each of these processes.

Initial Growth Rate of Cases

In the early phases of an epidemic, infections grow exponentially as a function of the force of infection. Because the force of infection can be directly related to R_0, empirical data describing the exponential increase in infections, along with information on the time-course of the infectious process, can be used to estimate R_0. The functional relationship between R_0 and the exponential rise in cases depends on the specific generation time of infection and its assumed distribution.[75,76] This approach is appropriate for estimating the basic reproductive number when the population is known to be entirely susceptible, or when the fraction that is susceptible is known. However, for endemic diseases, the fraction of the population that is susceptible may not be easy to obtain. Also for endemic infections, estimates may be linked to the particular season in which the epidemic began, limiting the utility of the estimate for certain applications such as estimating the critical vaccination fraction.

Final Outbreak Size

Analytic expressions of the final size of epidemics in a closed population have been derived for a large class of epidemic models. These expressions give an estimate of the final percentage or number of individuals infected in a setting as a function of the basic reproductive number. In epidemics in carefully observed populations, the observed final size of the outbreak can be equated to theoretical predictions where the basic reproductive number is a parameter:

$$R_0 = \frac{\ln(s_0/s_\infty)}{s_0 - s_\infty} \qquad \text{(Equation 15)}$$

where s_0 is the proportion of the population that is susceptible at the beginning of the epidemic, and s_∞ is the proportion susceptible at the end of the epidemic.[77] Note that $N(s_0 - s_\infty)$ is the final size of the epidemic.

Equilibrium Prevalence and Use of Average Age

At equilibrium, cases of disease are stable—that is, neither increasing nor decreasing. Thus R must be equal to 1. As stated earlier, $R = sR_0$ where s is the fraction of the population that is susceptible to infection. At equilibrium, $1 = R = sR_0$. If the fraction of the population that is susceptible can be estimated, it can be used to estimate the basic reproductive number through the expression $\frac{1}{s} = R_0$. The susceptible fraction can be obtained by serological survey or estimated using age-specific incidence of disease.[78] A gross estimate of the basic reproductive number can be determined using just the mean age of acquisition of infection or disease and the equation introduced earlier: $R_0 = \frac{L}{A} + 1$. This approach discards all information from the full age distribution of infections or cases. If age-stratified serological prevalence data can be obtained, the force of infection can be estimated by comparing age cohorts of age i to those of age $i - 1$. The additional seroprevalence in age class i provides an estimate of the hazard that cohorts experience in one year.[79] Estimates of the force of infection derived from this approach can be used to estimate the total fraction of the population susceptible to the disease (i.e., those escaping this hazard) to estimate the basic reproductive number.

Estimates derived using this approach are more robust in the face of secular changes in data collection methods. An additional advantage of using serological data is that estimates based on serological prevalence yield better estimates of the transmission of infection than estimates based on symptomatic surveillance.

Next Generation Matrix

As mentioned earlier, R_0 can be defined in two ways: (1) as the expected number of secondary infections attributable to a typical infectious individual in an entirely susceptible population and (2) as a threshold parameter indicating whether a pathogen successfully invades a population. Stated another way, R_0 is a threshold parameter describing the stability of a disease-free equilibrium of the system. These definitions are not inconsistent. If an infected individual causes less than 1 infection in an entirely susceptible population, the pathogen will not successfully invade that population. However, for diseases that lead to multiple types of infected individuals (e.g., hosts indexed by age or sexual activity class) who reside in multiple types of infectious compartments (e.g., active, latent, or treated tuberculosis), the specification of a typical infectious individual becomes difficult.

Diekmann et al. resolve this issue by formulating a definition of R_0 for an arbitrary model structure. They define R_0 as the spectral radius of the next generation matrix.[80] The next generation matrix describes the rate at which infectious individuals of a particular type (say, type i) infect individuals of a type j. If a transmission model has n types of infectious individuals, this matrix will have $n \times n$ entries. R_0 is the spectral radius, or largest-magnitude eigenvalue of this matrix. Detailed descriptions of this method appear work by in Diekmann et al.[80] and Van den Driessche and Watmough.[81]

Although this method provides an expression of the basic reproductive number as a function of model parameters for models of arbitrary complexity, a link must still be made with data. That link could be created by estimating each of the parameters of the transmission model using empirical data and solving the expression for R_0 to simply calculate this value. The expression may also be used with the approaches described previously of equating R_0 to some function of the equilibrium fraction of susceptible individuals or to an exponential increase in cases early in an epidemic.

INFECTIOUS DISEASE DYNAMICS AND PUBLIC HEALTH

Since its inception, the field of infectious disease dynamics has had an intimate relationship with public health practice. The promise of the ability to predict the course of outbreaks and the effects of interventions makes dynamic models an attractive and useful tool to policymakers. However, the most important contributions of dynamic models of infectious disease derive from how they affect thinking about the epidemic process, rather than any particular quantitative result. Here we present seven examples of the application of infectious disease dynamical theory to important public health problems, describing how these approaches informed the thinking about public health problems and influenced policy.

Malaria WHO Eradication

The model of malaria transmission that was developed by Ronald Ross and later refined by George MacDonald showed that it would not be necessary to completely eliminate the *Anopheles* vector to stop malaria transmission; instead, a substantial reduction in the mosquito population would be adequate. MacDonald postulated that "The worst conditions known in Africa could therefore be overcome by an increase in the daily mortality of the vector from about 5% to about 45%."[9] Based on this observation, the World Health Organization embarked on a DDT-focused mosquito reduction campaign that eliminated malaria transmission among 500 million people.[82]

That it is not necessary to eliminate all mosquitoes to eliminate transmission of malaria can be seen from examining Ross's basic model of malaria transmission (Box 6-2). The number of new infections occurring each month is given by the term $b^2 sai(1 - m_t) m_t p$, which implies that the basic reproductive number for malaria is

$$R_0 = b^2 sa \qquad \text{(Equation 16)}$$

A reduction in the number of mosquitoes surviving long enough to transmit disease (s) that is adequate to bring this value to less than 1 will eventually result in the elimination of malaria according to Ross's model. While the level needed may vary between locations based on the local mosquito biting rate (b) and the number of biting mosquitoes (a), in no case would it be necessary to reduce the mosquito population to zero bring to R_0 to less than 1 and so eliminate malaria.

Largely motivated by these models, the WHO and participating nations undertook malaria eradication efforts in the 1950s, 1960s, and 1970s. These programs were largely successes, resulting in large reductions in malaria transmission worldwide and eliminating the disease from many countries,[83] but ultimately failed in the face of the administrative and logistical challenges of a multidecade campaign.[84] Furthermore, the Ross–MacDonald model failed to account for some of the intricacies of malaria dynamics and their effect on elimination campaigns.[85] Nevertheless, modeling continues to play an important role in efforts to combat malaria, not only in informing malaria control strategies,[85] but also in shaping our understanding of the within-host dynamics of malaria infection and the emergence of drug resistance.[86]

Rubella Vaccination

Rubella (also known as German measles) is a disease that causes influenza-like symptoms and a mild rash.[46] However, when women are infected during the first trimester of pregnancy, rubella can cause congenital rubella syndrome (CRS) in the fetus; this severe disease often results in hearing impairment, congenital heart disease, and cataracts.[87,88] Rubella induces lifelong immunity, so women infected in childhood are protected from infection during their pregnancies. However, dynamic models of infectious disease show us that the introduction of a vaccine can increase the average age of infection to an infectious disease. Hence, the introduction a rubella vaccine at a level not adequate to induce complete herd immunity in the population could actually be injurious to public health by moving the average age of infection of those not vaccinated up to the childbearing years. The result would be to reduce the incidence of a relatively harmless childhood illness at the expense of causing more cases of CRS.

Because of the risk of increasing the burden of CRS, it becomes especially important to set rubella vaccination targets and meet these goals when deploying the vaccine. Dynamics-based models of infectious disease are the main tool used to understand what these targets should be and to compare the likely effects of different vaccination programs. Such models have been used to predict the effects of different vaccination levels on CRS and to contrast different strategies for deploying a fixed amount of vaccine.[16]

Recall that the average age of infection depends on both the reproductive number and the birth rate in the population. Vaccination reduces the number of susceptible individuals in the population, effectively reducing R_0 to $R_0' = R_0(1 - V)$, where V is the proportion of the population that has been vaccinated. We can use this relationship to derive an equation for the average age of infection, A, under different vaccination regimens:

$$A = \frac{1}{(R_0(1 - V) - 1)} \qquad \text{(Equation 17)}$$

We can apply this equation to a range of R_0 values consistent with estimates for rubella (3–11) and birth rates reflective of different countries worldwide, ranging from industrialized nations with stable populations (birth rates of approximately 7 per 1000) to developing nations with rapidly growing populations (birth rates of approximately 11 per 1000). **Table 6-2** shows the average age of infection expected in each of these contexts. If the R_0 for rubella is approximately 6, with no vaccination we would not see much CRS in high-birth-rate countries where the average age of infection is near 6 years old. Conversely, we may see significant numbers of CRS-affected children in low-birth-rate countries where the average age of infection would coincide with an age with high rates of fertility (29 years). If we introduce 50% vaccination in these two contexts, we would likely see a decrease

Table 6-2	Estimated Average Age of Infection for a Range of Birth Rates and R_0s Consistent with Rubella Transmission		
Birth rate/R_0	3	6	11
No Vaccination			
7 per 1000	71	29	14
15 per 1000	33	13	7
33 per 1000	15	6	3
50% Vaccination			
7 per 1000	285	71	31
15 per 1000	133	33	14
33 per 1000	60	15	7
80% Vaccination			
7 per 1000	—	714	119
15 per 1000	—	333	55
33 per 1000	—	151	25

in CRS cases in the low-birth-rate settings due the direct protection of those vaccinated and the fact that the average age of infection would be increased beyond the average childbearing age. Conversely, we would expect to see an increase in CRS cases in higher-birth-rate settings, where the average age of infection is increased closer to the average childbearing age. An increase to an 80% vaccination rate would reduce CRS in all of these contexts, moving the estimated average age of infection beyond the limit of the human life span (meaning the majority of people would never acquire rubella).

If we want accurate burden estimates, more sophisticated models of rubella transmission are necessary that take into account differential mixing by age, variations in vaccine uptake by age, and the transitory effects of a vaccination campaign, including possible increases and decreases in CRS incidence. Several such models have been developed, and used to evaluate raw coverage and more sophisticated vaccination strategies.[16,89] These modeling efforts have been used by the WHO to make recommendations on which countries should consider adding rubella to their vaccine schedules and what the risks of doing so are.[90]

Foot-and-Mouth Disease

A major outbreak of foot-and-mouth (FMD) disease occurred in 2001 in the United Kingdom. Foot-and-mouth disease is a disease of ruminants caused by an apthovirus of the picornavirus family. The virus causes fever, blisters on the mouth and hooves, and reduced weight and milk production in cattle, pigs, sheep, and other species.[91]

Though rarely causing mortality, outbreaks of FMD can have a dramatic economic impact as they can impose export bans and reduce production in livestock industries.[91] An effective vaccine is available that can produce a protective immune response 3–4 days after immunization.[91] The FMD-causative virus spreads readily from animal to animal as well as from farm to farm via high viral load droplets expelled from sick animals. Documented dispersal of virus has occurred at distances of 60 kilometers.[91] Restriction of movement of animals and culling or killing of animals on infected farms and on neighboring farms are measures that are often used to control spread.[92]

In 2001, FMD cases first appeared in a pig farm in Northumberland, United Kingdom, but the disease spread quickly to farms harboring other species. This outbreak was notable for real-time use of infectious disease models to inform outbreak responses that were performed by researchers on a scientific panel tasked with advising the official response. To minimize the economic impact of the outbreak, the government considered vaccination of animals, culling of animals only in infected farms, and culling of animals in neighboring farms. To compare these strategies, spatially explicit models of the transmission of FMD needed to be created.

Multiple approaches were taken to predict the potential impact of each strategy.[92–94] Because of the rapidity of spread within farms, transmission with farms was assumed to be effectively instantaneous, and the spread between farms became the focus of models. Multiple processes could spread virus between farms, including windborne and airborne transmission, movement of animals between farms and movement of equipment or staff between farms. Models created included deterministic and stochastic spatially explicit models that represented the potential infectious contact distribution as a local spatial kernel in which proximity to already infected farms dictated risk. On the basis of the modeling work, a change in policy was made from only culling animals on infected farms to include culling of animals on farms within a certain radius of infected farms. Many farmers opposed this decision, as they thought that culling of animals on infected farms was sufficient and that healthy animals would be killed unnecessarily under the proposed plan. Although the outbreak was controlled, the decision to cull animals on neighboring farms remains controversial.[95] This exercise highlighted many of the challenges to quantitative infectious disease dynamics in providing support to public health activities in real time, including the limited data available during the early phases of an epidemic and the challenge of communicating the results of detailed mathematical models in nontechnical forums.

The FMD outbreak in 2001 was an important milestone for infectious disease dynamics for reasons beyond the direct use of the work in real-time decision making. Work performed during the FMD outbreak and in subsequent analysis extended methods to parameterize spatially explicit models and to make statistical inferences about the spatiotemporal process of transmission.[96] The estimates of the farm-to-farm reproductive number of FMD represented some of the first work to use concepts from branching processes to estimate reproductive numbers in real time.[92,95]

Influenza Pandemic Preparedness and Response

Pre-2009: Pandemic Preparedness

Prompted by concerns over avian H5N1 influenza infections in humans, a concerted effort was made to use infectious disease models to help design pandemic preparedness policies in the mid-2000s. These efforts largely centered on two key questions: (1) Could a potential influenza pandemic be contained before it spread globally? and (2) Once a pandemic had begun to spread globally, how could countries mitigate its impact? Because many of the interventions available to control influenza must be targeted locally (e.g., antiviral prophylaxis and movement restrictions), these preparedness efforts made heavy use of agent-based models that could model the explicit spatiotemporal dynamics of infection at small scales.[42,97–99] The modeling efforts suggested that an influenza pandemic could be contained with the aggressive use of social distancing measures and antiviral prophylaxis, but only if R_0 was sufficiently low and the emerging pandemic was detected early enough, although the specifics differed between groups. Ferguson et al. estimated that a pandemic detected after the occurrence of 20 confirmed cases could be contained if R_0 was less than 1.8, and an antiviral stockpile of 3 million doses would be needed to do so.[97] Longini et al. estimated that 100,000 to 1 million courses of antiviral prophylaxis could contain a potentially pandemic influenza strain with an R_0 as high as 1.6 if the pandemic was detected and the intervention implemented within 21 days of the first human case.[100] These and other modeling efforts gave hope that, with adequate surveillance and antiviral stockpiles, it might be possible to detect and contain a pandemic before it spread.

At the same time, the models suggested that containment would not be possible unless detection of the emerging pandemic strain occurred very early and the global and local public health communities mounted a swift response. This observation sparked modeling efforts that focused on mitigating a pandemic that was already destined for global spread.[42,98] Of particular interest was minimizing the number of cases of a highly pathogenic influenza that would occur before a vaccine could be developed against the new strain. Three groups independently developed agent-based models of influenza transmission in parallel to examine the effectiveness of a "targeted layered containment" strategy combining antiviral treatment and prophylaxis along with school closure, quarantine, and other social distancing measures.[98] All three models showed that the targeted layered containment strategies could reduce the overall attack rate by 75% or more if $R_0 \approx 2$ or less.

2009: Pandemic Response

When a pandemic influenza strain did emerge in 2009, instead of an avian H5N1 strain arising in Southeast Asia, the world was confronted with a swine H1N1 strain emerging in North America.[101] The emerging strain was detected too late for any reasonable hope of containing it at its source, and was far less pathogenic than had been feared (low pathogenicity may be one reason for later detection of the virus).[102] Early efforts focused on characterizing the dynamic properties of this novel influenza—particularly its basic reproductive number, generation time, cross-immunity with previously circulating strains, and incubation period.[73,101,103] Along with more traditional epidemiological measures, such as the case-fatality ratio of the new strain, these measures were important to determine the potential impact of the emergent H1N1 2009 and to decide whether the assumptions typically used in influenza control still held. Initially, little was known about the virulence and transmissibility of this emerging virus, and these early efforts took place in close conjunction with, and in support of organizations such as the CDC and the WHO.

As early as May 2009, an initial assessment of most of these values had been made, indicating a R_0 and generation time fairly consistent with seasonal influenza and previous pandemic strains ($R_0 = 1.2–1.6$, mean generation time = 1.9 days) and a case-fatality rate of less than 0.5%.[101] Subsequent characterization of the dynamics of 2009 pandemic H1N1 were largely confirmatory of this initial analysis.[104,105] Efforts to evaluate the virus's transmission, attack rates, and the effectiveness of control measures in the 2009 pandemic continue, in an effort to better understand how novel influenza strains spread and establish themselves in the human population.

Estimating Trends in HIV Infection Using Backcalculation

In the late 1980s and early 1990s, the challenges of determining the overall burden of HIV infection in the United States and estimating the future course of the epidemic drew considerable interest from epidemiologists. Because of the long incubation period of HIV, counting AIDS cases is not an effective method of estimating the current burden of HIV infection, as persons with AIDS acquired HIV many years before. Knowing the current state of the epidemic was of critical importance, both for estimating the number of incubating AIDS cases and for predicting the epidemic's future course. Several methods were used to estimate HIV prevalence, including extrapolation of AIDS incidence curves and population-based serosurveys. Two important methods of estimation depended on an understanding of the dynamics of HIV infection: mathematical modeling and backcalculation.[22,106]

Backcalculation uses the distribution of the AIDS incubation period to estimate the number of underlying HIV infections necessary to produce the cumulative number of HIV infections observed by some time t, $a(t)$:[22]

$$a(t) = \int_0^t I(s)F(t - s\backslash s)\,ds$$

where (s) is the number of HIV infections in year s and $F(t - s\backslash s)$ is the cumulative distribution function of the incubation period of people infected in that year (**Figure 6-10**, part A). Year-specific incubation periods are needed because of the introduction of antiretroviral therapy, which increased the incubation period of HIV by preventing the development of AIDS. Using this relation, researchers produced estimates of HIV incidence between 1978 and 1990 (Figure 6-10, part B). Projections of AIDS incidence for the period 1991–1995 produced in 1991 using these estimates of underlying HIV infection rates were broadly consistent with the observed incidence.[22,107]

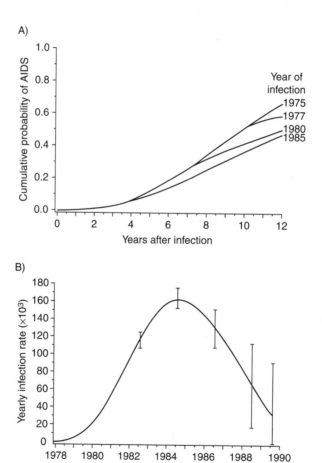

Figure 6-10 (a) Cumulative probability of developing AIDS based on year of HIV infection; (b) Reconstructed HIV infection rates in the United States, 1978–1990. From Brookmeyer R. Reconstruction and future trends of the AIDS epidemic in the United States. *Science* (New York, N.Y.). 1991;253(5015). Page 38, Figure 1. Reprinted with permission from AAAS.

HIV and Core Groups

The number of sexual partners and contacts is a central individual risk factor for acquisition of sexually transmitted disease.[108] At the population level, characteristics of sexual networks (that is, the characteristics of the population's sexual partnerships) can affect the dynamics of transmission.[109] The rate of sexual partnership formation of a person's sexual partners is important to determining that individual's risk. Early in the epidemic in many locations, there was recognition that a small group of individuals with a high rate of acquisition of sexual partners were important to spreading HIV.[110,111] The term "core group" was coined to describe groups of individuals with high rates of sexual activity.[112] Because of their increased sexual activity, core groups have an increased risk of acquisition and spread of the disease to others. The existence of a core group implies that equal distribution of screening and intervention efforts across the entire population are inefficient because this core group has a disproportionately important role in the transmission dynamics within the community. Considering the transmission of gonorrhea, Hethcote and Yorke estimated that screening efforts that target the core group are four times more effective in reducing incidence of gonorrhea than broadly targeted methods.[112]

Other theoretical work has suggested that specific features of core groups could explain disparities in the prevalence of STIs between communities, with a key feature being the level of assortativeness of individuals by the number of sexual partners they have.[113] Assortativity (and disassortativity) describes how similar people engaged in a sexual relationship are by some characteristic. It can describe this similarity based on race, economic class, or any other characteristic. In populations that are highly assortative by number of sexual partners (called degree assortativity), individuals form partnerships with people who have a similar number of partners as themselves. In disassortative populations by number of sexual partners, individuals are likely to form partnerships with individuals who have different numbers of partners than themselves (i.e., high sexually active individuals form partnerships with monogamous partners). The level of assortativity in a population dictates how isolated a core group is from the entire population. In highly assortative core groups, individuals are most likely to form partnerships with other members of the core group, which can act to restrict high prevalence to the core group.[114]

Efforts to understand the effect of higher-order network structure on STIs continue. Due to the difficulty of obtaining information about the sexual contacts of sexual contacts, many open questions remain in this area.

HPV Vaccination

Acute infection with human papillomavirus (HPV) is usually asymptomatic and occasionally causes warts (genital and otherwise).[46] Certain strains of HPV (16, 18, 31, and 45)[115] have been shown to cause cervical cancer in women, and a vaccine has been developed that protects against infection with some HPV strains (6, 11, 16, and 18). Men receive no benefit from the vaccine in terms of its most important effect: protection from cervical cancer (though more recent work has shown that other HPV-associated cancers may arise in men).[116] Nevertheless, vaccination of men may break transmission chains of HPV and help to induce herd immunity in the population, thereby protecting women from cervical cancer.

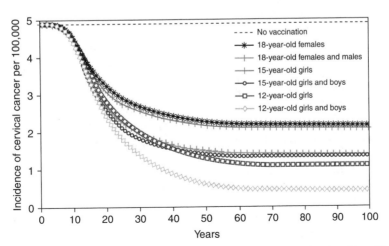

Figure 6-11 Projected incidence of cervical cancer under different vaccination strategies. Reproduced from Elbasha EH, Dasbach EJ, Insinga RP. Model for assessing human papillomavirus vaccination strategies. Emerging Infectious Diseases. 2007;13(1):28–41. Figure 8.

Recommendation of a vaccine that does not provide individual benefit to men is ethically concerning. Thus it is important to have a sense of the size of the additional reduction in mortality obtained by vaccinating both men and women versus vaccinating women alone. Several studies have attempted to use dynamic models of HPV transmission to address this question.[117–119] In one such analysis, Elbasha et al. created an age-structured compartmental model with 17 age groups, each of which was divided into three sexual activity levels (low, medium, and high) and two genders (male and female).[118] This model also incorporated progression to cervical cancer in infected women, so as to appropriately depict the burden of disease and the time delay between infection and clinical disease. This is a critical link not only in assessing the burden of disease, but also in linking the model to data, as available surveillance data for cervical cancer are much better than available surveillance data for HPV infections. Based on their model, the authors concluded that the vaccination of both boys and girls at 12 years of age would lead to the greatest reduction in HPV incidence and is the most cost-effective strategy for reducing the public health impact of HPV infection.

FUTURE TRENDS

The dominant trend in modern infectious disease dynamics is that of an increased coupling of models with data. Although the availability of greater computational power has created the possibility of ever more detailed and complex models, it has also enabled new powerful methods of fitting models to data using Monte Carlo methods and other approaches. Models that would have once been considered too complex to fit to data can now be fit using clusters of cheap computers and new methods of statistical inference.[48,120] At the same time as computational power has increased, so have the types of data available to use in the fitting process. Precise locations obtained from global positioning systems (GPS) provide relationships at small spatial scales, for example, while remote sensing data allow unprecedented understanding of the distribution of populations worldwide, and viral genetics raises the possibility of definitively identifying chains of infection and measuring the reproductive number using genetic data from pathogen populations.

These new types of data not only provide new tools for parameterizing traditional models of the epidemic process, but also open up new avenues of research that can benefit from the dynamic approach. The range of phenomena explored in infectious disease dynamics has expanded concomitantly, with increasing emphasis being placed on details of the transmission process, including explicit consideration of spatial spread and the evolution of the pathogen. Questions of genetic variation are intimately tied to our understanding of the immune pressures placed on pathogens through the immune process. As the number of questions benefiting from a dynamic approach expands and standard methodologies are developed, more nonspecialists in infectious disease modeling will almost certainly use tools of infectious disease dynamics. As the tools of infectious disease dynamics are more widely adopted and become more data driven, the identity of infectious disease dynamics as a distinct field may start to erode, but such a loss of identity would ultimately indicate the success and usefulness of the methods and approach to infectious disease epidemiology.

• • • REFERENCES

1. Blower S, Bernoulli D. An attempt at a new analysis of the mortality caused by smallpox and of the advantages of inoculation to prevent it. 1766. *Rev Med Virology*. 2004;14(5):275–288. Available at: http://www.ncbi.nlm.nih.gov/pubmed/15334536. Accessed September 8, 2011.

2. Langmuir AD. William Farr: founder of modern concepts of surveillance. *Int J Epidemiol*. 1976;5(1):13–18. Available at: http://www.ncbi.nlm.nih.gov/pubmed/770352.

3. Brownlee J. Historical note on Farr's theory of the epidemic. *Brit Med J*. 1915;2(2850):250–252. Available at: http://www.pubmedcentral.nih.gov/articlerender.fcgi?artid=2302838&tool=pmcentrez&rendertype=abstract. Accessed September 26, 2011.

4. Ransome A. On epidemics: studied by means of statistics of disease. *Brit Med J*. 1868;2(406):386–388. Available at: http://www.ncbi.nlm.nih.gov/pmc/articles/PMC2311055/. Accessed October 17, 2011.

5. Ransome A. On Epidemic Cycles. *Manchester Literary Philosophical Society Proceedings*. 1880;19:75–95.

6. Dietz K. The first epidemic model: a historical note on P. D. En'ko. *Austral J Stat*. 1988;30A(1):56–65. Available at: http://doi.wiley.com/10.1111/j.1467-842X.1988.tb00464.x. Accessed October 17, 2011.

7. En'ko PD. On the course of epidemics of some infectious diseases. *Int J Epidemiol*.

1989;18(4):749–755. Available at: http://www.ncbi.nlm.nih.gov/pubmed/2695472.

8. Fine PEM. Tropical disease: a challenge for epidemiology. *Proc. Roy. Soc. Med.* 1975;68:547–551.

9. Macdonald G. Eradication of malaria. *Public Health Rep.* 1965;80(10):870–879. Available at: http://www.pubmedcentral.nih.gov/articlerender.fcgi?artid=1919682&tool=pmcentrez&rendertype=abstract. Accessed October 17, 2011.

10. Frost WH. Some conceptions of epidemics in general by Wade Hampton Frost. *Am J Epidemiol.* 1976;103(2):141–151. Available at: http://www.ncbi.nlm.nih.gov/pubmed/766618.

11. Fine PEM. A commentary on the mechanical analogue to the Reed–Frost epidemic model. *Am J Epidemiol.* 1977;106(2):87–100.

12. Halloran ME, Longini IM, Struchiner CJ. *Design and Analysis of Vaccine Studies.* New York: Springer; 2010.

13. Heesterbeek H. The law of mass-action in epidemiology: a historical perspective. In: *Ecological Paradigms Lost: Routes of Theory Change.* 2005:81–106. Available at: http://books.google.com/books?hl=en&lr=&id=5J0MhQaiP-sC&oi=fnd&pg=PA81&dq=The+law+of+ mass-action+in+epidemiology:+a+historical+perspective&ots=eciukkO4Ig&sig= h9itoteIvZoilJIzu-MOoCMqwzDc. Accessed October 17, 2011.

14. McKendrick AG. The rise and fall of epidemics. *Paludism: Transactions of the Committee for the Study of Malaria in India.* 1912;1:54–66.

15. Kermack WO, McKendrick AG. Contributions to the mathematical theory of epidemics. I. *Proc Royal Soc London (Series A).* 1927;115A:700–721. Available at: http://rspa.royalsocietypublishing.org/content/138/834/55.full.pdf. Accessed October 17, 2011.

16. Anderson RM, May RM. Infectious disease of humans: dynamics and control. Oxford: Oxford University Press; 1991.

17. Dietz K. Models for parasitic disease control. *Bull Int Stat Inst.* 1975;46:531–544. Available at: http://scholar.google.com/scholar?hl=en&btnG=Search&q=intitle:Models+for+ parasitic+disease+control#0. Accessed October 26, 2011.

18. Bailey NTJ. *The Mathematical Theory of Epidemics.* New York: Hafner; 1957.

19. Bailey NTJ. *The Mathematics of Infectious Disease and its Applications.* London: Griffin; 1975.

20. Keeling MJ, Rohani P. *Modeling Infectious Diseases in Humans and Animals.* Princeton, NJ: Princeton University Press; 2007.

21. Sartwell PE. The incubation period and the dynamics of infectious disease. *Am J Epidemiol.* 1966;83(2):204. Available at: http://aje.oxfordjournals.org/content/83/2/204.full.pdf. Accessed October 17, 2011.

22. Brookmeyer R. Reconstruction and future trends of the AIDS epidemic in the United States. *Science (NY).* 1991;253(5015):37–42. Available at: http://www.ncbi.nlm.nih.gov/pubmed/2063206. Accessed September 15, 2011.

23. Lessler J, Reich NG, Brookmeyer R, et al. Incubation periods of acute respiratory viral infections: a systematic review. *Lancet Infect Dis.* 2009;9(5):291–300. Available at: http://www.ncbi.nlm.nih.gov/pubmed/19393959. Accessed June 8, 2011.

24. Nishiura H. Early efforts in modeling the incubation period of infectious diseases with an acute course of illness. *Emerg Themes Epidemiol.* 2007;4:2. Available at: http://www.pubmedcentral.nih.gov/articlerender.fcgi?artid=1884151&tool=pmcentrez&rendertype=abstract.Accessed March 9, 2011.

25. Sartwell PE. The distribution of incubation periods of infectious disease. *Am J Epidemiol.* 1950;51(3):310. Available at: http://aje.oxfordjournals.org/content/51/3/310.full.pdf. Accessed July 5, 2011.

26. Fraser C, Riley S, Anderson RM, Ferguson NM. Factors that make an infectious disease outbreak controllable. *Pro Natl Acad Sci USA.* 2004;101(16):6146–6151.

27. Gray RH, Wawer MJ, Brookmeyer R, et al. Probability of HIV-1 transmission per coital act in monogamous, heterosexual,

HIV-1-discordant couples in Rakai, Uganda. *Lancet.* 2001;357(9263):1149–1153. Available at: http://www.ncbi.nlm.nih.gov/pubmed/11323041.

28. Vittinghoff E, Douglas J, Judson F, et al. Per-contact risk of human immunodeficiency virus transmission between male sexual partners. *Am J Epidemiol.* 1999;150(3):306–311.

29. Forthal DN, Aarnaes S, Blanding J, de la Maza L, Tilles JG. Degree and length of viremia in adults with measles. *J Infect Dis.* 1992;166(2):421–424. Available at: http://www.ncbi.nlm.nih.gov/pubmed/1634814.

30. Carrat F, Vergu E, Ferguson NM, et al. Time lines of infection and disease in human influenza: a review of volunteer challenge studies. *Am J Epidemiol.* 2008;167(7):775–785. Available at: http://aje.oxfordjournals.org/cgi/content/full/167/7/775. Accessed July 29, 2011.

31. Fraser C, Donnelly C, Cauchemez S, et al. Pandemic potential of a strain of influenza A (H1N1) : early findings. *Science.* 2009;324:1557–1561.

32. Nishiura H, Wilson N, Baker MG. Estimating the reproduction number of the novel influenza A virus (H1N1) in a Southern Hemisphere setting: preliminary estimate in New Zealand. *N Z Med J.* 2009;122(1299):73–77. Available at: http://www.ncbi.nlm.nih.gov/pubmed/19684651.

33. Nishiura H, Castillo-Chavez C, Safan M, Chowell G. Transmission potential of the new influenza A (H1N1) virus and its age-specificity in Japan. *Euro Surveill.* 2009;14(22).

34. Earn DJ, Rohani P, Bolker BM, Grenfell BT. A simple model for complex dynamical transitions in epidemics. *Science (NY).* 2000;287(5453):667–670. Available at: http://www.ncbi.nlm.nih.gov/pubmed/10650003.

35. Bootsma MCJ, Ferguson NM. The effect of public health measures on the 1918 influenza pandemic in U.S. cities. *Proc Natl Acad Sci USA.* 2007;104(18):7588–7593.

36. Mossong J, Hens N, Jit M, et al. Social contacts and mixing patterns relevant to the spread of infectious diseases. *PLoS Med.* 2008;5(3):e74. Available at: http://www.pubmedcentral.nih.gov/articlerender.fcgi?artid=2270306&tool=pmcentrez&rendertype=abstract. Accessed July 15, 2010.

37. Schenzle D. An age-structured model of pre- and post-vaccination measles transmission, Institute for Medical Biometry, University of Tubingen, FRG has long been a favourite subject of stud. *Infection.* 1984:1;169–191.

38. Babad HR, Nokes DJ, Gay NJ, et al. Predicting the impact of measles vaccination in England and Wales: model validation and analysis of policy options. *Epidemiol Infect.* 1995;114(2):319–e44. Available at: http://www.pubmedcentral.nih.gov/articlerender.fcgi?artid=2271287&tool=pmcentrez&rendertype=abstract. Accessed October 17, 2011.

39. Ferguson NM, Anderson RM, Garnett GP. Mass vaccination to control chickenpox: the influence of zoster. *Proc Natl Acad Sci USA.* 1996;93(14):7231–7235. Available at: http://www.pubmedcentral.nih.gov/articlerender.fcgi?artid=38965&tool=pmcentrez&rendertype=abstract.

40. Morris M, Kretzschmar M. Concurrent partnerships and the spread of HIV. *AIDS (London).* 1997;11(5):641–648. Available at: http://www.ncbi.nlm.nih.gov/pubmed/9108946.

41. Epstein JM. *Generative Social Science: Studies in Agent-Based Computational Modeling.* Princeton, NJ: Princeton University Press; 2006.

42. Ferguson NM, Cummings DAT, Fraser C, et al. Strategies for mitigating an influenza pandemic. *Nature.* 2006;442(7101):448–452. Available at: http://dx.doi.org/10.1038/nature04795.

43. Longini IMJ, Nizam A, Xu S, et al. Containing pandemic influenza at the source. *Science.* 2005;309(5737):1083–1087. Available at: PM:16079251.

44. Hotchkiss JR, Strike DG, Simonson DA, Broccard AF, Crooke PS. An agent-based and spatially explicit model of pathogen dissemination in the intensive care unit. *Crit Care Med.* 2005;33(1):168–176. Available at: http://content.wkhealth.com/linkback/openurl?sid=WKPTLP:landingpage

&an=00003246-200501000-00025. Accessed September 8, 2011.

45. Eames KTD, Keeling MJ. Modeling dynamic and network heterogeneities in the spread of sexually transmitted diseases. *Proc Natl Acad Sci USA.* 2002;99(20):13330–13335. Available at: http://www.pubmedcentral.nih.gov/articlerender.fcgi?artid=130633&tool=pmcentrez&rendertype=abstract.

46. Howley PM, Knipe DM, Fields BN. *Fields Virology.* Philadelphia: Lippincott Williams & Wilkins; 2007.

47. Gans H, Yasukawa L, Rinki M, et al. Immune responses to measles and mumps vaccination of infants at 6, 9, and 12 months. *J Infect Dis.* 2001;184(7):817–826. Available at: http://www.ncbi.nlm.nih.gov/pubmed/11528592.

48. King AA, Ionides EL, Pascual M, Bouma MJ. Inapparent infections and cholera dynamics. *Nature.* 2008;454(7206):877–880. Available at: http://www.ncbi.nlm.nih.gov/pubmed/18704085. Accessed August 23, 2010.

49. Bridges CB, Kuehnert MJ, Hall CB. Transmission of influenza: implications for control in health care settings. *Clin Infect Dis.* 2003;37(8):1094–1101. Available at: http://www.ncbi.nlm.nih.gov/pubmed/14523774.

50. Li S, Eisenberg JNS, Spicknall IH, Koopman JS. Dynamics and control of infections transmitted from person to person through the environment. *Am J Epidemiol.* 2009;170(2):257–265. Available at: http://www.ncbi.nlm.nih.gov/pubmed/19474071. Accessed July 5, 2011.

51. Jones JH, Handcock MS. An assessment of preferential attachment as a mechanism for human sexual network formation. *Proc Biol Sci Royal Soc.* 2003;270(1520):1123–1128. Available at: http://www.pubmedcentral.nih.gov/articlerender.fcgi?artid=1691356&tool=pmcentrez&rendertype=abstract. Accessed July 5, 2011.

52. Gupta S, Trenholme K, Anderson RM, Day KP. Antigenic diversity and the transmission dynamics of *Plasmodium falciparum. Science (NY).* 1994;263(5149):961–963. Available at: http://www.ncbi.nlm.nih.gov/pubmed/8310293. Accessed October 17, 2011.

53. Cummings DAT, Schwartz IB, Billings L, Shaw LB, Burke DS. Dynamic effects of antibody-dependent enhancement on the fitness of viruses. *Proc Natl Acad Sci USA.* 2005;102(42):15259–15264.

54. Anderson RM, Jackson HC, May RM, Smith AM. Population dynamics of fox rabies in Europe. *Nature.* 1981;289(5800):765–771. Available at: http://www.ncbi.nlm.nih.gov/pubmed/7464941. Accessed October 17, 2011.

55. Antia R, Regoes RR, Koella JC, Bergstrom CT. The role of evolution in the emergence of infectious diseases. *Nature.* 2003;426(6967):658–661. Available at: ISI:000187132800040.

56. Fine PE, Jezek Z, Grab B, Dixon H. The transmission potential of monkeypox virus in human populations. *Int J Epidemiol.* 1988;17(3):643–650. Available at: http://www.ncbi.nlm.nih.gov/pubmed/2850277.

57. Lessler J, Cummings DAT, Fishman S, Vora A, Burke DS. Transmissibility of swine flu at Fort Dix, 1976. *J Royal Soc Interface/Royal Soc.* 2007;4(15):755–762. Available at: http://www.pubmedcentral.nih.gov/articlerender.fcgi?artid=2373398&tool=pmcentrez&rendertype=abstract. Accessed July 8, 2011.

58. Lipsitch M, Viboud C. Influenza seasonality: lifting the fog. *Proc Natl Acad Sci USA.* 2009;106(10):3645–3646. Available at: http://www.pnas.org/content/106/10/3645.long.

59. Fine PE, Clarkson JA. Measles in England and Wales—I: An analysis of factors underlying seasonal patterns. *Int J Epidemiol.* 1982;11(1):5–14. Available at: http://www.ncbi.nlm.nih.gov/pubmed/7085179.

60. Cummings DAT, Irizarry RA, Huang NE, et al. Travelling waves in the occurrence of dengue haemorrhagic fever in Thailand. *Nature.* 2004;427(6972):344–347. Available at: http://www.nature.com/nature/journal/v427/n6972/full/nature02225.html.

61. Shaman J, Pitzer VE, Viboud C, Grenfell BT, Lipsitch M. Absolute humidity and the seasonal onset of influenza in the continental United States. *PLoS Biol.* 2010;8(2):e1000316. Available at: http://www.pubmedcentral.nih.gov/articlerender.fc

gi?artid=2826374&tool=pmcentrez&rendert ype=abstract. Accessed July 15, 2011.

62. Ferrari MJ, Grais RF, Bharti N, et al. The dynamics of measles in sub-Saharan Africa. *Nature.* 2008;451(7179):679–684. Available at: http://www.ncbi.nlm.nih.gov/ pubmed/18256664. Accessed October 16, 2011.

63. Centers for Disease Control and Prevention. Fluview. Available at: http://www.cdc.gov/flu/ weekly/. Accessed September 10, 2011.

64. London WP, Yorke JA. Recurrent outbreaks of measles, chickenpox and mumps. I. Seasonal variation in contact rates. *Am J Epidemiol.* 1973;98(6):453–468. Available at: http://www. ncbi.nlm.nih.gov/pubmed/4767622. Accessed October 17, 2011.

65. Tsibris AMN, Korber B, Arnaout R, et al. Quantitative deep sequencing reveals dynamic HIV-1 escape and large population shifts during CCR5 antagonist therapy in vivo. *PloS One.* 2009;4(5):e5683. Available at: http:// www.pubmedcentral.nih.gov/articlerender.fcgi? artid=2682648&tool=pmcentrez&rendertype =abstract. Accessed October 18, 2011.

66. Smith DL, Dushoff J, Perencevich EN, Harris AD, Levin SA. Persistent colonization and the spread of antibiotic resistance in nosocomial pathogens: resistance is a regional problem. *Proc Natl Acad Sci USA.* 2004;101(10):3709–3714. Available at: http://www.pubmedcentral.nih.gov/articlerender. fcgi?artid=373527&tool=pmcentrez&rendertype =abstract. Accessed October 18, 2011.

67. Andreason V. Dynamics of annual influenza A epidemics with immuno-selection. *Math Biol.* 2003;46(504–536):33.

68. Gupta S. Chaos, persistence, and evolution of strain structure in antigenically diverse infec- tious agents. Science. 1998;280(5365):912–915. Available at: http://www.sciencemag.org/cgi/ doi/10.1126/science.280.5365.912. Accessed August 29, 2011.

69. Gog JR, Grenfell BT. Dynamics and selection of many-strain pathogens. *Proc Natl Acad Sci USA.* 2002;99(26):17209–14. Available at: http://www.pubmedcentral.nih.gov/articlerender. fcgi?artid=139294&tool=pmcentrez&rendertype =abstract. Accessed October 18, 2011.

70. Levin S. Community equilibria and stability, and an extension of the competitive exclusion principle. *Am Naturalist.* 1970;104(939): 413–423. Available at: http://www.jstor.org/ stable/2459310. Accessed October 18, 2011.

71. Lipsitch M, Dykes JK, Johnson SE, et al. Competition among *Streptococcus pneu- moniae* for intranasal colonization in a mouse model. *Vaccine.* 2000;18(25):2895–2901. Available at: http://www.ncbi.nlm.nih.gov/ pubmed/10812233. Accessed October 18, 2011.

72. Reich NG, Lessler J, Cummings DAT, Brookmeyer R. Estimating incubation period distributions with coarse data. *Stat Med.* 2009; 28(22):2769–2784. Available at: http:// onlinelibrary.wiley.com/doi/10.1002/ sim.3659/abstract. Accessed July 8, 2011.

73. Lessler J, Reich NG, Cummings DAT, et al. Outbreak of 2009 pandemic influenza A (H1N1) at a New York City school. *N Engl J Med.* 2009;361(27):2628–2636. Available at: http:// www.ncbi.nlm.nih.gov/pubmed/20042754.

74. White LF, Pagano M. A likelihood-based method for real-time estimation of the serial interval and reproductive number of an epi- demic. Stat Med. 2008;27(16):2999–3016. Available at: http://www3.interscience. wiley.com/journal/117354201/ abstract?CRETRY=1&SRETRY=0.

75. Wallinga J, Lipsitch M. How generation in- tervals shape the relationship between growth rates and reproductive numbers. *Proc Royal Soc B: Biol Sci.* 2007;274(1609):599–604. Available at: http://rspb.royalsocietypublishing. org/cgi/doi/10.1098/rspb.2006.3754. Accessed June 27, 2011.

76. Wearing HJ, Rohani P, Keeling MJ. Appropriate models for the management of infectious diseases. *PLoS Med.* 2005;2(7):e174. Available at: http://dx.doi.org/10.1371/journal. pmed.0020174.

77. Hethcote HW. The mathematics of infectious diseases. *Siam Rev.* 2000;42(4):599–653. Available at: ISI:000165673600003.

78. Cummings DAT, Iamsirithaworn S, Lessler JT, et al. The impact of the demographic transition

on dengue in Thailand: insights from a statistical analysis and mathematical modeling. *PLoS Med.* 2009;6(9):e1000139. Available at: http://www.pubmedcentral.nih.gov/articlerender.fcgi?artid=2726436&tool=pmcentrez&rendertype=abstract. Accessed July 7, 2011.

79. Grenfell BT, Anderson RM. The estimation of age-related rates of infection from case notifications and serological data. *J Hygiene.* 1985;95(2):419–436. Available at: http://www.pubmedcentral.nih.gov/articlerender.fcgi?artid=2129533&tool=pmcentrez&rendertype=abstract.

80. Diekmann O, Heesterbeek JA, Metz JA. On the definition and the computation of the basic reproduction ratio R_0 in models for infectious diseases in heterogeneous populations. *J Math Biol.* 1990;28(4):365–382. Available at: http://www.ncbi.nlm.nih.gov/pubmed/2117040. Accessed September 22, 2011.

81. Van den Driessche P, Watmough J. Reproduction numbers and sub-threshold endemic equilibria for compartmental models of disease transmission. *Math Biosci.* 180:29–48. Available at: http://www.ncbi.nlm.nih.gov/pubmed/12387915. Accessed September 26, 2011.

82. McKenzie FE. Why model malaria? *Parasitol Today.* 2000;16(12):511–516. Available at: http://www.pubmedcentral.nih.gov/articlerender.fcgi?artid=2173879&tool=pmcentrez&rendertype=abstract.

83. Brown PJ. Failure-as-success: multiple meanings of eradication in the Rockefeller Foundation Sardinia project, 1946–1951. *Parassitologia.* 1998;40(1–2):117–130. Available at: http://www.ncbi.nlm.nih.gov/pubmed/9653739. Accessed October 26, 2011.

84. Henderson DA. Eradication: lessons from the past. *Bull WHO.* 1998;76(suppl 2):17–21. Available at: http://www.pubmedcentral.nih.gov/articlerender.fcgi?artid=2305698&tool=pmcentrez&rendertype=abstract. Accessed October 26, 2011.

85. Smith DL, McKenzie FE, Snow RW, Hay SI. Revisiting the basic reproductive number for malaria and its implications for malaria control. *PLoS Biol.* 2007;5(3):e42. Available at: http://www.pubmedcentral.nih.gov/articlerender.fcgi?artid=1802755&tool=pmcentrez&rendertype=abstract. Accessed October 26, 2011.

86. Metcalf CJE, Graham AL, Huijben S, et al. Within-host malaria dynamics using the effective propagation number. *Science.* 2011;C:984–988.

87. Gregg NM. Congenital defects associated with maternal rubella. *Austral Hosp.* 1947;14(11):7–9. Available at: http://www.ncbi.nlm.nih.gov/pubmed/18914301. Accessed October 26, 2011.

88. Cooper LZ. The history and medical consequences of rubella. *Rev Infect Dis.* 1985;7(suppl 1):S2–S10. Available at: http://www.ncbi.nlm.nih.gov/pubmed/3890105. Accessed October 26, 2011.

89. Metcalf CJE, Bjørnstad ON, Ferrari MJ, et al. The epidemiology of rubella in Mexico: seasonality, stochasticity and regional variation. *Epidemiol Infect.* 2010:1–10. Available at: http://www.ncbi.nlm.nih.gov/pubmed/20843389. Accessed July 31, 2011.

90. World Health Organization. Rubella vaccines: WHO position paper—recommendations. *Vaccine.* 2011;(29):301–316. Available at: http://scholar.google.com/scholar?hl=en&btnG=Search&q=intitle:rubella+vaccines:+Who+position+paper#1. Accessed October 26, 2011.

91. Gloster J, Champion H. Airborne transmission of foot-and-mouth disease virus from Burnside Farm, Heddonon-the-Wall, Northumberland, during the 2001 epidemic in the United Kingdom. *Veterin Rec.* 2003:525–534. Available at: http://veterinary-record.bmj.com/content/152/17/525.abstract. Accessed October 18, 2011.

92. Woolhouse M, Chase-Topping M, Haydon D, et al. Epidemiology. Foot-and-mouth disease under control in the UK. *Nature.* 2001;411(6835):258–259. Available at: http://www.nature.com/nature/journal/v411/n6835/full/411258b0.html.

93. Ferguson NM, Donnelly CA, Anderson RM. Transmission intensity and impact of control policies on the foot and mouth epidemic in Great Britain. *Nature.* 2001;413(6855):

542–548. Available at: http://www.nature.com/nature/journal/v413/n6855/full/413542a0.html.

94. Keeling MJ, Woolhouse ME, Shaw DJ, et al. Dynamics of the 2001 UK foot and mouth epidemic: stochastic dispersal in a heterogeneous landscape. *Science (NY)*. 2001;294(5543):813–817. Available at: http://www.ncbi.nlm.nih.gov/pubmed/11679661.

95. Haydon DT, Kao RR, Kitching RP. The UK foot-and-mouth disease outbreak - the aftermath. *Nature reviews. Microbiology*. 2004;2(8):675–81. Available at: http://www.ncbi.nlm.nih.gov/pubmed/15263902. Accessed October 18, 2011.

96. Tildesley MJ, Deardon R, Savill NJ, et al. Accuracy of models for the 2001 foot-and-mouth epidemic. *Proc Biol Sci/Royal Soc*. 2008;275(1641):1459–1468. Available at: http://www.pubmedcentral.nih.gov/articlerender.fcgi?artid=2376304&tool=pmcentrez&rendertype=abstract. Accessed October 18, 2011.

97. Ferguson NM, Cummings DAT, Cauchemez S, et al. Strategies for containing an emerging influenza pandemic in Southeast Asia. *Nature*. 2005;437(7056):209–214. Available at: http://www.ncbi.nlm.nih.gov/pubmed/16079797. Accessed July 8, 2011.

98. Halloran ME, Ferguson NM, Eubank S, et al. Modeling targeted layered containment of an influenza pandemic in the United States. *Proc Natl Acad Sci USA*. 2008;105(12):4639–4644. Available at: http://www.pubmedcentral.nih.gov/articlerender.fcgi?artid=2290797&tool=pmcentrez&rendertype=abstract.

99. Germann TC, Kadau K, Longini IM, Macken CA. Mitigation strategies for pandemic influenza in the United States. *Proc Natl Acad Sci USA*. 2006;103(15):5935–5940.

100. Longini IM, Nizam A, Xu S, et al. Containing pandemic influenza at the source. Science (NY). 2005;309(5737):1083–1087. Available at: http://www.ncbi.nlm.nih.gov/pubmed/16079251. Accessed July 18, 2011.

101. Fraser C, Donnelly CA, Cauchemez S, et al. Pandemic potential of a strain of influenza A (H1N1): early findings. *Science (NY)*. 2009;324(5934):1557–1561. Available at: http://www.ncbi.nlm.nih.gov/pubmed/19433588. Accessed September 19, 2011.

102. Fraser C, Donnelly C, Cauchemez S, et al. Pandemic potential of a strain of influenza A (H1N1) : early findings. *Science*. 2009;324:1557–1561.

103. Cauchemez S, Donnelly CA, Reed C, et al. Supplementary material : household transmission of 2009 pandemic influenza A (H1N1) virus in the United States. *N Engl J Med*. 2009;361(27):1–19.

104. Yang Y, Halloran ME, Longini IM. A Bayesian model for evaluating influenza antiviral efficacy in household studies with asymptomatic infections. *Biostatistics (Oxford)*. 2009;10(2):390–403.

105. White LF, Wallinga J, Finelli L, et al. Estimation of the reproductive number and the serial interval in early phase of the 2009 influenza A/H1N1 pandemic in the USA. *Influenza Other Resp Virus*. 2009;3:1–10.

106. May RM, Anderson RM. Transmission dynamics of HIV infection. *Nature*. 1989;326 (6109):137–142. Available at: http://rstb.royalsocietypublishing.org/content/325/1226/45.short. Accessed September 16, 2011.

107. Report MW. HIV surveillance—United States, 1981–2008. *MMWR*. 2011;60(21):689–693. Available at: http://www.ncbi.nlm.nih.gov/pubmed/21637182. Accessed July 27, 2011.

108. Brookmeyer R, Williams GM. *AIDS Epidemiology: A Quantitative Approach*. New York: Oxford University Press; 1994.

109. Kretzschmar M, Morris M. Measures of concurrency in networks and the spread of infectious disease. *Math Biosci*. 1996;133(2):165–195. Available at: http://www.ncbi.nlm.nih.gov/pubmed/8718707. Accessed October 18, 2011.

110. Anonymous.

111. Bwayo J, Plummer F, Omari M, et al. Human immunodeficiency virus infection in long-distance truck drivers in east Africa.

Arch Intern Med. 1994;154(12):1391–1396. Available at: http://www.ncbi.nlm.nih.gov/ pubmed/8002691. Accessed October 18, 2011.

112. Hethcote HW, Yorke JA. Gonorrhea transmission dynamics and control. 1984. Available at: http://yorke.umd.edu/papers/Hethcote-Yorke-Gonorrhea-Transmission-and-Control-1984. pdf. Accessed October 17, 2011.

113. Morris M, Kurth AE, Hamilton DT, Moody J, Wakefield S. Concurrent partnerships and HIV prevalence disparities by race: linking science and public health practice. *Am J Public Health.* 2009;99(6):1023–1031. Available at: http:// www.pubmedcentral.nih.gov/articlerender.fcgi ?artid=2679771&tool=pmcentrez&rendertype =abstract. Accessed October 18, 2011.

114. Hamilton DT, Handcock MS, Morris M. Degree distributions in sexual networks: a framework for evaluating evidence. *Sex Transm Dis.* 2008;35(1):30–40. Available at: http:// www.ncbi.nlm.nih.gov/pubmed/18217224. Accessed October 18, 2011.

115. Stanley M. Pathology and epidemiology of HPV infection in females. *Gynecol Oncol.* 2010;117(2 suppl):S5–S10. Available at: http:// www.ncbi.nlm.nih.gov/pubmed/20304221. Accessed October 18, 2011.

116. Anic GM, Giuliano AR. Genital HPV infection and related lesions in men. *Prevent Med.* 2011;53(suppl 1):S36–S41. Available at: http:// www.ncbi.nlm.nih.gov/pubmed/21962470. Accessed October 18, 2011.

117. Kim JJ, Goldie SJ. Cost effectiveness analysis of including boys in a human papillomavirus vaccination programme in the United States. *Brit Med J.* 2009;339(2):b3884–b3884. Available at: http://www.bmj.com/cgi/doi/10.1136/bmj. b3884. Accessed July 6, 2011.

118. Elbasha EH, Dasbach EJ, Insinga RP. Model for assessing human papillomavirus vaccination strategies. *Emerg Infect Dis.* 2007;13(1):28–41. Available at: http://www.pubmedcentral.nih. gov/articlerender.fcgi?artid=2725801&tool= pmcentrez&rendertype=abstract.

119. Barnabas RV, Laukkanen P, Koskela P, et al. Epidemiology of HPV 16 and cervical cancer in Finland and the potential impact of vaccination: mathematical modelling analyses. *PLoS Med.* 2006;3(5):e138. Available at: http://www.pubmedcentral.nih.gov/articlerender.fcgi?artid=1434486&tool=pmcentrez&rendertype=abstract. Accessed July 18, 2011.

120. Cauchemez S, Valleron A-J, Boëlle P-Y, Flahault A, Ferguson NM. Estimating the impact of school closure on influenza transmission from Sentinel data. *Nature.* 2008;452(7188):750–754. Available at: http:// www.ncbi.nlm.nih.gov/pubmed/18401408. Accessed September 19, 2011.

121. Longini IM, Nizam A, Ali M, et al. Controlling endemic cholera with oral vaccines. *PLoS Med.* 2007;4(11):e336. Available at: http://www. pubmedcentral.nih.gov/articlerender.fcgi? artid=2082648&tool=pmcentrez&rendertype =abstract. Accessed October 2, 2011.

122. Chao DL, Halloran ME, Longini IM. Vaccination strategies for epidemic cholera in Haiti with implications for the developing world. *Proc Natl Acad Sci USA.* 2011;108(17):7081–7085. Available at: http:// www.pubmedcentral.nih.gov/articlerender. fcgi?artid=3084143&tool=pmcentrez&rende rtype=abstract. Accessed July 3, 2011.

123. Checchi F, Gayer M, Grais RF, Mills EJ. *Public Health in Crisis-Affected Populations: A Practical Guide for Decision Makers.* London: Overseas Development Institute; 2007.

124. Mari L, Bertuzzo E, Righetto L, et al. Modelling cholera epidemics: the role of waterways, human mobility and sanitation. *J Royal Soc Interface/Royal Soc.* July 2011. Available at: http://www.ncbi.nlm.nih.gov/ pubmed/21752809. Accessed July 26, 2011.

125. Johansson MA, Hombach J, Cummings DAT. Models of the impact of dengue vaccines: a review of current research and potential approaches. *Vaccine.* 2011;29(35):5860–5868. Available at: http:// www.ncbi.nlm.nih.gov/pubmed/21699949. Accessed October 18, 2011.

126. Hsieh Y-H, Ma S. Intervention measures, turning point, and reproduction number for dengue, Singapore, 2005. *Am J Trop Med Hygiene.* 2009;80(1):66–71. Available at: http://www. ncbi.nlm.nih.gov/pubmed/19141842.

127. Hsieh Y-H, Chen CWS. Turning points, reproduction number, and impact of climatological events for multi-wave dengue outbreaks. *Trop Med Int Health.* 2009;14(6):628–638. Available at: http://www.ncbi.nlm.nih.gov/pubmed/19392743. Accessed June 23, 2011.

128. Cowling BJ, Fang VJ, Riley S, Malik Peiris JS, Leung GM. Estimation of the serial interval of influenza. *Epidemiology.* 2009;20(3):344–347. Available at: http://www.ncbi.nlm.nih.gov/pubmed/19279492. Accessed June 24, 2010.

129. Smith DL, McKenzie FE, Snow RW, Hay SI. Revisiting the basic reproductive number for malaria and its implications for malaria control. *PLoS Biol.* 2007;5(3):e42. Available at: http://www.pubmedcentral.nih.gov/articlerender.fcgi?artid=1802755&tool=pmcentrez&rendertype=abstract. Accessed July 20, 2011.

130. Mossong J, Muller CP. Estimation of the basic reproduction number of measles during an outbreak in a partially vaccinated population. *Epidemiol Infect.* 2000;124(2):273–278. Available at: http://www.pubmedcentral.nih.gov/articlerender.fcgi?artid=2810911&tool=pmcentrez&rendertype=abstract.

131. Edmunds WJ, Gay NJ, Kretzschmar M, Pebody RG, Wachmann H. The pre-vaccination epidemiology of measles, mumps and rubella in Europe: implications for modelling studies. *Epidemiol Infect.* 2000;125(3):635–650. Available at: http://www.pubmedcentral.nih.gov/articlerender.fcgi?artid=2869647&tool=pmcentrez&rendertype=abstract.

132. Fine PEM. The interval between successive cases of an infectious disease. *Am J Epidemiol.* 2003;158(11):1039–1047. Available at: http://aje.oxfordjournals.org/cgi/content/full/158/11/1039.

133. Rios-Doria D, Chowell G, Munayco-Escate C, Castillo-Chavez C. Mathematical and statistical estimation approaches in epidemiology. In: Chowell G, Hyman JM, Bettencourt LMA, Castillo-Chavez C, eds. *Media.* 2009:1997–2006. Available at: http://www.springerlink.com/index/10.1007/978-90-481-2313-1. Accessed October 3, 2011.

134. Aycock WLl, Ingalls TH. Maternal disease as a principle in the epidemiology of congenital anomalies, with a review of rubella. *Am J Med Sci.* 1946:366–379.

135. Riley S, Fraser C, Donnelly CA, et al. Transmission dynamics of the etiological agent of SARS in Hong Kong: impact of public health interventions. *Science (NY).* 2003;300(5627):1961–1966. Available at: http://www.sciencemag.org/cgi/content/full/300/5627/1961. Accessed July 5, 2011.

136. Chowell G, Fenimore PWW, Castillo-Garsow MAA, Castillo-Chavez C. SARS outbreaks in Ontario, Hong Kong and Singapore: the role of diagnosis and isolation as a control mechanism. *J Theor Biol.* 2003;224(1):1–8. Available at: http://linkinghub.elsevier.com/retrieve/pii/S0022519303002285. Accessed September 8, 2011.

137. Lipsitch M, Cohen T, Cooper B, et al. Transmission dynamics and control of severe acute respiratory syndrome. *Science (NY).* 2003;300(5627):1966–1970. Available at: http://www.pubmedcentral.nih.gov/articlerender.fcgi?artid=2760158&tool=pmcentrez&rendertype=abstract. Accessed July 27, 2011.

138. Halloran ME, Longini IM, Nizam A, Yang Y. Containing bioterrorist smallpox. *Science.* 2002;298(5597):1428–1432. Available at: http://www.ncbi.nlm.nih.gov/pubmed/12434061. Accessed August 9, 2011.

139. Gani R, Leach S. Transmission potential of smallpox in contemporary populations. *Nature.* 2001;414(6865):748–751. Available at: http://www.ncbi.nlm.nih.gov/pubmed/11742399.

140. Eichner M, Dietz K. Transmission potential of smallpox: estimates based on detailed data from an outbreak. *Am J Epidemiol.* 2003;158(2):110–117. Available at: http://aje.oxfordjournals.org/cgi/content/full/158/2/110.

141. Nishiura H, Eichner M. Infectiousness of smallpox relative to disease age: estimates based on transmission network and incubation period. *Epidemiol Infect.* 2007;135(7):1145–50. Available at: http://www.pubmedcentral.nih.gov/articlerender.fcgi?artid=2870668&tool=pmcentrez&rendertype=abstract. Accessed October 2, 2011.

7

Geographic Information Systems

Gregory E. Glass

A common definition of geographic information systems (GIS) is that they are procedures to input, store, retrieve, manipulate, analyze, and output data that have spatial attributes associated with them.[1] Typically, the results are presented as maps or images that summarize the data or analyses performed on the data. Infectious disease epidemiology, almost by the very nature of the interaction of hosts and the pathogens within the environment (as well as vector and reservoir populations with vector-borne and zoonotic diseases), lends itself to GIS analysis, at least as a way to summarize the sometimes complex relationships associated with disease transmission.

Snow's classic study of cholera transmission around Broad Street in London in the mid-1850s is often summarized by referring to the map of deaths he plotted in relation to the Broad Street pump, as well as the pump's spatial relationship to other features such as workhouses, residences, and factories (**Figure 7-1**). As such, the manual construction of a map to present these data conforms to the definition of a GIS. Despite the convincing nature of the data when presented in this way, it is critical to keep in mind an important feature of Snow's analysis that generally characterizes the limited application of GIS in epidemiology: The map that he created did not lead him to conclude that (1) cholera was a waterborne illness and (2) the pump was the source of contagion (contrary to popular lore); rather, the map was a method that he used to summarize his data to his audience and a tool he used to try to convince others of his conclusions. As Vandenbroucke[2] recently noted, "As an historical example, it remains important to remember that Snow's theory on the communication of cholera was not derived from his epidemiologic observations, but preceded them." Although Snow applied the tool of GIS well, it was a relatively restricted application. The restriction has been due, historically, to technical limitations rather than to conceptual ones.

Although the spatial distribution of cases is recognized as important in understanding infectious disease transmission, the statistical and geographic tools have not been generally available to make the examination of spatial distributions of infectious diseases an important analytical method for epidemiologic investigations. The increased development of GIS as an analytical approach in epidemiology results from improved access to computer systems and their associated software. To date, most of the progress in spatial epidemiology has been made where point exposures to a single factor (e.g., a pollutant or radiation) are responsible for human disease. An analogous situation occurs during outbreak investigations that involve a single source of infection. Although the graphical presentation of these data is little removed from Snow's early representations, demonstrating the spatial consequences of epidemiologic processes deduced from more traditional means can be compelling.

For example, in 1979, an outbreak of anthrax was reported from the Sverdlovsk region in Russia involving deaths of both humans and domestic animals. Occasional anthrax outbreaks had been known from that region since at least the early 1900s. Anthrax is a disease caused by infection with *Bacillus anthracis*, and the severity of the disease caused by infection varies with the route of exposure. Cutaneous infection is least likely to cause mortality, whereas ingesting contaminated meat has a higher rate of mortality and inhalation of the agent is usually fatal. Official reports of the investigation indicated the 1979 outbreak was associated with contact with naturally infected animals. However, rumors persisted that the outbreak was related to an accidental release of bacteria from a military facility.

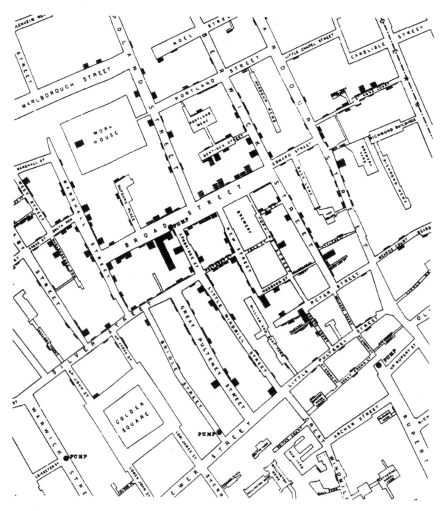

Figure 7-1 Map of the cholera outbreak in London around Golden Square and the Broad Street pump, indicating deaths, the pumps in the vicinity, and various land use features as drafted by John Snow. Courtesy of The Commonwealth Fund. In "Snow on Cholera" by John Snow, Commonwealth Fund: New York, 1936.

Subsequent epidemiologic investigations, summarized by Meselson et al.[3] with the mapping of human and animal cases, indicated both the locations and the timing (based on meteorologic conditions) were immediately downwind of the military facility. Furthermore, examination of autopsy materials confirmed the human cases resulted from inhalation rather than ingestion of the bacteria. Therefore, the cause of this outbreak was due to an aerosol containing anthrax organisms generated by the military facility, as subsequently concluded by Prime Minster Boris Yeltsin.

Probably one of the most striking early examples that moved beyond simple graphic representation and demonstrated the power of examining spatial patterns in infectious diseases was Maxcy's[4] implication of rodent arthropod vectors in the transmission of murine typhus. Comparison of the spatial distributions of typhus cases in Montgomery, Alabama,

from 1922 to 1925, based on places of residence and places of occupation, showed substantial aggregation by place of occupation rather than residence. Thus the differences in the spatial distributions of cases by alternative places of exposure provided a means to evaluate different epidemiologic hypotheses. Maxcy hypothesized that if human lice served as vectors of typhus (as was assumed by many people at that time), then multiple cases should occur in and around the same household because of close human contact. In reality, spatial clustering of cases was more evident when place of occupation was examined (**Figure 7-2**); typhus was especially common among workers associated with food services, leading Maxcy to propose that an arthropod vector associated with food services was responsible. Subsequent work[5] showed the vector of murine typhus to be the rat flea, whose hosts infested many of the food facilities at that time.

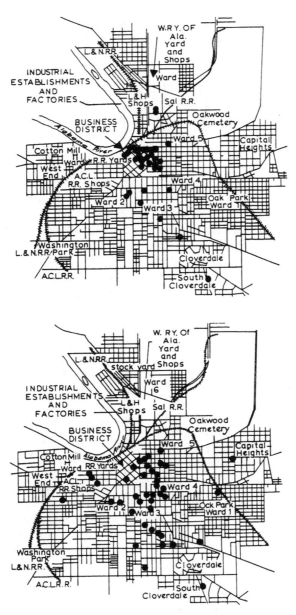

Figure 7-2 The distribution of cases of typhus fever in Montgomery, Alabama plotted by K. F. Maxcy in 1926. Top shows distribution of cases by place of work (or residence if unemployed); bottom by place of residence. The more focal distribution of cases by place of work (top) was used by Maxcy to infer that endemic typhus was not transmitted by lice. Reproduced from Maxcy, KF. 1926. An epidemiological study of endemic typhus (Brill's disease) in the Southeastern United States with special reference to its mode of transmission. *Pub Health Rep.* 41:2967–2995.

Clearly, one factor limiting the use of spatial data in earlier times was the methodological difficulties associated with manipulating spatial data. The problem with manually plotting information, such as Maxcy's data, multiplies significantly with each environmental factor examined, the spatial (and temporal) relationships of these factors, and the epidemiologic associations to be evaluated. These difficulties have been greatly reduced by the widespread introduction of relatively powerful computing systems in epidemiologic research and the development of dedicated

GIS software that is designed to perform functions associated with mapping spatial data. When coupled with spatial analytic methods that have developed during the past two decades, it seems that we may be able to use the spatial patterns of infectious diseases in an analytical fashion, rather than intuitively, to provide important clues to the epidemiology of infectious diseases. This is true even when multiple environmental factors interact to influence disease rates. The most intriguing possibility linked to these systems is that they might allow us to develop and test hypotheses about infectious disease epidemiology in ways that have previously been unfeasible.

This chapter provides an overview of GIS, with its structure discussed in functional terms. The influence of computer systems on the field means that many software systems have been developed to apply to spatial data, each with its own limitations. The field of GIS is rapidly growing and various textbooks exist as introductions to the methods and approaches of the technology.[6,7] Thus, after the brief overview of GIS, the rest of the chapter contains discussion of each of the major applications of GIS as they apply to infectious disease epidemiology. A series of case studies, from simple situations involving data storage through analysis and decision making, are provided. These examples represent studies that will provide some ideas of the broad scope of the technology's application.

OVERVIEW

Geographic information systems can be used for a variety of purposes in infectious disease epidemiology, and these functions are fairly general to any field using spatial data. In a broad sense, GIS can be used to help collect and store data, manage data, query data, model the processes generating data, and make programmatic decisions. It is important to realize that the latter tasks, especially modeling and decision making, are not independent of the earlier functions; the quality of modeling, for example, is critically influenced by how well data have been collected and managed.

An excellent recent synopsis of GIS can be found in the article by Vine et al.[8] Briefly, a major feature that distinguishes GIS from other computer-based systems is that GIS contain within the stored data information concerning the spatial relationships among geographic features, and provide methods to study the relationships among selected, relevant features. Two major formats are used to represent these features: vector format and raster format. Software systems tend to be predominantly one or the other, but more recent versions usually provide algorithms for alternating between formats.

Vector Format

Vector-format GIS represent features in two-dimensional space as points, lines, or polygons, whereas raster-format GIS represent features in two-dimensional space in (usually) a uniform grid. Other data formats, such as quadtrees, which are something of a hybrid format, also exist but are generally less commonly used.

The major conceptual difference between vector- and raster-based systems relates to how the data are represented. In vector format, points are located by specific x, y coordinates that typically represent a specific place on the earth's surface. Lines are interconnected points, linked one to another, whereas polygons represent features with areas and are joined line segments in which the first and last points have the same coordinates. These three types of features—points, lines, and polygons—are used to represent objects on a map. For example, points might be used to indicate the location of healthcare facilities, lines might be used to represent transportation networks (e.g., roads), and polygons might be used to indicate the geographic extent of service areas for the clinics. In vector formats, these elements are usually thought of as being fairly precisely located and, in the case of polygons, the area to the inside of the polygon's boundary is assumed to be homogeneous. These assumptions are only approximately true for most environmental features, however, which raises an issue of data quality that must be assessed in any analysis.

How objects are represented in vector format depends on the scale at which the data are gathered. For example, a clinic might be presented as a point at one scale; in contrast, as one moves to a larger scale (zooms in), floor plans and the outside walls of the buildings making up the clinic might be best represented by polygons. Issues related to choice of scale for GIS application are critical to the study design and outcome. The choice of scale, to some extent, is often determined by the initial resolution of the epidemiologic data. Consider, for example, that Lyme disease, a tick-borne bacterial infection, is a nationally reportable disease in the United States. However, the summary data may be available only at a state or, at best, county level. Consequently, the scale for the GIS applications of the problem may be no better than county resolution, with cases known to occur somewhere within the county boundary. A fairly small scale is most appropriate for presentation of these data, and it places limits on the types of questions that can be addressed. In properly maintained databases, the minimal mapping unit (or the extent of smallest feature identified) is indicated, which is an important consideration in the selection of databases for study.

Raster Format

Raster formats are typically represented as grids of a study area, and locations are determined by the row and column locations much like a Cartesian coordinate system so that each x, y coordinate represents the location of a cell. Probably the most obvious example of raster-based data is satellite imagery, in which reflected light from the earth is recorded by sensors on the satellite. The brightness of the reflected light is recorded for an area of the earth's surface. This area represents the spatial resolution of the image. No points or lines are used in raster formats, as all features have some minimal area assigned to them. Additionally, polygons, such as are used in vector formats, do not exist per se but rather are represented by large numbers of adjacent cells with the same data value.

This data format has two consequences in GIS. First, the locations of points, lines, and boundaries of areas are approximate, in that they are located somewhere within the specified cells but their precise locations are not identified. Thus the locations of features are somewhat "fuzzy"—which may be more realistic for natural features, such as habitat edges. Spatial accuracy of raster features is determined by the spatial resolution of the grid. The raster format sometimes provides a more detailed characterization of features in the inside of regions than vector formats, which assume features are uniform within a polygon.

Second, because the spatial resolution is determined by the interval distances between the rows and columns, the shorter the intervals, the finer the resolution. This produces a computational trade-off between improved spatial resolution, which is achieved by increasing the numbers of rows and columns, and the size of the database. Unlike in the vector format, the data value for each cell has to be recorded in the raster format. To minimize the sizes of files and the time needed to process data, various methods of data encoding have been developed in an effort to reduce the computational loads associated with raster formats.

Data Structure

The development of relational databases, in which different databases can be linked by a common key field, represented a major contribution to integrating GIS within infectious disease epidemiology. Relational database structures make it possible to use GIS as a tool within a larger, investigative analysis, rather than forcing studies to adhere to specified data frameworks.

Data Sources

Data for GIS can be derived from a variety of sources, both specifically for study (e.g., survey data) and as part of the regular duties of agencies (administrative data). As long as at least one of the variables in the gathered data can be linked to a geographic location (e.g., postal codes, addresses, census tracts, states, provinces, countries), the information can be incorporated into a GIS.

More typically, studies derive information from both administrative and specific study design sources. Information on environmental conditions (e.g., land-use or land-cover patterns, property ownership patterns, soils, watersheds) can be accessed from appropriate governmental agencies that gather such data as part of their administrative responsibilities. The resulting data can form a portion of the analysis, whereas specific survey data to study disease incidence, morbidity patterns, and so forth can be gathered as part of a specific study by investigators, who then attempt to link observed disease patterns with the spatial distribution of environmental covariates.

Remotely sensed information is a source of accurate, updated data for environmental analyses. Such information can be gathered from a variety of sources, such as airplanes, for survey studies, although most current sources that have a nearly administrative purpose rely on remotely sensed data recorded from satellites. Many different satellite platforms are actively gathering data today; they vary in their spatial resolution, temporal resolution, duration of data gathering, and the portions of the electromagnetic spectrum that are scanned. For example, the current Landsat Thematic Mapper platform surveys each region of the earth every 16 days. It scans in seven regions (bands) of the electromagnetic spectrum—three in the visible portion and four in the infrared region, with a spatial resolution of approximately 30 m. By contrast, the Advanced Very High Resolution Radiometer (AVHRR) system surveys each region twice daily, scanning in five bands of the electromagnetic spectrum, with a spatial resolution of 1.1 km.

Analysis of archived satellite imagery is a useful method to examine changes in environmental conditions over time or to review environmental conditions at the times of previous disease outbreaks. The choice of satellite data is influenced by both the time when the epidemiologic data were gathered and the spatial and temporal resolution needed for the environmental data. Interpretation of the satellite imagery—or any remotely sensed data, for that matter—can be a difficult task and requires substantial training. Thus, in GIS, the remotely sensed data serve as an updated data source on environmental conditions, but the quality of the interpretation relies on skills and techniques outside of GIS.[9]

Data Quality

Data quality, especially when those data were not gathered directly by the investigators, is a substantial, often ignored issue. Epidemiologists often encounter misclassification errors associated with attribution problems (false-positive and false-negative findings); however, four additional sources of error can be overlooked in GIS analyses: spatial, resolution, interpretive, and temporal errors.

Spatial errors involve misplacement of mapped features relative to their locations in the coordinate system. These errors can occur from simple data entry mistakes or from the methods used to locate the mapped features. One example of spatial errors introduced by the methodology used concerns address-matching algorithms that rely on digitized street maps. Digitized street map databases in vector formats often use an "arc–node" design to code information, where street intersections are nodes and the streets are the arcs. The numbering of the buildings is not done by actually locating each property boundary; instead, the "even" and "odd" sides of the streets are indicated in the file and the possible range of addresses is given. The geographic location of a residence is then determined by the linear interpolation of the building number relative to the range of numbers for the street.

Errors introduced by this coding method can be striking in some areas where block numbers have specific local meaning. In Baltimore, Maryland, blocks north and south of Baltimore Street are numbered in 100s north or south (e.g., 600 block of North Wolfe Street). At the intersection, the block changes in units of 100. Even if only 10 buildings, numbered 600 through 618 occupy one side of a block, on the next block the first building is numbered 700. Thus, with the arc–node format, all of the buildings will be mapped within the lower one fifth of each block even though they cover its entire length. If the spatial resolution of the study is not too fine, this error can be relatively insignificant; however, if exposures need to be specified with a high degree of spatial accuracy, the error could be substantial. Regardless, such errors need to be identified and empirically evaluated for each study.

Resolution errors can occur because the databases that make up the GIS inherently have some level of spatial resolution, or detail. This is sometimes known as a minimal mapping unit. That is, because of limitations related to resources or space, the databases are abstractions of the real world they represent. For example, a database of forest boundaries rarely, if ever, shows the exact location of each tree in the forest; rather, the edge of the forest is approximated

to some level of resolution. In addition, open spaces in the forest that support small meadows or grasslands may not be shown if these open spaces are too small (i.e., they are smaller than the minimal mapping unit). This abstraction is necessary but can limit the usefulness of a particular database for a specific study. Even if every environmental feature, such as each tree, could be located, epidemiologic investigations of infectious diseases rarely have sufficient accuracy themselves to make such detail meaningful. Consider Lyme disease, a bacterial infection transmitted by small, hard-bodied ticks. Clearly, an epidemiologic investigation that attempts to identify environmental risk factors of the disease requires identifying places of exposures for cases. However, the ticks associated with most disease transmission in the eastern United States are so small that only a few individuals can accurately identify where or when exposure occurred to any useful level of accuracy. Many people do not even recall getting tick bites.

The epidemiologic issue related to place of exposure is often a critical one with the application of GIS. Placing a "case" on a map has significant implications for any viewer of the data, but such conclusions may be incorrect. This is especially true when the place of exposure is unknown. The example of Maxcy's study[4] of murine typhus is a classic example of such a phenomenon. Recently, for example, Kitron et al. examined the risk of LaCrosse encephalitis (LAC) in Illinois.[10] This California group encephalitis virus is transmitted by mosquitoes and can produce severe disease, primarily in children. However, most cases are clinically not apparent and the symptoms vary widely, making diagnosis difficult. Consequently, it is difficult to identify where and when cases of LAC are likely to occur. Kitron et al. combined a GIS with spatial analyses to identify clusters of LAC cases, specifically seeking to determine whether regions existed where cases occurred at higher than expected frequencies. Their results showed significant spatial clustering in the state within three counties surrounding Peoria. Demonstration of this clustering then allowed the researchers to investigate which environmental factors occurred within the regions around these sites. Identifying these conditions might permit targeted interventions that would minimize environmental impacts associated with controlling mosquito vectors and eliminate most cases of LAC in the region.

Another condition in which the place of exposure is subject to significant error is when the time between exposure and onset of disease is relatively long, such as with human immunodeficiency virus (HIV), acquired immunodeficiency syndrome

(AIDS), and tuberculosis. Under this condition, use of current place of residence or place of work, for example, could give misleading results. This error factor is especially critical during the occurrence of syndromes whose causes are unknown. Thus workers using a GIS need to take special care in selecting which data are to be presented and how they are to be shown.

Interpretive errors are misclassification errors in the databases. In many cases when databases are obtained from other sources, such errors are difficult to estimate unless "ground truthing," in the case of environmental data, is conducted. Epidemiologists often fail to appreciate the level of error in these databases, especially when they are presented as maps. For example, remotely sensed data (e.g., those collected by satellites) can be used to interpret land-cover patterns. Land cover is classified based on the reflectance patterns from regions of the electromagnetic spectrum using various classification algorithms. However, when sites are "ground truthed" and compared with their predicted land cover, error rates of 15% to 20% have been commonly noted, especially in complex environments, such as residential or rural environments.[11]

Improvements in the classification algorithms remain a major research focus. For example, Gong[12] demonstrated that the use of evidential reasoning and artificial neural networks substantially improved classification rates of environmental data from multiple sources compared with the more traditional approaches.

All of the developed databases have a temporal aspect associated with their collection. This is evident for epidemiologic data gathered during an outbreak investigation, for example. Nevertheless, it is easy to forget that spatial databases gathered for a GIS also have temporal components that can change rather dramatically over various time scales. For example, soil databases may be relatively time invariant, whereas land cover, especially in rapidly developing areas, can change within a few years, and precipitation patterns can vary in a matter of hours. Consequently, the use of databases in GIS as part of infectious disease studies can produce classification errors if the environmental conditions during the time of the study differ substantially from those when the database was created.

Lack of Data

Finally, in many areas of the world, recently updated databases simply do not exist. This lack of information is one factor driving the interest in and application of remote sensing in GIS.

APPLICATION EXAMPLES

Data Collection and Storage

A major feature of computerized systems is their capacity to input and store large quantities of data with relative ease. When data are being collected to answer a specific focused research question, the data gathered are often limited to those variables needed to test the hypotheses associated with the question. In these cases, the data collection and storage needs may be relatively small and a GIS primarily serves to present the data visually.

By contrast, some agencies are required to gather certain data as part of their administrative responsibilities. These data files can be extensive, both in the number of records included and in the number of data fields incorporated into each record. If spatial attributes are associated with these data, especially if they are combined from multiple sources, a GIS can prove a useful system for organizing and updating the data.

As an example, consider schistosomiasis, a disease caused by infection with various species of parasitic worms of the genus *Schistosoma*. This disease causes substantial morbidity worldwide and is often associated with large-scale agro-ecosystem developments. Infection in humans requires contamination of water sources by infectious individuals, subsequent development in snail hosts, and then infection of susceptible people who contact contaminated water.

This complex interplay of hosts and environmental variables creates significant data storage issues when detailed epidemiologic studies of transmission patterns are undertaken. However, GIS can be exceptionally useful for such storage. For example, the Schistosomiasis Research Program (SRP)—a joint effort of the Egyptian Ministry of Health and the United States Agency for International Development (USAID)—undertook as part of its research program a detailed ecological study of environmental factors associated with schistosome transmission at six sites in Egypt. Irrigation canals at these sites represented the primary source of environmental exposure. The sites were sampled once a month for more than a year. The issues related to data storage involved the large number of environmental variables being recorded at a very fine spatial scale over the extended period of the project. Every 50 meters, 84 variables were recorded, including factors related to the type of canal, the abundance and size of host snails, the snails' transmissibility status (infectious versus not infectious), the abundance of other species of snails, water chemistry, aquatic vegetation, and temperature.

Because irrigation systems in these villages typically were 50 to 70 km long, it was usual to have 1400 collecting locations at each of the six sites. This resulted in the production of large volumes of data—nearly 50,000 sheets of data for each study site.

The longitudinal sampling of so many data variables at so many collecting locations for multiple sites presented a substantial data storage problem. Because collections were performed repeatedly at fixed collecting locations along the canals, a GIS provided a simple way of storing and organizing the data (**Figure 7-3**). Each collection location served as a key field in the data record, and those places were geocoded to their locations along the canals. Figure 7-3, a simple schematic of the study area, shows major features of one site, such as roads, canals, and collecting sites. The primary difference from many such hand-drawn schematics is that the locations of all the features are spatially accurate and are referenced to particular locations on the earth's surface. As a result, querying the data to identify where snail hosts were located and when transmission could occur became a simple process.

Data Management

Once data are entered, validated, and stored in the GIS, managing, updating, and editing them can be straightforward. GIS, in this sense, serves as a system to integrate data from various sources (e.g., paper maps, reports, administrative and test data) into a coherent system. Thus GIS can be especially helpful in quality control issues, both those related to

geographic locations and those used in evaluating consistency among different data sources.

In Baltimore, Maryland, the Baltimore City Health Department (BCHD) has as one of its responsibilities monitoring the number of cases of several reportable sexually transmitted diseases (STDs). The city has an area of approximately 240 square kilometers and a population of approximately 700,000 people; however, even in this small region, substantial ethnic, racial, and socioeconomic diversity exists. The administrative data are derived from several sources, including several public health care clinics where patients can be treated and offices of private physicians who diagnose their patients and take samples for laboratory workups; a network of public and private healthcare systems conducts laboratory diagnoses and reports the results to either the city or state health department (depending on the source of the specimen). The data include a required array of demographic and personal information. To coordinate all the information obtained from these various sources, the BCHD developed a data management scheme[13] that allows the information from laboratory tests and clinic records to be integrated and merged into a single large database (**Figure 7-4**). A GIS was incorporated into the data management scheme using place of residence as the geographic identifier.

The GIS provided an additional level of quality control for the database and healthcare delivery. For example, examination of the data showed substantial differences in the quality of data reporting by public and private providers for several important demographic variables. Public clinics reported racial data

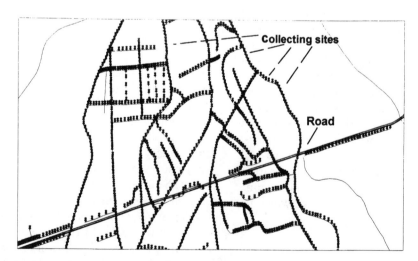

Figure 7-3 Collecting locations and selected features at one site in Egypt used to sample for snails that serve as host for schistosome parasites. Collecting sites are densely located along canals (thin lines). A major road (thick line) bisected the region. More than 1400 collecting locations were sampled each month during the study, but the same collecting locations were revisited each time, making data storage within a geographic information system feasible.

Collection Site	Date	Depth of Canal (Meters)	Site	Sampling Technique N = Canal Bed S = Surface	Non-Vector Snail Species			Schistosomiasis Vector Snail Species		
					Paspal	Phrag	Planor	Biomm9	Biom	Bioml 13
321.0000	6/29/93	0.10	1	N		1	0	0	0	0
321.0000	6/29/93	0.10	1	S		1	0	0	0	0
322.0000	6/29/93	0.10	2	N		1	0	0	0	0
322.0000	6/29/93	0.10	2	S		1	0	0	0	0
323.0000	6/29/93	0.10	3	N		2	0	0	0	0
323.0000	6/29/93	0.10	3	S		2	0	0	0	0
324.0000	6/29/93	0.10	4	N	2		0	1	0	0
324.0000	6/29/93	0.10	4	S	2		0	0	1	2
325.0000	6/29/93	0.10	5	N	1	1	0	0	0	2
325.0000	6/29/93	0.10	5	S	1	1	0	0	0	0
326.0000	6/29/93	0.10	6	N		1	0	1	0	0
326.0000	6/29/93	0.10	6	S		1	0	0	0	1
327.0000	6/29/93	0.10	7	N	1	1	0	0	0	0
327.0000	6/29/93	0.10	7	S	1	1	0	0	0	1
328.0000	6/29/93	0.20	8	N		1	0	0	0	1
328.0000	6/29/93	0.10	8	S		1	0	0	0	0
329.0000	6/29/93	0.10	9	N	1		0	0	0	0
329.0000	6/29/93	0.10	9	S	1		0	0	0	0
330.0000	6/29/93	0.10	10	N	1		0	0	0	0
330.0000	6/29/93	0.10	10	S	1		0	0	0	0
331.0000	6/29/93	0.10	11	N	1		0	0	0	0
331.0000	6/29/93	0.10	11	S			0	0	0	0

Figure 7-3 Continued

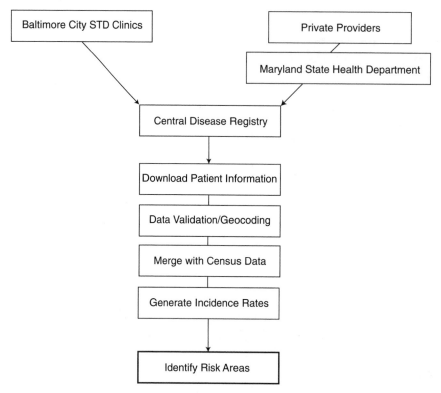

Figure 7-4 Data management of clinical information with the Baltimore City Health Department (BCHD) for sexually transmitted diseases. Cases could be seen initially at clinics run by BCHD or at private providers such as hospitals. If patients were seen by private providers, the information first was reported to the Maryland State Health Department before integration in the Central Disease Registry. The information then was downloaded to the georgraphic information system for validation, clearning, and geocoding. Subsequently, the information could be merged with census information, as shown here, to generate rate maps of selected sexually transmitted diseases (STDs) and identify high-risk areas.

for 99% of cases; by comparison, such data were reported for only 72% of cases by private providers. It is thought that STDs occur at substantially different rates in different portions of the population, but the extent to which reporting bias affects these results is uncertain. In general, if such administrative data were used to make programmatic decisions, such conclusions could be significantly in error.

Management of the data files using GIS also showed several places in the actual implementation of both services and the data management where problems had arisen. For example, a small subsample of patients with an STD were seen at both private healthcare systems and the public clinics for the same disease on a single day. This overlap was not identified in the previously used system because private and public clinics used different identification numbers for the same individuals. However, the GIS identified cases with identical demographic information at the same locality. Subsequent examination of confidential information by appropriate staff identified individuals who had been sent from the private facilities to the public clinics for treatment.

Querying

Once data management is ongoing within a GIS, its application in identifying disease patterns becomes of interest. Data querying in GIS, which represents an approach to examine past or current infectious disease patterns, is probably the most frequent use of a GIS. Querying takes advantage of many of the features specific to GIS, especially the spatial relationships of features to one another (topology). Such issues include how far cases of disease are from a potential site of transmission or how close they are to one another—a consideration often referred to as a "problem of adjacency." Querying often relies on taking survey and administrative data that have been collected and using the GIS to summarize and categorize the data. Such questions usually involve determining the numbers and geographic distributions of cases of disease within a region and their relationship to various features of interest.

Adjacency problems can be addressed by several methods in GIS. Typically, fairly "low-end" GIS technology can deal with many querying tasks;

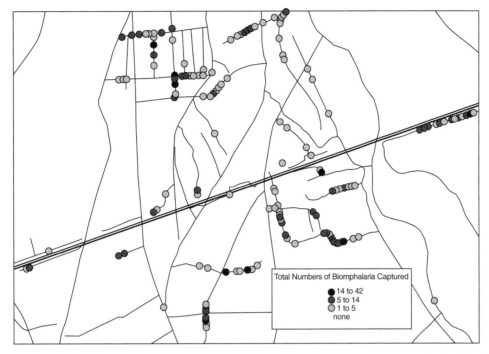

Figure 7-5 A data query of the schistosomiasis database for the map shown in Figure 7-3. This query involved locating all sites that captured *Biomphalaria,* one of the genera of snail that serves as a host for schistosoma in the region, for the entire collecting interval. Intensity of captures is shown by increasing darkness in the circles. Collecting localities that captured no snails are not indicated. Comparison with Figure 7-3 shows very few sites had any snails captured and only a few of these had significant numbers.

when fairly sophisticated relational aspects are investigated, more powerful systems are needed.

Consider the example of schistosomiasis discussed previously (Figure 7-3). An obvious question arises: Where are the snails found that serve as hosts for the schistosomes? Remembering how large the database was and how many sites were sampled, the utility of GIS queries is immediately obvious. When the database is queried for a simple tally of captures of *Biomphalaria*, the genus of the snail host for this disease of interest, throughout the year (**Figure 7-5**) and the results are compared with all the collecting sites (Figure 7-3), it becomes evident that the snails are very restricted in their distribution within the canals. If only sites with large numbers of snails (e.g., 14–42 snails) are considered, these sites are extremely limited. This finding raises several questions that then can be further queried. What is there about these 9 sites (out of 1450 sampled) that differs from the others? Does the difference relate to vegetation cover, water chemistry, other species of snails, or human activities? From a programmatic perspective, this finding also suggests that focused snail control in a very limited number of locations could have a substantial impact on the total abundance of the host snail population.

Other querying functions include extracting information from databases for specific geographic regions. This process of overlaying features is an often-used feature of GIS that has benefited from the development of relational database formats. The value of relational databases is that they permit the linking of data from multiple sources to obtain information that is not uniquely available in any one source. The STD data obtained by the city of Baltimore provide a useful example. An important concern is whether the rates of selected STDs differ substantially within the city. Estimating such rates requires a denominator consisting of the estimated population at risk. The STD database (Figure 7-4) does not include such information, but the U.S. Census Bureau can provide census data gathered in the city of Baltimore (**Figure 7-6**). A portion of its database is shown in Figure 7-6, along with a map of the census tracts in the city. Note that one of the data fields is the census tract number.

The distribution of gonorrhea cases for 1994 in Baltimore can be mapped on a similar base map to Figure 7-6 using place of residence (**Figure 7-7**). The geographic locations of these residences were determined by geocoding the addresses to another database of street addresses for the city. Rates of gonorrhea were estimated by overlaying the census

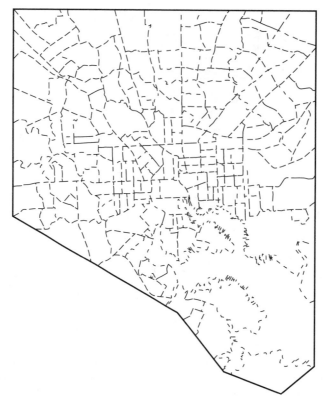

Tract90	Totalper	Perusamp	Per100	Pctinsam	Males	Females
010100	3508	477	3,508	13.6	1646	1862
010200	3435	494	3,431	14.4	1613	1822
010300	2414	344	2,418	14.2	1135	1279
010400	2244	292	2,218	13.2	1158	1086
010500	1942	285	1,968	14.5	962	980
020100	2078	260	2,148	12.1	1012	1066
020200	1863	264	1,916	13.8	987	876
020300	2088	240	1,965	12.2	1154	934
030100	1685	225	1,660	13.6	748	937
030200	2763	326	2,714	12.0	1461	1302
040100	1632	163	1,683	9.7	938	694
040200	1474	159	1,497	10.6	744	730
050100	3828	439	3,828	11.5	1568	2260
060100	3246	430	3,246	13.2	1530	1716
060200	4094	559	4,094	13.7	1910	2184

Figure 7-6 One database of census data for the city of Baltimore showing the geographic boundaries of census tracts within the city. Shown below the map is the database linked to the map indicating census tract number and population data.

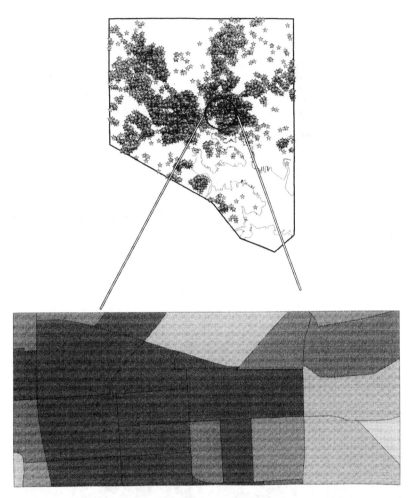

Figure 7-7 The geographic distribution of cases of gonorrhea for the city of Baltimore (top figure; cases have been randomly shifted to protect confidentiality). Using overlay procedures and census data (Figure 7-6), it is possible to link two unrelated databases to estimate disease rates for any portion of the city. An enlarged area is shown below. Rates of disease increase are shown with darker shading.

tract data on the locations of gonorrhea cases. The GIS was used first to count the numbers of cases in specific age–ethnicity–gender categories contained in the STD database, and then the appropriate categories from the census data were used as denominators to estimate rates. A large-scale portion of the data (Figure 7-7) shows that even in an area of intense transmission, substantial local variations in rates of disease are seen.[13] These data then might be used to identify and target regions where rates of disease are above some threshold for action.

Another important feature of GIS that involves data querying is the ability to measure distances from one feature of interest to another feature. If only two points are involved, this measurement can be done manually. In the situation of multiple cases or irregular features, however, the task becomes quite difficult, if not impossible. For example, Lyme disease is transmitted by hard-bodied ticks (genus *Ixodes*) that live

in forests. To assess the importance of peridomestic exposure, it would be of interest to know how far the residences of cases of human Lyme disease are from the edge of the nearest forest (**Figure 7-8**). Challenges abound, however: Forests have irregular boundaries, multiple cases of Lyme disease occur, and, practically, it would be impossible to measure the distance from the site of each Lyme disease case to the nearest forest edge. With aerial photographs and knowledge of where cases of disease occurred, it would be possible to estimate the distances with a ruler and a conversion method, although such an approach supposes that a procedure exists for identifying which forest edge is nearest to the site of each case. GIS can be used to measure the distances from the edges of all forests to each case by overlaying one data layer, the distribution of forests, with the distribution of Lyme disease cases in another layer, and calculating the distances between each case and the nearest forest edge.

(a)

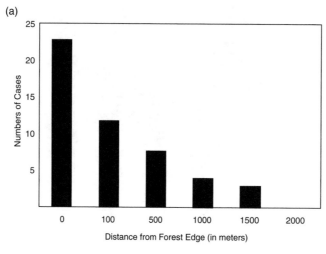

(b)

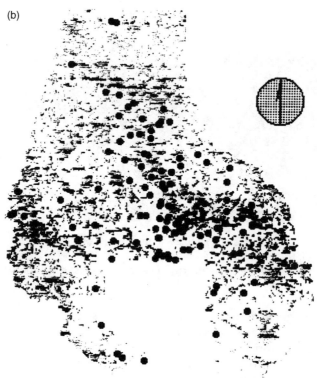

Figure 7-8 Geographic distirbution of the residences (dots) of Lyme disease in Baltimore County in relationship to forested areas (gray areas). (Places of residences have been randomly shifted to protect confidentiality). Using a buffer procedure it is possible to determine distances between the nearest forest edges and the residences of Lyme disease cases and summarize the results (graph above map). Results suggest nearness to forest edge may be a factor for disease.

In the county of Baltimore, the distribution of the residences of Lyme disease cases appears to be clustered along the edge of forested areas (Figure 7-8)—an observation confirmed by the histogram of cases relative to the distance from the edge of the forest. None of the persons infected resided more than 2000 m from the edge of the forest, and most lived within 100 m of the forest edge. Before confirming such a relationship, however, the distribution of all

residences from the forest edges would need to be determined, as residence in or near forests can be a culturally preferred behavior.

Modeling

One obvious feature of GIS database development is that a large number of potential environmental risk factors for a selected infectious disease can be evaluated. Any feature that can be given a geographic location can be considered in the epidemiologic investigation. Consequently, the investigator faces the task of selecting from among these features the most appropriate ones to examine and analyze.

In some cases of infectious diseases, the decision-making process can be straightforward, because the basic epidemiology is well understood and the environmental factors, both proximate and ultimate, are fairly clear. For many vector-borne diseases, for example, only one or a few vectors transmit the pathogen, and the environmental conditions that favor the vector have been characterized. These conditions are so well defined that all that needs to be done is to overlay the distributions of the appropriate conditions to identify the predicted distribution of disease. For example, Beck et al.[14] used information on the breeding, feeding, and flight habits of *Anopheles albimanus*, a major vector of malaria in the Americas, and the locations of villages to model the predicted risk of malaria in a region of coastal Mexico using satellite imagery to identify key environmental features.

It is not often appreciated, however, that the variables selected in the analysis and the way the biological information is used by the researcher represent a model of the disease process. This model is developed outside the GIS, and the GIS then is used to identify where the stated conditions exist. With such models, the GIS simply serves its query function. In contrast, for many infectious diseases with alternative hosts or vectors, such simple models cannot be developed. In addition, for many infectious diseases, the conditions that cause disease outbreaks are not clearly understood, in which case the GIS can be used as an exploratory data analysis tool to develop and test hypotheses about the potential importance of environmental factors. In this situation, statistical methods are used to identify "important" factors associated with disease. The GIS can be used to query the environmental data (Figure 7-8) associated with disease. This information can be exported and analyzed by various statistical procedures, with the GIS then being used to graphically represent the results.

Many infectious diseases with arthropod vectors are influenced by environmental conditions affecting the survival of the vector and any other hosts or reservoirs of the pathogen. Lyme disease, for example, is common along the coastal regions of northern and central North America (as well as elsewhere). The most common vector-borne disease in the United States, it is associated with substantial morbidity. In some areas, Lyme disease has a dramatic impact on outdoor activities of residents. Although exposure can be associated with recreational activities, a significant problem with Lyme disease in the northeastern United States is that much of the exposure appears to occur as part of daily activities around the place of residence.

Baltimore County, Maryland, is located along the western shore of the Chesapeake Bay, and surrounds Baltimore City on three sides. The county is a mixture of industrial, fairly high-density residential and rural environments. Since Lyme disease was recognized in Maryland, Baltimore County has had the largest number of cases reported annually. The county had a population of approximately 700,000 in 1990; in 1991, 38 cases of Lyme disease were reported.

To better understand the epidemiology of the disease, the areas within the county at high risk for the disease need to be identified. A number of environmental factors have been thought to influence the survival of the tick vector, the rodent reservoir of the Lyme disease spirochete, and the white-tailed deer, the host for the adult tick. Presumably, these factors interact to influence where and how intensely Lyme disease transmission occurs.

To model Lyme disease risk, a case-control design was developed using confirmed cases of Lyme disease. Place of residence was selected as the likely site of exposure. This decision was based on interviews conducted with patients, few of whom indicated any other likely site. Because residential site was used for exposure, control sites consisted of a randomly selected sample of all residential addresses within the county. A GIS was used to extract environmental variables (e.g., land-use characteristics, soil types, distance to forests, elevation, aquatic drainage systems) that were thought to influence Lyme disease risk from the areas around case residences, as well as randomly selected residential sites.[15] These data were analyzed by logistic regression analysis. The environmental variables, weighted by their appropriate regression coefficients, then were mapped throughout the region (**Figure 7-9**) as a measure of Lyme disease risk. The results of the risk map were evaluated on follow-up by comparing the numbers of cases of Lyme disease the following year, relative to a new set of randomly selected control sites. Follow-up showed that cases were 16 times more likely to occur in high-risk than in low-risk areas the following year.

A significant risk of modeling with GIS once the databases are developed is that in many situations the number of potential environmental variables is as great as, or greater than, the numbers of cases of disease. As such, the potential exists for the model to be unstable and dependent on idiosyncrasies of the data. This risk is not unique to GIS modeling; indeed, it is always present in exploratory data analysis. Nevertheless, because it is relatively easy to incorporate many variables once the databases are

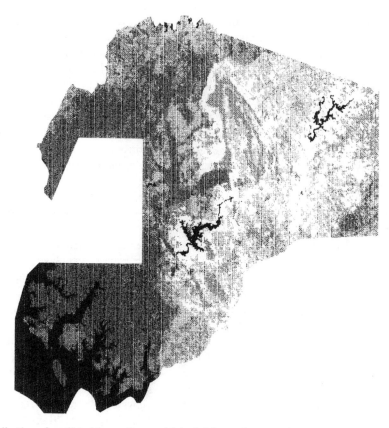

Figure 7-9 Geographic distribution of predicted Lyme disease risk in Baltimore County using a geographic information system to create an environmental database of potential risk factors for a case-control study design. Risk is mapped as four quartiles using the results of logistic regression analysis. Risk increases with increasing lightness. Reproduced from G E Glass, B S Schwartz, J M Morgan, III, D T Johnson, P M Noy, and E Israel. Environmental risk factors for Lyme disease identified with geographic information systems. *American Journal of Public Health* July 1995, Vol. 85, No. 7, p. 946, Figure 1.

constructed, it is an important aspect to remember with GIS.

Another potential problem with statistical modeling of spatial data is rarely explicitly considered in traditional epidemiologic analyses. In general, most traditional statistical methods assume that observations are independent of one another. However, this assumption is unlikely to be true, especially when considering the spatial distribution of infectious diseases. This point is fairly obvious for contagious diseases. Even when diseases, such as Lyme disease, are not contagious, significant spatial structure is generated by the underlying spatial correlation of environmental factors that influence the risk of disease. The major consequence for statistical models appears to be that the spatial structure creates a false sense of precision in the statistics.[16] A basic introduction to the measures and effects of spatial autocorrelation on data can be found in Griffith's book.[17]

Methods of analyzing spatially autocorrelated data have received special attention in geography. As such, many methods have been developed to estimate features that are spatially autocorrelated but have not been measured. For example, estimating the elevation of a particular point given the elevation at other points is a typical problem of spatial autocorrelation that is analogous to the problem of estimating the risk of disease at a particular location from which there are no data. Various methods have been developed to deal with this problem, such as "kriging," which attempts to use information about the internal spatial structure of the data to interpolate a "best" answer. A major practical problem with these approaches for public health is that they "smooth" the data, with sites that are at very low or very high risk being regressed toward the mean. As a result, very high-risk sites are predicted to have a lower risk, whereas very low-risk sites are predicted to have a higher risk than they actually do. Such tendencies are not desirable for practical public health problems. Additionally, simple spatial techniques (e.g., ordinary kriging) exclude information on the spatial distribution of other factors, such as environmental covariates, that may influence the distribution of the outcome in question.

An alternative approach is the explicit incorporation of spatial aspects of the data, as well as the other environmental data, and any information of the known biological processes. For example, Das et al.[18] used hierarchical linear modeling to develop a spatially explicit model of tick vector abundance for adult *Ixodes* found on the tick's principal host, white-tailed deer, that incorporated both spatial correlation of the data and overdispersion in the outcome variable, tick abundance. This hierarchical model had the advantage of identifying both environmental covariates of vector abundance and factors influencing the overdispersion of the tick vectors.

Decision Making

A major application of GIS technology that has been recognized, but little used in infectious disease epidemiology, is in decision making and targeted public health interventions. Throughout this chapter, the policy implications of the data collected for the various examples, such as targeting schistosomiasis control programs or developing STD interventions, have been mentioned. In principle, this use of a GIS would allow policymakers a better method of identifying areas at risk for the outcome of an infectious disease process, so that they could then direct resources toward preventing disease or targeting the at-risk population for screening and treatment while minimizing collateral (and potentially undesirable) impacts. In fact, development of accurate spatial models that incorporate the dynamics of infectious diseases might facilitate the testing of alternative strategies to identify the best strategy or combination of strategies for disease control. As noted previously, achieving this goal requires substantial, accurate databases that have been incorporated into a GIS, as well as a detailed understanding of disease processes. Given the lack of development of GIS in infectious disease epidemiology, it is not too surprising that few examples of this application exist. Even so, GIS should be extremely useful in targeting such interventions. The example discussed next demonstrates GIS's application in evaluation of vaccine trials by identifying target populations at risk for Lyme disease.

Until recently, public health interventions for Lyme disease primarily involved education and encouraging individuals to take appropriate personal protective measures to reduce exposure to vectors. However, recently several recombinant vaccines have been developed and tested. Although Lyme disease represents the most common vector-borne disease in North America and may be locally common, the number of individuals infected often represents only a very small portion of the entire population. For example, although the state of Maryland ranks fifth nationally in numbers of cases, the crude incidence in 1995 was approximately 9 per 100,000. A major problem in conducting population-based vaccine trials for diseases, such as Lyme disease, that lack a well-defined at-risk group is the large number of individuals who would need to be recruited to demonstrate the efficacy of a vaccine if individuals were recruited at random. Given the tremendous costs associated with recruiting patients for vaccine trials, testing them, and following up the population for evaluation, it would be nearly impossible to conduct vaccine trials by such a population-based recruitment strategy.

Maryland was included as a site for the evaluation of a double-blind trial for one candidate vaccine. Power estimates indicated that, assuming a vaccine efficacy of 80% and 4000 people in each of two arms of the study, it would be necessary to recruit from areas where the seasonal incidence was 500 per 100,000.[19] To identify an appropriate population, therefore, the GIS and the model of Lyme disease risk described previously were used to recruit individuals into the study. The map of Lyme disease risk (Figure 7-9) was overlaid with street maps of the region. Streets that overlaid high-risk areas were identified, and individuals who lived in these high-risk areas were contacted and asked to participate in the trial until 200 individuals were enrolled, the population size needed for the Maryland portion of the study (**Figure 7-10**). This approach reiterates the points made earlier that each use of GIS relies on the earlier applications: using databases that have been developed and checked, linking them with epidemiologic data, modeling the factors associated with disease, and then querying the results for specific conditions (residence in high-risk areas).

If this strategy was successful, we would expect to see a significant increase in the number of Lyme disease cases, compared with the crude population rate, making it possible to conduct the trial with substantially fewer participants and more power than would be possible otherwise. If the vaccine were successful, the cases should be (nearly) confined to the control group. As part of the 2-year surveillance, Lyme disease diagnostics were performed twice a year. By the end of the study, Lyme disease incidence in the control group was 2% per year. This rate was substantially higher than both the crude population level and the targeted incidence rate, and was sufficient to demonstrate the effectiveness of the vaccine with a limited sample size.

Figure 7-10 Application of geographic information system to decision making showing the high-risk area for Lyme disease whown in outlined region overlaid on street map. Street addresses falling in high-risk areas were selected to recruit individuals for vaccine trial based on the assumption that peridomestic risk was an indicator of individuals likely to be at high risk of disease.

CONCLUSION

The applications of GIS to infectious disease epidemiology are extremely diverse, ranging from data storage and management to modeling and programmatic decision making. As a tool for the field, GIS remains highly underutilized, although this situation is beginning to change. The opportunities to apply the technology are limited only by the users' abilities to apply the technology. For much of the practical infectious disease epidemiology, low-end data querying systems are perfectly adequate. These systems are fairly easily mastered in a short period of time. Most important, many services are being developed in which critical data layers are professionally constructed, which minimizes the time and resources needed to create and update needed data layers. Along with this expansion, however, comes the risk that data will be used inappropriately or beyond the level of their quality. Unlike many other investigative tools in epidemiology, because GIS produces derivative products, such as maps, these errors will be more difficult to detect. Despite this concern, the opportunities for a better understanding of infectious diseases using GIS outweigh the risks.

• • • REFERENCES

1. Aronoff S. *Geographic Information Systems: A Management Perspective.* Ottawa, Canada: WDL Publications; 1989.

2. Vandenbroucke JP. Re: "A new perspective on John Snow's communicable disease theory." *Am J Epidemiol.* 1997;146:363–364.

3. Meselson M, Guillemin J, Hugh-Jones M, et al. The Sverdlovsk anthrax outbreak of 1979. *Science.* 1994;266:1202–1208.

4. Maxcy KF. An epidemiological study of endemic typhus (Brill's disease) in the southeastern United States with special reference to its mode of transmission. *Public Health Rep.* 1926;41:2967–2995.

5. Woodward TE. President's address: typhus verdict in American history. *Trans Am Clin Climatology Assoc.* 1970;82:1–8.

6. Ripple WJ. GIS for resource management: a compendium. *Am Soc Photo Remote Sens.* 1987.

7. Antenucci JC, Brown K, Croswell PL, Kevany MJ. *Geographic Information Systems: A Guide to the Technology.* New York, NY: Van Nostrand Reinhold; 1991.

8. Vine MF, Degnan D, Hanchette C. Geographic information systems: their use in environmental epidemiologic research. *Environ Health Perspect.* 1997;105:598–605.

9. Sabins FF. *Remote Sensing: Principles and Interpretation.* 3rd ed. New York, NY: W. H. Freeman and Company; 1997.

10. Kitron U, Michael J, Swanson J, Haramis L. Spatial analysis of LaCrosse encephalitis in Illinois. *Am J Trop Med Hyg.* 1997;57:469–475.

11. Harris R. *Satellite Remote Sensing: An Introduction.* London: Routledge and Kegan Paul; 1987.

12. Gong P. Integrated analysis of spatial data from multiple sources: using evidential reasoning and artificial neural network techniques for geological mapping. *Photo Eng Remote Sens.* 1996;62:513–523.

13. Becker KM, Glass GE, Brathwaite W, Zenilman JM. Geographic epidemiology of gonorrhea in Baltimore, Maryland, using a geographic information system. *Am J Epidemiol.* 1998;147:709–716.

14. Beck LR, Rodriguez MH, Dister SW, et al. Assessment of a remote sensing-based model for predicting malaria transmission risk in villages of Chiapas, Mexico. *Am J Trop Med Hgy.* 1997;56:99–106.

15. Glass GE, Schwartz BS, Morgan JM, Johnson DT, Noy PM, Israel E. Environmental risk factors for Lyme disease identified with geographic information systems. *Am J Public Health.* 1995;85:944–948.

16. Breslow NE. Extra-Poisson variation in log-linear models. *Applied Statistics.* 1984;33:38–44.

17. Griffith DA. *Spatial Autocorrelation: A Primer.* Washington, DC: Association of American Geographers; 1987.

18. Das A, Lele SR, Glass GE, Shields T, Patz JA. Spatial modeling of vector abundance using generalized linear mixed models: application to Lyme disease. *Intl J GIS* 2002;16:151–166

19. Steere AC, Sikand VK, Meurice F, et al. Vaccination against Lyme disease with recombinant *Borrelia burgdorferi* outer-surface lipoprotein A with adjuvant. *N Engl J Med.* 1998;339:209–215.

8

Microbiology Tools for the Epidemiologist

Nicole M. Parrish and Stefan Riedel

Microbiology is the study of microorganisms, which are a diverse group of unicellular and multicellular organisms. Viruses, although they are strictly speaking acellular organisms, are included in this field. Medical microbiology is the study of interactions between organisms and their human and animal hosts that result in infectious disease manifestations. Despite our concentration on microorganisms that cause disease, the vast majority of microorganisms that we continuously interact with do not result in disease. In fact, many of these organisms are beneficial and essential for human health and well-being. Conversely, pathogenic bacteria, fungi, viruses, and parasites result in disease in a specific host by interactions of their cellular structures, products, or toxins with host tissue and cells. These components of organisms, which are collectively referred to as virulence factors, can be classified according to the function they provide for the microorganism:

1. Colonize
2. Evade host defense mechanisms
3. Invade and disseminate

Because humans and other animals have an abundance of microorganisms that colonize the external and internal surfaces of the body, it is important to identify and define which microorganisms cause disease. Despite the vast numbers of bacteria that inhabit our mouth, teeth, gastrointestinal tract, urogenital tract, and skin, only a small number of microorganisms cause disease. In addition to this normal flora, many pathogenic microorganisms can be found on body surfaces, whether as temporary colonizers or as a more permanent carrier state.

The prevention of infection and disease is in large part attributable to an array of defense mechanisms that have evolved to deal with these ongoing intimate interactions. *Mechanical barriers* are typically the first line of defense. Examples include skin and mucous membranes as a physical barrier, ciliated cells and mucus in the respiratory tract, and the washing action of tears and urine. *Chemical barriers* are produced (often by resident normal flora) at these sites that prevent colonization by pathogens; these barriers include fatty acids and propionic acid. Other compounds produced by the host that are inhibitory include lysozyme in tears, blood, urine, and sweat; acid in the stomach, vagina, and skin; basic polyamines and complement components in plasma; and acute-phase proteins, such as β-antitrypsin, fibrinogen, C-reactive protein, and β_2-microglobulin. In addition to mechanical and chemical mediators, *defensive cells* such as macrophages, polymorphonuclear neutrophils, monocytes, and eosinophils are all components of nonspecific host resistance or innate immunity. The fourth type of defense in humans and other vertebrates is *specific immunity*, which is a function of both the humoral immune system, involving antibody-mediated B-cell functions, and the cellular immune system, involving T-lymphocyte–mediated functions. A compromise in any of these defense mechanisms can lead to infection and disease in the host.

At times it can be difficult to determine that an organism is the cause of an infection. In 1884, Robert Koch, a German microbiologist, outlined his famous postulates for proving an organism is the cause of an infection (**Table 8-1**). Although Koch's postulates are not foolproof, they do describe a framework for understanding causation. The advent of modern and molecular microbiology has provided further methods to better determine the link between

Table 8-1	Guidelines Establishing the Etiology of Infectious Disease
Koch's Postulates	

1. The microorganism must be found in all cases of the disease, but must not be found in those not suffering from the disease.
2. The microorganism should be isolated from a diseased body and should be grown in vitro and in pure culture for several generations.
3. When the organism from a pure culture is introduced into a healthy body or animal, the typical disease must be the result.
4. The same organism must then be reisolated from the lesion/animal of such an experimentally caused disease.

a microorganism and disease. In the absence of a clearly identifiable microorganism, the host immune response to a specific organism can be a useful diagnostic tool.

Pathogenic microorganisms may cause disease either directly or indirectly. The pathology they cause can be another means of identifying them. The presence of a potentially pathogenic microorganism results in a host response (e.g., antibody production), which, in combination with the organism's virulence factors, can result in toxicity and host tissue damage characteristic of the specific infection. In other cases, microorganisms produce toxins that can be the sole cause of the pathology observed. In addition to true pathogenic microorganisms, some organisms of low virulence or pathogenicity can cause infections when the host is immunocompromised. Microorganisms that are only pathogenic in compromised hosts are referred to as opportunistic pathogens.

This chapter provides a broad overview of the classification, taxonomy, and structure of the various microorganisms. It also briefly describes the current and commonly used diagnostic tests for infectious diseases available to the clinical microbiologist. Although by no means comprehensive, the information presented here provides a basis of understanding for a further in-depth study of microbiology as it relates to infectious disease epidemiology.

TAXONOMY, CLASSIFICATION, AND STRUCTURE OF INFECTIOUS AGENTS

Early biologists realized that microorganisms such as algae, protozoa, fungi, and bacteria did not readily fit into the already-established plant and animal kingdoms. This recognition led to the proposal by Haeckel in 1886 of a third kingdom, the Protista. As viruses were still unknown at the time, they were not included in this classification system. Subsequent advances in the biologic sciences, specifically microscopy, led to a further subdivision of the Protista into eukaryotic cells, which included the algae, fungi, and protozoa, as well as members of the plant and animal kingdoms, and prokaryotic cells that represent the bacteria. The terms *eukaryotic* and *prokaryotic* reflect only the presence of a true nucleus (eukaryotic) or the absence of a well-delineated nucleus (prokaryotic). Significant structural and other biologic differences are described in **Table 8-2**, although the presence of transition forms can result in a blending of some of the listed characteristics.

The taxonomy of infectious agents is based on three concepts: classification, nomenclature, and identification. During the past 300 years of microbiology and since the invention of the microscope, a variety of characteristics have been used to name and identify microorganisms. Classification of microorganisms is a process by which microorganisms

Table 8-2	Comparison of Eukaryotic and Prokaryotic Cells	
	Eukaryotic Cell	**Prokaryotic Cell**
Form	Multicellular structures	Single cells
Nucleus	Nuclear membrane	DNA and chromosome(s) free in cytoplasm
Mitosis	Yes	No
Organelles	Membrane-bound organelles (e.g., mitochondria) present	No organelles present in cytoplasm
Ribosomes	80S = 40S + 60S	70S = 30S + 50S
Cell wall	Absent or cellulose	Peptidoglycan
Sterols	Yes, always	Only in *Mycoplasma* spp.

are systematically divided into groups; this process of grouping refers to the organization of organisms from (at the lowest level) phylum, class, order, and family, to genera and species (the highest level). Much of the organization of microorganisms continues to be based on phenotypic properties and morphology, such as size and shape, Gram stain and staining characteristics, and biochemical properties. Other criteria that may be useful for classification describe physiologic properties of specific organisms, their metabolism, or a unique ecologic niche (e.g., in the case of cyanobacteria). Recent advances in molecular technologies have also affected the traditional taxonomy of microorganisms, including molecular methods using DNA and RNA homology analysis, DNA sequencing, polymerase chain reaction (PCR) and micro-array technology, proteomic analysis, and nucleic acid base sequence similarity (e.g., pulsed-field gel electrophoresis). These methods are used to evaluate relatedness of microorganisms. Evidence from established phenotypic analyses, together with information from molecular and genetic analyses, is used to establish new taxa and reorganize existing groupings of microorganisms.

The naming of microorganisms follows a well-defined set of rules. With the exception of the viruses, nomenclature of microorganisms is typically binomial and includes the genus and species name—for example, *Staphylococcus aureus*. Beyond the species level, microorganisms can be further subdivided based on characteristics that do not warrant a separate species designation but do differentiate a specific member of a species or strain from other members of that particular strain or species. Differences or similarities used for subspecies or strain designation within a species can include a variety of parameters, such as structural or functional differences, phenotypic differences, antigenic differences in surface or subsurface structures, and genomic polymorphism. Strain differentiation is an important component of epidemiologic studies, as the significant diversity within species may result in different clinical manifestations or may be useful in defining a cluster of cases.

VIRUSES

Viruses are the smallest of the infectious agents, with the exception of prions, the agents of spongiform encephalopathies, such as scrapie and Creutzfeldt-Jakob disease. Viruses range in size from 20 to 200 nm and, as such, are not readily visible by light microscopy. They contain a single form or type of nucleic acid, either DNA or RNA, which functions as their genome. In addition to a single form of nucleic acid, viruses compositionally may contain proteins, lipids, and glycoproteins as structural components, depending on their level of complexity. Viruses are obligate intracellular parasites, and their replication is host-cell dependent, directed by their DNA or RNA. Viral subversion of the host's cellular machinery favors the synthesis of viral nucleic acid and structural proteins.

Viral infection is host-cell specific and depends on the presence of specific surface receptors (attachment molecules) for successful entry. Viruses specific for almost every organism have been identified. Even bacteria may be infected by phage viruses—an interaction that has proved useful in the laboratory for introducing genes into bacteria. The outcome for cells infected by a virus can vary and is often virus specific. For instance, some viruses cause rapid cell death (e.g., influenza), whereas others induce continued cellular growth with concomitant release of new virus particles (e.g., adenoviruses). Some viruses are capable of integrating their nucleic acid into the host cell's genome, thereby establishing a latent or quiescent state (e.g., herpesviruses). Latency can continue for long periods of time before reactivation followed by initiation of viral replication and subsequent lysis of the host cell (herpesviruses). Other viruses carry specific oncogenes capable of promoting cellular growth that can lead to transformation and immortalization of the cells. Such changes have been associated with human papillomavirus, the cause of cervical cancer.

In terms of classification, viruses are divided into families, genera, and species, as are other microorganisms. However, a typical binomial classification using genus and species is not used in a standardized fashion. Instead, viruses are referred to by their single names. Characteristics used for viral classification include the following:

- Viral genome: DNA or RNA; single- or double-stranded, linear or circular, segmented or nonsegmented; and genome capping with a protein or polynucleotide
- Size and shape of the capsid and whether it is enveloped or non-enveloped
- Method of replication
- Pathophysiology of the virus, such as host range, antigenic composition, vectors, and tissue tropism
- Physical/chemical features, such as susceptibility to acid or lipid solvents

DNA and RNA viruses of medical importance and some common disease associations are listed in **Table 8-3** and **Table 8-4**. These tables provide a broad overview of the more common viruses and

Table 8-3	Selected DNA Viruses of Medical Importance and Common Disease Associations	
Family	**Virus**	**Common Disease Associations**
Papillomaviridae	Papillomavirus	Common warts, genital warts, laryngeal papilloma, cervical cancer
Papovaviridae	BK virus	Ureteral stenosis, hemorrhagic cystitis
	JC virus	Progressive multifocal leukencephalopathy
Adenoviridae	Adenovirus	Pharyngoconjunctival fever, pharyngitis, respiratory infections, gastroenteritis
Herpesviridae	HSV-1	Cold sores, encephalitis
	HSV-2	Genital herpes
	Varicella zoster virus (VZV)	Chickenpox, shingles
	Epstein-Barr virus (EBV)	Infectious mononucleosis, Burkitt's lymphoma, nasopharyngeal carcinoma
	HHV-6	Roseola
	Cytomegalovirus (CMV)	Wide spectrum of disease in newborns and immunocompromised hosts
	HHV-7	Occasional roseola
	HHV-8	Kaposi's sarcoma
Poxviridae	Variola virus	Smallpox
Parvoviridae	Parvovirus (B19)	Fifth disease

Table 8-4	Selected RNA Viruses of Medical Importance and Common Disease Associations	
Picornaviridae	Poliovirus	Polio
	Coxsackie A virus	Undifferentiated fever, respiratory tract infections, herpangina, aseptic meningitis, acute hemorrhagic conjunctivitis, conjunctivitis
	Coxsackie B virus	Undifferentiated fever, respiratory tract infections, aseptic meningitis
	ECHO virus	Aseptic meningitis
	Rhinovirus	Common cold
Coronaviridae	Coronavirus	Common cold, severe acute respiratory syndrome (SARS)
Caliciviridae	Norwalk virus	Gastroenteritis
Paramyxoviridae	Measles virus	Measles
	Parainfluenza virus	Respiratory tract infections
	Mumps	Mumps
	Respiratory syncytial virus (RSV)	Lower respiratory tract infections, pneumonia, bronchiolitis
	Metapneumovirus	Respiratory tract infections
Orthomyxoviridae	Influenza virus	Influenza
Rhabdoviridae	Rabies	Rabies
Filoviridae	Ebola	Marburg and Ebola hemorrhagic fever
Reoviridae	Rotavirus	Gastroenteritis
	Coltivirus	Colorado tick fever
Togaviridae	Rubella virus	German measles
	Venezuelan encephalitis virus	Meningoencephalitis
	Eastern equine encephalitis virus	Meningoencephalitis
	Western equine encephalitis virus	Meningoencephalitis
Flaviviridae	Dengue fever virus	Dengue fever, dengue hemorrhagic fever
	Yellow fever virus	Yellow fever, hemorrhagic fever, hepatitis
	Japanese encephalitis virus	Encephalitis
	West Nile virus	Febrile illness, meningoencephalitis
	St. Louis encephalitis virus	Febrile illness, meningoencephalitis
Bunyaviridae	Hantavirus	Hemorrhagic fever with renal syndrome, hantavirus pulmonary syndrome
	California encephalitis virus	Meningoencephalitis
Arenaviridae	Lymphocytic choriomeningitis virus	Undifferentiated febrile illness
Retroviridae	Human immunodeficiency virus	AIDS

Table 8-5	Predominant Hepatitis Viruses of Medical Importance	
Family	**Virus**	**Genome**
Picornaviridae	Hepatitis A virus (HAV)	RNA
Hepadnaviridae	Hepatitis B virus (HBV)	DNA
Flaviviridae	Hepatitis C virus (HCV)	RNA
Hepeviridae	Hepatitis E virus (HEV)	RNA

some of the diseases they cause. **Table 8-5** lists the predominant hepatitis viruses, grouped the nature of the disease they cause, rather than by virus family or genome type and structure. The reader is referred to the references list at the end of this chapter for additional information.

Structure

The complete infectious virus is termed a *virion*. It is composed of its specific nucleic acid, DNA or RNA, surrounded by a protein coat known as the capsid. The capsid is further subdivided into capsomers, repeating identical morphologic protein subunits. Each capsomer subunit is composed of one or more polypeptides.

Viruses construct several different capsid shapes, depending on how these proteins combine. Arrangement of capsomers in the shape of an icosahedron (polygon with 20 faces), for example, results in cubic symmetry. In a cubically symmetrical virus, some capsomers are surrounded by five (penton) capsomers, whereas others are surrounded by six (hexon) capsomers. In helical viruses, the capsid proteins are arranged around a helical nucleic acid core. In addition to icosahedral and helical viruses, complex viruses have more intricate structural elements. The viral genome can have an associated protein complex that is referred to as the nucleocapsid and forms the viral core. Enveloped viruses possess a lipoprotein coat that surrounds the virion and is acquired from the infected host cell's membrane. Non-enveloped viruses are also referred to as naked viruses. Finally, viruses may possess glycoprotein spikes, known as peplomers, which protrude from the envelope and function in the attachment of the virus to target host cells.

BACTERIA

Classification

Classification of bacteria into taxonomic groups requires the use of both experimental and observational laboratory methods and techniques. As they were discovered earlier in history, bacteria have been subjected to human classification schemes for much longer than the viruses. Prokaryotic bacteria are named using the binomial system of genus and species (**Table 8-6**). Further subdivision can then occur among species, such as subspecies, serotype, and so on.

Table 8-6	Examples of Bacteria of Medical Importance	
Organism	**Clinical Features/Disease**	**Epidemiologic Features**
Aerobic and Facultatively Anaerobic Gram-Positive Cocci		
Staphylococcus aureus	Cutaneous infections (e.g., abscess, impetigo, wounds); pneumonia; bacteremia; osteomyelitis; arthritis; toxic shock syndrome; food poisoning	Colonize human skin and mucosal membranes (e.g., nares); resistance development (healthcare- and community-associated MRSA)
Staphylococcus, coagulase negative (e.g., *S. epidermidis*)	Opportunistic pathogen: bacteremia, endocarditis; prosthetic joint infects	Colonize human skin and mucosal surfaces
Enterococcus faecalis and *E. faecium*	Bacteremia, endocarditis; urinary tract infections; intraabdominal abscesses	Elderly patients; patients with long-term hospitalization and broad-spectrum antibiotic therapy
Streptococcus pyogenes (group A)	Pharyngitis; scarlet fever; sinusitis; impetigo, erysipelas, cellulitis, necrotizing fasciitis; glomerulonephritis; rheumatic fever; toxic shock syndrome	Diverse populations; carrier state
Streptococcus agalactiae (group B)	Neonatal disease (bacteremia, meningitis, pneumonia); urinary tract infections in adults	Diverse populations; carrier state
Viridans group streptococci	Abscess formation; subacute endocarditis; dental caries	Patients with abnormal or prosthetic heart valves
Streptococcus pneumoniae	Pneumonia and other respiratory tract infections; meningitis; bacteremia; endocarditis	Diverse populations: neonates, children, adults with chronic pulmonary disease, elderly

(Continued)

Table 8-6 (Continued)		
Organism	**Clinical Features/Disease**	**Epidemiologic Features**
Aerobic or Facultatively Anaerobic Gram-Positive Rods		
Bacillus anthracis	Anthrax (cutaneous, inhalational, gastrointestinal)	Animal workers; laboratory accidents; bioterrorism; consumption of infected meat
Bacillus cereus	Gastroenteritis, bacteremia, ocular infections	Contaminated food; traumatic eye injury; IV drug use
Corynebacterium diphtheriae	Diphtheria (respiratory or cutaneous)	Spread by respiratory droplets
Erysipelothrix rhusiopathiae	Erysipeloid (cellulitis)	Occupational disease (e.g., butchers, meat processors, farmers)
Listeria monocytogenes	Early-onset and late-onset neonatal disease (meningitis, sepsis); bacteremia in pregnant women	Ingestion of contaminated food (nonpasteurized dairy products); immunocompromised hosts; elderly women
Mycobacteria		
Mycobacterium tuberculosis	Tuberculosis	Opportunistic pathogen; emerging multidrug resistance
Mycobacterium avium complex	Localized pulmonary disease; also disseminated disease with multiorgan disease	Localized in patients with chronic pulmonary disease; disseminated in patients with HIV/AIDS
Mycobacterium leprae	Leprosy (Hansen's disease)	Spread by close contact with infected patients
Other Gram-Positive, Partially Acid-Fast Bacteria		
Nocardia species	Bronchopulmonary disease	Commonly found in soil and water; opportunistic pathogen in patients with underlying pulmonary disease
Rhodococcus equi	Lung abscess; opportunistic infections in immunocompromised patients	Commonly found in immunocompromised patients (e.g., AIDS, transplant recipients)
Aerobic Gram-Negative Cocci		
Neisseria meningitides	Meningitis, bacteremia	Carrier state; aerosol transmission
Neisseria gonorrheae	Gonorrhea, pelvic inflammatory disease, arthritis	Sexual transmission; asymptomatic carriers
Aerobic and Facultatively Anaerobic Gram-Negative Rods		
Escherichia coli	Urinary tract infections; bacteremia; meningitis	UTI: sexually active women; Meningitis: neonates
Escherichia coli, enterotoxic (STEC), enterohemorrhagic, and entoaggregative strains	Watery diarrhea, hemorrhagic colitis; watery diarrhea with mucus; hemolytic-uremic syndrome (HUS)	Foodborne or waterborne outbreaks; travelers' diarrhea; infants in developing countries
Klebsiella pneumonia	Pneumonia; urinary tract infections	Nosocomial infections; alcoholism
Serratia marcescens	Pneumonia; urinary tract infections; wound infections	Nosocomial infections
Enterobacter species		
Proteus species	Urinary tract infections; wound infections	Structural abnormalities in the urinary tract
Vibrio cholera	Cholera; severe watery diarrhea	Children and adults in developing countries
Vibrio vulnificus	Wound infections; primary septicemia	Immunocompromised patients; preexisting (chronic) hepatic disease
Vibrio parahaemolyticus	Watery diarrhea	Seafood-borne outbreaks

(Continued)

Table 8-6	(Continued)	
Organism	**Clinical Features/Disease**	**Epidemiologic Features**
Aerobic and Facultatively Anaerobic Gram-Negative Rods		
Salmonella species	Diarrhea; enteric fever (serovar *typhi*)	Contaminated food; immunocompromised patients are at risk for bacteremia
Shigella species	Bacillary dysentery	Contaminated food or water; person-to-person transmission
Yersinia pestis	Plague	Natural reservoir: rodents; transmitted to humans by rodent flea bites; bioterrorism
Yersinia enterocolitica and *Y. pseudotuberculosis*	Enterocolitis; mesenteric lymphadenitis	Worldwide distribution; contaminated food and water
Aeromonas species	Wound infections; gastroenteritis	Widely distributed in aquatic reservoirs; contaminated drinking water
Acinetobacter baumanii complex	Pneumonia; septicemia; wound infections; opportunistic infections	Nosocomial infections; patients with large wounds or burns are at increased risk; elderly
Pseudomonas aeruginosa	Pulmonary infections; primary skin infections; infections of urinary tract, ear, eye, and wounds; bacteremia	Nosocomial infections; ubiquitous organism in nature, in aquatic reservoirs, and on surfaces
Stenotrophomonas maltophilia	Wide variety of serious disseminated infections	Nosocomial infections
Burkholderia cepacia complex	Pulmonary infections; opportunistic infections	Compromised patients, especially those with cystic fibrosis and chronic granulomatous disease
Burkholdreia pseudomallei	Melioidosis	Opportunistic pathogen
Moraxella catarrhalis	Ear, eye, and respiratory tract infections	Children; patients with underlying pulmonary disease
Fastidious and Other Gram-Negative Bacilli		
Eikinella corrodens	Subacute endocarditis; wound infections	Human bite wounds; opportunistic pathogen in patients with damaged heart valves
Kingella kingae	Subacute endocarditis	Opportunistic pathogen
Haemophilus influenzae	Encapsulated type b strains: meningitis; septicemia; epiglottitis Nonencapsulated strains: otitis media; sinusitis; bronchitis; pneumonia	Aerosol transmission in young and unimmunized patients; possible spread from upper respiratory tract of elderly patients with chronic respiratory disease
Legionella pneumophilia	Legionnaires' disease (pneumonia) and Pontiac fever (flu-like illness)	Waterborne transmission; elderly and immunocompromised patients at increased risk
Francisella tularensis	Tularemia (pulmonary or skin infections)	Human infections via contact with wild rabbits, ticks, or deerflies; bioterrorism
Fastidious and Other Gram-Negative Bacilli		
Bordetella pertussis	Pertussis (whooping cough)	Aerosol transmission; pertussis toxin; severe disease in infants, milder in adults
Brucella species	Brucellosis	Exposure to infected goats, sheep, and cattle
Pasteurella multocida	Wound infections; pulmonary and disseminated infections	Cat bites; commensal in upper respiratory tract of animals, fowl, and perhaps humans
Campylobacter jejuni	Gastroenteritis	Contaminated food, milk, or water
Helicobacter pylori	Gastritis; peptic and duodenal ulcers; gastric adenocarcinoma	Infections are common (people in lower socioeconomic classes and in developing countries)

(Continued)

Table 8-6	(Continued)	
Organism	**Clinical Features/Disease**	**Epidemiologic Features**
Anaerobic Gram-Positive Organisms		
Clostridium perfringens	Cellulitis, necrotizing fasciitis, myonecrosis; food poisoning; septicemia	Ubiquitous in environment (e.g., soil, water, sewage)
Clostridium difficile	Antibiotic-associated diarrheal disease; pseudomembranous colitis	Colonizes human GI tract; nosocomial, hospital pathogen
Clostridium tetani	Tetanus	Ubiquitous in environment (e.g., soil, water, sewage)
Clostridium botulinum	Botulism (foodborne, infant, wound type)	Ubiquitous in environment (e.g., soil, water, sewage) and GI tract of animals; bioterrorism
Anaerobic Gram-Negative Organisms		
Bacteroides fragilis	Polymicrobial infection of the abdomen, skin, soft tissue, and female genitourinary tract	Colonizes human mucosal surface (oropharynx, intestine, vagina)
Spirochetes		
Treponema pallidum	Syphilis	Worldwide distribution; sexually transmitted disease
Borrelia burgdorferi	Lyme disease	Reservoir: rodents, deer, domestic pets, hard-shelled ticks Vector: hard-shelled ticks
Borrelia recurrentis	Epidemic, louse-borne relapsing fever	Reservoir: humans Vector: body louse
Leptospira	Leptospirosis (asymptomatic to influenza-like illness with yalgia); Weil syndrome (jaundice)	Worldwide distribution; rodents are common reservoir; soil is contaminated by rodent urine
Mycoplasma and Gram-Negative, Obligate Intracellular Bacteria		
Mycoplasma pneumoniae	Tracheobronchitis, pharyngitis, pneumonia	Strict human pathogen; asymptomatic carrier state
Chlamydophila pneumoniae	Asymptomatic respiratory tract infections to "atypical" pneumonia	Human pathogen
Chlamydophila psitacci	Psittacosis/ornithosis; pulmonary disease with hematogenous dissemination to liver and spleen	Exposure to dried excrement, urine, or secretions from psittacine birds (parrots, parakeets, macaws, cockatiels)
Chlamydia trachomatis	Trachoma and lymphogranuloma venerum (LVG)	Direct transmission by droplets via hands, eye-to-eye, or contaminated clothing; sexually transmitted
Ehrlichia chaffiensis	Human monocytic ehrlichiosis	Region: southeastern, central, and midwestern United States Reservoir: white-tailed deer, foxes, coyotes, wolves, domestic dogs Vector: Lone Star tick (*Amblyomma americanum*)
Anaplasma phagocytophilum	Human granulocytic ehrlichiosis	Region: northern United States central Midwest Reservoir: small mammals (mouse, chipmunks, voles) Vector: Lone Star tick and *Ixodes* tick
Rickettsia prowazekii	Epidemic typhus	Human body louse (*Pediculus humanus*)
Rickettsia rickettsia	Rocky Mountain spotted fever	More than 90% of infections in the United States occur from April to September Vector: dog tick (*Dermacentor variabilis*) and wood tick (*Dermacentor andersoni*)
Coxiella burnetii	Asymptomatic to flu-like symptoms; also pneumonia and hepatitis	Wide variety of hosts: cattle, sheep, goats, dogs, cats, and rabbits; exposure occurs via contaminated soil and milk

Originally, the taxonomic classification of bacteria was solely based on morphologic and biochemical characteristics. Today, the majority of microbiology laboratories continue to use bacterial microscopy, a variety of selective and nonselective growth media, and biochemical and immunologic tests for the identification and classification of bacterial organisms. In recent years, improvements in molecular technologies have afforded microbiology laboratories the opportunity to enhance, improve, and/or expedite the process of bacterial identification. Nevertheless, the use of established morphologic characterization of bacteria and basic phenotypic and biochemical tests remain valuable tools in the hands of experienced microbiologists.

Morphologic classification of bacteria is based on staining characteristics, shape, and size of the microorganism when visualized by light microscopy. The Gram stain reaction, which highlights a variation in cell wall structures of bacteria, has been used extensively for classification. Most of the clinical specimens for which bacterial culture is requested are smeared onto a glass slide, Gram stained, and reviewed at high-power magnification with a light microscope. The Gram stain procedure utilizes first gentian or crystal violet (purple dye) as the primary stain, then iodine, which serves as a mordant to bind the dye. These two steps are followed by decolorization with 95% ethanol or acetone–alcohol, and final counterstaining with safranin (a red dye). Crystal violet and iodine form large aggregates within the cell, which, depending on the nature of the cell wall, will be either retained or washed out by the action of alcohol. The decolorization is presumably due to the higher lipid content in the cell walls of such bacteria. Cells that retain the crystal violet–iodine complex will appear blue/purple when observed under the microscope and are called gram-positive. Conversely, bacteria that are decolorized by the alcohol and pick up the final safranin counter stain appear red/pink; they are called gram-negative. While the Gram stain procedure can be performed easily and quickly, specimen preparation and the interpretation of the stained slides under the microscope can be difficult.

Special stains are required for the evaluation of specimens that are submitted for the detection of mycobacteria, as these organisms have a different cell wall structure that resists regular staining methods; more importantly, once stained, their cell walls resist decolorization with strong organic solvents (e.g., acid-alcohol). Such stains are known as acid-fast stains, and the two most commonly used methods are the Ziehl-Nielsen stain and the Kinyoun stain. Acid-fast stains can differentiate members of the genus *Mycobacterium*, including the etiologic agents of tuberculosis (*M. tuberculosis*) and leprosy (*M. leprae*), from other bacteria. This differentiation is based on the ability of mycobacteria to retain a particular primary stain (carbolfuchsin) when decolorized with 95% alcohol containing 3% hydrochloride (hydrochloric acid). All other bacteria become decolorized during the acid wash. When these stains are applied, mycobacteria appear red against a green or blue background, depending on the counter stain used. Some other bacteria, such as *Nocardia* species and *Rhodococcus* species, exhibit a partial acid-fast staining characteristic appearance.

In addition to their differential staining characteristics, bacteria are morphologically classified on the basis of their shape and arrangement. Three general shapes have been identified:

- Cocci: round or spherical cells
- Bacilli: rod-shaped cells
- Curved, spiral forms

Further descriptive terms include coccobacilli, which are short, rod-shaped cells, and pleomorphic cells, which demonstrate variable morphologies.

Morphologically, bacteria are also categorized based on their arrangement when grown in cell culture. For example, *Streptococcus pneumoniae* is frequently described as gram-positive diplococci (pairs of cocci) because it grows in characteristic pairs, whereas *Staphylococcus aureus* is most often described as gram-positive cocci in clusters.

The ability of most bacteria to grow in vitro has allowed for their biochemical and morphologic classification. These taxonomic characteristics are based on the metabolic and physiologic differences between different groups of organisms and are most commonly referred to as phenotypic characteristics. A variety of methods have been developed to test for the presence or absence of particular enzymes, for example. Commonly used taxonomic classification tests based on this principle include determining whether bacteria can utilize specific nutrients for growth or whether they metabolize particular substrates, such as carbohydrates. Other phenotypic methodologies directly test for the presence of enzymes, such as catalase or oxidase. Catalase is an enzyme that breaks down H_2O_2 to water and oxygen; the test based on it involves applying hydrogen peroxide to a growing colony. If O_2 bubbles arise from the colony, the organism possesses the catalase enzyme. The presence of particular enzyme systems is most commonly detected by colorimetric assays; that is, if the enzyme is present, a pH change or production of a colored product in the culture medium will be evident. Similarly, antigen–antibody reactions have been used to distinguish between species, subspecies, or serotypes within a genus. In these tests, antibodies that bind to specific bacterial surface antigens can be used to identify bacteria that produce these proteins.

The most definitive classification and taxonomic organization of bacterial organisms is the latest edition of *Bergey's Manual of Systematic Bacteriology*. First published in 1923, this classification was solely based on morphologic and phenotypic characteristics of bacteria. Advances in genetics during the past 30 years have since resulted in reclassification of many of the bacteria to allow for more accurate reflection of evolutionary and phylogenetic relationships. Through the application of not only earlier serotyping methods but also molecular-based technologies (e.g., PCR, plasmid analysis, restriction endonuclease analysis, ribotyping), many of the bacterial organisms have been reclassified or renamed and bacterial taxonomy is more solidly based on nucleic acid profiles. These molecular methods themselves have gone through an evolution: whereas earlier tests used the measurement of DNA homology of the *entire* chromosome as the determinant of genetic relatedness, newer hybridization techniques using cloned or amplified *portions* of the genome have been developed to look for the presence of specific DNA sequences. These methods are now commonly used in diagnostic microbiology laboratories.

In particular, current genetic taxonomy has evolved to incorporate sequence analysis of highly conserved genes for determination of phylogenetic relationships. The most commonly used genes are the ribosomal RNA genes, which include the 16S, 23S, and 5S genes. These genes are found in all prokaryotes and contain both highly conserved as well as variable regions. Sequence, or base, changes in these genes reflect evolutionary and phylogenetic relationships among bacteria. As newer information will undoubtedly continue to emerge, the bacterial taxonomy and *Bergey's Manual* should always be understood as a "work in progress."

Bacterial microorganisms are present in all environments (e.g., soil, water, and air). They are part of all vital life functions of more complex life-forms and are found in association with both living and nonliving environments. Thus organisms of interest to the medical community represent only a part of the taxonomic classification of all bacteria. The work of Robert Koch and Louis Pasteur had dispelled many misconceptions about the causes of infectious diseases by the end of the nineteenth century. Subsequently, as the knowledge base grew, a clinically driven approach to classification of bacterial organisms emerged that relied on the concepts of pathogenicity and virulence.

Structure

Figure 8-1 illustrates the basic structure of a bacterial cell. Although all of the structures shown in the figure are involved in the life and survival of prokaryotic,

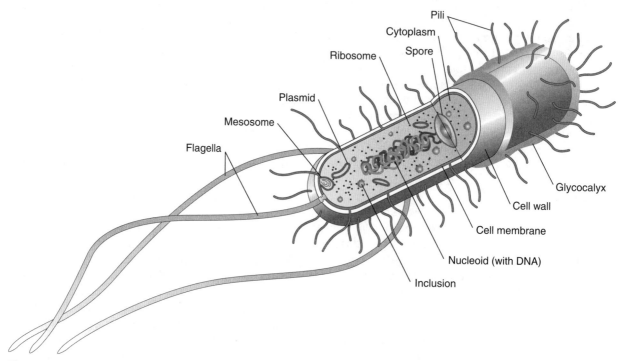

Figure 8-1 Structure and organelles of a basic bacteria. Note that they lack a nucleus.

bacterial cells, many are also important virulence factors and are briefly described here with emphasis on their roles in pathogenesis.

In contrast to eukaryotic cells, prokaryotes do not possess a true nucleus; instead, the genetic material—deoxyribonucleic acid (DNA)—of most bacteria is organized into a single, circular chromosome. However, a few bacteria may have two, three, or even four dissimilar chromosomes (e.g., *Vibrio cholera* has two chromosomes). The cytoplasm of all bacteria is surrounded by a cytoplasmic membrane and an additional bacterial cell wall, which provides structural rigidity, confers shape to the cell, and serves as the actual physical barrier against the outside environment. The cell membrane has several functions related to permeability and transport of solutes, electron transport systems, and receptor functions for chemotactic and other sensory transduction systems. The cell wall is an essential component of all bacteria, with the exception of mycoplasma. In addition to determining the size and shape of the cell, it serves as an exoskeleton, preventing lysis of the cell. As discussed earlier, differences in cell wall structure form the basis for taxonomic classification by use of the Gram stain.

As shown in **Figure 8-2**, an essential component all of bacterial cell walls is peptidoglycan. Peptidoglycan is a complex polymer composed of alternating units of *N*-acetyl-glucosamine and *N*-acetyl muramic acid in a β-1,4-linkage. The polysaccharide chains are cross-linked through peptide bonds between a pentapeptide chain (typically, four amino acids ending in D-alanine) and the muramic acid residue of *N*-acetyl muramic acid. This interlinked polymer forms the strong backbone for all other cell wall components. The gram-positive cell wall is composed of a very thick layer of peptidoglycan. Despite its thickness, this cell wall does not serve as a permeability barrier for the bacteria's cytoplasmic membrane. A unique component of the gram-positive cell wall is teichoic acid, a polymer composed of either glycerol or ribitol with phosphate linkages. It is frequently attached to the cytoplasmic membrane and can activate host macrophages through the release of interleukin 1 (IL-1) and tumor necrosis factor alpha (TNF-α).

Compared to gram-positive bacteria, gram-negative bacteria have a significantly more complex cell envelope. The outermost portion of the gram-negative cell wall is a lipid bilayer referred to

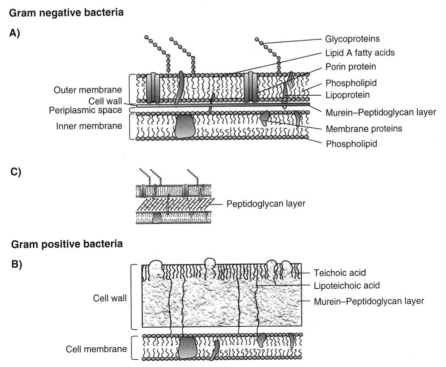

Figure 8-2 Gram negative (a) and gram positive bacteria (b) share similar structures including the phospholipid bilayer cell membrane and the presence of membrane proteins. The gram negative bacteria also has an outer membrane with extensive glycoproteins and porin structures. Note that the peptidoglycan layer is an intricate network of n-acetylglocosamine and N-acetylmuramic acid bound by glycosidic bonds. This is the site of action of the penicillin family of antibiotics. (c). In the gram positive bacteria the peptidoglycan layer is approximately twenty times thicker than in a gram negative, 20–80 nanometers (nm) versus 7–8 nm.

as the outer membrane. Underneath this outer membrane is an area called the periplasmic space, which contains a variety of enzymes related to metabolic and transport functions of the cell. The peptidoglycan layer of gram-negative bacteria is significantly thinner than that of gram-positive bacteria. The outer leaflet of the outer membrane contains lipopolysaccharide (LPS) or endotoxin, a three-component molecule that is a major virulence factor in gram-negative bacteria. Lipid A is the toxic component of LPS, which is located innermost in the lipid bilayer. Extending from lipid A is the core, an oligosaccharide composed of some unusual sugars. The composition of the core oligosaccharide is similar among all gram-negative bacteria. The outermost portion of LPS comprises a series of repeating oligosaccharides, the somatic antigen, which is a primary antigenic determinant of the cell. In addition to LPS, the outer membrane of gram-negative bacteria has a variety of proteins associated with it. One group of outer membrane proteins is known as porins; these proteins are frequently trimers (three identical proteins bound together) and have a central channel that provides for the passage of hydrophilic compounds through the hydrophobic outer membrane. Unlike the cell wall of gram-positive bacteria, the cell wall of gram-negative bacteria acts as a permeability barrier for the cell, owing to the presence of the hydrophobic outer membrane. Hydrophilic compounds with a molecular weight greater than approximately 800 kDa cannot pass through the porin protein channels.

Beneath the cell wall, all bacteria are surrounded by a cytoplasmic membrane, which serves as the primary osmotic barrier for the cell. The cytoplasmic membrane is a lipid bilayer composed of phospholipids and protein. Unlike eukaryotic cells, bacteria do not have sterols, such as cholesterol, in their membranes. Within the cytoplasm, ribosomes for protein synthesis and the bacterial chromosome are the essential structural components. In addition, many bacteria possess granules that can be visualized within the cytoplasm; these granules are most commonly storage depots for nutrients.

Some bacteria, such as those belonging to the *Mycobacterium*, *Nocardia*, and *Corynebacterium* genera, have a modified gram-positive cell wall structure; the cell walls of these organisms contain large amounts of waxes known as mycolic acids. In this case, the cell wall is composed of peptidoglycan and an external, asymmetric lipid bilayer. The inner leaflet of the cell wall contains mycolic acids that are linked to arabinoglycan. In addition, the outer leaflet contains several other extractable lipids. This cell wall structure confers hydrophobic properties upon

the bacteria and renders the organisms more resistant to harsh environmental conditions, including many chemicals such as detergents and strong acids.

Furthermore, some bacteria are capable of synthesizing large amounts of extracellular polymer structures. These structures are often referred to as capsules or slime layers, but the more inclusive term is glycocalyx. In general, capsules are nonessential cell structures. In the environment, their primary function is to prevent dehydration of the cell, but for many pathogens they also serve as a major virulence factor through interference in phagocytosis by the host.

Many bacteria also possess outermost structures such as flagella, fimbriae, and pili. Flagella are long, complex structures that are responsible for motility or movement. They are nonessential, and not all bacteria have them. Flagella are composed of protein, which is an important antigen (H antigen) for identification and classification among those bacteria that possess these structures. Fimbriae or pili are short, nonflexible structures that surround the surface of the cell. Like flagella, they are nonessential but function in adherence. In bacterial pathogens, these structures are responsible for adherence to host cells' membranes through a very specific interaction, which frequently determines the organotropism of a particular pathogen. A type of pili known as sex or F pili permits attachment and DNA transfer between similar species through a process known as conjugation—the most common method for acquisition of antibiotic-resistance determinants by bacteria.

Finally, some bacteria are capable of surviving in harsh environmental conditions by forming spores. The two most common endospores are the gram-positive rods: the obligately aerobic *Bacillus* species and the anaerobic *Clostridium* species. However, other bacteria are capable of endospore formation. Spore formation is usually triggered by depletion of nutrients in the environment. Bacteria then form a single, internal spore that is ultimately liberated when the cell dies by autolysis. Bacterial endospores are highly resistant to chemical agents, heat, and desiccation. When the environmental conditions again change to more favorable nutritional conditions, spores germinate to form single vegetative bacterial cells.

FUNGI

The study of pathogenic fungi and the diseases they cause is known as medical mycology. Fungi are eukaryotic organisms whose number includes a wide variety of forms, ranging from single-celled microscopic yeasts to the multicellular and macroscopic mushrooms and toadstools. All fungi are hetero-trophic, meaning they depend on organic nutrients for their metabolism and growth. The more than 100,000 species of fungi play an essential role in degrading organic waste in nature. Despite their ubiquity in nature, fewer than 400 fungi species are of medical importance, and fewer than 50 species are associated with more than 90% of all fungal infections in humans (**Table 8-7**). As eukaryotes, the fungi have a defined nucleus, surrounded by a nuclear membrane, a plasma membrane that contains sterols, mitochondria, Golgi apparatus, 80S ribosomes, and a cytoskeleton, as well as a cell wall or exoskeleton.

Classification

Historically, the fungi have been classified on the basis of morphologic characteristics and type of reproduction. As a group, the fungi are included in a separate biologic kingdom called Fungi. A fungal organism is classified within a specific phylum according to genus and species; further classification is according to class, order, and family according to the mode of sexual reproduction, morphology, physiologic properties, and phylogenetic relationships. Within the kingdom are four phyla: Chytridiomycota, Zygomycota, Ascomycota, and Basidiomycota. The largest phylum is the Ascomycota, which encompasses more than 60% of all known fungi, and some 85% of fungi pathogenic to humans.

Deuteromycota is a term formerly used to describe fungi that did not fit within the commonly established taxonomic classification, because their sexual reproductive forms had never been observed; these fungi were therefore described as *fungi imperfecti*. Because only their asexual reproductive form was known, the Deuteromycota were formerly considered a separate phylum. Although this term is no longer formally accepted as a taxon in mycology, many of the organisms previously included in this group have yet to find a place in the current taxonomic classification. Mycologists continue to rely on the asexual reproductive characteristics of molds, for example—at least for routine identification purposes of these organisms.

For the fungi in the phylum Zygomycota, sexual reproduction results in a zygospore and asexual reproduction produces numerous sporangia, which are produced in thin sac-like structures on top of specialized hyphae, called sporangiophores. Examples of these fungi include *Rhizopus*, *Absidia*, *Mucor*, *Rhizomucor*, and *Cunninghamella*. Organisms in the phylum Ascomycota produce ascospores sexually and conidia asexually. The latter forms are produced on specialized, often branched hyphal structures named conidiophores. Most yeast

(e.g., *Saccharomycetes* and *Candida*) and molds (e.g., *Trichophyton*, *Microsporum*, *Blastomyces*, *Coccidioides*, *Histoplasma*, and *Aspergillus*) are ascomycetes. Basidiomycota reproduce sexually by formation of a club-shaped basidium, and hyphae have complex septa. Among the basidiomycetes are mushrooms (*Amanita*) and *Cryptococcus* spp.

From a clinical point of view, fungi of medical importance can be grouped according to the type or location of infection that they cause. Whereas researchers have developed a substantial knowledge base related to the pathogenesis of bacterial and viral diseases, understanding of the molecular and genetic basis of pathogenesis in fungal infections remains limited. In general, immunocompetent patients have a high resistance against fungal infections including those from both endogenous (the patient's commensal flora) sources and exogenous (environmental) sources. Only a few fungi are sufficiently virulent to be considered primary pathogens. Among those are the organisms causing endemic mycoses: *Histoplasma capsulatum*, *Coccidioides immitis*, *Paracoccidioides brasiliensis*, *Blastomyces dermatitidis*, and *Penicillium marneffei*. These primary pathogens are capable of causing disease even in a healthy, immunocompetent host, when sufficiently large numbers of conidia are inhaled. They may also be thought of as opportunistic pathogens, as they cause more severe disease in patients with impaired immune systems. *Candida* spp., *Cryptococcus* spp., *Aspergillus* spp., and other filamentous molds are true opportunistic infections that cause disease only in patients with an impaired immune response or disrupted protective barriers (e.g., mucosal membranes). In some instances they may cause moderate to severe disease.

From yet another clinical point of view, fungal infections can be categorized based on the extent of the invasiveness of their disease. These groupings include the following categories:

- Superficial mycoses or infections that involve only the outermost layers of the skin and hair.

- Cutaneous mycoses that involve primarily the epidermis. Infections of the mucosal surfaces are also included in this group.

- Subcutaneous mycoses that cause infections of the dermis and subcutaneous tissue.

- Systemic mycoses, which are infections of internal organ systems following the inhalation of spores. The endemic mycoses caused by so-called dimorphic fungi are also included in this group.

Table 8-7 Common Fungi of Medical Importance

	Organism	Clinical Morphology		Natural Habitat	Infectious Form and Mode of Transmission	Common Sites of Infection
Superficial Mycoses	*Malassezia furfur*	Yeast		Part of human skin flora	Yeast; dissemination	Skin
Cutaneous Mycoses	*Epidermophyton floccosum*	Filamentous mold		Human disease	Conidia and hyphae; direct contact/ dissemination	Skin, hair, nails
	Microsporum canis			Animals		
	Microsporum gypseum			Soil		
	Trichophyton tonsurans			Human disease		
	Trichophyton rubrum			Human disease		
	Trichophyton mentagrophytes			Animals and human disease		
Subcutaneous Mycoses	*Sporothrix schenckii*	**Dimorphic**	Yeast within macrophages	Soil, plants	Conidia/hyphae; traumatic inoculation	Skin, subcutaneous tissue, lymphatics
Systemic (Primary), Endemic Mycoses	*Histoplasma capsulatum*		Yeast within macrophages	Soil, bat and bird droppings	Conidia; inhalation	Lung, bone marrow, blood
	Blastomyces dermatitidis		Yeast; broad-base budding	Soil, plant matter	Conidia; inhalation	Lung, skin, bones
	Coccidioides immitis		Spherules, endospores	Soil of arid regions	Arthroconidia; inhalation	Lung, skin, meninges
	Paracoccidioides brasiliensis		Multiple-budding yeast	Soil (?), plants	Conidia; inhalation/ trauma	Lung, skin, mucosal surfaces
	Penicillium marneffei		Yeast-like cells (nonbudding)	Soil, bamboo rat	Conidia; inhalation	Lung, skin, blood, CNS
Systemic, Opportunistic Mycoses	*Candida* spp. (*C. albicans, C. krusei, C. tropicalis, C. glabrata*)	Yeast		Human flora	Yeast with pseudohyphae; direct invasion/ dissemination	GI and GU tract, nails, viscera, blood
	Aspergillus spp. (*A. fumigatus, A. flavus, A. niger, A. terreus*)	Filamentous mold(s)		Ubiquitous in nature, plants	Conidia; inhalation	Lung, sinuses, eyes, skin, nails
	Fusarium spp.				Conidia; inhalation/ contact/ dissemination/ traumatic inoculation	Lung, eyes, blood, skin, nails
	Zygomycetes (*Rhizopus, Absidia, Mucor, Rhizomucor, Cunninghamella*)				Sporangia; inhalation/traumatic inoculation	Lung, sinuses, orbit, CNS, face
	Cryptococcus neoformans	Yeast		Soil, bird droppings	Yeast; inhalation	Lungs, CNS and meninges, skin

The systemic mycoses can be further subdivided into those caused by true or primary pathogens, which are capable of causing disease in healthy individuals, and opportunistic pathogens, which are marginally pathogenic to immunocompetent hosts but cause disseminated or deep-tissue infections in immunocompromised hosts.

Fungal infections of the skin and skin structures are usually described as superficial, cutaneous, or subcutaneous. Superficial mycoses are caused by fungi that typically colonize the keratinized layers of the skin, hair, and nails. These infectious are usually not associated with any host immune response and are nondestructive and, therefore, asymptomatic. In contrast, superficial mycoses are often of significant cosmetic concern to patients. Four fungi are known to cause superficial mycoses: *Malassezia furfur* (Pityriasis versicolor), *Hortaea werneckii* (Tinea nigra; formerly: *Exophiala werneckii*), *Trichosporon* spp. (White Piedra), and *Pedraia hortae* (Black Piedra). Pityriasis versicolor is a common superficial mycosis affecting many young adults worldwide. It is usually a disease of healthy people and has a higher prevalence in tropical and subtropical regions. Pityriasis presents with areas of hypopigmented and hyperpigmented macules on the chest, upper trunk, shoulders and arms, but any other part of the body can be affected as well. *M. furfur*, a lipophylic yeast, interferes with the melanin production in skin, and lesions are usually hypopigmented in dark-skinned individuals, whereas lesions in light-skinned people are usually pink to light brown and become more pronounced as they fail to tan after sunlight exposure. Diagnosis of *M. furfur* infection is typically made on clinical grounds; laboratory diagnosis involves visualization of the fungal elements in skin scrapings treated with KOH or calcofluor white. Tinea nigra and the Piedras are typically diseases in individuals residing in tropical areas.

Cutaneous mycoses are caused by a variety of fungi, including dermatophytes and nondermatophytic fungi. The majority of these infections are attributable to dermatophytes, which include the following organisms: *Epidermophyton floccosum*, *Microsporum* spp., and *Trichophyton* spp. *Candida* spp. are among the nondermatophytic agents causing infections of the skin, nails, and mucosal membranes. Dermatophytes present with a wide range of clinical syndromes, including diseases known as "ringworm" (Tinea corporis) and "athlete's foot" (Tinea pedis). In this nomenclature, "Tinea" refers to the disease caused by dermatophytes and is further described by the area of body affected: for example, Tinea capitis describes an infection of the hair/scalp, Tinea corporis is an infection of the body, and Tinea manum is an infection of the hand and palmar surfaces.

Dermatophytes can be further classified according to their natural habitat. Geophilic dermatophytes (e.g., *Microsporum gypseum*) live in the soil and are occasional pathogens in animals and humans; zoophilic dermatophytes (e.g., *Microsporum canis*, *Trichophyton metagrophytes*, *Trichophyton verrucosum*) are usually parasitic and live in the skin and hair of animals, but can be transmitted to humans. Among these organisms, *M. canis* is a common cause of ringworm in young adults and children. Finally, anthropophilic dermatophytes (e.g., *Epidermophyton floccosum*, *Trichophyton rubrum*, *Trichophyton tonsurans*, *Microsporum audouinii*) generally infect humans and are typically transmitted by direct body contact, or indirectly from the environment when an infected person sheds fungal elements/spores. Anthropophilic dermatophytes typically do not elicit a strong inflammatory host response, but instead cause indolent chronic infections that may prove difficult to cure (consider frequent exposure/reinfection). Zoophilic and geophilic dermatophytes, in contrast, commonly elicit a strong host response that includes highly inflammatory lesions; the lesions respond usually well to therapy. Most dermatophytic infections present as localized lesions and are amenable to topical treatment.

Subcutaneous mycoses are caused by a variety of fungi, which are found in soil and other environmental sources. Infection occurs by direct inoculation through broken skin, with the subsequent development of a localized infection, which rarely disseminates beyond the regional lymphatics. The most common cause of subcutaneous mycoses is *Sporothrix schenckii*, a thermally dimorphic fungus found on plant surfaces and in the soil. Infection is usually sporadic and most common in warmer climates. It occurs through implantation of microconidia of the filamentous stage into tissue through a puncture or abrasion, with subsequent conversion to the yeast form, resulting in a nodule that may ulcerate; secondary spread to the lymphatic system with formation of nodules occurs approximately 2 weeks after the initial lesion. Other subcutaneous mycoses include eumycotic mycetoma, chromoblastomycosis, and subcutaneous zygomycoses. The eumycotic mycetoma (in contrast to the bacterial actinomycotic mycetoma) is a subcutaneous infection, usually of the foot or ankle, as a result of traumatic inoculation. Rare in the United States, mycetomas are primarily seen in tropical areas of the world. The etiologic agents of the eumycotic mycetoma include common as well as relatively unusual fungi: *Fusarium*, *Phaeoacremonium*, *Curvularia*, *Exophiala*, and *Madurella*. Similar to the mycetomas, subcutaneous chromoblastomycosis is a disease commonly seen in the tropics. Etiologic agents include the pigmented (dematiaceous) fungi of the genera *Fonsecaea*, *Exophiala*, *Phialophora*, *Cladosporium*, and others. The disease manifests as a warty or cauliflower-like growth on the foot or ankle as a result of subcutaneous fungal growth. Subcutaneous zygomycoses are caused by *Conidiobolus coronatus* and *Basidiobolus ranarum* and are seen most commonly in Africa and, to a lesser extent, in India and South America.

Systemic mycoses can be viewed as those infections caused by dimorphic fungi (primary pathogens) in certain endemic areas (endemic mycoses), and those infections caused by opportunistic pathogens as they infect typically immunocompromised hosts. Etiologic agents of endemic mycoses include *Histoplasma capsulatum*, *Blastomyces dermatitidis*, *Coccidioides immitis*, *Paracoccidioides brasiliensis*, and *Penicillium marneffei*. These organisms are known as endemic pathogens because their natural habitats are confined to specific geographic regions. For example, *H. capsulatum* is found in the Mississippi and Ohio River valleys in the United States, but also in Mexico, Central America, and South America. *H. duboisii* causes African histoplasmosis in tropical areas of Kenya, Gabon, and Uganda. The natural habit for *H. capsulatum* is soil rich in nitrogen content, especially soil contaminated with bird or bat droppings; thus infections are associated with exposure to aerosolized soil and dust, bird roosts, caves, or decaying buildings. *Blastomyces dermatitidis* is found in the Mississippi and Ohio River valleys (southeastern and central United States), the Great Lakes area, and the Midwest, as well as in New York and Canada along the St. Lawrence River. This organism appears to grow in decaying organic matter, and the infection seems to be associated with exposure to aerosolized conidia present in soil and leafs.

Coccidiomycosis (*C. immitis*) is endemic in the arid southwestern United States, in northern Mexico, and in some areas of Central and South America. The mold and its arthroconidia (infective stage) are found in the soil, and the risk of exposure is greatest in the late summer to fall, when dry and dusty conditions are common. The growth of this fungus is enhanced by bat and rodent droppings. In contrast to *C. immitis*, *P. brasiliensis* is found only in South and Central America. The organism is commonly found in soil along the Amazon River valley and jungle and grows in areas characterized by high humidity, rich vegetation, and acid soil. The infection occurs either by inhalation of spores or by traumatic inoculation; infection is common in children and young adults, but overt disease is rather uncommon. In adults, *P. brasiliensis* infection is more common in men and

in people living in rural areas. Lastly, *P. marneffei* causes a disseminated disease involving tissues and organs of the reticulo-endothelial and mononuclear phagocytic system. This disease primarily affects HIV-infected individuals in Southeast Asia. The natural habitat for the pathogen appears to be the bamboo rat, but the organism has also been isolated from soil. As with all endemic mycoses, the infective stage is the microconidium of the mold form.

The route of entry for all of the primary systemic mycoses is the respiratory tract with subsequent dissemination to other organ systems, if infection is not controlled by the host. Person-to-person transmission does not occur.

The opportunistic systemic mycoses include a wide spectrum of fungi, including agents of the primary mycoses described previously, as well as usually saprophytic fungi such as *Aspergillus* spp., various zygomycetes (e.g., *Rhizopus* spp.), *Fusarium* spp., *Acremonium*, *Scopulariopsis*, *Scedosporium*, *Paecilomyces*, a variety of dematiaceous fungi, and yeast such as *Candida* spp. and *Cryptococcus*. Opportunistic fungi cause disease in immunocompromised hosts (e.g., patients with diabetes, hematologic malignancies, HIV/AIDS, elderly patients, or those receiving cytotoxic drug therapy). As a group, these fungi are ubiquitous in nature or can be found as part of the normal skin/mucosal flora (e.g., *Candida* spp.). Initial infection can progress to serious systemic diseases, depending on the degree and duration of immunosuppression of the host. The most common opportunistic fungi are members of the genus *Candida*, particularly *C. albicans*, which is now the fourth most common cause of nosocomial bloodstream infections. *Cryptococcus neoformans* is usually acquired by inhalation of aerosolized yeast cells, with subsequent dissemination to other organs, primarily the central nervous system (CNS). *C. neoformans* is a major opportunistic pathogen in patients with HIV/AIDS.

Structure

Fungi that are pathogenic to humans have been described in two distinct morphologic forms: yeasts, which are unicellular and reproduce by extension of buds from the mother cell, and molds, which are multicellular and multiply by sporulation. Molds grow as filamentous, branching strands of connected cells, which form what is called a hypha. The cumulative mass of intertwined hyphae is called a mycelium. Hyphae penetrating the nutritive media supporting the molds growth are called vegetative hyphae/mycelium, whereas hyphae that project above the surface are called aerial hyphae/mycelium and usually carry the reproductive structures of the mold. Hyphae may have intracellular divisions or septa, or they may lack them entirely. Zygomycetes are typically paucisepatate to aseptate molds.

The majority of fungi pathogenic to humans can be grown in vitro and form colonies that are either cottony or velvety in appearance. In contrast, yeast grow as moist, smooth colonies similar in appearance to bacteria. The majority of yeast reproduce by budding; some yeast species, however, produce buds that may not detach but rather become elongated. The continued budding process then produces elongated chains of cells termed pseudohyphae. **Figure 8-3** and **Figure 8-4** illustrate the morphology of yeast, budding yeast, and hyphal structures of molds.

For some fungi, both yeast and mold forms have been described; these fungi are termed to be dimorphic (e.g., *Histoplasma capsulatum* and *Coccidioides immitis*). Dimorphism is either associated with changes in temperature (filamentous at 25°C, yeast at 37°C) or temperature and nutrient dependent. The infectious or pathogenic form of the dimorphic fungi is the filamentous form (present in the environment), with infectious spores being acquired by inhalation and pulmonary disease being the primary disease stage.

All fungi have essentially a very rigid cell wall structure. These cell walls are composed of long

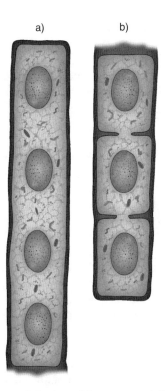

Figure 8-4 Somatic hyphae of fungus grow at the apices. Hyphae can be either (a) coenocytic: continuous multinucleated cells, or (b) septate: divided protoplasm with one or more nucleus per division.

chains of complex polysaccharides (approximately 85%), glycoproteins (approximately 10%), and lipids. Important components of fungal cell walls include chitin, glucans, and mannans. Some yeast and molds also contain melanin within their cell walls and appear black or brown; these fungi are termed dematiaceous. Unlike mammalian cell membranes, which contain cholesterol, fungal cell membranes typically contain ergosterol.

Aside from their morphologic appearance as colonies, fungi can be classified according to their type of reproductive mechanism—that is, sexual (teleomorph) or asexual (anamorph) reproduction. Most fungi (approximately 75%) are known to be capable of both sexual and asexual reproduction. In general, fungal organisms have been given different names based on their anamorphic and teleomorphic reproductive forms.

Sexual reproduction can be either homothallic (i.e., hermaphroditic = within a single strain) or heterothallic (i.e., between two genetically different fungal organisms within their species). The latter form of sexual reproduction occurs most commonly when mating-compatible strains of a species are stimulated by pheromones to undergo plasmogamy. In both types of sexual reproduction, plasmogamy is followed by

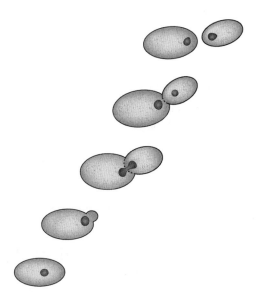

Figure 8-3 Asexual reproduction is the most common reproduction of yeast. A daughter cell is created from a bleb off the original cell resulting in two haploid cells. The daughter cell is often smaller than the first. Yeast may also undergo sexual reproduction where two cells fuse and then divide.

nuclear fusion, meiosis, and cell division, resulting in the exchange of genetic material. Therefore, fungi with capability for sexual reproduction must reduce the DNA content to half the DNA content found in their somatic cells and then fuse the gametes to make the next generation. The hemigenetic cells are known as spores, with a prefix that describes the origin of the spore. Examples include (1) zygosporangia, producing sporangiospores; (2) fusion of ascogonium and antheridium, producing ascospores; and (3) basidiocarps/basidia, producing basidiospores.

The fungi seen and isolated in the clinical laboratory typically reproduce by asexual means, producing spores named conidia or sporangia. Asexually derived spores are produced by mitosis, and their germination gives rise to an identical organism. The two major types of asexual spores produced by fungi are conidia and, in the zygomycetes, sporangiospores or sporangia. These spores are further described based on their morphology (e.g., size, shape, number of cells). In some fungi, the vegetative cells of the mycelium can transform into conidia, a process that occurs usually under certain environmental conditions (e.g., temperature change, nutrient depletion). Examples of these asexually derived spores are arthroconidia and chlamydospores.

MEDICAL PARASITOLOGY

The study of protozoan and animal parasites that infect humans is known as medical parasitology. Organisms considered in this field fall into two major categories: the protozoa and the helminths, in which the adult stage is a worm. A few parasites of medical importance from each of these categories are discussed in this section. Diagnosis of parasitic infections often involves direct examination of stool specimens for the presence of ova and parasites using standard light microscopy, which is described in greater detail in the next section.

Protozoa

The protozoa belong to a subkingdom, Protozoa, because they are neither plant nor animal. The morphology of protozoa varies widely and includes oval, spherical, and elongated cells that can range in size from 5–10 to 1–2 mm. Structurally, the protozoa resemble other eukaryotic cells in possessing a cytoplasmic membrane that encloses cytoplasm containing membrane-bound nuclei, mitochondria, 80S ribosomes, and a variety of specialized organelles associated with higher life-forms. The majority of protozoa are aquatic, living in wet soil, rivers, and

oceans, among other settings. However, a relatively small subset exists that are obligate parasites of animals and are capable of producing both acute and chronic disease.

Like fungi, many protozoa are capable of both asexual and sexual reproduction. Asexual reproduction usually involves division of a cell into two daughter cells of equal size and composition through transverse (crosswise) or longitudinal (lengthwise) fission. Some species are capable of unequal fission or division through budding or multiple fission. In contrast, the method of sexual reproduction involves the fusion of two morphologically disparate cells (conjugation) with exchange of nuclear material and segregation of two daughter cells. The reproductive cycles of some protozoa are complex, in that a part of the life cycle takes place in one host, such as a human or other vertebrate, and another stage takes place in an invertebrate host. In instances where two different hosts are required in the life cycle, the host in which sexual reproduction occurs is known as the definitive host, whereas the host in which only asexual multiplication occurs is termed the intermediate host. Not unlike spore-forming bacteria, some protozoa are capable of forming cysts that can survive in unfavorable environmental conditions. During conversion to the cyst form, protozoa become morphologically round or oval and secrete a protective coating around themselves that is resistant to temperature changes, toxic chemicals, and drying. Encysted protozoa are capable of survival outside of their specific host until they gain access to a new host, with subsequent resumption of growth and infection.

Classification

As with bacteria and fungi, only a limited number of the approximately 40,000 species of protozoa cause disease in humans. Pathogenic protozoa are found throughout the phylogeny of the subkingdom Protozoa. In the following sections, members of three phyla are discussed: Sarcomastigophora, Ciliophora, and Apicomplexa.

In the phylum Sarcomastigophora, amoebae make up a subphylum known as Sarcodina. Amoebic infections of humans are generally confined to the intestine but can occasionally be carried in the blood to other organs of the body, such as the liver, lungs, spleen, pericardium, and brain. Amoebae do not possess complex organelles and do not undergo sexual reproduction, but rather multiply by binary fission. They are known for their ability to acquire food through the use of fingerlike projections known as pseudopodia, meaning "false feet." These projections are also used for motility. Under adverse conditions, many species are capable of forming cysts that can change into actively feeding trophozoites when conditions are more favorable.

Of the Sarcodina, *Entamoeba* is the most prevalent genus found associated with humans. In most instances, species of this genus exist as normal flora of the human intestinal tract. However, one species, *Entamoebae histolytica*, is a notable pathogen in humans. Infections with *E. histolytica* are referred to as amebiasis and can be the cause of amebic dysentery. In such cases, actively growing organisms (trophozoites) invade the intestinal mucosa, resulting in lesions that can cause symptoms ranging from a few daily loose stools with small amounts of blood and mucus to acute cases with numerous intestinal ulcers causing severe diarrhea and substantial amounts of blood and mucus. In a small proportion of individuals, these intestinal ulcers may erode into adjoining blood vessels, allowing spread to other organs, especially the liver and lungs, and eventually leading to abscess formation.

Amebiasis is more prevalent in tropical and subtropical regions than in temperate zones and is often associated with poor sanitary conditions. In most instances, transmission is the result of ingestion of cysts from chronic carriers who shed the cyst form of the organism in their feces. Unlike acute cases, which tend to shed the trophozoite forms in feces, cysts are relatively resistant to harsh environmental conditions and, therefore, survive long enough to establish new infections.

Also in the phylum Sarcomastigophora, the subphylum Mastigophora comprises flagellated protozoa commonly divided into two groups: those causing disease in the intestinal or genital tracts of humans (intestinal flagellates) and those transmitted by blood-sucking insects (hemoflagellates). Intestinal flagellates can produce a spectrum of disease, ranging from asymptomatic to severe, whereas the hemoflagellates may produce severe disease that is often fatal.

Of the intestinal flagellates, *Giardia lamblia* is the only one that produces specific intestinal disease. The actively growing form of this organism is bilaterally symmetric, with two nuclei and four pairs of flagella that provide its motility. It also produces cysts. Infections in adults range from asymptomatic to mild, including abdominal cramps and diarrhea. In severe cases, malabsorptive deficiencies may result in the small intestine. This organism is ubiquitous throughout the world, including the United States, and may contaminate surface water. Furthermore, as it is resistant to chlorine, even treated water supplies can become contaminated if the water is not properly filtered.

Another flagellated protozoan, *Trichomonas vaginalis*, is the causative agent of trichomoniasis, a relatively common sexually transmitted disease infecting both men and women. Infection in both men and women can be asymptomatic or in women can cause a thin, watery, vaginal discharge, accompanied by burning and itching. The *T. vaginalis* parasite does not form cysts and has four anterior flagella with one posterior flagellum that forms the outer edge of an undulating membrane.

Hemoflagellates are those flagellated protozoa that are transmitted to humans by the bites of infected, blood-sucking insects. Two genera are of importance in this particular category: *Trypanosoma* and *Leishmania*. In both cases, cells of the protozoa pass through similar stages in their life cycles, including development in both vertebrate and invertebrate hosts. Four principal stages are typically involved in the life cycles of these parasites and are characterized by the presence or absence of an undulating membrane and flagella:

- Trypomastigotes, which characteristically possess an undulating membrane running the entire length of the organism, the outer edge of which is formed by a single flagellum that extends anterior to the cell
- Epimastigotes, in which the undulating membrane originates in the central part of the cell
- Promastigotes, which lack an undulating membrane but have a single anterior flagellum
- Amastigotes, which are rounded, nonmotile forms

It is important to remember that for each species of parasite, some forms develop in the vertebrate host and others develop in the invertebrate host.

Trypanosomes are the causative agents of West and East African sleeping sickness. Specifically, *Trypanosoma gambiense* is the etiologic agent of West African sleeping sickness, and *T. rhodesiense* is the etiologic agent of East African sleeping sickness (also known as Rhodesian trypanosomiasis). Transmission occurs as the result of a bite from an infected tsetse fly. The parasitic organisms then migrate through the blood, eventually invading the lymph nodes, which results in attacks of fever. These attacks can be intermittent and recur over a period of weeks to months, often resulting in heart damage. As the disease progresses, trypanosomes invade the central nervous system, causing meningoencephalitis, which is notable for slurred speech and difficulty walking. Later stages are characterized by convulsions, paralysis, mental deterioration, and increasing sleepiness that ultimately progresses to coma and death. This process may take several months to reach its ultimate conclusion. Although West and East African sleeping sickness are similar in clinical presentation, the East African form of the disease typically progresses much more rapidly, with death occurring well before the onset of the meningoencephalitis. Frequently, myocarditis is the cause of death.

Another disease caused by a trypanosome is American trypanosomiasis, also known as Chagas's disease. This disease is found in the southern United States and Central and South America, and its burden is particularly high in several South American countries. The causative agent of Chagas's disease is *T. cruzi*, which is transmitted to humans by reduviid bugs (also called kissing or assassin bugs). Reduviid adults can be more than 2 inches in length. They emerge from the walls and ceilings of substandard tropical housing to feed on humans at night. Their bite is painless and can occur on any exposed skin—commonly the face. Reduviid bugs shed trypanosomes in their feces. As the bugs feed, they continually defecate, contaminating the bite site and, therefore, infecting the host. Chagas's disease may also be transmitted by blood transfusion and vertically from mother to child.

T. cruzi is unable to multiply outside the cell in its vertebrate host; thus it undergoes a morphologic change to the amastigote form and is found multiplying in virtually every cell in every organ of the host's body. The organ most often affected in Chagas's disease is the heart, with growth of the parasite in this organ inducing an inflammatory reaction that enlarges the heart. The chronic phase of the disease is long and mostly asymptomatic. If left untreated, death occurs in approximately 30% of patients, usually from disturbances in heart rhythm or congestive heart failure.

The genus *Leishmania* includes another hemoflagellate that infects humans. All species of this parasite are transmitted from one animal to another by the bite of an infected sand fly of the genus *Phlebotomus*. In general, the form of the parasite introduced by the bite of the sand fly is the flagellated promastigotes (the form present in the insect's gut); they become transformed into nonmotile amastigotes, which then proliferate in cells of the reticuloendothelial system—specifically, macrophages and endothelial cells. Three species of this genus are of particular medical importance in humans: *Leishmania tropica*, the causative agent of cutaneous leishmaniasis; *L. braziliensis*, the causative agent of mucocutaneous leishmaniasis; and *L. donovani*, the causative agent

of visceral leishmaniasis. These diseases vary both in the regions of the world in which they are found and in their severity:

- Cutaneous leishmaniasis occurs primarily in the Near East, Mediterranean countries, Africa, southern Russia, and southern Asia. It is characterized by a papule that appears at the bite site and eventually develops into an ulcer. Secondary bacterial infection can be a problem but, in general, the ulcer heals within a year, leaving a depigmented scar.

- Mucocutaneous leishmaniasis is a variant of the cutaneous form, involving the mucous membranes of the nasopharyngeal area. If this disease is left untreated, the nasal septum, lips, and the soft palate may be destroyed, resulting in asphyxiation due to airway collapse or secondary bacterial infection. Mucocutaneous leishmaniasis is typically found in South America.

- Visceral leishmaniasis, also known as kala-azar, is a form of the disease in which the parasites are able to invade the reticuloendothelial system throughout the body, especially the liver and spleen. As a result, these organs become enlarged, causing abdominal swelling, and often culminating in death an average of 2 years after onset of initial symptoms.

In the phylum Ciliophora, only one of these free-living species, *Balantidium coli*, causes disease in humans. Actively growing trophozoites are covered in tiny, hairlike projections called cilia, which provide motility in aqueous environments. This organism has both a macronucleus that controls the metabolic activities of the cell and a micronucleus that is involved in sexual reproduction of the cell, which divides by transverse fission. In addition, this parasite is capable of forming cysts that provide a means of transmission upon ingestion of contaminated food or water. *B. coli* typically resides in the lumen of the intestine, obtaining food by ingesting bacteria. Occasionally, this organism can cause symptoms not unlike those seen in amebic dysentery.

The phylum Apicomplexa contains one class, the Sporozoa, which is of relevance to human disease. Members of this particular class are obligate parasites of animal hosts. Among the diseases caused by these organisms are malaria and toxoplasmosis, as well as intestinal infections. Because the life cycles of the Sporozoa are much more varied than those of the other protozoa, only a few of them are covered in this chapter.

Malaria is caused by one of four parasites belonging to the class Sporozoa: *Plasmodium vivax, P. ovale, P. malariae*, and *P. falciparum*. Although the clinical signs and symptoms vary with each species of malaria, in general they include chills and fever at intermittent, regular intervals, followed by profuse sweating. Because the life cycle of the malarial parasite is complex and varies by species, only a brief description is presented here. Transmission occurs when an individual is bitten by an infected female mosquito of the genus *Anopheles*. Sporozoites are released into the bloodstream of the host from the salivary glands of the mosquito as it feeds. Subsequently, the sporozoites migrate to the hepatocytes of the liver and undergo one or more rounds of asexual reproduction; they then return to the bloodstream as merozoites and invade red blood cells. Two species of this parasite, *P. ovale* and *P. vivax*, are associated with relapsing malaria—a form of disease caused by dormant parasites in the liver, which may erupt weeks, months, or years after the initial episode. Merozoites undergo several developmental stages and asexual reproduction within the red blood cells, eventually causing rupture of the cells and release of their contents into the bloodstream, where other red blood cells can then be infected and the process started again. It is during the time of red blood cell rupture and parasite release that the symptoms of the disease are present. In addition, after asexual reproduction has occurred in the red blood cells, some of the merozoites do not divide, but rather undergo a transition to male and female gametocytes. These, in turn, are ingested by a feeding mosquito, and the gametocytes are converted into male and female gametes that fuse, producing a zygote during sexual reproduction in the gut of the mosquito. The zygote undergoes several developmental transitions within the mosquito before once again reaching the sporozoite stage and repeating the infectious cycle.

In endemic areas, significant morbidity and mortality from malaria are the result of anemia, due to the high level of parasitized red blood cells. *P. falciparum*, the most dangerous of the malarial parasites, is especially adept at invading red blood cells. In addition, it can induce conformational changes in these cells that result in blocked capillaries, leading to hemorrhages in the brain, lungs, and kidneys. For this reason, severe infection with this species of parasite is often fatal.

Toxoplasmosis is caused by another member of the class Sporozoa, *Toxoplasma gondii*. This parasite is one of the most widespread in the world, infecting vertebrate hosts. Very often, the resulting disease is mild to asymptomatic in humans; however, it can present a particular threat in neonates and immunocompromised individuals. The *T. gondii* parasite is widespread throughout the animal kingdom and, therefore, is a common source of infection for humans through ingestion of undercooked or raw meat containing either the trophozoite or cyst forms. Notably, these parasites undergo their sexual reproduction in the intestinal cells of members of the cat family and are shed as oocysts in the feces of these animals. Infection can also result from ingestion of these oocysts, which release enclosed sporozoites that then travel to infect epithelial cells, leukocytes, the reticuloendothelial system, and the central nervous system. The parasites subsequently multiply within these cells.

Cryptosporidium, the causative agent of cryptosporidiosis, is also included in the class Sporozoa. Both the sexual and asexual reproductive cycles of this parasite occur in one host. Infectious oocysts are shed in the feces, which can then infect another susceptible host. Clinically, cryptosporidiosis is characterized by mild to severe diarrhea and nausea that spontaneously resolve in an average of 1–10 days. Although infection with *Cryptosporidium* produces asymptomatic to mild, self-limiting illness in most individuals, it can cause a persistent diarrhea in immunocompromised patients and may even be fatal.

Helminths

The numbers of invertebrates that parasitize humans are seemingly endless. Helminths are typically classified into two phyla: Platyhelminthes (flatworms) and Aschelminthes (roundworms). Generally speaking, many of these organisms live only in the intestinal tract of a parasitized host, whereas others invade organs such as the liver, lungs, blood, brain, and subcutaneous tissue. Most of these parasites are large, macroscopic organisms.

Platyhelminthes

The flatworms are the most primitive of the Platyhelminthes and characteristically have no digestive tract or only a rudimentary one. They are typically flat, and most contain both male and female reproductive organs (hermaphroditic). Although many require an alternation of hosts to complete their life cycles, humans are often the definitive host for the adult worms, whereas other animals serve as the hosts for the intermediate stages.

Intestinal cestodes, or tapeworms, of humans inhabit the intestinal tract. Adult tapeworms are long and ribbonlike, and are divided into segments with a head; the head has either suckers or hooks, which provide for attachment to the intestinal wall. In general, the animal in which the larval stage develops into an adult worm is the definitive host, and the animal in which the eggs develop into the larval stage is the intermediate host. Humans are the only definitive host for the beef and pork tapeworms—*Taenia saginata* and *T. solium*, respectively. Another tapeworm infection of humans is acquired by eating raw or undercooked fish infected with *Diphyllobothrium latum*, the fish tapeworm.

T. saginata is acquired by ingestion of beef infected with the larval stage of the parasite. Once the larvae reach the small intestine, the worm head emerges and attaches itself to the intestinal mucosa. Mature worms can reach a length of 8–12 m. Eggs are passed in the feces and can infect other animals, such as cattle. The eggs subsequently hatch, and the embryos disseminate throughout the body, particularly the muscles. There, they develop into the larval stage, or cysticercus, which will die in approximately 9 months if not ingested by the definitive host, humans. Most infections are asymptomatic, although malnutrition, anemia, and weight loss can result.

The adult pork tapeworm develops similarly to that of the beef tapeworm and can attain a length of 2–3 m. However, pigs can ingest eggs on fecally contaminated food. The larvae that develop can survive for several years in the musculature of the animal. If the larvae are ingested, very often no symptoms are present. Unlike the case for infection with the beef tapeworm, humans can serve as an intermediate host. They become involved in the pork tapeworm's life cycle when an individual ingests food or water contaminated with fecal material containing eggs from another human carrier. These eggs hatch, and the resulting larvae disseminate throughout the body, forming cysticerci. The resulting condition, cysticercosis, can cause an asymptomatic infection if either the subcutaneous tissues or muscles are involved. More severe complications and death can occur if vital organs (e.g., the CNS) become infected.

Other Platyhelminthes of human medical importance are the trematodes, also known as flukes. Adult worms are typically smaller than the cestodes, ranging in size from 1 mm to several centimeters; they use suckers to attach themselves to host tissue. These parasites are found worldwide, although most human infections occur in the Far and Near East. Trematodes require snails as their intermediate host. In general, parasite eggs hatch in fresh water and undergo several larval stages, one of which involves the snail, until the infective-stage larvae are formed. Humans become infected by ingestion of infective-stage larvae; alternatively, as in the case of the schistosomes, the larvae

may burrow directly through the skin of an individual standing in contaminated water. These parasites are typically classified as intestinal, liver, lung, or blood flukes. Intestinal flukes, such as *Fasciolopsis buski*, involve humans only accidentally. Liver flukes, such as *Fasciola hepatica*, mature into adult worms in the bile ducts of the liver. Lung flukes, such as *Paragonimus westermani*, cause a major disease of the lungs, paragonimiasis, and are found only in the Far East. Blood flukes of the genus *Schistosoma* cause schistosomiasis and vary in terms of the anatomic region in which the adult worms reside. For example, adult worms may reside in the inferior mesenteric veins of the large intestine (*S. mansoni*), the superior mesenteric veins of the small intestine (*S. japonicum*), or the rectal vessels and veins surrounding the bladder (*S. haematobium*). In the last case, ulceration of the bladder is common, leading to the presence of blood in the urine.

Aschelminthes

Nematodes, or roundworms, are small and possess functional digestive systems, including an anus. Human infections caused by these worms are largely divided into intestinal roundworms and blood and tissue roundworms. Of the intestinal roundworms, *Trichinella spiralis* is the cause of trichinosis in carnivorous animals. Human infection usually is the result of ingestion of the encysted larvae in undercooked or raw pork. After ingestion, the cysts reach the intestine, where the larvae are liberated and develop into adult worms. Adult female worms penetrate the intestinal mucosa, producing larvae that then migrate via the lymphatics to the muscles and other body parts, and become encysted. The severity of symptoms varies with the magnitude of the initial infection. Thus infection can be range from asymptomatic to severe, with initial symptoms including fever, diarrhea, and malaise, due to the activities of the adult worms in the intestines. In severe cases, muscle pain throughout the entire body can occur due to migration of the larvae into the skeletal muscles. However, this symptom is most commonly seen in cases of moderate to heavy infection. In addition, although encystment occurs only in muscle, larvae can infect other organs of the body, such as the lungs, heart, meninges, and brain. In particular, myocarditis—the most common cardiac lesion caused by the larvae—can lead to arrhythmias and congestive heart failure. The invasion of any of these organs during the early weeks of infection can be fatal.

Ascaris lumbricoides is the largest nematode infecting humans, often attaining a length of 20–30 cm. It is most frequently found in the tropics and some areas of the southern United States. Humans become infected by ingesting infectious eggs containing second-stage larvae. Once in the intestine, the larvae hatch, penetrate the intestinal mucosa, and eventually reach the lungs after the portal circulation picks them up. In the lung, the parasites undergo differentiation, are coughed up and swallowed, and eventually return to the small intestine, where adult worms remain attached. Only in cases of heavy infection are symptoms such as abdominal pain or complications arising from invasion of the liver seen.

Whipworm disease, caused by *Trichuris trichiura*, is found primarily in the tropics and occasionally in the southern United States. The adult worm lives in the human cecum and is attached to the intestinal mucosa. Eggs are passed in feces, and, as a result, transmission occurs via ingestion of contaminated food or water. Heavy infections are associated with chronic diarrhea, abdominal pain, vomiting, constipation, headache, and, in some cases, anemia.

Pinworms—*Enterobius vermicularis*—are strictly human parasites. Humans become infected by ingestion of fertilized eggs. As in the preceding example, adult worms live in the cecum. Female worms migrate to and lay their eggs in the perianal area, which produces an intense itching. Most infections are asymptomatic and resolve after all of the female worms have died.

Human hookworm disease is caused by *Necator americanus* and *Ancylostoma duodenale*. Both species are widely distributed in tropical regions; however, *A. duodenale* is also present in Europe. The eggs of both species are passed in the feces and develop into rhabditiform, or first-stage larvae, which are generally noninfectious. These larvae feed on vegetation and bacteria in the soil and subsequently develop into infectious, filariform larvae. Filariform larvae enter a host by direct penetration of the skin, usually of the foot, and migrate to the lungs, where they are coughed up and swallowed. Adult worms reside in the small intestine, attached to the mucosa. Although the life cycles of these two species are similar, only *N. americanus* has an obligatory requirement for development in the lungs, whereas *A. duodenale* can bypass this particular stage. In addition, *A. duodenale* can infect a host orally as well as by direct skin penetration. Symptoms of hookworm disease range from mild to severe and include headache, fever, nausea, and hemoptysis due to the migration of the larvae in the lungs, intestinal symptoms such as diarrhea and vomiting, and, in extreme cases, anemia due to the feeding activity of the worms in the intestines. Creeping eruption, also known as cutaneous larva migrans, can also result from the migration of the larvae beneath the skin.

Blood and tissue nematodes, unlike their intestinal counterparts, are not spread by fecal–oral transmission. Instead, most are carried from one host to another by the bite of an arthropod vector. In general, most worms in this category belong to the superfamily Filarioidea, and the human infection they cause is called filariasis. Adult worms generally range in size from 2 to 30 cm in length, and females are ordinarily twice the size of males. Unlike other nematodes, females do not lay eggs, but rather give birth to prelarval forms known as microfilariae. These microfilariae are subsequently picked up by a blood-sucking vector, which transmits the filariae from one host to another. These parasites are divided largely into two groups, based on the habitat of the adult worms: the lymphatic group (*Wuchereria bancrofti* and *Brugia malayi*) and the cutaneous group (*Loa loa* and *Onchocerca volvulus*).

Wuchereria bancrofti is the etiologic agent of elephantiasis. This mosquito-borne disease is typically found in the Pacific Islands and Africa, but also occurs sporadically in the Near and Far East and Central and South America. Within the human host, the larvae of this parasite enter the lymphatic vessels and nodes and eventually develop into adult worms. Because the adult worms tend to prefer the lymphatics of the lower extremities, in extreme cases, especially in endemic areas, fibrous tissue can develop around the worms, leading to an obstruction of lymphatic flow and the characteristic massive edema of the legs, scrotum, breasts, or female genitalia known as elephantiasis. This particular complication is relatively rare, however; more often, light infections cause only slightly enlarged lymph nodes. *Brugia malayi*, the causative agent of Malayan filariasis, is similar in life cycle to *W. bancrofti*. It is endemic on the Malay Peninsula, although it is also present in India, Indonesia, Thailand, Sri Lanka, and Vietnam.

Loa loa, often referred to as the African eye worm, is transmitted by mango or deer flies and is found only in Africa. Unlike other filarial parasites, adult worms of this particular species migrate through the subcutaneous tissue throughout the body and, in some cases, can affect the facial area. There they can be seen as they migrate across the bridge of the nose or the subconjunctival tissue of the eye.

River blindness is caused by *Onchocerca volvulus*, which is typically found in Central Africa and in some areas of Central and Northern South America. Infection is transmitted to humans by the bite of infected sand flies carrying infectious larvae. Adult worms reside in subcutaneous tissue and routinely become encased in a fibrous capsule that can often be seen beneath the skin. Microfilariae migrate from the capsules and move throughout the dermis and connective tissue and can cause ocular lesions, which may ultimately result in blindness.

DIAGNOSTIC MICROBIOLOGY

Since the study of microorganisms began with their initial observation in 1683 by Antony van Leeuwenhoek, using the first microscope, continuous progress has resulted in the discovery and identification of many more microscopic organisms and development of methods to detect and identify them. Historically, this process involved continuous improvements in microscopy and development of methods to cultivate microorganisms outside of their normal hosts. The subsequent discovery of the fields of immunology and molecular and genetic sciences led to the development of sensitive and specific of antigen–antibody reaction tests and ushered in the era of molecular science. The past 30 years have seen a rapid expansion of non-culture-based techniques for the detection and identification of microorganisms. These extraordinarily sensitive and specific molecular methodologies for detection of microbial pathogens, together with older established morphologic and phenotypic identification methods, have greatly improved the diagnostic capabilities and accuracy of clinical microbiology laboratory science. In the following section, the four major categories of microbial detection—microscopy, cultivation methods, immunology, and those utilizing molecular/nucleic acid methods—are briefly reviewed.

Microscopy

Light Microscopy

The current light microscope contains a built-in light source and a compound lens system, which means that at least two separate lenses are used. Specimens are visualized by transillumination, with light being focused on the object, which is then seen against a bright background. The major components of the microscope can be divided into lens systems and mechanical parts. The purposes of microscopy are threefold:

- Magnification of an image
- Maximization of resolution
- Optimization of the contrast between structures, organisms, cells, and background

The lens system in microscopes utilized today offers a variety of magnifications through a number of objective lenses in conjunction with a fixed (usually 10×) ocular lens. Light microscopes should be equipped with objective lenses of low-power (10×), high-dry (40×), and oil immersion (100×) formats, which will result in final magnifications, in conjunction with the ocular lens, of 100×, 400×, and 1000×, respectively.

As important as magnification, resolving power is also an essential component of microscopy. Resolving power is the ability of the lens system of the microscope to distinguish two objects as separate items, rather than one. Resolving power is dependent on the wavelength (L) of light used to illuminate the specimen or object and the numerical aperture of the microscopic system. Numerical aperture is a measure of the angle of the maximum cone of light that can enter the objective lens of the microscope. Resolving power of the microscope can be optimized through proper use of the condenser, which focuses light into the plane of the specimen. The most commonly used condensers produce a numerical aperture of 1.25. Resolving power can also be increased by adjusting the medium through which the light passes between the specimen or object and the objective lens. Special oils, termed immersion oil, have a refractive index similar to glass, permitting more light to be incorporated in the image, thereby improving resolving power. Visualization of bacteria usually requires the use of the 100× objective and immersion oil—a combination that results in a resolution of approximately 0.2 micron.

Optimization of resolving power and magnification may require further adjustment of contrast and must be incorporated into microscopic systems to differentiate or distinguish various elements within a microscopic field. This need arises because of the similar refractive indices of many microorganisms and the matrices in which they are being observed. Although some adjustment can be made through a decrease or increase in admitted light, the majority of biologic structures cannot be visualized without the use or application of differential stains. Biologic stains are dyes that improve the contrast between structures in specimens and objects. With this approach, the contrast is enhanced through a color differentiation—an attraction of a particular dye molecule, based on charge, pH, or other physiochemical interaction between a specific structural component and the dye.

Due to the relative nonspecific staining characteristics of dyes, most staining techniques involve a stepwise application of chemicals for differentiation. The primary stain, which is applied in the first step, is amphoteric and can act either as an acid or a base, depending on the predominance of anionic (acidic) or cationic (basic) moieties in the dye. In general, basic dyes stain structures that are acidic, such as nuclear chromatin, whereas acid dyes react with basic structures, such as cytoplasm and cell walls. The second step involves the application of mordant, which fixes the primary stain to its target. It is followed by decolorization, which removes unbound dye/stain from the structure in the microorganism. Finally, a secondary or counterstain is added to provide color to nontargeted structures or microorganisms. This process is best explained by the gram-stain and acid-fast staining of bacteria, described earlier in this chapter.

Variations on bright-field microscopy are employed in the diagnosis of infectious disease. Dark-field microscopy is utilized to increase the apparent resolving power of light microscopy below 0.2 micron. In dark-field microscopy, the condenser, which focuses light directly onto a plane, is replaced by a special dark-field condenser, which permits entry of light only from the periphery or circumference of the object or structure. As a result, objects within the field or specimen appear to glow. Although no real increase in resolution occurs, this technique does permit the visualization of microorganisms with diameters between 0.1 and 0.2 micron. This technique has been limited in application to visualization of spirochetes, such as *Treponema pallidum*, the causative agent of syphilis, in secondary syphilitic lesions; *Borrelia burgdorferi*, the agent of Lyme disease, in spinal fluid; and *Leptospira* species in urine or blood.

Fluorescence Microscopy

Fluorescence is a phenomenon that occurs when a molecule is impacted by a given wavelength of light and emits light at a wavelength longer than the one to which it was exposed. In fluorescent microscopy, specimens are labeled with a fluorescent dye (molecule) and exposed to ultraviolet (UV) light of a specific wavelength, which results in emission of longer-wavelength visible light. Specificity or selectivity depends on the nature of the fluorescent dye and the staining process. Examples of this direct fluorescence staining technique include auramine–rhodamine dye staining of mycobacteria and acridine orange staining of bacteria. The specificity of the mycobacterial fluorescent system reflects the staining technique, which takes advantage of the acid-fast nature of this group of bacteria. In contrast, acridine orange at low pH can intercalate into nucleic acids, with bacterial nucleic acids fluorescing green when the appropriate UV wavelength light is utilized. Fluorescent microscopy is significantly more sensitive than light microscopy because organisms that bind and retain dye are visualized as brightly glowing objects in a dark background.

Another powerful adaptation of this technique is direct florescent antibody (DFA) detection, which combines the sensitivity of fluorescent microscopy with the specificity of antigen–antibody reactions. In this technique, a fluorescent dye is linked to a specific antibody that binds only to a specific antigen. It is then possible to detect the presence and cellular location of any antigens because they literally "light up." Different antigens within a single specimen can be detected by using antibodies labeled with different florescent dye, also known as a fluorochrome. More commonly, indirect fluorescent antibody (IFA) methods are used to determine the presence of specific antigens. IFA uses a "second antibody," tagged with a fluorochrome, which binds to the antigen-specific antibody. The second antibody is derived from another species and is directed against multiple epitopes on the antibody class of the antigen specific antibody. As a result of this approach, IFA may be more sensitive than the direct method.

Electron Microscopy

The resolving power of any microscope is directly related to the wavelength of light, which is used for visualization. The use of an electron beam decreases the resolution from the 0.2 micron possible with a light microscope to 0.0005 micron in the electron microscope. Although the substantial increase in resolution of electron microscopy has led to significant scientific discoveries in the ultrastructure of microorganisms, a major disadvantage of this technology is its inability to examine living cells. In addition, the preparation process can result in the creation of artifacts.

Two types of electron microscopy are available: transmission and scanning. Transmission electron microscopy uses an electron beam that travels directly through the specimen, producing a two-dimensional image. Scanning electron microscopy produces a three-dimensional image of the specimen or object through the use of modified electron beams.

In electron microscopy, contrast is achieved through differences in electron density. As a result, specimens are treated with chemicals to accentuate the electron density differential. To optimize this electron density differential, three methods of preparation have been developed:

- Negative staining, which uses a heavy metal, such as uranium or gold, to stain the background, leaving the target structures lighter
- Freeze-etching, which involves rapid cooling of the specimen with subsequent fractures along planes of the object or specimen

- Osmium tetroxide or glutaraldehyde fixation and embedding in epoxy resins with very thin, fine sectioning of the specimen and, in some cases, enhancement with heavy metal treatment

Cultivation of Microorganisms

Almost all medically important bacteria and fungi can be cultivated outside of the host on artificial culture media. Due to the growth characteristics of bacteria, a single cell, when placed on appropriate culture medium and environmental conditions, will reproduce to numbers sufficient to be visible to the naked eye (i.e., a colony) or other means of detection (Table 8-8). Culture media can be prepared as a fluid (broth medium) or, alternatively, as a solid medium through the addition of a gelling agent—most commonly, agar. Agar is an acidic polysaccharide extracted from specific types of seaweed. Agar becomes liquid upon boiling and solidifies when cooled to a temperature less than 45°C. Once gelled, agar will not liquefy again unless heated to more than 80°C. In

Table 8-8	Commonly Media Used for Growth and Isolation of Pathogenic Bacteria		
Characteristic	**Medium**	**Primary Cultivation**	**Compounds/Comments**
Enrichment Media	Sheep blood agar	Cultivation of most bacteria	Determination of hemolytic reactions (therefore also differential)
	Chocolate agar	*Haemophilus* spp. and pathogenic *Neisseria* spp.	Peptone base, with solution of 2% hemoglobin or IsoVitaleX (BBL)
	Brain–heart infusion broth (BHI)	Cultivation of most bacteria	
	Thioglycollate broth	Obligate and falcultative anaerobes	Pancreatic digest of casein, soy broth, and glucose
	Buffered charcoal–yeast extract agar (BCYE)	*Legionella* spp. and other fastidious bacteria	Can be supplemented with antibiotics to inhibit growth of common gram-positive/gram-negative bacteria
Selective and Specialized Media	Phenylethyl alcohol agar (PEA)	Gram-positive cocci and anaerobic gram-negative bacilli	Phenylethanol inhibits growth of gram-negative organisms
	Columbia colistin–nalidixic acid agar (CNA)	Gram-positive cocci	Colistin and nalidixic acid inhibit growth of gram-negative organisms
	Cefsulodin–irgasan–novobiocin (CIN) agar	*Yersinia* spp.	Includes neutral red and crystal violet indicators
	Campy–blood agar	*Campylobacter* spp.	
	Thayer-Martin agar	*N. gonorrhoeae* and *N. meningitidis*	Antibiotics inhibit growth of contaminants
	Thiosulfate–citrate–bile–sucrose (TCBS) agar	*Vibrio* spp.	
	Regan-Lowe agar	*Bordetella pertussis*	Charcoal agar supplemented with horse blood
Selective and Differential Media	Hektoen enteric agar	*Salmonella* spp. and *Shigella* spp.	Bile salts, lactose, sucrose, salicin, ferric ammonium citrate, Bromthymol blue as indicators
	MacConkey agar	Lactose-fermenting and lactose-nonfermenting gram-negative bacilli	Lactose, neutral red as indicator; bile salts inhibit gram-positive organisms
	Eosin–methylene blue (EMB) agar		Peptone base with lactose and sucrose; eosin and methylene blue as indicators
	Lowenstein-Jensen agar	Mycobacteria	Glycerol, potato flour, coagulated whole eggs; malachite green inhibits gram-positive bacteria

addition, the basic nutrient agar can be enriched with various substrates (e.g., sheep blood, various sugars, or growth indicators and inhibitors) to allow use as an enhancing or selective growth medium.

The advantage of a solid agar medium is that clinical specimens (e.g., blood, sputum) can be "streaked" thin enough across the plate that single organisms may multiply to form visible colonies. Isolated colonies growing on a solid surface represent pure cultures, or a single strain, which may subsequently be identified and tested for organism identification and antimicrobial susceptibility to therapeutic antibiotic drugs.

The agar medium is also a primary diagnostic tool. Pathogenic microorganisms require a source of energy, electrons, carbon, nitrogen, oxygen, sulfur, and phosphorus to flourish. In addition, trace elements, such as potassium, calcium, magnesium, and iron, are required, as are very low concentrations of zinc, copper, manganese, nickel, boron, and cobalt. Many of the more fastidious microorganisms require specific vitamins, which function as coenzymes or precursors for coenzymes. The media utilized to cultivate microorganisms may be classified as either defined or undefined. Defined media are formulated from chemically known ingredients in known quantities; undefined media are prepared from ingredients in which not all of the components are known but do contain adequate amounts of essential or growth-promoting ingredients. Examples of ingredients frequently used in undefined cultures include partial digests of animal or vegetable protein, yeast extract, serum, or blood. The majority of diagnostic media are undefined because of their lower cost and their ability to support the growth of a broad range of pathogenic organisms. The use of complex media components, such as yeast extract, in media formulations for the routine growth and recovery of microbial pathogens obviates the need to add trace minerals and vitamins.

Enrichment media are formulated to encourage the growth of a wide variety of bacteria, although a single medium that will support the growth of all bacteria has not been found. Bacteriologic media are usually categorized into three groupings: enrichment, selective, and differential media. Examples of enrichment media used for the recovery of pathogenic bacteria include sheep blood agar, chocolate agar (a descriptor based on the color of the medium, not the ingredients), trypticase soy broth, and brain–heart infusion agar/broth. Selective media are used when specific pathogens are sought from specimens or sites that contain normal flora. In these instances, the pathogen of interest may be overgrown by normal flora, due to a slower growth rate or smaller numbers of the actual pathogen. Selective media usually contain chemicals, dyes, or antibiotics that are inhibitory to contaminating bacteria but not the specific pathogen of interest. Differential media contain indicator systems that permit the differentiation of groups of organisms based on a selective metabolic or physiologic characteristic. Commonly, a specific carbohydrate and a pH indicator is added to the base medium for this purpose. Fermentation of the carbohydrate results in a reduction of pH and a color change in the colony. Sheep blood (containing erythrocytes) added to base agar media can also be differential by indicating complete or partial hemolysis of erythrocytes and therefore the presence or absence of hemolysin, a common virulence factor in many bacteria.

Nonselective media for the isolation of mycobacteria are usually egg-based or agar-based enriched media that contain additives with fatty acids essential for the growth of mycobacteria. Likewise, many of the media supporting growth of fungi are enriched with substrates specific for the growth of fungi. Frequently, the properties of enrichment, selective, and differential media are combined in the same medium. Culture media commonly used in the clinical laboratory are listed in Table 8-7.

In addition to the nutritional requirements for in vitro growth of microorganisms, the optimal physical conditions for successful cultivation must be considered. Most human pathogens are mesophiles, which is to say they grow optimally at human body temperature, 37°C, and can tolerate only temperatures between 25°C and 40°C. Similarly, the ideal pH range for most bacteria lies between 6.5 and 7.5. The principal gases that affect bacterial growth are oxygen and carbon dioxide. Aerobic organisms require oxygen for growth and can be cultivated in an air atmosphere. In contrast, anaerobic bacteria cannot use oxygen as a terminal electron acceptor; oxygen is toxic to these organisms, and they cannot be cultivated in an air atmosphere. Facultatively aerobic bacteria do not require oxygen for growth, although if it is available, they are capable of using it as a terminal electron acceptor. Facultative anaerobes are capable of growth in the presence or absence of oxygen. Microaerophilic organisms require low levels of oxygen; they are cultivated in environments containing 5–10% CO_2, but cannot tolerate the level of oxygen present in atmospheric air. Thermophilic bacteria require higher temperatures (approximately 42°C) for optimal growth.

In addition to visualization of growth through colony formation on agar media or turbidity in broth media, several methods have been developed that do not depend on visual changes for detection of growth. These techniques include detection of carbon dioxide as a result of bacterial metabolism, bioluminescence, changes in electric impedance, and chromatographic detection of metabolic end products. All of these methods require growth or metabolism by the microorganism for successful detection.

Growth of Organisms Other Than Bacteria and Fungi

Viruses and some other microorganisms are obligate intracellular pathogens and, as such, cannot be cultivated using the techniques described in the preceding section. Because growth and replication of these pathogens require living cells, three techniques have been used for their culture: inoculation of tissue or cell culture, embryonated hens' eggs, and experimental animals.

Tissue culture is the method most commonly used to culture viruses. Cells of specific tissues are grown as monolayers in the presence of nutrient media until a confluent layer of cells is achieved. The resulting cell culture monolayers are of three basic types: primary cell culture, transformed haploid or heteroploid cell lines, and diploid cell lines or stains. In primary cell cultures, the cells have a normal chromosome count (diploid) and are derived from initial cell cultivation from a tissue source such as monkey or human embryonic kidney cells. Continued subculture and regrowth of primary cell lines usually result in one of two events: either the cells eventually die or they undergo spontaneous transformation. Transformed cell lines have altered growth characteristics; the chromosome count varies (haploid or heteroploid); and their susceptibility to viral infection can be altered. An important benefit of transformed cell lines is that they are immortal. Unlike primary cell lines, transformed cells can be subcultured or regrown through serial passage many times without dying. Transformed cells can also be obtained from malignant cells or tissue, or through mutagenesis in vitro. A common transformed cell line used diagnostically is Hep-2, which is derived from a human epithelial carcinoma. The third type of tissue culture is composed of diploid cells, usually of fibroblast origin, which can be subcultured or regrown through 30–40 passages, prior to dying out or transforming. The ability to cultivate viruses in vitro is highly dependent on the specific cell line in which a virus is placed. As a result, successful cultivation of human viral pathogens requires the use of a number of cell lines for diagnosis unless a specific viral pathogen is being sought.

Microbial growth in cell culture can be visualized or detected through a variety of methods. Most commonly, growth is detected by recognizing the cytopathic effect (CPE) that the pathogen has on the cell culture. Lytic or cytopathic viruses produce alterations in cell morphology during replication in susceptible cell lines, which can be observed directly by light microscopy. The morphologic changes observed are usually characteristic of a particular virus growing in a specific cell line. For example, as their name implies, respiratory syncytial viruses cause fusion of cells to produce multinucleated giant cells, termed syncytia. Other viruses produce proteins that are expressed on the membrane of infected cells; these viral proteins bind erythrocytes, and this binding can be detected by testing for hemadsorption or hemagglutination. Hemadsorption occurs when erythrocytes added to the infected cell culture adhere to the cell culture monolayer. Hemagglutination occurs when viruses released from infected cells cause the added erythrocytes to clump.

Detection and visualization of viruses that produce little or any CPE, do not possess hemagglutinins, or do not completely replicate in cell culture can be achieved through immunologic or nucleic acid probes. Most commonly, indirect fluorescent antibody (IFA) methods are used to detect viruses, although direct fluorescent antibody (DFA) techniques are used as well.

Another commonly utilized immunologic method for viral identification is neutralization. In this technique, viral infectivity is neutralized by mixing of subcultured virus with specific individual antibodies against different viruses and inoculation of cell lines with treated and untreated aliquots of the unknown viral agent. The identity of the virus is indicated by an inability of the virus to grow in the presence of specific antibodies compared to untreated controls.

Animal inoculation is used in the recovery of some microbes. For example, suckling mice in the first 48 hours of life are very susceptible to viral infection. Depending on the virus, such mice can be inoculated intracerebrally, subcutaneously, or intraperitoneally. Evidence of viral replication/infection is manifested by clinical disease. Confirmation and identification of the infecting virus can be achieved through histology, immunofluorescent staining, or detection of specific antibody response. Arboviruses and rabies virus are detected using this system.

Mycobacterium leprae, the cause of leprosy (Hansen's disease), is a noncultivable mycobacterium. Diagnosis of infection with this pathogen is usually made on the basis of clinical presentation and symptoms, visualization of the organism in skin-biopsy specimens, and the results of the skin-lepromin test. However, *M. leprae* has been shown to grow when material from a patient's lesion is inoculated in either mouse footpads or nine-banded armadillos. While it is interesting that these animals can be a host for leprosy, armadillo inoculation is not a common technique in the diagnostic laboratory.

Other bacterial organisms that are extremely difficult, or even impossible, to cultivate include members of the genera *Chlamydia*, *Chlamydophila*, *Rickettsia*, *Anaplasma*, *Orientia*, *Ehrlichia*, and *Coxiella*, and the spirochetes. For all these organisms, diagnostic approaches include immunologic testing methods, cell cultures, and molecular technology-based test methods.

Diagnostic Immunology

In the past, techniques used in the investigation of infectious diseases included culture, serologic tests, and biochemical assays. Initially, serodiagnosis was achieved through a variety of techniques, including antigen–antibody complex formation, agglutination, and complement fixation. However, these techniques were labor intensive and lacked specificity and sensitivity. These drawbacks improved significantly with the development of immunofluorescence, radioimmunoassays, and enzyme immunoassays.

In general, the use of immunoassays for the diagnosis of infectious diseases involves one of two main principles: testing for specific microbial antigens or testing for specific microbial–antigen antibodies. These assays may focus on the detection of a microbial antigen directly from a clinical specimen or the detection of a specific antigen, once an organism is cultured in vitro.

Tests for antibodies may be designed to detect any antibody isotype or a particular isotype, such as IgM or IgG. Precautions must be taken in using IgM or IgG, as markers for infection may result from the temporal expression of each of these isotypes. For example, in many infections levels of IgM rise rapidly following infection, peak within 7–10 days, and wane after several weeks. In contrast, detectable IgG requires at least 4–6 weeks to develop and persists longer than IgM. In general, the presence of IgM antibodies is indicative of recent infection. However, because IgM appears on second exposure to most agents and may persist in some individuals for long periods of time, interpretation of results must be undertaken carefully for each infectious agent. Therefore, in most cases, paired sera are required for the measurement of total antibody. Such testing includes both an early sample taken in the first week to 10 days after onset of symptoms and a subsequent sample taken during convalescence (3–4 weeks). In general, a fourfold or greater increase in antibody titer indicates a positive test.

Other antibody isotypes, such as IgA and IgE, are not routinely used in immunodiagnosis. Because IgA is primarily released at mucosal surfaces, its levels and persistence in sera are highly variable. IgE plays an important role in parasitic infections but has little role in the control of other infectious agents.

In terms of sensitivity and specificity in immunodiagnostics, several important terms should be remembered and their application understood. In addition to the traditional meaning of the term, *sensitivity*, in the context of immunodiagnostics, refers to the minimum level of antigen or antibody that can be detected by a given test. *Specificity* may also refer to the ability of a particular assay to distinguish one antigen from another. The following sections contain a brief summary and outline of several of the most commonly used immunodiagnostic methods.

Complement Fixation

Complement refers to series of serum proteins that become activated by a variety of biologic mechanisms. One of the functions of complement is lysis of red blood cells (RBCs) in the presence of RBC-specific antibody, which has become the basis for the complement fixation test. This assay involves incubation of test serum in the presence of a particular microbial antigen. If antibodies to that antigen are present (which indicates infection), complement is activated and depleted from the sample. As a result, reaction mixtures containing RBCs as an indicator of complement activity will not be lysed, due to the depleted complement in the sample. In the event that the test sample does not contain antigen-specific antibody, complement is not depleted, and the RBCs are lysed. This particular type of diagnostic assay has some inherent problems associated with it, including the fact that it is relatively labor intensive and can lack sensitivity. In addition, other factors in the serum can activate complement nonspecifically, producing false-positive results.

Agglutination Assays

Agglutination assays involve the immobilization of a particular antigen or antigen-specific antibody on polystyrene beads or latex particles, which are subsequently mixed with a test specimen. This specimen is then examined for evidence of clumping. Agglutination reactions are typically performed in a tube or on a slide and often are measured photometrically. In addition, agglutination assays can usually be completed within 30 minutes and the antigen- or antibody-coated beads are relatively stable for long periods of time.

This type of assay has been especially useful in the detection of soluble antigens from sterile body fluids, such as cerebrospinal fluid, urine, and serum, especially in the case of infections due to *Haemophilus influenzae*, *Streptococcus pneumoniae*, *Neisseria meningitidis, Cryptococcus neoformans*, and both group A and B streptococci. However, such assays have not been developed for rapid diagnosis of viral infections because the agglutination method lacks sensitivity for this particular type of agent.

Neutralization and Hemagglutination Inhibition Assays

Both of these assay types are used primarily for viral identification. Hemagglutination inhibition is used to detect viruses containing hemaglutinin, such as the influenza virus. This assay requires a mixture of viral hemaglutinin, RBCs, and a test sample. If virus-specific antibodies are present, they react with the viral hemaglutinin, preventing agglutination of the RBCs.

The neutralization assay is one of the most important standard techniques for the detection of cultivable viruses. In this approach, test samples are mixed with virus and subsequently incubated in the presence of a susceptible cell type.

Antibody Detection

Antibody detection is achieved largely through the use of competitive or noncompetitive EIAs. The noncompetitive EIA uses a solid support onto which the antigen has been fixed. The patient sample is added to the well, and antibodies specific to the antigen bind to it. The solid support is then washed so that only bound antibodies remain. Next, an enzyme-labeled antiglobulin directed against the class of antibody is added, along with a chromogenic enzyme substrate. The amount of color produced is directly proportional to the amount of specific antibody present in the test specimen.

The competitive version of this assay differs slightly from the preceding description, in that the test specimen is added simultaneously with an enzyme-labeled antibody specific for the antigen bound to the solid support. This step is followed by the addition of a chromogenic enzyme substrate. High levels of antibody in the test specimen will compete for antigen with the enzyme-labeled antibody; thus the amount of color produced is inversely proportional to the amount of antigen-specific antibody present in the test sample.

Radioimmunoassay

Radioimmunoassay (RIA) is a technique similar to EIA. However, a radioactive rather than an enzyme label is used, and specific binding is determined using a gamma- or beta-counter, depending on the isotope. Therein lie the disadvantages of RIA—adherence to radiation safety protocols and the restrictions that accompany working with radioactive substances. In addition, the immunoreagents used for RIAs are typically not stable for as long a period of time as those used in EIAs.

Fluorescent Antibody Techniques

Fluorescent antibody (FA) techniques have been widely used in the past for the detection of both microbial antigens and antigen-specific antibodies, and they continue to have many applications today. Tests can be either direct or indirect. In either case, antigen detection requires specimens that contain live virus and cannot be used to test patient serum or feces, which rarely contain virus. The microbe is grown, from a patient swab or other specimen, on glass slides and then fixed.

In the direct method, a fluorescein-labeled antibody specific for a particular antigen is incubated with a test specimen fixed on a glass microscope slide. If the antigen is present in the specimen, a bright yellow–green fluorescence will be seen under a fluorescent microscope.

The indirect method involves the use of a primary, unlabeled, antigen-specific antibody and a fluorescein-labeled anti-immunoglobulin specific for the primary antibody. Both are incubated with the test specimen, and results are interpreted in the same way as for the direct FA. Indirect florescent antibody techniques can also detect patient antibodies.

Because antiglobulin antibodies are directed against classes of antibodies, the indirect method allows for the differentiation of IgM and IgG; it is more sensitive and specific in identifying viruses, as compared with traditional cell culture. However, FA is commonly used for the detection of antibodies to *Legionella pneumophila* and serodiagnosis of several parasitic diseases, including malaria, leishmaniasis, African trypanosomiasis, pneumocystosis, toxoplasmosis, and schistosomiasis. It can also be used for the direct detection of antigen in clinical samples and in the diagnosis of respiratory syncytial virus, influenza virus type A, and parainfluenza viruses types 1 through 3.

Molecular Diagnostics

Advances in molecular biology have resulted in the application of molecular techniques in diagnostic microbiology. Although microscopy, culture, and phenotypic characterization remain the mainstay for microbial diagnosis in most laboratories, molecular techniques are changing the speed, sensitivity, and specificity of diagnosis and identification of etiologic agents. In addition, molecular methods offer greater safety, in that potentially dangerous organisms need not be grown in culture for detection. A variety of molecular techniques have evolved from initial hybridization and nucleic probes, including signal amplification, target amplification, and post-amplification technologies.

The underlying principle of nucleic acid probe technology is the selection of unique genomic sequences for a particular group of etiologic agents or specific genes with subsequent cloning, synthesis, and utilization. Probes can hybridize with either DNA or RNA, demonstrating high specificity to complementary sequences of the target nucleic acid. The hybridization is detected by labeling the probe with radioisotopes, enzymes, antigens, or chemiluminescent compounds that can be measured via instrumentation specific for the label.

Three nucleic acid probe hybridization methods have evolved: liquid-phase, solid-phase, and in situ hybridization.

- In liquid-phase hybridization, a single-stranded probe that does not hybridize to itself is utilized. The most commonly used method for diagnostic purposes is the hybridization protection assay. A labeled probe is mixed with the potential target and subjected to alkaline hydrolysis; the signal molecule is protected from hydrolysis, if hybridized, and is detected directly in the liquid specimens.

- In solid-phase hybridization, nucleic acid–bound nylon membranes or nitrocellulose are hybridized with the nucleic acid probe. Unbound probe is washed off, and hybridization can be detected using any of the signal systems mentioned earlier.

- In situ hybridization utilizes tissue or whole cells fixed to microscope slides. Probes are hybridized targets in the cells, using the same principles employed in solid-phase hybridization. The sensitivity of this method is limited by penetration of the probe into the cell, but does have the advantage of permitting visualization by microscopy of the location and cell type in which hybridization is occurring.

Nucleic acid probes have been used successfully for the detection of fastidious, slow-growing, and noncultivable organisms and antibiotic resistance genes, as well as for identification of phenotypically difficult microorganisms.

Signal amplification methods are designed to increase the signaling capacity of the hybridization reaction of a probe to its target through an increase in the concentration of the label. Such techniques increase the amount of signal generated by a fixed amount of probe/target hybrid, but do not increase the amount of target the way amplification methods do. As a consequence, these methods are less susceptible to contamination than target amplification but are comparatively limited in sensitivity. Two examples of signal amplification techniques are the solution hybridization antibody-capture assay, which uses chemiluminescent detection, and the branched DNA (bDNA) probe assay.

The hybridization antibody-capture assay uses RNA probes that hybridize with DNA target sequences to form an RNA–DNA hybrid. These hybrids are captured on a solid surface by attached antibodies specific for the RNA–DNA hybrids. The immobilized hybrids are then reacted with another enzyme-conjugated antibody specific for the hybrids. Signal amplification occurs through multiple antibody binding to the hybrid, with detection being achieved through the addition of a chemiluminescent substrate.

The branched DNA probe technique uses a branched multiple probe–enzyme complex. This system utilizes three probes for detection of a primary probe (target-specific), a branched secondary probe, and a short enzyme-labeled tertiary probe. The primary probes are used to capture the target on a solid surface. Branched oligonucleotide probes (bDNA amplifiers) specific for the hybridized primary probe are added, followed by the short enzyme-labeled tertiary probes. Chemiluminescent substrate is then added, and the signal can be quantified.

The polymerase chain reaction (PCR) method has in many ways revolutionized diagnostic microbiology. As the first amplification technology, it has been developed for the widest number of applications. Other target amplification systems that have been developed but are not yet as widely used include transcription-mediated amplification (TMA) and similar methodologies, and strand displacement amplification (SDA). As a target amplification method, PCR is based on the ability of DNA polymerase to copy a strand of DNA when two primers (oligonucleotides) bind to complementary strands of target DNA. The enzyme initiates elongation at the 3′ end of a primer bound to the target strand of DNA. The sequence between the two specific primers is amplified exponentially with each cycle of PCR. A cycle consists of three steps:

1. In the DNA denaturation step, the double-stranded target DNA is separated into single strands.
2. Primers anneal or bind to their complementary target sequences at a lowered temperature.
3. DNA polymerase synthesizes or extends the target sequences between the primers.

With each cycle, the PCR product or target sequences are doubled. The reaction is performed in a programmable thermal cycler, with 30–50 cycles usually being completed, resulting in amplification of more than 100 copies of the target sequence—a detectable level.

A variety of adaptations to PCR have been developed:

- RT-PCR, developed to amplify RNA targets through the initial use of the enzyme reverse transcriptase for conversion of the RNA target to cDNA

- Nested PCR, designed primarily to increase sensitivity through the use of two primer sets directed at the same target, one set within the other

- Multiplex PCR, in which two or more sets of primers specific for different targets are used in the same reaction

- Real-time PCR, involving simultaneous target amplification and detection

Other technologies for target amplification include transcription-mediated amplification systems and strand-displacement amplification. In addition to target amplification, two systems, QB replicase (QBR) and the DNA ligase reaction, are based on amplification of a probe.

The application of molecular technology to the diagnosis of infectious disease has enhanced the speed, sensitivity, and specificity of microbial diagnosis. Despite the improved ability to make some diagnoses associated with their use, however, these techniques currently remain more research tools than standard clinical diagnostic tools. Although significant strides have been made, false-positive results owing to contamination and false-negative results from a failure of the process are possible. Also, unlike culture systems, which are able to detect multiple pathogens, molecular tests are intended to identify only one pathogen. For the detection of more than one pathogen, additional tests must be performed. In addition, the cost of molecular diagnostics is higher than the cost of traditional culture. Nevertheless, use of molecular techniques is warranted in situations where currently available culture techniques are unable to recover or grow the organism in vitro, or instances where current methods are too insensitive, too costly, or too time consuming.

At this time, the "perfect" single diagnostic test for identification of microorganisms does not exist. Thus detection and identification of such organisms, along with determination of antibiotic susceptibility, requires multiple tests or combinations of tests for confirmation. Development of more rapid and more broadly applicable tests to identify unknown pathogens is a key priority in public health. While this goal was previously unattainable, advances in technology are increasing the possibility that such diagnostic tools might emerge in the future.

••• REFERENCES

1. Versalovic J, Carroll KC, Funke G, Jorgensen JH, Landry ML, Warnock DW. *Manual of Clinical Microbiology.* 10th ed. Washington, DC: ASM Press; 2011.

2. Mandell GL, Bennett JE, Dolin R. *Principles and Practice of Infectious Diseases.* 7th ed. Philadelphia, PA: Churchill Livingstone; 2010.

3. Anaissie EJ, McGinnis MR, Pfaller MA. *Clinical Mycology.* 2nd ed. Philadelphia, PA: Churchill Livingstone Elsevier; 2009.

4. Garcia LS. *Diagnostic Medical Parasitology.* 4th ed. Washington, DC: ASM Press; 2001.

5. Knipe DM, Howley PM. *Field's Virology.* 5th ed. Philadelphia, PA: Lippincott Williams & Wilkins; 2007.

6. de la Maza LM, Pezzlo MT, Shigei JT, Peterson EM. *Color Atlas of Medical Bacteriology.* Washington, DC: ASM Press; 2004.

7. Larone DH. *Medically Important Fungi.* 4th ed. Washington, DC: ASM Press; 2002.

8. Barrett JT. *Microbiology and Immunology Concepts.* Philadelphia, PA: Lippincott-Raven Publishers; 1998.

9. Persing DH, Tenover FC, Versalovic J, Tang YW, Unger ER, Relman DA, White TJ. *Molecular Microbiology: Diagnostic Principles and Practice.* Washington, DC: ASM Press: 2004.

10. Flint SJ, Enquist LW, Krug RM, Racaniello VR, Skalka AM. *Virology, Molecular Biology, Pathogenesis, and Control.* Washington, DC: ASM Press; 2000.

9

Molecular Epidemiology and Infectious Diseases

Susan M. Harrington, John S. Francis, William R. Bishai, and Karen C. Carroll

The past 20 to 30 years have seen significant advances in the ability of the clinical microbiologist to identify substrains of bacterial pathogens and use this information to track infectious diseases. Most strain typing has focused on bacteria, but fungi and viruses can also be typed. Medical diagnostic evaluations for a particular infectious disease usually end with identification of pathogens to their species; most clinical microbiology laboratories do not routinely identify organisms to the substrain level. For example, strains of *Staphylococcus aureus*, which are implicated in many hospital-acquired (nosocomial) infections, are identified to the species level, but are not routinely evaluated for evidence of belonging to a particular type. Similarly, *Streptococcus pneumoniae* isolates can be identified by serotype as well as by species, yet subtyping is not part of a routine microbiology culture result. Serotyping is occasionally performed to assess vaccine efficacy in immunized patients who develop invasive disease. Strain typing is used to determine how closely isolates of the same species are related to one another. When isolates from different patients are related or indistinguishable from one another, it may indicate a common source of the infection. This information is useful to epidemiologists who are responsible for tracking communicable diseases within a healthcare institution or a community. Such information helps them to identify point sources and transmission patterns of infections so that appropriate interventions may be applied. Likewise, when isolates are found to differ by subspecies analysis, it suggests a different source of infection. Hence, if two people are diagnosed with tuberculosis in the same community at the same time, differences by strain typing indicate that the individuals are highly unlikely to have passed the infection between each other.

In short, the goal of strain typing is to distinguish epidemiologically related isolates from those that are unrelated, based on the premise that related isolates share detectable characteristics that will distinguish them from others. Although strain typing is a very powerful tool for the epidemiologist, this procedure should be done with clear goals in mind and should be used to enhance a sound epidemiologic investigation. Many of the tools used to strain-type organisms involved in outbreaks and investigations conducted over a short time period are not applicable to population and evolutionary studies of genetic relationships between strains. It is important for the investigator to have an understanding of typing methods and the situations in which they are most applicable.

APPLICATION OF TYPING TECHNIQUES

Strain typing systems are widely used to characterize bacteria, fungi, and, more rarely, viruses. Many applications for typing methods exist, including studying the relationships between colonizing and infecting strains; documenting nosocomial transmission; distinguishing relapse from reinfection; establishing clonality of isolates within clusters of patients in the hospital or community; and tracking the spread of isolates between hospitals or communities over time.[1]

Often the laboratory is asked to subtype isolates when an epidemiologist notices increased incidence of disease associated with a specific pathogen or increased isolation of a microbe on routine surveillance of microbiology culture results. For example, during a 6-year period, an increased incidence of pediatric empyema was noted at a children's medical center in Salt Lake City associated with *Streptococcus pneumoniae* infection. Each pneumococcal strain was determined to be serotype 1, and pulsed-field gel electrophoresis (PFGE) indicated that the isolates were indistinguishable or at least closely related, supporting the hypothesis of clonal spread.[2]

Sometimes a relatively rare organism recovered over a short period of time from patients not obviously linked epidemiologically may be an indication of disease transmission. In one example, three cases of *Listeria monocytogenes* bacteremia, noted in two departments in the same hospital within a 2-week time period, led investigators to suspect a common source of contamination. Molecular typing quickly determined the isolates to be distinct; thus no further investigation was indicated.[3] Conversely, as part of a prospective study of tuberculosis transmission in Baltimore, two patients whose only link was the hospital in which they were treated were found to have the same *Mycobacterium tuberculosis* subtype. Upon further examination, the second patient was thought to have acquired tuberculosis from a contaminated bronchoscope that had been used on the other patient 2 days earlier.[4]

Reports of unusual pathogens (e.g., those with rare antimicrobial resistance patterns or unexpected isolates from environmental sources) alert microbiologists and epidemiologists to potential outbreaks. For example, molecular analysis of plasmid DNA proved useful in demonstrating clonality of a relatively rare strain of chloramphenicol-resistant *Salmonella* in California. The Los Angeles County Health Department Laboratory noticed a 4.9 times increase in this species; 87% of the cases involved chloramphenicol-resistant organisms. A case-control study showed the illness to be associated with consumption of ground beef derived from feedlots using antibiotics in cattle. The strain was further linked to contaminated beef, slaughterhouses, and dairy farms.[5] Likewise, use of polymerase chain reaction (PCR) and DNA sequencing was essential in identifying monkeypox (usually isolated in Africa) during an outbreak in the midwestern United States associated with individuals who had contact with pet prairie dogs exposed to an ill Gambian giant rat.[6] These molecular epidemiology–based techniques were also useful in the detection of a novel coronavirus as the causative agent of severe acute respiratory syndrome (SARS) during a worldwide outbreak originating from a single healthcare worker in China.[7,8]

Strain typing techniques are now used for other clinical applications as well. To determine if isolates of the same genus and species cultured from a patient weeks or months apart represent reinfection with a

new strain or recrudescence of a previous infection, they might be typed by molecular methods. In one report, an immunocompromised child had episodes of bacteremia 4 months apart with the same uncommon gram-negative bacterium, *Flavobacterium meningosepticum* (now called *Elizabethkingae meningoseptica*). Molecular analysis by PFGE showed the isolates to be indistinguishable; the two episodes of sepsis likely resulted from an indwelling central catheter that harbored small numbers of organisms.[9] In another example, 1 year after having been adequately treated for a *M. tuberculosis* infection, a patient with human immunodeficiency virus (HIV) was again found to have active disease. Was the therapy inadequate or had the patient been reinfected? Molecular studies showed the second strain recovered to be the same as the first, except for a mutation rendering it resistant to rifampin. The strain was presumed to have become resistant in vivo during rifabutin prophylaxis intended to prevent infection with *Mycobacterium avium*. Hence, molecular analysis proved reactivation of disease with a new antibiotic resistance pattern in the patient's original strain.[10]

Molecular techniques may also be used to determine if multiple blood cultures drawn over 1 or more days yielding coagulase-negative staphylococci or other skin flora represent a true bacteremia or culture contamination. Multiple strains isolated from a true bacteremia generally have the same molecular type, whereas skin contamination will likely produce heterogeneous strains.[11,12]

Finally, molecular typing techniques are being used to assist both healthcare institutions and communities at large with understanding the transmission and spread of multidrug-resistant gram-negative rods such as *Acinetobacter* spp. and carbapenemase-producing *Enterobacteriaceae*. In recent years, these organisms have become more prevalent within both acute care hospitals and extended care facilities. Understanding the dynamics of hospital-to-community-to-hospital spread is another critical role of molecular typing techniques.

DEFINITIONS AND BACKGROUND

Throughout this chapter, vocabulary known to the microbiologist and molecular biologist will be used. To create a framework for the reader, some basic concepts with respect to strain relatedness are defined in this section. In particular, strain typing methods that preceded molecular techniques are discussed. An overview of microbial nucleic acids and ways in which the genetic content of a microbe can vary is given as well. The laboratory techniques used to detect genetic change are also explained in this section before specific molecular typing methods are presented.

Relevant Concepts and Conventional Strain Typing Methods

An *isolate* refers to the bacterium or other microbe recovered from a primary microbiology culture. Typically, an isolate is characterized only by its source and its genus and species. The word *strain* is applied after some further testing is performed. Isolates may be grouped as a single strain based on characteristics they have in common—that is, if they give the same strain typing result. They can be considered unique strains if the typing technique distinguishes them from other strain types tested. *Clones* are isolates that have been derived from the same parent strain. Isolates are considered clones if they are indistinguishable from one another. Although progeny strains are produced from indistinguishable isolates, normally occurring genetic mutations will cause them to diverge gradually. Therefore, after multiple generations, daughter strains may no longer be identical, but will likely be clonally related.

Relationships among strains are to some extent relative. They may depend on which test is used for characterization. Different techniques provide information about different aspects of the organism. Also, isolates may be related to varying degrees depending on the amount of mutation within a species and the number of generations between the isolates.[13]

Before the advances in molecular biology of the past 20 to 30 years, the techniques used to characterize microorganisms were based on their phenotypic characteristics. The phenotype of an organism is derived from the expression of the genetic material. Biotyping, antimicrobial susceptibility patterns, serotyping, phage typing, bacteriocin typing, and protein-based methods are all examples of phenotypic tests. Each of these measures varies within a species, and each has observable properties. Although more discriminatory molecular methods have replaced these techniques owing to the new methods' ability to provide even more accurate strain typing, the information provided by phenotypic results should not be minimized.

Speciation of bacteria and yeasts has traditionally required testing for expression of metabolic functions with a series of biochemical tests. The results produced in these tests provide characteristic patterns for identification, and they are referred to as the "biotype." Biochemical identification is gradually being replaced by molecular methods, however, as it has not been a sensitive indicator of strain differences.

As pathogenic bacteria are identified to the species level, the clinical laboratory routinely performs testing of that microbe's susceptibility to a panel of antibiotics appropriate for therapy. The susceptibility results are reported as "susceptible," "intermediate," or "resistant" to each antibiotic. The susceptibility profile of the organism to the panel of antibiotics is termed the antibiogram. Two isolates found to have the same atypical antibiogram may be an early indicator that clonal dissemination is occurring. For highly resistant nosocomial species, such as vancomycin-resistant enterococci (VRE) or methicillin-resistant *S. aureus* (MRSA), antibiograms are of limited use because few changes will be seen in the susceptibility profile between isolates. Isolates with vastly different antibiograms are most likely unrelated. Sometimes, however, two antibiograms may differ by only one or a few antibiotic susceptibilities. Strains producing such patterns may be clonally related. Bacteria can become antibiotic resistant depending on the selective pressure of antibiotics in the environment or the presence of other resistant species that can transfer resistance genes. Conversely, organisms can also lose antibiotic resistance genes carried on extra-chromosomal DNA called plasmids. Overall, antibiograms provide highly standardized, prospective data and are an excellent place to start in making strain comparisons.

Some bacteria can be differentiated by serotype. Antigenic determinants (e.g., cell-surface carbohydrates, membrane proteins, and lipopolysaccharides) vary among organisms and can be detected with specific antibodies. Serotyping continues to be a useful method for species such as *Haemophilus influenzae*, *S. pneumoniae*, *Neisseria meningitidis*, *Salmonella* and *Shigella* species, *Escherichia coli*, and some viruses. Not only can serotyping differentiate stains, but certain serotypes also serve as markers of virulence. For example, *H. influenzae* type b causes severe invasive disease and *E. coli* O157:H7 can cause hemolytic uremic syndrome. Influenza viruses can be typed to determine which hemagglutinin (H) and neuraminidase (N) serotypes are circulating, for inclusion in yearly vaccine development. Serotyping, however, is limited as an epidemiologic typing method, because its discriminatory power is less than that of other, molecular methods. Additionally, serotyping can be expensive, and is useful for only a limited number of organisms for which antisera have been developed.[14]

Bacteriophage typing had long been the standard typing method for *S. aureus*. Unfortunately, this method is technically demanding and is generally available only in reference laboratories. Like phage typing, bacteriocin testing is expensive and technically difficult and is no longer performed in strain typing laboratories. Multilocus enzyme electrophoresis (MLEE) is a protein-based method. With this approach, extracts containing metabolic enzymes from the bacteria are separated by electrophoresis in starch gels. The location for each enzyme in the gel is then detected with a colorimetric substrate specific to that enzyme. Because the electrophoretic mobility of the enzymes depends on their exact amino acid content, it is strain specific. When evaluated as a profile, the electrophoretic mobilities or isoenzyme patterns are referred to as an electrophoretic type. Although it is moderately discriminatory, this technique is not in widespread use because it is technically demanding and has generally been replaced by multi-locus sequence typing (MLST), a method described later in this chapter.[15]

Like all living forms, microbes are composed of nucleic acid, protein, lipid, and carbohydrate. Methods exist for identifying intraspecies differences based on each of these four categories, some of which were discussed earlier in this chapter. In the last two decades, however, methods based on the presence, size, and sequence of nucleic acids have come to predominate in the field of molecular epidemiology. These methods are referred to as "genotypic" because they assess the genetic content of the microbe.

The Basics of Microbial Nucleic Acids and Mutational Change

The primary location of the genetic content of a microorganism is its chromosome. Bacteria are classified as prokaryotes, and they generally contain a single, circular chromosome consisting of double-stranded DNA (dsDNA). Fungi, in contrast, are eukaryotes that carry multiple linear chromosomes. An understanding of the components of DNA is essential to the basic theory of molecular epidemiology.

All dsDNA has two complementary strands, which pair by hydrogen bonding. Each strand consists of a sugar–phosphate backbone and the nucleotide bases adenine (A), guanine (G), thymidine (T), and cytosine (C). Adenine always pairs with thymidine, and guanine with cytosine. It is the order or sequence of these base pairings that determines the genetic content. The amino acids that make up proteins are encoded in nucleic acid triplets. Molecular biologists measure chromosomes, specific genes, or other DNA fragments by their length in base pairs (bp). Many genome-sequencing projects have been completed, allowing for the determination of the number of base pairs in the chromosome, and complete DNA sequence for these species. On average, bacterial chromosomes range in size from 800 kilobases (kb) to 10,000 kb.

In addition to the chromosome, there may be extra-chromosomal segments of DNA known as

---

> **Mutations in chromosomal DNA**
> - DNA point mutations
> - DNA insertions
> - DNA deletions
> - DNA rearrangements
>
> **Mobile genetic elements**
> - Insertion sequences
> - Transposons
> - Conjugative plasmids
> - Lysogenic phages
>
> **Excessory genetic material**
> - Multicopy plasmids
> - Single copy plasmids
> - Accessory chromosomes

Figure 9-1 Types of Alterations in DNA That Can Be Detected by Molecular Epidemiology

episomes or plasmids. Such DNA elements usually range in size from 1 to 200 kb.

The organism's total genetic content (i.e., chromosomal and episomal DNA together) is referred to as the genome. Molecular epidemiologists determine strain relatedness by detecting changes in the genome. Variations in the genetic content of a bacterium may occur in several different ways, as described next (**Figure 9-1**).

Mutational Changes

Mutations are mistakes that occur when the DNA of a parent bacterial strain is being copied during the replication process. The basal mutation rate for most bacterial species is about one error in 10^8 bp per generation. Hence, in an organism that has a genome size of 10^7 bp, a base pair replication error will be made once every 10 generations. Two general types of mutations are seen: (1) point mutations, which involve the substitution of one base for another, and (2) rearrangements of fragments of DNA, including insertions or deletions from the chromosome. Substitutions are further divided into two classes: synonymous and nonsynonymous single-nucleotide polymorphisms (sSNPs and nsSNPs, respectively). sSNPs do not alter the amino acid sequence of a protein, but nsSNPs lead to an amino acid replacement.[16]

Most mutations are inconsequential or silent (i.e., they do not lead to physiologic or functional changes in the mutated progeny cell). In organisms that replicate quickly and are present in large environmental reservoirs, however, significant genetic drift is observed. If the basal rate of genetic replication errors is assumed to be constant, then the more genetic differences between two isolates of the same species, the more time that has passed since the two originated from a common ancestor. Hence, it is possible to identify numerous changes of subspecies of most bacterial organisms, and to estimate the distance in evolutionary time between isolates.

Mobile Genetic Elements

Most bacterial species contain mobile genetic elements that create variability in the genome. A common type of mobile genetic element is the transposon. Duplicative transposons are capable of copying themselves and inserting a second copy at another site within the bacterial chromosome. Mobile genetic elements, such as transposons, lead to more easily detectable changes in the bacterial chromosome compared to point mutations resulting from the basal rate of mutation. Later in this chapter, we review how transposable elements may be used as part of a strain typing system.

Plasmids

Accessory genetic elements can be used to identify differences between species. In addition to the chromosome, many species contain relatively small, covalently closed, circular pieces of self-replicating DNA known as plasmids, which are present in single or multiple copies in the cytoplasm of the bacterial cell. Often these plasmids are nonessential and may come and go over time within a particular bacterial subpopulation. Some plasmids, however, carry elements that code for functional genes (e.g., metabolic enzymes, virulence factors, or antibiotic resistance). Antibiotic use can create selective pressure to maintain a plasmid. Likewise, absence of antibiotic can lead to loss of plasmids. Plasmids carried by a species (and their type and size) may be useful in identifying subspecies of the same strain.

MOLECULAR BIOLOGY TOOLS AVAILABLE TO THE MOLECULAR EPIDEMIOLOGIST

Some understanding of molecular biology laboratory techniques will be useful before the discussion of specific typing methods is presented. This section provides a brief overview of selected "tools." The reader is referred to *Molecular Cloning: A Laboratory Manual*[17] or *Molecular Microbiology: Diagnostic Principles and Practice*[18] for more details on specific procedures.

Restriction Endonucleases

Restriction endonucleases or restriction enzymes are often used for strain typing. These enzymes scan dsDNA, searching for specific sequences. When a specific recognition sequence innate to the restriction enzyme is found, the enzyme cleaves the dsDNA. **Table 9-1** shows several restriction enzymes and the sequences at which they cut.

In addition to having different recognition site sequence specificities, restriction endonucleases have different restriction site length specificities. Table 9-1 gives examples of restriction endonucleases that recognize four, six, or eight base pair sequences. As also shown in Table 9-1, endonucleases that recognize four base pairs will cleave DNA much more frequently than do those that recognize six or eight base pairs. For example, in DNA that is evenly distributed in it's A+T and G+C content (50:50), *Sau*A1, an enzyme that recognizes four base pairs, will be expected to cleave every 256 bp on average. The frequency of cutting depends not only on the number of bases in the recognition site, but also on the percent G+C and percent A+T of the organism.

Table 9-1	Some Common Restriction Endonucleases and Their Recognition Site Specificities		
Restriction Enzyme	Recognition Sequence	Base Pairs Recognized (N)	Approximate Frequency of Cutting (bp)
*Hae*III	5'—GG↓CC—3' 3'—CC↑GG—5'	4	256
*Sau*3AI	5'—↓GATC—3' 3'—CTAG↑—5'	4	256
*Eco*RI	5'—G↓AATTC—3' 3'—CTTAA↑G—5'	6	4,096
*Hind*III	5'—A↓AGCTT—3' 3'—TTCGA↑A—5'	6	4,096
*Pac*I	5'—TTAAT↓TAA—3' 3'—AAT↑TAATT—5'	8	65,530
*Not*I	5'—GC↓GGCCGC—3' 3'—CGCCGG↑CG—5'	8	65,530

Note: Arrows indicate the place in the DNA sequence where cutting occurs.

If a bacterial species is GC-rich, for instance, a restriction endonuclease whose recognition site is biased toward AT will be an infrequent cutter and a restriction endonuclease whose recognition site has a heavy G+C content will cleave much more often than expected. A good example of this behavior occurs in *M. tuberculosis,* which is 67% G+C and 33% A+T in its DNA content. The eight-base cutter *Pac*I, which recognizes the AT-rich sequence TTAATTAA, is expected to cut DNA containing equal amounts of AT and GC base pairs about every 65,537 bp. However, because of the heavy G+C content of *M. tuberculosis* DNA, *Pac*I fails to cut even once within its 4.7 million bp.

If a mutation has occurred at a restriction endonuclease site, the alteration of bases will prevent the enzyme from cutting. This situation is illustrated in **Table 9-2**, where a change from an AT base pair to a CG base pair in an *Eco*RI restriction site destroys the recognition sequence and prevents *Eco*RI cleavage. Likewise, insertion or deletion of DNA may lead to the creation or elimination of a restriction site. The use of restriction enzymes is fundamental to some molecular typing methods. Isolates that are clones will have the same DNA base sequence and, therefore, share the same spacing of restriction sites.

When the chromosome of a microbe is cut with a restriction enzyme, many DNA fragments of a variety of lengths are produced according to the spacing of the restriction enzyme recognition sites for that restriction endonuclease. Base mutations (i.e., insertions, deletions, or point mutations) that

Table 9-2	Sequence Recognized by Restriction Enzyme EcoRI
5′—G↓AATTC—3′ 3′—CTTAA↑G-5′	Recognition sequence for *Eco*RI. Arrows indicate site of enzyme cleavage.
5′—GCATTC—3′ 3′—CGTAAG—5′	A point mutation occurs. AT base pair changed to CG. Restriction site specificity is lost.
5′—GAAGCAATTC—3′ 3′—CTTCGTTAAG—5′	A DNA insertion occurs. Addition of four base pairs. Restriction site specificity is lost.

Note: Point mutations or DNA insertions or deletions cause loss of restriction specificity as shown.

alter restriction enzyme recognition sites will change the number and size of some of the restriction fragments. Also, nucleotides inserted or deleted between restriction sites will alter the length of restriction fragments.

Changes in the genome sequence (which may be detected by altered patterns of restriction enzyme cleavage) are called polymorphisms. *Restriction fragment length polymorphism* (RFLP) refers to variations in the lengths of restriction fragments; different RFLP patterns indicate genetic differences between strains and suggest that the strains are not clonal. **Figure 9-2** is a schematic diagram of the bacterial chromosome illustrating this principle. In the figure, organisms 1 and 2 are clones and, therefore, have an identical restriction site distribution as depicted by the lines cutting the circular chromosome. Organism 3 is

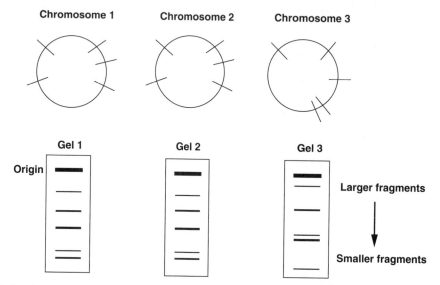

Figure 9-2 Restriction fragment length polymorphisms of three bacterial chromosomes. Lines on circles indicate sites for cutting with a restriction enzyme. Organisms 1 and 2 share restriction endonuclease sites and, therefore, have identical banding patterns on gel electrophoresis as depicted. Bacterium 3 has different restriction sites. The fingerprint for organism 3 is different from the other two.

unrelated and has a different restriction site pattern. The differences between organisms may be visualized by separating the fragments resulting from restriction enzyme digestion by gel electrophoresis. Nucleic acid probes and Southern hybridization can also be used to identify specific restriction fragment differences. Only restriction fragments with specificity for the probe are detected (highlighted bands in Figure 9-2). Southern hybridization using a DNA probe to a region known to be highly variable is an efficient, sensitive way of detecting RFLPs.

Gel Electrophoresis

A technique known as gel electrophoresis may be used to separate DNA molecules. In this method, agarose gels are formed with wells, into which small amounts of solutions containing DNA are placed. Agarose is a polysaccharide derived from seaweed, which forms a large matrix through which DNA fragments must migrate. DNA is negatively charged; thus, when a positive electrode is placed at the distal end of the gel and a negative electrode at the proximal end, the DNA migrates in a lane toward the positive charge (**Figure 9-3**). Usually, this migration occurs on the basis of size, such that small fragments run more rapidly than large fragments. After the separation under an electric charge, the gel is removed from the electrophoresis apparatus and stained using a variety of intercalating fluorescent chemicals such as ethidium bromide, which enable visualization of the DNA bands. Cameras attached to computer systems capture gel images and store or print these files. A molecular weight marker or size standard is always run on the same gel to determine DNA band size.

Standard agarose gel electrophoresis enables the separation of fragments of DNA ranging in size from 50 bp to approximately 15,000 bp. Beyond 15,000 bp, the DNA molecules are too large to fit easily through the agrose gel matrix and the fragments fail to migrate proportionally to their size. Thus, segments greater than 15,000 bp in size tend to accumulate at the origin of the agarose gel.

An adaptation of standard gel electrophoresis is capillary gel electrophoresis, in which separation is achieved by migration of DNA fragments through a capillary tube containing a polymer in solution. For this application, DNA molecules must have previously been tagged with fluorescent dyes. Instead of the nucleic acid bands being visualized within a gel, the molecules pass by a detector and a fluorescent signal is converted into an electronic signal. This signal is visualized as a series of peaks called an electropherogram. Smaller fragments pass through the capillary first and will appear at the beginning of the electropherogram, with peaks for successively larger fragments following them. Peak heights correlate to the amount of nucleic acid of that size present in the sample. Depending on the application, capillary gels can be used to separate DNA fragments as small as 15 bp and can distinguish between fragments that differ by only 1 bp in size. Automated DNA sequencing relies on capillary electrophoresis.

A modification of standard agarose gel electrophoresis is pulsed-field gel electrophoresis. PFGE enables large fragments of DNA, ranging from 10,000 bp to 5 million bp, to be separated on the basis of size. This technique uses standard agarose gels; however, the electric field in which the DNA migrates is

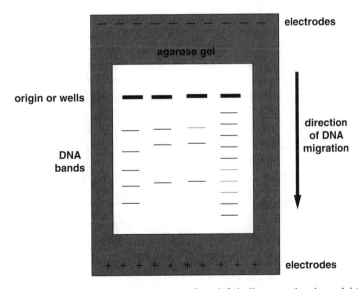

Figure 9-3 Conventional agarose gel electrophoresis. Fourth lane from left indicates molecular weight marker. © 2000, Susan M. Harrington.

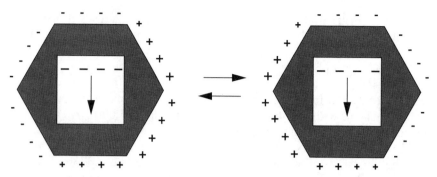

Figure 9-4 Schematic diagram of pulsed-field gel electrophoresis (PFGE) by the contour-clamped homogeneous electric fields (CHEF) technique. Alternation of current is shown. The figure on the left indicates current from northwest to southeast. The figure on the right shows the current from northeast to southwest. © 2000, Susan M. Harrington.

not applied in just one direction as in conventional electrophoresis. Instead, PFGE utilizes alternating electric fields, in which the current is applied for varying lengths of time in each direction, depending on the size of fragments to be separated. Several electrode configurations have been used by investigators; the most popular system is the contour-clamped homogeneous electric field (CHEF). The CHEF apparatus consists of a hexagonal array of electrodes producing two electric fields at 120° angles to each other (**Figure 9-4**). The length of time that the current is applied in each direction is referred to as the switch time or pulse time. Larger DNA molecules require longer pulse times, whereas smaller fragments are separated adequately with shorter pulse times. PFGE can be used to separate the fragments created by restriction endonuclease digestion of bacterial or fungal genomic DNA. Such digestion generally yields approximately 10 to 20 bands that have a range of fragment sizes. The array of small, medium, and large size fragments is separated by "ramping" the pulse time. With ramping, the pulse time is increased incrementally from just a few seconds up to several minutes over the course of the run.[19] Most users of PFGE purchase CHEF equipment, which can perform these intricate electrical switches with little programming by the operator.

Handling large pieces of DNA requires great care because such DNA fragments are fragile. For PFGE, DNA is extracted from cells that have been immobilized in agarose so that the DNA is not broken by agitation, vibration, or excessive pipetting.

Hybridization and Nucleic Acid Probes

Hybridization refers to the pairing or annealing of nucleic acids, both RNA and DNA, to complementary nucleic acid strands. Because of the rules of base pairing (A pairs with T; C pairs

with G), single strands of nucleic acid will anneal or hybridize to complementary strands that have the correct sequence of matching base pairs so as to form a complete set of Watson–Crick pairs. Nucleic acid probe technology, then, is based on the principle of hybridization. Sequences derived from specific genes or other DNA sequences can be used as probes to find places in the genome where their complementary sequences occur. The probe anneals to the genomic target sequences creating new, hybrid dsDNA.

In the process of Southern hybridization, target DNA, which has been digested with a restriction enzyme, is separated by size with agarose gel electrophoresis. The DNA bands are transferred by capillary action or "blotted" onto a nylon or nitrocellulose membrane and immobilized so that they will not come off even in liquid solutions (**Figure 9-5**). The target DNA, now on the membrane, is chemically treated to permit access to probe DNA. Probe DNA is then added, and hybridization is allowed to occur at the appropriate temperature. The probe DNA seeks out sequences that are complementary to it, and anneals to the target DNA bands immobilized on the membrane. Probe DNA is typically labeled with a radioisotope, or a fluorescent or chemiluminescent substrate. Following hybridization, the membrane is used to expose X-ray film (for radioisotope-labeled DNA) or treated with appropriate reagents to develop the indicator on the probe. This permits visualization of the target bands among the various bands on the membrane (Figure 9-5).

Polymerase Chain Reaction

Polymerase chain reaction is a tool used to amplify short sequences from among a diverse DNA pool such as a bacterial chromosome. The DNA length limits of PCR are sequences of approximately 10,000 bp.

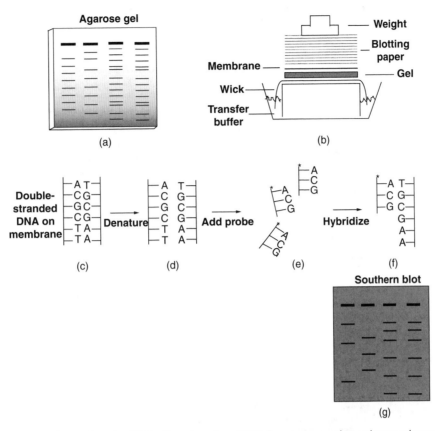

Figure 9-5 (a) Agarose gel electrophoresis. (b) Southern transfer of DNA from agarose gel to nylon membrane, steps involved in hybridization of probe DNA to target DNA on nylon membrane. Double-stranded DNA (c) is separated to the single-stranded form (d). Labeled probe (*) is added (e). Probe hybridizes to complementary DNA to form labeled dsDNA (f). Only bands from the agarose gel (a) with DNA sequence complementary to probe will hybridize. The hybridized Southern blot (g) shows target bands detected by labeled probe. © 2000, Susan M. Harrington.

In a standard PCR reaction, two specific oligonucleotide primers are mixed with template DNA. Oligonucleotides are very short segments of DNA, typically 15 to 30 bp in length. The template is the DNA that contains the sequences to be amplified. Template DNA is generated by lysing bacteria, fungi, or viral particles to release their respective genomes. The oligonucleotides are chosen based on the target sequence to be amplified within the template DNA. One oligonucleotide primer is complementary to the forward (top) strand at one end of the target sequence; the second oligonucleotide is complementary to the reverse (bottom) strand at the opposite end of the target sequence (**Figure 9-6**).

Polymerases are enzymes that facilitate DNA replication. Because PCR requires both high and low temperatures, thermostable polymerases (e.g., the DNA polymerase enzyme from *Thermus aquaticus* [Taq]) are used to amplify the target sequence. A typical PCR reaction mixture contains template DNA, oligonucleotide primers, polymerase, magnesium, deoxyribonucleotide triphosphate bases, and a suitable buffer. First, the template DNA is dissociated by heating to 94°C. Oligonucleotide primer annealing then occurs by cooling to a lower temperature such as 55°C; at this stage, the oligonucleotides have an advantage because of their high concentration, and they bind to the target more quickly than the original complementary strand. Finally, an extension phase occurs at 72°C, where the polymerase adds the correct nucleotides to the short primer oligonucleotide strand to create a new complementary strand. After 30–40 cycles of dissociation, annealing, and extension, the result is a large amplification of the target sequence—namely, the sequence between the two oligonucleotide primers called the PCR product or amplicon (Figure 9-6). The amplicon can then be analyzed by agarose or capillary gel electrophoresis, restriction endonuclease analysis, or Southern hybridization.

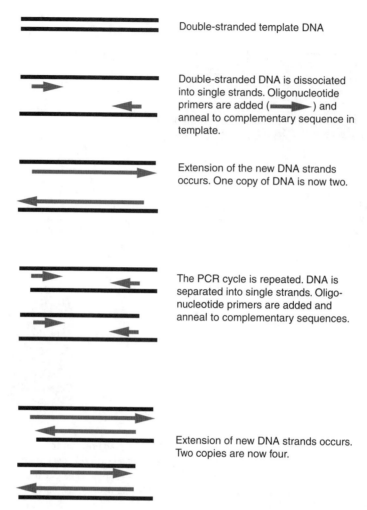

Double-stranded template DNA

Double-stranded DNA is dissociated into single strands. Oligonucleotide primers are added (➤) and anneal to complementary sequence in template.

Extension of the new DNA strands occurs. One copy of DNA is now two.

The PCR cycle is repeated. DNA is separated into single strands. Oligonucleotide primers are added and anneal to complementary sequences.

Extension of new DNA strands occurs. Two copies are now four.

Figure 9-6 Polymerase Chain Reaction Amplification of Template DNA. Two cycles of PCR are shown. Double-stranded DNA is separated into single strands. Primers anneal. New DNA strands are created through extension. Typical PCR reactions are 30 to 40 cycles long, creating millions of copies of double-stranded DNA.

DNA Sequencing

DNA sequencing is used to determine the exact order of nucleotide bases in DNA. This process has experienced many advances since the first DNA sequences were determined. Now a highly automated procedure, sequencing can be used in many applications, ranging from molecular cloning to strain typing and forensics to sequencing whole genomes.

To determine the sequence of a region of DNA, that region is often first amplified by PCR. Following PCR, the double-stranded DNA is separated, and one strand is used as a template for the sequencing reaction. Next, a primer that recognizes the product of the PCR reaction anneals specifically to the template. Nucleotide bases are added to extend the complementary strand. Some of these nucleotides are labeled with fluorescent dye-terminator tags (one color for each nucleotide A, C, G, or T). As these tagged

nucleotides (dideoxynucleotides) are incorporated, the extension of the sequence is terminated. The specificity of the added nucleotide is determined by the color of the label. This "sequencing" reaction occurs in cycles similar to PCR and yields products of varying lengths, each with a specific end label indicating the incorporated nucleotide. These DNA products are then separated according to size by capillary gel electrophoresis. The products pass a laser that determines which nucleotide has been incorporated based on the terminator dye fluorescence, and the resulting electropherogram displays the DNA sequence.

Microarrays

An oligonucleotide microarray (i.e., DNA chip) is an efficient method for detecting DNA sequences of interest. With this technique, more than 10,000 different oligonucleotides can be attached to a 1 cm² solid surface. The location of each DNA on the surface acts as an identifier. Unknown sequences that are complementary to known oligonucleotides on the DNA chip hybridize, allowing for their subsequent identification. Examples of the various formats used for SNP typing with microarrays include hybridization arrays and arrays with enzymatic processing. For hybridization arrays, alleles of known SNPs located at specific regions of a "chip" are allowed to hybridize with query SNPs present in fluorescently labeled PCR products. Hybridization results in positive signals that are detected by a computer, leading to identification of unknown SNPs. During arrayed primer extension, PCR products containing unknown SNPs are hybridized to the arrayed oligonucleotides. Bound oligonucleotides act as primers for a DNA polymerase extension reaction that incorporates fluorescently labeled dideoxynucleotides. The addition of enzymatic discrimination increases the specificity of the latter method.[20]

As typing methods are the focus of this chapter, the next section examines how these techniques use frequent and infrequent cutting enzymes, PFGE, hybridization, PCR, sequencing and microarrays to detect strain differences based on DNA sequence and/or restriction site specificities.

SPECIFIC TECHNIQUES OF MOLECULAR EPIDEMIOLOGY

This section describes the most commonly used nucleic acid molecular methods. Strengths and weakness of each method are highlighted, and examples are included. With the exception of methods that utilize DNA sequencing, these methods rely on visualization of DNA fragments, whether they are from plasmids, restriction digests, hybridization, or PCR products. These banding patterns serve as the "DNA fingerprints" used to compare one isolate to another.[21]

Evaluation of Typing Systems

Different typing systems measure different biologic properties and perform with varying degrees of success depending on the organism and technical requirements. No one system is best for all species, although several methods can be applied to almost all bacterial species, especially those causing the majority of hospital-associated outbreaks. As with other clinical laboratory methods, strain typing techniques must be carefully evaluated before they are used to answer epidemiologic questions. The specific question that

needs to be answered may lead to the selection of one method over another.

To be widely useful, a typing system must give an interpretable result for every isolate of a given species—a capacity referred to as typeability. Plasmid analysis—one of the earliest typing methods—detects the extra-chromosomal DNA of bacteria. However, not all strains within a species will contain plasmids, rendering them nontypeable by this method.

Reproducibility is another critical factor for typing systems. An assay cannot be considered reliable if the same results are not obtained when an isolate is tested multiple times in the system. Some molecular methods are highly technique dependent in this sense. For example, the reaction conditions, reagents, and template DNA used in the arbitrarily primed PCR reaction must be carefully standardized or a different result could be obtained with each run. Thus standardization is another important component. Interpretation of results is much more reliable when methods are performed in the same way from batch to batch.[14]

Discriminatory power is the ability of the typing technique to distinguish unrelated isolates from epidemiologically related strains. It is critical to include epidemiologically unrelated strains in the evaluation of new typing systems as controls. Many methods are able to link closely clustered isolates; however, the more challenging aspect of such analysis is to exclude unassociated strains. Often some isolates are found with a molecular link for which no epidemiologic link exists. The key is to minimize this phenomenon with the most powerful typing tool available.[14] It must also be understood that to some degree the ability to discriminate related from unrelated isolates is species dependent. For example, the number of different clones of MRSA is much more limited than the corresponding number for methicillin-susceptible strains, as a result of the way the methicillin resistance gene was acquired by some strains of the species.[22] The limited number of clones could cause the test operator to falsely link strains that are truly unrelated. For MRSA, then, it is important to compare isolates over a short time frame and to combine laboratory results with careful epidemiologic analysis.

Discriminatory power may be calculated with Simpson's index of diversity:

$$D = \frac{1}{N(N-1)} \sum_{i=1}^{K} n_i(n_i - 1)$$

where D is the index of diversity (0–1), N is the number of isolates tested, K is the number of strain types derived by the method, and n is the number of isolates of the ith type. Typing systems with a discriminatory index greater than 0.90 are considered to have effective power.[23] One caveat to consider when applying this formula, however, is that the definition of a strain type must be determined; that is, the number of band differences or mutations that must occur for two isolates to be considered different types must be known. Accepted definitions of strain type are defined in the literature for some methods, but not all.

The ease of interpretation or readability of DNA fingerprints varies. Some methods, such as chromosomal restriction endonuclease analysis, produce many bands that are difficult to distinguish because they are so close together. Faint or very bold bands can be equally difficult to discern. Interpretability can vary between methods or even between applications of a single method. For example, in Southern hybridization methods, one probe may yield a much more readable RFLP than another. In the last 10 years, more investigators have begun using sequence-based methods to ease the burden of interpreting the bands generated by fingerprinting methods.

Issues of cost-effectiveness, ease of use, ease of interpretation, and turnaround time must also be considered when selecting an analytical technique. As molecular methods have become more discriminatory, their use has come to require increasingly more expensive and sophisticated machinery, including PCR thermocyclers, PFGE equipment, DNA sequencers, and computer software for archiving data and comparing run-to-run results. The time to obtain results using these powerful techniques may range from 1 or 2 days for PCR to approximately 4 days for PFGE and RFLP. Likewise, the technical expertise needed to perform molecular techniques varies from simple DNA extraction to lengthy hybridization procedures. Finally, interpretation of banding patterns and results is method dependent as well.

The choice of a typing method depends on all of these parameters; it will vary with the needs and capabilities of individual laboratories. As each method is presented here, it is evaluated based on these criteria.

Plasmid Analysis

As described, some bacterial strains harbor extrachromosomal DNA called plasmids. Analysis of plasmid DNA is one of the oldest of the nucleic acid–based methods for strain typing and has been used in the evaluation of many outbreaks.[24] This method can easily be applied in many investigations, as plasmids are frequently present in bacterial cells and easily extracted for analysis with the inexpensive agarose gel electrophoresis equipment found in many laboratories.

On a practical level, some difficulties may be encountered when plasmid gel electrophoresis is performed. Plasmid DNA can range in size from just a few kilobases to almost 200 kb. Due to the size and secondary structure of plasmids, gels can have poor reproducibility and can be difficult to interpret. These problems can be overcome by cutting the plasmid DNA with a restriction enzyme. Referred to as plasmid restriction enzyme analysis (REA), this method creates smaller, linear fragments that migrate faithfully according to size, and the bands on the gels are then more easily interpreted. Cutting with a restriction endonuclease is dependent on DNA sequence; therefore, REA can distinguish whether single, large plasmids are the same in terms of both DNA content and size. The number of REA bands increases proportionately with the number of plasmids. Unfortunately, as band number increases, interpretation becomes more difficult.

When applying this method, the variable nature of plasmids must be appreciated. Depending on the environment and the antibiotic resistance genes or virulence factors encoded by the plasmids that a bacterium harbors, plasmids can be gained or lost because of selective pressures. Hence, depending on which antibiotic therapy is in use, strains involved in an outbreak can evolve through changes in plasmid content even as the outbreak is being evaluated.[25] Movement of plasmids (or the transposable elements that they carry) between strains of the same species and even between species has been observed.[26,27] Thus a plasmid epidemic could be encountered.[28] Plasmid results must be evaluated carefully in comparison to the susceptibility profiles of the organisms isolated at the time of an outbreak.

Two other factors should be considered when using plasmid analysis. First, not all strains will give a result because some do not carry plasmids. Second, because plasmid analysis focuses on only a small part of the genome, two bacterial strains might have the same plasmid content, yet possess unique chromosomes. With these comments in mind, it is probably best to apply this typing technique to studies that are relatively limited in time span and to combine plasmid analysis with other methods.

Restriction Endonuclease Analysis of Chromosomal DNA

Analysis of chromosomal DNA is an alternative to plasmid typing methods. The chromosome is the more stable genetic element, not subject to gain and loss as is the plasmid. Chromosomal REA is performed by extracting genomic DNA and cutting it with a restriction endonuclease that cuts frequently. Hundreds of fragments approximately 0.5 to 50 kb in length are produced, which are then separated by conventional gel electrophoresis. The advantages of chromosomal REA are twofold: (1) with the correct selection of restriction enzyme, all bacterial species are typeable, and (2) this technique is easy to perform. However, the large number of bands produced makes interpretation difficult.[15,29] Chromosomal REA has been largely replaced by newer methods.

RFLP Analysis Using REA with Southern Hybridization

The interpretability of chromosomal REA has been improved with the addition of nucleic acid probes targeted to specific multicopy genes, insertion sequences, or mobile genetic elements such as transposons. With this technique, DNA cut with a frequent-cutting restriction endonuclease is first separated in agarose. Next, the DNA fragments are transferred from agarose to a membrane by the Southern blotting technique. The DNA fragments immobilized on the membrane can then be hybridized with a nucleic acid probe. Only a small portion (ideally 10 to 20) of the thousands of restriction fragments will have specificity for the probe and will be detected. This technique—known as restriction fragment length polymorphism—detects the number of copies of sequence homologous to the probe and reflects the size of the restriction fragments containing those sequences. The number of bands will be proportional to the number of copies of the target as long as the target does not contain a restriction site. When a single restriction site is present within the target sequence, the probe will hybridize along both sides of the restriction site and two bands will be produced for each copy of target.

Several probes are most commonly used for RFLP typing; however, theoretically, any repetitive sequence with species specificity can work. For example, the *mec* A gene, which encodes methicillin resistance, and Tn554, a transposon, have both been used as probes of chromosomal digests for oxacillin-resistant *S. aureus*.[22,30] Other types of probes have included insertion sequences, toxin-producing genes, and even random chromosomal sequences.[18] Nevertheless, most of these probes are specific to only a single species, and sometimes only to strains within a species carrying the gene of interest.

Ribotyping has been a popular approach to RFLP typing, almost universally applicable to bacterial species. In this method, ribosomal RNA (rRNA) or DNA homologous to the ribosomal operon is used as the probe. The ribosomal operon, which encodes the rRNA transcripts essential to make a ribosome, is highly conserved within bacterial species and is usually present in multiple copies in the chromosome. Organisms such as *E. coli, Klebsiella,* and *Staphylococcus* species have 5–7 copies of this element, producing easily interpreted ribotype patterns with 10–15 bands.[31] Ribotyping is not of value for strain delineation of *M. tuberculosis* because only one copy of the ribosomal operon is present in this organism's chromosome.

Several repetitive elements have been studied as probes for RFLP.[32,33] IS6110, an insertion sequence present in 1 to 26 copies in *M. tuberculosis* complex organisms, has been widely used as a typing tool for this species.[34] Rarely, *M. tuberculosis* or related organisms will lack IS6110; most of these aberrant strains have come from cases in Southeast Asia. Additionally, as many as 25% of isolates have fewer than six bands when *M. tuberculosis* DNA is hybridized with IS6110.[35] **Figure 9-7** is an example of an IS6110-probed Southern blot of *M. tuberculosis*. Isolates with low band numbers are shown in lanes 3 and 5. The fewer the bands present, the less reliable the discrimination and other methods must be used. Mycobacterial interspersed repetitive units and spoligotyping, discussed later in this chapter, are alternatives to IS6110 fingerprinting for *M. tuberculosis*. RFLP with IS6110 has been used to study transmission in large cities and HIV-infected populations, epidemiology between nations, laboratory contamination, and outbreaks.[36-40] In Figure 9-7, lanes 1 and 10 contain DNA from a well-characterized *M. tuberculosis* strain that is used as a standard molecular-weight marker. Inclusion of a bacterium as a marker instead of purchasing one commercially is highly desirable. Not only does using DNA from a live organism serve as a determinant of molecular size, but it is also a useful extraction control. To be confident of the extraction process in the laboratory, every time this strain's DNA is extracted and cut with the indicated restriction enzyme, the same number and size of bands must be obtained.

Although ribotyping uses a commercially available standardized probe, the choice of restriction enzyme is not standardized. In fact, the most discriminatory enzyme varies between species. An increase in discrimination can be obtained by combining the results with two or more enzymes, but overall

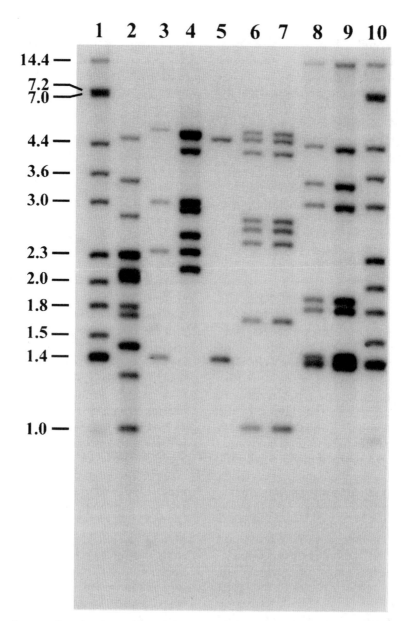

Figure 9-7 Restriction fragment length polymorphism of *Mycobacterium tuberculosis* with IS6110 probe. Lanes 2 to 9 contain clinical isolates. Lanes 1 to 10 are the molecular weight marker Mt 14323. Molecular weights are shown in kilobase pairs.

ribotyping is considered to be only a moderately discriminatory method.[30,41,42]

Ribotyping and other RFLP techniques generally produce interpretable banding patterns that are very reproducible. An advantage of these tests is that they do not require a lot of expensive equipment. They may take up to a week to perform, however, and require considerable technical expertise. An automated ribotyping instrument, known as the Riboprinter (DuPont-Qualicon), has been developed. As many as 32 organisms may be identified and typed in a single day using this device. However, the costs of the instrument and associated reagents are prohibitive for most clinical laboratories; thus the Riboprinter is mainly used by the pharmaceutical industry for environmental monitoring and clinical drug trials.

Pulsed-Field Gel Electrophoresis

First described in 1984 by Schwartz and Cantor, PFGE is one of the most widely used and discriminatory typing techniques.[19] Developed to separate large DNA molecules, it is the ideal method for electrophoresis of the fragments created by digestion of a genomic DNA extract with infrequent cutting restriction enzymes. Optimally, 10–20 bands are

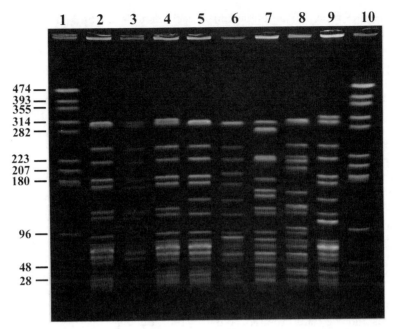

Figure 9-8 Pulsed-field gel electrophoresis of vancomycin-resistant *Enterococcus faecium*. Lanes 2 to 5, 7, and 8 are patient isolates recovered during an outbreak in an ICU. Lane 6 contains an isolate cultured from the surface of an IV machine. Lane 9 is a strain isolated 4 months later. The molecular weight maker, *Notl*-digested *E. faecalis* ATCC 47077, is in lanes 1 and 10. Molecular weights are in kilobase pairs.

produced. A major strength of PFGE is that probes and Southern blotting are usually not needed. The small number of bands produced can be visualized by staining and gel documentation with a computer imaging system.

With the appropriate restriction enzyme, PFGE can be used to type most bacteria and a number of fungal species. Rarely, DNA from isolates will be degraded during application of this technology, resulting in an uninterpretable pattern.[29] As with all strain typing methods, no one restriction enzyme is considered standard. Choice of the restriction enzyme depends on the percent G+C content of the organism, as previously described. Some enzymes inherently work better than others do. Lists of organisms and restriction enzymes used for PFGE have been published.[13,18]

Fungi have multiple individual chromosomes that vary in size and number within species. These may be extracted for separation as whole chromosomes or cut with restriction enzymes. Separation of intact chromosomes generates a type of fingerprint referred to as an electrophoretic karyotype. Interpreting karyotypes can be difficult if the chromosomes migrate closely to one another. Some investigators digest these DNAs with restriction enzymes, thereby yielding smaller, more readily distinguished bands.[43,44]

At the time of this writing, PFGE is probably the method most frequently used for outbreak investigations in the United States involving common hospital-associated pathogens. It has been shown to be highly discriminatory in outbreaks caused by many organisms such as *Staphylococcus*, *Candida*, *E. coli*, *Enterococcus*, and *Enterobacter*.[45–49] **Figure 9-8** shows some examples of VRE from a hospital ICU outbreak. A total of 13 VRE isolates were obtained from patient cultures over a 5-week period. Seven of these samples were characterized as belonging to the outbreak cluster. Lanes 2 to 4 in Figure **9-8** are indistinguishable outbreak isolates. The VRE isolate in lane 5 was considered a clonally related strain within the outbreak because it has only two bands different from the main outbreak strain. Lane 6 contains an environmental strain that was isolated from the surface of a bedside infusion pump. Because it shares many bands with the outbreak strain, this strain might also be related to the outbreak cluster. The strains in lane 7 and 8 are from patients who were not involved in the outbreak; these two patients were likely colonized before admission to the hospital. The isolate in lane 9 was recovered 4 months after the outbreak; its banding pattern suggests that it is a progeny isolate that has diverged from the outbreak strain.[13]

Because PFGE fingerprints are highly reproducible, their interpretation is fairly straightforward. However, a disadvantage of PFGE is the difficulty in comparing large numbers of isolates or results obtained from different laboratories.[49] In addition, interpretation can become time-consuming when several isolates that differ by only a few bands are compared, as illustrated in Figure 9-8. Many investigators use computer database and analysis software to compare large numbers of strains run on multiple gels. The Centers for Disease Control and Prevention has managed comparisons of large numbers of isolates with the highly successful PulseNet Program. This program utilizes a network of public health laboratories that receive organisms such as *E. coli* O157, *Salmonella*, and *Shigella*. Participating laboratories perform PFGE according to highly standardized protocols.[50] The resulting PFGE patterns are then analyzed with software and stored in a national database via the Internet. This database is regularly evaluated for matching strains, with the strain typing data being used in outbreak investigations around the country.

Other disadvantages of PFGE include the expense of the PFGE apparatus and the total time required to perform the testing. DNA extraction procedures may take 2–3 days, although more rapid methods have been developed.[51,52] The electrophoresis time is also lengthy; 20 hours is a typical running time, and a fair amount of technical expertise is necessary to carry out the procedure. Furthermore, DNA extraction takes great care. All extraction steps must be cautiously performed, with preparations being embedded in agarose to prevent mechanical breakage of chromosomal DNA.

PCR-Based Methods

All of the methods presented to this point require a fairly large amount of DNA for gel electrophoresis. In contrast, PCR-based strain typing techniques require only a small amount of DNA from the clinical isolate. In addition, DNA from organisms that cannot be grown by conventional culture methods can be amplified via PCR and then used to delineate strain differences. Compared with RFLP and PFGE, PCR fingerprinting is a rapid technology, with results becoming available within a day. Three basic variations of PCR fingerprinting are described in this subsection.

PCR-RFLP

PCR-RFLP utilizes PCR to amplify known variable regions of the genome. A restriction endonuclease is then used to digest these PCR products, yielding several smaller DNA fragments. For example, in a method called Vir typing, the *emm* gene for the antiphagocytic M protein in *Streptococcus pyogenes* is amplified and digested with *Hae*III, producing

characteristic RFLP patterns.[53] The DNA fragments are visualized by conventional gel electrophoresis. No hybridization or PFGE equipment is needed. Species-specific virulence genes such as *emm* of *S. pyogenes*, the coagulase gene of *S. aureus,* and genes coding for rRNA have proved useful for this method.[54] A related strain typing method based on sequencing of the 5' variable region of *emm* has also been developed.[55] Multilocus restriction fragment typing is a recently described method in which housekeeping genes are PCR amplified and digested with restriction enzymes[56]; this method is described further in a later section of this chapter.

Only well-characterized regions specific to a given species can be used as the basis for discrimination by PCR-RFLP. Hence, the discriminatory power of PCR-RFLP varies depending on both the organism and the gene being amplified. This method does, however, generate easily produced and interpreted, reproducible fingerprints.[14]

Repetitive Element PCR (Rep-PCR)

Rep-PCR uses PCR to amplify regions between known repetitive sequences.[57] Oligonucleotide primers, homologous to the ends of repetitive sequences, prime PCR reactions that amplify the sequences between these repeats. Repetitive sequences may be spaced somewhat randomly throughout the chromosome. It follows that the DNA fragment lengths between the repetitive elements are also variable. Rep-PCR produces a range of fragment lengths (or a DNA fingerprint) that is size fractionated by agarose gel electrophoresis. The repetitive extrapalindromic sequences of *E. coli* (rep), the enterobacterial repetitive intergenic consensus (ERIC) elements of *Enterobacteriaceae*, the BOX elements of gram-positive bacteria, and regions between rRNA genes are some of the repetitive elements used for this technique.[18,58]

Applicable to many bacterial species, rep-PCR is a discriminatory method, albeit one that is generally less discriminatory than PFGE and lacks reproducibility if attention to procedural details is not strictly followed.[59,60] This technique's discriminatory power can, however, be enhanced with multiple primer sets.[61] The DiversiLab System (bioMerieux, Inc., Durham, North Carolina), is a commercial variant of rep-PCR that improves the reproducibility of the method.[62] Commercial kits are available with primers specific to the organism to be typed. With this semi-automated platform, the products of the rep-PCR reaction are size fractionated on a microfluidics detection platform ("chip"), generating an electropherogram that is converted into a digitized gel image

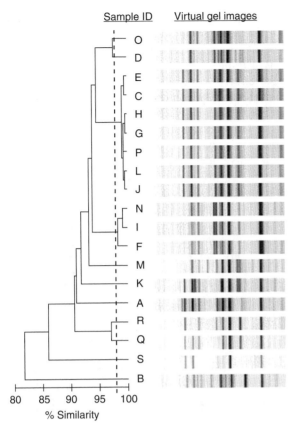

Sample ID   Virtual gel images

80 85 90 95 100
% Similarity

Figure 9-9 Dendrogram analysis and virtual gel image of rep-PCR fingerprint patterns of *N. meningitidis*. Vertical line indicates the similarity index characterizing related strains. Samples E, C, H, G, P, L, and J are serotype C from an outbreak. Samples O, D, M and S are serotype C isolates with no epidemiologic links. Samples N, I, and F are serotype B and were indistinguishable by PFGE. Samples K, A, R, Q, and B are various serotypes with no epidemiologic links. Healy M, Huong J, Bittner T, et al. Microbial DNA Typing by Automated Repetitive-Sequence-Based PCR. From *J Clin Microbiol*. 2005; 43:199–207. Reproduced with permission from American Society for Microbiology.

(**Figure 9-9**). The data are stored in an electronic database for between-run comparisons. This technology allows for collection of accurate, automated, reproducible data that can be archived allowing for comparisons over time or between laboratories via the Internet. As many as 12 isolates may be typed in an 8-hour shift. Its ease of use, accuracy, reproducibility, and rapid turnaround time have made rep-PCR the method of choice for routine strain typing by many clinical laboratories.

Arbitrarily Primed PCR or Random Amplified Polymorphic DNA

Arbitrarily primed PCR (AP-PCR) is the third PCR fingerprinting technique. With this method, a single, short oligonucleotide primer (8–10 bp) is selected

and is not intended to be specific for defined target sequences. The number of recognition sites for this primer in the template DNA is generally not known. PCR is performed at a low annealing temperature to facilitate binding of oligonucleotide to the template in regions that may lack perfect sequence homology. When primers anneal sufficiently close to each other (within approximately 1 kb), in the correct orientation and on opposite DNA strands, amplification of the region between the arbitrary primers takes place. These primers will anneal at multiple locations throughout the template. As with rep-PCR, products of various sizes result from the amplification process. The PCR products can then be separated by gel electrophoresis, yielding a fingerprint pattern.[63] An advantage of this method is that no sequence information about the organism is required. Many bacterial species, fungi, and some parasites have been typed successfully with AP-PCR.[61]

Whereas this method offers excellent typeability, batch-to-batch reproducibility is sometimes poor. Minor alterations in PCR reagents, the amount of template, or reaction conditions can result in nonspecific bands.[58] In general, AP-PCR is a more rapid method and is less technically demanding than RFLP or PFGE because fewer steps are involved. At the same time, AP-PCR can be more difficult to interpret than either RFLP or PFGE. The bands seen on AP-PCR gels generally vary in intensity, depending on reaction conditions, the ability of the arbitrary primers to anneal to template, and the efficiency of the elongation step. AP-PCR is probably best used with relatively small numbers of isolates that are compared within the same run on the same day.[14,27] A number of studies have demonstrated AP-PCR to have discriminatory power similar to PFGE and better than some other methods. Multiple primer sets have been used to increase discriminatory power.[64]

Interpretation of Results for Gel Electrophoresis-Based Methods

As molecular typing methods have been described, the interpretability or readability of the fingerprint has been mentioned repeatedly. This property is not the same as the interpretation of results. All of the gel electrophoresis-based methods produce a DNA fingerprint, or banding pattern, for each isolate. As the fingerprints are compared, the similarities or differences between them are evaluated. All of the bands from an isolate are compared with those in the other lanes on the gel.

The simplest comparison is that of two isolates having the same DNA fingerprint. These results are more accurately described as "indistinguishable" rather than identical. Each of the molecular typing methods evaluates only a portion of the genome (i.e., restriction endonuclease sites, a specific gene, or amplified sequence). It is impossible to say that two microorganisms are exact clones based on these types of tests. Clearly, mutations in the genome might occur that will not be detected by these methods. At the opposite extreme, it is fairly easy to decide that two isolates having vastly different fingerprints are not clonally related. The difficult interpretations are those in which isolates vary by just a few bands. Such strains may be related to each other, but how closely?

The relatedness of organisms can be expressed in terms of the number of genetic events or changes to the chromosome that occur from one generation to the next.[13] For example, two organisms that demonstrate changes in the chromosome produced by one genetic event may be categorized as "probably related." Strains that differ by two genetic events are characterized as "possibly related." Isolates differing by three or more genetic events are most likely "unrelated." It seems reasonable to categorize strains based on these definitions of relative relatedness, but it should be kept in mind that the rates of insertions/deletions and point mutations will vary for different species and that this logic will not apply to all bacteria.[13] However, if we accept these criteria, how many fingerprint band differences are required to place strains into these categories? Tenover et al. present a detailed discussion of molecular typing methods and the way in which mutations affect banding patterns.[27]

Some interpretive criteria used by investigators in molecular epidemiology can be found in the literature. The guidelines for PFGE have probably been those most widely applied.[13] For example, it is possible for one genetic change to cause up to three-band differences between two isolates. Hence, isolates with one- to three-band differences are probably related. Two genetic events would alter the PFGE pattern by anywhere from four to six bands. Strains with four-to six-band differences are possibly related. Unrelated strains differ by more than six bands.

Most investigators evaluating strain typing data in an outbreak will designate the most common type by a letter or number, such as strain A. Isolates that differ from A by one to three bands are subtypes of A. Isolates with more than three band differences are given new letter designations. In practice, as numerous fingerprints are compared, categorizing strains that "may be related" becomes complex. For example, two isolates may each be subtypes of strain A and

vary from each other by more than four bands. These subtype strains would represent new type strains B and C if evaluated apart from the type A strain. This example emphasizes the importance of evaluating strain types over a limited time period relative to an outbreak. Differences between epidemiologically unrelated strains will inevitably occur on a random basis. Two such strains could, therefore, have only minor molecular differences and be grouped as subtypes if no epidemiologic information is considered. Hence, interpretive guidelines can give misleading information if applied in a larger context without epidemiologic data.[13]

These interpretive criteria are valid for PFGE because the whole chromosome is assessed via this method. For other typing systems using gel electrophoresis, criteria for interpretation are less easily defined. Many genetic events can occur that will not be detected. For example, substitution mutations of DNA that do not alter restriction sites or target areas for probes will not be detected by RFLP methods.[27] Although no standard approach to RFLP interpretation has been proposed, some investigators have designated isolates with one-band difference subtypes of one another. Isolates with two or more band differences represent new strain types.[30]

For rep-PCR and AP-PCR, no standard approach has been established for analyzing minor differences in band patterns such as changes in intensity or a one-band size shift. Frequently, a second set of PCR primers is used to determine whether similar results are consistently obtained. Any mutational event may be responsible for the alterations seen in PCR fingerprints if that mutation occurs at a primer binding site. Additionally, insertions or deletions of DNA between primer binding sites might alter the banding pattern. Even so, not all mutations will be detected by this method. In a manner similar to the interpretation of RFLP results, isolates having a one-band difference by PCR fingerprinting may be considered subtypes of each other. PCR patterns having two or more bands different are generally categorized as different strains.[27,65]

Computer-Assisted Analysis of Fingerprinting Results

Sometimes the molecular epidemiologist needs to compare isolates in large populations or over a lengthy period of time. This circumstance requires between-gel comparisons, which cannot be done without strict standardization of the method (i.e., the same DNA extraction procedure, electrophoresis conditions, and molecular weight standards). For large data sets, computer assistance is a necessity. Such systems allow gels, photographs, or autoradiographic images to be scanned and stored as digitized images. A molecular size standard with a well-characterized pattern must be included in several lanes on the gel. Often the two end lanes and, depending on the size of the gel, at least one middle lane are used for standardization.

Currently, the most widely utilized computer program for fingerprint analysis is the BioNumerics software from Applied Mathematics (Sint-Martens-Latem, Belgium). With this program, analysis begins by defining the lanes to be analyzed. This step allows the user to compensate for lane curvatures or artifacts that might create distortions in the lane. The background of the gel can then be adjusted to enhance weak bands or alter contrast. In accordance with the settings defined by the user, the program defines the densitometric curves that represent the position and intensity of each band. The next step is normalization of the gel, during which the standards are used to align the lanes, compensating for distortions across the gel. The bands can then be identified automatically, based on user-defined filters for minimum area and band intensity. Alternatively, the software allows the user the flexibility to add, delete, or move bands after visual inspection. Most commonly, a combination of automatic and manual band finding is utilized.[66,67]

Within-gel and between-gel band matching can then be accomplished from the analyzed gel image. The user chooses an optimization setting for the fingerprint as a whole and a percent tolerance for matching around each band to enhance strain matching. The microprocessor applies various numerical indices to assign percent similarities or similarity coefficients to any or all pairs of isolates. For example, Dice coefficients are usually used for PFGE data and Pearson correlation coefficients for rep-PCR. Finally, graphical representation of the relatedness of isolates in the dataset can be accomplished in the form of dendrograms based on various grouping methods (e.g., Unweighted Pair Group Method with Arithmetic Mean [UPGMA], neighbor joining). (Examples are shown in Figures 9-9 and 9-12.) A dendrogram links isolates according to percent similarity in a manner similar to a phylogenetic tree. When used in a rigorously standardized fashion, fingerprinting software allows the user to make many comparisons that would otherwise be very time consuming. Detailed discussion of the mathematical analysis of fingerprint data is beyond the scope of this chapter, however, and the reader is referred to other texts for more information on this topic.[18,66]

Computerized analysis does have limitations. Although these systems can correct for differences that arise between gels, they do so imperfectly. For example, they are unable to correct for great variability. Furthermore, the extent of matching is determined by the tolerance and percent deviation selected by the operator. Overmatching or undermatching can occur, depending on this setting. Because the systems use mathematical methods to match strains, isolate 1 may match perfectly to isolate 2 and isolate 3, but isolates 2 and 3 may not match each other with 100% similarity. Even so, all three of these samples may be grouped together in a mathematical cluster.

Groupings of related strains based on similarity coefficients may also not correlate exactly with those that might be developed based on side-by-side comparison of band differences. In the previous section, one genetic event was correlated to a change in three or fewer bands on a PFGE gel. Depending on the total number of bands in the profile, the similarity coefficient associated with a three-band difference will vary. Mathematically, the smaller the total number of bands for each isolate, the lower the similarity (Dice) coefficient that will correlate with a three-band difference. Thus, for species that generate different average numbers of bands by PFGE, the similarity coefficient values for organisms that are placed into clusters or groups of the "same strain type" or "related strain types" within a given species will differ.

Cluster analysis must be carefully interpreted. It is sometimes helpful to allow the computer program to find strains that are closely related and then run these strains on the same gel in adjacent lanes.

A final cautionary note: the tree structure of a dendrogram is highly dependent on the grouping method chosen and can lead to false conclusions. Some grouping methods, such as UPGMA, give different tree structures depending on the order in which strains are added to the analysis. For strain typing applications, distances between strains on the tree are relative, not absolute. Dendrograms serve as graphical representations of relatedness of large groupings of strains and should not be interpreted as representative of genetic distance.

DNA Sequence-Based Methods

Sequence-based methods have emerged as significant tools for strain typing analysis. These methods generally rely on amplification of a gene by PCR, followed by DNA sequencing. Sequence data are analyzed by PCR product size and/or exact nucleotide content. Results are generally not the subject of banding pattern interpretation as are PFGE, RFLP, and PCR-based results. At least five approaches have been developed: (1) sSNP genotyping; (2) multilocus sequence typing (MLST); (3) a related method, multilocus restriction fragment typing (MLRFT); (4) sequencing of a single highly polymorphic locus; and (5) multilocus variable-number tandem repeat assays (MLVA).

sSNP Genotyping

Whole-genome DNA sequencing has opened the door for designing new methods for the typing of bacteria. Proteins capable of being produced from such DNA can be identified with computer programs (e.g., Gene Locator and Interpolated Markov Modeler [GLIMMER]). Analysis of the DNA sequences of different strains of bacteria and their predicted proteins allows for the discovery of numerous polymorphisms, of which sSNPs show distinct promise as a typing method. Once identified, sSNPs are verified by repeated DNA sequencing or use of mass spectrometry. Verified sSNPs for a particular organism can then be assayed for by microarray (e.g., GeneChip [Affymetrix Inc., Santa Clara, California]), mass spectrometry (e.g., Masscode [Qiagen Inc., Valencia, California]), gel electrophoresis (e.g., RFLP), and other methodologies.[16,20,68,69] Data generated from comparisons of sSNPs from different strains of a particular genus are then utilized for epidemiologic and phylogenetic studies.

sSNPs genotyping is efficient, amenable to automation, applicable to large bacterial populations, and predicted to have a significant impact, particularly in the epidemiology and evolution of *M. tuberculosis*. This method, however, is limited by its cost, need for prior DNA sequence knowledge, and effort required to establish an assay. Widespread use of sSNPs as a genotyping method in the future will likely depend on the introduction of less expensive, higher-throughput technologies.[20,68,69]

Multilocus Sequence Typing

MLST is based on the principles of MLEE and characterizes strains based on polymorphisms in a set of conserved housekeeping genes. For most applications, 7 to 10 genes are generally amplified by PCR and then sequenced. Strain comparisons are performed by aligning sequences. Each unique sequence becomes an allele and is assigned an allele number. The combination of alleles defines the sequence type (ST) (**Figure 9-10**).

Like other typing methods, MLST has both pros and cons. The cost of sequencing equipment and the technically demanding nature of the experiments are limitations. Conversely, a notable strength of MLST is that it is highly discriminatory, although it

generally has less discriminatory power than PFGE when used to type organisms involved in outbreaks. This limitation arises because the mutation rate in the housekeeping genes is slower than the rate of insertions, deletions, and other mutations that generate changes in PFGE patterns. MLST is best suited to the analysis of bacterial population genetics and has been applied to long-term epidemiology on both a local and worldwide basis.[70] Importantly, this technology generates discrete, objective data that are highly reproducible. MLST overcomes the difficulty of comparing results between laboratories without exchanging reference strains and allows for inter-laboratory comparisons through the Internet (http://www.mlst.net). This website has the added advantage of banking linked epidemiological associations by STs and has compiled allelic data from at least 25 countries, and for 27 genera of bacteria and fungi.[71–74] For *S. aureus*, more than 2000 isolates are represented in the MLST database, each with an assigned ST and allelic profile. The database can thus be mined for determining new STs and queried for molecular relationships between new and previously characterized strains.

A program developed by Fiel and Chan called BURST is widely used for analysis of MLST data.[75] An updated version, called eBURST (enhanced version Based Upon Related Sequence Types), is available via the Internet at http://eburst.mlst.net. Within the eBURST algorithm, isolates with the same allelic profile (ST) are considered clones. Isolates that differ at one locus from the ST are termed single-locus variants (SLV). If two loci differ, the isolate is called a double-locus variant (DLV). A clonal complex consists of a single dominant genotype (founder ST) and the related SLVs and DLVs. The strain that differs from the most STs at only one locus is considered the founding genotype of that clonal complex. The most parsimonious patterns of descent of all isolates in each clonal complex from the predicted founder are then displayed as a radial diagram, with the founder ST at the center of the diagram. Lines extend from the founder to the SLVs and from the SLVs to the DLVs, until a network of the relationships is created. The larger the number of isolates with a given ST, the larger the circle depicting the ST. Unlike with other analysis methods in which each isolate is compared to all the others, isolates that are distantly related by MLST are separated on an eBURST diagram with no joining lines, as the relationships between such strains are really unknown. eBURST diagrams can become very complicated when STs are similarly linked to multiple clonal complexes. As with other strain typing analyses, it must be kept in mind

a. Housekeeping genes for *S. aureus* MLST

Gene	Sequence Length bp	No. of Alleles	No. of Polymorphic Sites
arcC	456	17	19
aroE	456	17	23
glpF	465	11	14
gmk	429	11	13
pta	474	15	18
tpi	402	14	18
yqiL	516	16	19

b. Example alleles for *gmk*

| Allele | \multicolumn{13}{c}{Nucleotide base number in *gmk* gene with polymorphism} |

Allele	20	27	124	130	285	286	318	331	357	358	373	390	402
1	G	A	C	A	G	C	A	C	T	G	A	G	T
2	•	•	T	•	•	T	T	•	•	•	•	A	C
3	•	•	T	•	•	T	T	A	•	•	•	A	C
4	•	•	T	•	•	T	T	•	C	A	•	•	•
5	•	•	•	•	A	T	T	•	C	•	•	A	C
6	•	•	T	•	•	T	T	•	•	•	•	A	•
7	•	•	•	•	A	T	T	•	C	•	C	A	C
8	•	G	T	•	•	T	T	•	C	A	•	•	•
9	•	•	•	G	•	•	•	•	•	•	•	•	•
10	•	G	T	•	•	T	•	•	C	A	•	•	•
11	A	•	T	•	•	T	T	•	•	•	•	A	C

c. Example sequence types based on alleleic profiles

ST	*arcD*	*aroE*	*glpF*	*gmk*	*pta*	*tpi*	*yqiL*
1	1	1	1	1	1	1	1
2	1	1	1	8	1	1	1
3	1	1	1	9	1	1	12
4	3	1	1	8	8	8	1
5	1	4	1	4	12	1	10
6	12	4	1	4	12	1	3
7	5	4	1	4	4	6	3
8	3	3	1	1	4	4	3
9	3	3	1	1	1	1	10
10	3	3	1	2	1	1	10

Figure 9-10 Example MLST data for *S. aureus*. a. Housekeeping genes used for *S. aureus* MLST showing the number of sites in each gene with polymorphisms and the total number of alleles determined in this analysis. b. Example sequencing results for *gmk*. The original sequence is shown for allele 1. Polymorphic sites were found between nucleotide 20 and 402. A period indicates agreement with the sequence for allele 1. *For gmk* 11 alleles are derived from 13 nucleotide base sites with polymorphisms. c. Ten unique STs are characterized by the allele number determined at each locus. Adapted from Enright et al. Multilocus sequence typing for characterization of methicillin-resistant and methicillin-susceptible clones of *Staphylococcus aureus. J Clin Microbiol* 2000;38:1008–1015.

that eBURST diagrams are based on mathematical models. A quote from the Web site is instructive: "eBURST does not tell you the truth—it simply produces a hypothesis about the way each clonal complex may have emerged and diversified—and any additional phenotypic, genotypic, or epidemiological data that are available should be used to explore the plausibility of the proposed ancestry and patterns of descent."

Multilocus Restriction Fragment Typing

Diep et al.[76] have described a method for *S. aureus* typing called multilocus restriction fragment typing (MLRFT), based on the theory behind MLST. In this method, sequence variations in the same housekeeping genes used for MLST are detected by restriction fragment analysis (as opposed to sequencing). PCR is performed on the MLST-defined housekeeping genes, but the amplicons obtained are directly cut (without a purification step) by up to two restriction endonucleases, then analyzed by banding pattern after gel electrophoresis. Restriction alleles are assigned based on banding patterns expected from primary MLST banked sequences. It is predicted that MLRFT might have the ability to detect 95% of the diversity made available by MLST.

Compared to MLST, MLRFT is less expensive, is more time efficient, and requires less specialized equipment. It may, therefore, be more suitable for use in the routine clinical setting and in the developing world. In addition, because MLRFT is based on the same genes used for MLST, its results can be linked to the MLST Internet database. MLRFT has high discriminatory power and is believed to be portable between laboratories, because it is based on primary sequence data, with specific restriction endonuclease sites. Like MLST, it tends to detect slow changes in the genome and is unable to make fine strain distinctions, so its use in local outbreaks has been questioned.[56] Despite these potential limitations, MLRFT has been used in combination with PFGE and MLST in local molecular epidemiological investigations.[76,77]

Sequence Analysis of a Single Locus

Some organisms may be typed by sequencing of a single gene locus. The choice of the locus depends on knowledge of the variability of specific genes within a species. The variable nature of virulence elements makes the genes encoding these determinants attractive sequencing candidates.

Examples of genes used for strain typing include the *emm* gene of *S. pyogenes*, the coagulase (*coa*) and protein A (*spa*) genes of *S. aureus*, and the surface-layer protein A gene (*slpA*) of *C. difficile*.[55,78–81] Data analysis is specific for each method, as the genes and the proteins they encode are unique for each species. For strain delineation of *C. difficile* by *slpA* typing, for example, nucleotide sequencing is performed and the amino acid sequence is deduced from the sequence data. New strain types are then defined as those that differ by 20 amino acids or more.[82] When *emm* typing is performed, new sequence types are defined as those with less than 92% sequence identity within the first 90 amino acids.[66]

The number of repeats of a polymorphic 24-bp tandem repeat region within *spa* may vary between strains, which serves as the basis for *spa* typing (**Figure 9-11**).[80] A tandem repeat is a short region of DNA that is duplicated and inserted next to the original copy. Between 3 and 18 repeats have been detected in *spa*; thus *spa* typing may be referred to as a variable-number tandem repeat method (VNTR).[81] Additional diversity arises from point mutations

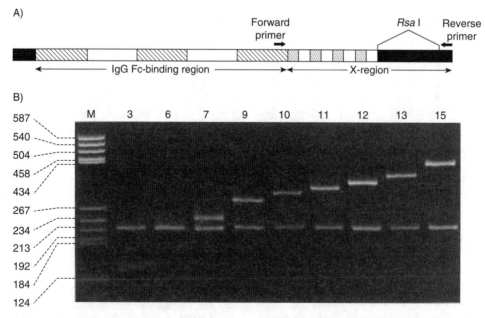

Figure 9-11 Physical map of protein. A) Primer binding sites and RsaI cleavage sites within the X-region are shown. B) After PCR, DNA is cleaved with RsaI and separated by agarose gel electrophoresis. Each strain has a 214 bp band consistent with the region between the RsaI site and the reverse primer. The size of the band generated from amplification of the region between the forward primer and RsaI site increases with additional 24-bp repeats. The number of repeats is shown above the lane. Frenay H, et al. Discrimination of epidemic and nonepidemic methicillin-resistant *Staphylococcus aureus* strains on the basis of protein A gene polymorphism. *J Clin Microbiol.* 1994; 32:846–847, Figure 1. Reproduced with permission of the American Society for Microbiology.

that may lead to amino acid substitutions within the repeat units. Increased discriminatory power is achieved by combining the number of tandem repeats with the nucleotide or amino acid sequence. *Spa* typing has been widely applied to the study of *S. aureus* strain relatedness, including in the setting of outbreaks, hospital-based epidemiology, and the regional prevalence of strain types.[80,81,83,84] Although standardization of interpretation of results in the literature had been lacking, at least one website (http://www.spaserver.ridom.de/) has been created to homogenize *spa* nomenclature and analysis; more recent publications utilize this scheme.[85]

Like other protocols based on DNA sequencing analysis, single-locus sequencing methods are desirable because they yield discrete data that are not subject to interpretation. Because they are based on only a single locus, they are generally rapidly performed. Their discriminatory power varies depending on the locus and species evaluated. Strain relatedness as analyzed by *spa* typing is generally similar to PFGE.[81,83,84] When single-locus sequencing methods display less discriminatory power than other methods such as PFGE or MLVA, they can be a useful screening tool for rapid evaluation of a potential outbreak.[86] Of note, *dru* typing, which assesses a direct repeat region within the chromosomal cassette that encodes methicillin resistance in staphylococci, increases discriminatory power among MRSA, which are typically highly clonal.[87]

Multilocus Variable-Number Tandem Repeat Analysis

MLVA was developed in an effort to create a strain typing technique that realizes the advantages of sequence-based methods (i.e., reproducible, objective results that can be shared electronically), yet achieves a discriminatory power for outbreak analysis similar to that provided by PFGE. Additional goals were to generate a method that can be performed rapidly and has applicability across many species, especially agents of bioterrorism and pathogens that are not easily cultivated. The MLVA genotype is based on the number of repeats of each of several different tandem repeat loci (VNTRs) within the genome of a particular species and is not dependent on the actual sequence of these regions.

Bacterial virulence genes—in particular, surface proteins—may be encoded by VNTR elements. Alterations in the number and/or sequence of the repeats contribute to antigenic diversity, allowing organisms to evade the immune response. Some VNTRs are found in noncoding, intergenic regions, whereas other useful VNTRs are located within open reading frames. To develop a MLVA assay, the VNTRs of the species under evaluation must be

selected. A number of programs for finding tandem repeats have been developed and can be accessed via the Internet.[88,89] Once a tandem repeat region is identified, the amount of polymorphism (i.e., the number of different alleles and allele frequency) within that region must be ascertained either experimentally or in silico from published genome sequences. The combination of VNTR loci most useful as part of a particular MLVA typing scheme is then determined through the evaluation of a well-defined collection of strains. Depending on the purpose of the evaluation, VNTRs of low- or high-level polymorphism will be most relevant.[90,91] Furthermore, the number of VNTR elements included in MLVA typing schemes is not standardized and will depend on the variability of the regions chosen for a given species and the epidemiologic application. For example, an initial panel with 6–8 VNTRs may be modified to include more elements if greater discriminatory power is needed.[18]

A database of tandem repeats identified from genome sequencing projects is available[92] (http://minisatellites.u-psud.fr/); this Web site is also a resource for identifying useful PCR primers and seeking assistance with the selection of tandem repeats based on sequence comparison of loci between isolates. To facilitate epidemiological investigations, results from previously published studies may also be queried for ongoing comparison to newly evaluated strains. While electronic data sharing for MLVA is not as standardized or as advanced as that for MLST, common sets of VNTRs for some species are becoming defined as electronic resources are utilized.

The first step in MLVA analysis is PCR amplification of the tandem repeat region. The size of the PCR product is determined by agarose gel or capillary electrophoresis. The number of repeats is inferred from the size of the PCR product by subtracting the combined length of the PCR primers and any other non-tandem repeat nucleotides included in the amplicon from the total size of the PCR product. This number is then divided by the number of base pairs in the repeat. PCR analysis may be conducted either for each tandem repeat locus separately or simultaneously within a multiplex PCR reaction for several loci. Fluorescent labeling of multiplex PCR products can improve the data output by clearly distinguishing products of similar sizes. The MLVA genotype consists of a set of numbers, where each number represents the number of repeats at each VNTR locus. Alternatively, results may be presented as the size of the PCR amplicon in base pairs (**Figure 9-12**).[91]

The number of loci at which isolates differ, independent of the number of repeats within a locus, is used to make comparisons. Interpretation of results

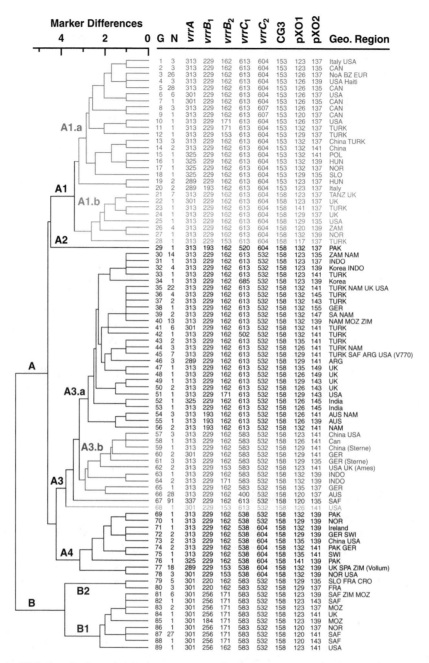

Figure 9-12 Example MLVA data for *B. anthracis*. G, genotype number; N, number of isolates with that genotype. PCR product size (bp) for each of 8 tandem repeat loci are shown. Dendrogram based on UPGMA cluster analysis. Genetic distance is presented as the absolute number of differences in marker alleles among genotypes. Keim P, et al. Multiple-locus variable-number tandem repeat analysis reveals genetic relationships within *Bacillus anthracis*. *J Bacteriol* 2000; 182:2928–2936, Figure 2. Reproduced with permission from American Society for Microbiology.

will depend on the type of epidemiologic analysis, the species, and the chosen VNTRs. Well-characterized outbreak isolates and those known to be unrelated must be used to develop relevant interpretation. Relationships may be diagramed as dendrograms usually using either UPGMA or neighbor–joining clustering methods (Figure 9-12).[18,90,93]

Protocols for MLVA have been published for agents of bioterrorism, organisms that are difficult to grow in culture, and organisms that cause nosocomial and foodborne outbreaks.[90,91,93–96] Reviews describing development of protocols are available.[18,97] MLVA typically has discriminatory power as good as or better than that of PFGE.[93,95] An adaptation of MLVA for typing of *M. tuberculosis* termed mycobacterial interspersed repetitive units (MIRU) has been widely adopted. Analysis of *M. tuberculosis* collections demonstrated MIRU to have discriminatory power superior to IS6110 RFLP, depending on the tandem repeat elements incorporated in the assay.[90,94] MIRU is a more rapid, nonsubjective method that is used as one of two preliminary typing methods for strain delineation of *M. tuberculosis*; it has replaced the labor-intensive IS6110 RFLP method as a typing tool for the U.S. National Tuberculosis Genotyping and Surveillance Network.

Spoligotyping

Spoligotyping (spacer oligotyping) is another method for strain typing of the *M. tuberculosis* complex (MTBC). This method is based on analysis of clustered, regularly interspaced short palindromic repeats (CRISPRs). Repeats are separated by unique spacers similar in size to the CRISPR. In the MTBC, this region is termed the DR locus. Conserved 36-bp repeats are separated by 43 spacer regions of 34–41 bp. Heterogeneity is introduced through recombination and insertion of IS elements. To perform spoligotyping analysis, the DR region of isolates is amplified by PCR. The PCR amplicon is hybridized to a membrane that is spotted with oligonucleotides representing the spacer regions. Strains are then differentiated based on the spacer regions to which they hybridize. Hybridization at each spacer is used to generate a digitized code for strain comparison.

Although less discriminatory than IS6110, spoligotyping is a useful screening method and provides results for strains with six or fewer bands by IS6110.[98] Spoligotyping is also an attractive method because it can be used to speciate mycobacteria within the MTBC.

NEW METHODOLOGIES

Several technologies that may have utility as strain typing methods are emerging. Raman spectroscopy and mass spectrometry are tools of analytical chemistry that are finding new applications in strain typing. Optical mapping, born from large-scale sequencing projects, is able to generate a whole-genome restriction map for a bacterium, fungus, or virus without DNA sequencing. How well these methods work to delineate strains and in which settings they may provide useful data are currently under exploration.

Raman Spectroscopy

The application of Raman spectroscopy to strain typing is a fairly recent development, but one considered to hold significant promise. This method generates a spectral fingerprint determined from the total biomass of an isolate and does not require prior knowledge of nucleic acid sequence characteristics. Laser light from the instrument interacts with molecular vibrations that are inherent in the electron cloud and bonds in the sample, resulting in excitation of molecules. Upon relaxation, a photon is emitted. The difference in energy of this photon is measured by the spectrophotometer. Minimal sample preparation is required and spectra are stored electronically, allowing strain relationships to be compared and represented graphically in a dendrogram format.[18] Comparative analyses are limited with this technology, but its discriminatory power has been shown to be similar to that of PFGE.[99,100]

The major advantages of Raman spectroscopy are that the data are rapidly generated and that test performance requires minimal technical skill. Throughput is so simple and easy that, if desired, every isolate generated in a clinical laboratory could be fingerprinted with real-time impact on hospital infection prevention practices.[99] The most significant drawback to this method is the cost of the instrumentation, which is several times greater than that for PFGE—a factor that might limit the usefulness of this method to larger academic centers and public health laboratories.

Optical Mapping

Optical mapping provides a whole-genome restriction map without the need for actually sequencing the organism. As with PFGE, DNA is first extracted in gel inserts. Using a microfluidics device, single DNA molecules representing the entire genome are aligned in parallel arrays and mounted on derivatized glass surfaces. The DNA is digested with a restriction endonuclease to generate adherent fragments, which are then each stained with a fluorochrome for visualization by fluorescence microscopy. The molecular size of each restriction fragment (kb) is inferred from fluorescence intensity. The order of the fragments in the genome is maintained owing to their immobilization on the glass and constitutes a single molecule map.

Next, fluorescence data for each molecule are converted to digital data. The data from the overlapping, single-molecule maps are then assembled by the software to generate a consensus optical restriction map for individual organisms. The restriction maps of two or more isolates are stored electronically and compared for differences in insertions, deletions, and rearrangements. The percentage difference between isolates may be calculated and visualized in dendrogram format, as with the results produced by other techniques.[101]

At this writing the use of optical mapping as a strain typing system is limited, but analyses of pathogenic *E. coli* and enterococcus demonstrate the robustness of the method.[102–104] Currently, the instrumentation for optical mapping is very expensive, but is available through OpGen Inc. (Gaithersburg, Maryland). Alternatively, customers may buy fairly inexpensive software, submit isolates to OpGen for analysis on a fee-for-service basis, and analyze the data provided by the company themselves.

Mass Spectrometry

Mass spectrometry (MS), a technology used to analyze proteins or DNA, has revolutionized the approach to microbial identification in clinical laboratories. This sea change has been made possible by advances in technology, such as matrix-assisted laser desorption ionization time-of-flight mass spectroscopy (MALDI-TOF MS). This adaption of MS enables the analysis of whole bacterial cells with minimal sample preparation and the analysis of proteins via soft ionization techniques.[105] A brief description of this technology adapted from the work by Emonent and colleagues follows.[105]

Colonies of the isolate to be identified are spread across the well of a conductive metallic plate. The specimen is then covered with a matrix (solution of acidic molecules). Next, the plate is placed in the instrument, where laser pulses hit the mixture. The small desorbed and deionized molecules are accelerated through an electrostatic field and drift through a "tunnel" until they contact the mass spectrometer's detector. Molecules of different masses and charges "fly" at different speeds ("time of flight"). A spectral signature, generally with a mass-to-charge ratio (*m/z*) in the range of 1000–20,000 is generated; this spectral signal is compared to others in the product database for genus or species assignment of the organism.[105]

Two commercial platforms—the MALDI Biotyper (Bruker Daltonics, Billerica, Massachusetts) and the Vitek MS (bioMerieux, Inc., Durham, North Carolina)—have expanded databases of MS results, and both target ribosomal proteins.[105] As mentioned earlier, both systems currently require culture of the isolate to be identified prior to the protein analysis. Species-level identification is based upon unique *m/z*

values observed in the MS fingerprint spectrum; discrimination at the strain level is defined by the relative abundance of shared *m/z* values among strains within a species.

Hundreds of manuscripts have been published dealing with the performance of these two systems for microbial identification, although fewer manuscripts have reported on their ability to perform strain typing for epidemiology studies (although theoretically this is possible).[106–109] Schlebusch et al. used MALDI-TOF MS for microbial typing of MRSA in a neonatal intensive care unit in Australia and found results comparable to a reference method that included SNP plus binary gene analysis.[106] Other researchers have investigated this technology's use for strain characterization of *Neisseria meningitidis*,[109] *Pantoea* species,[108] *Streptococcus pyogenes*,[107] and *Mycobacterium* species.[110] It is anticipated that as laboratories become more familiar with these platforms, their use in strain typing will be evaluated more fully.

Another use of MS is in the analysis of nucleic acids. Polymerase chain reaction–electrospray ionization mass spectroscopy (PCR/ESI-MS [Abbott Laboratories, Abbott Park, Illinois]) is a novel technology with broad applicability. In contrast to MALDI-TOF, it can be applied directly to clinical specimens, as well as to characterization of cultivated pathogens.

The PCR/ESI-MS works by a fundamentally unique principle. Briefly, for each genus of microbe, a set of PCR primers is designed that amplifies key regions of the microbial genome. Multiple PCR reactions are carried out in a microtiter plate for analysis of each sample, and some of the wells contain more than one primer pair. Following PCR, the microtiter plate is placed on the MS instrument (PLEX-ID) and a fully automated electrospray ionization mass spectrometry (PCR/ESI-MS) analysis is performed. The mass spectrometer is an analytical tool that effectively weighs the amplicons, or mixture of amplicons, with sufficient mass accuracy that the composition of A, G, C, and T can be deduced for each amplicon in the PCR reaction. Thus the mass spectrometer provides a great deal of information when analyzing PCR products, analogous to a microarray or parallel DNA sequencing instrument. However, in contrast to the latter methods, the mass spectrometer analyzes each PCR reaction in less than 1 minute, uses no consumable products, and can analyze more than 1400 PCR reactions in 24 hours in a completely automated (hands-off) fashion.[105,111]

The mass spectrometer weighs the PCR products, and the base compositions present are subsequently calculated. These base compositions provide the information needed to determine the species, the strain type, and the presence or absence of virulence factors or antibiotic resistance-determining factors and their mutational states. It is also possible to analyze the data in MLST databases (http://www.mlst.net/) and identify primer target sites where a small set of carefully selected primers provide sufficient resolving power to distinguish 99% of all the sequence types in the database. Such MLST-type analysis using Plex-ID enables rapid and high-resolution strain genotyping. This information can be used to establish clonality and to match a patient sample with a known strain.[112]

Numerous publications have described the use of PCR/ESI-MS technology for strain characterization of *S. aureus*, *Acinetobacter* spp., and other pathogens of interest to the hospital epidemiologist.[112,113] These studies have demonstrated comparable performance to PFGE, MLST, *spa* typing and other commercial systems such as the DiversiLab System. The major drawback to this system is the expense associated with both instrument acquisition and maintenance and reagent costs.[114]

CONCLUSION

Molecular strain typing has truly advanced the field of infectious disease epidemiology. Molecular methods are now considered standard components in ongoing infectious disease outbreak investigations and for evaluation of strains within populations. Additionally, strain typing has been used to answer clinical questions such as whether therapy should be altered because of relapse of an infection or if a new strain or resistance gene was acquired. Although strain typing is certainly a valuable tool to the infectious diseases epidemiologist, before it is initiated, epidemiologic investigations should always start with simple questions based on current case findings and microbiology. Controls known to be epidemiologically unrelated to cases should be included in the analysis to ensure adequate discrimination, and the most appropriate strain typing method for the situation should be applied. The method chosen will depend on the epidemiologic question, the species under investigation, and practical issues such as cost, ease of use, equipment availability, and time to results. By definition, different typing methods measure different biological properties, and they sometimes group isolates differently. This inconsistency is to be expected and emphasizes the need for clinical correlation.

The future of strain typing is exciting. Many genome-sequencing projects have already been completed, and others are under way. As detailed DNA sequence information is published, the structure and function of many more genetic elements may be determined. This information will likely prove useful for the rapid assessment of strain differences, which should have even greater impact on intervention and outcomes. The extent to which mass spectrometry, optical mapping, and Raman spectroscopy can be utilized within epidemiology remains to be seen, but these techniques may add to the current toolbox of widely used DNA-based methodologies or perhaps even change the approach to molecular strain typing altogether.

● ● ● **REFERENCES**

1. Pfaller MA. Molecular approaches to diagnosing and managing infectious diseases: practicality and costs. *Emerg Infect Dis.* 2001;7:312–318.

2. Byington CL, Spencer LY, Johnson TA, et al. An epidemiological investigation of a sustained high rate of pediatric parapneumonic empyema: risk factors and microbiological associations. *Clin Infect Dis.* 2002;34:434–440.

3. La Scola B, Fournier P, Musso D, et al. Pseudo-outbreak of listeriosis elucidated by pulsed-field gel electrophoresis. *Eur J Clin Microbiol Infect Dis.* 1997;10:756–760.

4. Michele T, Cronin W, Graham N, et al. Transmission of *Mycobacterium tuberculosis* by a fiberoptic bronchoscope. *JAMA.* 1997;278:1093–1095.

5. Spika J, Waterman S, Soo Hoo G, et al. Chloramphenicol-resistant *Salmonella newport* traced through hamburger to dairy farms. *New Engl J Med.* 1987;316:565–570.

6. Reed KD, Melski JW, Graham MB, et al. The detection of monkeypox in humans in the Western Hemisphere. *N Engl J Med.* 2004;350:342–350.

7. Ksiazek TG, Erdman D, Goldsmith CS, et al. A novel coronavirus associated with severe acute respiratory syndrome. *N Engl J Med.* 2003;348:1953–1966.

8. Drosten C, Gunther S, Preiser W, et al. Identification of a novel coronavirus in patients with severe acute respiratory syndrome. *N Engl J Med*. 2003;348:1967–1976.

9. Sader H, Jones R, Pfaller M. Relapse of catheter-related *Flavobacterium meningosepticum* bacteremia demonstrated by DNA macrorestriction analysis. *Clin Infect Dis*. 1995;21:997–1000.

10. Bishai W, Graham N, Harrington S, et al. Rifampin-resistant tuberculosis in a patient receiving rifabutin prophylaxis. *N Engl J Med*. 1996;334:1573–1576.

11. Zaidi A, Harrell L, Rost J, et al. Assessment of similarity among coagulase-negative staphylococci from sequential blood cultures of neonates and children by pulsed-field gel electrophoresis. *J Infect Dis*. 1996;174:1010–1014.

12. Hartstein A, Valvano M, Morthland V, et al. Antimicrobic susceptibility and plasmid profile analysis as identity tests for multiple blood isolates of coagulase-negative staphylococci. *J Clin Microbiol*. 1987;25:589–593.

13. Tenover F, Arbeit R, Goering R, et al. Interpreting chromosomal DNA restriction patterns produced by pulsed-field gel electrophoresis: criteria for bacterial strain typing. *J Clin Microbiol*. 1995;33:2233–2239.

14. Arbeit R. Laboratory procedures for the epidemiologic analysis of microorganisms. In: Murray P, Jo Baron E, Pfaller M, et al., eds. *Manual of Clinical Microbiology*. 6th edition. Washington, DC: ASM Press; 1995:190–208.

15. Maslow J, Mulligan M, Arbeit R. Molecular epidemiology: application of contemporary techniques to the typing of microorganisms. *Clin Infect Dis*. 1993;17:153–164.

16. Gutacker MM, Smoot JC, Lux Migliaccio CA, et al. Genome-wide analysis of synonymous single nucleotide polymorphisms in *Mycobacterium tuberculosis* complex organisms: resolution of genetic relationships among closely related microbial strains. *Genetics*. 2002;162:1533–1543.

17. Sambrook J, Russel D, eds. *Molecular Cloning: A Laboratory Manual*. 3rd edition. Cold Spring Harbor, NY: Cold Spring Harbor Laboratory Press; 2001.

18. Persing D, ed. in chief. *Molecular Microbiology: Diagnostic Principles and Practice*. 2nd ed. Washington, DC: ASM Press; 2011.

19. Schwartz D, Cantor C. Separation of yeast chromosome-sized DNAs by pulsed field gradient gel electrophoresis. *Cell*. 1984;37:67–75.

20. Gut IG. Automation in genotyping of single nucleotide polymorphisms. *Hum Mutat*. 2001;17:475–492.

21. Pfaller M, Herwaldt L. The clinical microbiology laboratory and infection control: emerging pathogens, antimicrobial resistance, and new technology. *Clin Infect Dis*. 1997;25:858–870.

22. Kreiswirth B, Kornblum J, Arbeit R, et al. Evidence for a clonal origin of methicillin resistance in *Staphylococcus aureus*. *Science*. 1993;259:227–230.

23. Hunter PR, Gaston MA. Numerical index of discriminatory ability of typing systems: an application of Simpson's index of diversity *J Clin Microbiol*. 1988;26:2465–2466.

24. Mayer L. Use of plasmid profiles in epidemiologic surveillance of disease outbreaks and in tracing the transmission of antibiotic resistance. *Clin Microbiol Rev*. 1988;1:228–243.

25. Locksley R, Cohen M, Quinn T, et al. Multiply antibiotic-resistant *Staphylococcus aureus*: introduction, transmission, and evolution of nosocomial infection. *Ann Intern Med*. 1982;97:317–324.

26. Rubens C, Farrar W, McGee Z, et al. Evolution of a plasmid mediating resistance to multiple antimicrobial agents during a prolonged epidemic of nosocomial infections. *J Infect Dis*. 1981;143:170–181.

27. Tenover F, Arbeit R, Goering R. How to select and interpret molecular strain typing methods for epidemiological studies of bacterial infections: a review for healthcare epidemiologists. *Infect Control Hosp Epidemiol*. 1997;18:426–439.

28. Tompkins L, Plorde J, Falkow S. Molecular analysis of R-factors from multiresistant nosocomial isolates. *J Infect Dis.* 1980;141:625–636.

29. Kristjansson M, Samore M, Gerding D, et al. Comparison of restriction endonuclease analysis, ribotyping, and pulsed-field gel electrophoresis for molecular differentiation of *Clostridium difficile* strains. *J Clin Microbiol.* 1994;32:1963–1969.

30. Tenover F, Arbeit R, Archer R, et al. Comparison of traditional and molecular methods of typing isolates of *Staphylococcus aureus. J Clin Microbiol.* 1994;32:407–415.

31. Hinojosa-Ahumada M, Swaminathan B, Hunter S, et al. Restriction fragment length polymorphisms in rRNA operons for subtyping *Shigella sonnei. J Clin Microbiol.* 1991;29:2380–2384.

32. van Soolingen D, Hermans P, de Haas P, et al. Occurrence and stability of insertion sequences in *Mycobacterium tuberculosis* complex strains: evaluation of an insertion sequence-dependent DNA polymorphism as a tool in the epidemiology of tuberculosis. *J Clin Microbiol.* 1991;29:2578–2586.

33. van Soolingen D, DeHaas W, Petra E, et al. Comparison of various repetitive DNA elements as genetic markers for strain differentiation and epidemiology of *Mycobacterium tuberculosis. J Clin Microbiol.* 1993;31:1987–1995.

34. van Embden J, Cave M, Crawford J, et al. Strain identification of *Mycobacterium tuberculosis* by DNA fingerprinting: recommendations for a standardized methodology. *J Clin Microbiol.* 1993;31:406–409.

35. Barman W, Reves R, Hawkes A, et al. DNA fingerprinting with two probes decreases clustering of *Mycobacterium tuberculosis. Am J Respir Crit Care Med.* 1997;155:1140–1146.

36. Small P, Hopewell P, Singh S, et al. The epidemiology of tuberculosis in San Francisco. *New Engl J Med.* 1994;330:1703–1709.

37. Alland D, Kalkut G, Moss A, et al. Transmission of tuberculosis in New York City. *New Engl J Med.* 1994;330:1710–1716.

38. Yang Z, Mtoni I, Chonde M, et al. DNA fingerprinting and phenotyping of *Mycobacterium tuberculosis* isolates from human immunodeficiency virus (HIV)–seropositive and HIV-seronegative patients in Tanzania. *J Clin Microbiol.* 1995;33:1064–1069.

39. Yang Z, de Haas P, van Soolingen D, et al. Restriction fragment length polymorphism of *Mycobacterium tuberculosis* strains isolated from Greenland during 1992: evidence of tuberculosis transmission between Greenland and Denmark. *J Clin Microbiol.* 1994;32:3018–3025.

40. Small P, McClenny N, Singh S, et al. Molecular strain typing of *Mycobacterium tuberculosis* to confirm cross-contamination in the mycobacteriology laboratory and modification of procedures to minimize occurrence of false-positive cultures. *J Clin Microbiol.* 1993;31:1677–1682.

41. Gordillo M, Singh K, Murray B. Comparison of ribotyping and pulsed-field gel electrophoresis for subspecies differentiation of strains of *Enterococcus faecalis. J Clin Microbiol.* 1993;31:1570–1574.

42. Martin I, Tyler S, Tyler K, et al. Evaluation of ribotyping as epidemiologic tool for typing *Escherichia coli* serogroup 0157 isolates. *J Clin Microbiol.* 1996;34:720–723.

43. King D, Rhine-Chalberg J, Pfaller M, et al. Comparison of four DNA-based methods for strain delineation of *Candida lusitaniae. J Clin Microbiol.* 1995;33:1467–1470.

44. Merz W. *Candida albicans* strain delineation. *Clin Microbiol Rev.* 1990;3:321–334.

45. Roman R, Smith J, Walker M, et al. Rapid geographic spread of a methicillin-resistant *Staphylococcus aureus* strain. *Clin Infect Dis.* 1997;25:698–705.

46. Diekema D, Messer S, Hollis R, et al. An outbreak of *Candida parapsilosis* prosthetic valve endocarditis. *Diagn Microbiol Infect Dis.* 1997;29:147–153.

47. Keene W, Sazie E, Kok J, et al. An outbreak of *Escherichia coli* 0157:H7 infections traced to jerky made from deer meat. *JAMA.* 1997;277:1229–1231.

48. Shi Z, Liu P, Lau Y, et al. Epidemiological typing of isolates from an outbreak of infection with multidrug-resistant *Enterobacter cloacae* by repetitive extragenic palindromic unit b1-primed PCR and pulsed-field gel electrophoresis. *J Clin Microbiol.*1996;34:2784–2790.

49. McDougal LK, Steward CD, Killgore GE, et al. Pulsed-field gel electrophoresis typing of oxacillin-resistant *Staphylococcus aureus* isolates from the United States: establishing a national database. *J Clin Microbiol.*2003;41:5113–5120.

50. Ribot EM, Fair MA, Gautom R, et al. Standardization of pulsed-field gel electrophoresis protocols for the subtyping of *Escherichia coli* O157:H7, *Salmonella*, and *Shigella* for PulseNet. *Foodborne Path Dis.*2006;3:59–67.

51. Matushek M, Bonten M, Hayden M. Rapid preparation of bacterial DNA for pulsed-field gel electrophoresis. *J Clin Microbiol.*1996;34:2598–2600.

52. Leonard RB, Carroll KC. Rapid lysis of gram-positive cocci for pulsed-field gel electrophoresis using achromopeptidase. *Diagn Mol Pathol.* 1997;6:288–291.

53. Hartas J, Hibble M, Sriprakash K. Simplification of a locus-specific DNA typing method (Vir typing) for *Streptococcus pyogenes*. *J Clin Microbiol.* 1998;36:1428–1429.

54. Goh S, Byrne S, Zhang J, et al. Molecular typing of *Staphylococcus aureus* on the basis of coagulase gene polymorphisms. *J Clin Microbiol.* 1992;30:1642–1645.

55. Facklam R, Beall B, Efstratio A, et al. *emm* typing and validation of provisional M types for group A streptococci. *Emerg Infect Dis.* 1999;5:247–253.

56. Diep BA, Perdreau-Remington F, Sensabaugh GF. Clonal characterization of *Staphylococcus aureus* by multilocus restriction fragment typing: a rapid screening approach for molecular epidemiology. *J Clin Microbiol.* 2003;41:4559–4564.

57. Versalovic J, Koeuth T, Lupski JR. Distribution of repetitive DNA sequences in eubacteria and application to fingerprinting of bacterial genomes. *Nucleic Acids Res.* 1991;19:6823–6831.

58. Tyler K, Wang G, Tyler S, et al. Factors affecting reliability and reproducibility of amplification-based DNA fingerprinting of representative bacterial pathogens. *J Clin Microbiol.* 1997;35:339–346.

59. Ross TL, Merz WG, Farkosh M, Carroll KC. Comparison of an automated repetitive sequence-based PCR microbial typing system to pulsed-field gel electrophoresis for analysis of outbreaks of methicillin-resistant *Staphylococcus aureus*. *J Clin Microbiol.* 2005;43:5742–5647.

60. Chuang YC, Wang JT, Chen ML, Chen YC. Comparison of an automated repetitive-sequence–based PCR microbial typing system with pulsed-field gel electrophoresis for molecular typing of vancomycin-resistant *Enterococcus faecium*. *J Clin Microbiol.* 2010;48:2897–2901.

61. van Belkum A. DNA fingerprinting of medically important microorganisms by use of PCR. *Clin Microbiol Rev.* 1994;7:174–184.

62. Healy M, Huong, J Bittner T, et al. Microbial DNA typing by automated repetitive-sequence–based PCR. *J Clin Microbiol.* 2005;43:199–207.

63. Welsh J, McClelland M. Fingerprinting genomes using PCR with arbitrary primers. *Nucleic Acids Res.* 1990;18:7213–7218.

64. van Belkum A, Kluytmans J, van Leeuwen W, et al. Multicenter evaluation of arbitrarily primed PCR for typing of *Staphylococcus aureus* strains. *J Clin Microbiol.* 1995;33:1537–1547.

65. Woods C Jr, Versalovic J, Koeuth T, et al. Analysis of relationships among isolates of *Citrobacter diversus* by using DNA fingerprinting generated by repetitive sequence–based primers in the polymerase chain reaction. *J Clin Microbiol.*1992;30:2921–2929.

66. Arbeit R, Arbique J, Beall B, et al. Molecular methods for bacterial strain typing: approved guideline. *Clin Lab Standards Inst.* 2007; 27(10).26-33

67. *BioNumerics Quick Guide v6.5.* Sint-Martens-Latem, Belgium: Applied Mathematics; 2010.

68. Fleishmann RD, Alland D, Eisen JA, et al. Whole-genome comparison of *Mycobacterium tuberculosis* clinical and laboratory strains. *J Bacteriol.* 2002;184:5479–5490.

69. Alland D, Whittmam TS, Murray MB, et al. Modeling bacterial evolution with comparative-genome–based marker systems: application to *Mycobacterium tuberculosis* evolution and pathogenesis. *J Bacteriol.*2003;185:3392–3399.

70. Peacock SJ, de Silva GDI, Justice A, et al. Comparison of multilocus sequence typing and pulsed-field gel electrophoresis as tools for typing *Staphylococcus aureus* isolates in a microepidemiological setting. *J Clin Microbiol.* 2002;40:3764–3770.

71. Enright MC, Robinson DA, Randle G, et al. The evolutionary history of methicillin-resistant *Staphylococcus aureus* (MRSA). *Proc Natl Acad Sci USA.* 2002;99:7687–7692.

72. Monk AB, Curtis S, Paul J, et al. Genetic analysis of *Staphylococcus aureus* from intravenous drug user lesions. *J Med Microbiol.* 2004;53:223–227.

73. Enright MC. The evolution of a resistant pathogen: the case of MRSA. *Curr Opin Pharmacol.* 2003;3:474–479.

74. Enright MC, Day NPJ, Daves CE, et al. Multilocus sequence typing for characterization of methicillin-resistant and methicillin-susceptible clones of *Staphylococcus aureus.* *J Clin Microbiol.* 2000;38:1008–1015.

75. Feil EJ, Li BC, Aanensen DM, et al. eBURST: inferring patterns of evolutionary descent among clusters of related bacterial genotypes from multilocus sequence typing data. *J Bacteriol.* 2004;186:1518–1530.

76. Diep BA, Sensabaugh GF, Somboona NS, et al. Widespread skin and soft-tissue infections due to two methicillin-resistant *Staphylococcus aureus* strains harboring the genes for Panton-Valentine leucocidin. *J Clin Microbiol.* 2004;42:2080–2084.

77. Carleton HA, An Diep B, Charlebois ED, et al. Community-adapted methicillin-resistant *Staphylococcus aureus* (MRSA): population dynamics of an expanding community reservoir of MRSA. *J Infect Dis.* 2004;190: 1730–1738.

78. Karjalainen T, Saumier N, Barc MC, et al. *Clostridium difficile* genotyping based on *slp*A variable region in S-layer gene sequence: an alternative to serotyping *J Clin Microbiol.* 2002;40:2452–2458.

79. Nahvi MD, Fitzgibbon JE, John JF, et al. Sequence analysis of *dru* regions from methicillin-resistant *Staphylococcus aureus* and coagulase negative staphylococcal isolates. *Microbial Drug Resist.* 2001;7:1–12.

80. Frénay HM, Theelen JP, Schouls LM, et al. Discrimination of epidemic and nonepidemic methicillin-resistant *Staphylococcus aureus* strains on the basis of protein A gene polymorphism. *J Clin Microbiol.* 1994;32: 846–847.

81. Walker J, Borrow R, Edwards-Jones V, et al. Epidemiological characterization of methicillin-resistant *Staphylococcus aureus* isolated in the north west of England by protein A (*spa*) and coagulase (*coa*) gene polymorphisms. *Epidemiol Infect.* 1998;21:517–514.

82. Kato H, Kato H, Ito Y, et al. Typing of *Clostridium difficile* isolates endemic in Japan by sequencing of *slp*A and its application to direct typing. *J Med Microbiol.* 2010;59: 556–562.

83. Harmsen D, Claus H, Witte W, et al. Typing of methicillin-resistant *Staphylococcus aureus* in a university hospital setting by using novel software for *spa* repeat determination and database management. J. *Clin Microbiol.* 2003;41:5442–5448.

84. Koreen L, Ramaswamay S, Graviss E, et al. *spa* typing method for discriminating among *Staphylococcus aureus* isolates: implications for use of a single marker to detect genetic micro- and macrovariation. *J Clin Microbiol.* 2004;42:792–799.

85. Babouee B, Frei R, Schultheiss E, et al. Comparison of the DiversiLab repetitive element PCR system with *spa* typing and pulsed-field gel electrophoresis for clonal characterization of methicillin-resistant *Staphylococcus aureus. J Clin Microbiol* 2011;49:1549–1555.

86. Killgore G, Thompson A, Johnson S, et al. Comparison of seven techniques for typing international epidemic strains of *Clostridium difficile*: restriction endonuclease analysis, pulsed-field gel electrophoresis, PCR-ribotyping, multilocus sequence typing, multilocus variable-number tandem-repeat analysis, amplified fragment length polymorphism, and surface layer protein A gene sequence typing. *J Clin Microbiol.* 2008;46:431–437.

87. Goering RV, Morrison D, Al-Doori Z, et al. Usefulness of *mec*-associated direct repeat unit (*dru*) typing in the epidemiological analysis of highly clonal methicillin-resistant *Staphylococcus aureus* in Scotland. *Clin Microbiol Infect.* 2008;14:964–969.

88. Benson G. Tandem repeats finder: a program to analyze DNA sequences. *Nucleic Acids Res.* 1999;27:573–580.

89. Merkel A, Gemmell N. Detecting short tandem repeats from genome data: opening the software black box. *Brief Bioinformatics.* 2008;9:355–366.

90. Supply P, Lesjean S, Savine E, et al. Automated high-throughput genotyping for study of global epidemiology of *Mycobacterium tuberculosis* based on mycobacterial interspersed repetitive units. *J. Clin. Microbiol.* 2001;39:3563–3571.

91. Keim P, Price LB, Klevytska AM, et al. Multiple-locus variable-number tandem repeat analysis reveals genetic relationships within *Bacillus anthracis. J Bacteriol.* 2000;182: 2928–2936.

92. Denoeud F, Vergnaud G. Identification of polymorphic tandem repeats by direct comparison of genome sequence from different bacterial strains: a web-based resource. *BMC Bioinformatics.* 2004;5:4.

93. Noller AC, McEllistrem MC, Pacheco A, et al. Multilocus variable-number tandem repeat analysis distinguishes outbreak and sporadic *Escherichia coli* O157:H7 isolates. *J Clin Microbiol.* 2003;41:5389–5397.

94. Sun YJ, Lee AS, Ng S, et al. Characterization of ancestral *Mycobacterium tuberculosis* by multiple genetic markers and proposal of genotyping strategy. *J Clin Microbiol.* 2004;42:5058–5064.

95. Sabat A, Krzyszton-Russjan J, Strzalka W, et al. New method for typing *Staphylococcus aureus* strains: multiple-locus variable number tandem repeat analysis of polymorphism and genetic relationships of clinical isolates. *J Clin Microbiol.* 2003;41:1801–1804.

96. Kimura M, Sakamuri RM, Groathouse NA. Rapid variable-number tandem-repeat genotyping for *Mycobacterium leprae* clinical specimens. *J Clin Microbiol.* 2009;47:1757–1766.

97. Lindstedt B. Multiple-locus variable number tandem repeats analysis for genetic fingerprinting of pathogenic bacteria. *Electrophoresis.* 2005;26:2567–2582.

98. Goyal M, Saunders NA, van Embden JD, et al. Differentiation of *Mycobacterium tuberculosis* isolates by spoligotyping and IS6110 restriction fragment length polymorphism. *J Clin Microbiol.* 1997;35:647–651.

99. Willemse-Erix DF, Scholtes-Timmerman, MJ, Jachtenberg JW, et al. Optical fingerprinting in bacterial epidemiology: Raman spectroscopy: a real-time typing method. *J Clin Microbiol.* 2009;47:652–649.

100. Willemse-Erix H, Jachtenberg J, Barutci H, et al. Proof of principle for successful characterization of methicillin-resistant coagulase-negative staphylococci isolated from skin by use of Raman spectroscopy and pulsed-field gel electrophoresis. *J Clin Microbiol.* 2010;48:736–740.

101. Zhou S, Kile A, Bechner M, et al. Single-molecule approach to bacterial genomic comparisons via optical mapping. *J Bacteriol.* 2004;186:7773–7782.

102. Schwan WR, Briska A, Stahl B, et al. Use of optical mapping to sort uropathogenic *Escherichia coli* strains into distinct subgroups. *Microbiology.* 2010;156:2124–2135.

103. Kotewicz ML, Jackson SA, LeClerc JE, Cebula TA. Optical maps distinguish individual strains of *Escherichia coli* O157:H7. *Microbiology.* 2007;153:1720–1733.

104. Johnson PD, Ballard SA, Grabsch EA, et al. A sustained hospital outbreak of vancomycin-resistant *Enterococcus faecium* bacteremia due to emergence of vanB *E. faecium* sequence type 203. *J Infect Dis.* 2010;202:1278–1286.

105. Emonent S, Shah HN, Cherkaoui A, Schrenzel J. Application and use of various mass spectrometry methods in clinical microbiology. *Clin Microbiol Infect.* 2010;16:1601–1613.

106. Schlebusch S, Price GR, Hinds S, et al. First outbreak of PVL-positive nonmultiresistant MRSA in a neonatal ICU in Australia: comparison of MALDI-TOF and SNP-plus-binary gene typing. *Eur J Clin Microbiol Infect Dis.* 2010;29:1311–1314.

107. Moura H, Woolfitt AR, Carvalho MG, et al. MALDI-TOF mass spectrometry as a tool for differentiation of invasive and non-invasive *Streptococcus pyogenes* isolates. *FEMS Immunol Med Microbiol.* 2008;53:333–342.

108. Rezzonico F, Vogel G, Duffy B, Tonolla M. Application of whole-cell matrix-assisted laser desorption ionization-time of flight mass spectrometry for rapid identification and clustering analysis of *Pantoea* species. *Appl Environ Microbiol.* 2010;76:4497–4509.

109. Lowe CA, Diggle MA, Clarke SC. A single nucleotide polymorphism assay for the genotypic characterization of *Neisseria meningitidis* using MALDI-TOF mass spectrometry. *Br J Biomed Sci.* 2004;61:8–10.

110. Hettick JM, Kashon ML, Slaven JE, et al. Discrimination of intact mycobacteria at the strain level: a combined MALDI-TOF MS and biostatistical analysis. *Proteomics.* 2006;6:6416–6425.

111. Ecker DJ, Sampath R, Massire C, et al. Ibis T5000: a universal biosensor approach for microbiology. *Nat Rev Microbiol.* 2008;6:553–558.

112. Hall TA, Sampath R, Blyn LB, et al. Rapid molecular genotyping and clonal complex assignment of *S. aureus* isolates by PCR/ESI-MS. *J Clin Microbiol.* 2009;47:1733–1741.

113. Wolk DM, Blyn LB, Hall TA, et al. Pathogen profiling: rapid molecular characterization of *Staphylococcus aureus* by PCR/ESI-MS and correlation with phenotype. *J Clin Microbiol.* 2009;47:3129–3137.

114. Whitman TJ, Qasba SS, Timpone JG, et al. Occupational transmission of *Acinetobacter baumannii* from a United States serviceman wounded in Iraq to a healthcare worker. *Clin Infect Dis.* 2008;47:439–443.

CHAPTER

10

The Immune System and Host Defense Against Infections

Joseph B. Margolick, Richard B. Markham, and Alan L. Scott

INTRODUCTION

The human immune system comprises a diverse array of cells found throughout the human body (**Box 10-1**) that protect it against the pathogenic effects of infectious organisms that may enter and threaten the body. The goal of this chapter is to describe (at a level appropriate for a non-immunologist) how this protection is provided. Astonishing insights into immunity have been realized in the last few decades, more than can be covered in an introductory overview chapter. Additional information is provided in feature boxes scattered throughout this chapter, along with referrals to other sources for those who may want to learn more detail. The last 30 years have been an exciting and challenging time for both immunology and infectious disease epidemiology. In this chapter, you will encounter the best of both worlds.

Research on immune functions uses many experimental methods, both in vivo and in vitro. In many cases, immunogenic cells perform the same functions in tissue culture, where they are relatively easy to measure, as they do in the body. Because these functions are generally similar across the immune systems of humans and of other animals, inferences from animal models of disease often have direct applicability to human host defense and immune function. Moreover, the advent of modern molecular microbiology and recombinant DNA methods has made it possible to isolate and characterize many of the molecules produced by immune cells that regulate and/or mediate the functions of the immune system, and also to gain insight into the functions of these molecules in animal models by inserting or deleting ("knocking out") the genes that code for these molecules. These studies have revealed a complex and dynamic interaction between cells of the immune system and pathogens.

The immune system is traditionally considered to have three defining characteristics. First, it can discriminate between self and non-self—that is, what is normally present in the host and what is not. Second, it remembers what it has encountered (memory). Memory allows the immune system to react more quickly and effectively to a stimulus it has encountered previously. Third, it responds only to the pathogen that is at hand (specificity). In this chapter, we also explain how the immune system attains these characteristics.

Two distinct but interrelated arms of the immune system—one general and one highly specific—have evolved for the recognition of pathogens and foreign molecules. Both arms involve a complex of cell surface receptors and soluble molecules that work in concert to identify a pathogen through unique aspects of its molecular makeup, and tag it for elimination.

Box 10-1	Cells of the Immune System

Cells of the immune system include lymphocytes, mononuclear phagocytes, and dendritic cells. These cells are derived from bone marrow precursors that circulate throughout the body in the bloodstream and populate the lymphoid organs, where they mature as described later in this chapter.

In the peripheral blood, approximately one-fourth of the white blood cells are lymphocytes and approximately one-twentieth are monocytes, the circulating form of mononuclear phagocytes. Less than 1% are dendritic cells. At any given time, only 2% of lymphocytes are found in the peripheral blood. The rest are present in the lymphoid tissues such as lymph nodes and collections of lymphoid aggregates that are found below mucosal surfaces in the body, such as gut-associated lymphoid tissue (GALT).

The first arm is designed to work within minutes after a pathogen establishes residency in the vertebrate host. It utilizes receptors that are constitutively expressed on mononuclear and polymorphonuclear phagocytic cells and on "killer" cells that recognize pathogen-associated molecular patterns (PAMPs). These receptors provide a general signal that certain types of microorganisms are present, and they initiate cellular mechanisms that can clear the foreign pathogen from the body. This ready-to-use capacity to rapidly recognize pathogens is referred to as the **innate** immune response. The term "innate" refers to the fact that these responses do not require time to develop but rather are ready to go at any time. The main cell types involved in innate immunity are macrophages, dendritic cells, and natural killer (NK) cells (**Box 10-2** and **Box 10-3**). Epithelial cells also play a role in the innate immune response.

Most encounters with microorganisms and toxins are not obvious to the person who experiences them because the innate immune response is able to eliminate the threat of infection. However, in those situations where cells and molecules of the innate immune response fail to control and eliminate a pathogenic organism, the role of the innate response shifts to one of initiating, modulating, and mediating the second, highly specific arm of the vertebrate defense system—the **adaptive** immune response. The term "adaptive" refers to the fact that these responses take time to develop and are modified over this time to best respond to the specific infection. The cells that regulate and carry out most of the major effector functions of the adaptive immune response are lymphocytes called T cells and B cells. These lymphocytes express cell surface antigen-specific receptors

that confer the inducibility and specificity that are the hallmarks of the adaptive immune response. In addition, after clearing the pathogen, the cells of the adaptive immune response develop a long-lived "memory" of the exposure that can be quickly mobilized upon re-exposure to the same antigens.

In the following review, we explore the cells and molecules that play key roles in the functions of both the innate and adaptive immune responses. The main cells involved in adaptive immunity are lymphocytes and macrophages (see Box 10-3).

Pathogens that reside inside cells pose a special challenge to the immune system, because they are not directly accessible to detection. However, cells containing pathogens are themselves altered at the cell surface, and these changes can be recognized by both the innate and the adaptive immune systems. As mentioned earlier, the innate immune system can recognize molecular patterns present on the pathogen itself. It can also recognize patterns on the surface of infected cells, which may be genetically altered as a result of being infected. For example, infection of a cell may cause a normal surface molecule to be expressed at abnormally high or low levels. This is yet another example of how innate immunity does not depend on the identity of the infecting pathogen. (Innate immunity is also triggered by non-infectious processes that affect the integrity of cells, such as heat injury, radiation, toxic exposures, or, in some cases, neoplastic transformation.)

Box 10-2   Macrophages and Dendritic Cells

Mononuclear phagocytes circulate in the peripheral blood as monocytes, and migrate into tissues where they become macrophages. Their functions are to ingest and eliminate infectious agents, process and present antigens, and regulate the functions of other immune cells, both innate and adaptive.

In tissues, dendritic cells have a characteristic shape with many long cytoplasmic processes (dendrites). They travel through the peripheral blood to tissues, where they persist in an immature form. When stimulated to mature by infection or injury, they become avid inducers of innate immunity. The mature cells also migrate to lymphoid organs carrying antigens bound to their cell surface, and function as potent antigen-presenting cells. Uniquely, these cells can induce a primary immune response. They also affect the cytokine secretion pattern of the antigen-activated T cells.

Box 10-3   Types and Names of Lymphocytes

Three types of lymphocytes are found in the peripheral blood: T cells, B cells, and natural killer (NK) cells. These cells are morphologically indistinguishable by conventional microscopic techniques, although NK cells are often a bit larger and have more granules in their cytoplasm than either T or B cells.

T and B cells are named after the organs that are necessary for their maturation. T cells mature in the thymus, a gland located underneath the breastbone or sternum, in mammals and rodents. B cells received their name from the bursa of Fabricius, an organ found in birds that is essential for B-cell maturation. Humans do not have this organ, so B cells mature in the bone marrow in humans. NK cells are described in Box 10-8.

Lymphocyte biology is a relatively new field (at least relative to the ages of the authors). Only in 1960 was it discovered (by Peter Nowell) that resting lymphocytes could be triggered to become activated, and only in 1964 was it discovered (by John Gowans) that lymphocytes recirculated in the body from blood to lymph and back to blood, even though recirculation of red cells had been demonstrated in 1628 by William Harvey.

The first step in the immune response to a pathogen is the recognition of the pathogen. It has long been known that the immune system can distinguish self from non-self or foreign antigens. How this was accomplished remained a fascinating mystery for many years, but the essential mechanisms have now been clarified, in work that resulted in at least seven Nobel Prizes.

RECOGNITION OF PATHOGENS

What does the immune system actually recognize, or react to? Substances that can trigger an immune response are called **antigens**. More specifically, the receptors on cells of the immune response recognize small sub-regions on each antigen, termed **epitopes** or **antigenic determinants**. A single antigen molecule can have many epitopes that can be recognized by different receptors. Epitopes can be made up of amino acids, sugars, lipids, or nucleotides. In adaptive immunity, lymphocyte receptors recognize highly unique epitopes on pathogen-derived antigens. Those antigens that are recognized during this response are not normally present in the body, because they are derived from particular molecules present in bacteria, viruses, parasites, or other organisms. In contrast, the receptors used in the innate immune response recognize pathogen-derived antigens that are not species-specific, but rather are representative of a class of microorganism, such as virus, bacteria, fungi, or parasite.

In recent years, much work has been directed at defining the precise chemical nature of antigens, including which characteristics an antigen must have to elicit an effective immune response. This work has been motivated by very practical concerns, such as the need to develop vaccines and understand immune responses to dangerous organisms.

Antigen Recognition in Adaptive Immunity: T and B Cells

The cells that are responsible for specific recognition of foreign antigens (i.e., adaptive immunity) are B and T lymphocytes (see Box 10-3). These cells have surface proteins that bind to (recognize) antigens with high specificity and affinity: each particular surface protein can bind effectively to one and only one antigen. These surface recognition proteins are called **antigen receptors**, and it is the precision of these receptors (they will bind to only one epitope out of all possible epitopes) that is responsible for the amazing specificity of the immune system. (**Box 10-4**). For T cells, the epitope is usually a small peptide; for

Box 10-4	Specificity of Antibodies

For many years, the specificity of antibodies produced by immunizing experimental animals has been exploited to identify substances in experiments and in clinical medicine. This has been particularly true since the development of methods for making monoclonal antibodies to any desired antigen. Monoclonal antibodies are derived from a single B cell and, therefore, cannot be contaminated by antibodies with other specificities.

B cells, it is frequently more than a small peptide that is recognized. When the antigen receptor binds its antigen, the B or T cell becomes activated and the immune response is initiated.

Both B and T cells can recognize any antigen that might possibly be encountered, including synthetic antigens that do not exist in nature. How such a vast array of receptors could exist was a puzzle to immunologists during the many years when it was believed that each unique antibody molecule was encoded by its own gene, because there is not enough DNA in the entire body to code for one gene for each possible antibody. The key to this diversity was determined first for B cells (**Figure 10-1**), and subsequently shown to apply to T cells (**Figure 10-2**) as well. One section of the receptor protein consists of relatively constant amino acid sequences that are shared by many receptors and coded for by a small number of genes. The second section is a highly variable part of the receptor

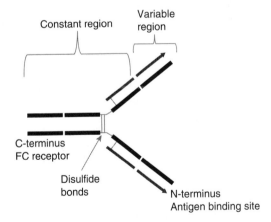

Figure 10-1 Schematic drawing of an antibody. The antibody molecule is composed of light (short) and long (heavy) chains. The N-terminus region contains the complimentarity defining regions which are highly variable giving the antibody the potential to bind to a nearly infinite number of foreign antigens. Near the C-terminus the constant region contains the FC receptor which is recognized by host immune cells and initiates further host responses against the antigen.

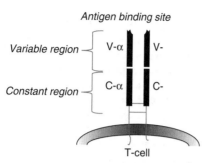

Figure 10-2 Schematic drawing of a T-cell receptor (TCR). The complimentarity defining region (CDR) is highly variable and is joined to the constant regions which are held to the cell surface by a long cytoplasmic tail. The variable region recognizes antigens in conjunction with host MHC.

that recognizes the vast diversity of antigens which is created by allowing rearrangement of gene segments to generate a huge number of permutations (**Box 10-5**). The genes coding for the constant and variable segments are assembled within a given B or T cell into a single DNA sequence that codes for the final receptor molecule that will be expressed by that cell (see **Box 10-7** for a more detailed description of this process).

Although generated by similar mechanisms, B- and T-cell antigen receptors work in different ways. The B-cell receptor recognizes antigens in their native form—that is, as they exist in nature. As a consequence, the antigen does not need to be manipulated

in any way, and the B cell can recognize the antigen by itself. This is true whether the B-cell receptor, which is an antibody molecule, is attached to the surface membrane of the B cell, or has been secreted from the cell and is free of the B cell entirely.

The T-cell antigen receptor differs from the B cell antigen receptor in two ways. First, it cannot recognize native antigens. Instead, it recognizes only antigens that have been broken down into short, epitope-sized peptide fragments. This process, which is referred to as **antigen processing**, can occur within the cytoplasm of many types of cells, called **antigen-presenting cells**. The processed antigen is then carried to the surface of the antigen-presenting cell by **major histocompatibility (MHC) proteins**. (**Box 10-6**) This leads to the second major difference between B- and T-cell recognition of antigens: the T-cell receptor binds not only to the processed peptide, but also to the carrier (MHC) protein on the surface of the antigen-presenting cell. This process of re-expressing the processed antigen on the surface of the antigen-presenting cell is called **antigen presentation**. In other words, the T-cell antigen receptor, even though it is specific for one peptide, is also specific for one MHC protein, and T-cells recognize an antigen only if it is bound to the correct MHC protein. (**Figure 10-3**). For this reason, antigen recognition by T cells is said to be **MHC-restricted**, and antigen-presenting cells and T cells must be **histocompatible** for T-cell activation to occur. Because of MHC-restriction, one person's T cells will not recognize any

Box 10-5	Generation of Receptor Diversity

The receptors for both T and B cells have a number of functional domains or regions. A large proportion of both of these receptors have common functions, such as anchoring the receptor to the cell membrane and binding to a number of accessory proteins both at the cell surface (to stabilize cell–cell interactions) and in the cytoplasm (where they act as a binding point for the proteins that participate in the transduction of signals from the cell membrane to the nucleus that result in cell activation and differentiation). These regions of the receptors are, therefore, termed constant regions.

Both T- and B-cell receptors have a domain that is specifically responsible for binding to a small portion of an antigen (i.e., an epitope). Some aspects of these receptors are illustrated in Figures 10-1, 10-2, and 10-3. This antigen-binding site is unique for each different B-cell receptor (i.e., antibody) or T-cell receptor and is the source of antigen specificity for a B cell or a T cell, respectively. This part of the receptor is, therefore, called the variable region.

The vast number of unique specificities used by the receptors of the adaptive immune response are generated by a random combinatorial mechanism that is independent of antigens. T-cell and B-cell receptors are composed of multiple protein chains. (See Figures 10-1, 10-2, and 10-3.) Each chain is encoded by a number of gene segments that are spliced together at the DNA level within a given T or B cell to form a complete gene for a specific receptor. A large number of germline gene segments encode the domains responsible for antigen recognition. These segments are assembled in a random fashion that, along with random insertions and deletions of nucleotides at splicing junctions, determines the final amino acid sequence of this variable region of the receptor protein, which in turn determines the antigen specificity of each receptor chain. Following molecular events that assemble the genes for the variable region of the receptor with those for the constant regions, the multiple protein chains are manufactured by the cell and joined to make the mature receptor. The interactions among the variable regions of these multichain molecules then determine the fine specificity of each receptor.

Current estimates of the number of different T-cell and B-cell receptors that are generated by the random use of multiple germline variable genes, imprecise joining of gene segments, and random use of different chains generated approach 10^{18}! This vast array of receptor molecules accounts for the astounding ability of the immune system to recognize any possible antigen.

Box 10-6   **General Function of MHC Proteins**

MHC proteins are part of a general protein-trafficking system within the cell. Intracellular proteins are continually being broken down into small peptides, and those peptides are taken up by MHC proteins within the cell and carried to the cell's surface. If a peptide being carried by the MHC protein is derived from a normal cellular protein, it does not elicit an immune response from T cells. Conversely, if the peptide is derived from a pathogen (or other foreign substance), T cells that recognize it (along with the MHC protein) are triggered and an immune response is initiated. Moreover, if a T cell were to encounter an MHC molecule from a different individual carrying a peptide from that individual, the foreign MHC–peptide combination would also be recognized, triggering an immune response. This latter circumstance arises when tissues from an individual of one MHC type are transplanted into an individual with another MHC type. Thus, when a T cell engages the MHC–peptide complex, it will initiate an immune response if either the peptide or the MHC molecule is derived from a "foreign" source.

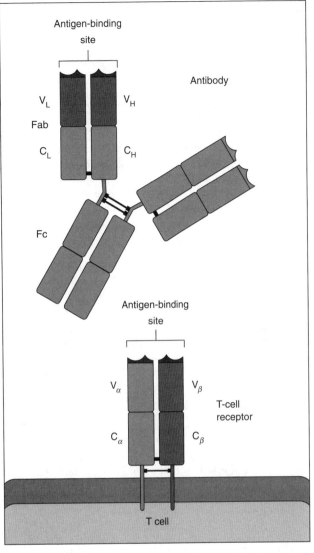

Figure 10-3 Diagrammatic representation of the structural similarity between the B-cell receptor (antibody molecule) and the T-cell receptor. Both have large constant regions and smaller variable regions, with the antibody-binding sites in the variable regions. Both are composed of disulfide-linked protein chains, called heavy and light for the B-cell receptor and chains for the T-cell receptor, which also have variable and constant regions.

antigens unless they are presented by that person's own antigen-presenting cells (or antigen-presenting cells from another person who happens to have some of the same particular MHC proteins). In summary, T-cell responses require the processing and presentation of antigens by an antigen-presenting cell to a histocompatible T cell.

MHC proteins are highly variable from person to person, and, in fact, are among the most variable proteins known (Box 10-7). It is this enormous variability from person to person that allows the immune system to distinguish self from non-self—that is, to differentiate between one's own cells and antigens and someone else's. Two broad classes of MHC molecules exist: Class I molecules, which are expressed on all nucleated cells in the body, and Class II molecules, which are primarily expressed by cells of the immune system (monocytes/macrophages, dendritic cells, B cells, and activated T cells). In humans, MHC proteins are also called human leukocyte antigens (HLA), and we refer to a person's "HLA type." MHC Class I proteins are the primary antigens responsible for graft rejection and must be expressed by a target cell for this cell to be killed by an antigen-specific CD8 T cell.[1] MHC Class II must be the same on the antigen-presenting cell and the CD4 T cells for the latter to be triggered.[2] In fact, all of the cells listed previously as expressing Class II MHC molecules are important antigen-presenting cells, even B cells. Of note, activated B cells can use their antigen-specific surface receptor to facilitate antigen uptake as the first step in antigen processing. For this reason, B cells can process antigens that are present in very

low concentrations, and they are important cells for presentation of antigens to T cells during mature immune responses.[3] However, B cells specific for a given antigen are much less numerous than other antigen-presenting cells, which explains why the non-specific antigen-presenting cells are essential.

Because they vary so widely among individuals, the MHC proteins from different people will interact differently with the foreign proteins or peptides encountered by those individuals. Most of the antigens

---

Box 10-7	Diversity of MHC Proteins

In humans, more than 2100 distinct MHC allele sequences have been described. Human Class I MHC proteins include HLA-A, HLA-B, and HLA-C proteins, which have 319, 609, and 161 known variants, respectively. Class II MHC proteins include HLA-DR, HLA-DQ, and HLA-DP; these have 406, 72, and 120 known variants, respectively. The number of distinct protein molecules that can be generated is not precisely known, but is certainly very large.

MHC proteins contain indentations or clefts that can accommodate small peptides (9–15 amino acids long). The characteristics of the amino acids surrounding the MHC cleft determine the peptide that can become bound in the cleft and, therefore, is presented to T cells.

Box 10-8	History of Natural Killer Cells

NK cells were discovered to be the cells responsible for the background killing that was detectable when peripheral blood cells were tested for cytotoxicity against various target cells. Researchers found that there was usually some level of cytotoxicity in such assays that did not depend on the presence of antigen in the assay, did not require priming of the cells, and was not mediated by the cytotoxic lymphocytes that were known at the time (i.e., the cytotoxic T cells). The cytotoxic cells turned out to be large granular lymphocytes. They were named natural killer (NK) cells because they did not need to be induced (primed) by in vitro treatments of the cells.

---

associated with pathogens are complex molecules that can be degraded by antigen-processing cells into many different peptides. Among individuals with different MHC proteins (i.e., different HLA types), therefore, different peptides may bind most efficiently to a given individual's repertoire of MHC proteins. For example, if a protein contains epitopes A and B, and individuals X and Y have different HLA types, then only epitope A may be presented by antigen-presenting cells in individual X and only epitope B may be presented by the corresponding cells in individual Y. Some individuals may have an MHC type that will not bind either of these epitopes; these individuals will not recognize this protein at all. This point means that immunizing a human population against a T-cell epitope (i.e., eliciting a cellular immune response at a population level) is much more difficult than eliciting a B-cell response, because B cells recognize native antigens, which are the same for everybody. Given the huge diversity of MHC proteins in the human population, development of vaccines that will induce general T-cell immunity represents an extremely formidable challenge. It is not a coincidence that almost all successful vaccines generated to date have depended largely on B-cell responses (i.e., antibodies) rather than T-cell responses.

Antigen Recognition in Innate Immunity

A third type of lymphocyte, termed natural killer (NK) cells, plays a key role in triggering innate immunity (**Box 10-8**).

The mechanism by which NK cells are triggered to kill has only recently been elucidated. Although they do not have antigen receptors, NK cells have surface receptors that inhibit their killing function. These inhibitory receptors, termed killer inhibitory receptors (KIRs), recognize abnormal levels of MHC

Class I molecules on all other nucleated cells in the body. Thus, if the target cell expresses MHC Class I to a normal degree, the NK cell is not triggered and the target cell is not killed. Conversely, downregulation of MHC Class I molecule expression (which is common in some virally-infected cells and some tumor cells) removes the inhibition of the NK cell, so that the target cell is killed.

This mechanism appears to be an important component of host defense against certain viral infections.[4,5] Many viruses interfere with expression of MHC molecules by the host cell (possibly as a means of evading cytotoxic CD8[+] T-cells, which require MHC Class I molecules to be expressed on the target cell, as discussed previously). Thus, NK cells help prevent the virus from getting away with this trick. This mechanism elegantly explains the function of NK cells.

After this understanding was reached, in somewhat of a surprise, stimulatory NK receptors were discovered by researchers. The function of NK cells is regulated by the balance of signals coming from the KIR and the stimulatory receptors. It has been hypothesized that stimulatory receptors on NK cells may be important in situations in which MHC proteins are over-expressed, which is uncommon in infectious diseases but may occur in neoplastic or pre-neoplastic conditions.

Macrophages and dendritic cells have been described in Box 10-2. How do they recognize antigens? In contrast to the specific recognition of particular antigens by T-cells, as described previously, macrophages and dendritic cells recognize molecules common to multiple pathogens, or structures derived from such antigens. For this reason, antigen receptors on these cells are referred to as pattern recognition receptors (**Box 10-9**).[6]

Examples of molecules that are recognized by their pattern are certain carbohydrates and lipopolysaccharides, including endotoxins. Another example is nonmethylated GpC motifs in bacterial DNA; these motifs are not present in mammalian DNA. These patterns are recognized by a family of receptors called toll-like receptors, so named because they resemble a type of receptor found in fruit flies called a toll receptor.[8,9]

AFTER ANTIGEN BINDING: IMMUNE ACTIVATION

Lymphocytes in the blood are generally in a **resting** state, which means the cell is structurally and functionally quiescent or inactive. Both B and T lymphocytes have the morphology one would expect of such cells (**Box 10-10**). When a lymphocyte encounters the antigen it is programmed to recognize (through its antigen-receptor), however, the cell becomes transformed into an activated cell. Activated cells can make important immune regulatory and effector molecules and can also proliferate, or multiply, by mitosis. Thus the resting state in which most lymphocytes are found in the peripheral blood is just a temporary phase, at least potentially. NK cells also circulate in a resting state, albeit with slightly more cytoplasm and pre-existing effector molecules than B or T cells.

The fact that immune cells generally exist in the resting state, along with the specificity of T- and B-cell receptors, allows the immune system to deploy its weapons only when and where they are needed. As discussed further in this section, the immune system includes powerful responses that can cause great damage to the host if not carefully controlled. Thus activation must be limited to those cells needed to neutralize a particular threat, and activation should be turned off as soon as possible after the threat has been removed or neutralized.

| Box 10-10 | Morphology of Lymphocytes |

Resting cells are characterized by condensed nuclear chromatin (i.e., nuclear DNA that is coiled and inaccessible to genetic machinery of the cell) and a minimal amount of cytoplasm (where cellular products such as antibodies and cytokines are made). In contrast, in activated cells, the nuclear DNA is dispersed and available for transcription into RNA, and the cytoplasm is more abundant and contains more organelles.

Activation of Adaptive Immunity

Both T- and B-cell receptors are anchored in the cell membrane, and are associated with adjacent molecules that cross through the cell membrane into the cytoplasm of the cell. When the antigen receptor binds its antigen, these associated molecules are altered in such a way that intracellular enzymes are activated to cause the lymphocyte to begin to carry out its programmed functions.

The ability of an *extracellular* antigen to cause activation of *intracellular* processes requires a signal to cross the cell membrane, a process called **signal transduction**. (Latin scholars will understand the reason for this name.) Signal transduction is not as simple as just binding the antigen to the receptor; factors such as the affinity of the antigen for the receptor are important, and in most cases an additional signal besides the antigen receptor-induced signal is required for the cell to become fully activated (referred to as **costimulation**). The second signal is not antigen-specific but can be mediated by binding of molecules on the antigen-presenting cell to other molecules on the surface of the lymphocyte.[7] The sequence of biochemical events in lymphocyte signal transduction has been extensively researched, and reviews can be found in textbooks of immunology, such as those listed at the end of this chapter.

The B and T cells that have been activated undergo cell division and begin to proliferate, giving rise to a clonal expansion of just those cells that are specific to the immune stimulus. This process of **clonal selection** is one of the most important mechanisms by which a careful control is maintained over immune reactions.

Activation of Innate Immunity

Activation of phagocytic cells through their pattern recognition receptors, or of NK cells through their activation and inhibitory receptors, occurs via a cascade of receptor-linked biochemical events similar to that which activates T cells through the T-cell receptor.

DEALING WITH THE PATHOGEN: IMMUNE EFFECTOR MECHANISMS

Once a foreign antigen enters the body, innate immunity serves as the first line of defense and an important regulation step in the development of the humoral and cellular arms of the adaptive immune response. There is an important time element to these responses. Several days are required for the full development of protective immunity in a naive host, because a very low number of antigen-specific T cells exist and these must be activated, clonally expanded, and converted from naive cells into activated effector cells and, eventually, into memory cells. One of the functions of the innate response is to provide a defense mechanism that will blunt the capacity of the pathogen to expand during the lag period between infection and the development of a mature adaptive immune response.

Broadly speaking, the effector functions of adaptive immunity include antibody production, activation and arming of immune cells capable of directly or indirectly killing microorganisms, killing of appropriate organisms and cells (such as cells infected with a virus), generation of delayed-type hypersensitivity responses, and regulation (induction and suppression) of these functions. Each of these aspects of adaptive immunity is carried out by specific subsets of cells, under the regulation of specific cytokines.

In innate immunity, NK cells and macrophages become activated, and in adaptive immunity T and B cells become activated, through their receptors. All of these processes are regulated by a complex tapestry of interconnecting cellular activations and production of hormone-like proteins (termed **cytokines; Box 10-11**) by the activated cells, which act on the same or other cells. Another way in which the actions of cytokines are controlled is through the regulation of expression of **cytokine receptors** (i.e.,

the proteins to which cytokines bind on target cells). These receptors are responsible for transduction of regulatory signals across cell membranes.

In other words, immune effector mechanisms, like immune activation, are stringently regulated by tight control of (1) the amount and type of cytokines that are produced, (2) the level of expression of cytokine receptors on cells of the immune response, (3) the different types of cells concerned, whose numbers can expand or contract by up to several orders of magnitude in just a few days, and (4) immunoglobulin proteins (termed **antibodies**) that can recognize and bind to the offending antigens. Cytokines are antigen-independent; that is, their structure and function do not depend on the antigen that elicits their production. More than 100 cytokines have been identified to date, and that number continues to grow. Some of the most important cytokines are described here.

Many cytokines have been given the name "interleukin," because they facilitate interactions between white blood cells (*leuko* = "white"). For example, interleukin-2 (IL-2) is a cytokine that promotes proliferation and growth of activated T cells, as well as other functions such as activation of cytotoxic T cells and natural killer cells to become more cytotoxic. Other related terms include "lymphokine" to describe cytokines made by lymphocytes, and "monokine" to refer to those cytokines made by mononuclear phagocytes.

Box 10-11	Cytokines

Cytokines are small proteins that function like hormones, except that as a general rule they do not circulate in the blood in meaningful quantities, but rather act over a distance of a few cell diameters. In other words, they act on cells adjacent, or in close proximity, to the secreting cell (this is called *paracrine* regulation, as distinguished from *endocrine* regulation, which implies circulation in the blood and action on distant cells). An example of paracrine function would be secretion by activated T-helper cells of cytokines that help nearby B cells differentiate into antibody-secreting cells, or cytokines that activate macrophages or killer T cells to become much more potent at killing microorganisms. In some cases, cytokines act on the secreting cell itself, which is called *autocrine* regulation. An example of autocrine regulation is the secretion by activated T-helper cells of cytokines that allow the activated T cells to proliferate and expand clonally.

The first cytokine was described in 1970, an event that was followed by the description of many immune functions (and other functions) that were mediated by possible cytokines. A major stumbling block to researchers in these early studies was the fact that cytokines are generally not present in the blood and, in fact, are extremely potent molecules with tiny physiological concentrations. Their relative rarity made biochemical purification and isolation of these molecules terribly difficult from a technical perspective, and greatly hampered the working out of cytokine networks. It was only with the advent of molecular biology, genetic cloning, and recombinant DNA methods that cytokines could be studied efficiently, because now genes for cytokines could be isolated and large quantities of pure proteins (i.e., uncontaminated by small amounts of other cytokines) could be generated. Such work ultimately allowed the identities, modes of action, and functional properties of unique cytokines to be defined.

The interleukin nomenclature is much more practical than naming proteins for their function. The latter is untenable because cytokines have many functions. For example, a cytokine that stimulated growth of B cells and one that stimulated metabolic activity of hepatocytes both turned out to have the same amino acid sequence as interleukin-6 (IL-6). In another case, a cytokine that killed certain tumor cells (tumor necrosis factor [TNF]) and a factor that caused wasting (cachectin) turned out to be identical proteins, and the name TNF won out.

Adaptive Immune Effector Mechanisms

Almost all T-cells belong to one of two major subsets. The first is helper T-cells, which induce or permit functions of other immune cells. These cells express a protein called CD4 (**Box 10-12**) on their cell surface, and, therefore, are called CD4 (or CD4+) lymphocytes. CD4 lymphocytes produce cytokines that increase the ability of macrophages to kill ingested organisms,[8] cause B cells to differentiate into antibody-producing cells,[9] activate other helper T-cells to expand clonally as mentioned previously, and increase the ability of cytotoxic T cells and NK cells to kill target cells. The other major subset of T cells is suppressor/cytotoxic T-cells, which generally inhibit other cells or kill them; they express a surface protein called CD8.[10] Adaptive immune mechanisms differ for extracellular versus intracellular pathogens.

Box 10-12	CD Nomenclature

The letters "CD" stand for "cluster designation" and are used to denote proteins recognized by sets or clusters of monoclonal antibodies. CD numbers have been assigned through CD363 based on data presented at several international workshops. CD4 was the fourth protein to be assigned a CD number.

Extracellular Immune Effector Mechanisms

Protection against free-living extracellular organisms is provided mainly by antibodies and phagocytic cells. As mentioned earlier, the production of antibodies is mediated by B cells. When B cells become activated, they begin rearranging the genes that code for antibodies, and the cells begin to differentiate into cells that are actually tiny antibody factories, called plasma cells. Plasma cells are produced in the secondary lymphoid tissues (e.g., lymph nodes, spleen, Peyer's patches) and eventually migrate to the bone marrow to secrete antibodies.

The antibodies produced by plasma cells are secreted proteins, although they are structurally similar to, and have the same antigen specificity as, the antibody molecules that are present in the membrane of the progenitor B cell. The function of antibodies is to bind to whole antigens, in their native forms, as mentioned previously. Antibodies are thus well designed to protect the host against extracellular antigens, such as bacteria that can grow outside cells. In many cases, these bacteria can grow quite rapidly, so it is important for the host defense to be able to mount a vigorous immune response as quickly as possible.

The main host defense against bacterial infection comprises ingestion of bacteria by white blood cells known as neutrophils. This process of ingestion (termed **phagocytosis**) is vastly more efficient if the bacteria have been coated with antibodies, because neutrophils have receptors on their cell surfaces that recognize the constant portion of the antibody molecule. The phenomenon of coating of bacteria by antibodies to facilitate phagocytosis is called **opsonization**. Other host proteins also facilitate phagocytosis and lysis of extracellular pathogens. For example, complement is a series of proteins that bind to microorganisms and to one another. The result is a cascade of reactions that generates membrane-bound proteins on the microorganism that can be recognized by phagocytic cells through complement receptors. (Complement proteins are not as efficient as antibodies in facilitating phagocytosis.) Antibodies can also directly interfere with replication of pathogens, binding of obligate intracellular pathogens to their target cells, and binding of toxins to their target molecules.

Antibodies are categorized into one of five classes: immunoglobulins M, D, G, A, and E. Antibodies in the various classes have different chemical structures, localization in the body, and functions. As might be expected given these distinctions, antibodies serve different roles in the host defense against infections, as described later in the sections on mucosal immunity and B-cell immune deficiency.

Intracellular Immune Effector Mechanisms

MHC Class I proteins, which are produced inside the cell and then move to the cell surface, carry with them peptides that are being produced inside the cell. If the cell has been infected by a virus and viral proteins are being produced, peptides derived from these viral proteins will be carried to the cell surface in this way. There, the MHC I–viral peptide complex can be recognized ("seen," in immunological parlance) by virus-specific CD8+ T cells that come in contact with the infected cell. These cells, in turn, will be activated by the interaction between the MHC Class I–viral peptide complex and the specific T-cell receptors, and the T-cells will kill the infected cell (**Box 10-13**). Because antigen processing and presentation outpace viral production after the virus enters a cell, the infected cell can be recognized and killed even before a new virus is produced or expressed on the cell surface. This factor is key to controlling the viral infection. The same pathway also explains why MHC Class I molecules are expressed on all (nucleated) cells in the body: it allows the immune system to "see" the internal state of all cells, a process termed **immune surveillance**.

In contrast to this "intracellular" pathway of antigen processing, Class II MHC molecules become

---

Box 10-13	T-Cell Killing Mechanisms

Two mechanisms by which T cells kill cells are known:

- In the first, a T-cell product, perforin, binds to the target cell membrane and causes pores to form in it. A second T-cell product, granzyme, facilitates this process and also induces programmed cell death in the target cell. (Programmed cell death is a mechanism by which cells can self-destruct.)

- In the second mechanism, T cell molecules termed Fas-ligand bind to Fas proteins on the target cell, again inducing programmed cell death.

Which mechanism kills the target cell is influenced by many factors, including the nature of the infection in the cell.[15]

---

loaded with peptides from antigens ingested from outside the cell, referred to as the "extracellular pathway." This factor explains why Class II MHC is expressed primarily by antigen-presenting cells, as mentioned earlier.

Killing of microorganisms occurs by several mechanisms. Cytotoxic T cells kill cells expressing microbial antigens. For example, activated cytotoxic T cells make proteins that function to kill target cells and organisms. Macrophages kill microorganisms they have ingested, but do so poorly if not activated by cytokines, of which the most important is interferon-gamma (IFNγ). In addition, a T-cell product called granulolysin can inhibit growth of both intracellular and extracellular microorganisms.[11] (This is an example of how the immune system tends to defy generalizations: it is not always true that antibodies protect against extracellular infections and cellular immunity protects against intracellular infections.)

During the course of a viral infection, CD8+ T cells may be activated in very large numbers. Because of their activated morphology, they look very different from the usual circulating lymphocyte, which, as has been mentioned, is a resting cell. For example, in acute infection with Epstein-Barr virus, so many of these "atypical lymphocytes" are present in the blood that this disease has been called infectious mononucleosis. Other viruses can cause this disease, too, and for the same reason—the florid activation of virus-specific T cells, primarily CD8+.

Innate Immune Cell Effector Mechanisms

NK cells become much more effective killers when exposed to certain cytokines[12,13] and can be stimulated to differentiate into lymphokine-activated killer cells after exposure to IL-2.[14,19] The cytotoxic mechanism of NK cells is similar to that by which cytotoxic

T cells kill—namely, perforin/granzyme- and Fas/Fas ligand-mediated induction of programmed cell death (apoptosis) of the target cells.[15,20] NK cells also play an immunoregulatory role through the production of cytokines—especially interferon, which enhances the immune response against viruses and other intracellular pathogens by activating macrophages.

Other effector mechanisms also contribute to innate immunity. Neutrophils and macrophages can ingest microorganisms, especially those that have been coated with antibody. (Because antibody is produced by the adaptive immune system, this is an example of co-operation of innate and adaptive immunity.) Antibody molecules can also bind to antibody receptors on the surface of killer cells (such as NK cells); this binding involves the constant end of the antibody molecule, so that the antigen receptor is free and can bind to antigen. The resulting antibody–effector cell unit can then recognize and kill a target cell, a process known as **antibody-dependent cellular cytotoxicity (ADCC)**. Finally, a series of serum proteins called **complement proteins** can bind to microorganisms and other target cells, either killing the cells outright (by forming large pores in their outer membranes) or rendering them susceptible to phagocytosis.

CYTOKINES OF THE INNATE AND ADAPTIVE IMMUNE SYSTEMS

Up to this point we have described innate and adaptive immunity separately. This separation is convenient conceptually, but substantial overlap in these systems is actually observed in the body, and this is certainly true for the cytokines involved in these aspects of immunity. In this section, we describe the most important cytokines in each system, but also point out how these cytokines overlap in function between innate and adaptive immunity.

Cytokines have several important characteristics. They are produced in tiny amounts, are short-lived, and generally act locally rather than systemically. They are synthesized only briefly after cell stimulation, due to transient gene expression and unstable RNA. Cytokines exert many activities, and many cytokines share the same activities (i.e., the cytokine network is redundant). Cytokines typically act via binding to very-high-affinity receptors, although some cytokines have intermediate- or low-affinity receptors that become activated only when very high concentrations of cytokine are present. Cytokine receptors sometimes can bind more than one cytokine, and also sometimes share component structures.

Among the many actions of cytokines on target cells are activation; stimulation of proliferation; production of other proteins, including other cytokines, cytokine receptors, or antibodies; production of one class of antibody rather than another; differentiation; and death. These processes may be either stimulated or inhibited depending on the combination and concentration of cytokines produced. Approximately 60 major (and many minor) cytokines have primary influence on the innate and adaptive immune response. Some of these cytokines, and some of their actions, are mentioned here.

Cytokines of the Innate Response

Cells of the innate immune system that produce cytokines include macrophages, NK cells, epithelial cells, endothelial cells (cells that form the blood vessel wall), dendritic cells, platelets, mast cells, and fibroblasts.

Tumor Necrosis Factor

Tumor necrosis factor (TNF) is produced primarily by macrophages in response to lipopolysaccharides of gram-negative bacteria, but also by T cells and NK cells. TNF receptors are expressed on most cell types, and binding of TNF to these receptors can lead to either cell activation or cell death (death occurs by activating cellular enzymes that cause the cell to degrade itself, a process known as apoptosis or programmed cell death). TNF recruits monocytes and neutrophils to sites of infection, where it then activates them to kill pathogens and to secrete other molecules that attract anti-inflammatory cells. Release of TNF causes fever; this cytokine is one of the most important mediators of septic shock, an often-fatal condition characterized by hypotension and intravascular coagulation. TNF also activates lipoprotein lipase in adipocytes, and for this reason chronic production of TNF can result in wasting (cachexia). Drugs that inhibit TNF have been reported to reduce tissue damage in inflammatory diseases such as rheumatoid arthritis but can increase susceptibility to tuberculosis, thus demonstrating the importance of TNF in host defense against this infection.[16]

Interleukin-1

Like TNF, IL-1 is produced by macrophages in response to microbial products, activates innate immune responses, induces fever, and causes cachexia. Unlike TNF, IL-1 is also produced by epithelial and endothelial cells, and does not induce programmed cell death. This interleukin helps to activate T cells. IL-1 release is stimulated by TNF. IL-1 exists in two forms, α and β, that stimulate the IL-1 receptor; a third form of IL-1 inhibits this receptor. The IL-1 receptor is present on T cells, fibroblasts, and epithelial and endothelial cells.

Interleukin-6

IL-6 is also produced by macrophages, but also by fibroblasts and endothelial cells. Production is enhanced by IL-1 and TNF. Receptors for IL-6 are present on activated B cells and hepatocytes, and IL-6 serves as a growth and differentiation factor for B cells and as a potent stimulator of production of acute-phase reactants by the liver.

Interleukin-12

IL-12 is produced by macrophages and dendritic cells stimulated by lipopolysaccharide, viral infections, and intracellular pathogens. This cytokine's production is also stimulated by interferon-α from NK cells and T cells. IL-12 is a major stimulator of the cell-mediated adaptive immune response and, therefore, is critical for the control of intracellular pathogens. This effect appears to be mediated through stimulation of production of interferon-gamma (IFN-γ) by NK cells and T cells, which in turn activates the cytotoxic function of macrophages. IL-12 is considered one of the main cytokines that directs the adaptive cellular immune response as opposed to the humoral response. The IL-12 receptor is present on NK and T cells exposed to IFN-γ and dendritic cells exposed to IL-15. Deficiency of this receptor has been associated with exacerbation of mycobacterial infections.[17]

Type I Interferons: Interferon-alpha and Interferon-beta

Early on in the study of immune responses to virus infection, researchers came to appreciate that certain secreted factors interfered with viral replication in previously uninfected cells. These factors were termed "interferons." Two classes of anti-viral, or type I, interferons exist: IFN-α, which is actually a family of approximately 20 closely related proteins all encoded on separate genes, and IFN-β, which is encoded by a single gene. IFN-β is the main secreted type I interferon.

While type I interferons are produced by a broad spectrum of cell types in response to nearly all virus species, some cells are specialized for their synthesis. For example, plasmacytoid dendritic cells can produce as much as 1000 times more type I interferon than other cells.

Type I interferons are an essential component of the innate immune response to virus challenge because they hold viral replication in check long enough that a specific and robust T-cell–mediated adaptive immune response can be generated to eliminate the virus from the body. Type I interferons use three main mechanisms to control virus replication and dissemination. First, they induce resistance in uninfected cells by activating mechanisms that result in the destruction of viral RNA and blocking of the production of viral proteins. Second, they activate NK cells, which are effective in detecting and killing virally-infected cells. Third, they induce the expression of Class I MHC molecules on the surface of infected cells, thereby rendering the infected cells more susceptible to killing by virus-specific cytotoxic CD8 T cells.

Chemokines

Chemokines are small proteins secreted by a variety of cells—not just immune cells—to attract or recruit immune cells to the site of an infection or inflammatory response. Lymphocytes and other immune cells respond to chemokines through the expression of chemokine receptors on their cell surface. (Chemokine receptors have become famous as the second receptors to which human immunodeficiency virus binds to enter cells.) Chemokines can be secreted into the extravascular tissues. They then diffuse into the bloodstream, where they activate endothelial cells so that intravascular cells such as lymphocytes, monocytes, and neutrophils are given a signal telling them to exit the blood where the endothelial cells are activated.

Interleukin-10

We have taken the dramatic step of listing this cytokine out of numerical order because, unlike the preceding cytokines, it was first described as an inhibitor, rather than a stimulator, of immune reactions. Specifically, IL-10 inhibits the functions of activated antigen-presenting cells, such as the production of IL-12 and IFN-γ and the expression of Class II MHC molecules and costimulatory molecules. Thus, it has a major effect on antigen presentation and T-cell activation.[18] Interestingly, no fewer than seven viruses, including Epstein-Barr virus and cytomegalovirus, produce proteins that mimic the effects of IL-10 by binding to IL-10 receptors.[19] Presumably the inhibition induced favors viral replication. In mice that lack IL-10 (IL-10 "knockouts"), immune regulation is abnormal, and a condition resembling inflammatory bowel disease develops.[20,21]

Cytokines of the Adaptive Response

These cytokines are produced primarily by T cells. They help T cells proliferate and differentiate into effector cells, thereby playing a critical role in cell-mediated immunity.

Interleukin-2

IL-2 is produced primarily by antigen-activated CD4+ T cells, with peak secretion occurring 8–12 hours after activation. Antigen-induced activation also results in the expression of high-affinity IL-2 receptors, so that antigen-activated T cells can preferentially respond to IL-2 production by proliferating. Thus IL-2 is an autocrine T-cell growth factor (and can be used to expand the numbers of T cells for several weeks in vitro). Lower-affinity IL-2 receptors are expressed by naive T cells, NK cells, and B cells.

Interleukin-4

IL-4 is produced by antigen-activated CD4+ T cells, but can also be made by mast cells, eosinophils, and basophils. This cytokine mediates expansion of CD4+ cells with a type 2 cytokine secretion pattern (also known as T_H2; functional T-cell subsets are discussed later in this chapter). To this end, IL-4 also inhibits type 1 (T_H1) responses such as IFN-γ production. It stimulates B cells to produce IgE and, along with IL-10, one subclass of IgG (IgG4). IL-4 is associated with responses to parasites, wound repair, and adaptive responses to environmental antigens that lead to allergic reactions.

Type II Interferon: Interferon-gamma

IFN-γ is produced by T cells and NK cells. It is a defining cytokine for type 1 T-helper cells (T_H1 cells, discussed later in this chapter), which produce it in response to antigen; in contrast, NK cells produce IFN-γ after exposure to pathogens. In both cases, IFN-γ production is amplified by IL-12, which for T cells is typically derived from the antigen-presenting cell. The functions of IFN-γ favor inflammation:

- Activation of cells that kill pathogens (e.g., macrophages, NK cells, neutrophils)
- Activation of antigen presentation including increased expression of MHC molecules (both Class I and Class II) by antigen-presenting cells
- Stimulation of production of IL-12, which in turn further amplifies inflammatory responses
- Stimulation (along with TNF) of endothelial cells to attract immune cells
- Stimulation of production of IgG1 and inhibition of IgG4 and IgE
- Inhibition of T_H2 and T_H17 responses

Deficiency of IFN-γ, or its receptor, as has been reported in a few cases of mutations in the gene encoding IFN-γ or the receptor, increases susceptibility to intracellular pathogens, pathogens that are killed by macrophages, and pathogens that are otherwise controlled by being walled off in granulomas.[22,23] Mycobacterial infections including tuberculosis are particularly affected.

Interleukin-17

This cytokine, officially designated IL-17A, is a member of an extended family of similar molecules (IL-17A through F). It is produced mainly by CD4 T cells (designated T_H17 cells), but can also be produced by CD8 T cells, NK cells, and neutrophils. Engaging the receptor for this cytokine on epithelial cells, endothelial cells, and fibroblasts results in the expression of cytokines and chemokines that recruit neutrophils and other cells that are important for the control of extracellular bacterial and fungal infections. In addition, members of the IL-17 family help to regulate the body's responses to commensal microorganisms and to mediate the pathology attendant to several autoimmune diseases.

THE ROLE OF CYTOKINE EXPRESSION IN DEFINING FUNCTIONALLY DIFFERENT EFFECTOR CD4 T-CELL LINEAGES

The cytokine response to pathogen challenge is complex and varies depending on a number of factors, including the genetics and immunological history of the host. However, within this variable response, patterns can be observed. These patterns have been used to help structure our understanding of the dynamics of the immune response, especially in relation to CD4 T cell responses.

Based on the cytokines they secrete, CD4 T cells have been classified into five subsets that carry out distinctive functions: T_H1, T_H2, T_H17, T_{FH} (T follicular helper cells), and T_{reg} (regulatory T cells).

T_H1 and T_H2 cells were the first of the CD4 subsets to be recognized. Th1 cells are characterized by the production of IFN-γ. They stimulate immune mechanisms that control intracellular pathogens such as viruses, certain bacteria (e.g., *Mycobacterium* and *Listeria*), and certain protozoan parasites (e.g., *Toxoplasma* and *Leishmania*). IFN-γ is a key cytokine for activating both cytotoxic CD8 T cells, which kill virus-infected cells, and macrophages, which are an essential cell type for killing intracellular eukaryotic pathogens. T_H2 cells are defined by IL-4, IL-13, IL-10, and IL-5, which stimulate B-cell maturation and the production of antibodies. Thus T_H2 cells are important for the control of extracellular helminth parasites—multicellular pathogens such as nematodes

(round worms) and flukes (flat worms)—through the activation of eosinophils, mast cells, and basophils. Importantly, T_H2 cytokines are required for production of IgE antibodies, which are responsible for the human response known as allergy and also play an important role in immunity against parasites. Recently, it has been appreciated that T_H2-derived cytokines promote macrophage and fibroblast differentiation into cells that produce matrix proteins at the site of tissue injury, thereby promoting tissue repair.

The third major subset is T_H17 cells, which produce mainly the IL-17 family of cytokines (i.e., IL-17A and IL-17F). This subset is induced early in the response against extracellular bacteria and fungi, and its release results in a rapid influx of neutrophils into the site of infection. T_H17 cells have also been shown to promote inflammation in a number of autoimmune diseases and have been implicated as playing a role in anti-tumor immunity.

The fourth major subset is T follicular helper cells (T_{FH}) cells, which were identified very recently. These cells carry out what has long been appreciated as one of the essential functions of CD4 T cells: to provide help to B cells for the production of antibody. T_{FH} cells are found in the secondary lymphoid tissues. They secrete the cytokine IL-21 and provide the cognate interactions required by B cells to proliferate and to switch from producing IgM to IgG, IgA, or IgE.

The final subclass of CD4 T cells is regulatory T cells. T_{reg} cells differ from the other CD4 cell subclasses, which activate and expand immune responses, in that they inhibit the magnitude and scope of immune responses. Specifically, T_{reg} cells limit immune responses against foreign antigens and prevent the induction of autoimmune responses that can lead to disease. T_{reg} cells produce regulatory cytokines such as IL-10, and can work either directly on the other CD4 T-cell subsets or indirectly by curtailing the function of antigen presenting cells. T_{reg} cells are also characterized by expression of the high-affinity IL-2 receptor and certain nuclear transcription factors.

MUCOSAL IMMUNITY

Most interactions between the human host and the microbial world occur either at the skin or at mucosal surfaces, such as the gastrointestinal tract and the respiratory tract. Immunity at these sites is referred to as **mucosal immunity**. Despite its importance, our understanding of mucosal immunity is quite limited, due to the difficulty of obtaining tissue or secretions from mucosal surfaces (in contrast to the ease of obtaining blood for study of systemic immune responses).

The gastrointestinal tract provides an ideal environment for bacterial growth and contains trillions of bacteria. The host must be protected from invasion by these bacteria, but this must be accomplished without the vigorous inflammatory response that maintains the sterility of the host's internal environment, because such a strong response would destroy the mucosal protective barrier. Thus, mucosal immunity differs in fundamental ways from systemic immunity, and mechanisms that operate in systemic immunity cannot be assumed to operate in the mucosal setting.

Epithelial cells are a key component of mucosal immunity. While not traditionally regarded as immune cells, these cells are linked by tight junctions that provide a physical barrier excluding bacteria from the systemic environment, and they secrete proteins that inhibit the growth of bacteria and reduce bacterial attachment to the epithelial surface, thereby promoting bacterial excretion from the gastrointestinal tract. Epithelial cells also bear toll-like receptors (TLRs), described earlier in this chapter, that recognize pathogen-associated molecular patterns (PAMPs) that are unique to bacteria or viruses. Engagement of TLRs causes epithelial cells to secrete products with antimicrobial and pro-inflammatory activity, such as alpha- and beta- defensins, which can disrupt bacterial cell walls.

Although TLRs can be triggered by both pathogenic and non-pathogenic bacteria, several mechanisms exist that reduce activation of mucosal immune responses by these receptors. First, the receptors tend to be located within or on the basolateral surface, of the epithelial cell, rather than its apical surface, so they become engaged only when bacteria have invaded the epithelial barrier. Second, TLRs that engage common bacterial components are present at reduced levels in epithelial cells compared with other cells with antibacterial activity, such as macrophages. Third, continuous exposure to bacterial products may downregulate the expression of TLRs on the luminal epithelial surface. In addition to these mechanisms, intestinal epithelial cells secrete proteins that directly inhibit their own production of pro-inflammatory factors following exposure to bacteria.

The transition from the innate immune response to the adaptive response depends on the ability of dendritic cells to present antigens to T cells involved in the induction of both cell-mediated and humoral immunity. The gastrointestinal tract contains a diverse array of dendritic cell populations with distinct functional capabilities. Some of these dendritic cells are clearly programmed, such as the epithelial cells at this site, to downregulate inflammatory responses. An important property of these cells is their ability to direct the humoral response to the production of immunoglobulin A (IgA), as opposed to immunoglobulin G (IgG), which has a greater propensity to induce inflammatory responses. Unlike IgG, for example, IgA does not activate the pro-inflammatory complement pathway. The attenuation of inflammatory responses by gastrointestinal dendritic cells has been attributed to their continuous exposure to microbial and dietary products.[24]

Thus IgA remains the mainstay of resistance to bacterial invasion from the mucosa of the gastrointestinal tract. Uniquely among immunoglobulins, IgA secreted into the gastrointestinal tract is linked to a protein termed secretory component, which protects the immunoglobulin from digestion and anchors it, through its Fc receptor, to the mucus covering the epithelial cells. Here, IgA can inhibit binding of pathogens to the epithelial surface, preventing colonization or invasion, and can also block bacterial toxins from interacting with host cells. Further, through engagement of its Fc receptor on phagocytic cells, IgA can promote uptake of pathogens without eliciting an inflammatory response.

Because exposure to viruses at mucosal surfaces tends to be episodic, rather than sustained as with bacteria, the need to attenuate the pro-inflammatory component of the T-cell-mediated responses following viral infection at mucosal surfaces is less critical. In turn, these responses more closely resemble those observed systemically. Antiviral IgA responses also contribute to the elimination of ongoing viral infection and provide protective immunity against subsequent infection.

Other mucosal sites share with the gastrointestinal tract a predilection toward mitigation of immune responses, but the patterns are not always the same as those of the GI tract. For example, because potent acquired immune responses might lead to rejection of a fetus or paternal sperm, the female genital tract has evolved as a site at which elicitation of humoral or cell-mediated immune responses is tightly regulated. In distinction to the GI tract, protection from microbial challenge depends more prominently on innate immune mechanisms. This difficulty in eliciting protective immunity may account, at least in part, for the widespread distribution of sexually transmitted infections (STIs) and the poor outcomes of efforts to develop STI-targeted vaccines.

RESPIRATORY IMMUNE ENVIRONMENT

Another important site of mucosal immunity is the respiratory system. Unlike the gastrointestinal tract, the respiratory tract, while not sterile, does not carry a massive microbial burden. Indeed, one of the main tasks of the respiratory mucosal immune system is to capture and prevent commensal and pathogenic microorganisms (as well as airborne environmental antigens) from reaching the delicate air spaces in the lungs, where inflammation can impair gas exchange with potentially dire consequences. (The hairs of the nose and the sweeping cilia on epithelial cells help by providing physical barriers to pathogen entry.) The respiratory immune defenses are sometimes termed the nasopharynx-associated lymphoid tissues (NALT; tonsils and nasal submucosal glands) and the bronchi-associated lymphoid tissues (BALT; bronchial submucosal glands and diffuse lymphoid follicles of the lower airways). The mucus coating the nasopharyngeal epithelium is another important physical barrier that traps microorganisms; it is rich in antimicrobial molecules (e.g., IgA, lactoferrin, and lysozyme).

As in the intestinal tract, the epithelial layers of the respiratory tract play a key role in local immune surveillance and regulation. When perturbed, the nasopharyngeal epithelia cells secrete pro-inflammatory cytokines (e.g., TNF, IL-1, IL-6) and chemokines that summon cells of the innate response. Bronchial epithelial cells generate cytokines such as IL-5, IL-6, IL-10, and transforming growth factor-beta (TGF-β) that both direct B-cell differentiation to IgA production and promote T-cell-mediated adaptive immunity in the respiratory tract.

COMMON MUCOSAL IMMUNE SYSTEM

An important attribute of mucosal immunity is the characteristic that a response generated at one mucosal site is transferred to other mucosal surfaces. Thus a pathogen-specific secretory IgA response generated initially in the small intestine will be propagated not only along the entire length of the small and large intestines, but also to the respiratory tract, salivary glands, mammary glands, ocular tissues, and other mucosal sites. This phenomenon has given rise to the concept of a **common mucosal immune system**. It is mediated by the ability of lymphocytes generated at one site to circulate via the blood and lymph to other mucosal sites that express common mucosal homing receptors. Lymphocytes that are activated in a mucosal environment are induced to express distinct receptors on their surface that allow them to move to any mucosal site. One of the advantages of a common mucosal immune system is that mothers can transfer protection against gastrointestinal pathogens to their newborns, via pathogen-specific IgA that is secreted into breast milk.

TOLERANCE AND THE REGULATION OF THE IMMUNE RESPONSE

One of the most remarkable qualities of the immune system is that it recognizes and responds to a seemingly infinite array of foreign and pathogen-associated molecules, but it does not respond to self molecules. This immunological unresponsiveness to self is referred to as **tolerance** or **self-tolerance**. Tolerance is maintained by several mechanisms. First, lymphocytes with receptors for self-antigens are eliminated in the thymus or bone marrow before they fully mature (producing **central tolerance**). Second, self-reacting lymphocytes are rendered functionally non-responsive (**anergy**) or induced to self-destruct (by **apoptosis**, a form of **programmed cell death**) when their receptors engage self-antigens without proper co-stimulation (producing **peripheral tolerance**). Imbalances in the regulation of tolerance can lead to autoimmune disorders.

Another important aspect of immune regulation is the down-regulation of the scope and duration of inflammatory responses. Again, multiple mechanisms come into play. Although immune-mediated elimination of antigens is important in limiting inflammatory responses, it has recently become clear that active mechanisms play a role in limiting these responses. In particular, **T-regulatory cells** (T_{reg}) suppress self-reactivity, thereby playing a key role in balancing reactivity and tolerance. Perturbation of T_{reg} function can lead to prolonged exuberant immune responses, tissue damage, and immune-mediated pathology.

SELECTIVE IMMUNE DEFICIENCIES: WINDOWS INTO THE NORMAL ROLES AND FUNCTIONS OF THE IMMUNE SYSTEM

As in other areas of medicine, much of what we know about the normal function and importance for human health of specific types of cells and specific proteins is derived from clinical syndromes in which these cells or proteins are absent or not functional (or experimental conditions designed to mimic these syndromes).

B-Cell Immune Deficiency

Syndromes exist in humans in which B cells fail to develop and the patient cannot produce antibodies. These syndromes are generally due to a mutation in one of the genes involved in the genetic rearrangements required for antibody generation. In birds, removal of the eponymous bursa of Fabricius leads to a virtually identical syndrome. Humans may develop a disease called common variable immune deficiency, in which the ability to produce some or all antibodies is lost. The mechanism of this disease is complex, but it is not due to congenital mutations because the patient made antibodies for many years before the onset of the disease. In at least some cases, the deficiency is due to overactive suppression of antibody production.

The primary symptom of antibody deficiency is recurrent bacterial infections with common extracellular bacteria such as *Staphylococcus* or *Streptococcus*. Pneumonia and sinusitis are especially common. The reason why a lack of antibodies predisposes individuals to this type of infection is that opsonization of these bacteria by antibodies is so important in allowing host phagocytic cells to ingest and kill the bacteria. Without antibodies, the phagocytic cells are outpaced by the rapidly growing bacteria and cannot do their job of clearing the infection. The types of infection may depend on the type of antibody that is missing. For example, if the deficiency is confined to IgA, the infections tend to be mucosal (e.g., sinusitis). (Recurrent infections are also seen when neutrophils are defective or absent.) However, if the missing antibodies are replaced by periodic injections of pooled antibodies, normal protection is restored and the clinical consequences of the underlying antibody deficiency can be prevented.

T-Cell Immune Deficiency

The clinical picture of selective T-cell deficiency was recognized based on animal experiments in which the thymus was removed, and on the clinical manifestations in human syndromes when the thymus fails to develop. It consists of recurrent infections with parasites, viruses, and intracellular bacteria. A similar picture has been recognized in transplant recipients whose cellular immunity is pharmacologically suppressed to prevent rejection of the graft (although this presentation can also be complicated by recurrent extracellular bacterial infections if neutrophils are depleted by the therapy). Congenital T-cell deficiencies can be due to mutations in the genes required for T-cell receptor rearrangement, T-cell signal transduction, or T-cell maturation. Clinical manifestations can vary according to the specific defect.

The clinical manifestations of cellular immune deficiency were sufficiently established that when the first clusters of cases of AIDS in the United States occurred in the late 1970s and early 1980s, researchers recognized almost immediately that it was a new disease characterized by acquired cellular immune deficiency.[25-27] Notably, only a few cases of *Pneumocystis carinii* pneumonia and other opportunistic illnesses were required for this recognition, because these illnesses were (and are) exceedingly rare in people with no known reason to be immunocompromised. In fact, the manifestations of AIDS are a perfect illustration of the consequences of cellular immune deficiency. No further description will be given here, because a very thorough description of AIDS appears elsewhere in this book.

Deficiencies in specific cytokines have also been reported, due to mutations in the gene for the cytokine or the receptor for the cytokine. These conditions usually manifest as difficulty controlling certain infections, as with tuberculosis in deficiency of IFN-γ.

Treatment of cellular immune deficiency is still in its infancy. In theory, these diseases can be treated by replacing missing cytokines or cells. In reality, replacement of cytokines has proved challenging because of the local nature of most cytokines' action, along with the toxicity of cytokines when administered systemically or in high concentrations. Bone marrow transplantation has been used successfully, and in one disease (adenosine deaminase deficiency) gene therapy has been tried with some success.

NK-Cell Immune Deficiency

For a long time after NK cells were discovered, researchers continued to debate whether they had any clinical importance. As so often happens, this question was answered by a clinical case.[28] The patient was a girl who presented at the age of 13 with a life-threatening infection with varicella-zoster virus. Before this event, she had experienced recurrent ear infections and low white blood cell counts. At age 17 she had disseminated cytomegalovirus infection, and at age 19 she developed an infection with herpes simplex virus with fever and generalized rash. Between infections, the patient's antibody levels, T-cell subset ratios, and T-cell responses in vitro (including the response to varicella-zoster virus) were normal, and live vaccines had caused no clinical problems for her. She was found to have a complete absence of NK cells, with no detectable NK cells in the blood and no detectable NK cell function in vitro. This case implicated NK cells in host defense against herpesviruses, as all of the patient's viral infections involved this class of virus. The patient remains the only case of NK cell deficiency that has been reported, but her presentation is important because it clearly demonstrates the in vivo function of NK cells.

Other functions of NK cells in host defense have been described, and were discussed earlier in this chapter, but their clinical importance is less clear. NK-cell function is reduced in HIV infection, and NK cells can directly lyse some intracellular pathogens such as *Toxoplasma gondii* and *Trypanosoma cruzi*.[29–31] NK cells also have antitumor activity in vitro.

Other Immune-Mediated Diseases Related to Infectious Organisms

Why do most lymphocytes circulate in a resting state? As discussed earlier, immune reactivity is a double-edged sword: the same mechanisms that kill microorganisms or infected cells can severely damage normal cells and body constituents.

A good example of this dual nature is seen in toxic shock syndrome, which is characterized by circulatory collapse, hypotension, shock, and, in some cases, death. Bacterial proteins can cause this syndrome by a variety of mechanisms. The common denominator of these mechanisms is the activation of very high numbers of T cells, resulting in excessive production of cytokines, which in turn leads to vasodilation and shock (**Box 10-14**).

Another demonstration of the risks of having an overactive immune system involves autoimmune disease. Autoimmunity in the thyroid gland and the pancreas, for example, can cause tissue damage leading to hypothyroidism and diabetes (due to lack of

---

Box 10-14	Consequences of Diffuse Activation of Cellular Immunity

In some infections, the reason why the bacterial proteins are able to activate so many T cells is that instead of binding only to antigen receptors specific for these proteins (which are present on only a tiny proportion of T cells—perhaps 0.01% or less), they bind to a relatively nonpolymorphic region of the T-cell antigen receptor (which is present on many T cells—as much as 5–10%). Proteins that can bind to the T-cell receptor in this way are called superantigens, because they activate so many T cells. Superantigens can activate a wide variety of T-cell receptors, far more than could be activated through the antigen-specific part of the receptor, which is highly polymorphic. This results in an enormous immune activation characterized by release of huge amounts of cytokines, which in turn cause the symptoms of the syndrome.

Box 10-15	Etiology of Autoimmune Disease

What triggers autoimmune disease is not known, but this topic has been intensively investigated since the description of the first autoimmune disease (thyroiditis leading to destruction of the thyroid gland and thus to hypothyroidism) in 1956. It is now clear that immune reactions normally involve self-recognition (through the requirement for MHC recognition in antigen presentation), so the problem is likely one of regulation rather than purely a failure to distinguish between self and non-self. Evidence clearly shows that some genetic factors are associated with a higher incidence of autoimmune disease (e.g., certain MHC alleles, female sex) and that environmental factors also play a role.

Some autoimmune diseases have been postulated to result from infectious organisms whose antigens are very similar to normal host antigens. Thus the immune system may be "tricked" by an infection into reacting against normal host antigens. This mechanism of initiation of autoimmune disease is called **molecular mimicry**.

---

insulin), respectively. Infections have been postulated to cause some autoimmune diseases (**Box 10-15**). Inflammation due to infections has also been hypothesized to contribute to the etiology of—if not cause—other diseases not traditionally considered infectious, such as atherosclerosis[32,33] and certain cancers.[34]

CONCLUSION

This chapter offered an introduction to the immune system and its role in host defense against infections. By necessity, many of the details of how immune reactions are regulated have been omitted. Keep in mind that most, if not all, of the principles and generalizations described here have exceptions, sometimes important ones. Curious readers can pursue their interests, which we hope have been stimulated (in a non-MHC restricted way, of course!).

• • • RECOMMENDED TEXTBOOKS OF IMMUNOLOGY

Delves, Martin, Burton and Roitt. *Roitt's Essential Immunology*. 12th ed. London: Blackwell; 2011.

Murphy K. *Janeway's Immunobiology: The Immune System in Health and Disease*. 8th ed. New York: Garland; 2011. A good introductory text.

Paul WE. *Fundamental Immunology*. Baltimore: Lippincott Williams and Wilkins; 2008. Especially Chapter 1 (The Immune System: An Introduction). A very detailed text.

• • • **REFERENCES**

1. Rouse BT, Norley S, Martin S. Antiviral cytotoxic T lymphocyte induction and vaccination. *Rev Infect Dis* 1988;10:16–33.

2. Katz DH, Hamaoka T, Benacerraf B. Cell interactions between histoincompatible T and B lymphocytes. II. Failure of physiologic cooperative interactions between T and B lymphocytes from allogeneic donor strains in humoral response to hapten-protein conjugates. *J Exp Med* 1973;137:1405–1418.

3. Lanzavecchia A. Antigen-specific interaction between T and B cells. *Nature* 1985; 314:537–539.

4. Lorenzo ME, Ploegh HL, Tirabassi RS. Viral immune evasion strategies and the underlying cell biology. *Semin Immunol* 2001;13:1–9.

5. Ploegh HL. Viral strategies of immune evasion. *Science* 1998;280:248–253.

6. Uthaisangsook S, Day NK, Bahna SL, Good RA, Haraguchi S. Innate immunity and its role against infections. *Ann Allergy Asthma Immunol* 2002;88:253–264.

7. Carreno BM, Collins M. The B7 family of ligands and its receptors: new pathways for costimulation and inhibition of immune responses. *Annu Rev Immunol* 2002;20:29–53.

8. Silva RA, Florido M, Appelberg R Interleukin-12 primes CD4+ T cells for interferon-gamma production and protective immunity during *Mycobacterium avium* infection. *Immunol* 2001;103:368–374.

9. Cantor H, Shen FW, Boyse EA. Separation of helper T cells from suppressor T cells expressing different Ly components. II. Activation by antigen: after immunization, antigen-specific suppressor and helper activities are mediated by distinct T-cell subclasses. *J Exp. Med* 1976;143:1391–1340.

10. Littman DR, Thomas Y, Maddon PJ et al. The isolation and sequence of the gene encoding T8: a molecule defining functional classes of T lymphocytes. *Cell* 1985;40:237–246.

11. Stenger S, Hanson DA, Teitelbaum R, et al. An antimicrobial activity of cytolytic T cells mediated by granulysin. *Science* 1998;282:121–125.

12. Carson WE, Giri JG, Lindemann MJ, et al. Interleukin (IL) 15 is a novel cytokine that activates human natural killer cells via components of the IL-2 receptor. *J Exp.Med* 1994;180:1395–1403.

13. Zhang T, Kawakami K, Qureshi MH, et al. Interleukin-12 (IL-12) and IL-18 synergistically induce the fungicidal activity of murine peritoneal exudate cells against *Cryptococcus neoformans* through production of gamma interferon by natural killer cells. *Infect Immun* 1997;65:3594–3599.

14. Rayner AA, Grimm EA, Lotze MT, et al. Lymphokine-activated killer (LAK) cells: analysis of factors relevant to the immunotherapy of human cancer. *Cancer* 1985;55:1327–1333.

15. Smyth MJ, Thia KY, Cretney E, et al. Perforin is a major contributor to NK cell control of tumor metastasis. *J Immunol* 1999;162:6658–6662.

16. Keane J, Gershon S, Wise RP, et al. Tuberculosis associated with infliximab, a tumor necrosis factor alpha-neutralizing agent. *N Engl J Med* 2001;345:1098–1104.

17. Altare F, Durandy A, Lammas D, et al. Impairment of mycobacterial immunity in human interleukin-12 receptor deficiency. *Science* 1998;280:1432–1435.

18. Moore KW, de Waal MR, Coffman RL, O'Garra A. Interleukin-10 and the interleukin-10 receptor. *Annu Rev Immunol* 2001;19:683–765.

19. Fickenscher H, Hor S, Kupers H, et al. The interleukin-10 family of cytokines. *Trends Immunol* 2001;23:89–96.

20. Chmiel JF, Konstan MW, Saadane A, et al. Prolonged inflammatory response to acute *Pseudomonas* challenge in interleukin-10 knockout mice. *Am J Respir Crit Care Med* 2002;165:1176–1181.

21. Takahashi I, Matsuda J, Gapin L, et al. Colitis-related public T cells are selected in the colonic lamina propria of IL-10-deficient mice. *Clin Immunol* 2002;102:237–248.

22. van Schaik SM, Obot N, Enhorning G, et al. Role of interferon gamma in the pathogenesis of primary respiratory syncytial virus infection in BALB/c mice. *J Med Virol* 2000;62:257–266.

23. Dorman SE, Picard C, Lammas D, et al. Clinical features of dominant and recessive interferon gamma receptor 1 deficiencies. *Lancet* 2004;364:2113–2121.

24. Villablanca EJ, Wang S, de CJ, et al. MyD88 and retinoic acid signaling pathways interact to modulate gastrointestinal activities of dendritic cells. *Gastroenterology* 2011;141:176–185.

25. Masur H, Michelis MA, Greene JB, et al. An outbreak of community-acquired *P. carinii* pneumonia: initial manifestation of cellular immune dysfunction. *N Engl J Med* 1981;305:1431–1438.

26. Gottlieb MS, Schroff R, Schander HM, et al. *Pneumocystis carinii* pneumonia and mucosal candidiasis in previously healthy homosexual men: evidence for a new acquired cellular immunodeficiency. *N Engl J Med* 1981;305:1425–1431.

27. Siegal FP, Lopez E, Hammer GS, et al. Severe acquired immunodeficiency in male homosexuals manifested by chronic perianal ulcerative herpes simplex lesions. *N Engl J Med* 1981;305:1439–1444.

28. Biron CA, Byron KS, Sullivan JL. Severe herpesvirus infections in an adolescent without natural killer cells. *N Engl J Med* 1989;320:1731–1735.

29. Hauser WE Jr, Tsai V. Acute toxoplasma infection of mice induces spleen NK cells that are cytotoxic for *T. gondii* in vitro. *J Immunol* 1986;136:313–319.

30. Cantor H, Boyse EA. Functional subclasses of T-lymphocytes bearing different Ly antigens. I. The generation of functionally distinct T-cell subclasses is a differentiative process independent of antigen. *J Exp.Med* 1975;141:1376–1389.

31. Martinez-Marino B, Shiboski S, Hecht FM, et al. Interleukin-2 therapy restores CD8 cell non-cytotoxic anti-HIV responses in primary infection subjects receiving HAART. *AIDS* 2004;18:1991–1999.

32. Arcari CM, Gaydos CA, Nieto FJ, et al. Association between *Chlamydia pneumoniae* and acute myocardial infarction in young men in the United States military: the importance of timing of exposure measurement. *Clin Infect Dis* 2005;40:1123–1130.

33. Danesh J, Whincup P, Walker M, et al. *Chlamydia pneumoniae* IgG titres and coronary heart disease: prospective study and meta-analysis. *BMJ* 2000;321:208–213.

34. Houghton J, Wang TC. *Helicobacter pylori* and gastric cancer: a new paradigm for inflammation-associated epithelial cancers. *Gastroenterology* 2005;128:1567–1578.

CHAPTER

11

Vaccines: Past, Present, and Future

Anita M. Loughlin and Steffanie A. Strathdee

INTRODUCTION

A vaccine is any biologically derived substance that elicits a protective immune response when administered to a susceptible host. The first documented account of vaccination is attributed to a Buddhist nun who described how smallpox scabs were dried, ground, and blown into the nostrils of susceptible persons in approximately AD 1000 to protect them from disseminated disease.[1] The first trial to evaluate the effects of vaccination occurred in 1796, when Edward Jenner proved that persons inoculated with cowpox were resistant to challenge with *Variola* virus, the etiologic agent of smallpox.

Worldwide improvements in sanitation and vaccination led to impressive declines in the incidence and mortality of many infectious diseases throughout the 1900s. Perhaps the greatest public health achievement of the modern era is the global eradication of smallpox in 1977 and the near elimination of polio. Despite these achievements, a significant proportion of the estimated 11.5 million deaths attributed to infectious and parasitic diseases in 1998 could have been prevented by existing vaccines (**Figure 11-1**). Barriers to achieving protective immunity in populations at the highest risk leave us far short of reaping the full potential of vaccines. In the world, 1 million children die from measles each year, 50% of whom live in Africa, despite the existence of highly effective vaccine. Furthermore, diseases such as tuberculosis may not come under control until an efficacious vaccine is developed.

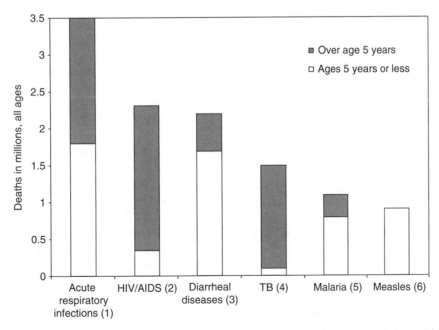

Figure 11-1 Leading causes of death worldwide from infectious diseases in 1998. Adapted from World Health Organization (1999). Report on Infectious Diseases: Leading Infectious Killers. http://www.who.int/infectious-disease-report/pages/graph5.html. Accessed February 29, 2012.

This chapter describes various types of traditional and experimental vaccines, the role of vaccines in the eradication of specific infectious diseases (e.g., smallpox, polio), and recent technological advances in vaccine development. In addition, it summarizes fundamental concepts relating to vaccine efficacy and effectiveness and barriers to achieving adequate vaccine coverage.

ACTIVE VERSUS PASSIVE IMMUNIZATION

Protection from many infectious diseases can be conferred by either passive or active immunization.

Passive immunity refers to the protection conferred by the transfer of animal or human antibody (immunoglobulin), by injection, in utero transfer, or breastfeeding, to a susceptible host. Passive antibody transfer from mother to child plays an important role in preventing disease in newborns. Although maternal antibodies do not necessarily provide full protection from infection, immunization of pregnant women against tetanus has led to dramatic reductions in the incidence of neonatal tetanus.[2] A disadvantage of passive immunity is that it is typically short lived. For example, protection conferred by immunoglobulin injection lasts only a few weeks; maternal antibodies can protect newborns for up to 6 months, especially if mothers continue to breastfeed.

Active immunity refers to protection produced by the host's own immune system and relies on the ability of the host to generate an immune response following exposure to specific antigen(s). In the field of immunology, antigens are described as being *self* if they are from the host or person, and *non-self* if they come from someone or something else. Immunogenic antigens are foreign bodies—commonly proteins or polysaccharides—that are recognized by the immune system as non-self and that then elicit a response. The goal of immunization is to elicit a protective immune response that confers protective immunity against natural infection with a wild-type (i.e., pathogenic) microorganism without causing serious clinical illness. For many pathogens, the immunologic response of people who have had natural infection and survived without chronic morbidity can guide in the development of a vaccine. Features of an ideal vaccine are listed in **Exhibit 11-1**.

Factors that affect the host immune response include the type and dose of antigen, the route of administration (e.g., intramuscular, subcutaneous, or oral), the presence or absence of maternal antibody, host factors (e.g., age, immunosuppression, genetics), and the characteristics of the vaccine (Exhibit 11-1). Timing of

Exhibit 11-1	Characteristics of an Ideal Vaccine

1. Produces a good humoral, cell-mediated, and local immune response, similar to natural infection, in a single dose.
2. Elicits protections against clinical disease and reinfection.
3. Provides protection for several years, preferably a lifetime.
4. Results in minimal immediate adverse effects or mild disease with no delayed effects that predispose to other diseases.
5. Induced immunity confers protections to multiple strains of organisms.
6. Can be administered simply in a form that is practically, culturally, and ethically acceptable to the target population.
7. Vaccine preparations do not require special handling (e.g., a cold chain).
8. Does not interfere significantly with the immune response to other vaccines given simultaneously.
9. Costs and benefits associated with receiving the vaccine clearly outweigh the costs and risks associated with natural infection.

immunization is another important consideration. For most vaccines, immunization must take place before natural infection occurs, with several weeks passing before the body is able to generate an adequate immune response. During some outbreaks (e.g., hepatitis A, measles), passive immunization offers effective short-term protection, especially when there is insufficient time for susceptible individuals' bodies to mount an adequate immune response following active immunization. The extent of the host's immune response has an important bearing on vaccine efficacy, which is discussed in detail later in this chapter.

TYPES OF VACCINES

The antigenic agent used in active immunization can be (1) a live organism that has been attenuated (i.e., weakened) or (2) an inactivated form that is either whole or fractionated (e.g., protein or polysaccharide component). A third type of vaccine, recombinant vaccines, is made by genetic manipulation of the organism's genomic material, and can be either live or inactivated. This section describes characteristics of the various types of vaccines, as well as a newer experimental approach involving vaccination with naked DNA. **Exhibit 11-2** depicts how vaccines are made and identifies examples of specific vaccines by type.

Whereas some vaccines are imagined as being able to prevent infection, many others prevent

Exhibit 11-2 | **Vaccine Manufacturing**

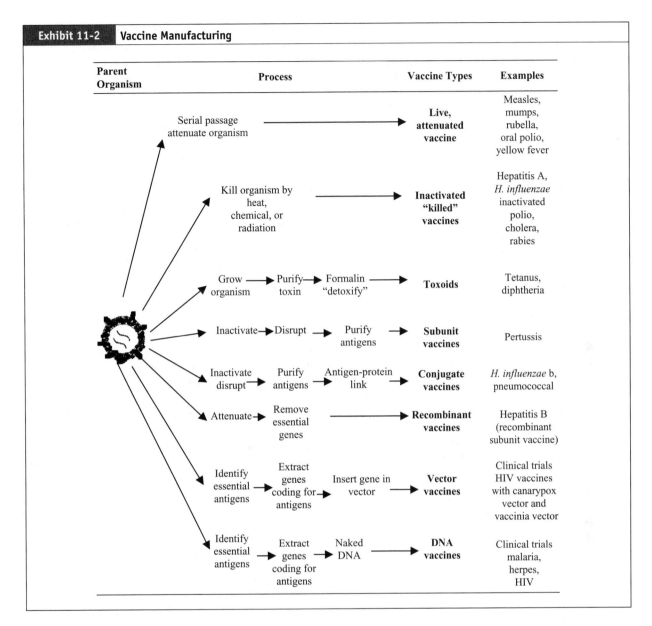

Parent Organism	Process	Vaccine Types	Examples
	Serial passage attenuate organism	**Live, attenuated vaccine**	Measles, mumps, rubella, oral polio, yellow fever
	Kill organism by heat, chemical, or radiation	**Inactivated "killed" vaccines**	Hepatitis A, *H. influenzae* inactivated polio, cholera, rabies
	Grow organism → Purify toxin → Formalin "detoxify"	**Toxoids**	Tetanus, diphtheria
	Inactivate → Disrupt → Purify antigens	**Subunit vaccines**	Pertussis
	Inactivate disrupt → Purify antigens → Antigen-protein link	**Conjugate vaccines**	*H. influenzae* b, pneumococcal
	Attenuate → Remove essential genes	**Recombinant vaccines**	Hepatitis B (recombinant subunit vaccine)
	Identify essential antigens → Extract genes coding for antigens → Insert gene in vector	**Vector vaccines**	Clinical trials HIV vaccines with canarypox vector and vaccinia vector
	Identify essential antigens → Extract genes coding for antigens → Naked DNA	**DNA vaccines**	Clinical trials malaria, herpes, HIV

or minimize the consequences of infection. For example, toxoid vaccine prevents tissue damage from bacterial toxins (e.g., tetanus or diphtheria toxin) but does not actually act against the bacteria themselves. Likewise, inactivated poliovirus vaccine does not prevent wild-type poliovirus from multiplying in the intestinal tract, but the immunity induced by this vaccine prevents the virus from causing central nervous system disease.

The public health burden of cancers caused by viral infection may be considerably reduced through the introduction of preventive or therapeutic vaccines. The inclusion of hepatitis B (HBV) vaccine in several national immunization programs will prevent primary disease as well as—is also hoped—reduce the incidence of liver cancer, although overcoming the barriers to achieving adequate coverage will be necessary. Preventive vaccines have also been licensed for human papillomavirus (HPV) infection. It is estimated that 50% of sexually active adults will have genital HPV at some point in their lives. HPV is highly prevalent among young men in the United States (25%)[3] and accounts for approximately 95% of all cervical cancers in women.[4]

Efforts to harness the specific targeting capacity of the immune system to selectively kill malignant cells has resulted in varying levels of success. Immunization with tumor antigen and stimulation of the immune system has been attempted as one approach. A novel gene therapy approach has reported results from a Phase 1 clinical trial. In this study, researchers used a modified, and crippled, HIV virus to insert genes to target the patient's leukemia into autologous T cells. These T cells were then returned to the patient. In three out of three patients, significant improvement was subsequently reported; two patients were described as cured of their leukemia. How durable this response will be is unknown at this time, but it is an exciting result that holds great promise.[5] Advances in this field are likely to lead to important victories in the war against cancer.[6]

Live Attenuated Vaccines

Bacteria and viruses are referred to as being *attenuated* if they have been rendered nonpathogenic. Bacteria can be attenuated through laboratory culture, and viruses through serial passaging in tissue culture or animal hosts. Both bacteria and viruses can be attenuated through genetic manipulation.

The potential role of attenuated organisms in vaccination was identified soon after Jenner's landmark smallpox vaccination study in 1796. In the 1870s, Louis Pasteur recognized that inoculating a weakened form of chicken cholera protected chickens against challenge with the wild-type virus. Pasteur then developed an attenuated anthrax bacilli vaccine that was first administered to livestock in 1881, and an attenuated live rabies vaccine that was used to immunize two human volunteers in 1885.[7] In 1909, the bacille Calmette-Guerin (BCG) tuberculosis vaccine was the first live attenuated bacterial vaccine developed for humans.

Live attenuated organisms must replicate, or multiply, in the host to induce an adequate immune response. These live vaccines typically generate a stronger immune response than inactivated vaccines, and immunity is considered lifelong due to immunologic memory. Live vaccines have the advantage of inducing both humoral and cell-mediated immunity. In simple terms, humoral immunity refers to antibody—specifically, immunoglobulin (Ig)—production. Antigen recognition by lymphocytes (T cells and B cells) leads to clonal expansion of specific B cells, the generation of memory cells, and production of specific antibodies that are directed against a particular antigen. The primary humoral immune response to a new antigen involves short-term production of IgM antibodies, which is replaced by longer-lasting, higher-affinity IgG antibodies. If the host is later reexposed to the same antigen, a rapid expansion of memory cells results in a secondary immune response involving production of specific IgG but not IgM antibodies. Cell-mediated immunity includes nonspecific first-line responses against invading organisms, such as phagocytes, natural killer cells, and complement as well as antigen-specific responses, such as activation of cytotoxic T lymphocytes (T cells that express CD8+ on their cell surface). These responses may be induced by live attenuated viral vaccines and potentially by naked DNA vaccines. **Figure 11-2** depicts humoral and cellular immune response pathways. For a detailed account of the

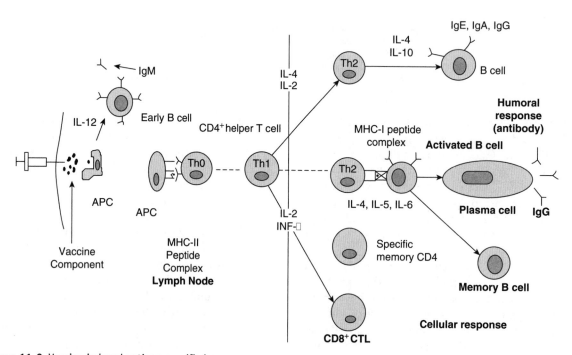

Figure 11-2 Vaccine induced antigen-specific immune response.

humoral and cell-mediated response to infectious agents, the reader is referred the referenced texts.[7–10]

Another potential advantage of live vaccines is the possibility of horizontal transmission, or indirect vaccination, which refers to the transmission of vaccine virus to other susceptible individuals. Horizontal transmission of vaccine virus has been described for live oral polio vaccine (OPV), for example.[12] Indirect vaccination has the significant benefit of enhancing vaccine coverage by exposing unvaccinated persons to the vaccine strain. However, the vaccine strain of polio reverts to the virulent strain in the gut of vaccinated patients over time. This conversion has resulted, on rare occasions, in vaccine-associated paralytic polio (VAPP) among the non-immune contacts of OPV recipients.[13] For this reason, horizontal transmission of vaccine strains requires careful monitoring and surveillance for the detection of disease cause by these strains. In countries where polio is no longer endemic, inactivated polio vaccine is recommended to eliminate the risk of VAPP. In the United States, OPV has not been used since 1999.[13]

Although attenuated vaccine strains may be controlled by immunocompetent persons, they may be poorly controlled by in the bodies of individuals with compromised immune systems (e.g., the elderly, infants, those on immunosuppressive drugs, persons with HIV/AIDS). In these populations, severe adverse events can occur with administration of such live vaccines. All unintended and serious consequences of vaccination are assessed through both clinical trials before approval and through surveillance mechanisms post licensure.

Antibody induction by live attenuated vaccines can sometimes be suppressed by circulating antibodies that cross-react with the attenuated organism. Interference can be caused by antibody produced during concurrent natural infections, immune globulin administered during recent passive immunization, or maternal antibodies. Measles vaccine is particularly sensitive to circulating maternal antibodies, which leads to the complicated measles immunization schedules used with preschool children.[14] In rare cases, antibodies induced by one vaccine can inhibit the immune response to another vaccine, a situation that bears watching when several vaccines are administered simultaneously. Previous concerns that administering yellow fever and cholera vaccines simultaneously could reduce the long-term immune response to both have not been borne out;[15] however, the Centers for Disease Control and Prevention (CDC) still recommends that these vaccines be administered at least 3 weeks apart. In addition, some antimalarial drugs (e.g., chloroquine) do interfere with live cholera vaccine.[16]

Immunization programs that incorporate live vaccines need to take appropriate measures to protect the vaccine from environmental conditions (e.g., heat, light). The system of vaccine storage and transport from manufacturer to client is called the *cold chain*, as constant refrigeration is one of the greatest challenges. Although stabilizing agents (e.g., magnesium chloride) can be used to safeguard the viability of live vaccines, failure to maintain the cold chain can compromise vaccine efficacy. When appropriate, simultaneous administration of several live virus vaccines (e.g., measles, mumps, rubella [MMR]) reduces cost by bundling the cumbersome handling, shipping, and storage requirements of the three vaccines.[16]

Inactivated Vaccines

In the recent past, *inactivated* vaccines were either whole viruses or bacteria that were "killed" using heat or chemicals (e.g., formalin). Today, most inactivated vaccines are not based on the whole virus, but rather use only extracted or purified protein or polysaccharide components of an organism.

As early as 1888, it was discovered that the diphtheria bacillus (*Corynebacterium diphtheriae*) produced a powerful toxin that caused the disease pathology.[17] In the early 1900s, chemical inactivation of bacterial toxins led to the first toxoids for diphtheria and tetanus that could be used for vaccination.

Another type of inactivated vaccine is based on polysaccharides that are typically derived from bacterial cell walls (e.g., pneumococcus, meningococcus, *Haemophilus influenzae* type b [Hib]). Purified polysaccharide-based vaccines are not consistently immunogenic for the elderly, immunocompromised persons, or infants, and are not recommended for children younger than 2 years of age. More successful vaccines have chemically linked, or conjugated, the polysaccharides to a protein carrier that can boost the immune response. This approach has been successfully used to maximize the immune response to Hib. Conjugate Hib vaccine was the first of this type of vaccine licensed for use in humans. Newer conjugate vaccines include the 7-serotype pneumococcal vaccine (PCV7) and the newly licensed 13-serotype pneumococcal vaccine (PCV13) that prevent many invasive *Streptococcus pneumoniae* infections, which replaced Hib as the most common bacterial cause of meningitis, bacteremia, and pneumonias.[18] A fourth quadrivalent conjugate vaccine, MCV4, was licensed in 2005 for the prevention of *Neisseria meningitides* sepsis, meningitis, and other severe disease caused by organism.[19] MCV4 is recommended for children, adolescents, persons living in close quarters such as students in dormitories or military recruits, and persons who have a complement deficiency or are asplenic.[20]

By definition, inactivated vaccines are not alive; thus they cannot replicate in the host or revert to virulence. These vaccines are not rendered ineffective by circulating antibody and require less stringent handling procedures. Inactivated vaccines are associated with fewer adverse effects, which, when they do occur, are commonly localized to the injection site. Although these properties are favorable, the immune response associated with inactivated vaccines is typically restricted to humoral immunity. Several doses are usually required to boost the specific antibody level, or *titer*. Immunity produced by inactive vaccines wanes with time, necessitating the administration of booster doses.

In cases where the antigenic component of the organism cannot be easily isolated, whole inactivated viruses or bacteria have formed the basis of vaccine preparations. Because these vaccines include many antigens, they are more likely to be *reactogenic*, meaning they induce more adverse effects. This problem arose with whole-cell pertussis vaccine, for example—use of the vaccine was associated with febrile seizures and allergic reactions. Newer inactivated acellular pertussis vaccines, which are component vaccines, have been developed and licensed since 1991. These vaccines are associated with fewer side effects and are considered very safe.

Recombinant Vaccines

In the last two decades, attention has focused on genetic manipulation of organisms to generate either live attenuated or inactivated vaccines. Several different approaches have been used.

Hepatitis B vaccine, the first recombinant DNA vaccine, was licensed in 1986. There was substantial interest in developing a new hepatitis B vaccine as an earlier vaccine; while it was highly efficacious, this vaccine was derived from human blood products, and it was later determined that some blood product donors were HIV infected. The vaccine production process was designed to inactivate HBV and, therefore, also inactivated HIV. Although no infections with either virus were ever documented, this near-miss encouraged the production of non-human-based vaccine components.

The recombinant vaccine harnessed the ability of *Saccharomyces cerevisiae*, yeast cells, to make proteins. The hepatitis B surface antigen (HBsAg)

genes were *transvected* (inserted) into the yeast cell genome. Once the genes were inserted, the yeast cells could be clonally expanded so that large quantities of HBsAg could be produced. This technique allows for high production of antigen without the use of human-derived materials and has been used to generate many new vaccines. For example, *Escherichia coli* has been used to express lipoprotein from *Borrelia burgdorferi*, the arbovirus responsible for Lyme disease.[21] The first human vaccine for Lyme disease was licensed in 1998.

In recent years, two new recombinant vaccines have been developed to prevent hepatitis E virus (HEV) infection. HEV is an enteric organism that is spread by fecal-contaminated water; it causes widespread outbreaks and sporadic cases of severe fulminant hepatitis. HEV infection has been predominantly identified in developing countries in Asia and Africa. This type of hepatitis has a high mortality rate, especially in infants and pregnant women.[22] The new recombinant vaccines induce antibody to a capsid protein (E_2) that prevents infection. In two large clinical trials, these vaccines have been shown to be 95% and 100% effective, respectively.[23,24] While neither vaccine has become commercially available, advocates are urgently demanding release of these vaccines for both prevention and outbreak control.[25-27]

Another approach to developing a recombinant vaccine involves deletion or modification of genes that are known to confer pathogenicity. This method has been used to construct an oral typhoid vaccine, among numerous other vaccines. Recently, genetic manipulation of rhesus monkey and human rotavirus genomes enabled the development of vaccines for rotavirus, the major etiologic agent responsible for diarrheal deaths in children. Development of rotavirus vaccines took advantage of the fact that human and animal (i.e., bovine, rhesus) strains of the virus readily underwent reassortment. The resultant multivalent vaccine increases the potential to provide protection against multiple serotypes.[28]

A third approach to recombinant vaccine development involves insertion of a gene from one organism to another, usually a live virus. The modified virus subsequently acts as a carrier, or vector, that expresses the foreign gene. Using this innovative approach, canarypox virus has been used to express HIV glycoproteins.[29] In 2009, a canarypox-based HIV vaccine was the first vaccine to demonstrate a small level of protection from infection. In a Thai trial that began in 2003, researchers tested a vaccine regimen that included a priming dose of a recombinant canarypox vector vaccine (ALVAC-HIV) followed by two booster doses of a recombinant glycoprotein 120-subunit vaccine (AIDSVAX B/E). A modest reduction in the risk of HIV infection (31.2%) was noted among vaccine recipients.[30] As the vaccine was effective enough to have an impact, it has raised hopes that a vaccine may someday be developed to control HIV.

Vaccinia virus and adenovirus have been used to express rabies G protein.[31,32] This vaccine vector has been used to immunize wildlife against rabies in a novel program in the southwestern United States.[31] Because the vaccine can be administered orally, meat sticks impregnated with vaccine were distributed in an aggressive campaign that used airplane drops as well as ground distribution to surround known cases of rabies. Coupled with an immunization campaign for domestic animals and an education campaign about the purpose and safety of the immunization meat sticks, the campaign was successful in slowing the spread of rabies in Texas.[31]

DNA Vaccines

DNA vaccines differ from traditional vaccines in that the naked DNA coding for a specific component of a disease-causing organism is injected directly into the body. The delivery system is either a saline solution injected through a hypodermic needle or DNA-coated gold beads propelled into the body using "gene guns." Although no DNA vaccine is currently licensed, DNA vaccination represents a considerable technological advance that may revolutionize immunization. Developed extensively throughout the 1990s, this approach offers the possibility of safer and cheaper vaccines, even for diseases where traditional vaccines have achieved only limited success. DNA vaccines are currently under development for malaria, West Nile virus, tuberculosis, and HIV, among other infections.

There are several potential advantages associated with DNA vaccines. First, the actual production of the immunizing protein takes place in the cells of the vaccinated host. This approach theoretically eliminates the risk of the vaccine causing the infection it is intended to prevent, which is a concern with traditional live attenuated vaccines. Second, like live vaccines, DNA vaccines have the ability to elicit a wide range of humoral and cell-mediated immune responses that might potentially have a long-term duration. Third, DNA vaccines are very stable and can be stored under a vast array of conditions, eliminating the need for a cold chain. For this reason, they may be particularly suitable for use in developing countries. Finally, DNA vaccines may lend themselves to generic production methods that will simplify and standardize vaccine production.

An important shortcoming of DNA vaccines is that they are limited to developing immune responses against protein components. As a consequence, they cannot substitute for traditional polysaccharide-based vaccines (e.g., pneumococcal vaccine). These vaccines also pose novel safety concerns. For example, they may cause long-term immunologic stimulation at the injection site, leading to chronic inflammation. DNA from the vaccine might also become incorporated into host chromosomes and could be oncogenic if their presence turned on oncogenes or turned off tumor suppressor genes. Clearly, the safety and efficacy of DNA vaccines need to be carefully evaluated to ensure that the potential risks of these new vaccines are well understood.

Novel Vaccines

Novel approaches in vaccine development include the identification of new targets, new adjuvants, and new vaccine delivery methods, as well as the development of new vaccine types and combination vaccines. Both disease severity and disease burden remain important criteria for selecting an organism for vaccine development. Notable infections influencing vaccine development include HIV, tuberculosis, and malaria—a virus, bacterium, and parasite, respectively. *The Jordan Report* lists many infectious agents for which vaccines are in the pipeline.[33] Viral vaccines include those focused on the hepatitis C virus and herpesvirus (HSV-1 and HSV-2). In addition to HSV and HPV vaccines, other vaccines are in development to prevent sexually transmitted infections including gonorrhea, syphilis, and chlamydia. Along with the two licensed rotavirus vaccines, vaccines to prevent *Escherichia coli*, *Salmonella typhi*, and *Shigella* species are among the many vaccines being developed to prevent the diarrheal diseases that account for 4.0% of all deaths and 5.7% of the disease burden worldwide.[34]

Enhancing the specific and protective immune response to a vaccine remains a significant challenge. Adjuvants, such as aluminum salt (alum), have been used since the 1920s to increase immunogenicity. The mechanism of action of these older adjuvants was to inhibit clearance of an antigen from the site of injection, thereby allowing better recognition of the antigen by antigen-presenting cells (APCs). Newer adjuvants that improve the delivery of antigens to APCs in the lymphoid tissue have been developed. For example, particulate adjuvants, such as liposomes and microspheres, protect antigens from being destroyed in the stomach and present antigens to macrophages in the gut to enhance mucosal immunity. Other adjuvants are being developed to direct the immune response toward either a cellular-mediated (T_H1) or an antibody (T_H2) immune response. These adjuvants include cytokines, such as interleukin and interferon-gamma, and chemokines.[35-37] Vaccines that target intracellular infections, such as HIV and *Mycobacterium tuberculosis*, or parasites, such as *Plasmodium* spp. (malaria), need to produce a strong T_H1 response. Strong antibody (T_H2) responses are the best defense for extracellular bacterial infections (e.g., *Haemophilus influenzae* type b) and toxin-mediated diseases (*Bordetella pertussis*).[35-37] Unfortunately, the incorporation of an adjuvant in a vaccine's formulation may increase the risk of an adverse reaction; therefore, separate animal studies and safety studies are needed to evaluate the adjuvant effects. For more in-depth discussion of adjuvants, the reader is referred to the article by Vogel and Alving in the 2002 *Jordan Report*.[36]

The way vaccines are administered is also changing. Combination vaccines have been developed to reduce the number of overall injections. The measles, mumps, and rubella (MMR) vaccine, the diphtheria–tetanus–acellular pertussis vaccine (DTaP), and the *Haemophilus influenzae* type b and hepatitis B vaccine (Hib-HepB) are a few examples of the many combination vaccines currently being administered. The newly licensed live attenuated influenza vaccine administered intranasally aims to produce both local (mucosal) and systemic immune responses. Likewise, orally administered vaccines (e.g., polio and cholera vaccines) are advantageous in that they produce mucosal immunity.

In the foreseeable future, edible vaccines may be used to administer vaccines more widely, safely, and cheaply. Transgenic plants such as potatoes, tomatoes, and bananas are being developed such that the plant gene will encode for the targeted vaccine antigens.[34,35] Among the edible vaccines in the development pipeline are vaccines that target measles, *E. coli*, Norwalk virus, and hepatitis B. It is hoped that such plants can be developed for the delivery of multivalent vaccines for protection against a broad range of diseases.

Lastly, transcutaneous immunization systems, including skin patches and gene guns, aim to deliver vaccine antigen and adjuvant across the epidermis to Langerhans cells, a specific class of dendritic APC.[35,37]

The development of DNA and other gene-based vaccines holds promise that new mechanisms to deliver antigen-encoding genomes to the host will result in novel vaccine types: vector vaccines, such as simple plasmids or more complex modified viral vaccines (e.g., *Vaccinia* or adenovirus) or bacterial vectors.[37] The newly licensed HPV vaccines include a piece of the HPV genome enclosed in a non-enveloped capsid, which creates a virus-like-particle (VLP).[38] VLPs are being developed for other viral infections such as avian influenza and HIV.[39]

IMMUNIZATION SCHEDULES

The goal of an effective immunization program is to vaccinate a high proportion of susceptible persons early in life (i.e., before they are potentially exposed to the infectious agent). In the United States, infants and children are immunized against hepatitis B, diphtheria, tetanus, pertussis, Hib, polio, measles, mumps, rubella, and varicella virus (**Exhibit 11-3**). Alternative immunization schedules are available from other sources for children who have missed primary immunization series or who were inadequately immunized.[28, 29]

Immunization schedules[40] differ from country to country, depending on the burden of disease in the population, the availability of an efficacious and effective vaccine, economic factors, and the level of priority that is placed on vaccine preventable diseases. Prevention of hepatitis B infection has become a worldwide priority; therefore, an HBV vaccine has been added to the World Health Organization's (WHO) Expanded Program on Immunization recommendations. The routine vaccinations recommended by WHO are diphtheria, tetanus, and pertussis vaccine; oral polio vaccine; and measles, mumps, and rubella vaccine. In addition, WHO recommends vaccination against tuberculosis (i.e., BCG) and yellow fever in countries where these diseases are endemic.

Target Populations

Vaccine programs must identify individuals before exposure to natural infection and must boost vaccination rates among these populations before immunity wanes and is no longer at protective levels. A failure to maintain vaccine levels has resulted in outbreaks of disease among school-aged children. Assessment of adolescents at routine healthcare visits is warranted to ensure completion of primary vaccine series for newer vaccines (e.g., varicella, hepatitis B vaccine) and provide boosters for MMR if necessary.[41] In 2005, two new vaccines were licensed and recommended for adolescents: a conjugate meningococcal vaccine and a DTaP vaccine.

In 2006 and 2009, two preventive vaccines were licensed for human papillomavirus (HPV). These vaccines were immediately recommended for adolescents

Exhibit 11-3   Recommended Childhood and Adolescent Immunizations Schedule, United States 2012

Vaccine ▼ \ Age ▶	Birth	1 month	2 months	4 months	6 months	9 months	12 months	15 months	18 months	19–23 months	2–3 years	4–6 years
Hepatitis B	Hep B	Hep B					Hep B					
Rotavirus			RV	RV	RV							
Diptheria, tetanus, pertussis			DTaP	DTaP	DTaP		*	DTaP				DTaP
Haemophilus influenzae type b			Hib	Hib	Hib		Hib					
Pneumococcal			PCV	PCV	PCV		PCV					PPSV
Inactivated poliovirus			IPV	IPV		IPV						
Influenza							Influenza (annually)					
Measles, mumps, rubella							MMR		*			MMR
Varicella							Varicella		*			Varicella
Hepatitis A							Dose 1				Hep A series	
Meningococcal									MCV4			

Range for all children — Range certain high-risk children — Range all children and for certain high risk groups

* The schedule has extensive footnotes that clarify the spacing between vaccination doses, and it generally allows a slightly earlier administration of a vaccine if the previous doses were given at the earliest possible time. Further adjustments are made for children at higher risk of measles.

This schedule includes the recommendations in effect as of December 23, 2011. Any dose not administered at the recommended age should be administered at a subsequent visit, when indicated and feasible. The use of a combination vaccine generally is preferred over separate injections of its equivalent component vaccines. Vaccination providers should consult the relevant Advisory Committee on Immunization Practices (ACIP) statement for detailed recommendations, available online at http://www.cdc.gov/vaccines/pubs/acip-list.htm. Clinically significant adverse events that follow vaccination should be reported to the Vaccine Adverse Event Reporting System (VAERS) online.

Modified from the Centers for Disease Control and Prevention (2012). Recommended immunization schedule for persons aged 0 through 6 years—United States, 2012. http://www.cdc.gov/vaccines/schedules/downloads/child/0-6yrs-schedule-pr.pdf. Updated May 31, 2012. Accessed June 25, 2012.

females as young as 9 years, with catch-up immunization through age 26 years. Gardasil, a HPV vaccine currently licensed for use in the United States, protects against HPV types 6, 11, 16, and 18. HPV vaccination provides nearly 100% protection against persistent infections, genital warts, and precancerous lesions of the cervix caused by HPV types 6, 11, 16, and 18,[42] and data indicate that the vaccine may partially protect against 10 additional HPV types that cause up to 90% of cancers.[42] On a national level, U.S. HPV immunization rates lag far behind the *Healthy People 2010* goals of 90% coverage for adolescent females. Public perception, parental health beliefs, and naïveté of adolescents' sexual behavior are barriers to HPV immunization. To further prevent the spread of HPV, in 2010 these vaccines were recommended for all adolescents, including young adult males. If developed, other vaccines to prevent sexually transmitted infections, including herpes simplex virus type 2 (HSV-2) and the human immunodeficiency virus (HIV), will likely be offered to adolescents in the future to assure vaccination prior to exposure to these viruses.

Adult vaccination is an important part of preventive medical care. Routine adult vaccines include pneumococcal vaccine, influenza, and tetanus toxoid. A newer varicella vaccine, Zostavax, was licensed in 2006 for use in people age 60 and older to prevent shingles. MMR, hepatitis B, and hepatitis A are recommended for adults at higher risk. The U.S. Public Health Service and the CDC provide immunization recommendations for international travelers, depending on the endemic diseases in the destination country (e.g., MMR, hepatitis A and B, yellow fever, meningococcal, typhoid, polio, rabies, plague, and Japanese encephalitis).[43] Hib, pneumococcal, and meningococcal vaccinations are recommended for immunosuppressed persons who are at high risk of invasive bacterial infections. However, vaccine-induced immune responses may not be optimal in immune-suppressed people, and some individuals may remain susceptible to the infections targeted by the vaccines.

Conditions that Contraindicate Vaccination

Immunization schedules are modified when an individual has a contraindication to a particular vaccine (**Exhibit 11-4**). Mild illnesses (e.g., low-grade fever, upper respiratory infection, otitis media, and mild diarrhea) or breastfeeding are not contraindications for immunization. Previous or suspected anaphylactic reaction to a vaccine component is the strictest contraindication to immunization. When a concurrent moderate or severe illness may be exacerbated

Exhibit 11-4	**Contradictions for Vaccination**

1. Severe allergy to any vaccine component
2. Severe illness
3. Immunosuppression (live vaccines only)
4. HIV infection (live virus vaccines except measles)
5. Pregnancy (especially live vaccines)
6. Encephalopathy
7. Recent receipt of blood products (MMR and varicella)

by a vaccine-induced immune response, immunization can be delayed. Contraindications are specific to live attenuated vaccines, which pose a threat to immunosuppressed individuals or to fetuses. Because measles can be a severe illness in an HIV-infected person, MMR immunization is recommended for HIV-infected persons before they become severely immunocompromised. Among blood-product recipients, circulating antibody present in transfused blood components can interfere with the replication of live vaccine virus. Therefore, it is recommended that MMR and varicella vaccinations be postponed for a period following blood or blood product transfusions.

VACCINE DEVELOPMENT

Vaccine innovation includes identification and characterization of antigens that induce neutralizing antibody or humoral response, identification of genetic clones that produce these antigens, vaccine biochemical formulation, numerous animal studies, and extensive manufacturing innovation to mass-produce vaccine. Vaccine science, innovation, and manufacturing are critical components in the development of safe and efficacious vaccines for all national immunization programs.

Licensure of any new vaccine requires that efficacy be demonstrated from preclinical studies. In the United States, the vaccine manufacturer begins this process upon filing an investigational new drug (IND) application with the U.S. Food and Drug Administration (FDA). All information concerning vaccine formulation, vaccine manufacturing, stability and sterility testing, and results of animal testing is submitted to the FDA. The FDA approves the implementation of human studies only if the new vaccine demonstrates preliminary potency, safety, and effectiveness in animal studies. The following section outlines the hierarchical process of preclinical and clinical research. At each point, the decision to progress to the next phase is based on promising results from the previous set of studies.

Preclinical Studies

Animal testing is used to develop assays that assess the humoral and cellular immune response to candidate vaccines. Through a series of studies, appropriate animal models are used to determine the dose-response relationship, to identify the optimal routes of administration, and to specify the dosing schedule necessary to achieve the maximum beneficial dose (i.e., the dose that maximizes the protective immune response and minimizes serious adverse events). Animal studies represent the first step in evaluating vaccine safety. A list of vaccine-induced toxicities is established, which may include severe systemic effects and organ systems damage, as well as the unlikely potential of a vaccine to be carcinogenic or teratogenic. Provided that its potential benefit is deemed to outweigh its potential harm, the product then proceeds to human studies.

Phase 1: Dose Finding and Safety

Following FDA review and approval by an institutional review board (IRB), early vaccine studies in humans are conducted to evaluate vaccine dose and safety and to assess whether the vaccine is biologically active. Specific toxicities (e.g., local and systemic reactions and hematological abnormalities) are evaluated in both Phase 1 and Phase 2 safety and immunogenicity studies. Rules for stopping an immunization series are established from the outset and are modified as more data are collected.

Most preventive vaccine clinical trials begin with trials in healthy, adult volunteers. Childhood vaccines are first tested in healthy adults and older children, prior to testing in infants. For some vaccines (e.g., HIV vaccines), initial clinical trials may be conducted in previously infected persons and subsequently among uninfected healthy adults. Adult studies typically begin with a single fixed dose of vaccine in a small number of volunteers (e.g., 5–10 subjects). Post-inoculation serologic assays measure the level and duration of the immune response. Adverse events are carefully enumerated and graded for severity, duration, and the relationship to vaccination. Small sequential studies may be conducted whereby the vaccine dose is increased until a beneficial dose is established. Additional Phase 1 or Phase 1/2 safety and immunogenicity studies are performed in children and infants to fine-tune the dose, define the vaccine schedule, and continue monitoring immune response and vaccine safety in these age groups.

Phase 2: Safety and Immunogenicity Trials

In Phase 2 studies, safety, benefit, and evidence of efficacy are the primary endpoints. Safety and immunogenicity endpoints are predefined based on preclinical and Phase 1 studies. The vaccine is tested in healthy persons representing the population for which the vaccine is indicated. In this phase of testing, the sample size needs to be sufficiently large to measure the vaccine's benefit (i.e., evidence of efficacy) without compromising the ability to estimate rates of adverse events. Studies enrolling 50–100 persons can measure adverse events at a rate of 10 in 100 doses and estimate the beneficial effect that occurs in 10% or more of the population.

As in Phase 1 studies, post-inoculation serologic assays are performed to measure the level and duration of the immune response. Participants are closely evaluated for severity and duration of adverse events. Expected adverse events and severity grades are listed in toxicity tables used to standardize safety evaluations. Correlates of protection provide evidence of vaccine clinical efficacy; they include immunologic markers of immune response to the vaccine, such as seroconversion (i.e., development of neutralizing antibodies), rise in antibody titer (i.e., booster response), and development of cell-mediated immune response (e.g., cytotoxic T lymphocytes).

Phase 3: Comparative Efficacy Trials

Comparative efficacy trials determine the impact of vaccination on prevention of infection and begin to assess the feasibility of administering vaccinations in at-risk populations. Vaccines that are shown to be safe and immunogenic in Phase 1 and 2 trials advance to Phase 3 randomized comparative trials to assess the true vaccine efficacy. Phase 3 trials involve large numbers of susceptible persons in more generalizable settings. The definitive study design for determining vaccine efficacy is the randomized, double-blinded, placebo-controlled trial. Often, multiple clinic sites are required to recruit a large enough sample to demonstrate vaccine efficacy with adequate study power. Sample size requirements depend on the incidence of infection in an unvaccinated population (or a similar vaccinated population if a standard vaccine is already available), as well as the expected reduction in the incidence in the vaccinated population. In Phase 3 trials, vaccine efficacy is calculated as the observed reduction in incidence (I) in the vaccinated (vac) versus the incidence in the unvaccinated (unv) population, expressed as a percentage.

Randomization strives to achieve comparability between vaccinated and unvaccinated groups with respect to demographic characteristics and risk factors for natural infection. Theoretically, randomization of a sufficient number of persons will ensure that characteristics that could affect the safety and efficacy of a vaccine will be evenly distributed across study arms. While investigators might know many factors that could influence a person's risk of disease, other unknown factors could also prove important. Randomization is intended to ensure that both *known* and, more importantly, *unknown* confounders are evenly distributed between the two arms. For example, risk factors for most childhood infections include other immunizations, attendance in daycare programs or school, exposure to infected individuals, and general health status. In vaccine trials of vaccines to prevent HIV, HBV, and hepatitis C infections, specific risk factors require consideration, such as the number of unprotected sexual acts and sharing of potentially contaminated drug-injection equipment. For infections such as malaria that are transmitted by a vector (e.g., *Aedes* spp.), it is important to take into account the level of endemicity of *Plasmodium* spp. and participants' use of mosquito nets and insect repellents.

Analysis of the distribution of these potential confounders is crucial, because differential exposure to the infectious agent across the vaccinated and unvaccinated (control) groups can bias estimates of vaccine efficacy. If known confounders are not evenly distributed, unknown confounders could also cause bias in the study results. The problem inherent in sample selection is that an investigator could use statistical methods to account for uneven distribution of known confounders if they were measured with sufficient detail, but there is no way to control for an unknown confounder. By design, a trial may strive to have equal distribution of key factors in each arm by stratifying participants prior to randomization. For example, a trial may separate participants by age groups and then randomize participants within each age group. This approach would ensure that the arms of the trial had a similar age distribution. Adjustments may be made in the analysis to account for known characteristics that, despite randomization, may not have been evenly distributed between the study arms.

VACCINE EFFICACY AND VACCINE EFFECTIVENESS

Measures of vaccine efficacy (VE) are calculated from prelicensure, randomized, double-blind, Phase 3 clinical trials. In contrast, results from postlicensure observational studies associate disease outcomes with vaccine failure in fully vaccinated and inadequately vaccinated individuals, and in populations with low vaccine coverage. Whereas vaccine trials measure efficacy, the overall estimate of protective effect calculated from an observational epidemiologic study is more accurately defined as vaccine effectiveness (VE*).[44,45] Overall vaccine effectiveness is the result of both the vaccine's direct effect, which refers to its ability to protect individuals from infection, and its indirect effect, which is its ability to reduce the spread of the infection in a population.[45,46] For a discussion of the ways in which vaccines can indirectly decrease the duration of disease, alter susceptibility, or reduce the infective period of an organism in a given population, refer to the publications of Halloran et al.[46–48]

In any given population, spread of disease is a function of the number of contacts (C), the probability of exposure to an infectious agent (E), and the probability that exposure leads to infection (P) (**Figure 11-3**). Determination of VE* generally assumes that infected, immune, and susceptible persons are

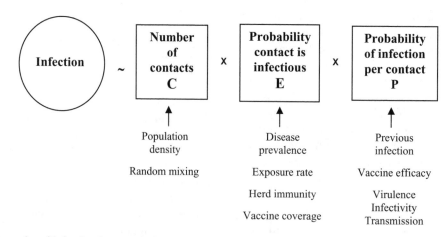

Figure 11-3 Dynamics of infection in a population

randomly mixed in the population and that the population is sufficiently dense so that contact (C) will be equal.[46–48] The probability of exposure is related to both the prevalence of disease and the number of immune persons in the population. *Herd immunity*, which refers to the overall level of immunity within a population, depends on the extent of immunity acquired from previous epidemics as well as other factors, such as vaccine coverage. The probability that contact with an infected person will result in infection is a function of an individual's susceptibility and the virulence of the organism. Individual susceptibility can be lower in those persons with protective immunity from either previous infection or vaccination.

In a randomized clinical trial, vaccine efficacy (VE) is the percent reduction in the incidence of disease in the vaccinated (I_{vac}) compared to the incidence of disease in the unvaccinated (I_{unv}):

$$VE = \frac{I_{unv} - I_{vac}}{I_{unv}} \times 100$$

The following equation is derived from dividing the previous expression by the incidence in the unvaccinated population:

$$VE = 1 - \frac{I_{vac}}{I_{unv}} = 1 - RR$$

As demonstrated by these equations, the ratio of incidence in the vaccinated to unvaccinated groups is a measure of relative risk (RR). The equation VE = 1 − RR is useful in epidemiological studies where vaccine effectiveness (VE*) can be assessed. Vaccine effectiveness (VE*) approximates vaccine efficacy (VE) when exposure (E) to the infectious agent is not dependent upon vaccination status and does not differ across comparison groups, and when the vaccinated and unvaccinated persons arise from the same population, such that the rate of contact (C) is equivalent.

$$VE^* = 1 - \frac{C_{vac} \times E_{vac} \times P_{vac}}{C_{unv} \times E_{unv} \times P_{unv}} = 1 - \frac{P_{vac}}{P_{unv}} = 1 - RR$$

If the comparison groups are similar, then vaccine effectiveness, VE* = 1 − P_{vac}/P_{unv}, is a function of the ratio of individual immunity in the vaccinated and unvaccinated groups, and can be estimated by VE* = 1 − RR.[45–47] **Table 11-1** summarizes equations for calculating vaccine effectiveness in observational studies.

Table 11-1	Vaccine Effectiveness Equations	
Prospective	**Cohort**	**VE* = 1 − RR**
Studies	**Outbreak investigation** (Attack rates or cumulative incidence)	VE* = 1 − AR$_{vac}$/AR$_{unv}$
	Household spread (Secondary attack rate)	VE* = 1 − SAR$_{vac}$/SAR$_{unv}$
	Longitudinal follow-up with time to event data	VE* = 1 − H$_{vac}$/H$_{unv}$
	Life-table (Hazard ratio)	VE* = 1 − CI$_{vac}$/CI$_{unv}$
	Person-time (Cumulative incidence)	VE* = 1 − OR
Retrospective Studies	**Case-control studies**	VE* = 1 − (a/c)/(b/d) ratio of the odds of vaccination in cases and controls.
	Unmatched	VE* = 1 − b/c ratio of discordant pairs
	Matched	
	Logistic regression model or proportional hazard model	VE* = 1 − e^{-vac}

Reproduced from Halloran ME, Struchiner CJ, and Longini IM, Study designs for evaluating different efficacy and effectiveness aspects of vaccines. *Am J Epidemiol* 146(10):790, Table 1. © 1997. By permission of Oxford University Press.

EPIDEMIOLOGIC STUDIES

After licensure, vaccines are administered to heterogeneous populations at risk of disease, who will vary in age, infirmity, access to health care, and risk of exposure. At this point, observational studies play an important role in assessing vaccine effectiveness. In contrast to randomized clinical trials evaluating vaccine efficacy, case-control and cohort studies evaluate the combination of vaccine efficacy and the success of a given immunization program. A significant decline in the overall incidence of disease is one indicator that the vaccine itself and the immunization campaign, which may include other disease prevention approaches such as hand washing messages, have contributed to the prevention of disease. A suboptimal vaccine effectiveness can also be due to a variety of vaccine and programmatic issues. Failure to vaccinate those populations at highest risk of infection could result in lower disease prevention than expected by the vaccine coverage rate. In addition, if a breakdown occurs in the handling of a vaccine (a live attenuated vaccine is not refrigerated properly) or manufacturing (a lot is poorly antigenic), then vaccine effectiveness would be compromised.

Seldom, if ever, do vaccine efficacy and/or coverage reach 100%. Therefore, outbreaks among vaccinated populations can and do occur. Observational studies can determine whether effectiveness was compromised overall in the general population or represented a more targeted problem within subgroups. Vaccine effectiveness can be measured within a population experiencing an outbreak, special populations at increased risk of infection (e.g., the elderly, children in daycare programs, people in refugee camps), or as part of community-wide surveillance of vaccine-preventable diseases.

Vaccine effectiveness can be determined by comparing risk of disease among vaccinated and unvaccinated groups. A study must compare groups with comparable susceptibility before vaccination, equal exposure to disease before and after vaccination, and equal risk of being diagnosed with disease during the study period.[45] As in randomized trials of vaccine efficacy, it is important to ensure that these groups are comparable with respect to known exposure, risk of infection, access to the vaccine, and opportunity for diagnosis. Potential bias may occur if any of the following conditions occur:

1. There is unequal exposure to disease that causes individuals to self-select for vaccination.
2. Vaccination status systematically differs between healthy and diseased persons.
3. Infection or disease is differentially diagnosed in the vaccinated versus the unvaccinated.[45–48]

Essential components to any epidemiologic study include definition of a case, standardized case finding, ascertainment of vaccine status, and level of exposure.

An a priori case definition or disease should be both sensitive and specific. A case definition that poorly represents the disease in question may lead to imprecise estimates of vaccine effectiveness.[48,49] When possible, rigorous studies should ensure laboratory confirmation of cases. Although it is not essential for every observational study, laboratory confirmation of cases increases the precision of the point estimate of vaccine effectiveness, which often yields a more favorable measure of a vaccine's effectiveness.[45,46]

In any study, it is crucial to assure that case finding occurs with the same degree of rigor in both the vaccinated and unvaccinated groups. Vaccination may prevent clinical disease but not infection, or it may reduce the severity of disease, resulting in a differential disease diagnosis in the vaccinated versus unvaccinated groups. Therefore, to avoid bias, a case definition must detect a spectrum of mild, moderate, and severe disease. The point estimate of vaccine effectiveness will be biased by the extent to which groups differ in assessment, medical care and diagnosis, validity of self-report or parental report of disease, and quality of medical records. Even among those persons who receive medical care for a vaccine-related event or breakthrough illness, the diligence of medical providers in reporting diseases is influenced by their perception of the importance of the report. Thus studies that rely on passive reporting systems may experience bias in the assessment of cases if clinicians feel it is more important to report cases of disease among those persons who have been vaccinated.

Equal effort must be made to confirm the vaccination status of both diseased and nondiseased persons. Reliance upon the self-reporting of vaccination status or inaccurate vaccination records (e.g., school records) may result in misclassification. When possible, self-reported vaccine histories should be confirmed through provider records, which are also important in confirming vaccination dates, vaccine type, manufacturer and lot number, and expiration dates.

The definition of *vaccination* must also be clear. When multiple doses of vaccine are required to develop full protection, the appropriate comparison is between persons who receive no vaccine and those who receive a complete course. If it is assumed that one or two doses induce some immunity, then inclusion of these persons in the unvaccinated group would enrich that group with nonsusceptibles, thereby lowering the attack rates in the unvaccinated group relative to the attack rates in the vaccinated group, and in turn decreasing the measured vaccine effectiveness. Alternatively, if the vaccinated group includes persons receiving less than the full series, the vaccinated group would be enriched with susceptibles, increasing attack rates and lowering measured effectiveness.[45,46] Vaccine effectiveness for one, two, and three doses compared to no vaccination can be calculated from prospective cohort and case-control studies.

Observational studies evaluating vaccine effectiveness are vulnerable to selection factors that can cause rates derived from diseased and nondiseased groups or vaccinated and unvaccinated groups to differ systematically. Factors such as age, sex, race, socioeconomic status, place of work or residence, attendance in school or daycare programs, and residence in jail or nursing homes may independently be related to both risk of disease and vaccination status. Therefore, researchers must diligently control for confounding factors in the design of the study (e.g., through stratification or matching), or preferably by ensuring sufficient sample size and collection of data on potential confounders so that statistical adjustments may be made.

In highly endemic areas and areas where there are adequate resources, surveillance is conducted among cohorts of vaccinated and unvaccinated persons. Upon establishing study participants' vaccination status at baseline, the cumulative incidence of infection in vaccinated persons (CI_{vac}) is compared to the cumulative incidence of infection in unvaccinated persons (CI_{unv}), thereby estimating the relative risk.[47] Other types of epidemiologic study designs that are used to evaluate vaccine effectiveness are described in detail in the remainder of this section. In-depth discussion on these field methods is found in publications by Halloran et al.[46-48]

Seroprevalence Cross-Sectional Studies

Evidence of vaccine efficacy and effectiveness are often correlated with a protective level of antibody in serum. In a cross-sectional study, a single serum sample is drawn and antibody levels are correlated with past records of vaccination and disease. The comparison of the proportion of subjects who have been vaccinated with protective antibody with the proportion of subjects who have not been vaccinated with protective antibody is a prevalence ratio (PR). In this case, the calculation of vaccine effectiveness is VE* = 1 − PR.

One advantage of seroprevalence studies is the ability to quickly assess vaccine-induced immunity, measured according to the length of time since vaccination. These results should be interpreted with caution, however, because antibody responses wane over time, and the absence of detectable antibody does not necessarily indicate susceptibility.

Prospective Studies

Populations at high risk of infection can be defined during an outbreak investigation, through a household contact study, or in a highly endemic area. Using methods such as personal interviews and medical records review, vaccination status can be confirmed and a cohort of vaccinated and unvaccinated persons followed for the purpose of identifying new cases of disease. Prospective studies yield valid estimates of RR when the disease is common and exposure is rare (i.e., vaccination coverage is high). In situations where the attack rate (AR) is expected to be high and the population contains a mixture of vaccinated and unvaccinated persons, a prospective study is useful for evaluating vaccine effectiveness.

In outbreak studies, vaccination status is established at baseline, and the RR is used to compare the AR in the vaccinated (AR_{vac}) and unvaccinated (AR_{unv}) groups. Households of primary cases represent highly exposed populations that warrant close observation. As high-risk households are identified, vaccination status is confirmed for each member of that household, and any secondary cases are identified. To estimate vaccine effectiveness, the RR is calculated as the ratio of vaccinated secondary cases (SAR_{vac}) to unvaccinated secondary cases (SAR_{unv}) from all households. Time-to-event analyses (i.e., survival analysis) are also useful for estimating RR. Using Cox proportional hazards models, the hazard ratio is an estimate of the instantaneous relative risk, which is the ratio of the probability of disease in the vaccinated group at some time point (H_{vac}) relative to the probability of disease in the unvaccinated (H_{unv}) at the same time point.[33-35]

In prospective studies, factors that erroneously increase the attack rate in the vaccinated group relative to the unvaccinated group will cause vaccine effectiveness to be underestimated, whereas any erroneous increase in the attack rate in the unvaccinated group relative to the vaccinated group will lead to an overestimate of vaccine effectiveness.

Case-Control Studies

Case-control studies can be an appropriate study design for assessing vaccine effectiveness when the disease is rare. One advantage of this approach is that data pertaining to multiple risk factors of vaccine failure can be collected and evaluated. Cases are often identified through a surveillance system, such as direct laboratory reporting or national surveillance databases. To avoid bias, controls should be selected from the same population as cases and should not significantly differ with respect to their probability of vaccination or exposure to infection. As in other case-control studies, a matched or unmatched design may be used.

The odds ratio (OR) is used to estimate RR or, in this case, VE*. The OR is calculated as the ratio of the odds of vaccination in the cases relative to the odds of vaccination in the controls, or the ratio of discordant pairs for unmatched and matched designs, respectively. Vaccine effectiveness is calculated as VE* = 1 − OR. When logistic models are used to calculate the OR for disease in the vaccinated group, the equation VE* = 1 − $e^{\beta_{vac}}$ is the measure of vaccine effectiveness, where $e^{\beta_{vac}}$ is the expotentiated log OR of disease in the vaccinated population. In case-control studies, VE* is underestimated when vaccination rates are erroneously over-reported in the cases relative to the controls; it is overestimated when controls are more likely to be misclassified as being vaccinated relative to cases.[48,49]

MONITORING ADVERSE EVENTS AND VACCINE SAFETY

In general, the risk of disease trumps the risk of vaccination. Some vaccines have been developed specifically to mitigate potential risks of vaccination. For example, recombinant hepatitis B vaccine replaced the theoretical risk of infection from the human serum-derived vaccine. Oral polio vaccine, which carried a rare risk of paralysis, has been replaced by inactivated polio vaccine in countries at low risk of natural infection. Most recently, acellular pertussis vaccines have replaced more reactogenic whole-cell pertussis vaccines. Unfortunately, as vaccine-preventable diseases become rarer, the perceived risk of severe adverse events from a particular vaccine can appear to outweigh the risk of natural infection among an uninformed public.

Comparative studies continue to collect information on adverse events. In the United States, additional postlicensure monitoring is achieved through the use of surveillance systems to track vaccine-related adverse events, as mandated by the National Childhood Injury Act of 1986. By 1998, a nationwide Vaccine Adverse Event Reporting System (VAERS) was established by the U.S. Department of Health and Human Services.[50,51] VAERS is a passive reporting system designed to collect case-series data

to detect rare events, to identify trends in commonly reported adverse events, and to detect early warning signals and generate hypotheses about possible new adverse events.[52] The strength of VAERS is its demonstrated feasibility as a cost-effective public health system for identifying potential harmful effects of mass vaccination. Healthcare providers and vaccine manufacturers are required to report all adverse events associated with the administration of a U.S. licensed vaccine. VAERS is especially important with newly licensed vaccines and in the assessment of new indications for vaccinations.

As in many passive reporting systems, VAERS case-series data are biased due to both under-reporting and over-reporting of suspected vaccine reactions.[50–52] Rates of adverse events cannot be calculated because the system does not collect denominator data (i.e., the number of persons vaccinated or the number of doses given).[52] Nevertheless, VAERS data can be used to identify clusters of rare adverse events, such as associations between oral polio vaccine and poliomyelitis, and between DTP and sudden infant death syndrome (SIDS). In further analysis of such clusters, DTP has been cleared of an association with SIDS.

After the licensure of the first rotavirus vaccine in 1998, VAERS detected a cluster of intussusception cases following administration of the vaccine (**Figure 11-4**).[53,54] Following identification of these kinds of adverse event clusters or signals, clinical, epidemiologic, and laboratory investigations are required to assess causality. Studies that substantiate severe adverse effects may lead to the withdrawal of vaccine, the development of safer vaccines, or compensation for persons who experienced the adverse events. In the cases of intussusception following rotavirus vaccination, subsequent investigations led the CDC to recommend suspension of the vaccine's use on July 16, 1999;[54] this move was followed by voluntary withdrawal of the vaccine from the market.[52] These preliminary findings were not confirmed, however. Moreover, while there was an increased risk of intussusception following rotavirus vaccination, overall rates of intussusception were dramatically reduced among vaccinated infants. After licensure of a new rotavirus vaccine, RotaTeq, the CDC implemented a large postlicensure safety study of this vaccine. The findings of this study concluded that this vaccine is not related to an increase risk of intussusception.[55]

The Vaccine Safety Datalink (VSD) project is another effort to improve postlicensure monitoring of vaccine-related adverse events. Beginning in 1991, the CDC, in partnership with health maintenance organizations (HMOs), established large cohorts

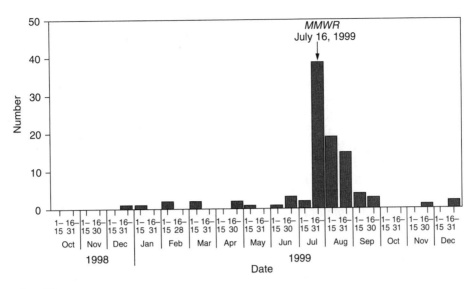

*n = 98.

Figure 11-4 Number* of confirmed cases of intussusception after implementation of rhesus-human rotavirus reassortant-tetravalent vaccine, by date reported to the Vaccine Adverse Event Reporting System—United States, October 1, 1998–December 31, 1999. Reproduced from the Centers for Disease Control and Prevention. Suspension of rotavirus vaccine after reports of intussusception-United States, 1999. *MMWR.* 2004 Sep 3;53(34):786–9.

of vaccinated children.[56] Subsequently, the VSD has expanded to monitor vaccine-related adverse events in adolescents and adults. VSD data are generated during routine healthcare visits and include both adverse event and denominator data (i.e., number vaccinated and doses administered) for large, stable populations. As such, the system is less subject to under-reporting or other biases common to passive surveillance systems. The VSD thus provides a rapid and economical means of conducting postlicensure comparative studies of vaccine safety.[56]

In a review of research tools to evaluate the causal association between vaccines and adverse events, Robert Chen, a CDC researcher, lists four criteria necessary to establish causality. First, laboratory confirmation (e.g., isolation of the vaccine virus strain from the pathogenic lesion) is required. Second, unique clinical syndromes specific to a vaccine (e.g., acute flaccid paralysis following OPV vaccine) must be identified. Third, the adverse event must recur upon rechallenge with the vaccine. Fourth, the adverse event must occur more often in the vaccinated group than in the unvaccinated group.[57] Adverse events that meet the first three criteria are rare. Clinical trials are often not sufficiently powered for safety studies to identify events that are rare; for example, intussusception occurs once per 10,000 doses of rotavirus vaccine, and acute encephalopathy occurs once in 100,000 doses of whole-cell pertussis vaccine. Despite the limitations of epidemiologic studies in quantifying extremely rare events, they serve to define an upper limit of risk of adverse events.[57]

Consistency in observational studies must be coupled with evidence of a biological mechanism by which a vaccine may cause the adverse event. Both of these criteria define the plausibility criteria set forth by the Institute of Medicine's (IOM) Immunization Safety Review Committee, which was convened to evaluate the plausibility and significance of many alleged vaccine adverse events.[57]

The association between autism and vaccines, specifically MMR vaccine, was one of the many vaccine-related adverse events scrutinized by the IOM committee. Two observations supported the hypothesis linking autism with MMR. First, an increased number of autism cases were being reported in the same time period when an increasing number of children were being vaccinated against measles (ecological association). Second, the signs of autism (e.g., loss of language skills) in the second year of life occurred close to the time when MMR was given. The latter factor indicated a temporal association between vaccine and disease, but it remained possible that the events are coincident and unrelated.[58]

The IOM investigated two potential causes of autism: the measles vaccine virus and the mercury-containing preservative, thimerosal.[59,60] In a 1998 study by Wakefield et al., researchers found measles virus RNA in the intestines of 8 of 12 children with neurological disorders, specifically autism. These findings suggested a potential biologic link between measles vaccine and autism, but did not provide specific evidence of a biologic mechanism.[61] The IOM considered this link along with the body of epidemiological data, which included nine controlled-observational studies, three ecological studies, and two studies based on the passive surveillance of systems; all of these studies consistently demonstrated no evidence of an association between MMR vaccine and autism. The committee concluded that the evidence favored rejection of a causal association between MMR vaccine and autism.[59] It is important to note that many years after its original publication, in 2010, *The Lancet* retracted and discredited Wakefield's article linking MMR vaccine with autism; the evidence that Wakefield committed fraud was presented in *British Medical Journal* in 2011.[62,63]

The situation with thimerosal was less clear. It has been well known that high doses of mercury exposure cause neurological damage. Studies of low-dose mercury exposure, ingested in seafood, on neurologic development have yielded inconclusive results. The IOM committee reported that no published or unpublished study that it reviewed linked thimerosal to autism. Despite this finding, the committee was concerned that children received many vaccines containing thimerosal and a cumulative effect was possible. Nevertheless, it concluded that there was insufficient evidence to accept or reject the causal association between thimerosal and autism.[59] By the year 2000 and despite the inconclusive evidence, but to alleviate parents' concerns about vaccine safety, vaccine manufacturers stopped making vaccines for infants and children that contained thimerosal.

For many rare and potential vaccine-related adverse events, the actual biological mechanisms are not yet known. Surveillance and epidemiologic studies might suggest such a mechanism, but further research is needed to establish the biologic bases for any event. In the United States, the CDC has funded seven Clinic Immunization Safety Assessment (CISA) centers.[64,65] A stated goal of these centers is to develop standard assessments of individuals who experience vaccine-related adverse events to advance the scientific understanding of the pathophysiology and risk factors associated with these reactions. This network will further augment the VAERS and VSD systems in the evaluation of vaccine safety.[54,57,64,65]

DIRECT IMPACT OF VACCINATION

"The impact of vaccination on the health of the people worldwide is difficult to exaggerate. With the exception of safe water, no modality, not even antibiotics, has had such a major effect upon reducing mortality and subsequent population growth."[66] The direct impact from widespread use of vaccines can be easily understood when one examines the incidence rates of specific diseases over time. This section highlights disease trends in poliomyelitis, measles, and invasive *Haemophilus influenzae* type b to illustrate the impact of effective vaccines and vaccine programs.

Polio

The increased incidence of paralytic poliomyelitis coincided with improvements in hygiene and societal development in the 1930s and 1940s (**Figure 11-5**). Prior to the development of sanitation systems, children acquired protective immunity when exposed to poliovirus in infancy. Polio infection in infants is restricted to the gastrointestinal tract because the human receptors necessary for poliovirus infection

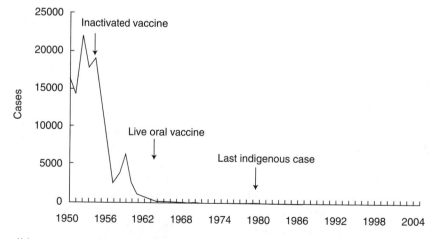

Figure 11-5 Poliomyelitis cases reported in the United States, 1950–2004. Reproduced from Poliomyelitis. In: Atkinson W, and Wolfe C, eds. Epidemiology and Prevention of Vaccine Preventable Diseases. 7th ed. Atlanta, GA: Public Health Foundation; 2002; p. 75.

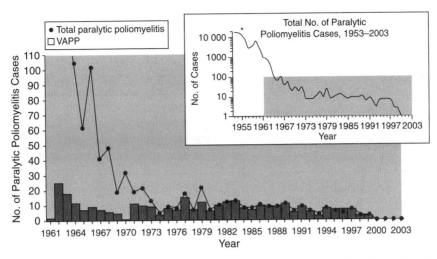

Figure 11-6 Reported cases of paralytic poliomyelitis, United States 1953–2003. Reproduced from Alexander, L.N. et al. Vaccine Policy Changes and Epidemiology of Poliomyelitis in the United States. *JAMA.* 2004;292:1696–1701.

of neurons are not expressed until later in childhood. Between 1940 and 1952, the incidence of paralytic polio in the United States rose from less than 12 cases per 100,000 persons to approximately 37 cases per 100,000 persons. Although the total number of cases declined before the first vaccine was introduced in 1955, the proportion of paralytic cases increased from a rate of 66% to 88% of all cases.[67]

In 1955, the Salk inactivated polio vaccine (IPV) was the first polio vaccine licensed. After its licensure, the United States began a mass-immunization campaign, and the incidence of poliomyelitis cases fell dramatically as more and more children were immunized. A 90% reduction in the number of poliomyelitis cases was attained with the Salk IPV alone. As a result, the death rate declined from 1.9 per 100,000 cases between 1915 and 1924 to 0.1 per 100,000 cases in 1961. The Salk IPV did not induce sufficient mucosal immunity to protect against reinfection, however, so outbreaks continued to occur, including a high number of cases in persons who were fully vaccinated.[67,68]

The Sabin oral live attenuated vaccine (OPV) was licensed for human use in 1961–1962, after which the incidence of poliomyelitis continued to decline further; in 1964, only 59 polio cases were reported in the United States. In 1960, a total of 2525 paralytic cases were reported, compared to 61 in 1965.[67,68] Thus the Sabin OPV quickly became the vaccine of choice in the United States and in most other parts of the world. In the United States, the last indigenously acquired poliovirus infection occurred in 1979,[69] and the last imported case occurred in 1993.[70]

Vaccine-associated paralytic poliomyelitis (VAPP) was recognized as early as 1962. Since the early 1970s, VAPP has accounted for almost all of the paralytic polio cases identified in the United States (**Figure 11-6**). Alexander et al. reviewed the U.S. paralytic polio cases between 1990 and 2003 and estimated VAPP incidence to be 0.34 case per 1 million OPV vaccines distributed to immunocompetent children; further, these researchers demonstrated that the risk of VAPP increased with increasing number of OPV doses received.[70] Persons with primary immunodeficiency who were indirectly vaccinated with vaccine poliovirus were at highest risk for VAPP. The authors estimated VAPP incidence within this population to be 3077 cases per 1 million immunocompromised individuals.[70] In 1999, the U.S. vaccine recommendation changed from an all-OPV immunization schedule to a two-dose IPV followed by OPV schedule. This modification in the schedule resulted in a 54% decline in VAPP. In 2000, an all-IPV schedule was implemented. The last case of VAPP in the United States occurred in 1999.[70]

Measles

Measles was an extremely important cause of childhood morbidity and mortality up to 5 years prior to vaccine licensure (1958–1962). At that time, the average annual number of reported measles cases in the United States was 503,282, with approximately 500 deaths attributable to measles occurring each year.[71] Epidemic cycles of measles occurred every 2–3 years, and the actual annual number of cases of measles was estimated to be in the range of 3 to 4 million. More than 50% of the population had experienced measles by age 6, and more than 90% had measles by age 15, with the highest incidence between ages 5 to 9 years.[72] The first live attenuated measles vaccine (Edmonston B strain) was licensed for use in 1963; the currently available vaccine, the Enderson-Edmonston

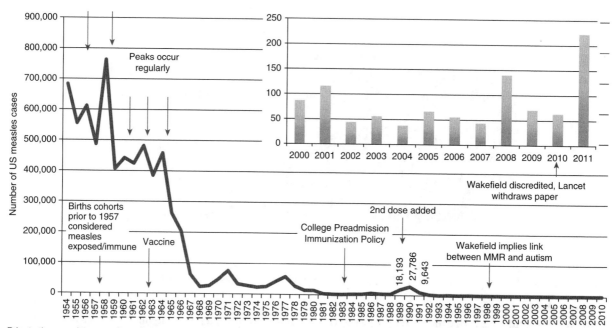

Prior to the use of the measles vaccine, large epidemics occurred every three years as the number of susceptible children became large enough to sustain large-scale transmission. Prior to the vaccine, exposure to measles was over 95% and those born before 1957 are considered immune. In May 1983, the American College Health Association responded to the high number of cases of measles among college students, recommending measles vaccination review and immunization, if deemed insufficient, for all matriculates. This recommendations was generalized to all children in 1989, when a second dose was added for children between 4–6 years of age.

Figure 11-7 Measles cases in the United States, 1954 to 2010, as reported to the Centers for Disease Control and Prevention. Data from MMWR Summary of Notifiable Diseases—United States, 2010 Weekly June 1, 2012 / 59(53);1–111; and MMWR Summary of Notifiable Diseases, United States, 1993 October 21, 1994/42(53);1–73; and MMWR Current Trends Measles on College Campuses – United States, July 26, 1985/34(29);445-9; and Godlee F, Smith J, Marcovitch H (2011). "Wakefield's article linking MMR vaccine and autism was fraudulent." http://www.bmj.com/content/342/bmj.c7452.full. Accessed June 25, 2012.

strain, was licensed in 1968. Following initial licensure, the incidence of measles decreased by more than 98%, and the 2- to 3-year epidemic cycles no longer occurred (**Figure 11-7**).[72]

Regional elimination of measles began in 1989, when the World Health Assembly resolved to reduce measles morbidity and mortality by 90% and 95%, respectively, by 1995. The goal to eliminate indigenous measles in the United States was set in 1978. In September 1999, the CDC reported a record low number of measles cases in the United States; only 100 measles cases were confirmed in 1998, most of which were imported or associated with an imported case.[71,73] In 2002, measles was recognized as nonendemic in the United States, with only 44 imported cases occurring in that year.[74]

In the United States, between 1985 and 1988, 42% of measles cases occurred in children who were vaccinated on or after their first birthday, and 68% of cases involved school-aged children who had been appropriately vaccinated as children and were vaccine failures. The measles outbreaks in 1985 and 1986 led to a recommendation in 1989 of universal reimmunization of children against measles, either at school

entry or at entry into middle school or junior high school.[75]

A resurgence of measles occurred between 1989 and 1991. There were 18,193 cases in 1989, 27,786 cases in 1990, and 9643 cases in 1991. During this resurgence, the age distribution changed, such that children 5 years and younger accounted for 45–48% of the new cases. The principal cause of the measles epidemic of 1989–1991 was failure to vaccinate children at the recommended age.[76,77] Pockets of low-immunization coverage were observed in inner-city communities, and the highest measles incidence occurred among Hispanic and African American children. Surveys conducted in areas experiencing preschool measles outbreaks indicated that as few as 50% of children had been vaccinated for measles by their second birthday, particularly among African American and Hispanic children. Intensive efforts to vaccinate preschool-age children were successful, and coverage among 2-year-old children increased from 70% in 1990 to 91% in 1996. Since 1993, fewer than 1000 cases have been reported annually.[72]

In 2011, along with outbreaks in Europe[78] and New Zealand,[79] the United States reported 156

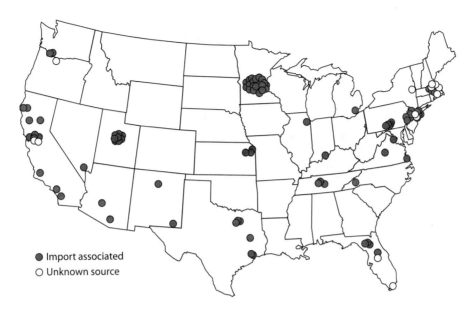

Figure 11-8 Distribution and origin of reported measles cases (N = 118)—United States, January 1–May 20, 2011. Reproduced from McLean H, Measles-United States, January–May 2011. *MMWR*. 2011;60(20):666.

confirmed measles cases, the highest number since 1996. These outbreaks occurred across the country (**Figure 11-8**). Most of the cases were associated with importations from measles-endemic countries. While a few cases had received appropriate MMR immunizations and represented vaccine failures, the CDC reports that 89% of the cases (including the cases among U.S. residents) were unvaccinated. Among the unvaccinated group, most claimed religious or personal exemptions, and a few cases represented missed opportunities for immunization.[80]

This resurgence of measles underscores that the risk of outbreaks persists, primarily among communities with religious and philosophical exemptions to vaccination. Smaller outbreaks were reported in unvaccinated preschool populations, vaccinated school populations (vaccine failures), college students, and adult communities. To enhance immunity levels, the CDC targets young adults born after January 1957 by encouraging MMR booster vaccination at colleges or other postsecondary educational institutions.

In contrast, some developing countries have not achieved high rates of measles immunization coverage, and measles accounts for nearly 50% of the 1.6 million vaccine-preventable deaths annually in children.[81] The 1990 World Summit for Children adopted a goal of vaccinating 90% of children worldwide against measles by the year 2000.[71] By 2002, immunization rates had increased worldwide, yet barriers remain to preventing high immunization rates in some countries. For

example, war and complex emergencies such as the devastating tsunami that hit Asia in late 2004 have been associated with outbreaks of measles, tetanus, and vaccine-preventable waterborne diseases (e.g., cholera). Work is needed to address these barriers, including changing the public's perception that vaccines are unsafe, building political and financial commitments, and development of effective partnerships.[58]

Haemophilus Influenzae Type b

Prior to the advent of an effective vaccine, it was estimated that 1 in every 200 children would develop an invasive *Haemophilus influenzae* type b (Hib) infection before the age of 5 years.[82] Subsequently, 60% of infected children developed bacterial meningitis; 10% of these children died, while many more suffered permanent impairments, ranging from hearing loss to mental retardation.

By 1993, invasive Hib disease had decreased by 95%, and the disease has been practically eliminated in the United States (**Figure 11-9**). This decline began with the introduction of bacterium capsular polysaccharide Hib vaccine in 1985. Upon its launch, the vaccine was recommended for children older than 2 years as it was poorly immunogenic in those less than 18 months. Young infants, however, are at greatest risk of developing this disease.[82] To overcome the poor immunogenicity of the polysaccharide-only vaccine, particularly in young infants, Hib polysaccharide-protein conjugates were developed. The first Hib conjugate vaccine was licensed

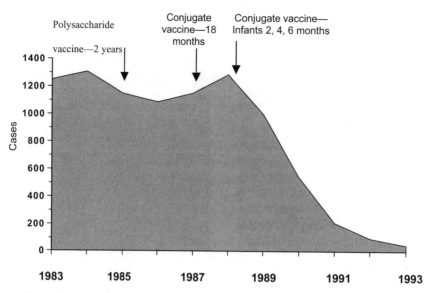

Figure 11-9 *Haemophilus influenzae* type b cases per year, United States 1983–1993. Adapted from the National Institute of Health. *The Jordan Report 1998: Accelerated Development of Vaccines.* Division of Microbiology and Infectious Diseases, National Institute of Allergy and Infectious Diseases.

in 1987 for children age 18 months and older. In 1988, similar vaccines were licensed for children as young as 2 months of age, based on clinical trials showing that these vaccines had more than 90% efficacy in fully immunized infants.[83] By 1997, 93% of all 2-year-old children in the United States had completed the Hib vaccine series. From 1989 to 1997, the race-adjusted incidence of Hib invasive disease among children younger than 5 years of age decreased by 99%, from 34 cases to 0.4 case per 100,000 children.[84]

While the number of cases of invasive Hib disease has decreased dramatically since Hib conjugate immunization was widely implemented, approximately 50 to 100 cases of invasive *H. influenzae* disease in children younger than age 5 years are reported to the CDC each year. At the end of 2007, a major manufacturer of Hib conjugate vaccine recalled two Hib vaccine lots and suspended production of its Hib vaccine. This action led to a shortage of Hib vaccine in the United States that lasted through 2009.[85,86] During the shortage, the CDC recommended that providers complete the primary series of Hib immunization in all children and defer the routine Hib vaccine booster that occurs between ages 12 and 15 months for children who were not at increased risk of Hib disease.[85,86] In 2008, the Minnesota Health Department reported 5 childhood cases of invasive Hib disease (the highest number of cases reported since the Hib conjugate vaccination began); 4 of 5 of these cases occurred

in under-immunized children, and 3 of these cases involved parental refusal of immunization.[87] Both in Minnesota and nationwide, it was shown later that the Hib immunization rate for the booster dose as well as the primary series had declined during the shortage.[88,89] Despite this finding, surveillance data did not reveal an increased incidence of invasive Hib disease in children younger than age 5 years during this time, but more than 50% of *H. influenzae* reported to the CDC was not serotyped and incidence could have been underestimated.[86] It is likely that high, sustained immunization coverage before the shortage had reduced Hib carriage and transmission in the population; during the time of the vaccine shortage, the prevalence of circulating Hib did not increase sufficiently to produce widespread outbreaks of disease.

Progress toward complete elimination continues in the United States and in Europe. Hib vaccines against strains circulating in the developing world have been tested in clinical trials. Despite the high burden of Hib pneumonia and invasive disease in developing countries, the cost of vaccine and sustainability of a Hib immunization program remain barriers to more extensive immunization. Since 2005, the Global Alliance for Vaccines and Immunization (GAVI) and its global partners have worked to improve Hib immunization worldwide.[90,91] By end of 2008, 66 countries in Central and South America, Central Europe, Africa, and Asia, had initiated Hib immunization program.[92]

THE ROLE OF VACCINES IN ERADICATION OF SPECIFIC DISEASES

Eradication of a given communicable disease brings total control over morbidity, disability, mortality, and subclinical disease, beyond control of the etiologic agent itself. As suggested by Evans, eradication is achieved when there is no risk of infection or disease in the absence of vaccination or any other control measures.[93] The need to immunize susceptible individuals before natural infection occurs represents a formidable obstacle in the case of many childhood diseases. Factors that favor the eradication of a communicable disease are identified in **Exhibit 11-5**.

An immunization program need not achieve 100% coverage to provide protection against disease in a community. Herd immunity implies that some level of immunity in a community can provide protection to susceptible (unimmunized) persons. This collective immunologic protection represents an indirect effect of a vaccine beyond the level of the individual to that of the population. As long as susceptible persons do not contact infected persons, transmission can be interrupted. However, the concept of herd immunity assumes that susceptible persons mix randomly within the population, which is often not the case. Groups of unimmunized persons who share common characteristics (e.g., age, religion, culture) often cluster together in relatively restricted geographic settings. The degree of herd immunity required to prevent an epidemic varies according to several factors: the specific disease, the extent to which an infected individual is capable of transmitting the infection, the duration of the infectious period, the size of the population, and mixing patterns within and between other populations.

The global eradication of smallpox serves as the gold standard against which other eradication programs are judged. Systematic application of smallpox vaccine began in Mexico and in Guatemala around 1805, and elsewhere in North America and Europe.[94] Initially, smallpox vaccine was offered to all age groups, but only those persons at risk (e.g., healthcare workers, travelers) were specifically targeted. As a result, incomplete coverage caused outbreaks to continue throughout the world. The first attempt at global immunization of smallpox came in 1956, but this effort was not successful in containing the disease. In 1967, there were still 10–15 million cases of smallpox per year causing at least 2 million

---

Exhibit 11-5	**Factors Associated with Potential for Eradication of a Communicable Disease**

Factors Associated with the Disease
- Ease of diagnosis and treatment
- Low prevalence of subclinical disease
- High disease burden and economic impact
- Long-term or lifelong immunity
- Disease cannot be reactivated
- Disease has predictable seasonality

Factors Associated with the Etiologic Agent
- Lack of an animal reservoir or vector
- Only one causative agent or serotype
- Short incubation period

Factors Associated with the Host or Target Population
- Correlates or protection can be demonstrated
- Host cannot be reinfected with the agent
- Host cannot shed the organism once infection is resolved
- High public acceptance of the vaccine and other control measures

Factors Associated with the Vaccine
- Can confer long-lasting protection in a few injections
- Minimal handling and storage requirements (e.g., cold chain)
- Simple administration
- Can be administered simultaneously with other vaccines or adapted to schedules and timing of the national childhood immunization programs
- Few short- or long-term adverse effects
- Low cost to produce and purchase vaccine

Adapted from Evans, AS. The Eradication of Communicable Diseases: Myth or Reality? *Am J Epidemiol* 1985;122(2):199–207.

deaths and 100,000 cases of blindness.[94] That year, the global smallpox eradication program was enhanced to utilize more sensitive surveillance and containment. Surveillance was particularly useful in the control of smallpox, as cases were always symptomatic—and always symptomatic before they were infectious. Furthermore, the vaccine prevents the development of symptomatic or infectious disease, even after exposure to an infectious case. Extensive case finding and tracking of the origins of smallpox outbreaks, coupled with immunization of remaining susceptible groups, proved able to stop transmission.[94] In addition, a standardized, lyophilized ("freeze-dried") vaccine had become available that did not require refrigeration, and the vaccine could be delivered rapidly by persons who were trained to use the bifurcated needles, a two-pronged instrument that essentially scratches the lyophilized vaccine powder into the skin.

Ultimately, a stable vaccine in an easily delivered form, combined with leadership, political will, and adequate resource allocation, led to the eradication of smallpox. The last known case of community transmission was observed in Somalia in 1977. Vaccination in the United States waned in the mid-1960s and was no longer recommended for the general population in 1965. U.S. military recruits were vaccinated for smallpox until 1982, although actual vaccination coverage was low. In 1980, WHO officially declared that smallpox had been eradicated, representing the most significant public health achievement of the 1900s. The threat of biologic weapons containing smallpox virus after the terrorist attacks of September 11, 2001, led the U.S. government to again recommend smallpox vaccine for all medical care providers, emergency first responders, and members of the US military.

Toward Global Eradication of Polio

Although incidence and prevalence of polio-induced paralysis decreased after the introduction of the Salk (IPV) and Sabin (OPV) vaccines in the 1950s, polio continued to take its toll in developing countries. In 1988, the World Health Assembly set a target to eradicate polio from the world by the year 2000, a goal that unfortunately was not met. The Global Polio Eradication Initiative (GPEI), which includes WHO, Rotary International, the CDC, and the United Nations Children's Fund (UNICEF), has spearheaded polio eradication efforts on a worldwide basis.

From the outset, eradication of polio appeared more difficult compared to smallpox. Three serotypes of poliovirus exist that do not share considerable cross-immunity. Polio infection has a high prevalence of subclinical infections, a longer incubation period, and multiple routes of exposure. Moreover, several doses of OPV or IPV are needed to induce immunity.

Despite these obstacles, progress toward eradication of polio over the last 22 years has been impressive. The four key strategies to stopping transmission of wild-type polio in areas affected by disease are presented in **Exhibit 11-6**. The virus was eradicated from the Western Hemisphere in 1991. In 1998, WHO estimated that global routine immunization coverage with three doses of OPV had reached 82%. Globally, numbers of cases have decreased by 99% since 1988. By 2003, the number of countries with endemic polio decreased from 125 to 7; by 2005 and continuing to present (2011), only 4 endemic countries remain—Pakistan, Afghanistan, India, and Nigeria—suggesting that eradication of polio may soon be a reality.[95–98]

A setback to the Global Polio Eradication Initiative was announced in June 2004, when WHO indicated that western and central Africa was at risk of a large polio outbreak. The vulnerable countries included those that border Nigeria, a country where the polio immunization programs were suspended in 2003 due to public fear of the vaccine's safety. At the beginning of 2003, only two sub-Saharan African countries had endemic polio. In 2004, paralytic polio cases had been identified in 10 previously polio-free countries across the continent. WHO began massive

---

Exhibit 11-6	**Four Core Strategies for Stopping Wild Poliovirus Transmission**

1. Strengthen routine childhood immunization, assuring high coverage with four doses of OPV in the first year of life.
2. Conduct supplemental immunization activities (SIAs)—mass campaigns to provide additional OPV doses to all children younger than age 5 years.
3. Conduct surveillance for wild-type poliovirus through laboratory testing of all cases of acute flaccid paralysis among children younger than age 15 years.
4. Conduct intensive house-to-house, targeted "mop-up" campaigns around recent infected cases.

Reproduced from *MMWR*. Progress toward interrupting wild poliovirus circulations in countries with reestablished transmission—Africa, 2009–2010.

immunization campaigns across the African continent in October and November of 2004, during the peak season for polio.[95] The campaign was successful in all but the poorest and most densely populated developing countries, where health delivery systems are inadequate, and where armed conflicts have interrupted routine vaccination campaigns. The major remaining reservoirs of polio are located in South Asia and West and Central Africa.[96]

Appropriate evaluation of an immunization program is essential for establishing whether control has been attained and whether a pool of susceptible individuals exists in which new outbreaks are possible. Evaluation should include surveys to assess vaccine coverage as well as clinical and/or serological confirmation of immunity. Sentinel surveillance should be maintained to identify the persistence of wild-type, indigenous, or imported virus, as well as live vaccine virus.[99] Highly specific serology tests can be used for diagnosis confirmation when available, but simpler measures that are highly sensitive markers of polio, such as acute flaccid paralysis and lameness, are also important surveillance tools. Only with systematic application of these methods will it be possible to determine whether polio or any other agent has been successfully eradicated.

The two remaining barriers to polio eradication are failure to vaccinate and vaccine failures. Despite intensive vaccination efforts, the factors related to having low vaccine coverage continue to be community resistance to the vaccine, poor ability to implement supplemental immunization activities (SIAs) in other areas, and a failure to engage hard-to-reach populations. OPV has been shown to have lower immunogenicity and effectiveness in tropical, developing countries. Specifically, trivalent OPVs have demonstrated lower vaccine efficacy and lower seroconversion rates to all strains compared to monvalent OPV (MOPV). Although immunization programs using trivalent vaccine were able to nearly eliminate wild type 2 poliovirus (WP2) infection,[100,101] vaccine failures following vaccination against wild types 1 (WP1) and 3 (WP3) continue to occur. Given that WP1 has been associated with more severe paralytic disease and large outbreaks, and in the absence of an effective trivalent or bivalent vaccine, monovalent type 1 OPV (MOVP1) vaccine was used solely in a wide-scale eradication effort in India. These efforts have led to remarkable progress in the interruption of transmission of WP1 in India; in 2010, only five cases of WP1 occurred in that country.[102] Outbreaks of WP1 continue to occur in Nigeria, Afghanistan, and Pakistan and a few other previously polio-free countries due to

persistent failure to fully vaccinate all children.[100] New vaccines strategies to eradicate both WP1 and WP2 in the remaining endemic countries may include a bivalent type 1 and 3 OPV vaccine.

Settling for a 99% reduction in polio is not an option. WHO states this point clearly: "As long as a single child remains infected, children in all countries are at risk of contracting polio."[98] This was evident in 2009 and 2010 when 23 previously polio free-countries were reinfected due to imports of the polio virus (**Figure 11-10**). Efforts continue to eradicate the disease, with the 2010–2012 GPEI strategic plan outlining the following goals:

- By mid-2010, stopping wild-type polio transmission following importation into countries with outbreaks in 2009
- Stopping WP1 transmission in subsequent outbreaks less than 6 months after confirmation
- Stopping wild-type poliovirus transmission in at least two of the four endemic countries by the end of 2011
- Stopping wild-type poliovirus transmission in all countries by the end of 2012[103]

Potential for Eradication of Other Communicable Diseases

The ability to control or attempt eradication of a communicable disease varies by country, according to demographic, environmental, hygienic, and economic factors. Apart from criteria that need to be taken into account when considering a specific communicable disease for eradication, such programs require political will, financial resources, and unwavering commitment to meet defined goals. In 1974, WHO created the Expanded Program on Immunization (EPI), which initially aimed to eliminate six diseases: tuberculosis, diphtheria, neonatal tetanus, whooping cough, poliomyelitis, and measles (**Table 11-2**). Prior to this initiative, fewer than 5% of children in developing countries were being immunized against these preventable childhood diseases. In more recent years, new vaccines have been added to EPI—namely, hepatitis B vaccine and yellow fever vaccine—and efforts are being made to include other underutilized vaccines such as Hib and pneumococcal conjugate (PCV) rotavirus vaccines, although the number of countries participating in these programs varies considerably. Since the establishment of EPI, major progress has been made toward eliminating other communicable diseases in various parts of the world. For example, routine administration of tetanus toxoid has virtually eliminated neonatal tetanus.

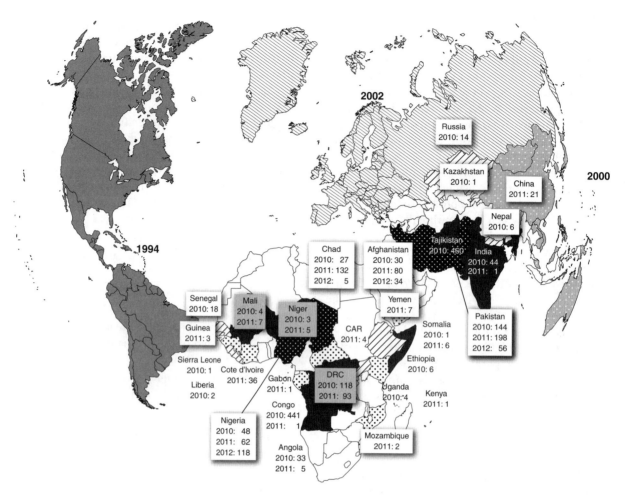

Only four countries reported polio in 2012: Nigeria, Chad, Afghanistan and Pakistan. Countries are shaded according to the last year of confirmed cases 2010 ◻, 2011 ▦, 2010 and 2011 ■, and 2010, 2011 and 2012 ▨. Annual case counts for 2010–2012 are also noted. Russia and China had contained epidemics in 2010 and 2011, respectively, but are still considered polio free. Three WHO regions are declared polio free: the Americas in 1994, the Western Pacific in 2000 and the European region in 2002.

Figure 11-10 "Every Last Child" the Polio Global Eradication Program as of June 30, 2012. Data from Polio Global Eradication Initiative. Polio this Week. http://www.polioeradication.org/Dataandmonitoring/Poliothisweek.aspx. Updated June 20, 2012. Accessed June 24, 2012; and World Health Organization (2011). Weekly Epidemiological Record (WER), Weekly epidemiologic report December 2011, 86th year No. 50, 2011, 86, 565–580 http://www.who.int/wer. Accessed June 24th, 2012.

In a response to poor vaccine coverage in preschool children, the United States launched the Childhood Immunization Initiative in 1993. It included five strategies:

1. Improve the quality and quantity of immunization services
2. Reduce vaccine costs
3. Increase community participation, education, and partnerships
4. Improve systems for monitoring diseases and vaccinations
5. Improve vaccines and vaccine use

Following establishment of this program, measles, diphtheria, mumps, tetanus, Hib, and congenital rubella have been virtually eliminated from the United States. Nevertheless, known subpopulations of unimmunized persons continue to represent the potential for new outbreaks.

Despite the successes described previously, the characteristics of some infectious agents make it unlikely that these diseases will be fully eradicated. In general, measles meets the criteria for eradication. By 2003, only 105 cases of measles were reported in the Western Hemisphere, raising hopes that measles might soon be eradicated in the Americas.[104] However, global eradication has proved to be difficult, as there is only a narrow window in time to vaccinate children after loss of protective maternal antibodies and exposure to natural infection. Meanwhile, control of

Table 11-2	Year of Introduction of Selected First-Generation Vaccines for Human Use and Year of First National and Expanded Immunization Program (EPI).		
Vaccine*	Year First Introduced	Year of First National Immunization Program	Year Beginning EPI
Smallpox	1798	1804	1956
Plague	1897	—	—
Diphtheria	1923	mid-1940s†	1974
Pertussis	1926	mid-1940s†	1974
Tuberculosis (BCG)	1921	1949	1974
Tetanus	1927	mid-1940s†	1974
Yellow fever	1935	1989	1989 (endemic countries)
Oral polio vaccine	1962	1974	1974
Measles	1964	1974	1985
Mumps	1967	1977	—
Rubella	1969	1970	—
Hepatitis B	1981	1990	1995
Haemophilus influenzae type b	1985	1985	pending
Varicella-zoster	1984	1989	—

Note: In 1974, EPI was established with six targeted diseases: diphtheria, pertussis, tetanus, measles, polio, and tuberculosis (BCG). Rubella and mumps vaccines were never adapted into the EPI as single antigen vaccines.
* Not necessarily the vaccine currently in use.
† Approximate time period of wide use in the United States.

influenza is hampered by the multiplicity of antigenic types, high contagiousness of the disease, and persistence of multiple reservoirs (i.e., swine, fowl) for the origin of new recombinant viruses. Yellow fever does not demonstrate the diversity of influenza virus, and an effective vaccine for this disease is in use. Nevertheless, yellow fever remains endemic due to the sylvan cycle, where mosquitoes transmit the virus to primates and to humans, making eradication unlikely.

BARRIERS TO VACCINE IMPLEMENTATION AND COVERAGE

Seemingly insurmountable barriers are encountered in the attempt to deliver proven vaccines to those populations who need them the most. Because most vaccines are developed and manufactured in developed countries, steps must be taken to ensure that live vaccines can be transported and stored in a developing country in a viable form, maintaining the cold chain where appropriate. Staff must be trained in vaccine administration, safe injection techniques, and program management. To increase vaccine acceptability, public education campaigns are required, using materials that are sensitive to the local language and culture.

Even in developed countries, proven vaccines do not necessarily reach those individuals who are at highest risk of infection. Although hepatitis B vaccine has been added to childhood immunization schedules in many developed countries, immunization levels remain low and risk of infection is high among injection drug users and homosexual/bisexual men, particularly those old enough to have missed the vaccine in childhood (**Exhibit 11-7**).

Exhibit 11-7	Barriers to Achieving High Coverage with Recombinant Hepatitis B Vaccine in the United States

1. One quarter of HBV-infected persons deny known risk factors for HBV infection.
2. Access to high-risk populations (e.g., homosexual/bisexual men, injection drug users, illegal aliens from endemic countries) is difficult because populations are "hidden"; high-risk behaviors are highly stigmatized.
3. Low awareness of HBV infection and consequences of disease (i.e., hepatitis, liver cancer).
4. Low acceptability of vaccine schedule.
5. Lack of third-party reimbursement to cover vaccine costs.
6. Rapid acquisition of HBV infection among high-risk populations.
7. Age-specific decline in immunogenicity of vaccine.
8. Waning of induced immunity over time (i.e., protection estimated to last 13 years).

Pockets of individuals with low coverage in most, if not all, countries are capable of perpetuating disease transmission. Even when adequate coverage has been achieved, births, immigration, waning immunity, and requirements for multiple doses mean that diligence is required to maintain herd immunity. Threats to achieving and maintaining coverage include wars, civil unrest, natural disasters, and other complex emergencies that can destroy the health infrastructure supporting immunization programs. The possibility of changes in the natural history of some diseases (e.g., new route of infection, new reservoir or host, reactivation of latent disease) underscores the need for continued sentinel surveillance in national and global immunization programs. The high cost of many proven vaccines also prevents many countries from adding these products to their national immunization programs. Apart from biologic considerations, some vaccines that have been proved both efficacious and effective have not been licensed due to their high cost, low public health priority, or lack of endorsement from pharmaceutical companies. If global eradication of major vaccine-preventable diseases is to be upheld as a realistic goal, developed countries, nongovernmental organizations, and pharmaceutical companies must fulfill their obligation to support immunization programs in resource-poor countries.

● ● ● REFERENCES

1. Hume EH. *Vaccines*. Baltimore, MD: W. B. Saunders Company; 1940.

2. Rappouli R. New and improved vaccines against diphtheria and tetanus. In: Levine MM, Woodrow GC, Kaper JB, Cobon GS, eds. *New Generation Vaccines*. 2nd ed. New York, NY: Marcel Dekker; 1997:417–436.

3. Smith JS, Gilbert PA, Melendy A, et al. Age-specific prevalence of human papillomavirus infection in males: a global review. *J Adolesc Health*. 2011;48(6):540–552.

4. Walboomers JM, Jacobs MV, Manos MM, et al. Human papillomavirus is a necessary cause of invasive cervical cancer worldwide. *J Pathol*. 1999;189(1):12–19.

5. Porter DL, Levine BL, Kalos M, et al. Chimeric antigen receptor–modified T cells in chronic lymphoid leukemia. *N Engl J Med*. 2011;365:725–733.

6. Hellstrom KE, Helstrom I, Chen L. Antitumor vaccines. In: Levine MM, Woodrow GC, Kaper JB, Cobon GS, eds. *New Generation Vaccines*. 2nd ed. New York, NY: Marcel Dekker; 1997:1095–1116.

7. Pasteur L. *Vaccines*. Paris: W. B. Saunders Company; 1885.

8. Abbas A, Lichtman A, Pober J. *Cellular and Molecular Immunology*. 3rd ed. Philadelphia, PA: W. B. Saunders Company; 1997.

9. Janeway C, Travers P. *Immunobiology*. 3rd ed. New York, NY: Garland Publishers; 1997.

10. Huston DP. The biology of the immune system. *JAMA*. 1997;22:1804–1814.

11. McDonnell WM, Askari FK. Immunization. *JAMA*. 1998;22:2000–2007.

12. Levine MM, Tacket CO, Galen JE, et al. Progress in the development of new attenuated strains of *Salmonella typhi* as live oral vaccines against typhoid fever. In: Levine MM, Woodrow GC, Kaper JB, Cobon GS, eds. *New Generation Vaccines*. 2nd ed. New York, NY: Marcel Dekker; 1997:437–446.

13. Alexander LN, Seward JF, Santibanez TA, et al. Vaccine policy changes and the epidemiology of poliomyelitis in the United States. *JAMA*. 2004;292:1692–1701.

14. Black F. Measles in acute viral infections. In: Evans AS, ed. *Viral Infections of Humans: Epidemiology and Control*. 2nd ed. New York, NY: Plenum Medical; 1989:521–522.

15. Kollaritsch H, Que JU, Kunz C, et al. Safety and immunogenicity of live oral cholera and typhoid vaccines administered alone or in combination with antimalarial drugs, oral polio vaccine, or yellow fever vaccine. *J Infect Dis*. 1997;175:871–875.

16. Guess HA. Combination vaccines: issues in evaluations of effectiveness and safety. *Epidemiol Rev*. 1999;2:89–95.

17. Roux E, Yersin A. Contribution a l'etude de la diptherie. *Ann Inst Pasteur*. 1888;2:629–661.

18. Black S, Shinefield H, Fireman B, et al. Efficacy, safety and immunogenicity of hepavalent pneumococcal conjugate vaccine in children. *Pediatr Infect Dis J.* 2000;19: 187–195.

19. Prevention and control of meningococcal disease. *MMWR.* 2005;54(RR07):1–21.

20. Updated recommendation from the Advisory Committee on Immunization Practices (ACIP) for revaccination of persons at prolonged increased risk of meningococcal disease. *MMWR.* 2009;58(37);1042–1043

21. Steere AC, Sikand VK, Meurice F, et al. Vaccination against Lyme disease with recombinant *Borrelia burgdorferi* outer-surface lipoprotein A with adjuvant. *N Engl J Med.* 1998;339:209–215.

22. Aggarwal R. Hepatitis E: historical, contemporary and future perspectives. *J Gastroenterol Hepatol.* 2011;26(suppl 1):72–82.

23. Shrestha MP, Scott RM, Joshi DM, et al. Safety and efficacy of recombinant hepatitis E vaccine. *N Engl J Med.* 20071;356(9):895–903.

24. Zhu FC, Zhang J, Zhang XF, et al. Efficacy and safety of a recombinant hepatitis E vaccine in healthy adults: large scale randomized, double-blind placebo-controlled, phase 3 trial. *Lancet.* 2010;376(9744):895–902.

25. Editorial. Hepatitis E vaccine: why wait? *Lancet.* 2010;376(9744):845.

26. Holmberg SD. Hepatitis E vaccine: not a moment too soon. *Lancet.* 2010;376(9744): 849–851.

27. Basnyat B. Neglected hepatitis E and typhoid vaccines. *Lancet.* 2010;376(9744):869.

28. Kapikian AZ, Hoshino Y, Chanock RM, Perez-Schael I. Efficacy of a quadrivalent rhesus rotavirus-based human rotavirus vaccine aimed at preventing severe rotavirus diarrhoea in infants and young children. *J Infect Dis.* 1996;174:S65–S72.

29. Clements-Mann ML, Weinhold K, Matthews TJ, et al. Immune responses to human immunodeficiency virus (HIV) type 1 induced by canarypox expressing HIV-1MN gp120, HIV-1SF2 recombinant gp120, or both vaccines in seronegative adults. *J Infect Dis.* 1998;177:1230–1246.

30. Rerks-Ngam S, Pitisuttithum P, Nitayaphan S, et.al. Vaccination with ALVAC and AIDSVAC to prevent HIV-1 infection in Thailand. *N Engl J Med.* 2009;361(23):2209–2220.

31. Brochier B, Kieny MP, Costy F, et al. Large-scale eradication of rabies using recombinant *Vaccinia*–rabies vaccine. *Nature.* 1991;354:520–522.

32. Prevec L, Campbell JB, Christie BS, et al. A recombinant human adenovirus vaccine against rabies. *J Infect Dis.* 1990;161:27–30.

33. National Institutes of Health (NIAID). *The Jordan Report* 20th anniversary: accelerated development of vaccines 2002. Appendix C: status of vaccine research and development. Available at: http://www .niaid. nih.gov/dmid/vaccines/jordan20/. Accessed January 13, 2005.

34. Pruss A, Kay D, Fewtrell L, Bartram J. Estimating the burden of diseases from water, sanitation, and hygiene at the global level. *Environ Health Perspect.* 2002;110: 537–542.

35. Ada G. Vaccine and vaccination. *N Engl J Med.* 2001;345:1042–1053.

36. Vogel FR, Alving CR. Progress in immunologic adjuvant development: 1982–2002. *The Jordan Report* 20th anniversary: accelerated development of vaccines 2002. Appendix C: status of vaccine research and development. Available at: http://www.niaid. nih.gov/dmid/vaccines/jordan20/. Accessed January 13, 2005.

37. Liu MA, Ulmer JB, O'Hagan D. Vaccine technologies. *The Jordan Report* 20th anniversary: accelerated development of vaccines 2002. Appendix C: status of vaccine research and development. Available at: http://www.niaid. nih.gov/dmid/vaccines/jordan20/. Accessed on January 13, 2005.

38. Pinto LA, Edwards J, Castle PE, et al. Cellular immune responses to human papillomavirus (HPV)-16 L1 in healthy volunteers immunized with recombinant HPV-16 L1 virus-like particles. *J Infect Dis.* 2003;188:327–338.

39. Roldão A, Mellado MC, Castilho LR, et al. Virus-like particles in vaccine development. *Expert Rev Vaccines.* 2010;9(10):1149–1176.

40. Recommended childhood and adolescent immunization schedule—United States, July–December 2004. *MMWR.* 2004;53: Q1–Q3.

41. Recommended childhood and adolescent immunization schedule: United States, 2005. *Pediatrics.* 2005;115:182.

42. Koutsky LA, Harper DM. Chapter 13: Current findings from prophylactic HPV vaccine trials. *Vaccine.* 2006;24(suppl 3):S114–S121.

43. National Center of Infectious Disease. Traveler's health. Available at: http://www.cdc.gov/travel. Accessed January 4, 2005.

44. Comstock GW. Vaccine evaluation by case-control or prospective studies. *Am J Epidemiol.* 1990;131:205–207.

45. Ornestein WA, Bernier RH, Hinman AR. Assessing vaccine efficacy in the field: further observations. *Epidemiol Rev.* 1988;10: 212–241.

46. Halloran ME, Haber M, Longini IM, Struchiner CJ. Direct and indirect effects in vaccine efficacy and effectiveness. *Am J Epidemiol.* 1991;133:323–331.

47. Halloran ME, Struchiner CJ, Longini IM. Study designs for evaluating different efficacy and effectiveness aspects of vaccines. *Am J Epidemiol.* 1999;146:789–803.

48. Halloran ME, Longini IM, Struchiner CJ. Design and interpretation of vaccine field studies. *Epidemiol Rev.* 1999;21:73–88.

49. Rodrigues LC, Smith PG. Use of the case control approach in vaccine evaluation: efficacy and adverse effects. *Epidemiol Rev.* 1999;21:56–72.

50. Chen RT, Rastogi SC, Mullen JR, et al. The Vaccine Adverse Event Reporting System (VAERS). *Vaccine.* 1994;5:542–549.

51. Braun MM, Ellenberg SS. Descriptive epidemiology of adverse events after immunization: reports of the Vaccine Adverse Event Reporting System (VAERS) 1991–1994. *J Pediatr.* 1997;131:529–535.

52. Varricchio F, Iskander J, Destefano F, et al. Understanding vaccine safety information from the Vaccine Adverse Event Reporting System. *Pediatr Infect Dis J.* 2004;23:287–294.

53. Haber P, Chen RT, Zanardi LR, et al. An analysis of rotavirus vaccine reports to Vaccine Adverse Event Reporting System: more than intussusception alone? *Pediatrics.* 2004;114:e353–e359.

54. Suspension of rotavirus vaccine after reports of intussusception—United States, 1999. *MMWR.* 2004;53:786–789.

55. Goveia MG, Ciarlet M, Owen KE, Ranucci CS. Development, clinical evaluation, and post-licensure impact of RotaTeq, a pentavalent rotavirus vaccine. *Ann NY Acad Sci.* 2011;1222:14–18.

56. Chen RT, Glasser JW, Rhodes PH, et al. Vaccine Safety Datalink Project: a new tool for improving vaccine safety monitoring in the United States. *Pediatrics.* 1997;99:765–773.

57. Chen RT. Evaluation of vaccine safety after the events of 11 September 2001: role of cohort and case control studies. *Vaccine.* 2004;22:2047–2053.

58. Meissner HC, Strebel PM, Orenstein WA. Measles vaccines and the potential for worldwide eradication of measles. *Pediatrics.* 2004;144:1065–1069.

59. Institute of Medicine. Immunization safety review. Available at: http://www.iom.edu/project.asp/id=4705. Accessed January 9, 2005.

60. McCormack MC. The autism "epidemic": impressions from the perspective of immunization safety review. *Ambulatory Pediatr.* 2003;3:119–120.

61. Wakefield AJ, Murch SH, Anthony A, et al. Illeal-lymphoid-nodular hyperplasia, non-specific colitis, and pervasive developmental disorders. *Lancet.* 1998;351:631–637.

62. Deer B. How the case against MMR vaccine was fixed. *BMJ.* 2011;342:c5347.

63. Godlee F, Smith J, Marcovitch H. Wakefield's article linking MMR vaccine and autism was fraudulent. *BMJ.* 2011;342:c7452.

64. Pless R, Casey C, Chen R. CISA: improving the evaluation, management and understanding of adverse events possibly related to immunizations. National Immunization Program, Centers for Disease Control and Prevention. Available at: http://www.cdc.gov/nip/vacsafe/cisa/introcisa.html. Accessed January 3, 2005.

65. LaRussa PS, Edwards KM, Dekker CL, et al. Understanding the role of human variation in vaccine adverse events: the Clinical Immunization Safety Assessment Network. *Pediatrics.* 2011;127(suppl 1):S65–S73.

66. Plotkin SL, Plotkin SA. A short history of vaccination. In: Plotkin SA, Mortimor EA, eds. *Vaccines.* 3rd ed. Pages 1–16. Philadelphia, PA: W. B. Saunders Company; 1999.

67. Ogra PL. Poliomyelitis as a paradigm for investment in the success of vaccination programs. *Pediatr Infect Dis J.* 1999;18:10–15.

68. Atkinson W, ed. Poliomyelitis. In: *Epidemiology and Prevention of Vaccine Preventable Diseases.* Atlanta, GA: Centers for Disease Control and Prevention; 1997:81–99.

69. Centers for Disease Control. Poliomyelitis—United States: 1975–1984. *MMWR.* 1986;35:180–182.

70. Alexander LN, Seward JF, Santibanez TA, et al. Vaccine policy changes and epidemiology of poliomyelitis in the United States. *JAMA.* 2004;292:1696–1701.

71. Measles. In Atkinson W, Furphy L, Humiston SG et al. eds. *Epidemiology and Prevention of Vaccine-Preventable Diseases.* 4th Ed. Atlanta, GA: Centers for Disease Control and Prevention, Department of Health and Human Services; 1997:117–137.

72. National Vaccine Advisory Committee. The measles epidemic: the problems, barriers, and recommendations. *JAMA.* 1991;266:1547–1552.

73. Centers for Disease Control and Prevention. Epidemiology of measles—United States, 1998. *MMWR.* 1999;48:749–753.

74. Centers for Disease Control and Prevention. Measles—United States 2000. *MMWR.* 2002;51:120–123.

75. Centers for Disease Control and Prevention. Impact of vaccine universally recommended for children. 1999. Available at: http://www.cdc.gov/od/oc/media/fact/impvacc.htm. Accessed November 12, 1999.

76. George P. Childhood immunizations. *N Engl J Med.* 1992;327:1794–1800.

77. Centers for Disease Control and Prevention. Progress toward global measles control and regional elimination, 1990–1997. *MMWR.* 1998;47:1049–1054.

78. Cottrell S, Roberts RJ. Measles outbreak in Europe. *BMJ.* 2011;342:d3724.

79. Notes from the field: multiple cases of measles after exposure during air travel—Australia and New Zealand, January 2011. *MMWR.* 2011;60(25):851.

80. McLean H. Measles—United States, January–May 2011. *MMWR.* 2011;60(20):666–668.

81. Strebel P, Cochi S, Grawbowski M, et al. The unfinished measles immunization agenda. *J Infect Dis.* 2003;187:S1–S7.

82. Cochi SL, Broome CV. Vaccine prevention of *Haemophilus influenzae* type b disease, past, present, and future. *Pediatr Infect Dis.* 1985;5:12–19.

83. Santosham M, Wolff M, Reid R, et al. The efficacy in Navajo infants of conjugate vaccine consisting of *Haemophilus influenzae* type b polysaccharide and *Neisseria meningitides* outer membrane protein complex. *N Engl J Med.* 1991;324:1767–1772.

84. McCollough M. Update on emerging infections from the Centers for Disease Control and Prevention. *Ann Emerg Med*. 1999;334:109–111.

85. Centers for Disease Control and Prevention. Interim recommendation for use of *Haemophilus influenzae* type b (Hib) conjugate vaccine related to recall of certain lots of Hib-containing vaccines (PedvaxHib® and Comvax®). *MMWR*. 2007;56:1318–1320.

86. Centers for Disease Control and Prevention. Continued shortage of *Haemophilus influenzae* type B (Hib) conjugate vaccines and potential implications for Hib surveillance—United States, 2008. *MMWR*. 2008;57(46):1252–1255.

87. Centers for Disease Control and Prevention. Invasive *Haemophilus influenza* type b disease in five young children—Minnesota 2008. *MMWR*. 2009;58(3):58–60.

88. Lowther SA, Shinoda N, Juni BA, et al. *Haemophilus influenzae* type b infection, vaccination, and *H. influenzae* carriage in children in Minnesota, 2008–2009. *Epidemiol Infect*. May 18, 2011:1–9.

89. White KE, Pabst LJ, Cullen KA. Up-to-date *Haemophilus influenzae* type b vaccination coverage during a vaccine shortage. *Pediatrics*. 2011;127(3):e707–e712.

90. The Hib initiative. Available at: www.Hibaction.org. Accessed June 2011.

91. The Hib initiative. Available at: www.gavialliance.org/vision/programme_support/new_vaccines/hib/index.php.

92. Hajjeh R. The Hib initiative. Available at: www.hibaction.org/resources/GAVI%20Partners%20Delhi%2005%20Final-rev.ppt. Accessed June 27, 2011.

93. Evans AS. The eradication of communicable diseases: myth or reality? *Am J Epidemiol*. 1985;122:1999–2007.

94. Fenner F, Henderson DA, Arita I, et al. *Vaccines*. Philadelphia, PA: W. B. Saunders Company; 1994.

95. World Health Organization. Polio experts warn of largest epidemic in recent years, as polio hits Darfur. Available at: http://www.who.int/mediacentre/news/releases/204/pr45/en. Accessed January 4, 2005.

96. World Health Organization. Polio eradication: the final challenge. In: *The World Health Report—Shaping the Future*. Available at: http://www.who.int/whr/2003/chapter4/en/. Accessed January 4, 2005.

97. Global Polio Eradication Initiative. Infected countries. Available at: www.polioeradication.org/infectedcountries.apsx. Accessed July 2011.

98. World Health Organization. Poliomyelitis Fact Sheet No. 114, 2010 November. Available at: www.who.int/mediacentre/factsheets/fs114/en/index.html. Accessed July 2011.

99. Evans A. Criteria for control of infectious diseases with poliomyelitis as an example. *Prog Med Virol*. 1984;29:141–165.

100. Cochi SL, Kew O. Polio today: are we on the verge of global eradication? *JAMA*. 2008;300(7):839–841.

101. Steinglass R. Global eradication of polio. *JAMA*. 2009;301(2):161–162.

102. Global Polio Eradication Initiative. Polio this week. Available at: www.polioeradication.org/Dataandmonitoring/Poliothisweek.aspx. Accessed July 7, 2011.

103. Centers for Disease Control and Prevention. Progress toward interruption of wild poliovirus transmission—worldwide, January 2010–March 2011. *MMWR*. 2011;60(18):582–586.

104. Pan American Health Organization. Progress towards measles elimination, Western Hemisphere, 2002–2003. *Wkly Epidemiol Rec*. 2004;79:149–151.

12

Nutrition and Infection

Alice M. Tang, Ellen Smit, and Richard D. Semba

INTRODUCTION

This chapter provides a practical introduction to the relationship between nutrition and infectious diseases. Over the past few decades, our knowledge of the interactions between nutrition, infection, and immune function has steadily expanded. It has been established that adequate nutritional status is necessary for the normal functioning of various components of the immune system.[1-3] Malnutrition may affect the course of infectious diseases through a variety of mechanisms, including compromising host immune function, diminishing response to therapies, and promoting comorbidities.[4]

The relationship between nutrition, infection, and immune function is generally cyclical in nature[5] (**Figure 12-1**). Even in a well-nourished host, the course of an infection will adversely affect nutritional status. If an infection is left untreated or becomes chronic, nutritional deficiencies may develop that further compromise the immune system, leading to more severe disease and increased susceptibility to other infections. If the host is already malnourished, acquiring an infection will lead to further nutritional deficiencies, such that the host rapidly progresses into a downward spiral leading to increased morbidity and mortality.

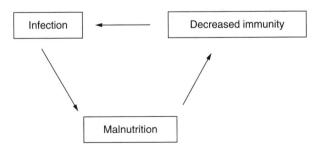

Figure 12-1 The relationship between nutrition, infection, and immune function is generally cyclical in nature

The nutritional consequences of infection, no matter which microorganism is causing the infection, tend to be predictable. Any infection, whether symptomatic or asymptomatic, is accompanied by losses of some nutrients from the body and redistribution of other nutrients. The magnitude of these changes depends on the severity and duration of the infection. Metabolic and nutritional responses that are specific to certain organisms occur when the infection becomes localized within a single organ system. For example, diarrheal infections cause sizable losses of fluid and electrolytes, whereas paralytic forms of infection result in wasting of bone and muscle. If the infection can be cured or eliminated naturally by the host immune system, lost body nutrients can then be replenished over a period of weeks to months. Conversely, if the infectious process is not eliminated and becomes chronic, body composition can become markedly altered and a new equilibrium of body nutrient balances is reached at a cachectic, or extremely wasted, level.

THE EFFECTS OF INFECTION ON NUTRITIONAL STATUS

Acute infections cause metabolic rates and oxygen consumption to increase. Both anabolic and catabolic processes are involved. The cells in the liver and lymphoid tissues rapidly increase their rates of synthesis of proteins needed for host defense mechanisms, and the proliferation of phagocytic and lymphoid cells is speeded up. To support these anabolic requirements and to maintain high metabolic rates in the presence of anorexia and a diminished food intake, catabolic processes are accelerated as well. The stores of available protein in muscle fibers and other tissues provide the additional supply of amino acid substrates, which are used for glucose production and the synthesis of new proteins required for host defense. To fuel the increased metabolic activity required to fight off the infection, the body appears to increase its utilization of glucose, but not lipids. As a result of the catabolic processes, the body loses weight and muscle mass, as nutrient stores are consumed in excess of intake. If the infection becomes chronic, available nitrogen stores are used up, fat depots are consumed, and a wasted, cachectic state develops. During the acute phase of fever, the body also retains water and salt.

THE EFFECTS OF MALNUTRITION ON HOST DEFENSE MECHANISMS

Malnutrition is best understood as a syndrome associated with variable losses of protein, carbohydrate, and fat stores, along with changes in micronutrients such as vitamins and minerals. It is often complicated by infection-induced anorexia and catabolism. A common finding in malnourished patients is the depletion of lymphocytes, particularly in T-cell regions of the thymus, spleen, and lymph nodes. Studies suggest that a relative reduction in circulating mature T lymphocytes (both T-helper and T-suppressor cells) occurs, so that plasma is enriched with immature and functionally defective cells.[6] As a result, there is a reduction in the efficacy of all host defenses that depend on T-cell function. Serum antibody levels are usually normal or elevated in the presence of malnutrition—an effect that may be due in part to the numerous infections and high antigenic loads faced by malnourished individuals in impoverished areas, and at the same time, a defect in T-suppressor cell function, which normally inhibits antibody production. One exception is that secretory IgA levels are often depressed in protein-energy malnutrition (PEM), causing more frequent mucosal infections of the gut and urinary tract. As a result, malnourished patients usually exhibit increased frequency and/or severity of certain bacterial, viral, fungal, and parasitic infections.

MALNUTRITION AND SPECIFIC INFECTIOUS DISEASES

Malnutrition is a major determinant of morbidity and mortality for many major infectious diseases, particularly among young children in developing countries, who often suffer from multiple serial infections.

Diarrheal Disease

Diarrheal disease is the second leading cause of death in children younger than 5 years of age, causing an estimated 1.5 million deaths each year worldwide.[7] Malnutrition and associated immunodeficiency are important risk factors for diarrheal disease among infants and young children in developing countries. The main causes of diarrheal diseases among children in developing countries are rotavirus, *Escherichia coli*, *Shigella*, *Vibrio cholerae*, *Salmonella*, and *Entamoeba histolytica*. Children who are malnourished (low weight-for-age, low mid-upper-arm circumference) have an increased prevalence of diarrhea, which in turn can exacerbate their malnutrition, resulting in more severe disease and a higher mortality rate.[7–9] Frequent episodes of diarrheal disease can also cause significant damage to the lining of the gut and disrupt normal gut flora colonization, which further exacerbates poor nutrition status and immune function.

Micronutrient deficiencies that have been described during diarrheal disease include deficits in vitamin A, vitamin D, vitamin B_{12}, folate, copper, iron, magnesium, selenium, and zinc.[10] Several clinical trials show that supplementation with vitamin A[11–13] or zinc[14–19] can reduce the morbidity and mortality of diarrheal disease in children, although the benefit of vitamin A appears to be limited to children who are vitamin A deficient or malnourished, or to children with shigellosis. The current recommendation from the World Health Organization (WHO) does not include vitamin A as part of treatment of diarrhea.

Lower Respiratory Infections

Acute respiratory infections (ARIs) are a major cause of morbidity and mortality among infants and children in developing countries. According to a 2009 WHO report, these infections account for an estimated 2 million deaths per year.[20] The main causes of acute lower respiratory infections in children are respiratory syncytial virus, adenovirus, parainfluenza virus, influenza virus, *Streptococcus pneumoniae*, and *Haemophilus influenzae*.[21] Zinc is essential for the growth and development of children, and randomized controlled trials have shown strong evidence that zinc supplementation reduces the incidence and prevalence of ARIs and pneumonia among children, especially in zinc-deficient populations.[22–28] Vitamin A deficiency causes pathologic alterations in the mucosal epithelium of the respiratory tract, including keratinization and loss of ciliated cells, mucus, and goblet cells. Epidemiologic studies have demonstrated that vitamin A deficiency is associated with lower respiratory infections,[11] although vitamin A supplementation appears to have little effect on reducing the incidence of either lower respiratory infections in children[29] or respiratory syncytial virus infection,[30,31] unless measles infection occurs at the same time.[12] Some evidence is emerging on the benefits of selenium, though further studies are needed to confirm this nutrient's role in the treatment of ARIs.[21]

Measles

An estimated 278,358 cases of measles and 164,000 measles-related deaths were reported in 2008.[32,33] This number reflects a decrease of 78% since the launch of the Measles Initiative in 2000; it is a vaccination campaign in high-risk countries jointly led by the American Red Cross, United Nations Foundation, U.S. Centers for Disease Control and Prevention (CDC), UNICEF, and WHO. Deaths from measles are largely the result of an increased susceptibility to secondary bacterial and viral infections, and the underlying mechanism includes immune suppression related to malnutrition.[34] Although most people recover from measles, those with malnutrition or coinfections are at increased risk of complications.[35–38] In the classic early investigation of a measles outbreak in the Faroe Islands by Peter Panum and August Manicus in 1846, the most severe diarrheal disease and highest mortality were described among those patients with greatest poverty and poor diet.[39] In general, malnourished children have more severe disease and higher mortality.[40,41] More persistent measles infection and viral shedding[37] have also been reported in malnourished children.[35]

A close synergism exists between measles and vitamin A deficiency. Low serum vitamin A levels are associated with higher mortality in acute, complicated measles infection.[42] Vitamin A supplementation for measles is one of the most important examples of the use of micronutrients as disease-targeted therapy. Randomized, placebo-controlled clinical trials show that such supplementation can reduce the mortality of measles by 50% or more, and high-dose vitamin A supplementation is now recommended as standard therapy for measles both in developing countries and in the United States.[11]

Tuberculosis

Approximately 1.8 billion individuals—nearly one-third of the world's population—are infected with *Mycobacterium tuberculosis*; most of these cases involve latent infection. In 2008 alone, an estimated 9.4 million new cases of tuberculosis (TB) occurred worldwide.[43] Malnutrition (along with poverty, overcrowding, and underlying human immunodeficiency virus [HIV] infection) is a major risk factor for the progression of latent tuberculosis infection to active infection.[44] Nevertheless, tuberculosis control programs tend to focus their efforts on chemoprophylaxis and chemotherapy alone, rather than upon improvement of host nutritional status.

Cod-liver oil—a rich source of vitamins A and D—was used as treatment for tuberculosis for more than 100 years, prior to the development of antibiotics.[45] Although the association between malnutrition and tuberculosis is well known, few controlled clinical trials have been conducted to investigate whether improved nutrition might reduce the risk of developing active disease or improve the clinical outcome of tuberculosis. A recent Cochrane review of randomized controlled trials comparing any oral nutritional supplement with no nutritional intervention, placebo, or dietary advice only among people being treated for active TB showed effects of high-energy supplements or combinations of multiple micronutrients including zinc and vitamin A on weight gain, but overall little evidence of effect on other clinical outcomes of TB.[46] The role of nutrition and tuberculosis remains a major area of neglect, despite the promise that micronutrients have shown as therapy for other types of infections and the long record of the use of vitamins A and D for treatment of pulmonary and miliary tuberculosis in both Europe and the United States.

Malaria

In 2008, there were an estimated 247 million cases of malaria and approximately 1 million deaths from this infection worldwide; more than 85% of all malaria cases occurred in Africa.[47] Vector control and antimalarial drugs have been the traditional strategy against malaria, and little attention, until recently, has been paid to improving host nutritional status.

Low levels of vitamin A, zinc, iron, and folate have been shown to be responsible for a substantial proportion of malaria morbidity and mortality.[48,49] Two separate randomized, placebo-controlled clinical trials conducted in Papua New Guinea demonstrated that vitamin A supplementation or zinc supplementation can reduce malarial morbidity in preschool children by 30–50%.[50,51] Iron-deficiency anemia is widespread among malaria-endemic regions, and iron supplementation is often a key component of relief efforts. A meta-analysis of iron supplementation in malaria endemic regions, however, showed a tendency toward higher parasite counts in individuals who received iron supplements.[52] In contrast, a

2011 Cochrane review reported that there was no increased risk of malaria with iron supplementation in areas that have regular malaria surveillance and where malaria treatment services were provided.[53] On this basis, it was recommended that iron supplementation should not be discontinued in areas that are malaria endemic.

Human Immunodeficiency Virus Infection

In 2009, there were an estimated 33.3 million persons infected with HIV worldwide, with 2.6 million new infections and 1.8 million deaths from this cause occurring in that year alone.[54] Currently, approximately half of the people living with HIV are women and 2.5 million are children younger than the age of 15. Malnutrition may affect the course of HIV infection through a variety of mechanisms, including compromising host immune function, diminishing response to therapies, and promoting comorbidities.[4] Wasting and malnutrition were routinely observed in AIDS patients in the early years of the HIV epidemic.[55,56] With the advent of highly active antiretroviral therapy (HAART) in the mid-1990s, however, many of the more severe nutritional problems associated with HIV infection declined in prevalence, particularly in resource-rich countries where patients had access to HAART. Given that most people with HIV infection live in resource-poor countries with limited access to HAART, HIV-related malnutrition remains of important concern on a global basis.

HIV wasting syndrome has been associated with increased opportunistic infections (OIs), lower CD4 counts, and hyperactivation of the immune system.[57-60] Weight loss of as little as 5% of total body weight is predictive of death.[61,62] Prior to the introduction of HAART, specific micronutrient abnormalities were more common in HIV-positive than HIV-negative individuals.[63-65] Low serum levels of many of these nutrients (particularly, vitamins A, B_6, and B_{12}, as well as zinc) were associated with more rapid disease progression,[66] increased mortality,[67] impaired neurologic function,[68] diminished lymphocyte response to mitogens,[64] and increased maternal–fetal transmission.[69] These micronutrients may be involved in the pathogenesis of HIV infection through their roles as antioxidants and in immune function.

Several clinical trials of multiple micronutrient supplementation in HIV-infected adults have been published.[70-77] The earliest and largest of these—a trial among HIV infected pregnant women in Tanzania—showed that multivitamin supplementation (compared to placebo) had several beneficial outcomes in HIV-infected pregnant women, including greater increases in T-cell counts during and after pregnancy, better birth outcomes (reduced fetal deaths and low birth weight),[78] and improved weight gain during pregnancy.[79] Further follow-up of the same women over several years' time demonstrated continued benefits of supplementation with multiple micronutrients in the form of higher T-cell counts, lower viral loads, slower HIV progression, and improved overall survival.[70] Additional analyses of these trial participants showed a beneficial effect of micronutrients on maternal wasting,[80] maternal and child hemoglobin status,[81] and maternal depression and quality of life.[82]

The other, more recent clinical trials showed mixed results. These trials were much smaller and were conducted in different geographic regions (Southeast Asia, Africa, United States) with differing population characteristics (including differing levels of micronutrient deficiency at baseline) and used different mixes and doses of multiple micronutrients, making it difficult to draw any generalizable conclusions. Some of these studies were conducted among pregnant women,[76] others involved people coinfected with TB,[73,74] and only one took place in a population treated with antiretroviral therapy.[77] Currently, many people living with HIV in resource-poor countries are gaining access to antiretroviral therapy, so the effects of micronutrient supplementation on HIV outcomes need to be reassessed in light of this fact.

In terms of energy requirements, a 2003 WHO report recommended that energy requirements should be increased by approximately 10% to maintain body weight and physical activity in asymptomatic HIV-positive adults and growth in asymptomatic HIV-positive children.[83] For persons in the symptomatic stages of HIV and AIDS, WHO recommended that energy requirements increase by approximately 20–30% to maintain adult body weight; for children experiencing weight loss, the recommendation was that energy intake increase by 50–100% over normal requirements. For patients on HAART, however, resting energy expenditure and energy requirements appear to be more variable[84-87]—an issue that requires further study.

MICRONUTRIENTS AND IMMUNITY TO INFECTIOUS DISEASES

The relationship between micronutrients and the immunity to different infections is a rapidly growing and promising area of investigation. Micronutrients

Table 12-1	Micronutrients Can Influence Immunity to Infectious Diseases Through Their Roles in the Immune Function
Vitamin A, carotenoids	Vitamin A refers to three types of compounds that exhibit biologic activity: the alcohol (retinol), the aldehyde (retinal or retinaldehyde), and the acid (retinoic acid). Plants contain a group of compounds called *carotenoids* that are converted to retinol in the body. Beta-carotene is the most biologically active carotenoid. Has essential roles in vision and various systemic functions, including normal cell differentiation and cell recognition, growth and development, bone development, immune functions, and reproduction.
Vitamin B$_6$	Coenzyme in numerous enzyme reactions particularly amino acid transport and metabolism. Direct effect on immune system through its role in protein and nucleic acid synthesis. Deficiency leads to a reduction in nucleic acid synthesis that restricts proliferation of lymphocytes.
Vitamin B$_{12}$	Coenzyme involved in transmethylation from methylfolate to homocysteine. Released unmethylated folate becomes available for nucleic acid synthesis.
Vitamin E	Most important lipid-soluble antioxidant in cell membranes. Protects unsaturated phospholipids of the membrane from oxidative degradation from Reactive Oxygen Species (ROS) by donating a hydrogen (called free-radical scavenging). Is important component of the cellular antioxidant defense system, which involves other enzymes (e.g., superoxide dismutases, glutathione peroxidases, glutathione reductase, catalase), many of which depend upon adequate levels of other antioxidants. Therefore the antioxidant function of vitamin E can be affected by the levels of other nutrients (zinc, selenium, copper, vitamin C).
Selenium	Active form functions as selenoenzyme. Major function as part of glutathione peroxidase that reduces cellular peroxides to H_2O and alcohol and prevents oxidative damage to proteins, lipid, lipoproteins, and DNA.
Zinc	Zinc binds to protein, forming zinc fingers that are involved in DNA transcription factors, hormone receptors, and enzymes. Zinc deficiency has been shown to impair a variety of immune functions: ↓ lymphocyte counts, loss of helper T-cell function, ↓ killer T lymphocyte activities, delayed dermal hypersensitivity responses, depressed humoral and cell-mediated immunity. Excess levels of zinc intake can have toxic effects on the immune system and may promote viral replication.

Reproduced from Tang, AM, Lanzillotti J, Hendricks K, Gerrior J, Gosh M, Woods M, Wanke C Micronutrients: current issues for HIV care providers. *AIDS.* 2055;19:848, Table 1.

can influence immunity to infectious diseases through their roles in the immune function (**Table 12-1**).[3] Micronutrient deficiencies, such as that of vitamin A and zinc, can have a major impact upon T- and B-cell function, generation of antibody responses, and function of other immune effector cells. Micronutrients such as vitamin E, vitamin C, zinc, and selenium act as strong antioxidants and can influence the clinical course of infections. Oxidative stress, which occurs during infections, refers to the condition when the balance between pro-oxidants and antioxidants is upset, leading to overproduction of free radicals and resulting pathology.[88] Activated macrophages and neutrophils have important roles in the killing of microorganisms through the generation of free radicals. Host bystander cells can also be damaged by free radicals, which can cause oxidation of nucleic acids,

chromosomal breaks, peroxidation of lipids in cell membranes, and damage to collagen, proteins, and enzymes.

Investigators who wish to study the relationship between micronutrients and infectious diseases must often focus upon one or two micronutrients for practical reasons. Considerable cost and complexity arise when attempting a comprehensive study of micronutrient status during infection, although a comprehensive approach would be ideal because micronutrient deficiencies often occur simultaneously. A brief overview of the relationship of specific micronutrients in immunity to infection follows.

Vitamin A

Vitamin A, or all-*trans* retinol, is an essential micronutrient for immunity, growth, cellular differentiation, maintenance of mucosal surfaces, reproduction, and vision.[11] Two main dietary forms of vitamin A are distinguished: preformed vitamin A, which is found in foods such as butter, egg yolks, and cod-liver oil; and provitamin A carotenoids, which are found in foods such as spinach, carrots, mangoes, and papayas. Approximately 90% of the vitamin A in the body is stored in the liver, and the adult liver can contain enough vitamin A to last for more than one year. Vitamin A acts as a regulator of more than 300 genes through its active metabolites, all-*trans* and 9-*cis* retinoic acid, and specific nuclear receptors (members of the steroid and thyroid hormone receptor superfamily).[89]

Vitamin A exerts a wide-ranging effect on different compartments of the immune system, including the growth, maturation, and function of T and B lymphocytes; the expression of certain cytokines; and the maintenance of mucosal surfaces of the respiratory, gastrointestinal, and genitourinary tracts.[90,91] Historically, the main clinical manifestations of vitamin A deficiency were known to be night blindness and xerophthalmia (changes in the conjunctiva and cornea of the eye),[11] but later research showed increased incidence and severity of infections as part of the spectrum of vitamin A deficiency effects. A hallmark of vitamin A deficiency is an impaired ability to mount an antibody response to protein antigens,[91] although recent research also shows an important role for vitamin A in T-cell development and activation.[92,93] Infants, preschool children, pregnant women, and lactating women are at the highest risk of developing vitamin A deficiency.[11] Abnormal urinary losses of vitamin A can occur during infections, however, which can accelerate the depletion of the body's vitamin A stores.[94] Because vitamin A is a fat-soluble vitamin, steatorrhea can interfere with intestinal absorption of vitamin A.

Vitamin D

Vitamin D includes steroids with the biological activity of vitamin D_3. This nutrient is produced in the skin upon exposure to sunlight, but is also available from dietary sources such as egg yolks and fish-liver oils. Vitamin D regulates calcium and phosphorus metabolism and bone mineralization; thus the clinical syndrome of vitamin D deficiency is manifested as rickets in children and osteomalacia in adults.[95] Immune cells, such as macrophages, produce an enzyme that converts circulating 25-OH vitamin D to the more active form of $1,25(OH)_2$ vitamin D. $1,25(OH)_2$ vitamin D, in turn, upregulates the vitamin D receptor (VDR), which induces the production of an anti-

mycobacterial peptide, cathelicidin.[96,97] Vitamin D deficiency has been most extensively studied in tuberculosis, and it is hypothesized that the increased risk of TB associated with this deficit is associated with a lack of appropriate VDR-dependent antimycobacterial activity.[98–100] A growing body of evidence also indicates that vitamin D deficiency plays a role in other viral infections, such as HIV, Epstein-Barr virus, and viral respiratory infections.[101] Furthermore, vitamin D acts to regulate genes via specific nuclear receptors, and VDR may interact with nuclear retinoic acid receptors, providing some basis for the hypothesized interaction between vitamins A and D.[102]

Vitamin E

Vitamin E refers to tocopherol and tocotrienol compounds, of which α-tocopherol is the most active and abundant isomer. Rich dietary sources of vitamin E include seeds, nuts, margarine, and vegetable oils. Vitamin E is a strong antioxidant that protects against cellular damage by inhibiting peroxidation of polyunsaturated fatty acids in cell membranes. A clear-cut deficiency syndrome of vitamin E has not been described in humans.[103] This nutrient may protect immune effector cells against free-radical reactions.[104–106] Results from randomized clinical trials have shown that vitamin E supplementation improves markers of immune function and reduces incidence of upper respiratory tract infections in elderly adults.[107,108]

B-Complex Vitamins

The B-complex vitamins include thiamin, riboflavin, niacin, vitamin B_6, vitamin B_{12}, and folate. These vitamins participate in the metabolism of carbohydrates, fats, and proteins, and in hematopoiesis. Given their essential role in nucleic acid and protein biosynthesis, it follows that deficiencies of these vitamins will have effects on the immune system. In particular, vitamins B_6, B_{12}, and folate are all required in the metabolism of antibodies and cytokines.[109–111] The possible role of these micronutrients in the pathogenesis of infectious disease needs further clarification, however.

Vitamin C

Vitamin C, or ascorbic acid, is involved in a variety of biological reactions, including conversion of dopamine to norepinephrine, carnitine synthesis, iron absorption, and folate metabolism. Citrus fruits, peppers, green vegetables, potatoes, and berries contain high amounts of vitamin C. Deficiency of vitamin C results in scurvy, a syndrome characterized by skin lesions, hemorrhages, joint effusions, and weakness. The therapeutic efficacy of vitamin C as treatment for symptoms of the common cold remains controversial.[112] Although some evidence indicates that the immune system is influenced by vitamin C, supplementation above the amount needed for repletion has not consistently been shown to be clinically beneficial.[113,114]

Iron

Iron plays an important role in oxygen transport, as an electron carrier in cytochromes and in certain iron metalloenzymes.[115] Iron deficiency is associated with anemia,[116] impaired psychomotor development,[117,118] lower work capacity,[119] prematurity,[120] and higher maternal mortality.[121,122] More than 30% of the world's population suffers from anemia, with many of these cases being related to iron deficiency.[123] Notably, pregnant women, women of childbearing age, infants, and children are at higher risk of developing iron-deficiency anemia. A high-cereal diet (which can interfere with iron absorption), chronic diarrhea, malabsorption, and blood loss from pregnancy, menstruation, and intestinal parasites[124] are all factors that can contribute to iron deficiency. Although iron deficiency may adversely affect neutrophil and lymphocyte function, the relationship between this deficit and infection remains unclear.[125] Some studies suggested that iron supplementation could increase susceptibility to malaria, but recent studies show that iron deficiency should be corrected in children with malaria.[126] There is insufficient evidence to support a role for iron supplementation in decreasing the incidence of infections,[127,128] and reducing iron deficiency remains a formidable challenge worldwide.

Selenium

Selenium, an essential trace element, is contained in the enzyme glutathione peroxidase and protects cells against oxidative damage.[129] This nutrient is found in seafoods, some meats, and grain products, depending on the selenium content of the soil. Keshan's disease, a cardiomyopathy, and Kashin-Beck disease, an osteoarticular disorder, occur in areas where the soil is low in selenium. Selenium may elicit cell-mediated and humoral immune responses and appears to influence the function of T lymphocytes.[130,131] Studies using a murine model for coxsackie B–induced myocarditis suggest that selenium deficiency can increase the virulence of the coxsackie B virus.[132] Some evidence suggests that selenium supplementation may

have benefits in HIV infection; however, this effect appears to be limited to those HIV-positive individuals who have initial low selenium levels.[133] The biological importance of selenium is complex, and the mechanism by which it may affect the immune system remains to be established.

Iodine

Iodine deficiency can result in goiter and a wide spectrum of mental, psychomotor, and growth abnormalities.[134] Iodine functions as a component of thyroxine (T_4), and 3,5,3'-triiodothyronine (T_3), two hormones that are required for normal growth, development, and metabolism. Nuclear thyroid hormone receptors can bind with retinoic acid receptors, suggesting that some interaction may occur between vitamin A and thyroid status.[135] Rich sources of iodine include seafood and iodized salt. Increased rates of stillbirths, abortions, infant mortality, and mental retardation have been noted in areas with endemic iodine deficiency, and studies suggest that iodine supplementation or iodination of irrigation water can reduce these risks.[136–138] It is estimated that 72% of households in developing countries now have access to iodized salt; the goal of the Universal Salt Iodination plan is to raise that rate to least 90%.[139] The role of iodine deficiency in immune function is not well established,[140] and further studies of the relationship between iodine deficiency and infections are needed.[141]

Zinc

Zinc is an important trace element that is needed for the function of more than 300 metalloenzymes, including those involved in metabolism of proteins, fats, and carbohydrates; for regulation of RNA synthesis through zinc fingers; for synaptic transmission; and for the function of protein kinase C.[142] Rich dietary sources of zinc include shellfish, beef, chicken, fish, nuts, and beans. Zinc deficiency is characterized by growth retardation, reproductive abnormalities, increased infections, and skin and neurological disorders. This deficit usually arises because of inadequate dietary intake of zinc, with pregnant and lactating women, infants, and preschool children being at the highest risk of zinc deficiency. Complicating the ability to determine the effect of zinc deficiency is the body's capacity to adapt to low zinc intakes; thus a person's appearance may not reflect a clinical deficiency of this nutrient.[141]

Zinc plays an important role in the growth, development, and function of neutrophils, macrophages, natural killer cells, and T and B lymphocytes.[143] As mentioned earlier, large series of randomized, placebo-controlled clinical trials suggest that zinc supplementation can reduce the morbidity of diarrheal disease, respiratory disease, and malaria, especially in areas where zinc deficiency is present.[144–148]

ASSESSMENT OF NUTRITIONAL STATUS

The previous sections have briefly illustrated the interrelationships between nutritional status, infection, and immune function. Due to the cyclical nature of the relationships, epidemiological studies can examine nutritional status as either a risk factor (exposure or determinant) of infectious diseases or as an outcome of infections. The tools used to assess nutritional disorders are at the core of a study's success in obtaining quality data, minimizing misclassification, and accurately estimating disease associations. The remainder of this chapter reviews the most commonly used methods for assessing nutritional status in epidemiologic studies.

Dietary Intake Assessment

Dietary intake assessments are based on information supplied either by the study participants themselves or by a surrogate. Most assessments focus on which foods were consumed, how much of those foods were consumed, how the foods were prepared, and how often the foods were consumed during a specific reference period. Some methods attempt to collect all of this information, whereas others focus on a selected few of these aspects. During the study design phase, investigators should try to select the method that will be most effective in getting the information needed for the specific research goals and for the specific study population. Sometimes a tool is selected because it is what others are using (good for comparisons across studies) or because it is the only option available. Although there is disagreement in the field about which tool is better, it is generally agreed that no perfect tool exists. The most commonly used methods for assessing dietary intake are reviewed in this section.

Food Records

A food record is a method of intake assessment in which a subject is asked to write down all foods and beverages consumed for a period of days (usually 3–7 days). Subjects are generally instructed on how to estimate the amount or serving size of each food item consumed, which can either be weighed or described. The food record is used as a quantitative way to describe the intake during the recording days, and often this method serves as the gold standard in validation or calibration studies. Portion sizes are thought to be more accurately recorded with this technique because they are written down at the time of consumption rather than relying on recall. Participants may, however, alter what they eat while reporting their intake. In addition, keeping a food record requires participants to be literate and compliant in recording everything they eat. Other disadvantages of this method are that the records need to be legible, they must be returned to the study investigator, and data entry of the food records can be time consuming. Some studies have also shown that food records tend to underestimate dietary intake.[149,150]

In deciding to use food records as a dietary assessment tool in a study of nutrition and infectious diseases, the following questions need consideration.

- How many days of record keeping will be sufficient to give an estimate of the usual intake of the study population?
- Will the study participants be compliant in keeping the records?
- Can the participants write legibly?
- Will participants not lose the food record?
- How will participants return the food records to the study investigators?
- Will study investigators (ideally trained nutritionists) be able to review the records with each participant for completeness and clarity?

Other methods of record keeping, such as using tape recorders, dictaphones, cell phones, or web-based applications may be options in some studies, but the higher cost associated with some of these techniques may be prohibitive. Thus, while food records may be a good method for the general population, they may not be a feasible option for specialized populations.

24-Hour Recall

A 24-hour recall is a method of intake assessment in which the subject is asked to recall everything consumed during the previous day or 24 hours. It is usually administered by a trained interviewer and may be done in person or by telephone. An advantage of the 24-hour recall is that the recall period is only one day, so most subjects are able to accurately recall their intake. Also, if the 24-hour recall is unannounced or unsuspected, the influence in food selection that might be observed with food records is eliminated. Data entry can be completed after the interview if the data have been recorded in pen-and-paper format, or the data can be entered during the interview using a computerized version of the interview format. The 24-hour recall can be completed on one occasion, or multiple 24-hour recalls can be completed on several days for each participant.

While the 24-hour recall is simpler and puts less of a burden on the participants, a single 24-hour recall does not provide good information on individual intake. Therefore, dietary information collected from 24-hour recalls should not be used to classify participants into deficient and nondeficient diets due to day-to-day within-person variation. This method can, however, be used to obtain reasonable estimates of average intakes of groups.[151,152]

For studies that require participants to be ranked individually according to nutrient intake, the single 24-hour recall is not the ideal method. Multiple 24-hour recalls may be considered, but such an approach requires participants to return to the study site for additional visits. This aspect of the study eliminates the "unexpectedness" of the assessment, and participants may then alter their food intake accordingly. Conducting 24-hour recalls over the phone may be feasible if study participants are accessible by telephone.

It is important that the 24-hour recall includes a full 24 hours. Many people consume foods during the middle of the night, and important nutrient data might be missed if one assumes that all food intake occurs between morning and evening hours. It is also important to customize serving sizes to the study population. In some populations, serving sizes may be described by the price or brand of the product, rather than the actual amount. Given the importance of customizing any dietary intake assessment tool to the target population, prior knowledge of eating and food buying habits in that community is essential.

Food Frequency Questionnaire

A food frequency questionnaire (FFQ) aims to get an estimate of usual intake by recalling intake from a list of a specific number of foods for a defined reference period, usually one year. This instrument generally asks subjects how often they ate certain foods, thinking back over the reference period. Some FFQs also include serving sizes, often as a specified portion or as a small, medium, or large portion size. Based on all the foods in the food list, participants' frequency

of intake, and serving size, nutrient intake values may then be calculated.

FFQs can be self- or interviewer-administered tools, and the processing time for FFQs versus food records or 24-hour recalls is generally shorter. Due to its ease of use, this data collection method is now commonly used in epidemiologic studies. FFQs depend on recollection of food intake during the reference period, however, and participants must have fairly regular eating habits. The value of the survey also depends heavily on the food list used. Some FFQs have been shown to provide reasonable estimates of group intakes, and some have been shown to be able to rank individual intake. Several investigators have described in detail issues to be considered when selecting, developing, and validating a FFQ.[153–159]

FFQs do not work well among study populations that have irregular eating habits—for example, among populations with extended periods of hospitalization, incarcerations, or homelessness. Irregular intakes, large variations in places of intake (i.e., a relative's house, a friend's house, soup kitchens, restaurants), and seasonal variations in intake may also make it difficult for participants to recall and average their food intake over a 12-month or even a 6-month period. Some FFQs allow study investigators to adapt the food list to their specific population. For example, based on pilot studies, an investigator might decide to eliminate some foods from the list that the population does not generally consume or add foods commonly consumed. Foods on the food list may also be grouped or ungrouped, depending on the frequency of consumption of each of the items. When altering the food list on a FFQ, the food and nutrient database must be updated according to the new food list. A FFQ should not be used indiscriminately with all populations.

Use of Technology in Dietary Intake Assessment

Recent advances in technology are enticing options that are being actively investigated for their use in assessing dietary intake. Examples include computer-administered versions of the 24-hour recall and food frequency questionnaire, web-based intake assessment methods, mobile food records, 3-D portion-size pictures, and the use of cell phones with digital cameras. ChooseMyPlate.gov is an example of a method that combines the U.S. government dietary guidelines with interactive web-based tools for tracking dietary intake and creating personalized meal plans that can be used at the individual

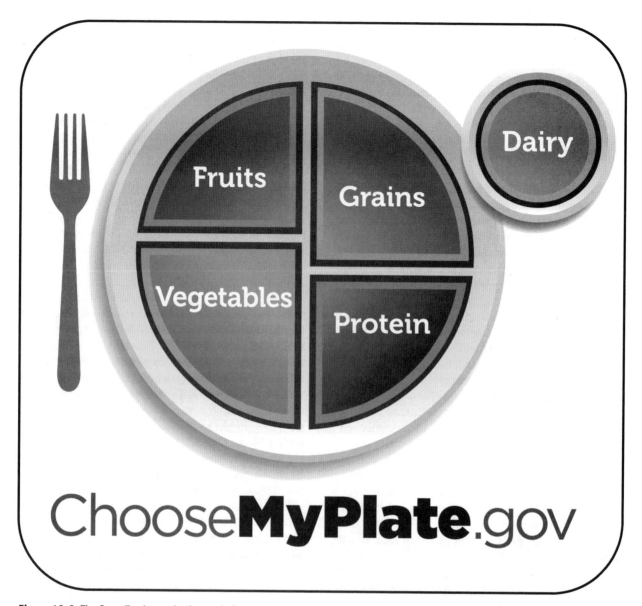

Figure 12-2 The SuperTracker and other tools for tracking diet and physical activity are available on ChooseMyPlate.gov. Courtesy of USDA.

level (**Figure 12-2**). Although these methods hold much promise, more studies are needed to determine their validity, reliability, and effectiveness as research tools.[160–162]

Translating Foods into Nutrients

The information obtained using any of the dietary intake assessments discussed previously may be translated into nutrient intake data through the use of databases that contain nutrient information for a range of foods. Foods consumed are first translated into food codes, which link the consumed foods to a nutrient database. A nutrient database contains the food codes and nutrient values for each code. After

the food code and the amount of food consumed have been entered, nutrient intakes can be computed.

A variety of government and commercial nutrient databases are available, and results may vary depending on which database is used. Not only can the databases used differ between methods—for example, the 24-hour recall and the FFQ—but different databases may also be used for the same method—for example, the 24-hour recall completed by different investigators. As with the assessment tools, no database is perfect. During the food coding process, because a database often includes many similar food items, incorrect selection or incorrect coding of the food items may occur. Databases also do not include all nutrients and non-nutrients. In addition, they need to be updated according to product availability in the food supply. For example, recent changes in the *trans*-fatty acid content of some foods and the introduction of low-carbohydrate foods need to be captured in the dietary assessment methods and then become part of the databases.

Other Intake Assessment Issues

Cognitive processes affect dietary intake assessments.[163] Although the impact of cognitive processes has been studied in the general U.S. population to some degree, little is known about the implications for specialized or international populations. For example, research indicates that asking questions and probes in neutral ways in the general U.S. population improves the quality of recalling dietary intake.[164] The effects of this relationship on the quality of dietary intake assessment in other populations, however, remains to be investigated.

Often, investigators are interested in the use of vitamin and mineral supplementation in addition to dietary intake. Assessments of supplement use can be done for a 24-hour recall period, for the same reference period as the FFQ, or as part of the food record. No standard method for collecting this information has been established. Although several dietary intake assessment tools have questions on vitamin–mineral supplementation, it is important to adapt these instruments to the population of interest. Ideally, the tool used will include detailed questions on type, brand name, frequency of use, and amount of each supplement used. Furthermore, multivitamins should be distinguished from single-vitamin supplements. However, people are often unable to recall brand names, other than the generic multivitamin, and may have difficulty answering questions about separate vitamins. For example, a participant who takes only a multivitamin and answers "yes" to a question about taking a multivitamin might also answer "yes" to a question about taking a vitamin C supplement, as vitamin C is included as part of the multivitamin. Participants might also have difficulty recalling the amount or dose of individual vitamins. When designing a questionnaire on vitamin and mineral supplements, questions should be carefully pilot-tested in the study population before incorporating them into the final questionnaire.

The analysis of dietary data can be complex, especially when trying to decide whether to adjust for energy intake or other dietary variables. This topic continues to be the topic of great epidemiologic debate, and there is not always a clear answer to the question.[165–167] Many dietary variables are collinear, so the investigator needs to take great care when using adjustment methods. For more detailed information, several good resources are available.[159,168]

Although the limitations of intake assessment might seem discouraging, it would be more discouraging to let these limitations stop us from doing important dietary intake research. We do need to be aware of the limitations of the tools we use and pretest them in the study population. Moreover, it is important for us to strive to improve current dietary intake assessment tools.

Body Composition

Measuring body composition can be as difficult as measuring dietary intake. Each method measures a different body compartment, and each has its advantages and disadvantages.

The most common methods used in research settings are height, weight, and body mass index (BMI) (weight in kilometers divided by height in meters squared), a height and weight index used as a measure of obesity. For example, the National Heart, Lung and Blood Institute's Obesity Education Initiative uses the following classification of overweight and obesity by BMI: less than 18.5, underweight; 18.5–24.9, normal weight; 25.0–29.9, overweight; 30.0–39.9, obese; and 40 or greater, extreme obesity.[169] Ideally, weight should be measured rather than self-reported, although self-reported weights can be reasonably used in some populations.[170–172] Interpreting weight as well as BMI can be problematic when individuals have edema or ascites, or, for example, in an obese patient who is protein-energy malnourished, yet still overweight. The waist circumference is used as a measure of abdominal fat content. For men, a waist circumference of greater than 102 cm is associated with an increased risk for obesity-associated risk factors; for women, the corresponding value is 88 cm.[169] This measurement requires locating the waist consistently for all subjects, which tends to be more difficult in obese individuals.

Densitometry measures the density of the body, which is then used to calculate percent body fat. One method to determine body density is underwater weighing, which is a measure of body volume and is often cited as the gold standard. The major limitation of this method is that it is cumbersome and expensive. Another method of densitometry is the whole-body plethysmograph (BODPOD), in which body volume is measured in a sealed chamber rather than underwater. This method appears to be as accurate as underwater weighing, but the equipment is complex and costly.[173]

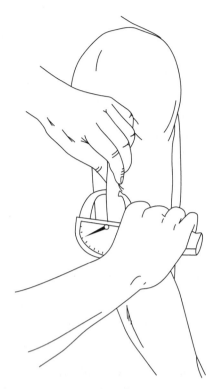

Grasp a double fold of skin and subcutaneous adipose tissue with the thumb and index finger of the left hand.

Place the caliper tips on the site where the sides of the skinfold are approximately parallel and 1 cm distal to where the skinfold is grasped.

Position the caliper dial so that it can be read easily. Obtain the measurement about 4 sec after placing the caliper tips on the skinfold.

Figure 12-3 Skinfold measurement as measurement of subcutaneous fat. Reproduced from Lee RD and Nieman DC. Nutritional Assessment. Page 139, Figure 6.17. © 2003 McGraw-Hill Publishers.

Skinfold measurements are used as a measure of subcutaneous fat (**Figure 12-3**). These measurements are obtained at a number of different body sites using special calipers. Use of this method requires trained, certified personnel who are regularly retrained, because the measurement is only as good as the measurer.[174] Measurements from three to seven sites on the body (usually a combination of triceps, subscapular, suprailiac, thigh, abdomen, chest, and midaxillary) are then combined using validated equations to obtain a measure of subcutaneous fat. When performed correctly, these measurements can correlate closely with underwater weighing.[175]

Bioelectrical impedance analysis (BIA) is a method used to estimate body cell mass, fat, and fat-free mass. The method is based on the principle that lean tissues, which consist primarily of electrolyte-containing water, are highly conductive and represent a low-impedance pathway. Fat and bone, in contrast, are nonconductive and have high impedance to current flow.[176] In practice, to obtain the BIA measurement, an imperceptible current (800 μA at a signal frequency of 50 kHz) is passed between the foot and hand of the subject and two components of impedance are measured—resistance and reactance. These values are then entered into any of several prediction equations to obtain estimates of total body water,

fat, fat-free mass, and body cell mass. The validity of BIA—particularly the equations used to calculate body fat—has been debated and continues to be investigated.[177,178] For optimal accuracy of measurements, subjects should not have consumed any alcohol within 12 hours or exercised vigorously within 8 hours of testing. The measurements should be taken on subjects 4 hours after eating and at least 1 hour after the last drink of water and within 30 minutes of voiding. Subjects remain clothed, with the exception of shoes and socks, and lie supine with limbs not touching their bodies. They should not be diaphoretic or soaked in urine, as the analyzer measures this fluid as fat-free mass. Gel electrodes are placed on the wrist, metacarpal region, ankle, and metatarsal region on the right side of the body. BIA is a quick, inexpensive, and portable method for assessing body composition, and its results appear to be reproducible.[179] However, results may be altered when hydration is abnormal (e.g., dehydration or edema).

Dual energy X-ray absorptiometry (DEXA) has become more popular in recent years for the measurement of body composition. DEXA scanners generate X rays at two energy levels to differentiate body weight into the components of fat, muscle, and bone mineral content. The results from DEXA scans have been shown to correlate well with underwater weighing.[180,181] Advantages of the DEXA method include the fact that it is based on a three-compartment model rather than a two-compartment model, as are most other methods. It can also distinguish regional as well as whole-body parameters of body composition. Disadvantages are that the equipment is expensive, and it often requires trained radiology personnel to operate.

Computed tomography (CT) scanning is another method for determining body composition. CT scans provide measures of body fat distributions and are used to obtain ratios of intra-abdominal to extra-abdominal fat. In addition to being costly, the radiation dose from a CT scan is higher than that from DEXA.[182] Other methods for determining body composition include magnetic resonance imaging (MRI), total body electrical conductivity (TOBEC), and near-infrared interactance (NIR), among others. The equipment needed for these methods is also complex and costly.

When deciding which method to use to assess body composition in studies of the relationship between nutrition and infectious diseases, consider using a combination of methods, which can strengthen the results. For example, to assess changes and redistribution of body fat in HIV infection, DEXA could be used to assess total body fat and CT scanning to assess the intra-abdominal to extra-abdominal fat ratio. For studies other than those with relatively small numbers of participants, some methods (e.g., underwater weighing) are clearly not feasible. Some methods, such as DEXA and CT scanning, may not be available within close proximity to the study clinic. Some studies may require methods that are quick and readily available, such as skinfold measurements and BIA, to maximize the number of individuals who are willing to participate.

In children, malnutrition has been defined as mildly underweight, or weight-for-age less than two standard deviations below the National Center for Health Statistics (NCHS) reference population mean.[183] Z-scores for weight-for-age, height-for-age, and weight-for-height are also used to classify malnutrition in children, and a wide variety of classification systems and cut-offs for malnutrition have been established.[184] Mid-upper-arm circumference can be used in screening for malnutrition when weight and height are difficult to obtain and the exact age of the child is unknown.[185]

Biochemical Measurements

Biochemical measurements may target a nutrient or its metabolite. Such a test may be used for examining metabolic pathways—for example, a particular dose may be orally administered and the appearance of metabolites in urine measured.[186] Ideally, the measurement should reflect nutrient status (the amount available to the body) so that the investigator can define a deficiency, excess, or adequacy of the nutrient. Some measurements can detect nutrient deficiencies before signs and symptoms appear, whereas others can reflect recent intake. For some nutrients, levels in the blood may also be used as an assessment of dietary intake.[187] Measures are most commonly done on samples of blood (whole blood, white cells, serum, or plasma) and urine, but for some nutrients, samples have included saliva, hair, nails, or tissue biopsies.

Many factors affect the measurement of a nutrient, and little is known about the exact influence of non-nutritional factors such as lifestyle, recreational drug use, medications, and the influence of disease. Quality control of any laboratory procedure needs to be stringent so that whichever measures are used will be reliable and valid. Many times multiple methods or assays are available for assessing the same nutrients, and it is important to keep in mind which methods were used in earlier research when comparing study results.

The same debate about the number of days necessary to determine average dietary intake may be argued for biochemical measures of nutrients as well, as intra-individual variations on a measure may require repeated measures. In addition, what might be an abnormal level for a "healthy" person might not be an abnormal level for a person with disease. For example, changes in biochemical measures can occur with infection or inflammation, which may not reflect real changes in general tissue nutrient status or dietary intake. It is also important to know how quickly changes in dietary intake affect changes in biochemical measurements—that is, whether the measurement responds within days or hours after changes in intake. Other factors, such as lifestyle or genetics, may also affect serum levels. The ability to control factors that affect the measurements need to be evaluated. For example, if a fasting specimen is needed, can the study participants reasonably be expected to have fasted when they come in for testing? If fecal or urinary analyses are required, can cooperation from study participants be expected?

Biochemical measurements are useful when combined with other indicators of nutritional status. Nevertheless, more research is needed to come up with better biochemical markers of nutritional status.

CONCLUSION

Nutrition is a major determinant of morbidity and mortality due to infectious diseases. Several micronutrients play essential roles in the growth, development, and function of the immune system and influence oxidative stress. For this reason, epidemiological studies of infectious diseases should include characterization of nutritional status. At a minimum, basic anthropometric indices such as weight and height should be a basic part of any epidemiological investigation of infectious diseases. Nutritional assessment can then be expanded into more sophisticated measures of specific micronutrients, dietary intake, and body composition. Major indicators of health, such as child mortality, birth weight, and maternal mortality, are influenced by host nutritional status. Likewise, micronutrients have been shown to influence the clinical course of diarrheal and lower respiratory disease, measles, malaria, and HIV. Nevertheless, supplementation with micronutrients may have varying effects depending on whether the level of supplementation is intended to correct deficiencies or represents a pharmacological dose. The potential role of micronutrients in the clinical course of tuberculosis, a major reemerging disease, remains especially neglected.

Although a variety of nutrition assessment tools are available, limited information is available on the appropriateness of their use in specialized populations. The decision on which tool(s) to use should be based on the study population and the specific research goals. Each tool should, to the extent possible, be customized to the target population. Few studies to date have focused on improving nutrition assessment methodology, and further research is needed to improve the existing tools used to assess nutritional status and develop innovative new ones.

• • • REFERENCES

1. Beisel WR. Role of nutrition in immune system diseases. *Comp Ther.* 1987;13(1):13–19.

2. Chandra RK. Symposium: History of nutritional immunology. Protein-energy malnutrition and immunological responses. *Am Inst Nutr.* 1992;597–600.

3. Beisel WR. Single nutrients and immunity. *Am J Clin Nutr.* 1982;35(suppl):417–468.

4. Guenter P, Muurahainen N, Simons G, et al. Relationships among nutritional status, disease progression, and survival in HIV infection. *J Acquir Immune Defic Syndr.* 1993;6: 1130–1138.

5. Dreizen S. Nutrition and the immune response. *Internat J Vit Nutr Res.* 1979;49:220–228.

6. Keusch GT. The history of nutrition: malnutrition, infection and immunity. *J Nutr.* 2003;133:336S–340S.

7. World Health Organization. *Diarrheal Disease.* 2009.

8. Black RE, Brown KH, Becker S. Malnutrition is a determining factor in diarrheal duration, but not incidence, among young children in a longitudinal study in rural Bangladesh. *Am J Clin Nutr.* 1984;39:87–94.

9. Chen LC, Huq E, Huffman SL. A prospective study of the risk of diarrheal diseases according to the nutritional status of children. *Am J Epidemiol.* 1981;114:284–292.

10. Lanata CF, Black RE. Diarrheal diseases. In: Semba RD, Bloem MW, eds. *Nutrition and Health in Developing Countries.* Totowa: Humana Press, 2008:139–178.

11. Sommer A, West KP Jr. *Vitamin A Deficiency: Health, Survival, and Vision.* New York: Oxford University Press; 1996.

12. Beaton GH, Martorell R, L'Abbe KA, et al. *Effectiveness of Vitamin A Supplementation in the Control of Young Child Morbidity and Mortality in Developing Countries.* Administrative Committee on Coordination/ Subcommittee on Nutrition, State-of-the-Art Nutrition Policy Discussion Paper No. 13. United Nations; 1993.

13. Bhandari N, Bahl R, Sazawal S, et al. Breastfeeding status alters the effect of vitamin A treatment during acute diarrhea in children. *J Nutr.* 1997;127:59–63.

14. Sazawal S, Black RE, Bhan MK, et al. Zinc supplementation reduces the incidence of persistent diarrhea and dysentery among low socioeconomic children in India. *J Nutr.* 1996;126:443–450.

15. Bhutta ZA, Bird SM, Black RE, et al. Therapeutic effects of oral zinc in acute and persistent diarrhea in children in developing countries: pooled analysis of randomized controlled trials. *Am J Clin Nutr.* 2000;72:1516–1522.

16. United Nations Children's Fund/World Health Organization. *Clinical Management of Acute Diarrhoea: Joint Statement.* 2004.

17. Ninh NX, Thissen JP, Collette L, et al. Zinc supplementation increases growth and circulating insulin-like growth factor I (IGF-I) in growth-retarded Vietnamese children. *Am J Clin Nutr.* 1996;63:514–519.

18. Rosado JL, Lopez P, Munoz E, et al. Zinc supplementation reduced morbidity, but neither zinc nor iron supplementation affected growth or body composition of Mexican preschoolers. *Am J Clin Nutr.* 1997;65:13–19.

19. Sazawal S, Black RE, Bhan MK, et al. Efficacy of zinc supplementation in reducing the incidence and prevalence of acute diarrhea: a community-based, double-blind, controlled trial. *Am J Clin Nutr.* 1997;66:413–418.

20. Initiative for Vaccine Research (IVR). Acute Respiratory Infections (Update September 2009). World Health Organization. Available at: http://www.who.int/vaccine_research/diseases/ari/en/index.html.

21. Lanata CF, Black RE. Acute lower-respiratory infections. In: Semba RD, Bloem MW, eds. *Nutrition and Health in Developing Countries.* Totowa, NJ: Humana Press, 2008:179–214.

22. Lassi ZS, Haider BA, Bhutta ZA. Zinc supplementation for the prevention of pneumonia in children aged 2 months to 59 months. *Cochrane Database Syst Rev.* 2010;CD005978.

23. Brown KH, Peerson JM, Baker SK, et al. Preventive zinc supplementation among infants, preschoolers, and older prepubertal children. *Food Nutr Bull.* 2009;30:S12–S40.

24. Ninh NX, Thissen JP, Collette L, et al. Zinc supplementation increases growth and circulating insulin-like growth factor I (IGF-I) in growth-retarded Vietnamese children. *Am J Clin Nutr.* 1996;63:514–519.

25. Sazawal S, Black RE, Jalla S, et al. Zinc supplementation reduces the incidence of acute lower respiratory infections in infants and preschool children: a double-blind, controlled trial. *Pediatrics.* 1998;102:1–5.

26. Meeks GJ, Witter MM, Ramdath DD. Zinc supplementation: effects on the growth and morbidity of undernourished Jamaican children. *Eur J Clin Nutr.* 1998;52:34–39.

27. Bhandari N, Bahl R, Taneja S, et al. Effect of routine zinc supplementation on pneumonia in children aged 6 months to 3 years: randomised controlled trial in an urban slum. *Br Med J.* 2002;324:1358–1360.

28. Penny ME, Marin RM, Duran A, et al. Randomized controlled trial of the effect of daily supplementation with zinc or multiple micronutrients on the morbidity, growth, and micronutrient status of young Peruvian children. *Am J Clin Nutr.* 2004;79:457–465.

29. Potential interventions for the prevention of childhood pneumonia in developing countries: a meta-analysis of data from field trials to assess the impact of vitamin A supplementation on pneumonia morbidity and mortality. The Vitamin A and Pneumonia Working Group *Bull World Health Organ.* 1995;73:609–619.

30. Dowell SF, Papic Z, Bresee JS, et al. Treatment of respiratory syncytial virus infection with vitamin A: a randomized, placebo-controlled trial in Santiago, Chile. *Pediatr Infect Dis J.* 1996;15:782–786.

31. Bresee JS, Fischer M, Dowell SF, et al. Vitamin A therapy for children with respiratory syncytial virus infection: a multicenter trial in the United States. *Pediatr Infect Dis J.* 1996;15:777–782.

32. Ebrahim GJ. Global measles situation. *J Trop Pediatr.* 2010;56:219–220.

33. Centers for Disease Control and Prevention. Global measles mortality, 2000–2008. *MMWR.* 2009;58:1321–1326.

34. Perry RT, Halsey NA. The clinical significance of measles: a review. *J Infect Dis.* 2004;189:S4–S16.

35. Dossetor J, Whittle HC, Greenwood BM. Persistent measles infection in malnourished children. *Br Med J.* 1977;1:1633–1635.

36. Chen LC, Rahman M, Sarder AM. Epidemiology and causes of death among children in a rural area of Bangladesh. *Int J Epidemiol.* 1980;9:25–33.

37. Koster FT, Curlin GC, Aziz KM, et al. Synergistic impact of measles and diarrhoea on nutrition and mortality in Bangladesh. *Bull World Health Organ.* 1981;59:901–908.

38. World Health Organization. *WHO Vaccine Preventable Diseases: Monitoring System, 2004 Global Summary.* Geneva, Switzerland: World Health Organization; 2004.

39. Manicus A. Maeslingerne paa Faeröerne i Sommeren 1846. *Ugeskrift Laeger.* 1847;6:189–210.

40. Smedman L, Lindeberg A, Jeppsson O, et al. Nutritional status and measles: a community study in Guinea-Bissau. *Ann Trop Paediatr.* 1983;3:169–176.

41. Alwar AJ. The effect of protein energy malnutrition on morbidity and mortality due to measles at Kenyatta National Hospital, Nairobi (Kenya). *East Afr Med J.* 1992;69:415–418.

42. Markowitz LE, Nzilambi N, Driskell WJ, et al. Vitamin A levels and mortality among hospitalized measles patients, Kinshasa, Zaire. *J Trop Pediatr.* 1989;35:109–12.

43. World Health Organization. Global tuberculosis control: a short update to the 2009 report. 2009. Available at: http://whqlibdoc.who.int/publications/2009/9789241598866_eng.pdf. Accessed November 29, 2010.

44. Hudelson P. Gender differentials in tuberculosis: the role of socio-economic and cultural factors. *Tuber Lung Dis.* 1996;77:391–400.

45. Williams CJB, Williams CT. *Pulmonary Consumption: Its Etiology, Pathology, and Treatment.* London: Longmans, Green, and Company; 1989.

46. Abba K, Sudarsanam TD, Grobler L, et al. Nutritional supplements for people being treated for active tuberculosis. *Cochrane Database Syst Rev.* 2008;CD006086.

47. World Health Organization. *Malaria.* 2010.

48. Caulfield LE, Richard SA, Black RE. Undernutrition as an underlying cause of malaria morbidity and mortality in children less than five years old. *Am J Trop Med Hyg.* 2004;71:55–63.

49. Friis H, Mwaniki D, Omondi B, et al. Serum retinol concentrations and *Schistosoma mansoni*, intestinal helminths, and malarial parasitemia: a cross-sectional study in Kenyan preschool and primary school children. *Am J Clin Nutr.* 1997;66:665–671.

50. Shankar AH, Genton B, Semba RD, et al. Effect of vitamin A supplementation on morbidity due to *Plasmodium falciparum* in young children in Papua New Guinea: a randomised trial. *Lancet.* 1999;354:203–209.

51. Shankar AH, Genton B, Baisor M, et al. The influence of zinc supplementation on morbidity due to *Plasmodium falciparum*: a randomized trial in preschool children in Papua New Guinea. *Am J Trop Med Hyg.* 2000;62:663–669.

52. International Nutritional Anemia Consultative Group. *Safety of Iron Supplementation Programs in Malaria-Endemic Regions.* Washington, DC: International Life Science Institute; 2000.

53. Okebe JU, Yahav D, Shbita R, Paul M. Oral iron supplements for children in malaria-endemic areas. *Cochrane Database of Systematic Reviews* 2011, Issue 10. Art. No.: CD006589. DOI: 10.1002/14651858.CD006589.pub3.

54. Joint United Nations Programme on HIV/AIDS. *Global Report: UNAIDS Report on the Global AIDS Epidemic 2010.* Geneva, Switzerland: UNAIDS; 2010. Available at: www.who.int/hiv/data/2009_global_summary.png.

55. Kotler DP, Goetz H, Lange M, et al. Enteropathy associated with the acquired immunodeficiency syndrome. *Ann Intern Med.* 1984;101:421–428.

56. Kotler DP, Wang J, Pierson RN Jr. Body composition studies in patients with the acquired immunodeficiency syndrome. *Am J Clin Nutr.* 1985;42:1255–1265.

57. Graham NMH, Munoz A, Bacellar H, et al. Clinical factors associated with weight loss related to infection with human immunodeficiency virus type 1 in the multicenter AIDS cohort study. *Am J Epidemiol.* 1993;137(4):1–8.

58. Graham NMH, Rubb S, Hoover DR, et al. Beta$_2$-microglobulin and other early predictors of human immunodeficiency virus type 1-related wasting. *Ann Epidemiol.* 1994;4:32–39.

59. Zangerle R, Reibnegger G, Wachter H, et al. Weight loss in HIV-1 infection is associated with immune activation. *AIDS.* 1993;7:175–181.

60. Grunfeld C, Feingold KR. Metabolic disturbances and wasting in acquired immunodeficiency syndrome. *N Engl J Med.* 1992;327(5):329–337.

61. Wheeler DA, Gibert CL, Launer CA, et al. Weight loss as a predictor of survival and disease progression in HIV infection. *J Acquir Immune Defic Syndr.* 1998;18:80–85.

62. Tang AM, Forrester J, Spiegelman D, et al. Weight loss and survival in HIV-positive patients in the era of highly active antiretroviral therapy. *J Acquir Immune Defic Syndr* 2002;31:230–236.

63. Beach RS, Mantero-Atienza E, Shor-Posner G, et al. Specific nutrient abnormalities in asymptomatic HIV-1 infection. *AIDS.* 1992;6:701–708.

64. Baum MK, Mantero-Atienza E, Shor-Posner G, et al. Association of vitamin B$_6$ status with parameters of immune function in early HIV-1 infection. *J Acquir Immune Defic Syndr.* 1991;4:1122–1132.

65. Bogden JD, Baker H, Frank O, et al. Micronutrient status and human immunodeficiency virus (HIV) infection. In: Bendich A, Chandra RK, eds. *Micronutrients and Immune Functions, Vol. 587.* New York: New York Academy of Sciences;, 1990:189–195.

66. Graham NMH, Sorenson D, Odaka N, et al. Relationship of serum copper and zinc levels to HIV-1 seropositivity and progression to AIDS. *J Acquir Immune Defic Syndr.* 1991;4:976–080.

67. Semba RD, Graham NMH, Caiaffa WT, et al. Increased mortality associated with vitamin A deficiency during HIV-1 infection. *Arch Intern Med.* 1993;153:2149–2154.

68. Mantero-Atienza E, Baum MK, Morgan R, et al. Vitamin B$_{12}$ in early human immunodeficiency virus-1 infection. *Arch Intern Med.* 1991;151:1019–1020.

69. Semba RD, Miotti PG, Chiphangwi JD, et al. Maternal vitamin A deficiency and mother-to-child transmission of HIV-1. *Lancet,* 1994;343:1593–1597.

70. Fawzi WW, Msamanga GI, Spiegelman D, et al. A randomized trial of multivitamin supplements and HIV disease progression and mortality. *N Engl J Med.* 2004;351:23–32.

71. Jiamton S, Pepin J, Suttent R, et al. A randomized trial of the impact of multiple micronutrient supplementation on mortality among HIV-infected individuals living in Bangkok. *AIDS.* 2003;17:2461–2469.

72. McClelland RS, Baeten JM, Overbaugh J, et al. Micronutrient supplementation increases genital tract shedding of HIV-1 in women: results of a randomized trial. *J Acquir Immune Defic Syndr.* 2004;37:1657–1663.

73. Range N, Changalucha J, Krarup H, et al. The effect of multi-vitamin/mineral supplementation on mortality during treatment of pulmonary tuberculosis: a randomised two-by-two factorial trial in Mwanza, Tanzania. *Br J Nutr.* 2006;95:762–770.

74. Semba RD, Kumwenda J, Zijlstra E, et al. Micronutrient supplements and mortality

of HIV-infected adults with pulmonary TB: a controlled clinical trial. *Int J Tuberc Lung Dis.* 2007;11:854–859.

75. Kelly P, Katubulushi M, Todd J, et al. Micronutrient supplementation has limited effects on intestinal infectious disease and mortality in a Zambian population of mixed HIV status: a cluster randomized trial. *Am J Clin Nutr.* 2008;88:1010–1017.

76. Kawai K, Kupka R, Mugusi F, et al. A randomized trial to determine the optimal dosage of multivitamin supplements to reduce adverse pregnancy outcomes among HIV-infected women in Tanzania. *Am J Clin Nutr.* 2010;91:391–397.

77. Kaiser JD, Campa AM, Ondercin JP, et al. Micronutrient supplementation increases CD4 count in HIV-infected individuals on highly active antiretroviral therapy: a prospective, double-blinded, placebo-controlled trial. *J Acquir Immune Defic Syndr.* 2006;42:523–528.

78. Fawzi WW, Msamanga GI, Spiegelman D, et al. Randomised trial of effects of vitamin supplements on pregnancy outcomes and T cell counts in HIV-1–infected women in Tanzania. *Lancet.* 1998;351:1477–1482.

79. Villamor E, Msamanga G, Spiegelman D, et al. Effect of multivitamin and vitamin A supplements on weight gain during pregnancy among HIV-1–infected women. *Am J Clin Nutr.* 2002;76:1082–1090.

80. Villamor E, Saathoff E, Manji K, et al. Vitamin supplements, socioeconomic status, and morbidity events as predictors of wasting in HIV-infected women from Tanzania. *Am J Clin Nutr.* 2005;82:857–865.

81. Fawzi WW, Msamanga GI, Kupka R, et al. Multivitamin supplementation improves hematologic status in HIV-infected women and their children in Tanzania. *Am J Clin Nutr.* 2007;85:1335–1343.

82. Smith Fawzi MC, Kaaya SF, Mbwambo J, et al. Multivitamin supplementation in HIV-positive pregnant women: impact on depression and quality of life in a resource-poor setting. *HIV Med.* 2007;8:203–212.

83. World Health Organization. *Nutrient Requirements for People Living with HIV/AIDS: Report of a Technical Consultation, 13–15 May 2003.* Geneva: World Health Organization; 2004. Available at: http://www.who.int/nutrition/publications/Content_nutrient_requirements.pdf.

84. Shevitz AH, Knox TA, Spiegelman D, et al. Elevated resting energy expenditure among HIV-seropositive persons receiving highly active antiretroviral therapy. *AIDS.* 1999;13: 1351–1357.

85. Fitch KV, Guggina LM, Keough HM, et al. Decreased respiratory quotient in relation to resting energy expenditure in HIV-infected and noninfected subjects. *Metabolism.* 2009;58:608–615.

86. Kosmiski LA, Kuritzkes DR, Lichtenstein KA, et al. Fat distribution and metabolic changes are strongly correlated and energy expenditure is increased in the HIV lipodystrophy syndrome. *AIDS.* 2001;15:1993–2000.

87. Kosmiski LA, Kuritzkes DR, Sharp TA, et al. Total energy expenditure and carbohydrate oxidation are increased in the human immunodeficiency virus lipodystrophy syndrome. *Metabolism.* 2003;52:620–625.

88. Baruchel S, Wainberg MA. The role of oxidative stress in disease progression in individuals infected by the human immunodeficiency virus. *J Leukoc Biol.* 1992;52:111–114.

89. Chambon P. A decade of molecular biology of retinoic acid receptors. *FASEB J.* 1996;10: 940–954.

90. Semba RD. Vitamin A, immunity, and infection. *Clin Infect Dis.* 1994;19:489–499.

91. Semba RD. The role of vitamin A and related retinoids in immune function. *Nutr Rev.* 1998;56:S38–S48.

92. Vaishnava S, Hooper LV. Eat your carrots! T cells are RARing to go. *Immunity.* 2011;34:290–292.

93. Hall JA, Cannons JL, Grainger JR, et al. Essential role for retinoic acid in the promotion of CD4(+) T cell effector responses via retinoic

acid receptor alpha. *Immunity.* 2011;34:
435–447.

94. Alvarez JO, Salazar-Lindo E, Kohatsu J, et al.
Urinary excretion of retinol in children with
acute diarrhea. *Am J Clin Nutr.* 1995;61:
1273–1276.

95. Fraser DR. Vitamin D. *Lancet.* 1995;345:
104–107.

96. Liu PT, Schenk M, Walker VP, et al.
Convergence of IL-1beta and VDR activation
pathways in human TLR2/1-induced antimicrobial responses. *PLoS One.* 2009;4:e5810.

97. Edfeldt K, Liu PT, Chun R, et al. T-cell cytokines differentially control human monocyte
antimicrobial responses by regulating vitamin
D metabolism. *Proc Natl Acad Sci USA.*
2010;107:22593–22598.

98. Chocano-Bedoya P, Ronnenberg AG. Vitamin
D and tuberculosis. *Nutr Rev.* 2009;67:
289–293.

99. Blumenthal A, Isovski F, Rhee KY.
Tuberculosis and host metabolism: ancient
associations, fresh insights. *Transl Res.*
2009;154:7–14.

100. Liu PT, Stenger S, Li H, et al. Toll-like
receptor triggering of a vitamin D–mediated
human antimicrobial response. *Science.*
2006;311:1770–1773.

101. Beard JA, Bearden A, Striker R. Vitamin
D and the anti-viral state. *J Clin Virol.*
2011;50:194–200.

102. Chambon P. A decade of molecular biology
of retinoic acid receptors. *FASEB J.*
1996;10:940–954.

103. Meydani M. Vitamin E. *Lancet.*
1995;345:170–175.

104. Meydani SN, Barklund MP, Liu S, et al.
Vitamin E supplementation enhances cell-
mediated immunity in healthy elderly
subjects. *Am J Clin Nutr.* 1990;52:557–563.

105. Meydani M, Meydani SN, Leka L, et al.
Effect of long-term vitamin E supplementation on lipid peroxidation and immune

responses of young and old subjects. *FASEB
J.* 1993;7:A415.

106. Meydani SN. Vitamin E enhancement of
T cell–mediated function in healthy elderly:
mechanisms of action. *Nutr Rev.* 1995;53:
S52–S58.

107. Meydani SN, Barklund MP, Liu S, et al.
Vitamin E supplementation enhances cell-
mediated immunity in healthy elderly subjects. *Am J Clin Nutr.* 1990;52:557–563.

108. Meydani SN, Leka LS, Fine BC, et al. Vitamin
E and respiratory tract infections in elderly
nursing home residents: a randomized controlled trial. *JAMA.* 2004;292:828–836.

109. Maggini S, Wintergerst ES, Beveridge S, et al.
Selected vitamins and trace elements support
immune function by strengthening epithelial
barriers and cellular and humoral immune
responses. *Br J Nutr.* 2007;98(suppl 1):
S29–S35.

110. Rall LC, Meydani SN. Vitamin B_6 and immune
competence. *Nutr Rev.* 1993;51:217–225.

111. Dhur A, Galan P, Hercberg S. Folate status
and the immune system. *Prog Food Nutr Sci.*
1991;15:43–60.

112. Hemila H. Vitamin C supplementation and
common cold symptoms: problems with inaccurate reviews. *Nutrition* 1996;12:
804–809.

113. Hemilä H, Chalker EB, Douglas RM.
Vitamin C for preventing and treating the
common cold. *Cochrane Database Syst Rev.*
2010;3:CD000980.

114. Heimer KA, Hart AM, Martin LG, et al.
Examining the evidence for the use of vitamin C in the prophylaxis and treatment of
the common cold. *J Am Acad Nurse Pract.*
2009;21:295–300.

115. Beard JL, Dawson H, Pinero DJ. Iron metabolism: a comprehensive review. *Nutr Rev.*
1996;54:295–317.

116. Viteri FE. Iron supplementation for the control of iron deficiency in populations at risk.
Nutr Rev. 1997;55:195–209.

117. Lozoff B, Brittenham GM, Wolf AW, et al. Iron deficiency anemia and iron therapy effects on infant developmental test performance. *Pediatrics.* 1987;79:981–995.

118. Walter T, De A, I, Chadud P, et al. Iron deficiency anemia: adverse effects on infant psychomotor development. *Pediatrics.* 1989;84:7–17.

119. Basta SS, Soekirman, Karyadi D, et al. Iron deficiency anemia and the productivity of adult males in Indonesia. *Am J Clin Nutr.* 1979;32:916–925.

120. Scholl TO, Hediger ML, Fischer RL, et al. Anemia vs iron deficiency: increased risk of preterm delivery in a prospective study. *Am J Clin Nutr.* 1992;55:985–988.

121. Alauddin M. Maternal mortality in rural Bangladesh: the Tangail District. *Stud Fam Plann.* 1986;17:13–21.

122. Harrison KA. Tropical obstetrics and gynaecology. 2. Maternal mortality. *Trans R Soc Trop Med Hyg.* 1989;83:449–453.

123. *Worldwide Prevalence of Anaemia 1993–2005: WHO Global Database on Anaemia.* Geneva, Switzerland: World Health Organization; 2008. Available at: http://whqlibdoc.who.int/publications/2008/9789241596657_eng.pdf. Accessed June 2, 2011.

124. Stoltzfus RJ, Dreyfuss ML, Chwaya HM, et al. Hookworm control as a strategy to prevent iron deficiency. *Nutr Rev.* 1997;55:223–232.

125. Walter T, Olivares M, Pizarro F, et al. Iron, anemia, and infection. *Nutr Rev.* 1997;55:111–124.

126. Menendez C, Kahigwa E, Hirt R, et al. Randomised placebo-controlled trial of iron supplementation and malaria chemoprophylaxis for prevention of severe anaemia and malaria in Tanzanian infants. *Lancet.* 1997;350:844–850.

127. Walter T, Olivares M, Pizarro F, et al. Iron, anemia, and infection. *Nutr Rev.* 1997;55:111–124.

128. Gera T, Sachdev HP. Effect of iron supplementation on incidence of infectious illness in children: systematic review. *Br Med J.* 2002;325:1142.

129. Foster LH, Sumar S. Selenium in health and disease: a review. *Crit Rev Food Sci Nutr.* 1997;37:211–228.

130. Roy M, Kiremidjian-Schumacher L, Wishe HI, et al. Supplementation with selenium restores age-related decline in immune cell function. *Proc Soc Exp Biol Med.* 1995;209:369–375.

131. Hoffmann PR, Berry MJ. The influence of selenium on immune responses. *Mol Nutr Food Res.* 2008;52:1273–1280.

132. Levander OA, Beck MA. Interacting nutritional and infectious etiologies of Keshan disease: insights from coxsackie virus B–induced myocarditis in mice deficient in selenium or vitamin E. *Biol Trace Elem Res.* 1997;56:5–21.

133. Irlam JH, Visser MME, Rollins NN, et al. Micronutrient supplementation in children and adults with HIV. *Cochrane Database Syst Rev.* 2010;12:CD003650.

134. Delange F. The disorders induced by iodine deficiency. *Thyroid.* 1994;4:107–128.

135. Chambon P. A decade of molecular biology of retinoic acid receptors. *FASEB J.* 1996;10:940–954.

136. Cobra C, Muhilal, Rusmil K, et al. Infant survival is improved by oral iodine supplementation. *J Nutr.* 1997;127:574–578.

137. Ren Q, Gr D, Cao X, et al. Effect of environmental supplementation of iodine on infant mortality and growth in children in Xinjiang, China. *Zhonghua Liu Xing Bing Xue Za Zhi.* 2002;23:198–202.

138. DeLong GR, Leslie PW, Wang SH, et al. Effect on infant mortality of iodination of irrigation water in a severely iodine-deficient area of China. *Lancet.* 1997;350:771–773.

139. UNICEF. *Sustainable Elimination of Iodine Deficiency: Progress since the 1990 World*

Summit for Children. New York, NY: United Nations Children's Fund; 2008.

140. Cobra C, Muhilal, Rusmil K, et al. Infant survival is improved by oral iodine supplementation. *J Nutr.* 1997;127:574–578.

141. Semba RD, Bloem MW, eds. *Nutrition and Health in Developing Countries.* Totowa, NJ: Humana Press; 2008.

142. Walsh CT, Sandstead HH, Prasad AS, et al. Zinc: health effects and research priorities for the 1990s. *Environ Health Perspect.* 1994;102(suppl 2):5–46.

143. Shankar AH, Prasad AS. Zinc and immune function: the biological basis of altered resistance to infection. *Am J Clin Nutr.* 1998;68:447S–463S.

144. Sazawal S, Black RE, Bhan MK, et al. Zinc supplementation reduces the incidence of persistent diarrhea and dysentery among low socioeconomic children in India. *J Nutr.* 1996;126:443–450.

145. Ninh NX, Thissen JP, Collette L, et al. Zinc supplementation increases growth and circulating insulin-like growth factor I (IGF-I) in growth-retarded Vietnamese children. *Am J Clin Nutr.* 1996;63:514–519.

146. Rosado JL, Lopez P, Munoz E, et al. Zinc supplementation reduced morbidity, but neither zinc nor iron supplementation affected growth or body composition of Mexican preschoolers. *Am J Clin Nutr.* 1997;65:13–19.

147. Sazawal S, Black RE, Bhan MK, et al. Efficacy of zinc supplementation in reducing the incidence and prevalence of acute diarrhea: a community-based, double-blind, controlled trial. *Am J Clin Nutr.* 1997;66:413–418.

148. Ruel MT, Rivera JA, Santizo MC, et al. Impact of zinc supplementation on morbidity from diarrhea and respiratory infections among rural Guatemalan children. *Pediatrics.* 1997;99:808–813.

149. Livingstone MB, Prentice AM, Strain JJ, et al. Accuracy of weighed dietary records in studies of diet and health. *BMJ.* 1990;300:708–712.

150. Mertz W, Tsui JC, Judd JT, et al. What are people really eating? The relation between energy intake derived from estimated diet records and intake determined to maintain body weight. *Am J Clin Nutr.* 1991;54:291–295.

151. Karvetti RL, Knuts LR. Validity of the 24-hour dietary recall. *J Am Diet Assoc.* 1985;85:1437–1442.

152. Gersovitz M, Madden JP, Smiciklas-Wright H. Validity of the 24-hr. dietary recall and seven-day record for group comparisons. *J Am Diet Assoc.* 1978;73:48–55.

153. Briefel RR, Flegal KM, Winn DM, et al. Assessing the nation's diet: limitations of the food frequency questionnaire. *J Am Diet Assoc.* 1992;92:959–962.

154. Sempos CT. Invited commentary: some limitations of semiquantitative food frequency questionnaires. *Am J Epidemiol.* 19921;135:1127–1132.

155. Rimm EB, Giovannucci EL, Stampfer MJ, et al. Authors' response to "Invited commentary: some limitations of semiquantitative food frequency questionnaires." *Am J Epidemiol.* 1992;135:1133–1136.

156. Kushi LH. Gaps in epidemiologic research methods: design considerations for studies that use food-frequency questionnaires. *Am J Clin Nutr.* 1994;59:180S–184S.

157. Thompson FE, Byers T. Dietary assessment resource manual. *J Nutr.* 1994;124:2245S–2317S.

158. Cade J, Thompson R, Burley V, et al. Development, validation and utilisation of food-frequency questionnaires: a review. *Public Health Nutr.* 2002;5:567–587.

159. Willett WC. *Nutritional Epidemiology.* New York, NY: Oxford University Press, 1998.

160. Thompson FE, Subar AF, Loria CM, et al. Need for technological innovation in dietary assessment. *J Am Diet Assoc.* 2010;110:48–51.

161. Long JD, Littlefield LA, Estep G, et al. Evidence review of technology and dietary assessment. *Worldviews Evid Based Nurs.* 2010;7:191–204.

162. Shriver BJ, Roman-Shriver CR, Long JD. Technology-based methods of dietary assessment: recent developments and considerations for clinical practice. *Curr Opin Clin Nutr Metab Care.* 2010;13:548–551.

163. Dwyer JT, Coleman KA. Insights into dietary recall from a longitudinal study: accuracy over four decades. *Am J Clin Nutr.* 1997;65:1153S–1158S.

164. Friedenreich CM. Improving long-term recall in epidemiologic studies. *Epidemiology.* 1994;5:1–4.

165. Willett WC, Howe GR, Kushi LH. Adjustment for total energy intake in epidemiologic studies. *Am J Clin Nutr.* 1997;65:1220S–1228S.

166. Freedman LS, Kipnis V, Brown CC, et al. Comments on "Adjustment for total energy intake in epidemiologic studies." *Am J Clin Nutr.* 1997;65(suppl):1229S–1231S.

167. Spiegelman D, McDermott A, Rosner B. Regression calibration method for correcting measurement-error bias in nutritional epidemiology. *Am J Clin Nutr.* 1997;65: 1179S–1186S.

168. *Design Concepts in Nutritional Epidemiology.* Margetts BM and Nelson M (eds.). Oxford, UK: Oxford University Press. 1991:1–420.

169. U.S. Department of Health and Human Services; National Heart, Lung, and Blood Institute. *Clinical Guidelines on the Identification, Evaluation, and Treatment of Overweight and Obesity in Adults: The Evidence Report.* NIH Publication No. 98-4083. Washington, DC: Public Health Service; 1998.

170. Kuczmarski MF, Kuczmarski RJ, Najjar M. Effects of age on validity of self-reported height, weight, and body mass index: findings from the Third National Health and Nutrition Examination Survey, 1988–1994. *J Am Diet Assoc.* 2001;101:28–34.

171. Villanueva EV. The validity of self-reported weight in US adults: a population based cross-sectional study. *BMC Public Health.* 2001;1:11.

172. Spencer EA, Appleby PN, Davey GK, et al. Validity of self-reported height and weight in 4808 EPIC-Oxford participants. *Public Health Nutr.* 2002;5:561–565.

173. Gundlach BL, Visscher GJ. The plethysmometric measurement of total body volume. *Hum Biol.* 1986;58:783–799.

174. Ruiz L, Colley JR, Hamilton PJ. Measurement of triceps skinfold thickness: an investigation of sources of variation. *Br J Prev Soc Med.* 1971;25:165–167.

175. Jackson AS, Pollock ML. Practical assessment of body composition. *Physician Sports Med.* 1985;13:76–90.

176. Ellis KJ. Human body composition: in vivo methods. *Physiol Rev.* 2000;80:649–680.

177. Chumlea WC, Guo SS. Bioelectrical impedance and body composition: present status and future directions. *Nutr Rev.* 1994;52:123–131.

178. Houtkooper LB, Lohman TG, Going SB, et al. Why bioelectrical impedance analysis should be used for estimating adiposity. *Am J Clin Nutr.* 1996;64:436S–448S.

179. Baumgartner RN. Electrical impedance and total body electrical conductivity. In: Roche AF, Heymsfield SB, Lohman TG, eds. *Human Body Composition.* Champaign, IL: Human Kinetics Books; 1996:79–108.

180. Roubenoff R, Kehayias JJ, Dawson-Hughes B, et al. Use of dual-energy x-ray absorptiometry in body-composition studies: not yet a "gold standard". *Am J Clin Nutr.* 1993;58:589–591.

181. Svendsen OL, Haarbo J, Hassager C, et al. Accuracy of measurements of body composition by dual-energy x-ray absorptiometry in vivo. *Am J Clin Nutr.* 1993;57:605–608.

182. Lohman TG. *Advances in Body Composition Assessment: Current Issues.* Exercise Science, monograph number 3. Champaign, IL: Human Kinetics Publishers; 1992.

183. Fishman SM, Caulfield LE, de Onis M, Blössner M, Hyder AA, Mullany L, and Black RE. Chapter 2. Childhood and maternal undernutrition. In: Comparative quantification of health risks: Global and regional burden of disease attributable to selected major risk factors. Ezzati M, Lopez AD, Rodgers A Murray CJL (eds.). Geneva: World Health Organization; 2004.

184. Gibson RS. *Principles of Nutritional Assessment.* New York: Oxford University Press; 1990.

185. Gibson RS. *Principles of Nutritional Assessment.* New York: Oxford University Press; 1990.

186. Lee RD, Nieman DC. *Nutrition Assessment.* St. Louis, MO: Mosby-Year Book;1996: 391–439.

187. Hunter D. Biochemical indicators of dietary intake. In: Willett WC, ed. *Nutritional Epidemiology.* New York: Oxford University Press; 1998:174–243.

13

Emerging and New Infectious Diseases

Kenrad E. Nelson

However secure and well-regulated civilized life may become, bacteria, protozoa, viruses, infected fleas, lice, ticks, mosquitoes, and bedbugs will always lurk in the shadows ready to pounce when neglect, poverty, famine, or war lets down the defenses. And even in normal times they prey on the weak, the very young, and the very old, living along with us, in mysterious obscurity waiting their opportunities. About the only genuine sporting proposition that remains unimpaired by the relentless domestication of a once free-living human species is the war against these ferocious little creatures, which lurk in the dark corners and stalk us in the bodies of rats, mice, and all kinds of domestic animals; which fly and crawl with the insects, and waylay us in our food and drink and even in our love.

—Hans Zinsser,
Rats, Lice and History, 1934

RESPONSES TO THE THREAT OF EMERGING INFECTIONS

Institute of Medicine

As with any public health problem, an effective plan to deal with the reality of new and emerging infections depends on the official recognition of the problem. The recognition that emerging infections constituted a substantial threat to the health of the American public and the population of the world was fostered by a meeting and subsequent report on emerging microbial threats to health. This committee was chaired by Nobel Laureate Dr. Joshua Lederberg, professor at Rockefeller University, and Dr. Robert E. Shope, professor of epidemiology and director of the Arbovirus Research Unit at Yale

University School of Medicine. The committee of the Institute of Medicine (IOM) met in February 1991 and convened an expert multidisciplinary committee to conduct an 18-month study of emerging microbial threats to health. The charge to the committee was "to identify significant emerging infectious diseases, determine what might be done to deal with them, and recommend how similar future threats might be confronted to lessen their impact on public health."[1] After reviewing evidence on the emergence of infectious diseases presented by numerous experts, the committee made a series of recommendations, including the following:

- Strengthened surveillance of infectious diseases through the Centers for Disease Control and Prevention (CDC), the National Institutes of Health (NIH), and the U.S. Department of Agriculture (USDA)
- Expansion of CDC's National Nosocomial Infection Surveillance (NNIS)
- The U.S. Public Health Service's development of a database on infectious disease surveillance and vaccine and drug availability
- An increase in creative and coordinated international infectious disease surveillance through the CDC, Department of Defense, NIH, and USDA
- Increased research on agent, host, vector, and environmental factors leading to the emergence of infectious diseases and expansion of the Epidemic Intelligence Service (EIS) and Field Epidemiology Training Program of the CDC
- Congressional funding of training in public health and related disciplines by the National Health Service Corps
- Development of a means for stockpiling selected important vaccines

- Development of procedures to ensure availability and usefulness of critical antibiotics to maintain human health
- Licensing by the Environmental Protection Agency of critical pesticides for use in infectious disease emergencies and funding priority for development of new pesticides
- Greater attention on developing more effective ways to use education to enhance behavior change in groups at high risk of developing infectious diseases

Since the release of the IOM report, several national and international health agencies have developed plans for dealing with the threat of new and emerging infections. The CDC plan focuses on more effective surveillance, improvements in the public health infrastructure, and applied research in public health prevention activities.[2] The NIH plan focuses on research and training. The Department of Defense plan focuses on surveillance and detection of new and emerging infectious diseases, especially in international settings, and the development of better vaccines. The World Health Organization (WHO) plans to improve international surveillance and communication to detect and monitor emerging infectious diseases.

The intensity of these efforts is crucial, as a range of issues facilitate the emergence of new pathogens that can pose a considerable threat to human populations on local and even global scales. This chapter describes several factors that promote the emergence of disease and highlights diseases that have followed this path to threaten humans.

FACTORS IN THE EMERGENCE OF INFECTIOUS DISEASES

Although the morbidity and mortality from infectious diseases declined dramatically during the 1900s related to the development and use of effective vaccines and antibiotics and a more hygienic environment, new infectious diseases have emerged, and old ones, such as tuberculosis, have reemerged. While factors influencing the balance between pathogens and host are always unique, some common factors can be described (**Table 13-1** and **Table 13-2**).

Population Growth

Perhaps the most important factor in the emergence of infectious diseases has been the growth of the human population beginning in the latter half of the 1800s. The human population and subsequent human crowding had been stable for several centuries, but then increased gradually with the urbanization and concentration of the labor force with industrialization. At the end of the 1900s, an accelerated increase in the population and a dramatic growth in large urban populations occurred. The necessary sanitary infrastructure to support these changes—such as sewage disposal, water supply, and food distribution and storage—has not kept pace with them. Nearly all large cities in both the developed and developing world have substantial populations living in crowded slums. In particular, such crowding and marginal sanitary conditions have been associated with increases in infectious diseases.

The world's population was declared to have reached 7 billion on October 31, 2011. Most predictions are that this population increase will continue, as will the growth of megacities—those with more than 10 million inhabitants. It is estimated that the world population will increase to between 10 billion and 15 billion inhabitants and then stabilize. When it reaches 2.5 times the current population, crowding and overburdened health infrastructures would make it a challenge to control the emergence and spread of infectious diseases. Thus, limiting population growth is a key public health priority (**Figure 13-1**).

Speed and Ease of Travel

Dramatic changes in the ability and ease of travel occurred in the 1900s. Airplane travel makes it possible to get from a tropical rainforest in Africa or South America to a suburban or rural area in the United States during the incubation period of Lassa fever, dengue, malaria, West Nile virus (WNV), encephalitis, and most other infectious diseases.[3] This factor has facilitated the introduction and spread of diseases from one area to another. In fact, autochthonous transmission of malaria has occurred occasionally in the temperate zone of the United States, secondary to the introduction of malaria by a visitor from an endemic area and subsequent focal transmission by local anopheline mosquitoes.[4]

The best example of the global spread of a new emerging infectious disease by airline travel was the severe acute respiratory syndrome (SARS) pandemic that affected 8450 persons and caused 850 deaths in 26 countries on 5 continents in 2003 before it was controlled. Also, air travel regularly effectively spreads new strains of influenza from one continent to another, typically from Asia to Australia, Europe, and North America, and then from North America to South America.[5,6]

Table 13-1	Emerging Infectious Diseases and Changes in Environment, Host, or Organism That Have Prompted Their Emergence
SARS	Human contact with exotic animals (civet cats), international travel
Monkey Pox	Human contact with exotic animals, animal contact
Anthrax	Bioterrorism

Arenaviruses
  Junin virus (Argentine hemorrhagic fever [HF])
  Machupo virus (Bolivian HF)
  Guanarito virus (Venezuelan HF)
	Changes in agriculture allowing closer contact with infected rodents

Hantavirus Sin Nombre virus (HPS)	Climatic changes allowing mice expansion
Rift Valley fever	Dams, irrigation, climate change
Filoviridae species Ebola-Marburg virus	Increased contact between infected primates and man; nosocomial spread, importation of animals
Dengue	Increased global travel, urbanization, increase in mosquito reservoir
Influenza	Integrated pig–duck agriculture, increase in global travel
HIV/(AIDS) HTLV	Changes in sexual behavior, urbanization, increase in illicit drug use, global shipment of blood products
Raccoon rabies	Shipment of infected raccoons
Cyclospora cayetanensis	International shipment of raspberries
Cholera	El Niño climate change, international travel, shipment of foods
Borrelia burgdorferi (Lyme disease)	Increased deer population, increased human contact with ticks in nature
Malaria	Growth and movement of human populations, declining use and effectiveness of insecticides, crowding
Escherichia coli O157:H7 (enterohemorrhagic *E. coli*)	Growth-centralized agriculture promoting cross-contamination, global distribution of foods
Pfisteria pisticida	Changes in agricultural practices leading to pollution of rivers and estuaries, overgrowth of dinoflagellates
Quinolone-resistant *Campylobacter*	Overuse and misuse of antibiotics in agriculture and in clinical settings
Multidrug-resistant *Mycobacterium tuberculosis*	Misuse of antibiotics, crowding in prisons, slums, hospitals, etc., allowing transmission
Cryptosporidium parvum	Contamination of municipal water supplies, increases in immunocompromised populations

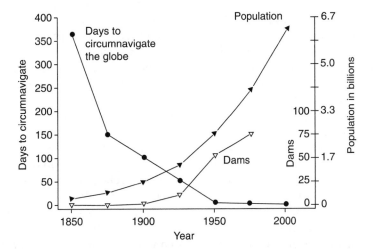

Figure 13-1 Over the last 150 years, there have been many global changes that have enhanced the probability of the emergence of new infectious diseases of humans and animals. This chart depicts three examples of such trends: the increase in the human population; the increased construction of large dams (over 75 meters high) built in the United States, 1890–1975; and the decrease in time needed to circle the globe. Reprinted from Seminars in Virology, Vol. 5, No. 2, Page 88, Murphy FA and Nathanson N. 'The Emergence of New Virus Diseases: An Overview.' © 1994, with permission from Elsevier.

Table 13-2	Some of the Factors Promoting the Emergence and Reemergence of Infectious Diseases
Increased Susceptibility of the Human Host	
AIDS, cancer, and other immunity-compromising conditions	
Aging	
Nutritional deficiencies	
Chronic diseases	
Antibiotic use	
Changes in Infectivity and Virulence of Pathogens	
Genetic changes in pathogens (e.g., recombination, genetic drift, and selection)	
Agriculture antibiotic use in animal feed	
Increased Exposure to Infectious Agents	
Changes in human behavior (e.g., sex, drug use, nutritional practices, and health care)	
Increased contact with animals (e.g., pets, exotic animals)	
Travel	
Climate change	
Dam building	
Crowding and population growth	
Changes in how people interact: day care, nursing homes, hospitals	
Ecosystem change: deforestation	
Bioterrorism	

Changes in the Food Industry

The global food supply can also be a source of infection. Fundamental changes in how food is produced have occurred over the last 100 years, such that today food is grown, processed, and delivered globally. Changes in global markets and the speed of transportation have made it economically profitable to transport food between the hemispheres—for example, enabling the U.S. consumer to have fresh fruits and vegetables on a year-round basis. The rise of agribusiness has also created extremely large farms and processing facilities. Because so much food passes through a relatively small number of facilities, the risk of cross-contamination is high. The United States also relies on a large population of migrant workers to perform manual labor on farms. These workers may come from other countries, and some may be carriers of pathogens from those countries. If proper hygiene is not maintained on the farms, these pathogens can enter the U.S. food supply.

Escherichia coli O157:H7

E. coli O157:H7 was first incriminated as the cause of infections in humans in 1982.[8] This organism has caused large-scale epidemics and sporadic cases of gastrointestinal illness in North America, Europe, and Japan.[9–16] In the United States, 79,000 illnesses and 61 deaths each year are due to *E. coli* O157:H7.[12] In contrast, this pathogen is not a significant problem in most developing countries.

This organism evolved from the ordinary intestinal flora of cattle by acquiring a large plasmid coding for two pathogenic traits—a hemolysin and Shiga toxin—and two traits that enhanced its survival—increased intestinal adhesion and acid stability (including survival in the human stomach).[9] Infections with *E. coli* O157:H7 are markedly more severe than infections with other pathogenic *E. coli*, being characterized by bloody diarrhea and, in some patients, hemolysis and acute renal failure, called *hemolytic-uremic syndrome* (HUS). Coupled with the fact that the infectious dose is very small (only 50 to 100 organisms), these traits gave this strain of *E. coli* some of the qualities of a "super-bug."

The *E. coli* O157:H7 organism is carried without symptoms in the intestinal tract of 1% to 10% of healthy cattle and sheep in the United States and throughout the world.[11] It can be transmitted by food, raw milk, and water, as well as by direct person-to-person spread. Large outbreaks of *E. coli* O157:H7 infection have occurred in the United States when hamburger contaminated during the slaughtering process was not thoroughly cooked. Contemporary food processing and distribution networks, collectively known as *corporate agribusiness*, mix meat from multiple locations; as a consequence, large quantities of hamburger may be contaminated by a single cow. The cultural preference for rare steak has been carried into a preference for poorly cooked hamburger, which increases the risk of pathogens on the surface of the meat being transferred to the inner uncooked portion of the meat thereby increasing infection with this pathogen. After a large outbreak of *E. coli* O157:H7 infection associated with a fast-food chain, the industry established standard cooking procedures and microbiologic monitoring of beef. No cases related to the fast-food industry have been reported since 1995.[13]

The *E. coli* O157:H7 organism has been implicated in other food-borne outbreaks when cow manure was used as a fertilizer. The risk is highest in foods that are normally consumed raw, such as alfalfa sprouts or fruit juices. Apples used to produce cider may include those that have been contaminated by falling from the tree. Because *E. coli* O157:H7 can cause disease when the initial inoculum is very small and it is acid stable, there have been several apple juice–related outbreaks. This risk has led to recommendations that apple juice be pasteurized.[10]

Escherichia coli 0104:H4

A novel variant of *E. coli*, *E. coli* O1O4:H4, caused a large epidemic of hemorrhagic gastroenteritis in Germany in 2011. On May 19, 2011, three hospitalized patients with acute renal failure and other symptoms of HUS were diagnosed in Hamburg, Germany. Active surveillance for acute hemorrhagic colitis and HUS identified 3222 cases and 39 deaths by June 18, 2011.[14] Of these cases, 810 (25%) involved HUS, adults (89%[5]) and women (68%). The estimated median incubation period was 8 days, with a median of 5 days from the onset of diarrhea to the development of HUS. The outbreak strains were typed as an enteroaggregative strain of *E. coli* that contained Shiga toxin and produced extended-spectrum beta-lactamase, conferring resistance to beta-lactam antibodies and third-generation cephalosporins (**Figure 13-2**).

This outbreak differed from previous outbreaks of hemorrhagic colitis and HUS from *E. coli* O157:H7 in several respects. Notably, it involved primarily adult women, whereas previous HUS cases reported in Germany and outbreak due to *E. coli* O157:H7

strains elsewhere were concentrated among children. Also, at 4 to 6 days, the incubation period was somewhat longer in this outbreak than had been reported in previous *E. coli* O157:H7 outbreaks. The proportion of patients with hemorrhagic colitis who developed HUS in this outbreak (25%) was also higher than in previous outbreaks (usually only 5% of cases). Importantly, enteroaggregative (EAEC) strains of hemorrhagic *E. coli* were present only in humans, which indicates that the source of the outbreak was human fecal contamination, believed to be on bean and seed sprouts from an organic sprout farm in lower Saxsony.[13] In addition, human-to-human transmission likely contributed significantly to the cases in this outbreak.[14] A review of 90 confirmed outbreaks found 20% secondary transmission from an infected case,[15] highlighting the importance of secondary transmission during an outbreak.

Antibiotic treatment of patients with enterohemorrhagic *E. coli* is contraindicated, because killing the organisms may cause increased release of the Shiga toxin. Instead, treatment of seriously ill patients includes hemodialysis, plasma exchange, and other strategies to remove circulating toxin. Recently, a few patients with HUS have been shown to improve after treatment with eculizumab, a monoclonal antibody to block complement complex formation.[16]

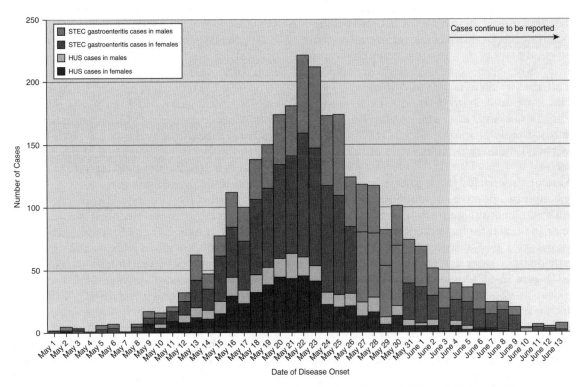

Figure 13-2 Shiga toxin producing *E. coli* outbreak in Germany. From Frank et al. (2011). Epidemic Profile of Shiga-Toxin–Producing Escherichia coli 0104:H4 Outbreak in Germany. *N Engl J Med* 2011; 365:1771–1780. © 2011 Massachusetts Medical Society. Reprinted with permission from Massachusetts Medical Society.

Cyclosporiasis

Before 1996, most documented cases of *Cyclospora cayetanensis* in North America occurred in travelers returning from overseas, and only three small U.S. outbreaks had been reported.[17] However, in 1998, several health departments reported cases of cyclosporiasis. Ultimately, 1465 cases, including 978 laboratory-confirmed cases, occurred in the spring and summer of 1996 and were reported to the CDC and the Canadian Health Department. Extensive investigation showed that raspberries imported from Guatemala were the source of these outbreaks.[18] Raspberries were first cultivated in Guatemala as a commercial crop in 1987, with exports markedly increasing in the mid-1990s. Another outbreak of cyclosporiasis related to Guatemalan raspberries occurred in 1997 (**Figure 13-3**).[19] Although the exact mode of contamination of the raspberries is unclear, it is likely that rinsing with contaminated water prior to export occurred. These outbreaks emphasize the difficulty of controlling pathogens when a food is eaten uncooked and is not easily monitored or disinfected before eating. With the expansion of international commerce and importation of foods from many countries, this type of problem is certain to become even more frequent in the future.

Whether changes in U.S. consumer food habits—for instance, expansion of organic farming, which to date has been mostly on smaller farms, or the emphasis on "eating local"—will change the overall pattern of large outbreaks across multiple states remains to be seen. Nevertheless, some ingredients are unlikely to be affected by these factors and, therefore, large epidemics are unlikely to disappear. Furthermore, large agribusiness is better able to establish safety standards. The elimination of *E. coli* O157:H7 from the fast-food industry is an example of success in this sector.

Variant Creutzfeldt-Jacob disease is an important example of a new type of foodborne illness that has affected humans (**Figure 13-4**). In this situation, a change in animal feeding practices resulted in the emergence of a new disease in humans—variant Creutzfeldt-Jacob disease in the United Kingdom in 1996[21] (**Figure 13-5**). This human epidemic followed an epidemic of bovine spongiform encephalopathy in which nearly 1 million cattle died because of the transmission of an agent contained in their feed. The infectious agent was a member of a new class of organisms named "prions" by Stanley Pruisener, a neurologist, as they are proteinaceous infectious agents. Pruisener had earlier studied a unique epidemic among the Fore linguistic people in New Guinea involving a disease called Kuru. Kuru was spread by ritual mortuary cannibalism when the Fore consumed the remains, especially the brains, of their dead relatives to immortalize them. Pruisener found that the infectious material could be transmitted from infected humans by inoculating their infected brain material into primates. Although Kuru does not have many of the common characteristics of an infectious disease, no inflammatory response occurs in the affected brain and the infectious material does not contain nucleic acid, so it is now accepted that the transmissible spongiform encephalopathies are caused by prions.[22,23]

Antibiotic Use and Abuse

Antibiotic use in both humans and animals is a force in the emergence of resistant pathogenic microorganisms. Antibiotics are widely used therapeutically and prophylactically in humans and for growth promotion in domestic animals.[24] A recent study of *Campylobacter jejuni* infections in Minnesota, between 1992 and 1998, linked human quinolone-resistant infections to the use of quinolones as a growth factor in chickens.[25] The widespread use of quinolone antibiotics in poultry feed, which began in the United States in 1995 and even earlier in Mexico, led to the emergence of these difficult-to-treat infections in humans in just a few years.[26]

That antibiotic resistance can develop quickly has been known since the development of penicillin. Penicillin inhibits the formation of the bacterial cell wall by interfering with peptidoglycan synthesis. Pencillinases render gram-negative bacteria resistant to penicillin. Methicillin, the next-generation antibiotic, was licensed in 1959 but methicillin-resistant *Staphylococcus aureus* (MRSA) organisms had already been identified by the 1960s.[24] While methicillin is no longer in use, the name of this antibiotic is still used to describe those bacteria that are resistant to the peptidoglycan inhibitors.

In the last few decades, MRSA organisms have emerged as the gram-positive organisms that are most frequently responsible for invasive bacterial infections among hospitalized patients and those infected in the community in the United States.[27] Some of these MRSA infections are responsible for significant morbidity and mortality.[28] Originally MRSA strains were classified as either "hospital associated" or "community associated" based on epidemiological criteria—that is, where the infection was acquired—but convergence of the strains found in the two settings has made this designation no longer useful.[29] MRSA organisms can be divided into eight distinct clusters that were identified by pulsed-field gel electrophoresis, named USA-100 through USA-800.[29] Strains

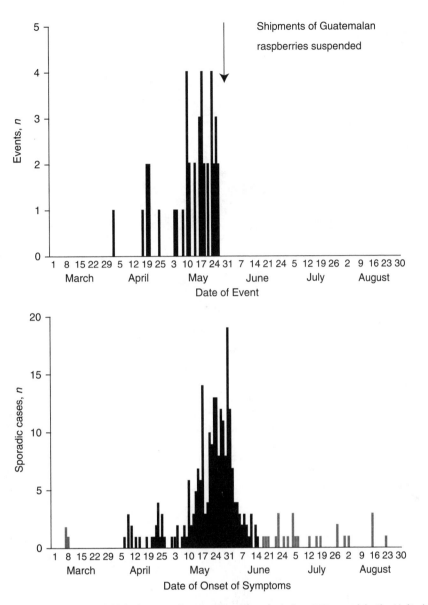

Figure 13-3 Dates of 41 events associated with clusters of cases of cyclosporiasis (n = 762 cases) in the United States and Canada in April and May 1997. For multiday events, the date of the first day of the event is shown. The last shipment of Guatemalan raspberries in the spring of 1997 was on May 28. Bottom. Dates of symptom onset for laboratory-confirmed sporadic cases of cyclosporiasis in the United States and Canada in 1997. The gray bars represent 31 case-patients who became ill during the period from March through August but not during the outbreak period of April through 15 June. The black bars represent 250 case-patients whose cases were classified as having occurred during the outbreak period. The median date of symptom onset for the 250 case-patients was May 26 (range, April 6 to June 15). Only 22 persons (8.8%) became ill in April, and most (225 [90.0%]) became ill by June 4. The date selected as the last date of the outbreak period was June 15 because Guatemalan raspberries exported in late May could still have been available for consumption in early June and because infected persons would have become symptomatic an average of 1 week after exposure. Not all of the sporadic cases of cyclosporiasis were necessarily due to consumption of raspberries. Reproduced from Herwaldt Bl., et al. The return of Cyclospora in 1997: another outbreak of cyclosporiasis in North America associated with imported raspberries. Cyclosporia Working Group. *Ann Intern Med*. 1999 Feb 2;130(3):213, Figure 1.

USA-300 and USA-400 were classified as community-associated MRSA (CA-MRSA), and the others were labeled as hospital-associated MRSA (HA-MRSA). All MRSA strains contain a gene coding for methicillin resistance, the mec-A gene complex, although the characteristics of the mec-A gene differ between strains. For example, strains USA-300 and -400 are similarly resistant to penicillinase-resistant antibiotics, but less frequently resistant to other antibiotics.[29] In addition, they more commonly carry a gene coding

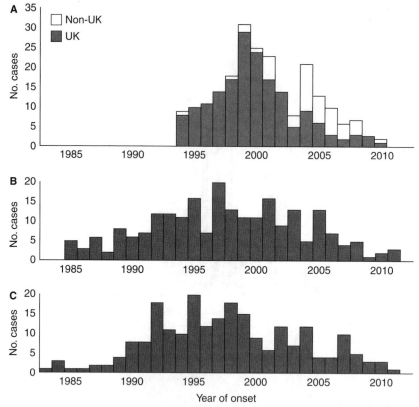

Figure 13-4 Annual incidence of variant Creutzfeldt-Jakob disease (vCJD) caused by ingestion of meat products contaminated with bovine spongiform encephalopathy agent (A) and iatrogenic CJD caused by contaminated dura matter (B) and cadaveric human growth hormone (C), 1982–2011. White bars in panel A represent cases from outside the United Kingdom, which were delayed in parallel with the later appearance of bovine spongiform encephalopathy outside the United Kingdom (not a second wave resulting from codon 129 genotype differences). Two patients are excluded: 1 presymptomatic patient from the United States who received human growth hormone and died of an intercurrent illness and 1 dura matter recipient from the United Kingdom with disease onset in 1978. Reproduced from Brown et al. Iatrogenic Creutzfeldt-Jakob disease, final assessment. *Emerg Infect Dis* [serial on the Internet]. June 2012. http://wwwnc.cdc.gov/eid/article/18/6/12-0116_intro.htm. Accessed August 29, 2012.

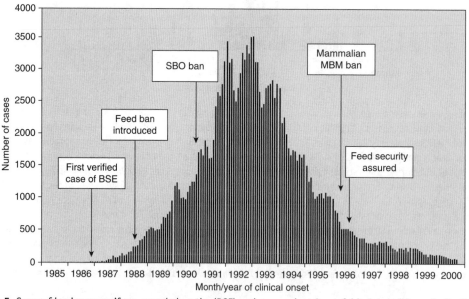

Figure 13-5 Cases of bovine spongiform encephalopathy (BSE) and new-variant Creutzfeldt-Jacob disease in the United Kingdom. The decline in the incidence of BSE began five years after the feed ban was enacted, prohibiting ruminant-derived feed to ruminants. Cases of vCJD have been reported since February, 1964. These cases were exposed to contaminated meat prior to the ban. There have been 175 cases of vCJD in the UK as of July, 2011. However, additional cases are likely because of the long incubation period. Four transfusion-transmitted vCJD cases have been diagnosed in the UK with incubation periods of 5.0–8.5 years after receiving a transfusion from a donor who subsequently developed vCJD, 1.4–3.5 years later. Reproduced from Brown P. Bovine spongiform encephalopathy and variant Creutzfelt Jacob disease: background, evolution, and current concerns. *Emerg Infect Dis*. 2001 Jan–Feb;7(1):6–16.

for the Panton-Valentine-leukocidin (PVL) toxin, which causes skin and soft-tissue necrosis.

In Europe, the rates of health care–associated MRSA infections are lower than in the United States.[30] However, one strain of MRSA, ST-398, has emerged in the Netherlands and Denmark as a zoonotic infection due to the incorporation of penicillinase-resistant antibiotics in pig feed for growth promotion.[31] The importance of the zoonotic reservoir of MRSA responsible for human infections in the United States has not been extensively studied.[32] This example illustrates the need for ecologic and public health-based decisions across health and agricultural industries to avoid new antibiotic-resistant human pathogens. Some studies suggest that restriction of the use of antibiotics in clinical settings might allow for the reemergence of an antibiotic-sensitive flora,[33] but such strategies have not proved entirely successful.

Dam Building

The construction of large dams to provide hydroelectric power to growing populations and irrigation for rural crops has had adverse consequences related to the emergence of infectious diseases. The number of large dams that were constructed in the United States, Asia, Africa, and elsewhere in the 1900s has increased in parallel with the population growth. The construction of such dams can displace rural and semirural populations and provide a propitious environment for the growth of mosquitoes and other vector species. The construction of the Aswan High Dam in upper Egypt, for example, was accompanied by a large expansion of the snail population and subsequently hundreds of thousands of *Schistosoma haematobium* infections in humans.

Expansion of Human Populations into Previously Uninhabited Forested and Suburban Areas

Not only has the number of humans increased, but their geographic dispersion has also expanded. Previously uninhabited areas may have disease cycles into which new inhabitants unwittingly intrude.

The emergence of Lyme disease, human granulocytic ehrlichiosis (HGE), human monocytic ehrlichiosis (HME), babesiosis, and Rocky Mountain spotted fever (RMSF) are linked to the growth of suburbia and recreation in tick-infested areas. In tropical Africa, the emergence of Ebola virus, Lassa fever, monkeypox, and HIV-1 and HIV-2 infections are related to the expansion of the human population into wilderness areas and increased exposure of humans to zoonotic pathogens.

Lyme Disease

Lyme disease was first recognized by Steere and colleagues in 1975, following the identification of a group of children living in Old Lyme, Connecticut, who were diagnosed with juvenile rheumatoid arthritis.[34] The geographic clustering of cases, the seasonal distribution with onset of illness in the summer, and a history of a prior distinctive skin lesion, erythema chronica migrans (ECM), eventually led to the hypothesis that Lyme disease was due to an infectious agent that was transmitted by ticks.[35] Willy Burgdorfer identified a spirochete organism, subsequently named *Borrelia burgdorferi*, in the salivary glands of the tick *Ixodes scapularis* on Shelter Island, New York. Lyme disease patients had immunofluorescent antibodies to this new organism, confirming its role as the causative agent of Lyme disease.[36]

In the 20 years since the recognition of Lyme disease, the number of reported cases has increased progressively, and the geographic areas of endemicity of the disease have expanded to include the coastal northeastern and mid-Atlantic states, several states in the Midwest (especially Minnesota, Wisconsin, and Michigan), and coastal California.[37,38] Although education has increased awareness and diagnosis of this condition, there has also been a clear increase in the incidence of the disease.[38] Factors promoting the emergence of Lyme disease include the encroachment of human populations into areas infected with tick vectors and the growth of the deer populations, the preferred terminal host of *Ixodes scapularis* ticks.[39]

Other Tick-Borne Infections

The same epidemiologic factors that led to an increase in Lyme disease have increased the incidence of other tick-borne diseases. For example, the incidence of Rocky Mountain spotted fever increased from about 200 to 400 cases per year from 1950 to 1960 to more than 1000 cases per year by 1980s.[46] Increased exposure to the disease vectors—primarily the Rocky Mountain wood tick (*Dermocenter andersonii*) in the western United States and the American dog tick (*Dermocenter variabilis*—in the eastern United States, occurred because of the expansion of human housing and recreation into the sylvan cycle.

Two forms of human ehrlichiosis—HME due to infection with *Ehrlichia chaffeeinsis* and HGE due to infection with *Ehrlichia ewingii*—have also been recognized with increased frequency in the past few years.[42] Like RMSF, these diseases are transmitted by ticks: HME by the dog tick and HGE by the deer tick. It is not unusual for a patient to be infected with Lyme disease and ehrlichiosis simultaneously.

Another tick-borne disease, babesiosis (an infection of red blood cells with *Babesia microti*), can be transmitted to humans by tick bites in the endemic areas in the coastal northeastern United States.[43]

While Lyme disease and Rocky Mountain spotted fever are the only reportable tick-borne infections in the United States, other tick-borne illnesses have likely increased as well.

Relocation of Animals

Movement of animal species, either through intentional transportation by humans or as a reaction to changes in their habitat, can increase human contact with their associated pathogens. For example, an epidemic of raccoon rabies was recognized in the northeastern United States; it was attributable to the intentional transportation of raccoons from the South, especially Georgia, Alabama, Florida, and the Carolinas, to Virginia and West Virginia for hunting by sportsmen.[44] Unfortunately, the raccoons were from rabies-endemic areas and raccoon rabies subsequently spread throughout the northeastern United States. Potential rabies exposure from raccoons is the most common cause of human postexposure rabies vaccine prophylaxis. For reasons that are unclear, despite more than 1000 documented exposures of humans to rabid raccoons in the northeastern United States, there has been only one documented transmission of rabies.[45] This outcome may represent either a success of the vaccine program or an unrecognized species barrier between this strain of rabies and humans.

More exotic viruses have also been introduced with animal importation. Ebola virus from Philippine rhesus macaques (*Macaca fascicularis*) caused an outbreak in a United States Army primate facility in Reston, Virginia.[46] In Germany, Marburg virus infected laboratory workers after exposure to infected monkeys imported from Africa.[47]

Contact with Exotic Animals

Exotic pets may also introduce new pathogens to communities. Monkeypox in humans was first identified in 1970 in the Democratic Republic of the Congo.[48] The causative agent is an Orthopox virus that is related to the smallpox (variola) virus and a number of other human and animal viruses. During May and June of 2003, the first cluster of human cases of monkeypox in the United States was reported.[49] The outbreak occurred across six Midwestern states—Wisconsin (39 cases), Indiana (16 cases), Illinois (12 cases), Missouri (2 cases), Kansas (1 case), and Ohio (1 case)[50]—and ended in early July 2003. Monkeypox was imported to the United States with African rodents that were shipped with prairie dogs to pet stores. While rodents were the source of infection, all 71 cases of human disease resulted from prairie dog contact (**Figure 13-6**).

All of the monkeypox cases were associated with prairie dogs purchased from an animal distributor in Illinois. These prairie dogs appear to have been infected with monkeypox virus through contact with Gambian rats and deer mice from Ghana. The CDC identified several animals with monkeypox from this shipment. A total of 178 (28%) African rodents could not be traced from the original shipments because records were not available. However, no cases of monkeypox were detected as a result of contact with these African rodents.

The Food and Drug Administration, CDC, and state regulatory authorities implemented several public health strategies to control this outbreak. These strategies included a joint order banning importation and movement of the implicated animal species as well as state-enacted measures to prohibit intrastate shipment and trade of the animals, establish premises quarantine, and begin animal euthanasia. The rapid diagnosis of monkeypox and coordinated public health response by CDC and FDA was effective in preventing the establishment of monkeypox as an epizootic disease in the United States. Many animals are susceptible to monkeypox, including squirrels, which are believed to be an important natural reservoir in Africa.[51] Additionally, smallpox vaccine was given to 30 persons who had been exposed to infected animals to prevent infection. One of these 30 persons developed a rash confirmed to be monkeypox within 2 weeks of immunization.[50]

The monkeypox epidemic emphasized, in a highly dramatic way, the potential for animal-to-human transmission of an unusual pathogen made possible by the unimpeded ability to transport animals from remote areas into the United States. The risk of introducing and spreading exotic diseases into a new environment by importation of infected animals has likely increased in the last few decades. The introduction of West Nile virus into the United States in 1999, for example, may have followed a similar pathway, although its origin has not been conclusively determined. How are future importations of new diseases to be prevented? It may not be easy to control these importations because of global trade and commerce.

Global Climate Change

Human activity has modified the climate of the planet. Climatologic researchers believe that greenhouse gases, such as carbon dioxide, methane, and nitrous oxide, have played a major role in the climate change experienced over the past several decades (**Figure 13-7**).

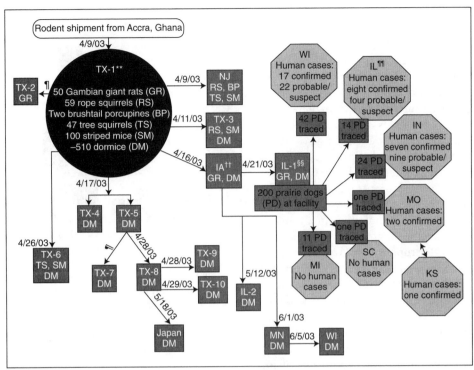

* Illinois (IL), Indiana (IN), Iowa (IA), Kansas (KS), Michigan (MI), Minnesota (MN), Missouri (MO), New Jersey (NJ), South Carolina (SC), Texas (TX), and Wisconsin (WI). Japan is included among sites having received shipment of rodents implicated in this outbreak.

† As of July 8, 2003.

§ Does not include one probable human case from Ohio; investigation is ongoing.

¶ Date of shipment unknown.

** Identified as distributor C in *MMWR* 2003; 52:561–564.

†† Identified as distributor D in *MMWR* 2003; 52:561–564.

§§ Identified as distributor B in *MMWR* 2003; 52:561–564.

¶¶ Includes two persons who were employees at IL-1.

Figure 13-6 Movement of imported African rodents to animal distributors and distribution of prairie dogs from an animal distributor associated with human cases of monkeypox – 11 states 2003. Reproduced from the Centers for Disease Control and Prevention. Multistate outbreak of monkeypox Illinois, Indiana, Kansas, Missouri, Ohio and Wisconsin, 2003. *MMWR.* 52(27):642–646.

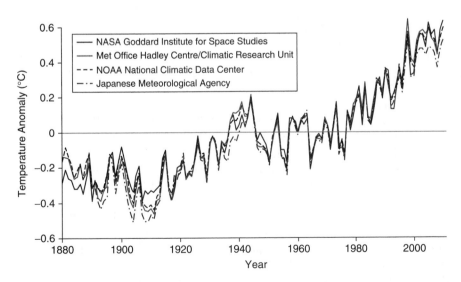

Figure 13-7 Global surface temperatures. Reproduced from the National Oceanic and Atmospheric Administration: Arctic Change. Global – Global Temperature Trends: 2011 Summation. http://www.arctic.noaa.gov/detect/global-temps.shtml. Accessed August 29, 2012.

Often referred to as *global warming,* these climactic changes are highly complex and are likely to include increases and decreases in temperatures and other changes in weather patterns. Currently, the planet is within 1°C of the previous maximum temperature, the Holocene maximum from 5000 to 9000 years ago; this suggests that further increases will result in dramatic changes in sea levels and extermination of species.[52] Global climate change might also lead to disruption in the earth's hydrologic cycle, leading to droughts in some areas and major increased rainfall with flooding in other areas. Storm intensity is also predicted to increase. These extreme weather conditions would affect human populations in a range of ways that could increase susceptibility to new and emerging diseases. Disruptions in farming, for example, could lead to food shortages and ultimately malnutrition. Emergency situations during and after storms could promote crowding in shelters and contaminated water sources. Vector populations may be enhanced as well. Whether global warming will continue at an accelerated rate, as some have predicted, and whether this trend will lead to an expansion of infectious diseases are not certain. However, the evolving scenario has sufficient biologic plausibility that it should be taken seriously.

Several epidemics have occurred in which climate change is believed to have been an important factor. In 1991, cholera occurred in Latin America after an absence of more than 100 years.[53] Within 2 years, cholera had spread from Peru to Mexico. Theories on the emergence of cholera pointed to a ship from Asia introducing the pathogen by release of contaminated bilge water. However, the cholera outbreak in Peru occurred simultaneously all along the western coast of the country, making this theory an unlikely explanation. Subsequently, Colwell et al. reported that the recent El Niño weather phenomenon was a critical factor in the rapid spread of cholera.[53] The 1993 El Niño warmed the surface of the South Pacific Ocean, leading to an algal bloom in the surface waters along the Pacific coast of South America. Zooplankton in the algal bloom can harbor *Vibrio cholera* in their exoskeleton[53] and gut, with as many as 10⁴ organisms per copepod being noted. These ubiquitous copepods disseminated cholera along coastal areas of Latin America soon after its reintroduction to this region.[53]

At the intersection of the states of New Mexico, Colorado, Arizona, and Utah, known as the Four Corners area, El Niño increases in rainfall led to increases in food supply for the mouse reservoir of Sin Nombre hantaviruses.[54] The resulting outbreak of hantavirus pulmonary syndrome was believed to be the first ever, as antibody serosurveys of persons

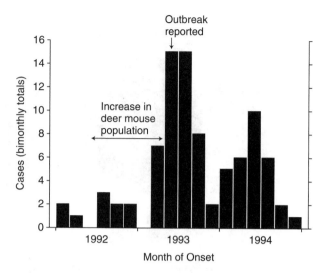

Figure 13-8 Cases of Hanta virus pulmonary syndrome by month of onset, United States, 1992–1994, omiting 16 cases with onsets prior to 1992. Reprinted from N. Nathanson and S. Nichol, Korean and Hemorrhagic Fever and Hanta Virus Pulmonary Syndrome: Two examples of Emerging Pathoviral Diseases in Emerging Infections, p. 370, R. M. Krause, ed., © 1998, with permission from Elsevier.

living in New Mexico were unable to document any previous infections (**Figure 13-8**).

To a point, mosquitoes will benefit from increases in temperature and rainfall. Large rainfalls in Tanzania in 1997 increased mosquito vector populations and were linked to an epidemic of Rift Valley fever (RVF). At least 478 deaths occurred, and an estimated 89,000 persons were infected.[55] The relationship among RVF epidemics, rainfall, and vector expansion has been shown to be present in previous east African epidemics as well.[56] Other mosquito species, such as various *Anopheles* species, *Aedes aegypti,* and *Aedes albopictus,* may expand their numbers or range under such circumstances, which could lead to epidemics of malaria, dengue, yellow fever, and viral encephalitis (such as Eastern encephalitis [EE]). Warmer temperatures also increase the epidemic's potential to spread through impact on the pathogens themselves. Dengue virus and the malaria virus have shortened extrinsic incubation periods at higher temperature, which means mosquitos are infectious sooner and for a longer percentage of their lives.[57,58]

War and Societal Disruption

Nearly every major war has been accompanied by significant epidemics of infectious diseases involving both the military combatants and the civilian populations in the war-torn regions. Often, casualties from infectious disease exceed the number of deaths in battle and overshadow military factors in the outcome of the conflict.[59]

Many examples of this interaction can be cited, but the "swine influenza" pandemic of 1918–1919 that occurred during World War I in Europe may be the most graphic one. The origin of this virus was likely a bird source in Kansas that was carried to the European theater by infected U.S. troops.[60] The resulting epidemic targeted healthy young adults, and was often rapidly fatal. The "swine influenza" was estimated to have infected 20% of the world's population and killed more than 20 million persons worldwide and at least 43,000 U.S. military personnel. More than 80% of the American war casualties were due to influenza.[59] Germany's General Erich Von Rudendroff blamed influenza for the defeat of the German army in the war, as more than 2000 men in each of his army divisions were ill in June 1918.

Other infectious diseases have affected troops as they are preparing to deploy or in the crowded and not always hygienic conditions of war. World War II soldiers were exposed to hepatitis B when they received yellow fever vaccine stabilized with human serum from an HBV carrier. During World War II, soldiers and civilians in the Pacific Rim experienced large epidemics of dengue. During the Soviet invasion of Afghanistan in 1979–1989, waterborne hepatitis was extremely common.[61] The causative agent was not identified until 1983, when Balyon described hepatitis E as a cause of enteric hepatitis in Asia.[62] In the first and particularly the second Gulf Wars, epidemics of visceral leishmaniasis due to *Leishmania tropica* occurred in U.S. troops.

Hantaviruses

A new viral infection first came to the attention of Western medicine during the Korean War in 1951, when U.S. troops stationed in Korea developed a new disease that was subsequently named *Korean hemorrhagic fever*. This disease was manifested by a febrile course with influenza-like symptoms. In approximately one-third of the cases, hemorrhagic symptoms and hypertension occurred, followed by severe renal failure. More than 3000 troops were infected, and the mortality rate was about 5%.[63] The etiologic agent was not identified until 1976, when Lee et al. working in Seoul, Korea, showed the etiologic agent to be a virus when it was isolated in Vero cell cultures.[84] The virus was named Hantan virus after the Hantan River, which transects the epidemic area at the demilitarized zone separating North and South Korea. It was isolated from the lungs of the striped field mouse, *Apodermus agrarius*. This common animal is now recognized as the major rodent host of the Hantan virus in rural Korea. The rodents commonly acquire the infection early in life and continuously excrete the virus in their urine for the rest of

their lives. Persons who may be exposed to infected rat urine, such as soldiers in a foxhole, are at risk of infection. There was no evidence of person-to-person spread of infection or of waterborne or foodborne transmission of Hantan virus in Korea.

Subsequently, another rodent-associated virus with some similarities to Hantan virus was isolated from urban rats (*Rattus norwegicus* and *Rattus rattus*).[84] Isolated cases of hemorrhagic fever were identified in urban residents and in laboratory workers who were exposed to these rats; the virus was named *Seoul virus*. It has now spread worldwide owing to rodents stowed away on commercial ships. In the United States, this virus has been identified in Baltimore and has been shown in a preliminary case-control study to have an association with hypertension and chronic renal disease[65]; however, these data are awaiting further confirmation.

Another related virus, Puumala virus, was isolated from patients in Sweden and voles in Finland. This virus caused a syndrome, termed nephropathica epidemica, consisting of an acute febrile disease with renal involvement.[66] Subsequently, WHO grouped the syndromes caused by these three related viruses together under the rubric *hemorrhagic fever with renal syndrome* (HFRS).

In almost all conflicts, civilians are at increased risk of disease. Displaced war refugees are at risk for malnutrition and diseases that flourish in crowded unsanitary conditions, such as cholera, shigellosis, and malaria. The United Nations High Commission on Refugees estimates that there are currently more than 16 million refugees and 5.4 million internally displaced persons throughout the world.[67] Many of these refugees are highly vulnerable to epidemics of infectious diseases. A massive outbreak of El Tor cholera occurred among Rwandan refugees in Goma, Zaire, during the war in Rwanda, resulting in 12,000 deaths—a 14.9% case-fatality rate in July 1994.[68] This outbreak once again demonstrated the potential for cholera to cause severe mortality in a situation of extreme civil disruption. In contrast, the cholera epidemic in Latin America at the same time had mortality of less than 1% because peaceful conditions allowed for good diagnostic and medical services, including oral dehydration therapy.[69]

Changes in the Susceptible Population
Growth of Day Care for Infants and Children Outside the Home

There has been a dramatic growth in the number of preschool children in daycare facilities. Clustering of children in daycare centers has facilitated the transmission of infectious agents between children, daycare staff, and others living in the child's household. As daycare centers have substantial populations of children in diapers, fecal–oral transmission is facilitated. Notably, infections from organisms such as rotavirus, *Giardia lamblia*, *Campylobacter jejuni*, *Shigella* species, and hepatitis A virus (HAV) have been transmitted in the daycare setting. In the late 1970s in Maricopa County (Phoenix), Arizona, a community-wide doubling of the reported cases of hepatitis due to HAV infection was linked to daycare transmission of this virus from infected infants to employees and household contacts.[70] Such outbreaks can have considerable morbidity. Outbreaks of HAV infections in daycare centers average 12 cases in size and last 3 months in duration.[75] While young children may be asymptomatic or have mild infections, adults often develop more severe clinical illnesses. Outbreaks are more often associated with larger centers that accept children in diapers.

Infections spread by the respiratory route and by direct contact are also common among children attending daycare centers. It has been estimated that approximately 10 respiratory infections occur each year among children at the peak age for respiratory infections (i.e., the second 6 months of life).[72] Most respiratory infections are viral, but bacterial infections can also be transmitted in daycare centers.

Efforts to reduce daycare-related transmission have emphasized improved hygiene; increased hand washing and disinfection of fomites, such as toys; and the use of preventive new vaccines, including those for HAV, varicella, *Haemophilus influenzae* type b, acellular pertussis, and *Streptococcus pneumoniae*. Traditional public health strategies to reduce exposure by excluding potentially infectious infants and children have proved less successful due to the difficulty of identifying ill children before they have transmitted their infection and the economic pressures on parents to go to work even when their children are ill.

Growth in Nursing Home Populations

The number of persons older than age 65 is growing rapidly in the U.S. population. In 2009, the Census Bureau estimated that 39 million U.S. residents were older than 65 years and 19 million were older than 75 years of age.[73] Of these older Americans, 4.9% lived in a group home facility (U.S. Census Bureau, 2008 American Community Survey). Elderly populations, especially those requiring nursing home care, are vulnerable to infectious diseases. Decline in immune function and crowding in extended-care facilities are key factors in their increased risk of emerging diseases. Hospital admission raises elderly individuals' risk of infection with nosocomial pathogens, some of which are antibiotic resistant. Nursing home residents may be important community reservoirs of staphylococci, enterococci, or gram-negative organisms that are resistant to multiple antibiotics.

Growth in Nonimmunized Populations

An important public health problem has surfaced recently related to persons who believe that the vaccines used to prevent childhood infections may be associated with hidden hazards. In particular, some children have not been immunized against measles, pertussis, and diphtheria based upon a false belief that these vaccines may increase the risk of autism and other health conditions. This decline in immunization has resulted in the reemergence of measles and pertussis, especially in Western Europe and Japan and recently in the United States. More than 25,000 cases of measles were reported among persons living in Europe in 2010, and many importations into the United States have occurred, especially in 2011.[74]

As the incidence of previously common diseases has decreased due to the successes achieved by public health interventions, large pools of susceptibles now exist in the developed world. In turn, epidemics of polio, measles, pertussis and malaria have occurred owing to lapses in vigilance in the setting of low incidence of naturally occurring disease. One of the most interesting examples of the development of a susceptible population came about from the cessation of smallpox vaccination because of the eradication of the virus in the 1980s. Vaccination ended between 1981 and 1985, and most young people are now susceptible to smallpox and other pox viruses against which they would have previously been vaccinated. While smallpox has not occurred, monkeypox (another pox virus) has reemerged in Africa in the past two decades since the cessation of smallpox vaccination. Studies of monkeypox in humans in Africa detected sporadic outbreaks in the 1970s and 1980s with only occasional human-to-human spread of infection, usually not beyond two generations.[74,75] In fact, monkeypox is much less infectious by person-to-person contact than smallpox; the longest transmission chain of human-to-human transmission reported has consisted of four transmission cycles.[76] Although severe, even fatal, disease from monkeypox can occur, the mortality in Africa is much lower than from smallpox. Also, human infections with monkeypox have usually required direct contact with an infected monkey.

Surveillance for monkeypox in several African countries has been conducted by WHO since the disease was recognized. The first recognized human case occurred in a child in the Democratic Republic of the Congo in 1970. Between 1970 and 1980, a total of 59 cases of monkeypox in humans were detected in Cameroon, Cote d'Ivoire, Liberia, Nigeria, Sierra Leone, and the Democratic Republic of the Congo.[77] Of the 47 cases in the Congo, all occurred in areas bordering the two tropical rainforests, and 8 (17%) of the infections were fatal. Serologic surveys in unvaccinated children done after 1980 in the endemic areas suggested that approximately 12% to 15% had antibodies to monkeypox, but most of the antibody-positive persons did not have a history of a compatible illness[77] (**Figure 13-9**).

Based partly on these data, WHO expert committees recommended against reinstitution of smallpox vaccine to control monkeypox. In 1996–1997, Medicens sans Frontiers reported an outbreak of monkeypox in the Congo to WHO.[78] Studies of the affected populations suggested that as many as 511 cases may have occurred. The reemergence of monkeypox in the Congo was facilitated by an ongoing war; the hostilities forced many persons to seek refuge in the forest. However, most cases of the disease were fairly mild, and the secondary attack rate was estimated to be 18%; it was 3% among those with a history of smallpox vaccination and 26% in those without a history of vaccination.[79] The possibility of reinstitution of smallpox vaccine to control monkeypox in the endemic area was reconsidered by WHO. However, it was decided not to use the vaccine in the general population in part because the prevalence of HIV infection was 7–10% or higher, and a fatal reaction to smallpox vaccine had been reported in a soldier with unrecognized HIV infection in the United States (although more recent data on smallpox vaccination of HIV infected military recruits did not find an increased risk).[80,81]

Issues Raised by Monkeypox

What should be done to prevent an increased incidence of monkeypox among African populations where the disease is endemic? Clearly, ongoing surveillance will be important to guide any future public health activities. Perhaps diluted smallpox vaccine might be useful to control outbreaks of monkeypox among isolated populations, but decisions should be made based on continued surveillance data. Do subjects need to be screened for HIV before giving smallpox vaccine? If so, what about their household contacts?

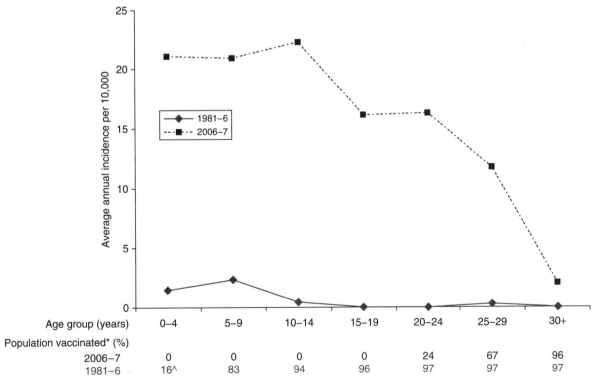

Age group (years)	0–4	5–9	10–14	15–19	20–24	25–29	30+
Population vaccinated* (%)							
2006–7	0	0	0	0	24	67	96
1981–6	16^	83	94	96	97	97	97

Figure 13-9 Monkeypox and Small Pox vaccination rates. Demonstrating a birth cohort effect. Reproduced from Rimoin et al (2010). NAS Proceedings: Major increase in human monkeypox incidence 30 years after smallpox vaccination campaigns cease in the Democratic Republic of Congo. Washington, DC. PNAS September 14, 2010 vol. 107 no. 37 16262–16267.

Human Immunodeficiency Virus

In addition to wreaking its own devastation, the spread of the human immunodeficiency virus (HIV) has led to the reemergence of several other infectious diseases. The optimistic forecasts of the 1960s and 1970s about control or elimination of most infectious diseases were erased by the emergence of HIV. This pandemic most likely arose from human contact with a modified or recombinant primate retrovirus from an infected chimpanzee in central Africa sometime in the late 19th or early 20th century.[82] Facilitated by international travel and the virus's long asymptomatic infectious period, once HIV expanded to urban areas of Africa, it spread around the world within a decade.[1,83] The targeting of critical cells of the immune system by HIV has led to the emergence of a large number of important secondary pathogens, or opportunistic infections, that cannot be controlled by the damaged immune system of infected individuals. Thus the HIV-1 pandemic has allowed the dramatic explosion of infections with several pathogens that had been rare or were under good control prior to the acquired immunodeficiency syndrome (AIDS) epidemic.

Before the identification of HIV as the cause of AIDS, clinicians and public health officials in Africa, Europe, and North America were concerned about the dramatic increase in several unusual infectious diseases. In sub-Saharan Africa, the emergence of AIDS was heralded by an increase in the number of patients with cryptococcal meningitis and Kaposi's sarcoma. In the United States and Europe, homosexual men were being diagnosed with Kaposi's sarcoma and *Pneumocystis carinii* (now called *Pneumocystis jarrovcci*) pneumonia, a previously rare infection seen primarily in children with congenital immunodeficiency diseases. Subsequently, the HIV virus was identified to be the cause of the immunocompromised state in patients with AIDS.

The global spread of HIV infections and AIDS has resulted in the emergence of many infectious diseases. These outcomes include a major reemergence of tuberculosis, especially in Africa. Infection with HIV increases the risk of tuberculosis disease after an infection with M. tuberculosis from 5% in an HIV-uninfected adult to 10–20% in an HIV-infected individual.[84] In addition, HIV infection has increased the number of persons with reactivated latent tuberculosis; such reactivation is estimated to occur in approximately 10% of persons with concomitant HIV infection and latent tuberculosis each year. In 2009, there were 1.6 million deaths from tuberculosis, with 360,000 of these deaths involving HIV-positive persons.

Many other infectious diseases have also emerged in HIV-infected populations, including visceral leishmaniasis in southern Europe;[85] disseminated histoplasmosis in the midwestern United States; *Penicillium marneffei* in Thailand, Vietnam, and southern China; and *Mycobacteria avium* complex (MAC) in patients throughout the world with severe immunosuppression.[86–87] Any infection that depends on intact and functional cellular immunity for its control is likely to be associated with an increased risk in patients with AIDS.

Increased Population of Immunosuppressed Persons

The number of persons receiving immunosuppressive therapy to treat cancers and autoimmune diseases and to prevent the rejection of a transplanted organ has increased in recent years. Furthermore, these patients are frequently treated in hospitals or other healthcare facilities where they have increased opportunities to acquire difficult-to-treat infections. Immunosuppressed patients are highly susceptible to disseminated infections with common fungi, such as *Candida* and *Aspergillus* species, and with gram-negative organisms.

Bioterrorism

Since the terrorist attacks in New York, Washington, D.C., and Pennsylvania on September 11, 2001, and the subsequent epidemic of anthrax transmitted through the U.S. Postal System, bioterrorism has become a more widely recognized concern.[88] Efforts have been made to strengthen the surveillance and early response systems in the United States. Even though smallpox has been eradicated, fears that it could be resurrected have led to continued vaccination of the military and consideration of voluntary vaccination of early medical responders, such as nurses, physicians, and others who work in emergency rooms, as they would likely be the first to see a case. To date, the Advisory Committee on Immunization Practices of CDC has advised against more widespread vaccination of the American public. The National Institutes of Health has established a large biodefense program to develop more sensitive means of detection as well as more effective vaccines and treatments against anthrax, smallpox, plague, tularemia, botulism, and other potential bioterrorism agents. In addition, efforts to develop broad-spectrum therapies to treat currently unknown agents are under way.

While attention has been focused recently on bioterrorism, the use of infectious agents against populations is not new. During the American colonial period, Native American tribes were given blankets intentionally contaminated with smallpox scabs containing variola virus in the hopes of causing disease in the recipients.[89] Even before that time, trebucheting (catapulting of corpses) was practiced in warfare. Gabriel de Mussi described in his memoir how plague was introduced to the city of Caffa in the Crimea by trebucheting.[90]

While bioterrorism has often been envisioned as a political tool of war, it is just as likely to be perpetrated by dissident groups of any size or carried out by unbalanced individuals. The uncertainties created by an unknown assailant will make it more difficult to prevent such attacks, detect bioterrorism in its early stages, and find the perpetrator. In Oregon during September and October of 1984, followers of Bhagwan Shree Rajneesh attempted to influence a local election by tainting salad bars with salmonella.[91] Interestingly, the intentional nature of the epidemic was neither suspected nor proven until nearly a year later.

The anthrax attacks of 2002 were similarly unexpected. The release of *Bacillus anthracis* (anthrax) spores into a public space, particularly one with a recirculating air supply, was feared by most public health officials. The actual attacks were even more difficult to contain, as they were not focused in time or geography. Anthrax spores were mailed to various targets, including United States senators, newscasters, and others. Five deaths and 22 cases of anthrax occurred (**Figure 13-10**). In addition to the individual health toll, significant disruptions and costs were associated with the attacks. Postal facilities and public buildings had to be decontaminated; mail delivery was stopped outright in some areas and greatly delayed in others. The episode caused considerable concerns, even panic, as to where and when the next attack would occur and who the enemy was.

Although the attacks soon stopped, the suspected culprit was not identified for several years. The prime suspect, a research microbiologist working at Ft. Detrick with a history of mental illness, committed suicide before being tried in court. This episode underscores the difficulties in anticipating and stopping future bioterrorism.

Prioritizing Bioterrorism Candidates The risk of a bioterrorism attack on the U.S. population had long been considered and feared. A defector from the Soviet Union reported that the Soviet military had undertaken a major effort to test and produce biological weapons, including smallpox, plague, anthrax, and other agents, during the 1960s through 1980s.[92] The instability of the former Soviet bloc region has raised fears that stockpiles from the program could be used by other states or dissident groups. Iraq was also believed to have prepared large stockpiles of biologic weapons, especially anthrax, and it was known that the country had used bioweapons to quell a Kurdish uprising.

In 1999, the U.S. Congress designated the CDC as the lead agency for overall public health planning to combat bioterrorism. That year, the CDC, working with military, WHO, and other experts, compiled a list of possible bioterrorism agents.[88] Organisms were placed in three categories based on four factors: (1) public health import based on morbidity and mortality, (2) ability to deliver the agent plus risk of secondary person-to-person transmission, (3) public perceptions and fear, and (4) special needs to deal with an attack, such as vaccine, drugs to treat illness, and surveillance needs. Category A was for agents of greatest potential, category B for agents that posed a significant threat but with less serious outcomes, and category C for other possible agents.[93]

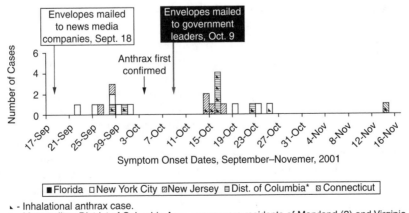

Figure 13-10 Anthrax epidemic curve. Reproduced from Jernigan DB et al. Investigation of bioterrorism-related anthrax, United States, 2001: epidemiologic findings. *Emerg Infect Dis.* 2002 Oct; 8(10):1019–28.

Table 13-3	Biodefense Categorization of Agents	
Category A Agents	Can be easily disseminated or transmitted from person to person Result in high mortality rates and have the potential for major public health impact	Might cause public panic and social disruption Require special action for public health preparedness
Anthrax (*Bacillus anthracis*) Botulism (*Clostridium botulinum toxin*)	Plague (*Yersinia pestis*) Smallpox (variola major) Tularemia (*Francisella tularensis*)	Viral hemorrhagic fevers (filoviruses [e.g., Ebola, Marburg] and arenaviruses [e.g., Lassa, Machupo])
Category B	Are moderately easy to disseminate Result in moderate morbidity rates and low mortality rates	Require enhanced diagnostic capacity and enhanced disease surveillance
Brucellosis (*Brucella* species) Epsilon toxin of *Clostridium perfringens* Food safety threats (e.g., *Salmonella* species, *Escherichia coli* O157:H7, *Shigella*) Glanders (*Burkholderia mallei*) Melioidosis (*Burkholderia pseudomallei*)	Psittacosis (*Chlamydia psittaci*) Q fever (Coxiella burnetii) Ricin toxin from *Ricinus communis* (castor beans) Staphylococcal enterotoxin B Typhus fever (*Rickettsia prowazekii*)	Viral encephalitis (alphaviruses [e.g., Venezuelan equine encephalitis, Eastern equine encephalitis, Western equine encephalitis]) Water safety threats (e.g., *Vibrio cholerae*, *Cryptosporidium parvum*)
Category C	Availability Ease of production and dissemination Potential for high morbidity and mortality rates and major health impact	
Emerging infectious diseases such as Nipah virus and hantavirus		

Reproduced from the Centers for Disease Control and Prevention, NCEH/ATSDR, NCIPC. Bioterrorism agents/diseases. Updated June 20, 2012 available at:. http://www.bt.cdc.gov/agent/agentlist-category.asp. Accessed June 24, 2012.

Six organisms were classified as being in category A, and another 10 organisms or groups of organisms were classified into category B (**Table 13-3**).

NOTABLE EMERGING INFECTIOUS DISEASES

Several examples of recent experiences with specific emerging infectious diseases are reviewed in this section. These diseases are notable for their severity and demonstrate the interplay between the factors discussed previously in the emergence of new human diseases.

Severe Acute Respiratory Syndrome

In contrast to diseases that have reemerged, Dengue or tuberculosis, or those which have spread to new areas, West Nile virus or monkeypox, SARS was a newly emergent zoonosis with the first human case occurring in 2002.[61,62]

Evolution of the Epidemic

In November 2002, an outbreak of an unusually severe atypical pneumonia occurred in Foshan, Guangdong Province, China. In January 2003, cases were seen in Guangzhou, the capital of the province; by February 2003, there were 305 cases with five deaths. Initially, WHO was concerned that the epidemic might be H5N1 influenza, which had caused respiratory infections with a high mortality rate in Hong Kong a few years earlier. On February 21, 2003, a 65-year-old physician checked into "Hotel M" in Hong Kong. He had been ill for six days and had traveled to Hong Kong from Guangdong province. The following day his health deteriorated, and he was admitted to a hospital in Hong Kong. He transmitted the infection to 13 other guests and visitors in the hotel with whom he had no direct contact. Another guest of Hotel M was admitted to the hospital in Hanoi on February 26; he was the source of an outbreak that included seven healthcare workers. Dr. Carlo Urbani, a greatly admired WHO physician, acquired SARS in Vietnam and died a few days later in a Bangkok hospital.[97] Subsequently, cases were reported from Singapore and Toronto among other guests at the hotel during the index patient's stay[98,99] (**Figure 13-11**).

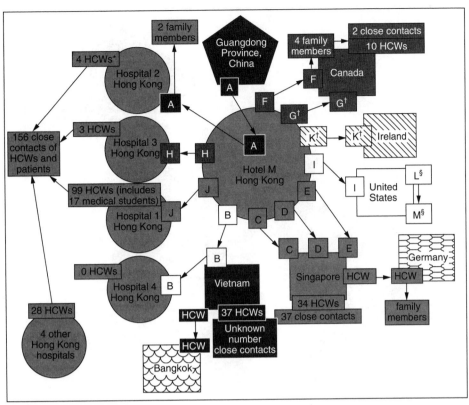

* Health care workers.

† All guests except G and K stayed on the 9th floor of the hotel. Guest G stayed on the 14th floor, and Guest K stayed on the 11th floor.

§ Guests L and M (spouses) were not at Hotel M during the same time as index Guest A but were at the hotel during the same times as Guests G, H, and I, who were ill during this period.

Figure 13-11 Chain of Transmission among guests at Hotel M Hong Kong. Reproduced from the Centers for Disease Control and Prevention. Update: Outbreak of Severe Acute Respiratory Syndrome-Worldwide, 2003. *MMWR*. March 28, 2003/52(12);241–248.

Amoy Gardens Epidemic

One of the most dramatic outbreaks of SARS occurred among residents of the Amoy Gardens housing complex in Hong Kong. A patient recovering from SARS visited his brother at the densely populated complex on two days in March. Subsequently, an epidemic of SARS occurred among the residents of the Amoy Gardens.[100] Overall, 330 persons in the complex and 128 people who lived near the Amoy Gardens became ill, accounting for 26.1% of the 1755 SARS cases in Hong Kong. A detailed evaluation of the outbreak in the complex implicated exhaust from the toilets and spread of the virus by aerosol transmission. This hypothesis was supported by assessments of the building structures, the toilet vents, wind patterns, and the distribution of cases throughout the complex (**Figure 13-12**).

The Singapore SARS Outbreak

The epidemic of SARS in Singapore followed closely after the epidemic in Hong Kong. On March 6,

2003, the Singapore Ministry of Health (MOH) was notified that three persons who had traveled to Hong Kong in February had been admitted to local hospitals for treatment of pneumonia. They had been guests at Hotel M in Hong Kong on February 20 and 21, coinciding with the stay of the index case. On March 14, the MOH was notified about six persons, including two healthcare workers, who were admitted to a local hospital after having had close contract with a case.

In the ensuing Singapore outbreak, five SARS patients were identified as "superspreaders," meaning that they had transmitted the infection to 10 or more persons.[101] Most of these cases resulted in continued transmission of the virus to one or more secondary cases, thereby expanding the chain of cases. The secondary cases did not also become superspreaders. Generally, the infected contacts spread the virus to only one or two persons. This pattern suggests that severe illness in these superspreaders (with excretion of large amounts of virus, coupled with delayed recognition of the infection), rather than an increase

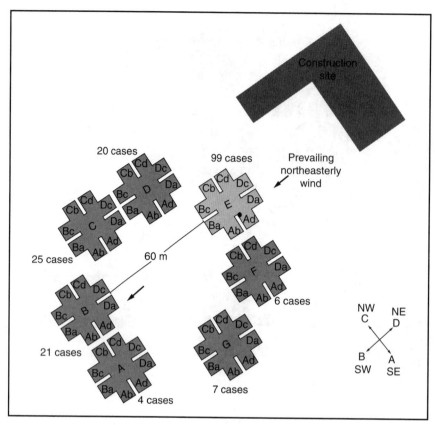

Figure 13-12 Amoy Garden SARS case distribution. The dot in building E shows the location of the apartment visited by the index case. Secondary cases were located primarily downwind in buildings B, C, and D. Upper case letters denote front facing windows and lower case letters denote side-facing windows. From Yu et al. Evidence of Airborne Transmission of the Sever Acute Respiratory Syndrome Virus. *N Engl J Med.* Apr 22;350(17):1733, Figure 1. © 2004 Massachusetts Medical Society. Reprinted with permission from Massachusetts Medical Society.

in infectivity of the virus, was likely responsible for these large clusters. Spread of SARS due to delayed diagnosis of infection was characteristic of the last three superspreaders in the Singapore outbreak; these three individuals had other medical conditions that caused the delay in the diagnosis and led to the spread of SARS to 62 persons (**Figure 13-13**). In contrast to these large clusters, 81% of SARS cases did not result in transmission to any of their contacts.

The occasional superspreaders played a major role in the propagation of the SARS outbreak and were involved in each of the cities that had large outbreaks. It was found that superspreaders in Hong Kong and Singapore accounted for 71.1% and 74.8% of SARS cases in those cities, respectively.[101] Superspreaders of SARS also played a major role in the Beijing outbreak.[102]

A detailed study of one superspreader was carried out in Hong Kong. He was a Hotel M guest and was admitted to the Prince of Wales Hospital in Hong Kong on March 4 after being ill since February 24.[103,104] During his hospitalization, there were an estimated 112 secondary cases and 26 tertiary cases within the facility; these cases included 20 doctors, 34 nurses,

15 allied health workers, and 16 medical students, as well as 53 patients or visitors to his ward.

A more detailed study of 66 medical students found that the rate of illness was highest among those who remembered entering the patient's room (10 out of 28), lower for those who were unsure (4 out of 18), and lowest in those who were only on the ward, but not in his cubical (1 out of 20). None of the remaining 268 medical students who did not enter the patient's ward developed SARS.[103] Furthermore, cases were much more common among students who examined patients for a longer duration and closer to the index patient. These data suggest that, despite the very large number of secondary cases, close contact was required for transmission. This episode also illustrates the importance of recognizing a disease rapidly and effectively isolating patients.

The Toronto Outbreak

The largest outbreak of SARS in North America occurred in Toronto, Canada; between February 23, 2003, and June 8, 2003, a total of 225 patients in the city were diagnosed as having SARS (**Figure 13-14**).

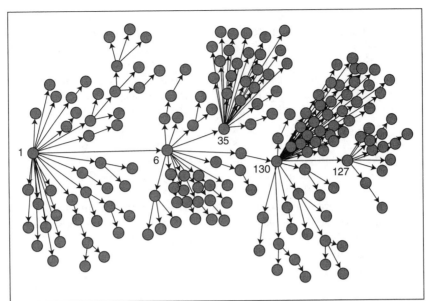

* Patient 1 represents Case 1; Patient 6, Case 2; Patient 35, Case 3; Patient 130, Case 4; and Patient
  127, Case 5. Excludes 22 cases with either no or poorly defined direct contacts or who were cases
  translocated to Singapore and the seven contacts of one of these cases.
Reference: Bogatti SP. Netdraw 1.0 Network Visualization Software. Harvard, Massachusetts:
Analytic Technologies, 2002.

Figure 13-13 SARS chains of transmission. Reproduced from the Centers for Disease Control and Prevention. Severe Acute Respiratory Syndrome – Singapore, 2003. *MMWR.* 52(18);405–411.

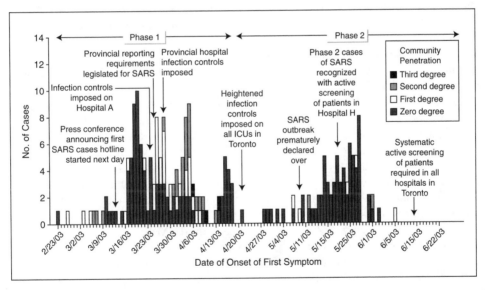

Figure 13-14 Toronto epidemic. From Svoboda T. Public Health Measures to Control the Spread of the Severe Acute Respiratory Syndrome during the Outbreak in Toronto. *NEJM.* 350:2354, Figure 1. © 2004 Massachusetts Medical Society. Reprinted with permission from Massachusetts Medical Society.

However, the Toronto Public Health Department investigated 2132 potential cases of SARS and identified 23,103 contacts of SARS patients who required quarantine.[105,106] The epidemic in Toronto was directly linked to Hotel M by a traveler who died at home on March 5, 2003. Her son died on March 13, and other household members succumbed and were admitted to four different hospitals on March 13, one day after

WHO issued a global alert concerning a severe respiratory outbreak in Hanoi, Vietnam, and Hong Kong that was spreading to other countries.

As was characteristic of SARS in every outbreak, the imported cases were linked back to the index case, and most infections occurred among close contacts either in hospitals or in household contacts of SARS cases. Only 20 cases were acquired in the community outside of a hospital or household contact with a case. However, transmission of the virus occurred in 11 (58%) of the acute care hospitals in Toronto.[106]

One unique feature of the Toronto epidemic was that it was bimodal. That is, a cluster of cases occurred between February 23, 2003, and April 20, 2003,[106] followed by a period of control, followed by another cluster of cases between April 27, 2003, and June 8, 2003, peaking on May 25, 2003. Rigorous infection control procedures were initially imposed in all ICUs in Toronto area hospitals, with isolation of SARS cases and contacts for 10 days, the outer limit of the incubation period. The number of cases declined after April 10, 2003, and the epidemic was prematurely declared over in early May 2003. However, after the decrease in cases, vigilance declined and the rigorous infection control procedures on general wards were lifted, although they were kept in place in the ICUs and emergency departments. Staff were no longer required to wear masks or respirators, except in high-risk areas and when caring for patients known to have SARS. This lessening of restrictions allowed for a resurgence of the epidemic when infection occurred in five patients at a rehabilitation hospital in Toronto. Because these patients had underlying illness, diagnosis was delayed. Seventy-eight new cases of SARS occurred among hospital staff, other patients, and visitors. To control the epidemic, the hospital was closed to all new admissions other than SARS patients, infection control was reinstituted, and healthcare workers were placed on a 10-day work quarantine. These moves brought control of the second wave of cases in Toronto.[106]

In March and early April 2003, laboratories in Germany, Hong Kong, Canada, and the CDC identified the new agent as the SARS coronavirus (SARS-CoV), unrelated to other known human coronaviruses.[107–110] Epidemiologic studies isolated SARS-CoV from civet cats and workers at animal markets in Guangdong Province.[111] The highest prevalence (72.7%) was found in those individuals who traded primarily in masked palm civets,[112] but other animals were also found to have antibodies.[78] That SARS-CoV was the cause of the epidemic was supported by evidence that patients seroconverted to SARS-CoV, whereas healthy contacts and controls did not. Subclinical infections were rarely documented.

Public Health Interventions

The pandemic of SARS eventually was controlled largely through several public health interventions that sought to interrupt the virus's transmission in countries experiencing epidemics. Interventions focused on isolation of cases, quarantine of exposed contacts, and protective equipment in the healthcare setting (N-95 filter-fitted masks, gloves, and gowns). Different countries took slightly different approaches to control spread. Beijing, being closely tied to the original cities, had multiple introductions of SARS and suffered the highest attack rate globally (2591 cases; 19/100,000 population).[113] In addition to establishing rigorous control measures in hospitals and prohibiting public events, the Chinese government rapidly built a special isolation hospital.[114] Overall, approximately 30,000 Beijing residents were quarantined in their homes or at another quarantine site for 14 days after possible exposure to a SARS patient.[114,115]

Beijing used a very strict definition of exposure that included persons with a 30-minute exposure to a SARS case or possible SARS case in the home, work, or hospital, or even on public transportation. An evaluation of these quarantine procedures found that only those persons who experienced direct contact with an infected individual developed SARS.[114,115] No cases occurred among persons who were quarantined because of contact with a contact or only during the incubation period. Overall, the attack rate in those who had cared for a SARS patient without precautions was 31.1%; it was 8.9% in those visiting a SARS patient, and 4.6% in those living with a SARS patient.

The Taiwanese government added persons who had traveled on an airplane and sat within three rows of a SARS patient to its quarantine list.[116] Overall, 131,132 persons were quarantined in Taiwan, and the attack rate ranged from 0.22% to 0.03% depending on their level of exposure. Taiwan was the last country to be declared SARS free on July 5, 2003.[116]

After two incubation periods (i.e., 20 days), the WHO declared the end of the SARS pandemic. Since that time there have been three cases of laboratory-acquired SARS.

Other Public Health Interventions

In addition to traditional public health procedures, new technologies were employed in some countries to detect and prevent SARS, including infrared "fever sensors" in airports and other public locations, cancellation of public events, increased education of travelers to notify health authorities if they developed a fever, and monitoring of travelers from countries with epidemics. It is difficult to evaluate the effectiveness of these additional measures. Although they increased the public awareness of the epidemic, they probably were not very effective as prevention measures.[117]

Conclusions

Altogether, 8450 persons became ill and 850 died in 26 countries on five continents as a result of the SARS epidemic. Although it was a devastating pandemic, several epidemiologic features of SARS enhanced the effectiveness of public health control of the epidemic. While the virus can be very infectious in some patients, the mean numbers of secondary cases acquiring infection from an infected person, i.e the mean number of persons who were infected by an infectious case among a susceptible population, or R_0, was estimated at 2.7, excluding superspreaders, by one group[117,118] and 2.2–3.6 by another group.[94] The infected person was infectious only *after* becoming symptomatic, with the highest viral loads occurring 7 days after the onset of symptoms. Virus was excreted in stool and respiratory secretions, but chronic excretion was uncommon. SARS was unusual in young children.

SARS can be quite contagious, however, and it became clear that the occasional superspreaders can effectively propagate an epidemic. Modern air travel was very effective in spreading the infection on a global scale. Aside from the occurrence of 8450 cases and 850 deaths, the SARS epidemic of 2003 caused major disruptions and panic in many modern societies, especially in Asia. While the travel advisory for Toronto lasted only one week, it had a profound economic impact on the business community and tourism industry.[119]

At the end of this global epidemic, naturally occurring human SARS appeared to have been eliminated. Cases of SARS did not continue to occur at a lower endemic level. However, SARS coronavirus is thought to have had a zoonotic reservoir in bats in China, so it could reemerge in humans if this animal reservoir has persisted.

Several important public health lessons emerged from the SARS epidemic:

- The importance of surveillance and international collaboration in controlling emerging infections
- The importance of travel in the global spread of infectious diseases
- The effectiveness of traditional methods to control the spread of infectious diseases (i.e., isolation of infectious cases and quarantine of contacts until the incubation period has passed)

Severe Fever with Thrombocytopenia Syndrome (SFTS)

As a result of the delayed recognition and investigation of SARS outbreak, the government of China increased surveillance activities to detect and control newly emerging infectious diseases. Between March and July 2009, several patients living in rural areas of Hubei and Henan provinces in Central China were identified with severe fever, thrombocytopenia, and leukopenia. The disease was initially thought to be caused by infection with *Anaplasma phagocytophilum*, but laboratory studies of sera from cases failed to confirm this diagnosis. Subsequently, a novel bunyavirus was identified as the cause of SFTS in 171 patients from Hobei and Henan provinces. This virus is related phylogenetically to the phlebovirus genus; it has also been identified in ticks. Patients with tick-borne SFTS have been identified in six provinces in north central China.[120] Another separate tick-borne phlebovirus was recently isolated from two patients in Missouri who had symptoms of fever, fatigue and leucopenia with onset 5–7 days after they had a tick bite.[121]

Enterovirus 71

Enterovirus 71 was first identified in California encephalitis patients in 1969.[122] Several epidemics of hand, foot, and mouth syndrome associated with enterovirus 71 infections have been reported.[123,124] While other viruses can cause hand, foot, and mouth syndrome, enterovirus 71 epidemics can be large and may be associated with encephalitis and severe morbidity or mortality.

Epidemics of hand, foot, and mouth syndrome, including among some patients with encephalitis, have occurred regularly in several Asian countries in the last two decades. In Taiwan in 1998, a large outbreak was studied by sampling from a panel of 818 sentinel physicians across Taiwan,[123] who reported 129,016 cases including 405 severe cases and 78 deaths; these data, when extrapolated over the entire country, would indicate there were more than 1 million cases. More than 60% of cases were caused by infection with enterovirus 71, 27.3% by coxsackie A16, and 10.6% by other enteroviruses. Outbreaks have been reported in recent years from other Asian countries, including Singapore, Thailand, Vietnam, and China[124] (**Figure 13-15**).

Cholera

Cholera reemerged as an epidemic disease in the 1990s. In 1992, a new epidemic strain, *Vibrio cholerae* 0139, appeared for the first time in India and Bangladesh.[125] There was a lack of cross-immunity between the Classic or El Tor *V. cholerae* 01 strains and the newly recognized *V. cholerae* 0139 strain, which enabled major outbreaks of cholera—estimated at more than 200,000 cases—to occur in India,

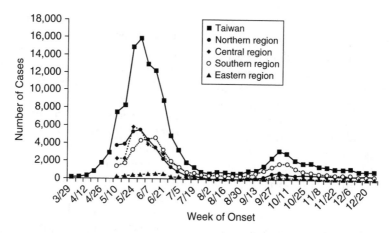

Figure 13-15 Enterovirus in Taiwan. From Ho, et al for the Taiwan Enterovirus Epidemic Working Group (1999). An Epidemic of Enterovirus 71 Infection in Taiwan. *N Engl J Med*. 341:929–935. Figure 1, Page 931. © 1999 Massachusetts Medical Society. Reprinted with permission from Massachusetts Medical Society.

Bangladesh, and several other countries in Southeast Asia. Travel-associated, imported cases were reported in the United States, Europe, and Japan.[125]

The most recent severe outbreak of cholera occurred in Haiti starting in October 2010. This outbreak appeared 10 months after a severe earthquake on January 2010 that killed an estimated 250,000 people, left 1.3 million homeless, and badly damaged the country's infrastructure. The outbreak was recognized when patients developed the hallmark acute, watery diarrhea and dehydration. Stool specimens revealed that the infectious agent was *Vibrio cholera* serogroup 0–1, serotype Ogawa, and that it was susceptible to some but not all antibiotics. The epidemic expanded rapidly. As of November 13, 2010, the Haitian Ministry of Health had reported 16,111 persons hospitalized and 993 cholera deaths.[126,127] By December 12, 2010, the epidemic had expanded nearly tenfold, with 121,581 cases, 63,711 hospitalizations, and 2591 deaths reported.[127] In addition, cholera spread to the Dominican Republic and Florida.

The rapid spread of the cholera epidemic in Haiti reflects the inadequate sanitation, extreme poverty, and general lack of access to clean water in the country.[128] In 2002 (before the earthquake struck), Haiti ranked last out of 147 countries for water security.[129] The country's public health infrastructure was also challenged by a lack of experience treating cholera, failure to use antibiotics at the recommended levels, and a lack of an effective vaccine.[129]

A study comparing the DNA sequences of *V. cholera* clinical isolates from Haiti with isolates from other epidemics found the organisms responsible for the Haiti epidemic to be closely related to strains from Bangladesh in 2002 and 2008 and more

distant from Latin America isolates.[130] This finding provoked political controversy, as peacekeeping troops from Southeast Asia were stationed in Haiti and were accused of initiating the outbreak.

Streptococcus Suis

Streptococcus suis infections are an important emerging disease in countries in Asia that support intensive swine-production industries. The first human case was reported in 1968, but the number of cases has increased dramatically in the last decade in China, Thailand, Vietnam, Hong Kong, and other Asian countries.[131,132] *S. suis* cases are geographically concentrated within countries in Asia where humans have contact with pigs on farms or where raw or undercooked pork, often including raw swine blood, is consumed. In northern Thailand, for example, a popular dish, labloo, is made from raw swine blood. *S. suis* patients present with sepsis, toxic shock syndrome, meningitis, and focal infections involving joints and endocarditis, but mortality is low when patients are treated appropriately with antibiotics. Mild to severe hearing loss can occur in as many as two-thirds of patients. Accurate surveillance of *S. suis* infection is hampered by the absence of a specific ICD-10 code for this infection.

Sichuan Province, China, experienced a large outbreak of 215 *S. suis* cases during a 2-month period in 2005; farmers who had direct contact with their pigs during slaughtering were infected.[131] In Thailand, 165 cases were reported between 2006 and 2008. A study of 450 adult patients with suspected bacterial meningitis in Vietnam found *S. suis* to be the most common pathogen, accounting for 151 (36%) of the cases.[132]

Waterborne Parasitic and Viral Infections and *Cryptosporidium* Species

The resurgence of cholera has primarily involved developing countries in Asia, Latin America, and Africa. However, waterborne infections from newly recognized parasitic agents are a significant and increasing problem in the United States as well. While U.S. municipal water supplies are chlorinated, not all of them use filtration to remove pathogens.[133] Some pathogens may even be transmitted in filtered water systems, as the number of microorganisms necessary to cause disease is extremely low for some pathogens.[133]

A massive outbreak of diarrhea occurred in the spring of 1993 in Milwaukee.[134] Between March 23 and April 9 of that year, an estimated 403,000 people became ill who had received water from one of two municipal water treatment plants. In early April, the Wisconsin Department of Health received reports of diarrhea and high rates of absenteeism among hospital employees, students, and school teachers. Later, *Cryptosporidium* oocysts were isolated from stool samples from 12 cases.[134] The detection of *C. parvum* in stools requires staining the stool with an acid-fast stain and examining the sample microscopically for *C. parvum* oocysts. Because of the complicated diagnostic process, *C. parvum* is not routinely included in diagnostic screens. Consequently, in the Milwaukee epidemic, only 12 cases were laboratory confirmed as involving *C. parvum*. Nevertheless, in this outbreak, other etiologies of diarrhea—such as *Salmonella*, *Shigella*, *Campylobacter*, *E. coli* O157:H7, and other common bacterial causes of diarrhea—were not found. The investigating epidemiologists isolated *C. parvum* from ice that had been frozen during the epidemic. In further analysis, it was suggested that *C. parvum* oocysts might have been endemic in the Milwaukee water supply, being present before the large outbreak in April 1993.[135] Subsequent studies have shown that contamination of domestic water supplies with *C. parvum* oocysts is not uncommon.[133,136] Milwaukee, like several other metropolitan areas in the U.S., treated the domestic water supply with chlorine but did not filter the water. Prior to the outbreak the water from one of the two systems exhibited increased turbidity but the colifom count did not increase above acceptible levels. This finding leaves open the possibility that waterborne outbreaks of cryptosporidiosis might be much more common than has been previously appreciated.[135]

The risk of disease or mortality among persons who are immunosuppressed, such as persons with AIDS, those on chemotherapy, and those with malignancies, is much higher than among healthy adults. *Cryptosporidium* infection is not effectively treatable in persons with AIDS. As a consequence, contamination of water, even at a low level, could cause significant morbidity and even mortality at the population level. Other parasitic pathogens that are resistant to chlorine and have a low infectious dose include *Microsporidium* species, *Cyclospora*, and *Giardia lamblia*. Prevention of these infections is important to protect this vulnerable population.

Noroviruses

Noroviruses are the most common cause of epidemic gastroenteritis; a major cause of foodborne illness, they are responsible for at least 50% of all gastroenteritis outbreaks worldwide. In the United States, approximately 21 million illnesses attributable to norovirus infection are estimated to occur annually.

The prototype norovirus was identified by electron microscopy as a cause of gastroenteritis in Norwalk, Ohio, in 1968.[137] These viruses do not grow well in culture; thus, until immunologic assays, followed by RT-PCR assays, were developed, their detection was difficult. Noroviruses are small (27- to 35-nm diameter), nonenveloped, single-stranded RNA viruses, which have been classified in the Caliciviridae genus. This genus contains at least 130 different genotypes, which are grouped into 5 genogroups (GI–GV). Genogroups 1, 2, and 4 infect humans, while genogroups 3 and 5 infect various animals.

Human norovirus infections are spread between infected humans, rather than from an animal reservoir. These viruses affect persons of all ages and are highly infectious. Stool samples from an infected individual can contain several billion viral particles per gram, and the infectious dose may be as low as 18 viral particles.

The illness typically begins after an incubation period of 12–48 hours. Symptoms onset is acute and includes nonbloody diarrhea, vomiting, nausea, and abdominal cramps. Immunity after an infection may be short-lived—only 6 months to 2 years. However, there is evidence indicating that some individuals may be relatively immune to infection. This natural immunity is based on the *FUT2* gene, which encodes 1,2-fucosyltransferase; 1,2-fucosyltransferase, in turn, produces the carbohydrate H-type 1 on the surface of epithelial cells and mucosal secretions. Secretion-negative individuals, who account for an estimated 21% of the population, do not express this antigen and are resistant to norovirus infection.[138]

Outbreaks of norovirus occur throughout the year, although a seasonal pattern of increased activity during the winter months has been observed. The virus can be transmitted by food, water, and person-to-person spread. Of the 600 norovirus outbreaks that were laboratory confirmed by the CDC during 1994–2006 in which the setting was known, 234 (35.4%) occurred in long-term care facilities (e.g., nursing homes); 205 (31.1%) were from restaurant, parties and events; 135 (20.5%) were from a vacation setting (including cruise ships); and 86 (13.0%) were from schools and communities.[139]

Ebola and Marburg Viruses

Ebola and Marburg viruses are members of the Filoviridae family and have elicited serious concern because of their high infectivity and mortality rates in human populations (**Table 13-4**). The unique pathology caused by these viruses is also notable. The disease is characterized by an abrupt onset with fever, diarrhea, dysphagia, severe weakness, hemorrhagic phenomena, and, in most outbreaks, high mortality.[140] Because coagulation is disrupted, patients in the advanced stages bleed from any wounds, along with their eyes and nose, and they may vomit blood from the loss of organ integrity. Hiccups occur in persons with the Ebola-Zaire strain; when it occurs, it is a predictor of death. These symptoms understandably cause considerable panic in outbreaks and the stigma associated with this panic has hindered the public health response during epidemics.

The first recognition of filoviruses was in 1967, when an epidemic of 31 cases and 7 deaths from viral hemorrhagic fever occurred in Marburg, Germany, among persons having contact with vervet or African green monkeys or their tissues that had been imported from Uganda.[141] The virus, named *Marburg virus*, was cultivated from the blood of sick humans who had become ill after exposure to the monkeys.

Outbreaks of Marburg virus have been unusual. In 1998, a 150-case outbreak of Marburg hemorrhagic fever occurred in the northeast Congo.[142] A cross-sectional serologic survey after the outbreak revealed that 15 (2%) of 912 participants were seropositive for Marburg virus antibodies, and 13 (87%) of the seropositive individuals had worked in a local gold mine.[143] No other risk factors for Marburg seropositivity were identified in this study. In 2005, another large outbreak of Marburg hemorrhagic fever occurred in Uige, Angola. In this outbreak, 374 cases were reported to WHO, of which 329 (88%) were fatal. This epidemic generated considerable fear in the involved communities, and ill persons often came to the hospital late and after other members of the household had been exposed and infected.

In 1976, two outbreaks of infection with Ebola virus occurred in Zaire and the Sudan; together, these outbreaks led to more than 550 cases and 430 deaths.[144–146] Since then 28 outbreaks of Ebola have been recognized and reported by CDC (http://www.cdc.gov/ncidod/dvrd/spb/mnpages/dispages/ebola/ebolatable.htm). Although most of these human epidemics have been initiated by contact with monkeys or other nonhuman primates, monkeys are unlikely to serve as the primary reservoir for Ebola virus, because they also have experienced high mortality from infection. Indeed, the Ebola virus is particularly devastating to gorillas; mortality from this cause has driven these giant apes closer to the brink of extinction. The linkage between Ebola virus and gorillas marks the first time a mammal has been placed on the critically endangered list because of an infectious disease. More than 5000 gorillas are estimated to have died in the Congo region of Africa in the past decade from this Ebola epizootic.

In Africa, where most of these epidemics have occurred, human-to-human transmission of the Ebola virus has been common. In the large outbreak in 1995 in Kikwit, Zaire (now the Congo), healthcare workers and relatives of cases acquired the disease and often succumbed to it.[147] Among the first 283 cases, 90 (32%) occurred in healthcare workers, and 28 (16%) of 173 members in the first 27 households developed disease, albeit only those who had direct contact with body fluids of the infected household member.[148,149] However, the institution of routine barrier precautions (including gowns and gloves) and the discontinuation of the ritual of bathing and cleaning of the corpse after death limited contact with infectious secretions and appeared to control further transmission.

Another outbreak of Ebola virus infection occurred in a monkey colony in Reston, Virginia. In this outbreak, the infected cynomolgus monkeys (*Macaca fascicularis*) had been imported from the Philippines, an area not known to be endemic for Ebola or other filoviruses. The monkeys were coinfected with another virus, Simian hemorrhagic fever (SMF) virus. In this outbreak, in contrast to previous outbreaks of Ebola virus, some evidence of aerosol transmission among the monkeys was noted.[46] Also, four laboratory workers who had used barrier precautions in handling the monkeys developed serologic evidence of infection but remained asymptomatic.[46] These outbreaks underscore the potential importance of differences between strains of Ebola virus in their infectivity and pathogenicity; four subtypes of Ebola virus have been identified to date.[150]

One apparent feature shared by persons who survive Ebola virus infections is that they appear not to develop high titers of neutralizing antibodies. Owing to this fact, an immune serum has not been developed for the therapy of persons with acute infections.

			Table 13-4	**Ebola Virus Infection**

Known Cases and Outbreaks of Ebola Hemorrhagic Fever (EHF), in Chronological Order

Year(s)	Country	Ebola Subtype	Number of Cases (Mortality, %)	Situation
1976	Zaire (DRC)	Ebola-Zaire	318 (88)	Spread by close personal contact and nosocomially by contaminated needles and syringes. First recognition of EHF.
1976	Sudan	Ebola-Sudan	284 (53)	Spread through close personal contact nosocomially. Many medical care personnel were infected.
1976	England	Ebola-Sudan	1 (0)	Laboratory infection by needle-stick.
1977	Zaire	Ebola-Zaire	1 (100)	Noted retrospectively.
1979	Sudan	Ebola-Sudan	34 (65)	Recurrence at 1976 Sudan epidemic site.
1994	Gabon	Ebola-Zaire	52 (60)	In gold-mining camps deep in the rainforest. Initially thought to be yellow fever.
1994	Ivory Coast	Ebola-Ivory Coast	1 (0)	Scientist who conducted an autopsy on a wild chimpanzee. Case treated in Switzerland.
1995	DRC	Ebola-Zaire	315 (81)	Index case worked in a forest adjoining the city. Spread through families and hospitals.
1996	Gabon	Ebola-Zaire	37 (57)	Chimpanzee found dead in the forest was eaten, 19 cases were involved in the butchery; other cases in family members.
1996–1997[1]	Gabon	Ebola-Zaire	60 (74)	Index case was a hunter who lived in a forest camp. Spread by close contact with infected persons. A dead chimpanzee concurrently found in the forest was infected.
1996	South Africa	Ebola-Zaire	2 (50)	A healthcare worker in the Gabon epidemic returned to South Africa; the nurse who took care of him also became infected and died.
2000–2001	Uganda	Ebola-Sudan	425 (53)	Risk factors were attending funerals of cases, being in the family of cases, and providing medical care without protection.
2001–2002	Gabon	Ebola-Zaire	65 (82)	Outbreak occurred on the border of Gabon and the Republic of the Congo.
2001–2002	Republic of Congo	Ebola-Zaire	57 (75)	First Ebola infection case in the Republic of the Congo.
2002–2003	Republic of Congo	Ebola-Zaire	143 (89)	
2003	Republic of Congo	Ebola-Zaire	35 (83)	
2004	Sudan	Ebola-Sudan	17 (41)	Concurrent with an outbreak of measles; several suspect cases reclassified as measles.
2007	DRC	Ebola-Zaire	264 (71)	
2007–2008	Uganda	Ebola-Bundibugyo	131 (37)	First reported occurrence of a new strain.
2008–2009	DRC	Ebola-Zaire	32 (47)	–
2011	Uganda	Ebola-Sudan	1 (100)	

[1]Epidemics were concentrated in time. Those noted as occurring in two years were only several months long, but crossed over the two calendar years.

(continues)

Table 13-4	(continued)		
Outbreaks of Ebola-Reston Hemorrhagic Fever All cases were linked to animals in or from the Philippines (monkeys and pigs). No human illnesses have been recorded, but antibody seroconversions have occurred.			
Year(s)	**Country**	**Animal**	**Situation**
1989	USA	Monkey	At quarantine facilities in Virginia and Pennsylvania, among monkeys imported from the Philippines. No human cases.
1990	USA	Monkey	At quarantine facilities in Virginia and Texas, in Philippine monkeys. Four humans developed antibodies asymptomatically.
1989–1990	Philippines	Monkey	High mortality among cynomolgus macaques. Three humans developed antibodies asymptomatically.
1992	Italy	Monkey	At quarantine facilities, among monkeys imported from the same export facility in the Philippines. No human cases.
1996	USA	Monkey	At quarantine facility in Texas, by Philippine monkeys. No human cases.
1996	Philippines	Monkey	At export facility in the Philippines. No human cases.
2008	Philippines	Pig	First known occurrence of Ebola-Reston in pigs. Six pig farm and slaughterhouse workers developed antibodies asymptomatically.

Modified from Centers for Disease Control (2011). Special pathogens branch: Known cases and outbreaks of ebola Hemorrhagic fever, in chronological order. http://www.cdc.gov/ncidod/dvrd/spb/mnpages/dispages/ebola/ebolatable.htm. Last modified October 12, 2011. Accessed August 28, 2012.

A chronic carrier state of Ebola virus has not been identified in any animal species.[151] The natural reservoir of filoviruses, including both the Ebola and Marburg viruses, is thought to be in several species of fruit bats. The genetic structures of Ebola isolates from the various outbreaks have considerable diversity, suggesting that they are not directly linked with one another, for example, through continued human-to-human transmission.

Because Ebola and Marburg viruses are classified as class A bioterrorism agents, considerable research has focused on vaccines and treatments for these viral diseases. Experimental vaccines have proved effective in protecting animals from potentially lethal infections. Designing a vaccine trial for a rare disease that emerges without warning will be difficult, however. Research teams must be prepared to respond rapidly and will face difficult ethical questions when randomizing populations at risk of disease to the vaccine or the control group given that there are no known treatments for these forms of hemorrhagic fever.

The U.S. National Institute of Allergy and Infectious Diseases is working with partners to bring a combined rabies/Ebola vaccine to human trials. This vaccine has been successful in animal studies in protecting them against both diseases.[152] By combining the two vaccines, researchers can test for benefit and efficacy in the rabies portion of the vaccine. They will also be able to test the safety of the Ebola portion but may not be able to demonstrate its efficacy, as it is unlikely there will be an Ebola outbreak at the time of the vaccine trials.

Arenaviruses

The arenaviruses are a group of negative-stranded, RNA viruses that are important causes of epidemic infections in tropical areas of Africa and South America. The prototype arenavirus, lymphocytic choriomeningitis virus (LCM), was discovered in 1933 and causes benign aseptic meningitis in humans in temperate areas of North America as well as in the tropics (**Table 13-5**). Other arenaviruses have also been identified, including those causing Argentine hemorrhagic fever (AHF), Bolivia hemorrhagic fever (BHF, Machupo virus),[153–155] and Venezuela hemorrhagic fever (VHF).[153] and Lassa fever virus.[156] The public health implication of a fifth arenavirus, Guanarito virus, is not clear. Various rodent species serve as the reservoir for the arenaviruses, including *Mus musclus* (the house mouse) for LCM, *Mastomys* species for Lassa fever, and *Calomys* species for AHF, BHF, and VHF.

In the 1960s and 1970s, Lassa fever virus caused several high-mortality epidemics in Nigeria, Liberia, Sierra Leone, and the United States. Mortality ranged from 77% in Nigeria to 20–60% in later epidemics.[156] Great concern arose after Lassa fever was first described that this virus might be the "Andromeda strain" that would spread rapidly to all human

Table 13-5	Ecologic Features of Arenaviruses Pathogenic for Humans		
Virus	Natural Host	Geographic Distribution	Disease
Lymphocytic choriomeningitis virus	*Mus musculus* (house mouse)	Europe, America	Aseptic meningitis
Junin virus	*Calomys musculinus*	Argentina	Argentine hemorrhagic fever
Machupo virus	*Calomys callosus*	Bolivia	Bolivia hemorrhagic fever
Guanarito virus	*Sigmodon alstoni*	Venezuela	Venezuela hemorrhagic fever
Lassa virus	*Mastomys natalensis*	West Africa	Lassa hemorrhagic fever

contacts, with high mortality. Subsequent investigation suggested that spread is preventable with ordinary respiratory precautions.

In recent decades, human-made changes in the environment have increased human exposure to virus-infected rodents. Junin virus emerged in Argentina when the pampas grassland that had been a grazing area for cattle was converted into cultivated farmland for the production of maize. This trend led to a major expansion of the population of a mouse, *Calomys musculinus*, that fed on the grain. Because these mice were frequently chronically infected with Junin virus, which they shed in their urine, the harvesting of the maize put humans in contact with the virus.

In Bolivia, an epidemic of BHF occurred in 1960 and was caused by a related virus, Machupo virus, when an area in eastern Bolivia was converted from cattle raising to subsistence agriculture. This ecologic change provided a suitable environment for the expansion of the population of a small mouse, *Calomys callosus*. This mouse invaded the homes and gardens of the local inhabitants and spread the virus that caused BHF. Unlike the case with AHF, this epidemic is now under control, due in part to the greater pathogenicity of the virus for the carrier mouse and the more limited contact of the human population with the reservoir host.

Zoonotic Paramyxovirus Infections

Several epidemics of human infection from two paramyxoviruses, Hendra virus and Nipah virus, have been documented in recent years. These epidemics have occurred in Australia and Asia from reservoirs in domestic animals.

Hendra Virus Epidemic in Australia

In September 1994, an outbreak of respiratory disease affected 18 horses, their trainer, and a stable hand in Queensland, Australia. Fourteen horses and one human died. A novel virus was isolated from the horses and humans, and originally was named *equine morbilivirus*.[157] One of the persons who had aseptic meningitis during the original outbreak recovered but became ill with encephalitis and died 13 months later.[158] During this illness, he developed seizures with distinctive changes on magnetic resonance imaging and histologic changes in the cerebral cortex. Polymerase chain reaction (PCR) analysis of his spinal fluid, brain, and serum yielded sequences identical to those obtained during the original outbreak. Subsequently, a second, unrelated outbreak was identified in Queensland, in which two horses died and one human became infected.[167] Laboratory studies have suggested that fruit bats (*Pteropus* species) in Australia and Papua New Guinea may be infected and serve as the natural reservoir for this newly recognized virus, which has been renamed *Hendra virus*.[160]

Nipah Virus

Between February and April 1999, a severe outbreak of viral encephalitis occurred in the Bakit Pelandok area of peninsular Malaysia that affected more than 200 individuals and a large number of pigs.[161] The outbreak was initially thought to be due to Japanese encephalitis virus (JE), as pigs are a reservoir of this virus. However, several features of the 1999 disease differed from JE infection. The outbreak involved only men who were in direct contact with pigs; it had a very high attack rate, pigs also became sick, and most of the human cases had been immunized against JE virus. There were 28 deaths among 91 patients admitted to the University of Malaya Medical Center in Kuala Lumpur.[162] A virus was isolated from cerebrospinal fluid (CSF) that stained positively with antibodies against Hendra virus by indirect immunofluorescence. Immunoglobulin M (IgM) capture enzyme-linked immunosorbent assay (ELISA) showed that several patients had IgM antibodies in their CSF against

Hendra virus antigens. No clinical evidence of pulmonary involvement was apparent, but inclusion bodies of probable viral origin were present in neurons. Electron microscopy revealed virus-like structures resembling paramyxoviruses, and nucleotide sequencing indicated that the virus was related, but not identical, to Hendra virus. Subsequently, 11 cases were reported from Singapore among workers on pig farms. By culling all pigs on farms with infected animals, the outbreaks were controlled.[162]

In 2001 and 2003, outbreaks of Nipah virus encephalitis were reported from Bangladesh.[163] In these outbreaks, no contact with pigs was reported. However, fruit bats tested positive for Nipah virus antibodies, and there was evidence of household clustering, suggesting human-to-human transmission.

Outbreaks of Nipah virus infections have been common in Bangladesh during the winter and early spring since these infections were first recognized in 2001. Among 23 introductions into human populations in Bangladesh between 2001 and 2009, 87 (71%) of 122 cases died.[164,165] Patients were infected from the consumption of raw date palm sap or by contact with another infected patient having respiratory symptoms. The natural reservoir for Nipah virus

is fruit bats, members of the *Pteropus* species. They spread the infection to humans by contaminating food, such as date palm sap, or by infecting pigs, cattle, goats, or other animals when they contaminate their feed with urine, saliva, or partially eaten food. An ingenious public health intervention has been developed and implemented in Bangladesh using a bamboo cover placed over the container collecting date palm sap to prevent its contamination by fruit bats.

Influenza Viruses

Perhaps the quintessential emerging viral infection of humans is influenza. This highly contagious acute respiratory illness has caused epidemics in humans since ancient times. Influenza viruses are named according to their hemagglutinin (H) and neuraminidase (N) proteins. The segmented RNA genome of the influenza virus has multiple strains that infect humans and bird species. While genetic drift occurs when the genome undergoes gradual changes, antigenic shift represents a dramatic change in the viral strain. Genetic shift occurs when a bird is infected with multiple strains. In that setting, it is possible for the eight separate RNA strands to become assembled using genes from different strains (**Figure 13-16**).

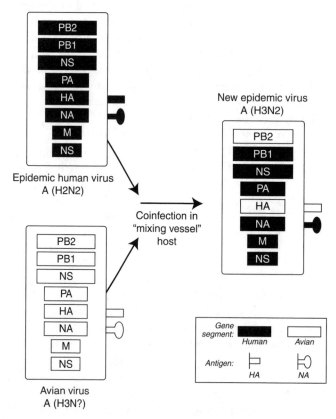

Figure 13-16 Diagram showing the antigenic shift in 1968, when a new avian gene was acquired. Gene segments are color-coded to represent avian or human species origin and their associated surface proteins. Copyright © Mark C. Steinhoff.

These genetic reassortments can create totally new strains that can cause pandemics. Because the human population lacks immunity to these viruses, there is great concern that these viruses may cause pandemics.

Global influenza surveillance programs closely monitor the emergence of new influenza viruses. Most strains will not be transmitted to humans, or may have limited pathogenicity in humans, but an influenza pandemic is inevitable. The most recent virus to cause concern was the H5N1 virus, which was first noticed in Hong Kong in 1997. This virus caused disseminated viremia in infected persons and resulted in death in 30% of cases.[167] While a widespread avian epidemic occurred, there was no evidence of person-to-person transmission. Millions of chickens and other birds were culled to contain the epidemic with substantial economic impact. Recently, outbreaks of H5N1 influenza have been widespread among aquatic and domestic birds with occasional spread to humans, and rare human-to-human transmission.[168]

NEWLY DISCOVERED PATHOGENS

Traditionally, infectious agents have been linked to specific diseases by the isolation of an organism on artificial media, a tissue culture, recovery of the organism after inoculation of infectious material into an animal, or visualization of the organism in tissues or excretions of an infected patient. However, in the last decade or so, molecular biologists have developed methods to identify the genetic material (DNA or RNA) of infectious organisms and even sequence the genome of pathogenic organisms without ever isolating the entire intact organism in vitro. One of the first examples of the genetic characterization of an organism using only molecular methods was the amplification of the nucleic acid of the hepatitis C virus (HCV) and the identification of this important cause of human hepatitis in 1989. Recently, additional successes have been reported in the use of molecular methods to identify the causative agents of infectious diseases. Also, epidemiologic methods have been applied to link new agents to well-studied chronic diseases. Both of these approaches have revolutionized thinking about infectious diseases and have identified "new" infectious diseases.

Whipple's Disease

In 1907, George Whipple described a disease characterized by chronic diarrhea, along with malabsorption, weight loss, polyarticular arthritis, and lymphadenopathy. The intestines and lymph nodes of patients with the disease had abnormal fat deposits, and the disease was often called *intestinal lipodystrophy*. Whipple, however, also noted bacilli in the walls of the intestines, but his repeated attempts to isolate and characterize the organisms by in vitro culture failed. Although steroids produced some temporary benefit, long-term antibiotic use sometimes was curative. With the advent of modern methods of molecular biology, it became possible to amplify the bacterial 16SrRNA gene and identify the causative organism in Whipple's disease as an actinomycete, which has been named *Tropheryma whippelii*.[171]

Cat Scratch Fever, Bacillary Angiomatosis, and Trench Fever

The clinical disease called cat scratch fever has been known to clinicians for some time. It is characterized by fever and unilateral necrotizing lymphadenopathy involving the epitrochlear and axillary nodes, with symptoms appearing after a cat scratch. Recently, another syndrome, bacillary angiomatosis (BA), has been recognized in AIDS patients. This disease is characterized by nodular vascular proliferative lesions in the skin, bone, or other organs. Infection of the liver results in the formation of angiomatous lesions known as *bacillary peliosis hepatitis*. Using both molecular techniques and cultures, an organism, *Bartonella henselii*, has been isolated from patients with cat scratch fever and those with BA. Apparently, the organisms causing the two diseases are similar, and host factors determine the clinical appearance of the resultant disease after infection. The organisms are sensitive to macrolide antibiotics, but the response is somewhat dependent on the immune competence of the infected patient. The reservoir for BA is the domestic cat, and the organisms are spread to humans by the cat flea.[172]

A related organism, *Bartonella quintana*, is the cause of trench fever, a disease that was common among soldiers serving in World War I; the disease was transmitted from one person to another by the body louse.[173] Although this disease has become very rare in modern times, cases have been described recently among homeless men.[174,175]

The last two decades have provided dramatically new challenges for infectious disease epidemiologists, yet much greater understanding of the complex multiplicity of factors leading to the emergence and spread of new infectious diseases. Almost certainly, this century will bring even greater challenges to the understanding and control of infectious diseases as the population grows and our relationship with the environment becomes even more complex and better understood than it is at present.

• • • **REFERENCES**

1. Institute of Medicine. *Emerging Infectious: Microbial Threats to Health in the United States*. Washington, DC: National Academies Press; 1992.

2. Centers for Disease Control and Prevention. Preventing emerging infectious diseases: a strategy for the 21st century. *MMWR Recomm Rep*. 1998;47(R8-15):1–14.

3. Murphy FA, Nathanson N. The emergence of new virus diseases: an overview. *Semin Virol*. 1994;5:87–102.

4. Zucker JR. Changing pattern of autochthonous malaria transmission in the United States. *Emerg Infect Dis*. 1996;2:37–43.

5. Guan Y, Zheng BJ, He YQ, et al. Isolation and characterization of viruses related to the SARS coronavirus from animals in southern China. *Science*. 2003;302:276–278.

6. Lee N, Hui D, Wu A, et al. A major outbreak of severe acute respiratory syndrome in Hong Kong. *N Engl J Med*. 2003;348:1986–1994.

7. Donnelly CA, Fisher MC, Fraser C, et al. Epidemiological and genetic analysis of severe acute respiratory syndrome. *Lancet Infect Dis*. 2004;4:672–683.

8. Armstrong GL, Hollingsworth J, Morris JG Jr. Emerging food-borne pathogens: *Escherichia coli* O157:H7 as a model of entry of a new pathogen into the food supply of the developed world. *Epidemiol Rev*. 1996;18:29–51.

9. Griffin PM, Tauxe RV. The epidemiology of infections caused by *Escherichia coli* O157:H7, other enterohemorrhagic *E. coli* and the associated hemolytic uremic syndrome. *Epidemiol Rev*. 1991;13:60–98.

10. Feng P. *Escherichia coli* O157:H7: novel vehicles of infection and emergence of phenotypic variants. *Emerg Infect Dis*. 1995;1:47–52.

11. Whittam TS, McGraw EA, Reid SD. Pathogenic *Escherichia coli* O157:H7: a model for emerging infectious diseases. Chapter 3, pgs. 123–165 in: Krause RM, ed. *Emerging Infections*. New York, NY: Academic Press; 1998.

12. Mead PS, Slutsker L, Dietz V, et al. Food-related illness and death in the United States. *Emerg Infect Dis*. 1005;5:607–625.

13. Kupferschmidt K. As *E. coli* outbreak recedes, new questions come to the fore. *Science*. 2011;333:27.

14. Kuijper EJ, Soonwala D, Vermont L, vanDissel JF. Household transmission of hemolytic uremic syndrome associated *E. coli* 0104:H4 in the Netherlands, May 2011. *Euro Surveill*. 2011;16:19897.

15. Snedeker KG, Shaw DJ, Locking ME, Prescott RJ. Primary and secondary cases in *E. coli* 0157 outbreaks: a statistical analysis. *BMC Infect Dis*. 2009;9:144–155.

16. Lapeyraque A-L, Malina M, Fremeavx-Bachi, et al. Eculizumab in severe Shiga toxin associated HUS. *N Engl J Med*. 2011;364:2561–2563.

17. Huang P, Weber JJ, Sosin DM, et al. The first reported outbreak of diarrheal illness associated with Cyclospora in the United States. *Ann Intern Med*. 1995;123:409–414.

18. Herwaldt B, Ackers MC, Cyclospora Working Group. An outbreak in 1996 of cyclosporiasis associated with imported raspberries. *N Engl J Med*. 1997;336:1548.

19. Herwaldt B, Beach MJ, Cyclospora Working Group. The return of Cyclospora in 1997: another outbreak of cyclosporiasis in N. America associated with imported raspberries. *Ann Intern Med*. 1999;130:210–220.

20. Griffiths JK. Human cryptosporidiosis: epidemiology, transmission, clinical disease, treatment and diagnosis *Adv Parasitol*. 1998;40:37–85.

21. Johnson RT, Gibbs CJ. Creutzfeldt-Jakob disease and related transmissible spongiform encephalopathies. *N Engl J Med*. 1998;339:1994–2004.

22. Prusiner SB. Novel proteinaceous infectious particles cause scrapie. *Science*. 1982;216:136–144.

23. Prusiner SB. Prions and neurodegenerative diseases. *N Engl J Med*. 1987;317:1571–1581.

24. Deresinski S. Methicillin-resistant *Staphylococcus aureus*: an evolutionary, epidemiologic, and therapeutic odyssey. *Clin Infect Dis*. 2005;40:562–573.

25. Smith KE, Besser JM, Hedberg CW et al. Quinolone-resistant *Campylobacter jejuni* infections in Minnesota 1992–1998. *N Engl J Med*. 1999;340:1525–1532.

26. Wegener HC. The consequences for food safety of the use of fluoroquinolones in food animals. *N Engl J Med*. 1999;340:1581–1582.

27. Klevens RM, Morrison MA, Nadle J, et al. Invasive methicillin-resistant *Staphylococcus aureus* infections in the United States. *JAMA*. 2007;298:1763–1771.

28. Klein E, Smith DL, Laxminaryan R. Hospitalizations and deaths caused by methicillin-resistant *Staphylococcus aureus*, United States, 1999–2005. *Emerg Infect Dis*. 2007;13:1840–1846.

29. Seybold U, Kourbatova EV, Johnson JG, et al. Emergence of community-associated methicillin-resistant *Staphylococcus aureus* USA300 genotype as a major cause of health care-associated blood stream infections. *Clin Infect Dis*. 2006;42:647–656.

30. Otter JA, French GL. Molecular epidemiology of community-associated methicillin-resistant *Staphylococcus aureus* in Europe. *Lancet Infect Dis*. 2010;10:227–239.

31. van Loo I, Huijsdens X, Tiemersma E, et al. Emergence of methicillin-resistant *Staphylococcus aureus* of animal origin in humans. *Emerg Infect Dis*. 2007;13: 1834–1839.

32. Silbergeld ER, Davis M, Leibler JH, Peterson AE. One reservoir: redefining the community origins of antimicrobial-resistant infections. *Med Clin N Am*. 2008;92:1391–1407.

33. Langlois BE, Dawson KA, Cromwell GI, Stahly TS. Antibiotic resistance in pigs following a 13 year ban. *J Animal Sci*. 1986;62:18–32.

34. Wyatt JD, Barker WH, Bennett NM, Hanlon CA. Human rabies post-exposure prophylaxis during a Raccoon rabies Epizootic in New York, 1993 and 1994. *Emerg Inf Dis*. 1999;5:415–423.

35. Steere AC, Malawista SE, Hardin JA, et al. Erythema chromium migrans and Lyme arthritis: the enlarging clinical spectrum. *Ann Intern Med*. 1977;86:685–698.

36. Burgdorfer W, Barbour AG, Hayes SF, et al. Lyme disease: a tick-borne spirochetosis. *Science*. 1982;216:1317–1319.

37. Steere AC. Lyme disease: a growing threat to urban populations. *Proc Natl Acad Sci USA*. 1994;91:2378–2383.

38. Bacon RM, Kugler KJ, and Mead PS. Surveillance for Lyme Disease—United States, 1992–2006. *Morb Mort Wkly Rep*. Oct 3,2008;57(55–10):1–9.

39. Centers for Disease Control and Prevention. Lyme Disease, United States, 1995. *MMWR*. 1996;45:481–484.

40. Steere AC. Lyme disease. *N Engl J Med*. 1989;321:586–596.

41. Woodward TE, Dumler JS. Rocky Mountain spotted fever. In: Evans AS, Brachman PS, eds. *Bacterial Infections of Humans*. 3rd ed. New York, NY: Plenum Press; 1998:597–612.

42. Anderson BS, Dawson JE, Jones DC, Wilson K. *Ehrlichia chaffeensis*, a new species associated with human ehrlichiosis. *J Clin Microbiol*. 1991;29:2838–2842.

43. Ruebush TR, Juranek DD, Chisholm ES, et al. Human babesiosis on Nantucket Island: evidence for self-limited and subclinical infections. *N Engl J Med*. 1977;297:825.

44. Rupprecht CE, Smith JJ. Raccoon rabies: the reemergence of an epizootic in a densely populated area. *Semin Virol*. 1994;5:155–164.

45. Wyatt JD, Barker WH, Bennett NM, Hanlon CA. Human rabies post-exposure prophylaxis during a raccoon rabies epizootic in New York, 1993–1994. *Emerg Inf Dis*. 1999;5:415–423.

46. Jahrling PB, Geisbert TW, Dalgard DW, et al. Preliminary report: isolation of Ebola virus from monkeys imported to the USA. *Lancet.* 1990;335:502–505.

47. Kissling RE, Robinson RQ, Murphy FA, Whitfield SG. Agent of disease contracted from green monkeys. *Science.* 1968;160:888–890.

48. Ladnyj ID, Ziegler P, Kima E. A human infection caused by monkeypox virus in Basankusu Territory, Democratic Republic of the Congo. *Bull WHO.* 1972;46:593–597.

49. Multistate outbreak of monkeypox—Illinois, Indiana, and Wisconsin, 2003. *MMWR.* 2003;52:537–540.

50. Update: multistate outbreak of monkeypox—Illinois, Indiana, Kansas, Missouri, Ohio, and Wisconsin, 2003. *MMWR.* 2003;52:642–646.

51. Khodakevich L, Szczeniowski M, Manbu MD, et al. The role of squirrels in sustaining monkeypox virus transmission. *Trop Geogr Med.* 1987;39:115–122.

52. Hansen J, Sato M, Ruedy R, et al. Global temperature change. *Proc Natl Acad Sci USA.* 2006;103;14288–14293. doi:10.1073/pnas.0606291103.

53. Colwell RR. Global climate and infectious disease: the cholera paradigm. *Science.* 1996;274:2025–2031.

54. Stone R. The mouse–pinon nut connection. *Science.* 1993;262:833.

55. Centers for Disease Control and Prevention. Rift Valley fever—East Africa, 1997–1998. *MMWR.* 1998;74:261–264.

56. Linthicum KJ, Anyamba A, Tucker CJ, et al. Climate and satellite indicators to forecast Rift Valley fever epidemics in Kenya. *Science.* 1999;285:397–400.

57. Watts DM, Burke DS, Harrison BA, et al. Effect of temperature on the vector efficiency of *Aedes aegypti* for dengue 2 virus. *Am J Trop Med Hyg.* 1987;36:143–152.

58. Paaijmans KP, Read AF, Thomas MB. Understanding the link between malaria risk and climate. *Proc Natl Acad Sci USA.* 2009;106:33.

59. Crosby AW. *Epidemic and Peace, 1918.* Westport, CT: Greenwood Press; 1976.

60. Taobenberger JK, Reid AH, Krafft AE, et al. Initial genetic characterizations of the 1918 "Spanish" influenza virus. *Science.* 1997;275:1793.

61. Grau IW, Jorgensen WA. Medical support in a counter guerilla war: epidemiologic lessons learned in the Soviet–Afghanistan war. *US Army Med Department J.* May–June 1995:41–49.

62. Balayan MS, Andjaparidza AG, Davinskaya SS, et al. Evidence for a virus in non-A, non-B hepatitis transmitted by the fecal–oral route. *Intervirology.* 1983;20:23–31.

63. Earle D. Symposium on epidemic hemorrhagic fever. *Am J Med.* 1954;16:619–709.

64. Lee H, Lee PW, Johnson KJ. Isolation of the etiologic agent of Korean hemorrhagic fever. *J Infect Dis.* 1978;137:298–308.

65. Glass GE, Watson NI, Leduc J, Kelen GD, Quinn TC. Infection with a rat-borne hantavirus in U.S. residents is consistently associated with hypertensive vascular disease. *J Infect Dis.* 1993;167:614–620.

66. Niklasson B. Leuc j. Epidemiology of Nephropathica epidemica in Sweden. *J Infect Dis.* 1987;155:269–276.

67. United Nations High Commission for Refugees. *The State of the World's Refugees: In Search of Solutions.* New York, NY: Oxford University Press; 1995.

68. Anderson C. Cholera epidemic traced to risk miscalculation. *Nature.* 1991;354:255.

69. Siddigue AK, Salam A, Islam MS et al. Why treatment centers failed to prevent cholera deaths among Rwanda refugees in Goma. *Lancet* 1995;345:359–361.

70. Hadler SC, Webster HM, Erben JJ, et al. Hepatitis A in day-care centers: a community-wide assessment. *N Engl J Med.* 1980;302:1222–1227.

71. Hadler SC, McFarland L. Hepatitis in day care centers: epidemiology and prevention. *Rev Infect Dis.* 1986;8:548–557.

72. Denny FW, Collier AM, Henderson FW. Acute respiratory infections in day care. *Rev Infect Dis.* 1986;8:523–532.

73. U.S. Census Bureau. *American Community Survey.* 2008.

74. Centers for Disease Control and Prevention Increased Transmission and Outbreaks of Measles—European region, 2011. *Morb Mort Wkly Rep.* 2011;60;1606–1610.

75. Breman JG, Nakano JH, Coffi E, et al. Human poxvirus disease after smallpox eradication. *Am J Trop Med Hyg.* 1977;26:273–281.

76. Jezek Z, Arita I, Mutombo M, et al. Four generations of probable person-to-person transmission of human monkeypox. *Am J Epidemiol.* 1986;123:1004–1012.

77. Jezek Z, Grab B, Szczeniowski MV, et al. Human monkeypox: secondary attack rates. *Bull WHO.* 1988;66:465–470.

78. Hutin YJ, Williams RJ, Malfait P, et al. Outbreak of human monkeypox, Democratic Republic of Congo, 1996 to 1997. *Emerg Infect Dis.* 2001;7:434–438.

79. Heymann DL, Szczeniowski M, Esteves K. Re-emergence of monkeypox in Africa: a review of the past six years. *Br Med Bull.* 1998;54:693–702.

80. Tasker SA, Schnepf GA, Lim M, et al. Unintended smallpox vaccination of HIV-1—infected individuals in the United States military. *Clin Infect Dis.* 2004;38(9):1320–1322.

81. Redfield RR, Wright DC, James WD, et al. Disseminated vaccinia in a military recruit with human immunodeficiency virus (HIV) disease. *N Engl J Med.* 1987;316:673–676.

82. Gao F, Bailes E, Robertson DL, et al. Origin of HIV-1 in the chimpanzee, *Pantroglodytes troglodytes. Nature.* 1999;196(3):336–341.

83. Barre-Sinoussi F, Chermann JC, Rey F, et al. Isolation of a T-lymphocyte retrovirus from patient at risk for acquired immunodeficiency syndrome (AIDS). *Science.* 1983;220:868–871.

84. Selwyn PA, Hartell D, Lewis VA, et al. A prospective study of the risk of tuberculosis among intravenous drug users with human immunodeficiency virus infection. *N Engl J Med.* 1989;320:545–550.

85. Montalban C, Calleja JC, Erice A, et al. Visceral leishmaniasis in patients infected with human immunodeficiency virus. *J Infect.* 1990;21:261–270.

86. Supparatpinyo K, Khamwan C, Baosoong V, et al. Disseminated *Penicillium marneffei* infection: an emerging HIV-associated opportunistic infection in Southeast Asia. *Lancet.* 1994;344:110–113.

87. Sepkowitz KA, Raffalli J, Riley C, et al. Tuberculosis in the AIDS era. *Clin Micro Rev.* 1995;8:180–199.

88. Rotz LD, Khan AS, Lillibridge SR, et al. Public health assessment of potential biological terrorism agents. *Emerg Infect Dis.* 2002;8:225–230.

89. Fenner F. *The History of Smallpox and Its Spread around the World.* Geneva, Switzerland: World Health Organization; 1988.

90. Wheelis M. Biological warfare at the 1346 siege of Caffa. *Emerg Infect Dis.* 2002;8:971–975.

91. Torok TJ, Tauxe RV, Wise RP, et al. A large community outbreak of salmonellosis caused by intentional contamination of restaurant salad bars. *JAMA.* 1997;278:389–395.

92. Alibek K. *Biohazard.* New York, NY: Random House; 1999.

93. The Biohazardous organisms and their classification currently listed by the US Center for Disease Control and Prevention can be viewed at the following website: http://www.bt.cdc.gov/agent/agentlist-category.asp

94. Poutanen SM, Low DE. Severe acute respiratory syndrome: an update. *Curr Opin Infect Dis.* 2004;17:287–294.

95. Peiris JS, Guan Y, Yuen KY. Severe acute respiratory syndrome. *Nat Med.* 2004;10: S88–S97.

96. Update: outbreak of severe acute respiratory syndrome—worldwide, 2003. *MMWR.* 2003;52:241–246,248.

97. Reilley B, van Herp M, Sermand D, Dentico N. SARS and Carlo Urbani. *N Engl J Med.* 2003;348:1951–1952.

98. Severe acute respiratory syndrome—Singapore, 2003. *MMWR.* 2003;52:405–411.

99. Update: severe acute respiratory syndrome—Toronto, Canada, 2003. *MMWR.* 2003;52:547–550.

100. Yu IT, Li Y, Wong TW, et al. Evidence of airborne transmission of the severe acute respiratory syndrome virus. *N Engl J Med.* 2004;350:1731–1739.

101. Li Y, Yu IT, Xu P, et al. Predicting superspreading events during the 2003 severe acute respiratory syndrome epidemics in Hong Kong and Singapore. *Am J Epidemiol.* 2004;160:719–728.

102. Shen Z, Ning F, Zhou W, et al. Superspreading SARS events, Beijing, 2003. *Emerg Infect Dis.* 2004;10:256–260.

103. Wong TW, Lee CK, Tam W, et al. Cluster of SARS among medical students exposed to single patient, Hong Kong. *Emerg Infect Dis.* 2004;10:269–276.

104. Leung GM, Hedley AJ, Ho LM, et al. The epidemiology of severe acute respiratory syndrome in the 2003 Hong Kong epidemic: an analysis of all 1755 patients. *Ann Intern Med.* 2004;141:662–673.

105. Booth CM, Matukas LM, Tomlinson GA, et al. Clinical features and short-term outcomes of 144 patients with SARS in the greater Toronto area. *JAMA.* 2003;289: 2801–2809.

106. Svoboda T, Henry B, Shulman L, et al. Public health measures to control the spread of the severe acute respiratory syndrome during the outbreak in Toronto. *N Engl J Med.* 2004;350:2352–2361.

107. Peiris JS, Lai ST, Poon LL, et al. Coronavirus as a possible cause of severe acute respiratory syndrome. *Lancet.* 2003;361:1319–1325.

108. Rota PA, Oberste MS, Monroe SS, et al. Characterization of a novel coronavirus associated with severe acute respiratory syndrome. *Science.* 2003;300:1394–1399.

109. Marra MA, Jones SJ, Astell CR, et al. The genome sequence of the SARS-associated coronavirus. *Science.* 2003;300:1399–1404.

110. Drosten C, Gunther S, Preiser W, et al. Identification of a novel coronavirus in patients with severe acute respiratory syndrome. *N Engl J Med.* 2003;348:1967–1976.

111. Guan Y, Zheng BJ, He YQ, et al. Isolation and characterization of viruses related to the SARS coronavirus from animals in southern China. *Science.* 2003;302:276–278.

112. Prevalence of IgG antibody to SARS-associated coronavirus in animal traders—Guangdong Province, China, 2003. *MMWR.* 2003;52:986–987.

113. Liang W, Zhu Z, Guo J, et al. Severe acute respiratory syndrome, Beijing, 2003. *Emerg Infect Dis.* 2004;10:25–31.

114. Efficiency of quarantine during an epidemic of severe acute respiratory syndrome—Beijing, China, 2003. *MMWR.* 2003;52:1037–1040.

115. Pang X, Zhu Z, Xu F, et al. Evaluation of control measures implemented in the severe acute respiratory syndrome outbreak in Beijing, 2003. *JAMA.* 2003;290:3215–3221.

116. Use of quarantine to prevent transmission of severe acute respiratory syndrome—Taiwan, 2003. *MMWR*. 2003;52:680–683.

117. Riley S, Fraser C, Donnelly CA, et al. Transmission dynamics of the etiological agent of SARS in Hong Kong: impact of public health interventions. *Science*. 2003;300:1961–1966.

118. Lipsitch M, Cohen T, Cooper B, et al. Transmission dynamics and control of severe acute respiratory syndrome. *Science*. 2003;300:1966–1970.

119. Svoboda T, Henry B, Shulman L, et al. Public health measures to control the spread of the severe acute respiratory syndrome during the outbreak in Toronto. *N Engl J Med*. 2004;350:2352–2361.

120. Yu X-J, Liang M-F, Zhang S-Y et al. Fever with Thrombocytopenia Associated with a Novel Bunyavirus in China. *N Engl J Med*. 2011;364;1523–32.

121. McMullin L K, Folk S M, Kelly A J et al. A New Phlebovirus Associated with Severe Febrile Illness in Missouri . *N Engl J Med*. 2012;367: 834–41.

122. McMinn PC. An overview of the evolution of enterovirus 71 and its clinical and public health significance. *FEMS Microbial Rev*. 2002;26:91–107.

123. Ho M, Chen E-R, Hsu K-H, et al. An epidemic of enterovirus 71 infection in Taiwan. *N Engl J Med*. 1999;341:929.

124. Zhang Y, Tan X-J, Wang H-Y, et al. An outbreak of hand, foot, and mouth disease associated with subgenotype C4 of human enterovirus 71 in Shandong, China. *J Clin Virol*. 2009;44:262–267.

125. Sack DA, Sack RB, Nair GB, Siddique AK. Cholera. *Lancet*. 2004;362:223–233.

126. Centers for Disease Control and Prevention. Update cholera outbreak—Haiti, 2010. *MMWR*. 2010;59(945):1473–1479.

127. Centers for Disease Control and Prevention. Update on cholera—Haiti, Dominican Republic and Florida, 2010. *MMWR*. 2010;59(50):1637–1641.

128. Farmer P, Almazor CP, Bahuson ET, et al. Meeting cholera's challenge to Haiti and the world: a joint statement on cholera prevention and care. PLOS *New Engl Trop Dis*. 2011;5:1145.

129. Farmer P. Political violence and public health in Haiti. *N Engl J Med*. 2004;350:1483–1486.

130. Chin C-S, Sovenson J, Harris JB, et al. The origin of the Haitian cholera outbreak strain. *N Engl J Med*. 2011;364:33–42.

131. Yu H, Jing H, Chen Z, et al. Human *Streptococcus suis* outbreak, Sichuan, China. *Emerg Infect Dis*. 2006;12:914–920.

132. Mai NTH, Hgo NT, Nga TVT, et al. *Streptococcus suis* meningitis in adults in Vietnam. *Clin Infect Dis*. 2008;46: 659–667.

133. Griffiths JK. Human cryptosporidiosis: epidemiology, transmission, clinical disease, treatment and diagnosis. *Adv Parasitol*. 1998;40:37–85.

134. MacKenzie WR, Hoxie NJ, Proctor ME et al. A massive outbreak in Milwaukee of Cryptosporidia infection transmitted through the public water supply. *N Engl J Med*. 1994;331:161–167.

135. Morris RD, Naumora EN, Griffiths JK. Did Milwaukee experience water-borne cryptosporidiosis before the large outbreak in 1993? *Epidemiology*. 1998;9:264–270.

136. Current WL, Garcia LS. Cryptosporidiosis (review). *Clin Microbiol Rev*. 1991;4: 325–358.

137. Kapikian AZ, Wyatt RG, Dulin R, et al. Visualization by immune electron microscopy of a 27nm particle associated with acute non-bacterial gastroenteritis. *J Virol*. 1972;10:1075–1081.

138. Lindesmith L, Moe C, Severing M, et al. *Nat Med*. 2003;9:548–553.

139. Centers for Disease Control and Prevention. Updated norovirus outbreak management and disease prevention guidelines. *MMWR*. 2011;60(3).

140. World Health Organization. Ebola haemorrhagic fever in Zaire, 1976: report of an international commission. *Bull WHO*. 1978;56:271–293.

141. Smith CEG, Simpson DIH, Bowen ETW. Fatal human disease from vervet monkeys. *Lancet*. 1967;2:1119–1121.

142. World Health Organization. Marburg fever, Democratic Republic of the Congo. *Wkly Epidemiol Rec*. 1999;74:145.

143. Bausch DG, Borchert M, Grein T, et al. Risk factors for Marburg hemorrhagic fever, Democratic Republic of the Congo. *Emerg Infect Dis*. 2003;9:1531–1537.

144. Bowen ETN, Lloyd G, Harris WJ, et al. Viral hemorrhagic fever in southern Sudan and northern Zaire. *Lancet*. 1977;1:571–573.

145. World Health Organization. Ebola haemorrhagic fever in Sudan 1976: report of World Health Organization International Study Team. *Bull WHO*. 1978;56:247–270.

146. Murphy FA, Peters CJ. Ebola virus: where does it come from and where is it going? In: Krause RM, ed. *Emerging Infections*. New York, NY: Academic Press; 1998:375–410.

147. Roels TH, Bloom AS, Buffington J, et al. Ebola hemorrhagic fever, Kikwit, Democratic Republic of the Congo, 1995: risk factors for patients without a reported exposure. *J Infect Dis*. 1999;179(suppl 1):S92–S97.

148. Dowell SE, Mukunu R, Ksiazek TG, et al. Transmission of Ebola hemorrhagic fever: a study of risk factors in family members, Kikwit, Democratic Republic of the Congo, 1995. *J Infect Dis*. 1999;(suppl 1):S87–S91.

149. Bwaka MA, Bonnet MJ, Calain P, et al. Ebola hemorrhagic fever in Kikwit, Democratic Republic of Congo: clinical observations in 103 patients. *J Infect Dis*. 1999;179 (suppl 1):S1–S7.

150. Le Guenno B, Formenty P, Wyers M, et al. Isolation and partial characterization of a new strain of Ebola virus. *Lancet*. 1996;345: 1271–1274.

151. Jezek Z, Szczeniowski MY, Mayembe-Tamfom JJ, et al. Ebola between outbreaks: intensified Ebola hemorrhagic fever surveillance in the Democratic Republic of the Congo, 1981–1985. *J Infect Dis*. 1999; (suppl 1):S60–S64.

152. Blaney JE, Wirblich C, Papaneri AB, et al. Inactivated or live-attenuated bivalent vaccines that confer protection against rabies and Ebola viruses *J Virol*. 2011;85: 10605–10616.

153. Johnson KM, Halstead SB, Cohen SN. Hemorrhagic fevers of Southeast Asia and South America: a comparative appraisal. *Prog Med Virol*. 1967;9:105–158.

154. World Health Organization. International symposium on arena viral infections of public health importance. *Bull WHO*. 1975;52: 318–766.

155. Salas R, Manziona N, Tesh RB, et al. Venezuelan hemorrhagic fever. *Lancet*. 1991;338:1033–1036.

156. Buckley SM, Casals J. Lassa fever, a new disease of man from West Africa III: isolation and characterization of the virus. *Am J Trop Hyg Med*. 1970;19:680–691.

157. Selrey LA, Wells RM, McCormick JG, et al. Infection of humans and horses by a newly described morbilli-virus virus. *Med J Aust*. 1995;162:642–645.

158. O'Sullivan JD, Allworth AM, Paterson DL, et al. Fatal encephalitis due to novel paramyxovirus transmitted from horses. *Lancet*. 1997;349:93–95.

159. Rogers RJ, Douglas IC, Baldock FC, et al. Investigation of a second focus of equine morbillivirus infection in a coastal Queensland. *Aust Vet J*. 1996;24:243–245.

160. Williamson MM, Hooper PT, Selleck PW, et al. Transmission studies of Hendravirus

(equine morbillivirus) in fruit bats, horses and cats. *Aust Vet J.* 1996;76:813–818.

161. Chua KB, Gohk J, Wong KT, et al. Fatal encephalitis due to Nipah virus among pig farmers in Malaysia. *Lancet.* 1999;354: 1257–1259.

162. Centers for Disease Control and Prevention. Outbreak of Hendra-like virus—Malaysia and Singapore, 1998–1999. *MMWR.* 1999;48:265–269.

163. Hsu VP, Hossain MJ, Parashar UD, et al. Nipah virus encephalitis reemergence, Bangladesh. *Emerg Infect Dis.* 2004;10:1082–1087.

164. Luby SP, Hossain MJ, Gurley ES. Recurrent zoonotic transmission of Nipah virus into humans, Bangladesh, 2001–2007. *Emerg Infect Dis.* 2009;15:1229–1235.

165. Luby SP, Gurley ES, Hassain MJ. Transmission of human infection with Nipah virus. *Clin Infect Dis.* 2009;49:1743–1748.

166. Nahar N, Sultana R, Gurley ES, et al. Date palm sap collection: exploring opportunities to prevent Nipah transmission. *EroHealth.* 2010;7:196–203.

167. Centers for Disease Control and Prevention. Isolation of avian influenza A (H5N1) viruses from humans—Hong Kong, May–December, 1997. *MMWR.* 1997;46:1204–1207.

168. Ungchusak K, Auewarakul P, Dowell SF, et al. Probable person-to-person transmission of avian influenza A (H5N1). *N Engl J Med.* 2005;352:333–340.

169. Choo QL, Kuo G, Weiner AJ, et al. Isolation of a cDNA clone derived from a blood-borne non-A non-B hepatitis genome. *Science.* 1989;244:359–362.

170. Whipple GH. A hitherto undescribed disease characterized anatomically by deposits of fat and fatty acids in the intestinal and mesenteric lymphatic tissues. *Johns Hopkins Hosp Bull.* 1907;18:382–391.

171. Relman DA, Schmidt TM, MacDermott RP, Falkow S. Identification of the uncultured bacillus of Whipples disease. *N Engl J Med.* 1992;327:293–301.

172. Koehler JE, Glaser CA, Tappero JW. Rochalimaea henselae infection: a new zoonosis with the domestic cat as reservoir. *JAMA.* 1994;271:531–535.

173. Strong RP, ed. *Trench Fever: Report of Commission, Medical Research Committee, American Red Cross.* Oxford, UK: Oxford University Press; 1918:40–60.

174. Drancourt M, Mainard JC, Brouqui P, et al. Bartonella (Rochalimaea) quintana endocarditis in three homeless men. *N Engl J Med.* 1995;332:419–423.

175. Spach DH, Kanter AS, Dougherty MJ, et al. Bartonella (Rochalimaea) quintana bacteremia in inner-city patients with chronic alcoholism. *N Engl J Med.* 1995;332: 424–428.

14

Healthcare-Associated Infections

Leilani Paitoonpong, Chun Kwan Bonnie Wong, and Trish M. Perl

INTRODUCTION

Healthcare-associated infections (HAIs) are infections that patients acquire during the course of receiving medical treatment for other conditions.[1] They are defined as localized or systemic conditions resulting from an adverse reaction to the presence of an infectious agent or its toxin(s) that has no evidence of being present or incubating at the time of admission to the care setting.[1] In general, infections are defined as associated with health care if they develop 48 hours after admission or receiving medical care or within 30 days of having a surgical procedure. They may be caused by a variety of infectious agents from endogenous and exogenous sources. Encapsulated in this general concept is the acquisition of organisms of epidemiologic significance that may not cause infection per se. In this case, the individual may become colonized with and harbor an organism that does not cause infection but could increase the risk of developing an infection. Such organisms include methicillin-resistant *Staphylococcus aureus* (MRSA), vancomycin-resistant enterococcus (VRE), and gram-negative rods (GNRs) that produce extended-spectrum beta-lactamases (ESBLs) or carbapenemases.

HAIs occur in all settings of care and across the continuum of care, including hospital acute care units, day procedure centers, ambulatory outpatient clinics, dialysis centers, long-term care facilities, nursing homes, and rehabilitation centers. To better reflect the diversity of the modern healthcare system that our patients encounter nowadays, the term HAIs has replaced older terms such as "nosocomial infections," "hospital-acquired infections," and "hospital-onset infections."

HAIs occur for primarily four reasons:

1. *Host factors*: Individuals may have a compromised immune system due to underlying disease or due to disruption of mucosal and skin surfaces that increases their risk of developing infections or acquiring organisms that are either high- and low-virulence organisms.

2. *Environment*: The hospital environment promotes the spread of microbial pathogens. The proximity to other patients, contamination of common equipment, exposure to water contaminated with microorganisms, presence of construction and renovation, tasks that healthcare providers (HCPs) perform, and the often-unwashed hands of HCPs contribute to creating the ideal conditions for transmission of infectious organisms.

3. *Technology*: Technology-based advances in health care provide sophisticated methods of monitoring and caring for patients. Unfortunately, these advances also provide new portals of entry for infection, alter normal host flora, and may increase antimicrobial resistance, thereby increasing the risk of HAIs.

4. *Human factors*: With the tremendous resource cuts that have occurred in the healthcare industry in recent years, the number and skill level of caregivers has decreased. Nontraditional and support staff now provide previously specialized nursing functions. HCPs are busier than ever, allowing them little time to observe simple infection prevention practices, such as hand washing. These changes may contribute substantially to healthcare-associated transmission of organisms and development of infections.

Bacteria cause approximately 90% of HAIs, with viruses, fungi, protozoa, and other classes of microorganisms causing the remaining infections. Based on surveillance data collected by the National Healthcare Safety Network (NHSN), the most common pathogens isolated from any HAIs are coagulase-negative staphylococci (CoNS, 15.3%), *Staphylococcus aureus* (14.5%), Enterococcus species (12.1%), *Escherichia coli* (9.6%), and *Pseudomonas aeruginosa* (7.9%).[2] As is true for community-acquired infections, the most frequently isolated organism depends on its source. *E. coli* most commonly causes urinary tract infections (UTIs; 21.4%); *S. aureus* most commonly causes surgical site infections (SSIs; 30%); CoNS most commonly causes central-line associated bloodstream infection (CLA-BSI; 34.1%); and *S. aureus* and *P. aeruginosa* cause 24.4% and 14.3%, respectively, of ventilator-associated pneumonia (VAP).[2]

THE MAGNITUDE OF PROBLEM OF HAIs

The problem of HAIs is a global issue. These infections are a major cause of morbidity and mortality in both pediatric and adult populations in the United States and worldwide. HAIs occasionally affect HCPs as well. The World Health Organization (WHO) estimates that 1.4 million people are affected with an HAI at any given moment (www.who.int/gpsc/country_work/summary_20100430_en.pdf). The prevalence of infection varies from 4.5% to 19.1%, with infection rates being higher in developing countries (**Table 14-1**). HAIs are becoming more of a challenge as modern medical care utilizes more invasive procedures and more sophisticated devices. Hence, much of the surveillance focus has been on infections associated with the placement of these devices. The emergence of antimicrobial-resistant pathogens and a lack of new antimicrobials in the pipeline has further fueled the problem. The increasing awareness of resistant pathogens has fostered a search for systems that can measure both colonization and infection. An aging population, the AIDS epidemic, the growth of chemotherapeutic options for cancer treatment, and a growing transplant population have also expanded the populations at risk for infection.[3]

In the United States, the Centers for Disease Control and Prevention (CDC) estimates that nearly 2 million patients experience an HAI each year, meaning 1 of every 10–20 patients hospitalized in the country develops such an infection.[4] These infections cause almost 100,000 deaths and are associated with an extra $4.5 billion to $6.5 billion in costs.[5] Based on these estimations, the number of deaths attributable to HAIs exceeds that for several of the top six leading causes of death in the United States. Of these infections, 36% occur in the urinary tract, 20% at the surgical site, 11% in the lung, and 11% in the bloodstream.[4]

Table 14-1	WHO Estimate of the Burden of Healthcare-Associated Infections Worldwide, 1995–2008
Country	**Estimated Prevalence**
Korea	3.7%
United States	4.5%
Norway	5.1%
Latvia	5.7%
France	6.7%
Lebanon	6.8%
Thailand	7.3%
United Kingdom and Ireland	7.6%
Cyprus	7.9%
Italy	8.3%
Finland	9.1%
Lithuania	9.2%
Greece	9.3%
Scotland	9.5%
Switzerland	10.1%
Canada	11.6%
Turkey	13.4%
Malaysia	13.9%
Brazil	14.0%
Tanzania	14.8%
Tunisia	17.8%
Morocco	17.8%
Mali	18.7%
Albania	19.1%

Data from World Health Organization (2011). The Burden of Health Care-Associated Infection Worldwide. www.who.int/gpsc/country_work/summary_20100430_en.pdf. Accessed February 29, 2012.

Multiple studies have shown that HAIs prolong the duration of hospitalization, and increase morbidity and mortality to patients.[6–12] They are costly both to the patient and to the healthcare system. It is estimated that at least 20% of all such infections could be prevented by better hygiene and infection control procedures.[13]

Worldwide, HAIs are now recognized as an important public health problem and warrant attention from policymakers, public health authorities, hospital leadership, and frontline healthcare personnel. Preventing these infections has now become a national priority for many countries, with initiatives in this area being led by healthcare organizations, professional associations, government and accrediting agencies, legislators, regulators, payers, and consumer advocacy groups.[14] Public reporting of HAIs occurs in many countries, including France, the United Kingdom, and the United States.

More than 4 million people in the European Union (EU) acquire a HAI annually, and approximately 37,000 die as a direct result of the infection. A point prevalence study conducted in 1417 intensive care units (ICUs) in 17 European countries demonstrated that as many as 44.8% patients were infected, and half of these patients (20.6%) acquired their infections in the ICU. Pneumonia was most common infection in this cohort, followed by urinary tract and bloodstream infections. Moreover, many of the infections were associated with multidrug-resistant organisms.[15]

The burden of HAIs is faced not only by developed countries, but also by resource-limited countries. While reports from developed countries are able to provide a glimpse into the scale of the problem of HAIs, few data are available from the developing world to quantify its scope. Nonetheless, the available data suggest that the prevalence of these infections, and hence the burden of disease, is higher in the developing world (Table 14-1).

Data collected in the 1980s in a WHO cooperative study, which included 55 hospitals in 14 countries from four WHO regions, revealed a mean prevalence of 8.7% for HAIs. The highest frequency of infection was noted in ICUs and acute surgical and orthopedic units. A slightly different epidemiology in terms of type of HAIs was used in this study—namely, surgical site infections contributed the most (25.1%), followed by urinary tract infections (22%) and pneumonia (20.5%).[16]

A 6-year surveillance study from 2003–2008 involving 173 ICUs in Latin America, Asia, Africa, and Europe, using the NHSN definitions, revealed a markedly higher rates of CLA-BSI, VAP, and catheter-associated urinary tract infections (CA-UTIs) in these regions than in comparable U.S. ICUs. The crude unadjusted excess mortality for device-related infections was reported to range from 23.6% (CLA-BSI) to 29.3% (VAP). The survey also reported higher frequencies of MRSA, *Klebsiella pneumoniae* resistant to third-generation cephalosporins, *Acinetobacter baumannii* resistant to imipenem, and *Pseudomonas aeruginosa* resistant to pipericillin.[17]

A more recent study from WHO estimated that the prevalence of HAIs, as derived from pooled data from countries outside Europe and the United States, was 15.5 per 100 patients (95% confidence interval [CI]: 12.6–18.9).[18] The pooled overall HAI density in adult ICUs was estimated at 47.9 per 1000 patient-days (95% CI: 36.7–59.1), at least three times as high as the density reported from the United States.[18] The lack of national infection control guidelines, the lack of a framework to reinforce compliance with guidelines when they are in place, and a lack of administrative and financial support and trained personnel in the settings of these resource-limited countries all contribute to their alarmingly higher rates of HAIs.[17]

While the burden of these infections varies from study to study because of the various methodologies used by investigators, several key points can be made:

- These infections are common.
- They are associated with significant morbidity and mortality.
- Multidrug-resistant organisms are commonly the cause of these infections and colonization.
- HAIs affect healthcare systems and patients worldwide.

Keeping these facts in mind, infection prevention programs should be organized to reduce HAIs and the spread of resistant organisms, along with their associated morbidity and mortality. The ultimate goal of these programs is to improve patient care, reduce hospital stays, and reduce healthcare-related costs. It is estimated that approximately one-third of HAIs might be prevented by well-organized infection control programs. Unfortunately, less than one-tenth (6% to 9%) of infections are actually prevented.[19,20] The following components of these programs are crucial in reducing HAIs:

- A trained physician with expertise in infection prevention and control (hospital epidemiologist)
- At least one infection control practitioner (ICP; now called an infection preventionist [IP]) per 250 beds[21]
- A computerized surveillance system
- A system of reporting HAI/colonization rates of hospitalized or at-risk patients to practicing physicians and surgeons[19]

HISTORY

The earliest advice regarding hospital hygiene was probably written in the fourth century B.C., in the *Charaka-Samhita*, a Sanskrit textbook of medicine, based on Indian Vedic medicine. The following excerpt demonstrates the early principles of hospital infection prevention and control:

In the first place a mansion must be constructed under the supervision of an engineer well conversant with the science of building mansions and houses. It shall be spacious and roomy. . . . One portion at least should be open to the current wind. It should not be exposed to smoke, or dust, or injurious sound or touch or taste or form or scent. . . . After this should be secured a body of attendants of good behavior, distinguished for purity and cleanliness of habits.[22]

The role of the facility and the environment continued to be recognized in medieval and renaissance Europe, where hospitals were overcrowded. Pioneers such as Theodoric of Bologna and Casper Stromayr reformed hospital practice by bathing their patients or shaving the site of operation, yet met with little success.[23] Toward the end of the 1700s, Madam Necker proposed "nursing the sick in a single bed." Prior to this time, as many as eight patients were nursed in a bed amid appalling squalor.[24]

Simpson, a Scottish surgeon, demonstrated an enduring concept that mortality following amputation was proportional to the size of the hospital and the degree of overcrowding.[25,26] And in the mid-1800s, Florence Nightingale, a nurse, published a dramatic report after her Crimean War experiences at the military hospitals, which demonstrated that far more soldiers died of HAIs than died from the primary effects of battle injuries.[27] Furthermore, Nightingale, with the help of John Farr, demonstrated a direct relationship between sanitary conditions at a hospital and postoperative complications.[28] She proposed that ward sisters maintain records of hospital patients who developed infections and introduced broad hospital hygiene, thereby pioneering the concept of HAI surveillance.

During the same era, Dr. Ignaz Semmelweis, the head of obstetrical service at the Royal Lying-In Hospital of Vienna, investigated the high maternal mortality rate at his facility. In doing so, he probably undertook the first hospital-based epidemiologic study.[29] Semmelweis recognized that rates of puerperal fever were higher in the ward staffed by physicians as opposed to the ward tended by nurse–midwives. A key difference between the two types of providers was that the physicians participated in autopsies of women with puerperal sepsis. They would then return to the wards to care for women in labor. Semmelweis observed this variation in care and linked the increased rates to a lack of hand washing after performing autopsies. Once hand washing was instituted after performing autopsies as a control measure, the ward-specific excess rate of puerperal sepsis and mortality associated with physicians declined and was equal to that for the midwives.[29]

Louis Pasteur continued to develop our understanding of microbiology and the role of organisms in infection when he demonstrated that air is contaminated with living germs and that growth of such organisms leads to spoilage.[30–32] Lister then reasoned that microbes were responsible for wound suppuration and introduced antisepsis to surgery.[33] He proposed controlling suppuration by preventing contaminated air from coming in contact with a wound. Similarly, in 1895, George Emerson Brewer, an American surgeon, recognized the problem of infections after surgery and undertook an intensive surveillance project to estimate the frequency of surgical wound infections, now called surgical site infections (SSIs).[34] He reported that SSI rates among patients after clean surgical operation was not 5% or less, but actually 39%—findings that inspired a review of surgical techniques and environmental risk factors. In 1915, Brewer reported in a follow-up a steady decline of SSIs to 1.2% among patients undergoing clean surgical procedures.[35]

In 1937, with the introduction of penicillin to treat serious staphylococcal and streptococcal infections, misconceptions developed that antimicrobial agents might be able to control and eventually eliminate all infectious diseases. Some physicians worried less about infections because nontoxic drugs could prevent serious complications and cure infections. In the 1940s, the concept of postsurgical antimicrobial prophylaxis was introduced, and widespread use of penicillin occurred. The increased use of penicillin resulted in the rapid emergence of resistant staphylococci. In the late 1950s, the first epidemics of healthcare-associated penicillinase-producing *Staphylococcus aureus* were reported in Europe and North America. In these outbreaks, patients—primarily neonates admitted to hospital nurseries without infections—subsequently developed staphylococcal sepsis.[36] These outbreaks generated greater interest in prevention practices within healthcare and regulatory agencies.

Over the ensuing decade, gram-positive organisms were the primary pathogens causing HAIs. Such infections increased in severity as treatment options shrank with the emergence of resistance to methicillin in *S. aureus*. By the 1970s, and perhaps in response to antibiotics with good gram-positive coverage, gram-negative organisms became most frequent cause of HAIs. However, the 1980s, new gram-positive organisms—specifically, CoNS, MRSA, and fungi, primarily *Candida* species—emerged as important HAI pathogens.[37] Since then, both bacteria and fungi causing HAIs have become increasingly resistant to antimicrobial agents.

For example, the prevalence of methicillin resistance among *S. aureus* isolates increased from 2.4% in 1975 to 29% in 1991.[38] Infections caused by MRSA are similar to those caused by methicillin-sensitive *S. aureus* (MSSA), in that they are life threatening and, in fact, are associated with increased mortality.[39] Vancomycin is the most commonly used antimicrobial agent against these resistant organisms, and its frequent empiric use has contributed to the development of vancomycin resistance among *S. aureus* and other organisms. Likewise, the incidence of VRE infection has also increased dramatically. Most concerning is the emergence of *S. aureus* strains with intermediate susceptibility to vancomycin or other glycopeptide antibiotics. Should glycopeptide-intermediate susceptibility (GISA) emerge as a major pathogen, we would essentially reenter the pre-antibiotic era with respect to their control.

In 1959, the first ICP was appointed in England to control hospital-acquired *Staphylococcus* infections.[40] It was not until 1963, however, that a full-time practitioner was hired to prevent HAIs in the United States.[41] In 1964, Boston City Hospital conducted some of the first modern prevalence studies and reported that 15% of inpatients had HAIs.[20,42] By 1968, the CDC was training ICPs in surveillance, prevention, and control of nosocomial infections, and in 1969, the Joint Commission for Accreditation of Healthcare Organizations (now The Joint Commission) mandated that all hospitals support an ICP. These trained professionals, who come from nursing, medical technology, and epidemiology backgrounds, are now called infection preventionists and are key to institutional program prevention and control efforts.

In 2003, the severe acute respiratory syndrome (SARS) epidemic catapulted the need for better infection control strategies and public health and institutional infrastructure into the public eye.[43-45] This epidemic killed more than 800 people and infected more than 8000 people worldwide.[46] With increasing visibility in the press, the emerging problem with antimicrobial resistance, and the demand for greater transparency, both patients and regulators worldwide have demanded that HAI rates, and in some cases process measures, be publicly reported. This trend has inspired a greater focus on patient safety, as HAIs are the primary complication that puts patients at risk. Fortunately, this has led to a call for zero infections. While this goal may not be achievable, we can have zero tolerance for practices and processes that are not supported by evidence to reduce patient risk.

SURVEILLANCE FOR HAIs

Definitions

HAIs are defined using a set of standard criteria that have been developed over time. In 2012, the definitions were undergoing revision. The CDC took the lead and developed the National Nosocomial Infection Surveillance (NNIS) system in 1970, which was composed of non-randomly selected hospitals that voluntarily submitted their data collected using standard methods and definitions. In 2005, NNIS was restructured into the National Health Safety Network (NHSN), which has almost 4000 participating hospitals. Today, the NNIS/NHSN is the most important source of national data on HAIs in the United States.[47] This system has also served as the model for systems and programs in other countries designed to ameliorate HAIs.

The CDC/NHSN has assumed a primary role in developing HAI definitions for the purposes of surveillance.[1] These definitions have been tested and validated for surveillance purposes in many acute care settings. Separate definitions have been developed for long-term care facilities.[48] Use of uniform definitions are critical if investigators are to identify patterns within hospitals and to compare rates of HAIs between hospitals or data systems. While not perfect, these definitions' persistence over the past 40 years has provided the infection prevention community with a standard way to identify complications that are associated with poor patient outcomes, to follow trends over time, and to measure the impact of prevention strategies. The definitions are often based on microbiologic, serologic, histologic results, although they may also use clinical criteria to differentiate a colonized body site versus one causing infections.

Measures of Frequency of HAIs

HAIs are evaluated by calculating rates, rather than the simple number of events or infections. For instance, the presence of six HAIs at a large institution (bed size > 500) has different implications than the same number of infections at a small institution (bed size < 25).

Crude Infection Rate

The most common measure of occurrence, the crude infection rate, is the ratio of infections per 100 admissions or discharges:

$$\text{Crude infection rate} = \frac{\text{Number of infections}}{100 \text{ admissions or discharges}}$$

The crude infection rate can also be site-specific. For example:

$$\text{Crude CLA-BSI} = \frac{\text{Number of CLA-BSI}}{100 \text{ admissions or discharge}}$$

Adjusted Infection Rate

To derive a rate that represents changes in the HAI rate from one period to another, the crude infection rate is often adjusted by patient-days or number of procedures. This step corrects for a patient being admitted in one month and discharged in another month. An example of an adjusted infection rate is the ratio of infections per 1000 patient-days or 100 surgical procedures.

$$\text{Adjusted infection rate} = \frac{\text{Number of infections}}{1000 \text{ patient-days}}$$

or

$$\text{Adjusted inection rate} = \frac{\text{Number of infections}}{100 \text{ surgical procedures}}$$

The crude infection rate does not adjust for risk factors for HAIs that vary among patients. The risk-adjusted infection rate adjusts the rate by the major risk factor for these device-related infections by the number of days that a medical device (e.g., central venous catheter, urinary catheter, ventilator) is used. A prospective study demonstrated that data collected for HAI rates should be adjusted for risk factors to correct for severity of illness.[49]

$$\text{Risk-adjusted infection rate} = \frac{\begin{array}{c}\text{Number of infections}\\\text{in question}\end{array}}{\begin{array}{c}\text{Number of days that}\\\text{a device is in place}\end{array}}$$

Device-Associated Infection Rates

A device-associated infection rate is a specific example of a risk-adjusted infection rate. The device-associated rate is most commonly reported as infections per 1000 device-days:

$$\text{Device-day infection rate} = \frac{\begin{array}{c}\text{Number of device-associated}\\\text{infections for specific site}\end{array}}{\text{Number of device-days}} \times 1000$$

Before calculating the risk-adjusted infection rate, certain steps should be followed:

1. Decide on the time period for the analysis (week, month, quarter, half-year, or year).
2. Select the patient population (ICU, surgical patients).
3. Choose the site of infection for which the rate is to be calculated (numerator).

The infection selected should be site specific and should occur in the selected population; the infection onset-days should occur during the time period selected. Once the device-days are determined, infections such as catheter-associated urinary tract infections would be calculated using the following formulation:

$$\text{CA-UTI rate (device-days)} = \frac{\begin{array}{c}\text{Number of urinary}\\\text{catheter-associated UTIs}\end{array}}{\begin{array}{c}\text{Number of urinary}\\\text{catheter-days}\end{array}} \times 1000$$

Calculation of the Number of Days That a Device Is in Place

In January 2011, on the first day of the month, suppose 20 patients had urinary catheters; 19 had catheters on day 2; 15 had catheters on day 3; 25 had catheters on day 4; 20 had catheters on day 5; 15 had catheters on day 6; and 15 had catheters on day 7. The number of patients with urinary catheters from days 1 to 7 is added (20 + 19 + 15 + 25 + 20 + 15 + 15), yielding 129 urinary catheter-days for the first week (**Table 14-2**). The total catheter-days for the entire month is the sum of the daily counts.

Device-Day Utilization

To determine the percentage of patient-days compared to device-days, the device utilization ratio can be calculated. The device-day utilization rate is specifically useful for measuring infection risk among patients in ICUs.

To calculate the number of patient-days, let us use another example. In January 2011, 20 patients were hospitalized at midnight on the unit on the first day; 20 on day 2; 18 on day 3; 25 on day 4; 24 on day 5; 20 on day 6; and 18 on day 7. To calculate the patient-days, add the number of patients in the unit from day 1 to day 7. The total number of patient-days for the week is 145 (Table 14-2). Remember that the patient-days are always calculated at the same time. Thus the patient-days are the total number of days that patients are in a unit during a selected time

Table 14-2	Comparison of Denominators: Device Utilization Days versus Patient Days	
Number of Day	**Number of Device-Days**	**Patient-Days**
1	20	20
2	19	20
3	15	18
4	25	25
5	20	24
6	15	20
7	15	18
Total	129	145

period. We had earlier calculated the total urinary catheter-days to be 129. Thus

$$\text{Device utilization} = \frac{129}{145} = 0.8897 \text{ or } 89\%$$

Eighty-nine percent of patient-days were also urinary catheter-days for the first week of the month.

Calculating the device-associated, device-day rate and utilization ratio helps IPs to evaluate how their hospital compares with the mean rates, such as those reported by the NHSN system. Some caveats apply. If the denominator is small (less than 50 device-days or patient-days), this ratio will not be a good estimate of the "true" device utilization. Therefore, a longer time period should be chosen. Also, not all hospitals are similar to the hospitals included in the comparison group. If huge variations in hospital infection rates are noted, reasons for these variations should be explored. Specialty care facilities, for example, may have higher rates of infection due to particularly vulnerable patients or types of surgery performed.

Incidence and Prevalence

To measure incidence and prevalence, surveillance surveys are performed. Incidence surveys determine the rate of new infections during a given time, whereas prevalence surveys determine the proportion of patients with infections at a given point in time. To calculate the incidence rate (I), the number of HAIs (during a given month) is divided by the number of patients discharged or admitted (during the same month), or by the number of patient-days[40,50]:

$$I = \frac{\text{Number of new HAIs (during a month)}}{\text{Number of patients discharged or admitted (during the same month) or patient-days}}$$

In addition, incidence rates can be site or organism specific, with the number of infections at a given site being used in the numerator, and the denominator as described previously.

Prevalence surveys are designed to measure all current HAIs. Because patients who experience HAIs are likely to have longer hospital stays, infected patients are typically over-represented in the hospital population. The prevalence rate then overestimates infection rates, compared with incidence rates. Nevertheless, prevalence surveys are often used because they are relatively easy to perform and provide a picture at a single point in time.[51] Prevalence surveys are useful in to determine the HAI rates in large populations of high-risk patients or to identify areas where targeted investigation may be useful.

During a prevalence survey, infection control personnel examine all patients' medical records and interview clinical staff to identify HAIs. The prevalence rate (P) is calculated by dividing the number of active (current) HAIs present on a given day in hospitalized patients by the number of patients hospitalized on the same day:

$$P = \frac{\text{Number of active HAIs}}{\text{Number of patients present}}$$

Methods to Evaluate Risk Factors for HAIs and the Impact of Interventions

Both observational and interventional epidemiologic studies can be used to study HAIs. Observational studies, such as case-control studies and cohort studies, are used to identify risk factors in outbreak investigations or epidemiologic studies and to assess outcomes. Intervention studies, such as clinical trials, are used to evaluate whether a given intervention is effective. Surveillance and outbreak investigations are routinely performed in most infection control programs. Randomized clinical trials are usually performed in infection control programs with active research programs.

Surveillance, a key component of infection control programs, has been defined as "a dynamic process for gathering, managing, analyzing, and reporting data on events which occur in specific populations."[52] Surveillance relies on four building blocks:

1. Collecting relevant data systematically for a specified purpose and during a defined period of time
2. Managing and organizing the data
3. Analyzing and interpreting the data
4. Communicating the results to those empowered to make beneficial changes

Surveillance is also a method used to measure the rate of HAIs events. The purpose of measuring the event is to determine the baseline rate, thereby enabling the investigator to compare the rate after an intervention has been instituted. Hence, surveillance is a necessary component of an intervention study.

Methods of Surveillance

Each institution should determine which method is best suited to its facility. The most common surveillance methods include the following:

- Hospital-wide surveillance
- Prevalence surveys
- Targeted surveillance
- Periodic surveillance[47]

Hospital-wide surveillance is the most comprehensive technique, but is also expensive and labor intensive. Prevalence surveys are inexpensive and can be applied to individual units or entire institutions.[47] Targeted surveillance focuses on selected areas of the hospital, selected patient populations, or selected organisms.[3] When based on the highest-risk areas or patients, it has been preferred over hospital-wide surveillance because it represents the most effective use of resources.[53] However, surveillance for certain epidemiologically important organisms may need to be hospital-wide.[53] Periodic surveillance is used when surveillance methods are done only during specified time intervals.[3]

Various methods or mixtures of methods are used to identify patients with HAIs:

- Total chart review
- Selective medical record review (e.g., chart summaries—either handwritten, such as the nursing summary notes, or stored in hospital databases)
- Reports of clinical symptoms from providers
- Clinical ward rounds
- Review of laboratory reports
- Extraction of data from pharmacy records, such as antimicrobial use
- Computer alerts and computer-based automated surveillance
- Follow-up letters/calls to providers[47]

The sensitivity and specificity vary for these methods of detecting HAIs when compared with the gold standard—total chart review. However, total chart review has not been shown to improve the sensitivity of detecting HAIs, compared with selective review of charts, based on review of laboratory reports and the nursing summary notes (74–94% versus 75–94%) and is very time intensive.[54] Case-finding methods must be applied systematically so that results are comparable over time. Most IPs choose their surveillance strategies based on the type of hospital, the patient population served, the resources available, and the "local" epidemiology and culture. New surveillance technologies using computer programs have been developed as well. For example, many institutions have computer programs or software that facilitate either surveillance or identification of patients colonized or infected with epidemiologically important organisms.[47,55] This software usually integrates the result from the microbiology, radiology, and pharmacy databases and clinical information from a variety of data sources.[3] Automated surveillance with user-definable control charts is more efficient at identifying potential outbreaks than routine surveillance.[56]

Outbreak investigations are the epidemiologic studies most closely identified with infection prevention programs, even though epidemic-related infections account for fewer than 5% of all HAIs.[57] Outbreak investigations begin with the identification of an unusual occurrence or an excessive rate of infections. Cases are defined and described in terms of place, person, and time. Organisms should be speciated and compared for similarity, using antimicrobial susceptibility and molecular technologies. If the cause of the outbreak is not overtly apparent or if a study is required to confirm the important exposures or causes, a case-control study is usually performed to determine risk factors. Steps for outbreak investigation are provided in **Table 14-3**.

Information about the risk factors for and the outcomes of HAIs is often obtained through different methods of investigation. Observational, case-control, and cohort studies are the most common study designs used. For example, knowledge of the risk factors for surgical site infections was obtained through a series of cohort studies in which surgical patients were followed postoperatively for SSIs.[58] Information on any potential risk factors for SSI was collected on all patients in the cohort, patients with

Table 14-3	Steps to Investigate an Outbreak

1. Determine the nature, location, and severity of the problem.
2. Identify cases.
3. Document notes regarding the outbreak in an orderly fashion.
4. Conduct a literature search.
5. Create a preliminary questionnaire.
6. Review medical records to establish a case definition.
7. Save isolates from cases, as well as from suspected cases and/or source.
8. Summarize the data into an easy-to-read line listing.
9. Form a hypothesis (source, mode of transmission, cause).
10. Test the hypothesis by either a case-control or cohort study.
11. Create an epidemic curve.
12. Demonstrate biologic plausibility.
13. Inform the appropriate individuals and agencies.
14. Institute emergency control measures:
    i. Eliminate the source, which could be the environment, a patient, or the HCP.
    ii. Protect exposed individuals by administering chemoprophylaxis or immunization.
15. Evaluate the control measures.
16. Document and report the outbreak.

and without SSIs were compared, and relative risks for the risk factors were calculated. The costs of HAIs have also been measured using matched case-control methods and cohort studies. For example, patients with CA-UTI have been matched to controls with similar diagnoses and severity of illness, and then costs and lengths of stay compared.[59,60]

Randomized controlled trials are the best study method to prove causation. In the setting of population-based analysis, two strategies are employed: those that randomize individuals to receive one treatment/intervention or not, and those that randomize units (cluster randomized) to a treatment or not. Cluster randomized studies are becoming more common, as they simplify study implementation; that is, units (rather than individual patients) are randomized to one intervention, which reduces the need to track individual patients while allowing the investigators to retain control over potential confounders through randomization. Clinical trials have been used to show the effects of sterilization and disinfection, closed urinary drainage systems, intravascular catheter care, dressing techniques, and care of respiratory therapy equipment related to HAIs.[61]

In addition, clinical trials have been important in showing what does *not* work. For example, a randomized clinical trial of antimicrobial prophylaxis for patients with chronic urinary catheters demonstrated no difference in the rate of UTIs and febrile episodes, compared with the control group, whose members did not receive prophylaxis.[62]

PATHOPHYSIOLOGY AND RISK FACTORS

Hospitalized patients, in general, are at high risk for infection, due to their underlying illness (immunosuppression, diabetes); hospitalization circumstances (trauma, burns); environmental, microbiologic, and virulence factors; procedure-related interventions, such as surgery or medical care (urinary catheter, vascular catheter, ventilators); and the process of care (patient/nurse ratios, inappropriate antibiotic use). Because patient characteristics are frequently beyond our control and difficult to alter, reduction in HAIs is best achieved by altering HCP behaviors, procedure-related techniques and conditions, or other processes of care.

Host Factors

Host factors that contribute to hospitalized patients developing infections include extremes of age, severity of underlying illnesses, immune dysfunction (T- or B-cell mediated), poor nutrition, genetic factors, and loss of the body's normal protective functions (skin integrity, microbial imbalance). Extremes of age are a major risk factor for HAIs.[49,63–65] In fact, data collated by the CDC indicated that 54% of all HAIs in adults occurred among those aged 65 years or older.[38] Thus, while those older than age 60 represented only 23% to 24% of discharges, they accounted for 37% to 64% of all HAIs.[66,67]

Several studies have shown that HAIs are related to underlying illness. In particular, pulmonary, cutaneous, and hematologic diseases alter host defenses by changing or modifying normal flora, breaching normal anatomic barriers, suppressing inflammatory responses, and modifying the reticuloendothelial system.[68–70] Underlying disease that causes immunosuppression, such as cancer or HIV infection, can make the host highly prone to HAIs.[71] In a 2-year study conducted in an oncology ICU, the overall infection rate was 50 cases per 100 patients, or 91.7 cases per 1000 patient-days.[72] Neutropenic patients have altered immunity, are exposed to many antimicrobial agents, and are hospitalized frequently for prolonged periods of time. These patients may be at a higher risk of developing HAIs due to bacterial colonization and catheter placement.[73–75] Other underlying diseases put certain groups of patients at higher risk for HAIs. For example, obese patients are at higher risk of postoperative infection in various kinds of surgical procedures.[76–83] Furthermore, obesity was found to be an independent risk factor for bloodstream catheter-related infection in ICU in a recent study.[84]

Environment

Air, water, and the inanimate surfaces surrounding the patient are referred to as the *environment*. Contamination of the floor, walls, bed frames, chairs, water, and air of the patient's environment may lead to HAIs.

Air

Malfunctioning or inadequate ventilation systems in healthcare facilities may not adequately filter air. *Aspergillus* species—one of the most invasive fungi—under appropriate environmental conditions can produce and disseminate several thousand spores per cubic meter of air.[85–87] These spores can remain suspended in air for long periods, but eventually they settle and can contaminate surfaces. The spores remain viable for months and can become airborne when dust-generating activities are performed, such as construction or demolition. If walls or surfaces become wet and are not replaced, molds can also grow and become sources of infection.

Water

Since the etiologic agent of Legionnaires' disease was first identified in 1976, numerous outbreaks of healthcare-associated Legionnaires' disease have been identified.[88–90] *Legionella* can colonize the water systems of large buildings and hospitals.[91] Hospital hot-water distribution systems and water-cooling towers for air conditioners have been implicated as sources of legionellosis outbreaks in patients.[92–109] Other water sources should also be considered as potential sources of contamination with pathogens, including ice machines, humidifiers, and areas where water accumulates and is maintained at the appropriate temperature.[110–120] Besides *Legionella*, the hospital water system or attached equipment can be a source of either an outbreak or pseudo-outbreak involving non-tuberculous *Mycobacterium*, fungi, and other nonfermenter gram-negative organisms (e.g., *Pseudomonas* spp., *Burkholderia* spp., *Stenotrophomonas* spp., *Acinetobacter* spp., *Ralstonia* spp., *Sphingomonas* spp., *Afipia felis*).[121–125] Whenever outbreaks of these organisms occur, the link to water reservoir should be on the priority list to investigate. An outbreak of Legionnaires' disease in hospitals in the fall of 2011 resulted in the elimination of water features from hospitals. While soothing and attractive, the risk of legionella contamination of these water reservoirs was high.

Inanimate Objects and Environmental Surfaces

Spread of resistant organisms has been linked to a contaminated environment or a fomite.[126] For example, *Clostridium difficile*, *Acinetobacter* species, VRE, and *S. aureus* have been cultured in the environment and in some cases linked to subsequent infections in patients.[127–130] Also, viral respiratory viruses have been found to contaminate fomites and have been a source of HAIs.[131]

Microbiologic Factors

The microbiologic factors that contribute to healthcare-associated transmission of infectious disease include virulence factors, the pathogen's ability to survive in the hospital environment, and antimicrobial resistance. While *S. aureus* and *Pseudomonas aeruginosa* are highly virulent pathogens, pathogens of relatively low virulence, such as *Acinetobacter* spp. can also cause HAIs in immunocompromised or critically ill patients. Many of these bacteria have characteristics (e.g., adhesions, resistance to disinfectants, spore formation) that facilitate their survival in the hospital environment so they can be transmitted to patients via thermometers, ventilators, urinary and vascular catheters, and other fomites. For example, microorganisms such as *Pseudomonas*, *Acinetobacter*, *Serratia*, and *Enterobacter* species can survive in hospital environments and can be relatively resistant to disinfectants.[132–135] These pathogens live in water and soil, where they are exposed to antimicrobial substances and may develop an inherent resistance to common antimicrobial agents. In another example, coagulase-negative staphylococci adhere to prosthetic devices and vascular catheters; this has become a major cause of bloodstream infections in patients with foreign bodies, such as prosthetic joints, valves, or permanent central venous catheters.

Extrinsic Factors

The extrinsic factors that contribute to HAIs include medical treatment and interventions, such as placement of invasive devices and operative procedures. The use of chemotherapy may cause immunosuppression and mucosal disruption and allow organisms a port of entry into the host. Equipment, such as dialysis machines or ventilators, may or may not be cleaned or maintained properly, and it may incorporate complicated reservoirs, filters, or mechanisms to prevent backflow—all features that can malfunction and lead to mechanisms of entry for organisms. Once organisms enter the body, infection may ensue. Nasogastric and endotracheal tubes have been shown to increase the risk of acquiring healthcare-associated pneumonia.[136] Although all of the previously mentioned extrinsic elements contribute to HAIs, the most frequently implicated extrinsic factors are surgical operations and invasive devices.

Another increasingly important factor is the use of antimicrobial agents that can lead to imbalances in the normal symbiotic relationship of organisms in the gastrointestinal (GI) tract, on the skin and other bodily surfaces. When the normal state of human endogenous flora is altered, selective pressure favors antimicrobial-resistant organisms. In fact, patients who received norfloxacin or fluconazole for GI tract decontamination during episodes of neutropenia have been shown to develop resistant organisms as a result of this type of selective pressure.[137,138] Organisms such as VRE can proliferate when broad-spectrum antimicrobials have killed the normal GI tract gram-negative and anaerobic flora.[139] Most importantly, *C. difficile* is an organism that emerges as a result of antibiotics and its disruption of the normal gastrointestinal balance.

ETIOLOGY AND TRANSMISSION

Endogenous versus Exogenous Organisms

There are four potential sources that can transmit microorganisms and lead to infections. Three of these are exogenous sources—fixed structures or the facilities of the hospital, devices or instruments used at the hospital, and healthcare personnel—and one is endogenous—the (source) patients. Exogenous infections are a direct result of pathogenic or non-pathogenic organisms directly acquired from the environment. These infections can be transmitted via the airborne route, through fomites or direct contact with carriers, by ingesting contaminated foods, or by parenteral inoculation. Endogenous source infections are divided into primary or secondary infections. Organisms that are a part of a patient's normal flora cause primary endogenous infections; organisms that become part of the patient's flora during the hospital stay cause secondary endogenous infections.[140]

Transmission of Microorganisms

Healthcare-associated transmission of organisms can occur by five routes: contact, droplet, airborne, common vehicle, and vector-borne.

Contact

The most frequent route that leads to the development of HAIs is direct or indirect contact.

Direct contact between body surfaces results in the transfer of microorganisms between a susceptible host and a colonized or infected individual. This type of transmission usually requires personal contact. It can occur between patient and HCP or between two patients, with one patient serving as the source of the infectious microorganisms and the other as a susceptible host. An example of such transmission would be transfer of organisms on the HCP's hands to another patient. In addition, HCPs are significant reservoirs of microorganisms. They can carry potentially infectious organisms on their skin, which can colonize their hands or nails. For example, increases in SSIs due to nasal carriage of *S. aureus* have been traced to HCPs who carry the organism.[141] Furthermore, outbreaks of *S. aureus*, *P. aeruginosa*, and *Candida* species infections have also occurred from colonized or infected HCPs.[141–148] HCPs and family members have been the sources of influenza, group A *streptococcus*, pertussis, and other organisms that have been transmitted nosocomially.[149–167]

Indirect-contact transmission involves contact of a susceptible host with a contaminated, usually inanimate object or fomites. Fomites can be medical devices (e.g., resuscitation bags, endotracheal tubes, suction devices, ventilators, endoscopes), instruments (e.g., rectal thermometers, blood pressure cuffs, stethoscopes), supplies such as dressings (especially in burn units), and toys (especially stuffed animals).[168] For example, Hughes and colleagues demonstrated that stuffed teddy bears used in a hand washing promotional campaign were heavily contaminated and colonized by organisms.[169]

Droplet

Organisms can be transmitted by respiratory droplets, especially respiratory viruses. Coughing, sneezing, and talking can produce droplets containing microorganisms that can be transmitted as far as 6 feet. Droplets are larger particles greater than 5 μm in size that are propelled a short distance through the air and can settle on the nasal mucosa, conjunctiva, or mouth of the host. Respiratory secretions may contain organisms that can be transmitted to HCPs or other patients while performing such tasks as suctioning, nebulization of medication, or bronchoscopy. Because these droplets are larger and heavier, they can contaminate inanimate surfaces as they land. Droplets transmit most respiratory viruses, pertussis, and meningococcus.[53]

Airborne

Organisms are also transmitted via air (airborne), by the spread of either the evaporated airborne droplets (5μm or smaller in size) that contain microorganisms or dust particles to which the infectious agent is attached. These small particles can remain suspended in the air for longer periods of time and can be propelled for greater distances than droplets. Transmission can occur in healthcare facilities that experience disruption of ventilation systems or inadequate respiratory protection.[170] *Mycobacterium tuberculosis* and viruses such as varicella, smallpox, and measles are transmitted in this fashion.[53]

Common Vehicle

Organisms can be transmitted extrinsically through common vehicles, such as food, water, medications, intravenous fluids, contaminated blood products, and medical equipment or devices. In health care, such infections can manifest as bloodstream infections or diarrhea. Contamination of medications mixed on wards is a common source of infection in the developing world; outbreaks of norovirus, for example, have been transmitted in this way.

Vector-Borne

Vector-borne transmission of microorganisms within hospitals or healthcare settings is unusual in developed countries. Vectors such as mosquitoes, flies, ticks, and others can transmit microorganisms if they are present in the facility.

MAJOR TYPES OF HAIs

HAIs can be classified according to the source and, more specifically, as being associated with either devices or procedures. In the United States, CDC/NHSN has grouped HAIs into 13 major categories to facilitate data analysis and comparison of data.[1] Four types of HAIs and their respective prevention guidelines, as issued by CDC, are discussed in further detail here, as they have been shown to cause the majority of HAIs.[4,171–173]

Urinary Tract Infection

A urinary tract infection is an infection involving any part of the urinary system, including the urethra, bladder, ureters, and kidney. UTIs are the most common type of HAI reported to the NHSN, accounting for more than 30% of HAIs in acute care hospitals and perhaps even more in long-term care facilities.[4] Among UTIs acquired in the hospitals, at least 75% are associated with a urinary catheter. Approximately 15% to 25% of hospitalized patients receive urinary catheters during their hospital stay. Urinary catheterization not only causes bacteriuria that commonly leads to unnecessary antimicrobial use, but the urinary drainage systems also serve as reservoirs for multidrug-resistant bacteria and as a source of transmission to other patients. Prolonged use of the urinary catheter is the most important risk factor for developing a catheter-associated urinary tract infection. Given this risk, catheters should be inserted only when clinically indicated and should be removed as soon as they are no longer needed. Owing to this practice, it is the rate of UTIs associated with indwelling urinary catheters that is commonly reported to national databases such as NHSN.[1]

The pathogens most frequently associated with CA-UTI in hospitals reporting to NHSN between 2006 and 2007 were *Escherichia coli* (21.4%) and *Candida* spp. (21.0%), followed by Enterococcus spp. (14.9%), *P. aeruginosa* (10.0%), *Klebsiella pneumoniae* (7.7%), and *Enterobacter* spp. (4.1%).[2] An increasing proportion of these organisms are becoming resistant to multiple antimicrobial agents.[174,175] CA-UTIs have been shown to be associated with increased morbidity, mortality, hospital cost, and length of stay.[176–178] Although morbidity and mortality from CA-UTIs are considered to be relatively low compared to other HAIs, such as central line–associated bloodstream infections and lower respiratory tract infections, the high prevalence of urinary catheter use leads to a large cumulative burden of infections. The CDC has estimated that as many as 139,000 hospital-onset, symptomatic CA-UTIs occurred in 2007, resulting in as much as $131 million in excess direct medical costs.[179]

In view of the magnitude of this problem, in the United States, the Department of Health and Human Services (DHHS) developed an action plan to prevent HAIs, with a 5-year national prevention target of a 25% decrease from baseline for CA-UTI rates as measured by the NHSN. The CDC updated its guideline for prevention of CA-UTI in 2009 to put greater emphasis on the following aspects of care:

1. Appropriate urinary catheter use
2. Proper techniques for urinary catheter insertion
3. Proper techniques for urinary catheter maintenance
4. Quality improvement programs
5. Administrative infrastructure
6. Surveillance

An estimated 17% to 69% of CA-UTIs may be preventable with these infection control measures.[180] In fact, with the introduction of more CA-UTI prevention efforts and improved general infection prevention strategies in recent years, a pervasive and sustained decline in the incidence rates of symptomatic UTI and asymptomatic bacteriuria was observed in all major adult ICU types reported under the prior National Nosocomial Infections Surveillance (NNIS) and current NHSN system.[179,180]

Bloodstream Infections

Healthcare-associated bloodstream infections (BSIs) develop in more than 250,000 patients in U.S. hospitals every year, with an estimated attributable mortality of 12% to 25% for each infection.[181–184] The marginal cost to the healthcare system is approximately $25,000 per episode.[185] Most BSIs result from a secondary source such as a postoperative wound or intra-abdominal infection, urinary tract infection, or pneumonia. Primary bacteremia occurs when the source is unrecognized; most of these cases are related to exposure to intravascular devices (IVDs).[184,186] A vast variety of IVDs are employed in modern medicine. For example, a catheter can be designated by the type of vessel it occupies; its intended life span; its site of insertion; its pathway from skin to vessel; its physical length; its function (dialysis, pressure measurement); or some special character of the catheter, each of which is associated with a different infection risk.[183]

The terminology used to define intravascular catheter-related infections can be confusing. The terms "catheter-related bloodstream infection" (CR-BSI) and "central line–associated bloodstream infection" (CLA-BSI) are most widely used in the literature, sometimes interchangeably. In fact, CR-BSI is a clinical definition that requires specific laboratory testing (e.g., quantitative blood cultures of differential time to positivity) to help identify the catheter as the source of the BSI. In contrast, the term CLA-BSI is typically used for surveillance purposes and is defined as a primary BSI in a patient who had a central line within the 48-hour period before the development of the BSI and is not bloodstream related to an infection at another site.[1]

The most common organisms causing healthcare-associated BSIs are coagulase-negative staphylococci (CoNS; 31% of isolates), *Staphylococcus aureus* (20%), enterococci (9%), and *Candida* species (9%). CoNS, *Pseudomonas* spp., *Enterobacter* spp., *Serratia* spp., and *Acinetobacter* spp. are more likely to cause infections in patients in ICUs. Gram-negative bacilli accounted for one-fifth of CLA-BSIs reported to CDC and the Surveillance and Control of Pathogens of Epidemiological Importance (SCOPE) database. The proportion of *S. aureus* isolates with methicillin resistance increased from 22% in 1995 to 57% in 2001. Similar to the trend observed in CA-UTIs, the proportion of healthcare-associated BSIs due to multidrug-resistant organisms is increasing in U.S. hospitals.[187]

With the implementation of different prevention strategies in a variety of clinical settings, studies have consistently shown a declining incidence rate of CLA-BSI in the United States.[188-191] In 2011, the CDC updated its guideline for prevention of intravascular catheter-related infections to emphasize performance improvement by implementing bundled prevention strategies[183]:

1. Educating and training healthcare personnel who insert and maintain catheters
2. Using maximal sterile barrier precautions during central venous catheter insertion
3. Using a greater than 0.5% strength chlorhexidine skin preparation with alcohol for antisepsis
4. Avoiding routine replacement of central venous catheters as a strategy to prevent infection
5. Using antiseptic/antibiotic-impregnated short-term central venous catheters and chlorhexidine-impregnated sponge dressings if the rate of infection is not decreasing despite adherence to the other strategies

The CDC guideline also emphasizes the importance of documenting and reporting rates of compliance with all components of the bundle as benchmarks for quality and performance improvement.[183] Since its publication, other, less expensive strategies such as chlorhexidine bathing have emerged as promising approaches.[192-195]

Healthcare-Associated Pneumonia and Ventilator-Associated Pneumonia

Healthcare-associated pneumonia (HCAP) is the leading cause of death among hospitalized patients.[196,197] Pneumonia is classified as HCAP when it occurs in any patient who (1) was hospitalized in an acute care hospital for 2 or more days within 90 days of the infection; (2) resides in a nursing home or long-term care facility; (3) received home intravenous antimicrobial therapy, chemotherapy, or home wound care within the past 30 days of the current infection; or (4) attended a hospital or hemodialysis clinic. HCAP may be further categorized as either early onset, in which pneumonia occurs during the first 4 days of hospitalization, and late onset, in which the disease occurs at least 4 days after admission.[1] HCAP typically increases the length of ICU stay from 5 to 7 days.[198]

Ventilator-associated pneumonia (VAP) arises in patients who have a device to assist or control respiration continuously through endotracheal tube or tracheostomy. This device must be present within the 48-hour period before the onset of infection.[1] A meta-analysis demonstrated that the incidence of VAP among patients receiving mechanical ventilation was 9.7% (95% CI: 7.0 –12.5) and incidence among patients in medical ICUs was 17.0% (95% CI: 5.9–28.0).[198] The additional cost for treating VAP was as high as $13,467 (in the year 2003).[198]

When microorganisms enter into and colonize the lower respiratory tract, HCAP can develop.[197] Under suitable circumstances, the pathogen can invade the mucosal and other host defenses, leading to disease.[197] Aspiration of oropharyngeal secretions plays an important role for developing HCAP. Any conditions that precipitate, aggravate, or influence the volume or severity of aspiration can contribute higher risk for infection—for example, supine position, swallowing difficulty, gastric overextension, depressed sensorium, and enteral feeding.[197,199,200] Proton pump inhibitors (PPIs), which are commonly used among hospitalized patients for stress ulcer prophylaxis, may increase the risk of pneumonia.[201-206] One hypothesis suggests that this agent decreases gastric acidity, an innate aspect of immunity, and then produces bacterial overgrowth.[207] Oropharyngeal colonization with multidrug-resistant organisms (MDROs) increases risk of pulmonary infection with these organisms. Risk factors for infection with MDROs have been extensively studied and include the following:

- Receiving antimicrobial treatment within the preceding 90 days[197,208-212]
- Current hospitalization of at least 5 days
- Previous hospitalization in the preceding 90 days for at least 2 days
- Immunosuppressive state
- High frequency of antimicrobial resistance in the community or in the specific unit
- The presence of risk factors for HCAP
- Residence in a nursing home or extended care facility
- Home infusion therapy (including antibiotics)
- Chronic dialysis within 30 days
- Home wound care
- A family member with multidrug-resistant pathogen[197]

Quasi-experimental studies have correlated the initiation of treatment with an inadequate spectrum of antimicrobial agent with increased mortality in HCAP/VAP patients.[213-216]

Intubation is the single most important risk factor: it increases the risk of developing pneumonia and VAP at least sixfold and increases mortality by 55%.[197,217,218] Once the first line of host defenses is breached by intubation and placement of an endotracheal tube, patients tend to aspirate organisms that colonize the oropharynx or upper gastrointestinal tract. Risk factors for developing VAP may be divided into those that can be modified and those that cannot be modified.[197] Nonmodifiable risk factors include advanced age, male gender, preexisting pulmonary disease, and severe underlying illness.[197,219-221] Modifiable risk factors include contaminated ventilator circuits, an endotracheal cuff with low pressure, multiple patient transfers, supine position of the patient, and gastric overextension.[197,220,221]

HCAP and VAP are mostly commonly caused by bacteria (multiple organisms), but can also be caused by fungi and viruses.[197] The most likely causative organism can be altered by the host's immune status.[197] The most common pathogens causing HCAP are *S. aureus*, *Streptococcus pneumoniae*, *P. aeruginosa*, and *Haemophilus influenzae*.[208,209,211,222,223] The pathogens causing early-onset HCAP resemble those organisms associated with community-acquired pneumonia, such as *S. pneumoniae*, *Moraxella catarrhalis*, and *H. influenzae*. Similarly, gram-negative bacilli or *S. aureus*, including MRSA, fungi, and *Legionella* spp., occur in late-onset HCAP.[1] Worldwide, the pathogens causing VAP are predominately gram negative, consisting of *P. aeruginosa*, *Acinetobacter baumannii*, and *Klebsiella* spp.[224-234] Compared with patients having HCAP, the prevalence of gram-negative pathogens is higher among VAP patients, while *S. aureus* is more common in patients with HCAP.[235] Respiratory viruses can cause pneumonia at any time of hospitalization and are likely underappreciated as a cause of HCAP and VAP.[1] HCAP among immunocompromised hosts can be caused by inhalation of aerosols or droplets contaminated with *Legionella* species, *Aspergillus* species and other molds, respiratory syncytial virus (RSV), influenza virus, and other respiratory viruses.[236-241]

Outbreaks of HCAP/VAP have been documented in numerous healthcare settings. Organisms associated with these outbreaks include influenza,[242-245] RSV,[246-249] human metapneumovirus,[250,251] adenovirus,[252] measles,[253] herpes simplex virus (HSV),[254] *P. aeruginosa*,[255-259] *A. baummannii*,[260-262] *Enterobacter cloacae*,[263,264] *K. pneumoniae*,[265,266] *B. cepacia*,[267,268] *Serratia marcescens*,[269] *M. catarrhalis*,[270] *Neisseria meningitides*,[271,272] *Flavobacterium meningosepticum*,[273] *S. aureus*,[257,274-276] *S. pneumoniae*,[277,278] *Legionella* spp.,[95,97,108,115,120,279-286] and *Pneumocystis jerovecii*.[287-289] Generally, in the setting of problems with ventilation or construction, *Aspergillus* spp. and *Mycobacterium tuberculosis* can also be associated with clusters in healthcare facilities (as discussed later in this chapter). The bacterial pathogens that cause HCAP or VAP may be multidrug resistant; in quasi-experimental studies, when an inadequate spectrum of antimicrobial agent was initiated as empiric therapy for HCAP/VAP, the mortality was increased.[213-216]

Many interventions to decrease HCAP/VAP have been investigated. In 2003, CDC published "Guidelines for Preventing Health Care–Associated Pneumonia." These guidelines outline the importance of (1) environmental controls to prevented invasive pulmonary aspergillosis and Legionellosis,

(2) standard precautions, (3) immunizations, (4) measures to prevent aspiration, and (5) surveillance.[221]

In 2008, Society for Hospital Epidemiology of America (SHEA) and Infectious Diseases Society of America (IDSA) published "Strategies to Prevent Ventilator-Associated Pneumonia in Acute Care Hospitals" in 2008.[290] To prevent VAP, these guidelines recommended interventions to decrease aspiration of secretions, including raising the head of bed, avoiding gastric overdistension, avoiding unintended extubation and reintubation, using a cuffed endotracheal tube with in-line or subglottic suctioning, and maintaining an endotracheal cuff pressure of at least 20 cm H_2O.[290] Furthermore, orotracheal intubation is preferable to nasotracheal intubation, as the latter may increase risk of sinusitis and VAP.[290] Three meta-analyses demonstrated the benefits of performing oral decontamination with antiseptic solution and favored chlorhexidine as the antiseptic of choice, although the impact was seen primarily in patients in cardiosurgical intensive care units.[291,292] However, an impact on mortality has not been demonstrated from this intervention.[291,293] It remains a standard of care to perform regular oral care with an antiseptic solution in mechanically ventilated patients.[290]

Surveillance for HCAP and VAP and process measures should be conducted in patients deemed at high risk for infection. The use of standard definitions is an important component of diagnosis of VAP, especially in ICU patients who have many risks for fever and pulmonary infiltrates. The VAP rate should be calculated by dividing the number of VAP cases by the number of ventilator-days.

Surgical Site Infection

Surgical site infection causes approximately one-fourth of all HAIs, making it a major HAI especially among surgical patients. In the United States, SSI is the second or third most frequent HAI, responsible for 29% of all HAIs and 14% of all healthcare-associated adverse events.[180] As many as 5% of surgical patients develop SSIs.[294] This rate may be higher in patients cared for in developing countries. SSIs cause significant morbidity and account for 55% of all the extra hospital days attributed to HAIs.[295] Such infections increase length of hospital stay, readmission rates, and medical costs.[296–305] Patients with an SSI have a 2 to 11 times higher risk of death, compared to surgical patients without an SSI.[306] These numbers highlight the tremendous burden of these infections and the importance of preventing them. Because of the frequency, morbidity, mortality, and economic burden of these infections, SSIs are given the high priority for surveillance.

The definition of an SSI has been debated for years. For the purposes of surveillance, a reasonable definition should be highly sensitive but must balance specificity. It should be applied systematically and used to analyze rates, examine risk factors, develop prevention strategies, and assess trends over time. Ideally, the definition chosen should remain unchanged to facilitate comparisons of data through the years and to determine whether interventions implemented reduce these rates. In 1992, a consensus group that included CDC, SHEA, and the Surgical Infection Society (SIS) modified how SSI was defined and changed the name from "surgical wound infection" to "surgical site infection."[307,308] The definition for NHSN is currently being revised.

SSIs are divided into incisional and organ-space SSIs. Incisional SSIs are further classified as involving only the skin and subcutaneous tissue (superficial incisional SSIs) or involving deep soft tissues of the incision (deep incisional SSIs). Superficial infections require that at least one of the following occur within 30 days of the operation[309]:

- Pus appears from the incision
- Organisms are isolated aseptically from cultured fluid or tissue
- At least one of the following signs and symptoms: pain or tenderness, localized swelling, redness, or heat when the surgeon deliberately opens the surgical incision
- The surgeon or attending physician diagnoses the infection

SSI secondary to prosthetic devices or foreign body can occur up to one year after the operation.

Only 33% to 67% of infected wounds are cultured, limiting the use of microbiologic case finding as a single case-finding strategy.[310] Direct inoculation is the most common pathway by which organisms cause infection. Endogenous flora can cause infections, especially those involving *S. aureus* (including MRSA). Carriers of *S. aureus* have a 2- to 14-fold increased risk of infection.[311,312] Approximately 85% of *S. aureus* infections are attributable to a carrier state, a fact that has led to the development of decolonization strategies including the use of intranasal mupirocin and chlorhexidine bathing.[312,313] Additionally, SSIs may result from exogenous sources—for example, a carrier healthcare worker (e.g., *S. aureus* and group A streptococci) contaminated equipment, and a defect in the ventilation system of the operative theater.[149,314–317] In those cases, the most common causes of SSI are *S. aureus,* enterococci, and coagulase-negative staphylococci. However, the infecting organisms vary according to the site of the surgical

Table 14-4	Surgical Site (Wound) Classification		
Wound Class	**Type of Wound**	**Definition**	**Example**
I	Clean	• Uninfected operative wound • No inflammation is encountered • No involvement of the respiratory, alimentary, genital, or uninfected urinary tract • Closed and, if necessary, drained with closed drainage • Operative incisional wounds that follow nonpenetrating (blunt) trauma (those meeting the criteria)	• Breast surgery • Vascular surgery (which is not infected) • Non-infected eye surgery • Splenectomy • Most orthopedic surgery • Lymph node biopsy/excision • Elective cesarean section with no premature rupture of membranes
II	Clean-contaminated	• Operative wound that enters the respiratory, alimentary, genital, or urinary tract under controlled conditions without unusual contamination • No evidence of infection or major break in technique	• GI surgery, including laparoscopy • Cholecystectomy • Vaginal hysterectomy • Head and neck surgery
III	Contaminated	• Open, fresh, accidental wounds • Operations with major breaks in sterile technique	• Open cardiac massage • Gross spillage from the gastrointestinal tract • Incisions involving acute inflammation
IV	Dirty/infected	• Old traumatic wounds with retained devitalized tissue involving an existing clinical infection or perforated viscus	• Debridement of infectious tissue

Adapted from Berard F, Gandon J. Postoperative wound infections: the influence of ultraviolet irradiation of the operating room and of various other factors. *Ann Surg.* 1964;160(suppl 2):1–192.

incision.[309,318] For operations that involve only skin or a clean wound, the most common pathogens are the skin flora (e.g., *S. aureus,* coagulase-negative staphylococci), while gram-negative and anaerobic organisms are often found in patients who undergo operations that involve the bowel, such as colon surgery.[309] **Table 14-4** shows the classification of surgical site infections.

Outbreaks of SSIs are rarely associated with HCPs (**Table 14-5**). For example, *S. pyogenes* (group A streptococci) is occasionally reported to cause SSIs, most commonly spread from asymptomatic individuals including HCPs.[149–158,320,321] In this case a single case should prompt increased surveillance and some investigation. Similarly, HCPs can be carriers of *S. aureus* and an investigation of HCP is indicated when fingerprinting of strains reveals they are clonal and suggests a single source. Outbreaks of *P. aeruginosa* have been caused by surgical staffs with onychomycosis.[144,147]

Risk factors that increase a patient's risk of developing an SSI can be categorized as intrinsic (patient related) or extrinsic (operation-related).[306] The patient's risk may increase if he or she has more than one risk factor. Patient characteristics, including the underlying medical condition(s) and the severity of the underlying disease, can increase the risk of developing an SSI. To date, very few controlled studies have examined the relative importance of these risk factors. Those additional risk factors that definitely increase the risk of developing an SSI include morbid obesity, smoking, old age, diabetes mellitus, a prolonged preoperative hospital stay, or a preoperative infection.[83,306,309,329–331] Several studies have shown that patients who are malnourished, have low albumin, have cancer, or are receiving immunosuppressive therapy are at increased risk of developing an SSI.[306,332–334] Unfortunately, it is frequently difficult to ameliorate these risks. If the patient's surgery is not urgent, and the health condition, such as diabetes, can be controlled or the patient surgery can be delayed, then a delay until the patient's health improves can improve his or her outcome.

Certain practices and procedures that occur in the operating room or during the perioperative period can increase the risk of SSI. In some cases, HCPs can alter their practices and potentially the patient's outcome. Those surgical and environmental factors that may

Table 14-5	Examples of Outbreaks of SSIs: Relationships Between Organisms and Sources	
Organisms	**Sources**	**Reference**
S. pyogenes	HCP (throat, vaginal, rectal, and skin colonization)	149–158, 320, 321
P. aeruginosa	HCP with onychomycosis	144, 147
MRSA	HCP (nasal, sinus, skin colonization)	145, 146
S. epidemidis	HCP	322
R. bronchialis	HCP's dog with fingernail contamination	323
P. mirabilis	Contaminated instruments	314
P. aeruginosa	Contaminated automated equipment	324
Aspergillus spp.	Defect in ventilation system of operating rooms	315
Nontuberculous mycobacterium	Contaminated instruments	316, 325
Nontuberculous mycobacterium	Contaminated skin marking	326, 327
Legionella spp.	Wound contaminated with tap water in postoperative period	328

alter the patient's risk of developing an SSI include a wound classified as contaminated or dirty (Table 14-4), a surgical procedure involving the abdomen, a long operative time, hair removal by razor (especially the night before surgery, so that preoperative colonization occurs), multiple surgical procedures, poor hemostasis during the procedure with blood loss and the need for transfusions, prolonged presence of drains, a less-skilled or inexperienced surgeon, and a low intraoperative body temperature.[335–341] Risk factors for SSIs are summarized in **Table 14-6**.

One of the most important interventions—if not the most important single intervention—is the appropriate use and timing of perioperative antimicrobial prophylaxis.[353] Pathogens that infect surgical sites during surgical procedures can be acquired from the patient, the hospital environment, or HCPs. The patient's endogenous flora are responsible for most infections. In surgical procedures involving the gastrointestinal, respiratory, genital, and urinary tracts, antimicrobial prophylaxis has proved efficacious in reducing SSIs. For many cardiac, neurosurgical, and orthopedic procedures, prophylaxis decreases the risk of developing an SSI. For most clean surgical procedures, antimicrobial prophylaxis remains controversial, although experts suggest giving patients a prophylactic antimicrobial agent when a foreign-body implant is inserted or if an infection occurring in a clean procedure would be associated with severe or life-threatening consequences (e.g., valve replacement).[306] Finally, if the perioperative antimicrobial agent is administered after the incision, the risk of an SSI increases sixfold above the risk when it is administered 30 minutes to 1 hour (2 hours is allowed

Table 14-6	Summary of Risk Factors for Surgical Site Infections[83,306,309,329–351]		
Patient Related		**Operation Related**	
Modifiable	**Nonmodifiable**		
• Diabetes, poor glucose control • Obesity • Smoking • Immunosuppressive agents • Malnutrition • Low albumin • Anemia • HIV (CD4 < 200/mm^3) • S. aureus colonization • Poor oral hygiene • Preoperative hospital stay • Preoperative infection • Poor hemostasis	• Age • ASA* score	• Wound class • Hair-removal • Preoperative infections • Operative time • Open surgery (compared to laparoscopic surgery) • Surgeon skill • Hypoxia • Hypothermia • Blood transfusion • Prolonged presence of a drain • Intra-operative administered fraction of inspired oxygen[309]	
*ASA: American Society of Anesthesiologists.			

for vancomycin and fluoroquinolones) before the incision.[306] Antimicrobial prophylaxis should be stopped within 24 hours after the surgery for most procedures.[306]

The patient's skin is a major source of intra-operative contamination and organisms. Resident flora such as coagulase-negative staphylococci can be found in the deeper layers of the dermis; hence, cleaning and disinfecting skin before operation by antiseptic reduces the risk of SSIs. A recent randomized study demonstrated the benefit of using a chlorhexidine-alcohol based preparation for skin antisepsis over povidone-iodine in patients undergoing clean-contaminated operations.[354]

Preoperative cleaning of the operative team's hands is equally important and is performed by the operative team. Recent studies have demonstrated that the time-consuming hand scrubbing with brushes for 10 minutes did not decrease SSI rate and that a shorter scrub or hand rubbing by aqueous alcohol solutions is adequate.[355] Scrubbing with brushes may damage the HCP's skin and result in increased shedding of bacteria.[356]

The operating facilities should be designed to promote best cleaning and disinfection practices, provide appropriate air handling, and assure that HCPs can follow best practices. The operating rooms should have a semi-sterile and sterile core, and the operating room itself must have higher pressure than the outside corridor (positive pressure). The doors to the operating room suite should remain closed at all times and the traffic in the room should be minimized.[357] Pass-throughs should be designed to minimize the traffic even further. Most exogenous wound contamination occurs during the operation through contact or airborne transmission of organisms; hence, events occurring after the operation (e.g., ward dressings and isolation techniques) are less likely to contribute to SSIs.

Finally, the importance of transparency and sharing SSI rates with surgeons, operating room staff, and leadership cannot be overemphasized. Reporting of surgeon-specific SSI rates can also have a role, although their use for credentialing purposes should be carefully considered. Programs that perform surveillance for SSIs may reduce these rates as much as 35% by reporting the rates associated with specific surgical teams.[308] To save resources, some programs have adopted methods that group the entire surgical population into patients who are at a higher or lower risk of developing SSIs. In risk stratification, procedures are classified and reported using a risk index. The NNIS risk index—the most commonly used stratification process—groups procedures into three categories.[358]

One of the major challenges in infection prevention and control is deciding when to include postdischarge surveillance for detecting SSIs. This strategy is important, as these infections can develop after the patient has been discharged home. Routine surveillance processes may not capture such SSIs (**Table 14-7**).[310,358-363] Thus surveying surgeons' offices to monitor each patient for a

Table 14-7	Percentage of SSIs Detected After Hospital Discharge	
Author (Year)	**Patient Population**	**SSIs Detected After Discharged (%)**
Roy (1994)[360]; Avato (2002)[364]; Noman (2011)[365]	Coronary artery bypass surgery	52–95
Mannian (2011)[347]	Cardiothoracic	61
Wójkowska-Mach (2008)[366]	Total knee or hip arthroplasty	59
Huotari (2006)[367]	Orthopedic surgery	28–90
Huenger (2005)[368]	Hip arthroplasty	25
Friedman (2001)[369]	Total knee arthroplasty	72
Sands (1996)[359]	Non-obstetrical	84
Simchen (1992)[370]	Herniography	51
Hulton (1992)[371]; Mitt (2005)[372]; Cardoso del Monte (2010)[373]	Cesarean section	42–95.4
Weigelt (1992)[374]	General surgery	35
Law (1990)[375]	Elective procedures	59
Reimer (1987)[376]; Manian (1990)[256]; Olson (1990)[334]	All procedures	2–73.7
Oliveira (2004)[378]; Prospero (2006)[379]; Bilimoria (2010)[363]	Appendectomy	71
Brown (1987)[362]	Major procedures	46

defined period after his or her surgery should be incorporated into surveillance strategies. Telephone surveys and questionnaires sent to patients and/or physicians have been used as well. Which method provides the most accurate data has not yet been determined.[308] While more difficult to perform, surveys that cover the postdischarge time period are important, as those SSIs that develop after either clean or clean-contaminated procedures are the most likely to occur after hospital discharge.

EPIDEMIOLOGICALLY IMPORTANT PATHOGENS AND EMERGING PATHOGENS

Bacteria

Methicillin-Resistant Staphylococcus aureus

Methicillin-resistant *Staphylococcus aureus* is resistant to many beta-lactam antibiotics.[381] Resistance to methicillin and other semi-synthetic penicillins was identified soon after this class of antibiotic was introduced into clinical care in the 1960s.[382] The first outbreak of MRSA in the United States was documented in late 1960s[42]; since then, MRSA organisms have become common gram-positive organisms, responsible for HAIs in many countries around the world.[383–388] The prevalence of MRSA varies in different parts of the world, however, and reflects the approach to antimicrobial stewardship and infection prevention practices.[389,390] Furthermore, MRSA has emerged in several continents as a zoonotic infection, and persons who contact animals may at increased risk for MRSA acquisition as compared to the general population.[391–395]

Infections with MRSA are associated with morbidity and mortality. Patients with MRSA bacteremia have higher mortality rate compare with patients with methicillin-sensitive *S. aureus* bacteremia.[396,397] However, this higher mortality rate may not result from increased virulence of resistant strains, but rather from other factors, including delays in the initiation of effective antimicrobial treatment, less-effective antimicrobial treatment, and higher severity of underlying illness among persons with antimicrobial-resistant strains.[397]

Traditionally MRSA was considered to be a healthcare-associated organism, but in the 1990s it was reported to be transmitted in previously healthy patients without a history of hospitalization—essentially members of the community.[398,399] The so-called community-associated MRSA (CA-MRSA) strains were less frequently resistant to other antibiotics than healthcare-associated MRSA strains (HA-MRSA).[382]

Both strains contain a gene coding for methicillin resistance, the *mec-A* gene. The *mec-A* gene is located on a mobile genetic element called the staphylococcal chromosome cassette (SCC mec); this cassette differs between CA-MRSA and HA-MRSA strains.[382] In addition, CA-MRSA strains commonly carry a gene coding for a toxin, with the most frequently discussed being the Panton-Valentine leukocidin (PVL) toxin that causes skin and soft-tissue necrosis.[382] Furthermore, phenotypically MRSA organisms are divided into eight distinct clusters identified by pulsed-field gel electrophoresis—that is, USA 100 through USA 800.[382] Strains USA 300 and USA 400 are classified as "community associated," and the others are classified as HA-MRSA.[400] The USA 300 strain was first reported in the United States and later spread to other parts of the world.[401,402] Recent epidemiologic studies indicate that USA 300 (HR-MRSA) strains have entered into healthcare facilities and are commonly transmitted to patients as an HAI.[403,404]

Thus the original designation of healthcare- versus community-associated MRSA is no longer as useful for differentiating the source of acquisition. For the purpose of surveillance, SHEA has proposed definitions that use time-based elements instead.[397] The terms "hospital-onset" and "community-onset" MRSA have been identified based on the time of specimen collection.[397] If MRSA is identified from a specimen obtained after the third day of hospitalization, this isolate is classified as "hospital-onset MRSA." Isolates identified before the third day of a patient's hospitalization are classified as "community-onset MRSA."[397]

S. aureus has a unique epidemiology that drives some of the prevention practices in healthcare settings. The nares and skin are the ecologic niches of the organism.[405,406] Controversy exists on whether the nares alone or the nares with additional sites (throat, perirectal, umbilical, or axilla/groin) are needed to determine colonization. Nonetheless, all agree that higher rates of nasal colonization with MRSA are seen in patients with diabetes mellitus, patients receiving hemodialysis, HIV-infected patients, and intravenous drug users.[407] MRSA colonization is the most important risk factor for infection[408–410]; the risk of developing an infection within 18 months after detection of MRSA colonization is as high as 29%.[411] Other risk factors include antimicrobial use, prolonged hospitalization, recent hospitalization or surgery, presence of foreign bodies, residence in a long-term facility, and frequent contact with the healthcare system or HCPs.[397,412–417] Colonization pressure or the amount of a resistant organism on the unit is also an independent risk factor for MRSA acquisition.[418–420]

Transmission of MRSA is associated with a complex web of events. First, multiple sites harbor the organism; thus, in a person with nasal colonization, the hands, fingers, and skin are also commonly colonized with the same MRSA strain.[421,422] Second, MRSA can spread by the contaminated HCP's hands after being acquired by direct contact with the MRSA-colonized patient or the MRSA-contaminated environment.[423,424] Third, HCPs are rarely the source of MRSA. A meta-analysis demonstrated prevalence of nasal colonization among HCPs was 4.6% (95% CI: 1.0–8.2%),[425] yet the number of outbreaks reported where HCPs were the source of MRSA is very small.[425–427] Several CA-MRSA outbreaks in healthcare settings have been reported in which healthy HCPs have been sickened.[428–442] Most of these outbreaks occurred in neonatal and maternal units.

The increased use of vancomycin to treat MRSA has contributed to the emergence of vancomycin-resistant organisms such as VRE and vancomycin (or glycopeptide)-intermediate *S. aureus* (VISA/GISA). GISA is thought to result from prolonged use of a glycopeptide antibiotic that leads to changes in cell-wall synthesis and decreases affinity for agents such as vancomycin. In contrast, vancomycin-resistant *S. aureus* (VRSA) strains have resulted from the acquisition of genetic material from enterococci, not antimicrobial pressure.[443–445] In the seven cases of VRSA were identified in the United States between 2002 and 2006, all of the patients had a history of prior MRSA and enterococcal infection/colonization.[446] Risk factors for VRSA include prior MRSA infection/colonization and antecedent vancomycin use.[447–449]

MRSA is a major problem globally and in most healthcare systems in North America.[450] Several approaches for its prevention have been developed and have proved successful, yet many issues remain unresolved.[312] Basic infection prevention measures such as hand hygiene, transmission-based precautions, and environmental cleaning should be applied to patients with MRSA colonization or infection. These patients should also be placed on contact precautions.[53] The duration of contact precautions necessary for patients with MRSA is disputed.[397] The patient's environment should have adequate cleaning and disinfection with U.S. Environmental Protection Agency (EPA)-registered hospital disinfectants. A hand hygiene compliance program and antimicrobial control program should be implemented.

Active surveillance screening for MRSA in high-risk (or sometimes all) patients is advocated by some sources.[451,452] Others advocate universal screening of asymptomatic patients and isolation of those who grow the organism, an approach known as the "search and isolate" strategy. This strategy seems to be more useful in an outbreak setting and for patients within certain high-risk groups.[453–459] The role of universal screening is one of the most controversial issues and has not yet been determined.[397,451,452,460–462] However, several recent U.S. studies do support the widespread use of active screening and decolonization with chlorhexidine in areas where MRSA is endemic.[451,452] In North America, screening of HCPs for MRSA should be considered in an outbreak setting if they are epidemiologically linked to a cluster of MRSA infections.[397]

Europeans have adapted a variety of approaches to preventing MRSA. The French have demonstrated the impact of a countrywide hand hygiene campaign on MRSA nationally and shown dramatic decreases in infection rates.[463] The Netherlands, a country with a low incidence of MRSA, has successfully controlled MRSA transmission by implementing a national "search-and-destroy" policy.[464] This policy moves beyond patient screening and contact isolation until the cultures are MRSA negative, and includes HCP screening, patient and HCP decolonization, ward closure, and intensive environmental cleaning.[464–466] The benefit of this policy in other countries with higher prevalence and different settings has not demonstrated.

HCPs should be educated about MRSA and preventive measures. Furthermore, patients and their family should be advised how to decrease spreading of the resistant organisms.

Vancomycin-Resistant Enterococcus

VRE is another emerging pathogen that is causing an increasing proportion of healthcare-associated enterococcal infections. Two of these two species are primary human pathogens: *E. faecalis* and *E. faecium* (most VRE are *E. faecium*).[467]

Enterococci are normal inhabitants of the GI tract and cause healthcare-associated urinary tract, bloodstream, wound, and intra-abdominal infections. Although less virulent than *S. aureus*, these bacteria are intrinsically resistant to multiple antimicrobial agents and can cause morbidity and mortality, especially in immunocompromised patients.[468–470] VRE is the most common cause of bacteremia in bone marrow and stem cell recipients in early post-transplant period (days 4–10).[470] This organism is associated with increased morbidity in such patients, and a meta-analysis demonstrated that VRE bacteremia increases mortality compared to bacteremia caused by vancomycin-sensitive enterococci.[471]

VRE strains were first described in the 1980s and became a significant healthcare problem in the 1990s.[472–474] Like many resistant organisms, these strains have become disseminated or emerged in a variety of settings.[475–509] The Clinical and Laboratory Standards Institute has defined the minimal inhibitory concentration (MIC) of vancomycin in any enterococci strains of 32 µg/mL as resistant to vancomycin.[510] Patients with serious underlying illnesses who have received multiple antimicrobial agents, including vancomycin, cephalosporins, and antianaerobic drugs, and who are colonized with VRE are at risk for developing a clinically significant VRE infection.[475,511–514] Colonization pressure is another important risk factor, defined as the proportion of VRE-colonized patients within a time-period; however, the definition of colonization pressure has varied among studies.[515–519] Other risk factors for infection include having an operation or a central line, characteristics of the patient's hospitalization (duration, ICU, transplant or oncology service admission, nursery), and contamination of the environment (proximity to a VRE-colonized patient, contaminated equipment, or supplies).[475–477,487,520–523]

Colonization with VRE may persist for long periods of time.[524] The organism has a predilection to contaminate the environment, so transmission of VRE can occur via direct contact with colonized patients or by indirect contact with HCPs, environmental surfaces, or inanimate objects.[525–527] Enterococci can persist on dry inanimate surfaces for as long as 4 months.[528]

One of the primary reasons that VRE is worrisome is that VRE can transfer vancomycin- or glycopeptide-resistance genes to other bacteria.[443,467] In 1992, VRSA was shown to develop in vitro by transfer of van A gene from *E. faecalis* to *S. aureus*, and the first clinical infection with VRSA was reported in 2002.[529,530]

Prevention measures are directed to the known sources of the organism and include the use and compliance with hand hygiene. Contact precautions should be applied for patients with VRE colonization/infection. Other preventive measures include cohorting of colonized patients, antimicrobial stewardship, and cleaning if contaminated environment and supplies.[513,531] Active surveillance culture may be performed in high-risk patients, with stool, rectal, or perirectal swabs generally being used for VRE detection.[532]

Clostridium difficile

Clostridium difficile infection (CDI) is a major healthcare-associated disease that has emerged internationally.[533,534] *C. difficile* bacteria colonize the intestinal tract in 1% to 3% of the normal population and cause disease by disrupting normal flora subsequent to antimicrobial therapy.[534,535] *C. difficile* is a spore-forming gram-positive bacterium that produces two important toxins: toxin A (enterotoxin) and toxin B (cytotoxin).[536,537] Although most pathogenic strains of *C. difficile* produce both toxins, 7% to 10% produce only toxin B—the toxin that is essential for virulence.[536,537] The primary mode of transmission is person-to-person spread through the fecal–oral route, although contamination of the environment is important for indirect transmission within hospitals and other healthcare settings.[538] The incubation period of CDI remains uncertain but has been estimated to be a median of 2–3 days after exposure to *C. difficile*.[538,539]

C. difficile was first identified as a pathogen associated with antimicrobial-associated diarrhea in 1978.[540] In the early years, its association with antibiotics was established and the common culprit agents were clindamycin, followed by ampicillin.[540] In the 1980s, cephalosporins superseded these agents as the most commonly implicated antibiotics linked to CDI.[540] Until 2003, *C. difficile* was viewed as an "annoyance"; in that year, however, the hypervirulence strain BI/NAP1/027 emerged and became associated with disease that was more severe, more refractory to standard therapy, and more likely to relapse.[533,534,540,541] The presumed virulence factor results from a deletion within the gene responsible for downregulation of toxin production.[533,534,540,541] This strain is strongly associated with use of fluoroquinolones.[541–543] The designations of this strain are based on different methods for strain typing: by its pulsed-field gel electrophoresis (PFGE) pattern, NAP1 (for North American PFGE type 1); by its restriction endonuclease analysis pattern, BI; and by its PCR ribotype designation, 027 strain.[534,538] This strain was first reported in North America, but has since spread to Europe and the rest of the world.[541,544–558] In a frightening twist, this epidemic strain has emerged in low-risk populations living in the community without extensive antibiotic or healthcare exposure.[559]

Risk factors for CDI include antimicrobial use, advanced age, prior hospitalization, severe underlying disease, immune suppression, use of feeding tubes, gastrointestinal surgery, chemotherapy, and use of proton pump inhibitors.[386,535,543,554,560–562] However, severe disease can occur in persons without established risk factor.[563] Although the antimicrobial agents that predispose individuals to CDI are typically fluoroquinolones, clindamycin, cephalosporins, and carbapenems, any antimicrobial agents can facilitate CDI—including vancomycin, the agent commonly used to treat the infection.[540,541,554,564,565] The spectrum of disease varies from asymptomatic, mild diarrhea to a fulminant colitis that may require a colectomy to death from toxic megacolon and sepsis.[537,561,566] Significant risk factors for mortality include advanced age and increasing lactate levels.[537,567,568] The gold standard for diagnosis CDI is cell culture, followed by identification of the toxogenic material isolated, but it is time-consuming process.[363] Polymerase chain reaction (PCR) testing for *C. difficile* and its toxins is increasing in popularity. A meta-analysis demonstrated that the mean sensitivity of PCR for diagnosing CDI was 90% (95% CI: 88–91%) and the specificity was 96% (95% CI: 96–97%).[569] Even so, many laboratories use older, less sensitive techniques and the method of diagnosis may be important for maximal case identification.

Minimizing exposures and preventable risk factors can prevent healthcare-associated *C. difficile* infection. In general, the approach combines antimicrobial stewardship with sound infection prevention practices.[570] Ways in which patients can acquire *C. difficile* during hospital stay include contact with contaminated HCPs' hands, medical equipment, and environmental surfaces, or direct contact with a patient with CDI. One published study demonstrated that *C. difficile* could be cultured from the hands and stools of asymptomatic patients with *C. difficile* colonization.[571] The bacteria can also easily contaminate the environment.[130,572] The vegetative forms of *C. difficile* can survive for 15 minutes on dry surfaces and up to 6 hours on moist surfaces.[130] Their spores can survive for as long as 5 months on environmental surfaces and are resistant to commonly used cleaning agents.[573] Hypochlorite-based solution is recommended for cleaning the environment because of its activity against the spore form.[538] Hand washing is preferred over alcohol hand hygiene solution in the setting of a CDI outbreak because alcohol has limited activity toward *C. difficile* spores.[538] However, no study has demonstrated a relationship between the increasing consumption of alcohol-based hand hygiene product and the incidence of CDI.[574–576] Patients with CDI should be isolated using contact precautions, but the duration of such isolation is controversial: some authors argue that this period should last until diarrhea stops, while others would extend precautions for the entire hospitalization. Patients with CDI should have single rooms, but cohorting may be used if needed.[538] Finally, offending antimicrobial agents should be discontinued when possible.[53]

Surveillance of CDI is essential for healthcare facilities in endemic areas. At a minimum, they should monitor for healthcare facility (HCF)–onset and HCF-associated CDI. One group of experts has characterized CDI based on the onset of symptoms. HCF-onset, HCF-associated disease is defined as a case patient whose symptom onset occurred at least 48 hours after admission.[538] In contrast, community-onset, HCF-associated disease is defined as a case patient whose symptom onset occurred within 4 weeks of discharge from a healthcare facility.[538] Infections are classified as community-acquired CDI when disease symptoms occur at least 12 weeks after discharge and no other healthcare exposures are documented.[538] If CDI occurs between 4 and 12 weeks after discharge, the source is classified as indeterminate.[538]

Multidrug-Resistant Gram-Negative Organisms

Multidrug-resistant organisms (MDROs) are those microorganisms that are resistant to one or more classes of antimicrobial agents. Primarily, MDRO refers to gram-negative bacteria.[532] Multidrug-resistant gram-negative organisms are emerging worldwide and cause all major HAIs, including CLA-BSI, CA-UTI, VAP, and SSI.[2,577,578] An NHSN study conducted during 2006–2008 demonstrated that drug resistance was common among *P. aeruginosa*, *A. baumannii*, and *K. pneumonia* and the MDR strain was most commonly found in *A. baumannii* (33–68%).[579] Resistance mechanisms found in gram-negative bacteria include the following features[580,581]:

- Enzyme production—the most common mechanism (e.g., extended-spectrum beta-lactamases [ESBLs], carbapenemase [CRE, KPC])
- Efflux pumps that remove antimicrobial agents from cells—a mechanism found in *P. aeruginosa* and *A. baumannii*
- Alteration of outer membrane proteins or porins, resulting in reduced drug permeability—a mechanism found in *P. aeruginosa* and *A. baumannii*
- Mutations at the antimicrobial binding site—a mechanism commonly found in gram-negative organisms against fluoroquinolones

Extended-spectrum beta-lactamases are enzymes that hydrolyze the beta-lactam ring that results in inactivation of penicillins, narrow-spectrum and third-generation cephalosporins, and monobactams.[582] ESBLs are more common among *K. pneumoniae* strains.[583] Latin America has the highest reported prevalence of ESBL-producing organisms, followed by Asia/Pacific Rim, Europe, and North America.[583] Risk factors for infection with ESBL-producing organisms include recent hospitalization, prior exposure to antimicrobial agents, previous history of urinary tract infection, older age, and diabetes mellitus.[584-589] Recently, incidence of community-onset ESBL-producing bacterial infections has been increasing, with urinary sources commonly being implicated.[588,590-592] Risk factors are not different from the hospital-onset infections: most patients have healthcare-associated disease, a previous history of hospitalization, a urinary catheter, and previous exposure to antimicrobial agents.[588,593-595] A prospective study in Sweden—an area not endemic for ESBLs—demonstrated that diarrhea during traveling to an endemic area is a risk factor for ESBL-producing organism acquisition.[596]

Carbapenem-resistant Enterobacteriaceae (CRE) is a type of gram-negative bacteria that is resistant to almost all available antimicrobial agents; it causes infections associated with significant morbidity and mortality.[597-600] Carbapenem-resistant *K. pneumoniae* (KPC) is the species of CRE most commonly found in the United States.[599] However, carbapenemase—which is transmitted via plasmids—can be found in other gram-negative organisms and species as well, including *K. oxytoca*, *E. coli*, *Enterobacter* spp., *Proteus mirabilis*, *S. marcescens*, and *Salmonella enterica*.[601] KPCs were first described in North Carolina in 1999 and have now been identified in 24 states; they are recovered routinely in the northeastern United States.[174,599] In 2006–2007, the NHSN reported carbapenem resistance in as many of 4% of *E. coli* isolates and 10.8% of *K. pneumoniae* infections.[2] Importantly, CREs and KPCs are endemic in countries such as Israel, Greece, and China, and have been reported in areas ranging from Brazil and Colombia to Norway, the United Kingdom, India, Sweden, Italy, and Finland.[601,602] Risk factors for KPCs include recent solid-organ or stem-cell transplantation, mechanical ventilation, prolonged hospital stay, an ICU stay, severe illness, and exposure to fluoroquinolones, cephalosporins, and carbapenems.[597,598,603,604]

NDM-1 is the most recently discovered carbapenemase.[605] It was first identified in 2008 from an Indian patient was transferred from a New Delhi Hospital to Sweden.[605] After this first identification, NDM-1 strains were reported from many countries around the world and the rapid dissemination has led to extreme concern in the public health community.[606-625] In the United States, the first three NDM-1 isolates were *E. coli*, *K. pneumoniae*, and *E. cloacae*; they were identified in patients who had recently received medical care in India.[626] It seems that the epicenter of the outbreak is in India and Pakistan, as most imported cases in other regions (including Australia, Canada, Japan, and countries in Europe) have been reported to be associated with healthcare contact in this region.[623,627-630] The rapid spread of the organism globally and resistance to broad-spectrum antimicrobials is driving global efforts to prevent transmission.

P. aeruginosa is a ubiquitous environmental gram-negative organism that has ability to develop resistance to antimicrobial agents by multiple mechanisms and is the major opportunistic pathogen among hospitalized patients.[631] This organism can be resistant to commonly used antiseptics (iodine-containing agents), and has been associated with outbreaks caused by *P. aeruginosa* with reduced susceptibility to disinfectants.[632] The epidemiology of these outbreaks points to water as an important reservoir for the pathogen. Possible sources in which it may lurk include shower heads, basins, sinks, bathtubs, faucets, bidets, toilets mouthwash and bath toys.[633-642] Additionally, the organism is transmitted via contamination of hands and artificial fingernails.[147,643,644] Although rare, outbreaks linked to infected HCPs have also been reported.[144,147,645]

Acinetobacter baumannii is a ubiquitous gram-negative organism that has emerged as major cause of HAIs in many hospitals and in injuries associated with war and trauma.[646] This organism has become the most common cause of VAP and ICU-related infection in healthcare institutions worldwide.[224,233,647-656] Besides VAP and bacteremia, *A. baumannii* has frequently been associated with wound infections.[657-661] It has been associated with outbreaks in field hospitals in Iraq and Kuwait.[662] Two important properties of this organism that contribute its ability to cause outbreaks in healthcare facilities are its ability to acquire antimicrobial-resistance genes and its ability to survive under a wide range of environmental conditions for prolonged periods of time.[646,660,663] An international multicenter study carried out between 2003 and 2008 demonstrated that 46.3% of *A. baumannii* isolates were resistant to carbapenems, as compared to 29.2% of such isolates reported to the CDC/NHSN network between 2006 and 2007.[17] Several *Acinetobacter* outbreaks have been reported from hospitals worldwide, and after repeated or prolonged outbreaks the causative organism commonly becomes endemic.[664-669] In the United States, healthcare-associated *Acinetobacter* infections have seasonal variation, with the rates being higher during summer time compared to other periods.[670-672] This organism is associated with hospital outbreaks, most commonly in ICUs, tropical environments, war, and natural disasters.[646,658,662]

Its ability to survive in the hospital environment and on equipment (especially respiratory equipment) has been identified as a common theme in *Acinetobacter* infections.[673-691] One study demonstrated that *Acinetobacter* strains had survived for 9 days after the infected patient was discharged from the studied unit.[683] A study of outbreaks associated with pulsatile wound treatment demonstrated that this treatment method could result in environmental contamination.[692] HCPs' hands can also be heavily contaminated by *A. baumannii*.[684,693,694] In a study relevant to modern medical care, researchers demonstrated that HCPs' cell phones can be contaminated with *Acinetobacter* strains that could be transmitted to patients.[695] Risk factors for *A. baumannii* infection/colonization include prolonged length of hospital stay, exposure to an ICU, mechanical ventilation, colonization pressure, antimicrobial use, recent surgery, invasive procedures, and underlying severity of illness.[646,660,696]

Patients with infections due to MDR *Acinetobacter* have increased hospital and ICU lengths of stay, and their treatment options are limited due to the bacteria's resistance to multiple antimicrobials.[11] Recently, an increasing number of *A. baumannii* strains resistant to all antimicrobials with therapeutic potential have been reported.[676,697–705]

Standard infection control measures are important to implement in patients with MDR gram-negative infection/colonization. These patients should be placed on contact precautions. Patient cohorting may be appropriated in an outbreak setting or with nosocomial transmission.[706] Widespread hand hygiene compliance is mandatory. Although active surveillance has been used successfully in the setting of outbreaks, no role for such surveillance has been established in non-outbreak settings.[532,707–709] Other measures in outbreak settings include molecular epidemiologic investigation to determine whether the situation involves clonal spreading, environmental culture, and enhanced environmental cleaning.[698,710–713] An antimicrobial stewardship program should be part of the interventions applied to control the outbreak.[714,715] In a non-outbreak setting, periodic microbiological surveillance—especially regarding specimens collected from high-risk patients—should be considered to identify unrecognized cases.[532] Internationally transferred patients from endemic areas or military settings should be screened for MDR gram-negative organisms before they are admitted to the new healthcare facility.

Pertussis

Pertussis is extremely contagious, with a greater than 80% secondary attack rate among susceptible household contacts.[716,717] In developed countries where universal pertussis immunization in infants has been implemented, the epidemiology of the disease

has changed: it now occurs more frequently among young adults—the primary reservoir—probably due to waning immunity.[718,719] Transmission occurs by contact with respiratory secretions or large aerosol droplets. The incubation period is between 7 and 21 days, and infectivity starts at the onset of the catarrhal stage through 3 weeks after the onset of symptoms.[720] Outbreaks in healthcare settings have been reported from both the United States and Europe.[159–162,721–732] In these settings, HCPs may play an important role in disease transmission, as the disease frequently goes unrecognized in the patient and waning immunity in HCPs makes them susceptible to this disease.[159–164,726,732–735] Because the clinical symptoms are less severe in adults, they may be unnoticed, with infectious HCPs transmitting the disease to their patients—a scenario that has resulted in spectacularly large healthcare-associated epidemics.[718,721] Neonates and infants younger than 1 year are at highest risk.[719] Commonly dismissed as unimportant, pertussis has high direct and indirect medical costs, all of which are preventable.[729,730]

The tetanus toxoid, diphtheria toxoid, and acellular pertussis vaccine (Tdap) licensed in 2005 for adolescent and adults is highly effective. Due to the high morbidity and costs associated with pertussis outbreaks in healthcare facilities, the Advisory Committee on Immunization Practices (ACIP) and the Healthcare Infection Control Practices Advisory Committee (HICPAC) recommend that all HCPs should receive Tdap if they have no contraindications.[736] Other prevention strategies directed toward pertussis transmission include early diagnosis and treatment, implementation of droplet precautions, exclusion of ill HCPs from caregiving duties, and postexposure prophylaxis (PEP) for exposed persons.[53,718,723] Postexposure prophylaxis with antibiotics (macrolides or trimethoprim-sulfamethazole) prevents the development of clinical disease among exposed individuals and may minimize subsequent transmission.[718,720,737] Newer macrolides are better tolerated than erythromycin and associated with higher compliance.[738,739] Exposed HCPs should be excluded from duty from the onset of the catarrhal stage through the third week after the onset of paroxysms or until 5 days after initiation of effective antimicrobial therapy.[53]

Mycobacteria
Tuberculosis

Outbreaks of *M. tuberculosis* (TB) involving patients and HCPs have been reported in a variety of healthcare settings, included long-term care facilities.

Many of these outbreaks involve multidrug-resistant tuberculosis (MDR-TB).[740–770] Coinfection with TB and HIV is common in these outbreaks.[749,755,771–774] Transmission has been linked to HCPs who did not use respiratory protection when they (1) performed aerosol-generating procedures and cough-producing procedures such as bronchoscopy, endotracheal intubation, sputum induction, and suction; aerosol treatment; irrigation of an open abscess; and autopsy; (2) cared for undiagnosed tuberculosis patients; and (3) worked in settings with poor ventilation systems or lack of environmental control measures including negative-pressure isolation.[170,744,745,747,749,769,775–780] Inadequate cleaning and disinfection of equipment was the most common cause of healthcare-associated outbreaks and pseudo-outbreaks via endoscopes.[329,775,777,778,781–783] Residents in long-term care facilities are at higher risk of acquiring tuberculosis compared to elderly people living in community, according to a 1984–1985 CDC study.[784] More importantly for both developed and developing country settings, a Canadian study demonstrated that risk of TB transmission within a facility was not correlated with number of tuberculosis patients, but instead with delayed diagnosis and treatment.[785] Overall TB-related mortality can be considered a yardstick for quality of care in health facilities.

M. tuberculosis is spread by the small-droplet nuclei (aerosols) expressed from the patient's upper and lower respiratory tract.[769] Draining abscesses can also be a source of disease transmission.[53,751,765] Of note, among organ transplant recipients, most TB disease is caused by reactivation of latent tuberculosis infection (LTBI) when individuals with such latent infection are immunosuppressed; however, transplantation-transmitted tuberculosis has also been reported.[786–790] Organs identified as transmitting TB have included the lung, kidney, and liver.[786–790]

HCPs worldwide are at increased risk of acquiring tuberculosis compared to the general population, in both endemic countries and those with low incidence of TB.[791] The units in the hospital that are associated with greater risk of exposure include medical wards (especially respiratory units), emergency departments, TB facilities, ambulatory units, laboratory/pathology units, and autopsy rooms.[792–797]

Preventive strategies for tuberculosis in healthcare settings can be divided into three levels: administrative controls, environmental controls, and respiratory protection[798,799] (**Table 14-8**). Administrative controls

Table 14-8	Preventive Strategies for Tuberculosis in Healthcare Settings
Administrative Controls	

- Assign responsibility for TB infection control in the setting
- Conduct a TB risk assessment
- Develop a plan/policy to ensure prompt detection of TB patients, provide airborne precautions, and implement adequate treatment of persons who have suspected or confirmed TB disease
- Implement effective work practices for the management of patients with suspected or confirmed TB disease
- Ensure use of the proper cleaning, disinfection, and sterilization process for contaminated endoscopes/equipment
- Train and educate HCPs about TB, with specific focus on prevention, transmission, and symptoms
- Develop a TB screening program for HCPs who are at risk for TB disease or who might be exposed to TB
- Apply epidemiologic-based prevention principles, including the use of setting-related infection control data
- Use appropriate signage advising respiratory hygiene and cough etiquette
- Coordinate efforts with the local or state health department

Environmental Controls

Primary environmental controls:

- Control the source of infection by using local exhaust ventilation (e.g., hoods, tents, or booths)
- Dilute and remove contaminated air by using general ventilation

Secondary environmental controls:

- Control airflow to prevent contamination of air in areas adjacent to the source (airborne infection isolation room)
- Clean air by using high-efficiency particulate air filtration or ultraviolet germicidal irradiation

Respiratory Protection Controls

- Implement a respiratory protection program
- Train HCPs on respiratory protection
- Train patients on respiratory hygiene and cough etiquette procedures

Source: Adapted from Centers for Disease Control and Prevention. Guidelines for preventing the transmission of *Mycobacterium tuberculosis* in health-care settings, 2005. *MMWR.* 2005;54(RR-17):1–141.

are the most important strategy.[798] The priority should be to develop strategies that minimize the amount of time that patients with tuberculosis spend in healthcare facilities, especially while they are undiagnosed.[799] Steps that facilities can take in this regard include the following measures:

- Implement triage of patients with symptoms consistent with tuberculosis
- Separate patients with suspected TB from other patients
- Diagnose patients with respiratory symptoms
- In the setting of suspected or probable TB disease, treat patients with the most effective antituberculosis treatment
- Educate patients with TB about protective measures to limit transmission
- Discharge patients safely but as fast as possible[798,799]

Adequate ventilation is the key for environmental control. Mechanical ventilation, natural ventilation, or mixed mode ventilation may be used in the healthcare setting depending on the resources and climate.[799] In the developed world setting, TB clinics are frequently separated from other healthcare facilities and patients wait for services in open areas, often completely outside.

Finally, the recommended respiratory protective device to prevent TB acquisition in the United States is the CDC/National Institute for Occupational Safety and Health (NIOSH)-certified nonpowered particulate filter respirator (N-, R-, or P-95, 99, or 100).[798] Disposable respirators or powered air respirators (PAPRs) with high-efficiency filters may also be used.[798] Fit testing should be part of the respiratory-protection program training, which is mandatory for all HCPs who will use respirators.[798] Of note, a plethora of observational data suggest that medical masks are adequate means of protection; they should be used in the absence of more advanced and expensive technologies.

New HCPs entering the workforce should undergo baseline screening for tuberculosis infection, followed up annually by use of either tuberculin skin tests or blood tests for *M. tuberculosis*.[798] Positive screening tests should be followed up by assessment for TB disease. HCPs with evidence of infectious TB disease should be furloughed and should be allowed to return to work when the following criteria are met:

1. Three consecutive sputum samples collected in 8- to 24-hour intervals are negative, with at least one sample taken in the early morning.

2. The HCP has responded to antituberculosis treatment.
3. The HCP is determined to be noninfectious by an expert.[798]

Contact investigation is commonly performed when a case of TB is discovered. It should be performed in the case of an HCP with TB in the following circumstances:

- New conversions in test results for TB infection
- Diagnosis of TB disease in an HCP
- Suspected person-to-person transmission of *M. tuberculosis*
- Breach in TB infection control practices that expose the HCP and patients to *M. tuberculosis*
- Possible TB outbreaks identified

The policy to prevent transmission of tuberculosis may vary acccording to the setting, the region of the world or country, the prevalence and incidence of TB in the general population, the types of facilities, and socioeconomic status. In 2009, WHO published a guide for infection control in healthcare facilities, congregate settings, and households that is available online at http://www.who.int/tb/publications/2009/infection_control/en/index.html. CDC guidelines for TB are available at http://www.cdc.gov/tb/publications/guidelines/infectioncontrol.htm.

Non-tuberculous Mycobacteria

Unlike with tuberculosis, the environment plays a crucial role in acquisition of non-tuberculous mycobacteria (NTM) infections.[121] Municipal water supplies and potable water systems and their supplies are the main reservoirs for these organisms.[121,122,800] NTM are relatively resistant to disinfection agents, elevated temperatures, and ultraviolet light compared with other pathogenic bacteria that may colonize potable water.[122]

A number of outbreaks and pseudo-outbreaks due to NTM have been reported in healthcare facilities.[122,800-816] The clinical presentations of such diseases include catheter-related infections, pulmonary infections, otitis, cutaneous infections, disseminated disease in immunocompromised patients, infections related to hemodialysis, peritonitis associated with continuous ambulatory peritoneal dialysis (CAPD), injection-related infection, and surgical site infections.[122,809,816-824] Inappropriate disinfection or sterilization is a commonly observed cause of both pseudo-outbreaks or infections.[802-805,825]

Viruses

Bloodborne Pathogens

The three most common healthcare-associated bloodborne pathogens are human immunodeficiency virus (HIV), hepatitis B virus (HBV), and hepatitis C virus (HCV). Nevertheless, the concepts discussed here can be generalized to nonviral pathogens transmitted by blood or other sterile body fluids, including those pathogens that cause malaria, syphilis, and other diseases.

Transmission of bloodborne pathogens in a healthcare facility is associated with failure in infection control practices or environmental controls. Transmission can occur via needle-sticks, contact with sharp objects, reuse of multidose medication vials, contact with mucous membranes, the dialysis process, blood transfusion, or organ transplantation.[826–860] Besides blood, other body fluids that can transmit viruses include cerebral fluid, synovial fluid, pleural fluid, pericardial fluid, peritoneal fluid, amniotic fluids, semen, and vaginal secretions.[861] HBV is the most infectious of the bloodborne pathogens, followed by HCV and HIV.[862] These pathogens have been transmitted to and from HCPs, and to and from patients.[863] One study demonstrated that the risk of needle-stick injuries in healthcare facilities was highest among housekeeping personnel (127/1000 persons) and laboratory personnel (104.7/1000 persons), followed by registered nurses (92.6/1000 persons).[864] Most injuries occurred during disposal of used needles, during drug injection, while drawing blood and recapping needles, or during handling of linens or trash containing uncapped needles.[864] Fortunately, the HBV vaccine is very effective; since it has come into widespread use, the incidence of hepatitis B in HCPs has declined by 95%.[866] Further declines are likely as the vaccine is now part of the U.S. pediatric vaccine schedule, which means that the prevalence of the virus will decrease among patients as well.

Standard precautions and education of staff members are crucial to prevent bloodborne pathogen exposures.[53] Education must cover when and where to use gloves, goggles, and other precautions and how to properly dispose of supplies contaminated with blood.[865] Other prevention measures include blood and organ donor screening, and proper cleaning and sterilization of reusable equipment and supplies.[3] Prompt care for HCPs exposed to blood includes wound management and cleaning, and reporting the exposure immediately after the incident. Postexposure prophylaxis against HIV and HBV is now the standard of care and decreases transmission,

particularly when PEP is administered rapidly after the exposure.[865] Healthcare facilities must have written protocols for reporting, evaluation, counseling, treatment, and follow-up of any occupational exposure.[865] Guidelines for prophylaxis are frequently updated and the most recent guidelines should be consulted for management of exposures.

SHEA has published guidelines for the management of HCPs who are infected with HBV, HCV, and/or HIV.[863] Under these guidelines, infected HCPs have only a few restrictions. HCPs with higher viral loads and those who are infected with certain viral strains that are deemed more infectious need to take additional precautions. HBV-infected HCPs with higher viral burdens (signaled by the presence of HBeAg or circulating viral burdens greater than 10^4 genome equivalents [GE] per milliliter for HBV, more than 10^4 GE/mL for HCV, and more than 5×10^2 GE/mL for HIV) should use two sets of gloves (double-gloving) for all invasive procedures and procedures that contact mucous membranes or nonintact skin and for all procedures where gloving is recommended.[863] In addition, they should not perform any procedures that are associated with a risk of HCP-to-patient transmission, such as those involving blind suturing.[863] These procedures include general surgery and all major surgery, general oral surgery, emergency procedures performed in the emergency department such as open resuscitation efforts and internal cardiac massage, interactions with patients in situations during which the risk of the patient biting the physician is significant, and any open surgical procedure lasting more than 3 hours.[863] HCPs with lower viral burdens may perform these high-risk procedures but they must be monitored by occupational health and a specific disease expert.[863]

Human Immunodeficiency Virus

Rates of transmission of HIV from patient to HCP and from HCP to patient declined dramatically after highly active antiretroviral therapy (HAART) came into widespread use.[867] The average risk for acquiring HIV from percutaneous injury is estimated to be 0.3% (95% CI: 0.2–0.5%); the risk after a mucous membrane exposure is estimated at 0.09% (95% CI: 0.006–0.5%).[861] Factors that increase the risk of HIV transmission from percutaneous injury are (1) deep injury, (2) a procedure that involved a needle being placed directly in a vein or artery, (3) a device visibly contaminated with the patient's blood, and (4) HIV viral load and stage of infection of the source.[861]

HCPs who are exposed to blood or body fluid containing HIV should be evaluated as soon as possible. HIV postexposure prophylaxis is selected based on the type of exposure (percutaneous or mucous membrane), the clinical status of the source patient, risk factors of transmission, and the risk of drug-resistant virus in the source patient.[3,861]

Hepatitis B Virus

Hepatitis B virus is only the healthcare-associated bloodborne pathogen for which infection is vaccine preventable. This virus can be transmitted parenterally, sexually, and perinatally.[868] Environmental surfaces play an important role in disease transmission, especially in hemodialysis units.[832–836] HBV carries a significant healthcare-associated transmission risk for HCPs who come in contact with blood or body fluids.[826–829,869–871] The most common causes of HBV transmission in healthcare settings have been identified as multidose vials and multipatient capillary blood sampling devices.[853] The risk of developing clinical hepatitis if the source patient is HBeAg positive ranges from 22% to 31%, and the risk of developing serologic evidence of HBV infection is as high as 37% to 62%. In case of an HBsAg-positive, HBeAg-negative source patient, the risk of acute hepatitis B is 1% to 6%, and the risk of developing serologic evidence of HBV infection ranges from 23% to 37%.[865] In the 1990s, HCPs accounted for 2% of all reported cases of HBV infection in the United States.[872]

Hepatitis B has been transmitted from patient to HCP, from HCP to patient, and from patient to patient; indeed, many healthcare-associated outbreaks have been documented.[830,831,837–843,849,853,871] The risk of transmission depends on the infected person's HBeAg status and/or the level of viremia in the source patient.[865] An HCP with percutaneous, mucous membrane, or nonintact skin exposure to blood or body fluid of any patient should be considered to have been exposed to HBV until proven otherwise.[865] A positive HBsAg test in the source patient confirms exposure.

Exposed, vaccinated HCPs should have their anti-HBs level measured; an antibody level of 10 mIU/mL or more indicates no need for prophylaxis.[868] The exposed, unvaccinated HCP and the HCP without evidence of immunity should receive intramuscular hepatitis B immunoglobulin (HBIG; 0.06 mL/kg) within 24 to 48 hours, with the first dose of hepatitis B vaccine given at a different site, followed by additional vaccine doses at 1 and 6 months.[868] HCPs whose anti-HBs levels have fallen below 10 mIU/mL with a previously documented protective level do not need to receive additional prophylaxis.[868]

Patients undergoing chronic hemodialysis are at risk of hepatitis B infection. Before initiating dialysis, their hepatitis B serologic status should be documented, and all susceptible patients should receive the complete series of hepatitis B vaccines.[873] To minimize the risk of HBV transmission, HBsAg-positive patients should be dialyzed in a separate room using separate machines, equipment, instruments, and supplies.[835]

Hepatitis C Virus

Healthcare-associated hepatitis C infections have been reported in various settings, including both patient-to-HCP and HCP-to-patient transmissions.[874–893] The risk of transmission after a percutaneous injury is 1.8% (range 0–7%).[865] Transmission rarely occurs when infectious blood contacts only mucous membranes.[865] Some studies suggest that environmental contamination may have role in HCV transmission, especially in hemodialysis clinics, but the contribution made by the environment in areas with lower potential contamination is unknown.[894–898] Standard precautions are required for HCV-infected patients.[53] Hemodialysis patients with HCV infection do not have to be isolated or dialyzed separately on dedicated machines.[835,873] Currently, no PEP regimen is effective for preventing HCV transmission, and a viable vaccine is not available.

Influenza Virus

Influenza is a major healthcare-associated pathogen, and transmission of this virus has been well documented from patients to HCPs, HCPs to patients, and HCPs to HCPs.[165–167,244,899–914] Influenza is associated with increased morbidity and mortality among patients in both long-term and acute care facilities.[915–917] Pandemic H1N1 influenza is associated with lower morbidity and mortality, but has been widely transmitted in healthcare settings,[918–927] including oseltamivir-resistant virus, especially among patients with hematologic malignancy.[919,928] Transmission predominantly occurs through contact with large, virus-laden droplets during close contact with infected individuals.[929–932] Indirect contact transmission by hands or inanimate objects may also occur.[932] The incubation period for influenza ranges from 1 to 4 days; viral shedding begins approximately 1 day prior to onset of symptoms, and continues for as long as 10 days.[932–935] Prolonged viral shedding has been reported among immunocompromised patients and children with severe disease.[936–938]

Persons at greatest risk of serious disease include the following groups:

- Children younger than age 5 years, but especially younger than age 2 years
- Adults older than 65 years

- Pregnant women (especially those in the second and third trimesters) and postpartum women (having given birth within the 2 weeks prior to influenza exposure)
- Individuals with chronic diseases, including pulmonary, cardiovascular, renal, hepatic, hematologic (including hemoglobinopathy), metabolic (including diabetes mellitus), and neurologic disorders
- Immunosuppressed persons (including immunosuppression caused by medications or by HIV)
- Morbidly obese (BMI ≥ 40) persons
- Persons younger than 18 years who require long-term aspirin therapy
- Person who reside in a nursing home or other chronic-care facility
- American Indians and Alaska Natives[932,941,942]

HCPs are often implicated as potential sources of influenza transmission,[166,167,913,920,922] as these healthy adults can be asymptomatic.[943] HCPs who use standard precautions and personal protective equipment (PPE) properly are not at increased risk of contracting influenza from patients, but they may contract influenza from community exposures and spread the virus to their immunocompromised patients.[944,945]

Studies have demonstrated that vaccinating HCPs for influenza reduces influenza transmission in healthcare settings, staff illness and absenteeism, and influenza-related morbidity and mortality among persons at increased risk for severe influenza illness.[915,946–949] In the Northern Hemisphere, influenza activity peaks between late December and early March. Thus the ideal time to vaccinate individuals with influenza vaccine is between October and mid-November. Currently, annual influenza vaccination is mandatory for HCPs in many hospitals and healthcare systems in the United States.[950–954]

By far, the best control measure in a healthcare setting is immunization against influenza; however, it is important that institutions engage in surveillance for early recognition and isolation of possibly infected individuals.[53] Other interventions should include strict hand hygiene, use of mask/respiratory protection, visitor screening, and postponement of nonessential admissions to any unit that has an outbreak.[955,956] Chemoprophylaxis with neuraminidase inhibitor (oseltamivir or zanamivir) may be used for postexposure prophylaxis.[932] HCPs who are suspected to have influenza should not work for 7 days or until their symptoms resolve.[934]

Norovirus

Norovirus refers to a group of viruses in the calicivirus family that are a major cause of outbreaks of nonbacterial gastroenteritis both in the community and in healthcare settings.[957–962] Norovirus infection has a short incubation period (2–48 hours), yet results in prolonged hospital stays and significant morbidity and mortality, particularly in immunocompromised persons and the elderly.[958,961,963–966] Norovirus is highly transmissible by the fecal–oral route and contaminates the environment and fomites.[959,961] Moreover, it can survive contact with chlorine and varying temperatures (freezing and heating to 60°C). Quaternary ammonium compounds and alcohols are ineffective in eliminating the virus.[959,967]

To prevent transmission, standard infection control practices with attention to the environment are critical. Strict hand washing with soap and water is imperative, as alcohol-based hand rubs may be ineffective against this pathogen.[959,961] Patients with norovirus infection should be placed on contact precautions.[961] The environment should be aggressively cleaned using a hypochlorite-based cleaning agent on nonporous environmental surfaces.[968] Cohorting and symptom screening may be instituted if ongoing transmission occurs. Finally, ward closure may be needed to terminate the outbreak.[958,961] One study demonstrated that the estimated cost of outbreak management of healthcare-associated norovirus infection was as high as $657,644 (in the year 2004).[958]

Fungi

Invasive fungal infections (IFIs) are important causes of morbidity and mortality, particularly in immunocompromised patients. Fungal pathogens are classified as either yeasts or molds. The most important yeasts are the *Candida* species; molds of epidemiologic importance include *Aspergillus*, *Zygomycetes*, and *Fusarium*. Infections due to *Candida* and *Aspergillus* species account for the vast majority of healthcare-associated fungal infections. Recently, the incidence of invasive fungal infections has increased—a trend that may be explained by factors including more hematopoietic stem-cell transplant and solid-organ transplant cases with consequent use of immunosuppressive agents; increased immunosuppression among other patients; improved diagnostic strategies to enhance surveillance; increased use of central venous catheters and parenteral nutrition; and large numbers of patients with HIV infection and burns.[969–971]

Candida Species

Candida species are the fourth most common cause of healthcare-associated BSIs in the United States. Furthermore, the associated mortality rate is the highest with *Candida* infection.[187] *Candida albicans* is the most common cause of invasive candidiasis (IC).[187] Risk factors for developing candidemia and IC include young age (infants younger than 1 year), advanced age, prolonged neutropenia (absolute neutrophil count less than 500/mm³), use of cytotoxic chemotherapy, use of broad-spectrum antimicrobial agents, use of steroids, presence of an indwelling catheter, receipt of total parenteral nutrition, a recent gastrointestinal operation, renal failure/hemodialysis, malnutrition, and prolonged length of hospitalization.[972–980]

Healthcare-associated transmission of *Candida* species may occur via indirect contact between patients by the contaminated hands of HCPs.[143,974,981] Although *Candida* species are normal flora, and infection due to these organisms arises from endogenous sources spreading via transmission from hands and contaminated fomites, as documented using molecular technology from various outbreaks.[982–986]

The use of fluconazole prophylaxis has changed the spectrum of *Candida* infections, from *C. albicans* previously being responsible for more than 50% of cases, to non-*C. albicans* species emerging as important infectious species, especially in hematology units.[987–991] Hand hygiene is the most effective procedure for preventing transmission of *Candida*, and this organism is killed by alcohol.[984,992] Antifungal prophylaxis should be preserved for patients undergoing allogeneic hematopoietic stem-cell transplantation (HSCT), those undergoing intensive remission-induction or salvage-induction chemotherapy for acute leukemia, and selected high-risk patients undergoing solid-organ transplantation.[993–995]

Aspergillus Species and Other Molds

Of all the molds causing human infections, *Aspergillus* is the most common and an important cause of morbidity and mortality in patients with hematologic malignancy and HSCT recipients.[996–1000] *A. fumigatus* is the species most commonly linked to human disease, although there has been an increase in non-*fumigatus* species of *Aspergillus* (e.g., *A. flavus* and *A. terreus*) over the past several decades.[1001–1003] Invasive aspergillosis (IA) generally involves the sinuses and the lungs, but can occasionally disseminate to other organs, including the brain and the skin.[1004–1011]

Both Zygomycetes and *Aspergillus* are ubiquitous molds that are found in decaying organic matter in the environment.[1003] Outbreaks of zygomycosis in healthcare settings have been associated with contaminated Elastoplast adhesive bandages, wooden tongue depressors, malfunctioning ventilation systems, ostomy bags, and disruption of the hospital environment.[387,1012–1022] Given that the organisms are found in soil, decomposing materials, and potentially water, the environment plays an important role in whether patients develop disease. Construction and/or renovation and suboptimal maintenance, cleaning, and protection of the environment have been the causes of multiple *Aspergillus* outbreaks.[1004,1023–1047] In addition to exposure, the most important risk factor for developing invasive mold infection is prolonged neutropenia, although patients with solid-organ transplants, advanced HIV, chronic granulomatous disease, cirrhosis and those receiving corticosteroids are at risk.[1003,1048–1058] Additional risk factors for zygomycosis include diabetes with or without ketoacidosis, iron overload, and use of desferoxamine.[1059]

Current guidelines recommended that HSCT recipients should be placed in protective environment units consisting of well-sealed rooms with high-efficiency particulate air (HEPA) filtration of incoming air, laminar airflow, positive room air pressure relative to the adjacent area, ventilation to provide more than 12 air changes per hour, and strategies to minimize dust.[53] Dried and fresh flowers and potted plants should be prohibited in these rooms.[53] At this point, there are no recommendations for protective environments for other types of immunocompromised patients.[53]

Recently, several reports have described breakthrough zycomycosis infections in HSCT patients and neutropenic hosts while receiving voriconazole.[1060–1062] Importantly, voriconazole has no antifungal activity against members of class Zygomycetes.[1060–1062]

Fusarium is another mold that has recently emerged as an important pathogen in this setting. One study demonstrated that hospital water system could serve as a reservoir of *Fusarium* species.[1063]

CONTROL AND PREVENTIVE STRATEGIES

Control and prevention of HAIs can occur at many levels. The Study of the Effectiveness of Infection Control (SENIC) demonstrated the utility of well-developed infection control programs that include IPs and hospital epidemiologists. Antimicrobial stewardship programs, which oversee the use of antibiotics in relationship to the microbial resistance seen in the facility, are of increasing importance and should now be included in infection prevention programs.

Surveillance and notifying clinicians of infection rates in their patients have been shown to enhance the effectiveness of infection control. Clearly, the development of policies and procedures to ensure infection prevention at all levels is necessary. Examples of such practices include hand hygiene among HCPs, immunization of HCPs, isolation of patients with communicable diseases, prevention of interactions between infectious hospital visitors and at-risk patients, cleaning of the environment, and installation and maintenance of water, heating, and air-conditioning systems.

Hand Hygiene

Because microorganisms may be transmitted from patient to patient or from environment to patient by contaminated hands, appropriate hand hygiene is the cornerstone for controlling the spread of many infectious agents.[1064-1068] The normal microbial flora of the skin (resident flora) help to prevent colonization with hospital-acquired microorganisms (transient flora). Resident microorganisms are most frequently found on the deeper skin layers, where they can survive, multiply, and be cultured.[1069] They usually consist of staphylococcal species (*S. epidermidis*, *S. hominis*, and *S. capitis*) and micrococci. In general, resident microorganisms tend not to be highly virulent, but they can cause infections in patients who are immunocompromised or who have implanted foreign devices. Organisms such as *S. aureus,* the *Klebsiella–Enterobacter* group, and *Acinetobacter* species have been reported to colonize the hands of HCPs and are considered transient flora in most cases.[1070-1075]

Transient microorganisms are acquired through accidental contamination and are characterized by their inability to multiply and persist. The hands of HCPs may acquire transient microorganisms from colonized or infected patients.

WHO and CDC have both produced guidelines that detail the data supporting the importance of hand hygiene, the appropriate techniques, and additional issues in prevention.[1081,1082] These guidelines advocate the use of soap and water or alcohol hand rubs. In general, alcohol-based products for hand disinfection are preferred over antimicrobial or plain soap and water because of their superior microbiocidal activity; they also require less time than hand washing with water, reduce drying of the skin, and are more convenient.[1068,1082] Several studies have demonstrated that introducing alcohol-based hand rubs can improve hand hygiene compliance in healthcare settings.[1083-1087] However, in the presence of visible soiling of hands (with blood or other body fluids or dirt, after using the toilet, or after exposure to spore-forming organisms such as *C. difficile* or *B. anthracis*), both guidelines recommend the use of hand washing with soap and water.[1068,1082]

WHO has described the "five moments"—events that should trigger hand hygiene. Hand hygiene should be performed routinely before and after contact with a patient and in the following scenarios:

1. Before performing any task involving an invasive device
2. After contact with body fluids or excretions, mucous membranes, nonintact skin, or wound dressings
3. If moving from a contaminated body site to another body site during care of the same patient
4. After contact with inanimate surfaces and objects (including medical equipment) in the immediate vicinity of the patient
5. After removing sterile or nonsterile gloves[1082]

Artificial fingernails are associated with increased colonization with gram-negative organisms and *S. aureus*. They have been associated with multiple hospital outbreaks.[643,1088,1089] HCPs who engage in patient contact or who handle sterile supplies should not be allowed to wear them.[1081]

Antimicrobial Stewardship Program

In recent years, antimicrobial resistance has become a worldwide problem. Excessive antimicrobial use in humans, animals, and agriculture has exerted intense pressure on microorganisms and their environment. The use of antimicrobials in any dosage over any period of time leads to selective pressure on the microorganisms. Recently, the emergence of virulent microbes owing to such selection has led to global epidemics.

In hospital formularies, antimicrobials represent the second most commonly used class of drugs. Between 23% and 40% of hospitalized patients receive systemic antimicrobial agents at any given time, and 40% to 50% of this use is inappropriate.[1103-1109] Antimicrobial stewardship programs monitor antimicrobial use in healthcare institutions and provide evidence-based approaches to prudent antimicrobial use.[1110]

To render such programs effective and to facilitate controlled antimicrobial usage, hospitals need an antimicrobial utilization committee. This committee should be composed of individuals with expertise in infectious diseases, pharmacy, microbiology, healthcare epidemiology and infection control, nursing, quality control and assurance, administration, information technology, and medicine (surgery, internal

Table 14-9	Strategies for Optimizing Antimicrobial Use in Hospitals[1077–1080]
Types of Stewardship	

- Restrictive formulary and restrictive use of formulary agents
- Therapeutic substitution
- Guidelines for appropriate use
- Pre-antibiotic use approval
- Selective reporting of antimicrobial susceptibilities
- Generic substitution
- Antimicrobial standardized order sheets
- Automatic antimicrobial stop orders
- Post-prescription review
- Computer-assisted management of certain antimicrobial agents or specific conditions

Strategies to Engage Clinicians
- Educate prescribers
- Use clinical guidelines

medicine, pediatrics, and obstetrics/gynecology). The chairperson of the infectious diseases department often heads this committee.

Strategies for optimizing antimicrobial use in healthcare settings are listed in **Table 14-9**.

Isolation and Barrier Precautions

Isolation and the use of barrier precautions are necessary to prevent patients, visitors, and HCPs from acquiring or transmitting communicable diseases or pathogenic microorganisms. Isolation and the use of barriers are based on our understanding of how diseases are transmitted. The CDC/HICPAC updated their guidelines for isolation precautions in 2007.[53] The guidelines are formulated using two levels of protection: one is standard and applied to all patients, and the other is based on the potential of disease or microorganism transmission. Contact, droplet, and airborne precautions are the most common forms of isolation that are implemented in addition to standard precautions. Standard precautions should be used for all patients and are designed to reduce the risk of transmission of microorganisms from both recognized and unrecognized sources of infection in the healthcare setting.

Standard precautions recognize that any body fluid may contain contagious microorganisms. They include hand hygiene; use of personal protective equipment; safe injection practices; respiratory hygiene/cough etiquette; and use of masks for insertion of catheters or injection of material into spinal or epidural spaces via lumbar puncture procedure.[53] Personal protective equipment, such as gown, gloves, mask or respiratory protection, and eye protection should be donned before entering a patient's room and discarded before leaving the patient's environment.[14,53]

Airborne precautions should be applied for patients with suspected or documented airborne infections such as pulmonary or laryngeal tuberculosis, varicella-zoster virus, and measles. Optimally, this practice would include placing patients in an airborne isolation infection room (AIIR). An AIIR is a single-patient room with negative air pressure and 6–12 air changes per hour (ACH). HCPs working within airborne precautions should be provided with N-95 or comparable high-level respirators.[53]

For droplet precautions, a single-patient room is preferred; if one is not available, a multi-bed room may be used with spatial separation at least 3 feet and drawing the curtain between patient beds.[53] HCPs should wear a mask when in close contact with a patient with a suspected disease transmitted by droplets, such as pertussis, meningococcus, influenza, and other respiratory diseases.[53]

Contact precautions are used for patients with disease that can be transmitted by direct contact, such as VRE, MRSA and *C. difficile* infection. This practice requires that the patient be placed in single-patient room if possible. HCPs caring for patients on contact precautions must wear a gown and gloves for all interactions that may involve contact with the patient or potentially contaminated areas in the patient's environment. PPE should be donned upon room entry and discarded before exiting the patient's room.[53]

Immunization

HCPs can potentially be exposed to a wide array of occupational-acquired infectious diseases, including vaccine-preventable diseases. The Advisory Committee on Immunization and Healthcare Infection Control Practices Advisory Committee strongly recommend HCP immunization for the following diseases: hepatitis B, influenza, measles, mumps, and rubella, varicella, and tetanus, diphtheria, and pertussis.[1124,1125]

Disinfection, Sterilization, and Environmental Control

Medical equipment used in procedures and treatments may expose patients to infectious organisms if not disinfected or sterilized properly. The literature provides many examples of the link between inappropriate disinfection or sterilization and outbreaks and pseudo-outbreaks in healthcare settings.[805,1126–1142]

Sterilization is a process intended to kill or eliminate all forms of microorganisms, including bacterial spores.[1143] Sterilization can be carried out using physical or chemical means, including steam under pressure, dry heat, ethylene oxide gas, hydrogen peroxide gas plasma, and liquid plasma.[1143]

Disinfection kills organisms but will not eliminate microbial spores.[1143] Disinfectants are classified as high, intermediate, or low level based on their ability to kill organisms. High-level disinfectants usually kill all microorganisms except microbial spores. Intermediate-level disinfectants can eliminate most viruses, most fungi, mycobacteria, and vegetative bacteria, but not microbial spores. Low-level disinfectants can destroy enveloped viruses, vegetative bacteria, and some fungi, but not mycobacteria and spores.[1143,1144]

The prion, which is a proteinaceous infectious agent causing Creutzfeldt-Jakob disease (CJD) and transmissible spongiform encephalopathies, is not readily inactivated by most conventional disinfection and sterilization procedures.[1145] A separate guideline for disinfection and sterilization of prion-contaminated medical instruments has been published.[1145] Of note, the North American guidelines differ from those used in Europe based on differences in data interpretation.

The Spaulding classification organizes patient care items and instruments into three categories: critical items, semi-critical items, and noncritical items. Critical items are those objects that enter sterile tissue or the vascular system and carry a high risk for transmitting infection.[1144] These items should be sterilized.[1144] Examples of critical items include surgical instruments, cardiac and urinary catheters, implants, and ultrasound probes used in sterile body cavities.[1144] Semi-critical items are instruments that contact mucous membranes or nonintact skin; the items in this category include respiratory therapy equipment, anesthesia equipment, endoscopes, bronchoscopes, laryngoscopes, prostate biopsy

probes, and endocavitary probes.[1144] Sterilization or high-level disinfection is needed to eliminate all pathogenic organisms and a majority of bacterial spores on semi-critical items.[1143] Equipment that has contact only with intact skin is considered noncritical.[1144] These items carry a minimal risk of transmitting infections, so low-level disinfectants may be used to clean them.[1144]

Recently published data have highlighted the role of the environment in contributing to healthcare-associated infections and outbreaks.[130,1146–1148] Consequently, environmental cleaning is an important method to reduce transmission of multidrug-resistant organisms.[526] Environmental surfaces are usually cleaned using an EPA (or other regulatory body)-registered hospital disinfectant.[1144] Isopropyl alcohol and most disinfectants (e.g., sodium hypochlorite, phenolic, and quaternary ammonium compounds) are effective against VRE and many other resistant bacteria.[1149] These compounds have activity against many viruses, including influenza and RSV, but may or may not have activity against *Mycobacterium tuberculosis*. However, to prevent transmission of *C. difficile*, chlorine-containing cleaning products with at least 1000 ppm available chlorine are recommended to decontaminate inanimate objects and environmental surfaces.[538] Chlorine bleach solution (1000–5000 ppm) is also recommended to prevent norovirus transmission.[130]

THE NEED FOR INTEGRATED INFECTION CONTROL PROGRAMS

Currently there is a trend to move from infection control to infection prevention, which highlights the primary function of professionals who run such programs. The key to controlling HAIs is the presence of an integrated program that includes the following services and trained individuals to perform these functions:

- Department of epidemiology and infection control/prevention
- Microbiology laboratory
- Occupational health services
- Pharmacy
- Informatics

Department of Hospital Epidemiology and Infection Control/Prevention

The role of this department is to measure the rates of HAIs, understand their epidemiology, and devise and evaluate effective strategies for their control and prevention. The components of this program are surveillance, outbreak investigation, education, healthcare system employee health, antimicrobial stewardship, product evaluation, cost–benefit analysis, and policy and procedure guidelines. More forward-thinking programs include process engineers, behavior psychologists, and project managers with training in Six Sigma or other quality management techniques. The organizational structure should include a trained hospital epidemiologist; one or more infection preventionists; one or more computer specialists; microbiology, data management and administrative support; infectious disease fellows; and an infection control committee. The infection control committee should be chaired by the hospital epidemiologist and should include representatives from the medical and surgical staff, hospital administration, employee health, pharmacy, microbiology, housekeeping, central supply, and engineering, as well as the IPs.

Microbiology Laboratory

Active involvement of the microbiology laboratory is crucial for the success of an infection control program. Culture reports from the microbiology laboratory are among the most important pieces of data included in surveillance. The infection prevention and control department and the microbiology laboratory must have a close working relationship. This interaction not only provides the IPs with timely microbiologic information, but also helps the laboratory determine the clinical significance of isolates and differentiate patients who are colonized from those with clinical infection. The microbiology laboratory can support the infection control department in the following ways:

- Ensure high-quality performance in the laboratory
- Designate a person to be a consultant to the infection control department
- Report relevant results in a timely, organized, and accessible way
- Provide basic microbiologic training to the infection control staff
- Monitor isolates of unusual pathogens, clusters of pathogens that might indicate an outbreak, and the emergence of multidrug-resistant pathogens
- Characterize antimicrobial susceptibility
- Perform special procedures and molecular fingerprinting studies

- Store isolates of epidemiologic importance
- Conduct environmental microbiologic studies
- Monitor commercial products, devices, or equipment that might become contaminated during manufacturing or transportation, when indicated

Employee Health Services

Exposure events are defined as occasions when patients or hospital employees are exposed to infectious microorganisms or ectoparasites. When an individual is exposed, the goal of the infection control department is to prevent further transmission of the organism. In the event of an exposure, all patients, visitors, and staff who might have been exposed must be identified, and appropriate measures should be initiated immediately. In most institutions, an employee health department evaluates whether an employee has been exposed to or remains susceptible to a contagious disease, examines that person, enforces work restrictions, and allows personnel to return to work. Infection control staff must collaborate with employee health services and develop protocols for triage, evaluation, prophylaxis, and follow-up after exposures to communicable diseases. The roles and responsibilities of both departments should be identified and clear lines of communication established.

Pharmacy Services

Pharmacy is also an essential partner in infection control and especially antimicrobial stewardship. This service identifies the quality, efficacy, safety, and cost-effectiveness of drugs. The use and availability of antimicrobial drugs may alter the susceptibility patterns of resistant pathogens.[1150] Interactions between pharmacists who confer with practitioners about treatment and IPs who are examining resistance patters can help develop synergistic approaches to emerging resistance problems. One of the easiest and the most cost-effective ways to determine the gross antimicrobial utilization is based on pharmacy data. High-risk drugs, units, and patients whose antimicrobial utilization rates exceed those expected or that correlate with resistant organisms can be identified. Antimicrobial use is the number of units, or defined daily doses, per 1000 population in a primary health setting or per patient-day in the hospital setting. Calculating this value allows trends in antimicrobial use to be evaluated and stratified by unit or service.

Computers and Information Systems

Nowadays, computer and information systems are essential for any infection control program. Especially when the healthcare facility faces the prospect of limited resources, computers and surveillance software can help IPs perform daily surveillance activity and manage their time more effectively. Administrative databases that contain patient demographics, clinical and pharmacy data, and microbiology and radiology reports are an important adjunct to surveillance and can now be integrated into several commercially available software programs. These data can be merged into a surveillance data system whose content can be stored and manipulated to facilitate surveillance. Personnel trained for data management and analysis are usually required to manage information systems. Such systems help to identify problems such as outbreaks, antimicrobial susceptibility trends, healthcare-associated pneumonias, SSIs, UTIs, BSIs, and the emergence of important pathogens, such as MRSA and VRE.

CONCLUSION

Healthcare-associated infections are likely to increase in frequency in the future, not only owing to the growth of the more vulnerable and older population but also because of broader use of more complicated procedures and more new treatment modalities that compromise immune system. More patients will encounter the healthcare system and will acquire infections, leading to further morbidity and mortality. Increases in antimicrobial resistance will complicate treatment courses and lengthen hospital stays. Hospital epidemiologists and infection control practitioners need to apply creative strategies for prevention of HAIs in a rapidly changing healthcare system. As the struggle to reduce the growth of healthcare costs continues, hospital epidemiology will play an important role in evaluating patients' outcomes and in improving the quality of their care.

• • • REFERENCES

1. Horan TC, Andrus M, Dudeck MA. CDC/NHSN surveillance definition of health care–associated infection and criteria for specific types of infections in the acute care setting. *Am J Infect Control.* 2008;36(5):309–332.

2. Hidron AI, Edwards JR, Patel J, et al. NHSN annual update: antimicrobial-resistant pathogens associated with healthcare-associated infections: annual summary of data reported to the National Healthcare Safety Network at the Centers for Disease Control and Prevention, 2006–2007. *Infect Control Hosp Epidemiol.* 2008;29(11):996–1011.

3. Sydnor ER, Perl TM. Hospital epidemiology and infection control in acute-care settings. *Clin Microbiol Rev.* 2011;24(1):141–173.

4. Klevens RM, Edwards JR, Richards CL Jr, et al. Estimating health care–associated infections and deaths in U.S. hospitals, 2002. *Public Health Rep.* 2007;122(2):160–166.

5. Stone PW, Braccia D, Larson E. Systematic review of economic analyses of health care–associated infections. *Am J Infect Control.* 2005;33(9):501–509.

6. Leu HS, Kaiser DL, Mori M, et al. Hospital-acquired pneumonia: attributable mortality and morbidity. *Am J Epidemiol.* 1989;129(6):1258–1267.

7. Kollef MH, Sharpless L, Vlasnik J, et al. The impact of nosocomial infections on patient outcomes following cardiac surgery. Chest. 1997;112(3):666–675.

8. Burgmann H, Hiesmayr JM, Savey A, et al. Impact of nosocomial infections on clinical outcome and resource consumption in critically ill patients. *Intensive Care Med.* 2010;36(9):1597–1601.

9. Muscedere JG, Day A, Heyland DK. Mortality, attributable mortality, and clinical events as end points for clinical trials of ventilator-associated pneumonia and hospital-acquired pneumonia. *Clin Infect Dis.* 2010;51(suppl 1): S120–S125.

10. Sanjay P, Fawzi A, Kulli C, et al. Impact of methicillin-resistant *Staphylococcus aureus* (MRSA) infection on patient outcome after pancreatoduodenectomy (PD): a cause for concern? *Pancreas.* 2010;39(8):1211–1214.

11. Sunenshine RH, Wright MO, Maragakis LL, et al. Multidrug-resistant *Acinetobacter* infection mortality rate and length of hospitalization. *Emerg Infect Dis.* 2007;13(1):97–103.

12. Rosenthal VD, Dwivedy A, Calderon ME, et al. Time-dependent analysis of length of stay

and mortality due to urinary tract infections in ten developing countries: INICC findings. *J Infect.* 2011;62(2):136–141.

13. Harbarth S, Sax H, Gastmeier P. The preventable proportion of nosocomial infections: an overview of published reports. *J Hosp Infect.* 2003;54(4):258–66.

14. Yokoe DS, Mermel LA, Anderson DJ, et al. A compendium of strategies to prevent healthcare-associated infections in acute care hospitals. *Infect Control Hosp Epidemiol.* 2008;29(suppl 1):S12–S21.

15. Vincent JL, Bihari DJ, Suter PM, et al. The prevalence of nosocomial infection in intensive care units in Europe: results of the European Prevalence of Infection in Intensive Care (EPIC) study. EPIC International Advisory Committee. *JAMA.* 1995;274(8):639–644.

16. Tikhomirov E. WHO programme for the control of hospital infections. *Chemioterapia.* 1987;6(3):148–151.

17. Rosenthal VD, Maki DG, Jamulitrat S, et al. International Nosocomial Infection Control Consortium (INICC) report, data summary for 2003–2008, issued June 2009. *Am J Infect Control.* 2010;38(2):95–104 e2.

18. Allegranzi B, Bagheri Nejad S, Combescure C, et al. Burden of endemic health-care–associated infection in developing countries: systematic review and meta-analysis. *Lancet.* 2011;377(9761):228–241.

19. Wenzel RP. Instituting health care reform and preserving quality: role of the hospital epidemiologist. *Clin Infect Dis.* 1993;17(5):831–834.

20. Kislak JW, Eickhoff TC, Finland M. Hospital-acquired infections and antibiotic usage in the Boston City Hospital—January, 1964. *N Engl J Med.* 1964;271:834–835.

21. Haley RW, Shachtman RH. The emergence of infection surveillance and control programs in US hospitals: an assessment, 1976. *Am J Epidemiol.* 1980;111(5):574–591.

22. Selwyn S. Hospital infection: the first 2500 years. *J Hosp Infect.* 1991;18(suppl A):5–64.

23. Major R. *A History of Medicine.* Oxford, UK: Blackwell Publishers; 1954.

24. Tenon J. *Memoires sur les Hopitaux de Paris.* Paris: Ph-D Pierres; 1788.

25. Simpson J. Some propositions on hospitalism, by the late Sir JY Simpsom, Bart. *Lancet.* 1870;2:698–700.

26. Simpson J. Presidential address on public health. *Trans Natl Assoc Promotion Soc Sci.* 1867:107–123.

27. Cohen IB. Florence Nightingale. *Sci Am.* 1984;250(3):128–137.

28. Nightingale F. *Notes on Hospitals.* 3rd ed. London: Longman; 1863.

29. Semmelweis IP. The etiology, the concept and the prophylaxis of childbed fever. *Med Classics.* 1861;5:334–773.

30. Absolon KB, Absolon MJ, Zientek R. From antisepsis to asepsis: Louis Pasteur's publication on "The germ theory and its application to medicine and surgery." *Rev Surg.* 1970;27(4):245–258.

31. Toledo-Pereyra LH, Toledo MM. A critical study of Lister's work on antiseptic surgery. *Am J Surg.* 1976;131(6):736–744.

32. Delaunay A. Centennial of the "germ theory and its applications to medicine and surgery," presented by Louis Pasteur in April of 1878. *Gac Med Mex.* 1979;115(3):145–149.

33. Lister J. A method of antiseptic treatment applicable to wounded soldiers in the present war. *Br Med J.* 1870;2(505):243–244.

34. Brewer G. Operative surgery at the city hosptial with preliminary report on the study of wound infection. *New York Med J.* 1896.

35. Brewer G. Studies in aseptic technique, with a report of some recent infections at the Roosevelt Hospital. *JAMA.* 1915;64:1369–1372.

36. Wise RI, Ossman EA, Littlefield DR. Personal reflections on nosocomial staphylococcal in

fections and the development of hospital surveillance. *Rev Infect Dis.* 1989;11(6):1005–1019.

37. Schaberg DR, Culver DH, Gaynes RP. Major trends in the microbial etiology of nosocomial infection. *Am J Med.* 1991;91(3B):72S–75S.

38. National Nosocomial Infections Surveillance (NNIS) report, data summary from October 1986–April 1996, issued May 1996: a report from the National Nosocomial Infections Surveillance (NNIS) System. *Am J Infect Control.* 1996;24(5):380–388.

39. Cosgrove SE, Sakoulas G, Perencevich EN, et al. Comparison of mortality associated with methicillin-resistant and methicillin-susceptible *Staphylococcus aureus* bacteremia: a meta-analysis. *Clin Infect Dis.* 2003;36(1):53–59.

40. Nosocomial infection rates for interhospital comparison: limitations and possible solutions: a report from the National Nosocomial Infections Surveillance (NNIS) System. *Infect Control Hosp Epidemiol.* 1991;12(10):609–621.

41. Wenzel K. The role of the infection control nurse. *Nurs Clin North Am.* 1970;5(1):89–98.

42. Barrett FF, Casey JI, Finland M. Infections and antibiotic use among patients at Boston City Hospital, February, 1967. *N Engl J Med.* 1968;278(1):5–9.

43. Shaw K. The 2003 SARS outbreak and its impact on infection control practices. *Public Health.* 2006;120(1):8–14.

44. Chen NH, Wang PC, Hsieh MJ, et al. Impact of severe acute respiratory syndrome care on the general health status of healthcare workers in taiwan. *Infect Control Hosp Epidemiol.* 2007;28(1):75–79.

45. Glasser JW, Hupert N, McCauley MM, Hatchett R. Modeling and public health emergency responses: lessons from SARS. *Epidemics.* 2011;3(1):32–37.

46. Summary of probable SARS cases with onset of illness from 1 November 2002 to 31 July 2003 [database on the Internet]. 2003. Available at: http://www.who.int/csr/sars/country/table2004_04_21/en/. Accessed January 9, 2012.

47. Perl TM, Chaiwarit R. Surveillance: an overview. In: Lautenbach E, Woeltje KF, Malani PN, eds. *Practical Healthcare Epidemiology.* 3rd ed. Chicago: University of Chicago Press; 2010:111–142.

48. McGeer A, Campbell B, Emori TG, et al. Definitions of infection for surveillance in long-term care facilities. *Am J Infect Control.* 1991;19(1):1–7.

49. Singh-Naz N, Sprague BM, Patel KM, Pollack MM. Risk factors for nosocomial infection in critically ill children: a prospective cohort study. *Crit Care Med.* 1996;24(5):875–878.

50. Freeman J, McGowan JE, Jr. Day-specific incidence of nosocomial infection estimated from a prevalence survey. *Am J Epidemiol.* 1981;114(6):888–901.

51. Rhame FS, Sudderth WD. Incidence and prevalence as used in the analysis of the occurrence of nosocomial infections. *Am J Epidemiol.* 1981;113(1):1–11.

52. Pottinger JM, Herwaldt LA, Perl TM. Basics of surveillance: an overview. *Infect Control Hosp Epidemiol.* 1997;18(7):513–527.

53. Siegel JD, Rhinehart E, Jackson M, Chiarello L. 2007 Guideline for isolation precautions: preventing transmission of infectious agents in health care settings. *Am J Infect Control.* 2007;35(10 suppl 2):S65–S164.

54. Haley RW, Hooton TM, Schoenfelder JR, et al. Effect of an infection surveillance and control program on the accuracy of retrospective chart review. *Am J Epidemiol.* 1980;111(5):543–555.

55. Woeltje KF, McMullen KM. Developing information technology for infection prevention surveillance. *Crit Care Med.* 2010;38(8 suppl):S399–S404.

56. Wright MO, Perencevich EN, Novak C, et al. Preliminary assessment of an automated surveillance system for infection control. *Infect Control Hosp Epidemiol.* 2004;25(4):325–332.

57. Haley RW, Tenney JH, Lindsey JO 2nd, et al. How frequent are outbreaks of nosocomial

infection in community hospitals? *Infect Control.* 1985;6(6):233–236.

58. Haley RW, Culver DH, Morgan WM, et al. Identifying patients at high risk of surgical wound infection: a simple multivariate index of patient susceptibility and wound contamination. *Am J Epidemiol.* 1985;121(2):206–215.

59. Givens CD, Wenzel RP. Catheter-associated urinary tract infections in surgical patients: a controlled study on the excess morbidity and costs. *J Urol.* 1980;124(5):646–648.

60. Coello R, Glenister H, Fereres J, et al. The cost of infection in surgical patients: a case-control study. *J Hosp Infect.* 1993;25(4):239–250.

61. Eickhoff TC. The Third Decennial International Conference on Nosocomial Infections. Historical perspective: the landmark conference in 1970. *Am J Med.* 1991;91(3B):3S–5S.

62. Warren JW, Anthony WC, Hoopes JM, Muncie HL Jr. Cephalexin for susceptible bacteriuria in afebrile, long-term catheterized patients. *JAMA.* 1982;248(4):454–458.

63. Freeman J, McGowan JE, Jr. Risk factors for nosocomial infection. *J Infect Dis.* 1978;138(6):811–819.

64. Stamm WE, Martin SM, Bennett JV. Epidemiology of nosocomial infection due to Gram-negative bacilli: aspects relevant to development and use of vaccines. *J Infect Dis.* 1977;136(suppl):S151–S160.

65. Saviteer SM, Samsa GP, Rutala WA. Nosocomial infections in the elderly: increased risk per hospital day. *Am J Med.* 1988;84(4):661–666.

66. Gross PA, Rapuano C, Adrignolo A, Shaw B. Nosocomial infections: decade-specific risk. *Infect Control.* 1983;4(3):145–147.

67. Emori TG, Banerjee SN, Culver DH, et al. Nosocomial infections in elderly patients in the United States, 1986–1990: National Nosocomial Infections Surveillance System. *Am J Med.* 1991;91(3B):289S–293S.

68. Barsic B, Beus I, Marton E, et al. Nosocomial infections in critically ill infectious disease patients: results of a 7-year focal surveillance. Infection. 1999;27(1):16–22.

69. Kampf G, Wischnewski N, Schulgen G, et al. Prevalence and risk factors for nosocomial lower respiratory tract infections in German hospitals. *J Clin Epidemiol.* 1998;51(6):495–502.

70. Berbari EF, Hanssen AD, Duffy MC, et al. Risk factors for prosthetic joint infection: case-control study. *Clin Infect Dis.* 1998;27(5):1247–1254.

71. Petrosillo N, Pagani L, Ippolito G. Nosocomial infections in HIV-positive patients: an overview. Infection. 2003 Dec;31 Suppl 2:28–34.

72. Velasco E, Thuler LC, Martins CA, et al. Nosocomial infections in an oncology intensive care unit. *Am J Infect Control.* 1997;25(6):458–462.

73. Dettenkofer M, Ebner W, Bertz H, et al. Surveillance of nosocomial infections in adult recipients of allogeneic and autologous bone marrow and peripheral blood stem-cell transplantation. *Bone Marrow Transplant.* 2003;31(9):795–801.

74. Elishoov H, Or R, Strauss N, Engelhard D. Nosocomial colonization, septicemia, and Hickman/Broviac catheter-related infections in bone marrow transplant recipients: a 5-year prospective study. *Medicine (Baltimore).* 1998;77(2):83–101.

75. Romano V, Castagnola E, Dallorso S, et al. Bloodstream infections can develop late (after day 100) and/or in the absence of neutropenia in children receiving allogeneic bone marrow transplantation. *Bone Marrow Transplant.* 1999;23(3):271–275.

76. Harrington G, Russo P, Spelman D, et al. Surgical-site infection rates and risk factor analysis in coronary artery bypass graft surgery. *Infect Control Hosp Epidemiol.* 2004;25(6):472–476.

77. Olsen MA, Higham-Kessler J, Yokoe DS, et al. Developing a risk stratification model

for surgical site infection after abdominal hysterectomy. *Infect Control Hosp Epidemiol.* 2009;30(11):1077–1083.

78. Lynch RJ, Ranney DN, Shijie C, et al. Obesity, surgical site infection, and outcome following renal transplantation. *Ann Surg.* 2009;250(6):1014–1020.

79. Pull ter Gunne AF, van Laarhoven CJ, Cohen DB. Incidence of surgical site infection following adult spinal deformity surgery: an analysis of patient risk. *Eur Spine J.* 2010;19(6):982–988.

80. Waisbren E, Rosen H, Bader AM, et al. Percent body fat and prediction of surgical site infection. *J Am Coll Surg.* 2010;210(4):381–389.

81. Daneman N, Lu H, Redelmeier DA. Discharge after discharge: predicting surgical site infections after patients leave hospital. *J Hosp Infect.* 2010;75(3):188–194.

82. Alam M, Siddiqui S, Lee VV, et al. Isolated coronary artery bypass grafting in obese individuals: a propensity matched analysis of outcomes. *Circ J.* 2011;75(6):1378–1385.

83. Wick EC, Hirose K, Shore AD, et al. Surgical site infections and cost in obese patients undergoing colorectal surgery. *Arch Surg.* 2011;146(9):1068–1072.

84. Dossett LA, Dageforde LA, Swenson BR, et al. Obesity and site-specific nosocomial infection risk in the intensive care unit. *Surg Infect (Larchmt).* 2009;10(2):137–142.

85. Rhame FS, Streifel AJ, Kersey JH Jr, McGlave PB. Extrinsic risk factors for pneumonia in the patient at high risk of infection. *Am J Med.* 1984;76(5A):42–52.

86. Rhame FS. Prevention of nosocomial aspergillosis. *J Hosp Infect.* 1991;18 (suppl A):466–472.

87. Thio CL, Smith D, Merz WG, et al. Refinements of environmental assessment during an outbreak investigation of invasive aspergillosis in a leukemia and bone marrow transplant unit. *Infect Control Hosp Epidemiol.* 2000;21(1):18–23.

88. Stout JE, Yu VL. Legionellosis. *N Engl J Med.* 1997;337(10):682–687.

89. Kirby BD, Snyder KM, Meyer RD, Finegold SM. Legionnaires' disease: report of sixty-five nosocomially acquired cases of review of the literature. *Medicine (Baltimore).* 1980;59(3):188–205.

90. Kugler JW, Armitage JO, Helms CM, et al. Nosocomial Legionnaires' disease. Occurrence in recipients of bone marrow transplants. *Am J Med.* 1983;74(2):281–288.

91. McGowan JE Jr. Environmental factors in nosocomial infection-a selective focus. *Rev Infect Dis.* 1981;3(4):760–769.

92. Best M, Yu VL, Stout J, et al. Legionellaceae in the hospital water-supply: epidemiological link with disease and evaluation of a method for control of nosocomial Legionnaires' disease and Pittsburgh pneumonia. *Lancet.* 1983;2(8345):307–310.

93. Johnston JM, Latham RH, Meier FA, et al. Nosocomial outbreak of Legionnaires' disease: molecular epidemiology and disease control measures. *Infect Control.* 1987;8(2):53–58.

94. Guiguet M, Pierre J, Brun P, et al. Epidemiological survey of a major outbreak of nosocomial legionellosis. *Int J Epidemiol.* 1987;16(3):466–471.

95. Le Saux NM, Sekla L, McLeod J, et al. Epidemic of nosocomial Legionnaires' disease in renal transplant recipients: a case-control and environmental study. *CMAJ.* 1989;140(9):1047–1053.

96. Tram C, Simonet M, Nicolas MH, et al. Molecular typing of nosocomial isolates of *Legionella pneumophila* serogroup 3. *J Clin Microbiol.* 1990;28(2):242–245.

97. Levin AS, Caiaffa Filho HH, Sinto SI, et al. An outbreak of nosocomial Legionnaires' disease in a renal transplant unit in Sao Paulo, Brazil. Legionellosis Study Team. *J Hosp Infect.* 1991;18(3):243–248.

98. Memish ZA, Oxley C, Contant J, Garber GE. Plumbing system shock absorbers as a source of *Legionella pneumophila*. *Am J Infect Control.* 1992;20(6):305–309.

99. Struelens MJ, Maes N, Rost F, et al. Genotypic and phenotypic methods for the investigation of a nosocomial *Legionella pneumophila* outbreak and efficacy of control measures. *J Infect Dis.* 1992;166(1):22–30.

100. Nechwatal R, Ehret W, Klatte OJ, et al. Nosocomial outbreak of legionellosis in a rehabilitation center: demonstration of potable water as a source. Infection. 1993;21(4): 235–240.

101. Colville A, Crowley J, Dearden D, et al. Outbreak of Legionnaires' disease at University Hospital, Nottingham: epidemiology, microbiology and control. *Epidemiol Infect.* 1993;110(1):105–116.

102. Patterson WJ, Seal DV, Curran E, et al. Fatal nosocomial Legionnaires' disease: relevance of contamination of hospital water supply by temperature-dependent buoyancy-driven flow from spur pipes. *Epidemiol Infect.* 1994;112(3):513–525.

103. Sustained transmission of nosocomial Legionnaires disease—Arizona and Ohio. *MMWR.* 1997;46(19):416–421.

104. Dondero TJ Jr, Rendtorff RC, Mallison GF, et al. An outbreak of Legionnaires' disease associated with a contaminated air-conditioning cooling tower. *N Engl J Med.* 1980;302(7):365–370.

105. Helms CM, Massanari RM, Wenzel RP, Pfaller et al. Legionnaires' disease associated with a hospital water system: a five-year progress report on continuous hyperchlorination. *JAMA.* 1988;259(16):2423–2427.

106. Garbe PL, Davis BJ, Weisfeld JS, et al. Nosocomial Legionnaires' disease: epidemiologic demonstration of cooling towers as a source. *JAMA.* 1985;254(4):521–524.

107. Berthelot P, Grattard F, Ros A, et al. Nosocomial legionellosis outbreak over a three-year period: investigation and control. *Clin Microbiol Infect.* 1998;4(7):385–391.

108. Lepine LA, Jernigan DB, Butler JC, et al. A recurrent outbreak of nosocomial legionnaires' disease detected by urinary antigen testing: evidence for long-term colonization of a hospital plumbing system. *Infect Control Hosp Epidemiol.* 1998;19(12):905–910.

109. Perola O, Kauppinen J, Kusnetsov J, et al. Nosocomial *Legionella pneumophila* serogroup 5 outbreak associated with persistent colonization of a hospital water system. *APMIS.* 2002;110(12):863–868.

110. Stout JE, Yu VL, Muraca P. Isolation of *Legionella pneumophila* from the cold water of hospital ice machines: implications for origin and transmission of the organism. *Infect Control.* 1985;6(4):141–146.

111. Woo AH, Yu VL, Goetz A. Potential in-hospital modes of transmission of *Legionella pneumophila*: demonstration experiments for dissemination by showers, humidifiers, and rinsing of ventilation bag apparatus. *Am J Med.* 1986;80(4):567–573.

112. Moiraghi A, Castellani Pastoris M, Barral C, et al. Nosocomial legionellosis associated with use of oxygen bubble humidifiers and underwater chest drains. *J Hosp Infect.* 1987;10(1):47–50.

113. Bangsborg JM, Uldum S, Jensen JS, Bruun BG. Nosocomial legionellosis in three heart-lung transplant patients: case reports and environmental observations. *Eur J Clin Microbiol Infect Dis.* 1995;14(2):99–104.

114. Graman PS, Quinlan GA, Rank JA. Nosocomial legionellosis traced to a contaminated ice machine. *Infect Control Hosp Epidemiol.* 1997;18(9):637–640.

115. Oren I, Zuckerman T, Avivi I, et al. Nosocomial outbreak of *Legionella pneumophila* serogroup 3 pneumonia in a new bone marrow transplant unit: evaluation, treatment and control. *Bone Marrow Transplant.* 2002;30(3):175–179.

116. Franzin L, Cabodi D, Scolfaro C, Gioannini P. Microbiological investigations on a nosocomial case of *Legionella pneumophila* pneumonia associated with water birth and review of neonatal cases. *Infez Med.* 2004;12(1):69–75.

117. Tercelj-Zorman M, Seljak M, Stare J, et al. A hospital outbreak of *Legionella* from a contaminated water supply. *Arch Environ Health*. 2004;59(3):156–159.

118. Schuetz AN, Hughes RL, Howard RM, et al. Pseudo-outbreak of *Legionella pneumophila* serogroup 8 infection associated with a contaminated ice machine in a bronchoscopy suite. *Infect Control Hosp Epidemiol*. 2009;30(5):461–466.

119. Pseudo-outbreak of Legionnaires disease among patients undergoing bronchoscopy—Arizona, 2008. *MMWR*. 2009;58(31):849–854.

120. Palmore TN, Stock F, White M, et al. A cluster of cases of nosocomial legionnaires disease linked to a contaminated hospital decorative water fountain. *Infect Control Hosp Epidemiol*. 2009;30(8):764–768.

121. Wallace RJ Jr, Brown BA, Griffith DE. Nosocomial outbreaks/pseudo-outbreaks caused by nontuberculous mycobacteria. *Annu Rev Microbiol*. 1998;52:453–490.

122. Phillips MS, von Reyn CF. Nosocomial infections due to nontuberculous mycobacteria. *Clin Infect Dis*. 2001;33(8):1363–1374.

123. Rutala WA, Weber DJ. Water as a reservoir of nosocomial pathogens. *Infect Control Hosp Epidemiol*. 1997;18(9):609–616.

124. Gebo KA, Srinivasan A, Perl TM, et al. Pseudo-outbreak of *Mycobacterium fortuitum* on a human immunodeficiency virus ward: transient respiratory tract colonization from a contaminated ice machine. *Clin Infect Dis*. 2002;35(1):32–38.

125. Maragakis LL, Winkler A, Tucker MG, et al. Outbreak of multidrug-resistant *Serratia marcescens* infection in a neonatal intensive care unit. *Infect Control Hosp Epidemiol*. 2008;29(5):418–423.

126. Astagneau P, Duneton P. [Management of epidemics of nosocomial infections]. *Pathol Biol (Paris)*. 1998;46(4):272–278.

127. Kaatz GW, Gitlin SD, Schaberg DR, et al. Acquisition of *Clostridium difficile* from the hospital environment. *Am J Epidemiol*. 1988;127(6):1289–1294.

128. Sexton T, Clarke P, O'Neill E, et al. Environmental reservoirs of methicillin-resistant *Staphylococcus aureus* in isolation rooms: correlation with patient isolates and implications for hospital hygiene. *J Hosp Infect*. 2006;62(2):187–194.

129. Zirakzadeh A, Patel R. Vancomycin-resistant enterococci: colonization, infection, detection, and treatment. *Mayo Clin Proc*. 2006;81(4):529–536.

130. Weber DJ, Rutala WA, Miller MB, et al. Role of hospital surfaces in the transmission of emerging health care–associated pathogens: norovirus, *Clostridium difficile*, and *Acinetobacter* species. *Am J Infect Control*. 2010;38(5 suppl 1):S25–S33.

131. Graman PS, Hall CB. Nosocomial viral respiratory infections. *Semin Respir Infect*. 1989;4(4):253–260.

132. Berthelot P, Grattard F, Mahul P, et al. Ventilator temperature sensors: an unusual source of *Pseudomonas cepacia* in nosocomial infection. *J Hosp Infect*. 1993;25(1):33–43.

133. Vesley D, Norlien KG, Nelson B, et al. Significant factors in the disinfection and sterilization of flexible endoscopes. *Am J Infect Control*. 1992;20(6):291–300.

134. Nosocomial infection and pseudoinfection from contaminated endoscopes and bronchoscopes—United States. *Can Dis Wkly Rep*. 1991;17(49):271–274.

135. Jawad A, Heritage J, Snelling AM, et al. Influence of relative humidity and suspending menstrua on survival of *Acinetobacter* spp. on dry surfaces. *J Clin Microbiol*. 1996;34(12):2881–2887.

136. Craven DE, Steger KA. Nosocomial pneumonia in mechanically ventilated adult patients: epidemiology and prevention in 1996. *Semin Respir Infect*. 1996;11(1):32–53.

137. Carratala J, Fernandez-Sevilla A, Tubau F, et al. Emergence of quinolone-resistant

Escherichia coli bacteremia in neutropenic patients with cancer who have received prophylactic norfloxacin. *Clin Infect Dis.* 1995;20(3):557–560.

138. Wingard JR, Merz WG, Rinaldi MG, et al. Increase in *Candida krusei* infection among patients with bone marrow transplantation and neutropenia treated prophylactically with fluconazole. *N Engl J Med.* 1991;325(18):1274–1277.

139. Sheretz RJ, Reagan DR, Hampton KD, et al. A cloud adult: the *Staphylococcus aureus*–virus interaction revisited. *Ann Intern Med.* 1996;124(6):539–547.

140. van Saene HK, Damjanovic V, Murray AE, de la Cal MA. How to classify infections in intensive care units: the carrier state, a criterion whose time has come? *J Hosp Infect.* 1996;33(1):1–12.

141. Boyce JM, Opal SM, Potter-Bynoe G, Medeiros AA. Spread of methicillin-resistant *Staphylococcus aureus* in a hospital after exposure to a health care worker with chronic sinusitis. *Clin Infect Dis.* 1993;17(3):496–504.

142. Foca M, Jakob K, Whittier S, et al. Endemic *Pseudomonas aeruginosa* infection in a neonatal intensive care unit. *N Engl J Med.* 2000;343(10):695–700.

143. Pfaller MA. Nosocomial candidiasis: emerging species, reservoirs, and modes of transmission. *Clin Infect Dis.* 1996;22(suppl 2): S89–S94.

144. McNeil SA, Nordstrom-Lerner L, Malani PN, et al. Outbreak of sternal surgical site infections due to *Pseudomonas aeruginosa* traced to a scrub nurse with onychomycosis. *Clin Infect Dis.* 2001;33(3):317–323.

145. Wang JT, Chang SC, Ko WJ, et al. A hospital-acquired outbreak of methicillin-resistant *Staphylococcus aureus* infection initiated by a surgeon carrier. *J Hosp Infect.* 2001;47(2):104–109.

146. Faibis F, Laporte C, Fiacre A, et al. An outbreak of methicillin-resistant *Staphylococcus aureus* surgical-site infections initiated by a healthcare worker with chronic sinusitis. *Infect Control Hosp Epidemiol.* 2005;26(2):213–215.

147. Mermel LA, McKay M, Dempsey J, Parenteau S. *Pseudomonas* surgical-site infections linked to a healthcare worker with onychomycosis. *Infect Control Hosp Epidemiol.* 2003;24(10):749–752.

148. Hernandez-Castro R, Arroyo-Escalante S, Carrillo-Casas EM, et al. Outbreak of *Candida parapsilosis* in a neonatal intensive care unit: a health care workers source. *Eur J Pediatr.* 2010;169(7):783–787.

149. Mastro TD, Farley TA, Elliott JA, et al. An outbreak of surgical-wound infections due to group A *Streptococcus* carried on the scalp. *N Engl J Med.* 1990;323(14):968–972.

150. Quinn RW, Hillman JW. An epidemic of streptococcal wound infections. *Arch Environ Health.* 1965;11:28–33.

151. Rountree PM, Bulteau VG. Hospital infection with tetracycline-resistant haemolytic streptococci. *Med J Aust.* 1965;2(11):446–448.

152. McKee WM, Di Caprio JM, Roberts CE Jr, Sherris JC. Anal carriage as the probable source of a streptococcal epidemic. *Lancet.* 1966;2(7471):1007–1009.

153. Holloway WJ, Scott EG. Nosocomial infection: report of an outbreak of wound infections due to tetracycline resistant group A *Streptococcus. Del Med J.* 1967;39(10):263–266.

154. McIntyre DM. An epidemic of *Streptococcus pyogenes* puerperal and postoperative sepsis with an unusual carrier site—the anus. *Am J Obstet Gynecol.* 1968;101(3):308–314.

155. Schaffner W, Lefkowitz LB Jr, Goodman JS, Koenig MG. Hospital outbreak of infections with group A streptococci traced to an asymptomatic anal carrier. *N Engl J Med.* 1969;280(22):1224–1225.

156. Gryska PF, O'Dea AE. Postoperative streptococcal wound infection: the anatomy of an epidemic. *JAMA.* 1970;213(7):1189–1191.

157. Richman DD, Breton SJ, Goldman DA. Scarlet fever and group A streptococcal surgical wound infection traced to an anal carrier. *J Pediatr.* 1977;90(3):387–390.

158. Stamm WE, Feeley JC, Facklam RR. Wound infections due to group A *Streptococcus* traced to a vaginal carrier. *J Infect Dis.* 1978;138(3):287–292.

159. Bassinet L, Matrat M, Njamkepo E, et al. Nosocomial pertussis outbreak among adult patients and healthcare workers. *Infect Control Hosp Epidemiol.* 2004;25(11):995–997.

160. Outbreaks of pertussis associated with hospitals—Kentucky, Pennsylvania, and Oregon, 2003. *MMWR.* 2005;54(3):67–71.

161. Ward A, Caro J, Bassinet L, et al. Health and economic consequences of an outbreak of pertussis among healthcare workers in a hospital in France. *Infect Control Hosp Epidemiol.* 2005;26(3):288–292.

162. Alexander EM, Travis S, Booms C, et al. Pertussis outbreak on a neonatal unit: identification of a healthcare worker as the likely source. *J Hosp Infect.* 2008;69(2):131–134.

163. Kurt TL, Yeager AS, Guenette S, Dunlop S. Spread of pertussis by hospital staff. *JAMA.* 1972;221(3):264–267.

164. Pascual FB, McCall CL, McMurtray A, et al. Outbreak of pertussis among healthcare workers in a hospital surgical unit. *Infect Control Hosp Epidemiol.* 2006;27(6):546–552.

165. Balkovic ES, Goodman RA, Rose FB, Borel CO. Nosocomial influenza A (H1N1) infection. *Am J Med Technol.* 1980;46(5):318–320.

166. Malavaud S, Malavaud B, Sandres K, et al. Nosocomial outbreak of influenza virus A (H3N2) infection in a solid organ transplant department. *Transplantation.* 2001;72(3):535–537.

167. Horcajada JP, Pumarola T, Martinez JA, et al. A nosocomial outbreak of influenza during a period without influenza epidemic activity. *Eur Respir J.* 2003;21(2):303–307.

168. Weber DJ, Rutala WA. Role of environmental contamination in the transmission of vancomycin-resistant enterococci. *Infect Control Hosp Epidemiol.* 1997;18(5):306–309.

169. Hughes WT, Williams B, Pearson T. The nosocomial colonization of T. Bear. *Infect Control.* 1986;7(10):495–500.

170. Menzies D, Fanning A, Yuan L, FitzGerald JM. Hospital ventilation and risk for tuberculous infection in canadian health care workers. Canadian Collaborative Group in Nosocomial Transmission of TB. *Ann Intern Med.* 2000;133(10):779–789.

171. Lanini S, Jarvis WR, Nicastri E, et al. Healthcare-associated infection in Italy: annual point-prevalence surveys, 2002–2004. *Infect Control Hosp Epidemiol.* 2009;30(7):659–665.

172. Gravel D, Taylor G, Ofner M, et al. Point prevalence survey for healthcare-associated infections within Canadian adult acute-care hospitals. *J Hosp Infect.* 2007;66(3):243–248.

173. Reilly J, Stewart S, Allardice GA, et al. Results from the Scottish National HAI Prevalence Survey. *J Hosp Infect.* 2008;69(1):62–68.

174. Srinivasan A, Patel JB. *Klebsiella pneumoniae* carbapenemase-producing organisms: an ounce of prevention really is worth a pound of cure. *Infect Control Hosp Epidemiol.* 2008;29(12):1107–1109.

175. Kallen AJ, Hidron AI, Edwards JR, Patel J, Srinivasan A, eds. *Antibiotic Resistance Among Important Gram-Negative Pathogens Causing Healthcare-Associated Infections Reported to the National Healthcare Safety Network, 2006–2007.* 18th Annual Scientific Meeting of the Society for Healthcare Epidemiology of America; Orlando, FL; 2008.

176. Saint S. Clinical and economic consequences of nosocomial catheter-related bacteriuria. *Am J Infect Control.* 2000;28(1):68–75.

177. Platt R, Polk BF, Murdock B, Rosner B. Mortality associated with nosocomial urinary-tract infection. *N Engl J Med.* 1982;307(11):637–642.

178. Tambyah PA, Knasinski V, Maki DG. The direct costs of nosocomial catheter-associated urinary tract infection in the era of managed care. *Infect Control Hosp Epidemiol.* 2002;23(1):27–31.

179. Burton DC, Edwards JR, Srinivasan A, et al. Trends in catheter-associated urinary tract infections in adult intensive care units-United States, 1990–2007. *Infect Control Hosp Epidemiol.* 2011;32(8):748–756.

180. Leape LL, Brennan TA, Laird N, et al. The nature of adverse events in hospitalized patients: results of the Harvard Medical Practice Study II. *N Engl J Med.* 1991;324(6):377–384.

181. Maki DG. Nosocomial bacteremia: an epidemiologic overview. *Am J Med.* 1981;70(3):719–732.

182. Banerjee SN, Emori TG, Culver DH, et al. Secular trends in nosocomial primary bloodstream infections in the United States, 1980–1989. National Nosocomial Infections Surveillance System. *Am J Med.* 1991;91(3B):86S–89S.

183. O'Grady NP, Alexander M, Burns LA, et al. Guidelines for the prevention of intravascular catheter-related infections. *Am J Infect Control.* 2011;39(4 suppl 1):S1–S34.

184. Maki DG, Kluger DM, Crnich CJ. The risk of bloodstream infection in adults with different intravascular devices: a systematic review of 200 published prospective studies. *Mayo Clin Proc.* 2006;81(9):1159–1171.

185. O'Grady NP, Alexander M, Dellinger EP, et al. Guidelines for the prevention of intravascular catheter-related infections. Centers for Disease Control and Prevention. *MMWR Recomm Rep.* 2002;51(RR-10):1–29.

186. Crnich CJ, Maki DG. The role of intravascular devices in sepsis. *Curr Infect Dis Rep.* 2001;3(6):496–506.

187. Wisplinghoff H, Bischoff T, Tallent SM, et al. Nosocomial bloodstream infections in US hospitals: analysis of 24,179 cases from a prospective nationwide surveillance study. *Clin Infect Dis.* 2004;39(3):309–317.

188. Frankel HL, Crede WB, Topal JE, et al. Use of corporate Six Sigma performance-improvement strategies to reduce incidence of catheter-related bloodstream infections in a surgical ICU. *J Am Coll Surg.* 2005;201(3):349–358.

189. Galpern D, Guerrero A, Tu A, et al. Effectiveness of a central line bundle campaign on line-associated infections in the intensive care unit. *Surgery.* 2008;144(4):492–495.

190. Costello JM, Morrow DF, Graham DA, et al. Systematic intervention to reduce central line–associated bloodstream infection rates in a pediatric cardiac intensive care unit. *Pediatrics.* 2008;121(5):915–923.

191. McKee C, Berkowitz I, Cosgrove SE, et al. Reduction of catheter-associated bloodstream infections in pediatric patients: experimentation and reality. *Pediatr Crit Care Med.* 2008;9(1):40–46.

192. Popovich KJ, Hota B, Hayes R, et al. Effectiveness of routine patient cleansing with chlorhexidine gluconate for infection prevention in the medical intensive care unit. *Infect Control Hosp Epidemiol.* 2009;30(10):959–963.

193. Munoz-Price LS, Hota B, Stemer A, Weinstein RA. Prevention of bloodstream infections by use of daily chlorhexidine baths for patients at a long-term acute care hospital. *Infect Control Hosp Epidemiol.* 2009;30(11):1031–1035.

194. Evans HL, Dellit TH, Chan J, et al. Effect of chlorhexidine whole-body bathing on hospital-acquired infections among trauma patients. *Arch Surg.* 2010;145(3):240–246.

195. Dixon JM, Carver RL. Daily chlorohexidine gluconate bathing with impregnated cloths results in statistically significant reduction in central line–associated bloodstream infections. *Am J Infect Control.* 2010;38(10):817–821.

196. Craven DE, Palladino R, McQuillen DP. Healthcare-associated pneumonia in adults: management principles to improve outcomes. *Infect Dis Clin North Am.* 2004;18(4):939–962.

197. Guidelines for the management of adults with hospital-acquired, ventilator-associated, and healthcare-associated pneumonia. *Am J Respir Crit Care Med.* 2005;171(4):388–416.

198. Safdar N, Dezfulian C, Collard HR, Saint S. Clinical and economic consequences of ventilator-associated pneumonia: a systematic review. *Crit Care Med.* 2005;33(10): 2184–2193.

199. El-Solh AA, Niederman MS, Drinka P. Nursing home–acquired pneumonia: a review of risk factors and therapeutic approaches. *Curr Med Res Opin.* 2010;26(12): 2707–2714.

200. Bekaert M, Timsit JF, Vansteelandt S, et al. Attributable mortality of ventilator associated pneumonia: a reappraisal using causal analysis. *Am J Respir Crit Care Med.* 2011;184(10):1133–1139.

201. Beaulieu M, Williamson D, Sirois C, Lachaine J. Do proton-pump inhibitors increase the risk for nosocomial pneumonia in a medical intensive care unit? *J Crit Care.* 2008;23(4):513–518.

202. Herzig SJ, Howell MD, Ngo LH, Marcantonio ER. Acid-suppressive medication use and the risk for hospital-acquired pneumonia. *JAMA.* 2009;301(20):2120–2128.

203. Miano TA, Reichert MG, Houle TT, et al. Nosocomial pneumonia risk and stress ulcer prophylaxis: a comparison of pantoprazole vs ranitidine in cardiothoracic surgery patients. *Chest.* 2009;136(2):440–447.

204. Dublin S, Walker RL, Jackson ML, et al. Use of proton pump inhibitors and H_2 blockers and risk of pneumonia in older adults: a population-based case-control study. *Pharmacoepidemiol Drug Saf.* 2010;19(8):792–802.

205. Ran L, Khatibi NH, Qin X, Zhang JH. Proton pump inhibitor prophylaxis increases the risk of nosocomial pneumonia in patients with an intracerebral hemorrhagic stroke. *Acta Neurochir Suppl.* 2011;111: 435–439.

206. Eom CS, Jeon CY, Lim JW, et al. Use of acid-suppressive drugs and risk of pneumonia: a systematic review and meta-analysis. *CMAJ.* 2011;183(3):310–319.

207. Fohl AL, Regal RE. Proton pump inhibitor-associated pneumonia: not a breath of fresh air after all? *World J Gastrointest Pharmacol Ther.* 2011;2(3):17–26.

208. Carratala J, Mykietiuk A, Fernandez-Sabe N, et al. Health care–associated pneumonia requiring hospital admission: epidemiology, antibiotic therapy, and clinical outcomes. *Arch Intern Med.* 2007;167(13):1393–1399.

209. Micek ST, Kollef KE, Reichley RM, et al. Health care–associated pneumonia and community-acquired pneumonia: a single-center experience. *Antimicrob Agents Chemother.* 2007;51(10):3568–3573.

210. Shorr AF, Zilberberg MD, Micek ST, Kollef MH. Prediction of infection due to antibiotic-resistant bacteria by select risk factors for health care–associated pneumonia. *Arch Intern Med.* 2008;168(20):2205–2210.

211. Shindo Y, Sato S, Maruyama E, et al. Health-care–associated pneumonia among hospitalized patients in a Japanese community hospital. *Chest.* 2009;135(3):633–640.

212. Cecere LM, Rubenfeld GD, Park DR, et al. Long-term survival after hospitalization for community-acquired and healthcare-associated pneumonia. *Respiration.* 2010;79(2):128–136.

213. Kollef MH. Inadequate antimicrobial treatment: an important determinant of outcome for hospitalized patients. *Clin Infect Dis.* 2000;31(suppl 4):S131–S138.

214. Micek ST, Lloyd AE, Ritchie DJ, et al. *Pseudomonas aeruginosa* bloodstream infection: importance of appropriate initial antimicrobial treatment. *Antimicrob Agents Chemother.* 2005;49(4):1306–1311.

215. Teixeira PJ, Seligman R, Hertz FT, et al. Inadequate treatment of ventilator-associated pneumonia: risk factors and impact on outcomes. *J Hosp Infect.* 2007;65(4):361–367.

216. Chang HC, Chen YC, Lin MC, et al. Mortality risk factors in patients with *Acinetobacter baumannii* ventilator: associated pneumonia. *J Formos Med Assoc.* 2011;110(9):564–571.

217. Cross AS, Roup B. Role of respiratory assistance devices in endemic nosocomial pneumonia. *Am J Med.* 1981;70(3):681–685.

218. Craven DE, Steger KA, Barber TW. Preventing nosocomial pneumonia: state of the art and perspectives for the 1990s. *Am J Med.* 1991;91(3B):44S–53S.

219. Kollef MH. Ventilator-associated pneumonia: a multivariate analysis. *JAMA.* 1993;270(16):1965–1970.

220. Cook DJ, Walter SD, Cook RJ, et al. Incidence of and risk factors for ventilator-associated pneumonia in critically ill patients. *Ann Intern Med.* 1998;129(6):433–440.

221. Tablan OC, Anderson LJ, Besser R, et al. Guidelines for preventing health-care—associated pneumonia, 2003: recommendations of CDC and the Healthcare Infection Control Practices Advisory Committee. *MMWR Recomm Rep.* 2004;53(RR-3):1–36.

222. Kollef MH, Shorr A, Tabak YP, et al. Epidemiology and outcomes of health-care–associated pneumonia: results from a large US database of culture-positive pneumonia. *Chest.* 2005;128(6):3854–3862.

223. Venditti M, Falcone M, Corrao S, et al. Outcomes of patients hospitalized with community-acquired, health care–associated, and hospital-acquired pneumonia. *Ann Intern Med.* 2009;150(1):19–26.

224. Kanafani ZA, Kara L, Hayek S, Kanj SS. Ventilator-associated pneumonia at a tertiary-care center in a developing country: incidence, microbiology, and susceptibility patterns of isolated microorganisms. *Infect Control Hosp Epidemiol.* 2003;24(11):864–869.

225. Rocha Lde A, Vilela CA, Cezario RC, et al. Ventilator-associated pneumonia in an adult clinical–surgical intensive care unit of a Brazilian university hospital: incidence, risk factors, etiology, and antibiotic resistance. *Braz J Infect Dis.* 2008;12(1):80–85.

226. Talha KA, Hasan Z, Selina F, Palash MI. Organisms associated with ventilator associated pneumonia in intensive care unit. *Mymensingh Med J.* 2009;18(1 suppl): S93–S97.

227. Walkey AJ, Reardon CC, Sulis CA, et al. Epidemiology of ventilator-associated pneumonia in a long-term acute care hospital. *Infect Control Hosp Epidemiol.* 2009;30(4):319–324.

228. Hu HB, Huang HJ, Peng QY, et al. Prospective study of colonization and infection because of *Pseudomonas aeruginosa* in mechanically ventilated patients at a neonatal intensive care unit in China. *Am J Infect Control.* 2010;38(9):746–750.

229. Werarak P, Kiratisin P, Thamlikitkul V. Hospital-acquired pneumonia and ventilator-associated pneumonia in adults at Siriraj Hospital: etiology, clinical outcomes, and impact of antimicrobial resistance. *J Med Assoc Thai.* 2010;93(suppl 1):S126–S138.

230. Kallel H, Dammak H, Bahloul M, et al. Risk factors and outcomes of intensive care unit–acquired infections in a Tunisian ICU. *Med Sci Monit.* 2010;16(8):PH69–PH75.

231. Joseph NM, Sistla S, Dutta TK, et al. Ventilator-associated pneumonia in a tertiary care hospital in India: role of multi-drug resistant pathogens. *J Infect Dev Ctries.* 2010;4(4):218–225.

232. Guanche-Garcell H, Requejo-Pino O, Rosenthal VD, et al. Device-associated infection rates in adult intensive care units of Cuban university hospitals: International Nosocomial Infection Control Consortium (INICC) findings. *Int J Infect Dis.* 2011;15(5):e357–e362.

233. Xie DS, Xiong W, Lai RP, et al. Ventilator-associated pneumonia in intensive care units

in Hubei Province, China: a multicentre prospective cohort survey. *J Hosp Infect.* 2011;78(4):284–288.

234. Japoni A, Vazin A, Davarpanah MA, et al. Ventilator-associated pneumonia in Iranian intensive care units. *J Infect Dev Ctries.* 2011;5(4):286–293.

235. Jones RN. Microbial etiologies of hospital-acquired bacterial pneumonia and ventilator-associated bacterial pneumonia. *Clin Infect Dis.* 2010;51(suppl 1):S81–S87.

236. Krowka MJ, Rosenow EC 3rd, Hoagland HC. Pulmonary complications of bone marrow transplantation. *Chest.* 1985;87(2):237–246.

237. Prodinger WM, Bonatti H, Allerberger F, et al. Legionella pneumonia in transplant recipients: a cluster of cases of eight years' duration. *J Hosp Infect.* 1994;26(3):191–202.

238. Harrington RD, Hooton TM, Hackman RC, et al. An outbreak of respiratory syncytial virus in a bone marrow transplant center. *J Infect Dis.* 1992;165(6):987–993.

239. Pannuti C, Gingrich R, Pfaller MA, et al. Nosocomial pneumonia in patients having bone marrow transplant: attributable mortality and risk factors. *Cancer.* 1992;69(11):2653–2662.

240. Philit F, Cordonnier C, Michallet M, Cordier JF. [Lung complications of hematopoietic stem cell transplantation]. *Rev Mal Respir.* 1996;13(5 suppl):S71–S84.

241. Singh N. Trends in the epidemiology of opportunistic fungal infections: predisposing factors and the impact of antimicrobial use practices. *Clin Infect Dis.* 2001;33(10):1692–1696.

242. Kapila R, Lintz DI, Tecson FT, et al. A nosocomial outbreak of influenza A. *Chest.* 1977;71(5):576–579.

243. Morens DM, Rash VM. Lessons from a nursing home outbreak of influenza A. *Infect Control Hosp Epidemiol.* 1995;16(5):275–280.

244. Gooskens J, Jonges M, Claas EC, et al. Morbidity and mortality associated with nosocomial transmission of oseltamivir-resistant influenza A(H1N1) virus. *JAMA.* 2009;301(10):1042–1046.

245. Buchbinder N, Dumesnil C, Pinquier D, et al. Pandemic A/H1N1/2009 influenza in a paediatric haematology and oncology unit: successful management of a sudden outbreak. *J Hosp Infect.* 2011;79(2):155–160.

246. Valenti WM, Clarke TA, Hall CB, et al. Concurrent outbreaks of rhinovirus and respiratory syncytial virus in an intensive care nursery: epidemiology and associated risk factors. *J Pediatr.* 1982;100(5):722–726.

247. Abdallah A, Rowland KE, Schepetiuk SK, et al. An outbreak of respiratory syncytial virus infection in a bone marrow transplant unit: effect on engraftment and outcome of pneumonia without specific antiviral treatment. *Bone Marrow Transplant.* 2003;32(2):195–203.

248. Visser A, Delport S, Venter M. Molecular epidemiological analysis of a nosocomial outbreak of respiratory syncytial virus associated pneumonia in a kangaroo mother care unit in South Africa. *J Med Virol.* 2008;80(4):724–732.

249. Kassis C, Champlin RE, Hachem RY, et al. Detection and control of a nosocomial respiratory syncytial virus outbreak in a stem cell transplantation unit: the role of palivizumab. *Biol Blood Marrow Transplant.* 2010;16(9):1265–1271.

250. Louie JK, Schnurr DP, Pan CY, et al. A summer outbreak of human metapneumovirus infection in a long-term–care facility. *J Infect Dis.* 2007;196(5):705–708.

251. Omura T, Iizuka S, Tabara K, et al. Detection of human metapneumovirus genomes during an outbreak of bronchitis and pneumonia in a geriatric care home in Shimane, Japan, in autumn 2009. *Jpn J Infect Dis.* 2011;64(1):85–87.

252. Hatherill M, Levin M, Lawrenson J, et al. Evolution of an adenovirus outbreak in a multidisciplinary children's hospital. *J Paediatr Child Health.* 2004;40(8):449–454.

253. Rivera ME, Mason WH, Ross LA, Wright HT Jr. Nosocomial measles infection in a pediatric hospital during a community-wide epidemic. *J Pediatr.* 1991;119(2):183–186.

254. Engelmann I, Gottlieb J, Meier A, et al. Clinical relevance of and risk factors for HSV-related tracheobronchitis or pneumonia: results of an outbreak investigation. *Crit Care.* 2007;11(6):R119.

255. File TM Jr, Tan JS, Thomson RB Jr, et al. An outbreak of *Pseudomonas aeruginosa* ventilator-associated respiratory infections due to contaminated food coloring dye: further evidence of the significance of gastric colonization preceding nosocomial pneumonia. *Infect Control Hosp Epidemiol.* 1995;16(7): 417–418.

256. Kerr JR, Moore JE, Curran MD, et al. Investigation of a nosocomial outbreak of *Pseudomonas aeruginosa* pneumonia in an intensive care unit by random amplification of polymorphic DNA assay. *J Hosp Infect.* 1995;30(2):125–131.

257. Ostrosky-Zeichner L, Baez-Martinez R, Rangel-Frausto MS, Ponce-de-Leon S. Epidemiology of nosocomial outbreaks: 14-year experience at a tertiary-care center. *Infect Control Hosp Epidemiol.* 2000;21(8):527–529.

258. Cezario RC, Duarte De Morais L, Ferreira JC, et al. Nosocomial outbreak by imipenem-resistant metallo-beta-lactamase–producing *Pseudomonas aeruginosa* in an adult intensive care unit in a Brazilian teaching hospital. *Enferm Infecc Microbiol Clin.* 2009;27(5):269–274.

259. Touati A, Achour W, Cherif A, et al. Outbreak of *Acinetobacter baumannii* in a neonatal intensive care unit: antimicrobial susceptibility and genotyping analysis. *Ann Epidemiol.* 2009;19(6):372–378.

260. Cox TR, Roland WE, Dolan ME. Ventilator-related *Acinetobacter* outbreak in an intensive care unit. *Mil Med.* 1998;163(6):389–391.

261. Frickmann H, Crusius S, Walter U, Podbielski A. [Management of an outbreak with cases of nosocomial pneumonia caused by a novel multi-drug–resistant *Acinetobacter baumannii* clone]. *Pneumologie.* 2010;64(11):686–693.

262. Ray A, Perez F, Beltramini AM, et al. Use of vaporized hydrogen peroxide decontamination during an outbreak of multidrug-resistant *Acinetobacter baumannii* infection at a long-term acute care hospital. *Infect Control Hosp Epidemiol.* 2010;31(12):1236–1241.

263. Harbarth S, Sudre P, Dharan S, et al. Outbreak of *Enterobacter cloacae* related to understaffing, overcrowding, and poor hygiene practices. *Infect Control Hosp Epidemiol.* 1999;20(9):598–603.

264. Manzur A, Tubau F, Pujol M, et al. Nosocomial outbreak due to extended-spectrum–beta-lactamase–producing *Enterobacter cloacae* in a cardiothoracic intensive care unit. *J Clin Microbiol.* 2007;45(8):2365–2369.

265. Gerding DN, Buxton AE, Hughes RA, et al. Nosocomial multiply resistant *Klebsiella pneumoniae*: epidemiology of an outbreak of apparent index case origin. *Antimicrob Agents Chemother.* 1979;15(4):608–615.

266. Martinez-Aguilar G, Alpuche-Aranda CM, Anaya C, et al. Outbreak of nosocomial sepsis and pneumonia in a newborn intensive care unit by multiresistant extended-spectrum beta-lactamase–producing *Klebsiella pneumoniae*: high impact on mortality. *Infect Control Hosp Epidemiol.* 2001;22(11):725–728.

267. Takigawa K, Fujita J, Negayama K, et al. Nosocomial outbreak of *Pseudomonas cepacia* respiratory infection in immunocompromised patients associated with contaminated nebulizer devices. *Kansenshogaku Zasshi.* 1993;67(11):1115–1125.

268. Martin M, Christiansen B, Caspari G, et al. Hospital-wide outbreak of *Burkholderia contaminans* caused by prefabricated moist washcloths. *J Hosp Infect.* 2011;77(3): 267–270.

269. Liu PY, Lau YJ, Hu BS, et al. Use of PCR to study epidemiology of *Serratia marcescens* isolates in nosocomial infection. *J Clin Microbiol.* 1994;32(8):1935–1938.

270. Patterson TF, Patterson JE, Masecar BL, et al. A nosocomial outbreak of *Branhamella catarrhalis* confirmed by restriction endonuclease analysis. *J Infect Dis.* 1988;157(5):996–1001.

271. Cohen MS, Steere AC, Baltimore R, et al. Possible nosocomial transmission of group Y *Neisseria meningitidis* among oncology patients. *Ann Intern Med.* 1979;91(1):7–12.

272. Rose HD, Lenz IE, Sheth NK. Meningococcal pneumonia: a source of nosocomial infection. *Arch Intern Med.* 1981;141(5):575–577.

273. Brown RB, Phillips D, Barker MJ, et al. Outbreak of nosocomial *Flavobacterium meningosepticum* respiratory infections associated with use of aerosolized polymyxin B. *Am J Infect Control.* 1989;17(3):121–125.

274. Iwahara T, Ichiyama S, Nada T, et al. Clinical and epidemiologic investigations of nosocomial pulmonary infections caused by methicillin-resistant *Staphylococcus aureus. Chest.* 1994;105(3):826–831.

275. Manhold C, von Rolbicki U, Brase R, et al. Outbreaks of *Staphylococcus aureus* infections during treatment of late onset pneumonia with ciprofloxacin in a prospective, randomized study. *Intensive Care Med.* 1998;24(12):1327–1330.

276. Sanchez Garcia M, De la Torre MA, Morales G, et al. Clinical outbreak of linezolid-resistant *Staphylococcus aureus* in an intensive care unit. *JAMA.* 2010;303(22):2260–2264.

277. Mandigers CM, Diepersloot RJ, Dessens M, et al. A hospital outbreak of penicillin-resistant pneumococci in the Netherlands. *Eur Respir J.* 1994;7(9):1635–1639.

278. Leggiadro RJ, Schaberg DR. Nosocomial pneumococcal infection: an outbreak. *Hosp Pract (Minneap).* 1999;34(10):77–78, 81–82, 86–92.

279. Marks JS, Tsai TF, Martone WJ, et al. Nosocomial Legionnaires' disease in Columbus, Ohio. *Ann Intern Med.* 1979;90(4):565–569.

280. Hanrahan JP, Morse DL, Scharf VB, et al. A community hospital outbreak of legionellosis: transmission by potable hot water. *Am J Epidemiol.* 1987;125(4):639–649.

281. Winter JH, McCartney AC, Fallon RJ, et al. Rapid diagnosis of an outbreak of Legionnaires' disease at Glasgow Royal Infirmary. *Thorax.* 1987;42(8):596–599.

282. Darelid J, Bengtsson L, Gastrin B, et al. An outbreak of Legionnaires' disease in a Swedish hospital. *Scand J Infect Dis.* 1994;26(4):417–425.

283. Knirsch CA, Jakob K, Schoonmaker D, et al. An outbreak of *Legionella micdadei* pneumonia in transplant patients: evaluation, molecular epidemiology, and control. *Am J Med.* 2000;108(4):290–295.

284. Darelid J, Lofgren S, Malmvall BE. Control of nosocomial Legionnaires' disease by keeping the circulating hot water temperature above 55 degrees C: experience from a 10-year surveillance programme in a district general hospital. *J Hosp Infect.* 2002;50(3):213–219.

285. Levy PY, Teysseire N, Etienne J, Raoult D. A nosocomial outbreak of *Legionella pneumophila* caused by contaminated transesophageal echocardiography probes. *Infect Control Hosp Epidemiol.* 2003;24(8):619–622.

286. Ozerol IH, Bayraktar M, Cizmeci Z, et al. Legionnaire's disease: a nosocomial outbreak in Turkey. *J Hosp Infect.* 2006;62(1):50–57.

287. de Boer MG, de Fijter JW, Kroon FP. Outbreaks and clustering of *Pneumocystis* pneumonia in kidney transplant recipients: a systematic review. *Med Mycol.* 2011; 49(7):673–680.

288. Cheung YF, Chan CF, Lee CW, Lau YL. An outbreak of *Pneumocystis carinii* pneumonia in children with malignancy. *J Paediatr Child Health.* 1994;30(2):173–175.

289. Gianella S, Haeberli L, Joos B, et al. Molecular evidence of interhuman transmission in an outbreak of *Pneumocystis jirovecii* pneumonia among renal transplant recipients. *Transpl Infect Dis.* 2010;12(1):1–10.

290. Coffin SE, Klompas M, Classen D, et al. Strategies to prevent ventilator-associated pneumonia in acute care hospitals. *Infect Control Hosp Epidemiol.* 2008;29(suppl 1):S31–S40.

291. Chan EY, Ruest A, Meade MO, Cook DJ. Oral decontamination for prevention of pneumonia in mechanically ventilated adults: systematic review and meta-analysis. *BMJ.* 2007;334(7599):889.

292. Labeau SO, Van de Vyver K, Brusselaers N, et al. Prevention of ventilator-associated pneumonia with oral antiseptics: a systematic review and meta-analysis. *Lancet Infect Dis.* 2011;11(11):845–854.

293. Tantipong H, Morkchareonpong C, Jaiyindee S, Thamlikitkul V. Randomized controlled trial and meta-analysis of oral decontamination with 2% chlorhexidine solution for the prevention of ventilator-associated pneumonia. *Infect Control Hosp Epidemiol.* 2008;29(2):131–136.

294. Leaper DJ. Surgical-site infection. *Br J Surg.* 2010;97(11):1601–1602.

295. Haley RW. Surveillance by objective: a new priority-directed approach to the control of nosocomial infections: the National Foundation for Infectious Diseases lecture. *Am J Infect Control.* 1985;13(2):78–89.

296. Perencevich EN, Sands KE, Cosgrove SE, et al. Health and economic impact of surgical site infections diagnosed after hospital discharge. *Emerg Infect Dis.* 2003;9(2):196–203.

297. Vegas AA, Jodra VM, Garcia ML. Nosocomial infection in surgery wards: a controlled study of increased duration of hospital stays and direct cost of hospitalization. *Eur J Epidemiol.* 1993;9(5):504–510.

298. Kirkland KB, Briggs JP, Trivette SL, et al. The impact of surgical-site infections in the 1990s: attributable mortality, excess length of hospitalization, and extra costs. *Infect Control Hosp Epidemiol.* 1999;20(11):725–730.

299. Boyce JM, Potter-Bynoe G, Dziobek L. Hospital reimbursement patterns among patients with surgical wound infections following open heart surgery. *Infect Control Hosp Epidemiol.* 1990;11(2):89–93.

300. Whitehouse JD, Friedman ND, Kirkland KB, et al. The impact of surgical-site infections following orthopedic surgery at a community hospital and a university hospital: adverse quality of life, excess length of stay, and extra cost. *Infect Control Hosp Epidemiol.* 2002;23(4):183–189.

301. McGarry SA, Engemann JJ, Schmader K, Sexton DJ, Kaye KS. Surgical-site infection due to *Staphylococcus aureus* among elderly patients: mortality, duration of hospitalization, and cost. *Infect Control Hosp Epidemiol.* 2004;25(6):461–467.

302. Coello R, Charlett A, Wilson J, et al. Adverse impact of surgical site infections in English hospitals. *J Hosp Infect.* 2005;60(2):93–103.

303. de Lissovoy G, Fraeman K, Hutchins V, et al. Surgical site infection: incidence and impact on hospital utilization and treatment costs. *Am J Infect Control.* 2009;37(5):387–397.

304. Broex EC, van Asselt AD, Bruggeman CA, van Tiel FH. Surgical site infections: how high are the costs? *J Hosp Infect.* 2009;72(3):193–201.

305. Mahmoud NN, Turpin RS, Yang G, Saunders WB. Impact of surgical site infections on length of stay and costs in selected colorectal procedures. *Surg Infect (Larchmt).* 2009;10(6):539–544.

306. Anderson DJ, Kaye KS, Classen D, et al. Strategies to prevent surgical site infections in acute care hospitals. *Infect Control Hosp Epidemiol.* 2008;29(suppl 1):S51–S61.

307. Horan TC, Gaynes RP, Martone WJ, et al. CDC definitions of nosocomial surgical site infections, 1992: a modification of CDC definitions of surgical wound infections. *Infect Control Hosp Epidemiol.* 1992;13(10):606–608.

308. Roy MC, Perl TM. Basics of surgical-site infection surveillance. *Infect Control Hosp Epidemiol.* 1997;18(9):659–668.

309. Mangram AJ, Horan TC, Pearson ML, et al. Guideline for prevention of surgical site infection, 1999. Hospital Infection Control Practices Advisory Committee. *Infect Control Hosp Epidemiol.* 1999;20(4):250–278.

310. Manian FA, Meyer L. Comprehensive surveillance of surgical wound infections in outpatient and inpatient surgery. *Infect Control Hosp Epidemiol.* 1990;11(10):515–520.

311. Perl TM, Roy MC. Postoperative wound infections: risk factors and role of *Staphylococcus aureus* nasal carriage. *J Chemother.* 1995;7(suppl 3):29–35.

312. Perl TM, Cullen JJ, Wenzel RP, et al. Intranasal mupirocin to prevent postoperative *Staphylococcus aureus* infections. *N Engl J Med.* 2002;346(24):1871–1877.

313. Bode LG, Kluytmans JA, Wertheim HF, et al. Preventing surgical-site infections in nasal carriers of *Staphylococcus aureus. N Engl J Med.* 2010;362(1):9–17.

314. Rutala WA, Weber DJ, Thomann CA. Outbreak of wound infections following outpatient podiatric surgery due to contaminated bone drills. *Foot Ankle.* 1987;7(6):350–354.

315. Mehta G. *Aspergillus* endocarditis after open heart surgery: an epidemiological investigation. *J Hosp Infect.* 1990;15(3):245–253.

316. Soto LE, Bobadilla M, Villalobos Y, et al. Post-surgical nasal cellulitis outbreak due to *Mycobacterium chelonae. J Hosp Infect.* 1991;19(2):99–106.

317. Anderson DJ. Surgical site infections. *Infect Dis Clin North Am.* 2011;25(1):135–153.

318. Emori TG, Gaynes RP. An overview of nosocomial infections, including the role of the microbiology laboratory. *Clin Microbiol Rev.* 1993;6(4):428–442.

319. Berard F, Gandon J. Postoperative wound infections: the influence of ultraviolet irradiation of the operating room and of various other factors. *Ann Surg.* 1964;160(suppl 2):1–192.

320. Schrack WD Jr, Miller GB, Parkin WE, Fontana DB. Four streptococcal infections traced to anal carrier. *Pa Med.* 1979;82(3):35–36.

321. Berkelman RL, Martin D, Graham DR, et al. Streptococcal wound infections caused by a vaginal carrier. *JAMA.* 1982;247(19):2680–2682.

322. Lark RL, VanderHyde K, Deeb GM, et al. An outbreak of coagulase-negative staphylococcal surgical-site infections following aortic valve replacement. *Infect Control Hosp Epidemiol.* 2001;22(10):618–623.

323. Richet HM, Craven PC, Brown JM, et al. A cluster of *Rhodococcus (Gordona) bronchialis* sternal-wound infections after coronary-artery bypass surgery. *N Engl J Med.* 1991;324(2):104–109.

324. Cruciani M, Malena M, Amalfitano G, et al. Molecular epidemiology in a cluster of cases of postoperative *Pseudomonas aeruginosa* endophthalmitis. *Clin Infect Dis.* 1998;26(2):330–333.

325. Rapidly growing mycobacterial infection following liposuction and liposculpture—Caracas, Venezuela, 1996–1998. *MMWR.* 1998;47(49):1065–1067.

326. Safranek TJ, Jarvis WR, Carson LA, et al. *Mycobacterium chelonae* wound infections after plastic surgery employing contaminated gentian violet skin-marking solution. *N Engl J Med.* 1987;317(4):197–201.

327. *Mycobacterium chelonae* infections associated with face lifts—New Jersey, 2002–2003. *MMWR.* 2004;53(9):192–194.

328. Lowry PW, Blankenship RJ, Gridley W, et al. A cluster of *Legionella* sternal-wound infections due to postoperative topical exposure to contaminated tap water. *N Engl J Med.* 1991;324(2):109–113.

329. Bronchoscopy-related infections and pseudoinfections—New York, 1996 and 1998. *MMWR.* 1999;48(26):557–560.

330. Moucha CS, Clyburn T, Evans RP, Prokuski L. Modifiable risk factors for surgical site

infection. *J Bone Joint Surg Am.* 2011;93(4): 398–404.

331. Koutsoumbelis S, Hughes AP, Girardi FP, et al. Risk factors for postoperative infection following posterior lumbar instrumented arthrodesis. *J Bone Joint Surg Am.* 2011 S;93(17):1627–1633.

332. Simchen E, Stein H, Sacks TG, et al. Multivariate analysis of determinants of postoperative wound infection in orthopaedic patients. *J Hosp Infect.* 1984;5(2):137–146.

333. Edmonston DL, Foulkes GD. Infection rate and risk factor analysis in an orthopaedic ambulatory surgical center. *J Surg Orthop Adv.* 2010;19(3):174–176.

334. Hennessey DB, Burke JP, Ni-Dhonochu T, et al. Preoperative hypoalbuminemia is an independent risk factor for the development of surgical site infection following gastrointestinal surgery: a multi-institutional study. *Ann Surg.* 2010;252(2):325–329.

335. Kurz A, Sessler DI, Lenhardt R. Perioperative normothermia to reduce the incidence of surgical-wound infection and shorten hospitalization. Study of Wound Infection and Temperature Group. *N Engl J Med.* 1996;334(19):1209–1215.

336. Vilar-Compte D, Mohar A, Sandoval S, et al. Surgical site infections at the National Cancer Institute in Mexico: a case-control study. *Am J Infect Control.* 2000;28(1):14–20.

337. Blasco-Colmenares E, Perl TM, Guallar E, et al. Aspirin plus clopidogrel and risk of infection after coronary artery bypass surgery. *Arch Intern Med.* 2009;169(8):788–796.

338. Vilar-Compte D, Rosales S, Hernandez-Mello N, et al. Surveillance, control, and prevention of surgical site infections in breast cancer surgery: a 5-year experience. *Am J Infect Control.* 2009;37(8):674–679.

339. Bernard AC, Davenport DL, Chang PK, et al. Intraoperative transfusion of 1 U to 2 U packed red blood cells is associated with increased 30-day mortality, surgical-site infection, pneumonia, and sepsis in general surgery patients. *J Am Coll Surg.* 2009;208(5):931–937.

340. Schwarzkopf R, Chung C, Park JJ, et al. Effects of perioperative blood product use on surgical site infection following thoracic and lumbar spinal surgery. *Spine (Phila Pa 1976).* 2010;35(3):340–346.

341. Hubner M, Diana M, Zanetti G, et al. Surgical site infections in colon surgery: the patient, the procedure, the hospital, and the surgeon. *Arch Surg.* 2011;146(11):1240–1245.

342. Kluytmans JA, Mouton JW, Ijzerman EP, et al. Nasal carriage of *Staphylococcus aureus* as a major risk factor for wound infections after cardiac surgery. *J Infect Dis.* 1995;171(1):216–219.

343. Weinstein HJ. The relation between the nasal-staphylococcal-carrier state and the incidence of postoperative complications. *N Engl J Med.* 1959;260(26):1303–1308.

344. Killian CA, Graffunder EM, Vinciguerra TJ, Venezia RA. Risk factors for surgical-site infections following cesarean section. *Infect Control Hosp Epidemiol.* 2001;22(10):613–617.

345. Ridgeway S, Wilson J, Charlet A, et al. Infection of the surgical site after arthroplasty of the hip. *J Bone Joint Surg Br.* 2005;87(6):844–850.

346. Gibbons C, Bruce J, Carpenter J, et al. Identification of risk factors by systematic review and development of risk-adjusted models for surgical site infection. *Health Technol Assess.* 2011;15(30):1–156.

347. Mannien J, Wille JC, Kloek JJ, van Benthem BH. Surveillance and epidemiology of surgical site infections after cardiothoracic surgery in the Netherlands, 2002–2007. *J Thorac Cardiovasc Surg.* 2011;141(4):899–904.

348. Howard DP, Datta G, Cunnick G, et al. Surgical site infection rate is lower in laparoscopic than open colorectal surgery. *Colorectal Dis.* 2010;12(5):423–427.

349. Romy S, Eisenring MC, Bettschart V, et al. Laparoscope use and surgical site

infections in digestive surgery. *Ann Surg.* 2008;247(4):627–632.

350. Varela JE, Wilson SE, Nguyen NT. Laparoscopic surgery significantly reduces surgical-site infections compared with open surgery. *Surg Endosc.* 2010;24(2):270–276.

351. Hellinger WC, Heckman MG, Crook JE, et al. Association of surgeon with surgical site infection after liver transplantation. *Am J Transplant.* 2011;11(9):1877–1884.

352. Maragakis LL, Cosgrove SE, Martinez EA, et al. Intraoperative fraction of inspired oxygen is a modifiable risk factor for surgical site infection after spinal surgery. *Anesthesiology.* 2009;110(3):556–562.

353. Classen DC, Evans RS, Pestotnik SL, et al. The timing of prophylactic administration of antibiotics and the risk of surgical-wound infection. *N Engl J Med.* 1992;326(5):281–286.

354. Darouiche RO, Wall MJ Jr, Itani KM, et al. Chlorhexidine-alcohol versus povidone-iodine for surgical-site antisepsis. *N Engl J Med.* 2010;362(1):18–26.

355. Parienti JJ, Thibon P, Heller R, et al. Hand-rubbing with an aqueous alcoholic solution vs traditional surgical hand-scrubbing and 30-day surgical site infection rates: a randomized equivalence study. *JAMA.* 2002;288(6):722–727.

356. Boyce JM, Pittet D. Guideline for hand hygiene in health-care settings: recommendations of the Healthcare Infection Control Practices Advisory Committee and the HIPAC/SHEA/APIC/IDSA Hand Hygiene Task Force. *Am J Infect Control.* 2002;30(8):S1–S46.

357. Sehulster L, Chinn RY. Guidelines for environmental infection control in health-care facilities: recommendations of CDC and the Healthcare Infection Control Practices Advisory Committee (HICPAC). *MMWR Recomm Rep.* 2003;52(RR-10):1–42.

358. Culver DH, Horan TC, Gaynes RP, et al. Surgical wound infection rates by wound class, operative procedure, and patient risk index. National Nosocomial Infections Surveillance System. *Am J Med.* 1991;91(3B):152S–157S.

359. Sands K, Vineyard G, Platt R. Surgical site infections occurring after hospital discharge. *J Infect Dis.* 1996;173(4):963–970.

360. Roy MC, Herwaldt LA, Embrey R, Kuhns K, Wenzel RP, Perl TM. Does the Centers for Disease Control's NNIS system risk index stratify patients undergoing cardiothoracic operations by their risk of surgical-site infection? *Infect Control Hosp Epidemiol.* 2000;21(3):186–190.

361. Simchen E, Rozin R, Wax Y. The Israeli Study of Surgical Infection of drains and the risk of wound infection in operations for hernia. *Surg Gynecol Obstet.* 1990;170(4):331–337.

362. Brown RB, Bradley S, Opitz E, et al. Surgical wound infections documented after hospital discharge. *Am J Infect Control.* 1987;15(2):54–58.

363. Bilimoria KY, Cohen ME, Ingraham AM, et al. Effect of postdischarge morbidity and mortality on comparisons of hospital surgical quality. *Ann Surg.* 2010;252(1):183–190.

364. Avato JL, Lai KK. Impact of postdischarge surveillance on surgical-site infection rates for coronary artery bypass procedures. *Infect Control Hosp Epidemiol.* 2002;23(7):364–367.

365. Noman F, Mahmood SF, Asif S, et al. A novel method of surgical site infection surveillance after cardiac surgery by active participation of stake holders. *Am J Infect Control.* 2012;40:479–480.

366. Wojkowska-Mach J, Jaje E, Romaniszyn D, et al. Comparison of SSI rates in endo-arthroplasty of hip and knee in a Cracow patient population and the importance of postdischarge surveillance. *Infection.* 2008;36(1):36–40.

367. Huotari K, Lyytikainen O. Impact of postdischarge surveillance on the rate of surgical site infection after orthopedic surgery. *Infect Control Hosp Epidemiol.* 2006;27(12):1324–1329.

368. Huenger F, Schmachtenberg A, Haefner H, et al. Evaluation of postdischarge surveillance of surgical site infections after total hip and knee arthroplasty. *Am J Infect Control.* 2005;33(8):455–462.

369. Friedman C, Sturm LK, Chenoweth C. Electronic chart review as an aid to postdischarge surgical site surveillance: increased case finding. *Am J Infect Control.* 2001;29(5):329–332.

370. Simchen E, Wax Y, Galai N, Israeli A. Discharge from hospital and its effect on surgical wound infections. The Israeli Study of Surgical Infections (ISSI). *J Clin Epidemiol.* 1992;45(10):1155–1163.

371. Hulton LJ, Olmsted RN, Treston-Aurand J, Craig CP. Effect of postdischarge surveillance on rates of infectious complications after cesarean section. *Am J Infect Control.* 1992;20(4):198–201.

372. Mitt P, Lang K, Peri A, Maimets M. Surgical-site infections following cesarean section in an Estonian university hospital: postdischarge surveillance and analysis of risk factors. *Infect Control Hosp Epidemiol.* 2005;26(5):449–454.

373. Cardoso Del Monte MC, Pinto Neto AM. Postdischarge surveillance following cesarean section: the incidence of surgical site infection and associated factors. *Am J Infect Control.* 2010;38(6):467–472.

374. Weigelt JA, Dryer D, Haley RW. The necessity and efficiency of wound surveillance after discharge. *Arch Surg.* 1992;127(1):77–81.

375. Law DJ, Mishriki SF, Jeffery PJ. The importance of surveillance after discharge from hospital in the diagnosis of postoperative wound infection. *Ann R Coll Surg Engl.* 1990;72(3):207–209.

376. Reimer K, Gleed C, Nicolle LE. The impact of postdischarge infection on surgical wound infection rates. *Infect Control.* 1987;8(6):237–240.

377. Olson MM, Lee JT Jr. Continuous, 10-year wound infection surveillance: results, advantages, and unanswered questions. *Arch Surg.* 1990;125(6):794–803.

378. Oliveira AC, Carvalho DV. Postdischarge surveillance: the impact on surgical site infection incidence in a Brazilian university hospital. *Am J Infect Control.* 2004;32(6):358–361.

379. Prospero E, Cavicchi A, Bacelli S, et al. Surveillance for surgical site infection after hospital discharge: a surgical procedure-specific perspective. *Infect Control Hosp Epidemiol.* 2006;27(12):1313–1317.

380. Krukowski ZH, Irwin ST, Denholm S, Matheson NA. Preventing wound infection after appendicectomy: a review. *Br J Surg.* 1988;75(10):1023–1033.

381. Centers for Disease Control and Prevention. MRSA infections. Available at: http://www.cdc.gov/mrsa/definition/index.html. Accessed November 14, 2011.

382. Deresinski S. Methicillin-resistant *Staphylococcus aureus*: an evolutionary, epidemiologic, and therapeutic odyssey. *Clin Infect Dis.* 2005;40(4):562–573.

383. Panlilio AL, Culver DH, Gaynes RP, et al. Methicillin-resistant *Staphylococcus aureus* in U.S. hospitals, 1975–1991. *Infect Control Hosp Epidemiol.* 1992;13(10):582–586.

384. Diekema DJ, Pfaller MA, Schmitz FJ, et al. Survey of infections due to *Staphylococcus* species: frequency of occurrence and antimicrobial susceptibility of isolates collected in the United States, Canada, Latin America, Europe, and the Western Pacific region for the SENTRY Antimicrobial Surveillance Program, 1997–1999. *Clin Infect Dis.* 2001;32(suppl 2):S114–S132.

385. Turnidge JD, Nimmo GR, Pearson J, et al. Epidemiology and outcomes for *Staphylococcus aureus* bacteraemia in Australian hospitals, 2005–06: report from the Australian Group on Antimicrobial Resistance. *Commun Dis Intell.* 2007;31(4):398–403.

386. Klevens RM, Morrison MA, Nadle J, et al. Invasive methicillin-resistant *Staphylococcus*

aureus infections in the United States. *JAMA.* 2007;298(15):1763–1771.

387. Antoniadou A. Outbreaks of zygomycosis in hospitals. *Clin Microbiol Infect.* 2009;15(suppl 5):55–59.

388. Jean SS, Hsueh PR. High burden of antimicrobial resistance in Asia. *Int J Antimicrob Agents.* 2011;37(4):291–295.

389. Sader HS, Streit JM, Fritsche TR, Jones RN. Antimicrobial susceptibility of gram-positive bacteria isolated from European medical centres: results of the Daptomycin Surveillance Programme (2002–2004). *Clin Microbiol Infect.* 2006;12(9):844–852.

390. Chen CB, Chang HC, Huang YC. Nasal meticillin-resistant *Staphylococcus aureus* carriage among intensive care unit hospitalised adult patients in a Taiwanese medical centre: one time-point prevalence, molecular characteristics and risk factors for carriage. *J Hosp Infect.* 2010;74(3):238–244.

391. Baptiste KE, Williams K, Willams NJ, et al. Methicillin-resistant staphylococci in companion animals. *Emerg Infect Dis.* 2005;11(12):1942–1944.

392. van Loo I, Huijsdens X, Tiemersma E, et al. Emergence of methicillin-resistant *Staphylococcus aureus* of animal origin in humans. *Emerg Infect Dis.* 2007;13(12):1834–1839.

393. Sing A, Tuschak C, Hormansdorfer S. Methicillin-resistant *Staphylococcus aureus* in a family and its pet cat. *N Engl J Med.* 2008;358(11):1200–1201.

394. Methicillin-resistant *Staphylococcus aureus* skin infections from an elephant calf—San Diego, California, 2008. *MMWR.* 2009;58(8):194–198.

395. Otter JA, French GL. Molecular epidemiology of community-associated meticillin-resistant *Staphylococcus aureus* in Europe. *Lancet Infect Dis.* 2010;10(4):227–239.

396. Engemann JJ, Carmeli Y, Cosgrove SE, et al. Adverse clinical and economic outcomes attributable to methicillin resistance among patients with *Staphylococcus aureus* surgical site infection. *Clin Infect Dis.* 2003;36(5):592–598.

397. Calfee DP, Salgado CD, Classen D, et al. Strategies to prevent transmission of methicillin-resistant *Staphylococcus aureus* in acute care hospitals. *Infect Control Hosp Epidemiol.* 2008;29(suppl 1):S62–S80.

398. Four pediatric deaths from community-acquired methicillin-resistant *Staphylococcus aureus*—Minnesota and North Dakota, 1997–1999. *MMWR.* 1999;48(32):707–710.

399. Lowy FD. Antimicrobial resistance: the example of *Staphylococcus aureus*. *J Clin Invest.* 2003;111(9):1265–1273.

400. McDougal LK, Steward CD, Killgore GE, et al. Pulsed-field gel electrophoresis typing of oxacillin-resistant *Staphylococcus aureus* isolates from the United States: establishing a national database. *J Clin Microbiol.* 2003;41(11):5113–5120.

401. Vandenesch F, Naimi T, Enright MC, et al. Community-acquired methicillin-resistant *Staphylococcus aureus* carrying Panton-Valentine leukocidin genes: worldwide emergence. *Emerg Infect Dis.* 2003;9(8): 978–984.

402. Tietz A, Frei R, Widmer AF. Transatlantic spread of the USA300 clone of MRSA. *N Engl J Med.* 2005;353(5):532–533.

403. Seybold U, Kourbatova EV, Johnson JG, et al. Emergence of community-associated methicillin-resistant *Staphylococcus aureus* USA300 genotype as a major cause of health care–associated blood stream infections. *Clin Infect Dis.* 2006;42(5):647–656.

404. Skov RL, Jensen KS. Community-associated methicillin-resistant *Staphylococcus aureus* as a cause of hospital-acquired infections. *J Hosp Infect.* 2009;73(4):364–370.

405. Sanford MD, Widmer AF, Bale MJ, et al. Efficient detection and long-term persistence of the carriage of methicillin-resistant *Staphylococcus aureus*. *Clin Infect Dis.* 1994;19(6):1123–1128.

406. Perl TM, Golub JE. New approaches to reduce *Staphylococcus aureus* nosocomial infection rates: treating *S. aureus* nasal carriage. *Ann Pharmacother*. 1998;32(1):S7–S16.

407. Weinke T, Schiller R, Fehrenbach FJ, Pohle HD. Association between *Staphylococcus aureus* nasopharyngeal colonization and septicemia in patients infected with the human immunodeficiency virus. *Eur J Clin Microbiol Infect Dis*. 1992;11(11):985–989.

408. Mest DR, Wong DH, Shimoda KJ, et al. Nasal colonization with methicillin-resistant *Staphylococcus aureus* on admission to the surgical intensive care unit increases the risk of infection. *Anesth Analg*. 1994;78(4):644–650.

409. Pujol M, Pena C, Pallares R, et al. Nosocomial *Staphylococcus aureus* bacteremia among nasal carriers of methicillin-resistant and methicillin-susceptible strains. *Am J Med*. 1996;100(5):509–516.

410. von Eiff C, Becker K, Machka K, Stammer H, Peters G. Nasal carriage as a source of *Staphylococcus aureus* bacteremia. Study Group. *N Engl J Med*. 2001;344(1):11–16.

411. Huang SS, Platt R. Risk of methicillin-resistant *Staphylococcus aureus* infection after previous infection or colonization. *Clin Infect Dis*. 2003;36(3):281–285.

412. Thompson RL, Cabezudo I, Wenzel RP. Epidemiology of nosocomial infections caused by methicillin-resistant *Staphylococcus aureus*. *Ann Intern Med*. 1982;97(3):309–317.

413. Brumfitt W, Hamilton-Miller J. Methicillin-resistant *Staphylococcus aureus*. *N Engl J Med*. 1989;320(18):1188–1196.

414. Boyce JM. Methicillin-resistant *Staphylococcus aureus*. Detection, epidemiology, and control measures. *Infect Dis Clin North Am*. 1989;3(4):901–913.

415. Lowy FD. *Staphylococcus aureus* infections. *N Engl J Med*. 1998;339(8):520–532.

416. Davis KA, Stewart JJ, Crouch HK, et al. Methicillin-resistant *Staphylococcus aureus* (MRSA) nares colonization at hospital admission and its effect on subsequent MRSA infection. *Clin Infect Dis*. 2004;39(6):776–782.

417. Rehm SJ, Tice A. *Staphylococcus aureus*: methicillin-susceptible *S. aureus* to methicillin-resistant *S. aureus* and vancomycin-resistant *S. aureus*. *Clin Infect Dis*. 2010;51(suppl 2): S176–S182.

418. Merrer J, Santoli F, Appere de Vecchi C, et al. "Colonization pressure" and risk of acquisition of methicillin-resistant *Staphylococcus aureus* in a medical intensive care unit. *Infect Control Hosp Epidemiol*. 2000;21(11):718–723.

419. Williams VR, Callery S, Vearncombe M, Simor AE. The role of colonization pressure in nosocomial transmission of methicillin-resistant *Staphylococcus aureus*. *Am J Infect Control*. 2009;37(2):106–110.

420. Verwer PE, Robinson JO, Coombs GW, et al. Prevalence of nasal methicillin-resistant *Staphylococcus aureus* colonization in healthcare workers in a Western Australian acute care hospital. *Eur J Clin Microbiol Infect Dis*. 2012;31(6):1067–1072.

421. Hare R, Ridley M. Further studies on the transmission of *Staph. aureus*. *Br Med J*. 1958;1(5062):69–73.

422. Solberg CO. A study of carriers of *Staphylococcus aureus* with special regard to quantitative bacterial estimations. *Acta Med Scand Suppl*. 1965;436:1–96.

423. Solberg CO. Spread of *Staphylococcus aureus* in hospitals: causes and prevention. *Scand J Infect Dis*. 2000;32(6):587–595.

424. Desai R, Pannaraj PS, Agopian J, et al. Survival and transmission of community-associated methicillin-resistant *Staphylococcus aureus* from fomites. *Am J Infect Control*. 2011;39(3):219–225.

425. Albrich WC, Harbarth S. Health-care workers: source, vector, or victim of MRSA? *Lancet Infect Dis*. 2008;8(5):289–301.

426. Vonberg RP, Stamm-Balderjahn S, Hansen S, et al. How often do asymptomatic healthcare

workers cause methicillin-resistant *Staphylococcus aureus* outbreaks? A systematic evaluation. *Infect Control Hosp Epidemiol.* 2006;27(10):1123–1127.

427. Bertin ML, Vinski J, Schmitt S, et al. Outbreak of methicillin-resistant *Staphylococcus aureus* colonization and infection in a neonatal intensive care unit epidemiologically linked to a healthcare worker with chronic otitis. *Infect Control Hosp Epidemiol.* 2006;27(6):581–585.

428. Healy CM, Hulten KG, Palazzi DL, et al. Emergence of new strains of methicillin-resistant *Staphylococcus aureus* in a neonatal intensive care unit. *Clin Infect Dis.* 2004;39(10):1460–1466.

429. Bratu S, Eramo A, Kopec R, et al. Community-associated methicillin-resistant *Staphylococcus aureus* in hospital nursery and maternity units. *Emerg Infect Dis.* 2005;11(6):808–813.

430. Regev-Yochay G, Rubinstein E, Barzilai A, et al. Methicillin-resistant *Staphylococcus aureus* in neonatal intensive care unit. *Emerg Infect Dis.* 2005;11(3):453–456.

431. Linde H, Wagenlehner F, Strommenger B, et al. Healthcare-associated outbreaks and community-acquired infections due to MRSA carrying the Panton-Valentine leucocidin gene in southeastern Germany. *Eur J Clin Microbiol Infect Dis.* 2005;24(6):419–422.

432. Community-associated methicillin-resistant *Staphylococcus aureus* infection among healthy newborns—Chicago and Los Angeles County, 2004. *MMWR.* 2006;55(12):329–332.

433. Sax H, Posfay-Barbe K, Harbarth S, et al. Control of a cluster of community-associated, methicillin-resistant *Staphylococcus aureus* in neonatology. *J Hosp Infect.* 2006;63(1):93–100.

434. David MD, Kearns AM, Gossain S, et al. Community-associated meticillin-resistant *Staphylococcus aureus*: nosocomial transmission in a neonatal unit. *J Hosp Infect.* 2006;64(3):244–250.

435. Saunders A, Panaro L, McGeer A, et al. A nosocomial outbreak of community-associated methicillin-resistant *Staphylococcus aureus* among healthy newborns and postpartum mothers. *Can J Infect Dis Med Microbiol.* 2007;18(2):128–132.

436. McAdams RM, Ellis MW, Trevino S, Rajnik M. Spread of methicillin-resistant *Staphylococcus aureus* USA300 in a neonatal intensive care unit. *Pediatr Int.* 2008;50(6):810–815.

437. Gould IM, Girvan EK, Browning RA, et al. Report of a hospital neonatal unit outbreak of community-associated methicillin-resistant *Staphylococcus aureus*. *Epidemiol Infect.* 2009;137(9):1242–1248.

438. Patrozou E, Reid K, Jefferson J, Mermel LA. A cluster of community-acquired methicillin-resistant *Staphylococcus aureus* infections in hospital security guards. *Infect Control Hosp Epidemiol.* 2009;30(4):386–388.

439. Maltezou HC, Vourli S, Katerelos P, et al. Panton-Valentine leukocidin-positive methicillin-resistant *Staphylococcus aureus* outbreak among healthcare workers in a long-term care facility. *Int J Infect Dis.* 2009;13(6):e401–e406.

440. Teare L, Shelley OP, Millership S, Kearns A. Outbreak of Panton-Valentine leucocidin-positive meticillin-resistant *Staphylococcus aureus* in a regional burns unit. *J Hosp Infect.* 2010;76(3):220–224.

441. Udo EE, Aly NY, Sarkhoo E, et al. Detection and characterization of an ST97-SCCmec-V community-associated meticillin-resistant *Staphylococcus aureus* clone in a neonatal intensive care unit and special care baby unit. I 2011;60:600–604.

442. Mine Y, Higuchi W, Taira K, et al. Nosocomial outbreak of multidrug-resistant USA300 methicillin-resistant *Staphylococcus aureus* causing severe furuncles and carbuncles in Japan. *J Dermatol.* 2011.

443. Vancomycin-resistant *Staphylococcus aureus*—Pennsylvania, 2002. *MMWR.* 2002;51(40):902.

444. Appelbaum PC. The emergence of vancomycin-intermediate and vancomycin-resistant *Staphylococcus aureus*. *Clin Microbiol Infect*. 2006;12(suppl 1):16–23.

445. Howden BP, Davies JK, Johnson PD, et al. Reduced vancomycin susceptibility in *Staphylococcus aureus*, including vancomycin-intermediate and heterogeneous vancomycin-intermediate strains: resistance mechanisms, laboratory detection, and clinical implications. *Clin Microbiol Rev*. 2010;23(1):99–139.

446. Sievert DM, Rudrik JT, Patel JB, et al. Vancomycin-resistant *Staphylococcus aureus* in the United States, 2002–2006. *Clin Infect Dis*. 2008;46(5):668–674.

447. Fridkin SK, Hageman J, McDougal LK, et al. Epidemiological and microbiological characterization of infections caused by *Staphylococcus aureus* with reduced susceptibility to vancomycin, United States, 1997–2001. *Clin Infect Dis*. 2003;36(4):429–439.

448. Charles PG, Ward PB, Johnson PD, et al. Clinical features associated with bacteremia due to heterogeneous vancomycin-intermediate *Staphylococcus aureus*. *Clin Infect Dis*. 2004;38(3):448–451.

449. Cosgrove SE, Carroll KC, Perl TM. *Staphylococcus aureus* with reduced susceptibility to vancomycin. *Clin Infect Dis*. 2004;39(4):539–545.

450. Clements A, Halton K, Graves N, et al. Overcrowding and understaffing in modern health-care systems: key determinants in meticillin-resistant *Staphylococcus aureus* transmission. *Lancet Infect Dis*. 2008;8(7):427–434.

451. Robicsek A, Beaumont JL, Paule SM, et al. Universal surveillance for methicillin-resistant *Staphylococcus aureus* in 3 affiliated hospitals. *Ann Intern Med*. 2008;148(6):409–418.

452. Jain R, Kralovic SM, Evans ME, et al. Veterans Affairs initiative to prevent methicillin-resistant *Staphylococcus aureus* infections. *N Engl J Med*. 2011;364(15):1419–1430.

453. Jernigan JA, Titus MG, Groschel DH, et al. Effectiveness of contact isolation during a hospital outbreak of methicillin-resistant *Staphylococcus aureus*. *Am J Epidemiol*. 1996;143(5):496–504.

454. Karchmer TB, Durbin LJ, Simonton BM, Farr BM. Cost-effectiveness of active surveillance cultures and contact/droplet precautions for control of methicillin-resistant *Staphylococcus aureus*. *J Hosp Infect*. 2002;51(2):126–132.

455. Wernitz MH, Swidsinski S, Weist K, et al. Effectiveness of a hospital-wide selective screening programme for methicillin-resistant *Staphylococcus aureus* (MRSA) carriers at hospital admission to prevent hospital-acquired MRSA infections. *Clin Microbiol Infect*. 2005;11(6):457–465.

456. Wernitz MH, Keck S, Swidsinski S, et al. Cost analysis of a hospital-wide selective screening programme for methicillin-resistant *Staphylococcus aureus* (MRSA) carriers in the context of diagnosis related groups (DRG) payment. *Clin Microbiol Infect*. 2005;11(6):466–471.

457. Khoury J, Jones M, Grim A, et al. Eradication of methicillin-resistant *Staphylococcus aureus* from a neonatal intensive care unit by active surveillance and aggressive infection control measures. *Infect Control Hosp Epidemiol*. 2005;26(7):616–621.

458. Shitrit P, Gottesman BS, Katzir M, et al. Active surveillance for methicillin-resistant *Staphylococcus aureus* (MRSA) decreases the incidence of MRSA bacteremia. *Infect Control Hosp Epidemiol*. 2006;27(10):1004–1008.

459. Huang SS, Yokoe DS, Hinrichsen VL, et al. Impact of routine intensive care unit surveillance cultures and resultant barrier precautions on hospital-wide methicillin-resistant *Staphylococcus aureus* bacteremia. *Clin Infect Dis*. 2006;43(8):971–978.

460. Pan A, Carnevale G, Catenazzi P, et al. Trends in methicillin-resistant *Staphylococcus aureus* (MRSA) bloodstream infections: effect of the MRSA "search and isolate" strategy

in a hospital in Italy with hyperendemic MRSA. *Infect Control Hosp Epidemiol.* 2005;26(2):127–133.

461. Harbarth S, Fankhauser C, Schrenzel J, et al. Universal screening for methicillin-resistant *Staphylococcus aureus* at hospital admission and nosocomial infection in surgical patients. *JAMA.* 2008;299(10):1149–1157.

462. Huskins WC, Huckabee CM, O'Grady NP, et al. Intervention to reduce transmission of resistant bacteria in intensive care. *N Engl J Med.* 2011;364(15):1407–1418.

463. Jarlier V, Trystram D, Brun-Buisson C, et al. Curbing methicillin-resistant *Staphylococcus aureus* in 38 French hospitals through a 15-year institutional control program. *Arch Intern Med.* 2010;170(6):552–559.

464. van Trijp MJ, Melles DC, Hendriks WD, et al. Successful control of widespread methicillin-resistant *Staphylococcus aureus* colonization and infection in a large teaching hospital in the Netherlands. *Infect Control Hosp Epidemiol.* 2007;28(8):970–975.

465. Spicer WJ. Three strategies in the control of staphylococci including methicillin-resistant *Staphylococcus aureus. J Hosp Infect.* 1984;5(suppl A):45–49.

466. Verhoef J, Beaujean D, Blok H, et al. A Dutch approach to methicillin-resistant *Staphylococcus aureus. Eur J Clin Microbiol Infect Dis.* 1999;18(7):461–466.

467. Werner G, Coque TM, Hammerum AM, et al. Emergence and spread of vancomycin resistance among enterococci in Europe. *Euro Surveill.* 2008 20;13(47).

468. Papanicolaou GA, Meyers BR, Meyers J, et al. Nosocomial infections with vancomycin-resistant *Enterococcus faecium* in liver transplant recipients: risk factors for acquisition and mortality. *Clin Infect Dis.* 1996;23(4):760–766.

469. Matar MJ, Tarrand J, Raad I, Rolston KV. Colonization and infection with vancomycin-resistant Enterococcus among patients with cancer. *Am J Infect Control.* 2006;34(8):534–536.

470. Kamboj M, Chung D, Seo SK, et al. The changing epidemiology of vancomycin-resistant Enterococcus (VRE) bacteremia in allogeneic hematopoietic stem cell transplant (HSCT) recipients. *Biol Blood Marrow Transplant.* 2010;16(11):1576–1581.

471. DiazGranados CA, Zimmer SM, Klein M, Jernigan JA. Comparison of mortality associated with vancomycin-resistant and vancomycin-susceptible enterococcal bloodstream infections: a meta-analysis. *Clin Infect Dis.* 2005;41(3):327–333.

472. Uttley AH, Collins CH, Naidoo J, George RC. Vancomycin-resistant enterococci. *Lancet.* 1988;1(8575–8576):57–58.

473. Leclercq R, Derlot E, Duval J, Courvalin P. Plasmid-mediated resistance to vancomycin and teicoplanin in *Enterococcus faecium. N Engl J Med.* 1988;319(3):157–161.

474. Sahm DF, Kissinger J, Gilmore MS, et al. In vitro susceptibility studies of vancomycin-resistant *Enterococcus faecalis. Antimicrob Agents Chemother.* 1989;33(9):1588–1591.

475. Livornese LL Jr, Dias S, Samel C, et al. Hospital-acquired infection with vancomycin-resistant *Enterococcus faecium* transmitted by electronic thermometers. *Ann Intern Med.* 1992;117(2):112–116.

476. Handwerger S, Raucher B, Altarac D, et al. Nosocomial outbreak due to *Enterococcus faecium* highly resistant to vancomycin, penicillin, and gentamicin. *Clin Infect Dis.* 1993;16(6):750–755.

477. Montecalvo MA, Horowitz H, Gedris C, et al. Outbreak of vancomycin-, ampicillin-, and aminoglycoside-resistant *Enterococcus faecium* bacteremia in an adult oncology unit. *Antimicrob Agents Chemother.* 1994;38(6):1363–1367.

478. Boyce JM, Opal SM, Chow JW, et al. Outbreak of multidrug-resistant *Enterococcus faecium* with transferable vanB class vancomycin resistance. *J Clin Microbiol.* 1994;32(5):1148–1153.

479. Edmond MB, Ober JF, Weinbaum DL, et al. Vancomycin-resistant *Enterococcus faecium* bacteremia: risk factors for infection. *Clin Infect Dis.* 1995;20(5):1126–1133.

480. Shay DK, Maloney SA, Montecalvo M, et al. Epidemiology and mortality risk of vancomycin-resistant enterococcal bloodstream infections. *J Infect Dis.* 1995;172(4):993–1000.

481. Wells CL, Juni BA, Cameron SB, et al. Stool carriage, clinical isolation, and mortality during an outbreak of vancomycin-resistant enterococci in hospitalized medical and/or surgical patients. *Clin Infect Dis.* 1995;21(1):45–50.

482. Quale J, Landman D, Atwood E, et al. Experience with a hospital-wide outbreak of vancomycin-resistant enterococci. *Am J Infect Control.* 1996;24(5):372–379.

483. Hwang YS, Brinton BG, Leonard RB, et al. Investigation of an outbreak of vancomycin-resistant *Enterococcus faecium* in a low prevalence university hospital. *J Investig Med.* 1998;46(9):435–443.

484. Nourse C, Murphy H, Byrne C, et al. Control of a nosocomial outbreak of vancomycin resistant *Enterococcus faecium* in a paediatric oncology unit: risk factors for colonisation. *Eur J Pediatr.* 1998;157(1):20–27.

485. Kirkpatrick BD, Harrington SM, Smith D, et al. An outbreak of vancomycin-dependent *Enterococcus faecium* in a bone marrow transplant unit. *Clin Infect Dis.* 1999;29(5):1268–1273.

486. Elsner HA, Sobottka I, Feucht HH, et al. Nosocomial outbreak of vancomycin-resistant *Enterococcus faecium* at a German university pediatric hospital. *Int J Hyg Environ Health.* 2000;203(2):147–152.

487. Falk PS, Winnike J, Woodmansee C, et al. Outbreak of vancomycin-resistant enterococci in a burn unit. *Infect Control Hosp Epidemiol.* 2000;21(9):575–582.

488. Kawalec M, Gniadkowski M, Hryniewicz W. Outbreak of vancomycin-resistant enterococci in a hospital in Gdask, Poland, due to horizontal transfer of different Tn1546-like transposon variants and clonal spread of several strains. *J Clin Microbiol.* 2000;38(9):3317–3322.

489. McCarthy KM, Van Nierop W, Duse A, et al. Control of an outbreak of vancomycin-resistant *Enterococcus faecium* in an oncology ward in South Africa: effective use of limited resources. *J Hosp Infect.* 2000;44(4):294–300.

490. Hanna H, Umphrey J, Tarrand J, et al. Management of an outbreak of vancomycin-resistant enterococci in the medical intensive care unit of a cancer center. *Infect Control Hosp Epidemiol.* 2001;22(4):217–219.

491. Byers KE, Anglim AM, Anneski CJ, et al. A hospital epidemic of vancomycin-resistant Enterococcus: risk factors and control. *Infect Control Hosp Epidemiol.* 2001;22(3):140–147.

492. Timmers GJ, van der Zwet WC, Simoons-Smit IM, et al. Outbreak of vancomycin-resistant *Enterococcus faecium* in a haematology unit: risk factor assessment and successful control of the epidemic. *Br J Haematol.* 2002;116(4):826–833.

493. Colak D, Naas T, Gunseren F, et al. First outbreak of vancomycin-resistant enterococci in a tertiary hospital in Turkey. *J Antimicrob Chemother.* 2002;50(3):397–401.

494. Sample ML, Gravel D, Oxley C, et al. An outbreak of vancomycin-resistant enterococci in a hematology-oncology unit: control by patient cohorting and terminal cleaning of the environment. *Infect Control Hosp Epidemiol.* 2002;23(8):468–470.

495. Christiansen KJ, Tibbett PA, Beresford W, et al. Eradication of a large outbreak of a single strain of vanB vancomycin-resistant *Enterococcus faecium* at a major Australian teaching hospital. *Infect Control Hosp Epidemiol.* 2004;25(5):384–390.

496. Knoll M, Daeschlein G, Okpara-Hofmann J, et al. Outbreak of vancomycin-resistant enterococci (VRE) in a hematological oncology ward and hygienic preventive measures: a

long-term study. *Onkologie.* 2005;28(4): 187–192.

497. Peta M, Carretto E, Barbarini D, et al. Outbreak of vancomycin-resistant *Enterococcus* spp. in an Italian general intensive care unit. *Clin Microbiol Infect.* 2006;12(2):163–169.

498. Kawalec M, Kedzierska J, Gajda A, et al. Hospital outbreak of vancomycin-resistant enterococci caused by a single clone of *Enterococcus raffinosus* and several clones of *Enterococcus faecium. Clin Microbiol Infect.* 2007;13(9):893–901.

499. Lucet JC, Armand-Lefevre L, Laurichesse JJ, et al. Rapid control of an outbreak of vancomycin-resistant enterococci in a French university hospital. *J Hosp Infect.* 2007;67(1):42–48.

500. Yang KS, Fong YT, Lee HY, et al. Predictors of vancomycin-resistant enterococcus (VRE) carriage in the first major VRE outbreak in Singapore. *Ann Acad Med Singapore.* 2007;36(6):379–383.

501. Comert FB, Kulah C, Aktas E, et al. First isolation of vancomycin-resistant enteroccoci and spread of a single clone in a university hospital in northwestern Turkey. *Eur J Clin Microbiol Infect Dis.* 2007;26(1):57–61.

502. Kurup A, Chlebicki MP, Ling ML, et al. Control of a hospital-wide vancomycin-resistant enterococci outbreak. *Am J Infect Control.* 2008;36(3):206–211.

503. Ergani-Ozcan A, Naas T, Baysan BO, et al. Nosocomial outbreak of vancomycin-resistant *Enterococcus faecium* in a paediatric unit at a Turkish university hospital. *J Antimicrob Chemother.* 2008;61(5):1033–109.

504. Drews SJ, Richardson SE, Wray R, et al. An outbreak of vancomycin-resistant *Enterococcus faecium* in an acute care pediatric hospital: lessons from environmental screening and a case-control study. *Can J Infect Dis Med Microbiol.* 2008;19(3):233–236.

505. Hoshuyama T, Moriguchi H, Muratani T, Matsumoto T. Vancomycin-resistant enterococci (VRE) outbreak at a university hospital in Kitakyushu, Japan: case-control studies. *J Infect Chemother.* 2008;14(5):354–360.

506. Zhu X, Zheng B, Wang S, et al. Molecular characterisation of outbreak-related strains of vancomycin-resistant *Enterococcus faecium* from an intensive care unit in Beijing, China. *J Hosp Infect.* 2009;72(2):147–154.

507. Servais A, Mercadal L, Brossier F, et al. Rapid curbing of a vancomycin-resistant *Enterococcus faecium* outbreak in a nephrology department. *Clin J Am Soc Nephrol.* 2009;4(10):1559–1564.

508. Nolan SM, Gerber JS, Zaoutis T, et al. Outbreak of vancomycin-resistant enterococcus colonization among pediatric oncology patients. *Infect Control Hosp Epidemiol.* 2009;30(4):338–345.

509. Pereira GH, Muller PR, Zanella RC, et al. Outbreak of vancomycin-resistant enterococci in a tertiary hospital: the lack of effect of measures directed mainly by surveillance cultures and differences in response between *Enterococcus faecium* and *Enterococcus faecalis. Am J Infect Control.* 2010;38(5):406–409.

510. Cockerill WM, Bush K, Dudley MN, et al. Performance standards for antimicrobial susceptibility testing; twenty-first informational supplement. Wayne, Pa: Clinical and Laboratory Standards Institute; 2011;31(1):84.

511. Fridkin SK, Edwards JR, Courval JM, et al. The effect of vancomycin and third-generation cephalosporins on prevalence of vancomycin-resistant enterococci in 126 U.S. adult intensive care units. *Ann Intern Med.* 2001;135(3):175–183.

512. Donskey CJ, Chowdhry TK, Hecker MT, et al. Effect of antibiotic therapy on the density of vancomycin-resistant enterococci in the stool of colonized patients. *N Engl J Med.* 2000;343(26):1925–1932.

513. Ostrowsky BE, Trick WE, Sohn AH, Quirk SB, Holt S, Carson LA, et al. Control of vancomycin-resistant enterococcus in health care facilities in a region. *N Engl J Med.* 2001 May 10;344(19):1427–33.

514. Minhas P, Perl TM, Carroll KC, et al. Risk factors for positive admission surveillance cultures for methicillin-resistant *Staphylococcus aureus* and vancomycin-resistant enterococci in a neurocritical care unit. *Crit Care Med.* 2011;39(10):2322–2329.

515. Bonten MJ, Slaughter S, Ambergen AW, et al. The role of "colonization pressure" in the spread of vancomycin-resistant enterococci: an important infection control variable. *Arch Intern Med.* 1998;158(10):1127–1132.

516. Riedel S, Von Stein D, Richardson K, et al. Development of a prediction rule for methicillin-resistant *Staphylococcus aureus* and vancomycin-resistant enterococcus carriage in a Veterans Affairs Medical Center population. *Infect Control Hosp Epidemiol.* 2008;29(10):969–971.

517. Drees M, Snydman DR, Schmid CH, et al. Antibiotic exposure and room contamination among patients colonized with vancomycin-resistant enterococci. *Infect Control Hosp Epidemiol.* 2008;29(8):709–715.

518. Cohen MJ, Adler A, Block C, et al. Acquisition of vancomycin-resistant enterococci in internal medicine wards. *Am J Infect Control.* 2009;37(2):111–116.

519. Ajao AO, Harris AD, Roghmann MC, et al. Systematic review of measurement and adjustment for colonization pressure in studies of methicillin-resistant *Staphylococcus aureus*, vancomycin-resistant enterococci, and *Clostridium difficile* acquisition. *Infect Control Hosp Epidemiol.* 2011;32(5):481–489.

520. Tornieporth NG, Roberts RB, John J, et al. Risk factors associated with vancomycin-resistant *Enterococcus faecium* infection or colonization in 145 matched case patients and control patients. *Clin Infect Dis.* 1996;23(4):767–772.

521. Porwancher R, Sheth A, Remphrey S, et al. Epidemiological study of hospital-acquired infection with vancomycin-resistant *Enterococcus faecium*: possible transmission by an electronic ear-probe thermometer. *Infect Control Hosp Epidemiol.* 1997;18(11):771–773.

522. Martinez JA, Ruthazer R, Hansjosten K, et al. Role of environmental contamination as a risk factor for acquisition of vancomycin-resistant enterococci in patients treated in a medical intensive care unit. *Arch Intern Med.* 2003;163(16):1905–1912.

523. Trillis F 3rd, Eckstein EC, Budavich R, et al. Contamination of hospital curtains with healthcare-associated pathogens. *Infect Control Hosp Epidemiol.* 2008;29(11):1074–1076.

524. Montecalvo MA, de Lencastre H, Carraher M, et al. Natural history of colonization with vancomycin-resistant *Enterococcus faecium*. *Infect Control Hosp Epidemiol.* 1995;16(12):680–685.

525. Duckro AN, Blom DW, Lyle EA, et al. Transfer of vancomycin-resistant enterococci via health care worker hands. *Arch Intern Med.* 2005;165(3):302–307.

526. Hayden MK, Bonten MJ, Blom DW, et al. Reduction in acquisition of vancomycin-resistant enterococcus after enforcement of routine environmental cleaning measures. *Clin Infect Dis.* 2006;42(11):1552–1560.

527. Hayden MK, Blom DW, Lyle EA, et al. Risk of hand or glove contamination after contact with patients colonized with vancomycin-resistant enterococcus or the colonized patients' environment. *Infect Control Hosp Epidemiol.* 2008;29(2):149–154.

528. Kramer A, Schwebke I, Kampf G. How long do nosocomial pathogens persist on inanimate surfaces? A systematic review. *BMC Infect Dis.* 2006;6:130.

529. Noble WC, Virani Z, Cree RG. Co-transfer of vancomycin and other resistance genes from *Enterococcus faecalis* NCTC 12201 to *Staphylococcus aureus*. *FEMS Microbiol Lett.* 1992;72(2):195–198.

530. *Staphylococcus aureus* resistant to vancomycin—United States, 2002. *MMWR.* 2002;51(26):565–567.

531. Muto CA, Jernigan JA, Ostrowsky BE, et al. SHEA guideline for preventing nosocomial

transmission of multidrug-resistant strains of *Staphylococcus aureus* and enterococcus. *Infect Control Hosp Epidemiol.* 2003;24(5):362–386.

532. Siegel JD, Rhinehart E, Jackson M, Chiarello L. Management of multidrug-resistant organisms in healthcare settings 2006. Available at: http://www.cdc.gov/hicpac/mdro/mdro_toc.html. Accessed November 11, 2011.

533. Dubberke ER, Gerding DN, Classen D, et al. Strategies to prevent *Clostridium difficile* infections in acute care hospitals. *Infect Control Hosp Epidemiol.* 2008;29(suppl 1): S81–S92.

534. Dubberke ER, Wertheimer AI. Review of current literature on the economic burden of *Clostridium difficile* infection. *Infect Control Hosp Epidemiol.* 2009;30(1):57–66.

535. Loo VG, Bourgault AM, Poirier L, et al. Host and pathogen factors for *Clostridium difficile* infection and colonization. *N Engl J Med.* 2011;365(18):1693–1703.

536. Lyras D, O'Connor JR, Howarth PM, et al. Toxin B is essential for virulence of *Clostridium difficile. Nature.* 2009;458(7242):1176–1179.

537. Ananthakrishnan AN. *Clostridium difficile* infection: epidemiology, risk factors and management. *Nat Rev Gastroenterol Hepatol.* 2011;8(1):17–26.

538. Cohen SH, Gerding DN, Johnson S, et al. Clinical practice guidelines for *Clostridium difficile* infection in adults: 2010 update by the Society for Healthcare Epidemiology of America (SHEA) and the Infectious Diseases Society of America (IDSA). *Infect Control Hosp Epidemiol.* 2010;31(5):431–455.

539. Otter JA, Yezli S, French GL. The role played by contaminated surfaces in the transmission of nosocomial pathogens. *Infect Control Hosp Epidemiol.* 2011;32(7):687–699.

540. Bartlett JG. Narrative review: the new epidemic of *Clostridium difficile*–associated enteric disease. *Ann Intern Med.* 2006;145(10):758–764.

541. McDonald LC, Killgore GE, Thompson A, et al. An epidemic, toxin gene-variant strain of *Clostridium difficile. N Engl J Med.* 2005;353(23):2433–2441.

542. Pepin J, Saheb N, Coulombe MA, et al. Emergence of fluoroquinolones as the predominant risk factor for *Clostridium difficile*–associated diarrhea: a cohort study during an epidemic in Quebec. *Clin Infect Dis.* 2005;41(9):1254–1260.

543. Stevens V, Dumyati G, Fine LS, et al. Cumulative antibiotic exposures over time and the risk of *Clostridium difficile* infection. *Clin Infect Dis.* 2011;53(1):42–48.

544. Smith A. Outbreak of *Clostridium difficile* infection in an English hospital linked to hypertoxin-producing strains in Canada and the US. *Euro Surveill.* 2005;10(6):E050630 2.

545. Tachon M, Cattoen C, Blanckaert K, et al. First cluster of *C. difficile* toxinotype III, PCR-ribotype 027 associated disease in France: preliminary report. *Euro Surveill.* 2006;11(5):E060504 1.

546. Kuijper EJ, van den Berg RJ, Debast S, et al. *Clostridium difficile* ribotype 027, toxinotype III, the Netherlands. *Emerg Infect Dis.* 2006;12(5):827–830.

547. Kato H, Ito Y, van den Berg RJ, Kuijper et al. EJ, Arakawa Y. First isolation of *Clostridium difficile* 027 in Japan. *Euro Surveill.* 2007;12(1):E070111 3.

548. Long S, Fenelon L, Fitzgerald S, et al. First isolation and report of clusters of *Clostridium difficile* PCR 027 cases in Ireland. *Euro Surveill.* 2007;12(4):E070426 3.

549. Pituch H, Bakker D, Kuijper E, et al. First isolation of *Clostridium difficile* PCR-ribotype 027/toxinotype III in Poland. *Pol J Microbiol.* 2008;57(3):267–268.

550. Soes LM, Brock I, Torpdahl M, et al. [First Danish case of *Clostridium difficile* ribotype 027]. *Ugeskr Laeger.* 2009;171(19):1579–1580.

551. Tae CH, Jung SA, Song HJ, et al. The first case of antibiotic-associated colitis by

Clostridium difficile PCR ribotype 027 in Korea. *J Korean Med Sci.* 2009;24(3):520–524.

552. Terhes G, Urban E, Konkoly-Thege M, et al. First isolation of *Clostridium difficile* PCR ribotype 027 from a patient with severe persistent diarrhoea in Hungary. *Clin Microbiol Infect.* 2009;15(9):885–886.

553. Riley TV, Thean S, Hool G, Golledge CL. First Australian isolation of epidemic *Clostridium difficile* PCR ribotype 027. *Med J Aust.* 2009;190(12):706–708.

554. Freeman J, Bauer MP, Baines SD, et al. The changing epidemiology of *Clostridium difficile* infections. *Clin Microbiol Rev.* 2010;23(3):529–549.

555. Lim PL, Ling ML, Lee HY, et al. Isolation of the first three cases of *Clostridium difficile* polymerase chain reaction ribotype 027 in Singapore. *Singapore Med J.* 2011;52(5): 361–364.

556. Kim H, Lee Y, Moon HW, et al. Emergence of *Clostridium difficile* ribotype 027 in Korea. *Korean J Lab Med.* 2011;31(3):191–196.

557. Richards M, Knox J, Elliott B, et al. Severe infection with *Clostridium difficile* PCR ribotype 027 acquired in Melbourne, Australia. *Med J Aust.* 2011;194(7):369–371.

558. Bishara J, Goldberg E, Madar-Shapiro L, et al. Molecular epidemiology of *Clostridium difficile* in a tertiary medical center in Israel: emergence of the polymerase chain reaction ribotype 027. *Isr Med Assoc J.* 2011;13(6):338–341.

559. Severe *Clostridium difficile*–associated disease in populations previously at low risk—four states, 2005. *MMWR.* 2005;54(47):1201–1205.

560. Emoto M, Kawarabayashi T, Hachisuga MD, et al. *Clostridium difficile* colitis associated with cisplatin-based chemotherapy in ovarian cancer patients. *Gynecol Oncol.* 1996;61(3):369–372.

561. Bartlett JG, Gerding DN. Clinical recognition and diagnosis of *Clostridium difficile* infection. *Clin Infect Dis.* 2008;46(suppl 1): S12–S18.

562. Naggie S, Miller BA, Zuzak KB, et al. A case-control study of community-associated *Clostridium difficile* infection: no role for proton pump inhibitors. *Am J Med.* 2011;124(3):276 e1–e7.

563. Surveillance for community-associated *Clostridium difficile*—Connecticut, 2006. *MMWR.* 2008;57(13):340–343.

564. Bignardi GE. Risk factors for *Clostridium difficile* infection. *J Hosp Infect.* 1998;40(1): 1–15.

565. Dubberke ER, Reske KA, Yan Y, et al. *Clostridium difficile*–associated disease in a setting of endemicity: identification of novel risk factors. *Clin Infect Dis.* 2007;45(12):1543–1549.

566. Pepin J, Vo TT, Boutros M, et al. Risk factors for mortality following emergency colectomy for fulminant *Clostridium difficile* infection. *Dis Colon Rectum.* 2009;52(3):400–405.

567. Karas JA, Enoch DA, Aliyu SH. A review of mortality due to *Clostridium difficile* infection. *J Infect.* 2010;61(1):1–8.

568. Morrison RH, Hall NS, Said M, et al. Risk factors associated with complications and mortality in patients with *Clostridium difficile* infection. *Clin Infect Dis.* 2011;53(12):1173–1178.

569. Deshpande A, Pasupuleti V, Rolston DD, et al. Diagnostic accuracy of real-time polymerase chain reaction in detection of *Clostridium difficile* in the stool samples of patients with suspected *Clostridium difficile* infection: a meta-analysis. *Clin Infect Dis.* 2011;53(7):e81–e90.

570. Aldeyab MA, Devine MJ, Flanagan P, et al. Multihospital outbreak of *Clostridium difficile* ribotype 027 infection: epidemiology and analysis of control measures. *Infect Control Hosp Epidemiol.* 2011;32(3):210–219.

571. Fekety R, Kim KH, Brown D, Batts DH, Cudmore M, Silva J, Jr. Epidemiology of antibiotic-associated colitis; isolation of

Clostridium difficile from the hospital environment. *Am J Med.* 1981 Apr;70(4):906–8.

572. Shaughnessy MK, Micielli RL, DePestel DD, et al. Evaluation of hospital room assignment and acquisition of *Clostridium difficile* infection. *Infect Control Hosp Epidemiol.* 2011;32(3):201–206.

573. Kim KH, Fekety R, Batts DH, et al. Isolation of *Clostridium difficile* from the environment and contacts of patients with antibiotic-associated colitis. *J Infect Dis.* 1981;143(1):42–50.

574. Boyce JM, Ligi C, Kohan C, et al. Lack of association between the increased incidence of *Clostridium difficile*–associated disease and the increasing use of alcohol-based hand rubs. *Infect Control Hosp Epidemiol.* 2006;27(5):479–483.

575. Vernaz N, Sax H, Pittet D, et al. Temporal effects of antibiotic use and hand rub consumption on the incidence of MRSA and *Clostridium difficile. J Antimicrob Chemother.* 2008;62(3):601–607.

576. Kaier K, Hagist C, Frank U, et al. Two time-series analyses of the impact of antibiotic consumption and alcohol-based hand disinfection on the incidences of nosocomial methicillin-resistant *Staphylococcus aureus* infection and *Clostridium difficile* infection. *Infect Control Hosp Epidemiol.* 2009;30(4):346–353.

577. Gaynes R, Edwards JR. Overview of nosocomial infections caused by gram-negative bacilli. *Clin Infect Dis.* 2005;41(6):848–854.

578. Albrecht SJ, Fishman NO, Kitchen J, et al. Reemergence of gram-negative health care–associated bloodstream infections. *Arch Intern Med.* 2006;166(12):1289–1294.

579. Kallen AJ, Hidron AI, Patel J, Srinivasan A. Multidrug resistance among gram-negative pathogens that caused health-care-associated infections reported to the National Healthcare Safety Network, 2006–2008. *Infect Control Hosp Epidemiol.* 2010;31(5):528–531.

580. Pfeifer Y, Cullik A, Witte W. Resistance to cephalosporins and carbapenems in Gram-negative bacterial pathogens. *Int J Med Microbiol.* 2010;300(6):371–379.

581. Ho J, Tambyah PA, Paterson DL. Multiresistant Gram-negative infections: a global perspective. *Curr Opin Infect Dis.* 2010;23(6):546–553.

582. Paterson DL, Bonomo RA. Extended-spectrum beta-lactamases: a clinical update. *Clin Microbiol Rev.* 2005;18(4):657–686.

583. Reinert RR, Low DE, Rossi F, et al. Antimicrobial susceptibility among organisms from the Asia/Pacific Rim, Europe and Latin and North America collected as part of TEST and the in vitro activity of tigecycline. *J Antimicrob Chemother.* 2007;60(5):1018–1029.

584. Rodriguez-Bano J, Navarro MD, Romero L, et al. Clinical and molecular epidemiology of extended-spectrum beta-lactamase–producing *Escherichia coli* as a cause of nosocomial infection or colonization: implications for control. *Clin Infect Dis.* 2006;42(1):37–45.

585. Tumbarello M, Spanu T, Sanguinetti M, et al. Bloodstream infections caused by extended-spectrum–beta-lactamase–producing *Klebsiella pneumoniae*: risk factors, molecular epidemiology, and clinical outcome. *Antimicrob Agents Chemother.* 2006;50(2):498–504.

586. Rodriguez-Bano J, Navarro MD, Romero L, et al. Risk-factors for emerging bloodstream infections caused by extended-spectrum beta-lactamase–producing *Escherichia coli. Clin Microbiol Infect.* 2008;14(2):180–183.

587. Wu UI, Yang CS, Chen WC, et al. Risk factors for bloodstream infections due to extended-spectrum beta-lactamase–producing *Escherichia coli. J Microbiol Immunol Infect.* 2010;43(4):310–316.

588. Rodriguez-Bano J, Picon E, Gijon P, et al. Community-onset bacteremia due to extended-spectrum beta-lactamase–producing *Escherichia coli*: risk factors and prognosis. *Clin Infect Dis.* 2010;50(1):40–48.

589. Lee JA, Kang CI, Joo EJ, et al. Epidemiology and clinical features of community-onset bacteremia caused by extended-spectrum beta-lactamase–producing *Klebsiella pneumoniae*. *Microb Drug Resist*. 2011;17(2):267–273.

590. Ho PL, Poon WW, Loke SL, et al. Community emergence of CTX-M type extended-spectrum beta-lactamases among urinary *Escherichia coli* from women. *J Antimicrob Chemother*. 2007;60(1):140–144.

591. Tian SF, Chen BY, Chu YZ, Wang S. Prevalence of rectal carriage of extended-spectrum beta-lactamase–producing *Escherichia coli* among elderly people in community settings in China. *Can J Microbiol*. 2008;54(9):781–785.

592. Meier S, Weber R, Zbinden R, et al. Extended-spectrum beta-lactamase–producing Gram-negative pathogens in community-acquired urinary tract infections: an increasing challenge for antimicrobial therapy. *Infection*. 2011;39(4):333–340.

593. Ben-Ami R, Rodriguez-Bano J, Arslan H, et al. A multinational survey of risk factors for infection with extended-spectrum beta-lactamase–producing enterobacteriaceae in nonhospitalized patients. *Clin Infect Dis*. 2009;49(5):682–690.

594. Rodriguez-Bano J, Alcala J, Cisneros JM, et al. *Escherichia coli* producing SHV-type extended-spectrum beta-lactamase is a significant cause of community-acquired infection. *J Antimicrob Chemother*. 2009;63(4):781–784.

595. Yang YS, Ku CH, Lin JC, et al. Impact of extended-spectrum beta-lactamase–producing *Escherichia coli* and *Klebsiella pneumoniae* on the outcome of community-onset bacteremic urinary tract infections. *J Microbiol Immunol Infect*. 2010;43(3):194–199.

596. Tangden T, Cars O, Melhus A, Lowdin E. Foreign travel is a major risk factor for colonization with *Escherichia coli* producing CTX-M-type extended-spectrum beta-lactamases: a prospective study with Swedish volunteers. *Antimicrob Agents Chemother*. 2010;54(9):3564–3568.

597. Schwaber MJ, Klarfeld-Lidji S, Navon-Venezia S, et al. Predictors of carbapenem-resistant *Klebsiella pneumoniae* acquisition among hospitalized adults and effect of acquisition on mortality. *Antimicrob Agents Chemother*. 2008;52(3):1028–1033.

598. Gasink LB, Edelstein PH, Lautenbach E, et al. Risk factors and clinical impact of *Klebsiella pneumoniae* carbapenemase-producing *K. pneumoniae*. *Infect Control Hosp Epidemiol*. 2009;30(12):1180–1185.

599. Guidance for control of infections with carbapenem-resistant or carbapenemase-producing Enterobacteriaceae in acute care facilities. *MMWR*. 2009;58(10):256–260.

600. Mouloudi E, Protonotariou E, Zagorianou A, et al. Bloodstream infections caused by metallo-beta-lactamase/*Klebsiella pneumoniae* carbapenemase-producing *K. pneumoniae* among intensive care unit patients in Greece: risk factors for infection and impact of type of resistance on outcomes. *Infect Control Hosp Epidemiol*. 2010;31(12):1250–1256.

601. Arnold RS, Thom KA, Sharma S, et al. Emergence of *Klebsiella pneumoniae* carbapenemase-producing bacteria. *South Med J*. 2011;104(1):40–45.

602. Nordmann P, Cuzon G, Naas T. The real threat of *Klebsiella pneumoniae* carbapenemase-producing bacteria. *Lancet Infect Dis*. 2009;9(4):228–236.

603. Hussein K, Sprecher H, Mashiach T, et al. Carbapenem resistance among *Klebsiella pneumoniae* isolates: risk factors, molecular characteristics, and susceptibility patterns. *Infect Control Hosp Epidemiol*. 2009;30(7):666–671.

604. Patel A, Calfee RP, Plante M, et al. Methicillin-resistant *Staphylococcus aureus* in orthopaedic surgery. *J Bone Joint Surg Br*. 2008;90(11):1401–1406.

605. Yong D, Toleman MA, Giske CG, et al. Characterization of a new metallo-beta-lactamase gene, bla(NDM-1), and a novel erythromycin esterase gene carried on a unique

genetic structure in *Klebsiella pneumoniae* sequence type 14 from India. *Antimicrob Agents Chemother.* 2009;53(12):5046–5054.

606. Bogaerts P, Verroken A, Jans B, et al. Global spread of New Delhi metallo-beta-lactamase 1. *Lancet Infect Dis.* 2010;10(12):831–832.

607. Kumarasamy KK, Toleman MA, Walsh TR, et al. Emergence of a new antibiotic resistance mechanism in India, Pakistan, and the UK: a molecular, biological, and epidemiological study. *Lancet Infect Dis.* 2010;10(9):597–602.

608. Poirel L, Lagrutta E, Taylor P, et al. Emergence of metallo-beta-lactamase NDM-1–producing multidrug-resistant *Escherichia coli* in Australia. *Antimicrob Agents Chemother.* 2010;54(11):4914–4916.

609. Poirel L, Revathi G, Bernabeu S, Nordmann P. Detection of NDM-1–producing *Klebsiella pneumoniae* in Kenya. *Antimicrob Agents Chemother.* 2011 Feb;55(2):934–6.

610. Poirel L, Ros A, Carricajo A, et al. Extremely drug-resistant *Citrobacter freundii* isolate producing NDM-1 and other carbapenemases identified in a patient returning from India. *Antimicrob Agents Chemother.* 2011;55(1):447–448.

611. Poirel L, Lascols C, Bernabeu S, Nordmann P. NDM-1–producing *Klebsiella pneumoniae* in Mauritius. *Antimicrob Agents Chemother.* 2012;56(1):598–599.

612. Zarfel G, Hoenigl M, Leitner E, et al. Emergence of New Delhi metallo-beta-lactamase, Austria. *Emerg Infect Dis.* 2011;17(1):129–130.

613. Kaase M, Nordmann P, Wichelhaus TA, et al. NDM-2 carbapenemase in *Acinetobacter baumannii* from Egypt. *J Antimicrob Chemother.* 2011;66(6):1260–1262.

614. Poirel L, Benouda A, Hays C, Nordmann P. Emergence of NDM-1–producing *Klebsiella pneumoniae* in Morocco. *J Antimicrob Chemother.* 2011;66(12):2781–2783.

615. Nordmann P, Poirel L, Toleman MA, Walsh TR. Does broad-spectrum beta-lactam resistance due to NDM-1 herald the end of the antibiotic era for treatment of infections caused by Gram-negative bacteria? *J Antimicrob Chemother.* 2011;66(4):689–692.

616. Ho PL, Lo WU, Yeung MK, et al. Complete sequencing of pNDM-HK encoding NDM-1 carbapenemase from a multidrug-resistant *Escherichia coli* strain isolated in Hong Kong. *PLoS One.* 2011;6(3):e17989.

617. Chan HL, Poon LM, Chan SG, Teo JW. The perils of medical tourism: NDM-1–positive *Escherichia coli* causing febrile neutropenia in a medical tourist. *Singapore Med J.* 2011;52(4):299–302.

618. D'Andrea MM, Venturelli C, Giani T, et al. Persistent carriage and infection by multidrug-resistant *Escherichia coli* ST405 producing NDM-1 carbapenemase: report on the first Italian cases. *J Clin Microbiol.* 2011;49(7):2755–2758.

619. Poirel L, Al Maskari Z, Al Rashdi F, et al. NDM-1–producing *Klebsiella pneumoniae* isolated in the Sultanate of Oman. *J Antimicrob Chemother.* 2011;66(2): 304–306.

620. Poirel L, Fortineau N, Nordmann P. International transfer of NDM-1–producing *Klebsiella pneumoniae* from Iraq to France. *Antimicrob Agents Chemother.* 2011;55(4):1821–1822.

621. Poirel L, Hombrouck-Alet C, Freneaux C, et al. Global spread of New Delhi metallo-beta-lactamase 1. *Lancet Infect Dis.* 2010;10(12):832.

622. Poirel L, Schrenzel J, Cherkaoui A, et al. Molecular analysis of NDM-1–producing enterobacterial isolates from Geneva, Switzerland. *J Antimicrob Chemother.* 2011;66(8):1730–1733.

623. Peirano G, Ahmed-Bentley J, Woodford N, Pitout JD. New Delhi metallo-beta-lactamase from traveler returning to Canada. *Emerg Infect Dis.* 2011;17(2):242–244.

624. Nordmann P, Couard JP, Sansot D, Poirel L. Emergence of an autochthonous and

community-acquired NDM-1–producing *Klebsiella pneumoniae* in Europe. *Clin Infect Dis.* 2011;54(1):150–151.

625. Sidjabat H, Nimmo GR, Walsh TR, et al. Carbapenem resistance in *Klebsiella pneumoniae* due to the New Delhi metallo-beta-lactamase. *Clin Infect Dis.* 2011;52(4):481–484.

626. Detection of Enterobacteriaceae isolates carrying metallo-beta-lactamase—United States, 2010. *MMWR.* 2010;59(24):750.

627. Deshpande P, Shetty A, Kapadia F, et al. New Delhi metallo 1: have carbapenems met their doom? *Clin Infect Dis.* 2010;51(10):1222.

628. Struelens MJ, Monnet DL, Magiorakos AP, et al. New Delhi metallo-beta-lactamase 1–producing Enterobacteriaceae: emergence and response in Europe. *Euro Surveill.* 2010;15(46):19716.

629. Mulvey MR, Grant JM, Plewes K, et al. New Delhi metallo-beta-lactamase in *Klebsiella pneumoniae* and *Escherichia coli,* Canada. *Emerg Infect Dis.* 2011;17(1):103–106.

630. Gupta N, Limbago BM, Patel JB, Kallen AJ. Carbapenem-resistant Enterobacteriaceae: epidemiology and prevention. *Clin Infect Dis.* 2011;53(1):60–67.

631. Stover CK, Pham XQ, Erwin AL, et al. Complete genome sequence of *Pseudomonas aeruginosa* PAO1, an opportunistic pathogen. *Nature.* 2000;406(6799):959–964.

632. Tschudin-Sutter S, Frei R, Kampf G, et al. Emergence of glutaraldehyde-resistant *Pseudomonas aeruginosa. Infect Control Hosp Epidemiol.* 2011;32(12):1173–1178.

633. Martino P, Venditti M, Papa G, et al. Water supply as a source of *Pseudomonas aeruginosa* in a hospital for hematological malignancies. *Boll Ist Sieroter Milan.* 1985;64(2):109–114.

634. Stephenson JR, Heard SR, Richards MA, Tabaqchali S. Gastrointestinal colonization and septicaemia with *Pseudomonas aeruginosa* due to contaminated thymol mouthwash in immunocompromised patients. *J Hosp Infect.* 1985;6(4):369–378.

635. Grigis A, Goglio A, Parea M, et al. Nosocomial outbreak of severe *Pseudomonas aeruginosa* infections in haematological patients. *Eur J Epidemiol.* 1993;9(4):390–395.

636. Blanc DS, Parret T, Janin B, et al. Nosocomial infections and pseudoinfections from contaminated bronchoscopes: two-year follow up using molecular markers. *Infect Control Hosp Epidemiol.* 1997;18(2):134–136.

637. Buttery JP, Alabaster SJ, Heine RG, et al. Multiresistant *Pseudomonas aeruginosa* outbreak in a pediatric oncology ward related to bath toys. *Pediatr Infect Dis J.* 1998;17(6):509–513.

638. Berrouane YF, McNutt LA, Buschelman BJ, et al. Outbreak of severe *Pseudomonas aeruginosa* infections caused by a contaminated drain in a whirlpool bathtub. *Clin Infect Dis.* 2000;31(6):1331–1337.

639. Gillespie TA, Johnson PR, Notman AW, et al. Eradication of a resistant *Pseudomonas aeruginosa* strain after a cluster of infections in a hematology/oncology unit. *Clin Microbiol Infect.* 2000;6(3):125–130.

640. Lyytikainen O, Golovanova V, Kolho E, et al. Outbreak caused by tobramycin-resistant *Pseudomonas aeruginosa* in a bone marrow transplantation unit. *Scand J Infect Dis.* 2001;33(6):445–449.

641. Reuter S, Sigge A, Wiedeck H, Trautmann M. Analysis of transmission pathways of *Pseudomonas aeruginosa* between patients and tap water outlets. *Crit Care Med.* 2002;30(10):2222–2228.

642. Aumeran C, Paillard C, Robin F, et al. *Pseudomonas aeruginosa* and *Pseudomonas putida* outbreak associated with contaminated water outlets in an oncohaematology paediatric unit. *J Hosp Infect.* 2007;65(1):47–53.

643. Moolenaar RL, Crutcher JM, San Joaquin VH, et al. A prolonged outbreak of *Pseudomonas aeruginosa* in a neonatal

intensive care unit: did staff fingernails play a role in disease transmission? *Infect Control Hosp Epidemiol.* 2000;21(2):80–85.

644. Yakupogullari Y, Otlu B, Dogukan M, et al. Investigation of a nosocomial outbreak by alginate-producing pan-antibiotic–resistant *Pseudomonas aeruginosa. Am J Infect Control.* 2008;36(10):e13–e18.

645. Zawacki A, O'Rourke E, Potter-Bynoe G, et al. An outbreak of *Pseudomonas aeruginosa* pneumonia and bloodstream infection associated with intermittent otitis externa in a healthcare worker. *Infect Control Hosp Epidemiol.* 2004;25(12): 1083–1089.

646. Fournier PE, Richet H. The epidemiology and control of *Acinetobacter baumannii* in health care facilities. *Clin Infect Dis.* 2006;42(5):692–699.

647. Dey A, Bairy I. Incidence of multidrug-resistant organisms causing ventilator-associated pneumonia in a tertiary care hospital: a nine months' prospective study. *Ann Thorac Med.* 2007;2(2):52–57.

648. Markogiannakis H, Pachylaki N, Samara E, et al. Infections in a surgical intensive care unit of a university hospital in Greece. *Int J Infect Dis.* 2009;13(2):145–153.

649. Erdem I, Ozgultekin A, Sengoz Inan A, et al. Incidence, etiology, and antibiotic resistance patterns of gram-negative microorganisms isolated from patients with ventilator-associated pneumonia in a medical–surgical intensive care unit of a teaching hospital in Istanbul, Turkey (2004–2006). *Jpn J Infect Dis.* 2008;61(5):339–342.

650. Johnson EN, Marconi VC, Murray CK. Hospital-acquired device-associated infections at a deployed military hospital in Iraq. *J Trauma.* 2009;66(4 suppl): S157–S163.

651. Rodrigues PM, Carmo Neto E, Santos LR, Knibel MF. Ventilator-associated pneumonia: epidemiology and impact on the clinical evolution of ICU patients. *J Bras Pneumol.* 2009;35(11):1084–1091.

652. Al Johani SM, Akhter J, Balkhy H, et al. Prevalence of antimicrobial resistance among gram-negative isolates in an adult intensive care unit at a tertiary care center in Saudi Arabia. *Ann Saudi Med.*;30(5):364–369.

653. Magret M, Amaya-Villar R, Garnacho J, et al. Ventilator-associated pneumonia in trauma patients is associated with lower mortality: results from EU-VAP study. *J Trauma.* 2010;69(4):849–854.

654. Ozdemir H, Kendirli T, Ergun H, et al. Nosocomial infections due to *Acinetobacter baumannii* in a pediatric intensive care unit in Turkey. *Turk J Pediatr.* 2011;53(3):255–260.

655. Tao L, Hu B, Rosenthal VD, et al. Device-associated infection rates in 398 intensive care units in Shanghai, China: International Nosocomial Infection Control Consortium (INICC) findings. Int *J Infect Dis.* 2011;15(11):e774–e780.

656. Gupta A, Kapil A, Lodha R, et al. Burden of healthcare-associated infections in a paediatric intensive care unit of a developing country: a single centre experience using active surveillance. *J Hosp Infect.* 2011;78(4):323–326.

657. Simor AE, Lee M, Vearncombe M, et al. An outbreak due to multiresistant *Acinetobacter baumannii* in a burn unit: risk factors for acquisition and management. *Infect Control Hosp Epidemiol.* 2002;23(5):261–267.

658. Zanetti G, Blanc DS, Federli I, et al. Importation of *Acinetobacter baumannii* into a burn unit: a recurrent outbreak of infection associated with widespread environmental contamination. *Infect Control Hosp Epidemiol.* 2007;28(6):723–725.

659. Babik J, Bodnarova L, Sopko K. *Acinetobacter*: serious danger for burn patients. *Acta Chir Plast.* 2008;50(1):27–32.

660. Maragakis LL, Perl TM. *Acinetobacter baumannii*: epidemiology, antimicrobial resistance, and treatment options. *Clin Infect Dis.* 2008;46(8):1254–1263.

661. Guerrero DM, Perez F, Conger NG, et al. *Acinetobacter baumannii*–associated skin

and soft tissue infections: recognizing a broadening spectrum of disease. *Surg Infect (Larchmt).* 2010;11(1):49–57.

662. Scott P, Deye G, Srinivasan A, et al. An outbreak of multidrug-resistant *Acinetobacter baumannii*–calcoaceticus complex infection in the US military health care system associated with military operations in Iraq. *Clin Infect Dis.* 2007;44(12):1577–1584.

663. Bergogne-Berezin E, Towner KJ. *Acinetobacter* spp. as nosocomial pathogens: microbiological, clinical, and epidemiological features. *Clin Microbiol Rev.* 1996;9(2):148–165.

664. Manikal VM, Landman D, Saurina G, et al. Endemic carbapenem-resistant *Acinetobacter* species in Brooklyn, New York: citywide prevalence, interinstitutional spread, and relation to antibiotic usage. *Clin Infect Dis.* 2000;31(1):101–106.

665. Villegas MV, Hartstein AI. *Acinetobacter* outbreaks, 1977–2000. *Infect Control Hosp Epidemiol.* 2003;24(4):284–295.

666. Lolans K, Rice TW, Munoz-Price LS, Quinn JP. Multicity outbreak of carbapenem-resistant *Acinetobacter baumannii* isolates producing the carbapenemase OXA-40. *Antimicrob Agents Chemother.* 2006;50(9):2941–2945.

667. Naas T, Coignard B, Carbonne A, et al. VEB-1 Extended-spectrum beta-lactamase–producing *Acinetobacter baumannii*, France. *Emerg Infect Dis.* 2006;12(8):1214–1222.

668. Coelho J, Woodford N, Afzal-Shah M, Livermore D. Occurrence of OXA-58–like carbapenemases in *Acinetobacter* spp. collected over 10 years in three continents. *Antimicrob Agents Chemother.* 2006;50(2):756–758.

669. Coelho JM, Turton JF, Kaufmann ME, et al. Occurrence of carbapenem-resistant *Acinetobacter baumannii* clones at multiple hospitals in London and Southeast England. *J Clin Microbiol.* 2006;44(10):3623–3627.

670. McDonald LC, Banerjee SN, Jarvis WR. Seasonal variation of *Acinetobacter* infections: 1987–1996. Nosocomial Infections Surveillance System. *Clin Infect Dis.* 1999;29(5):1133–1137.

671. Perencevich EN, McGregor JC, Shardell M, et al. Summer peaks in the incidences of gram-negative bacterial infection among hospitalized patients. *Infect Control Hosp Epidemiol.* 2008;29(12):1124–1131.

672. Eber MR, Shardell M, Schweizer ML, et al. Seasonal and temperature-associated increases in gram-negative bacterial bloodstream infections among hospitalized patients. *PLoS One.* 2011;6(9):e25298.

673. Irwin RS, Demers RR, Pratter MR, et al. An outbreak of *Acinetobacter* infection associated with the use of a ventilator spirometer. *Respir Care.* 1980;25(2):232–237.

674. Cunha BA, Klimek JJ, Gracewski J, et al. A common source outbreak of *Acinetobacter* pulmonary infections traced to Wright respirometers. *Postgrad Med J.* 1980;56(653):169–172.

675. Tankovic J, Legrand P, De Gatines G, et al. Characterization of a hospital outbreak of imipenem-resistant *Acinetobacter baumannii* by phenotypic and genotypic typing methods. *J Clin Microbiol.* 1994;32(11):2677–2681.

676. Go ES, Urban C, Burns J, et al. Clinical and molecular epidemiology of *Acinetobacter* infections sensitive only to polymyxin B and sulbactam. *Lancet.* 1994;344(8933):1329–1332.

677. Crowe M, Towner KJ, Humphreys H. Clinical and epidemiological features of an outbreak of *Acinetobacter* infection in an intensive therapy unit. *J Med Microbiol.* 1995;43(1):55–62.

678. Debast SB, Meis JF, Melchers WJ, et al. Use of interrepeat PCR fingerprinting to investigate an *Acinetobacter baumannii* outbreak in an intensive care unit. *Scand J Infect Dis.* 1996;28(6):577–581.

679. Riley TV, Webb SA, Cadwallader H, et al. Outbreak of gentamicin-resistant *Acinetobacter baumannii* in an intensive care unit: clinical, epidemiological and microbiological features. *Pathology.* 1996;28(4):359–363.

680. Kaul R, Burt JA, Cork L, et al. Investigation of a multiyear multiple critical care unit outbreak due to relatively drug-sensitive *Acinetobacter baumannii*: risk factors and attributable mortality. *J Infect Dis.* 1996;174(6):1279–1287.

681. McDonald LC, Walker M, Carson L, et al. Outbreak of *Acinetobacter* spp. bloodstream infections in a nursery associated with contaminated aerosols and air conditioners. *Pediatr Infect Dis J.* 1998;17(8):716–722.

682. Kapil A, Gulati S, Goel V, et al. Outbreak of nosocomial *Acinetobacter baumannii* bacteremia in a high risk ward. *Med Oncol.* 1998;15(4):270–274.

683. Catalano M, Quelle LS, Jeric PE, et al. Survival of *Acinetobacter baumannii* on bed rails during an outbreak and during sporadic cases. *J Hosp Infect.* 1999;42(1):27–35.

684. Roberts SA, Findlay R, Lang SD. Investigation of an outbreak of multi-drug resistant *Acinetobacter baumannii* in an intensive care burns unit. *J Hosp Infect.* 2001;48(3):228–232.

685. Mah MW, Memish ZA, Cunningham G, Bannatyne RM. Outbreak of *Acinetobacter baumannii* in an intensive care unit associated with tracheostomy. *Am J Infect Control.* 2001;29(5):284–288.

686. Das I, Lambert P, Hill D, et al. Carbapenem-resistant *Acinetobacter* and role of curtains in an outbreak in intensive care units. *J Hosp Infect.* 2002;50(2):110–114.

687. Aygun G, Demirkiran O, Utku T, et al. Environmental contamination during a carbapenem-resistant *Acinetobacter baumannii* outbreak in an intensive care unit. *J Hosp Infect.* 2002;52(4):259–262.

688. Huang YC, Su LH, Wu TL, et al. Outbreak of *Acinetobacter baumannii* bacteremia in a neonatal intensive care unit: clinical implications and genotyping analysis. *Pediatr Infect Dis J.* 2002;21(12):1105–1109.

689. Melamed R, Greenberg D, Porat N, et al. Successful control of an *Acinetobacter baumannii* outbreak in a neonatal intensive care unit. *J Hosp Infect.* 2003;53(1):31–38.

690. Wang SH, Sheng WH, Chang YY, et al. Healthcare-associated outbreak due to pan-drug resistant *Acinetobacter baumannii* in a surgical intensive care unit. *J Hosp Infect.* 2003;53(2):97–102.

691. Mirza IA, Hussain A, Abbasi SA, et al. Ambu bag as a source of *Acinetobacter baumannii* outbreak in an intensive care unit. *J Coll Physicians Surg Pak.* 2011;21(3):176–178.

692. Maragakis LL, Cosgrove SE, Song X, et al. An outbreak of multidrug-resistant *Acinetobacter baumannii* associated with pulsatile lavage wound treatment. *JAMA.* 2004;292(24):3006–3011.

693. El Shafie SS, Alishaq M, Leni Garcia M. Investigation of an outbreak of multidrug-resistant *Acinetobacter baumannii* in trauma intensive care unit. *J Hosp Infect.* 2004;56(2):101–105.

694. Morgan DJ, Liang SY, Smith CL, et al. Frequent multidrug-resistant *Acinetobacter baumannii* contamination of gloves, gowns, and hands of healthcare workers. *Infect Control Hosp Epidemiol.* 2010;31(7): 716–721.

695. Borer A, Gilad J, Smolyakov R, et al. Cell phones and *Acinetobacter* transmission. *Emerg Infect Dis.* 2005;11(7):1160–1161.

696. Playford EG, Craig JC, Iredell JR. Carbapenem-resistant *Acinetobacter baumannii* in intensive care unit patients: risk factors for acquisition, infection and their consequences. *J Hosp Infect.* 2007;65(3):204–211.

697. Hsueh PR, Teng LJ, Chen CY, et al. Pandrug-resistant *Acinetobacter baumannii* causing nosocomial infections in a university hospital, Taiwan. *Emerg Infect Dis.* 2002;8(8): 827–832.

698. Peleg AY, Seifert H, Paterson DL. *Acinetobacter baumannii*: emergence of a successful pathogen. *Clin Microbiol Rev.* 2008;21(3):538–582.

699. Falagas ME, Rafailidis PI, Matthaiou DK, et al. Pandrug-resistant *Klebsiella pneumoniae, Pseudomonas aeruginosa* and *Acinetobacter baumannii* infections: characteristics and outcome in a series of 28 patients. *Int J Antimicrob Agents.* 2008;32(5):450–454.

700. Saleem AF, Ahmed I, Mir F, et al. Pan-resistant *Acinetobacter* infection in neonates in Karachi, Pakistan. *J Infect Dev Ctries.* 2010;4(1):30–37.

701. Apisarnthanarak A, Mundy LM. Mortality associated with pandrug-resistant *Acinetobacter baumannii* infections in Thailand. *Am J Infect Control.* 2009;37(6):519–520.

702. Chuang YY, Huang YC, Lin CH, et al. Epidemiological investigation after hospitalising a case with pandrug-resistant *Acinetobacter baumannii* infection. *J Hosp Infect.* 2009;72(1):30–35.

703. Ben RJ, Yang MC, Hsueh JC, et al. Molecular characterisation of multiple drug-resistant *Acinetobacter baumannii* isolates in southern Taiwan. *Int J Antimicrob Agents.* 2011;38(5):403–408.

704. Magiorakos AP, Srinivasan A, Carey RB, et al. Multidrug-resistant, extensively drug-resistant and pandrug-resistant bacteria: an international expert proposal for interim standard definitions for acquired resistance. *Clin Microbiol Infect.* 2011;18(3):268–281.

705. Smani Y, Dominguez-Herrera J, Pachon J. Rifampin protects human lung epithelial cells against cytotoxicity induced by clinical multi and pandrug-resistant *Acinetobacter baumannii.* *J Infect Dis.* 2011;203(8):1110–1119.

706. Apisarnthanarak A, Warren DK, Fraser VJ. Creating a cohort area to limit transmission of pandrug-resistant *Acinetobacter baumannii* in a Thai tertiary care center. *Clin Infect Dis.* 2009;48(10):1487–1488.

707. Ben-David D, Maor Y, Keller N, et al. Potential role of active surveillance in the control of a hospital-wide outbreak of carbapenem-resistant *Klebsiella pneumoniae* infection. *Infect Control Hosp Epidemiol.* 2010;31(6):620–626.

708. Munoz-Price LS, De La Cuesta C, Adams S, et al. Successful eradication of a monoclonal strain of *Klebsiella pneumoniae* during a *K. pneumoniae* carbapenemase-producing *K. pneumoniae* outbreak in a surgical intensive care unit in Miami, Florida. *Infect Control Hosp Epidemiol.* 2010;31(10):1074–1077.

709. Munoz-Price LS, Hayden MK, Lolans K, et al. Successful control of an outbreak of *Klebsiella pneumoniae* carbapenemase-producing *K. pneumoniae* at a long-term acute care hospital. *Infect Control Hosp Epidemiol.* 2010;31(4):341–347.

710. Denton M, Wilcox MH, Parnell P, et al. Role of environmental cleaning in controlling an outbreak of *Acinetobacter baumannii* on a neurosurgical intensive care unit. *J Hosp Infect.* 2004;56(2):106–110.

711. Chan PC, Huang LM, Lin HC, et al. Control of an outbreak of pandrug-resistant *Acinetobacter baumannii* colonization and infection in a neonatal intensive care unit. *Infect Control Hosp Epidemiol.* 2007;28(4):423–429.

712. Dancer SJ. The role of environmental cleaning in the control of hospital-acquired infection. *J Hosp Infect.* 2009;73(4):378–385.

713. Wilson AP, Smyth D, Moore G, et al. The impact of enhanced cleaning within the intensive care unit on contamination of the near-patient environment with hospital pathogens: a randomized crossover study in critical care units in two hospitals. *Crit Care Med.* 2011;39(4):651–658.

714. Consales G, Gramigni E, Zamidei L, et al. A multidrug-resistant *Acinetobacter baumannii* outbreak in intensive care unit: antimicrobial and organizational strategies. *J Crit Care.* 2011;26(5):453–459.

715. Dortch MJ, Fleming SB, Kauffmann RM, et al. Infection reduction strategies including antibiotic stewardship protocols in surgical and trauma intensive care units are associated with reduced resistant gram-negative

healthcare-associated infections. *Surg Infect (Larchmt)*. 2011;12(1):15–25.

716. Mortimer EA Jr. Pertussis and its prevention: a family affair. *J Infect Dis*. 1990;161(3): 473–479.

717. Deen JL, Mink CA, Cherry JD, et al. Household contact study of *Bordetella pertussis* infections. *Clin Infect Dis*. 1995;21(5):1211–1219.

718. Weber DJ, Rutala WA. Management of healthcare workers exposed to pertussis. *Infect Control Hosp Epidemiol*. 1994;15(6):411–415.

719. Zepp F, Heininger U, Mertsola J, et al. Rationale for pertussis booster vaccination throughout life in Europe. *Lancet Infect Dis*. 2011;11(7):557–570.

720. Hewlett EL, Edwards KM. Clinical practice: pertussis—not just for kids. *N Engl J Med*. 2005;352(12):1215–1222.

721. Valenti WM, Pincus PH, Messner MK. Nosocomial pertussis: possible spread by a hospital visitor. *Am J Dis Child*. 1980;134(5):520–521.

722. Fisher MC, Long SS, McGowan KL, et al. Outbreak of pertussis in a residential facility for handicapped people. *J Pediatr*. 1989;114(6):934–939.

723. Christie CD, Glover AM, Willke MJ, et al. Containment of pertussis in the regional pediatric hospital during the Greater Cincinnati epidemic of 1993. *Infect Control Hosp Epidemiol*. 1995;16(10):556–563.

724. Deville JG, Cherry JD, Christenson PD, et al. Frequency of unrecognized *Bordetella pertussis* infections in adults. *Clin Infect Dis*. 1995;21(3):639–642.

725. Nennig ME, Shinefield HR, Edwards KM, et al. Prevalence and incidence of adult pertussis in an urban population. *JAMA*. 1996;275(21):1672–1674.

726. Calugar A, Ortega-Sanchez IR, Tiwari T, et al. Nosocomial pertussis: costs of an outbreak and benefits of vaccinating health care workers. *Clin Infect Dis*. 2006;42(7):981–988.

727. Bryant KA, Humbaugh K, Brothers K, et al. Measures to control an outbreak of pertussis in a neonatal intermediate care nursery after exposure to a healthcare worker. *Infect Control Hosp Epidemiol*. 2006;27(6): 541–545.

728. Vranken P, Pogue M, Romalewski C, Ratard R. Outbreak of pertussis in a neonatal intensive care unit—Louisiana, 2004. *Am J Infect Control*. 2006;34(9):550–554.

729. Baggett HC, Duchin JS, Shelton W, et al. Two nosocomial pertussis outbreaks and their associated costs—King County, Washington, 2004. *Infect Control Hosp Epidemiol*. 2007;28(5):537–543.

730. Zivna I, Bergin D, Casavant J, et al. Impact of *Bordetella pertussis* exposures on a Massachusetts tertiary care medical system. *Infect Control Hosp Epidemiol*. 2007;28(6):708–712.

731. Wright PW, Wallace RJ Jr, Wright NW, et al. Sensitivity of fluorochrome microscopy for detection of *Mycobacterium tuberculosis* versus nontuberculous mycobacteria. *J Clin Microbiol*. 1998;36(4):1046–1049.

732. Paterson JM, Sheppeard V. Nosocomial pertussis infection of infants: still a risk in 2009. *Commun Dis Intell*. 2010;34(4):440–443.

733. Gehanno JF, Pestel-Caron M, Marguet C, et al. [Pertussis outbreak in an outpatient hospital staff]. *Arch Pediatr*. 1998;5(1):92–93.

734. Cromer AL, Latham SC, Bryant KG, et al. Monitoring and feedback of hand hygiene compliance and the impact on facility-acquired methicillin-resistant *Staphylococcus aureus*. *Am J Infect Control*. 2008;36(9):672–677.

735. Hospital-acquired pertussis among newborns—Texas, 2004. *MMWR*. 2008;57(22):600–603.

736. Updated recommendations for use of tetanus toxoid, reduced diphtheria toxoid and

acellular pertussis (Tdap) vaccine from the Advisory Committee on Immunization Practices, 2010. *MMWR.* 2011;60(1):13–15.

737. Management of people exposed to pertussis and control of pertussis outbreaks. *CMAJ.* 1990;143(8):751–753.

738. Langley JM, Halperin SA, Boucher FD, Smith B. Azithromycin is as effective as and better tolerated than erythromycin estolate for the treatment of pertussis. *Pediatrics.* 2004;114(1):e96–e101.

739. Devasia RA, Jones TF, Collier B, Schaffner W. Compliance with azithromycin versus erythromycin in the setting of a pertussis outbreak. *Am J Med Sci.* 2009;337(3):176–178.

740. Ehrenkranz NJ, Kicklighter JL. Tuberculosis outbreak in a general hospital: evidence for airborne spread of infection. *Ann Intern Med.* 1972;77(3):377–382.

741. Stead WW. Tuberculosis among elderly persons: an outbreak in a nursing home. *Ann Intern Med.* 1981;94(5):606–610.

742. Tuberculosis in a nursing care facility—Washington. *MMWR.* 1983;32(9): 121–122, 128.

743. Stead WW, Lofgren JP, Warren E, Thomas C. Tuberculosis as an endemic and nosocomial infection among the elderly in nursing homes. *N Engl J Med.* 1985;312(23):1483–1487.

744. Lundgren R, Norrman E, Asberg I. Tuberculosis infection transmitted at autopsy. *Tubercle.* 1987;68(2):147–150.

745. Templeton GL, Illing LA, Young L, et al. The risk for transmission of *Mycobacterium tuberculosis* at the bedside and during autopsy. *Ann Intern Med.* 1995;122(12): 922–925.

746. Brennen C, Muder RR, Muraca PW. Occult endemic tuberculosis in a chronic care facility. *Infect Control Hosp Epidemiol.* 1988;9(12):548–552.

747. Kantor HS, Poblete R, Pusateri SL. Nosocomial transmission of tuberculosis from unsuspected disease. *Am J Med.* 1988;84(5):833–838.

748. *Mycobacterium tuberculosis* transmission in a health clinic—Florida, 1988. *MMWR.* 1989;38(15):256–258, 263–264.

749. Nosocomial transmission of multidrug-resistant tuberculosis to health-care workers and HIV-infected patients in an urban hospital—Florida. *MMWR.* 1990;39(40):718–722.

750. Haley CE, McDonald RC, Rossi L, et al. Tuberculosis epidemic among hospital personnel. *Infect Control Hosp Epidemiol.* 1989;10(5):204–210.

751. Hutton MD, Stead WW, Cauthen GM, et al. Nosocomial transmission of tuberculosis associated with a draining abscess. *J Infect Dis.* 1990;161(2):286–295.

752. Bentley DW. Tuberculosis in long-term care facilities. *Infect Control Hosp Epidemiol.* 1990;11(1):42–46.

753. From the Centers for Disease Control: nosocomial transmission of multidrug-resistant tuberculosis among HIV-infected persons—Florida and New York, 1988–1991. *JAMA.* 1991;266(11):1483–1485.

754. Transmission of multidrug-resistant tuberculosis from an HIV-positive client in a residential substance-abuse treatment facility—Michigan. *MMWR.* 1991;40(8):129–131.

755. Beck-Sague C, Dooley SW, Hutton MD, et al. Hospital outbreak of multidrug-resistant *Mycobacterium tuberculosis* infections: factors in transmission to staff and HIV-infected patients. *JAMA.* 1992;268(10):1280–1286.

756. Edlin BR, Tokars JI, Grieco MH, et al. An outbreak of multidrug-resistant tuberculosis among hospitalized patients with the acquired immunodeficiency syndrome. *N Engl J Med.* 1992;326(23):1514–1521.

757. Pearson ML, Jereb JA, Frieden TR, et al. Nosocomial transmission of multidrug-resistant *Mycobacterium tuberculosis*: a risk to patients and health care workers. *Ann Intern Med.* 1992;117(3):191–196.

758. Dooley SW, Jarvis WR, Martone WJ, Snider DE Jr. Multidrug-resistant tuberculosis. *Ann Intern Med.* 1992;117(3):257–259.

759. Jarvis WR. Nosocomial transmission of multidrug-resistant *Mycobacterium tuberculosis*. *Am J Infect Control.* 1995;23(2):146–151.

760. Zaza S, Blumberg HM, Beck-Sague C, et al. Nosocomial transmission of *Mycobacterium tuberculosis*: role of health care workers in outbreak propagation. *J Infect Dis.* 1995;172(6):1542–1549.

761. Jereb JA, Klevens RM, Privett TD, et al. Tuberculosis in health care workers at a hospital with an outbreak of multidrug-resistant *Mycobacterium tuberculosis*. *Arch Intern Med.* 1995;155(8):854–859.

762. Ikeda RM, Birkhead GS, DiFerdinando GT Jr, et al. Nosocomial tuberculosis: an outbreak of a strain resistant to seven drugs. *Infect Control Hosp Epidemiol.* 1995;16(3):152–159.

763. Lemaitre N, Sougakoff W, Coetmeur D, et al. Nosocomial transmission of tuberculosis among mentally-handicapped patients in a long-term care facility. *Tuber Lung Dis.* 1996;77(6):531–536.

764. Kenyon TA, Ridzon R, Luskin-Hawk R, et al. A nosocomial outbreak of multidrug-resistant tuberculosis. *Ann Intern Med.* 1997;127(1):32–36.

765. D'Agata EM, Wise S, Stewart A, Lefkowitz LB Jr. Nosocomial transmission of *Mycobacterium tuberculosis* from an extrapulmonary site. *Infect Control Hosp Epidemiol.* 2001;22(1):10–12.

766. Keijman J, Tjhie J, Olde Damink S, Alink M. Unusual nosocomial transmission of *Mycobacterium tuberculosis*. *Eur J Clin Microbiol Infect Dis.* 2001;20(11):808–809.

767. Nosocomial transmission of *Mycobacterium tuberculosis* found through screening for severe acute respiratory syndrome—Taipei, Taiwan, 2003. *MMWR.* 2004;53(15):321–322.

768. Malone JL, Ijaz K, Lambert L, et al. Investigation of healthcare-associated transmission of *Mycobacterium tuberculosis* among patients with malignancies at three hospitals and at a residential facility. *Cancer.* 2004;101(12):2713–2721.

769. *Mycobacterium tuberculosis* transmission in a newborn nursery and maternity ward—New York City, 2003. *MMWR.* 2005;54(50):1280–1283.

770. Huang WL, Jou R, Yeh PF, Huang A. Laboratory investigation of a nosocomial transmission of tuberculosis at a district general hospital. *J Formos Med Assoc.* 2007;106(7):520–527.

771. Di Perri G, Cruciani M, Danzi MC, et al. Nosocomial epidemic of active tuberculosis among HIV-infected patients. *Lancet.* 1989;2(8678–8679):1502–1504.

772. Wenger PN, Otten J, Breeden A, et al. Control of nosocomial transmission of multidrug-resistant *Mycobacterium tuberculosis* among healthcare workers and HIV-infected patients. *Lancet.* 1995;345(8944):235–240.

773. Guerrero A, Cobo J, Fortun J, et al. Nosocomial transmission of *Mycobacterium bovis* resistant to 11 drugs in people with advanced HIV-1 infection. *Lancet.* 1997;350(9093):1738–1742.

774. Moro ML, Gori A, Errante I, et al. An outbreak of multidrug-resistant tuberculosis involving HIV-infected patients of two hospitals in Milan, Italy. Italian Multidrug-Resistant Tuberculosis Outbreak Study Group. *AIDS.* 1998;12(9):1095–1102.

775. Nelson KE, Larson PA, Schraufnagel DE, Jackson J. Transmission of tuberculosis by flexible fiberbronchoscopes. *Am Rev Respir Dis.* 1983;127(1):97–100.

776. Wheeler PW, Lancaster D, Kaiser AB. Bronchopulmonary cross-colonization and infection related to mycobacterial contamination of suction valves of bronchoscopes. *J Infect Dis.* 1989;159(5):954–958.

777. Agerton T, Valway S, Gore B, et al. Transmission of a highly drug-resistant strain (strain W1) of *Mycobacterium tuberculosis*:

community outbreak and nosocomial transmission via a contaminated bronchoscope. *JAMA*. 1997;278(13):1073–1077.

778. Michele TM, Cronin WA, Graham NM, et al. Transmission of *Mycobacterium tuberculosis* by a fiberoptic bronchoscope: identification by DNA fingerprinting. *JAMA*. 1997;278(13):1093–1095.

779. Stuart RL, Bennett NJ, Forbes AB, Grayson ML. Assessing the risk of tuberculosis infection among healthcare workers: the Melbourne Mantoux Study. Melbourne Mantoux Study Group. *Med J Aust*. 2001;174(11):569–573.

780. Larson JL, Lambert L, Stricof RL, et al. Potential nosocomial exposure to *Mycobacterium tuberculosis* from a bronchoscope. *Infect Control Hosp Epidemiol*. 2003;24(11):825–830.

781. Wheeler AP, Graham BS. Atypical mycobacterial infections. *South Med J*. 1989;82(10):1250–1258.

782. Bryce EA, Walker M, Bevan C, Smith JA. Contamination of bronchoscopes with *Mycobacterium tuberculosis*. *Can J Infect Control*. 1993;8(2):35–36.

783. Weber DJ, Rutala WA. Lessons from outbreaks associated with bronchoscopy. *Infect Control Hosp Epidemiol*. 2001;22(7):403–408.

784. Prevention and control of tuberculosis in facilities providing long-term care to the elderly: recommendations of the Advisory Committee for Elimination of Tuberculosis. *MMWR Recomm Rep*. 1990;39(RR-10): 7–13.

785. Greenaway C, Menzies D, Fanning A, et al. Delay in diagnosis among hospitalized patients with active tuberculosis—predictors and outcomes. Am J Respir *Crit Care Med*. 2002;165(7):927–933.

786. Mourad G, Soulillou JP, Chong G, et al. Transmission of *Mycobacterium tuberculosis* with renal allografts. *Nephron*. 1985;41(1):82–85.

787. Ridgeway AL, Warner GS, Phillips P, et al. Transmission of *Mycobacterium tuberculosis* to recipients of single lung transplants from the same donor. *Am J Respir Crit Care Med*. 1996;153(3):1166–1168.

788. Winthrop KL, Kubak BM, Pegues DA, et al. Transmission of *Mycobacterium tuberculosis* via lung transplantation. *Am J Transplant*. 2004;4(9):1529–1533.

789. Transplantation-transmitted tuberculosis— Oklahoma and Texas, 2007. *MMWR*. 2008;57(13):333–336.

790. Edathodu J, Alrajhi A, Halim M, Althawadi S. Multi-recipient donor-transmitted tuberculosis. *Int J Tuberc Lung Dis*. 2010;14(11):1493–1495.

791. Baussano I, Nunn P, Williams B, et al. Tuberculosis among health care workers. *Emerg Infect Dis*. 2011;17(3):488–494.

792. Garcia-Garcia ML, Jimenez-Corona A, Jimenez-Corona ME, et al. Factors associated with tuberculin reactivity in two general hospitals in Mexico. *Infect Control Hosp Epidemiol*. 2001;22(2):88–93.

793. Driver CR, Stricof RL, Granville K, et al. Tuberculosis in health care workers during declining tuberculosis incidence in New York State. *Am J Infect Control*. 2005;33(9): 519–526.

794. Dimitrova B, Hutchings A, Atun R, et al. Increased risk of tuberculosis among health care workers in Samara Oblast, Russia: analysis of notification data. *Int J Tuberc Lung Dis*. 2005;9(1):43–48.

795. Jiamjarasrangsi W, Hirunsuthikul N, Kamolratanakul P. Tuberculosis among health care workers at King Chulalongkorn Memorial Hospital, 1988–2002. *Int J Tuberc Lung Dis*. 2005;9(11): 1253–1258.

796. Escombe AR, Huaroto L, Ticona E, et al. Tuberculosis transmission risk and infection control in a hospital emergency department in Lima, Peru. *Int J Tuberc Lung Dis*. 2010;14(9):1120–1126.

797. Trajman A, Menzies D. Occupational respiratory infections. *Curr Opin Pulm Med.* 2010;16(3):226–234.

798. Jensen PA, Lambert LA, Iademarco MF, Ridzon R. Guidelines for preventing the transmission of *Mycobacterium tuberculosis* in health-care settings, 2005. *MMWR Recomm Rep.* 2005;54(RR-17):1–141.

799. World Health Organization. *WHO Policy on TB Infection Control in Health-Care Facilities, Congregate Settings and Households.* Geneva, Switzerland: WHO; 2009. Available at: http://whqlibdoc.who.int/publications/2009/9789241598323_eng.pdf. Accessed October 31, 2011.

800. Kline S, Cameron S, Streifel A, et al. An outbreak of bacteremias associated with *Mycobacterium mucogenicum* in a hospital water supply. *Infect Control Hosp Epidemiol.* 2004;25(12):1042–1049.

801. Goodman RA, Smith JD, Kubica GP, et al. Nosocomial mycobacterial pseudoinfection in a Georgia hospital. *Infect Control.* 1984;5(12):573–576.

802. Lowry PW, Jarvis WR, Oberle AD, et al. *Mycobacterium chelonae* causing otitis media in an ear-nose-and-throat practice. *N Engl J Med.* 1988;319(15):978–982.

803. Nolan CM, Hashisaki PA, Dundas DF. An outbreak of soft-tissue infections due to *Mycobacterium fortuitum* associated with electromyography. *J Infect Dis.* 1991;163(5):1150–1153.

804. Gubler JG, Salfinger M, von Graevenitz A. Pseudoepidemic of nontuberculous mycobacteria due to a contaminated bronchoscope cleaning machine: report of an outbreak and review of the literature. *Chest.* 1992;101(5):1245–1249.

805. Maloney S, Welbel S, Daves B, et al. *Mycobacterium abscessus* pseudoinfection traced to an automated endoscope washer: utility of epidemiologic and laboratory investigation. *J Infect Dis.* 1994;169(5):1166–1169.

806. Camargo D, Saad C, Ruiz F, et al. Iatrogenic outbreak of *M. chelonae* skin abscesses. *Epidemiol Infect.* 1996;117(1):113–119.

807. Roy V, Weisdorf D. Mycobacterial infections following bone marrow transplantation: a 20 year retrospective review. *Bone Marrow Transplant.* 1997;19(5):467–470.

808. Gaviria JM, Garcia PJ, Garrido SM, et al. Nontuberculous mycobacterial infections in hematopoietic stem cell transplant recipients: characteristics of respiratory and catheter-related infections. *Biol Blood Marrow Transplant.* 2000;6(4):361–369.

809. Doucette K, Fishman JA. Nontuberculous mycobacterial infection in hematopoietic stem cell and solid organ transplant recipients. *Clin Infect Dis.* 2004;38(10):1428–1439.

810. Ferguson DD, Gershman K, Jensen B, et al. *Mycobacterium goodii* infections associated with surgical implants at Colorado hospital. *Emerg Infect Dis.* 2004;10(10):1868–1871.

811. Bettiker RL, Axelrod PI, Fekete T, et al. Delayed recognition of a pseudo-outbreak of *Mycobacterium terrae. Am J Infect Control.* 2006;34(6):343–347.

812. Tang P, Walsh S, Murray C, et al. Outbreak of acupuncture-associated cutaneous *Mycobacterium abscessus* infections. *J Cutan Med Surg.* 2006;10(4):166–169.

813. Wang SH, Mangino JE, Stevenson K, et al. Characterization of "*Mycobacterium paraffinicum*" associated with a pseudo-outbreak. *J Clin Microbiol.* 2008;46(5):1850–1853.

814. Wang SH, Pancholi P, Stevenson K, et al. Pseudo-outbreak of "*Mycobacterium paraffinicum*" infection and/or colonization in a tertiary care medical center. *Infect Control Hosp Epidemiol.* 2009;30(9):848–853.

815. Carbonne A, Brossier F, Arnaud I, et al. Outbreak of nontuberculous mycobacterial subcutaneous infections related to multiple mesotherapy injections. *J Clin Microbiol.* 2009;47(6):1961–1964.

816. Shachor-Meyouhas Y, Sprecher H, Eluk O, et al. An outbreak of *Mycobacterium mucogenicum* bacteremia in pediatric hematology–oncology patients. *Pediatr Infect Dis J.* 2011;30(1):30–32.

817. Pulliam JP, Vernon DD, Alexander SR, et al. Nontuberculous mycobacterial peritonitis associated with continuous ambulatory peritoneal dialysis. *Am J Kidney Dis.* 1983;2(6):610–614.

818. Nontuberculous mycobacterial infections in hemodialysis patients—Louisiana, 1982. *MMWR.* 1983;32(18):244–246.

819. Montoliu J, Gatell JM, Bonal J, et al. Disseminated visceral infection with *Mycobacterium fortuitum* in a hemodialysis patient. *Am J Nephrol.* 1985;5(3):205–211.

820. Bolan G, Reingold AL, Carson LA, et al. Infections with *Mycobacterium chelonei* in patients receiving dialysis and using processed hemodialyzers. *J Infect Dis.* 1985;152(5):1013–1019.

821. White R, Abreo K, Flanagan R, et al. Nontuberculous mycobacterial infections in continuous ambulatory peritoneal dialysis patients. *Am J Kidney Dis.* 1993;22(4):581–587.

822. Knox KR, Granick MS, Mitchell AT, Fonseca RB. Infection with nontuberculous *Mycobacterium* after injection of adulterated silicone fluid. *Aesthet Surg J.* 2004;24(4):342–345.

823. Keenan N, Jeyaratnam D, Sheerin NS. *Mycobacterium simiae*: a previously undescribed pathogen in peritoneal dialysis peritonitis. *Am J Kidney Dis.* 2005;45(5):e75–e78.

824. Sousa TS, Matherne RJ, Wilkerson MG. Case report: cutaneous nontuberculous mycobacterial abscesses associated with insulin injections. *J Drugs Dermatol.* 2010;9(11):1439–1442.

825. El Sahly HM, Septimus E, Soini H, et al. *Mycobacterium simiae* pseudo-outbreak resulting from a contaminated hospital water supply in Houston, Texas. *Clin Infect Dis.* 2002;35(7):802–807.

826. Scheiermann N, Kuwert EK, Pieringer E, Dermietzel R. High risk groups for hepatitis B virus infection in a university hospital staff as determined by detection of HB antigens, antibodies, and Dane particles. *Med Microbiol Immunol.* 1978;166(1–4):241–247.

827. Hadler SC, Doto IL, Maynard JE, et al. Occupational risk of hepatitis B infection in hospital workers. *Infect Control.* 1985;6(1):24–31.

828. Thomas DL, Factor SH, Kelen GD, et al. Viral hepatitis in health care personnel at the Johns Hopkins Hospital: the seroprevalence of and risk factors for hepatitis B virus and hepatitis C virus infection. *Arch Intern Med.* 1993;153(14):1705–1712.

829. Shapiro CN, Tokars JI, Chamberland ME. Use of the hepatitis-B vaccine and infection with hepatitis B and C among orthopaedic surgeons. The American Academy of Orthopaedic Surgeons Serosurvey Study Committee. *J Bone Joint Surg Am.* 1996;78(12):1791–1800.

830. Snydman DR, Hindman SH, Wineland MD, et al. Nosocomial viral hepatitis B: a cluster among staff with subsequent transmission to patients. *Ann Intern Med.* 1976;85(5):573–577.

831. Grob PJ, Bischof B, Naeff F. Cluster of hepatitis B transmitted by a physician. *Lancet.* 1981;2(8257):1218–1220.

832. Favero MS, Bond WW, Petersen NJ, et al. Detection methods for study of the stability of hepatitis B antigen on surfaces. *J Infect Dis.* 1974;129(2):210–212.

833. Lauer JL, VanDrunen NA, Washburn JW, Balfour HH Jr. Transmission of hepatitis B virus in clinical laboratory areas. *J Infect Dis.* 1979;140(4):513–516.

834. Bond WW, Favero MS, Petersen NJ, et al. Survival of hepatitis B virus after drying and storage for one week. *Lancet.* 1981;1(8219):550–551.

835. Recommendations for preventing transmission of infections among chronic

hemodialysis patients. *MMWR Recomm Rep.* 2001;50(RR-5):1–43.

836. Froio N, Nicastri E, Comandini UV, et al. Contamination by hepatitis B and C viruses in the dialysis setting. *Am J Kidney Dis.* 2003;42(3):546–550.

837. Rimland D, Parkin WE, Miller GB Jr, Schrack WD. Hepatitis B outbreak traced to an oral surgeon. *N Engl J Med.* 1977;296(17):953–958.

838. Ahtone J, Goodman RA. Hepatitis B and dental personnel: transmission to patients and prevention issues. *J Am Dent Assoc.* 1983;106(2):219–222.

839. From the Centers for Disease Control and Prevention: outbreaks of hepatitis B virus infection among hemodialysis patients—California, Nebraska, and Texas, 1994. *JAMA.* 1996;275(18):1394–1395.

840. Drescher J, Wagner D, Haverich A, et al. Nosocomial hepatitis B virus infections in cardiac transplant recipients transmitted during transvenous endomyocardial biopsy. *J Hosp Infect.* 1994;26(2):81–92.

841. Liang TJ, Hasegawa K, Rimon N, et al. A hepatitis B virus mutant associated with an epidemic of fulminant hepatitis. *N Engl J Med.* 1991;324(24):1705–1709.

842. Oren I, Hershow RC, Ben-Porath E, et al. A common-source outbreak of fulminant hepatitis B in a hospital. *Ann Intern Med.* 1989;110(9):691–698.

843. Coutinho RA, Albrecht-van Lent P, Stoutjesdijk L, et al. Hepatitis B from doctors. *Lancet.* 1982;1(8267):345–346.

844. Comstock RD, Mallonee S, Fox JL, et al. A large nosocomial outbreak of hepatitis C and hepatitis B among patients receiving pain remediation treatments. *Infect Control Hosp Epidemiol.* 2004;25(7):576–583.

845. Macedo de Oliveira A, White KL, Leschinsky DP, et al. An outbreak of hepatitis C virus infections among outpatients at a hematology/oncology clinic. *Ann Intern Med.* 2005;142(11):898–902.

846. Savey A, Simon F, Izopet J, et al. A large nosocomial outbreak of hepatitis C virus infections at a hemodialysis center. *Infect Control Hosp Epidemiol.* 2005;26(9):752–760.

847. De Schrijver K, Maes I, Van Damme P, et al. An outbreak of nosocomial hepatitis B virus infection in a nursing home for the elderly in Antwerp (Belgium). *Acta Clin Belg.* 2005;60(2):63–69.

848. Kondili LA, Genovese D, Argentini C, et al. Nosocomial transmission in simultaneous outbreaks of hepatitis C and B virus infections in a hemodialysis center. *Eur J Clin Microbiol Infect Dis.* 2006;25(8):527–531.

849. Rosenheim M, Cadranel JF, Stuyver L, et al. Nosocomial transmission of hepatitis B virus associated with endomyocardial biopsy. *Gastroenterol Clin Biol.* 2006;30(11): 1274–1280.

850. Gisselquist D, Upham G, Potterat JJ. Efficiency of human immunodeficiency virus transmission through injections and other medical procedures: evidence, estimates, and unfinished business. *Infect Control Hosp Epidemiol.* 2006;27(9):944–952.

851. Ganczak M, Barss P. Nosocomial HIV infection: epidemiology and prevention—a global perspective. *AIDS Rev.* 2008;10(1):47–61.

852. Ahn J, Cohen SM. Transmission of human immunodeficiency virus and hepatitis C virus through liver transplantation. *Liver Transpl.* 2008;14(11):1603–1608.

853. Lanini S, Puro V, Lauria FN, et al. Patient to patient transmission of hepatitis B virus: a systematic review of reports on outbreaks between 1992 and 2007. *BMC Med.* 2009;7:15.

854. Calderon GM, Gonzalez-Velazquez F, Gonzalez-Bonilla CR, et al. Prevalence and risk factors of hepatitis C virus, hepatitis B virus, and human immunodeficiency virus in multiply transfused recipients in Mexico. *Transfusion.* 2009;49(10):2200–2207.

855. Akiyama H, Nakamura N, Tanikawa S, et al. Incidence and influence of GB virus C and hepatitis C virus infection in

patients undergoing bone marrow transplantation. *Bone Marrow Transplant.* 1998;21(11):1131–1135.

856. Acute hepatitis C virus infections attributed to unsafe injection practices at an endoscopy clinic—Nevada, 2007. *MMWR.* 2008;57(19):513–517.

857. Candotti D, Allain JP. Transfusion-transmitted hepatitis B virus infection. *J Hepatol.* 2009;51(4):798–809.

858. Thompson ND, Perz JF, Moorman AC, Holmberg SD. Nonhospital health care–associated hepatitis B and C virus transmission: United States, 1998–2008. *Ann Intern Med.* 2009;150(1):33–39.

859. HIV transmission through transfusion—Missouri and Colorado, 2008. *MMWR.* 2010;59(41):1335–1339.

860. HIV transmitted from a living organ donor—New York City, 2009. *MMWR.* 2011;60(10):297–301.

861. Panlilio AL, Cardo DM, Grohskopf LA, et al. Updated U.S. Public Health Service guidelines for the management of occupational exposures to HIV and recommendations for postexposure prophylaxis. *MMWR Recomm Rep.* 2005;54(RR-9):1–17.

862. Panlilio AL, Shapiro CN, Schable CA, et al. Serosurvey of human immunodeficiency virus, hepatitis B virus, and hepatitis C virus infection among hospital-based surgeons. Serosurvey Study Group. *J Am Coll Surg.* 1995;180(1):16–24.

863. Henderson DK, Dembry L, Fishman NO, et al. SHEA guideline for management of healthcare workers who are infected with hepatitis B virus, hepatitis C virus, and/or human immunodeficiency virus. *Infect Control Hosp Epidemiol.* 2010;31(3):203–232.

864. McCormick RD, Maki DG. Epidemiology of needle-stick injuries in hospital personnel. *Am J Med.* 1981;70(4):928–932.

865. Updated U.S. Public Health Service guidelines for the management of occupational exposures to HBV, HCV, and HIV and recommendations for postexposure prophylaxis. *MMWR Recomm Rep.* 2001;50(RR-11):1–52.

866. Weber DJ, Rutala WA, Schaffner W. Lessons learned: protection of healthcare workers from infectious disease risks. *Crit Care Med.* 2010;38(8 suppl):S306–S314.

867. Do AN, Ciesielski CA, Metler RP, et al. Occupationally acquired human immunodeficiency virus (HIV) infection: national case surveillance data during 20 years of the HIV epidemic in the United States. *Infect Control Hosp Epidemiol.* 2003;24(2):86–96.

868. Mast EE, Weinbaum CM, Fiore AE, et al. A comprehensive immunization strategy to eliminate transmission of hepatitis B virus infection in the United States: recommendations of the Advisory Committee on Immunization Practices (ACIP) Part II: immunization of adults. *MMWR Recomm Rep.* 2006; 55(RR-16):1–33; quiz CE 1–4.

869. Pourkarim MR, Verbeeck J, Rahman M, et al. Phylogenetic analysis of hepatitis B virus full-length genomes reveals evidence for a large nosocomial outbreak in Belgium. *J Clin Virol.* 2009;46(1):61–68.

870. Dencs A, Hettmann A, Martyin T, et al. Phylogenetic investigation of nosocomial transmission of hepatitis C virus in an oncology ward. *J Med Virol.* 2011;83(3):428–436.

871. Burns K, Heslin J, Crowley B, et al. Nosocomial outbreak of hepatitis B virus infection involving two hospitals in the Republic of Ireland. *J Hosp Infect.* 2011;78(4):279–283.

872. Kane M. Epidemiology of hepatitis B infection in North America. *Vaccine.* 1995;13(suppl 1):S16–S17.

873. Kallen AJ, Arduino MJ, Patel PR. Preventing infections in patients undergoing hemodialysis. *Expert Rev Anti Infect Ther.* 2010;8(6):643–655.

874. Vaqlia A, Nicolin R, Puro V, et al. Needlestick hepatitis C virus seroconversion in a surgeon. *Lancet.* 1990;336(8726):1315–1316.

875. Schlipkoter U, Roggendorf M, Cholmakow K, et al. Transmission of hepatitis C virus (HCV) from a haemodialysis patient to a medical staff member. *Scand J Infect Dis.* 1990;22(6):757–758.

876. Seeff LB. Hepatitis C from a needlestick injury. *Ann Intern Med.* 1991;115(5):411.

877. Cariani E, Zonaro A, Primi D, et al. Detection of HCV RNA and antibodies to HCV after needlestick injury. *Lancet.* 1991;337(8745):850.

878. Marranconi F, Mecenero V, Pellizzer GP, et al. HCV infection after accidental needlestick injury in health-care workers. Infection. 1992;20(2):111.

879. Tsude K, Fujiyama S, Sato S, et al. Two cases of accidental transmission of hepatitis C to medical staff. *Hepatogastroenterology.* 1992;39(1):73–75.

880. Suzuki K, Mizokami M, Lau JY, et al. Confirmation of hepatitis C virus transmission through needlestick accidents by molecular evolutionary analysis. *J Infect Dis.* 1994;170(6):1575–1578.

881. Ridzon R, Gallagher K, Ciesielski C, et al. Simultaneous transmission of human immunodeficiency virus and hepatitis C virus from a needle-stick injury. *N Engl J Med.* 1997;336(13):919–922.

882. Mizuno Y, Suzuki K, Mori M, et al. Study of needlestick accidents and hepatitis C virus infection in healthcare workers by molecular evolutionary analysis. *J Hosp Infect.* 1997;35(2):149–154.

883. Nakano Y, Kiyosawa K, Sodeyama T, et al. Acute hepatitis C transmitted by needlestick accident despite short duration interferon treatment. *J Gastroenterol Hepatol.* 1995;10(5):609–611.

884. Esteban JI, Gomez J, Martell M, et al. Transmission of hepatitis C virus by a cardiac surgeon. *N Engl J Med.* 1996;334(9):555–560.

885. Noguchi S, Sata M, Suzuki H, et al. Early therapy with interferon for acute hepatitis C acquired through a needlestick. *Clin Infect Dis.* 1997;24(5):992–994.

886. Norder H, Bergstrom A, Uhnoo I, et al. Confirmation of nosocomial transmission of hepatitis C virus by phylogenetic analysis of the NS5-B region. *J Clin Microbiol.* 1998;36(10):3066–3069.

887. Sulkowski MS, Ray SC, Thomas DL. Needlestick transmission of hepatitis C. *JAMA.* 2002;287(18):2406–2413.

888. Transmission of hepatitis C virus from surgeon to patient prompts lookback. *Commun Dis Rep CDR Wkly.* 1999 29;9(44):387.

889. Brown P. Surgeon infects patient with hepatitis C. *BMJ.* 1999;319(7219):1219.

890. Duckworth GJ, Heptonstall J, Aitken C. Transmission of hepatitis C virus from a surgeon to a patient. The Incident Control Team. *Commun Dis Public Health.* 1999;2(3):188–192.

891. Cody SH, Nainan OV, Garfein RS, et al. Hepatitis C virus transmission from an anesthesiologist to a patient. *Arch Intern Med.* 2002;162(3):345–350.

892. Ross RS, Viazov S, Thormahlen M, et al. Risk of hepatitis C virus transmission from an infected gynecologist to patients: results of a 7-year retrospective investigation. *Arch Intern Med.* 2002;162(7):805–810.

893. Shemer-Avni Y, Cohen M, Keren-Naus A, et al. Iatrogenic transmission of hepatitis C virus (HCV) by an anesthesiologist: comparative molecular analysis of the HCV-E1 and HCV-E2 hypervariable regions. *Clin Infect Dis.* 2007;45(4):e32–e38.

894. Allander T, Gruber A, Naghavi M, et al. Frequent patient-to-patient transmission of hepatitis C virus in a haematology ward. *Lancet.* 1995;345(8950):603–607.

895. Le Pogam S, Le Chapois D, Christen R, et al. Hepatitis C in a hemodialysis unit: molecular evidence for nosocomial transmission. *J Clin Microbiol.* 1998;36(10):3040–3043.

896. Abacioglu YH, Bacaksiz F, Bahar IH, Simmonds P. Molecular evidence of nosocomial transmission of hepatitis C virus in a haemodialysis unit. *Eur J Clin Microbiol Infect Dis.* 2000;19(3):182–186.

897. Delarocque-Astagneau E, Baffoy N, Thiers V, et al. Outbreak of hepatitis C virus infection in a hemodialysis unit: potential transmission by the hemodialysis machine? *Infect Control Hosp Epidemiol.* 2002;23(6):328–334.

898. Michelin A, Henderson DK. Infection control guidelines for prevention of health care–associated transmission of hepatitis B and C viruses. *Clin Liver Dis.* 2010;14(1):119–136; ix–x.

899. Malanowicz W, Tyminska K, Czarniak S, Semenicki K. [Clinical picture of the 1971 influenza outbreak on the basis of hospital observation of 60 patients]. *Wiad Lek.* 1974;27(12):1049–1054.

900. Hall CB, Douglas RG Jr. Nosocomial influenza infection as a cause of intercurrent fevers in infants. *Pediatrics.* 1975;55(5):673–677.

901. Rivera M, Gonzalez N. An influenza outbreak in a hospital. *Am J Nurs.* 1982;82(12):1836–1838.

902. Arroyo JC, Postic B, Brown A, et al. Influenza A/Philippines/2/82 outbreak in a nursing home: limitations of influenza vaccination in the aged. *Am J Infect Control.* 1984;12(6):329–334.

903. Patriarca PA, Weber JA, Parker RA, et al. Efficacy of influenza vaccine in nursing homes: reduction in illness and complications during an influenza A (H3N2) epidemic. *JAMA.* 1985;253(8):1136–1139.

904. Saah AJ, Neufeld R, Rodstein M, et al. Influenza vaccine and pneumonia mortality in a nursing home population. *Arch Intern Med.* 1986;146(12):2353–2357.

905. Kashiwagi S, Ikematsu H, Hayashi J, et al. An outbreak of influenza A (H3N2) in a hospital for the elderly with emphasis on pulmonary complications. *Jpn J Med.* 1988;27(2):177–182.

906. Aktas F, Ulutan F, Artuk C, et al. [An outbreak of influenza in hospital personnel]. *Mikrobiyol Bul.* 1990;24(4):344–351.

907. Glezen WP, Falcao O, Cate TR, Mintz AA. Nosocomial influenza in a general hospital for indigent patients. *Can J Infect Control.* 1991;6(3):65–67.

908. Serwint JR, Miller RM. Why diagnose influenza infections in hospitalized pediatric patients? *Pediatr Infect Dis J.* 1993;12(3):200–204.

909. Whimbey E, Elting LS, Couch RB, et al. Influenza A virus infections among hospitalized adult bone marrow transplant recipients. *Bone Marrow Transplant.* 1994;13(4):437–440.

910. Nabeshima A, Ikematsu H, Yamaga S, et al. [An outbreak of influenza A (H3N2) among hospitalized geriatric patients]. *Kansenshogaku Zasshi.* 1996;70(8):801–807.

911. Evans ME, Hall KL, Berry SE. Influenza control in acute care hospitals. *Am J Infect Control.* 1997;25(4):357–362.

912. Adal KA, Flowers RH, Anglim AM, et al. Prevention of nosocomial influenza. *Infect Control Hosp Epidemiol.* 1996;17(10):641–648.

913. Chironna M, Tafuri S, Santoro N, et al. A nosocomial outbreak of 2009 pandemic influenza A(H1N1) in a paediatric oncology ward in Italy, October–November 2009. *Euro Surveill.* 2010;15(1).

914. Wong BC, Lee N, Li Y, et al. Possible role of aerosol transmission in a hospital outbreak of influenza. *Clin Infect Dis.* 2010;51(10):1176–1183.

915. Potter J, Stott DJ, Roberts MA, et al. Influenza vaccination of health care workers in long-term–care hospitals reduces the mortality of elderly patients. *J Infect Dis.* 1997;175(1):1–6.

916. McArthur MA, Simor AE, Campbell B, McGeer A. Influenza vaccination in long-term–care facilities: structuring programs for success. *Infect Control Hosp Epidemiol.* 1999;20(7):499–503.

917. Wendelboe AM, Avery C, Andrade B, et al. Importance of employee vaccination against influenza in preventing cases in long-term care facilities. *Infect Control Hosp Epidemiol.* 2011;32(10):990–997.

918. Liu C, Schwartz BS, Vallabhaneni S, et al. Pandemic (H1N1) 2009 infection in patients with hematologic malignancy. *Emerg Infect Dis.* 2010;16(12):1910–1917.

919. Moore C, Galiano M, Lackenby A, et al. Evidence of person-to-person transmission of oseltamivir-resistant pandemic influenza A(H1N1) 2009 virus in a hematology unit. *J Infect Dis.* 2011;203(1):18–24.

920. Chen LF, Dailey NJ, Rao AK, et al. Cluster of oseltamivir-resistant 2009 pandemic influenza A (H1N1) virus infections on a hospital ward among immunocompromised patients—North Carolina, 2009. *J Infect Dis.* 2011;203(6):838–846.

921. Mohty B, Thomas Y, Vukicevic M, et al. Clinical features and outcome of 2009-influenza A (H1N1) after allogeneic hematopoietic SCT. *Bone Marrow Transplant.* 2012;47:236–242.

922. Yeom JS, Lee JH, Bae IG, et al. 2009 H1N1 influenza infection in Korean healthcare personnel. *Eur J Clin Microbiol Infect Dis.* 2011;30(10):1201–1206.

923. Kharfan-Dabaja MA, Velez A, Richards K, et al. Influenza A/pandemic 2009/H1N1 in the setting of allogeneic hematopoietic cell transplantation: a potentially catastrophic problem in a vulnerable population. *Int J Hematol.* 2010;91(1):124–127.

924. George B, Ferguson P, Kerridge I, et al. The clinical impact of infection with swine flu (H1N109) strain of influenza virus in hematopoietic stem cell transplant recipients. *Biol Blood Marrow Transplant.* 2011;17(1):147–153.

925. Enstone JE, Myles PR, Openshaw PJ, et al. Nosocomial pandemic (H1N1) 2009, United Kingdom, 2009–2010. *Emerg Infect Dis.* 2011;17(4):592–598.

926. Magill SS, Black SR, Wise ME, et al. Investigation of an outbreak of 2009 pandemic influenza A virus (H1N1) infections among healthcare personnel in a Chicago hospital. *Infect Control Hosp Epidemiol.* 2011;32(6):611–615.

927. Fanella ST, Pinto MA, Bridger NA, et al. Pandemic (H1N1) 2009 influenza in hospitalized children in Manitoba: nosocomial transmission and lessons learned from the first wave. *Infect Control Hosp Epidemiol.* 2011;32(5):435–443.

928. Tramontana AR, George B, Hurt AC, et al. Oseltamivir resistance in adult oncology and hematology patients infected with pandemic (H1N1) 2009 virus, Australia. *Emerg Infect Dis.* 2010;16(7):1068–1075.

929. Alford RH, Kasel JA, Gerone PJ, Knight V. Human influenza resulting from aerosol inhalation. *Proc Soc Exp Biol Med.* 1966;122(3):800–804.

930. Moser MR, Bender TR, Margolis HS, et al. An outbreak of influenza aboard a commercial airliner. *Am J Epidemiol.* 1979;110(1):1–6.

931. Knight G. A simple method for determining size distribution of airborne dust by its settling velocity. *Am Ind Hyg Assoc J.* 1972;33(8):526–532.

932. Fiore AE, Fry A, Shay D, et al. Antiviral agents for the treatment and chemoprophylaxis of influenza: recommendations of the Advisory Committee on Immunization Practices (ACIP). *MMWR Recomm Rep.* 2011;60(1):1–24.

933. Cao B, Li XW, Mao Y, et al. Clinical features of the initial cases of 2009 pandemic influenza A (H1N1) virus infection in China. *N Engl J Med.* 2009;361(26):2507–2517.

934. De Serres G, Rouleau I, Hamelin ME, et al. Contagious period for pandemic (H1N1) 2009. *Emerg Infect Dis.* 2010;16(5):783–788.

935. Goins WP, Talbot HK, Talbot TR. Health care–acquired viral respiratory diseases. *Infect Dis Clin North Am.* 2011;25(1):227–244.

936. Gooskens J, Jonges M, Claas EC, et al. Prolonged influenza virus infection during lymphocytopenia and frequent detection of drug-resistant viruses. *J Infect Dis.* 2009;199(10):1435–1441.

937. Li CC, Wang L, Eng HL, et al. Correlation of pandemic (H1N1) 2009 viral load with disease severity and prolonged viral shedding in children. *Emerg Infect Dis.* 2010;16(8): 1265–1272.

938. Pinsky BA, Mix S, Rowe J, et al. Long-term shedding of influenza A virus in stool of immunocompromised child. *Emerg Infect Dis.* 2010;16(7):1165–1167.

939. Cowling BJ, Chan KH, Fang VJ, et al. Comparative epidemiology of pandemic and seasonal influenza A in households. *N Engl J Med.* 2010;362(23):2175–2184.

940. Suess T, Buchholz U, Dupke S, et al. Shedding and transmission of novel influenza virus A/H1N1 infection in households—Germany, 2009. *Am J Epidemiol.* 2010;171(11): 1157–1164.

941. Fiore AE, Uyeki TM, Broder K, et al. Prevention and control of influenza with vaccines: recommendations of the Advisory Committee on Immunization Practices (ACIP), 2010. *MMWR Recomm Rep.* 2010;59(RR-8):1–62.

942. Bautista E, Chotpitayasunondh T, Gao Z, et al. Clinical aspects of pandemic 2009 influenza A (H1N1) virus infection. *N Engl J Med.* 2010;362(18):1708–1719.

943. Jaeger JL, Patel M, Dharan N, et al. Transmission of 2009 pandemic influenza A (H1N1) virus among healthcare personnel-Southern California, 2009. *Infect Control Hosp Epidemiol.* 2011;32(12):1149–1157.

944. Williams CJ, Schweiger B, Diner G, et al. Seasonal influenza risk in hospital healthcare workers is more strongly associated with household than occupational exposures: results from a prospective cohort study in Berlin, Germany, 2006/07. *BMC Infect Dis.* 2010;10:8.

945. Moorthy M, Chacko B, Ramakrishna K, et al. Risk of pandemic (H1N1) 2009 virus infection among healthcare workers caring for critically ill patients with pandemic (H1N1) 2009 virus infection. *J Hosp Infect.* 2011;77(4):365–366.

946. Saxen H, Virtanen M. Randomized, placebo-controlled double blind study on the efficacy of influenza immunization on absenteeism of health care workers. *Pediatr Infect Dis J.* 1999;18(9):779–783.

947. Wilde JA, McMillan JA, Serwint J, et al. Effectiveness of influenza vaccine in health care professionals: a randomized trial. *JAMA.* 1999;281(10):908–913.

948. Carman WF, Elder AG, Wallace LA, et al. Effects of influenza vaccination of health-care workers on mortality of elderly people in long-term care: a randomised controlled trial. *Lancet.* 2000;355(9198): 93–97.

949. Pearson ML, Bridges CB, Harper SA. Influenza vaccination of health-care personnel: recommendations of the Healthcare Infection Control Practices Advisory Committee (HICPAC) and the Advisory Committee on Immunization Practices (ACIP). *MMWR Recomm Rep.* 2006;55 (RR-2):1–16.

950. Babcock HM, Gemeinhart N, Jones M, et al. Mandatory influenza vaccination of health care workers: translating policy to practice. *Clin Infect Dis.* 2010;50(4):459–464.

951. Rakita RM, Hagar BA, Crome P, Lammert JK. Mandatory influenza vaccination of healthcare workers: a 5-year study. *Infect Control Hosp Epidemiol.* 2010;31(9): 881–888.

952. Septimus EJ, Perlin JB, Cormier SB, et al. A multifaceted mandatory patient safety program and seasonal influenza vaccination of health care workers in community hospitals. *JAMA.* 2011;305(10):999–1000.

953. Karanfil LV, Bahner J, Hovatter J, Thomas WL. Championing patient safety through mandatory influenza vaccination for all healthcare personnel and affiliated physicians. *Infect Control Hosp Epidemiol.* 2011;32(4):375–379.

954. Kidd F, Wones R, Momper A, et al. From 51% to 100%: mandatory seasonal influenza vaccination. *Am J Infect Control.* 2012;40:188–190.

955. Jefferson T, Del Mar C, Dooley L, et al. Physical interventions to interrupt or reduce the spread of respiratory viruses. *Cochrane Database Syst Rev.* 2010;1:CD006207.

956. Cheng VC, Tai JW, Wong LM, et al. Prevention of nosocomial transmission of swine-origin pandemic influenza virus A/H1N1 by infection control bundle. *J Hosp Infect.* 2010;74(3):271–277.

957. Lynch M, Painter J, Woodruff R, Braden C. Surveillance for foodborne-disease outbreaks—United States, 1998–2002. *MMWR Surveill Summ.* 2006;55(10):1–42.

958. Johnston CP, Qiu H, Ticehurst JR, et al. Outbreak management and implications of a nosocomial norovirus outbreak. *Clin Infect Dis.* 2007;45(5):534–540.

959. Said MA, Perl TM, Sears CL. Healthcare epidemiology: gastrointestinal flu: norovirus in health care and long-term care facilities. *Clin Infect Dis.* 2008;47(9):1202–1208.

960. Harris JP, Edmunds WJ, Pebody R, et al. Deaths from norovirus among the elderly, England and Wales. *Emerg Infect Dis.* 2008;14(10):1546–1552.

961. MacCannell T, Umscheid CA, Agarwal RK, et al. Guideline for the prevention and control of norovirus gastroenteritis outbreaks in healthcare settings. 2011: Available at: http://www.cdc.gov/hicpac/norovirus/002_norovirus-toc.html.

962. Scallan E, Hoekstra RM, Angulo FJ, et al. Foodborne illness acquired in the United States—major pathogens. *Emerg Infect Dis.* 2011;17(1):7–15.

963. Lopman BA, Reacher MH, Vipond IB, et al. Clinical manifestation of norovirus gastroenteritis in health care settings. *Clin Infect Dis.* 2004;39(3):318–324.

964. Norovirus activity—United States, 2006–2007. *MMWR.* 2007;56(33):842–846.

965. Roddie C, Paul JP, Benjamin R, et al. Allogeneic hematopoietic stem cell transplantation and norovirus gastroenteritis: a previously unrecognized cause of morbidity. *Clin Infect Dis.* 2009;49(7):1061–1068.

966. van Asten L, Siebenga J, van den Wijngaard C, et al. Unspecified gastroenteritis illness and deaths in the elderly associated with norovirus epidemics. *Epidemiology.* 2011;22(3):336–343.

967. Barker J, Vipond IB, Bloomfield SF. Effects of cleaning and disinfection in reducing the spread of norovirus contamination via environmental surfaces. *J Hosp Infect.* 2004;58(1):42–49.

968. Duizer E, van Duynhoven Y, Vennema H, Koopmans M. Failure to detect norovirus in a large group of asymptomatic individuals by Marshall et al. *Public Health.* 2004;118(6):455–456; author reply 6–7.

969. Hadley S, Karchmer AW. Fungal infections in solid organ transplant recipients. *Infect Dis Clin North Am.* 1995;9(4):1045–1074.

970. Wingard JR. Fungal infections after bone marrow transplant. *Biol Blood Marrow Transplant.* 1999;5(2):55–68.

971. Ramirez E, Garcia-Rodriguez J, Borobia AM, et al. Use of antifungal agents in pediatric and adult high-risk areas. *Eur J Clin Microbiol Infect Dis.* 2012;31(3):337–347.

972. Wey SB, Mori M, Pfaller MA, et al. Hospital-acquired candidemia: the attributable mortality and excess length of stay. *Arch Intern Med.* 1988;148(12):2642–2645.

973. Goodrich JM, Reed EC, Mori M, et al. Clinical features and analysis of risk factors for invasive candidal infection after marrow transplantation. *J Infect Dis.* 1991;164(4):731–740.

974. Vazquez JA, Sanchez V, Dmuchowski C, et al. Nosocomial acquisition of *Candida albicans*: an epidemiologic study. *J Infect Dis.* 1993;168(1):195–201.

975. Vazquez JA, Dembry LM, Sanchez V, et al. Nosocomial Candida glabrata colonization:

an epidemiologic study. *J Clin Microbiol.* 1998;36(2):421–426.

976. Prentice HG, Kibbler CC, Prentice AG. Towards a targeted, risk-based, antifungal strategy in neutropenic patients. *Br J Haematol.* 2000;110(2):273–284.

977. Ostrosky-Zeichner L. New approaches to the risk of *Candida* in the intensive care unit. *Curr Opin Infect Dis.* 2003;16(6):533–537.

978. Diekema DJ, Pfaller MA. Nosocomial candidemia: an ounce of prevention is better than a pound of cure. *Infect Control Hosp Epidemiol.* 2004;25(8):624–626.

979. Puzniak L, Teutsch S, Powderly W, Polish L. Has the epidemiology of nosocomial candidemia changed? *Infect Control Hosp Epidemiol.* 2004;25(8):628–633.

980. Chang A, Neofytos D, Horn D. Candidemia in the 21st century. *Future Microbiol.* 2008;3(4):463–472.

981. Sanchez V, Vazquez JA, Barth-Jones D, et al. Nosocomial acquisition of *Candida parapsilosis*: an epidemiologic study. *Am J Med.* 1993;94(6):577–582.

982. Ruiz-Diez B, Martinez V, Alvarez M, et al. Molecular tracking of *Candida albicans* in a neonatal intensive care unit: long-term colonizations versus catheter-related infections. *J Clin Microbiol.* 1997;35(12):3032–3036.

983. Chowdhary A, Becker K, Fegeler W, et al. An outbreak of candidemia due to *Candida tropicalis* in a neonatal intensive care unit. *Mycoses.* 2003;46(8):287–292.

984. Clark TA, Slavinski SA, Morgan J, et al. Epidemiologic and molecular characterization of an outbreak of *Candida parapsilosis* bloodstream infections in a community hospital. *J Clin Microbiol.* 2004;42(10):4468–4472.

985. Viviani MA, Cogliati M, Esposto MC, et al. Four-year persistence of a single *Candida albicans* genotype causing bloodstream infections in a surgical ward proven by multilocus sequence typing. *J Clin Microbiol.* 2006;44(1):218–221.

986. Asmundsdottir LR, Erlendsdottir H, Haraldsson G, et al. Molecular epidemiology of candidemia: evidence of clusters of smoldering nosocomial infections. *Clin Infect Dis.* 2008;47(2):e17–e24.

987. Schaffner A, Schaffner M. Effect of prophylactic fluconazole on the frequency of fungal infections, amphotericin B use, and health care costs in patients undergoing intensive chemotherapy for hematologic neoplasias. *J Infect Dis.* 1995;172(4):1035–1041.

988. Trick WE, Fridkin SK, Edwards JR, et al. Secular trend of hospital-acquired candidemia among intensive care unit patients in the United States during 1989–1999. *Clin Infect Dis.* 2002;35(5):627–630.

989. Horn DL, Neofytos D, Anaissie EJ, et al. Epidemiology and outcomes of candidemia in 2019 patients: data from the prospective antifungal therapy alliance registry. *Clin Infect Dis.* 2009;48(12):1695–1703.

990. Lass-Florl C. The changing face of epidemiology of invasive fungal disease in Europe. *Mycoses.* 2009;52(3):197–205.

991. Leventakos K, Lewis RE, Kontoyiannis DP. Fungal infections in leukemia patients: how do we prevent and treat them? *Clin Infect Dis.* 2010;50(3):405–415.

992. Hautala T, Ikaheimo I, Husu H, et al. A cluster of *Candida krusei* infections in a haematological unit. *BMC Infect Dis.* 2007;7:97.

993. Marr KA, Bow E, Chiller T, et al. Fungal infection prevention after hematopoietic cell transplantation. *Bone Marrow Transplant.* 2009;44(8):483487.

994. Freifeld AG, Bow EJ, Sepkowitz KA, et al. Clinical practice guideline for the use of antimicrobial agents in neutropenic patients with cancer: 2010. Update by the Infectious Diseases Society of America. *Clin Infect Dis.* 2011;52(4):427–431.

995. Brizendine KD, Vishin S, Baddley JW. Antifungal prophylaxis in solid organ transplant recipients. *Expert Rev Anti Infect Ther.* 2011;9(5):571–581.

996. Denning DW, Marinus A, Cohen J, et al. An EORTC multicentre prospective survey of invasive aspergillosis in haematological patients: diagnosis and therapeutic outcome. EORTC Invasive Fungal Infections Cooperative Group. *J Infect.* 1998;37(2):173–180.

997. Williamson EC, Millar MR, Steward CG, et al. Infections in adults undergoing unrelated donor bone marrow transplantation. *Br J Haematol.* 1999;104(3):560–568.

998. Lortholary O, Ascioglu S, Moreau P, et al. Invasive aspergillosis as an opportunistic infection in nonallografted patients with multiple myeloma: a European Organization for Research and Treatment of Cancer/Invasive Fungal Infections Cooperative Group and the Intergroupe Francais du Myelome. *Clin Infect Dis.* 2000;30(1):41–46.

999. Paterson DL, Singh N. Invasive aspergillosis in transplant recipients. *Medicine (Baltimore).* 1999;78(2):123–138.

1000. Marr KA, Carter RA, Boeckh M, et al. Invasive aspergillosis in allogeneic stem cell transplant recipients: changes in epidemiology and risk factors. *Blood.* 2002;100(13):4358–4366.

1001. Baddley JW, Stroud TP, Salzman D, Pappas PG. Invasive mold infections in allogeneic bone marrow transplant recipients. *Clin Infect Dis.* 2001;32(9):1319–1324.

1002. Marr KA, Patterson T, Denning D. Aspergillosis: pathogenesis, clinical manifestations, and therapy. *Infect Dis Clin North Am.* 2002;16(4):875–894, vi.

1003. Alangaden GJ. Nosocomial fungal infections: epidemiology, infection control, and prevention. *Infect Dis Clin North Am.* 2011;25(1):201–225.

1004. Allo MD, Miller J, Townsend T, Tan C. Primary cutaneous aspergillosis associated with Hickman intravenous catheters. *N Engl J Med.* 1987;317(18):1105–1108.

1005. Landoy Z, Rotstein C, Shedd D. Aspergillosis of the nose and paranasal sinuses in neutropenic patients at an oncology center. *Head Neck Surg.* 1985;8(2):83–90.

1006. Schubert MM, Peterson DE, Meyers JD, et al. Head and neck aspergillosis in patients undergoing bone marrow transplantation: report of four cases and review of the literature. *Cancer.* 1986;57(6):1092–1096.

1007. Johnson AS, Ranson M, Scarffe JH, et al. Cutaneous infection with *Rhizopus oryzae* and *Aspergillus niger* following bone marrow transplantation. *J Hosp Infect.* 1993;25(4):293–296.

1008. Gerson SL, Talbot GH, Lusk E, et al. Invasive pulmonary aspergillosis in adult acute leukemia: clinical clues to its diagnosis. *J Clin Oncol.* 1985;3(8):1109–1116.

1009. Gerson SL, Talbot GH, Hurwitz S, et al. Discriminant scorecard for diagnosis of invasive pulmonary aspergillosis in patients with acute leukemia. *Am J Med.* 1985;79(1):57–64.

1010. Larkin JA, Greene JN, Sandin RL, Houston SH. Primary cutaneous aspergillosis: case report and review of the literature. *Infect Control Hosp Epidemiol.* 1996;17(6): 365–366.

1011. de Medeiros BC, de Medeiros CR, Werner B, et al. Central nervous system infections following bone marrow transplantation: an autopsy report of 27 cases. *J Hematother Stem Cell Res.* 2000;9(4):535–540.

1012. Gartenberg G, Bottone EJ, Keusch GT, Weitzman I. Hospital-acquired mucormycosis (*Rhizopus rhizopodiformis*) of skin and subcutaneous tissue: epidemiology, mycology and treatment. *N Engl J Med.* 1978;299(20):1115–1118.

1013. Hammond DE, Winkelmann RK. Cutaneous phycomycosis: report of three cases with identification of *Rhizopus. Arch Dermatol.* 1979;115(8):990–992.

1014. Abzug MJ, Gardner S, Glode MP, et al. Heliport-associated nosocomial mucormycoses. *Infect Control Hosp Epidemiol.* 1992;13(6):325–326.

1015. Levy V, Rio B, Bazarbachi A, et al. Two cases of epidemic mucormycosis infection in patients with acute lymphoblastic leukemia. *Am J Hematol.* 1996;52(1):64–65.

1016. Mitchell SJ, Gray J, Morgan ME, et al. Nosocomial infection with *Rhizopus microsporus* in preterm infants: association with wooden tongue depressors. *Lancet.* 1996;348(9025):441–443.

1017. Verweij PE, Voss A, Donnelly JP, et al. Wooden sticks as the source of a pseudoepidemic of infection with *Rhizopus microsporus* var. *rhizopodiformis* among immunocompromised patients. *J Clin Microbiol.* 1997;35(9):2422–2423.

1018. Holzel H, Macqueen S, MacDonald A, et al. *Rhizopus microsporus* in wooden tongue depressors: a major threat or minor inconvenience? *J Hosp Infect.* 1998;38(2):113–118.

1019. Maravi-Poma E, Rodriguez-Tudela JL, de Jalon JG, et al. Outbreak of gastric mucormycosis associated with the use of wooden tongue depressors in critically ill patients. *Intensive Care Med.* 2004;30(4):724–728.

1020. Christiaens G, Hayette MP, Jacquemin D, et al. An outbreak of *Absidia corymbifera* infection associated with bandage contamination in a burns unit. *J Hosp Infect.* 2005;61(1):88.

1021. LeMaile-Williams M, Burwell LA, Salisbury D, et al. Outbreak of cutaneous *Rhizopus arrhizus* infection associated with karaya ostomy bags. *Clin Infect Dis.* 2006;43(9):e83–e88.

1022. Garner D, Machin K. Investigation and management of an outbreak of mucormycosis in a paediatric oncology unit. *J Hosp Infect.* 2008;70(1):53–59.

1023. Sherertz RJ, Belani A, Kramer BS, et al. Impact of air filtration on nosocomial *Aspergillus* infections: unique risk of bone marrow transplant recipients. *Am J Med.* 1987;83(4):709–718.

1024. Ruutu P, Valtonen V, Tiitanen L, et al. An outbreak of invasive aspergillosis in a haematologic unit. *Scand J Infect Dis.* 1987;19(3):347–351.

1025. Aisner J, Schimpff SC, Bennett JE, et al. *Aspergillus* infections in cancer patients: association with fireproofing materials in a new hospital. *JAMA.* 1976;235(4):411–412.

1026. Lentino JR, Rosenkranz MA, Michaels JA, et al. Nosocomial aspergillosis: a retrospective review of airborne disease secondary to road construction and contaminated air conditioners. *Am J Epidemiol.* 1982;116(3):430–437.

1027. Rotstein C, Cummings KM, Tidings J, et al. An outbreak of invasive aspergillosis among allogeneic bone marrow transplants: a case-control study. *Infect Control.* 1985;6(9):347–355.

1028. Opal SM, Asp AA, Cannady PB Jr, et al. Efficacy of infection control measures during a nosocomial outbreak of disseminated aspergillosis associated with hospital construction. *J Infect Dis.* 1986;153(3):634–637.

1029. Perraud M, Piens MA, Nicoloyannis N, et al. Invasive nosocomial pulmonary aspergillosis: risk factors and hospital building works. *Epidemiol Infect.* 1987;99(2):407–412.

1030. Weems JJ Jr, Davis BJ, Tablan OC, et al. Construction activity: an independent risk factor for invasive aspergillosis and zygomycosis in patients with hematologic malignancy. *Infect Control.* 1987;8(2):71–75.

1031. Barnes RA, Rogers TR. Control of an outbreak of nosocomial aspergillosis by laminar air-flow isolation. *J Hosp Infect.* 1989;14(2):89–94.

1032. Hopkins CC, Weber DJ, Rubin RH. Invasive aspergillus infection: possible nonward common source within the hospital environment. *J Hosp Infect.* 1989;13(1):19–25.

1033. Arnow PM, Sadigh M, Costas C, et al. Endemic and epidemic aspergillosis associated with in-hospital replication of *Aspergillus* organisms. *J Infect Dis.* 1991;164(5):998–1002.

1034. Flynn PM, Williams BG, Hetherington SV, et al. *Aspergillus* terreus during hospital renovation. *Infect Control Hosp Epidemiol.* 1993;14(7):363–365.

1035. Oren I, Haddad N, Finkelstein R, Rowe JM. Invasive pulmonary aspergillosis in neutropenic patients during hospital construction: before and after chemoprophylaxis and institution of HEPA filters. *Am J Hematol.* 2001;66(4):257–262.

1036. Gerson SL, Parker P, Jacobs MR, et al. Aspergillosis due to carpet contamination. *Infect Control Hosp Epidemiol.* 1994;15:221–223.

1037. Anderson K, Morris G, Kennedy H, et al. Aspergillosis in immunocompromised paediatric patients: associations with building hygiene, design, and indoor air. *Thorax.* 1996;51(3):256–261.

1038. Loudon KW, Coke AP, Burnie JP, et al. Kitchens as a source of *Aspergillus niger* infection. *J Hosp Infect.* 1996;32(3):191–198.

1039. Leenders A, van Belkum A, Janssen S, et al. Molecular epidemiology of apparent outbreak of invasive aspergillosis in a hematology ward. *J Clin Microbiol.* 1996;34(2):345–351.

1040. Loo VG, Bertrand C, Dixon C, et al. Control of construction-associated nosocomial aspergillosis in an antiquated hematology unit. *Infect Control Hosp Epidemiol.* 1996;17(6):360–364.

1041. Gaspar C, Mariano A, Cuesta J, et al. [outbreak of invasive pulmonary mycosis in neutropenic hematologic patients in relation to remodelling construction work]. *Enferm Infecc Microbiol Clin.* 1999;17(3):113–118.

1042. Lass-Florl C, Rath P, Niederwieser D, et al. *Aspergillus terreus* infections in haematological malignancies: molecular epidemiology suggests association with in-hospital plants. *J Hosp Infect.* 2000;46(1):31–35.

1043. Lai KK. A cluster of invasive aspergillosis in a bone marrow transplant unit related to construction and the utility of air sampling. *Am J Infect Control.* 2001;29(5):333–337.

1044. Hahn T, Cummings KM, Michalek AM, et al. Efficacy of high-efficiency particulate air filtration in preventing aspergillosis in immunocompromised patients with hematologic malignancies. *Infect Control Hosp Epidemiol.* 2002;23(9):525–531.

1045. Panackal AA, Imhof A, Hanley EW, Marr KA. *Aspergillus ustus* infections among transplant recipients. *Emerg Infect Dis.* 2006;12(3):403–408.

1046. Chang CC, Cheng AC, Devitt B, et al. Successful control of an outbreak of invasive aspergillosis in a regional haematology unit during hospital construction works. *J Hosp Infect.* 2008;69(1):33–38.

1047. Kidd SE, Ling LM, Meyer W, et al. Molecular epidemiology of invasive aspergillosis: lessons learned from an outbreak investigation in an Australian hematology unit. *Infect Control Hosp Epidemiol.* 2009;30(12):1223–1226.

1048. Pagano L, Caira M, Candoni A, et al. The epidemiology of fungal infections in patients with hematologic malignancies: the SEIFEM-2004 study. *Haematologica.* 2006;91(8):1068–1075.

1049. Wallace MR, Kanak RJ, Newton JA, Kennedy CA. Invasive aspergillosis in patients with AIDS. *Clin Infect Dis.* 1994;19(1):222.

1050. Wallace JM, Lim R, Browdy BL, et al. Risk factors and outcomes associated with identification of *Aspergillus* in respiratory specimens from persons with HIV disease. Pulmonary Complications of HIV Infection Study Group. *Chest.* 1998;114(1): 131–137.

1051. Woitas RP, Rockstroh JK, Theisen A, et al. Changing role of invasive aspergillosis in AIDS: a case control study. *J Infect.* 1998;37(2):116–122.

1052. Libanore M, Prini E, Mazzetti M, et al. Invasive Aspergillosis in Italian AIDS patients. *Infection.* 2002;30(6):341–345.

1053. Singh N, Avery RK, Munoz P, et al. Trends in risk profiles for and mortality associated with invasive aspergillosis among liver transplant recipients. *Clin Infect Dis.* 2003;36(1):46–52.

1054. Denning DW. Aspergillosis in "nonimmunocompromised" critically ill patients. *Am J Respir Crit Care Med.* 2004;170(6): 580–581.

1055. Meersseman W, Vandecasteele SJ, Wilmer A, et al. Invasive aspergillosis in critically ill patients without malignancy. *Am J Respir Crit Care Med.* 2004;170(6):621–625.

1056. Singh N. Invasive aspergillosis in organ transplant recipients: new issues in epidemiologic characteristics, diagnosis, and management. *Med Mycol.* 2005;43(suppl 1): S267–S270.

1057. Meersseman W, Van Wijngaerden E. Invasive aspergillosis in the ICU: an emerging disease. *Intensive Care Med.* 2007;33(10):1679–1681.

1058. Segal BH, Romani LR. Invasive aspergillosis in chronic granulomatous disease. *Med Mycol.* 2009;47(suppl 1):S282–S290.

1059. Dimitrios P, Kontoyiannis REL. Agents of mucormycosis and entomophthoramycosis. In: Gerald L, Mandell JEB, Raphael Dolin, eds. *Mandell, Douglas, and Bennett's Principles and Practice of Infectious Diseases.* Philadelphia: Churchill Livingstone; 2010:3257–3269.

1060. Marty FM, Cosimi LA, Baden LR. Breakthrough zygomycosis after voriconazole treatment in recipients of hematopoietic stem-cell transplants. *N Engl J Med.* 2004;350(9):950–952.

1061. Siwek GT, Dodgson KJ, de Magalhaes-Silverman M, et al. Invasive zygomycosis in hematopoietic stem cell transplant recipients receiving voriconazole prophylaxis. *Clin Infect Dis.* 2004;39(4):584–587.

1062. Trifilio SM, Bennett CL, Yarnold PR, et al. Breakthrough zygomycosis after voriconazole administration among patients with hematologic malignancies who receive hematopoietic stem-cell transplants or intensive chemotherapy. *Bone Marrow Transplant.* 2007;39(7):425–429.

1063. Anaissie EJ, Kuchar RT, Rex JH, et al. Fusariosis associated with pathogenic *fusarium* species colonization of a hospital water system: a new paradigm for the epidemiology of opportunistic mold infections. *Clin Infect Dis.* 2001;33(11):1871–1878.

1064. Ayliffe GA. Nosocomial infection: the irreducible minimum. *Infect Control.* 1986; 7(2 suppl):92–95.

1065. Steere AC, Mallison GF. Handwashing practices for the prevention of nosocomial infections. *Ann Intern Med.* 1975;83(5):683–690.

1066. Lilly HA, Lowbury EJ. Transient skin flora: their removal by cleansing or disinfection in relation to their mode of deposition. *J Clin Pathol.* 1978;31(10):919–922.

1067. Bryan JL, Cohran J, Larson EL. Hand washing: a ritual revisited. *Crit Care Nurs Clin North Am.* 1995;7(4):617–625.

1068. Boyce JM, Pittet D. Guideline for hand hygiene in health-care settings: recommendations of the Healthcare Infection Control Practices Advisory Committee and the HICPAC/SHEA/APIC/IDSA Hand Hygiene Task Force. Society for Healthcare Epidemiology of America/Association for Professionals in Infection Control/Infectious Diseases Society of America. *MMWR Recomm Rep.* 2002;51(RR-16):1–45.

1069. Bolon M. Hand hygiene. *Infect Dis Clin North Am.* 2011;25(1):21–43.

1070. Casewell M, Phillips I. Hands as route of transmission for *Klebsiella* species. *Br Med J.* 1977;2(6098):1315–1317.

1071. Al-Khoja MS, Darrell JH. The skin as the source of *Acinetobacter* and *Moraxella* species occurring in blood cultures. *J Clin Pathol.* 1979;32(5):497–499.

1072. Larson E, McGinley KJ, Grove GL, et al. Physiologic, microbiologic, and seasonal effects of handwashing on the skin of health care personnel. *Am J Infect Control.* 1986;14(2):51–59.

1073. Pittet D, Dharan S, Touveneau S, et al. Bacterial contamination of the hands of hospital staff during routine patient care. *Arch Intern Med.* 1999;159(8):821–826.

1074. Larson EL. Persistent carriage of gram-negative bacteria on hands. *Am J Infect Control.* 1981;9(4):112–119.

1075. Noble W. Skin as a source for hospital infection. *Infect Control.* 1986;7(2 suppl): 111–112.

1076. Coovadia YM, Johnson AP, Bhana RH, et al. Multiresistant *Klebsiella pneumoniae* in a neonatal nursery: the importance of maintenance of infection control policies and procedures in the prevention of outbreaks. *J Hosp Infect.* 1992;22(3):197–205.

1077. Guiguet M, Rekacewicz C, Leclercq B, et al. Effectiveness of simple measures to control an outbreak of nosocomial methicillin-resistant *Staphylococcus aureus* infections in an intensive care unit. *Infect Control Hosp Epidemiol.* 1990;11(1):23–26.

1078. Isaacs D, Dobson SR, Wilkinson AR, et al. Conservative management of an echovirus 11 outbreak in a neonatal unit. *Lancet.* 1989;1(8637):543–545.

1079. Doebbeling BN, Li N, Wenzel RP. An outbreak of hepatitis A among health care workers: risk factors for transmission. Am J *Public Health.* 1993;83(12):1679–1684.

1080. Widmer AF, Wenzel RP, Trilla A, et al. Outbreak of *Pseudomonas aeruginosa* infections in a surgical intensive care unit: probable transmission via hands of a health care worker. *Clin Infect Dis.* 1993;16(3): 372–376.

1081. Boyce JM, Pittet D. Guideline for hand hygiene in health-care settings: recommendations of the Healthcare Infection Control Practices Advisory Committee and the HICPAC/SHEA/APIC/IDSA Hand Hygiene Task Force. *Infect Control Hosp Epidemiol.* 2002;23(12 suppl):S3–S40.

1082. Pittet D, Allegranzi B, Boyce J. The World Health Organization guidelines on hand hygiene in health care and their consensus recommendations. *Infect Control Hosp Epidemiol.* 2009;30(7):611–622.

1083. Girou E, Oppein F. Handwashing compliance in a French university hospital: new perspective with the introduction of hand-rubbing with a waterless alcohol-based solution. *J Hosp Infect.* 2001;48(suppl A): S55–S57.

1084. Pittet D, Hugonnet S, Harbarth S, et al. Effectiveness of a hospital-wide programme to improve compliance with hand hygiene. Infection Control Programme. *Lancet.* 2000;356(9238):1307–1312.

1085. Harbarth S, Pittet D, Grady L, et al. Interventional study to evaluate the impact of an alcohol-based hand gel in improving hand hygiene compliance. *Pediatr Infect Dis J.* 2002;21(6):489–495.

1086. Randle J, Clarke M, Storr J. Hand hygiene compliance in healthcare workers. *J Hosp Infect.* 2006;64(3):205–209.

1087. Souweine B, Lautrette A, Aumeran C, et al. Comparison of acceptability, skin tolerance, and compliance between handwashing and alcohol-based handrub in ICUs: results of a multicentric study. *Intensive Care Med.* 2009;35(7):1216–1224.

1088. Parry MF, Grant B, Yukna M, et al. *Candida* osteomyelitis and diskitis after spinal surgery: an outbreak that implicates artificial nail use. *Clin Infect Dis.* 2001;32(3):352–357.

1089. Gupta A, Della-Latta P, Todd B, et al. Outbreak of extended-spectrum beta-lactamase–producing *Klebsiella pneumoniae* in a neonatal intensive care unit linked to artificial nails. *Infect Control Hosp Epidemiol.* 2004;25(3):210–215.

1090. Doebbeling BN, Stanley GL, Sheetz CT, et al. Comparative efficacy of alternative hand-washing agents in reducing nosocomial infections in intensive care units. *N Engl J Med.* 1992;327(2):88–93.

1091. Swoboda SM, Earsing K, Strauss K, et al. Electronic monitoring and voice prompts improve hand hygiene and decrease nosocomial infections in an intermediate care unit. *Crit Care Med.* 2004;32(2):358–363.

1092. Won SP, Chou HC, Hsieh WS, et al. Handwashing program for the prevention of nosocomial infections in a neonatal intensive care unit. *Infect Control Hosp Epidemiol.* 2004;25(9):742–746.

1093. Zerr DM, Allpress AL, Heath J, et al. Decreasing hospital-associated rotavirus infection: a multidisciplinary hand hygiene campaign in a children's hospital. *Pediatr Infect Dis J.* 2005;24(5):397–403.

1094. Rosenthal VD, Guzman S, Safdar N. Reduction in nosocomial infection with improved hand hygiene in intensive care units of a tertiary care hospital in Argentina. *Am J Infect Control.* 2005;33(7):392–397.

1095. Johnson PD, Martin R, Burrell LJ, et al. Efficacy of an alcohol/chlorhexidine hand hygiene program in a hospital with high rates of nosocomial methicillin-resistant *Staphylococcus aureus* (MRSA) infection. *Med J Aust.* 2005;183(10):509–514.

1096. Pessoa-Silva CL, Hugonnet S, Pfister R, et al. Reduction of health care associated infection risk in neonates by successful hand hygiene promotion. *Pediatrics.* 2007;120(2):e382–e390.

1097. Harrington G, Watson K, Bailey M, et al. Reduction in hospitalwide incidence of infection or colonization with methicillin-resistant *Staphylococcus aureus* with use of antimicrobial hand-hygiene gel and statistical process control charts. *Infect Control Hosp Epidemiol.* 2007;28(7):837–844.

1098. Trick WE, Vernon MO, Welbel SF, et al. Multicenter intervention program to increase adherence to hand hygiene recommendations and glove use and to reduce the incidence of antimicrobial resistance. *Infect*

Control Hosp Epidemiol. 2007;28(1): 42–49.

1099. Grayson ML, Jarvie LJ, Martin R, et al. Significant reductions in methicillin-resistant *Staphylococcus aureus* bacteraemia and clinical isolates associated with a multisite, hand hygiene culture-change program and subsequent successful statewide roll-out. *Med J Aust.* 2008;188(11):633–640.

1100. Nguyen KV, Nguyen PT, Jones SL. Effectiveness of an alcohol-based hand hygiene programme in reducing nosocomial infections in the urology ward of Binh Dan Hospital, Vietnam. *Trop Med Int Health.* 2008;13(10):1297–1302.

1101. Herud T, Nilsen RM, Svendheim K, Harthug S. Association between use of hand hygiene products and rates of health care–associated infections in a large university hospital in Norway. *Am J Infect Control.* 2009;37(4):311–317.

1102. Aboumatar H, Ristaino P, Davis RO, et al. Infection prevention promotion program based on the PRECEDE model: improving hand hygiene behaviors among healthcare personnel. *Infect Control Hosp Epidemiol.* 2012;33(2):144–151.

1103. Jogerst GJ, Dippe SE. Antibiotic use among medical specialties in a community hospital. *JAMA.* 1981;245(8):842–846.

1104. Maki DG, Schuna AA. A study of antimicrobial misuse in a university hospital. *Am J Med Sci.* 1978;275(3):271–282.

1105. Castle M, Wilfert CM, Cate TR, Osterhout S. Antibiotic use at Duke University Medical Center. *JAMA.* 1977;237(26):2819–2822.

1106. Stevens GP, Jacobson JA, Burke JP. Changing patterns of hospital infections and antibiotic use: prevalence surveys in a community hospital. *Arch Intern Med.* 1981;141(5):587–592.

1107. Buckwold FJ, Ronald AR. Antimicrobial misuse: effects and suggestions for control. *J Antimicrob Chemother.* 1979;5(2):129–136.

1108. Kunin CM, Tupasi T, Craig WA. Use of antibiotics: a brief exposition of the problem and some tentative solutions. *Ann Intern Med*. 1973;79(4):555–560.

1109. Pallares R, Dick R, Wenzel RP, et al. Trends in antimicrobial utilization at a tertiary teaching hospital during a 15-year period (1978–1992). *Infect Control Hosp Epidemiol*. 1993;14(7):376–382.

1110. Tamma PD, Cosgrove SE. Antimicrobial stewardship. *Infect Dis Clin North Am*. 2011;25(1):245–260.

1111. Goldmann DA, Weinstein RA, Wenzel RP, et al. Strategies to prevent and control the emergence and spread of antimicrobial-resistant microorganisms in hospitals: a challenge to hospital leadership. *JAMA*. 1996;275(3):234–240.

1112. Price J, Ekleberry A, Grover A, et al. Evaluation of clinical practice guidelines on outcome of infection in patients in the surgical intensive care unit. *Crit Care Med*. 1999;27(10):2118–2124.

1113. Bantar C, Sartori B, Vesco E, et al. A hospitalwide intervention program to optimize the quality of antibiotic use: impact on prescribing practice, antibiotic consumption, cost savings, and bacterial resistance. *Clin Infect Dis*. 2003;37(2):180–186.

1114. Decker MD, Schaffner W. Immunization of hospital personnel and other health care workers. *Infect Dis Clin North Am*. 1990;4(2):211–221.

1115. Atkinson WL, Markowitz LE, Adams NC, Seastrom GR. Transmission of measles in medical settings—United States, 1985–1989. *Am J Med*. 1991;91(3B):320S–324S.

1116. Davis RM, Orenstein WA, Frank JA Jr, et al. Transmission of measles in medical settings. 1980 through 1984. *JAMA*. 1986;255(10):1295–1298.

1117. Poland GA, Nichol KL. Medical schools and immunization policies: missed opportunities for disease prevention. *Ann Intern Med*. 1990;113(8):628–631.

1118. Poland GA, Nichol KL. Medical students as sources of rubella and measles outbreaks. *Arch Intern Med*. 1990;150(1):44–46.

1119. Wurtz R, Check IJ. Breakthrough varicella infection in a healthcare worker despite immunity after varicella vaccination. *Infect Control Hosp Epidemiol*. 1999;20(8): 561–562.

1120. Behrman A, Schmid DS, Crivaro A, Watson B. A cluster of primary varicella cases among healthcare workers with false-positive varicella zoster virus titers. *Infect Control Hosp Epidemiol*. 2003;24(3):202–206.

1121. Ammari LK, Bell LM, Hodinka RL. Secondary measles vaccine failure in healthcare workers exposed to infected patients. *Infect Control Hosp Epidemiol*. 1993;14(2):81–86.

1122. Lane NE, Paul RI, Bratcher DF, Stover BH. A survey of policies at children's hospitals regarding immunity of healthcare workers: are physicians protected? *Infect Control Hosp Epidemiol*. 1997;18(6):400–404.

1123. Daskalaki I, Hennessey P, Hubler R, Long SS. Resource consumption in the infection control management of pertussis exposure among healthcare workers in pediatrics. *Infect Control Hosp Epidemiol*. 2007;28(4):412–417.

1124. Immunization of health-care workers: recommendations of the Advisory Committee on Immunization Practices (ACIP) and the Hospital Infection Control Practices Advisory Committee (HICPAC). *MMWR Recomm Rep*. 1997;46(RR-18):1–42.

1125. Kretsinger K, Broder KR, Cortese MM, et al. Preventing tetanus, diphtheria, and pertussis among adults: use of tetanus toxoid, reduced diphtheria toxoid and acellular pertussis vaccine recommendations of the Advisory Committee on Immunization Practices (ACIP) and recommendation of ACIP, supported by the Healthcare Infection Control Practices Advisory Committee (HICPAC), for use of Tdap among healthcare personnel. *MMWR Recomm Rep*. 2006;55(RR-17):1–37.

1126. Kellerhals S. A pseudo-outbreak of *Serratia marcescens* from a contaminated fiberbronchoscope. *APIC*. 1978;6(4):5–7.

1127. Gahrn-Hansen B, Alstrup P, Dessau R, et al. Outbreak of infection with *Achromobacter xylosoxidans* from contaminated intravascular pressure transducers. *J Hosp Infect*. 1988;12(1):1–6.

1128. Hartstein AI, Rashad AL, Liebler JM, et al. Multiple intensive care unit outbreak of *Acinetobacter calcoaceticus* subspecies *anitratus* respiratory infection and colonization associated with contaminated, reusable ventilator circuits and resuscitation bags. *Am J Med*. 1988;85(5):624–631.

1129. Hoffmann KK, Weber DJ, Rutala WA. Pseudoepidemic of *Rhodotorula rubra* in patients undergoing fiberoptic bronchoscopy. *Infect Control Hosp Epidemiol*. 1989;10(11):511–514.

1130. Hekker TA, van Overhagen W, Schneider AJ. Pressure transducers: an overlooked source of sepsis in the intensive care unit. *Intensive Care Med*. 1990;16(8):511–512.

1131. Nosocomial infection and pseudoinfection from contaminated endoscopes and bronchoscopes—Wisconsin and Missouri. *MMWR*. 1991 O4;40(39):675–678.

1132. Fraser VJ, Jones M, Murray PR, et al. Contamination of flexible fiberoptic bronchoscopes with *Mycobacterium chelonae* linked to an automated bronchoscope disinfection machine. *Am Rev Respir Dis*. 1992;145(4 Pt 1):853–855.

1133. Nicolle LE, McLeod J, Romance L, et al. Pseudo-outbreak of blastomycosis associated with contaminated bronchoscopes. *Infect Control Hosp Epidemiol*. 1992;13(6):324.

1134. Spach DH, Silverstein FE, Stamm WE. Transmission of infection by gastrointestinal endoscopy and bronchoscopy. *Ann Intern Med*. 1993;118(2):117–128.

1135. Flaherty JP, Garcia-Houchins S, Chudy R, Arnow PM. An outbreak of gram-negative bacteremia traced to contaminated O-rings in reprocessed dialyzers. *Ann Intern Med*. 1993;119(11):1072–1078.

1136. Mitchell DH, Hicks LJ, Chiew R, et al. Pseudoepidemic of *Legionella pneumophila* serogroup 6 associated with contaminated bronchoscopes. *J Hosp Infect*. 1997;37(1):19–23.

1137. Gray J, George RH, Durbin GM, et al. An outbreak of *Bacillus cereus* respiratory tract infections on a neonatal unit due to contaminated ventilator circuits. *J Hosp Infect*. 1999;41(1):19–22.

1138. Kressel AB, Kidd F. Pseudo-outbreak of *Mycobacterium chelonae* and *Methylobacterium mesophilicum* caused by contamination of an automated endoscopy washer. *Infect Control Hosp Epidemiol*. 2001;22(7):414–418.

1139. Gillespie JL, Arnold KE, Noble-Wang J, et al. Outbreak of *Pseudomonas aeruginosa* infections after transrectal ultrasound-guided prostate biopsy. *Urology*. 2007;69(5):912–914.

1140. Shimono N, Takuma T, Tsuchimochi N, et al. An outbreak of *Pseudomonas aeruginosa* infections following thoracic surgeries occurring via the contamination of bronchoscopes and an automatic endoscope reprocessor. *J Infect Chemother*. 2008;14(6):418–423.

1141. Rosengarten D, Block C, Hidalgo-Grass C, et al. Cluster of pseudoinfections with *Burkholderia cepacia* associated with a contaminated washer-disinfector in a bronchoscopy unit. *Infect Control Hosp Epidemiol*. 2010;31(7):769–771.

1142. Koh SJ, Song T, Kang YA, et al. An outbreak of skin and soft tissue infection caused by *Mycobacterium abscessus* following acupuncture. *Clin Microbiol Infect*. 2010;16(7):895–901.

1143. Rutula WA, Weber DJ. Guideline for disinfection and sterilization in healthcare facilities, 2008. 2008. Available at: http://www.cdc.gov/hicpac/Disinfection_Sterilization/17_00Recommendations.html.

1144. Rutala WA, Weber DJ. Sterilization, high-level disinfection, and environmental cleaning. *Infect Dis Clin North Am.* 2011; 25(1):45–76.

1145. Rutala WA, Weber DJ. Guideline for disinfection and sterilization of prion-contaminated medical instruments. *Infect Control Hosp Epidemiol.* 2010;31(2): 107–117.

1146. Boyce JM. Environmental contamination makes an important contribution to hospital infection. *J Hosp Infect.* 2007;65(suppl 2):50–54.

1147. Carling PC, Parry MF, Bruno-Murtha LA, Dick B. Improving environmental hygiene in 27 intensive care units to decrease multidrug-resistant bacterial transmission. *Crit Care Med.* 2010;38(4):1054–1059.

1148. Carling PC, Bartley JM. Evaluating hygienic cleaning in health care settings: what you do not know can harm your patients. *Am J Infect Control.* 2010;38(5 suppl 1):S41–S50.

1149. Saurina G, Landman D, Quale JM. Activity of disinfectants against vancomycin-resistant *Enterococcus faecium. Infect Control Hosp Epidemiol.* 1997;18(5):345–347.

1150. Goldstein EJ. Beyond the target pathogen: ecological effects of the hospital formulary. *Curr Opin Infect Dis.* 2011;24 (suppl 1):S21–S31.

2

Airborne Transmission

15

Epidemiology and Prevention of Influenza

Mark C. Steinhoff

INTRODUCTION

Influenza remains a major respiratory infection, responsible for a global total of 250,000 to 500,000 deaths per year. Influenza virus has a unique epidemiology in two aspects: (1) annual epidemics of this respiratory disease with attack rates of 10% to 30% occur in all regions of the world, and (2) it is the classical emerging infection, with global pandemics arising when new antigenic variants emerge. Influenza viruses are epizootic in avian and animal species, and analyses of nucleic acid sequences suggest that human influenza A viruses derive from avian influenza viruses. The antigenic variation of this virus is the key to its ability to cause annual epidemics and periodic pandemics. Because antigenic change is random and not predictable, the influenza virus will continue to cause widespread epidemics, although many aspects of the epidemiology and variability of this virus are understood and effective antivirals and vaccines are available. Current control strategies require reevaluation to achieve a true reduction in the toll of influenza morbidity and mortality, and enhanced pandemic preparedness is essential.

CLINICAL FEATURES OF INFLUENZA

The word *influenza* is from the Italian (derived from Latin *influentia*), referring to the influence of the stars, reflecting ancient concepts of the causation of influenza epidemics. The clinical disease influenza is familiar, because almost everyone has been infected. It is characterized by an abrupt onset of fever and respiratory symptoms, including rhinorrhea, cough, and sore throat.[1] Myalgia and headache are more common with influenza than with other respiratory viral infections, and the malaise and prostration of this disease are well known. Gastrointestinal symptoms are not common in adults, but 50% of infants and children may experience vomiting, abdominal pain, and diarrhea with influenza. Influenza disease is usually self-limited, lasting for 3 to 5 days, but complications, which are more frequent in the elderly and persons with chronic illnesses, can prolong illness. Some patients may develop a primary influenza viral pneumonia, which can be severe. More commonly, a secondary bacterial pneumonia may occur up to 2 weeks after the acute viral infection.[2,3] In infants and children, otitis media and croup are common complications. Other, less frequent complications include myocarditis, myositis, and encephalitis. Reye's syndrome, a hepatic and central nervous system (CNS) complication seen in children, is associated with the use of aspirin and other salicylates.

TRANSMISSION

Influenza virus spreads through respiratory secretions of infected persons, which may contain as many as 10^5 virus particles/mL. An infected person generates infectious aerosols of secretions during coughing, sneezing, and talking. In addition, infectious secretions are spread by direct (by kissing) or indirect (by nose–finger–doorknob) contact with respiratory mucosa. The inhaled virus attaches to columnar epithelial cells of the upper respiratory tract and initiates a new infection in the host. The incubation period is from 1 to 4 days, and infected hosts are capable of transmitting the virus from shortly before the onset of clinical disease up to the fourth or fifth day of illness.

DIAGNOSIS

Because of the clinical similarity of influenza virus infection to the manifestations of other respiratory viral infections, influenza virus infection cannot be reliably diagnosed from clinical signs and minor symptoms.[4] Although some clinicians and many laypersons use the term *flu* or *influenza* to describe respiratory illness, only viral culture or serology can prove the presence of influenza virus. Culture requires nasal or throat secretions obtained within 3 days of onset, which are then cultured in embryonated hens' eggs or tissue culture. Viral growth occurs in 2 to 3 days, after which the virus is identified using reagents for type and subtype. Influenza virus can also be identified rapidly within several hours in clinic settings using rapid antigen detection methods, such as immunofluorescence or enzyme-linked immunosorbent assay (ELISA) and other techniques, including polymerase chain reaction (PCR) amplification.

Infection has been proven by serology to show a fourfold increase in antibodies to influenza virus and requires acute and convalescent blood specimens obtained approximately 3 weeks apart. Standard techniques for detection of influenza antibodies include hemagglutination inhibition (HI), complement fixation (CF), and ELISA techniques.

THE VIRUS

Influenza virus was one of the first human viruses to be cultured and studied. In 1933, Wilson Smith, Andrews, and Laidlaw in the United Kingdom first isolated human influenza type A virus from an ill ferret (infected by secretions from an ill patient, Andrews).[5] Burnet developed the technique of culture in hens' eggs in 1936, which enabled study of the viruses and the development of vaccines. Influenza type B virus was isolated in 1940, and type C virus in 1947.

Influenza type A and B viruses contain eight segments of single-stranded RNA that code for 11 proteins. Influenza type C has seven RNA segments and a single surface glycoprotein. **Table 15-1** summarizes the gene segments and their associated proteins.

The hemagglutinin (HA) and neuraminidase (NA) are surface glycoproteins that are important in both pathogenesis and immune protection from infection. The HA functions as the attachment protein, mediating attachment to sialic acid–containing glycoproteins on columnar epithelial cells of the respiratory tract. HA has a binding site that is highly conserved and surrounded by five specific antigenic epitopes that manifest rapid changes. A specific antibody to these HA epitopes prevents attachment and entry of influenza viruses into host cells. HA specificity for receptor binding is a determinant of which species can be infected, or host range.[6] This protein is also a virulence determinant. It must be cleaved into H1 and H2 proteins by host proteases to create a hydrophobic tail necessary for fusion of viral and host cell membranes. The host proteases are found in human respiratory and avian enteric tissues. In avian viruses, the introduction of basic amino acids near the HA cleavage site permits cleavage by proteases of other tissues, which allows viral infection of vascular, CNS, and other tissues (pantropism) and a dramatic increase in virulence. The NA cleaves sialic acid residues to allow virus release

Table 15-1	The Genes of Influenza A Virus and Their Protein Products		
RNA Segment Number	**Gene Product**	**Protein**	**Proposed Functions of Protein**
1	PB1	Polymerase	RNA transcriptase
2	PB2	Polymerase	RNA transcriptase (host range determinant)
3	PA	Polymerase	RNA transcriptase
4	HA	Hemagglutinin	Viral attachment to cell membranes; major antigenic and virulence determinant
5	NA	Neuraminidase	Release from membranes; major antigenic determinant
6	NP	Nucleoprotein	Encapsidates RNA, type-specific antigen
7	M1	Matrix	Surrounds viral core; involved in assembly and budding
	M2	Ion channel	
8	NS1	Nonstructural	RNA binding, anti-interferon
	NS2	Nonstructural	Unknown

from the host epithelial cell; specific anti-NA antibody presumably diminishes release of virons from host cells.

Of the 8 influenza genome segments, five have been present in influenza viruses circulating globally since at least 1918. Three genome segments (HA, NA, and PB1 polymerase) have been newly acquired through reassortment with avian influenza viruses. Each reassortment with an acquisition of a new gene segment coincided with global pandemics (see Table 15-1).

The subtypes of influenza A virus are determined by these two surface antigens, NA and HA. Among influenza A viruses that infect humans, three different HA subtypes have classically been described—H1, H2, and H3. Three more subtypes—H5, H7, and H9—have also recently been shown to infect humans.

NOMENCLATURE

The nomenclature of influenza viruses is necessarily somewhat complex because of the need to name all new strains. Virus strains are named with (1) the virus type, (2) the geographic site of first identification of the specific virus, (3) the strain number from the isolating laboratory, (4) the year of virus isolation, and (5) the virus subtype (for influenza A). For example, one of the viruses in the influenza vaccine that was recommended for 2004–2005 was A California/7/2004(H3N2). This refers to a type A virus first isolated in California in 2004, as laboratory strain number 7, which is

subtype H3N2. The earliest isolate of influenza is A/WS(WilsonSmith)/33/H1N1.

EPIDEMIOLOGY OF EPIDEMICS AND PANDEMICS

The influenza virus causes annual epidemics of disease, and has caused five global pandemics in the last 100 years (*pandemic* from the Greek: *pan* = "all," *demos* = "people"). Pandemics of febrile respiratory disease that resemble influenza have been described since the days of Hippocrates (**Table 15-2**). The characteristic pattern of an influenza pandemic is initiation from a single geographic focus (often in Asia) and rapid spread, often along routes of travel.[7] High attack rates of all age groups are observed. Although case fatality rates are usually not increased substantially, because of the very large number of infections and cases, the number of hospitalizations and deaths is unusually high. In a pandemic, multiple waves of infections can sweep through a community, with each wave infecting sectors of the population different from those affected in the initial pandemic episode.

The 1918 Spanish influenza pandemic had an attack rate of 20% to 30% in adults, and 30% to 45% in children. The case fatality rate in adults was as high as 15% to 50%, with an unusual occurrence of deaths in young adults (**Figure 15-1**) and pregnant women. An estimated 20 to 50 million persons died in a single year in this global pandemic, many of them young adults (see the text box, "1918 Pandemic Flu").

Table 15-2	Antigenic Shifts of Influenza A Virus		
Years	Virus Description	Antigenic Change (Source)	Pandemic
1889	H3N2[a]	Not known	Severe
1900	H3N8[a]	Not known	Moderate
1918→1956	H1N1 "Spanish"	HA, NA (? swine)	Major; 50 million deaths in first year
1957→1968	H2N2 "Asian"	New HA, NA, PB1 (avian)	Severe
1968→	H3N2 "Hong Kong"	New HA,[b] PB1 (avian)	Moderate
1977→	H1N1 "Russian"	Apparently identical with 1956 H1N1[c]	Relatively mild[d]
2009→	H1N1 pdm 09	Triple reassortant (see text)	Moderate[e]

Notes:
[a]Data derived from serology; pandemic virus not available for study because influenza virus was first cultured in 1933.
[b]New human H3Ha varied by only six amino acids from parent avian H3HA, with all changes at sites important for receptor binding and antigenicity.
[c]May have escaped from a laboratory.
[d]Those aged more than 22 years had antibody from the 1918–1956 H1N1 strain.
[e]Those aged more than 60 years had antibody from the 1918 H1N1 strain of the 1940s.

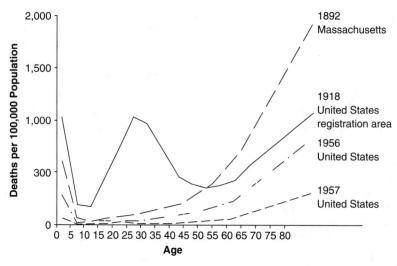

Figure 15-1 Age Distribution of Mortality of Selected Influenza Epidemics in the United States. Reproduced from C.C. Dauer and R.E. Sterling, 1961, Mortality from Influenza, *American Review of Respiratory Diseases*, vol. 82, Supplement, pp. 15–26. Official Journal of the American Thoracic Society.

Box 15-1	1918 Pandemic Flu

The influenza pandemic of 1918–1919, referred to as the "Spanish flu," caused more deaths globally than any pandemic since the Black Death (bubonic plague) of the 14th century. Estimates of the total number of deaths worldwide vary, but most sources estimate the pandemic caused at least 20 to 50 million deaths in the first 12 months. This estimate is an obvious underestimate because deaths in Asia and Africa were crudely estimated by colonial authorities.

First Wave

It appears influenza illness was first reported among American troops in the midwestern United States, from where it seems to have spread across the Atlantic with the movement of 1.5 million U.S. forces to the Western Front during World War I. Influenza was reported in March 1918 from Fort Riley, Kansas. In April, relatively mild influenza disease with low mortality was reported in troops on the East Coast. By April 15, U.S. troops in France were reporting influenza illnesses, as were troops in Britain. It is likely that crowding increased attack rates and mortality in the military; the U.S. Navy estimated that 40% of its seamen became ill. There were 54,000 battle deaths among U.S. forces in Europe and 43,000 influenza and pneumonia deaths. Battle lines were no barrier; German troops reported blitzkatarrh shortly after U.S. troops reported influenza, and German commanders complained that the disease disrupted their attack plans. By May and June 1918, most of Europe was experiencing the epidemic. Disease was reported in Africa in May, and in India and China in July and August—influenza had circled the world in 5 months.

During the summer, the character of the disease changed, showing higher rates of pneumonia in young adults with case-fatality rates of 50%. Some authorities suggest that the virus had mutated into a more virulent form. Isolated island populations suffered greatly. For example, in Tahiti 10% of the population died within 25 days of the onset of the epidemic. Similarly, in Western Samoa in November 1918, 20% of the population of 38,000 died within a 2-month period. In contrast, the Tristan da Cunha islands, isolated in the South Atlantic, did not experience the pandemic.

Second Wave

Beginning in August 1918, a second wave of severe disease, which was called "Spanish flu," swept the East Coast of the United States, following the European outbreaks. (Because of wartime censorship, British, French, German, and U.S. authorities did not report epidemic disease; Spain was neutral, and reported the epidemic and was awarded the name.) This time the United States experienced the severe influenza disease, with higher-case fatality rates seen in the European Western Front. A common description is of cyanosis and death from pneumonia within 2 to 3 days of illness onset.[17]

Surveys in the United States showed that 280 of every 1000 persons had clinical influenza symptoms. An estimated 550,000 excess deaths occurred in the United States, meaning approximately 1 of 200 persons died of influenza during the winter

(Continued)

of 1918–1919. Philadelphia reported the highest mortality rate: 12,897 influenza and pneumonia deaths in October and November of 1918, with a peak of 700 deaths per day in late October, and a 2-month mortality rate of 0.77%, leading to disruption of civic life, including a shortage of coffins. Desperate medical and public health authorities recommended many remedies and preventive actions now regarded as ineffective, including the use of gauze face masks, aerosol sprays, garlic or camphor necklaces, and legislation against public spitting. Mortality rates were lower in military and civilian African Americans than in whites, but approximately 2% of all Native Americans died during the epidemic.

The Spanish influenza epidemic of 1918 has been substantially ignored by historians until recently, perhaps because it occurred at the end of World War I. Katherine Anne Porter's novel, *Pale Horse, Pale Rider*, describes the experiences of young Americans during the pandemic.

1976 Swine Flu

When in January 1976 a similar swine H1N1 strain (A/New Jersey/76) was isolated in an ill soldier who died at Fort Dix, New Jersey, some U.S. public health authorities feared another pandemic and advised expanded immunization. Although not supported by all experts, a decision was reached to initiate mass immunization against swine flu, and the Swine Flu Program was announced in March 1976. A new national surveillance program for influenza disease and for vaccine adverse events was implemented. When liability issues were raised by the manufacturers, a special Swine Flu Tort Claims bill was passed by Congress, which specified that any claim arising from the Swine flu Program should be filed against the federal government. Vaccination started in October 1976, although no cases of swine flu disease had been reported. When, in December 1976, hundreds of cases of Guillain-Barre disease were reported following swine flu immunization, the vaccination program was suspended.[9]

The two major architects of the program, the Director of the CDC and the Assistant Secretary for Health of the Health, Education, and Welfare Department, resigned. A total of 48 million Americans received the swine flu vaccine, but only 6 cases of swine flu H1N1 disease were recorded, which suggests that the A/New Jersey/76 strain was not transmitted efficiently. More than 500 cases of Guillain-Barre syndrome were reported, apparently associated with the influenza vaccine, for which the federal government assumed liability and paid damages. Analysis suggested the risk of Guillain-Barre syndrome in 1976 vaccinees was 7 to 10 times increased over background risk, to about 10 cases for every 1 million vaccine recipients. A recent evaluation of Guillain-Barre syndrome associated with current influenza vaccine suggests a relative risk of 1.7, approximately 1 case per 1 million vaccinees.[10] This suggests the 1976 H1N1 vaccine had a unique association with Guillain-Barre syndrome.[10]

1918 Virus Resurrected

The 1918 pandemic virus was unique in its disease syndrome and epidemiology, but it was not available for study, as virology techniques did not exist at that time. In late 2005, the 1918 pandemic virus was re-created from viral RNA from a victim buried in permafrost and from autopsy material from two soldiers. Genomic viral RNA was obtained from these three sources and sequenced to generate a complete 1918 genomic sequence. These sequences show the avian heritage of the virus. Using plasmid-mediated reverse genetics, the 1918 pandemic virus was generated and studied in a high-containment laboratory. In comparison to current epidemic H1N1 viruses, the 1918 virus displayed high growth characteristics in human bronchial epithelial cells in culture. It caused death in 100% of mice within 4 days, whereas the control viruses killed none. In summary, the biologic tour de force of resurrecting the 1918 virus will allow detailed assessment of the molecular basis of its high pathogenicity and unique transmission patterns.[11,12]

Annual local epidemics follow a fairly predictable pattern. In North America, epidemics usually occur between November and March, manifested first by high rates of school and industrial absenteeism, followed by an increase in visits to healthcare facilities, an increase in pneumonia and influenza hospital admissions, and finally an increase in deaths from pneumonia or influenza. In any single locality, the influenza epidemic begins abruptly, reaches a peak within 3 weeks, and usually ends by 8 weeks. A city or region can experience two sequential or overlapping epidemics with different strains of viruses in a single winter. Epidemics in the Southern Hemisphere usually occur in the May to September winter season. The circulation of influenza viruses in the tropics links the two hemispheres[8,9] (as discussed later in this chapter). Virus spread during the winter season is said to be favored by the fact that the influenza virus survives better in environments of lower temperature and humidity. In tropical areas, its spread during the monsoon suggests that indoor crowding caused by weather may be a more important factor in transmission.[10]

A recent evaluation of the global patterns of seasonal activity of influenza virus analyzed data from the Northern and Southern Hemispheres from 1997 to 2005 in 19 temperate countries.[11] The important findings were that temporal overlaps of influenza activity between the two hemispheres occurred for the H3 and B types. Type B epidemics occurred significantly later in the season than H3 or H1 epidemics. Type H3 was the dominant or codominant virus in most seasons, and was the most widespread geographically. Countries more distant from the equator experienced influenza epidemics later in the year. This observation suggests that the later-winter seasonality of influenza epidemics may not be entirely related to winter environmental factors such as lower temperature, decreased humidity, or increased indoor crowding, because winter starts earlier in the year in the higher latitudes. It does suggest that transmission of specific virus strains from tropical regions might be an important factor accounting for later onset of epidemics in the higher latitudes.

INFLUENZA IN TROPICAL AND SUBTROPICAL REGIONS

Until recently, the burden of influenza in these regions has been underestimated because of the lack of laboratory capacity. The lack of laboratories able to diagnose influenza resulted in a reporting bias that artificially reduced the estimates of influenza incidence rates. In the last few years, increased concern has created increased awareness of the risk of pandemic influenza, which in turn has substantially expanded the ability to detect and characterize influenza viruses in tropical regions. This increased testing has provided new information regarding the epidemiology and disease burden.[12] In a review of these data,[9] it was reported that the major difference between tropical regions and the higher latitudes is that seasonality is less marked in tropical regions. Year-round surveillance has revealed that influenza viruses circulate for 9–12 months per year. Many settings show year-round presence, with seasonal increases in incidence, associated with monsoon or other climactic patterns. The perennial presence of influenza virus is related to the sequential circulation of many different virus types. The perennial presence and the number of types of circulating virus overall increase the exposure of the local population to influenza virus infection, as well as the burden of disease.[9] Incidence rates in Bangladesh show 102 infections per 1000 child-years for children younger than 5 years old—an annual 10% incidence. A detailed prospective serologic surveillance study showed an incidence rate of 32/100 infants.[13] These data suggest that children in this region have infection rate five times greater than that documented in the United States.

The constant presence and variety of influenza virus in the tropics suggest a mechanism for the generation and dissemination of new epidemic drifted influenza virus strains. A recent analysis of genetic and antigenic distribution and shifts showed temporally overlapping viral epidemics in East and Southeast Asia, which sustain a network of continuously circulating influenza viruses. Commonly, one of these viruses undergoes antigenic drift that favors local spread and migrates to Oceania, North America, Europe, and South America along the major air routes.[7] A comparison of phylogenetic relationships between influenza A/H3N2 viruses in 1999–2005 in New Zealand and New York concluded that global viral migration accounted for seasonal emergence of new strains.[14] The continuous presence of multiple influenza virus strains in tropical regions has implications for immunization policy, as neither Northern nor Southern Hemisphere vaccines may be ideal in tropical settings characterized by perennial circulation of diverse influenza viruses.

In general, rates of infection in infants and children are higher than those in adults, and the rates of hospitalization are highest in infants, lower in children, and high in the elderly.[15,16] Infants younger than 6 months old have the highest rates of seeking medical care for influenza illness. In some winters, as many as 9% of all infants are seen in clinics or admitted for such an infection.[15] Families with school-aged children have the highest rates of infection. These observations suggest that relatively immunologically naive children are important in the spread of epidemic strains.

Additional evidence that school transmission was the driver of community influenza transmission is provided by an analysis of the 2009 fall wave of the H1N1 pandemic. Analysis of local influenza-like illness (ILI) activity in relation to opening dates for public schools in 19 states showed that the pandemic increase in ILI activity did not occur until after schools opened, with a mean interval of 2 weeks between school opening and detection of widespread transmission.[17] These data suggest that immunization of schoolchildren should be undertaken shortly after school opening to affect community transmission.

Table 15-3	Influenza Disease by Age Group	
	Rate of Hospitalization/100,000	
Age (years)	**Normal**	**High Risk**
0–11 mo	496–1038	1900
1–2	186	800
3–4	86	320
5–14	8–41	92
15–44	20–30	56–110
45–64	13–23	392–635
≥65	125–228	399–518

Reproduced from the Centers for Disease Control and Prevention. *MMWR*, Vol. 52, RR06-, 2004; 1-40.

Table 15-3 summarizes recent U.S. data on rates for hospitalization for influenza.

Two metrics are useful to describe the transmission of influenza viruses: the basic reproduction number (R_0) and the generation time or serial interval. The reproductive number is the mean number of secondary cases per typical case; it ranged from 1.5 to 1.8 for the 1957 and 1968 pandemic viruses, and is estimated to have been in the range of 2.4–5.4 for the 1918 pandemic. An estimate of R_0 for the 2009 pandemic was 1.8–2.2. These data suggest that the 2009 H1N1 pandemic virus had a relatively low level of transmissibility. The mean serial interval for seasonal influenza has been estimated to be 3.6 days, and estimates for the 2009 H1N1 pandemic virus ranged from 2.6 to 3.2 days, suggesting a generation time less than that for seasonal influenza.[18]

Each epidemic and pandemic varies in size and impact, determined by the degree of the antigenic variation of the new virus, its virulence and transmissibility, and the level of existing protective immunity in the infected population. (Table 15-2 notes the association between the degree of antigenic difference and the size of the pandemic.) During average epidemics in North America, attack rates are often 10% to 20% in large populations, although certain population groups (e.g., school children or nursing home residents) and local outbreaks can have attack rates of 40% to 50%. More than 20,000 influenza-associated excess deaths occurred in the United States during each of nine epidemics between 1972 and 1991, and more than 40,000 deaths occurred during three of them. Analyses suggest the annual winter increase in all mortality is, in part, due to influenza.[19] Persons older than 65 years old

account for 90% of the excess deaths associated with annual epidemics.

Although pandemics cause many deaths over one or two winters, mortality from an emergent influenza strain is by no means restricted to the first two years after a new strain emerges. The cumulative deaths during successive annual epidemics of an interpandemic period often exceed the deaths in the pandemic period. For example, it has been estimated that the H3N2 virus in its first pandemic in 1968–1969 caused 34,000 deaths in the United States, but it has caused a total of more than 300,000 deaths in the annual epidemics in the subsequent 21 years during which it has circulated (from 1969 until the early 1990s).

Not only does influenza have a large impact on mortality, but morbidity from influenza is also significant. Since the 1990s, annual influenza has been associated with an average of 226,000 hospitalizations per year in the United States.[20]

Surveillance for influenza disease and for specific influenza viruses is necessary to track epidemic disease, to detect pandemics, and to determine virus serotypes for vaccine policy. In the United States, the Centers for Disease Control and Prevention (CDC) uses several surveillance systems:

- The collaborating laboratory surveillance system of 80 World Health Organization (WHO) collaborating laboratories and 60 other laboratories in the United States from October through May reports the total number of specimens received for respiratory virus testing and the number of positive isolates of influenza virus.
- An outpatient illness surveillance network uses a simple clinical definition of influenza-like illness, a fever greater than 100°F, plus cough or sore throat to tally the number of cases. Approximately 3000 physicians each week from October through May record the total number of patient visits for the week as well as the number of patients examined for influenza-like illness by age group.
- A 122-city mortality reporting system includes selected cities with a population of more than 100,000 and provides data on the percentage of deaths listed with pneumonia or influenza as the underlying cause or as being associated with influenza.
- Since 2004, influenza-associated deaths in children have been declared notifiable in the United States, and any laboratory-confirmed influenza-associated death is reported to CDC.

- Hospitalization surveillance: laboratory-confirmed influenza-associated hospitalizations are monitored and reported through the Influenza Hospitalization Network (Flu Serve-NET). This network covers 80 counties in 14 states by identifying cases the hospital records of influenza-positive cases.
- State and territorial epidemiologists report influenza activity levels. Each state epidemiologist reports the estimated level of influenza activity as no activity or sporadic (sporadically occurring cases of ILI or culture-confirmed influenza [CCI] without school or institutional outbreaks), regional (outbreaks of ILI or CCI in counties that total less than 50% of the state population), or widespread activity (outbreaks of ILI or CCI in counties that are larger than 50% of the total state population).

These data are summarized in the *Morbidity and Mortality Weekly Report* (*MMWR*) from the CDC and are found on its website (www.cdc.gov/flu/weekly).

MECHANISMS OF ANTIGENIC VARIATION

Because most epidemic and all 20th-century pandemic infections by influenza virus involve type A strains, the following discussion will focus on type A influenza. Although indistinguishable from type A in an individual patient, type B influenza disease is usually less severe, and it does not appear to cause pandemics. Type C disease is generally mild and not associated with widespread epidemics or pandemics.

The mutability or antigenic variation of influenza virus has been described by the term *antigenic drift*, denoting minor antigen changes through mutations. *Antigenic shift* describes major genetic and antigenic changes through reassortment.

Antigenic drift encompasses the frequent minor antigenic changes in the HA and NA surface antigens that account for the annual epidemics. This phenomenon is ascribed to the relatively high rate of spontaneous mutation in RNA viruses. RNA polymerase is a low-fidelity transcription enzyme without a proofreading function. The high rate of replication of these viruses with low fidelity generates many new amino acid substitutions in surface glycoproteins, some of which will be advantageous to the virus, allowing it to become an epidemic strain. Studies have shown that from 1968 to 1979,

7.9 nucleotide and 3.4 amino acid changes occurred per year, equivalent to an annual approximately 1% change in the amino acid composition of the HA. High rates of antigenic change are observed in the five specific epitopes of HA that surround the binding site; as noted previously, the binding site itself demonstrates little sequence variation. It is assumed that antibody to these epitopes sterically blocks access to the specific binding site, preventing attachment to and infection of host cells. Amino acid sequencing has shown that drift variants are sequential, suggesting selective pressure. For example, H3 sequential drift variants from 1968 to 1988 had four or more amino acid differences in at least two antigenic sites. The 1930s H1N1 virus strain (which was the first cultured influenza) shows substantial genetic drift from the ancestral 1918 H1N1 pandemic strain. It is also possible that changes in nonsurface proteins might influence replication, transmission, or tissue tropism (virulence), conferring a selective advantage to a specific strain. It is thought that after 10 to 30 years of circulation of a specific subtype, most members of the population will have antibody to that subtype, increasing the selection pressure for a new shift variant.

Antigenic shift comprises the major changes of HA, NA, or both of these surface antigens that create a new subtype. If the HA and NA determinants are novel, no antibody protection is present in human populations, and the stage may be set for a pandemic.

Viruses with segmented genomes can generate new variants rapidly by the random reassortment of the RNA segments in the mammalian cell. Coinfection of a single host cell by two influenza strains, each with a different eight-segmented genome, theoretically can generate 2^8 or 256 variants. The "mixing vessel" host for influenza is suspected to be swine, which are in contact with birds and humans, although humans can also serve in this role. Most new variants do not have a survival advantage and die out. However, if a shift variant (1) retains the ability to replicate well in humans, (2) is efficiently transmissible between humans, and (3) has new surface HA or NA determinants that evade existing influenza antibody profiles in the human population, a pandemic may ensue. Historically, serology and virology reveal that three antigenic shifts occurred during the 20th century, leading to three pandemics. Table 15-2 summarizes antigenic shifts of influenza A virus over the last 100 years. **Figure 15-2** demonstrates details of the antigenic shift of 1968, and **Figure 15-3** shows all pandemics.

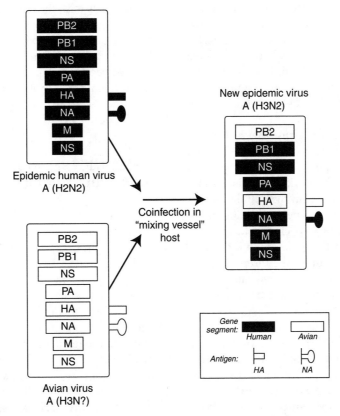

Figure 15-2 Diagram showing the antigenic shift in 1968, when a new avian gene was acquired. Gene segments are color-coded to represent avian or human species origin and their associated surface proteins. Copyright © Mark C. Steinhoff.

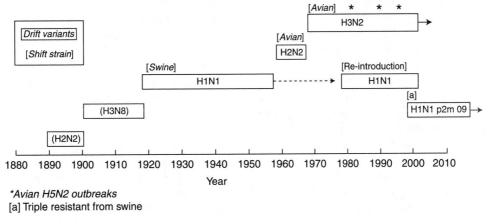

*Avian H5N2 outbreaks
[a] Triple resistant from swine

Figure 15-3 Twentieth century history of influenza antigenic shifts and pandemics, and interpandemic antigenic drift. Modified from Kilbourne, ED. Influenza pandemics of the 20th century. *Emerg Infect Dis*. 2006 Jan;12(1):9–14.

Five pandemics have occurred in the past 100 years. In 1918, the pandemic of influenza A H1N1 Spanish flu killed at least 50 million people in the first year; 500,000 died in the United States alone. In 1957, a major shift occurred with both new avian HA and NA (H1N1 to H2N2). In 1968, a new HA (H2N2 to H3N2) from an avian source was introduced, leading to a moderately severe pandemic. In 1977, the old 1951 H1N1 strain reappeared (likely having escaped from a laboratory), causing attack rates of more than 50% in younger members of the population who had been born after 1956 and, therefore, had no antibody to the earlier H1N1 subtype present from 1918 to 1957. Since 1977, both H1N1 and H3N2 subtypes have cocirculated worldwide (Figure 15-2 and Figure 15-3). A description of the 2009 H1N1 pandemic appears later in this chapter.

To summarize, influenza viruses with new surface antigens emerge, cause a pandemic, and become established in human populations. As the proportion of persons with antibodies against the specific pandemic strain increases within the population, the circulating influenza virus subtype must change or die out. Antigenic drift allows a specific influenza subtype to persist in the human population. It is assumed that annual epidemics occur in the inter-pandemic period because drift variant viruses with new minor antigenic changes can infect some members of the population.

A new pandemic occurs after an antigenic shift. This shift can result from genetic reassortment between human and animal influenza viruses or from direct transmission of an animal strain to humans, as was documented with influenza A (H5N1) in Hong Kong in the winter of 1997–1998.[13] This virus when isolated from humans had only avian genes, with no evidence of reassortment with human viruses. It is apparent that the novel avian influenza A (H5N1) virus did cause disease in at least 18 humans in Hong Kong (6 of whom died), but was not efficiently transmitted from human to human and, therefore, did not become pandemic. H5N1 has reappeared in humans several times.[21] This avian virus may at any time reassort with human-adapted viruses and acquire efficient transmissibility and could cause a pandemic in the near future. For this reason, public health authorities have begun development of H5 vaccines. H9N2 avian strains caused mild disease in Hong Kong in 1999 and 2003. Avian H7N7 caused poultry and human illness in the Netherlands in 2003.

The 1998 Hong Kong experience and the 1976 and 2009 swine influenza episode show that surface antigens, virulence, and transmissibility all vary independently and unpredictably. Not all new shift viruses with novel antigens will cause a pandemic; the criteria of transmissibility and human infectivity must also be met.

Genetic reassortment also occurs frequently in egg or tissue culture. Vaccine manufacturers take advantage of this viral characteristic to rapidly develop new vaccine strains. Two viruses are selected: a wild virus with the epidemic NA and HA antigens, and an egg-adapted virus (A/Puerto Rico/8/34) with the characteristics of vigorous growth in egg culture. Eggs are infected simultaneously with both viruses, and the reassortant progeny virus that exhibits both the epidemic HA and NA and the property of good growth in eggs is selected as the vaccine strain for production.

EPIZOOTIC INFECTIONS AND EVOLUTIONARY HISTORY

The current working hypothesis developed by Webster and others is that avian influenza strains are the source for all influenza viruses seen in birds and mammals.[22] Analysis of molecular relationships suggests that all A subtypes are descended from a primordial avian influenza virus. All of the known 15 HA and 9 NA influenza subtypes have been isolated from aquatic avian sources, which is likely their natural habitat, but only certain subtypes are found in mammalian species including swine, horses, dogs, seals, whales, and mink. Infection of feral (ducks, geese, gulls, terns, and shearwaters) or domestic (turkeys, chickens, geese, ducks, quail, and pheasants) avian species is usually asymptomatic, but occasionally has resulted in epidemics of avian disease, or "fowl plague." Ducks excrete up to 10^8 virus particles per gram of feces, and influenza virus is found in waters where ducks reside. The rate of antigenic drift is low in birds, suggesting stable adaptation between virus and avian host. Pigs have epithelial cell receptors for both human and avian HA; they are thought to be the mixing vessels or intermediate hosts of avian and mammalian influenza virus, providing an opportunity for reassortment and antigenic shift.

Although the virus of the 1918 pandemic has not been cultured, pandemic H1N1 viral RNA from bodies buried in permafrost in Alaska and from World War I autopsy material from the military has been analyzed and shows that the pandemic strain was unique and related to avian strains. Further analysis of the RNA sequence is being carried out to determine whether a genetic explanation for its high virulence can be obtained.[23,24] It is of note that the avian equivalent of H1N1 is still circulating in avian species and swine. The role of avian carriage of virus during annual waterfowl migration from the Northern Hemisphere to the Southern Hemisphere in the spread of new influenza variants is being investigated.

PREVENTION STRATEGIES AND TREATMENT

Vaccines to prevent infection and use of antiviral drugs either prophylactically or for treatment are the currently available strategies to reduce influenza disease. This section describes the recommended use of inactivated and live attenuated influenza vaccines, and of antiviral drugs.

Vaccines

Vaccines were developed soon after influenza virus was shown to grow in embryonated hens' eggs. An early vaccine trial in 1943 showed that a killed virus vaccine was effective in young adults. The current inactivated vaccine is derived from virus grown on chorioallantoic membranes of embryonated eggs. The allantoic fluids are ultracentrifuged to purify the virus particles, and the viruses are inactivated by formaldehyde or beta-propriolactone. Some manufacturers disrupt the virus particles to produce a "split virus vaccine" using detergents or ether. The potency is assessed by measuring HA antigen, and vaccines are standardized to contain 15 to 20 µg of HA antigen per dose. Egg-grown influenza viruses have been shown to have antigenic variation from the parent human strain, which may account for the variable protection offered by inactivated vaccines. When influenza is cultured in human cell lines, the derived influenza virus has identical amino acid sequences to the parent strain. In general, vaccines are immunogenic in adults after a single dose, but require two doses in infants and children who are immunologically naive. Current inactivated vaccines are 50% to 80% effective in preventing disease when the epidemic influenza virus matches the vaccine strains.[20]

The current egg-based influenza vaccine production process is laborious, and depends on the annual production of several hundred million eggs under strict standards of good manufacturing processes (GMP) that can be threatened by avian influenza disease in chicken flocks. It also has a limited surge capacity for production for new pandemic vaccines. Substantial effort is under way to develop new approaches for rapid production of influenza vaccines, which is needed for pandemics that can start at any time of the year. The use of adjuvants will reduce the dose for immunization, and vaccines with adjuvants have been approved in Europe but not by the U.S. Food and Drug Administration (FDA). Live attenuated vaccines designed to generate antibodies to the NS1 protein have been shown to be effective and are being developed.

Newer approaches include the following:

- Generation of recombinant HA proteins in baculovirus vectors, which are then purified, have shown safety and immunogenicity.
- Noninfectious virus-like particles can be generated from vectors that express the HA, NA, and matrix proteins, which spontaneously self-assemble into particles with the HA and NA proteins on the surface.
- A variety of viruses that can express virus proteins, but do not themselves infect or cause disease, have been developed into viral vector vaccines.
- DNA vaccines in which purified DNA segments coding for HA or NA peptides are injected are undergoing clinical trials.[25]

Cost-effectiveness analyses mostly support immunization of healthy subjects.[26] Over the past few years, infants and others have been added to the high-risk group. Pregnancy was associated with excess mortality in the 1918 influenza pandemic. Recent evaluations have shown a relative risk of 4.7 for influenza-related hospitalization of pregnant women in the third trimester, compared with postpartum controls[27,28] and the effectiveness of antepartum immunization in protection of pregnant women as well as their fetuses and infants.[29-32]

The current vaccine strategy in the United States has evolved from policies to protect persons at high risk for adverse outcomes from influenza infection to vaccinating healthy persons who may transmit the virus to high-risk persons and, after the 2009 pandemic, to universal immunization for all persons older than 6 months. (See **Box 15-2** summarizing current CDC recommendations as of August 2011.) The recommendations include a summary of persons at high risk who should be prioritized to receive vaccine if a shortage of vaccines arises, which may occur in some winters.

Virus mutability with antigenic shift and drift means a new vaccine must be produced each year to counter the new antigenic variants that continually arise. Each year in January, a review of circulating viruses in the Northern and Southern Hemispheres is undertaken by WHO, using data from a global network of surveillance laboratories, and the most likely epidemic influenza A (H1N1, H3N2) and a B strain are selected. The vaccine seed viruses are produced and distributed to manufacturers for production in eggs, clinical testing, licensing, packaging, and distribution by October before the winter influenza season. U.S. vaccine manufacturers produce as many as 250 million doses each year between February and

---

Box 15-2	CDC's Influenza Vaccine Recommendations, 2011

- All persons aged 6 months or older should be vaccinated annually.
- Protection of persons at higher risk for influenza-related complications should continue to be a focus of vaccination efforts as providers and programs transition to routine vaccination of all persons aged 6 months or older.
- When vaccine supply is limited, vaccination efforts should focus on delivering vaccination to the following persons:
  - Those aged 6 months to 4 years (59 months)
  - Those aged 50 years or older
  - Those with chronic pulmonary (including asthma), cardiovascular (except hypertension), renal, hepatic, neurologic, hematologic, or metabolic disorders (including diabetes mellitus)
  - Immunosuppressed persons (including those with immunosuppression caused by medications or by human immunodeficiency virus)
  - Those who are or will be pregnant during the influenza season
  - Those aged 6 months to 18 years who are receiving long-term aspirin therapy and, therefore, might be at risk for experiencing Reye syndrome after influenza virus infection
  - Residents of nursing homes and other chronic care facilities
  - American Indians and Alaska Natives
  - Morbidly obese persons (body mass index ≥40)
  - Healthcare personnel
  - Household contacts and caregivers of children younger than age 5 years and adults 50 years or older, with particular emphasis on vaccinating contacts of children younger than age 6 months
  - Household contacts and caregivers of persons with medical conditions that put them at higher risk for severe complications from influenza.

Reproduced from the Centers for Disease Control and Prevention, National Center for Immunization and Respiratory Diseases (NCIRD) (2011). Seasonal Influenza (Flu): Additional Information about Vaccination of Specific Populations. http://www.cdc.gov/flu/professionals/acip/specificpopulations.htm. Updated December 15, 2011. Accessed September 18, 2012.

October. This complex process is repeated annually and is usually effective, though in some years manufacturing problems have led to late or nondelivery of vaccine.[33]

The lessons learned in the 2009 H1N1 pandemic will be useful for future planning. Despite substantial government and private-sector effort to produce a pandemic vaccine, when the new pandemic H1N1 virus was identified in April 2009, the vaccine did not become widely available in the United States until December 2009. At that point, the pandemic had passed its peak activity. In the end, manufacturers were left with 70 million unused doses.

Usually this vaccine strategy is relatively effective in preventing disease and mortality in vaccinated persons in those years in which the vaccine composition closely matches the epidemic virus. Recent studies suggest that influenza immunization of healthy children will reduce all otitis media episodes by 40%, and immunization of children in daycare programs reduces the risk of illness in their families. Immunization of healthy adults can reduce reported respiratory illness by 20% and absenteeism by 36%.[34] The vaccine strategy to vaccinate healthy persons, especially children, is increasingly used and had been implemented in Japan until the early 1990s. Strategies to vaccinate a proportion of the children have the potential to disrupt epidemic transmission and protect adults.[35]

A recent randomized trial carried out in isolated Hutterite communities in Canada showed that immunization of children with TIV vaccine (Trivalent inactivated vaccine) resulted in substantial community protection of 59% among all members of the communities.[35] This prospective randomized trial confirmed observations from case-contact studies or nonrandomized comparisons of communities, and suggests that immunization of schoolchildren will substantially reduce community transmission of influenza.[36,37]

The inactivated influenza vaccines that are currently recommended and commercially available do not contain live viruses and cannot cause influenza disease. The most frequent side effect of vaccination is local soreness at the vaccination site, which can last for 1 or 2 days. Symptoms of fever, malaise, and myalgia have been infrequently reported, most often in persons who have had no exposure to influenza vaccine (e.g., young children). Allergic anaphylactic reactions, which can occur rarely after influenza vaccination, are related to hypersensitivity to residual egg protein in these vaccines or to thimerosal. The 1976 swine influenza vaccine was associated with an increased frequency of Guillain-Barre syndrome of ascending paralysis.[38] Recently, the association has been evaluated with current vaccines, and it is estimated to occur in approximately one case per million vaccinees—far less than the risk of severe influenza complications if not vaccinated.[39]

Live Influenza Vaccine

Live attenuated influenza viruses (LAIV) have been shown to be as effective as the inactivated virus vaccines.[40] The cold-adapted virus does not replicate effectively at 37°C; hence it can infect humans, but does not cause disease. The cold-adapted attenuated influenza virus is derived from an epidemic strain and an attenuated cold-adapted virus. After reassortment of the two viruses, progeny with the epidemic surface antigens and the characteristic of attenuated growth in humans are selected and produced.

These vaccine strains have been extensively tested in adults and children, and demonstrate protective efficacy of 92% against confirmed influenza infection and excellent safety characteristics.[20] Their chief advantage is that they can be administered as nose drops or aerosol and, therefore, are more acceptable to patients and do not require medical personnel for administration. The cold-adapted influenza vaccine (FluMist) was licensed in 2004 for use in people aged 5 years to 55 years in the United States with important exceptions (**Table 15-4** and **Table 15-5**).[20]

Recent studies show that the LAIV vaccines may be less effective than TIV in adults.[41] However, this must be balanced against the ease of administration of LAIV vaccines and their ready acceptance which may facilitate population vaccination to avert an epidemic.

Antiviral Drugs

The older antiviral agents, amantadine and rimantadine, inhibit the replication of type A influenza viruses

Vaccine*	Trade Name	Manufacturer	Presentation	Mercury Content (mcg Hg/0.5 mL dose)	Age Group	No. of Doses	Route
TIV[†]	Fluzone	Sanofi Pasteur	0.25 mL prefilled syringe	0.0	6–35 mos	1 or 2[§]	Intramuscular[¶]
			0.5 mL prefilled syringe	0.0	36 mos	1 or 2[§]	Intramuscular
			0.5 mL vial	0.0	36 mos	1 or 2[§]	Intramuscular
			5.0 mL multidose vial	25.0	6 mos	1 or 2[§]	Intramuscular
TIV	Fluvirin	Novartis Vaccine	5.0 mL multidose vial	24.5	4 yrs	1 or 2[§]	Intramuscular
			0.5 mL prefilled syringe	<1.0			
TIV	Fluarix	GlaxoSmithKline	0.5 mL prefilled syringe	0.0	3 yrs	1	Intramuscular
TIV	FluLaval	GlaxoSmithKline	5.0 mL multidose vial	25.0	18 yrs	1	Intramuscular
TIV	Afuria	CSL Biotherapies	0.5 mL prefilled syringe	0.0	6 mos	1	Intramuscular
			5.0 mL multidose vial	25.0			
TIV High Dose**	Fluzone High-Dose	Sanofi Pasteur	0.5 mL prefilled syringe	0.0	65 yrs	1	Intramuscular
LAIV[††]	FluMist[§§]	Medimmune	0.2 mL sprayer, divided dose	0.0	2–49 yrs	1 or 2[§]	Intranasal

* Immunization providers should check Food and Drug Administration–approved prescribing information for 2010–11 influenza vaccines for the most updated information.
† Trivalent inactivated vaccine.
§ Children aged 6 months–8 years who have never received a seasonal TIV before or who did not receive at least 1 dose of an influenza A (H1N1) 2009 monovalent vaccine should receive 2 doses, spaced ≥4 weeks apart. Those children aged 6 months–8 years who are vaccinated for the first time in the 2009–10 season with the seasonal 2009–10 seasonal vaccine but who received only 1 dose should receive 2 doses of the 2010–11 influenza vaccine formula, spaced ≥4 weeks apart.
¶ For adults and older children, the recommended site of vaccination is the deltoid muscle. The preferred site for infants and young children is the anterolateral aspect of the thigh.
** Trivalent inactivated vaccine high dose. A 0.5-mL dose contains 60 mcg each o A/California/7/2009 (H1N1)-like, A/Perth/16/2009 (H3N2)-like, and B/Brisbane/60/2008-like antigens.
†† Live attenuated influenza vaccine.
§§ FluMist is shipped refrigerated and stored in the refrigerator at 36°F–46°F (2°C–8°C) after arrival in the vaccination clinic. The dose is 0.2 mL divided equally between each nostril. Health-care providers should consult the medical record, when available, to identify children age 2–4 years with asthma or recurrent wheezing that might indicate asthma. In addition, to identify children who might be at greater risk for asthma and possibly at increased risk for wheezing after receiving LAIV, parents or caregivers of children age 2–4 years should be asked: "In the past 12 months, has a health-care provided ever told you that your child had wheezing or asthma?" Children whose parents or caregivers answer "yes" to this question and children who have asthma or who had a wheezing episode noted in the medical record within the past 12 months should not receive FluMist.

Reproduced from Centers for Disease Control and Prevention (2010). Prevention and Control of Influenza with Vaccines Recommendations of the Advisory Committee on Immunization Practices (ACIP). *MMWR* 2010;59(No RR-8) 1–62.

Table 15-5	Persons Who Should Not Be Vaccinated with LAIV

The following populations should not be vaccinated with LAIV:

- Persons younger than 5 years or those *older than* 50 years
- Persons with asthma, reactive airways disease, or other chronic disorders of the pulmonary or cardiovascular systems; persons with other underlying medical conditions, including such metabolic diseases as diabetes, renal dysfunction, and hemoglobinopathies; or persons with known or suspected immunodeficiency diseases or who are receiving immunosuppressive therapies
- Children or adolescents receiving aspirin or other salicylates (because of the association of Reye syndrome with wild-type influenza infection)
- Persons with a history of GBS
- Pregnant women
- Persons with a history of hypersensitivity, including anaphylaxis, to any of the components of LAIV or to eggs

Table 15-6	Antiviral Agents for Influenza Treatment and Prophylaxis			
	Amantadine	**Rimantadine**	**Zanamivir**	**Oseltamivir**
Types of influenza viruses inhibited	Influenza A	Influenza A	Influenza A and B	Influenza A and B
Route of administration	Oral (tablet, capsule, syrup)	Oral (tablet, syrup)	Oral inhalation*	Oral (capsule)
Ages for which treatment is approved	≥1 year	≥14 years	≥1 year	≥1 year
Ages for which prophylaxis is approved	≥1 year	≥1 year	Not approved for prophylaxis	≥1 year

*Zanamivir is administered by a plastic oral inhalation device.
Adapted from the Centers for Disease Control and Prevention, *MMWR*, Vol. 48, RR14, 1999.

(but have no effect on type B) by interfering with the M2 protein, which forms an ion channel. When taken prophylactically, these drugs have been shown to be 70% to 90% effective in preventing illness during influenza A epidemics. In addition, if begun within 48 hours of illness onset in healthy adults, these drugs can reduce the severity and duration of influenza A illness. Both drugs have CNS side effects of nervousness, anxiety, difficulty in concentrating, and lightheadedness. These drugs are advised for children older than 1 year of age (Table 15-5) and are not effective against HSN1.[20]

New drugs have been designed to inhibit NA activity.[20] An NA inhibitor, zanamivir (a sialic acid analogue), reduces disease duration by 1 or more days and prevents both type A and B disease with 67% to 82% effectiveness when taken prophylactically. Zanamivir (or Relenza) was licensed in the United States in July 1999 as inhalation therapy for persons older than 7 years. An oral NA inhibitor, oseltamivir (Tamiflu), is equally effective for prophylaxis and treatment for influenza in children older than 1 year (**Table 15-6**).

PANDEMIC 2009 H1N1 VIRUS

The pandemics recorded over the last 100 years have shown us that characteristics of age distribution, severity, and transmission parameters all vary unpredictably, and that pandemic influenza viruses may first appear on any continent at any time of the year.

The 2009 H1N1 pandemic occurred more than 39 years after the last global influenza pandemic. It involved the first H1N1 pandemic strain since the 1918 pandemic, and had a number of unique characteristics. The new virus was first detected in Mexico in April 2009 after observation of unusual influenza patterns. The initial isolates were submitted by Mexican authorities to reference laboratories in Canada and United States, and were recognized to be unique, new H1N1 viruses on April 15 of that year. The strain was given a number of names, but was eventually referred to as 2009 pH1N1. Recently, WHO suggested the standard terminology for this strain should be A(H1N1) pdm09. The new pandemic virus was classified as a triple reassortant because the gene segments in this virus were derived from three major sources:

- The HA, which has been circulating as an independent genetic lineage in swine since 1918
- The NA, which has been circulating in swine since 1979
- The PB1 and PB2, which have been circulating in swine since 1998

The pandemic strain first appeared in pigs in Mexico and was then transferred to humans.

The virus spread quickly throughout the United States, and from the United States to regions with direct flight connections, so that 32 countries in South America, Europe, and Asia had reported cases by the end of May 2009. WHO declared a pandemic alert level 5 in April 2009, and a level 6 alert in June 2009. By January 2010, more than 209 countries had laboratory-confirmed cases.

The 2009 H1N1 pandemic featured a lower level of severe illness than previous pandemics, with estimated case-fatality ratios ranging from 0.05% to 1.2%. The overall reduced mortality is partly due to the relative sparing of adults 65 years and older, likely due to their immunity due to previous exposure to the 1918 H1N1 lineage.

North America experienced two distinct pandemic waves. The initial wave lasted from May through July, and a second wave occurred from September through December. Overall, the attack rate in the United States was estimated to be 17%, with a higher attack rate in the younger age group compared to the older than age 65 years group.

Additional findings from a CDC review of the pandemic data[18] reveal that the highest rate of hospitalization was in the 0- to 4-year-old age groups, who experienced rates 3.5 times higher than the rate of hospitalization in the 65+-year-old group. Evaluations of those patients admitted to the hospital show that the majority of adults and children had one or more underlying medical conditions. Approximately 25% of admitted patients required ICU care, and obesity was identified as a risk factor for hospitalization, ICU admission, and death, independent of other chronic medical conditions. In some parts of the United States, hospitalization rates were higher for non-Hispanic blacks, Hispanics, and Asian Pacific Islanders, and mortality rates were greater in American Indians and Alaska Natives than in other ethnic groups.

The age distribution of pandemic influenza-associated deaths was strikingly different from that in seasonal influenza epidemics, with 96% of 2009 deaths occurring in persons younger than 65 years of age, in contrast to the usual 90% of deaths in persons older than age 65 years. The number of influenza-associated pediatric deaths was 4 times the average annual number since reporting began in 2004. The increased risk of influenza previously reported in pregnant women was evident during the 2009 pandemic, with pregnancy being associated with a 4.3-fold increased risk of hospitalization, and reports of increased rates of prematurity and reduced birth weight in influenza-affected pregnant women.

The CDC has developed a model that adjusts for likely under-ascertainment of laboratory-confirmed pandemic cases.[42] Using this statistical model, it is estimated that for every pandemic H1N1 case reported to CDC, 79 cases were not reported. Overall, between April 2009 and March 2010, pandemic H1N1 virus caused an estimated 60 million cases, 270,000 hospitalizations, and 12,000 deaths in the United States. These estimates suggest a cumulative attack rate in United States of 20%.

AVIAN INFLUENZA VIRUS

The H5N1 avian influenza strain has been causing disease and outbreaks in birds and humans in Asia since 1997. The majority of cases have come from Asia, including the countries of Cambodia, China, Indonesia, Thailand, and Vietnam; fewer cases have arisen in Africa in Egypt and Djibouti, and several cases have been noted in Europe and the Middle East, in Iraq, Turkey, and Azerbaijan. Overall mortality in these reported cases was 57%. Analysis of recent strains of H5N1 reveals that the virus has mutated substantially from the strain first seen in 1997. There is increasing concern regarding this avian virus that exhibits new surface antigen, has virulence in humans, but does not yet have efficient transmissibility between humans.[21,43] Eventually, the virus may acquire the human transmission phenotype properties needed to become the next pandemic strain.

The assumption that pandemics would likely originate in Southeast Asia and the close monitoring of new strains in that region were of no use when rapid identification and analysis of a new H1N1 strain were needed in Mexico in early 2009.[44] If a pandemic should occur before sufficient antiviral drugs are available, and few or no doses of specific vaccines are available,[45] epidemic control will have to rely on public health strategies that are centuries old—namely, physical restrictions of citizens. These measures include (1) isolation of those with influenza illness, (2) quarantine of all their contacts, and (3) banning of all public gatherings including schools, workplaces, shopping centers, churches, and bars.

● ● ● **REFERENCES**

1. Monto AS, Gravenstein S, Elliott M, et al. Clinical signs and symptoms predicting influenza infection. *Arch Intern Med* 2000;160:3243–3247.

2. Brundage JF. Interactions between influenza and bacterial respiratory pathogens: implications for pandemic preparedness. *Lancet Infect Dis* 2006;6:303–312.

3. O'Brien KL, Walters MI, Sellman J, et al. Severe pneumococcal pneumonia in previously healthy children: the role of preceding influenza infection. *Clin Infect Dis* 2000;30:784–789.

4. Ohmit SE, Monto AS. Symptomatic predictors of influenza virus positivity in children during the influenza season. *Clin Infect Dis* 2006;43:564–568.

5. Smith W, Andrews C, Laidlaw P. A virus isolated from influenza patients. *Lancet* 1933;2:66–68.

6. Matrosovich MN, Gambaryan AS, Teneberg S, et al. Avian influenza A viruses differ from human viruses by recognition of sialyloligosaccharides and gangliosides and by a higher conservation of the HA receptor-binding site. *Virology* 1997;233:224–234.

7. Russell CA, Jones TC, Barr IG, et al. The global circulation of seasonal influenza A (H3N2) viruses. *Science* 2008;320:340–346.

8. Viboud C, Alonso WJ, Simonsen L. Influenza in tropical regions. *PLoS Med* 2006;3:e89.

9. Brooks WA, Steinhoff MC. Epidemiology of influenza in tropical and subtropical low-income regions. In: Rappuoli R, Del Giudice G, eds. *Influenza Vaccines for the Future*, 2nd ed. Basel: Springer; 2011:55–76.

10. Lowen A, Palese P. Transmission of influenza virus in temperate zones is predominantly by aerosol, in the tropics by contact: a hypothesis. *PLoS Curr* 2009;1:RRN1002.

11. Finkelman BS, Viboud C, Koelle K, et al. Global patterns in seasonal activity of influenza A/H3N2, A/H1N1, and B from 1997 to 2005: viral coexistence and latitudinal gradients. *PLoS One* 2007;2:e1296.

12. Nair H, Brooks WA, Katz M, et al. Global burden of respiratory infections due to seasonal influenza in young children: a systematic review and meta-analysis. *Lancet* 2011;378:1917–1930.

13. Henkle E, Steinhoff MC, Omer SB, et al. Incidence of influenza virus infection in early infancy: a prospective study in South Asia. *Pediatr Infect Dis J* 2011;30:170–173.

14. Nelson MI, Simonsen L, Viboud C, et al. Phylogenetic analysis reveals the global migration of seasonal influenza A viruses. *PLoS Pathog* 2007;3:1220–1228.

15. Poehling KA, Edwards KM, Weinberg GA, et al. The underrecognized burden of influenza in young children. *N Engl J Med* 2006;355:31–40.

16. Neuzil KM, Zhu Y, Griffin MR, et al. Burden of interpandemic influenza in children younger than 5 years: a 25-year prospective study. *J Infect Dis* 2002;185:147–152.

17. Chao DL, Halloran ME, Longini IM, Jr. School opening dates predict pandemic influenza A (H1N1) outbreaks in the United States. *J Infect Dis* 2010;202:877–880.

18. Jhung MA, Swerdlow D, Olsen SJ, et al. Epidemiology of 2009 pandemic influenza A (H1N1) in the United States. *Clin Infect Dis* 2011;52(suppl 1):S13–S26.

19. Reichert TA, Simonsen L, Sharma A, et al. Influenza and the winter increase in mortality in the United States, 1959–1999. *Am J Epidemiol* 2004;160:492–502.

20. Fiore AE, Uyeki TM, Broder K, et al. Prevention and control of influenza with vaccines: recommendations of the Advisory Committee on Immunization Practices (ACIP), 2010. *MMWR Recomm Rep* 2010;59:1–62.

21. Beigel JH, Farrar J, Han AM, et al. Avian influenza A (H5N1) infection in humans. *N Engl J Med* 2005;353:1374–1385.

22. Webster RG. Influenza: an emerging disease. *Emerg Infect Dis* 1998;4:436–441.

23. Taubenberger JK, Reid AH, Lourens RM, et al. Characterization of the 1918 influenza virus polymerase genes. *Nature* 2005;437:889–893.

24. Tumpey TM, Basler CF, Aguilar PV, et al. Characterization of the reconstructed 1918 Spanish influenza pandemic virus. *Science* 2005;310:77–80.

25. Lambert LC, Fauci AS. Influenza vaccines for the future. *N Engl J Med* 2010;363:2036–2044.

26. Clements KM, Chancellor J, Nichol K, et al. Cost-effectiveness of a recommendation of universal mass vaccination for seasonal influenza in the United States. *Value Health* 2011;14:800–811.

27. Mak TK, Hesseling AC, Hussey GD, Cotton MF. Making BCG vaccination programmes safer in the HIV era. *Lancet* 2008;372:786–787.

28. Tamma PD, Steinhoff MC, Omer SB. Influenza infection and vaccination in pregnant women. *Expert Rev Respir Med* 2010;4:321–8.

29. Zaman K, Roy E, Arifeen SE, et al. Effectiveness of maternal influenza immunization in mothers and infants. *N Engl J Med* 2008;359:1555–1564.

30. Steinhoff MC, Omer SB, Roy E, et al. Influenza immunization in pregnancy: antibody responses in mothers and infants. *N Engl J Med* 2010;362:1644–1646.

31. Omer SB, Goodman D, Steinhoff MC, et al. Maternal influenza immunization and reduced likelihood of prematurity and small for gestational age births: a retrospective cohort study. *PLoS Med* 2011;8:e1000441.

32. Steinhoff MC, Omer SB, Roy E, et al. Neonatal outcomes after influenza immunization in pregnancy: a randomized controlled trial. *Can Med Assoc J* 2012 (in press).

33. Update: influenza vaccine supply and recommendations for prioritization during the 2005–06 influenza season. *Morb Mortal Wkly Rep* 2005;54:850.

34. Wilde JA, McMillan JA, Serwint J, et al. Effectiveness of influenza vaccine in health care professionals: a randomized trial. *JAMA* 1999;281:908–913.

35. Loeb M, Russell ML, Moss L, et al. Effect of influenza vaccination of children on infection rates in Hutterite communities: a randomized trial. *JAMA* 2010;303:943–950.

36. Monto AS, Davenport FM, Napier JA, Francis T, Jr. Modification of an outbreak of influenza in Tecumseh, Michigan by vaccination of schoolchildren. *J Infect Dis* 1970;122:16–25.

37. Hurwitz ES, Haber M, Chang A, et al. Effectiveness of influenza vaccination of day care children in reducing influenza-related morbidity among household contacts. *JAMA* 2000;284:1677–1682.

38. Langmuir AD, Bregman DJ, Kurland LT, et al. An epidemiologic and clinical evaluation of Guillain-Barre syndrome reported in association with the administration of swine influenza vaccines. *Am J Epidemiol* 1984;119: 841–879.

39. Lasky T, Terracciano GJ, Magder L, et al. The Guillain-Barre syndrome and the 1992–1993 and 1993–1994 influenza vaccines. *N Engl J Med* 1998;339:1797–1802.

40. Belshe RB, Nichol KL, Black SB, et al. Safety, efficacy, and effectiveness of live, attenuated, cold-adapted influenza vaccine in an indicated population aged 5–49 years. *Clin Infect Dis* 2004;39:920–927.

41. Monto AS, Ohmit SE, Petrie JG, et al. Comparative efficacy of inactivated and live attenuated influenza vaccines. *N Engl J Med* 2009;361:1260–1267.

42. Reed C, Angulo FJ, Swerdlow DL, et al. Estimates of the prevalence of pandemic (H1N1) 2009, United States, April–July 2009. *Emerg Infect Dis* 2009;15:2004–2007.

43. Stephenson I, Nicholson KG, Wood JM, et al. Confronting the avian influenza threat: vaccine development for a potential pandemic. *Lancet Infect Dis* 2004;4:499–509.

44. Harris KM, Maurer J, Kellermann AL. Influenza vaccine: safe, effective, and mistrusted. *N Engl J Med* 2010;363:2183–2185.

45. Barnett DJ, Balicer RD, Lucey DR, et al. A systematic analytic approach to pandemic influenza preparedness planning. *PLoS Med* 2005;2:e359.

16

Measles

William J. Moss and Martin O. Ota

INTRODUCTION

Measles is one of the most important infectious diseases of humans and has caused millions of deaths since its emergence as a zoonotic disease thousands of years ago. For infectious disease epidemiologists, measles has served as a model of an acute infectious disease, particularly for understanding the nature of epidemics. Kenneth Maxcy, the second chair of the Department of Epidemiology at the Johns Hopkins University School of Public Health, wrote in 1948, "The simplest of all infectious diseases is measles."[1] Despite the apparent simplicity, much has been learned about measles in the half-century since Maxcy's chapter was written. Detailed investigations of the virology, immunology, and transmission dynamics have shown measles to be a much more complex disease than Maxcy's statement indicates, and many questions remain unanswered. But this ignorance has not impeded enormous progress in global measles control.

DISEASE BURDEN

The disease burden caused by measles has decreased because of a number of factors. Measles mortality declined in developed countries in association with economic development, improved nutritional status, and supportive care, particularly antibiotic therapy to control secondary bacterial pneumonia. Remarkable progress in reducing measles incidence and mortality has been, and continues to be, made in resource-poor countries as a consequence of increasing measles vaccine coverage, provision of a second opportunity for measles vaccination through supplementary immunization activities (SIA), and efforts by the World Health Organization (WHO), the United Nations Children's Fund (UNICEF), and their partners to target endemic countries for accelerated and sustained measles mortality reduction. Specifically, this targeted strategy aims to achieve greater than 90% measles vaccination coverage in every district and to ensure that all children receive a second dose of measles vaccine. Provision of vitamin A through polio and measles SIA has contributed further to the reduction in measles mortality.

In 2003, the World Health Assembly endorsed a resolution urging member countries to reduce the number of deaths attributed to measles by 50% compared with 1999 estimates by the end of 2005. This global public health target was met, with estimated measles mortality reduced by 60% from an estimated 873,000 deaths in 1999 (uncertainty bounds: 634,000–1,140,000) to 345,000 deaths in 2005 (uncertainty bounds: 247,000–458,000) (**Figure 16-1**).[2] Further reductions in global measles mortality were achieved by 2008, during which there were an estimated 164,000 deaths due to measles (uncertainty bounds: 115,000–222,000) (Figure 16-1).[3] These achievements attest to the enormous public-health significance of measles vaccination. Prior to this effort, an estimated 30 million cases of measles occurred each year, with more than 1 million deaths. The revised global goal, as stated in the Global Immunization Vision and Strategy 2006–2015 by WHO and UNICEF,[4] is to reduce global measles deaths by 90% by 2015 compared to the estimated 733,000 deaths in 2000 (uncertainty bounds: 530,000–959,000).

The WHO Region of the Americas has eliminated measles, and four of the five remaining WHO regions have set measles elimination targets of or before 2020. In the Americas, intensive vaccination and surveillance efforts interrupted endemic measles virus transmission.[5] Progress in reducing measles incidence and mortality in sub-Saharan Africa[6] led to the proposal to eliminate measles in the WHO

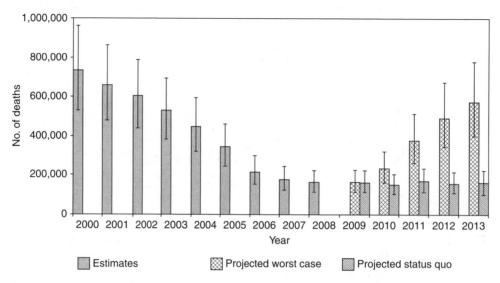

Figure 16-1 Estimated number of measles deaths, 2000–2008, and projections of possible resurgence of measles deaths, 2009–2013. Reproduced from the Centers for Disease Control and Prevention. Global Measles Mortality, 2000–2008. MMWR Weekly December 4, 2009;58(47):1321–1326.

African region by 2020.[7] Ironically, measles remains a public health problem in Europe.[8]

Even if achieved, numerous outbreaks highlight the challenges of sustaining measles elimination. Despite very high levels of measles vaccine coverage and population immunity, clustering of susceptible persons can lead to measles outbreaks.[9] Of greater concern are recent large measles outbreaks in countries of southern and eastern Africa,[10] reflecting the ease with which measles virus can reenter communities and cause large outbreaks if high levels of population immunity are not sustained. WHO projected that the number of measles deaths could reach 1.7 million between 2009 and 2013 if high-risk countries are unable to maintain current recommended strategies for measles control.[3]

Estimating Measles Mortality

Accurate assessment of the number of deaths attributable to measles is important in assessing progress in measles control. In the pre-vaccine era, almost all persons acquired measles, and the number of measles cases could be approximated by the number of births. Deaths due to measles could be estimated by multiplying the number of cases by age-specific case fatality proportions. This relatively simple method of counting measles cases and deaths (assuming the number of births and the case-fatality proportion could be accurately estimated) was no longer of use after the introduction of measles vaccination. More sophisticated methods of estimating measles mortality were needed.

The first obstacle in estimating the global number of measles deaths is defining those deaths attributable to measles. The difficulty arises from the fact that much of measles mortality is delayed until after resolution of the rash and is due to secondary infections that arise as a consequence of the prolonged state of immune suppression. A common method is to attribute a death to measles if it occurs within one month of the onset of rash.

The ideal method for estimating measles mortality is through accurate disease surveillance and registration of deaths. In the absence of accurate disease surveillance, measles mortality models were developed to estimate the global burden of measles and to monitor the progress of control programs. WHO used two different methods to estimate the global burden of measles in 2000.[11] In countries with an estimated measles vaccine coverage of greater than 80% and intensive case-based surveillance, measles incidence was estimated by adjusting the reported number of cases by a factor to correct for underreporting. This correction factor reflects the notification efficiency and was estimated to be between 5% and 40%. For countries with moderate to poor measles control, the number of children immune to measles in each country was estimated by multiplying the number of births, the estimated measles vaccine coverage, and the estimated vaccine effectiveness (the proportion of vaccinated children who develop protective immunity). All remaining susceptible children were assumed to develop measles, thereby providing an estimate of measles incidence. For both methods, the number of measles deaths was determined by multiplying the number of measles cases by a country- and age-specific case-fatality proportion. An advantage of this approach is that adjustments can be made for changes in vaccine coverage. A major weakness is the absence of reliable data to estimate several parameters, particularly the case-fatality proportions.[12]

Using a different approach, the proportion of all mortality caused by measles was derived from community-based studies in those countries with the highest mortality rates for children younger than age 5 years. These studies measured the specific cause of death in children younger than 5 years of age.[13] A meta-regression model was used to relate characteristics of the study population to the proportional mortality outcomes. From this model, the proportional distribution of child deaths by major cause, including measles, was estimated for the selected countries. The number of measles deaths was then calculated by multiplying the total number of deaths in children younger than 5 years of age (approximately 10 million) by the measles-specific proportional mortality. Using this method, measles was estimated to cause 1% of deaths in children younger than 5 years of age (uncertainty bounds: 1%–9%), compared to 5% of deaths as estimated by WHO.[14] These methods highlight the difficulties in accurately estimating measles mortality and in tracking the progress of control programs.[15]

BIOLOGIC CHARACTERISTICS OF THE MEASLES VIRUS

Measles virus is the causative agent of measles and was first isolated from the blood of David Edmonston in 1954 by John Enders and Thomas Peebles.[16] The development of vaccines against measles soon followed. Measles virus is a spherical, nonsegmented, single-stranded, negative-sense RNA virus and a member of the *Morbillivirus* genus in the family of Paramyxoviridae. Other members of the *Morbillivirus* genus, although not pathogenic to humans, are rinderpest virus and canine distemper virus. Rinderpest virus was eradicated in 2011—only the second pathogen eradicated by human intervention—and was the most closely related morbillivirus to measles. Rinderpest was a historically important pathogen of cattle and swine. It was responsible for devastating epidemics resulting in significant famines as animals necessary for feed, as a direct source of meat or milk, and for labor, such

as plowing fields, were killed. Measles was originally a zoonotic infection, arising from cross-species transmission from animals to humans by an ancestor morbillivirus.

Although RNA viruses have high mutation rates, measles virus is considered to be an antigenically monotypic virus, meaning that the surface proteins responsible for inducing protective immunity have retained their antigenic structure across time and space. The public health significance is that measles vaccines developed decades ago from a single measles virus strain remain protective worldwide. The virus is killed by ultraviolet light and heat, and attenuated measles vaccine viruses retain these characteristics, necessitating a cold chain for transporting and storing measles vaccines.

Measles Virus Genes and Proteins

The measles virus RNA genome consists of approximately 16,000 nucleotides and is enclosed in a lipid-containing envelope derived from the host cell. The genome encodes eight proteins, two of which (V and C) are nonstructural proteins that are expressed from the phosphoprotein (P) gene. Of the six structural proteins, P, large protein (L), and nucleoprotein (N) form the nucleocapsid housing the viral RNA. The hemagglutinin protein (H), fusion protein (F), and matrix protein (M), together with lipids from the host cell membrane, form the viral envelope. This relatively simple combination of proteins and ribonucleic acid has evolved to be one of the most highly infectious, directly transmitted agents known, and it remains the cause of millions of deaths.

In the epidemiology and control of measles, the two surface proteins F and H are most important. The H protein interacts with F to mediate fusion of the viral envelope with the host cell membrane.[17] The primary function of the H protein is to bind to the host cellular receptors for measles virus, the best known of which are CD46 and CD150 (SLAM). CD46 is a complement regulatory molecule expressed on all nucleated cells in humans. SLAM—an acronym for signaling lymphocyte activation molecule—is expressed on activated T and B lymphocytes and antigen-presenting cells. The distribution of these host proteins determines the cell types that can be infected by measles virus; in other words, they define the virus's tissue tropism. Wild-type measles virus enters cells primarily through the cellular receptor SLAM, and most vaccine strains bind to CD46, although wild-type measles virus may use both CD46 and SLAM as receptors during acute infection.[18] CD147/EMMPRIN (extracellular matrix metalloproteinase inducer) was recently identified as a measles virus receptor on epithelial cells.[19]

PATHOGENESIS

Respiratory droplets from infected persons transmit infection by carrying measles virus to epithelial cells of the respiratory tract of susceptible hosts. During the 10- to 14-day incubation period between infection and the onset of clinical signs and symptoms, the virus replicates and spreads within the infected host (**Figure 16-2**). Initial viral replication occurs in epithelial cells at the portal of entry in the upper respiratory tract, and the virus then spreads to local lymphatic tissue. Replication in local lymph nodes is followed by viremia (the presence of virus

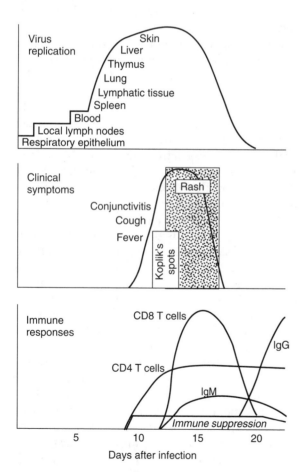

Figure 16-2 Measles virus replication, clinical manifestations and immune responses following infection. Reproduced from Knipe DM et al. Eds. Measles Virus. Fields Virology. 2001. 4th edition. Lippincott Williams and Wilkins.

in the blood) and the dissemination of measles virus to many organs, including lymph nodes, skin, kidney, gastrointestinal tract, and liver, where the virus replicates in epithelial and endothelial cells as well as monocytes and macrophages.

Although measles virus infection is clinically inapparent during the incubation period, the virus is actively replicating and the host immune responses are developing. Evidence of these processes can be detected. During the incubation period, the number of circulating lymphocytes is reduced (lymphopenia). Measles virus can also be isolated from the nasopharynx and blood during the later part of the incubation period and in the several-day prodromal period prior to the onset of rash when levels of viremia are highest. The prodrome ends with the appearance of the measles rash. This rash results from measles virus-specific cellular immune responses and marks the beginning of viral clearance from blood and tissue. Clearance of infectious virus from the blood and other tissues occurs within the first week after the appearance of the rash, although measles virus RNA can be detected in body fluids of some children for at least one month using a polymerase chain reaction (PCR)–based assay.[20]

Immune Responses to Measles Virus

Host immune responses to measles virus are essential for viral clearance, clinical recovery, and the establishment of long-term immunity (Figure 16-2). Early nonspecific (innate) immune responses occur during the prodromal phase of the illness. These innate immune responses contribute to the control of measles virus replication before the onset of more specific (adaptive) immune responses.[21] The adaptive immune responses consist of measles virus-specific humoral (antibody) and cellular responses. The protective efficacy of antibodies to measles virus is illustrated by the immunity conferred to infants from passively acquired maternal antibodies and the protection of exposed, susceptible individuals following administration of anti-measles virus immune globulin.[22]

The first measles virus-specific antibodies produced after infection are immunoglobulin M (IgM) subtype. The IgM antibody response is typically absent following reexposure or revaccination and serves as a marker of primary infection. Immunoglobulin A (IgA) antibodies to measles virus are found in mucosal secretions. The most abundant and most rapidly produced antibodies are against the nucleoprotein (N), and the absence of antibodies to N is the most accurate indicator of seronegativity to measles virus. Although not as abundant, antibodies to H and F proteins contribute to virus neutralization and are sufficient to provide protection against measles virus infection. The H protein elicits strong immune responses, and the lifelong immunity that follows infection is attributed to neutralizing antibodies against H.

Evidence for the importance of cellular immunity to measles virus is demonstrated by the ability of children with agammaglobulinemia (congenital inability to produce antibodies) to fully recover from measles, whereas children with severe defects in T-lymphocyte function often develop severe or fatal disease.[23] CD4+ T lymphocytes are activated in response to measles virus infection and secrete cytokines capable of modulating the humoral and cellular immune responses.[24] The initial predominant Th1 response (characterized by interferon-gamma [IFN-γ]) is essential for viral clearance, and the later Th2 response (characterized by interleukin-4 [IL-4]) promotes the development of measles virus-specific antibodies.

The duration of protective immunity following wild-type measles virus infection is generally thought to be lifelong.[25] The immunologic mechanisms involved in sustaining high levels of neutralizing antibody to measles virus are not completely understood, although general principles of immunologic memory probably govern this process. Immunologic memory to measles virus includes both continued production of measles virus-specific antibodies and the circulation of measles virus-specific CD4+ and CD8+ T lymphocytes.[26] Although immune protection is determined by measurement of anti-measles virus antibodies, long-lasting cellular immune response almost certainly plays an important role in protection from infection. Observations of the measles epidemic on the isolated Faroe Islands in 1846 demonstrated the long-term protective immunity conferred by measles. In this population, measles was reintroduced to the island decades after the last occurrence. Adults exposed earlier were protected despite having no exposure to measles between epidemics. Thus reexposure to measles virus was not necessary to maintain this long-term protection.[27]

Measles vaccine also induces both humoral and cellular immune responses. Antibodies first appear between 12 and 15 days after vaccination and peak at 21 to 28 days. IgM antibodies appear transiently in blood, IgA antibodies are predominant in mucosal secretions, and immunoglobulin G (IgG) antibodies persist in blood for years. Vaccination also induces measles virus-specific T lymphocytes. Although both humoral and cellular responses can be induced by measles vaccine, as is frequently the case with vaccine-induced responses they are of lower magnitude and shorter duration compared to those following wild-type measles virus infection.

Measles Virus-Associated Immune Suppression

The intense immune responses induced by measles virus infection are paradoxically associated with depressed responses to unrelated (non-measles virus) antigens, lasting for several weeks to months beyond resolution of the acute illness.[28] This state of immune suppression enhances susceptibility to secondary bacterial and viral infections causing pneumonia and diarrhea, and is responsible for much of the measles-related morbidity and mortality. Delayed-type hypersensitivity (DTH) responses to recall antigens, such as tuberculin, are suppressed[29] and cellular and humoral responses to new antigens are impaired following measles.[30] Reactivation of tuberculosis and remission of autoimmune diseases have been described and are attributed to this state of immune suppression.

Abnormalities of both the innate and adaptive immune responses have been described following measles virus infection. Transient lymphopenia with a reduction in CD4+ and CD8+ T lymphocytes occurs in children. Functional abnormalities of immune cells have also been detected, including decreased lymphocyte proliferative responses.[31] Dendritic cells—a key antigen-presenting cell—mature poorly, lose the ability to stimulate proliferative responses in lymphocytes, and undergo cell death when infected with measles virus in vitro.[32] The dominant Th2 response in children recovering from measles can inhibit Th1 responses and increase susceptibility to intracellular pathogens.[28] Engagement of CD46 and CD3 on monocytes has been shown to induce production of high levels of IL-10 and transforming growth factor (TGF)-β, an immunomodulatory and immunosuppressive cytokine profile characteristic of regulatory T cells.[33] The role of these cytokines in the immune suppression following measles is supported by in vivo evidence of elevated levels of IL-10 in the plasma of children after measles virus infection.[34]

Clinical Disease and Complications

Clinically apparent measles begins with a prodrome characterized by fever, cough, coryza (runny nose), and conjunctivitis (Figure 16-2). Koplik's spots—small white lesions on the buccal mucosa inside the mouth—may be visible during the prodrome and allow the

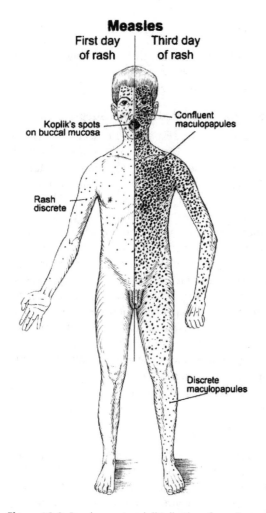

Figure 16-3 Development and distribution of measles rash. Reproduced from Perry RT and Halsey NA. The clinical significance of measles. J Infect Dis 2004;189(Suppl 1):S5. By permission of Oxford University Press.

astute clinician to diagnose measles prior to the onset of rash. The prodromal symptoms intensify several days before the onset of rash. The characteristic erythematous and maculopapular rash appears first on the face and behind the ears, and then spreads in a centrifugal fashion to the trunk and extremities (**Figure 16-3**). The rash lasts for 3 to 4 days and fades in the same manner as it appeared. Malnourished children may develop a deeply pigmented rash that desquamates or peels during recovery.

In uncomplicated measles, clinical recovery begins soon after appearance of the rash. Unfortunately, complications occur in as many as 40% of measles cases, and the risk of complication is increased by extremes of age and malnutrition.[35] Complications of measles have been described in almost every organ system. The respiratory tract is a frequent site of

complication, with pneumonia accounting for most measles-associated deaths.[36] Pneumonia is caused by secondary viral or bacterial infections or by measles virus itself. Pathologically, measles virus infection of the lung is characterized by multinucleated giant cells, which form when measles virus proteins on the cell surface allow cells to fuse. Other respiratory complications include laryngotracheobronchitis (croup) and otitis media (ear infection). Mouth ulcers, or stomatitis, may hinder children from eating or drinking. Many children with measles develop diarrhea, which further contributes to malnutrition. Eye disease (keratoconjunctivitis) is common after measles, particularly in children with vitamin A deficiency, and was a frequent cause of blindness in the past.

Because the rash of measles is a consequence of the cellular immune response, persons with impaired cellular immunity, such as those with acquired immunodeficiency syndrome (AIDS), may not develop the characteristic measles rash. These persons have a high case-fatality rate and frequently develop a giant-cell pneumonitis caused by measles virus. T-lymphocyte defects due to causes other than human immunodeficiency virus (HIV) infection, such as cancer chemotherapy, also are associated with increased severity of measles.

Rare but serious complications of measles involve the central nervous system. Post-measles encephalomyelitis complicates approximately 1 in 1000 cases, mainly in older children and adults. Encephalomyelitis occurs within two weeks of the onset of rash and is characterized by fever, seizures, and a variety of neurologic abnormalities. The finding of periventricular demyelination, the induction of immune responses to myelin basic protein, and the absence of measles virus in the brain suggest that post-measles encephalomyelitis is an autoimmune disorder triggered by measles virus infection.

Other central nervous system complications that occur months to years after acute infection are measles inclusion body encephalitis (MIBE) and subacute sclerosing panencephalitis (SSPE). In contrast to post-measles encephalomyelitis, MIBE and SSPE are caused by persistent measles virus infection. MIBE is a rare but fatal complication that affects individuals with defective cellular immunity; it typically occurs months after infection. SSPE is a slow progressive disease characterized by seizures and progressive deterioration of cognitive and motor functions, followed by death that occurs 5–15 years after measles virus infection. It most often occurs in persons infected with measles virus before 2 years of age.

LABORATORY DIAGNOSIS OF MEASLES

The characteristic clinical features of measles are of sufficient sensitivity and specificity to have high predictive value in regions where measles is endemic. However, laboratory diagnosis is necessary where measles virus transmission rates are low or in immunocompromised persons who might not have the characteristic clinical manifestations. Infection with rubella, parvovirus B19, human herpes virus 6, and dengue viruses may mimic measles. Detection of IgM antibodies to measles virus by enzyme immunoassay (EIA) is the standard method of diagnosing acute measles (Figure 16-2).[37] Alternatively, seroconversion using IgG-specific EIA or virus neutralization assays can be used to diagnose acute measles based on testing serum or plasma obtained during the acute and convalescent phases.

Measles virus can be isolated in tissue culture from white blood cells, respiratory tract secretions and urine, although the ability to isolate measles virus diminishes quickly after rash onset. Amplification and detection of measles virus RNA by reverse transcription–polymerase chain reaction (RT-PCR) from blood, urine, and nasal discharge is highly sensitive in detecting measles virus RNA and allows sequencing of the measles virus genome for molecular epidemiologic studies.

EPIDEMIOLOGIC CHARACTERISTICS

Mode of Transmission

Measles virus is transmitted primarily by respiratory droplets small enough to traverse several feet but too large to remain suspended in the air for long periods of time. The symptoms induced during the prodrome, particularly sneezing and coughing, enhance transmission. Measles virus also may be transmitted by the airborne route, suspended on small particles for a prolonged time. Direct contact with infected secretions can transmit measles virus, but the virus does not survive long on fomites, as it is quickly killed by heat and ultraviolet radiation.

Reservoir

Humans are the only reservoir for measles virus, a crucial fact for the potential eradication of measles. Nonhuman primates may be infected with measles virus and develop an illness similar to measles in humans, with rash, coryza, and conjunctivitis. However, populations of wild monkeys are not of sufficient size to maintain measles virus transmission.

Incubation Period

The incubation period for measles—that is, the time from infection to clinical disease—is approximately 10 days to the onset of fever and 14 days to the onset of rash, with a median of 12.5 days (95% confidence interval: 11.8–13.3 days).[38] The incubation period may be shorter in infants or following a large inoculum of virus, and it may be longer in adults. During this seemingly quiescent period, the virus is rapidly replicating and infecting target tissues as described earlier. The incubation period is best measured during outbreaks in which the time of exposure to the index case can be precisely determined. The first accurate measurement of the incubation period for measles was by the Danish physician Peter Panum during the measles outbreak on the sparsely populated Faroe Islands in 1846.

Infectious Period

The infectious period for measles is more difficult to measure than the incubation period, as it requires careful observation of the contacts of exposed persons prior to the onset of rash. Generally, persons with measles are infectious for several days before and after the onset of rash, when titers of measles virus in the blood and body fluids are highest (Figure 16-2). As with many other acute viral infections (severe acute respiratory syndrome [SARS] coronavirus being a notable exception*), the fact that measles virus is contagious prior to the onset of recognizable disease hinders the effectiveness of quarantine measures. Detection of measles virus in body fluids by a variety of means, including identification of multinucleated giant cells in nasal secretions or the use of RT-PCR, suggests the potential for prolonged infectious periods in persons immunocompromised by severe malnutrition or HIV infection.[20,39] However, whether the measles virus detected by these methods is infectious over this prolonged time is unclear.

Infectivity

Measles virus is one of the most highly contagious infectious agents, and outbreaks can occur in populations in which fewer than 10% of all persons are susceptible. Chains of transmission commonly occur among household contacts, school-age children, and healthcare workers. The contagiousness of measles virus is best expressed by the basic reproductive number R_0, which represents the mean number of secondary cases that arise if an infectious case is introduced into a completely susceptible population.[40] R_0 can be empirically measured, although the introduction of

---

* Patients with SARS coronavirus infection were not infectious until after symptoms developed, greatly aiding efforts to contain the epidemic.

measles virus into a completely susceptible population is rare. In the 1951 measles epidemic in Greenland, the index case attended a community dance during the infectious period resulting in an R_0 of 2000.[41] R_0 may also be estimated from the average age of infection (A), the life expectancy (L), and the duration of protection from maternally acquired antibodies (M) using the following equation:

$$R_0 = (L - M)/(A - M)$$

The estimated R_0 for measles virus is 12–18,[42] compared to only 5–7 for smallpox virus and 2–3 for SARS coronavirus. The high infectivity of the measles virus implies that a high level of population immunity is required to interrupt measles virus transmission, as described later in this chapter. Previously vaccinated children who acquire measles are thought to be less infectious than unvaccinated index cases.

Maternally Acquired Anti-measles Antibodies

Young infants in the first months of life are protected against measles by maternally acquired IgG antibodies. An active transport mechanism in the placenta is responsible for the transfer of IgG antibodies from the maternal circulation to the fetus starting at about 28 weeks' gestation and continuing until birth.[43] Three factors determine the degree and duration of protection in the newborn: (1) the level of maternal anti-measles antibodies; (2) the efficiency of placental transfer; and (3) the rate of catabolism in the child. Although providing passive immunity to young infants, maternally acquired antibodies can interfere with the immune responses to the attenuated measles vaccine by inhibiting replication of vaccine virus. In general, maternally acquired antibodies are no longer present in the majority of children by 9 months of age, the time of routine measles vaccination in many countries. The half-life of maternal anti-measles antibodies was estimated to be 48 days in the United States and Finland, but it is shorter in developing countries. Women with vaccine-induced immunity tend to have lower anti-measles virus antibody concentrations than women with naturally acquired immunity, and their children may be susceptible to measles at an earlier age.[44] Infants born to HIV-infected women may have lower levels of protective maternal antibodies independent of their own HIV infection status and also may be susceptible to measles at a younger age.[45]

Average Age of Infection

The average age of measles virus infection depends on the rate of contact with infected persons, the rate of decline of protective maternal antibodies, and the vaccine coverage rate. Infants in the first few months of life are protected by passively acquired maternal antibodies and measles is rare in this age group.

In densely populated urban settings with low vaccination coverage rates, measles is a disease of young children. The cumulative distribution can reach 50% by 1 year of age, with a significant proportion of children acquiring measles virus infection before 9 months, the age of routine vaccination. As measles vaccine coverage increases or population density decreases, the age distribution shifts toward older children. In such situations, measles cases predominate in school-age children. Infants and younger children, although susceptible if not protected by immunization, are not exposed to measles virus at a rate sufficient to cause a large disease burden in this age group. As vaccination coverage increases further, the age distribution of cases may be shifted into adolescence and young adults, necessitating targeted measles vaccination programs for these older age groups.

GEOGRAPHIC DISTRIBUTION

Measles is a global disease but may have been absent from the Americas prior to contact with Europeans. Measles, in combination with smallpox, likely was responsible for large numbers of deaths of Native Americans, facilitating European conquest.[46] Progress in measles elimination efforts has resulted in the interruption of measles virus transmission in large geographic regions, including the Americas. Because of its mode of transmission and high infectivity, this virus is most readily maintained in densely populated urban settings. Migration of infected persons to rural areas results in outbreaks in susceptible rural populations too small to maintain measles virus transmission. An extreme example occurs in isolated island populations where periodic introduction of measles virus results in widespread but self-limiting outbreaks.

POPULATION SIZE AND MEASLES VIRUS TRANSMISSION

To provide a sufficient number of new susceptibles through births to maintain measles virus transmission, a population size of several hundred thousand persons with 5000 to 10,000 births per year is required.[47] Measles virus is believed to have become established in human populations approximately 5000 to 10,000 years ago when human populations achieved sufficient size in the Middle Eastern river valley civilizations to maintain virus transmission. Measles virus presumably was a zoonotic infection, resulting from the cross-species transmission of an ancestral morbillivirus, likely from domesticated cattle.

Transmission Dynamics

Measles incidence has a typical temporal pattern characterized by yearly seasonal epidemics superimposed upon longer epidemic cycles of 2 to 5 years or more (**Figure 16-4**). These epidemic cycles have been well documented over many decades in different geographic locations and have been characterized analytically in both simple and sophisticated mathematic

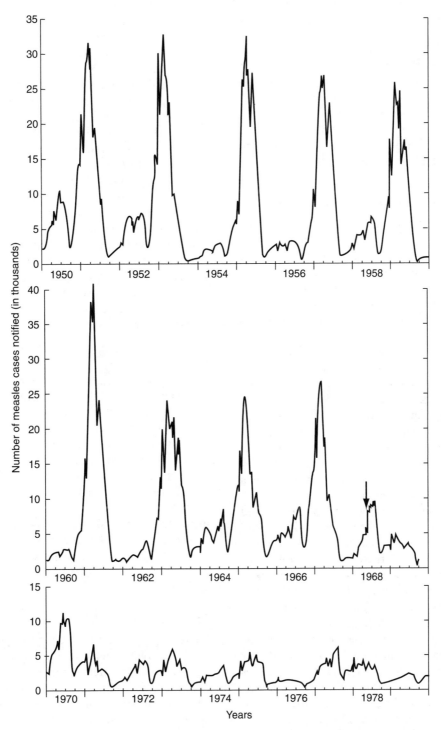

Figure 16-4 Epidemic cycles of measles cases in England and Wales by week, 1950–1979. The arrow indicates the beginning of the national measles vaccination program in 1968. Reproduced from Fine PE and Clarkson JA. Measles in England an Wales – I. An analysis of factors underlying seasonal patterns. *Int J Epidemiol* 1982;11;5–14, by permission of The Oxford University Press.

models. In temperate climates, annual measles outbreaks typically occur in the late winter and early spring. These annual outbreaks are likely the result of social networks facilitating transmission (e.g., congregation of children at school) and environmental factors favoring the viability and transmission of measles virus.[48] Measles cases continue to occur during the interepidemic period in large populations but at low incidence. The longer cycles occurring every several years result from the accumulation of susceptible persons over successive birth cohorts and the subsequent decline in the number of susceptibles following an outbreak. Measles vaccination programs that achieve coverage rates in excess of 80% extend the interepidemic period from the typical 2–5 years to 4–8 years by reducing the number of susceptibles.

Modeling Measles Virus Transmission Dynamics

Because of characteristic epidemic cycles, measles has served as a model for understanding the transmission dynamics of an acute infectious disease and the impact of different vaccination strategies. Mathematic modeling of measles dynamics was first attempted 100 years ago by Sir William Hamer.[49] The basic principle underlying early models was the law of mass action, in which the periodicity of measles incidence was described as a function of the changing number of infectious and susceptible persons as they contact one another. The number of susceptible persons, in turn, was determined by the introduction of new susceptibles through birth and the removal of susceptibles through the acquisition of protective immunity following infection. However, the epidemic cycles generated by these simple deterministic models approached a steady state, losing their periodicity.

The introduction of stochastic (chance) and seasonal processes resulted in models of measles epidemics that closely resembled observed data. Further development of these models allowed for predictions of the impact of vaccination strategies on various epidemiologic characteristics of measles virus transmission, including the increase in the average age of infection and the interepidemic period.[42] More sophisticated models of measles virus transmission dynamics have investigated the role of nonlinear dynamics in temporal and spatial patterns of measles incidence,[50] traveling waves of infection originating in large cities and spreading to small towns,[51] seasonality,[52] and the loss of spatial synchrony in measles epidemics following the introduction of measles vaccination.[53]

MEASLES MORTALITY AND CASE FATALITY

Measles case-fatality proportions vary widely, depending on the average age of infection, nutritional status of the population, measles vaccine coverage, and access to health care.[34] In developed countries, such as the United States, fewer than 1 in 1000 children with measles die. In endemic areas in sub-Saharan Africa, by comparison, the measles case-fatality proportion may be 5%. Measles is a major cause of child deaths in refugee camps and in internally displaced populations. Its case-fatality proportions in children in complex emergencies have been as high as 20% to 30%. During a famine in Ethiopia, measles alone or in combination with wasting accounted for 22% of 159 deaths among children younger than 5 years of age, and 17% of 72 deaths among children aged 5 to 14 years.[54]

The measles case-fatality proportion is highest at extremes of age. Vaccinated children, should they develop disease after exposure, have less severe disease and significantly lower mortality rates. Vaccination programs, by increasing the average age of infection, shift the burden of disease out of the age group with the highest case fatality (infancy), further reducing measles mortality.

Nutritional Status

Measles and malnutrition have important bidirectional interactions. Measles is more severe in malnourished children, although separating the independent effects of nutritional and socioeconomic factors is often difficult. Children with severe malnutrition, such as those with marasmus or kwashiorkor, are at particular risk of death following measles. Measles, in turn, can exacerbate malnutrition by decreasing intake (particularly in children with mouth ulcers), increasing metabolic demands, and enhancing gastrointestinal loss of nutrients as a consequence of a protein-losing enteropathy.[55] Measles in persons with vitamin A deficiency leads to severe keratitis, corneal scarring, and blindness.[56]

Sex Differences

Interestingly, some data suggest that measles mortality may be higher in girls. Among persons of different ages and across different regions, measles mortality in girls was estimated to be 5% higher than in boys.[57] Although older historical data and recent surveillance data from the United States do not support this conclusion,[58] if true, the higher mortality in girls is in contrast to most infectious diseases, in which disease severity and mortality is highest in males. Supporting the hypothesis of biologic differences in the response to measles virus was the observation that girls were more likely than boys to have delayed mortality following receipt of high-titer measles vaccine.[59] The underlying mechanisms are likely differences in immune responses to measles virus between girls and boys, although no cogent theory has been developed.[60]

Host Genetics

All persons without preexisting protective immunity are believed to be susceptible to infection with measles virus, and geographic differences in disease severity and mortality are almost certainly due to environmental and nutritional factors rather than genetic differences. Nevertheless, genetic factors (e.g., genes regulating cytokine production) may explain some of the differences in response to measles virus between individuals. The host genetics underlying immune responses to measles vaccine have been more extensively studied and suggest that polymorphisms in human leukocyte antigen (HLA) genes are associated with differences in antibody responses.[61]

MEASLES VACCINES

Attenuation of measles virus is commonly achieved by serial passage in chick embryo cells. The first attenuated measles vaccine licensed in the United States was called Edmonston B. This vaccine was safe and immunogenic but frequently was associated with fever and rash. The Schwarz and Moraten ("more attenuated Enders") strains were derived from the original Edmonston strain but further attenuated through passage in chick embryo fibroblasts. Despite differences in their passage history, these vaccine strains have identical genomic sequences.[62] The Moraten vaccine (Merck) is the only measles vaccine used in the United States, whereas the Schwarz vaccine is used in many countries throughout the world. Other attenuated measles vaccines have been produced from locally derived wild-type strains, particularly in Russia, China, and Japan. One vaccine strain, the Edmonston-Zagreb vaccine, was passaged in human diploid cells rather than chick embryo fibroblasts, which may be responsible for its increased immunogenicity and reactogenicity. Measles vaccines are relatively heat stable in the lyophilized (dry) form, but rapidly lose potency when exposed to heat after reconstitution.[63]

Measles vaccines are administered by subcutaneous injection, necessitating the availability of needles, syringes, and trained healthcare workers. Proper disposal of used needles and syringes can be a major logistic problem, particularly after mass vaccination campaigns. Autodestruct syringes are widely used in mass measles vaccination campaigns to prevent reuse. Aerosol administration of measles vaccine was first evaluated in the early 1960s in several countries, including the former Soviet Union and the United States. More recent studies have shown that aerosol administration of measles vaccine is highly effective in boosting antibody titers, although the primary immune response to aerosol measles vaccine is lower than following subcutaneous administration.[64] Administration of measles vaccine by aerosol has the potential to greatly facilitate measles vaccination during mass campaigns.

Formalin-Inactivated Measles Vaccine and Atypical Measles

In the 1960s, a formalin-inactivated, alum-precipitated measles vaccine (FIMV) was licensed and administered to children in the United States. Three doses of inactivated vaccine elicited a protective antibody response that waned within months.[65] However, as many as 60% of immunized children exposed to measles developed atypical measles, characterized by high fever, pneumonitis, and a petechial rash on the extremities,[66] leading to withdrawal of the FIMV in 1967.

High-Titer Measles Vaccines

Seroconversion rates with attenuated measles vaccines in young infants are low because of immunologic immaturity and the interference of transplacentally acquired maternal antibodies with replication of vaccine virus.[67] To protect young infants against measles, high-titer preparations containing 10–100 times the standard dose of vaccine virus were evaluated in several countries. Seroconversion rates in 4- to 6-month-old infants immunized with high-titer measles vaccine were comparable to those of 9- to 15-month-old children vaccinated with standard-titer measles vaccine, and the protective antibody response persisted for more than 2 years. Unfortunately, the high-titer measles vaccine resulted in a poorly understood increase in mortality in immunized girls 1 to 2 years after vaccination compared to girls immunized with standard-titer measles vaccine.[68] The increased mortality was attributable to infections such as diarrhea and pneumonia. Although these studies were carried out in countries with different levels of socioeconomic development, excess mortality was observed only in countries with poor socioeconomic conditions and frequent malnutrition (Senegal, Haiti, and Guinea Bissau). The basis for the increased mortality in girls is not understood.

Measures of Protection

Measles vaccine efficacy (VE) under study conditions, or effectiveness under field conditions, is measured as 1 minus a measure of the relative risk in the vaccinated group compared to the unvaccinated group (VE = 1 − RR). A number of field methods and study designs can be used to measure measles vaccine efficacy.[69,70] For example, measles vaccine efficacy can be estimated by measuring the proportion of measles cases occurring in vaccinated persons and the proportion of the population that is vaccinated. Measles vaccine efficacy can then be calculated using the following equation:

$$VE = \frac{PPV - PCV}{PPV - (PCV \times PPV)}$$

where PPV is the proportion of the population that is vaccinated against measles and PCV is the proportion of measles cases that are vaccinated.

Immunologic markers of protective immunity are commonly used to assess measles vaccines. Measurement of antibodies to measles virus by the plaque reduction neutralization assay is best correlated with protection from infection and remains the gold standard for determination of protective antibody

titers. Neutralizing antibody levels of 120 mIU/mL (or 200 mIU/mL depending on the WHO reference serum used) are considered protective following vaccination.[71]

Determinants and Duration of Protection

The proportion of children who develop protective antibody titers following measles vaccination depends on the presence of inhibitory maternal antibodies and the immunologic maturity of the vaccine recipient, as well as the dose and strain of vaccine virus. Frequently cited figures are that approximately 85% of children develop protective antibody titers when given measles vaccine at 9 months of age and 90% to 95% respond when vaccinated at 12 months of age.[72] Concurrent acute infections may interfere with the immune response to measles vaccine, although this effect is probably uncommon.[73] Polymorphisms in human immune response genes also determine immune responses to measles vaccine.[61]

The duration of immunity following measles vaccination is more variable and shorter than following wild-type measles virus infection, with an estimated 5% of children developing secondary vaccine failure at 10 to 15 years after vaccination.[74]

Optimal Age of Vaccination

The optimal age of measles vaccination is determined by consideration of the age-dependent increase in seroconversion following measles vaccination and the average age of infection (**Figure 16-5**). In regions

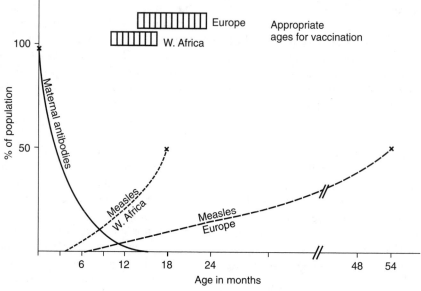

Figure 16-5 Estimation of the optimal age of measles vaccination based on the rate of loss of maternal antibodies and the age of measles virus infection. Reproduced from Walsh JA. Selective primary health care: Strategies for control of disease in the developing world. IV Measles. *Rev Infect Dis* 1983;5: 330–340. Page 336, Figure 3.

of intense measles virus transmission, the average age of infection is low and the optimal strategy is to vaccinate against measles as young as possible. However, both maternally acquired antibodies and immunologic immaturity reduce the protective efficacy of measles vaccination in early infancy. In many parts of the world, 9 months is considered the optimal age of measles vaccination and is the age recommended by the Expanded Program on Immunization (EPI). Most countries following the EPI schedule administer measles vaccine alone, although more countries are introducing combined measles and rubella vaccines as rubella control programs expand.

In communities with intense measles virus transmission, a significant proportion of children may acquire measles before 9 months of age. Under some circumstances, provision of an early dose of measles vaccine at 6 months of age (e.g., in outbreaks or to HIV-infected children) is appropriate. In contrast, in regions that have achieved measles control or elimination, and where the risk of measles in infants is low, the age of measles vaccination is increased to ensure that a higher proportion of children develop protective immunity. For example, in the United States the first dose of measles vaccine is administered at 12–15 months of age, as a combined measles, mumps, and rubella (MMR) vaccine.

Adverse Events Associated with Measles Vaccine

Fever occurs in approximately 5% to 15% of recipients 6 to 12 days following measles vaccination, and a rash occurs in approximately 5% of recipients. These signs and symptoms are a consequence of the host immune response to replicating measles vaccine virus but do not result in serious morbidity or mortality. Rarely, thrombocytopenia (low platelets) may occur.

Although assumed to be rare, the risk of disease caused by attenuated measles vaccine virus in HIV-infected persons is unknown.[75] The only documented case of disease induced by vaccine virus in an HIV-infected person was in a 20-year-old man who died 15 months after receiving his second dose of measles vaccine.[76] He had a very low CD4+ T-lymphocyte cell count but no HIV-related symptoms at the time of vaccination. Ten months later he developed a giant-cell pneumonitis, and measles vaccine virus was identified in his lung. Fatal, disseminated infection with measles vaccine virus has been reported rarely in persons with other impairments of immune function.

Much public attention has focused on a purported association between the MMR vaccine and autism since the publication of a report in 1998 hypothesizing that this vaccine might cause a syndrome of autism and intestinal inflammation. The events that followed, and the public concern over the safety of MMR vaccine, led to diminished vaccine coverage in the United Kingdom and provide important lessons in the misinterpretation of epidemiologic evidence and the communication of scientific results to the public.[77] Several comprehensive reviews and additional epidemiologic studies rejected evidence of a causal relationship between MMR vaccination and autism.[78] One of the most conclusive studies was a large retrospective cohort study of more than 500,000 Danish children that found the relative risk of MMR vaccine to be 0.92 (95% confidence interval: 0.68–1.24) for autistic disorder.[79] Subsequently, the original research that falsely linked MMR to autism was found to be fraudulent and *The Lancet* renounced the article.

MEASLES CONTROL, ELIMINATION, AND ERADICATION

Different goals for measles control have been established, necessitating different vaccination strategies. Three broad goals can be defined: mortality reduction, regional elimination, and global eradication.

Mortality Reduction

Mortality reduction—the least demanding of the three goals—calls for a reduction in measles mortality from a predetermined level through reductions in incidence, case fatality, or both. Although a reduction in case-fatality rates through appropriate case management (discussed later in this chapter) is an important component, measles mortality reduction is achieved largely through a reduction in incidence. To reduce incidence, measles vaccine is administered as a single dose through routine immunization services in child health clinics, with the optimal age of immunization determined by the transmission intensity and rate of decline of maternal antibodies. The EPI recommends a single dose of measles vaccine at 9 months of age. If vaccination coverage is sufficiently high, substantial reductions in incidence and mortality occur, the interepidemic period lengthens, and the age distribution shifts toward older children, further contributing to a reduction in case fatality.

Regional Elimination

Measles elimination is the interruption of measles virus transmission within a defined geographic area, such as a country, continent, or WHO region. Small outbreaks of primary and secondary cases may still occur following importation from outside the region, but sustained transmission does not occur. Because of the high infectivity of measles virus and the fact that not all persons develop protective immunity following vaccination, a single dose of measles vaccine does not achieve a sufficient level of population immunity to eliminate measles. A second dose of measles vaccine is necessary to eliminate measles by providing protective immunity to children who failed to respond to the first dose and to those who were not previously vaccinated.

Two broad strategies to administer the second dose have been used. In countries with sufficient infrastructure, the second dose of measles vaccine is administered through routine immunization services, typically prior to the start of school (4–6 years of age). High coverage levels are ensured by school entry requirements. A second approach, first developed by the Pan American Health Organization (PAHO) for South and Central America,[80] involves mass immunization campaigns (called supplementary immunization activities [SIA]) to deliver the second dose of measles vaccine. This strategy was successful in eliminating measles in South and Central America and has resulted in a marked reduction in measles incidence and mortality in parts of sub-Saharan Africa.[32]

The PAHO strategy consists of four subprograms: catch-up, keep-up, follow-up, and mop-up (**Figure 16-6**).[80] The *catch-up* phase is a one-time, mass immunization campaign that targets all children within a broad age group regardless of whether they have previously had wild-type measles virus infection or measles vaccination. The goal is to rapidly achieve a high level of population immunity and interrupt measles virus transmission. These campaigns are conducted over a short period of time, usually over several weeks, and during a low transmission season.

Under the PAHO strategy, children 9 months to 14 years of age are targeted for vaccination. In many countries, this age group represents a substantial proportion of the total population. The appropriate target age range depends on the age distribution of measles seropositivity. In regions endemic for measles, the vast majority of older children are likely to be immune. Nevertheless, seroprevalence studies usually are not conducted prior to catch-up campaigns, and this broad age range first adopted by PAHO has been widely used in sub-Saharan Africa. These campaigns require large investments of financial resources and personnel; extensive logistical planning to transport and store vaccines, maintain cold chains, and dispose of syringes and needles; and community mobilization to ensure participation. If they are successful, however, supplementary immunization activities are cost-effective and can abruptly interrupt measles virus transmission, with dramatic declines in incidence and mortality being observed.[81]

Keep-up refers to the need to maintain greater than 90% routine measles vaccine coverage through improved access to measles vaccination and a reduction in missed opportunities (e.g., because of a belief in false contraindications to vaccination). *Follow-up* refers to periodic mass campaigns to prevent the accumulation of susceptible children. Follow-up campaigns typically target children 1 to 4 years of age, a narrower age group than targeted in catch-up campaigns. Follow-up campaigns should be conducted when the estimated number of susceptible children reaches the size of one birth cohort, generally every 3 to 5 years after the catch-up campaign. *Mop-up*

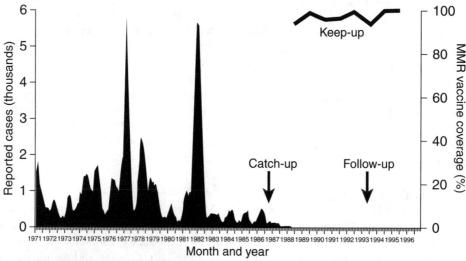

Note: Measles cases reported through 31 December 1996.

Figure 16-6 Impact of Catch-Up, Keep-Up and Follow-Up measles vaccination campaigns on measles incidence in Cuba. Reproduced from the Pan American Health Organization. Measles Eradication Field Guide. Technical Paper No. 41. Washington DC, 1999, Figure 1, page 2.

campaigns target difficult-to-reach children in sites of measles outbreaks or low vaccine coverage, including those living on the street or in areas of conflict.

Two doses of measles vaccine are recommended in two situations apart from an elimination strategy. In communities where measles occurs in a significant proportion of children younger than 9 months of age, measles vaccine should be administered at 6 months of age and a repeat dose given at 9 months of age. Such a situation may arise in a refugee camp or densely populated urban slum area with intense measles virus transmission. Two doses of measles vaccine also are recommended for HIV-infected children. Although there are limited data at present to support this recommendation, HIV-infected children are at risk of severe and fatal measles and likely are less immunocompromised at 6 months of age than later. However, in much of sub-Saharan Africa where HIV prevalence rates are highest, most HIV-infected children are not diagnosed until later in life, when they present with severe illness. This may change with increased access to HIV diagnostic testing and antiretroviral drugs.

Global Eradication

Eradication refers to the global interruption of transmission of an infectious agent. The pathogen need not be extinct (e.g., laboratory isolates of smallpox exist), but human infection and disease have ceased. Following eradication, control efforts such as vaccination programs and disease surveillance can cease.

The possibility of measles eradication has been discussed for almost 40 years.[82] Serious discussion of measles eradication began in the late 1960s as smallpox eradication was nearing completion and the effective, long-term immunity induced by measles vaccine became apparent. Measles virus meets many of the biologic criteria for disease eradication.[83] The virus has no nonhuman reservoir, the infection is accurately diagnosed, and measles vaccination is a highly effective intervention. Although measles virus displays sufficient genetic variability to conduct molecular epidemiologic analyses, the antigenic epitopes against which protective antibodies develop have remained stable. In this sense, measles virus is a monotypic virus: vaccines derived from a measles virus isolate from the United States in the 1950s remain protective across space and time. The reason measles virus has not mutated significantly is not fully known, but presumably the antigenic epitopes that confer protective immunity are critical to viral entry and replication.[84] Where measles virus differs from smallpox and polio viruses is that it is more highly infectious, necessitating much higher levels of population immunity to interrupt transmission.

The vaccination strategy necessary for measles eradication is not different from that of elimination, except that the target population is global. The success of measles elimination in large geographic regions suggests that measles eradication is possible. Two doses of measles vaccine, administered through routine immunization services or via supplementary immunization activities, would need to be administered to the children of the world. Many believe this to be a realistic and morally imperative goal,[85,86] but, as polio eradication efforts have shown, the endgame may be full of challenges.

Case Management

Although the most important strategy to reduce the number of measles deaths is primary prevention through vaccination, secondary prevention of deaths is also important. No specific antiviral drug is used routinely to treat measles virus infection, although the broad antiviral agent ribavirin has been used to treat immunocompromised persons or persons with SSPE, alone or in combination with interferon-γ or intravenous immunoglobulin.[87,88] Intravenous immunoglobulin also has been used to prevent severe measles in high-risk individuals following exposure, but as with ribavirin, this agent's high cost precludes its use in most regions where measles is endemic.

The major components of case management include provision of vitamin A, prompt treatment of secondary bacterial infections, and nutritional support. Several placebo-controlled trials have demonstrated marked reductions in morbidity and mortality in hospitalized children with measles treated with vitamin A.[89] WHO recommends administration of two daily doses of 200,000 IU of vitamin A to all children with measles 12 months of age or older. Lower doses (100,000 IU) are recommended for children less than 12 months of age. Overall, this regimen results in a 64% reduction in the risk of mortality (RR = 0.36; 95% CI: 0.14–0.82).[90] Pneumonia-specific mortality is reduced, and the impact is greatest in children younger than 2 years of age. The mechanisms by which vitamin A reduces measles morbidity and mortality are not known, but likely these effects are mediated through beneficial effects on epithelial cells and host immune responses.

Secondary bacterial infections are a major cause of morbidity and mortality following measles, and effective case management involves prompt treatment with antibiotics. Various strategies have been used to guide antibiotic therapy in children with measles.[91] Antibiotics are indicated for children with measles who have clinical evidence of bacterial infection, including pneumonia, otitis media, skin infection, eye infection, or severe mouth ulcers. Whether all children with measles, or all hospitalized children with measles, should be given prophylactic antibiotics remains controversial. Limited evidence suggests that antibiotics administered as prophylaxis to all children presenting with measles may reduce the incidence of pneumonia but not mortality.[22] The potential benefits of antibiotic prophylaxis need to be weighed against the risks of accelerating antibiotic resistance.

Vitamin A Prophylaxis

Vitamin A has been widely distributed through polio and measles SIAs as well as through routine child health services. Pooled analysis of community-based studies of vitamin A supplementation of apparently healthy children resulted in a 39% reduction in measles-associated mortality.[92] Thus vitamin A is not only effective in reducing mortality when used to treat hospitalized children with measles, but community-based supplementation programs can result in measles mortality reduction.

Surveillance and Outbreak Investigation

Disease surveillance is an important component of measles elimination programs, providing estimates of measles incidence and mortality, the effectiveness of the control program, and information to support targeted interventions.[37] Case-based surveillance with laboratory confirmation of suspected cases should be the gold standard. Not all suspected cases in an outbreak need to be laboratory confirmed if they can be epidemiologically linked to a confirmed case. As the incidence of measles declines, other viral causes of fever and rash may be mistaken for measles. Many surveillance programs test specimens for rubella virus-specific IgM antibodies. Although confirmation typically requires detection of anti-measles virus IgM antibodies in plasma or serum, less invasive specimen collection methods, including oral fluid swabs and dried blood spots collected on filter paper, may be more acceptable to patients.[23]

Molecular Epidemiology

Although measles virus is considered to be monotypic, variability within the genome is sufficient to allow for molecular epidemiologic investigation. Genetic characterization of wild-type measles viruses is based on sequence analysis of the genes coding for the N and H proteins.[93] One of the most variable regions of the measles virus genome is the 450-nucleotide sequence at the carboxy-terminal of the N protein, with as much as 12% variability being observed between wild-type viruses. WHO recognizes eight clades of measles virus (designated A through H) and 23 genotypes (**Figure 16-7**). New genotypes will be identified with enhanced surveillance and molecular characterization. As measles control efforts intensify, molecular surveillance of circulating measles virus strains can be used to document interruption of measles virus transmission and to identify the source and transmission pathways of measles virus outbreaks.

Obstacles to Measles Control and Prospects for Eradication

> The build-up of susceptible children over time in a population is the most serious obstacle to measles eradication.
> —*PAHO Measles Eradication Field Guide*[80]

Herd Immunity Threshold

Interruption of measles virus transmission does not require that all persons be immunized and protected. If a sufficient proportion of the population is immune, the chance that an unprotected person will encounter an infectious individual is reduced to almost zero. Protection of unvaccinated persons by a reduction in the risk of exposure is referred to as herd immunity,[94,95] and the level of population immunity necessary to interrupt transmission is known as the herd immunity threshold (H). The herd immunity threshold can be derived using analytical models of infectious disease dynamics from the following equation:

$$H = 1 - 1/R_0$$

where R_0 is the basic reproductive number.[42] A number of assumptions are made in deriving this formula, including the unrealistic assumption of homogenous mixing of the population (i.e., an individual has an equal chance of coming into contact with any other individual). Nevertheless, this simple equation provides a means of assessing the level of population immunity required to interrupt transmission based on a measure of infectivity (R_0). For measles, with a R_0 of 12–18, the herd immunity threshold is 93% to 95%. This does not represent vaccine coverage but rather the proportion of the population protected against measles. As noted earlier, this level of population immunity cannot be achieved with a single dose of measles vaccine for which the primary vaccine failure rate is approximately 15% when administered at 9 months of age. In contrast, for smallpox and polio viruses, each with a R_0 of 5–7, the herd immunity threshold is estimated to be 80% to 85%. Clearly, much higher levels of population immunity

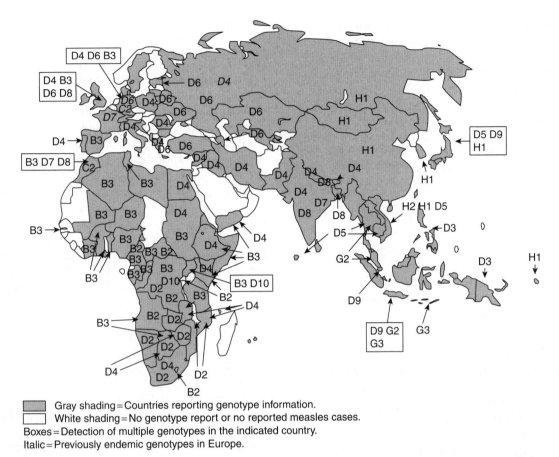

Figure 16-7 Distribution of measles virus genotypes associated with endemic transmission. Reproduced from Rota P, Bellini WJ. Update on the Global Distribution of Genotypes of Wild Type Measles Viruses. *Journal of Infectious Diseases* 2003;187(Suppl 1): S274, Figure 2. By permission of Oxford University Press.

are required to interrupt transmission of measles virus than for smallpox or polio virus.

Measles Outbreaks in Highly Vaccinated Populations

Measles outbreaks have been reported in populations with high vaccine coverage, demonstrating the highly contagious nature of measles and the inability of a single dose of vaccine to provide sufficient levels of population immunity to prevent measles virus transmission. Furthermore, in several carefully investigated measles outbreaks in highly vaccinated persons, mild or asymptomatic measles virus infection was demonstrated by a boosting of anti-measles virus antibodies in vaccinated persons—evidence that prior immunity can prevent disease manifestations but not necessarily infection. How infectious such asymptomatic cases are remains unclear.

Failure to Vaccinate

The most important reason for not achieving high levels of population immunity is the failure to vaccinate

susceptible persons.[96] Underlying this failure are several causes, including insufficient resources, lack of political will, populations who are difficult to reach (e.g., street children, nomadic persons), fear of real or perceived adverse events, and religious or philosophical objections to vaccination.

The problem of limited resources remains an important one for many countries with a high burden of disease caused by measles, particularly in parts of sub-Saharan Africa. Many of these countries have high child and adult mortality rates, and are attempting to deal with epidemics of tuberculosis, HIV, and malaria in addition to the common causes of child mortality from pneumonia, diarrhea, and undernutrition. However, efforts to generate funds for measles control have been successful. By 2005, the Africa Measles Initiative, led by the American Red Cross, Centers for Disease Control and Prevention, UNICEF, WHO, and the United Nations Foundation, had mobilized resources for African countries to reduce measles mortality and vaccinate millions of children against measles.

The political commitment to control measles is high in much of sub-Saharan Africa and Asia, where measles is known to be a major cause of child mortality, but low in some industrialized countries, including Japan, Italy, France, and Germany, where measles vaccine coverage is low. Measles eradication requires the full political commitment of all countries.

Following the public scare surrounding the alleged association between MMR vaccine and autism, measles vaccine coverage in the United Kingdom declined. The decline in measles vaccine coverage coincided with several large measles outbreaks and the potential for the basic reproductive number to exceed 1 and the reestablishment of endemic measles.[97] Measles outbreaks have been reported in religious communities with low vaccine coverage,[98] further highlighting the ability of measles virus to cause disease and death in pockets of susceptible persons.

Vaccine Failure

A less common cause for not achieving high levels of population immunity is vaccine failure. As noted earlier, primary vaccine failure occurs in approximately 15% of children vaccinated at 9 months of age and 5% to 10% of children vaccinated at 1 year of age.[99] Improper administration of measles vaccine and loss of immunogenicity because of inadequate storage are less common causes of measles vaccine failure. It is important to recognize that as measles vaccine coverage increases, the proportion of cases in vaccinated children also increases. This relationship is sometimes misinterpreted as demonstrating a loss of vaccine potency (e.g., because of inadequate vaccine storage), but merely reflects the fact that with sufficiently high vaccination coverage rates, a greater proportion of cases will occur in children who did not respond to the first dose of measles vaccine than in children who were never vaccinated.

Subclinical Measles

Subclinical measles is defined as a fourfold rise in measles virus-specific IgG antibodies following exposure to wild-type measles virus in an asymptomatic individual with some prior measles immunity. Subclinical infection may be important in boosting protective antibody levels in children with waning immunity,[100] but it raises the concern that persons with incomplete immunity and subclinical infection might be capable of transmitting measles virus. Whether partially immune individuals with subclinical infection can sustain measles virus transmission is unknown.

HIV Epidemic

In regions of high HIV prevalence and crowding, such as urban centers in sub-Saharan Africa, HIV-infected children could play a role in the sustained transmission of measles virus.[101] HIV-infected mothers may have defective transfer of IgG antibody across the placenta, resulting in lower titers of protective antibodies in the infant and enlarging the period of susceptibility to measles virus infection prior to routine immunization. HIV-infected children may not have an adequate primary response to measles immunization and may lose immunity with progressive immunosuppression, so that they remain susceptible to measles virus despite immunization.[75] Children with defective cell-mediated immunity may not develop the characteristic measles rash, and infection may go unrecognized, with the potential for widespread transmission of measles virus, particularly in healthcare settings. Finally, HIV-infected children may have prolonged shedding of measles virus,[6] increasing their period of infectivity and the spread of measles virus to secondary contacts. Counteracting the increased susceptibility of HIV-infected children to measles is the high mortality rate, particularly in sub-Saharan Africa, such that these children do not live long enough to build up a sizeable pool of susceptible children.[102] This may change with increased access to antiretroviral drugs, such that HIV-infected children receiving antiretroviral therapy may need to be revaccinated against measles.[103,104]

New Tools for Measles Eradication

The ideal measles vaccine would be inexpensive, safe, heat-stable, immunogenic in neonates or very young infants, and administered as a single dose without needle or syringe.[105] The age at vaccination should coincide with the EPI schedule to maximize compliance and share resources. Finally, a new vaccine should not elicit atypical measles upon exposure of immunized individuals to wild-type measles virus and should not be associated with prolonged immunosuppression, adversely affecting immune responses to subsequent infections.

A number of vaccine candidates with some of these characteristics are undergoing preclinical studies. Naked cDNA vaccines are thermostable, are inexpensive, and could theoretically elicit antibody responses in the presence of passively acquired maternal antibody. DNA vaccines encoding either or both the measles hemagglutinin and fusion proteins are safe, immunogenic, and protective against measles challenge in naive, juvenile rhesus macaques.[106] Dry-powder delivery of live, attenuated measles vaccine was also effective in a macaque model.[107] Alternative techniques for administering measles DNA, such as alphavirus, parainfluenza virus, or enteric bacterial vectors, also are under investigation.

CONCLUSION

The elimination of measles in large geographic areas, such as the Americas, suggests that global eradication of this disease is feasible with current vaccination strategies. Potential barriers to eradication include (1) lack of political will; (2) difficulties of measles control in densely populated urban environments; (3) the HIV epidemic; (4) waning immunity and the potential transmission from subclinical cases; (5) transmission among susceptible adults; (6) the risk of unsafe injections; and (7) unfounded fears of disease caused by measles vaccine.[83,96] Whether the threat from bioterrorism precludes stopping measles vaccination after eradication is a topic of debate, but, at the least, a single-dose rather than a two-dose measles vaccination strategy could be adopted. Serious discussion of measles eradication likely will take place after polio eradication is achieved and will be a focus of infectious disease epidemiologists in the years to come.

ACKNOWLEDGMENTS

We thank Dr. Diane E. Griffin for helpful comments on the first edition of this chapter.

• • • REFERENCES

1. Maxcy KF. Epidemiology. In: Rivers TM, ed. *Viral and Rickettsial Infections of Man.* Philadelphia: Lippincott; 1948:128–146.

2. Wolfson LJ, Strebel PM, Gacic-Dobo M, et al. Has the 2005 measles mortality reduction goal been achieved? A natural history modelling study. *Lancet* 2007;369:191–200.

3. World Health Organization. Global reductions in measles mortality 2000–2008 and the risk of measles resurgence. *Weekly Epidemiol Rec* 2009;84:509–516.

4. World Health Organization, United Nations Children's Fund. *Global Immunization Vision and Strategy 2006–2015.* Geneva, Switzerland: Author; 2005.

5. de Quadros CA, Andrus JK, Danovaro-Holliday MC, Castillo-Solorzano C. Feasibility of global measles eradication after interruption of transmission in the Americas. *Expert Rev Vaccines* 2008;7:355–362.

6. Centers for Disease Control and Prevention. Progress toward measles control: African region, 2001–2008. *Morb Mortal Wkly Rep* 2009;58:1036–1041.

7. World Health Organization, Regional Committee for Africa. *Towards the Elimination of Measles in the African Region by 2020: Report of the Regional Director.* 2009.

8. Muscat M, Bang H, Wohlfahrt J, et al. Measles in Europe: an epidemiological assessment. *Lancet* 2009;373:383–389.

9. Parker AA, Staggs W, Dayan GH et al. Implications of a 2005 measles outbreak in Indiana for sustained elimination of measles in the United States. *N Engl J Med* 2006;355:447–455.

10. World Health Organization. Measles outbreaks and progress towards meeting measles pre-elimination goals: WHO African Region, 2009–2010. *Wkly Epidemiol Rec* 2011;86:129–136.

11. Stein CE, Birmingham M, Kurian M, et al. The global burden of measles in the year 2000: a model that uses country-specific indicators. *J Infect Dis* 2003;187(suppl 1):S8–S14.

12. Wolfson LJ, Grais RF, Luquero FJ, et al. Estimates of measles case fatality ratios: a comprehensive review of community-based studies. *Int J Epidemiol* 2009;38:192–205.

13. Morris SS, Black RE, Tomaskovic L. Predicting the distribution of under-five deaths by cause in countries without adequate vital registration systems. *Int J Epidemiol* 2003;32(6):1041–1051.

14. Black RE, Morris SS, Bryce J. Where and why are 10 million children dying every year? *Lancet* 2003;361:2226–2234.

15. World Health Organization. Monitoring progress towards measles elimination. Weekly Epidemiol Rec 2010; 85:490–495.

16. Enders JF, Peebles TC. Propagation in tissue cultures of cytopathic agents from patients with measles. *Proc Soc Exp Biol Med* 1954;86:277–286.

17. Hashiguchi T, Ose T, Kubota M, et al. Structure of the measles virus hemagglutinin bound to its cellular receptor SLAM. *Nat Struct Mol Biol* 2011;18:135–141.

18. Schneider U, von Messling V, Devaux P, Cattaneo R. Efficiency of measles virus entry and dissemination through different receptors. *J Virol* 2002;76:7460–7467.

19. Watanabe A, Yoneda M, Ikeda F, et al. CD147/EMMPRIN acts as a functional entry receptor for measles virus on epithelial cells. *J Virol* 2010;84:4183–4193.

20. Permar SR, Moss WJ, Ryon JJ, et al. Prolonged measles virus shedding in human immunodeficiency virus-infected children, detected by reverse transcriptase–polymerase chain reaction. *J Infect Dis* 2001;183:532–538.

21. Hahm B. Hostile communication of measles virus with host innate immunity and dendritic cells. *Curr Top Microbiol Immunol* 2009;330:271–287.

22. Black FL, Yannet H. Inapparent measles after gamma globulin administration. *JAMA* 1960;173:1183–1188.

23. Good RA, Zak SJ. Disturbances in gamma globulin synthesis as "experiments of nature." *Pediatrics* 1956;18:109–149.

24. Naniche D. Human immunology of measles virus infection. *Curr Top Microbiol Immunol* 2009;330:151–171.

25. Amanna IJ, Carlson NE, Slifka MK. Duration of humoral immunity to common viral and vaccine antigens. *N Engl J Med* 2007;357:1903–1915.

26. Walker JM, Slifka MK. Longevity of T-cell memory following acute viral infection. *Adv Exp Med Biol* 2010;684:96–107.

27. Panum PL. *Observations Made During the Epidemic Of Measles on the Faroe Islands in the Year 1846.* New York: Delta Omega Society; 1940.

28. Griffin DE. Measles virus-induced suppression of immune responses. *Immunol Rev* 2010;236:176–189.

29. Tamashiro VG, Perez HH, Griffin DE. Prospective study of the magnitude and duration of changes in tuberculin reactivity during uncomplicated and complicated measles. *Pediatr Infect Dis J* 1987;6:451–454.

30. Coovadia HM, Wesley A, Henderson LG, et al. Alterations in immune responsiveness in acute measles and chronic post-measles chest disease. *Int Arch Allergy Appl Immunol* 1978;56:14–23.

31. Hirsch RL, Griffin DE, Johnson RT, et al. Cellular immune responses during complicated and uncomplicated measles virus infections of man. *Clin Immunol Immunopathol* 1984;31:1–12.

32. Schneider-Schaulies S, Schneider-Schaulies J. Measles virus-induced immunosuppression. *Curr Top Microbiol Immunol* 2009;330:243–269.

33. Kemper C, Chan AC, Green JM, et al. Activation of human CD4+ cells with CD3 and CD46 induces a T-regulatory cell 1 phenotype. *Nature* 2003;421:388–392.

34. Moss WJ, Ryon JJ, Monze M, Griffin DE. Differential regulation of interleukin (IL)-4, IL-5, and IL-10 during measles in Zambian children. *J Infect Dis* 2002;186:879–887.

35. Morley D. Severe measles in the tropics. *Brit Med J* 1969;1:297–300.

36. Duke T, Mgone CS. Measles: not just another viral exanthem. *Lancet* 2003;361:763–773.

37. Bellini WJ, Helfand RF. The challenges and strategies for laboratory diagnosis of measles in an international setting. *J Infect Dis* 2003;187(suppl 1):S283–S290.

38. Lessler J, Reich NG, Brookmeyer R, et al. Incubation periods of acute respiratory viral infections: a systematic review. *Lancet Infect Dis* 2009;9:291–300.

39. Dossetor J, Whittle HC, Greenwood BM. Persistent measles infection in malnourished children. *BMJ* 1977;1:1633–1635.

40. Gay NJ. The theory of measles elimination: implications for the design of elimination strategies. *J Infect Dis* 2004;189(suppl 1): S27–S35.

41. Christensen PE, Schmidt H, Bang HO, et al. An epidemic of measles in southern Greenland, 1951. Measles in virgin soil. II. The epidemic proper. *Acta Med Scand* 1953;144:430–449.

42. Anderson RM, May RM. *Infectious Diseases of Humans. Dynamics and Control.* Oxford, UK: Oxford University Press; 1992.

43. Crowe JE Jr. Influence of maternal antibodies on neonatal immunization against respiratory viruses. *Clin Infect Dis* 2001;33(10): 1720–1727.

44. Gagneur A, Pinquier D. Early waning of maternal measles antibodies: why immunization programs should be adapted over time. *Expert Rev Anti Infect Ther* 2010;8:1339–1343.

45. Scott S, Moss WJ, Cousens S, et al. The influence of HIV-1 exposure and infection on levels of passively acquired antibodies to measles virus in Zambian infants. *Clin Infect Dis* 2007;45:1417–1424.

46. McNeill WH. *Plagues and Peoples.* London: Penguin; 1976.

47. Black FL. Measles endemicity in insular populations: critical community size and its evolutionary implication. *J Theor Biol* 1966;11:207–211.

48. Fine PE, Clarkson JA. Measles in England and Wales. I: An analysis of factors underlying seasonal patterns. *Int J Epidemiol* 1982;11:5–14.

49. Hamer WH. The Milroy lectures on epidemic disease in England: The evidence of variability and persistence of type. *Lancet* 1906;1:733–739.

50. Earn DJ, Rohani P, Bolker BM, Grenfell BT. A simple model for complex dynamical transitions in epidemics. *Science* 2000;287(5453):667–670.

51. Grenfell BT, Bjornstad ON, Kappey J. Travelling waves and spatial hierarchies in measles epidemics. *Nature* 2001;414(6865):716–723.

52. Ferrari MJ, Grais RF, Bharti N, et al. The dynamics of measles in sub-Saharan Africa. *Nature* 2008;451:679–684.

53. Rohani P, Earn DJ, Grenfell BT. Opposite patterns of synchrony in sympatric disease metapopulations. *Science* 1999;286(5441):968–971.

54. Salama P, Assefa F, Talley L, et al. Malnutrition, measles, mortality, and the humanitarian response during a famine in Ethiopia. *JAMA* 2001;286:563–571.

55. Dossetor JF, Whittle HC. Protein-losing enteropathy and malabsorption in acute measles enteritis. *Br Med J* 1975;2(5971):592–593.

56. Semba RD, Bloem MW. Measles blindness. *Surv Ophthalmol* 2004;49:243–255.

57. Garenne M. Sex differences in measles mortality: a world review. *Int J Epidemiol* 1994;23:632–642.

58. Perry RT, Halsey NA. The clinical significance of measles: a review. *J Infect Dis* 2004;189(suppl 1):S4–S16.

59. Halsey NA. Increased mortality after high-titre measles vaccines: too much of a good thing. *Pediatr Infect Dis J* 1993;12:462–465.

60. Brown AC, Moss WJ. Sex, pregnancy and measles. In: Klein SL, Roberts C, eds. *Sex Hormones and Immunity to Infection.* Berlin/ Heidelberg: Springer-Verlag; 2010: Chapter 11, pages 281–302.

61. Poland GA, Ovsyannikova IG, Jacobson RM. Vaccine immunogenetics: bedside to bench to population. *Vaccine* 2008;26:6183–6188.

62. Parks CL, Lerch RA, Walpita P, et al. Comparison of predicted amino acid sequences of measles virus strains in the Edmonston vaccine lineage. *J Virol* 2001;75:910–920.

63. World Health Organization. Measles vaccines. *Weekly Epidemiol Rec* 2009;84:349–360.

64. Low N, Kraemer S, Schneider M, Restrepo AM. Immunogenicity and safety of aerosolized measles vaccine: systematic review and meta-analysis. *Vaccine* 2008;26:383–398.

65. Carter CH, Conway TJ, Cornfeld D, et al. Serologic response of children to inactivated measles vaccine. *JAMA* 1962;179:848–853.

66. Fulginiti VA, Eller JJ, Downie AW, Kempe CH. Altered reactivity to measles virus: atypical measles in children previously immunized with inactivated measles virus vaccines. *JAMA* 1967;202:1075–1080.

67. Gans HA, Arvin AM, Galinus J, et al. Deficiency of the humoral immune response to measles vaccine in infants immunized at age 6 months. *JAMA* 1998;280:527–532.

68. Aaby P, Samb B, Simondon F, et al. Child mortality after high-titre measles vaccines in Senegal: the complete data set. *Lancet* 1991;338:1518–1519.

69. Orenstein WA, Bernier RH, Dondero TJ, et al. Field evaluation of vaccine efficacy. *Bull World Health Organ* 1985;63:1055–1068.

70. Halloran ME, Struchiner CJ, Longini IM J. Study designs for evaluating different efficacy and effectiveness aspects of vaccines. *Am J Epidemiol* 1997;146:789–803.

71. Cohen BJ, Audet S, Andrews N, Beeler J. Plaque reduction neutralization test for measles antibodies: description of a standardised laboratory method for use in immunogenicity studies of aerosol vaccination. *Vaccine* 2007;26:59–66.

72. Moss WJ, Scott S. *WHO Immunological Basis for Immunization Series: Measles.* Geneva, Switzerland: World Health Organization; 2009.

73. Scott S, Cutts FT, Nyandu B. Mild illness at or after measles vaccination does not reduce seroresponse in young children. *Vaccine* 1999;17:837–843.

74. Anders JF, Jacobson RM, Poland GA, et al. Secondary failure rates of measles vaccines: a metaanalysis of published studies. *Pediatr Infect Dis J* 1996;15:62–66.

75. Scott P, Moss WJ, Gilani Z, Low N. Safety and immunogenicity of measles vaccine in HIV-infected children: systematic review and meta-analysis. *J Infect Dis* 2011; 204 Suppl 1: S164–178.

76. Angel JB, Walpita P, Lerch RA, et al. Vaccine-associated measles pneumonitis in an adult with AIDS. *Ann Intern Med* 1998;129:104–106.

77. Offit PA, Coffin SE. Communicating science to the public: MMR vaccine and autism. *Vaccine* 2003;22:1–6.

78. DeStefano F. Vaccines and autism: evidence does not support a causal association. *Clin Pharmacol Ther* 2007;82:756–759.

79. Madsen KM, Hviid A, Vestergaard M et al. A population-based study of measles, mumps, and rubella vaccination and autism. *N Engl J Med* 2002;347:1477–1482.

80. Pan American Health Organization. *Measles Eradication: Field Guide.* Washington, DC: Author; 1999.

81. Dayan GH, Cairns L, Sangrujee N, et al. Cost-effectiveness of three different vaccination strategies against measles in Zambian children. *Vaccine* 2004;22:475–484.

82. Sencer DJ, Dull HB, Langmuir AD. Epidemiologic basis for eradication of measles in 1967. *Public Health Rep* 1967;82:253–256.

83. Moss WJ, Strebel P. Biological feasibility of measles eradication. *J Infect Dis* 2011;204 Suppl 1:S47–53.

84. Frank SA, Bush RM. Barriers to antigenic escape by pathogens: trade-off between reproductive rate and antigenic mutability. *BMC Evol Biol* 2007;7:229.

85. Orenstein WA, Strebel PM, Papania M, et al. Measles eradication: is it in our future? *Am J Public Health* 2000;90:1521–1525.

86. de Quadros CA. Can measles be eradicated globally? *Bull World Health Organ* 2004;82:134–138.

87. Forni AL, Schluger NW, Roberts RB. Severe measles pneumonitis in adults: evaluation

of clinical characteristics and therapy with intravenous ribavirin. *Clin Infect Dis* 1994; 19:454–462.

88. Solomon T, Hart CA, Vinjamuri S, et al. Treatment of subacute sclerosing panencephalitis with interferon-alpha, ribavirin, and inosiplex. *J Child Neurol* 2002;17(9):703–705.

89. Sudfeld CR, Navar AM, Halsey NA. Effectiveness of measles vaccination and vitamin A treatment. *Int J Epidemiol* 2010;39(suppl 1):i48–i55.

90. D'Souza RM, D'Souza R. Vitamin A for the treatment of children with measles: a systematic review. *J Trop Pediatr* 2002; 48(6): 323–327.

91. Kabra SK, Lodha R, Hilton DJ. Antibiotics for preventing complications in children with measles. *Cochrane Database Syst Rev* 2008;CD001477.

92. Villamor E, Fawzi WW. Vitamin A supplementation: implications for morbidity and mortality in children. *J Infect Dis* 2000;182(suppl 1): S122–S133.

93. Rota PA, Featherstone DA, Bellini WJ. Molecular epidemiology of measles virus. *Curr Top Microbiol Immunol* 2009;330:129–150.

94. Fine PEM. Herd immunity: history, theory, practice. *Epidemiologic Rev* 1993;15:265–302.

95. Fine P, Eames K, Heymann DL. "Herd immunity": a rough guide. *Clin Infect Dis* 2011;52:911–916.

96. Moss WJ. Measles control and the prospect of eradication. *Curr Top Microbiol Immunol* 2009;330:173–189.

97. Jansen VA, Stollenwerk N, Jensen HJ, et al. Measles outbreaks in a population with declining vaccine uptake. *Science* 2003;301:804.

98. Feikin DR, Lezotte DC, Hamman RF, et al. Individual and community risks of measles and pertussis associated with personal exemptions to immunization. *JAMA* 2000;284:3145–3150.

99. Cutts FT, Grabowsky M, Markowitz LE. The effect of dose and strain of live attenuated measles vaccines on serological responses in young infants. *Biologicals* 1995;23:95–106.

100. Whittle HC, Aaby P, Samb B, et al. Effect of subclinical infection on maintaining immunity against measles in vaccinated children in West Africa. *Lancet* 1999;353:98–101.

101. Moss WJ, Cutts F, Griffin DE. Implications of the human immunodeficiency virus epidemic for control and eradication of measles. *Clin Infect Dis* 1999;29:106–112.

102. Scott S, Mossong J, Moss WJ, et al. Predicted impact of the HIV-1 epidemic on measles in developing countries: results from a dynamic age-structured model. *Int J Epidemiol* 2008;37:356–367.

103. Sutcliffe CG, Moss WJ. Do HIV-infected children receiving HAART need to be revaccinated? *Lancet Infect Dis* 2010;10: 630–642.

104. Rainwater-Lovett K, Moss WJ. Immunologic basis for revaccination of HIV-infected children receiving HAART. *Future Virol* 2011;6:59–71.

105. Griffin DE, Pan CH, Moss WJ. Measles vaccines. *Front Biosci* 2008;13:1352–1370.

106. Polack FP, Lee SH, Permar S, et al. Successful DNA immunization against measles: neutralizing antibody against either the hemagglutinin or fusion glycoprotein protects rhesus macaques without evidence of atypical measles. *Nat Med* 2000;6:776–781.

107. Lin WH, Griffin DE, Rota PA, et al. Successful respiratory immunization with dry powder live-attenuated measles virus vaccine in rhesus macaques. *Proc Natl Acad Sci USA.* 2012;109:14989–14994.

Global Epidemiology of Meningococcal Infections

Mark C. Steinhoff and Kenrad E. Nelson

INTRODUCTION

Meningococcal disease is a global problem, with an epidemiology that varies widely by region and causes an estimated 500,000 cases and 50,000 deaths each year according to the World Health Organization (WHO). The meningococcus bacteria cause severe disease with rapid onset and poor outcomes, even with treatment. Although the endemic disease is relatively rare, epidemic meningococcal disease occurs in outbreaks in the "meningitis belt" in sub-Saharan Africa as well as in other regions. Because of the varied and dynamic epidemiologic patterns of disease, control strategies are substantially different between geographic regions, and change within single countries over time.

This chapter describes meningococcal disease and control strategies related to it in both industrial and developing regions. Because of continued endemic meningitis and the potential for epidemics, vaccines are the mainstay of control efforts. Recent development and licensure of new vaccines in Europe and the United States, and the development of a vaccine tailored for the African meningitis belt, suggest better control can be expected in the future.

THE ORGANISM

Epidemic meningitis was described in Switzerland in 1805 and in the United States in 1806.[1] The bacterium *Neisseria meningitidis*, also called meningococcus, was first isolated in 1887 at the beginning of the era of discovery of infectious organisms.[2] Reviews of historical data from sub-Saharan Africa have shown large epidemics in that setting since the early 1900s,[3] but likely not before then.

Worldwide, approximately 500,000 cases of meningitis occur each year; in the United States, the incidence is approximately 3000 cases per year.[4] Because of the success of vaccines against *Haemophilus* and pneumococcal meningitis, meningococcal meningitis is now the most important cause of endemic bacterial meningitis in children in the United States.[5]

The meningococcus is a gram-negative encapsulated aerobic bacterium. The capsular polysaccharide is a major virulence factor and defines 14 serogroups, among which 6 groups (A, B, C, W135, X, and Y) cause the most diseases. Meningococci are further classified by *serotypes*, defined by the PorB outer membrane proteins, and by *serosubtype*, defined by the PorA proteins. In addition, immunotypes related to lipopolysaccharides are used to classify strains. The genomes for isolates of group A and group B have been published,[6,7] and a group C genome is currently being sequenced. For epidemiologic purposes, many other strain classifications are used, including electropherotyping and multilocus sequence typing (MLST).[8] Sequence typing focuses on 7 housekeeping genes that classify several hypervirulent lineages.

Meningococci have multiple mechanisms by which they generate new antigenic variations and evade host defenses; capsular switching and other genetic variance generate new epidemic strains.[9,10] Genetic sequence data suggest that genes have been acquired from other meningococci and other respiratory commensals such as *H. influenzae*, and the presence of many repeating sequences of DNA specifying surface proteins allows generation of antigenic variations.[11]

The meningococcus colonizes and infects humans, and there are no other hosts. It usually resides as a harmless commensal in the nasopharynx in

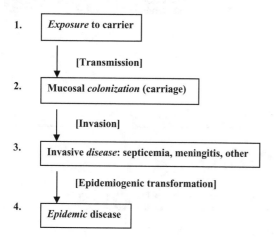

Figure 17-1 Stages and process of meningococcal infection and disease

10% to 20% of adults. Transmission from person to person occurs either by direct contact with respiratory secretions (kissing), by indirect contact (sharing of eating utensils), or by aerosol droplets (coughing, sneezing). Only a small proportion of persons who are colonized in the nasopharynx develop invasive disease. Invasive disease is related both to virulence characteristics of the particular strain and to host factors.

The major unknowns regarding meningococcal disease are the factors determining (1) acquisition and transmission of organisms, (2) the development of invasive disease in a small proportion of all persons who have nasopharyngeal colonization, (3) the development of epidemics, and (4) the shifting serogroups, subtypes, and clones that cause epidemics in various geographic settings. **Figure 17-1** summarizes the processes and stages of meningococcal infection and epidemics. Recent genomic analyses of invasive strains compared to colonizing strains in a large collection in the Czech Republic showed that the invasive strains all had a specific phage DNA gene cluster, compared to only 10% of the carried strains. This finding suggests that the phage DNA mediates invasiveness and possibly determines epidemic clones.[12]

ACQUISITION AND CARRIAGE

Rates of meningococcal carriage in European children are generally less than 3%, increasing to 20% to 30% in the 15- to 24-year-old age group. Carriage rates among military recruits and contacts of cases are generally much higher, ranging from 20% to 70%. Respiratory infections by influenza and other viruses and exposure to tobacco smoke are associ-

ated with increased carriage.[13] The heterogeneity of subtypes and immunotypes is greater among carriers than among patients with invasive disease during epidemics. Colonization of the nasopharynx by meningococci usually produces an antibody response several weeks after acquisition of the organism. Because carriage of meningococcus and related nonpathogenic *N. lactamica* results in natural bactericidal antibody, 65% to 85% of adult individuals have naturally acquired protective bactericidal serum antibody titers.[14–17]

DISEASE

Invasive disease usually occurs within 1 to 4 days of acquisition. Approximately 60% of all patients presenting with acute cases of meningococcal disease have less than 24 hours of illness before hospitalization. In the endemic pattern disease, 30% of meningococcal disease is meningitis, which, even with therapy, has a mortality rate of 10% to 15% and neurologic and other sequelae in a high proportion of survivors. Septicemia without meningitis (meningococcemia) occurs in 10% to 20% of cases and can lead to loss of limbs and death. Pneumonia (5% to 10% of all meningococcal disease) and other syndromes including arthritis, pericarditis, endocarditis, pharyngitis, urethritis, and cervicitis have been described.[5,18]

TREATMENT

Before the use of antibiotics, mortality from meningococcal disease was as high as 85%. Flexner and others showed that passive antibody treatment with specific animal sera was effective in reducing mortality.[19] Treatment with penicillin is effective, because resistance to penicillin among meningococcal isolates is rare. Antibiotic treatment with broader-spectrum drugs, including ceftriaxone, to cover additional bacteria is often used for empirical treatment of bacterial meningitis and is effective. Chloremphenicol is also an effective therapy in many settings, though resistance has been reported.[20] In addition to antibiotic treatment, good supportive care to treat shock and disseminated intravascular coagulation reduces mortality, though this rate remains between 10% and 15% in wealthy countries.[21]

In the setting of endemic disease, *chemoprophylaxis* can be effective to prevent illness in family members and other close contacts. In the United States, chemoprophylaxis of close contacts is recommended

Feet (Scale t)	1		2		3

| Inches 3 | | 6 | | 9 | | 0 | | 3 | | 6 | | 9 | | 0 | | 3 | | 6 | | 9 | | 0 |

Beds less than 9″ apart
Carrier Rate = 30% or more.

Beds less than one foot apart.
Carrier Rate = 20% or more.

Beds 1′4″ apart (The usual distance in mobilisation standard strictly observed) Carrier Rate = 9%

Beds 2′6″ apart (as in "spacing out" Caterham) Carrier Rate = under 5%

Beds 3 feet apart. Carrier Rate = under 2%

Figure 17-2 Glover in 1920 reported on the effect of crowding in the British Army Guards Depot at Caterham in 1916. These barracks were designed for 800 men, but with World War I mobilization up to 13,000 were housed in the barracks and in huts and tents around it. The normal military rule for bed separation was three feet, but "there were great temptations to hygenically unprincipled authorities . . . to put in more beds." Glover was able to show that decreased distance between beds (crowding) was correlated with increased carriage rates of meningococcus A, and eventually with an outbreak of meningococcal disease in the barracks. The figure shows his graph of data relating bed separation with carriage rates in the recruits. Reproduced from Glover JA. Observation of the meningococcus carrier rate, and their application to the prevention of cerebrospinal fever. In Medical Research Council. Cerebrospinal fever Special Report Series no 50 London: His Majesty's Stationery Office, 1920:133–65.

for prevention of sporadic meningococcal disease. Close contacts are defined as household members, daycare center contacts, and anyone directly exposed to the oral secretions of the index case. Antimicrobial chemoprophylaxis should be administered to these contacts as soon as possible, because the risk of invasive disease is greatest within a few days of the index case. The Centers for Disease Control and Prevention (CDC) website provides information on the dose and duration of the recommended drugs, which include rifampin, ciprofloxacin, and ceftriaxone.[22]

RISK FACTORS

Important host factors for meningococcal disease are the absence of bactericidal antibodies in serum, the absence of a normal complement cascade, and the presence of certain mannose-binding lectins.[23] A variety of human genetic polymorphisms are associated with severity of disease without apparently affecting the risk of acquisition.[24] Other biological risk factors include complement deficiencies, anatomic or functional asplenia, and chronic disease. For meningococcal disease in the United States, risk factors include age younger than 11 months, household crowding, viral infection,[13] active and passive smoking,[25] residence in college dormitories, and chronic underlying illnesses. During outbreaks in the United States, bar or nightclub patronage and alcohol use have been associated with increased risk of acquisition.[26] In African settings, risk factors include exposure to

cooking fire smoke and sharing a bedroom with a case.[27] During World War I, the importance of spacing of beds in sleeping quarters to reduce transmission and carriage of meningococci was understood and led to bed spacing regulations in military barracks (see **Figure 17-2**).

EPIDEMIOLOGY

In the past, meningococcus caused large epidemics in North America and Europe, but these types of outbreaks have not occurred in industrial countries (except for Norway and New Zealand) for the last 60 years. Rates of endemic meningococcal disease of all groups in the United States recently ranged from 1 to 1.5 per 100,000 population.[22] In Europe, rates have been higher,[28–30] and childhood rates of 5 per 100,000 in Great Britain prompted universal use of vaccine.[31] **Table 17-1** compares the characteristics

Table 17-1	Comparison of Meningococcal Disease Epidemiology	
Characteristic	High-Income Regions	Low Income; Meningitis Belt
Serogroups	B,C	A, C, now W135
Epidemiology	Endemic, winter	Endemic/epidemic, dry season
Incidence (per 100,000)	1–5	20/600
Peak Age	College age	School age
Case Fatality	5–15%	>15%

of meningococcal disease in wealthier countries and in countries with limited resources. In general, the nature and quality of surveillance define the reported incidence of meningococcal disease. [32]

The epidemiology of meningococcal disease varies by the major serogroups, geography, and chronology. Group A historically has been the cause of large epidemic outbreaks and is associated with endemic and epidemic outbreaks in the meningitis belt of Africa. Group A disease is rare in the United States and Europe. [33]

Group B disease is the most important cause of endemic disease in developed countries, causing approximately 30% to 40% of cases in the United States and as many as 80% of cases in European countries. Norway, Cuba, and New Zealand have experienced epidemic group B disease in the recent past. Meningococcal group C disease has variable rates of endemic disease, and currently accounts for approximately 30% of disease in the United States and in Europe. Group Y has become more frequently found in the United States. Group W135 disease has become increasingly important and has been related to the Hajj pilgrimage since the late 1990s. [34]

In the United States, in recent years serogroup Y has caused 39% of disease, serogroup C 31%, serogroup B 23%, and W135 2%; group A has not been found in cases (**Figure 17-3**). [33] In Canada and Europe, serogroups B and C predominate (**Figure 17-4**), but in Africa serogroups A and W135 are most common. The distribution of serogroups in the United States changed during the 1990s. [35] For example, group Y represented 9% of all cases between 1990 and 1992, but from 1997 to 2003, it accounted for 28% of all cases. Group B rates ranged from 43% to 34%. [36] *Epidemic meningitis* was a feature in the North American and European countries until the middle of the last century. During the last decades, large epidemics have occurred in the African meningitis belt and within China. [37]

Serogroup A, subgroup III has caused two large global pandemics. The first occurred from the 1960s to 1970s in China, Russia, Scandinavia, and Brazil. A second group A(III) pandemic was associated with epidemics in the 1980s in China and an outbreak from 1982 to 1984 in Kathmandu, Nepal. [37,38] In 1985, epidemics occurred in New Delhi, India, and in Pakistan. During the 1987 Hajj in Mecca, Saudi

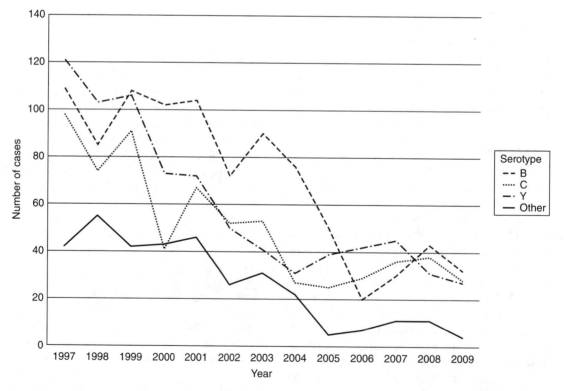

Figure 17-3 N. menigitides reported to Active Bacterial Core Surveillance (ABC): Emerging Infections Program Network 1997–2009. Reproduced from the Centers for Disease Control and Prevention (2009). Active Bacterial Core Surveillance Report, Emerging Infections Program Network, Neisseria meningitidis, 1997–2009. http://www.cdc.gov/abcs/reports-findings/survreports/mening08.pdf. Accessed September 17, 2012.

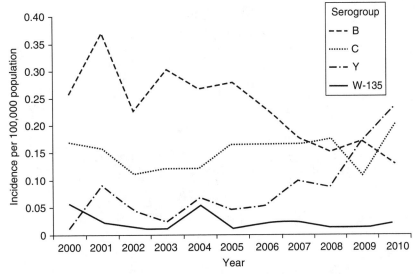

^aIn 2010, the number of *N. meningitidis* isolates were: 12 (serogroup B), 19 (serogroup C), 22 (serogroup Y) and 2 (serogroup W-135).

Figure 17-4 Incidence of invasive *Neisseria meningitidis* caused by serogroups B, C, Y, and W-134, Sweden, 2000–2010. Thulin Hedberg S, Törös B, Fredlund H, Olcén P, Mölling P. Genetic characterisation of the emerging invasive Neisseria meningitidis serogroup Y in Sweden, 2000 to 2010. Euro Surveill. 2011;16(23):pii=19885. Available from: http://www.eurosurveillance.org/ViewArticle. aspx?ArticleId=19885

Arabia, the same strain caused an outbreak among pilgrims and later was found in epidemics in the meningitis belt in Africa, including the 1996 epidemic, which involved the largest number of cases of all recorded episodes. This A(III) ST5 strain caused epidemic disease in tropical regions not historically in the sub-Saharan belt, including Kenya, Tanzania, Zambia, and South Africa, as late as 1998.[39-41]

It is possible the use of group A/C vaccine among pilgrims has modified the transmission of these serogroups during the Hajj. In 2001, serogroup W135 caused 400 cases of meningococcal disease in Hajj pilgrims and their contacts. The W135 clone is thought to have been spread through returning Hajj pilgrims, and has been described in the meningitis belt and in many other countries ranging from North America and Europe through the Far East.[34,42,43] In report, Saudi authorities have modified the immunization regulations for Hajj pilgrims, who must now show evidence of immunization with A, C, Y, W135 vaccine.[44]

THE MENINGOCOCCAL BELT

The meningitis belt in Africa was defined by Lapeyssonie in 1963 when he described a sub-Saharan region, stretching from Ethiopia to Senegal, characterized by periodic large epidemics of meningococcal

meningitis.[45] This region, which is characterized by dry grassland and scrub with subsistence farming, stretches across 16 sub-Saharan Sahel countries. It is home to 170 million people, with a per capita gross national product (GNP) between $100 and $800 per person, putting the meningitis belt in the least developed category economically. The region is delimited by a northern boundary of the Sahara Desert and a southern boundary of humid savannah and rainforest. It has limited rainfall, mostly confined to May to November of the year. Few epidemics occur in regions within the rainfall isohyet* of 300–1000 millimeters or with mean humidity greater than 10 g/m³.[46-48] Typically, epidemics occur during the dry season and end with onset of the rain season.[46] The endemic incidence ranges from 3 to 60 cases per 100,000 population (rates that would be considered epidemics elsewhere), increasing to 200 to 600 cases per 100,000 population during the epidemics. In the 1996–1997 epidemic, there were more than 214,000 cases and 21,800 deaths reported.[44] In this region, it estimated that during the decade of the 1990s, approximately 700,000 cases and at least 100,000 deaths from meningococcal disease occurred. In contrast, in the United States during this same time period there were 22,000 cases and approximately 2000 deaths.

* Isohyet is a cartography word from Greek ίσος *isos* ("equal") and ύετος or *huetos* ("rain"). An isohyet is a line joining points of equal precipitation on a map.

Meningitis Belt

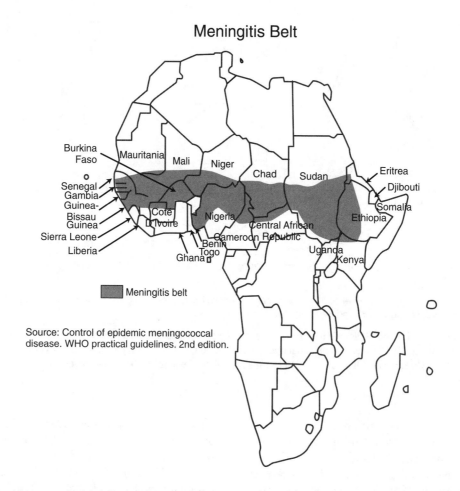

Source: Control of epidemic meningococcal disease. WHO practical guidelines. 2nd edition.

Figure 17-5 The African meningitis belt. Reproduced from the World Health Organization. Control of epidemic meningococcal disease, WHO practical guidelines, 2nd edition. http://www.who.int/csr/resources/publications/meningitis/whoemcbac983.pdf. Accessed September 10, 2012.

Historically, groups A and C have caused epidemics in this region; group W135 of ST-11 clonal complex appeared in Hajj pilgrims in 2000, and has now spread widely.[49,50] The ST-11 clonal complex was earlier seen in group C epidemics, suggesting a capsular switch has occurred in the meningococcal organism.

Surveillance data in 13 countries in the Africa meningitis belt are now available weekly through the WHO Multi-diseases Surveillance Center in Ougadougou, Burkina Faso.[51]

VACCINES

Polysaccharide capsules of serogroups A, C, Y, and W135 elicit bactericidal antibodies that are serogroup specific. These antibodies have been shown to correlate with protection from disease. Studies in the 1960s demonstrated that the serum bactericidal antibodies are important in protection of military recruits from epidemic disease. Recruits who arrived in boot camp with detectable bactericidal serum antibody levels did not develop disease even though colonized, whereas recruits who did not have antibody had attack rates as high as 38%.

In contrast, serogroup B polysaccharide capsule is poorly immunogenic, likely because of its similarity to sialic glycopeptides expressed on the surface of developing neural cells. For this reason, vaccines against serogroups B meningococci utilize noncapsular antigens, often surface proteins that have a high level of diversity.[52] Each group B vaccine is developed to match a specific epidemic strain.

A number of meningococcal vaccines have been available since at least the 1960s.[53,54] These vaccines consist of the purified polysaccharide capsule and vary based on the number of serogroups they contain and whether they consist of polysaccharide alone or polysaccharide conjugated to a protein. As with other capsular polysaccharide vaccines, the meningococcal polysaccharide is less immunogenic in children and does not appear to stimulate long-term immunologic memory. Also similar to developments for other bacterial capsular polysaccharides, chemical conjugation of protein to polysaccharides appears to result in improved immunogenicity, enhanced immunologic memory, and longer-term protection, especially in infants and children. The enhanced immunogenicity and high effectiveness of polysaccharide conjugate vaccines in young infants have allowed effective vaccines for infants to be made available in the United States and the United Kingdom. Conjugation does not improve the poor immunogenicity of the group B polysaccharide, so the outer membrane protein (OMP) and outer membrane vesicle remain the optimal vaccine antigens.

The efficacy of the polysaccharide vaccines has been shown to range from 80% to 100% in military recruits and epidemic situations. The conjugate group C vaccine as used in Great Britain has an overall efficacy greater than 90% for all vaccinated age groups.[55] The use of this vaccine has also resulted in reduction of carriage of group C strains in the entire population, suggesting a herd effect. **Table 17-2** summarizes the availability of vaccines for meningococcal disease. The quadrivalent (groups A, C, Y, and W135) conjugate vaccine was licensed by the Food and Drug Administration (FDA) for use in United States in February 2005 and was recommended for children 11 years of age or older, students entering high school, and college

freshmen living in dormitories. The quadrivalent PS vaccine in the United States is sold for approximately $60; the PS vaccine for Hajj pilgrims is sold for around $5. The trivalent PS vaccine licensed in 2002 for use only in Africa costs approximately $1.50.

Because group B organisms now cause a substantial proportion of disease in the United States and have caused outbreaks elsewhere, development of a noncapsular vaccine has been of recent interest. To date, vaccines have been produced using outer membrane proteins from epidemic strains in Norway and Cuba. These vaccines were relatively effective in reducing disease in those epidemics.[56–58] New Zealand experienced an outbreak of group B meningococcal disease in 2000 and responded with an epidemic-specific OMP vaccine; it effectively controlled spread of the infection, such that the vaccine was discontinued in 2008.

Because of the heterogeneity of OMP antigens, there is interest in additional strategies for vaccines. The genome sequence of a group B strain has been analyzed and an assessment of the open reading frames yielded 570 surface exposed proteins; 5 were expressed as recombinant proteins and were able to prevent disease in a rodent model, and 2 induced bactericidal antibody when used as vaccines in mice.[59] This identification of potential vaccine antigens from genome sequencing has been termed *reverse vaccinology* because it identifies potentially protective surface proteins from genome sequence data directly, rather than from the classical sequence of detection, and isolation of the surface proteins and testing for natural antibody.[6, 57]

Table 17-2		Current Meningococcal Vaccines		
Serogroup Polysaccharide Vaccines	Protein	Producer Vaccines	Licensed in	Licensed
A/C	—	Sanofi (Aventis)	Europe, Asia, Africa	1978
A, C, Y, W135	—	Sanofi (Aventis)	Widely used, but not in the United States	1981
A, C, Y, W135	—	GSK		
A, C, W135	—	GSK	Africa only	2002
Conjugate Vaccines				
C	Variable	Wyeth, Chiron, Baxter	United Kingdom, Europe, Canada	2001
A, B, C, W135	DT	Sanofi Pasteur (Aventis)	United States pending	2005
A	TT	MVP		NA

Notes: DT, diphtheria toxoid; TT, tetanus toxoid; MVP, Meningococcal Vaccine Program.

VACCINE STRATEGIES

Three strategies for utilization of meningococcal vaccines have been proposed: (1) immunization of high-risk populations; (2) universal immunization, usually as part of infant immunization; and (3) epidemic response, or mass immunization of an affected population to curtail an epidemic (**Table 17-3**). Because disease patterns vary widely by regions and through time, these strategies and their adoption/relation to local disease patterns are discussed here.

High-Risk Populations

The experience of the epidemics in the U.S. military recruits in 1960s and 1970s resulted in the development of the quadrivalent polysaccharide vaccine. This vaccine is still received by all military recruits in the United States and those in many other countries.

In the United States, college freshmen have been identified as a high-risk group, and immunization with polysaccharide quadrivalent PS vaccine has been recommended since 2000.[60] Recently, the licensure of a quadrivalent conjugate polysaccharide vaccine has led to the recommendation of its use in children older than age 11 years, those starting high school, or those living in dormitories in a university.[61,62]

In January 2011, the FDA lowered the approval age range for the use of conjugate quadrivalent A, C, Y and W135 vaccine to include persons aged 2 through 55 years.[63,64] There are currently two licensed conjugate quadrivalent vaccines in the United States, both of which have equivalent safety and efficacy. The Advisory Committee on Immunization Practices (ACIP) of the CDC recommends that children ages 2 to 10 years who are at increased risk of meningococcal disease should be immunized. A two-dose primary series is recommended for children with a terminal complement deficiency or anatomic or functional asplenia. A single dose is recommended for children who are at increased risk because they are travelers to or residents of countries in which meningococcal disease is hyperendemic or epidemic. The ACIP did not recommend the routine use of conjugate meningococcal vaccine for children aged 2 through 10 who were not at increased risk of disease.[65] Routine immunization of children with the quadrivalent conjugate meningococcal vaccine at age 11 is recommended by the ACIP.

Because the highest rates of meningococcal disease in the Unites States occur in 0- to 1-year-olds, when a suitable vaccine is available, it is likely that infant universal immunization will be considered in the United States. Such policies are already in place in Canada and the United Kingdom.[66]

Universal Immunization

In 1992, the Egyptian Ministry of Health initiated a vaccination program for all school children using a bivalent A/C polysaccharide vaccine at school entry, and a second dose three years later. This strategy disrupted a previously observed pattern of outbreaks of illness approximately every 8 years with incidences of 20/100,000.[67,68]

A policy of universal immunization with type C conjugate vaccine of infants and 15- to 17-year-olds was adopted by Great Britain in 1999 in response to high rates of group C disease among infants and adolescents in that country. There was an initial 90% effectiveness of vaccine in recipients, although it became apparent that booster doses were needed in infants to maintain protection. This program has been successful in curtailing the epidemic of group C disease (see **Table 17-3**) in Great Britain and has now been adopted by Spain, the Netherlands, and several provinces in Canada.[69,70]

Table 17-3	National Immunization Policies: Examples in Four Countries			
Country	Income (GNP per capita)	Incidence per 100,000	Vaccine Policy	Vaccine Used	Groups
United States	$25,850	1.1	High risk College age	PS, now Cj	A, C, Y, W135
United Kingdom	$16,561	5	Universal infant	Cj	C
Egypt	$1,200	20	High risk School age	PS	A/C
Benin	$380	65.9	Epidemic response	PS	A/C or A, C, W135

Notes: PS, polysaccharide; Cj, conjugate polysaccharide.

Epidemic Response

Norway, Cuba, and New Zealand adopted a strategy of mass immunization for their specific group B epidemics. Each country developed a protein vaccine with specific proteins to match its own epidemic strains.

The vaccine strategy of *epidemic response* in the meningitis belt has been the subject of much discussion.[71–75] Until recently, the WHO strategy suggested enhanced surveillance for meningococcal disease to detect the onset of meningococcal epidemic, followed by mass vaccination with current polysaccharide vaccines in the affected regions. It was claimed that epidemic response of mass immunization can curtail epidemics.[76–78] However, this approach meant that vaccine control procedures started weeks after the epidemics were recognized, so it was not optimal.[79] Furthermore, polysaccharide vaccines do not reduce carriage of meningococci or induce herd immunity, so epidemics often recur. The strengthening of both surveillance and routine Expanded Program on Immunization (EPI) systems to achieve high coverage of immunization among young children has made preventive immunization a more attractive strategy.

WHO currently proposes a threshold for epidemics of 10/100,000 inhabitants per week. A lower alert threshold of 5/100,000 inhabitants allows time to prepare for an epidemic and initiate mass vaccination if appropriate. For populations numbering less than 30,000, the alert threshold is 2 cases per week.[77,78] The CDC defines an outbreak of serogroup C meningococcus as 3 or more confirmed or probable cases during a period of less than 3 months, representing a primary attack rate of at least 10/100,000 population.[22]

The availability of an affordable conjugate polysaccharide vaccine has enabled universal infant immunization in the meningitis belt. The Meningococcal Vaccine Project (MVP) was established in 2001 to develop an inexpensive conjugate group A meningococcus vaccine for the meningitis belt of Africa. MVP is a collaboration between the Gates Foundation, which funded the Program for Appropriate Technology in Health (PATH), and WHO.[80] It supported the technical transfer to enable development of the group A vaccine by the Serum Institute of India (SII) and testing for safety and immunogenicity in India.

Subsequently, studies in Mali, Gambia, and Senegal found the vaccine to be immunogenic, to have an acceptable safety profile and to induce immunologic memory.[81] Mass vaccination campaigns using the meningococcal group A conjugate vaccines targeting persons aged 1–29 began in Burkina Faso, Mali, and Niger in September 2010. The potential public health benefit from MVP has already been suggested by the record low number of meningitis A cases in the countries where this program has been introduced.[82] With distribution of MenAfriVac in Nigeria, Cameroon, and Chad in late 2011, the total number of vaccinated persons is now 55 million (www.meningvax.org).

More recently serogroup W135 has been spread across Africa by Hajj pilgrims returning from Mecca. The introduction of W135 has prompted development of a low-cost, specially formulated trivalent vaccine containing A, C, and W135 for use in the meningococcal belt. Should the group W135 organisms become more prevalent in the meningococcal belt, the MVP program will consider making a bivalent conjugate polysaccharide vaccine available in its program.[80, 81]

• • • REFERENCES

1. Vieusseux M. Memoire sur la maladie qui a regné a Genêve au printemps de 1805. *J Med Chir Pharmacol* 1805;11:163.

2. Weichselbaum A. Ueber die aetiologie der akuten meningitis cerebrospinalis. *Fortschr Med* 1887;5:573–583.

3. Greenwood B. Manson lecture. Meningococcal meningitis in Africa. *Trans R Soc Trop Med Hyg* 1999;93:341–353.

4. Sharip A, Sorvillo F, Redelings MD, et al. Population-based analysis of meningococcal disease mortality in the United States 1990–2002. *Pediatr Infect Dis J* 2006;25:191–194.

5. Rosenstein NE, Perkins BA, Stephens DS, et al. Meningococcal disease. *N Engl J Med* 2001;344:1378–1388.

6. Pizza M, Scarlato V, Masignani V, et al. Identification of vaccine candidates against serogroups B meningococcus by whole-genome sequencing. *Science* 2000;287:1816–1820.

7. Parkhill J, Achtman M, James KD, et al. Complete DNA sequence of a serogroup A strain of *Neisseria meningitidis* Z2491. *Nature* 2000;404:502–506.

8. Maiden MC, Bygraves JA, Feil E, et al. Multilocus sequence typing: a portable approach to the identification of clones within populations of pathogenic microorganisms. *Proc Natl Acad Sci USA* 1998;95:3140–3145.

9. Swartley JS, Marfin AA, Edupuganti S, et al. Capsule switching of *Neisseria meningitidis*. *Proc Natl Acad Sci USA* 1997;94:271–276.

10. Harrison LH, Shutt KA, Schmink SE, et al. Population structure and capsular switching of invasive *Neisseria meningitidis* isolates in the pre-meningococcal conjugate vaccine era—United States, 2000–2005. *J Infect Dis* 2010;201:1208–1224.

11. Schoen C, Blom J, Claus H, et al. Whole-genome comparison of disease and carriage strains provides insights into virulence evolution in *Neisseria meningitidis*. *Proc Natl Acad Sci USA* 2008;105:3473–3478.

12. Bille E, Zahar J-R, Perrin A, et al. A chromosomally integrated bacteriophage in invasive meningococci. *J Exp Med* 2005;201:1905–1913.

13. Moore PS, Hierholzer J, DeWitt W, et al. Respiratory viruses and mycoplasma as cofactors for epidemic group A meningococcal meningitis. *JAMA* 1990;264:1271–1275.

14. Yazdankhah SP, Caugant DA. *Neisseria meningitidis*: an overview of the carriage state. *J Med Microbiol* 2004;53:821–832.

15. Broome CV. The carrier state. *Neisseria meningitidis*. *J Antimicrob Chemother* 1986;18(suppl A):25–34.

16. Maiden MC. Dynamics of bacterial carriage and disease: lessons from the meningococcus. *Adv Exp Med Biol* 2004;549:23–29.

17. Caugant DA, Hoiby EA, Magnus P, et al. Asymptomatic carriage of *Neisseria meningitidis* in a randomly sampled population. *J Clin Microbiol* 1994;32:323–330.

18. Apicella MA. *N. meningitidis*. In: Mandell GL, Bennet JE, Livingston RDC, eds. *Principles and Practice of Infectious Disease*. Philadelphia, PA: Churchill, Livingston; 2000:2228–2241.

19. Flexner S. The results of serum treatment in thirteen hundred cases of epidemic meningitis. *J Exp Med* 1913;17:553–576.

20. Tondella ML, Rosenstein NE, Mayer LW, et al. Lack of evidence for chloramphenicol resistance in *Neisseria meningitidis*, Africa. *Emerg Infect Dis* 2001;7:163–164.

21. Kirsch EA, Barton RP, Kitchen L, Giroir BP. Pathophysiology, treatment and outcome of meningococcemia: a review and recent experience. *Pediatr Infect Dis J* 1996;15:967–978; quiz 979. Comment in: *Pediatr Infect Dis J.* 1997;16:540–542.

22. Centers for Disease Control and Prevention. Prevention and control of meningococcal disease and meningococcal disease and college students: recommendation of the Advisory Committee on Immunization Practices (ACIP). *MMWR.* 2000;49(RR-7):1–22.

23. Hibberd ML, Sumiya M, Summerfield JA, et al. Association of variants of the gene for mannose-binding lectin with susceptibility to meningococcal disease. *Lancet* 1999;353:1049–1053.

24. Emonts M, Hazelzet JA, de Groot R, Hermans PW. Host genetic determinants of *Neisseria meningitidis* infections. *Lancet Infect Dis* 2003;3:565–577.

25. Stuart JM, Cartwright KA, Robinson PM, Noah ND. Effect of smoking on meningococcal carriage. *Lancet* 1989;2:723–725.

26. Harrison LH, Dwyer DM, Maples CT, Billmann L. Risk of meningococcal infection in college students. *JAMA* 1999;281:1906–1910.

27. Hodgson A, Smith T, Gagneux S, et al. Risk factors for meningococcal meningitis in northern Ghana. *Trans R Soc Trop Med Hyg* 2001;95:477–480.

28. Cartwright K, Noah N, Peltola H, Meningococcal Disease Advisory Board. Meningococcal disease in Europe: epidemiology, mortality, and prevention with conjugate vaccines. Report of a European advisory board meeting Vienna, Austria, 6–8 October 2000. *Vaccine* 2001;19:4347–4356.

29. Greenwood BM, Greenwood AM, Bradley AK, et al. Factors influencing susceptibility to meningococcal disease during an epidemic in the Gambia, West Africa. *J Infect* 1987;14:167–184.

30. Noah N, Henderson B. *Surveillance of Bacterial Meningitis in Europe 1999/2000*. London: PHLS; 2002:1–47. Available at: http://www.phls.org.uk/topics_az/meningo/m_surveillance9900.pdf. Accessed April 25, 2005.

31. Ramsay ME, Andrews N, Kaczmarski EB, Miller E. Efficacy of meningococcal serogroup C conjugate vaccine in teenagers and toddlers in England. *Lancet* 2001;357:195–196.

32. Halperin SA, Bettinger JA, Greenwood B, et al. The changing and dynamic epidemiology of meningococcal disease. *Vaccine* 2011. doi: 10.1016/j.vaccine.2011.12.032.

33. Harrison LH. Epidemiological profile of meningococcal disease in the United States. *Clin Infect Dis* 2010;50(suppl 2):S37–S44.

34. Lingappa JR, Al-Rabeah AM, Hajjeh R, et al. Serogroup W-135 meningococcal disease during the Hajj, 2000. *Emerg Infect Dis* 2003;9:665–671.

35. Rosenstein NE, Perkins BA, Stephens DS, et al. The changing epidemiology of meningococcal disease in the United States, 1992–1996. *J Infect Dis* 1999;180:1894–1901.

36. Tondella MLC, Popovic T, Rosenstein NE, et al. Distribution of *Neisseria meningitidis* serogroup B serosubtypes and serotypes circulating in the United States. *J Clin Microbiol* 2000;38:3323–3328.

37. Wang J-F, Caugant DA, Li X, et al. Clonal and antigenic analysis of serogroup A *Neisseria meningitidis* with particular reference to epidemiological features of epidemic meningitis in the People's Republic of China. *Infect Immun* 1992;60:5267–5282.

38. Zhu P, van der Ende A, Falush D, et al. Fit genotypes and escape variants of subgroup III *Neisseria meningitidis* during three pandemics of epidemic meningitis. *Proc Natl Acad Sci* 2001;98:5234–5239.

39. Moore PS. Meningococcal meningitis in sub-Saharan Africa: a model for the epidemic process. *Clin Infect Dis* 1992;14:515–525.

40. Riou JY, Djibo S, Sangare L, et al. A predictable comeback: the second pandemic of infections caused by *Neisseria meningitidis* serogroup A subgroup III in Africa, 1995. *Bull WHO* 1996;74:181–187.

41. Leimkugel J, Hodgson A, Forgor AA, et al. Clonal waves of *Neisseria* colonisation and disease in the African meningitis belt: eight-year longitudinal study in northern Ghana. *PLoS Med* 2007;4:e101.

42. Dull PM, Abdelwahab J, Sacchi CT, et al. *Neisseria meningitidis* serogroup W-135 carriage among US travelers to the 2001 Hajj. *J Infect Dis* 2005;191:33–39.

43. Wilder-Smith A, Goh KT, Barkham T, Paton NI. Hajj-associated outbreak strain of *Neisseria meningitidis* serogroup W135: estimates of the attack rate in a defined population and the risk of invasive disease developing in carriers. *Clin Infect Dis* 2003;36:679–683.

44. Tikhomirov E, Santamaria M, Esteves K. Meningococcal disease: public health burden and control. *World Health Stat Q* 1997;50:170–177.

45. Lepeyssonnie L. La méningite cérébrospinale en Afrique. *Bull WHO* 1963;28(suppl):53–114.

46. Cheesbrough JS, Morse AP, Green DR. Meningococcal meningitis and carriage in western Zaire: a hypoendemic zone related to climate? *Epidemiol Infect* 1995;114:75–92.

47. Sultan B, Labadi K, Guégan JF, Janicot S. Climate drives the meningitis epidemics onset in West Africa. *PLoS Med* 2005;2:0045–0049.

48. Molesworth AM, Cuevas LE, Connor SJ, et al. Environmental risk and meningitis epidemics in Africa. *Emerg Infect Dis* 2003;9:1287–1293.

49. Nicolas P, Norheim G, Garnotel E, et al. Molecular epidemiology of *Neisseria meningitidis* isolated in the African meningitis belt between 1988 and 2003 shows dominance of sequence type 5 (ST-5) and ST-11 complexes. *J Clin Microbiol* 2005;43:5129–5135.

50. Teyssou R, Muros-Le Rouzic E. Meningitis epidemics in Africa: a brief overview. *Vaccine* 2007;25(suppl 1):A3–A7.

51. WHO web site for reports of meningococcal disease in Africa. Available at: http://www.who.int/csr/disease/meningococcal/epidemiological/en/.

52. Sacchi CT, Whitney AM, Popovic T, et al. Diversity and prevalence of PorA types in *Neisseria meningitidis* serogroup B in the United States, 1992–1998. *J Infect Dis* 2000;182:1169–1176.

53. Danzig L. Meningococcal vaccines. *Pediatr Infect Dis J* 2004;23: S285–S292.

54. Jódar L, Feavers IM, Salisbury D, Granoff DM. Development of vaccines against meningococcal disease. *Lancet* 2002;359:1499–1508.

55. Balmer P, Borrow R, Miller E. Impact of meningococcal C conjugate vaccine in the UK. *J Med Microbiol* 2002;51:717–722.

56. Sierra GVG, Campa HC, Varcacel NM, et al. Vaccine against group B *Neisseria meningitidis*: protection trial and mass vaccination results in Cuba. *NIPH Ann* 1991;14:195–210.

57. Bjune G, Hoiby EA, Gronnesby JK, et al. Effect of outer membrane vesicle vaccine against group B meningococcal disease in Norway. *Lancet* 1991;338:1093–1096.

58. Holst J, Feiring B, Fuglesang JE, et al. Serum bactericidal activity correlates with the vaccine efficacy of outer membrane vesicle vaccines against *Neisseria meningitidis* serogroup B disease. *Vaccine* 2003;21:734–737.

59. Rappuoli R. Reverse vaccinology: a genome-based approach to vaccine development. *Vaccine* 2001;19:2688–2691.

60. Centers for Disease Control and Prevention. Prevention and control of meningococcal disease recommendations of the Advisory Committee on Immunization Practices (ACIP). *MMWR.* 2005;54(RR-7):1–21.

61. Raghunathan PL, Bernhardt SA, Rosenstein NE. Opportunities for control of meningococcal disease in the United States. *Annu Rev Med* 2004;55:333–353.

62. Committee on Infectious Diseases. Prevention and control of meningococcal disease: recommendations for use of meningococcal vaccines in pediatric patients. *Pediatrics* 2005;116: 496–505.

63. Centers for Disease Control and Prevention. Licensure of a meningococcal conjugate vaccine and guidance for use—Advisory Committee on Immunization Practices (ACIP), 2010. *MMWR* 2010;59:223.

64. Centers for Disease Control and Prevention. Updated recommendations for use of meningococcal conjugate vaccines—Advisory Committee on Immunization Practices (ACIP) 2010. *MMWR* 2011;60:72–76.

65. Centers for Disease Control and Prevention. Licensure of a meningococcal conjugate vaccine for children aged 2 through 10 years and updated booster dose guidance for meningococcal disease—Advisory Committee in Immunization Practice (CIP) 2011. *MMWR* 60:1018–1019.

66. Cohn AC, MacNeil JR, Harrison LH, et al. Changes in *Neisseria meningitidis* disease epidemiology in the United States, 1998–2007: implications for prevention of meningococcal disease. *Clin Infect Dis* 2010;50:184–191.

67. Nakhla I, Frenck RW Jr, Teleb NA, et al. The changing epidemiology of meningococcal meningitis after introduction of bivalent A/C polysaccharide vaccine into school-based vaccination programs in Egypt. *Vaccine* 2005;23;3288–3293.

68. Hausdorff WP, Hajjeh R, Al-Mazrou A, et al. The epidemiology of pneumococcal, meningococcal, and *Haemophilus* disease in the Middle East and North Africa (MENA) region: current status and needs. *Vaccine* 2007;25:1935–1944.

69. Trotter CL, Andrews NJ, Kaczmarski EB, et al. Effectiveness of meningococcal serogroup C conjugate vaccine 4 years after introduction. *Lancet* 2004;364:365–367.

70. Snape MD, Pollard AJ. Meningococcal polysaccharide-protein conjugate vaccines. *Lancet Infect Dis* 2005;5:21–30.

71. World Health Organization. Detecting meningococcal meningitis epidemics in highly endemic African countries. *Wkly Epidemiol Rec* 2000;38:306–309.

72. Robbins JB, Towne DW, Gotschlich EC, Schneerson R. "Love's labours lost": failure to implement mass vaccination against group A meningococcal meningitis in sub-Saharan Africa. *Lancet* 1997;350:819,880–882.

73. Robbins JB, Schneerson R, Gotschlich EC. A rebuttal: epidemic and endemic meningococcal meningitis in sub-Saharan Africa can be prevented now by routine immunization with group A meningococcal capsular polysaccharide vaccine. *Pediatr Infect Dis J* 2000;19:945–953.

74. Robbins JB, Schneerson R, Gotschlich EC, et al. Meningococcal meningitis in sub-Saharan Africa: the case for mass and routine vaccination with available polysaccharide vaccines. *Bull WHO* 2003;81:745–750.

75. See responses to 57 in *Bull WHO* 2003;81:751–755.

76. Miller MA, Wenger J, Rosenstein N, Perkins B. Evaluation of meningococcal meningitis vaccination strategies for the meningitis belt in Africa. *Pediatr Infect Dis J* 1999;18:1051–1059.

77. Lewis R, Nathan N, Diarra L, et al. Timely detection of meningococcal meningitis epidemics in Africa. *Lancet* 2001;358: 287–293.

78. Leake JA, Kone ML, Yada AA, et al. Early detection and response to meningococcal disease epidemics in sub-Saharan Africa: appraisal of the WHO strategy. *Bull WHO* 2002;80:342–349.

79. LaForce FM, Ravenscroft M, Djingarey M, Vivani S. Epidemic meningitis due to group A *Neisseria meningitidis* in the African meningitis belt: a persistent problem with an imminent solution. *Vaccine* 2009;27(suppl 2B):13–19.

80. Hargreaves JR, Greenwood B, Clift C, et al. Making new vaccines affordable: a comparison of financing processes used to develop and deploy new meningococcal vaccines an pneumococcal conjugate vaccines. *Lancet* 2011;378:1885–1893.

81. Sow SO, Okoho BJ, Diallo A, et al. Immunogenicity and safety of a meningococcal A conjugate vaccine in Africans. *N Engl J Med* 2011;364;2293–2304.

82. Meningitis Vaccine Project. Dramatic fall in cases of meningococcal group A meningitis in three West African Countries after a new vaccine introduction in 2011. Available at: http://www.meningvax.org/files/PR_MemAfrVacTMimpact-9June2011_EN_pdf.

● ● ● **FOR FURTHER READING**

WHO website for reports of meningococcal disease in Africa. Available at: http://www.who.int/csr/disease/meningococcal/epidemiological/en/.

CHAPTER

18

Tuberculosis

Jonathan E. Golub, Jacqueline S. Coberly, and Richard E. Chaisson

INTRODUCTION

The ancient Greeks called it *phthisis*, the Romans *tabes*, and the Hindus *rajayakshma*; in Victorian England, it was known as *consumption*.[1] All of these names referred to the wasting illness that is characteristic of the disease we now call *tuberculosis* (TB). Tuberculosis is a complex communicable disease of humans caused by the tubercle bacilli, a group of genetically related mycobacteria also known collectively as the *Mycobacterium tuberculosis* complex. The tubercle bacilli are a group of slow-growing mycobacteria that include *M. tuberculosis*, *M. africanum*, *M. canettii*, *M. bovis*, and *M. microti*. The first three members of this group are, at least to date, strictly human pathogens.

M. bovis causes illness in a variety of animals as well as in humans.[2–4] Similarly, *M. microti* generally causes disease in rodents, but has been linked retrospectively to infections in llamas, ferrets, and cats. It has also been implicated as the cause of pulmonary tuberculosis in a small number of humans.[5] With the advent of effective drug treatment in the 1950s and preventive therapy (or chemoprophylaxis, as it was then called) in the 1960s, many in the medical and public health communities, particularly in industrialized countries, assumed tuberculosis was conquered. This hubris led to several decades of neglect by the biomedical community, during which control efforts were ignored or deliberately weakened.[6] Unfortunately, the economic, social, and public health factors that foster the propagation of tuberculosis had not been eliminated, not even from the industrialized nations. Thus, in the 1980s and 1990s, as the deterioration of control programs coincided with the burgeoning epidemic of human immunodeficiency virus (HIV), tuberculosis rebounded. Numerous outbreaks were seen in the larger cities of the United States that had the highest incidence

of HIV.[7] More serious, however, was the fact that in some areas of the developing world where tuberculosis and HIV are both endemic, the incidence of tuberculosis doubled, and healthcare facilities became overwhelmed by the dual epidemic.[6]

The World Health Organization (WHO) declared tuberculosis to be a global emergency in 1993.[6] Eighteen years later, considerable progress has been made in managing this infection, but tuberculosis remains a leading cause of premature death in young adults around the world.[8] Roughly one third of the world's inhabitants are latently infected with *M. tuberculosis*. WHO has estimated that 8.8 million people developed tuberculosis and 1.45 million died from it in 2010, representing a significant decline from the 9.4 million cases reported in 2009.[8] Efforts to promote tuberculosis control have more than doubled since 1993, and the tuberculosis incidence rate has continued to decline annually since 2002 when it peaked at 142 cases per 100,000 population. Moreover, TB mortality has fallen by more than a third since 1990 and all WHO regions, other than the African Region, are on track to halve their 1990 mortality rates by 2015. Control efforts, highlighted by the DOTS (directly observed therapy, short course)/Stop TB Strategy, have saved almost 7 million lives by successfully treating 46 million of 55 million TB patients treated in DOTS programs.[8] The global success has been driven to a significant extent by China's overwhelming achievements since 1990. That country has seen an annual 3.4% decline in its TB incidence, a halving of prevalence, and an 80% reduction in TB mortality.[8]

Despite this success, China and India account for one third of the world's TB cases, with the primary drivers of the epidemic in these countries being social determinants such as tobacco exposure, diabetes, malnutrition, alcohol abuse, and indoor air pollution.[9] Meanwhile, in Africa, the high prevalence of

latent TB infection and HIV infection, a high prevalence of multidrug-resistant TB, and the complex
epidemiology and natural history of tuberculosis
continue to make control of the disease on this continent particularly challenging.[10]

THE ORGANISM

The family Mycobacteriaceae, of the order
Actinomycetales, is composed of a number of slow-
growing, acid-fast bacilli. Most are saprophytes—
useful inhabitants of soil and water that fix nitrogen
and help degrade organic material. Some are pathogens in animals and occasionally cause opportunistic
infection in humans.[11,12] Only four species are highly
pathogenic in humans: *Mycobacterium leprae* (which
causes leprosy) and three of the tubercle bacilli. The
tubercle bacilli, or *Mycobacterium tuberculosis*
complex, comprise a group of five closely related
mycobacteria that cause tuberculosis (**Table 18-1**).
M. tuberculosis, *M. africanum*, and *M. bovis* are the
most common cause of human tuberculosis, although
M. bovis is also known to cause disease in a variety of animal species. The other two members of the
complex, *M. canettii* and *M. microti*, do cause tuberculosis in humans, albeit infrequently.[1,3–5,12] In fact,
M. microti has been identified as a human pathogen
only relatively recently.[5] Although they vary widely
by favored host, phenotype, and pathogenicity, the

Table 18-1	Species of *Mycobacteria*		
	Microbe	**Reservoir**	**Clinical Manifestation**
Always pathogenic in man	M. tuberculosis	Man	Pulmonary and disseminated TB
	M. bovis	Cattle, man	TB-like disease
	M. leprae	Man	Leprosy
	M. africanum	Man, monkey	Rarely TB-like pulmonary disease
Potentially pathogenic in man	M. avium complex	Soil, water, birds, fowl, swine, cattle, and environment	Disseminated and pulmonary TB-like disease
	M. canettii	Man, possibly others	Rarely TB-like pulmonary disease
	M. microti	Rodents, llamas, cats, ferrets, and possibly man	Rarely TB-like pulmonary disease
	M. kansasii	Water, cattle	TB-like disease
Uncommon or rarely pathogenic in man	M. genavense	Possibly man and pet birds	Blood-borne disease with AIDS
	M. haemophilum	Unknown	Subcutaneous nodules and ulcers primarily with AIDS
	M. malmoense	Environment, possibly others	Adults: TB-like pulmonary Children: Lymphadenitis
	M. marinum	Fish, water	Skin infections
	M. scrofulaceum	Soil, water	Cervical lymphadenitis
	M. simiae	Monkey, water	TB-like pulmonary and disseminated disease with AIDS
	M. szulgai	Unknown	TB-like pulmonary disease
	M. ulcerans	Man, environment	Skin infections (Buruli ulcer)
	M. xenopi	Water, birds	TB-like pulmonary disease

Adapted from Brooks GF et al, editors. Jawetz, Melnick & Adelberg's Medical Microbiology, 21st Edition. Stamford: Appleton & Lange: 1998; and
Niemann S et al. (2000). Two cases of *Mycobacterium microti*-derived tuberculosis in HIV-negative immunnocomptent patients. *Emerging Infectious
Diseases* 6(5): 539–42; and Pffyer, G et al (1998). *Mycobacterium canettii*, the smooth variant of M. *tuberculosis*, isolated from a Swiss patient
exposed in Africa. *Emerging Infectious Diseases* 4(4): 631–4.

bacteria that make up the *M. tuberculosis* complex share more than 90% of their genome and have identical 16S rRNA sequences.[2,13] With the advent of the HIV epidemic, several other mycobacteria—most notably, *M. avium* complex (MAC)— have emerged as common opportunistic pathogens and, in people infected with HIV, cause illness that is clinically similar to disseminated tuberculosis.[1,13]

The bacteria that make up the *M. tuberculosis* complex are slender, slightly curved, rod-shaped bacteria averaging 4 by 0.3 µm in size.[1,3,13] *M. tuberculosis* is strictly aerobic; in contrast, *M. bovis* is microaerophilic and adapts more easily to nonpulmonary sites of infection. Like other mycobacteria, the tubercle bacilli have an unusual concentration of high-molecular-weight lipids in their cell wall, accounting for approximately 50% of their dry weight. This high lipid content makes these organisms hydrophobic and resistant to aqueous bactericidal agents and drying. It is also responsible for their acid-fast nature, a characteristic that is essentially synonymous with mycobacteria.[3,13]

Mycobacteria are slow growing and fastidious in culture. Indeed, because *M. tuberculosis* has a very long generation time (approximately 24 hours), culture is a slow process, often resulting in diagnostic delays and sometimes misdiagnosis.[5] Traditionally mycobacteria are grown on solid, enriched media, where colonies appear 4 to 6 weeks after inoculation. They can also be grown in liquid culture, where they form characteristic strings that can be seen by light microscopy. Rapid liquid culture systems (e.g., BACTEC) have been adapted for use with mycobacteria and allow identification of organisms in as little as 9–16 days, depending on the concentration of microbes in the specimen being tested.[3,14] DNA probes speed speciation of organisms following growth. Alternatively, a number of biochemical tests can be used to speciate mycobacteria, though these approaches are time consuming.[3,15]

In 1998, a consortium of scientists deciphered and published the genome map of the H37Rv strain of *M. tuberculosis* (**Figure 18-1**). The complete genome was revealed to be 4,411,529 base pairs

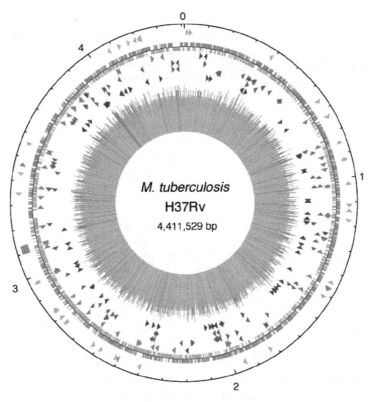

Figure 18-1 Circular map of the chromosome of *M. tuberculosis* H37Rv. The outer circle shows the scale in Mb, with 0 representing the origin of replication. The first ring from the exterior denotes the positions of stable RNA genes and the direct repeat region; the second ring inward shows the coding sequence by strand; the third ring depicts repetitive DNA; the fourth ring shows the positions of the PPE family members; the fifth ring shows the PE family members; and the sixth ring shows the positions of the PGR5 sequences. The figure was generated with software from DNASTAR. Reprinted by permission of Macmillan Publishers Ltd: Nature. Cole ST, et al. Deciphering the biology of mycobacterium tuberculosis from the complete genome sequence. June 11; 393(6685):538. Copyright © 1998.

long and contains approximately 4000 genes.[16] Since then, advances in genotyping technology have been rapidly applied to studies of the molecular epidemiology of the tubercle bacilli. Genotyping methods have been rapidly adopted, including restriction fragment-length polymorphism (RFLP), polymerase chain reaction (PCR)–based spoligotyping, and profiling of the mycobacterial interspersed repetitive units based on the number and size of the variable number tandem repeats in the genome (MIRU-VNTR). Most recently, the application of whole-genome sequencing analysis has been shown to be optimal, though this technique remains too costly for universal use. These methods vary in sensitivity and specificity, so some caution is needed when interpreting results.[18]

Genotyping studies are providing some interesting insights into the epidemiology of tuberculosis. For example, 15 years ago it was dogma that *M. tuberculosis* was a mutated form of *M. bovis*; the assumption being that around 7000–4000 BCE, when humans began domesticating animals, they were exposed to *M. bovis*, which, over time, mutated into a human pathogen.[19] In a recent fingerprinting

study, however, the genomes of 100 strains of *M. tuberculosis* complex were mapped and compared. The genetic lineage developed from these analyses provides evidence that human *M. tuberculosis* is not a mutation of *M. bovis*; rather, both bacteria diverged from a common ancestor long before either infected humans[2,13] (**Figure 18-2**).

DNA fingerprinting is also being used with traditional field epidemiology to help link index and secondary cases and to distinguish active disease resulting from reactivation versus recent transmission. When distinguishing between reactivation and recent transmission, the presumption is that the genotype of cases due to reactivation will not match the genotype of other cases in the community because the infection was acquired at some distant point in the past. Conversely, in cases involving recent infection, the genotype of the organism should be shared with at least the index case and probably other cases in the community resulting from the same index case. Note, however, that the "orphan" isolates that do not share a genotype with any other organism from the community could still be related to other cases

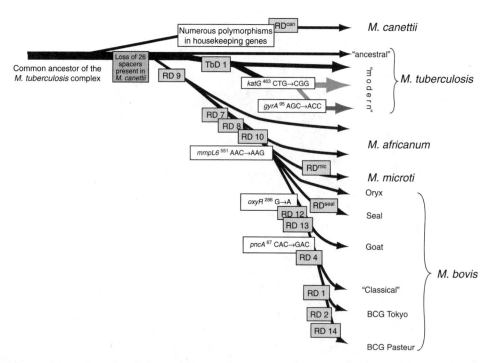

Figure 18-2 Scheme of the proposed evolutionary pathway of the tubercle bacilli illustrating successive loss of DNA in certain lineages (gray boxes). The scheme is based on the presence or absence of conserved deleted regions and on sequence polymorphisms in five selected genes. Note that the distances between certain branches may not correspond to actual phylogenetic differences calculated by other methods. The top five dark arrows indicate that strains are characterized by katG463. CTG (Leu), gyr A95 ACC (Thr), typical for group 1 organisms. The bottom seven arrows indicate the strains belong to group 2 characterized by katG463 CGG (Arg), gyrA95 ACC (Thr). The light gray arrow indicates that strains belong to group 3, characterized by katG463 CGG (Arg), gyrA95 AGC(Ser), as defined by Sreevatsan et al. Reprinted from Brosch, R, AS Pym, SV Gordon, ST Cole. The evolution of mycobacterial pathogenicity: clues from comparative genomics. Trends Microbiol. Sep;9(9):452–8. Copyright © 2001, with permission from Elsevier.

in the community, but the link cannot be identified with traditional epidemiology; this can happen when the index case is sputum negative, or when the DNA fingerprint of the index is obtained for other reasons. Nevertheless, cluster analysis is fairly reliable and has provided new and interesting epidemiologic information about tuberculosis.

Before fingerprinting was commonly available, it was believed that most infections in immunosuppressed people in low-prevalence areas represented reactivation of latent infection. The populations at risk were often transient, and linking cases epidemiologically was difficult. More recently, DNA fingerprinting studies of community cohorts have identified some surprising clusters and helped guide the shoe-leather epidemiology needed to confirm the linkages suggested by fingerprint evidence.[20] Fingerprinting studies have also helped characterize the global distribution of genotypes, clarify patterns of transmission in communities, detect laboratory transmission, and prioritize control activities.[21–26] A U.S. study helped dispel the dogma that TB can be transmitted only through prolonged contact, and that casual transmission frequently occurs.[27] DNA fingerprinting is also being used to investigate the origins of susceptibility to the tuberculosis bacilli and innate host immunity to it.[18,28,29]

HISTORY

Evolution of the Tubercle Bacilli

Mycobacteria are ancient organisms that probably first appeared more than 1 million years ago in soil and water and gradually adapted to animal hosts during the Paleolithic period*.[19,30] Until recently, it was hypothesized that when humans began domesticating cattle, they began to be exposed to M. bovis, which eventually mutated into the human pathogen M. tuberculosis. A recent comparison of the genotype of 100 tubercle bacilli showed, however, that M. bovis, M. tuberculosis, and the other members of the M. tuberculosis complex all diverged from a common ancestor through successive loss of DNA (Figure 18-2).[2]

Regardless of the evolutionary path of the tubercle bacilli, at some point in early prehistory tuberculosis became pathogenic for humans. Skeletal remains of Neolithic humans with deformities suggestive of

* The Paleolithic (Greek, "old stone age") era began approximately 2.6 million years ago, when Hominis (from Homo habilis through to Homo Sapiens sapiens) began to congregate in small groups and used basic stone tools. The era ends around 10,000 BP (Before Present—fixed at 1950 when carbon dating was developed).

tuberculosis have been found in Germany, France, Italy, Denmark, and Jordan and are dated from 8000 to 5000 BCE.[1,31] It cannot be conclusively proved that these deformities are the result of infection with the tubercle bacillus, as the organism cannot be cultured from the bone. Nevertheless, the deformities are strongly suggestive of spinal tuberculosis or Pott's disease.[1,19]

Traces of tuberculosis-like disease have also been identified in Egyptian mummies dating from 3500 to 400 BCE.[3,30] One particularly well-preserved mummy of a 5-year-old boy from about 1000 BCE was discovered with the lungs intact. Again, the causative organism could not be conclusively identified, but a diagnosis of tuberculosis was made based on the observation of pleural adhesion, blood in the trachea, and the presence of acid-fast bacilli in the lung tissue.[3] Egyptian artifacts from this period also begin to show people with the spinal deformities characteristic of Pott's disease.[3]

Based on available evidence, tuberculosis appears to have initially been a sporadic disease in humans. This is difficult to verify, however, because relatively few large collections of skeletal remains of prehistoric human are available for examination. What is known with certainty is that as civilization developed and people began to gather together in ever increasing numbers, reports of tuberculosis became more numerous, leading to the establishment of tuberculosis as an endemic disease of humans by the beginning of the first millennium.[1,19]

Global Evolution of the Epidemic

By CE 100, tuberculosis was well established in the Mediterranean states and Western Europe. It remained relatively sporadic for centuries, until people began settling in larger communities.[19] The advent of the Industrial Revolution and the great migrations to the cities that followed created an ideal environment for the spread of tuberculosis.[30,32] In 1662, 1 of every 6 northern Europeans had tuberculosis; 100 years later, this figure had doubled.[3] Tuberculosis was so common that most of the population became infected, and 25% of all deaths were attributed to tuberculosis.[19] Thomas Sydenham was quoted in 1682 as saying, "Two thirds of those who die of chronic diseases . . . [are] . . . killed by phthisis."[32] The epidemic peaked in England in 1780s and in Western Europe by 1800.[30]

Although sporadic, M. bovis infections were not uncommon in the largely agrarian societies of the New World. However, it was the English and European colonists who are mostly likely responsible for spreading M. tuberculosis throughout the world.

Tuberculosis came to North America on the *Mayflower* and was well established in the colonies by the early 1700s.[1,30] The epidemic passed through the United States in a wave, pushing south and west with the spread of industrialization, and by the early 1900s it was endemic in North America.[30] Tuberculosis was also spread to South America by colonists, but because the Spanish quarantined consumptives in the 1600s and 1700s, its introduction in that region was slowed.[1] Tuberculosis also spread into Eastern Europe, Asia, and Africa from Western Europe. The epidemics in Russia came in the late 1800s and those in Asia in the early 1900s. Tuberculosis was still largely unknown in Africa at the beginning of the 1900s and spread slowly through the interior with the colonizing Europeans.[1,19]

Herd immunity to tuberculosis develops slowly because of the long incubation period of the TB organism. Differences in the epidemiology in different parts of the world may be related to when tuberculosis was introduced to the population, with the most serious disease present in Africa where tuberculosis was introduced latest, leaving the least amount of time for herd immunity to develop.[19,33]

CLINICAL MANIFESTATIONS

As discussed in more detail later, tuberculosis begins with latent infection that can progress to active disease. Latent tuberculosis infection (LTBI) causes no symptoms, and most latently infected people are unaware that they harbor tubercle bacilli. Tuberculosis disease generally affects the lungs and respiratory tract, but can strike nearly any organ system in the body. Both primary and reactivation tuberculosis disease can result in pulmonary or extrapulmonary manifestations. In immunocompetent people, approximately 80% of tuberculosis is pulmonary, whereas extrapulmonary disease is less common. Extrapulmonary disease is much more common in immunodeficient individuals and children.[34,35] A small percentage of immunocompetent patients and many more immunodeficient ones develop both pulmonary and extrapulmonary tuberculosis.[35]

The onset of active tuberculosis is insidious, and the symptoms can be nonspecific. Pulmonary disease causes symptoms ranging from very mild to severe and can present with productive cough with or without bloody sputum, fatigue, anorexia, weight loss, fever, sweating and/or chills, and chest pain.[13,34,35] Extrapulmonary tuberculosis also causes fatigue and night sweats, but generally other symptoms specifically related to the affected organ system

will be prominent.[13,34–36] The most frequent sites of extrapulmonary infection include the pleura, pericardium, larynx, lymph nodes, skeleton (particularly the spine), genitourinary tract, eyes, meninges, gastrointestinal tract, adrenal glands, and skin.[3,37–39] Systemic infection with tubercle bacilli occurs when hematogenous or lymphatic dissemination spreads the organism throughout the body, producing small nodules of infection in essentially every organ. Early researchers named disseminated disease *miliary tuberculosis* because they thought the tiny nodules resembled grains of millet, particularly when seen by chest radiography.[13,35,40] Miliary tuberculosis is especially common in children and in people with immunosuppression.[7,34,41]

DIAGNOSIS

Latent Tuberculosis Infection

Latent tuberculosis infection is asymptomatic; therefore, diagnosis is based on clinical tests that identify signs of infection or immunologic responses to tuberculosis antigens. In the past, tuberculosis infection was often diagnosed radiographically, with calcified lesions interpreted as evidence of infection.[3,42] This technique has been shown to lack both sensitivity and specificity and has now been abandoned. Serologic diagnosis of tuberculosis infection has been extensively investigated but also lacks sensitivity because the number of tubercle bacilli in latent tuberculosis is very small, and antibody responses are limited.[43] Identification of specific cellular immune responses through the induction of delayed-type hypersensitivity with a tuberculin skin test (TST) remains the most widely used method for diagnosing latent infection.[43,44]

Purified protein derivative (PPD) of tuberculin is a solution prepared from cultures of tubercle bacilli.[45,46] It was developed by Robert Koch in 1890 and touted as a cure for tuberculosis. The curative value of tuberculin was soon disproved, but further studies showed that it could be used to identify people with tuberculosis infection.[42,46,47] The Mantoux method of intracutaneous injection of a standardized dose of PPD has been widely validated, whereas other methods (e.g., the Tine test) have not. Individuals with LTBI develop a zone of induration when a standardized amount of tuberculin is injected intracutaneously, whereas uninfected people react minimally or not at all. The TST result is reported as the width of induration that surrounds the test site observed at a minimum of 48–72 hours following injection.[48] The test is usually applied to the volar surface of the forearm and read by a trained observer, who measures induration by marking the edge of the hardened area of skin, either visually or manually, to demarcate the border, and recording the distance across in millimeters. Induration of the injection site is the result of a delayed-type hypersensitivity response in which activated T cells and macrophages migrate to the site of antigen injection and mount a localized cellular immune response. It is essential that at least 48 hours be allowed for this process to mature; earlier readings may produce falsely negative or positive results. Erythema of the site is nonspecific and, except in Japan, is not used to determine test results. Positive results remain measurable for more than one week in most instances.[49]

The performance characteristics of the tuberculin test were standardized in the 1940s in an important study conducted by Carroll Palmer, in which varying concentrations of tuberculin were administered to a group of patients with active tuberculosis and to controls who were unlikely to have ever encountered tuberculosis.[50] The currently used standard dose of 5 tuberculin units of PPD-S was found to elicit a reaction of greater than 10 mm of induration in almost 98% of tuberculosis patients and in less than 5% of controls. A smaller dose of another preparation (i.e., 2 tuberculin units of RT-23 tuberculin) produces similar results.

Exposure to non-tuberculous mycobacteria may induce cross-reactivity to the tuberculin, which can result in a falsely positive reaction.[46] Similarly, vaccination against tuberculosis with bacillus Calmette-Guérin (BCG) vaccine can induce a response. The strength and durability of the reaction produced by BCG is less than with tuberculosis infection, and after three to five years it does not generally interfere with PPD testing.[34,51,52] Skin test results can also be falsely negative when the cellular immune system is impaired. People with active tuberculosis who are coinfected with HIV, have cancer, or have other immunosuppressive illnesses are frequently unable to mount a response to any skin test antigen, so tuberculin results in these people should be interpreted with some care.[36,37,46,50] Moreover, malnutrition and micronutrient deficiencies interfere with immunity and can inhibit response to tuberculin, as can acute viral infections such as measles.[13,34,42,53-56] In addition, between 10% and 25% of people with active tuberculosis fail to respond to tuberculin.[46,57] The size of the tuberculin response is not, however, associated with the patient's stage of disease, as the size of reaction in active cases and their close contacts is similar.[37,46]

In summary, the size of the reaction to tuberculin varies considerably depending on the individual's exposure to the tubercle bacilli and other non-tuberculous mycobacteria, BCG vaccination history, and immune status.[46]

Although the sensitivity and specificity of tuberculin testing can be evaluated in people with active tuberculosis, determining the accuracy of the test in people with latent infection is more difficult, as no gold standard for diagnosis exists. In studies of U.S. Navy recruits undertaken in the 1950s and 1960s, a tuberculin reaction of greater than 10 mm was strongly associated with the subsequent risk of tuberculosis. Nonetheless, because some people with negative tests develop tuberculosis and many people with positive tests do not, the interpretation of test results must be modified on the basis of clinical and epidemiologic knowledge. Perhaps more so than with most clinical tests, interpretation of the tuberculin test is highly dependent on prior probability of tuberculosis infection and clinical consequences of misreading the result.

As shown in **Table 18-2**, the reaction size that is considered positive varies depending on the clinical

Table 18-2	Cut-Points for Positive Tuberculin Skin Test (TST)
Category	**Induration = TST Positive**
• Coinfected with HIV • Close contacts of known active case • People with fibrotic changes consistent with prior tuberculosis • People with organ transplants or other immunosuppression	≥5 mm
• Recent immigrants (<5 yrs) • Injection drug users (IDUs) • Prolonged exposure to high-risk congregate settings • Mycobacterial laboratory personnel • People with clinical conditions that put them at increased risk • Infant, children, and adolescent contacts exposed to adults in high-risk categories	≥10 mm
• People with no known risk factors for TB, but recommend only targeted skin testing	≥15 mm

Adapted from Centers for Disease Control and Prevention, D. o. T. E. (2005). Tuberculin skin testing, document #250140.

status of the person being tested.[48] For example, people likely to have been recently exposed to tuberculosis, such as household contacts of an active infectious case, have a high prior probability of infection and the cut-off point for a positive test is reduced to 5 mm. Similarly, an HIV-infected person has a very high risk of developing active tuberculosis if infected, so a 5-mm reaction is considered positive because the consequences of misinterpreting the result are severe and because HIV infection suppresses the cellular immune response and can diminish the size of the reaction to PPD.[49] People who come from an area where tuberculosis is prevalent have a lower risk than household contacts but a higher risk than someone who lives in a low-incidence country; therefore, a 10-mm response is considered positive. For people with a low prior probability of tuberculosis exposure, the cut-off point for a positive test is 15 mm of induration.[48]

In recent years, attempts to modernize the diagnosis of latent tuberculosis have focused on assays that detect the production of interferon-gamma (IFN-γ) by T cells in response to stimulation with mycobacterial antigens, collectively referred to as interferon-gamma release assays (IGRAs). These "indirect tests" do not directly detect the presence of actual TB bacilli, but rather identify an immune response that suggests recent or remote exposure to TB bacilli.[50,51] Such immunodiagnostic assays promise to improve on the tuberculin test by eliminating skin test placement and reading errors, obviating the need for patients to return for interpretation of results, and standardizing the assessment of results with objective measurements in a laboratory. T cells obtained from individuals who have been infected with *M. tuberculosis* will produce IFN-γ when cocultivated with tuberculous antigens, whereas T cells from uninfected individuals will not. Detection of the produced IFN-γ is possible with either an enzyme-linked immunosorbent assay (ELISA) that measures soluble cytokines or an enzyme-linked immunospot assay (ELISPOT) that stains intracellular IFN-γ in T cells. Two commercial applications of this approach have been developed: an ELISA-based method called Quantiferon-Gold In-Tube (QGIT) and an ELISPOT assay called T SPOT TB. Early versions of these assays relied on PPD-S as the antigen and, therefore, were associated with false-positive results in people who had been vaccinated with BCG or who had non-tuberculous mycobacterial infections.[50] Second- and third-generation assays, now commercially available in a number of countries, rely on *M. tuberculosis*-specific antigens from a region of the mycobacterial genome known as RD-1 that

is absent in BCG and most non-tuberculous mycobacteria.[51] Studies of these tests show that they have excellent agreement with the tuberculin skin test, but appear to be more specific, as they are less likely to be positive in individuals with a history of BCG vaccination who are otherwise at low risk for tuberculosis infection.[51,52] QGIT is now recommended for determining LTBI status in the United States, and its utility has been verified in a variety of settings.[53] However, in low- and middle-income countries, these tests have not been endorsed by WHO, as insufficient data exist to prove their utility in these settings, particularly in those countries with high TB and/or HIV prevalence.[54]

Surprisingly, IGRAs are no more likely to predict risk of developing active tuberculosis than the TST, though data available on follow up for IGRA studies pale in comparison to the wealth of data from TST follow up studies.[55] While a positive result for either test indicates a doubling of risk for active TB, IGRAs tend to produce fewer false-positive results, so they are a more efficient test in TB control programs that seek to implement preventive therapy.

As the literature for IGRAs has exploded over the past 10 years, several systematic reviews have assessed the assays' potential usefulness in different settings and populations. These tests have been conclusively shown not to aid in the diagnosis of active TB disease.[56] Although they represent an enormous step forward in diagnosing latent TB, their use is limited by their high cost, exacting technical requirements (fresh blood must be put into cell culture within several hours of being collected), and lack of prospective validation. Nonetheless, IGRAs are a welcome addition to the diagnostic arsenal and will play a valuable role in both clinical practice and epidemiologic research in the coming years.

Active Tuberculosis Disease

In active tuberculosis, clinical signs and symptoms result from the replication of large numbers of tubercle bacilli and the ensuing inflammatory host response. Diagnosis of active tuberculosis is based on evaluation of epidemiologic assessment of tuberculosis risk, clinical findings and symptoms, and laboratory tests including chest radiographs, tuberculin skin tests, microscopic examination, and culture of tissues such as sputum or biopsy specimens.

The signs and symptoms of active tuberculosis are nonspecific and overlap with a number of other pulmonary and systemic diseases. Fever, sweats, and weight loss are prominent systemic findings and are usually of several weeks' or months' duration. Cough is a principal feature of pulmonary tuberculosis and can be associated with sputum production or hemoptysis. The symptoms of extrapulmonary tuberculosis are highly variable and depend on the specific organ involved.

Chest radiographs are critically important in diagnosing pulmonary tuberculosis. Classically, patients with reactivation tuberculosis have upper-lobe cavitary infiltrates or involvement of the superior segments of the lower lobes, whereas patients with primary tuberculosis have mostly lower or mid-lung infiltrates and hilar adenopathy. Recent studies using molecular epidemiologic techniques, however, have shown that both primary and reactivation tuberculosis can present with chest X-ray findings that are classic for the other form of disease. In the setting of clinical symptoms consistent with tuberculosis and an abnormal chest radiograph, specific diagnostic tests for tuberculosis should be undertaken. With HIV infection and tuberculosis, however, the chest X-ray in some patients may be normal.

Diagnosis of tuberculosis is confirmed by identification of acid-fast bacilli by smear or by isolation of *M. tuberculosis* in cultures of sputum or other tissues. Zeihl-Nielsen staining is the standard method used globally for microscopic identification of acid-fast bacilli. In this process, a fixed smear is exposed to hot carbol fushin dye for 2 to 3 minutes, rinsed, and decolorized with a dilute acid-alcohol solution. Mycobacteria absorb the carbol fushin dye but resist decolorization because of the high lipid content in their cell walls—hence the name acid-fast bacilli.[15] Fluorescent staining with auraminerhodamine is a more sensitive but more expensive technique. Unfortunately, the number of tubercle bacilli present in sputum may be very low, particularly in noncavitary disease, so direct microscopic observation is a fairly insensitive way to diagnose tuberculosis. Only approximately 60% of culture-confirmed cases of tuberculosis are smear positive. Also, positive microscopy simply proves the presence of acid-fast bacilli, which could include nonpathogenic species of mycobacteria or other acid-fast bacteria such as *Nocardia*.[36,37]

Several types of tests, including nucleic acid amplification assays (e.g., PCR), mass spectrometry or gas-liquid chromatography for tuberculostearic acid, and immunoassays for mycobacterial antigens and antibodies, have been evaluated, but with mixed results. Nucleic acid amplification tests have been approved in the United States for the diagnosis of tuberculosis in patients with positive sputum smears. Both the positive and negative predictive value of these tests are high if the sputum smear is positive, but in patients with negative sputum smear the positive predictive value of nucleic acid amplification is only in the vicinity of 50%. In many parts of the world where tuberculosis is endemic, culture and radiography are unavailable or extremely limited. In these areas, diagnosis relies primarily on clinical history and microscopic examination of sputum. New, simple, rapid diagnostic techniques are desperately needed in these areas and would also be valuable in more industrialized areas. Research in this area is ongoing, and advances have recently been made.

Significant advancements in diagnosing TB have evolved over the past several years, particularly in diagnosing TB and multidrug-resistant TB simultaneously. Line probe assays (LPAs) are a strip test that can detect TB bacteria from smear-positive sputum specimens or culture isolates using PCR amplification, while detecting drug resistance to rifampicin and/or isoniazid simultaneously.[57] Two LPAs are currently on the market: one made by Innogenetics in Belgium (INNO-LiPA Rif.TB) and another produced by Hain Life Science GmbH in Germany (GenoType MTBDR). Rifampin resistance is detected through mutations in the *rpoB* gene, while isoniazid resistance is identified through mutations in the *katG* and *inhA* genes.[58,59] When assessing *M. tuberculosis* isolates from culture, the LPAs' sensitivity and specificity are consistently high.[60] With clinical specimens (including sputum) and culture isolates, the sensitivity and specificity for rifampicin resistance are high for both LPAs across multiple subpopulations, at 98.1% and 98.7% for the Belgian and German tests, respectively.[61] Accuracy for isoniazid was considerably lower (84.3%) and varied widely across groups, while specificity was high for all populations (99.5%).

More recently, the Xpert MTB/RIF assay has been called a game-changer in the TB diagnostic world. Xpert MTB/RIF is a fully automated system that allows the operator to perform sample processing, DNA amplification, and detection of *M. tuberculosis* and of rifampicin resistance in less than 2 hours time with very little hands-on operation.[62] Boehme et al. evaluated Xpert in a multicountry study and showed that with a single test, 98% of patients with smear-positive and culture-positive TB were correctly identified, while the same proportion of rifampin-resistant isololates were detected.[62] Moreover, 72.5% of smear-negative, culture-positive patients were detected. This assay has created considerable excitement, and many studies investigating the full capacity of this assay are currently under way, including use of Xpert outside of the traditional laboratory setting because of its minimal operator and laboratory requirements. The test is more costly than traditional diagnostics, so the cost-effectiveness in various settings needs to be evaluated. WHO recently recommended Xpert as the initial diagnostic test in individuals suspected of having HIV-associated TB and has published several documents designed to aid implementation of this diagnostic tool by TB programs.[73,64]

Ultimately, the diagnosis of tuberculosis involves a synthesis of clinical and laboratory findings. The case definition of tuberculosis used for surveillance purposes accepts the diagnosis if there is a positive culture, a positive acid-fast smear with compatible clinical findings, or a characteristic illness with other evidence suggestive of tuberculosis and an appropriate response to anti-tuberculosis therapy.

THERAPY

History of Therapy

The history of tuberculosis therapy is divided into three eras: the pre-sanatorium, sanatorium, and chemotherapeutic eras. From earliest recognition of tuberculosis as a disease until the middle of the 1800s, therapy for tuberculosis was based on the prevailing medical dogma.[65] When ill airs were thought to cause tuberculosis, patients were told to move to mild, mountain, or seaside climates. When imbalance of bodily humors was thought to be the cause of all disease, bloodletting was recommended for tuberculosis. Rest or mild exercise and different variations in diet were also recommended at various times. Although most of these treatments did the patient no harm, they also did little to deter the progress of the infection.

In the 1850s, a number of physicians observed that a prolonged rest in quiet, mountainous, rural areas had cured their patients of tuberculosis, and the sanatorium movement was born. The underlying premise of this approach was that clean air combined with rest or mild exercise and good food would stimulate the body to heal itself. Consequently, patients were isolated in rural institutions built solely for the treatment of tuberculosis.[42,65] The first sanatorium was established by Brehmer in 1854 in the mountains of Germany; as the idea took hold, additional sanatoria were built throughout Europe, the United States, and England.[42,65] Isolation of tuberculosis cases in sanatoria, although perhaps no more beneficial to patients than extended rest at home, decreased the spread of tuberculosis in the community, contributing to the large decline

in tuberculosis incidence seen in the late 1800s and early 1900s in Europe and the United States.[65] Developments in the basic sciences during the sanatoria movement also contributed to this decline. During this time Koch discovered the causative agent of tuberculosis, and radiographic technology and surgical techniques were developed that greatly enhanced physicians' ability to diagnose and treat tuberculosis.

Unfortunately, sanatorium care had its limitations, and in the early 1900s tuberculosis was still a major cause of death. In 1938, Rich and Follis showed that sulfanilamide inhibited the growth of *M. tuberculosis* in guinea pigs, and the search for effective chemotherapeutic agents for tuberculosis began. Dapsone was tested against tuberculosis in 1940, and in 1943 streptomycin was found to have anti-tuberculosis action. The identification of other anti-tuberculosis drugs, including para-aminosalicylic acid (PAS) and isoniazid (INH), soon followed.[65]

The tradition of randomized clinical trials has a prominent place in the history of tuberculosis research. The scarcity of streptomycin in the early 1940s led the British Medical Research Council to perform the first multicenter, randomized, controlled clinical trial to estimate the efficacy of streptomycin against a placebo.[66] This elegant trial showed the profound efficacy of streptomycin against the tubercle bacilli but also the limitations of single-drug therapy in the treatment of tuberculosis. More trials followed the first rapidly as new drugs were identified, each building on the information provided by earlier work. A series of trials over several decades proved the value of combination therapy for curing tuberculosis and preventing drug resistance: the efficacy of dual therapy with streptomycin and PAS[67,68]; the efficacy of combined therapy using isoniazid[67]; the utility of multidrug therapy in shortening the duration of tuberculosis treatment[68]; the minimum treatment time needed for effective cure of tuberculosis[65–67]; the optimal drug combination for therapy[67–73]; the efficacy of intermittent (twice or thrice weekly) treatment[71,74–76,]; and the efficacy of treatment for tuberculosis in HIV-infected people.[77–80]

Current Therapy

The drugs most commonly used in treatment of tuberculosis today and their mode of action are shown in **Table 18-3**. Because the bacillary population in an infected person consists of actively growing, semi-dormant, and dormant mycobacteria,[81] effective chemotherapy is complex. Some drugs that kill actively growing bacilli cannot kill those in the latent, resting phase. Drug treatment must, therefore,

Table 18-3	First-Line Anti-Tuberculosis Drugs and Their Modes of Action	
Agent	**Activity**	**Toxicity**
Isoniazid	Bactericidal	Liver, peripheral nerve, hypersensitivity
Rifampin	Bactericidal and sterilizing	Liver, gastrointestinal, discoloration of body fluids, nausea, hematological
Rifapentine	Bactericidal and sterilizing	Liver, gastrointestinal, discoloration of body fluids, nausea, hematological
Pyrazinamide	Sterilizing	Liver, hyperuricemia, gout, malaise, gastrointestinal
Ethambutol	Bacteriostatic (dose dependent)	Liver, optic neuritis, skin
Streptomycin	Bactericidal	Ototoxicity, kidneys

Data from AD Harris and AD Maher. TB/HIV: A Clinical Manual. Copyright 1996, World Health Organization; and RH Alford, Antimycobacterial Agents. Principles and Practice of Infectious Diseases, 3rd Ed., pp. 350–360, GL Mandell et al. eds., © 1990, Churchill Livingstone.

continue for a minimum of six months to allow the majority of latent organisms to be exposed to the drugs during periods of metabolic activity and to be killed. Unfortunately, this long period of treatment also allows sufficient time for mutant bacilli to emerge that are resistant to the drug being used for treatment. When a single drug is used for treatment of tuberculosis, mutants resistant to that drug rapidly emerge and eventually become the predominant bacilli, and therapy fails. Use of at least two drugs to which the organisms are susceptible reduces the probability of developing drug-resistant microbes to essentially zero.

Key to treatment success is adherence to the full drug regimen, which reduces the risk of treatment failure and the emergence of drug resistance.[82] The Centers for Disease Control and Prevention (CDC) and other authorities recommend that directly observed therapy (DOT) be used for tuberculosis therapy. DOT implies that a healthcare worker monitors each tuberculosis patient closely and observes the patient take each dose of anti-tuberculosis medication. Historical analysis suggests that use of DOT contributes to reductions in tuberculosis incidence and dramatically reduces the incidence of drug-resistant tuberculosis[8, 83]

WHO currently recommends a short-course DOT drug regimen (DOTS) for treatment of tuberculosis that includes treatment with four drugs—generally isoniazid, rifampin, pyrazinamide, and ethambutol—for two months, followed by four months of treatment with isoniazid and rifampin[84] (**Table 18-4**). Review of many studies showed that less than six months of drug therapy results in unacceptably high treatment failure or relapse rates, yet longer treatment regimens do not yield substantially better outcomes, with relapse rates of 5% or less.[69,] [85]Of increasing concern is the drug–drug interaction

Table 18-4	Components of an Effective WHO DOTS Program

- Political commitment with increased and sustained financing
- Case detection through quality-assured bacteriology
- Standardized treatment with supervision and patient support
- An effective drug supply and management system
- Monitoring and evaluation system and impact measurement

Adapted from Harries AD, Maher D. TB/HIV A Clinical Manual. Geneva: World Health Organization; http//www.who.int.

between rifamycins and antiretroviral therapy, particularly protease inhibitors and non-nucleoside protease inhibitors.[86]

EPIDEMIOLOGY: GLOBAL PREVALENCE AND INCIDENCE

The magnitude of the global tuberculosis epidemic is staggering. One third of the world's population, or roughly 2.2 billion people, are infected with *M. tuberculosis*.[8] Tuberculosis is the eighth leading cause of death in the world and causes more deaths each year (approximately 1.4 million in 2010) than all other infectious agents except HIV.[8] Although tuberculosis reemerged in the 1980s as a public health problem in the United States and other industrialized nations, the majority of all tuberculosis cases occur in the developing world[8] (**Figure 18-3**).

Global Variations in Disease

WHO collects and reports global tuberculosis incidence data annually. Although reporting to WHO is voluntary, nearly all countries in the world comply.

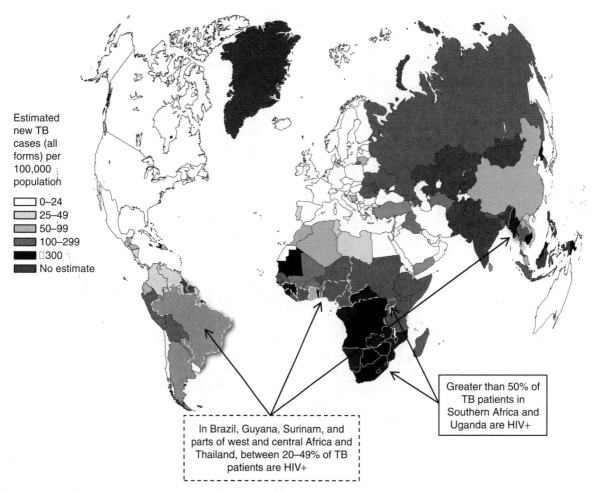

Estimated
new TB
cases (all
forms) per
100,000
population

- 0–24
- 25–49
- 50–99
- 100–299
- ☐300
- No estimate

In Brazil, Guyana, Surinam, and
parts of west and central Africa and
Thailand, between 20–49% of TB
patients are HIV+

Greater than 50% of
TB patients in
Southern Africa and
Uganda are HIV+

Figure 18-3 Estimated TB Incidence Rates and Corresponding HIV Prevalence Rates by Country, 2010. Adapted from WHO (2010). Global Tuberculosis Control: Surveillance planning financing. Geneva, Switzerland. http://www.who.int/tb/publications/global_report/en/index/ html. Accessed February 29, 2012.

Types of data provided include the number of new tuberculosis cases of all types, the number of new smear-positive cases, age and sex information for smear-positive cases, the number of cases coinfected with HIV, and information on the status of the country's tuberculosis control program.[8] The quality of the data reported to WHO varies. To compensate for these differences, WHO now reports these estimates with uncertainty intervals, although estimates are becoming more precise as more countries are providing numbers from direct measurements.[8]

WHO presents data annually by geographic regions of the world. Although convenient and logical, some of the six regions include countries with very different risks of tuberculosis. This diversity confuses the epidemiologic picture somewhat, but the WHO regions are the only available source of standardized global information. As shown in Figure 18-3 and **Table 18-5**, the incidence and prevalence of tuberculosis vary greatly around the world.[8]

The South East Asia Region (SEAR) has the largest number of TB cases of any of the WHO regions (WHO estimate: 3,200,000 cases in 2010). The per capita rate of disease is highest in the Africa region (AFR), however: 276/100,000 in 2010 versus 193/100,000 for SEAR. Together, SEAR and AFR account for roughly 66% of all tuberculosis cases in the world, and as many as 60% to 70% of adults in these regions are latently infected with TB. The rates of disease in the Eastern Mediterranean region (EMR) and the Western Pacific Region (WPR) are also high, but only about one third of the rate seen in AFR.

The number of cases and rate of disease are lowest in the Americas (AMR) and European (EUR) regions, although there is fairly wide variation by country within these regions. Incidence and mortality curves show two peaks in these regions as well. The first occurs in infancy, and males predominate. The second peak occurs in adolescence and early

Table 18-5	Number of Estimated Incident Tuberculosis Cases (All Types), Prevalent Tuberculosis Cases (All Types), Deaths due to TB, and Estimated Incidence Rate, Worldwide and by WHO Region, 2010			
	Estimated Incidence	Estimated Prevalence	Estimated Deaths	Estimated Annual Incidence Rate (per 100,000 Population)
Africa (AFR)	2,300,000	2,800,000	250,000	276
Americas (AMR)	270,000	330,000	20,000	29
Eastern Mediterranean (EMR)	650,000	1,000,000	95,000	109
European (EUR)	420,000	560,000	61,000	47
South East Asia (SEAR)	3,500,000	5,000,000	500,000	193
Western Pacific (WPR)	1,700,000	2,500,000	130,000	93
Global Total	8,800,000	12,000,000	1,100,000	128

Adapted from the World Health Organization (2011). WHO Global Tuberculosis Report 2011, Table 2.1 page 12. http://www.who.int/tb/publications/global_report/en/index.html. Last updated October 31, 2011. Accessed February 29, 2012.

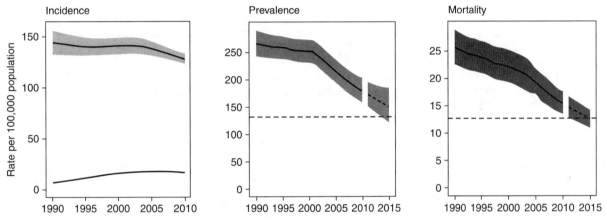

Figure 18-4 Trends in tuberculosis case notification rates, all types of tuberculosis. Reproduced from the World Health Organization (2011). Global Tuberculosis Control: Surveillance, Planning, Financing. Geneva, Switzerland, http://www.who.int/tb/publications/global_report/en/index.html. Accessed September 18, 2012.

adulthood, and females predominate. As rates decline after the second peak, the incidence and mortality in males surpass the corresponding rates in females at about 35 years of age (lower than in AFR and SER) and remain higher until death.[8,30]

Figure 18-4 shows global trends in estimated TB incidence, prevalence, and mortality from 1990 to 2010. The prevalence and mortality figures are reported relative to the Stop TB Partnership target of a 50% reduction in prevalence and mortality by the year 2015 compared to the year 1990. The incidence figure includes trends for all TB and TB among HIV-infected persons. Global incidence has steadily declined, albeit quite slowly, since reaching a peak in 2004, whereas prevalence and mortality have markedly declined over the past 10 years. **Figure 18-5**

stratifies TB incidence by WHO region for the period 1990–2010.

Since 1990, all regions have been on a steady or downward trend in terms of TB cases, except for Africa, where the increase in cases has been fueled by the HIV epidemic. In the Americas, incidence has declined sharply, with the most significant declines coming from Brazil. The significant declines in TB cases in the Western Pacific are due primarily to successful control efforts in China.

Disease trends in Africa vary depending on HIV prevalence. In high-prevalence areas, notification rates continue to increase, as they have since the mid-1980s. In some countries, this increase has been mitigated by effective tuberculosis control activities.

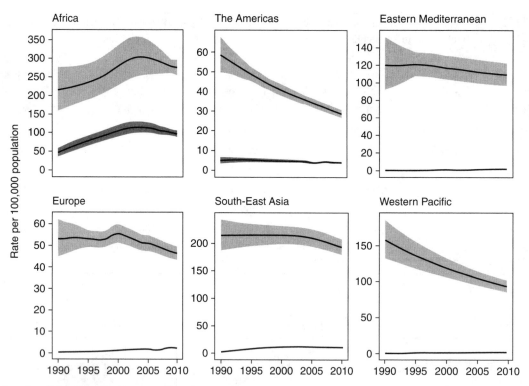

Figure 18-5 Trends in tuberculosis case notification rates, by region. Reproduced from the World Health Organization (2011). Global Tuberculosis Control: Surveillance, Planning, Financing. Geneva, Switzerland, http://www.who.int/tb/publications/global_report/en/index.html. Accessed September 18, 2012.

NATURAL HISTORY OF TUBERCULOSIS

The tubercle bacilli are only moderately infectious; some 20% to 30% of people exposed to an active case become infected.[87] As with most other infectious diseases, development of clinical tuberculosis is a two-step process: infection of the host with the microorganism occurs first, followed by development of active disease caused by unchecked microbial replication and the body's immune response. What is different about the tubercle bacillus is that after it infects tissues, it can remain dormant for 20 to 30 years before active disease develops.

In a classic infection, *M. tuberculosis* enters the body via minute droplet nuclei deposited in the air when a person with active tuberculosis coughs, talks, or sneezes.[13,87] The droplet nuclei travel through the airways and are deposited on the alveolar surface, where the microbe is ingested by alveolar macrophages and begins replication. Activated macrophages release cytokines, which in turn recruit more macrophages and activated T cells in an effort to control the infection.[12,13,35] At this point, either the inflammation infection cycle continues and active primary tuberculosis develops

(5% to 10% of people[65,88]), or the immune system contains the primary infection. A sizeable, but unknown, proportion of the 90% to 95% of people whose immune systems contain the primary infection develop latent infection.[13,65] In these people, the microbe can remain in macrophages and other cells for decades in a quiescent, yet viable state. In 5% to 10% of people with a latent infection, some later waning of cellular immunity allows these dormant bacilli to begin growing again, resulting in an active infection that is referred to as *reactivation tuberculosis*.[12,13,15]

The propagation of tuberculosis within a population can be viewed as a series of steps related to the natural history of tuberculosis infection in individuals, as illustrated in **Figure 18-6**.[89] Within a population, a reservoir of tuberculosis exists within people with latent tuberculosis infection (Stage 1). Each year, a proportion of these latently infected individuals develop active tuberculosis (Stage 2). Reactivation of latent tuberculosis is facilitated by recent infection, malnutrition, immunosuppression, and other medical conditions that affect cellular immunity. Thus, in a population with a high prevalence of HIV infection, a large proportion of tuberculosis

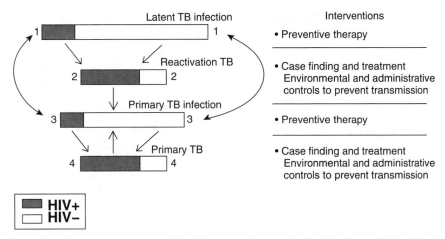

Figure 18-6 Dynamics of TB in a population with high HIV prevalence. Reprinted with permission of the International Union Against Tuberculosis and Lung Disease. Copyright © The Union.

cases will be HIV-infected individuals (Figure 18-6, shaded area). People with reactivation tuberculosis transmit infection to their contacts, causing tuberculosis infection (Stage 3). Rapid diagnosis of infectious cases and effective therapy reduce the number of contacts who are infected, but even in the best of circumstances an average of 10 contacts are infected before the case is sterilized with appropriate chemotherapy. Five percent to 10% of these contacts will develop active tuberculosis within the next year or two (Stage 4), and then will pass infection 1 active tuberculosis infection on to a number of their contacts (Stage 3). The remainder of the newly infected persons will enlarge the pool of latently infected individuals (Stage 1).

MECHANISM OF TRANSMISSION

Airborne transmission via the respiratory tract is the primary and most efficient mode of transmitting tuberculosis. People with active pulmonary or laryngeal tuberculosis discharge minute particles of sputum into the air when coughing, talking, sneezing, or singing.[43,90-92] The liquid in these sputum droplets evaporates, leaving droplet nuclei that contain the solid parts of the droplet and sometimes a few mycobacteria.[93] The speed of evaporation depends primarily on the size of the droplet, although environmental factors, such as humidity, also affect the process. Large droplets evaporate more slowly, so they quickly drop out of the air. Smaller droplets, 1 to 10 μm in diameter, dry more quickly and can remain in the air for long periods of time.[93] It is the floating droplet nuclei that cause infection. They are

inhaled by uninfected people and lodge in the alveoli or terminal bronchioles to form the nidus of infection.[30] The size of the droplet nuclei is critical, as larger ones lodge in the lining of the nose and trachea, whereas very tiny ones may be expired before they lodge in the respiratory tract.[94]

The infectivity of an individual with pulmonary tuberculosis is a function of the virulence of the bacteria, the frequency of the person's cough, and the degree of pulmonary cavitation. Loudon and colleagues showed that coughing, talking, and singing produced both different quantities and different sizes of droplet nuclei and that both properties are important components of infectivity.[90,92] The degree of pulmonary cavitation is important because it correlates with the bacterial load in the sputum. Logically, the more open lesions, or cavities, in the lung, the greater the probability that bacteria will be expired. Similarly, laryngeal tuberculosis is particularly infectious because all exhalations are forced through infected tissue.[30,37,95-97]

M. tuberculosis can also enter the body through mucous membranes in the gut, genitourinary tract, and conjunctiva, or through abrasions or breaks in the skin. Infection via these routes produces an infection at the site of entry that may remain localized or may spread to other organs and tissues via the lymphatic or blood system.[15,38,39] Transmission through these portals is relatively rare, especially in industrialized areas where the incidence of tuberculosis is low. These routes of infection are more common in developing countries where the prevalence of tuberculosis is higher. The respiratory route is still the most efficient and common mode of tuberculosis transmission in all parts of the world.

RISK FACTORS ASSOCIATED WITH INFECTION

The risk of infection is a function of exposure to the tubercle bacilli, which in turn is controlled by the infectivity of the patient, and the probability of contact with infectious organisms. Characteristics of the infectious case, such as severity of disease,[97,98] frequency of cough and other vocal activities, consistency of sputum, and initiation of chemotherapy,[99] affect the number and viability of the microbes expelled into the environment. Factors in the environment that increase the probability of contact with infected air, such as decreased ventilation, increased duration or intimacy of contact with the case, amount of ultraviolet light available, and crowding, increase the risk of acquiring infection.[42, 96, 100]

The risk of exposure refers to the probability that a susceptible person will come in contact with the tubercle bacilli. Factors associated with exposure are external to the host and include the prevalence of infectious tuberculosis in the population, population density, living conditions, and, sometimes, cultural practices. In areas where tuberculosis is endemic, the risk of exposure to the bacteria is higher simply because more people are infectious at any given time. Similarly, crowding forces people into more frequent contact with one another and increases the risk of exposure to an infectious case. Poverty has been associated with exposure, but it is so closely linked to crowding that it is difficult to tell whether it is a surrogate for crowding or a true risk factor for exposure. Chapman and Dyerly noted the association between poverty and tuberculosis but concluded that poverty was probably a surrogate for crowding and increased prevalence.[98] Studies in New York City and Washington County, Maryland, tend to disagree, however.[101,102] These studies examined factors associated with the prevalence of latent tuberculosis as measured by a positive tuberculin skin test reaction and showed that LTBI was more common in impoverished areas, even after adjustments for age and, in New York, for race. When control measures in a population are inadequate, the average duration of infectivity of a case lengthens, and the risk of exposure increases because more susceptible people can be exposed even if crowding is minimal. Cultural factors that control exposure to the public or otherwise modify exposure to an infectious case, such as sequestering women, can also affect the risk of exposure, either positively or negatively.

Risk of infection, given that exposure has occurred, is more difficult to study. Several investigations have shown that people with severe tuberculosis, as defined by cavitation or smear positivity, are more infectious than those with milder disease, presumably because they excrete more bacilli. One classic study examined the environmental and social factors associated with acquisition of infection by children living in a household with one or more tuberculous adults. The researchers found that the severity of disease in the index case was the strongest predictor of infection in the children.[99] Another study done in British Columbia and Saskatchewan found that children exposed to smear-positive cases were more likely to become infected with TB than those exposed to smear-negative cases, regardless of duration of contact.[97]

The way in which the index case expels bacteria also affects the number of mycobacteria expelled during exhalation and the risk of acquiring infection given exposure. Coughing is the best way for an index case to spread tuberculosis. A cough produces roughly four to seven times as many droplet nuclei as talking or singing, although singing produces a slightly greater proportion of small droplet nuclei that may be more infectious.[90,92] It is also clear that effective treatment of tuberculosis rapidly eliminates mycobacteria in the lungs and decreases the risk of transmission.[99,100]

It seems, therefore, that the risk of infection is a function of exposure to the tubercle bacilli, which in turn is controlled by the infectivity of the patient and the probability of contact with infectious organisms. Factors in the patient, such as severity of disease, frequency of cough, consistency of sputum, and initiation of chemotherapy, affect the number and viability of the microbes expelled into the environment. Factors in the environment that increase the probability of contact with infected air, such as decreased ventilation, increased duration or intimacy of contact with the case, amount of ultraviolet light available, and crowding, increase the risk of acquiring infection.[42,96,100] Fortunately, under normal household circumstances, tuberculosis is not highly infectious. The secondary attack rate for tuberculosis in 5- to 9-year-old household contacts was found to be approximately 48%, two-thirds lower than the corresponding attack rate for measles, mumps, or pertussis.[98] The risk of infection increases dramatically in crowded conditions, such as prisons,[103] naval vessels,[104] and nursing homes,[105] and spread can be explosive in this type of confined setting.

RISK FACTORS ASSOCIATED WITH DEVELOPMENT OF DISEASE

In the general population, only 5% to 10% of people infected with the tubercle bacillus develop active, clinical disease.[106] The risk factors that control progression from infection to disease are complex and intertwined, but differ from those that control infection. Logically these factors tend to be intrinsic because the time between infection and development of disease can vary significantly.[87]

Time Since Infection

Most cases of active tuberculosis develop within the first 2 years after infection, although the risk of infection is elevated through the fifth year after exposure.[87, 91] In a public health study of tuberculin-positive contacts of tuberculosis cases in the United States, the risk of developing tuberculosis was 1% in the first year after exposure versus 0.07% 8 to 10 years later.[87] Similarly, in a cohort of tuberculin-negative adult Norwegians followed longitudinally for tuberculin conversion and development of tuberculosis, radiographic changes associated with tuberculosis were observed in 130 of 272 tuberculin converters (48%), all within the first year after converting to a positive tuberculin reaction.[47] The question, however, is whether the time since infection is a true risk factor or a marker for another risk factor. Most likely it is a marker for the true risk factors, which may include the virulence of the infecting strain of tuberculosis and the person's inherent susceptibility to developing active disease.

Fibrotic Lesions

The presence of healed fibrotic lesions increases the risk of tuberculosis, presumably from reactivation disease, although this is nearly impossible to prove. In studies of individuals with healed fibrotic lesions, the incidence of tuberculosis ranged from 2 to 4 cases per 1000 person-years.[91,107] In a Danish study, reactors with calcified lesions were twice as likely to develop tuberculosis as reactors without calcifications.[30]

Age

The main question to be answered is whether the risk of developing active disease varies with age. It might seem logical to tackle this question by examining graphs plotting tuberculosis incidence and mortality by age (**Figure 18-7**). Such graphs are cross-sectional, however, showing the rates of disease in many different birth cohorts at a particular instant in time, and the risk of tuberculosis can vary drastically for different birth cohorts. To clarify this issue, birth cohort analyses have been done in different populations to examine the risk of disease throughout life in cohorts of people born at the same time.[47,91,101]

Figure 18-8 shows a cohort analysis done by Comstock from data collected and reported by the United States Public Health Service.[87,108] It shows that as a birth cohort ages, people susceptible to tuberculosis are eliminated by disease or mortality, eventually leaving a cohort that is more resistant to disease. Thus the incidence of tuberculosis actually declines as a specific birth cohort ages. This elimination of susceptible people also has an effect on the overall susceptibility to tuberculosis in the community, eventually producing a community that is more resistant to disease. Thus the risk of infection, and consequently disease, is lower for each successive birth cohort in the community. If you view the

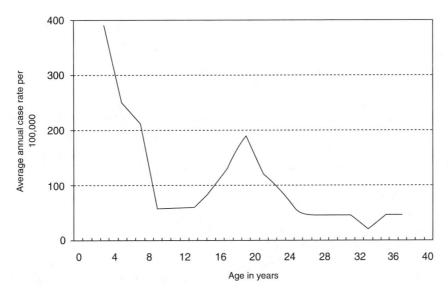

Figure 18-7 Standard tuberculosis incidence or mortality by age. Reproduced from G.W. Comstock, Frost Revisited: The Modern Epidemiology of Tuberculosis, American Journal of Epidemiology, Vol. 101, pp. 363–382. Copyright © 1975 by permission of Oxford University Press.

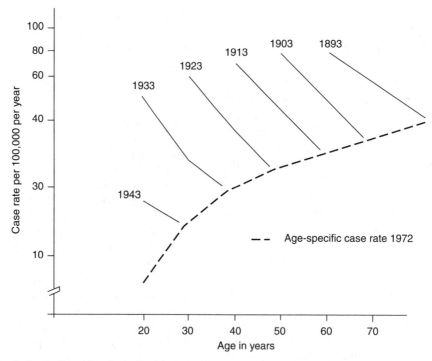

Figure 18-8 Cohort analysis of effect of age on tuberculosis incidence. Reproduced from G.W. Comstock, Frost Revisited: The Modern Epidemiology of Tuberculosis, American Journal of Epidemiology, Vol. 101, pp. 363–382. Copyright © 1975 by permission of Oxford University Press.

disease incidence cross-sectionally by age, the oldest birth cohorts (i.e., the oldest ages) have the highest incidence of infection. This is because their risk of infection has been higher since birth, not because the incidence of tuberculosis increases with age. If you look instead at the tuberculosis incidence curve for each birth cohort, you see that the risk of tuberculosis declines steadily with age within each cohort.

Sex

Numerous studies, both cross-sectional and longitudinal, have shown that the development of active tuberculosis varies by sex. Incidence and mortality curves show two peaks. The first occurs in infancy, when rates are higher in boys than girls. This differential equalizes later in childhood. In late adolescence, the curves again rise sharply, with the rates in women exceeding those in men. After about age 60, the rates flip once more, and the incidence in men exceeds that in women for the remainder of life.[30]

In a prospective study in Puerto Rico, tuberculin-positive, tuberculosis-free people aged 1 to 19 years at enrollment were followed for more than 18 years for the development of active disease. In young children aged 1 to 6 years, the incidence of tuberculosis was higher in males than in females of the same age. After 6 years of age, however, the incidence was higher in females at all ages. This cohort was followed only

until the oldest members were 40 years of age, however, so the authors could not comment on the risk of disease in older adults.

In a similar prospective study conducted in Bangalore, India, a cohort of people was actively screened for tuberculosis annually for 8 years. The authors found that women aged 10 to 44 years had a 130% higher risk of developing tuberculosis than men the same age, but that after age 44 the risk in men was as much as 250% higher than in women.[54]

In a similar study in Gedde-Dahl, Norway, a cohort of tuberculin-negative adults was followed for tuberculin conversion and development of tuberculosis. The observed incidence of tuberculosis was equal in males and females younger than age 19 years; 25% to 30% higher in women at age 20 to 29; and 17% to 25% higher in males than females after age 40. In the mass screening campaign in Denmark, investigators found that the incidence of tuberculosis was 71% higher in females than males at 24 to 34 years of age; 22% higher in females aged 35 to 44; and 67% higher in males older than age 45.[47,54,109]

The effect of sex on development of disease was also studied in a population of Alaskan Inuits. Essentially everyone in the population was tuberculin positive by age 15. The investigators found that the incidence of tuberculosis was similar in males and females until about age 10; 25% higher in females from age 10 to 39; and similar in males and females 40 years of age and older.[54,110]

In 2010, women accounted for 36% of all TB cases globally, for a global male-to-female ratio of 1.78.[8] In most countries of the world, a high ratio is observed, though Afghanistan, Iran, and Pakistan have consistently remained exceptions with ratios of 0.47, 1.03 and 1.05, respectively.[111] In countries with high HIV prevalence in sub-Saharan Africa, the ratio favors women, as they are more likely to be HIV infected and TB disproportionally affects those individuals with HIV/AIDS.[112] HIV/AIDS prevalence is very low in Afghanistan, Iran, and Pakistan, however, so this factor is unlikely to account for the sex-ratio differences in those countries. A recent analysis of data from Pakistan and India suggests that many more females are being diagnosed with TB in younger age groups (before age 45); although this ratio reverses at older ages, it is not as skewed as in India, Pakistan's geographical neighbor.[113] The reasons for the increased rates of TB among females in these countries need to be better understood.

In summary, the risk of developing tuberculosis, given infection, appears to be higher in males than females during infancy and again after about age 45 to 60, but higher in females than males during adolescence and early adulthood. The reason for this divergence is not clear. The peak in women during reproductive years suggests that hormonal factors may be involved, although pregnancy in itself does not seem to affect the risk of developing tuberculosis.[114] It has also been suggested that the excess prevalence in men at older ages is due to increased immune suppression related to increased smoking and drinking, but the evidence for this hypothesis is sketchy.[54]

Genetics

Genetic factors clearly play some role in the development of tuberculosis in humans, but the extent of this role is unclear. Lurie has shown there is some genetic basis for resistance to tuberculosis in rabbits,[115] and a variety of evidence suggests the same is true for humans. In a tragic accident in 1926, 249 infants in Lubeck, Germany, were vaccinated with live *M. tuberculosis* instead of BCG vaccine. Seventy-six of the infants died and 173 survived after suffering various levels of illness. None of the infants had been previously vaccinated with BCG, none was old enough to have acquired immunity from natural exposure to tuberculosis, and all infants received the same dose of mycobacteria. The variation in their responses to the infection may be partially due to nutritional status and other factors, but some of it must have been due to differences in innate susceptibility to tuberculosis.[33,65]

It has also been suggested that some of the racial and geographic differences observed in tuberculosis incidence result from differences in population resistance to tuberculosis.[19,116] Population resistance to a specific microbe presumably develops over time as natural selection favors hosts who are better able to resist or cope with infection. This phenomenon was observed when tuberculosis was introduced for the first time in the Qu'Appelle Indians in the late 1800s. Initially 10% of the population died annually from tuberculosis. Half of the families in the community died out within two generations, but the annual tuberculosis death rate in the remaining population was only 0.2%.[117] A similar scenario occurred when tuberculosis was introduced to the Yanomami Indians in the Amazon.[57] Epidemic tuberculosis arrived in Europe in the 1300s and 1400s and was a major cause of premature death from the Industrial Revolution through the middle of the 1900s. European colonists brought tuberculosis with them to Asia and Africa, where epidemic tuberculosis was essentially unknown before 1900.

If the notion of population resistance, as seen in the Qu'Appelle and Yanomami Indians, is correct, then present-day people of European ancestry should have more resistance to tuberculosis than people of African origin. In the United States, African Americans have historically had much higher rates of tuberculosis than Caucasians, but they have also traditionally had higher rates of poverty, crowding, and malnutrition—all factors that are strongly associated with exposure to tuberculosis. It is, therefore, difficult to determine whether the difference in incidence is due to exposure or genetics. A study of tuberculin sensitivity in New York City showed that at every socioeconomic level, African American and Puerto Rican residents were more likely to have evidence of LTBI than Caucasian residents.[101] In another study, African American nursing home residents were twice as likely to become infected with *M. tuberculosis* as white residents in the same nursing homes. Again, the difference remained after correction for socioeconomic and environmental factors.[118] None of these studies is conclusive, but collectively they suggest that genetics has some effect on population-level resistance to tuberculosis.

Perhaps the strongest evidence that genetics plays a role in susceptibility to tuberculosis comes from twin studies, which examine the incidence of disease in pairs of twins. When both twins in a pair develop a disease, they are called concordant; they are discordant when only one of the twins is diseased. If genetics plays no role in a disease, the concordance rate should be the same in monozygotic twins and dizygotic twin pairs.

If genetics is important, then concordance should be higher in monozygotic twins because they have identical genomes. Several twin studies have shown that the concordance for tuberculosis is roughly twice as high in monozygotic twins as in dizygotic twins.[119–121] Many of these studies were done before multiple regression was widely available, but Comstock reanalyzed the Prophit twin study data using multiple logistic regression. He found that concordance remained more than twice as high in monozygotic twins even after adjustment for sex, age, infectivity of the index, type of tuberculosis, and years of contact.[119] Although environment must play a role in the development of disease in twin pairs, it seems clear that monozygotic twins are at greater risk of disease.

Other types of studies have also suggested a genetic component in tuberculosis. Edwards and colleagues examined U.S. Navy recruits who had been exposed to tuberculosis.[108] They found that men who had close—generally family—contact with a tuberculosis case were taller and thinner than those without such exposure regardless of their tuberculin status. This suggests that lean body build may be a marker for a familial risk for tuberculosis.[87, 108]

In a well-executed study by Overfield and Klauber, the prevalence of a positive tuberculin response and active tuberculosis was correlated with ABO and MN blood types in a random sample of Alaskan Eskimos with a very high tuberculosis infection rate. The authors reported that people with blood types AB and B were three times more likely to have moderate to severe tuberculosis compared to people with blood types O and A.[122] There also appears to be some correlation between development of tuberculosis and histocompatibility types.[30]

Several studies have also shown that genetic polymorphisms may be associated with tuberculosis risk. A case-control study in the Gambia found that allelic variation in the gene *nramp-1* was associated with tuberculosis risk, though wild-type alleles were present in the majority of cases and polymorphisms in a large proportion of controls.[123] Another study from Cambodia identified a specific HLA-DQ haplotype associated with tuberculosis.[124]

Interferon-γR1 deficiency has also been shown to be associated with increased susceptibility to tuberculosis. In a study of French children who developed disseminated BCG after vaccination, a small proportion of children with no other underlying immune defect had a specific autosomal recessively inherited mutation in the gene coding for interferon-γR1.[33,125,126] Studies have also suggested that several other genes or chromosome regions may affect susceptibility to tuberculosis, and research continues in this area.[33]

Stress

It has long been suggested that stress may affect the development of tuberculosis,[18,100] probably by weakening the cell-mediated immune response that holds latent disease in check and prevents new infection. A study in Denmark showed that among tuberculin reactors, the risk of developing active tuberculosis was lowest in married men, who presumably had the highest level of social support; intermediate in single and widowed men; and highest in divorced men, who had the least social support. A similar but less dramatic trend was seen in women. In addition, married people who developed tuberculosis had less severe disease than did unmarried people.[30,109] A study of tuberculosis incidence in the U.S. Navy shortly after World War II showed that rates were especially high in personnel from the Philippines. The difference in rates has been attributed to psychosocial stress caused by social isolation and separation from family and other support structures.[100]

Tuberculosis has long been associated with poverty,[65,98,102] even after adjustment for other pertinent factors.[99] Some evidence suggests that poverty is probably a marker for increased risk of infection with tuberculosis,[98] but it is possible that poverty imposes a psychological stress on the body that reduces immune capacity and increases the risk of reactivation or of development of disease given exposure.

Nutrition

The association between poverty, crowding, and malnutrition is well established. It is no surprise, then, that tuberculosis—which is strongly associated with crowding and poverty—has also been associated with malnutrition.[42,65] A number of studies have examined the association of specific micronutrients with the development of tuberculosis. In one study, mean plasma vitamin A levels were lower in children with pulmonary tuberculosis than in those without it. More extensive or more severe disease was also associated with low vitamin A levels. High-dose treatment with vitamin A had no effect on the course of the tuberculosis, however.[55] Low vitamin A and selenium levels have also been associated with an increased risk of developing tuberculosis in a cohort of HIV-infected, adult reactors in Haiti.[127]

A study in tuberculin reactors found that reaction size increased as nutritional status improved, and severe malnutrition has also been associated with anergy to tuberculin skin test following BCG vaccine.[53] In times of war, food deprivation has been associated with increased tuberculosis incidence and mortality; incidence decreased when food became available again. These data suggest that the deprivation caused an increase in reactivation disease, probably by inhibiting cell-mediated immunity.[42,47]

Similarly, a study in Muscogee County, Georgia, measured the thickness of subcutaneous fat over the trapezius ridges in baseline photofluorograms of tuberculosis-free people. The investigators found that people with less than 5 mm of fat over the ridge were twice as likely to develop tuberculosis over the next 14 years than people with 10 mm or more of fat.[87] This is in keeping with the considerable body of literature suggesting that tall, thin men are more likely to develop tuberculosis than are shorter, heavier men.

A systematic review of six studies reported a strong and consistent log-linear relationship between TB incidence and BMI across diverse settings,[128] and this association has been seen in HIV-infected patients as well.[129] It seems clear, therefore, that the risk of tuberculosis is higher in thinner people. What is not clear is whether thinness is the risk factor for disease or a marker of genetic susceptibility, as suggested by Edwards's studies in navy recruits.[87,108]

Occupation

Few studies have examined occupation as a risk factor for tuberculosis. The notable exception is studies of people exposed to silica at their work sites. Silicosis has been shown to lower resistance to tuberculosis infection in animals, and tuberculosis is more common among people exposed to silica on the job than to those who are unexposed.[42] There also appears to be an interaction between silicosis, HIV infection, and tuberculosis in South African miners. Those individuals with both silicosis and HIV are more likely to develop tuberculosis than those with only one of the two risk factors.

Inhalation therapists and funeral home workers have been found to have increased risk for tuberculosis infection and disease.[130–132] Healthcare workers, in general, appear to have varying rates of tuberculosis. In some settings, the incidence in such employees is similar to or lower than rates in other occupational groups[131]; in other cases, rates are actually increased.[133]

Smoking

Although a link between smoking and tuberculosis seems obvious, the evidence supporting the association was lacking until recently, when several prospective studies were published. A study in India showed that male smokers were three times more likely to report a history of tuberculosis than nonsmokers.[134] A large prospective study in Korea investigated the association of cigarette smoking with TB incidence, recurrence, and mortality in a cohort of more than 1 million South Koreans.[135] Compared to never smokers, both male and female current smokers had a 60% increased risk of death from TB, whereas an increased risk of incident TB was found only among men. These results were adjusted for alcohol consumption and age, and were reduced when adjusted for BMI.

A prospective study in Hong Kong examined the incidence of tuberculosis in smokers and non-smokers and found that it was highest in current smokers (735/100,000), lowest in never smokers (174/100,000), and intermediate in ex-smokers (427/100,000). The trend was significant ($P < .001$) and persisted after adjustment for multiple factors. In addition, current smokers who developed tuberculosis smoked more cigarettes than those who did not (13.43 cigarettes per day versus 7.87; $P = .01$), and a significant dose response was observed.[136]

A study of response to treatment in patients diagnosed with tuberculosis in Kuwait suggests that smoking may delay sputum conversion in some people.[137] How smoking worsens tuberculosis is unclear, but it has been suggested that iron loading of pulmonary macrophages secondary to smoking may damage the cells and make them more susceptible to infection with *M. tuberculosis*.[138]

Evidence on the association between smoking and tuberculosis has been assembled in several systematic reviews, all of which have found that cigarette smoking is associated with an approximate doubling of risk for tuberculosis infection, for having clinical evidence of disease, and for tuberculosis mortality.[139–144] A recent modeling analysis suggests that tobacco smoking would produce an excess of 18 million tuberculosis cases and 40 million deaths between 2010 and 2050 if smoking trends continue along their current trajectories.[145] Recently, efforts have been directed toward reducing smoking among newly diagnosed TB patients, with the hope that smoking cessation in these individuals will lead to better treatment outcomes.[146,147]

Diabetes

The association between diabetes mellitus (DM) and TB, and their synergistic role in causing human disease, has been recognized for centuries, though interest in the intersection of these diseases has been renewed in recent years.[148] Recent analyses have suggested that type 2 DM increases TB risk 3.1-fold,[149], and 10.2% of TB in WHO's 22 countries with the highest TB burden among adults is attributable to DM.[150] DM may impair immunologic responses to TB, leading to more severe disease and higher risk of mortality. In one study in Maryland,[151] after adjustment for many confounding factors, the odds of death were 6.5 times greater in patients with DM compared to those without DM (aOR 95% confidence interval: 1.1–38.0), but sample size limited the precision of this estimate. Because causes of death are not reported in most studies, we do not know whether excess mortality is explained by increased severity of TB in DM patients or by the existence of comorbidities attributable to DM compounded by more advanced age.

HIV Infection and AIDS

Infection with HIV has been identified as the most potent biologic risk factor for developing tuberculosis. In HIV-infected people with evidence of prior tuberculosis infection, the annual risk of reactivation is between 3% and 14%.[152] Among people already infected with HIV, newly acquired tuberculosis infection progresses to active disease within several months in a high proportion (approximately 40%).[153] WHO estimates that the risk of TB increases 20-fold among HIV-infected individuals living in high HIV-prevalence countries.[8] Approximately 25% of all HIV-related TB occurs in South Africa, where TB rates now approach 1000 cases per 100,000 population.[8]

The risk of TB following HIV seroconversion is seen in **Figure 18-9**.[154] TB incidence doubled in the first year after HIV seroconversion in a cohort of more than 20,000 South African miners.[155] Decreasing CD4 counts corresponds with increased risk of TB, though TB occurs at higher CD4 counts than most

other opportunistic infections.[155] Antiretroviral therapy for HIV-infected patients reduces TB risk by as much as 81% and reduces mortality significantly as well.[155–161] Although ART initiation results in rapid recovery of immune function, HIV-infected patients receiving ART remain at high risk for TB disease and TB immune reconstitution disease (TB-IRIS).[162–164]

An important question that has been conclusively answered recently is the optimal time to initiate highly active antiretroviral therapy (HAART) in patients with HIV-related tuberculosis.[165,166] Recent WHO recommendations state that HIV-infected patients with active TB should initiate HAART as soon as possible after TB treatment, irrespective of CD4 cell count,[167] though the quality of the evidence supporting these recommendations is characterized as low or moderate. The SAPiT trial in South Africa reported a 56% mortality reduction among patients starting HAART during TB treatment, within 4 weeks after the start of TB therapy, or within 4 weeks of completion of the intensive phase of TB therapy, compared to those initiating HAART within 4 weeks after TB treatment completion.[168,169] The recent STRIDE trial reported no mortality difference between those starting HAART within 2 weeks of TB treatment initiation and those starting within 8–12 weeks after TB treatment start.[170] Both the SAPiT and STRIDE trials reported a significant drop in mortality among early starters of HAART with advanced immunosuppression.

The CAMELIA clinical trial in Cambodia evaluated when to start HAART among severely immunosuppressed patients, 72% of whom had T-cell counts

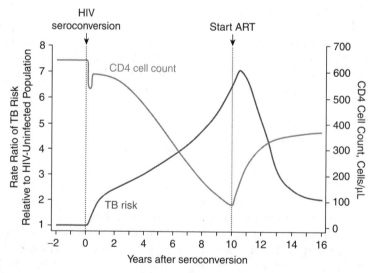

Figure 18-9 The risk of tuberculosis following HIV seroconversion varies with level of immune suppression. Reproduced from Havlir DV, et al. Opportunities and challenges for HIV care in overlapping HIV and TB epidemics. *JAMA* 300(4):424. Copyright © 2008 American Medical Association. All rights reserved.

less than 50 cells/mm³. The study found a reduction of 34% among patients starting HAART 2 weeks after TB treatment initiation compared to those starting HAART within 8 weeks.[171] Studies in developed countries have shown that patients with very advanced HIV disease have better survival if HAART is given during TB treatment,[172–175] though the risks of immune reconstitution inflammatory syndrome (IRIS),[176,177] drug interactions, and additive drug toxicity raise concerns about early initiation of HAART in TB/HIV coinfection.[178]

Collectively, these three clinical trials (SAPiT, STRIDE, and CAMELIA) suggest that HAART be initiated very early for those persons with advanced immunosuppression. In contrast, those with higher CD4 counts at the time of TB diagnosis can wait to initiate HAART and not compromise risk of survival, while also reducing their risk of IRIS and other complications.

In areas where tuberculosis infection is common and HIV has become prevalent, rapidly escalating rates of tuberculosis have occurred and the DOTS approach has not held it in check (**Figure 18-10**).[179] HIV-related immune deficiency compromises host response to tubercle bacilli, thereby raising the likelihood of reactivation of latent infection. Among HIV-infected people, the most important risk factors for reactivation of tuberculosis are a positive tuberculin skin test and a low CD4 lymphocyte count.[180] Although HIV infection can cause anergy to antigens such as tuberculin, a high proportion of HIV-infected patients with tuberculosis have a positive skin test, and the presence of

a positive test is a powerful predictor of subsequent tuberculosis risk. Several early studies suggested that anergy was associated with a very high risk of developing tuberculosis, and it was hypothesized that the lack of response to tuberculin indicated an inability of host immune response to contain tubercle bacilli.[181,182] Subsequent studies have failed to confirm an association between anergy and reactivation tuberculosis,[183] and it has been suggested that anergy is a marker for severe immune deficiency that increases the risk of *primary* tuberculosis in areas where transmission of infection is common. As the CD4 count falls, the incidence of reactivation and primary tuberculosis rises, and extrapulmonary sites of disease become more frequent.[80] Unlike most other opportunistic infections in HIV disease, however, tuberculosis can occur at a relatively high CD4 level and may be a first manifestation of HIV in many patients.[154] In addition, active tuberculosis can be transmitted by the airborne route between HIV-infected people, contributing to microepidemics of institutional and community outbreaks of disease.

The growth of the HIV epidemic over the past two decades has occurred largely in areas of the world where tuberculosis infection is endemic. As a result, tuberculosis has become one of the major opportunistic diseases associated with HIV infection and a leading cause of death in developing countries. As discussed later in this chapter, the HIV epidemic now seriously undermines tuberculosis control in many developing countries, and new and more aggressive strategies are needed to reduce the high incidence of tuberculosis seen in populations with high levels of HIV infection.

Other Factors

A variety of other factors, most of which have a negative impact on the immune system, are known to increase the risk of developing tuberculosis. Those factors include malignancies, renal failure, gastrectomy, jejunoileal bypass, corticosteroid treatment, and measles.[91,95]

BACILLUS CALMETTE-GUÉRIN

Tuberculosis was one of the first diseases for which a vaccine was developed. In 1921, Albert Calmette and Camille Guérin attenuated a virulent strain of *M. bovis* through serial passage on glycerinated bile potato media.[40,184,185] The final product, BCG, was tested in a human subject later that year and put into common use in France in 1924 to protect child contacts of active TB cases.[186,187]

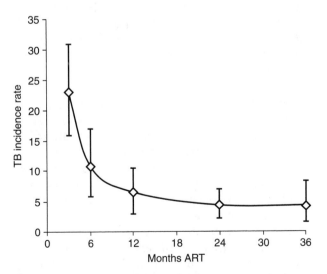

Figure 18-10 Tuberculosis incidence rates in South African patients receiving antiretroviral therapy. Reprinted with permission of the International Union Against Tuberculosis and Lung Disease. Copyright © The Union.

Use of BCG in Europe soon became fairly common, but its efficacy was questioned by some, particularly in the United States. In 1930, more than 50% of a cohort of children vaccinated with BCG in Lubeck, Germany, contracted tuberculosis and many died. It was subsequently shown that the children had accidentally been vaccinated with virulent tubercle bacilli from a culture stored in the same incubator as the BCG culture.[65,185] The Lubeck disaster, combined with the disruption of Europe during World War II, discouraged the use of BCG for a time. Tuberculosis morbidity and mortality increased markedly during World War II,[47] however, and after the war, vaccination was quickly reinstituted in Europe and became the norm.[40] Today BCG vaccine is one of the standard vaccines in WHO's Expanded Program on Immunization[34] and is used in nearly every country in the world, with the notable exceptions of the United States and the Netherlands.[42] Nevertheless, in recent years many countries have reconsidered their BCG strategy and have stopped administering this vaccine.[188]

Bacillus Calmette-Guérin is one of the safest vaccines in use.[185] It is given at birth to infants in more than 100 countries throughout the world and is recommended for some healthcare workers at risk of exposure to tuberculosis. The BCG vaccine is rarely given to healthy adult populations because its efficacy in this group is uncertain. It is administered intradermally or percutaneously and generally causes a superficial, crusted ulcer at the site of administration. This lesion heals in 2 to 3 months, generally leaving a 4- to 8-mm concave scar.[43] A small proportion of vaccinees get suppurative axillary or cervical lymphadenopathy, which generally heals best without treatment. Persistent or disseminated BCG is a rare complication of vaccination that occurs in 3 to 6 infants per 1 million vaccinations and in 1 to 14 cases per 1 million vaccinations in people aged 1 to 20 years.[34,52] The risk is higher in immunocompromised individuals, such as those with HIV infection[189]; thus WHO recently stopped recommending BCG vaccination for children with symptomatic HIV infection.[190]

Although the precise risk of disseminated BCG in HIV-infected individuals is unknown, BCG is contraindicated if HIV infection is present[51] as well as in people with other forms of immune compromise and in those with skin infections or burns.[33,51]

Controlled studies to measure the efficacy of BCG have been ongoing since 1926 and have included observational and case-control studies and clinical trials. Case-control studies have been used to measure the efficacy of BCG vaccine in specific geographic regions. In these studies, the reported cases of tuberculosis in an area are matched to controls, and the efficacy is estimated from the tuberculosis incidence rate in vaccinated and unvaccinated cases and controls, where[191]

$$\% \text{ Efficacy} = [1 - (R)] \times 100$$

Incidence in vaccinated R = Incidence in the unvaccinated

The underlying assumption is that fewer than 80% of people have received vaccine; otherwise, there are too few unvaccinated cases and controls to reliably estimate efficacy.

Case-control studies have also been used to measure the relative efficacy of two different BCG vaccines given to the same population.[192,193] In these studies it was possible to determine the relative efficacy of the different vaccines because they were given one after the other to the same population using the same delivery methods. The efficacy for the time period covering each vaccine was estimated separately. Case-control studies are observational, and the lack of randomization means there is a potential for bias. The assumption in a case-control study is that, apart from the effect of the vaccine, the risk of developing tuberculosis is equal in the vaccinated and unvaccinated groups. If this is not true, then the estimated efficacy may be incorrect.

In contact studies, cohorts of children living with newly diagnosed tuberculosis cases are followed for the development of tuberculosis. The incidence of tuberculosis is estimated in vaccinated and unvaccinated children, and vaccine efficacy is computed as in a case-control study.[40] As with the case-control studies, these cohort studies are not randomized, and results are subject to questions if the probability of vaccination varies with the risk of developing tuberculosis.

Many clinical trials—some randomized and some not—have also been carried out to determine the efficacy of BCG vaccine. At first glance, the results of these studies are confusing. The efficacy of BCG as estimated in the different studies ranges from −22% to +85%. The difficulty is that the studies have measured different products in different populations. BCG was developed in 1921, during the infancy of microbiology. It came not from a single colony, but rather from a culture of mycobacteria; thus it is not a "strain" in the strictest sense of the word. In addition, the original BCG "strain" was distributed to and subcultured in laboratories around the world, producing a large number of daughter strains, some of them with very different characteristics from the original.[40] As a consequence, the organism used in the many BCG vaccine studies has varied markedly. The route of administration and the dose of vaccine have also varied in different studies, and the effect that these differences have had on efficacy is difficult to predict. Furthermore, several studies have shown that exposure to non-tuberculous mycobacterium provides some protection against infection with *M. tuberculosis* and may reduce the efficacy of BCG for a given population.[106]

To summarize, it appears that BCG provides some protection in infants against miliary disease and tuberculosis meningitis, but a good estimate of the efficacy is not available. The vaccine does not appear to confer good protection in adults and should probably be used only in extreme circumstances.

New, effective vaccines against tuberculosis are needed badly. Research in the field is expanding, and some new candidate vaccines are beginning clinical trials. Testing the new vaccines will be challenging. BCG vaccination is entrenched in developing countries where the risk of tuberculosis is highest and the need for new tuberculosis vaccines is greatest. WHO has made a determined effort to ensure high coverage rates in infants in areas where tuberculosis is endemic. In these areas, where preventive therapy is rare and treatment for tuberculosis can be problematic, it would be unethical to deprive infants of an available vaccine even though it provides at best minimal protection against disseminated disease. Therefore, it is improbable that the new vaccine(s) will be tested in placebo-controlled efficacy trials; studies will have to measure some, as yet unknown, biologic marker of protection, or compare the efficacy of the new vaccine against the efficacy of BCG and infer the relative efficacy of the two vaccines from those measurements.

TUBERCULOSIS CONTROL STRATEGIES: CASE FINDING AND TREATMENT

In 1994, WHO declared tuberculosis a global emergency and developed the DOTS program to combat disease globally. Although short-course directly observed therapy is the cornerstone of the strategy, the WHO DOTS program encompasses a series of policies that are meant to result in effective tuberculosis control (Table 18-4). The program aims to encourage governments to develop the political will to support tuberculosis control, a strong surveillance system that records and monitors cases, sufficient laboratory components to ensure diagnosis, effective short-course treatments that are at least partially delivered to patients under healthcare professional observation, and a reliable supply of anti-tuberculosis drugs.

The DOTS strategy originally called for country programs to detect 70% of smear-positive tuberculosis cases and to treat 85% of those cases successfully, though this goal has since been determined to not be sufficient to control the epidemic. It is assumed that implementation of the DOTS strategy and achievement of these goals would make a substantial impact on tuberculosis incidence and contribute to effective tuberculosis control. Indeed, when DOTS is implemented well in a country, large proportions of active tuberculosis cases can be treated and cured, and drug resistance can be prevented.[179] Implementation of a DOTS program requires the establishment of a registration system, microscopy services, a stable drug supply, and adequate staffing to permit supervision of therapy for at least 2 months, but many countries with the greatest tuberculosis burden are the least able to undertake this kind of commitment. Although the per capita cost of effective tuberculosis treatment services is relatively low (e.g., $0.23 per year in Peru), mobilization of resources to create an integrated national program is difficult. A larger problem, however, is the generation of political will to support tuberculosis control. Even in countries where substantial foreign assistance has been provided for tuberculosis services, control efforts frequently lag for many reasons, including governmental disorganization and disruption, competing needs, and lack of interest or commitment in tuberculosis as a public health problem.

Despite these challenges, progress to control TB has been made. As part of WHO's Stop TB Strategy, DOTS has been provided to 55 million people and 46 million have successfully completed treatment.[8] Case detection rates have improved in some areas, although case finding remains a difficult task. WHO estimates that globally approximately 65% of new cases were identified in 2010.[8] In 2000, the United Nations' Millennium Development Goals (MDGs) provided a framework to evaluate the implementation and impact of disease control programs, including tuberculosis. The targets for tuberculosis are to reduce tuberculosis incidence and to halve tuberculosis prevalence and mortality by 2015. WHO's recent estimates suggest that in much of the world these goals can be met, but the HIV and multidrug-resistant TB epidemics will make it very difficult to meet those goals in Africa and Eastern Europe.[8]

In areas with generalized HIV epidemics, in particular, it is clear that the DOTS strategy is insufficient to control tuberculosis. Sub-Saharan Africa

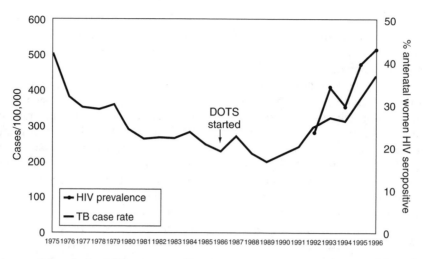

Figure 18-11 Despite a well-functioning DOTS program and low levels of anti-TB resistance in Botswana, the epidemic of tuberculosis has continued to grow due to the severe epidemic of HIV. Reprinted with permission of the International Union Against Tuberculosis and Lung Disease. Copyright © The Union.

is experiencing devastating increases in tuberculosis rates as a consequence of high levels of HIV infection in the general population. Countries such as South Africa, Botswana, Zambia, Malawi, and others have seen threefold to fivefold increases in TB incidence over the past 10–15 years as HIV prevalence has increased (Figure 18-5).[179] Botswana, a country with a well-functioning and highly efficient DOTS program in place since 1985, has rates of TB that are now well above 500/100,000, illustrating the limitations of the DOTS strategy in holding down tuberculosis incidence in the face of an extensive HIV epidemic (**Figure 18-11**).[179] Aggressive public health strategies that extend beyond DOTS, such as active tuberculosis case finding, widespread use of preventive therapy, and other novel approaches, are required to contain tuberculosis in these settings. In response, WHO has implemented the "three I's" approach toward controlling the HIV/TB epidemic: isoniazid preventive therapy, infection control, and intensified case finding.[194]

Epidemiologic Basis of Tuberculosis Control

Control of tuberculosis implies a reduction in the number of cases that occur each year within a community or population. In mathematical terms, tuberculosis control means that the reproductive rate of the disease must be less than 1.0, meaning each case of tuberculosis must produce less than one secondary case. This simple and necessary goal of control has been largely overlooked in most international tuberculosis programming until recently. Instead, programs were largely focused on intermediary goals

such as case detection and cure rates. Although there is great medical and humanitarian value in finding, treating, and curing cases of tuberculosis, the perspective of public health requires that the principal aim of tuberculosis control be to reduce the incidence of the disease.

The propagation of tuberculosis within a population can be viewed as a series of steps related to the natural history of tuberculosis infection in individuals, as illustrated in Figure 18-6.[89] The reservoir of tuberculosis in a community is the group of latently infected people at risk of developing tuberculosis (Stage 1). Some change in immunity in the latently infected allows the tubercle bacillus to begin active growth and reactivation tuberculosis develops (Stage 2). These new cases are infectious, and each will infect a minimum of 8 to 15 contacts (Stage 3) before their infection is sterilized by appropriate chemotherapy. Rapid diagnosis and treatment of the new infectious cases reduces the number of infected contacts. Five to 10 percent of these infected contacts will develop primary tuberculosis within 2 years (Stage 4), and the remainder will fuel the pool of latently infected people (Stage 1).

A variety of factors moderate the dynamics of this model in a community. The most obvious is HIV infection. People coinfected with HIV and the tubercle bacillus have a dramatically increased risk of developing tuberculosis and contribute disproportionately to reactivation and new tuberculosis infections (Stages 2 and 3). In areas where HIV and tuberculosis are endemic, this increased risk of disease from reactivation and primary infection substantially increases the case rate (Stages 2 and 4). Other factors that prolong infectivity, such as poor case detection, lack of effective treatment, and drug resistance, also increase case rates.

Current Tuberculosis Control Strategies

On a community level, tuberculosis can be controlled through the use of an effective vaccine, detection and treatment of infectious cases, and screening for and treatment of latent tuberculosis infection.[195] In developing countries, control measures have emphasized BCG vaccination and case detection and treatment.[195] BCG vaccination of uninfected individuals is intended to provide protection against active tuberculosis infection and does not necessarily protect against latent infection (Figure 18-6, Stage 3). Even when BCG vaccine is highly efficacious, new cases of tuberculosis continue to arise from the latently infected pool until all at-risk individuals die. An increasing body of evidence also indicates that the efficacy of current BCG vaccines is attenuated. Thus, while BCG vaccination is widespread, the epidemiologic benefit gained from this intervention is limited.

The predominant method of case detection for TB has relied on passive detection of individuals seeking care for their TB symptoms. Implementation of a strong passive case detection program along with DOTS in Peru, for example, resulted in an annual 6% decrease in TB incidence following an initial substantial increase in detected cases.[196] A strong national commitment was required and resulted in a marked increase in sputum examinations. The successes in Peru were not, however, repeated in regions where HIV significantly changed the epidemiologic picture of TB.[196]

More recently, active case finding has become a strategy that has gained momentum as a method to decrease TB incidence, particularly in areas with an HIV epidemic. Corbett et al. describe two intensified case-finding strategies in Harare, Zimbabwe, that significantly reduced TB prevalence over a 3-year period. Driving a mobile van through the communities that publicized sputum collection for symptomatic individuals detected 1.5 times as many TB patients, and the overall reduction in culture-positive TB prevalence in the communities was 44%.[197] Active case finding for tuberculosis has been a strategy for tuberculosis for more than 100 years, though slowing declining TB incidence rates globally will require an intensification of effort, particularly in HIV-infected populations.[198]

Detection of tuberculosis cases and institution of effective chemotherapy are widely held to be the most important strategies for controlling tuberculosis and are the backbone of tuberculosis control. Rapid identification of cases and institution of effective treatment eliminate ongoing transmission of infection and limit the number of secondary cases, although an average of 8 to 15 contacts are infected before a newly identified infection can be sterilized with chemotherapy. It is, therefore, more accurate to state that case detection and treatment reduce, but do not eliminate, transmission of infection to susceptible individuals.

Treatment of latent tuberculosis infection with isoniazid (INH) or other anti-tuberculosis medications reduces the risk of subsequent tuberculosis by 60% to 90%.[199] Recommendations in the United States state that 9 months of daily INH is the most effective duration,[200] based primarily on Comstock's analysis of INH clinical trial outcomes.[201] Adherence to a 9-month regimen is challenging, so shorter courses of therapy are desired. Most recently a study conducted in several countries with low to moderate TB incidence reported a 3-month once-weekly combination of rifapentine and isoniazid to not be inferior to the standard 9-month INH regimen.[202] The 3-month regimen also had a higher adherence rate. Provision of treatment for latent infection to people at high risk of developing tuberculosis is an important adjunct to case identification and treatment in reducing tuberculosis incidence in a community and is a strategy that has been used extensively in the United States and Europe. In the United States, INH preventive therapy is targeted at close contacts of infectious cases, individuals with HIV and latent tuberculosis infection, recent tuberculin converters, and other tuberculin-positive people at high risk of developing active tuberculosis.[48] The use of treatment for latent infection is very limited in resource-poor areas, however, and is usually directed only at young children living in households with smear-positive cases. Shorter regimens were also seen to be just as effective in reducing TB as longer regimens among HIV-infected patients in South Africa.[203]

The HIV epidemic has changed the dynamics of tuberculosis in many resource-poor areas, and evidence now suggests that provision of INH to HIV-infected patients receiving HAART can significantly reduce TB risk.[158,159] Effective control of tuberculosis in HIV-endemic areas requires treatment of latent infection if control is to be achieved, though the feasibility of 6 months of isoniazid preventive therapy (IPT) for HIV-infected patients in areas of high TB prevalence is unknown. Three randomized trials of long-term isoniazid (3 years or more) have produced conflicting results. In a trial in

Botswana, a 56% reduction in TB incidence was seen in HIV-infected patients randomized to receive IPT for 3 years, though the protection conferred was limited to TST-positive participants.[204] A South Africa study, which included only TST-positive patients, reported no benefit of long-term IPT in the intent-to-treat analysis, but an as-treated analysis reported 58% protection among patients who were actively receiving long-term IPT compared with those who received only 6 months of IPT.[203] A trial in India found no benefit of long-term IPT compared to a 6-month regimen of isoniazid and ethambutol.[205] India has considerable lower incidence and prevalence of TB, which may have influenced the risk of reinfection. Durability of IPT in the pre-HIV era was shown clearly in early trials in Alaska, where annual infection rates and TB incidence rival those in present-day South Africa, and protection from TB disease persisted for 20 years.[206] However, the impact of HIV on progression of TB infection, along with recent trial results, suggests that lifetime preventive therapy may be required for HIV-infected patients living in high TB incident areas.

In 2010, among the world's 12 million prevalent tuberculosis cases, 650,000 were estimated to be resistant to at least isoniazid and rifampin, the definition for multidrug-resistant TB (MDR-TB).[207] Drug sensitivity testing is not done for most TB isolates in resource-poor countries, if at all, so reliable prevalence data for this form of TB are not available.

Dramatic outbreaks of MDR-TB in HIV-infected patients and among healthcare workers in the United States in the early 1990s focused international attention on the emergence of strains of *M. tuberculosis* resistant to antimycobacterial drugs. Infections involving strains resistant to multiple drugs are difficult to cure, and the necessary treatment is much more toxic and expensive. As noted previously, good tuberculosis control programs prevent emergence of drug-resistant tuberculosis in patients with susceptible strains but may fail to cure and prevent secondary cases in individuals with resistant strains, whether previously treated or not.

Currently, there are a number of "hot spots" around the world where MDR-TB prevalence is high. The greatest proportion of new TB cases consisting of MDR-TB are seen in European regions, whereas estimates of MDR-TB's incidence throughout Africa are quite low.[8] WHO estimates that the rate of MDR-TB among new TB patients is relatively stable at the global level, increasing in the African and European regions, and dropping in the Eastern Mediterranean, South East Asia, and Western Pacific regions—though these estimates have wide

confidence limits. The Russian Federation reported MDR-TB rates between 23.8% and 28.3% among new TB cases in the northwest part of the country, compared to 5.4% in other oblasts (provinces).[207] Prisoners in Russia have high rates of MDR-TB, and transmission within penal colonies is high. Other areas with high levels of MDR-TB include Belarus, Estonia, Kazakhstan, and Ukraine.

The evolution of extensively drug-resistant (XDR) TB is of growing concern globally. XDR-TB came to light with an outbreak among HIV-infected patients in Tugela Ferry, South Africa, in which 52 of 53 patients with XDR died; their median survival was 16 days from time of diagnosis.[208] Since this outbreak, XDR-TB has been detected in every country where surveillance has been conducted.[207]

Aggressive tuberculosis control measures that include prevention of institutional transmission of infection, DOTS, screening, and treatment of latent infection can dramatically reduce the prevalence of MDR-TB.[209] In New York City, for example, such an approach was extremely successful in reversing a disastrous epidemic of MDR-TB that affected that city in the early 1990s.[210] However, in other areas of the world, mobilization of resources to combat drug-resistant disease is more difficult, and community and institutional transmission of MDR strains continues, resulting in escalating levels of resistant cases and more treatment failures and deaths.

CONCLUSION

Tuberculosis is one of the most prevalent and deadly infections on Earth. Because humans are the primary reservoir of infection and transmission is via the aerosol route, eradication of tuberculosis is theoretically possible. Recent strategies aimed at increasing case detection of TB in an effort to ultimately reduce TB incidence and prevalence have been encouraging,[197] and models suggest that TB can be reduced if control strategies are widely implemented. Recent advances in molecular epidemiology have improved our understanding of tuberculosis dynamics, though the fundamental measures for controlling the disease have been known and available for decades. New drugs are needed to shorten the duration of treatment, new diagnostics must be developed to detect more cases more efficiently, and innovative strategies are required to maximize the impact of current and new technologies. Tuberculosis continues to threaten humanity, and aggressive, comprehensive global efforts to control it must expand and adapt to meet this threat.

● ● ● **REFERENCES**

1. Haas F, Haas SS. The origins of *Mycobacterium tuberculosis* and the notion of its contagiousness. In: Rom W, Garay SM, eds. *Tuberculosis*. New York: Little, Brown; 1996:3–19.

2. Brosch R, Pym AS, Gordon SV, Cole ST. The evolution of mycobacterial pathogenicity: clues from comparative genomics. *Trends Microbiol* 2001;9:452–458.

3. Haas D, des Prez RM. *Mycobacterium tuberculosis*. In: Mandell G, Bennett JE, Dolin R, eds. *Mandell, Douglas and Bennett's Principles and Practice of Infectious Diseases*. New York: Churchill Livingstone; 1995:2213–2243.

4. Pfyffer G, Auckenthaler R, van Embden JDA, van Soolingen D. *Mycobacterium canettii*, the smooth variant of *M. tuberculosis*, isolated from a Swiss patient exposed in Africa. *Emerg Infect Dis* 1998;4:631–634.

5. Niemann S, Richter E, Dalugge-Tamm H, et al. Two cases of *Mycobacterium microti*-derived tuberculosis in HIV-negative immunocompetent patients. *Emerg Infect Dis* 2000;6:539–542.

6. World Health Organization, Global Tuberculosis Control. *Global Tuberculosis Control, WHO Report 1998*. Geneva, Switzerland: Author; 1998.

7. Pitchenik A, Cole C, Russell BW, et al. Tuberculosis, atypical mycobacteriosis, and the acquired immunodeficiency syndrome among Haitian and non-Haitian patients in south Florida. *Ann Intern Med* 1984;101:641–645.

8. World Health Organization, Global Tuberculosis Control. *Global Tuberculosis Control, WHO Report 2011*. Geneva, Switzerland: Author; 2011.

9. Lonnroth K, Jaramillo E, Williams BG, Dye C, Raviglione M. Drivers of tuberculosis epidemics: the role of risk factors and social determinants. *Soc Sci Med* 2009;68(12):2240–2246.

10. Chaisson RE, Martinson NA. Tuberculosis in Africa: combating an HIV-driven crisis. *N Engl J Med* 2008;358:1089–1092.

11. Brooks G, Butel JS, Morse SA, eds. *Jawetz, Melnick and Adelberg's Medical Microbiology*. 21st ed. Stanford, CA: Appleton and Lange; 1998.

12. Robbins S, Angell M, Kumar V, eds. *Basic Pathology*. 3rd ed. Philadelphia, PA: WB Saunders; 1981.

13. Brosch R, Gordon V, Marmiesse M, et al. A new evolutionary scenario for the *Mycobacterium tuberculosis* complex. *PNAS* 2002;99:3684–3689.

14. Freeman B. *Burrows Textbook of Microbiology*. 22nd ed. Philadelphia, PA: WB Saunders; 1985.

15. Pediatrics, tuberculosis. In: Peter G, ed. *1997 Red Book: Report of the Committee on Infectious Diseases*. Elk Grove Village, IL: American Academy of Pediatrics; 1997:541–567.

16. Cole S, Brosch R, Parkhill J, et al. Deciphering the biology of *Mycobacterium tuberculosis* from the complete genome sequence. *Nature* 1998;393:537–544.

17. Schurch A, van Soolingen D. DNA fingerprinting of *Mycobacterium tuberculosis*: From page typing to whole-genome sequencing. *Infect Genetics Evol* 2011; epub.

18. Daley C. Molecular epidemiology: a tool for understanding control of tuberculosis transmission. *Clin Chest Med* 2005;26:217–231.

19. Stead W, Bates JH. Geographic and evolutionary epidemiology of tuberculosis. In: Rom W, Garay SM, eds. *Tuberculosis*. New York: Little, Brown; 1996:77–83.

20. Daley C. Tuberculosis contact investigations, please don't fail me now. *Am J Resp Crit Care Med* 2004;169:779–781.

21. Easterbrook P, Gibson A, Murad S, et al. High rates of clustering of strains causing tuberculosis in Harare, Zimbabwe: a molecular epidemiological study. *J Clin Micro* 2004;42:4536–4544.

22. Borgdorff M, van der Werf MJ, de Haas PEW, et al. Tuberculosis elimination in the Netherlands. *Emerg Infect Dis* 2005;11:597–602.

23. Bennett D, Onorato IM, Ellis BA, et al. DNA fingerprinting of *Mycobacterium tuberculosis* isolates from epidemiologically linked case pairs. *Emerg Infect Dis* 2002;8:1224–1229.

24. Ellis B, Crawford JT, Braden CR, et al. Molecular epidemiology of tuberculosis in a sentinel surveillance population. *Emerg Infect Dis* 2002;8:1197–1209.

25. Centers for Disease Control and Prevention. Human tuberculosis caused by *Mycobacterium bovis*—New York City, 2001–2004. *MMWR* 2005;54:605–608.

26. van Deutekom H, Hoijng SP, de Haas PEW, et al. Clustered tuberculosis cases: do they represent recent transmission and can they be detected earlier? *Am J Resp Crit Care Med* 2004;169:806–810.

27. Golub JE, Cronin WA, Obasanjo OO, et al. Transmission of *Mycobacterium tuberculosis* through casual contact with an infectious case. *Arch Intern Med* 2001;161:2254–2258.

28. Pan H, Yan B-S Rojas, M, et al. Ipr1 gene mediates innate immunity to tuberculosis. *Nature* 2005;434:767–772.

29. Narvskaya O, Mokrousov I, Limeschenko E, et al. Molecular characterization of *Mycobacterium tuberculosis* strains from the northwest region of Russia. *EpiNorth J* 2005;11:18.

30. Stead W, Dutt AK. Epidemiology and host factors. In: Schlossberg D, ed. *Tuberculosis.* New York: Springer-Verlag; 1994:1–16.

31. Formicola V, Milanesi Q, Scarsini C. Evidence of spinal tuberculosis at the beginning of the fourth millennium BC from Arene Candide Cave (Liguria, Italy). *Am J Phys Anthropol* 1987;72:1–6.

32. Pesanti E. A history of tuberculosis. In: Lutwick L, ed. *Tuberculosis.* New York: Chapman and Hall Medical; 1995.

33. Bellamy R. Genetic susceptibility to tuberculosis. *Clin Chest Med* 2005;26:233–246.

34. Tuberculosis. In: Peter G, ed. *1997 Red Book: Report of the Committee on Infectious Diseases.* Elk Grove Village, IL: American Academy of Pediatrics; 1997:541–567.

35. Pitchenik A, Fertel D, Block AB. Mycobacterial disease epidemiology, diagnosis, treatment and prevention. *Clin Chest Med* 1988;9:425–441.

36. Cohen FJD, ed. *Tuberculosis: A Sourcebook for Nursing Practice.* New York: Springer; 1995.

37. Isselbacher K, Braunwald E, Wilson JD, et al. *Harrison's Principles of Internal Medicine Companion Handbook.* 13th ed. New York: McGraw-Hill; 1995.

38. Abebe M, Lakew M, Kidane D, et al. Female genital tuberculosis in Ethiopia. *Int J Gyn Obstet* 2004;84:241–246.

39. Wong H, Tay YK, Sim CS. Papular eruption on a tattoo: a case of primary inoculation tuberculosis. *Australasian J Dermatol.* 2005;46:84.

40. ten Dam H. BCG vaccination. In: Reichman L, Hershfield ES, eds. *Tuberculosis: A Comprehensive International Approach.* New York: Marcel Dekker; 1993:251–274.

41. Raviglione M, Snider DE, Kochi A. Global epidemiology of tuberculosis: morbidity and mortality of a worldwide epidemic. *JAMA* 1995;273:220–226.

42. Comstock G, O'Brien RJ. Tuberculosis. In: Evans A, Brachman PS, eds. *Bacterial Infections of Humans, Epidemiology and Control.* New York: Plenum Medical Book; 1991:745–772.

43. Starke J. Tuberculosis in children. *Curr Opin Pediatr* 1995;7:268–277.

44. ATS/CDC. Control of tuberculosis in the United States. *Am Rev Respir Dis* 1992;146:1623–1633.

45. Thomas C, ed. *Taber's Cyclopedic Medical Dictionary.* Philadelphia, PA: FA Davis; 1977.

46. Schein M, Huebner RE. Tuberculin skin testing. In: Rossman M, MacGregor RR, eds. *Tuberculosis Clinical Management and New Challenges.* New York: McGraw-Hill; 1995:73–88.

47. Sutherland I. Recent studies in the epidemiology of tuberculosis based on the risk of being infected with tubercle bacilli. *Adv Tuberc Res* 1976;19:1–63.

48. ATS/CDC. Targeted tuberculin testing and treatment of latent tuberculosis in latent tuberculosis infection. *MMWR* 2000;49(RR06):1–54.

49. Johnson M, Coberly J, Clermont H, et al. Tuberculin skin test reactivity among adults infected with human immunodeficiency virus. *J Infect Dis* 1992;166:194–198.

50. Bellete B, Coberly JS, Barnes GL, et al. Evaluation of a whole-blood interferon-gamma release assay for the detection of *Mycobacteriumtuber culosis* infection in 2 study populations. *Clin Infect Dis* 2002;34:1449–1456.

51. Pai M, Riley LW, Colford JM Jr. Interferon-gamma assays in the immunodiagnosis of tuberculosis: a systematic review. *Lancet Infect Dis* 2004;4:761–776.

52. Kang YA, Lee HW, Yoon HI, et al. Discrepancy between the tuberculin skin test and the whole-blood interferon-gamma assay for the diagnosis of latent tuberculosis infection in an intermediate tuberculosis-burden county. *JAMA* 2005;293:2756–2761.

53. Mazurek M, Jereb J, Vernon A, et al. Updated guidelines for using interferon gamma release assays to detect *Mycobacterium tuberculosis* infection—United States, 2010. *MMWR Recomm Rep* 2010;59(RR-5):1–25.

54. World Health Organization. *Use of Tuberculosis Interferon-Gamma Release Assays (IGRAs) in Low- and Middle-Income Countries: Policy Statement.* WHO/HTM/TB/2011.18.

55. Rangaka MX, Wilkinson KA, Glynn JR, et al. Predictive value of interferon-γ release assays for incident active tuberculosis: a systematic review and meta-analysis. *Lancet ID* August 14, 2011. [Epub ahead of print]

56. Metcalfe JZ, Everett CK, Steingart KR, et al. Interferon-γ release assays for active pulmonary tuberculosis diagnosis in adults in low- and middle-income countries: systematic review and meta-analysis. *J Infect Dis* 2011;204(4):S1120.

57. World Health Organization, Stop TB Partnership. *Tuberculosis Prevention, Care and Control: A Practical Directory of New Advances.*

58. Rossau R, Traore H, De Beenhouwer H, et al. Evaluation of the INNO-LiPA Rif.TB assay, a reverse hybridization assay for the simultaneous detection of *Mycobacterium tuberculosis* complex and its resistance to rifampin. *Antimicrob Agents Chem Other* 1997;41:2093–2098.

59. Hain Lifescience GmbH. GenoType MTBDRplus, version 1.0. May 1, 2008. Available at: www.hain-lifescience.com/pdf/304xx_pbl.pdf.

60. Morgan M, Kalantri S, Flores L, Pai M. A commercial line probe assay for the rapid detection of rifampicin resistance in *Mycobacterium tuberculosis*: a systematic review and meta-analysis. *BMC Infect Dis* 2005;5:62.

61. Ling DI, Zwerling AA, Pai M. GenoType MTBDR assays for the diagnosis of multidrug-resistant tuberculosis: a meta-analysis. *Eur Respir J.* 2008;32:1165–1174.

62. Boehme CC, Nabeta P, Hillemann D, et al. Rapid molecular detection of tuberculosis and rifampin resistance. *N Engl J Med* 2010;363(11):1005–1015.

63. *Policy Statement: Automated Real-Time Nucleic Acid Amplification Technology for Rapid and Simultaneous Detection of Tuberculosis and Rifampicin Resistance: Xpert MTB/RIF System.* WHO/HTM/TB/2011.4. Geneva, Switzerland: World Health Organization; 2011.

64. *World Health Organization Monitoring of Xpert MTB/RIF Roll-out.* Geneva, Switzerland: World Health Organization.

65. Dubos R, Dubos J. *The White Plague: Tuberculosis, Man and Society.* Boston: Little, Brown; 1952.

66. BMRC. Streptomycin treatment of pulmonary tuberculosis. *BMJ* 1948;2:769–782.

67. BMRC, Hong Kong Chest Service. Controlled trial of 4 three-times-weekly regimens and a daily regimen all given for 6 months for pulmonary tuberculosis; second report: the results up to 24 months. *Tubercle* 1982;63:89–98.

68. BMRC. Treatment of pulmonary tuberculosis with streptomycin and p-aminosalicylic acid. *BMJ* 1950;2:1073–1108.

69. Hong Kong Chest Service/Tuberculosis Research Centre, M.B. A controlled trial of 3-month, 4-month and 6-month regimens of chemotherapy for sputum-smear-negative pulmonary tuberculosis, results at 5 years. *Am Rev Respir Dis* 1989;139:871–876.

70. Hong Kong Chest Service, B. Five-year follow-up of a controlled trial of five 6-month regimes of chemotherapy for pulmonary tuberculosis. *Am Rev Respir Dis* 1987;136:1339–1342.

71. Singapore Tuberculosis Service, B. Long-term follow-up of a clinical trial of six-month and four-month regimens of chemotherapy in the treatment of pulmonary tuberculosis. *Am Rev Respir Dis* 1986;133:779–783.

72. Singapore Tuberculosis Service, B. Five-year follow-up of a clinical trial of three 6-month regimens of chemotherapy given intermittently in the continuation phase in the treatment of pulmonary tuberculosis. *Am Rev Respir Dis* 1988;137:1147–1150.

73. Azia A, Ishaq M, Jaffer NA, et al. Clinical trial of two short-course (6-month) regimes and a standard regimen (12 month) chemotherapy in retreatment of pulmonary tuberculosis in Pakistan. *Am Rev Respir Dis* 1986;134: 1056–1061.

74. Hong Kong Chest Service, B. Controlled trial of 6-month and 8-month regimens in the treatment of pulmonary tuberculosis: the results up to 24 months. *Tubercle* 1979;60:201–210.

75. East African, B. Controlled clinical trial of five short-course (4-month) chemotherapy regimens in pulmonary tuberculosis, second report of the 4th study. *Am Rev Respir Dis* 1981;123:165–170.

76. Castelo A, Jardim JRB, Goihman S, et al. Comparison of daily and twice-weekly regimens to treat pulmonary tuberculosis. *Lancet* 1989;2:1173–1176.

77. Okwere A, Whalen C, Byckwaso F, et al. Makerene University–Case Western Reserve University research collaboration. *Lancet* 1994;344:1323–1328.

78. Perriens J, St. Louis ME, Mukadi YB, et al. Pulmonary tuberculosis in HIV-infected patients in Zaire: a controlled trial of treatment for either 6 or 12 months. *N Engl J Med* 1995;332:779–784.

79. Chaisson R, Clermont HC, Holt EA, et al., JHU-CDS Research Team. Six-month supervised intermittent tuberculosis therapy in Haitian patients with and without HIV infections. *Am J Respir Crit Care Med* 1996;154:1034–1038.

80. Alwood K, Keruly JC, Moore-Rice K, et al. Effectiveness of supervised, intermittent therapy for tuberculosis in HIV infected patients. *AIDS* 1994;8:1103–1108.

81. Harries A, Maher D. *TB/HIV: A Clinical Manual.* Geneva, Switzerland: World Health Organization; 1996.

82. American Thoracic Society, Centers for Disease Control and Prevention. Treatment of tuberculosis: official joint statement of the American Thoracic Society, CDC, and the Infectious Diseases Society of America. *Am J Resp Crit Care Med* 2003;167:602–662.

83. Chaisson R, Coberly JS, DeCock KM. DOTS and drug resistance: a silver lining to a darkening cloud. *IJTLD* 1999;3:1–3.

84. World Health Organization. *The STOP TB Strategy: Building on and Enhancing DOTS to meet the TB-Related Millennium Development Goals.* WHO/HTM/TB/2006.368.

85. Chang KC, Leung CC, Yew WW et al. Dosing schedules of 6-month regimens and relapse for

pulmonary tuberculosis. *Am J Respir Crit Car Med* 2006;174:1153–1158.

86. Burman WJ. Issues in the management of HIV-related tuberculosis. *Clin Chest Med* 2005;26:283–294.

87. Comstock G. Frost revisited: the modern epidemiology of tuberculosis. *Am J Epidemiol* 1975;101:363–382.

88. Murray C, Styblo K, Rouillon A. Tuberculosis in developing countries: burden, intervention and cost. *Bull Int Union Against Tuberc Lung Dis* 1990;65:1–20.

89. De Cock K, Chaisson RE. Will DOTS do it? A reappraisal of tuberculosis in countries with high rates of HIV infection. *Int J Tuberc Lung Dis* 1999;3:457–465.

90. Loudon R, Roberts RM. Singing and the dissemination of tuberculosis. *Am Rev Respir Dis* 1968;98:297–300.

91. Rieder H. Epidemiology of tuberculosis in Europe. *Europ Respir J* 1995;20(suppl):620–632.

92. Loudon R, Roberts RM. Droplet expulsion from the respiratory tract. *Am Rev Respir Dis* 1966;95:435–442.

93. Wells W. On air-borne infection. Study II. Droplets and droplet nuclei. *Am J Hyg* 1934;20:611–618.

94. Sonkin LS. The role of particle size in experimental air-borne infection. *Am J Hyg* 1951;53:337–354.

95. Rieder H, Cauthen GM, Comstock GW. Epidemiology of tuberculosis in the United States. *Epidemiol Rev* 1989;11:79–98.

96. Rieder H. *Epidemiologic Basis of Tuberculosis Control.* 1st ed. Paris, France: International Union Against Tuberculosis and Lung Disease; 1999.

97. Grzybowski S, Barnett GD, Styblo K. Contacts of cases of active pulmonary tuberculosis. *Bull Int Union Tuberc* 1975;50:107–121.

98. Chapman J, Dyerly MD, Powell DR. Social and other factors in intrafamilial transmission of tuberculosis. *Am Rev Respir Dis* 1964;90:48–60.

99. Kamat S, Dawson JJY, Devadatta S, et al. A controlled study of the influence of segregation of tuberculosis patients for one year on the attack rate of tuberculosis in a 5-year period in close family contacts in south India. *Bull WHO* 1966;34:517–532.

100. Comstock G. Epidemiology of tuberculosis. *Am Rev Respir Dis* 1982;125(suppl):8–15.

101. Reichman L, O'Day R. Tuberculous infection in a large urban population. *Am Rev Respir Dis* 1978;117:705–712.

102. Kuemmerer J, Comstock GW. Sociologic concomitants of tuberculin sensitivity. *Am Rev Respir Dis* 1967;96:885–892.

103. Stead W. Undetected tuberculosis in prison. *JAMA* 1978;240: 2544–2547.

104. Houk V, Baker JH, Sorensen K, Kent DC. The epidemiology of tuberculosis infection in a closed environment. *Arch Environ Health* 1968;16:26–35.

105. Stead W, Lofgren JP, Warren E, Thomas C. Tuberculosis as an endemic and nosocomial infection among the elderly in nursing homes. *N Engl J Med* 1985;312:1483–1487.

106. Comstock G, Livesay VT, Woolpert SF. Evaluation of BCG vaccination among Puerto Rican children. *Am J Pub Health* 1974;64: 283–291.

107. IUAT. Efficacy of various durations of isoniazid preventive therapy for tuberculosis: five years of follow-up in the IUAT trial. *Bull WHO* 1982;60:555–564.

108. Edwards L, Livesay VT, Acquaviva FA, Palmer CE. Height, weight, tuberculosis infection and tuberculous disease. *Arch Environ Health* 1971;22:106–112.

109. Horwitz O. Epidemiologic basis of tuberculosis eradication. 10. Lung studies on the

risk of tuberculosis in the general population of a low-prevalence area. *Bull WHO* 1969;41:95–113.

110. Comstock G, Cauthen GM. Epidemiology of tuberculosis. In: Reichman L, Hershfield ES, eds. *Tuberculosis: A Comprehensive International Approach*. New York: Marcel Dekker; 1993:23–48.

111. Word Health Organization. *Global Tuberculosis Control: Epidemiology, Strategy, Financing*. WHO/HTM/TB/2009.411.

112. Joint United Nations Programme on HIV/AIDS (UNAIDS). *Global Report: UNAIDS Report on the Global AIDS Epidemic 2010*. Geneva, Switzerland: UNAIDS; 2010.

113. Codlin AJ, Khowaja S, Chen Z, et al. Short report: gender differences in tuberculosis notification in Pakistan. *Am J Trop Med Hyg* 2011;85(3):514.

114. Horwitz O. Tuberculosis risk and marital status. *Am Rev Respir Dis* 1971;104:22–31.

115. Lurie M. *Resistance to Tuberculosis: Experimental Studies in Native Acquired Defensive Mechanisms*. Cambridge, MA: Harvard University Press; 1984.

116. O'Brien S. Ghetto legacy. *Curr Biol* 1991;i:209–211.

117. Motulsky A. Metabolic polymorphisms and the role of infectious disease in human evolution. *Hum Biol* 1960;32:28–62.

118. Stead W, Senner JW, Reddick WT, et al. Racial differences in susceptibility to infection by *Mycobacterium tuberculosis*. *N Engl J Med* 1990;322:422–427.

119. Comstock G. Tuberculosis in twins: a re-analysis of the Prophit survey. *Am Rev Respir Dis* 1978;117:621–624.

120. Kallmann F, Reisner D. Twin studies on the significance of genetic factors in tuberculosis. *Am Rev Tuberc* 1942;47:549–574.

121. Simonds B. *Tuberculosis in Twins*. London: Pitman Medical Publishing; 1963.

122. Overfield T, Klauber MR. Prevalence of tuberculosis in Eskimos having blood group B gene. *Hum Biol* 1980;52:87–92.

123. Bellamy R, Ruwende C, Corrah T, et al. Variations in the NRAMP1 gene and susceptibility to tuberculosis in West Africans. *N Engl J Med* 1998;338:640–644.

124. Goldfeld A, Delgado JC, Thim S, et al. Association of an HLA-DQ allele with clinical tuberculosis. *JAMA* 1998;279:226–228.

125. Casanova J-L, Blanche S, Emile J-F, et al. Idiopathic disseminated bacillus Calmette-Guerin infection: a French national retrospective study. *Pediatrics* 1996;98:774–778.

126. Jouanguy E, Altare F, Lamhamedi S, et al. Interferon-γ-receptor deficiency in an infant with fatal bacille Calmette-Guerin infection. *N Engl J Med* 1996;335:1956–1961.

127. Rwangabwoba J, Humphrey J, Coberly J, et al. Vitamin A status and development of tuberculosis and or mortality. In: *The XI International Conference on AIDS*. Vancouver, Canada: International Conference on AIDS; 1996.

128. Lonnroth K, Williams BG, Celielski P, Dye C. A consistent log-linear relationship between tuberculosis incidence and body mass index. *Int J Epidemiol* 2009;39:149–155.

129. Hanrahan CF, Golub JE, Mohapi L, et al. Body mass index and risk of tuberculosis and death. *AIDS* 2010;24(10):1501–1508.

130. Sterling T, Pope DS, Bishai WR, et al. Transmission of *Mycobacterium tuberculosis* from a cadaver to an embalmer. *N Engl J Med* 2000;342:246–248.

131. Geisseler J, Nelson KE, Crispen RG, Moses VK. Tuberculosis in physicians: a continuing problem. *Am Rev Respir Dis* 1986;133:733–738.

132. McKenna M, Hutton M, Cauther G, Onorato IM. The association between occupation and tuberculosis: a population-based survey. *Am J Respir Crit Care Med* 1996;154:587–593.

133. Barrett-Connor E. The epidemiology of tuberculosis in physicians. *JAMA* 1979;241:33–38.

134. Gajalakshmi V, Peto R, Kanaka TS, Jha P. Smoking and mortality from tuberculosis and other diseases in India: retrospective study of 43000 adult male deaths and 35000 controls. *Lancet* 2003;362:507–515.

135. Jee SH, Golub JE, Jo J, et al. Smoking and risk of tuberculosis incidence, mortality, and recurrence in South Korean men and women. *Am J Epidemiol* 2009;170:1478–1485.

136. Leung C, Li T, Lam TH, et al. Smoking and tuberculosis among the elderly in Hong Kong. *Am J Resp Crit Care Med* 2004;170:1027–1033.

137. Abal A, Jayakrishnan B, Parwer S, et al. Effect of cigarette smoking on sputum smear conversion in adults with active pulmonary tuberculosis. *Respir Med* 2005;99:415–420.

138. Boelaert J, Gomes MS, Gordeuk VR. Smoking, iron, and tuberculosis. *Lancet* 2003;362:1243–1244.

139. Davies PDO, Yew WW, Ganguly D, et al. Smoking and tuberculosis: the epidemiological association and immunopathogenesis. *Trans R Soc Trop Med Hyg* 2006;100(4):291–298.

140. Bates I, Fenton C, Gruber J, et al. Vulnerability to malaria, tuberculosis, and HIV/AIDS infection and disease. Part 1: determinants operating at individual and household level. *Lancet Infect Dis* 2004;4(5):267–277.

141. Chiang C, Slama K, Enarson DA. Associations between tobacco and tuberculosis [Educational Series: tobacco and tuberculosis. Serialised guide. Tobacco cessation interventions for tuberculosis patients. Number 1 in the series]. *Int J Tuberc Lung Dis* 2007;11(5):258–262.

142. Lin HH, Ezzati M, Murray M. Tobacco smoke, indoor air pollution and tuberculosis: a systematic review and meta-analysis. *PLoS Med* 2007;4(1):e20.

143. Pai M, Mohan A, Dheda K, et al. Lethal interaction: the colliding epidemics of tobacco and tuberculosis. *Expert Rev Anti-infective Therap* 2007;5(3):385–391.

144. Slama K, Chiang CY, Enarson DA, et al. Tobacco and tuberculosis: a qualitative systematic review and meta-analysis. *Int J Tuberc Lung Dis* 2007;11(10):1049–1061.

145. Basu S, Stuckler D, Bitton A, Glantz SA. Projected effects of tobacco smoking on worldwide tuberculosis control: mathematical modeling analysis. *BMJ* 2011;343:d5506.

146. Chiang YC, Lin YM, Lee JA, et al. Tobacco consumption is a reversible risk factor associated with reduced successful treatment outcomes of anti-tuberculosis therapy. *Int J Infect Dis* 2011 [Epub ahead of print].

147. Awaisu A, Nik Mohamed MH, Mohamad Noordin N, et al. The SCIDOTS Project: evidence of benefits of an integrated tobacco cessation intervention in tuberculosis care on treatment outcomes.

148. Dooley KE, Chaisson RE. Tuberculosis and diabetes mellitus: convergence of two epidemics. *Lancet Infect Dis* 2009;9(12):737–746.

149. Jeon CY, Murray MB. Diabetes mellitus increases the risk of active tuberculosis: a systematic review of 13 observational studies. *PLoS Med* 2008;5(7):e152.

150. Lonnroth K, Castro KG, Chakaya JM, et al. Tuberculosis control and elimination 2010–50: cure, care, and social development. *Lancet* 2010;375(9728):1814–1829.

151. Dooley KE, Tang T, Golub JE, et al. Impact of diabetes mellitus on treatment outcomes of patients with active tuberculosis. *Am J Trop Med Hyg* 2009;80(4):634–639.

152. Hopewell P, Chaisson RE. Tuberculosis and human immunodeficiency virus infection. In: Reichman L, Hershfield ES, eds. *Tuberculosis: A Comprehensive International Approach.* New York: Marcel Dekker; 2000.

153. Daley C, Small PM, Schecter GF, et al. An outbreak of tuberculosis with accelerated

progression among persons infected with human immunodeficiency virus: an analysis using restriction-fragment-length polymorphisms. *N Engl J Med* 1992;326:321–325.

154. Havlir DV, Getahun H, Sanne I, Nunn P. Opportunities and challenges for HIV care in overlapping HIV and TB epidemics. *JAMA* 2008;300:423.

155. Sonnenberg P, Glynn JR, Fielding K, et al. How soon after infection with HIV does the risk of tuberculosis start to increase? A retrospective cohort study in South African gold miners. *J Infect Dis* 2005;191(2):150–158.

156. Badri M, Wilson D, Wood R. Effect of highly active antiretroviral therapy on incidence of tuberculosis in South Africa: a cohort study. *Lancet* 2002;359(9323):2059–2064.

157. Lawn SD, Harries AD, Williams BG, et al. Antiretroviral therapy and the control of HIV-associated tuberculosis: will ART do it? *Int J Tuberc Lung Dis* 2011;15(5):571–81.

158. Golub JE, Saraceni V, Cavalcante SC, et al. The impact of antiretroviral therapy and isoniazid preventive therapy on tuberculosis incidence in HIV-infected patients in Rio de Janeiro, Brazil. *AIDS* 2007;21(11):1441–1448.

159. Golub JE Pronyk P, Mohapi L, et al. Isoniazid preventive therapy, HAART and tuberculosis risk in HIV-infected adults in South Africa: a prospective cohort. *AIDS* 2009;23(5): 631–636.

160. Lawn SD, Myer L, Bekker LG, Wood R. Burden of tuberculosis in an antiretroviral treatment programme in sub-Saharan Africa: impact on treatment outcomes and implications for tuberculosis control. *AIDS* 2006;20(12):1605–1612.

161. Lawn SD, Badri M, Wood R. Tuberculosis among HIV-infected patients receiving HAART: long term incidence and risk factors in a South African cohort. *AIDS* 2005;19(18):2109–2116.

162. Lawn SD, Myer L, Bekker LG, Wood R. Tuberculosis-associated immune reconstitution disease: incidence, risk factors and impact in an antiretroviral treatment service in South Africa. *AIDS* 2007;21:335–341.

163. Lawn SD, Bekker LG, Miller RF. Immune reconstitution disease associated with mycobacterial infections in HIV-infected individuals receiving antiretrovirals. *Lancet Infect Dis* 2005;5:361–373.

164. Schluger NW, Perez D, Liu YM. Reconstitution of immune responses to tuberculosis in patients with HIV infection who receive antiretroviral therapy. *Chest* 2002;122(2):597–602.

165. Piggot DA, Karakousis PC. Timing of antiretroviral therapy for HIV in the setting of TB treatment. *Clin Dev Immunol* 2011;

166. Nachega JB, Rosenkranz B, Simon G, et al. Management of adult active tuberculosis disease in era of HIV pandemic, current practices and future perspectives. *Infect Disord Drug Targets* 2011;11(2):134–43.

167. World Health Organization. *Antiretroviral Therapy for HIV Infection in Adults and Adolescents: Recommendations for a Public Health Approach—2010 Revision.*

168. Abdool Karim SS, Naidoo K, Grobler A, et al. Timing of initiation of antiretroviral drugs during tuberculosis therapy. *N Engl J Med* 2010;362(8):697–706.

169. Abdool Karim S, Naidoo K, Padayatchi N, et al. Integration of antiretroviral therapy with tuberculosis treatment. *N Engl J Med* 2011;365:1492–1501.

170. Havlir D, Kendal M, Ive P, et al. Timing of antiretroviral therapy for HIV-1 infection and tuberculosis. *N Engl J Med* 2011;365:1482–1491.

171. Blanc FX, Sok T, Laureillard D, et al. Earlier versus late start of antiretroviral therapy in HIV-infected adults with tuberculosis. *N Engl J Med* 2011;365:1471–1481.

172. Dean GL, Edwards SG, Ives NJ, et al. Treatment of tuberculosis in HIV-infected persons in the era of highly active antiretroviral therapy. *AIDS* 2002;16(1):75–83.

173. Velasco M, Castilla V, Sanz J, et al. Effect of simultaneous use of highly active antiretroviral therapy on survival of HIV patients with tuberculosis. *J Acquir Immune Defic Syndr* 2009;50(2):148–152.

174. Zachariah R, Fitzgerald M, Massaquoi M, et al. Does antiretroviral treatment reduce case fatality among HIV-positive patients with tuberculosis in Malawi? *Int J Tuberc Lung Dis* 2007;11(8):848–853.

175. Westreich D, MacPhail P, Van Rie A, et al. Effect of pulmonary tuberculosis on mortality in patients receiving HAART. *AIDS* 2009;23(6):707–715.

176. Meintjes G, Rabie H, Wilkinson RJ, Cotton MF. Tuberculosis-associated immune reconstitution inflammatory syndrome and unmasking of tuberculosis by antiretroviral therapy. *Clin Chest Med* 2009;30(4): 797–810.

177. Burman W, Weis S, Vernon A, et al. Frequency, severity and duration of immune reconstitution events in HIV-related tuberculosis. *Int J Tuberc Lung Dis* 2007;11(12):1282–1289.

178. Piscitelli SC, Gallicano KD. Interactions among drugs for HIV and opportunistic infections. *N Engl J Med* 2001;344:984–996.

179. Kenyon TA, et al. Low levels of drug resistance amidst rapidly increasing tuberculosis and human immunodeficiency virus co-epidemics in Botswana. *Int J Tuberc Lung Dis* 1999; 3(1):4–11.

180. Markowitz N, Hansen N, Hopewell PC, et al. Incidence of tuberculosis in the United States among HIV-infected patients. *Ann Intern Med* 1997;126:123–132.

181. Antonucci G, Girardi E, Raviglione MC, Ippilito G. Risk factors for tuberculosis in HIV infected persons: a prospective cohort study. *JAMA* 1995;274:143–148.

182. Selwyn P, Sckell BM, Alcabes P, et al. High risk of active tuberculosis among intravenous drug users with cutaneous anergy. *JAMA* 1992;268:504–509.

183. Caiaffa W, Graham NHM, Vlahov D, et al. Instability of delayed-type hypersensitivity (DTH) skin test anergy in human immunodeficiency infection. *Arch Int Med* 1996;155:2111–2117.

184. Ten Dam H. BCG vaccination: an old idea revisited. In: Rossman M, MacGregor RR, eds. *Tuberculosis*. New York: McGraw-Hill; 1995:109–128.

185. Ayvazian L. History of tuberculosis. In: Reichman L, Hershfield ES, eds. *Tuberculosis: A Comprehensive International Approach*. New York: Marcel Dekker; 1993:1–22.

186. Fine P, Sterne JAC, Ponnighaus JM, Rees RJW. Delayed-type hypersensitivity, mycobacterial vaccines and protective immunity. *Lancet* 1994;344:125–1249.

187. Hagwood B. Doctor Albert Calmette 1863–1933: founder of antivenomous serotherapy and antituberculous BCG vaccination. *Toxicon* 1999;37:1241–1258.

188. Zwerling A, Pai M. The BCG world atlas: a new, open-access resource for clinicians and researchers. *Expert Rev Anti Infect Ther* 2011;9(8):559–561.

189. Hesseling AC, Johnson LF, Jaspan H, et al. Disseminated bacilli Calmette-Guerin disease in HIV-infected South African infants. *Bull WHO* 2009;87:505–511.

190. Safety of BCG vaccine in HIV-infected children. *Wkly Epidemiol Rec* 2007;82:22.

191. Smith P. Case-control studies of the efficacy of BCG against tuberculosis. In: *XXVIth IUAT World Conference, 1986*. Professional Post Graduate Services, International; 1987.

192. Shapiro C, Cook N, Evans D, et al. A case-control study of BCG and childhood tuberculosis in Cali, Colombia. *Int J Epidemiol* 1985;14:441–446.

193. Sutrisna B, Utomo P, Komalarini S, Swatriani S. Penelitian efekitfitas vaksin BCG dan beberapa factor lainnya pada anak yang mederita TBC berat di 3 Rumah sakit di Jakarta 1981–1982. *Medika* 1983;9:143–150.

194. World Health Organization. *WHO Three I's Meeting: Intensified Case Finding (ICF), Isoniazid Preventive Therapy (IPT) and TB Infection Control (IC) for people living with HIV.* Report of a joint World Health Organization HIV/AIDS and TB Department meeting. April 2–4, 2008, Geneva, Switzerland.

195. International Union Against Tuberculosis and Lung Disease. *Tuberculosis Guide for Low Income Countries.* 3rd ed. Paris, France: Author; 1994.

196. Suarez PG, Watt CJ, Alarcon E, et al. The dynamics of tuberculosis in response to 10 years of intensive control effort in Peru. *J Infect Dis* 2001;184:473–478.

197. Corbett EL, Bandason T, Duong T, et al. Comparison of two active case-finding strategies for community-based diagnosis of symptomatic smear-positive tuberculosis and control of infectious tuberculosis in Harare, Zimbabwe (DETECTB): a cluster-randomized trial. *Lancet* 2010;376:1244–1253.

198. Golub JE, Mohan C, Comstock GW, Chaisson RE. Active case-finding of tuberculosis: historical perspective and future prospects. *Int J Tuberc Lung Dis.* 2005; 9:1183–1203.

199. Ferebee S. Controlled chemoprophylaxis trials in tuberculosis: a general review. *Adv Tuberc Res* 1970;17:28–106.

200. American Thoracic Society, Centers for Disease Control and Prevention. Targeted tuberculin testing and treatment of latent tuberculosis infection. *MMWR* 2000;49(RR06):1–54.

201. Comstock GW. How much isoniazid is needed for prevention of tuberculosis among immunocompetent adults? *Int J Tuberc Lung Dis*

202. Sterling TR, Villarino ME, Borisov AS, et al. Three months of rifapentine and isoniazid for latent tuberculosis infection. *N Engl J Med* 2011;365:23.

203. Martinson NA, Barnes GL, Moulton LH, et al. New regimens to prevent tuberculosis in adults with HIV infection. *N Engl J Med* 2011;365:11–20.

204. Samandari T, Agizew TB, Nyirenda S, et al. 6-month versus 36-month isoniazid preventive treatment for tuberculosis in adults with HIV infection in Botswana: a randomized, double-blind, placebo-controlled trial. *Lancet* 2011;377:1588–1598.

205. Swaminathan S, Menon P, Perumal V. *Efficacy of a 6-Month vs a 36-Month Regimen for Prevention of TB in HIV-Infected Persons in India: A Randomized Clinical Trial.* Presented at the 17th Conference on Retroviruses and Opportunistic Infections. February 16–19, 2010, Montreal, Canada. Abstract103.

206. Comstock GW, Baum C, Snider DE Jr. Isoniazid prophylaxis among Alaskan Eskimos: a final report of the Bethel isoniazid studies. *Am Rev Respir Dis* 1979;119(5):827–830.

207. World Health Organization. *Multidrug and Extensively Drug-Resistant TB (M/SDR-TB): 2010 Global Report on Surveillance and Response.*

208. Gandhi NR, Moll A, Sturm AW, et al. Extensively drug-resistant tuberculosis as a cause of death in patients co-infected with tuberculosis and HIV in a rural area of South Africa. *Lancet* 2006;368:1575.

209. Weis SE, Slocum PC, Blais FX, et al. The effect of directly observed therapy on the rates of drug resistance and relapse in tuberculosis. *N Engl J Med* 1994;330:1179–1184.

210. Frieden TR, Fujiwara PI, Washko RM, Hamburg MA. Tuberculosis in New York City: turning the tide. *N Engl J Med* 1995;333:229–233.

19

The Epidemiology of Acute Respiratory Infections

Kenrad E. Nelson and Mark C. Steinhoff

INTRODUCTION

As recently as 1997, acute respiratory infections (ARI) were termed a "forgotten pandemic."[1] These infections, which include pneumonia, bronchitis, bronchiolitis, otitis media, sinusitis, pharyngitis, laryngitis, measles, and pertussis, continue to cause 18% of all deaths worldwide among children younger than 5 years old and 8.2% of all disability and premature mortality.[1] Children living in developing countries have especially high morbidity and mortality rates. Despite the global prominence of acute lower respiratory infections, research investment in this area has lagged, with an inadequate proportion of all health-related research and development dollars being devoted to ARI. Recently, this situation has improved with the renewed concern about a global pandemic of influenza.[1]

Although slow in coming, substantial gains in the battle against acute respiratory infections have been made by implementing a public health approach to prophylaxis and treatment. Major advances have occurred in understanding of the epidemiology and etiology of these infections. Data about risk factors continue to accumulate, with most information coming from the developed world, where funding, logistics, and infrastructure are available to support large, multidimensional epidemiologic studies related to ARI. Epidemiologic studies of the risk factors for lower respiratory tract infections have been pursued since the 1980s, with studies of nutrition, the effects of indoor and outdoor air pollution, and active and passive smoking being undertaken, and effective new vaccines being developed for the most important pathogens. In this chapter, the effects on public health, etiology, and risk factors of acute respiratory infections are

reviewed, and the major methodological problems and requirements for future research are delineated.

IMPACT ON PUBLIC HEALTH

Developing Countries

Over the past 25 years, published data have indicated huge differences in ARI mortality rates between developing and developed countries. A World Health Organization (WHO) study in 1990 revealed that, in the world as a whole, the number of deaths attributable to ARI was 12 times greater in developing countries than in developed countries.[2] A recent WHO report estimated that in 2008 18% of all mortality in children aged younger than 5 years was attributable to acute respiratory infections (**Table 19-1**).[3] The burden of mortality falls heaviest on developing countries. Those countries where infant mortality rates exceed 25 per 1000 suffer 98% of the world's deaths from ARI in infants and 99% of those deaths in children aged 1 to 4 years.[4] Furthermore, countries with infant mortality of approximately 100 per 1000 can be expected to contribute 58% of the ARI-related deaths in infants and 66% of those in children aged 1 to 4 years.[4] As these estimates are based on national mortality reporting systems of varying quality, underestimation of the true mortality rate from ARI is possible.

Recent Estimates of Total Pneumonia Mortality and Morbidity

A systematic analysis of the global, regional, and national mortality in children younger than 5 years of age in 2008 was published recently.[3] According to this analysis, an estimated 8.795 million deaths

Table 19-1	Causes of Mortality in Children Younger than 5 Years of Age in 2008
	Estimated Number (UR; millions)
Neonates aged 0–27 days	
Preterm birth complications	1.033 (0.717–1.216)
Birth asphyxia	0.814 (0.563–0.997)
Sepsis	0.521 (0.356–0.735)
Other	0.409 (0.318–0.883)
Pneumonia*	0.386 (0.264–0.545)
Congenital abnormalities[†]	0.272 (0.205–0.384)
Diarrhoea[‡]	0.079 (0.057–0.211)
Tetanus	0.059 (0.032–0.083)
Children aged 1–59 months	
Diarrhoea[‡]	1.257 (0.774–1.886)
Pneumonia*	1.189 (0.789–1.415)
Other infections	0.753 (0.479–2.830)
Malaria	0.732 (0.601–0.851)
Other non-communicable diseases	0.228 (0.143–0.606)
Injury	0.279 (0.174–0.738)
AIDS[§]	0.201 (0.186–0.215)
Pertussis[¶]	0.195 (......)
Meningitis	0.164 (0.110–0.728)
Measles	0.118 (0.075–0.180)
Congenital abnormalities[†]	0.104 (0.078–0.160)

Uncertainty range (UR) is defined as the 2.5–97.5 centile. ··=data unavailable.

* Estimated number of deaths in children younger than 5 years overall is 1.575 million (UR 1.046 million–1.874 million.)
[†] Estimated number of deaths in children younger than 5 years overall is 0.376 million (UR 0.283 million–0.580 million).
[‡] Estimated number of deaths in children younger than 5 years overall is 1.336 million (UR 0.822 million–2.004 million).
[§] [6] Uncertainty range is based on UNAIDS' estimated lower and upper bounds for deaths in children younger than 15 years.
[¶] Crowcroft and colleagues' sensitivity analysis presents extreme upper and lower values for various inputs.

Reprinted from The Lancet, 375, Black et al, Global, regional, and national causes of child mortality in 2008: a systematic analysis, 1969–87, Copyright 2010, with permission from Elsevier.

occurred in children younger than 5 years in 2008. Of these deaths, 68% (5.970 million) were due to infectious diseases, with the largest proportion due to pneumonia (18%; 1.575 million), followed by diarrhea (15%; 1.335 million), and malaria (8%; 0.732 million). Neonatal deaths accounted for 41% of deaths and included preterm birth complications and deaths from a variety of other causes, including 386,000 deaths due to pneumonia in this age group.

A previous systematic review of under-5 mortality in 2000 estimated the total global mortality in this age group to be 10.6 million, with 19% of these deaths due to pneumonia.[1] Estimates of the global burden of disease caused by infection with two major respiratory pathogens, *Streptococcus pneumoniae* and *Haemophilus influenzae* group B, have been published as well.[5,6] One study estimated that *S. pneumoniae* caused approximately 826,000 deaths (range: 582,000–926,000) in children aged 1–19 months in 2000.[5] Of these deaths, 91,000 (range: 63,000–102,000) occurred in human immunodeficiency virus (HIV)–positive children and 735,000 (range: 519,000–926,000) in HIV-negative children; more than 61% of these deaths occurred in 10 African countries. *S. pneumoniae* infection was

estimated to cause approximately 11% of all deaths in children 1–59 months of age. Acceleration of the use of protein-conjugated *S. pneumoniae* vaccines in these high-risk populations in Africa and Asia is a critical public health priority at present.

The global burden of disease of *H. influenzae* type b (Hib) in children 1–59 months of age was estimated to include approximately 8.13 million serious illnesses per year in 2000.[6] Infections with this organism were estimated to have caused some 371,000 deaths (range: 247,000–527,000) in children 1–59 months of age in 2000. A highly effective and safe vaccine to prevent Hib infection is available, so these infections are almost entirely preventable. Fortunately, by 2006, 108 countries had implemented routine childhood vaccination with Hib vaccine.[6]

Global Alliance for Vaccines and Immunization

After the successful eradication of smallpox with a well-organized, coordinated public health program, which relied on an effective vaccine as a central component of the campaign, interest in using vaccines to control other infectious diseases increased. The first international vaccine effort after smallpox eradication in 1980 was the Childhood Vaccine

Initiative (CVI), which began in 1990 and functioned in collaboration with UNICEF and WHO's Expanded Program on Immunization (EPI). The CVI was organized to help develop and provide preventive vaccines for developing country populations by providing a link between the pharmaceutical industry and public health authorities from developing country populations.[7] Subsequently in 2000, the Global Alliance for Vaccines and Immunization (GAVI) was formed as a successor to CVI.

GAVI is a public–private partnership between the relevant experts and political decision makers in vaccines and immunization. It includes developing and donor countries, international development agencies and financial organizations (e.g., WHO, UNICEF and the World Bank), philanthropic organizations (i.e., the Bill and Melinda Gates Foundation), academia, the vaccine industry in both industrialized and developing countries, and representatives from civil society and the business community. GAVI was born and launched at the World Economic Forum in Davos in January 2000.

Developing countries can apply for funds from GAVI to support their immunization activities. Eligibility requirements include a gross domestic product per capita of less than $1500/year; a clear commitment to immunization, as shown by coverage of at least 50% children in each birth cohort with the six EPI vaccines; and a population of fewer than 150 million persons.[8–10]

Over its first 10 years of operation, GAVI received and distributed $4.5 billion to process and buy vaccines and strengthen the health systems for 72 developing countries. A major success of this alliance has been a dramatic increase in the use of Hib vaccine. Use of this vaccine has resulted in an estimated 5.4 million future deaths prevented.[9,10] In addition, a vaccine to prevent meningococcal meningitis type A infections in the meningitis belt in Africa has been developed and distributed. Future challenges include the use of protein-conjugated polysaccharide vaccines for *S. pneumoniae*, typhoid fever and rotavirus vaccines, and other preventive vaccines.

Morbidity in Developing and Developed Countries

In contrast to the mortality data, ARI-related morbidity is similar for children in both developing and developed countries.[4,11] In India, Ethiopia, and Costa Rica, the mean number of episodes of respiratory illness per year for children younger than 3 years of age was reported as 7.3, 7.9, and 4.9, respectively. In older children (3–5 years of age), the rates were also similar across India, Ethiopia, and Costa Rica—6.2, 6.6, and 5.7 episodes/year, respectively.[11–14] Similarly, in the developed world, data

from National Research Council studies of respiratory infection in young children in 12 countries suggest that the incidence of such disease in the first year of life ranges from 5 to 9 episodes.[11] Older data from the Seattle Virus Watch found that from 1965 to 1969, infants experienced a mean of 4.5 episodes per year.[15] In Tecumseh, Michigan, infants experienced a mean of slightly more than 6 episodes of respiratory illness per year, and children aged 1 to 4 years experienced a mean of just more than 5 episodes per year.[16] Caution is in order when considering these data, however: the studies from which these data were culled used widely differing methodologies and were reported several years ago. Thus prevalence rates might not be directly comparable or might have changed in recent years.

The incidence of chronic bronchitis (chronic obstructive pulmonary disease) is generally similar in developing and developed countries.[17] For example, Lai et al. found 6.8% of an elderly group of Chinese living in Hong Kong to have chronic bronchitis,[18] and pharmaceutical research indicated a 6.9% incidence in Taiwan.[17] However, Pandey found a high incidence of chronic bronchitis (18%) in Nepal,[19] with women and men equally affected by the disease. Indonesia also appears to have an especially high incidence of chronic bronchitis, although available data do not differentiate chronic bronchitis from acute bronchitis or account for multiple episodes during the observation period.[17] An age profile in a sample of nearly 250,000 persons in Indonesia noted the incidence of chronic bronchitis was 15.7% in those persons aged 30 to 39 years, 19.3% in those aged 40 to 54 years, and approximately 6% in those aged 55 years or older.[17]

Developed Countries

In developed countries, ARI is the leading cause of morbidity, accounting for 20% of medical consultations, 30% of absences from work, and 75% of all antibiotic prescriptions.[1] Of all the ARIs, pneumonia has been the most thoroughly studied.

In 1900, pneumonia was the second leading cause of death in the United States, after tuberculosis.[20] Mortality rates per 100,000 population between 1910 and the present are shown in **Figure 19-1**.[17] In 1918, pneumonia mortality skyrocketed due to complications from the great influenza pandemic, which that year killed more than 540,000 Americans. Since that time, the pneumonia-related mortality rate has fallen significantly because of better hygiene practices and the availability of effective treatment, including antipneumococcal serum, sulfa drugs, penicillin, and other antibiotics, as well as the use of influenza Hib and pneumococcal vaccines. The slight increase in

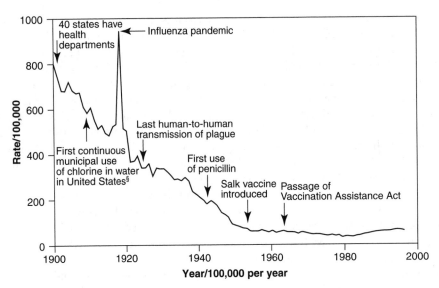

Figure 19-1   Crude death rates for infectious diseases, United States 1990–1996. Reproduced from the Centers for Disease Control and Prevention (1999). *MMWR*, Vol. 48 No. 29 pp. 621–648.

pneumonia-related deaths since 1990 primarily reflects the increase in proportion of Americans who are elderly and who have a high pneumonia risk.[17] Mortality rates from influenza and pneumonia in the United States declined between 1999 and 2008, especially in persons older than age 75 and after 2003 (**Table 19-2**). This decline may be due in part to more widespread use of conjugated pneumocccal vaccines in children and more extensive use of influenza vaccines, in addition to the absence of a major influenza pandemic during these years. The sharp rise in influenza seen in the figure for 2009 reflects the severity of the 2009 influenza season. Currently, in the United States, mortality rates from community-acquired pneumonia range from 1% to 5% in outpatients and from 15% to 30% in inpatients, making it the eighth leading cause of death.[21–24] Community-acquired pneumonia results in hospitalization in 20% of patients and 65 million days of restricted activity.[21]

Figure 19-2 pinpoints where in the United States deaths from pneumonia occurred between 1979 and 1992.[20] Although it was long theorized that a higher mortality rate from pneumonia occurred during winter and that cold temperatures promote pneumonia, these ideas are not consistent with the pattern of mortality.[20] Indeed, no definitive pattern with regard to climate is apparent in the United States from the 1979–1992 data: California had the highest pneumonia-related mortality rates; Georgia and Massachusetts had high rates; and North Dakota had the third lowest rate. The apparent contradiction raised by Florida, a state known as

a retirement destination, being among those states with low rates of pneumonia is believed to be due to the "healthy retiree" effect. Healthy older people are able to retire to places such as Florida, whereas less healthy people in the older age group remain at home (Figure 19-2).[20]

Hospital-acquired (nosocomial) pneumonia is the second most common nosocomial infection in the United States, but it is the type of nosocomial infection most frequently associated with a fatal outcome.[26] The annual incidence is 5 to 10 cases per 1000 hospital admissions, and up to 20 times this figure in patients on ventilators.[26] Mortality rates run as high as 33% to 50% in patients on ventilators.[27,28] The availability of penicillin, macrolides, and other antibiotics to treat pneumonia has greatly reduced the mortality and morbidity associated with this infection.

Age-specific incidence rates of minor episodes of respiratory illness (primarily upper respiratory tract infections) in the United States have varied little since 1933, as indicated by the results of studies that evaluated populations of varying compositions and used differing study methodologies and definitions of acute respiratory illness.[29] Over this period, however, pneumonia mortality rates have decreased in all age groups, except the elderly (Table 19-2). Indeed, since 1981, mortality rates have increased in pneumonia patients aged 55 years or older. It is unclear why this trend is occurring, although alterations in the types and pathogenicity of organisms causing pneumonia and changing host factors may be contributory factors.[29]

Table 19-2	Influenza and Pneumonia Mortality Rates for the United States 1995–2009. A gradual decline in influenza and pneumonia related deaths is seen in the sparklines. The decline is accented by a sharp drop in pneumonia deaths following the introduction of the vaccine in 1999. There is also a recent increase in influenza in 2009 related to a more intense influenza season that year. Sparklines are simple graphical representations of data. Note they are not scaled relative to each other, but give a visual representation of the data in each age and disease category over the 15-year period.

Year	Age	All ages (age-adjusted)	18–24	25–44	45–54	55–64	65+ (age-adjusted)	65–74	75–84	85+
1995	Influenza and pneumonia	33.4	0.6	2.5	6.6	16.2	237.2	56.9	231.5	1020.9
1995	Influenza	0.2	*	*	*	0.1	1.6	0.4	1.2	8.2
1995	Pneumonia	33.2	0.6	2.5	6.5	16.1	235.5	56.5	230.3	1012.7
1996	Influenza and pneumonia	32.9	0.6	2.4	6.4	16.7	233.5	56.3	228.7	1002.1
1996	Influenza	0.3	*	0	0.1	0.2	2	0.4	1.6	9.6
1996	Pneumonia	32.6	0.6	2.4	6.3	16.6	231.5	55.8	227.1	992.5
1997	Influenza and pneumonia	33.3	0.7	2.3	6.5	17	236.3	56.4	231.6	1015.7
1997	Influenza	0.3	*	0	*	0.1	1.9	0.4	1.4	9.4
1997	Pneumonia	33	0.7	2.2	6.5	16.9	234.4	56	230.2	1006.3
1998	Influenza and pneumonia	34.6	0.7	2.3	6.2	16.8	247.4	59.3	240.1	1069.5
1998	Influenza	0.7	*	*	0.1	0.3	4.8	0.8	4.3	23
1998	Pneumonia	33.9	0.7	2.2	6.1	16.5	242.6	58.4	235.9	1046.5
1999	Influenza and pneumonia	23.5	0.5	1.6	4.6	11	167.4	37.2	157	751.8
1999	Influenza	0.6	*	0	0.1	0.3	4.4	0.9	3.7	21.2
1999	Pneumonia	22.9	0.5	1.6	4.6	10.7	163	36.4	153.3	730.6
2000	Influenza and pneumonia	23.7	0.6	1.7	4.7	11.9	168.6	39.1	160.3	744.1
2000	Influenza	0.6	*	0	0.1	0.4	4.5	1.1	4	20.2
2000	Pneumonia	23.1	0.6	1.6	4.6	11.5	164.2	38	156.4	723.9
2001	Influenza and pneumonia	22	0.5	1.6	4.6	10.7	155.8	36.3	148.5	685.6
2001	Influenza	0.1	*	*	*	0.1	0.5	0.1	0.4	2.2
2001	Pneumonia	21.9	0.5	1.5	4.6	10.6	155.3	36.2	148.1	683.4
2002	Influenza and pneumonia	22.6	0.5	1.6	4.8	11.2	160.7	37.5	156.9	696.6
2002	Influenza	0.2	*	*	*	0.1	1.7	0.3	1.4	8.8
2002	Pneumonia	22.4	0.4	1.5	4.7	11.1	159	37.2	155.5	687.8
2003	Influenza and pneumonia	22	0.6	1.6	5.2	11.2	154.8	37.3	151.1	666.1
2003	Influenza	0.6	0.1	0	0.1	0.3	3.9	1	3.6	17
2003	Pneumonia	21.4	0.6	1.6	5.1	10.9	150.9	36.3	147.5	649.1
2004	Influenza and pneumonia	19.8	0.5	1.4	4.6	10.8	139	34.6	139.3	582.6
2004	Influenza	0.4	*	0	0.1	0.2	2.5	0.5	2.2	11.4
2004	Pneumonia	19.4	0.5	1.4	4.5	10.7	136.5	34	137	571.2
2005	Influenza and pneumonia	20.3	0.5	1.5	5.1	11.3	141.9	35.5	142.2	593.9
2005	Influenza	0.6	*	0	0.1	0.2	4.1	0.7	3.7	19.3
2005	Pneumonia	19.7	0.4	1.5	5	11.1	137.8	34.8	138.5	574.7
2006	Influenza and pneumonia	17.8	0.5	1.4	4.6	10	123.7	32	127.8	502.5
2006	Influenza	0.3	*	*	0.1	0.1	1.7	0.4	1.8	7
2006	Pneumonia	17.5	0.5	1.4	4.6	9.8	122	31.6	125.9	495.5
2007	Influenza and pneumonia	16.2	0.5	1.3	4.4	9.6	112.3	28.7	114.1	463.2
2007	Influenza	0.1	*	0	*	0.1	0.6	0.2	0.6	2.5
2007	Pneumonia	16.1	0.4	1.3	4.3	9.5	111.7	28.5	113.5	460.7

(Continued)

Table 19-2	*(Continued)*								
Year	Age	All ages (age-adjusted)	18–24	25–44	45–54	55–64	65+ (age-adjusted)	65–74	75–84	85+
2008	Influenza and pneumonia	16.9	0.6	1.5	5.1	11.1	115.6	31.1	119.1	465.2
2008	Influenza	0.5	*	0.1	0.2	0.4	3.2	0.6	3.2	14.3
2008	Pneumonia	16.4	0.5	1.4	4.9	10.7	112.3	30.4	115.9	450.9
2009	Influenza and pneumonia	16.2	1.1	2.6	6.5	11.9	104	30.1	105.9	413.5
2009	Influenza	0.9	0.5	0.8	1.5	1.4	1.6	1.1	1.6	3.6
2009	Pneumonia	15.3	0.6	1.7	5	10.5	102.5	29	104.4	409.8

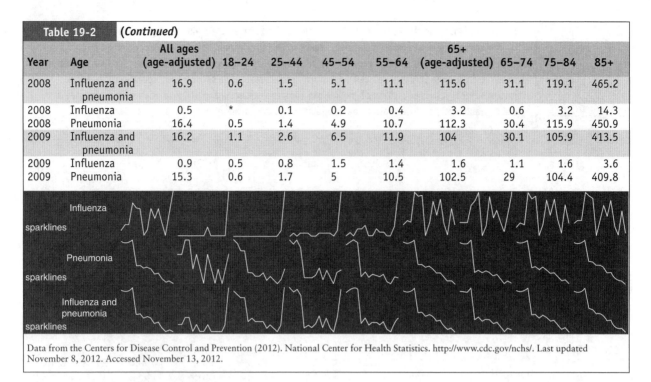

Data from the Centers for Disease Control and Prevention (2012). National Center for Health Statistics. http://www.cdc.gov/nchs/. Last updated November 8, 2012. Accessed November 13, 2012.

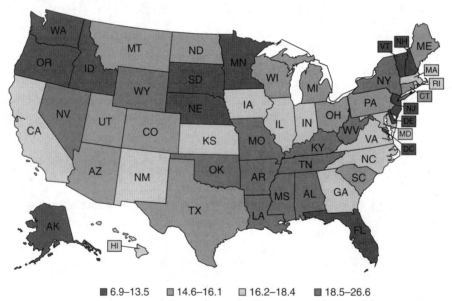

6.9–13.5   14.6–16.1   16.2–18.4   18.5–26.6

Figure 19-2 Influenza and pneumonia death rate per 100,000. "Number of Deaths per 100,000 Population Caused by Influenza and Pneumonia, 2009", statehealthfacts.org, The Henry J. Kaiser Family Foundation, May 2009.

Despite decreasing mortality rates for pneumonia and influenza in young children and infants, lower respiratory tract illness (croup, bronchitis, bronchiolitis, and pneumonia) remains an important cause of morbidity in this age cohort, annually affecting approximately 25% of children aged less than 1 year and 18% of children aged 1 to 4 years.[30–35] In 1989, Wright et al. reported the cumulative incidence of first episodes of lower respiratory tract infection in infants to be 32.9% in children of families participating in a prepaid health plan.[36] This higher rate might have been seen because of differing diagnostic criteria compared with previous studies,[32–34] an active rather than a passive follow-up regimen, and increased physician attendance because of lack of a financial disincentive in a prepaid health plan. In older children and adults in the United Kingdom, ARI accounted for almost one fourth of all primary care contacts, and one third of days taken off work.[37] In a survey in Australia, 17% of patients aged 15 years or older and 43% of children aged less than 15 years consulted a doctor for respiratory symptoms during the 2 weeks preceding the survey.[38] A study in Adelaide, South Australia, showed that children younger than 5 years experienced a mean of seven episodes of respiratory illness per year, which prompted three doctor visits, 15 days of medication, and 52 days of respiratory symptoms annually.[38,39]

The incidence of chronic bronchitis is similar in the United States and Europe.[20] In 1994, Enright et al. reported that 5.1% to 5.4% of the middle-aged to elderly population in the United States have chronic bronchitis, with a lower prevalence in nonsmokers.[40] In Europe, chronic bronchitis has been reported to affect 3.7% of people in Denmark,[41] 4.5% in Norway,[42] 6% and 6.4% in Barcelona and Valencia, Spain, respectively,[44] and 6.7% in Sweden.[45]

In the United States in 1998, community-acquired pneumonia accounted for an estimated $3.6 billion in expenditures for treating patients younger than age 65 years and $4.8 billion for treating patients aged 65 years or older.[46] In 1999, costs associated with acute exacerbations of chronic bronchitis were $419 million in patients younger than 65 years and three times that much ($1.2 billion) for patients aged 65 years and older.[47]

CLASSIFICATION OF ACUTE RESPIRATORY INFECTIONS

Two basic systems are most commonly used to classify acute respiratory infections: the case-management classification system and the "traditional" clinical classification system (**Table 19-3**).

Table 19-3	Classification of Acute Respiratory Infection Clinical Syndromes		
Case-Management Classification (children aged 2 months to 4 years)			**"Traditional" Classification**
Stridor	**Wheezing**	**No wheezing**	
Mild	Mild	Mild	Upper respiratory tract syndromes
Hoarseness plus "barking" cough; no stridor when calm = mild croup	Improves with bronchodilator; respiratory rate <50/min = mild bronchiolitis or asthma	Cough; nasal obstruction; respiratory rate <50/min = URI,* cold	Common cold; URI* Acute otitis media Pharyngitis/tonsillitis Acute sinusitis
Home care; no antibiotic	Oral salbutamol Moderate	No antibiotic; home care Moderate	Middle respiratory tract syndromes
	Improves with bronchodilator; respiratory rate 50–70/min = mild bronchiolitis or asthma Consider antibiotic; oral salbutamol; home care	Respiratory rate >50/min; no chest indrawing = pneumonia Antibiotic; home care	Croup Laryngotracheo-bronchitis Epiglottitis Laryngitis Tracheitis
Severe	Severe	Severe	Lower respiratory tract syndromes
Stridor when calm; chest indrawing = severe croup or epiglottitis	No improvement with bronchodilator; respiratory rate >70/min = severe bronchiolitis or asthma	Respiratory rate >50/min; chest indrawing = severe pneumonia	Bronchiolitis Bronchitis Pneumonia
Admit; antibiotic; manage airway	Admit; bronchodilators; consider oxygen and antibiotics Very severe	Admit; antibiotic Very severe	
	Cyanosis or inability to drink = very severe bronchiolitis or asthma Admit; bronchodilators; oxygen and consider antibiotic	Cyanosis or inability to drink = very severe pneumonia Antibiotic; admit; oxygen	

* URI, upper respiratory infection.

Reproduced from NMH Graham, The Epidemiology of Acute Respiratory Infection in Children and Adults: A Global Perspective, Epidemiologic Reviews, Vol. 12, p. 152, Table 2. © 1990. By permission of Oxford University Press.

Case-Management Classification

In an effort to reduce pneumonia-related mortality, WHO has developed a simple case-management approach to be followed by village healthcare workers. Before 1988, simplified case classifications, as used in India,[48] Papua New Guinea,[49] and other developing countries,[50] were applied successfully by health workers to determine when children should be given antibiotics or referred to secondary or tertiary level care. Adherence with these classifications resulted in reductions in both pneumonia-related mortality and in overall mortality. The simplified case definitions were based on respiratory rates recorded among children with symptoms of respiratory infections. The sensitivity and specificity of increased respiratory rate were determined using clinically confirmed or chest radiograph-confirmed pneumonia (or "lower respiratory tract infection") as the putative gold standard. For example, using receiver operating characteristic (ROC) curves, Cherian et al. showed that higher respiratory rates were more sensitive and specific for infants than for older children aged less than 5 years (**Figure 19-3**).[51]

In 1988, changes were made to improve the specificity of case-management guidelines.[50,52-55] Although the primary focus remained on pneumonia, classification and management of syndromes causing stridor and wheezing were directly addressed, and otitis media was classified separately (Table 19-3). Other major differences from the earlier classification were in the younger-than-2-month-old age group, for whom the newer classification recognized that a respiratory rate greater than 50 breaths/minute and some chest in-drawing could be considered normal[52]; with regard to cough, which is often absent in neonates with pneumonia, the newer classification specified that this sign is not sufficiently sensitive to be used as an indicator of severe disease. The newer case-management classification recommended that signs of general sepsis should be sought (i.e., fever, feeding problems, drowsiness, convulsions, abdominal distention, hypothermia) as well as more specific signs of pneumonia (respiratory rate greater than 60 breaths/minute, severe chest in-drawing, respiratory grunt) when determining whether to prescribe antibiotics and to hospitalize patients.[52]

Clinical Classification

Acute respiratory infections can be classified by the site of primary pathology (Table 19-3). This system is preferred by most physicians, and it is compatible with the International Classification of Diseases

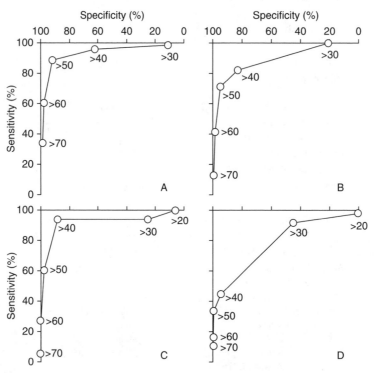

Figure 19-3 Receiver operating characterisitcs (ROC) curves for respiratory rates as indicators of lower respiratory tract infections in infants and children. Reprinted from The Lancet, 322, Cherian et al. Evaluation of simple clinical signs for the diagnosis of acute lower respiratory tract infection, 126, Copyright 1988, with permission from Elsevier.

(ICD) system. However, such classification can lead to some confusion because infections are not always limited to one part of the respiratory tract. Moreover, clinicians may disagree on whether an acute respiratory infection can be termed "upper," "middle," or "lower." Stridor-causing conditions often have been classified as upper respiratory tract infections, thus suggesting mild disease, which can be a misleading assumption. Because stridor can cause severe, and possibly fatal, respiratory distress, consideration has been given to classifying stridor-causing conditions as acute lower respiratory infections.[55]

PATHOGENS RESPONSIBLE FOR ACUTE RESPIRATORY INFECTIONS

In a large percentage of patients with acute respiratory infections, the pathogens responsible for infection are not known. This problem is especially notable with regard to community-acquired pneumonia, for which the causative organism is unknown in approximately 98% of those individuals treated as outpatients and 50% to 60% of those persons treated as hospital inpatients.[56,57]

Viruses

Many upper respiratory viral infections in children and adults are caused by rhinoviruses (30% to 50%) or coronaviruses (5% to 20%), with the remainder (30% to 65%) due to influenza virus, parainfluenza virus, respiratory syncytial virus, adenoviruses, and certain enteroviruses.[58] These infections are generally mild, are self-limiting, and do not involve respiratory distress.

In children, viral causes of the acute lower respiratory tract infections, pneumonia, bronchiolitis, and croup generally appear to be similar in both developed and developing countries.[59-69] The primary pathogens are respiratory syncytial virus; parainfluenza virus types 1, 2, and 3; influenza virus types A and B; adenoviruses; metapneumovirus; and enteroviruses. Respiratory syncytial virus is most commonly associated with bronchiolitis, and parainfluenza virus (especially type 1) is more often associated with croup.[70-73] In developing countries, measles contributes to croup and serious morbidity in other lower respiratory infections more than it does in the developed world.[69,74,75] Approximately 90% of cases of acute bronchitis are caused by viruses, including influenza virus, parainfluenza virus, and rhinovirus.[68,76]

In adults, viral causes of pneumonia are generally less important than nonviral causes. Nevertheless,

influenza has been associated with a significant proportion of cases in adults, perhaps causing as many as half of all virus-associated cases and approximately 8% to 10% of all pneumonias in general.[32,79,80] Respiratory syncytial virus and parainfluenza also have been identified in some adult cases of pneumonia, but these viruses are less common than influenza.[80] In developed countries, influenza epidemics in elderly patients (older than 65 years of age) are associated with especially high mortality and hospitalization rates from acute respiratory infections; thus influenza poses a major health risk to this age group.[79] More than 50% of excess hospitalizations and more than 80% of influenza-related deaths occur in persons aged 65 years and older, in whom mortality is 30 to 50 times greater than in younger adults and adolescents.[79,80] In developing countries, viral causes of adult lower respiratory tract infections have not been widely studied. No indication is seen that viral pathogens are implicated to any greater degree in pneumonia cases in developing countries than they are in developed countries, although the mode of transmission in the poorer nations (unwashed hands, contaminated water) can differ from those in the developed world (daycare facilities, contaminated aerosols).[76,80]

Several viruses have been identified recently to be important causes of acute respiratory infection. The severe acute respiratory syndrome (SARS) coronavirus caused a major pandemic when it emerged in southern China in 2002. This virus is a new human pathogen that crossed species to infect humans—that is, a zoonotic infection. While no new cases of SARS have been seen since this epidemic, its emergence reminds us of the potential for zoonosis and the risk of previously unknown viruses infecting humans. The epidemiology of the SARS pandemic is covered in detail in the chapter on emerging infections.

In 2001, investigators in the Netherlands isolated a new virus from children and adults with acute respiratory tract infection.[81] This RNA virus is closely related to avian pneumovirus. In the last few years, metapneumovirus has been isolated from patients with acute respiratory infection in the United States, Australia, Canada, and the United Kingdom.[82-86] A study was published recently from Vanderbilt University in Nashville, Tennessee, in which nasal washes were collected prospectively from 463 infants and children who were seen for acute lower respiratory infection between 1976 and 2001.[87] A viral cause other than metapneumovirus was detected in 41% of these children. Of 248 specimens available for which no other pathogen was detected, 49 (20%) contained metapneumovirus[86]; 28% of illnesses occurred

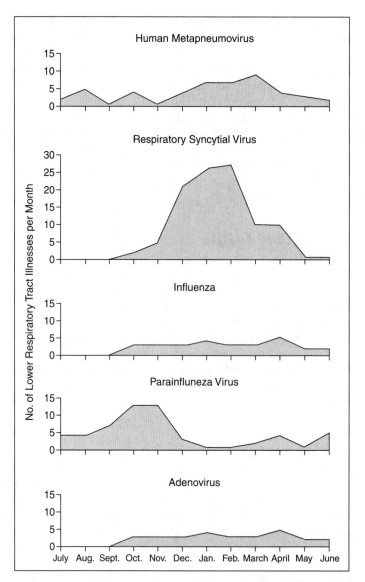

Figure 19-4 Epidemiologic pattern of lower respiratory tract infections with human metapneumovirus and other viruses. From Williams et al. Human metapneumovirus and lower respiratory tract disease in otherwise healthy infants and children. *N Engl J Med.* Vol. 350(5):446, Figure 1. © 2004 Massachusetts Medical Society. Reprinted with permission from Massachusetts Medical Society.

between December and April; and 2% of infected children were hospitalized. The seasonal distribution of metapneumoviruses and other viral pathogens in this study is shown in **Figure 19-4.**

In 2005, a human parvovirus was identified in pooled respiratory secretions using host DNA depletion, random polymerase chain reaction (PCR) amplification, sequencing, and bioinformatics.[87] This newly identified virus was named human bocavirus (HBoV). It was subsequently identified in respiratory secretions of 17 additional children with clinical lower respiratory tract infection. Following this initial report, investigators from countries around the world have identified HBoV in respiratory secretion

of 5% to 10% of children with pneumonia.[88–92] In addition, HBoV has been identified in fecal samples of children with gastroenteritis.[93,94]

Sinnombre virus is another recently identified virus that is responsible for lower respiratory infections during epidemic or endemic transmission from its reservoir in rodents. The epidemiology of the hantavirus pulmonary syndrome associated with sinnombre virus infections is discussed in the chapter on emerging infections.

Prior to the use of molecular diagnostic methods to identify the agents causing acute respiratory tract infection, most epidemiologic studies had been hampered by the limited laboratory techniques available to isolate viral pathogens. Isolation of virus from 20% to 25% of specimens has been the maximal rate in several well-conducted studies.[31,76,95–99] Recent improvements in these techniques might be expected to result in higher isolation rates becoming more common. When combinations of viral culture and immunofluorescence techniques were used in one study of lower respiratory infections in infants to identify viral pathogens from throat and nasopharyngeal swabs, a 66% isolation rate was reported.[32]

The use of nucleic acid amplification methods to identify respiratory viruses has increased the proportion of illnesses in which a viral pathogen has been identified to substantially more than 50%.[80,81]

Bacteria

Microbiologic isolation of the specific pathogen that is responsible for community-acquired pneumonia is difficult and is rarely done in current medical practice. Expectorated sputum is commonly contaminated with bacterial flora from the upper airway.[98] Examination of a Gram-stained sputum is very rarely done at present because of the belief that it is an insensitive test.[99] In addition, the Clinical Laboratory Integrity Act (CLIA) regulations have discouraged the routine microscopic examination of a stained sputum because they require such examinations be performed only by a licensed medical technician.[99] Sputum obtained by transtracheal aspiration or bronchoscopy is more likely to identify the infecting pathogen, but these procedures carry some risks for the patients, are more difficult to implement, and may be susceptible to some contamination. Percutaneous needle aspirates of the lung have been reported to be a sensitive method to identify the pathogen in patients with lobar pneumonia.[100,101]

Whereas the specific pathogen responsible for an adult patient with community-acquired pneumonia (CAP) was identified in 50% to 80% of cases prior to the mid-1980s, it is identified in less than 10% of cases in current medical practice.[99] This trend has implications for treatment. A prospective study was done comparing the outcome (i.e., mortality, length of hospital stay, resolution of fever, and clinical treatment failure) in 262 patients who were randomized to receive either empirical broad-spectrum antibiotic treatment to treat the major pathogens in pneumonia cases or initial identification of the infecting organism followed by pathogen-directed treatment[102]; this study found no difference in these outcomes between the two groups of patients. Another study compared the outcome of 18,209 Medicare patients who were hospitalized for CAP according to when antibiotic treatment was started after hospital admission.[103] This study found a reduction in in-hospital mortality and

length of stay among patients in whom antibiotics were begun within 4 hours of admission.[103] Initiation of antibiotic therapy for CAP has been utilized subsequently as one of the measures of quality of care of hospitalized patients with pneumonia.[104] As rapid antibiotic use is now considered a measure of quality care for this indication, health providers have been pressured to start therapy as quickly as possible after pneumonia diagnoses, promoting the use of broad-spectrum empirical therapy over the strategy of first identifying the infecting organism and then tailoring the therapy for the causative pathogen.[104] On the one hand, this practice has resulted in some unnecessary use of some antibiotics in patients with CAP, thereby increasing the risk of the development of antibiotic resistance strains of pathogens. On the other hand, earlier therapy may improve the outcome for some patients.

One consideration in selecting the therapy for CAP patients is whether they might be infected with an "atypical agent," such as *Mycoplasma pneumoniae hominis*, *Legionella pneumophila*, *Chlamydia pneumoniae*, or a viral pathogen. Of these difficult-to-diagnose microorganisms by culture or a stained sputum exam, *Legionella* may be the most significant because it requires specific therapy to avoid significant morbidity or mortality. *Legionella* should be considered if the patient acquired pneumonia on a cruise ship or in a hotel.[105] A recent outbreak of *Legionella* infection was reported among persons exposed to the pathogen from a decorative "water wall."[106] These waterfalls had been installed in hospital waiting areas as attractive and relaxing features; however, it is likely most will now be removed to prevent Legionnaires' disease. Rapid antigen detection tests have been approved by the Food and Drug Administration (FDA) to detect *S. pneumoniae* or *Legionella pneumonphila* type 1 antigens in the urine.[106,108] In addition, a multiplex reverse transcription–polymerase chain reaction (RT-PCR) assay to detect 12 viral pathogens simultaneously in patients with CAP has been licensed.[109] The more frequent use of these assays in the future should facilitate more rapid initiation of effective therapy in patients with acute respiratory infection and improve outcomes.

Active Bacterial Core Surveillance of the Emerging Infections Program Network

To better understand the epidemiology of several important bacterial pathogens that cause acute community-acquired lower respiratory infections, sepsis, and meningitis, the Centers for Disease Control and Prevention (CDC) established the Active Bacterial Core (ABC) Surveillance Program in 1995.[110] This program collects and analyzes microbiologic and molecular data on five organisms that are isolated in cultures from usually sterile sites (i.e., blood, cerebrospinal fluid, joint fluid) by 600 laboratories in all or part of seven states that are participating in the CDC-funded Emerging Infections Program (EIP). The pathogens that are evaluated include *S. pneumoniae, H. influenzae, N. meningitides,* group A *Streptococcus* (*S. pyogenes*) and group B *Streptococcus.*

Data collected in the ABC study have allowed evaluation of the effectiveness of three vaccines: pneumococcal, *H. influenzae* type b, and meningococcal. The emergence of serotypes not contained in the *S. pneumoniae* and *N. meningitis* vaccines and the antibiotic sensitivity patterns of these important pathogens also have been evaluated in the ABC program. An estimated 6% to 10% of untreated pulmonary infections involving *S. pneumoniae* or *H. influenzae* result in sepsis or meningitis, so the ABC system will identify only a minority of pneumonia caused by these pathogens. Nevertheless, many of the more serious infections will be detected.

Developing Countries

Bacteria-caused lower respiratory infections are more common in children in developing countries than in the developed world, where viral infections are more often encountered.[33] Reliable data regarding the pathogens responsible for pneumonia in adults in developing countries have come chiefly from hospital studies. *Streptococcus pneumoniae* is by far the most important cause of pneumonia in adults: it is associated with as many as 70% of cases in which a

pathogen is isolated,[111] with *Haemophilus influenzae* and *Staphylococcus aureus* being relatively less important in adults than in children (together accounting for approximately 10% of cases). *Streptococcus pyogenes* and *Corynebacterium diphtheriae* most commonly cause pharyngitis and tonsillitis. Acute epiglottitis is caused chiefly by *H. influenzae* type b, and whooping cough by *Bordetella pertussis.*[112,113] In otitis media, *S. pneumoniae* and *H. influenzae* are the most commonly isolated bacteria,[113,114] but *Moraxella catarrhalis* has been isolated in 27% of patients in some series.[115] *S. pneumoniae* and *H. influenzae* are also important in acute sinusitis in children[116,117] and in adults.[118]

Berman and McIntosh[119] have reviewed studies of bacteria isolated from children in developing countries using lung aspiration techniques. The most frequently isolated pathogens were *H. influenzae, S. pneumoniae* (together accounting for 54% of isolates), and *S. aureus* (accounting for 17% of isolates). A subsequent study in Zimbabwe found a similar pattern of pathogens responsible for lower respiratory infections.[120]

Developed Countries

The key bacterial pathogens responsible for CAP in the developed world appear to be the same as those in developing countries. A literature review of 15 published reports from North America showed the most common bacterial pathogens to be *S. pneumoniae* (20% to 60% of isolates) and *H. influenzae* (3% to 10%) (**Table 19-4**). A meta-analysis of 122 published studies between 1966 and 1995 ($N = 7057$) indicated that *S. pneumoniae* was responsible for 66% of

Table 19-4	Microbiological Characteristics of Community-Acquired Pneumonia (CAP)	
	Prevalence, %	
Origin	**North America**[a]	**British Thoracic Society**[b]
Streptococcus pneumoniae	20–60	60–75
Haemophilus influenzae	3–10	4–5
Staphylococcus aureus	3–5	1–5
Enterobacteriaceae	3–10	Rare
Legionella	2–8	2–5
Mycoplasma pneumoniae	1–6	5–18
Chlamydophila pneumoniae	4–6	–
Aspiration	6–10	–
Viruses	2–15	8–16

Note: Data from Mundy et al. [8].

[a]Based on 15 reports from North America.
[b]Based on an analysis of 453 adults in a prospective study of CAP in 25 British hospitals. Ellipses indicate that no studies were performed to detect the designated agent.

Reproduced from Bartlett (2011). Diagnostic tests for agents of Community Acquired Pneumonia, Clinical Infectious Diseases 2011:52(S4);S296–S304.

			Meta-analysis[‡]	
Microbial Agents	**Literature Review* (%)**	**The British Thoracic Society[†] (%)**	**Cases (%)**	**Deaths (%)**

Table 19-5   Pathogens Most Commonly Involved with Health Care Associated Pneumonia

Microbial Agents	**Literature Review* (%)**	**The British Thoracic Society[†] (%)**	**Cases (%)**	**Deaths (%)**
Bacteria				
–*Streptococcus pneumoniae*	20–60	60–75	65	66
–*Haemophilus influenzae*	3–10	4–5	12	7
–*Staphylococcus aureus*	3–5	1–5	2	6
–Gram-negative bacilli	3–10	Rare	1	3
–Miscellaneous agents[§]	3–5	(Not included)	4	9
Atypical pathogens	10–20	—	12	6
–*Legionella* sp.	2–8	2–5	4	5
–*Mycoplasma pneumoniae*	1–6	5–18	7	1
–*Chlamydia pneumoniae*	4–6	(Not included)	1	<1
Viral	2–15	8–16	3	≤1
Aspiration pneumonia	6–10	(Not included)	—	—
No diagnosis	30–60	—	—	—

*Based on analysis of 15 published reports from North America.[98] Low and high values are deleted.

[†]Estimates are based on analysis of 453 adults in prospective study of community-acquired pneumonia in 25 British hospitals.[98]

[‡]Meta-analysis of 122 published studies of community-acquired pneumonia in the English language literature 1966 to 1995; data are limited to 7057 patients who had an etiologic diagnosis.[98] Percentage of death column refers to percentage of all deaths attributed to the designated pathogen.

[§]Includes *Moraxella catarrhalis,* group A streptococcus, and *Neisseria meningitidis* (each 1% to 2%).

J.G. Bartlett (1998). Approach to the Patient with Pneumonia. Ed. Gorbach, Infectious Disease, 2nd edition. pp. 553–564. By permission of Oxford University Press.

deaths in CAP cases.[121] A review of health care associated pneumonia indicated that gram-negative bacteria account for 50% to 70% of cases (**Table 19-5**).[121] The most frequently isolated pathogen is *Pseudomonas aeruginosa,* followed by a diverse array of Enterobacteriaceae. These bacteria reach the lower airways by aspiration of gastric contents. Patients being treated with ventilators are at the highest risk of health care associated pneumonia.

Approximately 50% to 75% of infective exacerbations of chronic bronchitis are bacterial in origin.[17] Studies conducted in the Northern Hemisphere have consistently shown *H. influenzae* to be the major pathogen and *M. catarrhalis* to be the second most common pathogen.[76]

Other Pathogens

Mycoplasma pneumoniae, Chlamydia species, *Legionella* species, and *Pneumocystis carinii* are the nonviral respiratory pathogens most frequently responsible for pneumonia and acute bronchitis in both children and adults.[122–124]

M. pneumoniae can also cause upper respiratory infections.[122,123,125] Of the *Chlamydia* species, *C. trachomatis* is implicated more in cases of pneumonia in young infants,[126] and *C. pneumoniae* (also called TWAR, based on the names of the first two isolates, TW-183 and AR-39) is responsible primarily for pneumonia cases among older children and adults.[127,128] Most of the cases of *P. carinii* pneumonia that have been reported since the early 1980s have occurred in patients with acquired immunodeficiency syndrome (AIDS).[124]

P. carinii pneumonia occurs as an opportunistic infection in patients with AIDS most frequently when their CD4[+] lymphocyte counts fall below 200 cells/mm^3. Approximately 60% to 80% of AIDS patients will develop *P. carinii* pneumonia at some stage during the course of their illness.[124] In developed countries, both children and adults with AIDS and other conditions associated with immunosuppression are at significant risk of *P. carinii* pneumonia. In countries in sub-Saharan Africa, AIDS-associated *P. carinii* pneumonia is less common, but the reasons for this lower incidence are unclear.[124] HIV-infected patients also have a greater incidence of CAP caused by the intracellular bacterial pathogens *Salmonella* and *Legionella* than patients not infected with HIV.[124]

RISK FACTORS

The risk factors for community-acquired pneumonia and hospital acquired pneumonia are summarized in **Table 19-6** and **Table 19-7**, respectively.[110] Specifics pertaining to key risk factors are provided in this section.

Table 19-6 Acute Repiratory Infection Morbidity Rates in Four U.S. Cohort Studies

Investigators	Years	Population	Mean Incidence per Year by Age Group (years)											
			<1	1–2	3–4	5–9	10–14	15–19	20–24	25–29	30–39	40–49	50–59	≥60
van Volkenburgh and Frost[25]	1924	Public health service families		3.0		2.7	1.9	1.4		2.0*	1.8†	1.6†	1.4§	
	1928–1929	Baltimore, MD, families		4.5		3.5	3.5	2.4	2.8		2.7	2.4	1.7	
	1929–1930	Baltimore, MD, families		4.5		3.8	2.8	2.3	2.7		2.6	2.3	2.1	
Gwaltney et al.[26]	1963–1966	Insurance company employees						2.5		2.1	2.2	1.7		
Fox et al.[27]	1965–1969	Seattle, WA, families	5.1	5.8	5.8	3.8	2.3							
Monto and Ullman[13]	1969–1971	Tecumseh, MI, families	6.1	5.7	4.7	3.5	2.7	2.4	2.8	2.7	2.3	1.7	1.6	1.3

*25–34 years of age.
†35–44 years of age.
‡45–54 years of age.
§≥55 years of age.
¶≥45 years of age.

Reproduced from NMH Graham, The Epidemiology of Acute Respiratory Infection in Children and Adults: A Global Perspective, Epidemiologic Reviews, Vol. 12, pp. 149–178, © 1990, by permission of Oxford University Press.

Table 19-7	Risk Factors of Community-Acquired Pneumonia

1. Old age
2. Smoking (>20 cigarettes a day)
3. Air pollution
4. Chronic diseases (e.g., diabetes, chronic hepatopathies, renal, cardiac, respiratory failure)
5. Malnutrition, precarious social and economic situations
6. Acute and chronic alcoholism
7. Chronic obstructive pulmonary disease
8. Primitive ciliary dyskinesia, bronchiectasis, cystic fibrosis
9. Congestive cardiomyopathies
10. Neuromuscular diseases
11. Dementia
12. Autoimmune diseases (LES, rheumatoid arthritis, and other collagen diseases)
13. Malignancy
14. Immunodeficiencies
15. Splenectomy
16. Immunosuppressive therapies
17. Drug addiction
18. Inadequate use of antibiotics

Courtesy of the Journal of Chemotherapy.

Table 19-8	Risk Factors for Health Care Associated Pneumonia

1. Mechanical ventilation (the most important risk factor for health care associated pneumonia)
2. Advanced age (>65 years)
3. Chronic diseases (e.g., diabetes, cardiopathies, chronic obstructive pulmonary disease, chronic hepatopathies, chronic alcoholism, respiratory, cardiac, renal failure, obesity)
4. Malignancy
5. Prolonged immobilization (stroke, neuromuscular diseases)
6. Immunosuppressive therapies (cytotoxics, steroids)
7. Immunodeficiency
8. Thoracic and abdominal surgery
9. Burns
10. Traumas (thorax and abdomen, multiple, rib fractures, pulmonary contusions, pneumothorax, hemothorax)
11. Treatment with antacids and/or H2 blockers
12. Antibiotic therapy and prophylaxis
13. Increase in number of hospitalized patients susceptible to infections
14. Increase in invasive techniques for diagnosis and therapy
15. Mechanical ventilation (MV):—Reintubation—MV duration (>3 d)—Positive end-expiratory pressure—Persistence of coma during MV—Severity of underlying disease—Gastric content aspiration—Oropharyngeal aspiration—Intensive care unit
16. Airway instrumentation
17. Previous intubations and endotracheal prostheses
18. Ultrasound nebulizers and humidifier systems
19. Increase in number of staff members caring for the patient
20. Visitors, relatives, friends, and so on
21. Moving the patient inside the hospital
22. Health staff not adequately educated to prevent nosocomial infections
23. Inadequate hospital structures and facilities
24. Organ transplantation
25. Periodontitis, dental caries, gingivitis

Courtesy of the Journal of Chemotherapy.

Demographic Factors

Age

The incidence of viral respiratory illness peaks in infancy and early childhood and steadily decreases with age because of changes in patterns of exposure and age-related acquisition of specific immunity to an increasing number of virus types encountered over time (**Table 19-8**).[15,16,33–37,96,97]

On examination of markers of more severe conditions (e.g., pneumonia and influenza mortality rates), a different pattern of age-related change is observed. Although infants are at greater risk from pneumonia than older children and young to middle-aged adults, mortality rates are highest in the elderly (Table 19-2). Elderly patients have reduced vital capacity, lesser respiratory muscle strength, and impaired local and general immune defenses, all of which render them more susceptible than younger adults to severe acute lower respiratory infection. Pneumonia and influenza mortality rates, in particular, have increased in the elderly population over the past 15 years (Table 19-2). The most likely explanation for this trend is that many more at-risk persons (e.g., those with cardiovascular disease and chronic airways obstruction) are surviving into old age and suffering pneumonia as a terminal event.

It is also possible that some of these deaths might be attributable to changing virulence of respiratory pathogens and increased cumulative exposures to environmental factors, such as smoking and air pollution.

In developing countries, data on pneumonia-related mortality rates over the entire age range are sparse because many nations, especially those in Africa and Asia, do not report information to WHO. However, Costa Rica and Cuba have contributed data to the WHO database, and both developing countries show an excess burden of mortality in infants and young children. Mortality rates in older children and young adults in Costa Rica are not much higher than those in the United States. As in the United States, mortality rates rise rapidly in the elderly in Costa Rica and Cuba, with this increase being especially pronounced in Cuba.

Gender

The incidence of acute respiratory infections has been known to vary according to gender since the 1920s. In Baltimore, between 1928 and 1930, van Volkenburgh and Frost reported higher rates of acute respiratory infections in boys aged younger than 9 years, and the reverse pattern beyond that age.[29] Similar findings were reported by Monto and Ullman, who found higher rates of infection in boys aged less than 3 years, but lower rates in older age groups.[16] Gwaltney et al. found that young women aged 16 to 24 years experienced more upper respiratory tract illness than did young men of similar age, even after adjusting for number of children and smoking status, with no differences being seen in patients older than age 24 years.[30] A review of pneumonia cases between 1979 and 1992 showed men to be at greater risk of pneumonia than women; this finding was considered partly due to men being more susceptible because of increased exposure to two key pneumonia risk factors—alcoholism and nicotine.[20]

Fox et al. found that mothers in Seattle families experienced more upper respiratory illness than did their husbands, but not more lower respiratory illness.[31] This could have been due to the mothers' more frequent exposure to young children. However, a subsequent study of viral chest infections in infants found no differences in incidence by sex.[36] Pneumonia-related mortality rates in older adults are higher in men than in women, although this is not the case with mortality rates from upper respiratory tract infection. The reason for the greater susceptibility of older men is not certain, but it may reflect their generally higher rates of cardiovascular disease and chronic airway obstruction as compared to women.

Outdoor Air Pollution

Outdoor air pollution has been known to affect the incidence of acute respiratory infections since the early 1930s. Historically, episodes of acute, severe, particulate air pollution in the Meuse Valley, Belgium (1930); Donora, Pennsylvania (1948); New York City (1953 and 1962); and greater London (1948, 1952, and 1956) were associated with increases in all-cause mortality, primarily because of more deaths from pneumonia and cardiovascular disease.[133] An estimated 4000 excess deaths were reported in the disastrous London fog of 1952,[129] with the elderly and very elderly in greater London being the groups most severely affected.

These studies prompted research to evaluate the effects of much lower levels of air pollution on the outcomes of acute respiratory illnesses. The components of air pollution most widely studied have been suspended respirable particulates, sulfur dioxide, nitrogen dioxide, and ozone. Although studies in the 1960s and 1970s provided somewhat contradictory results,[134] they were instrumental in changing the focus on outcomes from mortality to both mortality and morbidity. Indeed, morbidity was considered a more sensitive outcome measure than mortality in studies of relatively low levels of air pollution. In 1964, Toyama reported a correlation between bronchitis mortality and level of suspended particulates in all ages.[135] He also found that respiratory morbidity rates were higher for all age groups and ventilatory function poorer in children in air-polluted cities compared with relatively nonpolluted rural areas. Lunn et al. studied respiratory illness patterns in children exposed to relatively high and low levels of particulate matter (smoke) and sulfur dioxide in Sheffield, United Kingdom.[136,137] These investigators found a relationship between exposure to high levels of particles and sulfur dioxide in air and repeated episodes of acute upper and lower respiratory tract illness, after adjusting for socioeconomic status. Conversely, Colley and Reid found a relationship between air pollution (urban/rural comparison) and acute lower (but not upper) respiratory illness in children.[138] This effect was most marked in the lower social classes. Cassel et al. also found no relationship between air pollution and upper respiratory illness.[139] In infants in England and Wales who were examined and followed between 1958 and 1964, pneumonia and respiratory disease mortality were strongly associated with air pollution.[140] In 1970, Lawther et al. related acute exacerbations of chronic bronchitis to daily variations in smoke and sulfur dioxide.[141]

Health effects in adults have been estimated to occur with atmospheric levels of more than 500 µg/m³ of sulfur dioxide and 250 µg/m³ of particulates in adults, and 180 µg/m³ and 120 µg/m³, respectively, in children older than age 4 years.[134] A weaker but still significant relationship was also seen in children aged 1 to 4 years. In the Great Salt Lake Basin and the Rocky Mountains, high levels of sulfur dioxide and suspended sulfate were associated with excess reports of croup in children (age-, sex-, and social class-adjusted rates) who resided in a high-pollution area for more than 3 years.[142] Durham found that upper respiratory symptoms reported by Los Angeles college students presenting to campus health centers were significantly correlated with sulfur dioxide and nitrogen dioxide levels independent of the effects of age, weather, and smoking levels.[143] Levy et al. found that high levels of sulfur dioxide and particulate matter—but not nitrogen dioxide, carbon monoxide, or pollen—predicted hospital admission for acute respiratory disease in children and adults, after adjusting for the effects of temperature.[144] In Chicago, acute upper and lower respiratory tract illness attack rates were reported to be higher in both adults and children, but in New York only lower respiratory tract illness attack rates were significantly higher in residents of high-pollution areas.

Studies in the 1980s sought to examine the effects of air pollution at much lower levels than earlier studies and tried to determine which components of air pollution are of primary importance. Studies designed to allow concurrent comparisons of similar demographic areas and adjustment for confounding factors (e.g., the Six Cities Study[145]) were instrumental in clarifying the role of outdoor air pollution in increasing susceptibility to acute respiratory illness. Ware et al. found that between-city annual mean differences in particulate and suspended sulfate concentrations as small as 80 $\mu g/m^3$ doubled the risk of acute cough and substantially increased the risk of bronchitis and other lower respiratory illness in children.[145] These investigators also found significant, albeit weaker, associations with sulfur dioxide. Mean monthly peaks of sulfur dioxide did not exceed a range of 80 to 200 $\mu g/m^3$. In a study by Pope, 24-hour fine-particulate levels as low as 50 $\mu g/m^3$ were associated with significantly increased hospitalization rates in children and adults for acute respiratory disease.[146] The associations were stronger for bronchitis and asthma than for pneumonia and pleurisy, and persisted when adjustments were made for meteorologic variables. Derriennic et al. observed that sulfur dioxide levels, but not levels of particulates or nitrogen dioxide, predicted deaths from respiratory disease in adults older than 65 years of age.[147] Other studies have confirmed the importance of the association between particulates, sulfur dioxide, and respiratory symptoms in children.[148,149]

The evidence is now supportive of the hypothesis that suspended particulates, suspended sulfates, and sulfur dioxide at levels currently being measured in ambient air significantly increase the risk of morbidity from acute respiratory illness in adults and children alike. Because most studies do not include virologic sampling, it is unclear whether such morbidity is chiefly caused by bronchial reactivity and respiratory tract irritation or by infection. Studies

supported by virologic culture and serology are needed to answer this question. Ozone exposures below the U.S. ambient air quality standard have been associated with acute changes in ventilatory function[150] and increased risk of cough and lower respiratory illness.[151] The importance of ambient levels of nitrogen dioxide as a risk factor for respiratory illness is less clear.[144,152]

Indoor Air Pollution

Indoor air pollution from passive smoke, nitrogen dioxide from gas cooking or heating, and smoke from biomass fuels have been investigated for their impact on acute respiratory infections.

A 1999 review of studies published during the 1990s showed that the incidence of respiratory illnesses and middle ear infection was greater in children living in homes where either parent smoked, with odds ratios between 1.2 and 1.6.[153] The odds ratios were much higher in preschool children than in school-aged children. For sudden infant death syndrome, the odds ratio for maternal smoking was approximately 2. Exposure to maternal cigarette smoke approximately doubles the risk of lower respiratory tract infection in children aged less than 2 years.[154,155] Paternal smoking seems less contributory to infection rates, possibly because fathers are generally around their children less than mothers during their children's first 2 years of life.[156,157] Passive smoking is believed to increase respiratory infection rates in children by reducing mucociliary clearance.[153] Although negative studies have also been reported,[158–160] these investigations either involved small numbers of patients[160] or did not report on smoking effects in children younger than age 2 years.[158,159]

In studies linking maternal smoking during pregnancy with respiratory infections in infants, prenatal smoking was found to be a stronger risk factor for bronchitis in infants than postnatal smoking.[161,162] As relatively few women change their smoking habits during or after pregnancy, it is difficult to identify sufficiently large comparison groups to fully settle this question.

Heating stoves and natural gas cooking increase exposure of household members to nitrogen dioxide.[163,164] However, studies designed to investigate the relationship between the low levels of nitrogen dioxide and enhancement of risk of acute respiratory illness have yielded equivocal results.[165–169] One study showed that children in Adelaide who lived in homes using gas heating were more likely to develop acute respiratory illness than those living in homes with electric heating, but the level of significance was marginal (odds ratio [OR] = 1.6; 95% confidence interval [CI]: 1.0–2.6).[163] Based on current data, any effects attributable to nitrogen dioxide exposures are likely to be very small, if they exist at all.[170]

In developing countries, the negative public health impact of smoke from biomass fuels used for cooking is well established. Exposure to fire wood or other biomass smoke during cooking occurs in as many as 50% of the world's households.[171] Wood smoke, in particular, is thought to be responsible for almost 50% of all cases of obstructive airway disease.[17] In 1996, a multivariate analysis of a case-control study in Colombia found wood smoke to be more highly associated (OR = 3.43) with development of chronic bronchitis in women than either tobacco use or passive smoking (OR = 2.22 and 2.05, respectively).[172] Children in many developing countries are exposed to respirable particles from these fuels at peak and daily indoor concentrations approximately 20 times greater than the levels present in developed countries where two packs of cigarettes are smoked per day[170] (a level at which the risk of many respiratory symptoms approximately doubles[155]). In a study in Nepal, Pandey et al. found a relationship between hours per day spent near a stove and episodes of severe acute lower respiratory tract illness in children aged less than 2 years.[173] However, this study was flawed by the lack of adjustment made for confounding factors, such as parental smoking. In a small, poorly controlled study, Kossove found that Zulu infants presenting to a medical clinic with acute lower respiratory illness were more likely to be exposed to cooking smoke at home than children without respiratory illness.[174] Campbell et al. reported that children carried on their mother's back during cooking periods were at 2.8 times greater risk of an episode of "fast or difficult breathing" (predictive of acute lower respiratory infection) than children who were not carried in this way.[175,176] All of these studies had methodologic problems because they were conducted in areas with high acute respiratory infection incidence where exposure to indoor smoke is universally high and the exposure dose was not measured. Intervention studies in high-incidence areas need to be conducted to evaluate respiratory infection rates in persons living in homes using wood fuel compared with those living in homes using smokeless fuel or fluted stoves.

In the developed world, one U.S. study of children from homes with wood-burning stoves found children experienced more acute upper and lower respiratory tract illness than children from homes without such stoves.[177,178] Levels of the many gases, chemicals, and respirable particulates in wood smoke were not reported, which would have been desirable to assess the stove–illness connection in more detail. However, the greater incidence of respiratory illness was not explained by social class, smoking, or other indoor sources of air pollution. Another study in the United States, using a retrospective design, failed to find any relationship between wood smoke exposure and respiratory illness in school-aged children.[178] By inference, this lack of relationship suggests that preschool children may be more at risk of acute respiratory infection in living environments heated by wood-burning stoves than are older children.[179]

A systematic review and meta-analysis of studies of indoor air pollution from unprocessed fuel use and pneumonia risk in children younger than 5 years concluded that this exposure increased the risk of pneumonia by 89% (OR = 1.79; 98% CI: 1.45–2.18). However, only two intervention trials were included in this meta-analysis; the OR of the intervention studies was 1.28 (95% CI: 1.06–1.54).[344]

Smoking

A relationship between smoking and acute respiratory infection was first established in several prospective studies conducted in the late 1950s.[180–186] These data indicated that smokers were at increased risk of dying from pneumonia and influenza, with their overall pneumonia–influenza mortality ratio being 1.4 (range: 0.7–2.6). Four subsequent studies showed that smoking is associated with increased severity and incidence of influenza.[187,190] Kark et al. reported that the attributable proportion of influenza ascribable to smoking was 31% for all influenza cases and 41% for severe influenza cases.[189] Tobacco smoking is undoubtedly the most common cause of chronic bronchitis.[17]

In the Tecumseh family-based study, Monto et al. assessed the incidence of respiratory illness in smokers and nonsmokers.[191] In otherwise healthy index cases, both male and female smokers experienced more episodes of acute respiratory illness than nonsmokers. Studies in adolescents and young adults have also reported more respiratory symptoms in smokers than nonsmokers.[192–194] Reingold found that smoking significantly increased the incidence of pneumonia and pneumonia-related mortality, and that smoking is an important independent risk factor for Legionnaires' disease.[195] Lipsky et al. found that smoking independently increased the risk of pneumococcal infections fourfold in their study of "high-risk" adults.[196] Petitti and Friedman also found smokers to be at greater risk of pneumonia and influenza, although this risk was lower in those persons who smoked low-tar cigarettes.[197] Conversely, Simberkoff et al. found no relationship between pneumonia mortality and smoking in patients at high risk.[198] In a community-based study in which the prevalence of smoking was assessed among patients with pneumonia, Woodhead et al. reported that 100 of 236 patients with pneumonia (42%) were current smokers, and that 175 of them (74%) had smoked "at some time."[199] However, a control group was not used in this study to see if smoking was associated with higher pneumonia rates.

In the American Cancer Society's 25-state study from 1959 to 1965, male smokers were determined to be at greater risk of dying from influenza and pneumonia (International Classification of Diseases, 7th revision, codes 480–481, 490–493) than male nonsmokers (relative risk [RR] = 1.82; 95% CI: 1.45–2.27).[200] This study did not show female smokers to be at increased risk. However, in the 50-city study conducted in 1982–1986, risk of mortality from pneumonia and other respiratory diseases (International Classification of Diseases, 9th revision, codes 010–012, 480–489, 493) was significantly increased in current female smokers (RR = 2.18; 95% CI: 1.60–2.97) as well as in current male smokers (RR = 1.99; 95% CI: 1.52–2.61) aged 35 years and older.[200]

Crowding

Crowding favors the propagation of respiratory infections, as is true for all contagious diseases. As early as 1927, a highly significant correlation was seen between the proportion of overcrowded houses in a borough (two or more persons per room) and pneumonia mortality in England and Wales.[201] The strongest correlation was found in the age group 0–5 years, although an effect was also seen in the age groups 45–64 and 65–74 years. Pneumonia epidemics were observed in crowded living conditions in South African mining camps, during the construction of the Panama Canal, and in Civilian Conservation Corps barracks.[202] In 1945, Payling-Wright and Payling-Wright showed strong correlations between crowding (number of persons per room and number of children per family) and mortality from bronchopneumonia in children younger than age 2 years.[203] Another study demonstrated a significant correlation between crowding and death from bronchopneumonia in infants, although the investigators cautioned that the relationship was confounded by indices of air pollution, social class, and educational status.[140]

Family Size

Since the 1970s, studies have focused on family size as a measure of crowding. The number and age of

siblings in families predict the rates of acute lower respiratory tract infection in infants,[160] incidence of bronchitis and pneumonia in infants,[204] and rates of acute respiratory illness in older children and adults.[205] In developing countries, given the extreme level of confounding between malnutrition and crowding as risk factors for acute respiratory infection, it is difficult to separate out the relative contribution of each variable.

Daycare Centers

In developed countries, increased reliance on daycare centers for children has led to another type of crowding. Children attending group daycare centers are at increased risk of acute upper and lower respiratory tract infections.[160,206] In particular, daycare attendance greatly increases the risk of acute otitis media in children.[207–210]

Refugee Camps

During the 1990s, acute respiratory infections, along with measles and diarrheal disease, were the most frequent causes of death among refugees who escaped Somalia during the 1992–1993 famine[211] and among Bhutanese refugees emigrating into southeastern Nepal during 1991–1992 to escape ethnic persecution.[212] Marfin et al. examined the morbidity and mortality among 73,500 Bhutanese refugees who emigrated into southeastern Nepal (six refugee camps) between February 1991 and June 1992 to escape ethnic persecution in Bhutan.[212] Crude mortality rates up to 1.15 per 10,000 deaths per day were reported during the first 6 months of surveillance. The leading causes of death were measles, diarrhea, and acute respiratory infections.

Nutrition

As malnutrition is so closely correlated with poverty, crowding, poor housing, and poor education in developing countries, it has proved difficult to identify an independent effect of this factor on risk for respiratory infection.[213–215] Nevertheless, epidemiologic studies evaluating certain nutritional interventions (vitamin A and breastfeeding) have shown that malnutrition is at least a contributory factor when it comes to respiratory health.

In a study in Costa Rica, James assessed the relationship of malnutrition (comparison of weight with standard measures) and respiratory illness in poor children younger than the age of 5 years.[14] His unadjusted analysis indicated that malnourished children experienced 2.7 times more bronchitis and 19 times more pneumonia, and they were far more likely to be hospitalized than well-nourished children. Children of low weight experienced no more upper respiratory illness than did children of normal weight, but their episodes lasted longer. Tupasi et al. reported a 27-fold increased relative risk for pneumonia-related mortality in hospitalized children with third-degree malnutrition, with relative risks of 11.3 and 4.4 for second- and first-degree malnutrition, respectively.[215] However, these researchers' multivariate analyses indicated that malnutrition was not related to incidence of respiratory morbidity, possibly because of strong confounding from socioeconomic status. Berman et al. found a significant relationship between malnutrition and pneumonia, but not between malnutrition and bronchitis or tracheobronchitis, in children attending health centers in Cali, Colombia.[74] Escobar et al. observed that in children hospitalized with lower respiratory illness, mortality increased in relation to the level of malnutrition (weight for age).[61]

In a case-control study reported in 1996, Fonseca et al. used a risk factor questionnaire to determine key factors contributing to childhood pneumonia among 650 children younger than 2 years living in urban poor areas of Forteleza, Brazil.[216] Age-matched controls were recruited from the neighborhood where the children with pneumonia lived. Malnutrition was the most important risk factor, although low birth weight, nonbreastfeeding, attendance at a daycare center, crowding, high parity, and incomplete vaccination status each posed a significant risk. Children who had suffered from previous episodes of wheezing or who had been hospitalized for pneumonia had a greater than threefold increased risk of contracting the disease. Pneumonia risk in this study was not influenced by socioeconomic status or by environmental variables.

In the early 1980s, vitamin A deficiency in children was found to be a risk factor associated with both increased morbidity from respiratory infection and increased overall mortality.[217,218] In Thailand, children with deficient serum retinol were four times more likely to experience respiratory morbidity than children who were not deficient in this nutrient.[219] This study also found that supplementation with vitamin A offered some protection against respiratory illness, although this effect varied by age and length of follow-up, probably because of the small sample size. In well-nourished children in Adelaide, Australia, Pinnock et al. conducted two placebo-controlled vitamin A intervention studies.[220,221] In the first study, respiratory morbidity in children with a history of frequent respiratory illness

was reduced by 19% in those taking the supplement.[220] However, in the second study, vitamin A supplementation did not affect respiratory morbidity significantly in children aged 2 to 7 years who had an episode of bronchiolitis in the first year of life and who were followed for 12 months.[221] In view of the disparate findings between retinol-deficient and well-nourished children, the beneficial effects of vitamin A supplementation are likely to be limited to populations whose diets are significantly deficient.

In developing countries, breastfeeding has been shown to confer a protective effect against respiratory infections. In Brazil, for instance, breastfeeding reduced the incidence of upper respiratory morbidity, otitis media, and pneumonia in young infants in one study,[222] and respiratory infection mortality in children in another.[223] It is unclear whether the protective effect of breastmilk derived from its conferred anti-infective properties,[224] from improved hygiene, or from nutritional factors per se. Similarly, in Rwanda, mortality from acute lower respiratory infections in hospitalized children younger than 2 years was lower in those who were breastfed.[225] In developed countries, breastfeeding appears to offer a clearly protective benefit against the risk of acute otitis media[224,225] but perhaps not against other types of respiratory morbidity. Many studies in which bivariate analyses were conducted have reported that breastfed babies were at significantly lower risk of respiratory illness, but the relationship was not seen after adjustments were made for confounding factors.[226–230]

Certain other nutritional factors have been suggested as possibly influencing respiratory health, although these links all appear to be weak or inconclusive. Obesity was reported to be associated with increased incidence of respiratory illness in infants in one study,[231] but these findings were confounded by the fact that the normal-weight comparison group was of higher socioeconomic status and had been breastfed much longer. Although vitamin C supplementation has been suggested to prevent or to treat upper respiratory tract infections, the results of placebo-controlled trials have been too unimpressive to prompt a global recommendation for use of this vitamin.[232–234]

Lower Respiratory Tract Infection in Early Infancy

Several studies have reported a relationship between acute lower respiratory tract infection in the first 2 years of life and the development in adulthood of chronic cough,[193,235] reduced ventilatory function,[224–227] and increased bronchial reactivity.[236–239] In a case-control study reported in 1985,[240] young children who experienced high levels of respiratory illness morbidity were 11 times more likely to have experienced an episode of bronchitis, bronchiolitis, or pneumonia in the first year of life than children who had experienced low levels of morbidity (controls). The relationship remained strong (OR = 9.5; 95% CI: 5.5–16.6) even after adjustments were made for number of siblings, use of child care, sex, parental history of respiratory illness, breastfeeding, maternal stress levels, exposure to gas heating, parental occupational status, and low birth weight. In a 3-year study of pneumococcal vaccine in young children, the strongest predictor of acute respiratory morbidity (recorded in respiratory symptom diaries by the mothers) in any 6-month period was the level of morbidity the previous 6 months.[221,241] In England and Wales, Barker and Osmond found an increased incidence of mortality among people with chronic bronchitis who had a history of childhood respiratory infection.[242]

It is unclear whether lower respiratory infection in early life acts as a true risk factor by causing long-term damage to the lower respiratory tract or whether it acts as an early marker for genetically preprogrammed subsequent respiratory morbidity (chronic or acute). It will be difficult to determine which factor is more important until an effective intervention is available (e.g., a vaccine for respiratory syncytial virus). If previous respiratory morbidity predicts the level of subsequent morbidity from respiratory infections, implications also are seen for statistical analyses of these types of data. For autocorrelation of this type, a need is seen to control or adjust for repeated episodes of acute lower respiratory illness; alternatively, the first episode can be used as the outcome for analysis. In prospective studies, Kaplan-Meier curves and Cox regression analysis are then often used to estimate "survival time."[37] Where frequent outcomes occur, as with upper respiratory tract infections, use of the first episode as an outcome would result in loss of too much data. Auto-regression techniques,[243] which have not been widely used in studies of acute respiratory infections, allow adjustment for autocorrelated variables in multivariate models.

Psychosocial Factors

The relationship between psychosocial factors and respiratory infections has been investigated in cross-sectional and retrospective studies,[243–249] in prospective epidemiologic studies,[250–252] and in experimental settings.[253–255] Upper respiratory infections or illnesses were the outcomes of interest in these studies, and no data regarding lower respiratory illness were presented.

Two cross-sectional studies reported a relationship between respiratory infection and social isolation, life changes, illness behavior, maladaptive coping, and unresolved role crises.[256,257] However, these studies did not address the effect of psychosocial factors on respiratory infection rates. Another cross-sectional study indicated a relationship between anxiety and upper respiratory illness, but it was unclear how the outcome was measured.[243] In a longitudinal study that controlled for the effects of age, sex, race, family income, and family size in the analyses by Boyce et al., high life-event scores and strict family routines were associated with increased duration and severity of acute respiratory illness in children.[246] However, these investigators did not measure stress levels or rigidity of family routines until the end of the study. Other cross-sectional studies have found relationships between poor family functioning and doctor visits for acute respiratory infections in children,[249] type A personality and respiratory illness in college students,[247] and maternal stress and bronchitis in children.[248] None of these three studies controlled for confounding factors, however, nor did they address the temporal relationship between psychosocial factors and respiratory illness.

Several prospective studies have shown that psychosocial factors can increase susceptibility to upper respiratory tract infections.[251] Kasl et al. evaluated the relationship between a combination of high motivation and poor academic performance with clinical infectious mononucleosis in U.S. Military Academy cadets at West Point, New York.[251] Over a 4-year period, cadets who seroconverted to Epstein-Barr virus were monitored, and those with high motivation, a poor academic record, and an "overachieving" father were significantly more likely to have clinical infectious mononucleosis than a subclinical infection. Poor academic record and high motivation interacted in this study to increase the risk of clinical disease significantly. Disease severity was confirmed by ascertaining the heterophil antibody titers in the clinical and subclinical cases.

In a series of studies involving experimentally induced colds at the Common Cold Unit in the United Kingdom, introversion was associated with higher symptom and virus-shedding scores and certain life changes that resulted in decreased activity predicted virus shedding; cognitive dissonance was associated with increased symptoms.[253–255] Although patients who appear to be more introverted and those reporting higher stress or anxiety levels might be expected to report more symptoms, the finding that these factors were also associated with virus shedding in two of the studies substantiates objective validation of a psychosocial–illness relationship.

Graham et al.[250] studied the relationship between stress and upper respiratory tract infection in a prospective study in Adelaide, Australia. In a blinded fashion, episodes of illness were divided into definite, uncertain, and doubtful, which were confirmed, where possible, by a study nurse, virologic culture, or both. To optimize the precision of stress measurement, a combination of three measures (major life events, minor life events, and psychological distress) was used in the initial analyses. Pre-study stress variables predicted nurse-confirmed episodes and symptom days in "definite" episodes even after adjusting for a range of confounding factors. Pre-study stress levels also predicted both episodes and symptom days of respiratory illness.

Finally, in a longitudinal study of 16 families ($N = 100$), Meyer and Haggerty reported that stressful life events in families were four times more likely to precede an episode of streptococcal pharyngitis than to follow it.[252] High stress levels were also significantly associated with increased levels of anti-streptolysin O titer in this study. Although no adjustments were made for confounding factors, the objective outcome measures and prospective design were strengths of this study.

Two mechanisms have been suggested to explain why stress and anxiety might predispose individuals to respiratory infection.[4] First, because psychological stress and other psychological factors appear to suppress many components of immune function,[256] this dampening of the immune response may lead to increased susceptibility to respiratory infection. However, it is possible that the immune function fluctuations observed to be associated with psychological factors may not have high clinical relevance. Second, high stress levels or anxiety may lead to reduced adherence to normal hygiene measures (e.g., hand washing and use of tissues) usually used to reduce transmission of respiratory viruses.[254–259] This mechanism is questionable, however, because in experimental cold studies, these transmission factors were controlled.[253–255]

Socioeconomic Status

In general, socioeconomic status—whether measured by rankings of occupational prestige,[11,38,193] level of income,[203] or educational status[129]—appears to be associated with increased susceptibility to acute lower, but not upper, respiratory tract infections. Gardner et al. used a combined measure of family income, insurance status, and parental educational level to measure socioeconomic status, which they found

to be related only to lower respiratory illness.[147,160] Measures of the proportion of families with incomes below the poverty line and of occupational prestige have been linked with increased mortality from bronchitis and pneumonia in children,[191,203] as has educational status.[127,140] The differentials in pneumonia and influenza mortality observed between economically developing and developed countries reflect the association of low socioeconomic development with susceptibility to pneumonia, in particular. Conversely, the relatively similar levels of upper respiratory illness reported in developing and developed countries lends support to findings in developed countries that low socioeconomic status does not increase the risk of these conditions.[12–16,29,318]

The results of a retrospective study by Schenker et al. differ from those of the preceding studies.[260] These investigators found a relationship between low socioeconomic status (occupational status or educational level of parents) and severe chest illness in the first 2 years of life, as well as with chronic respiratory symptoms, but not with pneumonia or bronchitis. The disparity between the conclusions of this study and the others may be attributed to its presentation of differential symptom reporting rates by lower and high educational groups. This illustrates how differently alternate measures of socioeconomic status can behave in predicting respiratory illness; it may also indicate that lower social class could be a stronger risk factor for lower, rather than upper, respiratory illness. Tupasi et al. confirmed that low socioeconomic status within developing countries also strongly predicts risk of acute respiratory infection.[215] However, these investigators did not differentiate between upper and lower tract respiratory infections, nor did they separate out the effects of factors such as crowding, malnutrition, and immunization status. This adjustment is very important in analyzing the results from epidemiologic studies investigating socioeconomic risk factors. Indeed, bivariate analyses performed in a study in Adelaide showed that children of parents of lower occupational status had increased susceptibility to respiratory illness.[261] However, after adjusting for factors such as sex, maternal smoking, number of siblings, parental history of respiratory illness, breastfeeding, use of child care, and maternal stress levels, the relationship between social class and increased risk of respiratory infection was no longer observed.

Meteorologic Factors

Epidemics of acute respiratory infections have been most closely correlated with low temperature, humidity, precipitation, or all of those factors, which are associated with increased time spent indoors, either at home or at school.[262-264] Any situation in which crowding is present facilitates efficient viral transmission. It is not clear whether meteorologic factors alone cause increased host susceptibility or enhanced viral integrity, or whether crowding must be a concomitant variable. The effects of low temperature or "chilling" on host susceptibility has been well studied.[265-267] In studies conducted in the United States and the United Kingdom, volunteers experimentally infected with rhinoviruses and exposed to combinations of cold temperatures, wet clothes, and fatigue had no greater than normal susceptibility to infection.[265-267] Studies as early as the 1920s suggested a correlation between low temperatures and increases in mortality from pneumonia and bronchitis[203,268]; however, the results of these studies were confounded by increased time spent indoors (resulting in crowding) and higher levels of air pollution during winter. The latter factor may be an important contributor to respiratory illness. After all, in the Northern Hemisphere, peak levels of respirable particulate air pollution occur in midwinter, presumably because condensation, cloud cover, and precipitation prevent dispersal of particulates and gases; thus trapped pathogens in the ambient air would be more likely. In a study by Pope,[133] low temperature was the meteorologic variable most closely correlated with hospitalization for respiratory disease and together with mean fine particulate levels explained 83% of the variance in total monthly hospital admissions for respiratory disease.

Humidity could also be a meteorologic factor contributing to respiratory morbidity. Given that rhinoviruses have better survival rates at higher humidities, Gwaltney has postulated that rhinovirus-caused infections may be more easily transmitted in places where, or in seasons when, humidity is high.[269] As high humidity is often associated with the rainy season in temperate or warm climates, meteorologic studies investigating a humidity–respiratory infection correlation would need to factor the effect of crowding into analyses, as more of the study population would be expected to stay indoors to avoid the rain, thus confounding study results.

Care-Seeking Behavior

The care-seeking behavior of families and their expectations regarding appropriate treatment affect the morbidity and mortality associated with acute respiratory infections.[270] Factors influencing the choice of provider include the mother's perceptions of the cause of illness, distance from a provider, cost of care, availability and accessibility of a provider, and past experience with that provider. Some families demonstrate a "wait-and-see attitude" because of limited funds, distance from a health provider, failure to recognize the severity of the illness, waiting for home remedies to work, or local custom prohibiting a mother to leave her home for any purpose.[271-273] In developing countries, patients can seek care from several different people (e.g., physicians, healers, shamans), making assessment of treatment difficult.

Human Immunodeficiency Virus Infection

Human immunodeficiency virus infection predisposes people to several types of acute respiratory infections, the most common of which is *Pneumocystis carinii* pneumonia.[274] In 60% of newly diagnosed cases of AIDS, *P. carinii* pneumonia is the initial AIDS-defining illness, and an additional 20% of patients with AIDS will develop *P. carinii* pneumonia during the course of their illness.[274] Children with AIDS are also at risk from *P. carinii* albeit at a slightly lower rate than adults.[275-277] *P. carinii* pneumonia does not appear to be an important pulmonary complication of AIDS in Africa.[278] This lack of association in Africa may, in part, reflect the difficulty of diagnosing this condition when bronchoscopy is not readily available. However, introduction of sputum induction techniques currently used in developed countries may prove useful in improving the diagnostic accuracy of studies in Africa.[279] Adoption of such diagnostic methods should lead to a more definitive picture of the incidence of *P. carinii* pneumonia in HIV-infected persons on that continent.

Adults and children infected with HIV are also at increased risk from bacterial pneumonia.[125,280] *Streptococcus pneumoniae* and *Haemophilus influenzae* are the most commonly isolated organisms in community-acquired, HIV-associated bacterial pneumonia. The risk of pneumonia appears to be increased in HIV-infected patients with and without AIDS.[281-285] The most common viral pulmonary infection found in both adults and children with AIDS is cytomegalovirus.[276,277] However, the pathogenicity of this virus in the lung is not always entirely clear, because it is sometimes isolated in the absence of histologic evidence of cytopathic change to lung parenchyma.[286] The causative agents of acute lower respiratory tract infections in HIV-infected patients in Africa have yet to be completely elucidated.

In general, gastrointestinal and dermatologic complications of HIV infection are more common in Africa than in the United States; in the latter, pulmonary complications most often manifest in HIV-infected patients.[278] In one study, only 14% of HIV-infected Africans living in Europe had *P. carinii* pneumonia.[287] The most common pulmonary complication of HIV infection in Africa appears to be tuberculosis,[288,289] although few studies have used appropriate microbiologic techniques to establish accurate estimates of risk in comparison with other organisms. It seems likely that HIV-infected children and adults in Africa will be at greatly increased risk from pneumonia caused by pyogenic bacteria such as *S. pneumoniae*, *H. influenzae*, and *Staphylococcus aureus*, because these organisms are already important causes of pneumonia in that part of the world.

Whether HIV infection is associated with increased susceptibility to upper respiratory tract infections or respiratory viruses in general is not known. It is also not known whether these less serious conditions can predispose patients with AIDS to secondary bacterial invasion and pneumonia. If immune system activation is important in the pathogenesis of AIDS, as has been postulated, another issue that needs to be explored is whether viral respiratory infections play a role in accelerating disease progression.

Low Birth Weight

Low birth weight may be an important risk factor for acute respiratory infections, as evidenced by the higher mortality rates from ARI in infants with low birth weight compared to normal-weight infants in developing countries in the first year of life.[1,3] Drillien reported that babies with low birth weight (less than 4 lb, 8 oz [less than 2000 g]) experienced higher rates of respiratory illness in the first 2 years of life.[290] This relationship persisted when this investigator stratified the results by a "maternal care" index, although what was meant by maternal care was not well defined. After stratification by quality of housing and maternal care, low birth weight did not predict respiratory illness. In a 7-year birth cohort study, Chan et al. found that low birth weight (less than 2000 g) was associated with subsequent chronic cough, but not wheeze.[291] As acute respiratory symptoms were not reported in this study, the effect of low birth weight on respiratory infection rate could not be assessed.

Victora et al. found that a birth weight of less than 2500 g was associated with increased mortality from respiratory infections, and this relationship persisted after adjustment for parental employment status, income, and education.[292] In a study in India, Datta et al. observed that, during the first year of life, infants with low birth weights (less than 2500 g) had the same respiratory illness attack rate as normal-weight infants (4.65 versus 4.56 episodes), but a much higher case-fatality rate (24.6 versus 3.2 per

100 episodes of moderate or severe respiratory illness).[293] These data suggest that low-birth-weight children may experience more severe respiratory infections; however, these infections are no more frequent than in normal-weight control populations. Given that low birth weight is associated with crowding, poverty, and poor nutritional status, these factors may cause too much confounding to allow any conclusions to be drawn about the independent contribution of low birth weight to respiratory health.

Overprescribing of Antibiotics and Misuse of Medication

It has been estimated that 75% of all antibiotic prescriptions are written for acute respiratory infections.[105] Most of these prescriptions are probably unnecessary, as many of the infections treated are viral in origin and, therefore, unresponsive to drugs directed against bacterial pathogens. Overprescribing of antibiotics poses a public health risk because it hastens the development of antibiotic resistance.

In developing countries, overprescribing of antibiotics by unqualified medical practitioners is especially common.[270] Self-medication with drugs that can mask the symptoms of respiratory infections, inappropriate courses of medication prescribed by healthcare providers, and premature discontinuation of therapy also contribute to increased morbidity in cases of acute respiratory infections.[271,294–296]

In China, herbal remedies are still commonly used to treat these infections. Liu and Douglas identified 27 articles published primarily in Chinese-language journals between 1985 and 1996 that described favorable effects of herbal remedies for acute respiratory infections.[297] These authors found limitations in the study design and data presentation of the clinical trials. They believed that definitive conclusions about efficacy could not be made in view of insufficient information on randomization and baseline comparisons, the use of outcome measures that were either complicated or of doubtful validity, the use of poorly defined terms to connote efficacy (e.g., "effect rate"), and inadequate or missing statistical analysis. Therefore, it is possible that millions of Chinese individuals are currently receiving inadequate treatment of acute respiratory infections.

Increasing Resistance to Antibiotics

Clinical response to antibiotics, especially penicillins and oral cephalosporins, has been greatly affected by the emergence of antibiotic resistance since the 1980s. Resistance rates of *H. influenzae* to penicillin and amoxicillin have been reported to range from 30% to 40% in Singapore, Indonesia, Thailand, Taiwan, Hong Kong, and the Philippines, and to be 15% in Malaysia and Korea.[17] In Latin America, the prevalence of amoxicillin resistance to *H. influenzae* varies greatly among countries. It has been reported to be almost 50% in hospital isolates in Guatemala, 25% to 30% in the general population of Argentina and Venezuela, 10% in Colombia and Uruguay, and 2.5% in Ecuador.[17] Pneumococcal resistance is more than 70% among patients in hospitals in Manila, Philippines; 30% to 40% in Hong Kong, Korea, and Taiwan; and 10% to 20% in Singapore and Malaysia.[17] The prevalence of pneumococcal resistance is generally lower in Latin America than Southeast Asia, although it has reached 15% to 25% in some areas.[14,17]

Other Host Factors

Primarily uncontrolled studies have mentioned many other factors as possibly increasing the risk of pneumonia in adults. In high-risk outpatients, Simberkoff et al. found that chronic pulmonary, cardiac, and renal disease predicted the incidence of pneumonia, but they did not observe an association with hepatic disease, alcoholism, or diabetes mellitus.[198] Lipsky et al. noted that dementia, cerebrovascular disease, and institutionalization independently predicted pneumonia.[196] These researchers also confirmed that increasing age, smoking, chronic obstructive lung disease, and congestive cardiac failure increased pneumonia risk, but that diabetes mellitus, malignancy, or heavy alcohol use did not.

Maternal antibodies to respiratory syncytial and influenza viruses in cord blood appear to be protective against subsequent infection in infants.[298,299] If maternal immunity can be passively transferred to infants, it would be expected that vaccination of pregnant women would be beneficial in protecting the infant against these viruses.

A family history of asthma is associated with increased risk of bronchiolitis in infancy, and it appears to strongly interact with exposure factors such as presence of an older sibling in the house and passive smoking.[300]

The contribution of genetic factors to the risk of respiratory infection in children appears to be supported by other studies reporting increased rates of wheeze-related respiratory infection in infants with higher virus-specific immunoglobulin E responses to respiratory syncytial viruses,[301] in those with parainfluenza viruses,[302] and in those with small airway diameters.[303]

EFFICIENT METHODS OF DATA COLLECTION TO EVALUATE RESPIRATORY EPIDEMIOLOGY

No standardized questionnaires exist for collection of acute respiratory infection symptom data, although standardized instruments developed by the American Thoracic Society and the British Medical Research Council are available to measure chronic respiratory symptomatology.[304,305] As the focus of the latter questionnaires is on symptoms of airway reactivity and allergy, these instruments cannot be readily adapted for studies of acute respiratory infections. This situation has prompted many researchers to create and use either nonstandardized respiratory symptom diaries (**Figure 19-5**) or recall questionnaires. Respiratory diaries have three advantages over questionnaires: (1) they practically eliminate recall bias; (2) they are useful in studies in which specific symptom complexes are important; and (3) they are more likely to be accurate records of symptom duration. The main drawback of respiratory symptom diaries is that they require daily recording by the study participant, which could be viewed by participants as such a burden that they may stop making entries, as happens especially in multiyear studies.

Alternatively, research assistants can call or visit study participants on a weekly or biweekly basis to inquire via a questionnaire about symptom frequency and duration in the preceding period. Although this approach has all the problems associated with recall data, it has advantages of sustainability over long periods and the ability of the interviewer to define symptoms more clearly than would otherwise be possible using a diary approach. Questionnaires, which are easier to standardize than symptom diaries, have been shown to be associated with higher compliance rates over a 2-year period in patients with lower respiratory infections.[306,307]

Standardized questionnaires are especially needed in developing countries.[294,308] Often, the clinical and laboratory expertise and facilities are not available to confirm a diagnosis, and many difficulties exist regarding standardizing measures of exposure between studies. The National Research Council's project in 12 countries was a major attempt to standardize data collection and study protocols.[11] Although some variation in methods was inevitable, these data are probably the most comparable of any collected to date.

Much effort has been devoted to developing criteria for identifying acute lower respiratory infections from simple clinical signs. Several studies have now

RESPIRATORY EVENTS IN EARLY CHILDHOOD

CHILD'S NAME				ID																										
DECEMBER 1998	1	2	3	4	5	6	7	8	9	10	11	12	13	14	15	16	17	18	19	20	21	22	23	24	25	26	27	28	29	30 31
Is he/she completely well? Y=Yes N=No																														
Do you think he/she has a cold? Y or N																														
Record each symptom he/she experiences each day. Mark with X.																														
Runny nose																														
Stopped-up nose																														
Hoarse throat																														
Wheezy/noisy breathing																														
Moist cough																														
Dry cough																														
Fever (feels hot)																														
Pulling at ears																														
Medication given (M)*																														
* Doctor visits (D)*																														
Hospital visits (V)/ Hospital stays (S)* (*more details on back)																														
OTHER ILLNESSES (give brief details)																														

Figure 19-5 Examples of acute respiratory illness symptom diary used in a 2-year cohort study of infects in Adelaide, Australia, 1988–1990. Reproduced from the Centers for Disease Control and Prevetion (2005). Direct and indirect effects of routine vaccination of children with 7-valent pneumococcal conjugate vaccine on incidence of invasive pneumococcal disease – United States, 1998–2003. *MMWR* Spt 16, 2005/54(36):893–897.

shown that tachypnea and a history of fast breathing[49,308,309] are highly sensitive and specific predictors of lower respiratory tract infections in both community and hospital settings.[49,308–310] The sensitivity and specificity of tachypnea as a diagnostic criterion is improved when chest in-drawing is considered.[310] Campbell et al. reported that the best predictors of lobar pneumonia in infants were temperature greater than 38.5°C and a respiratory rate greater than 60 breaths per minute.[311] Diagnoses more specific than "acute lower respiratory infection," such as severe pneumonia, may not be predictable based only on the presence of a respiratory rate of more than 50 breaths per minute. Nevertheless, to conduct epidemiologic studies in developing countries, the high sensitivity and specificity of maternal history of fast breathing as a predictor of acute lower respiratory tract infection is still very valuable.

PREVENTION OF RESPIRATORY INFECTIONS

The epidemiology of acute respiratory infections is well understood today primarily because of research that has been conducted during the past three decades. Clear associations between acute respiratory infections and factors such as chronic disease in adults, direct smoking, passive smoking, crowding, and breastfeeding have been well documented. The relatively higher incidence of acute respiratory infections in developing countries compared with the developed world results from a combination and interaction of factors associated with poverty and lower social status—large family size, crowded living conditions, less access to medical care, higher smoking rates, potential for nutritional deficit, lower breast-feeding rates, exposure to environmental pollutants (tobacco smoke, wood smoke, urban air pollution), and stressful living environments.

In developed countries, certain issues remain to be better defined, including the relationship between air pollution and acute respiratory infections, the relationship between maternal antibody levels and passive immunity in infants, and the reasons for the increase in pneumonia mortality in older age groups. Standardization of acute symptom questionnaires and symptom diaries still needs to be done to facilitate more complete and thorough epidemiologic studies in both developing and developed countries.

The knowledge gained about the epidemiology and risk factors associated with ARI has been accompanied by public health programs to prevent ARI.

Cigarette Smoking

In the United States, many successful programs have been initiated to reduce the prevalence of cigarette smoking. These have involved health education programs targeted to individuals, laws regulating or prohibiting smoking in public places, increased taxes on cigarettes, and successful court cases that forced tobacco companies to pay some of the health costs incurred from cigarette-related illnesses. These efforts reduced the prevalence of current smoking in the United States to 20.3% among an age-adjusted sample of adults older than 18 years in 2009, down from 23.4% in 2000. In the 2009 National Health Interview Survey (NHIS), men were more likely to be current smokers, with 22.6% of men acknowledging current smoking as compared to 18% of women. The reduction in smoking in the United States will impact ARI rates as smoking is an important risk factor for morbidity and mortality.[312]

Similar programs to prevent tobacco smoking in developing countries have not been either comprehensive or successful to date. For example, an estimated 68% of the adult male population of China smokes cigarettes at present.[313] In the same survey that identified this rate, only 9.5% of those who had ever smoked cigarettes had quit, only 10% of current smokers said they intended to quit, and individuals' knowledge of many of the adverse health effects of smoking was much less than that of comparable populations in the United States.[314] In contrast, in the United States more than half of those who had ever smoked had quit and most current smokers said they would like to quit.[312]

Vaccines

Pneumococcal Conjugate Vaccine

In 2000, a seven-valent pneumococcal (PCV-7) conjugate vaccine was licensed in the United States for routine use in children younger than 5 years of age.[315] The seven serotypes in the vaccine were selected to include 80% to 90% of pneumococcal serotypes causing invasive disease in U.S. children. Surveillance data from 2001–2007 indicate that substantial declines in invasive pneumococcal disease have occurred in children and adults compared to pre-vaccine years.[316] The effectiveness of PCV-7 at the population level has been evaluated using population-based data from the Active Bacterial Core (ABC) of the Emerging Infections Program Network, a cooperative surveillance program conducted by eight state health departments and the CDC.[317]

This surveillance includes active identification of invasive pneumococcal disease (IPD) by health department staff who contact microbiology laboratories for reports of *S. pneumoniae* isolates in eight states, and from several counties in California, representing a catchment area of approximately 16 million persons.[317] This surveillance has shown that 7 years after the initiation of routine immunization of young children with PCV-7, there has been a 45% decline in the incidence of invasive pneumococcal disease (from 24.4 to 13.5 cases per 100,000 population) and a 94% reduction in the incidence of PCV-7 type invasive infections (from 15.5 to 1.0 cases per 100,000 population) among U.S. children (**Figure 19-6**). Furthermore, the vaccine prevented more than twice as many cases of invasive pneumococcal disease in adults between 2000 and 2007 through indirect effects on pneumococcal transmission (i.e., herd immunity) than through its direct effect of protecting vaccinated children. Among adults, the greatest absolute decrease in overall IPD rates was seen among those persons older than 65 years of age[316,318] (rate difference of −22.2 cases per 100,000 population; **Figure 19-7**).

Increases in the number of cases caused by pneumococcal serotypes not included in the vaccine (i.e., replacement disease), especially type 19A, occurred; however, this increase was smaller than the declines in vaccine-serotype disease. Declines in the incidence of IPD were observed among vaccine-related serotypes among children younger than 5 years of age. The rates of IPD associated with these strains were stable for older children and adults, however, they increased significantly among persons older than age 50 years (**Table 19-9**).

The PCV-7 vaccine is expensive (estimated at $56 per dose in the United States) but has been calculated to be cost-effective in terms of disability-adjusted life-years (DALYs) in developed industrialized countries.[319] The Global Alliance for Vaccines and Immunization (GAVI) has begun a new program that aims to accelerate development and introduction of pneumococcal vaccine, making it more widely available in middle- and low-income countries. Vaccines have been developed to include additional serotypes to better cover the strains causing invasive disease globally. A 10-valent conjugate vaccine (PCV-10) has been licensed and includes serotypes 1, 5, and 7F in addition to the serotypes in the 7-valent vaccine; a 13-valent vaccine (PCV-13) also includes types 3, 6A, and 19A. The addition of 19A to the vaccine is important, because this serotype has accounted for the largest proportion of replacement disease since the PCV-7 vaccine was introduced.[316,318]

The results of a randomized, placebo-controlled, double-blind trial of an investigational 9-valent pneumococcal conjugate vaccine among children aged 6–51 weeks in the Gambia was reported in 2005.[320] This vaccine included the serotypes in the 7-valent vaccine licensed in the United States, plus serotypes 1 and 5, which are important causes of invasive pneumococcal disease among children in Africa. In this study, 8218 children received vaccine and 8219 were given placebo. The efficacy of the vaccine against WHO-defined radiological pneumonia was 37% (95% CI: 27–45%). The efficacy of the vaccine against any invasive pneumococcal disease caused

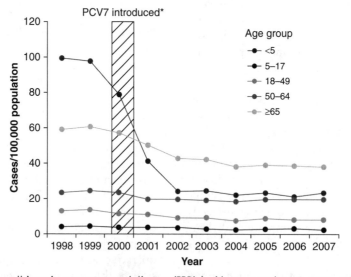

Figure 19-6 Changes in overall invasive pneumococcal disease (IPD) incidence rates by age group, 1998–2007. Seven valent pneumococcal conjugate vaccine (PCV7) was introduced in the United States for routine use among young children and infants in the second half of 2000. Reproduced from Tamara Pilishvili et al. Sustained Reductions in Invasive Pneumococcal Disease in the Era of Conjugate Vaccine. *Journal of Infectious Diseases* 2010;201;32–41. By permission of Oxford University Press.

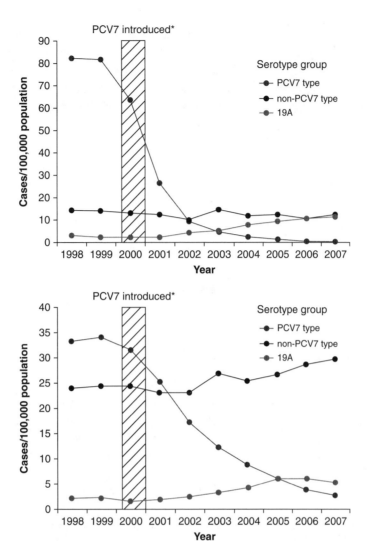

Figure 19-7 Changes in invasive pneumococcal disease (IPD) incidence by serotype group among children aged <5 (A) and adults aged >65 years (B), 1998–2007. Seven-valent pneumococcal conjugate vaccine (PCV7) was introduced in the United States for routine use among young children and infants in the second half of 2000. Reproduced from Tamara Pilishvili et al. Sustained Reductions in Invasive Pneumococcal Disease in the Era of Conjugate Vaccine. Journal of Infectious Diseases 2010;201;32–41. By permission of Oxford University Press.

by vaccine serotypes was 72% (95% CI: 51–90%), and it was 50% (95% CI: 21–69%) against all serotypes and 16% (95% CI: 3–28%) against nonvaccine serotypes.

Another randomized, placebo-controlled trial of three doses of 9-valent pneumococcal conjugate vaccine among 39,836 children was conducted in Soweto, South Africa.[321] In this study, vaccine efficacy was measured in children with and without HIV infection and in the setting of frequent antibiotic-resistant invasive pneumococcal infections. Among children who were HIV negative, the vaccine efficacy was 83% (95% CI: 39–97%) in preventing invasive pneumococcal disease from serotypes included in the vaccine; among HIV-positive children, the efficacy was 65% (95% CI: 24–86%) against

the same serotypes. The episodes of radiographically confirmed pneumonia among HIV-negative children were reduced by 20% (95%:CI, 2–35%). The incidence of invasive pneumococcal disease caused by penicillin-resistant strains was reduced by 67%, and the incidence of that disease caused by trimethoprim-sulfamethoxazole–resistant strains was reduced by 56%.

These two studies among high-risk infants and children in Africa suggest that the routine use of a proposed pneumococcal vaccine containing 11 of the most prevalent serotypes could be an important strategy to reduce the most important cause of childhood mortality in developing countries. The diagnosis of pneumonia by health workers in the field and antibiotic treatment, together with referral of

Table 19-9	Changes in Projected Numbers of Invasive Pneumococcal Disease (IPD) Cases by Age Group and Serogroup Category – Active Bacterial Core Surveillance (ABCs), United States, 1998–1999, 2003			
Age Group (yrs)	Serotype Category*	1998–1999 Average Projected No. of Cases[†]	2003 Projected No. of Cases[†]	Change in Annual Projected No. of Cases
<5				
	Vaccine	14,293	876	−13,417
	Nonvaccine	2,947	3,578	631
	Total	17,240	4,454	−12,786
5–17				
	Vaccine	1,195	569	−626
	Nonvaccine	880	824	−56
	Total	2,075	1,393	−682
18–39				
	Vaccine	5,023	1,610	−3,413
	Nonvaccine	3,419	3,407	−12
	Total	8,442	5,017	−3,425
40–64				
	Vaccine	8,945	4,167	−4,778
	Nonvaccine	7,545	10,237	2,692
	Total	16,490	14,404	−2,086
≥65				
	Vaccine	11,595	4,230	−7,365
	Nonvaccine	9,169	10,635	1,466
	Total	20,764	14,865	−5,899
All ages				
	Vaccine	41,051	11,452	−29,599
	Nonvaccine	23,960	28,681	4,721
	Total	65,011	40,133	−24,878

*Serotypes included in the 7-valent pneumococcal conjugate vaccine are defined as vaccine serotypes (4, 6B, 9V, 14, 18C, 19F, and 23F). All other serotypes are considered nonvaccine serotypes.
[†]Annual national projections of IPD cases were calculated by applying age- and race-specific disease rates for the aggregate ABCs surveillance area to the age and racial distribution of the U.S. population on the basis of 2000 U.S. Census data.

Reproduced from the Centers for Disease Control and Prevetion (2005). Direct and indirect effects of routine vaccination of children with 7-valent pneumococcal conjugate vaccine on incidence of invasive pneumococcal disease – United States, 1998–2003. *MMWR* Spt 16, 2005/54(36):893–897.

those patients with severe infections for treatment, as described earlier in this chapter, are also important components of the public health strategy to reduce mortality from childhood pneumonia. Unfortunately, the emergence of invasive pneumococcal infections involving organisms resistant to trimethoprim-sulfamethoxazole or penicillin might somewhat limit the effectiveness of antibiotic treatment.[322] Therefore, the use of an effective conjugated pneumococcal vaccine with appropriate spectrum of serotypes (i.e., a 9- or 11-valent vaccine) would be an important part of the strategy to reduce pneumonia mortality among children in developing countries.

Conjugated *Haemophilus influenzae* Vaccines

Haemophilus influenza type b (Hib) was the pathogen most commonly causing bacterial meningitis in infants and children between 1 month and 5 years of age worldwide prior to the routine use of conjugated Hib vaccines to prevent these infections.[6] These organisms were responsible for meningitis rates of 50 cases per 100,000 persons younger than 5 years of age in the United States.[2,19,307] Among Native Americans and Alaskan populations, rates of 150 to 200 cases per 100,000 population per year were reported.[323]

The first vaccines available for the prevention of Hib disease consisted of multivalent Hib polysaccharides and were developed in the 1970s . A large clinical trial in Finland found an efficacy of 90% for one dose of a polysaccharide vaccine in the prevention of invasive Hib disease in 18- to 71-month-old children.[324] Unfortunately, this vaccine was infective in children 3 to 17 months of age—the population with the highest incidence of invasive Hib disease.

In 1990, Hib conjugate vaccines were licensed in the United States for use in infants at least 2 months of age.[325] After licensure of the Hib conjugate vaccines, a dramatic decrease in invasive Hib diseases among infants and children younger than 5 years of age was observed; the incidence declined from 37 cases per 100,000 persons in 1989 to 11 cases per 100,000 persons in 1991.[325] This decline continued with further expanded use of the Hib conjugate vaccine, with more than a 95% decline to 1.3 cases per 100,000 children younger than 5 years of age occurring by 1997.[326] Of the children with invasive Hib in 1996–1997, 41% were younger than 6 months of age and, therefore, were too young to have received a second dose of vaccine. Similar decreases in the incidence of invasive Hib have been reported from European countries after the introduction and use of conjugated vaccines.[327]

The rates of utilization of conjugated Hib vaccines in low-income developing countries in Africa, Asia, and Latin America lagged behind the routine use of the vaccine in the United States and Western Europe. In part, the important contribution of invasive Hib infections in causing pneumonia and meningitis mortality was not appreciated by policymakers. In addition, the cost of adding another vaccine to the National Immunization program was an impediment. One randomized clinical trial compared a Hib conjugate vaccine plus DPT to DPT alone in a study involving 42,848 infants and children in the Gambia between 1993 and 1995. This study found a 95% efficacy of invasive Hib in children who had received three doses of Hib vaccine and a 21% reduction overall in radiologically diagnosed pneumonia.[328]

A few other countries in Africa introduced conjugate Hib vaccines into their national immunization program in the next several years. These vaccines were utilized for routine infant and child immunization in Kenya in 2000.[328] Prior to the use of the conjugated Hib vaccine, the median age of invasive Hib was 8 months and the mortality was 23%. Three years after the vaccine was introduced, the incidence of invasive Hib in children younger than age 5 had decreased from 66 per 100,000 to 7.6 per 100,000. Conjugated Hib vaccine was introduced into the national immunization program in Uganda in 2002. The incidence of bacterial meningitis due to Hib infection decreased from 88 cases per 100,000 children under age 5 years in the pre-vaccine years (2001–2002) to 13 cases per 100,000 4 years later and near zero 5 years later.[329]

Despite these impressive experiences, the inclusion of conjugate Hib vaccines in the national immunization programs of most countries in Africa and Asia increased slowly until 2005. In that year, GAVI created the Hib initiative to accelerate evidence-based decision making for Hib vaccine introduction in GAVI-eligible counties. The Hib initiative is a consortium that consists of four academic and public health organizations: the Johns Hopkins Bloomberg School of Public Health, the London School of Hygiene and Tropical Medicine, WHO, and CDC.[330] This consortium, with support from GAVI for the costs of the vaccine, had persuaded 66 (92%) of 72 GAVI-eligible countries to include conjugated Hib vaccines in their national immunization programs by 2010.[330] The GAVI Hib Initiative has resulted in the inclusion of Hib vaccine in the immunization programs of a higher proportion of GAVI-eligible countries than in higher-income, upper-middle-income, or lower-middle-income countries.[331] A concern expressed by some countries was that non-group B strains of *H. influenzae* might replace group B strains if population immunity was high to *H. influenzae* type b. To date, replacement of group B strains has not been found to have occurred among populations in Europe after the introduction of the conjugated Hib vaccines.[332]

In summary, the wide use of conjugated Hib vaccines for childhood immunization globally has been an impressive success in reducing mortality in children younger than age 5. These vaccines have the potential to reduce overall mortality among such children by 4% worldwide, which will make an important contribution to achieving Millennium Development Goal 4—namely, reducing under-five mortality by 60% between 1990 and 2015.[333] The remaining challenge is to expand the use of the 13-valent pneumococcal conjugate vaccine among lower-income and middle-income countries worldwide. In contrast to the widespread adoption of Hib vaccine, only 41 (21%) of 160 countries had introduced conjugated pneumococcal vaccines into their national immunization programs by 2010.[334]

Pertussis

Despite being preventable by vaccination for several decades, pertussis remains one of the top 10 causes of death worldwide in childhood, with mortality occurring mainly among unvaccinated children.[335] Even in some countries with strong vaccination programs, this disease continues to occur and to kill young infants and children, as the diagnosis is often missed. Reliable epidemiologic data on pertussis are sparse, however. It is estimated that this disease causes nearly 300,000 deaths in children every year, mostly in developing countries.[335]

Some countries have reported an increase in pertussis among adolescents, adults, and young infants prior to vaccination. Infants may not develop typical paroxysms of cough or a whoop but rather may present with apnea or sudden swollen airways at death. Often an infant may acquire infection from an unvaccinated adult or older sibling, especially a mother whose immune status has waned after a series of DPT vaccines given in infancy or a remote pertussis infection. Because of the risk to unvaccinated infants, in 2008 the Advisory Committee on Immunization Practices (ACIP) of the CDC recommended vaccination of pregnant women with Tdap (i.e., tetanus, reduced-dose diphtheria, and acellular pertussis vaccine) in the immediate postpartum period; this recommendation applies to women who have not received a booster dose of Tdap in the past 2–3 years.[336] Other family members and close contacts of a newborn infant, including health care workers, should also be vaccinated with Tdap to prevent transmission of pertussis to a newborn prior to the infant receiving routine immunization beginning at 2 months after birth.

This strategy to protect newborn infants from infection has been termed "cocooning." Unfortunately, there are several problems with the cocooning strategy. First, immunizing pregnant women immediately after delivery leaves the newborn susceptible to infection for at least 7–10 days before the woman responds to the vaccine. Most deaths from pertussis (approximately 80%) occur in the first 3 months of life. Second, it is very difficult to ensure that all of the persons who will have close contact with an infant in the home and healthcare institution are vaccinated. Although more than 50% of cases of transmission of pertussis to infants involve the mother, siblings, fathers, and healthcare personnel have also transmitted the infection to newborn infants. Because of this risk, the ACIP recently recommended that a dose of Tdap be given to pregnant women during the third trimester of pregnancy to provide passive antibody protection to the infant.[337]

This strategy for the prevention of exposure of newborn infants to pertussis might also be applied in developing countries. However, the cost and very limited availability of acellular pertussis vaccine in developing countries represent significant barriers to its adoption. The pertussis component of the DPT vaccine utilized in most developing countries is the cheaper whole-cell pertussis vaccine, which might pose significant safety concerns for use in pregnant women. It is also unknown whether immunization of women during pregnancy would provide sufficient passive antibody protection to an infant or whether it would just complicate the development of active immunity—the maternal antibodies could, for example, diminish the infant's antibody response to DPT. Some recent data suggest there may be a modest depressive effect by passively acquired antibodies from the mother on the level of responses to pertussis (i.e., DPT or Tdap) vaccine in the infant.[337] More likely, the passive antibodies transferred from a pregnant woman who was immunized in late pregnancy to her fetus would provide protection from severe pertussis in the first two months of life.

Measles Vaccines

Measles has been a major contributor to morbidity and mortality from pneumonia in children worldwide. Data from WHO indicate that in 1999, this disease was responsible for 10% of deaths worldwide in children younger than 5 years of age. An estimated 40 million cases of measles and 800,000 deaths occurred annually during the 1980s and early 1990s, with half of these deaths taking place in Africa.[338]

In the past 10 years, a major effort has been made by a coalition of partners including WHO, UNICEF, CDC, and national ministries of health in the affected countries to reduce measles mortality. The strategies employed resemble the public health methods that were successful in eliminating endemic measles from the Americas in 2000. The coalition's program includes four components:

- Increasing routine coverage for the first dose of measles-containing vaccine (MCV-1) for all children, starting in infants at 9 months of age
- Providing a second opportunity for measles vaccination through supplemental immunization activities (SIAs)
- Improving measles case management
- Establishing case care-based surveillance with laboratory confirmation[338]

During the interval from 2001 to 2008, MCV-1 coverage increased from 57% to 73%, SIAs vaccinated approximately 398 million children, and reported measles cases decreased by 93% in Africa, down from 492,116 cases in 2001 to 32,278 cases in 2008. Unfortunately, the number of measles cases in Africa increased in 2009 to 83,464 cases and again in 2010 to 172,824 reported cases (**Figure 19-8**). Of the cases reported in 2010, 14% were confirmed by laboratory testing and 63% by epidemiological linkage.[339] Clearly the measles control program during the last decade has had a major impact in reducing measles mortality and morbidity, yet the resurgence of measles in 2009 and 2010 in Africa underscores the

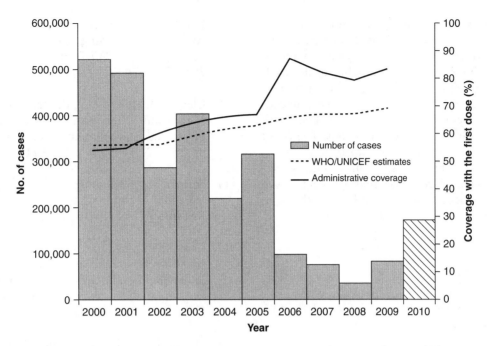

a Confirmed cases of measles during 2000–2009 were reported by Member States to WHO and UNICEF through the Joint Reporting Form.

b Data are from WHO and UNICEF estimates of coverage of measles vaccination; these estimates are based on reviews of surveys and national reports of administrative coverage, and adjusted for biases. Administrative coverage is calculated by dividing the number of doses administered by the total estimated number in the target population (children aged <1 year).

c The 2010 data are from monthly measless case-based surveillance reported to the WHO Regional Office for Africa; data from the Joint Reporting Form are not included.

Figure 19-8 The relationship between measles vaccination coverage and measles cases in Africa. Reproduced from the World Health Organization (2011). Weekly Epidemiologic Record. 1 April 2011, vol. 86, 14(pp. 129–140).

necessity of maintaining and intensifying important public health programs to continue to protect new cohorts of infants.

Despite the elimination of endemic transmission of measles in the United States in 2000, each year 80 to 200 cases of imported measles are reported in the country, the majority of which are imported by visitors to areas where measles remains endemic.[340] Many of the cases of measles that are imported into the United States have acquired their infection in Europe, where endemic transmission remains common.[341] Some of these imported cases have resulted in significant spread to unvaccinated contacts . In 2006–2007, a total of 12,132 cases of measles were reported in European countries.[341,342] The data from North America, Europe, and Africa indicate that dramatic reductions in measles morbidity and mortality can be achieved, but only if aggressive public health efforts are maintained to continue high rates of vaccine coverage after they are initially established.

Malaria

Malaria contributes to mortality from community-acquired pneumonia in areas where this disease is endemic. WHO's recent program that seeks to "Roll Back Malaria" has resulted in significant reductions in malaria mortality.

SUMMARY

Acute respiratory infections are a major cause of mortality, especially in children younger than age 5 in developing countries. Many different organisms are responsible for these infections. Among the bacteria, *S. pneumoniae*, *H. influenzae* type b, and *B. pertussis* are the most common causative sources. A variety of viruses are also important, especially respiratory syncytial virus, influenza viruses, parainfluenza viruses, and measles; all of these pathogens are important causes of morbidity and mortality.

Effective vaccines are available for the prevention of many of these infections. However, the delivery of these multiple vaccines to young infants in developing countries has been a public health challenge. Nevertheless, significant progress has been made in the past decade as the developed countries have devoted increased attention to the public health problems of the least developed nations. The GAVI coalition has played an important role in the progress that has been made to date and will likely continue to provide the resources that will help reduce morality from acute respiratory infections throughout the world.

• • • REFERENCES

1. Bryce J, Boschi-Pinto C, Shibuyo K, et al. WHO estimates of death in children. *Lancet* 2005;365:1147–1150.

2. Murray CJL, Lopez AD. *Global Comparative Assessments in the Health Sector.* Geneva, Switzerland: World Health Organization; 1994.

3. Black RE, Cousens S, Johnson HL, et al. Global, regional and national causes of child morality in 2008: a systematic analysis. *Lancet* 2010;375:1969–1987.

4. Graham NMH. The epidemiology of acute respiratory infection in children and adults: a global perspective. *Epidemiol Rev* 1990;12:149–178.

5. O'Brien KL, Wolfson LJ, Watt JP, et al. Burden of disease caused by *Streptococcus* pneumonia in children younger than 5 years: global estimates. *Lancet* 2009:374:893–902.

6. Watt JP, Wolfson LJ, O'Brien HL, et al. Burden of disease caused by *Haemophilus influenza* type b in children younger than 5 years: global estimates. *Lancet* 2009;374:903–911.

7. Muraskin W. Origins of the children's vaccine initiative: The political foundation. *Soc Sci Med* 1996;42:1721–1734.

8. Sandberg KI, Andersen S, Bjune G. A new approach to global health institutions? A case study of new vaccine introduction and the formation of the GAVI Alliance. *Soc Sci Med* 2010;31:1349–1356.

9. Lab-Levy TJ. Contribution of the GAVI Alliance to improving health and reducing poverty. *Phil Trans Royal Soc* 2011;366:2743–2747.

10. Clemens J, Holmgren J, Kaufman SHE, Mantovani A. Ten years of the Global Alliance of Vaccines and Immunization: challenges and progress. *Nat Immunol* 2010;11:1069–1072.

11. Berman S. Epidemiology of acute respiratory infections in children of developing countries. *Rev Infect Dis* 1991;13(suppl 6):S454–S462.

12. Kamath KR, Feldman RA, Sundar Rao PSS, et al. Infection and disease in a group of South Indian families. II. General morbidity patterns in families and family members. *Am J Epidemiol* 1969;89:375–383.

13. Freij L, Wall S. Exploring child health and its ecology: the Kirkos study in Addis Ababa: an evaluation of procedures in the measurement of acute morbidity and a search for causal structure. *Acta Paediatr Scand Suppl* 1977;267:1–18.

14. James JW, Longitudinal study of the morbidity of diarrheal and respiratory infections in malnourished children. *Am J Clin Nutr* 1972;25:690–694.

15. Fox JP, Cooney MK, Hall CE. The Seattle virus watch. V. Epidemiologic observations of rhinovirus infections, 1965–1969, in families with young children. *Am J Epidemiol* 1975;101:122–143.

16. Monto AS, Ullman B. Acute respiratory illness in an American community. *JAMA* 1974;227:164–169.

17. Ball P, Make B. Acute exacerbations of chronic bronchitis. An international comparison. *Chest* 1998;113(suppl 3):199S–204S.

18. Lai CKW, Ho SC, Lau J, et al. Respiratory symptoms in elderly Chinese living in Hong Kong. *Eur Respir J* 1995;8:2055–2061.

19. Pandey MR. Domestic smoke pollution and chronic bronchitis in a rural community of the hill region in Nepal. *Thorax* 1984;39:337–339.

20. Doyle R. U.S. deaths from pneumonia. Available at: http://www.sciam.com/

0297issue/0297scicit6.html. Accessed February 22, 2006.

21. Centers for Disease Control and Prevention. Mortality from pneumonia by age in the United States, 1910–2010. *MMWR* 2012;63:175–184.

22. Meeker DP, Longworth DL. Community-acquired pneumonia: an update. *Cleve Clin J Med* 1996;63:16–30.

23. Fine MJ, Chowdhry T, Ketema A. Outpatient management of community-acquired pneumonia. *Hosp Pract (Off Ed)* 1998;3:123–133.

24. Marrie TJ. Community-acquired pneumonia: epidemiology, etiology, treatment. *Infect Dis Clin North Am* 1998;13:723–740.

25. Farber MO. Managing community-acquired pneumonia: factors to consider in outpatient care. *Postgrad Med* 1999;105:106–114.

26. Mandell LA, Campbell GD Jr. Nosocomial pneumonia guidelines: an international perspective. *Chest* 1998;113(suppl 3):188S–193S.

27. Fagon JY, Chastre J, Hance A, et al. Nosocomial pneumonia in ventilated patients: a cohort study evaluating attributable mortality and hospital stay. *Am J Med* 1993;94:281–288.

28. American Thoracic Society. Hospital-acquired pneumonia in adults: diagnosis, assessment of severity, initial antimicrobial therapy, and preventative strategies. *Am J Respir Crit Care Med* 1996;153:1711–1725.

29. van Volkenburgh VA, Frost WH. Acute minor respiratory diseases prevailing in a group of families residing in Baltimore, Maryland, 1928–1930: prevalence, distribution and clinical description of observed cases. *Am J Hyg* 1933;17:122–153.

30. Gwaltney JM Jr, Hendley JO, Simon C, et al. Rhinovirus infections in an industrial population. I. The occurrence of illness. *N Engl J Med* 1966;275:1261–1268.

31. Fox JP, Hall CE, Cooney MK, et al. The Seattle virus watch. II. Objectives, study population and its observation, data processing and summary of illnesses. *Am J Epidemiol* 1972;96:270–285.

32. Bates JH. Microbiologic etiology of pneumonia. *Chest* 1989;95(suppl 5):194S–197S.

33. Glezen W, Denny FW. Epidemiology of acute lower respiratory disease in children. *N Engl J Med* 1973;288:498–505.

34. Henderson FW, Clyde WA, Collier AM, et al. The etiologic and epidemiologic spectrum of bronchiolitis in pediatric practice. *J Pediatr* 1979;95:183–190.

35. Denny FW, Clyde WA. Acute lower respiratory tract infections in non-hospitalized children. *J Pediatr* 1986;108:635–646.

36. Wright AL, Taussig LM, Ray CC, et al. The Tucson children's respiratory study. II. Lower respiratory tract illness in the first year of life. *Am J Epidemiol* 1989;129:1232–1246.

37. Cole P, Wilson R. Host–microbial inter-relationships in respiratory infection. *Chest* 1989;95(suppl):217S–221S.

38. Australian Bureau of Statistics. *Australian Health Survey*. Preliminary bulletin no. 1. Canberra, Australia: Author; 1977.

39. Douglas RM. ARI: the Cinderella of communicable diseases. In: Douglas RM, Kerby-Eaton E, eds. *Acute Respiratory Infections in Children*. Proceedings of an international workshop. Adelaide, South Australia: University of Adelaide; 1985:1–2.

40. Enright PL, Krumla RA, Higgins MW, et al. Prevalence and correlates of respiratory symptoms in the elderly. *Chest* 1994;106:827–834.

41. Lange P, Groth S, Nyboe J, et al. Chronic obstructive lung disease in Copenhagen: cross-sectional epidemiological aspects. *J Intern Med* 1989;226:25–32.

42. Bakke PS, Baste V, Hanoa R, et al. Prevalence of obstructive lung disease in a general population: relation to occupational title and exposure to some airborne agents. *Thorax* 1991;46:863–870.

43. Alonso J, Anto JM. *Encuesta de salut de Barcelona. 1986* [Government publication]. Barcelona, Spain; 1989.

44. Brotons B, Perez JA, Sanchez-Toril F, et al. Prevalencia de la enfermedad obstructiva

cronica y el asma: estudio transversal. *Arch Bronconeumol* 1994;103:481–484.

45. Lundback B, Nystrom L, Rosenhall L, et al. Obstructive lung disease in northern Sweden: respiratory symptoms assessed by postal questionnaire. *Eur Respir J* 1991;4:257–266.

46. Niederman MS, McCombs JS, Unger AN, et al. The cost of treating community-acquired pneumonia. *Clin Ther* 1998;20:820–837.

47. Niederman MS, McCombs JS, Unger AN, et al. Treatment cost of acute exacerbations of chronic bronchitis. *Clin Ther* 1999;21: 576–591.

48. McCord C, Kielmann AA. A successful programme for medical auxiliaries treating childhood diarrhea and pneumonia. *Trop Doct* 1978;8:220–225.

49. Shann FA, Hart K, Thomas D. Acute lower respiratory tract infections in children: possible criteria for selection of patients for antibiotic therapy and hospital admission. *Bull WHO* 1984;62:749–753.

50. World Health Organization. *Case Management of Acute Respiratory Infections in Children: Intervention Studies* WHO/ARI/88.2. Geneva, Switzerland: Author; 1988.

51. Cherian T, John TJ, Simoes E, et al. Evaluation of simple clinical signs for the diagnosis of acute lower respiratory tract infection. *Lancet* 1988;2:125–128.

52. World Health Organization. *ARI Programme Report, 1988.* WHO/ ARI/89.3. Geneva, Switzerland: Author; 1989.

53. World Health Organization. *Programme of Acute Respiratory Infections: Report of the Fourth Meeting of the Technical Advisory Group.* WHO/ARI/89.4. Geneva, Switzerland: Author; 1989.

54. World Health Organization. *Case Management of Acute Respiratory Infections in Children in Developing Countries.* WHO/RSD/85.151. Geneva, Switzerland: Author; 1985.

55. World Health Organization. *Proposal for the Classification of Acute Respiratory Infections and Tuberculosis for the Tenth Revision of the International Classification of Diseases.* WHO/RSD/88.25. Geneva, Switzerland: Author; 1985.

56. Bartlett JG, Breiman RF, Mandell G, et al., for the Infectious Diseases Society of America. Community-acquired pneumonia in adults: guidelines for management. *Clin Infect Dis* 1998;26:811–838.

57. Reimer LG, Caroll KC. Role of the microbiology laboratory in the diagnosis of lower respiratory tract infections. *Clin Infect Dis* 1998;26:742–748.

58. Reed SE. The etiology and epidemiology of common colds and the possibilities of prevention. *Clin Otolaryngol* 1981;6:379–387.

59. Berman S, McIntosh K. Selective primary healthcare: strategies for control of disease in the developing world. XXI. Acute respiratory infections. *Rev Infect Dis* 1985;7:674–691.

60. Berman S, Duenas A, Bedoya A, et al. Acute lower respiratory tract illnesses in Cali, Colombia: a two-year ambulatory study. *Pediatrics* 1983;71:210–218.

61. Escobar JA, Dover AS, Duenas A, et al. Etiology of respiratory tract infections in children in Cali, Colombia. *Pediatrics* 1976;57:123–130.

62. Shann F, Gratten M, Germer S, et al. Aetiology of pneumonia in children in Goroka Hospital, Papua New Guinea. *Lancet* 1984;2:537–541.

63. Sobeslavsky O, Sebikari SRK, Harland PSEG, et al. The viral etiology of acute respiratory infections in children in Uganda. *Bull WHO* 1977;55:625–631.

64. Ogunbi O. Bacterial and viral etiology of bronchiolitis and bronchopneumonia in Lagos children. *J Trop Med Hyg* 1970;73:138–140.

65. Monto AJ, Johnson KM. Respiratory infections in the American tropics. *Am J Trop Med Hyg* 1968;17:867–874.

66. Chanock R, Chambon L, Chang W, et al. WHO respiratory disease survey in children: a serological study. *Bull WHO* 1967;37:363–369.

67. Spence L, Barratt N. Respiratory syncytial virus associated with acute respiratory infections in Trinidadian patients. *Am J Epidemiol* 1968;88:257–266.

68. Kloene W, Bang FB, Chakraborty SM, et al. A two-year respiratory virus survey in four villages in West Bengal, India. *Am J Epidemiol* 1970;92:307–320.

69. Olson LC, Lexomboon U, Sithisarn P, et al. The etiology of respiratory tract infections in a tropical country. *Am J Epidemiol* 1973;97:34–43.

70. Belshe RB, Van Voris LP, Mufson MA. Impact of viral respiratory diseases on infants and young children in a rural and urban area of southern West Virginia. *Am J Epidemiol* 1983;117:467–474.

71. Foy HM, Cooney MK, Maletzky AJ, et al. Incidence and etiology of pneumonia, croup and bronchiolitis in preschool children belonging to a prepaid medical care group over a four-year period. *Am J Epidemiol* 1973;97:80–92.

72. Mufson MA, Krause HE, Mocega HE, et al. Viruses, *Mycoplasma pneumoniae* and bacteria associated with lower respiratory tract disease among infants. *Am J Epidemiol* 1970;91:192–202.

73. Murphy TF, Henderson FW, Clyde WA Jr, et al. Pneumonia: an eleven-year study in a pediatric practice. *Am J Epidemiol* 1981;113:12–21.

74. Berman S, Duenas A, Bedoya A, et al. Acute lower respiratory tract illnesses in Cali, Colombia: a two-year ambulatory study. *Pediatrics* 1983;71:210–218.

75. Wesley AG. Indications for intubation in laryngotracheobronchitis in black children. *S Afr Med J* 1975;49:1126–1128.

76. Bariffi F, Sanduzzi A, Ponticiello A. Epidemiology of lower respiratory tract infections. *J Chemother* 1995;7:263–276.

77. MacFarlane JT. Treatment of lower respiratory infections. *Lancet* 1987;2:1446–1449.

78. Marrie TJ, Durant H, Yates L. Community-acquired pneumonia requiring hospitalization: 5 year prospective study. *Rev Infect Dis* 1989;11:586–599.

79. Clezen WP. Serious morbidity and mortality associated with influenza epidemics. *Epidemiol Rev* 1982;4:25–44.

80. Hayden FG. Respiratory viral infections. In: Federman DD, ed. *Scientific American Medicine*. New York: Scientific American; 1997:1–12.

81. van de Hoogen BG, de Jong JC, Groen J, et al. A newly discovered human pneumovirus isolated from young children with respiratory tract disease. *Nat Med* 2001;7:719–724.

82. Peret TC, Bolvin G, Li Y, et al. Characterization of human metapneumoviruses isolated from patients in North America. *J Infect Dis* 2002;185:1660–1663.

83. Nissen MD, Siebert DJ, Mackay IM, Sloots TP, Withers SJ. Evidence of human metapneumovirus in Australian children. *Med J Aust* 2002;176:188.

84. Stockton J, Stephenson I, Fleming D, Zambon M. Human metapneumovirus as a cause of community-acquired respiratory illness. *Emerg Infect Dis* 2002;8:897–901.

85. Esper F, Boucher D, Weibel C, et al. Human metapneumovirus infestations associated with a newly emerging respiratory infection in children. *Pediatrics* 2003;111:407–410.

86. Williams JV, Harris PA, Tollefson SJ, et al. Human metapneumovirus and lower respiratory tract disease in otherwise healthy infants and children. *N Engl J Med* 2004;350:443–450.

87. Allander T, Tammi MT, Kriksson M, et al. Cloning of a human parvovirus by molecular screening of respiratory tract samples. *PNAS* 2005;102:12891–12912.

88. Hender T, Jartti T, Gupta S, et al. Human bocavirus and acute wheezing in children. *CID* 2007;44:904–910.

89. Fry AM, Lu X, Chittaganpitch M, et al. Human bocavirus: a novel parvovirus epidemiologically associated with pneumonia

requiring hospitalization in Thailand. *J Infect Dis* 2007;195:1038–1045.

90. Kesebir D, Vazquez M, Weibel C, et al. Human bocavirus infection in young children in the United States: molecular epidemiological profile and clinical characteristics of a newly emerging respiratory virus. *J Infect Dis* 2006;194:1276–1282.

91. Manning A, Russel V, Eaststick K, et al. Epidemiological profile and clinical associations of human bocavirus and other human parvoviruses. *JIB* 2006;194:1283–1290.

92. Fabrizio M, Andreoli E, Pifferi M, et al. Human bocavirus in Italian patients with respiratory diseases. *J Clin Virol* 2007;38:321–325.

93. Vicente D, Cilla G, Montes M, et al. Human bocavirus: a respiratory and enteric virus. *Emerg Infect Dis* 2007;13:636–637.

94. Lau SKP, Yip CCY, Que T-I, et al. Clinical and molecular epidemiology of human bocavirus in respiratory and fecal samples from children in Hong Kong. *J Infect Dis* 2007;196:986–993.

95. Monto AS, Napier JA, Metzner HL. The Tecumseh study of respiratory illness. I. Plan of study and observations on syndromes of acute respiratory disease. *Am J Epidemiol* 1971;94:269–279.

96. Monto AS, Cavallaro JJ. The Tecumseh study of respiratory illness. II. Patterns of occurrence of infection with respiratory pathogens. 1965–1969. *Am J Epidemiol* 1971;94:280–289.

97. Maletzky AJ, Cooney MK, Luce R, et al. Epidemiology of viral and mycoplasma agents associated with childhood lower respiratory illness in a civilian population. *J Pediatr* 1971;78:407–414.

98. Barrett-Connor E. The nonvalue of sputum culture in the diagnosis of pneumococcal pneumonia. *Am Rev Resp Dis* 1971;103:845–848.

99. Bartlett JG. Diagnostic tests for agents of community-acquired pneumonia. *Clin Infect Dis* 2011;32(suppl 4):S296–S304.

100. Bollows JGM. The reliability of sputum typing and its relation to serum therapy. *JAMA* 1935;105:1512–1523.

101. Sullivan RJ Jr, Dawdle WR, Merine WM, Hierholzer JC. Adult pneumonia in a general hospital: etiology and host risk factors. *Arch Intern Med* 1972;129:935–942.

102. Van Eerden MM, Vlaspolder F, deGraaf CS, et al. Comparison between pathogen directed antibiotic treatment and empirical broad spectrum antibiotic treatment in patients with community-acquired pneumonia: a prospective randomized study. *Thorax* 2005;60:672–678.

103. Houck PM, Bratzler DW, Nea W, et al. Timing of antibiotic administration and outcomes for Medicare patients hospitalized with community-acquired pneumonia. *Arch Intern Med* 2004;164:627–644.

104. Linenaaver PK, Remoss D, Romas S, et al. Public reporting and pay for performance in hospital quality improvement. *N Engl J Med* 2007;356:486–496.

105. Bartlett JG. Is activity against "atypical" pathogens necessary in the treatment protocols for community-acquired pneumonia? Issues with combination therapy. *Clin Infect Dis* 2008;47:S232–S236.

106. Thomas E, Haupt RT, Hefferman RT, et al. An outbreak of Legionnaires disease associated with a decorative water wall fountain in a hospital. *Control Hosp Epidemiol* 2012;30:185–191.

107. Johansson N, Kalin M, Tiveljunge-Lindell J, et al. Etiology of community-acquired pneumonia: increased microbiological yield with new diagnostic methods. *Clin Infect Dis* 2010;50:202–209.

108. Weatherall C, Pooloni R, Gogglieb T. Point-of-care urinary pneumococcal antigen test in the emergency department for community-acquired pneumonia. *Emerg Med J* 2008;25:144–148.

109. Mahoney J, Chong S, Merantc F, et al. Development of a respiratory virus panel test for detection of twenty human respiratory

viruses by use of multiplex PCR and a fluid microbial-based assay. *J Clin Microbiol* 2007;45:2965–2970.

110. Schucat A, Hilger T, Zell E, et al. Active bacterial core surveillance of the emerging infections program network. *Emerg Infect Dis* 2001;7:92–99.

111. Marrie TJ, Durant H, Yates L. Community-acquired pneumonia requiring hospitalization: 5 year prospective study. *Rev Infect Dis* 1989;11:586–599.

112. Molleni RA. Epiglottitis: incidence of extra-epiglottic infection. Report of 72 cases and review of the literature. *Pediatrics* 1976; 58:526–531.

113. Miller DL, Alderslade R, Ross EM. Whooping cough and whooping cough vaccine: the risks and benefits debate. *Epidemiol Rev* 1982;4:1–24.

114. Howie VM, Ploussard JH, Lester RL Jr. Otitis media: a clinical and bacteriological correlation. *Pediatrics* 1970;45:29–35.

115. Engelhardt D, Cohen D, Strauss N, et al. Randomized study of myringotomy, amoxy-cillin/clavulanate or both for acute otitis media in infants. *Lancet* 1989;2:141–143.

116. Wald ER, Milmoe GJ, Bowen A, et al. Acute maxillary sinusitis in children. *N Engl J Med* 1981;304:749–754.

117. Evans FO, Sydnor JB, Moore WEC, et al. Sinusitis of the maxillary antrum. *N Engl J Med* 1975;293:735–739.

118. Hamory BH, Sande MA, Snydor A, et al. Etiology and antimicrobial therapy of acute maxillary sinusitis. *J Infect Dis* 1979;139:197–202.

119. Berman S, McIntosh R. Selective primary healthcare: strategies for control of infectious diseases in the developing world XXI. Acute respiratory infections. *Rev Infect Dis* 1985;7:674–691.

120. Ikeogu MO. Acute pneumonia in Zimbabwe: bacterial isolates by lung aspirations. *Arch Dis Child* 1988;63:1266–1267.

121. Bartlett JG. Approach to the patient with pneumonia. In: Gorbach SL, Bartlett JG, Blacklow NR, eds. *Infectious Diseases*. 3rd ed. Pgs. 470–479. Philadelphia, PA: WB Saunders; 2004.

122. Grayston JT, Alexander E, Kenny G, et al. *Mycoplasma pneumoniae* infections. *JAMA* 1965;19:369–374.

123. Jansson E, Wager O, Stenstrom R, et al. Studies on Eaton PPLO pneumonia. *Br Med J* 1964;1:142–145.

124. Cunha BA. Community-acquired pneumonia in human immunodeficiency virus-infected patients. *Clin Infect Dis* 1999;28:410–411.

125. Komaroff AL, Aronson MD, Pass TM, et al. Serologic evidence of chlamydia and mycoplasma pharyngitis in adults. *Science* 1983;222:927–929.

126. Stagno S, Brasfield DM, Brown MB, et al. Infant pneumonitis associated with cytomegalovirus, chlamydia, pneumocystis and ureaplasma. *Pediatrics* 1981;68:322–329.

127. Grayston JT, Kuo CC, Wang SP, et al. A new *Chlamydia psittaci* strain, TWAR, isolated from acute respiratory tract infections. *N Engl J Med* 1986;315:161–168.

128. Marrie TJ, Grayston JT, Wang SP, et al. Pneumonia associated with TWAR strain of chlamydia. *Ann Intern Med* 1987;106:507–511.

129. Logan WPD. Mortality in the London fog incident, 1952. *Lancet* 1953;1:336–338.

130. Firket J. The cause of the symptoms found in the Meuse Valley during the fog of December, 1930. *Bull Acad R Med Belg* 1931;11:683–741.

131. Gore AT, Shaddick CW. Atmosphere pollution and mortality in the county of London. *Br J Prev Soc Med* 1958;12:104–113.

132. Ciocco A, Thompson DJ. A follow-up of Donora ten years after: methodology and findings. *Am J Public Health* 1961;51:155–164.

133. Greenberg L, Erhardt C, Field F, et al. Intermittent air pollution episodes in

New York City, 1962. *Public Health Rep* 1963;78:1061–1064.

134. Holland WW, Bennett AE, Cameron IR, et al. Health effects of particulate air pollution: reappraising the evidence. *Am J Epidemiol* 1979;110:527–659.

135. Toyama T. Air pollution and its effects in Japan. *Arch Environ Health* 1964;8:153–173.

136. Lunn JR, Knowelden J, Handyside AJ. Patterns of respiratory illness in Sheffield infant school children. *Br J Prev Soc Med* 1967;21:7–16.

137. Lunn JE, Knowelden J, Roe JW. Patterns of respiratory illness in Sheffield infant school children. *Br J Prev Soc Med* 1970;24:223–228.

138. Colley JRT, Reid DD. Urban and social origins of childhood bronchitis in England and Wales. *Br Med J* 1970;2:213–217.

139. Cassel EJ, Lebowitz M, McCarroll JR. The relationship between air pollution, weather, and symptoms in an urban population. *Am Rev Respir Dis* 1972;106:677–683.

140. Collins JJ, Kasap HS, Holland WW. Environmental factors in child mortality in England and Wales. *Am J Epidemiol* 1971;93:10–22.

141. Lawther PJ, Waller RE, Henderson M. Air pollution and exacerbations of bronchitis. *Thorax* 1970;25:525–539.

142. French JC, Lowrimore C, Nelson WC, et al. The effect of sulphur dioxide and suspended sulphates on acute respiratory disease. *Arch Environ Health* 1973;27:129–133.

143. Durham WH. Air pollution and student health. *Arch Environ Health* 1974;28:241–254.

144. Levy D, Gent M, Newhouse MT. Relationship between acute respiratory illness and air pollution levels in an industrial city. *Am Rev Respir Dis* 1977;116:167–173.

145. Ware JH, Ferris BC, Dockery DW, et al. Effects of ambient sulphur oxides and suspended particles on respiratory health of preadolescent children. *Am Rev Respir Dis* 1986;133:834–842.

146. Pope CA. Respiratory disease associated with community air pollution and a steel mill, Utah Valley. *Am J Public Health* 1989;79:623–628.

147. Derriennic F, Richardson S, Mollie A, et al. Short-term effects of sulphur dioxide pollution on mortality in two French cities. *Int J Epidemiol* 1989;18:186–187.

148. Dockery DW, Speizer FE, Stram DO, et al. Effects of inhalable particles on respiratory health of children. *Am Rev Respir Dis* 1989;139: 587–594.

149. Dales RE, Spitzer WO, Suissa S, et al. Respiratory health of a population living downwind from natural gas refineries. *Am Rev Respir Dis* 1989;139:595–600.

150. Kinney PL, Ware JH, Spangler JD, et al. Short-term pulmonary function change in association with ozone levels. *Am Rev Respir Dis* 1989;139:56–61.

151. Schwartz J, Dockery DW, Wypii D, et al. Acute effects of air pollution on respiratory symptom reporting in children [Abstract]. *Am Rev Respir Dis* 1989;139(suppl):A27.

152. Goings SAJ, Kulla TJ, Bascom R, et al. Effect of nitrogen dioxide exposure on susceptibility to influenza A virus infection in healthy adults. *Am Rev Respir Dis* 1989;1075–1081.

153. Cook DG, Strachan DP. Summary of effects of parental smoking on the respiratory health of children and implications for research. *Thorax* 1999;54:357–366.

154. Fergusson DM, Horwood LJ, Shannon FT. Parental smoking and respiratory illness in infancy. *Arch Dis Child* 1980;55:358–361.

155. Ferris BG, Ware JH, Berkey CS, et al. Effects of passive smoking on health of children. *Environ Health Perspect* 1985;62:289–295.

156. Colley JRT, Holland WW, Corkhill RT. Influence of passive smoking and parental

phlegm on pneumonia and bronchitis in early childhood. *Lancet* 1974;2:1031–1034.

157. Fergusson DM, Horwood LJ. Parental smoking and respiratory illness during early childhood: a six-year longitudinal study. *Pediatr Pulmonol* 1985;1:99–106.

158. Lebowitz MD, Burrows B. Respiratory symptoms related to smoking habits of family adults. *Chest* 1976;69:48–50.

159. Love GJ, Lan S, Shy CM, et al. The incidence and severity of acute respiratory illness in families exposed to different levels of air pollution, New York metropolitan area, 1971–2. *Arch Environ Health* 1981;36:66–73.

160. Gardner G, Frank AL, Taber L. Effects of social and family factors on viral respiratory infection and illness in the first year of life. *J Epidemiol Community Health* 1984;38:42–48.

161. Taylor B, Wadsworth J. Maternal smoking during pregnancy and lower respiratory tract illness early in life. *Arch Dis Child* 1987;62:786–789.

162. Comstock GW, Meyer MB, Helsing KJ, et al. Respiratory effects of household exposures to tobacco smoke and gas cooking. *Am Rev Respir Dis* 1981;124:143–148.

163. Melia RJW, Florey C duV, Darby SC, et al. Differences in NO_2 levels in kitchens with gas or electric cookers. *Atmospheric Environ* 1978;12:1379–1381.

164. Spangler JD, Duffy CP, Letz R, et al. Nitrogen-dioxide inside and outside 137 homes and implications for ambient air quality standards and health effects research. *Environ Sci Technol* 1983;17:164–168.

165. Ware JH, Dockery DW, Spiro A, et al. Passive smoking, gas cooking and respiratory health of children living in six cities. *Am Rev Respir Dis* 1984;129:366–374.

166. Melia RJ, Florey C duV, Altman DC, et al. Association between gas cooking and respiratory disease in children. *Br Med J* 1977;2:149–152.

167. Melia RJ, Florey C duV, Chinn S. The relation between respiratory illness in primary school children and the use of gas for cooking. I. Results from a national survey. *Int J Epidemiol* 1979;8:333–338.

168. Keller MD, Lanese RR, Mitchell RI, et al. Respiratory illness in households using gas and electricity for cooking. I. Survey of incidence. *Environ Res* 1979;19:495–503.

169. Keller MD, Lanese RR, Mitchell RI, et al. Respiratory illness in households using gas and electricity for cooking. II. Symptoms and objective findings. *Environ Res* 1979;19:504–515.

170. Samet JM, Marbury MC, Spangler JD. Health effects and sources of indoor air pollution. Part 1. *Am Rev Respir Dis* 1987;136:1486–1508.

171. Smith KR, Aggarwal AL, Dave RM. Air pollution and rural biomass fuel in developing countries: a pilot study in India and implications for research and policy. *Atmospheric Environ* 1983;17:2343–2362.

172. Dennis RJ, Maldonado D, Norman S, et al. Woodsmoke exposure and risk for obstructive airways disease among women. *Chest* 1996;109:115–119.

173. Pandey MR, Boleij JSM, Smith KR, et al. Indoor air pollution in developing countries and acute respiratory infection in children. *Lancet* 1989;1:427–429.

174. Kossove D. Smoke-filled rooms and lower respiratory disease in infants. *S Afr Med J* 1982;61:622–624.

175. Campbell H, Armstrong JRM, Byass P. Indoor air pollution in developing countries and acute respiratory infection in children. *Lancet* 1989;1:1012.

176. Campbell H, Byass P, Greenwood BM. Simple clinical signs for the diagnosis of acute respiratory infections. *Lancet* 1988;2:742–743.

177. Honicky RE, Osborne JS, Akpom CA. Symptoms of respiratory illness in young children and the use of wood-burning

stoves for indoor heating. *Pediatrics* 1985;75:587–593.

178. Osborne JS III, Honicky RE. Chest illness in young children and indoor heating with wood [Abstract]. *Am Rev Respir Dis* 1989;139(suppl):A29.

179. Tuthill RW. Woodstoves, formaldehyde, and respiratory disease. *Am J Epidemiol.* 1984;120:952–955.

180. Doll R, Hill AB. Lung cancer and other causes of death in relation to smoking. *Br Med J* 1956;2:1071–1081.

181. Hammond EC, Horn D. Smoking and death rates: report on forty-four months of follow-up on 187,783 men. I. Total mortality. *JAMA* 1958;166:1159–1172.

182. Hammond EC, Horn D. Smoking and death rates: report on forty-four months of follow-up on 187,783 men. II. Death rates by cause. *JAMA* 1958;166:1294–1308.

183. Dorn HF. The mortality of smokers and nonsmokers. *Am Stat Assoc Proc Soc Stat Sect* 1958;1:34–71.

184. Dunn JE, Linden G, Breslow L. Lung cancer mortality experience of men in certain occupations in California. *Am J Public Health* 1960;50:1475–1487.

185. Bes EWR, Josie GH, Walker CB. A Canadian study of mortality in relation to smoking habits, a preliminary report. *Can J Public Health* 1961;52:99–106.

186. U.S. Public Health Service. *Smoking and Health: Report of the Advisory Committee to the Surgeon General of the Public Health Service.* PHS publication no. 1103. Atlanta, GA: U.S. Department of Health, Education and Welfare, Public Health Service, Centers for Disease Control; 1964.

187. Finklea JF, Sandifer SH, Smith DD. Cigarette smoking and epidemic influenza. *Am J Epidemiol* 1969;90:390–399.

188. Mackenzie JS, Mackenzie IM, Holt PG. The effect of cigarette smoking on susceptibility to epidemic influenza and on serological responses to live attenuated and killed subunit influenza vaccines. *J Hyg (Camb)* 1976;77:409–417.

189. Kark JD, Lebuish M. Smoking and epidemic influenza-like illness in female military recruits: a brief survey. *Am J Public Health* 1981;71:530–532.

190. Kark JD, Lebuish M, Rannon L. Cigarette smoking as a risk factor for epidemic A (H1N1) influenza in young men. *N Engl J Med* 1982;307:1042–1046.

191. Monto AS, Higgins MW, Ross HW. The Tecumseh study of respiratory illness. VIII. Acute infection in chronic respiratory disease and comparison groups. *Am Rev Respir Dis* 1975;111:27–36.

192. Holland WW, Elliott A. Cigarette smoking, respiratory symptoms and antismoking propaganda. *Lancet* 1968;1:41–43.

193. Colley JRT, Douglas JWB, Reid DD. Respiratory disease in young adults: influence of early childhood lower respiratory tract illness, social class, air pollution and smoking. *Br Med J* 1973;3:195–198.

194. Rush D. Respiratory symptoms in a group of American secondary school students: the overwhelming association with cigarette smoking. *Int J Epidemiol* 1974;3:153–165.

195. Reingold AL. Role of *Legionellae* in acute infections of the lower respiratory tract. *Rev Infect Dis* 1988;10:1018–1028.

196. Lipsky BA, Boyko EJ, Inui TS, et al. Risk factors for acquiring pneumococcal infections. *Arch Intern Med* 1986;146:2179–2185.

197. Petitti DB, Friedman GD. Respiratory morbidity in smokers of low and high yield cigarettes. *Prev Med* 1985;14:217–225.

198. Simberkoff MS, Cross AP, Al-Ibrabim M, et al. Efficacy of pneumococcal vaccine in high risk patients: results of a Veterans Administration cooperative study. *N Engl J Med* 1986;315:1318–1327.

199. Woodhead MA, MacFarlane JT, McCracken JS, et al. Prospective study of the aetiology and outcome of pneumonia in the community. *Lancet* 1987;1:671–674.

200. U.S. Department of Health and Human Services. *Reducing the Consequences of Smoking: 25 Years of Progress.* DHHS publication no. (CDC)89-8411. Atlanta, GA: U.S. Department of Health and Human Services, Public Health Service, Centers for Disease Control; 1989.

201. Woods HM. The influence of external factors on the mortality from pneumonia in childhood and later adult life. *J Hyg (Camb)* 1927;26:36–43.

202. Finland M. Pneumococcal infections. In: Evans AS, Feldman HA, eds. *Bacterial Infections in Humans: Epidemiology and Control.* Chapter 23, pgs. 417–433. New York, NY: Plenum; 1982.

203. Payling-Wright G, Payling-Wright H. Etiological factors in broncho-pneumonia amongst infants in London. *J Hyg (Camb)* 1945;44:15–30.

204. Leeder S, Corkhill R, Irwig LM, et al. Influence of family factors on the incidence of lower respiratory illness during the first year of life. *Br J Prev Soc Med* 1976;30:203–212.

205. Monto AS, Ross HW. Acute respiratory illness in the community: effect of family composition, smoking and chronic symptoms. *Br J Prev Soc Med* 1977;31:101–108.

206. Strangert K. Respiratory illness in preschool children with different forms of day care. *Pediatrics* 1976;57:191–196.

207. Bell DM, Gleiber UW, Mercer AA, et al. Illness associated with child day care: a study of incidence and cost. *Am J Public Health* 1989;79:479–484.

208. Strangert K. Otitis media in young children in different types of day-care. *Scand J Infect Dis* 1977;9:113–123.

209. Vinther B, Pederson CB, Elbrond O. Otitis media in childhood: sociomedical aspects with special reference to day care conditions. *Clin Otolaryngol* 1984;9:3–8.

210. Silipa M, Karma P, Pukander J, et al. The Bayesian approach to the evaluation of risk factors in acute and recurrent otitis media. *Acta Otolaryngol* 1988;106:94–101.

211. Moore PS, Marfin AA, Quenomoen LE, et al. Mortality rates in displaced and resident populations of central Somalia during the famine of 1992. *Lancet* 1993;341: 935–938.

212. Marfin AA, Moore J, Collins C, et al. Infectious disease surveillance during emergency relief to Bhutanese refugees in Nepal. *JAMA* 1994;272:377–381.

213. Aaby P, Bukh J, Lisse IM, et al. Decline in measles mortality: nutrition, age at infection or exposure. *Br Med J* 1988;296:1226–1228.

214. Aaby P. Malnutrition and overcrowding/intensive exposure in severe measles infection: review of community studies. *Rev Infect Dis* 1988;10:478–491.

215. Tupasi TE, Velmonte MA, Sanvictores MEG, et al. Determinants of morbidity and mortality due to acute respiratory infections: implications for intervention. *J Infect Dis* 1988;157:615–623.

216. Fonseca W, Kirkwood BR, Victora CG, et al. Risk factors for childhood pneumonia among the urban poor in Fortaleza, Brazil: a case-control study. *Bull WHO* 1996;74: 199–208.

217. Sommer A, Tarwotjo I, Hussaini G, et al. Increased mortality in mild vitamin A deficiency. *Lancet* 1983;2:585–588.

218. Sommer A, Katz J, Tarwotjo I. Increased risk of respiratory disease and diarrhea in children with pre-existing mild vitamin A deficiency. *Am J Clin Nutr* 1984;40:1090–1095.

219. Bloem MW, Wedel M, Egger RJ, et al. Mild vitamin A deficiency and risk of respiratory tract diseases and diarrhea in preschool and school children in northeastern Thailand. *Am J Epidemiol* 1990;131:332–339.

220. Pinnock CB, Douglas RM, Badcock NR. Vitamin A status in children who are prone to respiratory tract infections. *Aust Paediatr J* 1986;22:95–99.

221. Pinnock CB, Douglas RM, Martin AJ, et al. Vitamin A status of children with a history of respiratory syncytial virus infection in infancy. *Aust Paediatr J* 1988;24:286–289.

222. Forman MR, Gravbard BI, Hoffman HJ, et al. The Pima infant feeding study: breast feeding and respiratory infections in the first year of life. *Int J Epidemol* 1984;13:447–453.

223. Victora C, Smith PG, Vaughan JP, et al. Evidence of protection by breast feeding against infant deaths from infectious diseases in Brazil. *Lancet* 1987;2:319–322.

224. Saarinen UM. Prolonged breast feeding as a prophylaxis for recurrent otitis media. *Acta Paediatr Scand* 1982;71:567–571.

225. Teele DW, Klein JO, Rosner B, et al. Epidemiology of otitis media during the first seven years of life in children in greater Boston: a prospective cohort study. *J Infect Dis* 1989;160:83–94.

226. Pullan CR, Toms GL, Martin AJ, et al. Breast feeding and respiratory syncytial virus infection. *Br Med J* 1980;281:1034–1036.

227. Watkins CJ, Leeder SR, Corkhill RT. The relationship between breast and bottle feeding and respiratory illness in the first year of life. *J Epidemiol Community Health* 1979;33:180–182.

228. Taylor B, Wadsworth J, Golding J, et al. Breast-feeding, bronchitis, and admissions for lower respiratory illness and gastroenteritis during the first five years. *Lancet* 1982;1:1227–1229.

229. Fergusson DM, Horwood LJ, Shannon FT, et al. Infant health and breast feeding during the first 16 weeks of life. *Austr Paediatr J* 1978;14:254–258.

230. Fergusson DM, Horwood LJ, Shannon FT, et al. Breast feeding, gastrointestinal and lower respiratory illness in the first two years. *Austr Paediatr J* 1981;17:191–195.

231. Tracey VV, De NC, Harper JR. Obesity and respiratory infection in infants and young children. *Br Med J* 1971;1:16–18.

232. Wright AL, Holberg CJ, Martinex FD, et al. Breast feeding and lower respiratory tract illness in the first year of life. *Br Med J* 1989;229:946–949.

233. Tyrell DAJ, Wallace-Craig J, Meade TW, et al. A trial of ascorbic acid in the treatment of the common cold. *Br J Prev Soc Med* 1977;31:189–191.

234. Pitt HA, Costrini AM. Vitamin C prophylaxis in marine recruits. *JAMA* 1979;241:908–911.

235. Strachan DP, Anderson HR, Bland JM, et al. Asthma as a link between chest illness in childhood and chronic cough and phlegm in young adults. *Br Med J* 1988;296:890–893.

236. Weiss ST, Tager IB, Muñoz A, et al. The relationship of respiratory infections in early childhood to the occurrence of increased levels of bronchial responsiveness and atrophy. *Am Rev Respir Dis* 1985;131:573–578.

237. Woolcock AJ, Leeder SR, Pear JK, et al. The influence of lower respiratory illness in infancy and childhood and subsequent cigarette smoking on lung function in Sydney school children. *Am Rev Respir Dis* 1979;120:5–14.

238. Kattan M, Keens TG, Lapierre JG, et al. Pulmonary function abnormalities in symptom-free children after bronchiolitis. *Pediatrics* 1977;59:883–888.

239. Mok JYQ, Simpson H. Outcome for acute bronchitis, bronchiolitis, and pneumonia in infancy. *Arch Dis Child* 1984;59:306–309.

240. Graham NMH. *Psychosocial Factors in the Epidemiology of Acute Respiratory Infection* [MD thesis]. Adelaide, South Australia: University of Adelaide; 1987.

241. Douglas RM, Miles HB. Vaccination against *Streptococcus pneumoniae* in childhood: lack

of a demonstrable benefit in young Australian children. *J Infect Dis* 1984;149:861–869.

242. Barker DJP, Osmond C. Childhood respiratory infection and adult chronic bronchitis in England and Wales. *Br Med J* 1986;293:1271–1275.

243. Belfer ML, Shader RI, DiMascio A, et al. Stress and bronchitis. *Br Med J* 1968;3:805–806.

244. Jacobs MA, Spilken AZ, Norman MM, et al. Life stress and respiratory illness. *Psychosom Med* 1970;32:233–242.

245. Belfer ML, Shader RI, DiMascio A, et al. Stress and bronchitis. *Br Med J* 1968;3:805–806.

246. Boyce WT, Jensen EW, Cassel JC, et al. Influence of life events and family routines on childhood respiratory tract illness. *Pediatrics* 1977;60:609–615.

247. Stout CW, Bloom LJ. Type A behavior and upper respiratory infections. *J Human Stress* 1981;8:4–7.

248. Hart H, Bax M, Jenkins S. Health and behavior in preschool children. *Child Care Health Dev* 1984;10:1–16.

249. Foulke FG, Reeb KG, Graham AV, et al. Family function, respiratory illness and otitis media in urban black infants. *Fam Med* 1988;20:128–132.

250. Graham NMH, Douglas RM, Ryan P. Stress and acute respiratory infection. *Am J Epidemiol* 1986;124:389–401.

251. Kasl SV, Evans AS, Niederman JC. Psychosocial risk factors in the development of infectious mononucleosis. *Psychosom Med* 1979;41:445–466.

252. Meyer RJ, Haggerty RJ. Streptococcal infections in families: factors altering susceptibility. *Pediatrics* 1962:29:539–549.

253. Totman R, Kiff J, Reed SE, et al. Predicting experimental colds in volunteers from different measures of life stress. *J Psychosom Res* 1950;24:155–163.

254. Totman R, Reed SE, Craig JW. Cognitive dissonance, stress and virus-induced common colds. *J Psychosom Res* 1977;21:51–61.

255. Broadbent DE, Broadhent MHP, Philpotts RJ, et al. Some further studies on the prediction of experimental colds in volunteers by psychological factors. *J Psychosom Res* 1984;28:511–523.

256. Kiecolt-Glaser JK, Glaser R. Psychological influences on immunity. *Psychosomatics* 1986;27:621–624.

257. Dick EC, Houssain SV, Mink KA, et al. Interruption of transmission of rhinovirus colds among human volunteers using virucidal paper handkerchiefs. *J Infect Dis* 1986;153:352–356.

258. Gwaltney JM, Moskolski PB, Hendley JO. Hand-to-hand transmission of rhinovirus colds. *Ann Intern Med* 1978;88:463–467.

259. Gwaltney JM Jr, Hendley JO. Transmission of experimental rhinovirus infection by contaminated surfaces. *Am J Epidemiol* 1982;116:828–833.

260. Schenker MB, Samet JM, Speizer FE. Risk factors for childhood respiratory disease: the effect of host factors and home environmental exposures. *Am Rev Respir Dis* 1983;128:1038–1043.

261. Graham NMH, Woodward AJ, Ryan P, et al. Acute respiratory illness in Adelaide children. II. The relationship of maternal stress, social supports and family functioning. *Int J Epidemiol* 1990;19:937–944.

262. Dingle JM, Badger GF, Jordan WS Jr. *Illness in the Home: A Study of 25,000 Illnesses in a Group of Cleveland Families.* Cleveland, OH: Western Reserve University; 1964.

263. Beem MO. Acute respiratory illness in nursery school children: a longitudinal study of the occurrence of illness and respiratory viruses. *Am J Epidemiol* 1969;90:30–44.

264. Hendley JO, Gwaltney JM Jr, Jordan WS Jr. Rhinovirus infections in an industrial population. IV. Infections within families of employees

during two fall peaks of respiratory illness. *Am J Epidemiol* 1969;89:184–196.

265. Douglas RG Jr, Lindgram KM, Cough RB. Exposure to cold environment and rhinovirus cold: failure to demonstrate an effect. *N Engl J Med* 1968;279:742–747.

266. Christie AB. *Infectious Diseases: Epidemiology and Clinical Practice.* Edinburgh, Scotland: Churchill Livingstone; 1974.

267. Jackson GG, Muldoon RL, Johnson GC, et al. Contribution of volunteers to studies of the common cold. *Am Rev Respir Dis* 1963;88(suppl):120–127.

268. Young M. The influence of weather conditions on the mortality from bronchitis and pneumonia in children. *J Hyg* 1924;23:151–175.

269. Gwaltney JM. Epidemiology of the common cold. *Ann N Y Acad Sci* 1980;353:54–60.

270. D'Souza RM. Care-seeking behavior. *Clin Infect Dis* 1999;28:234.

271. D'Souza RM. *Household Determinants of Childhood Mortality: Illness Management in Karachi Slums.* Canberra, Australia: National Centre for Epidemiology and Population Health, the Australian National University; 1997:316.

272. Kundi MZM, Anjum M, Mull DS, Mull JD. Maternal perceptions of pneumonia and pneumonia signs in Pakistani children. *Soc Sci Med* 1993;37:649–660.

273. Rahaman MM, Aziz KMS, Munshi MH, et al. A diarrhea clinic in rural Bangladesh: influence of distance, age and sex on attendance and diarrheal mortality. *Am J Public Health* 1982;72:1124–1128.

274. Hughes WT. *Pneumocystis carinii* pneumonia. *N Engl J Med* 1987;317:1021–1023.

275. Rubinstein A, Sicklick M, Gupta A, et al. Acquired immunodeficiency with reversed T4/T8 ratios in infants born to promiscuous and drug addicted mothers. *JAMA* 1983;249:2350–2356.

276. Oleske J, Minnefar AB, Cooper B, et al. Immune deficiency syndrome in children. *JAMA* 1983;249:2345–2349.

277. Scott GB, Buck BE, Leterman JG, et al. Acquired immunodeficiency syndrome in infants. *N Engl J Med* 1984;310:76–81.

278. Quinn TC, Mann JM, Curran JW, et al. AIDS in Africa: an epidemiologic paradigm. *Science* 1986;234:955–963.

279. Leigh TR, Parsons P, Hume C, et al. Sputum induction for diagnosis of *Pneumocystis carinii* pneumonia. *Lancet* 1989;2:205–206.

280. Bernstein LJ, Krieger BZ, Novick B, et al. Bacterial infection in the acquired immunodeficiency syndrome. *Pediatr Infect Dis J* 1985;4:472–475.

281. Schlamm HT, Yancowitz SR. *Haemophilus influenzae* pneumonia in young adults with AIDS, ARC, or risk of AIDS. *Am J Med* 1989;86:11–14.

282. Rolston KVI, Uribe-Botero G, Mansell PWA. Bacterial infections in adult patients with the acquired immune deficiency syndrome (AIDS) and AIDS-related complex. *Am J Med* 1987;83:604–605.

283. Witt DJ, Craven DE, McCabe WR. Bacterial infections in adult patients with the acquired immune deficiency syndrome (AIDS) and AIDS-related complex. *Am J Med* 1987;82:900–906.

284. White S, Tsou E, Waldhorn RE, et al. Life-threatening bacterial pneumonia in male homosexuals with laboratory features of the acquired immunodeficiency syndrome. *Chest* 1985;87:486–488.

285. Selwyn PA, Feingold AR, Martel D, et al. Increased risk of bacterial pneumonia in HIV-infected intravenous drug users without AIDS. *AIDS* 1988;2:267–272.

286. Murray JF, Garay SM, Hopewell PC, et al. Pulmonary complications of the acquired immunodeficiency syndrome: an update. *Am Rev Respir Dis* 1987;135:504–509.

287. Biggar RJ, Bouvet E, Ebbeen P, et al. Clinical features of AIDS in Europe. *Eur J Cancer Clin Oncol* 1984;20:165–167.

288. Hira SK, Ngandu N, Wadhawan D, et al. Clinical and epidemiological features of HIV infection at a referral clinic in Zambia. *J AIDS* 1990;3:87–91.

289. Piot P, Laga M, Ryder R, et al. The global epidemiology of HIV infection: continuity, heterogeneity, and change. *J AIDS* 1990;3:403–412.

290. Drillien CM. A longitudinal study of the growth and development of prematurely and maturely born children. Part IV. Morbidity. *Arch Dis Child* 1959;14:210–217.

291. Chan KN, Elliman A, Bryan E, et al. Respiratory symptoms in children of low birth weight. *Arch Dis Child* 1989;64: 1294–1304.

292. Victora CG, Smith PG, Barros FC, et al. Risk factors for deaths due to respiratory infections among Brazilian infants. *Int J Epidemiol* 1989;18:918–925.

293. Datta N, Kumar V, Kumar L, et al. Application of a case management approach to the control of acute respiratory infections in low birth weight infants: a feasibility study. *Bull WHO* 1987;65:77–82.

294. Caldwell JC, Reddy PH, Caldwell P. The social component of mortality decline: an investigation in South India employing alternative methodologies. *Population Studies* 1983;37:185–205.

295. Abosede OA. Self-medication: an important aspect of primary health care. *Soc Sci Med* 1984;19:699–703.

296. Colson AC. The differential use of medical resources in developing countries. *J Health Soc Behav* 1971;12:226–237.

297. Liu C, Douglas RM. Chinese herbal medicine in the treatment of acute respiratory tract infections: review of randomized and controlled clinical trials. *Clin Infect Dis* 1999;28:235–236.

298. Puck JM, Glezen WP, Frank AL, et al. Protection of infants from infection with influenza A virus by transplacentally acquired antibody. *J Infect Dis* 1980;142:844–849.

299. Glezen WP, Paredes A, Allison JE, et al. Risk of respiratory syncytial virus infection for infants from low income families in relationship to age, sex, ethnic group and maternal antibody level. *J Pediatr* 1981;98:708–715.

300. McConnochie KM, Roghmann KJ. Parental smoking, presence of older siblings and family history of asthma increase risk of bronchiolitis. *Am J Dis Child* 1986;140:806–812.

301. Welliver RC, Wong DT, Sun M, et al. The development of respiratory syncytial virus specific IgE and the release of histamine in nasopharyngeal secretions after infection. *N Engl J Med* 1981;305:841–846.

302. Welliver RC, Wong DT, Middleton E, et al. Role of parainfluenza virus specific IgE in pathogenesis of croup and wheezing subsequent to infection. *J Pediatr* 1982;101: 889–896.

303. Martinez FD, Morgan WJ, Wright AL, et al. Diminished lung function as a predisposing factor for wheezing respiratory illness in children. *N Engl J Med* 1988;319:1112–1117.

304. Speizer F, Comstock G. Recommended respiratory disease questionnaires for use with adults and children in epidemiological research. *Am Rev Respir Dis* 1978;118:7–53.

305. Fletcher CM. Standardized questionnaire on respiratory symptoms: a statement prepared for and approved by the Medical Research Council's Committee on the Etiology for Chronic Bronchitis. *Br Med J* 1960;2:1665.

306. Gold DR, Weiss ST, Tager IB, et al. Comparison of questionnaire and diary methods in acute childhood respiratory

illness surveillance. *Am Rev Respir Dis* 1989;139:847–849.

307. Miller DL. *Some Problems in the Classification of Acute Respiratory Infection in Young Children and Questionnaire Design.* WHO/RSD/81.8. Geneva, Switzerland: World Health Organization; 1981.

308. Leventhal JM. Clinical predictors of pneumonia as a guide to ordering chest roentgenograms. *Clin Pediatr* 1982;21:730–734.

309. Cherian T, John TJ, Simoes E, et al. Evaluation of simple clinical signs for the diagnosis of acute lower respiratory tract infection. *Lancet* 1988;2:125–128.

310. Campbell H, Byass P, Greenwood BM. Simple clinical signs for the diagnosis of acute lower respiratory infections. *Lancet* 1988;2: 742–743.

311. Campbell H, Byass P, Lamont AC, et al. Assessment of clinical criteria for identification of severe acute lower respiratory tract infections in children. *Lancet* 1989;1:297–299.

312. Centers for Disease Control and Prevention. Cigarette smoking among adults—United States, 2003. *MMWR* 2005;54:509–512.

313. Yang G, Fan L, Tan J, et al. Smoking in China: findings of the 1996 National Prevalence Survey. *JAMA* 1999;282: 1247–1253.

314. Yang G, Ma J, Chen A, et al. Smoking cessation in China: findings from the 1996 National Prevalence Survey. *Tobacco Control* 2001;10:170–174.

315. Centers for Disease Control and Prevention. Preventing pneumococcal disease among infants and young children: recommendations of the Advisory Committee on Immunization Practices (ACIP). *MMWR* 2000;49(RR-9).

316. Centers for Disease Control and Prevention. Direct and indirect effects of routine vaccination of children with 7-valent pneumococcal conjugate vaccine on incidence of invasive pneumococcal disease—United States, 1998–2003. *MMWR* 2005;54:893–897.

317. Centers for Disease Control and Prevention. Behavioral Risk Factor Surveillance System (BRFSS). Available at: http://www.cdc.gov/ brfss/ index.htm. Accessed February 22, 2006.

318. Pilishvili T, Lexau C, Farley MM, et al. Sustained reductions in invasive pneumococcal disease in the era of conjugate vaccine. *J Infect Dis* 1010;201:32–41.

319. Lieu TA, Ray GT, Black SB. Projected cost-effectiveness of pneumococcal conjugate vaccination of healthy infants and young children. *JAMA* 2000;283:1460–1468.

320. Cutts FT, Zaman SMA, Enware G, et al. Efficacy of nine-valent pneumococcal conjugate vaccine against pneumonia and invasive pneumococcal disease in the Gambia: randomized, double-blind, placebo-controlled. *Lancet* 2005;365:1139–1146.

321. Klugman KP, Madhi SA, Huebner RE, et al. A trial of a 9-valent pneumococcal conjugate vaccine in children with and those without HIV infection. *N Engl J Med* 2003;349:1341–1348.

322. Straus WL, Qazi SA, Kundi Z, et al. Antimicrobial resistance and clinical effectiveness of cotrimoxazole versus amoxicillin for pneumonia among children in Pakistan: randomized controlled trial. *Lancet* 1998;352:270–274.

323. Levine OS, Schwartz B, Pierce N, Kane M. Development, evaluation and implementation of *Haemophilus influenzae* type B vaccines for young children in developing countries: current status and priority actions. *Pediatr Infect Dis J* 1998;17: S95–S113.

324. Peltola H, Kayhty M, Virtanen M, Makela PH. Prevention of *Haemophilus influenza* type b bacteremic infections with capsular polysaccharide vaccine. *N Engl J Med* 1984; 310:1561–1566.

325. Adams WG, Deaver KA, Cochi SL, et al. Decline of childhood *Haemophilus influenza* type b (Hib) disease in the Hib vaccine era. *JAMA* 1993;269:221–226.

326. Centers for Disease Control and Prevention. Progress toward eliminating *Haemophilus influenza* type b disease among infants and children—United States, 1987–1997. *MMWR* 1998;41:993–998.

327. Peltola H. Worldwide *Haemophilus influenza* type b disease at the beginning of the 21st century: global analysis of the disease burden 25 years after the use of the polysaccharide vaccine and a decade after the advent of conjugates. *Clin Microb Rev* 2000;13:302–317.

328. Adegobola RA, Secka O, Lahai G, et al. Elimination of *Haemophilus influenza* type b (Hib) disease from the Gambia after the introduction of routine immunization with a Hib conjugate vaccine: a prospective study. *Lancet* 2005;366:144–150.

329. Cowgill KD, Ndiritu M, Nyiro J, et al. Effectiveness of *Haemophilus influenza* type b conjugate vaccine introduction into routine childhood immunization in Kenya. *JAMA* 2006;246:671–678.

330. Hajjeh R. Accelerating introduction of new vaccines barriers to introduction and lessons learned from the recent *Haemophilus influenza* type b vaccine experience. *Trans R Soc B* 2011;386:2827–2832.

331. Sandberg KI, Andersen S, Bjune G. A new approach to global health institutions? A case study of new vaccine introduction and the formation of the GAVI Alliance. *Soc Sci Med* 2010;71:1349–1356.

332. Ladhani S, Ramay ME, Chandra M, Slack MP. No evidence for *Haemophilus influenza* serotype replacement in Europe after introduction of the Hib conjugate vaccine. *Lancet Infect Dis* 2008;8:275–276.

333. Oje LR, O'Loughlin RE, Cohen AL. Global use of *Haemophilus influenza* type b conjugate vaccine. *Vaccine* 2010;28:7117–7132.

334. Levine OS, Knoll MD, Jones A, et al. Global status of *Haemophilus influenza* type b and pneumococcal conjugate vaccines: evidence, policies, and introductions. *Curr Opin Infect Dis* 2010;23:236–241.

335. Crowcroft NS, Stein L, Duclos P, Birmingham M. How best to estimate the global burden of pertussis? *Lancet Infect Dis* 2003;3:413–418.

336. Prevention of pertussis, tetanus, and diphtheria among pregnant and postpartum women and their infants: recommendation of the Advisory Committee on Immunization Practices. *MMWR* 2008;57(RR-4):1–51.

337. Centers for Disease Control and Prevention. Updated recommendations for use of tetanus toxoid, reduced diphtheria toxoid and acellular pertussis vaccine (Tdap) in pregnant women and persons who have or anticipated moving close contact with an infant aged <12 months: Advisory Committee on Immunization Practices (ACIP), 2011. *MMWR* 2011;60(41):1413–1444.

338. World Health Organization. Global reductions in measles mortality 2000–2008 and risk of measles resurgence. *Wkly Epidemiol Rec* 2009;84:505–516.

339. World Health Organization. Measles outbreaks and progress towards meeting measles pre-elimination goals: WHO-African Region 2009–2010. *Wkly Epidemiol Rec* 2011;86:129–140.

340. Parker AA, Staggs W, Dayan GH, et al. Implication of a 2005 measles outbreak in Indiana for sustained elimination of measles in the United States. *N Engl J Med* 2006;355:447–455.

341. Muscat M, Bang H, Wohlfahrt J, et al. Measles in Europe: an epidemiological assessment. *Lancet* 2009;373:387:389.

342. Centers for Disease Control and Prevention. Measles among unvaccinated US residents, aged 6–23 months who have travelled outside the United States 2001–2011. *MMWR* 2011;60:397–400.

343. Dherani M, Pope D, Mascarenhas M, et al. Indoor air pollution from unprocessed solid fuel use and pneumonia risk in children aged under five years: a systematic review and meta-analysis. *Bull WHO* 2008;86:390–398.

344. Smith KR, McCracken JP, Weber MW, et al. Effect of reduction in household air pollution on childhood pneumonia in Guatemala (RESPIRE): a randomized controlled trial. *Lancet* 2011;378;1717–1726.

345. Wang W, Ren P, Sheng T, et al. Simultaneous detection of respiratory viruses in children with acute respiratory infection using two different multiplex reverse transcription-PCR assays. *J Virol Methods* 2009;162:40–48.

3

Oral Transmission of Infection

20

Diarrheal Diseases

Robert E. Black, Christa L. Fischer Walker, and Claudio F. Lanata

INTRODUCTION

Diarrheal diseases are an important global problem, causing high rates of morbidity and mortality, particularly in developing countries.[1] Diarrhea occurs most frequently in conditions of poor environmental sanitation and hygiene, inadequate water supply, poverty, and limited education. Over the last century, many countries experienced economic growth and overall environmental conditions improved dramatically, which in turn decreased the burden of diarrheal diseases in developed countries.[2] As middle-income and developing countries continue to undergo similar economic, social, and epidemiologic transitions, it is likely that the burden of diarrheal disease will continue to decline. Unfortunately, the benefits of economic and social transitions are slow to reach the poorest of the poor, among whom high rates of diarrhea morbidity and mortality remain problematic, especially among children younger than 5 years of age.

Although infectious diarrheal diseases rarely cause death in economically developed countries, diarrhea continues to cause substantial morbidity, and the associated costs of treatment and lost wages continue to be problematic.[3,4] In addition, high rates of diarrhea in some settings, such as hospitals and daycare centers, and outbreaks of foodborne diarrhea have resulted in increased concerns about this disease.[5,6]

From the beginning of the 1980s, substantial global efforts were directed at reduction of diarrheal disease mortality.[7] It was recognized that dehydration as a result of diarrhea played a substantial part in the case-fatality rate for this illness and that such dehydration could be prevented or treated with oral fluid and electrolyte replacement, along with continued feeding. This low-tech approach made effective therapy more widely available through national diarrheal disease control programs in developing countries. Similar clinical approaches have also improved the management of diarrhea in the United States, resulting in improved therapy and a reduction in diarrhea-related mortality. Now, with the introduction of zinc supplementation for the treatment of diarrhea, there is yet one more inexpensive and simple tool for preventing diarrhea mortality. In addition, increased efforts are being directed at prevention of diarrhea through research on the etiology, epidemiology, and transmission patterns of diarrheal diseases.

GENERAL EPIDEMIOLOGY DEFINITIONS

Diarrhea is a symptom complex characterized by stools of decreased consistency and increased number. Although it is possible to define diarrhea as the occurrence of these symptoms simply in comparison to that individual's prior bowel pattern, epidemiologic studies have generally used a more generalizable definition.[8] Most studies now define diarrhea as three or more loose or watery stools during a 24-hour period. At least 2 days free of diarrhea are usually required to define an episode as terminated. Dysentery is a diarrheal disease defined by the presence of blood in loose or liquid stools.

Although most diarrheal episodes resolve within a week, a small proportion continue for 2 weeks or more.[9] Studies in many countries show that the distribution of episode durations is continuous, but skewed toward the longer durations. Thus any definition of "persistent" diarrhea is an arbitrary threshold but a useful indicator of severe disease for diarrhea control programs. The World Health Organization (WHO) operationally defines persistent diarrhea as an episode that lasts for at least 14 days.[10,11] The term *persistent diarrhea*, as used by WHO, encompasses episodes that begin acutely and continue for longer than their expected duration; it is not intended to include infrequent diarrheal disorders, such as hereditary syndromes, gluten-sensitive enteropathy, or other noninfectious conditions.

SOURCES OF DATA

Data to describe the epidemiology of diarrheal diseases come from three main sources: (1) prospective studies in households and health facilities, (2) passive or active surveillance systems, and (3) outbreak investigations. Cross-sectional surveys may also provide limited types of information.

Prospective studies in households in developing countries have generally used visits by health workers at an interval of no more than one week to collect data on symptoms and to obtain specimens of stool for etiologic testing. Such studies in more developed countries often use a combination of household visits and telephone contacts. Prospective studies in health facilities may be done in general outpatient clinics, hospital wards, or special populations; an example of the last is studies of nosocomial infections in newborn nurseries.

Passive surveillance is based on routine reports of a specified disease to public health officials by healthcare workers. In active surveillance, cases are identified by the researcher querying health workers or laboratories about a specific disease. Passive surveillance can be done on a wide scale and is relatively inexpensive, but its value may be limited by reporting that is incomplete, biased, and delayed. Active surveillance of selected diseases might be appropriate if more complete and timely information is needed. In general, developing countries do not have useful passive or active surveillance as a routine system for diarrheal diseases; disease surveillance systems are weak and rates of care-seeking for diarrheal disease are low. In the United States, surveillance systems exist for only a limited number of diarrheal disease pathogens that are reported through laboratory-based passive surveillance.

Investigation of outbreaks of diarrheal diseases can be very useful to rapidly develop information on the risk factors, transmission patterns, and control measures for enteric pathogens. Such investigations can lead to controls to contain that outbreak, as well as help develop measures to prevent future outbreaks.

In developing countries, cross-sectional surveys are commonly conducted to obtain information about health conditions and the use of health services. Although information on the presence of diarrhea in the respondent on the day of survey can be reported accurately, these data may be a biased indicator of the incidence of infectious diarrhea because the symptom of diarrhea is frequent, commonly mild, and may be affected by seasonal variations. Surveys of patients or their families may provide information on recent more clear and memorable events such as hospitalization or death from diarrheal diseases or medical care received for current episodes.

INCIDENCE

A summary of prospective, community-based studies in developing countries concluded that the median annual incidence of all diarrhea in children younger than 5 years of age was 3.4 episodes in 1990 and 2.9 episodes in 2010.[12] Diarrheal incidence has varied in the different settings in which it has been studied (**Table 20-1**). This variation could be due to methodologic differences, such as the definition of diarrhea, or surveillance techniques used in the study. In community-based studies, the incidence has been highest in studies that included a small number of children under surveillance and more frequent home visiting, suggesting that the other studies may have found lower rates because of underreporting.[13] At the same

Table 20-1	Median Age-Adjusted Diarrhea Incidence Rates (Episodes per Child Year) for Children Under 5 Years of Age in Selected WHO Regions of the World	
World Health Organization Region	Number of Prospective Studies Included in Estimate	Age-Adjusted Incidence Rate for Children 0–4 Years of Age
Sub-Saharan Africa	7	5.0
Latin America	14	5.0
Eastern Mediterranean	4	4.9
South-East Asia	6	3.1
Western Pacific	3	3.3
Global	**33**	**3.5**

Reproduced from Boschi-Pinto, C., C.F. Lanata, and R.E. Black, The Global Burden of Childhood Diarrhea in Maternal and Child Health Global Challenges, Programs, and Policies, J. Ehiri, Editor. 2009, p. 225–243, with kind permission from Springer Science+Business Media B.V.

time, it is likely that actual differences in the incidence of diarrhea in different populations exist because of different environmental and host risk factors, as well as the relative frequency of various enteropathogens. Both methodologic- and setting-specific differences may also affect the distribution of diarrheal episode duration. Studies that have the most intensive and frequent surveillance are most likely to identify mild and short-duration episodes that might not otherwise be reported with less intensive case finding.

In developing countries, the incidence of diarrhea varies greatly with age. Generally the first 2 years of life have the highest incidence, followed by a decline with increasing age. Peak incidence is often at 6–11 months of age (**Figure 20-1**). The incidence in boys and girls is generally similar, or slightly higher in boys; however, in some countries boys may be taken to health facilities more often, giving the appearance of higher rates of diarrhea among that group.

In the United States, the Centers for Disease Control and Prevention (CDC) has estimated that there are 21–37 million episodes of diarrhea each year in children younger than 5 years of age; approximately 10% of these illnesses led to a visit to a physician.[14] A prospective community-based study found an annual incidence rate of diarrhea in persons of all ages of 0.63 episodes per person-year of observation.[15]

The highest incidence occurred in infants, who had a rate of 1.43 episodes per person-year. Children, especially those attending daycare centers, have a higher incidence of diarrheal disease, due to a naïve immune system and person-to-person transmission within these settings. However, these rates may be declining, especially among children 6–23 months of age, as the widespread uptake of rotavirus vaccine decreases the incidence and severity of rotavirus diarrheal episodes.[16]

Older children, adolescents, and adults typically have lower incidence rates of diarrhea than children younger than 5 years of age. In a systematic review of prospective and cross-sectional surveys in both developing and developed countries, incidence of diarrhea was less than 1 episode per person per year (**Table 20-2**).[17] The elderly are often thought to be at particular risk of diarrheal diseases because of decreased immune function. This effect can be more pronounced in developed countries among adults in long-term care facilities with unsanitary conditions or increased risk of nosocomial transmission.

Another group of individuals from developed countries who are at increased risk of diarrhea are those who travel to developing countries.[18] Numerous studies have demonstrated that approximately half of such travelers will develop diarrhea during a trip of approximately 2 weeks.

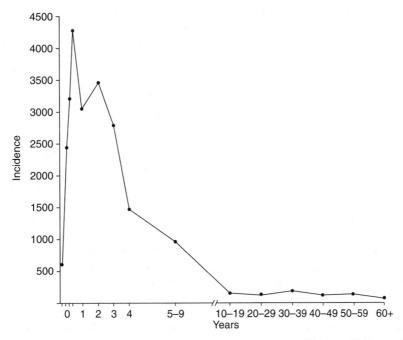

Figure 20-1 Annual age-specific incidence of diarrhea per 1000 person-years assessed by household surveillance. Reprinted from THE LANCET, Vol. 1, RE Black et al. Incidence and severity of Rotavirus and Escherichia coli Diarrhea in Rural Bangladesh. Page 142, © 1981, with permission from Elsevier.

Table 20-2	Median Diarrhea Incidence Rates (Episodes per 100 Person-Years) by Age for Children > 5 Years of Age, Adolescents, and Adults in Selected Regions of the World		
World Health Organization Region	**Number of Studies Included in Estimate**	**Episodes per 100 Person-Years**		
		5–14 Years	**15–54 Years**	**≥ 55 Years**
Americas	6	50.8	62.1	39.5
Eastern Mediterranean	3	88.4	88.4	66.4
Europe	3	56.4	37.2	78.7
South-East Asia	6	67.5	29.9	30.1
Western Pacific	5	26.5	44.3	50.4
Sub-Saharan Africa*	NA	NA	NA	NA

*No data were available from Sub-Saharan Africa.

Walker, C.L. and R.E. Black (2010). Diarrhoea morbidity and mortality in older children, adolescents, and adults. Epidemiol Infect. 138(9): p. 1215–26. Reproduced with permission.

IMPACT OF DIARRHEA

It is well appreciated that diarrheal diseases are important causes of death in developing countries. In 2010, there were approximately 800,000 diarrheal-related deaths among children younger than 5 years of age.[1]

This number represents a substantial reduction from the estimated 3.3 million diarrheal-related deaths per year in the 1980s[13] or from the 2.5 million diarrhea deaths per year in the 1990s.[20] The diarrheal mortality rate is highest in the first year of life.

The case-fatality rates in children in developing countries have been reported to range from 0.1% to 0.5% in settings as diverse as urban Central African Republic, rural Egypt, rural northern India, and rural Indonesia. Overall, the diarrheal case-fatality rate in children younger than 5 years of age in developing countries is estimated to be 0.2%. The case-fatality rate is highest in the youngest children. In rural India, the case-fatality rate for persistent diarrhea was reported to be 20 times higher than that for acute diarrhea.[21]

In more developed countries, the diarrhea mortality rate and the illness case-fatality rate are very low.[3,14] In developed countries, diarrhea deaths are rare among children; for example in the United States, fewer than 50 diarrhea deaths occur each year among children younger than 5 years of age.[19]

Diarrhea mortality among adults has not been widely studied in developing countries where vital registration data are not available to record the cause of death. In low- and middle-income countries, diarrhea mortality rates have been estimated to be in the range of 0.1–2.88/1000 person-years in African countries and 0.3–1.0/1000 person-years in Asian countries.[17] Although diarrhea deaths among older children, adolescents, and adults are rare in developed countries, such disease remains an important cause of death among the elderly. In the United States in 2007, there were 6771 diarrhea deaths among older children, adolescents, and adults, with 82% of these deaths occurring in people 65 years of age and older.[22]

In developing countries, the infectious diseases of childhood have an adverse effect on growth. Diarrheal diseases have the greatest effect of all the infectious diseases, possibly because of the concomitant reduction in appetite, altered feeding practices, and decreased absorption of nutrients, along with the very high prevalence of diarrhea in young children in these settings.[23] The magnitude of the effect of diarrheal diseases on growth seems to be modified by a number of factors. Continued breastfeeding and continued feeding during diarrhea can prevent weight faltering. In addition, children who consume a good diet will not only better withstand the illness, but also have the potential to grow more rapidly after the illness and thereby recover from any weight loss. Because most children in developed countries usually receive appropriate treatment and consume an adequate diet, the growth effects of diarrhea—especially given the low prevalence of the illness—is probably very small. However, in developing countries where children suffer from repeated episodes, the cumulative detrimental effect on growth can be substantial.[24]

Diarrheal diseases impose an economic burden because of the costs of medical care, medications, and lost work. Because the illnesses can largely be managed by fluid and nutritional therapy, much of the medication use, such as antibiotics and so-called antidiarrheal drugs, are an unnecessary expense and are potentially hazardous. Current recommendations for the treatment of diarrhea among children younger than 5 years of age include oral rehydration salts (ORS) and zinc supplementation, both of which are inexpensive and should be available for home management.[25]

MICROBIAL ETIOLOGIES

Relative Importance of Enteropathogens

A large number of bacterial, viral, and parasitic agents have been associated with diarrhea in both developing and developed countries. Because the highest rates of diarrheal diseases and the most severe consequences generally occur in young children, most studies have focused on this age group. Older children and adults may become ill from the same enteropathogens, but the relative frequencies with which these organisms are encountered varies because of immunity acquired from prior infection or from differential exposure to the various pathogens.

Community-based studies are those in which household visits are made to identify cases of diarrhea and to collect fecal specimens for identification of enteropathogens. These studies give the best measure of the overall incidence of diarrheal disease because they are not based on severity or care-seeking and are not subject to bias in the ascertainment of cases. In a review of 61 studies (published 1990–2002) with comprehensive microbiology from developing countries, enterotoxigenic *Escherichia coli* (ETEC) constituted the largest proportion of episodes with a median of 14.1% (**Table 20-3**). The next most commonly found organism has been *Giardia lamblia*. *Campylobacter* species, enteropathogenic *E. coli* (EPEC), and rotavirus were identified in 7–8% of these diarrheal episodes. Other organisms were less frequently observed. The relative importance of these organisms was rather variable in the different studies.

Noroviruses are emerging as an important pathogens leading to diarrhea and vomiting. Because this kind of infection is typically epidemic and seasonal, it is often not included in yearlong studies prospective studies. In the United States, norovirus causes more than 21 million gastrointestinal illnesses each year, many of which will manifest as severe acute diarrhea disease.[26]

Studies in health facilities—either outpatient clinics or hospital wards—involve a more selected group of patients who have sought care because of an illness of greater severity. A review of 98 studies done in outpatient health facilities in developing countries found that rotavirus was the most

frequent enteropathogen, with a median incidence of 18% (Table 20-3). However, these studies demonstrated that bacterial pathogens predominated overall, accounting for approximately 40% of illnesses. Of these, the most common was *C. jejuni*. As illustrated in the range of percentage identification in **Table 20-4**, each of these bacterial pathogens can be very frequent in some settings. Among the parasites, *C. parvum* and *G. lamblia* were the most frequently identified. A review of 107 studies in hospitalized children found that rotavirus was the most common

Table 20-3	Percentage Identification of Selected Enteropathogens in Children with Diarrhea in Outpatient Clinic Studies in Developing Countries (98 studies)	
Enteropathogen	**Median (%)**	**Interquartile Range (%)**
Campylobacter sp	12.6	4.0–16.7
Cryptosporidium parvum	2.5	0.8–4.0
Entameba histolytica	0.6	0.1–1.4
Enteropathogenic *Escherichia coli*	9.1	4.5–19.4
Enterotoxigenic *Escherichia coli*	8.7	5.2–15.3
Giardia lamblia	3.0	1.2–5.7
Rotavirus	18.0	13.3–30.7
Salmonella sp	3.2	1.3–6.7
Shigella sp	5.8	2.4–11.0

Table 20-4	Percentage Identification of Selected Enteropathogens in Children with Diarrhea in Community-Based Studies in Developing Countries (61 studies)	
Enteropathogen	**Median (%)**	**Interquartile Range (%)**
Campylobacter sp	7.6	3.9–13.4
Cryptosporidium parvum	5.7	3.8–8.5
Entameba histolytica	3.5	0.8–5.8
Enteropathogenic *Escherichia coli*	8.8	6.6–13.2
Enterotoxigenic *Escherichia coli*	14.1	6.7–22.6
Giardia lamblia	10.2	7.4–18.8
Rotavirus	8.0	4.2–15.3
Salmonella sp	0.9	0.2–3.1
Shigella sp	4.6	2.2–7.6

Table 20-5	Percentage Identification of Selected Enteropathogens in Children with Diarrhea in Hospital Studies in Developing Countries (107 studies)	
Enteropathogen	Median (%)	Interquartile Range (%)
Campylobacter sp	4.5	2.3–9.9
Cryptosporidium parvum	3.4	1.3–7.9
Entameba histolytica	0.7	0.2–3.7
Enteropathogenic *Escherichia coli*	15.6	8.3–27.5
Enterotoxigenic *Escherichia coli*	9.5	6.4–16.1
Giardia lamblia	1.6	0.5–5.5
Rotavirus	25.4	17.0–37.7
Salmonella sp	4.4	2.9–8.4
Shigella sp	5.6	2.8–10.4

pathogen, followed by EPEC and ETEC (**Table 20-5**). A number of recent studies in hospitalized children with diarrhea in East Asian countries have found that 40–60% had rotavirus identified.[27,28]

In general, community-based studies identified an enteropathogen in approximately half of the episodes, and the health facility–based studies identified an enteropathogen in nearly 75% of the episodes—although these rates are difficult to estimate from the studies available, because most studies do not set out to test for all possible pathogens. The detection tests for many of the enteropathogens do not have optimal sensitivity, so these studies may have underestimated their incidence. Although it is likely that these enteropathogens individually account for only a small proportion of the episodes, collectively they may cause many of the episodes not associated with one of the more common enteropathogens. Other enteropathogens of interest are adenovirus and astrovirus,[29,30] as well as *Bacteroides fragilis* and *Clostridium difficile*,[31] particularly among patients taking antibiotics.[32]

The identification of an enteropathogen from feces during diarrhea does not necessarily mean that that organism is causing the illness. In fact, studies that have performed comprehensive microbiology analyses have often found two or more enteropathogens simultaneously, making it difficult to assign causality. These mixed infections could occur because the individual is exposed simultaneously or sequentially, or an individual may have an asymptomatic infection with one enteropathogen at the time of exposure to another disease-causing agent.

Asymptomatic enteric infections are common in developing country populations but less so in developed country settings. In community-based studies, routine assessment of enteropathogens allows for a comparison between times when the children have diarrhea and when they are healthy. Community-based studies often find a similar rate of identification of enteropathogens in children when they have diarrhea and when they do not. For example, in nine community-based studies in developing countries, the median identification of *Campylobacter* species was 8% during diarrhea, compared to 7% when patients did not have diarrhea (**Table 20-6**). Some enteropathogens, such as rotavirus, may have a higher rate of identification during diarrhea episodes. In health facility-based studies, children who came to the same facility for a reason other than diarrhea may be used as controls. Often the relative prevalence of different enteropathogens is more distinct between diarrhea cases and controls in these studies.

The pathogenicity (i.e., the number of infections with diarrhea divided by the total number of infections) varies by enteropathogen and in some cases by age (**Table 20-7**). For example, the pathogenicity of rotavirus is lower in the first 6 months of life than in the second 6 months, presumably due to passive protection from maternally derived antibody in early infancy.[33] In contrast, some pathogens, such as *Shigella* species, have a higher pathogenicity early in childhood. This difference may arise because the initial infection induces some immunity, which protects more effectively against subsequent illness than against infection.

Table 20-6	Median Percentage Identification of *Campylobacter* sp and Rotavirus from Cases of Diarrhea and Controls without Diarrhea in Community-Based Studies in Developing Countries					
	Community-Based Studies			Health Facility–Based Studies		
Enteropathogen	(*N*)	Diarrhea	Control	(*N*)	Diarrhea	Control
Campylobacter sp	9	8	7	29	7	2
Rotavirus	11	4	1	31	21	4

Reproduced from Black, R.E., et al., Incidence and etiology of infantile diarrhea and major routes of transmission in Huascar, Peru. *Am J Epidemiol*, 1989. 129(4): p. 785–99. By permission of Oxford University Press.

Table 20-7	Pathogenicity of Selected Enteropathogens by Age Group in Peruvian Infants in a Community-Based Study					
	Age 0–5 Months			Age 6–11 Months		
Enteropathogen	Infections with Diarrhea (*N*)	Total Infections	Pathogenicity	Infections with Diarrhea (*N*)	Total Infections	Pathogenicity
Campylobacter sp	73	177	0.41	65	188	0.35
Enterotoxigenic *Escherichia coli*	42	119	0.35	40	103	0.39
Rotavirus	18	33	0.55	23	28	0.82
Shigella sp	14	17	0.82	16	34	0.47

Reproduced from Black, R.E., et al., Incidence and etiology of infantile diarrhea and major routes of transmission in Huascar, Peru. *Am J Epidemiol*, 1989. 129(4): p. 785–99. By permission of Oxford University Press.

Table 20-8	Percentage of Children <5 Years Experiencing Dehydration During Diarrheal Episodes by Enteropathogen in Two Community-Based Studies in Rural Bangladesh			
Enteropathogen	Episodes (*N*)	Dehydration (*N*)	Dehydration (%)
Rotavirus	78	28	36
Vibrio cholerae	3	1	33
Enterotoxigenic *Escherichia coli*	322	17	5
Other	843	17	2
Total	1246	63	76

Data from Black, R.E., et al., Incidence and severity of rotavirus and *Escherichia coli* diarrhoea in rural Bangladesh. Implications for vaccine development. *Lancet*, 1981. 1(8212): p. 141–3 and Black, R.E., et al., Longitudinal studies of infectious diseases and physical growth of children in rural Bangladesh. II. Incidence of diarrhea and association with known pathogens. *Am J Epidemiol*, 1982. 115(3): p. 315–24.

The virulence (i.e., the number of severe illnesses divided by the total number of illnesses) may also vary by enteropathogen. This can be illustrated by the propensity of the organism to cause an illness that leads to dehydration. In community-based studies in Bangladesh,[34,35] children with rotavirus diarrhea or cholera are most likely to develop dehydration (**Table 20-8**). Those persons with ETEC had a modestly increased rate of dehydration compared with all other types of diarrhea.

In the United States, the relative importance of the various enteropathogens differs from that in developing countries (**Table 20-9**). In studies done in health facilities, rotavirus is the most important enteropathogen associated with diarrhea, just as it is in developing countries, but this is expected to change owing to the widespread use of the rotavirus vaccine since 2006.[36] In general, the bacterial causes of diarrhea are less important in developed countries, although *Campylobacter* species and *Salmonella* species may be important in some settings. This pattern may be shifted closer to a developing country pattern in certain higher-risk populations. For example,

residents of Indian reservations in the United States have shown higher rates of diarrhea than the general population, although good access to medical care has now reduced the diarrheal mortality to a very low level.[37,38] In such settings (**Table 20-10**), rotavirus is still the most important pathogen, but other organisms such as ETEC and *Campylobacter* species may play a more prominent role than they do in the general U.S. population.

In the United States, it is estimated that each year there are 1300 deaths, 56,000 hospitalizations, and 9.4 million illnesses caused by foodborne infections, counting both outbreaks and sporadic cases caused by 31 major enteric pathogens.[39] In 2006, the CDC reported more than 1200 outbreaks of foodborne disease.[40] In the 49% of cases for which a cause was identified, norovirus was the pathogen most often identified, being responsible for 54% of the outbreaks. Traditionally, *Salmonella*, *Staphylococcus*, and *Clostridium perfringens* have been considered the main responsible organisms, and they continue to be important. A number of other organisms that are commonly spread by the foodborne route (notably

Table 20-9	Percentage Identification of Selected Enteropathogens in Children with Diarrhea and Controls Attending an Outpatient Clinic in the United States	
Enteropathogen	Diarrhea Cases (N = 246)	Controls (N = 155)
Adenovirus (enteric)	4	0
Aeromonas sp	6	7
Campylobacter sp	<1	<1
C. parvum	<1	0
ETEC	0	0
G. lamblia	<1	0
Rotavirus	22	10
Salmonella sp	5	0
Shigella sp	0	—
Vibrios	<1	0

Reproduced from Kotloff KL, Wasserman SB, Steciak JY et al. Acute diarrhea in Baltimore children attending an outpatient clinic. *The Pediatric Infectious Disease Journal*, Lippincott Williams & Wilkins. 1988;7:752–9.

Table 20-10	Percentage Identification of Selected Enteropathogens in Children with Diarrhea in Different Settings on a U.S. Indian Reservation		
Enteropathogen	Home	Outpatient Clinic (N = 535)	Hospital (N = 488)
Adenovirus	2	3	5
Aeromonas sp	1	1	2
Campylobacter sp	5	4	3
Enterotoxigenic Escherichia coli	5	5	14
Rotavirus	8	6	24
Salmonella sp	<1	1	1
Shigella sp	7	6	5
Vibrios	0	0	<1

Adapted from RB Sack et al. (1995). Diarrhoeal Disease in the White Mountain Apaches: Clinical Studies. *J Diarrhoeal Dis Res*. Mar 13(1):12–17.

Campylobacter and *E. coli* O157:H7) have also caused substantial morbidity.

In an investigation of an outbreak of diarrhea possibly related to consumption of contaminated food, it is important to consider the different clinical presentations of these pathogens.[41] For example,

staphylococcal illness often features severe vomiting along with diarrhea, does not usually present with fever, and generally lasts about a day. *C. perfringens* is usually characterized by diarrhea without fever and also lasts less than a day. Salmonella is often associated with diarrhea, vomiting, and fever that may last for several days. The incubation period of the causes of infectious foodborne diarrhea also differs: *Staphylococcus* has an incubation period of 2–7 hours, but *C. perfringens* has an incubation of 8–14 hours and *Salmonella* an incubation of 2–3 days.

Specific Enteropathogens
Bacterial Agents

Campylobacter jejuni and *Campylobacter coli* cause watery diarrhea and sometimes dysentery, especially in young children.[42] Immunity acquired from previous *Campylobacter* infections is the likely explanation for the low rate of illness in adults and the high prevalence of asymptomatic infection in developing countries. In the United States, *Campylobacter* species infection occurs in all age groups, with peak incidence being noted in the first year of life and in young adults. The higher rate of disease in young adults has been linked to food-handling errors made by these individuals when cooking. There is often a summer seasonality with *Campylobacter* species infections.

Escherichia coli can produce diarrhea by a variety of mechanisms.[43] Although *E. coli* organisms are part of the normal flora of the intestine, this organism may also possess a variety of virulence properties. The diarrheagenic potential of *E. coli* was recognized decades ago with the so-called enteropathogenic *E. coli* (EPEC).[44] Previously, these organisms were identified by their serotypes once they were implicated in a diarrhea outbreak. This nomenclature has now been superseded. Diarrheagenic *E. coli* are designated based on the demonstration of virulence properties or laboratory characteristics felt to be associated with virulence properties. Only some of the strains previously identified by serology such as EPEC have been found to produce "attaching and effacing" lesions in the intestine and patterns of adherence in tissue culture assays.[43] EPEC strains are now identified by their adherence pattern in tissue cultures or by the presence of plasmids that confer that capacity. The pathogenic role of subgroups of adherent *E. coli* in acute or persistent diarrhea has been well established; the role of other variants is still in question.[45-47] Persistent diarrhea in association with HIV infection is usually linked to the same enteropathogens as diarrhea in HIV-negative persons, but some additional organisms can be found.[48,49]

Other strains of enterotoxigenic *E. coli* produce a heat-labile toxin (LT) or heat-stable toxin (ST), or both, and a number of assays can now be used to evaluate these organisms for toxin production or the genetic capability to produce these toxins.[43] Although these assays are not optimally sensitive because they require testing of a small number of organisms in the feces, ETEC remains the most frequent cause of diarrheal illnesses in children in developing countries. It has been demonstrated further that many ETEC strains produce colonization factors that are important in pathogenesis, indicating that not all toxin-producing *E. coli* are necessarily pathogens.[43] This may be a partial explanation for the high frequency of asymptomatic infections with ETEC in developing countries, but it is also clear that acquired immunity may protect individuals from illness, but not colonization.[50] An enteroinvasive type of *E. coli* has been described as resulting in dysentery and as having a pathogenesis similar to that found with *Shigella* species. These organisms may occasionally cause outbreaks but do not appear to be frequent causes of endemic diarrheal diseases.

In the early 1980s, *E. coli* O157:H7 was identified as an important cause of hemorrhagic colitis.[51] These organisms produce exotoxins, which resemble the Shiga toxin of *S. dysenteriae* type 1. Such entero-hemorrhagic *E. coli* (EHEC) has developed into a major public health problem in the United States and Canada, but appears to be very infrequent in developing countries. Large outbreaks of EHEC infection have occurred in which some cases developed hemolytic uremic syndrome or other serious complications, which can lead to death in approximately 2% of patients.[52] The primary reservoir for EHEC is cattle, and transmission to humans has been most commonly related to consumption of undercooked ground beef or unpasteurized milk. Outbreaks have also been traced to other foods and person-to-person transmission, predominately in daycare centers and other types of institutions.

Salmonella species continue to be an important public health problem in developed countries, but their importance varies in developing countries. In the United States, the highest attack rate for salmonellosis is in infants, but elderly and immunosuppressed individuals are also at higher risk of this disease.[53] *Salmonella* species are found in animal hosts, especially poultry. In fact, *S. enteritidis* can colonize the ovaries of egg-laying hens, which can result in infection of the egg before it is laid.[54] The rates of salmonellosis have increased in developed countries in the

last decade, and nearly all of this increase is due to foodborne transmission. Salmonellosis often has a summer seasonality.

Four serogroups of *Shigella* have been identified. In developing countries, *S. flexneri* is the most common infectious agent, followed by *S. sonnei*, *S. boydii*, and *S. dysenteriae*; however, outbreaks of *S. dysenteriae* type 1 (or Shiga's bacillus) have occurred in many countries.[55,56] The resulting illnesses are often severe, resulting in a high case-fatality rate, and these organisms may be resistant to most commonly used antibiotics. In the United States and most other developed countries, *S. sonnei* is the most common serogroup, with *S. flexneri* accounting for most of the remaining cases.[57] In endemic situations, shigellosis is primarily a disease of children, reflecting the likelihood of fecal–oral transmission in this age group. Foodborne and waterborne outbreaks occur occasionally, but the predominant route of transmission is from person to person. Shigellosis has a seasonality in which it is predominantly observed in the warm months, although in developing countries this pattern may also be influenced by the availability of water and changes in the level of personal hygiene.

Cholera is a diarrheal illness caused by infection of the small intestine with *Vibrio cholerae*. It has been feared for centuries because cholera epidemics can result in high mortality and social disruption.[58] A series of global pandemics of cholera have occurred. The seventh pandemic, which is still continuing, is generally thought to have begun in 1961. This pandemic, caused by the *V. cholerae* biotype El Tor, spread from Sulawesi throughout Asia, the Middle East, the Soviet Union, and Africa, and into a few countries of Europe. North America did not have any indigenous cases of cholera in this century until a single case was detected in Texas in 1973. It has subsequently been discovered that *V. cholerae* El Tor is endemic in the Gulf Coast area of Texas and Louisiana, with cases sporadically occurring in that area. Latin America had been spared from cholera epidemics since the end of the last century, but in 1991 cholera reappeared in Peru. It subsequently spread throughout much of South and Central America, with some cases being imported into the United States.[59]

All previous cholera pandemics had been due to *V. cholerae* serotype O1 until 1992, when cases of cholera associated with a *V. cholerae* strain that did not include agglutinate with O1 antisera were reported from India and Bangladesh. This strain, which was subsequently designated serotype O139, caused epidemic disease throughout India and Bangladesh and cases in a number of other countries of Asia.[60] After the initial outbreaks due to this organism, the rates of disease have decreased, but the strain persists, along with *V. cholerae* O1. These outbreaks demonstrate the potential for strains of *V. cholerae* other than serotype O1 to cause epidemic cholera and may represent the beginning of a new pandemic; the threat is especially great immediately following natural or human-made disasters—as was seen in the 2010 cholera outbreaks in Haiti and Pakistan, both of which occurred after major earthquakes.

In endemic areas, cholera predominantly affects children 2–15 years of age, but may also cause a large proportion of severe watery diarrheal diseases in adults during the season of transmission.[58] Immunity develops after initial infection, although asymptomatic infections may still occur. In areas that have not had exposure to *V. cholerae* previously, the entire population is susceptible to this infection, resulting in high outbreak attack rates in children and adults. *V. cholerae* may have an environmental reservoir in marshes and rivers and is commonly spread by seafood, as well as directly by water.

A number of other *Vibrio* species may cause diarrhea, as well as bacteremia and other serious illness.[61] *V. parahemolyticus* can cause diarrhea, including outbreaks. These illnesses occur with low frequency in most countries, but in Japan *V. parahemolyticus* is a frequent cause of diarrhea and outbreaks.[62] There is recent evidence documenting that *V. parahemolyticus* serotype O3:K6 is spreading from Asia in a pandemic that has reached Africa and more recently South America.[63] In North America, as well as other countries, *V. vulnificus* and non-O1 *V. cholerae* also cause diarrhea and systemic infection.[61,64]

Aeromonas hydrophila is often found, and *Plesiomonas shigelloides* is less frequently found, during diarrhea outbreaks in developing countries.[65,66] These organisms appear to be much less frequent in developed country settings. At least for *A. hydrophila*, the higher rate of isolation of the organism during diarrhea compared with controls suggests a causative role.[67] However, the importance of these organisms and the mechanisms by which they may cause diarrhea are unknown.

Yersinia enterocolitica may cause diarrhea and other abdominal symptoms. It is a common cause of disease in Western Europe, and outbreaks have occurred in the United States as well, primarily from contaminated meat and milk.[68] This organism has been assayed for in a number of developing countries, but has been rarely found in cases of diarrhea.[69]

Clostridium difficile causes colitis associated with the use of a variety of antibiotics. Although this organism can be found in acute diarrhea, the causative relationship is unclear.[70]

A number of other bacterial enteropathogens are associated with diarrheal diseases. These organisms are primarily involved in foodborne disease outbreaks, but may also cause sporadic cases of diarrhea. *Bacillus cereus* has been associated with outbreaks related to consumption of cooked rice, and *Clostridium perfringens* is usually associated with outbreaks in which the spores of the organism germinate in anaerobic conditions after cooking of meat, resulting in the production of the toxin that causes diarrhea.[71] *Staphylococcus aureus* outbreaks of diarrhea may be caused by an infected food handler contaminating food. *S. aureus* produces a heat-stable enterotoxin that, when ingested, causes the illness.

Strains of *Bacteroides fragilis* that produce an enterotoxin have recently been associated with diarrheal diseases, both in the United States and in Bangladesh.[31,72] Because of limited availability of the diagnostic assay, the importance of this enteropathogen is unknown.

Viral Agents

Rotaviruses are the most important viral agents causing diarrheal diseases. This type of illness largely occurs in the first two years of life throughout the world.[73] Rotavirus diarrhea has a winter seasonality in most developed countries, but the seasonality in developing countries is less marked, with disease generally occurring throughout the year. In addition to reflecting the role of rotavirus as an endemic enteropathogen, outbreaks have occurred in daycare centers and hospitals. The organism may be a cause of a small proportion of disease in adults, such as caregivers for small children and in travelers from developed countries to developing countries.[74]

Enteric adenoviruses of serotypes 40 and 41 are the second most important cause of viral diarrhea.[75,76] These organisms appear to occur worldwide. Norovirus (previously referred to as Norwalk agent and related 27-nm caliciviruses, such as Hawaii and Snow Mountain agents) causes watery diarrhea and/or vomiting.[30,77] Several studies indicate that norovirus agent alone may account for 2–5% of childhood diarrheas in developing countries.[78] It may have a similar or greater importance in the United States.

Other viruses or viruslike particles have been proposed as causes of diarrhea. For example, coronaviruses, astroviruses, and small round virus-like particles have all been found during diarrhea.[29,79,80] Pestivirus has also been reported in association with diarrhea.[81] The causative role of these agents and their importance are unknown.

Parasitic Agents

Cryptosporidium parvum, a coccidian parasite, is likely the most important parasitic cause of diarrheal diseases.[82] It has a global distribution as an endemic disease, but may also occur in outbreaks, including large waterborne outbreaks from municipal water systems. Cryptosporidial cysts are very resistant to chlorine and must be removed from drinking water by filtration. Related organisms of the true coccidia, such as *Isospora belli*, may cause diarrhea but appear to be uncommon except in association with HIV/AIDS[83] immune suppression. Diarrhea associated with microsporidia also occurs with HIV/AIDS, but the role of this organism in immunocompetent individuals has not been described.[84]

Cyclospora cayetanensis, previously referred to as "cyanobacterium-like bodies" and by other names, is a newly described enteropathogen.[85] These coccidian parasites have been found in a number of developing countries and may be of comparable importance to *C. parvum*. In developed countries, these organisms have been known to cause diarrheal disease in HIV/AIDS patients and in travelers to developing countries.[85,86] Outbreaks have been reported from consumption of imported raspberries.

Giardia lamblia is a common protozoan with a very high carriage rate in many developing country populations, particularly in children.[87] This organism does not appear to be an important diarrheal pathogen in most developing countries, however.[88,89] In developed countries, *G. lamblia* may be a frequent parasitic cause of diarrhea.[90] Infections are passed from person to person and are common in daycare centers and other institutions. Waterborne or foodborne outbreaks have also occurred. Like *C. parvum*, *G. lamblia* is resistant to chlorine, particularly in cold water, and prevention of waterborne giardiasis depends on adequate water filtration to remove the parasitic cysts.

E. histolytica can cause amebiasis and may be associated with extra-intestinal complications, such as liver abscess.[91,92] This parasite appears to be an infrequent cause of childhood diarrhea or dysentery in developing countries, but is rare in developed countries. Other protozoan infections can be associated with diarrhea, including those due to *Balantidium coli* and *Chilomastix mesnili*. *Blastocystis hominis* is of uncertain pathogenicity.[93]

Most intestinal helminthic infections are not associated with diarrhea, but dysentery and even rectal prolapse have been associated with severe *Trichuris trichiura* infections and diarrhea with other intestinal parasites.[94]

TRANSMISSION ROUTES

General Factors

Diarrheal diseases result from exposure of a susceptible host to a pathogenic organism. Nearly all enteropathogens are transmitted by direct contact with human feces or indirectly through contact with feces through water, food, or eating utensils. Some enteropathogens have an animal or environmental reservoir, and contact with the pathogen from these sources may then result in infection. It is clear that populations of lower socioeconomic status or educational level may have a higher exposure to enteropathogens due to residence in poorer environmental conditions or less hygienic practices, particularly in child care.

Water

Waterborne transmission has been documented for most enteropathogens.[95] For some organisms, such as *V. cholerae* and norovirus, this may be the predominant form of transmission, but even for these pathogens foodborne transmission may also be common. The use of contaminated sources of water for bathing, washing, swimming, cleaning, and cleaning feeding utensils have been implicated in transmission, as well as consumption of contaminated water.[96]

In developing country settings without access to tap water in the home, poor handling practices of water stored in the house—mainly involving introduction of contaminated hands or utensils into water containers—have been linked to an increased risk for diarrheal diseases.[97] Studies have now documented that water quantity is more important than water quality in determining risk of diarrheal disease, which highlights the importance of access to a source of water within a short walk from the home (i.e., less than 30 minutes round trip).[95,98] This factor arises because water availability is important for hygienic behaviors that would prevent much of the transmission by person to person or through food.

Food

Breastfeeding, especially exclusive breastfeeding in the first 6 months of life, protects against diarrheal diseases.[99,100] Breastfed children are exposed to fewer enteropathogens than might be in food or water. Furthermore, breastmilk may provide passive immunologic protection against some of the organisms. Especially in developing countries, the incidence of diarrheal diseases increases sharply with the introduction of weaning foods.[101] These foods are often heavily contaminated, and studies have demonstrated the relationship between consumption of more contaminated foods and illness related to organisms such as ETEC.[102]

The level of bacterial contamination may vary by the type of food and by food-handling practices.[103] It is strongly influenced by the storage time between initial preparation and consumption because many of the bacterial enteropathogens can multiply in the food during storage at ambient temperature.[102] Food may be contaminated in the home or before it reaches the home. In developing countries, most uncooked foods should be assumed to be contaminated. Fruits and vegetables can be contaminated during irrigation with water contaminated with sewage (intentionally as a fertilizer or unintentionally) or through improper handling. In the United States and other developed countries, some foods, such as chicken, must also be assumed to be contaminated with *Salmonella* species and *Campylobacter* species.[71] In addition, the recent outbreaks of *E. coli* O157:H7 suggest that all ground beef must be considered potentially contaminated with this organism. Until further control of these infections in the reservoir and at the processing level is implemented, thorough cooking of food is the primary means of preventing disease.

In developing countries, much of the food production is still done on a small scale at the local level. In contrast, in developed countries, there is an increasing trend toward large-scale production and distribution of food. These production and slaughtering techniques—most notably in the poultry industry and production of hamburger—make contamination with enteropathogens much more widespread. In addition, developed countries are increasingly importing food from all over the world.[71] As a consequence of this practice, consumers are at risk of exposure to contaminated fruits and vegetables, as well as other products.

Feeding Utensils

In developing countries, baby bottles, bottle nipples, cups, spoons, and food containers are frequently contaminated with fecal bacteria, as well as specific enteropathogens.[33,104] These utensils are difficult to keep clean in unhygienic environments. Although boiling or application of a sterilizing solution is effective in eliminating contamination, the use of these methods may be inconsistent. The risk of contamination of feeding utensils, as well as of water and food, makes exclusive breastfeeding for infants younger than 6 months of age and continued breastfeeding for older babies vital in settings with poor environmental sanitation.

Animals

Animals may be the reservoir for a variety of enteropathogens.[52,105,106] Poultry is the primary source for *C. jejuni* and *Salmonella* species; the main animal reservoir for *E. coli* O157:H7 is cattle. *C. perfringens* is also commonly associated with animals and *Y. enterocolitica* commonly with pigs and cows. Shellfish may be a reservoir for *V. cholerae* and other *Vibrio* species.

Flies

A variety of enteropathogens have been isolated from flies, including bacteria, viruses, and parasites.[107] The organisms may be carried on the external surface of the fly or may be ingested, in which case the survival of bacteria may be prolonged. Flies may contaminate food or even water in a house when feeding. Evidence for flies as a means of transmission is inconclusive, however.[107,108] Intervention studies have shown that fly control at a military camp in Israel decreased diarrhea, and particularly shigellosis.[109] These findings were subsequently confirmed through a study conducted in Pakistan.[110] More such studies are needed to evaluate the value of fly control as a major public health intervention in developing countries.

Hygiene

Personal hygiene practices are closely linked with person-to-person transmission of diarrhea.[111] Of the various hygiene practices, hand washing is probably the most widely studied. The increased risk of diarrhea with inadequate hand washing, in particular after defecation or cleaning a child, has been documented. Intervention studies have confirmed this relationship by demonstrating a reduction in the incidence of diarrhea with proper hand washing.[112]

Hand washing with soap is effective in eliminating fecal contamination, even viruses. In developing countries where soap may not be available, hand washing with mud, ash, or other agents that facilitate removal of contaminants from the hands has also been found to be effective, but rinsing with water alone less so.[113] Hand-washing promotion programs seem effective in reducing diarrheal diseases as well as respiratory and skin diseases, but require further evaluation before they are widely implemented.[114,115]

Another important hygiene behavior is proper disposal of fecal material. In developing countries with poor sanitation, defecation in the yard or in open areas as well as nonhygienic methods of feces disposal are demonstrated risk factors for diarrhea.[116] Crawling infants who may come in contact with the feces on the ground are at particular risk of such disease.[117] The need for proper sanitation facilities is great in the home and especially in places, such as schools, where young children are at particular risk.

HOST RISK FACTORS

Malnutrition

Malnutrition and diarrheal diseases are often found together in developing countries because they coexist in children living in poor socioeconomic and environmental conditions. In addition, malnutrition may be a direct risk factor for diarrheal diseases through compromised immunologic function and tissue regenerative capability. Malnourished children in developing countries have been found to have a 70% higher risk of diarrhea.[118–120] Other studies have found no increase in diarrheal incidence in malnourished children.[121] Nearly all studies show that malnourished children have diarrheal episodes of longer duration and often greater severity.[121]

Micronutrient Deficiencies

In addition to general malnutrition, specific micronutrient deficiencies may result in either a higher incidence or a greater severity of diarrhea. Vitamin A deficiency is associated with more severe diarrhea, and in populations deficient in vitamin A, supplementation with this nutrient reduces diarrheal mortality.[122,123] Zinc deficiency is also related to diarrhea. Zinc supplementation in populations presumed to be deficient in this nutrient reduces the incidence and duration of diarrheal episodes.[124] Other micronutrients may be related to diarrhea as well. As with malnutrition in general, these specific micronutrient deficiencies may result in immunologic compromise or reduced ability to repair damaged intestinal mucosa.

Gastric Acid

The acidic contents of the stomach are an important barrier to ingested enteropathogens, especially many of the bacterial agents. Hypochlorhydria may increase the likelihood that sufficient quantity of the pathogen would reach the small intestine and cause infection.[125] Thus medical conditions that reduce gastric acid or medications that neutralize the acid may lead to a greater frequency or severity of diarrheal diseases. Furthermore, *Helicobacter pylori* infection in the stomach is common in children in developing countries.[126] Because this infection may result in hypochlorhydria, it may lead to a greater risk of diarrhea.

Genetic Factors

There may be some genetic predisposition to diarrheal diseases, but current evidence on this front is very limited. Persons of blood group O have a greater risk of developing cholera and experience more severe illness than persons of other blood groups.[127] Few studies have been done to examine such a relationship between blood group and other enteropathogens, but the limited data available do not demonstrate a strong relationship for ETEC or *Vibrio* species other than *V. cholerae* O1.[128,129]

Immunity

Immunity plays an important role in susceptibility to enteropathogens. Maternal antibody is provided to the infant through breastmilk; it protects against a variety of enteric infections. Transplacental antibody may also play a role in some individuals. Acquired immunity is established after an episode of diarrheal disease or, in some cases, after even an asymptomatic infection.

Persons with compromised immune systems, such as those resulting from micronutrient deficiencies, have a reduced resistance to enteric infection. Studies have shown that depressed cell-mediated immunity is associated with an increase in both acute and persistent diarrhea.[119,130] Immunocompetence in a child can be compromised by previous viral infections, such as measles or influenza, or by other infections, such as tuberculosis or typhoid fever. These infections, along with micronutrient deficiencies, can increase the risk of diarrhea through alteration in immune function or by other mechanisms.

Cholera was the first diarrheal disease for which a vaccine became available. A parenteral cholera vaccine provides approximately 50% protection lasting for less than 6 months. New killed or live *V. cholerae* vaccines may offer greater efficacy and duration of protection. An oral vaccine consisting of killed *Vibrio* species may provide 50–60% efficacy for 2 years after vaccination.[131] When tested in Bangladesh, one variation of the killed whole-cell vaccine also proved to be effective in mass vaccination against cholera,[132] although its public use to date has been limited to travelers and in the control of outbreaks in refugee populations.

An effective rhesus-based rotavirus vaccine introduced in the United States in 1998 was withdrawn from the market in 1999 due to rare side effects (intussusception). Currently, two human-based rotavirus vaccines are on the market in the United States; these vaccines have been shown to be highly efficacious, albeit less so when tested in developing country settings.[133] Of course, because of the high rates of rotavirus disease in low-income settings, even a vaccine with lower efficacy is still an important public health tool. Vaccines for many of the other important enteropathogens, such as ETEC and *Shigella*, are also in development and under evaluation.

ANTIMICROBIAL RESISTANCE

Among the bacterial enteropathogens, a progressive increase in resistance to antibiotics has been observed.[134] For some of the enteropathogens that have an associated animal reservoir, this resistance may result from the large-scale use of antimicrobial agents to prevent or treat infections in the animals. Also, the use of low-dose antibiotics in animal feed to enhance weight gain is suspected to increase the risk of the emergence of antibiotic resistance.

In addition, extensive use of antibiotics for human infections plays a part in the development of antimicrobial resistance. Especially problematic is the extensive use of antibiotics in developing countries without prescription or medical supervision. This practice has resulted in outbreaks caused by organisms such as *V. cholerae* and *Shigella dysenteriae* type 1 that are resistant to most commonly used antibiotics. Unfortunately, in developing countries, alternative antibiotics are often unavailable or unaffordable.

STRATEGIES FOR CONTROL

Reduction of mortality from diarrheal diseases by appropriate treatment is the mainstay of diarrheal disease control programs.[135] Correction of dehydration by oral rehydration salts (ORS), or intravenous therapy if necessary; zinc supplementation; and maintenance of nutrition by continued feeding during illness are important tools for reducing diarrheal disease mortality throughout the world. The addition of zinc supplements to the treatment regimen offers an inexpensive and effective alternative to the use of unnecessary antibiotics.[136] Antibiotic therapy should be used only in cases of dysentery with presumed shigellosis or for cholera; in these circumstances, it can reduce the illness severity and the case-fatality rate. In addition, a few of the parasitic agents can be specifically treated with antimicrobial agents.

For developing countries, reduction in the incidence of diarrheal diseases is a continuing challenge. Reviews of intervention research concluded that promotion of breastfeeding and improved weaning practices are a high priority for diarrheal prevention

in such areas.[137] Successful breastfeeding promotion programs that encourage exclusive breastfeeding (nothing else given to the infant—especially not water, which may be contaminated) during the first 6 months of life and any breastfeeding in children from 6 to 23 months of age will reduce diarrheal incidence early in infancy and improve childhood diarrheal mortality rates.[138] Improved weaning practices could have the added advantage of improving the nutritional content of the diet as well as decreasing microbial contamination.[139,140] Improved water supply, sanitation, and hygiene behaviors would also be expected to reduce diarrheal incidence. Hand washing with soap had been shown to reduce diarrhea by 48%, while improved sanitation may reduce diarrhea incidence by another 36%. Although traditional randomized trials are difficult to execute for water and sanitation interventions, no one will dispute that improving water quality and quantity will also decrease diarrhea incidence.[112] The recent demonstration that disinfection of water at the point of use can reduce diarrhea points to another feasible means of improving water quality and thereby reducing diarrhea incidence.[141]

Measles causes transient immunosuppression, and measles immunization, which is currently being widely implemented in developing country programs, may result in a slight reduction in diarrheal incidence and subsequent measles-related diarrheal mortality.[142] The use of cholera vaccines may have a role in the control of this disease in selected populations.[143] The newly developed rotavirus vaccines could potentially have widespread applicability throughout all regions of the world, as rotavirus remains the leading cause of diarrhea mortality among children younger than 5 years of age.[133] Because rotavirus diarrhea is also an important cause of morbidity and healthcare costs in developed countries, this vaccine is now part of the routine vaccination schedule for young children in such countries.[144]

Routine zinc supplementation has been found to reduce diarrhea incidence, as well as pneumonia and other infectious diseases, and to reduce mortality.[124] Although reduction in the incidence of diarrhea and its complications will follow from general economic development and improved environmental conditions, it is clear that particular interventions could speed progress in this regard. Efforts must continue to provide effective case management for diarrhea, but increased emphasis should be given to prevention of diarrheal morbidity. This approach is feasible, even in developing countries, through improved feeding practices and nutrition combined with enhanced water supply, sanitation, and hygiene. Because numerous enteropathogens cause diarrhea, especially in developing countries, and because vaccines protect only against specific organisms, these more general control measures are essential.

Diarrhea remains the second leading cause of death around the world.[19] The evidence supporting individual prevention and treatment interventions is solid. In a recent analysis, key diarrhea interventions including ORS, zinc, antibiotics for dysentery, vitamin A supplementation, rotavirus vaccine, improved water and sanitation, and breastfeeding were modeled using the Lives Saved Tool (*LiST*).[145] In this analysis of 68 priority UNICEF countries, with nearly 100% coverage of all diarrhea interventions, the authors demonstrated that diarrhea mortality could be reduced by 92% for an additional $84.8 billion or $3.24 per capita.[146] If water and sanitation costs are borne by the individual or private sector, the costs would be lowered to $12.5 billion, or $0.80 per capita. Given the current tools available, diarrhea morbidity and mortality could be significantly reduced if attention was paid to appropriate delivery strategies and a commitment was made to sustainable programs by governments and policy leaders around the world.

● ● ● REFERENCES

1. Liu L, et al. Global, regional, and national causes of child mortality: an updated systematic analysis for 2010 with time trends since 2000. Lancet, 2012. 379(9832):p.2151–2161.

2. Newsholme A, ed. *Fifty Years in Public Health*. London: G. A. A. Unwin; 1939:321–360.

3. Kilgore PE, et al. Trends of diarrheal disease–associated mortality in US children, 1968 through 1991. *JAMA* 1995;274(14):1143–1148.

4. Smith JC, et al. Cost-effectiveness analysis of a rotavirus immunization program for the United States. *Pediatrics* 1995;96(4 Pt 1): 609–615.

5. Holmes SJ, Morrow, AL, Pickering LK. Child-care practices: effects of social change on the epidemiology of infectious diseases and antibiotic resistance. *Epidemiol Rev* 1996;18(1):10–28.

6. Voetsch AC, et al. FoodNet estimate of the burden of illness caused by nontyphoidal *Salmonella* infections in the United States. *Clin Infect Dis* 2004;38(suppl 3):S127–S134.

7. Claeson M, Merson MH. Global progress in the control of diarrheal diseases. *Pediatr Infect Dis J* 1990;9(5):345–355.

8. Baqui AH, et al. Methodological issues in diarrhoeal diseases epidemiology: definition of diarrhoeal episodes. *Int J Epidemiol* 1991;20(4):1057–1063.

9. Black RE. Persistent diarrhea in children of developing countries. *Pediatr Infect Dis J* 1993;12(9):751–761; discussion 762–764.

10. McAuliffe JF, et al. Prolonged and recurring diarrhea in the northeast of Brazil: examination of cases from a community-based study. *J Pediatr Gastroenterol Nutr* 1986;5(6):902–906.

11. Baqui AH, et al. Epidemiological and clinical characteristics of acute and persistent diarrhoea in rural Bangladeshi children. *Acta Paediatr* 1992;381(suppl):15–21.

12. Fischer Walker, C.L. et al. Diarrhoea incidence in low- and middle-income countries in 1990 and 2010: a systematic review. BMC Public Health, 2012. 12: p.220–227.

13. Bern C, et al. The magnitude of the global problem of diarrhoeal disease: a ten-year update. *Bull World Health Organ* 1992;70(6):705–714.

14. Glass RI, et al. Estimates of morbidity and mortality rates for diarrheal diseases in American children. *J Pediatr* 1991;118 (4 Pt 2):S27–S33.

15. Monto AS, Koopman JS. The Tecumseh Study. XI. Occurrence of acute enteric illness in the community. *Am J Epidemiol* 1980;112(3):323–333.

16. Tate JE, et al. Sustained decline in rotavirus detections in the United States following the introduction of rotavirus vaccine in 2006. *Pediatr Infect Dis J* 2011; 30(1 suppl):S30–34.

17. Walker CL, Black RE. Diarrhoea morbidity and mortality in older children, adolescents, and adults. *Epidemiol Infect* 2010;138(9):1215–26.

18. Black RE. Epidemiology of travelers' diarrhea and relative importance of various pathogens. *Rev Infect Dis* 1990;12(suppl 1):S73–S79.

19. Black RE, et al. Global, regional, and national causes of child mortality in 2008: a systematic analysis. *Lancet* 2010;375(9730):1969–1987.

20. Kosek M, Bern C, Guerrant RL. The global burden of diarrhoeal disease, as estimated from studies published between 1992 and 2000. *Bull World Health Organ* 2003;81(3):197–204.

21. Bhan MK, et al. Major factors in diarrhoea related mortality among rural children. *Indian J Med Res* 1986;83:9–12.

22. World Health Organization Mortality Database. March 25, 2011. Available at: http://www.who.int/whosis/mort/download/en/index.html. Access May 8, 2011.

23. Black RE. Would control of childhood infectious diseases reduce malnutrition? *Acta Paediatr Scand* 1991;374(suppl):133–140.

24. Checkley W, et al. Multi-country analysis of the effects of diarrhoea on childhood stunting. *Int J Epidemiol* 2008;37(4):816–830.

25. World Health Organization, United Nations Children's Fund. *WHO/UNICEF, Geneva, Switzerland, Joint Statement. Clinical Management of Acute Diarrhoea.* 2004.

26. Updated norovirus outbreak management and disease prevention guidelines. *MMWR Recomm Rep* 2011;60(RR-3):1–18.

27. Fang ZY, et al. Sentinel hospital surveillance for rotavirus diarrhea in the People's Republic of China, August 2001–July 2003. *J Infect Dis* 2005;192(suppl 1):S94–S99.

28. Van Man N, et al. Epidemiological profile and burden of rotavirus diarrhea in Vietnam: 5 years of sentinel hospital surveillance, 1998–2003. *J Infect Dis* 2005;192(suppl 1): S127–S132.

29. Unicomb LE, et al. Astrovirus infection in association with acute, persistent and nosocomial diarrhea in Bangladesh. *Pediatr Infect Dis J* 1998;17(7):611–614.

30. Parashar UD, et al. Human caliciviruses as a cause of severe gastroenteritis in Peruvian children. *J Infect Dis* 2004;190(6):1088–1092.

31. San Joaquin VH, et al. Association of *Bacteroides fragilis* with childhood diarrhea. *Scand J Infect Dis* 1995;27(3):211–215.

32. Thomas C, et al. *Clostridium difficile*-associated diarrhea: epidemiological data from Western Australia associated with a modified antibiotic policy. *Clin Infect Dis* 2002;35(12):1457–1462.

33. Black RE, et al. Incidence and etiology of infantile diarrhea and major routes of transmission in Huascar, Peru. *Am J Epidemiol* 1989;129(4):785–799.

34. Black RE, et al. Incidence and severity of rotavirus and *Escherichia coli* diarrhoea in rural Bangladesh: implications for vaccine development. *Lancet* 1981;1(8212):141–143.

35. Black RE, et al. Longitudinal studies of infectious diseases and physical growth of children in rural Bangladesh. II. Incidence of diarrhea and association with known pathogens. *Am J Epidemiol* 1982;115(3):315–324.

36. Kotloff KL, et al. Acute diarrhea in Baltimore children attending an outpatient clinic. *Pediatr Infect Dis J* 1988;7(11):753–759.

37. Sack RB, et al. Diarrhoeal diseases in the White Mountain Apaches: clinical studies. *J Diarrhoeal Dis Res* 1995;13(1):12–17.

38. Santosham M, et al. Diarrhoeal diseases in the White Mountain Apaches: epidemiologic studies. *J Diarrhoeal Dis Res* 1995;13(1): 18–28.

39. Scallan E, et al. Foodborne illness acquired in the United States—major pathogens. *Emerg Infect Dis* 2011;17(1):7–15.

40. Surveillance for foodborne disease outbreaks—United States, 2006. *MMWR* 2009; 58(22):609–615.

41. Horwitz MA. Specific diagnosis of foodborne disease. *Gastroenterology* 1977;73(2):375–381.

42. Nachamkin IBM, Tompkins LS, eds. Campylobacter jejuni: *Current Status and Future Trends*. Washington, DC: American Society for Microbiology; 1992.

43. Levine MM. *Escherichia coli* that cause diarrhea: enterotoxigenic, enteropathogenic, enteroinvasive, enterohemorrhagic, and enteroadherent. *J Infect Dis* 1987;155(3):377–389.

44. Robins-Browne RM. Traditional enteropathogenic *Escherichia coli* of infantile diarrhea. *Rev Infect Dis* 1987;9(1):28–53.

45. Clausen CR, Christie DL. Chronic diarrhea in infants caused by adherent enteropathogenic *Escherichia coli. J Pediatr* 1982;100(3):358–361.

46. Korzeniowski OM, et al. A controlled study of endemic sporadic diarrhoea among adult residents of southern Brazil. *Trans R Soc Trop Med Hyg* 1984;78(3):363–369.

47. Lanata CF, et al. Epidemiologic, clinical, and laboratory characteristics of acute vs. persistent diarrhea in periurban Lima, Peru. *J Pediatr Gastroenterol Nutr* 1991;12(1):82–88.

48. Carcamo C, et al. Etiologies and manifestations of persistent diarrhea in adults with HIV-1 infection: a case-control study in Lima, Peru. *J Infect Dis* 2005;191(1):11–19.

49. Bern C, et al. The epidemiology of intestinal microsporidiosis in patients with HIV/AIDS in Lima, Peru. *J Infect Dis* 2005;191(10):1658–1664.

50. Black RE, et al. Enterotoxigenic *Escherichia coli* diarrhoea: acquired immunity and transmission in an endemic area. *Bull World Health Organ* 1981;59(2):263–268.

51. Riley LW, et al. Hemorrhagic colitis associated with a rare *Escherichia coli* serotype. *N Engl J Med* 1983;308(12):681–685.

52. Griffin PM, Tauxe RV. The epidemiology of infections caused by *Escherichia coli* O157:H7, other enterohemorrhagic *E. coli*, and the associated hemolytic uremic syndrome. *Epidemiol Rev* 1991;13:60–98.

53. Chalker RB, Blaser MJ. A review of human salmonellosis: III. Magnitude of *Salmonella* infection in the United States. *Rev Infect Dis* 1988;10(1):111–124.

54. Gast RK, Beard CW. Production of *Salmonella enteritidis*–contaminated eggs by experimentally infected hens. *Avian Dis* 1990;34(2):438–446.

55. Khan MU, et al. Fourteen years of shigellosis in Dhaka: an epidemiological analysis. *Int J Epidemiol* 1985;14(4):607–613.

56. Ebright JR, et al. Epidemic Shiga bacillus dysentery in Central Africa. *Am J Trop Med Hyg* 1984;33(6):1192–1197.

57. Lee LA, et al. Hyperendemic shigellosis in the United States: a review of surveillance data for 1967–1988. *J Infect Dis* 1991;164(5):894–900.

58. Glass RI. The epidemiology of cholera. In: Baurua GWI, ed. Cholera. New York: Plenum Medical Book Company; 1992:129–154.

59. Ries AA, et al. Cholera in Piura, Peru: a modern urban epidemic. *J Infect Dis* 1992;166(6):1429–1433.

60. Large epidemic of cholera-like disease in Bangladesh caused by *Vibrio cholerae* O139 synonym Bengal. Cholera Working Group, International Centre for Diarrhoeal Diseases Research, Bangladesh. *Lancet* 1993;342(8868):387–390.

61. Blake PA, Hollis DG. Diseases of humans (other than cholera) caused by vibrios. *Ann Rev Microbiol*, 1980;34:341.

62. Fukami T, Saku K. Clinical epidemiology of infectious enteritis of outpatients at Tokyo Metropolitan Bokuto General Hospital. In Saito M, Nakaya R, Matsubara Y, eds. *Infectious Enteritis in Japan*. Tokyo: Saikon Publishing; 1986:211–220.

63. Matsumoto C, et al. Pandemic spread of an O3:K6 clone of *Vibrio parahaemolyticus* and emergence of related strains evidenced by arbitrarily primed PCR and toxRS sequence analyses. *J Clin Microbiol* 2000;38(2):578–585.

64. Levine WC, Griffin PM. *Vibrio* infections on the Gulf Coast: results of first year of regional

surveillance. Gulf Coast Vibrio Working Group. *J Infect Dis* 1993;167(2):479–483.

65. Holmberg SD, Farmer JJ 3rd. *Aeromonas hydrophila* and *Plesiomonas shigelloides* as causes of intestinal infections. *Rev Infect Dis* 1984;6(5):633–639.

66. Rennels MB, Levine MM. Classical bacterial diarrhea: perspectives and update— *Salmonella, Shigella, Escherichia coli, Aeromonas* and *Plesiomonas. Pediatr Infect Dis* 1986;5(1 suppl):S91–S100.

67. Gracey M, Burke V, Robinson J. *Aeromonas*-associated gastroenteritis. *Lancet* 1982;2(8311):1304–1306.

68. Black RE, et al. Epidemic *Yersinia enterocolitica* infection due to contaminated chocolate milk. *N Engl J Med* 1978;298(2):76–79.

69. Samadi AR, et al. An attempt to detect *Yersinia enterocolitica* infection in Dacca, Bangladesh. *Trop Geogr Med* 1982;34(2):151–154.

70. Torres AR, et al. Differentiation of *Neisseria gonorrhoeae* from other *Neisseria* species by use of the restriction endonuclease HaeIII. *J Clin Microbiol* 1984;20(4):687–690.

71. Bean NH, et al. Foodborne disease outbreaks, 5-year summary, 1983–1987. *MMWR CDC Surveill Summ* 1990;39(1):15–57.

72. Sack RB, et al. Enterotoxigenic *Bacteroides fragilis*: epidemiologic studies of its role as a human diarrhoeal pathogen. *J Diarrhoeal Dis Res* 1992;10(1):4–9.

73. Anderson EJ, Weber SG. Rotavirus infection in adults. *Lancet Infect Dis* 2004;4(2):91–99.

74. Fischer Walker CL, Sack D, Black RE. Etiology of diarrhea in older children, adolescents and adults: a systematic review. *PLoS Negl Trop Dis* 2010;4(8):e768.

75. Gary GW Jr, Hierholzer JC, Black RE. Characteristics of noncultivable adenoviruses associated with diarrhea in infants: a new subgroup of human adenoviruses. *J Clin Microbiol* 1979;10(1):96–103.

76. Uhnoo I, et al. Importance of enteric adenoviruses 40 and 41 in acute gastroenteritis in infants and young children. *J Clin Microbiol* 1984;20(3):365–372.

77. Greenberg HB, et al. Prevalence of antibody to the Norwalk virus in various countries. *Infect Immun* 1979;26(1):270–273.

78. Black RE, et al. Acquisition of serum antibody to Norwalk virus and rotavirus and relation to diarrhea in a longitudinal study of young children in rural Bangladesh. *J Infect Dis* 1982;145(4):483–489.

79. Tiemessen CT, et al. Infection by enteric adenoviruses, rotaviruses, and other agents in a rural African environment. *J Med Virol* 1989;28(3):176–182.

80. Kurtz JB, Lee TW, Pickering D, Astrovirus associated gastroenteritis in a children's ward. *J Clin Pathol* 1977;30(10):948–952.

81. Yolken R, et al. Infantile gastroenteritis associated with excretion of pestivirus antigens. *Lancet* 1989;1(8637):517–520.

82. Leav BA, Mackay M, Ward HD. *Cryptosporidium* species: new insights and old challenges. *Clin Infect Dis* 2003;36(7):903–908.

83. Guerrant RL, Bobak DA. Bacterial and protozoal gastroenteritis. *N Engl J Med* 1991;325(5):327–340.

84. Shadduck JA. Human microsporidiosis and AIDS. *Rev Infect Dis* 1989;11(2):203–207.

85. Ortega YR, et al. *Cyclospora* species—a new protozoan pathogen of humans. *N Engl J Med* 1993;328(18):1308–1312.

86. Elder GH, Hunter PR, Codd GA. Hazardous freshwater cyanobacteria (blue-green algae). *Lancet* 1993;341(8859):1519–1520.

87. Stevens DP. Selective primary health care: strategies for control of disease in the developing world. XIX. Giardiasis. *Rev Infect Dis* 1985;7(4):530–535.

88. Gilman RH, et al. Rapid reinfection by *Giardia lamblia* after treatment in a hyperendemic Third

World community. *Lancet* 1988;1(8581): 343–345.

89. Sullivan PS, et al. Illness and reservoirs associated with *Giardia lamblia* infection in rural Egypt: the case against treatment in developing world environments of high endemicity. *Am J Epidemiol* 1988;127(6):1272–1281.

90. Flanagan PA. *Giardia*: diagnosis, clinical course and epidemiology. A review. *Epidemiol Infect* 1992;109(1):1–22.

91. Wanke C, Butler T, Islam M. Epidemiologic and clinical features of invasive amebiasis in Bangladesh: a case-control comparison with other diarrheal diseases and postmortem findings. *Am J Trop Med Hyg* 1988;38(2): 335–341.

92. Nanda R, Baveja U, Anand BS. *Entamoeba histolytica* cyst passers: clinical features and outcome in untreated subjects. *Lancet* 1984;2(8398):301–303.

93. Casemore DP. Foodborne protozoal infection. *Lancet* 1990;336(8728):1427–1432.

94. Genta RM. Diarrhea in helminthic infections. *Clin Infect Dis* 1993(16 suppl 2): S122–S129.

95. Esrey SA, Feachem RG, Hughes JM. Interventions for the control of diarrhoeal diseases among young children: improving water supplies and excreta disposal facilities. *Bull World Health Organ* 1985;63(4):757–772.

96. Hughes JM, et al. Epidemiology of eltor cholera in rural Bangladesh: importance of surface water in transmission. *Bull World Health Organ* 1982;60(3):395–404.

97. Swerdlow DL, et al. Waterborne transmission of epidemic cholera in Trujillo, Peru: lessons for a continent at risk. *Lancet* 1992;340(8810):28–33.

98. Waddington H, et al. *Water, Sanitation, and Hygiene Interventions to Combat Childhood Diarrhoea in Developing Countries*. 3rd ed. International Initiative for Impact Evaluation. London: Intiative for Impact Evaluation; 2009.

99. Arifeen S, et al. Exclusive breastfeeding reduces acute respiratory infection and diarrhea deaths among infants in Dhaka slums. *Pediatrics* 2001;108(4):E67.

100. Bhandari N, et al. Effect of community-based promotion of exclusive breastfeeding on diarrhoeal illness and growth: a cluster randomised controlled trial. *Lancet* 2003;361(9367):1418–1423.

101. Barrell RA, Rowland MG. Infant foods as a potential source of diarrhoeal illness in rural West Africa. *Trans R Soc Trop Med Hyg* 1979;73(1):85–90.

102. Black RE, et al. Contamination of weaning foods and transmission of enterotoxigenic *Escherichia coli* diarrhoea in children in rural Bangladesh. *Trans R Soc Trop Med Hyg* 1982;76(2):259–264.

103. Lanata CF. Studies of food hygiene and diarrhoeal disease. *Int J Environ Health Res* 2003;13(suppl 1):S175–S183.

104. Cherian A, Lawande RV. Recovery of potential pathogens from feeding bottle contents and teats in Zaria, Nigeria. *Trans R Soc Trop Med Hyg* 1985;79(6):840–842.

105. Rodrigue DC, Tauxe RV, Rowe B. International increase in *Salmonella enteritidis*: a new pandemic? *Epidemiol Infect* 1990;105(1):21–27.

106. Blaser MJ, et al. Reservoirs for human campylobacteriosis. *J Infect Dis* 1980;141(5):665–669.

107. Esrey S. *Interventions for the Control of Diarrhoeal Diseases among Young Children: Fly Control*. Geneva, Switzerland; World Health Organization; 1991.

108. Nichols GL. Fly transmission of *Campylobacter*. *Emerg Infect Dis* 2005;11(3):361–364.

109. Cohen D, et al. Reduction of transmission of shigellosis by control of houseflies (*Musca domestica*). *Lancet* 1991;337(8748):993–997.

110. Chavasse DC, et al. Impact of fly control on childhood diarrhoea in Pakistan:

community-randomised trial. *Lancet* 1999;353(9146):22–25.

111. Feachem RG. Interventions for the control of diarrhoeal diseases among young children: promotion of personal and domestic hygiene. *Bull World Health Organ* 1984;62(3):467–476.

112. Cairncross S, et al. Water, sanitation and hygiene for the prevention of diarrhoea. *Int J Epidemiol* 2010;39(suppl 1):i193–i205.

113. Hoque BA, Briend A. A comparison of local handwashing agents in Bangladesh. *J Trop Med Hyg* 1991;94(1):61–64.

114. Luby SP, et al. Effect of intensive handwashing promotion on childhood diarrhea in high-risk communities in Pakistan: a randomized controlled trial. *JAMA* 2004;291(21):2547–2554.

115. Luby SP, et al. Effect of handwashing on child health: a randomised controlled trial. *Lancet* 2005;366(9481):225–233.

116. Huttly SR, et al. Feces, flies, and fetor: findings from a Peruvian shantytown. *Rev Panam Salud Publica* 1998;4(2):75–79.

117. Zeitlin MF, Klein RE, Ahmad N, Ahmad K. *Sanitary Conditions of Crawling Infants in Rural Bangladesh*. Report to the USAID Asia Bureau and to the HHS Office of International Health, Bangladesh.

118. Sepulveda J, Willett W, Munoz A. Malnutrition and diarrhea: a longitudinal study among urban Mexican children. *Am J Epidemiol* 1988;127(2):365–376.

119. Baqui AH, et al. Malnutrition, cell-mediated immune deficiency, and diarrhea: a community-based longitudinal study in rural Bangladeshi children. *Am J Epidemiol* 1993;137(3):355–365.

120. Checkley W, et al. Effects of nutritional status on diarrhea in Peruvian children. *J Pediatr* 2002;140(2):210–218.

121. Black RE, Brown KH, Becker S. Malnutrition is a determining factor in diarrheal duration,

but not incidence, among young children in a longitudinal study in rural Bangladesh. *Am J Clin Nutr* 1984;39(1):87–94.

122. Sommer A, Katz J, Tarwotjo I. Increased risk of respiratory disease and diarrhea in children with preexisting mild vitamin A deficiency. *Am J Clin Nutr* 1984;40(5):1090–1095.

123. Sommer A, et al. Impact of vitamin A supplementation on childhood mortality: a randomised controlled community trial. *Lancet* 1986;1(8491):1169–1173.

124. Yakoob MY, et al. Preventive zinc supplementation in developing countries: impact on mortality and morbidity due to diarrhea, pneumonia and malaria. *BMC Public Health* 2011;11(suppl 3):S23.

125. Schiraldi O, et al. Gastric abnormalities in cholera: epidemiological and clinical considerations. *Bull World Health Organ* 1974;51(4):349–352.

126. Sullivan PB, et al. *Helicobacter pylori* in Gambian children with chronic diarrhoea and malnutrition. *Arch Dis Child* 1990;65(2):189–191.

127. Glass RI, et al. Predisposition for cholera of individuals with O blood group: possible evolutionary significance. *Am J Epidemiol* 1985;121(6):791–796.

128. Black RE, et al. Association between O blood group and occurrence and severity of diarrhoea due to *Escherichia coli*. *Trans R Soc Trop Med Hyg* 1987;81(1):120–123.

129. van Loon FP, et al. ABO blood groups and the risk of diarrhea due to enterotoxigenic *Escherichia coli*. *J Infect Dis* 1991;163(6):1243–1246.

130. Black RE, Lanata CF, Lazo F. Delayed cutaneous hypersensitivity: epidemiologic factors affecting and usefulness in predicting diarrheal incidence in young Peruvian children. *Pediatr Infect Dis J* 1989;8(4):210–215.

131. Sinclair D, et al. Oral vaccines for preventing cholera. *Cochrane Database Syst Rev* 2011;3:CD008603.

132. Lucas ME, et al. Effectiveness of mass oral cholera vaccination in Beira, Mozambique. *N Engl J Med* 2005;352(8):757–767.

133. Fischer Walker CL, Black RE. Rotavirus vaccine and diarrhea mortality: quantifying regional variation in effect size. *BMC Public Health* year;11(suppl 3):S16.

134. Lederberg JSR, Oaks SC Jr, eds. *Emerging Infections: Microbial Threats to Health in the United States.* Washington, DC: National Academies Press; 1992.

135. Santosham M, et al. Progress and barriers for the control of diarrhoeal disease. *Lancet* 2010;376(9734):63–67.

136. Fischer Walker CL, et al. Zinc and low os-molarity oral rehydration salts for diarrhoea: a renewed call to action. *Bull World Health Organ* 2009;87(10):780–786.

137. Lamberti LM, et al. Breastfeeding and the risk for diarrhea morbidity and mortality. *BMC Public Health* 2011;11(suppl 3):S15.

138. Imdad A, Yakoob MY, Bhutta ZA. Effect of breastfeeding promotion interventions on breastfeeding rates, with special focus on developing countries. *BMC Public Health* 2011;11(suppl 3):S24.

139. Research on improving infant feeding practices to prevent diarrhoea or reduce its severity: memorandum from a JHU/WHO meeting. *Bull World Health Organ* 1989;67(1):27–33.

140. Ashworth A, Feachem RG. Interventions for the control of diarrhoeal diseases among young children: weaning education. *Bull World Health Organ* 1985;63(6):1115–1127.

141. Mintz ED, Reiff FM, Tauxe RV. Safe water treatment and storage in the home: a practical new strategy to prevent waterborne disease. *JAMA* 1995;273(12):948–953.

142. Feachem RG, Koblinsky MA. Interventions for the control of diarrhoeal diseases among young children: measles immunization. *Bull World Health Organ* 1983;61(4):641–652.

143. Reyburn R, et al. The case for reactive mass oral cholera vaccinations. *PLoS Negl Trop Dis* 2011;5(1):e952.

144. Tate JE, et al. Uptake, impact, and effectiveness of rotavirus vaccination in the United States: review of the first 3 years of postlicensure data. *Pediatr Infect Dis J* 2011;30(1 suppl):S56–S60.

145. Stover J, McKinnon R, Winfrey B. Spectrum: a model platform for linking maternal and child survival interventions with AIDS, family planning and demographic projections. *Int J Epidemiol* 2010;39(suppl 1):i7–i10.

146. Walker CL, et al. Scaling up diarrhea prevention and treatment interventions: a lives saved tool analysis. *PLoS Med* 2011;8(3):e1000428.

21

Transmissible Spongiform Encephalopathies

Kenrad E. Nelson

INTRODUCTION

In the last 38 years, a radically new class of infectious agents—the spongiform encephalopathies—has been recognized as the cause of several diseases of humans and animals (**Exhibit 21-1**). The infectious agents causing these diseases appear to differ from viruses in that they do not contain nucleic acids, but only proteins; they have been labeled *prions*, or *proteinaceous infectious particles* by Stanley Prusiner.[1,2] The spongiform encephalopathies are unique among the infectious diseases in that they exhibit none of the traditional hallmarks of an infectious disease. The brain tissue of animals with these infections show spongiform changes in the cytoplasm of nerve cells without an inflammatory infiltrate; the patient or animal does not have a fever, high white cell count, or a rise in acute-phase reactants or cytokines; nor is there a measurable immune response to the infectious agent.[3] Therefore, these diseases originally were believed to be degenerative, rather than infectious, and due to genetic factors, rather than infectious agents.

Exhibit 21-1	Transmissible Spongiform Encephalopathies of Animals and Humans (Prion Diseases)

A. Animal Diseases
- Scrapie (sheep and goats)
- Transmissible mink encephalopathy
- Wasting disease of deer and elk
- Bovine spongiform encephalopathy*
- Transmissible spongiform encephalopathy of captive wild ruminants*
- Feline spongiform encephalopathy*

B. Human Diseases
- Kuru
- Sporadic Creutzfeldt-Jakob disease
- Familial Creutzfeldt-Jakob disease
- Gerstmann-Straussler-Scheinker disease
- Fatal familial insomnia
- New variant Creutzfeldt-Jakob disease*

* These diseases all appear to have a common source.

From R.T. Johnson and C.J. Gibbs, Creutzfeldt-Jacobs Disease and Selected Transmissable Spongiform Encephalopathies, *N Engl J Med*. Vol. 339, pp. 1994–2004, © 1998 Massachusetts Medical Society. Reprinted with permisison from Massachusetts Medical Society.

SCRAPIE

The disease of sheep called *scrapie* has been known for at least 200 years. It is widespread among sheep in Europe, Asia, and the Americas, and is also seen among goats cohabiting with affected sheep. The Scottish term "scrapie" comes from the characteristic feature of the disease, which is marked by areas of the skin denuded of fleece, due to the animals rubbing their irritated skin against fixed objects. The disease is insidious in onset but is characterized eventually by a progressive, eventually fatal, ataxia that leads to death of the affected animals in a matter of months. The affected sheep are afebrile and have normal cerebrospinal fluid (CSF) and no overt signs of infection. Pathologic lesions are limited to the central nervous system and show the characteristic non-inflammatory spongiform lesions with nerve loss, cytoplasmic vacuolization of degenerating nerves, and a striking astrocytosis. Scrapie initially was believed to be an autosomal dominant genetic disease until two French investigators transmitted the disease to uninfected animals and found the agent to be a filterable agent.[4]

Subsequently, it was demonstrated that the disease also could be transmitted to mice.[5]

The scrapie agent is unusual in that it contains no nucleic acids and is resistant to chemicals that normally inactivate nucleic acids, such as formaldehyde, ethanol, ultraviolet (UV) radiation, alkylating agents (such as B-propriolactone), proteases, and nucleases. However, the organism can be inactivated by autoclaving at 121°C under pressure or by exposure to extremes of pH, detergents, or phenol. This led to the hypothesis that the infectious agent was an infectious protein, or prion, which is a proteinase-resistant isoform of a normal cellular protein—that is, it is a normal protein, but is abnormally folded. The prion protein that causes disease has an abnormal structure characterized by a large beta-sheet configuration, in contrast to the alpha-helical structure of the normal protease-sensitive host prion protein. It has sometimes been characterized as PrP[res] or PrP[sc] compared to PrP[c], the normal host prion protein.[1,2]

KURU

In the 1950s, a disease was recognized among the primitive Fore people living in a remote area of highland New Guinea. This disease was called *Kuru*, meaning "shivering" or "trembling" in the Fore language. Kuru is characterized by an insidious onset of truncal ataxia. The ataxia progresses and becomes incapacitating. Eventually, ataxia occurs with every effort of voluntary movement, and death occurs uniformly 3 to 24 months after the onset of symptoms. The pathology shows spongiform changes in the brain similar to that caused by scrapie.

Because of the ability to transmit scrapie to laboratory animals, William Hadlow, a veterinarian who had worked with the scrapie agent, suggested that Kuru might also be due to a transmissible agent.[6] Subsequently, brain tissue from Kuru patients was inoculated into chimpanzees, which resulted in disease.[7] Epidemiologic studies subsequently indicated the likelihood that Kuru was due to ritual postmortem cannibalism by the relatives of patients who died from Kuru. While men participated in the cannibalism, Fore adult women and children prepared the body for consumption (see **Table 21-1**).[7,8] Consequently, the disease was more common in adult women, but male and female children were affected equally, because the women fed infectious material to their children, regardless of their sex.

With the suppression of cannibalism by Australian missionaries and settlers in the 1950s, Kuru has virtually disappeared. There were 11 persons diagnosed with Kuru between 1996 and 2004, indicating an incubation period of more than 50 years.[9]

Table 21-1	Transmission of Prion Diseases from Human to Human	
Mode of Transmission	**Example (no. of cases reported)**	**Incubation Period (years)**
1. Intracranial transplantation or inoculation	a. Dural grafts (>80 cases)	1.3–17
	b. Inadequately sterilized instruments (several cases)	0.6–2.2
		1.3–1.8
2. Extracranial transplantation	Corneal grafts (2 cases)	1.3–1.5
3. Extracranial inoculation of neural tissue	a. Human growth hormone and gonadotropin (>100 cases)	4–19*
	b. Arterial embolization with lyophilized dura mater (2 cases)	3.5–7.5
4. Extracranial inoculation or oral exposure	a. Possible exposure to bovine spongiform encephalopathy prion (40 cases)	5–10*
	b. Transmission of Kuru by ritual cannibalism (several thousand cases)	4.40 or more

* Numbers represent minimum incubation periods since hormone was given over periods of years (time from midpoint of treatment to onset = 12 years).

From R.T. Johnson and C.J. Gibbs, Creutzfeldt-Jacobs Disease and Selected Transmissable Spongiform Encephalopathies, *N Engl J Med*. Vol. 339, pp. 1994–2004, © 1998 Massachusetts Medical Society. Reprinted with permision from Massachusetts Medical Society.

CREUTZFELDT-JAKOB DISEASE

Creutzfeldt-Jakob disease (CJD) presents as a dementia, characterized by rapidly progressive mental deterioration, myoclonic jerking, and other neurologic signs. Classic CJD commonly begins between 55 and 70 years of age, but rare cases have occurred in younger adults, even in adolescents. The disease often begins with fatigue, insomnia, and other nonspecific signs or sometimes with focal signs, such as ataxia, visual loss, or aphasia. These symptoms are followed by progressive and relentless dementia, myoclonus, and other neurologic signs. The mean duration of survival is only 5 to 6 months, and more than 80% of patients die within 12 months. As in the other spongiform encephalopathies, there is no fever or other signs of infection, the patient's spinal fluid is normal, and the brain has characteristic spongiform changes. However, the 14-3-3 brain protein has been reported to be present in the spinal fluid in nearly all patients with CJD.

Approximately 10% of patients with CJD have a family history consistent with an autosomal dominant inheritance. In most, but not all, of these affected families, persons with CJD have a point mutation in the gene coding for the prion protein. The majority of CJD cases (90%) have no other affected family members. CJD occurs at a rate of approximately 1 case per million persons per year without evident clustering (aside from the 10% attributable to familial cases), in virtually all populations.

This disease has been inadvertently transmitted by the transplantation of dural and corneal grafts from infected donors. A total of 230 cases have been recognized worldwide since the first case was reported in 1974; 142 of the 228 cases transmitted by dural grafts occurred in Japan. It has been estimated that as many as 20,000 dural grafts were implanted annually in Japan in the decade before the risk of CJD was recognized. The mean incubation period has been 12 years (range 1.3–30 years) for symptoms of CJD after the graft was placed.[10] CJD has also been transmitted by the intracerebral use of a stereotactic electrode to control an epileptogenic focus. Six cases of CJD have resulted from transmission by neurosurgical instruments or electrodes.[10] The electrode had been used previously in a CJD patient and subsequently was disinfected only by soaking in alcohol; the CJD prion, like the prion causing scrapie, is resistant to disinfection by virucidal compounds.

In addition to these cases resulting from implants or invasive neurosurgical procedures 226 iatrogenic cases of CJD have been transmitted by the use of human growth hormone (HGH) prepared from pools of human pituitary tissue obtained from cadavers. The first three cases of CJD due to growth hormone were reported in 1985. Subsequently, 29 cases have occurred in the United States, 65 cases in the United Kingdom, 119 cases in France, and 13 cases in 6 additional countries.[10,11] In France all 119 cases occurred in a cohort of 1170 patients who received HGH during a 20 month period from December 1985 and July 1985, an attack rate of 10.2%. In the United States CJD has not developed in any patient who started treatment after 1977 when a highly selective column chromatography step was introduced into the purification protocol.[10] An estimated 2700 patients received HGH prior to 1997, so the attack rate among patients in the U.S. is estimated at 1.1%. The attack rate in the UK has been estimated at 3.6%.[10] Fortunately, HGH is now prepared synthetically, rather than by extraction from pools of human pituitary glands, so no further patients should acquire CJD by this route. However, additional clinical cases may still appear from previous exposure, due to the potentially long incubation period of CJD.

Bovine Spongiform Encephalopathy

In April 1985, a dairy farmer in the south of England observed a previously healthy cow that became apprehensive, was ataxic, and developed aggressive behavior. Progressive ataxia developed, and eventually the cow died. When tissues were sent to the central veterinary laboratory in the United Kingdom, the brain exhibited the typical features of bovine spongiform encephalopathy (BSE), a disease of cattle known to be caused by infection with a prion. Over the next few years, the number of cases of BSE in cattle in the United Kingdom grew rapidly. Sixteen cases were found in 1986, and more than 7000 cases were found in 1989. The epidemic peaked in 1992, when 36,000 cases of BSE were reported throughout Great Britain, Scotland, and Ireland (**Figure 21-1**).[10]

Eventually, more than 220,000 cases of BSE were reported from more than 34,000 herds in the United Kingdom.[12] The cattle herds with cases of BSE were scattered throughout the United Kingdom, and there was no evidence of horizontal transmission of the disease between cattle in the same herd. The epidemiologic pattern of disease was that of a common-source, foodborne outbreak. Researchers eventually concluded that the most likely source was from contaminated meat and bone meal (MBM) that had been used for cattle feed. Meat and bone meal had been prepared in the United Kingdom from the

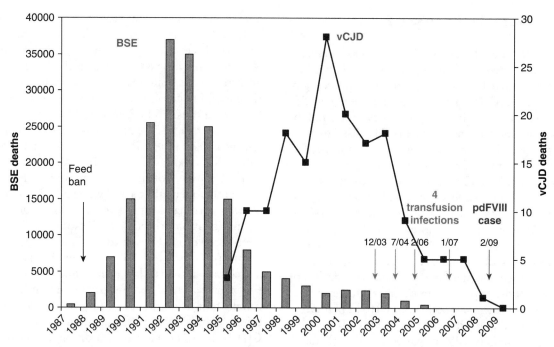

Figure 21-1 BSE and vCJD deaths in UK. Adapted from Johnson RT et al. Creutzfeldt-Jacobs Disease and Related Transmissable Spongiform Encephalopathies. *N Engl J Med*. 1998 Dec 31;339(27):1994–2004. © 1998 Massachusetts Medical Society.

rendered carcasses of sheep and other livestock, including cattle. Sheep had long been known to have an endemic level of infection with a prion disease, scrapie, in the United Kingdom. However, BSE did not appear in cattle until the 1980s. On investigation, it was concluded that prions from scrapie-infected sheep and BSE-infected cattle were identical.[13,14]

The BSE epidemic followed changes in the cattle rendering process that had occurred in the late 1970s. At that time, changes were introduced into the rendering process for the preparation of bone meal from animal remains (offal), due in part to an oil crisis in the Middle East. The use of continuous heating of offal, as opposed to batch heating, was substituted to save fuel. Also, the sale of tallow became unprofitable because of public concern about the health effects of animal fat consumption. The collapse of the tallow market resulted in most of the rendered fat remaining with the offal; in the past, it had been separated from the offal to be sold. The added fat content probably acted to prevent the disinfection of prion proteins in the animal carcasses. Further amplification of the epidemic was probably related to the use of animal carcasses, including neural tissues from animals such as cattle and sheep that succumbed to BSE or scrapie, for the preparation of animal feed. As a result of these factors, the dose of BSE/scrapie prions in cattle feed probably increased dramatically in the late 1970s.

Bovine spongiform encephalopathy and other prion diseases have been transmitted experimentally to a number of species by the oral route; oral transmission has been accomplished with various species of rodents and nonhuman primates.[15] These experimental data supported the hypothesis that BSE could be a foodborne outbreak in the cattle. The theory that the BSE agent in cattle had originated from sheep scrapie was strengthened considerably when molecular genetic studies of the BSE prion protein found it to be identical to the scrapie protein.[14]

Concern about the growing epidemic of BSE increased until the U.K. government instituted a ban against the use of carcasses from animals at risk for spongiform diseases for the preparation of animal feed. In 1988, a ban on feeding animal-derived feed (such as MBM from rendered sheep, goats, or cattle) to ruminants was instituted in the United Kingdom. This intervention proved to be the critical public health strategy in controlling the BSE epidemic. Nevertheless, as the epidemic evolved, disturbing evidence appeared suggesting cross-species infection from the BSE prion might have occurred. Domestic cats, as well as captive and exotic ruminants, died of BSE after eating animal feed containing possibly infected cattle tissues.[16] However, the public health actions that were taken— especially the animal feed ban in 1988—had a dramatic effect on controlling the epidemic after a lag period of approximately 5 years, which is the median incubation period of the disease in cattle. The epidemic peaked in 1992 and has declined progressively since then (Figure 21-1).

The occurrence of BSE in species other than cattle heightened concerns as to whether humans might also be susceptible to transmission of this disease.[16,17] Although no evidence demonstrated that humans were susceptible to scrapie, which had been endemic in sheep in the United Kingdom for two centuries, passage of prions through another animal might have altered the host range. Good evidence related to other prion diseases shows that passage of a prion through one species may alter the host susceptibility in a third species. Experimentally, mouse-adapted strains of scrapie passed through hamsters altered their transmissibility to other rodents,[18] human strains of Kuru or CJD could not be transmitted to ferrets until passed through primates or cats,[19] and a bovine strain of BSE could not be transmitted to hamsters until it was passed through mice.[20] Although the reasons for the species barrier in prion diseases is not known, the theory is that the likelihood of successful interspecies transmission is influenced by the degree of homology between the pathologic prion protein and the host endogenous prion protein.

Variant Creutzfeldt-Jakob Disease

In 1989, specified types of bovine offal (including brain, spinal cord, and organ meats) were banned from human food in the United Kingdom. However, because of concern about the potential transmission of BSE to humans, national surveillance of CJD was instituted in the United Kingdom in 1990. During the interval between 1990 and 1994, no unusual cases or clusters of CJD in humans were encountered.[18] Beginning in 1994, however, patients with CJD with an unusual clinical presentation, course, laboratory findings, and brain histopathology were identified. Furthermore, these cases of atypical CJD were much younger than the classic cases. Because of their unusual demographic, clinical, and pathologic features, they were called *variant Creutzfeldt-Jakob disease* (vCJD).[21,22] The clinical and pathologic differences between classic and variant CJD made it possible to classify patients (**Table 21-2**). The cases could then be classified definitively by molecular analysis of their prion to determine whether it was a BSE or classic prion protein.

Between 1995 and 2004–2010, 175 deaths from vCJD occurred in the United Kingdom, 24 deaths occurred in France, and 18 deaths occurred in eight other countries including Portugal, the Netherlands, Spain, Ireland, Italy, Saudi Arabia, and Japan (**Table 21-3**). Cases of vCJD from citizens of countries other than the United Kingdom who had lived in the United Kingdom for at least 6 months prior to becoming ill were probably exposed in that country and were assigned to the U.K. epidemic. Importantly, the numbers of cases of classic CJD and hereditary CJD in the United Kingdom remained about the same during this interval (**Table 21-4**).

The patients with vCJD are strikingly different from those with classic CJD. They are quite young, with a mean age of 29 years versus 60 years for sporadic cases of classic CJD. They also present with prominent psychiatric and behavioral manifestations, and have persistent painful paresthesia; the skin sensations may be similar to the sensory abnormalities leading to the scrapie lesions in sheep. Cerebellar ataxia uniformly develops, and the clinical course is prolonged, with an average survival of 14 months, compared with only 5 months in classic sporadic CJD.[2,22] The electroencephalogram fails to show the typical periodic complexes of classic CJD, although some EEG abnormalities may occur. The histopathology of the brain lesions in vCJD differs from that in

Table 21-2	Comparison of New-Variant and Sporadic Creutzfeldt-Jakob Disease	
Characteristic	**Variant**	**Sporadic**
Mean age at onset (yr)	29	60
Mean duration of disease (mo)	14	5
Most consistent and prominent early signs	Psychiatric abnormalities, sensory symptoms	Dementia, myoclonus
Cerebellar signs (% of patients)	100	40
Electroencephalographic periodic complexes (% of patients)	0	94
Pathological changes	Diffuse amyloid plaques	Sparse plaques in 10%

From Johnson RT et al. Creutzfeldt-Jacobs Disease and Related Transmissable Spongiform Encephalopathies. *N Engl J Med.* 1998 Dec 31;339(27):1994–2004. © 1998 Massachusetts Medical Society.

Table 21-3	vCJD Cases per Estimated Population, 2011		
Country	vCJD Cases[a]	Estimated Population, 2011[b]	Crude Rate[c]
United Kingdom	175	62,688,000	2.8×10^{-6}
Ireland	2	4,671,000	4.3×10^{-7}
France	24	65,103,000	3.7×10^{-7}
Portugal	2	10,760,000	1.9×10^{-7}
The Netherlands	3	16,847,000	1.8×10^{-7}
Spain	5	46,755,000	1.1×10^{-7}
Saudi Arabia	3	26,132,000	1.1×10^{-7}
Italy	2	61,017,000	3.3×10^{-8}
Japan	1	126,476,000	7.9×10^{-9}

[a] Cases resident in the United Kingdom for 6 months or longer are attributed to the United States.
[b] U.S. Census Bureau estimates mid-2011.
[c] Not corrected for population age distribution or efficiency of case recognition/reporting.

Adapted from the World Health Organization (2012). Variant Creutzfeldt-Jakob disease, Fact sheet N°180. http://www.who.int/mediacentre/factsheets/fs180/en/. Revised February 2012. Accessed October 2, 2012.

Table 21-4	Deaths from Definite and Probable CJD, 1990–2004							
Referrals of Suspect CJD		**Deaths of Definite and Probable CJD**						
Year	Referrals	Year	Sporadic	Iatrogenic	Familial	GSS	vCJD	Total Deaths
1990	[53]	1990	28	5	0	0	—	33
1991	75	1991	32	1	3	0	—	36
1992	96	1992	45	2	5	1	—	53
1993	78	1993	37	4	3	2	—	46
1994	118	1994	53	1	4	3	—	61
1995	87	1995	35	4	2	3	3	47
1996	134	1996	40	4	2	4	10	60
1997	161	1997	60	6	4	1	10	81
1998	154	1998	63	3	3	2	18	89
1999	170	1999	62	6	2	0	15	85
2000	178	2000	50	1	2	1	28	82
2001	179	2001	58	4	3	2	20	87
2002	163	2002	72	0	4	1	17	94
2003	162	2003	76	5	4	2	18	105
2004	112	2004	46	1	2	1	9	59
Total		**Total**						
Referrals	1920	**Deaths**	757	47	43	23	148	1018

Data from the National Creutzfeldt-Jakob Disease Research & Surveillance Unit (NCJDRS). Creutzfeldt-Jakob Disease Surveillance in the UK: Thirteenth Annual Report 2004. http://www.cjd.ed.ac.uk/Archive%20reports/report13.pdf. Accessed October 2, 2012.

classic CJD in containing diffuse amyloid plaques called *florid plaques* (or daisy plaques) (Table 21-2). When brain tissue from patients with vCJD is inoculated into mice by the intracerebral route, the incubation period of vCJD and BSE are identical and differ from that of classic CJD.[23]

All of the patients with vCJD had a history of eating meat prior to their illnesses. One patient reported becoming a vegetarian within 1 year of onset of symptoms of vCJD, but he had eaten beef previously. None of the patients reported eating cattle brains but, prior to the ban on the inclusion of cattle brain tissues (or specific bovine offal [SBO]) in human food in 1989, these tissues were commonly included in sausages, meat pies, and other human foods.

As a result of the epidemiologic, clinical, histopathologic, and animal inoculation data cited previously, it is now clear that vCJD represents human infection with the prions of BSE, due to oral ingestion of the agent in food.[23] If this theory is correct, it raises several difficult public health issues. How many cases of vCJD will eventually occur in the United Kingdom after the limit of the incubation period has been reached? How many people are now incubating the disease in the United Kingdom, where more than 200,000 cases of BSE in cattle have been reported and many more infected cattle were slaughtered and eaten by humans before they became symptomatic?

Predicting the number of cases of vCJD that might eventually occur in the United Kingdom has proved problematic. Different scientists have used different sets of data at various times during the epidemic and different assumptions about the biology, transmissibility, and incubation period of BSE to predict the eventual numbers of cases of vCJD that might occur.[24–27] These estimates have ranged from high estimates of 6.1–13.7 million cases (a prediction made in the late 1990s) to 300–400 cases (in the most recent and probably more realistic prediction made in 2003).

Epidemiologists face several difficulties in modeling the number of human cases. First, the number of cattle infected with BSE was large; 200,000 cases were diagnosed and reported, but several million asymptomatic cattle older than 30 months of age were also consumed prior to the report of the first human cases of vCJD. The precise risk to humans of consuming meat from an infected cow is unknown. However, this risk likely varies greatly according to whether neurologic tissue or organ meats are consumed, as the BSE prion is not present in muscle but rather is localized to neural tissue and lymphoid-containing organs. However, several popular cuts of meat, such as T-bone steak, often contain intercostal nerves. If

the animal was killed by first stunning the cow with an air gun, this practice could drive brain and CNS tissue into blood vessels and muscle. In addition, mechanically recovered meat often contains neural tissue.[28] When meat is mechanically recovered, instruments are used to scrape the meat from the bone after the carcass has been cut into steaks, and this often results in the inclusion of nerve tissue.

The second problem in predicting the number of cases is that the incubation period can be quite long in prion diseases. It is assumed that vCJD usually has an incubation period of 10–15 years, with some cases occurring after much longer periods, perhaps up to 50 years, as has been observed with Kuru.

Third, it appears that only a proportion of the human population is fully susceptible to vCJD. Susceptibility is related to the amino acid composition of the prion protein gene in humans; all of the human cases studied to date have been homozygous for methionine at the prion protein codon (codon 129). Only approximately 40% of the British population is homozygous for methionine (Met/Met) at prion codon 129; 50% are heterozygous for methionine/valine, and 11% are homozygous for valine at the prion protein codon 129 (**Table 21-5**). Among those cases of sporadic CJD in the United Kingdom that occurred between 1990 and 2001, 69% involved Met/Met, 15% involved Met/Val, and 17% involved Val/Val. Also, in the 51 cases of iatrogenic CJD in France, which involved patients who were infected by contaminated human growth hormone, 32 (61%) were Met/Met, 6 (12%) were Met/Val, and 13 (25%) were Val/Val at codon 129; the non-Met/Met cases were smaller in number and had a 5-year longer incubation period.[29] Therefore, it is possible that persons who are not homozygous for Met/Met at codon 129 might have reduced susceptibility to vCJD but might have a longer incubation period.

Nevertheless, the number of cases of vCJD has declined since peaking in 2000, when 28 cases were diagnosed, while the number of cases of sporadic,

Table 21-5	Percentage of Codon 129 Genotypes in CJD and in the Normal Population		
	Met/Met	Met/Val	Val/Val
Normal population	39%	50%	11%
Sporadic CJD	68%	15%	18%
hGH-related CJD	48%	20%	32%
vCJD	100%	—	—

Reproduced from Will, RG. Acquired Prion Disease: Iatrogenic CJD, variant CJD, kuru. British Medical Bulletin. 2003;66:255–65, by permission of the Oxford University Press.

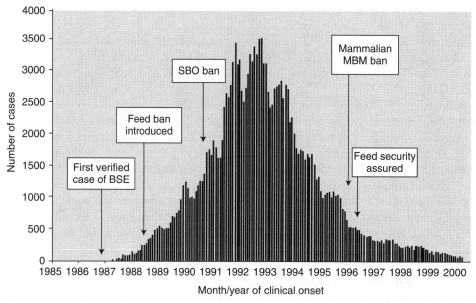

Figure 21-2 Time course of epidemic bovine spongiform encephalopathy in the United Kingdom, 1986–2000, with dates of major precautionary interventions. The mammalian ban on meat and bone meal in March 1996 extended a 1994 ban for farmed food animal species to include *all* mammalian species. Reproduced from Brown P. Bovine spongiform encephalopathy and variant Creutzfeldt-Jakob disease: background, evolution, and current concerns. *Emerg Infect Dis*. 2001 Jan–Feb;7(1):6–16.

iatrogenic, and familial CJD has remained stable (Table 21-4). These data suggest that the eventual number of cases will be in the hundreds, rather than in the thousands or millions as was predicted earlier. The declining number of BSE cases in the United Kingdom and the extensive public health procedures to eliminate human exposure to BSE-infected cattle probably combined to limit any human exposure in persons in the United Kingdom to the period 1980–1996 (**Figure 21-2**).

Since the BSE epidemic among cattle in the United Kingdom was first recognized, however, other countries have reported BSE in their cattle.[30] From 1986 through 2001, more than 98% of BSE cases worldwide were reported from the United Kingdom, where the disease was first described. During this period, four other European countries reported at least one indigenous case. By 1998, the number of countries with cattle-derived BSE increased to 8, and then expanded to 18 by 2001. From 2001 to 2003, three countries outside Europe—Canada, Japan, and Israel—reported cases of BSE. In 2004, a case of BSE was reported in a cow in the United States that had been imported from Canada. By 2003, more than 55% of BSE cases worldwide were reported outside the United Kingdom.[30] This apparent diffusion of BSE cases reflected a marked decline of BSE among cattle in the United Kingdom, as well as improved surveillance for the disease and larger number of cases in many other countries. It is also

possible that contaminated cattle feed, such as MBM, was imported from the United Kingdom by several other countries after the laws were enacted prohibiting the use of MBM in the United Kingdom. Also, cattle from the United Kingdom may have been imported by other countries. The U.S. Food and Drug Administration (FDA) denies that either MBM or cattle from the United Kingdom were ever imported into the United States, however.

An interesting study to estimate the number of U.K. residents who may be incubating vCJD but are now asymptomatic was published by Hilton and colleagues.[31-33] These researchers collected samples of appendices and tonsils from the general population of the United Kingdom and tested the tissues for the presence of the abnormal scrapie prion protein PRP^{sc}. To date, they have detected PRP^{sc} in 3 of 12,674 appendix samples.[32] This gives an estimate of 237 possibly infected persons per 1 million population in the United Kingdom, with a 95% confidence interval of 49–692 cases per 1 million population (**Table 21-6**).

In Hilton et al.'s work, studies of tissues from diagnosed vCJD cases taken 3 years and 4 years prior to the onset of clinical vCJD were positive for PRP^{sc} using their methods, but a sample taken 11 years prior to the onset of clinical disease from another patient was negative.[31] Clearly, more data of this type are needed to estimate the number of persons who might have subclinical BSE infections, given the wide confidence

Table 21-6	Prevalence of Disease Related Prion Protein PRP^CJD in Britain by Birth Cohort (Positive/Total; Rate per Million with 95% Confidence Intervals*)		
	Current (2004-September 2008) National Tissue Survey	**Earlier 1995–9 National Tissue Survey**	
Birth Cohort	**Tonsils**	**Appendices**	**Tonsils**
1940 and before	NA	NA	0/225
1941–60	NA	0/573	0/266
1961–85	0/12 753; 0 (0-289)	3/10 278; 292 (60 to 853)	0/694
1986–90	0/9 564; 0 (0-386)	0/396	0/119
1991–5	0/10 344; 0 (0-357)	NA	1/106
1996–2000	0/15 708; 0 (0-253)	NA	1/17
2001–7	0/14 638; 0 (0-252)	NA	NA
Total	0/63 007; 0 (0-59)	3/11 247; 267 (55 to 779)	0/1 427; 0 (0 to 2 582)

Reproduced from Clewley et al. Prevalence of disease related prion protein in anonymous tonsil specimens in Britain; cross sectional opportunistic survey. BMJ 2009; 338:b1442 with permission from BMJ Publishing Group Ltd.

interval of currently available data. Nevertheless, these data suggest that the vCJD epidemic may well continue for at least another decade or so.

Possible Transfusion-Transmitted vCJD

Soon after the recognition of vCJD, concerns were expressed that the infection might be more likely than classic CJD to be spread by blood or blood product transfusion. Patients with vCJD routinely show evidence of prions in lymphatic tissues of the gastrointestinal tract, such as the appendix and tonsils. In contrast, in patients with classic CJD, the infectious prions are concentrated in the central nervous system. No evidence has been obtained to suggest that classic CJD was spread by transfusion,[34,35] despite the fact that one study found it possible to transfer CJD to mice by intracerebral injection of buffy coat cells from an infected animal.[36] A few investigators have also detected the CJD agent in the buffy coat cells of experimentally infected guinea pigs or mice. In contrast, the prion is usually not present in human blood in patients with classic CJD.

In addition, no cases of classic CJD have been reported from multiply transfused patients with clotting disorders or hemoglobinopathies. If an infectious CJD agent was present in the blood of patients prior to their development of symptoms, patients with hemophilia and related disorders would have been transfused with infected blood during the era when Factor VIII pools contained blood from as many as 10,000 donors. Furthermore, recipients of blood transfusions from more than 200 persons who donated blood shortly prior to the onset of clinical classic CJD have remained free of the disease—some for many years.[35] Despite these reassuring data from persons transfused

with blood from patients with classic CJD, substantial concern has been expressed about the possible risks of the transfusion transmission of vCJD due to the different distribution of PRP^sc, which involves the peripheral lymphatic tissues, in infected patients who are incubating the disease.

The United Kingdom transfusion service made efforts soon after the epidemic of vCJD was recognized to obtain all of its blood products from sources outside the United Kingdom to reduce this risk. In 1999, the FDA recommended that potential blood donors who had lived in the United Kingdom 6 months or more between 1980 and 1996 be excluded as donors, while the potential risk of the transfusion transmission of vCJD was being evaluated.[13] The choice of 6 months' residency in the United Kingdom to exclude donors was made to limit the exposure of transfusion recipients to potentially infected donors while maintaining an adequate donor pool. A survey of donors from several large Red Cross blood banks found that the 6-month deferral would exclude approximately 80% of donors who had lived or visited the United Kingdom, while reducing the total donor pool by only 2–3%.[13]

Subsequently, BSE was reported among cattle from many other countries in Europe, albeit at rates far lower than in the United Kingdom (**Table 21-7**). The apparent spread of BSE to other European countries led the FDA to recommend the exclusion of blood donors who had visited or lived in the United Kingdom for 3 months as well as persons who had lived or visited other European countries for a total of 5 years between 1980 and 1996. Recently, this exclusion was extended to members of the U.S. military who were stationed in Europe south of the Alps for 6 months between 1980

Table 21-7	Reported Cases of Bovine Spongiform Encephalopathy in the United Kingdom and Other Countries, as of December 2000		
Country	Native Cases	Imported Cases	Total Cases
United Kingdom	180,376[a]	—	180,376
Republic of Ireland	487	12	499
Portugal	446	6	452
Switzerland[b]	363	—	363
France[b]	150	1	151
Belgium	18	—	18
The Netherlands	6	—	6
Liechtenstein	2	—	2
Denmark	1	1	2
Luxembourg	1	—	1
Germany	3	6	9
Oman	—	2	2
Italy	—	2	2
Spain[c]	—	2	2
Canada	—	1	1
The Falklands (UK)	—	1	1
The Azores (Portugal)[d]	—	1	1

[a] Includes 1287 cases in offshore British islands.
[b] Includes cases detected by active surveillance with immunologic methods.
[c] Origin and dates of imported cases are under investigation.
[d] Case imported from Germany.

Reproduced from Brown P. Bovine spongiform encephalopathy and variant Creutzfeldt-Jakob disease: background, evolution, and current concerns. *Emerg Infect Dis.* 2001 Jan–Feb;7(1):6–16.

and 1996, as the U.S. military purchased beef from the United Kingdom for U.S. troops during this time.

The decision to exclude blood donors based on the theoretical risk of transmission of the vCJD agent was quite difficult and controversial when it was made, because it was based solely on the distribution of the prion in peripheral tissues, presumably including circulating blood cells, and the theoretical risk that transfusion transmission might be possible. No transfusion-transmitted cases had occurred from vCJD, and fairly convincing data showed that the risk of transfusion transmission of classic CJD was very low or absent when the decision was being considered. Nevertheless, a substantial concern remained that a large proportion of the U.K. population could be incubating vCJD and, therefore, might be infectious. The stakes of a delayed decision that was later found to be incorrect were felt to be quite high in light of the prognosis of vCJD infection after clinical symptoms appeared.

To evaluate the risk of transfusion-transmitted vCJD, the data from the CJD surveillance unit and the U.K. blood donor services were linked in 1997. This study identified 48 recipients of blood from a total of 15 donors who later developed vCJD.[37] In one of these cases, transfusion transmission of vCJD probably occurred. The recipient was a 62-year-old individual who had been transfused with red cells from a 24-year-old donor in 1996. The donor developed vCJD in 2000, 3 years and 4 months after the donation. The recipient developed symptoms of vCJD in late 2002, 6.5 years after the blood transfusion. As of July 2011, a total of four patients had developed vCJD after a transfusion from a donor who was in the incubation period of vCJD when donating blood. These cases were identified using look-back tracing of persons who had been transfused with blood products from a donor who subsequently developed vCJD.

One very interesting probable transfusion-transmitted infection occurred in the United Kingdom.[38] This patient had received a unit of non-leuko-depleted red blood cells from a donor who developed vCJD 18 months after his donation. Five years after the transfusion, the recipient died from a ruptured aortic aneurysm. At the postmortem exam, the protease-resistant scrapie protein was detected in the patient's spleen and cervical lymph node, but not in his brain. Thus the patient was infected but had not yet developed vCJD. He was found to be heterozygous at prion protein codon 129; the codon contained both methionine and valine. This case raises the possibility that heterozygotes might be susceptible to infection but might have longer incubation periods prior to the onset of clinical symptoms of vCJD. The incubation period in some of the exposed patients who are homozygous for valine at codon 129 of the prion protein could even be several decades.

Remaining Questions

Several important questions about this continuing epidemic remain unanswered. First, how many vCJD cases will eventually occur in the United Kingdom? Will cases occur among persons who are heterozygous, or who have Val/Val amino acids at codon 129? Will additional cases occur in countries outside the United Kingdom? Will additional transfusion-transmitted cases of vCJD be detected? Will human cases of vCJD occur in populations outside the United Kingdom where cattle BSE has been identified? Is there a risk of nosocomial transmission by contaminated instruments used for surgery in patients who are incubating vCJD but are not yet clinically ill? How long will this tragic epidemic persist?[39]

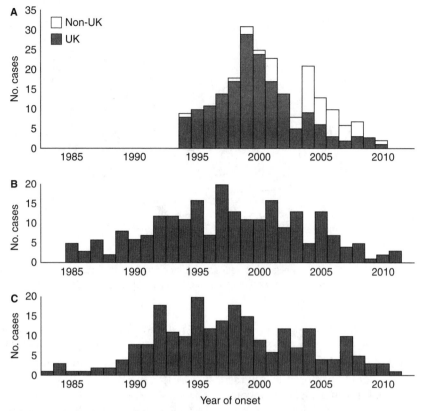

Figure 21-3 Annual incidence of variant Creutzfeldt-Jakob disease (vCJD) caused by ingestion of meat products contaminated with bovine spongiform encephalopathy agent (A) and iatrogenic CJD caused by contaminated dura matter (B) and cadaveric human growth hormone (C), 1982–2011. White bars in panel A represent cases from outside the United Kingdom, which were delayed in parallel with the later appearance of bovine spongiform encephalopathy outside the United Kingdom (not a second wave resulting from codon 129 genotype differences). Two patients are excluded: 1 presymptomatic patient from the United States who received human growth hormone and died of an intercurrent illness and 1 dura matter recepient from the United Kingdom with disease onset in 1978. Reproduced from Brown et al. Iatrogenic Creutzfeldt-Jakob disease, final assessment. *Emerg Infect Dis* [serial on the Internet]. June 2012. http://wwwnc.cdc.gov/eid/article/18/6/12-0116_intro.htm. Accessed August 29, 2012.

The epidemic curves depicting the number of cases of CJD from dural grafts and HGH and vCJD from consumption of meat by year is shown in **Figure 21-3**.

CHRONIC WASTING DISEASE OF MULE DEER AND ELK

Several prion diseases affect animals but have not been found to be transmissible to humans to date. One such disease of concern is chronic wasting disease (CWD) of deer and elk. This disease affects only deer (*Odocoileus* species) and Rocky Mountain elk (*Cervus elaphus nelsoni*).[40] CWD was first identified as a fatal wasting syndrome of captive mule deer in the 1960s in research facilities in Colorado, but was recognized to be a transmissible spongiform encephalopathy only in 1978.[41] The disease was first recog-

nized in wild, free-ranging elk in Colorado in 1981.[42] Subsequently, it was found among deer and elk in a contiguous area in northeastern Colorado and southeastern Wyoming (**Figure 21-4**). Based on surveillance of hunter-harvested animals from 1996–1999, it has been estimated that 5% of mule deer, 2% of white-tailed deer, and fewer than 1.0% of elk may be infected.[43] The diagnosis of preclinical or clinical CWD can be made based on immunohistochemical studies.[44,45]

CWD can be transmitted horizontally from one animal to another, in contrast to BSE. In addition, the environment can be contaminated with prions from an animal that has died. This can cause recurring epidemics among captive animals that are housed in an area where CWD-positive animals have previously died. The contamination in the field where CWD-affected animals grazed can persist for years.

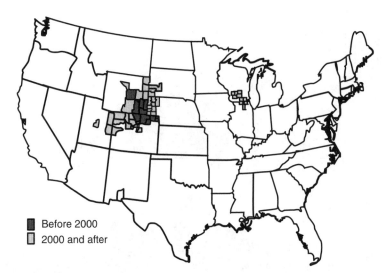

Figure 21-4 Chronic wasting disease among free-ranging deer and elk by county, United States. Reproduced from Belay, ED et al. Chronic wasting disease and potential transmission to humans. *Emerg Infect Dis*. 2004 Jun;10(6):977–84.

In the past few years, CWD has spread beyond its previous locale to include areas in Utah, southern Wisconsin, and New Mexico.[46] It is not clear how the disease spread, but it could have been by migration or transport of animals for hunting. Out of concern about CWD spread among wild deer and elk in Wisconsin, and in response to fears that CWD could eventually be transmitted to humans, the Wisconsin Department of Natural Resources launched a culling program by providing special hunting permits to eliminate the disease in the area where it was detected.[46] So far, no humans have been found to be infected with the CWD prion. Nevertheless, public health officials remain concerned because of the example set by BSE, the long incubation period of prion diseases, the difficulty of diagnosing prion diseases prior to symptoms, and the frequent human consumption of venison among persons living in the endemic area for CWD. A few cases of encephalopathy in young persons exposed to venison have been reported, but on careful study they were found to be classic CJD with onset at a young age and not infection with the CWD prion.[47] However, it is not certain at this point that CWD could not be spread to humans if larger numbers of persons consumed CWD-infected animals. Continued surveillance is essential.

● ● ● REFERENCES

1. Prusiner SB. Novel proteinaceous infectious particles cause scrapie. *Science* 1982;216:136–144.

2. Prusiner SB. Prions and neurodegenerative diseases. *N Engl J Med* 1987;317:1571–1581.

3. Johnson RT, Gibbs CJ. Creutzfeldt-Jakob disease and related transmissible spongiform encephalopathies. *N Engl J Med* 1998;339:1994–2004.

4. Cuille J, Chelle PL. La maladic die "tremblante du mouton" est-elle inoculable. *CR Acad Sci (Paris)* 1936;203:1552–1554.

5. Chandler RC. Encephalopathy in mice produced by inoculation with scrapie brain material. *Lancet* 1961;1:378–379.

6. Hadlow WJ. Scrapie and Kuru. *Lancet* 1959;2:289–290.

7. Gajdusck DC, Gibbs CJ, Alpers M. Experimental transmission of a Kuru-like syndrome to chimpanzees. *Nature* 1966;209:794–796.

8. Glasse R. Cannibalism in the Kuru region of New Guinea. *Trans NY Acad Sci* 1967;29:748–754.

9. Johnson RT. *Viral Infections of the Nervous System*. 2nd ed. Philadelphia: Lippincott-Raven Press; 1998:356.

10. Brown P,Brandel J-P,Sato T,et al. Iatrogenic Creutzfeldt-Jakob Disease, Final Assessment. *Emerg Infect Dis*. 2012;18;901–907.

11. Brown P, Gajdusek DC, Gibbs C, Asher DM. Potential epidemic of Creutzfeldt-Jakob disease

from human growth hormone therapy. *N Engl J Med* 1985;313:728–731.

12. Nathanson N, Wilesmith J, Griot C. Bovine spongiform encephalopathy (BSE): causes and consequences of a common source epidemic. *Am J Epidemiol* 1997;145:959–969.

13. Collinge J, Sidle KC, Meads J, et al. Molecular analysis of prion strain variation and the aetiology of "new variant" CJD. *Nature* 1996;383:685–690.

14. Bruce ME, Will RG, Ironside JW, et al. Transmissions to mice indicate that "new variant" CJD is caused by the BSE agent. *Nature* 1997;389:498–501.

15. Gibbs CJ Jr, Amyx HL, Bacote A, Masters CL, Gajdusek DC. Oral transmission of Kuru, Creutzfeldt-Jakob disease, and scrapie to nonhuman primates. *J Infect Dis* 1980;142:205–208.

16. Wyatt JM, Pearson GR, Smerdon T, et al. Spongiform encephalopathy in a cat. *Vet Rec* 1990;126:513.

17. Kirkwood JK, Wells GA, Wilesmith JW, et al. Spongiform encephalopathy in an Arabian oryx (*Oryx leucoryx*) and a greater kudu (*Tragelaphus strepsiceros*). *Vet Rec* 1990;127:418–420.

18. Kimberlin RH, Walker CA, Fraser H. The genomic identity of different strains of mouse scrapie is expressed in hamsters and preserved on reisolation in mice. *J Gen Virol* 1989; 70(Pt 8):2017–2025.

19. Gibbs CJJ, Gajdusek DC, Amyx H. Strain variation in viruses of Creutzfeldt-Jakob disease and Kuru. In: Hadlow WJ, ed. *Slow Transmissible Diseases of the Nervous System.* New York: Academic Press; 1979:87–110.

20. Foster JD, Hope J, McConnell I, et al. Transmission of bovine spongiform encephalopathy to sheep, goats, and mice. *Ann NY Acad Sci* 1994;724:300–303.

21. Cousens SN, Zeidler M, Esmonde TF, et al. Sporadic Creutzfeldt-Jakob disease in the United Kingdom: analysis of epidemiological surveillance data for 1970–96. *BMJ* 1997;315:389–395.

22. Will RG, Ironside JW, Zeidler M, et al. A new variant of Creutzfeldt-Jakob disease in the UK. *Lancet* 1996;347:921–925.

23. Scott MR, Will R, Ironside J, et al. Compelling transgenetic evidence for transmission of bovine spongiform encephalopathy prions to humans. *Proc Natl Acad Sci USA* 1999;96:15137–15142.

24. Cousens SN, Vynnycky E, Zeidler M, et al. Predicting the CJD epidemic in humans. *Nature* 1997;385:197–198.

25. Ghani AC, Ferguson NM, Donnelly CA, et al. Epidemiological determinants of the pattern and magnitude of the vCJD epidemic in Great Britain. *Proc Biol Sci* 1998;265: 2443–2452.

26. Donnelly CA, Fisher MC, Fraser C, et al. Epidemiological and genetic analysis of severe acute respiratory syndrome. *Lancet Infect Dis* 2004;4:672–683.

27. Ghani AC, Ferguson NM, Donnelly CA, Anderson RM. Predicted vCJD mortality in Great Britain. *Nature* 2000;406:583–584.

28. Bruce ME, McConnell I, Will RG, Ironside JW. Creutzfeldt-Jakob disease infectivity in extra-neural tissues. *Lancet* 2001;358:208–209.

29. Deslys JP, Jaegly A, d'Aignaux JH, et al. Genotype at codon 129 and susceptibility to Creutzfeldt-Jakob disease. *Lancet* 1998;351:1251.

30. Will RG. Acquired prion disease: iatrogenic CJD, variant CJD, Kuru. *Br Med Bull* 2003;66:255–265.

31. Hilton DA, Ghani AC, Conyers L, et al. Accumulation of prion protein in tonsil and appendix: review of tissue samples. *BMJ* 2002;325:633–634.

32. Hilton DA, Ghani AC, Conyers L, et al. Prevalence of lymphoreticular prion protein accumulation in UK tissue samples. *J Pathol* 2004;203:733–739.

33. Hilton DA, Fathers E, Edwards P, et al. Prion immunoreactivity in appendix before clinical onset of variant Creutzfeldt-Jakob disease. *Lancet* 1998;352:703–704.

34. Wilson K, Code C, Ricketts MN. Risk of acquiring Creutzfeldt-Jakob disease from blood transfusions: systematic review of case-control studies. *BMJ* 2000;321:17–19.

35. Esmonde TF, Will RG, Slattery JM, et al. Creutzfeldt-Jakob disease and blood transfusion. *Lancet* 1993;341:205–207.

36. Manuelidis EE, Kim JH, Mericangas JR, Manuelidis L. Transmission to animals of Creutzfeldt-Jakob disease from human blood. *Lancet* 1985;2:896–897.

37. Llewelyn CA, Hewitt PE, Knight RS, et al. Possible transmission of variant Creutzfeldt-Jakob disease by blood transfusion. *Lancet* 2004;363:417–421.

38. Peden AH, Head MW, Ritchie DL, et al. Preclinical vCJD after blood transfusion in a PRNP codon 129 heterozygous patient. *Lancet* 2004;364:527–529.

39. Head MW, Ironside JW. Mad cows and monkey business: the end of vCJD? *Lancet* 2005;365:730–731.

40. Williams ES, Miller MW. Chronic wasting disease of deer and elk: a review with recommendations for management. *J Wildl Manage* 2002;66:551–563.

41. Williams ES, Young S. Chronic wasting disease of captive mule deer: a spongiform encephalopathy. *J Wildl Dis* 1980;16:89–98.

42. Spraker TR, Miller MW, Williams ES, et al. Spongiform encephalopathy in free-ranging mule deer (*Odocoileus hemionus*), white-tailed deer (*Odocoileus virginianus*) and Rocky Mountain elk (*Cervus elaphus nelsoni*) in north-central Colorado. *J Wildl Dis* 1997;33:1–6.

43. Miller MW, Williams ES, McCarty CW, et al. Epizootiology of chronic wasting disease in free-ranging cervids in Colorado and Wyoming. *J Wildl Dis* 2000;36:676–690.

44. O'Rourke KI, Baszler TV, Besser TE, et al. Preclinical diagnosis of scrapie by immunohistochemistry of third eyelid lymphoid tissue. *J Clin Microbiol* 2000;38:3254–3259.

45. Wild MA, Spraker TR, Sigurdson CJ, et al. Preclinical diagnosis of chronic wasting disease in captive mule deer (*Odocoileus hemionus*) and white-tailed deer (*Odocoileus virginianus*) using tonsillar biopsy. *J Gen Virol* 2002;83:2629–2634.

46. Belay ED, Maddox RA, Williams ES, et al. Chronic wasting disease and potential transmission to humans. *Emerg Infect Dis* 2004;10:977–984.

47. Belay ED, Gambetti P, Schonberger LB, et al. Creutzfeldt-Jakob disease in unusually young patients who consumed venison. *Arch Neurol* 2001;58:1673–1678.

Blood and Body Fluid as A Reservoir of Infectious Diseases

Human Immunodeficiency Virus Infections and the Acquired Immunodeficiency Syndrome

Kenrad E. Nelson and David D. Celentano

INTRODUCTION

The human immunodeficiency virus (HIV) epidemic is as modern an epidemic as it is large. This epidemic has advanced with the cultural and technological transformations of the 20th century. However, research, treatment, and (one hopes) a cure have also proceeded incredibly rapidly, as the full force of modern science was turned on the pandemic.

A zoonotic infection of humans occurring in Congo in the 1890s, HIV infection simmered slowly in Africa, manifested by increases in cryptococcal meningitis and disseminated tuberculosis. However, these were always common infections in Africa. Later, modern transportation allowed the infection to spread across the continent. Serological evidence of HIV infection was found in stored serum samples from subjects from Zaire that had been collected in 1959.[1] The probable origin of HIV-1 was from *Pan troglodytes* (chimpanzees) in West and Central Africa, with the infection then being transmitted to humans during hunting for "bush meat."[2] Another human immunodeficiency virus, HIV-2, was discovered subsequently in African green monkeys in the wild in West Africa.[3] Humans can be infected either by HIV-1 or HIV-2, and both viruses can cause immunodeficiency and acquired immunodeficiency syndrome (AIDS), although the prevalence and virulence of HIV-2 are considerably less than those associated with HIV-1.[4-5] From there, airline travel took the virus to Haiti, as this island nation has close cultural ties to West Africa. From Haiti, it spread to popular holiday destinations in the Dominican Republic. In particular,

the Dominican Republic was a preferred holiday destination for the increasingly visible and sexually active community of men who have sex with men (MSM). The sexual revolution of the late 1960s and 1970s created an ideal environment for the virus to spread.

AIDS, as it became known, is the severe state of immune depression caused by years of HIV infection. AIDS was first identified in the United States in 1980–1981 among MSM. Pentamadine availability was managed by the Centers for Disease Control and Prevention (CDC), as it was a rarely used drug for *Pneumocystis* pneumonia treatment in children whose immune systems were suppressed by cancer chemotherapy. When CDC received multiple requests for pentamadine to treat adult men, the cluster of illness was noted. Early epidemiology studies identified clusters of *Pneumocystis carinii* pneumonia (PCP) and Kaposi's sarcoma (KS) (or both) occurring in MSM in Los Angeles, New York, and a few other cities, many of whom had reported sexual contact with another case (**Figure 22-1**).[6-9] Subsequently, similar patterns of disease were noted among injection drug users, persons with hemophilia, and some transfusion recipients.[10,11]

Several research groups investigated the causes of the immunosuppression underlying the occurrence of these opportunistic infections. In 1984, Robert Gallo and colleagues at the National Cancer Institute of the National Institutes of Health (NIH) and Luc Montagnier and coworkers at the Pasteur Institute independently reported the discovery of the cause of AIDS, a novel human retrovirus, the human immunodeficiency virus.[12,13]

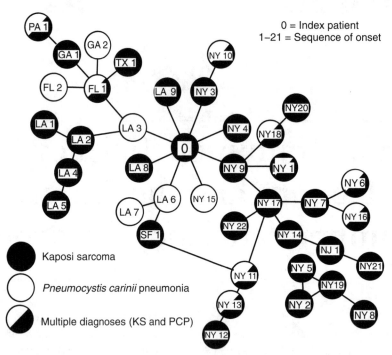

Cities: LA, Los Angeles; NY, New York City; SF, San Francisco.
States: FL, Florida; GA, Georgia; NJ, New Jersey; PA, Pennsylvania;
           TX, Texas.

Figure 22-1 Sexual contacts among homosexual men with AIDS. Each circle presents an AIDS patient. Lines connecting the circles represent sexual exposures. Indicated city or state is place of residence of a patient at the time of diagnosis. "0" indicates Patient 0 (described in text). Reprinted from Auerbach et al. Cluster of Cases of the Acquired Immune Deficiency Syndrome. Patients linked by Sexual Contact. *American Journal of Medicine*. Vol., 76, pp. 487–492, © 1984, with permission from Elsevier.

THE AIDS PANDEMIC

Since AIDS was originally identified in the early 1980s, the disease has spread to nearly every country in the world. AIDS has become a global pandemic of extraordinary importance. An estimated 34 million people were living with HIV infection worldwide in 2010, an increase of 17% since 2001.[14] The disease is most frequently encountered in sub-Saharan Africa, where the population prevalence among adults is estimated to be more than 5%.[14] These population-level numbers mask the severity of the epidemic in some countries and subpopulations, however. Swaziland has the highest rates in the world, with nearly 30% of its people 15–49 years old being infected; moreover, women are disproportionally infected, with more than 40% being HIV positive. Globally, the epidemic is most severe among women, and the prevalence among young women (15–24 years old) is 10% or greater in many countries in sub-Saharan Africa. Because of its relentless growth, involving mostly adolescents and young adults during the prime of life, the AIDS epidemic has had a catastrophic effect on many societies and economies.

THE HIV VIRUS

HIV is a retrovirus, a double-stranded RNA virus that undergoes reverse transcription to form double-stranded DNA in the cytoplasm of an infected cell (**Figure 22-2**). The viral genome consists of three structural genes, termed *env*, *pol*, and *gag*. The genome codes for several regulatory proteins, including Tat, Rev, Vif, Vpu, Vpr, and Nef. The p16/p14 Tat proteins activate viral transcription. The p14 Rev protein is responsible for the transport and stability of viral RNA. The p27/p25 Nef proteins are active in the downregulation of CD4 cells.[15]

The HIV virus attaches to the CD4 cell surface molecule through high-affinity interactions between the viral envelope protein, Gp120, and a specific region of the CD4 molecule (**Figure 22-3**). The CD4 molecule is present in abundance on both immature T lymphocytes and mature CD4+ helper T lymphocytes. It is also present in lower concentrations on monocytes, macrophages, and antigen-presenting dendritic cells. HIV also binds to one of two co-receptors, CCR5 or CXCR4. Once the CD4 molecule and the co-receptor are engaged,

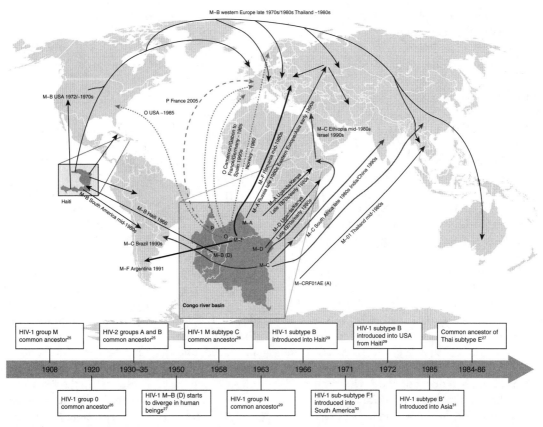

Figure 22-2 Global emergence of HIV strains over time. Reprinted from The Lancet. Tebit, D and Arts, E. Tracking a century of global expansion and evolution of HIV to drive understanding and to combat disease. *Lancet Infect Dis,* 2011;11:45–56, with permission from Elsevier.

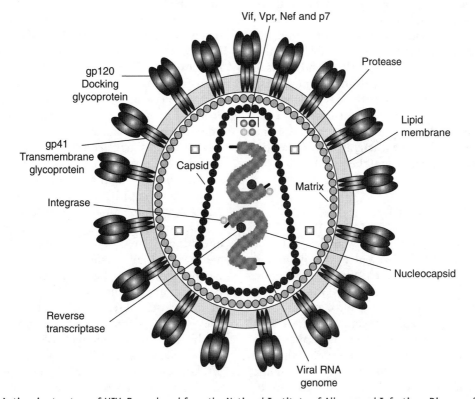

Figure 22-3 Antigenic structure of HIV. Reproduced from the National Institute of Allergy and Infectious Diseases (2004). How HIV Causes AIDS. http://www.niaid.nih.gov/topics/hivaids/understanding/howhivcausesaids/Pages/cause.aspx. Accessed October 16, 2012. Last updated November 19, 2004.

the viral attachment complex shifts conformation, thereby allowing the membrane fusion complex to fuse with the cell wall and the viral capsid to enter the cell. Cells of monocyte/macrophage origin generally express only CCR5; however, many lymphocyte populations express both receptors.

After the virus enters the cell, the viral RNA is converted to DNA using the viral enzyme reverse transcriptase. The double-stranded DNA molecules then enter the nucleus and are integrated into the host cell chromosomal DNA. In resting cells, the transcription and integration may be incomplete and viral DNA may remain in the cytoplasm. The unintegrated DNA is short-lived; in contrast, integrated DNA can persist for long periods in resting T lymphocytes.[16]

Subsequently, transcription of the HIV genome occurs to form RNA transcripts, which leave the nucleus. Modification of the viral polyproteins by cellular and viral enzymes (proteases) is essential for viral assembly. The virus is then spliced and re-packaged near the cell surface and released from the host cell.

HIV has a high replication rate, with approximately 10 billion viral particles produced each day.[16,17] As an RNA virus, it does not undergo RNA polymerase editing, and the reverse transcriptase results in a huge error rate in viral replication. It has been estimated that every day every possible amino acid is mutated in the production of so many viral particles. The result is a swarm of viable and non-viable viruses causing high levels of immune system activation, but with only a fraction of the viruses actually being able to productively infect other cells. Although HIV itself is not long-lived (its half-life is estimated at 6 hours), the genome is integrated into both activated immune cells and incredibly long-lived central memory T cells. These long-lived cells serve as the viral reservoir and enable the virus to become reactivated even after decades of effective antiretroviral therapy.[18]

HIV NATURAL HISTORY

After HIV infection either by sexual contact or parenterally, the virus is present in the blood and the viral RNA can be detected within 7–10 days. Approximately 7–21 days later, HIV antibodies appear in the blood. Early in the infection, the viral load is usually very high.[19] Infection of gut-associated lymphoid tissue (GALT) occurs rapidly, and the destruction of GALT is complete within the first few weeks of infection. Subsequently an immune response occurs, which includes the appearance of antibodies and a cellular response consisting of CD8+

cytotoxic T lymphocytes directed against the virus. At this point, the level of viremia declines and a viral "set point" is established in 3–4 months (**Figure 22-4**). The level of the viral set point can vary considerably and is predictive of the rate at which the disease will progress. The AIDS mortality among untreated persons with very high viral load at the set point—that is, more than 100,000 copies/mL—is quite rapid and averages about 4.5 years, whereas persons with lower viral loads at the set point survive more than 10 years after their infection.[20]

After the set point is reached, a gradual decline in the level of CD4+ T lymphocytes occurs along with an increase in the level of CD8+ T lymphocytes, so that the total number of CD3+ T cells is relatively stable for several years. Nevertheless, the CD4/CD8 lymphocyte ratio is significantly decreased (i.e., less than 1.0) compared to the uninfected state. During this time, the body experiences an ongoing, destructive war between the immune system and the virus. Massive numbers of viral particles are produced, and the immune system responds to their presence. Activated immune cells are susceptible to infection, so the very response to the virus accelerates infection of additional cells. Cells traffic to the lymph nodes to perform immune surveillance, but the lymph architecture is increasingly scarred by the severity of the immune response: as fibrosis increases, the lymph nodes become less and less able to perform their vital functions.[21]

Approximately 18–24 months prior to the development of clinical AIDS, the level of total CD3+ cells decreases more rapidly, meaning there is loss of T-cell homeostasis.[22] The loss of T-cell homeostasis heralds the patient's inability to keep up with the virus-induced destruction of the immune system. This phenomenon is often accompanied by a "switch" in the co-receptor utilization of the dominant HIV, from a CCR5, or non-syncitium-inducing cell type, to a CXCR-4 (syncitium-inducing or duotropic) type. Rarely, CXCR-4 viruses are transmitted initially and predominate even early in the infection; in such cases, the progression to clinical AIDS occurs more rapidly (**Figure 22-5**).[23]

During the acute stage, which occurs 2–4 weeks after the initial infection when HIV levels in the blood are maximal, an "acute HIV infection syndrome" commonly occurs; this phenomenon has been reported in approximately 50% or more of patients in some closely observed cohorts in developed countries.[24-26] The symptoms noted during this time resemble infectious mononucleosis and include fever (95%), adenopathy (75%), pharyngitis (70%), rash (70%), and other systemic symptoms, including meningitis, Guillain-Barré syndrome, peripheral neuropathy, and Bell's palsy.[24-26] Generally, HIV

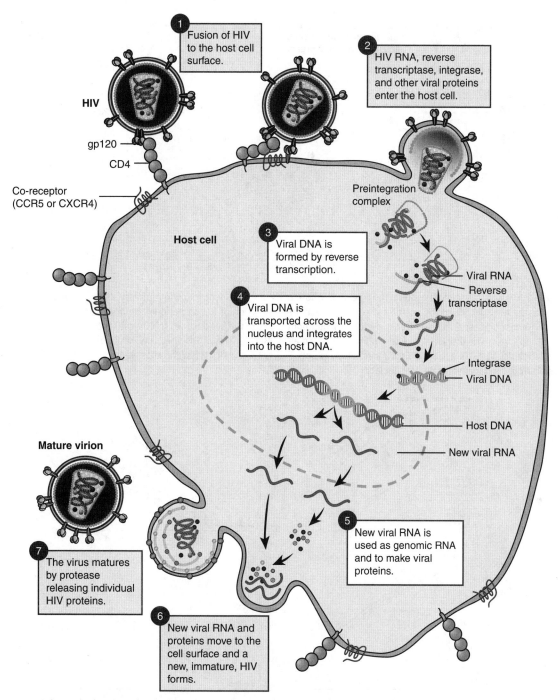

Figure 22-4 Schematic drawing of the HIV life cycle. Reproduced from the National Institute of Allergy and Infectious Diseases (2012). HIV Replication Cycle. http://www.niaid.nih.gov/topics/HIVAIDS/Understanding/Biology/Pages/hivReplicationCycle.aspx. Updated April 3, 2012. Accessed October 2, 2012.

serology is negative during this acute seroconversion syndrome, but patients have demonstrable viremia. Seroconversion occurs within a few weeks after the prodromal phase resolves.

A meta-analysis of the time from HIV-1 seroconversion to AIDS and death (before the widespread use of highly active antiretroviral therapy [HAART]) among 13,030 HIV-1 seroconverters enrolled in

38 studies in Europe, North America, and Australia—the CASCADE study[27]—has provided the most comprehensive evaluation of the time to AIDS and death among persons in developed countries in the pre-HAART era. The CASCADE investigators found that the median time to AIDS was 9.5–11.0 years, and the median survival was 10.5–11.8 years after infection in untreated patients (**Figure 22-6**). There were no

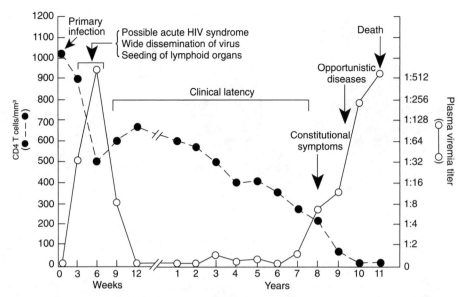

Figure 22-5 Typical course of HIV infection in persons who receive no treatment following primary infection, a chain of events occurs over the next decade of the person's life—widespread dissemination of HIV in peripheral blood accompanied by an abrupt fall in CD4+ lymphocytes; a clinical latency period lasting about 5 years; further declines in CD4 cells marked by consititutional symptoms, opportunistic diseases, and death. From Pantaleo et al. Mechanisms of Disease: The Immuno-pathogenesis of Human Immunodeficiency Virus Infection. *N Engl J Med.* Vol. 328, pp. 327–335. © 1993 Massachusetts Medical Society. Reprinted with permission from Massachusetts Medical Society.

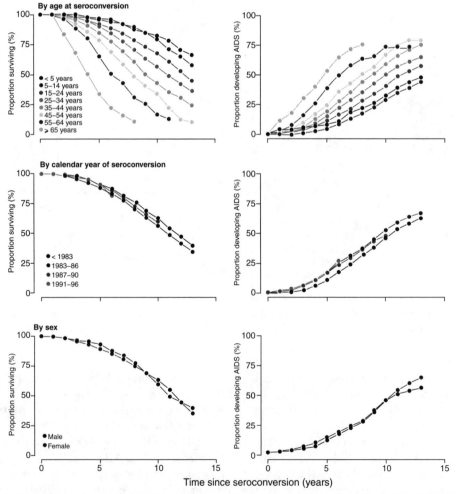

Figure 22-6 Survival and development of AIDS from seroconversion. Reprinted from The Lancet, 355, CASCADE study. Time from HIV seroconversion to AIDS and death before widespread use of highly-active antiretroviral therapy: a collaborative re-analysis. 1131–1137, Copyright 2000, with permission from Elsevier.

significant differences in progression by exposure category, gender, or year of infection between 1983 and 1996. However, the age of the person at the time of infection substantially affected the progression rate. Persons who were older when they were infected progressed more rapidly. Among persons aged 15–24 years at the time of infection, the median survival was 12.5 years (95% confidence interval [CI]: 12.0–12.9 years), and the median time to AIDS was 12.0 years (95% CI: 10.7–11.7 years). In contrast, among persons 45–54 years old at seroconversion, the median AIDS-free interval was 7.7 years (95% CI: 7.1–8.6 years) and the median survival was 11.0 years (95% CI: 10.7–11.7 years). After it became possible to quantitate HIV viral RNA in the plasma, it was shown that the levels of virus in the plasma at the set point were predictive of the subsequent rate of HIV progression and could be combined with the CD4+ count to more accurately predict the time of onset of AIDS and death in HIV-infected patients.[19,20] In fact, the combination of the viral RNA (i.e., viral load) with the CD4+ count more accurately predicts the time to AIDS than the CD4+ count alone.[20] This relationship reflects how the CD4 count indicates the degree of immunosuppression, and the viral load indicates the level of immune control versus viral replication and pathogenesis.

Fewer data are available on the rate of progression among persons in developing countries. Because death is the result of uncontrolled infections, the exposure of patients to pathogens is a key element of survival. In areas of the world characterized by a higher prevalence of aggressive infectious diseases, such as tuberculosis or untreated cancer, life expectancy is much shorter. A study in Thailand found that progression was more rapid among young adults compared to HIV-infected persons of comparable age in developed industrialized countries, with median survival of 7.4–8.4 years after seroconversion among infected Thais.[28]

AIDS-RELATED OPPORTUNISTIC INFECTIONS

The diagnostic hallmark of untreated HIV is the development of AIDS and its accompanying opportunistic infections (OIs). A large number of OIs have been identified in immunosuppressed HIV-infected persons and have been classified as "AIDS-defining illnesses." The CDC lists 28 conditions as "AIDS-defining illnesses." In the United States, *Pneumocystis carinii* pneumonia, the HIV wasting syndrome, Kaposi's sarcoma, oropharyngeal and esophageal candidiasis, extrapulmonary cryptococcus, and tuberculosis account for most initial AIDS-defining OIs in patients (**Table 22-1**).

The frequency of the initial AIDS-defining diagnosis among cases reported to the CDC in 1990, 1995, and 1997, using the pre-1993 clinical definition, is shown in Table 22-1. AIDS-related OIs in developing countries often have a different distribution at the onset of AIDS than has been reported among patients in the United States and other industrialized countries. In Thailand, for example, the distribution of the top 10 AIDS-defining illnesses among 101,945 cases of symptomatic AIDS that were reported between 1994 and 1998 is shown in **Table 22-2**.[29]

Thailand is similar to many other developing countries in Asia and Africa in that tuberculosis is the most frequent AIDS-defining illness, followed closely by the wasting syndrome and several systemic fungal infections—namely, candidiasis, cryptococcosis, and penicilliosis. Also, PCP, which has been classified as a fungal infection caused by *Pneumocystis jiroveci* (formerly known as *P. carinii*), is common in Thailand. The frequent occurrence of PCP differs from the clinical reports of AIDS in Africa, where PCP among adults has been reported to be rare, although it appears to occur commonly in pediatric AIDS cases.[30] Infection with *Penicillium marneffei* is limited to AIDS patients in Southeast Asia, where the organism is endemic and is geographically localized to this area.[31] Kaposi's sarcoma is relatively rare among AIDS patients in Asia but is quite common among such patients in Africa and the Caribbean.[29,32] Disseminated histoplasmosis is a common AIDS-defining illness among patients in the histoplasmosis belt in the U.S. Midwest.[33] Leishmaniasis is a common AIDS-related OI in Spain and other areas where this organism is endemic.[34]

Timing of AIDS-Related Opportunistic Infections

The time of occurrence of AIDS-related opportunistic infections during the natural history of HIV infection varies with each OI (**Figure 22-7**). Typically, oropharyngeal and esophageal candidiasis, oral hairy-cell leukoplakia, and tuberculosis occur relatively early in an HIV infection, when the CD4+ count may be 200–300 cells/μL or higher. Disseminated cytomegalovirus infections (CMV), toxoplasmosis, and *Mycobacterium avium* infections usually do not occur until the CD4+ cell count falls below 50–100 cell/μL. This knowledge of the natural history of HIV has been used to develop antibiotic protocols to prevent frequently occurring OIs in patients with HIV. In some cases, antibiotic prophylaxis of an opportunistic infection has been shown to delay the progression of HIV/AIDS and to prolong survival of HIV-positive patients. Prolonged survival has been shown for prophylaxis of PCP,

Table 22-1	Incidence of CD4+ Counts Associated with Opportunistic Infection and Cancer in HIV-Infected Patients					
Variable			**CD4+ Count[†]**			
	Incidence [95% CI][†]	**Mean**	**Median**	**First Quartile[‡]**	**Third Quartile[§]**	
	n (%)	◄────────────	cells/mm3	──────────────►		
Candida esophagitis	186 (13.3) [11.5 to 15.5]	79	30	9	103	
Cytomegalovirus	102 (6.9) [5.7 to 8.5]	37	15	5	46	
Cryptosporidiosis	12 (0.8) [0.4 to 1.4]	92	28	2	124	
Cryptococcosis	34 (2.3) [1.5 to 3.2]	63	32	12	115	
AIDS dementia complex	87 (5.8) [4.6 to 7.3]	61	18	4	77	
Herpes simplex virus infection	19 (1.2) [0.7 to 1.9]	195	107	17	350	
Herpes zoster	51 (3.8) [2.8 to 5.0]	171	154	38	275	
Kaposi sarcoma	37 (2.5) [1.7 to 3.4]	87	34	10	117	
Mycobacterium avium complex bacteremia	109 (7.4) [6.0 to 9.0]	26	9	3	18	
Mycobacterium tuberculosis infection	6 (0.4) [0.1 to 0.9]	176	171	17	261	
Non-Hodgkin lymphoma	24 (1.6) [1.0 to 2.4]	59	27	7	80	
Primary *Pneumocystis carinii* pneumonia	110 (8.9) [7.4 to 1.0]	79	36	12	101	
Secondary *Pneumocystis carinii* pneumonia	76 (5.1) [4.0 to 6.4]	34	10	1	30	
Progressive multifocal leukoencephalopathy	9 (0.6) [0.5 to 0.7]	42	39	32	57	
Toxoplasmosis	34 (2.3) [1.5 to 3.2]	44	22	8	50	
The wasting syndrome	37 (2.5 [1.7 to 3.4]	38	22	7	56	

* AIDS = acquired immunodeficiency syndrome: HIV = human immunodeficiency virus.
† CD4+ count obtained within 6 months before the opportunistic infection was diagnosed.
‡ Per 100 person-years. Based on a range of 1231 of 1498 person-years of follow-up. First quartile = 25th percentile.
§ Third quartile = 75th percentile.

Reproduced from Richard Moore and Richard Chaisson. Natural History of Opportunistic Disease in an HIV-Infected Urban Clinic Cohort, Annals of Internal Medicine 1996;124;633–642.

Table 22-2	AIDS-Defining Illnesses Among Patients >10 Years of Age in Thailand, 1994–1998	
Illness	**Number**	**%**
Tuberculosis	29,437	28.9
Wasting syndrome	28,729	28.2
Pneumocystic carinii pneumonia	20,145	19.8
Disseminated cryptococcosis	18,821	18.5
Esophageal candidiasis	5,989	5.9
Pneumonia, bacterial	3,691	3.6
Penicillium marneffei	3,054	3.0
Cerebral toxoplasmosis	3,133	3.1
HIV encephalopathy	1,987	1.9
Cryptosporidiosis	895	0.9

Reproduced from Chariyalertsak S et al. Clinical presentation and risk behaviors of patients with acquired immunodeficiency syndrome in Thailand, 1994–1998: regional variation and temporal trends. *Clin Infect Dis* 2001:32;955–62. By permission of Oxford University Press.

tuberculosis, and *M. avium* infections.[35] It is equally likely (although no clear data have been reported) that prevention of fungal infections may prolong survival of antiretroviral-naive patients (**Table 22-3**).

Because of increasing availability of antiretroviral therapy (ART), emphasis has shifted to treatment of the underlying immune suppression with effective ART rather than prophylaxis in immune-suppressed patients. Unfortunately, not all patients will effectively respond to ART, and many will still need prophylactic regimens to prevent illness. A CDC task force has reviewed the published literature and the available scientific evidence and published recommendations for the use of prophylactic regimens for the prevention of specific AIDS-related OIs.[35] Immune reconstitution following ART is also not complete; while CD4 cell counts may rise to levels that would seem sufficient, some patients have immune deficiency previously associated with lower absolute T-cell counts. Thus these patients require closer clinical follow-up.

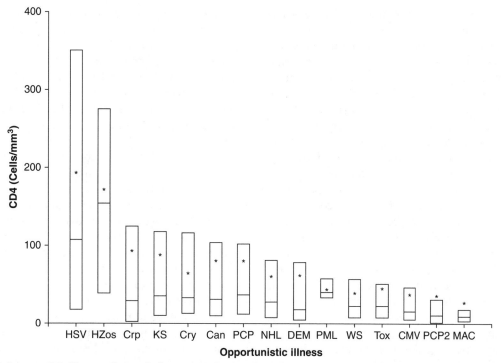

Figure 22-7 Opportunistic illnesses that typically occur as the CD4+ lymphocyte count in peripheral blood progressively decreases over time in an untreated HIV-infected patient. Can = *Candida* esophagitis; CMV = Cytomegalovirus infection; Crp = cryptosporidiosis; Cry = cryptococcal meningitis; DEM = acquired immunodeficiency virus dementia complex; HSV = herpes simplex virus infection; HZos = herpes zoster; KS = Kaposi sarcoma; MAC = *Mycobacterium* avium complex bacteremia; NHL = non-Hodgkin lympoboma; PCP = primary *Pneumocystis carinii* pneumonia; PCP2 = secondary *Pneumocystis carinii* pneumonia; PML = progressive multifocal leukoencephalopathy; Tox = *Toxoplasma gondii* encephalitis; WS = the wasting syndrome. Reproduced from Richard Moore and Richard Chaisson. Natural History of Opportunistic Disease in an HIV-Infected Urban Clinic Cohort, Annals of Internal Medicine 1996;124;633–642.

Table 22-3	Diseases for Which CDC Task Force Recommends Prophylaxis in HIV-Infected Patients to Prevent AIDS-Related OIs and Progression	
Disease	**Prophylaxis**	**Level**
Tuberculosis (latent), i.e., PPD+	INH and pyramethamine	Strong
Pneumocystis carinii pneumonia	TMP-SMX	Strong
Toxoplasmosis (*T. gondii* antibody-positive pts)	Toxoplasma-IgG antibody pos TMP-SMX	Strong
M. avium complex	(<100 CD4+) clarithromycin or azithromy-cin	Strong
Strep. pneumonia	Pneumovax	General
Influenza	Influenza vaccine	General
Hepatitis B virus	HBV vaccine	General
Hepatitis A virus	HAV vaccine	General (esp. for HCV carriers)

Note: Consult CDC. *MMWR.* 2002;51:RR-6 for details of recommendations.

HOST FACTORS IN SUSCEPTIBILITY OR RESISTANCE TO HIV INFECTION AND DISEASE PROGRESSION

After infection with HIV, the host mounts an immune response consisting of both cellular and humoral immunity. This response usually results in some control of viral replication with a substantial decrease in the viral load.

Because HIV transmission rates are low, an effective immune response—either innate or adaptive—must be mounted against the virus in many exposed people. Innate antiviral factors and physical characteristics of the body surface repel the virus in most cases. Mucosal IgA and IgG antibodies and CD8+ T cells may inhibit HIV at the mucosal surface and prevent or clear HIV infection after exposure. Also, CD8+ and CD4+ T cells may clear infection after the virus has penetrated the mucosal barrier early in infection. Clearance of virus may occur prior to the appearance of neutralizing antibodies; however, exposed persons may harbor T lymphocytes that respond specifically to HIV peptides by proliferation and cytokine secretion.[36,37] Documentation of these events is difficult and highly disputed in HIV transmission research circles. HIV dogma states that infection is irreversible and that there are no cases of viral clearance after infection. However, acquired immunity after HIV exposure has been demonstrated among frequently exposed persons— for example, in a cohort of Kenyan commercial sex workers—and nonprogression of the infection for prolonged periods has been observed in other infected persons. These so-called "elite controllers" of their HIV infection may have normal levels of CD4+ T lymphocytes and undetectable HIV RNA while not receiving specific antiretroviral therapy for many years. These findings give rise to optimism that these protective mechanisms could be enhanced to produce a sterilizing or pathogenesis-controlling vaccine.

In addition to the acquired immune response, several genetic host factors have been discovered that influence resistance or susceptibility to infection. Among these host factors is a common genetic mutation involving the deletion of 32 base pairs in the chemokine receptor CCR5. Persons who are homozygous for this mutation are resistant to infection with CCR5-utilizing viruses.[38] Persons who are heterozygous for the deletion have lower viral loads and slower progression to AIDS.[39] In 2007, an HIV-positive U.S. citizen living in Germany, Timothy Brown, developed leukemia and required a bone marrow transplant. Because the German healthcare system has a more generous system for picking an ideal match, his physician, G. Hütter, was able to search for a donor candidate who was both an HLA match and had the CCR5 deletion (donor 61). Brown stopped taking HIV medication before his bone marrow transplant and has not had detectable virus since the transplant. He did suffer a relapse of his leukemia, but received a second transplant from the same donor and has remained in remission. He is apparently cured of his HIV infection. Numerous questions remain in this case. In particular, why the virus completely disappeared is unclear. Despite aggressive ablative therapy prior to the transplant, this patient still has CCR5-carrying cells in his body, and no amount of radiation would eliminate all the immune cells. Furthermore, the patient had CXCR4 viruses detected prior to the transplant, and these viruses have not emerged. This result has energized the search for a cure to HIV infection.[40]

Additional host genetic factors have been identified that affect the resistance or susceptibility to HIV-1 infection or the rate of progression to AIDS after infection. These include a mutation in the CCR5 promoter, a CCR2–641 mutation, and a mutation in the stromal-derived factor (SDF13'A/3'A).[41,42] The number of segmental duplications of two CC chemokine genes, CCL3L1 and CCL4L1, on chromosome 17q were recently shown to be associated with the susceptibility to HIV infection and the rate of progression after infection in several human populations.[43]

Persons who are homozygous at one, two, or three HLA class 1 loci or have a polymorphism for interleukin 10 (IL-10+/5'A or 5'A/5'A) have more rapid progression after they are infected with HIV.[44] However, homozygosity of class 1 HLA alleles has not been shown to increase the risk of HIV infection. In contrast, HLA class 1 allele sharing between an infected person and an exposed seronegative recipient (through either a sexual contact or a mother–infant pair) has been shown to increase the risk of transmission.[45,46] Also, one study has found discordance of an HLA class II allele, HLA-DRB3, to be protective for the sexual transmission of HIV-1 among a sample of couples.[47]

Specific HLA alleles have also been shown to influence the genetic susceptibility to HIV-1 infection. The alleles HLA-B*27 and B*57 have been consistently associated with a favorable prognosis after infection, mostly by influencing early viral equilibration,[44] although they do not protect against HIV infection. In contrast, HLA-B*35 and HLA-B*53 have been associated with an unfavorable prognosis and higher viral load in infected individuals.[44] To date, no other single HLA-B allele has been shown to have a significant influence on the disease progression, nor have any associations between HLA-A or HLA-C alleles and natural history been demonstrated convincingly. However, research in the genetic influences on HIV susceptibility and natural history is being pursued by several research groups at present.

The combined effect of several of these genetic host factors on the natural history of HIV infection has been studied among 525 homosexual men in the Multicenter AIDS Cohort Study cohort who seroconverted between 1984 and 1996, prior to the advent of HAART.[48] On the basis of a regression tree analysis using a Cox proportional hazard model for times to AIDS, it was estimated that 30% of the men enrolled in MACS had one or more genetic resistance factors. The participants with the genetic resistance determinants experienced slower progression early after their infection, although the effect was limited to the first four years after infection. Clearly, additional evaluation of host resistance factors influencing HIV infection and progression will be important. Such studies require large cohorts of carefully followed subjects in various populations in whom genetic diversity can be evaluated. The Center for HIV AIDS Vaccine Immunology (CHAVI) is an example of one of a large collaboration of geneticists and other basic scientists working to bring together the wealth of genetic samples to answer these key questions in HIV vaccinology and cure. Some of the host factors currently believed to be related to susceptibility or resistance to HIV-1 infection and progression are listed in **Table 22-4.**

Research has discovered several cellular factors that suppress HIV-1 replication. It has been known for some time that several human and primate cell lines were naturally resistant to infection with HIV-1. One mechanism of this natural resistance has been identified as being due to a protein called tripartite motif (TRIM) 5-alpha, which has ubiquiton ligase activity. When the TRIM 5-alpha gene from monkey cells that were resistant to HIV-1 infection was transferred into and expressed by normally susceptible human cells, resistance to HIV-1 infection was induced.[49] This finding could eventually prove important for the development of new therapeutic approaches to control HIV-1 infection.

Another cellular mechanism to defend against infection with HIV-1 and other retroviruses has been described. This resistance is mediated by a cytidine deaminase termed APOBEC3G.[50] APOBEC3G mutates deoxycytidine to deoxyuridine in the negative strand of viral DNA; these multiple mutations render the virus inactive. However, many retroviruses, including HIV, have evolved the *vif* (viral infectivity factor) gene to inactivate APOBEC3G. The successful replication of HIV-1 in cells is determined by a balance between cellular APOBEC3G and *vif*. Recently, important mutations in APOBEC3G have been discovered.[51] One such mutation, H186 RR, has been associated with a more rapid decline in T lymphocytes and progression to AIDS. This codon-changing variant gene was found to be common among African Americans ($f = 37\%$) but is rare in European Americans ($f = 5\%$) with HIV-1 infection.[52]

Researchers continue to study genetic polymorphisms that influence HIV infection, transmission, and risk of progression. Despite the information gained through extensive genetic exploration, however, it is likely that HIV is affected by a broad constellation of host genes interacting with viral genes. This complex interaction between multiple genes complicates efforts to understand all the relevant interactions.

Table 22-4	Association Between Human Genetic Markers and Polymorphisms and Susceptability to HIV-1 Infection and Progression
Genetic Marker	**Effect on Risk**
CCR5	
Homozygous 32 base pair deletion	Absolute protection from CCR5 viruses
Heterozygous 32 base pair deletion	Slower progression
Promoter P1/-P1	Slower progression
CCR2-641	Slower progression
Increased CCL3L1 segmented duplication	Increased resistance
HLA Class 1 homozygous	Rapid progression
HLA-DR B3+ homozygous (couples)	Increased transmission
HLA concordance (in couples)	Increased transmission
HLA-B*57, HLA-B*27	Slower progression
HLA-B*35, HLA-B*53	More rapid progression
HLA-A2/6802 and HLA-A0205/6802	Decreased transmission
TRIM 5a	Slower progression associated with some SNPs due to an uncoating block
APOBEC3G (RR Genotype)	More rapid disease progression
NK (natural killer) KIR alleles (e.g., 3DS1 and 3D1 in pts. with BW4 genotype)	Slower progression

INFLAMMATION AND MICROBIAL TRANSLOCATION

As HIV-infected patients are now living longer thanks to effective therapy to suppress their HIV, their risk for chronic diseases is of increasing concern. Diabetes, cardiovascular disease, liver and kidney failure, and cancer are the leading causes of morbidity and mortality among this population. Not only are the rates of these diseases elevated compared to HIV-negative persons, but there is also an indication they may occur at younger ages. Given this pattern, HIV has been postulated to be a model of accelerated aging. It is not yet clear if this increase in morbidity and mortality is a direct result of the viral infection and the immune response or to drug toxicity.

Research is ongoing to investigate immune activation or inflammation as the underlying cause of these pathologies. For instance, cardiovascular disease is now recognized to be the result of inflammation that causes macrophages to traffic into arterial walls, form foamy cells, and eventually create plaques, which can subsequently rupture. Evaluation of inflammation markers among HIV-positive patients has found increased levels of chronic inflammation markers, including C-reactive Protein (hsCRP), D-dimer, interleukins 6 and 10 (IL-6 and IL-10), and many other biological markers.

The underlying cause of this inflammation remains under study as well. The infection with loss of gut-associated T lymphocytes (GALT) in early infection disrupts gut mucosal integrity and results in elevated plasma levels of bioactive bacterial lipopolysaccharide (LPS) and bacterial DNA—specifically, conserved sequences of DNA coding the 16s rRNA subunit (16s DNA). This increase leads to chronic inflammation and depletion of CD4+ T memory cells. This pathogenetic sequence of events, which is termed microbial translocation, is only partially reversed by effective antiviral therapy. Even in patients with well-controlled viremia, some replication is ongoing, which may also contribute to inflammation. Attempts to eliminate the last reservoirs of virus with intensification regimens and the addition of anti-inflammatory drugs to the antiviral regimen are under study. [53]

HIV GENOTYPES

HIV-1 has been classified into three groups, based on genetic relatedness—namely, groups M, N, and O. The latter two groups are geographically limited to countries in West Africa. Group M strains of HIV-1 have been divided into 11 genetic subtypes, designated A–K. Particular subtypes are found more commonly in certain areas of the world. In the Americas and Europe, subtype B strains have predominated, whereas in Africa various subtypes have been more common in different countries. In India, subtype C has predominated, and in Thailand and other countries in Southeast Asia, subtype E (now called CRF01_AE) has predominated.

Recombinants are becoming more common over time, and genetic subtypes are showing significant dynamism between and across countries, risk groups, and regions. Data from Africa, Asia, and South America have shown that a significant percentage of circulating strains represent mosaics of two or more subtypes. Coinfection by different subtypes is apparently not uncommon, leading to the conclusion that infection with HIV does not protect individuals from reinfection. Packaging of RNA from different subtypes into the same viral particle, coupled with the strand-switching activity of reverse transcriptase, generates recombinant HIV in coinfected individuals. Since full-length viral sequencing became more efficient in the past 5 years, it has become clear that subtypes and recombinants are equally important in the pandemic. Recombinant viruses are now identified as circulating recombinant forms (CRFs), if the same recombinants are commonly found in different geographic regions, or unique recombinant forms (URFs), if they are found in only a few individuals. The distribution of HIV-1 genotypes in three East African countries (Uganda, Tanzania, and Kenya) has been found to include 35–45% URFs, emphasizing the frequency of coinfections or super-infections with different HIV-1 genotypes in these populations. [54] Subtype E has been classified as a recombinant subtype since the first full-genome sequences were done; several other strains have been recognized as recombinants based on full-length or partial sequences. [54] HIV is a rapidly changing virus and the original subtypes can be imagined to be snapshots of the virus at the time they were defined and not actual specific types that are maintained due to some unknown selective advantage.

The relationship between HIV subtypes and clinical progression has been investigated in several populations with diverse strains. For example, in more than 2000 hospitalized patients in Thailand, the level of immune suppression, spectrum of opportunistic infections, and mortality were similar with subtype B-infected and CRF01_AE-infected patients. [55] However, a study of survival after infection with subtype CRF01_AE strains among Thai military conscripts found significantly shorter median survival (7.8–8.4 years) than has been reported among cohorts of persons from Western countries infected with subtype B strains (9.5–11 years).[56] Whether the decreased survival was due to viral, host, or environmental factors is not clear. In Kenya, where subtypes A, C, and D cocirculate, the plasma RNA levels were highest and the CD4 counts were lowest in persons infected with subtype C viruses.[57] In Uganda, subtype D infection has been reported to be associated with more rapid progression than subtype A.[58] In contrast, a study in Sweden showed no differences in the rate of CD4 cell decline or clinical progression among persons infected with subtypes A, B, C, or D.[59] In a prospective study in Senegal, persons infected with subtypes C, D, or G were eight times more likely to develop AIDS during follow-up than those infected with subtype A.[60] It is difficult to determine whether the apparent variation in progression among persons infected with different subtypes is due to genetic differences in the viruses, host characteristics, or other factors.

Studies of the genetic diversity of HIV strains have proved very useful in tracing epidemiologic patterns of HIV-1 transmission in populations. Among injection drug users (IDUs) in Russia, several subtypes of HIV-1—namely, subtype A, subtype B, and a recombinant A/B strain—have demonstrated drug trafficking links between Kaliningrad, a Russian enclave on the Baltic Sea[61] and more distant areas of Russia. Similarly, four overland heroin-trafficking routes in southeast Asia have been defined in this manner (Figure 22-7).[62]

IMPACT OF COINFECTIONS ON HIV

It is now widely accepted that the progression to AIDS among HIV-1–infected individuals is highly correlated with HIV-1 viral load and the CD4 cell count.[63,64] It is also likely that differential immune activation is the primary driver of the variability in progression to AIDS in persons infected with HIV-1.[65,66] Over the last several years, evidence has accumulated in support of the theory that coinfections, through chronic immune activation and its consequent effect on host immunity and HIV progression, may account for the enhanced HIV infection rate, accelerated progression of disease, and reduced survival seen in sub-Saharan Africa.[67]

Tuberculosis

Worldwide, tuberculosis (TB) is the most serious opportunistic infection among HIV-infected individuals. Previous advances to control the disease

were eliminated by the HIV epidemic, allowing for a resurgence of tuberculosis.[68] HIV has also fueled the current epidemics of multidrug- and extremely drug-resistant TB.

Tuberculosis most often comes under immunologic control in an HIV-positive patient and remains latent. There is an elevated risk of disease in the first year after infection, which then drops substantially to yield a 10% lifetime risk of active disease. The dominant cytokine response in M. tuberculosis infection is Th1, and 90% of individuals newly infected with M. tuberculosis do not develop active TB, in part, due to the Th1 immune response. However, when there is a Th1/Th2 shift, the predominant Th2 response may predispose such individuals to an increased risk of both HIV and active M. tuberculosis when they are exposed.[69] HIV-infected patients are then at high risk of active disease (10%) in the first year, and face an additional 2% risk each year that they will progress to active disease. Patients are also at higher risk of acquiring TB again. HIV-positive persons living in high TB incidence areas are also at an extremely high risk of TB, TB activation, and TB reinfection. Complicating this picture is the fact that TB diagnosis in HIV-positive patients is more difficult, as these individuals are often smear negative and, therefore, may be falsely screened as negative.

Because the TB and HIV epidemics have substantial geographic overlap, control of each disease is dependent on control of the other. Treatment of HIV before advanced immune suppression, treatment of TB for a year, and prophylaxis of patients with isoniazid (INH) are necessary to control the disease. Development of novel TB drugs that will shorten treatment times in HIV-positive patients and point-of-care diagnostic tools are active areas of research.

Treatment of Patients Who Are Coinfected with Tuberculosis and HIV

Patients with AIDS frequently are diagnosed when they have active, often disseminated, tuberculosis. Despite the availability of effective therapy for tuberculosis, it is the most common cause of death in AIDS patients in South Africa. The optimal timing of antituberculous chemotherapy and highly active antiretroviral therapy (HAART) was unclear until recently because of the common appearance of immune reconstitution syndrome (IRIS) in such patients during HAART treatment and drug interactions between rifampin and some classes of antiretroviral drugs. Also, the high pill burden, overlapping side effects, and programmatic difficulties in monitoring and managing therapy were common challenges.

To define the optimal course of therapy for patients coinfected with HIV and tuberculosis, a randomized controlled trial was done in South Africa, known as the Starting Antiretroviral Therapy at Three Points in Tuberculosis (SAPIT) trial. In this study, 642 patients were enrolled to evaluate the outcome among those who were treated with integrated TB and anti-HIV therapy compared to those in whom therapy was sequential, with TB therapy given first, followed by anti-HIV treatment. This trial found that mortality was 56% lower (5.4/100 person-years) when antiretroviral therapy began soon after TB therapy than when antiretroviral therapy was delayed until the completion of TB therapy (12.1/100 person-years). It is now recommended that HAART therapy be initiated soon after initiating TB therapy—for example, 4–6 weeks, after beginning anti-TB therapy in coinfected patients.[70]

Helminths

It has been hypothesized that parasitic infections—specifically, infections with helminths (schistosomiasis, ascaris, bookworm, and taenia)—may be responsible, in part, for the increased susceptibility and spread of HIV in the developing world.[71] Specifically, the immune activation caused by helminthic infections is thought to increase the susceptibility to and progression of HIV in coinfected persons. The evidence supporting this hypothesis comes in part from studies of Ethiopian Jews who have emigrated to Israel, as well as residents of the Western Cape region of South Africa. The majority of Ethiopian immigrants were infected with helminths, and their immunological profiles were dominated by activation of a Th2 response.[71-74] Some evidence indicates that Th2 clones are more permissive for HIV-1 infection, and a Th2 predominance or a Th2 immune activation may impede the development of antiviral immunity.[73] This immune activation is also marked by increased expression of HIV co-receptors and decreased secretion of β–chemokines in vitro.[73] Further, studies in some populations have found that anti-helminthic treatment has been associated with decreased HIV plasma viral load. However, the reduction in HIV viral load after anti-helminthic therapy has not been observed in all African populations.[75]

Malaria

Together, malaria and HIV cause more than 4 million deaths per year, with more than 90% of these deaths occurring in sub-Saharan Africa. These highly disease-burdened regions overlap geographically, prompting further speculation about the possibility of a direct interaction between HIV and malaria.

Early studies failed to find a significant direct impact of malaria on the prevalence or progression of HIV.[76] However, children with severe anemia due to malaria are at risk of transfusion-transmitted HIV. With the creation of the World Health Organization's (WHO) Roll Back Malaria partnership in 1998, as well as increased funding for both of these diseases from the Global Fund for HIV, Tuberculosis, and Malaria, increased attention has been paid to these three significant diseases. The possibility of interactions between HIV and malaria has major public health implications, and the growing body of evidence lending support to this possibility justifies the need to better understand these interactions (**Table 22-5**). Recent studies have demonstrated an increased HIV-1 viral load in persons with malaria, which decreased with successful treatment of malaria.[77] Studies of pregnant women have found an increased rate of mother-to-child transmission (MTCT) of HIV-1 associated with placental malaria.[78] A study in Uganda of patients with partial immunity to malaria found that HIV-1-infected persons more frequently developed clinical malaria and had higher parasite levels than those who were HIV negative.[79]

Hepatitis C Virus

Because of shared routes of transmission, hepatitis C virus (HCV) infection is common in HIV-positive individuals and is considered an opportunistic infection of HIV.[80-82] In the United States, 15–30% of HIV-infected persons are also infected with HCV; however, the prevalence of HIV-HCV coinfection varies markedly by the route of acquisition of HIV infection (risk category). For example, among HIV-positive patients seen at the Johns Hopkins HIV Clinic (*n* = 1955), HCV coinfection prevalence rates were as follows: 85.1% of those reporting injection drug use, 14.3% of those reporting heterosexual contact, and 9.8% of those reporting male homosexual contact.[78]

HCV infection in patients with HIV infection has been associated with higher HCV RNA viral load and accelerated progression of HCV-related liver disease.[81-83] One study reported that HCV RNA levels were higher in persons with hemophilia who became infected with HIV than in those who did not, and that liver failure occurred exclusively in those coinfected with HIV and HCV.[83] In a study of liver disease and hepatocellular carcinoma among 4865 men exposed to HCV-contaminated blood products, at all ages the risk for liver-related death after HCV

Table 22-5	Overview of the Interactions Between HIV and Malaria		
Type of Interaction	Pregnant Women	Children	Adult Men and Non-Pregnant Women
The effect of HIV on malaria			
— Increased risk of infection with malaria	+	?	+
— Increased malaria parasite density	+	?	+
— Decreased response to standard antimalarial treatment	+	?	+
The effect of malaria on HIV			
— Increased HIV viral load	+	?	+
— Increased risk of HIV transmission	?(1)	+(2)	?
Effects of dual infection			
— Increased risk of illness	+	+	+
— Increased risk of anemia	+	+	+
— Increased risk of low birth weight	+	-	-

Notes:
+ Evidence for interaction available
? Lack of direct evidence of data
− Interaction is not applicable
(1) Through mother-to-child transmission
(2) Through unscreened blood transfusions to treat anaemia
Reproduced from *Malaria and HIV/AIDS: Interactions and Implications: Conclusions of a Technical Consultation*, June 2004, © Roll Back Malaria/WHO. http://whqlibdoc.who.int/hq/2004/WHO_HIV_2004.08_eng.pdf. Accessed October 24, 2012.

exposure was 1.4% and 6.5% for HIV-negative and HIV-positive individuals, respectively.[84] Data from most studies confirm the detrimental impact of HIV infection on hepatitis C infection. As survival of HIV-infected persons has been extended due to HAART and the prophylaxis of traditional OIs, it is likely that hepatitis C morbidity and mortality will increase.[85]

A significant challenge in HCV research has been the difficulty encountered when trying to measure the state of liver pathology. Although serum markers of liver function have been developed to evaluate the functional capacity of the liver, they have considerable variability and their predictive value is more complex in dual infection. Liver biopsy remains the gold standard, but it is an invasive procedure that measures the status of the liver only in the location of the biopsy. One new technique that shows promise in evaluating the entire liver is an ultrasound scan of the liver, known as fiberscan. This device is licensed in Europe, but as of 2012 had not yet secured U.S. approval. If approved by the U.S. Food and Drug Administration (FDA), it provide give a less invasive measure of liver function across the entire organ.

The issue of whether HCV infection also adversely affects progression of HIV disease remains controversial.[82] In a prospective study of 416 HIV seroconverters in Italy, those with and without HCV infection progressed to AIDS at similar rates.[86] Among the 1955 men seen at the Johns Hopkins HIV Clinic, there was no difference in progression to AIDS or death associated with HCV infection after adjusting

for HAART and HIV suppression.[79] Conversely, one study of 3111 persons receiving HAART reported that HCV-infected persons had a modestly increased risk for progression to a new AIDS-defining event or death, even among the subgroup with continuous suppression of HIV replication.[87] This same study found that CD4 increases were smaller after effective anti-HIV therapy in persons with HCV infection than in those without such coinfection. However, a review of the literature—including two subsequent studies evaluating the immunologic response to potent antiretroviral therapy—failed to confirm these observations.[88–90]

Recent advances in HCV therapy have resulted in significantly higher cure rates for all HCV-infected patients. These treatments raise the possibility that many coinfected patients can clear their HCV infection. To date, uptake of HCV therapy has been slow, but is gaining momentum. Advances in the next few years may change the HCV/HIV epidemic considerably.

GB Virus C

GB virus C (GBV-C) is a flavivirus that is closely related to hepatitis C virus. Although GBV-C was first detected by nucleic acid amplification in patients with non-A, non-B hepatitis, the virus does not replicate in hepatocytes and is not a hepatitis virus. In fact, GBV-C has not been associated consistently with any human disease (it is not even screened from the U.S. blood supply), although infections are quite common among injection drug users and homosexual men.

GBV-C replicates in CD4+ T cells.[91] Numerous studies have shown no effect or a beneficial effect for patients coinfected with GBV-C and HIV.[92–101] Most of these studies were done among cohorts of prevalent HIV-1-infected persons, in whom the duration of HIV-1 infection was not precisely known but was estimated by modeling.[87–98] The impact of GBV-C on untreated HIV required a study with known date of HIV acquisition.

The longstanding Multicenter AIDS Cohort Study (MACS) has known dates of seroconversion. In this cohort, it was found that there was no effect of GBV-C on survival when it was measured shortly after seroconversion; when measured 5 to 6 years after HIV seroconversion, however, men without GBV-C viremia were 2.78 times more likely to die than men with persistent GBV-C infection. Men in the MACS cohort who cleared their GBV-C viremia had more rapid progression and poorer survival than either those with persistent infection or HIV-positive men who never experienced a GBV-C coinfection.[102]

At the same time, a report from the Amsterdam cohort of homosexual men found no association between GBV-C persistent viremia and survival or progression to AIDS; instead, men who lost their GBV-C viremia were three times more likely to progress than men who never had GBV-C virus infection in their cohort.[101] These authors postulated that loss of GBV-C viremia was a marker for loss of sufficient CD4+ T cells to support continued GBV-C replication. Data were reported recently from the Viral Activation Transfusion Study in which patients with advanced HIV infection who needed transfusions were randomized to receive either leukoreduced or non-leukoreduced red cell transfusions. The mortality was 78% lower (HR = 0.22) among patients who acquired incident GBV-C infections in this study despite similar CD-4+ cell counts and HIV viral load at baseline prior to their GBV-C incident infection.[374] These prospective data were free of the bias associated with higher GBV-C infection prevalence in subjects with higher CD-4+ cells in several other observational studies.

These studies highlight the importance of understanding the full longitudinal history of a disease. Without multiple samples to evaluate changes in GBV-C status over time, the apparent inconsistencies in the relationship could not have been elucidated. Interest in GBV-C has waned considerably as the protective effect of the coinfection has been demonstrated to be substantially weaker than the effect of ART. Previous protocols to intentionally infect participants with GBV-C who have limited drug options due to resistance have not been pursued as new drug classes have been licensed.

Laboratory research into mechanisms of viral interference of GBV-C has continued. In vitro experiments have found that GBV-C-infected CD4+ T cells are more resistant to infection with HIV-1.[103] Also, the expression of a gene for the chemokines RANTES, MIP 1-α, MIP-1-β, and SDF-1 and secretion of the chemokines into the culture supernates were higher in GBV-C-infected cells. Surface expression of CCR5 was also significantly lower in GBV-C-infected cells.[103]

Other Agents

Several other coinfections have been reported to be associated with transient decreases in HIV-1 viral load, including measles,[104,105] dengue fever,[106] and scrub typhus.[107] The mechanism of the suppression of HIV replication during these acute infections is believed to be associated with immune activation and elevated cytokine and/or chemokine levels from the coinfection. However, these acute infections are associated with only transient reductions in the viral load. In addition some investigators have reported HIV-2 co-infections to be associated with slower progression and lower viral load among patients with HIV-1 infections.[375]

ANTIRETROVIRAL THERAPY

No Therapy to Monotherapy/Dual Therapy

HIV therapy can be loosely divided into several time periods. The pre-therapy period was from zoonosis until 1983, when the disease was recognized. Treatment of opportunistic infections and prophylaxis for OIs was the only option until AZT's licensure. From 1987 until 1996, a few more nucleoside reverse transcriptase inhibitors (NRTIs) came to the market; thus this era is called the "monotherapy" or "dual-therapy" era.

There has been a marked improvement in the natural history of HIV infections when responses are measured at the population level. An evaluation of the proportion of men in the Multicenter AIDS Cohort Study who were receiving various forms of therapy between 1986 and 1999 and their progression to AIDS documented the benefits of various regimens in a cohort of HIV-infected men. A comparison of the progression of infection among HIV-positive MACS participants, after adjusting for the duration of infection at baseline, found the relative hazard of progression to AIDS during the era of no treatment to be 1.52 (95% CI: 0.93–2.49) compared with men in the monotherapy era.[108] The hazard of progression in the era of combination therapy was 1.03 (95% CI: 0.77–1.38), and during the era of HAART it has been 0.31 (95% CI: 0.21–0.45).[108]

Mortality from AIDS in the general population in the United States declined dramatically with the availability of HAART after 1996. A CDC-sponsored HIV outpatient study (HOPS) reported the use of HAART therapy and mortality among 1000 patients with AIDS

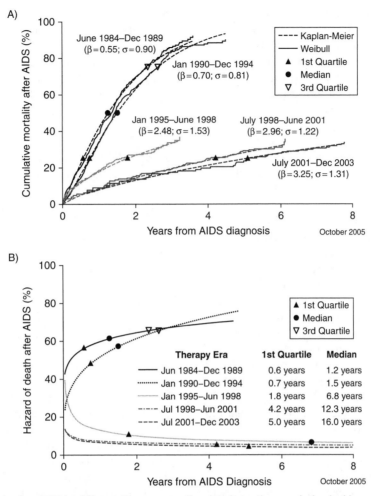

Figure 22-8 Risk of death after AIDS in different therapy eras. Figure A shows the cumulative incidence of death among persons with an AIDS diagnosis. Figure B shows that before ARVs after AIDS the risk of death continued to increase. In contrast, in the latest therapy eras, while there is a large hazard at the time of the event, once a person survives 2 years after AIDS, the hazard of death is very low. Modified from Schneider et al. Patterns of the hazard of death after AIDS through the evolution of antiretroviral therapy: 1984–2004. *AIDS* 2005;19:2009–2018.

and CD4+ cell counts less than 100 cells/mm³. In these patients, approximately 80% were using protease inhibitors (PIs) by 1997, and the mortality declined from 29.4 deaths per 100 person-years in 1995 to 8.8 deaths per 100 person-years in 1997 (**Figure 22-8**). In addition to decreased mortality, the incidence of AIDS-defining opportunistic infections have been reduced dramatically in the HAART era.[109]

HIV therapy is in constant evolution and the reader interested in the latest recommendation should go to Internet sources to find the most up-to-date recommendations. There are also several excellent references that are frequently updated, including *The Johns Hopkins Hospital 2012 Edition, Medical Management of HIV infection*, by John G. Bartlett and Joel E. Gallant (hopkins-aids.edu/mmhiv/order.html.) In addition, the International Antiviral Society-USA panel makes updated recommendations for therapy on a regular

basis. Their recommendations are published in the Journal of the American Medical Association.[378]

As a retrovirus, HIV has numerous pathways that are not used by the human host and, therefore, are good drug targets. The first antiretroviral to show any success in clinical trials was zidovudine (AZT). AZT is an NRTI that was developed in cooperation between Burroughs Wellcome and the National Cancer Institute out of cancer therapy programs that had been interested in retroviruses as causes of cancer. AIDS activism and the Ronald Reagan administration's drive to reduce federal regulation synergistically pushed for an accelerated approval process so that AZT moved from the laboratory to approval in a little more than two years. AZT was approved for use in HIV patients on March 20, 1987, and as a postexposure prophylaxis in the 1990s. Early optimism, which emerged as patients were rescued literally from death's door, was crushed by HIV's ability to rapidly develop resistance to this therapy. To effectively treat this rapidly mutating virus, it became clear, a multipronged treatment approach would be necessary. In the early 1990s the protease inhibitor class began clinical trials, and on December 6, 1995, saquinavir was approved.

Hit Early, Hit Hard

While many patients received HIV medications prior to licensure because they were enrolled in clinical trials and received drugs under "compassionate use" clauses, the highly active antiretroviral therapy (HAART)—in Europe, called combination antiretroviral therapy (CART)—era began in earnest in 1996. Most patients were able to suppress the virus to levels below the threshold of detectability with the licensed viral load assays (i.e., fewer than 50 copies/µL). This led to the hypothesis that with aggressive therapy for several years, the infection might be "cured" through the combined effects of the drugs and the host's immune system. The catchphrase for HAART during this period became "Hit hard, hit HIV early."[110]

Subsequently, the latent viral reservoir in long-lived resting lymphocytes and macrophages was described, leading to a change in thinking about appropriate antiretroviral therapy. Modeling the time to the natural elimination of this reservoir of latent virus suggested that the reservoir of these cells or their daughter cells would persist for 60 years or more.[111] Adding to this discovery of the latent reservoir was the recognition that patients who were treated for several years with repeatedly undetectable viral loads commonly returned to their pretreatment viral loads within a few weeks after withdrawal of treatment. This observation led to the rejection of the hypothesis that HIV infection could be cured with currently available drugs.

Unfortunately, the new drug regimens had severe toxicities. Complications of such therapy include a variety of conditions, especially lactic acidosis, lipodystrophy, visceral fat accumulation, insulin resistance, and diabetes, especially with thymidine analogs, such as d4T (stavudine), AZT (zidovudine), and protease inhibitors. Also, peripheral neuropathy, hepatitis, rash (including Stevens-Johnson syndrome), and renal toxicity have been reported as complications of therapy with antiretroviral drugs. The reader should consult references describing HIV/AIDS therapy for more details.

Treatment-Sparing Regimens

Because of the cost of antiretroviral therapy, the pill burden, and the side effects, it was considered possible to give intermittent treatment relief to patients whose virus was suppressed and in whom the CD4+ cell count had recovered. In addition, prospective studies determined that many patients taking antiretroviral drugs often interrupted their therapy. Therefore, it was proposed to purposefully interrupt therapy in selected patients who had controlled their HIV infection, in a practice called "structured treatment interruption."

To determine whether structured treatment interruptions were associated with adverse outcomes, two large clinical trials were conducted. The first trial, called Strategies for Management of Antiretroviral Therapy (SMART), enrolled 5472 patients. In 2720 of these individuals, therapy was interrupted when the CD4+ cell count exceeded 350 cells/mm^3 and restarted after it fell below 250 cells/mm^3 (the treatment-sparing arm of the trial). In the control group of 2752 patients, therapy was continued uninterrupted (the viral suppression arm). The study ended early in January 2006 when it was found that opportunistic disease or death occurred in 120 patients in the treatment-sparing group (3.3 events per 100 person-years) and in 47 patients in the viral suppression group (1.3 events per 100 person-years).[112]

In the other trial, known as the Staccato trial, 450 subjects with CD4+ cell counts greater than 350 cells/mm^3 and HIV viral load less than 50 copies/mL were randomized to receive either continuous treatment or interrupted therapy. This smaller study also found that adverse events were more common in those patients with interrupted therapy, although they experienced cost savings and their HIV viruses did not become resistant to drugs.[113]

After the results of the SMART trial were reported, an expert committee of the International AIDS Society recommended against treatment interruptions.[114]

Viral Suppression and Cure

Today, supported by studies that demonstrate the lasting damage the HIV virus has on the immune system, and facilitated by new, more convenient regimens with better toxicity profiles, the pendulum has swung back to earlier treatment. Some sources even advocate treatment at the time of infection to preserve as much immune function as possible. In fact, the most recent recommendations of the Expert Committee on Antiretroviral Therapy of the International AIDS Society are to consider offering treatment to any patient with HIV infection despite the CD-4+ cell count .

The North American AIDS Cohort Collaboration Observational Research Database (NA-ACCORD) study reported on the risk of AIDS and death among patients starting ART in Canada and the United States. Using a marginal structural method (MSM) analysis, these researchers evaluated survival according to the CD4 cell count at which 17,571 participants initiated ART. MSM analysis allows the study team to structure the data as though patients were entering a hypothetical clinical trial in which patients who started with between 500 and 351 CD4 cells/mm³ were compared to those who started fewer than 350 cells/mm³. Those who started at the lower CD4 cell count were found to have a 69% increased risk of death. In a second analysis, those who initiated therapy with fewer than 500 CD4 cells/mm³compared to those who started therapy with higher CD4+ cell counts had a 94% higher risk of death.[114]

The HIV Causal Collaboration gathered data on more than 20,000 patients in the United States and Europe. In a more robust analysis using a dynamic marginal structural model pioneered by Hernan and Robins, this team modeled a hypothetical clinical trial in which multiple CD4 strata were defined and patients were assigned a status of "initiated" or "deferred" within each strata. The team found that the risk of AIDS or death was increased by 38% for those who delayed treatment until after their CD4 cell counts fell below 350 cells/mm³ and by 90% for those who delayed treatment until their CD4 cell counts fell below 200 cells/mm³.[115]

These novel statistical methods have been difficult to explain to the broader medical community, but the consistency of the finding that AIDS and death are reduced when ART is initiated earlier is reassuring. As these methods are further refined and strengthened, it is likely that observational data will increasingly be used to inform clinical effectiveness.

Now that the virus can be well controlled with antiviral medications, emphasis has shifted to finding "the cure." A cure for HIV could be achieved either by completing eliminating the virus or by developing a robust immune response that could control the virus in a latent state indefinitely.

The Guidelines

The most important questions regarding antiretroviral therapy in an HIV-infected treatment-naive patient are when to start treatment, which drugs to start with, when to change drugs, and which drugs to change to. In 1995, physicians with specific expertise in HIV-related basic science and clinical research were invited by the International AIDS Society—USA to serve on a volunteer panel to evaluate the scientific evidence on therapy and to make broad recommendations. This panel, which has augmented since 1999 with international experts, meets periodically to evaluate the evidence and update its recommendations. The reader should refer to the panel's reports, which are usually published in the *Journal of the American Medical Association*, for these detailed recommendations. The recently published recommendation for when to start and what to start with are presented in **Table 22-6**.

Table 22-6	When to Start Antiretroviral Therapy (ART) in Persons with HIV Infection: U.S. Recommendations and Those of the World Health Organization

International Antiviral Society – USA Panel recommends:
1. Treatment of ART should be offered to all HIV-infected persons regardless of CD4 Cell count
2. ART is especially indicated for the following patients:
   A. Pregnant women
   B. Patients with an opportunistic infection
   C. Chronic hepatitis B virus or hepatitis C virus infection
   D. Age above 60 years
   E. HIV-associated nephropathy
   F. Acute HIV infection
   G. CD4 count below 500 cells/up
   H. Tuberculosis infection
Start ART within 2 weeks if CD4 cell count below 50ul and by at least 8-12 weeks if CD4 count is higher in patients with TB meningitis

Early ART in patients with Cryptococcal meningitis has been associated with higher mortality, so these patients should be managed in consultation with an expert
World Health Organization recommends:
   A. Antiretroviral Therapy (2)
   B. In patients with CD4 count below 350 cells/ul
   C. In patients with AIDS or Constitutional Symptoms of HIV, i.e. weight loss >10%, diarrhea or fever lasting >1 month regardless of CD4 cell count

Data from Thompson et al. *Antiretroviral Treatment of Adult HIV Infection. JAMA* 2012; 308: 387–402; and the World Health Organization (2008). *Scaling up Antiretroviral Therapy in Resource-limited Settings.* www.who.int/hiv/pub/arv/pub18/en. Accessed August 3, 2012.

In keeping with the multipronged approach to HIV to maximize efficacy and limit the emergence of resistant virus, the guidelines generally recommend at least two classes of drugs in a regimen. Only recently has the abacavir, zidovudine, and laimivudine (three-NRTI) combination been accepted as a regimen.

The panel does not recommend a single drug combination as optimal therapy, but rather lists several combinations of antiretroviral drug classes that are recommended:

- Two NRTIs and one NNRTI
- Two NRTIs and one PI
- Three NRTIs (e.g., abacavir, zidovudine, and lamivudine)

It is important to consider the fact that HAART therapy has delayed the progression and mortality from HIV/AIDS, but the treatment is not without toxicities. HIV-infected patients appear to have an elevated risk of many chronic diseases, including diabetes, cardiovascular disease, cancer, and neurologic decline, among others. The individual contributions of the HIV virus, coinfections, high-risk behaviors such as drug use and smoking, and therapy to the development of these diseases are not known.

Perhaps patients who have used only the lowest-toxicity HAART regimens will be found to have a lower burden of these diseases. Alternatively, perhaps those patients who have the most fully suppressed levels of virus will benefit the most.

Studies to understand this most likely multifactorial disease risk profile will require large sample sizes, long-term follow-up, and novel epidemiologic designs and statistical analysis. Several large cohort studies (50,000–500,000 patients) have been developed in the last decade: the EuroCoord collaboration of European clinical databases, the Center for AIDS Research Network Clinical Study (CNICS), the International Epidemiologic Databases to Evaluate AIDS (IeDEA), and others. These studies have been built upon the clinical programs that treat patients globally. By improving the quality of medical records, maximizing the use of electronic medical records, improving harmonization of data collection across multiple sites, and using advanced statistical methods such as marginal structural modeling, these studies hope to be able to provide the least biased estimates of therapy effectiveness in the most generalizable populations.

Table 22-7 lists the drugs approved for use in the United States and the date of their approval for

Table 22-7	Antiretroviral Drugs Approved by the FDA			
Brand Name	**Generic Name**	**Manufacturer Name**	**Approval Date**	**Time to Approval**
Multi-class Combination Products				
Atripla	efavirenz, emtricitabine and tenofovir disoproxil fumarate	Bristol-Myers Squibb and Gilead Sciences	12-Jul-06	2.5 months
Complera	emtricitabine, rilpivirine, and tenofovir disoproxil fumarate	Gilead Sciences	10-Aug-11	6 months
Nucleoside Reverse Transcriptase Inhibitors (NRTIs)				
Combivir	lamivudine and zidovudine	GlaxoSmithKline	27-Sep-97	3.9 months
Emtriva	emtricitabine, FTC	Gilead Sciences	02-Jul-03	10 months
Epivir	lamivudine, 3TC	GlaxoSmithKline	17-Nov-95	4.4 months
Epzicom	abacavir and lamivudine	GlaxoSmithKline	02-Aug-04	10 months
Hivid	zalcitabine, dideoxycytidine, ddC (no longer marketed)	Hoffmann-La Roche	19-Jun-92	7.6 months
Retrovir	zidovudine, azidothymidine, AZT, ZDV	GlaxoSmithKline	19-Mar-87	3.5 months
Trizivir	abacavir, zidovudine, and lamivudine	GlaxoSmithKline	14-Nov-00	10.9 months
Truvada	tenofovir disoproxil fumarate and emtricitabine	Gilead Sciences, Inc.	02-Aug-04	5 months
Videx EC	enteric coated didanosine, ddI EC	Bristol Myers-Squibb	31-Oct-00	9 months
Videx	didanosine, dideoxyinosine, ddI	Bristol Myers-Squibb	9-Oct-91	6 months
Viread	tenofovir disoproxil fumarate, TDF	Gilead	26-Oct-01	5.9 months
Zerit	stavudine, d4T	Bristol Myers-Squibb	24-Jun-94	5.9 months
Ziagen	abacavir sulfate, ABC	GlaxoSmithKline	17-Dec-98	5.8 months

(Continued)

Table 22-7	(Continued)			
Brand Name	**Generic Name**	**Manufacturer Name**	**Approval Date**	**Time to Approval**
Nonnucleoside Reverse Transcriptase Inhibitors (NNRTIs)				
Edurant	rilpivirine	Tibotec Therapeutics	20-May-11	10 months
Intelence	etravirine	Tibotec Therapeutics	18-Jan-08	6 months
Rescriptor	delavirdine, DLV	Pfizer	4-Apr-97	8.7 months
Sustiva	efavirenz, EFV	Bristol Myers-Squibb	17-Sep-98	3.2 months
Viramune (Immediate Release)	nevirapine, NVP	Boehringer Ingelheim	21-Jun-96	3.9 months
Viramune XR (Extended Release)	nevirapine, NVP	Boehringer Ingelheim	25-Mar-11	9.9 months
Protease Inhibitors (PIs)				
Agenerase	amprenavir, APV	GlaxoSmithKline	15-Apr-99	6 months
Aptivus	tipranavir, TPV	Boehringer Ingelheim	22-Jun-05	6 months
Crixivan	indinavir, IDV,	Merck	13-Mar-96	1.4 months
Fortovase	saquinavir (no longer marketed)	Hoffmann-La Roche	7-Nov-97	5.9 months
Invirase	saquinavir mesylate, SQV	Hoffmann-La Roche	6-Dec-95	3.2 months
Kaletra	lopinavir and ritonavir, LPV/RTV	Abbott Laboratories	15-Sep-00	3.5 months
Lexiva	Fosamprenavir Calcium, FOS-APV	GlaxoSmithKline	20-Oct-03	10 months
Norvir	ritonavir, RTV	Abbott Laboratories	1-Mar-96	2.3 months
Prezista	darunavir	Tibotec, Inc.	23-Jun-06	6 months
Reyataz	atazanavir sulfate, ATV	Bristol-Myers Squibb	20-Jun-03	6 months
Viracept	nelfinavir mesylate, NFV	Agouron Pharmaceuticals	14-Mar-97	2.6 months
Fusion Inhibitors				
Fuzeon	enfuvirtide, T-20	Hoffmann-La Roche & Trimeris	13-Mar-03	6 months
Entry Inhibitors – CCR5 co-receptor antagonist				
Selzentry	maraviroc	Pfizer	06-August-07	8 months
HIV integrase strand transfer inhibitors				
Isentress	raltegravir	Merck & Co., Inc.	12-Oct-07	6 months

Reproduced from the U.S. Food and Drug Administration (2011). For Consumers: Antiretroviral drugs used in the treatment of HIV infection. http://www.fda.gov/ForConsumers/ByAudience/ForPatientAdvocates/HIVandAIDSActivities/ucm118915.htm. Last updated August 25, 2011. Accessed October 1, 2012.

the HIV/AIDS indication. More antiviral drugs are approved for the treatment of HIV/AIDS than for any other viral infection in humans. However, the fairly large number of drugs available for the treatment of HIV infections in the United States, in part, reflects the fact that none is capable of eradicating the virus or producing a permanent cure, and many have significant toxicity, are expensive, or are difficult to take. The development of viral resistance to many drugs is quite common, especially when adherence is not excellent (i.e., more than 80%). In addition, adverse drug reactions are quite common, meaning that drug regimens must be changed frequently.

Nevertheless, antiretroviral therapy has had a profound effect on the natural history of HIV in countries where HAART is available. The success of antiretroviral therapy in decreasing AIDS mortality in industrialized countries has fueled the development of strategies by WHO to provide effective treatment for resource-limited countries. Effective antiretroviral drugs have now been combined in a single tablet that is effective, is simpler to use, and improves adherence. The most recent of these drugs, Atripla, was licensed by the FDA in July 2006. It combines three drugs into a single tablet, which effectively treats HIV as a single daily dose (**Table 22-8**).

Immune Reconstitution Disease

A particularly devastating side effect of HIV/AIDS treatment is immune reconstitution inflammatory syndrome (IRIS). Patients in whom effective antiretroviral therapy is begun, and particularly those who were severely immunosuppressed with CD4+ T-cell counts below 100 cells/mm^3, can develop disseminated immune reactions. As the functioning immune system is restored and the CD4+ T-cell count increases, symptoms often

Table 22-8	WHO and U.S. Guidelines for PMTCT		
WHO 2012 Guidelines			**US Perinatal Guidelines 2012**
Treatment for CD4 count ≤350 cells/mm³		Prophylaxis for CD4 count >350 cells/mm³	Preconception counseling: Discuss childbearing intentions with all women of childbearing age, inform about effective and appropriate contraceptive methods to reduce unintended pregnancy, include information on safer sexual practices, evaluate ARVs with consideration of the women's health and therapy effectiveness
Option A			**All HIV-Infected Pregnant Women**
Triple ARVs starting as soon as diagnosed continued for life		Antipartum: AZT starting as early as 14 weeks gestation Itrapartum: at onset of labor sdNVP and first dose AZT/3TC Postpartum: daily AZT/3TC through 7 days	Counseled about and administered antiretroviral drugs during pregnancy for prevention of perinatal transmission, regardless of their HIV RNA levels
Option B same initial ARVs for both:			**Serodiscordant Couples**
Triple ARV's starting as soon as diagnosed, continued for life		Triple ARVs starting as early as 14 weeks gestation and continued intrapartum and through childbirth if not breastfeeding or until 1 week after cessation of all breastfeeding	• Treatment of the infected partner may not be fully protective against sexual transmission of HIV. • Techniques to prevent exposure of the uninfected partner including artificial or self-insemination methods, donor sperm or sperm preparation techniques if the male partner is HIV+ should be discussed.
Option B+: Same treatment and prophylaxis. Regardless of CD4 count, triple ARVs starting as soon as diagnosed, continued for life			• HIV positive members of a discordant couple are strongly recommended to receive ARVs if their CD4 cell count <550 and are moderately recommended at higher CD4
Infant			
Option A: Daily NVP from birth through 1 week after cessation of breastfeeding. If mother is on treatment or not breastfeeding AZT/NVP through 4–6 weeks	Option B/B+ AZT or NVP through 4–6 weeks regardless of infant feeding method		• 6 weeks of Zidovudine with three doses of NVP at birth, 48 hours later, and 96 hours after second dose. • Breastfeeding is not recommended for all HIV-1 infected women in the U.S., including those taking antiretrovirals

Data from the Panel on Treatment of HIV-Infected Pregnant Women and Prevention of Perinatal Transmission. Recommendations for Use of Antiretroviral Drugs in Pregnant HIV-1-Infected Women for Maternal Health and Interventions to Reduce Perinatal HIV Transmission in the United States. Available at http://aidsinfo.nih.gov/contentfiles/lvguidelines/PerinatalGL.pdf. Accessed October 16, 2012; and the World Health Organization (2012). Programmatic Update Use of Antiretroviral Drugs for Treating Pregnant Women and Preventing HIV Infection for Infants; Executive Summary April 2012. http://www.who.int/hiv/PMTCT_update.pdf. Accessed October 16, 2012.

appear from an inflammatory response to an infection that was previously tolerated during the time of severe immunosuppression.[117] Signs and symptoms of IRIS include fever, pleural effusions, ascites, pulmonary infiltrates, osteomyelitis, meningitis, renal failure, and occasionally mortality. IRIS most commonly occurs in patients who are coinfected with HIV and TB.

The first reports of *M. tuberculosis*–associated IRIS were published in 1998 after the advent of HAART.[118] Since them, IRIS has been reported in

M. avium-infected patients,[119] patients infected with *M. leprae* or *M. kansasii*,[120] and patients who received bacillus Calmette-Guerin (BCG) vaccine when they were immunosuppressed.[121] This syndrome has also been seen with a range of other opportunistic infections, including cytomegalovirus, hepatitis B and C viruses, *Cryptococcus neoformans*, *Pneumocystis jaroveckil carinii* progressive multifocal leukoencephalopathy (caused by JC virus), leishmaniasis, and cerebral toxoplasmosis. Control of severe IRIS reactions can usually be managed with the use of corticosteroids, in addition to specific anti-infection therapy directed at the opportunistic pathogen.[122]

MODES OF TRANSMISSION AND RISK FACTORS

HIV infection may be transmitted by sexual intercourse, injection drug use or other parenteral exposures, transfusion of blood or blood products, organ transplantation, and occupational exposure to HIV-contaminated blood or body fluids.

Sexual Transmission

Transmission of HIV through sexual intercourse is estimated to account for 75–80% of the global HIV infections that have occurred to date.[123] Unprotected receptive anal intercourse is the most effective means of sexual transmission. The risk varies according to various factors but probably is on the order of 0.5–1.0% per contact.[123] Both males and females are equally vulnerable to infection by anal intercourse. The transmission from infected males to females by vaginal intercourse has been estimated to occur at an average rate of 0.3% per contact, and transmission from an infected female to a male at a somewhat lower rate.[123] However, a study in Uganda found similar rates of transmission from men to women, and vice versa.[124] Traumatic sex, such as from fisting among MSM or rough heterosexual sex, is associated with an increased rate of transmission. Sociocultural situations that increase the likelihood of traumatic sex, such as rape, use of vaginal tightening agents, or sex while under the influence of cocaine or alcohol, increase the risk of HIV transmission. The presence of a sexually transmitted infection in either partner increases the risk of transmission by approximately fivefold.[125] The increased risk is greatest with a genital ulcer disease, such as syphilis, herpes, or chancroid. However, nonulcerative sexually transmitted diseases (STDs) also increases the risk of transmission in part because of the activated inflammatory cells in the genital tract, many of which may be quite susceptible to HIV infection.[126]

Another important factor in the risk of HIV-1 transmission is the viral load in the infected partner. Studies in Uganda and Thailand have estimated a 2.5-fold increased risk of transmission for each log increment in the viral load.[124,127] No transmission occurred in these populations when the viral load was less than 1500 copies/μL, despite unprotected sex.

Because of the high viral load occurring in primary infection prior to an immune response, the risk

of transmission is high at this time.[128] It has been postulated that early in an epidemic, the risk per sexual contact may be higher than it is in a more mature epidemic because a higher proportion of infected persons has recent infections with high viral loads.[129] High viral load also occurs late in the natural history, after the onset of AIDS. However, at this time patients are frequently quite ill, so unprotected sex is less frequent. In addition, most persons are well aware of their HIV infection after the onset of AIDS and may be more likely to use barrier precautions during sex.

Cervical ectopy (replacement of the multilayered squamous cells at the cervical os with single-layered columnar epithelium) increases the risk of HIV transmission.[130] The higher prevalence of cervical ectopy in adolescent girls after menarche may partially explain the higher HIV seroprevalence among 15- to 24-year-old females compared to older women in sub-Saharan African countries.[131]

Hormonal contraceptives (in the absence of condom use) have been shown in some studies to increase the risk of HIV transmission,[132,133] whereas other studies have failed to confirm this association.[134] Women using hormonal contraceptives may have more frequent intercourse or use barrier methods less often, which may confound this association. However, it is biologically plausible that some hormonal contraceptives could increase the risk of HIV transmission by increasing cervical ectopy. The specific hormonal composition of the contraceptive may also influence the risk and explain some of the discrepant results reported by various researchers. Contraceptives containing progesterone, which have a greater effect on the cervical epithelium, may be associated with a greater risk.[133] Unprotected sex during pregnancy and menstruation has been shown to increase the risk of transmission in some studies.[135]

In all regions of sub-Saharan Africa, the predominant means of transmission of HIV-1 is believed by most experts to be heterosexual. However, there is considerable heterogeneity in the prevalence of HIV infection in different regions of the continent. In particular, the rates of infection in populations in Western Africa are considerably lower than those in Eastern and Southern Africa.[136] To explore some of the determinants of these regional differences, an ecological study was done in four cities in sub-Saharan Africa.[137] This study enrolled 900–1000 persons in Catonou, Benin, and in Yaoundé, Cameroon, where the adult population HIV prevalence was approximately 4%, compared to Kisumu, Kenya, and Ndola,

Zambia, where the prevalence was in the range of 25–30%. The participants were questioned about their sexual practices, condom use, STD history, and other potential factors that might explain the differences in HIV-1 prevalence in their country. Although sexual behavior variables were strongly correlated with HIV-1 prevalence at the individual level, only moderate differences were noted in the frequency of these factors at the population level that might explain the variation in country-level HIV-1 prevalence. A stronger ecological association was seen with HSV-2 infection and male circumcision rates and adult HIV-1 prevalence than with sexual behavior variables. The prevalence of HSV-2 was higher and circumcision rates were lower in areas with higher HIV-1 prevalence, possibly explaining some of the differences seen.[138] Although many of the important factors that affect HIV-1 transmission have been identified, their combined interaction at the population level can be complex.

Injection Drug Use

Injection drug use is the second most important risk behavior associated with HIV infection worldwide. This mode of transmission accounts for an estimated 15–25% of HIV infections globally. However, in some areas of the world, especially Eastern Europe, the Russian Federation, Southern China, East Asia, and the Middle East, IDUs account for the great majority of HIV-infected persons.[139]

The predominant risk behavior associated with HIV transmission among injection drug users is sharing of contaminated injection equipment.[140,141] Most IDUs initiate the injection of illicit drugs with another experienced drug user, who is often older. At the time of initiation of drug injection and early after starting to inject, drugs and injection equipment are commonly shared. Therefore, IDUs are at especially high risk of HIV infections early in their injection careers.

Social situations that increase the likelihood that injection equipment will be shared, such as injection in "shooting galleries" (defined as places such as abandoned buildings, private homes, or other areas where drugs and equipment can be purchased or rented for injection), put a drug user at especially high risk of acquiring HIV.[140] Injection of drugs in shooting galleries is necessitated by paraphernalia laws that define carrying syringes as a crime and, therefore, discourage IDUs from having their own injecting equipment on their person.

Some drug injection practices, such as "booting" (the practice of drawing a small amount of blood into the syringe prior to injection), can increase the risk of HIV transmission to those who share equipment. Also, the "cooker" (the equipment used to dissolve the drugs) can become contaminated when the dissolved drugs are drawn into several syringes. Both "back loading," where the syringe is used to mix and measure out aliquots of drugs, and "front loading," where the needle is replaced between syringes, can lead to transmission of HIV from one user to another.[142]

In addition to these specific injection practices, the risk of infection increases with a larger number of needle-sharing partners. Also, injection of cocaine compared to heroin is associated with a higher risk of infection among drug users in the northeastern United States. These users commonly inject both heroin and cocaine (commonly referred to as "speedballing").[143] Cocaine has a shorter half-life than heroin and is often injected more frequently, sometimes in binges, with a larger number of needle-sharing partners.[143] Injection of cocaine, which is a stimulant, is commonly associated with concomitant high-risk sexual practices. Crack cocaine use has been linked to outbreaks of syphilis and other STDs.[144]

Treatment of drug abuse with methadone or bupernorphine replacement has been shown to decrease the risk of HIV infection.[145] However, there is insufficient access to methadone or other drug treatment programs in the United States and many other countries to accommodate the numbers of persons injecting drugs. Furthermore, methadone treatment is most effective for persons using opiates alone rather than those also injecting cocaine or other illicit drugs. In addition, many drug users do not feel "ready" to enroll in a treatment program.

Given these factors, a public health strategy of "harm reduction" has been developed to decrease the risk of HIV, other infections, and other adverse consequences of using contaminated injection equipment.[146] These programs offer clean syringes in exchange for used injection equipment to out-of-treatment injection drug users. Such programs have generated political controversy in the United States and many developing countries by persons who believe they condone, tolerate, or support illegal injection drug behavior.[147,148] Because of these concerns, no syringe-exchange harm-reduction programs were funded by the federal government in the United States until 2009. Nevertheless, many syringe-exchange programs are operating in the United States with funding by foundations, nongovernmental organizations (NGOs), or local governments and recently by the federal government as well.[149] Evaluation of these programs has indicated that they commonly attract the heaviest drug users, who are not in drug treatment.[150–153] These programs allow medical and public health contact with a seriously addicted population, who can sometimes be referred for needed medical care as well as reduce their high-risk behavior for HIV transmission.[150–153] An evaluation of the evidence of their effectiveness by a committee of the Institute of Medicine concluded that harm-reduction programs were effective in reducing transmission of HIV.[154–158]

The epidemic of HIV among drug users in the United States is geographically diverse. In most large cities in the northeastern United States the HIV prevalence is higher than in western or midwestern cities. The HIV prevalence among IDUs in several northeastern cities such as Hartford, New York, Newark, Philadelphia, Baltimore, and Washington, D.C., ranges from 25% to 40%, whereas in western cities such as Denver, Phoenix, San Diego, Los Angeles, and Portland, only 2.7–12.0% of IDUs are HIV positive.[156,158] These discrepant seroprevalence rates among IDUs have persisted from the mid-1980s to the present, whereas the prevalence of HIV among MSM does not differ widely in large cities in the United States.[156]

One study of sexual and drug use variables among 1528 East Coast IDUs compared to 1149 West Coast IDUs found a nearly 10-fold higher prevalence in HIV positivity (21.5%) among East Coast IDUs compared to West Coast IDUs (2.3%). However, the differences in reported sexual or injection behaviors were insufficient to explain the difference in HIV infection rates.[157]

Another study raised the novel hypothesis that differences in the types of heroin available in West Coast and East Coast cities could explain much of the difference in HIV infection rates.[158] Heroin on the West Coast commonly is grown and processed in Mexico and is called "black tar heroin." It is quite viscous and requires fairly extensive heating to dissolve the drug prior to injection. It is also likely to clot in the syringe, so extensive rinsing is necessary after it is injected. Furthermore, it is likely to sclerose veins, so IDUs commonly transition rapidly from intravenous injection to subcutaneous or intramuscular injection, and sharing or reuse of syringes is less feasible. All of these behavioral characteristics of the injection routine differ from drug users on the East Coast, where the heroin originates in South Asia and South America and consists primarily of a white or light brown powder. This heroin is more easily dissolved and may not require heating or subsequent extensive rinsing of syringes after an injection.[158]

The epidemic of HIV related to injection drug use is strongly affected by the sociocultural environment.[159] Several researchers have demonstrated that being in prison constitutes a high risk for exposure to HIV through injection drug use.[159,160] Other high-risk urban environments in inner-city populations facilitate the transmission of HIV directly or are indirectly related to drug use. Therefore, preventive interventions directed only at individual behavior are likely to be less successful than structural interventions directed at changing the social environment in preventing drug use-related HIV epidemics.[159]

An estimated 15.9 million (11.0–21.2 million) people inject drugs worldwide; of these persons, nearly 20%—an estimated 3 million—are living with HIV infection. Access to HIV prevention services has increased yet remains quite low; UNAIDS and a recent review have published data on the global coverage of prevention and treatment services for injection drug users. Nevertheless, the prevention of HIV infection has been quite successful among several populations of IDUs, such as in Australia, Vancouver, Taiwan, and elsewhere.[161,162]

Perinatal Transmission

The risk of perinatal transmission from an HIV-infected woman to her infant was first recognized in 1982. Approximately 90% of HIV/AIDS cases in children are perinatally acquired; the remainder occur in children with hemophilia or those who have received a contaminated blood transfusion. In the absence of a preventive intervention, 20–25% of HIV-infected women who deliver vaginally in the United States or Europe and 25–40% of such women in sub-Saharan Africa transmit the infection to their infants.[163–167] Approximately 20% of HIV transmission from a mother to her infant occurs in utero, 60–65% during delivery, and 12–15% from breastfeeding. Transmission in utero is operationally defined as detection of HIV by culture or nucleic acid amplification in the infant within the first 48 hours after birth.[168] Peripartum infection is defined as children who were not breastfed and who have negative HIV culture and/or nucleic acid amplification (polymerase chain reaction [PCR]) tests in the first few days of life, followed by a positive test on days 7 to 90.

Transmission by breastfeeding can occur at any time. The risk appears to be greatest during the early weeks after birth but continues throughout the duration of breastfeeding.[169,172] Most breastfeeding transmission occurs in developing countries, where breastfeeding is common, formula is expensive, or no clean water supply is available to facilitate formula feeding. In developing countries, where the absence of breastfeeding is associated with very high infant mortality, exclusive breastfeeding has been shown to be associated with a lower risk of HIV transmission than when other foods are given to the infant who is being breastfed.[172]

Elective cesarean section performed prior to rupture of the membranes appears to reduce the risk of HIV transmission. A meta-analysis that included data from 8533 mother–infant pairs from 15 international cohorts of non-breastfeeding women showed that, after adjustment for receipt of antiretroviral therapy, maternal disease stage, and infant birth weight, elective cesarean section decreased HIV transmission by approximately 50% (adjusted odds ratio: 0.43; 95% CI: 0.33–0.56).[167] When elective cesarean section was combined with zidovudine during the antepartum, intrapartum, and neonatal periods, HIV transmission was reduced by approximately 87%, compared with vaginal delivery and nonuse of zidovudine therapy (adjusted OR: 0.13; 95% CI: 0.09–0.19).[167] With effective therapy of the mother with HAART regimens that have resulted in very low viral loads at the time of delivery (fewer than 400 copies/µL), cesarean section probably has no added benefit. The perinatal transmission rate with effective HAART therapy of the mother is approximately 1.2%.[173,174]

Risk factors that increase the risk of mother-to-infant transmission include internal fetal monitoring, prolonged labor and delivery, chorioamnionitis, high viral load in the mother, primary HIV infection during pregnancy, and advanced HIV disease in the mother. Several studies have shown that women with low serum vitamin A levels are more likely to transmit HIV to their infant during delivery. However, controlled trials of vitamin A supplementation during pregnancy failed to decrease the transmission rate.[175,176] Thus vitamin A deficiency is now regarded as a marker of increased risk rather than as a cofactor for perinatal transmission of HIV. Irrigation of the birth canal with chlorhexidine to lower the HIV viral load in the birth canal prior to delivery also did not reduce HIV transmission to the infant.[177,178] Rates of bacterial neonatal sepsis, however, were significantly reduced by vaginal cleansing.[179] Treatment of chorioamnionitis during pregnancy also did not decrease the rates of maternal-to-child transmission of HIV.

A landmark study that was published in 1994, known as the ACTG-076 trial, found that zidovudine given to pregnant women after the first trimester, during delivery, and to the infant for the first 6 weeks of life decreased the mother-to-child HIV transmission rate by 67%, from 25% in those receiving placebo to 8% in those given AZT.[180] Only a modest decrease

in the viral load in the mother from baseline was seen (median decrease of 0.28 log copies/µL).[181] This landmark study found that most infections were transmitted during the last trimester or during labor and delivery into this non-breastfeeding population and that reductions in the viral load explained only a part of the protective efficacy.[181] This complex and expensive regimen, although effective, was not suitable for implementation in developing countries, where most mother-to-child infections were occurring. Therefore, a study was done in Thailand with a modified AZT regimen. In this study, AZT was started in pregnant women at the 36th week of pregnancy and given during delivery but not to the infant. This simpler regimen had a 50% efficacy and reduced HIV transmission from 18.9% to 9.4% at a fraction of the cost of the ACTG-076 regimen.[182] The Thai infants in this study were fed formula after delivery.

Another important study focused on a simpler regimen and was conducted in Uganda (HIVNET 012). In this study, a single dose of nevirapine was given during labor and another dose was given to the infant during the first week of life.[183] Despite breastfeeding, the maternal–infant transmission rate was reduced from 25.1% to 13.1% (47% efficacy) at 14–16 weeks and persisted until 18 months, at which time the infants who had received nevirapine had a 15.2% infection rate compared to 25.8% of the controls (41% efficacy).[184] This greatly simplified regimen was well tolerated. Resistance mutations to nevirapine (especially $K^{103}N$) were demonstrated at 6 weeks' postpartum in approximately 20% of women who had received a single dose of the drug.[185] although the mutant virus became less frequent in untreated women after several months.[186] This finding raised concerns that widespread use of nevirapine might eventually increase the risk of the transmission of resistant viruses or that subsequent therapy of women with those resistance mutations with other non-NRTI agents might fail.[187] Despite these concerns, a review of the risks and benefits of single-dose nevirapine for the prevention of mother-to-child transmission by a WHO committee concluded that the benefits of this approach outweigh the risk in resource-limited settings.[188]

The positive results of these prevention trials have raised hopes that mother-to-child transmission of HIV could be prevented or reduced dramatically at the population level. Several additional trials were conducted with antiretroviral (ARV) treatment of pregnant women in developing countries aimed at improving the efficacy, simplifying the regimen, or reducing the cost or toxicity.

Current Guidelines for Prevention of MTCT of HIV in the United States

A U.S. Public Health Service task force has reviewed the evidence relating to the prevention of vertical transmission of HIV and developed guidelines for the United States (Table 22-8).[189] These guidelines aim to maximally reduce the rates of transmission according to existing evidence. If the viral load is greater than 1000 copies/μL, elective cesarean section should be done prior to the onset of labor. In women who have not received antepartum or intrapartum antiviral therapy, the committee recommended prophylactic therapy of the infant.

A critically important component of the successful prevention of mother-to-child transmission of HIV in the United States is the identification of HIV-infected pregnant women. It is currently recommended that all pregnant women be tested for HIV regardless of their perceived risk. The most effective strategy to obtain informed consent for testing is the "opt out" strategy, in which women are told they will be tested unless they decline, rather than an "opt in" strategy, in which women are counseled and asked if they wish to be tested. The former strategy has resulted in testing of approximately 85% of pregnant women.[190]

Developing Countries

Despite the availability of several effective regimens to prevent mother-to child transmission of HIV, an estimated 640,000–700,000 new HIV infections occurred in children younger than 15 years of age in 2004, and 510,000 children died from AIDS that year. Nearly all of these new HIV infections in children occurred in developing countries, especially in sub-Saharan Africa.[191] The dramatic increase in HIV infections among young women 15–24 years old in sub-Saharan African countries has escalated the problem of infant and childhood infections. Approximately 90% of all HIV infections in children are caused by maternal-to-infant transmission. Overall, in sub-Saharan Africa, the ratio of female:male HIV infection is approximately 1.3:1.0.[191] In several countries in Southern Africa, the HIV prevalence among 15- to 24-year-old females is 30% or higher. Therefore, it is especially urgent to implement programs to detect and treat HIV-infected pregnant women to prevent transmission to their infants.

Several obstacles stand in the way of implementing an effective public health program to prevent MTCT of HIV. Among these are the fact that most deliveries in sub-Saharan Africa occur at home, especially in rural areas. Many women do not receive prenatal care. The availability of screening for HIV is far from universal, and many women are fearful of being screened because of the stigma of being identified as HIV positive. Nevertheless, prevention of MTCT of HIV was a major component of WHO's "3 by 5" program ("Treat 3 Million Persons by 2005"). Access to HIV testing continues to expand. The availability of reliable rapid tests has been important in identifying HIV-positive women, especially when their first contact with health care comes when they are in labor.

Another barrier to preventing transmission to infants is the high rate of incident HIV infection in pregnant women. A high proportion of infections occur during pregnancy and breastfeeding because couples stop using condoms for contraception. Pregnant women may also be at higher risk of infection due to hormonal factors, through a mechanism as yet not fully explained. Whatever the reason, the rates of infection are high among pregnant women, and increasing testing rates both at the time of delivery and during the breastfeeding period is crucial to lowering infections in infants. In Botswana, incidence rates among pregnant women who previously tested negative for HIV were found to be 2% in the third trimester and postpartum period. Based on these results, Lu L et al. estimated that 43% of MTCT infections in Botswana in 2007 may be due to undetected HIV infection late in pregnancy and postpartum.[192]

Today the emphasis in prevention of MTCT (PMTCT) is on expanding the availability of combination ART therapy to women during pregnancy and the breastfeeding period. WHO has proposed the following steps to optimize prevention:

- For HIV-infected pregnant women, the initiation of ART for their own health is recommended for all women who have CD4 cell counts of 350 cells/mm³ or less, irrespective of WHO clinical staging, and for all women in WHO clinical stage 3 or 4, irrespective of the CD4 cell count.
- Maternal ART should be coupled with the daily administration of nevirapine (NVP) or twice-daily AZT to infants from birth or as soon as feasible thereafter until 4 to 6 weeks of age, irrespective of the mode of infant feeding.

The Kesho Bora study ("A better future," Swahili) found that giving HIV-positive mothers a combination of three antiretroviral drugs (ARVs) during pregnancy, delivery, and breastfeeding cut HIV infections in infants by 43% by the age of 1 year and reduced transmissions during breastfeeding by

54% compared with the previously recommended ARV drug regimen stopped at delivery.[193]

At the United Nations General Assembly Special Session on HIV/AIDS in June 2001, governments from 189 countries committed themselves to a comprehensive program of international and national action to fight the HIV/AIDS pandemic by adopting the Declaration of Commitment on HIV/AIDS. This declaration established specific goals, including reducing the proportion of infants infected with HIV by 20% by 2005 and by 50% by 2010.[194]

A successful program to prevent MTCT of HIV was implemented nationally in Thailand in 2000 after a successful pilot study in seven provinces. Between October 2000 and September 2001, data were reported from 822 public health hospitals in all regions in Thailand. Among 573,655 women giving birth during that period, 96.7% received prenatal care; of those, 93.3% were tested for HIV prior to delivery. Among 6646 HIV-seropositive women, 70.1% received prophylactic antiretroviral therapy prior to delivery, 88.7% of the neonates of these seropositive women received prophylactic antiretroviral therapy, and 83.2% of the neonates received infant formula.[195] These encouraging results suggest that rapid implementation of a public health program to prevent maternal-to-infant transmission in a developing country is feasible.

A report from UNAIDS in 2010 indicated there has been significant progress in reducing mother-to-child transmission of HIV in recent years. Worldwide, 59% of pregnant women living with HIV in low- and middle-income countries received antiretroviral medication to prevent mother-to-child transmission in 2010[196]—up from only 15% in 2005.[197] Several countries have achieved more than 80% coverage levels, including Botswana, Namibia, South Africa, and Swaziland. Unfortunately, others lag far behind, including Nigeria and the Democratic Republic of the Congo. The UNAIDS goal is to reach more than 80% coverage in the next few years (**Figure 22-9**).[196]

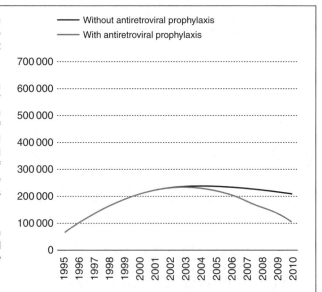

Figure 22-9 Success of ARVs for Prevention of Mother to Child Transmission. Reproduced from the World Health Organization (2011). Global HIV AIDS Response, Epidemic update and health sector progress towards universal access: Progress report 2011. Page 18.; http://whqlibdoc.who.int/publications/2011/9789241502986_eng.pdf. Accessed October 2, 2012.

Transmission by Blood Transfusion, Blood Products, and Organ Transplantation

The transfusion of HIV-contaminated blood is the most effective way to transmit the virus. More than 90% of seronegative recipients are infected by transfusion of a single contaminated unit of blood.[198] The risk of transmission of HIV through the transfusion of blood or blood products was recognized very early in the AIDS epidemic. After this risk was recognized, and prior to the identification of the HIV virus, blood banks established procedures to exclude any man who had sex with another man since 1978 and other potential donors at high risk of infections from heterosexual or drug-use exposures. These donor exclusion criteria have remained in place to the present, despite the implementation of serological and nucleic acid testing (NAT) of all donations.

Exclusion of potential donors at high risk and screening of all units with sensitive antibody and nucleic acid tests have collectively resulted in a very low risk of HIV transmission by blood transmission in the United States and other industrialized countries at present. Lackritz et al. estimated the risk of transmission of an HIV-infected unit of blood to be 1 in 450,000–660,000 donations among 41 million blood donations in 19 American Red Cross centers in 1992–1993.[199]

The risk of transfusion-related transmission has been further reduced with the development of more sensitive enzyme-linked immunosorbent assays (ELISA) and the implementation of nucleic acid testing (NAT) to identify infected donors (those in the window period) prior to seroconversion. The risk of an HIV-infected unit being accepted for transfusion was estimated to be only 1 in 2,135,000 units in 2001 after the implementation of a fairly extensive behavioral interview to screen donors, followed by enzyme immunoassay (EIA) and NAT screening of their blood.[200] In the first 3 years after NAT screening of all blood donations was introduced in 1999, the Red Cross Blood Collection Centers in the United States identified 12 NAT-positive, antibody-negative units among 37,164,054 units screened, or 1 in 3.1 million donations.[200] A cost-effectiveness analysis found that NAT screening for HIV and hepatitis C virus (HCV) costs $4.7–11.2 million per quality-adjusted life-year (QALY) saved.[201] Despite this high cost, it is the current philosophy of FDA and other regulatory authorities that transfusion should be as close as possible to "100% safe" for the recipient, even though it is not possible to achieve perfect safety. Another advantage of the introduction of NAT is that such testing can be multiplexed fairly easily by introducing additional primers to detect nucleic acids from other infectious agents. This was done during the West Nile virus (WNV) epidemic, after it was recognized that the incidence of WNV infectious donors was fairly high in some areas during the height of the transmission season.[202,203] More than 1000 WNV viremic donors were identified in 2003 and 2004.[203]

Before HIV screening became available, 75–90% of recipients of Factor VIII concentrate and 30% of all Factor IX recipients had been infected with this virus.[204] The risk of HIV transmission from transplantation of a whole organ from an HIV-infected donor is nearly 100%.[205–207] Fresh-frozen, unprocessed bone from a donor who is HIV positive is highly likely to transmit an HIV infection if marrow elements and adherent tissue are not removed. Relatively avascular solid tissue poses a lower risk for HIV transmission, especially if it has been processed by techniques that might inactivate HIV.[207]

The CDC recommends that all organ donors be screened for HIV, hepatitis B, and hepatitis C prior to transplanting their organs into a recipient. The transmission of HIV from a living donor who donated a kidney to the recipient was reported in New York City in 2009. The donor had been screened for HIV antibodies 10 weeks prior to donating his kidney but had sex with another man in the interval between the negative serological test and donation.[208] A survey of organ procurement centers found that all donors are screened for HIV antibodies by EIA and Western blot but that 52% of centers screened deceased donors and only 24% of centers screened living donors using HIV NAT.[209] The CDC now recommends that all donors be screened by EIA and HIV NAT and that living donors be screened as close to the time of donation as possible, but no longer than 3 days before donating organs.[210]

Despite the safety of the blood supply in industrialized countries, blood transfusion in many developing countries still carries a significant risk of HIV transmission. In some resource-poor countries, antibody screening of blood donors is not universal because of an inconsistent supply of testing reagents. Furthermore, donors are commonly paid or are replacement donors for individual patients. First-time donors, who are at higher risk of transmitting HIV than repeat donors, are more common in most developing countries. Paid and first-time donors have been found to be at higher risk of HIV, hepatitis B, and hepatitis C virus infections in most populations. Importantly, the HIV risk in many developing countries is not concentrated in populations of MSM and IDUs, but rather in the general heterosexual population. This complicates the development of a strategy to select a low-risk donor population. Outbreaks of HIV infection have been reported among plasmapheresis donors in China, Mexico, and other developing countries.[211,212]

Transmission in the Healthcare Setting

HIV infection is a risk for healthcare workers and laboratory personnel who handle sharp instruments or who may be exposed to body fluids from HIV-infected patients. Needle-stick accidents pose a far greater risk than does intact skin or mucous membrane exposure to HIV-contaminated blood or body fluids. A 0.4% HIV seroconversion rate has been reported in healthcare workers who had percutaneous injuries with HIV-contaminated surgical instruments.[213,215] Most of these injuries have occurred in emergency situations involving resuscitation attempts and during surgery. The risk of HIV infection is greatest when the healthcare worker has been exposed to a quantity of blood from patients with advanced HIV disease and very high viral load. Exposure of mucosal and nonintact skin to HIV-contaminated body fluids accounts for a lower infection risk (less than 0.1%) than does penetrating exposures.[213–215] One large prospective study evaluating 2712 intact cutaneous exposures detected no infections,[216] although there have been reports of HIV transmission in cases where there was cutaneous exposure to HIV-contaminated fluids or blood splashes.[217]

Early in the epidemic, an outbreak of six cases of HIV occurred among patients of an HIV-infected dentist.[218] Genetic sequencing of the viruses from the infected patients and the dentist indicated the viruses were from a common source.[219] The only reasonable explanation was transmission from the dentist to his patient.[218] This outbreak generated considerable concern and anxiety and prompted a more rigorous approach to sterilization in dental offices. Fortunately, this outbreak was an unusual event.

In some developing countries, inadequate infection control practices regarding contaminated syringes and needles have resulted in HIV transmission to patients. The relative importance of parenteral versus sexual exposures in the transmission of HIV in developing countries has recently been debated.[220–221] Nevertheless, the adoption of universal precautions is strongly advocated to reduce occupational exposures among healthcare workers.

Environmental and Casual Contact Transmission

Environmental transmission of HIV is not believed to occur. Although studies of HIV survival in the environment revealed that HIV could be recovered by tissue culture 1–3 days after drying,[222] the clinical relevance of this finding is dubious because the virus concentration in this report was several thousand-fold higher than that in the blood in persons with HIV infection. However, environmental contamination could pose a risk for persons working in a research laboratory where concentrated virus preparations exist; at least one transmission has occurred in this setting.[223] Environmental spread of HIV is also unlikely, as inactivation of HIV is quite rapid. CDC studies have demonstrated that drying causes HIV concentrations to decrease 90–95% within several hours.[224] There have been no reports of HIV infection due to contact with an environmental surface because HIV is unable to reproduce, spread, or maintain infectivity outside its living host. There is no evidence to support the transmission of HIV by insects,[225–227] despite the common belief in many populations that this poses a risk.

Household transmission of HIV in the absence of sexual or percutaneous exposure is rare. HIV has not been shown to be transmitted through the sharing of household items, such as towels, plates, sheets, glasses, toilet, or bath or shower facilities that have been soiled by feces, saliva, urine, or tears from an infected patient. Studies in the United States and Europe of nonsexual, non-needle-sharing household contacts of persons with HIV infection have indicated no evidence of infection among family members.[228–230] HIV transmission has been reported in households where needles were shared for medical injections at home and where there was mucocutaneous exposure to blood or other body substances during home health care.[231–233] In one unusual case reported to the CDC involving HIV transmission between two brothers with hemophilia, the putative spread of infection was due to sharing the same shaving razor.[234]

Postexposure Prophylaxis and Preexposure Prophylaxis

Occupational Exposure

As of June 2003, CDC had received voluntary reports of 57 U.S. healthcare workers with documented seroconversion temporally associated with an occupational exposure to an HIV-infected patient. An additional 138 seroconversions in healthcare workers are considered possibly due to occupational exposures.[235]

In a retrospective case–control study of occupational exposure, several factors were associated with an increased risk of HIV transmission.[236] Risk was increased if the exposure involved a larger quantity of blood, a device visibly contaminated with blood, a hollow-bore device as compared to a solid needle, a procedure that involved a needle being placed directly in a vein or artery, or a deep injury. The risk was also increased for exposure to blood from source persons with terminal illness.

Some evidence suggests that host defenses might influence the risk for HIV infection. Studies of HIV-exposed but uninfected healthcare workers and sex workers demonstrated that several persons had an HIV-specific cytotoxic T-lymphocyte (CTL) response or mucosal IgA HIV-specific antibodies.[237,238]

Studies in animals suggest that postexposure prophylaxis (PEP) might have some prophylactic efficacy.[239] Although a randomized clinical trial comparing PEP to no treatment in humans cannot be conducted for ethical and logistical reasons, observational data comparing infection rates after known exposures among healthcare workers who received prophylaxis and those who did not after a known exposure indicate that PEP with ZDV was associated with an 81% (95% CI: 43–94%) decrease in transmission.[240]

The efficacy of prevention of maternal-to-child transmission by treatment of either mother or infant suggests that prophylaxis after exposure might be capable of preventing transmission under some circumstances. Nevertheless, failures of PEP to prevent HIV transmission have been reported in at least 21 cases, despite the prompt initiation of antiretroviral therapy.[241] Currently, CDC recommends a two-drug regimen be provided within 1–2 hours (if possible) for a less-severe exposure (e.g., solid needle, asymptomatic source case) for 28 days. The two drugs selected could be AZT/3TC (Combivir), 3TC and Stavudine, or Didanosine and D4T.[242] For more severe exposures or if the source patient has a known resistant virus, lopinavir, invirase, atazanavir, or tenofovir can be added to the 28-day regimen. Minor to moderate adverse reactions are commonly experienced by patients receiving these PEP regimens. However, serious side effects are unusual.

Nonoccupational Exposures

In the past several years, a substantial number of MSM have taken PEP following a possible exposure to HIV. There has been no clear evidence to date that the availability of PEP after a high-risk exposure has reduced the use of condoms or promoted other high-risk sexual behavior. However, this remains an issue of public health concern.

The results of a randomized trial of the daily use of a combination of two oral antiretroviral drugs, emtricitabine and tenofovir, among 2499 HIV-seronegative men or transgender women compared to placebo found a 44% reduction in the incidence of HIV (95% CI: 15–63%; $p = 0.005$) after a median follow-up of 1.2 years in those taking the antiretroviral drugs. These important findings have stimulated additional studies as well as more widespread usage of antiretroviral prophylaxis on both a preexposure and postexposure basis among persons at high risk of infection.[243]

Preexposure prophylaxis (PrEP) was recently tested and found to be efficacious in patients at high risk of infection with HIV. The iPrEX study was conducted by researchers at the David Gladstone Institute among patients from the United States and Peru. Participants were men who have sex with men, and transgender women who have sex with men. In this study, the risk of transmission was reduced by nearly 44% among all participants, and by even more (73%) among those who reported high adherence to the treatment regimen. On July 16, 2012, the FDA approved the use of the HIV drug combination tenofovir and emtricitabine (brand name Truvada) for HIV prevention. Of note, some studies have not shown PrEP regimens to be as effective in preventing infection among women, highlighting the differences in the transmission process for women and men who have sex with men. The efficacy of the use of antiretroviral drugs taken as pre-exposure prophylaxis to HIV uninfected persons at high risk of infection to prevent HIV transmission has been evaluated in several populations recently.

Rapid HIV Tests

HIV testing is a critical point of entry for providing information regarding HIV transmission, prevention, counseling, and referral. Unfortunately, almost one-third of patients who have tested positive for HIV at CDC-funded public testing sites did not return for their results[244] and many high-risk patients often do not get tested because of various factors, including the number of visits required to be tested and obtain their result. Because of the need for accurate, noninvasive, and inexpensive rapid testing for HIV, the use of rapid point-of-care tests has become the standard of care throughout sub-Saharan Africa in recent years. Rapid tests for HIV have important applications in several testing situations, including in social venues such as bars, in acute care settings such as emergency rooms, and for military use in the field.[245] Rapid tests are believed to be an essential component of the WHO scale-up access program for antiretroviral therapy in Africa. To address these needs, rapid tests have been in development for more than a decade. At present, in excess of 60 rapid HIV tests have been developed and are available worldwide; four of these have been approved by the FDA for use in the United States.[246]

The first FDA-approved rapid HIV test, Oraquick Advance, received FDA approval in November 2002. This test can be performed using whole blood, oral fluid, or plasma; it can detect HIV-1 and HIV-2 and results are available in 20 minutes. Several other point-of-care tests are now widely available and used routinely in the field for HIV testing using finger-stick blood or oral fluid. Home-based testing using the over-the-counter Orasure rapid test was approved in July 2012; this approach greatly expands the diversity of ways in which people may monitor their

HIV status. How the availability of rapid tests influences HIV status awareness overall, and whether it increases the frequency of testing and thus reduces the time an individual is unaware of his or her HIV status and potentially transmitting the virus to others, remain to be seen.

GLOBAL PREVALENCE OF HIV

UNAIDS has estimated that 34 million persons were living with HIV infection at the end of 2010. These numbers represented a 17% increase in prevalence since 2001. In 2010, there were an estimated 2.7 million newly infected persons, including an estimated 390,000 among children. This total was 15% less than the incidence in 2001 and 21% less than the number of new infections at the peak of the epidemic in 1997. The number of deaths in 2010 from HIV/AIDS was 1.8 million persons. A total of 2.5 million deaths have been prevented in low- and middle-income countries since 1995 owing to the introduction of antiretroviral therapy, according to calculations by UNAIDS. The proportion of women living with HIV has remained stable at 50% globally, although women are more affected in sub-Saharan Africa (59%) and the Caribbean (53%) (**Figure 22-10** and **Figure 22-11**).[247]

AIDS epidemics are classified by UNAIDS as follows:

- *Generalized*—when the HIV prevalence among the general population (i.e., pregnant women) is greater than 1%
- *Concentrated*—when the prevalence in pregnant women is less than 1%, but the prevalence is greater than 5% in populations at higher risk (e.g., IDUs, CSWs, MSM, or STD patients)
- *Nascent*—in countries with some HIV infections but with prevalence less than 5% in high-risk populations

Sub-Saharan Africa

Sub-Saharan Africa is the region most dramatically affected by the global AIDS epidemic. It has been estimated that 68% of all people living with HIV are in sub-Saharan Africa, despite the fact that this region contains only 12% of the global population. Sub-Saharan Africa also accounted for 70% of all new HIV infections in 2010. Nevertheless, the number of new infections in this region has substantially declined in the last decade. South Africa is the country with the largest number of people living with HIV in the world—5.6 million.[247]

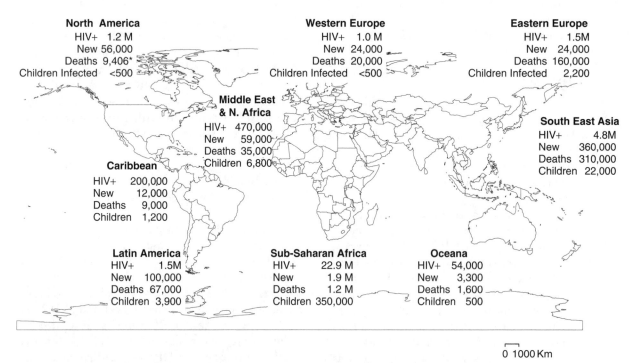

North America
HIV+   1.2 M
New 56,000
Deaths 9,406*
Children Infected <500

Western Europe
HIV+   1.0 M
New 24,000
Deaths 20,000
Children Infected <500

Eastern Europe
HIV+   1.5M
New   24,000
Deaths 160,000
Children Infected   2,200

Middle East & N. Africa
HIV+   470,000
New   59,000
Deaths 35,000
Children 6,800

Caribbean
HIV+   200,000
New   12,000
Deaths 9,000
Children 1,200

South East Asia
HIV+   4.8M
New   360,000
Deaths 310,000
Children 22,000

Latin America
HIV+   1.5M
New 100,000
Deaths 67,000
Children 3,900

Sub-Saharan Africa
HIV+   22.9 M
New   1.9 M
Deaths 1.2 M
Children 350,000

Oceana
HIV+   54,000
New   3,300
Deaths 1,600
Children 500

0 1000 Km

Figure 22-10 Global HIV/AIDS Indicators. Data from the World Health Organization (2011). Global HIV AIDS Response, Epidemic update and health sector progress towards universal access: Progress report 2011. http://whqlibdoc.who.int/publications/2011/9789241502986_eng.pdf. Accessed October 2, 2012.

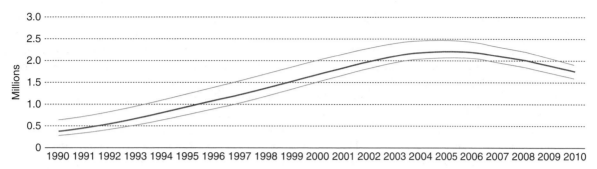

Figure 22-11 Number dying of HIV/AIDS-related causes globally. Reproduced from the World Health Organization (2011). Global HIV/AIDS Response, Epidemic update and health sector progress towards universal access: Progress report 2011. Page 18.; http://whqlibdoc.who.int/publications/2011/9789241502986_eng.pdf. Accessed October 2, 2012.

Almost half of all deaths from AIDS-related illnesses occur in sub-Saharan Africa—1.2 million in 2010. However, the number of deaths has declined in the last decade due to the wide availability of free, effective antiretroviral therapy. HIV prevalence among adults is approximately 5.0% in this region. However, the HIV prevalence among young persons aged 15–24 years is more than twice as great among females (3.3%) as among males (1.4%). This difference reflects sexual patterns of older men with higher prevalence having sex with younger females. It also reflects gender inequality and possibly the effect of hormonal contraceptives increasing the transmission of HIV during unprotected sex.

The total number of new HIV infections in sub-Saharan Africa has dropped by more than 26%, falling to 1.9 million from the estimated 2.6 million at the height of the epidemic in 1997. The annual HIV incidence in South Africa, though still high, dropped by one-third between 2001 and 2009, from 2.4% to 1.5%. The HIV prevalence in Swaziland is the highest of any country in the world.

The Caribbean

The Caribbean is the second-most affected region in the world. Among persons 15–44 years of age in this geographic area, AIDS is now the leading cause of death. The adult HIV prevalence has been estimated to be 0.9%, and approximately 200,000 adults and children are living with HIV infection. In the Caribbean region, new HIV infections have been reduced by one-third from 2001 levels. HIV incidence has decreased by an estimated 25% in the Dominican Republic and Jamaica since 2001, but by only 12% in Haiti. The epidemic in the Caribbean is occurring largely through heterosexual intercourse, although sex between men, which is stigmatized, is a significant contributor. Cuba is notable for having a very low HIV prevalence in a region characterized by a high HIV burden.[247]

Asia

While national HIV rates in many Asian countries are much lower than those in most of sub-Saharan Africa, the population of Asia is very large and heterogeneous. Large numbers of persons are infected with HIV, and many are at high risk of becoming infected. Asia comprises both well-established, generalized epidemics (i.e., general population HIV prevalence ≥ 1%) and recent concentrated epidemics (i.e., HIV prevalence ≥ 5% in risk groups), each having unique epidemiologic features and HIV prevention and control needs. Long-term generalized epidemics are found in Thailand, Cambodia, and Myanmar. Other regions, such as selected areas in India and China, have localized but significant epidemics in specific populations, particularly migrants, sex workers, and drug users. Some countries have experienced expanding epidemics only recently. These countries include Indonesia, Nepal, Vietnam, Malaysia, and several provinces in China. Other Asian countries continue to have low rates of HIV, even among persons at high risk of HIV, including Bangladesh, East Timor, Laos, Pakistan, and the Philippines. Overall, UNAIDS has estimated that 4.9 million adults and children were living with HIV in Asia as of December 2010, compared with 4.1 million in 2001. In South and Southeast Asia, the estimated 270,000 new infections in 2010 was 40% lower than the incidence at the epidemic's peak.[247]

In China, HIV has spread to all 31 provinces, autonomous regions, and principalities. An estimated 740,000 persons were living with HIV in 2009. In some areas, such as Henan, Anhui, and Shandong, HIV spread extensively in the early 1990s among rural adults who sold their plasma repeatedly to supplement their incomes and acquired HIV through contaminated plasmapheresis equipment coupled with the practice of infusing donors with red blood cells, pooled from many donors, to alleviate anemia caused by frequent donation.[247,248] In southern and western China, the prevalence of HIV is highest among injection drug users and commercial sex workers. In addition, a growing number of MSM living in China are infected with HIV.

In India, the HIV epidemic is more diverse. In 2009, an estimated 2.4 million persons were living with HIV—a prevalence second only to South Africa in terms of the number of persons with HIV/AIDS.[249] A severe epidemic of HIV among injection drug users has been under way for several years in the state of Manipur in northeastern India. However, HIV prevalence is high among IDUs elsewhere—notably in Chennai, where 64% of IDUs were reported to be HIV positive in one study.[250] The HIV epidemic is more severe in southern India than in the very populous northern states at present and is fueled primarily by heterosexual transmission. The course of the HIV/AIDS epidemic in India—and in China, and Indonesia—will be a major determinant of the size of the future global pandemic because of the very large populations potentially at risk of infection in these areas.

The HIV/AIDS epidemic emerged rapidly among injection drug users in Thailand in early 1988. It was followed soon thereafter by increasing HIV prevalence among sex workers and their clients seen at STD clinics, especially in the upper northern provinces of the country. In 1991, the Thai government instituted an aggressive and successful prevention program to prevent the heterosexual transmission of HIV during commercial or casual sex.[251,252] This program has often been called the 100% Condom Program, because it emphasized the use of condoms during commercial sex to prevent HIV infection. However, the promotion of condoms was only one feature of the AIDS prevention effort in Thailand: the campaign also included a strong and integrated political and financial commitment to the prevention of HIV at all levels of Thai society.

Thailand is the only country in Asia with a generalized epidemic at present. The HIV prevalence in pregnant women was 1.2% in 2009. In recent years, there has been a resurgence of HIV infections among MSM. For example, the prevalence of HIV/AIDS increased from 17% in 2003 to 31% in 2008 among MSM in Bangkok.

Thailand launched a nationwide semiannual HIV seroprevalence sentinel surveillance system that included anonymous surveys of HIV prevalence in several populations at risk (i.e., "direct" or brothel-based female sex workers and "indirect" female sex workers, STD patients, injection drug users, blood donors, and pregnant women) in June 1989; the system was expanded nationally in 1991. The prevalence data gathered through this system allowed monitoring of the temporal trends and spread of HIV infection in the various risk groups throughout the country and helped to evaluate the needs and progress of the control program. The sentinel surveillance data showed decreasing HIV prevalence among all of these populations, except for injection drug users, during the mid- and late 1990s (**Figure 22-12**).[253]

The effective HIV prevention program in Thailand was partially replicated in neighboring Cambodia and has been associated with reduced HIV prevalence among high-risk groups.[254] In addition to public health programs to prevent HIV by reducing the frequency of high-risk sex, programs to prevent transmission through injection drug use and

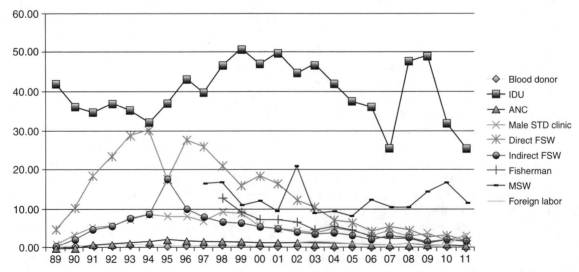

Figure 22-12 Thailand HIV Sentinel Surveillance: 1989–2011. Reproduced from Saengwonloey et al. (2003). Thailand Report: HIV/AIDS Surveillance 1998. Journal of Acquired Immune Deficiency Syndromes: February 2003. Vol. 32, pp. S63–S67.

expanded voluntary counseling and testing and treatment programs are needed in Asia to more effectively control the epidemic. Antiretroviral therapy is available free of charge to Thai citizens. In 2009, an estimated 67% of the 530,000 persons living with HIV were receiving therapy.[255]

Eastern Europe and Central Asia

The number of persons infected with HIV in Eastern Europe has increased by 25% in the past decade, reaching an estimated 1.5 million by the end of 2009.[256] The Russian Federation and Ukraine account for almost 90% of the epidemic in this region. An estimated 27,000 people in the region, excluding the Russian Federation, were newly infected with HIV in 2009, with an additional 58,500 cases being noted in the Russian Federation. Outside of Russia, the epidemic in the Ukraine is the most severe and illustrates an epidemic fueled by widespread injection of illicit drugs. An estimated 80% of HIV-infected injecting drug users are young adults (i.e., younger than age 30). Drug users commonly reuse injection equipment in the Ukraine. In some areas, drug users are females who frequently engage in commercial sex to obtain money to support their drug use. All of the elements are in place for an explosive epidemic.[257]

There is little indication that the epidemic has stabilized in this region, as new HIV infections and AIDS-related deaths continue to increase. It has been estimated that there are 1.5–3.0 million drug users in Russia. Methadone replacement therapy for opiate users is illegal in Russia, as is buprenorphine, and harm-reduction programs are not widely available. In addition, the number of female sex workers has expanded significantly in the decades since the breakup of the former Soviet Union. The proportion of prisoners with a history of drug use has increased, which has fueled epidemics of HIV and tuberculosis in the prison system. The future of the HIV epidemic in Russia and Eastern Europe will be influenced substantially by the movement of HIV infections from drug users to sex workers and their clients and the numbers of new drug users.

Latin America

An estimated 1.5 million people are living with HIV infection in Latin America. In 2010, approximately 67,000 people in this region died of AIDS, and 100,000 people were newly infected.[247] The epidemic in Latin America has stabilized in recent years.

Two countries in the region, Guatemala and Honduras, have relatively high HIV prevalence rates in the general population. However, several other countries have substantial focal epidemics.

Brazil accounts for more than one-third of the total number of people with HIV infections in Latin America. The HIV epidemic in Brazil has spread to all regions of the country. Originally, the main risk behavior for HIV infection was anal intercourse between men. More recently, injection drug use, especially in southern Brazil,[258] and heterosexual transmission have become important factors in perpetuating the epidemic. Infection is significantly associated with lower socioeconomic status among drug users and persons who have acquired HIV through sexual contact.[259] Bisexuality is significantly more common among men who have sex with men in Latin America than in North America or Europe. Moreover, anal intercourse is more common among heterosexual couples in Latin America, thereby increasing the risk of male-to-female transmission of HIV.[260]

The national AIDS program in Brazil is unique among developing countries in that it was the first to integrate HIV/AIDS prevention with care and treatment of persons with HIV/AIDS.[261]

Spread of HIV has been common in Latin America among MSM, especially in Costa Rica, Venezuela, Panama, and Nicaragua. Many men who have a history of male sex in Latin America are bisexual, placing their regular female partners at risk.[262] Most countries in Latin America have focused their official HIV/AIDS prevention efforts on populations of female commercial sex workers, so there is often a mismatch between prevention spending priorities and the main epidemiological features of the epidemic.[263]

Oceania

An estimated 54,000 persons in Oceania are infected with HIV. Although 1600 persons are believed to have died of AIDS, an estimated 3900 persons were newly infected with HIV in 2010.[247] Among young people 15–24 years of age, an estimated 0.2% of women and 0.1% of men were infected with HIV by the end of 2010.[247]

The annual number of new HIV diagnoses in Australia has gradually increased from 650 in 1998 to about 900 in 2009. Transmission of HIV in Australia and New Zealand continues to occur mainly through sexual intercourse between men, which accounted for more than 85% of new HIV diagnoses between 1997 and 2002. Remarkably, injection drug use was responsible for only 2% and heterosexual intercourse for 8.5% of newly required HIV infections in that period. Australia is perhaps the best example of prevention of spread of HIV among injection drug users through a well-organized and functional harm-reduction program to prevent HIV among injection drug users. New Zealand began offering needle-exchange services in 1987.[264]

Papua New Guinea has the highest prevalence of HIV infection in the Pacific. An estimated 0.6% of adults—roughly 16,000 people in an adult population of about 2.6 million—were living with HIV at the end of 2003.[247] The number of new HIV infections has been increasing annually since the mid-1990s. In 2003, 1.4% of pregnant women at antenatal clinics in the capital city of Port Moresby tested HIV positive. The main risk factor for transmission in New Guinea is commercial and casual heterosexual sex. New Guinea is also known for a high incidence of rape, sexual aggression, and other forms of violence against women. In one study, as many as 70% of women were found to have experienced domestic violence.[265]

Middle East and North Africa

An estimated 310,000 persons in the Middle East and North Africa were infected with HIV at the end of 2008.[266] This prevalence increased from an estimated 200,000 in 2001 and reflects the nascent status of the epidemic in this region. An estimated 35,000 adults and children were newly infected in 2004, and the adult HIV prevalence was 0.3%. There were some 20,000 deaths among adults and children due to AIDS in 2008. All routes of transmission have been reported, although surveillance is not adequate in most countries of the region.

The most severely affected country in the region is Sudan, which has been wracked by a civil war and humanitarian crises. Recent estimates indicate that 1% of the adult population was living with HIV at the end of 2008; approximately 220,000 persons were infected, and they accounted for nearly 80% of all HIV infections in the entire region.[267]

Injection drug use has accounted for a large proportion of the persons known to be HIV infected in several countries in North Africa and the Middle East. This appears to be the case in Libya, Algeria, Egypt, Iran, Bahrain, Kuwait, and Oman.[268] In surveys, 7.8% to 9.3% of men who have sex with men were HIV positive in the Sudan, 6% in Egypt, and 4% in Morocco.

Western and Central Europe

UNAIDS and WHO have estimated that 840,000 people were living with HIV in Western and Central Europe at the end of 2010. Many have been infected for several years, and approximately 20% have AIDS. An estimated 30,000 adults and children were newly infected with HIV in 2010, similar to the estimated number of newly infected persons in 2001. The adult

HIV prevalence is estimated at 0.2%. Despite substantial reductions in HIV-related morbidity and mortality in the countries of Western and Central Europe, HIV remains a major public health problem in the region.[247,269]

The number of new infections among men who have sex with men has increased in the last several years, while the incidence among injection drug users has decreased. Migrants from countries with generalized HIV epidemics, especially from sub-Saharan Africa, account for a large and increasing proportion of infections in Western Europe. In the 12 countries with available data, two-thirds of all heterosexually acquired HIV infections during 2005 occurred in people who had immigrated to Europe from countries in Africa with generalized HIV epidemics. Western Europe is the destination of many migrants from sub-Saharan Africa, where the HIV epidemic is most severe and the HIV genotypes most diverse.[270]

Available data indicate that although HIV/AIDS is widely distributed throughout Europe, the epidemic is most severe in the countries of southern Europe.[271] Several challenges have been noted regarding the future control of the epidemic in Western Europe. Among them are the evidence of increased risky sexual behavior among MSM based on the belief that HIV can be prevented with postexposure prophylaxis or that AIDS is now easily treatable. Since the late 1990s, increases in the rates of syphilis and gonorrhea have been reported among homosexual and bisexual men in Europe and other industrialized countries. These increases in STDs among MSM are very troubling and suggest that the rate of risky behaviors remains high—which means that the HIV epidemic is not under control despite the declining AIDS mortality. Many of the STD cases occurred among older MSM, which suggests that the fear of AIDS morbidity and mortality has declined with the advent of successful HIV therapy.[272]

The detection and control of HIV among migrants is a continuing challenge, as these populations often have substantial barriers to HIV prevention and care services. Providing effective HIV prevention and treatment to migrant populations will be an important goal to prevent the future spread of HIV in Europe.

North America
United States

In the United States, all 50 states, the District of Columbia, and 6 dependent areas—American Samoa, Guam, the Northern Mariana Islands, Palau, Puerto Rico, and the U.S. Virgin Islands—report HIV surveillance data to the CDC via the same name-based system. The CDC recommended this type of reporting in 1999, and states gradually adjusted their practices to adopt the new standard. Previously, states had reported AIDS diagnoses but advances in therapy made use of AIDS statistics problematic. HIV patients who are well treated for their infection should not develop AIDS. In the 21st century, AIDS is more a marker of inadequate health care than infection status in the United States. Comparisons of data from previous years are complicated by the uneven reporting standards, however, and care must be taken when using these data as not all jurisdictions reported in an equivalent manner in the past.

The new HIV infections among adults and adolescents reported to the CDC from 37 states and 5 U.S. respondent areas with name- and risk-based reporting in 2008 included 31,595 males and 10,662 females. Among females, 84% acquired the virus by heterosexual contact and 15% acquired it from injection drug use. Among males, 72% of new infections derived from male-to-male sexual contact, 15% were from heterosexual contact, and 9% were from injection drug use (**Figure 22-13**). Overall, the majority of new infections (54%) were from male-to-male sex, 32.3% were from heterosexual contact, and 10.5% were due to injection drug

use. Only 190 (0.5%) of newly reported infections involved other types of exposures.

Among males with newly reported infections, 45% were African American, 31% were white, and 21% were Hispanic. Among females, 65% were African American, 17% were white, and 16% were Hispanic. Overall, 51.9% of newly reported infections were in African Americans, despite the fact that members of this racial group account for only 12% of the U.S. population. The incidence of HIV infection among African American males was 131.9 cases per 100,000 person-years; in Hispanic males, the incidence was 52.3 cases per 100,000 person-years. Non-white U.S. infection rates among adults and adolescents were highest in New York (59.8/100,000) and Florida (50.3/100,000). The reported incidence of HIV in nine Southern states exceeded 20/100,000[5] in 2008.[273]

In 37 states and 5 U.S. dependent areas, 433,944 male adolescents and adults and 162,844 females were HIV positive in 2007. Among males, 40% were African American, 37% were white, and 20% were Latino. Among females, 61% were African American, 19% were Latino, and 18% were white. Among males, 62% had acquired their infection by male-to-male sexual contact, 17% by injection drug use, 13% by heterosexual contact, and 7% by male-to-male sex and injection drug use.

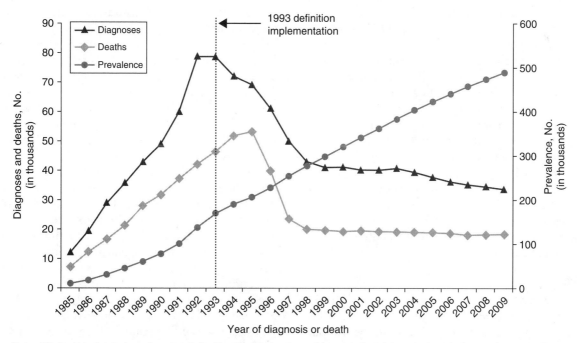

Note: All displayed data have been statistically adjusted to account for reporting delays, but not for incomplete reporting. Death may be due to any cause.

Figure 22-13 AIDS Diagnoses, Deaths, and Persons Living with AIDS 1985–2009—United States and 6 U.S. Dependent Areas. Reproduced from the Centers for Disease Control and Prevention (2012). AIDS Surveillance – Trends (1985–2010). www.cdc.gov/hiv/topics/surveillance/resources/slides/trends/index.htm. Last Modified July 16, 2012. Accessed October 2, 2012.

Among females, 73% acquired their infection by heterosexual contact, 26% by injection drug use, and 1% by other means. As noted earlier, these surveillance numbers are incomplete, particularly given that the states that did not report HIV status were some of the most heavily impacted states: California, Oregon, Washington, Illinois, and Pennsylvania. The proportion of adults and adolescents living with HIV is highest in Washington, D.C. (1781/100,000). The five states with the highest rates of HIV infection are New York, Maryland, Florida, Georgia, and Louisiana.

Mexico

The first AIDS cases in Mexico were reported in 1983. Since then, approximately 50,000 cases of AIDS have been reported nationwide, and it has been estimated that more than 150,000 persons are HIV infected.[274] The epidemic in Mexico is less intense than that in the United States: approximately 0.3% of the general adult population is infected. An estimated 220,200 persons are living with HIV in Mexico, which has a total population of 113 million persons. An estimated 20,000 new HIV infections and 10,000 AIDS-related deaths occur each year. Overall, approximately 40% of reported cases are in homosexual or bisexual men, 7% in transfusion recipients, 20% in heterosexuals, 30.8% in IDUs, and 1% in paid plasma donors. Mexico experienced a significant epidemic of HIV infections among paid plasmapheresis donors in the early and mid-1980s, when donors were infected during donation by contaminated blood collection equipment.[275] More than 400 cases of AIDS among paid donors and more than 2500 cases have been reported among transfusion recipients in Mexico.[276] Many of these transfusion-acquired cases were among pregnant women who required blood transfusions for bleeding during delivery. The epidemic related to plasma donation and blood transfusions was controlled by closing commercial plasmapheresis centers, outlawing paid donors, and establishing licensed state blood transfusion centers with adequate infection control procedures.

Canada

An estimated 90,000 persons are living with HIV in Canada. Approximately 3000 new HIV infections are reported each year. The HIV prevalence is about 0.2%. The highest proportion of reports involve persons 15–29 years of age; MSM represent the highest-risk group. Injecting drug use was the second exposure category until 1998, peaking at 33% of all new infections in 1996 and 1997 but decreasing to 18% in 2003 and 2004. Harm-reduction services have effectively decreased the incidence of new HIV infections in injecting drug users, especially in Vancouver.[247]

ESTIMATING HIV INCIDENCE

Estimating the incidence of HIV-1 infection is important to evaluate the current status of transmission dynamics, to identify high-risk populations, and to evaluate prevention programs. Incidence estimates are also critical for calculating the sample sizes needed for clinical trials of vaccines or other preventive interventions.

The traditional method of measuring the incidence of HIV-1 infection involves repeated testing of cohorts of persons at risk periodically during extended periods of follow-up. These groups could be cohorts of persons enrolled in a study or those who undergo routine repeated screening, such as for blood donation, pregnancy, or other indications. These selected populations may not provide reliable data for other groups in the population who are at higher risk (e.g., STD clinic patients, sex workers). Cohort members are repeatedly counseled to prevent infection, and those at higher risk may be more likely to be lost to follow-up, leading to an underestimate of the incidence. Prospective studies are expensive, and the data may not be generalizable to key subgroups in the population. Blood donors are screened for behavioral risks and selected by blood banks so they are at significantly lower risk of infection, whereas younger pregnant women are sexually active and, therefore, may be at greater HIV risk. UNAIDS uses seroprevalence rates of pregnant women to estimate the seroprevalence in the general population in developing countries.[277,278]

Various models have been described to estimate the incidence and total numbers of HIV-infected members of a population. The "back-calculation model" was first described in the 1980s.[279] This model relied on accurate reporting of AIDS cases and an assumption that trends in new AIDS cases reflected existing and past trends in HIV infection. The incidence of AIDS, together with the incubation period from HIV infection to AIDS, allowed the size of the HIV-positive population to be estimated. Unfortunately, these models are not useful if AIDS case reporting is incomplete.

As the availability of effective antiretroviral therapy has changed the natural history of HIV/AIDS, prolonged the incubation period, and decreased the mortality from AIDS, these original models are no longer applicable in populations with access to HAART. Various statistical models have been developed to estimate incidence from cross-sectional, prevalence surveys. The simplest of these models assumes that HIV incidence rates in the population are stable over time and that the prevalence increases linearly with age, so that the slope of the regression line provides a crude estimate of HIV incidence.[280] More complex models adjust for mortality, cohort effects, or other factors.

Other methods to estimate the incidence of HIV-1 take advantage of virological or serological markers; for example, p24 antigen prevalence among HIV-negative persons in the population can be used to estimate incidence. A study in India reported a 19.6% 1-year incidence in a high-risk population based on the p24 antigen-positive/antibody-negative prevalence, compared to a 11.7% annual incidence based on the seroconversion rate among prospectively followed STD patients.[281] In this study, the duration of the p24 antigen-positive window prior to EIA seroconversion was estimated as.22.5 days, and the p24 antigen-positive/EIA-negative prevalence was used to calculate the incidence, which was then compared with the seroconversion rate in prospective follow-up. Other investigators have utilized HIV RNA prevalence among seronegative subjects (the seronegative window period) to estimate the incidence of infection.[282]

The most common method for estimating HIV incidence at present relies on a sensitive/less-sensitive serological testing strategy. In this algorithm, sera that are reactive with a sensitive EIA are retested using an EIA in which the sera have been diluted on a 1:20,000 basis instead of 1:400, and the incubation period is shortened from 60–120 minutes to 30 minutes to make the assay less sensitive.[283] These tests are based on the weaker antibody response that occurs early after infection compared to the stronger response noted in those patients who have been infected longer. Recent infections would be positive on the standard test, but not on the detuned or less sensitive test. Different HIV subtypes have been found to have different "incubation periods," which in turn affects the time a patient has to be infected to be found positive on both the sensitive and the detuned assays. The original sensitive/less-sensitive testing strategy (also called "detuned" or standard algorithm for recent HIV-1 seroconversion [STARHS] assay) used a modified commercial HIV-1 antibody assay (Abbott 3A11) and calculated an incubation period of 129 days for the seroconversion from the more sensitive standard assay to the detuned, less-sensitive

assay among persons with HIV subtype B infections.[283] Subsequently, the assay was modified to use the licensed Vironostika EIA assay after the Abbott 3A11 assay was no longer available.[284] However, when sera were studied from persons in Thailand who were infected with subtype E infections, the window period was found to be much longer and variable—that is, 270–350 days.[285,286] Because the window period varies with different viral subtypes, the test is less reliable in areas with greater viral diversity.

An IgG capture enzyme immunoassay (BED-EIA) has been developed that indirectly measures an increasing proportion of HIV IgG in the serum.[287,288] This assay captures both HIV and non-HIV IgG in the same proportion present in the serum and includes a multi-subtype-derived branched synthetic peptide (BED) from the gp41 immunodominant region of HIV-1. This assay has been shown to detect recent infections with various subtypes of HIV, including subtypes B and E in Thailand; subtypes A, D, and C, in Africa; and subtype B in the United States and Europe with a similar duration of the seroconversion window (approximately 160 days).[288] Because of the loss of antibody-producing cells with advanced HIV infection, these sensitive/less-sensitive antibody assays can become positive among some patients with advanced AIDS or low viral load due to use of HAART or in participants who control this infection naturally. However, these persons can be identified by their very low CD4 counts or AIDS symptoms. The duration of the window period in which RNA or p24 antigen is present before HIV EIA positivity and the BED detects incident HIV is shown in **Figure 22-14**.[289]

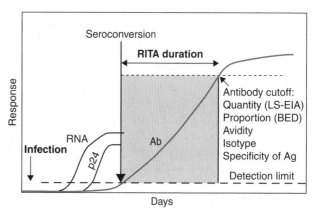

Figure 22-14 Recent Infection Testing Algorithm (RITA). Reproduced from Mastro et al. Estimating HIV Incidence in Populations Using Tests for Recent Infection: Issues, Challenges and the Way Forward. *J HIV and Surveill Epidemiol* 2010 January 1;2(1):1–14.

Other investigators have reported on the evolution of antibody patterns during infection and have used these patterns to estimate recent infections. Antibodies to *gag* (p24 and p17) and *env* (gp120 and gp47) usually appear earlier than those to polymerase gene products (p31, p51, and p66). Antibody affinity and avidity also vary during the course of infection and can be used to differentiate recent infections from more chronic infections.[290]

It has been reported that anti-p24 IgG3 antibodies are elicited only early in HIV-1 infection.[291] The IgG3 antibodies to p24 disappeared by approximately 4 months after infection and were present only 34 to 120 days after infection (total duration: 86 days) among sera from 17 seroconversion panels. If these data can be generalized to persons infected with different subtypes, this assay could become a very useful epidemiological tool. A study in Africa found that the highest specificity was obtained by combining the results from the BED, avidity assay, CD4 count, and viral level.[292]

SOCIAL AND CULTURAL FACTORS

Urbanization has been associated with a higher prevalence of STDs in many parts of the world. Urban environments increase the opportunity for mixing between populations; they attract young people for economic reasons who are likely to be sexually active, and they may be associated with increases in sexual risk taking as more traditional and conservative practices are dropped in the fast-paced and anonymous urban environment. In the United States, HIV/AIDS has been observed more frequently in urban areas than in rural areas.

Sexual mixing patterns can also define how rapidly HIV-1 spreads in a population. In cities with a high male/female ratio, such as Nairobi, Bombay, and Harare, the rate of casual and commercial sex has increased. This has led to high HIV-1 prevalence rates in sex workers and their clients, and ultimately to an increased incidence of HIV infection in the general population of these cities.

Sexual practices certainly vary between countries and regions of the world. For example, unprotected receptive anal intercourse is unusual in sub-Saharan Africa, whereas it plays a significant role in the spread of HIV in the United States, Latin America, and some Caribbean countries.[293,294] Bisexuality appears to be more common in Latin American than in many other Western countries.[295] In many countries, however, expression of a homosexual lifestyle is repressed;

therefore, MSM in these countries may be more hesitant to report same-sex intercourse, making accurate evaluation of risk behaviors difficult. Cultural conceptions of sexual identity vary considerably and must be considered when reviewing the local epidemiology of HIV prevalence and incidence.

Significant rural-to-urban migration is occurring throughout the developing world. The use of migrant labor (which may be seasonal or for weeks at a time) exposes the worker to long absences, increasing the possibility of family breakdown and both members of a sexual dyad seeking out other sexual partners.[296] Higher HIV incidence is seen among women who are poor and who have few options to make money other than commercial sex. Poverty predisposes populations to commercial sex, homelessness in adults, the presence of street children, poor education, and migration—all of which may enhance the possibility of spreading HIV infection.

UNAIDS and WHO conducted an international study in 1998 to evaluate the effect of literacy on HIV incidence.[297] In 161 countries for which literacy and HIV data were available, higher rates of literacy were strongly correlated with lower rates of HIV infection. Better-educated people have greater access to information about HIV, how it is spread, and how it can be avoided. However, in sub-Saharan Africa, the opposite literacy–HIV incidence pattern also has been observed.[297] In this region, the rapid social changes that have accompanied development and increased educational opportunities have promoted behaviors that increase the risk of HIV infection. Higher-paying jobs among the educated population in this region have served to support high-risk behaviors, which may include increased alcohol consumption, supporting a younger female partner, or visiting sex workers. Education has provided access to income and has emancipated many women of sub-Saharan Africa, resulting in their greater social mobility and increased likelihood of being involved in more sexual relationships, albeit not usually concurrently.

PREVENTION OF HIV/AIDS

In the three decades since the emergence of HIV/AIDS, this pandemic has become part of the context of contemporary life. The tens of millions of deaths and the millions of people on antiretroviral therapy attest to the toll that this disease has exacted globally and its impact on the world. In sub-Saharan Africa, the toll has been especially devastating, distorting the population pyramid and dampening the economic development of the region. Early prevention successes were collectively developed by the affected communities—persons living with HIV/AIDS—who confronted significant stigma and discrimination. Nevertheless, they reduced the epidemic through normative sexual behavior change.[291] Early government intervention, such as that seen in Thailand in 1991,[292-293] has been associated with national-level prevention success and has been determined to be key in a sustained and effective response, in contrast to the widespread denial seen in most countries. However, individual behavior change associated with sexual behavior risk reduction through the use of condoms, reduction in the number of sex partners, or seeking HIV testing has proved difficult to sustain over time. [294] Other strategies for more effective risk reduction have been sought.

In the past decade, a remarkable series of research findings have been reported that offer new promise for controlling the HIV/AIDS epidemic.[295] Until recently, almost all HIV prevention strategies relied on individual behavior change. The first positive successes associated with biomedical prevention are now generating renewed excitement in the HIV/AIDS community. Among the developments supporting these biomedical prevention strategies are the following:

- Consistent results from three randomized controlled trials involving medical male circumcision in sub-Saharan Africa
- New evidence on microbicides that can be used on a precoital basis by both females and males
- Preexposure prophylaxis success among men who have sex with men around the world
- Data showing that treatment of STDs does not reduce the risk of HIV acquisition
- A consistent finding on the success of treatment for the prevention of mother-to-child transmission that points to implementation barriers that must be overcome
- HIV prophylactic vaccine findings from Thailand that suggest we can identify the correlates of prevention
- Most recently, antiretroviral treatment as prevention, which was heralded as the scientific breakthrough of 2011 by *Science* magazine[296]

Of course, all of these prevention strategies require that HIV-uninfected but high-risk persons be identified; thus they rely heavily on HIV testing.

Similar to the biomedical prevention field, behavioral prevention has also matured. The hallmark of behavioral prevention at the turn of the century was voluntary HIV counseling and testing, which was considered to be the first step in HIV prevention. More recently, voluntary HIV counseling and testing has evolved in many communities to provider-initiated counseling and testing, or the "opt-out" strategy, in which all clients in health services are provided an HIV test unless they actively refuse such testing. Key to the successes of antiretroviral treatment strategies to control HIV transmission from an infected person to an uninfected partner is adherence to medication use. A variety of new research findings suggest that new technologies can be utilized to remind patients to take their medicines on time, and hence boost treatment adherence. The effectiveness of male condoms has been accepted worldwide, but sustaining consistent use has proved difficult. Nevertheless, all counseling and testing strategies include messages about the effectiveness of male condom use. Finally, new findings on targeting social and behavioral change communications suggest that communication strategies can augment and support both biomedical and behavioral interventions.

The third strategy for HIV prevention is based on making structural changes that reduce risk. Several promising research findings indicate that interventions to retain young women in school in sub-Saharan Africa can lead to reduced HIV infection. Thus this strategy can both improve women's educational attainment and increase their employment options, leading to longer-term success in society.

Perhaps the greatest promise for ending the HIV epidemic is associated with a new HIV prevention strategy—HIV combination prevention. This approach culls the best results from each of the three prevention modalities, and combines biomedical, behavioral and structural approaches to synergistically reduce the risk of HIV transmission within populations. It also incorporates a treatment strategy known as "community viral load," in which effective HIV antiretroviral treatment reduces transmission by controlling HIV viral load in infected persons, along with effective behavioral strategies.

Biomedical Prevention Modalities

Biomedical prevention is traditionally under the control of the medical community. These approaches require interaction between high-risk members of the community and healthcare providers. Hence, the first step in promoting biomedical prevention is reducing the barriers to access to healthcare providers. Achieving this goal may present several challenges, including distance to healthcare facilities (if they exist), transportation, losing a day's work, and awareness of both the existence of services and their perceived success rates. The first step in virtually all biomedical prevention strategies is HIV testing (covered in the "Behavioral Prevention Strategies").

Condoms and Other Barrier Prevention Methods

Condoms   A great body of evidence exists that the use of male condoms reduces sexual transmission of HIV.[297–300] Male latex condoms are the recommended type. Other male condoms such as those made of plastic or lambskin in exist, but latex condoms are the most effective against HIV and are also the most studied.[301] It is now well known that water-based lubricants are the only appropriate lubricant or additive to be used with condoms. Petroleum-based lubricants render latex condoms less effective against HIV transmission, and nonoxynol-9 has been implicated in increasing the risk of HIV transmission.

Latex condoms have been shown, via in vitro permeability tests, to block the passage of HIV.[302] However, studies of effectiveness, as opposed to laboratory or efficacy studies, are the most useful in determining the real-life (or use-effectiveness) potential of condoms to prevent HIV transmission. A large European prospective study of serodiscordant subjects who were stable partners showed the following rates of transmission according to reported condom use:

- None (0%) of the HIV-negative partners became infected among couples who consistently and correctly used condoms, despite a cumulative 15,000 episodes of intercourse when the negative partner was at putative risk.
- Among couples who used condoms inconsistently, the rate of seroconversion was 4.8/100 person-years (95% CI: 2.5–8.4).[300]

The risk of transmission increased with advanced stages of HIV infection in the positive partner (*P*<.04), and withdrawal to avoid ejaculation in the vagina had a protective effect in uninfected women (*P* <.02).[309]

Because randomized controlled trials of condom use for the prevention of HIV transmission are not considered ethical, the best data on condom effectiveness come from observational studies comparing subjects who were "always users" as compared to "never users" of condoms. A recent meta-analysis of studies conducted with subjects who either always (100%) or never (0%) use condoms provides the most convincing evidence of condoms' effectiveness.[300] Studies included in this meta-analysis that involved "always users" yielded a homogenous HIV

infection incidence of 1.14 (95% CI: 0.56–2.04) per 100 person-years. References to "never users" were more heterogeneous, but yielded an incidence rate of 5.75 (95% CI: 3.16–9.66). The preventable fraction (proportionate reduction) of HIV infection with consistent condom use was approximately 80%.

A Cochrane review of the effectiveness of male condoms found they were approximately 85% effective in reducing the heterosexual transmission of HIV among HIV-discordant couples.[301] Model-based estimates concur with this estimate, indicating that condoms decrease the per-contact probability of male-to-female transmission of HIV by approximately 95%. Even occasional condom use, based on some statistical models, has been shown to be of significant value, with a roughly linear relationship between the proportion of sexual contacts in which a condom is used and the resultant reduction in the risk of infection. For example, using a condom half the time will result in about half the potential reduction obtained through consistent condom use. Such results suggest that harm-reduction strategies need to be reconsidered to include the message that some condom use can be protective, for those persons who are unable to use condoms 100% of the time.[313] Most risk reduction counseling protocols currently recommend using condoms for all sexual acts, and do not take into consideration the protection provided by at least some condom use. This more complex message is important to convey, as effective and consistent use of condoms within established partnerships has been demonstrated to be a continuing challenge.[314] Because a condom is needed for protection from HIV at each coital act, a consistent and ample supply is also required.

Female condoms have the same mode of protective action as male condoms—that is, they serve as a physical barrier preventing exposure to secretions. Although clinical trials have demonstrated effectiveness of female condoms relative to sexually transmitted infections,[302,303] their effectiveness in preventing HIV infection has not been directly determined.[304] Based on STD and pregnancy prevention studies, it is estimated that the female condom is 94–97% effective in HIV risk reduction when used correctly and consistently.[304] High cost has been cited as a barrier to effective uptake of female condoms in international settings.[295,305] As with male condoms, the female condom must be used at each coital act (although it can be inserted earlier in the sexual act than a male condom and might be less disruptive for that reason), and the recommendation by the manufacturer is that it be a single-use device. Finally, the female condom provides a female-controlled prevention method, which is an urgent need

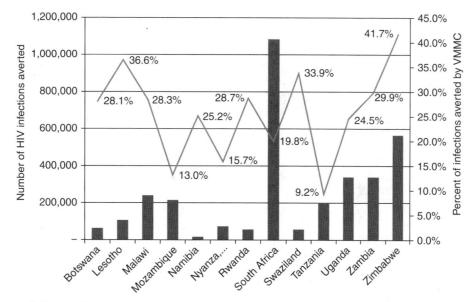

Figure 22-15 Cumulative number and percentages of HIV infections averted between 2011 and 2025 by scaling up adult VMMC to reach 80% coverage in five years. Reproduced from Hankins C, Forsythe S, Njeuhmeli E (2011) Voluntary Medical Male Circumcision: An Introduction to the Cost, Impact, and Challenges of Accelerated Scaling Up. PLoS Med 8(11):e1001127.

given the increasing feminization of the global HIV/AIDS epidemic.

A WHO expert committee reviewed the evidence in the role of condoms in the control of HIV and other STDs. It concluded, "Condom use is a critical element in a comprehensive, effective and sustainable approach to HIV prevention and treatment."

The female diaphragm was evaluated in the MIRA (Methods for Improving Reproductive Health in Africa) trial in Durban and Johannesburg, South Africa, and Harare, Zimbabwe, among sexually active women aged 18–49 who were recruited for the study between September 2003 and September 2005. The incidence of HIV was virtually identical in the intervention and control groups using an intention-to-treat analysis.[306] The proportion of women reporting condom use was significantly lower in the intervention group (54%) than in the control group (85%), attenuating whatever effect the diaphragm might have provided.

Male Medical Circumcision Adult male medical circumcision has been well established as a means to reduce the risk of HIV acquisition by approximately 60%.[307–309] Data have also been published indicating that adult male medical circumcision significantly reduces the incidence of herpes simplex virus, type 2, and the prevalence of human papillomavirus infection, demonstrating the broader public health benefits of the procedure.[310] A recent review[311] of the published evidence of the association of male circumcision and

HIV/STDs in men and women suggests that this procedure has a long-term benefit for women in HIV-discordant partnerships. Few data suggest that risk compensation (unsafe practices or increased risky behavior) occurs among men who undergo medical male circumcision, which was also reported in a meta-analysis of the three randomized controlled trials.[312] The cost-effectiveness of this one-time procedure is considered to be quite high (**Figure 22-15**).[313,314]

As countries in sub-Saharan Africa scale up male medical circumcision services, operational research issues have emerged. Key elements identified as critical to program scale-up include the following: "leadership and partnerships; situational analysis; advocacy; enabling policy and regulatory environment; cost and impact analyses; strategy and operational plans for national implementation; quality assurance and improvement; human resource development; commodity security; and social change communication, and monitoring and evaluation."[311]

Adult male medical circumcision among men who have sex with men has not been evaluated in a randomized controlled trial (although a trial is under way among MSM in China). A recent Cochrane Collaboration[315] conducted a systematic review of male circumcision for prevention of homosexual acquisition of HIV in men, including 21 observational studies with more than 71,000 participants. The pooled-effect estimate for HIV acquisition was not statistically significant, with considerable heterogeneity seen. Subgroup analysis did detect significance of circumcision for men who reported the insertive role but not for those who reported a receptive role.

Microbicides and HIV Prevention   In recent years, almost half of new HIV infections occurred in persons 15–24 years of age, with two-thirds found in women.[316] Among the myriad of social, behavioral, and biological factors that expose women to enhanced susceptibility to HIV infection, early sexual initiation with older partners seems particularly risky for women's vulnerability. Condom use, safer sexual practices, and prevention of STDs are often not under the control of women. Vaginal microbicides are considered in this context to be a critical female-controlled strategy to prevent HIV infection.[317]

Microbicides are topical products that are applied to the vagina or rectum to prevent HIV and other STDs. The design of products was based on animal studies and laboratory investigations of compounds that demonstrated activity against HIV and bacterial and other viral infections.[318] Gel formulations have been the most widely used in trials, but films, rings, and tablets have also been evaluated.[319] Recent reviews of microbicides are widely available,[320,321] and updates on the status of trials is available on several advocacy websites (www.global-campaign.org; www.popcouncil.org/topics/microbicides.asp; www.hivresourcetracking.org; www.ipmglobal.org; www.womenshealth.gov).

First-generation HIV microbicides focused on surfactants (detergents, such as non-oxynol-9, SAVVY, and sodium lauryl surfate), anionic polyanions (Carageenan, Cellulose sulfate, Pro 2000, CAP), and acidifying agents (Buffergel), which were generally well tolerated but not efficacious.[319] Second-generation HIV microbicides include reverse transcriptase inhibitors (non-nucleosides and nucleotides—for example, tenofovir) and early inhibitors (CCR5 ligands, lectins, and monoclonal antibodies).[319] Because this field is changing so rapidly, the reader is referred to updated trial information found on the websites.

Whether one or more microbicides will be necessary is currently unknown, as its depends on whether one agent can reduce initial replication or whether viral entry inhibition will also be needed. The issue of how HIV viral resistance may influence the efficacy of microbicides as antiretroviral drugs come into greater use, especially in low- and middle-income settings, is also not known. Additionally, how microbicides are used outside of the clinical trial setting is not known, although use rates are certainly lower than prescribed and condoms may not be consistently used, as demonstrated quite routinely in trials.[320]

Chemoprophylaxis for HIV Prevention   There is growing awareness that antiretroviral drugs can be an effective strategy for HIV prevention. A recent review[321] of the current and future clinical use of antiretroviral chemoprophylaxis before and after high-risk exposure to HIV suggests that this approach may be useful in some populations. The use of antiretroviral therapy in high-risk uninfected persons remains somewhat controversial, however. The use of antiretroviral therapy for postexposure prophylaxis has been widely recommended in occupational settings for a number of years[322] and has a strong evidence base supporting its effectiveness.

In cases where the likelihood of HIV exposure is high, chemoprophylaxis via oral or topical formulations may be an effective strategy for prevention. Animal studies have provided the scientific basis for preexposure prophylaxis.[323] More than a dozen studies are currently being conducted in the field with a number of agents, with the majority evaluating the effectiveness of tenofovir alone or in combination with emtricitabine (Truvada). Tenofovir, a chemoprophylactic agent that has a long intracellular half-life, achieves high concentrations in genital tissue, and has demonstrated antiviral activity in monocytes/macrophages.[324] Tenofovir is a viral replication inhibitor that suppresses the replication of HIV in the vagina or rectum during intercourse exposures. Most of the current trials are using tenofovir given as a daily dose, either in combination with emtricitabine (daily oral) or coitally dependent.

The AIDS Vaccine Advocacy Coalition (www.avac.org) has a PrEPWatch site that provides continuous updates on the status of all current clinical trials involving PrEP and PEP. In 2010, the iPrEx study team[325] released the results of its PrEP study for HIV prevention in men who have sex with men, in which 2499 HIV-seronegative men or transgender women were assigned to emtricitabine and tenofovir disoproxil fumarate or placebo daily. The intervention arm experienced a 44% reduction in the incidence of HIV infection. This finding has reenergized the chemoprophylaxis field, but the modest protection delivered by this means calls for renewed focus on behavioral prevention in support of the study medication.[325]

On May 10, 2012, an expert panel convened by the FDA recommended that Truvada receive a change of label so that it can be sold as an HIV preventive medication.[329] As more PrEP findings emerge, the issue of who should prescribe these drugs, how providers should be trained, and who should pay will come to the fore. Certainly, there are concerns about unsupervised use of chemoprophylactic medications, especially the fear that tenofovir resistance emergence in the community might compromise their effectiveness. As with adult male medical circumcision, there is also concern about risk compensation.[349] Three studies of PrEP to prevent the heterosexual transmission of HIV in high risk populations in Africa were reported in August, 2012 with discrepant results.[326-328] A study of 2120 HIV negative women at high risk for HIV infection living in 3 African countries with high HIV infection rates were randomized to take Tenofovir-Emtricitabine (TDF-FTC) or placebo on a daily basis for a year. The HIV incidence in TDF-FTC group, 4.7 per 100 person years, and the control group, 5.0 per 100 person years were not different in this study.[327] Another study of 4747 couples from Kenya and Uganda who were discordant for HIV infection evaluated once daily TDF, or TDF-FTC in comparison to placebo. A total of 82 HIV infections occurred during follow-up; there were 17 in the TDF group, 13 in the TDF-FTC group and 52 in the placebo group. This was a relative reduction of HIV incidence of 67% (95% CI 44–81%; P<0.001) in the TDF group and of 75% (95% CI = 55-87%; P<0.001) in the TDF-FTC group.[326] The third study enrolled 1219 men and women in Botswana to receive either daily TDF-FTC or placebo.[328] The study participants were followed for 1563 person years (median 1.1 years, maximum 3.7 years). This study was discontinued because of poor retention. However, 33 participants became infected with HIV; of these 9 were in the TDF = FTC group and 24 were in the placebo group. The incidence was 1.2 and 3.1 infections per 100 person years respectively. The efficacy of TDF-FTC in this study was 62.2% (95%CI = 21.5-83.4%, P = 0.03). The study subjects who received TDF-FTC in this study had higher rates of side effects including nausea, vomiting dizziness, and a significant decline in bone mineral density. However, these were not regarded as major side effects from the therapy. While PrEP will probably not be a major component of biomedical prevention, it certainly has a place within the prevention toolbox in selected situations.

Treatment of Sexually Transmitted Infections The HIV epidemic in sub-Saharan Africa has developed in a population with a preexisting burden of infectious diseases, and these concurrent infections appear to have important interactions with HIV. STDs are known to have a direct effect on HIV-1 transmission—especially those that involve genital ulceration, such as *Treponema pallidum*, HSV-2, and *Haemophilus ducreyi*.[386] Both ulcerative and non-ulcerative STDs also have been associated with an increased viral load in the genital tract.[387,388] Non-ulcerative STDs have been shown to increase HIV-1 transmission as well, possibly via increased CD4+ cell recruitment and activation at the genital tract.[389] In vitro studies have shown that *T. pallidum* can induce HIV gene expression in monocytes through a nuclear factor NF-κ B pathway.[390] Studies have found a substantially increased concentration of HIV in the genital tract of persons infected with *Neisseria gonorrhoeae* or other STDs, which decreased after successful treatment of the STD.[389] The increased HIV viral load in the genital tract of HIV-positive persons noted with frequently encountered STDs has been postulated to explain, in part, the rapid dissemination of HIV in sub-Saharan Africa and Asia.[316]

Five major trials focusing on the treatment of sexually transmitted infections as a means to reduce HIV acquisition have been reported in the past 15 years, but provide mixed evidence on HIV incidence. Four community-randomized trials were conducted in sub-Saharan Africa to evaluate improved case detection and treatment of symptomatic diseases[333-335] or periodic mass treatment of common sexually transmitted infections.[336] The design of these trials differed, however, as did the types of STDs affected by the intervention. Only the Mwanza trial demonstrated a reduction in HIV incidence; the trials in Uganda and Zimbabwe showed no effect of case detection or treatment on HIV incidence. Speculation suggests that the epidemic was more established in Uganda.[337]

In a similar fashion, epidemiologic evidence suggests a strong link between herpes simplex virus, type 2—the most common cause of genital ulcers and a leading infection worldwide—and HIV among women and men who have sex with men. HSV-2 coinfection is exceptionally common among people with HIV infection. Longitudinal cohort studies demonstrated a nearly threefold increase in HIV infection among heterosexual men and women with herpes and a nearly twofold increase in HIV infection among MSM.[338,339] Based on these observational data and biological plausibility, the HIV Prevention Trial Network (HPTN) 039[340] was launched to test whether acyclovir treatment of HSV-2 might reduce HIV incidence. HIV-negative women in Zambia, Zimbabwe, and South Africa and MSM in Peru and the United States who were HSV-2 infected were treated with acyclovir to control their HSV-2 infection. Although this trial failed to prevent HIV transmission, it did reduce genital ulcers from HSV-2 by 37%. The failure to lower HIV incidence in the acyclovir arm was a disappointment for the HIV prevention field and may reflect the lack of a true association between HSV-2 and HIV transmission, a failure of acyclovir to prevent all ulcers, or the role of HSV-2 in HIV transmission outside of genital ulcers.

A review of the literature[341] on treatment of sexually transmitted infections as a strategy for HIV prevention identified a number of issues that must be addressed in future studies. Important issues include trial design and conduct, epidemic stage, and statistical power. Bacterial vaginosis and recognition and adjustment for HIV treatment must also be taken into account.

Prevention of Mother-to-Child Transmission

One of the heralded success stories in HIV prevention is that of the dramatic worldwide reduction in the transmission of HIV-1 from mothers to children. The use of effective antiretroviral treatments of mothers has reduced the transmission to their newborns from 25% in 2011 to 1–5% today. Breastfeeding transmission can also be substantially prevented.[342–343] There is no question that in low- and middle-income countries, primary prevention works.[344] The only remaining questions today are operational research questions:

- How we can identify women in cases where antenatal care is substandard or not available
- How to better optimize PMTCT to assess women early in antenatal care
- How to deal with mothers who select home-based birth
- How to assure a steady supply of effective antiretroviral drugs in resource-constrained contexts
- How to assure breastfeeding while avoiding further HIV transmission

These steps in the provision of care are known collectively as the "care cascade"—and keeping people on the cascade is a vital implementation step in improving care. The success of each step in the cascade is necessary to ensure the success of the overall program, as the success rates must be multiplied together to get the final success rate. For example, if 75% of mothers are tested, 80% get their test results, 80% receive HIV treatment, 90% take the medication, and 80% of infants receive their medication, then the success rate of the PMTCT program through birth is 0.75 (tested) × 0.80 (get results) × 0.80 (enroll in treatment) × 0.90 (take medication) × 0.80 (infant gets medication) = 35%. Intensive research along the treatment cascade is urgently needed.

HIV Prophylactic Vaccines

The development of an effective, safe, and affordable HIV vaccine has been a cornerstone of HIV prevention research since 1985. Many trials to date have proved vaccines to be ineffective—among drug users, among men who have sex with men in the United States who received an HIV-1 envelope glycoprotein 120 subunit vaccine, and in international trials of T-cell–based vaccines.[345] A vaccine trial (the STEP study) was done using an adenovirus type 5 vectored vaccine designed to stimulate cell-mediated immune responses, i.e., RKAd5 HIV-1 gag/pol/nef vaccine, among 3000 volunteers who were randomly assigned to receive 3 doses of the vaccine or a placebo and followed for HIV incident infection. In this study the vaccine was ineffective in preventing HIV-1 infections among subjects with adenovirus 5 antibody titers >1:200 at baseline. But in those with higher adenovirus 5 titers at baseline and in subjects who were uncircumcised the incidence of HIV-1 infection was significantly increased. The hazard ratio for incident HIV-1 infection was 2.3 (95% CI = 1.2–4.3) in those with adenovirus infection and 3.8 (95% CI = 1.5–9.3) among uncircumcised men but was not increased in circumcised men or those with absent or low adenovirus titers at baseline. Therefore, this study was stopped due to this unanticipated result.[373] However, one recent report[346] of a Phase 2b clinical trial evaluated a pox virus prime followed by a glycoprotein 120 boost, the RV144 trial in Thailand. Among 16,000 low-risk volunteers, 31% efficacy was achieved in reducing HIV incidence. While a somewhat modest result, this study was the first to demonstrate any efficacy for an HIV vaccine. After this trial it was hypothesized that the infected subjects had suboptimal vaccine responses or more frequent exposures.[347] A case-control study to evaluate the immune correlates of protection from HIV-1 infection in this trial found that the level of binding IgG antibodies to variable regions 1 and 2 of HIV-1 envelope proteins correlated inversely with the rate of HIV-1 infection (estimated odds ratio, 0.57 per 1-SD increase; P = 0.02; q = 0.08). Also the binding of plasma IgA antibodies to Env correlated directly with the rate of infection (estimated odds ratio = 1.54 per SD increase; P = 0.03; q = 0.08). This analysis suggested that Env-specific antibodies may mitigate the effects of potentially protective antibodies.[377] Clearly more data are needed to confirm this intriguing finding and to determine what type of immune response might prevent infection or control viral replication. A major challenge to the development of an effective HIV vaccine has been the extensive genetic diversity of the viral envelope proteins. Current vaccine research is focused on designing immunogen that will elicit broadly reactive neutralizing antibodies to envelope proteins.[380] Broadly reacting envelope neutralizing antibodies have been identified in some patients with chronic HIV infection, including some 'elite controllers,' who have infections with low or undetectable viral load and maintain normal immune function despite chronic HIV infection.[381,382]

Because clinical trials are moving at a very rapid pace, consult the International AIDS Vaccine Initiative website (www.iavi.org) or the NIH (www.nih.gov) website for updates on current trials. A recent review[348] of the current status of HIV vaccine studies, particularly in Africa, identifies the major challenges to this rapidly emerging field.

Treatment as Prevention

Several observational studies have reported decreased HIV transmission in HIV-discordant couples when the index partner was treated with antiretroviral therapy. In July 2011, HPTN 052 results were published in the *New England Journal of Medicine*.[349] This study enrolled 1763 couples where one partner was infected with HIV and the other was not; half of infected partners were men, and approximately half the couples were from Africa. Participants with CD4 counts between 350 and 550 cells were randomly assigned to either immediate treatment or treatment after a decline in CD4 to > 350 cells/ul or the onset of HIV-related symptoms. Of 28 linked HIV

transmissions, 27 occurred in the delayed therapy arm as compared to 1 in the early treatment group (for a hazard rate of 0.04). This finding of 96% efficacy in preventing transmission associated with early initiation of HIV treatment has been called by *Science* magazine the medical breakthrough of 2011. Clearly, this finding is now recognized internationally as the standard of treatment that we must now try to implement.

A number of scientific reviews of treatment as prevention (TasP) have been published recently.[350,351,366,382,385] Among the issues covered is the gap between treatment and prevention, the point at which to start treatment, HIV counseling and testing, and future steps for the field. Issues that need to be addressed include longer-term adherence support strategies, delays in initiation of treatment following obtaining test results, continuing issues with stigma and discrimination that discourage patients from coming forward for treatment, and concerns noted with long-term behavior change. As with the PMTCT treatment cascade, a similar treatment cascade can be enumerated for HIV-positive patients initiating care. The challenges of the treatment cascade are numerous, and this is an area of intense research (**Figure 22-16**).

Behavioral Prevention Strategies

Until the past several years, behavioral prevention for HIV infection was considered to consist of health education and counseling, strategies to implement and

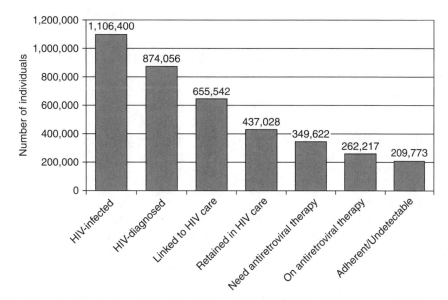

Figure 22-16 Wasted Opportunities to Improve Health of Persons Living with HIV and Help Prevent HIV Transmission. Reproduced from Gardner EM, McLees MP, Steiner JF, Del Rio C, Burman WJ. The spectrum of engagement in HIV care and its relevance to test-and-treat strategies for prevention of HIV infection. *Clin Infect Dis*. 2011 Mar 15;52(6):793–800.

sustain individual behavior change decisions (partner reduction, avoidance of anonymous partners, improved and consistent condom use and skills), and strategies to improve adherence to medical recommendations, particularly regarding antiretroviral use. Theoretically based interventions relying on psychology, social change, and communication were prominent features of this approach. However, there has been much criticism of how much behavioral prevention strategies have been involved in slowing the HIV epidemic. In this section, we review the major challenges to HIV behavioral prevention research and implementation at the community level.

In March 2011, the American Foundation for AIDS Research (amfAR)[352] issued a clarion call for HIV prevention, and outlined a "roadmap" to reinvigorate the HIV prevention effort. The report noted that prevention must remain a central component of the longer-term response to HIV/AIDS, and it noted the challenges to treatment scale-up in the currently challenging economic conditions. It is clear that prevention is the most cost-effective defense against HIV, as estimates indicate that each HIV infection prevented in the United States saves $355,000 in medical care costs.[353]

The amfAR roadmap identifies the key elements of a successful behavioral prevention strategy. First, its focuses on education and behavior change strategies that address diverse populations. Prevention can change behavior such that exposure to HIV is reduced. Indeed, virtually all biomedical prevention strategies depend on adherence to recommendations of use. Conditional cash transfer programs in Malawi and Tanzania supported by the World Bank use financial incentives to encourage positive behaviors. While they have not yet addressed HIV prevention in randomized controlled trials, early evidence appears suggestive of significant risk reduction with better adherence.

The second strategy in behavioral prevention is HIV counseling and testing. Voluntary HIV testing has been a hallmark of HIV prevention since testing first became available in 1985. To access HIV prevention services, knowing one's HIV status is the first step. To date, the majority of HIV infections in Africa have not been identified. The CDC estimates that 20% of all HIV infections in the United States have not been detected. To overcome this gap, there has been a call to move from voluntary HIV counseling and testing to "opt-out" testing, or provider-initiated testing and counseling.[354] A corollary of this strategy is the new prevention concept termed "seek, test, and treat," which addresses the goal of early diagnosis and prompt linkage to care for persons early in the course of a confirmed HIV infection. This strategy has two components: provision of universal, annual voluntary testing of all adults and immediate provision of antiretroviral therapy.[355,385]

A recent review[356] of behavioral strategies to reduce HIV transmission identified five behavioral strategies to make them work better. First, HIV prevention is neither simple nor simplistic—and sustainability is a major challenge to overcome. Second, combination prevention—that is, combining behavioral and biomedical strategies—will be essential if any broad-stroke effort is to be successful. Third, prevention program must have multiple targets and outcomes and use multiple levels of intervention: one size most definitely does not fit all. Fourth, behavioral interventions alone are probably insufficient to affect this epidemic. Finally, we need to adequately fund, implement, and evaluate interventions. The amfAR report notes the low priority level that behavioral prevention requires compared to HIV treatment. An update of a recent systematic review[357] of HIV prevention interventions focused on trials that use HIV infection status as an outcome. Trials generally were found wanting on a number of key factors: interventions were inherently ineffective, they were inadequately implemented, or there were problems in measurement of effectiveness. The behavioral prevention community notes the inherent difficulties in its research methodologies and is striving to become increasingly rigorous and relevant.

Structural Approaches to HIV Prevention

One of the enduring criticisms of behavioral prevention (which applies to biomedical prevention as well) is that it relies on individual behavior change that is constrained by broader structural factors, which may constrain choice. The drivers of HIV epidemics are widely viewed as being factors such as gender and age, poverty and wealth, and policy and power.[358] These root causes of individual risk and vulnerability are clearly at play in most epidemics, yet there little has been done to address these most fundamental causes.

Structural approaches to HIV prevention include changes in the law to allow access to services or to overcome discrimination. Microcredit programs to assist vulnerable women to address economic disparities, for example, might lead to decreased gender-based violence. Syringe-exchange programs are widely viewed as falling under this rubric.[359] Structural approaches include the 100% condom campaign in Thailand and the Dominican Republic[360] and gender-based violence initiatives. While quantifying the effects of these approaches might be difficult, they offer strong evidence that a population-level approach may be far more cost-effective than individual behavior change strategies. As part of a package of prevention initiative, they may be attractive to policymakers.

The Way Forward: Combination HIV Prevention

With the success of HPTN 052 and some of the recent gains in biomedical prevention, it has become increasingly recognized that combination HIV prevention is the way forward.[296,361–364] The former argument about care and treatment versus prevention has now been replaced by treatment as prevention.[385] Most policymakers, opinion leaders, and prevention specialists now recognize that prevention is a multifaceted issue, and that no one approach on its own can lead to the desired endpoint—the prevention of future cases of HIV/AIDS. In this time of constrained economies, we must wrest the full benefit from each of our strategies to meet our goal. Thus the new watchword for HIV has become combination prevention. While this is a lofty goal, three new international projects in sub-Saharan Africa are soon to be launched to test this strategy in reducing or eliminating HIV. While these studies will take years to answer the research question, all three are combining biomedical and behavioral prevention approaches in community randomized trials with HIV incidence as the endpoint.

ADDRESSING THE AIDS PANDEMIC

As described earlier in this chapter, the HIV/AIDS pandemic represents an unprecedented crisis affecting human health. Virtually every country in the world has been affected to some extent by the AIDS epidemic. In particular, many countries in sub-Saharan Africa have been devastated by this scourge, with the life expectancy of their populations declining by 20 years or more and substantial proportions of young adults dead or seriously ill from the disease. The AIDS epidemic has destabilized societies as it has spread.

In recognition of the societal impact of the AIDS pandemic, a United Nations General Assembly Special Session (UNGASS) on HIV/AIDS was held on June 25–27, 2001, the first special session of the UN General Assembly devoted to coping with the effects of a single disease. At this session, governments from 189 countries committed themselves to a comprehensive program of international and national action to fight the HIV/AIDS pandemic by adopting the Declaration of Commitment on HIV/AIDS.[393] The declaration also included a pledge on the part of the UN General Assembly that it would devote itself at least one full day annually to reviewing the progress achieved in realizing the goals of the commitment. To facilitate this review, the joint United Nations Programme on HIV/AIDS (UNAIDS, www.unaids.org) and its partners have developed a set of core indicators for monitoring the progress of the various international and national organizations in meeting the goals.

Numerous serious barriers exist to implementation of the commitment to reverse the effects of the AIDS pandemic in resource-limited countries in sub-Saharan Africa and other regions of the world. Effective antiretroviral drug combinations are very expensive, associated with some toxicity, and difficult to take, and they require a high degree of adherence to be effective. Even more important, the absence of an adequate public health and medical infrastructure for diagnosing and treating HIV infections, monitoring the response, and minimizing the stigmatization of persons who are HIV infected in many developing countries poses a serious barrier to the development of an effective global AIDS control program.

Despite these obstacles, the United Nations followed the UNGASS meeting with the establishment of a Global Fund to Control HIV, Tuberculosis, and Malaria (the three major lethal epidemic infectious diseases affecting less-developed countries). Contributions were solicited from developed industrialized countries to support the global fund. Developing countries could develop a disease control plan directed at one or more of these diseases and submit a request for funding to the UN Global Fund. By the end of 2003, the global fund had approved 227 grants totaling $2.1 billion to 124 countries and had already disbursed $232 million; approximately 60% of these grants were for AIDS prevention.

In 2001, scientists at UNAIDS, WHO, and other organizations calculated that, under optimal conditions, 3 million people living in developing countries with HIV infection could be provided with antiretroviral therapy and access to medical services by the end of 2005.[392] Despite these estimates, treatment enrollment among persons in developing countries continued to lag. In 2003, only an estimated 400,000 (7%) of the 5,900,000 individuals believed to need antiretroviral therapy in developing countries were receiving treatment.[392] On September 22, 2003, the "Treat 3 Million Persons by 2005" ("3 by 5") initiative was announced by Dr. Lee Jung-Wok, Director General of WHO.[394] This important initiative helped energize the urgent effort to deal with the AIDS crisis in sub-Saharan Africa and other developing, resource-limited countries with major AIDS epidemics. The challenge was put forward to meet a specific goal—treat 3 million persons within 2 years.

Implementation of the 3 by 5 Program

When the "3 by 5" program was announced by WHO in 2003, major hurdles existed to its implementation, including the expense and difficulties of using HAART, inadequate public health and medical infrastructure, widespread stigmatization of AIDS, and uncertain and uneven political commitment. Although most developed-market-economy countries supported the 3 by 5 program philosophically, their level of financial support for the program was uncertain.

To begin implementation of the 3 by 5 program, WHO developed a series of guidelines at a meeting in Lusaka, Zambia, in November 2003 as follows[43,94]:

- Strengthen and expand prevention, care, treatment support, and other services provided directly by communities.
- Promote and protect the human rights of people living with HIV/AIDS and everyone affected by HIV, especially poor and vulnerable populations, including sex workers, injection drug users, men who have sex with men, displaced persons, and migrant workers. This must be done in an environment in which people living with HIV/AIDS are encouraged and supported to volunteer, learn, and disclose their HIV status.
- Assure quality of care by involving communities in monitoring and evaluating antiretroviral services.
- HIV testing and counseling should be available in health facilities at all levels.
- Simple rapid finger-prick tests should be the test of choice to scale up testing and counseling services.
- Strengthen existing HIV prevention services while antiretroviral therapy is being introduced.
- Ensure that people living with HIV/AIDS receive key HIV prevention services and commodities.

WHO recommended initial therapy with a simplified first-line drug combination of stavudine, lamivudine, and nevirapine in a fixed-dose combination. This multidrug tablet has been produced, along with various second-line combinations, by several private and government pharmaceutical firms in India, Thailand, China, and Brazil at a cost of $300–500 per patient per year, and treatment costs continue to decline globally. The Clinton Foundation's Clinton Health Access Initiative (CHAI) has negotiated drug pricing and drug distribution agreements with industry to secure affordable drug access to its partner countries. The UNITAID international organization, founded in 2006 with leadership from Brazil and France, also purchases drugs for HIV/AIDS, malaria, and tuberculosis for the Global Fund and other WHO programs. These global alliances have substantially increased the negotiating capacity of countries, have raised funds in innovative ways (e.g., a surcharge on airline tickets), and have increased access to ART for HIV-infected persons.

As of June 2005, approximately 1 million persons in resource-limited countries were receiving combination antiretroviral therapy.[392] In the last 6 years, access to ART has expanded dramatically in sub-Saharan Africa. At the end of 2011, an estimated 6.7 million of the total 11 million persons needing therapy were receiving it.[316] Their treatment costs have been supported by the UNAIDS Global Fund, PEPFAR, and the World Bank. WHO now recommends therapy for any HIV-infected person with a CD4+ cell count of less than 350 cells/µL.

PEPFAR Program

A major boost to the global effort to control the AIDS pandemic came in January 2003, when President George W. Bush announced in his State of the Union message the intention of the United States to initiate the President's Emergency Plan for AIDS Relief (PEPFAR), with funding of $15 billion over the next 5 years.[394] The initial funds were provided by the U.S. Congress in 2003. The political motivation was one of compassion and security, as HIV was declared a global emergency and a threat to political stability. PEPFAR is administrated through the Office of the Global AIDS Coordinator (OGAC) under the OGAC Ambassador. Giving the head of OGAC Ambassador status facilitated access to world leaders as the program reached out globally. Initially the plan started slowly: PEPFAR treated only 155,000 people with antiretroviral treatment in the first 8 months of its operation. However, efforts directed at prevention, care for orphans and vulnerable children, and care for people with HIV prior to their needing ARV medications were all expanded simultaneously. More than 1 million women were provided services to prevent mother-to-child transmission of HIV, and more than 1.7 million persons received some health care through the PEPFAR program.

Initially, the PEPFAR program was targeted to 15 "focus countries" in Africa, the Caribbean, and Vietnam.[394] PEPFAR worked in concert with global partners to build a health infrastructure by establishing care and treatment centers and providing testing and prevention services. In contrast to the UN Global Fund and the 3 by 5 program, the antiretroviral drugs paid for by PEPFAR must be licensed by the FDA. In response to this requirement, the FDA created a mechanism for the rapid review and licensure of antiretroviral drug combinations, allowing for the use of cheaper, simpler-to-use, generic drug combinations in countries included in PEPFAR programs. PEPFAR also focused its treatment dollars on second-line regimens, which included licensed drugs, leaving the Global Fund to purchase first-line medications.

Understandably, the first years of PEPFAR were difficult. Many groups were trying address the global catastrophe and overlap, duplication, and disorganization were more common than wished. Even within the U.S. government, multiple agencies were involved. The United States Agency for International Development (USAID), the CDC's Global AIDS Program (GAP), the National Institutes of Health, and many other agencies were involved in program development, implementation, technical consultation, program evaluation, and resource delivery. The PEPFAR unilateral decision-making process, which concentrated solely on meeting implementation goals, was in conflict with the multipartner approach used previously. Nevertheless, the bold approach of the PEPFAR program overcame global stagnation and profoundly changed the attitude toward the feasibility of providing ARV drugs.

At first, the prevention activities in PEPFAR were modeled after the ABC program that had successfully reduced HIV incidence in Uganda. This program initially included a focus on abstinence (A), being faithful (B), and current and consistent use of condoms (C), as appropriate with a focus on the first two. The program has evolved over time, so that the prevention program is now more multifaceted than it was in its early years. In 2008, President Barack Obama announced the intention to provide $48 billion to support PEPFAR in the next 6 years. The "Tom Lantos and Henry J. Hyde United States Global Leadership Against HIV/AIDS, Tuberculosis and Malaria Reauthorization Act of 2008"[395] expanded PEPFAR to include tuberculosis and malaria and drops the focus-country concept. However, those countries previously designated as "focus countries" remain those in greatest need and receive the largest support. The PEPFAR program has been remarkably successful in providing antiretroviral treatment for a large proportion of those in need. A modeling study published in 2009 estimated that PEPFAR averted 1.1 million deaths and reduced the overall death rate in those countries by 10%.[394]

In addition to the United Nations program and PEPFAR, a number of bilateral collaborations between developed and developing countries in sub-Saharan Africa have been established. For example, the Bill and Melinda Gates Foundation, in collaboration with the CDC, the Harvard AIDS Institute, and the Merck Research Foundation, has developed an HIV/AIDS prevention and treatment program in Botswana, the country with the highest proportion of adults who are HIV positive. To improve the capacity of sub-Saharan African countries to begin to deal with the AIDS pandemic, there is a critical need to greatly improve their medical and public health capability.

THE FUTURE

The HIV/AIDS epidemic has been transformed over the last 30 years from an invisible plague in rural Africa to a global pandemic that has penetrated every corner of the world. But its ravages did not go unchallenged, and modern research and care have begun to turn the tide of the epidemic. With no other disease has such progress been made in so short a time. Therapeutics for HIV can now restore health and for many will ensure only a small reduction in life span. Transmission is understood and it is well known how to prevent infection. Prevention and treatment require robust testing programs and people who are willing to be tested. Testing requires that the test is available and is accurately administered and that stigma does not make people fearful of being tested. Research to improve prevention approaches for those at highest risk—men and women who have anal sex—must continue. Stigma continues to deter patients from seeking treatment; moreover, when they want it, such therapy is not always available or affordable. Therapy programs remain threatened from the retraction of resources because of the global economic depression that began in 2010. Drug resistance remains a cloud on the horizon that could undermine treatment programs globally. Continued research may yield a cure for HIV, or a vaccine or microbicide to effectively shut off transmission, and we must continue to search for these answers. However, we can make significant progress on the HIV/AIDS epidemic with the knowledge we have today, if we have the will.

● ● ● **REFERENCES**

1. Nahmias AJ, Weiss J, Yao X, et al. Evidence for human infection with an HTLVII/LAV-like virus in Central Africa, 1959. *Lancet* 1986;1:1297.

2. Gau F, Bailes E, Robertsen DL, et al. Origin of HIV-1 in the chimpanzee, *Pan troglodytes*. *Nature* 1999;397:436–437.

3. Hirsch VM, Olnsted RA, Murphey-Corb M, et al. An African primate lentivirus (SIVson) closely related to HIV-2. *Nature* 1989;339:389–392.

4. Marlink R, Kanki P, Thior I, et al. Reduced rate of disease development after HIV-2 infection as compared to HIV-1. *Science* 1994;265:1587–1590.

5. DeKock KM, Adjorlolo G, Ekpini E, et al. Epidemiology and transmission of HIV-2: why there is no HIV-2 pandemic. *JAMA* 1993;270:2083–2086.

6. Centers for Disease Control. Pneumocystic pneumonia: Los Angeles. *MMWR* 1981;30:250–252.

7. Centers for Disease Control. Kaposi's sarcoma and pneumocystic pneumonia among homosexual men: New York City and California. *MMWR* 1981;30:305–308.

8. Gottlieb M, Schroff R, Schanker HM, et al. Pneumocystic pneumonia and mucosal candidiasis in previously healthy homosexual men. *N Engl J Med* 1981;305:1425–1431.

9. Auerbach DM, Darrow WM, Jaffe HW, Curran JW, . Cluster of cases of the acquired immune deficiency syndrome: patients linked by sexual contact. *Am J Med* 1984;76:487–492.

10. Selik RM, Haverkos HH, Curran JW. Acquired immune deficiency syndrome (AIDS) trends in the United States, 1978–1982. *Am J Med* 1984;76:493–500.

11. Chamberland MO, Lastrok G, Haverkos HH, et al. Acquired immunodeficiency in the United States: an analysis of cases outside high-incidence groups. *Ann Intern Med* 1984;101:617–623.

12. Gallo RL, Salahuddin SZ, Popovic M, et al. Frequent detection and isolation of cytopathic retroviruses (HTLV-III) from patients with AIDS and at risk for AIDS. *Science* 1984;224:497–500.

13. Klatzmawn D, Barre-Sinousi F, Nugeyre MT, et al. Selective tropism of lymphadenopathy associated virus (LAV) for helper-inducer T lymphocytes. *Science* 1984;225:59–63.

14. UNAIDS/World Health Organization. AIDS epidemic update, December, 2005. Geneva, Switzerland.

15. Levy J. *HIV and the Pathogenesis of AIDS* (2nd ed.). Washington, DC: ASM Press; 1998.

16. Perelson AS, Neumann AU, Markowitz M, et al. HIV-1 dynamics in vivo: virion clearance rate, infected cell life span and viral generation time. *Science* 1996;271:1582–1586.

17. Perelson AS, Essunger P, Lao YZ, et al. Decay characteristics of HIV-1 compartments during combination therapy. *Nature* 1997;387:188–191.

18. Siliciano JD, Kajdas J, Finzi D, et al. Long-term latent reservoir for HIV-1 in resting CD4+ T cells. *Nat Med* 2003;9:727–728.

19. Lyles R, Munoz A, Yamashita TE, et al. Natural history of human immunodeficiency virus type-1 viremia after seroconversion and proximal to AIDS in a large cohort of homosexual men, in the Multicenter AIDS Cohort Study. *J Infect Dis* 2000;18:872–880.

20. Mellors JW, Munoz A, Giorgi JV, et al. Plasma viral load and CD4+ lymphocytes as prognostic markers of HIV-1 infection. *Ann Intern Med* 1997;126:946–954.

21. Van Grevenynghe J, Halwani R, Chomont N, et al. Lymph node architecture collapse and consequent modulation of FOXO3a pathway on memory T and B-cells during HIV infection. *Semin Immunol* 2008;20(3):196–203.

22. Margolick JB, Munoz A, Donnenberg AD, et al. Failure of T-cell homeostasis preceding AIDS in HIV-1 infection. The Multicenter AIDS Cohort Study. *Nat Med* 1995;1:674–680.

23. Tersmette M, Lange JME, De Goede REY, et al. Differences in risk for AIDS and AIDS mortality associated with biological properties of HIV variants. *Lancet* 1989;1:983–985.

24. Kassatto S, Rosenberg ER. Primary HIV type 1 infection. *Clin Infect Dis* 2004;38:1447–1453.

25. Schacker T, Collier AC, Hughes J, et al. Clinical and epidemiologic features of primary HIV infection. *Ann Intern Med* 1996;125: 257–264.

26. Niu MT, Stein DS, Schnittman SM. Primary HIV type-1 infection: review of pathogenesis and early treatment interventions in humans and animal retrovirus infections. *J Infect Dis* 1994;168:1490–1501.

27. CASCADE study. Time from HIV seroconversion to AIDS and death before widespread use of highly-active antiretroviral therapy: a collaborative re-analysis. *Lancet* 2000;355: 1131–1137.

28. Rangsin R, Chio J, Khamboonruang C, et al. The natural history of HIV-1 infection in young Thai men after seroconversion. *J AIDS* 2004;36:622–629.

29. Chariyalerksak S, Sirisanthana T, Nelson KE, et al. Clinical presentation and risk behaviors of AIDS patients in Thailand, 1994–1998: regional variation and temporal trends. *Clin Infect Dis* 2001;32:955–962.

30. Davis JL, Fei L, Huang L. Respiratory infection complicating HIV infection. *Curr Opin Infect Dis* 2008;21(2):184–190.

31. Supparatpinyo K, Uthammachai C, Nelson KE, et al. Disseminated *Penicillium marneffei*: an emerging HIV-associated opportunistic infection in SE Asia. *Lancet* 1994;344:110–113.

32. Ablashi D, Chatlynne L, Cooper H, et al. Seroprevalence of human herpes virus 8 in countries of Southeast Asia, compared to the USA, Caribbean and Africa. *Br J Cancer* 1999;81:893–897.

33. Wheat CJ, Connolly-Stringfield PA, Baker RL. Disseminated histoplasmosis in the acquired immunodeficiency syndrome: clinical findings diagnosis and treatment and review of the literature. *Medicine* 1990;60:361–375.

34. Alvar J, Canavete C, Gutierrez-Sohr E, et al. Leishmania and human immunodeficiency virus, co-infection: the first 10 years. *Clin Microbiol Rev* 1997;10:298–319.

35. Centers for Disease Control and Prevention. Recommendations for the prophylaxis of opportunistic infection in patients with HIV infection. *MMWR* 2002;51:RR-6.

36. Rowland-Jones SL, Doug T, Fowke KR, et al. Cytotoxic T cell responses to multiple conserved HIV epitopes in HIV-resistant prostitutes in Nairobi. *J Clin Invest* 1998;102:1758–1765.

37. Promedej N, Costello C, Wernett MM, et al. Broad human immunodeficiency virus–specific T cell responses to conserved HIV proteins in HIV-seronegative women highly exposed to a single HIV-infected partner. *J Infect Dis* 2003;187:1053–1063.

38. Dean M, Carrington M, Winkler C, et al. Genetic restriction of HIV-1 infection and progression to AIDS by a deletion allele of the CCR5 structural gene. *Science* 1996;273:1856–1862.

39. Huang Y, Paxton WA, Wolinsky SM, et al. The role of a mutant CCR5 allele in HIV-1 transmission and disease progression. *Nat Med* 1996;2:1240–1243.

40. Rosenberg T. The man who was cured of HIV and what it means for a cure. *New York Magazine*, May 29, 2012. Available at: nymag.com/health/features/aids-cure-2011-6/. Accessed May 22, 2012.

41. Smith MW, Dean M, Carrington M, et al. Contrasting genetic influence of CCR2 and CCR5 variants in HIV-2 infection and disease progression. *Science* 1997;277:959–965.

42. Winkler C, Medi W, Smith MW, et al. Genetic restriction of AIDS pathogenesis by an SDF-1 chemokine gene variant. *Science* 1998;279:389–393.

43. Gonzalez E, Kulkarni H, Boivar H, et al. The influence of CCL3L1 gene-containing segmental duplications on HIV-1/AIDS susceptibility. *Science* 2005;307:1434–1440.

44. Kaslow RA, Dorak T, Tang J. Influence of host genetic variation on susceptibility to HIV type 1 infection. *J Infect Dis* 2005;191(suppl 1):S68–S77.

45. MacDonald KS, Embree J, Njenga S, et al. Mother–child class 1 HLA concordance increases perinatal human immunodeficiency type-1 transmission. *J Infect Dis* 2000;182:123–132.

46. Dorak MT, Tang J, Penman-Aguilar A, et al. Transmission of HIV-1 and HLA-B allele sharing within serodiscordant heterosexual Zambian couples. *Lancet* 2004;363: 2132–2139.

47. Hader SL, Hodge TW, Buchacz KA, et al. Discordance at human leukocyte antigen-DR-B3 and protection from human immunodeficiency virus type 1 transmission. *J Infect Dis* 2002;185:1729–1735.

48. Silverberg MJ, Smith MW, Chimiel JS, et al. Fraction of cases of acquired immunodeficiency syndrome prevented by interactions of identified restriction gene variants. *Am J Epidemiol* 2004;159:239–241.

49. Stremlau M, Owens CM, Perron MJ, et al. The cytoplasmic body component TRIM 5a restricts HIV-1 infection in Old World monkeys. *Nature* 2004;427:848–857.

50. Sheehy AM, Gaddis NC, Choi JD, Malim MH. Isolation of a human gene that inhibits HIV-1 infection and is suppressed by the viral Vif protein. *Nature* 2002;418:646–650.

51. Harris RS, Liddament MT. Retroviral restriction by APOBEC proteins. *Nat Rev Immunol* 2004;4:868–876.

52. An P, Blieber G, Duggal P, et al. APOBEC3G genetic variants and their influence on the progression to AIDS. *J Virol* 2004;78: 11070–11076.

53. Hunt PW. HIV and inflammation: mechanisms and consequences. *Curr HIV/AIDS Rep* 2012;9(2):139–147.

54. McCutchan FE. Understanding the genetic diversity of HIV-1. *AIDS* 2000;14(suppl 3): S31–S44.

55. Amornkul PN, Tansuphaswadikul S, Limpakarnjanarat K, et al. Clinical disease associated with HIV-1 subtype B and E infection among 2104 patients in Thailand. *AIDS* 1999;13:1963–1969.

56. Chariyalerksak S, Sirisanthana T, Saengwonloey O, Nelson KE. Clinical presentation and risk behaviors of AIDS patients in Thailand, 1994–1998: regional variation and temporal trends. *Clin Infect Dis* 2001;32:955–962.

57. Neilson JR, John GL, Carr JK, et al. Subtypes of human immunodeficiency virus type 1 and disease stage among women in Nairobi, Kenya. *J Virol* 1999;73:4393–4403.

58. Kaleebu PFN, Mahe C, Yirrell D, et al. The role of HIV-envelope subtypes A and D on disease progression in a large cohort of HIV-1 positive individuals in Uganda. 13th International Conference on AIDS, Durban, S. Africa, July 2000 (abstract A 3079).

59. Aleus A, Lidman K, Bjorkmon A, et al. Similar rate of disease progression among individuals infected with HIV-1 genetic subtypes A–D. *AIDS* 1999;13:901–907.

60. Kanki PJ, Hamel DJ, Sankale JL, et al. Human immunodeficiency virus type 1 subtypes differ in disease progression. *J Infect Dis* 1999;179:68–73.

61. Bobkov A, Kazenna E, Selimova L, et al. A sudden epidemic of HIV type 1 among injecting drug users in the former Soviet Union: identification of subtype A, subtype B and novel gag A/env B recombinants AIDS. *Res Hum Retroviruses* 1998;14:669–676.

62. Beyrer C, Razak HH, Lisam K, et al. Overland heroin trafficking routes and HIV-1 spreading in south and south-east Asia. *AIDS* 2000;14:75–83.

63. Graziosi C, Soudeyns H, Rizzardi GP, et al. Immunopathogenesis of HIV infection. *AIDS Res Hum Retroviruses* 1998;14: S135–S142.

64. Bentwich Z, Maartens G, Torten D, et al. Concurrent infections and HIV pathogenesis. *AIDS* 2000;14:2071–2081.

65. Lawn SD. AIDS in Africa: the impact of coinfections on the pathogenesis of HIV-1 infection. *J Infection* 2004;48:1–12.

66. Bentwich Z, Kalinkovich A, Weisman Z, et al. Can eradication of helminthic infections change the face of AIDS and tuberculosis? *Immunol Today* 1999;20:485–487.

67. Roussanov BV, Taylor JM, Giorgi JV. Calculation and use of an HIV-1 disease progression score. *AIDS* 2000;14(17):2715–2722.

68. Dolin PF, Raviglione MC, Kochi A. Global tuberculosis incidence and mortality during 1990–2000. *Bull WHO* 2004;72:213–220.

69. Schluger NW, Rom WN. The host immune response to tuberculosis. *Am J Respir Crit Care Med* 1998;157:679–691.

70. Abdool Karim SS, Naidoo K, Grobler A, et al. Integration of antiretroviral therapy with tuberculosis treatment. *N Engl J Med* 2011;365(16):1492–1501.

71. Modjarrad K, Zulu I, Redden DJ, et al. Treatment of intestinal helminthes does not reduce plasma concentrations of HIV-1 RNA in coinfected Zambian adults. *J Infect Dis* 2005;192:1277–1283.

72. Bentwich Z, Kalinkovich A, Weisman Z, et al. Can eradication of helminthic infections change the face of AIDS and tuberculosis? *Immunol Today* 1999;20:485–487.

73. Bentwich Z , Maatens G, Torten Q, et al. Concurrent infections and HIV pathogenesis. *AIDS* 2000;14:2071–2081.

74. Lawn SD. AIDS in Africa: the impact of coinfections on the pathogenesis of HIV-1 infection. *J Infection* 2004;48:1–12.

75. Modjarrad K, Zulu I, Redden DJ, et al. Treatment of intestinal helminthes does not reduce plasma concentrations of HIV-1 RNA in coinfected Zambian adults. *J Infect Dis* 2005;192:1277–1283.

76. Greenburg AL, Ryder RW, Medi M, et al. *Plasmodium falciparum* malaria and perinatally acquired human immunodeficiency virus type 1 infection in Kinshasa, Zaire. *N Engl J Med* 1991;325:105–109.

77. Kublin JG, Patnaik P, Jere CS, et al. Effect of *Plasmodium falciparum* malaria on concentration of HIV-1 RNA in the blood of adults in rural Malawi: a prospective cohort study. *Lancet* 2005;365:233–240.

78. Xiao L, Owen SM, Rudolph DL, et al. *Plasmodium falciparum* antigen-induced human immunodeficiency virus type 1 replication is mediated through induction of tumor necrosis factor-alpha. *J Infect Dis* 1998;177:437–445.

79. French N, Nakiyingi J, Lugada E, et al. Increasing rates of malarial fever with deteriorating immune status in HIV-1 infected Ugandan adults. *AIDS* 2001;15:899–906.

80. Sulkowski M, Mehta SH, Torbenson MS, et al. Rapid fibrosis progression among HIV/hepatitis virus co-infected adults. *AIDS* 2007;21:2209–2216.

81. Monga HK, Rodriguez-Barradas MC, Breaux K, et al. Hepatitis C virus infection-related morbidity and mortality among patients with human immunodeficiency virus infection. *Clin Infect Dis* 2001;33:240–247.

82. Rockstroh JK, Spengler U. HIV and hepatitis C virus co-infection. *Lancet Infect Dis* 2004;4:437–444.

83. Eyster Fried MW, Di Bisceglie AM, Goedert JJ, et al. Increasing hepatitis C virus RNA levels in hemophiliacs: relationship to human immunodeficiency virus infection and liver disease. Multicenter Hemophilia Cohort Study. *Blood* 1994;84:1020–1023.

84. Darby SC, Ewart DW, Giangrande PL, et al. Mortality from liver disease in haemophilic men and boys in the UK given blood products contaminated with hepatitis C. UK Haemophilia Centre Directors' Organisation. *Lancet* 1997;350:1425–1431.

85. Palella FJ Jr, Delaney KM, Moorman AC, et al. Declining morbidity and mortality among

patients with advanced human immunodeficiency virus infection. HIV Outpatient Study Investigators. *N Engl J Med* 1998;338: 853–860.

86. Dorrucci M, Pezzotti P, Phillips AN, et al. Coinfection of hepatitis C virus with human immunodeficiency virus and progression to AIDS. Italian Seroconversion Study. *J Infect Dis* 1995;172:1503–1508.

87. Greub G, Ledergerber B, Battegay M, et al. Clinical progression, survival, and immune recovery during antiretroviral therapy in patients with HIV-1 and hepatitis C coinfection: the Swiss HIV Cohort Study. *Lancet* 2000;356:1800–1805.

88. Sulkowski MS, Moore RD, Mehta SH, et al. Hepatitis C and progression of HIV disease. *JAMA* 2002;288:199–206.

89. Chung RT, Evans SR, Yang Y, et al. Immune recovery is associated with persistent rise in hepatitis C virus RNA, infrequent liver test flares, and is not impaired by hepatitis C virus in co-infected subjects. *AIDS* 2002;16:1915–1923.

90. Gonzalez SA, Talal AH. Hepatitis C virus in human immunodeficiency virus-infected individuals: an emerging comorbidity with significant implications. *Sem Liver Dis* 2003;23:149–166.

91. Limketka BV, Mehta SH, Sutcliffe CG, et al. Relationship of liver disease stage and antiviral therapy with liver-related events and death in adults coinfected with HIV/HCV. *JAMA* 2012;308:370–378.

92. Fierer DS, Uriel AJ, Carriero DC, et al. Liver fibrosis during an outbreak of f acute hepatitis C virus infection in HIV-infected men;A prospective cohort study. *J Infect Dis* 2008;198: 663–666.

93. Fierer DS, Mullen MP, Dieterich DT, et al. Early-onset liver fibrosis due to primary hepatitis C virus infection is higher over time in HIV-infected men. *Clin Infect Dis* 55:887. Vogel M, Page E, Boeseke C, et al. Liver fibrosis progression after acute hepatitis C virus infection in HIV-positive individuals. *Clin Infect Dis* 2012;54:556–559.

94. Bottie AE, Stugie SV, Harle ST, et al. Hepatitis C virus infection in HIV-infected men who have sex with men: sustained rising incidence in Antwerp, Belgiom, 2011–2009. *Eurosurveillance* September 2010. Available at: www.eurosvveillunce.org.

95. Thompson MA, Abeng JA, Hey JF, et al Antiretroviral treatment of adult HIV infection, 2012: Recommendations of the International Antiviral Society USA Panel. *JAMA* 2012;308:387–402.

96. Xiang J, Wunschmann S, Schmidt WN, et al. Full-length GB virus C (hepatitis G virus) RNA transcripts are infectious in primary CD4-positive T cells. *J Virol* 2000;74:9125–9133.

97. Heringlake S, Ockenga J, Tillmann HI, et al. GB virus C/hepatitis G virus infection: a favorable prognostic factor in human immunodeficiency virus-infected patients? *J Infect Dis* 1998;177:1723–1726.

98. Toyoda H, Fukuda Y, Hayakawa T, et al. Effect of GB virus C/hepatitis G virus coinfection on the course of HIV infection in hemophilia patients in Japan. *J Acquir Immune Defic Syndr Hum Retrovirol* 1998;17:209–213.

99. Lefrère JJ, Roudot-Thoraval F, Morand-Joubert L, et al. Carriage of GB virus C/hepatitis G virus RNA is associated with a slower immunologic, virologic, and clinical progression of human immunodeficiency virus disease in coinfected persons. *J Infect Dis* 1999;179:783–789.

100. Yeo AET, Matsumoto A, Hisada M, et al. Effect of hepatitis G virus infection on progression of HIV infection in patients with hemophilia: Multicenter Hemophilia Cohort Study. *Ann Intern Med* 1000;132:959–963.

101. Xiang J, Wunschmann S, Diekema DJ, et al. Effect of coinfection with GB virus C on survival among patients with HIV infection. *N Engl J Med* 2001;345:707–714.

102. Tillman HL, Heiken H, Knapik-Botor A, et al. Infection with GB virus C and reduced mortality among HIV-infected patients. *N Engl J Med* 2001;345:715–724.

103. Sabin CA, Devereux H, Kinson Z, et al. Effect of coinfection with hepatitis G virus on HIV disease progression in hemophilic men. *J Acquir Immun Defic Syndr Human Retrovirol* 1998;19:546–548.

104. Birk M, Lindback S, Lidman C. No influence of GB virus C replication on the prognosis in a cohort of HIV-1 infected patients. *AIDS* 2002;16:2482–2485.

105. Brust D, Jagannatha S, Herpin B, et al. Hepatitis G virus (HGV) infection does not prolong survival of patients with early-stage HIV disease: importance of baseline HIV viral load as a predictor of mortality. In: *Abstracts of the 14th International AIDS Conference,* Barcelona, Spain, July 7–12, 2002.

106. Van der Bij AK, Kloosterboen N, Prins M, et al. GB virus C coinfection and HIV-1 disease progression: the Amsterdam Cohort Study. *J Infect Dis* 2005;181:678–685.

107. Williams CF, Kliazman D, Yamashita TE, et al. Persistent GB virus C infection and survival in HIV-infected men. *N Engl J Med* 2004;350:980–990.

108. Xiang J, George SL, Wunshchmann S, et al. Inhibitors of HIV-1 replication by GB virus C infection through increases in RANTES, MIP-1a, MIP-1b and SDF-1. *Lancet* 2004;363:2040–2046.

109. Moss WJ, Ryan JT, Monze M, et al. Suppression of human immunodeficiency virus replication during acute measles. *J Infect Dis* 2002;185:1035–1042.

110. Grivel JC, Garcia M, Moss WJ, Margolis LB. Inhibition of HIV-1 replication in human lymphoid tissues ex vivo by measles virus. *J Infect Dis* 2005;192:71–78.

111. Watt G, Kanti-Pong P, Jongsakul K. Decrease in human immunology virus type 1 load during acute dengue fever. *Clin Infect Dis* 2003;36:1067–1069.

112. Watt G, Kant-Pong P, de Souza M, et al. HIV-1 suppression during acute scrub-typhus infection. *Lancet* 2000;356:475–479.

113. Tarwater P, Mellors J, Gore ME, et al. Methods to assess population effectiveness of therapies in human immunodeficiency virus incident and prevalent cohorts. *Am J Epidemiol* 2001;154:675–681.

114. Palella FJ Jr, Delaney KM, Moorman AC, et al. Declining morbidity and mortality among patients with advanced human immunodeficiency virus infection. HIV Outpatient Study Investigators. *N Engl J Med* 1998;338(13):853–860. PubMed PMID: 9516219.

115. Ho DD. Time to hit HIV, early and hard. *N Engl J Med* 1995;333:450–451.

116. Siliciano JD, Kajdas J, Finzi D, et al. Long-term latent reservoir for HIV-1 in resting CD4+ T cells. *Nat Med* 2003;9:727–728.

117. Strategies for Management of Antiretroviral Theory (SMART) Study Group. CD4+ count-guided interruption of antiretroviral treatment. *N Engl J Med* 2006;355:2289–2296.

118. Ananworanich J, Gayet-Ageron A, Le Broz M, et al. CD4-guided scheduled treatment interruptions compared with continuous therapy for patients with HIV-1: results of the Staccato randomized trial. *Lancet* 2006;368:459–465.

119. Hammer SM, Eron JJ, Reiss P, et al. Antiretroviral treatment of adult HIV infection: 2008 recommendation of the International AIDS Society—USA Panel. *JAMA* 2008;300:555–570.

120. Kitahata MM, Gange SJ, Abraham AG, et al. Effect of early versus deferred antiretroviral therapy for HIV on survival. *N Engl J Med* 2009;360(18):1815–1826.

121. HIV-CAUSAL Collaboration, Cain LE, Logan R, Robins JM, et al. When to initiate combined antiretroviral therapy to reduce mortality and AIDS-defining illness in HIV-infected persons in developed countries: an observational study. *Ann Intern Med* 2011;154(8):509–515.

122. Lawn SD, Bekker L-G, Miller RF. Immune reconstitution disease associated with

mycobacterial infections with HIV-infections in HIV-infected individuals receiving antiretrovirals. *Lancet Infect Dis* 2005;5:361–377.

123. Michailidis C, Pozniak AL, Mandalia S, et al. Clinical characteristics of IRIS syndrome in patients with HIV and tuberculosis. *Antivir Ther* 2005;10(3):417–422.

124. Centers for Disease Control and Prevention. Recommendations for the prophylaxis of opportunistic infection in patients with HIV infection. *MMWR* 2002;51:RR-6.

125. Kesseling AC, Scharf HS, Hanellar NA, et al. Danish bacille Calmette-Guerin vaccine-induced disease in human immunodeficiency virus infected children *Clin Infect Dis* 2003:37:1226–1233.

126. French MA, Lenzo M, John M, et al. Immune restoration disease after the treatment of immunodeficient HIV-infected patients with highly active antiretroviral therapy. *HIV Med* 2000;1:107–113.

127. Lesho E. Evidence base for using corticosteroids to treat HIV-associated immune reconstitution syndrome. *Expert Rev Anti Infect Ther* 2006;4:469–478.

128. European Study Group on Heterosexual Transmission of HIV. Comparison of female to male and male to female transmission of HIV in 563 stable couples. *BMJ* 1992;304:809–813.

129. Wawer MJ, Gray RH, Serwadda NK, et al. Rates of HIV-1 transmission per coital act, by stage of HIV-1 infection, Rakai, Uganda. *J Infect Dis* 2005;191:1403–1409.

130. Pilcher CD, Tien HC, Eron JL, et al. Brief but efficient: acute HIV infection and the sexual transmission of HIV. *J Infect Dis* 2004;189:1785–1792.

131. Nicolosi A, Correa Leite ML, Musico M, et al. The efficiency of male–female and female to male sexual transmission of HIV: a study of 730 stable couples. *Epidemiology* 1994;5:570–575.

132. Nagachinta T, Duerr A, Suriyanon V, et al. Risk factors for HIV-1 transmission from seropositive male blood donors to their regular female partners in northern Thailand. *AIDS* 1997;11:1763–1772.

133. Wawer MJ, Gray RH, Serwadda NK, et al. Rates of HIV-1 transmission per coital act, by stage of HIV-1 infection, Rakai, Uganda. *J Infect Dis* 2005;191:1403–1409.

134. Royce RA, Sena A, Cates W, Cohen MS. Sexual transmission of HIV. *N Engl J Med* 1997;336:1072–1078.

135. Laga M, Schwartlander B, Risani E, et al. To stem HIV in Africa, prevent transmission to young women. *AIDS* 2001;15:931–934.

136. Mati SK, Hunter DJ, Maggwn BN, Tukei PM. Contraceptive use and the risk of HIV infection in Nairobi, Kenya. *Int J Gynacecol Obstet* 1995;48:61–67.

137. Marx PA, Spira AL, Gettie A, et al. Progesterone implants enhance HIV vaginal transmission and early virus load. *Nat Med* 1996;2:1084–1089.

138. Mati SK, Hunter DJ, Maggwn BN, Tukei PM. Contraceptive use and the risk of HIV infection in Nairobi, Kenya. *Int J Gynacecol Obstet* 1995;48:61–67.

139. Henin Y, Mendelbrot I, Henrion R, et al. Virus excretion in the cervicovaginal secretions of pregnant and nonpregnant HIV-infected women. *J AIDS* 1993;6:72–75.

140. Asamoah-Odei E, Garcia-Callga JM, Boerma T. HIV prevalence and trends in sub-Saharan Africa: no decline and large subregional differences. *Lancet* 2004;364:35–40.

141. Buve A, Carael M, Hayes RJ, et al. The multicenter study to determine the differential spread of HIV in four cities in Africa: summary and conclusions. *AIDS* 2001;suppl 4:S127–S131.

142. Auvert B, Buve A, Lagarde E, et al. Male circumcision and HIV infection in four cities in sub-Saharan Africa. *AIDS* 2001;15(suppl 4): S31–S40.

143. UNAIDS/World Health Organization. AIDS epidemic update, December, 2005. Geneva, Switzerland: 2005.

144. Vlahov D, Munoz A, Anthony JC, et al. Association of drug-injection patterns with antibody to HIV type-1 among injection drug users in Baltimore. *Am J Epidemiol* 1990;132:847–856.

145. Schoenbaun EE, Harter D, Selwyn PA, et al. Risk factors for human immunodeficiency virus infection in intravenous drug users. *N Engl J Med* 1989;321:874–879.

146. Jose B, Friedman SR, Neaigus A, et al. Syringe-mediated drug-sharing (backloading): a new risk factor for HIV among injecting drug users. *AIDS* 1993;7:1653–1660.

147. Anthony JC, Vlahov D, Nelson KE, et al. New evidence on intravenous cocaine use and the risk of infection with HIV. *Am J Epidemiol* 1991;134:1179–1184.

148. Chirgwin K, DeHovitz JA, Dillion S, et al. HIV infection, genital ulcer disease and crack cocaine use among patients attending a clinic for sexually transmitted diseases. *Am J Public Health* 1991;81:1576–1579.

149. Metzger DS, Woody GE, McClellan AT, et al. Human immunodeficiency virus seroconversion among intravenous drug users in- and out-of-treatment: an 18 month prospective follow-up. *J AIDS* 1993;6:1049–1056.

150. van Ameijden EJC, van den Hock JAR, Hangtrecht HJA, Coutinho RA. The harm reduction approach and risk factors for human immunodeficiency virus seroconversion in injecting drug users, Amsterdam. *Am J Epidemiol* 1992;136:236–243.

151. Ball AL, Rana S, Dehne K. HIV prevention among injecting drug users: responses in developing and transitional countries. *Public Health Rep* 1998;113(suppl 1):170–181.

152. Lurie P, Drucker E. An opportunity lost: HIV infections associated with lack of a national needle-exchange program in the USA. *Lancet* 1997;349:604–608.

153. Centers for Disease Control and Prevention. Update: syringe exchange programs— United States, 2002. *MMWR* 2005;54: 673–676.

154. Strathdee SA, Celentano DD, Shah N, et al. Needle exchange attendance and health care utilization promote entry into detoxification. *J Urban Health* 1999;98: 448–453.

155. Han JA, Vranizam KM, Moss AR. Who uses needle exchange? A study of injection drug users in San Francisco, 1989–1990. *J AIDS* 1997;15:157–164.

156. Archibald CP, Ofner M, Strathdee SA, et al. Factors associated with frequent needle exchange program attendance in injection drug users in Vancouver, Canada. *J AIDS* 1998;17:160–166.

157. Vlahov D, Unge B, Brookmeyer R, et al. Reductions in high-risk drug use behaviors among participants in the Baltimore needle exchange program. *J AIDS* 1997;16: 400–406.

158. Normand J, Vlahov D, Moses LE. *Preventing HIV Transmission: The Role of Sterile Needles and Bleach.* Washington, DC: National Academies Press; 1995.

159. Lurie P, Reingold A, Bower B, et al. *The Public Health Impact of Needle Exchange Programs in the United States and Abroad.* Vol. 1. Atlanta, GA: Centers for Disease Control and Prevention; 1996.

160. Holmberg SD. The estimated prevalence and incidence of HIV in 96 large U.S. metropolitan areas. *Am J Public Health* 1996;86: 642–654.

161. Garfein RS, Monterroso ER, Tong TC, et al. Comparison of HIV injection risk behaviors among injection drug users from East and West Coast US cities. *J Urban Health* 2004;81:260–267.

162. Ciccarone D, Bourgois P. Explaining the geographic variation for HIV among injection drug users in the United States. *Substance Use Abuse* 2003;14:2049–2063.

163. Rhodes T, Singer M, Bourgois P, et al. The social structural production of HIV risk among injecting drug users. *Soc Sci Med* 2005;61:1026–1044.

164. Beyrer C, Jittiwutikarn J, Teokol W, et al. Drug use, increasing incarceration rates and prison-associated HIV risks in Thailand. *AIDS Behavior* 2003;7:153–161.

165. Mathers BM, Degenhardt L, Ali H, et al. HIV prevention, treatment, and care services for people who inject drugs: a systematic review of global, regional, and national coverage. *Lancet* 2010;375(9719):1014–1128.

166. Huang YF, Kuo HS, Lew-Ting CY, et al. Mortality among a cohort of drug users after their release from prison: an evaluation of the effectiveness of a harm reduction program in Taiwan. *Addiction* 2011;106(8): 1437–1445.

167. Blanche S, Rouzioux C, Guihard Moscato ML, et al. A prospective study of infants born to women seropositive for human immunodeficiency virus type 1. *N Engl J Med* 1989;320:1643–1648.

168. European Collaborative Study. Mother-to-child transmission of HIV infection. *Lancet* 1988;2:1039–1043.

169. European Collaborative Study. Risk factors for mother-to-child transmission of HIV-1. *Lancet* 1992;339:1007–1012.

170. Hutton C, Parks WP, Lai SH, et al. A hospital-based prospective study of perinatal infection with human immunodeficiency virus type. *J Pediatr* 1991;118:347–353.

171. International Perinatal HIV Group. The mode of delivery and the risk of vertical transmission of human immunodeficiency virus type 1: a meta-analysis of 15 prospective cohort studies. *N Engl J Med* 1999;340: 977–987.

172. Bryson YJ, Luzuriaga K, Sullivan JL, Wara DW. Proposed definitions for in utero versus intrapartum transmission of HIV-1. *N Engl J Med* 1992;326:1246–1247.

173. Van de Perre P, Simonon A, Msellati P, et al. Postnatal transmission of human immunodeficiency virus type-1 from mother to infant. *N Engl J Med* 1991;325:593–598.

174. Wiktor SZ, Ekpini E, Nduati RW. Prevention of mother-to-child transmission of HIV-1 in Africa. *AIDS* 1997;11(suppl B):S79–S87.

175. Nduati R, John G, Mobori-Ngacha D, et al. Effect of breastfeeding and formula feeding on transmission of HIV-1: a randomized trial. *JAMA* 2000;283:1167–1174.

176. Coutsoudis A, Pillay K, Kuhn L, et al. Method of feeding and transmissions of HIV-1 from mothers to children by 15 months of age: prospective cohort study from Durban, South Africa. *AIDS* 2001;15: 379–387.

177. Cooper ER, Charurat M, Mofenson L, et al. Combination antiretroviral strategies for treatment of pregnant HIV-1 infected women and prevention of prenatal HIV-1 transmission. *J AIDS* 2002;484–494.

178. Centers for Disease Control and Prevention. Successful implementation of perinatal HIV guidelines: a multistate surveillance evaluation. *MMWR Recomm Rep* 2001;50:17–28.

179. Fawzi WW, Msamanga G, Hunter D, et al. Randomized trial of vitamin supplements in relation to vertical transmission of HIV-1 in Tanzania. *J AIDS* 2000;23:246–254.

180. Coutsoudis A, Pillay K, Spooner E, et al. Randomized trial testing the effect of vitamin A supplementation on pregnancy outcomes and early mother to child HIV-1 transmission in Durban, South Africa. *AIDS* 1999;13:1517–1524.

181. Biggar RJ, Miotti PG, Taha TE, et al. Perinatal intervention trial in Africa: effects of a birth canal cleansing intervention to prevent HIV transmission. *Lancet* 1996;347:1647–1650.

182. Gallard P, Mwanyumba F, Verhofstede C, et al. Vaginal lavage with chlorhexidine during labor to reduce mother-to-child HIV

transmission: clinical trial in Mombasa, Kenya. *AIDS* 2001;15:389–396.

183. Taha TE, Biggar RJ, Broadhead RL, et al. Effect of cleansing the birth canal with antiseptic solution on maternal and newborn morbidity and mortality in Malawi: clinical trial. *BMJ* 1997;315:216–220.

184. Connor EM, Sperling RS, Gelber R, et al. Reduction of maternal–infant transmission of human immunodeficiency virus type-1 with zidovudine treatment. *N Engl J Med* 1994;331:1173–1180.

185. Sperling RS, Shapiro DE, Coombs RW, et al. Maternal viral load, zidovudine treatment, and the risk of transmission of human immunodeficiency virus type-1 from mother to infant. *N Engl J Med* 1996;335:1621.

186. Shaffer N, Chuachoowong PA, Mock C, et al. Short-course zidovudine for perinatal HIV-1 transmission in Bangkok, Thailand: a randomized controlled trial. *Lancet* 1999;353:773–780.

187. Guay L, Musoke P, Fleming T, et al. Intrapartum and neonatal single-dose nevirapine compared with zidovudine for prevention of mother–child transmission of HIV-1 in Kampala, Uganda: HIVNET 012 randomized trial. *Lancet* 1999;354:795–802.

188. Jackson JB, Musoke P, Fleming T, et al. Intrapartum and neonatal nevirapine compared with zidovudine for prevention of mother-to-child transmission of HIV-1 in Kampala, Uganda: 18 month follow-up of the HIVNET 012 randomized trial. *Lancet* 2003;362:859–868.

189. Jackson JB, Backer-Pergola G, Guay LA, et al. Identification of the K103N resistance mutation in Ugandan women receiving nevirapine to prevent vertical HIV-1 transmission. *AIDS* 2000;14:F111–F115.

190. Eschleman SH, Mracna M, Guay L, et al. Selection and fading of resistance mutations in women and infants receiving nevirapine to prevent HIV-1 vertical transmission (HIVNET 012). *AIDS* 2001;15:1951–1957.

191. Nolan M, Fowler MG, Mofenson LM. Antiretroviral prophylaxis of perinatal HIV-1 transmission and the potential impact of antiretroviral resistance. *J AIDS* 2002;30:216–229.

192. World Health Organization. *Antiretroviral Drugs and the Prevention of Mother-to-Child Transmission of HIV Infection in Resource-Limits Settings.* Report of a Technical Consultation. Geneva, Switzerland: February 5–6, 2004.

193. Mofenson LM. Advances in the prevention of vertical transmission of human immunodeficiency virus. *Sem Pediatr Infect Dis* 2003;14:295–308.

194. Centers for Disease Control and Prevention. HIV testing among pregnant women—United States and Canada, 1998–2001. *MMWR Recomm Rep* 2002;51:1013–1016.

195. UNAIDS/World Health Organization. AIDS epidemic update, December, 2005. Geneva, Switzerland: Author; 2005.

196. Kebaabetswe PM. Barriers to participation in the prevention of mother-to-child HIV transmission program in Gaborone, Botswana: a qualitative approach. *AIDS Care* 2007;19(3):355–360.

197. Kesho Bora Study Group, de Vincenzi I. Triple antiretroviral compared with zidovudine and single-dose nevirapine prophylaxis during pregnancy and breastfeeding for prevention of mother-to-child transmission of HIV-1 (Kesho Bora study): a randomised controlled trial. *Lancet Infect Dis* 2011;11(3):171–180.

198. http://www.un.org/ga/aids/coverage/FinalDeclarationHIVAIDS.html

199. Amornwichet P, Teeraratkul A, Simonds RJ, et al. Preventing mother-to-child HIV transmission: the first year of Thailand's national program. *JAMA* 2002;288:245–248.

200. http://www.childinfo.org/hiv_aids_mother_to_child.html

201. http://www.avert.org/pmtct-hiv.htm

202. Busch MP, Operskalski EA, Mosley JW, et al. Factors influencing human immunodeficiency virus type 1 transmission by blood transfusion. *J Infect Dis* 1996;174:26–33.

203. Lackritz EM, Satten GA, Aberle-Grasse J, et al. Estimated risk of transmission of the human immunodeficiency virus by screened blood in the United States. *N Engl J Med* 1995;333:1721–1725.

204. Dodd RY, Notari EP, Stramer SL. Current prevalence and incidence of infectious disease markers and estimated window-period risk in the American Red Cross blood donor population. *Transfusion* 2002;42:973–979.

205. Jackson JB, Busch MP, Stramer SL, Aubuchon JP. The cost-effectiveness of NAT for HIV, NCV and HBV in whole blood donations. *Transfusion* 2003;43(6):721–729.

206. Pealer LN, Marfin AA, Petersen LR, et al. Transmission of West Nile virus through blood transfusion in the United States in 2002. *N Engl J Med* 2003;349:1236–1245.

207. Busch MP, Laglio HS, Robertson EE, et al. Screening the blood supply for West Nile virus RNA by nucleic acid amplification testing. *N Engl J Med* 2005;353:460–467.

208. Caussy D, Goedert J. The epidemiology of human immunodeficiency virus and acquired immunodeficiency syndrome. *Sem Oncol* 1990;17:244–250.

209. Simonds RJ, Holmberg SD, Hurwitz RL, et al. Transmission of human immunodeficiency virus type 1 from a seronegative organ and tissue donor. *N Engl J Med* 1992;326: 726–732.

210. Centers for Disease Control and Prevention. Guidelines for preventing transmission of human immunodeficiency virus through transplantation of human tissues and organs. *MMWR* 1994;43:RR-8.

211. Ratijan GA, Strengers PEW, Persijn HM. Prevention of transmission of HIV by organ and tissue transplantation. *Transpl Int* 1993;6:165–172.

212. Simonds RJ, Holmberg SD, Hurwitz RL, et al. Transmission of human immunodeficiency virus type 1 from a seronegative organ and tissue donor. *N Engl J Med* 1992;326: 726–732.

213. Jackson JB, Busch MP, Stramer SL, Aubuchon JP. The cost-effectiveness of NAT for HIV, NCV and HBV in whole blood donations. *Transfusion* 2003;43(6):721–729.

214. http://www.cdc.gov/media/releases/2011/s0921_organ_transplant.html. Updated September 21, 2011; accessed May 23, 2012.

215. Shan H, Wang J-X, Reu F-R. Blood banking in China. *Lancet* 2002;360:1770–1775.

216. Volkow P, Del Rio L. Paid donation and plasma trade: unrecognized forces that drive the AIDS epidemic in developing countries. *Int J STD AIDS* 2005;16:5–8.

217. Tokars JI, Marcus R, Culver DH, et al. Surveillance of HIV infection and zidovudine use among health care workers after occupational exposure. *Ann Intern Med* 1993;48:913–919.

218. Centers for Disease Control and Prevention. Public Health Service guidelines for the management of occupational exposures to HBV, HCV and HIV and recommendations for post exposure prophylaxis. *MMWR* 2001;50: RR-11.

219. Ippolito G, Puro V, DeCarli G. The risk of occupational human immunodeficiency virus infection in health care workers: the Italian Study Group on occupational risk of HIV infection. *Arch Intern Med* 1993;153: 1451–1458.

220. Henderson DK, Fahey BJ, Willy M, et al. Risk for occupational transmission of human immunodeficiency virus type 1 (HIV-1) associated with clinical exposures: a prospective evaluation. *Ann Intern Med* 1990;113: 740–746.

221. Ippolito G, Puro V, Petrosillo N, et al. Simultaneous infection with HIV and hepatitis C virus following occupational conjunctive blood exposure. *Scand J Infect Dis* 1993;25:270–271.

222. Ciesielski C, Marianos D, Ou CY, et al. Transmission of human immunodeficiency virus in a dental practice. *Ann Intern Med* 1992;116:798–805.

223. Ou C-Y, Ciesielski C, Myers G, et al. Molecular epidemiology of HIV transmission in a dental practice. *Science* 1992;256:1165–1171.

224. Gisselguist D, Rothenberg RB, Potterat J, et al. HIV infections in sub-Saharan Africa not explained by sexual or vertical transmission. *Int J STD AIDS* 2002;13:657–666.

225. Kiwanaka N, Gray RH, Serwadda D, et al. The incidence of HIV-1 associated with injecting and transfusions in a prospective cohort, Rakai, Uganda. *AIDS* 2004;18:341–344.

226. Reinik L, Verea K, Salahoddin SZ, et al. Stability and inactivation of HTLV-III/LAV under clinical and laboratory environments. *JAMA* 1986;255:1887–1891.

227. Beaumont T, van Nuenen A, Broersen S, et al. Reversal of human immunodeficiency virus type 1 IIIB to a neutralization-resistant phenotype in an accidentally infected laboratory worker with a progressive clinical course. *J Virol* 2001;75:2246–2252.

228. Centers for Disease Control. Recommendation for prevention of HIV transmission in healthcare settings. *MMWR* 1987;36:28.

229. Webb PA, Happ CM, Maupin G, et al. Potential for insect transmission of HIV: experimental exposure of *Limex hemipterus* and *Toxobychites amboinensis* to human immunodeficiency virus. *J Infect Dis* 1989;160:970–977.

230. Srinivasan A, York D, Bohen C. Lack of HIV replication in arthropod cells. *Lancet* 1987;1:1094–1095.

231. Jupp PG, Lyons SF. Experimental assessment of bedbugs and mosquitoes as vectors of human immunodeficiency virus. *AIDS* 1987;1:171–174.

232. Friedland GH, Saltzman BR, Rogers MF, et al. Lack of transmission of HTLV-III/LAV infection to household contacts of patients with AIDS or AIDS-related complex with oral candidiasis. *N Engl J Med* 1986;314:344–349.

233. Friedland GH, Klein RS. Transmission of the human immunodeficience virus. *N Engl J Med* 1987;317:1125–1131. Rogers ME, White C, Sanders T, et al. Lack of transmission of human immunodeficiency virus from infected children to their household contacts. *Pediatrics* 1990;84:210–214.

234. Wahn V, Kramer H, Voit T, et al. Horizontal transmission of HIV infection between two siblings. *Lancet* 1986;2:694.

235. *Koeni*g RE, Gautier T, Levy JA. Unusual intrafamilial transmission of human immunodeficiency virus. *Lancet* 1986;2:627.

236. Fitzgibbon JE, Gaur S, Frenkel CD, et al. Transmission from one child to another of human immunodeficiency virus type 1 with a zidovudine-resistance mutation. *N Engl J Med* 1993;329:1835–1841.

237. Centers for Disease Control and Prevention. HIV transmission between two adolescent brothers with hemophilia. *MMWR* 1993;42:948–951.

238. Gerberding JC. Occupational exposure to HIV in health care settings. *N Engl J Med* 2003;348:826–833.

239. Cardo DM, Culuer DH, Ciesielski LA, et al. A case-control study of HIV seroconversion in health care workers after percutaneous exposure. *N Engl J Med* 1997;337:1485–1490.

240. Clerici M, Levin JM, Kessler HA, et al. HIV-specific T-helper activity in seronegative health care workers exposed to contaminated blood. *JAMA* 1994;221:42–46.

241. Broliden K, Hinkula J, Devito C, et al. Functional HIV-1 specific IgA antibodies in HIV-1 exposed, persistently IgG seronegative female sex workers. *Immunol Letter* 2001;79:29–36.

242. Scientific basis for PEP rests in animal trials. *AIDS Alert* 1997;12(9):100–101.

243. Centers for Disease Control and Prevention. Antiretroviral postexposure prophylaxis after injection-drug use or other nonoccupational exposure to HIV in the United States. *MMWR* 2005;54(RR-02):1–20.

244. Gerberding JC. Occupational exposure to HIV in health care settings. *N Engl J Med* 2003;348:826–833.

245. Centers for Disease Control and Prevention. Public Health Service guidelines for the management of occupational exposures to HBV, HCV and HIV and recommendations for post exposure prophylaxis. *MMWR* 2001;50:RR-11.

246. Grant RM, Lama JR, Anderson PL, et al., and the iPrEx Study Team. Preexposure chemoprophylaxis for HIV prevention in men who have sex with men. *N Engl J Med* 2010;363(27):2587–2599.

247. Chon R, Hoffman LH, Fu R, et al. Screening for HIV: a review of the evidence for the U.S. Preventive Services Task Force. *Ann Intern Med* 2005;143:85–93.

248. AMFAR. CDC quick facts: rapid testing. HHS approves wider access to rapid HIV test. February 4, 2003. Available at: http://www.amfar.org. Accessed July 25, 2005.

249. Branson BM. Point-of-care rapid tests for HIV antibodies. *J Lab Med* 2003;27:288–295.

250. UNAIDS global report 2010. Available at: http://www.unaids.org/globalreport/global_report.htm.

251. Zhang M, Shang H, Wang Z, et al. Natural history of HIV infection in former plasma donors in rural China. *Front Med China* 2010;4(3):346–350.

252. UNAIDS World AIDS Day Report, December 2011. WHO: Geneva, Switzerland.

253. Solomon SS, Srikrishman AK, Mehta SH, et al. High prevalence of HIV, HIV/hepatitis C coinfection and risk behaviors among injection drug users in Chenai, India: a cause for concern. *J AIDS* 2008;49:317–332.

254. Rojanapithayakurn W, Hanenberg R. *The 100% condom program in* Thailand. *AIDS* 1996;10:1–7.

255. Nelson KE, Celentano DD, Eiumtrakul S, et al. Changes in sex and behavior and a decline in HIV infection among young men in Thailand. *N Engl J Med* 1996;335:297–303.

256. Onloey O, Jiraphongsa C, Foy H. Thailand report: HIV/AIDS surveillance 1998. *J AIDS* 2003;32:S63–S67.

257. Kruglov YV, Kobyshcha YV, Salyuk T, et al. The most severe HIV epidemic in Europe: Ukraine's national HIV prevalence estimates for 2007. Sex Transm Infect 2008;84:i37–i41.

258. Caiaffai WJ. The dynamics of the human immunodeficiency virus epidemics in the south of Brazil: increasing role of injection drug users. *Clin Infect Dis* 2003;37(suppl 5):5376–5381.

259. Granato N, Morell MGG, Areco K, Peres CA. Association factors for HIV infection in commercial sex workers in Sao Paolo, Brazil [Abstract]. XV International AIDS Conference, Bangkok, Thailand; July 11–16, 2004. WePcC6202.

260. Guimaraes MD, Munoz A, Boschi-Pinto C, Castilho CA. HIV infection among female partners of seropositive men in Brazil. *Am J Epidemiol* 1995;142:538–547.

261. Galvao J. Brazil and access to HIV/AIDS drugs: a question of human rights and public health. *Am J Public Health* 2005;95:1110–1016.

262. Parker RG, Tawil O. Bisexual behavior and HIV transmission in Latin America. Chapter 3: pages 75–94, In: Tielman R, Caballo M,

Hendriks A, eds. *Bisexuality and HIV/AIDS.* New York: Prometheus Press; 1991.

263. Brouwer C, Harris BM, Tanaka S. Violence against women in Papua New Guinea. Chapter 4: pages 93–108, In: *Gender Analysis in Papua, New Guinea, 1998.* Washington, DC: World Bank; 1998.

264. Hamers FF, Downs AM. The changing face of the HIV epidemic in Western Europe: what are the implications for public health policies? *Lancet* 2000;364:83–94.

265. Centers for Disease Control and Prevention. *HIV/AIDS Surveillance Report, 2003.* Vol. 15. Atlanta, GA: ; 2004:1–46.

266. Del Rio C, Sepulvida J. AIDS in Mexico: lessons learned and implications for developing countries. *AIDS* 2002;16:1445–1457.

267. Schwartlander B, Stanecki K, Brown T, et al. Country-specific estimates and models of HIV and AIDS: methods and limitations. *AIDS* 1999;13:2445–2458.

268. Walker N, Stanecki K, Brown T, et al. Methods and procedures for estimating HIV/AIDS and its impact: the UNAIDS/WHO estimates for the end of 2001. *AIDS* 2003;17:2215–2225.

269. Brookmeyer R, Gail MH. *AIDS Epidemiology: A Quantitative Approach.* New York: Oxford University Press; 1992.

270. Williams B, Gouws E, Wilkinson D, Karim SA. Estimating HIV incidence rates from age prevalence data in epidemic situations. *Statis Med* 2001;20:2003–2016.

271. Brookmeyer R, Quinn T, Shepherd M, et al. AIDS epidemic in India: a new method for estimating current human immunodeficiency virus (HIV) incidence rates. *Am J Epidemiol* 1995;142:209–213.

272. Busch M, Satten GA, Henrard DR, et al. Time course of detection of viral and serological makers for HIV infection. *Transfusion* 1995;35:91–97.

273. Janssen RS, Satten GA, Stramer SL, et al. New testing strategy to detect early infection for use in incidence estimates and for clinical and prevention purposes. *JAMA* 1998;280:42–48.

274. Rawal BD, Degola A, Lebedeoa L, et al. Development of a new less-sensitive enzyme immunoassay for detection of early HIV-a infection. *J AIDS* 2003;33:349–355.

275. Young CL, Hu DJ, Byers R, et al. Evaluation of a sensitive/less sensitive testing algorithm using the Biomerieux Vironostika-LS assay for recent HIV-1 subtype B1 or E infection in Thailand. *AIDS Res Hum Retroviruses* 2003;19:481–486.

276. Parekh BS, Hu DJ, Vanichseni S, et al. Evaluation of a sensitive/less sensitive testing algorithm using the 3 A11-LS assay for detecting recent HIV seroconversion among individuals with HIV-1 subtype B or E infection in Thailand. *AIDS Res Hum Retrovirus* 2001;17:453–458.

277. Dobbs T, Kennedy S, Pau C-P, et al. Performance characteristics of the immunoglobulin G-capture BED-enzyme immunoassay, an assay to detect recent human immunodeficiency virus type 1 seroconversion. *J Clin Micro* 2004;42:2623–2628.

278. Parekh BS, McDoug JS. Application of laboratory method's for estimation of HIV-1 incidence. *Indian J Med Res* 2005;121:510–518.

279. Kim AA, McDougal JS, Hargrove J, et al. Evaluating the BED capture enzyme immunoassay to estimate HIV incidence among adults in three countries in sub-Saharan Africa. *AIDS Res Hum Retroviruses* 2010;26:1051–1061.

280. Guy R, Gold J, Calleja JM, et al. Accuracy of serological assays for detection of recent infection with HIV and estimation of population incidence: a systematic review. *Lancet Infect Dis* 2009;9:747–759.

281. Thomas HI, Wilson S, O'Toole CM, et al. Differential maturation of avidity of IgG antibodies to gp41, p24 and p14 following

infection with HIV-1. *Clin Exper Immun* 1996;103:185–191.

282. Wei X, Liu X, Dobbs T. Development of two avidity-based assays to detect recent HIV type 1 seroconversion using a multisubtype gp41 recombinant protein. *AIDS Res Hum Retroviruses* 2010;26:61–71.

283. Duong YT, Qiu M, De AK, et al. Detection of recent HIV-1 infection using a new limiting-antigen avidity assay: potential for HIV-1 incidence estimates and avidity maturation studies. *PLOS One* 2012;7: e33328.

284. Cousins MM, Laeyendeekev O, Beauchamp G, et al. Use of high resolution melting (ARM) assay to compare gap, pol and env diversity in adults with different stages of HIV infection. *PLOS One* 2011;6:e27211.

285. Centers for Disease Control and Prevention. *HIV/AIDS Surveillance Report*, Vol. 22. Atlanta, GA: 2012.

286. Baily MC, Anderson RM. Sexual contact patterns between men and women and the spread of HIV-1 in urban centers in Africa. *IMA J Math Appl Med Biol* 1991;8:221–247.

287. Quinn TL, Mann JM, Curran JW, et al. AIDS in Africa: an epidemiological paradigm. *Science* 1986;16:516–519.

288. Parker RG, Tawil O. Bisexual behavior and HIV transmission in Latin America. In: Tielman R, Caballo M, Hendriks A, eds. Bisexuality and HIV/AIDS. New York: Prometheus Press; 1991.

289. Hunt CW. Migrant labor and sexually transmitted disease and AIDS in Africa. *J Health Soc Behav* 1989;30:353–373.

290. UNAIDS/World Health Organization. *Report on the Global HIV/AIDS Epidemic.* Geneva, Switzerland: WHO; 1998.

291. Merson MH, O'Malley J, Serwadda D, Apisuk C. HIV prevention: the history and challenge of HIV prevention. *Lancet* 2008;372:475–488.

292. Hannenberg R, Rojanapithayakorn W. Prevention as policy: how Thailand reduced STD and HIV transmission. *AIDS Captions* 1996;3:24–27.

293. Nelson KE, Celentano DD, Eiumgrakol S, et al. Changes in sexual behavior and a decline in HIV infection among young men in Thailand. *N Engl J Med* 196; 335:297–303.

294. Becker MH, Joseph JG. AIDS and behavioral change to reduce risk: a review. *Am J Public Health* 1988;78:394–410.

295. Padian NS, Buve A, Balkus J, et al. Biomedical interventions to prevent HIV infection: evidence, challenges, and way forward. *Lancet* 2008;372:585–599.

296. Scientific breakthrough of the year. *Science*, December 23, 2011.

297. Conant M, Hardy D, Sernatinger J, et al. Condoms prevent transmission of AIDS-associated retrovirus. *JAMA* 1986;255: 1706.

298. Weller S, Davis K. Condom effectiveness in reducing heterosexual HIV transmission. *Cochrane Database Syst Rev* 2002;1:CD003255.

299. Holmes KK, Levine R, Waver M. Effectiveness of condoms in prevention sexually transmitted infections. *Bull World Health Organ* 2004;82:454–461.

300. Pinkerton SD, Abramson PR. Effectiveness of condoms in prevention HIV transmission. *Soc Sci Med* 1997;44:1303–1312.

301. Foss AM, Hossain M, Vickerman PT, Watts CH. A systematic review of published evidence on intervention impact on condom use in sub-Saharan Africa and Asia. *Sex Transm Infection* 2007;83:510–516.

302. Fontanet AL, Saba J, Chandelying V, et al. Protection against sexually transmitted diseases by granting sex workers in Thailand the choice of using the male or female condom: results from a randomized controlled trial. *AIDS* 1998;12:1851–1859.

303. Feldblum PJ, Kuyoh MA, Bmayo JJ, et al. Female condom introduction and sexually transmitted infection prevalence: results of a community intervention trial in Kenya. *AIDS* 2001;15:1037–1044.

304. French PP, Latka M, Gollub EL, et al. Use-effectiveness of the female versus male condom in preventing sexually transmitted disease in women. *Sex Transm Dis* 2003;30:433–439.

305. Buck J, Kang MS, van der Straten A, et al. Barrier method preferences and perceptions among Zimbabwean women and their partners. *AIDS Behav* 2005;9:415–422.

306. Padian NS, van der Straten A, Ramjee G, et al. Diaphragm and lubricant gel for prevention of HIV acquisition in southern African women: a randomized controlled trial. *Lancet* 2007;370:251–261.

307. Gray RH, Kigozi G, Serwadda D, et al. Male circumcision for HIV prevention in men in Rakai, Uganda: a randomized trial. *Lancet* 2007;369:657–666.

308. Bailey RC, Moses S, Parker CB, et al. Male circumcision for HIV prevention in young men in Kisumu, Kenya: a randomized controlled trial. *Lancet* 2007;369:643–656.

309. Auvert B, Taljaard D, Lagarde E, et al. Randomized, controlled intervention trial of male circumcision for reduction of HIV infection risk: the ANRS 1265 Trial. *PLoS Med* 2005;2:e298.

310. Tobian AR, Serwadda D, Quinn TC, et al. Male circumcision for the prevention of HSV-2 and HPV infections and syphilis. *N Engl J Med* 2009;360:1298–1309.

311. Weiss HA, Dickson KE, Agot K, Hankins CA. Male circumcision for HIV prevention: current research and programmatic issues. *AIDS* 2010; 24(suppl 4):S61–S69.

312. Mehta SD, Gray RH, Aubert B, et al. Does sex in the early period after circumcision increase HIV-seroconversion risk? Pooled analysis of adult male circumcision clinical trials. *AIDS* 2009;23:1557–1564.

313. Gray RH, Li X, Kigozi G, et al. The impact of male circumcision on HIV incidence and cost per infection prevented: a stochastic simulation model from Rakai, Uganda. *AIDS* 2007;21:845–850.

314. Kahn JG, Marseille, E, Aubert B. Cost-effectiveness of male circumcision for HIV prevention in a South African setting. *PLoS Med* 2006;3:e517.

315. Wiysonge CS, Kongnyuy EJ, Shey M, et al. Male circumcision for prevention of homosexual acquisition of HIV in men. *Cochrane Database Syst Rev* 2011;6:CD007496.

316. UNAIDS. *AIDS Epidemic Update*. Geneva: UNAIDS/World Health Organization; 2011.

317. Ramjee G, Kamali A, McCormack S. The last decade of microbicide clinical trials in Africa: from hypothesis to facts. *AIDS* 2010;24 (suppl 4):S40–S49.

318. Balzarini J, Van Damme L. Microbicide drug candidates to prevent HIV infection. *Lancet* 2007;369:787–797.

319. Buckheit RW, Watson KM, Morrow KM, Ham AS. Development of topical microbicides to prevent the sexual transmission of HIV. *Antiviral Res* 2010;85:142–158.

320. Morris GC, Lacey CJN. Microbicides and HIV prevention: lessons from the past, looking to the future. *Curr Opin Infect Dis* 2010;23:57–63.

321. Mayer KH, Venkatesh KK. Chemoprophylaxis for HIV prevention: new opportunities and new questions. *J AIDS* 2010;55(suppl 5):S122–S127.

322. Division of STD Prevention, National Center for HIV/AIDS, Viral Hepatitis, STD, and TB Prevention, Centers for Disease Control and Prevention. Sexually transmitted diseases treatment guidelines, 2006. *MMWR Recomm Rep* 2006;55(RR11):1–94. Erratum: *MMWR Recomm Rep* 2006;55:997.

323. Mayer K, Venkatesh KK. Antiretroviral therapy for HIV prevention: current status

and future prospects. *Am J Public Health* 2010;100:1867–1876.

324. Adamson P, Marcus J, Pipkin S, et al. Characteristics of and HIV seroconversion among patients receiving non-occupational HIV post-exposure prophylaxis in a sexually transmitted disease clinic: San Francisco, 2007 to 2009. Paper #958. Presented at: 17th Conference on Retroviruses and Opportunistic Infections; San Francisco, CA; February 16–19, 2010.

325. Grant RM, Lama JR, Anderson PL, et al. Preexposure chemoprophylaxis for HIV prevention in men who have sex with men. *N Engl J Med* 2010;364:137–1375.

326. Baeten JM, Donnell D, Ndase P, et al. Antiretroviral prophylaxis for HIV prevention in heterosexual men and women *N Engl J Med* 2012;367:399–410.

327. Van Damme I, Corneli A, Ahmed K, et al. Preexposure prophylaxis for HIV infection among African women. *N Engl J Med* 2012;367:411–422.

328. Thigpen MC, Kehaabetswe PM, Paxton LA, et al. Antiretroviral preexposure prophylaxis for heterosexual HIV transmission in Botswana. *N Engl J Med* 2012;367;423–434.

329. Grady D. FDA advisory panel backs preventive use of HIV drug. *New York Times* May 10, 2012;D5.

330. Paltiel A, Freedberg KA, Scott CA, et al. HIV preexposure prophylaxis in the United States: impact on lifetime infection risk, clinical outcomes, and cost-effectiveness. *Clin Infect Dis* 2009;48:806–815.

331. Fleming D, Wasserheit J. From epidemiologic synergy to public health policy and practice: the contribution of other sexually transmitted diseases to sexual transmission of HIV infection. *Sex Transm Infect* 1999;75:3–17.

332. Rottingen J-A, Cameron D, Garnett G. A systematic review of the epidemiologic interactions between classic sexually transmitted diseases and HIV: how much really is known? *Sex Transm Dis* 2001;28:579–597.

333. Grosskurth H, Mosha F, Todd J, et al. Impact of improved treatment of sexually transmitted diseases on HIV infection in rural Tanzania: randomized controlled trial. *Lancet* 1995;346:530–536.

334. Gregson S, Adamson S, Papaya S, et al. Impact and process evaluation of integrated community and clinic-based HIV-1 control: a cluster-randomised trial in Eastern Zimbabwe. *PLoS Med* 2007;4:e102.

335. Kamali A, Quigley M, Nakiyingi J, et al. Syndromic management of sexually-transmitted infections and behavior change interventions on transmission of HIV-1 in rural Uganda: a community randomized trial. *Lancet* 2003;361:645–652.

336. Wawer MJ, Sewankambo NK, Serwadda D, et al. Control of sexually transmitted diseases for AIDS prevention in Uganda: a randomized community trial. Rakai Project Study Group. *Lancet* 1999;353:525–535.

337. Korenromp E, White R, Orroth K, et al. Determinants of the impact of sexually transmitted infection treatment on prevention of HIV infection: a synthesis of evidence from the Mwanza, Rakai and Masaka intervention trials. *J Infect Dis* 2005;191(suppl 1): S168–S178.

338. Freeman EE, Weiss HA, Glynn JR, et al. Herpes simplex virus 2 infection increases HIV acquisition in men and women: systematic review and meta-analysis of longitudinal studies. *AIDS* 2006;20:73–78.

339. Wald A, Link K. Risk of human immunodeficiency virus infection in herpes simplex virus type 2-seropositive persons: a meta-analysis. *J Infect Dis* 2002;185:45–52.

340. Celum C, Wald A, Hughes J, et al. Effect of acyclovir on HIV-1 acquisition in herpes simplex virus 2 seropositive women and men who have sex with men: a randomized, double-blind, placebo-controlled trial. *Lancet* 2008;371:2109–2119.

341. Hayes R, Watson-Jones D, Celum C, et al. Treatment of sexually transmitted infections for HIV prevention: end of the road or new

beginning? *AIDS* 2010;24(suppl 4): S15–S26.

342. Coorvadia H, Kindra G. Breastfeeding HIV transmission and infant survival: balancing pros and cons. *Curr Opin Infect Dis* 2008;21:11–15.

343. Wilfert CM, Fowler MG. Balancing maternal and infant benefits and the consequences of breastfeeding in the developing world during the era of HIV infection. *J Infect Dis* 2006;195:165–167.

344. Current issues in prevention of mother-to-child transmission of HIV-1. *Curr Opin HIV AIDS* 2009;4:319–324.

345. Diffenbach CW, Fouci AS. Thirty years of HIV and AIDS: future challenges and opportunities. *Ann Intern Med* 2011;154:154–160.

346. Rerks-Ngarm S, Pitisuttithum P, Nitayaphan S, et al. Vaccination with ALVAC and AIDSVAX to prevent HIV-1 infection in Thailand. *N Engl J Med* 2009;361: 2209–2220.

347. Shattock RJ, Warren M, McComack S, Hankins CA. Turning the tide against HIV. *Science* 2011;333:42–43.

348. Fast PE, Kaleebu P. HIV vaccines: current status worldwide and in Africa. *AIDS* 2010; 24 (Supp 4):S50–S60.

349. Cohen MS, Chen YQ, McCauley M, et al. Prevention of HIV-1 infection with early antiretroviral therapy. *N Engl J Med* 2011;365:493–505.

350. Granich R, Crowley S, Vitoria M, et al. Highly active antiretroviral treatment as prevention of HIV transmission: review of scientific evidence and update. *Curr Opin HIV AIDS* 2010;5:298–304.

351. El-Sadr WM, Affrunti M, Gamble T, Zerbe A. Antiretroviral therapy: a promising HIV prevention strategy? *J AIDS* 2010;55(suppl 2): S116–S121.

352. amfAR—The Foundation for AIDS Research. *Accelerating an HIV Prevention Revolution: A Roadmap. Issue Brief.* Washington, DC: amfAR Public Policy Office; March 2011.

353. Centers for Disease Control and Prevention. HIV prevention in the United States at critical crossroads. 2009. Available at: http://cdc.gov/hiv/resources/reports/pdf/hiv_prev_us.pdf.

354. Bartlett JG, Branson BM, Fenton K, et al. Opt-out testing for human immunodeficiency virus in the United States: progress and challenges. *JAMA* 2008;300:945–951.

355. Granich R, Gilks C, Dye C, et al. Universal voluntary HIV testing with immediate antiretroviral therapy as a strategy for elimination of HIV transmission: a mathematical model. *Lancet* 2009;373:48–57.

356. Coates TJ, Richter L, Caceres C. Behavioural strategies to reduce HIV transmission: how to make them work better. *Lancet* 2008;372:669–684.

357. Ross DA. Behavioural interventions to reduce HIV risk: what works? *AIDS* 2010; 24(suppl 4):S4–S14.

358. Gupta GR, Parkhurst JO, Ogden JA, et al. Structural approaches to HIV prevention. *Lancet* 2008;372:764–775.

359. Des Jarlais DC. Structural interventions to reduce HIV transmission among injection drug users. *AIDS* 2000;14:41–46.

360. Kerrigan D, Moreno L, Rosario S, et al. Environmental–structural interventions to reduce HIV/STI risk among female sex workers in the Dominican Republic. *Am J Public Health* 2006;96:120–125.

361. Pronyk P, Hargreaves JR, Kim JC, et al. Effects of a structural intervention for the prevention of intimate partner violence and HIV in rural South Africa: results of a cluster randomized trial. *Lancet* 2006;368: 1973–1983.

362. Vermund SH, Allen KL, Abdool Karim Q. HIV-prevention science at a crossroads: advances in reducing sexual risk. Curr Opin HIV/AIDS 2009;4 (4):266–273.

363. Hankins CA, de Zalduondo BO. Combination prevention: a deeper understanding of effective HIV prevention. *AIDS* 2010;24(suppl 4):S70–S80.

364. Burns DN, Dieffenbach CW, Vermund SH. Rethinking prevention of HIV type 1 infection. *Clin Infect Dis* 2010;51:725–731.

365. Piot P, Bartos M, Larson H, et al. Coming to terms with complexity: a call to action for HIV prevention. *Lancet* 2008;372: 845–859.

366. Cohen MS, Fidler S. HIV prevention 2010: where are we now and where are we going? *Curr Opin HIV AIDS* 2010;5:265–268.

367. Kurth AE, Celum C, Baeten J, et al. Combination HIV prevention: significance, challenges, and opportunities. *Curr HIV/AIDS Rep* 2011;8:62–72.

368. Padian NS, McCoy SI, Abdool Karim SS, et al. HIV prevention transformed: the new prevention research agenda. *Lancet* 2011:378:269–278.

369. World Health Organization/UNAIDS. *Progress on Global Access to HIV Antiretroviral Therapy: An Update on "3 by 5."* Geneva Switzerland: Author; 2005.

370. Bendavid E, Bhattacharya J. The President's Emergency Plan for AIDS Relief in Africa: an evaluation of outcomes. *Ann Intern Med* 2009;150:688–695.

371. Gardner EM, McLees MP, Steiner JF, et al. The spectrum of engagement in HIV care and its relevance to test-and-treat strategies for prevention of HIV infection. *Clin Infect Dis* 2011;52(6):793–800.

372. Lynch S, Ford N, van Cutsem G, et al. Getting HIV treatment to the most people. *Science* 2012;337:298–300.

373. Buchbinder SP, Mehrotra DV, Duerr A et al. Efficacy assessment of a cell-mediated immunity HIV-1 vaccine (the Step Study): a double-blind ,randomized, placebo-controlled,test-of-concept trial. *Lancet* 2008;372;1881–1893.

374. Vahidnia F, Peterson M, Stapleton JT, Rutherford GW, Busch M, Custer B. Acquisition of GBVirus Type C and Lower Mortality in Patients with Advanced HIV Disease, *Clin Infect Dis* 2012;55:1012–1019.

375. Esbjornsson J, Mansson F, Kvist A et al. Inhibition of HIV-1 Disease Progression by Contemporaneous HIV-2 infection. *N Engl J Med* 2012;367:224–232.

376. Pitisuttithun P, Gilbert P, Gurwith M et al. Randomized,double-blind placebo-controlled efficacy trial of a trivalent recombinant glycoprotein 120 HIV-1 vaccine among injection drug users in Bangkok. *J Infect Dis* 2006;194:1661–1671.

377. Haynes BF, Gilbert PB, McElrath J et al. Immune-Correlates Analysis of an HIV-1 Vaccine Efficacy Trial. *N Engl J Med* 2012;366;1275–1286.

378. Thompson MA, Aberg JA, Hoy JF et al. Antiviral Treatment of Adult HIV Infection; 2012 Recommendations of the International Antiviral Society-USA Panel. *JAMA* 2012;308:387–402.

379. Shattock RJ, Warren M, McCormack S. Hankins CA. Turning the tuda against HIV. *Science* 2011; 333: 42–43.

380. Burton DR, Ahmed R, Barouch DH et al. Blueprint for HIV Vaccine Discovery. *Cell Host & Microbe* 2012; 12:396–407.

381. Binley JM, Lybarger EA, Crooks ET et al. Profiling the specificity of neutralizing antibodies in a large panel of plasmas from patients chronically infected with human immunodeficience virus type 1 subtype B and C. *J Virol* 2008;82;11651–11668.

382. Simek MD, Rida W, Priddy FH et al. Human Immunodeficiency virus type 1 "elite controllers" individuals with broad ad potent neutralizing activity identified by using a high throughput neutralizing assay together with an analytic selection algorithim. *J Virol* 2009;83;7337–7348.

383. Cohen MS, Muessig KE, Kumi-Smith M, Powesr KA, Kashuba ADM. Antiviral agents

and HIV prevention: Controversies, conflicts, and consensus. *AIDS* 2012;26:1585–1598.

384. Juusola JL, Brandeau ML, Owens DK, Bendavid E . The cost-effectiveness of Preexposure Prophylaxis for HIV Prevention in the United States in Men who Have Sex with Men. *Ann Intern Med* 2012;156:541–55.

385. Montaner JSG .Treatment as prevention—a double hat-trick. *Lancet* 2011;378:208.

386. Wasserheit.JN, Epidemiological synergy: Interrelationship between human immuno-deficiency virus infection and other sexu-ally transmitted infections. *Sex Trans Dis* 1992;19:61–77.

387. Laga M, Manuka R, Kivuva M et al. Non-ulcerative sexually transmitted diseases as risk factors for HIV-1 transmission in women: results from a cohort study. *AIDS* 1993;7:95–102.

388. Nelson KE, Suriyanon V, Rongruangthanakit K et al. High rate of transmission of subtype E human immunodeficiency virus type 1 in heterosexual couples in Thailand: Role of sexually transmitted diseases and immune compromise. *J Infect Dis* 1999;337:337–343.

389. Cohen M S, Hoffman I E, Reyes RA et al. reduction in concentration of HIV-1 in semen after treatment of urethritis: Implications for

the prevention of sexual transmission of HIV-1. *Lancet* 1997;349:1868–1873.

390. Theus SA, Harrich DA, Gaynor R, Redolf JD, Norgard MV. Treponma pallidum lipoprotein and synthetic lipoprotein analogues induce human immunodeficiency virus type 1 gene expression in monocytes via NFK-B activa-tion. *J Infect Dis* 1998;177:941–951.

391. Schwartlander B,Stover J.,Walker N. et al. AIDS. Resource needs for AIDS. *Science* 2001;292: 2436.

392. Schwartlander B, Grubb I, Perriens J. The 10 year struggle to provide antiretroviral treatment to people with HIV in the developing world. *Lancet* 2006;368;541–546.

393. United Nations. Declaration of Commitment on HIV/AIDS—Global crisis, global action. Available at http://www.un.org/ga/aids/coverage/FinalDeclarationHIVAIDS,html. Accessed December 3, 2012.

394. Lyerla R, Merrill CS, Ghys PD, Calleja-Garcia JMC, DeCock KM. The Use of Epidemiological Data to Inform the PEPFAR response. *J Acquir Immune Defic Syndr* 2012;60(Suppl 3):S57–S62.

395. Emanuel EJ. PEPFAR and Maximizing the Effects of Global Health Assistance. *JAMA* 2012;307:2097–2099.

CHAPTER

23

Viral Hepatitis

Kenrad E. Nelson and David L. Thomas

INTRODUCTION

Hepatitis is inflammation of the liver, which may be caused by viral or other infections, toxins, and a number of other conditions. This chapter considers the epidemiology of the five diverse viruses that cause hepatitis as their primary clinical syndrome and, therefore, share the name *hepatitis virus*. Two of these viruses—hepatitis A virus (HAV) and hepatitis E virus (HEV)—are transmitted by fecal–oral exposure from an infected to a susceptible individual, or, in the case of HEV genotype 3 or 4, from a foodborne infection that is acquired from a zoonotic reservoir. The other hepatitis viruses—hepatitis B virus (HBV), hepatitis C virus (HCV), and hepatitis delta virus (HDV)—are parenterally transmitted by exposure to infected blood, or through sexual or perinatal contact.

Other viruses, such as cytomegalovirus (CMV), Epstein-Barr virus (EBV), yellow fever virus, Lassa fever virus, Ebola virus, and other agents, may also infect the liver and cause hepatitis (**Table 23-1**). However, the clinical pathology of these viruses includes infection of other tissues, so they are not considered to be hepatitis viruses.

As early as the 1600s, epidemics of jaundice and other manifestations of liver disease were associated with military campaigns and were especially problematic during World War II.[1] Hepatitis following use of glycerinated human lymph to prevent smallpox was described in 1885.[2] Outbreaks of jaundice related to the administration of pooled human serum to prevent mumps[3] or to prepare a yellow fever vaccine[4] suggested that a transmissible agent was present in human blood. Blood transmission of hepatitis was also suggested by the frequent recognition of hepatitis in syphilis patients treated in clinics where injection equipment was not sterilized between patients.[5]

Conversely, hepatitis was uncommon in patients attending clinics with good infection control practices.[5]

Along with the appreciation that human blood could transmit hepatitis came the recognition that many cases of hepatitis, including epidemics of the disease, did not follow blood exposure.

Table 23-1	Conditions that Cause Hepatitis in Humans

Hepatitis viruses
  Hepatitis A virus
  Hepatitis B virus
  Hepatitis C virus
  Hepatitis D virus
  Hepatitis E virus
Other viruses
  Epstein-Barr virus
  Human immunodeficiency virus
  Lassa fever virus
  Yellow fever virus
  Adenovirus
  Herpes simplex virus
  Human herpes-6 virus
  Ebola virus
Nonviral infectious agents
  Pneumococcal pneumonia
  Leptospirosis
  Syphilis
  Coxiella burnetti
  Toxoplasmosis
Noninfections
  Alcohol
  Medications
    Dilantin
    Isoniazid
    Ritonavir
    Chlorpromazine
    Rifampin, etc.
  Anesthesia (halothane)

The suspicion that there were at least two different epidemiologic types of hepatitis virus was confirmed by studies conducted by Krugman et al. at the Willowbrook State School in New York.[6] These studies showed that viruses the researchers labeled MS-2 strains were exclusively transmitted parenterally, whereas other MS-1 strains could be transmitted orally. Furthermore, heat-inactivated convalescent sera obtained after MS-2 infection could prevent MS-2 infection. These studies laid the foundation for the classification of hepatitis into serum hepatitis (MS-2 viruses) and infectious hepatitis (MS-1 viruses).

In the 1950s and 1960s, numerous attempts were made to isolate the viruses or infect experimental animals with the agents responsible for hepatitis. In 1965, the "Australia antigen" was isolated from the blood of Australian aboriginals by Blumberg and associates.[7] This antigen was subsequently found to be the hepatitis B surface antigen (HBsAg).[8]

Within a decade of this discovery, the HBV virus and its major antigens had been fully characterized, and serologic tools became available for epidemiologic studies. After the introduction of the routine screening of blood donors for HBsAg in 1973, the incidence of post-transfusion hepatitis decreased by approximately 50%—yet post-transfusion hepatitis that was not due to hepatitis B continued to occur, indicating that another parenterally transmitted hepatitis virus existed.[9] HCV was discovered in 1989 and was shown to be the cause of most parenterally transmitted non-A, non-B (PT-NANB) hepatitis worldwide.[10–12]

The hepatitis delta virus (HDV) was discovered by Rizzetto in 1977 and was initially described as a new antigen detectable in patients with HBV-associated chronic liver disease.[13] Studies in chimpanzees subsequently established that HDV was a unique RNA virus that was transmissible but dependent on the presence of active HBV infection to cause infection in humans.[14]

Viral particles of HAV were identified in stool samples of patients with infectious hepatitis in 1973.[15] Over the next several years, the immunologic and virologic aspects of HAV and its natural history were more clearly defined. In 1979, HAV was first grown in tissue culture[16]; subsequently, vaccines were developed from cell culture-derived virus and shown to be effective.[17,18]

However, large epidemics of waterborne hepatitis—most notably a very large epidemic that occurred in New Delhi, India, in 1955—were found not to be due to HAV.[18] Researchers found that convalescent sera from persons who were infected during this large epidemic did not have HAV antibodies.[19] The agent of these outbreaks was called enterically transmitted non-A, non-B hepatitis (ET-NANB).[20] Virus-like particles were identified in the feces of patients by immune electron microscopy in the early 1980s and named hepatitis E virus (HEV). Subsequently, an animal model of hepatitis E was developed in cynomolgus monkeys.[20,21]

BIOLOGIC BASIS FOR TRANSMISSION

The five hepatitis viruses differ markedly in their genetic composition and biology. The viral characteristics can explain differences in transmission routes. HBV, HCV, and HDV are not transmitted through fecal–oral exposure, as their lipid envelopes are unstable in the biliary excretory tract, rendering them noninfectious in stool. HAV and HEV do not have envelopes, are infectious in stool, and are relatively stable under environmental conditions. In contrast, the capability of hepatitis viruses to be spread by blood relates to the total time and viral levels in serum. All hepatitis viruses can cause infection if they are percutaneously inoculated. However, HAV and HEV exist in blood for very brief intervals and, therefore, only rarely contaminate percutaneous transmission vehicles, such as blood products or needles. In contrast, HBV, HCV, and HDV may be detected in the blood of asymptomatic carriers for decades.

CLINICAL SYNDROME

All hepatitis viruses may cause the same general syndrome (**Table 23-2**). After exposure, there is an incubation period lasting from 2 to 10 weeks for HAV and HEV, from 4 to 10 weeks for HCV, and from 6 to 20 weeks for HBV. This may be followed by a flulike prodromal illness with fever, chills, anorexia, vomiting, and fatigue. A few patients with HBV infection develop an urticarial rash, arthralgia, arthritis, or glomerulonephritis during the acute illness that are caused by immune complexes. As the systemic symptoms improve, jaundice may occur, followed by a period of convalescence. The hallmark of hepatitis is an elevation of liver enzymes in the blood—specifically, alanine aminotransferase (ALT) and aspartate aminotransferase (AST). The blood bilirubin may also rise, with levels greater than 3.0 mg/dL causing jaundice. Rarely, patients will develop acute fulminant hepatic necrosis and liver failure. This outcome is less frequent with HCV than with the other hepatitis viruses.

Table 23-2	Characteristics of Hepatitis Viruses			
Virus	**Nucleic Acid**	**Routes of Transmission**	**Mortality**	**Risk of Chronic Illness**
HAV	Non-enveloped single-stranded RNA	Fecal–oral	Low	None
HBV	Enveloped double-stranded DNA	Parenteral (sex, perinatal)	Moderate-High	High
HCV	Enveloped single-stranded RNA	Parenteral (sex, perinatal)	Moderate-High	High
HDV	Enveloped single-stranded RNA	Parenteral (sex)	High	High
HEV	Non-enveloped single-stranded RNA	Fecal–oral	Low-moderate	Low

HEPATITIS A VIRUS

Virology

The hepatitis A virus (HAV) is a small (27 nm) non-enveloped RNA virus belonging to the family Picornaviridae. The virus, which has icosohedral symmetry and contains approximately 7478 nucleotides, is composed of at least four major structural polypeptides, designated as VP1 to VP4. The genomic organization and replication of HAV are similar to that of poliovirus and other picornaviruses. However, HAV has little nucleotide or amino acid homology with other enteroviruses, and there is less evidence that HAV replicates in intestinal tissues. HAV was originally classified in the genus *Enterovirus*, but it is now classified in a separate genus, *Hepatovirus*.

HAV is quite stable in the environment after it is shed in the feces, retaining infectivity for at least 2 to 4 weeks at room temperatures. The virus is resistant to non-ionic detergents, chloroform, or ether, and it retains infectivity at pH 1.0 at 38°C for 90 minutes. It is only partially inactivated at 60°C for 1 hour. Temperatures of 85°C to 95°C for 1 minute are required to inactivate HAV in shellfish. The virus is also relatively resistant to free chlorine, especially when it is associated with organic matter. These features explain the occurrence of HAV outbreaks from consumption of shellfish and other foods or beverages and outbreaks associated with swimming pools.

HAV exists as a single serotype, and HAV infection—whether symptomatic or not—confers lifelong immunity in people infected with strains from any location worldwide. Only humans and several nonhuman primates (e.g., marmosets, tamarins, owl monkeys, and chimpanzees) are known to be naturally infected with HAV.

In 1979, HAV was cultured in fetal rhesus monkey kidney cells after the virus had been passaged multiple times in marmosets.[16] Since then, HAV has been cultivated directly from clinical or environmental samples, but adaptation periods of 4 to 10 weeks have been required for detection of significant amounts of HAV antigen in infected cells. Generally, HAV isolates do not produce cytopathology in tissue cultures, although cytopathic variants have been isolated that produce plaques in cell culture. The isolation of the virus has allowed comparative virologic studies and diagnostic reagents to be developed to confirm current or past infection and immunity.

Clinical Features and Diagnosis

In the individual, the clinical features of acute HAV infection are not sufficiently distinctive to allow differentiation from other types of acute viral hepatitis. However, prodromal symptoms, including anorexia, nausea, abdominal discomfort, diarrhea, and fever, may be more prominent in persons infected with HAV than in patients infected with HBV or HCV, and they often begin abruptly. Rarely, arthritis, urticarial rash, arteritis, or aplastic anemia has been reported in patients with acute HAV infection. HAV infection can cause 2.0% to 27% of cases of acute fulminant hepatitis in developed countries.[22,23] Unlike HBV and HCV infections, there is no evidence that HAV causes chronic hepatitis. However, 10% to 15% of patients with acute HAV have a relapse of their illness within a few weeks of their recovery. These relapses include excretion of virus in the stool, indicating that patients are infectious during a clinical relapse.[24]

An important clinical feature of HAV infection is the inverse relationship between symptoms and age of the patient. Most infants and children younger than age 6 years are asymptomatic or have nonspecific symptoms. Among children younger than age 3 with HAV infection, only 5% develop jaundice; this percentage increases to 10% in children 4 to 6 years of age. In contrast, most HAV-infected adolescents and adults develop jaundice, and 75% develop characteristic prodromal symptoms. The public health importance of HAV infections in developed countries is related to the high rates of morbidity, which can persist for a few weeks. As noted previously, some patients will have a recurrence of symptoms that prolongs morbidity.

The specific diagnosis of HAV infection is confirmed by immunoglobulin M (IgM) serum antibodies to HAV. The antibody assay is highly sensitive and specific. Antibodies of the IgM class usually develop by the time the patient is symptomatic and persist for 3 to 6 months. Total Ig or IgG antibodies in the absence of IgM antibodies is usually considered to signify previous infection. Most patients—even those who are not icteric—will have elevated serum ALT and AST levels during the acute infection. Although HAV is present in the stool in the pre-symptomatic and pre-icteric phases of the illness, viral cultures are not generally done because of the difficulty in isolating this virus in tissue culture.[25]

Transmission Routes

The principal means of HAV transmission is by ingestion of infectious feces. Infection can occur by direct person-to-person transfer of virus on hands or fomites, or by consumption of contaminated food or water. As noted earlier, bloodborne transmission is uncommon, as HAV is present in the blood only from the middle of the incubation period until early in the clinical illness. Infectivity titers in the stool are very high, as much as 10^8 infectious units per gram of feces in the late incubation period and first week of the illness.[26] Virus can also be present in saliva at titers of 10^{2-3} or less per milliliter.[27] Household or sexual contact with a person with hepatitis is the most common exposure reported to the Centers for Disease Control and Prevention (CDC), accounting for approximately 22% of cases [28] To be counted as a secondary case, the most recent exposure to a case of hepatitis should have been 2 to 6 weeks before onset of illness. Transmission among homosexual men has been well documented; whether this occurs through sexual contact or simply by nonsexual intimate contact is not clear.[29,30]

Transmission of HAV by blood occurs infrequently.[31,32] However, a large outbreak of parenterally transmitted HAV was reported in 1994 among European hemophiliacs infected by contaminated clotting factor concentrates.[33] The clotting factor concentrate was purified from a large pool of plasma donors who had not yet developed neutralizing antibodies, so the HAV in the preparation was infectious.[34] Injection-drug users are believed to be at increased risk of infection, but the route of transmission could be parenteral or fecal–oral transmission from poor hygienic practices.[29,35,36]

Common-source outbreaks have occurred from contamination of food and water supplies.[37,38] Foodborne outbreaks usually result from contamination of food by an infected food handler. Uncooked foods, such as salads, fruit, lettuce, sandwiches, glazed or iced pastries, and some dairy products, are particularly susceptible to such contamination.[39,40] Some foodborne outbreaks have involved consumption of shellfish harvested from sewage-contaminated waters that have been eaten with little or no cooking.[41,42] Bivalve mollusks, such as clams, oysters, and mussels, are particularly risky because they filter large volumes of water and, therefore, concentrate infectious HAV and other viruses in their digestive system.[43] In addition, outbreaks of HAV have been reported from consumption of foods contaminated at the time of harvest or processing that were subsequently served raw, such as lettuce, onions, strawberries, and raspberries.[39,40] Nevertheless, hepatitis traced to contaminated food or water accounts for only some 8% of HAV cases reported to the CDC.[44,45]

Daycare settings, especially those that enroll children in diapers, may have hepatitis A outbreaks. Adult contacts of 1- to 2-year-old children are at highest risk of infection, and adults are more likely to be symptomatic overall. In daycare centers not enrolling children in diapers, outbreaks are much less common.[46] In addition to the absence of symptoms in infected children, prolonged viral secretion in infants has been linked to transmission in daycare centers and hospitals. More than 15% of all HAV infections reported to the CDC have been related to daycare center transmission.

International travel to developing countries with potentially contaminated food or poor water sanitation infrastructure may also result in HAV infection. The risk of HAV infection during international travel is highest among long-term residents of developing countries, such as missionaries, Peace Corps volunteers, and military and peacekeeping force personnel.[49–51] Although short-term tourists are at increased risk of HAV, the risk is not great, as most of these travelers can avoid potentially contaminated water and foods during short travel periods.

Worldwide Epidemiology

The epidemiology of HAV infections varies greatly in different populations throughout the world (**Figure 23-1**). Seroprevalence studies in various countries have been used to define the prevalence of prior infection to classify areas into those with high, intermediate, or low endemicity. Areas with high endemicity for HAV include countries in Africa, Asia, Central and South America, and the Middle East. In these areas, the prevalence of HAV antibody reaches 90% among adults, and most children become infected by age 10. However, persons in the upper socioeconomic classes may not become infected until

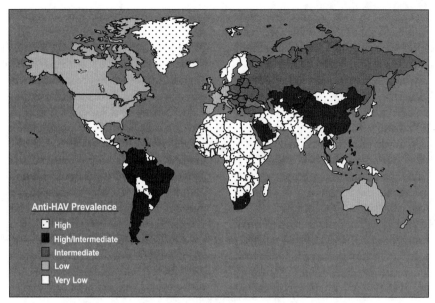

Figure 23-1 Global distribution of Hepatitis A. Data from the World Health Organization. Global Alert and Response, Hepatitis A: Surveillance and Control. http://www.who.int/csr/disease/hepatitis/whocdscsredc2007/en/index4.html#endemicity. Accessed October 25, 2012.

they reach adolescence or adulthood. Paradoxically, prevention of disease among young children increases the risk of morbidity.[51]

In more developed countries in Europe and Asia, the endemicity of HAV is intermediate, and the prevalence of HAV antibody varies widely. In countries such as Italy, Greece, Thailand, Taiwan, and Korea, the prevalence of HAV antibody in adults reaches 80% or higher, but in children younger than age 10, antibody prevalence is only 20% to 30%, and the major increase in antibody occurs in persons between the ages of 10 and 20 years (**Figure 23-2**).[52–55] These data indicate a cohort effect in which older adults belong to cohorts that were infected in childhood.

In Europe and the United States, HAV antibody prevalence in adults varies from 30% to 50% but is less than 10% in children under age 10. However, low socioeconomic status is associated with high rates of infection.[56]

In some northern European countries and in Japan, HAV infection has become rare. The antibody prevalence is less than 10% in children and adolescents in such areas. By comparison, adults older than age 40 have antibody prevalence of 30% to 60%, indicating a cohort effect where older persons were infected as children when HAV infections were more common.

Despite the fact that the United States is considered to be a country where the endemicity of HAV is low, there is considerable geographic variation among HAV incidence rates within the country. In the United States, low socioeconomic status is associated with high rates of infection.[57] Counties with significant minority populations have high incidence rates. Studies have demonstrated that counties with more than 10% American Indian residents or 15% or more Hispanic residents had 3.5 and 2.1 times the rate of HAV found in other counties, respectively.[56,57]

In countries with high endemicity of HAV infection, most acute hepatitis in children younger than age 15 is due to HAV; however, HAV is rarely the cause of hepatitis in adults. In areas of intermediate endemicity, studies have shown that a relatively high proportion (50% to 60%) of adult cases of hepatitis are due to HAV. In low-endemicity areas in Western Europe and the United Sates, the majority of acute hepatitis cases in children are caused by HAV, but in adults, the proportion varies from 10% to 50%.[56]

In the United States and many other countries with low or intermediate endemicity, HAV incidence is cyclical, with 7- to 10-year peaks in the number of reported cases (**Figure 23-3**). Recent peak years include 1971 (59,000 cases; 29/100,000), 1989 (36,000 cases; 14/100,000), and 1995 (31,582 cases; 12/100,000).[44,58–60] The cyclical pattern of HAV is even more apparent in surveillance data from Shanghai, China (**Figure 23-4**). These data show a substantial epidemic of HAV in 1989—more than 300,000 cases—due to consumption of contaminated raw clams.[42] This large foodborne epidemic illustrates the potential for explosive epidemics of

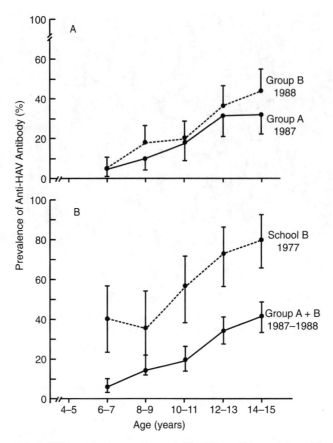

Figure 23-2 Age-specific hepatitis A (HAV) antibody prevalence (with 95% confidence intervals) among school children in Bangkok: A, rates measured in 1987 (group A) and 1988 (group B); B, combined antibody prevalence rates for groups A and B contrasted to those in the group school in 1977. Reproduced from BL Innis, R Snitbhan, and CH Hoke et al., The Declining Transmission of Hepatitis A in Thailand, *Journal of Infectious Diseases*, Vol. 163, pp. 989–995, © 1991, by permission of Oxford University Press.

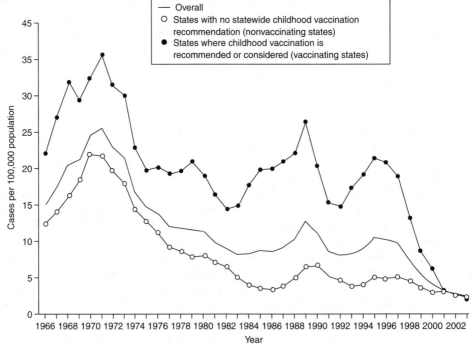

Figure 23-3 U.S. hepatitis A incidence by year, 1966–2003. Reproduced from Wasley et al. Incidence of Hepatitis A in the United States in the Era of Vaccination. *JAMA*. Vol. 294 No. 2. 194–201. Copyright © 2005 American Medical Association. All rights reserved.

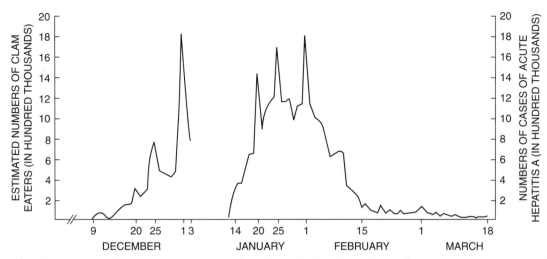

Figure 23-4 Distribution of the estimated numbers of persons who ate clams from 9 December 1987 to 3 January 1988 and the number of cases of hepatitis A between 14 January and 18 March 1988 in 12 districts of Shanghai. Reproduced from Halliday et al. An Epidemic of Hepatitis A Attributable to the Ingestion of Raw Clams in Shanghai, China. *J Infect Dis*. 164 (5): 852–859. Figure 1. © 1991 by permission of Oxford University Press.

HAV in a country where the endemicity has been reduced in recent years by improvements in the hygiene. Low transmission results in the accumulation of a large susceptible population in which a large outbreak can occur.

Prevention

Improved environmental sanitation to prevent fecal contamination of food and water has been the most important means of preventing infection.[52–55] Prior to development of a vaccine for HAV, passive immunization with pooled human immunoglobulin (IG) was used as postexposure or preexposure prophylaxis against hepatitis A. IG is highly effective in preventing symptomatic HAV infections up to 6 months if given before or within 2 weeks after exposure to the virus,[61,62] but if given after exposure, IG is only 75% to 85% effective[63]; HAV infection may occur, but symptoms are rare, and fecal shedding of the virus is limited. The decreased symptoms in patients who receive IG after infection may be due to control of the spread of HAV within the liver until a protective immune response is mounted. The use of IG as postexposure prophylaxis is also called passive-active immunization.[37]

IG is often not recommended or is ineffective in common-source foodborne or waterborne outbreaks when exposure is identified too late for infection to be prevented.[64,65] Prior to the licensure of effective HAV vaccines, repeated preexposure prophylaxis with IG was recommended at 6-month intervals for persons who continued to be at high risk of exposure, such as Peace Corps volunteers and medical missionaries.[63] However, active immunization is now a much preferable preventive strategy. Two inactivated HAV vaccines have been licensed in the United States. These vaccines were tested in 1- to 16-year-olds in Thailand[18] and in 2- to 16-year-olds living in a Hassidic Jewish community in New York state.[17] Both vaccines proved highly effective. Although the long-term durability of the immune response is uncertain, the high efficacy in preventing acute HAV raises the possibility that HAV morbidity could be reduced dramatically with selective vaccination of high-risk populations.

While the panel initially recommended targeting high-risk populations and geographical areas,[60,65] in 2006 the Advisory Committee on Immunization Practices (ACIP) of the CDC recommended that all children be given HAV vaccine at 2 years of age.[66] Subsequently, this recommendation was changed to vaccinate children at 1 year of age, so that HAV vaccine was included in the routine immunization schedule. The expanded use of HAV vaccine resulted in a 10-fold reduction in the number of reported cases of HAV infection, from an average of 28,000 cases reported annually during 1987–1997 to 2979 acute symptomatic cases reported in 2007 (**Figure 23-5**).[56] These data suggest that young children are the most important reservoir for HAV infection of the entire population.

An immunization program was started in Israel in 1999 in which toddlers aged 18–24 months were given two doses of HAV vaccine. This program resulted in a 95% reduction in reported hepatitis A infections, from 50.4 per 100,000 in 1993–1998 to 2.4 per 100,000, suggesting a profound effect of herd immunity by vaccination of toddlers.[67]

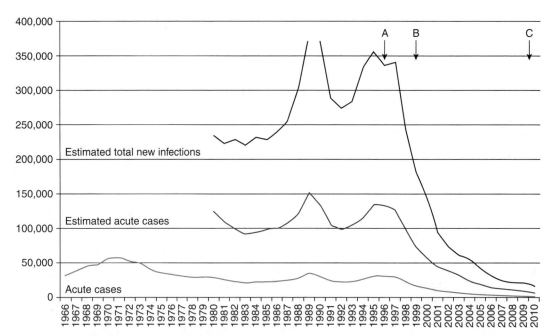

Hepatitis A vaccination recommendations have sought to increase coverage since 1996 (A) when recommended for children in high disease areas, 1999 (B) included areas with high rates of infection and today (C) recommended for all children 12–23 months.

Figure 23-5 United States Hepatitis A Reported and Estimated Cases. Data from the Centers for Disease Control and Prevention (2010). Viral Hepatitis Surveillance Program. http://www.cdc.gov/hepatitis/Statistics/2008Surveillance/Table1a.htm. Updated June 25, 2010. Accessed November 19, 2012.

The impact of immunizing a reservoir population, children, was also seen in the United States. Data from the Third National Health and Nutrition Examination Survey (NHANES), conducted during 1988-1994 indicated that approximately 30% of US population had serologic evidence of immunity to HAV, reaching a high of 70% among persons aged over 70 years of age.[68] The effective vaccination of 1- to 2-year-old children results in substantial herd immunity for the remainder of the population of the United States such that exposure rates are much lower for adults today than for those over 70 years.

The widespread use of HAV vaccine has resulted in a change in the groups who are presently at greatest risk of infection. Currently, sexual contact with an HAV-infected patient, especially among men having sex with men (MSM), and international travel to areas where HAV is common are the most important risk factors for infection.[67] The ACIP has advised that HAV vaccine be administered prior to travel to endemic areas for HAV. To prevent infection after exposure to HAV, immunoglobulin has generally been recommended by the ACIP. However, a recent study of 1090 susceptible persons who were randomized to receive either HAV vaccine or immunoglobulin within 14 days after exposure found no difference in the two regimens.[69] Therefore the ACIP recommended that

HAV vaccine could be used to prevent hepatitis A infection among persons aged 2–40 years, if it could be given within 14 days of exposure.[70] The advantages of using HAV vaccine over immunoglobulin are its greater availability and the fact that the vaccine can induce active immunity with longer protection. Immunoglobulin is still preferred to prevent hepatitis A on a postexposure basis for those persons older than 40 years of age.

Several countries, including Korea, China, and Thailand, among others, have transitioned from developing to developed industrialized countries in the past two decades. Consequently, a large proportion of their adult population is now susceptible to HAV infection.[71–73] These countries will need to decide whether to include HAV vaccine in the routine childhood immunization schedule.

HEPATITIS B VIRUS

Virology

Hepatitis B virus is a partially double-stranded DNA virus that is a member of the family Hepadnaviridae. This family includes several other animal viruses, including woodchuck hepatitis virus, duck hepatitis virus, and ground squirrel hepatitis virus[74]. Humans are the only natural host for HBV infection. The chimpanzee is the primary experimental model for infection, but the disease has also been studied in gibbons, marmosets, and other primates.[74] HBV can retain infectivity for at least 1 month at room temperature and much longer when frozen. Heating to 90°C for 1 hour renders HBV noninfectious.

The HBV genome has approximately 3200 nucleotides and replicates through an RNA intermediate that is transcribed by a gene product with reverse transcriptase activity. The proteins encoded by the HBV genome are the envelope, the nucleocapsid, the X protein, and a DNA polymerase. The envelope proteins encoded by the HBV genome includes the surface proteins, pre-S, pre-S2, and the HBsAg. HBsAg is a glycosylated lipoprotein that contains the major site for binding of neutralizing antibody. It can circulate as a part of the complete virion (called the Dane particle) or independently of viral particles. Four subtypes of HBsAg have been identified, which are designated adw, ayw, adr, and ayr. The "a" epitope, which is common to all HBsAg subtypes, is the binding epitope for neutralizing antibodies. Therefore, antibodies to HBsAg are protective for all subtypes.[75] Nonlethal mutations can also occur in the S gene, sufficiently altering the expression of this protein to permit viral escape from neutralizing antibodies. The occurrence of the other subtype determinants varies geographically, such that HBsAg subtyping has been used in epidemiology studies to establish patterns of transmission.[76] The subtypes do not appear to differ in infectivity or virulence.

The HBV nucleocapsid proteins—HBeAg and HBV core antigen (HBcoreAg)—are also used to delineate between important disease states. HBeAg is a marker for current active viral replication. However, mutations can occur that truncate expression of "e" antigen without substantially altering virion production. The resultant viral phenotype results in clinical infection with HBV DNA and HBsAg but no detectable HBeAg in the blood. Some individuals infected with these HBeAg-negative mutant viruses have developed fulminant hepatitis.[77–80] The HBcoreAg is the major nucleocapsid protein and is not detected in the serum but is present in the liver. The cellular immune response to HBcoreAg in the liver is believed by some investigators to be responsible for hepatic necrosis associated with chronic liver disease in HBV carriers.[80–84] Persons infected with HBV form antibodies to HBcoreAg that are persistent, making them useful in the diagnosis of current or previous infection.

Clinical Features and Diagnosis

The clinical features of HBV infection are similar to those of other hepatitis viruses and range from asymptomatic infection to jaundice following a flu-like prodromal illness. However, persons with acute HBV infection are more likely to develop a serum sickness-like illness (arthritis, arthralgia, urticarial rash), and chronic infection is associated with glomerulonephritis or vasculitis resembling periarteritis nodosa.[85]

Like HAV infection, HBV infection in infants and children rarely results in jaundice, and such young patients usually remain completely asymptomatic; in contrast, 10% to 20% of children older than age 6 and 40% to 50% of adults develop jaundice with acute HBV infection.[86] However, a lack of jaundice during acute infection increases the risk that a patient will fail to clear the virus and becomes chronically infected. In infants born to a mother who is an HBeAg-positive carrier, the risk of infection with chronic carriage (defined as carriage for more than 1 year) is approximately 80% if HBV vaccination is not initiated soon after birth.[87] The risk of chronic infection decreases with increasing age.[88] By age 6, chronic infection occurs in 5% to 10% of individuals, and 1% to 5% of adolescents and adults. Persons who are immunosuppressed, HIV-positive patients, patients on dialysis, and oncology and transplant patients have a high risk of developing chronic HBV.

Most persons with chronic HBV infection do not develop chronic liver disease, and a spectrum of histologic disease has been described.[89–91] Some patients have normal liver biopsies. Chronic persistent hepatitis consists of low-grade focal inflammation; chronic active hepatitis is diffuse active inflammation with bridging necrosis between hepatic lobules. The most serious form of chronic infection is cirrhosis, which is characterized by scarring, diffuse necrosis, and regeneration and disruption of hepatic lobular architecture.

The probability of clinically significant chronic liver disease is highest in those persons who were infected as infants or children, as compared to persons in whom infection occurs during adult life.[92] Prospective studies in Taiwan have estimated that 25% of persons infected as infants or children who become chronic HBV carriers develop primary hepatocellular carcinoma (PHC) during their lifetime.[93–95]

Hepatitis B Virus and Primary Liver Cancer

In the last 30 years, considerable evidence has been published describing chronic HBV infection as a cause of PHC in humans.[94] This evidence includes ecologic data indicating those geographic areas with

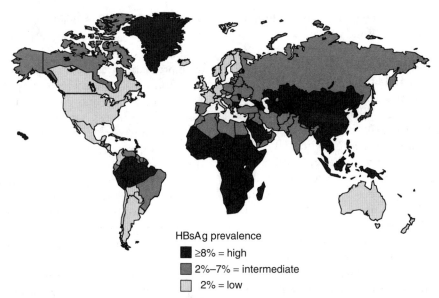

HBsAg prevalence

■ ≥8% = high
■ 2%–7% = intermediate
□ 2% = low

Figure 23-6 Geographic distribution of chronic HBV infection. These areas constitute 45% of the global population and include China and Southeast Asian countries, sub-Saharan Africa, and several areas in the Artic, including Alaska, Northern Canada, and Greenland. Reproduced from the Centers for Disease Control and Prevention (2011). Testing and Public Health Management of Persons with Chronic Hepatitis B Virus Infection. http://www.cdc.gov/hepatitis/HBV/PDFs/HBV_figure3map_08-27-08.pdf. Updated April 27, 2011. Accessed November 19, 2012.

the highest HBV carrier rates (**Figure 23-6**) as well as the areas where PHC is most common. More persuasive are several prospective cohort studies of infection with HBV and the subsequent development of PHC. In the first, largest, and most comprehensive of these studies, Beasley et al. studied 22,707 male civil servants between the ages of 40 and 59 in Taiwan between March 15, 1976, and June 3, 1978.[95] These men were all healthy and free of liver cancer at baseline. By December 1985, 151 of these men had experienced incident PHC in a cumulative 186,000 person-years of follow-up, for an average of 8.2 PHC cases per 100 person-years. Overall, 141 of the men who developed PHC were HBsAg carriers at baseline, giving a rate of PHC in the HBsAg carriers of 505 per 100 person-years versus 5.3 per 100 person-years in HBsAg-negative patients. The relative risk of PHC for HBsAg carriers was 104 times higher than for noncarriers at baseline.

Additional prospective studies of the risk of PHC in areas where this neoplasm is common have shown similar strong associations with chronic HBV infection.[94] The risk is especially high in China, and prospective studies suggest that 40% of Chinese males with chronic HBV infection will die from PHC.[894] The World Health Organization (WHO) has estimated that 80% of all PHC cases in the world occur in persons with chronic HBV infection.[94]

Although the precise molecular mechanism of carcinogenesis is not known, HBV DNA is

often clonally integrated into the cellular DNA of carcinoma cells, indicating that these tumors have arisen by a clonal expansion in a cell with HBV integration.[96–98] The oncogenic potential of HBV is supported by data from studies of carcinogenesis of other animal hepadnaviruses. Chronic hepatitis and liver cancer have been documented in woodchucks in the United States and in ducks in China that are infected with other hepadnaviruses closely related to HBV. The association of PHC with persistent hepadnavirus infections in woodchucks and the Beachey ground squirrel is even stronger than the association between HBV and PHC in humans. In fact, the risk of liver cancer in animals that have carried these hepadnaviruses for 3 years or longer approaches 100%.[99–103] Oncogenesis may also be the result of HBV-induced increased cell turnover. Other chronic liver diseases are linked to PHC, which may be a common mechanism for development of cancer.

From a public health perspective, the most encouraging and persuasive data linking HBV infection to PHC document the reduction in the incidence of PHC associated with immunization for HBV in Taiwan.[104] In that country, a nationwide hepatitis B vaccination program of all newborn infants of HBsAg-carrier mothers began in July 1984. The program was expanded to include all newborns in 1987, then to include children and adults who were HBV uninfected between 1987 and 1990. The rates of primary liver cancer reported to the tumor registry among 6- to 9-year-olds fell from 0.52 per 100,000 (82 cases among 15,739,570 children) born between July 1978 and June 1984, to 0.13 per 100,000 (3 cases among 2,281,106 children) in those born between July 1984 and June 1986. This significant decrease was not seen for other neoplasms and strongly suggests that HBV immunization of newborns prevented subsequent liver cancer in this cohort of immunized children.

Aflatoxin consumption is another important risk for PHS. A study in Shanghai, China, found a synergistic interaction between chronic HBV infection and aflatoxin biomarkers in the urine of patients with PHC.[105] The relative risk for PHC was 7.3 in those with HBsAg alone and 3.4 in subjects with aflatoxin biomarkers only, but it was 59.4 in subjects who were positive for both aflatoxin and chronic HBV infection.

Diagnosis

The diagnosis of HBV infection is usually confirmed using serologic tests. Testing is performed to measure viral products, antigens, and antibodies against these antigens. The glycoprotein coat of HBV contains HBsAg, which is produced in excess and can circulate independent of the virus. Detection of HBsAg is done currently using enzyme immunoassay (EIA).

The presence of HBsAg indicates active HBV infection, but testing for IgM antibody to hepatitis B core (anti-HBc) is needed to determine whether the HBV infection is recent or chronic. Detection of HBsAg is possible in acute infections during the incubation period prior to the increase in liver enzymes or the appearance of jaundice and for several weeks thereafter (**Figure 23-7**). In persons who develop

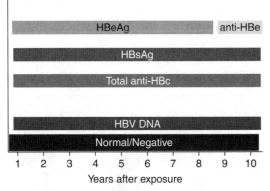

Figure 23-7 Progression to chronic hepatitis B infection. Reproduced from the Centers for Disease Control and Prevention (2012). Viral Hepatitis Resource Center, Part I - Animated Graph Tutorials: Chronic Hepatitis B. http://www.cdc.gov/hepatitis/Resources/Professionals/Training/Serology/training.htm#one. Updated August 6, 2012. Accessed November 19. 2012.

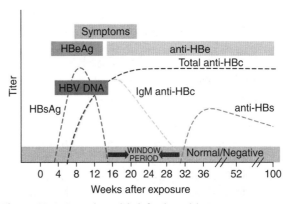

Figure 23-8 Acute hepatitis infection with recovery. Reproduced from the Centers for Disease Control and Prevention (2012). Viral Hepatitis Resource Center, Part I – Animated Graph Tutorials: Acute Hepatitis B. http://www.cdc.gov/hepatitis/Resources/Professionals/Training/Serology/training.htm#one. Updated August 6, 2012. Accessed November 19. 2012.

chronic HBV infection, HBsAg persists in the serum (**Figure 23-8**).

Anti-HBs appears with recovery from acute infection and after immunization with HBV vaccine. Anti-HBs titers have been measured to document the levels of protective antibodies after immunization, and an anti-HBs level of 10 IU/mL or more is believed to be protective. In many patients, anti-HBs levels may not rise for several months after acute HBV infection, and initially they complex with HBsAg and may be undetectable.

Hepatitis B core antigen is part of the viral nucleocapsid. No serologic test for HBcAg is available because this antigen is localized within hepatic cells and not secreted. However, anti-HBc are commonly used to diagnose current or past HBV infection. Anti-HBc develops soon after HBV infection and persists for the lifetime of an individual.[106–107] IgM anti-HBc is a serological marker of recent infection—that is, within the past 6 to 9 months.

Although the diagnosis of recent HBV infection is made by detecting HBsAg and/or IgM anti-HBc, other methods can also be used to document active HBV infection. A third antigen–antibody system involves HBeAg, which is a soluble conformational antigen that consists of a secreted portion of the HBcAg. HBeAg is found in the blood during acute or chronic HBV infection and is a marker of infectivity. For example, 90% of pregnant women whose blood is positive for HBeAg at the time of delivery will transmit HBV to their newborn infants if there is no prophylaxis of the infant with immunoglobulin or vaccine.[87] Because positivity for HBeAg signifies active HBV infection with a high viral load (i.e., more than 10,000 copies/mL), infants born to HBeAg-positive women should receive anti-HBs immunoglobulin as well as HBV vaccine when possible. However, because infants whose mothers are HBsAg positive but HBeAg negative at delivery also may become infected, decisions to use HBV vaccine for prevention of transmission are not based on the HBeAg status of the mother; that is, all infants of HBsAg-positive women should be given HBV vaccine and anti-HBs starting as soon after birth as possible. In contrast, the potential infectivity of healthcare personnel and subsequent work restrictions are judged largely by HBeAg results. The enzyme HBV DNA polymerase can also be measured in the serum and, like HBeAg, is a marker of active replication of HBV. The interpretation of the various serological tests for HBV infection and susceptibility in general use is summarized in **Table 23-3**.

In addition to the serologic methods described previously, HBV DNA can be quantified in serum by a variety of molecular tests. Monitoring of HBV DNA levels can be useful in the treatment of patients with chronic HBV infection, in following patients receiving antiviral therapy, and in screening for HBsAg mutants. HBV DNA can also be detected in tissue by *in situ* hybridization or PCR amplification. The dynamics of the appearance of HBV antigens and antibody responses to infection are depicted in Figure 23-7 and Figure 23-8.

Transmission Routes

HBV can be transmitted by percutaneous blood exposure, sexual intercourse, and from a mother to her infant (**Figure 23-9**). The risk of transfusion-transmitted HBV infections in the United States declined substantially starting with HBsAg screening of blood donors in 1973, followed by exclusion of high-risk populations for HBV, HCV, and HIV

Table 23-3	Interpretation of Hepatitis B Serologic Test Results	
HBsAg	negative	Susceptible
anti-HBc	negative	
anti-HBs	negative	
HBsAg	negative	Immune due to natural infection
anti-HBc	positive	
anti-HBs	positive	
HBsAg	negative	Immune due to hepatitis B vaccination
anti-HBc	negative	
anti-HBs	positive	
HBsAg	positive	Acutely infected
anti-HBc	positive	
IgM anti-HBc	positive	
anti-HBs	negative	
HBsAg	positive	Chronically infected
anti-HBc	positive	
IgM anti-HBc	negative	
anti-HBs	negative	
HBsAg	negative	Interpretation unclear; four possibilities: 1. Resolved infection (most common) 2. False-positive anti-HBc, thus susceptible 3. "Low level" chronic infection 4. Resolving acute infection
anti-HBc	positive	
anti-HBs	negative	

Reproduced from the Centers for Disease Control and Prevention (2012). Interpretation of Hepatitis B Serologic Test Results. http://www.cdc.gov/hepatitis/HBV/PDFs/SerologicChartv8.pdf. Updated August 1, 2011. Accessed November 19, 2012.

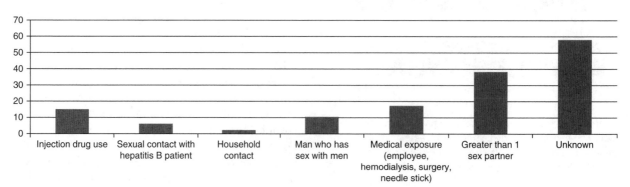

Figure 23-9 Percent of Hepatitis B Cases by Transmission Risk Category. Data from the Centers for Disease Control and Prevention (2009). MMWR Surveillance for Acute Viral Hepatitis- United States, 2007. Vol. 58, No SS-3.

infection as blood donors and in 2010 routine utilization of nucleic acid testing by PCR to detect HBV DNA among blood donors. Also, blood centers in the United States and Europe routinely test donated blood for anti-HBc. These testing procedures have virtually eliminated transfusion-transmitted HBV in the countries adopting this policy. However, screening donated blood for anti-HBc is not feasible in many countries in Asia or Africa because the rate of anti-HBc is so high that 40% to 70% of possible donors would be excluded. Therefore, transfusion-transmitted HBV is more frequent in these areas.[105] Also, parenteral transmission still occurs in some situations. Persons who inject illicit drugs commonly share injection equipment and have a very high prevalence and incidence of HBV infection.[108,109] Persons receiving pooled blood products may likewise be at risk high rates for HBV infection because very large pools may include a rare donor who was in the seronegative window period or had a false-negative test for HBsAg or very low levels of HBV DNA at the time of donation.

In many developing countries, where the HBsAg carrier rate is very high (i.e., 10% or higher) in the general population and disposable injection equipment is not available, HBV transmission by medical injections continues to be common. Also, parenteral exposures, such as acupuncture, tattoos, and body piercing, are risks for HBV transmission. Because of the very high concentration of virus in some persons with acute or chronic HBV infection (as much as 10^{10} virions/mL), exposures to minute amounts of blood that occur from activities such as sharing of toothbrushes, razors, wash cloths, or towels and the presence of eczematous skin lesions that exude serum can result in transmission in the household setting.[110–112] HBV transmission has also been demonstrated to occur between children and teachers in a classroom.[113] Other populations who are at high risk of HBV infection include clients of institutions for the developmentally disabled and prisoners.

HBV is also transmitted commonly by sexual intercourse. Numerous studies in various populations have shown that the prevalence of HBV increases with the number of sex partners.[114–116] Populations with large numbers of sex partners, such as commercial sex workers and both homosexuals and heterosexuals with multiple partners, can have a high prevalence of HBV infection.[114–116] In households, the sexual partners of an HBsAg carrier are at greater risk of HBV infection than are others in the household.[114–116] Virologic studies have shown that HBV is present in semen and other secretions,

although at levels 100- to 1000-fold lower than in the blood.

In many parts of the world, HBV infection is acquired during the perinatal period or in early childhood. Infants born to a mother who is an HBsAg carrier and is HBeAg positive have a 90% risk of acquiring an HBV infection if they are not given hepatitis B immunoglobulin (HBIG) and HBV vaccine soon after birth.[86, 87] However, if HBIG is given within a few hours of birth along with an initial dose of HBV vaccine, the transmission rate is reduced by as much as 90%. HBV vaccination alone reduces the risk of transmission by 70%. Limited data also suggest that antiviral therapy of the pregnant woman with high HBV DNA levels (more than 10^8 IU/mL) may further reduce transmission to infants. Infants of women who are HBsAg positive but HBeAg negative have a lower risk.

Worldwide Epidemiology

The prevalence of HBV infection varies greatly worldwide. In some areas of the world, HBV infections are highly endemic, and 8% or more of the total population are chronic carriers of HBsAg. These areas encompass 45% of the global population and include China and Southeast Asian countries, sub-Saharan Africa, and several areas in the Arctic, including Alaska, northern Canada, and Greenland (Figure 23-6). The First Nation people of Canada and the United States have high rates of HBV. In most of these areas, primary liver cancer is also very common and is often the most frequent cancer in adult males. Nearly all HBV infections occur during the perinatal period or in early childhood in these areas. Because acute HBV infections in infancy and early childhood result in a high rate of chronic carriage, the high endemicity is perpetuated from one generation to the next. The perinatal transmission of HBV among Alaska natives has been reduced dramatically in the last several years by the implementation of an effective program to vaccinate newborns immediately after they were born.[117]

In developed countries of North America, Western Europe, Australia, and some areas of South America, the rates of HBV infection are much lower. Less than 2% of the population are chronic carriers, and the overall infection rate, measured by the prevalence of anti-HBc, is 5% to 20%. In these areas, which constitute 12% of the global population, the frequency of perinatal or early childhood infection is low; however, they may account for a disproportionately high number of chronic HBV infections. Some subgroups also have higher rates, such as those living in the Amazon basin, and immigrants from areas with higher population prevalence. These immigrant populations may contribute substantially to the subset of HBV infections that are transmitted during the perinatal and early childhood period.[118–120] In these areas, most infections occur among high-risk adult populations, including injection-drug users; homosexual men; persons with multiple sex partners; patients with multiple exposures to pooled blood products, such as hemophiliacs; and healthcare workers.[115,119,121]

The remaining parts of the world, which constitutes 43% of the global population, have an intermediate rate of HBV infection. The prevalence of HBsAg positivity ranges from 2% to 8%, in these regions and serologic evidence of past infection is found in 20% to 60% of the population. In these areas, there are mixed patterns of infant, early childhood, and adult transmission. In many countries in sub-Saharan

Africa, for example, transmission of HBV commonly occurs during childhood rather than the perinatal period. Another risk for populations in developing countries is that posed by contaminated blood products or medical equipment. Nosocomial transmission in developing countries where HBV is highly endemic remains common.

In the United States, the CDC has conducted a detailed assessment of behaviors in the Sentinel Counties Study of viral hepatitis to estimated the risk factors for acute HBV infection. The CDC estimate of the proportion of persons with acute HBV infections associated with known risk factors in 1992–1993 was as follows: heterosexual contact, 41%; injection-drug use, 15%; homosexual contact, 9%; household contact, 2%; healthcare employment, 1%; other, 1%; and unknown, 31% (**Table 23-4**, Figure 23-9). It is likely that the relative contribution of injection-drug

Table 23-4	Number and Percentage of Patients with Acute Hepatitis B who Reported Selected Epidemiologic Characteristics, by Age Group, United States, 2007					
	Age group (yrs)					
	<45		≥45		Total	
Characteristic[†]	No.	(%)	No.	(%)	No.	(%)
Cases reported with risk factor data						
Injection-drug use	229/1,200	(19.1)	55/688	(8.0)	**284/1,888**	**(15.0)**
Sexual contact with hepatitis B patient	62/851	(7.3)	22/505	(4.4)	**84/1,356**	**(6.2)**
Household contact of hepatitis B patient	19/851	(2.2)	12/505	(2.4)	**31/1,356**	**(2.3)**
Homosexual activity (male)[§]	46/400	(11.5)	16/189	(8.5)	**62/589**	**(10.5)**
Medical employee with blood contact	5/1,236	(0.4)	6/719	(0.8)	**11/1,955**	**(0.6)**
Hemodialysis	1/1,032	(0.1)	2/589	(0.3)	**3/1,621**	**(0.2)**
Had >1 sex partner	322/744	(43.3)	118/405	(29.1)	**440/1,149**	**(38.3)**
Heterosexual	293/708	(41.4)	110/390	(28.2)	**403/1,098**	**(36.7)**
Homosexual or bisexual (male)	29/36	(80.6)	8/15	(53.3)	**37/51**	**(72.5)**
Blood transfusion	1/1,221	(0.1)	8/709	(1.1)	**9/1,930**	**(0.5)**
Surgery	102/1,165	(8.8)	112/671	(16.7)	**214/1,836**	**(11.7)**
Percutaneous injury (e.g., needlestick)	52/1,080	(4.8)	21/631	(3.3)	**73/1,711**	**(4.3)**
Unknown	757/1,363	(55.5)	483/775	(62.3)	**1,240/2,138**	**(58.0)**
Cases reported with no risk factor data available	1,468		893		2,361	
Total cases reported	**2,831**		**1,668**		**4,499**	

* The percentage of cases for which a specific risk factor was reported was calculated on the basis of the total number of cases for which any information for that exposure was reported. Percentages might not total 100% because multiple risk factors might have been reported for a single case.
† Exposures that occurred during the 6 weeks–6 months before onset of illness.
§ Among males, 18% reported homosexual behavior.

Reproduced from the Centers for Disease Control and Prevention (2009). MMWR Surveillance for Acute Viral Hepatitis- United States, 2007. Vol. 58, No SS-3.

use to HBV infections may be higher in populations with a high burden of drug use.

The incidence of hepatitis B infection has declined in the United States since the mid-1980s. In 2007, it was estimated to be 1.5 cases per 100,000 population, which was the lowest rate since active surveillance began in 1996 and represents an estimated decline of more than 80% from the rate in 1990, when a national strategy was implemented to reduce the incidence of HBV infections.[118] (**Figure 23-10**) CDC has estimated that 38,000 new HBV infections occurred in the U.S. population in 2008, which represents a sharp decline from an estimated 73,000 cases in 2003. The greatest decline in incidence has occurred among the cohort of children in whom the recommendations for routine infant and adolescent vaccination have been implemented. Vaccination coverage among young adults (19–35 years of age) is estimated at 93%. The incidence among children younger than age 15 years declined 98% from 1.2 cases per 100,000 population in 1990 to 0.02 cases per 100,000 in 2007.[118]

The incidence of HBV among adults has also declined, albeit to a lesser extent than among infants and children. Few cases are now reported in certain populations that previously were considered to be at high risk, e.g. dialysis patients and health care workers. These declines are a result of improvements in infection control and routine use of hepatitis B vaccination in these populations. A high proportion of the new HBV infections occur among injection drug users, MSM, and persons with multiple sex partners[117–123]

In recent years, however, a new high-risk group has been identified. During 1999–2007, 16 outbreaks of hepatitis B were detected and investigated in the United States, involving 157 persons. In nearly all of these outbreaks, the cases involved diabetics in nursing or assisted care facilities sharing glucose-monitoring equipment.[124–125] CDC has estimated that 38,000 new HBV infections occurred in the U.S. population in 2008, which declined from an estimated 73,000 cases in 2003. Overall, 4.35% to 5.6% of the U.S. population is estimated to have been infected with HBV, which gives an estimated 800,000 to 1.4 million persons with HBV in the United States[118]

The risk of transfusion-transmitted HBV infections in the Untied States has declined substantially in the last few decades. Screening of blood donors for HBsAg was instituted in 1972. More effective screening of blood donors for drug use or sexual risk behavior and exclusion of men who have sex with men was implemented to reduce the risk of HIV transmission in the early 1980s. Most blood collection centers in the United States implemented routine nucleic acid testing to detect HBV DNA among blood donors in 2010. Also, blood

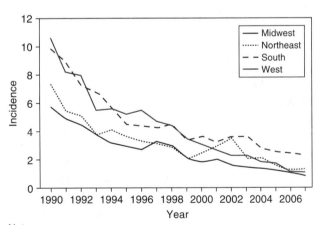

Notes:
1. Incidence per 100,000 population.
2. *Midwest*: Illinois, Indiana, Iowa, Kansas, Michigan, Minnesota, Missouri, Nebraska, North Dakota, Ohio, South Dakota, and Wisconsin; *Northeast*: Connecticut, Maine, Massachusetts, New Hampshire, New Jersey, New York, Pennsylvania, Rhode Island, and Vermont; *South*: Alabama, Arkansas, Delaware, District of Columbia, Florida, Georgia, Kentucky, Louisiana, Maryland, Mississippi, North Carolina, Oklahoma, South Carolina, Tennessee, Texas, Virginia, and West Virginia; and *West*: Alaska, Arizona, California, Colorado, Hawaii, Idaho, Montana, Nevada, New Mexico, Oregon, Utah, Washington, and Wyoming.

Figure 23-10 Incidence of Acute Hepatitis B, by Region and Year—United States, 1990–2007. Reproduced from the Centers for Disease Control and Prevention (2009). MMWR Surveillance for Acute Viral Hepatitis- United States, 2007. Vol. 58, No SS-3.

centers in the United States and Europe routinely test donated blood for antibodies to anti-HBc. Anti-HBc is a very sensitive test for HBV as any persons ever infected would be removed from the blood supply, but a less specific test as not all persons with anti-HBc are viremic for HBV. These testing procedures virtually eliminated transmission-transmitted HBV. However, screening donated blood for anti-HBc is not feasible in many countries in Asia or Africa because the rate of anti-HBc is so high that 40% to 70% of possible donors would be excluded. Therefore, transfusion-transmitted HBV is more frequent in these areas.[114,121,122]

Although the incidence of HBV has declined in the United States, the prevalence of chronic HBV infection has not changed; this steady state is largely related to immigration of individuals from countries with endemic HBV.[117] Chronic HBV infections are recognized especially among several populations in the United States—namely, First Nations people from Canada and the United States, injection-drug users, persons with multiple sex partners, immigrants from Asia[118] and Africa, and immunocompromised patients with AIDS and other causes of immunosuppression whose HBV infection has reactivated.[114,118,121]

A recent study of the incidence of hepatocellular carcinoma in the United States estimated that the number of cases increased by 46% between 1976–1980 and 1991–1995.[126] This increased incidence of liver cancer probably reflects the effects of an increased rate of chronic HBV and HCV infections, combined with the effects of alcohol use among carriers of these viruses. The incidence of hepatocellular carcinoma tripled in the United States between 1975 and 2005, increasing from 1.6 to 4.9 cases per 100,000 population.[129] Worldwide, primary cancer of the liver is the third leading cause of cancer mortality among men and the sixth leading cause among women.[126]

Screening Hepatitis B Virus Carriers for Cirrhosis and Hepatocellular Carcinoma

It is particularly important to periodically screen persons who are chronic HBV carriers for hepatocellular carcinoma (HCC). In 2007, an expert committee of the American Association for the Study of Liver Disease (AASLD) published recommendations for screeing of HBV carriers, i.e., persons who are HBsAg positive.[127] The committee recommended screening the following HBsAg positive patients at 6 month intervals with ustrasound to detect early liver cancer: Asian over 40 years of age, African patients over 20 years of age, all patients with cirrhosis, and patients with a family history of HCC. These recommendations were based, in part, on a randomized control trail in Shanghai which found a reduction of mortality from liver cancer by 37% from 131.5 to 83.2 per 100,000 population in a population of 18,816 HBsAg carriers whose HCC was detected at an earlier stage by screening.[128] Most of these patients, in addition to screening would be candidates for treatment of their chronic HBV infection with anti-viral drugs to suppress their viral replication. More recent studies have found that pre-core mutations in the X gene of HBV may precede the occurrence of HCC by several years.[129,130] These data suggest that it might be possible to prevent or delay the onset of HCC by screening chronic carriers of HBV to detect high-risk mutations and treating such patients to reduce their viral load.

Although these screening recommendations may appear straightforward, it is sometimes difficult to determine whether a patient with chronic HBV infection might have cirrhosis. Many would argue that liver biopsy is the gold standard for diagnosis, and although histologic examination of a liver biopsy may be the best method to detect cirrhosis, a biopsy is invasive and occasionally causes complications. Moreover, it represents only a small sample of the liver, so it may not always detect early cirrhosis. Recently, other noninvasive diagnostic methods have become available, including fibroscan, which allows for more frequent assessment. Whereas fibroscan abnormalities reliably detect advanced fibrosis or cirrhosis they are less sensitive in detecting early stages of fibrosis. In addition, biochemical methods have been used to diagnose cirrhosis; these include measurements of elevated liver enzymes, AST/platelet ratio, haptoglobin, apolipoprotein-A1 and other methods that evaluate the functional status of the liver.[129]

Risk Factors and Biomarkers for Hepatocellular Carcinoma

Several viral, host, and environmental factors have been found to be associated with an increased risk of hepatocellular carcinoma among persons with chronic HBV infection. Host factors include older age, male sex, the presence of cirrhosis, a family history of liver cancer, and coinfection with HIV, HDV, or HCV. Virus factors include high levels of HBV replication, infection with HBV genotype C versus genotype B or A, a common double mutation in the core-promoter region of the virus (nucleotides 1762 A to T and 1764 G to A mutation), and several other mutations in the x gene, or pre-core genome of HBV. Environmental factors include frequent high alcohol consumption, aflatoxin exposure, cigarette smoking, diabetes, and obesity.[130]

Among these risk factors, the association between the acquired double mutation in the HBV genome 1762^T/1764^A may be especially useful as a biomarker for the prediction of increased risk of subsequent liver cancer, as prospective studies have detected such mutations 5 or more years prior to the appearance of a cancer.[131]

Although the presence of cirrhosis is an important risk factor for the subsequent development of liver cancer, it is important to recognize that HCC may sometimes develop among HBV chronic carriers in the absence of cirrhosis. Only 40% to 50% of liver cancer among chronically HBV-infected patients in Africa have cirrhosis, whereas cirrhosis precedes liver cancer in 90% of such patients in Asia, the United States, and Europe.[132]

An increased rate of HCC among males has been found in every population. In a study of more than 2 million pregnancies between 1983 and 2000 in Taiwan, 17% of the women were HBsAg positive at the time of delivery. By 2005, 294 of these women had died from HCC.[133] The relative risk (RR) of HCC among HBsAg carriers was 42% lower (RR = 0.58; 95% confidence interval [CI], 0.42–0.74) in women having two pregnancies and 52% lower (RR = 0.48; 95% CI, 0.34–0.72) in women having three or more pregnancies.[136] In addition to these data among women, a nested case-control study among men with chronic HBV infection who subsequently developed HCC found higher levels of androgenic hormones among the men several years prior to the diagnosis of HCC.[134] These data lend support to the hypothesis that the levels of female and male hormones may be cofactors in the pathogenesis of HCC among persons with HBV infections and may partially explain the sex difference in HCC.

Staging of Liver Disease

The natural history of chronic HBV infection is now recognized to have four phases, although not all patients go through all phases. These phases of HBV infection are most prominent when infection is acquired in infancy or childhood.

The first phase is the "immune tolerant phase," which is characterized by the presence of HBeAg, high levels of serum DNA, normal serum transaminases, and minimal or no inflammation on liver biopsy. During this phase, which may last several decades in patients with infection acquired perinatally, spontaneous or treatment-induced HBeAg clearance is unusual and patients rarely progress to cirrhosis or liver cancer.[130] In patients who acquire HBV infection during late childhood or as adults, this phase may be short-lived.

The second phase, immune clearance, is characterized by the presence of HBeAg, elevated HBV DNA levels, persistent or intermittent elevation in serum liver enzymes, and active inflammation in the liver. The elevated liver enzymes reflect immune-cytolysis of infected hepatocytes. Some of the flares in liver enzymes may lead to hepatic decompensation. The immune response in this phase may lead to clearance of HBeAg from the serum.

The third phase, known as the "immune control" phase, is characterized by the absence of HBeAg, presence of anti-HBe, normal aminotransferase levels, and low levels of serum HBV DNA (i.e., less than 10^5 IU/mL). Liver biopsy at this stage may show mild hepatitis and minimal fibrosis. However, some patients may have cirrhosis if the liver inflammation during the immune clearance phase was severe or persistent. The use of sensitive assays to detect HBV DNA has revealed that replication is ongoing,[138] but when this immune control stage persists, the patient is at minimal risk of progression to severe liver disease or cirrhosis.

Some inactive carriers have "reactivation" of their HBV infection, a fourth stage. This may occur spontaneously or as a result of immunosuppression.

A study of 283 patients in Taiwan who were followed for approximately 9 years after they developed antibodies to HBeAg (the third phase) found that 67% had a sustained remission, 4% had HBeAg revision to positivity, and 24% had HBeAg-negative chronic hepatitis.[135] Cirrhosis developed in 8% and HCC in 25% of these patients; these conditions occurred more frequently in those patients with active hepatitis after their loss of HBeAg. In fact, the core-promoter double mutation[131] and a stop codon mutation in the pre-core region of the HBV genome, NT/896,[131] will turn off production of HBeAg. The double mutation commonly precedes the onset of hepatocellular carcinoma in patients with HBeAg-negative chronic HBV infection.[131]

The data from follow-up of patients after HBV infection indicate that the virus is not generally directly cytopathic, but that the sequelae of cirrhosis and liver cancer are primarily immune mediated. Furthermore, HBV infections are not curable. Thus the goal of antiviral therapy of chronic HBV infection is the prevention of liver fibrosis, cirrhosis, and liver cancer. The main stages of the infection when inflammation, fibrosis, and cirrhosis develop are during the immune clearance and reactivation stages. Antiviral therapy should be used in patients during the immune clearance or reactivation stages of this infection when inflammation and fibrosis of the liver may occur. The goal of treatment during these stages is to suppress viral replication and liver inflammation and fibrosis.

Prevention

Studies of strategies to prevent HBV infection began in the 1970s. Krugman et al.[147] showed that heat-inactivated whole-virus preparations from HBV carriers could prevent infection. Also, it was shown that immunoglobulin containing high titers of antibodies to surface antigen was effective in preventing infection after acute exposure.

The initial vaccines were prepared from the plasma of persons chronically infected with HBV. These plasma-derived vaccines were found to be highly effective and safe.[148,149] The overall preventive efficacy was 92%; however, nearly 100% of subjects who developed anti-HBs levels greater than 10 MIU/mL were protected, especially from developing chronic HBV infection.[148–152]

Currently, hepatitis B vaccines are produced using recombinant DNA technology to express HBsAg in yeast or mammalian cells.[149] These subunit vaccines are quite effective after three doses in stimulating a protective immune response, and stimulated immune memory has been found to be comparable to plasma-derived vaccines in preventing acute and chronic infections. Because the vaccine is highly purified, free of other viral components, and not derived from pooled human sera, it cannot accidentally expose recipients to other human-derived contaminates. This was the first successful use of molecular genetic methods to produce a human vaccine.

Preexposure vaccination requires three or more doses to induce a protective immune response. Although it is currently not known whether HBV vaccine provides a lifelong immunity to infections, available data suggest that persons who respond well to vaccine are protected for at least 15 or more years.[153] In persons whose level of antibody declines, exposure to HBV rarely results in clinically apparent acute or chronic infection. However, some individuals develop anti-HBc, and a few develop HBsAg.

A recently published study from Taiwan found that approximately one-third of subjects who originally responded well to an HBV vaccine series failed to develop a booster response when revaccinated 25 or more years after the primary series.[154] Thus it is unclear whether revaccination with a full course series will be necessary or successful and requires further study.

HBV vaccines must be given intramuscularly (in the deltoid muscle in adults), as they are poorly immunogenic if given subcutaneously.[155,156] Also, when HBV vaccines are frozen, their immunogenicity declines. Even with proper handling and administration, some persons respond poorly to HBV vaccines, based on genetic factors. One study found that persons who were homozygous for a certain major histocompatibility haplotype (HLA-B8, SCO1, DR 3) responded poorly to HBV vaccines.[157] Although most persons responded to vaccine, as many as 50% of vaccine responders have anti-HBs titers less than 10 MIU/mL several years later. These true responders are protected against disease but years later are difficult to distinguish from nonresponders. Thus, when checking vaccine response, it is necessary to measure anti-HBs titers approximately 2 months after the third vaccine dose.

Strategies for the use of HBV vaccines to prevent HBV infections must consider the epidemiology of the infection and populations in whom the risk of infection is greatest. In many developing countries—especially in Asia, where the endemicity of HBV is high and perinatal infection accounts for a large proportion of HBV infections—vaccine should be given as soon after birth as possible.

WHO has recommended that HBV vaccines be included with the vaccines given in the Expanded Programme of Immunization (EPI) for countries having high or moderate endemicity of hepatitis B virus infection.[158] Unfortunately, some countries in sub-Saharan Africa have not yet included HBV vaccine in their EPI programs because of economic constraints and lack of appreciation of the sequelae of chronic HBV infections in their countries. However, substantial progress has been made in the last few years in HBV vaccine coverage in Africa.

Initially, in the United States, HBV vaccine was used selectively. However, as it proved difficult to identify and immunize persons who were at risk for this infection, the strategy has been expanded to all children, in addition to targeted immunization of persons at higher risk, such as illicit drug users, persons with multiple sex partners, and healthcare workers. An economic analysis of the routine use of HBV vaccine for the immunization of infants found this strategy to be cost-effective in the United States over a wide range of assumptions.[153] Evidence indicates that the incidence of HBV has declined in the United States in the past few years. This decline may not be due entirely to a change in vaccination policy, but rather may also reflect wider implementation of methods to prevent the sexual and parenteral transmission of other infectious diseases.

Treatment

Treatment of HBV can suppress replication of the virus but does not eradicate the infection. Thus the

Table 23-5	Approved Treatments for Hepatitis B			
Brand Name	**Generic Names**	**Manufacturer Name**	**Indication**	**Additional Information**
Baraclude	Entecavir	Bristol-Myers Squibb	Chronic hepatitis B virus infection with evidence of active viral replication	High barrier to resistance first line oral regime
Epivir-HBV	Lamivudine	GlaxoSmithKline	Chronic hepatitis B associated with hepatitis B viral replication and active liver inflammation	Can be used in patients with decompensated liver
Hepsera	Adefovir dipivoxil	Gilead Sciences	Chronic hepatitis B in patients greater than or equal to 12 years of age	Improvement in fibrosis, necroinflammatory scores, reduced HBV DNA lowered ALT, and cleared HBeAg, some renal toxicity
Intron A	Interferon apha-2b	Schering	Chronic hepatitis B in patients 1 year of age or older with compensated liver disease	Essentially replaced by pegylated interferon[160]
Pegasys	Pegylated interferon	Roche	Treatment of adult patients with HBeAg positive and HBeAg negative chronic hepatitis B who have compensated liver disease and evidence of viral replication and liver inflammation	Anti-viral and immune activation activity
Tyzeka	Telbivudine	Novartis	Chronic hepatitis B in adult patients with evidence of viral replication and either evidence of persistent elevations in serum aminotransferases (ALT or AST) or histologically active disease	none
Viread	Tenofovir	Gilead Sciences	Chronic hepatitis B in adults.	High barrier to resistance, some renal toxicity, first line oral regimen

Modified from the U.S. Food and Drug Administration (2011). For Consumers, Hepatitis Therapies. http://www.fda.gov/ForConsumers/ByAudience/ForPatientAdvocates/ucm151494.htm. Updated May 25, 2011. Accessed November 6, 2012.

goal of treatment is to suppress active infection to prevent or delay the onset or progression of liver damage (**Table 23-5**). The permanent eradication of HBV infection cannot be accomplished because of the integration of HBV DNA into the host genome and the presence of an intracellular conversion pathway that replenishes the pool of transcripts and templates (i.e., covalently closed circular HBV DNA) in the hepatocytes.[159] Because of treatment toxicity, cost, and the development of resistance to the drugs, therapy is generally targeted to patients with elevated alanine aminotransferase levels or histologic evidence of moderate or severe inflammation or fibrosis. The goal of treatment is to prevent cirrhosis, hepatic failure, or hepatocellular carcinoma.

Seven therapeutic regimens have been licensed for the treatment of chronic HBV infection: two interferon regimens and five nucleoside/nucleotide analogs.[160] (**Figure 23-11**) Controlled trials have demonstrated that liver fibrosis can be reversed with antiviral drug therapy in patients with chronic HBV infections.[156] In addition, a randomized controlled trial of lamivudine therapy in patients with significant fibrosis or cirrhosis found that the patients who were treated with lamivudine had a significantly lower incidence of HCC, cirrhosis, and mortality from liver-related causes. This improvement in outcome was sustained despite the fact that drug-resistant mutations emerged from 15% to 32% in the first year to about 70% by the fifth year of treatment.[162] This indicates

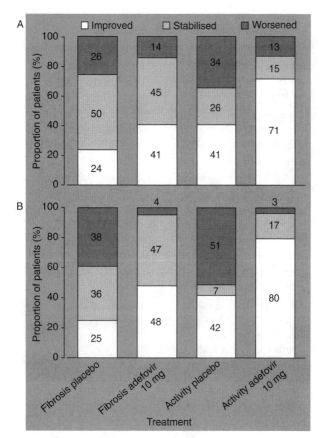

Figure 23-11 Effect of 10mg adefovir on fibrosis stage and necroinflammatory activity grade in patients with chronic hepatitis B. (A) HBeAg positive: 168 patients with baseline biopsy given adefovir, 161 given placebo, (B) HBeAg negative: 121 patients with baseline biopsy given adefovir, 57 given placebo. There was a significant difference (P < .001) both for fibrosis and necroinflammatory (activity) scores. Reprinted from The Lancet, 362, Lai Cl. et al., Viral Hepatitis B, 2089–94, Copyright 2003, with permission from Elsevier.

that the mutation reduces fitness of the virus[163,164] Currently, several drugs are available for treating patients with chronic HBV infections that are much less likely to promote resistance mutations in HBV viruses, but lamivudine remains an important medication as it can be used and often improves live function in patients with decompensated liver disease.[161]

The decision to treat a patient with chronic HBV infection should consider the activity and stage of the liver disease, the HBV replication stage, and the predicted risk of the development of cirrhosis and liver cancer in the foreseeable future. This information should be balanced against the possible adverse effects and cost of treatment, the risk of development of viral drug resistance, and the likelihood of spontaneous remission.

Treatment is clearly indicated for patients with acute liver failure, for patients with decompensated

or compensated cirrhosis, and for patients receiving immunosuppressive therapy. Treatment should be considered in patients with liver fibrosis or inflammation and cirrhosis, in those with chronic hepatitis with serologic or histologic evidence of liver inflammation or fibrosis, and in patients with HBeAg-negative hepatitis.[160]

Hepatitis B Genotypes

There are eight major genotypes of HBV (designated A to H), each of which has a different geographic distribution. Genotype A is pandemic, B and C are found in Asia, D in southern Europe and the United States, E in Africa, F in the United States, G in the United States and France, and H in Central and South America.[159] Somewhat conflicting data have been published on the association of HBV genotypes with differing natural history. Most information on the association of the HBV genotype with the natural history has come from studies in Asia, where genotype B and C predominate. As most chronic HBV infections in Asia arise from perinatal infections, the duration of infection is somewhat easier to assess. Most studies in Asia have found that compared to genotype C, genotype B infections are associated with spontaneous HBeAg seroconversion at a younger age, less active liver disease, a slower rate of progression to cirrhosis, and better responses to interferon treatment.[150–155] Most studies have reported that genotype C is more common than B in patients with hepatocellular carcinoma in Asia.[169–172]

Considerably fewer data have been published on the natural history of chronic HBV infection in genotypes other than B and C. However, studies have suggested that patients infected with genotype A compared to those with genotype D have a higher rate of clearance of HBeAg and HBV DNA and a more favorable histologic appearance on liver biopsy. A cluster of fulminant hepatitis among American Indians in Montana was associated with infection with a genotype D strain of HBV.[173,174] However, many of these patients with fulminant hepatitis had also taken acetaminophen, a potentially hepatotoxic drug, which could have worsened the HBV infection. This outbreak illustrates the difficulty in assessing the role of viral genotypes because of the possible effect of other hepatotoxins in many infected patients.

HBV-HIV Coinfection

Because HBV and HIV have similar modes of transmission, coinfection with these two viruses is very common. Whereas 40 million persons worldwide are estimated to be infected with HIV, almost 400 million persons are chronic HBV carriers.[175]

Coinfection is especially common in sub-Saharan Africa and Asia, but is also common elsewhere. In the United States, chronic HBV infections occurs nearly 10 times more frequently in HIV-positive persons than in persons who are HIV negative.[175] Active HBV infection was associated with a two-fold increased rate of HIV seroconversion among homosexual men in the Multicenter AIDS Cohort Study (MACS).[176]

Persons with anti-HBc are at increased risk of reactivation of HBsAg after they develop HIV infection.[175] Coinfection adversely affects the chronic viral illnesses associated with infection with either virus. The liver-related mortality among participants in the MACS was 17 times greater in men who were HIV positive than in those who were only HBsAg carriers.[177] Also, HBV infection can increase the toxicity of antiretroviral medications. Several studies have reported that the incidence of grade 3–4 hepatotoxicity among HBV-HIV coinfected persons was 9–10 times greater than among those persons with only HIV infection.[175]

The treatment of either HBV or HIV in persons who are coinfected is further complicated by the fact that some drugs are effective against both viruses, so that single-drug therapy for HBV may lead to resistance mutations in HIV. Drugs with these characteristics include lamivudine and tenofovir. Also, concerns have arisen that the use of adefovir as monotherapy for HBV could induce resistance to tenofovir.[167-169] For this reason, most experts recommend the use of tenofovir or entecavir along with a fully suppressive HIV regimen.

Clearly, more data are needed on the short-term and long-term effectiveness of various treatment regimens for coinfected individuals. The recommendations of an expert panel that examined the complex issues in the care of patients with HIV-HBV coinfections was published recently.[178]

DELTA HEPATITIS VIRUS

Virology

Hepatitis delta virus (HDV) was discovered by Rizzetto and colleagues in Italy in 1977.[13] The virus was originally described as a new antigen in patients with chronic HBV infection. The virus could be transmitted to chimpanzees only if they were infected with HBV.[14] It was then recognized that HDV virus relies on HBV for essential viral components and cannot cause infection in those who are not also infected with HBV. HDV infections can be established in other species, such as woodchucks, ducks, and ground squirrels, which are chronically infected with their respective hepadnaviruses. However, natural HDV infections have not been identified in these animals.

The HDV is a 35- to 38-nm enveloped particle that contains a small circular single-stranded RNA; the internal protein is the delta antigen, and the outer coat is the HBsAg. The virus appears to be related to some disease-causing viruses of plants. Only one serotype of HDV is known to occur. However, three genotypes have been described, based on nucleic acid homology of isolates from different locations: one from North America, Europe, and Asia; one from Japan; and one from tropical South America.

Clinical Features and Diagnosis

The clinical features of acute and chronic HDV infection are similar to those with other forms of hepatitis. However, persons who are coinfected with HBV and HDV from the same source may have more severe acute hepatitis than persons who have only HBV infection.[179] Anicteric hepatitis (non-jaundice hepatitis) occurs in only 20% to 30% of adult patients with HBV and HDV coinfections, but it is found in more than 50% of adults who are infected with HBV alone.[180] Also, some persons who are coinfected with HDV and HBV may have a biphasic illness.[179] Fulminant hepatitis may occur in some persons who are coinfected with these two viruses and appears to be much more common than in persons infected with only HBV.

Superinfection occurs in persons chronically infected with HBV who are exposed to HDV. Jaundice and further elevation in the liver enzymes may occur very soon after HDV superinfection. However, serologic evidence of HDV infection may not occur for 2 to 6 weeks (**Figure 23-12**). Jaundice precedes serologic evidence of infection, due to the fact that liver cells are already infected with HBV. Such patients generally develop chronic infection and are at high risk of severe chronic liver disease.[181] Some data suggest that patients who are coinfected with HDV have a higher risk of developing primary liver cancer than do those with HBV infection alone; however, the risk of liver cancer in such patients has not been clearly defined.

HDV infection can be diagnosed serologically. Enzyme immunoassay tests are available for testing for HDV antigen and antibodies in serum. Persons who are coinfected will be positive for anti-HBc and a marker of delta infection. Although delta antigen is detectable in liver tissue, it is not always observed

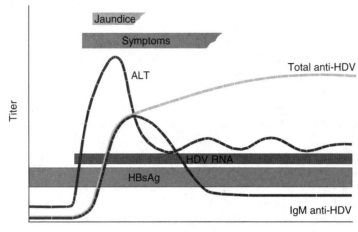

Figure 23-12 HBV-HDV superinfection. Reproduced from the Centers for Disease Control and Prevention (2009). Hepatitis D Information for Health Professionals. http://www.cdc.gov/hepatitis/HDV/index.htm. Updated November 10, 2009. Accessed November 19, 2012.

in blood. Likewise, HDVAb can be undetectable in some instances of acute self-limited infection. Antibodies to HDV appear soon after acute HDV infection, so coinfected patients may also be positive for the HDV antibody.

HDV superinfection of HBsAg carriers will be HDV antigen or antibody positive and IgM anti-HBc negative. HDV antigen is usually cleared, but HDV antibody can persist for years. Also, patients infected with HDV will have HDV RNA in their serum.

Transmission Routes

HDV transmission can occur either by parenteral exposure to blood from HDV-infected persons or by sexual contact with a carrier. Outbreaks of HDV

have been reported among injection-drug users in Los Angeles and in Worcester, Massachusetts.[182] Indirect exposure to infected blood may account for most of the cases in epidemic areas of South America.[183] Sexual transmission is much less efficient, and HDV infections are uncommon in homosexual men who are HBsAg carriers.

Worldwide Epidemiology

Infections with HDV have been reported throughout the world, but generally correspond to areas where HBV is highly endemic, with some exceptions (**Figure 23-13**). The regions with the highest prevalence of HDV are in northern Colombia, Venezuela, the Amazon basin of Brazil, Romania, Italy, and parts of Africa.[183] The prevalence of HDV

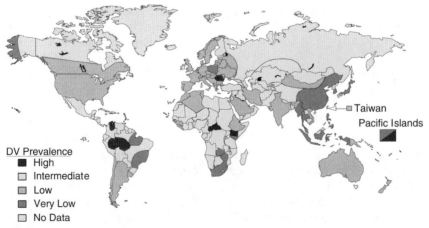

Figure 23-13 Geographic distribution of HDV. Reproduced from the Centers for Disease Control and Prevention (2009). Hepatitis D Information for Health Professionals. http://www.cdc.gov/hepatitis/HDV/index.htm. Updated November 10, 2009. Accessed November 19, 2012.

is low in the United States and Western Europe but is higher among some populations of injection drug users in these areas.[179] The prevalence of HDV is very low in China and Southeast Asia, despite the high level of HBV endemicity in this region.

Prevention

Methods for the control and prevention of HDV infection are the same as those used to prevent hepatitis B virus infection. Successful immunization with HBV vaccine of persons at risk for HBV would also prevent HDV. In addition, the risk of HDV superinfection should be a major incentive for injection-drug users who are HBsAg carriers to avoid further high-risk exposures. All HBsAg carriers should be counseled to avoid parenteral or sexual exposure to possible HBV-HDV carriers.

HEPATITIS C VIRUS

Virology

HCV is a spherical, enveloped, RNA virus approximately 50 nm in diameter that contains a positive-sense, single-stranded genome approximately 9.7 kb (**Figure 23-14**) in length.[184,185] HCV is a member of the family Flaviviridae, classified within its own *Hepacivirus* genus. The RNA contains a single large (approximately 3000 bp) open reading frame (ORF) flanked by highly conserved 5′ and 3′ untranslated

regions.[186] The approximately 9.0-kb ORF encodes a polyprotein that is cotranslationally processed into at least 10 proteins. These include, from the amino terminus, structural proteins (the viral nucleocapsid or "core" protein, the envelope proteins E1 and E2, and a short, possibly transmembrane protein, p7 or NS2A), and six nonstructural proteins that are involved in replication of the viral RNA (Figure 23-14).

The liver is presumed to be the primary source of virus present in blood, as HCV-specific antigens and both negative- and positive-strand HCV RNA have been identified within hepatocytes.[184,187,188] Some data suggest that the virus may also replicate within peripheral mononuclear cells of lymphoid or perhaps bone marrow origin.[189,190] However, when assays are done with strand-specific reverse transcriptase, Landord et al. showed that extra hepatic replication is insufficient to explain HCV RNA detected in blood.[191] Mathematical models of viral kinetics suggest that virions have a half-life of approximately 2.5 hours in the bloodstream and that as many as 10^{12} virions are produced each day in a chronically infected human.[192] This rate exceeds comparable estimates of the production of HIV by more than an order of magnitude. The high level of virus turnover, coupled with the absence of proofreading by the NS5B RNA polymerase, results in relatively rapid accumulation of mutations within the viral genome. Multiple HCV variants can be recovered from the plasma and liver

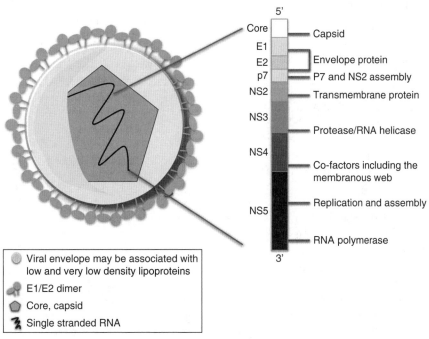

Figure 23-14 Hepatitis C Virus Structure. Data from Popescu. Hepatitis C Virus Assembly Imaging. Viruses 2011 Nov; 2(11):2238–2254.

of an infected individual at any time. Thus, like many RNA viruses, HCV exists in each infected person as a quasi-species, or "swarm" of closely related but distinct genetic sequences.[193,194] For example, in the blood of a recently infected individual, as many as 85% of cDNA clones recovered from viral RNAs may represent unique genetic variants.[195]

HCV infections are often persistent, indicating that the virus has evolved mechanisms to escape immune surveillance. Because of limitations in experimental models and the infrequent recognition of natural acute infection, these mechanisms are poorly understood. It has been proposed that the quasi-species nature of the infection is responsible for its persistence, and individuals with a more complex infection were more likely to have persistent infection in one study.[196] Nevertheless, because single clone infections of chimpanzees can persist, viral complexity is clearly not necessary and could be a result of persistence, rather than the cause of it.[197] One paradox is that HCV persistence occurs despite a broad humoral and cellular immune response. It has been suggested that, HCV sequence variation may contribute to viral persistence. Mutations may alter the amino acid sequences of critical epitopes, leading to the escape of a new quasi-species variant from a previously suppressive immune response, either cellular or humoral.[198-200] Viral escape from a cytotoxic lymphocyte clone has been reported in a persistently infected chimpanzee and was shown to correlate with a single NS3 amino acid substitution.[200]

Biology of Transmission

HCV transmission requires that infectious virions contact susceptible cells that sustain replication. It is difficult to ascertain which body fluids contain infectious hepatitis C virions. Using sensitive techniques, HCV RNA can be detected in blood (including serum and plasma), saliva, tears, seminal fluid, ascitic fluid, and cerebrospinal fluid.[201-205] HCV RNA-containing blood is infectious when administered intravenously—for example, by transfusion or experimental inoculation of chimpanzees. In addition, one chimpanzee was infected by intravenous inoculation of saliva.[206] Very little information regarding the potential infectivity of other body fluids has been published, both because the experiments have not been performed and because accidental percutaneous exposures to nonblood body fluids are rare.

The second requirement for transmission is contact of infectious virions with a susceptible cell. HCV replication occurs in the hepatocyte and possibly elsewhere. Multiple HCV coreceptors have been identified that appear to in part explain some

of the tissue (and host) tropism.[207,208] Seminal fluid may contain HCV RNA, but sexual transmission is uncommon. Whether this discrepancy is due to a paucity of infectious virions in seminal fluid or insufficient numbers of susceptible cells in the genital mucosa is unknown.

HCV diversity can be exploited for epidemiologic research. The nucleotide sequence corresponding to the HCV envelope and some nonstructural proteins is highly variable, and at least six distinct HCV genotypes have been described.[209,210] The genetic heterogeneity of HCV strains is sufficiently high that detection of the same or nearly identical nucleotide sequences in two individuals represents strong evidence for a common source of infection. These comparisons have been used to demonstrate HCV transmission between sexual partners, within families, among patients, and from healthcare workers to patients.[211-214] HCV genotype/subtype classification also may be used epidemiologically but is less specific than nucleotide sequence analysis.

HCV Genotypes

Based on sequence analysis, at least 6 genotypes of HCV have been defined, numbered 1–6. Knowledge of the genotype or serotype is helpful for prediction of a response to antiviral therapy and the choice and duration of therapy. Viral clearance rates after treatment with the combination of pegylated interferon and ribavirin are in the range of 70% to 80% for genotypes 2 and 3, but are only approximately 48% for genotypes 1, 4, 5, and 6 (**Figure 23-15**).[215,216] As discussed later in this section, treatment of patients with genotype 1 HCV infection with protease inhibitors in addition to peginterferon and ribavirin has

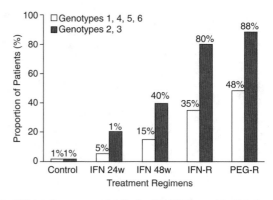

Note: IFN, interferon; w, weeks, R, ribavirin; PEG, pegylated interferon.

Figure 23-15 Viral clearance rates after treatment with the combination of pegylated interferon and ribavirin are about 70–80% for genotypes 2 and 3 but only about 48% for genotypes 1, 4, 5, and 6. Reprinted from The Lancet, 362, Poynard T et al., Viral Hepatitis C, 2095–2010, Copyright 2003, with permission from Elsevier.

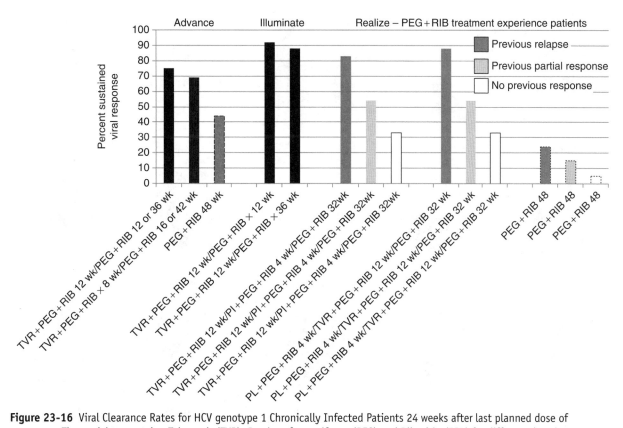

Figure 23-16 Viral Clearance Rates for HCV genotype 1 Chronically Infected Patients 24 weeks after last planned dose of treatment. Three trials comparing Telaprevir (TVR), Peg interferon alfa-2a (PEG) and Ribavirin (RIB) for different durations. (Outlined bars are for those who did not receive any TVR.) Data from Perry, C. Telaprevir: A review of its use in the management of Genotype 1 Chronic Hepatitis. *AIDS Drug Evaluation*. 2012 72(5) 619–641.

improved response rates to near the same level as with genotypes 2 and 3 (**Figure 23-16**). The severity of the disease, as measured by the fibrosis stage, is not related to the genotype. However, genotype 3 is associated with higher rates of hepatic steatosis and higher ALT levels.[216]

The genotypes are distributed geographically (**Figure 23-17**). Genotypes 1, 2, and 3 account for approximately 90% of infections in the United States and are the most common sources of HCV infection in Europe. Genotype 4 accounts for nearly all of the HCV infections in Egypt.[217] In Asia, genotypes 1, 3, and 6 each account for approximately one-third of HCV infections.[218] Genotype 5 is focused in Madagascar, South Africa, and France.[217] Viral recombination has been reported among injection-drug users in St. Petersburg, Russia, but appears to be very uncommon with HCV, in contrast to HIV infection.[219]

Clinical Features and Diagnosis

Acute HCV infection is usually unnoticed. Fewer than one-fifth of persons will have jaundice or sufficient symptoms to seek medical care. When symptoms do occur, they are indistinguishable from those caused by other hepatitis viruses. After the acute infection, 60% to 85% of persons will have persistent viremia, and more than half will demonstrate elevated liver enzyme levels.[220-223] HCV infection may persist over 10 to 50 years without symptoms or with symptoms, such as malaise, that are too general to be attributed to HCV infection.

Approximately 2% to 25% of individuals with persistent HCV infection will develop life-threatening cirrhosis and/or liver cancer.[223-226] Cirrhosis can cause liver failure, which manifests as esophageal varices, ascites, hypoprothrombinemia, and hepatic encephalopathy. HCV infection is also associated with vasculitis, essential mixed cryoglobulinemia,[227,228] membranoproliferative glomerulonephritis,[228,229] and sporadic porphyria cutanea.[230,231] Approximately 10,000 persons die of HCV infection each year in the United States.[232]

The laboratory diagnosis of HCV infection is based principally on detection by enzyme immunoassay of antibodies to recombinant HCV peptides.[233-235] The sensitivity of the latest, third-generation, HCV

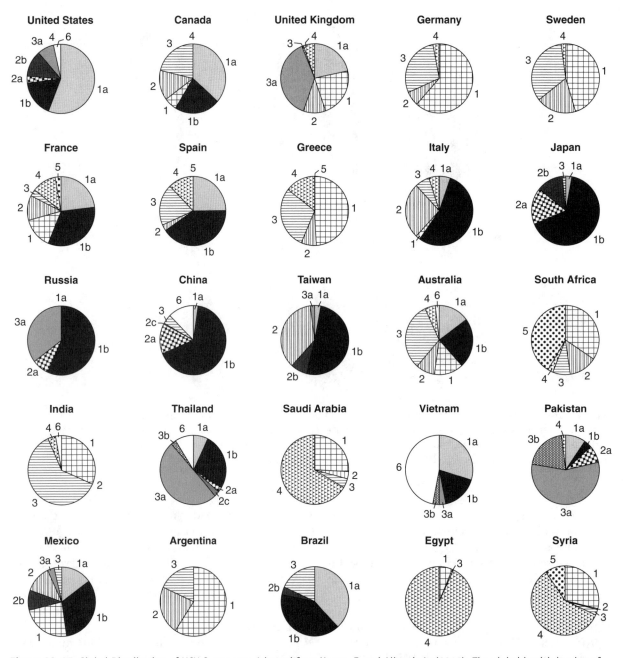

Figure 23-17 Global Distribution of HCV Genotypes. Adapted from Negro, F. and Alberti, A. (2011). The global health burden of hepatitis C virus infection. *Liver International,* 31:1–3.

antibody assay is estimated to be 97%, and it can detect HCV antibody within 6 to 8 weeks of exposure.[236,237] These assays are measures of HCV infection, not immunity. Assays for IgM HCV antibodies are not clinically useful. The FDA has licensed the recombinant immunoblot assay (RIBA; Ortho Diagnostic Systems, Raritan, New Jersey) as a supplemental test to the enzyme immunoassay.[238,239] The RIBA identifies the specific antigens to which antibodies are reacting in the EIA and may be positive (2 or more antigens), indeterminate (1 antigen), or negative. The RIBA assay can be used to confirm the specificity of a positive

EIA test. The specificity of a positive EIA can also be assessed by considering the magnitude of the optical density of the sample relative to a control, the so-called signal-to-cutoff ratio. Results reported above the signal-to-cutoff ratio for a given lab usually will also give a positive result on RIBA.[240,241]

HCV RNA can be detected in plasma and serum by reverse-transcription PCR, real-time PCR, and other nucleic acid amplification and detection systems.[240,242,245] Detection of HCV RNA indicates ongoing infection, whereas clearance of serum HCV RNA, either spontaneously or following treatment, correlates with ALT normalization and improvement in liver histology.[223,241] Most newer HCV RNA assays provide information on both the presence and the quantity of HCV RNA in serum or plasma. HCV quantification is important for assessment of treatment outcomes. Thus HCV infection is usually diagnosed by detection of HCV antibody by enzyme immunoassay, followed detection of HCV RNA because that algorithm provides information about exposure, indicates whether infection is ongoing or resolved, and serves as a baseline for assessment of treatment response.

Transmission Routes

Transfusion of Blood Products

Transfusion of blood or organs positive for HCV RNA almost always results in transmission.[241,246–249] Prior to screening blood donations for HCV antibodies and surrogate markers, approximately 17% of HCV infections in the United States were caused by transfusion.[259] After routine screening was implemented, the risk of transfusion transmission of HCV dropped significantly.[251,252] In 1987, routine screening of blood donors for elevations in alanine aminotransferase (ALT—a liver enzyme) and anti-HBc were instituted primarily to decrease the risk of transmitting HCV. It is estimated that these surrogate markers for HCV infection reduced the risk of transfusion transmission of HCV by approximately 50%.[251]

In May 1990, the first-generation two-antigen serologic test for HCV was licensed and used to screen all blood donors in the United States. The use of this specific HCV screening test further reduced the risk of the transmission of HCV by blood products.

The probable rate of transmission of viral infections by transfusion has been estimated by calculating the number of donors who were in the seronegative window period at the time of donation in 1991–1993 by modeling data from seroconverters among repeat donors at five large Red Cross blood banks. This study estimated that approximately 1 in 63,000 donors who were HBV infected and 1 in 103,000 who were HCV infected were in the seronegative window period at the time of their donation.[253]

In 1999, transfusion transmission was reduced further because blood donations in the United States were tested for HCV (and HIV) RNA in a mini-pool format (i.e., pools of 16 or 24 samples) with the use of one of two nucleic acid-amplification tests.[254] Both assays are highly specific and sensitive, with 50% detection limits of 14 copies of HCV per milliliter.[213] Among 39,721,404 donors screened between March 1999 and April 1, 2002, 170 (4.3 per million) were

HCV RNA positive and 105 (2.9 per million) of these persons donated blood that was otherwise "transfusible" (i.e., had no other infectious markers).[254] Today, the rate of transfusion-transmitted HCV is extremely low in both the United States and Europe, where RNA amplification is used for donor screening, and the prevalence of HCV infections in the donor population is low in general because of exclusion of high-risk donors (i.e., injection-drug users). Among 6,658,537 blood donations at American Red Cross collection sites in 2008, only 1276 (0.036%) were positive for markers of HCV infection, a rate of 1 per 2769 donations[246]; however, the residual risk after screening donors for antibodies and HCV RNA is less than 1 per million.[255] In contrast, in many developing countries, where screening is not done or utilizes only EIA, transfusion-transmitted HCV infections are much more common. The prevalence of HCV infection in the general population of many developing countries is higher than in the United States and Western Europe due to illicit drug use and more frequent exposures to potentially contaminated injections.

HCV also has been transmitted by intravenous administration of contaminated blood products, including immunoglobulin (IG) and clotting factors, as illustrated in several large outbreaks.[256–260] Current IG viral inactivation procedures and recombinant clotting factor use have further decreased the risk of transmission by these products.

Needle-stick and Nosocomial Transmission

HCV can be transmitted by percutaneous contaminated needle-sticks, as occurs among illicit-injection-drug users and inadvertently in the practice of medicine. With a single needle-stick exposure, the risk of HCV transmission to a susceptible person is approximately 1% to 3%, intermediate between the risk for transmission of HBV (30%) and HIV (0.3%). Because of multiple needle-stick exposures, 50% to 95% of persons acknowledging a history of illicit drug use have HCV infection.[261–266] Injection-drug users may acquire HCV infection by sharing contaminated needles and drug-use equipment, sometimes among groups of persons, such as in "shooting galleries." New initiates into drug use are at the highest risk for HCV infection because they are susceptible and they are likely to be sharing injecting equipment and using it after more experienced users.[267] HCV infection that occurs in the context of drug use but without acknowledged injection use may be due to other blood exposures (such as sharing straws for intranasal ingestion of cocaine).[268] However, unacknowledged injection drug use is difficult to exclude, and the extent to which HCV transmission can occur through intranasal cocaine use remains unclear.

HCV transmission occurs in 1% to 3% of healthcare workers who experience needle-stick exposures to HCV-infected patients.[268–271] Whereas hollow-bore needle-stick exposures (which can contain a higher volume of body fluids than solid needles) account for most transmission from patients to healthcare workers, HCV infection has also been reported from blood splashed on the conjunctiva and a solid-bore needle-stick.[272] Nonetheless, the prevalence of HCV infection among dental and medical healthcare workers is similar to that among the general population, demonstrating that chronic infection is uncommon after such exposures.[273–281]

Other forms of bloodborne nosocomial transmission also occur. Patient-to-patient HCV transmission has been documented, for example. In one report, two patients were noted to have acquired HCV infection 8 to 10 weeks after a colonoscopic procedure, which was performed with the same colonoscope as had been used hours earlier on an HCV-infected patient.[211] HCV isolates from all three patients had high nucleotide identity in a variable HCV genomic segment, essentially proving a common source of infection. Nosocomial HCV transmission also has been suggested by identification of clusters of non-transfused patients with similar HCV nucleotide sequences. In one Swedish hematology ward, five clusters of identical or closely related viruses were found. All patients in each cluster had overlapping hospitalizations but not common sources of blood.[214] Similarly, evidence of patient-to-patient HCV transmission has been found in several dialysis centers.[281–283]

Nosocomial transmission of HCV is uncommon and sporadic in developed countries, where recent receipt or provision of health care is not commonly reported by patients with new HCV infections.[285] However, in developed countries, traditional and nontraditional medical practices are probably the leading source of HCV transmission (as discussed in the "Worldwide Epidemiology" section). Breaks in infection control practices have been detected in some instances of nosocomial HCV transmission and are impossible to exclude in others. Strict adherence to infection control guidelines must be rigorously maintained, especially when mucosal barriers are frequently broken, such as in dialysis units. For example, in one report from Spain, 67% of acute HCV infections were linked to receipt of medical care.[286] WHO estimates that unsafe injections continue to cause 2.3 to 4.7 million new HCV infections each year.[287]

HCV has also been transmitted from healthcare providers to patients, although such cases remain rare. In one instance, HCV infection was detected in six patients after cardiac surgery.[212] Blood donors for these patients were HCV negative. Five of six patients had a genetically similar, unusual HCV strain that was later found in the surgeon as well. No infection control breaches were identified. However, the surgeon did have percutaneous injuries when tying wires to close the sternum.

Miscellaneous Percutaneous Exposures

HCV can be transmitted by other unusual percutaneous exposures. Tattooing has been associated with HCV infection.[289,290] A human bite, acupuncture, and scarification rituals have also been associated with HCV infection.[291]

Sexual Transmission

HCV is probably infrequently transmitted by sexual intercourse. Biologic plausibility exists for sexual transmission, as evidenced by detection of HCV RNA in semen and saliva.[201–204] However, as mentioned earlier, we do not know whether these fluids contain infectious virions in sufficient quantity to transmit infection or whether the mucosal barrier is protective. Evidence for sexual transmission of HCV is indirect. High rates of HCV infection have been found in persons with multiple sexual partners and commercial sex workers,[213,292–295] and acute HCV infection has been reported in instances where sexual, but not other exposures, are recognized.[287,298] In studies of families of HCV-infected patients, sexual partners are generally the only contacts at increased infection risk—a risk that increases with the duration of the relationship.[299–302,304] High nucleotide identity is often found in the HCV strains of the sexual partners.[213,300–302] Although sexual transmission could explain these findings, it is almost impossible to exclude other common exposures, such as sharing razors, other subtle percutaneous exposures, or unacknowledged drug use.

The importance of the "indirect" nature of the evidence is underscored by studies that found sexual transmission in heterosexual couples to be rare. Studies of long-term sexual partners of HCV-infected hemophiliacs and transfusion recipients generally show little or no incidence of HCV transmission, even if there had been frequent unprotected sexual intercourse.[305–308] In one study, 895 monogamous sexual partners of persons with chronic hepatitis C were followed for more than 8000 person-years, and there were no instances of sexual HCV transmission, despite unprotected intercourse occurring an average of 1.8 times per week.[309]

In contrast, HCV infection occurs in persons acknowledging high-risk sexual practices, and multiple outbreaks have occurred among HIV-infected men who have sex with men (MSM).[310–312] HCV outbreaks among MSM have been reported from multiple countries and are associated with sexual practices that increase the risk of exposure to body fluids. In recent years, improvements in HIV treatment have lowered the perceived risk of sexual contact without condoms. Sexual partners have also sought to lower their risk of HIV infection by having sex only with partners of the same HIV status—a practice known as sero-sorting. These practices may or may not lower an individual's risk of HIV, but sexual contact without a condom certainly increases the risk of HCV transmission.

It is difficult to reconcile all of the apparent contradictions in the data regarding sexual transmission of HCV. Mucosal tears and consequent blood exchange or HIV infection of donor and/or recipient might account for the greater incidence in MSM. It is also possible that, as with HIV, the risk of sexual HCV transmission is greater during the acute phase of infection, when viremia peaks and prior to formation of neutralizing antibodies. That hypothesis would explain why high rates of incident sexual transmission are seen in settings in which exposures to newly infected persons are most likely, compared to the rare/nonexistent risk observed in long-term stable partnerships of chronically infected persons.

Perinatal Transmission

HCV infection occurs in 2% to 8% of infants born to HCV-infected mothers.[315–321] Because of passive transfer of maternal HCV antibody, infant HCV infection must be diagnosed through detection in infant serum of HCV RNA or HCV antibody after the child has reached 18 months of age. HIV coinfection has been associated with more frequent transmission of HCV from mother to infant in some studies.[318–322] Higher maternal HCV viral load also has been associated with transmission of HCV from mother to infant.[327,323–326] The effect of maternal HIV on perinatal HCV transmission may occur through increased HCV viral load.[327–330] HCV RNA has been detected in breastmilk,[317,331,332] but the risk of transmission does not appear to be high in breastfeeding infants.[333]

Two large prospective studies of the perinatal transmission of HCV have been reported. The rates of perinatal transmission in these studies varied from 4.7% in 190 infants born to infected mothers in a U.S. study to 6.2% in 1479 infants in a collaborator European study.[334,335] Both studies found an increased rate of transmission among women who were coinfected with HIV, had prolonged labor (i.e., more than 6 hours), or had internal fetal monitoring.

Worldwide Epidemiology

It is estimated that more than 170 million persons are infected with HCV worldwide.[336] Through August 1997, 130 countries had reported HCV prevalence rates to the WHO or in the literature. HCV infection was found in all but three countries, and it is difficult to imagine that infection would not be found there with further investigation. In developed nations, HCV prevalence rates are less than 3%; among volunteer blood donors, however, they are less than 1% (Figure 23-17 and **Figure 23-18**).

Several highly endemic regions for HCV have been identified. In most of these countries, HCV

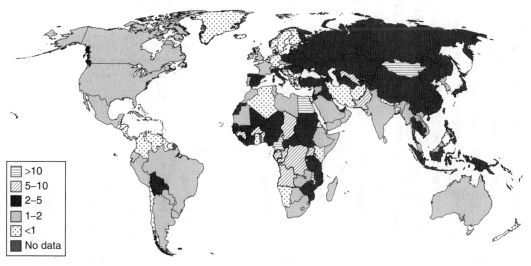

Figure 23-18 Global prevalence of HCV. Reproduced from Lavanchy, D (2011). Evolving Epidemiology of Hepatitis C Virus. *Clinical Microbiology and Infection* 17:107–115.

infection is prevalent among persons older than 40 years of age but uncommon in those younger than 20 years of age.[337–340] This cohort effect suggests a time-restricted exposure that, in many instances, appears to have been receipt of a medical procedure. In Egypt, HCV prevalence rates ranging from 10% to 30% have been reported.[341–345] A national campaign to treat schistosomiasis infections was responsible for a major epidemic of HCV infections. Until the 1970s, parenteral anti-schistosomiasis therapies were administered to entire villages, and injection equipment was frequently not sterilized between injections. Similarly, in several areas in Italy and Japan, a high HCV prevalence among older persons was linked to contaminated injections.[337,338,346,347] In the isolated Arahiro region of Japan, 45% of individuals older than 41 years of age had HCV infection, whereas in another area the same-age prevalence was 2%.[348] Folk remedies, such as acupuncture and cutting of skin with nonsterilized knives, were identified as likely transmission modes for the infection. Percutaneous folk practices have occurred for thousands of years and were surely important in the worldwide dissemination of HCV.

High rates of HCV infection also have been reported in urban areas of developed countries. In Baltimore, Maryland, HCV infection was found in 18% of patients attending an inner-city emergency department and 15% attending a nearby clinic for sexually transmitted diseases.[293,349] Injection-drug use—not medical procedures—was chiefly responsible for transmission in this setting.

The epidemiology of HCV infection has been carefully studied in several developed nations, including the United States and France. In the United States, the yearly incidence of HCV infection has declined since the 1980s (**Figure 23-19**).[232,350] At least two-thirds of community-acquired HCV infections are related to injection-drug use. Injection-drug use in the 6 months prior to infection is acknowledged by approximately 38% of subjects.[285,351] However, non-injection-drug use and other indicators of injection use are acknowledged by another 44%. Sexual or household exposure to HCV is detected in approximately 10% of individuals with acute HCV infection, whereas transfusions, occupational exposures, and other factors are infrequently (less than 4%) identified as sources of infection.

The epidemiology and overall burden of HCV infection in the United States has been further characterized using the Third National Health and Nutrition Examination (NHANES) data.[352] A total of 23,527 persons, who were representative of the general population of the United States, were

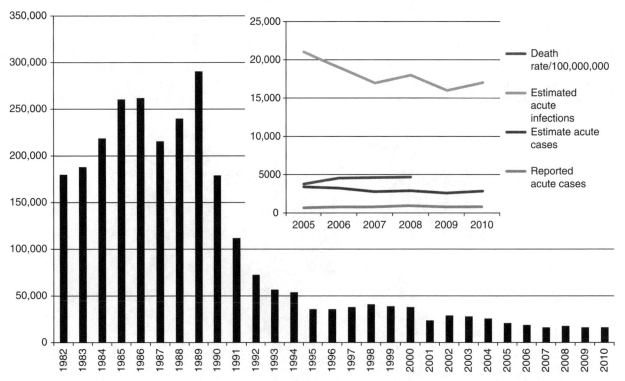

Figure 23-19 United States HCV incidence has declined from 1982 to 2010. Inset details 2005–2010 data with HCV mortality rate. Data from the Centers for Disease Control and Prevention (2011). Viral Hepatitis Statistics & Surveillance. http://www.cdc.gov/hepatitis/ Statistics/. Last Updated June 22, 2012. Accessed November 6, 2012.

tested for HCV infection. Antibodies to HCV were detected in 1.8%, which can be extrapolated to suggest almost 4 million Americans have hepatitis C. Active infection (HCV RNA) was detected in 74% of those who were HCV antibody (RNA) positive, suggesting that 2.7 million persons in the United States had ongoing infection. Illegal drug use and high-risk sexual exposures were associated with HCV infection, as were low socioeconomic indices, low levels of education, and poverty. This large-scale representative sampling study improved our understanding of the burden and distribution of infection, but because a history of the injection of illicit drugs was not included in the NHANES interview, it is difficult to estimate the contribution of current or remote drug-injection practice to the HCV prevalence in this sample. Also, because the NHANES survey included only persons with a stable residence, and excluded the homeless and imprisoned populations, the measured prevalence of HCV likely underestimated the true rate.[353]

A survey of HCV prevalence was repeated in the 1999–2002 NHANES population.[354] In that study, the HCV prevalence was 1.6% and the peak prevalence of HCV was in persons 40–49 years of age. Significant risk factors for HCV included the following: (1) any history of injection-drug use, (2) a blood transfusion prior to 1992, and (3) an elevated ALT level. Taken together, these three risk factors identified 85.1% of HCV-infected persons.

Trends in the disease burden of HCV parallel the epidemiology. In the United States, HCV infection causes 8000 to 10,000 deaths per year, and is the leading cause of liver failure leading to transplantation.[355,356] However, because HCV-related morbidity and mortality generally take decades to become manifest, HCV-related liver morbidity and mortality are expected to rise in the United States in the coming decade, reflecting aging of the large cohort born from 1945 to 1964 who were infected 20 to 30 years ago. Using multistate disease models, one group recently estimated that HCV-related liver failure and cancer will continue to increase until 2020–2023 if infected persons do not receive widespread treatment.[357] Liver-related mortality was predicted to rise from 146,667 cases in 2000–2009 to 254,550 cases in 2010–2019 and again to 283,378 cases in 2020–2029. WHO is trying to obtain reliable global estimates of prevalence and disease burden, but they are not currently available.

Factors Affecting HCV Natural History

Although the viral genotype and level of viral RNA are not useful as predictors of the rate of progression of HCV to severe liver disease, several host characteristics are important in this regard. In one investigation, the progression of fibrosis in liver biopsies was evaluated among 2235 HCV-infected patients in France.[358] In this study, the stage of fibrosis was graded using a 5-point scale, the METAVIR scale, with 0 being normal and 4 being cirrhosis. The factors associated with more rapid progression were age of infection older than 40 years, daily alcohol consumption of 50 grams or more, and male sex. These risk factors for more rapid progression after infection have been confirmed in other populations.[217,359]

In addition, HCV-infected patients with HIV infection and severe immunosuppression (i.e., CD4 T-cell counts < 200 cells/μL) progress more rapidly than HIV-uninfected subjects, after adjusting for age, sex, and alcohol consumption.[350,358–360] Also, patients with a high body mass index and diabetes mellitus appear to experience more rapid progress of their HCV infection.[177]

HCV-Related Hepatocellular Carcinoma

Despite the reduced incidence of HCV infections in the last several years, the burden of chronic disease from previous infections is increasing in the United States. The incidence of mortality from HCC increased by 41% in 1991–1995 compared to 1976–1980.[130] Also, hospitalizations for liver cancer increased by 46% in Veterans Administration hospitals between 1983 and 1997. Analysis of hospitalizations for primary liver cancer among veterans found a threefold increase in the age-adjusted rates associated with hepatitis C virus infection in the 1990s, whereas the rates for liver cancer associated with hepatitis B virus infection and alcoholic cirrhosis remained relatively stable.[361] Modeling the national HCV seroprevalence data from the NHANES study suggested that the number of persons with chronic HCV infection for 30 or more years, who are at risk for liver cancer or cirrhosis, will continue to increase until 2020.[362]

Treatment

HCV infection can be eliminated with treatment, an outcome called a sustained virologic response (SVR) or cure. However, relapses can occur after the completion of a course of antiviral therapy. The responses to therapy of HCV infection are classified as either sustained virological response (SVR), meaning clearance of HCV RNA that persists for 24 weeks after cessation of treatment (which equates to a cure of the HCV infection); rapid virologic response (RVR), meaning HCV RNA undetectable after 4 weeks; early virological response (EVR), meaning HCV undetectable after 12 weeks; partial response, meaning a more than 2 log decrease after 24 weeks; and nonresponse, meaning a less than 2 log decrease after 24 weeks of treatment. The degree and rapidity of the response to treatment serve as useful clinical markers for the eventual cure with a full course (24–48 weeks) of therapy.

Since 1991, when interferon-alfa was first licensed for use to treat HCV infection, slow improvements in HCV treatments have occurred, such that SVR rates have increased from less than 10% in the early 1990s to 70% in 2011 with the approval of HCV protease inhibitors.[363–366] SVR rates vary substantially according to factors such as the viral genotype, HCV viral load, age, weight, HIV status, race/ethnicity, and gender. A less frequent sustained virological response to treatment of HCV among African Americans and Hispanics has been consistently observed.[363,364] Because these racial/ethnic groups responded less well than Caucasians when they were infected from a common source, investigators suspected that host genetic factors may be involved in these differences.

Three groups reported the results of genome-wide association studies (GWAS) studies comparing the frequency of single-nucleotide polymorphisms (SNPs) between responders and nonresponders to therapy.[367–369] Each of these studies reported that nucleotide sequences near the IL-28-B gene were associated with responses to therapy. Persons who responded were more likely to be homozygous for cytidine (CC), whereas nonresponders were more likely to be heterozygous or homozygous for thymidine (CT or TT). In addition, the nucleotide sequence near *IL28B*, the gene for lambda interferon-3, has a marked impact on the likelihood of responding to interferon-alfa and ribavirin-based HCV treatment.[367] The mechanism of this association is not known, but it is interesting that the same association has been detected in cases involving spontaneous resolution of HCV infection.[370] Interestingly, these genetic findings also explain some of the ethnic differences in HCV outcomes, as the geographic distribution of allele frequencies parallels the outcome likelihood, which were found to be most favorable in Asia and least favorable in Africa.

From 2002 to 2011, the standard of care for treatment of chronic HCV infection was administration of peginterferon-alfa and ribavirin. Although chronic HCV infections could be cured in approximately half of all patients with 12 months of interferon and ribavirin therapy, many patients did not accept or complete a course of treatment because of drug toxicity and the need for frequent (i.e., weekly) injections. In 2011, two HCV protease inhibitors were approved for treatment of genotype 1 HCV infection.[365,366] These new drugs can reduce the duration of treatment to 6 months or less in some patients, while increasing the overall cure rate to approximately 70%. However, the recently licensed protease inhibitors must be used in combination with interferon and ribavirin because when they are used alone drug-resistant strains of the virus emerge rapidly.

Additional medications are under development, including combinations that would allow persons to be cured without administration of interferon-alfa. It is possible that development of more effective and better-tolerated medications will result in expanded testing and treatment of chronic hepatitis C worldwide, as has occurred with HIV. However, current estimates of the rates of HCV testing and treatment, even in economically developed countries, are extremely low.[371,372]

Prevention

HCV prevention is chiefly accomplished through efforts to prevent exposure. There are no vaccines available to prevent HCV infection. Exploratory vaccine development efforts are ongoing, but the complexity of the infection and poor understanding of the immune response have complicated this work. Postexposure administration of immunoglobulin to prevent HCV infection is not currently recommended because little evidence supports its effectiveness in the past, and there is even more reason to doubt the effectiveness of the newer products that do not contain HCV antibody.[232] Nevertheless, the incidence of HCV infection has declined in the United States, largely because of the practice of screening blood donations for HCV antibody and surrogate markers. In some (but not all) studies, use of needle exchange programs has also been associated with reductions in HCV incidence.[373,374]

In Baltimore, HCV incidence has declined among injection-drug users (IDUs) in recent years, albeit not as much as the incidence of HIV.[375] This difference underscores the need for more intensive efforts among IDUs to prevent HCV, which is more transmissible than HIV by percutaneous exposures. Because most HCV infections in developed nations are due to illicit-injection-drug use, expanded efforts to treat and prevent drug dependence are urgently needed as well as expansion of HCV treatment among infected drug users.[376] In developing nations, it is urgent to begin programs to alter attitudes regarding blood exposures and to improve the safety of necessary percutaneous practices.

HEPATITIS E VIRUS

Virology

Hepatitis E virus (HEV) is a single-stranded, positive sense RNA virus that is approximately 32 nm in diameter.[375-377] The virus is relatively sensitive to inactivation, being inactivated by cesium chloride, freeze–thawing, and pelleting. Like HAV, HEV lacks an envelope, making it stable in bile and, therefore, transmissible by ingestion of fecally-contaminated water. HEV is resistant to the pH extremes of the gastrointestinal tract, although it is assumed that water chlorination decreases infectivity. Hepatitis E virus was first visualized by Balayan. He investigated an epidemic in Asia in 1980 and purposely ingested infectious stool. Subsequently he was able to visualize viral particles in his own stool using electron microscopy.[401]

The HEV genome is approximately 7.2 kb in length and consists of three open reading frames (ORFs). Recombinant antigens synthesized from the second and third ORFs are used in diagnostic assays. HEV isolates may have as little as 75%

homology, and four major genotypes have been identified, within one serotype (**Figure 23-20**). Isolates collected in the Western Hemisphere are especially heterogeneous, but phylogenetically cluster with a highly related virus from swine.[366] Genotypes 1 and 2 have a human reservoir and are transmitted as a waterborne infection from person to person during periods of monsoon rains and in contaminated water supplies, often in very large epidemics, in countries in Southeast Asia. Epidemics of hepatitis from genotype 1 HEV have also been reported among refugee populations in Africa.[379-380] Genotypes 3 and 4 have a zoonotic reservoir, especially in pigs and are acquired by humans as an endemic foodborne or contact infection throughout the world.[381] HEV shares certain morphologic and biophysical properties with caliciviruses, yet its genomic organization is notably different from other members of this family.[375] Hepatitis E virus shows highest, but limited, amino acid similarity in its replicative enzymes with the rubella virus and alphaviruses of the family Togaviridae and with the plant Furovirus. However, recently, HEV has been classified as a hepevirus in the family Hepeviridae.

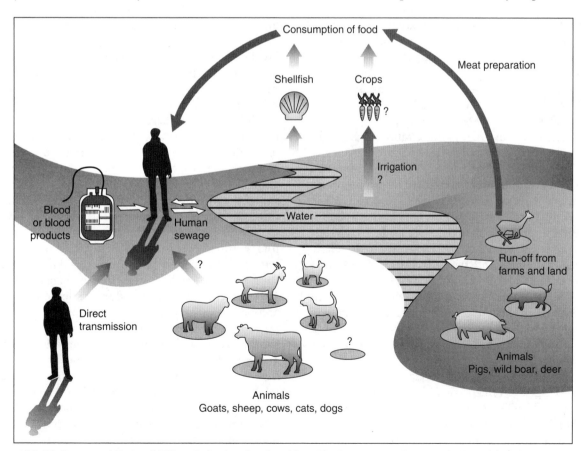

Figure 23-20 Source and Route of HEV1-4 Infection. Reprinted from The Lancet, 379, Kamar et al., Hepatitis E, 2477–88, Copyright 2012, with permission from Elsevier.

Although HEV does not proliferate well in cell culture, animal models have been developed. Most experiments have been conducted in nonhuman primate species using the cynomolgus macaque, *Macaca fascicularis*, or swine.[382] Laboratory infections of chimpanzees, tamarins, owl monkeys, rhesus monkeys, and other animals have also been reported.[383,384] Pigs are commonly infected with genotypes 3 and 4 but are resistant to infection with genotypes 1 and 2.[375]

Clinical Features and Diagnosis

Acute HEV infection is impossible to distinguish from other hepatitis virus infections. As with HAV infection, the disease is usually self-limited, and most patients recover completely without complications or sequelae. The typical incubation period ranges from 15 to 60 days (mean = 40 days) from the time of exposure.[385] The liver is the main site of replication. Although the mortality during acute HEV infection is generally low in healthy persons, severe and often fatal disease is common among women infected during pregnancy in developing countries.[386-388] Mortality rates ranging from 15% to 30% have been reported among pregnant women infected during several outbreaks.[379,380,386-388] Recently, chronic hepatitis due to HEV infection has been observed among transplant recipients and other immunocompromised patients.[379] Genotypes 1 and 2 have a human reservoir and are transmitted by contaminated water in countries in Asia and Africa, often involving thousands of cases during periods of contaminated water supplies in India, Pakistan, and Nepal. During a 1993–1994 Pakistan HEV outbreak, attack rates of fulminant icteric hepatitis increased by trimester of pregnancy.[387]

As with all hepatitis virus infections, viremia can be detected before the onset of symptoms or liver enzyme elevations. HEV RNA is detectable in blood for 14 to 28 days in most patients with clinical disease, although it may be prolonged.[375] HEV has been detected in stool up to 9 days prior to the icteric phase of disease and typically lasts 7 to 14 days thereafter.[375,385]

The serologic course of HEV infection has been determined using nonhuman primate models, human volunteer studies, and outbreak investigations. Both IgG and IgM antibody responses occur soon after HEV infection, with peak antibody titers occurring 2 to 4 weeks after infection, though they may persist much longer—even for years—in some transplant patients.[375,385] The HEV IgM titers decline rapidly within 3 to 6 months after infection.

Some immunocompromised patients may not develop antibodies to HEV after infection. Diagnosis in these patients depends on the detection of HEV RNA in the serum. Several investigators have found significant variability in the performance of serologic assays for HEV antibody.[391-393] Consequently, there are no FDA-approved and -licensed serological assays for this virus available in the United States. This lack of diagnostics is likely responsible for the rarity of recognized cases of HEV in the United States. In contrast, several countries in Western Europe have reported an increasing number of cases in recent years.[394-398]

The transmission of HEV genotype 1 is primarily by ingestion of contaminated water. Monsoon rains may cause epidemics when they overwhelm water sanitation in Asia where the virus is endemic. The first large epidemic that was subsequently shown (27 years later) to be due to HEV occurred in Delhi, India, in December 1955–January 1956.[387] This epidemic included more than 30,000 cases (most among adults) and 65 deaths, half of whom were pregnant women. There was no evidence of person-to-person spread, so the epidemic was short-lived. This epidemic was followed by frequent rainy-season epidemics of HEV in the Indian subcontinent.[368]

Two large epidemics of hepatitis due to HEV genotype 1 infections have been reported from Africa recently. An epidemic in Darfur, Sudan, involved more than 9000 persons.[379] Another epidemic in a refugee population in Kitgun, Uganda, in 2007 involved more than 7000 persons and lasted nearly a year.[380] In this epidemic, evidence of person-to-person transmission was seen, as was infection from ingestion of contaminated water.

In contrast to these large epidemics, individual patients or small clusters of hepatitis from genotype 3 or 4 strains of HEV have been reported from several countries in Europe, North America, Japan, Taiwan, China, and other industrialized countries. The sources of infection in these cases are often not identified, although a food source for the infection was implicated in several outbreaks. Japanese investigators reported severe acute HEV infection in a patient after he consumed the meat from a wild boar he had shot.[400] Three small clusters of acute hepatitis from HEV infection were reported from southern France among persons attending wedding parties who ate figatella, a pig liver sausage that is traditionally consumed raw or lightly smoked. In these outbreaks, anti-HEV IgM was found in 7 of 13 persons who ate figatella and 0 of 5 persons attending the same meal who did not eat figatella. HEV RNA found in the patients' sera was identical to the genotype 3 HEV RNA amplified from figatella that was purchased at a local market.[402]

Another investigator from Japan reported four persons who developed acute HEV after eating sushi prepared from a Sitka deer.[403] A portion of the deer meat, which had been stored frozen for future consumption, contained HEV genotype 3 RNA with nucleotide sequences identical to these found in the patients.

Another potential source of HEV infection is shellfish, which is often eaten raw. An outbreak of 37 cases of HEV occurred among passengers on a cruise ship on a worldwide tour in which shellfish were identified as the probable source of infection.[404]

A prevalence study of 18,695 subjects enrolled in the Third National Health and Nutrition Evaluation Survey (NHANES) in the United States found an HEV seroprevalence of 21%, with a significantly higher prevalence of anti-HEV IgG in persons who reported consuming organ meats more than once per month.[405] Studies in the United States, Europe, and Japan have found an increased prevalence of HEV antibodies among farmers who have frequent direct contact with pigs.[406–408] These recent data clearly indicate that HEV has a zoonotic reservoir in pigs, deer, and possibly other animals. Infectious HEV has been detected in about 10% of pig liver for sale in grocery stores in the United States.[409] Cooking infectious meat to an internal temperature of 71C (161F) for 20 minutes is required to inactivate HEV.[410] Furthermore, chronic infection of pigs, which then excrete infectious virus in their stool, could lead to environmental contamination with HEV. Animal feces is often used to fertilize vegetable crops, which may then be eaten without cooking.

Other routes of transmission of HEV have also been reported. The virus can be transmitted by transfusion or organ transplantation, albeit much less frequently than by ingestion of contaminated food or water.[411]

Worldwide Epidemiology

Large epidemics of hepatitis among adults from HEV infection are noted to occur frequently in the Indian subcontinent.

HEV is one of the most frequent causes of viral hepatitis globally due to the large outbreaks that occur in the densely populated areas in southern Asia. In Africa and the Middle East, epidemics occur but are much less extensive. (**Figure 23-21**).

Moreover, there is an increasing recognition of sporadic cases of acute hepatitis from HEV in many countries in Western Europe. Some of these cases are among travelers who have acquired their infection in endemic countries in Asia before entering Europe. In the United Kingdom, 186 cases of hepatitis from HEV were reported between 1996 and 2003.[397] A total of 129 (69%) of these infections were acquired during travel to Asia—but 17 (9%) were not associated with travel. The travel-associated cases were infected with

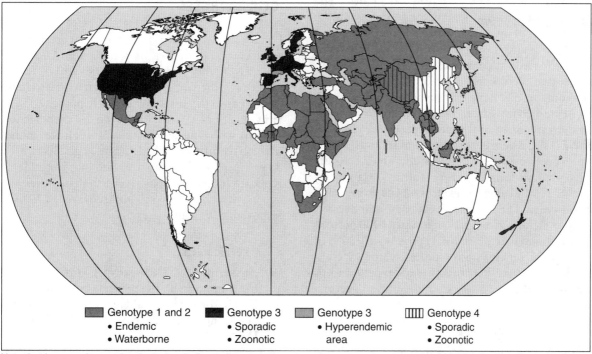

Note that in several countries, including in South America, there have been occasional reports of HEV3 infection. Countries left blank are those with insufficient data.

Figure 23-21 Global distribution of HEV. Reprinted from The Lancet, 379, Kamar et al., Hepatitis E, 2477–88, Copyright 2012, with permission from Elsevier.

genotype 1 viruses, whereas the locally acquired cases were infected with genotype 3 HEV strains. Locally acquired HEV infections appear to be common in southern France as well. A survey of hospitals in France was done to detect diagnosed cases of HEV in 2007.[396] This survey found 53 documented cases, of whom 47 had not traveled out of France prior to their infection. In Germany, HEV infection has been a notifiable disease since 2001. The number of reported cases has increased each year since reporting began. A study of 66 of 96 cases that were reported between May 2006 and August 2007 identified 45 (68%) with autochthonous infection and 21 (32%) with travel-associated disease.[397] HEV genotype 3 was present in all tested patients with autochthonous infection, and genotype 1 was present in 8 of 9 of the travel-associated cases.

In contrast to the situation in the European countries, symptomatic autochthonous cases of acute hepatitis from HEV are very rare in the United States. The reason for this discrepancy is unclear. However, the lack of an FDA-licensed serological test available to clinicians and laboratories in the United States certainly promotes under-recognition of this infection. Because most acute infections are self-limited (except among pregnant women and immunocompromised patients), clinicians are not often motivated to seek assistance from the CDC or a research laboratory to confirm a diagnosis. The CDC has confirmed a small number of cases in the United States. However, the high seroprevalence of HEV IgGAb and the identification of HEV RNA in pig liver for sale at commercial markets combine to suggest that HEV infections may occur much more commonly in U.S. patients than are diagnosed.

Acute hepatitis from HEV appears to be quite common in Japan and other industrialized countries in Asia, where genotype 4 strains are endemic. A prospective epidemiologic study among adults in Bangladesh found a seroprevalence of approximately 25% and a seroincidence of 64 cases per 1000 person-years. The incidence was highest in persons 20–40 years of age, but was only 5 per 1000 person-years in children in this study. Approximately 35% of seroconverters in this study reported symptoms compatible with acute hepatitis.[412] Genotype 1 strains were isolated from a few symptomatic subjects in this population.

Prevention and Treatment

Although severe acute HEV infections are much less common in populations in developed industrialized countries, there is accumulating evidence of foodborne transmission of this virus. Therefore, high-risk persons, such as pregnant women and immunocompromised patients, should avoid eating raw or undercooked organ meats, including some sausages. Consumption of raw shellfish may also pose a risk, although more data are needed to evaluate this risk. Avoiding drinking contaminated water in countries where HEV is endemic is an important recommendation that will be difficult to follow for the populations in these countries.

Two controlled trials of HEV vaccine prepared from ORF 2 of a genotype 1 strain have been reported. One study done among military personnel in Nepal found an efficacy of 96% in preventing clinical hepatitis from HEV.[413] Another study of an HEV polypeptide ORF-2 subunit vaccine in more than 100,000 participants in China found an efficacy of 100% in subjects who received all three doses of the vaccine.[414]

It will be a major challenge to prepare and deliver an HEV vaccine to the populations who need it. Two different investigators have recently reported cases in which ribavirin or interferon-2b therapy reduced the viral load in immunocompromised patients with chronic HEV infection.[415,416] However, neither of these drugs could be used to treat pregnant women because of the risk of teratogenicity.

OTHER VIRUSES

For 5% to 20% of persons with acute hepatitis syndromes, no etiology is found (non-A to non-E hepatitis). Other viruses, such as GB virus C (briefly identified as hepatitis G virus until it was determined to not cause hepatitis nor infect hepatocites), TTV virus, and SEN-V virus, have been discovered among patients with clinical hepatitis.[417–419] However, most of these recently described viruses (e.g., GB-C, TTV) do not usually cause hepatitis and the viruses do not replicate in hepatic cells. Nevertheless, other viral agents, which are as yet undiscovered, are likely responsible for some cases of hepatitis.

• • • REFERENCES

1. Zuckerman AJ. The history of viral hepatitis from antiquity to the present. In: Deinhardt F, Deinhardt J, eds. Viral Hepatitis Laboratory and Clinical Science. New York, NY: Marcel Dekker; 1983:3–32.

2. Lürman A. Eine icterus epidemic. *Berl Klin Worchenschr.* 1885;22: 20–23.

3. Beeson PB, Chainey G, McFarlan AM. Hepatitis following injection of mumps convalescent plasma. *Lancet.* 1944;1: 814–821.

4. Zucker JR. Changing pattern of autochthonous malaria transmission in the United States. *Emerg Infect Dis.* 1996;2:37–43.

5. MacCallum FO. Jaundice in syphilitics. *Br J Vener Dis.* 1943;19:63.

6. Krugman S, Giles JP, Hammond J. Infectious hepatitis: evidence for two distinctive, clinical, epidemiological and immunological types of infections. *JAMA.* 1967;200:365–373.

7. Blumberg BS, Alter HJ, Visnich S. A "new" antigen in leukemia sera. *JAMA.* 1965;191:541–546.

8. Prince AM. An antigen detected in the blood during the incubation period of serum hepatitis. *Proc Natl Acad Sci USA.* 1968;60: 814–821.

9. Feinstone SM, Kapikian AZ, Purcell RH, Alter AJ, Holland PV. Transfusion-associated hepatitis not due to viral hepatitis type A or B. *N Engl J Med.* 1975;292:767–770.

10. Alter HJ, Purcell RH, Shih JW, et al. Detection of antibody to hepatitis C in prospectively followed transfusion recipients with acute and chronic non-A, non-B hepatitis. *N Engl J Med.* 1989;321: 1494–1500.

11. Choo QL, Koo G, Weiner AJ, Overby LR, Bradley DW, Houghton M. Isolation of a cDNA clone derived from a blood borne non-A, non-B viral hepatitis genome. *Science.* 1989;244:351–362.

12. Kuo G, Choo QL, Alter HJ, et al. An assay for circulating antibodies to a major etiologic virus of human non-A, non-B hepatitis. *Science.* 1989;244:362–364.

13. Rizzetto M, Canese MC, Arico S, et al. Immunofluorescence detection of a new antigen-antibody system associated to the hepatitis B virus in the liver and in the serum of HBsAg carriers. *Gut.* 1977;18: 997–1003.

14. Rizzetto M, Canese MC, Gerin JC, et al. Transmission of the hepatitis virus associated delta antigen to chimpanzees. *J Infect Dis.* 1980;141:590–601.

15. Feinstone SM, Kapikian AZ, Purcell RH. Hepatitis A: detection by immune electron microscopy of a virus-like antigen association with acute illness. *Science.* 1973;182: 1026–1028.

16. Provost PJ, Hilleman MR. Propagation of human hepatitis A virus in cell culture in vitro. *Proc Soc Exp Biol Med.* 1979;160:213.

17. Werzberger A, Mensch B, Kuter B, et al. A controlled trial of formalin-inactivated hepatitis A vaccine in healthy children. *N Engl J Med.* 1992;327:453–457.

18. Innis BL, Snitbban R, Kunasol P, et al. Protection against hepatitis A by an inactivated vaccine. *JAMA.* 1994;271: 1328–1334.

19. Wong DL, Purcell RH, Sreentvasan MA, Prasad SR, Parri KM. Epidemic and endemic hepatitis in India: evidence for non A/non B hepatitis virus etiology. *Lancet.* 1980;2: 876–878.

20. Bradley DW, Krawczynski K, Cook EH, et al. Enterically transmitted non-A, non-b hepatitis: serial passage of disease in cynomolgus monkeys and tamarins, and discovery of disease associated with 27 to 34 nm virus-like particles. *Proc Natl Acad Sci USA.* 1987;84: 6277–6281.

21. Kane MA, Bradley DW, Shrestha SM, et al. Epidemic non-A, non-B hepatitis in Nepal: recovery of a possible etiologic agent and transmission to marmosets. *JAMA.* 1984;252:3140–3145.

22. Acute Hepatic Failure Study Group. Etiology and prognosis in fulminant hepatitis. *Gastroenterology.* 1979;77:A33.

23. Mathieson CR, Skinholj P, Nielsen JO, Purcell RH, Wong DC, Ranek C. Hepatitis A, B and non-A, non-B in fulminant hepatitis. *Gut.* 1980;21:72–77.

24. Sjogren MH, Tanno H, Fay O, et al. Hepatitis A virus in stool during clinical relapse. *Ann Intern Med.* 1987;106:221.

25. Andre FE, D'Hondt E, Delem A, Safary A. Clinical assessment of the safety and efficacy of an inactivated hepatitis A vaccine. Rationale and summary of findings. *Vaccine.* 1992;10(suppl 1): S160–S163.

26. Conlepis AG, Locarnini SA, Lehmann NC, Gust D. Detection of hepatitis A virus in the feces of patients with naturally acquired infections. *J Infect Dis.* 1980;141:151.

27. Cohen JL, Feinstone S, Purcell RH. Hepatitis A virus infection in a chimpanzee: duration of viremia and detection of virus in saliva and throat swabs. *J Infect Dis.* 1989;180:887.

28. Shapiro CN, Coleman PJ, McQuillan GM, Alter MJ, Margolis HS. Epidemiology of hepatitis A: seroepidemiology and risk groups in the USA. *Vaccine.* 1992;10:S59–S62.

29. Villano SA, Nelson KE, Vlahov D, et al. Hepatitis-A among homosexual men and injection drug users: more evidence for vaccination. *Clin Infect Dis.* 1997;25:726–728.

30. Corey L, Holmes HK. Sexual transmission of hepatitis A in homosexual men. *N Engl J Med.* 1980;302:345–438.

31. Noble RC, Kane MA, Reeves SA, Roeckel I. Post transfusion hepatitis A in a neonatal intensive care unit. *JAMA.* 1984;252: 2711–2715.

32. Rosenblum LS, Villarino ME, Nainan OV, et al. Hepatitis A outbreak in a neonatal intensive care unit: risk factors for transmission and evidence of prolonged viral excretion among preterm infants. *J Infect Dis.* 1991;164:476–482.

33. Mannucci PM, Gdorin S, Gringeri A, et al. Transmission of hepatitis A to patients with hemophilia by factor VIII concentrates treated with organic solvent and detergent to inactivate viruses. *Am Intern Med.* 1994;120:1–10.

34. Lemon SM, Murphy PC, Smith A, et al. Removal/neutralization of hepatitis A virus during manufacture of high purity, solvent/ detergent factor VIII concentrate. *J Med Virol.* 1994;43:44–48.

35. Widell A, Hansson BG, Moestrup T, Nordenfelt E. Increased occurrence of hepatitis A with cyclic outbreaks among drug addicts in a Swedish community. *Infection.* 1983;11:198–204.

36. Centers for Disease Control and Prevention. Hepatitis A among drug users. *MMWR.* 1988;37:297.

37. Lemon SM. Type A viral hepatitis. New developments in an old disease. *N Engl J Med.* 1985;313:1059–1067.

38. Bergeisen GH, Hinds MW, Skaggs JW. A waterborne outbreak of hepatitis A in Meade County, Kentucky. *Am J Public Health.* 1985;75:161–168.

39. Niu MT, Polish LB, Robertson BH, et al. A multi-state outbreak of hepatitis A associated with frozen strawberries. *J Infect Dis.* 1992;166:518–529.

40. Rosenblum LS, Mirkin IR, Allen DT, Safford S, Hadler SC. A multifocal outbreak of hepatitis A traced to commercially distributed lettuce. *Am J Public Health.* 1990;80: 1075–1079.

41. Desenclos JA, Klontz KC, Wilder MH, Nainan OV, Margolis HS, Gunn RA. A multistate outbreak of hepatitis A caused by the consumption of raw oysters. *Am J Public Health.* 1991;81:1268–1272.

42. Halliday ML, Kang L, Lao Y, et al. An epidemic of hepatitis A attributable to the ingestion of raw clams in Shanghai, China. *J Infect Dis.* 1991;164:852–859.

43. Enriquez R, Frosner GG, Hochstein-Montzel V, Riedemann S, Reinhardt G. Accumulation and persistence of hepatitis A virus in mussels. *J Med Virol.* 1992;37:174–179.

44. Centers for Disease Control and Prevention. Hepatitis Surveillance Report. 1994;55: 1–35.

45. Shapiro CM, Shaw FE, Mendel EI, Hadler SC. Epidemiology of hepatitis in the United States. In: Hollinger FB, Lemon SM, Margolis HS, eds. Viral Hepatitis and Liver Disease. Baltimore, Md: Williams & Wilkins; 1991:214–220.

46. Hadler SC, McFarland L. Hepatitis in day care centers. Epidemiology and prevention. *Rev Infect Dis*. 1985;8:548–557.

47. Hadler SC, Webster HM, Erben JJ, et al. Hepatitis A in daycare centers. A community-wide assessment. *N Engl J Med*. 1980;302:1222–1230.

48. Gingrich GA, Hadler SC, Elder HA, Ash KA, Owen SA. Serologic investigation of an outbreak of hepatitis A in a rural daycare center. *Am J Public Health*. 1983;83:1190–1198.

49. Lange WR, France JD. High incidence of viral hepatitis among American missionaries in Africa. *Am J Trop Med Hyg*. 1990;43:527–533.

50. Steffen R. Risk of hepatitis A in travelers. *Vaccine*. 1992;30: 569–572.

51. Bancroft WH, Lemon SM. Hepatitis A from the military perspective. In: Gerety RJ, ed. Hepatitis A. New York, NY: Academic Press; 1984:81–100.

52. Innis BL, Snithban R, Hoke CH, Muniudhorn W, Laorakpongse T. The declining transmission of hepatitis A in Thailand. *J Infect Dis*. 1991;163:989–995.

53. Hsu HY, Chang MH, Chen DS, Lee CY, Sung JL. Changing seroepidemiology of hepatitis A virus infection in Taiwan. *J Med Virol*. 17:297–301.

54. Kremastinis J, Kalapothaki V, Trichopoulos D. The changing epidemiologic pattern of hepatitis A infection in urban Greece. *Am J Epidemiol*. 1984;120:203–206.

55. Stroffolini T, Decrescenzo L, Giammacco A, et al. Changing patterns of hepatitis virus infection in children in Palermo, Italy. *Eur J Epidemiol*. 1990;6:84–87.

56. Shapiro CN, Coleman PJ, McQuillan GM, Alter HJ, Margolis HS. Epidemiology of hepatitis A: seroepidemiology and risk groups in the USA. *Vaccine*. 1992;10:S59–S62.

57. Shaw FGJ, Shapiro CN, Welty TK, Dill W, Reddington J, Hadler SC. Hepatitis transmission among the Sioux Indians of South Dakota. *Am J Public Health*. 1990;80: 1091–1094.

58. Centers for Disease Control and Prevention. Hepatitis Surveillance Report. 1996;56: 15–27.

59. Wasley A, Samandari T, Bell BP. Incidence of hepatitis A in the United States in the era of vaccination. *JAMA*. 2005;294: 194–201.

60. Centers for Disease Control and Prevention. Prevention of hepatitis A through active or passive immunization: recommendations of the Advisory Committee on Immunization. Practices (ACID). *MMWR*. 1999;48 (RR-12):1–37.

61. Krugman S, Ward R, Giles JP, Jacobs AM. Infectious hepatitis, study on effect of gammaglobulin and on the incidence of apparent infection. *JAMA*. 1960;174:823–883.

62. Winokur PC, Stapleton JT. Immunoglobulin prophylaxis for hepatitis A. *Clin Infect Dis*. 1992;14:580–586.

63. Advisory Committee on Immunization Practices CDC. Recommendations for protection against viral hepatitis. *MMWR*. 1985;34:315–316.

64. Carl M, Francis DP, Maynard JE. Food-borne hepatitis: recommendations for control. *J Infect Dis*. 1983;148(6):1133–1135.

65. Centers for Disease Control and Prevention. Protection against viral hepatitis: recommendation of the immunization practices advisory committee. *MMWR*. 1990;39:5–27.

66. Centers for Disease Control and Prevention. Prevention of hepatitis A through active or passive immunization: recommendations of the Advisory Committee on Immunization Practice (ACIP)/*MMWR* 2006; 55 (No.RR-7).

67. Centers for Disease Control and Prevention. Surveillance for acute viral hepatitis - United States, 2007. *MMWR*; 58:No.SS-3.

68. Bell BP, Kruszon-Moran D, Shapiro CN et al. Hepatitis A virus infection in the United States: Serologic results from the Third National Health and Nutrition Survey. *Vaccine* 2005;25:5798–5806.

69. Victor JC, Monto AS, Surdina TY et al. Hepatitis A virus vaccine verses immune globulin for post exposure prophylaxis. *N Engl J Med* 2007; 357 (17):1685–1694.

70. Centers for Disease Control and Prevention. Update: Prevention of hepatitis A after exposure to hepatitis A virus and in international travelers. Updated recommendations of the Advisory Committee on Immunization Practices (ACIP). *MMWR* 2007; 56(41):1080–1084.

71. Park G-H, Cho Y-Y, Park J-H et al. Changes in the age-specific prevalence of hepatitis A virus antibodies: A 10-year cohort study in Jinju, South Korea. *Clin Infect Dis* 2006; 42:1148–1150.

72. Barzaga BN. Hepatitis A shift epidemiology in south-East Asia and China. *Vaccine* 2000; 18;suppl 1;S61–64.

73. Nelson KE. Global changes in the epidemiology of Hepatitis A virus infections. *Clin Infect Dis* 2006; 42:1151–1152.

74. Deinhardt F. Hepatitis in Primates, In Lauffer M. ed. Advances in Virus Research. Vol 29. Chapter 4:113–167. New York, NY: Academic Press.

75. Szmuness W, Stevens CE, Harley EJ, et al. Hepatitis B vaccine in medical staff on hemodialysis units: efficacy and subtype cross-protection. *N Engl J Med*. 1982;307:1481–1486.

76. Coursaget-Pauty AM, Plancoa A, Soulier JP. Distribution of HBsAg subtypes in the world. *Vox Sang*. 1983;44:197–211.

77. Brown JC, Carman WF, Thomas HC. The clinical significance of molecular variation within the hepatitis B virus genome. *Hepatology*. 1992;15:144–148.

78. Hawkins AE, Gilson RJC, Beath SV, et al. Novel application of a point mutation assay: evidence for transmission of hepatitis B viruses with precore mutations and their detection in infants with fulminant hepatitis B. *J Med Virol*. 1994;44:13–21.

79. Fingerote RJ, Bain VG. Fulminant hepatic failure. *Am J Gastroenterol*. 1993;88:1000–1010.

80. Terazawa S, Kojsma M, Yamanaka T, et al. Hepatitis B virus mutants with pre-core region defects in two babies with fulminant hepatitis and their mothers positive for antibodies to hepatitis B e antigen. *Pediatr Res*. 1991; 29:5–9.

81. Penna A, Chisani FV, Bertolotti A, et al. Cytotoxic T lymphocytes recognize an HLA-DZ-restricted epitope within the hepatitis B virus nucleocapsid antigen. *J Exp Med*. 1991;174:1568–1570.

82. Ando K, Moriyama T, Guidotti LG, et al. Mechanism of class I restricted immunopathology. A transgenic mouse model of fulminant hepatitis. *J Exp Med*. 1993;178:1541–1554.

83. Yoakum GH, Korba BE, Lechner JR, et al. High-frequency transfusion and cytopathology of hepatitis B virus core antigen gene in human cells. *Science*. 1983;22:385–389.

84. Pignattelli M, Waters J, Brown D, et al. HLA class I antigens on hepatocyte membrane during recovery from acute hepatitis B virus infection and during interferon therapy in chronic hepatitis B virus infection. *Hepatology*. 1986;6:349–355.

85. Deinstag JL. Immunogenesis of the extra hepatic manifestation of hepatitis B virus infection. Springer *Semin Immunopathol*. 1981;3: 461–475.

86. McMahon BJ, Alward WLM, Ball DB, et al. Acute hepatitis B virus infection: relation of age to the clinic expression of disease and subsequent development of the carrier state. *J Infect Dis*. 1985;157:599–603.

87. Stevens CE, Neurath RA, Bensley RP, Szmuness W. HBeAg and anti-HBe detection by radioimmunoassay: correlation of vertical

transmission of hepatitis B virus in Taiwan. *J Med Virol.* 1979;3: 237–241.

88. Ganem D. Persistent infection of human with hepatitis B virus, mechanisms and consequences. *Rev Infect Dis.* 1982;4:1026–1047.

89. Hoofnagle JH, Shafritz DA, Popper H. Chronic type B hepatitis and the "healthy" HBsAg carrier state. *Hepatology.* 1987;7: 758–763.

90. McMahon BJ, Alberts SR, Wainwright RB, Bulkow L, Lanier AP. Hepatitis B related sequelae. Prospective study in 1400 hepatitis B surface antigen positive Alaska Native carriers. *Arch Intern Med.* 1990;150:1051–1054.

91. Beasley RP, Hwang LY, Stevens CE, et al. Efficacy of hepatitis B immunoglobulin for prevention of perinatal transmission of the hepatitis B virus: final report of a randomized double-blind, placebo-controlled trial. *Hepatology.* 1983;3:135–141.

92. Hsieh CC, Tzonoa A, Zaritsanos K, Kalaman E, Lan SJ, Trichopulos D. Age at first establishment of chronic hepatitis B virus infection and hepatocellular carcinoma risk. A birth order study. *Am J Epidemiol.* 1992;136:1115–1121.

93. Beasley RP. Hepatitis B virus. The major etiology of hepatocellular carcinoma. *Cancer.* 1988;61:1942–1956.

94. El-Serag HB. Hepatocellular carcinoma. *N Engl J Med.* 2011: 365:118–27

95. Beasley RP, Hwong LY, Lin CC, Chicu CS. Hepatocellular carcinoma and hepatitis B virus. A prospective study of 22,207 men in Taiwan. *Lancet.* 1981;2:1129–1133.

96. Aoki N, Robinson WS. Hepatitis B virus in cirrhosis and hepatocellular carcinoma nodules. *Mol Biol Med.* 1989;6:398–408.

97. Shih C, Burke K, Chou MJ, et al. Tight clustering of human hepatitis B virus integration sites in hepatomas near a triple-stranded region. *J Virol.* 1987;61:3491–3498.

98. Safritz DA, Shoural D, Sherman H, Hadziyannis S, Kew M. Integration of hepatitis B virus DNA into the genome of liver cells in chronic liver disease and hepatocellular carcinoma. *N Engl J Med.* 1981;305:1067–1075.

99. Gerin JL. Experimental WHV infection of woodchucks: an animal model of hepadnavirus-induced liver cancer. *Gastroenterol Jpn.* 1990;25(suppl):38–42.

100. Korba BE, Weks FU, Baldwin B, et al. Hepatocellular carcinoma in woodchuck hepatitis virus-infected woodchucks: presence of viral DNA in tumor tissue from known carriers and animals serologically recovered from acute infections. *Hepatology.* 1989;9: 465–470.

101. Marion PL, Van Davelano MJ, Knight SS, et al. Hepatocellular carcinoma in ground squirrels persistently infected with ground squirrel hepatitis virus. *Proc Natl Acad Sci USA.* 1983;33:4543–4546.

102. Popper HJ, Roth L, Purcell RH, Tennant BC, Gerin JH. Hepatocarcinogenicity of the woodchuck hepatitis virus. *Proc Natl Acad Sci USA.* 1987;84:855–870.

103. Popper HJ, Shih JW, Gerin JH, et al. Woodchuck hepatitis and hepatocellular carcinoma: correlation of histologic with virologic observations. *Hepatology.* 1981;1:91–98.

104. Chang M-H, Chen C-J, Lai M-S, et al. Universal hepatitis B vaccination in Taiwan and the incidence of hepatocellular carcinoma in children. *N Engl J Med.* 1997;336: 1855–1859.

105. Qian G-S, Ross RK, Yu MC, et al. A follow-up study of urinary markers of Aflatoxin exposure and liver cancer, risk in Shanghai, People's Republic of China. *Cancer, Epidemiol, Biomarkers Prev.* 1994;3:3–10.

106. Hoofnagle JH, Di Bisceglie AM. Serologic diagnosis of acute and chronic hepatitis. *Semin Liver Dis.* 1991;11:73–83.

107. Seeff LB, Beebe BW, Hoofnagle JH, et al. A serologic follow-up of the 1942 epidemic of post-vaccination hepatitis in the United States Army. *N Engl J Med.* 1987;316:965–970.

108. Levine OS, Vlahov D, Nelson KE. Epidemiology of hepatitis B virus infections among injecting drug users: seroprevalence, risk factors and viral interactions. *Epidemiol Rev.* 1994;16:418–436.

109. Garfein R, Vlahov D, Galai N, Doherty MC, Nelson KE. Prevalence of hepatitis C virus, hepatitis B virus, human immunodeficiency virus and human T-lymphotrophic virus infections in short term injection drug users. *Am J Public Health.* 1996;86:655–661.

110. Bernier RH, Sampliner R, Gerety R, Tabor E, Hamilton F, Nathanson N. Hepatitis B infection in households of chronic carriers of hepatitis B surface antigen: factors associated with prevalence of infection. *Am J Epidemiol.* 1982;116:199–211.

111. Franks AL, Berg CJ, Kane MA, et al. Hepatitis B infection among children born in the United States to Southeast Asian refugees. *N Engl J Med.* 1089;321:1301–1305.

112. Hurie MB, Mart EE, Davis JP. Horizontal transmission of hepatitis B virus infection to United States-born children of Hmong refugees. *Pediatrics.* 1992;89:269–274.

113. Williams I, Smith MG, Sinha D, et al. Hepatitis B virus transmission in an elementary school setting. *JAMA.* 1997;278:2167–2169.

114. Margolis AS, Alter MJ, Hadler SC. Hepatitis B: evolving epidemiology and implications for control. *Semin Liver Dis.* 1991;11:84–92.

115. Alter MJ, Hadler SC, Judson FN, et al. The changing epidemiology of hepatitis B in the United States: need for alternative vaccination strategies. *JAMA.* 1990;263:1218–1222.

116. McQuillan GM, Coleman PJ, Kruszon-Maran D, Moyer LA, Lambert SB, Margolis HS. Prevalence of hepatitis B virus infection in the United States: The National Health and Nutrition Examination Surveys, 1976 through 1994. *Am J Public Health.* 1999;89:14–18.

117. McMahon BJ, Bulkow LR, Singleton RJ. Elimination of hepatocellular carcinoma and acute hepatitis B in children 25 years after hepatitis B newborn and catch-up immunization program *Hepatology.* 2011; 54(3):801–7

118. Surrell ME, Belongia EA, Coste J, et al. National Institutes of Health Consensus Development Conference Statement: Management of hepatitis B. *Ann Intern Med.* 2009; 150:104–110

119. McQuillan GM, Townsend TR, Fields HA, et al. The seroepidemiology of hepatitis B virus in the United States 1976–89. *Am J Med.* 1989;87:5–10.

120. Bogomolski-Yahalom V, Granot E, Linder N, et al. Prevalence of HBsAg carriers in native and immigrant pregnant female populations in Israel and passive/active vaccination against HBV of newborns at risk. *Isr J Med.* 1991;34:217–222.

121. McMahon BJ, Schoenberg S, Bulkow L, et al. Seroprevalence of hepatitis B viral markers in 52,000 Alaskan Natives. *Am J Epidemiol.* 1993;138:544–549.

122. Fay OH, Hadler SC, Maynard JE, Pinherro F. Hepatitis in the Americas. *Bull Pan Am Health Org.* 1985;19:401–408.

123. Cohen C, Evans AA, London WT et al. Underestimation of chronic hepatitis B virus infection in the United States of America. *J Virol Hepat.* 2008; 15:12–13.

124. Centers for Disease Control and Prevention. Transmission of hepatitis B virus among persons undergoing blood glucose monitoring in long-term care facilities. Mississippi, North Carolina, Los Angeles County, California, 2003–2004. *MMWR.* 2005,54 (9):220–223.

125. Centers for Disease Control and Prevention. Deaths from acute hepatitis B virus infection associated with assisted blood glucose monitoring in an assisted-living facility - North Carolina August-October 2012. *MMWR.* 2011(6):182.

126. Carl M, Blakey DL, Francis DP, Maynard JE. Interruption of hepatitis B transmission by modification of gynecologists' surgical technique. *Lancet.* 1982;1:731–733.

127. Shaw FE Jr, Barrett CI, Hamm R, et al. Lethal outbreak of hepatitis B in a clinical practice. *JAMA*. 1986;255:3260–3264.

128. Elephantitis and Liver cancer: A Matopma; Strategy for Prevention and Control of Hepatitis B and C. Institute of Medicine, Washington, DC. Jan 2010.

129. Lee KG, Seo YS, An H et al. Usefulness of non-invasive markers predicting liver cirrhosis in patients with chronic hepatitis B. *Jour Gastroentero and Hepato*. 2010; 29: 94–100.

130. El-Serag HB, Mason AC. Rising incidence of hepatocellular carcinoma in the United States. *N Engl J Med*. 1999;340:745–750.

131. McGlynn KA, Tarone RE, and El-Serag H.B. Comparison of trends in the incidence of hepatocellular carcinoma and intrahepatic cholangiocarcinoma in the United States. *Cancer, Epidemiol Prev Biomarkers, Prev*. 2006; 15:1197–1203.

132. El-Serag H and Rudolph KC. Hepatocellular carcinoma epidemiology and molecular carcinogenesis. *Gastroenterology*. 2007; 132:2557–2576.

133. McMahon BJ, Lanier A, Wainwright RB, Kilkenny JJ. Hepatocellular carcinoma in Alaska Eskimos: epidemiology, clinical features and early detection. *Prog Liver Dis*. 1990;9:643–655.

134. Kuang S-Y, Lekawanvijut S, Maneekarn N, et al. Hepatitis B 1762T/1764A mutations, hepatitis C infection and codon 249 p53 mutations in hepatocellular carcinoma in Thailand. *Cancer, Epidemiol, Biomarkers Prev*. 2005;14:380–384.

135. Kuang SY, Jackson PE, Wang JB, et al. Specific mutations of hepatitis B virus in plasma predict liver cancer development. *Proc Natl Acad Sci USA*. 2004;101: 3575–3580.

136. LeeKG, Seo US, An H et al. Usefulness of non-invasive markers predict liver cirrhosis in patients with chronic hepatitis B. *Jour Gastroentero and Hepato*. 2010; 29:94–100.

137. Yim HJ and Lok A. Natural History of chronic hepatitis B virus infection: what we knew in 1981 and what we know in 2005. *Hepatology*. 2006; 43:S173–S181.

138. Munoz A, Chen JG, Egner PA et al. Predictive power of hepatitis B 1762T/1764A/ mutations in plasma for hepatocellular carcinoma risk in Qiding, China. *Carniogeneis*. 2011; 27:2070–2082.

139. Kirk GD, Bah E, Montesano R. Molecular epidemiology of human liver cancer: insights into etiology, pathogenesis and prevention from the Gaskin, West Africa. *Carcinogenesis*. 2006; 27:2070–2082.

140. Fwu C-W, Chein Y-C, Yang S-Y, et al. Determination of immune memory to hepatocellular carcinoma among parous women in Taiwan. Nationwide Cohort Study. *J Nat'l Cancer Inf*. 2009; 101:1019–1027.

141. Yu M-W, Yang Y-C, Yang S-Y, et al. Hormonal markers and hepatitis-B virus-related hepatocellular carcinoma risk: A nested case-control study among men. *J Nat Cancer Inst*. 2001; 93:1644–1651.

142. Hsu YS, Chien RN, Yeh LT et al. Long-term outcome after spontaneous HBeAg seroconversion in patients with chronic hepatitis B. *Hepatology*. 2002;35= 1522–1527.

143. Carmen WF, Jaeyna MR, Hadziyannis S, et al. Mutation preventing formation of hepatitis B e antigen in patients with chronic hepatitis B infection. *Lancet*. 1989; 334:588–591.

144. Okamoto H, Tsuda T, Rkaharc Y, et al. Hepatitis B virus with mutations on the core promoter for an e antigen negative phenotype in carriers with antibody to e antigen. *J Virol*. 1994; 68:8102–8110.

145. Lok A and McMahon BJ. Chronic Hepatitis B. *Hepatology*. 2007; 45:503–539.

146. Hoo TI, Wu TC, Lee PL, et al. Seroclearence of hepatitis B surface antigen in chronic carriers does not necessarily imply a good prognosis. *Hepatology*. 1998; 28:231–236.

147. Krugman S, Giles JP, Hammond J. Hepatitis virus effect of heat on the infectivity and antigenicity of MS-1 and MS-2 strain. *J Infect Dis*. 1970;122:423–436.

148. Szmuness W, Stevens CE, Harley EJ, et al. Hepatitis B vaccine: demonstration of efficacy in a controlled clinical trial in a high-risk population in the United States. N Engl J Med. 1980;303:833–841.

149. Francis DP, Hadler SC, Thompson SE, et al. Prevention of hepatitis B with vaccine. Report from the Centers for Disease Control multi-center efficacy trial among homosexual men. *Ann Intern Med*. 1982;97: 362–366.

150. Yu ZY, Liu CB, Francis DP, et al. Prevention of perinatal acquisition of hepatitis B virus carriage using vaccine: preliminary report of a randomized double-blind placebo-controlled and comparative trial. *Pediatrics*. 985;76:713–718.

151. Pooduotawan Y, Sanpayat S, Pongpuniert W. Protective efficacy of a recombinant DNA hepatitis B vaccine in neonates of HBe antigen-positive mothers. *JAMA*. 1989;261:3278–3281.

152. Stevens CE, Taylor PR, Tong MJ, et al. Yeast-recombinant hepatitis B vaccine. Efficacy with hepatitis B immunoglobulin in prevention of perinatal hepatitis B virus transmission. *JAMA*. 1987;257: 2612–2616.

153. Centers for Disease Control and Prevention. Update: recommendations to prevent hepatitis B virus transmission—United States. *MMWR*. 1995;44:574–575.
    a. Jan C-F, Huang R-C, Chien Y-C et al. Determination of immune memory to hepatitis B vaccination through early booster response in college students. *Hepatology*. 2010; 51:1547–1554.

154. Ukena T, Esber H, Bessette R, et al. Site of injection and response to hepatitis B vaccine. *N Engl J Med*. 1985;313:579–580.
    a. Anzola M. Hepatocellular carcinoma: a role of hepatitis B and hepatitis C viruses proteins in hepatocarcinogenesis. *J Virol Hep*. 2004;11:383–393.

155. Centers for Disease Control and Prevention. Suboptimal responses to hepatitis B vaccine given by injection in the buttock. *MMWR*. 1985;34:105–108.

156. Alper CA, Kruskall MS, Marcus-Bagley D, et al. Genetic prediction of non response to hepatitis B vaccine. *N Engl J Med*. 1989;321: 708–712.

157. World Health Organization. Progression and control of viral hepatitis: memorandum from WHO meeting. *Bull WHO*. 1988;66: 443–455.

158. World Health Organization. Progression and control of viral hepatitis: memorandum from WHO meeting. *Bull WHO*. 1988;66:443–455.

159. Lee SM. Hepatitis B virus infection. *N Engl J Med*. 1997;337: 1733–1745.

160. Kwon H and Lok AS. Hepatitis B therapy. *Nature Reviews, Gastroenterology and Hepatology*. 2011; 8:275–284.

161. Liaw Y-F, Sung JJY, Chow WC, et al. Lamivudine for patients with chronic hepatitis B and advanced liver disease. *N Engl J Med*. 2004;351:1521–1531.

162. Lai C-L, Dienstag J, Schiff E, et al. Prevalence and clinical correlates of YMDD variants during lumivudine therapy for patients with chronic hepatitis B. *Clin Infect Dis*. 2003;36:687–696.

163. Perrillo RP, Lai C-L, Liaw Y-F, et al. Predictors of HBeAg loss after lamivudine treatment for chronic hepatitis B. *Hepatology*. 2002;36:186–194.

164. Fung SK, Wong F, Hussain M, Lok ASF. Sustained response after a 2 year course of lamivudine treatment of hepatitis Be antigen-negative chronic hepatitis B. *J Viral Hepatitis*. 2004;11:432–438.

165. Yiaw Y-F, Sung JJ, Chow WC, et al. Lamiuvdine for patients with advanced liver disease. *N Engl J Med*. 2004;351:1521–1531.

166. Fung SK, Lok ASF. Management of hepatitis B patients with antiviral resistance. *Antivir Ther.* 2004;9:1013–1026.

167. Perrilo R, Schiff E, Yoshida E, et al. Adefovir dipivoxil for the treatment of lamivudine-resistant hepatitis B mutants. *Hepatology.* 2000;32:129–134.

168. Hadziyannis SJ, Tassopoulos MC, Heathcote EJ, et al. Adefovir dipivoxil for the treatment of hepatitis Be antigen-negative chronic hepatitis B. *N Engl J Med.* 2003;348: 800–807.

169. Yuen M-F, Sablon E, Yuan H-J, et al. Significance of hepatitis B genotype in acute exacerbation, HBeAg seroconversion, cirrhosis-related complications and hepatocellular carcinoma. *Hepatology.* 2003;37: 562–567.

170. Wai CT, Chu C-J, Hussain M, Lok ASF. HBV genotype B is associated with better response to interferon therapy in HBeAg(+) chronic hepatitis than genotype C. *Hepatology.* 2002;36:1425–1430.

171. Kao J-H, Wa N-H, Chen P-J, Lai M-Y, Chen D-S. Hepatitis B genotypes and the response to interferon therapy. *J Hepatol.* 2000;33:998–1002.

172. Chu C-J, Hussain M, Lok ASF. Hepatitis B virus genotype B is associated with earlier HBeAg seroconversion compared with hepatitis B virus genotype C. *Gastroenterology.* 2002;122:1756–1762.

173. Sanchez-Tapias JM, Costa J, Mas A, Bruguera M, Rodes J. Influence of hepatitis B virus genotype on the long-term outcome of chronic hepatitis B in western patients. *Gastroenterology.* 2002;123:1848–1856.

174. Garfein RS, Bower WA, Loney CM, et al. Factors associated with fulminant liver failure during an outbreak among injecting drug users with acute hepatitis B. *Hepatology.* 2004;40:865–873.

175. Thio CL. Hepatitis B in the human immunodeficiency virus infected patient: epidemiology, natural history and treatment. *Sem Liver Dis.* 2003;3:125–136.

176. Twu SJ, Detels R, Nelson KE, et al. Relationship of hepatitis B virus infection to human immunodeficiency virus type 1 infection. *J Infect Dis.* 1993;167:299–304.

177. Thio CL, Seaburg EC, Skolasky R, et al. HIV-1, hepatitis B virus and risk of liver-related mortality in the Multicenter AIDS Cohort Study (MACS). *Lancet.* 2002;360:1921–1926.

178. Soriano V, Puoti M, Bonacini M, et al. Care of patients with chronic hepatitis B and HIV coinfection: Recommendations from an HIV-HBV international panel. *AIDS.* 2005;19:221–240.

179. Fields HA, Hadler SC. Delta hepatitis: a review. *J Clin Immunol.* 1986;9:128–142.

180. Kwon H and Lok AS. Hepatitis B therapy. *Nature Reviews, Gastroenterology and Hepatology.* 2011; 8:275–284.
    a. Arico S, Aragona M, Rizzetto M, et al. Clinical significance of antibody to the hepatitis delta virus in symptomless HBsAg carriers. *Lancet.* 1985;2:356–357.

181. Caredda F, Antinoni S, Re T, Pastechia C, Moroni M. Course and prognosis of acute HDV hepatitis. *Prog Clin Biol Res.* 1987;234: 267–276.

182. Lettau L, McCarthy JG, Smith MH, et al. An outbreak of severe hepatitis due to delta and hepatitis B virus in injection drug users and their contacts. *N Engl J Med.* 1987;317:1256–1261.

183. Hadler SC, De Monson M, Ponzotto A, et al. Delta virus infection and severe hepatitis: an epidemic in the Yupca Indians of Venezuela. *Ann Intern Med.* 1984;100: 339–344.

184. Shimizu YK, Feinstone SM, Kohara M, Purcell RH, Yoshikura H. Hepatitis C virus: detection of intracellular virus particles by electron microscopy. *Hepatology.* 1996;23:205–209.

185. Kaito M, Watanabe S, Tsukiyama-Kohara K, et al. Hepatitis C virus particle detected by immunoelectron microscopic study. *J Gen Virol.* 1994;75:1755–1760.

186. Choo QL, Richman KH, Han JH, et al. Genetic organization and diversity of the hepatitis C virus. *Proc Natl Acad Sci USA*. 1991;88:2451–2455.

187. Negro F, Pacchioni D, Shimizu Y, et al. Detection of intrahepatic replication of hepatitis C virus RNA by in situ hybridization and comparison with histopathology. *Proc Natl Acad Sci USA*. 1992;89:2247–2251.

188. Krawczynski K, Beach MJ, Bradley DW, et al. Hepatitis C antigens in hepatocytes. Immunomorphologic detection and identification. *Gastroenterology*. 1992;103:622–629.

189. Lerat H, Berby F, Trabaud MA, et al. Specific detection of hepatitis C virus minus strand RNA in hematopoietic cells. *J Clin Invest*. 1996;97:845–851.

190. Shimizu YK, Igarashi H, Kanematu T, et al. Sequence analysis of the hepatitis C virus genome recovered from serum, liver, and peripheral blood mononuclear cells of infected chimpanzees. *J Virol*. 1997;71:5769–5773.

191. Lanford RE, Chavez D, Von Chisari F, Sureau C. Lack of detection of negative-strand hepatitis C virus RNA in peripheral blood mononuclear cells and other extrahepatic tissues by the highly strand-specific rTth reverse transcriptase PCR. *J Virol*. 1995;69: 8079–8083.

192. Neumann AU, Lam NP, Dahari H, et al. Hepatitis C viral dynamics in vivo and the antiviral efficacy of interferon-alpha therapy. Science. 1998;282:103–107.

193. Martell M, Esteban JI, Quer J, et al. Hepatitis C virus (HCV) circulates as a population of different but closely related genomes: quasi-species nature of HCV genome distribution. *J Virol*. 1992;66:3225–3229.

194. Kato N, Ootsuyama Y, Tanaka T, et al. Marked sequence diversity in the putative envelope proteins of hepatitis C viruses. *Virus Res*. 1992;22:107–123.

195. Wang Y, Ray SC, Laeyendecker O, Ticehurst JR, Thomas DL. Assessment of hepatitis C virus sequence complexity by the electrophoretic mobility of both single- and double-stranded DNA. *J Clin Micro*. 1998;36:2982–2989.

196. Ray SC, Wang YM, Laeyendecker O, Ticehurst J, Villano SA, Thomas DL. Acute hepatitis C virus structural gene sequences as predictors of persistent viremia: hypervariable region 1 as decoy. *J Virol*. 1998;73: 2938–2946.

197. Major ME, Mihalik K, Fernandez J, et al. Long-term follow-up of chimpanzees inoculated with the first infectious clone for hepatitis C virus. *J Virol*. 1999;73:3317–3325.

198. Weiner AJ, Geysen HM, Christopherson C, et al. Evidence for immune selection of hepatitis C virus (HCV) putative envelope glycoprotein variants: potential role in chronic HCV infections. *Proc Natl Acad Sci USA*. 1992;89:3468–3472.

199. Shimizu YK, Hijikata M, Iwamoto A, Alter HJ, Purcell RH, Yoshikura H. Neutralizing antibodies against hepatitis C virus and the emergence of neutralization escape mutant viruses. *J Virol*. 1994;68:1494–1500.

200. Weiner A, Erickson AL, Kansopon J, et al. Persistent hepatitis C virus infection in a chimpanzee is associated with emergence of a cytotoxic T lymphocyte escape variant. *Proc Natl Acad Sci USA*. 1995;92: 2755–2759.

201. Liou TC, Chang TT, Young KC, Lin XZ, Lin CY, Wu HL. Detection of HCV RNA in saliva, urine, seminal fluid, and ascites. *J Med Virol*. 1992;37:197–202.

202. Chen M, Yun Z-B, Sällberg M, et al. Detection of hepatitis C virus RNA in the cell fraction of saliva before and after oral surgery. *J Med Virol*. 1995;45:223–226.

203. C Wang JT, Wang TH, Sheu JC, Lin JT, Chen DS. Hepatitis C virus RNA in saliva of patients with posttransfusion hepatitis and low efficiency of transmission among spouses. *J Med Virol*. 1992;36:28–31.

204. Fiore RJ, Potenza D, Monno L, et al. Detection of HCV RNA in serum and seminal fluid from HIV-1 co-infected intravenous drug addicts. *J Med Virol*. 1995;46:364–367.

205. Mendel I, Muraine M, Riachi G, et al. Detection and genotyping of the hepatitis C RNA in tear fluid from patients with chronic hepatitis C. *J Med Virol.* 1997;51:231–233.

206. Abe K, Inchauspe G. Transmission of hepatitis C by saliva. *Lancet.* 1991;337:248.

207. Pileri P, Uematsu Y, Campagnoli S, et al. Binding of hepatitis C virus to CD81. *Science.* 1998;282:938–941.

208. Dorner M, Horwitz JA, Robbins JB, et al. A genetically humanized mouse model for hepatitis C virus infection. *Nature.* 2011; 478:208–214.

209. Bukh J, Miller RH, Purcell RH. Genetic heterogeneity of hepatitis C virus: quasispecies and genotypes. *Semin Liver Dis.* 1995;15: 41–63.

210. Simmonds P, Holmes EC, Cha T-A, et al. Classification of hepatitis C virus into six major genotypes and a series of subtypes by phylogenetic analysis of the NS-5 region. *J Gen Virol.* 1993;74: 2391–2399.

211. Bronowicki JP, Venard V, Botté C, et al. Patient-to-patient transmission of hepatitis C virus during colonoscopy. *N Engl J Med.* 1997;337:237–240.

212. Esteban JI, Gómez J, Martell M, et al. Transmission of hepatitis C virus by a cardiac surgeon. *N Engl J Med.* 1996;334:555–560.

213. Thomas DL, Zenilman JZ, Alter HJ, Shih JW, Galai N, Quinn TC. Sexual transmission of hepatitis C virus among patients attending Baltimore sexually transmitted diseases clinics—an analysis of 309 sexual partnerships. *Infect Dis.* 1995;171:768–775.

214. Allander T, Gruber A, Naghavi M, et al. Frequent patient-to-patient transmission of hepatitis C virus in a haematology ward. *Lancet.* 1995;345:603–607.

215. Fried MW, Shiffman MI, Reddy RK et al. Pegylated interferon alpha Za in combination with ribauirin: efficacy and safely results from a phase III randomized multicenter trial. *Gastroenterology.* 2001; 120 (suppl 1):288.

216. Manns MP, McHutchinson JG, Gordon SC, et al. Peginterferon alfa-2b plus ribavirin compared with interferon alfa-2b plus ribavirin for initial treatment of chronic hepatitis C: a randomized trial. *Lancet.* 2001;358: 958–965.

217. Poynard T, Yuen MF, Ratzine V, Lai CL. Viral hepatitis C. *Lancet.* 2003;362:2095–3000.

218. Doi H, Apichartpiyatul C, Ohba KI et al. Hepatitis C virus subtype prevalence in Chaing Mai, Thailand and Identification of a novel subtupe of genotype 6. *J Clin Microbial.* 1996; 34:569–74.

219. Kalinina O, Norder H, Mukomolor S, Magnias LO. A natural intergenotypic recombinant of hepatitis C virus identified in St. Petersburg. *J Virol.* 2002;76:4034–4043.

220. Villano SA, Vlahov D, Nelson KE, Cohn S, Thomas DL. Persistence of viremia and the importance of long-term follow-up after acute hepatitis C infection. *Hepatology.* 1999;29:908–914.

221. Inglesby TV, Rai R, Astemborski J, et al. A prospective, community-based evaluation of liver enzymes in individuals with hepatitis C after drug use. *Hepatology.* 1999;29: 590–596.

222. Farci P, Alter HJ, Wong D, et al. A long-term study of hepatitis C virus replication in non-A, non-B hepatitis. *N Engl J Med.* 1991;325: 98–104.

223. Alter MJ, Margolis HS, Krawczynski K, et al. The natural history of community acquired hepatitis C in the United States. *N Engl J Med.* 1992;327:1899–1905.

224. Tong MJ, El-Farra NS, Reikes AR, Co RL. Clinical outcomes after transfusion-associated hepatitis C. *N Engl J Med.* 1995;332: 1463–1466.

225. Kiyosawa K, Sodeyama T, Tanaka E, et al. Interrelationship of blood transfusion, non-A, non-B hepatitis and hepatocellular carcinoma: analysis by detection of antibody to hepatitis C virus. *Hepatology.* 1990;12: 671–675.

226. Kenny-Walsh E. Clinical outcomes after hepatitis C infection from contaminated anti-D immune globulin. Irish Hepatology Research Group. *N Engl J Med.* 1999;340: 1228–1233.

227. Agnello V, Chung RT, Kaplan LM. A role for hepatitis C virus infection in Type II cryoglobulinemia. *N Engl J Med.* 1992;327: 1490–1495.

228. Misiani R, Bellavita P, Fenili D, et al. Hepatitis C virus infection in patients with essential mixed cryoglobulinemia. *Ann Intern Med.* 1992;117:573–577.

229. Johnson RJ, Gretch DR, Yamabe H, et al. Membranoproliferative glomerulonephritis associated with hepatitis C virus infection. *N Engl J Med.* 1993;328: 465–470.

230. Fargion S, Piperno A, Cappellini MD, et al. Hepatitis C virus and porphyria cutanea tarda: evidence of a strong association. *Hepatology.* 1992;16:1322–1326.

231. DeCastro M, Sanchez J, Herrera JF, et al. Hepatitis C virus antibodies and liver disease in patients with porphyria cutanea tarda. *Hepatology.* 1993;17:551–557.

232. Centers for Disease Control and Prevention. Recommendations for prevention and control of hepatitis C virus infection and HCV-related chronic disease. *MMWR.* 1998;47(RR-19):1–39.

233. McHutchinson JG, Person JL, Govindarajan S, et al. Improved detection of hepatitis C virus antibodies in high-risk populations. *Hepatology.* 1992;15: 19–25.

234. Nakatsuji Y, Matsumoto A, Tanaka E, Ogata H, Kiyosawa K. Detection of chronic hepatitis C virus infection by four diagnostic systems: first generation and second-generation enzyme-linked immunosorbent assay, second-generation recombinant immunoblot assay and nested polymerase chain reaction analysis. *Hepatology.* 1992;16:300–305.

235. Chien DY, Choo QL, Tabrizi A, et al. Diagnosis of hepatitis C virus (HCV) infection using an immunodominant chimeric polyprotein to capture circulating antibodies: reevaluation of the role of HCV in liver disease. *Proc Natl Acad Sci USA.* 1992;89:10011–10015.

236. Couroucé A-M, Le Marrec N, Girault A, Ducamp S, Simon N. Anti-hepatitis C virus (anti-HCV) seroconversion in patients undergoing hemodialysis: comparison of second- and third-generation anti-HCV assays. *Transfusion.* 1994;34:790–795.

237. Vallari DS, Jett BW, Alter HJ, Mimms LT, Holzman R, Shih JW. Serological markers of posttransfusion hepatitis C viral infection. *J Clin Micro.* 1992;30:552–556.

238. van der Poel CL, Cuypers HTM, Reesink HW, et al. Confirmation of hepatitis C virus infection by new four-antigen recombinant immunoblot assay. *Lancet.* 1991;337: 317–319.

239. Buffet C, Charnaux N, Laurent-Puig P, et al. Enhanced detection of antibodies to hepatitis C virus by use of a third-generation recombinant immunoblot assay. *J Med Virol.* 1994;43:259–261.

240. McGuinness PH, Bishop GA, Lien A, Wiley B, Parsons C, McCaughan GW. Detection of serum hepatitis C virus RNA in HCV antibody-seropositive volunteer blood donors. *Hepatology.* 1993;18:485–490.

241. Vrielink H, van der Poel CL, Reesink HW, et al. Look-back study of infectivity of anti-HCV ELISA-positive blood components. *Lancet.* 1995;345:95–96.

242. Zaaijer HL, Cuypers HTM, Reesink HW, Winkel IN, Gerken G, Lelie PN. Reliability of polymerase chain reaction for detection of hepatitis C virus. *Lancet.* 1993;341: 722–724.

243. Bresters D, Cuypers HT, Reesink HW, et al. Comparison of quantitative cDNA-PCR with the branched DNA hybridization assay for monitoring plasma hepatitis C virus RNA levels in haemophilia patients participating a controlled interferon trial. *J Med Virol.* 1994;43:262–268.

244. Gretch DR, Dela Rosa C, Carithers RL Jr, Willson RA, Williams B, Corey L. Assessment of hepatitis C viremia using molecular amplification technologies: correlations and clinical implications. *Ann Intern Med.* 995;123:321–329.

245. Miskovsky EP, Carella AV, Gutekunst K, Sun C, Quinn TC, Thomas DL. Clinical characterization of a competitive PCR assay for quantitative testing of hepatitis C virus. *J Clin Microbiol.* 1996;34:1975–1979.

246. Esteban JI, Lopez-Talavera JC, Genesca J, et al. High rate of infectivity and liver disease in blood donors with antibodies to hepatitis C virus. *Ann Intern Med.* 1991;115: 443–449.

247. Pereira BJG, Milford EL, Kirkman RL, et al. Prevalence of hepatitis C virus RNA in organ donors positive for hepatitis C antibody and in the recipients of their organs. *N Engl J Med.* 1992;327:910–915.

248. Terrault NA, Wright TL. Hepatitis C virus in the setting of transplantation. *Semin Liver Dis.* 1995;15:92–100.

249. Pereira BJG, Milford EL, Kirkman RL, Levey AS. Transmission of hepatitis C virus by organ transplantation. *N Engl J Med.* 1991;325:454–460.

250. Centers for Disease Control and Prevention. Public Health Service interagency guidelines for screening blood, plasma, organs, tissue and semen for evidence of hepatitis B and C. *MMWR.* 1991;40:1–23.

251. Donahue JG, Munoz A, Ness PM, et al. The declining risk of post-transfusion hepatitis C virus infection. *N Engl J Med.* 1992;327: 369–373.

252. Blajchman MA, Bull SB, Feinman SV. Post-transfusion hepatitis: impact of non-A, non-B hepatitis surrogate tests. *Lancet.* 1995;345: 21–25.

253. Schreiber GB, Busch MP, Kleinman SH, Korelitz JJ. The risk of transfusion-transmitted viral infections. *N Engl J Med.* 1996;334: 1685–90.

254. Stramer SL, Glynn SA, Kleinman SH, et al. Detection of HIV-1 and HCV infection among antibody-negative blood donors by nucleic acid-amplification testing. *N Engl J Med.* 2004;351:760–768.

255. Zou S, Stramer SC, and Dodd RV. Donor testing and risk: Current prevalence, incidence and residual risk of transfusion-transmissible agents in US allogeneic donations. Transfusion Med Rev, 2011.

256. Widell A, Elmud H, Persson MH, Jonsson M. Transmission of hepatitis C via both erythrocyte and platelet transfusions from a single donor in serological window-phase of hepatitis C. *Vox Sang.* 1996;71: 55–57.

257. Yap PL, McOmish F, Webster ADB, et al. Hepatitis C virus transmission by intravenous immunoglobulin. *J Hepatol.* 1994;21: 455–460.

258. Bjoro K, Froland SS, Yun Z, Samdal HH, Haaland T. Hepatitis C infection in patients with primary hypogammaglobulinemia after treatment with contaminated immune globulin. *N Engl J Med.* 1994;331:1607–1611.

259. Power JP, Lawlor E, Davidson F, Hepatitis C. Viraemia in recipients of Irish intravenous anti-D immunoglobalin. *Lancet.* 1994;344: 1166–1167.

260. Bresee JS, Mast EE, Coleman FJ, et al. Hepatitis C virus infection associated with administration of intravenous immune globulin—a cohort study. *JAMA.* 1996;276:1563–1567.

261. Thomas DL, Vlahov D, Solomon L, et al. Correlates of hepatitis C virus infections among injection drug users in Baltimore. *Medicine.* 1995;74:212–220.

262. Bolumar F, Hernandez-Aguado I, Ferrer L, Ruiz I, Aviñó M, Rebagliato M. Prevalence of antibodies to hepatitis C in a population of intravenous drug users in Valencia, Spain, 1990–1992. *Int J Epidemiol.* 1996;25: 204–209.

263. Girardi E, Zaccarelli M, Tossini G, Puro V, Narciso P, Visco G. Hepatitis C virus

infection in intravenous drug users: prevalence and risk factors. *Scand J Infect Dis.* 1990;22:751–752.

264. Bell J, Batey RG, Farrell GC, Crewe EB, Cunningham AL, Byth K. Hepatitis C virus in intravenous drug users. *Med J Aust.* 1990;153: 274–276.

265. Van Ameijden EJ, van den Hoek JA, Mientjes GH, Coutinho RA. A longitudinal study on the incidence and transmission patterns of HIV, HBV and HCV infection among drug users in Amsterdam. *Eur J Epidemiol.* 1993;9:255–262.

266. Patti AM, Santi AL, Pompa MG, et al. Viral hepatitis and drugs: a continuing problem. *Int J Epidemiol.* 1993;22:135–139.

267. Garfein RS, Doherty MC, Brown D, et al. Hepatitis C virus infection among short-term injection drug users. *JAIDS.* 1998;18: S11–S19.

268. Conry-Cantilena C, Vanraden MT, Gibble J, et al. Routes of infection, viremia, and liver disease in blood donors found to have hepatitis C virus infection. *N Engl J Med.* 1996;334:1691–1696.

269. Kiyosawa K, Sodeyama T, Tanaka E, et al. Hepatitis C in hospital employees with needlestick injuries. *Ann Intern Med.* 1991;115:367–369.

270. Ridzon R, Gallagher K, Ciesielski C, et al. Simultaneous transmission of human immunodeficiency virus and hepatitis C virus from a needle-stick injury. *N Engl J Med.* 1997;336:919–922.

271. Mitsui T, Iwano K, Masuko K, et al. Hepatitis C virus infection in medical personnel after needlestick accident. *Hepatology.* 1992;16:1109–1114.

272. Sartori M, La Terra G, Aglietta M, Manzin A, Navino C, Verzetti G. Transmission of hepatitis C via blood splash into conjunctiva. *Scand J Infect Dis.* 1993;25:270–271.

273. Thomas DL, Gruninger SE, Siew C, Joy ED, Quinn TC. Occupational risk of hepatitis C infections among general dentists and oral surgeons in North America. *Am J Med.* 1996;100:41–45.

274. Thomas DL, Factor S, Kelen G, Washington AS, Taylor E, Quinn TQ. Hepatitis B and C in health care workers at the Johns Hopkins Hospital. *Arch Intern Med.* 1993;153: 1705–1712.

275. Gerberding JL. Incidence and prevalence of human immunodeficiency virus, hepatitis B virus, hepatitis C virus, and cytomegalovirus among health care personnel at risk for blood exposure: final report from a longitudinal study. *J Infect Dis.* 1994;170: 1410–1417.

276. Kuo MY, Hahn LJ, Hong CY, Kao JH, Chen DS. Low prevalence of hepatitis C virus infection among dentists in Taiwan. *J Med Virol.* 1993;40:10–13.

277. Martinez-Bauer E, Forns X, Armellis M, et al. Hospital admission is a relevant source of hepatitis C virus acquisition in Spain. *J Hepatol.* 2008; 48:20–27.

278. Campello C, Majori S, Poli A, Pacini P, Nicolardi L, Pini F. Prevalence of HCV antibodies in health-care workers from northern Italy. *Infection.* 1992;20:224–226.

279. Polish LB, Tong MJ, Co RL, Coleman PJ, Alter MJ. Risk factors for hepatitis C virus infection among health care personnel in a community hospital. *Am J Infect Control.* 1993;21:196–200.

280. Puro V, Petrosillo N, Ippolito G, et al. Occupational hepatitis C virus infection in Italian health care workers. *Am J Public Health.* 1995;85:1272–1275.

281. Schvarcz R, Johansson B, Nyström B, Sönnerborg A. Nosocomial transmission of hepatitis C virus. *Infection.* 1997;25:74–77.

282. Munro J, Biggs JD, McCruden EAB. Detection of a cluster of hepatitis C infections in a renal transplant unit by analysis of

sequence variation of the NS5a gene. *J Infect Dis.* 1996;174:177–180.

283. Stuyver L, Claeys H, Wyseur A, et al. Hepatitis C virus in a hemodialysis unit: molecular evidence for nosocomial transmission. *Kidney Int.* 1996;49:889–895.

284. Sampietro M, Badalamenti S, Salvadori S, et al. High prevalence of a rare hepatitis C virus in patients treated in the same hemodialysis unit: evidence for nosocomial transmission of HCV. *Kidney Int.* 1995;47:911–917.

285. Alter MJ. Epidemiology of hepatitis C. *Hepatology.* 1997;26:62S–65S.

286. Martinez-Bauer E, Forns X, Armellis M, et al. Hospital admission is a relevant source of hepatitis C virus acquisition in Spain. *J Hepatol.* 2008; 48:20–27.

287. Koten JW, Hauri AM, Armstrong KL. Use of injections in healthcare settings world-wide (2000): literature review and regional estimates. *BMJ.* 2003; 329: 1075.

288. Hutin YJ, Hauri Aon, Armstrong GL. Use of Injectious in health care settings world wide, 2000: Literature review and regional estimates. *BMJ.* 2003; 327: 1075–87.

289. Ko YC, Ho MS, Chiang TA, Chang SJ, Chang PY. Tattooing as a risk of hepatitis C virus infection. *J Med Virol.* 1992;38:288–291.

290. Sun DX, Zhang FG, Geng YQ, Xi DS. Hepatitis C transmission by cosmetic tattooing in women. *Lancet.* 1996;347:541.

291. Dusheiko GM, Smith M, Scheuer PJ. Hepatitis C virus transmission by human bite. *Lancet.* 1990;336:503–504.

292. van Doornum GJJ, Hooykaas C, Cuypers MT, van Der Lind MMD, Coutinho RS. Prevalence of hepatitis C virus infections among heterosexuals with multiple partners. *J Med Virol.* 1991;35:22–27.

293. Thomas DL, Cannon RO, Shapiro C, Hook EWI, Alter MJ, Quinn TC. *J Infect Dis.* 1994;169:990–995.

294. Petersen EE, Clemens R, Bock HL, Friese K, Hess G. Hepatitis B and C in heterosexual patients with various sexually transmitted diseases. *Infection.* 1992;20:128–131.

295. Nakashima K, Kashiwagi S, Hayashi J, et al. Sexual transmission of hepatitis C virus among female prostitutes and patients with sexually transmitted diseases in Fukuoka, Kyushu, Japan. *Am J Epidemiol.* 1992;136:1132–1137.

296. Utsumi T, Hashimoto E, Okumura Y, et al. Heterosexual activity as a risk factor for the transmission of hepatitis C virus. *J Med Virol.* 1995;46:122–125.

297. Capelli C, Prati D, Bosoni P, et al. Sexual transmission of hepatitis C virus to a repeat blood donor. *Transfusion.* 1997;37: 436–440.

298. Healey CJ, Smith DB, Walker JL, et al. Acute hepatitis C infection after sexual exposure. *Gut.* 1995;36:148–150.

299. Akahane Y, Kojima M, Sugai Y, et al. Hepatitis C virus infection in spouses of patients with type C chronic liver disease. *Ann Intern Med.* 1994;120:748–752.

300. Kao JH, Chen PJ, Yang PM, et al. Intrafamilial transmission of hepatitis C virus: the important role of infections between spouses. *J Infect Dis.* 1992;166:900–903.

301. Kao JH, Hwang YT, Chen PJ, et al. Transmission of hepatitis C virus between spouses: the important role of exposure duration. *Am J Gastroenterol.* 1996;91: 2087–2090.

302. Chayama K, Kobayashi M, Tsubota A, et al. Molecular analysis of intraspousal transmission of hepatitis C virus. *J Hepatol.* 1995;22: 431–439.

303. Piazza M, Sagliocca L, Tosone GM, et al. Sexual transmission of the hepatitis C virus and efficacy of prophylaxis with intramuscular immune serum globulin—a randomized controlled trial. *Arch Intern Med.* 1997;157:1537–1544.

304. Thaikruea L, Nelson KE, Thongsawat S, Maneekarn N, Netski D, Thomas DL. Risk factors for hepatitis C virus infection among blood donors in Northern Thailand. *Transfusion.* 2004;44:1433–1440.

305. Bresters D, Mauser-Bunschoten ED, Reesink HW, et al. Sexual transmission of hepatitis C. *Lancet.* 1993;342:210–211.

306. Everhart JE, Di Bisceglie AM, Murray LM, et al. Risk for non-A, non-B (Type C) hepatitis through sexual or household contact with chronic carriers. *Ann Intern Med.* 1990;112:544–555.
    a. Beasley RP. Nature usually favors females. *J Infect Dis.* 2005;192:1865–1866.

307. Brettler DB, Mannucci PM, Gringeri A, et al. The low risk of hepatitis C virus transmission among sexual partners of hepatitis C infected hemophilic males: an international, multicenter study. *Blood.* 1992;80:540–543.

308. Gordon SC, Patel AH, Kulesza GW, Barnes RE, Silverman AL. Lack of evidence for the heterosexual transmission of hepatitis C. *Am J Gastroenterol.* 1992;87:1849–1851.

309. Vandelli C, Renzo F, Romano L, et al. Lack of evidence of hepatitis C among monogamous couples: results of a 10-year prospective follow-up study. *Am J Gastroenterology.* 2004;99:855–9.

310. Melbye M, Biggar RJ, Wantzin P, Krogsgaard K, Ebbesen P, Becker NG. Sexual transmission of hepatitis C virus: Cohort study (1981–1989) among European homosexual men. *Br Med J.* 1990;301:210–212.

311. Danta M, Brown D, Bhagani S et al. Recent epidemic of acute hepatitis C virus infections in HIV-positive men who have sex with men linked to high-risk sexual behavior *AIDS.* 2007;21:983–91.

312. van de Laar T, Pybus O, Bruistan S, et al. Evidence of a large, international network of HCV transmission in HIV-positive men who have sex with men. *Gastroenterology.* 2004;136:1609–17.

313. Osmond DH, Charlebois E, Sheppard HW, et al. Comparison of risk factors for hepatitis C and hepatitis B virus infection in homosexual men. *J Infect Dis.* 1993;167:66–71.

314. Bodsworth NJ, Cunningham P, Kaldor J, Donovan B. Hepatitis C virus infection in a large cohort of homosexually active men: independent associations with HIV-1 infection and injecting drug use but not sexual behaviour. *Genitourin Med.* 1996;72:118–122.

315. Roudot Thoraval F, Pawlotsky JM, Thiers V, et al. Lack of mother-to-infant transmission of hepatitis C virus in human immunodeficiency virus-seronegative women: a prospective study with hepatitis C virus RNA testing. *Hepatology.* 1993;17:772–777.

316. Reinus JF, Leikin EL, Alter HJ, et al. Failure to detect vertical transmission of hepatitis C virus. *Ann Intern Med.* 1992;117:881–886.

317. Ohto H, Terazawa S, Nobuhiko S, et al. Transmission of hepatitis C virus from mothers to infants. *N Engl J Med.* 1994;330:744–750.

318. Zanetti AR, Tanzi E, Paccagnini S, et al. Mother-to-infant transmission of hepatitis C virus. *Lancet.* 1995;345:289–291.

319. Lam JPH, McOmish F, Burns SM, Yap PL, Mok JYQ, Simmonds P. Infrequent vertical transmission of hepatitis C virus. *J Infect Dis.* 1993;167:572–576.

320. Novati R, Thiers V, Monforte AD, et al. Mother-to-child transmission of hepatitis C virus detected by nested polymerase chain reaction. *J Infect Dis.* 1992;165:720–723.

321. Wejstal R, Widell A, Mansson A-S, Hermodsson S, Norkrans G. Mother-to-infant transmission of hepatitis C virus. *Ann Intern Med.* 1992;117:887–890.

322. Weintrub PS, Veereman Wauters G, Cowan MJ, Thaler MM. Hepatitis C virus infection in infants whose mothers took street drugs intravenously. *J Pediatr.* 1991;119:869.

323. Thomas DL, Villano SA, Reister K, et al. Perinatal transmission of hepatitis C virus

from human immunodeficiency virus type 1-infected individuals. *J Infect Dis.* 1998;177:1480–1488.

324. Matsubara T, Sumazaki R, Takita H. Mother-to-infant transmission of hepatitis C virus: a prospective study. *Eur J Pediatr.* 1995;154: 973–978.

325. Lin H-H, Kao J-H, Hsu H-Y, et al. Possible role of high-titer maternal viremia in perinatal transmission of hepatitis C virus. *J Infect Dis.* 1994;169:638–641.

326. Moriya T, Sasaki F, Mizui M, et al. Transmission of hepatitis C virus from mothers to infants: its frequency and risk factors revisited. *Biomed Pharmacother.* 1995;49:59–64.

327. Telfer PT, Brown D, Devereux H, Lee CA, Dusheiko GM. HCV RNA levels and HIV infection: evidence for a viral interaction in haemophilic patients. *Br J Haematol.* 1994;88:397–399.

328. Sherman KE, O'Brien J, Gutierrez G, et al. Quantitative evaluation of hepatitis C virus RNA in patients with concurrent human immunodeficiency virus infections. *J Clin Microbiol.* 1993;31: 2679–2682.

329. Eyster ME, Fried MW, Di Bisceglie AM, Goedert JJ. Increasing hepatitis C virus RNA levels in hemophiliacs: relationship to human immunodeficiency virus infection and liver disease. *Blood.* 1994;84:1020–1023.

330. Thomas DL, Shih JW, Alter HJ, et al. Effect of human immunodeficiency virus on hepatitis C virus infection among injecting drug users. *J Infect Dis.* 1996;174:690–695.

331. Ogasawara S, Kage M, Kosai K, Shimamatsu K, Kojiro M. Hepatitis C virus RNA in saliva and breast-milk of hepatitis C carrier mothers. *Lancet.* 1993;341:561.

332. Ohto H, Okamoto H, Mishiro S. Vertical transmission of hepatitis C virus. Reply. *N Engl J Med.* 1994;331:400.

333. Lin H-H, Kao J-H, Hsu H-Y, et al. Absence of infection in breast-fed infants born to hepatitis C virus-infected mothers. *J Pediatr.* 1995;126:589–591.

334. Hepatitis C Virus Network. A significant sex—but not elective cesarean section—effect on mother-to child transmission of hepatitis C virus infection. *J Infect Dis.* 2005;192: 1872–1879.

335. Mast EE, Huvang L-Y, Seto DSY, et al. Risk factors for perinatal transmission of hepatitis C virus (HCV) and the natural history of HCV acquired in infancy. *J Infect Dis.* 2005;192:1880–1889.

336. World Health Organization. Hepatitis C: global prevalence. *Weekly Epidemiological Record.* 1997:341–348.

337. Osella AR, Misciagna G, Leone A, Di Leo A, Fiore G. Epidemiology of hepatitis C virus infection in an area of southern Italy. *J Hepatol.* 1997;27:30–35.

338. Chiaramonte M, Stroffolini T, Lorenzoni U, et al. Risk factors in community-acquired chronic hepatitis C virus infection: a case-control study in Italy. *J Hepatol.* 1996;24: 129–134.

339. Nakashima K, Ikematsu H, Hayashi J, Kishihara Y, Mitsutake A, Kashiwagi S. Intrafamilial transmission of hepatitis C virus among the population of an endemic area of Japan. *JAMA.* 1995;274: 1459–1461.

340. Guadagnino V, Stroffolini T, Rapicetta M, et al. Prevalence, risk factors, and genotype distribution of hepatitis C virus infection in the general population: a community-based survey in southern Italy. *Hepatology.* 1997;26:1006–1011.

341. Arthur RR, Hassan NF, Abdallah MY, et al. Hepatitis C antibody prevalence in blood donors in different governorates in Egypt. *Trans R Soc Trop Med Hyg.* 1997;91: 271–274.

342. Sulkowski MS. Hepatitis C virus infection as an opportunistic disease in persons infected with the human immunodeficiency virus. *Clin Infect Dis.* 2000;30:S77–S84.

a. Abdel-Wahab MF, Zakaria S, Kamel M, et al. High seroprevalence of hepatitis C infection among risk groups in Egypt. *Am J Trop Med Hyg.* 1994;51:563–567.

343. Eyster ME, Diamondstone LS, Lien JM, Ehrmann WC, Quan S, Goedert JJ. Natural history of hepatitis C virus infections in multitransfused hemophiliacs: effect of coinfection with human immunodeficiency virus. The Multicenter Hemophilia Cohort Study. *JAIDS.* 1993;6:602–610.
    a. Kamel MA, Ghaffar YA, Wasef MA, Wright M, Clark LC, Miller FD. High HCV prevalence in Egyptian blood donors. *Lancet.* 1992;340:427.

344. Hibbs RG, Corwin AL, Hassan NF, et al. The epidemiology of antibody to hepatitis C in Egypt. *J Infect Dis.* 1993;168:789–790.

345. El-Sayed NM, Gomatos PJ, Rodier GR, et al. Seroprevalence survey of Egyptian tourism workers for hepatitis B virus, hepatitis C virus, human immunodeficiency virus, and Treponema pallidum infections: association of hepatitis C virus infections with specific regions of Egypt. *Am J Trop Med Hyg.* 1996;55:179–184.

346. Prati D, Capelli C, Silvani C, et al. The incidence and risk factors of community-acquired hepatitis C in a cohort of Italian blood donors. *Hepatology.* 1997;25:702–704.

347. Noguchi S, Sata M, Suzuki H, Mizokami M, Tanikawa K. Routes of transmission of hepatitis C virus in an endemic rural area of Japan— molecular epidemiologic study of hepatitis C virus infection. *Scand J Infect Dis.* 1997;29:23–28.

348. Kiyosawa K, Tanaka E, Sodeyama T, et al. Transmission of hepatitis C in an isolated area in Japan: community-acquired infection. *Gastroenterology.* 1994;106:1596–1602.

349. Kelen GD, Green GB, Purcell RH, et al. Hepatitis B and hepatitis C in emergency department patients. *N Engl J Med.* 1992;326:1399–1404.

350. Alter MJ. Epidemiology of hepatitis C in the West. *Semin Liver Dis.* 1995;15:5–14.

351. Alter MJ, Hadler SC, Judson FN, et al. Risk factors for acute non-A, non-B hepatitis in the United States and association with hepatitis C virus infection. *JAMA.* 1990;264: 2231–2235.

352. Alter MJ, Kruszon-Moran D, Nainan OV, et al. The prevalence of hepatitis C virus infection in the United States, 1988 through 1994. *N Engl J Med.* 1999;341: 556–562.

353. Murphy EL, Bryzman PA, Williams AE. Prevalence of Hepatitis C Virus Infection in the United States. *N Engl J Med* 1999; 341:2093–2095.

354. Ge D, Fellay J, Thompson HJ etal. Genetic variation in IL28B predicts hepatitis C treatment-induced viral clearance. *Nature.* 2009; 461:399–401.

355. Everhart JE, Ruhl CE. Burden of digestive diseases in the United States-Part III: liver, biliary tract and pancreas. *Gastroenterology.* 2009;136:1134–44.

356. Wise M, Bialek S, Firelli C, Bell BP, Survillo F. Changing trends in hepatitis C-related mortality in the United States 1995–2004. Hepatology 2008;47: 1128–1135.

357. Davis GL, Alter MJ, El-Serag H, Poynard T, Jennings LW. Aging of hepatitis C virus (HCV) – infected persons in the United States: a multiple cohort model of HCV prevalence and disease progression. *Gastroenterology.* 2010;138:513–521.

358. Poynard T, Bedossa P, Opolon P, et al. Natural history of liver fibrosis progression in patients with chronic hepatitis C. *Lancet.* 1997;349: 825–832.

359. Thomas DL, Astembroski J, Rai R, et al. The natural history of hepatitis C virus infection: host, viral and environmental factors. *JAMA.* 2000;284:450–456.

360. Benhamon Y, Bocket M, DiMartino V, et al. Liver fibrosis progression in HIV and HCV coinfected patients. The Multivirc Group. *Hepatology.* 1999;30:1054–1058.

361. El-Serag HB, Mason AC. Risk factors for the rising rates of primary liver cancer in the United States. *Arch Intern Med.* 2000;160: 3222–3230.

362. Armstrong GL, Alter MJ, McQuillan GM, Margolis HS. The past incidence of hepatitis C virus infection: implication for the future burden of chronic liver disease in the United States. *Hepatology.* 2000;31: 772–782.

363. Muir AJ, Bornstein JD, Killenberg PG. Peginterferon alfa-2b and ribavirin for the treatment of chronic hepatitis C in blacks and non-Hispanic Whites. *N Engl J Med.* 2004; 350:2265–2271.

364. Conjecvaram HS, Fried MW, Jeffers IJ et al. Peginterferon and ribavirin treatment in African-American and Caucasian American patients with hepatitis C genotype 1. *Gastroenterology.* 2006;131:470–477.

365. Pooydad F, McLone J, Bacon BR et al. Boceprevir for untreated chronic HCV genotype 1 infection. *N Engl J Med.* 2011; 364:1195–1206.

366. Jacobson IM, McHutchison JG, Ousheiko G, et al. Telaprivir for previously untreated chronic hepatitis C virus infection. *N Engl J Med.* 2011;364:2405–2416.

367. Ge D, Fellay J, Thompson AJ et al. Genetic variation in IL28B predicts hepatitis C virus treatment induced viral clearance. *Nat Genetics.* 2009;41:399–401.

368. Suppint V, McKowan M, Malenetial G, et al. IL28B is associated with response to chronic hepatitis C interferon alpha and ribavirin therapy. *Nat Genetic.* 2009;41:1100–1104.

369. Tanaka Y, Nishida N, Sugiyama M, et al. Genome-wide association of IL28B with response to pegylated interferon alpha and ribavirin therapy for chronic hepatitis C. *Nat Genetics.* 2009;41:1106–1109.

370. Thomas DL, Thio CL, Martin MP, et al. Genetic variation in IL28B and spontaneous clearance of hepatitis C virus. *Nature.* 2009; 461:798–801.

371. Labrique AR, Thomas DL, Stoszek SK, Nelson KE. Hepatitis E: A new emerging infectious disease. *Epidemiol Rev.* 1999; 21:162–178.

372. Bradley DW. Hepatitis E virus: A brief review of the biology, molecular virology, and immunology of a novel virus. *J Hepatol.* 1995;22(suppl 1):140–145.

373. Hagan H, Jarlais DCD, Friedman SR, Purchase D, Alter MJ. Reduced risk of hepatitis B and hepatitis C among injection drug users in the Tacoma syringe exchange program. *Am J Public Health.* 1995;85:1531–1537.

374. Hagan H, McGough JP, Thiede H, Weiss NS, Hopkins S, Alexander ER. Syringe exchange and risk of infection with hepatitis B and C viruses. *Am J Epidemiol.* 1999;149: 203–213.

375. Mehta SH, Astemborski J, Kirk GD, Strathdee SA, Nelson, KE, Vlahov D and Thomas DL. Changes in blood-borne infection risk among injection drug users. *J Infect Dis.* 2011;203:587–594.

376. Ticehurst J. Identification and characterization of hepatitis E virus. In: Hollinger FB, ed. Viral Hepatitis and Liver Disease. Baltimore, MD: Williams & Wilkins; 1991:501–513.

377. Labrique AR, Kuniholm MH, Nelson KE. Global impact of hepatitis E. New horizons for an emerging virus: Emerging Infections, edited by Scheld WM, Grayson ML, Hoghen JM. RSM Presi, Washington DC. 9:2010; 53–93

378. Meng XJ, Purcell RH, Halbur PG, et al. A novel virus in swine is closely related to the human hepatitis E virus. *Proc Natl Acad Sci USA.* 1997;94:9860–9865.

379. Guthmann JP, Klovstad H, Boccia D, et al. A large outbreak of hepatitis E among a displaced population in Darfur, Sudan, 2004: The role of water treatment methods. *Clin Infect Dis.* 42:1685–1691.

380. Teshale EH, Howard CM, Grytdal SP, et al. Hepatitis E epidemic, Uganda. *Emerg Infect Dis.* 16:126–129.

381. Nelson KE, Kmush B, Labrique AB. The emerging threat of hepatitis E virus infections in developed countries and among immuno-compromised populations. *Expert review of infectious diseases.* 2011; 9(12): 1133–1148.

382. Longer CF, Denny SL, Caudill JD, et al. Experimental hepatitis E: pathogenesis in cynomolgus macaques (Macaca fascicularis). *J Infect Dis.* 1993;168:602–609.

383. Maneerat Y, Clayson ET, Myint KS, Young GD, Innis BL. Experimental infection of the laboratory rat with the hepatitis E virus. *J Med Virol.* 1996;48:121–128.

384. Bradley DW, Krawczynski K, Cook EH, et al. Enterically transmitted non-A, non-B hepatitis: serial passage of disease in cyno-molgus macaques and tamarins and recovery of disease-associated 27 to 34 nm virus-like particles. *Proc Natl Acad Sci USA.* 1987;84: 6277–6281.

385. Chauhan A, Jamell S, Dilawari JB, Chawla YK, Kaur U, Ganguly NK. Hepatitis E transmission to a volunteer. *Lancet.* 1993;341:149–150.

386. Nanda SK, Yalcinkaya K, Panigrahi AK, Acharya SK, Jameel S, Panda SK. Etiological role of hepatitis E virus in sporadic fulminant hepatitis. *J Med Virol.* 1994;42:133–137.

387. Rab MA, Bile MK, Mubarik MM, et al. Water-borne hepatitis E virus epidemic in Islamabad, Pakistan: A common source out-break traced to the malfunction of a modern water treatment plant. *Am J Trop Med Hyg.* 1997;57:151–157.

388. Teo CG. Fatal outbreaks of jaundice in preg-nancy and the epidemic history of hepatitis E. *Epidemiol Infect.* 2012;140:767–787.

389. Karmar N, Selves J, Mansuy JM, et al. Hepatitis E virus and chronic hepatitis in organ-transplant recipients. *N Engl J Med.* 2008;358(8), 811–817.

390. Kamar N, Mansuy JM, Cointault O, et al. Hepatitis E virus-related cirrhosis in kidney and kidney-pancreas-transplant recipients. *Am J Transplant.* 2008;8(8), 1744–1748.

391. Bendall R, Ellis V, Ijaz S, Ali R, Dalton H. A comparison of two commercially avail-able anti-HEV IgG kits and a re-evaluation of anti-HEV IgG seroprevalence data in de-veloped countries. *J Med Virol.* 2010;82(5), 799–805.

392. Mast EE, Alter MJ, Holland PV, Purcell RH. Evaluation of assays for antibody to hepatitis E virus by a serum panel. Hepatitis E Virus Antibody Serum Panel Evaluation Group. *Hepatology.* 1998;27(3), 857–861.

393. Drobeniuc J, Meng J, Reuter G, et al. Serologic assays specific to immunoglobu-lin M antibodies against hepatitis E virus: pangenotypic evaluation of performances. *Clin Infect Dis.* 2010;51(3) e24–7.

394. Dalton HR, Stableforth W, Thurairajah P, et al. Autochthonous hepatitis E in Southwest England: natural history, complications and seasonal variation, and hepatitis E virus IgG seroprevalence in blood donors, the elderly and patients with chronic liver disease. *Eur J Gastroenterol Hepatol.* 2008;20(8), 784–790.

395. Lewis HC, Wichmann O, Duizer E. Transmission routes and risk factors for autochthonous hepatitis E virus infection in Europe: a systematic review. *Epidemiol Infect.* 2010;138(2), 145–166.

396. Hepatitis E in the South West of France in in-dividuals who have never visited an endemic area. *J Med Virol.* 2004;74:419–424.

397. Ijaz S, Arnold E, Banks M, et al. Non-travel-associated hepatitis E in England and Wales: demographic, clinical and molecular epidemiologic characteristics. *J Infect Dis.* 2005;192:1166–1172.

398. Clemente-Casares P, Pina S, Buti M, et al. Hepatitis E virus epidemiology in indus-trialized countries. *Emerg Infect Dis.* 2003;9:448–454.

399. Wong DC, Purcell RH, Sreennivasan MA, Prasad SR, Parvi KM. Epidemic and endemic hepatitis in India: evidence for non-A, non-B hepatitis virus etiology. *Lancet.* 1980;2: 876–878.

400. Labrique AB, Thomas DL, Stoszck SK, Nelson KE. Hepatitis E: new emerging infectious disease. *Epidemiol Rev.* 1999;21: 162–178.
    a. Matsuda H, Okada K, Takahashi K, Misbiro S. Severe hepatitis E virus infection after ingestion of uncooked liver from a wild boar. *J Infect Dis.* 2003;188:944.

401. Balayan MS, Andjaparidze AG, Savinskaya SS, et al. Evidence for a virus in non-A, non-B hepatitis transmitted via the fecal-oral route. *Intervirology.* 1983;20(1), 23–31.

402. Colson P, Borentain P, Queyriaux B, et al. Pig liver sausage as a soruce of hepatitis E virus transmission to humans. *J Infect Dis.* 2010;202(6), 825–834.

403. Tei S, Kitajima N, Takahashi K, Mishiro S. Zoonotic transmission of hepatitis E virus from deer to human beings. *Lancet.* 2003;362(9381), 371–373.

404. Said B, Ijaz S, Kafatos G, et al. Hepatitis E outbreak on cruise ship. *Emerg Infect Dis.* 2009;15(11), 1738–1744.

405. Kuniholm MH, Purcell RH, McQuillan GM, et al. Epidemiology of hepatitis E virus in the United States: Results from the Third National health and Nutrition Examination Survey, 1988–1994. *J Infect Dis.* 2009;200(1), 48–56.

406. Christensen PB, Engle RE, Hjort C et al. Time trend of the prevalence of hepatitis E, antibodies among farmers and blood donors: A potential zoonosis in Denmark. *Clin Infect Dis.* 2008;47(8), 1026–1031.

407. Withers MR, Correa MT, Morrow M, et al. Antibody levels to hepatitis E virus in North Carolina swine workers, non-swine workers, swine, and murids. *Am J Trop Med Hyg.* 2002;66(4), 384–388.

408. Meng XJ, Wiseman B, Elvinger F, et al. Prevalence of antibodies to hepatitis E virus in veterinarians working with swine and in normal blood donors in the United States and other countries. *J Clin Microbiol.* 2002;40(1), 117–122.

409. Feagins AR, Opriessing T, Guenetle DK, Halbur PG, Meng XJ. Detection and Characterization of infectious Hepatitis E virus from commercial pig livers sold in local grocery stores in the USA. *J Gen Virol.* 2007; 88:912–917.

410. Barnard E, Hogee S, Garry P, Rose N, Pavio N. Thermal inactivation of infectious hepatitis E virus in experimentally contaminated food. *Appl Environ Microbiol.* 2012;78: 5153–9.

411. Baylis SA, Nick S, Blumel J, Micha Nubling C. Hepatitis E virus and blood donors in Germany. *Vox Sang.* 2010;98(3 Pt 2), 479.

412. Labrique AB, Zaman K, Hossian Z, et al. Epidemiology and risk factors for incident hepatitis E Virus infections in rural Bangladesh. *Am J Epidemiol.* 2010;172:952–961.

413. Shrestha, MP, Scott RM, Joshi DM, et al. Safety and efficacy of a recombinant hepatitis E vaccine. *N Engl J Med.* 2007;356:895–903.

414. Simons JN, Leary TP, Dawson GJ, et al. Isolation of novel virus-like sequences associated with human hepatitis. *Nature Med.* 1995;1:564–569.

415. Alter HJ, Nakatsuji Y, Melpolder JC, et al. The incidence and disease implications of transfusion associated hepatitis G virus infection. *N Engl J Med.* 1997;336:747–754.

416. Linnen J, Wages J Jr, Zhang-Keck ZY, et al. Molecular cloning and disease association of hepatitis G virus: a transfusion-transmissible agent. *Eur J Biochem.* 1996;271:505–508.

24

Sexually Transmitted Diseases

Charlotte A. Gaydos

INTRODUCTION

In the United States, 19 million new cases of sexually transmitted diseases (STDs) occur annually, costing $10–17 billion per year and primarily affecting adolescents and young adults.[1–3] This chapter reviews the epidemiology of STDs, the assessment of personal risk factors, and the community factors that contribute to STD morbidity. A number of specific diseases are considered, focusing on the most common organisms, including *Chlamydia trachomatis*, *Neisseria gonorrhoeae*, *Treponema pallidum* (syphilis), *Haemophilus ducreyi* (chancroid), *Trichomonas vaginalis*, bacterial vaginosis, and chronic viral infections, including herpes simplex virus (HSV) and human papillomavirus (HPV) (**Table 24-1**).

Understanding the epidemiology of STDs is a critical step in developing rational diagnostic, treatment, and control strategies. In recent years, molecular assays such as nucleic acid amplification assays have revolutionized diagnostic testing modalities.[4] At the same time, treatment has become more complex, especially in bacterial infections, because of the emergence of antimicrobial resistance.[5] STDs have been conclusively linked to increased risk of HIV transmission and acquisition.[6–9] Traditional disease control program approaches have included clinic-based screening and partner notification. These measures have been augmented by community-based STD control, including use of computerized disease surveillance systems, geographic mapping, and use of noninvasive new diagnostic specimens and molecular assays, as well as population-based screening in the nonclinical setting. Additionally, issues of health inequity and health disparities make STDs a prime target for management and control. STDs present numerous barriers to routine clinical care and diagnosis, because of the associated stigma, costs, and confidentiality issues.[10]

Table 24-1	Sexually Transmitted Diseases
Bacterial Infection	
Gonorrhea (*Neisseria gonorrhoeae*)	
Syphilis (*Treponema pallidum*)	
Chlamydia (*Chlamydia trachomatis*)	
Chancroid (*Hemophilus ducreyi*)	
Granuloma inguinbale (*Campylobacter granulomatis*)	
Lymphogranuloma venereum (*Chlamydia trachomatis LGV serovars*)	
Bacterial vaginosis (ecological disturbance of the vaginal flora)	
Viral	
Genital herpes (herpes simplex type 1 and type 2)	
Human herpesvirus 8 (Kaposi sarcoma)	
Human papillomavirus infection	
Condylomata acuminate (genital warts)	
Cervical/anal dysplasia and epithelial cancers	
Hepatitis B infection	
Human immunodeficiency virus	
Human T-cell lymphotropic virus type 1 (HTLV-1)	
Cytomegalovirus	
Parasitic	
Trichomonas	
Scabies	
Pediculosis	

TRANSMISSION MODES: THE DEFINITION OF A SEXUALLY TRANSMITTED DISEASE

Sexually transmitted diseases are transmitted through sexual intercourse, which is defined as sexual contact including vaginal intercourse, oral intercourse (i.e., fellatio or cunnilingus), or rectal intercourse. These diseases can be transmitted between either heterosexual or homosexual partners. Different types of sexual activity may result in increased risks. Receptive rectal intercourse and vaginal intercourse carry the highest risks of STD transmission.

CHLAMYDIA

Chlamydia trachomatis infection is the most common bacterial STD in the United States, with approximately 2–3 million cases estimated to occur annually.[11] In 2010, there were 1,307,893 cases of chlamydia reported to the Centers for Disease Control and Prevention (CDC) (**Figure 24-1**).[3]

Chlamydiae are obligate intracellular bacteria, which cause a wide variety of diseases in humans and animals.[12,13] The infections, causes by serovars D–K, are associated with many clinical syndromes, ranging from cervicitis, salpingitis, acute urethral syndrome, endometritis, ectopic pregnancy, infertility, and pelvic inflammatory disease (PID) in the female; to conjunctivitis and pneumonia in infants; to urethritis, proctitis, and epididymitis in the male.[14] Serovars A–C are associated with trachoma, a cause of infectious blindness in the developing world.[13]

Gender Differences

Men

In men, chlamydia urethritis accounts for approximately 40% of all cases of nongonococcal urethritis in the United States.[14] Urethritis in men typically presents as a mucoid discharge, associated often with dysuria. Asymptomatic infection occurs in more than 30% of cases. The time from infection to development of symptoms is usually in the range of 7–14 days.

Rectal chlamydia infection occurs predominantly in homosexual men who have had receptive rectal intercourse.[15] As with other infections in gay men, rectal chlamydia has been increasing. Lymphogranuloma venereum (LGV) is a chlamydia syndrome causing inflammatory and ulcerative disease and is caused by the L1, L2, and L3 serovars. From 2003 to 2005, LGV outbreaks causing severe rectal inflammation, mostly in men having sex with men (MSM) with HIV, were reported from the Netherlands and a number of U.S. cities.[16]

Women

Women bear the burden of most of the morbidity due to chlamydia infections because of the seriousness of the sequelae of infections, especially pelvic inflammatory disease (PID). In women, cervical infection is the most commonly reported syndrome.[17] More than half of women with cervical infection are asymptomatic. When symptoms occur, they may manifest as vaginal discharge or poorly differentiated abdominal or lower abdominal pain. At clinical examination, there are often no clinical signs present. When they are present, however, signs include mucopurulent cervical discharge, cervical friability, and cervical edema.[18]

Left untreated, approximately 30% of women with chlamydial infection will develop pelvic inflammatory disease.[18] The PID seen in conjunction with chlamydia is associated with lower rates of clinical symptoms than the PID seen with gonorrhea. However, this subacute PID is associated with higher rates of subsequent infertility because chlamydia induces an inflammatory reaction characterized by fibrosis.

Epidemiology

The epidemiology of chlamydia is interesting because the reporting scheme includes a number of artifacts. Reported chlamydia infections are more common in women (610.6/100,000) than in men

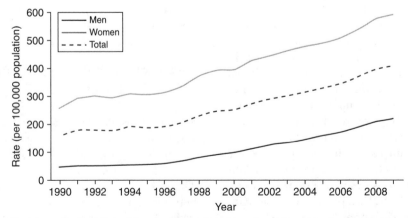

Figure 24-1 Chlamydia—Rates by Sex, United States, 1990–2009. Reproduced from the Centers for Disease Control and Prevention. 2010 Sexually Transmitted Diseases Surveillance. http://www.cdc.gov/std/stats10/figures/7.htm, Last Updated November 17, 2011. Accessed October 26, 2012.

(233.7/100,000), and rates have increased substantially since 1984 (Figure 24-1).[3] Both of these trends may be somewhat artificial, however. The rate differential between women and men is mainly due to different ascertainment and reporting practices. Women are typically diagnosed with an etiologic diagnosis of chlamydia on the basis of a chlamydia screening test performed at physical examination. Clinical practice guidelines strongly recommend routine chlamydia screening for sexually active women younger than the age of 25.[5,19] This practice has also been incorporated into quality assurance guidelines for managed care organizations (HEDIS).[20] In contrast, men are often treated for chlamydia infection on the basis of presentation of a syndrome of urethritis or as a contact to a woman with chlamydia, with definitive etiologic diagnoses never being made. As a consequence, these cases may not meet surveillance definitions for chlamydia and may not be reported.

The trend of increasing incidence of infection likely results from increased screening activity, because women are routinely screened for this STD (and men are not).[3] The ascertainment bias favors increased disease reporting in women. A true estimate of chlamydia prevalence is not known, which presents major problems in evaluating trends.[11]

The rates of chlamydia are highest in adolescent women and drop off steeply past that age. For example, the reported rate for women between the ages of 15 and 19 is 3,378.2/100,000, but drops off to 530.9/100,000 for women ages 30–34.[3] There is a strong hypothesis that this steep decline in incidence may not be related solely to behavior, but rather may also reflect the development of partial immunity to clinical infection through periodic repeated exposures.

Diagnosis

Advances in chlamydia testing technology since the early 1980s have resulted in easy, assessable chlamydia screening being available. Before 1984, chlamydia testing was available only by tissue culture, which was expensive and cumbersome, or by direct fluorescent antibody (DFA) testing, which was labor intensive. The nonculture tests that were developed were not sensitive. Currently, molecular nucleic acid amplification tests (NAATs) can be performed both on urogenital specimens, such as cervical and urethral swabs, as well as vaginal swabs, and on urine.[4,13,21–29] The development of new, non-invasive urine- and vaginal-based, nucleic acid-based technologies has resulted in substantial expansion of screening activities because of the reduced need to perform clinical pelvic exams. Most test formats have combined the gonorrhea and chlamydia assays into a single test platform. Many of the new assays can also be performed robotically.[30–32]

Chlamydia screening programs have been demonstrated to be cost-effective.[33–35] Screening intervention programs can affect chlamydia prevalence and be instrumental in preventing PID and sequelae such as hospitalization by removing infected individuals from the prevalent pool of the population.[36–39]

GONORRHEA

Gonorrhea is a bacterial exudative infection caused by *Neisseria gonorrhoeae*, a fastidious gram-negative bacteria.[40] *N. gonorrhoeae* was first described by Neisser in 1879, and is a gram-negative, nonmotile, non-spore-forming diplococcus, belonging to the family Neisseriaceae. Gonorrhea is one of the oldest diseases known to humans; the term, which is Greek and means "flow of seed," was first coined by Galen; clinically, gonorrhea was described in the Old Testament of the Bible as well as in ancient Chinese, Greek, Roman, and Egyptian writings.[40,41] The other pathogenic species is *N. meningitidis*, to which *N. gonorrhoeae* is genetically closely related. Although *N. meningitidis* is not usually considered to be an STD, it may infect the mucous membranes of the anogenital area of homosexual men.[42]

Gender Differences
Men

In men, urethritis is the most common syndrome associated with gonorrhea. Discharge or dysuria usually appears within one week of exposure, although as many as 5–10% of patients never have signs or symptoms. Asymptomatic disease can exist in men for as long as several weeks after infection.[40] Nevertheless, during this time the infectious organism is potentially transmissible to sexual partners. Epididymitis and epididymo-orchitis can occur as a complication of untreated gonococcal infections, but can also be caused by chlamydia, coliforms, or *Pseudomonas*. The incidence of epididymitis is estimated to be in the range of 1–4 cases per 1000 men per year.[43]

Symptomatic anorectal gonococcal disease occurs in persons with a history of receptive rectal intercourse.[44] Approximately 50% of these patients have symptoms of rectal pain, discharge, constipation, and tenesmus. Anorectal disease can also occur in women who have endocervical gonorrhea and who have not necessarily had receptive rectal intercourse. In these cases, infection is presumed to have occurred via tracking of secretion across the perineum. Indeed, as many as 30% of such women often have coexistent rectal infection, though it is usually asymptomatic.

Because rectal gonorrhea in men implies a history of unprotected rectal intercourse, surveillance of rectal gonorrhea has been useful as a surrogate marker for HIV risk in MSM. Starting in 1997, troubling reports of an increase of gonorrhea in MSM surfaced, with this trend continuing into the present.[3] From 1990 to 2010, the proportion of isolates from MSM in selected STD clinics from the Gonococcal Isolate Surveillance Project (GISP) has increased steadily from 4.6% to 28.9%, with the largest proportion of isolates being noted on the West Coast.[3]

Pharyngeal gonorrhea also occurs among those who practice oral sex and has been detected more frequently in the era of molecular tests, as these diagnostics are more sensitive than culture.[45,46]

Women

In women, gonorrhea typically causes cervical disease (cervicitis). Women with untreated gonococcal cervicitis, as well as untreated chlamydia infections, develop upper tract infection and/or pelvic inflammatory disease.[47,48] Other organisms, such as anaerobes, *Gardnerella vaginalis*, enteric gram-negative rods, and other pathogens, such as *Mycoplasma genitalium* and bacterial vaginosis-associated microflora, may also be associated with PID.[5]

Epidemiology

In 2010, 309,341 cases of gonorrhea in the United States were reported to the CDC by local and state health departments, representing a nationwide population-based rate of 110.8/100,000; this rate has been fairly stable since 1997.[3] An additional 1–2 cases are thought to occur for every officially reported case. The highest rates are seen in adolescent women (age 15–19 years) and young adult men (20–24 years), representing, in part, sexual behavior patterns.

One of the problems with the CDC-reported data is that they are based on a passive case-based reporting system. Population-based studies have demonstrated that the epidemiology of *incident* symptomatic disease, as represented by passive reporting, is different from *prevalent* asymptomatic infection. For example, in a survey conducted in Baltimore in 1997–1998, a population-based sample of individuals aged 18–35 years were interviewed in their households, and urine samples were assayed by NAAT for chlamydia and gonorrhea. Gonorrhea

estimates using this population were more than three times greater than the rates reported by health departments.[49] Although gonorrhea incidence has decreased by nearly 70% since the peak of the gonorrhea epidemic in the mid-1970s, the infection has become increasingly prevalent in inner-city areas affected by other social problems, especially drug use and pregnancy. In these areas, incidence rates among adolescents often exceed 15% per year.

Disseminated gonococcal infection (DGI), or gonococcal septicemia, occurs in approximately 0.5–3% of untreated gonococcal cases.[40] DGI is more commonly seen in women, in particular during pregnancy, and is also more common in persons with complement deficiencies.

Perinatal Disease

Perinatal infection with gonorrhea is relatively rare in the United States, but is often found in the developing world. Perinatal gonococcal disease is transmitted by direct exposure, as an infant passes through the birth canal of an infected cervix.

Gonococcal ophthalmia is a severe public health problem in the developing world and can be effectively prevented with inexpensive prophylaxis. The incidence of gonococcal ophthalmia is estimated to be 42% of infants exposed to an infected cervical canal. These infants develop a purulent conjunctivitis that can then rapidly progress to keratitis and subsequent corneal blindness. Because of the severe sequelae of this infection, public health authorities instituted postnatal prophylaxis with ophthalmic silver nitrate as early as 1910, effectively preventing corneal infection in 95% of exposed infants. Prevention of perinatal infection is the rationale for aggressive screening programs in pregnant women.

The same perinatal ophthalmia can be caused by *C. trachomatis*. Ophthalmia is also occasionally seen in adults, usually as a result of self-inoculation.

Diagnosis

The gold-standard diagnostic approach for gonorrhea has traditionally been culture; culture involves many operational considerations, such as logistical requirements and environmental requirements. Specimens should be inoculated onto nonselective media (chocolate agar), upon which all *Neisseria* spp. will grow, or selective media, such as modified Thayer-Martin (MTM). Selective media contain antimicrobial agents that inhibit the growth of commensal bacteria, nonpathogenic *Neisseria* spp., and fungi. Because pathogenic *Neisseria* spp. are nutritionally and environmentally fastidious, the ideal method for transporting organisms for culture is to plate the specimens directly onto the culture medium and immediately incubate the plates in an increased humidity atmosphere of 3–5% CO_2, at a temperature of 35–37°C.

A direct Gram stain may be performed as soon as the specimen is collected on site, or a smear may be prepared and transported to the laboratory. Urethral smears from males with symptomatic gonorrhea usually contain intracellular gram-negative diplococci in polymorphonuclear leukocytes (PMNs). Extracelllular organisms may be seen as well, but a presumptive diagnosis of gonorrhea requires the presence of intracellular diplococci. The sensitivity of such smears in males ranges from 90% to 95.0%.[50] However, endocervical smears from females and rectal specimens require diligent interpretation, owing to colonization of these mucous membranes with other gram-negative coccobacillary organisms. In females, the sensitivity of an endocervical Gram stain is estimated to be 50% to 70.0%.[50]

Nucleic acid amplification tests, such as polymerase chain reaction (PCR), standard displacement amplification (SDA), transcription-mediated amplification (TMA), and real-time PCR, are now widely used and are the most common gonorrhea (and chlamydia) tests performed in the United States today.[29,51] NAATs are more sensitive in certain situations and can be used on nongenital samples, such as urine and vaginal swabs. The use of urine as a diagnostic technique has facilitated expansion of gonorrhea screening efforts, especially in populations where clinical service provision is difficult and/or inadequate.

Treatment

Treatment for mucosal gonorrhea infections is based on providing single-dose regimens, preferably oral, that are effective against most or all of the known resistant determinants.[5] Current regimens include either a quinolone (see the discussion of resistance in the next subsection) or a third-generation cephalosporin. All patients treated for gonorrhea should also be treated for chlamydia, with either azithromycin 1 gram (single dose) or doxycycline 100 mg twice daily for 1 week. The chlamydia recommendation is based on the high rate of gonorrhea/chlamydia coinfection, which may be as high as 30–40%.[5]

N. gonorrhoeae has tremendous capacity to develop antimicrobial resistance. For 30 years after World War II, penicillin was the antimicrobial therapy of choice. In 1976, the first case of plasmid-medicated penicillinase-producing N. gonorrhoeae (PPNG) was reported. PPNG rapidly developed into a major public health problem and made the penicillin class of antibiotics obsolete by the mid-1980s. Chromosomally mediated resistance to penicillin (CMRNG) was described in the early 1980s, high-level plasmid-mediated tetracycline resistance (TRNG) developed in 1986, and quinolone antibiotic resistance (QRNG) appeared in the late 1990s.[52]

Development of standardized effective gonococcal treatment strategies has required accurate surveillance, which has occurred since the mid-1980s with the implementation of the national gonorrhea surveillance network. This multisite surveillance system has provided standardized mechanisms for determining antimicrobial resistance. As a by-product of that system, the CDC's Gonococcal Isolate Surveillance Project (GISP) recently described increased incidence of anorectal infection in the GISP cohort, suggesting that unprotected anal intercourse was increasing within the homosexual community surveyed by the GISP program. This trend presents a very troubling public health issue, as it indicates a higher risk profile for all STDs, including HIV.

Quinolone Resistance

Quinolone resistance has rapidly emerged as a major public health problem in gonorrhea treatment. Quinolone resistance is mediated by mutations in the gyrase and topoisomerase genes in the gonococcal genome, which render high-level resistance to the quinolone class of drugs. This development has had major implications. For example, in parts of Southeast Asia, more than 50% of gonococcal isolates consist of QRNG.[53] From 2002 to 2004, this development rapidly spread to the western United States and Hawaii. More recently, QRNG has been associated with as many as 10–15% of isolates in the United States in homosexual men. For this reason, quinolones are no longer recommended as first-line therapy for gonorrhea.[5] Recently, ceftriaxone-resistant gonorrhea has been isolated and cefixime treatment failures have occurred, leading to the disturbing forecast of a future era with untreatable gonorrhea.[54–56]

Population-Based Surveys for Chlamydia and Gonorrhea Diagnostic Testing

The availability of nucleic acid amplification tests has revolutionized gonorrhea and chlamydia diagnostics. NAATs are highly sensitive and are able to detect as few as 10 organisms per specimen. These tests have been applied in a large number of field settings, including emergency departments, job centers, middle and high schools, and military training sites. The largest studies have been done in military recruits being inducted at large bases in the eastern United States that processed inductees from all 50 states; these investigations found prevalences of 10% in females and approximately 5% in male recruits.[39,57-59] In another sample, consisting of more than 12,000 adolescents in the United States, the overall prevalence of chlamydial infection was estimated to be 4.2%.[60] Hospital emergency departments have also been sites for urine screening of young adults presenting for reasons other than reproductive health care and have demonstrated high prevalence as well.[61-63]

Combining the NAAT technology with population-based surveys provides new insights into the burden of these STDs in the general population. A survey in Baltimore provided estimates representative of adults living in the city between the ages of 18 and 35 years.[49] The prevalence of gonococcal infection overall was 3.0% in all adults aged 18 to 35 years; it ranged from 8% in 19- and 20-year-olds to 0.5% in 33- to 35-year-olds.

PELVIC INFLAMMATORY DISEASE

PID is most often considered to be a result of gonorrhea, chlamydia, enteric organisms, and anaerobic organisms, but is a poorly defined syndrome, in part because it affects multiple organs and is not associated with any clearly defined diagnostic criteria (**Figure 24-2**). Semantically, PID represents infection of the soft tissues of upper genital tract structures and includes endometritis, salpingitis, oophoritis, and pelvic peritonitis. Fatalities from PID are rare,

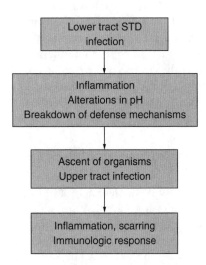

Note: STD, sexually transmitted disease.

Figure 24-2 Pelvic inflammatory disease pathogenesis model.

but severe disease may lead to tubo-ovarian abscess and at times the necessity for hysterectomy. Chronic complications are more common. Women with previous history of PID are more likely to have tubal-factor infertility and are at higher risk for ectopic pregnancy.[64-71] The overall direct economic impact of PID alone has been estimated to be $4.2 billion.[72]

The consequences of PID were eloquently shown by Westrom in a large cohort of Swedish women.[68,73-75] He diagnosed all cases of PID by laparoscopy (the gold-standard diagnostic procedure) and followed them for over 25 years—from adolescence through the childbearing years. According to these data, 10% of women with one PID episode had tubal infertility, 25% of those who had two episodes had tubal infertility, and more than 60% of women with three episodes had tubal infertility. The relative risk of ectopic pregnancy was greater than 10 compared to women without one episode of PID. Because these complications occur long after the initial infective process, the epidemics of infertility and ectopic pregnancy track the initial epidemic of gonorrhea or chlamydial infection by a substantial latency period.

In the United States, an estimated 500,000 to 1,000,000 cases of PID occur annually.[3] Estimates of PID incidences vary and are made more difficult by the lack of prospective studies, as well as the difficulty in clinical diagnosis.[48] Ascertainment of disease burden is difficult because PID syndrome is not a reportable disease. The CDC reported 113,000 cases of PID from Initial Visits to Physicians' Offices and the National Disease and Therapeutic Index Surveillance for 2010, but the actual burden of cases is estimated to be much higher.[3] Changes in the U.S. healthcare system in recent decades have emphasized outpatient management of STDs. Therefore, although hospital discharges for PID since 1990 have dropped sharply, these data are considered unreliable because of the confounding caused by changing practice patterns.

PID is associated with adolescence, increased number of sexual partners, a previous episode of PID, use of an intrauterine device, and douching.[76-79] Clinical criteria that have been traditionally used for diagnosis include two of three major criteria: lower abdominal pain, adnexal tenderness, or fever.[78] Some sources have also added the presence of a lower tract infection (gonococcal or chlamydial cervicitis). Careful studies of clinical criteria that have used laparoscopy as the standard for diagnosis of PID found that the sensitivity and specificity of clinical criteria is 60–70% in expert hands.[80] As many as one-fourth of PID cases may not demonstrate symptoms, especially disease associated with chlamydia. Given this fact, many practitioners currently treat women with mild cervical motion tenderness with treatment regimens effective against PID under the assumption that the benefit of preventing pelvic inflammatory disease or curing early pelvic inflammatory disease outweighs the costs in terms of increased cost of treatment and potential side effects.

Treatment strategies for PID are based on the underlying microbiology, including antimicrobial coverage for *N. gonorrhoeae*, *C. trachomatis*, streptococci, gram-negative rods, and anaerobes.[81] Treatment regimens are complex (and beyond the scope of this chapter), but guidelines are issued every two years by the CDC.[5]

Despite the strides made in developing effective antimicrobial regimens, treatment efficacy has proved difficult to assess. Most clinical treatment studies use clinical criteria for determination of efficacy, despite the limitations of clinical diagnosis. Therefore, these studies are subject to both type I and type II statistical errors. Furthermore, although the morbidity of PID is a long-term phenomenon, few treatment studies have correlated effective antimicrobial therapy with better long-term outcomes in terms of reduced incidence of infertility and ectopic pregnancy. Treatment of acute PID is considered to be secondary prevention. The consensus regarding primary prevention is that reducing gonococcal and chlamydial infections is the most effective approach.[82] Screening interventions for chlamydia have demonstrated reductions in PID prevalence of more than 60%.[36]

SYPHILIS

Syphilis is a bacterial sexually transmitted disease caused by *Treponema pallidum*.[83] Traditionally, syphilis has been divided into three clinical stages: primary, secondary, and late (including tertiary and late benign syphilis). Latent syphilis is a serological diagnosis for which symptoms are not apparent and which is differentiated into early (infection duration less than 1 year) or late (infection duration greater than 1 year).[84]

Epidemiology

Transmission of syphilis is relatively inefficient. Studies have demonstrated that the transmission efficiency of this disease between an infected partner and an uninfected partner is only 20%. After the initial exposure, a latency period of three weeks passes prior to the development of the initial symptoms. During this latency period (or, in epidemiologic terms, the "critical period"), a newly infected individual is not

infectious to his or her sexual partners. However, this status changes rapidly after development of the initial genital ulcerative lesion (chancre). The chancre is a primary syphilis ulceration that occurs at the site of mucosal inoculation.

Syphilis occurs in settings where there is high turnover of sex partners. Commercial sex workers and other transient individuals with multiple sex partners are at increased risk. In developed countries, moreover, syphilis has been associated with a variety of social and behavioral factors, including bathhouses frequented by homosexual men, prostitution related to drug abuse, and poor access to health care.[85] In the developing world, more important issues are prostitution, transience, and poor access to health care.

Syphilis rates in the United States reached a plateau in the late 1960s and continued to drop until 1975. At this time, the epidemiology of syphilis reflected the broader, societal social trends in the United States (**Figure 24-3**). During 1975–1980, rates increased nearly 50%, but nearly all of the increase was due to greater incidence among homosexual men. MSM culture was undergoing the "gay revolution" at this time, with homosexual men demonstrating increased sexual openness and pride in their sexual orientation. During 1980–1985, rates declined by 40% as men dramatically reduced their sexual risk practices in response to the HIV epidemic. Rates again increased nearly 100% between 1985 and 1991 (Figure 24-3).[86] This epidemic was due to increased rates among heterosexuals, especially racial and ethnic minorities, and corresponded to increased use of crack cocaine, which was introduced to the United States in 1985. Aggressive control programs, especially a large national syphilis elimination effort in African American communities that included extensive medical ethnography and grassroots efforts, led to a sustained decrease in syphilis rates in this community since 1991.[5,87]

More recently, as described earlier, syphilis has again increased in MSM, just as it did in the 1970s. Increased rates of risky sexual behavior in MSM have been correlated with a reduction in concern about HIV due to the development of highly effective antiretroviral therapy and "safe-sex fatigue," where men are tired of maintaining safe sexual practices.[3]

Clinical Course

Initial infection with *T. pallidum* occurs through sexual contact at a mucosal membrane. The incubation period for this infection ranges between 10 and 30 days.[84] Typically, 3 weeks after the initial

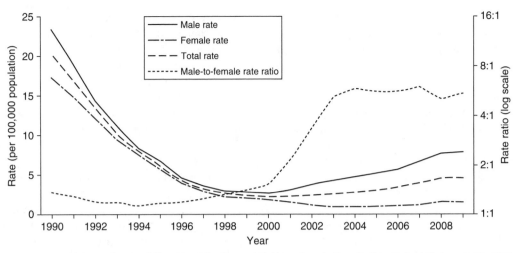

Figure 24-3 Primary and Secondary Syphilis—Rates by Sex and Male-to-Female Rate Ratios, United States, 1990–2009. Reproduced from the Centers for Disease Control and Prevention. 2010 Sexually Transmitted Diseases Surveillance. http://www.cdc.gov/std/stats10/figures/35.htm, Last Updated November 17, 2011. Accessed October 26, 2012.

exposure, a chancre develops at the site of contact. The chancre is a painless lesion with an indurated border and has associated painless lymphadenopathy. Syphilis is a systemic disease, however—even in primary syphilis, systemic dissemination may occur. In some studies, 10% to 15% of patients with early primary syphilis have demonstrated cerebrospinal fluid (CSF) abnormalities.[88] Left untreated, the chancre spontaneously heals within 2–3 weeks.

Four to eight weeks later, the secondary syphilis syndrome develops. Secondary syphilis consists of a systemic vasculitis caused by high levels of *T. pallidum* in the blood and associated immunologic responses. The most characteristic findings are dermatological in nature, including the classic palmar plantar rash, but patterns may include papular, maculopapular, papulosquamous, and psoriasiform lesions. Patchy alopecia may develop, especially on the scalp. On the mucosal surfaces, mucous patches may be noted. Condyloma lata—large, fleshy, wart-like lesions—may develop on the genitalia. Condyloma lata and mucous patches are highly infectious. Left untreated, the secondary syphilis syndrome spontaneously resolves usually within 1–2 months of onset.

Late complications of syphilis, such as neurosyphilis, cardiovascular syphilis, and gummatous syphilis, do not develop until 10–20 years after the resolution of early syphilis. In HIV patients, case reports have suggested that late complications may occur earlier.[89]

Early latent syphilis is a serologic diagnosis in which a fourfold increase in titer (i.e., two dilutions) occurs within 1 year with previous documentation of the earlier serology. Late latent syphilis is a serologic diagnosis of syphilis occurring more than 1 year after baseline diagnosis. The differentiation between early latent and late latent syphilis has both treatment and public health implications.

Diagnosis

Diagnosis of syphilis is complex because the organism cannot be cultured, and serological tests have been largely unchanged for half a century. In primary cases, the organism can be visualized by dark-field microscopic examination, but realistically this procedure is not available in most settings.

Serological diagnosis of syphilis is a two-step procedure.[90] Previously, a nontreponemal screening test was performed as the initial step, which would be followed by a more specific treponemal test as the confirmation test. The advent of new enzyme immunoassay treponemal tests recently has resulted in an increase of the use of a treponemal test, using recombinant antigens, as the initial test in many laboratories, however.[91] This test is then followed by a non-treponemal test to determine a titer. This practice has resulted in some confusion among clinicians when the initial treponemal test is positive, but the non-treponemal test is negative regarding the serological status of the patient. The CDC and others have recommended algorithms to be followed for interpretation in such cases. Implications for clinical management include the need for analysis of patient risk factors, further confirmatory testing by another treponemal test such as the *Treponema pallidum* particle agglutination (TP-PA) assay, and determination of whether the patient may have had prior treated syphilis.[91–94]

The most widely used non-treponemal tests are the Venereal Disease Research Laboratory (VDRL) and rapid plasma reagin (RPR) tests. Results for these tests are reported as titers (i.e., the dilutions required to achieve a negative reaction using standard reagents). Patients with a positive non-treponemal test should have a confirmatory test such as TP-PA assay, the fluorescent treponemal antibody-absorbed (FTA-ABS) test, or microhemagglutination (MHATP) test. As many as 20% of patients with positive non-treponemal tests have negative confirmatory tests; these are termed *benign false positives* (BFP). Most frequently, these outcomes are seen in patients with past series of intravenous drug abuse, pregnancy, systemic disorders such as lupus, and other infectious processes such as Lyme disease. Patients with BFP results and with titers greater than 1:16 are extremely unusual.

In primary syphilis, the sensitivity of serologic testing is 85%. In this setting, false-negative cases may occur because seroconversion may occasionally take longer to develop than the genital ulcer. In secondary syphilis, sensitivity of serological diagnosis is close to 100%. Titers in secondary syphilis may be extremely high. In latent syphilis, the serological tests are positive, but patients do not have corresponding clinical symptoms.

Syphilis in HIV-Infected Patients

All stages of syphilis are seen more commonly in HIV-infected patients. Studies in STD clinics have demonstrated that HIV prevalence in patients with syphilis is as much as three times higher than the number of nonsyphilis patients in these settings.[83,89] However, the serologic manifestations and serologic response to treatment are largely unaffected by HIV status. Because of initial reports of treatment failure, many experts believed that all patients with syphilis, and especially patients with coexistent HIV infection, should be aggressively treated. Prospective studies by CDC investigators have demonstrated that in the majority of cases, such therapy is not necessary.[95]

Congenital Syphilis

In women who have untreated primary or secondary syphilis, the vertical transmission rate is estimated to be in the range of 75–95%.[96] Late congenital syphilis is rarely seen in today's antibiotic era. Transmission does occur transplacentally. Screening and treatment for congenital syphilis during pregnancy can effectively prevent this disorder, however. Thus congenital syphilis is completely preventable through screening, diagnosis, and treatment during the prenatal period. Therefore, congenital syphilis is considered a sentinel public health event and warrants an investigation. These cases occur almost exclusively in situations where there was inadequate prenatal care or where there are deviations from medical practice.

Treatment

Treatment of primary, secondary, and early latent syphilis is recommended to consist of benzathine penicillin.[97] In patients who are allergic to penicillin, doxycycline may be used. Pregnant women with syphilis should be treated only with penicillin-based regimens. An increased number of case reports have described syphilis that is resistant to macrolides, so these medications are not recommended.[98]

Intervention approaches to syphilis control have long capitalized on the unique clinical aspects of the disease:

- After treatment, an individual is noninfectious to sexual partners. With the advent of penicillin therapy, this concept has become a major tool in developing intervention strategies.
- The long latency period from time of infection to time of infectiousness offers an opportunity for reducing secondary spread contacts. This understanding has been the basis of syphilis control programs based on partner notification and screening programs. In STD control programs, such practice is known as "surrounding the epidemic."
- The availability of an inexpensive diagnostic screening test (the syphilis serological test) allows widespread screening opportunities.
- Because treatment during pregnancy prevents vertical transmission, prenatal screening and treatment programs have been established.

Role of the Syphilis Registry

All state and many local health departments in the United States maintain a syphilis "reactor registry." Positive serological tests are reportable by law (by the laboratory); therefore, reporting is reasonably complete. Reactor registries compile test results and histories of treatment and can be useful in determining whether an individual patient had a previous serology and whether a positive test represents early latent, late latent, or previously treated disease. Useful epidemiological databases are also available to conduct operational and clinical research.

Partner Notification

Syphilis presents the prototype disease for the use of partner notification and presumptive treatment of partners.[99] Although the empirical evidence strongly suggests that this strategy has been an effective approach in syphilis control, no randomized trials to date have been performed to demonstrate this relationship. Furthermore, partner notification is complicated in situations where large numbers of anonymous sex partners are the secondary spread contacts—a consideration that has been especially problematic in evaluation of disease intervention approaches in the homosexual bathhouses and in crack cocaine-associated epidemics.[100,101] In these situations, many public health intervention strategies have revolved around aggressive screening and presumptive treatment of partners.

Another intriguing aspect of syphilis is the relationship of immunology to infectiousness. The infectiousness of syphilis to sexual partners is largely concentrated in the primary and secondary stages. Individuals who are in late stages of syphilis (late latent, tertiary) are *infected* but not *infectious* and cannot be reinfected themselves during that time.[102] Theoretically, then, it is possible to "saturate" a community to the point where there are so many latent infections that the pool of susceptibles decreases and "burns out" the outbreak. Paradoxically, in this situation, treating infected persons would revert many individuals back to a susceptible state.

GENITAL HERPES INFECTION

Genital herpes (from the Greek, meaning "to creep") is typically due to herpes simplex type 2 (HSV-2), but may also be caused by HSV-1, and is widely prevalent in the adult U.S. population.[103–106] Because of the problem in differentiating recurrences versus new infection, accurate incidence data are difficult to enumerate. Seroprevalence studies using type-specific research-grade assays have demonstrated that approximately 1 in 6 married sexually active Americans (40 million people) is infected with the herpes simplex virus; most of these individuals are asymptomatic (**Figure 24-4**).[103,105] Seropositivity has been associated with increased numbers of sexual partners, minority race, and socioeconomic status. Interestingly, even when adjusting for reporting artifacts in socioeconomic differences, African Americans still have substantially higher rates of HSV-2 seropositivity than other ethnic groups.[106]

An intriguing aspect of herpes epidemiology has been the shift in primary genital disease from HSV-2

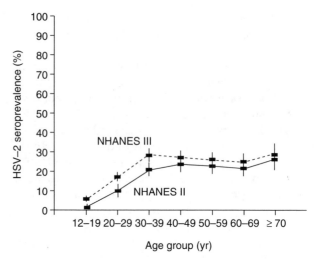

Figure 24-4 Herpes simplex virus 2 (HSV-2) seroprevalence according to age in NHANES ll (1976 to 1980) and NHANES lll (1988 to 1994). Bars indicate 95% confidence intervals (CIs). From Fleming et al. Herpes Simplex Virus Type 2 in the United States, 1976 to 1994, *N Engl J Med*. Vol. 337, 1105–1111, © 1997 Massachusetts Medical Society. Reprinted with permisison from Massachusetts Medical Society.

to HSV-1.[105] HSV-1 usually causes orofacial herpes (cold sores). HSV-2 still causes the bulk of prevalent genital infections, because recurrences due to HSV-2 are much more common. Nevertheless, studies from a variety of geographical regions have demonstrated that HSV-1 can cause just as many primary genital outbreaks as HSV-2. Two hypotheses have been suggested to explain this epidemiological trend. One hypothesis posits that increased HSV-1 genital infection results from increased oral sexual behavior. An alternative hypothesis is based on immunologic susceptibility. Individuals from previous generations were more likely to be exposed to HSV-1 as young children and, therefore, would be immune to genital HSV-1. In contrast, many of today's young adults are susceptible to HSV-1 because of their lack of prior exposure as children.

Genital herpes is almost exclusively sexually transmitted.[104] Approximately 90% of genital herpes is caused by HSV-2; 10% is caused by HSV-1. The reversed ratio is seen in cases of orofacial herpes. Orofacial herpes due to HSV-1 is transmitted as an upper respiratory tract infection, usually in early childhood.

HSV-1 and HSV-2 cause similar clinical syndromes at their respective mucosal sites. Acute infection with herpes simplex occurs after inoculation of virus to the mucosal site. Primary infection is often asymptomatic. When symptomatic cases occur, a mucosal or epidermal ulcer develops. Simultaneously, viral particles enter the sensory nerve roots supplying the area and travel along the nerve axons to the dorsal root ganglia (DRG), where latency develops. For genital herpes, latency develops in the lumbosacral dorsal root ganglia; for orofacial herpes, the trigeminal ganglia are the source of the latent virus. When recurrences develop, viral particles begin replication in the DRG and travel centripetally to the periphery, exit at the mucosa or skin surface, and cause a repeat genital ulceration. Because of prior priming of the humoral and cellular immune systems, outbreaks are typically shorter than primary infections.

Clinical Features

Genital herpes can occur at any mucosal exposed site (genitalia, rectum, and mouth). In primary disease, the ulceration develops 5–10 days after exposure; there may also be associated systemic signs, such as fever, myalgias, headache, and occasionally meningeal irritation.[104] Recurrent herpes can develop at any time after the primary infection. In many settings, patients report a prodrome, which may consist of low-grade fever, pruritus, and tingling at the site of recurrence. Patients often report that they are able to feel the recurrence developing with nonspecific signs and symptoms, which is most likely related to irritation of the peripheral nerve roots.

Because many patients have asymptomatic primary infection, differentiation of a clinical first episode into primary disease or recurrence (in patients who have had an asymptomatic primary episode) is often not possible. In the research setting, *primary* infections are defined as an initial clinical episode with no serological evidence of prior infection. Most patients, however, when presenting with their initial episode, actually have serological evidence of prior infection.[107] This condition is termed *first clinical episode of recurrent disease.* This distinction is often a very confusing point to clinicians and can be diagnosed by using type-specific serological tests. In some studies, more than 90% of persons with recurrent herpes diagnosed serologically could not identify a primary outbreak occurrence in the past. Symptomatic recurrences are less symptomatic and heal more rapidly than the primary episode. Recurrences are most frequent within the first year after primary infection and decrease thereafter. The factors involved in inducing recurrent episodes are not well characterized.[104] Physical and physiological stresses have been classically cited as important cofactors, but there are few well-controlled studies that have been able to clearly elucidate these relationships.

Asymptomatic shedding plays a major role in transmission of HSV. This type of shedding occurs between clinical outbreaks, especially in the first few years after diagnosis.[107] Initial culture studies of women with a recent diagnosis of primary herpes found that asymptomatic shedding occurred approximately 1% of the time. The asymptomatic culture-diagnosed shedding represents a potential infectious inoculum (approximately 10^4 viral particles). Further recent work with PCR demonstrated that shedding detectable by PCR occurred almost on a daily basis.[108] Asymptomatic shedding rates are increased in persons with HIV or other immunodeficiencies.[109]

Diagnosis of Genital Herpes

Culture or other direct viral-specific tests from a lesion specimen establish the virological diagnosis of herpes. The highest yield of samples is that from the base of a wet genital ulcer or an aspirate of a vesicular eruption prior to breakdown. Serological testing using recombinant type-specific antigens is useful in ascertaining the presence of an IgG response to HSV-2.[110] This response is typically detectable 4–6 weeks after exposure. The most commonly used commercial test has been shown to have acceptable sensitivity and specificity in African countries if the cutoff level is increased from 1.1 to 2.1.[111]

Persons who have positive cultures but who are seronegative are defined as having *primary HSV infection.* In contrast, persons with a first clinical outbreak, but who are HSV-2 seropositive, have *recurrent infection.* Serology can also be useful in defining whether an individual will benefit from suppressive therapy to reduce transmission.

Herpes Simplex in Pregnancy

The major concern with herpes simplex in pregnant women is preventing transmission to the neonate.[112] Recurrent herpes during pregnancy is not a severe clinical problem unless lesions are present in the birth canal at time of delivery, which is an indication for a cesarean section. Another approach advocated by some obstetricians and perinatologists is routine cultures of the birth canal at parturition. If herpes simplex is diagnosed within 1–2 days, the infant may be started on prophylactic antiviral therapy.

The major risk in pregnant women is development of primary herpes during the last trimester of pregnancy. In those cases, as many as one-third of infants will be born with neonatal herpes syndrome, which may be fatal or lead to disability.[104] Fetal infection is presumed to occur transplacentally. Primary infection during pregnancy can occur *only* if the pregnant woman is previously uninfected and has an infected male partner. This is the type of setting where serologic diagnoses of previously unrecognized HSV are useful.

Treatment

In acute primary or recurrent genital herpes, treatment with nucleoside analogs results in more rapid healing of symptoms and more rapid resolution of viral shedding and of the ulcer.[113] Treatment, however, is not curative. Acyclovir has been used for treatment since 1982, has a long track record of efficacy and safety, and has recently become available in generic formulations. Newer drugs for the treatment of genital herpes include famciclovir and valacyclovir, which offer the advantages of less frequent dosing.[114]

Suppressive Therapy

In individuals who have more than six recurrences per year or who are profoundly immunosuppressed and have recurrent disease (such as those with advanced HIV disease, transplant recipients, and patients undergoing chemotherapy), suppressive therapy is indicated. Suppressive regimens are more than 90% protective in preventing recurrences.[113] Suppressive therapy also has a public health benefit. Studies of *discordant* couples (couples in which one partner is HSV-2 seropositive and the other is not) have shown that suppressive treatment of the *infected* partner, even if asymptomatic, reduces transmission of symptomatic disease by more than 90%; in addition, a 60% reduction of asymptomatic transmission occurs.[115] This finding has profound impact because it sets a paradigm for treatment of an infected individual—not to benefit the patient, but to benefit an exposed second party (the sexual partner).

From an epidemiologic and control perspective, the following factors are associated with increased HSV transmission:

- Asymptomatic viral shedding is implicated in more than half of the cases of new primary herpes transmission. Individuals with previous HSV-2 infection have asymptomatic shedding approximately 1–3% of the time, with an increased proportion of days that are positive in the year following the initial outbreak. From a clinical standpoint, there are no specific lesions or symptoms that are associated with asymptomatic shedding. Therefore, patients who are under the impression that if they are asymptomatic, they are unlikely to shed virus, can actually transmit the infection to their sexual partners.

- Especially in women, herpes recurrences may be confused with other vaginal infections, especially "yeast infections." This misclassification of herpes symptoms may lead to unprotected sexual encounters among misdiagnosed individuals, resulting in increased transmission.
- Studies in monogamous couples in which one partner is infected and the other uninfected (discordant) indicate that approximately 11% of partners will seroconvert per calendar year of exposure.[104] Studies have demonstrated that seroconversion may be less likely to occur in the face of antiviral therapy.
- Prevention recommendations in the long term are difficult to implement because of the issue of asymptomatic shedding and the high prevalence of disease.

Despite methodological challenges, condom efficacy in preventing HSV transmission has been measured. The challenges include the need to evaluate discordant couples, the relatively low seroconversion rate in discordant couples (8–11% per year), the need for periodic serological monitoring, and the reliance on self-reports for the independent variable. Nevertheless, by nesting behavioral measures into Phase 3 vaccine studies for preventive HSV vaccines, condom efficacy has been shown to exceed 90% for consistent users, and to exceed 60% for inconsistent users.[116]

HSV-2 has also been conclusively implicated in HIV transmission. Prospective and retrospective studies in the United States and abroad have demonstrated that presence of HSV-2, even only serologically, is an independent predictor of increased HIV seroconversion.[117] The presence of a genital ulcer or primary infection in these cases potentiates that risk. A large meta-analysis evaluated 31 studies examining the association between HSV-2 infection and the risk for HIV acquisition, and found that HSV independently increased the risk or odds ratio to 2.9–5. Furthermore, incident HSV results in even greater risk. The per-contact probability of HIV acquisition was five times greater if the susceptible partner was HSV-2 seropositive compared with partners who were HSV-2 seronegative (**Table 24-2**).[118] These findings, coupled with the overall consistent macro-epidemiology, prompted clinical trials of prophylactic antiviral medication as a potential prevention intervention for HIV transmission. Unfortunately, the results were disappointing, as they failed to find a reduction in HIV transmission.[119] Daily acyclovir therapy did not reduce the risk of transmission of

Table 24-2 **Per-Contact Probability of HIV-1 Acquisition in HIV-1 Discordant Couples by HSV-2 Serology**

Couple Status	Per-Contact Probability
Overall	0.0011
Susceptible HIV-1 partner, HSV-2 seropositive	0.002
Susceptible HIV-1 partner, HSV-2 seronegative	0.004 ($P = .01$)
Susceptible HIV-1 partner, HSV-2 seropositive with symptomatic GUD	0.0031
Susceptible HIV-1 partner, HSV-2 seropositive without GUD	0.0019
Susceptible HIV-1 partner, HSV-2 seronegative without GUD	0.0004 ($P = .01$)

Reproduced from Corel L, Wald A, Celum CA, et al. The effects of herpes simplex virus-2 on HIV-1 acquisition and transmission: a review of two overlapping epidemics. *J Acquir Immune Defic Syndr.* 2004;35(5):435–445.

HIV-1, despite a reduction in plasma HIV-1 RNA of 0.25 log(10) copies per milliliter and a 73% reduction in the occurrence of genital ulcers due to HSV-2.

CHANCROID

Chancroid is a genital ulcer disease caused by *Haemophilus ducreyi* and is predominantly seen in the developing world.[120] In the United States, fewer than 1000 cases are seen annually; those cases are usually associated with prostitution and drug use.[121] Chancroid was critically important in fomenting the spread of HIV in sub-Saharan Africa and South Asia. This genital ulcer disease is highly associated with increasing HIV transmission and acquisition risk.[122]

Chancroid is the most common genital ulcer disease in developing parts of the world, especially sub-Saharan Africa.[123] In addition, HIV has been successfully cultivated from the base chancroidal ulcers. Vertical transmission does not appear to occur with *H. ducreyi*. In the United States, outbreaks of chancroid have been generally associated with heterosexual, drug-using activity.[120] No homosexually related epidemics have been reported in the United States. Other risk factors that appear to play a role in the epidemiology of chancroid include alcohol use, intravenous drug use, and contact with commercial sex workers. Chancroid should also be considered in travelers to endemic areas presenting with a genital ulcer.

The incubation of chancroid is 4–7 days. The ulcer develops initially as a tender papule with erythema. Over the next 1–2 days, pustular erosion develops, leading to ulceration. The ulcer typically is undermined; in contrast to syphilis, it is often painful and is not indurated, and has a purulent exudate. Painful, large adenopathy is seen in as many as 50% of patients. These lesions can develop into large purulent nodes that can spontaneously develop

sinus tracts and rupture (buboes). Chancroid does not disseminate or cause systemic disease. The classic identifying features of chancroidal ulcers are short incubation period; painful, tender ulcerations with an undermined, beefy appearance; purulent exudate; and rapid resolution with appropriate antimicrobial treatment.

Diagnosis of chancroid is difficult because the organism grows only on special medium at 33°C.[124] Culture media are not widely available outside of infectious disease reference centers. Newer diagnostic tests using DNA amplification techniques of ulcer exudates have been developed but are not yet widely available.[124–126]

In the United States, chancroid should be considered as a potential etiology of genital ulcer in the following groups:

- Patients with genital ulcers in an area where chancroid is known to be endemic. Outbreaks over the past 20 years have occurred in New York City; Philadelphia, Pennsylvania; South Florida; Southern California; and Mississippi.
- Patients with genital ulcer disease who have recent travel or exposure to an individual with travel to developing countries.

If there is any doubt about the diagnosis, presumptive treatment may be an option, as it is extremely effective.

Treatment

Chancroid is effectively treated with azithromycin.[5] Widespread resistance has developed to penicillin and single-dose ceftriaxone or trimethoprim-sulfamethoxazole.

Epidemiological approaches in chancroid control are based on detection of disease and aggressive treatment. No studies have been performed to demonstrate effectiveness of partner notification. In addition, the issues of diagnosis are a major problem. Therefore, surveillance of cases of genital ulcer disease that do not respond to traditional therapies is useful for detecting the emergence of chancroid within a defined population. Subsequent to identification, aggressive partner notification and even presumptive treatment approaches have been successful in reducing outbreaks in the United States.

Chancroid can be differentiated from syphilis and from herpes in that the genital ulcers do not respond to penicillin or to antiviral drugs, they do not spontaneously resolve, and they respond very rapidly to ceftriaxone and the other recommended antichancroid therapies.[124] In the United States, chancroid should be considered as a sentinel event and prompt an epidemiologic investigation including evaluation of travel patterns of potential partners.

HUMAN PAPILLOMAVIRUS INFECTION

Human papillomaviruses are small DNA viruses that have the unique capacity of causing chronic infection, and that can cause malignant transformation and cervical cancer, but also cannot be cultured in vitro, making diagnosis of subclinical infection difficult.[127] Nearly 100% of cervical cancers are suspected to be associated with human papillomavirus (HPV).[128] Although no significant variation in HPV positivity occurs among countries, rates of cervical cancer vary widely.[128]

More than 100 subtypes of HPV have been identified. The HPV types that most commonly infect the genital tract are HPV-6, -11, -16, and -18. HPV-6 and HPV-11 have been termed low-risk types, as they are seldom associated with malignancy, but instead occur on external surfaces of the vulva, anus, and vagina. In contrast, HPV-16, -18, -31, and -45, among others, are associated with invasive cervical and other epithelial cancers and, therefore, are classified as high-risk types.[129,130]

The vast majority of HPV infections are asymptomatic. Moreover, only a fraction of women will develop cytological changes that progress to cervical malignancy (**Figure 24-5**). The genital HPV viruses are transmitted sexually and have been identified in skin as well as genital secretions. The incubation period for infection is not well defined, although most authorities estimate that it is approximately 3 months, with a reported range of 3 weeks to 8 months.[131,132] A small proportion of patients infected with genital subtypes 6 and 11 will develop *condyloma acuminata*, or genital warts.[129] These

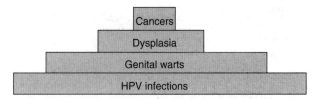

Figure 24-5 Human papillomavirus (HPV) pyramid.

lesions are fleshy, nonvascular warts that are caused by proliferation of the keratinized epithelium and that may occur anywhere on the external genitalia. In women, cervical warts are occasionally observed; in men, besides the external warts, lesions may be present inside the urethra.

HPV is a sexually transmitted infection. It is not a systemic disease, however, and transmission is thought to occur through mechanical abrasion of an infected epithelial surface with an uninfected epithelium. HPV DNA can be detected in vulvar, vaginal, cervical, oral, and anal samples in women, and in penile shaft, glans, foreskin, scrotum, oral, and anal samples in men; even so, most cases of HPV are clinically asymptomatic.[133] The various types of HPV also demonstrate different tropism: HPV-2 and -4 are associated with warts on the hand; types 6 and 11 are associated with genital warts; and types 16 and 18 are associated with a high proportion of cervical cancers.[133]

Estimates of infection rates range from 20% to more than 90%, depending on the specific populations studied, with college students, adolescents, and commercial sex workers demonstrating the highest rates.[134] The National Health and Nutrition Examination Survey (NHANES) estimated the prevalence of HPV by PCR of vaginal swabs in a representative sample of 1921 women aged 14–59 years, reporting an overall prevalence of 26.8%.[135] It is generally accepted that HPV infections in women are detected periodically and that most new infections resolve in 1 to 2 years.[133] Trend data collected by the CDC suggest that the incidence of this STD has increased over the past 30 years. In men, HPV infection rates were estimated to range from 1.3% to 72.9% in a review of 40 publications, of which 15 reported prevalences greater than 20%.[136] In this meta-analysis, prevalence varied by sampling methods, processing methods, anatomic sites sampled, and the population studied.[136]

Genital warts and cervical dysplasia represent only a small proportion of persons with infection (Figure 24-5). Prevalence and incidence studies have found that HPV infection is extremely common in women, with incidence rates greater than

20% per year being observed. The highest-risk period appears to be within the year after initiating sexual intercourse.[131] Immunity resulting from natural infection is only type specific; therefore, repeated infections and even simultaneous infection with multiple subtypes are possible.

High-risk types of HPV, especially types 16 and 18, have been conclusively shown to be the cause of cervical and other epithelial squamous cell cancers.[130] The sexually transmitted epithelial cancers include cervical carcinoma, vulvar carcinoma, some oral carcinomas, penile carcinoma, and anal carcinoma. Sexually transmitted HPV-associated anal and oral carcinomas are seen predominantly in homosexual men and are associated with HIV infection.[127]

In cervical cancer, HPV infection of the transition zone may cause a number of changes leading to malignant transformation. The hallmark of HPV infection is koilocytosis, a ballooning of the nuclear portion of the cervical epithelial cells. Left unchecked, this condition may lead to cervical atypia, early cervical malignant dysplasia, or frank malignant transformation. In most cases involving an immunocompetent host, the latency period from development of HPV infection to development of early cervical cancer is often 5–10 years. Advanced cervical cancer cases often take more than 20 years to develop. Although there are no parallel lesions in men, HPV infection is associated with anogenital cancers, especially in MSM.[137,138]

The strength of association between high-risk HPV (HR-HPV) infection and invasive cervical cancer is unprecedented in cancer epidemiology, with odds ratios exceeding 45 in most cases. Development of cancer occurs only with *persistent* infection and has a latency period of years. However, this association must be considered in the context of the high prevalence of transient HPV infection among sexually active women and the frequent resolution of HPV-associated lesions. Thus it can be concluded that HR-HPV infection is a necessary but insufficient cause of invasive cervical cancer.

Besides infection with HR-HPV, the other factors influencing risk for progression to invasive cervical cancer are less well defined. Cigarette smoking has been consistently found to increase this risk.[139] In addition, long-term use of oral contraceptives (longer than 5 years), coinfection with other sexually transmitted diseases (e.g., *Chlamydia trachomatis* or herpes simplex virus), host immune defects such as coinfection with HIV, and inflammation have been found to increase the risk for HPV-associated cervical cancer, although these observations are generally less consistent than those demonstrated for smoking.[140,141]

Treatment

Treatment for condylomata (genital warts) is based on tissue-destructive therapy.[5] Genital warts are a proliferative epithelial process that is caused by HPV stimulation. Treatment should be guided by the preference of the patient, available resources, and the experience of the clinician, as the primary reason for treating warts is cosmetic and relief of symptoms.[5] In most cases, the proliferation of the epithelium is benign. Eradication of HPV-containing tissue is difficult because grossly and histologically appearing tissues may be infected with HPV and cannot be detected unless specifically probed for by DNA analysis. Therefore, the treatment of genital wart lesions due to HPV by traditional destructive methods such as liquid nitrogen or surgery leads to substantial recurrence rates because HPV infection is often present in the histologically normal surgical margins.

Clinical Screening for High-Risk HPV: The Pap Smear Approach

Because of the long latency period and the slow, local progression of squamous cell cervical cancer, screening for the disease is an effective prevention measure. Development of advanced cervical cancer should be considered to be a sentinel event and cause one to evaluate the cancer prevention program. For most persons, Pap smear screening is recommended every 3 years.[142–146] These programs have been found to be extremely effective in reducing the population-based morbidity and mortality from cervical cancer, but are expensive interventions and require access to highly trained cytotechnologists. In HIV-infected women, screening is recommended every 6 months because of the more aggressive disease seen in these patients. If cervical abnormalities are found, then further evaluation may include colposcopy and possibly biopsy. The Pap smear approach has been traditionally oriented toward identification of HPV-adverse outcomes (i.e., cervical malignancy).

Specific HPV Testing

HPV tests detect a pool of high-risk HPV subtypes (i.e., those associated with development of cervical cancer). There is consensus that these tests are appropriate for use in two major circumstances. The first is in the low-grade Pap smear abnormality (e.g., atypical cells of undetermined significance [ASCUS]), in which case the presence or absence of a diagnostic HPV test can help determine whether the woman needs further workup (i.e., colposcopy), or can be defined as having an inflammatory, low-risk Pap smear. A positive HPV test in this setting would indicate the need for colposcopic intervention, whereas a negative HPV test would indicate continuation of normal follow-up.[147] HPV testing is also useful in diagnosing women as low risk. Women older than 30 years, who are monogamous, and who have negative HPV tests, can be assigned to a much more infrequent Pap smear screening algorithm.[148]

HPV Vaccines

The HPV vaccine is the first vaccine explicitly designed to prevent cancer induced by a virus.[149] The rationale and technical approach for the HPV vaccine was innovative, in that it utilized artificially prepared virus-like particles (VLPs) as the viral antigen in an appropriate adjuvant. The development of the first vaccine and efficacy standards for licensure have been reviewed by Barr et al.[150] In studies of thousands of women, the vaccine was demonstrated to have an efficacy of more than 99% for the types of disease associated with the HPV types covered by the vaccine.[151] When both HPV and high-grade cervical lesions cytological outcomes are used as assessment criteria, the efficacy of this approach has been extremely high (98–100%).[151–155]

There are now two commercially available HPV vaccines: one that provides protection against HPV types 6, 11, 16, and 18, and one that covers types 16 and 18.[156] Results of efficacy trials with these vaccines have been consistently high over 4 years of follow-up.[157] Models of vaccination in the United States have shown this approach to be cost-effective.[158]

Recommendations for Vaccination

The CDC recommends the HPV vaccine for females aged 11–12 years, but it can be given to girls as young as age 9 years and as catch-up vaccination for females aged 13–26 years.[159] Recently, the vaccine has also been recommended for males, but modeling studies report that increasing vaccine uptake in pre-adolescent girls is more effective in reducing HPV infection than including boys in existing vaccination programs.[160] The vaccine is administered intramuscularly at three separate 0.5 mL doses, with the second dose administered 2 months after the first dose and the third dose given 6 months after the first dose.

HPV also causes 83–95% of anal cancer cases, 20–50% of vulvar cancer cases, 60–65% of vaginal cancer cases, 30–42% of penile cancer cases, and a growing body of evidence suggests that it causes oropharyngeal and head and neck cancer.[150,161,162] An intriguing aspect of HPV vaccination, therefore,

is a policy question: Given these statistics, which population would be most appropriate to vaccinate? Consensus among STD experts is that this vaccine should be utilized universally for women and potentially for men as well, at ages 11–12 years (i.e., before both females and males initiate sexual activity). From a policy standpoint, this recommendation has presented challenges in convincing parents/guardians that STD vaccination is appropriate for this young population. Qualitative work has revealed a dichotomy between population groups' attitudes toward HPV vaccination, in that African American inner-city mothers tend to approve STD vaccination much more readily than suburban non-African American mothers.[163] Actual uptake of the vaccine has been lower than hoped for.[164]

Primary prevention of transmission of HPV infection by condom use appears to be of limited effectiveness, likely because of the broad range of epithelial targets for infection in men and women, the absence of detectable symptoms to identify an infected partner, and inconsistent condom use (e.g., lack of use during abrasive foreplay).[165] However, evaluation of condom effectiveness in preventing HPV transmission is complicated by the difficulty in obtaining a reliable diagnosis of HPV infection in men to confirm exposure and in accurately ascertaining proper condom use.

VAGINAL INFECTIONS

When evaluating individuals with vaginal infections or vaginal discharge, it is imperative to differentiate primary vaginal infections from cervical infections presenting as vaginitis.[166] Clinically, women often present with nonspecific symptoms of vaginal discharge or low abdominal pain; this condition needs to be differentiated from vaginal disease, cervical disease, or both. Gonococcal and chlamydial infections are the most common cause of cervical disease. Vaginitis has a number of causes including trichomoniasis, bacterial vaginosis, and candidiasis. Because *Candida* is not a sexually transmitted infection and has very few long-term health effects, it will not be considered here.

Trichomoniasis

Trichomoniasis infections, caused by the flagellated parasite *Trichomonas vaginalis* (TV), are highly prevalent STDs worldwide, with estimates of 7–8 million infections annually in the United States and 180 million globally.[167] As such, trichomoniasis represents the most common curable STD in young, sexually active women.[2,168] Signs and symptoms include a watery vaginal discharge, punctate hemorrhagic lesions on the cervix, and occasionally a frank cervicitis occurring in response to the vaginal infection.[169] Symptoms are exacerbated during menses because the organism can ingest hemoglobin and replication is increased during that time. *Trichomonas* syndromes in men have not been systematically described until recently[170] because clinical practice was (and still is) to presumptively treat all male contacts of women with trichomoniasis.[169] Trichomoniasis does not produce systemic disease in the host.

Diagnosis

Microscopic examination of a wet mount is the most inexpensive and widely used method for diagnosis of trichomoniasis. However, culture or newer DNA-based methods may be as much as 50% more sensitive, especially in women with asymptomatic infection and in men.[170–174] Currently, there is only one FDA-approved NAAT assay for the detection of *Trichomonas*.[175] The development of new testing techniques has resulted in alternative sampling strategies as well. Traditional approaches to STD diagnosis in women necessitate a direct speculum examination, which is necessary to visualize the vaginal mucosa and cervix, and for sampling of the fornix. The availability of nucleic acid–based diagnostic technology for gonorrhea and chlamydia diagnosis has led to suggestions that a speculum examination is not necessary and that a swab of the distal vaginal can provide adequate specimen material.[176] Sampling can also be performed with self-collected vaginal swabs.[177,178]

Treatment

Treatment for trichomoniasis is metronidazole, 2 grams as a single dose—a regimen that is also considered safe in pregnancy.[5] Metronidazole resistance is occasionally reported. Tinidazole, 2 grams orally in a single dose, is also recommended.

Epidemiology

Despite the availability of better diagnostic tests, basic understanding of the epidemiology of trichomoniasis has not changed greatly. The National Health and Nutrition Examination Survey of 2001–2004 (NHANES) estimated that 3.1% of women in the United States have *Trichomonas vaginalis* (TV).[179] Miller et al. reported that 2.8% of women 18 to 26 years in the National Longitudinal Study of Adolescent Health cohort were positive for trichomoniasis, with infection rates in black

women ranging from 10.5% to 13%.[180] Data from the National Health and Nutrition Examination Surveys, combining the 2001–2002 and 2003–2004 waves, demonstrated that TV was associated with other STDs among women in the civilian, non-institutionalized U.S. population in a sample of 3648 women, representing a weighted sample of the experience of 65,563,298 women between the ages of 14 and 49 years.[181] The prevalence of trichomoniasis was 3.2%, with more than 80% of cases being asymptomatic. Nevertheless, large population-based studies of prenatal clinic attendees and STD clinic attendees have continued to find high rates of *Trichomonas* infection (10–15%).[168,171] *Trichomonas* infections have been documented to be of much higher prevalence in blacks than in whites.[179,180,182]

Trichomonas infection has been associated with a number of complications, such as potential facilitation of HIV infection.[7,182–188] Repeat infections are common in HIV-infected women, and treatment of *Trichomonas* has been reported to reduce HIV shedding.[8,9] *Trichomonas* infections have been associated with poor reproductive outcomes such as low birth weight (LBW) and premature birth.[185,189] In a cohort of more than 13,000 women, there was an attributable risk of trichomoniasis associated with LBW in blacks of 11% versus 1.6% in Hispanics and 1.5% in whites.[189] Other data indicate that *Trichomonas* infections are associated with pelvic inflammatory disease.[186,190] Additionally, it has been estimated that the overall annual economic burden of trichomoniasis on the private sector amounts to $18.9 million among all U.S. women.[191]

In men, studies from different locales have confirmed the role of *Trichomonas* in urethritis.[169,170,192,193] For many years, trichomoniasis was considered to be a nuisance. Although the infection causes symptoms that may even occasionally be disabling, it does not cause upper tract disease, nor does it cause systemic disease. In an immunocompromised host, the organism load of *Trichomonas* may be higher (such as in HIV-infected women), but no systemic disease occurs.

Bacterial Vaginosis

Bacterial vaginosis (BV) is a disorder that occurs as a result of ecological disturbances among the vaginal flora; it is the most prevalent cause of vaginal symptoms in women of childbearing age.[194] The normal vaginal flora overwhelmingly consists of lactobacilli. As a result, the vaginal host environment is acidic, with a pH less than 4.5. In bacterial vaginosis, alteration of the microflora occurs, such that the population of lactobacilli is replaced by gram-negative rods and anaerobes. As a result, the pH increases to more than 4.5, often to 7 or higher. Gram stain of normal vaginal fluid demonstrates predominately lactobacilli, whereas Gram stain from a woman with BV shows mostly gram-variable cocobacilli, such as *Gardnerella vaginalis* or anaerobic gram-negative bacilli, with a decrease or absence of normal lactobacilli.[194] Culture of vaginal fluid reveals mixed flora with the presence of *G. vaginalis, Mobiluncus* spp., *Prevotella* spp., peptostreptococcus, and other anaerobes. New molecular methods have revealed many unculturable organisms to be associated with BV.[195,196]

Clinical manifestations include development of vaginal odor and discharge, along with the microscopic appearance of clue cells, which are epithelial cells with numerous anaerobes or *G. vaginalis* bound to the surface, creating a "ground glass" appearance for the cell. A fish-like odor is often present due to the production of amine compounds by the anaerobic bacteria. Bacterial vaginosis most frequently presents as secondary to another infectious, metabolic, or iatrogenic event.

Diagnosis of BV is made by one of two methods: (1) Nugent criteria-evaluation of a vaginal smear Gram stain, demonstrating the characteristic alteration of the vaginal flora, by enumerating the absence of lactobacilli and the presence of clue cells and typical anaerobic bacilli[197,198]; or (2) Amsel clinical criteria, which include at least three of the four following indications: homogenous white adherent vaginal discharge, pH greater than 4.5, presence of an amine odor with the addition of KOH to vaginal fluid, and presence of clue cells.[199]

Treatment of BV uses antimicrobial agents that are effective against anaerobes, such as metronidazole, clindamycin, or tinidazole, which results in reestablishment of the normal vaginal microflora.[5] Recurrences are common.[200]

BV can occur as a secondary disorder and can be caused by infection, douching, or antibiotics (**Figure 24-6**). The most common causes of secondary BVs include the following:

- Alteration of vaginal microflora as a result of cervical infection and subsequent inflammation. In many of these cases, resolution of the primary cervical infection may result in resolution of the bacterial vaginosis.
- Alteration of vaginal microflora as a result of antibiotic use. Tetracyclines and other commonly used broad-spectrum antibiotics are especially implicated in these disorders.

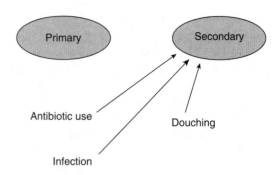

Figure 24-6 Bacterial vaginosis.

- Direct instillation into the vagina of microbicides and douches.[201] Douching is particularly associated with development of BV. Vaginal douching is associated with increased risk of chlamydia and BV and has no clinical benefit. Consequently, clinical recommendations should always include specific recommendations not to douche.

Some patients may have primary bacterial vaginosis, meaning BV without any identifiable cause. These patients do resolve the infection with treatment; however, BV recurs frequently in this population. Rapid fluctuation of the vaginal microbiota has been demonstrated to occur as well, which has been associated with rectal sex and lubricant use the day before specimen collection.[202] The epidemiologic issues with BV are further complicated by the fact that the infection occurs more frequently in sexually active women and is frequently seen in women who have sex with women.[203] However, correlative infectious conditions in the male host have never been demonstrated.

In pregnant women, BV has been demonstrated to be a risk factor for premature rupture of membranes and premature delivery.[204] A large, multicenter study found that in a population of more than 10,000 women, the prevalence of BV was 16%. The adjusted odds ratio of BV and delivery of a preterm, low-birth-weight infant was 1.4. A follow-up study found that treatment of BV in pregnancy reduced the BV-associated preterm risk by one-half to two-thirds.

BV has also been demonstrated to be more common in black women, for reasons that are not completely clear. The adjusted odds ratio for blacks compared to whites is 2.9 for bacterial vaginosis.[205] The study was controlled for maternal parity, age, education, insurance status, marital status, smoking, age at first intercourse, and number of male partners in the past year.

In addition, BV has been associated with an increased incidence of postsurgical infections, including increased PID incidence after first-trimester abortion and cellulitis after hysterectomy.[206] It has recently been demonstrated to be a risk factor for HIV infection in women, especially when *Trichomonas* is present.[207,208] In HIV-positive women, 51.4% had BV and 28% had *Trichomonas* infection; among women who were HIV positive and *Trichomonas* positive, the rate of BV was 61.0%.[208]

CONTROL OF SEXUALLY TRANSMITTED DISEASES AS AN HIV PREVENTION INTERVENTION

Epidemiological Relationships

Sexual HIV transmission is facilitated by the same risk behaviors as are associated with the traditional STDs: multiple sexual partners, sex with prostitutes, and drug-using sexual partners.[6,209,210] Despite these behavioral confounders, the link between STDs and HIV infection has been conclusively demonstrated. Some examples have already been summarized in this chapter. Multiple factors contribute to this biological relationship:

- Facilitation of STD organisms' access to the vascular portal of entry.
- Recruitment of target cells. STDs such as syphilis and chlamydia induce a lymphocytic response. Theoretically, recruitment of an increased number of CD4 target lymphocytes into an area that is exposed to HIV could facilitate infection. STDs also increase HIV receptors.
- Potentiation of HIV replication. Studies have demonstrated that HIV replication is potentiated by presence of herpes simplex virus (viral transactivation).
- Increased viral load in the infected partner. In particular, acute HIV infection is associated with viral loads in the range of 10^5–10^6, but it is paradoxically seronegative because not enough time has elapsed for seroconversion.[211] A large study in North Carolina public clinics used HIV DNA detection of pooled specimens to identify acute HIV seroconverters; 43% of HIV transmission was estimated to occur during primary infection.[212]

Use of Epidemiologic Models to Guide Control Efforts

Epidemiologic models for STD control are based on the May-Anderson model of microparasites.[213,214] STDs form a unique subset because exposure risk is not random, but rather is determined by exposure to new sexual partners. These sexual partner characteristics, or "mixing," become critically important. Consequently, the models are based on the reproductive rate equation $R_0 = BCD$, where B equals the transmission coefficient, C equals the turnover of partners, and D equals the duration of infection. As long as the reproductive rate remains greater than 1, the number of cases is expected to increase. Conversely, control efforts are directed toward decreasing either one or all of the constituent terms of the reproductive rate equation to drive the reproductive rate to less than 1.

Interventions specifically designed to decrease the transmission efficiency (B) include the use of barrier methods of contraception, use of microbicides, and recommended use of condoms. Although most interventions reduce the transmission efficiency, public health epidemiologists need to be aware that occasionally unanticipated effects may occur. For example, vaginal microbicides have been developed that reduce the transmission efficiency of gonococcal and chlamydial infection; however, use of these microbicides may result in increased HIV transmission. Although vaginal microbicides are in development to prevent HIV and other STDs, development of a product that is acceptable to users, does not disrupt the beneficial balance of the vagina, and prevents pathogen transmission has proved to be quite a challenge. Similarly, hormonal contraceptives may also increase the potential for HIV transmission among women who are exposed to the virus. Likewise, STDs appear to increase the transmission efficiency of HIV in most settings.

Partner turnover (C) includes components that are related to the number of different partners to whom a person is exposed, thereby increasing both the statistical risk of STD exposure and the number of exposures with each partner (or dose). This variable actually encompasses a complex term. From a simplistic standpoint, the most effective intervention is to reduce this term to 0, which would negate the entire reproductive rate equation. This abstention model is impractical in most circumstances. Nevertheless, by reducing the number of partner exposures through risk intervention, risk reduction, education, and counseling, the reproductive rate equation can be substantially affected.

Reducing the duration of infection (D) can also decrease the reproductive rate. Reducing the duration of infection is a practical option for diseases that are curable—which essentially excludes chronic viral diseases such as HIV, herpes simplex, and HPV. One could argue that antiviral medications, which reduce the viral load burden and shedding, actually affect transmission efficiency (B). Interventions that diminish the duration of infection, remove individuals from the infected pool, and reduce exposure opportunities for the population include population-based screening programs, development of effective treatment guidelines based on population base data, and partner notification. All of these strategies are driven by the goal of removing asymptomatic infected individuals from the population pool.

EPIDEMIOLOGY AND BEHAVIOR

STDs are unique in the infectious disease world in that they are completely dependent on behavioral factors for transmission. Abstinent individuals will not contract an STD. Acquisition of STDs is also dependent on the probability that a person will come into contact with an STD-infected partner, susceptibility of the host, and efficiency of transmission of the organism through sexual intercourse. Therefore, the epidemiological risk of the sexual *partner* is a key determinant of infection risk.

STD incidence is highest in adolescents and young adults. For gonorrhea and chlamydia infections—the STDs for which the largest bodies of data are available—more than 95% of incident infections occur between the ages of 15 and 39.[3] The highest rates of incidence are seen in adolescent women (age 15–19) and in men who are between the ages of 20 and 24. These findings correlate very closely with sexual behavior patterns such as sexual partner turnover in the adolescent and young adult age groups.[215]

Not only is the *number* of sexual partners important, but the *type* of sexual partner also contributes to potential infection risk. The constellation of an individual's sexual partners and their partners' partners constitute a sexual network.[216] Individuals with partners who are more likely to be infected with STDs, such as those involved in commercial sex work or drug use, are much more likely to contract an STD than individuals who do not have high-risk sexual partners—even though the index patient may perceive himself or herself to be at low risk. Similarly, persons with serial partners, but having only one sexual partner at a time, are less likely to spread STDs than persons who have multiple concurrent sexual partners.

STDs need to be evaluated within the context of overall morbidity attributable to unprotected sexual behavior.[217] Risky sexual behavior patterns also result in morbidity such as unintended pregnancy, low-birth-weight infants, the cost of pregnancy terminations,

sexually transmitted diseases, direct costs attributable to STD care, and the long-term STD costs including complications of STDs such as pelvic inflammatory disease and ectopic pregnancy, HIV, and STD-facilitated HIV transmission. **Table 24-3** shows common perinatal complications caused by STDs.

Developing effective prevention control management strategies requires public health officials and clinicians to understand the patterns of sexual behavior of patients. The particular activities that are important in contributing to risk include age of sexual debut; number of partners, including delineation between serial partners or number of concurrent partners and development of an interlinked sexual network; features of sex partners that convey greater risk, such as anonymous sexual partners, commercial sex workers, and sexual contacts in gay bathhouses or drug use environments; travel to areas of high prevalence; and use of barrier protection methods including condom use patterns.[218] Travel is particularly important for some populations. In parts of the world such as Western Europe where STD rates are low, travelers to highly endemic areas account for more than half of the new bacterial STD infections.[219]

Assessing sexual behavior is critical to the development of behavior and disease control interventions. Major challenges in designing and implementing intervention strategies include using appropriate assessment tools, defining an individual's or population baseline status, and implementing an intervention. Individual patient management involves taking a good sexual risk history, yet many primary care clinicians in the United States do not even ask their patients if they are sexually active.[220] In a survey of 718 patients in an adult care clinic about their provider, 44% had never been asked about sexual

Table 24-3	Perinatal Complications of STDs
Gonorrhea, Chlamydia	Ophthalmia Neonata
	Pneumonia
	Low birth weight
Syphilis	Congenital syphilis
Trichomonas	Premature rupture of membranes
	Premature delivery
Bacterial vaginosis	Premature rupture of membranes
	Premature delivery
Herpes simplex	Congenital herpes syndrome
Human papillomavirus	Laryngeal papillomatosis
Hepatitis B	Perinatal transmission
HIV	HIV infection in infant

health by their provider; 18% had never had a gender-specific genital exam; one-third had never been tested for HIV; 33% stated they would not use a condom at their next sexual act; and 32% were uncomfortable discussing STDs with their provider.[220] Education of primary care clinicians about STDs, including their diagnosis, treatment, and management, is often needed.

National Surveys

A number of large cross-sectional national surveys have been very useful in assessing behavior and trends. In the United States, these studies have included the National Health and Nutritional Examination Surveys (NHANES); the Sexual Behavior, Sexual Attraction, and Sexual Identity in the United States study; data from the 2006–2008 National Survey of Family Growth; and the Youth Risk Behavioral Surveillance (YRBS) study.[2,215,221] Trends in these data strongly suggest that the overall median age of sexual debut has stabilized at 15.5–16 years. Nationwide, 46.0% of high school students report ever having sexual intercourse; this rate is higher in blacks (65.2%) than in whites (42.0%).[221] By grade, rates range from 31.6% of 9th graders to 62.3% of 12th graders. Among 34.2% currently sexually active youth, 61.1% report that they or their partner used a condom at last intercourse.[221]

Data from the National Survey of Family Growth demonstrated that among adults aged 25–44, approximately 98% of females and 97% of males have ever had vaginal intercourse, 89% of females and 90% of males have ever had oral sex with an opposite-sex partner, and 36% of females and 44% of males have ever had anal sex with an opposite-sex partner. More women (13%) than men (5.2%) reported same-sex contact in their lifetime.[215] Knowledge of these behaviors is important to designing control methods.

Social Determinants of Health

Socioeconomic status has been linked to increased incidence of STDs in a number of different settings, including rural and urban areas in the United States. Areas where there has been a decrease in available health services—especially preventive health services—have also been associated with increased incidence of STDs.[3]

Sexual and Social Context

Sexual context also affects interventions for STDs. Epidemiological risk assessment of STDs frequently evaluates *individual-based risk*. A challenge in using STDs as intervention measures is that risk is also determined by environmental and contextual factors that are beyond the immediate sexual encounter. In other words, qualitative aspects not of the individual himself or herself, but of the individual's sexual partners, play an important role. For example, the risk profile of a partner may dictate an individual's STD risk, independent of his or her own sexual behavior.

In the United States, drug use is particularly associated with STD incidence, especially syphilis, and especially in men who have sex with men.[5,222] In this country, when STDs are examined by race or ethnicity, very wide discrepancies are also demonstrated between racial and ethnic groups.[223] Race and ethnicity in the United States often correlate with other, more fundamental determinants of health status such as socioeconomic status, access to good quality medical care, and efforts to receive good-quality medical care. Reporting biases may be at play as well, although these differences occur even when these biases are controlled.

Syphilis demonstrates the interaction of disease and the social partner circumstances. Between 1999 and 2003, overall syphilis rates in the United States increased 20%. This increase was related to high-risk sexual behavior observed in MSM men since the late 1990s. As many as 40–50% of homosexual men with incident syphilis are HIV positive. Furthermore, the syphilis increase has changed the male/female ratio of this disease from nearly 1:1 in 1991 to greater than 3:1 in 2004, reflecting the shift to a predominantly homosexual population.[100] Hypotheses that have been proposed to explain this trend include the availability of highly active antiretroviral therapy that essentially changed the perception of HIV/AIDS from that of a fatal disease to a chronic disease, as well as "prevention fatigue" among MSM after 30 years of prevention messages. These trends are particularly troubling because of their implications for HIV transmission.

Interventions to Reduce STDs by Promoting Condom Use

Promoting condom use has been one of the central doctrines of the HIV and STD risk-reduction strategy in the United States. Numerous programs, which have been developed to promote marketing and wide distribution of large numbers of condoms and instructions for their use, have long been part of national and international STD guidelines. Condoms are effective—when used correctly and consistently—in reducing the risk of STDs,[116] including HIV. Studies of HIV-discordant heterosexual couples have demonstrated that consistent use in controlled settings results in a decrease in HIV seroconversions.[224]

Studies of condom use have focused on understanding the determinants and issues related to their use, especially considering the low consistent-use rate indicated by national surveys. Increased condom usage is influenced by knowledge of a perceived benefit (i.e., STD/HIV prevention), peer-group social norms, and sex education with specific instruction in condom use. One challenge to maintaining continued use of condoms is the need to continually reinforce the perceived benefit. As with sex education programs, condom promotion has not been demonstrated to increase sexual activity in adolescents or to result in earlier sexual debut. Effective condom promotion requires continual integration of public health and social marketing efforts.

Behavioral Models as Interventions

When developing STD/HIV interventions, behavioral models are necessary for their design and evaluation. Behavioral models are deterministic constructs of sexual behavior.[225] These constructs are usually delineated in sequential steps, with each step being (1) an environmental factor, (2) a behavioral attitude (e.g., positive or negative attitude for condom use), (3) an individual's area knowledge, or (4) a previous behavior. Risk behavior is a necessary precursor step to acquisition of an STD. These contextual behavioral elements affect whether the outcome, or the end result, is a risky or prevention behavior.

Behavior models provide a deterministic basis and underlying justification for intervention. They also provide a process for evaluation, as the predecessor key behavioral determinants can also be measured.[225] Theories of behavioral change include the Health Belief Model; stages of change theory; theory of reasoned action; social learning and social cognitive theory; social networks; social influence and peer norm theory; and diffusion of innovations theory. When defined as a multistep process, these behavioral models allow for logical points for intervention.[225] Behavioral models also facilitate multiple-step intervention approaches to provide synergy. Behaviors do not occur in a social vacuum, of course. Thus structural and environmental factors related to STD control and prevention can affect an individual's ability to implement prevention behaviors, with the peer group often being most important determinant of an individual's success.

Temporal sequence is also important to model development and interventions. The stages of change theory is a construct that has been used in a number of interventions, including the widely reported project known as RESPECT (risk-reduction counseling to prevent human immunodeficiency virus and sexually transmitted diseases).[226] This model has proved particularly attractive in intervention development because it divides a behavior into five stages that are arranged along a continuum[225]:

1. *Pre-contemplation* is the stage before an individual is beginning to think of adopting safer sexual behaviors.
2. *Contemplation* is the stage at which an individual is considering a behavior change, but is not ready to act on it.
3. *Preparation* ("ready for change") is the stage at which an individual is actively considering changing behavior and is taking steps to actualize that behavior change.
4. *Action* is the process of changing behavior and moving toward a preventive behavior mode.
5. *Maintenance* is the process of maintaining behavior change once it has occurred.[225]

Programs based on stages of change theory usually involve efforts such as continual education, booster sessions, or encouragement. The advantage of this model is that it offers intervention designers an opportunity to develop measures that can be adapted to an individual based on understanding of that person's particular "stage" along the five-step continuum. From a population basis, this type of model offers the potential for attacking a risk behavior at multiple key decision points.[225]

EDUCATION

Because STD rates are much higher in adolescents and in some ethnic minorities, special tools, such as better education, are needed to address this "hidden epidemic."[217] Many persons—especially adolescents, but also some clinicians—are reluctant to discuss sexual health issues openly because of the social implications, issues of privacy, and confidentiality.[220] Many barriers exist in getting persons tested and treated for STDs. Focusing on sexual health rather than sexual disease is one solution to addressing this epidemic.[227] However, barriers both for clinicians and for patients must be overcome to realize this goal.

Barriers for providers:

- Lack of reimbursement for time required to address sexual health issues
- Lack of awareness that patients are sexually active
- Lack of knowledge that screening can be performed without a pelvic exam

Barriers for patients:

- Inability to pay copayment for the diagnostic test
- Lack of knowledge of the asymptomatic nature of STDs, high prevalence, and possible adverse long-term reproductive effects of STDs

Facilitating educational awareness of noninvasive specimen types and the ability to easily and quickly diagnose and treat these infections without a painful examination by a clinician can aid in rapid diagnosis and treatment. Many clinicians are not aware, for example, that the CDC, the U.S. Preventive Services Task Force, and other professional organizations recommend screening for chlamydia in all sexually active women younger than age 25 years and in those women 25 years and older with STD risk factors.[19,20] In the United States, it is estimated that fewer than 50% of all women who should be screened are currently being screened for chlamydia.[20]

PREVENTION ISSUES SPECIFIC TO WOMEN

Women are at higher risk for HIV and STD transmission for both biological and behavioral factors. During unprotected intercourse, women are potentially exposed to a higher inoculum, through ejaculation, than their male partner. Changes in the vaginal and cervical mucosa through inflammation or hormonally induced changes can increase the tissue's friability. Hormonal contraceptives have been epidemiologically associated with increased risk of HIV transmission, which coincidentally causes a major policy dilemma in developing countries where overpopulation and the HIV epidemic coexist. Nevertheless, women are at significant risk. In many sexual relationships, women may not be able to refuse sexual relations or require their male partner to use a condom because of either economic circumstances or fear of physical and/or emotional abuse. For example, commercial sex workers may be at an

economic disadvantage if the client's preference is for unprotected intercourse. These issues have intensified the need to develop female-controlled disease-prevention methods. Female condoms are available but are not widely used. Effective vaginal microbicides still await development.

CORE GROUPS AND TARGETING

Besides the mathematical approaches, designing control strategies also requires assessing the impact of sociogeographic effects. STDs predominantly affect specific demographic subgroups. Within the broad population strata, these diseases are often concentrated in areas where poverty and other limitations on healthcare access exist. This factor has resulted in development of the "core group" concept.[228,229]

Core groups are population subgroups that are disproportionately affected by STDs and that often act as the endemic reservoir of disease within a community. These cohorts may be either sociologically or geographically defined. For example, in developing countries, the predominant core groups are long-distance truck drivers and commercial sex workers; in the United States, there is often a direct link to drug use. In the United States and Western Europe, core groups are often defined geographically as being residents of defined core areas that typically are socioeconomically depressed. In the urban environment, core areas in the United States have been well documented for gonorrhea, syphilis, and HIV.[230,231] Within a core area, disease incidence may be 20–30 greater than that of surrounding areas. For example, in Baltimore, researchers have identified discrete core areas where the reported gonorrhea rate in 1994 for persons aged 15–39 years was 6821/100,000 for men and 4341/100,000 for women, and areas where primary and secondary syphilis incidence had similar disproportionately high rates (**Figure 24-7**). The geographic core concept appears to be most relevant to incident STDs such as gonorrhea, syphilis, and chancroid, but is probably not as relevant in the chronic viral STDs. At present, chlamydia has the characteristics of a chronic infection with diffuse population-based prevalence patterns. However, with the institution of control programs, this distribution will probably change.

The transmission efficiency of gonorrhea and syphilis through unprotected sexual exposure has been empirically estimated to be 30–50% per exposure, and treatment effectively breaks the transmission chain. Therefore, under most circumstances, introduction

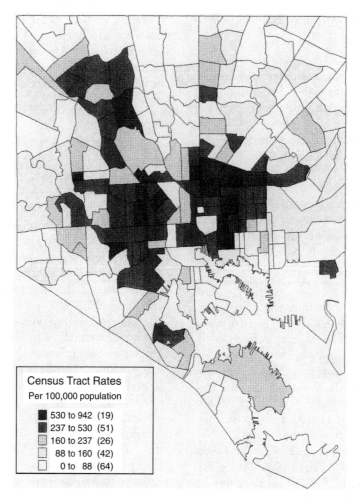

Figure 24-7 Early syphilis, Maryland, 1996. Data generated in Baltimore City Health Department laboratory.

of gonorrhea into a community free of infection should not result in a sustained epidemic. In turn, community-based models of STD transmission postulate that core areas or epidemiologically defined core groups are critical to maintaining high rates of gonorrhea.[232] In these models, cores are characterized by a high transmission density—an empirical function that is dependent on characteristics of the sexual network. In contrast to many other infectious diseases, STD transmission is dependent on behavior—specifically, sexual intercourse. Thus STD transmission is limited to sexual networks, meaning the interrelated sexual connections of a defined social group.

Analyses of sexual networks provide a rational basis for defining transmissibility to susceptible sexual partners.[233] A sexual network is the interrelated sexual connections of a defined social group. In a dense sexual network, multiple pathways exist between sexual partners, leading to multiple sources for disease exposure.[234] These core group ideas have

facilitated two branches of research activity in STD intervention approaches that may have profound implications for STD control.

Social Networks

Traditional STD intervention approaches have used partner notification as a major tool in control programs. As discussed earlier, for diseases for which the incubation period is short, such as gonorrhea, and for diseases with prolonged latency periods (asymptomatic infection) that are efficiently transmitted, such as chlamydia, partner notification may not work. In contrast, syphilis has been traditionally controlled with partner notification using the rationale of the "critical period." As a control tool, however, partner notification has never been fully and formally evaluated. In settings where partners are not named, such as in drug-related prostitution, this process typically fails. New approaches have utilized understanding the social network, meaning the individuals who are associated with the syphilis patient in a variety of everyday activities, and not limited to the sex partners. These approaches appear to be successful in identifying additional infected persons.

Geographically Directed Screening

STDs, especially syphilis and gonorrhea, are associated with a host of adverse socioeconomic indicators. In the United States, these factors are often correlated with residential housing patterns. In highly impacted areas, STD rates, as evaluated by census tract, may be an order of magnitude higher than the corresponding rates in surrounding areas. For example, gonorrhea rates in adolescents in the inner-city areas of Baltimore, Maryland; Washington, D.C.; Miami, Florida; and similar settings may be as high as 10,000–15,000/100,000 (**Figure 24-8** and **Figure 24-9**). In these densely populated, highly impacted areas, geographically directed screening interventions represent a potential control option.

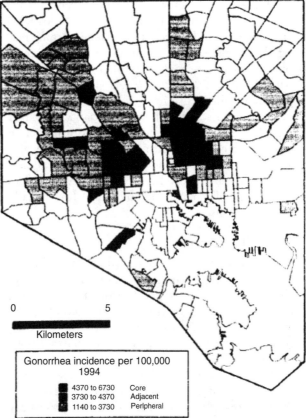

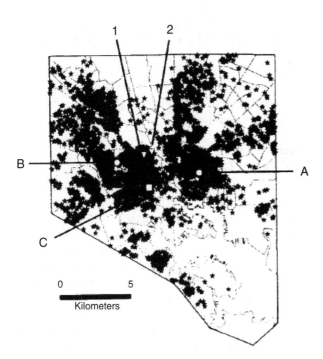

Figure 24-8 Dot map of reported gonorrhea for cases with valid residential addresses (N = 6,831), Baltimore City, Maryland, 1994. The Baltimore City Health Department sexually transmitted disease (STD) program operates two STD clinics located within high incidence areas (A & B). Point C represents the geographic centroid of the city. Point 1 represents the mean vector of private sector cases from the geographic centroid; point 2 represents the mean vector of public sector cases (see text). The scalar distance between point 1 and point 2 is 299 m. Reproduced from Becker et al. Geographic Epidemiology of Gonorrhea in Baltimore, Maryland, Using a Geographic Information System. *Am J Epi*, Vol. 147(7), 1998:709–716. By permission of Oxford University Press.

Figure 24-9 Gonorrhea incidence per 100,000 by census tract, for census tracts with >30 cases (1990 census), Baltimore City, Maryland, 1994. Definitions of core, adjacent, and peripheral areas are given in the text. Note that when rates are calculated, disease density is highest in the inner-city core areas. Reproduced from Becker et al. Geographic Epidemiology of Gonorrhea in Baltimore, Maryland, Using a Geographic Information System. *Am J Epi*, Vol. 147(7),1998:709–716. By permission of Oxford University Press.

PRACTICAL ISSUES

Guides for Healthcare Providers

Guides for clinicians can provide practical information for encouraging providers to screen and manage patients with STDs and to use practical tools to enhance screening for STDs. These guides are another method to enhance control measures. One such popular guide in use is *Why Screen for Chlamydia? An Implementation Guide for Healthcare Providers*, published by Partnership for Prevention (www.prevent.org/ChlamydiaScreening).[235] This guide offers practical management techniques including sexual history taking; testing and counseling; treatment; patient management; and partner notification.

Other resources for chlamydia and STD healthcare providers are available and freely downloadable at www.prevent.org/ncc. They include learning materials and guides such as healthcare for adolescents online STD cases; materials for professionals and tribal healers; *Safe in the City*, a video intended to promote condom use for STD prevention; tips for preventing loss of youth confidentiality; a trigger for a health survey for adolescents; information on minors' access to confidential reproductive health services; billing and coding for confidential adolescent health services; and, importantly, several guides for expedited partner therapy (EPT) for sexually transmitted diseases.

Partner Notification

Sexual partners who had sexual contact with the STD-infected patient in the preceding 60 days should be notified to seek health care for testing and treatment. Partners can be notified either by the patient or by the treating physician. Previously, traditional partner management and partner notification methods have been used successfully, especially for syphilis, where they are still used today. However, finding partners can be particularly difficult in areas where commercial sex workers or gay men with anonymous sex partners are operative. Another challenge, especially in the management of gonorrhea and chlamydia infections, has not been in identifying partners, but rather in accessing them, especially in areas where there is poor resource availability.

Most health departments in the United States no longer have resources for routine partner notification except for gonorrhea, syphilis, and HIV. The method of using a disease intervention specialist is labor intensive and costly—a major roadblock given today's shrinking budgets. Thus several Internet-accessible methods of notifying partners that they may have been exposed to a sexually transmittable infection have become popular in the United States; the most widely used is inSPOT.[236,237] Also available are CDC's e-cards (http://www2a.cdc.gov/ecards/message/message.asp?cardid=292).

Expedited partner therapy may be an alternative in some locations in the United States.[238]

Expedited Partner Therapy

In some states, it is legal for a diagnosed patient to deliver medications or a prescription directly to sexual partners without the partner being clinically assessed. EPT may be especially beneficial in situations in which the patient doubts that a partner will seek medical care.[238] This practice is growing in the United States, to the point where it is now legal or permissible to provide EPT in many states. Up-to-date, detailed information about the legal status of EPT in each state can be found at www.cdc.gov.

INNOVATIVE STD CONTROL METHODS

Treatment to Control Transmission of STDs

Another modality for controlling transmission of STDs that has received much press attention in recent years has been the use of various treatment regimens. For example, once-daily valacyclovir to reduce the risk of transmission of genital herpes has been shown to reduce transmission to partners.[239] For HIV, a recent report demonstrated prevention of HIV transmission in 1763 sero-discordant couples with early antiretroviral therapy.[240] Only one of 28 linked transmissions occurred in the early therapy group, and the relative dearth of clinical events in the early therapy group indicated both individual and public health benefits from this strategy.[240] Future studies will add much information to the knowledge base related to using treatment to control STDs and HIV.

Vaccination to Prevent Transmission of HPV and Prevent Cervical Cancer

One of the most recent and potentially most successful control programs for STDs is the initiative to vaccinate young women against acquisition of human papillomavirus infections, thereby preventing cervical cancer.[150,151] Two recently developed prophylactic cervical cancer vaccines, both of which exploit the viral-like particle (VLP) technology of HPV, have the ability to decrease a large proportion of cervical cancer cases worldwide.[156] Both vaccines confer protection against cervical cancer on the order of 70–75%, which represents the percentage of invasive cancers attributable to HPV-16 and -18. Challenges to ensuring the successful control of this largely preventable disease require endorsement of the vaccines by governments and policymakers, affordable prices, education at all levels, overcoming the barriers to vaccination, and continued adherence to screening programs.[156]

Home Collection of Urogenital Specimens

There has been much interest recently in the possibility of using samples collected at home for direct mailing to a laboratory for testing, thereby completely bypassing the clinic for routine screening when an individual does not have symptoms. Although home collection is not yet an FDA-approved option, the focus of current research has shown that vaginal swabs can be collected at home and sent through the U.S. mail to a laboratory for testing.[241-245] Several studies have indicated that home collection is preferred by many to most women.[244,246]

Innovative Internet Recruitment for Home-Collected Vaginal Swabs as STD Control

Recently, two ongoing studies—*I Want the Kit* (IWTK; http://www.iwantthekit.org/female/default.html), which is available in several states, and *I Know* (https://www.dontthinkknow.org), which operates in Los Angeles, California—have recruited women, through specially designed websites that offer information and a test kit, to collect samples at home and mail them to a testing laboratory.[178,247-249] Both of these projects mail a home collection kit to users after self-requests, thereby facilitating screening through education and self-empowerment or responsibility for one's own sexual health. Each program reports results back to the participant and links users directly with treatment services. Women have reported satisfaction with this method of screening, indicating that they would use the Internet again to obtain a screening kit. Among women tested in these studies, high prevalence (9–10%) of chlamydia and of high-risk sexual behavior have been reported. These web-based sites have been designed with input from focus groups of young women.[249,250] IWTK is also available for men.[251]

Circumcision to Reduce HIV Transmission

While circumcision studies in Africa[252,253] have shown benefit in reducing acquisition of HIV and even HPV, HSV-2, and syphilis,[254,255] further uptake of voluntary medical male circumcision (VMMC) is unlikely to affect the HIV epidemic in the United States, as MSM remain a key risk group in that country. Circumcision has not been shown to reduce the risk of HIV transmission among MSM. That said, because VMMC has been confirmed to reduce the risk of HIV by more than 60%, it remains a powerful tool in an individual's prevention package and should be considered by men who are at risk for their individual benefit. VMMC is being promoted in countries with high rates of HIV among heterosexuals and low rates of current male circumcision. Mathematical models of the impact of VMMC in Africa have shown that it can significantly alter the trajectory of the epidemic.[256]

FUTURE CONSIDERATIONS

The Affordable Care Act (ACA) in the United States stresses that primary care clinicians and health directors in Federally Qualified Health Centers (FQHC) will be essential in the provision of routine STD and HIV testing and care. Under this federal legislation, diagnosis and treatment of STDs will shift from specialty STD clinics to the primary care setting. To improve the sexual health of the general population, it will be necessary to provide and expand training from clinicians in STD clinics to primary care clinicians to meet their identified needs. Because preventive services keep people healthy, save lives, and reduce eventual future healthcare costs, especially with regard to STDs and HIV, education and training will necessarily need to be centered in the federal health reform efforts.

The ACA requires "private health plan coverage for sexual health preventive services," which is an excellent step toward minimizing the STD burden. Such services include chlamydia tests for all sexually active women 24 years and younger, all pregnant women, and women at high risk who are 25 years or older; gonorrhea and syphilis testing for women at risk; syphilis and HBV tests for all pregnant women; and HIV tests for all high-risk adults and at-risk adolescents.

Primary care clinicians working in FQHC will require expanded training to increase their awareness and acquire the necessary skills to institute screening for sensitive issues such as STDs and HIV. As an example of the need to raise awareness and educate primary care providers on these topics, recent data on the trends in achieving the 21 critical national health objectives for adolescents and young adults by 2010 demonstrated that although some progress was made, the United States regressed in achieving two of these goals—those related to chlamydia infections and obesity.[257] Clearly, much future work will be necessary to achieve better sexual health in the United States.[227]

SUMMARY

- STDs have major health impacts, including direct medical costs, indirect medical costs, and facilitation of HIV infection.
- STDs are predominantly asymptomatic.
- Traditional intervention strategies for STDs have been oriented toward four goals:
  - Reducing the potential for exposure through modifying risky behavior patterns and primary STD prevention

- Reducing the infected pool of individuals through screening programs
- Providing treatment based on regimens that are known to be effective
- Treatment of infected partners through contact notification

● ● ● **REFERENCES**

1. Chesson HW, Blandford JM, Gift TL, Irwin KL. The estimated direct medical cost of sexually transmitted diseases among American youth, 2000. *Perspect Sex Repro Health.* 2004;36:11–19.

2. Weinstock H, Berman S, Cates W. Sexually transmitted disease among American youth: incidence and prevalence estimates. *Perspect Sex Repro Health.* 2004;36:6–10.

3. Centers for Disease Control and Prevention. *Sexually Transmitted Disease Surveillance, 2010.* Atlanta, GA: U.S. Department of Health and Human Services; 2010. *CDC* 2011;1–155.

4. Gaydos CA. Nucleic acid amplification tests for gonorrhea and chlamydia: practice and applications. *Infect Dis Clin North Am.* 2005;19:367–386.

5. Centers for Disease Control and Prevention. Sexually transmitted disease treatment guidelines 2010. *MMWR* December 17, 2010. Available at: www.cdc.gov/std/treatment/2010. CDC. 2010;59:1–110.

6. Fleming DT, Wasserheit J. From epidemiological synergy to public health policy and practice: the contribution of other sexually transmitted diseases to sexual transmission of HIV infection. *Sex Transm Infect.* 1999;75:3–17.

7. Van Der Pol B, Kwok C, Pierre-Louis B, et al. *Trichomonas vaginalis* infection and human immunodeficiency virus acquisition in African women. *J Infect Dis.* 2008;197:548–554.

8. Kissinger P, Amadee A, Clark RA, et al. *Trichomonas vaginalis* treatment reduces vaginal HIV-1 shedding. *Sex Transm Dis.* 2009;36:11–16.

9. Kissinger P, Secor WE, Leichliter JS, et al. Early repeated infections with *Trichomonas vaginalis* among HIV-positive and HIV-negative women. *Clin Infect Dis.* 2008;46:994–999.

10. Centers for Disease Control and Prevention. CDC health disparities and inequalities report—United States, 2011. *MMWR.* 2011;60(suppl):1–113.

11. Miller WC, Zenilman JM. Epidemiology of chlamydial infection, gonorrhea, and trichomoniasis in the United States. *Infect Dis Clin North Am.* 2005;19:281–296.

12. Campbell LA, Kuo C-C, Gaydos CA. Chlamydial infections. In: Detrick B, Hamilton RG, Folds JD, eds. *Manual of Molecular and Clinical Laboratory Immunology.* 7th ed. Washington, DC: ASM Press; 2006;518–525.

13. Gaydos CA. Chlamydiae. In: Spector S, Hodinka RL, Young SA, Wiedbrauk DL, eds. *Clinical Virology Manual.* 4th ed. Washington, DC: ASM Press; 2009;630–640.

14. Gaydos CA, Quinn TC. Chlamydia infections. In: Longo D, Fauci AS, Kasper DL, et al, eds. *Harrison's Principles of Internal Medicine.* 18th ed. New York: McGraw-Hill Medical; 2011:1421–1431.

15. Stamm WE. Lymphogranuloma venereum. In: Holmes KK, Sparling PF, Stamm WE, et al., eds. *Sexually Transmitted Diseases.* 4th ed. New York: McGraw-Hill; 2008; 595–605.

16. Centers for Disease Control and Prevention. Lymphogranuloma venereum among men who have sex with men—Netherlands, 2003–2004. *MMWR.* 2004;53:985–988.

17. Marrazzo JM. Mucopurulent cervicitis: no longer ignored, but still misunderstood. *Infect Dis Clin North Am.* 2005;19:333–349.

18. Stamm WE. *Chlamydia trachomatis* infections of the adult. In: Holmes KK, Sparling PF, Stamm WE, et al., eds. *Sexually Transmitted Diseases.* 4th ed. New York: McGraw-Hill; 2008;575–593.

19. U.S. Preventive Services Task Force. Screening for chlamydial infection: U.S. Preventive Services Task Force recommendation statement. *Ann Intern Med.* 2007;147:128–134.

20. National Committee for Quality Assurance. *The State of Health Care Quality 2010: HEDIS Measures of Care.* Washington, DC: Author; 2010:43-44. Available at: http://www.ncqa.org/portals/0/state%20of%20health%20care/2010/SOHC%202010%20-%20Full2 pdf.

21. Jaschek G, Gaydos C, Welsh L, Quinn TC. Direct detection of *Chlamydia trachomatis* in urine specimens from symptomatic and asymptomatic men by using a rapid polymerase chain reaction assay. *J Clin Microbiol.* 1993;31:1209–1212.

22. Gaydos CA, Quinn TC, Willis D, et al. Performance of the APTIMA Combo 2 assay for the multiplex detection of *Chlamydia trachomatis* and *Neisseria gonorrheae* in female urine and endocervical swab specimens. *J Clin Microbiol.* 2003;41:304–309.

23. Schachter J, McCormick WM, Chernesky MA, et al. Vaginal swabs are appropriate specimens for diagnosis of genital tract infection with *Chlamydia trachomatis. J Clin Microbiol.* 2003;41:3784–3789.

24. Gaydos CA, Theodore M, Dalesio N, et al. Comparison of three nucleic acid amplification tests for detection of *Chlamydia trachomatis* in urine specimens. *J Clin Microbiol.* 2004;42:3041–3045.

25. Gaydos CA, Quinn TC. Urine nucleic acid amplification tests for the diagnosis of sexually transmitted infections in clinical practice. *Curr Opin Infect Dis.* 2005;18:55–66.

26. Schachter J, Chernesky MA, Willis D,E et al. Vaginal swabs are the specimens of choice when screening for *Chlamydia trachomatis* and *Neisseria gonorrhoeae*: results from a multicenter evaluation of the APTIMA assays for both infections. *Sex Transm Dis.* 2005;32:725–728.

27. Schachter J, Moncada J, Liska S, et al. Nucleic acid amplification tests in the diagnosis of chlamydial and gonococcal infections of the oropharynx and rectum in men who have sex with men. *Sex Transm Dis.* 2008;35:637–642.

28. Gaydos CA, Ferrero DV, Papp J. Laboratory aspects of screening men for *Chlamydia trachomatis* in the new millennium. *Sex Transm Dis.* 2008;35(suppl):S45–S50.

29. Gaydos CA. Sexually transmitted infections screening and diagnostic practices. In: Somesh Gupta BK, ed. *Sexually Transmitted Infections.* 2nd ed. New Delhi, India: Elsevier; 2011:1242–1250.

30. Gaydos CA, Cartwight CP, Colaninno P, et al. Performance of the Abbott RealTime CT/NG for the detection of *Chlamydia trachomatis* and *Neisseria gonorrhoeae. J Clin Microbiol.* 2010;48:3236–3243.

31. Taylor SN, Van Der Pol B, Lillis R, et al. Clinical evaluation of the BD ProbeTec™ *Chlamydia trachomatis* (CT) Q^x amplified DNA assay on the BD Viper™ system with XTR™ technology. *Sex Transm Dis.* 2011;38:603–609.

32. Gaydos CA, Essig A. *Chlamydiaceae.* In: Murray PR, Baron EJ, Jorgensen JH, et al., eds. *Manuel of Clinical Microbiology.* 10th ed. Washington, DC: American Society for Microbiology; 2011;986–1000.

33. Howell MR, Quinn TC, Gaydos CA. Screening for *Chlamydia trachomatis* in asymptomatic women attending family planning clinics: a cost effectiveness analysis of three preventive strategies. *Ann Intern Med.* 1998;128:277–284.

34. Hu D, Hook EW III, Goldie SJ. Screening for *Chlamydia trachomatis* in women 15 to 29 years of age: a cost-effectiveness analysis. *Ann Intern Med.* 2004;141:1501–1513.

35. Blake D, Maldeis N, Barnes MR, et al. Cost-effectiveness of screening strategies for *Chlamydia trachomatis* using cervical swabs, urine, and self-obtained vaginal swabs in a sexually transmitted disease clinic setting. *Sex Transm Dis.* 2008;35:649–655.

36. Scholes D, Stergachis A, Heidrich FE, et al. Prevention of pelvic inflammatory disease by

screening for cervical chlamydial infection. *N Engl J Med.* 1996;334:1362–1366.

37. Howell MR, McKee JKT, Gaydos JC, et al. Point-of-entry screening for *C. trachomatis* in female army recruits: who derives the cost savings? *Am J Prev Med.* 2000;19:160–166.

38. Howell MR, Gaydos JC, McKee JKT, et al. Control of *Chlamydia trachomatis* in female army recruits: cost-effective screening and treatment to prevent pelvic inflammatory disease. *Sex Transm Dis.* 1999;26:519–526.

39. Clark KL, Howell RM, Li Y, et al. Hospitalization rates in female U.S. Army recruits associated with a screening program for *C. trachomatis. Sex Transm Dis.* 2002;29:1–5.

40. Hook EW III, Handsfield HH. Gonococcal infections in the adult. In: Holmes KK, Sparling PF, Stamm WE, et al., eds. *Sexually Transmitted Diseases.* 4th ed. New York: McGraw-Hill Medical; 2008:627–645.

41. Sparling PF. Biology of *Neisseria gonorrhoeae.* In: Holmes KK, Sparling PF, Stamm WE, et al., eds. *Sexually Transmitted Diseases.* 4th ed. New York: McGraw-Hill Medical; 2008: 607–626.

42. Janda WM, Morello JA, Lerner SA, Bohnhoff M. Characteristics of pathogenic *Neisseria* spp. isolated from homosexual men. *J Clin Microbiol.* 1983;17:85–91.

43. Clark RB, Lewinski MA, Leoffelholz MJ, Tibbetts RJ. Verification and validation of procedures in the clinical microbiology laboratory. *Cumitech.* 2009;31A:1–24.

44. Tsunoe H, Tanaka M, Nalayama H, et al. High prevalence of *Chlamydia trachomatis, Neisseria gonorrhoeae,* and *Mycoplasma genitalium* in female commercial sex workers in Japan. *Inter J STD AIDS.* 2000;11:790–794.

45. Schachter J, Moncada J, Liska S, et al. Nucleic acid amplification tests in the diagnosis of chlamydial and gonococcal infections of the oropharynx and rectum of men who have sex with men. *Sex Transm Dis.* 2008;35:637–642.

46. Bachmann LH, Johnson RE, Cheng H, et al. Nucleic amplification tests for diagnosis of *Neisseria gonorrhoeae* oropharyngeal infections. *J Clin Microbiol.* 2009;42: 902–907.

47. Paavonen J, Westrom L, Eschenbach D. Pelvic inflammatory disease. In: Holmes KK, Sparling PF, Stamm WE, et al., eds. *Sexually Transmitted Diseases.* 4th ed. New York: McGraw-Hill Medical; 2008:1017–1050.

48. Ross JDC. Pelvic inflammatory disease. In: Somesh Gupta BK, ed. *Sexually Transmitted Infections.* 2nd ed. New Delhi: Elsevier; 2011:557–568.

49. Turner CF, Rogers SM, Miller HG, et al. Untreated gonococcal and chlamydial infection in a probability sample of adults. *JAMA.* 2002;287:726–733.

50. Hook EW III, Handsfield HH. Gonococcal infections in the adult. In: Holmes KK, Mardh P, Sparling PF, et al., eds. *Sexually Transmitted Diseases.* 2nd ed. New York: McGraw-Hill; 1990:149–165.

51. Kuypers J, Gaydos CA, Peeling RW. Principles of laboratory diagnosis of STIs. In: Holmes KK, Sparling PF, Stamm WE, et al., eds. *Sexually Transmitted diseases.* 4th ed. New York: McGraw-Hill; 2008:937–957.

52. Centers for Disease Control and Prevention. Fluoroquinolone-resistance in *Neisseria gonorrhoeae,* Hawaii, 1999 and decreased susceptibility to azithromycin in *N. gonorrhoeae.* Missouri, 1999. *MMWR.* 2000;49:833.

53. Tapsall JW. Implications of current recommendations for third-generation cephalosporins use in the WHO Western-Pacific region following the emergence of multi-resistant gonococci. *Sex Transm Infect.* 2009. doi:10.1136/sti.2008.035337.

54. Ohnishi M, Golparian D, Shimuta K, et al. Is *Neisseria gonorrhoeae* initiating a future era of untreatable gonorrhea? Detailed characterization of the first strain with high-level resistance to ceftriaxone. *Antimicrob Agents Chemother.* 2011;55:3538–3545.

55. Ohnishi M, et al. Spreading of a chromosomal cefixime-resistant *penA* gene among different *Neisseria gonorrhoeae* lineages. *Antimicrob Agents Chemother.* 2010;54:1060–1067.

56. Ohnishi M, et.al. Ceftriaxone-resistant *Neisseria gonorrhoeae*, Japan. *Emerg Infect Dis.* 2011;17:148–149.

57. Gaydos CA, Howell MR, Pare B, et al. *Chlamydia trachomatis* infections in female military recruits. *N Engl J Med.* 1998;339:739–744.

58. Cecil JA, Howell MR, Tawes JJ, et al. Features of *Chlamydia trachomatis* and *Neisseria gonorrhoeae* infection in male army recruits. *J Infect Dis.* 2001;184:1216–1219.

59. Gaydos CA, Howell MR, Quinn JC, et al. Sustained high prevalence of *Chlamydia trachomatis* infections in female army recruits. *Sex Transm Dis.* 2003;30:539–544.

60. Miller WC, Ford CA, Morris M, et al. Prevalence of chlamydial and gonococcal infections among young adults in the United States. *JAMA.* 2004;291:2229–2236.

61. Mehta SD, Rothman RE, Kelen GD, et al. Unsuspected gonorrhea and chlamydia in patients of an urban adult emergency department: a critical population for STD control. *Sex Transm Dis.* 2001;28:33–39.

62. Mehta SD, Rothman RE, Kelen GD, et al. Clinical aspects of diagnosis of gonorrhea and *Chlamydia* infection in an acute care setting. *Clin Infect Dis.* 2001;32:655–659.

63. Finelli L, Schillinger JA, Wasserheit JN. Are emergency departments the next frontier for sexually transmitted disease screening? *Sex Transm Dis.* 2001;28:40–42.

64. Washington AE, Aral SO, Wolner-Hanssen P, et al. Assessing risk for pelvic inflammatory disease and its sequelae. *JAMA.* 1991;266: 2581–2586.

65. Westrom L. Pelvic inflammatory disease. *JAMA.* 1991;266:2612.

66. Westrom L, Joesoef R, Reynolds G, et al. Pelvic inflammatory disease and fertility. *Sex Transm Dis.* 1992;19:185–192.

67. Hillis SD, Joesoef R, Marchbanks PA, et al. Delayed care of pelvic inflammatory disease as a risk factor for impaired fertility. *Am J Obstet Gynecol.* 1993;168:1503–1509.

68. Westrom L, Joesoef R, Reynolds G, et al. Pelvic inflammatory disease and fertility: a cohort study of 1844 women with laparoscopically verified disease and 657 control women with normal laparoscopic results. *Sex Transm Dis.* 1992;152:1275–1282.

69. Westrom LV. Sexually transmitted diseases and infertility. *Sex Transm Dis.* 1994;21 (suppl 2):S32–S37.

70. Hillis SD, Wasserheit JN. Screening for *Chlamydia* a key to the prevention of pelvic inflammatory disease. *N Engl J Med.* 1996;334:1399–1401.

71. Hillis SD, Owens LM, Marchbanks PA, et al. Recurrent chlamydial infections increase the risks of hospitalization for ectopic pregnancy and pelvic inflammatory disease. *Am J Obstet Gynecol.* 1997;176:103–107.

72. Washington AE, Katz P. Cost of and payment source for pelvic inflammatory disease: trends and projections, 1983 through 2000. *JAMA.* 1991;266:2565–2569.

73. Westrom L. Incidence, prevalence, and trends of acute pelvic inflammatory disease and its consequences in industrialized countries. *Am J Obstet Gynecol.* 1980;138:880–892.

74. Westrom L, Bengtsson L, Mardh P-A. Incidence, trends, and risks of ectopic pregnancy in a population of women. *Brit Med J.* 1981;282:15–18.

75. Westrom L. Effect of pelvic inflammatory disease on fertility. *Venereology.* 1995;8:219–222.

76. Washington AE, Cates W, Wasserheit J. Preventing pelvic inflammatory disease. *JAMA.* 1991;266:2574–2580.

77. Ness RB, Randall H, Richter H,E et al. Condom use and the risk of recurrent pelvic inflammatory disease, chronic pelvic pain,

or infertility following an episode of pelvic inflammatory disease. *Am J Public Health.* 2004;94:1327–1329.

78. Centers for Disease Control and Prevention. Pelvic inflammatory disease: guidelines for prevention and management. *MMWR.* 1991;40(RR-5):1–25.

79. Nelson DB, Ness RB, Peipert JF, et al. Factors predicting upper genital tract inflammation among women with lower tract infection. *J Womens Health.* 1998;7:1033–1040.

80. Sellors J, Mahony J, Goldsmith C, et al. The accuracy of clinical findings and laparoscopy in pelvic inflammatory disease. *Am J Obstet Gynecol.* 1991;164:113–120.

81. Ledger WJ. Effectiveness of inpatient and outpatient treatment strategies for women with pelvic inflammatory disease. *Am J Obstet Gynecol.* 2002;188:598–600.

82. Owusu-Edusei K, Bohm M, Chesson H, Kent C. *Chlamydia* screening and pelvic inflammatory disease: insights from exploratory time-series analyses. *Am J Prev Med.* 2010;38:652–657.

83. Hook EW III, Marra CM. Acquired syphilis in adults. *N Engl J Med.* 1992;326:1060–1069.

84. Sparling PF, Swartz MN, Musher DM, Healy BP. Clinical manifestations of syphilis. In: Holmes KK, Sparling PF, Stamm WE, et al., eds. *Sexually Transmitted Diseases.* 4th ed. New York: McGraw-Hill; 2008:661–684.

85. Centers for Disease Control and Prevention. Primary and secondary syphilis—United States, 2002. *MMWR.* 2003;52:1117–1120.

86. Rolfs RT, Nakashima AK. Epidemiology of primary and secondary syphilis in the United States, 1981 through 1989. *JAMA.* 1990;264:1432–1437.

87. St. Louis ME, Wasserheit JN. Elimination of syphilis in the United States. *Science.* 1998;281:353–354.

88. Lukehart SA, Hook EWI, Baker-Zander SA, et al. Invasion of the central nervous system by *Treponema pallidum*: implications for diagnosis and treatment. *Ann Intern Med.* 1988;109:855–862.

89. Rompalo AM, Lawlor J, Seaman P, et al. Modification of syphilitic genital ulcer manifestations by coexistent HIV infection. *Sex Transm Dis.* 2001;28:448–454.

90. Larson SA, Steiner BM, Rudolph AH. Laboratory diagnosis and interpretation of tests for syphilis. *Clin Microbiol Rev.* 1995;8:1–21.

91. Centers for Disease Control and Prevention. Syphilis testing algorithms using treponemal tests for initial screening—four laboratories, New York City, 2005–2006. *MMWR.* 2008;57:872–875.

92. Senã AC, White BL, Sparling F. Novel *Treponema pallidum* serologic tests: a paradigm shift in syphilis screening for the 21st century. *Clin Infect Dis.* 2010;51:700–708.

93. Park IU, Chow JM, Boland G, et al. Screening for syphilis with treponemal immunoassay: analysis of discordant serology results and implications for clinical management. *J Infect Dis.* 2011;204:1297–1304.

94. Hoover KW, Radolf JD. Serodiagnosis of syphilis in the recombinant era: reversal of fortune. *J Infect Dis.* 2011;204:1295–1296.

95. Rolfs RT, Joesoef MR, Hendershot EF, et al. A randomized trial of enhanced therapy for early syphilis in patients with and without human immunodeficiency virus infection. The Syphilis and HIV Study Group. *N Engl J Med.* 1997;337:307–314.

96. Centers for Disease Control and Prevention. Congenital syphilis—United States, 2002. *MMWR.* 2004;53:716–719.

97. Pew Internet & American Life Project. November 30–December 30, 2006. Available at: http://www.pewinternet.org/report. Accessed April 16, 2007.

98. Lukehart SA, Godornes C, Molini BJ, et al. Macrolide resistance in *Treponema pallidum* in the United States and Ireland. *N Engl J Med.* 2004;351:154–158.

99. Andrus JK, Flemming DW, Harger DR, et al. Partner notification: can it control epidemic syphilis? *Ann Intern Med.* 1990;112:539–543.

100. Centers for Disease Control and Prevention. Trends in primary and secondary syphilis and HIV infections in men who have sex with men—San Francisco and Los Angeles, California, 1998–2002. *MMWR.* 2004;53:575–578.

101. Klausner JD, Wolf W, Fischer-Ponce L, Katz MH. Tracing a syphilis outbreak through cyberspace. *JAMA.* 2000;284: 447–449.

102. Grassly NC, Fraser C, Garnett GP. Host immunity and synchronized epidemics of syphilis across the United States. *Nature.* 2005;43:417–421.

103. Fleming DT, McQuillan GM, Johnson RE, et al. Herpes simplex virus type 2 in the United States, 1976–1994. *N Engl J Med.* 1997;337:1105–1111.

104. Corey L, Wald A. Genital herpes. In: Holmes KK, Sparling PF, Stamm WE, et al., eds. *Sexually Transmitted Diseases.* 4th ed. New York: McGraw-Hill Medical; 2008:399–437.

105. Xu F, Sternberg MR, Kottiri BJ, et al. Trends in herpes simplex virus type 1 and type 2 seroprevalence in the United States. *JAMA.* 2006;296:964–973.

106. Gottlieb SL, Douglas JM Jr, Foster M, et al. Incidence of herpes simplex virus type 2 infection in 5 sexually transmitted disease (STD) clinics and the effect of HIV/STD risk-reduction counseling. *J Infect Dis.* 2004;190:1059–1067.

107. Wald A, Zeh J, Selke S, et al. Reactivation of genital herpes simplex virus type 2 infection in asymptomatic seropositive persons. *N Engl J Med.* 2000;342:844–850.

108. Trotstein E, Johnston C, Huang ML, et al. Genital shedding of herpes simplex virus among symptomatic and asymptomatic persons with HSV-2 infection. *JAMA.* 2011;305:1441–1449.

109. Augenbraun M, Feldman J, Chirgwin K, et al. Increased genital shedding of herpes simplex virus type 2 in HIV-seropositive women. *Ann Intern Med.* 1995;123: 845–847.

110. Wald A, Ashley-Morrow R. Serological testing for herpes simplex virus (HSV-1 and HSV-2 infection. *Clin Infect Dis.* 2002;35(suppl 2):S173–S182.

111. Mujugira A, Morrow RA, Celum C, et al. Performance of the Focus HerpeSelect-2 enzyme immunoassay for the detection of herpes simplex virus type 2 antibodies in seven African countries. *Sex Transm Infect.* 2011;87:238–241.

112. Brown ZA, Wald A, Morrow RA, et al. Effects of serologic status and cesarean delivery on transmission rates of herpes simplex virus from mother to infant. *JAMA.* 2003;289:203–209.

113. Rooney JF, Straus SE, Mannis ML, et al. Oral acyclovir to suppress frequently recurrent herpes labialis: a double-blind, placebo-controlled trial. *Ann Intern Med.* 1993;118:268–272.

114. Wald A, Selke S, Warren T, et al. Comparative efficacy of famciclovir and valacyclovir for suppression of recurrent genital herpes and viral shedding. *Sex Transm Dis.* 2006;33:529–533.

115. Corey L, Wald A, Patel R, et al. Once-daily valacyclovir to reduce the risk of trans-mission of genital herpes. *N Engl J Med.* 2004;350:11–20.

116. Wald A, Langenberg AG, Link K, et al. Effect of condoms on reducing the transmis-sion of herpes simplex virus type 2 from men to women. *JAMA.* 2001;285:3100–3106.

117. Wald A, Corey L. How does herpes simplex virus type 2 influence human immunodefi-ciency virus infection and pathogenesis? *J Infect Dis* 2003;187:1509–1512.

118. Corey L, Wald A, Celum CA, et al. The effects of herpes simplex virus-2 on HIV-1 acquisition and transmission: a review

of two overlapping epidemics. *J AIDS.* 2004;35:435–445.

119. Celum C, Wald A, Lingappa LR, et al. Acyclovir and transmission of HIV-1 from persons infected with HIV-1 and HSV-2. *N Engl J Med.* 2010;362:427–439.

120. Spinola SM. Chancroid and *Haemophilus decreyi.* In: Holmes KK, Sparling PF, Stamm WE, et al., eds. *Sexually Transmitted Diseases.* 4th ed. New York: McGraw-Hill Medical; 2008:689–699.

121. Mertz KJ, Weiss JB, Webb RM, et al. An investigation of genital ulcers in Jackson, Mississippi, with use of a multiplex polymerase chain reaction assay: high prevalence of chancroid and human immunodeficiency virus infection. *J Infect Dis.* 1998;178:1060–1066.

122. Greenblatt RM, Lukehart SA, Plummer FA, et al. Genital ulceration as a risk factor for human immunodeficiency virus infection. *AIDS.* 1988;2:47–50.

123. Steen R. Eradicating Chancroid. *Bull WHO.* 2001;79:818–826.

124. Lewis D. Chancroid: clinical manifestations, diagnosis, and management. *Sex Transm Dis.* 2003;79:68–71.

125. Suntoke TR, Hardick A, Tobian AAR, et al. Evaluation of multiplex, real-time PCR for detection of *Haemophilus ducreyi, Treponema pallidum,* herpes simplex virus type 1 and 2 in the diagnosis of genital ulcer disease in the Rakai District, Uganda. *Sex Transm Dis.* 2009;85:97–101.

126. Risbud A, Chan-Tack K, Gadkari D, et al. The etiology of genital ulcer disease by multiplex polymerase chain reaction and relationship to HIV infection among patients attending sexually transmitted disease clinics in Pune, India. *Sex Transm Dis.* 1999;26:55–62.

127. Bosch FX, Lorincz A, Munoz N, et al. The causal relationship between human papillomavirus and cervical cancer. *J Clin Pathol.* 2002;55:244–265.

128. Egelkrout EM, Galloway DA. The biology of genital human papillomaviruses. In: Holmes KK, Sparling PF, Stamm WE, et al., eds. *Sexually Transmitted Diseases.* 4th ed. New York: McGraw-Hill; 2008:463–487.

129. Koutsky L. Epidemiology of genital human papillomavirus infection. *Am J Med.* 1997;102(suppl 5A):3–8.

130. Munoz N, Bosch FX, de Sanjose S, et al. Epidemiological classification of human papillomavirus types associated with cervical cancer. *N Engl J Med.* 2003;348:518–527.

131. Moscicki AB, Hills N, Shiboski S, et al. Risks for incident human papillomavirus infection and low-grade squamous intraepithelial lesion development in young females. *JAMA.* 2001;285:2995–3002.

132. Moscicki AB, Hills N, Shiboski S, et al. Regression of low-grade squamous intraepithelial lesions in young women. *Lancet.* 2004;364:1678–1683.

133. Winer RL, Koutsky LA. Genital human papillomavirus infection. In: Holmes KK, Sparling PF, Stamm WE, et al., eds. *Sexually Transmitted Diseases.* 4th ed. New York: McGraw-Hill Medical; 2008:489–508.

134. Bauer HM, Ting Y, Greer CE, et al. Genital human papillomavirus infection in female university students as determined by a PCR-based method. *JAMA.* 1991;265:472–477.

135. Dunn EF, Unger ER, Sternberg M, et al. Prevalence of HPV infection among females in the United States. *JAMA.* 2007;297:813–819.

136. Dunn EF, Nielson CM, Stone KM, et al. Prevalence of HPV infection among men: a systemic review of the literature. *J Infect Dis.* 2006;194:1044–1057.

137. Palefsky JM, Giuliano AR, Goldstone S, et al. HPV vaccine against anal HPV infection and anal intraepithelial neoplasia. *N Engl J Med.* 2011;365:1576–1585.

138. Hoots BE, Palefsky JM, Pimenta JM, Smith JS. Human papillomavirus type distribution in anal cancer and anal intraepithelial lesions. *Int J Cancer.* 2009;124:2375–2383.

139. Bleakley A, Hennessy M, Fishbein M. Public opinion on sex education in US Schools. *Arch Pediatr Adolesc Med.* 2006;160:1151–1156.

140. Smith JS, Munoz N, Herrero R, et al. Evidence for *Chlamydia trachomatis* as a human papillomavirus cofactor in the etiology of invasive cervical cancer in Brazil and the Philippines. *J Infect Dis.* 2002;185:324–331.

141. Smith JS, Herrero R, Boseiit C, et al. Herpes simples virus-2 as a human papillomavirus cofactor in the etiology of invasive cervical cancer. *J Natl Canter Inst.* 2002;94: 1604–1613.

142. American College of Obstetricians and Gynecologists. ACOG Practice Bulletin number 66, September 2005: management of abnormal cervical cytology and histology. *Obstet Gynecol.* 2005;106:645–664.

143. Vesco K, Whitlock EP, Eder M, et al. *Screening for Cervical Cancer: A Systematic Evidence Review for the U.S. Preventive Services Task Force.* Evidence Synthesis No. 86. AHRQ Publication No. 11-05156-EF-1. Rockville, MD: Agency for Healthcare Research and Quality; 2011.

144. American Cancer Society. Cervical cancer: prevention and early detection. *American Cancer Society* [serial online] 2011. http://www.cancer.org/search/index?QueryText=Cervical+cancer%3A+prevention+and+early+detection. Accessed December 16, 2011.

145. Feldman S. Making sense of the new cervical-cancer screening guidelines. *N Engl J Med.* 2011;365:2145–2147.

146. ACOG Practice Bulletin no. 109. Cervical cytology screening. *Obstet Gynecol.* 2009;114:1409–1420.

147. Cox J. The clinician's view: role of human papillomavirus testing in the American Cancer Society guidelines for colposcopy and cervical cytology and cervical cancer precursors. *Arch Pathol Lab Med.* 2003;127:950–958.

148. Goldie SJ, Kim JJ, Wright TC. Cost-effectiveness of human papillomavirus DNA testing for cervical cancer screening in women aged 30 years or more. *Obstet Gynecol.* 2004;103:619–631.

149. Koutsky LA, Ault KA, Wheeler CM, et al. A controlled trial of a human papillomavirus type 16 vaccine. *N Engl J Med.* 2002;347: 1645–1651.

150. Barr E, Tamms G. Quadrivalent human papillomavirus vaccine. *Clin Infect Dis.* 2007;45:609–617.

151. The FUTURE II Study Group. Quadrivalent vaccine against human papillomavirus to prevent high-grade cervical lesions. *N Engl J Med.* 2007;356:1915–1927.

152. Garland SM, Hernandez-Avila M, Wheeler CM, et al. Quadrivalent vaccine against human papillomavirus to prevent anogenital disease. *N Engl J Med.* 2007;356:1928–1942.

153. Paavonen J, Jenkins D, Bosch FX, et al. Efficacy of a prophylactic adjuvanted bivalent L1 virus-like particle against infection with human papillomavirus types 16 and 18 in young women: an interim analysis of a Phase III double-blind, randomized controlled trial. *Lancet.* 2007;369: 2161–2170.

154. Joura EA, Leodolter S, Hernandez-Avila M, et al. Efficacy of a quadrivalent prophylactic human papillomavirus (types 6, 11, 16,18) L1 virus-like–particle vaccine against high-grade vulval and vaginal lesions: a combined analysis of three randomised clinical trials. *Lancet.* 2007;369:1693–1702.

155. Paavonen J, Naud P, Salmeron J, et al. Efficacy of human papillomavirus (HPV)-16/18 ASO4-adjuvanted vaccine against cervical infection and precancer caused by oncogenic HPV types (PATRICIA): final analysis of a double-blind, randomized study in young women. *Lancet.* 2009;374:301–314.

156. Garland SM, Smith JS. Human papillomavirus vaccines: current status and future prospects. *Drugs.* 2010;70:1079–1098.

157. FUTURE I/II Study Group, Dillner J, Kjaer SK, Wheeler CM, et al. Four year efficacy of prophylactic human papillomavirus quadrivalent vaccine against low grade cervical, vulvar, and vaginal intraepithelial neoplasia and anogenital warts: randomised controlled trial. *BMJ.* 2010;341:c3493. doi: 10.1136/bmj.c3493.

158. Chesson HW, Ekwueme DU, Sayaiya M, Markowitz LE. Cost-effectiveness of human papillomavirus vaccination in the United States. *Emerg Infect Dis.* 2008;14:244–251.

159. Centers for Disease Control and Prevention. Quadrivalent human papillomavirus vaccine: recommendations of the Advisory Committee on Immunization Practices (ACIP). *MMWR.* 2007;56:1–24.

160. Bogaards J, Kretzschmar M, Xiridou M, et al. Sex-specific immunization for sexually transmitted infections such as human papillomavirus: Insights from mathematical models. *PLoS Medicine.* 2011;8:e1001147.

161. Syrjanen S. Human papillomaviruses in head and neck carcinomas. *N Engl J Med.* 2007;356:1993–1995.

162. D'Souza G, Kreimer A, Viscidi R, et al. Case-control study of human papillomavirus and oropharyngeal cancer. *N Engl J Med.* 2007;356:1944–1956.

163. Mays RM, Sturm LA, Zimet GD. Parental perspectives on vaccinating children against sexually transmitted infections. *Soc Sci Med.* 2004;58:1405–1413.

164. Manhart LE, Holmes KK, Koutsky LA, et al. Human papillomavirus infection among sexually active young women in the United States: implications for developing a vaccination strategy. *Sex Transm Dis.* 2008;33:508.

165. Manhart L, Koutsky LA. Do condoms prevent HPV infection, external genital warts, or cervical neoplasia? A meta analysis. *Sex Transm Dis.* 2002;29:725–735.

166. Holmes KK, Stamm WE, Sobel JD. Lower genital tract infection syndromes in women. In: Holmes KK, Sparling PF, Stamm WE, et al., eds. *Sexually Transmitted Diseases.* 4th ed. New York: McGraw-Hill Medical; 2008;987–1016.

167. World Health Organization. *Trichomonas.* 2010. http://www.who.int/reproductivehealth/publications/rtis/2008_STI_estimates.pdf. Accessed August 15, 2012.

168. Van Der Pol B, Williams JA, Orr DP, et al. Prevalence, incidence, natural history, and response to treatment of *Trichomonas vaginalis* infection among adolescent women. *J Infect Dis.* 2005;192:2039–2044.

169. Hobbs M, Sena AC, Schwebke J. *Trichomonas vaginalis* and trichomoniasis. In: Holmes KK, Sparling PF, Stamm WE, et al., eds. *Sexually Transmitted Diseases.* 4th ed. New York: McGraw-Hill Medical; 2008:771–793.

170. Wendel KE, Erbelding EJ, Gaydos CA, Rompalo AM. Use of urine polymerase chain reaction to define the prevalence and clinical presentation of *Trichomonas vaginalis* in men attending an STD clinic. *Sex Transm Infect.* 2003;79:151–153.

171. Wendel KA, Erbelding EJ, Gaydos CA, Rompalo AM. *Trichomonas vaginalis* polymerase chain reaction compared with standard diagnostic and therapeutic protocols for detection and treatment of vaginal trichomoniasis. *Clin Infect Dis.* 2002;35:576–580.

172. Burstein GR, Waterfield G, Joffe A, et al. Screening for gonorrhea and chlamydia by DNA amplification in adolescents attending middle school health centers: opportunity for early intervention. *Sex Transm Dis.* 1998;25:395–402.

173. Huppert JS, Mortensen JE, Reed JL, et al. Rapid antigen testing compares favorably with transcription-mediated amplification assay for the detection of *Trichomonas vaginalis* in young women. *Clin Infect Dis.* 2007;45:194–198.

174. Nye MB, Schwebke JR, Body BA. Comparison of APTIMA *Trichomonas vaginalis* transcription-mediated amplification to wet mount microscopy, culture, and polymerase chain reaction for diagnosis of trichomoniasis in men and women. *Am J Obstet Gynecol*. 2009;200:188.e1–188.e7.

175. Schwebke JR, Hobbs M, Taylor S, et al. Molecular testing for *Trichomonas vaginalis* in women: results of a pivotal US clinical trial. *J Clin Microbiol*. 2011;49:4106–4111.

176. Blake DR, Duggan A, Quinn JC, et al. Evaluation of vaginal infections in adolescent women: can it be done without a speculum? *Pediatrics*. 1998;102(4 Pt 1):939–944.

177. Crucitti T, Van Dyck E, Tehe A, et al. Comparison of culture and different PCR assays for detection of *Trichomonas vaginalis* in self collected vaginal swab specimens. *Sex Transm Infect*. 2003;79:393–398.

178. Gaydos CA, Hsieh Y-H, Barnes M, et al. *Trichomonas vaginalis* infection in women who submit self-collected vaginal samples after Internet recruitment. *Sex Transm Dis*. 2011;38:828–832.

179. Sutton M, Sternberg M, Koumans EH, et al. The prevalence of *Trichomonas vaginalis* infection among reproductive-age women in the United States, 2001–2004. *Clin Infect Dis*. 2007;45:1319–1326.

180. Miller WC, Swygard H, Hobbs MM, et al. The prevalence of trichomoniasis in young adults in the United States. *Sex Transm Dis*. 2005;32:593–598.

181. Allsworth JE, Ratner JA, Peipert JF. *Trichomonas* and other sexually transmitted infections: results from the 2001–2004 National Health and Nutrition Examination Surveys. *Sex Transm Dis*. 2009;36:738–744.

182. Miller M, Liao Y, Gomez A, et al. Factors associated with the prevalence and incidence of *Trichomonas vaginalis* infection among African American women in New York City who use drugs. *J Infect Dis*. 2008;197:503–509.

183. Hardick A, Hardick J, Wood BJ, Gaydos CA. Comparison between the prototype Gen-Probe TMA *Trichomonas vaginalis* assay and a real-time PCR for *Trichomonas vaginalis* using the Roche Lightcycler instrument in female self-administered vaginal swabs and male urine samples. *J Clin Microbiol*. 2006;44:4197–4199.

184. McClelland RS, Sangare L, Hassan WM, et al. Infection with *Trichomonas vaginalis* increases the risk of HIV-1 acquisition. *J Infect Dis*. 2007;195:698–702.

185. Schwebke JR, Burgess D. Trichomoniasis. *Clin Microbiol Rev*. 2004;17:794–803.

186. Moodley P, Wilkinson D, Connolly C, et al. *Trichomonas vaginalis* is associated with pelvic inflammatory disease in women infected with human immunodeficiency virus. *Clin Infect Dis*. 2002;34:519–522.

187. Van Der Pol B. *Trichomonas vaginalis* infection: the most prevalent nonviral sexually transmitted infection receives the least public health attention. *Clin Infect Dis*. 2007;44:23–25.

188. Mavedzenge SN, Van Der Pol B, Cheng H, et al. Epidemiological synergy of *Trichomonas vaginalis* and HIV in Zimbabwean and South African women. *Sex Transm Dis*. 2010;37:460–466.

189. Cotch MF, Pastorek JG, Nugent RP, et al. *Trichomonas vaginalis* associated with low birth weight and preterm delivery. *Sex Transm Dis*. 1997;24:353–360.

190. Cherpes TL, Weisenfeld HC, Melan MA, et al. The associations between pelvic inflammatory disease, *Trichomonas vaginalis* infection, and positive herpes simples virus type 2 serology. *Sex Transm Dis*. 2006;33:747–752.

191. Owusu-Edusei K, Tejani MN, Gift TL, et al. Estimates of the direct cost per case and overall burden of trichomoniasis for the employer-sponsored privately insured women population in the United States, 2001 to 2005. *Sex Transm Dis*. 2009;36:395–399.

192. Kaydos-Daniels SC, Miller WC, Hoffman I, et al. Validation of a urine-based PCR-enzyme–linked immunosorbent assay for use in clinical research settings to detect *Trichomonas vaginalis* in men. *J Clin Microbiol.* 2003;41:318–323.

193. Hobbs MM, Kazembe P, Reed AW, et al. *Trichomonas vaginalis* as a cause of urethritis in Malawian men. *Sex Transm Dis.* 1999;26:381–387.

194. Hillier S, Marrazzi J, Holmes K. Bacterial vaginosis. In: Holmes KK, Sparling PF, Stamm WE, et al., eds. *Sexually Transmitted Diseases.* 4th ed. New York: McGraw-Hill Medical; 2008:737–768.

195. Fredricks DN. Molecular methods to describe the spectrum and dynamics of the vaginal microbiota. *Anaerobe.* 2011;17:191–195.

196. Fredricks D, Fiedler T, Marrazzo J. Molecular identification of bacterial associated with bacterial vaginosis. *New Engl J Med.* 2005;353:1899–1911.

197. Nugent RP, Krohn MA, Hillier SL. Reliability of diagnosing bacterial vaginosis improved by a standardized method of Gram stain interpretation [Abstract]. *J Clin Microbiol.* 1991;29:297–301.

198. Spiegel C. Diagnosis of bacterial vaginosis by direct Gram stain of vaginal fluid. *J Clin Microbiol.* 1983;18:170.

199. Amsel R, Totten PA, Spiegel CA, et al. Nonspecific vaginitis: diagnostic criteria and microbial and epidemiologic association [Abstract]. *Am J Med.* 1983;74:14–22.

200. Sobel J, Ferris D, Schwebke J, et al. Suppressive antibacterial therapy with 0.75% metronidazole vaginal get to prevent recurrent bacterial vaginosis. *Am J Obstet Gynecol.* 2006;194:1283–1289.

201. Luong M, Libman M, Dahhou M, et al. Vaginal douching, bacterial vaginosis, and spontaneous preterm birth. *J Obstet Gynaecol Can.* 2010;32:313–320.

202. Brotman R, Ravel J, Cone R, Zenilamn J. Rapid fluctuation of the vaginal microbiota measured by Gram stain analysis. *Sex Transm Infect.* 2010;86:297–302.

203. Marrazzo J, Thomas KK, Agnew K, Ringwood K. Prevalence and risks for bacterial vaginosis in women who have sex with women. *Sex Transm Dis.* 2010;37:335–339.

204. Hillier S, Nugent R, Eschenbach D, et al. Association between bacterial vaginosis and preterm delivery of a low-birth-weight infant. The Vaginal Infections and Prematurity Study Group. *New Engl J Med.* 1995;333:1737–1742.

205. Royce R, Jackson T, Thorp JJ, et al. Race/ethnicity, vaginal flora patterns, and pH during pregnancy. *Sex Transm Dis.* 1999;26:96–102.

206. Larsson P, Platz-Christensen J, Thejls H, et al. Incidence of pelvic inflammatory disease after first-trimester legal abortion in women with bacterial vaginosis after treatment with metronidazole: a double-blind, randomized study. *Am J Obstet Gynecol.* 1992;166(Pt 1):100–103.

207. Gatski M, Martin D, Levison J, et al. The influence of bacterial vaginosis on the response to *Trichomonas vaginalis* treatment among HIV-infected women. *Sex Transm Infect.* 2011;87:208.

208. Gatski M, Martin D, Clark R, et al. Co-occurrence of *Trichomonas vaginalis* and bacterial vaginosis among HIV-positive women. *Sex Transm Dis.* 2011;38:163–166.

209. Wasserheit JN. Epidemiological synergy: interrelationships between human immunodeficiency virus and other sexually transmitted diseases. *Sex Transm Dis.* 1992;19:61–77.

210. Royce R, Sena A, Cates WJ, Cohen M. Sexual transmission of HIV. *N Engl J Med.* 1997;226:1072–1078.

211. Pilcher C, Tien H, Eron JJ, et al. Brief but efficient: acute HIV infection and the

sexual transmission of HIV. *J Infect Dis.* 2004;89:1785–1792.

212. Oh MK, Cloud GA, Baker SL, et al. Chlamydial infection and sexual behavior in young pregnant teenagers. *Sex Transm Dis.* 1993;20:45–50.

213. Garnett GP, Hughes JP, Anderson RM, et al. Sexual mixing patterns of patients attending sexually transmitted diseases clinics. *Sex Transm Dis.* 1996;3:248–257.

214. Brunham R, Plummer F. A general model of sexually transmitted disease epidemiology and its implication for control. *Med Clin North Am.* 1990;74:1339–1352.

215. Centers for Disease Control and Prevention. Sexual behavior, sexual attraction, and sexual identity in the United States: data from the 2006–2008 National Survey of Family Growth. *Natl Health Stat Rep.* 2011;36.

216. Potterat JJ, Rothenburg RB, Muth SQ. Network structural dynamics and infectious disease propagation. *Int J STD AIDS.* 1999;10:182–185.

217. Eng TR, Butler WT. The neglected health and economic impact of STDs. In: Eng TR, Butler WT, eds. *The Hidden Epidemic: Confronting Sexually Transmitted Diseases.* Washington, DC: National Academy Press; 1997:28–68.

218. Manhart LE, Aral SO, Holmes KK, Foxman S. Sex partner concurrency: measurement, prevalence, and correlates among urban 18–39-yearolds. *Sex Transm Dis.* 2002;29:133–143.

219. Hawkes S, Hart GJ, Bletsoe E, et al. Risk behaviour and STD acquisition in genitourinary clinic attenders who have travelled. *Genitourin Med.* 1995;71: 351–354.

220. Nurutdinova D, Rao S, Shacham E, et al. STD/HIV risk among adults in the primary care setting: are we adequately addressing our patients' needs? *Sex Transm Dis.* 2010;38:30–32.

221. Centers for Disease Control and Prevention, Surveillance Summaries. Sexual identity, Socioeceonomic Status of sexual contacts, and health-risk behaviors among students in grade 9–12—youth risk behavior surveillance, selected sites, United States, 2001–9. *MMWR.* 2011;60:1–133.

222. Branson B, Handsfield H, Lampe M, et al. Revised recommendations for HIV testing of adults, adolescents, and pregnant women in health-care settings. *MMWR Recomm Rep.* 2006;55:1–17.

223. Zenilman JM. Ethnicity and sexually transmitted infections. *Curr Opin Infect Dis.* 1998;11:47–52.

224. NIMH Multisite HIV/STD Prevention Trial for African American Couples Group. Concordant and discordant reports on shared sexual behaviors and condom use among African American serodiscordant couples in four cities. *AIDS Behav.* 2010;14:1011–1022.

225. Zenilman JM. Behavioral interventions: rationale, measurement, and effectiveness. In: Zenilman JM, Moellering RC Jr, eds. *Sexually Transmitted Infections.* Philadelphia: W.B. Saunders Company; 2005:541–562.

226. Kamb ML, Fishbein M, Douglas JM, et al. Efficacy of risk-reduction counseling to prevent human immunodeficiency virus and sexually transmitted diseases: a randomized controlled trial. *JAMA.* 1998;280:1161–1167.

227. Centers for Disease Control and Prevention. *A Public Health Approach for Advancing Sexual Health in the United States: Rationale and Options for Implementation. Meeting Report of an External Consultation.* Atlanta, GA: Author; December 2010.

228. Rotherberg R, Potterat J, Woodhouse D. Personal risk taking and the spread of disease: beyond core groups. *J Infect Dis.* 1996;174(suppl):S144–S149.

229. Rothernberg R, Long D, Sterk C, et al. The Atlanta Urban Networks Study: a blueprint for endemic transmission. *AIDS.* 2000;14:2191–2200.

230. Bernstein K, Curriero F, Jennings J, et al. Defining core gonorrhea transmission utilizing spatial data. *Am J Epidemiol.* 2004;160:51–58.

231. Zenilman J, Ellish N, Fresia A, Glass G. The geography of sexual partnerships in Baltimore: application of core theory dynamics using a geographical information system. *Sex Transm Dis.* 1999;26:75–81.

232. Rothenberg R, Potterat J. Temporal and social aspects of gonorrhea transmission: the force of infectivity. *Sex Transm Dis.* 1988;15:88–92.

233. Rothenberg R, Narramore J. The relevance of social network concepts to sexually transmitted disease control. *Sex Transm Dis.* 1996;23:24–29.

234. Rothenberg R, Potterat J, Woodhouse D, et al. Social network dynamics and HIV transmission. *AIDS.* 1998,12:1529–1536.

235. Maloney SK, Johnson C. *Why Screen for Chlamydia? An Implementation Guide for Healthcare Providers.* Washington, DC: Partnership for Prevention; 2008:1–12.

236. Rietmeijer CA, Westergaard B, Mickiewicz TA, et al. Evaluation of an online partner notification program. *Sex Transm Dis.* 2011;38:359–364.

237. Levine D, Woodruff AJ, Mocello AR, et al. inSPOT: the first online STD partner notification system using electronic postcards. *PLoS Med.* 2008;5:e213.

238. Golden MR, Whittington WLH, Handsfield HH, et al. Effect of expedited treatment of sex partners on recurrent or persistent gonorrhea or chlamydial infection. *N Engl J Med.* 2005;352:676–685.

239. Corey L, Wald A, Patel R, et al. Once-daily valacyclovir to reduce the risk of transmission of genital herpes. *N Engl J Med.* 2011;350:11–20.

240. Cohen MS, Chen YQ, McCauley M, et al. Prevention of HIV-1 infection with early antiretroviral therapy . *N Engl J Med.* 2011;365:493–505.

241. Knox J, Tabrizi SN, Miller P, et al. Evaluation of self-collected samples in contrast to practitioner-collected samples for detection of *Chlamydia trachomatis, Neisseria gonorrhoeae*, and *Trichomonas vaginalis* by polymerase chain reaction among women living in remote areas. *Sex Transm Dis.* 2002;29:647–654.

242. Hsieh Y-H, Howell MR, Gaydos JC, et al. Preference among female army recruits for use of self-administered vaginal swabs or urine to screen for *Chlamydia trachomatis* genital infections. *Sex Transm Dis.* 2003;30:769–773.

243. Hobbs MM, Van Der Pol B, Totten P, et al. From the NIH: proceedings of a workshop on the importance of self-obtained vaginal specimens for detection of sexually transmitted infections. *Sex Transm Dis.* 2008;35:8–13.

244. Grasek AA, Secura GM, Allsworth JE, et al. Home-screening compared with clinic-based screening for sexually transmitted infections. *Obstet Gynecol.* 2010;115:745–752.

245. Cook RL, Ostergaard L, Hillier SL, et al. Home screening for sexually transmitted diseases in high risk young women: randomized controlled trial. *Sex Transm Infect.* 2007;83:285–291.

246. Xu F, Stoner B, Taylor SN, et al. Use of home-obtained vaginal swabs to facilitate rescreening for *Chlamydia trachomatis* infections: two randomized controlled trials. *Fujie Obstet Gynecol.* 2011;118:231–239.

247. Gaydos CA, Barnes M, Aumakhan B, et al. *Characteristics of Users of the Internet Who Submit Self-Obtained Urogenital Samples Through the Mail for Testing Sexually Transmitted Infections.* 2008 National STD Prevention Conference; Chicago, IL; March 10–13, 2009. Abstract B8b, p110.

248. Gaydos CA, Barnes M, Aumakham B, et al. Can e-technology through the Internet be used as a new tool to address the *Chlamydia trachomatis* epidemic by home sampling and vaginal swabs? *Sex Transm Dis.* 2009;36:577–580.

249. Kerndt P. "I Know": Combining home testing technology, social marketing, and lessons from e-commerce to fight chlamydia and gonorrhea disparities among young women. *National STD Prevent Conf.* March 8–10, 2010.

250. Gaydos CA, Rizzo-Price PA, Barnes M, et al. The use of focus groups to design an Internet-based program for chlamydia screening with self-administered vaginal swabs: What women want. *Sexual Health.* 2006;3:209–215.

251. Chai SJ, Aumakham B, Barnes M, et al. Internet-based screening for sexually transmitted infections to reach nonclinic populations in the community: risk factors for infection in men. *Sex Transm Dis.* 2010;37:756–763.

252. Bailey RC, Moses S, Parker CB, et al. Male circumcision for HIV prevention in young men in Kisumu, Kenya: a randomised controlled trial. *Lancet.* 2007;369:643–656.

253. Gray RH, Kigozi G, Serwadda D, et al. Male circumcision for HIV prevention in men in Rakai, Uganda: a randomised trial. *Lancet.* 2007;369:657–666.

254. Gray RH, Serwadda D, Kong X, et al. Male circumcision decreases acquisition and increases clearance of high-risk human papillomavirus in HIV-negative men: a randomized trial in Rakai, Uganda. *J Infect Dis.* 2010;201:1455–1462.

255. Tobian AA, Serwadda D, Quinn TC, et al. Male circumcision for the prevention of HSV-2 and HPV infections and syphilis. *N Engl J Med.* 2009;360:1298–1309.

256. Hankins C, Forsythe S, Njeuhmeli E. Voluntary medical male circumcision: an introduction to the cost, impact, and challenges of accelerated scaling up. *PLoS Med.* 2011;8(11):e1001127.

257. Jiang N, Kolbe LJ, Seo D-C, et al. Health of adolescents and young adults: trends in achieving the 21 critical national health objectives by 2010. *J Adolesc Health.* 2011;49:124–132.

5

Vector-Borne and Parasite Diseases

25

Emerging Vector-Borne Diseases

Kenrad E. Nelson

INTRODUCTION

In the last two decades, several vector-borne infections have emerged as major causes of human morbidity and mortality. A dramatic recent example is the spread of West Nile virus (WNV) into the Western Hemisphere from endemic foci in the Middle East, Africa, and eastern Europe. Moreover, the recent epidemic activity of WNV has also increased and expanded, even in the areas where the virus previously was endemic.

Other examples of the spread of vector-borne infections include the emergence of all four serotypes of dengue virus in the Caribbean and Central and South America, the expansion of the geographic foci of Japanese encephalitis virus to western India and Pakistan, and the emergence of yellow fever in West Africa.[1–3] In addition, the incidence of Lyme disease in the United States and that of tick-borne encephalitis virus in eastern and central Europe and Russia have increased in the last decade.

Malaria remains a major cause of infectious morbidity and mortality in sub-Saharan Africa and other tropical countries in Asia, the Middle East, and South America. However, despite the continued major public health impact of malaria on morbidity and mortality, especially in infants and children, there appears to have been a reduction in the incidence of the disease in some areas in Africa in the past few years.

Although the emergence of each of these vector-borne infections is linked to unique changes in human activity and the environment, several cross-cutting factors facilitate the emergence of infectious diseases:

- The increased ease and frequency of global travel allow infected persons to efficiently spread an infection to a new area.
- Rapid urbanization in the major cities of the tropics has created slums characterized by extreme density of human populations.
- The profusion of nonbiodegradable containers (i.e., mostly plastic) has created breeding sites for many mosquitoes, especially *Aedes aegypti*, in proximity to large human populations.
- The public health infrastructure has deteriorated, and vector-control programs have been abandoned, due in part to the pressures to "privatize" the economies of many developing countries.

In addition to these proximate causes for the emergence of arthropod-borne viruses, several other factors may have played a role in their emergence in the past or could become more important in the future:

- Building of large dams and water projects that provide breeding sites for mosquito vectors
- Deforestation and changes in land use associated with expansion of human habitation
- Introduction of new virus-amplifying hosts or efficient vectors into new areas (e.g., introduction of *Aedes albopictus* into the Americas)

Also, climatic changes (global warming) could amplify endemic transmission by expanding mosquito breeding sites to new temperate areas and potentially decreasing the extrinsic incubation period of the virus in the mosquito.[4]

ARTHROPOD-BORNE VIRUS INFECTIONS

Arboviruses are important causes of encephalitis and hemorrhagic fever in many parts of the world. Only specific species of mosquitoes or ticks that are present in specific ecologic systems can transmit these viruses. Because they depend on transmission by the arthropod host, these diseases are seasonal in temperate climates, yet occur on a year-round basis in tropical climates. The virus must replicate in the vector and travel from the mosquitoes' stomach to their salivary glands before transmission can occur. The interval between infection of the vector when blood is ingested from a viremic host until the virus appears in the salivary gland of the arthropod is referred to as the extrinsic incubation period. This period is shorter at higher temperature, but averages 6–10 days for most arboviral infections.

Arboviruses are classified into four families: Togaviridae, Flaviviridae, Bunyaviridae, and Reoviridae. The vectors, animal reservoir, and geographic distribution of some important representatives of these four viral families are shown in **Table 25-1**. The viruses generally are not cytopathic to the infected mosquitoes. However, some arboviruses are neurotropic in the mosquito, as well as in humans. This factor is especially true for Japanese encephalitis (JE) virus and may increase transmission by enhancing biting of CO_2-emitting targets, such as humans and other animals, by JE-infected mosquitoes.

The transmission of these viruses may occur throughout the year in tropical areas but increases during the rainy seasons. In contrast, in temperate climates, infections occur only during the warmer months. The mechanism of survival of arboviruses over the winter in cold temperatures is of considerable epidemiologic interest. Although it is possible that a female mosquito could hibernate after a blood meal and reemerge the following season, this behavior is believed to be uncommon. Generally, only nulliparous mosquitoes hibernate. Nevertheless, hibernating mosquitoes infected with West Nile virus have been found in storm sewers during the winter in the New York area.[5] The virus could also be reintroduced by migrating birds. In southern areas in the United States, virus-infected mosquitoes have been found year-round.[6] Another mechanism for wintering over is the vertical transmission of the viral genome to the eggs of an infected female mosquito. This pattern has been shown to occur among most of the viruses in the *Bunyavirus* and *Phlebovirus* groups. Also, experimental evidence indicates that vertical transmission of several flaviviruses is possible, as is sexual transmission of these viruses from male to female mosquitoes.[7,8] Ticks do survive for several years and can spread infection during subsequent seasons after they are infected.

FLAVIVIRUSES

The Flaviviridae family contains approximately 68 single-stranded RNA viruses, most—but not all—of which are transmitted by arthropods. Several flaviviruses have been especially prominent among the important emerging human infections in the past decade or two. Notably, West Nile virus has spread dramatically in the Western Hemisphere, dengue in the Caribbean and Central and South America, and Japanese encephalitis virus in Asia.[9]

DENGUE AND OTHER MOSQUITO-BORNE INFECTIONS

Although dengue has been known as a human disease for more than 200 years, in the last 20 years, dengue fever, dengue hemorrhagic fever (DHF), and dengue shock syndrome (DSS) have emerged as the most important arthropod-borne viral disease of humans worldwide.[10] It is estimated that as many as 100 million cases of dengue fever occur annually on a global basis. Approximately 250,000 cases of DHF are officially reported each year, but the actual number is probably several times higher. The syndrome of DHF/DSS was first reported as an epidemic disease in the Philippines in 1954, and it gradually spread to other areas in Southeast Asia.[11] This more severe form of dengue is associated with a mortality rate of 5% to 15% and is believed to be caused by immune complexes formed when a person with a history of one dengue serotype becomes infected with a different serotype.[12] The robust immune response is not specific enough to prevent disease, but is strong enough to cause vascular damage by creating immune complexes on FC receptors of vascular endothelial cells. The vascular leakage from the damaged vessels can then cause hemorrhage and fluid accumulation, leading to DHF or DSS.

Immune enhancement was suggested as the cause of DHF in the 1997 dengue 2 outbreak in Cuba.[13] That country had been free of dengue since the outbreak of dengue 1 infection in 1981. Overall, it was estimated that 5208 cases of dengue fever and 205 cases of DHF occurred. In sharp contrast to outbreaks in Asia, nearly all dengue fever and DHF cases in this outbreak arose in adults; all except three of the DHF cases were in adults who had been infected with dengue 1 in 1981 and experienced a secondary dengue infection in 1997.[14,15] In another outbreak of dengue in Rayong, Thailand, in 1980, researchers found that all cases of DHF had a secondary immune response, indicating they had had a prior dengue infection.[16]

In contrast, an outbreak of dengue 2 infection occurred in Peru in 1993 in a population that had previously been infected with other dengue genotypes; however, no cases of DHF occurred.[17] This outbreak

Table 25-1	Arboviruses That Cause Encephalitis			
Family Genus Complex Virus Species	**Vector**	**Animal Reservoir**	**Geographical Location**	**Importance in Encephalitis[a]**
Togaviridae				
Alphavirus[b]				
Eastern encephalitis	Mosquitoes (*Culiseta, Aedes*)	Birds	Eastern and gulf coasts of US, Caribbean, and South America	++
Western encephalitis	Mosquitoes (*Culex*)	Birds	Widespread; but disease in western US and Canada	++
Venezuelan equine encephalitis	Mosquitoes (*Aedes, Culex, Mansonia,* etc.)	Horses and small mammals	South and Central America, Florida, and southwest US	+
Flaviviridae[c]				
St. Louis complex				
St. Louis	Mosquitoes (*Culex*)	Birds	Widespread in US	+++
Japanese	Mosquitoes (*Culex*)	Birds	Japan, China, Southeast Asia, and India	++++
Murray Valley	Mosquitoes (*Culex*)	Birds	Australia and New Guinea	++
West Nile	Mosquitoes (*Culex*)	Birds	Africa, Middle East, and southern Europe	++
Liheus	Mosquitoes (*Psorphora*)	Birds	South and Central America	+
Rocio	Mosquitoes (?)	Birds	Brazil	++
Tick-borne complex				
Far Eastern tick-borne encephalitis[d]	Ticks (*Ixodes*)	Small mammals and birds	Siberia	+++
Central European tick-borne encephalitis	Ticks (*Ixodes*)	Small mammals and birds	Central Europe	+++
Kyasanur Forest	Ticks (*Haemophysalis*)	Small mammals and birds	India	++
Louping III	Ticks (*Ixodes*)	Small mammals and birds	North England, Scotland, and Ireland	+
Powassan	Ticks (*Ixodes*)	Small mammals and birds	Canada and northern US	+
Negishi	Ticks (?)	Small mammals and birds	Japan	+

(Continued)

Table 25-1   (Continued)

Family Genus Complex Virus Species	Vector	Animal Reservoir	Geographical Location	Importance in Encephalitis[a]
Bunyaviridae[e]				
Bunyavirus				
California group				
California encephalitis	Mosquitoes (Aedes)	Small mammals	Western US	+
La Crosse	Mosquitoes (Aedes)	Squirrels, chipmunks	Midwestern and eastern US	+++
Jamestown Canyon	Mosquitoes (Culiseta)	White-tailed deer	US and Alaska	+
Cache Valley	Mosquitoes (Culiseta)	Livestock and large mammals	North and South America	+
Snowshoe hare	Mosquitoes (Culiseta)	Snowshoe hare	Canada, Alaska, northern US, and Russia	+
Tahnya	Mosquitoes (Aedes, Culiseta)	Small mammals	Central Europe	+
Inkoo	Mosquitoes (?)	Reindeer, moose	Finland and Russia	+
Phlebovirus				
Rift Valley	Mosquitoes (Culex, Aedes)	Sheep, cattle, camels	East Africa	+
Reoviridae				
Coltivirus				
Colorado tick fever	Ticks (Dermacentor)	Small mammals	Rocky Mountain area	+

[a] ++++, over 10,000 cases/year; +++, common outbreaks of >100 cases/year; ++, irregular outbreaks; +, rare occurrences.

[b] Formerly group A arboviruses.

[c] Formerly group B arboviruses.

[d] Formerly Russian spring–summer encephalitis.

[e] Several other Bunyaviridae (Arbia and Toseana viruses of genus *Phlebtovirus*; Erve virus of genus *Nairovirus*), Reoviridae (Lipovnik and Tribec viruses of genus *Orbivirus*; Eyach of genus *Coltivirus*), and single tick-borne members of Bunyaviridae (Bhyanjavirus) and Orthomyxoviridae (Thogotovirus) have been tentatively associated with CNS disease in Europe, Asia, and Africa (Dobler, 1996).

Adapted from Richard T. Johnson, Viral Infections of the Nervous System, © 1982. Raven Press, Lippincott Williams & Williams.

supports the second major hypothesis concerning the cause of DHF/DSS—namely, that the virulence of the dengue strain is a critical factor in the pathogenesis of DHF and more severe dengue infections. This hypothesis has been put forward by Rosen and colleagues, who have reported DHF in patients during a primary dengue infection.[18–20] The pathogenesis of DHF/DSS is not completely understood, but various data favor both immune enhancement from a secondary infection and high virulence of some dengue viruses and the combination of these factors to be related to severe life-threatening dengue infections, meaning DHF and DSS.[21]

Factors Favoring Dengue Emergence

Several factors have promoted the emergence of dengue and its spread to new geographic areas. Increases in the use and disposal of nonbiodegradable containers and their storage in peridomestic locations have provided a wealth of breeding places for the mosquito vector *Aedes aegypti* in close proximity to humans. A program to eradicate *A. aegypti* from the Americas was initiated by the Pan American Health Organization (PAHO) in 1947 to control yellow fever, which is also spread by the same mosquito. Efforts were successful in a number of countries. By 1972, *A. aegypti* had been eliminated from 19 countries in the Americas, representing 73% of the area originally infected (**Figure 25-1**).

Unfortunately, the campaign gradually lost steam, and funding was withdrawn.[22] This occurred in part because of the identification of a jungle cycle

of yellow fever and the recognition that, even with the elimination of *A. aegypti* from urban areas, a focus of yellow fever would persist. Hence, the disease was no longer felt to be eradicable. Within about 10 years, *A. aegypti* had reestablished itself in virtually all of South and Central America (**Figure 25-2**).

In 1981, a severe epidemic of dengue type 2 infection, including the first cases of DHF/DSS in the Western Hemisphere, occurred in Cuba.[23] In 1986, an explosive outbreak of dengue type 1, involving more than 1 million cases, occurred in Rio de Janeiro. Subsequently, dengue epidemics were observed in Paraguay, Bolivia, Peru, Ecuador, Colombia, and Venezuela. More recently, dengue outbreaks have been reported for the first time in Argentina.[24] All four dengue serotypes are currently endemic in Latin America. Their continued importance was evident when a large epidemic of dengue type 2 virus, including cases of DHF, occurred in Cuba in 1997.[25–27]

Reports of dengue in Africa were unusual in the 1960s and 1970s or prior to that time. In the mid-1980s, however, dengue appeared first along the coast of Kenya, then in the Ivory Coast and Burkina Faso. Dengue has spread to other African countries in recent years. Also, in Asia, dengue has spread westward into India, Pakistan, and the Middle East in the last decade (**Figure 25-3**).

Another factor that has raised considerable concern about the potential for further spread of mosquito-borne viruses in the Americas was the introduction of *Aedes albopictus* into Houston in used truck tires imported from Southeast Asia for recapping

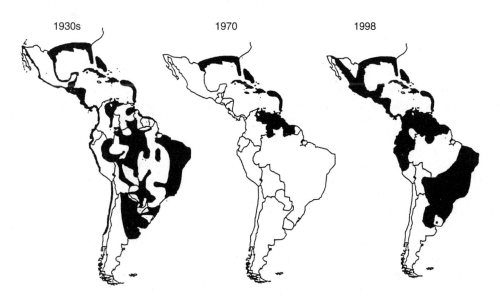

Figure 25-1 Aedes aegypti distribution in the Americas during the 1930s and in 1970 and 1998. Gubler D. Dengue and dengue hemorrhagic fever. Clin Microbiol Rev. 1998 July; 11(3);480–96. Reproduced with permission from American Society for Microbiology.

Prior to 1981   1981–1998

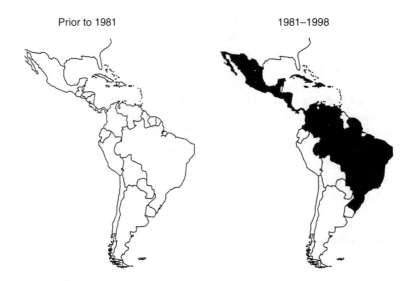

Figure 25-2 DHF in the Americas before 1981 and from 1981 to 1998. Gubler D. Dengue and dengue hemorrhagic fever. Clin Microbiol Rev. 1998 July; 11(3);480–96. Reproduced with permission from American Society for Microbiology.

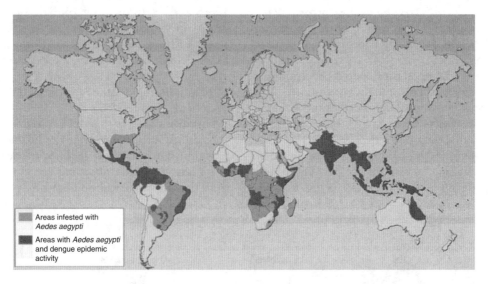

Areas infested with
Aedes aegypti

Areas with *Aedes aegypti*
and dengue epidemic
activity

Figure 25-3 Dengue: its current distribution and countries with a. aegypti and at risk of introduction. Reprinted by permission from Macmillan Publishers Ltd: *Nature Medicine*. Mackenzie, J. et al. Emerging flaviviruses: the spread and resurgence of Japanese encephalitis, West Nile and dengue viruses. *Nat. Med.* 2004 Dec; 10(12 Suppl): S98–109. Copyright © 2004.

in 1985.[28] These spare tires collected rainwater and served as excellent breeding sites for these mosquitoes, which could transmit dengue and yellow fever, as well as other arthropod viruses, such as eastern equine encephalitis. *A. albopictus* mosquitoes have also been introduced into Brazil in a similar manner; these effective vector mosquitoes are now widely distributed in 19 states of the United States (**Figure 25-4**). Each year, more than 100 cases of dengue are reported in persons in the United States who have acquired their infections in the endemic areas of Asia, Latin America, or Africa.[29] It is quite possible that these viremic

individuals might eventually provide a sufficient reservoir to reestablish dengue as an endemic disease in the southern United States, with either *A. aegypti* or *A. albopictus* as the vector.

Control and Prevention of Dengue

The prevention of dengue in areas where the disease is endemic is directed at avoiding contact with an infected *A. aegypti* or *A. albopictus* vector. Dengue epidemics tend to be geographically localized where both *A. aegypti* and infected humans reside. An infected mosquito remains infected for its entire life and

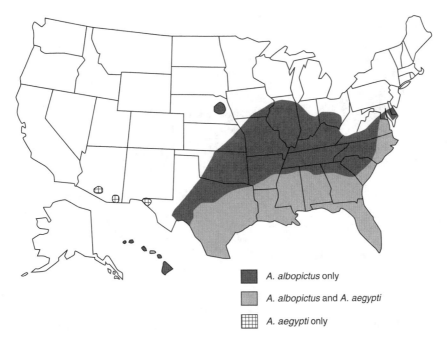

Figure 25-4 A. aegypti and A. albopictus distribution in the United States in 1998. Gubler D. Dengue and dengue hemorrhagic fever. Clin Microbiol Rev. 1998 July; 11(3);480–96. Reproduced with permission from American Society for Microbiology.

may bite repeatedly, so it can be a highly effective vector. Because these mosquitoes are found both around homes (peridomestic) and in homes, and because they may bite at any time, especially during the daytime, prevention is difficult. The most effective means of prevention involves destroying sites where larvae develop, such as water-filled containers in and around the house, and using strategies to prevent larval development when water-filled containers are present. Outdoor spraying to kill adult mosquitoes is much less effective than attacking the larval breeding sites, as adult A. aegypti may be indoors when the spraying is done.[30]

While it is possible to control dengue by eliminating larval breeding sites,[31] this approach requires a very labor-intensive effort. Household screens, air-conditioning, and other methods to seal the living area from mosquitoes are also effective in preventing dengue.

A recent report described a coordinated program to control dengue in several communities in Vietnam.[32] This program involved support from the central government (vertical) plus local community action (horizontal approach). It focused on destroying larval breeding sites where possible and the use of predacious copepods of the genus *Mesocyclops* as a biological agent to control A. aegypti larval development in water-filled containers. The program has eliminated dengue from the target area for the past two years.

Several researchers have been working for more than a decade on developing an effective dengue vaccine.[33–35] One problem in development of a vaccine to prevent dengue is that the vaccine needs to be equally effective against all four serotypes and protection needs to last until dengue is no longer endemic in an area. If either of these criteria is not met, use of a vaccine could potentially increase the risk of DHF or DSS when the protective immunity wanes. This theoretical risk is based on the hypothesis that DHF/DSS could occur when the level of protective antibodies wanes over time. Tetravalent dengue vaccines have been developed and are currently undergoing clinical trials in humans.

WEST NILE VIRUS IN NORTH AMERICA

West Nile virus (WNV) is a flavivirus that was first isolated in 1937 from the blood of a febrile patient in the West Nile district of northern Uganda.[36] Subsequently, in the 1950s, the virus was recognized as a cause of severe meningoencephalitis in the elderly. Equine disease due to WNV was reported in the 1960s in Egypt and France.[37] Outbreaks of WNV infection were reported in Israel, France, Russia, South Africa, and Romania in the 1970s.[38,39] Studies of these outbreaks found that birds were the reservoir and amplifying host, that infections were transmitted by mosquitoes, and that horses, birds, and humans were susceptible.[40]

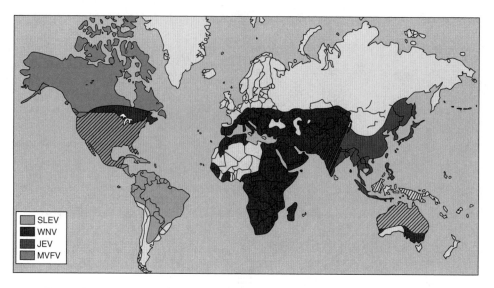

Figure 25-5 The global distribution and spread of the major Japanese encephalitis serological group members. Reprinted by permission from Macmillan Publishers Ltd: *Nature Medicine*. Mackenzie, J. et al. Emerging flaviviruses: the spread and resurgence of Japanese encephalitis, West Nile and dengue viruses. *Nat. Med.* 2004 Dec; 10(12 Suppl): S98–109. Copyright © 2004.

During 1994–2000, many outbreaks of WNV occurred in North America, Europe, and the Middle East as the geographic area for endemic WNV expanded.[40] The virus is now recognized to have an extensive distribution in Africa, the Middle East, Eastern Europe, the former Soviet Union, and South Asia, as well as in Australia, where it is known as Kunjin virus (**Figure 25-5**).[40]

West Nile virus is antigenically related to Japanese encephalitis virus, St. Louis encephalitis virus, and Murray Valley fever virus. However, unlike the other members of the Japanese encephalitis serogroup, WNV can be divided into two lineages. Lineage 1 viruses are more pathogenic for humans, whereas lineage 2 viruses cause only mild human disease or no symptoms. Lineage 1 viruses have circulated recently in Romania (1996), Tunisia (1997), and Russia (1999) and are now epidemic in the United States and Canada.

Probably the best recent example of the introduction and rapid emergence of a human mosquito-borne viral infection from one geographic region to another is the emergence and spread of West Nile virus in North America after its introduction in the summer of 1999 into the borough of Queens, New York.[41] Subsequent genetic analysis work has shown that the genetic structures of the North American WNV isolates and those from Israel are virtually identical.[42]

The original outbreak was recognized and reported by an infectious diseases physician, who cared for six patients with encephalitis in August 1999.[41] He suspected an outbreak of viral encephalitis based on the patients' similar clinical presentation.

Initial serological investigation of the cases detected immunoglobulin M (IgM) antibodies to viruses in the St. Louis encephalitis group of flaviviruses. In fact, initially the outbreak was thought to be due to St. Louis encephalitis (SLE) virus, as SLE had been endemic in North America, although it had never been reported from New York. Subsequently, 62 cases of meningoencephalitis, with 8 deaths, were reported in the New York area in 1999.

Another unusual feature of this epidemic was the deaths of several bird species at the Bronx zoo in September 1999. Deaths occurred in a cormorant, two Chilean flamingoes, and an Asian pheasant. In addition to the deaths of birds in the zoo, the 1999 outbreak and subsequent outbreaks of WNV were accompanied by extensive mortality among wild birds, especially crows and other corvid species. The extensive bird mortality associated with WNV infection has differentiated this virus from other arbovirus epidemics. In the 2002 WNV epidemic, a total of 124,854 dead birds were reported to state and local health departments, 31,514 were tested for WNV, and 15,745 (50%) were positive. West Nile virus has been isolated from 138 species of birds in the United States.[43] In fact, bird mortality has proved a sensitive method of epidemiologic surveillance of the geographic extension of WNV activity in each of the annual epidemics since 1999.[44,45] Bird mortality has generally preceded cases of WNV infection in humans and has been used for sentinel surveillance of WNV activity (**Figure 25-6**). In addition, in common with several other North American arboviruses, WNV infection is commonly fatal for horses. The impact

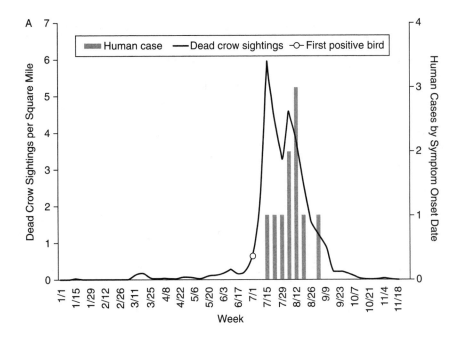

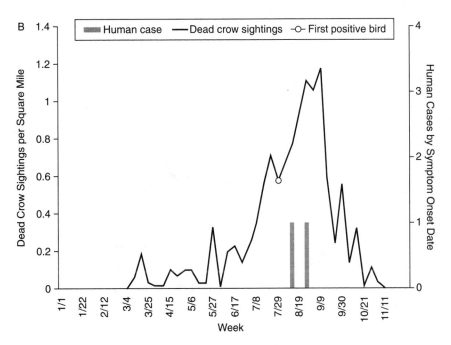

Figure 25-6 Dead crow density (number of dead crow sightings per square mile) compared with number of human cases, by week. A. Staten island, axis scale for weekly dead crow density 0 to 7; B. Brooklyn, axis scale for weekly dead crow density 0 to 1.4; C. Queens, axis for weekly dead crow density 0 to 0.7; D. Manhattan, axis scale for weekly dead crow density 0 to 1.4. Reproduced from Eidson et al. Dead crow densities and human cases of West Nile virus, New York State, 2000. *Emerg Infect Dis*. 2001;7:662–4.

(Continued)

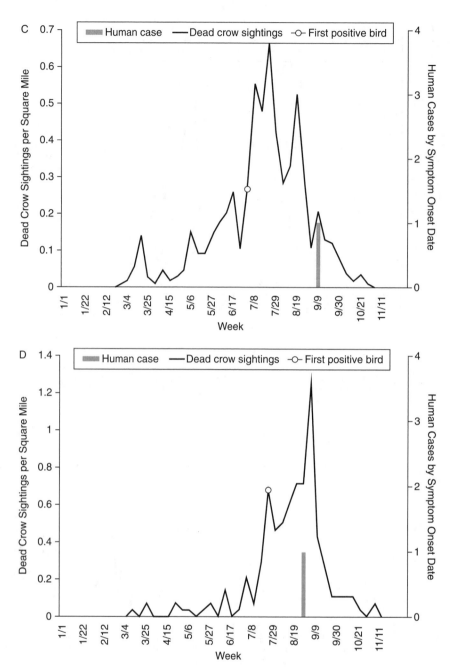

Figure 25-6 (*Continued*)

of WNV emergence in other species is an evolving story. The near-elimination of corvid species from areas of the United States will alter the distribution of many other bird species. Ornithologists are actively working to determine susceptibility to WNV and minimize morbidity and mortality among endangered birds, such as the whooping crane.

After the localized epidemic in New York in the summer and fall of 1999, seasonal epidemics spread to other areas of the United States in subsequent years. In 2001, 64 cases of WNV meningoencephalitis were reported, but the cases were in 38 counties in 10 states in the eastern United States. In 2002, a major epidemic of WNV occurred, in which 4156 cases and 284 deaths were reported. The human cases in 2002 were concentrated in several midwestern (i.e., Michigan, Illinois, and Ohio) and southern states (i.e., Louisiana, Texas, and Mississippi).[46] In the summer and fall of 2003, another large epidemic occurred that was especially severe in several western states, including Nebraska, Colorado, North and South Dakota, and New Mexico.[47] Overall, 9862 symptomatic human WNV infections and 264 deaths were reported in 2003 (**Table 25-2**). In 2004, the

Table 25-2	Species of Mosquito Positive for WNV by Year	
1999	**2002**	**2003**
Aedes vexans	Ae. aegypti	Ae. aegypti
Culex pipiens	Ae. albopictus	Ae. albopictus
Cx. restuans	Ae. vexans	Ae. cinereus
2000	An. atropos	Ae. vexans
Ae. vexans	An. barberi	An. atropos
Anopheles punctipennis	An. crucians/bradleyi	An. barberi
Cx. pipiens pipiens	An. punctipennis	An. crucians/bradleyi
Culiseta melanura	An. quadrimaculatus	An. punctipennis
Ochlerotatus cantator	An. walkeri	An. quadrimaculatus
Oc. japonicus	Cq. perturbans	An. walkeri
Oc. triseriatus	Cx. erraticus	Cq. perturbans
Psorophora ferox	Cx. nigripalpus	Cx. erraticus
2001	Cx. pipiens	Cx. nigripalpus
Ae. albopictus	Cx. quinquefasciatus	Cx. pipiens
Ae. cinereus	Cx. restuans	Cx. quinquefasciatus
Ae. vexans	Cx. salinarius	Cx. restuans
An. punctipennis	Cx. tarsalis	Cx. salinarius
An. quadrimaculatus	Cx. territans	Cx. tarsalis
Coquillettidia perturbans	Cs. inornata	Cx. territans
Cx. nigripalpus	Cs. melanura	Cs. inornata
Cx. pipiens	Deinocerites cancer	Cs. melanura
Cx. quinquefasciatus	Oc. atropalpus	Deinocerites cancer
Cx. restuans	Oc. atlanticus/tormentor	Oc. atropalpus
Cx. salinarius	Oc. canadensis	Oc. atlanticus/tormentor
Cs. melanura	Oc. cantator	Oc. canadensis
Oc. canadensis	Oc. japonicus	Oc. cantator
Oc. cantator	Oc. sollicitans	Oc. dorsalis
Oc. japonicus	Oc. taeniorhynchus	Oc. infirmatus
Oc. sollicitans	Oc. triseriatus	Oc. fitchii
Oc. trivattatus	Oc. trivattatus	Oc. japonicus
Orthopodomyia signifera	Or. signifera	Oc. provocans
Ps. columbiae	Ps. ciliata	Oc. sollicitans
Uranotaenia sapphirina	Ps. columbiae	Oc. sticticus
	Ps. ferox	Oc. stimulans
	Ur. sapphirina	Oc. taeniorhynchus
		Oc. triseriatus
		Oc. trivattatus
		Or. signifera
		Ps. ciliata
		Ps. columbiae
		Ps. ferox
		Ps. howardii

epidemic was centered in Arizona and California, and 2470 cases and 88 deaths were reported.[48] It is somewhat curious that although WNV has spread to Central America and the Caribbean, encephalitis is less frequent there than in North America.

Population surveys following epidemics of WNV have allowed the spectrum of clinical diseases associated with WNV to be better understood. It is now believed that only 1 infected person in 150 will develop frank encephalitis, whereas 20% will develop fever, headache, or milder symptoms, and 80% of infected persons will remain asymptomatic. Similar to outbreaks of St. Louis encephalitis in the United States, older persons and those who are immunosuppressed are at much greater risk of neurological disease. Extrapolation from the number of reported meningoencephalitis cases suggests that approximately 400,000–500,000 human infections actually occurred in the United States in 2003. Serosurveys of human populations in an area that has recently experienced an epidemic of WNV often detect antibodies in approximately 5% of the population.[49] These data indicate that despite the occurrence of large epidemics in each of the past 12 years in the United States, human immunity (i.e., herd immunity) is not likely to be a significant factor in the occurrence, size, or absence of subsequent epidemics. Conversely, the density of infected birds that can maintain high levels of viremia and abundant and suitable vector mosquitoes are probably critical factors in driving epidemics. Nevertheless, geographic studies are needed to elucidate the impact of human immunity in the specific environments that have both the susceptible bird populations and the appropriate mosquito vectors. Low overall immunity may mask high densities of immunity in those communities at highest risk.

Another unique feature of the recent WNV epidemics in North America has been the broad range of mosquito species from which the virus has been isolated. In the first 4 years of the recurring epidemics, WNV was isolated from 43 different species of mosquitoes plus several tick species (Table 25-2). The virus is primarily transmitted by *Culex* species mosquitoes. These mosquitoes are capable of hibernating during the winter and maintaining a pool of virus for the following season.[50] During the first few epidemic years in the eastern United States, *Culex pipiens* mosquitoes were believed to be the main vector transmitting the virus among birds. Transmission from birds to humans may have involved not only *C. pipiens* but other culicine mosquitoes, such as *C. restuans* and *C. quinquefasciatus*. However, when the epidemic moved to the Midwest and the West, *C.*

tarsalis became a major vector. *C. tarsalis* is known to be a more avid human biter than *C. pipiens* and is more difficult to eradicate from its outdoor breeding sites. During the westward march of the epidemic center in recent years, WNV activity continued in the areas that were previously epidemic, albeit at a lower level. Because of the continued activity in many areas of the United States, the broad range of mosquito vectors, and recurring summer/fall epidemics for the past 12 years, most experts believe that yearly seasonal epidemics will continue to occur, similar to the yearly epidemics of the related virus Japanese encephalitis in many countries of southeast Asia.

St. Louis encephalitis virus is another human flavivirus that has been endemic in the United States for the past 60 years. However, in contrast to JE and WNV, SLE tends to occur as a rare endemic infection with occasional large-scale epidemics, often separated by several years or even decades.

To more effectively monitor the epidemiology of West Nile virus infections in the United States, the Centers for Disease Control and Prevention (CDC) established an electronic passive reporting system in 2000 called ArboNET in collaboration with state and local health departments. This system monitored WNV infections in humans, mosquitoes, birds, and other animals. Neuroinvasive disease became nationally notifiable in 2004.

During 1999–2008 in the United States, 28,961 cases of WNV disease were reported from 1869 countries in 47 states and the District of Columbia (**Figure 25-7**). Of all cases reported, 11,822 (41%) were classified as neuroinvasive disease and 17,139 (59%) as non-neuroinvasive disease; a total of 1134 deaths were noted (**Figure 25-8**). If the assumption is made that the reporting of neuroinvasive disease is complete, then 1,655,080 WNV infections occurred during the period 1999–2008. During the years 2004–2011 sporadic cases and small outbreaks occurred in most states during the transmission season (**Figure 25-9**). This led some experts to question whether annual epidemics on WNV would persist. However, one of the largest epidemics on record occurred in 2012 with 3142 cases including 1630 patients with neuroinvasive disease from 45 states reported to the CDC by September 18, 2012 (**Figure 25-10**).[105] Almost 40% (1225 cases) were reported from Texas. It is not clear what caused this dramatic increase in cases. Experts have proposed theories related to climate and weather changes, distributions of susceptible birds, and the rate of viral replication in mosquitoes.[106] Neuroinvasive diseases from WNV occurs in all age groups but

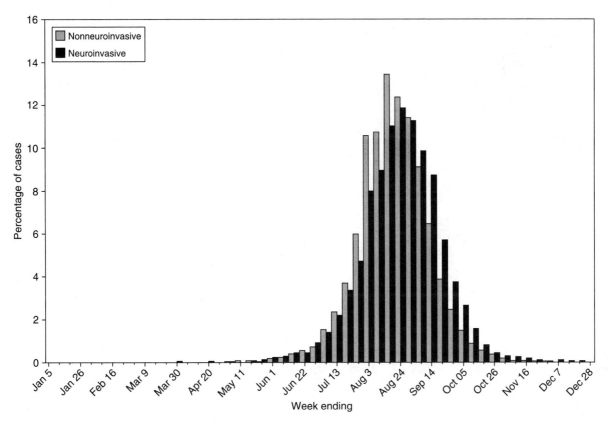

Figure 25-7 West Nile virus disease cases (N=26962) by week of illness onset–United States 1999–2008. Reproduced from the Centers for Disease Control and Prevention (2010). Lindsey N, Staples J, Lehman J, Fischer, M. Surveillance for Human West Nile Virus Disease—United States, 1999–2008. *MMWR* April 2, 2010 / 59(SS02);1–17.

disproportionally affects older persons; more than 1 case per 100,000 population was noted in the western mountainous states.[51]

Of the neuroinvasive arboviral infections reported to the CDC through ArboNET or other mechanisms

between 1999 and 2007, the majority were due to West Nile virus. However, six other groups of neuroinvasive arboviral infections were reported, including 895 California virus infections and 188 from St. Louis encephalitis virus (**Table 25-3**).

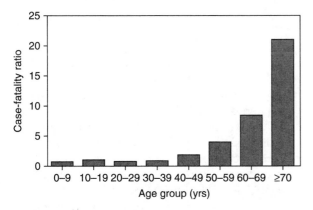

Figure 25-8 West Nile virus neuroinvasive disease case-fatality ratios, by age group–United States, 1999–2008. Reproduced from the Centers for Disease Control and Prevention (2010). Lindsey N, Staples J, Lehman J, Fischer, M. Surveillance for Human West Nile Virus Disease—United States, 1999–2008. *MMWR* April 2, 2010 / 59(SS02);1–17.

Table 25-3	Number of Cases of Neuroinvasive Domestic Arboviral Diseases Reported in the United States from 1999–2011	
	Cases Per Year	
Virus	**Median**	**(Range)**
West Nile	689	(19–2946)
La Crosse	73	(46–167)
St. Louis encephalitis	8	(2–79)
Eastern equine encephalitis	6	(3–21)
Powassan	1	(0–12)

Reproduced from the Centers for Disease Control and Prevention (2012). West Nile Virus: Information and Guidance for Clinicians; Clinician Outreach and Communication Activity (COCA). http://emergency.cdc.gov/coca/ppt/2012/08_30_12_WNV_INT.pdf. Updated August 30, 2012. Accessed January 7, 2013.

*No cases were reported from Alaska, Hawaii, Maine, or any U.S. territories.

Figure 25-9 Year of First Reported Human West Nile Virus Disease Case, by State–United States, 1999–2008. Reproduced from the Centers for Disease Control and Prevention (2010). Lindsey N, Staples J, Lehman J, Fischer, M. Surveillance for Human West Nile Virus Disease—United States, 1999—2008. *MMWR* April 2, 2010 / 59(SS02);1–17.

Other (Non-mosquito) Routes of WNV Transmission

Another unique feature of WNV infection has been the identification of the importance of non-mosquito transmission of the virus. This possibility was first recognized when an organ donor acquired WNV after several transfusions and subsequently donated several organs, which transmitted WNV to four transplant recipients.[52] Subsequently, in 2002, surveillance of symptomatic WNV-infected patients detected 23 persons in whom the virus had been transmitted by transfusion from one of 16 viremic blood donors (**Figure 25-11**).[53] This was likely a significant underestimate of the risk of transfusion transmission of WNV, as only symptomatic recipients for whom the donor could be traced and shown

to have been viremic when the donation occurred were detected and counted. Transmission of WNV by breastfeeding, transplacentally, and by occupational exposure has also been reported. Biggerstaff and Petersen have estimated the risk of transmission of WNV through blood transfusion during the epidemic period in various geographic areas of the United States in 2002, prior to donor screening. They estimated the risks of WNV transmission by transfusion to be 1.46–12.33 per 10,000 donations for selected high incidence areas during the 2002 epidemic (**Figure 12-12**).[54] These rates fluctuated markedly over time as the local epidemic peaked and waned.

The U.S. Food and Drug Administration (FDA) and the American Association of Blood Banks encouraged the pharmaceutical industry to develop

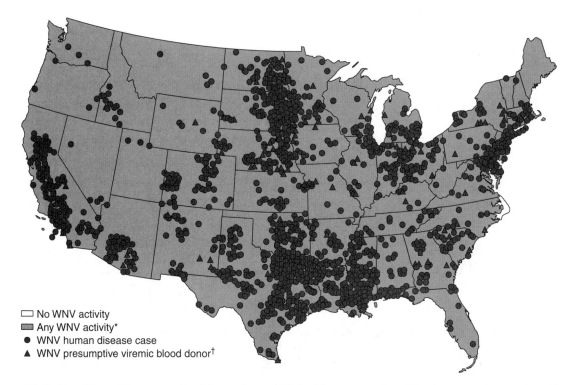

☐ No WNV activity
▨ Any WNV activity*
● WNV human disease case
▲ WNV presumptive viremic blood donor†

Figure 25-10 West Nile activity reported by Arbonet, by state, United States, 2012 (as of October 9, 2012). Reproduced from the Centers for Disease Control and Prevention (2012). National Center for Emerging and Zoonotic Infectious Diseases (NCEZID) Division of Vector-Borne Diseases (DVBD): Statistics, Surveillance, and Control. http://www.cdc.gov/ncidod/dvbid/westnile/ Mapsactivity/surv&control12MapsAnybyState.htm. Accessed October 15, 2012. Last modified October 9, 2012.

screening tests for WNV nucleic acids (NAT) by July 1, 2003, the start of the next WNV transmission season. A strategy to screen all blood donors with a NAT assay was felt to be feasible, as similar nucleic acid–based assays were already being used to screen donors for HIV and hepatitis C virus. Fortunately, the effort proved to be successful when two manufacturers developed NAT screening assays that were used for screening all blood donors in the United States during the 2003 WNV transmission season.

Among 6.0 million donors screened during June–December 2003, 818 WNV NAT-positive

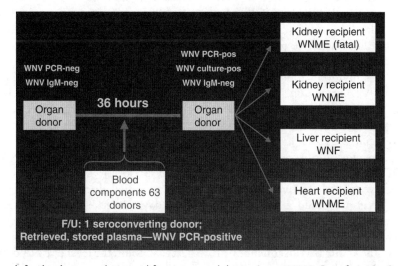

Figure 25-11 WN virus infection in organ donor and four organ recipients, August 2002. Data from the Centers for Disease Control and Prevention (2002). Public Health Dispatch: West Nile Virus Infection in Organ Donor and Transplant Recipients—Georgia and Florida, 2002. *MMWR* September 6, 2002;51(35);790.

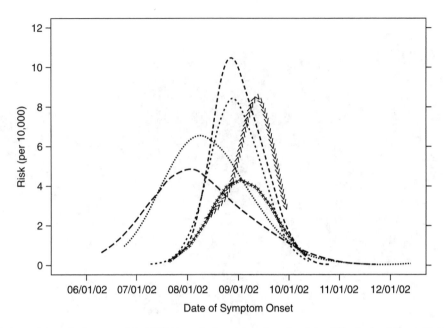

Figure 25-12 Estimated transfusion-associated WNV transfusion risk curbers by state: Illinois, Louisiana, Michigan, Mississippi, Nebraska, Ohio. Reproduced from Biggerstaff et al. (2003). Estimated risk of transmission of the West Nile virus through blood transfusion in the US, 2002. *Transfusion*. 2002 Aug;42(8):1019–26.

donors were detected and deferred.[55] Another six transfusion-transmitted WNV infections occurred when the screening NAT assays gave false-negative results because the level of viremia in the donor was below the limit of detection using either the minipool NAT screening assay for testing 6 or 16 donor samples in a pool or individual donor screening.[54] The level of WNV RNA in generally asymptomatic viremic donors is often modest to quite low (i.e., fewer than 50–2000 copies/mL) compared to that found in donors infected with HIV or HCV. The use of minipool samples for donor screening can occasionally result in a false-negative test. Because of this problem, many blood banks switch from minipool screening to individual donor screening during the height of WNV transmission. The decision to switch from minipool to individual screens is based on increases in the rates of NAT-positive donations at a blood collection facility.[56]

Clearly, the implementation of screening blood donors during the WNV transmission season in the United States has been very cost-effective. It is likely that donor screening has prevented at least 1500 cases of WNV transmission to transfusion recipients. Because transfusion recipients are often immunocompromised or elderly, the clinical consequences of transfusion-acquired WNV infection are much more serious in this population than in generally healthy persons who acquire the disease by mosquito bite. For example, all four recipients of organ transplants from the 2002 case were symptomatic; three had meningoencephalitis, and one died.

The surveillance of blood donors for WNV infection has provided extremely important clinical and epidemiological data. First, because donors are usually asymptomatic, their NAT prevalence has allowed a better estimate of the extent and geographic localization of the WNV epidemic than data limited to clinical reports of meningoencephalitis cases. Second, quantitation of WNV RNA has provided a better understanding of the natural history of WNV infection in humans.

A model based on screening of blood donors has been developed by Busch, who estimated that the level of virus increases after infection from a mosquito bite. In the first day or so after infection, the level of WNV RNA may be below the limit of detectability using an individual donation NAT assay. Then for a day or so, the level of RNA can be detected only by individual donor NAT screening. For the next 3–5 days, the level of RNA increases so that it is detectable by minipool NAT screening, using pools of 10–16 donors developed for the commercial assays. At that point, the level of RNA declines, and first IgM and then IgG antibodies appear. Overall, approximately 7–10 days pass after an infectious mosquito bite before antibodies appear. No cases of transfusion transmission of virus from donors after WNV antibodies appeared have been reported. However, more data are needed to determine whether IgM antibodies renders a NAT-positive donor noninfectious. Another unusual feature of WNV infection is that IgM antibodies commonly persist for a long time, perhaps for 500 days or more. Thus it is not possible to interpret the presence of IgM antibodies to WNV as indicative of a recent infection.

Remaining Questions

Many questions remain about the unusual introduction and spread of WNV throughout North America. First, how was the virus introduced from its endemic focus in the Middle East? This answer will never be known for certain, but several possibilities have been suggested. The virus could have been transported from Israel to New York aboard a plane by an infected mosquito, bird, or (less likely) human. Infected birds could have migrated across the Atlantic. It has been documented that birds can cross the Atlantic aided by the wind. Alternatively, birds could have been transported by ship or might have been imported illegally as a part of the trade in exotic pets. It is unlikely that an infected traveler could have started the epidemic in North America, as the levels of virus in humans usually are not sufficient for them to act as a reservoir. Intentional introduction or bioterrorism has been postulated by some sources but seems very unlikely.

The next question is why WNV spread so extensively in North America. The answer to this question is also uncertain. However, it should be noted that severe epidemics of WNV and expansion of the areas of endemicity in Europe, the Middle East, and Africa have also occurred in recent years. In addition, other flaviviruses, especially dengue, Japanese encephalitis virus, and yellow fever virus have emerged and expanded their geographic range in the past decade. The westward spread of WNV has probably resulted from migrating infected birds. Clearly, there is need for better surveillance, more effective mosquito control, and the development of a protective vaccine or antiviral treatment to control WNV in North America, Europe, and the Middle East in the years to come.

JAPANESE ENCEPHALITIS VIRUS

Japanese encephalitis virus (JE) is a mosquito-borne flavivirus that is endemic in eastern, southern, and southeast Asia, Papua New Guinea, and the Torres Strait of northern Australia (**Figure 25-13**). It is the most important infection causing childhood neurological disease in Asia. Each year 35,000–50,000 cases of encephalitis due to JE and 10,000 deaths are reported. However, it is likely that cases may be underreported from some endemic areas. Although 25–30% of cases of JE are fatal and 50% of survivors develop permanent neurological sequelae, most JE infections are asymptomatic; the ratio of symptomatic to asymptomatic infections ranges from 1:250 to 1:1000.[57]

The incubation period of JE is 5–15 days. Clinical disease can vary from a nonspecific febrile illness to severe meningoencephalitis with ensuing coma and seizures or aseptic meningitis with flaccid paralysis.[57] Most clinical cases occur in infants and children in the endemic areas, although adults, including travelers to rural areas, can become infected. In the rural areas that are endemic for JE, most older children and adults are immune because of subclinical infections experienced during childhood.

Epidemiology of JE Viruses

Epidemics of JE were recognized as early as 1871 in Japan and were common in Japan, Korea, and China in the first half of the 1900s.[58] However, widespread use of the inactivated JE vaccine in Korea, Japan, and Taiwan since 1965 has reduced the number of human cases substantially. Nevertheless, the enzootic cycle of JE continues to infect wild birds and pigs in these countries. During the last several decades, JE has spread widely in Asia from the originally recognized foci in Japan, Korea, and China. Although occasional cases of encephalitis had been noted in Thailand, epidemic JE was not a recognized health problem in Southeast Asia until 1969, when an epidemic of 685 cases was reported in the Chiang Mai valley in northern Thailand.[59] Subsequently, yearly outbreaks involving thousands of cases and hundreds of deaths occurred in northern Thailand. The disease continued to spread throughout Asia and is now endemic in Indonesia, the Philippines, northern Australia, and south Asia, including Sri Lanka, most of India, and Nepal (Figure 25-5).

JE virus was first isolated from the brain of a human case in 1935 and from *Culex tritaeniorhynchus* mosquitoes in 1938. These mosquitoes breed in irrigated rice fields and other stationary water sources throughout Asia. It was subsequently established that the JE cycle in nature included transmission of the virus to aquatic birds, such as herons, egrets, and ducks. The virus titer is amplified by

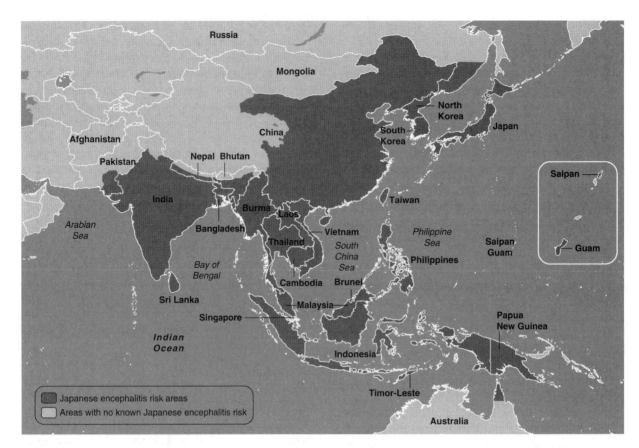

Figure 25-13 Geographic distribution of Japanese Encephalitis Virus. Reproduced from the Centers for Disease Control and Prevention National Center for Emerging and Zoonotic Infectious Diseases (2011). Infectious Diseases Related to Travel. http://wwwnc.cdc.gov/travel/pdf/yellowbook-2012-map-03-08-geographic-distribution-japanese-encephalitis.pdf. Last updated September 1, 2011. Accessed November 27, 2012.

infection of pigs and can then be spread by mosquitoes to humans (**Figure 25-14**). Because of the large populations of people living in the endemic areas of rural Asia and the serious sequelae of JE, this virus is one of the most important emerging infections in humans.

Japanese encephalitis is largely a rural disease in Asia, with C. *tritaeniorhynchus* mosquitoes breeding in rice fields and pigs providing the major source of blood meals. Seasonal epidemiologic patterns of JE infection have also been observed. In tropical areas, the virus circulates in most months, but the number of infections increases during times of rice field irrigation and the rainy season. In temperate areas, the disease is more common in the summer and absent during the cold months in the winter. The expansion of rice cultivation and pig husbandry in rural areas of Asia in response to the tremendous population growth and need for food in the 20th century were

important factors leading to the increased numbers of JE infections in humans and the expansion of the areas of endemicity.

Control of JE disease has largely rested on routine immunization of infants and children with an inactivated mouse-brain–derived vaccine that was originally developed in Korea. Studies of this vaccine among children in Thailand found the vaccine to be quite efficacious.[60] Several countries—including Korea, Japan, China, Taiwan, and Thailand—have introduced JE vaccine into the routine childhood immunization schedule, and this practice has substantially reduced the number of cases. Nevertheless, large populations in rural South Asia remain susceptible to JE disease. More recently cell-derived JE vaccines have been developed and licensed to avoid the rare complication of allergic encephalomyelitis from the mouse-brain vaccines. However, these newer vaccines are more expensive.

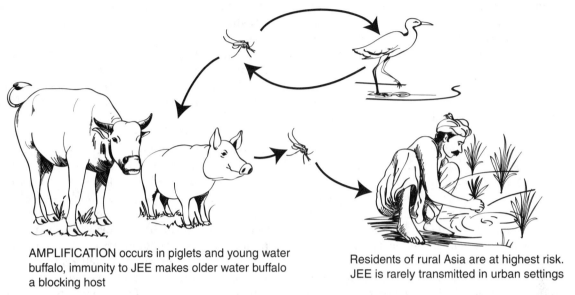

The NATURAL CYCLE is between water birds, herons particularly, and *Culex tritaeniorhynchus*. Birds are the virus reservoir

AMPLIFICATION occurs in piglets and young water buffalo, immunity to JEE makes older water buffalo a blocking host

Residents of rural Asia are at highest risk. JEE is rarely transmitted in urban settings

Figure 25-14 Japanese Encephalitis Transmission includes a Natural Cycle, an Amplification Cycle and Zoonotic Transmission Primarily in Rural Asia.

YELLOW FEVER

Yellow fever is the prototype member of the Flaviviridae family. Infection with yellow fever virus results in a severe systemic illness characterized by hemorrhage; hepatic, renal, and myocardial injury; and very high mortality, ranging from 20% to 60% or higher. The inapparent illness to clinical illness ratio of yellow fever infections is approximately 7:1. The disease occurs in several phases, with an incubation period of 3–6 days following a bite from an infected mosquito. The acute phase is characterized by sudden onset of fever, headache, myalgia, nausea, and vomiting and lasts for approximately 3 days. This stage is followed by a toxic phase consisting of jaundice, hematemesis, melena, coma, and death in 25–50% of the cases who progress to this stage.

Historical records indicate that yellow fever epidemics appeared in the New World in Yucatan, Cuba, and the Caribbean area in the middle of the 1600s, probably introduced into the Americas by the slave trade from Africa. During the 1700s, major epidemics occurred throughout North America, accompanied by high mortality.[61] The disease initially was believed to be transmitted as a "miasma" from sewage and rotting material, until the hypothesis of Dr. Carlos Finley of Cuba in 1881 and the subsequent experiments of Walter Reed and his group on human

volunteers in Cuba demonstrated that the agent was a filterable virus that was transmitted by the bite of infected *Aedes aegypti* mosquitoes.[62,63]

In the 1920s and 1930s, researchers in the United States, England, and France worked on developing a protective vaccine for yellow fever. Theiler and Smith at the Rockefeller Foundation developed a live vaccine, the 17D strain, which had been attenuated by serial passage in cell cultures and embryonated chicken eggs.[64] The 17D strain vaccine was tested in more than 1 million persons in Brazil and found to be highly effective.[64] Subsequently, the French mouse-brain–derived yellow fever vaccine and the 17D vaccine were widely used in areas of previous epidemic disease. By the late 1940s, control of yellow fever had been achieved at a population level in francophone Africa.

With the knowledge that the disease was spread to humans by the bite of *A. aegypti* mosquitoes, comprehensive public health programs were implemented to control the disease by elimination of the vector. Early success in the control of yellow fever epidemics by eliminating sites for *A. aegypti* larval development were led by Gorgas and colleagues in Cuba and the Panama Canal zone. Prior to the leadership of Gorgas, efforts to build the canal had to be abandoned because more than 55,000 workers had died from yellow fever or malaria.[65] Subsequently, Soper spearheaded control programs in Brazil and other neighboring countries in South America.[66] However, these successful programs to control urban yellow fever were periodically interrupted by reintroduction of yellow fever from the jungle. It was discovered in the 1930s in Rio de Janeiro that two yellow fever transmission cycles operate in nature: (1) The urban cycle involves transmission from a viremic human to another susceptible person by *A. aegypti*; (2) the jungle, or sylvan, cycle involves transmission of the virus among nonhuman primates by different mosquitoes. In South America, the enzootic cycle involves monkeys and diurnally active tree-hole breeding mosquitoes, such as the *Haemagogus* species. In Africa, *A. africanus* is an important vector of jungle yellow fever.

Brazil developed an active program to control yellow fever by eliminating the *A. aegypti* vector from key urban centers into the 1920s. This program was quite successful, but occasionally *A. aegypti* was reintroduced in the country from neighboring countries. In 1947, Brazil proposed to the Pan American Health Organization that a plan of regional elimination of *A. aegypti* from the Americas be undertaken. The other countries of Latin America signed on to this effort, and in the subsequent years *A. aegypti* was reduced or eliminated from many areas in the region. Once again, however, small outbreaks of yellow fever occurred periodically due to reintroduction of the virus from the jungle areas.

Based in part on the inability to control the jungle cycle of yellow fever transmission and an assessment of the cost-effectiveness of the *A. aegypti* eradication effort, the mosquito elimination program was abandoned in the 1970s. At this time *A. aegypti* mosquitoes were limited to islands in the Caribbean, the southeastern United States, and a few areas in northern South America. In the following two decades, *A. aegypti* became reestablished throughout South and Central America and the Caribbean (Figure 25-1).

Since the 1980s, yellow fever has reemerged across Africa and in South America (**Figure 25-15**).[66–68] In the period from 1987 to 1995, a total of 18,735 yellow fever cases and 4522 deaths were reported to the World Health Organization (WHO)—the largest number of cases reported since reporting began in 1948 (**Figure 25-16**). Because many of the cases occur in rural areas or in children in areas where diagnostic facilities are unavailable, it is likely that the number of cases actually is 10–500 times greater than the number reported. WHO estimates that 200,000 cases occur every year.[66] Almost all of the cases arise in sub-Saharan Africa, especially West Africa. The disease has never been reported from Asia, despite the abundance of *A. aegypti* vectors and widespread dengue epidemics. The last epidemic in the United States occurred in New Orleans in 1905, when 5000 cases and 1000 deaths occurred.[62]

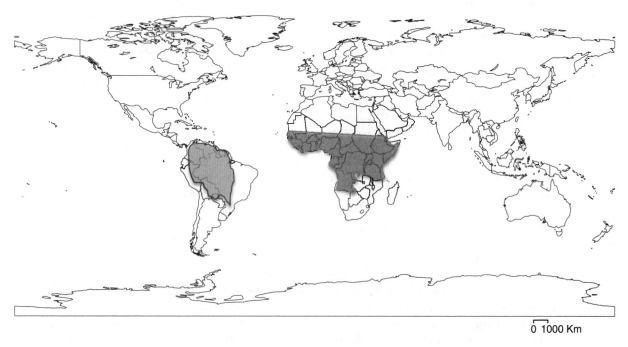

Figure 25-15 Areas of the World with Yellow Fever. Data from the World Health Organization. Global Alert and Response (GAR). Yellow fever: a current threat. http://www.who.int/csr/disease/yellowfev/impact1/en/. Accessed October 17, 2012.

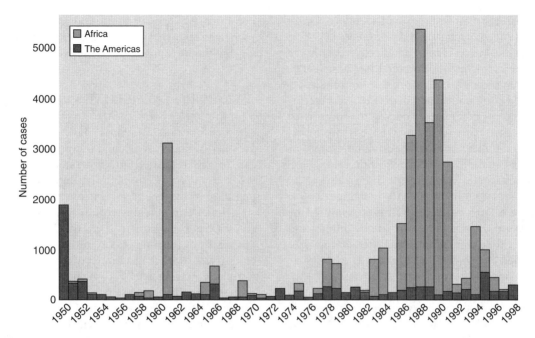

Figure 25-16 Reported number of cases of yellow fever, 1950–1998. Reproduced from the World Health Organization. WHO Report on Global Surveillance of Epidemic-prone Infectious Diseases—Yellow fever. http://www.who.int/csr/resources/publications/yellowfev/CSR_ISR_2000_1/en/index4.html. Accessed October 17, 2012.

In Africa, both sylvan and urban transmission cycles occur. Thirty-three African countries in a band from 15° north to 10° south of the equator are at risk for yellow fever epidemics (Figure 25-12). In the past decade, Nigeria has had the largest number of cases in this region; several other West African countries have experienced urban epidemics. Yellow fever had not been reported from east Africa for 50 years until 1992, when an outbreak of jungle type yellow fever occurred in Kenya. This outbreak was controlled with a large-scale immunization campaign.

In South America, the sylvan transmission cycle predominates. Outbreaks have been reported from Bolivia, Brazil, Ecuador, and Peru during the last decade. Cases are often seen among forest workers who have not been immunized. One small outbreak of urban yellow fever was reported from Santa Cruz, Bolivia, in 1998, which was the first urban-type outbreak in South America since 1954.[69]

Experts are very concerned that the reemergence of urban-type epidemics of yellow fever in the Western Hemisphere is a real possibility.[66–68] The factors that might promote reemergence are the wide distribution of *A. aegypti* throughout the region; the ease and frequency of travel from yellow fever endemic areas, which could place a viremic person in an area conducive to transmission; and the generally low levels of immunity of the population from vaccine or natural infection.

In addition to vector control, vaccination is an important tool in yellow fever control. A cost–benefit analysis of the introduction of yellow fever vaccine into the Expanded Programme on Immunization (EPI) has been done.[70] Routine use of the 17D yellow fever vaccine for infants older than 6 months of age and children would be more effective in preventing deaths than the current strategy of using the vaccine only during epidemics. While quite safe and highly effective in older children, the vaccine cannot be used in infants younger than 6 months because of a higher risk of adverse reactions, such as encephalitis in young infants.

CHIKUNGUNYA VIRUS

Chikungunya is a mosquito-borne disease caused by an alpha virus of the Togaviridae family. Chikungunya means "that which bends up" in the Makonde language of Kenya; this name refers to the joint inflammation and typical posture that are characteristic of this infection. Chikungunya virus was first identified from both humans and mosquitoes in 1952 during an epidemic of febrile arthralgia in Tanzania.[71] Following this initial isolation, chikungunya virus has caused numerous epidemics in Africa, India, and Southeast Asia that have included thousands of cases.[72–74] The virus is transmitted by mosquitoes of the genus *Aedes*, including both *A. aegypti* and *A. albopictus*.

The clinical illness is characterized by an abrupt onset of fever, polyarthralgia, and often a rash. The articular symptoms are distinctive and often debilitating. They often resolve within days to a few weeks, but in some cases they may persist for months or years.[75] Occasional patients may have neurological or cardiac complications, but the articular symptoms are much more typical for this infection. The population attack rate of symptomatic disease during an epidemic is often very high—50% or higher. The virus has a human reservoir and is transmitted by *Aedes* mosquitoes directly from viremic humans to other susceptibles. In rural tropical Africa, the virus is maintained by a sylvatic cycle involving *Aedes* mosquito transmission between primates.

In August 2004, an outbreak of chikungunya was reported in a community in Kenya; the attack rate in the population of exceeded 50%. Over the next several months, the outbreak spread to other areas in Kenya, where it demonstrated very high population incidences. In March 2005, the first cases were reported from Reunion Island in the Indian Ocean, where the disease had never been reported previously. In December 2005, at the beginning of the rainy season, an explosive outbreak occurred that was estimated to involve 260,000 people in a population of 770,000 residents of the island.[76] Subsequently, the epidemic spread to other islands in the Indian Ocean, India (with an estimated 1.5 million cases), France, and Italy. *A. aegypti* had become very rare on Reunion Island after an intensive DDT spraying program to control malaria in the 1950s. However, *A. albopictus* replaced *A. aegypti* after the program was discontinued; indeed, this vector was responsible for a large dengue outbreak in 1977. Studies of virus isolates from the Reunion Island outbreak disclosed a single amino acid mutation at position 226 of the glycoprotein ol-protein EL (A226V) of the epidemic virus, which rendered the virus more infectious for *A. albopictus* mosquitoes.[77,78]

An outbreak in Italy was introduced by a viremic traveler who was infected in India. Because the vector, *A. albopictus*, was well established, this single introduction resulted in 208 documented cases in northern Italy. This raises the possibility that chikungunya virus could be imported and cause epidemics in other countries in Europe or North America where *A. albopictus* is a common resident mosquito.

There is no effective treatment for chikungunya. Due to its high attack rate and wide distribution in east Africa, India, and southern Europe and its severe, often chronic, morbidity, it would be important to develop an effective vaccine to prevent this infection.

Preliminary data have been reported on a virus-like particle vaccine that appears to be effective in preventing chikungunya infection in rhesus monkeys.[79]

TICK-BORNE ENCEPHALITIS VIRUS

The tick-borne encephalitis (TBE) virus is another member of the Flaviviridae family. The TBE viruses can be differentiated into a western and far eastern subtype using monoclonal antibodies, specific peptides, or by genetic sequencing.

Human disease due to infection with the TBE viruses has been known since the 1930s. Seasonal outbreaks of meningitis due to the western subtype of TBE were described among populations in Europe, especially Austria in 1931.[80] A survey in 1958 found that 56% of all virus diseases of the central nervous system in Austria were due to TBE.[81] The far eastern subtype of TBE is more virulent, often leading to severe encephalitis with higher mortality than the western subtype.[82]

Ticks are the vectors and reservoir hosts of TBE in nature. Several species of ticks have been found to be infected, but *Ixodes ricinus*, the common castor bean tick, is the major vector of the western TBE subtype and *Ixodes persulcatus* of the far eastern TBE subtype.[82] These ticks parasitize many species of mammals, reptiles, and birds in addition to humans. Small mammals tend to have higher levels of viremia—sufficient to infect ticks. During the viremic stage, milk from goats, cows, and sheep may be infectious and a source of infection to humans if they consume raw milk from these animals. Infection by the oral route has been reported from Slovakia after consumption of nonpasteurized cheese from infected animals.[83] Inactivated vaccines have been prepared against both the western and far eastern subtypes of TBE virus.[82] These vaccines are quite immunogenic and effective in preventing infection in humans at risk of disease caused by TBE viruses.[82,84,85]

OTHER MOSQUITO-BORNE ENCEPHALITIS VIRUSES IN NORTH AMERICA

La Crosse Virus

The next most frequent cause of arboviral encephalitis in the United States is a member of the California family of bunyaviruses, known as La Crosse virus. In 1960, La Cross was first isolated from a child with fatal encephalitis in Wisconsin.[86] Since then, this virus has been identified in states throughout the midwestern and eastern United States (**Figure 25-17**).

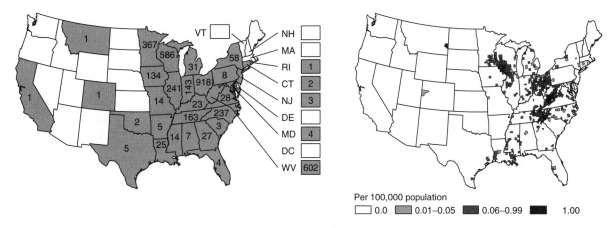

Figure 25-17 The geographic distribution of California encephalitis due to the La Crosse strain of the virus. Figure A shows cumulative cases of neuroinvasive disease. Figure B shows average cases per county per year. Reproduced from the Centers for Disease Control and Prevention National Center for Emerging and Zoonotic Infectious Diseases (2011). La Crosse Encephalitis: Epidemiology & Geographic Distribution. http://www.cdc.gov/lac/tech/epi.html#map. Updated September 9, 2011. Accessed November 27, 2012.

Since 1964, when La Crosse encephalitis was first reported, cases have been reported every year; a mean of 75 cases per year were reported between 1964 and 2000 (**Figure 25-18**). In 2000, a total of 114 cases were reported from 14 states. The natural cycle of La Crosse virus involves transmission between *Ochlerotatus triseriatus* mosquitoes and small mammals, especially chipmunks and tree squirrels (**Figure 25-19**). This mosquito has a limited flight range and lives in tree holes in wooded areas. Persons living in suburban areas with trees on or near their property are at highest risk of infection. A prevention strategy is to fill tree holes with concrete,

tar, or other filler to eliminate breeding areas for vector mosquitoes and to dispose of used containers that could serve as breeding sites.

La Crosse virus and other related viruses can be maintained in nature by transovarial transmission by an infected female mosquito. Virus survival over winter by transovarial transmission has allowed some arboviruses in the *Bunyavirus* genus to become endemic in far northern latitudes. For example, the snowshoe hare habitat is the subarctic, where the summer season during which mosquitoes can hatch and develop is very short. Unless the eggs were infected when they hatched, it might not be possible for mosquitoes

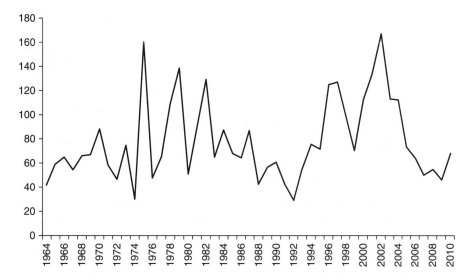

Figure 25-18 California Serogroup Virus Neuroinvasive Disease Cases Reported by Year, 1964–2010. Reproduced from the Centers for Disease Control and Prevention (2010). La Crosse Encephalitis: Epidemiology & Geographic Distribution. http://www.cdc.gov/lac/tech/epi.html. Last Updated September 9, 2011. Accessed October 17, 2012.

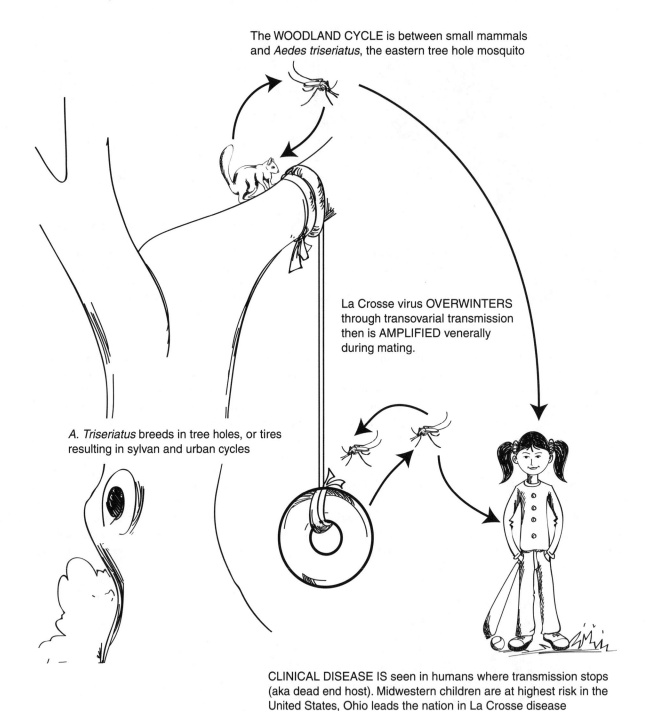

The WOODLAND CYCLE is between small mammals and *Aedes triseriatus*, the eastern tree hole mosquito

La Crosse virus OVERWINTERS through transovarial transmission then is AMPLIFIED venerally during mating.

A. Triseriatus breeds in tree holes, or tires resulting in sylvan and urban cycles

CLINICAL DISEASE IS seen in humans where transmission stops (aka dead end host). Midwestern children are at highest risk in the United States, Ohio leads the nation in La Crosse disease

Figure 25-19 La Crosse Virus Transmission includes a Natural Cycle, an Amplification Cycle and Zoonosis in both Urban and Rural Areas of the U.S.

to acquire infection from snowshoe hares at a rate sufficient to maintain the endemic cycle from year to year.

St. Louis Encephalitis Virus

St. Louis encephalitis virus has become a frequent cause of arboviral encephalitis in the United States since it was originally identified in the 1940s. For the next several decades, SLE was the most frequent cause of epidemics of viral encephalitis during the summer in the United States. Large epidemics of SLE have occurred in Florida and Texas, for example. An epidemic involving more than 2000 cases of encephalitis with 171 deaths occurred in 1975 in the United States; persons from 31 states became ill

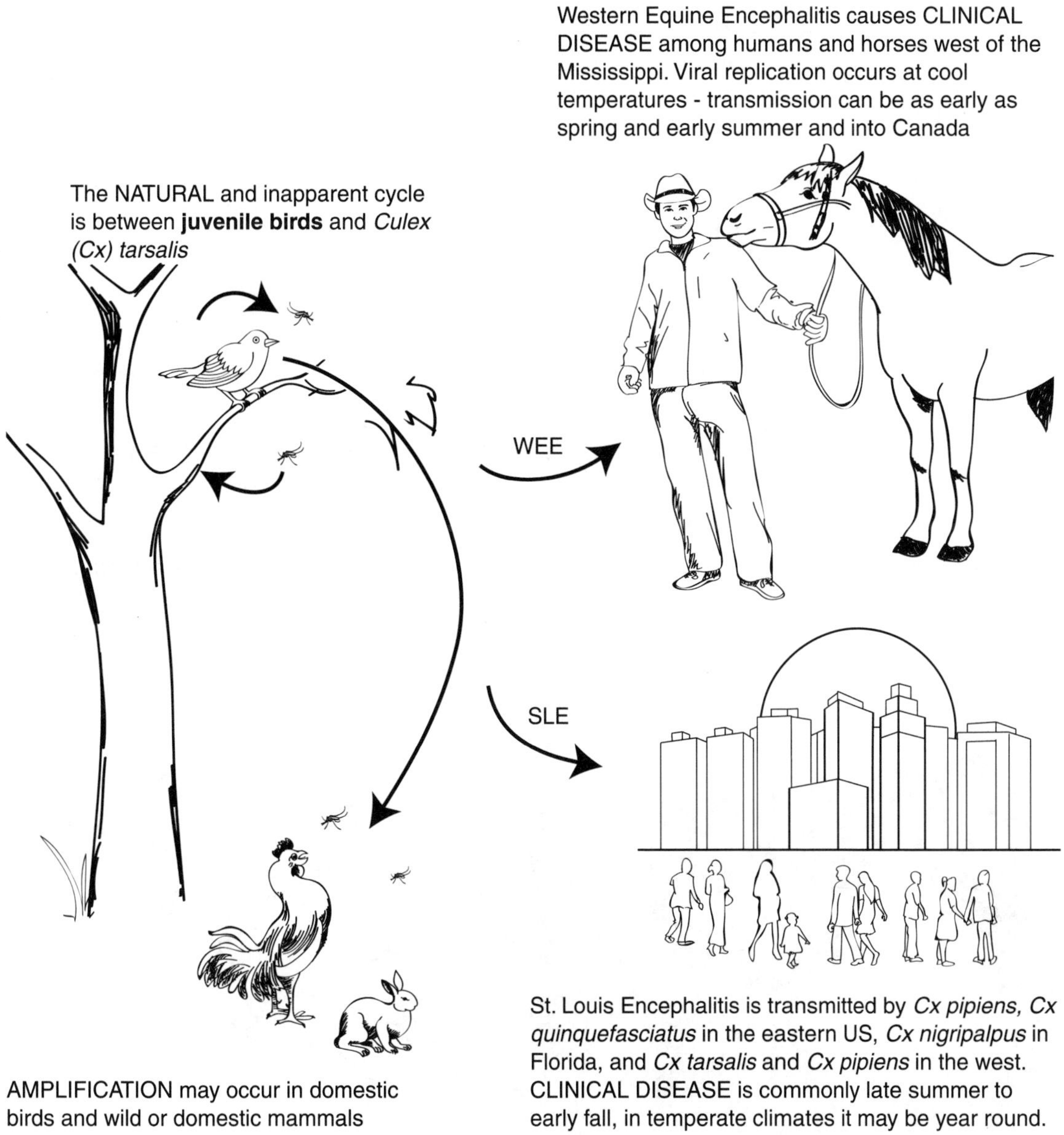

Western Equine Encephalitis causes CLINICAL DISEASE among humans and horses west of the Mississippi. Viral replication occurs at cool temperatures - transmission can be as early as spring and early summer and into Canada

The NATURAL and inapparent cycle is between **juvenile birds** and *Culex (Cx) tarsalis*

WEE

SLE

AMPLIFICATION may occur in domestic birds and wild or domestic mammals

St. Louis Encephalitis is transmitted by *Cx pipiens, Cx quinquefasciatus* in the eastern US, *Cx nigripalpus* in Florida, and *Cx tarsalis* and *Cx pipiens* in the west. CLINICAL DISEASE is commonly late summer to early fall, in temperate climates it may be year round.

Figure 25-20 Western Equine Encephalitis and St. Louis Encephalitis share a similar transmission cycle.

during this epidemic but the incidence was highest in the Midwest, especially Illinois.[86] Encephalitis cases due to SLE were reported from as far north as Canada during this outbreak.

The SLE virus can be transmitted in different cycles in different locations. In the western United States, it is spread from the reservoir in passerine birds, such as the house sparrow, by *Culex tarsalis* mosquitoes. This cycle is similar to that for western encephalitis transmission in rural areas of the western United States (**Figure 25-20**). In the Midwest, SLE is spread by other culicine mosquitoes, especially *Culex pipiens*. In Florida, a rural cycle involves transmission by *Culex*

nigrapalpus. The epidemic activity of urban SLE is greatest in drought years, where dirty water collects due to poor drainage. However, rural SLE tends to occur more frequently in years with heavy rainfall.[87]

The inapparent to apparent infection ratio is 60–100:1. However, clinical encephalitis occurs more frequently in the elderly, similar to West Nile virus encephalitis. Urban epidemics tend to occur more frequently in lower-socioeconomic areas. Apart from years in which major urban epidemics occur, SLE is noted only sporadically. Between 1964 and 2000, a mean of 121 cases (median 26 cases) were reported annually (**Figure 25-21**).

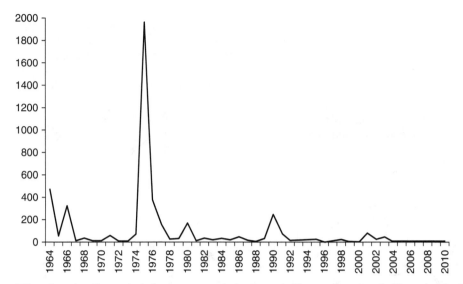

* Neuroinvasive disease includes cases reported as encephalitis, meningoencephalitis, or meningitis.

Figure 25-21 Reported Cases of St. Louis Encephalitis 1964–2010. Reproduced from the Centers for Disease Control and Prevention (2010). Saint Louis Encephalitis: Epidemiology & Geographic Distribution. http://www.cdc.gov/sle/technical/epi.html#moremapschartstables. Last Updated June 13, 2011. Accessed October 17, 2012.

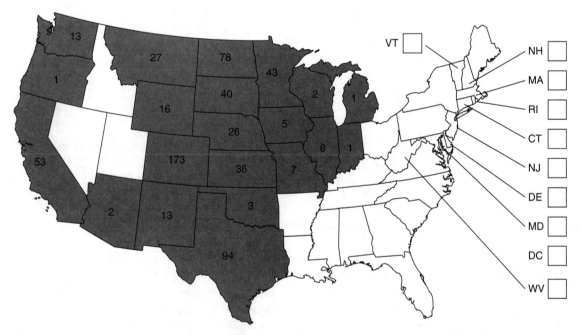

* Neuroinvasive disease includes cases reported as encephalitis, meningoencephalitis, or meningitis. Cases are
  reported by state of residence.

Data table: From 1964 through 2010, WEEV neuroinvasive disease cases have been reported in Arizona (2), California (53), Colorado (173), Illinois (6), Indiana (1), Iowa (5), Kansas (36), Michigan (1), Minnesota (43), Missouri (7), Montana (27), Nebraska (26), New Mexico (13), North Dakota (78), Oklahoma (3), Oregon (1), South Dakota (40), Texas (94), Washington (13), Wisconsin (2) and Wyoming (16).

Figure 25-22 Western Equine Encephalitis Virus Neuroinvasive Disease Cases Reported by State, 1964–2010. Reproduced from Centers for Disease Control and Prevention (2010). Western Equine Encephalitis Virus Neuroinvasive Disease Cases* Reported by State, 1964–2010. http://www.cdc.gov/ncidod/dvbid/arbor/arbocase/wee_map.pdf. Accessed October 18, 2012.

Western Encephalitis Virus

Western encephalitis (WE) virus causes sporadic cases of encephalitis in the rural areas of the western United States (**Figure 25-22**). This virus has been called western equine encephalitis virus because it often causes clinical encephalitis and death in horses as well as humans. The incidence of WE encephalitis increases with heavy rainfall. The virus is transmitted from the reservoir in birds to humans and horses by *Culex tarsalis*. The inapparent to apparent infection ratios ranges from 25:1 to 50:1 in children and is 1000:1 or greater in adults. Most cases of clinical encephalitis from WE infection occur in children younger than 2 years of age.[88]

The most recent epidemic of western encephalitis occurred in Colorado in 1987. The reasons for the absence of epidemic transmission since then are not known. During 1964–2000, an average of 17 cases (median of 3 cases) were reported per year in the United States. However, even endemic transmission of this virus has not been documented in the past decade. The last case was reported in 1999. The reasons for the apparent disappearance of WE virus in the United States are not known.

Eastern Encephalitis Virus

Eastern encephalitis virus is found in the eastern half of the United States, especially in the freshwater marshes along the shores of the Atlantic and Gulf coasts (**Figure 25-23**). Human infections are rare because the natural cycle occurs in remote areas and the mosquito vector, *Culiseta melanura*, does

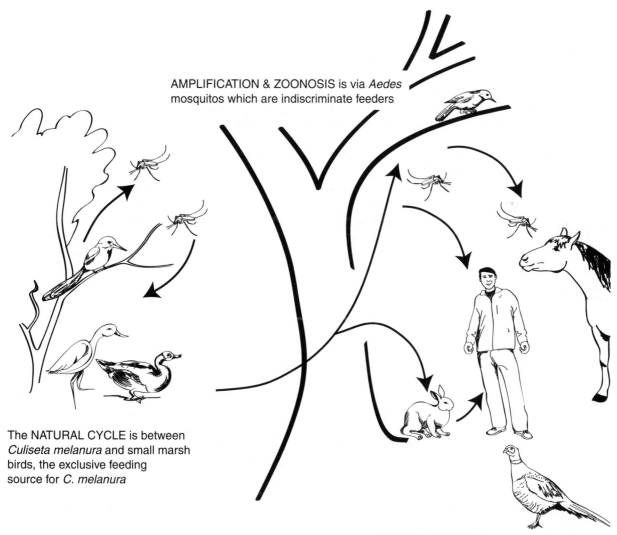

AMPLIFICATION & ZOONOSIS is via *Aedes* mosquitos which are indiscriminate feeders

The NATURAL CYCLE is between *Culiseta melanura* and small marsh birds, the exclusive feeding source for *C. melanura*

CLINICAL DISEASE is transmitted by *Aedes* mosquitos. Humans, horses and pheasants can have symptoms of EEV.

Figure 25-23 Eastern Equine Encephalitis Transmission includes a Natural Cycle, an Amplification Cycle and Subsequent Zoonosis.

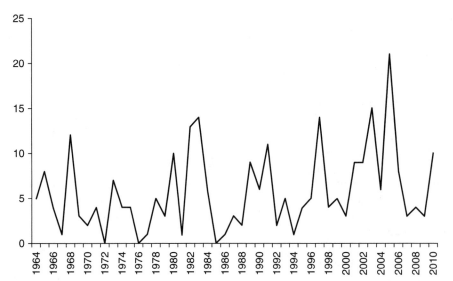

* Neuroinvasive disease includes cases reported as encephalitis, meningoencephalitis, or meningitis.

Data table: In the United States, the annual number of reported Eastern equine encephalitis virus neuroinvasive disease cases reported varies. From 1964 through 2010, an average of 6 cases were reported annually (range 0–21). This graph demonstrates how the number of cases can vary markedly from year to year.

Figure 25-24 Eastern Equine Encephalitis Virus Neuroinvasive Disease Cases Reported by Year, 1964–2010. Reproduced from the Centers for Disease Control and Prevention (2010). Eastern Equine Encephalitis: Epidemiology & Geographic Distribution. http://www.cdc.gov/sle/technical/epi.html#moremapschartstables. Last Updated June 10, 2011. Accessed October 17, 2012.

not commonly feed on humans. However, when human infection occurs, it often results in severe encephalitis with high mortality (i.e., more than 20%). The inapparent to clinical infection rates ranges from 2:1 to 8:1 in children and from 4:1 to 50:1 in adults. During 1964–2010, an average of five human cases were reported each year in the United States (**Figure 25-24**).

Venezuelan Encephalitis

Venezuelan encephalitis (VE) is localized in the United States to southern Florida, especially the Everglades, and south Texas. Infections caused by VE are also endemic in Central and South America. The virus can be spread by both *Aedes* and *Culex* genera mosquitoes. Major epidemics have been reported from South America and typically involve horses, which can serve as the reservoir of the virus. As with several other arboviruses, human infections are more severe in children.

OTHER TICK-BORNE INFECTIONS

Other tick-borne infections that are endemic in the United States have been described in recent years, and these diseases may have increased in frequency

as well. However, the temporal trends related to their incidence are less clear because the only reportable tick-borne infections in the United States are Rocky Mountain spotted fever (RMSF) and Lyme disease. The number of patients with RMSF increased from approximately 200 to 400 cases per year in the 1950s and 1960s to more than 1000 cases per year in the late 1970s and 1980s. Increased opportunities for human exposure to the vectors—primarily the Rocky Mountain wood tick (*Dermocenter andersonii*) in the western United States and the American dog tick (*Dermocenter variabilis*) in the eastern United States—occurred because of the expansion of suburban housing into wooded, tick-infested areas and the increased opportunities for exposure associated with recreational activities. Currently, RMSF is more common in the eastern United States.

Two forms of human ehrlichiosis—human monocytic ehrlichiosis (HME), caused by infection with *Ehrlichia chaffeeinsis*, and human granulocytic ehrlichiosis (HGE), caused by infection with *Ehrlichia ewingii*—have also been recognized with increased frequency in the past few years. HME is transmitted by the dog tick and HGE by the deer tick. Another tick-borne disease, babesiosis, an infection of red blood cells with *Babesia microti*, can be transmitted to humans by tick bites in the endemic areas in the coastal northeastern United States. It is not unusual for a patient to be seen who has both Lyme disease and ehrlichiosis after exposure to tick habitats in an endemic area. It seems likely that these other tick-borne diseases have increased in frequency, similar to the increases in incidence documented with Lyme disease. However, without surveillance, the documentation of this increased incidence has been difficult to interpret.

A tick-borne encephalitis virus was isolated from the brain of child who died from encephalitis after receiving a tick bite while on a vacation near Powassan, Ontario, Canada.[89] The Powassan virus, a member of the flavivirus group of viruses, occasionally causes encephalitis in Canada and the northern areas of the United States.

A new virus was isolated from patients in Central China in 2009 who had symptoms of severe fever with thrombocytopenia, leucopenia, and multiple organ dysfunction. This was an RNA virus in the genus phlebovirus in the Bunyaviradae family. It was named the Severe Fever and Thrombocytopenia Syndrome Virus (SFTS-V). SFTS-V RNA was also identified in several ticks in the Ixodidae family of the species *H. longicornis* that were obtained from animals in the area of the epidemic.[100–101] Person to person transmission of SFTS-virus has been reported among persons having contact with blood from infected patients.[102–103]

Another new tick-borne virus in the Bunyavirus family was isolated recently from a patient in Missouri who had symptoms of encephalitis. This virus was named the Heartland virus.[104]

Lyme Disease

Lyme disease was first recognized by Steere and colleagues in 1975 following the identification of a group of children living in Old Lyme, Connecticut, who were diagnosed with juvenile rheumatoid arthritis.

In the 50 years since the recognition of Lyme disease, the number of reported cases has increased progressively, and the geographic areas of endemicity of the disease have expanded to include the coastal northeastern and mid-Atlantic states, several states in the Midwest (especially Minnesota, Wisconsin, and Michigan), and coastal California.

Colorado Tick Fever Virus

Colorado tick fever virus is transmitted in the Rocky Mountain area by the tick *Dermacentor andersoni*; this tick is endemic in the region. Typically, the disease occurs among hikers in rural areas in the western United States during May through July. The symptoms include a febrile illness and macular papular rash occurring 3–6 days after a tick bite. Recovery without sequelae is the rule, but occasionally severe, even fatal, disease has been reported.

TRYPANOSOMIASIS

American Trypanosomiasis (Chagas's Disease)

The pathogenic organism responsible for American trypanosomiasis, *Trypanosome cruzi* and the vector, *Triatoma* species, were discovered by Carolos Cruz approximately 100 years ago. Infections with *T. cruzii* remain the most important parasitic disease in South and Central America and Mexico at present. The organism is spread from the feces of various *Triatoma* species (also known as "kissing bugs"). These organisms do not penetrate intact skin, but their bite causes an itching sensation that often results in inoculation of the organisms or transfer of the organisms to the mucosa of the eyes, mouth, or nose. The result is an acute infection, most commonly in children, after a short incubation period of 5–14 days. The acute infection can involve the myocardium and also may produce painless bipalpebral edema (Romana's sign) as well as other skin lesions, hepatomegaly diarrhea, and meningoencephalitis. The acute disease may occasionally be fatal but usually resolves; the infection becomes chronic, with 20% to 30% of patients developing myocardial fibrosis or gastrointestinal disease, such as megaesophagus.[90]

Major international efforts have been made to control the vector and prevent transfusion transmission of Chagas's disease in the past 25 years. The incidence of this disease has dropped from an estimated 700,000 new cases per year to 40,000 cases today, and the annual number of deaths has fallen from more than 45,000 to 12,500.[91]

The infectious organism can be transmitted by the insect vector, by blood transfusion or transplantation from an infected donor, congenitally from mother to infant, or as a foodborne infection. The insect vector is present in southern Texas, Arizona, and California. The pathogen has been imported by the estimated 100,000 to 300,000 persons with chronic *T. cruzii* infections who have immigrated to the United States. A total of 8 transfusion-transmitted *T. cruzii* infections have been documented in the United States and Canada.[90] In the past three years, blood donors in the United States have been screened for *T. cruzii* antibodies. The seroprevalence of *T. cruzii* has been estimated as approximately 1 in 33,000 U.S. blood donors.

Remaining issues in the control of *T. cruzii* infection in Latin America include urban migration with establishment of an urban reservoir in some areas, deforestation, a sylvatic reservoir, and insecticide resistance. The region of Gran Chaco (southern Bolivia, northern Argentina, and western Paraguay) remains at high risk for *Triatoma* spp. infestation, with a high prevalence of infection being noted in children. However, Chile, Uruguay, and Brazil have declared that *T. cruzii* transmission by the vector *T. infestans* has been eliminated.

Infected persons can be treated with benznidazole or nifutimox. A randomized clinical trial—the Benznidazole Evaluation for Interrupting Trypanosomiasis (BENEFIT)—is under way to determine whether treatment will decrease adverse cardiac outcomes.

Human African Trypanosomiasis

The number of human African trypanosomiasis cases exploded in the early 1900s during the era of European colonization. Massive epidemics occurred involving large areas of sub-Saharan Africa.[92] This phenomenon, in turn, led to a concerted public health effort to control the disease using vector control and treatment of human infections. By the early 1960s, the disease was nearly eradicated. In the last three decades, however, the disease has reemerged and is now a serious health problem in Africa (**Figure 25-25**).[92–95]

African sleeping sickness is caused by two subspecies of *Trypanosoma brucei*, an extracellular protozoan parasite. *T. brucei gambiense* is focally distributed in western and central Africa and is transmitted by riverine species of the tsetse fly (*Glossina* species). *T. brucei rhodesiense* is distributed in eastern and southern Africa and is transmitted by savannah species of the tsetse fly. Although the two species of trypanosomes are morphologically indistinguishable, the epidemiology and clinical illness in humans infected with the two parasites differ. *T. brucei rhodesiense* is a zoonotic parasite that infects a variety of domestic and wild animals, especially cattle, which serve as the reservoir. In contrast, *T. brucei gambiense* has a human reservoir. The tsetse fly vector of *T. brucei gambiense* inhabits humid and dark areas of vegetation along fast-moving streams. Human activities, such as washing, fishing, or collecting firewood, bring humans into contact with the habitat of the tsetse fly vector.[96]

Thirty-two human infections with *T. brucei rhodesiense* have been reported to CDC in the last 35 years among visitors to game preserves in Africa.[95] Nearly all of the imported cases since 1990 were acquired in Tanzania.

Infection with either *Trypanosoma* subspecies leads to encephalitis; however, infection with *T. brucei rhodesiense* is usually more acute. The encephalitis is usually fatal if not treated. Therapy is usually

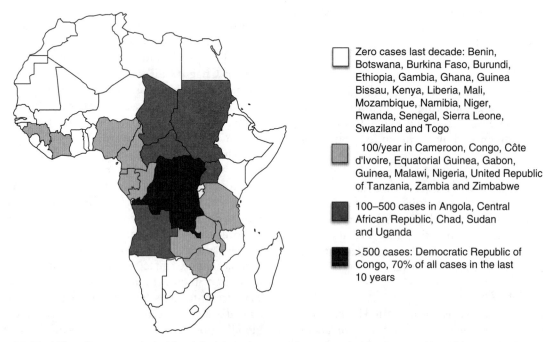

Figure 25-25 African Trypanosomiasis (sleeping sickness), reported cases 2012. Data from World Health Organization (2012). Human African trypanosomiasis (sleeping sickness). http://www.who.int/mediacentre/factsheets/fs259/en/. Accessed October 17, 2012.

successful with melarsopol, an organic arsenic, compared to treatment with suramin, eflornithine, or nifurtimox. However, drug toxicity during treatment is common.

Sleeping sickness emerged in Africa as a major health problem in the 1990s, fueled by wars, social disruption, and a shortage of drugs to treat the disease. However, lobbying by Medecins Sans Frontieres for improved access of developing countries to essential medicines and funding by the Gates Foundation resulted in an agreement by Aventis both to provide efleflornithine free of charge and to support control activities.[93] As a result, the number of cases of sleeping sickness has decreased from an estimated 450,000 in 1997 to 50,000 currently. If the current level of support can be maintained, experts at WHO now believe human African trypanosomiasis could be eliminated as a public health problem.[97-99]

RIFT VALLEY FEVER

Rift Valley fever (RVF) is a phlebovirus that has been recognized for many years as a cause of disease in domestic ruminants and humans in African countries south of the Sahara. In 1978, a major epidemic of RVF occurred in Egypt. This event was followed by an outbreak in 1987 in Senegal after the opening of a new dam. The 1997 epidemic of RVF associated with the increased rainfall accompanying El Niño weather conditions has already been discussed.

SUMMARY

Many of the vector-borne diseases are experiencing an expansion of their range. Control of vectors, vaccination, and mitigation of illness through effective therapy are all needed to reduce levels of these diseases. Considerable progress has been made toward eliminating some diseases (e.g., malaria, sleeping sickness) but others are, in fact, expanding (e.g., Lyme, West Nile virus, and dengue). Vector-borne diseases know no international boundaries. and increased cooperation between countries will be required to eradicate them.

• • • REFERENCES

1. MacKenzie JS, Gubler DJ, Petersen LR. Emerging flaviviruses: the spread and resurgence of Japanese encephalitis, West Nile and dengue viruses. *Nat Med* 2004;10:S98–S109.

2. Solomon T. Flavivirus encephalitis. *N Engl J Med* 2004;351:370–378.

3. Weaver SC, Barrett AD. Transmission cycles, host range, evolution and emergence of arboviral disease. *Nat Rev Microbiol* 2004;2:789–801.

4. Patz JA, Epstein PR, Burke TA, Balbus JM. Global climate change and emerging infectious diseases. *JAMA* 1996;275:217–223.

5. Nasci RS, Savage HM, White DJ, et al. West Nile virus in overwintering *Culex* mosquitoes, New York City, 2000. *Emerg Infect Dis* 2001;7:742–744.

6. Tesh RB, Parsons R, Siirin M, et al. Year-round West Nile virus activity, Gulf Coast region, Texas and Louisiana. *Emerg Infect Dis* 2004;10:1649–1652.

7. Rosen L, Shroyer DA, Tesh RB, et al. Transovarial transmission of dengue viruses by mosquitoes: *Aedes albopictus* and *Aedes aegypti*. *Am J Trop Med Hyg* 1983;32:1108–1119.

8. Rosen L. Sexual transmission of dengue viruses by *Aedes albopictus*. *Am J Trop Med Hyg* 1987;37:398–402.

9. MacKenzie JS, Gubler DJ, Petersen LR. Emerging flaviviruses: the spread and resurgence of Japanese encephalitis, West Nile and dengue viruses. *Nat Med* 2004;10:S98–S109.

10. Gubler DJ, Clark GG. Dengue/dengue hemorrhagic fever: the emergence of a global health problem. *Emerg Infect Dis* 1995;1:55–57.

11. Halstead SB. Dengue haemorrhagic fever: a public health problem and a field for research. *Bull WHO* 1980;58:1–21.

12. Halstead SB. Observations related to pathogenesis of dengue hemorrhagic fever. VI. Hypotheses and discussion. *Yale J Biol Med* 1970;42:350–362.

13. Vaughn DW. Invited commentary: dengue lessons from Cuba. *Am J Epidemiol* 2000;152:800–803.

14. Guzman MG, Kouri G, Valdes L, et al. Epidemiologic studies on dengue in Santiago de Cuba, 1997. *Am J Epidemiol* 2000;152:793–799.

15. Kouri G, Guzman MG, Valdes L, et al. Reemergence of dengue in Cuba: a 1997 epidemic in Santiago de Cuba. *Emerg Infect Di.* 1998;4:89–92.

16. Sangkawibha N, Rojanasuphot S, Ahandrik S, et al. Risk factors in dengue shock syndrome: a prospective epidemiologic study in Rayong, Thailand. I. The 1980 outbreak. *Am J Epidemiol* 1984;120:653–669.

17. Watts DM, Porter KR, Putvatana P, et al. Failure of secondary infection with American genotype dengue 2 to cause dengue haemorrhagic fever. *Lancet* 1999;354:1431–1434.

18. Barnes WJ, Rosen L. Fatal hemorrhagic disease and shock associated with primary dengue infection on a Pacific island. *Am J Trop Med Hyg* 1974;23:495–506.

19. Rosen L. The Emperor's New Clothes revisited, or reflections on the pathogenesis of dengue hemorrhagic fever. *Am J Trop Med Hyg* 1977;26:337–343.

20. Rosen L. The pathogenesis of dengue haemorrhagic fever: a critical appraisal of current hypotheses. *S Afr Med J* 1986;(suppl):40–42.

21. Vaughn DW, Green S, Kalayanarooj S, et al. Dengue viremia titer, antibody response pattern, and virus serotype correlate with disease severity. *J Infect Dis* 2000;181:2–9.

22. Gubler DJ. Dengue and dengue hemorrhagic fever. *Clin Microbiol Rev* 1998;11:480–496.

23. Guzman MG, Kouri GP, Bravo J, et al. Dengue haemorrhagic fever in Cuba. I. Serological confirmation of clinical diagnosis. *Trans R Soc Trop Med Hyg* 1984;78:235–238.

24. Gubler DJ. Dengue and dengue hemorrhagic fever. *Clin Microbiol Rev* 1998;11:480–496.

25. Guzman MG, Kouri G, Valdes L, et al. Epidemiologic studies on dengue in Santiago de Cuba, 1997. *Am J Epidemiol* 2000;152:793–799.

26. Kouri G, Guzman MG, Valdes L, et al. Reemergence of dengue in Cuba: a 1997 epidemic in Santiago de Cuba. *Emerg Infect Dis* 1998;4:89–92.

27. Vaughn DW. Invited commentary: dengue lessons from Cuba. *Am J Epidemiol* 2000;152:800–803.

28. Craven RB, Eliason DA, Francy DB, et al. Importation of *Aedes albopictus* and other exotic mosquito species into the United States in used tires from Asia. *J Am Mosq Control Assoc* 1988;4:138–142.

29. Rigau-Perez JG, Gubler DJ, Vorndam AV, Clark GG. Dengue surveillance—United States, 1986–1992. *MMWR CDC Surveill Summ* 1994;43:7–19.

30. Gubler DJ. *Aedes aegypti* and *Aedes aegypti*–borne disease control in the 1990s: top down or bottom up. Charles Franklin Craig Lecture. *Am J Trop Med Hyg* 1989;40:571–578.

31. Gubler DJ. Dengue and dengue hemorrhagic fever. *Clin Microbiol Rev* 1998;11:480–496.

32. Kay B, Vu SN. New strategy against *Aedes aegypti* in Vietnam. *Lancet* 2005;365:613–617.

33. Guirakhoo F, Weltzin R, Chambers TJ, et al. Recombinant chimeric yellow fever–dengue type 2 virus is immunogenic and protective in nonhuman primates. *J Virol* 2000;74:5477–5485.

34. Kinney RM, Huang CY. Development of new vaccines against dengue fever and Japanese encephalitis. *Intervirology* 2001;44:176–197.

35. Vaughn DW, Hoke CH Jr, Yoksan S, et al. Testing of a dengue 2 live-attenuated vaccine (strain 16681 PDK 53) in ten American volunteers. *Vaccine* 1996;14:329–336.

36. Smithburn KC, Hughes TP, Burke AW, Paul JU. A neotropic virus isolated from the blood of a native of Uganda. *Am J Tropic Med Hyg* 1940;20:471–492.

37. Hurlbut HS, Rizk F, Taylor RM, Work TH. A study of the ecology of West Nile virus in Egypt. *Am J Trop Med Hyg* 1956;5:579–620.

38. McIntosh BM, Jupp PG, Dos Santos I, Meenehan GM. Epidemics of West Nile and Sindbis viruses in South Africa with *Culex univittaatus Theobald* as vector. *Lancet Infect Dis* 1976;72:295–300.

39. Work TH, Hurlbut HS, Taylor RM. Indigenous wild birds of the Nile Delta as potential West Nile virus circulating reservoirs. *Am J Trop Med Hyg* 1955;4:872–888.

40. Murgue B, Murri S, Triki H, et al. West Nile in the Mediterranean basin: 1950–2000. *Ann N Y Acad Sci* 2001;951:117–126.

41. Nash D, Mostashari F, Fine A, et al. The outbreak of West Nile virus infection in the New York City area in 1999. *N Engl J Med* 2001;344:1807–1814.

42. Lanciotti RS, Roehrig JT, Deubel V, et al. Origin of the West Nile virus responsible for an outbreak of encephalitis in the northeastern United States. *Science* 1999;286:2333–2337.

43. Marfin AA, Petersen LR, Eidson M, et al. Widespread West Nile virus activity, eastern United States, 2000. *Emerg Infect Dis* 2001;7:730–735.

44. Eidson M, Komar N, Sorhage F, et al. Crow deaths as a sentinel surveillance system for West Nile virus in the northeastern United States, 1999. *Emerg Infect Dis* 2001;7:615–620.

45. Kulasekera VL, Kramer L, Nasci RS, et al. West Nile virus infection in mosquitoes, birds, horses, and humans, Staten Island, New York, 2000. *Emerg Infect Dis* 2001;7:722–725.

46. Campbell GL, Marfin AA, Lanciotti RS, Gubler DJ. West Nile virus. *Lancet Infect Dis* 2002;2:519–529.

47. Granwehr BP, Lillibridge KM, Higgs S, et al. West Nile virus: where are we now? *Lancet Infect Dis* 2004;4:547–556.

48. Centers for Disease Control and Prevention. ArboNET Database. 2005. Available at: http://www.cdc.gov.

49. Mostashari F, Bunning ML, Kitsutani PT, et al. Epidemic West Nile encephalitis, New York, 1999: results of a household-based seroepidemiological survey. *Lancet* 2001;358:261–264.

50. Nasci RS, Savage HM, White DJ, et al. West Nile virus in overwintering *Culex* mosquitoes, New York City, 2000. *Emerg Infect Dis* 2001;7:742–744.

51. Centers for Disease Control and Prevention. Surveillance for human West Nile virus disease—United States, 1999–2008. *MMWR* 2010;59(SS-2):1–17.

52. Iwamoto M, Jernigan DB, Guasch A, et al. Transmission of West Nile virus from an organ donor to four transplant recipients. *N Engl J Med* 2003;348:2196–2203.

53. Pealer LN, Marfin AA, Petersen LR, et al. Transmission of West Nile virus through blood transfusion in the United States in 2002. *N Engl J Med* 2003;349:1236–1245.

54. Biggerstaff BJ, Petersen LR. Estimated risk of transmission of the West Nile virus through blood transfusion in the US, 2002. *Transfusion* 2003;43:1007–1017.

55. Centers for Disease Control and Prevention. Update: West Nile virus screening of blood donations and transfusion-associated transmission—United States, 2003. Reported by Klienman S, Busch M, Caglioti S et al. *MMWR* 2004;53:282–284.

56. Custer B, Tomasulo PA, Murphy EL, et al. Triggers for switching from minipool testing by nucleic acid technology to individual-donation nucleic acid testing for West Nile virus: analysis of 2003 data to inform 2004 decision making. *Transfusion* 2004;44:1547–1554.

57. Solomon T, Vaughn DW. Pathogenesis and clinical features of Japanese encephalitis and West Nile virus infections. *Curr Top Microbiol Immunol* 2002;267:171–194.

58. Mackenzie JS, Gubler DJ, Petersen LR. Emerging flaviviruses: the spread and resurgence of Japanese encephalitis, West Nile and dengue viruses. *Nat Med* 2004;10:S98–S109.

59. Grossman RA, Edelman R, Willhight M, et al. Study of Japanese encephalitis virus in Chiangmai Valley, Thailand. 3. Human

seroepidemiology and inapparent infections. *Am J Epidemiol* 1973;98:133–149.

60. Hoke CH, Nisalak A, Sangawhipa N, et al. Protection against Japanese encephalitis by inactivated vaccines. *N Engl J Med* 1988;319:608–614.

61. Monath TP. Yellow fever vaccine. In: Plotkin S, Orenstein W, Offit PA eds. *Vaccines*. 5th ed Philadelphia, PA: Saunders; 2008;959-1056.

62. Bres PL. A century of progress in combating yellow fever. *Bull WHO* 1986;64:775–786.

63. Carter HR. *Yellow Fever: An Epidemiological and Historical Study of Its Place of Origin.* Baltimore, MD: Williams & Wilkins; 1931.

64. Monath TP. Yellow fever: Victor, Victoria? Conqueror, conquest? Epidemics and research in the last forty years and prospects for the future. *Am J Trop Med Hyg* 1991;45:1–43.

65. Soper FL. The 1964 status of *Aedes aegypti* eradication and yellow fever in the Americas. *Am J Trop Med Hyg* 1965;14:887–891.

66. Robertson SE, Hull BP, Tomori O, et al. Yellow fever: a decade of reemergence. *JAMA* 1996;276:1157–1162.

67. Monath TP. Yellow fever: an update. *Lancet Infect Dis* 2001;1:11–20.

68. Tomori O. Yellow fever: the recurring plague. *Crit Rev Clin Lab Sci* 2004;41:391–427.

69. Van der SP, Gianella A, Pirard M, et al. Urbanisation of yellow fever in Santa Cruz, Bolivia. *Lancet* 1999;353:1558–1562.

70. Ross RW. The Newala epidemic III. The virus: isolation, pathogenic properties and relation to the epidemic. *J Hyg* 1956;54:177–191.

71. Thaung U, Ming CK, Swe T, Thein S. Epidemiological features of dengue and chikungunya infection in Burma. *SE Asian J Med Public Health* 1975;6:276–283.

72. Thaikruea L, Charearnsook O, Reanphumkarnkit S, et al. Chikungunya in Thailand: a re-emerging disease? *SE Asian J Trop Med Public Health* 1997;28:359–364.

73. Lam SK, Chua KB, Hooi PS, et al. Chikungunya infection: an emerging disease in Malaysia. *SE Asian J Trop Med Public Health* 2001;32:447–451.

74. Bright SW, Prozesky OW, De La, Harpe AL. Chikungunya virus infection: a retrospective study of 107 cases. *S Afr Med J* 1983;63:313–315.

75. Borgherini G, Pouheau P, Staikowsky F, et al. Outbreak of chikungunya on Reunion Island: early clinical and laboratory features in 157 adult patients. *Clin Infect Dis* 2007;44:1401–1407.

76. Tsetsarkin KA, Vanlandingham DL, McGee CE, et al, A single mutation in chikungunya virus affects vector specificity and epidemic potential. *PLoS Pathog* 2007;3:e201.

77. Vazelille M, Moutailler S, Coudrier D, et al. Two chikungunya isolates from the outbreak of La Reunion (Indian Ocean) exhibit different patterns of infection in the mosquito, *Aedes albopictus. PLoS One* 2007;2:e1168.

78. Rezza G, Nicoletti L, Angelini R. Infection with chikungunya virus in Italy: an outbreak in a temperate region. *Lancet* 2007;370:1840–1846.

79. Akahata W, Yang Z-Y, Anderson H, et al. A virus-like particle vaccine for epidemic chikungunya virus protects non-human primates against infection. *Nat Med* 2010;16:334–338.

80. Monath TP, Nasidi A. Should yellow fever vaccine be included in the expanded program of immunization in Africa? A cost-effectiveness analysis for Nigeria. *Am J Trop Med Hyg* 1993;48:274–299.

81. Schneider K. Uber epidemische meningitis serosa. *Wien Klin Wochenschr* 1931;44:350–352.

82. Kausler J, Kraus P, Moritsch H. Klinische and Virologisch-serologische. *Wein Klin Wochenschr* 1958;70:634–637.

83. Barrett PN, Dorner F, Plotkin SA. Tick-borne encephalitis vaccine. In: Plotkin SA, Orenstein WA Offit PA , eds. *Vaccines*. 5th ed. Philadelphia, PA: Saunders; 2008:841–856.

84. Gresikova M, Sekeyova M, Stupalova S, Necas S. Sheep milk-borne epidemic of tick-borne encephalitis in Slovakia. *Intervirology* 1975;5:57–61.

85. Klockmann U, Krivanec K, Stephenson JR, Hilfenhaus J. Protection against European isolates of tick-borne encephalitis virus after vaccination with a new tick-borne encephalitis vaccine. *Vaccine* 1991;9:210–212.

86. Kunz C, Heinz FX, Hofmann H. Immunogenicity and reactogenicity of a highly purified vaccine against tick-borne encephalitis. *J Med Virol* 1980;6:103–109.

87. Creech WB. St. Louis encephalitis in the United States, 1975. *J Infect Dis* 1977;135:1014–1016.

88. Shope RE. Arbovirus-related encephalitis. *Yale J Biol Med* 1980;53:93–99.

89. Earnest MP, Goolishian HA, Calverley JR, et al. Neurologic, intellectual, and psychologic sequelae following western encephalitis: a follow-up study of 35 cases. *Neurology* 1971;21:969–974.

90. Reimana CA, Hayes EB, Diguiseppi C, et al. Epidemiology of neuroinvasive arboviral disease in the United States, 1999–2007. *Am J Trop Med Hyg* 2008;79(6):974–979.

91. Mclean DM, Donohue WL. Powassan virus: isolation of virus from a fatal case of encephalitis. *Can Med Assoc J* 1959;80:708–711.

92. Lescure F-X, LeLoup G, Freilij H, et al. Chagas disease: changes in knowledge and management. *Lancet* 2010;10:556–570.

93. Moncayo A, Silverira AC. Current epidemiological trends for Chagas disease in Latin America and future challenges in epidemiology, surveillance and health policy. *Men Inst Oswaldo Crus* 2009;104:17–30.

94. Ekwanzala M, Pepin J, Khonde S, et al. In the heart of darkness: sleeping sickness in Zaire. *Lancet* 1996;348:1427–1430.

95. Barrett MP. The fall and rise of sleeping sickness. *Lancet* 1999;353:1113–1114.

96. Fevre EM, Picozzi K, Fyfe J, et al. A burgeoning epidemic of sleeping sickness in Uganda. *Lancet* 2005;366:745–747.

97. Moore AC. Human Africa trypanosomiasis: a reemerging public health threat. In: Scheld WM, Murray BE, Hughes JH, eds. *Emerging Infections*. Washington, DC: ASM Press; 2004:143–157.

98. Barrett MP, Borahmore RJS, Stich A, et al. The trypanosomiases. *Lancet* 2003;362: 1469–1480.

99. Human African trypanosomiases (sleeping sickness): epidemiological update. *Wkly Epidemiol Res* 2006;81:71–80.

100. Yu X-J, Liang M-F, Zhang S-Y et al. Fever with Trobocytopenia Associated with a Novel Bunyavirus in China *N Engl J Med* 2011;364:1523–1532.

101. Zhang Y-Z, He Y-W, Dai Y-A et al. Hemmorhagic Fever Caused by a Novel Bunyavirus in China: Pathogenesis and Correlates of a Fatal Outcome. *Clin Infect Dis* 2012;54:527–533.

102. Liu Y, Hu W, Wu J et al. Person-to-Person Transmission of Severe Fever with Thrombocytopenia Syndrome Virus. *Vector-Borne and Zoonotic Dis* 2012;12:156–160.

103. Gui Z, Liang M, Zhang Y et al. Person-to-Person Transmission of Severe Fever with Thrombocytopenia Syndrome Bunyavirus Through Blood Contact. *Clin Infect Dis* 2012;54:249–252.

104. McMullin LK, Folk SM, Kelly AJ et al. A New Phlebovirus Associated with Severe Febrile Illness in Missouri. *N Engl J Med* 2012;367:834–841.

105. Petersen LR and Fischer M. Unpredictable and Difficult to Control—the Adolescence of West Nile Virus. *N Engl J Med* 2012;367:1281–1284.

106. Reisen WK. Landscape epidemiology of vector-borne diseases. *Annu Rev Entomol* 2010;55:461–483.

CHAPTER 26

Lyme Disease

Diane E. Griffin

INTRODUCTION

In 1975, a concerned mother from Old Lyme, Connecticut (**Figure 26-1**), reported to the Connecticut State Health Department that 12 children in her small town of 5000 residents had an illness that had been diagnosed as juvenile rheumatoid arthritis. At approximately the same time, a mother from nearby East Haddam told physicians at the Yale Rheumatology Clinic in New Haven that there was an epidemic of arthritis occurring in her family and neighbors. In response to this information, investigators established a system of surveillance in the communities east of the Connecticut River to identify all cases of "Lyme arthritis" and determine the cause of this new disease, which was suspected to be of infectious etiology. Fifty-one individuals (39 children and 12 adults) with similar symptoms of arthritis were identified. Seventeen of the 39 children lived on just four country roads and, on those roads, 10% of children had the illness. Many families had more than one affected member.[1]

The disease these individuals described began with the sudden onset of pain and swelling in a knee or other large joint. The first attack of arthritis lasted about a week, but many individuals had recurrent

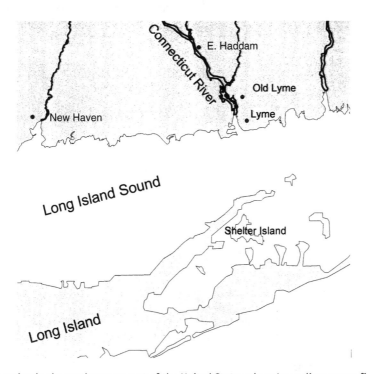

Figure 26-1 Map of the region in the northeastern part of the United States where Lyme disease was first recognized, where the epidemiology of the disease was defined and where Borrelia burgdorferi was first isolated from Ixodes scapularis ticks. Modified from Wallis et al, Erythema Chronicum Migrans and Lyme Arthritis: Field Study of Ticks. *Am J Epidemiol.* 108:323. © 1978 by permission of Oxford University Press.

attacks, usually involving large joints, with a similar distribution to that of initial attacks. More than half of those interviewed reported other flu-like symptoms suggestive of an infectious disease, such as headache, chills, fever, and malaise. In addition, 13 patients said that approximately one month before the arthritis began, they had noticed a red skin papule; this lesion had developed into a large annular lesion with red margins and central clearing that continued to expand. This unique skin lesion usually appeared on an extremity, was not painful, lasted 2–3 weeks, and was consistent with a previously described disease, erythema migrans (EM). EM was recognized primarily in Europe and had been associated with bites of the sheep tick *Ixodes ricinus*, but had not been associated with subsequent arthritis.[2] One patient remembered having been bitten by a tick at the site where the lesion developed.

These early data suggested that the disease often had manifestations other than, or in addition to, arthritis; was probably due to an infectious agent; was likely to be arthropod borne; and was potentially related to a previously described disease in Europe.[1]

CLINICAL PICTURE AND BIOLOGICAL INFORMATION

The Vector

Cases of Lyme disease occur primarily in the summer (**Figure 26-2**), indicating that the disease is seasonal and consistent with the possibility suggested by one of the original patients that it was tick borne. Therefore,

in the summers of 1976 and 1977, ticks and patients in the areas around the Connecticut River were studied.[3–5] A surveillance system was established using healthcare providers in the area around Old Lyme, Connecticut, including both sides of the river. To enhance surveillance, introductory lectures were conducted at three southern Connecticut hospitals, and specialists in dermatology, rheumatology, pediatrics, and internal medicine were contacted.

The broad scope of the surveillance program was intended to reduce bias in the collection of cases. A case was defined as a recent episode of EM or a diagnosis of Lyme arthritis. Forty-three new cases of Lyme disease were identified, mostly on the east side of the Connecticut River, where the incidence was 2.8 cases/1000 residents. The incidence was 0.1 case/1000 residents on the west side of the river—a difference of almost 30-fold. Nine of these 43 individuals (21%) remembered a tick bite at the site of the initial skin lesion within the 3 previous weeks. One individual had saved the tick, which was identified as the deer tick *Ixodes scapularis*.

For each case, 2 control participants were chosen from neighbors who lived within 150 feet of the case. In addition to matching on local environmental conditions, cases and controls were matched by age and sex. Epidemiologic investigation (**Table 26-1**) revealed that the patients with Lyme disease had more cats and farm animals and had more often noted ticks on their pets and themselves than their neighbors without disease.[4]

Analysis of the ticks collected showed that *Ixodes scapularis* (occasionally referred to as *I. dammini*) was much more abundant on the east than

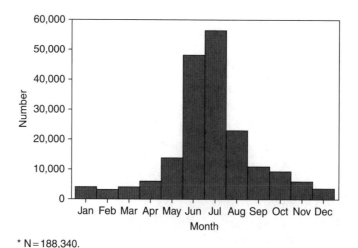

* N = 188,340.

Figure 26-2 Seasonal incidence of Lyme disease in the United States, 1992–2006. Reproduced from Bacon RM, Kugeler KJ, Mead PS, Centers for Disease Control and Prevention (CDC). Surveillance for Lyme disease—United States, 1992–2006. *MMWR* Surveill Summ. 2008;57:1–9.

on the west side of the Connecticut River. Immature *I. scapularis* were 13 times more abundant on white-footed mice (*Peromyscus leucopus*) and adult *I. scapularis* were 16 times more abundant on white-tailed deer (*Odocoileus virginianus*) in communities on the east side compared to the west side of the river (**Table 26-2**). Although no pathogen was isolated from the ticks or the people with Lyme disease, these data provided strong epidemiologic evidence for a tick-transmitted agent as the cause of Lyme disease.[5]

Extensive searches for the etiologic agent of Lyme disease using a wide variety of culture techniques proved unsuccessful. However, the agent was identified in the summer of 1981 when Willy Burgdorfer, a medical entomologist specializing in the study of ticks

as vectors of infectious agents, was analyzing ticks from various parts of Long Island, New York. As part of his studies, he noted the presence of spirochetes in the midguts of most *Ixodes* ticks collected on Shelter Island, which is located directly across Long Island Sound from the mouth of the Connecticut River (**Figure 26-1**). In an indirect immunofluorescent assay, these spirochetes were stained by sera from patients with Lyme disease, but not by sera from individuals without a history of Lyme disease,[6] suggesting an etiologic link to the disease. In retrospect, organisms morphologically characteristic of spirochetes had been associated with EM in Europe in 1948,[7] but had not become accepted as the EM infectious agent. Subsequently, the Lyme disease spirochete was isolated from the blood and tissues of patients with Lyme disease[8,9] and was identified as a new species of *Borrelia, Borrelia burgdorferi*.[10]

I. scapularis, like most hard ticks, has a complicated life cycle that requires 2 years to complete and includes progression through the stages of egg, six-legged larvae, eight-legged immature nymph and the eight-legged reproductively mature adult tick (**Figure 26-3**). At each stage, a blood meal is required for morphogenesis and progression to the next stage. Adult ticks lay eggs in the early spring that hatch to become larvae. *Ixodes,* like all tick species, walk to the ends of grasses and tree leaves, where they "quest," front legs waving in the air, until a suitable host brushes past them (**Figure 26-4**). Ticks do not fly, hop, drop, or jump to their next meal. The larvae feed once and then rest for the remainder of the year. The following spring, nymphs emerge and feed once.

The white-footed mouse is a primary host for immature *I. scapularis* and develops persistent infection with *B. burgdorferi*,[11] but other mammals,

| Table 26-1 | Risk Factors for Contracting Lyme Disease: Comparison of Patients with Their Neighbors, Connecticut, 1977 |

Risk Factor	Cases (%)	Neighbors (%)	Statistical Significance (P value)
Male	53	44	ns
Rural environment	47	45	ns
Activities in woods	77	61	ns
Farm animals	26	11	<.05
Pets	86	81	ns
Cats	63	39	<.01
Ticks on pets	70	27	<.0001
Tick bites	44	25	<.05
Mosquito bites	72	70	ns

Reproduced from Steere et al. Erythema Chronicum Migrans and Lyme Arthritis: Epidemiologic Evidence for a Tick Vector. *Am. J. Epidemiol.* 108(4): 317. © 1978 by permission of Oxford University Press.

| Table 26-2 | Numbers and Types of Ticks Collected from Various Sources East and West of the Connecticut River, 1977 |

	West			East		
Source	Number	Ixodes	Dermacentor	Number	Ixodes	Dermacentor
Humans	21	8	37	27	33	20
Dogs	26	2	78	16	27	96
Cats	10	12	17	4	3	5
White-footed mice	143	29	26	197	498	143
Other mammals	10	3	15	9	9	77
Dragging	0	0	0	1	8	43
Totals	210	54	173	254	578	384

Reproduced from Wallis et al, Erythema Chronicum Migrans and Lyme Arthritis: Field Study of Ticks. *Am J Epidemiol.* 108:325. © 1978 by permission of Oxford University Press.

Figure 26-3 Adult and nymph *Ixodes scapularis* tick. Courtesy of CDC/Michael L. Levin, Ph. D.

Figure 26-4 *Ixodes,* as do all tick species, walk to the end of grasses and tree leaves where they "quest," front legs waving in the air, until a suitable host brushes past them. Courtesy of CDC/Anna Perez.

reptiles, and birds, which are variably susceptible to persistent infection with *B. burgdorferi,* are also fed upon by *I. scapularis* ticks. Both nymphs and adults will feed on humans and can transmit Lyme disease.[12] After the nymph feeds, the adult emerges and feeds once in the summer/fall. Usually, adults feed on large mammals such as domestic pets, humans, and deer. Adults mate preferably on white-tailed deer. The male tick dies, while the female overwinters and lays eggs the following spring.

Interstage and vertical transmission of *B. burgdorferi* is rare (less than 0.1%), so eggs are not commonly infected.[13] The larvae may acquire the spirochete at the first feeding, and tick saliva contains proteins that facilitate acquisition of *Borrelia* from an infected vertebrate host.[13] The chance of the first host being infected depends on its susceptibility to *B. burgdorferi* infection and on being previously bitten by an infected tick. The white-footed mouse,

for example, has many litters of pups each year. Because vertical transmission is rare, mice infected in the previous year will not pass their infection on to the next generation. Instead, nymphal ticks, which emerge in the spring, are responsible for transmitting *B. burgdorferi* to the next generation of mice. If nymphal forms of the tick emerge and feed before the larvae hatch, as is the case in the northern United States and Canada, host populations have a higher prevalence than in regions where larvae may hatch and feed before the nymphs, which is the case in the southern United States. This order of feeding, combined with feeding on *B. burgdorferi*-incompetent hosts in the southeast United States, explains the high prevalence of *B. burgdorferi* in *Ixodes* ticks from the northeastern United States (50%) as compared to the southeastern United States (1%).[14]

The distribution of *I. scapularis* is probably determined by the need for high humidity and availability of host species, particularly deer.[15] Populations of this tick are abundant in the United States in the northeast and upper Midwest and in southern Canada.[15,16] Related ticks—*I. pacificus,* the western black-legged tick; *I. ricinus,* the sheep tick; and *I. persulcatus*—are the primary vectors for Lyme disease along the Pacific Coast of North America, in Europe, and in Asia.[14,15,17] The enzootic cycles of *B. burgdorferi* on the Pacific coast and in the southeastern United States are maintained primarily between reservoir rodents and species of *Ixodes* ticks (e.g., *I. spinipalpis, I. affinis, I. minor*) that rarely bite humans.[18] The immature forms of bridge vector ticks that do bite humans (e.g., *I. scapularis, I. pacificus*) have a variety of suitable hosts including lizards, which are not susceptible to *B. burgdorferi,*[19] resulting in a low penetrance of *B. burgdorferi* in these regions.[14]

The Infectious Agent

Borrelia are motile, helical, gram-negative spirochetal bacteria that are maintained in zoonotic cycles involving a variety of wild mammals and birds as reservoirs. By definition, reservoir species are hosts that are commonly infected with an organism and remain infectious for the vector for prolonged periods of time.[11,20] For *B. burgdorferi,* this is determined largely by ability of the host complement system to inactivate the spirochetes.[21–23] *B. burgdorferi* has been isolated from the blood of white-footed mice (*Peromyscus leucopus*), which are abundant, highly susceptible to persistent infection, and a preferred host of *I. scapularis* at early stages of the life cycle (**Figure 26-5**), and do not become resistant to repeated tick feeding.[11,18,24] Vector competence describes the inherent ability of an

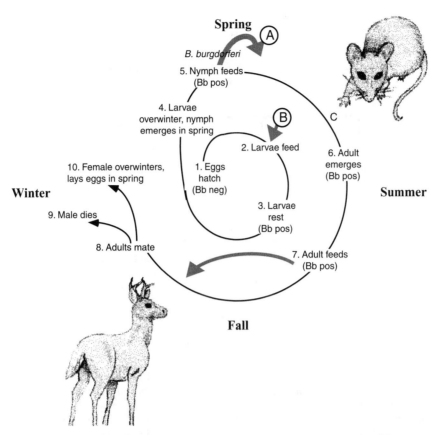

Figure 26-5 Life cycle of *Ixodes scapularis* indicating principal seasonal activity and hosts. The tick must overwinter twice and take 3 blood meals on two different vertebrate hosts (white-tailed deer [B] and white-footed mice [C]) to complete the life cycle. Ticks become infected by feeding on mice infected with *Borrelia burgdorferi* (Bb), the reservoir species. Ticks remain infected and can transmit infection to uninfected mice and to humans. © 1999, Carolyn Masters Williams.

arthropod to become infected with the organism and subsequently to transmit the infectious agent to a new vertebrate host. Larval ticks acquire *B. burgdorferi* when they feed on infected mice, persistent infection is established in the tick, and all subsequent stages of the vector remain infected unless *Borrelia* in the midgut are inactivated through subsequent feeding on an incompetent host.[20,22,25] Infected nymphal ticks then transmit *B. burgdorferi* to uninfected mice. Data indicate that mice are the most important reservoir species for maintaining the invertebrate cycle of infection and that the abundance of this host in endemic areas correlates with the risk of infection.[26] Deer, although important for the tick life cycle, have blood that can inactivate *Borrelia* and are dead-end hosts.[15,22]

The genome of *B. burgdorferi* is small (fewer than 1.5 megabases) and consists of an unusual linear chromosome and more than 20 linear and circular plasmids that encode a variety of virulence factors, including lipoproteins.[27] The structure includes an inner membrane, an outer membrane, and periplasmic flagella. The primary outer surface lipoproteins (Osp) vary antigenically between strains and can undergo phase shifts as an important means of organism adaptation to growth in vertebrate and invertebrate hosts.[28–30] OspA, which has multiple distinct antigenic variants, and OspB are encoded on a bicistronic operon and expressed on the surface of spirochetes within the midgut of unfed ticks. OspA binds to a tick receptor TROPSA and, along with OspB, promotes adherence and survival in the tick midgut that is essential for *B. burgdorferi* colonization.[31–34] When infected nymphs take a blood meal, the *Borrelia* cease expression of OspA, thus releasing them from the gut, and begin to express OspC (**Figure 26-6**). This switch is induced in part by the increase in temperature and decrease in pH in the tick midgut associated with taking a blood meal.[35]

Infected ticks have several hundred *B. burgdorferi* in the gut lumen. When a blood meal is taken, the organisms begin to proliferate and increase their numbers more than a hundred-fold. The members of this expanded population of *Borrelia* cross the midgut epithelium into the hemolymph, and then enter the salivary glands. It takes approximately 60 hours after tick attachment for sufficient numbers of organisms

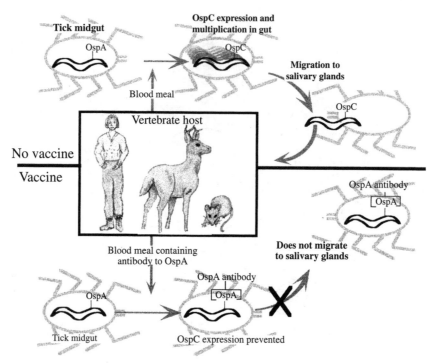

Figure 26-6 Schematic diagram of the changes in the expression of Osp proteins by *B. burgdorferi* (Bb) in infected ticks after taking a blood meal from an unvaccinated individual (top) and an individual previously vaccinated against OspA (bottom). When the blood meal contains no OspA antibody *B. burgdorferi* is induced to express OspC, multiply and spread to the salivary gland of the tick which allows transmission to the host on which the tick is feeding. When the blood meal contains antibody to OspA, *B. burgdorferi* expression of OspC is inhibited and neither multiplication nor spread to the salivary glands occurs. © 1999, Carolyn Masters Williams.

to be present in salivary glands for infection of a new host.[36–39] OspC is the primary surface antigen expressed by *B. burgdorferi* in vertebrate hosts and is important for successful infection and subsequent dissemination.[40–44] This lipoprotein is polymorphic, with specific versions of OspC being associated with infection of different vertebrate hosts and potentially with severity of human disease.[29,45–48]

Other lipoproteins expressed by *B. burgdorferi* that are important during tick feeding and host infection include proteins that bind complement regulatory factors in host plasma. *Borrelia* are susceptible to immobilization and lysis through the alternative complement pathway.[21] Resistance to complement-dependent lysis depends on the ability of *Borrelia* to bind factor H and/or factor H-like proteins in the blood meal through complement regulatory-acquiring surface proteins (CRASPs). Complement regulatory factors in host plasma control the alternative pathway of complement activation at the level of C3b and prevent lysis by complement bound to a surface.[49] *B. burgdorferi* produces three families of CRASPs that confer resistance to complement present in plasma.[50–52] This circumvention of innate immunity allows persistent infection in the vertebrate host and prevents lysis in the tick's gut.

Eighteen genospecies of *B. burgdorferi sensu lato* are now recognized, of which three—*B. burgdorferi sensu stricto*, *B. afzelii*, and *B. garinii*—are associated with human disease.[53] Each of these genospecies has a different reservoir host and is associated with different clinical manifestations of infection.[54,55] An important determinant of vertebrate host and tick infection is susceptibility of the *Borrelia* genospecies to complement-dependent lysis.[22] For instance, sera from lizards and deer can lyse *B. burgdorferi s.s.* and *B. afzelii*, while sera from mice and humans cannot. In contrast, *B. garinii* is lysed by serum from mice, but not by serum from birds, the reservoir host for this genospecies.[23]

CLINICAL MANIFESTATIONS

Figure 26-7 graphically summarizes the clinical manifestations of Lyme disease.

Early Disease

As noted earlier, *B. burgdorferi* is introduced into the skin of a susceptible host by the saliva from an infected tick. The earliest manifestation of infection is usually a slowly expanding skin lesion that appears

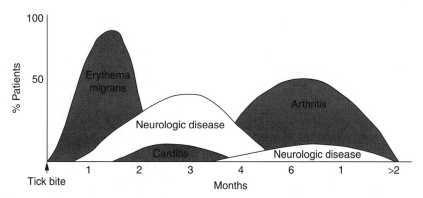

Figure 26-7 Schematic drawing of the clinical phases of Lyme disease indicating the approximate percentage of infected individuals that will develop the various manifestations of infection if left untreated. © Diane E Griffin.

within days to weeks at the site of the bite. This lesion starts as a red macule or papule. The later appearance of the lesion, which may become very large, is characteristic of an EM lesion with an erythematous border and a clearing center. The lesion is usually warm, but not particularly painful or pruritic. *B. burgdorferi* can be isolated from this lesion.[8,55] This stage of Lyme disease is often accompanied by flu-like symptoms including fever, chills, malaise, stiff neck, and headache,[17,56] and *B. burgdorferi* can often be isolated from the blood.[8,9,57] Even without treatment, these early signs and symptoms generally resolve within 3–4 weeks.

Secondary Disease

The secondary disseminated phase of the disease usually occurs within 1–6 months after exposure and may be manifested as more generalized EM lesions, myocarditis, or neurological disease.[17] Dissemination to form multiple secondary annular skin lesions is usually accompanied by more intense systemic manifestations with severe lethargy, encephalopathy, myalgias, generalized lymphadenopathy, and splenomegaly. A second type of skin eruption, known as lymphocytoma or lymphadenosis benigna cutis, may also be seen, particularly in Europe. This condition consists of a solitary red or violaceous lesion most commonly located on the ear lobe in children or on the nipple in adults. It may be accompanied by regional lymphadenopathy as well as other manifestations of Lyme disease.[58] Carditis occurs in 5–16% of untreated individuals with disseminated Lyme disease and presents with palpitations associated with atrioventricular conduction abnormalities and occasionally ST-segment and T-wave changes on the electrocardiogram. These signs and symptoms usually resolve within 6 weeks, but temporary pacing may be required.[59,60]

B. burgdorferi frequently invades the central nervous system,[61] and neurological complications occur in approximately 10–15% of untreated patients. These complications include meningitis, meningoencephalitis, cranial nerve palsies, and radiculitis. Systemic symptoms may be present, but skin lesions and lymphadenopathy have usually resolved by this point in the disease course. Approximately half of the patients with meningitis have some symptoms of encephalitis, such as depressed consciousness, impaired concentration, seizures, ataxia, or behavioral abnormalities. The most characteristic neurological abnormalities are cranial and peripheral neuropathies, most commonly Bell's palsy.[62,63]

Late Disease

The later stages of Lyme disease occur weeks to months after the initial infection. The most common manifestation is arthritis, which may be monoarticular or oligoarticular, and which occurs in approximately 60% of untreated patients. Large joints, particularly the knees, are most frequently affected, but occasionally involvement of small joints is also noted. The arthritic attacks last weeks to months and can be recurrent over years.[64] *B. burgdorferi* can often be detected in synovial fluid aspirated from affected joints. Chronic arthritis develops in a subset of patients with a genetic susceptibility to this complication and probably has an autoimmune component.[65] OspA is upregulated in inflammatory foci and OspA-reactive T cells are found in the joint fluid from patients with Lyme arthritis resistant to treatment.[66,67]

Late Lyme disease can also have a characteristic skin eruption, acrodermatitis chronica atrophicans, which is most commonly seen in elderly European women infected with *B. afzelii*. This chronic skin disease begins insidiously on the distal portions of the extremities with redness and swelling, followed by atrophy and ultimately loss of fingers and toes. The skin disease is associated with persistent infection and is often accompanied by joint deformities or polyneuropathy.[68,69] Neurological manifestations of late

Lyme disease are less well defined but include chronic progressive leukoencephalitis (which may resemble multiple sclerosis and is seen most often in Europe associated with *B. garinii* infection), generalized encephalopathy, and generalized polyneuropathy.[68,70,71]

DIAGNOSIS

The diagnosis of Lyme disease during the early phases of the disease is based primarily on the characteristic clinical presentation. The history of tick exposure is often helpful, although because of the small size of the tick, the bite may not be recognized by the patient. Therefore, the season of the year and a history of living or vacationing in a known endemic area are important information. The EM rash is characteristic and usually sufficient for the diagnosis of primary disease.[58,72] The clinical presentation of secondary disease, especially the combination of meningitis and cranial or peripheral neuropathy, should suggest Lyme disease as the leading diagnosis. Culturing the organism provides a definitive diagnosis, but is positive primarily early in disease.[17,73-75] Borrelia DNA can be detected by polymerase chain reaction (PCR) in synovial fluid, cerebrospinal fluid (CSF), and blood with varying levels of success.[73,74,76]

Antibody to *B. burgdorferi* develops slowly after infection, and *Borrelia*-specific IgM may not be present early in disease.[77,78] IgG antibody to the organism, as measured by enzyme immunoassay or immunoblot, is usually, but not always, present at the time of development of carditis, neurologic disease, or disseminated skin lesions. In neurologic disease, antibody may also be present in CSF.

Currently, a two-tier approach that combines enzyme immunoassay with a confirming immunoblot is recommended for serologic diagnosis.[78] Enzyme immunoassays using recombinant or peptide antigens (e.g., VlsE, C6) are more specific than those using whole-cell sonicates of *B. burgdorferi* and may allow use of a single test.[57,79,80]

Other Diseases Associated with Lyme Disease

In addition to those symptoms and conditions associated with Lyme disease, a wide range of conditions have been suggested to be associated with infection with *B. burgdorferi*; these conditions are often referred to as post-Lyme disease syndrome or chronic Lyme disease.[68,81] Although there are no scientific data to support the claims, chronic fatigue syndrome, dyslexia, and other degenerative, inflammatory, and neuropsychiatric conditions have been

linked to Lyme disease. Epidemiologic research studies designed to examine the risk of disease for specific populations have not been able to supply answers to individuals who want to know the cause of their symptoms. Several characteristics of Lyme disease have encouraged speculative claims about its implications: it is an emerging disease; symptoms of Lyme-associated disease can occur long after the initial infection; definitive tests for its diagnosis are lacking; and the high prevalence of the disease in endemic areas ensures that there are persons with both a diagnosis of Lyme disease and another condition. Only continued epidemiologic investigation coupled with improvements in diagnosis will ensure that these questions are satisfactorily answered.

TREATMENT

The generally accepted treatment for early Lyme disease, including facial nerve palsy and mild carditis, for most adults is orally administered tetracycline, usually in the form of doxycycline, amoxicillin, or cefuroxime axetil, and as amoxicillin or cefuroxime axetil for pregnant or lactating women and young children.[68,82] Treatment usually lasts for 10–21 days, and has several benefits: it shortens the course of EM; greatly reduces the later manifestations of arthritis, carditis, and neurological disease; and results in a decrease in the levels of antibody to OspC and VlsE.[68,83-86] Patients with more severe cardiac or neurologic disease or with arthritis are often treated with intravenous antibiotics, usually ceftriaxone or cefuroxime for 14 days, although oral doxycycline may be sufficient.[68,87] Symptoms of pain or fatigue that persist after treatment do not benefit from repeated or prolonged antibiotic treatment,[88] although this remains a matter of discussion.[89] Chronic arthritis that is unresponsive to antibiotic therapy is associated with an immune response to OspA and is autoimmune in nature.[65-67]

EPIDEMIOLOGY

Lyme disease is endemic in several areas of the United States (**Figure 26-8**), Canada, eastern and central Europe, and Russia.[16,90] Although this disease was first recognized in 1975, *B. burgdorferi* is not new to North America or Europe. In retrospect, at least one case of Lyme disease occurred on Cape Cod in 1962,[91] and in 1970 the case of a Wisconsin physician who developed EM at the site of a tick bite was reported.[92] Museum ticks collected in Europe in

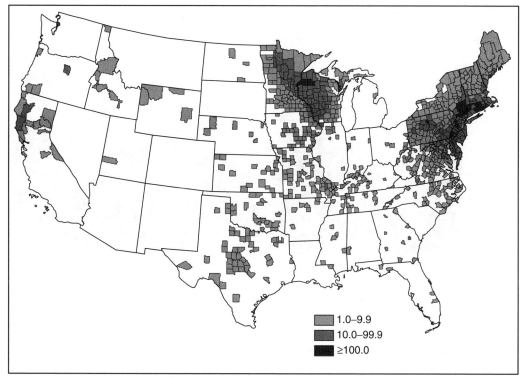

*Per 100,000 population.

Figure 26-8   Map of the United States with average rate of Lyme disease by county for 1992–2006. Reproduced from Bacon RM, Kugeler KJ, Mead PS, Centers for Disease Control and Prevention (2008). Surveillance for Lyme disease—United States, 1992–2006. *MMWR* 2008;57:1–9.

1884 and on Long Island in the 1940s were positive when examined by PCR for *B. burgdorferi* DNA,[93,94] and it is likely that the organism has been present in these locations for many centuries.[95] However, cases of Lyme borreliosis have been increasing in both America (**Figure 26-9**) and Europe.[96,97]

The incidence of Lyme disease and seropositivity as evidence of prior infection varies dramatically between geographic regions (Figure 26-8), which undoubtedly correlates with the prevalence of *Ixodes* ticks that feed on humans, the proportion of these ticks that are infected, the virulence of the *Borrelia*, and the opportunity for human exposure to infected ticks.[98–101] Several possible reasons for the emergence of Lyme disease have been examined. There is little evidence that climate change in the form of increasing temperatures is an important factor.[102] Nevertheless, weather can play a role because ticks require a moist environment and precipitation in the spring affects tick abundance by increasing nymph survival.[103,104]

United States

Those areas of the United States in which frequent transmission of *B. burgdorferi* to humans is observed include the Northeast and upper Midwest. However,

a zoonotic cycle is maintained in many other parts of the United States, and cases of Lyme disease are seen by physicians in many regions because of occasional transmission and summertime vacation travel to areas of high risk. Essentially all cases of Lyme disease in North America are due to infection with *B. burgdorferi sensu stricto*, although more than 12 OspC sequence types have regional heterogeneity in their distribution.[101,105] The ratio of apparent-to-inapparent infections is 1:1.[91] The age distribution is bimodal, with peaks in children from 5 to 14 years of age (8.6 cases/100,000 population/year) and adults 50 to 59 years of age (7.8 cases/100,000 population/year).[97] Males and females are approximately equally affected (53% male).[97]

In the United States, the vector for human infection in the Northeast, Southeast, and Midwest is *I. scapularis*, while along the Pacific coast it is *I. pacificus*. Transmission occurs primarily in the spring and early summer, when ticks are most abundant and active. Disease follows a few weeks later (Figure 26-7). In some areas, virtually 100% of the ixodid ticks are infected with the Lyme disease *Borrelia*. The incidence of Lyme disease has been steadily increasing since its recognition in 1975 (Figure 26-9), and the zones of

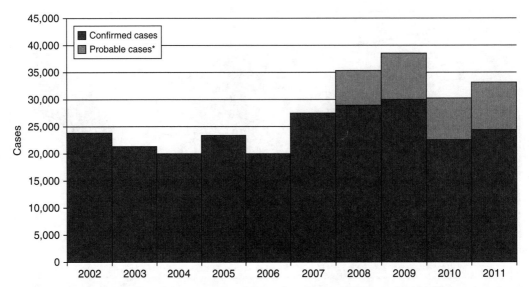

The graph displays the number of reported cases of Lyme disease from 2002 through 2011. The number of confirmed cases ranged from a low of 19,804 in 2004 to high of 29,959 in 2009.

Figure 26-9 Numbers of reported cases of Lyme disease in the United States from 2002–2011. Reproduced from the Centers for Disease Control and Prevention Centers for Disease Control and Prevention National Center for Emerging and Zoonotic Infectious Diseases (2012). Lyme Disease. http://www.cdc.gov/lyme/stats/chartstables/casesbyyear.html. Updated September 12, 2012. Accessed November 27, 2012.

relatively high incidence are expanding. Lyme disease is currently the most common arthropod-borne disease in the United States.

The numbers of cases fluctuate from year to year. In the Northeast, this variation is likely linked to the fluctuating abundance of white-footed mice, a primary host for *I. scapularis* and the primary reservoir of *B. burgdorferi* (**Exhibit 26-01**). An important food source for mice is acorns, which are naturally produced in increased abundance every 2–5 years. Another food source for mice is the pupae of gypsy moths. Recent experimental studies have shown that in oak forests in the eastern United States, defoliation by gypsy moths and the risk of Lyme disease are determined by local interactions between acorn abundance and the numbers of white-footed mice, moths, deer and ticks.[106] Moth increases are caused by reductions in mouse density that occur when there are no acorns; during those times of hardship for mice, moth pupae are more likely to survive. Conversely, an increase in acorns increases the numbers of mice and the densities of *I. scapularis*, predicting increased numbers of cases of Lyme disease.

On the Pacific coast and in the Southeast, the transmission cycle for *B. burgdorferi* differs from that seen on the Atlantic coast. In California and Oregon, western gray squirrels—rather than white-footed mice—are the primary reservoir hosts,[107] and *I. spinipalpis*, a non-human-biting tick, maintains

B. burgdorferi in the enzootic cycle. The primary vector of *B. burgdorferi* to humans is *I. pacificus*,[108] which feeds on a wide variety of hosts; thus only 1–2% of these ticks become infected.[109] In the Southeast, cotton rats, eastern woodrats, and cotton mice are reservoir hosts, and *I. minor* and *I. affinis* are important enzootic vectors that rarely feed on humans.[18,110] The primary vector of *B. burgdorferi* to humans is *I. scapularis*, as in the Northeast, but many fewer are infected.

Europe and Asia

The EM skin lesion was first described in Sweden in 1909.[2] The distribution of EM disease in Europe correlates with the distribution of *I. ricinus*, the transmitting vector, and extends from north and central Europe into eastern Europe and Russia.[90,111] *I. persulcatus* is the most important vector in Asian Russia, China, and Japan.[54] Strains of *Borrelia* causing infection in Europe are much more varied than in North America and include all three genospecies of *B. burgdorferi sensu lato* (*B. burgdorferi s. s.*, *B. garinii*, and *B. afzelii*),[54] while in Asia, *B. garinii* and *B. afzelii* are the most common pathogens. The major reservoir hosts for *B. afzelii* are *Apodemus* mice and *Clethrionomys* voles, while *B. garinii* is maintained predominantly in a bird–tick cycle.[54]

In studies performed in southern Sweden, where 10–30% of ticks are infected with *Borrelia*, the

Exhibit 26-1	The White-Footed Mouse

Published in 1967, long before the importance of the mouse would be recognized in the transmission of Lyme disease, this description by Roger Caras predicts some of the difficulties faced in control of Lyme disease:

- The mouse will build multiple nests, foiling attempts to line the nest with insecticide-impregnated cotton balls.
- There will be fluctuations in the number of mice, and thus fluctuations in the incidence of Lyme disease.
- Eradication of the mouse is unlikely.

Caras's text also reminds us that understanding the transmission of infectious diseases may take us far from the clinics, laboratories, and computer models in which epidemiologic research can become entrenched:

Their habits range from the arid Southwest to the forests of New England. Despite the northern latitudes to which they have spread, none of them hibernate. They may nest in the ground or adapt one that they find. They are very clean about themselves, frequently washing and grooming, but they are very careless about their nests—so careless that they must often abandon a nest and construct another every few weeks.

The white-footed mouse is not a quiet animal and has many things to say to and about the world around him. He has various high-pitched squeaks, trills, and chitters for a variety of occasions, but he is most dramatic when he buzzes. His shrill buzz can last for five to ten seconds and can be heard up to fifty feet away. When really excited, he drums his forefeet in a wild fury.

The white-footed mice are not only nocturnal; they generally won't move around even on bright moonlit nights. For them, the dark world is the only safe one. The white-footed mouse is a very important link in the chain that connects the meat-eaters to the world of vegetable matter. Almost every animal that will eat meat (even just on occasion) hunts the white-footed mouse. Therefore, the mouse is always on guard. He survives as an individual by his wits (but usually doesn't get to see old age, however witty he may be) and as a species by his fecundity.

The population of white-footed mice in a given area runs in cycles. In the long-term cycle, the population will hit a peak every three or five years. On the short term, there are peak months. When white-footed mice are scarce, other animals suffer as the predators look elsewhere to meet their needs. Appetite is not cyclical.

Breeding can be year round if the winters are mild. Litter size varies from one to nine, with three or four being usual. A healthy female in an area where the food supply is good can deliver ten or eleven litters a year. Young born in the early spring can breed before the first day of summer. And so, prey as the predators might, there will always be more white-footed mice to carry on.

Reprinted with permission from *North American Mammals: Fur-Bearing Animals of the United States and Canada,* Copyright © 1967 Roger G. Caras.

highest rates of EM were found to be among children 4–9 years old and adults 60–74 years old. There was no difference in the incidence between males and females. In children, tick bites were more often about the head and neck than in adults, and bites in these regions increased the risk of neuroborreliosis.[112]

EXPOSURE/RISK FACTORS

Because Lyme disease is transmitted by ticks, it is not surprising that living, working, or vacationing in a woodsy, rural environment increases an individual's risk of developing this disease.[98] In a particular location, the risk of infection is determined by the density of infected nymphal ticks.[113] The probability of contracting Lyme disease after a tick bite in an area of endemic disease ranges from 0.012 to 0.05.[114] Once exposed to an infected tick, the likelihood of becoming infected with *B. burgdorferi* depends on how long the tick is attached. In mice, transmission of infection requires attachment for at least 36 hours and is most efficient between 48 and 72 hours.[36,38] In humans,

the incidence of Lyme disease is significantly higher (20% versus 1.1%) if the duration of attachment is greater than 72 hours.[39] This need for prolonged attachment is explained by the time required for the *Borrelia* in the tick midgut to shift from expressing OspA to OspC, multiply, and migrate to the tick salivary glands in sufficient numbers for transmission (Figure 26-6).

CONTROL MEASURES

Prevention of a vector-borne zoonotic disease such as Lyme disease in humans can take the form of controlling the reservoir host species (mice), controlling the host species required for maintenance of the vector (deer), controlling the vector (ticks), preventing human exposure to the vector, or prophylaxis or immunization of humans against infection.[115–117] Essentially all of these approaches have been or are being explored as mechanisms to prevent Lyme disease.

Control of reservoir species is difficult. *Peromyscus* populations fluctuate with food supply,[106] but the abundance of food in woodlands is not really amenable to human control measures. Furthermore, the diversity of hosts for the immature forms of the tick make elimination of these hosts unfeasible. The availability of diverse hosts of varying ability to serve as reservoirs will decrease the likelihood of tick infection and prevalence of disease in a community.[118]

Deer are an important host for adult ticks, as they are the preferred site for mating. Deer populations have burgeoned in many regions, a trend that is associated with increased *I. scapularis* populations.[119] Several studies have shown that decreasing or eliminating deer populations can reduce the numbers of infected ticks after several years.[119–121]

Strategies for directly reducing the tick populations have been successful in limited areas. Acaricides have been delivered to white-footed mice in cotton balls or bait boxes scattered over a wooded area or topically to deer at four-poster feeding stations. These approaches have resulted in as much as 95% reduction of *I. scapularis* populations in treated areas.[113,122] Another approach has been to trap and vaccinate mice with OspA to prevent infection. This approach decreased tick infection by 19–23%.[123] A long-term effect on infected *I. scapularis* populations using either of these approaches requires a sustained effort that is expensive and impractical for large areas.

Preventing exposure to the vector is inexpensive and universally applicable. Wearing light clothing so ticks are visible, avoiding grass and shrubbery where questing ticks are likely to be waiting, applying insecticide, and limiting access to skin surfaces by wearing a long-sleeved shirt and long pants tucked into socks all decrease the likelihood of tick bite. Daily "tick checks" will result in removal of ticks before the 36–48 hours of attachment needed to transmit *B. burgdorferi*. These preventive measures are reasonable and effective when the risk of exposure to ticks arises only during certain activities.[124,125] However, residents of rural areas, or those with wooded areas near their homes, are potentially exposed to ticks every day. In areas of the country where infection rates in ticks are also high, such as the northeastern United States from Maryland to Maine, people may be at risk of Lyme disease whenever they are outside. With summertime temperatures exceeding 80°F, long-sleeved shirts and long pants are not a realistic solution. In the spring, when the nymphal forms of the tick are active, daily "tick checks" are also difficult because the nymphal tick is both light colored and minute.

Antibiotic prophylaxis after exposure to ticks has been studied by several investigators and is effective, but generally not recommended.[126] An analysis of cost-effectiveness concluded that empiric treatment for anyone with a tick bite is indicated if the probability of infection is greater than 0.036. Under this formula, prophylaxis is not recommended in any region where the prevalence of infected ticks is less than 10%.[114] A trial of antimicrobial prophylaxis (amoxicillin for 10 days) concluded that even in highly endemic areas, the risk of infection is so low that the number of adverse reactions to antimicrobial treatment was equivalent to, or greater than, the number of cases prevented.[127] Another study showed that a single dose of doxycycline within 72 hours of exposure prevented EM, but side effects occurred in 6–8 individuals for every case of Lyme disease prevented.[128]

VACCINE

A vaccine based on the OspA protein—the Osp expressed by *B. burgdorferi* in the infected unfed tick—was licensed in the United States in 1998. Antibody to OspA in the blood meal blocks *Borrelia* development in the tick and the subsequent transmission of *B. burgdorferi* from the vector to the host (Figure 26-6) and protects mice and humans from *B. burgdorferi* infection.[129–131] Thus the OspA vaccine is a transmission-blocking Lyme disease vaccine. Studies of OspA vaccines reported vaccine efficacy of 76–100% after three doses with only mild to moderate side effects in the vaccine recipients.[130,131] However, vaccine acceptance by the public and by physicians was limited, and the product was withdrawn from the market in 2002. Reasons for its removal from marketing included concerns about OspA-induced autoimmune disease, low risk of Lyme disease in most parts of the country, need for frequent booster injections, and high cost compared to antibiotic treatment of early infection.[95,132,133]

New vaccines are under development. Candidate proteins for transmission-blocking vaccines have been identified in tick saliva;[134–136] in addition, proteins, including OspC, that induce protective immunity in vertebrate hosts have been identified in *B. burgdorferi*.[137,138] It is likely that a new vaccine will employ multiple immunogens.[139]

CONCLUSIONS

Lyme disease is an example of a zoonotic vector-borne disease. Its "emergence" as a cause of human disease is a product of human exposure to an existing natural transmission cycle. Analyses of museum specimens have shown that *Borrelia* have infected *Ixodid* ticks for decades and are not new pathogens.

The factors that have contributed to the emergence of Lyme disease are instead changes in the host–vector–environment relationship. The environmental movement has brought increased attention to preservation of natural areas and increased occupation of suburban, semi-rural housing. Deer populations have burgeoned since they were almost eliminated from the United States at the turn of the century. As deer are fringe woodland dwellers, they have adapted well to the suburban environment. The availability of deer as the preferred mating host has in turn allowed for an increase in the number of ticks. Humans intrude on the sylvan cycle of Lyme disease when they camp, hike, and otherwise enjoy the woodland areas around them.

The epidemiologic questions surrounding the late complications of Lyme disease are difficult to answer. It is difficult to determine which diseases are truly associated with *B. burgdorferi*, as the length of time between infection and disease makes causation difficult to prove.

• • • REFERENCES

1. Steere AC, Malawista SE, Snydman DR. Lyme arthritis: an epidemic of oligoarticular arthritis in children and adults in three Connecticut communities. *Arthritis Rheum* 1977;29:7–17.

2. Afzelius A. Erythema chronicum migrans. *Acta Dermatol Venereol* 1921;2:120–125.

3. Steere AC, Malawista SE, Hardin JA, et al. Erythema chronicum migrans and Lyme arthritis: the enlarging clinical spectrum. *Ann Intern Med* 1977;86:685–698.

4. Steere AC, Broderick TF, Malawista SE. Erythema chronicum migrans and Lyme arthritis: epidemiologic evidence for a tick vector. *Am J Epidemiol* 1978;108:312–321.

5. Wallis RC, Brown SE, Kloter KO, Main AJ. Erythema chronicum migrans and Lyme arthritis: field study of ticks. *Am J Epidemiol* 1978;108:322–327.

6. Burgdorfer W, Barbour AG, Hayes SF, et al. Lyme disease: a tick borne spirochetosis? *Science* 1982;216:1317–1319.

7. Lennhoff C. Spirochaetes in aetiologically obscure diseases. *Acta Dermatol Venereol* 1948;28:295–324.

8. Steere AC, Grodzicki RL, Kornblatt AN, et al. The spirochetal etiology of Lyme disease. *N Engl J Med* 1983;308:733–740.

9. Benach JL, Bosler EM, Hanrahan JP, et al. Spirochetes isolated from the blood of two patients with Lyme disease. *N Engl J Med* 1983;308:740–742.

10. Johnson RC, Schmid GP, Hyde FW, et al. *Borrelia burgdorferi* sp. *nov.*: etiologic agent of Lyme disease. *Int J System Bacteriol* 1984;34:496–497.

11. Bunikis J, Tsao J, Luke CJ, et al. *Borrelia burgdorferi* infection in a natural population of *Peromyscus leucopus* mice: a longitudinal study in an area where Lyme borreliosis is highly endemic. *J Infect Dis* 2004;189: 1515–1523.

12. Schulze TL, Bowen GS, Lakat MF, et al. The role of adult *Ixodes dammini* (Acari: Ixodidae) in the transmission of Lyme disease in New Jersey, USA. *J Med Entomol* 1985;22:88–93.

13. Narasimhan S, Sukumaran B, Bozdogan U, et al. A tick antioxidant facilitates the Lyme disease agent's successful migration from the mammalian host to the arthropod vector. *Cell Host Microbe* 2007;2:7–18.

14. Barbour AG, Fish D. The biological and social phenomenon of Lyme disease. *Science* 1993;260:1610–1616.

15. Lane RS, Piesman J, Burgdorfer W. Lyme borreliosis. *Annu Rev Entomol* 1991;36: 587–609.

16. Ogden NH, Bouchard C, Kurtenbach K, et al. Active and passive surveillance and phylogenetic analysis of *Borrelia burgdorferi* elucidate the process of Lyme disease risk emergence in Canada. *Environ Health Perspect* 2010;118:909–914.

17. Steere AC. Lyme disease. *N Engl J Med* 2001;345:115–125.

18. Oliver JH Jr, Lin T, Gao L, et al. An enzootic transmission cycle of Lyme borreliosis spirochetes in the southeastern United States. *Proc Natl Acad Sci USA* 2003;100:11642–11645.

19. Eisen L, Eisen RJ, Mun J, et al. Transmission cycles of *Borrelia burgdorferi* and *B. bissettii* in relation to habitat type in northwestern California. *J Vector Ecol* 2009;34:81–91.

20. Telford SR III, Mather TN, Moore SI, et al. Incompetence of deer as reservoirs of the Lyme disease spirochete. *Am J Trop Med Hyg* 1988;39:105–109.

21. Kuo MM, Lane RS, Giclas PC. A comparative study of mammalian and reptilian alternative pathway of complement-mediated killing of the Lyme disease spirochete (*Borrelia burgdorferi*). *J Parasitol* 2000;86:1223–1228.

22. Kurtenbach K, De Michelis S, Etti S, et al. Host association of *Borrelia burgdorferi sensu lato*: the key role of host complement. *Trends Microbiol* 2002;10:74–79.

23. Kurtenbach K, Sewell HS, Ogden NH, et al. Serum complement sensitivity as a key factor in Lyme disease ecology. *Infect Immun* 1998;66:1248–1251.

24. Bosler EM, Coleman JL, Benach JL, Massay DA. Natural distribution of the *Ixodes dammini* spirochete. *Science* 1993;220: 321–322.

25. Matuschka FR, Heiler M, Eiffert H, et al. Diversionary role of hoofed game in the transmission of Lyme disease spirochetes. *Am J Trop Med Hyg* 1993;48:693–699.

26. Ostfeld RS, Canham CD, Oggenfuss K, et al. Climate, deer, rodents, and acorns as determinants of variation in Lyme-disease risk. *PLoS Biol* 2006;4:e145.

27. Rosa PA, Tilly K, Stewart PE. The burgeoning molecular genetics of the Lyme disease spirochaete. *Nat Rev Microbiol* 2005;3: 129–143.

28. Anguita J, Hedrick MN, Fikrig E. Adaptation of *Borrelia burgdorferi* in the tick and the mammalian host. *FEMS Microbiol Rev* 2003;27:493–504.

29. Templeton TJ. *Borrelia* outer membrane surface proteins and transmission through the tick. *J Exp Med* 2004;199:603–606.

30. Scheckelhoff MR, Telford SR, Wesley M, Hu LT. *Borrelia burgdorferi* intercepts host hormonal signals to regulate expression of outer surface protein A. *Proc Natl Acad Sci USA* 2007;104:7247–7252.

31. Yang XF, Pal U, Alani SM, et al. Essential role for OspA/B in the life cycle of the Lyme disease spirochete. *J Exp Med* 2004;199:641–648.

32. Neelakanta G, Li X, Pal U, et al. Outer surface protein B is critical for *Borrelia burgdorferi* adherence and survival within *Ixodes* ticks. *PLoS Pathog* 2007;3:e33.

33. Pal U, Li X, Wang T, et al. TROSPA, an *Ixodes scapularis* receptor for *Borrelia burgdorferi*. *Cell* 2004;119:457–468.

34. Battisti JM, Bono JL, Rosa PA, et al. Outer surface protein A protects Lyme disease spirochetes from acquired host immunity in the tick vector. *Infect Immun* 2008;76: 5228–5237.

35. Schwan TG, Piesman J, Golde WT, et al. Induction of an outer surface protein on *Borrelia burgdorferi* during tick feeding. *Proc Natl Acad Sci USA* 1995;92:2909–2913.

36. Hojgaard A, Eisen RJ, Piesman J. Transmission dynamics of *Borrelia burgdorferi s.s.* during the key third day of feeding by nymphal *Ixodes scapularis* (Acari: Ixodidae). *J Med Entomol* 2008;45:732–736.

37. Piesman J. Dynamics of *Borrelia burgdorferi* transmission by nymphal *Ixodes dammini* ticks. *J Infect Dis* 1993;167:1082–1085.

38. des VF, Piesman J, Heffernan R, et al. Effect of tick removal on transmission of *Borrelia burgdorferi* and *Ehrlichia phagocytophila* by *Ixodes scapularis* nymphs. *J Infect Dis* 2001;183:773–778.

39. Sood SK, Salzman MB, Johnson BJB, et al. Duration of tick attachment as a predictor of the risk of Lyme disease in an area in which Lyme disease is endemic. *J Infect Dis* 1997;175:996–999.

40. Tilly K, Bestor A, Jewett MW, Rosa P. Rapid clearance of Lyme disease spirochetes lacking

OspC from skin. *Infect Immun* 2007;75: 1517–1519.

41. Seemanapalli SV, Xu Q, McShan K, Liang FT. Outer surface protein C is a dissemination-facilitating factor of *Borrelia burgdorferi* during mammalian infection. *PLoS One* 2010;5:e15830.

42. Radolf JD, Caimano MJ. The long strange trip of *Borrelia burgdorferi* outer-surface protein C. *Mol Microbiol* 2008;69:1–4.

43. Grimm D, Tilly K, Byram R, et al. Outer-surface protein C of the Lyme disease spirochete: a protein induced in ticks for infection of mammals. *Proc Natl Acad Sci USA* 2004;101:3142–3147.

44. Xu Q, McShan K, Liang FT. Essential protective role attributed to the surface lipoproteins of *Borrelia burgdorferi* against innate defenses. *Mol Microbiol* 2008;69:15–29.

45. Brisson D, Dykhuizen DE. ospC diversity in *Borrelia burgdorferi*: different hosts are different niches. *Genetics* 2004;168: 713–722.

46. Strle K, Jones KL, Drouin EE, et al. *Borrelia burgdorferi* RST1 (OspC type A) genotype is associated with greater inflammation and more severe Lyme disease. *Am J Pathol* 2011;178:2726–2739.

47. Wormser GP, Brisson D, Liveris D, et al. *Borrelia burgdorferi* genotype predicts the capacity for hematogenous dissemination during early Lyme disease. *J Infect Dis* 2008;198:1358–1364.

48. Alghaferi MY, Anderson JM, Park J, et al. *Borrelia burgdorferi* ospC heterogeneity among human and murine isolates from a defined region of northern Maryland and southern Pennsylvania: lack of correlation with invasive and noninvasive genotypes. *J Clin Microbiol* 2005;43:1879–1884.

49. Kenedy MR, Akins DR. The OspE-related proteins inhibit complement deposition and enhance serum resistance of *Borrelia burgdorferi*, the Lyme disease spirochete. *Infect Immun* 2011;79:1451–1457.

50. Hellwage J, Meri T, Heikkila T, et al. The complement regulator factor H binds to the surface protein OspE of *Borrelia burgdorferi*. *J Biol Chem* 2001;276:8427–8435.

51. Kraiczy P, Hellwage J, Skerka C, et al. Complement resistance of *Borrelia burgdorferi* correlates with the expression of BbCRASP-1, a novel linear plasmid-encoded surface protein that interacts with human factor H and FHL-1 and is unrelated to Erp proteins. *J Biol Chem* 2004;279:2421–2429.

52. Hartmann K, Corvey C, Skerka C, et al. Functional characterization of BbCRASP-2, a distinct outer membrane protein of *Borrelia burgdorferi* that binds host complement regulators factor H and FHL-1. *Mol Microbiol* 2006;61:1220–1236.

53. Stanek G, Reiter M. The expanding Lyme Borrelia complex: clinical significance of genomic species? *Clin Microbiol Infect* 2011;17:487–493.

54. Wang G, van Dam AP, Schwartz I, Dankert J. Molecular typing of *Borrelia burgdorferi sensu lato*: taxonomic, epidemiological, and clinical implications. *Clin Microbiol Rev* 1999;12:633–653.

55. Logar M, Ruzic-Sabljic E, Maraspin V, et al. Comparison of erythema migrans caused by *Borrelia afzelii* and *Borrelia garinii*. *Infection* 2004;32:15–19.

56. Wormser GP. Clinical practice: early Lyme disease. *N Engl J Med* 2006;354:2794–2801.

57. Wormser GP, Nowakowski J, Nadelman RB, et al. Impact of clinical variables on *Borrelia burgdorferi*–specific antibody seropositivity in acute-phase sera from patients in North America with culture-confirmed early Lyme disease. *Clin Vaccine Immunol* 2008;15:1519–1522.

58. Mullegger RR. Dermatological manifestations of Lyme borreliosis. *Eur J Dermatol* 2004;14:296–309.

59. Rostoff P, Gajos G, Konduracka E, et al. Lyme carditis: epidemiology, pathophysiology, and clinical features in endemic areas. *Int J Cardiol* 2010;144:328–333.

60. Costello JM, Alexander ME, Greco KM, et al. Lyme carditis in children: presentation, predictive factors, and clinical course. *Pediatrics* 2009;123:e835–e841.

61. Luft BJ, Steinman CR, Neimark HC, et al. Invasion of the central nervous system by *Borrelia burgdorferi* in acute disseminated infection. *JAMA* 1992;267:1364–1367.

62. Halperin JJ. Neurologic manifestations of Lyme disease. *Curr Infect Dis Rep* 2011;13:360–366.

63. Skogman BH, Croner S, Nordwall M, et al. Lyme neuroborreliosis in children: a prospective study of clinical features, prognosis, and outcome. *Pediatr Infect Dis J* 2008;27:1089–1094.

64. Steere AC, Gibofsky A, Patarroyo ME, et al. Chronic Lyme arthritis: clinical and immunogenetic differentiation from rheumatoid arthritis. *Ann Intern Med* 1979;90:896–901.

65. Steere AC, Dwyer E, Winchester R. Association of chronic Lyme arthritis with HLA-DR4 and HLA-DR2 alleles. *N Engl J Med* 1990;323:219–223.

66. Steere AC, Klitz W, Drouin EE, et al. Antibiotic-refractory Lyme arthritis is associated with HLA-DR molecules that bind a *Borrelia burgdorferi* peptide. *J Exp Med* 2006;203:961–971.

67. Meyer AL, Trollmo C, Crawford F, et al. Direct enumeration of *Borrelia*-reactive CD4 T cells ex vivo by using MHC class II tetramers. *Proc Natl Acad Sci USA* 2000;97:11433–11438.

68. Wormser GP, Dattwyler RJ, Shapiro ED, et al. The clinical assessment, treatment, and prevention of Lyme disease, human granulocytic anaplasmosis, and babesiosis: clinical practice guidelines by the Infectious Diseases Society of America. *Clin Infect Dis* 2006;43:1089–1134.

69. Asbrink E, Hovmark A, Olsson I. Clinical manifestations of acrodermatitis chronica atrophicans in 50 Swedish patients. *Zentralbl Bakteriol Mikrobiol Hyg A* 1986;263:253–261.

70. Oschmann P, Dorndorf W, Hornig C, et al. Stages and syndromes of neuroborreliosis. *J Neurol* 1998;245:262–272.

71. Henningsson AJ, Malmvall BE, Ernerudh J, et al. Neuroborreliosis: an epidemiological, clinical and healthcare cost study from an endemic area in the south-east of Sweden. *Clin Microbiol Infect* 2010;16:1245–1251.

72. Stanek G, Fingerle V, Hunfeld KP, et al. Lyme borreliosis: clinical case definitions for diagnosis and management in Europe. *Clin Microbiol Infect* 2011;17:69–79.

73. Cerar T, Ogrinc K, Cimperman J, et al. Validation of cultivation and PCR methods for diagnosis of Lyme neuroborreliosis. *J Clin Microbiol* 2008;46:3375–3379.

74. Cerar T, Ruzic-Sabljic E, Glinsek U, et al. Comparison of PCR methods and culture for the detection of *Borrelia* spp. in patients with erythema migrans. *Clin Microbiol Infect* 2008;14:653–658.

75. Liveris D, Schwartz I, Bittker S, et al. Improving the yield of blood cultures from patients with early Lyme disease. *J Clin Microbiol* 2011;49:2166–2168.

76. Babady NE, Sloan LM, Vetter EA, et al. Percent positive rate of Lyme real-time polymerase chain reaction in blood, cerebrospinal fluid, synovial fluid, and tissue. *Diagn Microbiol Infect Dis* 2008;62:464–466.

77. Branda JA, Guero-Rosenfeld ME, Ferraro MJ, et al. 2-tiered antibody testing for early and late Lyme disease using only an immunoglobulin G blot with the addition of a VlsE band as the second-tier test. *Clin Infect Dis* 2010;50:20–26.

78. Steere AC, McHugh G, Damle N, Sikand VK. Prospective study of serologic tests for Lyme disease. *Clin Infect Dis* 2008;47:188–195.

79. Jobe DA, Lovrich SD, Asp KE, et al. Significantly improved accuracy of diagnosis of early Lyme disease by peptide enzyme-linked immunosorbent assay based on the borreliacidal

antibody epitope of *Borrelia burgdorferi* OspC. *Clin Vaccine Immunol* 2008;15:981–985.

80. Burbelo PD, Issa AT, Ching KH, et al. Rapid, simple, quantitative, and highly sensitive antibody detection for Lyme disease. *Clin Vaccine Immunol* 2010;17:904–909.

81. Feder HM Jr, Johnson BJ, O'Connell S, et al. A critical appraisal of "chronic Lyme disease." *N Engl J Med* 2007;357:1422–1430.

82. Treatment of Lyme disease. *Med Lett Drugs Ther* 2010;52:53–54.

83. Kowalski TJ, Tata S, Berth W, et al. Antibiotic treatment duration and long-term outcomes of patients with early Lyme disease from a Lyme disease–hyperendemic area. *Clin Infect Dis* 2010;50:512–520.

84. Philipp MT, Wormser GP, Marques AR, et al. A decline in C6 antibody titer occurs in successfully treated patients with culture-confirmed early localized or early disseminated Lyme borreliosis. *Clin Diagn Lab Immunol* 2005;12:1069–1074.

85. Jobe DA, Kowalski TJ, Bloemke M, et al. Rapid decline of OspC borreliacidal antibodies following treatment of patients with early Lyme disease. *Clin Vaccine Immunol* 2011;18:1034–1037.

86. Marangoni A, Sambri V, Accardo S, et al. A decrease in the immunoglobulin G antibody response against the VlsE protein of *Borrelia burgdorferi sensu lato* correlates with the resolution of clinical signs in antibiotic-treated patients with early Lyme disease. *Clin Vaccine Immunol* 2006;13:525–529.

87. Halperin JJ, Shapiro ED, Logigian E, et al. Practice parameter: treatment of nervous system Lyme disease (an evidence-based review): report of the Quality Standards Subcommittee of the American Academy of Neurology. *Neurology* 2007;69:91–102.

88. Auwaerter PG. Point: antibiotic therapy is not the answer for patients with persisting symptoms attributable to Lyme disease. *Clin Infect Dis* 2007;45:143–148.

89. Stricker RB. Counterpoint: long-term antibiotic therapy improves persistent symptoms associated with Lyme disease. *Clin Infect Dis* 2007;45:149–157.

90. Schmid GP. The global distribution of Lyme disease. *Rev Infect Dis* 1985;7:41–50.

91. Steere AC, Taylor E, Wilson ML, et al. Longitudinal assessment of the clinical and epidemiological features of Lyme disease in a defined population. *J Infect Dis* 1986;154:295–300.

92. Scrimenti RJ. Erythema chronicum migrans. *Arch Derm* 1970;102:104–109.

93. Persing DH, Telford SM, Rys PN, et al. Detection of *Borrelia burgdorferi* DNA in museum specimens of *Ixodes dammini* ticks. *Science* 1990;249:1420–1423.

94. Matuschka FR, Ohlenbusch A, Eiffert H, et al. Characteristics of Lyme disease spirochetes in archived European ticks. *J Infect Dis* 1996;174:424–426.

95. Steere AC, Coburn J, Glickstein L. The emergence of Lyme disease. *J Clin Invest* 2004;113:1093–1101.

96. Kampen H, Rotzel DC, Kurtenbach K, et al. Substantial rise in the prevalence of Lyme borreliosis spirochetes in a region of western Germany over a 10-year period. *Appl Environ Microbiol* 2004;70:1576–1582.

97. Bacon RM, Kugeler KJ, Mead PS, Centers for Disease Control and Prevention (CDC). Surveillance for Lyme disease—United States, 1992–2006. *MMWR Surveill Summ*. 2008;57:1–9.

98. Gustafson R, Svenungsson B, Gardulf A, et al. Prevalence of tick-borne encephalitis and Lyme borreliosis in a defined Swedish population. *Scand J Infect Dis* 1990;22:297–306.

99. Daniels TJ, Boccia TM, Varde S, et al. Geographic risk for Lyme disease and human granulocytic ehrlichiosis in southern New York state. *Appl Environ Microbil*. 1998;64:4663–4669.

100. Brisson D, Vandermause MF, Meece JK, et al. Evolution of northeastern and midwestern *Borrelia burgdorferi*, United States. *Emerg Infect Dis* 2010;16:911–917.

101. Qiu WG, Bruno JF, McCaig WD, et al. Wide distribution of a high-virulence *Borrelia burgdorferi* clone in Europe and North America. *Emerg Infect Dis* 2008;14:1097–1104.

102. Randolph SE. Evidence that climate change has caused "emergence" of tick-borne diseases in Europe? *Int J Med Microbiol* 2004;293(suppl 37):5–15.

103. McCabe GJ, Bunnell JE. Precipitation and the occurrence of Lyme disease in the northeastern United States. *Vector Borne Zoonotic Dis* 2004;4:143–148.

104. Subak S. Effects of climate on variability in Lyme disease incidence in the northeastern United States. *Am J Epidemiol* 2003;157:531–538.

105. Bunikis J, Garpmo U, Tsao J, et al. Sequence typing reveals extensive strain diversity of the Lyme borreliosis agents *Borrelia burgdorferi* in North America and *Borrelia afzelii* in Europe. *Microbiology* 2004;150:1741–1755.

106. Jones CG, Ostfeld RS, Richard MP, et al. Chain reactions linking acorns to gypsy moth outbreaks and Lyme disease risk. *Science* 1998;279:1023–1026.

107. Salkeld DJ, Leonhard S, Girard YA, et al. Identifying the reservoir hosts of the Lyme disease spirochete *Borrelia burgdorferi* in California: the role of the western gray squirrel (*Sciurus griseus*). *Am J Trop Med Hyg* 2008;79:535–540.

108. Merten HA, Durden LA. A state-by-state survey of ticks recorded from humans in the United States. *J Vector Ecol* 2000;25:102–113.

109. Brown RN, Lane RS. Lyme disease in California: a novel enzootic transmission cycle of *Borrelia burgdorferi*. *Science* 1992;256:1439–1442.

110. Maggi RG, Reichelt S, Toliver M, Engber B. Borrelia species in *Ixodes affinis* and *Ixodes scapularis* ticks collected from the coastal plain of North Carolina. *Ticks Tick Borne Dis* 2010;1:168–171.

111. Dekonenko EJ, Steere AC, Berardi VP, Kravchuk LN. Lyme borreliosis in the Soviet Union: a cooperative US-USSR report. *J Infect Dis* 1988;158:748–753.

112. Berglund J, Eitrem R, Ornstein K, et al. An epidemiologic study of Lyme disease in southern Sweden. *N Engl J Med* 1995;333:1319–1324.

113. Hoen AG, Rollend LG, Papero MA, et al. Effects of tick control by acaricide self-treatment of white-tailed deer on host-seeking tick infection prevalence and entomologic risk for *Ixodes scapularis*–borne pathogens. *Vector Borne Zoonotic Dis* 2009;9:431–438.

114. Magid D, Schwartz B, Craft J, Schwartz JS. Prevention of Lyme disease after tick bites: a cost-effective analysis. *N Engl J Med* 1992;327:534–541.

115. Hayes EB, Piesman J. How can we prevent Lyme disease? *N Engl J Med* 2003;348:2424–2430.

116. Clark RP, Hu LT. Prevention of Lyme disease and other tick-borne infections. *Infect Dis Clin North Am* 2008;22:381–96, vii.

117. Fish D, Childs JE. Community-based prevention of Lyme disease and other tick-borne diseases through topical application of acaricide to white-tailed deer: background and rationale. *Vector Borne Zoonotic Dis* 2009;9:357–364.

118. LoGiudice K, Ostfeld RS, Schmidt KA, Keesing F. The ecology of infectious disease: effects of host diversity and community composition on Lyme disease risk. *Proc Natl Acad Sci USA* 2003;100:567–571.

119. Rand PW, Lubelczyk C, Lavigne GR, et al. Deer density and the abundance of *Ixodes scapularis* (Acari: Ixodidae). *J Med Entomol* 2003;40:179–184.

120. Rand PW, Lubelczyk C, Holman MS, et al. Abundance of *Ixodes scapularis* (Acari:

Ixodidae) after the complete removal of deer from an isolated offshore island, endemic for Lyme disease. *J Med Entomol* 2004;41: 779–784.

121. Jordan RA, Schulze TL, Jahn MB. Effects of reduced deer density on the abundance of *Ixodes scapularis* (Acari: Ixodidae) and Lyme disease incidence in a northern New Jersey endemic area. *J Med Entomol* 2007;44:752–757.

122. Dolan MC, Maupin GO, Schneider BS, et al. Control of immature *Ixodes scapularis* (Acari: Ixodidae) on rodent reservoirs of *Borrelia burgdorferi* in a residential community of southeastern Connecticut. *J Med Entomol* 2004;41:1043–1054.

123. Tsao JI, Wootton JT, Bunikis J, et al. An ecological approach to preventing human infection: vaccinating wild mouse reservoirs intervenes in the Lyme disease cycle. *Proc Natl Acad Sci USA* 2004;101:18159–18164.

124. Connally NP, Durante AJ, Yousey-Hindes KM, et al. Peridomestic Lyme disease prevention: results of a population-based case-control study. *Am J Prev Med* 2009;37:201–206.

125. Vazquez M, Muehlenbein C, Cartter M, et al. Effectiveness of personal protective measures to prevent Lyme disease. *Emerg Infect Dis* 2008;14:210–216.

126. Warshafsky S, Lee DH, Francois LK, et al. Efficacy of antibiotic prophylaxis for the prevention of Lyme disease: an updated systematic review and meta-analysis. *J Antimicrob Chemother* 2010;65:1137–1144.

127. Shapiro ED, Gerber MA, Holabird NB, et al. A controlled trial of antimicrobial prophylaxis for Lyme disease after deer-tick bites. *N Engl J Med* 1992;327:1769–1773.

128. Nadelman RB, Nowakowski J, Fish D, et al. Prophylaxis with single-dose doxycycline for the prevention of Lyme disease after an *Ixodes scapularis* tick bite. *N Engl J Med* 2001;345:79–84.

129. Fikrig E, Barthold SW, Kantor FS, Flavell RA. Protection of mice against the Lyme disease agent by immunizing with recombinant OspA. *Science* 1990;250:553–556.

130. Steere AC, Sikand VK, Meurice F, et al. Vaccination against Lyme disease with recombinant *Borrelia burgdorferi* outer-surface lipoprotein A with adjuvant. Lyme disease vaccine study group. *N Engl J Med* 1998;339:209–215.

131. Sigal LH, Zahradnik JM, Lavin P, et al. A vaccine consisting of recombinant *Borrelia burgdorferi* outer-surface protein A to prevent Lyme disease. Recombinant Outer-Surface Protein A Lyme Disease Vaccine Study Consortium. *N Engl J Med* 1998;339:216–222.

132. Hanson MS, Edelman R. Progress and controversy surrounding vaccines against Lyme disease. *Expert Rev Vaccines* 2003;2:683–703.

133. Poland GA. Vaccines against Lyme disease: what happened and what lessons can we learn? *Clin Infect Dis* 2011;52(suppl 3):s253–s258.

134. Narasimhan S, Deponte K, Marcantonio N, et al. Immunity against *Ixodes scapularis* salivary proteins expressed within 24 hours of attachment thwarts tick feeding and impairs *Borrelia* transmission. *PLoS One* 2007;2:e451.

135. Dai J, Wang P, Adusumilli S, et al. Antibodies against a tick protein, Salp15, protect mice from the Lyme disease agent. *Cell Host Microbe* 2009;6:482–492.

136. Hovius JW, van Dam AP, Fikrig E. Tick–host–pathogen interactions in Lyme borreliosis. *Trends Parasitol* 2007;23:434–438.

137. Earnhart CG, Buckles EL, Marconi RT. Development of an OspC-based tetravalent, recombinant, chimeric vaccinogen that elicits bactericidal antibody against diverse Lyme disease spirochete strains. *Vaccine* 2007;25:466–480.

138. Livey I, O'Rourke M, Traweger A, et al. A new approach to a Lyme disease vaccine. *Clin Infect Dis* 2011;52(suppl 3):s266–s270.

139. Schuijt TJ, Hovius JW, van der PT, et al. Lyme borreliosis vaccination: the facts, the challenge, the future. *Trends Parasitol* 2011;27:40–47.

CHAPTER

27

The Epidemiology and Control of Malaria

William J. Moss and Richard H. Morrow

BACKGROUND, HISTORY, AND PUBLIC HEALTH IMPORTANCE

History of Malaria Control

Vertebrates, mosquitoes, and plasmodia have been interacting and evolving together for tens of thousands of years, and humans have been afflicted with malaria as long as there have been humans. Documentation of what is certainly malaria dates back to 2700 BCE in China, and malaria is featured in the writings of Homer, Plato, Aristotle, Chaucer, Pepys, and Shakespeare. It has been more than 100 years since the discovery that malaria is caused by a protozoan parasite that infects red blood cells and is transmitted by mosquitoes from human to human. In 1902, Ronald Ross was awarded the Nobel Prize in medicine for his work on malaria and its transmission cycle. Since then, major scientific advances have continued to understand the parasite, its life cycle within anopheline mosquitoes, and its pathogenesis in humans.[1]

The Greeks had known of the relationship between fever and swamps and low-lying water since the sixth century BCE. Control of mosquito breeding through drainage and environmental control was a key aspect in the development of the Panama Canal and continued to be the major approach to malaria control until after World War II. During World War II, two major biochemical and pharmaceutical advances in unrelated fields revolutionized malaria control and its treatment: dichlorodiphenyltrichloroethane (DDT) as an insecticide was found to be highly effective against anopheline vectors, and chloroquine replaced quinine as the principal antimalarial drug.

With these new tools, plans for the reduction and control of malaria were envisioned, but beyond that the prospect of total eradication of this horrendous disease was proposed. Fundamentally, achieving this goal required the elimination of every parasite of all human malaria species, principally by stopping the transmission by the vector from one human to the next. Residual spraying of DDT on the walls of households was the major weapon employed and, in nearly all early trials, proved remarkably effective in killing mosquitoes that had just taken a blood meal from a sleeping household resident. The availability of chloroquine—a rapidly and uniformly curative drug with a wide margin of safety and very low cost—for treatment provided an additional tool.

Following World War II, the newly formed World Health Organization (WHO) formulated a malaria eradication plan at the 8th World Health Assembly in 1955. It was estimated that eradication using DDT residual spraying could be accomplished at a cost of less than 25 cents per person per year; the total cost for the first 5 years would be $500 million.[2]

Plans were put into action in many areas of the world, and truly dramatic success was achieved in some regions. By the late 1950s, the most inspirational, ambitious, complex, and costly health campaign ever undertaken was well under way.[3] Early campaign efforts in many countries in Europe, Asia, and Latin America were enormously successful. Indeed, in Malta the anopheline vector was completely eliminated. In contrast, little effect was seen in many continental tropical countries of Asia and South America. In Africa, where malaria was by far of greatest importance, virtually nothing was even attempted. Unfortunately, the emphasis on logistics and organization was accompanied by a comparable de-emphasis on scientific research.[3] Over a period extending for 20 years, virtually no innovative research on malaria was undertaken—the general opinion, frequently and loudly expressed, was that

"We know what has to be done; let us get on with it!" As a consequence, an entire generation of malaria researchers was lost.

Even by the mid-1960s, it was clear that the eradication campaign would fail. The complex logistical and operational needs were too much for the weak infrastructures in most tropical countries; moreover, basic biological developments emerged, including anopheline resistance to insecticides and parasite resistance to antimalarials.[4] Over time, the malaria eradication campaign came to be viewed as a major failure. In the wisdom of hindsight, the failure was a result of scientific arrogance and lack of foresight. Nevertheless, it should not be forgotten that large numbers of lives were saved in many countries, and major economic activities were spurred.

After the failed malaria eradication efforts, most countries greatly reduced their expenditures on malaria programs; in many areas, the result was an epidemic resurgence of malaria. However, with a shift in focus to reducing mortality and serious morbidity, rather than seeking eradication, came the gradual emergence of researchers seeking a fuller understanding of malaria parasites, the pathogenesis of malaria disease, and new approaches to control. By the end of the 1990s, major advances had been made in understanding the molecular biology of the malaria parasite, parasite and vector genomics and proteomics, vector control methods, the immunological responses to malaria infection, the rational development of novel antimalarial agents and vaccines, and a variety of innovative strategies for malaria control.

WHO, UNICEF, the United Nations Development Programme, and the World Bank came together to provide a coordinated international approach to fighting malaria when they launched the Roll Back Malaria (RBM) Partnership in 1998. The RBM Partnership is a global initiative of more than 90 partners whose activities include coordinating the many stakeholders; working toward an in-depth understanding of the ecology, biology, and epidemiology of malaria, particularly in Africa; developing comprehensive and cohesive planning; and raising funds and political support. Other important efforts to reduce malaria morbidity and mortality include the Multilateral Initiative on Malaria (MIM), the Malaria Vaccine Initiative (MVI), the President's Malaria Initiative (PMI), and the Global Fund to Fight AIDS, Tuberculosis, and Malaria. The Bill and Melinda Gates Foundation has challenged the public health community by calling for renewed efforts to achieve malaria eradication and committed enormous resources to this goal.

The terms "control," "elimination," and "eradication" for malaria are now defined[5] as follows:

- *Malaria control*: reducing the disease burden to a level at which it is no longer a public health problem.
- *Malaria elimination*: interrupting local mosquito-borne malaria transmission in a defined geographical area—that is, zero incidence of locally contracted cases, although imported cases will continue to occur. Continued intervention measures are required.
- *Malaria eradication*: permanent reduction to zero of the worldwide incidence of malaria infection.

Although the goal of global eradication per se remains contentious, prospects have been brightened such that organizations can now realistically work toward malaria elimination in many parts of the globe. It is vital that such malaria elimination and eradication efforts be based on detailed understanding of local malaria epidemiology and transmission dynamics, effective use of current tools and strategies, and, likely, new tools, particularly with the threat of the spread of drug and insecticide resistance.[6]

Public Health Importance

The impact of malaria in human populations varies greatly in different parts of the world. Wherever there is *Plasmodium falciparum*, there will be dire consequences, but the public health consequences will vary according to the intensity of transmission. Traditionally, geographical areas are classified into four levels of endemicity (intensity of transmission) as set forth in **Table 27-1**. **Figure 27-1** shows a map of the distribution of *Plasmodium falciparum* malaria created by the Malaria Atlas Project.[7]

Although *P. vivax* malaria is a major cause of morbidity in parts of China, Southeast and Central Asia, Latin America, and the Caribbean, the overwhelming burden of disease occurs in those countries subjected to *P. falciparum* malaria, especially in sub-Saharan Africa. Most of the discussion of this type of malaria in this chapter will focus on issues related to tropical Africa, where malaria is of greatest importance and where approaches to control have had, until recently, the least success.

The public health significance of a disease depends on its incidence and resulting disability and mortality. In addition, this impact depends on epidemiological characteristics such as those related to person (age, sex, and other demographic variables such as occupation, education, and socioeconomic group), place (urban and rural, or particular

Table 27-1	Malaria Endemicity			
	Transmission	Children 2–9 Yrs with Enlarged Spleens & Parasites	Parasitemia	Entomologic Infectious Rate (EIR) Bites/Person/Year
Holo-endemic	Intense, everyone has malaria parasites all the time.*	>75%	>75%	>20** SouthAmerica/Asia = 20–50, very rare >50 Africa >50 -100s
Hyper-endemic	Regular, often seasonal transmission.	50–75%	50–75%	5–20
Meso-endemic	Regular, but much lower than hyper. Danger of occasional epidemics with fairly high morbidity and mortality.	10–50%	10–50%	>10
Hypo-endemic	Population will have little or no immunity. Danger of severe epidemics involving all age groups.	<10%	<10%	Not detected except when epidemic

*detection of parasites may be very difficult because of high levels of immunity, but sufficient search will reveal presence of parasites

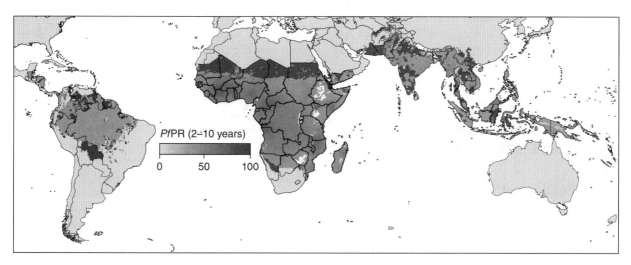

PfPR (2÷10 years)

0   50   100

Figure 27-1 The Spatial Distribution of P. falciparum Malaria Endemicity. Reproduced from Hay et al. A World Malaria Map: Plasmodium falciparum Endemicity in 2007. PLOS Medicine: San Francisco, CA.

ecological zones), and time (including seasonal or other cyclical variation or secular trends). In infectious diseases, the incidence of a disease is commonly expressed in terms of episodes per time period or the number of persons affected per time period. In many places where malaria is hypoendemic or mesoendemic, the incidence of malaria has meaning and can be expressed as the number of episodes per thousand persons per year or as the number of persons having episodes per thousand persons per year. In holoendemic areas, however, with an entomological inoculation rate ranging from dozens to hundreds of infectious bites per person per year, everyone is infected all the time and is reinfected every few days. The very concept of incidence, or indeed prevalence, has little meaning in this context. Instead, the health status of an individual in these situations results from a balance between the parasite and host immunity. Clearance of parasites from the host occurs with reasonable certainty only when an individual is given an effective antimalarial drug. Reinfection and, therefore, "a new incident" case occurs as soon as the level of the antimalarial drug drops below the effective therapeutic level and recently injected sporozoites develop into blood-stage parasites. Further discussion of different measures of malaria transmission is found in the "Malaria Metrics" section later in this chapter.

Since rates were first reported by WHO in the 1950s, childhood malaria mortality has been estimated at 1–2 million children per year. In the past decade, however, two important trends have taken place: the quality of malaria mortality data has improved and, even more notably, increased effectiveness of antimalarial efforts has become evident. In a 2004 WHO report, global deaths from malaria were estimated to have dropped to 1,272,000 (with 1,136,000 in Africa).[8] A continuing decline in mortality is supported by the estimates for 2009 of 781,000 deaths from malaria worldwide (including 709,000 in Africa).[9]

An indirect indicator of the importance of malaria mortality is the relative frequency of sickle-cell trait (AS) in tropical Africa. This deleterious trait is maintained in the population because of the protection it provides against malaria. The high proportion of adults with the AS genotype in West Africa is a reflection of the selective mortality, 15–20%, among children with the AA genotype (see the section on "Human Genetic Factors").[10]

THE BIOLOGY OF MALARIA PARASITES AND ANOPHELINE VECTORS

Malaria Parasites and Their Life Cycle

Five species of protozoan parasites of the genus *Plasmodium* infect humans: *P. falciparum*, *P. vivax*, *P. ovale*, *P. malariae*, and *P. knowlesi*. *P. knowlesi*, whose natural vertebrate host is the monkey *Macaca fascicularis*, was recently recognized as a zoonotic infection of humans in Malaysia, Indonesia, and other parts of Southeast Asia.[11,12] Although *P. vivax* is the most widespread form of malaria infection in the world, *P. falciparum* causes the most severe

disease and is responsible, by far, for most deaths and serious morbidity due to malaria (**Table 27-2**).

The complex life cycle of the malaria parasite is shown in **Figure 27-2**. The parasite undergoes multiple transformations within the mosquito and human host; at least a dozen separate steps have been defined. The parasite is transmitted to humans as the sporozoite form in the saliva of an infected female anopheline mosquito taking a blood meal (1). Sporozoites enter the venous blood system from the subcutaneous tissues through the capillary bed, and within minutes those that avoid the defending reticuloendothelial system invade liver cells (2). Over the next 5 to 15 days, each sporozoite nucleus replicates thousands of times to develop into a hepatic schizont within the liver cells (3). When released from the swollen liver cells, each schizont splits into tens of thousands of daughter parasites called merozoites (4). Merozoites attach to specific erythrocyte surface receptors (Duffy blood group antigen for *P. vivax*, glycophorins for *P. falciparum*)[13] and penetrate the erythrocyte (5). Each intraerythrocytic merozoite differentiates into a trophozoite that ingests human hemoglobin, enlarges, and divides, into 6 to 24 intraerythrocytic merozoites, forming a schizont. The red cell swells and bursts, releasing the next batch of approximately 20 merozoites (6), which then attach and penetrate new erythrocytes to begin this cycle again.

Along with the liberation of merozoites, the resultant hemolysis and release of pyrogens from infected red cells and the host's response to these toxins correspond with clinical paroxysms of fever and chills; when synchronous, the simultaneous release from many red cells accounts for the periodicity of these symptoms in some patients. This second stage of asexual division takes approximately 48 hours for *P. falciparum*, *P. vivax*, and *P. ovale*, and 72 hours for *P. malariae*. A single *P. falciparum* merozoite potentially can lead to 10 billion new parasites through these recurrent cycles.

After a number of cycles within red cells, some merozoites differentiate into sexual forms called gametocytes (7)—macrogametocytes (female) and microgametocytes (male)—that are then available

Table 27-2	Malaria Parasites of Humans				
Species	**Intra-RBC Schizont Period**	**Type of RBC**	**Relapse (hypnozyte)**	**Global Distribution**	
P. vivax	48 hours	Reticulocytes	Yes	Everywhere except Africa	
P. ovale	48 hours	Reticulocytes	Yes	Africa	
P. malariae	72 hours	Older RBCs	No	Everywhere	
P. falciparum	48 hours (±)	All	No	Tropical regions	

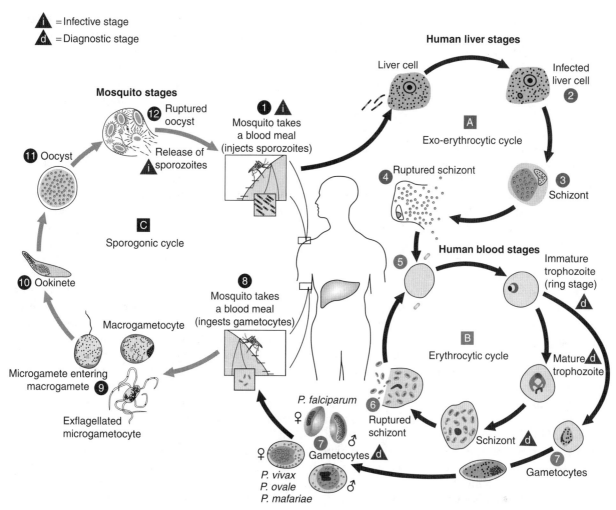

Figure 27-2 Life cycle of the malaria parasite. Reproduced from the Centers for Disease Control and Prevention. Laboratory Identification of Parasites of Public Health Concern. Life cycle of malaria at: http://www.dpd.cdc.gov/dpdx/images/ParasiteImages/M-R/Malaria/Malaria_LifeCycle.gif. Last modified July 20, 2009. Accessed January 24, 2012.

to be ingested by an anopheline mosquito during its blood meal (8). Factors related to gametogenesis include the species of parasite, length of infection or number of intraerythrocytic cycles, density of parasitemia, drug treatment, and age or immune status of the infected individuals.[14]

Sporogonic Development

Once in the mosquito, the red cells are digested, freeing the gametocytes, which then begin sexual reproduction leading to sporogonic development.[15] The male and female gametes fuse, providing for genetic recombination, to form a zygote (9). Over the next 12 to 14 hours, the zygote elongates and forms an ookinete (10), which in turn penetrates the wall of the mosquito's stomach and becomes an oocyst (11). During the next several days, the oocyst enlarges,

forming more than 10,000 sporozoites. After the oocyst ruptures into the coelomic cavity of the mosquito (12), the sporozoites migrate to the salivary glands (1), ready to be injected back into the human host to complete their life cycle. Once infected with malaria, a female anopheline remains infected for life and can transmit sporozoites with each blood meal.

The phases of parasite development—from ingestion of gametocytes to when sporozoites in the salivary glands are poised for reinoculation into the human host—constitute the extrinsic cycle or sporogonic phase, which generally takes 7–12 days. The time required depends on the species of parasite and the ambient temperature. For example, under optimal conditions with the temperature at 30°C, *P. falciparum* requires 9 days to complete the sporogonic phase; at 20°C, however, it takes 23 days—a difference of 14 days for a temperature differential of 10°C. With an average life span for most anophelines of less than 3 weeks, the ambient temperature is critical to transmission of the malarial infection.

During sporogonic development, each female–male pair of gametocytes potentially can produce more than 10,000 sporozoites for inoculation. Because dozens to thousands of gametocytes can be ingested with one blood meal, the potential exists for millions of sporozoites to be injected with one bite. Perhaps related to damage to the mosquito from such heavy loads or insufficient nutrients and metabolites available to support these levels of parasitemia, such high inocula counts are not observed. Limited studies of naturally infected mosquitoes have found sporozoite loads (the number of sporozoites in the salivary glands of an anopheline) to range from 10 to more than 100,000.[16]

In vitro studies using experimentally infected mosquitoes have shown that most infected mosquitoes transmit fewer than 25 sporozoites per bite, but approximately 5% of these mosquitoes can transmit hundreds.[17] Epidemiological studies comparing sporozoite rates (the proportion of anopheline females with sporozoites in their salivary glands) with infant infection have demonstrated that less than 20% of sporozoite inoculations result in infection. However, great variation in the ratio of the infant conversion rate (ICR—the rate at which infants acquire malaria) to the entomological inoculation rate (EIR—roughly the number of infectious bites per person) has been found between places, between seasons, and for evaluation of vector control.[18,19] In general, far lower numbers of sporozoites are delivered than are found in the salivary glands. Nevertheless, some bites do transmit high numbers of infective sporozoites, and although speculative, high inocula may lead to more severe disease.

Biological Differences Among Malaria Species

Important species-specific differences are found in the generic life cycle described in the preceding discussion. With *P. vivax* and *P. ovale*, some sporozoites entering hepatic cells do not immediately proceed to tissue schizogony, but rather become hypnozoites and lie dormant for months to years.[20] Later, these hypnozoites can differentiate into hepatic schizonts, leading to the cycle of erythrocytic schizogony and consequent relapse of symptoms. This biologic capability accounts for the relapses characteristic of *P. vivax* and *P. ovale* and the need for specific drug treatment targeted to the hypnozoite stage (primaquine). Different strains of *P. vivax* from diverse areas of the world are known to have characteristic relapse patterns. In general, following acute infection with either *P. vivax* or *P. ovale*, patients are at risk of having a relapse for as long as 3 to 4 years. No diagnostic test is available to determine whether individuals have hepatic hypnozoites.

P. falciparum, P. malariae, and *P. knowlesi* (despite the phylogenetic relatedness of the latter to *P. vivax*) do not produce hypnozoites and do not lead to relapse, but untreated or inadequately treated infections may cause persistent low-grade parasitemia leading to recrudescent clinical disease. The term "relapse" refers to renewed infection from survival of the parasite in hepatic cells as hypnozoites, whereas "recrudescence" refers to renewed infection from surviving erythrocytic forms.

The different species of human malaria parasites have affinities for particular types of erythrocytes. *P. vivax* and *P. ovale* parasites invade young reticulocytes; thus the density of peripheral parasitemia in these infections rarely exceeds 3%. In contrast, *P. malariae* is limited to older red cells. However, *P. falciparum* infects erythrocytes of all ages, and for this reason it is able to produce high-density parasitemias with serious morbidity and high mortality. *P. knowlesi* also infects erythrocytes of all ages, completes its intraerythrocytic life cycle in 24 hours (faster than other human malaria parasites), and can reach high levels of parasitemia, resulting in severe disease similar to *P. falciparum*.[21]

Important differences in gametocyte production are also noted among species.[22] After infection with *P. vivax*, infective gametocytes appear in the peripheral blood almost as soon as the asexual blood-stage schizonts form. Gametocytes are usually present when *P. vivax* malaria is first diagnosed and before antimalarial treatment has been started. *P. vivax* can be transmitted prior to symptomatic disease, and its gametocytes will not have been exposed to drug pressure that would select for drug-resistant mutants; as a consequence, drug-sensitive parasites are not at a disadvantage in competition with the drug-resistant strains. In contrast, following infection with *P. falciparum*, gametocytes appear only after several intraerythrocytic cycles, first appearing at least 10 days after the onset of clinical symptoms. Early treatment of *P. falciparum* with an effective drug will kill blood-stage schizonts, preventing gametocytes from developing and blocking transmission. However, those gametocytes that do develop will be derived from malaria parasites that survived drug treatment and may carry drug resistance genes. This pattern strongly facilitates the selection and spread of drug-resistant parasites. The difference in timing of gametocyte emergence may be a factor accounting for the much higher rate of drug resistance in *P. falciparum* as compared to *P. vivax*.

Aspects of the Molecular Biology of the Malaria Parasite

Understanding of the molecular biology of malaria parasites was advanced by the publication of the genome sequence of *P. falciparum* in 2002[23] and the *P. vivax* genome in 2008.[24] Functional and comparative genomics and proteomics of the malaria parasite during different stages of its life cycle will lead to improved understanding of *Plasmodium* biology and pathogenesis, and the identification of potential new drug and vaccine targets.[25]

The genome of *P. falciparum* consists of 14 chromosomes containing more than 5000 predicted genes. Several aspects of the molecular biology of *P. falciparum* are relevant to malaria epidemiology and control. A large proportion of identified genes are involved in immune evasion and host–parasite interactions. *P. falciparum* contains three families of highly variable genes, the most important of which is the *var* gene family, comprising approximately 60 genes encoding for the *P. falciparum* erythrocyte membrane protein 1 (PfEMP1). Transcriptional switching between different *var* genes allows the parasite to evade immune responses directed against PfEMP1. These genes may also be modified by the exchange of material between chromosome ends, where these genes are located. PfEMP1 is located on the surface of infected red blood cells and mediates adherence to endothelial cells. One *var* gene encodes a protein that mediates adherence to chondroitin sulfate A in the placenta and is partly responsible for the severe disease observed in pregnant women.[26] Specifically, a conserved parasite *var* gene (*var2csa*) is associated with placental malaria and mediates adherence of parasitized erythrocytes to the placenta.[27] Thus this gene family encodes for an important virulence factor responsible for the sequestration of infected red blood cells in various organs of the infected human.[28]

Genome sequencing of *P. falciparum* has led to the identification of plasmodia-specific metabolic pathways. These pathways are ideal targets for novel antimalarial drugs. For example, enzymes involved in fatty acid synthesis or protein degradation in food vacuoles may be ideal drug targets. Genomic research may also identify antigens for vaccine development, particularly conserved sequences expressed on cell surfaces during different stages of parasite development.[29] However, *P. falciparum* geneticists caution, "genome sequences alone provide little relief to those suffering from malaria," and work must be done to convert this knowledge into effective interventions.[23]

The malaria genome project focused on a single clone of *P. falciparum*, and further work is needed to define the genetic diversity found among parasites from different geographical regions. Improved understanding of strain genetic differences will provide insights into transmission, pathogenesis, and drug resistance.[30]

Anopheline Mosquitoes and Their Life Cycle

Malaria is transmitted only by the genus *Anopheles* mosquitoes. More than 70 species of *Anopheles* are known to be capable of transmitting malaria to humans, with approximately 40 considered important vectors. The female anopheline requires protein derived from host blood for egg production; therefore, only the female feeds on blood, and she is the only vector for malaria.

There is great variation among different species in host feeding preference, biting, and resting behavior, and in selection of larval habitat for laying the eggs, and these differences determine the local epidemiology of malaria. Some anophelines are opportunistic feeders on a variety of vertebrates (zoophilic), whereas others are very particular and take blood meals only from humans (anthropophilic). Some feed only indoors (endophagic), whereas others may occasionally or exclusively feed outdoors (exophagic). Whether they rest indoors (endophilic) or outdoors (exophilic) after feeding is critical to understanding the potential impact of indoor insecticide spraying. Nearly all anophelines prefer clean water in which to breed, but some have very specific preferences for the aquatic environment in which they lay their eggs. For example, *Anopheles stephensi* breeds in tin cans and in confined water systems, whereas *Anopheles gambiae*—the most important malaria vector in Africa—prefers small, open, sunlit pools. Knowledge of this variation is critical for effective vector control.

The mosquito goes through four stages of growth during its life cycle, from egg to larva to pupa to adult. Shortly after emerging as an adult (eclosion) and before the first blood meal, adult anopheline females mate. They usually mate only once and store the sperm, laying a total of 200–1000 eggs in 3 to 12 batches over their lifetime. A fresh blood meal is required for development of each egg batch. After hatching, an anopheline larva feeds at the water's surface and develops over 5–15 days before pupation. Within 2–3 days, an adult mosquito emerges from the pupal case. The entire cycle requires a total of 7–20 days, depending on the anopheline species and the environmental conditions. Under favorable conditions of high humidity and moderate temperatures, female anophelines can survive at least one month—time enough for the parasite to go through the sporogonic cycle of 7–12 days needed to develop sporozoites in the salivary glands for injection with the next blood meal. Thereafter, the mosquito is capable of transmission with each subsequent human blood meal, often taken every 2–3 days for the remainder of its life. Therefore, the longevity of the anopheline mosquito is critically important in determining the efficiency of transmission.

Mosquitoes are able to seek out their host in response to a combination of chemical and physical stimuli, including carbon dioxide, body odors, warmth, and movement. The odorant receptors of *A. gambiae* have been characterized, and this knowledge could lead to strategies to block the ability of mosquitoes to track human hosts.[31] Most anopheline mosquitoes feed at night, but some species may feed in late afternoon or early morning. During feeding, the mosquito injects salivary fluid containing enzymes into the subcutaneous tissue. These enzymes diffuse through the surrounding tissue and increase blood flow, facilitating both the blood meal and the transfer of sporozoites to the capillary bed. Anophelines generally feed on people sleeping indoors. Some species, however, bite outdoors, especially those that are forest dwellers, such as *Anopheles dirus*. After feeding, the engorged female seeks a resting place on a nearby wall or in a secluded spot outdoors. Some species alter their behavior in the presence of DDT or other insecticides, becoming irritated and flying outside to seek refuge. Engorged mosquitoes usually rest for 24–36 hours to digest the blood meal before they search for an oviposition site.

Vector identification involved in malaria transmission serves as the starting point for entomological investigation of local malaria epidemiology. Measurement of the entomological inoculation rate (EIR; described later in this chapter) for each of the potential vectors is important for determining the relative contribution of each species to transmission as well as for determining the intensity of transmission in the area.

Enormous spatial and temporal variation in vector species is evident. Ecological change induced by human activities such as urbanization, deforestation, and irrigation may modify mosquito habitats and vector distribution. A major obstacle to species identification is the existence of species complexes, in which genetically distinct sibling groups are morphologically indistinguishable. Sibling species may vary in their potential as vectors due to differences in susceptibility to parasitic infection, resistance to insecticides, breeding habitat, geographic distribution, host preference, or biting and resting habits. For example, the *A. gambiae* complex consists of seven species, including two of the most important vectors in sub-Saharan Africa: *A. gambiae* and *A. arabiensis*. In contrast to *A. gambiae*, *A. arabiensis* often feeds on cattle, rests outdoors, and is tolerant of low humidity. Another member of this species complex, *A. quadriannulatus*, feeds only on animals and is not a vector of human malaria. Even within *A. gambiae*, genetic heterogeneity occurs in conjunction with geographic and seasonal variations. Further advances in understanding local ecological, vector, host, and parasite factors should translate into improved approaches to malaria control.

Concurrent with the publication of the genome sequence of *P. falciparum*, a first draft of the genome sequence of *A. gambiae* was published in 2002.[32] Identification of polymorphisms within the *A. gambiae* genome will aid in the detection of insecticide resistance (e.g., detoxifying enzymes), genetic factors responsible for transmission efficiency of malaria parasites, and gene flow within mosquito populations. Genetic studies should lead to a better understanding of the determinants of anopheline behaviors, including the mechanisms by which the mosquito identifies human hosts as well as metabolic targets for insecticide development. Components of the mosquito's innate immune system have been identified that allow for a better understanding of the coevolution of parasite and vector, and potential reasons for different transmission efficiencies.[33] Interestingly, bacteria within the mosquito midgut, including *Enterbacter*[34] and *Wolbachia*,[35] inhibit *P. falciparum* oocyst development.

MALARIA METRICS

Understanding the dynamics of malaria transmission is fundamental to understanding how best to reduce transmission through vector control and other antimalarial measures.[36] Sir Ronald Ross (1857–1932) and George Macdonald (1903–67) pioneered the quantification of variables related to the transmission dynamics of malaria. Their work laid the foundation for the worldwide malaria eradication described in the "History of Malaria Control" section; these measures and their use in defining critical points of action for malaria control are now of renewed interest as countries are strengthening their control efforts and are reconsidering the prospects of malaria elimination and eradication.[5,36]

The starting point for Ross and Macdonald in understanding the determinants of malaria transmission was to consider the basic reproduction rate (R, or Z_0 in their nomenclature) as the number of new cases of malaria generated by a single case of malaria in a given period of time. For malaria to be eliminated, R must be reduced to less than 1.

The critical variables that determine R are those detailed later in this section for the entomological inoculation rate (EIR) and vectorial capacity (VC). These basic indices of malaria transmission are closely related; both are applied to a defined ecological zone or geographical area, and both vary greatly in place and time.[37] The EIR is the number of infected bites that each person receives per night (or time period) and is calculated by multiplying the human landing rate (HLR) by the sporozoite rate (SR) and usually expressed on an annual basis as the annual EIR. The HLR, previously termed the "human biting rate," is obtained by capturing all mosquitoes that land on a person (the "bait") during a night and is expressed as the number of mosquitoes landing (bites) per person per night. The SR is determined by microscopic examination of dissected salivary glands to detect sporozoites in these captured mosquitoes, expressed as the ratio of infected anophelines to the total anophelines collected. More recently, serologic and molecular techniques have been developed to measure the SR, including rapid dipstick methods that are easily used under field conditions to detect circumsporozoite proteins.[38] Even with these advances, measuring the HLR and the SR is difficult, tedious, and costly. Only a fraction (perhaps 20%) of the sporozoites inoculated are infectious. The EIR provides a direct measure of malaria transmission and the risk of human exposure to the bites of infected mosquitoes.

In contrast, the VC measures the rate of *potentially* infective contact, meaning the potential for malaria transmission, and is based solely on key vector parameters in a particular area. In theory, it is independent of whether humans are actually present (to obtain variable a in the VC formula below, of course, requires that some humans have been bitten). The VC is the number of potentially infective contacts an individual human could acquire in an area, through the vector population, per unit of time.[39] The formula for its calculation is as follows:

$$VC = ma^2p^n/-\log p$$

where m is the density of vectors in relation to humans (obtained by standardized sampling methods to give the number of female anophelines caught in a collection per person per night); a is the human biting habit (the proportion of blood meals taken from humans to the total number of blood meals taken from any animal), so that a person is bitten by ma vectors in 1 day; p is the daily survival probability of the vector; and n is the extrinsic incubation (or sporogonic) period of the vector measured in days, so that a fraction p^n of the vectors survive the extrinsic cycle (incubation period). The vectors still have an expectation of life of $1/-\log p$ (the expectation of life is assumed to be independent of age): each of the surviving vectors bites a persons per day. In principle, the VC can predict the extent to which anopheline populations must be reduced to reduce transmission.

It is important to understand the nonlinear relation among these variables. In **Figure 27-3**, the prevalence of parasitemia in the human population is charted against the average annual VC.[40] Note that at low levels of VC, small increases result in a rapid rise in parasite prevalence; thereafter, a long plateau

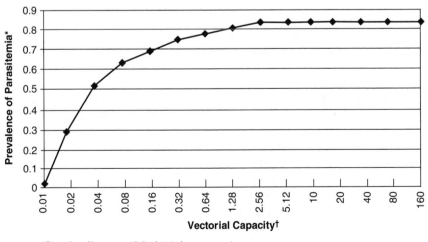

*Proportion of human population infected.
†Number of potentially infectious contacts per person per day.

Figure 27-3 Prevalence of parasitemia as related to vectorial capacity. Data from Garki Project Molineaux and Gramiccia, WHO, Geneva, 1980, p. 281.

is reached, where large changes in the VC do not change the parasite prevalence. This is the situation in much of tropical Africa. In these areas, reduction of several 100-fold or even 1000-fold in the VC will not change the prevalence of malaria (although it may change the frequency and nature of severe malaria).

Current antimalarial interventions reduce transmission (i.e., the reproductive rate) as follows: effective treatment of people with parasitemia reduces human infectivity (SR in the EIR, no effect on VC); indoor residual spraying reduces the daily survival rate of the mosquito (SR in the EIR, *ma* in the VC); and insecticide-treated mosquito nets reduce the human biting rate of the mosquito (HLR in the EIR, *ma* in the VC) and its daily survival rate (SR in the EIR, expectation of vector life in VC).

Geographical Areas According to Intensity of Transmission

As indicated in the section on the public health importance of malaria and outlined in Table 27-1, traditionally geographical patterns of transmission have been classified into four broad categories according to the intensity of transmission: holoendemic, hyperendemic, mesoendemic, and hypoendemic. Further classification schemes have been devised in efforts to simplify the complex epidemiological factors of malaria and to better target strategies for malaria control.[36]

PATHOGENESIS IN INDIVIDUAL HUMANS

Infection and Disease

The distinction between infection and disease is particularly important in malaria. Infection with the malaria parasite does not necessarily result in disease, especially in highly endemic areas. In these regions, children may have parasitemia prevalence rates of 50% or more, yet few will have symptoms.

Disease is the result of the combination of parasite multiplication and the host reaction to the parasite. The classic description of periodic shaking chills, severe fever, and drenching sweats every two or three days can be seen in non-immune adults infected with *P. vivax* (every other day) or *P. malariae* (every third day). The symptoms in these cases result from the host response to synchronous lysis and release of pyrogens from infected red cells. However, with *falciparum* malaria, clinical manifestations, particularly in children, range from asymptomatic parasitemia to severe overwhelming disease and rapid death.[41] Children may present with drowsiness, coma, convulsions, or simply listlessness and fever with nonspecific symptoms. Abdominal cramping, cough, headaches, muscle pains, and varying levels of mental disorientation are common. Severe and complicated malaria due to *falciparum* malaria is a medical emergency.

Host Response

Malaria, on a population basis, is the most intense stimulator of the human immune system known. Many immunologic defense systems are activated in response to malaria infections, including the reticuloendothelial system with enhanced phagocytosis in the spleen, lymph nodes, and liver to remove infected RBCs; an intense production of antibodies (humans can develop several grams per liter of immunoglobulin directed against malaria); and a range of cellular immune responses and cytokine cascades. Some of these responses are protective, whereas others contribute to pathology; often they have both effects. For example, pro-inflammatory cytokines, severe metabolic acidosis, and the classical sequestration of infected RBCs that causes cerebral anoxia all may contribute to the pathogenesis of cerebral malaria; at the same time, however, this pro-inflammatory response and acidosis evidently account for why some patients survive without neurological complications.[42]

The host response to malaria can go wrong in several ways. For example, the pathogenesis of "big spleen disease" (tropical splenomegaly) is caused by an excessive and inappropriate host response to malaria. Tropical splenomegaly is fairly common among relatively non-immune populations who, because they move to a malarious area or experience a change in climate, are exposed to more intense transmission. The disease starts in childhood, progressing through adolescence to young adulthood with severe anemia, high levels of immunoglobulin M (IgM) and antimalarial antibodies, a decrease in platelets, and a huge spleen. Malaria parasites are rarely detected. If untreated, tropical splenomegaly is often fatal, usually from a secondary infection. Two lines of evidence indicate this outcome is directly the result of an abnormal reaction to malaria: (1) those persons with sickle trait (hemoglobin SA) do not develop big spleen disease,[43] and (2) individuals with tropical splenomegaly who take long-term antimalarial prophylaxis have gradual reduction in spleen size and anemia, and return to normal health after many months.

Malaria parasites have evolved complex mechanisms to evade host immune responses and establish persistent or repeated infections. Understanding the basis of effective immune responses that either prevent infection or reduce disease severity is important for vaccine development. Protective immunity following natural infection takes years to develop.[44] However, no immunodominant response has been identified, and an effective immune response is likely the sum of cellular and humoral responses to multiple parasite antigens. Antibodies to the circumsporozoite protein can prevent the binding of sporozoites to liver cells. Cellular immune responses—specifically interferon-γ secreting T cells—are important in killing infected liver cells.[45] Antibodies play a role in killing parasitized red blood cells and can protect the host from sporozoite challenge, although cell-mediated immunity contributes to blood-stage protection as well. The great antigenic variability of *P. falciparum*, as described previously, is in large part responsible for the ability of the parasite to evade effective host immune responses.

Human Genetic Factors

As humans, mosquitoes, and malaria parasites have evolved, many human genetic characteristics that provide partial protection against malaria have emerged. These genetic polymorphisms mostly involve the red blood cell, and include structural variants in the β globin chain of hemoglobin such as sickle-cell trait (hemoglobin S) and hemoglobins C (West Africa) and E (Southeast Asia); altered α and β globin chain production leading to the α and β thalassemias (Mediterranean anemia); erythrocyte enzyme deficiencies including glucose-6-phosphate dehydrogenase (G6PD); red cell cytoskeletal abnormalities such as ovalocytosis; and changes in the red cell membrane such as the absence of the Duffy blood group factor (West Africa).[46] The mechanism that provides protection seems clear for sickle-cell trait—when red cells are invaded, they sickle and are preferentially removed by the reticuloendothelial system, thereby reducing parasite density levels[47]—but mechanisms have not been fully elucidated for many other genetic polymorphisms. In addition to genetic changes involving hemoglobin, red cell membrane proteins, or red cell metabolism, polymorphisms in human immune response genes may affect infection and disease, and polymorphisms in cytokine genes or their promoters have also been associated with disease susceptibility and severity.[48]

Many polymorphisms place a heavy burden on the homozygous individual, such as hemoglobin SS or sickle-cell disease. Accounting for the frequency of sickle-cell trait (AS) in tropical Africa (ranging from 15% to 30% AS hemoglobin in adults), the historical case-fatality rate attributable to malaria is approximately 10–20% of all children with AA hemoglobin genotype.[10] For example, if 28% of the adult population has sickle trait, then the S gene allele frequency in the adult gene pool would be half of 28%. The

Hardy-Weinberg law gives a selection coefficient for the AA genotype of $0.14/(1.00 - 0.14) = 0.1628$. The ratio of AS-genotype individuals to AA-genotype individuals for survivorship to adulthood would be $1/(1.00 - 0.1628) = 1.194$, which is equivalent to nearly a 20% excess death rate for those with the AA genotype before adulthood. Because the only advantage of AS over AA is protection from severe malaria, the case-fatality rate due to malaria in those persons with AA hemoglobin is 19.4%.

Another way to calculate the mortality rate attributable to malaria among AA children is to compare the prevalence of difference genotypes in adults and children. The sharp age-specific rise in prevalence of sickle-cell trait in West Africa from 20–24% in newborns to 26–29% in adults indicates that many infants born without the "protective" sickle-cell trait die before adulthood. This differential survival can be expressed as the ratio of the proportion of AS in adults to the proportion of AS in newborns, or as the proportion of AA in adults divided by the proportion of AA in newborns. In the Garki study area, which is characterized by very high malaria transmission and sickle-trait rates, adults were found to be 28.96% AS and 70.2% AA (0.84% were classified as "other," including those with AC and SC hemoglobin), whereas newborns were 23.6% AS and 73.78% AA (2.62% were "other," including 2.1% SS and 0.5% AC), giving a ratio of 3.86/2.99 = 1.29. This ratio indicates that there is a 29% case-fatality rate in persons with the AA genotype because of malaria.[19]

Undernutrition and Micronutrient Deficiencies

Malaria is prevalent in regions where childhood undernutrition is common, and nutritional deficiencies interact with malaria infection in complex ways. Early observational studies suggested that undernourished children suffered lower morbidity and mortality than adequately nourished children. These early reports often involved selected groups or were conducted during famine, and refeeding severely malnourished children may worsen apparent disease severity. However, more recent studies have not confirmed this association. Pooled analyses of two cohort studies that examined the relationship between underweight and the severity of malaria found that malnourished children were more likely to die from malaria than adequately nourished children.[49] Malaria chemoprophylaxis should be provided to famine victims or severely malnourished child in malarious areas when treating severe protein-energy malnutrition.

Iron deficiency is the most common micronutrient deficiency and is associated with defects in immune responses and a number of poor health outcomes. Early observations suggested that infants with iron deficiency had less severe malaria than children without iron deficiency, and that providing iron supplementation might increase disease severity.[50] A more recent systematic review concluded that oral iron supplementation for preventing or treating anemia among children in malaria-endemic areas did not increase the risk of clinical malaria or death when adequate malaria surveillance and treatment were in place.[51] However, the increase in hemoglobin was variable.

Vitamin A is essential for proper immune function in response to malaria. A trial of vitamin A supplementation in preschool children in Papua New Guinea found that vitamin A reduced clinical episodes of malaria, splenic enlargement, and parasite density, particularly in children 1 to 3 years of age.[52] However, vitamin A may not affect severe malaria or mortality. Extrapolating from this single trial, the fraction of malaria morbidity attributable to vitamin A deficiency was estimated to be 20% worldwide.[49] Complicating interpretation of such studies is the fact that low serum retinol levels are commonly found in children with malaria, but this condition may be due to preexisting vitamin A deficiency, a contribution of malaria to vitamin A deficiency, or merely an acute effect of malaria on retinol metabolism or binding.[53]

Zinc is another micronutrient essential for both cell-mediated and humoral immunity. In randomized trials in Papua New Guinea and the Gambia, the effects of zinc supplementation on malaria morbidity and mortality were investigated.[54,55] The fraction of malaria morbidity attributable to zinc deficiency was estimated to be 20% worldwide—similar to that for vitamin A.[49] In Papua New Guinea, zinc supplementation reduced malaria-attributable clinic attendance by 38% and had its greatest effect on attacks having high-density parasitemia. In the Gambia, the effect of zinc supplementation was less pronounced, but the treatment group did have fewer clinic visits for malaria compared to the placebo group. In contrast, a recent review of five clinical trials concluded that zinc had no effect on malaria incidence or mortality.[56]

THE DIVERSITY OF *FALCIPARUM* MALARIA DISEASE

Advances have been made in differentiating distinctive forms of severe *falciparum* malaria and in understanding underlying pathogenic factors— for example, inoculum size, differing strains of *falciparum*, differing immunologic responses, and various host factors. These discoveries, in turn, have contributed to an appreciation of distinctive epidemiological features of different forms of clinical disease, based on an understanding of the relation of disease manifestations to intensity and constancy of transmission due to ecological factors, genetic characteristics of the parasite, and genetic and acquired immune mechanisms in humans.

Severe Malaria

In areas of Africa with very high transmission rates (EIR >50), severe disease in children does not progress from mild or moderate illness; instead, it strikes abruptly without warning. Mothers are frequently unable to get their infants and young children to a health center in time to provide treatment before the child dies, even when facilities with trained health workers are readily available. If they do manage to reach a hospital, many patients die within 24 hours of admission despite treatment efforts.

Rapid progression to severe disease is not characteristic in areas with less intense transmission. In southeast Asia, malaria typically slowly progresses in severity over several days in both children and adults, and does so in both major types of severe disease that occur there: cerebral malaria, which has a median time of 5 days from onset to cerebral symptoms, and multiple organ dysfunction syndrome (MODS), which is somewhat slower in development and has a median time of progress of 8 days.[59] Early effective treatment before the onset of the severe phase is the key to reducing mortality in these circumstances. Although these slowly progressive types are also seen in Africa, they are less common in high-transmission areas than the rapid severe forms in children.

Disease caused by *P. falciparum* is a major cause of death in children wherever there is a high intensity of malarial infection. Results from community-based intervention studies indicate that malaria may account for nearly half of the mortality rate in children younger than 5 years in holoendemic areas. In hospitals throughout much of tropical Africa, a large proportion of under-5 admissions and deaths are due to malaria. However, drawing conclusions about the burden of disease based on hospital data is problematic. Hospital data substantially underestimate childhood malaria deaths, as only a small proportion of patients are brought to the hospital and most deaths are at home. The pattern of disease in hospitals is determined by access and health-seeking behavior as well as the nature of the disease and, therefore, may not provide a good estimate of the pattern of disease in the broader community. Furthermore, although malaria is a major cause of high fever in young children, recent studies have shown that bacteremia (particularly invasive pneumococcal infection) is also a major cause of fever requiring immediate antibiotic therapy (not antimalarial agents).[58] Understanding the true community epidemiology of malaria as well as effectively reducing childhood morbidity and mortality from fever will require community surveillance and rapid differential diagnostic capacity.

Clinical Patterns

The first important clinical distinction to be made is between severe and nonsevere disease caused by *P. falciparum*.[57] It is important to recognize that severe malaria among children in holoendemic areas behaves as a different disease than nonsevere malaria. This section focuses on the distinctive features of the various forms of severe malaria, particularly those of cerebral malaria and of severe anemia with and without respiratory distress.

The starting point for understanding the pathogenesis of severe malaria is a clear description of the clinical course of the disease. A number of systematic clinical studies have described the presenting symptoms and clinical characteristics of African children younger than 5 years old from low moderate to highly intensive transmission areas hospitalized with severe malaria.[60,61] Most children with severe malaria can be classified as having one of three distinctive syndromes: two syndromes that are readily delineated clinically—those with neurological deficit (20% of admissions with 15% mortality) and those with respiratory distress (15% of admissions with 15% mortality)—plus a third life-threatening syndrome, not so readily apparent clinically when first seen, of severe anemia (20% of admissions with 5% mortality).

The roles of hypoglycemia and metabolic acidosis in the pathogenesis of severe disease are central.[62] Hypoglycemia, which is difficult to diagnose clinically, can have a prevalence equivalent to that of respiratory distress and an even higher mortality (approximately 22%). Hypoglycemia associated with cerebral malaria is certainly a contributory factor in deaths from unarousable coma and probably those with acidosis.[63] In addition, children with malaria have an increased incidence of non-typhoidal *Salmonella* infection;[64] consequently, a reduction in the incidence of non-typhoidal *Salmonella* invasive disease in the Gambia was associated with the decline in malaria disease.[65]

Cerebral Malaria

The classical histopathological picture of cerebral malaria is intense sequestration of infected cells in the cerebral microvasculature, and clinically is associated with case-fatality ratios ranging from 10% to 50%. However, cerebral malaria is heterogeneous,[66] and different pathogenic mechanisms underlie the four overlapping WHO-defined syndromes: (1) prolonged postictal state, characterized as deep sleep, headache, confusion, and muscle soreness; (2) covert status epilepticus, characterized by continual seizures; (3) severe metabolic derangement (particularly with hypoglycemia and metabolic acidosis); and (4) children with a primary neurological syndrome. Patients commonly present with more than one of these conditions. A child may be acidotic, have hypoglycemia, and be in status epilepticus; recognition and proper management of all three syndromes as well as treatment of the malaria are critical. These distinctions are important for selecting the appropriate therapy, of course, but careful delineation also may help in differential diagnosis of children. Encephalopathy due to *P. falciparum* causes a distinctive retinopathy—a patchy retinal whitening and focal changes of vessel color—and can be used to distinguish cerebral malaria from other causes of encephalopathy in children.[67]

Hypoglycemia is especially common in severe pediatric malaria. Of pediatric patients admitted for severe malaria in Thailand, 23% had hypoglycemia;[68] in Malawi, 33% of such patients had hypoglycemia.[69] The outlook was grim for these patients. In the Malawi study, 37% with hypoglycemia died and 26% were discharged with brain damage—a rate many times higher than the rate in pediatric patients diagnosed with cerebral malaria but with normal blood sugar levels. The combination of hypoglycemia with lactic acidosis is particularly devastating. Survivors of cerebral malaria have higher rates of epilepsy and cognitive impairment than survivors of other forms of severe malaria.[70]

Respiratory Distress

Pulmonary edema, which is often seen with acute respiratory distress syndrome (ARDS), is included in the WHO criteria for severe malaria and is a serious, frequently fatal complication of malaria in non-immune adults. The clinical signs of hyperventilation, driven by efforts to reduce CO_2, are highly sensitive and specific for the diagnosis of respiratory distress.[71]

Cardiac failure, coexistent pneumonia, direct sequestration of malaria parasites in the lungs, and increased central drive to respiration in association with cerebral malaria all contribute to respiratory distress. Nevertheless, the main factor is metabolic acidosis, which arises largely from lactate production caused by reduced oxygen supply to the tissues. In addition, several factors increase lactic acidemia: the metabolic processes of the malaria parasite itself; reduced hepatic blood flow leading to reduced lactate clearance; and high levels of cytokines that directly impair cellular metabolism and increase lactate production.

Severe Anemia

The third major clinical manifestation of severe malaria is severe anemia;[72] it, too, has a complex pathogenesis and varies considerably geographically, partly reflecting the extent of interaction with undernutrition and iron deficiency.[73] Severe anemia tends to be the predominant form in areas of the most intense transmission and is common in the youngest age groups.[74]

Different manifestations of severe malaria arise from interaction of a limited number of pathogenic processes: metabolic acidosis, red cell destruction, toxin-mediated activation of cytokine cascades, and infected cell sequestration in tissue microvascular beds. All lead to reduced tissue oxygenation as a unifying process in the pathogenesis of these major clinical syndromes of severe malaria. Other severe, but less common, causes of malarial mortality include renal failure, pulmonary edema with acute respiratory distress syndrome, and disseminated intravascular coagulopathy (DIC).

Epidemiological Features of Severe Malaria in Children

Most descriptions of severe malaria in African children have focused on differentiating those with severe anemia from those with cerebral and neurological involvement. Clear epidemiological differences parallel these distinctive clinical forms of severe malaria. As the intensity of transmission increases, the proportion of the population having severe malaria as compared to nonsevere malaria shifts increasingly to younger age groups. Thus, in the areas with the most intense transmission, severe malaria and death are restricted largely to children younger than 5 years, and most clinical disease is seen in those younger than age 10.[41]

Within any endemic area, the pattern of severe morbidity varies with age; severe anemia predominates in younger children with a median age of 15 to 24 months, whereas cerebral malaria is more common in older children with a median age of 36 to 48 months. Between endemic areas with different levels of transmission intensity, there may be a marked difference in the age distributions of children with severe malaria and in the relative importance

of different clinical syndromes. An additional factor that apparently affects the nature of severe malaria in a population is the constancy of transmission. Areas of intense perennial transmission have a high incidence of severe anemia, whereas areas with intense seasonal transmission have a high incidence of cerebral malaria.

In areas of intense transmission, the prevalence and density of both asexual and gametocyte stages of *P. falciparum* reach a peak in early childhood and decline thereafter. Density of parasitemia drops off before prevalence, and density of gametocytes declines before that of asexual stages. The density of asexual parasites at which symptoms appear increases in early life and declines thereafter. This pattern indicates a separate immune response to toxic products of red cell rupture as compared to the response to the parasites themselves. The antitoxic immunity builds rapidly with early infections, but declines thereafter as effective immune responses to the parasites themselves slowly develop and then directly reduce toxic products.[75,76]

Many questions remain about superinfection, defined as infection concurrent with an already existing infection. Superinfection is common in holoendemic malaria areas with an EIR of dozens to hundreds each year. An important epidemiological point is that the incidence of malarial disease, whether mild or severe, is limited to the period of transmission in areas of holoendemic seasonal malaria. This point can be interpreted as saying that disease onset must require a recent inoculation. In some way, the newly inoculated parasite must differ from those parasites already present in that particular child. Quantitatively, there are more parasites already in the blood than will be released from the liver cells derived from the new batch of sporozoites. During the low-transmission season, each child continues to harbor the same parasite type and remains without symptoms. In contrast, during the high-transmission season, parasite isolates are quite diverse, and rapid shifting of types within each child occurs. Those patients who become symptomatic do so only with the acquisition of a new parasite type. Only some of the new types are associated with symptoms, but these types vary from child to child.[77]

Some evidence indicates that those patients with severe malaria have not received a higher inocula than those with nonsevere malaria,[78] but much work remains to be done to relate the number of sporozoites injected by individual inoculum to clinical disease. Reports on the effectiveness of insecticide-impregnated bednets indicate that the impact on mortality, or on severe malaria, is greater than the impact on nonsevere malaria; likewise, there is a greater reduction in clinical disease than in prevalence of asymptomatic parasitemia.[79]

Malaria in Pregnancy

Women who become infected with malaria while pregnant are at much greater risk of serious consequences than women who are not pregnant (or than men); host defense mechanisms apparently are dampened during and for several weeks postpartum, with reductions in both cell-mediated and humoral responses being noted.

In all areas endemic for malaria, pregnant women are more likely to be bitten by malaria vectors.[80] This increased risk of exposure has been hypothesized to be related to the higher metabolic rate of pregnancy that increases body temperature and CO_2 release, both of which serve as attractants for mosquitoes. However, in a study of risk behaviors, researchers also noted that pregnant women were more exposed to mosquitoes when they left the home to urinate at night. Pregnant women are also at higher risk of infection with malaria of all types, and are more likely to develop severe, complicated malaria and die, compared to nonpregnant women. Adverse outcomes of their pregnancies are also higher, due to active malarial infection of the placenta.[81]

The maternal mortality ratio (MMR) for women infected with malaria ranges from 100 to more than 1000 deaths per 100,000 live births, and relative risks of death for pregnant women with malaria are increased at least twofold. The MMR is as high in low-transmission areas as it is in high-transmission areas, but the nature of the complications and those at greatest risk are different. In low-transmission areas, pregnant women across the spectrum of parity die from severe, complicated malaria, particularly with cerebral symptoms, hypoglycemia, and acute respiratory distress syndrome. MMRs as great as 1000 per 100,000 live births have been reported during malaria epidemics in low-transmission areas. In areas of high transmission, the risk of severe disease and death is increased mainly among women in their first pregnancy (more than 1000 per 100,000 MMR), even though they may have had a high level of immunity prior to their pregnancy. Mortality is mainly related to severe anemia.[82]

The prevalence of parasitemia is highest during the second trimester of pregnancy regardless of the transmission intensity. In low-transmission areas, pregnant women with malaria virtually always have symptoms and generally have parasitemia regardless of parity. In contrast, in high-transmission areas, pregnant women often have asymptomatic parasitemia; it is only primigravidae who have symptoms and a high risk of complications.[83]

Malaria infection during pregnancy commonly leads to infection of the placenta. The pathogenic activity of the parasite and the often-intense host responses combine to contribute to the high fetal mortality due to malaria. When malaria is caused by *P. falciparum*, there may be a discrepancy in parasitemia between the placenta and the peripheral blood. Such a concentration of parasites in the placenta is not seen with *P. vivax*. *P. falcipirum*'s tendency to concentrate in the placenta is most notable in high-transmission areas where pregnant women may demonstrate an intense placental parasitemia but few, if any, parasites are found in the peripheral blood. Although this phenomenon is not fully understood, the condition seems to be related to the expression of unique variant surface antigens on parasitized cells within the placenta, as well as the distinctive placental and uterine immunological and biochemical responses and associated immunological memory.[84] Local uterine and placental responses apparently are least effective in first pregnancies, but increase in subsequent pregnancies. In high-transmission areas, women, when pregnant for the first time, lose their high levels of malaria immunity, yet somehow retain their immunity during subsequent pregnancies. This differing level of protection may be due to the younger age of women during their first pregnancies, such that their own immunity to *Plasmodium* is not fully developed, or it may relate to other, not fully understood mechanisms. HIV infection has profound effects on infant and maternal morbidity and mortality, increases susceptibility to maternal malaria, impairs the ability of pregnant women to control parasitemia, and increases this risk among all pregnant women, not just the primigravidae.[85]

Malaria increases the rates of low-weight births and of stillbirths.[86] The proportion of low-birth-weight (LBW) infants is elevated in both low-transmission and high-transmission areas, but the reasons for the low weight may be different in the two areas: preterm delivery (PTD) is common in low-transmission areas, especially in association with acute febrile episodes caused by malaria in the third trimester, whereas in high-transmission areas intrauterine growth retardation (IUGR) is associated with chronic placental inflammatory damage. In addition, maternal malaria leads to a higher perinatal and infant mortality rate—though whether this difference reflects the low birth weight or other factors is not yet clear. In areas of moderate transmission, women with malaria of all parities have a substantially higher risk of low birth weight and severe anemia. The risk of low birth weight is particularly high in children whose mothers had chronic placental malaria, is more common in

P. falciparum infection, and is increased with severe anemia.

Malaria and HIV

Early investigations did not find interactions between HIV and malaria coinfection, with the exception of HIV-infected pregnant women. More recently, HIV-infected Ugandan adults were observed to have twice as many episodes of symptomatic parasitemia as HIV-uninfected adults, and the parasite density and clinical signs and symptoms were correlated with the degree of immunosuppression.[87] In Malawi, plasma HIV-1 RNA levels in adults were almost twice as high during periods of malaria parasitemia but returned to baseline within a few weeks after antimalarial treatment, suggesting malaria may enhance HIV disease progression and increase infectivity.[88] Fewer studies have investigated malaria in HIV-infected children—the age group at greatest risk of morbidity and mortality caused by malaria. Although not definitive, these studies suggest malaria may be more severe and less responsive to therapy in HIV-infected children and, further, that malaria may adversely affect HIV disease progression. HIV-infected children receiving cotrimoxazole prophylaxis for pneumocystis pneumonia and bacterial infection, however, derive some protection against malaria.[89]

HUMAN ACTIVITIES, CLIMATE CHANGE WITH GLOBAL WARMING, AND THE EPIDEMIOLOGY OF MALARIA

Human activities—particularly at the population level, but also at the individual behavioral level—strongly influence the epidemiological pattern of malaria and the efforts to control it. Agricultural development, population movement, and urbanization are important determinants of the pattern of malaria transmission, and control measures involve the interplay of broad social, cultural, and economic factors.

Malaria has long been linked to farming practices. In sub-Saharan Africa, the clearing of forest for crop production led to increased breeding of *A. gambiae*, the most efficient vector of human malaria, which prefers sunlit open pools of standing water to the full shade of tropical forest. The formation of small towns, dams, and irrigation schemes arising in concert with agricultural development in much of Africa has concentrated populations of humans and vectors in relatively confined areas near water supplies. Additionally, agricultural use of pesticides has been a major factor in the development and spread of insecticide-resistant vectors. Thus the very efforts to promote economic development and improve human conditions have increased the intensity of malaria transmission.

Population movements throughout Africa have also contributed to increased malaria transmission. Traditionally, in many parts of Africa, seasonal migration has been a part of life, with people moving from their village settlements to rural farms during the early months of the wet season when cultivation, planting, and weeding are carried out. Often intensity of transmission is much higher in these areas than in their settled home villages, where water supplies are controlled. In a similar way, many pastoral Africans are exposed to higher transmission as they move their livestock between highland and lowland pastures with the seasons.

Other reasons for population movement are related to population expansion, with movement of humans into previously unoccupied and more marginally productive areas. The living and working conditions in these areas often result in greater exposure to malaria vectors. Africa has been especially afflicted with drought, famine, war, and political upheavals resulting in mass population displacement and refugee movements, all of which are frequently associated with increased malaria transmission. These groups frequently are poorly served by government health and malaria control programs, and have less access to antimalarial agents and other aspects of health care.

Climate Change, Global Warming and Malaria Transmission

Although climate warming is occurring in many areas of the globe and may lead to increased transmission of malaria in some areas, the consequences of this trend are likely to be quite variable and the magnitude of the impact remains controversial.[90] One study estimated an overall increase of 20–25% in malaria globally attributable to global warming by 2100. This estimate was based on both prolonged transmission seasons in the current endemic areas and geographical expansion of the endemic areas.[91] Other analyses suggest the impact will be significantly less dire, given the shrinking malaria map over the past century in the face of rising global temperatures, current declines in malaria incidence, and the effectiveness of control interventions.[92]

Malaria in Areas of Conflict and Humanitarian Emergencies

Disasters and conflicts, so prominent in Africa for decades, greatly contribute to the transmission of malaria and inhibition of antimalaria control efforts. Approximately one-third of malaria deaths in sub-Saharan Africa occur in countries affected by conflict and humanitarian emergencies. Factors facilitating malaria mortality in humanitarian emergencies include migration of non-immune people to hyperendemic areas, overcrowding, interruption of vector-control programs, and inadequate access to health care.[93] Multiple interventions, including provision of shelter, vector control, case management, and surveillance, are required for malaria control in these settings. Insecticide-treated plastic sheeting may be an effective means of vector control among refugee and internally displaced populations.[94]

Urban Migration

In contrast to the types of population movement described previously, the major secular migrations to urban areas throughout Africa generally have little influence on malaria transmission.[95] Although malaria in Africa is principally a rural rather than an urban disease, some anopheline species have become well adapted to city life. For example, *A. arabiensis* has become a transmitter of malaria in many cities of Nigeria. Generally, this vector is restricted to semi-urban slum areas rather than the highly concentrated populations in urban centers.

Social Class

Although malaria can infect and cause severe disease in anyone, it is principally a disease of the poor and uninformed. Loss of healthy life due to malaria is much higher in poor rural areas of Africa than in the better-developed urban areas.

Some notion of the difference in impact on different social groups can be seen in the studies by Oduntan in Nigeria,[96] who found that the prevalence of sickle-cell trait among elite school children in Ibadan was less than 20%, whereas in rural children not attending school, the prevalence of AS was 26.3%. This disparity shows malaria's selective pressure on poor children, who tend to experience high malaria mortality due to exposure, nutrition, and access to health care. If one assumes that the AA, AS, and SS genotypes were equally distributed at birth, and that there is a zero mortality rate among elite AA-genotype children by the time they reach school age, the observed distribution would indicate that 29.9% of those with the AA genotype in the non-elite group would have died from malaria.

In reality, the assumption that the distributions are the same at birth is probably unlikely to hold true, as there is a strong tendency for social classes to intermarry. Thus it is likely that some of this marked difference in gene distribution could be attributed

to selective pressure over several generations. The interplay between environmental factors (malaria) and genetics (hemoglobin genotypes) ensures that the prevalence of the sickle-cell trait will decline among those for whom the selective pressure of malaria has abated. The dramatic differential in mortality from malaria by social class reinforces the public health imperative to improved equity in health.

Health-Seeking Behavior

Individual and community behavior are important factors influencing the population effects discussed previously and are crucial in determining the success of malaria control. In Africa, great diversity in cultures and community structures is apparent. Understanding and acting in accord with the prevailing belief systems are essential for malaria control efforts; otherwise, these beliefs may serve as barriers to adoption of effective interventions. Health-seeking behavior, which is key for obtaining timely treatment, depends on understanding the need for treatment; thus people's perceptions of malaria and its causes are very important. Even in communities that have an appreciation of the importance of malaria and the need to obtain appropriate treatment, the symptoms of cerebral malaria may be misunderstood because this form of the disease produces convulsions and confusion. People frequently do not recognize these as signs for urgent treatment for malaria; indeed, such symptoms often are attributed to belief of supernatural causes, not something that modern medicine can affect, and the advice of traditional healers may be sought.[97] As detailed in the section on antimalarial interventions, virtually all approaches to control require a good understanding of which factors contribute to malaria and the active participation of the community, families, and individuals.

DIAGNOSIS AND TREATMENT

Diagnosis

A definitive diagnosis of malaria is made by demonstration of parasites in red blood cells. The standard technique is microscopic examination of Giemsa-stained thick and thin smears of blood on glass microscope slides. The thick smear is the more sensitive method for the detection of parasites. With thin films, skilled technicians can not only determine the species of malaria, but also obtain reliable estimates of the number of parasites (parasite density). The ability to detect parasites depends on the number of fields examined and the experience of the technician viewing the slide.

Although this approach continues to be standard practice, problems of practical implementation and interpretation exist. At the practical level, Giemsa-stained blood smears examined with standard light microscopes have been used for decades in every area in the world. Yet the work is tedious and requires continuous concentration; delays in viewing smears can result in delayed treatment; maintenance of the microscope and staining materials requires rigorous control; and standards related to training technicians and supervising their activities can be difficult to maintain. Quality control methods are essential, and approaches to maintain good morale among the technicians are critical.

The problems of interpretation of blood smears are twofold. First, peripheral smears may be falsely negative in two circumstances: (1) before red blood cells are infected and (2) later during schizogony, when infected red blood cells are sequestered in the capillary beds. Second, the peripheral smear may be "falsely" positive in the sense that the presence of parasites in a blood smear from a febrile patient in an endemic area does not necessarily mean that the symptoms are due to malaria. Most school-aged children in holoendemic areas will have malaria parasites in their blood all the time. Thus there is no specific approach to diagnosing clinical disease in this situation. In highly endemic areas, patients are often treated on the basis of clinical symptoms alone. Usually a clinician, quite appropriately and in accordance with Integrated Management of Childhood Illness (IMCI) guidelines, will give antimalarial agents to any child with fever. Such an approach may be necessary to provide early treatment to young children with severe malaria, but also can result in overdiagnosis, the misuse of antimalarial medications, and the inappropriate treatment of other causes of fever.[98] With the introduction of more expensive artemisinin-combination therapy (ACT), many national guidelines now require confirmation of malaria with a rapid diagnostic test prior to treatment.

Many efforts have been expended to develop rapid, point-of-care methods of diagnosis that do not involve such demanding discipline and technical skills. Several immunochromatographic assays have been developed that detect a variety of malaria antigens, including histidine-rich protein 2 (HRP2) and lactate dehydrogenase (LDH).[99] These rapid diagnostic tests have been designed for use as dipsticks and are easy to use in health centers or the community without equipment and with minimal training. Generally, these tests have high sensitivity and specificity at moderate parasite densities, but demonstrate reduced sensitivity at lower parasite densities. The use of simple, inexpensive, and rapid diagnostic tests for malaria has been of increasing importance as countries in Africa shift from the use of low-cost antimalarial agents (chloroquine and sulfadoxine/pyrimethamine) to more expensive drugs (ACT) in the face of widespread drug resistance.

Although not appropriate for the diagnosis of malaria in endemic areas, the use of polymerase chain reaction (PCR)-based assays can provide high sensitivity in persons with low-level parasitemia.[100] These molecular diagnostic tools can distinguish infections with multiple *Plasmodia* species and can provide quantitative measures using real-time PCR that may prove useful in following up on responses to treatment. PCR-based genotyping is valuable in the analysis of malaria parasites in drug efficacy trials because it enables researchers to distinguish between recrudescence and reinfection. Molecular epidemiology also assists in analyzing parasite populations resulting from vector control or environmental alterations.[101]

Treatment

The history of drug treatment of malaria goes back hundreds of years. In the early 1600s, Jesuit missionaries brought back to Europe cinchona bark used by Peruvian healers against fevers for generations. In 1820, the active ingredient was identified as the alkaloid quinine, the first highly active drug against a specific infection. Even today, it remains an important therapeutic agent for drug-resistant *falciparum* malaria. In China, extracts of the plant *Artemisia annua* (wormwood) have been in use for centuries as a malaria therapy. A family of highly effective antimalarial drugs, the artemisinins, was derived from this plant and is in widespread use in combination with other antimalarial agents.

At the time of World War II, several compounds were found to be highly effective against malaria, including chloroquine, primaquine, and sulfadoxine-pyrimethamine. Chloroquine was synthesized in the late 1930s in Germany. During the war, the Allies captured some chloroquine and found it to be highly effective against malaria. Chloroquine is rapidly absorbed after oral administration and is active against the asexual stages of all human-infective species except for resistant strains of *P. falciparum* and *P. vivax*. Chloroquine interferes with the degradation of heme, allowing the accumulation of toxic metabolic products that kill the parasite within the red blood cell. In appropriate doses, it is well tolerated even when taken for long periods, and it is safe for young children and pregnant women. The only important side effect is intense pruritus reported uniquely but frequently by black Africans. Because of low toxicity, low cost, and effectiveness, chloroquine was the drug of choice to treat malaria for decades following World War II. Only after parasite resistance to chloroquine was demonstrated were serious efforts focused on developing alternative antimalarial agents.

Primaquine was developed by the U.S. Army during World War II and is the only drug that is effective against hypnozoites. Primaquine can be used to prevent infection in the liver (referred to as a "causal" prophylaxis) and to eliminate the hypnozoite stages of *P. vivax* and *P. ovale* that lead to relapse (antirelapse treatment). It is also effective in eliminating gametocytes and, at least theoretically, could play a role in reducing transmission and preventing the spread of drug-resistant strains.[102] Primaquine causes hemolysis in persons with glucose-6-phosphate dehydrogenase (G6PD) deficiency, a condition that is common in individuals of African and Mediterranean descent.

Sulfadoxine-pyrimethamine (SP, Fansidar), originally developed and promoted for its efficacy against chloroquine-resistant *P. falciparum*, was widely used as a replacement for chloroquine in areas in which drug resistance emerged. Both compounds inhibit enzymes in the folic acid synthesis pathway. Because it is single-dose therapy and inexpensive, SP was widely used in Africa to treat malaria before the emergence and spread of resistance. It remains the preferred antimalarial for pregnant women and can be used for intermittent preventive treatment of young children. Adverse reactions, some of which are severe, including Stevens-Johnson syndrome, have been reported when SP is used for prophylaxis.

The U.S. Army developed mefloquine, a synthetic compound structurally related to quinine and quinidine, for its activity against chloroquine-resistant *P. falciparum* by the late 1960s. Mefloquine has an unusually long half-life and is used for chemoprophylaxis and for treatment in combination with artesunate in Thailand. However, resistance to mefloquine emerged in Southeast Asia. Frequent reports of adverse mental reactions have led to a reduction in its use.

Artemisinin and related compounds (e.g., artesunate, arthemether), the agent of the Chinese herbal medicine, are metabolized to the active form, dihydroartemisinin, and act in part by inhibiting a calcium-pumping enzyme *P. falciparum* ATP6.[103] These drugs quickly clear blood-stage parasites and gametocytes and stimulate a rapid clinical response. When one of these agents is used alone, recrudescence is common and the development of resistance is fostered, and so these drugs are combined with other antimalarial agents with a longer half-life.

Thus the most significant change in the treatment of malaria has been not the introduction of novel antimalarial medications, but rather the use of older drugs in combination. Because of rapid and widespread emergence of resistant parasites in Southeast Asia, combination therapy has been used in that region for many years. In sub-Saharan Africa, combination therapy was introduced more recently. Not only is combination therapy more effective in regions where resistance to chloroquine and sulfadoxine-pyrimethamine is widespread, but combination therapy can also improve compliance by shortening the duration of therapy. Importantly, combination therapy can decrease the risk of resistant mutations arising during therapy, similar to the principles guiding combination therapy for HIV-1 infection and tuberculosis. Many combinations of antimalarial agents have been used, and some do not include an artemisinin compound, such as the clindamycin/quinine, chlorproguanil/dapsone, and atovaquone/proguanil regimens. However, the most widely used combinations include an artemisinin, so that the regimen is referred to as artemisinin-based combination therapy. Examples include artemether/lumefantrine (available as a fixed-dose formulation), artesunate/amodiaquine, and artesunate/mefloquine. The major disadvantage of ACT is the higher cost of artemisinin derivatives.

DRUG RESISTANCE

The emergence and spread of drug-resistant malaria, particularly of chloroquine- and sulfadoxine-pyrimethamine-resistant *P. falciparum* (and more recently the potential spread of artemisinin resistance), are of major public health importance and are currently monitored through the World Antimalarial Resistance Network (WARN).[104] These once highly effective, affordable, and safe drugs are no longer useful in many malaria-endemic regions, forcing countries to switch to more expensive artemisinin-based combination therapies. Resistance to more recently introduced antimalarial agents, such as mefloquine and atovaquone, developed quickly. Tragically, delayed parasite clearance ("resistance") following treatment with ACT has been detected along the Thai–Cambodian border.[105] Antimalarial drug resistance is largely a problem with *P. falciparum* infection, although chloroquine-resistant *P. vivax* is prevalent in Papua New Guinea and Irian Jaya. Clinically, relevant drug resistance in *P. malariae* and *P. ovale* has not been documented.

Many factors contribute to the emergence and spread of antimalarial drug resistance, including pharmacologic properties of the drug, use of counterfeit drugs with inadequate concentrations, host immunity, parasite genetics, and transmission characteristics.[106] For example, use of antimalarial drugs with a prolonged half-life (such as sulfadoxine-pyrimethamine), poor compliance, or inappropriate use can expose parasites to subtherapeutic drug levels, which in turn increases the risk of emergence of drug-resistant parasites.

Antimalarial drug resistance can be assessed in several ways, including evaluation of therapeutic responses in vivo, measurement of parasite growth ex vivo, and identification of genetic mutations associated with resistance. However, there is great need for a rapid, simple, and inexpensive field test to detect antimalarial drug resistance. WHO developed the traditional method of in vivo resistance testing. In this approach, infected patients are given an antimalarial drug according to an established regimen, and parasite counts are performed at the start of therapy, at 24 hours, at 7 days, and at 28 days after the start of treatment. If parasites are not detectable at the end of 7 days (and still not detectable at 28 days), the malaria parasites are considered sensitive to the drug. If clearance of parasites occurs at 7 days, but recrudescence appears 8 or more days after the start of treatment, the parasites are stage RI resistant. If there is reduction in parasitemia but not complete clearance at 7 days, the parasites are considered stage RII resistant. If there is no evidence of response, the parasites are considered to be fully resistant, designated as RIII.

In the absence of molecular epidemiologic tools, however, distinguishing recrudescence from reinfection is not possible. To overcome this limitation in regions of intense transmission, WHO introduced a modified protocol based on clinical response rather than parasitemia. Adequate clinical response is distinguished from early and late treatment failure. A limitation in interpreting in vivo testing is that persons with immunity will improve even if the parasites are moderately resistant to the drug.

In vitro testing of P. falciparum drug resistance relies on short-term culture of malaria parasites.[107] Blood from a parasitemic individual is prepared for culture and incubated with increasing concentrations of an antimalarial drug. Several assay endpoints have been developed to measure parasite growth in the presence of different drug concentrations, including schizont maturation, radioisotope incorporation, and detection of the parasite enzyme LDH or HRP2. The major advantage of in vitro resistance testing is that these assays are not influenced by individual variations in drug levels and immune responses.

In vivo and in vitro test systems provide two complementary approaches to determine malaria drug resistance and are useful in monitoring the geographic distribution and levels of drug resistance. Such monitoring provides a basis for selecting effective antimalarial agents for use in the area, but affords little basis for certainty that a specific drug will be effective in a specific individual. Particularly for severe malaria in children, which strikes with great speed, neither of these test systems is rapid enough to guide treatment choices.

Genetic polymorphisms are associated with drug resistance and are best characterized for chloroquine and sulfadoxine-pyrimethamine resistance. Chloroquine resistance is associated with mutations in the *pfcrt* gene, which codes for a membrane transporter protein that allows the parasite to excrete chloroquine so that intracellular concentrations do not reach toxic levels.[108] One particular mutation—the substitution of threonine for lysine in codon 76 (K76T)—is highly associated with chloroquine resistance.

Multiple mutations decrease the binding affinity of P. falciparum enzymes to sulfadoxine-pyrimethamine. At least five different point mutations in the gene encoding the enzyme dihydropteroate synthetase (*dhps*) confer resistance to sulfadoxine, for example. Resistance to pyrimethamine is caused by specific point mutations in the gene encoding dihydrofolate reductase (*dhfr*). The *pfdhps* double mutant and the *pfdhfr* triple mutant form the *pfdhfr/pfdhps* quintuple mutant, which is associated with SP treatment failure.[109] Mutations in the *pfmdr1* gene are associated with resistance to mefloquine, chloroquine, and other antimalarial drugs.

The molecular basis of artemisinin partial resistance is as yet unknown, although an increased *pfmdr* copy number has been suggested as a genetic basis for this effect. Parasite exposure to artemisinin monotherapies in subtherapeutic doses for more than 30 years and the availability of substandard artemisinins likely led to the selection for resistance along the Thai–Cambodian border.[110] Containment strategies include enhanced surveillance and vector control, along with early diagnosis of cases and treatment with combination therapy.

Epidemiology of Drug Resistance in Malaria

Chloroquine resistance in P. falciparum was first reported in the late 1950s in South America in areas between Venezuela and Colombia and in Southeast Asia along the Thai–Cambodian and Thai–Burmese borders.[111] Although it was nearly 20 years later that resistance was first demonstrated in Africa,[112] chloroquine-resistant malaria is now widespread there as well. Areas that remain free of chloroquine resistance include Mexico, parts of Central America and the Caribbean, and parts of central Asia: in these areas intensity of transmission is generally low and predominantly due to *P. vivax*.[113] Of great interest and possibly of importance, removal of the selective drug pressure resulted in the return of chloroquine sensitivity in Malawi.[114] In other settings, declining prevalence of chloroquine resistance is associated with low levels of chloroquine use in communities, possibly in response to a decrease in selective pressure.[115]

Along the Thai–Cambodian border, *P. falciparum* was first noted to be resistant to sulfadoxine-pyrimethamine in the mid-1960s, with more widespread resistance reported in the late 1970s after the drug was introduced into the malaria control program.[111] In Africa, resistance to sulfadoxine-pyrimethamine was first noted in the late 1980s, with high-level resistance and treatment failures most common in East Africa. Mefloquine resistance also was first observed near the Thai–Cambodian border in the late 1980s. Clinically significant resistance to mefloquine is rare in Africa, although treatment failures associated with *pfmdr1* amplification have been reported in West Africa.[116]

The origins and mechanisms of spread of drug-resistant strains of *P. falciparum* are of great public health importance. Resistance to chloroquine appears to have originated only four times, and to have spread from Asia to Africa.[117] Resistance to sulfadoxine-pyrimethamine was thought to have multiple, independent origins. However, genotyping of microsatellite markers flanking the *dhfr* gene suggests that high-level resistance to sulfadoxine-pyrimethamine (i.e., triple or quadruple mutant *dhfr* alleles) originated in Southeast Asia and subsequently spread to Africa.[118]

Of considerable debate is whether drug resistance evolves more rapidly in areas of high or low malaria transmission.[119,120] This question has important public health implications, as interventions to reduce transmission could affect rates of drug resistance. Lower transmission was hypothesized to increase rates of drug resistance by enhancing parasite inbreeding, thereby lowering the rate of genetic recombination and increasing the probability that drug-resistance mutations would spread in the parasite population. Inbreeding is more frequent when transmission rates are lower, as infection with multiple different strains is less likely. The frequent emergence of resistance along the Thai–Cambodian border supports the hypothesis that lower transmission facilitates the emergence of drug resistance.

However, the true situation is more complex than this simple analysis suggests. Reduced transmission in Zimbabwe through residual insecticide spraying of households was associated with suppressed levels of drug resistance, suggesting that malaria control measures that reduce transmission will not increase drug resistance.[121]

VACCINES AGAINST MALARIA

Prospects for a successful vaccine against malaria have been considered bright for several decades; unfortunately, they have remained simply prospects, and to date no vaccine has been sufficiently effective to warrant widespread use. However, progress has been made, including a multicountry, Phase 3 trial of a circumsporozoite vaccine involving more than 16,000 children in Africa.[122]

Vaccine development has largely focused on *P. falciparum*, although efforts have also been made to develop vaccines against *P. vivax*. The overwhelming evidence that humans develop protective immune responses against *P. falciparum* when repeatedly exposed to infection indicates that development of an effective vaccine should be possible. By the age of 6 years, most children in holoendemic regions have acquired substantial immunity against the disease. These children are protected from severe and fatal malaria, even though they may have parasitemia and occasional bouts of fever. The population will have paid a high price for this protection, however, as under-5 mortality from malaria is very high. Early studies by Ian McGregor et al. demonstrated that serum from immune adults in the Gambia could be used to treat young children with malaria in East Africa.[123] In the early 1970s, David Clyde and others demonstrated that injection of sporozoites derived from irradiated *P. falciparum*-infected mosquitoes provided protective immunity against challenge.[124,125] However, the immunologic basis of protection induced by natural infection or irradiated sporozoites is not completely understood.

In addition to the empirical evidence for an effective acquired immune response, genomic and proteomic work based on sequencing the genomes of *P. falciparum*, the *Anopheles gambiae* vector, and the human host may spur novel vaccine development. Moreover, progress has been made in understanding the immunology and pathogenesis of malaria, and advances have been made in vaccinology. Subunit vaccines composed of synthetic peptides or recombinant proteins, newer vaccine strategies (e.g., prime-boost and the targeting of dendritic cells), and novel adjuvants give hope that the formidable impediments to malaria vaccine development will be overcome.[126]

Several high-risk groups would greatly benefit from a malaria vaccine that decreases morbidity and mortality, including young children and primigravida women in endemic areas. In addition, immunologically naive travelers to malaria-endemic regions would benefit from a vaccine that prevents infection. These different risk groups necessitate the development of different types of vaccine. The different stages of the malaria parasite outlined in Figure 27-2 represent potential targets for immunization. To date, vaccine development has focused largely on three parasite stages: (1) pre-erythrocytic sporozoite and hepatic forms to prevent infection; (2) asexual erythrocytic forms to reduce morbidity and mortality; and (3) sexual forms within the mosquito to prevent transmission. **Table 27-3** outlines malaria vaccine strategies according to the strategy for protection, the stage in the malaria life cycle with presumed time period of exposure, and the target antigens with examples of vaccine candidates.

Much effort has gone into development of sporozoite vaccines because immunity was induced by immunization with irradiated sporozoites, even though there is little evidence of effective natural immunity to sporozoites. However, a single sporozoite that evades the immune response could potentially generate thousands of merozoites capable of infecting red blood cells. Efforts to develop a pre-erythrocytic vaccine have focused largely on targeting the circumsporozoite (CS) protein, a major component of the sporozoite surface. One of the more promising CS vaccines, RTS,S/AS02A, consists of recombinantly expressed *P. falciparum* CS peptides fused to a portion of the hepatitis B virus surface antigen and administered with an adjuvant (AS02A). In a much-publicized clinical trial, both the first clinical episode of malaria and episodes of severe malaria were reduced in Mozambican children for 6 months following vaccination.[127] However, protective efficacy for the first clinical episode of malaria was only 30%, and antibody titers decayed rapidly. A Phase 3 multicenter efficacy trial of the RTS,S/AS01 malaria vaccine is now under way in different transmission settings within Africa.[128] In addition to this subunit vaccine, other vaccine constructs targeting the pre-erythrocytic stages include using viral vectors or plasmid DNA to express recombinant CS,

Table 27-3	Malaria Vaccine Strategies		
Vaccine Strategy			
Target		**Stage in Malaria Life Cycle**	**Vaccine Targets (examples)**
Prevent infection			
Sporozoites		Sporozoite Intra-vascular (3–5 minutes)	Sporozoite antigens: circumsporozoite protein (CSP) (RTS,S/AS02A), (TRAP)
⇓			
Liver stage		Liver stage Intra-hepatocytic (1–2 weeks)	Liver stage antigens (LSA)1
⇓			
Prevent disease			
Infected red blood cells		Asexual blood stage Intra-erythrocytic (2+ day cycle)	Merozoite Surface Protein (MSP)-1 Apical Merozoite Antigen (AMA)-1 Schizont antigens *P. falciparum* erythrocyte membrane protein (PfEMP-1)
⇓			
Prevent transmission			
Gametocytes		Sexual blood stage	Gametocyte antigens *P. falciparum* sexual stages (Pfs 45/48)
⇓			
Sexual stages within the mosquito		Anopheles mosquito Intra-mosquito mostly (10–14 days)	Sexual stage antigens (Pfs 25/28)

thrombospondin-related adhesion protein (TRAP), and liver-stage antigen (LSA). Additional approaches include pursuit of a radiation-attenuated sporozoite vaccine and vaccines based on genetically modified sporozoites.[129]

Vaccines against asexual blood stages of *P. falciparum* would seem a promising approach, as passive transfer of immunity has been shown with antimerozoite immunoglobulin. As noted earlier, however, the *P. falciparum* genome contains a number of highly polymorphic gene families, most importantly the *var* genes encoding the surface protein PfEMP1, which allows successive waves of parasites to express new variant surface antigens. Thus antibodies directed against these variable surface proteins are unlikely to remain effective for long. A limited number of conserved surface antigens also appear to exist, against which protective immunity might be established.[130] Children surviving malaria eventually mobilize a sufficiently diverse set of antibodies that provide protection against severe disease. In holoendemic Africa, where the entomological inoculation rate may be in the hundreds per year, protective immunity takes place over several years, through thousands of inoculated parasites. The hope is to develop a vaccine that can induce similar levels of immunity in weeks or months, and by age 6 months rather than 6 years.

Finally, substantial work has been done on vaccines directed against gametocytes that block parasite development within the mosquito, termed "transmission blocking" vaccines.[131] These vaccines represent an interesting approach, in that the vaccine would not protect the vaccinated individual but rather would reduce transmission from those who are infected, analogous to the use of residual insecticides in households. Preclinical studies have demonstrated that antibodies against sexual-stage antigens expressed by *P. vivax* and *P. falciparum* can prevent the development of infectious sporozoites in the mosquito salivary gland. Newer approaches target critical mosquito proteins in the midgut.[132] Actual interruption of malaria transmission in communities, however, would require sustained high levels of vaccine coverage.[133]

APPROACHES TO CONTROL

The complexities of the malaria transmission cycle and the host–parasite interactions that lead to disease in the human host provide a wide variety of opportunities to stop or slow transmission of parasites and to reduce disease manifestations. Historically, though based on the flawed theory of miasma, the major public health approach to malaria entailed the establishment of communities away from low-lying swamps to reduce vector contact.

Current approaches to malaria control include a variety of strategies directed against both the vector and the parasite. Detailed knowledge of the local ecological and epidemiological circumstances; of the human economic, cultural, and social situation; and of the pathogenesis of human malaria disease is as vital for determining how best to intervene, as are the specifics of the vector, parasite, and intervention tool itself. Control strategies that may be of particular value in Africa and new tools to support them are outlined in **Table 27-4**.

Vector Control Methods

The array of vector control methods is based on the premise of attacking the mosquito in various stages of its life cycle: control of breeding sites to reduce vector density by drainage and waterway engineering and application of specific larvacides and biological agents; the use of mosquito netting, screens, and repellents for personal protection from bites; aerosol distribution of insecticides to reduce adult mosquito densities; killing adult mosquitoes after they have taken a blood meal by use of residual insecticides within households, and thereby reducing further transmission; and the development of insecticide-impregnated bednets and curtains that kill adult mosquitoes as they seek a blood meal.

Breeding Site and Larva Control

After the discovery of the role of mosquito vectors in malaria, efforts were directed toward elimination or reduction of vector breeding sites by swamp drainage and environmental control, including water source diversion, water management with flushing and sluicing, covering of wells, clearing vegetation, and reforestation. Application of DDT, other insecticides, and larvacides also served as breeding site control methods, particularly in urban settings. In addition to these engineering and insecticide approaches, various biological methods—including larva predators, such as larvivarous fish and bacteria such as *B. thuriagensis* that produce specific antilarval toxins—have been selectively used. Approaches to vector control through reduction of breeding sites continue to play a role in malaria control strategies.

Table 27-4	Control Strategies for Malaria in Africa

What can be done now:
- General infrastructure/institution improvement
- Role of vector control with
  - Environmental improvements to reduce breeding
  - Impregnated bed nets
  - Personal protection
- Household use of antimalarials for those under 5 years of age
- Intermittent preventive treatment for infants and pregnant women
  - Monitoring for antimalarial resistance
- Strengthened nutrition programs
- Improved immunization coverage especially in remote areas in anticipation of effective vaccines

New tools:
- Vaccine development, especially asexual phase
- Drug development and acceleration of those in the pipeline
- Understanding of the molecular biology of the parasite
- Understanding of the sporogonic cycle to aid in reengineering of the anopheline
- Improved entomological field methods for better understanding of microepidemiological variation
- Understanding mechanisms of drug resistance and factors that contribute to its spread
- Better diagnostic tests that rapidly and inexpensively indicate drug resistance

Adult Vector Control

The use of DDT for household residual spraying had great impact on malaria control in many areas of the world, and this strategy's initial successes served as the rationale for the malaria eradication efforts undertaken in the 1950s and 1960s. The conceptual foundation for eradication through use of residual insecticides was based on anopheline resting behavior after a blood meal. The success of this approach depends on the biting and resting behavior of the mosquito and on the willingness of the human population to have their households sprayed. DDT works by killing mosquitos when they rest after engorgement. The higher the intensity of transmission, the more difficult it is to achieve a sufficient level of coverage. Success with residual household spraying was achieved in large areas of Europe, Asia, and Latin America, but in areas with EIRs of dozens per year (as in much of tropical Africa), control by residual spraying alone was not possible.

Where residual spaying was successful, a different obstacle to its use arose: anopheline resistance to DDT became widespread. Although other insecticides were substituted, they were generally difficult to formulate for residual spraying and were much more expensive and toxic to humans and other mammals. Unfortunately, DDT was also an excellent agricultural insecticide, and its widespread use

in agriculture has been implicated as the cause of anopheline resistance. Residual spraying of DDT for malaria control required a minute amount of pesticide that was not used outside and did not disperse into the environment, as it was absorbed by the wall material. Given these facts, antimalaria use of DDT likely was not a factor either in the development of anopheline resistance or in the devastation of bird populations by DDT thinning of egg shells. The ecological effects of agricultural use led to major restrictions and, in many countries, complete banning of DDT for any use. As production dropped, the cost of DDT increased. These restrictions, and their accompanying economic realities, affected antimalarial residual spraying programs, ultimately curtailing an effective public health tool. However, in 2006, WHO and the U.S. Agency for International Development endorsed indoor DDT spraying to control malaria.[134] The use of household residual insecticides, including DDT in some countries, continues as an important vector control measure in many countries.[135,136]

Long-Lasting Insecticide Treated Bednets

Widespread use of long-lasting, insecticide-treated impregnated bednets (LLITNs) leads to reductions in transmission of malaria, clinical disease, and overall childhood mortality. Although not all studies have demonstrated such positive benefits, a sufficient body of evidence was collected for the Roll Back Malaria global partnership to recommend LLITNs as a key method for reducing the burden of malaria in high-transmission areas of Africa. The distribution of LLITNs is a major component of malaria control programs and great progress has been made in the widespread distribution of LLITNs.[9]

The three key determinants of effectiveness are coverage (proportion of households with LLITNs), adherence (the proportion of individuals properly deploying LLITNs each night), and net treatment care (the proportion of nets properly treated with insecticide). These three determinants should serve as the foundation for implementation of national programs, and efforts should continue to improve the intervention tools (the net, the insecticide, and methods for durable treatment and retreatment) and their deployment.[137] Of increasing concern is the emergence and spread of insecticide (pyrethroid) resistance, which could render LLITNs ineffective.[138]

Personal and Household Protection

Repellants of various types, protective clothing, screening, bednets, and other forms of personal protection against the bite of mosquitoes are all of importance and widely recommended. Nevertheless, aside from educational campaigns and exhortations, this approach has never been viewed as a major component in malaria control programs.

Treatment Strategies

Passive Case Finding and Treatment

In tropical Africa, the principal approach employed by antimalaria programs has been the use of antimalarial drugs in passive case finding and treatment of those who present to clinics or pharmacies with symptoms of malaria. This approach may be reactive or passive in regard to the health system, but it requires active seeking of health care at appropriate health facilities on the part of patients, families, and communities. Health workers in Africa are taught about the major symptoms of malaria and the need to treat it promptly with an appropriate antimalarial drug. Treatment of malaria in childhood is accorded a prominent place in the Integrated Management of Childhood Illnesses (IMCI). This important provider-oriented, facility-based approach focuses on assessment and treatment of the major causes of child mortality. With the introduction of ACT, many national programs now require confirmation of malaria using a rapid diagnostic test (RDT), resulting in less misclassification and overtreatment, but also increasing costs and likely causing some delays in treatment.[139]

Unfortunately, severe malaria kills children so rapidly in much of Africa that often mothers cannot get their children to facility-based treatment in time. An effective case treatment strategy for reducing under-5 mortality must include community mobilization and education for families, particularly for the mother or caretaker, to help them understand the urgency of obtaining treatment of their sick child. The range of IMCI activities extends beyond the health facility to include critical family and community aspects. The extension of intermittent preventive treatment to children younger than age 5 years within the context of IMCI has yielded promising results.[140]

Home Treatment

A relatively untried strategy for timely provision of antimalarial therapy is to teach mothers to recognize symptoms of malaria in their children and to treat those children immediately at home. If mothers could be taught to recognize and promptly treat their children, and if they had an appropriate antimalarial supply immediately at hand, it seems reasonable to expect that many children could be saved in high-transmission areas, where patients are often dying under current health care conditions.

This approach was tested in a randomized trial in Tigray, Ethiopia. Village-based mother coordinators (MCs) received training and supervision to teach neighboring mothers to recognize symptoms of malaria in their children and promptly administer chloroquine. Overall under-5 mortality was reduced by 40% at very low cost.[160]

Home treatment of children by their mothers had not been seriously considered as a viable approach by most malaria experts because of concerns that "illiterate women" would misuse, sell, or waste the drugs; that they would not know when or at which dose to give the medications; and that indiscriminant use of antimalarial agents would lead to increased drug resistance. This study gave dramatic evidence refuting this view, demonstrating the high degree of effectiveness of home treatment by mothers in the circumstances in Tigray.

Prophylaxis

Prophylaxis with antimalarial agents has been the standard procedure for travelers and short-term residents of endemic areas. It has also been an effective approach for selected "captive" populations, such as plantation workers or miners. From a public health viewpoint, prophylaxis has been shown to be highly beneficial in pregnancy, both for the pregnant woman and for the fetus, especially for first and second pregnancies. However, this strategy has been replaced in pregnant women by intermittent preventive (full) treatment (IPTp), which involves administration of a full-treatment course each month during antenatal care.

Intermittent Preventive Treatment

An alternative strategy to prevent malaria in pregnant women and young children involves the use of intermittent preventive treatment. This strategy differs from chemoprophylaxis in that infants and children receive periodic treatment doses of antimalarial drugs, rather than continuous prophylactic regimens. Intermittent treatment can be offered at the time of routine childhood immunization, a strategy referred to as intermittent preventive treatment in infants (IPTi).

Two large trials of intermittent preventive treatment were conducted in Tanzania. In the first study, children were randomly assigned to receive sulfadoxine-pyrimethamine or placebo at 2, 3, and 9 months of age along with routine vaccinations.[141] During the first year of life, the protective efficacy against clinical malaria was 59%, and the incidence of severe anemia was cut in half. In the second trial, amodiaquine was administered three times over 6 months to infants in the first year of life.[142] Its protective efficacy was 65% against malaria fevers and 67% against anemia.

Logic would suggest that IPT need not be limited to infancy, but rather that IPT be given to every child younger than 5 years of age when seen for any other reason. No evidence exists that IPTi interferes with the immune responses to childhood vaccines and trials demonstrate added benefits from the use of LLITNs.[143,144] As with chemoprophylaxis, intermittent preventive treatment potentially could adversely affect drug resistance rates and the development of protective immunity, but studies to date have not demonstrated these outcomes. If the much-needed improvements in the parts of sub-Saharan Africa with low childhood vaccination coverage rates can be achieved, it would also lead to a greater impact of IPTi.

Strategies for Vaccine Use

Even after development of one or several vaccines, the most appropriate vaccine and its use will depend on the epidemiological situation. With the success in malaria control achieved through current measures, some have suggested that the threshold for using a partially effective vaccine has been raised.[145]

A sporozoite vaccine is designed to prevent infection. A potential danger, however, is that if any sporozoite bypasses host defenses and invades a liver cell, a full-blown malaria episode could follow. An asexual stage vaccine, in contrast, would mimic natural immunity, and could be targeted to children and pregnant women in holoendemic areas. Natural infection could provide the booster effect. In such a situation, it could be counterproductive to reduce transmission, as transmission would be the method for vaccine boosting.

Vaccines directed against the sexual, gamete forms ("transmission blocking" vaccines) might be useful as an additional control component in areas of relatively unstable malaria where other control measures are in place. Such vaccines might be a particularly useful supplement to reduce the spread of drug-resistant parasites. Mathematical modeling suggests transmission-blocking vaccines could play an important role in ensuring malaria elimination and in preventing the reestablishment of transmission after cessation of vector control activities.[146]

Although this section has discussed approaches to control that are separately focused on vector control, antimalarial treatment, or use of vaccines, most malaria control programs need to use a combination of antimalarial measures tailored to fit the epidemiological and ecological circumstances.

THE FUTURE OF MALARIA CONTROL AND ELIMINATION

Doing Better with What We Have

The first priority for reducing the continuing, appallingly high mortality from malaria in Africa is to improve and extend coverage of currently available tools. To do so requires strengthened planning based on detailed, local epidemiological data combined with improved management and operational research capacity of the health system, particularly that of primary health care and its support systems at the local community and district levels. It also requires basic human development improvements, including strengthened infrastructural and institutional support for enhanced employment opportunities, strengthened women's groups, better access to microcredit, augmented community and family education, and better communication and transport systems. These general development improvements are needed because the strategies to achieve effective malaria control require understanding and concerted action at the household and community levels. The fundamental institutional and profound structural reconstruction required to achieve these basic changes have begun to be enacted in a few African countries, demonstrating that these changes can be successfully accomplished. The apparent reduction in the number of deaths attributed to malaria in these countries may demonstrate that these changes can improve population health. Even so, there is a very long way to go. Globally, the need for improved equity to generate the capacity for all countries and locales to make decisions for themselves not only must be recognized, but the wealthy nations (and their voters) must also be convinced that it is in their long-term interest.

Operational research to support better planning and management, largely country and even locale specific, is needed, with special attention being paid to quality management and support supervision to enhance health worker performance. In particular, if the antimalarial strategies discussed earlier are to be effective, more work must be devoted to the following:

- Increased use of intermittent preventive treatment of malaria in children (IPTc) as well as IPT in pregnancy and in infants, especially in conjunction with community-based efforts directed toward distribution of LLITNs in high-transmission areas
- Increased use of RDTs for malaria for symptomatic children
- Training of community health workers to properly diagnose malaria with RDTs and treat infected children with ACT
- Training of trainers in the distribution and use of antimalarial agents by mothers in the household to treat their children
- Community-based programs for distribution, use, and continuing retreatment of insecticide-treated bednets
- Increased monitoring for drug and insecticide resistance
- Support for communities to work through their own approaches to control malaria, including reduction of vector habitats, especially in areas with marginal or highly variable transmission
- Continued improvement in immunization coverage, particularly to the underserved populations in anticipation of an effective antimalarial vaccine

New Tools at Last

Certainly, better intervention tools directed at malaria are needed. Research on nearly all aspects of control measures against parasites and vectors is needed, and a detailed research agenda for malaria elimination and eradication has been developed,[147] including research sub-agendas for vector control,[148] diagnostics,[149] drugs,[150] vaccines,[151] modeling,[152] surveillance,[153] and health systems.[154]

Basic research priorities include the following:

- Development of asexual-phase vaccines, especially now that health infrastructures in many African countries are sufficiently developed to deliver childhood vaccines to at least 75% of their population. Many consider this concern to be the first priority related to malaria.
- Continued efforts for drug development.
- Continued work to understand the molecular biology of the parasite, especially the metabolic pathways contributing to virulence that might be amenable to rational drug development.
- Further work on the much-neglected sporogonic cycle, which may aid in efforts to reengineer anophelines so that they are unable to support transmission.
- Continued development of mathematical modeling done in direct concert with field investigations, which may facilitate a deeper understanding of the critical quantitative relationships involved in transmission control.
- Improved entomological field methods for better understanding of micro-epidemiological variation and for local anopheline control efforts.
- Better understanding of the mechanisms underlying drug resistance and factors contributing to its spread, which will likely require a combined understanding of genetics, entomology, and epidemiology.
- Simple, inexpensive, rapid, and robust diagnostic tests that can provide for quantification of parasite density and that can indicate drug sensitivity (or resistance).

Reduction of the continuing high mortality and morbidity from malaria in Africa will require both better use of current control measures (necessitating better epidemiological and ecological information for better planning); better management of control programs; increased direct involvement of families and communities; accelerated research toward vaccines, drugs, and vector control approaches; and fundamental understanding of the biology of parasite, vector, and human host.

In recent years, the burden of malaria has decreased dramatically in parts of sub-Saharan Africa.[155] This decline has led to renewed interest in the possibility of malaria eradication.[156–159] One strategy for regional elimination is a stepwise approach starting with countries at the margins of endemic transmission.[160] Nevertheless, in regions of declining malaria transmission, new strategies for malaria control are needed to further reduce transmission and achieve elimination. These tasks will be the work of the next generation of infectious disease epidemiologists.

• • • **REFERENCES**

1. Packard RM. *The Making of a Tropical Disease: A Short History of Malaria.* Baltimore, MD: Johns Hopkins University Press; 2007.

2. International Development Advisory Board. *Malaria Eradication: Report and Recommendations of the International Development Advisory Board.* 1956.

3. Najera JA, Gonzalez-Silva M, Alonso PL. Some lessons for the future from the Global Malaria Eradication Programme (1955–1969). *PLoS Med* 2011;8:e1000412.

4. World Health Organization. *Re-examination of the Global Strategy of Malaria Eradication.* WHO Official Records No. 176. Geneva, Switzerland: Author; 1969.

5. World Health Organization. *Global Malaria Control and Elimination: Report of a Technical Review.* Geneva, Switzerland: Author; 2008.

6. Greenwood B. Can malaria be eliminated? *Trans R Soc Trop Med Hyg* 2009;103(suppl 1): S2–S5.

7. Hay SI, Guerra CA, Gething PW, et al. A world malaria map: *Plasmodium falciparum* endemicity in 2007. *PLoS Med* 2009;6:e1000048.

8. World Health Organization. *World Malaria Report.* Geneva, Switzerland: Author; 2004.

9. World Health Organization. *World Malaria Report 2010.* Geneva, Swtizerland: Author; 2010.

10. Morrow RH. The application of a quantitative approach to the assessment of the relative importance of vector and soil transmitted diseases in Ghana. *Soc Sci Med* 1984;19: 1039–1049.

11. Singh B, Kim Sung L, Matusop A, et al. A large focus of naturally acquired *Plasmodium knowlesi* infections in human beings. *Lancet* 2004;363:1017–1024.

12. White NJ. *Plasmodium knowlesi*: the fifth human malaria parasite. *Clin Infect Dis* 2008;46:172–173.

13. Oh SS, Chishti AH. Host receptors in malaria merozoite invasion. *Curr Top Microbiol Immunol* 2005;295:203–232.

14. Bousema T, Drakeley C. Epidemiology and infectivity of *Plasmodium falciparum* and *Plasmodium vivax* gametocytes in relation to malaria control and elimination. *Clin Microbiol Rev* 2011;24:377–410.

15. Aly AS, Vaughan AM, Kappe SH. Malaria parasite development in the mosquito and infection of the mammalian host. *Annu Rev Microbiol* 2009;63:195–221.

16. Beier JC, Davis JR, Vaughan JA, et al. Quantitation of *Plasmodium falciparum* sporozoites transmitted in vitro by experimentally infected *Anopheles gambiae* and *Anopheles stephensi. Am J Trop Med Hyg* 1991;44:564–570.

17. Beier JC. Malaria parasite development in mosquitoes. *Annu Rev Entomol* 1998;43: 519–543.

18. Beadle C, McElroy PD, Oster CN, et al. Impact of transmission intensity and age on *Plasmodium falciparum* density and associated fever: implications for malaria vaccine trial design. *J Infect Dis* 1995;172:1047–1054.

19. Molineaux L, Gramiccia G. *The Garki Project: Research on the Epidemiology and Control of Malaria in the Sudan Savanna of West Africa.* Geneva, Switzerland: World Health Organization; 1980.

20. Markus MB. The hypnozoite concept, with particular reference to malaria. *Parasitol Res* 2011;108:247–252.

21. Kantele A, Jokiranta TS. Review of cases with the emerging fifth human malaria parasite, *Plasmodium knowlesi. Clin Infect Dis* 2011;52:1356–1362.

22. Baker DA. Malaria gametocytogenesis. *Mol Biochem Parasitol* 2010;172:57–65.

23. Gardner MJ, Hall N, Fung E, et al. Genome sequence of the human malaria parasite *Plasmodium falciparum*. *Nature* 2002;419:498–511.

24. Carlton JM, Adams JH, Silva JC, et al. Comparative genomics of the neglected human malaria parasite *Plasmodium vivax*. *Nature* 2008;455:757–763.

25. Winzeler EA. Malaria research in the post-genomic era. *Nature* 2008;455:751–756.

26. Rowe JA, Kyes SA. The role of *Plasmodium falciparum var* genes in malaria in pregnancy. *Mol Microbiol* 2004;53:1011–1019.

27. Rogerson Sj, Hviid L, Duffy PE, et al. Malaria in pregnancy: pathogenesis and immunity. *Lancet Infect Dis* 2007;7:105–117.

28. Fairhurst RM, Wellems TE. Modulation of malaria virulence by determinants of *Plasmodium falciparum* erythrocyte membrane protein-1 display. *Curr Opin Hematol* 2006;13:124–130.

29. Takala SL, Plowe CV. Genetic diversity and malaria vaccine design, testing and efficacy: preventing and overcoming "vaccine resistant malaria." *Parasite Immunol* 2009;31:560–573.

30. Mackinnon MJ, Marsh K. The selection landscape of malaria parasites. *Science* 2010;328:866–871.

31. Carey AF, Wang G, Su CY, et al. Odorant reception in the malaria mosquito *Anopheles gambiae*. *Nature* 2010;464:66–71.

32. Holt RA, Subramanian GM, Halpern A, et al. The genome sequence of the malaria mosquito *Anopheles gambiae*. *Science* 2002;298:129–149.

33. Cirimotich CM, Dong Y, Garver LS, et al. Mosquito immune defenses against *Plasmodium infection. Dev Comp Immunol* 2010;34:387–395.

34. Cirimotich CM, Dong Y, Clayton AM, et al. Natural microbe-mediated refractoriness to *Plasmodium* infection in *Anopheles gambiae*. *Science* 2011;332:855–858.

35. Hughes GL, Koga R, Xue P, et al. *Wolbachia* infections are virulent and inhibit the human malaria parasite *Plasmodium falciparum* in *Anopheles gambiae*. *PLoS Pathog* 2011;(5):e1002043.

36. Hay SI, Smith DL, Snow RW. Measuring malaria endemicity from intense to interrupted transmission. *Lancet Infect Dis* 2008;8:369–378.

37. Macdonald G. The measurement of malaria transmission. *Proc R Soc Med* 1955;48: 295–302.

38. Coleman RE, Barth JF, Turell MJ, et al. Development and evaluation of a dipstick assay for detection of *Plasmodium falciparum* and *P. vivax* sporozoites in mosquitoes (Diptera: Culicidae). *J Med Entomol* 2000;37:581–587.

39. Garrett-Jones C. The human blood index of malaria vectors in relation to epidemiological assessment. *Bull World Health Organ* 1964;30:241–261.

40. Dietz K, Molineaux L, Thomas A. A malaria model tested in the African savannah. *Bull World Health Organ* 1974;50:347–357.

41. Crawley J, Chu C, Mtove G, Nosten F. Malaria in children. *Lancet* 2010;375:1468–1481.

42. Mishra SK, Newton CR. Diagnosis and management of the neurological complications of *falciparum* malaria. *Nat Rev Neurol* 2009;5:189–198.

43. Hamilton PJ, Morrow RH, Ziegler JL, et al. Absence of sickle trait in patients with tropical splenomegaly syndrome. *Lancet* 1969;2:109.

44. Doolan DL, Dobano C, Baird JK. Acquired immunity to malaria. *Clin Microbiol Rev* 2009;22:13–36, Table.

45. Overstreet MG, Cockburn IA, Chen YC, Zavala F. Protective CD8 T cells against *Plasmodium* liver stages: immunobiology of an "unnatural" immune response. *Immunol Rev* 2008;225:272–283.

46. Wellems TE, Hayton K, Fairhurst RM. The impact of malaria parasitism: from corpuscles to communities. *J Clin Invest* 2009;119:2496–2505.

47. Luzzatto L, Nwachuku-Jarrett ES, Reddy S. Increased sickling of parasitised erythrocytes as mechanism of resistance against malaria in the sickle-cell trait. *Lancet* 1970;1:319–321.

48. Vannberg FO, Chapman SJ, Hill AV. Human genetic susceptibility to intracellular pathogens. *Immunol Rev* 2011;240:105–116.

49. Caulfield LE, Richard SA, Black RE. Undernutrition as an underlying cause of malaria morbidity and mortality in children less than five years old. *Am J Trop Med Hyg* 2004;71(suppl 2):55–63.

50. Smith AW, Hendrickse RG, Harrison C, et al. The effects on malaria of treatment of iron-deficiency anaemia with oral iron in Gambian children. *Ann Trop Paediatr* 1989;9:17–23.

51. Ojukwu JU, Okebe JU, Yahav D, Paul M. Oral iron supplementation for preventing or treating anaemia among children in malaria-endemic areas. *Cochrane Database Syst Rev* 2009;CD006589.

52. Shankar AH, Genton B, Semba RD, et al. Effect of vitamin A supplementation on morbidity due to *Plasmodium falciparum* in young children in Papua New Guinea: a randomised trial. *Lancet* 1999;354:203–209.

53. Sanjoaquin MA, Molyneux ME. Malaria and vitamin A deficiency in African children: a vicious circle? *Malar J* 2009;8:134.

54. Shankar AH, Genton B, Baisor M, et al. The influence of zinc supplementation on morbidity due to *Plasmodium falciparum*: a randomized trial in preschool children in Papua New Guinea. *Am J Trop Med Hyg* 2000;62:663–669.

55. Bates CJ, Evans PH, Dardenne M, et al. A trial of zinc supplementation in young rural Gambian children. *Br J Nutr* 1993;69:243–255.

56. Yakoob MY, Theodoratou E, Jabeen A, et al. Preventive zinc supplementation in developing countries: impact on mortality and morbidity due to diarrhea, pneumonia and malaria. *BMC Public Health* 2011;11(suppl 3):S23.

57. Bejon P, Berkley JA, Mwangi T, et al. Defining childhood severe *falciparum* malaria for intervention studies. *PLoS Med* 2007;4:e251.

58. Berkley JA, Lowe BS, Mwangi I, et al. Bacteremia among children admitted to a rural hospital in Kenya. *N Engl J Med* 2005;352:39–47.

59. Alles HK, Mendis KN, Carter R. Malaria mortality rates in South Asia and in Africa: implications for malaria control. *Parasitol Today* 1998;14:369–375.

60. Okiro EA, Al-Taiar A, Reyburn H, et al. Age patterns of severe paediatric malaria and their relationship to *Plasmodium falciparum* transmission intensity. *Malar J* 2009;8:4.

61. Carneiro I, Roca-Feltrer A, Griffin JT, et al. Age-patterns of malaria vary with severity, transmission intensity and seasonality in sub-Saharan Africa: a systematic review and pooled analysis. *PLoS One* 2010;5:e8988.

62. Planche T, Dzeing A, Ngou-Milama E, et al. Metabolic complications of severe malaria. *Curr Top Microbiol Immunol* 2005;295:105–136.

63. Maitland K, Marsh K. Pathophysiology of severe malaria in children. *Acta Trop* 2004;90:131–140.

64. Were T, Davenport GC, Hittner JB, et al. Bacteremia in Kenyan children presenting with malaria. *J Clin Microbiol* 2011;49:671–676.

65. Mackenzie G, Ceesay SJ, Hill PC, et al. A decline in the incidence of invasive non-typhoidal *Salmonella* infection in the Gambia temporally associated with a decline in malaria infection. *PLoS One* 2010;5:e10568.

66. Idro R, Marsh K, John CC, Newton CR. Cerebral malaria: mechanisms of brain injury and strategies for improved neurocognitive outcome. *Pediatr Res* 2010;68:267–274.

67. Beare NA, Lewallen S, Taylor TE, Molyneux ME. Redefining cerebral malaria by including

malaria retinopathy. *Future Microbiol* 2011;6:349–355.

68. White NJ, Warrell DA, Chanthavanich P, et al. Severe hypoglycemia and hyperinsulinemia in falciparum malaria. *N Engl J Med* 1983;309:61–66.

69. Taylor TE, Molyneux ME, Wirima JJ, et al. Blood glucose levels in Malawian children before and during the administration of intravenous quinine for severe falciparum malaria. *N Engl J Med* 1988;319:1040–1047.

70. Idro R, Carter JA, Fegan G, et al. Risk factors for persisting neurological and cognitive impairments following cerebral malaria. *Arch Dis Child* 2006;91:142–148.

71. Mohan A, Sharma SK, Bollineni S. Acute lung injury and acute respiratory distress syndrome in malaria. *J Vector Borne Dis* 2008;45:179–193.

72. Calis JC, Phiri KS, Faragher EB, et al. Severe anemia in Malawian children. *N Engl J Med* 2008;358:888–899.

73. Boele van Hensbroek M., Calis JC, Phiri KS, et al. Pathophysiological mechanisms of severe anaemia in Malawian children. *PLoS One* 2010;5:e12589.

74. Casals-Pascual C, Roberts DJ. Severe malarial anaemia. *Curr Mol Med* 2006;6:155–168.

75. Molineaux L. *Plasmodium falciparum* malaria: some epidemiological implications of parasite and host diversity. *Ann Trop Med Parasitol* 1996;90:379–393.

76. Smith T, Genton B, Baea K, et al. Relationships between *Plasmodium falciparum* infection and morbidity in a highly endemic area. *Parasitology* 1994;109(Pt 5):539–549.

77. Lines J, Armstrong JR. For a few parasites more: inoculum size, vector control and strain-specific immunity to malaria. *Parasitol Today* 1992;8:381–383.

78. Adiamah JH, Koram KA, Thomson MC, et al. Entomological risk factors for severe malaria in a peri-urban area of the Gambia. *Ann Trop Med Parasitol* 1993;87:491–500.

79. Alonso PL, Lindsay SW, Armstrong Schellenberg JR, et al. A malaria control trial using insecticide-treated bed nets and targeted chemoprophylaxis in a rural area of the Gambia, west Africa. 6. The impact of the interventions on mortality and morbidity from malaria. *Trans R Soc Trop Med Hyg* 1993;87(suppl 2):37–44.

80. Lindsay S, Ansell J, Selman C, et al. Effect of pregnancy on exposure to malaria mosquitoes. *Lancet* 2000;355:1972.

81. Rogerson Sj. Malaria in pregnancy and the newborn. *Adv Exp Med Biol* 2010;659:139–152.

82. Milner DA Jr, Montgomery J, Seydel KB, Rogerson SJ. Severe malaria in children and pregnancy: an update and perspective. *Trends Parasitol* 2008;24:590–595.

83. Davis TM, Mueller I, Rogerson SJ. Prevention and treatment of malaria in pregnancy. *Future Microbiol* 2010;5:1599–1613.

84. Rogerson Sj, Mwapasa V, Meshnick SR. Malaria in pregnancy: linking immunity and pathogenesis to prevention. *Am J Trop Med Hyg* 2007;77(6 suppl):14–22.

85. Briand V, Badaut C, Cot M. Placental malaria, maternal HIV infection and infant morbidity. *Ann Trop Paediatr* 2009;29:71–83.

86. Umbers AJ, Aitken EH, Rogerson SJ. Malaria in pregnancy: small babies, big problem. *Trends Parasitol* 2011;27:168–175.

87. Whitworth J, Morgan D, Quigley M, et al. Effect of HIV-1 and increasing immunosuppression on malaria parasitemia and clinical episodes in adults in rural Uganda: a cohort study. *Lancet* 2000;356:1051–1056.

88. Kublin JG, Patnaik P, Jere CS, et al. Effect of *Plasmodium falciparum* malaria on concentrations of HIV-1-RNA in the blood of adults in rural Malawi: a prospective cohort study. *Lancet* 2005;365:233–240.

89. Sandison TG, Homsy J, Arinaitwe E, et al. Protective efficacy of co-trimoxazole prophylaxis against malaria in HIV exposed children

in rural Uganda: a randomised clinical trial. *BMJ* 2011;342:d1617.

90. Paaijmans KP, Blanford S, Bell AS, et al. Influence of climate on malaria transmission depends on daily temperature variation. *Proc Natl Acad Sci USA* 2010;107:15135–15139.

91. Tanser FC, Sharp B, le Sueur D. Potential effect of climate change on malaria transmission in Africa. *Lancet* 2003;362:1792–1798.

92. Gething PW, Smith DL, Patil AP, et al. Climate change and the global malaria recession. *Nature* 2010;465:342–345.

93. Connolly MA, Gayer M, Ryan MJ, et al. Communicable diseases in complex emergencies: impact and challenges. *Lancet* 2004;364:1974–1983.

94. Graham K, Mohammad N, Rehman H, et al. Insecticide-treated plastic tarpaulins for control of malaria vectors in refugee camps. *Med Vet Entomol* 2002;16:404–408.

95. Tatem AJ, Guerra CA, Kabaria CW, et al. Human population, urban settlement patterns and their impact on *Plasmodium falciparum* malaria endemicity. *Malar J* 2008;7:218.

96. Oduntan SO. The health of Nigerian children of school age (6–15 years). I. Design of the study, general appearance, heights and weights, nutritional status and haematalogical findings. *Ann Trop Med Parasitol* 1974;68:129–143.

97. Winch PJ, Makemba AM, Kamazima SR, et al. Local terminology for febrile illnesses in Bagamoyo District, Tanzania and its impact on the design of a community-based malaria control programme. *Soc Sci Med* 1996;42:1057–1067.

98. Gwer S, Newton CR, Berkley JA. Over-diagnosis and co-morbidity of severe malaria in African children: a guide for clinicians. *Am J Trop Med Hyg* 2007;77(6 suppl):6–13.

99. World Health Organization. Malaria rapid diagnostic test performance: results of WHO product testing of malaria RDTs: round 1 (2008). France: Author; 2009.

100. Hawkes M, Kain KC. Advances in malaria diagnosis. *Expert Rev Anti Infect Ther* 2007;5:485–495.

101. Greenwood B. The molecular epidemiology of malaria. *Trop Med Int Health* 2002;7:1012–1021.

102. White NJ. The role of anti-malarial drugs in eliminating malaria. *Malar J* 2008;7 (suppl 1):S8.

103. Golenser J, Waknine JH, Krugliak M, et al. Current perspectives on the mechanism of action of artemisinins. *Int J Parasitol* 2006;36:1427–1441.

104. Sibley CH, Barnes KI, Plowe CV. The rationale and plan for creating a World Antimalarial Resistance Network (WARN). *Malar J* 2007;6:118.

105. Dondorp AM, Nosten F, Yi P, et al. Artemisinin resistance in *Plasmodium falciparum* malaria. *N Engl J Med* 2009;361: 455–467.

106. Mita T, Tanabe K, Kita K. Spread and evolution of *Plasmodium falciparum* drug resistance. *Parasitol Int* 2009;58:201–209.

107. Laufer MK, Djimde AA, Plowe CV. Monitoring and deterring drug-resistant malaria in the era of combination therapy. *Am J Trop Med Hyg* 2007;77(6 suppl):160–169.

108. Wellems TE, Plowe CV. Chloroquine-resistant malaria. *J Infect Dis* 2001;184:770–776.

109. Kublin JG, Dzinjalamala FK, Kamwendo DD, et al. Molecular markers for failure of sulfa-doxine-pyrimethamine and chlorproguanil-dapsone treatment of *Plasmodium falciparum* malaria. *J Infect Dis* 2002;185:380–388.

110. Dondorp AM, Yeung S, White L, et al. Artemisinin resistance: current status and scenarios for containment. *Nat Rev Microbiol* 2010;8(4):272–280.

111. Talisuna AO, Bloland P, D'Alessandro U. History, dynamics, and public health importance of malaria parasite resistance. *Clin Microbiol Rev* 2004;17:235–254.

112. Campbell CC, Chin W, Collins WE, et al. Chloroquine-resistant *Plasmodium falciparum* from East Africa: cultivation and drug sensitivity of the Tanzanian I/CDC strain from an American tourist. *Lancet* 1979;2:1151–1154.

113. http://www.cdc.gov/malaria/travelers/country_table/a.html

114. Laufer MK, Thesing PC, Eddington ND, et al. Return of chloroquine antimalarial efficacy in Malawi. *N Engl J Med* 2006;355:1959–1966.

115. Frosch AE, Venkatesan M, Laufer MK. Patterns of chloroquine use and resistance in sub-Saharan Africa: a systematic review of household survey and molecular data. *Malar J* 2011;10:116.

116. Witkowski B, Iriart X, Soh PN, et al. *pfmdr1* amplification associated with clinical resistance to mefloquine in West Africa: implications for efficacy of artemisinin combination therapies. *J Clin Microbiol* 2010;48: 3797–3799.

117. Wootton JC, Feng X, Ferdig MT, et al. Genetic diversity and chloroquine selective sweeps in *Plasmodium falciparum*. *Nature* 2002;418:320–323.

118. Roper C, Pearce R, Nair S, et al. Intercontinental spread of pyrimethamine-resistant malaria. *Science* 2004;305:1124.

119. Hastings IM. Malaria control and the evolution of drug resistance: an intriguing link. *Trends Parasitol* 2003;19:70–73.

120. Mharakurwa S. *Plasmodium falciparum* transmission rate and selection for drug resistance: a vexed association or a key to successful control? *Int J Parasitol* 2004;34:1483–1487.

121. Mharakurwa S, Mutambu SL, Mudyiradima R, et al. Association of house spraying with suppressed levels of drug resistance in Zimbabwe. *Malar J* 2004;3:35.

122. Regules JA, Cummings JF, Ockenhouse CF. The RTS,S vaccine candidate for malaria. *Expert Rev Vaccines* 2011;10:589–599.

123. McGregor IA, Carington SP CS. Treatment of East African *P. falciparum* malaria with West African gammaglobulin. *Trans R Soc Trop Med Hyg* 1963;57:170–175.

124. Clyde DF, Most H, McCarthy VC, Vanderberg JP. Immunization of man against sporozite-induced falciparum malaria. *Am J Med Sci* 1973;266:169–177.

125. Clyde DF. Immunization of man against *falciparum* and *vivax* malaria by use of attenuated sporozoites. *Am J Trop Med Hyg* 1975;24:397–401.

126. Crompton PD, Pierce SK, Miller LH. Advances and challenges in malaria vaccine development. *J Clin Invest* 2010;120:4168–4178.

127. Alonso PL, Sacarlal J, Aponte JJ, et al. Efficacy of the RTS,S/AS02A vaccine against *Plasmodium falciparum* infection and disease in young African children: randomised controlled trial. *Lancet* 2004;364:1411–1420.

128. Leach A, Vekemans J, Lievens M, et al. Design of a Phase III multicenter trial to evaluate the efficacy of the RTS,S/AS01 malaria vaccine in children across diverse transmission settings in Africa. *Malar J* 2011;10:224.

129. Hoffman SL, Billingsley PF, James E, et al. Development of a metabolically active, non-replicating sporozoite vaccine to prevent *Plasmodium falciparum* malaria. *Hum Vaccin* 2010;6:97–106.

130. Gratepanche S, Gamain B, Smith JD, et al. Induction of crossreactive antibodies against the *Plasmodium falciparum* variant protein. *Proc Natl Acad Sci USA* 2003;100:13007–13012.

131. Lavazec C, Bourgouin C. Mosquito-based transmission blocking vaccines for interrupting *Plasmodium* development. *Microbes Infect* 2008;10:845–849.

132. Dinglasan RR, Jacobs-Lorena M. Flipping the paradigm on malaria transmission-blocking vaccines. *Trends Parasitol* 2008;24:364–370.

133. Tediosi F, Maire N, Penny M, et al. Simulation of the cost-effectiveness of malaria vaccines. *Malar J* 2009;8:127.

134. Eskenazi B, Chevrier J, Rosas LG, et al. The Pine River statement: human health consequences of DDT use. *Environ Health Perspect* 2009;117:1359–1367.

135. Sadasivaiah S, Tozan Y, Breman JG. Dichlorodiphenyltrichloroethane (DDT) for indoor residual spraying in Africa: how can it be used for malaria control? *Am J Trop Med Hyg* 2007;77(6 suppl):249–263.

136. van den Berg H. Global status of DDT and its alternatives for use in vector control to prevent disease. *Environ Health Perspect* 2009;117:1656–1663.

137. Sexton AR. Best practices for an insecticide-treated bed net distribution programme in sub-Saharan eastern Africa. *Malar J* 2011;10:157.

138. Ranson H, N'guessan R, Lines J, Moiroux N, et al. Pyrethroid resistance in African anopheline mosquitoes: what are the implications for malaria control? *Trends Parasitol* 2011;27:91–98.

139. d'Acremont V, Malila A, Swai N, et al. Withholding antimalarials in febrile children who have a negative result for a rapid diagnostic test. *Clin Infect Dis* 2010;51:506–511.

140. Wilson AL. A systematic review and meta-analysis of the efficacy and safety of intermittent preventive treatment of malaria in children (IPTc). *PLoS One* 2011;6:e16976.

141. Schellenberg D, Menendez C, Kahigwa E, et al. Intermittent treatment for malaria and anaemia control at time of routine vaccinations in Tanzanian infants: a randomised, placebo-controlled trial. *Lancet* 2001;357:1471–1477.

142. Massaga JJ, Kitua AY, Lemnge MM, et al. Effect of intermittent treatment with amodiaquine on anaemia and malarial fevers in infants in Tanzania: a randomised placebo-controlled trial. *Lancet* 2003;361:1853–1860.

143. Konate AT, Yaro JB, Ouedraogo AZ, et al. Intermittent preventive treatment of malaria provides substantial protection against malaria in children already protected by an insecticide-treated bednet in Burkina Faso: a randomised, double-blind, placebo-controlled trial. *PLoS Med* 2011;8:e1000408.

144. Dicko A, Diallo AI, Tembine I, et al. Intermittent preventive treatment of malaria provides substantial protection against malaria in children already protected by an insecticide-treated bednet in Mali: a randomised, double-blind, placebo-controlled trial. *PLoS Med* 2011;8:e1000407.

145. Greenwood B, Targett G. Do we still need a malaria vaccine? *Parasite Immunol* 2009;31:582–586.

146. Smith TA, Chitnis N, Briet OJ, Tanner M. Uses of mosquito-stage transmission-blocking vaccines against *Plasmodium falciparum*. *Trends Parasitol* 2011;27:190–196.

147. Alonso PL, Brown G, Arevalo-Herrera M, et al. A research agenda to underpin malaria eradication. *PLoS Med* 2011;8:e1000406.

148. malERA Consultative Group on Vector Control. A research agenda for malaria eradication: vector control. *PLoS Med* 2011;8:e1000401.

149. malERA Consultative Group on Diagnoses and Diagnostics. A research agenda for malaria eradication: diagnoses and diagnostics. *PLoS Med* 2011;8:e1000396.

150. malERA Consultative Group on Drugs. A research agenda for malaria eradication: drugs. *PLoS Med* 2011;8:e1000402.

151. malERA Consultative Group on Vaccines. A research agenda for malaria eradication: vaccines. *PLoS Med* 2011;8:e1000398.

152. malERA Consultative Group on Modeling. A research agenda for malaria eradication: modeling. *PLoS Med* 2011;8:e1000403.

153. malERA Consultative Group on Monitoring EaS. A research agenda for malaria eradication: monitoring, evaluation, and surveillance. *PLoS Med* 2011;8:e1000400.

154. malERA Consultative Group on Health Systems and Operational Research.

A research agenda for malaria eradication: health systems and operational research. *PLoS Med* 2011;8:e1000397.

155. O'Meara WP, Mangeni JN, Steketee R, Greenwood B. Changes in the burden of malaria in sub-Saharan Africa. *Lancet Infect Dis* 2010;10:545–555.

156. Feachem RG, Phillips AA, Hwang J, et al. Shrinking the malaria map: progress and prospects. *Lancet* 2010;376:1566–1578.

157. Tatem AJ, Smith DL, Gething PW, et al. Ranking of elimination feasibility between malaria-endemic countries. *Lancet* 2010;376:1579–1591.

158. Moonen B, Cohen JM, Snow RW, et al. Operational strategies to achieve and maintain malaria elimination. *Lancet* 2010;376:1592–1603.

159. Sabot O, Cohen JM, Hsiang MS, et al. Costs and financial feasibility of malaria elimination. *Lancet* 2010;376:1604–1615.

160. Feachem R, Sabot O. A new global malaria eradication strategy. *Lancet* 2008;371:1633–1635.

28

Epidemiology of Helminth Infections

Clive J. Shiff

INTRODUCTION

Parasitism is a way of life. Over evolutionary time, the niche by which one species depends on another for subsistence has been elaborated in countless ways. Not only have parasitic species developed a means to adapt to existence in the gut, in the tissues, and within the cells of their hosts, but these species have also evolved mechanisms to distribute their progeny so that they can readily find and be taken up by a new host. Parasites have adopted a variety of forms, some of which may appear grotesque. They have evolved stratagems to evade the immune defenses of their hosts, and they have coevolved with their hosts to the extent that they adapt to the behavior patterns of normal life and exploit these so as to migrate to other sources of hosts. All of these factors influence in some way the epidemiology of parasitic infections.

Transmission and acquisition of parasites by any naive host involves three factors: (1) a source of infection or reservoir must be present from which the parental generation of the parasite radiates; (2) a means of transmission must exist by which the parasite gains access to the host; and (3) a susceptible host must be available. As these factors bear directly on the severity of parasitic infections and their importance in the communities of humans, they must be considered in any study on the epidemiology, health impact, and control of the infection. Parasites have evolved numerous strategies to be successful within their various hosts, but transmission essentially involves two types of cycle. The first is the direct cycle, where transmission is from person to person, usually through fecal waste in the environment. The second is the indirect cycle, which involves additional hosts or vectors that actively transfer the parasite from one host to another.

To demonstrate the complexity of this process, one example of each cycle will be discussed in this chapter in detail. The direct cycle will be explained through consideration of the life cycle and epidemiology of hookworms. The indirect cycle will consider the complex epidemiology of schistosomes. The hookworms affecting humans belong to two species of nematode parasites, which produce similar infections, but because they are difficult to differentiate clinically and epidemiologically, they usually are considered together. Transmission of these parasites depends on fecal contamination of the environment, absence of acceptable latrines, and a barefoot lifestyle. The schistosome parasite is a blood-dwelling trematode that has a complex life cycle involving living in freshwater molluscs as well as in the bloodstream of its definitive host. This parasite has coevolved in tandem with its aquatic and human hosts, producing a well-balanced association. However, the recent settling of human populations in new areas, with their need for water and their changing agricultural activities, as well as the burgeoning of these human populations, has increased the transmission of the parasite and, therefore, has produced severe and debilitating infections. Indeed, overt disease caused by these parasites often results when the ecological balances to which the various populations have been adapted become unstable or break down, resulting in increasingly severe levels of infection.

HOOKWORM PARASITES OF HUMANS

Hookworms belong to the phylum Nematoda. Nematodes are tubular animals, diecious, with a definite body cavity in which the various organs are suspended. Their gut is tubular, commencing in a complex oral region where the mouth and pharynx may have cutting teeth or plates, and the pharynx may be adapted for sucking and ingesting food. A hookworm's body is covered with an outer cuticle, which is a complex structure consisting of several layers that serves as a protective cover for the worm. These parasites are equipped only with longitudinal muscles, which accounts for the sinuous movements characteristic of the group.

In parasitic nematodes, the female is usually larger and packed with large ovaries and uterus. The males may exhibit complex external copulatory structures, which are characteristic of some species and which are used in identification. Eggs, which are usually characteristic for each species, are laid in large numbers; they may be embryonated or contain developing larvae. Usually the larval development takes several days, after which a first-stage larva emerges. This stage is able to ingest food and will proceed through two molts to reach the L3 stage, which in hookworms is infective; at this point larvae can no longer ingest food. The infective L3 larva (called the filariform stage) is able to attach to and penetrate the skin of the next host by using proteolytic enzymes secreted in the apical area of the worm. Altogether, four larval molts occur before the adult develops, and it is always the third-stage larva that is infectious.

Life Cycle

Two species of hookworm are known to infect humans: *Ancylostoma duodenale* and *Necator americanus*. The life cycles of these two parasites are similar and, therefore, will be discussed together (**Figure 28-1**). Embryonated eggs are passed in the feces of an infected person. In a suitable environment—one that is shady or dark, moist, and warm (22°C to 32°C)—the eggs will hatch within 24 to 48 hours, releasing first-stage larvae. These forms are not infective; they can ingest food, and will soon molt into second-stage larvae after approximately 3 days. A second molt occurs after about 6 days, and the resulting third-stage larva is infectious—at the filariform stage. These larvae are unable to feed; however, under ideal conditions, they can survive and remain infectious for several weeks.

Larvae invade by penetrating the skin between the toes or through the feet or ankles. However, they can also be transmitted through eating or handling unwashed, contaminated vegetables. Evidence also suggests that *A. duodenale* can be transmitted to suckling infants through breastmilk. The filariform larvae secrete proteolytic enzymes that facilitate the penetration through the skin; they then enter the

blood circulation and usually molt once more as they pass through the lungs. From the alveolar spaces, the larvae are coughed up in sputum, are swallowed, and thus gain entry to the human gut. The worms then reach the intestine where, as adults, they mate. They adhere to and lacerate the intestinal mucosa with their strong oral plates or teeth, they pump blood into the gut by means of the powerful muscular pharynx, and they can continue to flush their gut with a stream of blood from the intestinal vessels they have penetrated. Thus, apart from consuming blood as a source of food, the parasites cause considerable amounts of blood to be lost and voided in the feces of the host. Egg production commences 4 to 8 weeks after the initial infection and the worms can live approximately 3 years.

Epidemiology of Hookworm Infections

Hookworm infection is a worldwide problem that is most prevalent in warm, humid areas or environments. It is widespread in the tropics, but is also common in warm, wet areas of the temperate zones; it is frequently associated with anemia in the affected populations.

Vulnerable populations include children, pregnant and lactating women, and women who menstruate heavily. The prevalence of geohelminth infections is age related, possibly because of immunologic factors or specific activities or behavior patterns related to age. The prevalence of hookworm is found to be lower among children younger than 5 years, but gradually increases with age; by age 8 years, a marked increase in prevalence occurs, which diminishes in later life. A clustering of infections is seen in certain children: evidence shows that heavily or lightly infected children have a statistical predisposition to acquire similar infection intensities following deworming procedures if patterns of exposure have not changed.

The highest prevalence of hookworm infection is found in males, teenagers, and young adults, which may be related to occupational hazards. For example, tending crops such as in rice paddies, where one must stand in the fields for many hours, increases the exposure to hookworm and the likelihood of becoming infected. Other risk factors are associated with the extent of outdoor defecation, presence of defecation fields, and the type of soil, which should be loose and hold moisture well, thereby providing a refuge for the infective larvae. Poor standards of living and sanitation are the major determinants of hookworm prevalence. Infection rates are usually higher in rural areas than in urban areas, and higher in

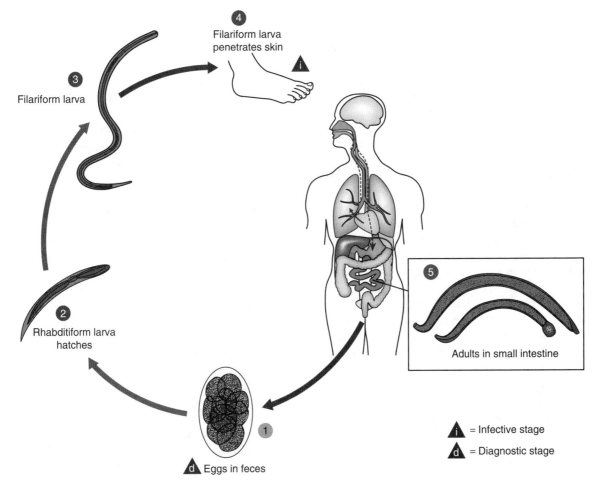

Figure 28-1 Life Cycle of the Hookworm. Reproduced from the Centers for Disease Control and Prevention DPDx. Parasites and Health: Hookworm. http://www.dpd.cdc.gov/dpdx/HTML/Hookworm.htm. Accessed December 4, 2012.

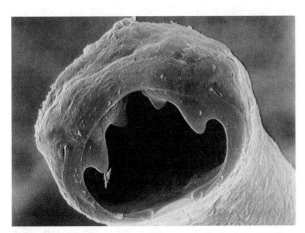

Figure 28-2 Shows a photograph of Ancylostoma duodenale. Courtesy of Dr. G. Schad.

people who rank low on the socioeconomic scale. In parts of Europe and North America where hookworm was previously common, the infections have been all but eradicated because of improved access to effective sanitation and improved living conditions, including the wearing of shoes. **Figure 28-2** shows a photograph of *Ancylostoma duodenale*.

Control Measures

No prophylactic drugs are available for hookworm infections, although iron therapy is useful in preventing serious nutritional depletion, especially in women and children. Mebendazole is often used to treat both hookworm and other geohelminth infections. Mass chemotherapy is effective in reducing the prevalence of all geohelminths, but its effects are short-lived if no improvements are made in sanitation and health education.

Considerable lack of knowledge exists about the transmission of intestinal parasites in many parts of the world. A study of mothers in urban slums in Sri Lanka demonstrated that 42% of mothers thought that parasites were acquired through eating sweets, 25% thought that they were transmitted through other children, and 25% did not know how the parasites were acquired. None of the study participants were aware of the relationship between contamination of soil with feces and transmission of the worms.[1] Kendall et al.[2] also mention that some societies consider that worms are normal symbiotes of the gut, which when mistreated (e.g., during a period of starvation or low food intake) can cause illness such as diarrhea.

One of the best measures an individual can take to avoid hookworm infection is wearing adequate footwear. This practice reduces the risk of infection, especially if shoes are worn in latrines, in the vicinity of human habitation, and during agricultural work. The appropriate use and maintenance of latrines also makes a difference. Hookworm eggs and larvae do not survive more than 1 or 2 months in soil, even under ideal conditions. Use of latrines helps reduce contamination of soil with the parasite and, therefore, reduces transmission. Additionally, minimizing the use of night soil as a fertilizer helps prevent the contamination of vegetables with parasites. Measures that can be used to prevent the transmission of all geohelminths include cleaning up stools of infants too young to use latrines; maintaining personal hygiene and care in preparing food, especially vegetables; the use of adequate footwear; and public education in elementary sanitation.

Potential for Vaccines?

There is much similarity between hookworm parasites of dogs and humans not only in terms of parasite morphology, but also in terms of the host response; therefore it is appropriate to study the immune responses in dogs and extrapolate the findings to humans. This subject is well reviewed by McSoreley and Loukas.[3] In experimental conditions, strong antibody responses representing all classes of immunoglobulins are noted, with parasite-specific immunoglobulin M (IgM) becoming detectable 6 weeks post infection, and immunoglobulin G (IgG) increasingly being detectable 8 weeks after infection. Immunoglobulin E (IgE) response develops slowly after multiple infections and appears to afford protection to further infection. Cytokine responses are complex and induce polarized TH2 responses, although this relationship is not clear in all instances. Finally, in the immune repertoire, cellular responses have been noted, again with much complexity.

Much of the work investigating the human response to hookworm infection has been done in the search for a hookworm vaccine. In fact, irradiated L3-stage larvae of *Ancylostoma caninum* have been used

as a vaccine in dogs. Although this vaccine achieved high levels of protection, its use was discontinued because it did not achieve sterilizing immunity and was expensive to produce.[4] The approach to hookworm vaccination in humans is directed against the invasive larval stage of *Necator americanus* termed NA-ASP-2, and the resulting product has been through safety trials in both the United States and Brazil. However, the efficacy and production of such a vaccine have not yet been tested.[5]

SCHISTOSOME PARASITES IN HUMANS

Three important species of schistosomes infect humans, with an additional two that occur in restricted areas.

Schistosoma haematobium occurs primarily in Africa, with extensions into the Middle East and western Asia. This species lives in the vesicular veins and capillaries of the bladder mucosa and causes the condition known as urinary schistosomiasis (bilharzia).

Schistosoma mansoni occurs primarily in Africa, but is also found in the northern parts of South America (Brazil) and the Caribbean. Adults of this species normally live in the capillaries that drain the mesenteries; also sometimes found in the liver sinuses, they can produce the condition called intestinal schistosomiasis (also known as intestinal bilharzia).

Schistosoma japonicum occurs mainly in China and parts of Southeast Asia, particularly in the Philippines. This species, which occupies the same region of the body as *S. mansoni*, is a more virulent form of the parasite, and it frequently produces severe sequelae.

The other human-infective species are *S. meekongi*, which is related to *S. japonicum*, found in Vietnam and adjoining territories, and *S. intercalatum*, which is related to *S. haematobium*, found in Cameroon and parts of West Africa.

Because of their reliance on freshwater snails as aquatic intermediate hosts, the entire distribution of these parasites is associated with water resources in which the appropriate snail species are found.

Life Cycle

Adult schistosomes differ from typical trematode worms in their narrow, elongated shape and separate sexes. The male is the larger of the two sexes, approximately 1.0 to 1.5 cm in length, with a cylindrical body folded to form a ventral gynecophoric canal in which the longer, slender female is embraced for most of the time. Both worms have two suckers—an oral sucker surrounding the mouth and a ventral sucker or acetabulum. The mouth leads into a blind gut that bifurcates along most of the length of the body. In the female, this area is dark with hematin derived from the digestion of blood cells. The number of testes in the male, the length of the uterus, and the shape of the eggs in females are distinctive to the species.

Eggs are deposited in the fine capillaries of the organ in which the worms are living. In vesicular schistosomiasis, this is the bladder; in the intestinal form, it is the intestinal mucosa. The eggs break through into the lumen of the bladder or gut, usually with a small amount of bleeding, and are passed to the exterior in the urine or feces. Many eggs do not break through the mucosa and remain in the tissue or are flushed into the liver, where they form a nidus for granulomata to develop. In severe infections, these granulomata damage the affected organ. In some cases of ectopic egg deposition, severe long-term paraplegia can occur when the base of the spinal cord is involved.

If the schistosome eggs are deposited in freshwater, or in a place where they can be soon washed into the water, the cycle continues. The eggs hatch, and a free-living, ciliated form, known as the miracidium, emerges. These miracidia use a number of environmental cues to seek out appropriate intermediate host snails. Miracidia move quite rapidly and can cover great distances in their search for snails. In some recent studies in Egypt, S. mansoni miracidia were shown commonly to infect snails 5 to 6 m distant, and some infected snails more than 20 m distant. The association is specific, so only the correct species of mollusc will sustain the infection. The miracidia do not ingest food and so have an infective life limited to approximately 5 to 6 hours. During this time, they must find the appropriate snail. The miracidium attaches to the snail and secretes proteolytic enzymes that penetrate into the tissues of the snail. The parasite then commences a process of asexual development. The miracidium enlarges into a mother sporocyst, a saclike organism that later buds off additional daughter sporocysts from layers of germinal epithelium. These daughter sporocysts migrate to the digestive gland of the snail, where they grow and finally produce copious numbers of the next larval stage, the cercaria.

Cercariae emerge from infected snails in response to sunlight after a prepatent period of approximately 30 days, although this could be much longer in cool weather. Cercariae normally emerge around midmorning, and continue emerging from the snails throughout the day, although by afternoon the numbers soon decline. The cercariae are furcocercous (**Figure 28-3**) and move by vibrating their forked

tail. Their main movement is up and down—that is, vertical rather than horizontal—and their target is the skin of a nearby human being. They respond to appropriate skin lipids that stimulate the process of penetration, a process that must occur within 6 to 12 hours after emergence, as cercariae, too, have no means to ingest nutrients.

When they commence penetration, cercariae secrete proteolytic enzymes, bore through the skin of the victim, then shed the tail, and, by contortions, penetrate into the subdermis, invade the lymphatic system, and move via the circulatory system to the lungs. In the lungs, the developing form, known as the schistosomulum, remains for a few days before continuing in the circulatory system to the liver. In the liver, the schistosomula mature and move to the end organ system in pairs.

Epidemiology of Schistosomiasis
Reservoir of the Parasite Population
Of the various important species of schistosome that affect human populations, S. haematobium and S. mansoni are primarily anthropophilic. Their reservoir is almost entirely confined to humans, although occasional episodes of transmission have been ascribed to other primates. With S. intercalatum, the picture is unclear; however, with S. japonicum and the related species, the parasites are found in a wide range of animals as well as in the human population. The source of the reservoir fundamentally affects the epidemiology of schistosomiasis and, in turn, influences attempts to control the disease.

As with most other parasitic infections, schistosomes are over-dispersed or aggregated in the reservoir population. That is, many hosts harbor few parasites, whereas a few hosts harbor many parasites, with the distribution fitting a negative binomial curve. This aggregated distribution has been ascribed to numerous factors: the degree of individual susceptibility, patterns of exposure to transmission foci, age difference in susceptibility, and the development of acquired resistance to further infection. Each of these factors should be considered in the epidemiology of schistosomiasis.

Age Prevalence of Schistosomiasis
Examination of the prevalence of Schistosoma infection in any population living in an endemic region will show a typical distribution (**Figure 28-4**). The proportion of infected persons increases with age, reaching a peak in childhood and adolescence. After the early 20s, age prevalence declines. In adult life, it remains approximately one-third as high as at the peak

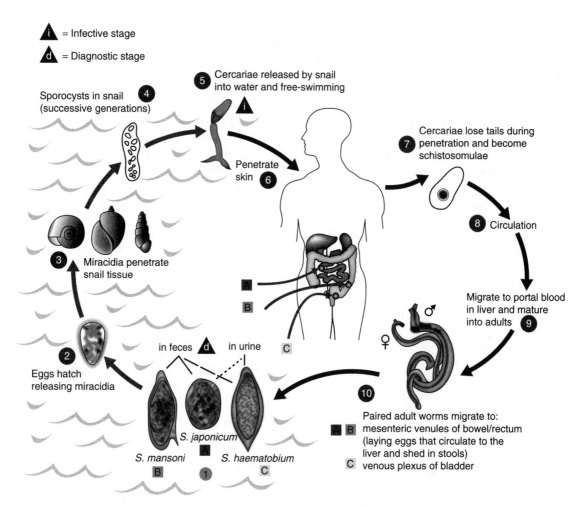

Figure 28-3 Illustration of the schistosomes, miracidia, and cercariae life cycles. Reproduced from the Centers for Disease Control and Prevention DPDx. Parasites and Health: Schistosomiasis. http://www.dpd.cdc.gov/dpdx/HTML/Schistosomiasis.htm. Accessed December 4, 2012.

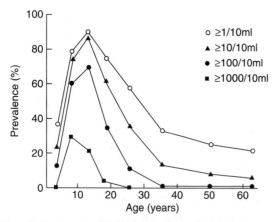

Figure 28-4 Prevalence and distribution of *Schistosome haematobium* egg output in relation to age in a Gambian community. Reprinted from Transactions of the Royal Society of Tropical Medicine and Hygeine, Vol. 73. HA Wilkens et al, The Significance of Pro-teinuria and Haematuria in Schistosoma Haematobium Infection, p. 75, © 1979, with permission from the Royal Society of Tropical Medicine and Hygiene.

until old age, when it declines further. The peak seen in these age prevalence curves is a factor of the endemicity or transmission rate (incidence) of infection, as can be seen in **Figure 28-5** and **Figure 28-6**, which show the pattern of infection in three regions of Zimbabwe wherein a high, medium, or low level of transmission occurs. These data clearly illustrate that prevalence in the community is age specific and that it is strongly influenced by the transmission rate, which itself is a function of the amount of surface water in the area and the extent of human contact with the water.

Schistosomes are long-lived parasites. Estimations based on die-off of infections under conditions where snail control operations were carried out suggest that they have a mean life span of 5 to 6 years; in numerous instances, however, parasites have been found to live several decades. The decline in the level of infection seen in adults living in endemic areas may be related to acquired resistance induced by the current

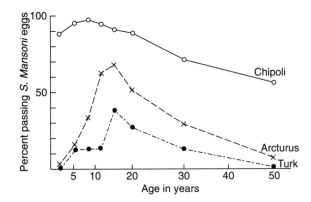

Figure 28-5 Prevalence of *Schistosome haematobium* infections in relation to age in three communities of Zimbabwe. Reprinted from V. de V. Clarke, The Influence of Acquired Resistance in the Epidemiology of Bilharziases, Central African Journal of Medicine, Vol. 12, No. 6, Supplement, p. 9, © 1966.

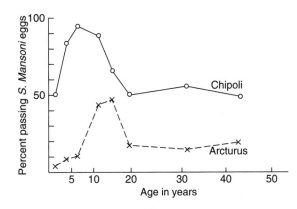

Figure 28-6 Prevalence of *Schistosome mansoni* infections in relation to age in two communities of Zimbabwe. Reprinted from V. de V. Clarke, The Influence of Acquired Resistance in the Epidemiology of Bilharziases, Central African Journal of Medicine, Vol. 12, No. 6, Supplement, p. 9, © 1966.

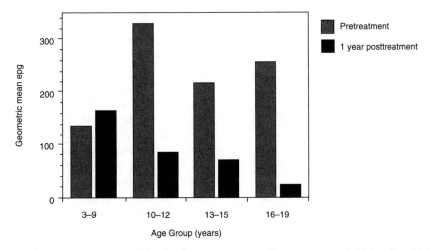

Figure 28-7 Geometric mean intensities of re-infection by age, one year after treatment of children in a high-transmission area (Mbugua et al. in preparation). Reprinted from New Strategies in Parasitology, Butterworth et al., Immunity and Morbidity in Human Schistosomiasis, p. 201, © 1989, with permission from Elsevier.

infection. This condition, which is known as premunition, comprises acquisition of immunity in people subjected to infection by this parasite. Certainly, antibodies are produced by people, even those who no longer show evidence of infection by passage of parasite eggs in the excreta. Furthermore, treatment of the infection does not appear to annul this protection, and the rate of acquisition of new infections among recently treated people, although high in children, declines abruptly in older children and adults (**Figure 28-7**). Recently, it has been suggested that the onset of puberty and the sexual maturation of the human host affect the ability of the parasite to invade its target. Numerous studies on human behavior and

water contact have failed to show that this decline in prevalence in adults is a function of decreased water contact with age. When naive adults become infected with schistosomes, acute sequelae develop rapidly, which suggests that sexual maturity plays little role in acquisition of infection.

Compiling of age prevalence curves of schistosome infection is necessary to determine the public health impact of the disease. Overall figures taken from a community as a whole might mask the severe impact that such disease has on children, for example. Furthermore, one must have some indication about the intensity (severity) of the infection—an understanding that can be obtained by estimating the intensity of infection or the associated worm burden. Actually, it is not possible to get an approximation of the number of worms infecting a patient; however, if the number of eggs passed in urine or feces is counted and expressed as a rate per 10 mL urine or 1 g feces, then it is possible to predict where and in whom the most serious pathology may develop. Also, these estimates provide a good indication of the extent of the reservoir for the next generation of parasites.

Egg burden in relation to age is clearly shown in Figure 28-7. In an intensive study in Zimbabwe, Clarke[6] translated this feature into a parameter he called the "infection potential." He showed that in high-endemicity areas, between 82% and 92% of *S. haematobium* eggs passed in a community were from children younger than 12 years of age. The pattern with *S. mansoni* was similar, although in areas of lower prevalence, the egg load appeared to be more evenly distributed in the population. Studies in the Philippines and China indicated that age-related egg passage does not follow changes in prevalence as consistently as in *S. haematobium*.[7]

Transmission and the Role of the Intermediate Host

Knowing about the distribution of the intermediate host snails is a key to understanding the epidemiology of schistosomiasis. In all instances, the snails involved are freshwater gastropod molluscs; they are entirely aquatic, although they can survive dry periods in small number within mud refuges. They belong to the family Planorbidae and the genera Biomphararia (*S. mansoni*) and Bulinus (*S. haematobium*). In the *S. japonicum* cycle, the snails are prosobranchs, which have an operculum to close the main aperture of the snail; thus they are amphibious and can survive periods of dryness and spend part of their life out of water. These snails are pioneering species with rapid rates of reproduction, so their populations can reach huge numbers when conditions are ideal. Because they are detritus feeders, in their environment they are seldom restricted by shortages of food. Although certain predacious animals consume snails, under natural conditions the predators have little impact on the snail populations.

Snails are cold-blooded and reproduce more rapidly in summer than in winter. They lay eggs in small batches on plant surfaces, stones, or other objects—even plastic sheets floating in the water. Each snail can produce several hundred eggs per week. These eggs will hatch in approximately 7 days, and the emerging snails will mature in about 6 weeks. Snails surviving dry periods can repopulate ponds within a short time.

Factors Affecting Snail Infection Rates

Miracidia emerge from schistosome eggs passed into water, and they will detect and infect snails nearby. The process of development in the snails is temperature dependent and proceeds more rapidly in warmer weather. In Zimbabwe, it has been shown that the rising temperatures of spring shorten the prepatent period, producing a heavy load of cercariae in the water in early summer. Patterns of snail population fluctuation and presence of infected snails in Egypt show peaks in spring and again in autumn. The intense heat of summer and the cold in winter negatively affect both the overall snail populations and the number of infected snails. These factors produce a seasonal pattern to the risk of infection in endemic areas.[8]

The Susceptible Human

Transmission of schistosomes requires contact of a susceptible host with cercariae-infested water. Such contact with water can involve ritual ablution, domestic chores, agricultural activities, gardening or fishing, or even recreation and bathing. Occasionally, an infection will occur from casual contact with water, even if the host is unaware of the contact. In most endemic areas, however, water contact is regular and systematic and part of a daily routine of life that entails a sustained exposure to the water and the risk of acquiring an infection when cercariae are present. It might be assumed that the longer the duration of contact, the heavier the worm burden. This is not always the case, however—as people get older, the likelihood of reinfection diminishes, as discussed earlier.

The actual incidence of infection in a community is difficult to assess because in an endemic area, a large proportion of the people will be infected and it is challenging to assess acquisition of new infections. It is possible to treat a cohort of people and reexamine them after a period of time to assess the number of reacquired cases. However, because a strong immune response militates against reinfection, measurement of incidence in this way can be done only in young children who are still susceptible to reinfection. Recently, researchers have shown that a circulating antigen can be detected in active cases, which may make further epidemiologic studies easier to carry out. However, currently few data exist to assess the value of this test under field conditions.[9]

Schistosomiasis in the Community

Schistosome parasites have evolved a well-adapted association with their human hosts. This association has probably developed over evolutionary time, particularly because of humans' nomadic lifestyle. However, with the more recent development of agriculture and settling of the human population in village communities, infection severity has increased and the ill effects of the disease have become more noticeable. Where new dams have been constructed, where population movements have occurred bringing naive hosts into contact with the parasite, and where conditions have led to expansions of snail populations, the cycle of transmission has been exacerbated and the local human population has developed disease. Thus the public health problem of schistosomiasis is a product of perturbed ecological processes, and control of the disease needs to focus on reducing the level of contact between host, snail, and parasite. To do so, a careful consideration of all aspects of schistosomes' complex life cycle and its various components must figure high in the development of control strategies.[10]

OTHER GEOHELMINTHS

Worms with Direct Life Cycles

A life cycle is considered direct when no intermediate host is involved and transmission occurs directly from one human host to another. The following species are transmitted directly, and they provide examples of direct cycles: *Strongyloides stercoralis*, *Trichuris trichiura*, *Ascaris lumbricoides*, and *Enterobius vermicularis*. Life cycles and brief notes on the epidemiology are discussed here.

Strongyloidiasis

The life cycle of *Strongyloides stercoralis* is similar to that of hookworm, albeit with some important modifications. This organism may experience both a free-living cycle and a parasitic cycle. In the free-living cycle, larvae are passed in the feces of infected people. In the presence of waterlogged soil and abundant feces, the larvae mature into rhabditiform males and females—a nonparasitic, noninfective form. Under ideal conditions, the adults mate and produce several cycles of free-living worms; however, as food declines or the habitat desiccates, a filariform generation will develop, leading to a third stage— filariform larvae—that will remain on the fecal mass and penetrate through the skin of anyone contacting the larvae. The larvae then circulate through the pulmonary alveolae, are coughed up, and migrate to the pharynx and finally to the intestine. They penetrate the mucosa in the duodenum and upper jejunum, molt twice, and become mature females in

approximately 2 weeks. There are no parasitic males, so reproduction is parthenogenetic at this stage.

The female is a delicate filariform worm, 2 to 3 mm in length and 30 to 40 microns in width. Females produce an indeterminate number of embryonated eggs daily; these usually hatch in the mucosa, and the larvae escape in the feces. Autoinfection can occur if the emerging first-stage larvae molt twice internally and develop into the third filariform stage. These organisms may reinvade the mucosa and proceed to reestablish a secondary infection. In immunocompromised hosts, this represents a severe stage of the infection. With the advent of human immunodeficiency virus (HIV) infection and in cases of decreasing immunocompetence (particularly associated with old age, cancer, and use of immunosuppressive drugs), strongyloidiasis has become increasingly important. In such immunocompromised hosts, dormant or new infections can disseminate and spread throughout the body. The infection is sporadic, particularly in communities where sanitation facilities are inadequate or defective.

Several species of *Strongyloides* occur in animals, and the infection is known to be a zoonosis with reservoir populations in a variety of animals. This makes the infection difficult to control with chemotherapy alone. The best approach is treatment of positive cases, together with emphasis on general use of latrines as a sanitary measure.

Trichuriasis (Human Whip Worm Infection)

Adults of *Trichuris trichiura* live attached to the wall of the cecum, and humans are the only source of infection. The adult worms have a large fleshy body and are attenuated in the anterior two-thirds of the length, giving the picture of a whip. The mouth, which is located at the distal end of the whip, is provided with a stylus that is connected to a thin, capillary-like esophagus. This thin portion of the worm becomes insinuated into the mucosa of the cecum and large bowel, and it anchors the worm in place. The presence of such worms causes irritation, probably as a result of the feeding process, which seems to involve tissue lysis by the parasite.

The female *T. trichiura* is 35 to 50 mm in length, with the male slightly smaller. Eggs are produced in situ and passed in the feces. They are characteristically barrel-shaped and robust and are laid unembryonated. Development of the larvae takes approximately 3 weeks, after which the eggs are infective. Eggs are not resistant to desiccation or bright sunlight. Transmission is most efficient in warm, humid, moist conditions, and infection results from swallowing infective eggs.

In areas of high endemicity, small children seem most vulnerable to this disease, and they can develop heavy infections, which may be caused by geophagy. *Trichuris* infection does not respond well to treatment, probably because its favored habitat is the lower bowel, a site difficult to reach with active drugs.

Ascariasis

Ascariasis is caused by *Ascaris lumbricoides*, the large roundworm infecting humans. One of the world's most ubiquitous parasites, it has been recognized from ancient times. The adults, which are free-living organisms in the intestine, are very large; the female is 20 to 35 cm in length and 3 to 6 mm in diameter, and the male is slightly smaller. The severity of infection depends on the number of worms a patient carries; however, the worms produce prodigious amounts of eggs on a continuous basis—approximately 200,000 eggs per female can be passed in a daily stool. The eggs may be either fertile or infertile. Fertile eggs are encased in a thick shell consisting of three layers. The eggshell is remarkably stable and resistant to desiccation. It also prevents toxic substances from reaching the developing embryo. Thus the eggs of *A. lumbricoides* can survive the rigors of sewage treatment and remain infective for many months, even years under ideal conditions.

The eggs produced are unembryonated and, as such, are not infective. A period of development and two molts occur in the egg prior to it becoming infective. This takes place by ingestion, either in fecally contaminated food or in water, or even inhaled through dust. The larvae emerge in the intestine and immediately penetrate the gut epithelium, then circulate through the blood system to the lungs, where they may remain for 9 to 15 days. They are then coughed up and swallowed, and finally return to the gut. In 8 to 10 weeks, worms are mature; if males and females are present, the females will start to produce fertile eggs.

Pinworm

Pinworm is caused by *Enterobius vermicularis*, a cosmopolitan parasite more common in temperate climates than in warmer areas, when less frequent bathing and infrequent washing of underclothes occurs. The worms are small nematodes, with the male being somewhat smaller (2–5 mm in length and not more than 0.2 mm wide) than the female (2–13 mm long and as much as 0.5 mm in diameter). The worms live in the cecum, appendix, and adjacent areas of the ascending colon. They occupy the mucous layer between the mucosa and the fecal matter.

The gravid female becomes distended, and is packed with eggs. At this time, it migrates down the colon and out the anus. Normally, the eggs are deposited at one time, after which the female disintegrates. Eggs are not commonly laid in the bowel, although they are sometimes found in the feces. Usually, eggs are smeared over the perianal region; they can best be seen and identified by the "Scotch tape" test. For this test, a 6-cm length of clear tape is placed over the anal area, pressed against the skin, and removed. The tape is then placed on a glass microscopic slide, with the tacky side to the glass. Eggs adhering to the adhesive can be seen by observing the glass slide under a low-power microscope.

The eggs are elongate-ovoidal, distinctly compressed laterally, and flattened on one side; they measure 50–60 by 20–30 microns. The shell is relatively thick and colorless. The eggs embryonate and become infective a few hours after being laid. They are robust and resistant to disinfectants and drying, and may remain viable for as long as 2 weeks. Eggs that are swallowed hatch when they reach the intestine, and the development to adult usually takes approximately 1 month.

The epidemiology of pinworm infection is associated with contact between individuals usually living together or people who handle soiled clothing, particularly night-clothes. Frequently, this type of contact occurs within families. Eggs are transferred from hand to mouth, particularly following scratching the perianal area after females have emerged and laid eggs, through inhalation of dust particles in bedrooms where an infected person may sleep, or similar person-to-person contact. Transmission is efficient and can lead to very severe infestations.

Control is a matter of treatment and prevention. As the eggs are resistant to disinfection, it is best to consider any contaminated area as infective for as long as 2 weeks after treatment of any cases, and to maintain a high level of cleanliness and hygiene to prevent the cycle from restarting.

Worms with Indirect Cycles (Including a Vector-Borne Stage)

The parasites with indirect cycles belong to a group (or superfamily) of nematode worms called the Filarioidea. They live in the tissues or body cavity of a mammalian host and are transmitted by the bite of an arthropod vector. The females produce microfilariae, which are unique in that they are less differentiated than the first-stage larvae of other nematodes. Highly motile and threadlike, they exist in the blood or subcutaneously in the mammalian host. The microfilariae in blood exhibit diurnal periodicity and are usually present in the peripheral circulation synchronized with the biting behavior of the insect vector. When taken up by an arthropod vector, they migrate first through the gut wall into the hemocoel, and then into the thoracic muscles of the insect. They proceed through two stages of development, finally emerging as the third-stage larva (L3), which is infective and invades a new mammalian host during the next blood meal. Seldom are more than two or three L3 forms found in one mosquito.

Bancroftian Filariasis (Elephantiasis)

Elephantiasis is a condition caused by one of two parasites: *Wucheraria bancrofti*, which is widespread in most tropical areas, and *Brugia malayi*, which is an important human parasite in Southeast Asia and the Pacific Islands. In most of their distribution, both species exhibit nocturnal periodicity and microfilariae are in the peripheral circulation only at night.

The adults of these two species are threadlike and long; males are approximately 40 mm in length, whereas the females are approximately 100 mm in length. They are normally found coiled in lymph nodes in the inguinal region, although they can also occur in axillary nodes. Infiltration of plasma cells, macrophages, and eosinophils around the infected nodes occurs and eventually results in inflammation and swelling. In time, the nodes become blocked and proximal lymphatic vessels become stenotic and obstructed, which leads to lymphedema and thickening of the subcutaneous tissue and eventually to elephantiasis. Approximately 8 to 12 months after an active infection is established, the worms become sexually mature; at that point, microfilariae appear in the blood and circulate in the peripheral blood according to the diurnal periodicity described previously. It appears from experimental work with animal models that the microfilariae can live as long as 200 days.

The epidemiology of this infection is very much associated with the local distribution of mosquito vectors. However, as several genera of mosquitoes can transmit microfilariae, the endemic areas are extensive. Peridomestic breeding places for culicine mosquitoes are becoming increasingly important, particularly in urban areas. Infection occurs in young people; however, because the vectors carry small numbers of infective parasites, it normally takes many years before noticeable sequelae of the infection occur.

Control of the disease depends on reducing the number of breeding sites of the vectors, particularly those in close proximity to houses. In areas where sewage treatment is inadequate and wastewater is allowed to stand in pools, and where effluent from domestic water usage occurs, mosquito populations abound and present serious problems. Control by various methods—for example, vector control, reduction of potential mosquito breeding sites, the use of insect repellents, and extensive chemotherapy—needs to be implemented. Researchers have recently shown that use of the drug ivermectin will reduce considerably the level of microfilaremia and, in this way, restrict the reservoir of infection. A combination of these various approaches will likely be successful in reducing the prevalence of both these parasites.[11]

Onchocerca volvulus

Onchocerca volvulus is associated with the condition known as river blindness. The adult forms live in subcutaneous nodules where they lie in tangled masses of male and female worms. They reproduce by producing unsheathed microfilariae, which migrate through the skin intradermally. These forms are not found in the blood, but they frequently occur in the vitreous humor of the eye. The microfilariae are ingested during the process of feeding by blackflies (*Simulium* species), which breed in well-oxygenated, fast-flowing water, and are pests to people living near streams and rivers.

The microfilariae pass through two molts in the blackfly, and after approximately 6 to 8 days exist as L3 forms in the thoracic muscles of the fly; finally they migrate to the mouth-parts of the fly. At the next blood meal, the larvae leave the fly and penetrate the wound caused during the feed. Once in the skin of a new host, the larvae migrate to various parts of the body, penetrate through the subcutaneous tissue, molt further, and finally mature into adults. The prepatent period in humans is 3 to 15 months. The parasites reside in nodules, which may be located in the deep fascia or in subcutaneous tissue. They are frequently palpable and can be removed surgically. The onchocercal nodules usually cause no symptoms, although they can be somewhat deforming. The main problems from the infection come from the long-lived microfilariae in the skin and eye. In chronic infections, a progressive loss of subcutaneous connective tissue occurs and the skin becomes loose and depigmented. Dermatitis and infiltration by lymphocytes can occur, adding to the irritation and disfigurement of the host.

Severe ocular pathology is frequently associated with savannah onchocerciasis transmitted by blackflies of the *Simulium damnosum* species group. Transmission in the forest environment can be intense, and the prevalence of infection in such areas is high; however, blinding onchocerciasis is seen less frequently in people exposed to the forest-dwelling species of blackflies.

The distribution of onchocerciasis is extensive in West and Central Africa, and stretching into East Africa, as far south as Malawi. It also exists in the Arabian peninsular, Yemen, Central America, and the northern part of South America. However, in the Americas, although ocular infiltration and damage occur, little blindness is associated with the infection.

To understand the epidemiology of onchocerciasis, it is important to know something about the vector. The blackfly belongs to the genus *Simulium*. Members of this genus, which are voracious blood feeders, are cosmopolitan in distribution. Both males and females take blood, and both are worrisome nuisance pests associated with strong-flowing water. Not all *Simulium* species carry *Onchocerca*, however. In Africa, the vectors belong to the *S. damnosum* complex and *S. neavei* group, whereas in South America, several anthropophilic species transmit the parasite.

The flies lay their eggs in water, preferably on rocks or emergent vegetation washed with fast-flowing, usually well-oxygenated water. The larval and pupal forms of the insect live on firm substrates immersed in the water, where they feed on plankton and suspended particles. The adult flies do not normally venture far from their breeding sites; hence transmission of this parasite is associated with rivers. In parts of Africa, prior to the major control efforts of the Onchocerciasis Control Programme, villages near rivers and the associated lands were abandoned by peasant farmers who feared the infection.

Control of the disease has consisted of a two-front attack using both chemical control of the vector and treatment of the infection among humans. Because of their restricted breeding habits, blackflies can be controlled by treating the rivers with specially formulated insecticides. The insecticide is adsorbed on clay particles suspended in the fast-flowing water and is selectively toxic to filter-feeding insects. This strategy has been used for the past 20 years in a large part of West Africa, and it has been successful in reducing both the blackfly population and the transmission of *O. volvulus*. More recently, ivermectin—a drug that eliminates the microfilariae from the skin of infected people for as long as a year—has been used to augment the vector control efforts. Collectively, this work has reduced morbidity and blindness in a large section of the West African population. Because the drug does not kill adult worms, treatment has to be repeated every 12 months; however, methods to overcome this drawback are being developed and some hope exists that the infection will decline in importance as a public health problem.[12]

CONTROL OF NEGLECTED TROPICAL DISEASES

The parasites considered in this chapter fall into the group now known as "neglected tropical diseases." They are "neglected" in the sense that they are not included in the major disease initiatives launched by donors and major agencies that provide funding for treatment and control of HIV/AIDS, malaria, and tuberculosis. However, their public health burden is extremely large, as they afflict a large proportion of the world's population, cause considerable morbidity and growth retardation among children, and produce high mortality among rural adults, especially from bladder cancer.[13] These helminthiases are easily and inexpensively treated, however, and for the most part they can be targeted and treated while children are at school.[14]

Currently, several programs are under way in selected endemic countries that are having a considerable effect on the morbidity and mortality associated with neglected tropical diseases. These are mainly donor-driven efforts, and the programs' long-term sustainability is doubtful unless they can secure support within their own communities and evolve into country-owned programs. Furthermore, the penetrance of control programs is diminished when school children are the main target for programs, as many infected individuals are not in school. These remaining individuals will sustain the reservoir for parasites, allowing them to spread easily if control efforts wane.

● ● ● **REFERENCES**

1. De Silva NR, Chan MS, Bundy DA. Morbidity and mortality due to ascariasis: re-estimation and sensitivity analysis of global numbers at risk. *Trop Med Int Health* 1997;2:519–528.

2. Kendall C, Foote D, Martorell R. Ethnomedicine and rehydration therapy: a case study of ethno-medical investigation and program planning. *Soc Sci Med* 1984;19:253–260.

3. McSoreley JM, Loukas DS. The immunology of hookworm infections. *Parasite Immunol* 2010;32:549–559.

4. Diemart DJ, Bethony JM, Hotez PJ. Hookworm vaccines. *Clin Infect Dis* 2008;46:282–288.

5. Bethony JM, Cole RN, Guo X, et al. Vaccines to combat the neglected tropical diseases. *Immunol Rev* 2011;239:237–270.

6. Clarke V de V. The influence of acquired resistance in the epidemiology of bilharziasis. *Cent Afr J Med* 1966;12(suppl 6):1–30.

7. Jordan P, Webbe G. Epidemiology: In: Jordan P, Webbe G, Sturrock RW, eds. *Human Schistosomiasis.* Oxford, UK: CAB International; 1993:87–158.

8. Shiff CJ, Coutts WCC, Yiannakis C, et al. Seasonal patterns in the transmission of *Schistosoma haematobium* in Rhodesia. *Trans R Soc Trop Med Hyg* 1974;73:375–380.

9. Ndhlovu P, Cadman H, Gunderson H, et al. Circulating anodic antigen levels in a Zimbabwe rural community endemic for *Schistosoma haematobium* using the magnetic beads antigen-capture enzyme linked immunoassay. *Am J Trop Med Hyg* 1996;54:637–642.

10. Gryseels B. Human resistance to schistosome infections. *Parasitol Today* 1994;10:380–384.

11. Nicholas L, Plichart C, Nguyen LN, Moulia-Pelat JP. Reduction of *Wucheraria bancrofti* adult worm circulating antigen after annual treatments of dethylcarbamazine combined with ivermectin in French Polynesia. *J Infect Dis* 1997;175:489–492.

12. Molyneux DH, Davies JB. Onchocerciasis control: moving towards the millennium. *Parasitol Today* 1997;13:418–425.

13. Shiff C, Naples JM, Ishaarwal S, et al. Non-invasive methods to detect schistosome-based bladder damage: is the association sufficient for epidemiological use?" *Trans R Soc Med Hyg* 2010;104:2–5.

14. Hotez P, Fenwick A. Schistosomiasis in Africa: an emerging tragedy in our new global health decade. *PLoS Neg Trop Dis* 2009;3(9):e485.

Index